The Scots peerage

Founded on Wood's edition of Sir Robert Douglas's peerage of Scotland

Containing an historical and genealogical account of the nobility of that kingdom

Sir James Balfour Paul

Alpha Editions

This edition published in 2019

ISBN : 9789353898090

Design and Setting By
Alpha Editions
email - alphaedis@gmail.com

THE

SCOTS PEERAGE

FOUNDED ON WOOD'S EDITION
OF SIR ROBERT DOUGLAS'S

Peerage of Scotland

CONTAINING
AN HISTORICAL AND GENEALOGICAL ACCOUNT
OF THE NOBILITY OF THAT KINGDOM

EDITED BY

SIR JAMES BALFOUR PAUL, C.V.O., LL.D.
LORD LYON KING OF ARMS

VOLUME IX
INDEX

EDINBURGH: DAVID DOUGLAS

1914

EDITORIAL NOTE

This, the concluding volume of the *Scots Peerage*, completes a work, the first volume of which was published in 1904. It contains, in the first place, a long list of *addenda et corrigenda*: the latter may, it is hoped, serve to put right some at all events of the actual errors which have occurred in the work; the former, and they are the larger class of the two, contain a good deal of information which has come to light since the publication of the several articles. The editor has to thank many kind correspondents and contributors for information supplied, and especially he may name his friends Mr. J. Maitland Thomson, LL.D., and Col. the Hon. R. E. Boyle, both of whom have been unremitting in their helpful endeavours to increase the usefulness and accuracy of the *Peerage*. Nobody is more aware of the many shortcomings of this work than the editor himself, but perhaps he may be allowed to claim that at all events it is an advance on what has gone before. No doubt, with increased facilities of investigation and the further publication of national records and the contents of private charter-chests, a future generation may be able to produce a fuller and still more accurate account of individual families, but it is hardly probable that a history of the Scottish Peerage on a scale similar to that of the present work will be attempted for many years to come.

The full and elaborate Index, with which the greater part of this volume is occupied, is the work of Mrs. Alexander Stuart, who has brought towards its completion an enthusiasm, energy, and ability which are beyond all praise. Not only does it contain a list of between forty and fifty thousand names, but each person is definitely described by the mention of his or her title, occupation, or relationship. In itself, indeed, the Index forms a valuable compendium of Scottish family history, which will be found useful even without reference to the pages of the *Peerage*. But it goes without saying that such an Index doubles the usefulness of a work like the present. It is not often that an editor meets with a compiler who is so fully in accord with him as to the standard to be aimed at in an index, and who is so capable of carrying it to a successful conclusion. It is difficult for the editor adequately to express the obligations he is under to Mrs. Stuart for her services in this matter.

The Index has been compiled on the following principles:—

1. A Peerage title is given, in capitals, with its holders in alphabetical order, and their respective wives.
2. If the name of the title is changed, *e.g.* from Lyon to Glamis, it is given a separate heading.
3. The surname of the holder of a Peerage title is given in capitals with the various Peerages, in alphabetical order, pertaining to it.
4. After Peers, owners of lands are given in alphabetical order; those of the same Christian name are put in chronological order.
5. Ordinary persons then come in alphabetical order and according to the paging in the volumes.
6. Women are given under their maiden names: if married, as 'wife of ——'; if unmarried as 'dau. of ——.'
7. As a rule, children who died in infancy are not inserted.

In taking leave of a task which has been a congenial if a somewhat strenuous one for the last twelve years, the editor has to express his appreciation of the amicable relations which have subsisted between him and his contributors (some now, alas, beyond the reach of acknowledgments). It is a pleasure to have worked with such colleagues.

JAMES BALFOUR PAUL.

EDINBURGH, *June* 1914.

ADDENDA ET CORRIGENDA

ADDENDA ET CORRIGENDA

VOL. I.

KINGS OF SCOTLAND

p. **4**, l. 26, for 'Annandale,' read 'Carrick (vol. ii. p. 433).'

p. **4**, l. 2 from foot, after Bohun, insert 'father of the first,' after 'Hereford' insert 'of that family (*Complete Peerage*).'

p. **6**, l. 29, for '17 January,' read '28 January (*Scottish Kings*, p. 97).'

p. **8**, l. 19, for '1547' read '1347.'

p. **9**, l. 6, after '1362,' add 'She had left King David on account of his infidelity, and received Hertford Castle from King Edward as a residence.'

p. **10**, l. 2, after 'St.,' insert 'Florent de.'

p. **10**, l. 3, for 'Brittany' read 'Anjou.'

p. **10**, l. 12, for 'Brittany' read 'Touraine.'

p. **10**, l. 21, after 'Priory of,' insert 'Lehon, a Priory of the abbey of.'

p. **10**, l. 22, for 'title' read 'tithe.'

p. **12**, l. 2, after 'known,' add 'Walter had also a daughter, *Margaret*, buried at Paisley (*Regist. de Passelet*, 74).'

p. **12**, l. 5, after 'Eva,' add note, 'Her name was certainly Eva (*Reg. Prior S. Andree*, 257), but her parentage is unknown.'

p. **12**, l. 9, after 'leaving,' add 'issue,' and delete 'at least two sons.'

p. **12**, between ll. 12 and 13, add

'3. *Leonard*, designed son of Alan, Steward of the King of Scots, who is noted in the *Liber Vitæ* of Durham as bestowing a bezant yearly on the convent, was probably also a son (*Illustrations of Scottish History*, 18).

4. *Avelina*, who was, in 1200, carried off by Duncan, son of Gilbert, afterwards Earl of Carrick (Hoveden, *Rolls Series*, iv. 145).'

p. **12**, l. 24, delete 'He appears to have died soon after 13th June 1292,' and insert 'He was summoned by Edward I. to attend him into France, 1st September 1294, and died soon after that date.'

p. **12**, between ll. 36 and 37, insert

'7—— a daughter, married to Donald Lord of the Isles. *See* Isles.'

p. **12**, l. 37, for '7' read '8.'

p. **14**, l. 23, for '1326' read '1327.'

Note.—Bower, the only authority, is so confused at this point that he may be read to mean either year. Walter witnessed several royal charters after 9 April 1326, the latest being dated 31 March 1327 (Polmaise Charter-Chest).

p. **15**, l. 4 from foot, after 'her,' add 'who was buried in the church of the Blackfriars of Perth (*Blackfriars of Perth*, 38).'

p. **17**, ll. 26 and 27, delete 'about the year 1367,' and insert 'Papal dispensation, dated 13 March 1365-66' (cf. vol. vii. 37).'

p. **18**, l. 16, for '1409' read '1405.'

p. **18**, l. 17, after 'Kennedy;[4]' add 'In July 1409 there was a papal dispensation for her marriage with Sir William Cunningham of Kilmaurs (cf. vol. iv. 230).'

p. **18**, l. 17, delete 'third,' and insert 'on 13 November 1413 she was married.'

p. **19**, l. 16, after '1496,' add note, 'The Duchess Eleanor's arms are still in the Burg at Meran. See Baillie-Grohman's *The Land in the Mountains.*'

p. **22**, l. 36, for 'John, Lord Gordon' read 'John, styled Lord Gordon.'

p. **22**, l. 3 from foot, for 'Isabella' read 'Agnes.'

p. **22**, l. 2 from foot, after 'Buchan,' add 'afterwards Countess of Bothwell (see charter cited in *Geneaologist*, N.S., viii. 185, 186).'

p. **23**, l. 4, after 'Barthélemy,' insert 'She was living 22 August 1560.'

p. **24**, l. 9, after 'He,' insert 'was born about 1529, as a dispensation granted by Pope Clement VII. on 30 August 1534 states that he was then in his fifth year (*Sixth Report Hist. MSS. Com.*, 670) and.'

p. **24**, l. 5 from foot, after 'Coldingham,' insert 'He was born about 1531 (Dispensation *ut cit.*).'

p. **24**, ll. 4 and 5 from foot, delete '28 December 1561,' and insert '11 January 1561-62 (*Cal. of Scot. Papers*, i. 590).'

p. **25**, l. 7, after 'Whithorn,' insert 'He was born about 1533 (Dispensation *ut cit.*).'

p. **29**, l. 15, after 'Maria,' insert note, 'Her name was originally Henrietta only, as recorded in the baptismal register at Exeter. She took the name of Anna on joining the Roman Catholic faith when she married the Duke of Orleans' (*ex inform.* Hon. James Hope).

ABERCORN

p. **37**, l. 27, after '1543' add note, 'Claud was probably baptized June 1546. (Cf. *Treasurer's Accounts*, viii. 461.)'

p. **39**, l. 19, for '24,' read '29.'

p. **39**, ll. 27, 28, delete 'High Treasurer of Scotland.' William Hamilton, though frequently so styled never appears to have held this office. He does not appear even to have been a knight.

p. **39**, l. 28, delete 'March,' and insert 'a few days before 18 February (*Complete Peerage*, viii. 488).'

p. **40**, l. 13, for '1662,' read '1622,' and add '(contract dated 20 July 1619) (*Reg. of Deeds*, ccxciv. 160).'

p. **40**, note 3, l. 4 from foot, for 'Robert Lauder of the Bass,' read 'Maurice Lauder of Dunbar.'

p. 42, l. 11, after 'issue,' add 'Warrant for his burial in Holyrood Church 17 April 1696 (*Privy Council Acta*).'

p. 42, ll. 20 and 21, delete 'Campbell,' and insert after of, 'Sir Archibald Campbell of Glencarradale' (cf. vol. v. 504).'

p. 47, l. 7. Boyd of Trochrig gives the date of Lord Abercorn's death as Monday, 2 April 1618 (Bannatyne Club *Misc.*, i. 289). The date in the text is taken from his funeral entry in the Lyon Office.

p. 47, l. 17, after 'Hamilton,' delete comma, and insert full stop. 'He chose curators 19 July 1621, his next-of-kin on the father's side being Sir George Hamilton of Greenlaw and Sir Frederick Hamilton; on the mother's side, William Boyd of Bonshaw and Adam Boyd of Templeton (*Acts and Decreets*, ccclvi. 103).'

p. 48, l. 21, after 'contract,' add 'She was buried in Holyrood church on or after 9 June 1696 (Warrant in *Privy Council Acta*).'

p. 49, l. 24, delete 'William Lenthall of Burford, in the county of Oxford, Speaker in the House of Commons in the Long Parliament,' and insert 'Sir John Lenthall, Marshal of the King's Bench, by Hester, daughter of Sir Thomas Temple, first Baronet of Stowe, which Sir John was the Speaker's brother (*Complete Peerage*, viii. 253).'

p. 54, l. 34, for '1735' read '1735-36.'

p. 54, l. 2 from foot, delete 'at Paris, 17 March 1731, was buried in the Scots College there,' and insert 'in Dublin, 6, was buried in St. Patrick's Cathedral there 9, March 1730-31. Michel, on whose authority the statement in the text was given, is wrong, and the inscription he quotes must belong merely to a memorial tablet.'

p. 55, l. 28, delete the notice of John Hamilton, and insert 'John Hamilton was made a major-general in 1690-91, and died a prisoner in Dublin of wounds received at the battle of Aughrim. He married at Sixmile Bridge, co. Clare, in January 1690, Elizabeth M'Can, daughter of Glesney M'Can by Eleanor, daughter of William Folliard. They had an only child, *Margaret*, who became a chanoinesse of Poussay, in Lorraine, of which her cousin, Elizabeth de Gramont, was Abbess. She married, first, 16 September 1715, Pierre, Comte de Réance, etc.; and, secondly, 18 July 1718, François Philippe, Comte de Marmier, and had a son, Philippe François, created Marquis de Marmier 1740, from whom the present Marquis de Marmier descends (*ex. inform.* G. D. Burtchaell, Esq., Athlone Pursuivant).'

p. 62, l. 15, after 'son,' insert 'She had a pardon for violating the Acts of Parliament against marriage with Papists in December 1734 (Signet Bills, Public Record Office).'

p. 63, l. 17, for 'in November' read '13 October.'

p. 63, l. 2 from foot, for 'eighty' read 'seventy.'

p. 64, l. 23, after '1789,' insert 'the Patent, a most unusual one, as neither her father nor any of his issue could have succeeded to the title, was obtained with great difficulty through the influence of her cousin, the first Marquess, with whom she was on terms of intimacy. The King was most averse to granting it (Cf. Wraxall's *Posthumous Memoirs*, 163, and Lady Charlotte Bury's *Diary*, ii. 157).'

p. **68**, l. 28, after 'Jane,' insert 'Gore.'

SANDILANDS, LORD ABERCROMBIE

p. **75**, l. 17, for 'third' read 'fourth.'

p. **75**, last line, after 'Garden,' add 'He was killed at the battle of Pinkie, 1547, and his widow married, secondly, John Shaw of Broich (*Exch. Rolls*, xviii. 468; *Acts and Decreets*, xxii. 397).'

p. **76**, l. 24, after 'Janet,' insert 'natural.'

p. **76**, l. 25, for 'Andrew' read 'Patrick (see *Reg. Mag. Sig.*, 13 April 1541).'

p. **76**, last line, after 'Pittedie,' add 'married Isobel Cuninghame and left a son and heir *John*, who was served heir to his father 26 May 1610 (*Fife Retours*).'

p. **76**, note 14, for 'xxxiii.' read 'lxxxiii.'

p. **77**, after l. 11, add

'9. *Isobel*, married, before 12 December 1562, to John Boswell of Balmuto (*Reg. Mag. Sig.*, 2 March 1562-63). By contract dated 28 October 1554, he had become bound to marry Grisel or Isobel, whichever he pleased, when he had completed his fourteenth year (*Reg. of Deeds*, i. 249).'

p. **77**, l. 21, after 'had,' add 'besides *James*, accidentally killed at St. Andrews in April 1574 by George, son of John Shaw of Lethangie, both being children (*Reg. Sec. Sig.*, lvi. 140).'

p. **77**, note 4, for '393' read '293.'

p. **78**, l. 15, delete 'before June 1593,' and insert 'contract 1590 (*Reg. of Deeds*, clxviii. 227).'

p. **78**, l. 18, after 'William,' insert 'married Catherine Cranstoun (*Reg. of Deeds*, ccccxxxii. 47), and had a son *William*, and a daughter, married to James Carstairs (*Ibid.*, DLix. 327). He is also said to have had an eldest son, *John*, of Rashiehill, father of another John, father of John of Breadshaw, whose son Thomas was served heir of Sir James Sandilands of St. Monance, first Lord Abercrombie (*sic*), brother-german of his great-great-grandfather, in 1734 (Canongate Services of Heirs). Thomas's claim to be Lord Abercrombie was rejected by the House of Lords in 1739 (*Stewartiana*, 127).'

p. **78**, l. 24, delete whole line.

p. **78**, l. 25, after 'Catherine,' insert 'married (contract 5 April 1628) to Mr. Adam, son of Adam Bothwell of Glencorse, and died before 21 March 1632 (cf. vol. iv. 435).'

p. **78**, l. 27, after 'Jean,' insert 'Died 1647, Mr. Andrew, her brother, being served heir to her 26 January 1648 (Fife Sheriff-Court Books).'

p. **78**, ll. 31 and 32, delete 'and predeceased his father, dying in 1644 or 1645,' and insert 'was alive 1 January 1645 (*Reg. of Deeds*, DLix. 326).'

p. 79, l. 2, after 'Catherine,' insert 'married to Sir Robert Dalzell, first Baronet of Glenae (discharge for tocher dated 20 June 1644, *Reg. of Deeds*, DLVII. 70).'

p. 79, after l. 3, insert

'7. *Mary*, baptized 9 May 1638 (Canongate Reg.), probably identical with that Marion who calls herself sister of James, Lord Abercrombie, and daughter of Dame —— Carnegy and Sir James Sandilands, in a deed renouncing certain rights she had over lands belonging to her brother, which she had apprised. The date is 17 November 1658, and at that time she was "appearand" wife of Mr. David Lyall, minister of Banchory-Devenick, afterwards of Aberdeen and Montrose, where he died in 1696' (*ex inform.* Dr. W. A. Macnaughton, Stonehaven; deed recorded in Register of Bonds, etc., Sheriff-Court Books, Stonehaven).'

p. 79, l. 4, for 'father's' read 'mother's.'

p. 79, l. 5 from foot, for 'Crichton,' read 'Lichtoun.'

p. 80, l. 22, after 'Falkland,' insert 'Lord Abercrombie ultimately divorced his wife, apparently on 13 March 1663 (*Edin. Com. Decreets*, but the Decreet is not engrossed in the Register). On 18 October 1663 he produced extract of his divorce before the kirk-session of Kinneff, and was thereafter contracted and proclaimed with Christian Fletcher (Kinneff Register).'

p. 81, l. 17, for 'VII.' read 'II.'

p. 81, l. 31, after 'proper,' insert 'on a chief azure three mullets of the first.'

ABERDEEN

p. 83, l. 28, for 'Lomnay' read 'Lonmay.'

p. 87, l. 27, after 'Charles,' insert 'apprenticed to Bailie George Reid, merchant, Edinburgh, 6 July 1659 (Edinburgh Apprentice Register).'

p. 89, l. 22, delete '7 May 1691,' and insert '1694 (*ex inform.* Hon. Vicary Gibbs).'

p. 89, ll. 26, 27, delete 'died before June 1709,' and insert 'was buried 16 December 1708 (*Complete Peerage*, s.v. Eglinton).'

p. 90, l. 28, for '1 April,' read '25 April.'

p. 90, l. 29, delete 'Anna.'

p. 90, l. 31, for 'pence,' read 'pounds.'

p. 91, l. 6, after 'thirdly,' insert 'banns proclaimed at Bellie 15 November 1729.'

p. 91, l. 8, after '1791,' insert 'and was buried in St. Cuthbert's Churchyard, Edinburgh.'

p. 93, l. 18, for '1793,' read '1795.

p. 95, l. 34, after 'Morton,' add note, 'The present wife is reckoned agreeable and clever, but how unlike her predecessor in beauty and charm (Lady Charlotte Bury's *Diary*).'

p. 100, last l. after 'daughter,' insert '*Henrietta.*'

p. 102, l. 22, after 'in,' insert 'March.'

p. 103, l. 9, after 'George,' insert 'entered Douai College 5 November 1685, aged ten. Studied Philosophy at Paris, and became a religious, but renounced in 1699.'

'4. *Patrick*, entered Douai 10 April 1681, aged nine.'

p. 103, l. 10, delete '4,' and insert '5.'

p. 103, l. 10, after '*John*,' insert 'entered Douai 5 November 1685, aged eight (*Records of Scots Colleges*).'

p. 103, l. 11, delete '5,' and insert '6.'

p. 103, l. 14, after '1698,' insert 'for adultery with a Frenchman Lavelette or Laballot (*Consistorial Processes*, Scot. Rec. Soc., No. 86).

p. 103, l. 15, delete 'succeeded his father 1681 and on,' and insert 'entered Douai 10 April 1681, aged eleven. Became a religious (probably Jesuit) at Rome, "a sweet youth and humble like the dust of the street" (*Letters of James, Earl of Perth*, Camden Soc., 1845, p. 18). On 4 Sep- September 1694 Aboyne was in Scotland, having been captured on his return from France, and sent down from London on bail. He was, 19 October 1694, confined to one of the houses of Glamis or Castle Lyon, whichever the Earl of Strathmore should be residing at for the time (*Privy Council Acta*). On'.

p. 103, line 16, after '1698,' insert 'he.'

p. 103, l. 27, after 'married,' insert 'as his first wife.'

p. 103, l. 28, after 'Kinnaird,' insert 'She was dead before 3 November 1731 (*Consistorial Processes*, Scot. Rec. Soc., No. 293).'

p. 103, last line, after 'married,' insert '20 June 1724 (*Complete Peerage*).'

p. 104, l. 6, after 'Glentanner,' insert 'born 19 June 1728.'

p. 104, l. 12, after 'Baronet,' insert 'She died 31 March and was buried at Restalrig 6 April 1803 (Restalrig Reg.).'

p. 104, l. 15, after 'company,' insert 'Born 8 July 1765, died 26 December 1832.'

p. 104, l. 16, after 'R.N.', insert 'Born 9 April 1769, died 23d August 1799, and was buried at Restalrig (*Ibid*).'

p. 104, l. 17, delete 'died young,' and insert 'was buried at Restalrig, 23 February 1781 (*Ibid.*).'

p. 104, l. 18, after 'Clementina,' insert 'born 6 May 1763.'

p. 104, l. 18, delete 'at Exmouth, 13 December 1801, aged 33,' and insert 'after 9 July 1804, when she was served heir to her mother.'

p. 104, l. 20, after '*Grace*,' insert '*Margaret*, born 27 September 1766.'

p. 104, l. 22, after 'Lockhart,' insert 'born 1732.'

p. 104, l. 26, after 'first,' insert '25 April 1753.'

p. 104, l. 26, after 'Levi,' insert 'She died *s.p.* 17 March 1754.'

p. 104, l. 26, delete 'and,' and insert 'He married.'

p. 104, l. 26, after 'secondly,' insert ' 4 October 1770.'

p. 104, l. 27, after 'Portsmouth,' insert 'She died 29 May 1813, having thrown herself out of the window in the house of her daughter, Mrs. Williams, 39 Somerset Street, Portman Square. They had seven children, of whom four came of age (*Notes and Queries*, 10 S. ix. 449; x. 38).'

p. **104**, l. 28, delete 'and left,' and insert 'By his second wife he had issue :—'

p. **104**, l. 29, after 'Gordon,' insert 'born 28 July 1775.'

p. **104**, l. 30, after 'Gordon,' insert 'born 9 May 1780, was in the Royal Artillery, and afterwards in the 56th Regiment. He was living in 1828 at Laverstock, Salisbury. For an account of the elopement of these two brothers with Mrs. Lee, see Bulloch's *Earls of Aboyne*, App.'

p. **104**, l. 31, after '(3) *Catherine*,' insert '(4) *Caroline*, died at Exmouth, 13 December 1801.'

p. **104**, l. 41, for 'CHARLES,' read 'GEORGE.'

p. **104**, last line, after 'Catherine,' insert 'born at Holyrood 31 March 1760, and died at Restalrig 5 June 1764 (Restalrig Reg.).'

p. **105**, l. 2, delete '26 May 1766,' and insert 'at the Castle de la Tour, in the Pays de Vaud, 23 May 1786 (*Rambles about Bath*, 317).'

p. **105**, l. 4, for '23 April' read '14 May (Reg. St. George's, Hanover Square).'

p. **105**, l. 20, for 'CHARLES' read 'GEORGE.'

p. **105**, ll. 11 and 12, delete 'Royal Scots, the 113th Regiment, and 3rd Foot Guards,' and insert 'the 22nd Foot and Grenadier Guards (*Army Lists*).'

AIRLIE

p. **106**, l. 23, for 'Kynmethan,' read 'Kinminethen.'

p. **111**, after l. 16, insert

'4. *Henry*, a natural son, had a dispensation to take orders and hold two benefices, 30 July 1405 (*Reg. Avenion.*, 320, 604). He was provided to the canonry and prebend of Tulynestyn in Aberdeen Cathedral, 19 August 1413 (*Cal. Pet. to the Pope*, i. 600).'

p. **113**, l. 22, delete 'or William Lord Seton.'

p. **113**, l. 23, after 'statement,' add 'He certainly married Isobel Forbes, who survived him. On 1 August 1489, she executed a revocation of deeds done by him in prejudice of her rights (*Aberdeen Burgh Sasines*).'

p. **114**, delete ll. 7 and 8.

p. **114**, l. 27, delete 'is known to have,' and insert after married, 'secondly, before May 1478.'

p. **114**, l. 28, after '1486.[7]' insert 'She was the widow of William, second Lord Graham, and daughter of William, second Earl of Angus, and by her he had a son, *Oliver* (*Reg. de Aberbrothock*, ii. 176, 300).'

p. **114**, l. 34, delete '*Walter*, stated to be,' and insert '*Oliver*, who was.' After Balfour, insert 'He married Felicia Fentoun (*Reg. de Aberbrothock*, ii. 176, 300, 390).'

p. **114**, note 5, add 'He was dead three and a half years before 2 May 1508 (Aberdeen Sheriff Court Diet Book, vol. i. at date).'

p. **115**, after l. 5, insert

'7. *Thomas* (probably by first marriage), bailie in a Sasine 8 July 1483 (Bamff Charters).'

'8. *Margaret* (by first marriage), married, contract 10 April 1482, to Gilbert Ramsay younger of Bamff (*Ibid*). She is incorrectly given in the text as belonging to the previous generation.'

p. **115**, ll. 6, 11, and 17, for '7, 8, 9,' read '9, 10, 11.'

p. **117**, l. 19, delete 'previous to the Reformation,' and insert 'before 15 May 1556 (See writ in Protocol Book of James Harlaw, f. 114).

p. **117**, after l. 29, add

'(2) *Janet*, married (contract 14 October 1572) to James Anderson, maltman, burgess of Perth (*Reg. of Deeds*, xl. 277). In 1577 she is called Thomas's daughter and heir, and there is mention of *John Ogilvie* of Easter Bogside, brother and heir of tailzie of Archibald, Thomas's lawful son (*Acts and Decreets*, lxxi. 311). His retour to Archibald was, however, reduced, February 1578-79 (*Ibid.*, lxxv. 25).'

p. **117**, l. 31, for '(2),' read '(3).'

p. **117**, last l., after 'James,' insert 'fifth.'

p. **118**, l. 20, after 'to,' insert 'Thomas, son of.'

p. **118**, l. 29, after 'husband,' insert 'and as his second wife.'

p. **118**, l. 30, delete '1574,' and insert '1 October 1578.'

p. **122**, l. 3, after 'Montgomerie,' insert 'daughter of Robert Montgomerie in Haltoun, and Euphame Guthrie, his wife (Brechin Com. Deeds at Forfar, 14th March 1594-95: cf. *Reg, Mag. Sig.*, 8 May 1601).'

p. **122**, l. 25, for 'instituting,' read 'substituting.'

p. **122**, l. 29, delete 'before 1588,' and insert '11 November 1581, with great solemnity and triumph, in Holyrood House.'

p. **123**, l. 8, after 'Newbigging,' insert 'styled second son in 1620 (*Reg. of Deeds*, cccxx. 41).'

p. **124**, l. 15, after 'died,' delete 'soon afterwards,' and insert 'in 1666 (*Reg. of Retours*, xxxix. 183).'

p. **125**, l. 3, for '*Helen*' read '*Elizabeth*.'

p. **125**, l. 3, after 'married,' insert 'as his first wife.'

p. **125**, l. 6, after 'good,' add 'She died in 1654, after a lingering illness (Oxenfoord Writs).'

p. **127**, after l. 30, insert

'(3) *Elizabeth*.

(4) *Helen*, married, at Edinburgh, 4 March 1759, to Roger Robertson of Ladykirk (Wood's Douglas's *Peerage*), with issue.'

p. **128**, l. 14, delete '1813,' and insert '1803. Testament recorded 5 April 1803.'

p. **129**, l. 8, after 'first,' insert 'on or before 31 May 1648.'

p. **129**, l. 13, after 'Inshewan,' insert 'She raised an action of divorce against her husband in 1798 (*Consistorial Processes*, Scot. Rec. Soc., No. 1133).'

p. **130**, l. 23, after '1835,' insert 'and was buried in the Canongate Churchyard.'

p. **130**, l. 24, after '1838,' insert 'at 6 Heriot Row, Edinburgh.'

p. **130**, l. 6 from foot, for '1838,' read '1831.'

p. **130**, l. 4 from foot, delete '*s.p.*'

p. **131**, l. 16, after 'Alderley,' insert note, 'Nature but rarely moulds such a nature in which knowledge, intelligence, and charity are so excellently blended and combined (Lady Dorothy Neville's *Reminiscences*, 156).'

AIRTH

p. **137**, l. 25, after '1612,' add note, 'In *Reg. Mag. Sig.* (30 July 1613, the date of this contract is given as 30 January 1610.'

p. **137**, l. 28, delete 'alive in 1683,' and insert 'died in 1687 or 1688.'

p. **137**, l. 5 from foot, after 'Bramhall,' insert 'Archbishop of Armagh.'

p. **137**, l. 4 from foot, after '*Eleanor*,' insert 'born 17 January 1661-62 (Parish Register, St. Peter's, Drogheda, Ireland).'

p. **137**, l. 4 from foot, after 'married,' delete remainder of sentence, and insert 'licence 15 February 1682, to Arthur, afterwards Sir Arthur Rawdon, Bart., and died 17 March 1710, and was buried at St. Andrew's, Dublin (*Complete Baronetage*).'

p. **138**, l. 6, after '*Archibald*,' insert 'baptized 25 April 1631 (Canongate Reg.).'

p. **138**, note 1. The reference is '*Reg. of Deeds*, DXXIV. 358.'

p. **138**, note 2, for 'lii.' read 'DLII.'

p. **139**, l. 22, for '1632' read '1633 (*Gen. Reg. Sas.*, xxxvii. 188, 191).'

p. **141**, l. 17, for 'charter' read 'warrant.'

p. **141**, l. 34, after 'married,' insert 'contract 13 December 1681, tocher 4000 merks (*Stirlings of Keir*, 172).'

p. **141**, l. 4 from foot, delete 'prior to 28 April 1677,' and insert 'in November 1661 (*Privy Council Decreta*, 25 June 1674).'

p. **141**, l. 3 from foot, after '1684,' insert 'for adultery with Robert Ross, younger of Auchlossen (*Edin. Com. Consist. Decreets*, i. 1).'

p. **142**, l. 1. *Note*.—The correct date of the second marriage of the Earl of Airth and Menteith with Katherine Bruce was 4 April 1685 (Edinburgh Reg.). It was solemnised by warrant of the Bishop of Edinburgh to Mr. Alexander Ramsay.

p. **142**, l. 25, after 'married,' insert 'in 1686 (*Privy Council Decreta*, 21 July 1691).'

p. **142**, l. 26, after 'issue,' insert 'buried at Arbuthnott, 19 April 1699.'

p. **142**, l. 4 from foot, for 'on' read 'in.'

p. **144**, l. 9, after 'Surrey,' insert 'her footman and the co-respondent in the divorce case' (*Consistorial Processes*, Scot. Rec. Soc., No. 1005).'

p. **145**, l. 19, after 'husband,' add 'with three other children :—'

ALBANY

p. **149**, l. 1, for 'six' read 'seven.'

p. 149, ll. 11 and 12, delete 'and, secondly, to Robert Stewart of Lorne, by both of whom,' and add

'4. *Joanna*, married to Sir John Stewart of Ennerme [Innermeath], as is shown by a commission from Pope Benedict XIII. to the Bishop of St. Andrews to dispense with the marriage, dated at Avignon 5 Kal. October Anno 3 (A.D. 1397) (*Regesta Avenionensia*, 303, f. 556). They had issue.'

p. 149, l. 13, for '4' read '5.'

p. 149, l. 14, 'delete 'before February 1407-8,' and insert, '8 May 1402' (cf. vol. vii. 242).

p. 149, l. 15, after 'secondly,' insert 'before 1406 (cf. vol. iv. 334).'

p. 149, l. 17, for '5' read '6.'

p. 149, l. 19, for '6' read '7.'

p. 150, l. 20, after 'married,' insert 'first, a lady whose Christian name was Joanna, but whose surname is not stated. She is referred to as his former wife in the dispensation, dated 9 June 1392, for the marriage of Murdac and Isobel (*Regesta Avenion.*, 269, f. 397). She may have been a Douglas, as explained in vol. v. 342 *n.* He married, secondly' (etc., as in text).

p. 150, l. 26, after '1421,[3]' add 'Robert had dispensation on 4 May 1414 to marry Euphemia Stewart, Countess of Strathearn (*Reg. Avenion.*, 344, f. 670), but the marriage did not take place.'

p. 150, l. 29, after 'papal,' insert 'dispensation on 5 September 1415, for a marriage with Euphemia Stewart, Countess Palatine of Strathearn, they being in second and third degrees from the common stem and in the third and fourth degrees of affinity (*Regesta Avenion.*, 335, f. 649). She had been contracted to his brother Robert. Walter had another' (dispensation, as in text).

p. 153, l. 10, after 'Breadalbane,' add 'He had another daughter, *Janet*, married to Thomas Charteris of Kinfauns, but divorced from him (*Acts and Decreets*, xiii. 129, 344).'

p. 153, l. 28, after 'Arran,' insert 'and had issue a son *James*.'

p. 153, l. 29, after '1542,' add 'Margaret Stewart survived Sir Patrick and became the wife and widow of David Ross of Balnagown, who died in 1527 (*Acta Dom. Conc.*, xxxvii. f. 180 (189)).'

p. 153, l. 3 from foot, for 'd'Bouillon' read 'de Bouillon.'

p. 154, l. 28, delete '8,' and insert 'contract 13 (*L'Art de verifier les dates*, ii. 372).'

ALTRIE

p. 159, l. 3, for '13 July 1594' read '18 March 1595-96 (Benholm Charters).'

p. 159, l. 10, for '1556' read '1566 (*Reg. of Deeds*, viii. 361).'

p. 159, l. 12, after '1584),' add 'She was divorced from him, and in 1617 was the wife of James Allardes (Slains Charters; see Riddell's *Tracts*, 114).'

p. **159**, l. 13, delete 'prior to 28,' and insert 'contract 25.'

p. **159**, l. 17, after '*Margaret*,' delete 'and secondly,' and insert 'John Erskine died 21 October 1592, and she was married, secondly, before 1 February 1596-97 (Benholm Charters).'

p. **159**, l. 18, for 'ninth,' read 'tenth.'

ANGUS

p. **167**, l. 10, for 'Richard, the son of a,' read 'the son of a Richard.'

p. **168**, l. 2, delete '1246,' and insert '2 December 1247, before which date she had married Richard of Dover, son of Richard Fitzroy, a natural son of King John. By him she had issue a son *Richard* and a daughter *Isabel*, afterwards wife of David, Earl of Athol (*Genealogist*, new series, xxii, 109).'

p. **168**, l. 10, delete 'in,' and insert 'before 8 November (Patent Rolls).'

p. **168**, l. 11, after 'issue,' add 'He married Elizabeth, daughter of Alexander Cumyn, Earl of Buchan. She died in 1369 (cf. vol. ii. 256).

p. **168**, l. 17, delete 'in 1325,' and insert '30 March 1325 and was buried in the Abbey of Newminster. He married, first, before 20 September 1303, Lucy, daughter, and in her issue heir of Sir Philip de Kyme of Kyme, co. Lincoln, by Joan, daughter of Sir Hugh de Bigod, Chief Justiciar of England; and, secondly, Alianore ——, who survived him and married, secondly, before 16 August 1327, Sir Roger Mauduit of Eshot and Bockenfield, co. Northumberland. She died 31 March 1358' (Article by G. W. Watson in *Genealogist*, N.S. vol. xxvi. p. 193).'

p. **168**, l. 18, delete 'and,' and insert 'Earl Robert.'

p. **168**, l. 25, delete 'in,' and insert '6 or 7 January 1380-81.'

p. **168**, l. 25, after 'without,' insert 'surviving.'

p. **168**, l. 26, after 'issue,' insert 'He married, first, Joan, daughter of Sir Robert Willoughby d'Eresby. She died 13 July 1350, and he married, secondly, before October 1369, Maud, only daughter of Sir Thomas de Lacy of Cockermouth. She survived him and married, secondly, before 1 May 1383, as his second wife, Henry Percy, first Earl of Northumberland, and died *s.p.s.* 18 December 1398 (*Genealogist, ut supra*).'

p. **170**, l. 24, for 'William' read 'John.'

p. **171**, l. 2, and note 1, 'This is the only known son of Earl Thomas. Douglas, followed by the *Complete Peerage*, gives him a son Thomas, Earl of Angus from 1361 to 1377, but his statement is founded on wrong premises.'

p. **173**, l. 7 from foot, for '1409' read '1405.'

p. **173**, l. 5 from foot, after 'third,' insert '13 November 1413.'

p. **174**, l. 5 from foot, for '1435' read '1436.'

p. **175**, l. 10, for 'three' read 'four.'

p. **175**, l. 10, after 'sons,' insert 'and a daughter.'

p. **175**, after l. 23 insert

'4. *Hugh*, who, in a Papal Bull of 7 June 1455, is said to be brother-german of the then Earl of Angus, in the twentieth year of his age, and in the second and third degrees of consanguinity with James, King of Scots (*Reg. Vaticana*, ccccIxxvii. 141). He had several provisions to canonries, etc., between 1449 and 1455, was archdeacon of St. Andrews in 1458 (*Reg. Mag. Sig.*), and rector of St. Andrews University 1466 (*Reg. of Papal Petitions*, 590, 116).'

5. *Helen*, married, first, to William, second Lord Graham; secondly, to James, first Lord Ogilvie of Airlie (see addenda to Airlie article).'

p. **178**, l. 5, delete '3 *Anne* to issue,' and insert 'The wife of William, second Lord Graham, was named Helen, and was a sister, not a daughter of Earl George.'

p. **178**, ll. 8, 10, 13, 17, 22, and 23, for '4, 5, 6, 7, 8, 9,' read '3, 4, 5, 6, 7, 8.'

p. **178**, l. 28, after 'father,' insert 'comma,' and add 'to whom he was served heir 12 April 1468 (*Harl. MS.*, 6443).'

p. **180**, l. 15, for 'at' read 'on.'

p. **183**, l. 1, delete 'before May 1468,' and insert 'on 4 March 1467-68.'

p. **184**, l. 14, after 'was,' insert 'Margaret, daughter of John Carmichael of Meadowflat, to whom and his children by her he granted a Bond of Provision 28 January 1553-54 (*Acts and Decreets*, x. 164). He married, thirdly.'

p. **185**, l. 2, after 'Keith,' add 'Agnes was married (contract 14 January 1571-72) to William Hay of Urie (*Reg. Sec. Sig.*, xli. 45). They were divorced before 1587 (*Reg. of Deeds*, xxviii. 125).'

p. **185**, line 5, after 'Katherine,' insert 'She was married to John Carmichael, Captain of Crawford (*Harl. MS.*, 6443).'

p. **185**, l. 16, delete 'in September 1522,' and insert 'between 10 September, when his will was executed, and 15 September 1522, when it received probate (Small's *Poetical Works of Gavin Douglas*, i. p. cxvii; *Scottish Historical Review*, ii. 63).'

p. **186**, note 4, after '149,' add, 'but see vol. iv. p. 406, where further details as to the Herries marriage are given.'

p. **188**, l. 23, delete 'in 1560,' and insert 'on 12 December 1573, when her liferent was reserved in a charter to her grandson (*Reg. Mag. Sig.*, at date).'

p. **192**, line 22, after 'first,' insert 'contract 26 June 1509 (Buccleuch Charter-Chest).'

p. **192**, l. 25, after 'Tudor,' insert 'whom he married 4 (or 6) August 1514 at the Church of Kinnoull (*Scottish Kings*, at date)' and.'

p. **192**, l. 27, after 'wife,' insert 'whom he married before 9 April 1543 (*Reg. Mag. Sig.*, at date).'

p. **193**, l. 6, after 'and,' insert 'by, it is said, a daughter of Stewart of Traquair.'

p. **193**, l. 4 from foot, after 'first,' insert 'contract 19 January 1567-68 (*Acts and Decreets*, xlii. 22).'

p. **196**, l. 6 from foot, delete 'in the beginning of 1587. In July,' and insert '12 July 1587, and in the same month (*Hatfield Col.*, iii. 268).'

p. **196**, l. 4 from foot, for 'seventh Earl of,' read 'eighth Lord.'

p. 196, l. 2 from foot, after '1583,' insert note, 'The exact date of Robert Douglas's death is doubtful. See *post*, vol. vi. 550.'

p. 197, l. 3, after '*Margaret*,' delete remainder of sentence, and insert 'who was served heir of line to her father 13 July 1590 (*Reg. of Deeds*, xlvi. 142A). She was alive in 1591 (*Ibid.*, xxxvii. 276; *Harl. MS.*, 6442).'

p. 198, l. 26, after 'Gavin,' insert 'styled of Raquarrall.'

p. 198, l. 32, after 'married,' insert 'first, contract 27 October 1598 (*Reg. of Deeds*, cccxxxi. 211) Jean, sister of Robert Menzies, burgess of Aberdeen, and widow of Gilbert Menzies of Auldquhat; secondly.'

p. 199, l. 1, delete 'who,' and insert 'entered Douai College in 1596 and afterwards went to Rome, where he graduated in philosophy in 1598 (*Records of Scots Coll.*, 7). He.'

p. 199, l. 12, after 'married,' insert 'contract 5 January 1567-68, (*Aberdeen Hornings*, 25 June 1584).'

p. 204, l. 26, delete 'in,' and insert '11 September.'

p. 205, l. 3 from foot, after 'Isabel,' insert 'baptized 21 May 1642 (Canongate Reg.). She was the third daughter by the second marriage (*Lanark Sasines, Upper Ward*, i. 134). She was.'

p. 206, l. 6, after 'daughter,' insert 'She died 8 January 1713.'

p. 206, last line, delete 'or about 15,' and substitute 'Tuesday 16 (MS. [1659] by his widow at Kilkerran).'

p. 207 l. 3, delete 'In,' and insert 'On 26 April.'

p. 207, after l. 10, insert
'2. *Charles*, baptized 9 February 1637 (Canongate Reg.).'

p. 207, l. 11, for '2' read '3.'

p. 207, l. 15, for '3' read '4'; after 'death,' delete remainder of sentence, and insert 'Baptized 1 April 1655, and buried in April 1656 (*Ibid*).'

p. 207, l. 17, for '4 and 5' read '5 and 6.'

p. 207, after l. 18, insert
'7. *Ann*, baptized 8 January 1650 (*Ibid*).'

p. 207, l. 19, for '6' read '8.'

p. 208, l. 11, after 'Dundee,' add 'On the abolition of heritable jurisdictions, the Duke received £5104, 5s. 1d. as his compensation for the regalities of Kirriemuir, Abernethy, Selkirk, Jedburgh Forest, Bonkle and Preston, Bothwell, Douglas and Dudhope (*Treasury Money Book*, xliii. 149, P.R.O.).'

p. 208, l. 15, insert at beginning of line, 'He was engaged to the daughter of widow Jack, a taverner in Perth, but this was apparently broken off (Lamont's *Diary*).'

p. 210, l. 5, for 'August' read 'April.'

p. 211, l. 2, delete 'in' and insert 'on 1.'

p. 211, line 6, after 'beautiful,' insert note, 'Her "beauty" was doubtful, but she was very free and outspoken, and quite a character. She was the last of the nobility to be attended by halberdiers when going about the country. When she visited, she left her dress behind her as a present. She left certain estates to Archibald Douglas and other heirs of entail to be called Douglas Support; and provided that the person succeeding should bear the name and arms of Douglas, with the addition of a woman with a child in her arms and a snake under her feet: but these have never been officially recorded. There was a picture at Douglas of her holding a medallion of Archibald in her right hand and a pair of scales in her left. On a pedestal the heads of Lords Mansfield and Camden, and, crouching on the ground in an attitude of terror, a figure with a mask in his right hand, supposed to be the Duke of Hamilton.'

p. **213**, l. 25, after 'Macdowall,' read '(*sic* in Lyon Register, but probably for Galloway).'

MURRAY, EARL OF ANNANDALE

p. **220**, ll. 12, 13, 'for John, Master of Maxwell,' read 'Maister John of Maxwell.'

p. **221**, l. 18, for 'sixth' read 'fifth.'

p. **221**, l. 22, for 'seventh' read 'sixth.'

p. **222**, note 13, for '218' read '281.'

p. **224**, l. 19, after 'married,' insert 'contract 2 January 1547 (*Acta Dom. Conc. et Sess.*, xxvi. 36).'

p. **226**, l. 9, delete 'Drumlanrig,' and insert 'Hawick.' See vol. vii. 129.

p. **228**, l. 11, delete 'in,' and insert '22 (Sir Thomas Hope's *Diary*).'

p. **229**, ll. 21, 22, delete 'and Lord St. John of Torphichen in the county of Perth.'

JOHNSTONE, EARL OF ANNANDALE

p. **236**, l. 25, for 'whom' read 'who.'

p. **239**, l. 10, after 'issue,' delete 'a son, Adam Scott,' and add 'two sons, *Robert* and *Adam*. Robert, the elder, was infeft in the lands of Rysholm, co. Ayr, as heir to his mother, 10 November 1541 (Sasine in Kelburn Charter-Chest). She had died in 1524 (*Acts and Decreets*, vi. 111, 26 January 1551). Robert died before 19 January 1549, when his brother Adam sold Wamphray, with his father's consent (*Reg. Mag. Sig.*, 24 January 1549).'

p. **245**, l. 31, delete '1576,' and insert 'in 1598, as she is referred to in a writ of 1 November in that year (*Reg. Sec. Sig.*, lxx. f. 90).'

p. **246**, l. 2 from foot, after 'will,' delete remainder of paragraph, and insert 'She married, first, John Carmichael, younger of Meadowflat; secondly, William Weir, younger of Stonebyres; and, thirdly, William Livingston of Jerviswood (cf. vol. viii. 371).'

p. **247**, l. 7, for '1570' read '1570-71.'

p. **248**, l. 7, delete 'at a date which has not been ascertained,' and insert 'about March 1543-44 (*Treasurer's Accounts*, viii. 267).'

p. **248**, l. 2 from foot, after '1577,' add 'She was married, secondly, to Alexander (Abernethy), sixth Lord Saltoun, and thirdly, in or before

1589, to William, son of Mark Ker, Commendator of Newbattle (cf. vol. vii. 412; v. 455).'

p. **254,** l. 25, after '1609,' delete to end of paragraph, and insert 'She was dead before 1624 (*Gen. Reg. Inhibs.*, 22 November 1624).'

p. **258,** l. 4, after 'residence,' add note, 'See a sonnet on him by Arthur Johnston in *Musa Latina Aberdonensis*, vol. ii. p. 46 (New Spalding Club).'

p. **258,** l. 15, after 'Carnegie,' insert 'They were married in the Kirk of Holyroodhouse, 25 February 1647 (Canongate Reg.).'

p. **258,** l. 16, after 'year,' add 'Her will is dated 4 July 1648.'

p. **263,** l. 8, after 'Annandale,' add 'But apparently he was buried in Greyfriars, Edinburgh, 30 July 1672 (Greyfriars' Burial Reg.).'

p. **264,** l. 16, for 'fifteenth' read 'eighteenth.'

p. **264,** l. 16, after 'issue,' insert 'Albert Johnstone Campbell, who died April 1907, the last male of the Campbells of Glen Saddell and Newfield, is said to have claimed through Lady Mary, as heir of line, the Annandale and Hartfell Peerages.'

p. **264,** after l. 29, insert 'There is a tradition that there was a daughter, Christian, who made a runaway match with James Willison, in Elvanfoot, first writing to him proposing marriage, and then riding with him to Edinburgh, where they were married. See a note on the family of Black of Over Abington by W. G. Black, Glasgow, p. 9. The name, however, does not appear in the Edinburgh Marriage Register.'

p. **265,** l. 1, for 'these' read 'the.'

p. **268,** l. 28, after 'Westerhall,' insert 'He was killed at Carthagena, 1741.'

p. **268,** l. 28, for '1772' read '1762.'

ARBUTHNOTT

p. **273,** last l., delete 'another son,' and insert 'his grandson.'

p. **280,** l. 13, after 'Ilk,' insert 'with issue (*Ninth Rep. Hist. MSS. Com.*, 192).'

p. **280,** l. 25, delete 'prior to February 4, 1576, when his,' and insert 'in January 1573. His.'

p. **280,** l. 26, after 'recorded,' insert '4 February 1576.'

p. **280,** l. 28, after '*James*,' insert 'Collector of Cess for Angus and Mearns (*Reg. of Deeds*, vii. 196).'

p. **281,** note 13, after '*Origines*,' insert

'In 1469 Guille Arbutnot was an Archer of the Scots Guard in France (Forbes Leith, i. 162).'

p. **282,** l. 30, after 'first,' insert 'prior to 5 August 1468.'

p. **285,** l. 5 from foot, delete '1626,' and insert '1 March 1642 (*Aberdeen Reg. of Inhibitions*).'

p. **285,** after l. 3 from foot, insert

'iii. *Mr. Peter*, designed brother german to Mr. Andrew Arbuthnott, heir apparent of Little Fiddes, on 6 January 1597-98, was pedagogue to Lord Thirlestane in 1607, obtained a Crown charter of certain lands in Lauderdale 1 April 1633 (*Reg. Mag. Sig.*), and died *s.p.*'

p. **285**, l. 2 from foot, for 'iii.' read 'iv.'

p. **286**, l. 1, after 'Fiddes,' insert 'married, first, Sara Strachan; and, secondly, Janet Gordon, who survived him.'

p. **286**, l. 2, delete 'by his wife, Janet Gordon,' and insert 'issue.'

p. **286**, l. 9 from foot, for '[11]' read '[10].'

p. **286**, l. 7 from foot, after '[11],' insert 'He was a merchant in Dundee. He was twice married, and died in 1690, leaving by his first wife, Janet Gordon, who died in 1680, James, Alexander, and Elizabeth, to whom their uncle Patrick was served tutor at law (*Retours*).'

p. **286**, l. 5 from foot, after '1651,' insert 'became a Writer to the Signet in 1678, and died 6 March 1704.'

p. **286**, l. 2 from foot, for 'and' read 'He.'

p. **287**, l. 32, for 'Robert' read 'Henry.'

p. **288**, l. 17, after '1532,' add 'He had letters of legitimation 15 February 1530-31 (*Reg. Sec. Sig.*, viii. 237).'

p. **290**, l. 7 from foot, delete '13 April 1558,' and insert 'in September 1553.'

p. **290**, note 7, delete note and insert '*Treasurer's Accounts*, vol. x.'

p. **292**, l. 6, after 'Andrew,' insert 'apprentice with James Dalziel, merchant and bailie of Edinburgh, 14 March 1610. He is.'

p. **292**, l. 13, after '(5),' insert '*Mr.*'

p. **292**, l. 26, after 'Arbuthnott,' add 'In confirmation as executor dative to his mother he is designed Mr. Robert Arbuthnott at the Kirk of Fordoun.'

p. **293**, l. 6, after 'secondly,' insert 'as his second wife.'

p. **293**, l. 21, for '1557' read '1557-58.'

p. **294**, l. 5, after 'first,' insert 'contract 8 October 1556.'

p. **296**, note 12, after 'vol.', insert 'xvi.'

p. **297**, l. 6, after '16,' delete to end of paragraph and insert '*Margaret*, married, before 1582, to David Ogilvy of Persie (*Reg. of Deeds*, cccxxi. 141; see also *Laing Charters*, 1053). She died 10 June 1614 (St. Andrews Tests., 25 June 1614).'

p. **297**, l. 21, delete 'Crown.'

p. **299**, l. 27, after 'Elizabeth,' insert 'eldest daughter (*Forfar Sasines*, ii. 72).'

p. **300**, l. 26, delete '20.'

p. **300**, l. 27, after 'recorded,' insert '31 May 1619 and.'

p. **301**, l. 27, after 'on,' insert '31.'

p. **302**, l. 12 from foot, for 'Torlairtoun' read 'Tortairstoun.'

p. **302**, l. 6 from foot, before 'Melville,' insert 'Richard.'

p. **303**, l. 16, delete 'born,' and insert 'baptized 4 April.'

p. **303**, l. 18, delete 'born 1657,' and insert 'baptized 20 October 1654 (Kinneff Reg., *ex inform.* W. A. Macnaughton, M.D.).'

p. **306**, l. 17, after 'died,' insert '13 August.'

p. **308**, l. 19, after 'peculiar,' insert 'She died 4 November 1692 (*Ibid.*).'

p. 309, l. 8, after 'Elizabeth,' insert 'died 16 April 1755 (Aberdeen *Com. Reg.*, 3 February 1768).'

p. 309, l. 11, after 'Ann,' insert 'died 15 February 1777 (*Annual Register*).'

p. 310, l. 12, after 'first,' insert 'contract 20 and 21 January 1687 (*Part. Reg. Sas. Aberdeen and Kincardine*, xii. 468).'

p. 310, l. 13, after 'secondly,' insert 'contract 8 September 1694 (*Part. Reg. Sas. Aberdeen and Kincardine*, xv. 113; *Gen. Reg. Sas.*, xci. 408).'

p. 310, l. 15, after 'Anne,' insert '(or Agnes)'; after 'married,' insert 'contract 20 and 25 November 1693 (*Part. Reg. Sas. Aberdeen*, xiv. 463).'

p. 310, l. 34, delete '*William*, who both,' and insert '*William Henry*, baptized 13 February 1691 (Canongate Reg.). Both he and his immediate elder brother.'

p. 311, after line 6, insert

'11. *Janet*, "sister to the present Viscount Arbuthnott," died at Prestonpans, July 1706 (Funeral Entry Lyon Office).'

p. 312, ll. 4 and 5, delete 'in 1710,' and insert '8, and was buried 10 May 1710 in the Abbey there (*Complete Peerage*).'

p. 313, l. 1, for '*prisc fideiæ*,' read '*priscæ fidei*.'

p. 313, l. 32, after 'married,' insert 21 April 1769.'

p. 314, l. 5, after 'married,' insert '27 December 1775.'

p. 314, l. 32, for '1808' read '1805.'

p. 315, l. 6, after 'had,' insert 'with other issue.'

p. 315, l. 17, for 'Thomson' read 'Morison.'

p. 315, l. 21, after '1888,' insert 'married, 21 November 1911, to N. D Beatson Bell, C.I.E.'

p. 315, l. 32, after 'Madras,' insert 'retired 1908. Married Gertrude Forbes, daughter of C. E. F. Nash, Barrister-at-law, with issue.'

p. 315, l. 36, for '1891,' read '1894,' and insert 'John Sinclair, born 1898; Donald Charles, born 1902; Hugh Forbes, born 1906.'

p. 315, l. 37, delete 'Margaret, born 1896,' and insert 'Anne, Eliza Mary. Mary Frances Clementina.'

p. 315, l. 2 from foot, after 'of,' insert '(1) James Vaughan Allen of Inchmartine; and (2).'

p. 315, last line, after '1902,' add 'without issue. She died 1904.'

p. 316, l. 3, after '1903,' insert 'without issue.'

p. 316, l. 24, after '1847,' insert 'He died 1906, unmarried.'

p. 317, l. 5, for 'wyverns' read 'dragons.'

ARGYLL

p. 320, l. 11, delete 'first.'

p. 320, note 2, for '204' read '203*.'

p. 321, note 6, delete 'Robertson's *Index*, 14,' and insert '*Cal. Doc. Scot.*, ii. 200.'

p. 323, l. 25, delete 'His only recorded wife is,' and insert 'He married, first, before 1303, the younger daughter of Andrew Crawford (*Cal. of Docs. Scot.*, ii. 1406); and, secondly.'

p. **324**, l. 22, for 'Robert, Lord Erskine' read 'Sir Robert Erskine.'

p. **327**, ll. 7 and 6 from foot, delete 'said to have been married, first, to John Macdonald, Earl of Ross,' and insert 'married, first, to John, eldest son of John, Lord of the Isles.'

p. **327**, l. 6 from foot, after 'Lennox,' insert 'Her first marriage is referred to in a dispensation for her second, dated 30 March 1373 (Theiner, p. 348, No. 700; cf. vol. v. of this work, p. 340).'

p. **329**, l. 11, after '326,' add '"Sir" John or Ian Campbell was rector of Kilmartin, and as "frater noster" witnessed, on 4 June 1414, a charter of his brother Duncan at "Innyschonelle" Castle (Argyll Charter-Chest).'

p. **329**, l. 20, after 'Lochwinnoch,' insert 'Kildalvan, Dunloskin.'

p. **329**, after line 29, insert

'6. *Patrick*, a priest, who, as vicar of Kilmartin, and brother to Duncan Cambell, Lord de Cambell and Lord of Lochawe, witnessed a charter at Inchconnell Castle, 20 November 1420 (Argyll Charter-Chest).

7. *Celestine*, who, along with his brother Patrick, witnessed a charter 6 July 1403 (*Ibid.*).'

p. **329**, l. 30, for '6' read '8.'

p. **329**, after l. 32, insert

'9. *Mor*. On 30 May 1393 there was a mandate to the Bishop of Sodor to grant dispensation for the marriage of Hector Macgilleoin and Mor, daughter of Colin Cambel of Sodor and Argyll dioceses who had married although in the third and fourth degrees of consanguinity (*Reg. Avenion.*, cclxxii. 403).'

p. **329**, l. 34, delete 'sometimes called Neil.'

p. **331**, l. 5 from foot, after 'secondly,' insert '(under dispensation of date 17 January 1422-23, they being in the second and third degrees of affinity and third and fourth of consanguinity (*Cal. Papal Letters*, vii. 259).'

p. **331**, l. 2 from foot, delete 'born *c.* 1406.'

p. **331**, note 9, for '187,' read 'p. clxxvii.' and add 'Marcellina was still alive in February 1419-20, when she and her husband were granted the privilege of a portable altar (*Cal. Papal Letters*, vii. 336).'

p. **332**, l. 20, after '1440,' add 'probably before 1439.'

p. **332**, ll. 23 and 24, delete 'this last unless she was a natural daughter,' and insert 'of either of these marriages. He probably did marry Mariota of the Isles, daughter of Sir Donald, Lord of the Isles and Ross, as, on 13 February 1419-20, the Pope granted a dispensation for their union, as though they were betrothed they could not marry without his permission (*Ibid.*, vii. 151). She is probably the Mariota of the Isles, who about 1439 married Alexander Sutherland of Dunbeath (*The Thanes of Cawdor*, 16).'

p. **334**, l. 2 from foot, for '*Margaret*,' read '*Marion*.'

p. **334**, l. 2 from foot, delete 'after 1469,' and insert 'contract dated at

Edinburgh 14 September 1469, when she was twelve years of age; 1000 merks in tocher, one of the largest of the time (MS. *penes* Editor). They were certainly married before 23 April 1475, when they had a grant of lands in Midlothian from his grandfather, the first Lord Seton.'

p. **334**, l. 2 from foot, after 'George,' insert 'second.'

p. **335**, ll. 2 and 3, delete 'generally said to have been executed in his father's lifetime, 1490,' and insert 'before 5 March 1478-79, on which date he granted a discharge of part of her tocher to the Earl (Argyll Charter-Chest).'

p. **335**, l. 5, 'On 14 September 1469 Helen is styled second daughter (*Harl. MSS.*, 4693, f. 9a, printed in the *Family of Seton*, ii. 845). She was living 23 January 1528-29 (*Complete Peerage*).'

p. **335**, l. 6, for 'June' read 'September.'

p. **335**, after l. 6 insert

'6. *Margaret*, married to Patrick Buchanan, younger of Buchanan, tocher 600 merks. The marriage-contract, dated at Stirling 22 June 1486, bears that my lord shall pay so much of this sum at Michaelmas "if he may gudlie gett it" (*Third Rep. Hist. MSS. Com.*, 390; Fraser's *Lennox Book*, ii. 127, 128; Argyll Charter-Chest).'

p. **335**, ll. 7, 9, 13, and 16, for '6, 7, 8, 9,' read '7, 8, 9, 10.'

p. **335**, l. 18, after 'Maclean,' add 'Either this Catherine or another daughter of the same name, and styled "second dochter," was contracted at Stirling, 6 February 1464-65, to James Haldane, eldest son and heir of John Haldane of Gleneagles, it being provided that if she died he should have any younger daughter of the Earl (Argyll Charter-Chest).'

p. **336**, l. 7, after '1511,' insert 'He married, first, Jonet, daughter of James Stewart, Sheriff of Bute, from whom he was divorced (cf. vol. ii. of this work, 288).'

p. **336**, l. 7, delete 'an only child,' and insert 'a son *John*, who, as son and heir of the deceased Archibald Campbell of Skipinche, had in 1542 (*Reg. Sec. Sig.*, xvi. f. 33) an order from the King under the Privy Seal for the restoration of his father's property. His superior alleged that he had no title to the lands because his father had not died at the faith and peace of the King inasmuch as being in ward in the Castle of Edinburgh he broke out of it and rendered null an order of the King for his enlargement. John married Marion Montgomery, daughter of Hugh Montgomery of Hazelhead, widow of Thomas Crawford of Auchinames and of William, second Lord Sempill (cf. vol. vii. of this work, 535). Archibald Campbell had also.'

p. **336**, l. 28, for 'fourth' read 'fifth.'

p. **336**, l. 32, after 'John' insert 'Stewart.'

p. **336**, l. 33, after 'died,' insert 'before.'

p. **336**, l. 35, after 'married,' insert 'before 10 November 1522 (when she is called Moir).'

p. **336**, l. 35, delete 'of that Ilk,' and insert 'of Inveryne (*ex inform.* John Macgregor, W.S.).'

p. **337**, delete ll. 10 and 11, and accompanying note, and insert 'This Earl, or possibly his father, had another daughter, married to Iain "Brayach" M'Iain of Ardnamurchan, with issue. His eventual heiress, Mariota M'Iain, in 1538 resigned her lands ln favour of Archibald, fourth Earl of Argyll, and to this deed her seal, showing the Campbell arms of her mother impaled with those of Ardnamurchan, is appended (Argyll Charter-Chest).'

'He also had two other daughters, *Katherine* and *Elizabeth*, as on 27 March 1501 a marriage-contract was entered into at Edinburgh between George, Earl of Huntly, and Alexander, Lord Gordon, on the one part, and Archibald, Earl of Argyll, on the other, whereby Alexander's son and apparent heir George Gordon (whose existence has been previously unknown) was to marry which of the two best pleased him, whilst Colin, third Earl, was to marry either Janet or Margaret Gordon. He did marry the former, but George Gordon must have died young, and his projected marriage did not take place (Argyll Charter-Chest).'

p. **337**, last line, delete 'towards the end of,' and insert '9 October (Chronicle of Fortingall).'

p. **338**, l. 21, after 'first,' insert 'James Stewart, Sheriff of Bute, but her marriage must have been annulled (*Acts and Decreets*, vi. 474). She was married, secondly.'

p. **338**, l. 24, 'after 'Glen,' delete 'secondly,' and insert 'He died in 1565, and she married, thirdly.'

p. **338**, l. 26, after 'captivity' insert 'Her legitimacy is doubtful; she is called "base sister" to the Earl of Argyll (*State Papers, Ireland*, 296).'

p. **340**. l. 9, after 'Maclean,' insert 'contract dated 12 March 15— -6, year illegible, but perhaps 1545-46; in it her father is styled Hector Maclean of Doward, and it appears she married the Earl to appease the great feud between her house and his (Argyll Charter-Chest).'

p. **340**, l. 10, after 'her,' insert 'She is stated to have married, secondly, Callough O'Donell, Lord of Tyrconnel, and to have been taken prisoner with him by John O'Neill prior to 30 May 1561 (*Carew State Papers*, 1515-74, p. 314; *Calendar of State Papers, Ireland*, 172; cf. also *Irish Statutes*, i. 323, 324; *Carew Papers*, fifth series, 204, 209). To O'Neill she bore two sons (*Misc.* Maitland Club, pt. I.), and her kinsmen, the Macleans, endeavoured to get her released (*State Papers, Ireland*, 29 September 1562). After O'Neill's death she returned to Scotland, married John Stewart of Appin (writ in Reg. Ho., Edinburgh, No. 2352, where she is styled Katherine M'Lane, Countess of Argyll), and died not many years prior to 1595.'

p. **340**, l. 13, after '1575,' insert 'The Earl had another natural son, *John*, who was Provost of the Collegiate Church of Kilmun. In a charter of 14 November 1566 the fifth Earl calls him his brother (Argyll Charter-Chest); a third natural son, *Archibald*, was the progenitor of the Glendaruel family.'

p. **342**, l. 30, for '5 July,' read '1 July (*Eleventh Rep. Hist. MSS. Com.*,

Duke of Hamilton's MS., App. vi. 54), and after '1553,' insert 'bearing to be in fulfilment of another contract of 10 December 1538, when both parties must have been infants (Moray Writs).'

p. 343, l. 1, after 'dying,' insert '7 January 1587-88 (Edin. Tests., 26 March 1588).'

p. 343, l. 5, after 'Glencairn,' delete 'but had no issue by her,' and insert 'and had a son, who died at birth (30 June 1574, *Cal. of Scottish Papers*, v. 13).'

p. 343, l. 10, delete from '1. *John*, to end of sentence (see corrigenda on p. 340).'

p. 343, l. 12, for '2' read '1.'

p. 343, l. 20, after 'Earl,' insert 'He was aged fifteen in 1573, when he was a hostage in England. On 18 June 1592 he granted a precept at Stirling, in which he is styled Lord of Craignish, and his mother's name Beatrix Campbell is mentioned (Argyll Charter-Chest; *Acts and Decreets*, cxvii. 346).'

p. 343, ll. 21 and 24, for '3' and '4,' read '2' and '3.'

p. 343, l. 31, for 'a daughter,' read 'two daughters, *Jean* (styled sister's daughter of Colin, Earl of Argyll) and.'

p. 344, l. 6, for '5' read '4'; after 'will,' insert 'She was married, before 6 June 1590, to Iain Macfarlane, fiar of Arrochar, who then granted a discharge to the seventh Earl for the complete tocher payment of £500 (Argyll Charter-Chest).'

p. 345, l. 28, after 'age,' insert 'They had a previous contract 21 February 1547-48 (*Acta Dom. Conc. et Sess.*, xxvi. 35).'

p. 345, l. 28, after 'secondly,' insert 'between May 1571 and 26 February 1571-72 (*Complete Peerage*).'

p. 345, last line, after 'who,' insert 'chose curators 5 July 1592, the next-of-kin on father's side being John, Bishop of the Isles, and Archibald Campbell of Lochnell, and on mother's side George, Earl Marischal, and Robert, Lord Altrie (*Acts and Decreets*, cxxxvii. 349). He.'

p. 346, after l. 5 insert
'4. *Jean* (*Acts and Decreets*, lxxi. 95).'

p. 349, l. 4, after 'faith,' insert note, 'Alexander Craig wrote the following lines on the Earl becoming a Roman Catholic:—

"Now Earl of Guile and Lord Forlorn then goes,
Quitting the Prince to serve his foreign foes,
No faith in plaids, no trust in Highland trews,
Cameleon-like they change to many hues."

(*Staggering State*).'

p. 349, l. 14, after '1638,' add, 'Will dated 9 October, proved 29 November 1638 (Somerset House Wills, *ex inform.* Hon. Vicary Gibbs).'

p. 349, l. 15, delete 'before October 1594,' and insert '24 July 1592.'

p. 349, l. 24, for '1659,' read '1649.'

p. 349, l. 25, delete 'in 1611,' and insert 'Contract 24, 25, and 27 May 1611 (*Reg. of Deeds*, cci. 230).'

p. **349**, l. 29, after 'first,' insert 'contract dated 1624 (*Reg. Mag. Sig.*, as in note).'

p. **349**, l. 29, for 'Robert,' read 'John.'

p. **349**, l. 32, for 'September,' read 'February (Edinburgh Marriage Reg.).'

p. **349**, note 4, delete '*The Complete Peerage* gives the date of the marriage as 1628.'

p. **349**, last line, insert bracket after '1617.'

p. **350**, l. 8, after 'had,' insert 'by her, who died 12 January 1635.'

p. **350**, l. 9, delete 'born 1611.'

p. **350**, l. 9, after 'Chapel Royal,' insert '25 September 1610 (*Reg. of Chapel Royal*).'

p. **350**, l. 11, the reference number [3] should be inserted after 'sponsors,' and deleted from the next line.

p. **350**, note 6, delete '*Ibid.*', and insert 'Check-book *ut sup.*'

p. **350**, ll. 15, 16, delete 'after 21 September 1644,' and insert 'in France about 15 September 1645 (*Complete Peerage*).'

p. **350**, l. 17, delete 'and 9'; delete from 'and,' down to end of paragraph and relative notes, and insert 'born at Ashley House, Waltham, Surrey, 14 November 1611, died young (List of Children of seventh Earl by his second wife, from a document in his own handwriting).'

p. **350**, after l. 22, insert

'9 and 10. *Frederick* and *Charles*, evidently the twins christened at Somerset House, 31 December 1616, for whom Queen Anne and Prince Charles stood sponsors (List., *ut sup.*). Charles died young. Frederick may have been the son who died 1636, having been "in warrs."

11. *Charles* (*secundus*), born at Stirling about 1618; died before 1636 (List, *ut sup.*).

12. *Eugene*, born in the winter of 1619 at Brussels; died before 1636.

13. *Charles* (*tertius*), born in St. Martin's Lane, London, about 1629, and died young before 1636.'

p. **350**, l. 23, for '10' read '14.'

p. **350**, l. 23, after '*Mary*,' insert 'born in Brussels about 1622 (List, *ut sup.*).'

p. **350**, l. 25, for '11' read '15.'

p. **350**, l. 28, after '1694,' insert 'as an Augustinian Canoness, under the name of Isabelle Claire d'Arguille. She is not mentioned in her father's list of his children.'

p. **350**, l. 29, for '12' read '16.'

p. **350**, l. 29, after 'Victoria,' insert 'born at Brussels 1627 (List, *ut sup.*). "A very fine lady," she.'

p. **350**, l. 31, after 'sister,' insert 'She is mentioned as "dead lately" in a letter of 9 August 1694 (*Letters from James, Earl of Perth*, Camden Society, 40).'

p. **350**, l. 32, for '13' read '17.'

p. **350**, l. 32, after '*Barbara*,' insert 'born at Brussels about 1624.'

p. **350**, l. 33, after 'Brussels,' insert 'afterwards in a nunnery at

Louvain, where she was known in religion as Barbara Meliora Campbell.'

p. **350**, l. 33, after 'yearly,' insert 'She died before 9 August 1694 (Letter, *ut cit.*).'

p. **350**, l. 34, for '14' read '18.'

p. **350**, l. 34, delete '1619,' and insert 'at Fisher's Folly in S. Botolph's, Bishopsgate, and christened 6 December 1614.'

p. **350**, after l. 37 insert—

'The following additional daughters are also mentioned in their father's list

19. *Elizabeth*, born at Brussels 1621.

20. *Constance*, born at Brussels about 1625 or 1626. Became a Benedictine nun as Anne Constance d'Arguille.

21. A daughter, born at Leith in Scotland, who died unbaptized, 1617.'

p. **351**, after l. 3, insert 'The Earl had also a natural daughter Anna, married, first, as his second wife, to Sir Donald Campbell, Baronet, of Ardnamurchan, who died 1651; and, secondly, in or before 1652, to Alexander Campbell of Inverliver; both are named in a bond dated 1652 (Argyll Charter-Chest).'

p. **351**, l. 10, after '1623,' insert 'He chose curators 27 March 1622, the next-of-kin on the father's side being Colin Campbell of Lundie, Alexander Campbell of Lochenzell, Colin Campbell of Kirktowchmachill, and Sir John Campbell of Calder, on mother's side William, Earl of Morton, and Sir Archibald Douglas of Killour (*Acts and Decreets*, ccclìv. 270).'

p. **360**, l. 20, delete 'who,' and insert 'eldest, not second son, was born at Roseneath, 14 December 1668, and (see a curious attestation to his having been baptized, a fact which was doubted, *Scottish Antiquary*, i. 13).'

p. **360**, l. 23, after 'married,' insert 'as his second wife (contract 11 April 1694).'

p. **360**, l. 25, after '1744,' insert 'leaving eight sons and seven daughters.'

p. **360**, l. 29, after '*Jean*,' add 'married in 1700 to George Maxwell of Dalswinton, and had issue (*Decreets* (Mackenzie), 21 January 1747; Fraser's *Maxwells of Pollok*. i. 453).'

p. **361**, l. 1, after 'marriage,' read 'Admitted advocate in 1704.'

p. **361**, l. 7, after 'unmarried,' delete 'probably before 1660,' insert 'and died insane at Inveraray after 29 January 1712, at a great age. She is said to have fallen into a melancholy on account of King Charles II. having refused to marry her. She was kept at Dunoon Castle.'

p. **361**, l. 17, delete 'before 19 October 1663,' and relative note, and insert 'at Edinburgh 1691, unmarried (*ex inform.* Niall D. Campbell, Esq.).'

p. **366**, l. 2 from foot, after 'Earl,' insert 'was contracted in his youth, about 1641 or 1642, to Lady Ann Hamilton, daughter of James, first Duke of Hamilton, and afterwards Duchess, with a tocher of 100,000 merks; but the marriage did not take place (*Eleventh Rep. Hist. MSS. Com.*, App. vi. 55). He.'

p. 367, l. 1, delete 'May 1668,' and insert 'in 1706, aged eighty-five (Willcock's *Scots Earl*).'

p. 368 l. 3, after 'outrage,' insert 'Miss Wharton ultimately married Colonel Brierly, who commanded a regiment of horse in the service of William III. (*Patrician*, v. 276).'

p. 368, ll. 9 and 10, delete 'at least one son.'

p. 368, l. 10, after '*Charles*,' insert 'born 20 March 1703 (Canongate Reg.).'

p. 368, l. 11, after '1718,' insert '*John*, born 1 February 1705 (*Ibid.*).'

p. 368, l. 11, for 'two' read 'three.'

p. 368, l. 12, after '*Mary*,' insert 'born 25 October 1695.'

p. 368, l. 14, after 'Saltoun,' add 'and *Anna* (*secunda*), born 7 August 1700 (*Ibid.*).'

p. 368, l. 15, after '1657,' add 'Probably the Lady Mary Campbell, "daughter of Orgyel," buried in Greyfriars, Edinburgh, 12 January 1695 (Greyfriars Reg.).'

p. 368, after l. 21, insert

'8. *Margaret*, baptized 12 January 1692 (Canongate Reg.).'

p. 368, l. 28, after 'Argyll,' insert 'baptized 25 July 1658 (*Ibid.*).'

p. 370, l. 2, after '1703,' insert 'He left his estate of Charton, near North Shields, to his mistress, Mrs. Alison. The Duchess and her son disputed the settlement (see Maidment's *Scottish Elegiac Verses*, Edinburgh, 1842; also *Argyll Papers*, privately printed; and the privately printed part of Maidment's *Scottish Pasquils*).'

p. 370, l. 6, after 'married,' insert '12.'

p. 370, l. 14, after 'Anne,' insert 'born 12 January 1692 (Canongate Reg.).

p. 370, l. 21, delete paragraph, and insert

'4. *Margaret*, born 2 June 1690 (Canongate Reg.).'

5. *Katherine*, baptized 11 February 1697. Lady Katherine Campbell, daughter of John (*sic*), Earl of Argyll, was buried in Petersham, Surrey, 25 January 1699-1700 (*ex inform.* Keith W. Murray, Esq.).'

p. 371, l. 4, for 'Mackay' read 'Macky.'

p. 377, l. 1, after '*Caroline*,' insert 'born 7 November 1717.'

p. 377, l. 7, for 'Marquess of Townshend' read 'Marquess Townshend.'

p. 380, l. 26, 'after 'married,' insert 'Licence 19 January 1713.

p. 380, l. 26, delete 'the daughter of Mr.' and insert 'Anne, daughter of Major Walter.'

p. 381, l. 12, for 'Charles' read 'Archibald.'

p. 382, l. 6, for 'Philip' read 'Edward.'

p. 382, ll. 24 and 25, delete 'and had issue, and,' and insert 'who.'

p. 382, l. 25, after '1756,' add 'His widow died at Bath 3 December 1783.'

p. 382, l. 3 from foot, after 'issue,' add 'Jean raised an action of declarator of marriage in 1747 and got decree. A Margaret Cochrane, widow of Lewis Kennedy, Collector of Customs at Irvine, alleged marriage with Captain John at the seat of Lord Dundonald at Paisley, 3 July 1724; the claim, however, failed. Captain John and his wife had four children, the first, Elizabeth, being born 10 October 1726; the youngest, Jean, born 19 November 1729, was the only one alive at the time of raising the process (*Consistorial Processes*, Scot. Rec. Soc., No. 372).'

p. **382**, l. 2 from foot, after '*Primrose*,' insert 'born 1710.'

p. **383**, l. 2, after 'issue,' add 'She had a half-witted grandson who poisoned her porridge, but she did not eat it, and her cousin, Mrs. Elphinstone, took it instead and died, (*ex inform.* Lady Constance Russell).'

p. **384**, last line, delete 'divorced.'

p. **385**, l. 2, after '1760,' insert 'and from whom she obtained a judicial separation on account of cruelty.'

p. **385**, l. 3, for '24 July' read '25 June.'

p. **385**, l. 4, after '1807,' insert 'aged about seventy (Miss Berry's *Journal*, ii. 229; Lady Constance Russell's *Three Generations of Fascinating Women*). Miss Berry says she was burned to ashes in the only room in the house that was burned. It is supposed she took a fit (both her sisters died in fits) and fell with her head on the candle.'

p. **385**, ll. 5 and 7, '*Mary* and *Jane* are both said to have been illegitimate (*ex inform.* John Ferrier, Esq.).'

p. **385**, l. 14, after '1773,' insert 'but did not go out till 1775 (*ex inform.* L. Camphell Johnstone, Esq.).'

p. **385**, l. 27, for '*Anne*' read '*Louisa* (*ex inform.* L. Campbell Johnston, Esq.).'

p. **386**, l. 3, for 'George' read 'John.'

p. **386**, l. 5, delete 'died without issue,' and insert 'was a spendthrift, and shot himself at the Bedford Arms, Covent Garden, 15 August.'

p. **386**, l. 8, after 'fortune,' insert 'She died, 28 May 1828, at Upper Brook Street, London. Lady Caroline died 17 January 1803, aged eighty-two.'

p. **387**, l. 15, for '3 March' read 'Saturday, 3 February (*Notes and Queries*, 10th ser. iv. 384).'

p. **387**, l. 19, after 'she,' insert 'born 1733, at Hemingford Gray, co. Huntingdon.'

p. **387**, l. 24, for '20' read '21' (Miss Berry's *Journal*, i. 269).'

p. **387**, l. 31, after 'married,' insert 'without her parents' consent.'

p. **387**, line 35, after '*Maria*,' add note, 'For an account of her under the title of A Bygone Beauty, see Lady Constance Russell's *Three Generations of Fascinating Women*. Her birth is there given as on 28 January 1775. There is a portrait of her by Tischbein at Swallowfield; another by Anna Tonelli, and a drawing of her and her husband by Edridge. She was also painted by Hoppner and by Alexander Blackley.'

p. **388**, line 3, for '17 March' read '23 March,' and add note, Miss Berry (*Journal*, iii. 157), who was there, says the marriage took place at Lord Burghersh's house in Florence, he being the English minister there.'

p. **388**, l. 26, after 'offspring,' add note, 'A natural daughter, Catherine Black Campbell, was born April 1806. She was engaged successively to the Duke of Newcastle and the Duke of Marlborough, but married neither, and died in obscurity and poverty in a lodging house in Brompton Row about 1862 (See Lady Constance Russell's *Three Generations of Fascinating Women*).'

p. **391,** l. 1, for 'Assory' read 'Ascog.'

p. **391,** l. 20, after '1895,' add 'Lady Colin Campbell died in London 2 November 1911.'

p. **391,** line 28, after '1854,' add 'died at Edinburgh 6 July 1910.'

p. **392,** l. 22, for 'President of the Council for India,' read 'Secretary of State for India.'

ARRAN

p. **397,** l. 5, after 'Societie,' insert '"A lewd, fascinating woman." She died "miserablie" in September 1595 (*Wardlaw MS.*, Scot. Hist. Soc., p. 221).'

p. **397,** last line, after '*Elizabeth*,' add 'married, contract 9 December 1602, to Duncan Bayne of Tulloch (*Reg. of Deeds*, clxxxvii. 35).'

p. **397,** after last line, add
'5. *Marie* (*P. C. Reg.*, 2nd ser. iv. 403), married to Mr. John Finlayson of Killeith (*Reg. of Deeds*, cccvi. 293).'

p. **398,** for 'Fife' read 'Galloway.'

ASTON OF FORFAR

p. **401,** l. 1, for '1651,' insert '1615.'

p. **402,** l. 12 from foot, after 'had,' insert 'issue' and remove ':—'

p. **403,** l. 21, after '1763,' insert 'She died 11 August 1764.'

p. **404,** l. 14 from foot, after 'died,' insert '24 August.'

p. **411,** l. 29, after 'secondly,' insert 'apparently after 1680.'

p. **412,** l. 16, after 'married,' insert 'about 1 October 1698 (*Complete Peerage*).'

p. **413,** l. 22, for 'October,' read '9 November.'

CELTIC EARLS OF ATHOLL

p. **415,** ll. 14 and 20, delete 'Norwegian,' and insert 'Icelandic

p. **416,** l. 20, Same correction.

p. **419,** l. 9 of notes, delete 'and successor.'

p. **422,** l. 30, after 'house,' insert 'He was buried in the graveyard of the Franciscans at Haddington (*Chron. de Lanercost*).'

p. **423,** l. 22, after 'Ferneleth,' insert note, 'In the original charter among the Cupar Abbey writs in possession of the Earl of Moray, the Countess's name is written Forueleth, which is the Gaelic Forbhflaith, "perfect princess" (*ex inform.*, W. J. Watson, LL.D., Rector, High School, Edinburgh). Another Forveleth, "filia Keraldi," occurs about 1240 (*Reg. Episc. Glasg.*, No. 177).'

p. **425,** l. 13, for 'quarelled' read 'quarrelled.'

p. **425**, l. 4 from foot, after 'Chilham,' delete 'who,' and insert 'the granddaughter of Richard Fitzroy. (See *corrigenda*, p. 168, line 2, *supra.*) She died 18 March 1292, and was buried, 24 March, in the church of Canterbury, near the altar of St. Edward (*Hist. Works, Gervase of Canterbury*, ii. 300). She.'

p. **429**, l. 8, after 'manors,' insert 'On 16 November 1316 he had a pardon as David, Earl of Asceles (*Patent Rolls* [1313-17], 567).'

p. **429**, l. 22, delete 'before,' and insert 'between 8 February and.'

p. **430**, l. 18, after 'Atholl,' insert note, 'See *Archæologia Æliana*, 3rd ser., vol. iii.'

p. **433**, last l., insert after or, 'but the quartering for Atholl in the more modern arms is given as Paly of six or and sable.'

CAMPBELL, EARL OF ATHOLL

p. **435**, last line, after 'Atholl,' add 'Moray died 17 October 1346, and Joanna married, fourthly, dispensation dated 5 Id. November 1347, as his second wife, William, Earl of Sutherland (*See that title* and *Cal. of Papal Reg. Letters*, vol. iii.).'

p. **435**, at end of note 1, add 'Cf. also another copy recorded in *Reg. of Deeds* (Durie's Div.), 103, 9 Aug. 1704.'

STEWART, EARL OF ATHOLL

p. **436**, ll. 12, 13, 14, 15, and 16, delete from 'The' down to 'Crown,' and insert

'On 31 May 1367 King David II. granted a charter of the earldom to Robert's son, John Stewart of Kyle (afterwards King Robert III.), and Annabella, his wife, on the resignation of his father (*Exch. Rolls*, iv. p. clxx, where 3d is a misprint for 31st). He is called Earl of Atholl in a charter by Robert II. to Cupar Abbey (*Reg. Avenion.* ccix. 377). The Earldom remained in his hands.'

p. **437**, l. 14, delete 'May 1409,' and insert '8 June 1404,' adding note—

'He is described on the last-mentioned date as Walter Stewart, Earl of Atholl and Caithness, in a safe-conduct by the English King (Rymer's *Fœdera*, viii. 361; *Cal. Doc. Scot.*, iv. No. 656).'

p. **438**, l. 23, after 'known,' delete 'but,' and insert, 'though it must have been before 1 August 1404, when he had a dispensation to marry Margaret (or Elizabeth) Grahame, daughter of Sir William Grahame of Kincardine (cf. vol. vi. 218), though this marriage did not take place, and.'

p. **438**, l. 24, for 'her' read 'his wife's.'

p. **442**, l. 6, after 'Caithness' read 'She died 21 March 1518, and was buried with him (*Complete Peerage*).'

p. **442**, l. 12, delete 'before 1482,' and insert 'contract dated 14 October 1474 (Menzies Charter-Chest; cf. *Herald and Genealogist*, vi. 596).'

p. **442**, l. 18, after 'consanguinity [5],' add 'She was married again (contract

9 December 1529) to Ninian, third Lord Ross (vol. vi. 252; cf. *Acta Dominorum Concilii*, xli. f. 25).'

p. **443**, l. 14, after 'Ruthven,' add 'and, possibly fifthly, James, son of (Gilbert?) Grey of Foulis, but the only authority for this is Sir Robert Gordon in his *Genealogy of the Earls of Sutherland*, 106.'

p. **443**, l. 22, for 'Colin' read 'Kenneth.'

p. **443**, l. 31, after 'first,' insert 'before December 1533 (*Fourth Rep. Hist. MSS. Com.*, 536).'

p. **443**, l. 32, after 'Grizel,' delete 'daughter,' and insert 'granddaughter and senior heir of line (*ex inform.* Rev. John Ferguson of Aberdalgie; Rattray Writs in Dupplin Charter-Chest).'

p. **443**, note 2, 'The note in the Sutherland Book here referred to is wrong. It does not refer to the deed mentioned in the text of that volume, and the authority there quoted should be the seventh, not the eighth, Report of the *Hist. MSS. Com.* In that Report (pp. 711 and 713) there are two retours showing that Janet Campbell was wife of John Stewart, second Earl of Atholl.'

p. **444**, l. 4, for '1536' read '1556.'

p. **444**, l. 13, after 'Redhall,' insert as note, 'The marriage must have taken place before January 1545-46. Cf. Letter by Countess of Atholl 14th January 1545-46 (Gen. Reg. Ho. See also *Comm. Decreets*, iii. 347).'

p. **445**, l. 9, after 'Erskine,' insert 'She was living 15 August 1584 (*Complete Peerage*).'

p. **445**, l. 15, after 'first,' insert 'contract 24 December 1567; for 'sixth' read 'fifth.'

p. **445**, l. 24, delete 'about,' and insert 'in December.'

p. **445**, l. 24, after '1581,' insert '(contract registered 18 January 1583).'

p. **446**, l. 5, for 'James' read 'John.'

p. **446**, l. 6, delete 'and had issue,' and insert 'She married, thirdly, James Stewart, eldest son of James, Master of Buchan, son of John, third Earl of Buchan. By her first husband she had issue.'

p. **446**, l. 17, after 'Standenflat,' insert 'She died 19 July 1623.'

p. **446**, l. 20, for 'first,' read 'second.'

p. **446**, note 5, for '950' read '280.'

p. **447**, l. 15, for 'IV.' read 'VI.'

p. **447**, l. 20, after 'Leslie,' insert reference number [3] and semicolon.'

p. **447**, l. 21, delete reference number [3].

p. **447**, l. 23, for '1580' read '1582.'

MURRAY, DUKE OF ATHOLL

p. **454**, l. 2 of notes, for '1284' read '1319-33.'

p. **462**, l. 29, for '1562' read '1562-63.'

p. **462**, l. 31, after 'him,' insert 'and was still alive on 17 December 1577' (James Harlaw's Protocol Book, Gen. Reg. Ho., f. 223).'

p. **462**, l. 34, for '1596' read '1596-97.'

p. **462**, last l., for '1565' read '1565-66.'

p. **463,** l. 6, after '1599,' add 'He married, contract 20 and 22 January 1600, Agnes, daughter of Robert Bruce of Blairhall (*Reg. of Deeds*, lxxxiv. 354).'

p. **466,** ll. 22 and 23, delete 'He was living 28 May 1618,' and insert 'He was buried in March 1621 (Canongate Reg.), having married Katherine Preston (*Reg. of Deeds*, cxlii. 126).'

p. **467,** l. 4, delete 'Sir.'

p. **467,** last l., after 'married,' insert 'first.'

p. **468,** l. 3, after 'London,' add 'She married, secondly, Col. Patrick Robertson of Sir Patrick Livingstone's Regiment of Dragoons before 24 February 1694 (*Reg. of Deeds*, Mackenzie, lxxiv., 29 June 1694).'

p. **468,** after line 8, insert

'ii. *John*, baptized 31 March 1633 (St. Andrews Reg.).

'iii. *Elizabeth*, married to Simon Fraser of Inverallochy, with issue a son, Simon, baptized 3 May 1639 (*Wardlaw MS.*, Scot. Hist. Soc., p. 512).'

p. **468,** l. 9, for 'ii.' read 'iv.'

p. **469,** l. 29, after 'issue,' insert 'besides a son James, baptized 5 July 1580 (Perth Reg.), but who must have died young.'

p. **469,** note 12, add to note, 'The Dunfermline Parish Register, 4 February 1584-85, gives her name as Margaret, not Catherine.'

p. **470,** l. 8, after 'son,' insert 'born at Dunfermline 14 February 1584-85 (Dunfermline Par. Reg.).'

p. **470,** l. 26, for '*Catherine*,' read '*Annabella* (*Inverness Sas., Secretary's Reg.*, i. 139)'

p. **470,** l. 28, after 'married,' insert 'contract 27 January and 9 February 1607 (*Reg. of Deeds*, ccvi. 340).'

p. **471,** l. 21, delete 'before 30 January 1628.'

p. **471,** l. 22, delete 'in the Chapel of Tullibardine,' and insert 'at St. Margaret's, Westminster, 30 July 1627.'

p. **472,** after line 3, insert

'2. *Mungo*, baptized 23 February 1617 (Canongate Reg.).'

p. **472,** l. 4, for '2' read '3.'

p. **480,** l. 4, after 'time,' insert note, 'For a quaint medical certificate see Fraser's *Melville Book*, ii. 227.'

p. **480,** l. 16, The date of the Duke's death is given as 12 November in Maidment's *Scottish Elegiac Verses*.

p. **480,** l. 21, According to the last-mentioned authority the Duchess died 9 January.

p. **480,** l. 30, *Scot. Eleg. Verses* gives 1 September as the date of Tullibardine's death at Mons.'

p. **487,** l. 11, for 'fourth' read 'third.'

p. **491,** l. 9 from foot, delete '10 November 1786.'

p. **493,** l. 5, after '1789,' delete 'and,' and insert 'Both Lord William and his wife were buried in St. George's Cemetery, Tyburn (*Notes and Queries*, 10th ser., xi. 217, quoting F. A. Crisp's *Visitations*, vol. xv.).'

p. **493,** l. 6, after '1827,' insert 'he.'

p. 494, l. 30, for '8' read '4.'
p. 495, l. 15, for 'EARL OF STRANGE' read 'EARL STRANGE.
p. 499, l. 24, for 'uncle' read 'granduncle.'
p. 500, l. 7 from foot, delete '*Stewart.*'
p. 501, l. 8, delete '*Stewart.*'

BADENOCH

p. 503, delete pp. 503, 504, and down to 'Kilbride' on l. 22 of p. 505, and insert

'The traditional origin of the Comyns given by Sir Robert Douglas and other writers, and followed in this article, seems open to serious question. All that can safely be said is probably this:—the first of the family known in Scotland was William the Chancellor. He had three nephews, sons of a brother whose name is uncertain:—

'1. *William*, killed *circâ* 1144.

'2. *Richard*, who acquired the castle and honour of Northallerton as part of the settlement of his uncle's claims to the Bishopric of Durham.

'3. *Walter*.

'This Richard and his wife Hextilda had certainly four sons, John, William, Odinell, and Simon (as in text), and probably a fifth son David, and from them the various Scots families of the name appear to be descended.'

p. 505, after l. 22, insert

'6. *Idonea*, married to Adam FitzGilbert, with issue a daughter *Christian* (*Reg. Hon. de Morton*, ii. 4; *Origines Parochiales*, i. 189).'

p. 507, after l. 20 insert

'4. *Alexander*, named in two charters of his brother John in 1278 (*Chart. of Inchaffray*, pp. 100, 101, 291). He was taken prisoner at Dunbar, and afterwards liberated on mainprise to serve King Edward beyond seas (*Cal. of Docs. Scot.*, ii. 177).

'5. *Robert*, also taken and liberated as above (*Ibid.*). Slain at Dumfries along with his nephew the Red Cumyn (*Ibid.*, ii. 1747)'

p. 508, note 7, for 'lxvi.' read 'lvi.'

BALCARRES

p. 512, l. 9 from foot, for '23 February 1574' read '21 October 1572.'
p. 512, ll. 3 and 2 from foot, delete 'succeeded to the earldom,' and insert 'was created Earl.'
p. 513, after l. 3, insert

'8. *Jonet* (natural daughter), married, first (contract 13 March 1562-63), to William, son of George Marshall of Auchnacree, and secondly, before 22 August 1594, to David Jameson (*Reg. of Deeds*, ccxxviii. 458).'

p. 513, l. 21, after 'dated,' insert '1 and 2 (*Reg. of Deeds*, xi. 384).'

p. **514**, l. 6, for 'May' read 'March (*Reg. Mag. Sig.*, 19 March 1619).'

p. **515**,, after l. 3, insert

'2. *Margaret*, daughter of David Lindsay of Edzell, was married to Sir James Keith of Benholm, contract 13, 21, and 22 February 1618 (*Reg. of Deeds*, cccxxxvi. 394).'

p. **517**, last line, after '1639' add 'He married Margaret Elphinstone (Stirling Tests., 15 November 1625), without issue. She died in July 1625, within a year after her marriage, and names a brother Michael and a sister Marie in her will.'

p. **518**, l. 11, after *Margaret*, insert 'second daughter (Moray Writs, vol. iv. No. 52.

p. **519**, l. 1, delete 'before 31 January 1642,' and insert 'in March 1642.

p. **519**, l. 17, delete '11 June,' and insert '10 January (Lamont's *Diary*).'

p. **519**, l. 22, delete reference number [4], and insert it after 1643 on next line.

p. **520**, l. 3 from foot, after '1689,' add 'She died in the Canongate, Edinburgh, and was buried at Balcarres in March 1698 (Funeral Entry, Lyon Office).'

p. **521**, l. 2, delete 'in,' and insert '15 October.'

p. **521**, l. 7, delete reference number [1], and insert it after Kilconquhar, on line 5.

p. **522**, l. 6 from foot, after 'Wigtown,' insert 'She was divorced by him 7 December 1708 (*Consistorial Processes*, Scot. Record Soc., No. 162).'

p. **523**, l. 4 from foot, delete 'who,' and insert 'She was forty years his junior, and rejected his offer at first, whereupon he took to his bed, and became so ill that his life was despaired of. He made his will, by which he left half his estate to Miss Dalrymple, and she, hearing of this, relented, and married him. She.'

p. **528**, l. 3 from foot, after 'Hope,' insert, 'As a young woman, she was admired by Mr. Atkinson, a great army contractor, and a supporter of Pitt. He died, however, in 1785, leaving her a considerable portion of his fortune (Wraxall's *Posthumous Memoirs*, i. 120).'

p. **528**, line 2 from foot, after '*Margaret*,' insert '*Janet*' (Kilconquhar Reg.

p. **529**, l. 1, after 'banker,' insert 'son of George Fordyce, Provost of Aberdeen, who died at Hammersmith, 8 September 1789, aged sixty.'

p. **529**, l. 4, after 'issue,' add, 'Burges was an old lover of Lady Margaret, but monetary difficulties prevented their union, and she married Fordyce, a wealthy but rather elderly person, whereupon her sister Ann wrote her well-known ballad of "Auld Robin Gray," "Jamie," it is said, being James Bland Burges. The latter married, first, Elizabeth, daughter of Edward, first Viscount Wentworth, 19 June 1777. She died 25 January 1779, and he married, secondly, Anne Montoline, daughter of Baron de St. Hyppolite. He survived her, and then, Lady Margaret's first husband being dead, he married his first love, as stated in the text. . . . Fordyce, her first husband, was a reckless speculator, and ruined many other people besides himself. His firm of Neall, James, Fordyce & Downe failed in June 1772.'

p. **529**, l. 21, after 'sable,' insert 'all.'

BALFOUR OF BURLEIGH

p. 531, l. 25, after 'death,' add 'but it was previous to February 1499-1500 (*Acta Dom. Conc.*, ix. 101).'

p. 531, l. 27, after 'Treasurer,' insert 'He, or possibly his son Michael, also married, in 1476, Elizabeth, daughter of Douglas of Lochleven (*Harl. MS.*, 6433).'

p. 532, l. 20, delete 'probably other issue,' and insert 'at least another son, Robert (*Acta Dom. Conc. et Sess.*, i. 36).'

p. 532, l. 31, after 'Forrester,' insert '(who survived him, and was married, secondly, to James Pringle of the Tynnes) (*Acta Dom. Conc. et Sess.*, i. 36).'

p. 533, l. 22, after 'her,' insert '(who survived him, and was married, secondly, to Patrick Kinninmont of Craighall, contract 3 July 1579) (*Reg. of Deeds*, xvii. 263).'

p. 533, l. 24, for 'Michael' read 'Andrew (*Reg. of Deeds*, v. 515).'

p. 533, l. 25, after 'Montquhanny,' insert as note, 'From a writ dated 24 August 1568, it clearly appears that Andrew Balfour of Montquhanny was father of *Michael* (then deceased), *Gilbert* of Westray, *Sir James* of Pittendreich, *George*, Prior of Charterhouse, *John*, *Andrew*, *Robert*, and *David* Balfours (*Reg. Acts and Decreets*, xlii. f. 331).'

p. 536, l. 19, after 'secondly,' insert 'in the Old Kirk of Aberdeen, June 1604.'

p. 536, l. 22, after '1597;[8]' insert 'she also obtained a divorce from her second husband, Balfour, 24 March 1620 (*Edin. Com. Decreets*).'

p. 536, l. 23, for 'Blaney' read 'Blayney.'

p. 536, l. 24, after 'daughters,' add 'one of whom, *Anne*, married Archibald Hamilton of Ballygelly, etc., ancestor of the Hamiltons, Barons of Glenawley (*Gen. Reg. Sasines*, liv. f. 333; Burke's *Ext. Peerage*, 259).'

p. 537, l. 10, after '*David*,' insert 'baptized 1 September 1577. He was apparently named after David, eleventh Earl of Crawford. who was the first witness to the ceremony (Anstruther Wester Reg.). He was.'

p. 537, l. 20, after 'Collairnie,' add 'She was certainly granted the marriage of David Barclay of Collairnie, 13 August 1587 (*Reg. Sec. Sig.*, lvi. 2).'

p. 537, l. 21, delete this line and substitute 'Agnes Balfour, who married John Henderson of Fordell, is erroneously stated to be a daughter of Margaret Balfour, but she was a daughter of David Balfour of Balbuthie (*Reg. of Deeds*, lxiv. f. 406).'

p. 542, l. 7, after 'married,' insert 'contract 12 July 1591 (*Reg. of Deeds*, lxxxiv. 504).'

p. 542, l. 7, after 'of,' insert 'William.'

p. 542, l. 11, delete 'in,' and insert 'contract 30 August (*Reg. of Deeds*, ccxxii. 156).'

p. 542, l. 16, after 'Balfour, add 'being styled Sir Robert Balfour of Star during his father-in-law's lifetime (*Gen. Reg. Inhibs.*, v. 380).'

p. 544, note 3, add to note 'Charter to her as his future spouse, 22 February 1633 (*Gen. Reg. Sasines*, xxxvii. 275).'

p. **546,** l. 4, after 'married,' insert 'contract 3 July 1680 (Fife Sheriff-Court Reg. of Deeds, 10 July 1680).'

p. **546,** l. 8, after 'first,' insert 'contract 16 April 1684 (Gask Charters).'

p. **546,** ll. 10, 11, 12, 13, delete from 'The' down to '1684.'

p. **546,** l. 16, delete 'said to have been.'

p. **546,** l. 16, after 'married,' insert 'contract 28 September 1688 (*Fife Sasines*, xv. 427).'

p. **547,** l. 3, after '*Mary*,' insert 'baptized 7 July 1790 (Canongate Reg.).'

p. **547,** l. 9, delete 'Miss Robertson,' and insert 'Janet Thomson (Inverkeithing Par. Reg., 17 November 1705), niece of Andrew Thomson, minister of Orwell.' *Note.*—Stenhouse and she were proclaimed at the latter place, 17 November 1705, and were married on 6 December.

p. **549,** l. 27, after 'Laffrie,' insert 'or Lafriese (Edin. Mar. Reg.).'

p. **550,** l. 8, after 'married,' insert '8 April 1669.'

p. **550,** l. 2 from foot, delete '1670, or,' and insert 'after 4 October.'

p. **551,** l. 22, for '1784' read '1684.'

p. **552,** l. 7 from foot, for 'fifth' read 'fourth.'

p. **552,** l. 2 from foot, after 'Margaret,' insert 'born 4 October 1716 (Edin. Reg.).'

p. **553,** l. 22, after 'married,' insert '(proclaimed in the Canongate Church 12 October 1792).'

p. **553,** l. 25, 'He was sometime a merchant in China.'

p. **553,** l. 26, after 'married,' insert '13 February 1793.'

p. **553,** l. 27, after 'Glasgow,' delete 'and,' and insert 'By her, who was born at Killearn, near Glasgow, 13 August 1768, and died at Edinburgh in December 1851, he.'

p. **553,** l. 4 from foot, after '1817,' insert note 'For an amusing story of Laurence Dundas Bruce while a midshipman aboard the *Bellerophon* on the day that Napoleon surrendered see *Memoirs of an Aristocrat.* (by George Home), 218.'

p. **555,** l. 14, for '7 August' read '16 July.'

p. **555,** l. 20, after 'First,' insert 'on a rock.'

BALMERINO

p. **561,** l. 21, after '1612,' insert note, 'The evidence for the first Lord's death on this date is precarious: Calderwood's date, about the end of May, is more probable. At all events he was dead by 2 June 1612 (*Gen. Reg. Inhibitions*, 2nd series, iii. 344).'

p. **562,** l. 5, after 'first,' insert 'after 10 April 1589, when a testimonial was directed to Alva as to their having been proclaimed in Stirling on.'

p. **562,** l. 9, for 'another son,' read 'issue.'

p. **562,** ll. 10 and 11, delete 'and three daughters.'

p. **562,** after line 11 insert,

'3. *Alexander*, baptized 6 May 1603 (Canongate Reg.). He must have died young.'

p. **562,** ll. 12, 13, 14, for '3, 4, 5,' read '4, 5, 6.'

p. 562, after l. 15, insert 'Lord Balmerino had a natural son *Robert*, witness to a deed 4 June 1604 (*Reg. of Deeds*, cxix).'

p. 569, l. 7 from foot, delete '16,' and insert 'at Holyroodhouse, 15 (Canongate Reg.).'

p. 569, l. 3 from foot, insert

'1. *James*, born before 3 March 1673, to whom the third Lord Balmerino on that day disponed his books (Moray Writs, Box 40, No. 1124). This James must have died in infancy.' For '1.' read '2,' and on p. 570, for '2, 3, 4, 5,' read '3, 4, 5, 6.'

p. 569, l. 3 from foot, after 'eldest,' insert 'surviving.'

p. 570, l. 8, after '16 February 1692,' add note, 'This date is given by Wood but the marriage did not take place till after 30 April 1701, the date of the marriage contract (Earl of Moray's Writs), followed by a charter of same date made in contemplation of the marriage (cf. *Fife Sasines*, xx. f. 68).'

p. 570, after l. 12, insert 'One of these children was baptized at Leith 3 September 1674 (South Leith Kirk-Session Minutes).'

p. 570, l. 13, for '7 June' read '12 June (Edin. Mar. Reg.).'

p. 571, l. 4, after '5,' insert 'and was buried at Restalrig 9.'

p. 571, l. 7, after '1767,' insert 'She was buried at Restalrig 27 September (Restalrig Burial Reg.).'

p. 571, l. 8, for brother' read 'half-brother.'

p. 575, l. 5, after 'Tower,' insert 'The inscription on his coffin plate was "Arthurus dominus Balmerino decollatus 18 die Augusti 1746, ætatis sue 58" (*Historical Papers*, New Spalding Club, i. Plate xi.).'

p. 575, l. 15, after '1765,' insert 'aged fifty-seven, and was buried there.'

VOL. II.

BANFF

p. **8**, ll. 18 and 19, delete 'when her eldest son George is mentioned.'

p. **9**, l. 6, after 'thanked,' insert 'He was provided to the parsonage of Cruden by Pope Paul IV., 26 May 1555 (Slains Inventory).'

p. **13**, l. 18, for 'Demptsr' read 'Dempster.'

p. **15**, l. 18, for 'Tilbertie' read 'Tibbertie.'

p. **15**, l. 18, for 'Torfaulds' read 'Forfaulds.'

p. **15**, ll. 18, 26 and 31, for 'Oatlaw' read 'Outlaw.'

p. **15**, l. 29, for 'Monteoffer,' read 'Montcoffer,' and insert 'he.'

p. **18**, l. 14, after 'married,' insert 'contract 25 June 1635 (Forglen Writs).'

p. **19**, l. 17, after 'married,' insert 'contract 12 August and 2 September 1648 (Forglen Writs).'

p. **19**, l. 18, after 'and,' insert 'by her, who died in March 1708.'

p. **21**, l. 4, after 'annum,' add note, 'There was apparently an action of adherence by him against her in 1686 (*Edin. Consistorial Processes*, Scot. Record Soc., No. 40).'

p. **21**, l. 6, after '*Anne*,' insert 'or *Anna*, married to James Law (Forglen Writs).'

p. **21**, l. 10 from foot, delete 'and had by Helen Lauder (who,' and insert, 'having married, 11 January 1712, Helen, daughter of Sir John Lauder of Fountainhall. She.'

p. **21**, l. 6 from foot, after '1742' insert 'having had by her first husband :—'

p. **22**, l. 8, after 'London,' insert 'She died 31 January 1784, aged sixty-nine, and was buried at Cheam, Surrey.'

p. **22**, l. 13, after 'Navy,' insert note, 'An account of his outfit for Navy in January 1732-33 including "a lac'd hat," six "fine cheque shirts," six nightcaps, "a fair wigg," a silver hilted sword, and a prospect glass, is given in *The Genealogist* for April 1909.'

p. **22**, l. 29, after '1746,' insert 'He was buried, 10 May 1747, at St. Martin's-in-the-Fields.'

p. **22**, note 1, for 'Brim's' read 'Burn's.'

BARGANY

p. **27**, l. 19, after '1637,' delete 'By his wife,' and insert 'He married, first, Katherine, daughter of John Carnegie of that Ilk. She died 17 February 1595-96 (Edinburgh Tests.); and he married, secondly, in 1596 (Bargany MSS.).'

p. **27**, l. 21, insert full stop instead of comma after 'family.'

p. **27**, l. 21, for 'had' read 'left.'

p. **27**, after line 24 insert

'4. *Alexander*, who was in Germany in 1635 (*Reg. of Deeds*, DXIII. 340).

5. *Margaret*, eldest daughter, married (contract 11 January 1615, tocher 11,000 merks), to John (afterwards Sir John) Hamilton of Bearcrofts, eldest son of Sir John Hamilton of Grange (*Reg. of Deeds*, ccxciv. 293).'

p. **27**, l. 25, for '4' read '6.'

p. **27**, l. 25, after 'married,' insert 'contract 5 and 7 March 1619, tocher 10,000 merks (*Reg. of Deeds*, ccxciv. 302).'

p. **27**, l. 27, for '5' read '7'; after 'married,' insert 'in 1623 (Nisbet's *Heraldry*).'

p. **27**, ll. 29, 30, for '6 and 7' read '8 and 9.'

p. **27**, after l. 30, insert—

'10. *Jean*, married (contract 18 and 20 December 1632) to Thomas Hay of Park (Bargany MSS.).'

p. **28**, l. 20, for 'Elliott' read 'Alyth.'

p. **28**, l. 4 from foot, after 'married,' insert 'contract 1660 (Bargany MSS.).'

p. **28**, l. 2 from foot, after 'Grizel,' insert 'died May 1678 (*Ibid.*).'

p. **29**, l. 4, before 'December,' insert '28 (*Reg. of Deeds*, Durie, 29 January 1680).'

p. **31**, l. 8, for 'in' read 'contract 23 August (*Edinburgh Sasines*, v. 188).'

p. **32**, l. 5, after 'married,' insert 'as his first wife.'

p. **32**, l. 17, after 'issue,' insert 'Some years after Sophie Johnston asserted that she was married to Lord Bargany, and was accused of having suborned witnesses to prove her case (*P. C. Decreta*, 16 December 1684).'

p. **32**, l. 23, after 'first' insert 'about 1694 (Bargany MSS.).'

BARRET OF NEWBURGH

p. **35**, l. 10, for '17 October 1627' read 'before 18 July 1618.'

p. **35**, l. 15, after 'secondly' insert 'in August 1635 (*Cal. of State Papers*).'

p. **35**, l. 20, after '1664, dying 22 July 1674 (*Families of Lennard and Barret*, 402).'

BELHAVEN

p. **40**, l. 8 from foot, for 'Gairnie' read Gairnsay in Orkney.'

p. **40**, after l. 5 from foot, insert

'4. *Elizabeth*, married as his third wife, to Alexander, first Viscount Kingston (*Haddington Inhibitions*, xviii. 412).'

p. **43**, l. 16, after 'married,' insert '17 March 1653 (Edin. Mar. Reg.).'

p. **43**, l. 25, after 'died,' insert '30 May (*Scottish Elegiac Verses*).'

p. **44**, after l. 13, insert
'(6) *Rachel*, married to Sir William Weir of Blackwood, Baronet (Douglas's *Baronage*).'

p. **44**, l. 18, delete notice of Daniel Hamilton, and insert '*Daniel*, appointed Clerk of the Admiralty Court 10 December 1702, and died *s.p.* before 20 November 1717, when his testament was recorded in Edinburgh. He did not marry Mary Hamilton, as stated in the text, and probably did not marry at all. Mary was the wife of another Daniel Hamilton, a writer in Edinburgh, brother of Gavin Hamilton, depute-clerk of the Court of Session 1687-1714, and laird of Inverdovat, co. Fife. They had issue six children. Mary died 2 December 1717, and Daniel about 20 August 1718 (*ex. inform.* W. H. C. Hamilton).'

p. **44**, l. 25, after 'Edinburgh,' insert 'President of the College of Surgeons 1704-5 and 1710-11.'

p. **44**, l. 25, after 'married,' insert 'in September 1700 (Edin. Mar. Reg.).'

p. **44**, l. 25, delete 'died *s.p.m.*' and insert 'Testament recorded at Edinburgh 12 June 1713 (Edin. Tests.). He had a son *James* Hamilton of Swanston, who was served heir to his mother 9 April 1740.'

p. **44**, l. 32, after '1661,' insert 'married 16 March 1682 to Hew Dalrymple, Advocate, ultimately Sir Hew Dalrymple of North Berwick, Lord President of the Court of Session (Edin. Mar. Reg.).'

p. **44**, l. 7 from foot, after 'married,' insert 'as his second wife 25 August 1693 (Edin. Mar. Reg.).'

p. **46**, l. 9 from foot, after 'married,' insert 'proclamation 17 January (Edin. Reg.), contract 5 February 1697 (*Edin. Sasines*, lxvii. 318).'

p. **46**, l. 7 from foot, after 'and,' insert 'by her, who died 17 August 1707 and was buried at Stenton.'

p. **47**, l. 7 from foot, for 'third of Wishaw' read 'first of Wishaw.'

p. **49**, l. 6 from foot, for 'George' read 'James.'

p. **52**, after last line insert
'7. *Euphemia*, married to Col. Alexander Baillie (see p. 51).'

p. **59**, l. 10, after '1884,' insert 'married 29 March 1910 to William Michael Jamieson Martin, R.A.'

BELLENDEN

p. **64**, after line 18, insert note, 'Adam Bothwell, Bishop of Orkney, writing to Napier of Merchiston in February 1660-61, seems to say that two sisters of Sir John Bellenden, the Justice-Clerk, were married through his influence with two Sinclairs (Napier's *Memoirs*, 68).'

p. **65**, l. 9, after '1576,' insert 'aged fifty-six (*Foulis Account Book*, Scot-Hist. Soc., p. xliv).'

p. **65**, l. 20, after 'Fordel,' add 'and of Nicol Cairncross, burgess of Edinburgh (*Acts and Decreets*, xlix. 168).'

p. **65**, l. 23, after '*Mary*,' delete 'These both died young,' and insert 'who was her mother's executor before 8 July 1569 and she and her sister Catherine were both dead before 14 June 1571 (*Acts and Decreets*, xlix. f. 168).'

p. 65, l. 5 of notes, at the end of note 5 insert 'Katherine Bellenden is styled "spous to Robert Crag" in July 1541 (*Treasurer's Accounts,* vii. 463).'

p. 71, after note 11, add 'He appears to have been Treasurer by 30 February 1660-61. See original bond by Charles II. to him for £4000 (*penes* J. Mackenzie, Esq. Edinburgh).'

p. 72, l. 1, for '1602' read '1662.'

p. 73, l. 9, after '1707,' insert note, 'The following is a copy of the invitation to Lord Bellenden's funeral: "The honour of your presence to accompany the corps of my Lord Bellenden, my father, from his lodgings in Paterson's Land, near the Canongate foot, to his burial-place, the Abbey Church, upon Sunday the 3rd inst. at eight of the clock in the morning is earnestly desired by John Bellenden." Lady Constance Russell states that this was sent out in *November* 1706 (*Notes and Queries*, 10th series, vi. 54).'

p. 74, l. 11, after '*Mary,*' insert 'baptized at Edinburgh 4 May 1685 (Edin. Reg.).'

BLANTYRE

p. 84, l. 38, for 'William' read 'Alexander.'

p. 85, after l. 1, insert

'5. *Alexander* (*Reg. of Deeds*, ccclxvii. 393).

6. *Ludovic*, (*Ibid.*, 20 November 1622).'

p. 85, ll. 2 and 8, for '5' and '6' read '7' and '8.'

p. 86, l. 2, for 'Margaret' read 'Marie (*Gen. Reg. Sas.*).'

p. 86, l. 3, after 'Rowallan,' delete from 'sasine' to 'was,' and insert 'He granted a charter to her as his future wife on 24 September 1641, where she is designed Marie Muir, daughter of the late Sir William Muir of Rowallan, and Sara Brisbane, his spouse, and she had sasine 2 October 1641, but he died in that month. She married, secondly, in terms of disposition 14 May 1644, John Brisbane, younger of Bishoptoun, and is there designed relict of Walter, Lord Blantyre (*Gen. Reg. Sas.*, liv. 250). He was, etc.'

p. 86, l. 24, after '1690,' insert '"Grenok yr." writes to "the laird of Kelburne" 2 May 1676 about Lord Blantyre then apparently dying in Bute. Asks Kelburne to see him buried and secure the bed clothes and drugget. Complains of the neglect of many friends. He probably died of smallpox (*ex inform.* Col. the Hon. R. E. Boyle).'

p. 88, l. 21, after 'married,' insert 'in 1725 (Dunbar's *Social Life in Former Days*, 121).

p. 88, l. 4 from foot, after 'married,' add note 'He was reported in 1725 as about to be married to Lady Catherine Cochrane, afterwards Lady Galloway (*Ibid.*, 119).'

BORTHWICK

p. 95, l. 20, after 'him' add note, 'On 1 May 1411 a dispensation was issued for the marriage of William Borthwick and Beatrice Sinclair, but there is no clue as to which William Borthwick is meant (*Reg. Aven.*, 337,

f. 170). He had a daughter, Janet Borthwick, for whose marriage to Adam Hepburn, lord of Hailes, a Papal dispensation was granted on 2 November 1411 (*Reg. Aven.*, 339, f. 549).'

p. **99**, note 7, add 'He was the son and heir of David Borthwick, burgess of Haddington (*Twelfth Rep. Hist. MSS. Com.*, App. viii. 112).'

p. **100**, l. 3, after 'married,' insert 'first.'

p. **100**, l. 4, after 'and,' insert 'secondly, in or before 1625, Helen Preston, widow of Henry Forrester of Corstorphine (cf. vol. iv. 90). He.'

p. **100**, l. 18, after 'married,' delete 'Janet Lies,' and insert 'contract 25 January 1622, Janet, eldest daughter of William Leyis, merchant burgess of Edinburgh (*Reg. of Deeds*, cccxciii. 95).

p. **103**, l. 28, after '1659,' insert 'chaplain of John, Lord Borthwick, 1667 (*Justiciary Records*, Scot. Hist. Soc., xlviii. 245, 251).'

p. **105**, l. 11, add 'died 12 July 1907.'

p. **106**, l. 12, for 'M. L. L.' read 'H. L. L.'

p. **107**, l. 6, for 'Cairnsmuir' read 'Cairnmuir.'

p. **107**, after l. 18, insert—

'*e. Beatrice*, contracted, about September 1556, to John, son of William Lithgow of Drygrange (Protocol Book of Gilbert Grote, f. 20).'

p. **107**, after l. 25 insert—

'6. *Cristine*, named with her sister Catherine in a letter under the Privy Seal 21 May 1502 (*Reg. Sec. Sig.*, i. 832).'

p. **107**, lines 26, 27, for '6, 7' read '7, 8.'

p. **108**, l. 24, for '28 November 1528,' read 15 December 1530 (*Acta Dom. Conc. et Sess.*, iii. 152). His marriage with Mariot Seton was annulled by the Pope.'

p. **108**, l. 25, for 'his widow' read 'Mariot Seton.'

p. **108**, l. 26, after 'Eglinton,' insert 'whom she survived, and married, thirdly, Alexander Graham of Wallaston (cf. vol. iii. p. 439).'

p. **109**, l. 10, after 'married,' insert 'contract 28 May 1538 (*Acts and Decreets*, xliv. 159).'

p. **109**, l. 24, for 'in March' read '27 February.'

p. **110**, l. 16, for 'in March' read '28 March' (Retour of his son, Canongate Court Book, 31 December 1573).'

p. **111**, l. 3, after 'Castle' add note, 'When, on 11 June 1567, certain of the nobility suddenly beset the castle and demanded the delivery of Bothwell, Lord Borthwick answered that he was fled to Dunbar (Birrel's *Diary*, 9).'

p. **112**, l. 16, for 'in 1582' read 'contract 26 October 1582 (*Reg. of Deeds*, xx. pt. ii. 309).'

p. **113**, l. 13, after 'William,' insert semicolon; delete 'and,' and insert 'he was of full age in July 1612 (*Reg. of Deeds*, cxcviii. 296), though.'

p. **114**, l. 2 from foot, delete between '13 March 1674 and 27 November 1675,' and insert 'in November 1674 (cf. Service of John Dundas of Harvieston, 28 January 1674, Arniston Writs, p. 157).'

p. **116**, l. 3, after '1772,' add 'and was buried there 9 September (St. Nicholas Burial Reg.).'

p. **119**, l. 4, after 'Freeland,' add 'and died 13 June 1910.'

p. **119**, l. 15, after 'Wigtown,' add 'He was elected a Representative Peer, 30 January 1906.'

p. **119**, after l. 19, add 'Lord Borthwick died 4 October 1910, when the Peerage became dormant, if not extinct.'

MORAY AND RAMSAY, LORDS BOTHWELL

p. **128**, after l. 5 from foot, insert—

3. Possibly *Maurice* (Macfarlane's *Gen. Coll.*, ii. 505, quoting Kilravock MS.).'

p. **128**, note 4, delete from 'Thomas' on line 5 from foot of notes to 'to *Scotiæ*' on line 2 from foot.

p. **133**, line 24, for 'Fife' read 'Forfar.'

p. **134**, last l., for 'in' read 'on.'

HEPBURNE, EARL OF BOTHWELL

p. **135**, l. 19, after 'had,' insert 'with Marion Fourhuire or Fourbour, his spouse.'

p. **136**, l. 1, after 'Berwickshire,' insert 'This charter was confirmed by David II. about 1343 (*Reg. Mag. Sig.*, vol. i., new ed., App. i. No. 117).'

p. **137**, l. 19, for 'inherited his father's title of,' read 'was created (cf. p. 437).

p. **137**, note 7, add at end of note '*Cal. Papal Letters*, iv. 222.'

p. **139**, l. 2, after '1443-44.' insert 'On 2 November 1411 a Papal dispensation was issued for a marriage between Adam Hepburne and Janet Borthwick, daughter of Sir William Borthwick (*Reg. Avenionensia*, cccxxxix. f. 549).'

p. **141**, l. 15, after 'chest,' add 'Annes (Agnes) Hepburne, by the contract cited, was affianced to Alexander Home, son and apparent heir of Sir Alexander Home of that Ilk, and on 2 January 1450-51 a Papal mandate was issued to grant a dispensation for the marriage of Alexander Home and Agnes Hepburne who had married, knowing themselves to be in the third and third degrees of affinity, and that her father was Alexander's godfather (*Reg. Vaticana*, ccccxvi. f. 122). This Alexander was son of the first and father of the second Lord Home.'

p. **142**, l. 20, delete 'who is not known to have married,' and insert 'who married Margaret, sister of William Douglas of Whittingham; They appear in a contract 22 November 1521. It is added that an action of divorce by the said Margaret against the said John then depended (*ex inform.* W. Keith Murray from fragment of a record of the Court of the official of St. Andrews *penes* Lord Bolton).'

p. **143**, note 2, after '94a,' insert 'see also Gilbert Grote's Protocol Book, f. 43b.'

p. **144**, l. 15, after 'Galloway,' delete '[7],' and insert 'on 15 January 1509-10.[7]'

p. **144**, after l. 31, insert—

'(5) *Jean Hepburne*, married, as second wife, to William, Master of Ruthven (cf. vol. iv. 259), (MS. at Newhailes; Wood's Douglas's *Peerage*, i. 661).'

p. **144**, note 7, after '205' add 'Earlston Charters, *penes* E. Rainsford Murray.'

p. **145**, l. 16, after '1544-45,' add 'and may have been his wife.'

p. **147**, l. 26, after '1506-7,' insert 'The bulls of the Priory of St. Andrews were delivered to him 26 May 1483 (Roman Transcripts, Public Record Office).'

p. **147**, ll. 33 and 34, delete 'within a few months thereafter,' and insert '15 January 1525-26 (*Black Book of Taymouth*).'

p. **148**, l. 6, after '1451,' insert 'in terms of a Papal dispensation granted 6 July 1448 (*Reg. Vat.*, DXXII. fol. 56).'

p. **148**, l. 22, delete '(afterwards created Lord Home).'

p. **149**, l. 31, after 'married,' insert 'first, before 1511, to Sir William Preston of that Ilk (New Hailes Muniments; *Reg. Mag. Sig.*, 13 February 1510-11); and secondly.'

p. **149**, l. 32, delete 'He,' and insert 'The latter.'

p. **150**, last two lines, delete the whole sentence. See note above, page 141.

p. **156**, l. 4 from foot, for '1523' read '1523-24.'

p. **156**, note 9, after '50,' insert 'contract in Wigtoun Charter-chest, (Scot. Rec. Soc., p. 44.)'

p. **158**, l. 6 from foot, after '1544.' insert note, 'He appears to have been taken prisoner in September 1544 (cf. *Treasurer's Accounts*, viii. 315).'

p. **159**, l. 21, for 'first,' read 'third (cf. vol. vii. 571).'

p. **160**, l. 8 from foot, for '28 December 1561,' read '11 January 1561-62 (*Cal. of Scot. Papers*, i. 190),' and delete note 8.

p. **165**, l. 16, after 'married,' insert '24 February (Canongate Reg.).'

p. **166**, l. 25, after '1567,' insert reference number [7].

STEWART, EARL OF BOTHWELL

p. **168**, l. 19, for '4 January,' read '11 January (*Cal. of Scot. Papers*, i. 190).'

p. **169**, l. 29, after 'Hamilton,' insert 'described in 1643 as "indweller in Canongate" (Treasury Precepts, H. M. Reg. Ho., 27 Feb. 1643).'

p. **169**, l. 30, after 'Ferguslie,' add 'and secondly, before November 1638, to John Hamilton, brother-german to the late James Hamilton of Peill (son of James Hamilton of Corshill) (*Reg. of Deeds*, DXVI. f. 354).'

p. **171**, l. 4 from foot, after 'Coldingham,' insert 'styled in 1615 of Springkell (*Reg. of Deeds*, CCLXX. 141).'

p. **171**, last line, after 'Home,' delete 'and,' and insert 'daughter of Sir

Alexander, and sister of Sir George Home of Manderston (*Gen. Reg. Inhibitions*, 26 September 1621). They.'

p. **172**, l. 6, after '1679,' insert comma, and add, 'but this is a mistake, as he must have died before 1658, when Francis Stewart, presumably his son, was charged to enter heir to John Stewart of Coldingham, his grandfather (*Gen. Reg. Inhibs.*, 8 July 1675). It must have been this younger Francis who fought at Bothwell Brig. His commission as Lieutenant of Dragoons is dated 27 September 1678, as Captain, 24 July 1679 (Dalton's *Scots Army*, 106). Captain Francis Stewart's testament was confirmed 20 February 1684: he must have died before 17 March 1683, when Sir Patrick Home, his executor, petitioned the Privy Council for possession of his effects (*P. C. Decreta*).'

p. **172**, l. 16, after 'Margaret,' insert 'eldest daughter.'

p. **172**, l. 16, after 'married,' insert 'contract August 1621 (cf. vol. ii. 517, note 6).'

p. **172**, after l. 25 insert

'9. *Christian*, married to Edward Withrington of Kirkington (*Gen. Reg. Inhibitions*, 7 November 1635).'

p. **173**. l. 11, after '*Robert*,' insert 'He was in 1656 charged to enter heir to his father and elder brother. He died before 8 July 1675 (*Gen. Reg. Inhibitions*).'

BREADALBANE

p. **174**, l. 19, after 'Ardgowan,' insert 'He must therefore have been born after February 1522-23, about which time the marriage took place.'

p. **177**, l. 6 from foot, after 'Clandonoquhy,' add note, 'Further research shows that she was apparently not married to Sir John. John, Bishop of the Isles, had a dispensation for illegitimacy in connection with his provision to the Bishopric (*Vatican Index*). On 26 March 1466 Pope Paul II. dealt with the petition of Sir Colin Campbell, then ambassador from James III. to the Holy See, on behalf of John Campbell, scholar, of Lismore diocese, of baronial race on both sides, born of said Colin, a married man, and an unmarried woman, then in his seventh year, for dispensation to hold two canonries: which the Pope granted when he should reach his ninth year (Reg. of Petitions to the Pope, DLXXXV. 206). This may well have been the future bishop (*ex inform.* J. Maitland Thomson, LL.D).'

p. **177**, line 2 from foot, after 'Merchiston,' insert 'who died before 10 July 1552 (St. Giles' Charters, 115).'

p. **180**, l. 17, after 'Merchiston,' add 'She was married, secondly, to Robert Fairlie of Braid (*Acts and Decreets*, iii. 50).'

p. **182**, l. 24, after 'married,' insert 'probably about October 1559, when she was infeft in certain lands in virtue of their marriage-contract (Lawers Inventory).'

p. **182**, l. 26, after '*Margaret*,' insert 'adopted in 1561 by Patrick M'Athair (*Black Book of Taymouth*, 205), and afterwards.'

p. **182,** l. 28, delete 'before 15 June 1551,' and insert '28 January 1550-51.'

p. **182,** note 10, after '10,' insert '*Black Book of Taymouth.*'

p. **182,** note 12, delete '*Reg. Mag. Sig.*,' and insert '*Acta Dom. Conc. et Sess.*, xxvii. 36.'

p. **183,** l. 2, delete 'on 16 January 1610,' and insert 'by 25 February 1607.'

p. **183,** l. 3, after 'son,' delete comma, and insert 'chose curators. (*Acts and Decreets*, ccxxvi. 46).'

p. **183,** l. 4, after '*Colin*,' insert 'his son,' after 'him,' delete full stop, and insert '16 January 1610.'

p. **183,** l. 12, after 'issue [6],' insert 'before 20 August 1622, when his brother Archibald had a precept of clare constat in certain lands in Lismore as his brother and nearest heir.'

p. **183,** l. 26, for '1589,' read '1587 (*Reg. of Deeds*, xxx. 164).'

p. **184,** l. 11, after '1575,' insert 'On 26 November 1578 on the narrative that "our cusenge Duncane Campbell fiar of Glenurquhay for his serves and gudwill borne touertis us is to be put at be his father," the Earl of Argyll granted an undertaking to protect him against his father (*Black Book of Taymouth*, 221).'

p. **186,** l. 6, after '1614,' insert reference '(*Reg. of Deeds*, cclxxxi. 381).'

p. **187,** note 14, after '*Deeds*,' insert 'lxv. 239.'

p. **188,** l. 1, delete 'had been.'

p. **188,** l. 2, after 'married,' insert 'contract 19 November 1625, Margaret, eldest daughter of Colin Campbell of Aberuchill (*Reg. of Deeds*, ccclxxxiii. 154).'

p. **188,** l. 6, delete 'and others,' and insert

(3) *Patrick.*

(4) *James.*

(5) *Elizabeth*, styled youngest lawful daughter. She had come of age before 4 March 1662, and is mentioned along with Patrick, James and John as "oyes of Elizabeth Sinclair," in February 1654 (*Stirlingshire Sasines*).'

p. **188,** l. 17, after 'married,' insert 'contract 3 and 7 April 1628 (*Reg. of Deeds*, ccccl v. 326).

p. **189,** l. 26, after 'and,' insert 'by her who died 24 December 1667, aged eighty-four (Auchlyne Family Bible).'

p. **189,** l. 3 from foot, after 'married,' insert 'contract 10 and 11 March 1641 (*Reg. Mag. Sig.*, 20 June 1642.)'

p. **189,** note 10, add to note, 'the Auchlyne Family Bible gives the date of his death as 16 November 1658, at the age of eighty.

p. **190,** l. 18, after 'married,' insert 'as her first husband.'

p. **190,** l. 23, after '1772,' insert reference '*Scots Mag.*, 1772, p. 226.'

p. **190,** l. 25, after 'Stonefield,' insert 'She died 16 April 1813 (*Lairds and Lands of Loch Tayside*, p. 12).'

p. **190,** l. 34, after 'married,' insert 'John, second son of Andrew,' and after 'Gartartan,' add 'A marriage contract of date 18 June 1719 states she was then his spouse.'

p. **191,** l. 9 from foot, after 'issue,' insert 'besides five daughters.'

p. **191**, l. 8 from foot, after 'died,' delete 'without issue,' and insert '10 May 1713 (Auchlyne Family Bible).'

p. **191**, l. 4 from foot, after 'Regiment,' insert 'was wounded at the battle of Fontenoy.'

p. **192**, l. 9, delete ——, and insert 'Duncan.'

p. **192**, l. 10, after 'Macpherson,' insert 'in Cult or in Glenorchy (*Court of Sess. Minute-Book*, ii. 106, 107).'

p. **192**, l. 12, after 'Hellsglen,' insert 'with issue a son *Archibald*.'

p. **192**, l. 2 from foot, after 'Lochdochart,' insert '(They gave in their names for marriage 8 November 1800. [Killin Parish Register]).'

p. **193**, l. 4, after 'Campbell,' insert 'born 2, and baptized 10 October 1801 (Callander Par. Reg.).'

p. **198**, l. 9, after '1794,' insert 'ensign 96th Regiment of Foot,' and after 'unmarried,' insert 'on 5 March 1813, in Jersey, aged 18 (*Scots Mag.*).'

p. **198**, l. 13, delete 'exchanged into 42nd Regiment.'

p. **198**, l. 14, delete from 'for,' down to 'Regiment,' in line 17, and insert 'he served as an officer in the 60th, 91st, and 9th North British Militia Regiments, and became captain in the 21st Royal North British Fusiliers, 12 June 1806.'

p. **198**, l. 8 from foot, after '1720,' insert 'was a subaltern in the 43rd Regiment in 1745 (Brown's *Hist. of the Highlands*, iv. 150).'

p. **199**, l. 22, after 1730.[12],' insert 'besides the before-named nine sons Colin had five daughters, Susanna, born 28 June 1717, Mary, 3 August 1727, Christian, 6 December 1728, Lucie, 26 February 1730, and Jean, 13 September 1731 (Glenfalloch Family Bible).'

p. **199**, l. 27, after 'issue,' insert note, 'These daughters are mentioned in Court of Session Minute-Book (ii. 9), where they are mistakenly said to be the daughters of Archibald, son of William.'

p. **199**, l. 6 from foot, delete 'between 1648 and 1651,' and insert 'in 1648 or 1649.'

p. **199**, l. 2 from foot, after 'Lochdochart,' insert 'of which he had sasine, 28 March 1650 (*Part. Reg. of Sasines, Perthshire*, i. 40). He died 8 November 1699 aged seventy-two (Auchlyne Family Bible).'

p. **200**, l. 3, after 'issue,' insert

'(1) *John*, who had sasine of Loragen and Lochdochart (Sheriff Court Books, Perth).

i. *William*, his son, had sasine of these lands 16 January 1743; Crown charter 12 March 1744 (*Part. Reg. of Sasines, Perth*, xxiii. 230-231; *Reg. Mag. Sig.* lib. xcviii. 140).

(i) *Charles*, his eldest son, had also sasine of the above lands, 1763. Late in life he married a second wife, Catherine Buchanan, by whom he had a son:—

a. Charles Archibald, M.D., Montreal, baptized 30 September 1814 (Perth

Par. Reg.). He married Marjorie M'Gillivray of Salrevors, Canada, with issue *James*, *Charles*, and *Robert* (marriage, births, and baptisms, registered in Perth, 1861-62).

(*a*) *James*, of Montreal, married Louise V. Phillips of Chicago, U.S.A., and has issue, *Marion*, *Rosyln*, and *Norman* (marriage, births, and baptisms recorded in St. James' Parish Church, Chicago, 1878-86.'

p. **200**, l. 6, after 'He died' delete 'in,' and insert '24 February.'

p. **200**, l. 6, after 'she died,' delete 'in 1698,' and insert '17 January 1693, aged fifty-three (*Ibid.*).'

p. **200**, l. 8, after 'married,' insert 'contract 26 October 1626 (*Reg. of Deeds*, DX. 234).'

p. **200**. l. 17, delete 'before 5 July 1625,' and insert 'contract 8 June 1624 (*Reg. of Deeds*, cccci. 407).'

p. **200**, l. 3 from foot, after '1637,' insert 'She died in March 1660, leaving issue (Dunblane Tests.).'

p. **201**, l. 12, delete 'in,' and insert '24.'

p. **201**, l. 12, after '1686,' insert 'aged seventy nine (Auchlyne Family Bible).'

p. **201**, l. 27, after 'Tulloch,' insert 'He was alive 18 April 1692.'

p. **202**, l. 1, for 'Robert,' read 'Gilbert' (*Perth Sasines*, iii. 272 and other evidence).'

p. **202**, after l. 9 insert

'15. *Elizabeth*, married, contract dated at Ardchattan 16 April 1701, to John Darroch, minister of the parish of Craignish,' and add one to subsequent numbers of children.

p. **202**, l. 18, after 'Company,' insert 'In the *Gen. Reg. of Inhibs.*, 20 November 1679, William is named before Colin, so he may have been older.'

p. **202**, l. 26, after 'had,' insert note, 'In the Register mentioned above the order of children by third wife is given thus:—Charles, Susanna, Mary, Jean, Sopbia, Grisel and Anna.'

p. **202**, l. 3 from foot, after 'married,' insert 'as his third wife, probably on 10 October 1697 (Killin Par. Reg.).'

p. **207**, l. 4 from foot of notes, after 'sister,' insert 'She is designed "only lawful daughter to the deceast John, Earle of Brodalbine" (Canongate Reg. of Marriages).'

p. **207**, l. 7 from foot, for 'Abbey' read 'Palace (*Scots Mag.*).'

p. **210**, l. 7 from foot, after 'Berwick,' add note, 'David Gavin, or perhaps his father, made a large fortune as a tailor in Holland: he married, first, a Miss Hearsey, whose father lived in Middleburg, Zeeland.'

p. **210**, last line, after 'married,' insert 'as his second wife.'

p. **211**, l. 3 from foot, after '1677,' add 'He left about £300,000 personalty divided between the issue of his two sisters.'

p. **213**, l. 16, delete 'Assistant' and 'Deputy.'

p. **213**, l. 11 from foot, after 'Watch,' insert 'A.D.C. to the King.'

p. **213**, l. 7 from foot, delete 'who.'

p. **213**, l. 6 from foot, delete 'was an extra lady-in-waiting to H.R.H. the Duchess of Albany.'

p. **214**, l. 12, after '2nd,' insert 'argent.'

BRECHIN

p. **221**, l. 1, for 'lenient' read 'venial.'

p. **223**, l. 16, after 'Seton,' delete from 'Neither' to 'identified,' and insert 'She was the wife of Sir William Seton of that Ilk. Her son, Alexander, became Lord of Gordon. (*See title* Huntly).'

p. **223**, last line, after '1369[8],' add 'He had, 27 June 1358, a dispensation to marry Elizabeth Ramsay, daughter of William Ramsay, Earl of Fife, but it does not appear that the marriage took place (*Papal Petitions*, i. 331).'

BUCCLEUCH

p. **228**, l. 19, after 'Angus,' insert 'who married, secondly, before October 1488, George, second Earl of Rothes. (*See that title.*)'

p. **228**, note 3, for 'i. 74' read 'ii. 74.'

p. **228**, note 5, for '*Ibid*' read '*Scotts of Buccleuch*, ii. 71.

p. **231**, ll. 6 and 7, delete 'shortly before 19 May 1552,' and insert 'between 20 August 1550, when he signed a deed as curator of a son of his stepmother, Janet Beatoun, by a former husband (*Scotts of Buccleuch*, ii. 199), and 9 February 1551-52, when his widow had married again (see vol. iii. 503; *Reg. Mag. Sig.*, 9 February 1551-52).'

p. **231**, l. 3 from foot, before 'contract,' insert 'post-nuptial.'

p. **236**, l. 4, after 'failing,' insert 'the eldest heir-female of his body, whom failing' (it was thus, of course, that his daughter Mary succeeded).

p. **239**, l. 14, after 'state,' insert 'She was very crooked, and had one leg shorter than the other' (from an accident at dancing at the Court of Charles II. *v. Pepys's Diary*). 'She was the last lady in Scotland who had as pages, young gentlemen of good birth, who learned their breeding in attending on persons of quality (Sir Walter Scott's letters to R. Chambers, privately printed, 1904).'

p. **239**, l. 14, delete 'there,' and insert 'at Dalkeith.'

p. **239**, l. 15, delete 'at Dalkeith,' and insert 'there.'

p. **243**, l. 7, after 'died,' insert 'of inoculation for smallpox (Fraser's *Melville Book*, ii. 265).'

p. **243**, l. 9 from foot, after 'issue,' insert 'The Duchess gives her £20,000, the Duke £10,000, and they settle £15,000 more (Horace Walpole to Miss Berry, 17 October 1790).'

p. **247**, l. 8 from foot, for 'third' read 'first.'

BUCHAN

p. **251**, l. 23, after '1182,' add note, 'Magnus, "son of Earl Colbeyn," is a witness to two charters by W. Comyn, Earl of Buchan (*Antiq. Aberdeen and Banff*, ii. 427, 428).'

p. **252**, note 2, delete 'may have been,' and insert 'was,' adding after 'Fergus' '(see *Antiq. Aberdeen and Banff*, ii. 427, 428).'

p. **256**, l. 17, for '*Emma*,' read '*Agnes* (*see title* Strathearn).'

p. **256**, l. 23, delete '——,' and insert 'Margaret,' and after 'Soulis' insert 'the Competitor (*Cal. Doc. Scot.*, ii. No. 870).'

p. **262**, after 'note 3,' add 'cf. vol. vii. 159.'

p. **266**, l. 14, for '1 March 1466' read '27 March 1459.'

p. **266**, note 1, delete note, and insert '*Acta Dom. Conc.*, xvi. 264.'

p. **267**, ll. 22 and 23, for 'probably in 1498-99,' read 'in 1499 (*Acts and Decreets*, xxvii. 360).'

p. **267**, l. 24, for 'only one' read 'a.'

p. **267**, after l. 25, insert 'He is also said to have had a daughter married to Alexander Abernethy, fourth Lord Saltoun (*Frasers of Philorth*, ii. 50; see also vol. vii. of this work, p. 409), and another, *Marion*, contracted in 1505 to Sir Thomas Ogilvy (*Acts and Decreets*, xvi. 233).'

p. **267**, l. 7 from foot, after 'Bothwell,' insert 'another, *Elizabeth*, married Mungo Home of Ersiltoun (cf. vol. iv. 469).'

p. **268**, l. 23, delete 'in,' and insert '5 April (Dun *obits*).'

p. **268**, l. 3 from foot, for '1551,' read '1561,' and add 'He was alive on 13 February 1560-61, when he entered into a contract with a John Mortimer as to certain lands (Protocol Book of Duncan Gray, f. 19).'

p. **269**, l. 1, after 'first,' delete from 'Mary' down to 'Kennedy' on l. 3, and insert 'Elizabeth Stewart, natural daughter of James, Earl of Moray (see vol. vi. 312; the Earl of Moray's testament there quoted makes no mention of any legitimate issue). On 12 September 1546 there was an agreement between John, Master of Buchan, and Elizabeth Stewart his putative spouse, whereby she obliged herself to furnish proof that before their marriage she had cohabited with a gentleman who was in the fourth degree of kinship with the Master, so that they might be divorced; for which (she having never received maintenance, meat, or clothing of him to this day) she was to be paid 100 merks, with a gown and kirtle with suitable trimming (Moray Writs, box ii. No. 34). After the Master's death an action of bastardy against Christian, his daughter, was raised before the Commissary-general of Aberdeen, on the ground that Elizabeth Stewart, the Master's wife, having survived him, his daughter, by Margaret Ogilvy, must have been born in adultery (*Ibid.*, box ii. Nos. 17 and 20). But in 1549 James, Master of Buchan, renounced the process of bastardy, and consented that Christian should be served heir to her father, also that James, Commendator of the Priory of St. Andrews, should, after the decease of the Earl and of Christian, enjoy the earldom of Buchan, and might, if he so pleased, have Christian to wife. All which the Master ratified by a notarial instrument, dated 3 August 1550 (*Ibid.*, box ii. No. 35).'

p. **269,** ll. 5 and 6, delete 'two years at least,' and insert 'and married secondly, after 16 December 1549, George Barclay of that Ilk (*Acts and Decreets*, xx. 436; *Reg. Mag. Sig.*, 27 June 1551).'

p. **269,** l. 15, after '1618,' add 'He married Mary, daughter of William Ruthven, first Earl of Gowrie, and relict of John Stewart, fifth Earl of Atholl, and of John Stewart, sixth Lord Innermeath, afterwards Earl of Atholl (see vol. i. 446, 447).'

p. **269,** l. 18, after 'Denmark,' add note, 'Adrian Damaan was a Professor in the University of Leyden, and was in 1594 agent for the States General at the Scottish Court.'

p. **269,** after l. 19 insert

'3. *Eleanor*, said to have been married to Dempster of Muiresk (Douglas's *Peerage*, 95; Dempster's *Hist.*, sec. ii. 173).'

'The Earl had also a natural son, *Robert*, who, on 12 January 1558-59 had a tack from his father of part of the lands of Nevay, Forfarshire (Protocol Book of Duncan Gray, fol. 18b.).'

p. **269,** l. 21, for '1551,' read '1561.'

p. **269,** l. 8 from foot, after 'was married,' insert '6 October 1652 (*Harl. MSS.*, 6437).'

p. **270,** l. 14, after 'married,' insert 'contract 22 and 28 February 1590-91 (*Reg. of Deeds.* xxxvi. 336), proclamation of banns 4 July 1591 (Aberdeen Reg.).'

p. **271,** ll. 3, 4 and 5, delete 'about 1580. He succeeded to his father in 1586,' and insert 'perhaps in or about November 1565, at which time his mother is said to have been "travelland with child" (*P. C. Reg.*, i. 396).'

p. **271,** l. 11, delete 'Margaret, second,' and insert 'in 1598 Anne, eldest (*Harl. MSS.*, 6442).'

p. **271,** l. 18, after married,' insert 'contract 2 December 1608.'

p. **271,** ll. 18 and 19, delete 'probably about 1608 and had by him an only child.'

p. **271,** l. 20, delete 'who.'

p. **271,** l. 21, after 'married,' insert '18 June 1615 (*Reg. of Deeds*, cccxxxvi. 299).'

p. **272,** l. 18, delete 'in 1628,' and insert 'at Holyrood, and was buried at Auchterhouse 20 August 1628 (Funeral entry, Lyon Office).'

p. **272,** after l. 28, insert

'5. *Anna* (*Gen. Reg. Sasines*, xxxix. 350).'

p. **272,** l. 9 from foot, for '5' read '6.'

p. **272,** l. 5 from foot, after '1638-39,' insert 'Crawfurd states that they had a daughter *Dorothy* married to —— Walker, co. Middlesex (*Peerage*, 48), and several other children who died young.'

p. **273**, l. 12, after 'married,' insert 'after 11 April 1655, when she is described as his future wife (*Banff Sasines*, vii. 125).'

p. **273**, after l. 22, insert

'2. *Margaret*, married to William Gray of Innereichty (*Forfar Sasines*, vi. 264).'

p. **273**, ll. 23, 26, 27 for '2, 3, 4' read '3, 4, 5.'

p. **273**, l. 23, for 'Margaret' read '*Mary* or *Marjory* (*Aberdeen Sasines*, vi. 286, xii. 533).'

p. **273**, l. 27, after 'married,' insert '3 January 1684 (Edinburgh Reg.)'

p. **274**, l. 1, for '5' read '6.' After 'Halkerton,' insert 'Sheriff Clerk of Angus: she married, secondly, Alexander Carnegie, second son of Sir John Carnegie of Balnamoon (Macfarlane's *Gen. Coll.*, ii. 181).'

p. **274**, l. 8, for 'the soldiers of William III.' read 'the Master of Forbes (Edinburgh Letters of 13 July in *London Gazette*, 17-21 July 1690).'

p. **274**, l. 9, delete 'unmarried,' and insert 'having married at the Chapel in Duke's Place, St. James's, London, 4 September 1683, Marjorie Foulis, widow of William, eighth Earl of Morton (certificate of marriage and other papers, Misc. Documents H. M. Register House). She was dead before 1690 (Edinburgh Tests., 19 February 1690).'

p. **275**, line 4 from foot, delete 'in 1745' and insert '14, and was buried at Hampstead, 17 October 1745.'

p. **275**, l. 3 from foot, for 'in' read '11 February.'

p. **275**, last line, delete ——, and insert 'Anne.'

p. **276**, l. 24, after 'born,' insert '7 December (Edin, Reg.),' after 'married insert '11 July 1726 (Edinburgh Mar. Reg.).'

p. **276**, l. 5 from foot, after '1739,' insert 'in Lady Huntingdon's Chapel at Bath.'

p. **276**, l. 3 from foot, after 'Bart,' insert note, 'There was a Scotch Countess of Buchan who is carrying a pure, rosy, vulgar face to Heaven (Horace Walpole's *Letters*, 10 October 1766).'

p. **277**, l. 6 from foot, after 'Buck,' delete 'who,' and insert 'against whom he unsuccessfully raised an action of divorce 1820. She.'

p. **279**, l. 16, delete 'Bart.'

BURNTISLAND

p. **282**, l. 23, after 'London,' insert note, 'He satisfied for fornication committed with one . . . Weymes at the Chapel of the Weymes in Fife, Mr. Harie Weilkie, minister of the Weymes did receave him in the Church of the Weymes. This cheild was gotten by him before he went into England with the armie. He went backe to London again March 1654 (Lamont's *Diary*).'

p. **283**, l. 9 from foot, after '1705,' insert note, 'Her body was taken from Roystoun to Burntisland at 12 at night with a great many flambeaux: thence to Easter Wemyes where she was buried in the beginning of June (?) (*Edinburgh Courant*).'

BUTE

p. **292**, l. 20, for 'Mary' read 'Agnes.' *Note.*—'In 1552 she is described as sometime spouse to James Stewart, Sheriff of Bute, now to James M'Donald of Donyveig and Glens (*Acts and Decreets*, vi. 474). Her marriage with the Sheriff of Bute must therefore have been annulled. See vol. i. 338, where she is said (following Gregory) to have been daughter of Colin, third Earl of Argyll.'

p. **293**, l. 14, for 'Mary' read 'Jean (*Reg. Sec. Sig.*, lv. 35).'

p. **293**, l. 19, delete 'before 15 September 1595,' and insert 'contract 11 June 1593 (*Reg. of Deeds*, cxxix. 126).'

p. **295**, l. 4 from foot, after 'married,' insert 'contract 9 March 1631 (*Reg. of Deeds*, DXXVIII. 262).'

p. **297**, l. 7, after 'had,' insert 'by her, who survived him and was on 1 August 1672 the wife of Robert M'Neill of Illandrow (*Reg. of Deeds*, Durie, 14 Feb. 1673).'

p. **297**, note 4, after '*Peerage*,' insert '; Edinburgh Mar. Reg.'

p. **299**, l. 23, delete 'marriage,' and insert 'first wife, who was buried 16 July 1696 (Greyfriars Reg.).'

p. **303**, l. 12, after 'he,' insert 'died 1 March 1818, having.'

p. **304**, l. 9 from foot, after '1822,' insert note, 'His wife gave him by mistake a lotion which had been ordered for a footman's leg, which poisoned him (Mrs. Warenne Blake's *Memoirs of a Vanished Generation*, 108).'

p. **305**, l. 14, delete reference number '[1].'

p. **305**, l. 15, for reference '[2]' read '[1].'

p. **305**, l. 29, after 'Rothesay,' insert '[2].'

p. **309**, l. 24, for 'Phillipps' read Phillippo.'

p. **312**, l. 12, after '3rd,' insert 'argent.'

CAITHNESS

p. **323**, l. 5 from foot, after 'Blaknes[5],' add 'He married —— daughter and heiress of Duncan Cairns of Cairns and acquired the lands of Cairns and Whitburn (*History of the Family of Cairns*, by H. C. Lawlor, Killyfaddy, Belfast, 2 and Table at p. 16).'

p. **333**, l. 25, delete 'sometime between the date of the charter and 29 March 1482 (*see below*)' and insert 'between Martinmas 1479 and Whitsunday 1480 (*Exch. Rolls*, viii. 48).'

p. **334**, after l. 14, insert

'3. *Elizabeth* called also *Marjory*, married to Andrew, Master of Rothes, who died before January 1477-78; she died about 1508.'

p. **334**, l. 20, for '3' read '4' and add one to each number thereafter.

p. **334**, l. 32, after 'Atholl,' insert 'and died 21 March 1518.'

p. **337**, l. 14, for 'Mary, daughter of Sir William,' read 'Margaret, daughter of Sir Gilbert (*Acta Dom. Conc.*, xxiii. 101).'

p. **338**, after l. 19, insert

'3. *Archibald* (*Acta Dom. Conc. et Sess.*, xxii. 41).'

p. 338, l. 20, for '3' read '4.'

p. 338, l. 27, after '*David*,' insert 'also *Matthew* (*Reg. Mag. Sig.*, 19 May 1585).'

p. 340, l. 7, after 'who,' insert 'was born in 1543, as he was twenty years of age or thereby on 8 November 1563 (Gilbert Grote's Protocol Book, 96). He.'

p. 340, ll. 14 and 15, for 'about 1577-78' read 'in September 1575 (Edin. Tests.).'

p. 340, l. 26, after 'married,' insert 'first.'

p. 340, l. 28, delete 'by whom,' and insert 'and secondly, contract 6 October 1621, Grisel, daughter of Mr. Robert Crichton of Eliok, widow of Thomas Dunbar, Dean of Moray (*Reg. of Deeds*, cccxvii. 141; *Elgin Sasines*, 163, 164). She survived him, and is designed his widow 7 March 1633 (*Inverness Sasines*, 11 April 1633).'

p. 340, l. 5 from foot, after 'first,' insert 'before 2 September 1626, when Sir James, being about to go abroad on military service, granted a factory in her favour (*Reg. of Deeds*, cccxci. 62).'

p. 340, l. 4 from foot, after '1633),' insert 'daughter of Sir Walter Dundas of that Ilk and widow of Sir William Sharp of Ballindoch (*Reg. of Deeds*, cclxxxix. 97).'

p. 341, l. 3 from foot, after 'issue,' add 'He married, 5 January 1764, Catherine, daughter of John Rose in Keiss, parish of Wick. She raised an action of declarator of the marriage in 1783 and divorced him in 1786 (*Consistorial Processes, etc.*, Scot. Rec. Soc., Nos. 791, 842).'

p. 342, l. 11, after '1582,' insert 'married, contract 10 December 1587, to Sir John Home of Cowdenknowes (cf. vol. iv. 474; *Reg. of Deeds*, xxvi. 271).'

p. 342, l. 12, after 'issue,' insert 'having been, it is said, slain by his elder brother John, who bruised him to death with his fetters during his imprisonment in Girnigo (Catherine Sinclair's *Shetland and the Shetlanders*, 35).'

p. 342, l. 13, delete 'but leaving,' and insert 'He had.'

p. 342, l. 20, after 'age,' add 'in 1572 (cf. vol. viii. 334). She was married, secondly, to Alexander Innes of that Ilk, after 10 September 1574, and died before 25 November 1575 (*Reg. of Deeds*, xvi. 369).'

p. 342, l. 22, after 'secondly,' insert 'contract 10 April 1580 (*Reg. of Deeds*, xlvii. 24).'

p. 342, ll. 25 and 26, delete entire sentence.

p. 342, l. 27, for '9' read '8.'

p. 342, l. 27, for 'about 1574,' read 'contract 20 and 21 September 1581.'

p. 342, ll. 28 and 29, delete 'She was living 15 June 1598,' and insert 'She married, secondly, contract 1588, Alexander Gordon of Strathaven, and died 6 November 1619 (cf. vol. iii. 571).'

p. 342, after line 29, insert

'9. *Jonet*, married, contract 20 October 1573, to William Sutherland younger of Dunbeath (*Reg. of Deeds*, xiii. 115).'

p. 343, l. 13, delete '10 December 1606,' and insert '29 December 1615 (*Reg. Mag. Sig.*, 6 June 1616).'

p. **343,** l. 25, delete 'in,' and insert 'contract 21 May (cf. vol. iii. 34).

p. **344,** l. 3, delete 'between May 1633 and October 1634,' and insert 'contract 17 and 25 December 1633 (*Reg. of Deeds*, cccclxxxi. 445).'

p. **348,** l. 25, after 'her,' insert 'who survived him and was alive in 1684 (*Gen. Reg. Sasines*, 25 September 1684).'

p. **350,** after l. 11 from foot, insert

'8. *Jean*, baptized 10 April 1764 (Dunnet Par. Reg.).'

p. **351,** l. 9 from foot, delete 'before 1583,' and insert 'contract 13 December 1578 (cf. *Reg. Mag. Sig.*, 16 February 1578-79; *Reg. of Deeds*, xvii. 3),' and add note, 'There was an abortive proposal that he should marry Jean Gordon, sister to the Earl of Sutherland (see vol. viii. 343, note 1).'

p. **358,** l. 6 from foot, after 'Baronet,' insert 'to whom he was served heir-male general 7 January 1890.'

CALLANDER

p. **362,** line 4 from foot, after 'Helena,' insert 'the latter of whom was married to John Stirling of Herbertshire (*Reg. of Deeds*, lxxxiii. 222; *Linlithgow Inhibs.*, x. 227).'

p. **363,** l. 7, for 'third' read 'second (*Maitland Club Misc.*, iv. pt. i. p. 202; Hamilton Papers, *Eleventh Rep. Hist. MSS. Com.*, App. vi. 59).'

CARDROSS

p. **365,** ll. 22 and 23, delete 'shortly after 14 December 1625,' and insert 'on 18 April 1626 (contract 8 December 1625) (*Reg. of Deeds*, cccxcvi. 202; Canongate Reg.).'

p. **365,** l. 24, after 'issue,' add 'along with a daughter *Mary*, baptized 22 April 1628 (Canongate Reg.), married to John Buchanan of that Ilk after 21 October 1654, when she had a charter as his future wife (*Gen. Reg. Sasines*, viii. 325).'

p. **365,** l. 2 from foot, for '18' read '10.'

p. **366,** l. 3, after '1671,' insert 'and was buried in Holyrood Church, 25 July 1671 (Canongate Reg.).'

p. **366,** l. 8, after 'Kincardine,' delete 'and had issue,' and insert 'She survived him, and there was a warrant to bury her in Holyrood Church 28 December 1696 (*P. C. Acta*).'

p. **366,** l. 13, after 'marriage,' insert 'along with two twins, William and David, who were baptized 9 March 1662 (Canongate Reg.), but who must have died young:—'

p. **366,** ll. 16 and 17, delete '5 October 1700 (a date erroneously given in the *Services of Heirs*),' and insert 'in April 1697, and was buried in Holyrood (*P. C. Acta*).'

p. **367,** l. 21, after 'undergone,' add 'and was buried at Holyrood.'

p. **367,** l. 28, after 'married,' insert contract 14 August 1721 (*Perth Sasines*, xviii. 186).'

CARLYLE

p. 375, l. 27, after 'recorded,' insert 'but there is some reason to suppose that she may have been a daughter of Robert or Adam Crosby who lived at Corby, Cumberland. She was lady of Ormesby previously referred to (*ex inform.* by C. H. Herries Crosbie).'

p. 382, last line of note 9, add 'Edward Carlyle of Limekilns was, in 1596-97, a brother of Herbert Carlyle of Brydekirk (*P. C. Reg.*, v. 743).'

p. 386, after line 25, insert

'7. *Elizabeth*, contracted in 1492 to Robert Herries, son and apparent heir of George Herries of Terrauchty (*Acta Dom. Conc.*, 296).'

p. 389, last line, delete 'whose daughter Grizel he married, and.'

p. 390, l. 4, after 'wife,' insert Grizel, a sister of Edward Maxwell of Hills (*Drumlanrig Writs*).'

CARNWATH

p. 405, l. 16, after 'tombstone,' insert 'in Abercorn Church.'

p. 405, l. 19, after 'Carnwath,' add 'It is stated that he left a son (the General) and a daughter, married to William Drummond of Riccarton. His wife was Janet, daughter (Crawfurd says a natural daughter) of Edward, first Lord Bruce of Kinloss (cf. vol. iii. 477).'

p. 406, l. 10, delete '13 August 1607, when his son was still apparent of that Ilk,' and insert '2 January 1609 (*Reg. of Deeds*, cci. 317).'

p. 408, l. 2, after '1632,' insert 'He was alive 11 July 1635 (*Reg. Mag Sig.*) but died before July 1636 (*Lanark Sasines*, iii. 542).'

p. 408, l. 2, delete from 'In June' down to 'his body' on line 8, and insert same after 'Carnwath' on last line of p. 411. Note 'The information refers to the second Lord Dalzell, who, and not his father, was the first Earl of Carnwath.'

p. 408, l. 8, delete 'Died 1639.'

p. 408, l. 9, for 'Sir' read 'Mr.'

p. 408, l. 12, for 'second' read 'first.'

p. 409, l. 2, delete 'before 1625,' and insert 'contract 8 July 1624 (*Reg. of Deeds*, ccccxvi. 240).'

p. 409, l. 16, after '1685,[6]' insert 'He was captain of a company of Foot in the Earl of Mar's Regiment (*Warrant Book for Scotland*, iv.).'

p. 409, l. 20, delete 'between 13 May 1685 and 29 April 1686,' and insert '2 September 1685 (*Notes and Queries*, 10th ser., viii. 402).'

p. 409, l. 22, delete 'Miss Sandilands of the family of Torphichen,' and insert 'Catherine, daughter of Sir James Sandilands of St. Monans (Discharge for tocher 20 June 1644; *Reg. of Deeds*, Dlvii. 70; cf. vol. i. 78, 79).'

p. 409, note 14, add to note 'see also *Privy Council Acta*, 19 January and

3 August 1697, when he was cited as a Jacobite. He is said to have married —— Graham and left issue (cf. vol. v. 129).'

p. **410**, after l. 7, insert

'*b. Robert*, born and baptized 1 June 1704 (Canongate Reg.).'

p. **410**, ll. 8 and 10, for '*b*, *c* and *d*' read '*c*, *d* and *e*.'

p. **410**, l. 12, for '1652' read '1662.'

p. **410**, l. 22, after '1685,' insert 'He had a commission, dated at Whitehall 12 December 1679, as captain of the company of Foot formerly commanded by Sir Robert Dalzell, his father, in the Earl of Mar's Regiment (*Warrant Book for Scotland*, iv.). In 1686 Sir John appears in the list of that Regiment (*Notes and Queries*, 10th ser., viii. 445).'

p. **410**, l. 31, for 'sixth' read 'fifth.'

p. **410**, l. 4 from foot, for 'seven' read 'seventeen.'

p. **410**, l. 3 from foot, after '1734,' insert 'He left very shortly and became a soldier (*Scots Colleges*, New Spalding Club, i. 201).'

p. **410**, l. 2 from foot, for '(*b*)' read '*c*.' Mary was daughter, not granddaughter of the second Baronet.

p. **411**, l. 1, after 'son,' insert 'He was in a Scots Danish Company raised for service in Germany (*Reg. of Deeds*, cccc. 217).'

p. **411**, l. 14, after '*William*,' insert 'of Chisholm (*Reg. of Deeds*, DX. 167).'

p. **411**, l. 18, after 'merks,' insert 'He married (contract 2 and 5 July 1629) Margaret, daughter of John Stirling of Glorat (*Ibid.*, Dlxxxiii. 58).'

p. **411**, l. 25, delete 'Earl of Carnwath,' and insert 'Lord Dalzell.'

p. **411**, note 10, after 'cccxxxvi.' insert '127.'

p. **412**, l. 1, after 'Holyrood,' insert 'He succeeded his father as Lord Dalzell and, as appears from his son's marriage-contract on 21 July 1537 (*Reg. of Deeds*, cxxvi. 69) it was he (and not his father as generally supposed) who was on 21 April 1639 created at York EARL OF CARNWATH, BARON DALZELL AND LIBERTON, with remainder to heirs-male of his body.'

p. **412**, l. 10, after 'day,' insert note 'Baillie calls him "that monster of profanitie" (*Letters*, ii. 78).'

p. **413**, ll. 10 and 15, for 'third' read 'second.'

p. **413**, l. 15, after 'Carnwath,' insert 'had, as son of Sir Robert Dalzell on 15 September 1633 a licence to pass beyond seas (*Genealogist*, April 1909). He.'

p. **413**, note 5, after 'DXXX.', insert '151.'

p. **414**, l. 9, for 'merks' read 'pounds Scots.' *Note.*—The *Carnegie Book ut cit.* erroneously says merks as in the text.

p. **414**, ll. 15 and 24, for 'fourth' read 'third.'

p. **414**, l. 17, for 'fifth' read 'fourth.'

p. **414**, l. 5 from foot, for '1684' read 'January 1682, by a charter confirmed 15 February 1684 (*Reg. Mag. Sig.*), the Earl being then described as deceased.'

p. **414**, l. 5 from foot, for '1688' read '1683.'

p. **414**, l. 5 from foot, after 'married,' insert '10 December 1676 (Pencaitland Reg.).'

p. **414**, ll. 3 and 4 from foot, delete 'who died January 1713, and by whom,' and insert 'By her, who died 15 January 1698 (Funeral entry, Lyon Office), and was buried at Holyrood.'

p. **414**, last line, delete 'first.'

p. **414**, note 16, last line, for '23' read '229, 230.'

p. **415**, l. 1, delete from 'and' to end of paragraph and relative note.

p. **415**, l. 4, for 'fifth' read 'fourth.'

p. **415**, l. 5, after '1659,' insert 'captain of a company in the Guards 1686; lieutenant-colonel, 1691.'

p. **415**, l. 18, for 'sixth' read 'fifth.'

p. **417**, ll. 8 and 6 from foot, for 'seventh' read 'sixth.'

p. **418**, l. 11, for 'eighth' read 'seventh.'

p. **418**, l. 12, for 'tenth' read 'ninth.'

p. **418**, l. 17, for 'eleventh' read 'tenth.'

p. **419**, l. 5, for 'eighth' read 'seventh.'

p. **419**, l. 9, for 'Blackford' read 'Becford.'

p. **419**, ll. 14 and 15, for 'ninth' read 'eighth.'

p. **419**, l. 18, for 'tenth' read 'ninth.'

p. **419**, l. 23, for 'eleventh' read 'tenth.'

p. **420**, l. 1, for 'twelfth' read 'eleventh.'

p. **420**, l. 3, after '1892,' insert 'He died suddenly on his way to the House of Lords in Great Smith Street, Westminster, 8 March 1910.'

CARRICK

p. **426**, l. 15, after 'Margaret,' insert 'or Isabel,' and add note, 'Neil, Earl of Carrick, and Isabel, Countess of Carrick, granted a charter to the Abbey of Saddell in Cantyre (*Reg. Mag. Sig.*, 1 January 1507-8).'

p. **431**, l. 32, for 'third' read 'first.'

p. **431**, l. 32, for 'Hereford' read 'Hertford.'

p. **431**, l. 34, for '1284' read '1264 (*Cal. Doc. Scot.*, i. No. 2356).'

p. **432**, note 3, for '369' read '373.'

p. **435**, note 4, for '375' read '379.'

p. **437**, l. 6, for '1373' read '1370 (*Reg. Mag. Sig.*, vol. i., No. 356, new edition).'

p. **439**, l. 2, delete '28 April 1398.'

p. **442**, l. 1, delete from '1639' down to 'Carrick' on line 4, and relative note, and insert '22 June 1643 and 3 March 1646, the date of the grant of his wife's administration.'

p. **442**, l. 12, for 'John' read 'Matthew (see grant of administration above cited).'

p. **442**, l. 16, after 'and,' add 'another *Jean*, married, contract 23 July 1622, to John Campbell, son of Patrick Campbell of Balsalloch (*Gen. Reg. Sasines*, xvii. 116).'

p. **442**, l. 19, after '1639,' add 'He married Barbara Bannatyne (*Edinburgh Burgh Reg. of Deeds*, 9 July 1661).'

p. **442**, after l. 19, insert 'There was another son (presumably natural), *Adam*, mentioned 1627 (*Reg. of Deeds*, ccccxi. 48).'

CASSILLIS

p. **445**, note 6, l. 3 from foot, for 'Kenredy' read 'Kennedy.'

p. **448**, l. 4 from foot, for 'daughter' read 'half-sister.'

p. **448**, last line, for '1405' read '1409.'

p. **448**, note 3, for 'p. 440' read 'p. 444.'

p. **449**, l. 19, for 'fourth' read 'fifth.'

p. **449**, transpose notes 8 and 9; for 'clxxi.' in present note 8 read 'clxxiv.'; for '129, 130' in present note 9 read '159, 160.'

p. **451**, l. 17, delete 'a fleur-de-lys,' and insert 'three fleurs-de-lys.'

p. **454**, l. 3 from foot, delete 'who it is said had no issue,' and insert 'Gilbert, third Earl, was infeft as his heir November 1532 (Culzean Charters, No. 316).'

p. **458**, l. 24, for '23' read '3.'

p. **458**, note 8, delete note, and insert '*Reg. Sec. Sig.*, No. 1754.'

p. **459**, l. 14, after 'part,' insert 'They had, however, a daughter, Janet Gordon, described in 1515 as Sir Alexander's daughter and heir (see vol. v. 103, 104).'

p. **462**, l. 22, for '1 May 1547,' read '18 March, 1546-47.'

p. **462**, l. 29, for 'January' read 'February.'

p. **465**, l. 9, for 'following' read 'same (*Reg. Sec. Sig.*, i. 3878).'

p. **465**, note 5, for '*Trials*, 7' read '*Trials*, i. 242*.'

p. **467**, last line, delete 'a daughter,' and insert '*Marion*.'

p. **467**, last line, after 'Bomby,' insert 'She married secondly, before 1562, William Campbell, younger of Skeldon (*Acts and Decreets*, xxiv. 245).'

p. **470**, at end of note 7 add 'He was Treasurer on 30 January 1553-54 (Cartulary of Holyrood, 290).'

p. **471**, l. 18, delete from 'ane particular manne' to end of sentence, and insert 'ane werry wyse manne, and veil beluiffit of all.[3]'

p. **471**, note 3, after '*Kennedyis*,' insert 'The character of "ane particular manne,' etc., belongs to the fourth, not the third Earl.'

p. **473**, ll. 6 and 7 from foot, delete 'a boy of eight years old.'

p. **473**, l. 6 from foot, transfer reference number '[7]' to after 'Arran' on line 4 from foot.

p. **474**, end of note 3, insert 'He must have died before 11 July 1604 (cf. *Acta Parl. Scot.*, iv. 268 and 271).'

p. **475**, after l. 6, insert

'(3) *Jean*, described in 1665 as sister of John, Lord Cassillis, married to William Stewart of Carragan, co. Tyrone. His will 9 April 1665 (*ex inform.* J. Stewart Kennedy).'

p. **475**, l. 7, delete 'was only eight years old when he succeeded his father, who,' and insert 'was probably born between Martinmas 1574 and April 1575, as on 14 August 1589 he chose curators (*Acts and Decreets*, cxxi. 144); and on 2 April 1596 he had sasine of many lands which had been in the superior's hands for nineteen years by reason of ward (*Exch. Rolls*, xxiii. 377). His father.'

p. **475**, ll. 14 and 15, delete 'the following year.'

p. 477, after l. 22, insert 'He was contracted to Jean Cunningham, daughter of James, seventh Earl of Glencairn, who deceased 23 November 1597 "in her virginitie" (M. I. at Kilmaurs).'

p. 477, l. 31, after 'wealthy,' insert 'ane very unmeet match for she was past bairns bearing. . . . The King and Court mockit the same marriage, and made sonnets in their contempt, and specially his Majesty took his pastime of that sport (*Chronicles of the Kings of Scots*).'

p. 482, l. 17, after 'daughter,' insert 'Mr. Thomas Kennedy, son of the deceased Sir John Kennedy of Culzean and Lady Elizabeth Kennedy, daughter of the deceased John, Earl of Cassillis, were proclaimed with a view to marriage 10 September 1699, but "stopt by her order under hand 24 September 1699" (Edin. Mar. Reg.; cf. p. 490).'

p. 482, l. 23, for '1666' read '1668.'

p. 484, l. 13, for '20' read '26 (*Reg. Sec. Sig. Latin Reg.* iv. pt. ii. 182; *Gen. Reg. Sas.*, xxi. 129).'

p. 484, l. 15, after '1697-98,' insert 'post-nuptial contract 9 November 1698 (*Reg. of Deeds*, Dalrymple, 3 July 1710).'

p. 484, l. 30, delete 'She died 10 March 1734-35,' and insert 'She is called daughter of Sir Thomas Hutcheson, Knight, by his wife, a daughter of Sir Thomas Boteler, Knight, in her Funeral entry, Lyon office. She died at Barnton 10, and was buried at Holyrood, 16 March 1734. She is called Jean in the Holyrood Register.'

p. 485, l. 1, after 'married,' insert '26 (Canongate Reg.).'

p. 485, l. 19, for '7 March' read '8 August.'

p. 485, l. 22, for '1739' read '1738 (cf. vol. viii. 362; the *Gentleman's Mag.* gives the marriage as in October 1738).'

p. 487, l. 4, after 'wife,' insert 'contract 4 April and 15 May 1605.'

p. 487, l. 5, after 'Rowallan,' insert 'She died in January 1622 (Glasgow Tests.): in her testament she leaves Agnes Mure her "oye" certain sums of money which had been left by another Agnes Mure styled sister of the legatee in case of her decease before her marriage. Agnes was evidently the daughter of the William Mure, junior, mentioned in the charter of 20 June 1616 referred to in note 2.'

p. 488, l. 10, after '1629,' add 'He married, contract 15 February 1617, Margaret, daughter of Hew Kennedy of Garrihorn (*Reg. of Deeds*, ccccxlv. 1).'

p. 488, l. 15, after 'first,' insert 'contract 11 October 1600 (*Reg. of Deeds*, lxxxiv. 216).'

p. 488, l. 5 from foot, after '1643,' insert 'He was knighted at Holyrood 12 July 1633 (Balfour's *Annals*, iv. 366).

p. 489, l. 17, after 'married,' delete 'to James,' and insert 'in 1650 to Gilbert (*Ayr Sasines*, viii. 342).'

p. 489, l. 19, after 'married,' insert 'contract 12 April 1648 (*Ayr Sasines*, viii. 164).'

p. 493, l. 6, after '488.),' add note, 'A claim to the title is mentioned in the *General Evening Post* of 1-3 January 1793. It was made by Samuel Paterson, junior, a clerk in the Sun Fire Office, eldest son of Samuel

Paterson, librarian to the Marquess of Lansdowne. The wife of the elder Samuel, Mrs. Hamilton Lewis Paterson, died 29 November 1790, and is said (Ayre's *London Sunday Gazette*, 19 December 1790) to have been "a granddaughter of the noble houses of Kennedy and Cochrane, a niece of the late all accomplished Susanna, Countess of Eglinton, and cousin-german to the present Earls of Cassillis and Eglinton" (*Notes and Queries*, 11th ser., ii. 325). She was probably a granddaughter of Lewis Kennedy and Magdalene Cochrane (see p. 491). The claim of her son was of course never pressed. Both Patersons, senior and junior, are noticed in the *Dict. Nat. Biog.*'

p. 497, l. 3 from foot, delete entire line and accompanying note and insert 'and in 1793 a troop of yeomanry in Carrick, from which the Ayrshire Yeomanry (Earl of Carrick's Own), took its rise.'

p. 498, l. 11 from foot, delete 'and has,' and insert 'He died 10th April 1905, leaving issue.'

p. 500, l. 10 from foot, for 'March' read 'May.'

CATHCART

p. 516, l. 19, for 'before his father' read '15 May 1602.'

p. 516, l. 26, for 'a' read 'two.'

p. 516, l. 27, for 'daughter' read 'daughters.'

p. 516, l. 27, after '*Margaret*,' insert 'and *Jean*, the latter of whom was married, first, to Thomas, brother of William Cathcart of Bardarroch, and secondly, before 1626, to Archibald, brother of David Dunbar of Enterkin (*Reg. of Deeds*, ccclxxxiii. 8).'

p. 518, note 10, for '1572' read '1672.'

p. 519, l. 26, for '31' read '21 (*Caledonian Mercury*, 22 March 1733).'

p. 520, l. 2, after 'Bart,' delete 'by whom she had a daughter,' and insert 'She had a decreet of separation and aliment 7 March 1750 (*Consistorial Processes*, etc., Scot. Rec. Soc., No. 391; cf. vol. iii. 457).'

p. 520, l. 26, after 'Ireland,' insert 'On her wedding ring at her fourth marriage she had engraved "If I survive, I will have five."'

p. 521, l. 8, for '31 May' read '30 April (O.S.) or 11 May (N.S.).'

p. 522, l. 10 from foot, after '1764,' insert 'Bred at Glasgow, "very much under the eye of the Principal": graduated at Balliol College, Oxford, 1786.'

p. 522, l. 7 from foot, after '1802,' insert 'died 1841.'

p. 524, l. 6, for '1776' read '1796.'

p. 527, l. 7 from foot, for 'November' read 'December (*Patrician*, iii. 93).'

p. 530, l. 3 from foot, after 'Cambridge,' insert 'He died 30 October 1905.'

p. 531, l. 3, for 'and has,' read 'having had.'

p. 531, l. 6, after 'Scots Guards,' add 'He succeeded his father as fourth Earl, and died, unmarried, in London 2 September 1911, being succeeded, as fifth Earl, by his brother George.'

COLVILLE OF CULROSS

p. 542, after l. 11, insert—

'5. *Janet*, married Alexander *de jure* third Lord Boyd; there was a dispensation for the marriage, legitimising the children already born, 23 November 1505 (cf. vol. v. 151).'

p. **543,** l. 1, after 'Ersiltoun,' insert '(Dispensation about 29 November 1502).'

p. **543,** l. 2, delete 'Crichton, widow of —— Campbell,' and insert 'daughter of Sir Robert Crichton of Sanquhar, and widow of William Douglas, third of Drumlanrig, and of James Campbell of West Loudoun' (cf. vol. vii. 116).

p. **543,** l. 18, after 'Drumskeath,' add 'who was in 1522 parish clerk of Erskine (*Culzean Inventory*, No. 258).'

p. **543,** note 1, after '31,' add 'Margaret Ker must have been divorced and married again, as on 16 February 1508-9, she was the wife of a Robert Rynde (*Acta Dom. Conc.*, xx. f. 136).'

p. **557,** l. 18, after '1630,' add 'She married secondly, on 27 January 1622, Laurence, afterwards Sir Laurence Mercer of Aldie, and had issue (Mercer Pedigree in Lyon Office).'

p. **557,** after l. 22, insert—

'(3) *Mary*, married to Duncan Campbell of Glenlyon (*Reg. of Deeds*, DXXVI. 57).'

p. **557,** l. 2 from foot, after 'marriage,' add 'She was married to John Moncrieff of Balcaskie, and had a charter as his future spouse 16 October 1626 (*Fife Sasines*, vi. 176).'

COLVILLE OF OCHILTREE

p. **571,** l. 5, after '1596,' insert 'He married Katherine Douglas, who survived him and married, secondly, William Stewart of Egilshay.'

p. **572,** l. 2, after '*Elizabeth*,' add 'married (contract 1 November 1592) to James Lindsay of Dowhill (*Reg. of Deeds*, xlv. 255).'

p. **572,** l. 3, after '*Janet*,' insert 'married Robert Douglas.'

p. **572,** l. 3 from foot, after '*William*,' insert 'He was minister of Cramond, 1635, and subsequently of Greyfriars, Trinity College, and the Tron Kirks, all in Edinburgh (see Scott's *Fasti, passim*): deposed 26 July 1649, for favouring the "engagement," but reponed 8 November 1654 (Mar and Kellie Papers, *Hist. MSS. Com. Rep.*, 206). He was.'

p. **573,** l. 21, after 'secondly,' insert 'in the Kirk of Carnock, 25 February 1656 (Dumfermline Reg.).'

COUPAR

p. **577,** l. 13, after '1666,' insert 'when she was very young and subject to great pressure (*Athenæum*, 26 June 1905).'

CRANSTOUN

p. **586,** l. 20, after 'confirmed,' insert 'by that King about 1339, and.'

p. **586,** l. 21, after '1441,' insert 'He had also a grant from David II. on 24 July 1370 of the lands of New Cranstoun on his own resignation, to be held blench instead of ward (original at Oxenfoord).'

p. **586,** l. 23, after 'grants,' insert 'to him.'

p. **586**, l. 26, delete 'these,' and insert 'grants by William of Seton of certain.'

p. **586**, l. 29, delete 'by William of Seton; and of the,' and insert 'and another grant by Thomas, son of Duncan of Symondston, of that.'

p. **586**, l. 31, delete 'by Thomas, son of Duncan of Symondston.'

p. **587**, l. 6, after 'CRANYSTOUN,' insert 'had from Robert III. charters of Cranstoundaw and Whitehope 29 April, and of New Cranstoun 21 September 1396, both on his father's resignation (Oxenfoord Writs). He.'

p. **590**, l. 1, after 'Hume,' insert '(Dispensation granted about June 1503).'

p. **590**, l. 10, after 'Macgill,' insert 'daughter of Sir James Macgill of Rankeillor.'

p. **594**. l. 5, after 'Riccarton,' insert 'She was buried in the Kirk of Currie, 5 September 1702 (Funeral entry, Lyon Office).

p. **594**, l. 21, after 'Wauchope,' insert 'daughter of Adam Wauchope of Keckmure, and widow of Sir John Murray of Blackbarony (*Gen. Reg. Sasines*, vii. 89; cf. Douglas's *Baronage*, 71).'

p. **595**, l. 15, after 'secondly,' insert, 'contract 7 April 1623 (*Reg. of Deeds*, ccccIxxxvii. 66).'

p. **596**, last line, for 'second,' read 'fifth.'

p. **598**, l. 7, after '1752,' insert note, 'There is a full account of the circumstances in the *Patrician*, vol. vi., and in the *Wonderful Magazine*, vol. i. 209. The latter says of him "His person was diminutive: he was so marked with the smallpox that his face was in seams and he squinted, but he possessed the faculty of small talk which is but too prevailing with many of the fair sex."'

p. **601**, l. 7 from foot, for 'Forfarshire,' read 'Kincardineshire.'

VOL. III.

CRAWFORD

p. 8, l. 22 for 'Bene' read 'Beneyt.'

p. 11, l. 3 from foot, after '1369,' insert '(mandate for dispensation for this marriage dated 12 January 1365-66) (*Reg. Aven.*, clxiii. 176).'

p. 13, l. 23, after 'married,' insert '(mandate for dispensation of this marriage dated 18 May 1357) (*Reg. Aven.*, cxxxv. 386).'

p. 15, l. 22, after '1385,' delete 'a lady variously named Jean, Kathrina and.

p. 15, l. 24, after 'regis[10],' insert 'A dispensation for the marriage was issued 22 February 1374-75 (*Reg. Aven.*, cxcvii. 34).'

p. 16, l. 14, for 'Gasclune' read 'Glasclune.'

p. 18, l. 21, after 'married,' insert '(mandate for dispensation of this marriage, dated 26 February 1422-23) (*Cal. of Papal Letters*, vii. 260).'

p. 20, l. 6, after 'issue,' add 'He died before 10 May 1558, leaving *David*, *Jonet*, and *Christian*. His wife married, secondly, before that date, Abraham Crichton (*Acts and Decreets*, xvi. 301; xvii. 206).

p. 23, note 10, after 'Charters,' add 'The spouses had precept of sasine of lands in the barony of Alyth 10 June 1480 (Gray Inventory).'

p. 24, after l. 11, insert

'5. *Jonet*, mentioned in her mother's will (Edin. Tests).'

p. 25, l. 11, after 'David,' add 'He married Matilda, daughter of William Graham of Fintry (*Acts and Decreets*, xvii. 165).'

p. 26, after l. 3 from foot, insert

'The "Wicked Master" had also two sons, possibly illegitimate, *Alexander* and *Patrick* (*Acts and Decreets*, xix. 439; liii. 356).'

p. 27, l. 12, after 'afterwards,' insert 'before 10 April 1543.'

p. 27, l. 16, after 'first,' insert 'contract 28 May 1538 (*Acts and Decreets*, xliv. 129).'

p. 28, l. 16 delete 'Lord,' before Gray, and insert 'Patrick, Master of.'

p. 28, l. 16, after 'widow of,' insert 'Alexander Blair of Balthayock (Gray Inventory, 511) and of.'

p. 29, l. 12, for '1580' read '1582.'

p. 31, l. 5 from foot, after 'Crawford,' insert 'was baptized 8 March 1575-76 (Perth Reg.) and.'

p. 32, note 4, after '1618,' insert 'His wife, indeed, was suing for divorce in 1610 (*Gen. Reg. of Inhibitions*, i. 212).'

p. 32, note 5, for 'Haig' read 'Haigh.'

p. 33, l. 8 from foot, after 'Crawford,' add note 'He was probably older than Henry, as he is mentioned before him in a bond of provision by his father to his sons and daughters, dated 17 February 1616 (*Reg. of Deeds*, ccxci. 445).'

p. **33,** l. 4 from foot, after '1631,' insert 'She was married (contract 22 December 1626 (*Reg. of Deeds*, ccclxxxvii. 434) to Robert Fletcher of Balmirmer.'

p. **33,** after l. 4 from foot, insert

'10. *Annas*, probably second daughter, as she is mentioned after Margaret in the bond of provision above quoted.

11. *Lilias*, also mentioned in the bond.'

p. **35,** l. 5 from foot, for '1613' read '1633.'

p. **36,** l. 13, after 'Windsor Castle, insert note 'Lamont (*Diary*, August 1652) says he was imprisoned in the Tower. Lady Crawford went up from Leith by the ordinary coach to see him.'

p. **36,** l. 5 from foot, after 'buried,' add 'in August 1640 (Hope's *Diary*, 113).'

p. **36,** after last line insert

'6. *James*, baptized 12 January 1649 (Canongate Reg.).'

p. **37,** ll. 1, 4, 7, 9 and 11, for '6, 7, 8, 9, 10' read '7, 8, 9, 10, 11.'

p. **37,** l. 1, after 'Anna,' insert 'baptized 1 September 1631, and named after Anna, Marchioness of Hamilton (St. Andrews Reg.).'

p. **37,** l. 1, after 'married,' insert 'at the Kirk of Holyroodhouse 11 April 1648 (Canongate Reg.).'

p. **37,** l. 4, after 'married,' insert 'two days after her eldest sister (*Ibid.*).'

p. **37,** l. 21, after 'government,' insert 'The Earl figures in Pitcairn's comedy of *The Assembly* as Lord Whigridden, a Presbyterian Peer, a rigid fool. See also Maidment's *Scottish Elegiac Verses*.'

p. **38,** l. 1, after '*Thomas*,' insert 'born 12 January 1694 (Canongate Reg.).'

p. **40,** l. 11, for 'Cupar' read 'Ceres.'

p. **40,** l. 29, for '1769' read '1759.'

p. **43,** l. 26, delete 'left,' and insert 'died 15 August 1825, leaving.'

p. **46,** l. 30, for '1878' read '1873.'

p. **46,** l. 4 from foot, after 'George' delete 'comma'; for 'Baron' read 'Barons.'

p. **51,** l. 4, delete 'The arms anciently borne by the Lindsays were usually an Eagle,' and insert 'The Lindsays in ancient times seem to have borne an eagle as a device.'

CRICHTON

p. **57,** l. 8, after 'Gilberton,' insert note 'Recent research has brought to light the fact that on 1 July 1364 a grant of dispensation for the marriage of William de Krechtoun and Margaret, daughter of the late Sir John Preston, Knight, was issued (*Regesta Vaticana*, ccli. f. 302). If this lady be the Margaret Crichton who obtained the charter of Gilberton it would seem that she must have been the mother of all the sons.'

p. **57,** l. 25, after 'appears,' insert 'as the grantee of a bond on 1 March 1422. He is next mentioned.'

p. 64, l. 20, after 'Wardlaw,' insert 'of Kilbaberton (*Acta Dom. Conc.*, ix. 37).'

p. 67, l. 3 from foot, for 'at least one child,' read 'several children, including.'

p. 67, l. 2 from foot, after 'Rothes' insert 'By Patrick Panter, presumably the Abbot of Cambuskenneth, and Secretary to King James IV., she had a son David Panter, who was legitimated 12 August 1513 (*Reg. Mag. Sig.*, 19 January 1539-40), and became Bishop of Ross (Dowden's *Bishops of Scotland*, 228).'

CROMARTIE

p. 71, l. 7, after 'Macleod,' insert 'eldest daughter of Torquil Macleod of the Lewis (contract 6 May 1605).'

p. 71, after l. 22, insert

'6. *Torquil*, described as brother of Mr. Alexander and Charles in a writ of 1636, after his death (*Reg. of Deeds*, DXLIX. 215).'

p. 71, l. 24, after 'married,' insert 'contract 23 and 27 February 1633 (*Reg. of Deeds*, CCCCXCI. 40).'

p. 71, ll. 23, 24, for '6 and 7,' read '7 and 8.'

p. 72, l. 13, delete 'in,' and insert 'contract 25 July.'

p. 73, after l. 6, insert

'5. *Torquil*, baptized 28 September 1647 (Kinghorn Reg.).'

p. 73, l. 7, for '5' read '6.'

p. 73, l. 7, after '*Kenneth*,' insert 'baptized 26 November 1648 (*Ibid.*).'

p. 73, after l. 8, insert

'7. *Charles*, baptized 9 April 1650 (*Ibid.*).'

p. 73, ll. 9, 11, 14, 16, 18, and 20, for '6, 7, 8, 9, 10, 11' read '8, 9, 10, 11, 12, 13.'

p. 73, l. 18, after 'married,' insert 'contract 4 March 1670,'

p. 73, l. 20, after 'married,' insert 'contract 19 August 1667.'

p. 75, l. 29, after 'first,' delete 'in,' and insert 'contract 6 July 1654.'

p. 75, l. 30, for 'Moy' read 'Mey.'

p. 76, l. 6, after 'married,' insert 'first, Mary, sister of David Kinnear of that Ilk (*P. C. Decreta*, 4 December 1690); secondly.'

p. 76, l. 6, after 'Campbell,' insert 'thirdly, contract 14 January 1726, Elizabeth Edwards, widow, first, of Charles Graydon, and, secondly, of Alexander Sutherland of Kinminitie (see *infra*, p. 204).'

p. 76, l. 8 from foot, after 'married,' insert 'July 1674.'

p. 76, l. 7 from foot, after 'issue,' insert 'She raised an action of divorce against her husband 21 August 1694 (*Consistorial Processes*, Scot. Rec. Soc., No. 65). She died aged seventy, and was buried 29 September 1726 (Canongate Reg.).'

p. 76, l. 5 from foot, after 'issue,' insert 'Sir George and his two sons were drowned in Colston Water, near his own house, on Wednesday, 5 May 1703, "the lady who was in the coach with them was very miraculously preserved" (Turnbull's *Diary*, Scot. Hist. Soc. *Misc.*, i. 431).'

p. **77**, l. 3, for '11,' read '29 (*Wemyss Book*, i. 318).'
p. **77**, l. 5, for 'but,' read 'and.'
p. **77**, l. 6, delete 'no issue,' and insert 'a daughter Sophia, who died 15 August 1727, aged twenty-five (Canongate Reg.).'
p. **78**, l. 13, for 'May 1726' read 'at the age of nineteen, and was buried 7 June 1728 (Canongate Reg.).'
p. **81**, after l. 25, insert '9. *Amelia*,' and alter numeration of subsequent children accordingly.
p. **81**, l. 2 from foot, after 'Baronet,' insert 'full stop,' and delete 'and.' Insert 'She was divorced in 1791 for adultery with Robert Harrup, surgeon, Dumfries (*Consistorial Processes*, Scot. Rec. Soc., No. 963).'
p. **83**, l. 10, for '1597' read '1797.'
p. **83**, l. 4 from foot, for '11 March 1869' read '14 March 1895, aged ninety-nine.'
p. **86**, l. 4, after '1st,' insert 'or.'

DALHOUSIE

p. **88**, after l. 2 from foot, insert 'In light of more recent research the pedigree and statements given on pp. 89, 90 fall to be revised. The William Ramsay de Dalwolsy mentioned above was probably the father of:—

1. Sir William, of whom below.

2. *Alexander*, who had from his brother, Sir William, a charter of the lands of Kernok, confirmed by David II. 11 November 1341 (note of Carnock charters communicated by Horatius Bonar, W.S.). About the same time he had from the same king a charter of the lands of Hawthornden, forfeited by Laurence Abernethy (*Reg. Mag. Sig.* i. new ed. App. 2, p. 563). He was, no doubt, the hero of the exploits recounted on p. 89 of text, and the victim of the Knight of Liddesdale's revenge. He was buried in Newbattle Church, see text p. 90, l. 29. He left a son Alexander, of whom below.

Sir William Ramsay was at Berwick in 1338 as in text; granted Carnock to his younger brother as above; and was on the assize who tried Malise, Earl of Strathearn for treason in 1344 (Roll of Parliament, printed in *Scottish Historical Review* for April 1912). He had from David II. a charter of the lands of Inverleith about 1346 (Robertson's *Index*, 36). He left issue:—

1. Sir Patrick, of whom below.

2. *Sir William*, Sheriff of Lothian in 1357, when he is styled brother of Patrick (Reg. of Newbattle, 309). He had from David II. a grant of £20 sterling yearly, 9 September 1362 (*Reg. Mag. Sig.*, vol. i. new ed. No. 109), and another to him (as of Dalwolsy) and Agnes his wife of the lands of Nether Liberton on 24 October 1369 (*Ibid.*, No. 334). He is styled thus probably to distinguish him from his contemporary Sir William Ramsay of Culluthy; he is never styled *dominus* de Dalhousie. He and his wife sold Nether Liberton to Adam Forrester of Corstor-

phine, 10 April 1384; he styles himself in the charter "lord of Inverleith" (notes from Corstorphine Charters by Thomas Thomson, W.S.). On 6 June 1377 he had a safe-conduct from Edward III., being infirm of body and under the care of the prior of Bermondsey (*Rot. Scot.*, i. 982). He was alive in 1388-89 (*Exch. Rolls*, iii. 188, 693). He had a son David, who had from Robert II. a charter of Inverleith, on his father's resignation, 2 July 1384 (*Reg. Mag. Sig.*, vol. i. new ed. No. 791).

SIR PATRICK was lord of Dalwolsy before 1353 and in 1357 as in text. He styles Alexander his uncle at the latter date (see text). In 1367 (not 1357 as text) he resigned the barony of Dalwolsy in favour of his cousin Alexander (see below). Thereafter he is styled of Kerynton (Charter of 1369 quoted in text). His wife's name was Margaret (see text), and he had a son James, a substitute in the Dalwolsy charter of 1367 (see below).

ALEXANDER, son of Alexander Ramsay of Kernok, had from David II. a charter of the barony of Dalwolsy to himself and the heirs of his body, whom failing, to James, son of Sir Patrick Ramsay and the heirs of his body, whom failing, Sir Patrick's nearest heirs bearing his surname; on Sir Patrick's resignation, dated 15 June 1367 (Original charter belonging to the Earl of Dalhousie), Alexander's charter granting the Blindhalch to Newbattle Abbey, quoted in text, is undated, but must have been granted between 1369 and 1374. It does not appear whether the later lords of Dalhousie were descended from Alexander or from his cousin James.'

p. **92**, l. 3, after 'issue,' insert '(besides a daughter Jonet, to whom her grandfather on 3 April 1456 granted a bond to pay her 500 merks Scots in the event of her brother Alexander dying without issue, in which case she would have succeeded to the estates but for the tailzie of the day before) (original in Dalhousie Charter-chest).'

p. **92**, l. 19, after 'Elizabeth,' insert 'more correctly Isabel.'

p. **92**, l. 20, after 'Angus,' delete 'and,' and insert 'who survived him and was married, secondly, to Thomas Livingstone (*Liber Sententiarum Officialis S. Andree infra Laudoniam*, fol. 55). By her Alexander.'

p. **92**, l. 22, after '*Elizabeth*,' insert 'married to Sir Alexander Boswell of Balmuto (*ex inform.* Marquis de Ruvigny),'

p. **92**, l. 8 from foot, after 'married,' insert 'first, Elene Home, whom he divorced (notarial instrument *penes* Fraser Trustees); secondly.'

p. **94**, l. 2, after 'complainer,' insert 'He was a burgess of Edinburgh: he married Janet Wycht and had issue *William* and *Nicol* (*Edinburgh Burgh Reg. of Deeds*, vol. vi., 19 September 1595), and *John* (Reg. Ho. Charters, 24 September 1595).'

p. **94**, l. 7, after 'Agnes Stewart,' insert 'Countess of Bothwell.'

p. **94**, l. 18, for 'married to' read 'mothers of.'

p. **95**, l. 8 from foot, after 'Berwick,' add 'She was certainly in 1598 the wife of Lawrence Howburn, styled "apparent of Tullibole" (*Reg. of Deeds*, lxxiii. 70).'

p. **95,** l. 2 from foot, after '1570,' add 'He is also styled son of George Ramsay of Dalhousie in a writ of 29 July 1570 (Protocol Book of Gilbert Grote, f. 132), but nothing more is known of him.'

p. **95,** delete last sentence on page, as the statement applies to the William Ramsay mentioned on pp. 93, 94.

p. **97,** l. 18, after 'marriage,' insert 'of date 16 April 1593 (*Reg. of Deeds*, xlvi. 53).'

p. **99,** l. 7, for 'and' read 'OF.'

p. **99,** l. 2 from foot, after '*John*,' insert 'He married, in or before 1660, Marjorie Spence, and had by her at least one son,

WILLIAM, afterwards sixth Earl of Dalhousie.'

p. **100,** l. 27, delete 'He married,' and the whole of ll. 28, 29, 30.

p. **101,** after l. 14, insert

'4. *James*, mentioned in his brother Robert's testament.'

p. **101,** l. 15, for '4' read '5.'

p. **101,** after l. 15, insert

'6. *Lydia*, mentioned with her brothers and sisters in Robert's testament.'

p. **101,** l. 16, for '5' read '7.'

p. **101,** l. 16, after 'first,' insert 'in 1665 (cf. vol. vi. 600).'

p. **101,** l. 16, for 'tenth' read 'eleventh.'

p. **101,** l. 17, after 'secondly,' insert 'contract 26 December 1684.'

p. **101,** l. 19, for '6' read '8.'

p. **101,** l. 21, for '7' read '9.'

p. **101,** ll. 7 and 8 from foot, delete 'and, thirdly, to Samuel Collins, M.D.' (The statement to this effect in Wood's Douglas's *Peerage* is erroneous.)

p. **102,** l. 21, delete 'Captain.'

p. **102,** l. 22, delete 'full stop' and 'Captain Ramsay was the,' and insert comma.

p. **102,** l. 23, for 'second' read 'first.'

p. **102,** l. 23, after 'was,' insert 'baptized at Dundee 2 December 1660 (Dundee Par. Reg.); became.'

p. **103,** l. 17, for '3rd' read '1st' (Hamilton's *Hist. of the Grenadier Guards*).'

p. **104,** l. 4, after '1831,' insert 'He died 13 April 1852, having married, first, 1 December 1794, Patricia Heron, daughter of Gilbert Gordon of Halleaths, who died 11 May 1821, and, secondly, in 1822, Elizabeth, daughter of John William Barton. She survived him and married, secondly, 25 April 1856, Bonamy Mansell Power of Guernsey, and died at Paris 25 June 1867.'

p. **104,** l. 15, for '1743' read '1793.'

p. **104,** l. 22, for 'second' read 'served.'

p. **105,** l. 10, delete 'full stop,' and insert 'comma, a daughter *Charlotte*, who married Marcus Slade, colonel 50th Regiment, and died at Hampton Court 23 February 1909, aged eighty-six.'

p. **105,** l. 4 from foot, delete 'and was present at the battle of Waterloo.'

p. **106,** l. 19, for '76th Foot' read '26th Foot.'

p. **107,** l. 23, for '19 October' read '22 December (Cockpen Par. Reg.).'

p. **107,** l. 26, for '1850' read '1853.'

p. **110,** l. 3, for 'CREST' read 'CRESTS.'

p. **110,** l. 4, after 'or,' for full stop put comma, and insert 'for *Ramsay*: a double-headed wyvern with wings erect, spouting fire before and behind, proper, for *Maule*.'

DINGWALL

p. **117,** l. 20, after 'Knight,' insert 'On 21 June 1338 he had a grant from his (half?) sister Christian of the lands of Myles, East Lothian, to which she had succeeded as heir of her brother Laurence de Preston, and which Edward III. had treated as forfeited (Craigmillar Charters; *Cal. of Docs. Scot.*, iii. 337, 385).'

p. **118,** l. 2, after 'Edinburgh,' delete 'His son,' and insert 'He died before 1 July 1364. He had two sons and a daughter:—

1. SIMON, of whom after.

2. *William*, who had from Robert III. a charter of the lands of Wester Benyne *circâ* 1399 (*Reg. Mag. Sig.*, vol. i. new ed. p. 642, No. 1884). He as Knight and Lord of Benyne granted some subjects in Musselburgh to Andrew, son of his deceased brother-german, Sir Simon, 28 May 1420 (Craigmillar Charters).

3. *Margaret* (see *ante* corrigend., on vol. iii. p. 57, l. 8).'

p. **118,** l. 16, after 'Robert III.,' insert 'He had from his father a charter of Loganraw and others in 1395 (*Ibid.*), which was witnessed by his brother Andrew and by a hitherto unknown brother, *John*.'

p. **118,** l. 17, after 'Craigmillar,' insert 'He died 22 August 1421 (*Ibid.*).'

p. **118,** l. 18, and l. 4 of footnotes, for '1421' read '1426.'

p. **119,** l. 11, after 'right,' insert 'He had a grant, on 21 June 1497, from his cousin, Sir Simon Preston of that Ilk, of the lands of Loganraw and others (Craigmillar Charters).'

p. **119,** l. 19, after 'day,' insert 'He had a precept of clare constat as heir of Archibald, his father, in Loganraw 12 October 1526 (*Ibid.*).'

p. **119,** l. 4 from foot, after '1532,' insert 'and another as heir of his father in Loganraw 16 October 1531 (*Ibid.*).'

p. **124,** ll. 5, 7 and 27, for 'Gray' read 'Grey.'

p. **124,** l. 20, for 'Julien' read 'Julian.'

MAXWELL, EARL OF DIRLETON

p. **131,** after l. 3, add

'3. *Jane*, married to —— Wharwood.

4. *Anne*, married, in or before 1642, as his third wife, to Sir Thomas Bowyer, first Baronet of Leythorne. Both these children are mentioned in their mother's will, dated 22 August 1657, and proved in C.P.C. 20 August 1660 (*ex inform.* G. E. Cokayne).'

DOUGLAS, EARL OF DOUGLAS

p. **140,** l. 21, after '1305,' insert 'But before the end of that year she was married, secondly, to Sir William Bagot of the Hyde (*Collections for a*

History of Staffordshire by Major-General the Hon. George Wrottesley: London, 1908; *Genealogist*, xxv. 140).'

p. 141, l. 8, for 'Aberdeenshire,' read 'Banffshire.'

p. 152, l. 2 from foot, for '1584' read '1384-85.'

DOUNE

p. 186, l. 6 from foot, for 'Whitsunday 1547' read 'Whitmonday 1544, three years before the remission (*Reg. Sec. Sig.*, xxi. f. 40*b*, 4 September 1547).'

p. 187, l. 2, after 'Aichisoune,' delete full stop, and insert 'who had previously been the wife of —— Fraser (by whom she had a daughter Margaret, her executor), of John Logan (*Reg. of Deeds*, ii. 20), and of William Berry, burgess of Edinburgh (Moray Writs, Box i. No. 57).'

p. 187, l. 7, after 'ward,' insert 'He died 2 September 1584. His wife survived him and died 26 March 1585 (Edin. Tests.).'

p. 187, l. 11, after 'Buchlivie,' insert 'He died in August 1576 (*Edin. Sasines*).'

p. 187, l. 13, after 'Aberdour,' insert '(who is styled in 1582 Elizabeth Robertson or Downie (Moray Writs, Box i. No. 24), and who married, secondly, before 18 October 1597, John Wemyss of Cutkillhill (*Ibid.*, Box iv. No. 114).'

p. 187, l. 15, for '*Janet*' read '*Barbara* (*ex inform.* Niall Campbell, Esq.).'

p. 187, after l. 19, insert

'(2) *John*, mentioned in his father's will. He died before 10 November 1595, leaving a widow, Esther Thomson (Moray Writs, Box iv. No. 97).'

p. 187, l. 20, after '1619,' insert 'married (contract 7 April 1614), Agnes, eldest daughter of William Shaw of Lethangie, with issue.'

p. 187, ll. 20 and 21, for '(2)' and '(3)' read '(3)' and '(4).'

p. 187, l. 2 from foot, for 'II.' read 'I.'

p. 188, l. 5 from foot, after 'Revenues,' insert 'He and his wife had a charter of the lordship of Doune, 6 January 1587-88, ratified to his grandson, James, Earl of Moray, in 1592 (*Acta Parl. Scot.*, iii. 628; *Reg. Mag. Sig.*). She was at Donibristle when it was burned on 7 February 1591-92, and she was so suffocated by the fire that she died shortly after (Moray Writs, Box iv. No. 58).'

p. 188, note 11, after '258,' add 'His will, dated 5 May 1590, is among the Moray Writs (Box i. No. 52).'

p. 189, after l. 24, insert, 'In a note of the names of Lady Doune's executors (Moray Writs, Box iv. No. 59) Alexander is named before John; Archibald is not named, so was probably dead. The daughters mentioned are *Margaret*, *Jean* and *Agnes*.'

p. 189, l. 25, for 'III.' read 'II.'

DUFFUS

p. 194, l. 22, after 'issue,' insert 'She married, secondly, Sir Thomas Lundie of Pratis.'

p. **194**, l. 23, after 'Oliphant,' add 'and, thirdly, Sir William Keith of Inverugy (*Acta Dom. Concilii*, xxviii. f. 71; cf. ff. 181, 192).'

p. **195**, after l. 19, insert

'5. *Muriel* Sutherland, wife of Alexander Seton of Meldrum, was, it is said, another daughter. She was also the wife of Andrew Fraser of Stanywood. (*See title* Fraser, vol. iii. 109; cf. *Reg. Mag. Sig.*, ii. No. 2507; *Thanage of Fermartyne*, 688).'

p. **202**, l. 2, after 'him,' insert 'being styled domina de Duffus 13 October 1579 (*Reg. Mag. Sig.*, 6 December 1579), and.'

p. **202**, l. 27, after 'Rearquhar,' add note 'William Sutherland of Rearquhar died before 10 March 1707. He left two daughters, *Christian* and *Margaret*. He is described as brother-german of Hugh Sutherland of Kinnauld (*Abbreviate of Adjudications*, vol. lvii. 10 March 1707).'

p. **204**, l. 1, delete 'before 1604,' and insert 'contract 21 December 1604 (Bulloch's *House of Gordon*, 84; *Reg. Mag. Sig.*, 25 November 1608).'

p. **204**, l. 25, delete 'was apparently twice married, his second wife being,' and insert 'styled of Mosstowie, married, first, Barbara Guthrie, daughter of Sir Henry Guthrie of Kingedward, widow of William Lindsay of Culsh (*Abbreviate of Adjudications*, lxvii. pt. ii. 775), and had issue; secondly.'

p. **204**, l. 32, after 'married,' insert '(contract dated 30 April 1715) (Durie *Decreets*, vol. 486).'

p. **204**, l. 32, after 'Edwards,' insert 'of Monmouth, widow of Charles Graydon, Receiver-General of Customs in Scotland (by whom she had issue a son, *Charles*).'

p. **204**, l. 33, after 'Grandvale,' add note 'On 4 October 1727 she assigned to Sir Kenneth, *inter alia*, her share of thirty-two shares of 100 guineas each assigned by Archibald, Earl of Argyll, on 28 March 1691, giving right to a share of all manner of guns, sums of money, gold, silver, jewels, treasure, etc., which at any time had been wrecked or at any time found near or about the island of Mull or elsewhere upon or adjoining to Argyllshire on the coast of Scotland (*Reg. of Deeds*, M'Ken. Office, 143, 19 January 1728. The writer is indebted to Mr. D. Murray Rose for directing attention to this fact, and other additions to this article).'

p. **209**, l. 18, after 'thirdly,' insert '(contract dated 26 August 1654; tocher £8000 and any jewels left her by her grandmother) (Moray Writs).'

p. **209**, after l. 29, insert 'On 3 April 1666 Lord Duffus writes that his youngest son was dead. Robin and Marie were unwell on 6 March 1666 (*ex inform.* John Macgregor, W.S.).'

p. **212**, l. 1, after '*Elizabeth*,' insert 'fourth daughter. She was in 1704 taught dancing by William Badhame, dancing master, Edinburgh, who received £50 for his tuition (Dunbar's *Social Life in Former Days*, 14). She was married (contract 21 November 1709) as daughter of James, Lord Duffus, and sister-german of William Sutherland of Roscommon, to Sir John Gordon of Embo (*Inverness Sasines*, vii. 47).'

p. **212**, after l. 7, add

'11. *Isabel*, buried in Greyfriars, Edinburgh, 26 July 1694 (Greyfriars Reg.).

12. *Esther*, married to John Rose in Balvraid; they were infeft in the lands of Easter Balvraid 22 November 1711.'

p. **213**, l. 3, after 'executors,' insert 'Married to Baron Otto Gustaff Wrede of the kingdom of Sweden (Summons, Sutherland *v.* Sutherland, 3 April 1778, in *Extinct Processes*, Sale of Skelbo (Dal.), 29 June 1787).'

p. **214**, l. 9, after 'Army,' insert 'In 1771 he eloped (being then a Captain in the 26th Foot) with Lady Mary Hay, daughter of James, Earl of Erroll, and wife of Major-General John Scott of Balcomie, whom she had married in November of the previous year (*Consistorial Processes, etc.*, Scot. Rec. Soc., No. 583).'

p. **215**, l. 20, for 'surmounted' read 'surrounded.'

DUMBARTON

p. **217**, l. 17, after 'issue,' insert 'besides two daughters.'

DUMFRIES

p. **221**, l. 7 from foot, after 'Elgin,' insert 'On 8 May 1472 he had from George, Lord Haliburton, a charter of the lands of Rossie (now Rossieochil) (Rossie Charters). He was styled of Rossie, and died before 2 February 1502-3, leaving a son and heir *John* (*Reg. Mag. Sig.*, 3 March 1502-3), who died before March 1507-8, leaving a widow Katherine Ross (*Acta Dom. Conc.*, xix. 231), and a daughter *Margaret*, his heir, who married Andrew Stewart of Calzebrochan, and had issue (Rossie Charters).'

p. **224**, l. 7, after 'craig,[2]' add as note 'Robert Crichton had probably another daughter. At least in a charter of 1509 Robert, second Lord Crichton describes Thomas Kilpatrick of Closeburn as his brother-in-law. A Margaret Sinclair, widow of the late Patrick Crichton of Petlandy, is described on 6 February 1523-24 as sister of the late Robert (second) Lord Crichton. She had a son *Robert* (*Acta Dom. Conc.*, vol. xxxiv. 84).'

p. **228**, l. 5, after '1677,' insert 'and was then probably the eldest surviving son.'

p. **228**, l. 6, after '*William*,' insert 'eldest son (*Reg. of Deeds*, DLX. 108).'

p. **228**, after l. 8, insert

'iii. *John*, second son, mentioned 1646 (*Ibid.*) and 22 May 1649 (*Reg. Mag. Sig.*).'

p. **228**, ll. 9 and 12, for 'iii' and 'iv' read 'iv' and 'v.'

p. **228**, note 6, for '*Dumfries Retours*' read '*Ayr Retours.*'

p. **231**, l. 23, after '1612,' insert 'Robert Carlyle and James Irving were hanged in Fleet Street for their share of the crime on 24 June (Craik's *Romance of the Aristocracy*, iii. 344).'

p. 231, l. 26, after 'issue,' insert 'It is stated that he had been divorced from his wife only two days before the murder was committed. She, however, came and stayed with him in prison (Craik, *ut supra*, 357). It is also said (Winwood, iii. 385) that she married in a few weeks after Crichton's execution, "one Sands of Buckinghamshire."'

p. 231, l. 5 from foot, after 'lady,' add note 'A base courtesan in Paris (Spotswood).'

p. 231, note 2, add 'Apparently £500 was offered for Crichton alive and £300 dead (Sloane, MS. 4173 f. 318, cited in Craik's *Romance, etc.*, iii. 342).

p. 234, l. 11, delete 'in 1642 and 1643,' and insert 'on 19 December 1637 (*Reg. Mag. Sig.*, 16 January 1638).'

p. 235, l. 21, after '1618,' add note, 'They were married by Mr. John Guthrie, minister of Perth on "ane Sunday after the afternoon's sermon" (*Chronicles of Perth*).'

p. 236, l. 10, after 'Alexander' read 'afterwards.'

p. 236, l. 10, after 'Eglinton,' insert 'He "ran away without any advice," and married her, the daughter of "a broken man," when he was sure of Lady Buccleuch's marriage, "the greatest match in Britain. This unexpected prank is worse to all his kin than his death would have been" (Baillie's *Letters*, iii. 366).'

p. 236, l. 30, for 'French' read 'Freugh.'

p. 236, l, 5 from foot, after '1803,' insert 'They had issue a son

i. *William*, Prebendary of Peterborough, who, by his wife Euphemia Gauden had issue:—

(i) *John Crichton Stuart* of New Freugh, N.S.W. He married, first, in 1841, Helen Maria, daughter of R. A. Fitzgerald; secondly, in 1864, Susan Mary, daughter of the Rev. Edward Hartigan, with issue by first wife:—

a. William Sutherland, Rector of Owsden, Suffolk.'

p. 237, l. 19, for '26 July' read '19 June (*Annual Reg.*).'

p. 238, l. 11, for '*Vallange*' read '*Ross*.' (The name in the text is that given in the Lyon Register.)

DUNBAR, EARL OF DUNBAR

p. 252, l. 27, for 'Bruce' read 'Brice.'

p. 273, l. 24, delete whole line, and insert 'to have been a Seton but may have been the daughter of Alan de Wyntoun who married the heiress of Seton and seems to have taken her name (*ex inform.* Colonel the Hon. R. E. Boyle).'

p. 278, l. 13, delete from 'probably' to 'Colluthie' inclusive with note 7, and insert after 'Wemyss' 'whose parentage is not known. She married, before 1566, a John Wemyss and was his wife in 1570 (*Acts and Decreets*, xxxix. 431; xlv. 289).'

HOME, EARL OF DUNBAR

p. 280, l. 2 from foot, delete from 'married' to end of sentence.

p. 282, l. 23, for 'a son' read 'four sons and five daughters.'

p. 282, l. 14 from foot, after 'sons,' add 'by his second wife, besides a daughter *Isobel* by his first (*Gen. Reg. Hornings*, 18 October 1676).'

p. 283, after l. 7, insert
'ii. *Patrick.*'

p. 283, l. 8, for 'ii' read 'iii.'

p. 283, after l. 15, insert
'iv. *Alexander.* v. *Margaret.* vi. *Jonet.* vii. *Anne.* viii. *Elspeth.* ix. *Helen.* (*Reg. of Deeds*, cccxliii. 318).'

p. 284, l. 16, after 'secondly,' insert 'contract 14 August 1610 (*Reg. of Deeds*, cccxi. 16).'

p. 284, l. 18, after 'Edinburgh,' insert 'and widow of Isaac Morison, bailie of Edinburgh (Laing Hist. MS. Bibl. Univ. Edin. Div. ii. No. 473). She obtained decree of Adherence against him 22 June 1620 (*Edin. Com. Decreets*).'

p. 285, after l. 32, insert
'viii. *Margaret*, married to John Stewart of Coldingham (*Gen. Reg. Inhibs.*, 26 September 1631; cf. vol. ii. 171).'

p. 286, l. 12, after '1628,' insert 'married Christian Cockburn.'

VISCOUNT OF DUNBAR

p. 298, l. 8, delete 'She was living at the date of her husband's will,' and insert 'She married, secondly, John Dalton of Swine, co. York (*Genealogist*, new ser., xxvii. 220).'

SCRYMGEOUR, EARL OF DUNDEE

p. 304, l. 25, after 'Baliol,' insert 'He died in 1306, being executed by order of King Edward I. (*Cal. Doc. Scot.*, ii. No. 1811). He married Tiphanie, daughter of David de Inchesirth (*Scrymgeour Invent.*, Scot. Rec. Soc., No. 782).'

p. 305, l. 2, after '*reddendo*,' insert 'for the lands.'

p. 305, l. 3, after 'spurs,' insert note, 'A Richard Scrymgeour is mentioned as Constable of Dundee in 1329 (Inventory *ut sup.*, No. 147).'

p. 306, after l. 7, insert
'2. *John* (secundus) of Henristoun, styled *scutifer* in 1459; married Janet Stag and had issue *John* and *James* (charter of 20 July 1431. *Lauderdale Charter Chest*).

3. *James*, mentioned in 1418 (*Lauderdale Writs*).

4. *David*, mentioned in 1452 and had a charter of Balmakewan (Inventory *ut sup.*, No. 857).'

p. 306, l. 8, for '2' read '5.'

p. 306, ll. 20, 21, delete 'He died between January 1459-60 and August 1463,' and insert 'He was still alive on 8 August 1466 (*Acta Parl. Scot.*, vii. 160), and the date of his death is not exactly known.'

p. 306, l. 24, after 'Marion,' insert 'de Abernethy.'

p. 306, after l. 28, insert

'4. *John* (by third wife) (*Lauderdale Writs*).'

p. 306, last line, delete 'He had succeeded his father before,' and insert 'On.'

p. 307, l. 1, delete 'when.'

p. 307, l. 11, after 'Glassary,' insert '(by second wife) (*Acta Dom. Conc.*, 118).'

p. 308, l. 7, delete '1503,' and insert '4 April 1504 (Fife Sheriff-Court Book, f. 40).'

p. 308, l. 14, delete '——,' and insert '4. *Giles* (Benholm Writs).'

p. 309, l. 4, delete 'before 17 December 1551,' and insert 'in February 1543-44 (*Acts and Decreets*, xlix. 38*b*).'

p. 309, l. 9, for '1583' read '1533.'

p. 309, l. 18, after 'Kirkton,' insert 'It appears that they contracted marriage without her father's consent (*Acta Dom. Conc. et Sessionis*, vi. f. 111*b*).'

p. 309, l. 22, for 'to' read 'of.'

p. 309, l. 10 from foot, after 'inserted,' insert note, 'Since the above was written, the House of Lords (*App. Cases*, 1910, p. 342), reversing the decision of the Court of Session, has found that the office of Standard Bearer belonged *jure sanguinis* to the male representative of the house of Scrymgeour. The descent of Mr. Henry Scrymgeour Wedderburn from David Scrymgeour of Sonahard was admitted. Who this David of Sonahard was has not been definitely proved, but there is a presumption that he may have been identical with that David of Balmakewan mentioned above (*corrig*, on p. 306, line 7). Meanwhile, unless and until an heir is found with undoubted nearer descent, the effect of the House of Lords' judgment is that Mr. Scrymgeour Wedderburn has, as representative of the House of Scrymgeour, acted as the Hereditary Standard Bearer of Scotland at the coronation of King George v.

p. 309, l. 3 from foot, after 'Scrimgeour,' insert 'by his second wife, Margaret Maitland.'

p. 311, l. 6, after 'married,' insert 'contract 1583 (Moray Writs, Box xv., No. 1800).'

p. 312, l. 11, after 'uncle,' insert 'comma.'

p. 313, after l. 15, insert

'4. *Elspeth*, married to John Campbell of Lundie, without issue (Moray Writs, box xv. No. 1574).'

p. 313, ll. 24, 25, for '13 March' read '15 November.'

p. 313, l. 28, for 'George' read 'Sir David.'

p. 314, l. 2, after '*Margaret*,' insert '(afterwards wife of James Alexander, son of the first Earl of Stirling).'

p. 314, l. 11, after 'married,' insert 'contract 2 and 30 July 1617 (*Reg. of Deeds*, cclxxxiv. 1497).'

p. 315, l. 6, for '1486' read '1686.'

p. 315, l. 7, after '1686-87,' insert 'She was buried at Holyrood in 1697 (Warrant of 24 February; *P. C. Acta*).'

p. 315, note 7, for 'Fordell' read 'Fardill.'

GRAHAM, VISCOUNT OF DUNDEE

p. 316, l. 11, after 'issue,' add

'1. *David*, who had issue a son (*Douglas Book*, iii. 119).'

p. 316, l. 23, for 'Dudhope' read 'Glassary.'

p. 319, l. 14, delete 'after 3 June,' and insert 'contract 20 May (*Reg. of Deeds*, xlvii. 74).'

p. 321, l. 18, for '*circâ* 1616-17' read 'contract 13 March 1617 (*Reg. of Deeds*, ccclxxxvii. 384).'

p. 324, l. 21, after 'to,' insert 'Robert, son of (*Aberdeen and Kincardine Sasines*, 23 April 1665).'

p. 324, l. 22, delete 'was his second wife,[9] and,' with relative note.

p. 324, l. 4 from foot, delete 'Sir.'

DUNDONALD

Since the present article was written, the *Inventory of the Writs of the Earldom of Dundonald* has been published by the Scottish Record Society, and the information therein contained makes some changes on the pedigree given in the text necessary.

p. 336, l. 10, after 'assessment of,' insert 'a.'

p. 336, l. 12, after '1603,' insert note, 'The "four merk land of Linclive" appears to have been part of Wester Cochrane, and is mentioned in a wadset of 2 April 1583 (*Dundonald Inventory*, No. 24). It is not clear that the John Cochrane living there in 1460 was John Cochrane of that Ilk. In 1522 there is mention of a John Cochrane and Margaret Morton, his spouse, as joint tenants of Lincliff (Paisley Rental Book).'

p. 336, l. 16, delete 'issue as far as recorded,' and insert on next line

'Robert of Cochrane, who, on 5 March 1456-57, resigned the lands of Cochrane in favour of his son Allan (*Dundonald Inventory*, No. 2).'

p. 336, l. 17, insert 'Robert' after 'father.'

p. 336, l. 21, after 'Armiger,' insert 'He had a charter of the lands of Cochrane from King James II. on the resignation of his father Robert, as above stated (*Dundonald Inventory*, No. 2).'

p. 336, ll. 23, 24, 25, delete 'comma' after '1476,' and insert 'full stop'; delete 'and must have succeeded his father by 1480, as on 8 May of that year,' and insert 'On 8 May 1480.'

p. **336,** l. 10 of notes, after '1488,' delete remaining lines and insert 'Peter married Isobel Spreull (*Acta Dom. Conc.*, xxii. 61) and was succeeded by John Cochrane, though there is nothing to show that John was his son. John Cochrane had sasine of Nether (or Easter) Cochrane in 1505 (*Exchequer Rolls*, xii. 717), and as "John Cochrane of that Ilk" entered into a contract with Isobel Spreull, "relict of Peter Cochrane, now spouse of Patrick Dunyng, anent her terce of Pitfour and others" (*Acta Dom. Conc.*, xxii. 61). Easter Cochrane was sold in 1519 to Archbishop James Beaton by a licence granted under the Privy Seal in 1509 (*Reg. Sec. Sig.*, i. 1943), and John Cochrane, was thereafter styled "of Pitfour," and held the lands under the superiority of the Earl of Crawford, by whom he had been infeft 2 May 1510. He was succeeded by his son *Peter*, who is named in a charter under the Great Seal to George Rollok of Duncrub in 1572, and who was followed by his son David. *David* died 1598, leaving nine children, and his will was proved in Edinburgh 23 January 1598-99. His successor, *Francis Cochrane* of Pitfour, is named in a cause that came before the Privy Council 1605. He was seised in the lands of Pitfour 4 September 1607, and is the last of that line. The Cochranes of Easter Cochrane and of Pitfour may have been descended from a Roger or Robert Cochrane who had a charter of Pitfour and others from King David II. about 1360 (*Reg. Mag. Sig.*, vol. i., new ed., App. 2, 1356).'

p. **337,** delete ll. 10, 11 and 12, and insert 'He died *vitâ patris s.p.*'

p. **337,** l. 13, delete from 'Robert Cochrane' down to 'of that Ilk' on l. 5 from foot of p. 338 and accompanying notes, and insert as follows:—

'ROBERT COCHRANE of that Ilk must have succeeded about 1488, as in that year he had sasine of the lands of Cochrane by command of Matthew, Earl of Lennox (*Dundonald Inventory*, No. 4). He was alive 2 January 1516-17, when he gave sasine of the lands to his son John and his wife (*Ibid.*, No. 7).

JOHN COCHRANE of that Ilk was seised in the lands of Cochrane by Robert, his father, 10 January 1492 (*Ibid.*, No. 5) and had a charter of the same lands 13 January 1498 (*Ibid.*, No. 6). He married Elizabeth Semple, before 20 January 1486-87, when they had a charter of Corsefoord (*Ibid.*, No. 26).

JOHN COCHRANE of that Ilk, served heir to his grandfather in the lands of Wester Cochrane 8 May 1520 (*Ibid.*, No. 8), and married Marion Stewart, who was his widow 27 November 1540 (*Acts and Decreets*, xxxiv. 385), and who, in 1556, was the wife of John Gibson (*Ibid.*, xii. 248). He had issue JOHN, who succeeded him, *William*, who is mentioned with Marion Stewart, his mother, in a renunciation dated 1 April 1565 (*Inventory*, No. 22), and *David*, who occurs in a mortgage on the lands of Cochrane with his brother William, 28 May 1536 (*Laing Charters*, 409).

JOHN COCHRANE of that Ilk succeeded his father 12 May 1539 (*Inventory*, No. 11). He is stated by Crawfurd to have married Mary, daughter of Lindsay of Dunrod, of which marriage no evidence has been found. He certainly married Elizabeth Semple of Fulwood, and with her had a charter of the lands of Craigton, dated 5 April 1529 (*Ibid.*, No. 9). By her he had issue:—

1. WILLIAM, who succeeded him.
2. *Janet*, named in the will of Elizabeth Montgomery, her sister-in-law. She may have been the daughter who was married to —— Maxwell, and had a son, William, mentioned in the will of William Cochrane of that Ilk.'

p. **339**, l. 9 from foot, for 'Alexander' read 'John.'

p. **340**, second last line of notes, delete 'Charles Home Cochran of Ashkirk, Hawick, N.B., Captain R.N,' and insert 'Alexander Charles Purves Cochran, born September 1879, captain 40th Pathans.'

p. **340**, add to end of note, 'The Cochranes of Rochsoles, which was acquired by Patrick Cochrane in 1579, are stated by Nisbet to be descended from Barbachlaw.'

p. **342**, after l. 6, insert

'ii. *Hugh*, who took the name of Peebles, and died after 1717. He is mentioned in the will of his half-sister Eupheme, proved in Glasgow, 1749. The estate of Mainshill passed to the Earl of Eglinton.'

p. **342**, ll. 7, 8, 10 and 11, for 'ii, iii, iv, v,' read 'iii, iv, v, and vi.'

p. **342**, l. 24, after 'relict of,' insert 'Col. Walter.'

p. **342**, l. 26, after 'him,' insert 'Her will was proved in Edinburgh, 1677, by Walter Scott of St. Leonards and Harlawood, her son by her first marriage.'

p. **342**, l. 28, after 'navy,' add 'Died in Ireland before 1661 (*Books of Protestant Owners, Ireland*).'

p. **345**, l. 6, for 'the' read 'James.'

p. **345**, l. 7, after 'Lennox' read 'and Esmé, his son.'

p. **346**, l. 23, after 'married,' insert 'after 14 April 1633, when she is styled his future wife (*Reg. of Deeds*, DXXVI. 205), and.'

p. **349**, l. 24, delete 'only.'

p. **350**, l. 23, after '1766,' insert 'Married —— Turnbull (*Reg. of Deeds*, Mackenzie, 1766).'

p. **350**, after l. 25, insert

'(3) *Thomas*, baptized at Ochiltree, 1 September 1664.

(4) *Charles*, baptized at Ochiltree, 2 August 1669.

(5) *Eupheme*, baptized at Ochiltree, 24 June 1660.'

p. **350**, l. 26, delete '(3),' and insert '(6).'

p. **350**, l. 26, after 'married,' insert 'in London, 18 February 1686 (Mar. Licences, Faculty Office).'

p. **350**, l. 26, after 'Berwick,' insert 'Her husband died 27 September 1691, aged twenty-nine. She survived till 21 March 1748, when she died, and was buried with her husband in Legerwood Churchyard (cf. Turnbull's *Diary*, Scot. Hist. Soc. *Misc.*, i. 328). Their daughter, *Elizabeth*, married the eighth Earl of Dundonald. The story of Grizel Cochrane's robbery of the postbags containing the warrant for her father's execution appears to be mythical.'

p. **350**, after l. 26, insert

'3. *James*, for whose burial at Holyrood a warrant was granted 13 February 1694 (*P. C. Acta*).'

p. **350**, l. 27, for '3' read '4.'

p. **351**, l. 10, after 'Glen,' insert 'Lady Katherine Kennedy died in 1700, and was buried in Greyfriars Churchyard, Edinburgh, 15 February (Commissary Rec.). By her.'

p. **351**, l. 26, for 'Smith' read 'Smythe.'

p. **351**, l. 27, after 'issue' delete to end of sentence and insert 'Her grand-daughter, Catherine Smythe, became heiress of her grand-aunt, Christian Cochrane.'

p. **352**, l. 2, after '1694,' add 'when William Cochrane of Kilmaronock succeeded to the estate of Polkellie.'

p. **352**, l. 13, after 'married,' insert 'as his first wife, 28 April 1680 (Dundonald Par. Reg.).'

p. **354**, l. 17, for '1689' read '1687 (Paisley Par. Reg.).'

p. **354**, l. 18, for 'twelve' read 'fourteen.'

p. **355**, l. 19, after 'issue,' insert 'a *Pastoral* on their nuptials was written by Alexander Pennecuik and published at Edinburgh, 1723.'

p. **357**, l. 22, for '1790,' read '1740.'

p. **358**, l. 23, after 'Dundonald,' insert 'baptized at Ochiltree, 23 July 1691.'

p. **359**, l. 13, for 'James,' read 'John.'

p. **360**, after l. 2 from foot, insert

'15. *Catherine*, married William Wood, and died 4 October 1776, and was buried at Holyrood.'

p. **360**, last line, for 'second' read 'third.'

p. **363**, l. 21, after 'fleet,' insert note, 'Napoleon called him "Le Loup des Mers."'

p. **368**, l. 5, delete '27 March,' and insert '26 December.'

p. **368**, l. 8, after 'ARMS,' insert '(recorded in Lyon Register).—1st and 4th.'

p. **368**, l. 9, after 'azure,' insert 'for *Cochrane*: 2nd and 3rd, argent, on a saltire sable nine lozenges of the field, for *Blair*.'

DUNFERMLINE

p. **372**, l. 5 from foot, after 'married,' insert 'in Holyrood Abbey Chapel, 5 June 1614 (Canongate Reg.).'

p. **373**, l. 4, for '1621' read '1624 (cf. vol. viii. 449).'

p. **373**, delete ll. 12 and 13.

p. **373**, ll. 14, 15, for '1608' read 'towards the end of November 1615,' and for 'fourteen' read 'six.'

p. **373**, l. 28, after 'army,' insert 'On 14 January 1637 he describes himself as now of the age of twenty-one years complete (*Reg. of Deeds*, Di. 177).'

p. **373**, l. 28, for '1607' read '1637.'

p. **374**, l. 12, after 'married,' insert 'contract 29 March, 2 April and 9 November 1632 (*Reg. of Deeds*, 14 May 1450).'

p. **374**, l. 14, after 'born,' insert '13 June (Dunfermline Reg).'

p. **374**, l. 19, delete 'in September 1670,' and insert 'contract 8 September 1670; tocher 20,000 merks (*Wigtown Inventory*, Scot. Rec. Soc., No. 349).'

p. **374**, l. 24, after 'Dunfermline,' add 'born 12 June 1642 (Dunfermline Reg.).'

p. **374**, l. 25, delete 'in 1675,' and insert 'between 23 August and 27 October 1677 (*Reg. Sec. Sig.*, 2nd ser., iii. f. 159; *Paper Register of Great Seal*, x. 11).'

p. **375**, l. 11, after 'married,' insert 'contract 6 July 1682 (*Reg. of Deeds*, Durie, 12 January 1608).'

DUNKELD

p. **381**, l. 14, after '*Mary*,' delete 'who' and insert 'baptized 5 February 1701 at St. Germain—Marie d'Este, titular Queen of Great Britain, being her godmother (*Reg. of St. Germain en Laye*, p. 70). She.'

p. **381**, after l. 15, insert 'Lord Dunkeld had a natural son *Claude* by Estelaine Pen, said to be a Scotswoman, baptized 2 June 1697 (*Ibid.*).'

DUNMORE

p. **384**, l. 4 from foot, for 'Mastyr' read 'Martyr.'

p. **385**, l. 26, delete 'unmarried.'

p. **385**, l. 28, after '1731,' insert 'Mary Halket, daughter of Sir Charles Halket of Pitfirran, raised an action of declarator of marriage, alleged to have taken place in 1708, against him, and got decreet 10 October 1717. They had a daughter *Catherine*, baptized at Dunfermline in January 1709 (*Consistorial Processes*, etc., No. 199). He appointed Mary Megott of St. Olave, Southwark (probably his mistress) his sole executrix. He gave a factory to "his beloved spouse" in 1709 (*Reg. of Deeds*, Mackenzie, 14 February 1711).'

p. **386**, l. 12, for 'Drummie' read 'Drimmie.'

DYSART

p. **398**, l. 3, after 'Oliphant,' insert 'He was, no doubt, that Alexander Murray, Canon of Inchaffray, who signs various feu charters of the lands of that Abbey, *e.g. Lib. Insule Missarum*, p. 120.'

p. **398**, delete from 'He' on l. 17 to 'issue' on l. 23 and insert 'He married, first, Marion, daughter of Alexander Alexander of Menstrie (cf. vol. viii. 168), who died in January 1595 (Edin. Tests., 10 March 1597); secondly, Barbara, daughter of John Murray of Arbenie. She died

15 September 1600 (Edin. Tests.); and he married, thirdly, Agnes, daughter of Nairn of Strathord. By his first wife he had issue :—'

p. **398,** l. 26, delete entire line, and insert 'in February 1643, leaving issue.'

p. **398,** l. 28, after 'married,' insert 'his cousin Jean, daughter of Mr. Anthony Murray, parson in England' (*Funeral Escutcheons*, Lyon Office, Scot. Rec. Soc., 42).'

p. **398,** after l. 5 from foot, insert

'By his second wife he had :—

(6) *Mungo.*

(7) *Margaret*, mentioned in her mother's will.

By his third wife he had :—

(8) *Margaret* (*secunda*).

(9) *Janet* (*Reg. of Deeds*, ccix. 165).'

p. **401,** l. 1, for 'Murray' read 'Conall (Gask Writs, Bundle cxxxi. No. 13[2]).'

p. **401,** after l. 27, insert

'7. *Anthony*, parson of Utricton (or Urthrisholm) in Kent (*Genealogist*, xxviii. 23).'

p. **401,** l. 27, after 'father,' insert 'styled servitor to the Countess of Nottingham; died before 23 September 1611 (*Reg. of Deeds*, cxcii. 269).'

p. **401,** l. 28, for '7' read '8.'

p. **401,** after l. 28, insert

'9. *Janet*, baptized 15 January 1575 (Par. Reg. Perth), married to Archibald Napier (*Genealogist*, xxviii. 23).'

p. **402,** l. 17, for 'probably died about 1651,' read 'died after 11 September 1653 (Birch's *Transcripts of Nicholas' Letters*).'

p. **402,** l. 2 from foot, after '*Anne*,' insert 'who had, in consideration of her bounty towards officers and soldiers who were in straits in and about London and Westminster after the battle of Worcester, on 18 November 1676, a pension of £200 (*P. C. Eng. Reg.*, iii. 89).'

p. **402,** note 4, after 'Elizabeth,' add 'He appears, however, in the Register of the Great Seal after 1643 merely as William Murray.'

p. **402,** note 6, delete from 'but no authority is quoted' down to end of note, and insert 'and this latter statement is correct, *vide The Nicholas Papers*.'

p. **405,** last line, delete 'before February 1708' and corresponding note 8, and insert 'about 1705 (*Sutherland Book*, i. 367).'

p. **405,** last line, after 'first,' delete 'on Wednesday.'

p. **406,** l. 1, for 'before 1 January 1677-78,' read '26 December 1677.'

p. **409,** l. 5, 'In the epitaphs from the "Abbey of Kilhampton" (*a jeu d'esprit* published in 1780) it is stated that "the loveliness of her disposition was clouded with remorse and sorrow as having provoked the slander of a V(illain) who dared justify his insult with the sword, and though she survived the fatal issue, the remainder of her days was known only to solitude and marked with lamentation," evidently referring to the circumstances of her husband's death.'

p. **409,** l. 20, for 'February' read 'March,' and after '1751,' insert 'baptized 25 April following at St. James's, Piccadilly.'

p. **410,** l. 1, after '*Jane*, insert 'born 26 March and baptized 29 April 1750 at St. James's, Piccadilly.'

p. **411,** l. 10, after '1789,' insert 'Horace Walpole wrote the following epitaph on her:—

"Adieu, sweet shade, complete was thy career,
Though lost too soon and premature thy bier:
For each fair character endowed thy life
Of daughter, sister, friend, relation, wife.
Yet lest unaltered fortune should have seemed
The source whence virtues so benignly beamed,
Long mining illness proved thy equal soul,
And patience like a martyr's, crowned the whole.
Pain could not sour, whom blessings had not spoil'd,
Nor death affright, whom not a vice had soil'd."

Journal of Miss Berry, i. 190.'

p. **413,** l. 21, after 'Munro,' insert '109 Princes Street, Edinburgh.'

p. **413,** l. 22, after 'issue,' insert '*Lionel Alexander Arthur*, who married Louisa Margaret Hope. On 15 October 1912 his domicile was declared to be Scottish (*Chancery Division*).'

p. **414,** l. 35, for '3' read '2.'

p. **420,** l. 18, for 'with' read 'between two.'

p. **420,** l. 19, after 'expanded' insert 'or.'

EGLINTON

p. **426,** l. 3 from foot, after '*John*,' add note 'John MacHenry had on 14 August 1394 a dispensation to marry Margaret, daughter of Thomas de Kirkpatrick, Knight. He had a previous intercourse with Evota, daughter of —— "Meclelan" laic (*Regesta Vaticana*, cccvii. f. 567).'

p. **428,** third line of note 5, after '1357,' insert '(The dispensation for their marriage is dated 19 February 1362-63) (*Regesta Vaticana*, cclxi. f. 21).'

p. **432,** l. 24, delete 'and it is doubtful if he survived his grandfather.'

p. **432,** l. 31, after 'heir,' insert 'He appears to have died in 1468, as in the retour of his son Hugh as his heir in Bonington and Pilton (Coupar Writs in Moray Charter-chest, Div. 5, No. 87) these lands are said to have been in the hands of Katherine Kennedy for eighteen years by reason of conjunct fee, and thereafter for one year in non-entry.'

p. **437,** l. 22, after 'Argyll,' insert 'He died before 29 August 1538, when his brother Neil was infeft as his heir in Milnestaneflat and other lands (*Acts and Decreets*, 1. 387).'

p. **437,** note 8, after '1523,' insert 'cf. *Reg. Sec. Sig.*, i., No. 3024, 31 July 1518.'

p. **442,** l. 19, after 'married,' insert 'apparently on 19 May 1583 (*Bowes Correspondence*, Surtees Soc., 440).'

p. **443,** l. 22, after 'death,' insert 'He was born about 1584 (*Edin. Comm. Decreets*, 11 March 1612). He chose curators 3 August 1598 (Fife Sheriff Court Books).'

p. **444,** l. 6 from foot, after 'grants,' insert 'On 3 March 1610 the Earl petitioned the Privy Council for a summons against Hew Campbell, Lord Loudoun and Jean Campbell, Duchess of Lennox, requiring them to produce the Countess, who had been carried off in June 1608 by emissaries of theirs to Loudoun House, where she was still detained a prisoner (*P. C. Reg.*, viii. 820).'

p. **446,** l. 17, after 'first,' insert 'contract 6 June 1612 (*Reg. of Deeds*, cciv. 161).'

p. **447,** ll. 3 and 4 from foot, delete 'widow of John Hamilton of Letham, but also described in her husband's testament as.' *Note.*—John Hamilton of Bardanoch never possessed Letham, which was purchased by his son William about 1716.'

p. **448,** l. 3 from foot, for 'tenth' read 'fifth.'

p. **450,** ll. 16, 17, for '24 January 1688' read '27 November 1686 (*Seafield Correspondence*, Scot. Hist. Soc., 34).'

p. **452,** l. 1, after '*Montgomerie*,' insert 'baptized 11 September 1680, (Canongate Reg.).'

p. **452,** l. 4 from foot, after 'unmarried,' insert 'she married, secondly in December 1682, Sir Patrick Ogilvie of Boyne, Lord Boyne (*Seafield Correspondence*, Scot. Hist. Soc., xiii.).'

p. **452,** note 3, for '*Memorials*, i. 93' read '*Memorials*, i. 95.'

p. **453,** l. 6 from foot, after '1678,' add note 'She is said to have died 5 December 1675, which is so far corroborated by a reference to her funeral in Glasgow weaver's accounts, 1675-76.'

p. **454,** l. 27, for 'before 15 June 1687' read 'in August 1686 (*Seafield Correspondence*, Scot. Hist. Soc., 34).'

p. **456,** l. 12 from foot, after 'unmarried,' insert 'The Glasgow Council accounts, under date 11 April 1696, refer to the expenses of the Magistrates for one night at Kilwinning when at the burial of *two* Masters of Montgomerie. It would appear, therefore, that one of his two immediate younger brothers died at the same time as he did.'

p. **457,** l. 9, after 'issue,' insert 'Her third daughter Catherine was seduced by a blackguard Sir John Houston of Houston, Bart. (see vol. ii. 520) (though his wife divorced him for impotency). She went on the town, and wrote her own memoirs, *The Amours and Adventures of Miss Katty M.* (cf. *Letters of C. K. Sharpe and Sir Walter Scott to Robert Chambers*, p. 34, privately printed, 1904).'

p. **457,** l. 8 from foot, after '14,' insert 'and was buried at Restalrig, 16.'

p. **457,** l. 3 from foot, delete 'in,' and insert '24 (Reg. of Old St. Paul's, Edinburgh; *Scottish Antiquary*, v. 14).'

p. **458,** l. 5, for 'about' read 'on (*Ibid.*).'

p. **460,** l. 17, after '1788,' read 'for adultery with the Duke of Hamilton (*Consistorial Processes, etc.*, Scot. Rec. Soc., No. 882).'

p. **460,** l. 18, for '1734' read 1794.'

p. **462,** l. 4 from foot, for 'the elder brother' read 'grandnephew.'

p. **463,** l. 4, delete 'daughter of Charles Newcomen, Clonahard, co. Longford,' and insert 'one of the eight illegitimate daughters of Thomas, second Viscount Newcomen, by Harriet Holland (*Scottish Historical Review*, v. 103).'

p. **464,** l. 2 from foot, for '25' read '24.'

ELGIN AND AILESBURY

p. **468,** l. 24, for 'consecration' read 'enthronement.'

p. **470,** l. 17, after 'Rosyth,' insert '(she afterwards married —— Auchmuty, and had a son Henry (*Acta Dom. Conc.*, xiv. 105).'

p. **474,** l. 6 from foot, for 'nephew' read 'son.'

p. **474,** ll. 4 and 5 from foot, delete 'afterwards second Lord Bruce of Kinloss.'

p. **474,** l. 4 from foot, after 'him,' insert 'William, married Margaret Cruickshank (*Records of Sheriff-Court of Aberdeen*, ii. 22), with issue a son, as above stated.'

p. **475,** l. 3, after 'Kinloss,' insert 'of which he was appointed Commendator, 26 July following (*Reg. Sec. Sig.*, xlix. 135).'

p. **475,** l. 5, delete 'the position of Commendator of Kinloss, with.'

p. **477,** l. 19, delete 'Sir.'

p. **479,** l. 17, for '1872' read '1672.'

p. **482,** l. 18, for 'Allan' read 'Allen.'

p. **482,** l. 28, after 'her,' insert note 'Horace Walpole's name for her was "one more game at cribbage" (Miss Berry's *Journal*, i. 412).'

p. **483,** l. 12, for '1 August 1642' read 29 July 1641.'

ELGIN AND KINCARDINE

p. **485,** l. 17, delete 'Margaret, daughter of Archibald Primrose of Burn-Brae,' and insert 'Euphame, daughter of David Primrose in Culross (cf. vol. vii. 216).'

p. **485,** after l. 25, insert

'4. *Christina*, or *Christian*, "eldest lawful daughter," married, first, to Robert, Master of Colville (vol. ii. 557), who died before December 1614; secondly, after 29 December 1617, when she had a sasine as his future wife (Protocol Book of James Primrose, H.M. Reg. Ho., f. 153), Laurence, afterwards Sir Laurence Mercer of Aldie, with issue.'

p. **485,** ll. 26 and 29, for '4' and '5' read '5' and '6.'

p. **485,** delete ll. 31 and 32, with accompanying note.

p. **486,** l. 7, for 'Robert' read 'John.'

p. **486,** l. 11, delete 'to Sir John Arnot of Fernie, Fife,' and insert 'contract 31 May 1664, to Sir James Nicolson, younger of Cockburnspath.'

p. **486,** after l. 15, insert

6. *Grisel*, married, before 3 January 1642, to Sir Robert Arnot, eldest son of Sir James Arnot of Fernie (Fife Sheriff-Court Deeds, 20 January 1713).'

p. **486,** note 1, for '1635' read '1638.'

p. **486**, note 3, for '*Ibid*' read 'Wood's Douglas's *Peerage*, i. 518.'

p. **486**, note 4, for '*Ibid*,' read '*Gen. Reg. of Sasines*, x. 102.'

p. **487**, after l. 12, insert

'2. *Cornelius*, baptized 13 June 1663 (Culross Reg.); died young.

3 and 4. *Alexander* and *Cornelius* (*secundus*), twins, baptized 13 September 1664 (*Ibid.*); also died young.'

p. **487**, ll. 13, 14 and 17, for '2, 3, 4' read '5, 6, 7.'

p. **487**, after l. 18, insert

'8. *Lucy*, baptized 1 September 1669 (Canongate Reg.).'

p. **487**, l. 19, for '5' read '9.'

p. **487**, l. 21, for 'second' read 'fifth,' and after 'son,' insert 'baptized 5 June 1666 (Culross Reg.).'

p. **488**, l. 20, after 'Allan,' insert 'It was probably he who became Rector of Wath, co. York, in 1716, and died 27 May 1723, aged eighty-one (*ex inform.* H. B. M'Call, Esq.).'

p. **488**, l. 21, after '*Helen*,' insert 'baptized 30 November 1643.'

p. **488**, l. 24, after '*Janet*,' insert 'baptized 18 January 1638.'

p. **488**, after l. 27, insert

'5. *Margaret*, baptized 6 August 1639.'

p. **488**, l. 28, for '5' read '6.'

p. **488**, l. 28, after '*Rachel*,' insert 'baptized 24 October 1648 (Edin. Reg.).'

p. **492**, l. 26, after '1816,' add 'He, who was born 1763, married, secondly, Ann Henderson, heiress of Fordel.'

p. **496**, after line 5, insert

'(4) *Richard Frederick David*, born 2 March 1894.'

p. **496**, ll. 6, 7, 8, 9, for '(4), (5), (6), (7)' read '(5), (6), (7), (8).'

p. **496**, l. 30, for '18' read '8.'

p. **496**, l. 32, for '9' read '29.'

ELIBANK

p. **500**, ll. 5 and 28, for '1485' read '1485-86.'

p. **501**, l. 12, after 'Register,' insert 'He was Clerk of Council in 1509 (charter *penes* Rev. A. T. Grant).'

p. **502**, l. 13, for '22 April 1507' read '31 January 1503-4 (Protocol Book of J. Foular).'

p. **502**, l. 14. after 'Hoppar,' insert 'daughter of Richard Hoppar, burgess of Edinburgh (*Acta Dom. Conc.*, xxii. 93).'

p. **502**, l. 19, for 'Archibald' read 'Alexander (*Ibid.*, xxxv. 103).'

p. **502**, l. 21, after '*Margaret*,' insert 'first contracted to Henry Wardlaw of Torry, which contract he was personally called on to implement by Andrew Murray her brother, 22 March 1530-31 (Edin. Council Records).'

p. **502**, l. 25, for '1513' read '1513-14.'

p. **503**, ll. 20 and 22, for '1551' read '1551-52.'

p. **503**, l. 23, after 'lands,' insert 'The Governor Arran gave her on her marriage a tocher of £133, 6s. 8d. (*Treas. Accounts*, x. 115).'

p. **504**, l. 8, delete 'is said to have.'

p. **504,** note 4, after '184,' add '(*Reg. Sec. Sig.*, xliv. 17).'

p. **507,** l. 4, after 'married,' insert 'contract 18 January 1628 (*Reg. of Deeds*, ccciii. 144).'

p. **507,** l. 4, delete 'Skene, by whom,' and insert 'second daughter of John Skene of Halyards, Clerk of Session. By her.'

p. **509,** l. 8 from foot, after 'secondly,' insert '13 February 1670 (Edin. Reg.).'

p. **509,** l. 24, delete from 'lieutenant' down to 'captain 1685-88' on l. 26.

p. **510,** l. 13, for '1638' read 'contract 24 March 1638 (*Reg. of Deeds*, DXviii. 289).'

p. **516,** ll. 16 and 17, delete 'Miss Collier,' and insert 'a daughter and co-heir of John Collier of Hastings, Sussex (who died 9 December 1760).'

p. **516,** l. 17, for 'who' read 'She.'

p. **518,** note 2, after 'son,' insert 'was, in 1776, a member of the Council of Revenue at Patna, Bengal. He is mentioned as a substitute next after his half-brother Patrick in the entail of Simprim after noted (see next paragraph). He.'

p. **519,** l. 7, after 'Aberlady,' insert note 'Besides William Young mentioned in the preceding paragraph, Lord Elibank had four other natural sons, one of whom *Patrick* was five years old on 9 November 1776, when his father, with whom he was living at Ballincreiff, entailed on him the estate of Simprim (*Reg. of Entails*, xix. 339).'

p. **521,** l. 8, for '1833' read 'at Edinburgh 6 January 1834.'

p. **523,** l. 8, after '1871,' insert 'created, 3 July 1911, VISCOUNT ELIBANK OF ELIBANK, co. Selkirk, in the Peerage of the United Kingdom.'

p. **523,** l. 19, Created BARON MURRAY OF ELIBANK, co. Selkirk, 13 August 1912.

p. **524,** l. 20, after '1643,' insert 'Viscount Elibank of Elibank, co. Selkirk, 3 July 1911.'

ELPHINSTONE

p. **527,** l. 11, delete 'The name of Sir William Elphinstone's wife is unknown, but,' and insert 'He married, *ante* 6 November 1421, Margaret Hepburne. On that date the spouses had a charter from James Douglas, Lord of Dalkeith (Moray Charters, Box ii. No. 22).'

p. **529,** last line, for '1578' read '1518.'

p. **530,** l. 10, for '1524' read '1504.'

p. **530,** note 1, delete note and insert 'Original in Elphinstone Charter-chest.'

p. **531,** l. 7, for 'death' read 'baptism.'

p. **531,** l. 15, after 'Forbes,' insert 'and died in 1518, her *obit* being celebrated on 10 September (Spalding Club *Misc.*, i. 74).'

p. **532,** l. 26, for 'fourth' read 'fifth.'

p. **533,** ll. 6 and 7, delete 'before 8 August 1590,' and insert '10 June 1589 (cf. vol. vii. 463).'

p. **533,** l. 3 from foot, 'after 'married,' insert 'proclamation 15 April 1592 (Stirling Reg.).'

p. **534,** l. 15, for 'Lundrassie' read 'Findrassie.'

p. **536**, l. 17, after 'issue,' insert 'and, secondly, to James Stewart of Ryland (*Reg. of Deeds*, ccccxviii. 345).'

p. **536**, note 8, add to note 'According to *Records of the Scots Colleges* (New Spalding Club), p. 190, he was Rector of the Scots College at Rome from 8 September 1622 to the beginning of January 1644.'

p. **538**, l. 14, after 'married,' insert 'contract 27 October and 24 November 1613 (*Reg. of Deeds*, cccclxxxvii. 253).'

p. **538**, l. 25, after '*Jean*,' insert 'contracted to Alexander Elphinstone of Dunlugus, 29 April 1644 (*Banff Sasines*, v. 185).'

p. **538**, l. 30, after '*Anna*,' insert 'contracted to Thomas, eldest son of Walter Kinnaird of Cowbin 2 May 1653 (*Elgin Sasines*, iv. 130).'

p. **539**, l. 22, after 'Quarrell,' add 'while a daughter Marion was married to George Norvell of Boghall, Advocate.'

p. **542**, after l. 16, add

'*Jean Elphinstone*, married, 16 November 1673, to Robert Mylne, Provost of Linlithgow, created Baronet 1686, is said to have been a a daughter of Lord Elphinstone but nothing has been found to prove the statement (Edin. Mar. Reg.; *ex inform.* Rev. R. S. Mylne).'

p. **545**, l. 15, after '1784,' add (see vol. i. p. 383 *Corrigenda*).'

p. **549**, l. 4, for 'titles' read 'two baronies.'

p. **549**, after l. 9, insert

'By his second wife the Viscount had also a daughter:—

Georgiana Augusta Henrietta, married, first, 20 September 1831, to the Hon. Augustus John Villiers, second son of George, fifth Earl of Jersey. He died 1837, and she was married secondly, 10 May 1870, to Lord William Godolphin Osborne, and died 21 September 1892.'

p. **550**, l. 28, for 'Torriedale' read 'Torrisdale.'

ERROLL

p. **559**, l. 12, delete 'June 1306,' and relative note, and insert '3 September of that year, when his son Gilbert is styled Lord of Erroll (Coupar Charters *penes* Earl of Moray, Div. 4, No. 32).'

p. **562**, l. 7, for '1416' read '3 July 1416 (*Reg. Vat.*, cccxxviii. 453).'

p. **562**, after l. 14, insert

'(3) *John*.'

p. **563**, l. 2, for '1436' read '1437.'

p. **563**, after l. 9, insert

'3. *Nicholas*, who died before 1452, leaving three sons, *Gilbert*, *Nicholas* and *Alexander*, substitutes in the charter of 1452 (see *infra*).

4. *Alexander* of Mouchale, also a substitute in that charter.'

p. **563**, delete ll. 10 to 15. 'These were brothers, not uncles of the first Earl.'

p. **563**, after l. 29, insert

'2. *Walter*. He and the rest of the younger sons are substitutes in the undermentioned charter of 1452, and he is a witness with his brothers David and Thomas to a charter of confirmation by their nephew William, third Earl of Erroll, to Allan Kynard of that Ilk, 14 March 1470-71.'

p. **563**, l. 7 from foot, for '2' read '3. *Mr.*'

p. **564**, after l. 2, insert

'4. *David*, in 1470-71 *Mr. David.*

5. *Nicholas.*

6. *Thomas*, in 1470-71 *Mr. Thomas.*'

p. **564**, l. 7, after 'resignation,' insert 'He was raised to the rank of a Lord of Parliament before 10 April 1450, on which date, as well as in the September following, he is styled Lord the Hay (Writs in Erroll Charter-chest; *Acta. Parl. Scot.*, 6 July 1451, ii. 67, 69).'

p. **564**, note 2, l. 4 from foot of notes, delete 'and no copy of them has been discovered,' and insert 'but transcripts have recently been discovered in H.M. Register House. The charter of the Lordship of Erroll contains a destination to the Earl and the heirs-male of his body, with remainder successively to Walter, Mr. Gilbert, David, Nicholas, and Thomas, the Earl's brothers, William Hay of Ury, his uncle, and Gilbert, Nicholas, and Alexander, sons of his uncle Nicholas, Alexander Hay of Dronlaw, Gilbert and John Hay, brothers of the last, Alexander of Mouchale, the Earl's uncle, Sir David Hay of Lochorwart, Edmund Hay of Tallou and the heirs-male of their bodies respectively.'

p. **565**, l. 10, after '1471,' add 'After Huntly's death she married, secondly, Andrew, second Lord Gray, who died in 1514, and she was apparently alive in 1517 (*Acta Dom. Conc.*, xxix. 38, 39).'

p. **567**, l. 3 from foot, after 'Calder,' insert 'She is named as Countess of Erroll in an order of Court, dated 9 July 1532, at which date she was dead, and her sons Mr. Peter and James Sandilands of Cruvie were her executors (*Acta Dom. Conc. et Sess.*, i. f. 58).'

p. **568**, l. 6, after '1511,' add as note 'This conclusion is wrong. They were the same person (cf. vol. vii. 411).'

p. **568**, l. 25, after 'Sutherland,' add note 'On 26 May 1541 the Countess got from the King six ells Paris black and four ells French black for "dule weed." On 12 May 1542 she got thirteen ells of red velvet to be a gown "agane hir marriage" (*Treasurer's Accounts*, vii. 449; viii. 77).'

p. **569**, l. 2 from foot, after 'Essilmont,' insert 'dying in February 1608 (Slains Charters).'

p. **571**, l. 14, after 'secondly,' insert 'at Aberdeen in June 1604.'

p. **571**, l. 16, after 'Burleigh,' add 'She obtained decree of divorce against him, 24 March 1620 (*Edin. Comm. Decreets*).'

p. **572**, l. 13, after 'Earl,' insert note 'In a note on the Scots nobility of 10 April 1589 Francis is said to be third son, the two elder being deaf and dumb (Grampian Club, *Estimate of Scots Nobility*, 56).'

p. **573**, l. 5, after '1626,' insert 'and died in September 1657 (Dunblane Tests.), having.'

p. **573**, l. 9, for 'before 1672' read 'in July 1670 (Dunblane Tests.).'

p. **574**, l. 2, after 'married,' insert 'contract 23 July 1602 (Slains Charters).'

p. **574**, l. 3, after 'Erroll,' insert 'was baptized 30 April 1564 (Erroll Reg.), and.'

p. **575**, l. 6 from foot, after 'time,' insert 'He was afterwards warded within a certain distance of his own house; but in order to make arrangements with his creditors he got a licence, 9 November 1615, to "repair to Edinburgh and there to remain in some lodging, not kything onyway in daylicht upon the heich street" (*P. C. Reg.*, x. 405).'

p. **576**, note 2, add to note 'There is, however, in the same Charter-chest another will of this Earl, dated 12 November 1630.'

p. **577**, l. 14, after 'secondly,' insert 'before 20 May 1643 (*Reg. of Deeds*, DXLIX. 364).'

p. **577**, l. 21, after '*Margaret*,' insert 'baptized 11 April 1611.'

p. **577**, l. 25, delete 'baptized 11 April 1611.'

p. **577**, l. 28, delete from 'which' down to end of sentence, and insert 'probably intended to secure consideration for her on her travels as she was an invalid and obliged to live abroad for her health. She was one of the three noble ladies whom Gilbert Blakhal served (see his *Brief Narration*, Spalding Club). She died unmarried.'

p. **577**, l. 31, for 'in' read '8 September'; and for 'ten' read 'twelve.'

p. **578**, l. 14, for '7 December 1636' read 'December 1637 (Spalding's *Memorials*, i. 84).'

p. **579**, l. 27, for '1 October' read '21 October (Slains Charters).'

p. **579**, l. 7 from foot, after '*s.p.*' insert 'after November 1693 (*Perth's Letters*, Camden Society, 15).

p. **580**, l. 7, after 'Edinburgh,' insert 'He spent three years, 1712-15, travelling abroad. His accounts for his tour are in the Slains Charter-chest.'

p. **580**, l. 22, after 'Dalgaty,' insert 'He predeceased his wife, dying in July 1745 (Slains Charters).'

p. **581**, l. 17, for 'mother' read 'aunt.' See previous page.

p. **581**, l. 5 from foot, after 'divorced,' insert 'in 1771, she having eloped with Captain James Sutherland of Duffus of the 26th Foot (*Consistorial Processes*, etc., Scot. Rec. Soc., No. 583).'

p. **583**, last line, after '1812,' insert 'and was buried in Bath Abbey (M.I.), aged thirty-four.'

p. **587**, l. 19, for '1315' read '1314.'

FAIRFAX

p. **606**, l. 5, after '1900,' insert 'He made out his claim to the title before the House of Lords, 17 November 1908.'

p. **606**, l. 9, for 'gules' read 'sable.'

FALKLAND

p. **610**, l. 4, after '1633,' insert note 'He broke his leg while out shooting; it had to be amputated, and in the absence of the doctors hemorrhage set in. When medical assistance was procured nothing could be done, and he bled to death. Another account says he died from blood poisoning, the result of the amputation, after a week's illness (Marriott's *Life and Times of Lord Falkland*, 2nd ed., 72).'

p. **610**, l. 8, after 'fifty-four,' add 'The effigies of her and her husband appear at the head and foot of the tomb of Lord Tanfield in the Parish Church of Burford, co. Oxford.'

p. **610**, l. 15, after '1642,' add 'while pursuing the enemy at the head of a troop of Royalist Horse in an obscure village in Devonshire (Clarendon's *Life*; for notices of Lorenzo and his elder brother see Godfrey's *Social Life under the Stuarts*).'

p. **610**, l. 28, after 'Scott,' insert 'He was buried 15 March 1656 (Funeral entry, Ulster's Office).'

p. **610**, l. 6 from foot, after 'her,' insert 'who died 25, and was buried 27 July, 1658, her will as Dame Susan Cary, widow, relict of Patrick Cary, late of Dublin, being dated 25 July 1658, and proved that year (*ex inform.* G.D. Burtchaell, Esq., Athlone Pursuivant).'

p. **610**, l. 4 from foot, delete 'born about 1656,' and insert 'baptized 25 April 1656 at St. John's, Dublin (Par. Reg., *ex inform.* G. D. Burtchaell, Esq., Athlone Pursuivant).'

p. **611**, l. 2, after 'her,' insert 'who was buried in Westminster Abbey 11 April 1719 (cf. vol. iv. 382).'

p. **611**, after l. 9, insert

'(3) *Susanna Patricia*, baptized at St. John's, Dublin, 2 April 1657.

(4) *Patricia*, mentioned along with her sister in her mother's will.'

p. **611**, l. 5 from foot, after 'man,' insert note 'Aubray says "I have heard Dr. Ralph Bathurst say that when he was a boy my Lord Falkland lived at Coventry (where he had then a house) and that he would sit up very late at night in his study, and many times came to the library at the school there." His teacher was Philemon Holland, "the Translator-General" (Whibley's *Literary Portraits*, p. 149).'

p. **614**, l. 6, after '*Dorothy*,' insert 'born 3, and baptized 21 October, 1705, at St. Gregory's by St. Paul's, London.'

p. **614**, l. 11, after '1804,' insert 'in the house of her uncle, Arthur Richard Dillon, sometime Archbishop of Narbonne, Somerset Street, Portman Square. Her relations with him gave rise to some scandal (*Notes and Queries*, 10th ser., viii. 102; see also *Memoirs of the Comtesse de Boigne*.)'

p. **614**, l. 4 from foot, for '1799' read '1779,' and after 'Chapman,' add 'of Tarrant Gunville, Dorset, who was buried in Bath Abbey, 12 January 1798. They left issue.'

VOL. IV.

FIFE

p. 8, after l. 9, insert

'2. *Annabella*, married to Sir Hugh. . . . (Inv. of Titles, H.M. Reg. Ho., iii. 16).'

FINDLATER

p. 19, l. 3, after 'Ythane,' insert 'She was married, secondly, to Alexander Irvine of Drum, and died in 1532, her obit being celebrated 19 May (Spalding *Misc.*, i. 68).

p. 19, l. 22, after Aberdeen delete 'she,' and transfer the remainder of the paragraph to new line, and insert

'11. *Margaret*, who, etc.' as in text.

p. 19, l. 24, for '11' read '12.'

p. 20, l. 6, after 'Moray,' insert 'An Elizabeth Ogilvy, daughter of the Laird of Findlater, is said to have been the wife of Alexander Irvine of Drum, who fell at the battle of Pinkie 1547 (*The Irvines of Drum*, by Col. Forbes Leslie, 66, 168).

p. 26, l. 12 from foot, for '1615' read '1616.'

p. 29, l. 22, for 'ninth' read 'eighth.'

p. 29, note 5, after 'clxxxii.' add '229.'

p. 32, l. 2 from foot, after '*David*' add 'of Templehall. He died before 27 January 1575-76, having married, before 10 April 1556, Christina Galychtlie, heiress of Ebrux, who survived him. They had issue a son *Gilbert* (Protocol Book of Duncan Gray, f. 7b; *Acts and Decreets*, lx. 453).'

p. 33, l. 4, after '1535' add 'He was alive 31 March 1558 (Protocol Book of Duncan Gray, f. 15).'

p. 34, note 7, for 1161' read 1611.'

p. 35, l. 14, for 'p. 30' read 'p. 29.'

p. 35, l. 17, delete 'Inchmartin.'

p. 35, l. 18, for 'was sold in that year' read 'had been sold in 1650.'

p. 35, l. 23, for '30 March 1658' read 'in May 1659 (*Seafield Correspondence*, Scot. Hist. Soc., ix.).'

p. 35, l. 27, for 'Innes' read 'Irvine.'

p. 36, l. 5, after 'She,' insert '(who died in August 1687) (*Seafield Correspondence*, Scot. Hist. Soc., 39).'

p. 36, l. 8, after 'married,' insert 'in October 1703 (Edin. Reg.).'

p. 36, l. 15, after 'were,' insert '(besides other children, who died young).'

p. **36**, l. 17, for 'June 1698' read 'May 1699 (*Seafield Correspondence*, Scot. Hist. Soc., 265).'

p. **36**, l. 7 from foot, after 'married,' insert 'first, Elizabeth, daughter of Sir James Baird of Auchmedden, and widow of Sir Alexander Abercrombie of Birkenbog.'

p. **37**, l. 5, for '(4)' read '4.' After l. 5 insert

'5. A son born before 19 April 1672 died young.'

'6. *Robert*, born February 1673 (*Seafield Correspondence*, Scot. Hist. Soc., p. xv.), a cornet of Dragoons, died before 19 October 1693 (*Ibid.*, 124).'

'7. A daughter, born before July 1666, died young.'

p. **37**, l. 6, for '(5)' read '8,' and after '*Mary*,' insert 'married, first, in 1698, to a son of George Leslie of Burdsbank, much to the annoyance of her family; and, secondly, on 25 September 1704, to George, son of Alexander Barclay in Banff (*Seafield Correspondence*, Scot. Hist. Soc., 247, 248, 381).'

p. **37**, l. 7, for '(6)' read '9.'

p. **37**, l. 8, for '1698' read '1692 (*Ibid.*).' *Note.*—The above were children not of Col. Patrick but of the third Earl.

p. **38**, l. 3, for '1' read '21 (*Warrant Books*, xviii. 239).'

p. **38**, l. 9 from foot, for '6 May' read 'shortly after 12 May (*Seafield Correspondence*, Scot. Hist. Soc., 266).'

p. **38**, l. 8 from foot, after '*George*,' insert 'probably born about January 1695 (*Seafield Correspondence*, Scot. Hist. Soc., 157, 158).'

p. **40**, l. 14, after 'Atholl,' insert note, 'She was a very capable woman, who saved the estate from being sold, through excellent management. She built from her own funds the bridge sixty feet high and with a span of eighty-two feet, across the Burn of Deskford to Cullen House. As a mark of respect, her portrait was hung in the County Rooms at Aberdeen (C. Sinclair's *Shetland and the Shetlanders*, 279).'

p. **40**, l. 23, for '1729' read '1779.'

p. **40**, l. 28, after '1813,' insert note, 'She became blind during the last years of her life, and was very badly off. Caroline, Princess of Wales, writes to Lady Charlotte Bury saying that she has no more than £300 a year. The Duchess of Brunswick gave her £250 a year and an allowance for candles, coals, and the rent of a small lodging in Manchester or Baker Streets (*Diary of a Lady in Waiting*, ii. 392).'

FORBES

p. **44**, l. 1, after 'is,' insert 'said to be.'

p. **44**, ll. 6 and 7, delete these lines and insert 'but the document is injured at the place where the name occurs. The surname is certainly not de Forbes: it is del . . ., and probably del Ard.'

p. **54**, l. 4, for 'John' read 'James.'

p. **54**, l. 8 from foot, after '1565,' insert 'It is also stated (*History of the Family of Burnett of Leys*, New Spalding Club, p. 29; Macfarlane's *Gen. Coll.*, ii. 244) that she was ultimately married to Alexander or Arthur Forbes of Echt, who survived her.'

p. 54, after l. 7 from foot insert

'5. *Alexander*, who, with his brother William, was tried and acquitted for art and part in the slaughter of Alexander Seton of Meldrum 27 January 1527-28 (Forbes Charters).'

p. 54, ll. 6, 5, and 2 from foot, for '5, 6, 7' read '6, 7, 8.'

p. 54, l. 2 from foot, after 'Brux' insert 'She is also said to have married as his second wife, Alexander Burnett of Leys (*Acts and Decreets*, xxxix.; *Family of Burnett of Leys*, New Spalding Club, p. 25).'

p. 55, l. 2, after 'her,' insert 'who died 1518.'

p. 56, l. 22, after 'issue,' insert 'He was instituted to the parsonage and prebend of Forbes 26 February 1562-63 (Forbes Charters).'

p. 59, l. 2 from foot, after 'divorce,' insert 'On 22 July 1577 William Douglas of Glenbervy had a remission for adultery with Margaret Gordon, sister of umquhile George, Earl of Huntly (*Reg. Sec. Sig.* xliv. 87).'

p. 62, l. 5, after 'married' insert 'contract 22 and 23 January 1628 (*Reg. of Deeds*, ccccIxxvii. 224).'

p. 62, l. 21, delete 'Sir.'

p. 62, after l. 29 insert

'4. *Robert*, youngest son, captain in the Scottish service in 1666 (Forbes Charters).'

p. 62, ll. 30, 31, and 35, for '4, 5, 6' read '5, 6, 7.'

p. 63, l. 12, after 1675, insert 'as his first wife.'

p. 63, l. 15, after 'secondly,' insert 'contract dated 26 March 1668.'

p. 64, l. 9, after '1730,' insert 'She was alive in 1766.'

p. 68, l. 18, delete 'Bart. of Nova Scotia.'

FORBES OF PITSLIGO

p. 72, l. 3, insert 'great' before 'grandfather.'

p. 74, l. 5 from foot, after 'daughter' add 'married, contract 3 November 1620, to Walter Ogilvy of Boyne (*Reg. of Deeds*, ccccIxxxviii. 274).

p. 74, l. 3 from foot, delete line.

p. 74, l. 2 from foot, for '6' read '5.'

p. 75, l. 6 from foot, after 'first,' insert 'contract 4 and 5 February 1706, tocher 10,000 merks (*Reg. of Deeds*, Dalrymple, 4 January 1711).'

FORRESTER

p. 82, after l. 15 insert 'He apparently had another daughter, J—— whose arms impaled with those of her husband, William Napier of Wrightshouses, and bearing date 137– is over the gateway of St. Margaret's, North Queensferry. William Napier acquired part of Wrightshouses from Adam Forrester in 1390 (Robertson's *Index*, 137, No. 9).'

p. 84, after l. 27 insert

'3. *John* (*secundus*) mentioned in the charter of 1430-31 (see preceding paragraph).

p. **84,** ll. 28 and 32, for '3 and 4' read '4 and 5.'

p. **85.** ll. 18 and 19, delete 'whose name is unknown, but.'

p. **85,** l. 20, after 'husband,' insert 'and indicate her to have been a member of the well-known Edinburgh burgess family of Wigmore (*Eccles. Architecture of Scot.*, Macgibbon and Ross, iii. 261).'

p. **85,** l. 30, after 'witnesses' insert 'He was served heir to his grandfather in Longniddry 12 October 1451 (Wintoun Inventory, No. 77).

p. **85,** l. 33, after 'before,' insert '16 March 1466-67, when his son was served heir to him, On [20, etc.]'

p. **85,** l. 33, delete 'when.'

p. **86,** l. 17, after 'Corstorphine,' insert 'was served heir to his father 16 March 1466-67 (Wintoun Inventory, No. 77), and.'

p. **87,** l. 5, after 'Calder,' insert 'She died in March 1562 (Edin. Tests.).'

p. **88,** l. 2 from foot, after 'Corstorphine,' insert 'had a precept of clare constat from George, Lord Seton, 26 June 1548, as heir of his father (Wintoun Inventory, No. 79). He.'

p. **89,** l. 29, delete 'one daughter' and insert 'issue :—'

'1. *James*, who died in the lifetime of his father, leaving a natural son *James*, to whom, as his grandson, Sir James, on 28 April 1587, granted the lands of Nether Barnton, Langnudrie, and others (Charter *penes* Earl of Moray).'

p. **90,** l. 28, after '8,' delete '——' and insert '*Katherine*, married, contract 1621, to Robert son of James Douglas, Commendator of Melrose (*Reg. of Deeds*, cccxii. 295).'

p. **92,** l. 15, for 'in 1654' read 'before 10 August 1652 (*Gen. Reg. Inhibs.*).'

p. **92,** l. 22, delete lines 22 and 23. Helen, Lady Ross, was the daughter of Sir James Forrester of Torwoodhead (*see title* Ross).

p. **92,** ll. 24, 27, 32, 36, for '3, 4, 5, 6,' read '2, 3, 4, 5.'

p. **92,** note 1, after 'cxcviii.,' insert '333.'

p. **93,** last line for 'Brawford' read 'Brainfoord.'

p. **94,** l. 15, for 'Lilian' read 'Lilias.'

p. **94,** after l. 17, insert

'2. *Margaret* (*P. C. Reg.*, 3rd ser., ii. 569, where there is a narrative of the conjugal relations of Lilias Forrester and her husband).'

p. **99,** l. 24, after 'stars,' insert 'argent.'

FORTH

p. **101,** l. 24, for '1566' read '1556.'

p. **102,** l. 7, after '*Alexander*,' insert 'styled Captain Alexander, died before 1615, leaving a daughter Elizabeth (*Reg. of Deeds*, ccclv. 415).'

p. **102,** l. 5 from foot, after '1655,' insert 'Sir Francis had a natural daughter, *Margaret*, married to James Henderson (*Gen. Reg. Inhibs.*, 16 November 1676).'

p. **103,** after l. 18, insert

'(4) *James*, (5) *Elizabeth*, (6) *Christian* (*Gen. Reg. Inhibs.*, 5 November 1674).'

p. **105,** l. 15, after 'Church,' insert 'Sir Philip Warwick in his memoirs describes the Earl as "a Scot, an experienced commander, and a man of natural courage: purely a soldier, and of a most loyal heart, which his countrymen remembered, for they used both him and his widow with all extremity afterwards." The number of the wound marks which the Earl bore is said to have been greater than the number of battles in which he was engaged (*Memoirs of Ann, Lady Fanshawe*, 348 *n*.).'

p. **105,** l. 21, after 'wife,' insert 'She was godmother to Lady Fanshawe's daughter Anne, born in Jersey in 1646.

FRASER

p. **109,** l. 10, after '1505,' add 'He married, contract 28 October 1501, (*Aberdeen Burgh Sasines*), Muriel Sutherland, widow of Alexander Seton of Meldrum. She must have been his second wife.'

p. **109,** ll. 11 and 12, delete these lines and insert 'He left issue:—'

p. **109,** ll. 5 and 6 from foot, delete 'is not ascertained,' and insert 'was Stewart as appears from a charter to himself and his wife of the lands of Blayrneill, 30 September 1505 (*Aberdeen Burgh Sasines*).

p. **116,** after l. 6 from foot, insert

'4. *James*, witness to a deed in 1648 (*Reg. of Deeds*, DLXVI. 26), died *v.p.*, *s.p.*, and alter succeeding numbers of children accordingly.'

p. **118,** after line 22, insert 'Andrew, third Lord Fraser, had also a natural daughter *Marjory* (*Reg. of Deeds* (Durie), 16 March 1681).'

FRENDRAUGHT

p. **125,** l. 25, after '1599,' insert 'He married Isobel Chalmers, with issue a son *George*. He was alive in 1637 (*Reg. of Deeds*, DXVIII. 371).'

p. **126,** l. 19, after 'Craig,' insert 'She was alive 1664 (*P. C. Reg.*, 3rd ser. i. 501).'

p. **128,** l. 24, for '2' read '3.'

p. **129,** l. 5, after 'married,' insert 'contract 9 May 1642 (*Reg. of Deeds*, DLII. 160).'

p. **134,** after l. 2, insert note

'The following are said to have been children of James Crichton of Auchingone.'

William, born 16 April 1710.
Elspet, born 10 December 1711.
George, born 7 February . . .
Janet, born 21 September 1719.
Margaret, born 4 January 1723.
Anna, born 21 May 1726.
Alexander, born 3 May 1729.

(*ex inform.* Douglas Crichton, Esq. Lincoln's Inn Fields).'

STEWART, EARL OF GALLOWAY

p. **149,** l. 4, after 'preserved,' add note 'Her Christian name was Isobel (*Patent Rolls*, Henry IV. for 1400).'

p. **150**, ll. 5 and 6 from foot, delete 'is believed to have died about 1479,' and insert 'was alive 8 October 1485 (Protocol Book of James Young).'

p. **150**, l. 3 from foot, delete 'is said to have.'

p. **150**, last line, after 'Menteith,' insert 'She was alive 23 October 1495 (*Acta Dom. Conc.*, 401).'

p. **151**, l. 26, for 'about 1479-80' read 'between 1485 and 1495.'

p. **151**, l. 6 from foot, for 'about 1500' read 'in 1496.'

p. **152**, l. 5, after 'Kirkmaho,' delete down to 'Fintalloch' on l. 16.'

p. **152**, after l. 24, insert

'ALEXANDER STEWART, fourth of Garlies, succeeded his father in 1496, having sasine of these lands in that year (*Exch. Rolls*, x. 771). He died in 1500, having married Janet Gordon, who survived him and married, secondly, Sir William Keith of Inverugie (*Acta Dom. Conc.*, xvii. 176). He had issue :—

1. ALEXANDER.
2. *Walter*, ancestor of Barclye. 3. *Janet*.
4. *Elizabeth* (*Acta Dom. Conc.*, xxii. 161).'

p. **152**, l. 25, for 'fourth' read 'fifth.'

p. **153**, ll. 2 and 3, delete 'was one son,' and insert 'were.'

'1. ALEXANDER.
2. *Thomas*, alive in 1584 (*Reg. Sec. Sig.*, li. 76).'

p. **153**, l. 4, for 'fifth' read 'sixth.'

p. **155**, l. 6, for 'fourth' read 'sixth.'

p. **155**, l. 25, after 'families,' insert 'He died 10 August 1592, having married Margaret Stewart, with issue (Edin. Tests.).'

p. **155**, l. 10 from foot, after 'Barbara,' as note, insert 'Barbara Gordon survived her husband and married again, before 2 September 1592, Alexander Agnew of Ardoch (Cal. of Charters, Reg. Ho. at date).'

p. **156**, l. 23, for 'Mureford' read Penninghame (cf. vol. v. 108).'

p. **156**, l. 26, for 'fourth' read 'sixth.'

p. **158**, l. 7, delete 'she married, secondly, John Wallace of Dundonald.'

p. **158**, after l. 9, insert

'2. *Thomas*. 3. *William*.
4. *James*, all mentioned in mutual bonds of caution (*P. C. Reg.*, v. 574). The last named was his mother's executor (*v. post*, p. 408).'

p. **158**, ll. 10 and 11, for '2' and '3' read '5' and '6.'

p. **158**, l. 18, for 'fifth' read 'seventh.'

p. **159**, l. 3, delete 'before 10 October 1576,' and insert 'contract 21 April 1574 (*Reg. of Deeds*, xiv. 350).'

p. **159**, l. 4, for 'William' read 'James.'

p. **159**, l. 5, after 'Queensberry' insert 'who died 13 Aug. 159—, and was buried at Glasserton (*Fourth Rep. Hist. Monuments Com.* i.).'

p. **159**, l. 11, delete entire entry.

p. **159**, l. 14, for '3' read '2.'

p. **159**, delete ll. 23, 24, 25.

p. **159**, ll. 26, 27, 28, 29, for '4, 5, 6, 7' read '3, 4, 5, 6.'

p. **159**, l. 7 from foot, for 'sixth' read 'eighth.'

p. **161**, after l. 16, add
'4. *Janet* (probably illegitimate) appears in the Charity Rolls of 1694 and 1696.'

p. **163**, l. 25, for '1761' read '1701.'

p. **163**, l. 27, for '1761' read '1701.'

p. **165**, l. 14, after 'January,' insert note 'The marriage took place on 7 January according to a contemporary account (*Red Book of Grandtully*, ii. 324).

p. **165**, l. 20, for 'proved' read 'recorded (*Reg. of Deeds*, ccxlv. 286).'

GARNOCK

p. **174**, l. 23, for '1681' read '1680 (Edin. Tests.).'

GLASGOW

p. **184**, note 2, for 'Fordun' read 'Bower.'

p. **185**, after l. 17, insert
Robert Boyl, layman of Glasgow diocese, had an indult to choose a confessor 6 June 1372 (*Reg. Aven.*, clxxxiii. 551).

p. **187**, note 9, after '*Reg. Mag. Sig.*,' insert 'Edin. Tests., 26 February 1584-85.'

p. **189**, l. 10 from foot, after '1583,' insert 'and was living 26 December 1584 (Kelburne Writs).'

p. **197**, note 5, delete '189.'

p. **198**, l. 24, delete '15 October 1673,[16]' and insert '1 March 1688 [16].'

p. **199**, l. 21, delete 'in,' and insert '23 April.'

p. **199**, l. 21, delete 'is said to have.'

p. **200**, l. 16, after 'Mr. William,' insert 'who had.'

p. **200**, l. 18, after 'afterwards,' insert 'bought on the death of Sir Alexander.'

p. **200**, l. 2, from foot, delete 'had,' and insert 'died 30 June 1730, leaving (original letter at Kelburne).'

p. **203**, l. 22, for 'elder' read 'eldest.'

p. **204**, l. 13, after 'issue,' insert '(besides two sons, both named *David*, who died young (correspondence at Kelburne).'

p. **204**, l. 4 from foot, for '1721' read '1720.'

p. **205**, l. 3 from foot, after '1729,' insert 'and was buried at Rowallan (original letter at Kelburne).

p. **205**, l. 2 from foot, for '29 March 1720 [17]' read '9 July 1724 [17].'

p. **205**, note 17, delete note and substitute 'Correspondence at Kelburne.'

p. **209**, l. 6, after '1865,' add 'He died at Twyssenden Manor, Goudhurst, Kent, 29 September, and was buried at Kilndoun 2 October 1909.

p. **209**, l. 16, for 'St. Helen's' read 'Middleton, near Freshwater.'

p. **210**, l. 39, for 'Alister' read 'Alastair.'

p. **210**, l. 9 from foot, after '1886,' add 'married at the Cathedral, Christchurch, to Agar Williams of Wellington, New Zealand, and has issue.'

p. **211**, l. 23, for 'is' read 'became.' After 'barrister-at-law,' add 'He died at Horsington House, Templecombe, 22, and was buried at Horsington 27 March, 1907.'

p. **211**, l. 26, after 'and,' insert 'by her, who survived him, and died at Parkstone, Dorset, 2, and was buried at Horsington 6, February 1911.'

p. **211**, l. 27, for 'has' read 'had.'

p. **213**, l. 12, after 'Hagley,' add 'She died at Salisbury 7, and was buried beside her husband 9, January 1907.'

p. **213**, l. 21, after 'and,' insert 'by her who died at Fleet, Hants, 14, and was buried there 17, November 1909.'

p. **213**, l. 3 from foot, delete 'has' and insert 'by her, who died at Tokio, Japan, 10 May 1910, aged forty-six, had.'

p. **214**, l. 27, after 'was,' insert 'born at Craig, 17 July 1766 (Kilmaurs Par. Reg.), and was.'

p. **215**, l. 1, for '25 September' read '5 November (Canongate Reg.).'

p. **215**, l. 3, after 'Bart.,' insert 'Rear.'

p. **215**, after l. 9, insert
'13, Grissell, died young.'

p. **216**, l. 1, after '1791,' insert 'aged sixty-three.'

p. **216**, l. 1, for '*Jane*' read '*Jane Mary*.' For '30' read '13'; after '1823,' add 'aged fifty-nine; buried at Renfrew (Coffin plate).'

p. **218**, l. 3, after 'died,' insert 'at Edinburgh.'

p. **218**, l. 4, after '1868,' insert 'aged seventy-one.'

p. **220**, l. 19, after '1897,' insert 'Commander.'

p. **220**, l. 22, after 'Surrey,' add 'and has issue:—
(1) *David William Maurice*, born at Kelburne 24 July 1910.'

p. **220**, l. 4 from foot, after '1906,' insert 'He married, 15 September 1908 at Holy Trinity Church, Sloane Street, Katherine Isabel Salvin, daughter of Edward Salvin Bowlby of Gilston Park, Herts, and Knoydart, Inverness, and has issue:—
'(1) *Patrick John Salvin*, born at Melbourne, Victoria, 21 March 1910.'

GLENCAIRN

p. **226**, l. 24, after 'brother,' insert 'On 16 March 1365-66 a Papal commission was granted to dispense in Nigel Cunningham's marriage with a lady named Joanna Douglas, of St. Andrews diocese, not otherwise designed, to whom he was related in the third degree of affinity (*Reg. Aven.*, clxiii. f. 217).'

p. **230**, last line, after '1417,' add in note, 'See *Acta Dom. Concilii*, xix. f. 15, for charter by Robert, Duke of Albany (dated at Stirling 17 December 1415), confirming a charter of 23 November 1400, by William of Cunynghame, knight, Lord of Redhall, granting to his natural son, William, the lands of Bonaly and Wodehall in the barony of Redhall and sheriffdom of Edinburgh.'

p. **230**, note 3, after '1639,' insert 'see also *Reg. Mag. Sig.*, vol. i. (new ed.), App. 2, No. 1952, and *Ibid.*, 21 Nov. 1450.'

p. **234,** l. 8, for 'fifteenth' read 'fourteenth.'

p. **235,** l. 15, delete 'he was succeeded by his son,' and insert 'He had issue:—

'1. CUTHBERT, who succeeded.

2. *Archibald* (Protocol Book of James Young 1 November 1497).'

p. **236,** l. 8 from foot, for 1499' read 1509.'

p. **238,** l. 1, delete 'soon after' and insert 'in.' Add to note 1 '*Acts and Decreets*, xxxviii. 227.'

p. **241,** l. 17, after 'Craigie' add 'She had a tocher of £466, 13s. 4d. from the Earl of Arran the Governor, which was paid to her husband in November 1552 (*Treasurer's Accounts*, x. 130).'

p. **242,** ll. 22, 23, for '18 October 1580' read '24 February 1579-80 (*Reg. Sec. Sig.* xlvi. 106).'

p. **242,** note 14, after 'Lyon Office' add 'see also Fraser's note books No. vi. (Lyon Office MSS.) note of contract and discharge of tocher by Earl of Glencairn 26 July 1549.'

p. **243,** l. 2, after 'name' add 'He died in July 1610, his executors being two daughters *Ann* and *Marion* (Glasgow Tests., 20 January 1613).'

p. **243,** ll. 12, 13, delete after '15 August' and insert 'contract 24 April (*Reg. of Deeds*, xviii. pt. i. 8).'

p. **243,** l. 20, after 'married,' insert 'contract 30 December 1577 (Hutton Coll. Adv. Lib., vii. 103).'

p. **244,** l. 23, after '1574,' insert 'Margaret.'

p. **245,** l. 7, after 'Lennox,' insert 'He was dead before 23 February 1629 (*Reg. of Deeds*, ccccxiv. 274).'

p. **245,** l. 8, after 'married,' insert contract 28 January 1618 (*Reg. of Deeds*, cclxxxviii. 231).'

p. **245,** l. 8, after 'daughter of' delete to end of paragraph, and insert 'Andrew Knox, Bishop of the Isles. By her, who survived him, he had a son *John*, mentioned above, who died *s.p.*, and three daughters. *Margaret* was married to Sir Alexander Cunningham of Robertland; *Anna* to Robert Wallace, Bishop of the Isles; and *Elizabeth* to William Wallace of Helenton, Advocate (*Retours*, *Ayr*, 327, 394, 421, 539; *Fasti Eccl. Scot.*, iii. 449; *Ayr Sasines*, viii. 179; Edin. Tests.).'

p. **246,** l. 4. after 'Mary,' insert 'youngest daughter.'

p. **246,** after l. 7, insert

'By his second wife the Earl had a son

'10. *James*, baptized 21 January 1612 (Canongate Reg.). He died young (*Acts and Decreets*, cclxxxi. 402).'

p. **246,** l. 23, delete 'before 26 July 1614,' and insert 'about 1609.'

p. **247,** l. 1, after 'married,' insert 'in Cornwall 1660.'

p. **247,** l. 2, after 'Minto,' insert 'against whom she raised an action of divorce in 1668 (*Consistorial Processes, etc.*, Scot. Rec. Soc., No. 12).'

p. **247,** l. 5, after 'secondly,' delete 'to,' and insert 'contract 29 May 1661 (*Perth Sasines*, i. 152) to John.'

p. **247,** l. 7, after '*Jean*,' insert 'married to John Blair of that Ilk, with whom, as his future spouse, she had a charter of lands 5 August 1646 (*Reg. Mag. Sig.*).'

p. **247**, l. 12, delete 'as,' and insert 'being buried in Holyrood Church in January 1661 (Canongate Reg.) and.'

p. **248**, l. 2 from foot, for '25 July' read '27 January.'

p. **249**, l. 16, for 'Colestoun' read 'Orbistoun.'

p. **249**, l. 28, for 'third' read 'fifth.'

p. **250**, l. 4 from foot, delete '2,' and insert 'proclamation 23 (Edin. Reg.).'

p. **251**, l. 1, delete '20,' and insert 'proclamation 27 (Edin. Reg.) as his second wife.' (Cf. vol. v. 509.)

p. **251**, l. 14, for '24' read '25.'

p. **251**, l. 14, after 'June,' insert 'and was buried in Restalrig 30.'

p. **252**, l. 24, for '1469' read '1463.'

GOWRIE

p. **257**, note 4, for '33' read '83.'

p. **260**, l. 15, after 'Ilk,' insert 'who died 7 December 1592 (Edin. Tests.).'

p. **260**, l. 20, for 'about 1612' read 'contract 28 April 1621 (*Reg. of Deeds*, clxxx. 229).'

p. **260**, l. 25, after '1600,' add 'He was a burgess of Perth, and married, contract 14 October 1593, Bessie Mathow (*Reg. of Deeds*, clxxx. 229).'

p. **260**, l. 26, after 'conspiracy,' add 'He married, contract 15 February 1598-99, Agnes, daughter of Henry Adamson, merchant, Perth (*Reg. of Deeds*, cxlii. 168).'

p. **260**, l. 27, delete after '*Jean*' to end of sentence, and insert 'married, contract 23 May 1587, Laurence Mercer of Clevage, eldest son of James Mercer of Newton (*Reg. of Deeds*, xxxiii. 286).'

p. **260**, l. 28, after '*Barbara*,' delete to end of sentence, and insert 'married contract 1611, to Henry Rattray of Kincarrochy (*Reg. of Deeds*, clxxx. 235).'

p. **260**, after l. 30, insert

'(7) *Beatrix*, named with her sisters Annas and Dorothy in her mother's testament.

(8) *Annas.*

(9) *Dorothy*, married to James Ruthven in Feu (*Perth Sasines, Secretary's Reg.*, vi. 411).

There was also a son *John* (perhaps illegitimate) named in his eldest brother's testament.'

p. **260**, note 8, for '*Ibid.*' read 'Wood's Douglas's *Peerage*.'

p. **261**, l. 24, after 'secondly,' insert 'contract 9 April.'

p. **261**, l. 29, after 'Dowager,' insert 'She survived Lord Ruthven, and is said to have married, fifthly, James, son of Gilbert Gray of Foulis, but the only authority for this is Sir Robert Gordon's *Genealogy of the Earls of Sutherland*.'

p. **262**, l. 9, after 'Ruthven,' insert 'born about 1560 (*Cal. of Scottish Papers*, i. No. 707).'

p. **262**, l. 26, after '*Alexander*,' insert 'of Halieland.'

p. **262,** l. 27, after 'He,' insert 'married Elizabeth Wemyss (*Reg. of Deeds*, clxxxi. 150), and.'

p. **264,** l. 6, after 'Anna,' read 'and the father of Charles I.'

p. **266,** l. 17, for 'George' read 'Hugh.'

p. **266,** l. 27, after '*Lilias*,' insert 'baptized 27 January 1568-69 (Perth Reg.).'

p. **266,** l. 29, after '*Dorothea*,' insert 'baptized 30 April 1570 (*Ibid.*).'

p. **266,** after l. 30, insert

'14. *Katherine*, baptized 28 February 1571-72 (*Ibid.*) Died young.

p. **266,** l. 31, for '14' read '15.'

p. **266,** note 2, after '1595,' add '*Reg. of Deeds*, xlvi. 444.'

GRAY

p. **272,** l. 4, for 'May' read 'December.'

p. **274,** l. 13 from foot, the words 'and grandson of Sir Patrick' should be in brackets.

p. **276,** l. 1, after 'Balnamoon,' insert reference '(*Registrum de Panmure*, i. xxix.).'

p. **276,** l. 5 from foot, after 'completed,' insert 'till much later.'

p. **277,** l. 3, after 'Lyle,' add 'He married again, after 1501, Elizabeth Hay, relict of George, second Earl of Huntly, the lady to whom he had been contracted (*Acta Dom. Conc.*, xxix. ff. 38, 39).'

p. **277,** l. 13, after '1500,' insert 'She was then contracted to Walter Drummond, grandson of the first Lord Drummond, but the contract was discharged in January 1501-2 (*Acta Dom. Conc.*, xii. 39).'

p. **278,** l. 5, for 'secondly' read 'thirdly,' and for ('? Alexander)' read 'William (cf. vol. vi. 34).'

p. **278,** l. 6, for 'thirdly' read 'secondly. *See title* Wemyss.'

p. **281,** l. 8, for '1562' read '1558.'

p. **281,** l. 8 from foot, after 'issue,' insert 'She survived him and was married, secondly, to William Rollock of Balbegie (cf. vol. v. 220).'

p. **282,** l. 18, after 'Invergowrie,' insert 'as Patrick Gray, son of Patrick, Lord Gray, was, on 31 May 1567, instituted as perpetual vicar of the church of Rossie (Protocol Book of Duncan Gray, f. 41). He.'

p. **285,** l. 2, delete 'before 18 August 1604,' and insert 'November 1603.'

p. **285,** l. 6 from foot, delete 'in 1612,' and insert '4 September 1611 (*Synod of Fife*, Abbotsford Club, 36).'

p. **287,** l. 27, delete 'said to be widow of Sir John Sydenham, Bart. of Brompton, and to be aged eighty,' and insert 'daughter of Sir Thomas Guldeford of Hemsted in Cranbrook, Kent. She had married, first, John Baker of Sissinghurst, Kent; secondly, as his second wife, Sir John Sydenham, Knight, of Brimpton, Somerset, who died 1626. The following year she married, when she was about eighty, Lord Gray (cf. Pedigree of Sydenham in *Misc. Gen. et Her.*, 2nd ser., iii. 327; *Complete Baronetage*, i. *sub* Baker; *State Papers, Dom.*, 1628-29, 28, 447; *Notes and Queries*, 10th ser., xi. 54).'

p. 287, note 3, for '28' read '58.'

p. 288, l. 1, after 'married,' insert 'first, to Captain Archibald Douglas, who was killed by the Dutch at Chatham, 11 June 1667 (*ex inform.* Patrick Gray, Esq.), and, secondly.'

p. 291, l. 14, after 'Gray,' insert born 9 Feb. 1671 (Perth Bap. Reg.).'

p. 292, last line, for 'thirteenth' read 'twelfth.'

p. 293, ll. 1 and 2, for 'fourteenth' and 'fifteenth' read 'thirteenth' and 'fourteenth.'

VISCOUNT OF HADDINGTON

p. 299, l. 5 from foot, for '1831' read '1631.'

p. 299, note 6, for 'Adjournals' read 'Adjournal.'

p. 300, after l. 4, insert

'8. *James* or *Jacob*, a general-major in the Swedish service, married, before 1614, Isobel, daughter of James Spens, Count of Hoya, Swedish Ambassador to England. In 1647 he raised a regiment.

9. *Jane*, married to Robert More, who had letters of denization in September 1661 (*Forty-third Rep. of Deputy Keeper of Records*, App. 193).'

p. 300, l. 9, after '1605,' insert 'of these, George was infeft in the barony of Wyliecleugh in 1632 (*Gen. Reg. Sas.*, xxxiii. 89), and was dead *s.p.* before 1645 (*Reg. Mag. Sig.*, 22 June 1635 and 26 November 1647).'

p. 301, l. 8 from foot, for '1 June' read '11 June.'

EARL OF HADDINGTON

p. 306, l. 16, for 'Cosmus' read 'Cosmas.'

p. 307, l. 25, after 'Newbyres,' insert 'She was buried 23 November 1612 (Canongate Reg.).'

p. 308, l. 10, delete 'about 1604,' and insert 'contract 26 June 1602 (Oxenfoord Writs).'

p. 308, l. 12, for 'at least one daughter' read 'six daughters.'

p. 308, after l. 13, insert

'(1) *Elizabeth*, married (contract 8 September 1619) to Robert Hamilton of Bathgate (*Reg. Mag. Sig.*, 25 October 1620).

(2) *Agnes*, married, as in text.

(3) *Christian*, married (contract 21 February 1630) to Mr. John Scharp of Houstoun (*Reg. Mag. Sig.*, 28 July 1632).

(4) *Margaret.*

(5) *Jean*, married to Cornet John Home (*Reg. of Deeds*, DLiii. 140).

(6) *Rebecca.*'

p. 308, l. 14, delete from 'Probably' down to '1627' on l. 16.

p. 308, l. 19, for '30' read '20.'

p. 308, l. 20, for 'teacher of the St. Mary Magdalene School,' read 'Preceptor of the Magdalene Hospital.'

p. 309, l. 24, after 'thirdly,' insert 'contract 13 January 1649 (*Gen. Reg. of Inhibs.*, 6 September 1675).'

p. **309**, after l. 25, insert

'6. *Marion*, eldest daughter, married, in 1582, to James Ross, merchant, Edinburgh (Protocol Book of A. Lawson, i. 81).'

p. **309**, ll. 26, 29 and 31, for '6, 7, 8' read '7, 8, 9.'

p. **315**, l. 22, for 'young' read 'in November 1619 (Canongate Reg.).'

p. **317**, after l. 7, insert

'7. *Mary*, baptized 5 May 1629 (Canongate Reg.).'

p. **317**, ll. 8, 9, for '7, 8' read '8, 9.'

p. **317**, after l. 12, insert

The earl had also a son, presumably natural, Mr. Thomas of Parkley, who married, first, Helen Stewart, eldest daughter of William, second Lord Blantyre (cf. vol. ii. 85); secondly, Janet Foulis (*Edin. Sasines*, vii. 371, 437). He was keeper of the General Register of Sasines in 1657 (*Acts and Decreets* (Durie) 23 June 1677). Will dated 17 May 1668 (Edin. Tests.).

p. **317**, l. 30, after 'romance,' insert 'She was an intimate friend of Ninon de l'Enclos, and was included in the *Portraits* written by Mlle. de Scudery.'

p. **318**, l. 14, after 'married,' insert 'in the Kirk of Holyroodhouse 13 April 1648 (Canongate Reg.).'

p. **321**, l. 4 from foot, for 'David' read 'James.'

p. **322**, l. 15, for 'in or before 1720' read 'before 1719.'

p. **323**, after l. 40, insert the names of the following children of Charles, Lord Binning, which have been accidentally omitted :—

'3. *Charles*, born 6 October 1725, died in infancy.

4. *John*, born 22 October 1726, died 1730.

5. *Charles*, born 3 October 1727; lieutenant 3rd Dragoon Guards 29 July 1751; captain 1st Dragoon Guards 12 March 1755; major 19 May 1762; retired with rank of lieut.-col. 1776; Governor of Blackness Castle 1792, till his death, which took place at Tynninghame 28 September 1806.

6. *Grisell*, married, at London 24 July 1745, Philip, second Earl Stanhope, and died at Ovenden, Kent, 28 December 1811, in her ninety-third year.

7. *Helen Mary*, born 8 October 1724, and died young.

8. *Rachel*, died, unmarried, at Mellerstain 20 October 1797.'

p. **324**, l. 8, after 'secondly,' insert 'proclamation of banns 4 March 1786 (Canongate Reg.).'

p. **326**, l. 25, for 'younger brother' read 'great uncle.'

p. **327**, l. 11 from foot, for '1836' read '1863.'

p. **327**, l. 10 from foot, after 'Baronet' place full stop; delete 'with' and insert 'She died 16 January 1908, and he died May 1910, leaving.'

HALIBURTON OF DIRLETON

p. **332**, l. 20, delete from 'married' down to 'He' in line 23 and insert 'who (*Exch. Rolls*, ii. 175).'

p. **332**, l. 24, delete from 'his' down to 'presently' on l. 26.

p. **332,** l. 27, for 'Adam' read 'Alexander.'

p. **332,** l. 9 from foot, for '1372' read '1377.'

p. **333,** l. 9, for '1372' read '1377.'

p. **333,** l. 11, after '1378-79,' insert 'He was alive 1388 (see below), and had a son *John*, his successor, and a daughter *Jean*, married to Henry St. Clair, first Earl of Orkney of the St. Clair line; in the charter of 1388 quoted below, Henry, Earl of Orkney is styled brother of Sir John Haliburton, which proves that Jean in the text is placed a generation too low.'

p. **333,** l. 12, for 'nephew' read 'son.'

p. **333,** l. 19, after '1397,' insert 'On 24 July 1388 he granted license to mortify the lands of Cameron to the Lady altar of Musselburgh; in this deed he styles himself Lord of Drylton, while his father witnesses it as Walter, Lord of that Ilk (Craigmillar Charters). This indicates that he must have married Christian Vaus, heiress of Dirleton, but he may have also married the Cameron heiress referred to in the text; unless Christian Vaus was also co-heiress of the Camerons through her mother. John certainly used a seal quartering the arms of both Cameron and Vaus in 1384 during his father's lifetime.'

p. **333,** delete lines 3 and 4 from foot.

p. **334,** l. 3 from foot, after 'of,' insert 'Sir.'

p. **334,** l. 2 from foot, delete 'first Lord Haliburton' and insert 'There was a papal dispensation for his marriage 18 August 1427 (*Cal. of Papal Letters*, vii. 527).'

p. **335,** l. 4, after '1439,' insert 'He married Johanna, daughter of John Congalton of that Ilk. She appears as his widow 1446-47 (*Munimenta de Melros*, 567).'

p. **335,** l. 22, after 'Congalton,' insert 'second son of John Congalton (cf. vol. viii. 575 and authorities there cited).'

p. **335,** after l. 25, insert

'3. *Walter.*

4. *John.* Both mentioned in a charter of 1464 (*Hutton Coll.*, Haddington, f. 16).'

p. **335,** l. 3 from foot, for '1448' read '1458,' and after 'marriage,' insert '(already consummated).'

p. **335,** note 12, for 'Vatican' read 'Lateran.'

p. **336,** l. 27, for 'Sauchie' read 'Sauchieburn.'

p. **337,** l. 10, for 'was dead before 10 February 1506-7' read 'died 6 December 1505 (*Exch. Rolls*, xii. 432).'

p. **337,** l. 16, after 'Stevenston,' insert 'widow of Andrew Mowbray, burgess of Edinburgh (Robertson's *Parl. Records*, 500)'; and for 'secondly' read 'thirdly.'

HAMILTON

p. **341,** l. 18, for 'Lambert' read 'Larbert.'

p. **346,** l. 4 from foot, after '1402,' insert 'He was certainly dead before

1410, when his widow had a dispensation to marry William Douglas of Drumlanrig (*Reg. Aven.*, ccc. f. 641; cf. vol. vii. 114).'

p. **349,** l. 17, after 'Hamilton,' insert 'He had also another son *James* and a daughter *Eupham.*'

p. **353,** l. 10, after 'Crawford,' add 'The marriage was dissolved, and in 1503 she was the wife of John Forrester of Niddrie (*Acta Dom. Conc.*, xii. 166, 173).'

p. **354,** l. 26, after 'Albany,' insert 'and had by her a son *James.*'

p. **354,** l. 26, after 'and,' insert 'married, secondly, David Ross of Balnagown, who died 20 May 1527 (*Acta Dom. Conc.*, xxxvii. 189). She.'

p. **361,** l. 2 from foot, after 'Somerville,' insert *Grisel*, married (contract 28 June 1548), to Andrew, Lord Rothes, was also a daughter, but whether by this marriage is not known. A son *Cuthbert* is mentioned at the Scottish Court in 1544 (*Treasurer's Accounts*, viii. 357).'

p. **362,** l. 3, after 'Ilk,' insert 'She was alive in March 1557-58 (Protocol Book of John Robeson, f. 226, where her husband is called *William*).

p. **363,** l. 7, after 'Lothian,' insert 'He was Sheriff of Lanark in 1543 (*Treasurer's Accounts*, viii. 192).'

p. **363,** l. 12, after 'first,' insert 'in 1544 (she had a trousseau in March 1543-44 (*Treasurer's Accounts*, viii. 267).'

p. **363,** l. 19, after 'Lindsay,' insert 'He had a grant of the lands of Parkhill 1 September 1547 (*Reg. Sec. Sig.*), and is styled of Parkhill in 1550, when he had a royal grant (*Ibid.*, xxiv. 8).'

p. **363,** l. 6 from foot, after '*James*,' insert 'of Kinnell.'

p. **364,** ll. 2, 3, delete 'The name of his wife has not been ascertained.' and insert 'He married Janet Murray (Canongate Court Book), who died before 1 October 1572, and had (1) *William*; (2) *Paul*, captain of Arran, ancestor of the Hamiltons of Coats (*Reg. of Deeds*, ccccxcv. 264); (3) *Gavin* (*Acts and Decreets*, ccxxxiv. 86) mentioned in 1608.'

p. **364,** l. 10, for 'fifth' read 'fourth.'

p. **365,** l. 10, after '12,' insert 'and were married 15.'

p. **365,** l. 13, after '1563' add 'She was married, thirdly, to John Crawford in Shaw (*Acts and Decreets*, lii. 96, A.D. 1573).'

p. **365,** l. 18, for 'fifth' read 'fourth.'

p. **365,** i. 21, after 'Finnart' add 'She was still alive in 1557-58 (Protocol Book of J. Robeson, f. 220).'

p. **365,** at end of note 10 add 'A "half-sister of the Governor's" is in December 1547 said to be wife of John Wemyss (*Cal. Scot. Papers*, i. 48).'

p. **368,** l. 27, after '1572-73,' insert 'He received the Order of the Cockle (St. Michael) from the King of France, apparently as a kind of pledge for an advance of money, as in his will he directs it to be delivered again to the King, so that his son Claud might receive payment of the sums advanced (Edin. Tests.).'

p. **368,** l. 7 from foot, for '1579' read '6 December 1580, when an inquest found that she ought to be interdicted from administering her property, being, and having been for twenty-four years, excessively profuse (Moray Writs, box 15, No. 1209).'

p. **369,** l. 6 from foot, delete 'apparently without issue.'

p. **369,** l. 3 from foot, after 'Fife,' add 'He appears to have left issue, as in his father's will of 16 January 1574 his "tua bairns" are consigned to the care of his brother John. In view of the above-mentioned service they must either have died young or have been illegitimate.'

p. **369,** last line, after 'older,' insert note, 'There was a "bairn" of the Lord Governor baptized 9 June 1546, who may have been Claud (*Treasurer's Accounts*, viii. 461).'

p. **370,** l. 12, after 'lands,' insert note 'She was undoubtedly married to him. On 2 February 1545-46 she got an extensive trousseau "at her departure to the northland with the Earl of Huntlie" (*Treasurer's Accounts*, viii. 436), and her marriage is alluded to as an accomplished fact in 1548-49 (*Ibid.*, ix. 282). She had a tocher of 5000 merks, of which, however, only 2000 were actually paid as Huntly owed Arran 3000 (Cf. also Letter in H.M. Reg. Ho. (Corr. Mary of Guise), 11 February 1545-46).'

p. **370,** l. 15, after 'contracted,' insert 'on 10 July 1546 to Gilbert Kennedy, son of Gilbert, Earl of Cassillis (*P. C. Reg.*, i. 42) and.'

p. **373,** l. 19, after 'married,' insert 'first, about 1594, Catherine, daughter of John Carnegie of that Ilk (*Carnegie Book*, i. 50). She died before 24 May 1597. Testament confirmed 21 January 1602 (Edin. Tests.); secondly.'

p. **373,** l. 22, for '*Margaret*' read '*Jean* (*See Chiefs of Colquhoun*, and Glasgow Tests., 13 September 1633).'

p. **377,** l. 22, after 'Castle,' insert note 'At Pendennis "he has not changed a sheet for sixteen weeks time; they took all from him when he was put into that hole and left him neither money nor clothes, linen, nor woollen, but what was on his back; onlie they permitted his dog to go with him" (Dunbar's *Social Life in Former Days*, ii. 44).'

p. **380,** l. 15, after 'him,' insert 'and married, secondly, 19 June 1655, Thomas Dalmahoy of the Priory of Guildford, and was buried 2 September 1659 (cf. vol. iii. 130).'

p. **380,** l. 5 from foot, after 'thirdly,' insert 'in October 1703 (Edin. Reg.).'

p. **382,** l. 27, delete 'an Irish lady, name unknown, who,' and insert 'Anne, daughter and co-heir of Charles, Lord Lucas of Shenfield, and widow of Edward, son of Patrick Cary, and grandson of Henry, first Viscount Falkland. She (cf. vol. iii. 610).'

p. **383,** l. 6, after 'married,' insert '5 February 1687 (Canongate Reg.).'

p. **391,** l. 13 from foot, after '*Catharine*,' insert 'born 31 October and baptized 17 November 1700, being named after her aunt, the Countess of Tullibardine (Canongate Reg.).'

p. **391,** after l. 9 from foot, insert

'7. *Henrietta*, born 19 April 1704 (Canongate Reg.).'

p. **391,** l. 8 from foot, for '7' read '8.'

p. **391,** l. 8 from foot, after '*Susan*,' insert 'born 26 September 1706 (*Ibid.*).'

p. **393,** l. 3, for '10' read '5 (Canongate Reg.).'

p. **395,** l. 9, after '1846,' insert 'in a small house in White Lion Street, Pentonville. She was at one time in the household of Queen Caroline, upon whose death she retired into private life. A portion of her remaining days was embittered by the fact of a person having insinuated himself into her confidence and obtained many of her letters and papers; and having then daringly published, without her sanction, *A Secret History of the Court of England from the Accession of George III. to the death of George IV.*, under her name. The legal difficulties that ensued caused her much vexation, and obliged her to reside for a time in France (*The Patrician*, ii. 297).'

p. **396**, l. 1, after '1863,' insert note 'While in Paris he slipped on a polished stair and got concussion of the brain. The Empress nursed him to the end with much devotion (Lord Lamington's *Days of the Dandies*).'

HERRIES

p. **398**, l. 17, for 'Vandosine' read 'Vandosme.'

p. **404**, l. 12, after 'David,' insert 'On the dismissal of a later curator, George Herries of Terraughtie, for certain crimes, "Andro Heris sone and apparend are to Herbert, Lord Heris," and "Thomas M'K[l]ellane of Bondby" were appointed in his place, 27 May 1500 (*Reg. Sec. Sig.*, i. 532, 684).'

p. **404**, l. 7 from foot, after '*John*,' add 'He had a remission, along with his brother Mungo, for certain debts owing to the King 12 December 1508 (*Reg. Sec. Sig.*, i. 1778).'

p. **405**, l. 13, delete 'but was in favour again before,' and insert 'for the slaughter of George Sinclair of Highfield but was pardoned before 12 December 1508 at the request of the Queen of France (*Reg. Sec. Sig.*, i. 1498, 1721, 1778, 1854). On.'

p. **405**, l. 13, delete 'when.'

p. **406**, at end of note 2, add 'In an inventory of writs in the Angus Charter-chest (drawn up in March 1588-89, *Acts and Decreets*, cxx. 23b) is a note of "Ane charter maid vnder the gret and previe seill to Jonet Douglas, dochter to Archibald, Erl of Angus of Tarrigillis and Kirkgunzie, xxij of December 1^{m} $iiij^{c}$ lxxxxv yeiris.'

p. **407**, after l. 11, insert

'2. *Andrew*, "brother to William, Lord Hereis," and others had a respite for arson and other crimes 26 May 1528 (*Reg. Sec. Sig.*, i. 3966).'

p. **407**, l. 12, for '2' read '3.'

p. **407**, l. 22, for '3' read '4.'

p. **409**, l. 4, after 'Skirling,' insert 'contract 1 May 1552 (*Acts and Decreets*, vi. 267).'

p. **415**, l. 15, after '*James*,' add 'It was probably he who married Ælitia Collins and had a son *Robert*, aged nineteen in 1647, and a daughter *Alice* living in 1665 (*Records of Scots Colleges, etc.*, New Spalding Club, i. 197; *Carlaverock Book*, i. 388).'

p. **415**, l. 20, after 'married,' insert 'contract 31 October 1603 (*Reg. of Deeds*, clviii. 422).'

p. 416, l. 24, delete entire paragraph after '*Frederick*,' and insert 'educated at Douai at the charges of Colonel Semple from 29 July 1629 to November 1632, when he went to Spain and entered the Society of Jesus. He was Rector of the Scots College at Madrid from 1656 till his death on 9 May 1659 (*Records of Scots Colleges*, New Spalding Club, 25, 195, 202).'

p. 416, note 12, for '3 August 1642' read '13 August 1649.'

p. 417, l. 3, for '23' read '16.'

p. 418, l. 9 from foot, for 'young' read 'in 1836.'

p. 418, l. 4 from foot, for '1901' read '1891.'

p. 423, l. 25, after '1884,' insert 'He died 5 October 1908, when the barony of the United Kingdom became extinct and his Scottish honours descended to his eldest daughter.'

p. 423, l. 7 from foot, after '1905,' insert 'and a son Bernard Marmaduke, Earl of Arundel and Surrey, born 30 May 1908.'

HOLYROODHOUSE

p. 433, l. 26, after 'respectively,' add 'He had also a natural son *John*, apprenticed 4 March 1640 to Robert Chrystie, barber, Edinburgh (*Edin. Reg. of Apprentices*, Scot. Rec. Soc.).'

p. 435, l. 2, for '1628' read '1623.'

p. 435, l. 5 from foot, after 'married,' insert 'contract dated 22 and 24 September 1629 (*Reg. of Deeds*, ccccclxi. 342).'

p. 435, l. 3 from foot, for '1639' read '1629.'

p. 436, l. 8, after 'issue,' add 'In 1678 she was the wife of Mr. William Gray (*Reg. of Deeds* (Durie), 17 May, 1680).'

p. 438, l. 18, after 'Glencorse,' insert 'born 10 July 1736 (Canongate Reg.).'

p. 439, l. 1, delete 'married, according to Home Drummond's MS., to John Menzies, surgeon in Perth. *Note.*—It was no doubt Mary who was married to a Menzies. Anne was buried at Holyrood as Miss Anne Bothwell.'

p. 439, l. 5, after '*Mary*,' delete 'who' to 'named,' and insert 'married to Neil Menzies, son of James Menzies of Comrie, and had issue.'

HOME

p. 445, l. 4 from foot. According to a genealogy *penes* Sir William Fraser's Trustees, dated 1664, this George was ancestor of the Homes of Spott.

p. 447, l. 16, delete from 'He is said' down to '1436' on l. 28, and then take in from 'Sir Alexander' on p. 448, l. 5 from foot, onwards.

Note.—Recent investigation shows that previous writers on this pedigree, including Sir William Fraser in his Report (followed by the writer of this article), to the Historical MSS. Comm. (*Twelfth Report*,

App. pt. viii. 78-79), have been wrong in making the first Lord Home a separate personage from Sir Alexander. The mistake arose from the supposed necessity of finding a husband for Marion, heiress of Landells, and not perceiving that she was really identical with Marion Lauder. In view of this the following rearrangement and alteration of the text falls to be made:

p. 447, l. 5 from foot, delete from 'They had issue' to end of page.

p. 448, l. 18, after 'in,' insert 'or before.'

p. 448, l. 22, delete from 'I. SIR ALEXANDER' down to 'father' on next line. *Note.*—The information contained from the words 'a charter' on line 23, to 'Crown' on l. 5 from foot of same page, apply to Alexander, eldest son of Lord Home. (See *infra.*)

p. 449, after l. 4 from foot, delete down to 'Hepburn' on p. 450, l. 2, and insert

'Lord Home married, first, before 1424, Marion, daughter of John Lauder and his wife, Katherine, daughter of William de Landells and his wife Jouet. In 1425 she got sasine of the lands of Swynset, as heir of her mother, Katherine, who must have succeeded to them through her father, who, along with his wife, had a royal charter of these and other lands 4 January 1390-91 (*Reg. Mag. Sig.*, vol. i. new ed. No. 813). Sir Alexander and Marion were related in the fourth degree of consanguinity, etc., as on p. 447. They had issue :—

1. *Alexander*, who had a charter, etc., as on l. 23, p. 448, down to 'Crown' on l. 5, from foot of same page. He died *v.p.* about 1456. He married, contract 2 February 1448 (*Scotts of Buccleuch*, ii. 39), Annes or Agnes, daughter of Sir Adam Hepburn of Hailes: they had a papal dispensation for the marriage, 2 January 1450-51, on the ground that they were within the third and third degrees of affinity (*Reg. Vat.* ccccxvi. 122). They had issue, as on p. 450, ll. 4-6.
2. *George*, who seems to have been originally destined for the Church: he had papal provision of canonries of Glasgow and Dunkeld 14 June 1447, and was in his fifteenth year in 1450-51 (*Reg. Vat.*, ccccxvi. 124, 126). He had a confirmation charter, etc., as in text on p. 450.
3. *John*, Prior of Coldingham, as in text on p. 450.
4. *Sir Patrick*, of Fastcastle, as in text on p. 450.

5, 6, and 7. *Nicholas*, *Katherine*, and *Elyne*, as in text on p. 448.'

p. 451, l. 4, after 'married,' insert 'about January 1496-97 (cf. vol. vi. 357).'

p. 454, l. 5, from foot. According to the genealogy of 1664, there were eight daughters in all.

p. 456, l. 27, after 'forth.),' insert 'They had a dispensation for their marriage, which had been carried out *per verba de futuro*, they being within the third and fourth degrees of affinity, 24 and 25 February 1513-14 (*Laing Charters*, No. 301).'

p. 460, l. 18, after '1589' add 'He had a natural son George, who in 1574 was in Sweden (*Edin. Burgh Reg. of Deeds*, 7 Aug, 1574).'

p. 462, l. 8 from foot, for 'before February 1582-83' read 'contract 4, 15, 24, and 25 February 1580-81 (*Reg. of Deeds*, xix. 180).'

p. 463, after l. 10, insert

'The existence of two other daughters in 1578 is mentioned in the retour of the Commendator of Jedburgh as tutor to his nephew in that year (see below).'

p. 463, l. 14, after 'Home,' insert 'was for some time a student at St. Leonard's College, St. Andrews (*Reg. of Deeds*, xix. 90). He.'

p. 465, l. 7 from foot, after 'married,' insert 'contract 18 October 1627 (*Reg. of Deeds*, ccccIxxvii. 440).'

p. 465, l. 5 from foot, after 'married,' insert 'contract 23 August and 6 September 1632 (*Ibid.*, ccccIxxvii. 447).'

p. 467, l. 10, for 'Jane' read 'Fane.'

p. 468, l. 22, after 'her,' insert 'who survived him and married, secondly, before 1503, Sir William Colville of Ochiltree (cf. vol. ii. 543).'

p. 470, l. 4, from foot after '1584,' insert 'In 1586 he is styled Chanter of Ross (*Reg. of Deeds*, xxiv. 409).'

p. 471, l. 3, after 'Graden, and another son *John*, styled servitor to Lord Newbattle, who was dead in 1595 (*Edin. Inhibs.*, vii. 141).'

p. 471, l. 24, after 'Blyndlie,' insert 'who survived him (*Reg. of Deeds*, cxxxvii.).'

p. 471, l. 25, delete 'He married, secondly,' and insert

'5. *William* (*secundus*) of Bellitaw (*Reg. of Deeds*, ci. 11 July 1604) married.'

p. 471, l. 28, after 'Mellerstain,' insert 'He apparently murdered his step-son, John Haitlie of Mellerstaines, at the Salt Tron in Edinburgh 3 January 1602 (Birrell's *Diary*, 57).'

p. 471, ll. 29, 35, for '5, 6' read '6, 7.'

p. 472, after l. 14, insert

'8. *Barbara*, married to Robert Cairncross of Colmeslie (*Reg. of Deeds*, ii. 87).'

p. 473, l. 17, delete 'or before 22' and relative note, and insert '16 (Edin. Tests.).'

p. 474, l. 4 from foot, after 'first,' insert 'contract 10 December 1587 (*Reg. of Deeds*, xxvi. 271).'

p. 478, l. 24, delete 'was living 13 April 1683,' and insert 'died in 1694. (Her son Charles had licence to attend her funeral, 26 June. *P. C. Acta*.)'

p. 478, after last line, insert

'6. *Anna* (*Privy Seal, English Reg.*, ii. 342).

7. *Margaret*, married, contract 21 July 1662 (*Reg. of Deeds*, Durie, 16, 17 June 1670), to Alexander Home of Ayton.'

The genealogy of 1664 gives five daughters, *Anna*, *Margaret*, *Isabel*, *Jean*, and *Elizabeth*, all living in 1664.

p. 479, l. 4, after '1671,' insert note, 'The Duke of Lauderdale's daughter Mary was offered to him as a wife, but she was so deformed he would not have her. From that time Lauderdale would pay no more attention to the claim of Home of Wedderburn for repayment of money lent to the King (*Hist. MSS. Com.*, Milne-Home MSS., 106).'

p. 479, l. 6, for 'Withyam' read 'Withyham.'

p. 479, l. 19, after 'sustained,' insert 'In 1693 he was a prisoner in Edinburgh Castle, and on 22 June his Countess was allowed to remain there with him (*Privy Council Acta*). On 13 March 1694 he was liberated, and confined to his house of Hirsel and two miles about it on this side Tweed (*Ibid.*).'

p. 481, l. 5, after 'Jamaica,' insert 'He deserted her 24 February 1743 (*Chancery Roll*, Jamaica, 19 August 1752).'

p. 482, l. 24, for '1873' read '1875.'

p. 484, l. 4, after 'vert,' insert 'beaked gules.'

HOPETOUN

p. 486, l. 12, for '20 April 1579' read '4 August 1580.'

p. 486, l. 19, after '*Katherine*' add 'married to Mr. Richard Brown, minister of Tynron, and had issue a son, Mr. *Daniel* (*Fasti Ecclesiæ Scoticanæ*, by Hew Scott, D.D., i. 685; *P. C. Reg.*, 2nd ser., vii. 304).'

p. 486, after last line, insert

'4. *Elizabeth*, married to Patrick Rig, merchant, Edinburgh; she died 28 October 1578 (Edin. Tests.; Hope's *Diary*, 31).'

p. 487, l. 8, for '1591' read '1609.'

p. 489, l. 10 from foot, for 'fourteen' read 'fifteen.'

p. 489, after l. 9, from foot, insert

'1. *George*, of St. Albans, Herts, who granted a power of attorney to his father's clerk to uplift certain moneys, 27 April 1633 (*Reg. of Deeds*, cccclxi. 481). If eldest son he must have predeceased his father.'

p. 489, l. 8 from foot *et seq.*, The numbers attached to the names of Sir Thomas Hope's children fall to be increased by one.

p. 491, l. 17, for 'was dead before 1655' read 'died in May 1653.'

p. 492, l. 15, for 'Magalen' read 'Magdalen.'

p. 493, l. 21, after '1682' insert note, 'The family tradition is that in the wreck of the *Royal Gloucester* Hope got a seat in a boat, but gave it up to the Duke of York, and was in consequence drowned. On this account Queen Anne gave his son a Peerage almost immediately after he came of age (*ex inform.* Miss Jessie Hope).'

p. 494, last line, after 'army,' insert 'died at Clifton 1861, having.'

p. 504, l. 6, after 'Sleat, insert 'by Louise Maria La Coast, illegitimate daughter of H.R.H. the Duke of Gloucester, by Lady Almeria Carpenter, daughter of the Earl of Tyrconnel.'

HUNTLY

p. 517, note 7, add 'There was a commission to grant dispensation for the marriage of Thomas Somerville and Elizabeth Gordon 2 Nov. 1411 (*Reg. Aven.*, cccix. 549).'

p. 518, l. 7 from foot, after 'brother,' insert note, 'She appears to have been heiress in part at least during her brother's life. Her ward and marriage are said to have been bestowed by Robert III. on Sir Walter Buchanan 2 February 1403-4 (*Harl. MSS.*, No. 4693).'

p. **529,** l. 21, after 'Lindsay,' insert 'she married, secondly, some time after Huntly's death, Andrew, second Lord Gray, in violation of a contract between her and Huntly (*Acta Dom. Conc.*, xxix. 38, 39). She had originally been contracted to Gray half a century previous (cf. *ante*, p. 276).'

p. **531,** l. 10, for 'John Crichton of Invernyte' read 'the son and heir of Thomas, second Lord Innermeath. (Original Bond at Slains.)'

p. **532,** l. 19, for '20 October' read '14 October.'

p. **532,** after l. 5 from foot, insert

'1. *George.* The existence of this son has been hitherto unknown; but by contract between his father and grandfather on the one part, and Archibald, second Earl of Argyll, on the other, dated 27 March 1501, he (styled son and apparent heir of his father) was to marry either Katherine or Elizabeth Campbell, daughters of the said Earl, whichever of the two best pleased him, while Colin Campbell (afterwards third Earl) was to marry either Janet or Margaret Gordon, his sisters. The Earl did marry Janet, but George must have died young, and the marriage did not take place (Argyll Charter-chest).'

p. **532,** l. 4 from foot, for '1' read '2.'

p. **533,** l. 22, for 'a son' read 'two sons.'

p. **533,** l. 22, after '*George*,' insert 'and *John*, the latter of whom became Dean of Salisbury, and died 3 September 1619, in the seventy-fifth year of his age. He married Genevieve Petaw, daughter of Gideon Petaw, Lord of Mauld, in the Isle de France, who died at Gordonstoun 6 December 1643, in her eighty-third year; their only child, *Louise*, married, in 1613, Sir Robert Gordon of Gordonstoun, Bart.'

p. **533,** l. 24, for '2' read '3.'

p. **533,** l. 28, for '3' read '4.'

p. **533,** l. 34, for '4' read '5.'

p. **533,** l. 5 from foot, for '5' read '6.'

p. **533,** l. 5 from foot, for '1503' read '1505' (Adv. Lib. MS. 32.2.4. vol. 4, p. 274).

p. **533,** after l. 4 from foot, insert

'7. *Margaret* (*Acts and Decreets*, xx. 182).'

p. **536,** l. 8, for 'daughter' read 'sister.' (The title of the marriage-contract given in the Spalding Club *Miscellany* is wrong.)

p. **536,** l. 19, after '370,' insert note, 'There is no doubt that he married her, and she went north with him in 1545-46 (*Treasurer's Accts.*, viii. 436).'

p. **538**, last line, after 'married,' insert 'first, shortly before 4 February 1577-78, Jane Leslie, "Lady Moyness" daughter of John Leslie of Parkhill and widow of Sir Alexander Dunbar of Cumnock (Moray Writs, Box xv. No. 850: cf. *Records of the Family of Leslie*, ii. 151; Douglas's *Baronage*, 120). She died in August 1579 (Edin. Tests.). He married, secondly.'

p. **539,** l. 2, after 'widow of,' insert 'James Ochterlony younger of that Ilk (*Acts and Decreets*, xlix. 126; *Reg. of Deeds*, xxvi. 420) and of.'

p. **539**, note 1, for '1584' read '1585.'

p. **540**, last line, after 'football' add note 'The Protocol Book of John Mushet, Stirling, contains the following: "The xix of October 1576, George, Erle of Huntly, etc. etc., decessit vpone ane haistie maladie at x hours nycht or thairby I being present with him, his secretar and familiar servand."'

p. **547**, headline, for 'Marquess of Gordon' read 'Marquess of Huntly.'

p. **547**, l. 25, for '1641' read 'contract 28 and 31 October 1639 (*Reg. of Deeds*, DXXIV. 62).'

p. **547**, l. 3 from foot, for 'in December 1650' read 'in childbed at Traquair June 1651 (Balfour's *Annals*, iv. 351).'

p. **549**, l. 9, after 'Crouly,' insert 'She died at sea on her way to Scotland (Letter at Slains, 22 February 1715).'

p. **549**, l. 17, after 'Huntly,' insert was born in 1649 (*Addl. MSS.*, 23, 122, f. 80); but in a letter to Lauderdale 4 July 1664 he says he is almost fourteen (*Notes and Queries*, 10th ser., x. 7).'

p. **549**, l. 18, after 'boy,' insert 'he.'

p. **550**, l. 7 from foot, for '1697' read '1696 (*Consistorial Processes etc.*, Scot Rec. Soc., No. 74).'

p. **551**, l. 2, for 'James' read 'Robert.'

p. **551**, after l. 9, insert

'1. *George*, born 1680, died young (Letter at Gordon Castle).'

p. **551**, ll. 10, 11, for '1, 2' read '2, 3.'

p. **552**, l. 16, for 'Inverary' read 'Inverury.'

p. **554**, line 4, after 'wife,' insert note, 'Catherine Gordon had been sent by her father (who did not approve of the match, as he was already brother-in-law to his proposed son-in-law) to her grandfather the Duke of Atholl. She wrote to him "My dear Father, I beg to inform you that I was married this day to the Duke of Gordon. We propose in a few days to present ourselves at Haddo House when I have no doubt we shall receive your blessing (*The Gay Gordons*, by J. M. Bulloch, 92).'

p. **554**, l. 12, for 'George' read 'Alexander.'

p. **554**, l. 18, After 'Bunbury,' insert note, 'She was a daughter of the second Duke of Richmond: was born 14 February 1744, and married, 2 June 1762, Sir Thomas Charles Bunbury, Bart. He divorced her 17 May 1776, and she married, secondly, 27 August 1781, as his second wife, Col. the Hon. George Napier, son of the sixth Lord Napier, and died blind, but still beautiful, in 1826.'

p. **554**, l. 6 from foot, delete '(died 1831)' and insert '(born 6 March 1782, died 2 September 1831).'

p. **557**, l. 12, after 'Lennox,' insert 'they were married in her mother's dressing-room at Gordon Castle, and nobody knew of it except two women servants till three days later, when it was announced at a big dance party by the Marquess of Huntly (Bulloch's *Gay Gordons*, 92).

p. **557**, l. 23, delete 'of.'

p. **559**, l. 18, After 'ninety-one,' insert note, 'He danced till he was eighty or more (Mrs. Warenne Blake's, *Memoirs of a Vanished Generation*, 124).

p. **559**, after l. 28, insert 'There was a son born 11 January 1796 who probably died young.'

p. **559**, l. 5 from foot, after 'Munster,' insert 'and natural daughter of William IV., and widow of the Hon. John Kennedy Erskine, second son of the first Marquess of Ailsa.'

p. **560**, l. 1, Bulloch gives 1806, so does Burke.

p. **560**, l. 6, Bulloch gives 1902, so does Burke.

p. **560**, l. 9, Bulloch gives 3 July, Burke as in text.

p. **561**, l. 1, for '29' read '28.'

p. **561**, l. 8, delete '(*heir presumptive*).'

p. **561**, l. 11, after '1900,' insert 'He died at sea 14 June 1907.

p. **562**, l. 2, for 'second' read 'third.'

p. **562**, l. 21, after '2nd,' insert 'or.'

HYNDFORD

p. **565**, last line, after 'issue,' insert 'before 1556, when his brother David is described as of Balmedie (*Reg. of Deeds*, i. 462).'

p. **566**, l. 10, after 'John,' insert 'born about 1564.'

p. **566**, l. 10, after 'minister,' insert 'of Newburn 1595.'

p. **566**, l. 10, after 'Kilconquhar,' insert '1603. Died at Edinburgh 1622.'

p. **566**, l, 10, for 'a son' read 'two sons.'

p. **566**, l. 11, after '*Frederick*,' insert 'β. *William*.'

p. **566**, l. 21, delete 'Sir.'

p. **566**, l. 33, delete 'no' before 'issue.'

p. **566**, l. 33, for 'before 1622' read '15 September 1621.'

p. **566**, l. 37, delete 'leaving issue,' and insert 'having had issue by his first wife:—

(*a*) *William*.

(*b*) *Jean*.

(*c*) *Katrine*.

all mentioned in their mother's will.

And by his second wife:—'

p. **567**, l. 7, delete 'of Balvaird,' and insert 'Doctor of Medicine in Perth.'

p. **567**, l. 12, delete 'before 1800,' and insert 'at Balmblae 15 January 1786' (*Scots Mag.*).'

p. **567**, after line 21 insert

(*e*) *William* (*P. C. Reg.*, 3rd ser., vol. iii. 585).'

p. **568**, l. 13, after 'He,' insert 'died at Craigpotty, Perthshire, 7 September 1761, aged eighty-six (*Scots Mag.*), having.'

p. **568**, l. 14, after 'had,' insert 'by her, who died 1731.'

p. **568**, l. 18, after 'married,' insert '3 October 1725 (*Edin. Mar. Reg.*).'

p. **568**, l. 23, after 'died,' insert 'at Pitcallan near Perth, 29 September 1783 (*Scots Mag.*).'

p. **573**, l. 12 from foot, delete from 'was succeeded by,' down to 'dominus de Carmichael,' on l. 6 from foot.

Note.—Recent investigation renders it probable that the John Carmichael mentioned in the text was identical with the John mentioned on p. 563, and that the two Williams on p. 573 are the same person.

p. **575**, after l. 19 insert

'3. *David*, described in 1505 as brother of the laird of Carmichael (*Acta Dom. Conc.*, xvii. 40).'

p. **575**, ll. 20 and 21, delete 'in 1474 when,' and insert 'on 23 April 1465, when he acted along with his father as attorney for Gilbert, Lord Kennedy (*Culzean Inventory*). In 1474.'

p. **576**, l. 23, delete 'he was succeeded by his,' and insert. 'Besides a daughter *Jean*, mentioned in 1554 (*Acts and Decreets*, viii. 450), he had an.'

p. **577**, l. 15, for 'He died about 1585,' read 'He survived till after 11 August 1586 (*P. C. Reg.*, iv. 94).'

p. **578**, after l. 6, add

'4. *Margaret*, married to Robert Wardlaw, fiar of Kilbaberton (*Acts and Decreets*, lxxix. 185).'

5. *Abigail*, married, contract 17 April and 4 May 1590, to Hugh Weir, younger of Clowburn (*Reg. Mag. Sig.*, 20 August 1617). She was a widow 9 March 1595-96 (*Reg. of Deeds*, lii. 108), which proves that she was a generation older than she is represented in the text (p. 580).'

p. **579**, l. 2, after 'Carmichael,' insert 'On 2 December 1585 he was appointed the King's Master Stabler (*Reg. Sec. Sig.*, liii. 73).'

p. **579**, last line, after 'married,' insert 'contract 5 September 1561 (*Reg. of Deeds*, iv. 373).'

p. **580**, l. 1, delete 'Sir George Douglas of Pittendreich,' and insert 'James, fourth Earl of Morton (*Ibid.*).'

p. **580**, l. 2, delete 'who survived him certainly to the year 1620,' and accompanying reference, and insert 'She died in 1625 (Edin. Tests.).'

p. **580**, ll. 26 and 27, delete this entry. See above, p. 578.

p. **580**, l. 28, for '5' read '4.'

p. **580**, after l. 29 insert

'5. *Helen* (*Reg. of Deeds*, xxv. 11).'

p. **581**, l. 22, delete 'before 12 June 1624' and accompanying reference and insert 'contract 25 March 1613 (*Reg. of Deeds*, ccxvi. 327).'

p. **581**, after l. 27, insert 'Hugh had also a natural son, *John* (*P. C. Reg.*, 2nd ser. vi. 612).'

p. **582**, after line 3, insert, 'He married Elizabeth, daughter of Sir Patrick Home of Polwarth (cf. vol. vi. 11).'

p. **582**, l. 24, after 'issue,' insert '(besides a natural son, *John*). (*Gen. Reg. Inhibs.*, xxxii. 56).'

p. **582**, last line, delete 'a son,' and insert 'three sons :—

1. WALTER.

2. *John*, who was alive in 1632, being then about eighty, and who had a son, *John* (*Reg. of Deeds*, ccccliv. 118), Commissary of Lanark, to whom Lord Carmichael was served heir 17 June 1656 (*Inq. Gen.*). He died 3 March 1656 (Lanark Tests.).
3. *Gavin*, died *ante* 16 May 1656 (Edin. Tests.), having had—
   (1) *Gavin*, died 1625, without issue (Edin. Tests.).
   (2) *Margaret* (*Ibid.*).
   (3) *Elizabeth*, married John Fleming, schoolmaster in Edinburgh (*Ibid.*).'

p. 583, l. 21, for '1608' read 'contract 11 September 1598 (*Reg. of Deeds*, lxvi. 235).'

p. 583, l. 6 from foot, after 'she,' insert 'married, secondly, after 6 April 1635, John Muir, elder of Annestoun and.'

p. 583, l. 5 from foot, delete 'and had a son, *John*,' and insert 'By her first husband she had three sons, *Walter*, *William*, and *John* (Lanark Tests., 2 July 1638).'

p. 587, l. 21, after 'He,' delete 'was dead before 4 November 1681,' and insert 'died December 1680 (Lanark Tests., 7 June 1681).'

p. 588, l. 9, for '*Agnes*' read '*Rachel* (*Reg. Mag. Sig.*, 16 July 1649).'

p. 588, l. 9, after 'married,' insert 'contract 17 June 1642 (*Reg. of Deeds*, DXXXIV. 113).'

p. 588, after l. 17, insert
'10. *Marion* (*Gen. Reg. of Inhibs.*, 30 June 1669).'

p. 591, l. 8 from foot, for '18' read '9 (*Scots Mag.*).

p. 591, l. 6 from foot, for '2' read '21.'

p. 592, l. 18, for '1769' read '1789.'

p. 592, l. 25, for 'sixth' read 'fifth.'

p. 592, l. 27, for 'seventh' read 'sixth.'

p. 592, after l. 13 from foot, insert
'vii. *Grace* (Lanark Tests., 16 January 1786).'

p. 593, l. 2, after '*Beatrix*,' add note, 'She is called Barbara in her funeral entry in the Lyon Office.'

p. 593, l. 2, after '1700,' insert 'as his first wife.'

p. 593, l. 4, after 'Admiralty,' insert semicolon, 'she died 1 August 1702.'

p. 594, l. 16, for 'second' read 'first.'

VOL. V.

INNERMEATH

p. 3, l. 23, for 'eighth' read 'first.'

p. 5, l. 17, after 'secondly,' insert 'in June 1573 (see *Decreet* cited in note 8).'

p. 6, l. 4 from foot, after 'Robert,' insert 'married Janet Leslie (*Reg. of Deeds*, ccccciii. 84), perhaps daughter of Robert Leslie of Auldcraig (*Family of Leslie*, iii. 383).'

p. 7, l. 24, after 'secondly,' add 'contract 11 February 1608 (*Reg. of Deeds*, cxlviii. 212).'

IRVINE

p. 11, ll. 16, 17, delete from 'baptized' down to '1616,' and relative reference.

p. 22, l. 28, for 'John' read 'Colin.'

LORD OF THE ISLES

p. 39, l. 9, delete 'about 1337,' and insert 'Papal dispensation for the marriage 4 June 1337 (*Regesta Avenionensia*, li. f. 125).'

p. 39, l. 10, after 'her,' insert 'whom he subsequently divorced (*Proc. Soc. Antiq. Scot.*, viii. 276).'

p. 42, after last l., insert

'5. *Marion.* There was a commission from the Pope 13 February 1419-20 for her marriage with Celestine Campbell (*Cal. of Papal Letters*, vii. 151), but it does not seem to have taken place. She is stated to have married Alexander Sutherland (Douglas's *Peerage*).'

p. 42, note 3, for '*Avinionensis*' read '*Avenionensia*.'

p. 45, after l. 10, insert 'He had three natural sons, Hugh, Alexander and Donald, legitimated by the Pope 29 June 1445 (*Cal. Papal Letters*, ix. 523).'

p. 47, l. 17, after 'issue,' insert 'A Papal Bull in April 1478 exempted her from ordinary jurisdiction during the controversy between her and her husband (*Roman Transcripts*, Public Record Office).'

JEDBURGH

p. 54, last l. of notes, insert '9' before '*Reg. Mag. Sig.*'

p. 59, l. 4 from foot, delete 'She was alive in 1546' and relative note, and insert 'She married, secondly (contract January 1529-30), Sir Walter Scott of Branxholm, from whom she was divorced (cf. vol. ii. 230).'

p. 67, ll. 28, 29, for 'in March 1685-86' read '30 March 1586 (Spalding Club *Misc.*, ii. 58).'

p. 68, l. 7, after 'Scotland,' insert 'and previously the wife of Patrick, sixth Lord Gray, whom she had divorced (cf. vol. iv. 285).'

p. 68, l. 32, after 'married,' insert 'contract dated at Oxnamcraig 6 November 1587 (Blackbarony Writs).'

p. 68, l. 36, for '1587' read '1587-88.'

p. 68, note 8, add to note 'She was a daughter of her father's second wife, not of his first as indicated in the text.'

p. 70, l. 15, after 'married,' insert 'contract 4 December 1660 (*Reg. of Deeds*, Mack, 17 Oct. 1667).'

p. 72, last l., for '1591' read '19 February 1584-85 (*Reg. Sec. Sig.*, lii. 12).'

p. 75, l. 26, delete 'died in 1631,' and insert 'was still alive on 20 April 1633 (see *post*, p. 76, l. 22 *corr.*).'

p. 75, l. 26, after 'married,' insert 'first.'

p. 75, l. 29, after 'Ochiltree,' insert 'He married, secondly (contract dated 2 July 1621), Katherine M'Culloch, widow of William Houston of Cottreoch, by whom she had a son, *William*, to whom, on 8 July 1645, she assigned her rights under her marriage-contract with Lord Jedburgh. She died between that date and 1 July 1647 (*ex inform.* John MacGregor, Esq., W.S.).'

p. 75, l. 29, for 'they' read 'by his first wife he.'

p. 76, l. 14, after 'married,' insert 'contract 2 and 5 March 1614 (*Reg. of Deeds*, ccciii. 51).'

p. 76, l. 18, after 'Alison,' insert '(styled fifth daughter in a charter to her of 1 May 1627) (*Reg. Mag. Sig.*, 5 February 1628).'

p. 76, l. 18, after 'married,' insert 'contract 21 and 24 July 1620 (*Ibid.*).'

p. 76, l. 19, after '1648,' insert 'buried in Greyfriars, 24 April 1671.'

p. 76, l. 20, after '1648,' insert 'buried in Holyrood Church, 8 March 1664 (Canongate Reg.).'

p. 76, l. 21, after '1648,' insert 'buried in Greyfriars, 3 May 1663.'

p. 76, l. 22, delete 'married to —— M'Culloch, and,' and insert 'married, but whether for her first or second husband is not known, Nicholas Lewin, eldest son of Thomas Lewin of Warkworth, Northumberland, by whom she had a son Thomas of Amble, who married his cousin, Helen Rutherford. On 20 April 1633 a receipt was granted to Andrew, Lord Jedburgh, for 600 merks of her tocher. She (*ex inform.* T. E. Watson, Monmouth; cf. vol. vii. 379); (*Reg. Mag. Sig.*, 4 April 1649, Chancery Depositions, Record Office (Bridges), 171-4, 1685).'

p. 78, l. 32, for 'without issue' read 'without surviving issue. A daughter Mary was born at Redbraes 17 November 1656, and died 3 October 1658 (Family Bible at Marchmont).'

p. 79, second last l. of note, for 'field' read 'chevron.'

KELLIE

p. 81, l. 1, after 'second,' insert 'surviving.'

p. 81, l. 2, for 'fourth' read 'fifth.'

p. **85**, l. 2 from foot, for 'ERSKINE' read 'DIRLTOUN.'

p. **86**, l. 2, after 'first,' add '30 November 1587 (Stirling Reg.).'

p. **86**, l. 5 from foot, for 'third' read 'second.'

p. **88**, l. 19, after 'died,' delete '1734,' and insert 'at Edinburgh, 17 July 1735 (Edin. Tests., 16 June 1736).'

p. **89**, note 2, for 'Canongate' read 'Carnbee.'

p. **92**, l. 21, delete 'Sir.'

p. **92**, l. 24, after 'there,' insert 'Agatha Gigli.'

p. **92**, l. 25, after '*Charles*,' insert 'born at Rome 1739.'

p. **92**, l. 26, after 'ultimately,' insert '(17 January 1803).'

p. **92**, l. 26, after 'Paris,' insert '20.'

p. **93**, l. 6, after 'married,' insert '24 April 1743.'

p. **93**, l. 6, for 'Laverockland' read 'Laverocklaw.'

p. **96**, l. 6 from foot, for 'ERSKINE' read 'DIRLTOUN.'

p. **97**, after l. 5, add

'The Earl of Mar and Kellie recorded the following arms in the Lyon Office :—

Quarterly : 1st and 4th, argent, a pale sable, for *Erskine* ; 2nd and 3rd, azure, a bend between six cross crosslets fitchée or, for *Mar* ; over all an inescutcheon gules, charged with the Royal Crown of Scotland proper within a double tressure flory counterflory or, as a coat of augmentation for the Earldom of *Kellie*.

CRESTS.—1st, a dexter hand holding a skene dhu in pale argent, hilted and pommelled or, for *Erskine*; 2nd, a demi-lion rampant guardant gules, armed argent, for *Kellie*.

SUPPORTERS.—Two griffins gules, armed, beaked and winged or.

MOTTOES.—*Je pense plus*, for *Erskine* ; *Decori decus addit avito* for *Kellie*.'

KENMURE

p. **99**, l. 20, after 'David II.' insert as note, 'These three writs are recorded at length in *Reg. of Deeds* (Dalrymple's Office), vol. cxli., 3 March 1738.'

p. **100**, l. 15, after '1403,' as note, 'Recorded in same register.'

p. **102**, l. 3, after 'Borgue,' insert 'and also of Kirkconnell in the parish of Tongland.'

p. **104**, l. 5 from foot, before 'in Crosherie,' insert 'of Mundork.'

p. **105**, l. 14, after '1492,' insert 'She was married, secondly, to Patrick Sinclair of Spotts and Woodhouselee (*Acta Dom. Conc.*, xx. 195).'

p. **105**, after l. 14, insert

'9. *Annabel*, contracted to Cuthbert, son and heir of Andrew M'Dowell of Spotts (*Acta Dom. Conc.*, xix. 103).'

p. **106**, last l., for 'Sir William' read 'James.'

p. **108**, l. 22, after 'Glendonwyn,' insert 'daughter of John Glendonwyn of Drumrash (Earlston MS. Lyon Office).'

p. **108,** l. 27, after 'married,' insert 'contract 24 August and 19 September 1622 (*Reg. of Deeds*, ccclviii. 49),'

p. **108,** after l. 5 from foot, insert

'(iii) *Marion*, styled eldest daughter, married (contract 9 July 1689) to Alexander Lennox of Callie (*Reg. of Deeds*, DXXIX. 65; DXLVII. 266).'

p. **109,** after l. 2, insert

'iv. *Elizabeth*, married, contract 4 January 1612, to Alexander Gordon of Airds (Earlston MS., Lyon Office).

v. *Jean*, married, contract 17 May 1622, to David Arnot of Chapel (*Reg. of Deeds*, cccxcviii. 432).'

p. **109,** l. 25, after '*James*,' insert 'probably the second son (*Acts and Decreets*, vi. 23).'

p. **109,** l. 25, after '1540,' insert 'In 1555 he is styled titular of Glenluce (*Reg. of Deeds*, i. 258). He died in April 1559 (*Acts and Decreets*, xxix. 78).'

p. **109,** note 8, add to note, 'One of these Janets (or a third sister of the same name) was contracted in 1533 to Archibald Mure of Torhousmure (*Acta Dom. Conc. et Sess.*, ii. 184).'

p. **110,** ll. 1, 2, delete 'or 1561.'

p. **110,** l. 5, after 'to,' insert 'William, son of.'

p. **110,** l. 6, after 'from,' insert 'the latter of.'

p. **111,** l. 21, after 'intestate,' add note, 'He executed a testament and codicil a few days before his death, confirmed 3 September and 10 October 1605 (*Kenmore Inventory*. The confirmation mentioned in the text was not till 3 February 1610.'

p. **112,** l. 5, for 'in' read '24 July.'

p. **112,** l. 18, after 'married,' insert 'contract October 1615 (*Reg. of Deeds*. cccvi. 254).'

p. **112,** after l. 8 from foot, insert

'(4) *William*. (5) *Elizabeth*.'

p. **112,** l. 2 from foot, for 'Mary' read 'Margaret (*Kenmore Inventory*).'

p. **112,** note 6, for 'v. 226' read 'iv. 226.'

p. **116,** l. 22, delete '1 January 1597' and relative note, and insert '1 February 1597-98 (*Reg. of Deeds*, lxi. 201).

p. **116,** l. 24, delete 'whom,' and insert 'her (who divorced him for adultery 11 August 1608) (*Edin. Comm. Decreets*).'

p. **117,** l. 7, for 'two' read 'three.'

p. **117,** l. 8, after 'daughters,' insert '*Margaret*, alive in 1639 (*Reg. of Deeds*, DXX. 470).'

p. **120,** l. 17, after 'Kenmure,' insert 'baptized after his father's death, 10 December 1634 (Canongate Reg.),' and for 'who' read 'He.'

p. **121,** l. 14, after 'homes,' insert 'In March 1651 Lord Kenmure was under the discipline of the Church for *inter alia* fornication with Margaret Seytoune.'

p. **121,** note 1, for '*Unique Traditions*, 1833' read '*Lights and Shadows*, 1824, 249.'

p. **123**, l. 4, for 'his heir' read 'the heir'; after 'line, insert 'of the first Viscount.'

p. **123**, l. 27, for 'preceding' read 'first.'

p. **124**, l, 10 from foot, for 'before 7 September 1698 intestate and' read '20 April 1698.'

p. **125**. l. 20, after 'secondly,' insert 'contract 1 and 3 October 1693 (*Reg. of Deeds* (Mackenzie), 28th May 1733).'

p. **125**, l. 11 from foot, after 'adjoining' insert note, 'By this contract it was provided that the heirs-male of the marriage should succeed, not only to all the lands but also to the title and dignities, the latter an obviously impossible provision. By his *mortis causa* settlement, however, the Viscount left Kenmure to his eldest son and successor, the other estates going to his younger sons. It was not without difficulty that this was ultimately carried out; and in 1727 Mr. John sold Greenlaw to his sister-in-law, Mary, Viscountess of Kenmure. (Observ. by W. Gordon of Culvennan, *ex inform.* Mrs Walker; *Answers on behalf of the Publick*, on Forfeited Estate Proceedings, 26 August 1719).'

p. **131**, l. 5 from foot, for 'fourth' read 'only.'

KILMARNOCK

p. **137**, l. 5 from foot, for 'in' read 'dated 20 September (*Muniments of Burgh of Irvine*, Ayrshire and Galloway Arch. Assoc. 1890, No. 1).'

p. **139**, l. 2 from foot, for 'third' read 'second,' and for 'fourth' read 'fifth.'

p. **141**, l. 8. after '1451,' insert 'He is stated to have been ancestor in the direct line (*ergo* illegitimate) of Edward Boyd of Merton Hall, in Wigtown, who died 27 August 1846 (*Patrician*, ii. 193).'

p. **152**, l. 21, for 'third' read 'fourth.'

p. **155**, note 3, after '399,' insert 'Nisbet's *Heraldry*, App. ii. 276.'

p. **168**, l, 7, after 'Conyngham,' insert 'of Auchenharvie, widow of Thomas Boyd of Pitcon (*Reg. of Deeds*, cxcviii. 241; cf. *Reg. Mag. Sig.*, 7 February 1587-88).'

p. **171**, l. 10, for '*circâ* 29' read '26 April and 11 (*Reg. of Deeds*, DXXIX. 244).'

p. **171**, l. 17, for 'Ardross' read 'Harden.'

p. **171**, l. 7 from foot, for '1626' read '1628.'

p. **172**, l. 5, after '1639,' insert 'tocher 35,000 merks, which was not fully paid till after Boyd's death (*Wigtown Inventory*, Scot. Rec. Soc., No. 342).'

p. **174**, l. 14, after '1737,' insert 'He married Katherine Van Beest, and had a son Malcolm, ensign in the Army, who married Mary Collins (Slains Writs).'

p. **175**, l. 27, after 'Baronet,' insert note, 'Her paternity is confirmed by the registration of an agreement between Margaret, Marchioness of Lothian, Mrs. Helenor Boyd, widow of Mr, Thomas (*sic*) Boyd,

Advocate, brother-german of the deceased William, Earl of Kilmarnock, and Mrs. Isabel Brisbane *alias* Nicolson, three of the four daughters and heirs of line of the deceased Sir Thomas Nicolson of Kemnay (*Reg. of Deeds*, Durie, 4 July 1730; *ex inform.* Ernest Axon, Esq.)'

p. **179**, l. 2, for 'Gulielmus' read 'Wilhelmus.'

p. **179**, l. 3, for 'ætat' read 'ætatis.'

p. **179**, l. 4, after '42' insert note, 'There is a *facsimile* of the coffin plate in *Historical Papers*, New Spalding Club, i. 339.'

p. **179**, l. 7 from foot, after 'issue,' insert note, 'Charles must have married twice, as his widow was the stepmother of his son Major Charles (see will of the latter).'

p. **180**, l. 8, after '1792,' insert 'His will is dated Falmouth, 10 July 1790 (Slains Writs). He evidently left neither widow nor legitimate issue, as his natural son Charles, born at Halifax, Nova Scotia, was his residuary legatee.'

KILSYTH

p. **185**, l. 23, for 'three' read 'four.'

p. **186**, last line, for 'three' read 'four.'

p. **187**, l. 2, after '(secundus)' add

'4. *Patrick* (*Hist. MSS. Com. Report* on Edmondstone of Duntreath MS., p. 86).'

p. **188**, l. 11, after '*John*,' insert 'who under the designation of John Livingston in Falkirk, received from his nephew Sir William Livingston of Kilsyth, on 27 May 1580, an annualrent of 20 merks, to himself and Elizabeth Fleming, his spouse (*Hist. MSS. Com.* Edmondstone MSS. 102).

p. **188**, after l. 11, insert

'7. *George*, who had a feu-charter of part of Falkirk, 14 February 1552-53 (Holyrood Chart, H.M. Reg. Ho., fol. 77).'

p. **188**, ll. 12, 14, 15, for '7, 8, 9,' read '8, 9, 10.'

p. **188**, l. 16, delete entire line. The Baillies did not acquire Jerviswood till the time of Charles II.

p. **189**, l. 17, delete from 'died' down to '1595-96,' in l. 18, and insert 'been alive up at least to 26 January 1596-97, when his son and successor is still styled of Darnchester (Protocol Book of A. Ker, Linlithgow).

p. **189**, last line of note 4, after 'period,' insert 'It has since been discovered that the true year of the writ in question is 1599 (Cf. *Reg. of Deeds*, lxix. f. 16).'

p. **190**, l. 11 from foot, delete 'a son.'

p. **190**, after l. 10 from foot, insert

'(2) *Lilias*, married (contract 2 November 1631) to John Hamilton younger of Kinglass (*Reg. of Deeds*, DXviii. 232).'

p. **190**, l. 6 from foot, for 'by whom,' read 'and by her, who married, secondly, in 1630, John Cornwall, younger of Bonhard (*Reg. of Deeds*, DVI. 346).'

p. **191**, l. 10, after 'married,' insert 'contract 25 February 1617 (Oxenfoord Writs).'

KINGSTON

p. **196**. ll. 8 and 9, delete from 'said' down to 'family,' and insert 'daughter of Sir Andrew Fletcher of Inverpeffer (*Gen. Reg. of Inhibitions*, 31 August 1670).'

p. **196**, ll. 13, 14, delete 'is said to have,' and after 'Hamilton' insert reference '(*Haddington Inhibs.*, xviii. 412).'

KINNAIRD

p. **203**, l. 5 from foot, after 'of' add as a note,

'In an old Inventory of Kinuaird writs, dated March 1630 (*Acts and Decreets*, ccccxxxiii. f. 231, etc.), there is an entry of "ane chartour grantit be Allan of Kynnaird to Michaell Scot of Balverie of the landis of Flacraig and Craighall, quhilkis wer callit of befoir Dunnoir and Kinbrichour.' No date is given, but it was apparently before 1328, the date of the next writ.

p. **204**, l. 3, for '7' read '17.'

p. **204**, l. 5, for 'Walter' read 'Robert.'

p. **204**, note 1, delete last sentence of note, and insert 'It is now in the Dalhousie Charter-chest: it is granted to Richard de Kynnard and to Richard his son and the heirs of his body, with remainder successively to *Alan*, *Reginald*, *Hugh*, *William*, *Thomas*, and *David*, brothers of Richard the younger, and the heirs of their bodies respectively.'

p. **206**, l. 1, for 'name' read 'surname.'

p. **206**, l. 2, after 'but,' insert 'by her, whose Christian name was Margaret, (*Reg. Mag. Sig.*, 28 October 1486).'

p. **208**, l. 15, for 'Bertram' read 'Betoun.'

p. **208**, l. 27, for 'Partick' read 'Patrick.'

p. **209**, l. 12, for 'John' read 'Andrew.'

p. **210**, l. 8, after 'married,' delete 'in' and insert 'contract 29 September (*Reg. of Deeds*, 25 February 1687).'

p. **211**, l. 15, for 'July' read 'January (*Edin. Comm. Decreets*).'

p. **211**, l. 29, after 'her,' insert 'who was dead before 11 March 1735.'

p. **211**, l. 4 from foot, delete 'and,' and insert 'daughter of George Gordon, Doctor of Medicine in Banff. They were married 3 November 1731 in Dundee. She raised an action of Declarator of Marriage 11 March 1735, by which time George Kinnaird was dead, and got decree (*Consistorial Processes*, etc., Scot. Rec. Soc. No. 293).'

p. **212**, l. 30, delete 'before majority,' and insert '12 February 1779.'

p. **213**, l. 8, delete 'in,' and insert '23 December.'

p. 213, l. 19, delete 'in,' and insert '1 December.'

p. 214, l. 9 from foot, after 'and,' insert 'by her, who died 20 March 1910, aged ninety-two.'

p. 214, last line, after 'Victoria,' insert 'He died 12 March 1910.'

p. 215, l. 18, delete 'an infant in 1846,' and insert '14 May 1846, aged two years.'

KINNOULL

p. 220, after line 10, insert
'2. *Peter*, baptized 9 November 1555.'

p. 220, l. 11, delete line.

p. 220, l. 12, after '*Peter*,' insert '(*secundus*), baptized 23 April 1557.'

p. 220, l. 14, after '*William*,' insert 'baptized 5 July 1560.'

p. 220, after line 15, insert
'5. George, baptized 4 December 1570, of whom afterwards.'

p. 220, l. 16, for '5,' read '6.'

p. 220, l. 16, after 'Janet,' insert 'baptized 19 November 1554.'

p. 220, after line 16, insert
'7. *Margaret*, baptized 16 February 1558-59.'
'8. *Isobel*, baptized 13 May 1564.'

p. 220, line 17, for '6' read '9.'

p. 220, l. 17, after '*Elizabeth*,' insert 'baptized 29 March 1566.'

p. 220, l. 25, for '7' read '10.'

p. 220, l. 25, after '*Katherine*' insert '(third daughter), baptized 24 December 1561.'

p. 220, after line 25, insert
'11. *Marjory*, baptized 14 November 1568.' *Note*.—The baptisms of these children are from the Errol Register, which, though not contemporary, appears to be based on authentic materials.'

p. 220, l. 26, for 'second' read 'fifth.'

p. 224, after line 25, insert
'3. *Archibald*, baptized 23 May 1635 (Perth Reg.),' and alter numbers of succeeding children accordingly.

p. 224, line 26, after '*James*,' insert 'who married, and had a daughter, Grizel, married, *c*. 1668, to Lieut.-Col. Alexander, eighth son of first Earl of Stirling.'

p. 225, l. 1, after '*Elizabeth*' insert 'baptized 28 May 1636 (Perth Reg.).'

p. 230, after line 28, insert
'There was also a natural daughter, *Isobel*, mentioned in the testament of George Hay of Balhousie.'

p. 230, l. 31, delete 'of Carnock.'

p. 230, i. 31, after 'Advocate,' insert 'brother of Sir James Nicolson of Cockburnspath.'

p. 232, l. 9, for '11 December' read '31 December.'

p. 233, l. 9, for 'Miles' read 'Milnes.'

p. 239, l. 13, after 'gules,' insert 'surmounted by a scimitar in pale argent.'

KINTORE

p. 240, ll. 21, 22, for 'INVERUGIE' read 'INVERURIE.'

p. 241, l. 2 from foot, for '9' read '19.'

p. 243, l. 15, after '1504,' insert 'As Sir George Falconer aftermentioned had a charter of Lethens in 1506-7, it is not improbable that this Alexander is identical with the Alexander who was father of Sir George.'

p. 244, line 7 from foot, for '*Janet*' read '*Marjorie* (*Reg. Mag. Sig.*, 2 October 1557).'

p. 244, note 10, after 'Kilravock 72;' insert 'She is there called *Janet* in error.'

p. 245, after line 3, insert
'5. *Isobel*, married to John Middleton of Kilhill (cf. vol. vi. 173).'

p. 245, l. 11, delete 'only' and 'Sir (cf. vol. i. 184).'

p. 246, after l. 13, insert
'4. *Marjorie*, married, shortly after 27 November 1598, to Angus Macintosh of Termett (*Reg. of Deeds*, cclxxii. 145; cf. also Moray Writs, box. iv. No. 143, where he is called Angus Williamson).'

p. 246, ll. 14 and 16, for '4' and '5' read '5' and '6.'

p. 247, l. 12, after 'married,' delete 'Margaret, daughter of Robert Graeme of Crigie,' and insert 'first, Marjory Irvine, who died before Easter 1661. Her executors brought an action against his daughter and executor, Lady Balmain, with reference to her share in Sir Alexander's estate in 1719 (Sheriff Court Books of Kincardineshire, *ex inform.* Dr. Macnaughton, Stonehaven). He married, secondly, Helen, daughter of John Grahame of Crigie.

p. 247, ll. 13 and 14, delete 'and had issue ALEXANDER, fourth Lord,' and insert 'He had one daughter, *Elizabeth*, married, contract 1678, to Sir Charles Ramsay of Balmain, Baronet, as above mentioned.'

p. 248, l. 14, after 'child,' insert 'probably *David*, referred to as son of John Falconer of the Cunzie House (Factory in his favour, by David Barclay, Kincardine Sheriff-Court Books, 25 October 1666).'

p. 249, after l. 12, insert
'2. *Thomas* (*Acts and Decreets*, cccxci. 111, A.D. 1626).'

p. 249, l. 13, for '2' read '3.'

p. 249, l. 13, after '*Agnes*,' insert '(called *Grisel* in her Funeral entry in the Lyon Office).'

p. 249, l. 5 from foot, after 'married,' insert 'proclamation of banns 24 February 1766 (Edin. Mar. Reg.).'

p. 250, l. 6, delete from 'IV. ALEXANDER' down to end of paragraph. *Note.*—As David, Lord Falconer, who died in 1751, served heir to his cousin David, third (not fourth as in text) Lord in 1724, the existence of an Alexander, fourth Lord, seems impossible. His name occurs in Wood's Douglas's *Peerage*, but he is not mentioned in the first edition by Sir Robert Douglas, and Sir Alexander of Glenfarquhar, of whom he is alleged to have been a son, died in 1717, his executor being his daughter (and probably only child) Elizabeth, wife of Sir Charles Ramsay of Balmain.

p. **250,** l. 11, for 'V.' read 'IV.' for 'fifth' read 'fourth.'
p. **250,** l. 14, for 'fourth' read 'third.'
p. **250,** l. 20, for 'sixth' read 'fifth.'
p. **250,** l. 21, for 'seventh' read 'sixth.'
p. **251,** l. 2, after 'married,' insert 'proclamation of banns 16 December 1750 (Edin. Mar. Reg).'
p. **251,** l. 12 for 'VI.' and 'sixth' 'read 'V.' and 'fifth.'
p. **251,** l. 25, for 'VII.' and 'seventh' read 'VI.' and 'sixth.'
p. **251,** line 30, for 'eighth' read 'seventh.'
p. **251,** line 33, for 'VIII.' and 'eighth,' read 'VII.' and 'seventh.'
p. **252,** l. 15, for 'IX.' and 'ninth' read 'VIII.' and 'eighth.'
p. **252,** l. 20, after '1826,' insert 'aged fifty-six.'
p. **252,** l. 31, for 'X.' read 'IX.'
p. **253,** l. 32, for 'tenth' read 'ninth.'
p. **253,** l. 7 from foot, for 'XI.' read 'X.'
p. **253,** l. 6 from foot, for 'eleventh' read 'tenth.'
p. **254,** l. 17, for 'XII.' read 'XI.'
p. **254,** l. 18, for 'twelfth' read 'eleventh.'
p. **255,** l. 2, for 'Inverugie' read 'Inverurie,'

KIRKCUDBRIGHT

p. **268,** l. 15, after 'married,' insert 'contract 28 July 1640 (*Reg. of Deeds*, DXXXI. 45).'
p. **270,** after l. 22, insert

'6. *Elizabeth*, married in 1589 to John, eldest son of John Herries of Maidenpaup, great-grandson of Herbert, first Lord Herries (Herries Peerage Case, Min. of Evidence, 119, No. 74).'

LAUDERDALE

p. **285,** l. 21, for 'Lonchquerwart' read 'Louchquerwart.'
p. **291,** l. 17, for 'fourth' read 'second.'
p. **298,** l. 15, after 'married,' insert 'contract 30 May 1555 (*Acts and Decreets*, xix. 11).'
p. **298,** l. 8 from foot, for 'Frances' read 'Francis.'
p. **301,** l. 14, after 'Fleming,' insert 'daughter of James, fourth Lord Fleming (*Wigtown Inventory*, Scot. Rec. Soc., No. 569).'
p. **301,** l. 20, for '23' read '22.'
p. **301,** l. 8 from foot, for 'Novembris quintilis' read 'nonas quintilis (misquoted in *Family of Seton*, i. 220).'
p. **306,** after l. 9, insert

'2. *Isobel*, baptized 3 September 1635 (Canongate Reg.). She must have died young.'

p. **306,** l. 6 from foot for 'fell' read 'were assumed to fall.'

p. 307, l. 1, delete from 'And' down to 'Birkhill' on l. 4, and insert 'But in subsequent proceedings with regard to the office of Standard Bearer, the House of Lords, reversing the Court of Session, held on 7 April 1910 that the office had not been effectually acquired by Lord Halton (1910, *Sess. Cases*, *H.L.*, p. 35).'

p. 308, l. 29, after 'Earl,' add 'He joined James VII. and died 12 Septem- 1691, at St. Germain-en-Laye (*Reg. of St. Germain*, i. 98, 158).

p. 309, l. 9, for '1705' read '1706, recorded 29 March 1706.'

p. 309, ll. 21 to 24. *Note.—Isobel* and *Mary* were sisters, not daughters of William Maitland. They should in consequence be numbered 7 and 8, and the notices should be in large type.

p. 311, l. 8 from foot, after 'her' insert '(who was born on or before 6 May 1692 (*Seafield Cor.*, Scot. Hist. Soc., 82, 83), and died at Bath, 24 September 1778).'

p. 312, l. 36, for '1883' read '1833.'

p. 317, l. 9, delete 'in,' and insert 'proclamation of banns 1 April (Edin. Mar. Reg.).'

p. 319, l. 24, after 'Lords,' insert note, '"One of those active, bustling spirits who will rather engage in perils and even mischiefs, than remain in a state of torpid tranquillity" (Lady Holland's *Journal*, i. 101).'

p. 319, l. 27, after 'Office,' insert note,
'A nice little painted doll, a cipher as to intellect . . . amiable and obedient (*Memoirs of a Highland Lady*, 293).'

p. 319, l. 5 from foot, after 'Torbreck,' insert note, 'She eloped with him; "poor, silly and not wealthy" (*Ibid.*).'

p. 321, l. 26, after 'in the,' insert '8th and (*Army Lists*).'

p. 321, l. 27, for '1874' read '1869 (*Ibid.*).'

p. 321, l. 8 from foot, delete 'and Hereditary Royal Standard Bearer for Scotland.'

THE CELTIC EARLS OF LENNOX

p. 330, note 3, l. 6 from foot of notes, delete from 'with Cristinus' down to 'witness' on l. 4 from foot.

p. 330, l. 3 from foot of notes, delete 'therefore a separate personage,' and insert 'as Cristinus Judex de Levenax and Gilchrist or Cristinus the son of Earl Alwin appear as witnesses to the same charter they must be distinct persons (*Cart. de Levenax*, 96).'

STEWART, DUKE OF LENNOX

p. 346, note 5, after '*Aubigny*,' insert 'by Lady Elizabeth Cust.'

p. 350, l. 8 from foot, after 'Halkhead,' insert 'They had a charter 15 November 1515 (*Reg. Sec. Sig.*, i. 2661). Chronologically it is more likely that she was a daughter of the second Earl.'

p. 352, l. 13, after 'issue,' add 'She married, secondly, before March 1529-30, Ninian, third Lord Ross of Halkhead (*Acta Dom. Conc.*, xli. 25, 30).'

p. 352, ll. 7 and 5 from foot, for 'Queulle' read 'Queuille (*ex inform.* Lady Elizabeth Cust).'

p. 353, after l. 4, insert
'5. *Margaret*, mentioned A.D. 1542 (*Rec. Sec. Sig.*, xvi. 58).'

p. 353, l. 14, for '1543' read '1544.'

p. 353, l. 31, after 'killed,' insert 'by one James Cadell or Cawdor (John Scott's Protocol Book).'

p. 354, l. 5, after 'sons,' insert note, 'Their first child *Henry* was born in February 1545 and died 28 November in same year. M.I. in Stepney Church (Craik's *Romance of the Aristocracy*, ii. 353).'

p. 354, l. 6 from foot, after 'and,' insert 'by her who died at Sheffield Castle 21 January 1582 (*Ibid.*, ii. 355).'

p. 355, l. 26, delete '29 March 1586,' and insert '29 August 1586 (Monday between two and three p.m.) (Protocol Book of John Scott, notes, corroborated by tombstone in St. Leonard's Chapel; cf. Hay Fleming's *Reformation in Scotland*, 634).'

p. 356, l. 22, after 'Balsac,' insert note, 'Katharine de Balsac was descended from the Viscomtes of Milan and also from the Scaligers of Verona (*ex inform.* Lady Elizabeth Cust).'

p. 357, l. 5 from foot, delete 'in 1621,' and insert '16 June 1621, the Earl of Hertford, her former husband, having died 5 April previous (Craik's *Romance of the Aristocracy*, ii. 392; *Complete Peerage*, iv. 225).'

p. 358, l. 8, after '1620,' add 'He married a lady named Margaret Hamilton, whom he treated very badly, as appears from the *Register of Privy Council*, 2nd ser., vol. i. *passim*.'

p. 358, l. 26, delete '3. *Francis*, died young.' (There was no such son.)

p. 359, l. 6, after 'secondly,' insert 'within three months of her husband's death.'

p. 359, l. 14, after '1674,' add note, 'The statement in the text is incorrect It was Lady Katherine O'Brien, and not her daughter, who was allowed the Barony of Clifton. At the time of the decision of the House of Lords her daughter was only eight years old (*ex inform.* Lady Elizabeth Cust), but according to the *Complete Peerage* (ii. 277) she was born 29 January 1673, and was therefore then only one year old.'

p. 359, l. 18, for 'Newton' read 'Leighton.'

LENNOX, DUKE OF LENNOX

p. 371, l. 8, after '4th' insert 'quarterly, 1st and 4th.'

p. 371, l. 10, after '2nd' insert 'counterquarter.'

p. 371, l. 11, after '3rd,' insert 'counterquarter.'

LEVEN

p. 373, l. 24, after 'tocher,' insert note, 'Andrew, Earl of Rothes, is said to have had an illegitimate son, Alexander, by Christina Scott in Strathkiness. It was baptized by a layman, John Downy, who got into great trouble on account of his action with the Kirk-Session of St. Andrews. It has been suggested that this child was the Earl of Leven. The date of the birth is not recorded, but the baptism was in 1586, rather late for the accuracy of the theory (cf. *Records of Kirk-Session of St. Andrews*, Scot. Hist. Soc., 563, 567-70, 572).'

p. 378, l. 30, after 'married,' insert 'contract 5 September 1639 (*Reg. of Deeds*, DLI. 55).'

p. 378, l. 3 from foot, for '*Margaret*' read '*Janet* (cf. vol. iv. 130). She was older than Anne.'

LINDORES

p. 382, l. 11, for 'Turnberry' read 'Lumbenny.'

p. 383, l. 12 from foot, for 'between 1606 and 1609' read 'between 22 May and 5 October 1608 (*Gen. Reg. Inhibs.*, 2 December 1608).'

p. 383, l. 2 from foot, delete from 'It' to end of sentence, and insert 'He appears to have married twice, his second wife being Catherine Basset. As his widow she was, 17 November 1676, granted a pension of £100 sterling (*Privy Seal, English Reg.*, iii. 126).'

p. 384, l. 4, delete 'Loch of Lindores,' and insert 'River Tay.'

p. 384, l. 9, after '*s.p.*', insert 'and was buried at Holyrood in May 1668 (Canongate Reg.).'

p. 384, after l. 10, insert

'6. *George*.

7. *Henry* (*Reg. Mag. Sig.*, 11 August 1614).'

p. 384, ll. 11, 13, 15, 18, 20, for '6, 7, 8, 9, 10' read '8, 9, 10, 11, 12.'

p. 384, l. 11, for '1622' read '1609 (*Reg. of Deeds*, clxii. 146, and cccxxvii. 488, correcting *Reg. Mag. Sig.*, 13 January 1625).'

p. 384, l. 14, for 'Moy' read 'Mey.'

p. 384, l. 15, for '*Jean*' read '*Anna* (*Reg. Mag. Sig.*, 20 August 1618).' *Note.*—She, or another sister of the same name, had previously been married to James Leslie, fiar of Otterstoun, who, in 1614, is styled the second lord's brother-in-law (*Reg. of Deeds*, ccxx. 295; *Reg. Mag. Sig.*, 11 August 1614).

p. 385, l. 10, after 'first,' insert 'contract 10 April 1673 (*Perth Sasines*, vii. 248).'

p. 385, l. 11, after 'Innernytie,' insert 'who died at Edinburgh, 22 February 1680 (*Red Book of Grandtully*, ii. 251).'

p. 385, note 2, after '*Annals*, iii. 423,' insert 'of his natural children four sons are known: *James*, a lieutenant in the Army; *Robert* and *Ludovic*, who went to Barbadoes; and *Francis*, who lived at Weems. A natural daughter, *Anna*, was married to Captain James Drummond, and, as his widow, figures on the Royal Charity Rolls from Whitsunday 1683 onwards.'

p. 386, l. 25, for '8 and 15 September 1603' read '28 April 1616.'

p. 386, l. 10 from foot, delete 'killed along with his father at Dundee, 1651,' and insert 'also a knight, and died between August 1676 and February 1677 (*Privy Seal, English Reg.*, iii. 130).'

p. 386, l. 9 from foot, for '1550 the' read '1650 Jonet.'

p. 386, l. 7 from foot, after '*s.p.*,' insert 'in March 1686 (St. Andrews Tests.), and a daughter Elizabeth, who was married to William Dick of Grange. (See below, No. 5, where she is erroneously entered as as a sister instead of a daughter of John).'

p. 386, l. 2 from foot, after '5' transfer entire entry to No. 1, Elizabeth being a daughter of John Leslie and Janet Hay.

p. 386, l. 2 from foot, after '5,' insert '*Anna*, married to Robert Kirkcaldy of Grange after 7 April 1637, when she was his "future spouse" (*Gen. Reg. Sas.*, xlvi. 156).'

p. 386, note 8, for '472' read '479.'

p. 387, after l. 8, insert

'7. *Margaret*, married (contract 17 September 1649) to John Grant of Ballindalloch (*Chiefs of Grant*, i. 520).'

p. 388, l. 14, after 'her,' insert 'who survived him, and was married, secondly, to Patrick Forbes (Fife Sheriff-Court Book, 23 May 1682).'

LINDSAY.

p. 394, l. 8, for 'John' read 'George, first.'

p. 394, note 4, for '157' read '167.'

p. 394, l. 12, delete 'Alexander,' and insert 'Robert, afterwards second (cf. vol. iv. 235).'

p. 398, l. 11, after '1563,' insert 'He was contracted to marry Marjory, daughter and heiress of George Lindsay, but the marriage did not take place (*Acta Dom. Conc.*, xxix. 108).'

p. 398, l. 13, after 'Moncur,' insert note, 'There was "stop" to the marriage intimated by her son Patrick on 10 January 1564-65, and parties were ordered by the Kirk Session of St. Andrews to compear on the 21st of that month, but there is no further record of the ultimate issue of the case.'

p. 398, note 6, for 'xxxii' read 'lxxxii.'

p. 404, l. 6, for 'under' read 'over.'

p. 404, l. 8, for 'under fourteen' read 'above twelve.'

LIVINGSTON, EARL OF LINLITHGOW

p. 426, l. 6, for 'Barnton' read 'Banton.'

p. 426, after l. 14, add

'6. *Sir Henry*, Preceptor of Torphichen (cf. *ante*, p. 184, and *Hist. MSS. Comm. Report* on Duntreath Papers, 83).

p. 429, l. 20, delete from 'This' to end of paragraph, and insert 'He had issue, a son,

(1) *Alexander* of Dunipace. He was a member of the Town

Council of Stirling in 1527-28. He married Alison Gourlay (*Reg. Mag. Sig.*, 24 December 1521), and had issue:—

i. *David* of Bantaskine, died *vitâ patris*, having married Elizabeth Shaw, with issue.

ii. *Mr. Alexander* of Dunipace and Fildes. He married Elizabeth, daughter of Sir Adam Hepburn of Craigs (cf. *ante*, vol. ii. 149; *Reg. Mag. Sig.*, 24 July 1525) with issue (*Lands and Lairds of Larbert and Dunipace Parishes*, by J. C. Gibson, 1908).'

p. **429**, l. 24, delete 'Sir Robert Bruce of Airth' and accompanying note, and insert 'James Hamilton of Cadzow (*Eleventh Rep. Hist. MSS. Comm.*, App. vi. 14, 15; cf. vol. iv. 348).'

p. **433**, ll. 22, 23, for 'is supposed to have been' read 'was (see next entry).'

p. **434**, l. 7, after 'Kilsyth,' insert 'On 28 May 1498 he had a precept of clare constat as heir of his uncle James, Lord Livingstone, in the lands of Catscleuch from George Sinclair of Herbertshire (*Wigtown Charter-chest*, Scot. Rec. Soc., 719).'

p. **434**, l. 11, after '1503,' insert 'He appears on 1 November 1472 to have entered into an obligation to marry Elizabeth, daughter of Robert, Lord Fleming (*Wigtown Charter-chest*, Scot. Rec. Soc., 44), but it is doubtful if the marriage took place, though in a pedigree of 1625 in the Livingstone Charter-chest it is stated that it did, and that William was Elizabeth Fleming's son.'

p. **434**, note 7, delete 'probably first wife of Patrick Hepburn, first Lord Hailes.'

p. **435**, l. 5, for 'Whitson' read 'Whitsome.'

p. **435**, l. 8, after 'James,' insert 'He is said to have married and to have had a son, Alexander, minister of Monyabrock, whose great-grandson, Robert, born 13 December 1654, went to America, and was ancestor of the Livingstones of Livingstone Manor.'

p. **435**, l. 12, after '1553' add 'He appears on 16 October 1563 as Captain of the Royal Castle of Kirkwall, and demanding restitution of certain gear and writs formerly belonging to his deceased wife, Margaret Strang (Protocol Book of Gilbert Grote, f. 94).'

p. **435**, note 2, for 'iii.' read 'ii.'

p. **436**, l. 22, after 'Queen,' add as a note, 'He was at St. Germains in France, 25 July 1549 (*Reg. Mag. Sig.*, 20 April 1550), also in April 1550 (letter in H.M. Reg. Ho.).'

p. **436**, l. 24, after '1551,' note, 'He was perhaps dead before 1 October 1550. (Cf. letter from his son to the Queen Regent in H. M. Reg. Ho.).'

p. **436**, l. 13 from foot, after 'Janet Stewart,' insert 'perhaps a daughter of Alexander, second Earl of Buchan (Pedigree (A.D. 1625) in Livingstone Charter-chest).'

p. **439**, note 4, after '389' add '*Cal. of State Papers*, v. 248.'

p. **442**, l. 20, delete from 'Whether' to 'ascertained' in l. 22, and insert 'Lady Livingstone survived her husband, but appears to have been murdered before 18 October 1597, when Alexander, Master of Elphinstone, is charged to produce a certain Maws Livingstone suspect of the crime (*Ninth Rep. Hist. MSS. Comm.*, pt. ii. No. 59).'

p. 442, ll. 30 and 31, delete 'believed to have been of the family of Innernytie,' and insert 'Crichton, probably a daughter of William Crichton of Drumcrocemuir (*Part. Reg. of Sasines, Linlithgow and Bathgate*, i. 306).'

p. 442, l. 4 from foot, for 'Mary' read 'Margaret.'

p. 442, l. 3 from foot, for 'Bailie' read 'Baillie.'

p. 442, l. 2 from foot, after 'Dundrennan,' add note, '[6] *Reg. Mag. Sig.*, 21 February 1610.'

p. 442, l. 2 from foot, after 'William,' insert 'also married a Margaret Baillie (*P. C. Reg.*, ix. 19, 154), and had a son, also William, who.'

p. 447, l. 17, after 'first,' insert 'contract 22 August 1648 (*ex inform.* Ernest Axon, Esq.).'

p. 448, l. 7, delete '23 November 1660,' and insert 'in September 1662, when the regiment was raised.'

p. 448, l. 7, insert 'lieutenant' before 'colonelship.'

p. 448, l. 9, after 'Council,' insert 'He was promoted Colonel in July 1666 (Dalton's *The Scots Army*, 1661-88, pt. ii. 13, 15).'

LOTHIAN

p. 452, l. 5, for 'second' read 'third (cf. vol. vii. 324).'

p. 452, l. 7, for 'Jedburgh' read 'Roxburghe.'

p. 452, l. 15, after 'Altonburn,' insert note, 'It is pointed out that Brigadier-General Walter Ker of Littledean was allowed by the House of Lords the character of heir-male and representative of the Kerrs of Cessford, and that his line is not exhausted. But see vol. vii. 331. (*ex inform.* William D. Kerr, Esq., Glasgow).'

p. 457, l. 14, after '*s.p.*', add 'having married Jean, daughter of James Donaldson, Advocate, widow of William Eigge, merchant, Edinburgh.'

p. 458, l. 4, after 'December,' insert '1614.'

p. 467, after line 28, insert

'1. *Robert*, died in infancy.'

p. 467, l. 29, for '1' read '2.'

p. 467, after line 29, insert

'3. *Margaret.*'

p. 467, l. 31, for '2' read '4.'

p. 467, l. 33, for '3' read '5.'

p. 468, after line 8, insert

'6. *Robert.*'

p. 468, l. 9, for '4' read '7.'

p. 468, after l. 10, insert

'8. *Henrietta Maria.*'

p. 468, l. 11, for '5' read '9.'
delete ll. 20 and 21, and insert
'10. *Anna.*
11. *Katherine.*'

p. 468, l. 22, delete 'These two,' and insert 'Two.'

p. 475, l. 16, after 'unmarried,' insert 'in 1717.'

p. 480, l. 19, after 'first,' insert 'contract dated at Edinburgh and Newbattle, 7 and 8 December 1711: tocher £3000 stg. (*Reg. of Deeds*, Durie, cxxx., 4 February 1713).'

p. 480, l. 20, for 'Nicholson' read 'Nicolson.'

p. 483, l. 25, for 'July' read 'April.'

p. 487, l. 11, for '28 October 1587,' read '15 October 1591.'

p. 487, l. 21, for 'in' read 'on.'

p. 487, l. 23,, delete 'and.'

p. 487, l. 23, for 'sable' read 'of the first.'

LOUDOUN

p. 499, l. 21, for 'fourth' read 'third.'

p. 504, l. 13, after 'Clathick,' insert 'married, first, 18 June 1590, Margaret Donaldson (Stirling Reg.). He must have married again as he.'

p. 507, l. 2 from foot, after 'and,' insert 'by her, who died before 22 February 1686 (*Seafield Correspondence*, Scot. Hist. Soc., 20).'

p. 508, l. 10, delete 'in 1714,' and insert '7 March 1707.'

p. 509, l. 7, for 'only' read 'third.'

p. 509, l. 8, delete 'born 4 February 1677,' and insert 'baptized 25 August 1684 (Kirkliston Reg.).'

p. 509, l. 9, for '1777' read '1779.'

p. 509, l. 10, delete 'aged oue hundred.'

p. 509, l. 16, after 'married,' insert 'proclamation of banns, 4 August 1728 (Edin. Reg.).'

p. 511, l. 11, for 'Kilmarnock' read 'Rowallan.'

p. 512, l. 17, for 'Rawdon' read 'Hastings.'

LOVAT

p. 525, l. 24, after 'Margaret,' insert 'perhaps the Margaret Lady Mackay, wife of John Mackay of Strathnaver (*The Book of Mackay*, 85).'

p. 527, l. 17, after 'will,' insert 'She married (contract dated at Kirktoun of Ferneway, 26 March 1562), Allan M'Ranald of Leyis, and had issue. (Sheriff-Court Book of Inverness, at date; *The Clan Donald*, iii. 228).'

p. 529, l. 27, after '1581,' insert 'She married James Cuming of Altyre before November 1602, with a tocher of 5000 merks. (*Reg. of Deeds*, cxci. f. 233; charters quoted in *The Bruces and the Comyns*, 464, 465.).'

p. 529, l. 28, delete whole line and relative note.

p. 529, l. 29, for '6' read '5.'

p. 529, note 10, delete note and insert 'Edin. Tests., 21 December 1597.'

p. 534, l. 21, after 'married,' insert 'contract, 29 September 1679 (*Reg. of Deeds*, 25 February 1687).'

p. 534, l. 24, after 'married,' insert 'contract 29 April 1684.'

p. 534, l. 27, for 'Mackenzie,' read 'Macdonell.'

p. 540, l. 2, after 'married,' insert 'contract dated at various places, according as the different consenters signed, from 3 April to 9 July 1733 (*Forfeited Estates Papers*, Scot. Hist. Soc. 46).'

p. 540, l. 19, after 'married,' insert 'in August 1742 (*Inverness Gaelic Society's Transactions*, xix. 192 *n.*).'

p. 540, l. 26, after '1726,' insert, 'He was educated at the University of St. Andrews, under the care of Prof. Thomas Craigie, 1744-45.'

p. 543, l. 6 from foot, for '1645,' read '1648. (*Reg. Inhibitions, Inverness*, 2 series, vol. 2, f. 139).'

p. 544, after line 2, insert

'3. *William*, named in 1656 as uncle of Thomas [fourth] Laird of Strichen.

4. *George*, also so named.

5. *Walter*, also so named. He also appears as a witness on 5 August 1651. (*Aberdeen Sasines*, xv. f. 162; Book of Debts, H.M. Reg. Ho., 28 August 1656).

6. *Margaret*, married to John Forbes of Corsindae (*Aberdeen Sasines*, ix. ff. 4-7).'

p. 544, l. 4, for '1645' read '1648.'

p. 544, l. 8, after 'in,' insert 'or before August.'

p. 544, l. 7 from foot, for 'her' read 'his wives.'

p. 545, l. 23, after 'son, insert 'besides one daughter, *Isabella*, married (proclamation of banns, 27 May 1784), to Lieutenant Æneas Mackay, late of Rhenorea (Canongate Reg.).'

p. 547, l. 18, after 'Buckinghamshire,' insert 'died at Bournemouth, 17 August 1912.'

LYLE

p. 551, l. 3, for '1365' read '1366.'

p. 551, l. 8, for 'Buchanan' read 'Boquhan.'

p. 551, last line, delete 'his brother-in-law.'

p. 552, l. 24, for 'Magaretum' read 'Margaretam.'

p. 552, l. 4 from foot, for 'Andrew' read 'Alexander.'

p. 553, l. 16, for 'Lisle' read 'Lyle.'

p. 554, l. 18, delete 'There is no evidence for the statement that' and relative note.

p. 554, l. 19, after 'married,' insert 'first, Margaret.'

p. 554, l. 19, after 'Seton,' add note, 'Since the above was written evidence has been found of the marriage, and that Lord Lyle had by his first wife at least one son, *George* (cf. vol. viii. 578, and authority there quoted).'

p. **555**, l. 20, after 'Dunrod,' insert 'She was married, secondly, to William Menzies of Roro (*Acta Dom. Conc.*, xliii. 103).'

p. **556**, l. 11, for 'Fymont' read 'Finnart.'

p. **556**, l. 16, for 'Buchanan' read 'Boquhan.'

p. **556**, l. 30, after 'married,' insert 'contract 28 August 1549 (*Acta Dom. Conc. et Sess.*, xxvi. 90). She got £1000 tocher and gifts of sundry dresses from the Governor Arran (*Treasurer's Accounts*, ix. 335-336).'

p. **557**, l. 21, for 'quidam certam summam pecunia' read 'quadam certa summa pecunie.'

ANCIENT EARLS OF MAR

p. **589**, l. 4, after 'issue,' insert 'and was buried in the Greyfriars Church, Inverness, 26 July (*Cal. of Papal Letters*, viii. 601).'

p. **589**, after line 6, insert 'The Earl had another natural son, David, canon of Ross and treasurer of Moray (*Cal. Papal Letters*, ix. 484, 530).'

ERSKINE, EARL OF MAR

p. **597**, l. 28, after 'father,' insert 'In 1388 he was "guardian of the Temple in Scotland" (Brit. Mus., *MS. Harl.*, 6439).'

p. **608**, l. 3, after 'before,' insert '15 July (cf. vol. iv. 448).'

p. **608**, l. 4, for 'Alexander, first Lord Home' read 'Sir Alexander Home of that Ilk. For 'Sir Adam Hepburn of Hales' read 'Adam, Master of Hales (*Ibid.*).'

p. **621**, ll. 9, 10, delete from 'The' down to 'but,' and insert 'She died 23 December 1587, and was buried at Alloa 9 January 1587-88 (Funeral letter, Moray Writs, box 3, No. 241).'

p. **621**, l. 26, after 'Hague,' insert 'In 1630 he is styled Captain Alexander Erskine of Cambuskenneth (*Reg. of Deeds*, ccccxxxv. 284).'

p. **621**, l. 34, after 'so,' add 'Tradition identifies him (and rightly) with "the faithless lover" of "Lady Ann Bothwell's Lament." He probably did marry the Croft lady (Mar and Kellie MS. Rep. 178; *Fourth Rep. Hist. MSS. Com.*, 527). He refers to his wife in a letter to his mother, and after his death his brother Arthur does the same. She survived, and probably died between 1640 and 1643. They had three or perhaps four children. Two sons—*Alexander*, who was at Scots Craig with his uncle Arthur in May 1643 and was then sent to the wars abroad, and *Thomas*, who was about ten in 1646, and was sent by his uncle Charles, who was then in London, to his wife in Edinburgh. A daughter was kept by some one in England who was anxious to get rid of her by sending her to her father's representatives.'

p. **622**, l. 25, after 'married,' insert 'first.'

p. **622**, l. 27, after 'issue,' insert 'secondly (contract 1638), to Patrick Maule, first Earl of Panmure.'

p. **622**, note 3, for '1671' read '1677.'

p. **634**, l. 19, for 'father' read 'grandfather.'

VOL. VI.

MARCHMONT

p. 5, l. 19, delete 'first,' and insert after 'wife,' 'Margaret Crichtoun.'

p. 6, l. 11, delete 'second,' and insert after 'wife,' 'Margaret Lauder.'

p. 10, l. 4, for 'He' read 'She.'

p. 11, l. 6 from foot, for 'Sir James' read 'Sir John.'

p. 12, l. 19 from foot. The following list of Sir Patrick's family is from an old Family Bible at Marchmont:—

'1. *John*, born at Ballincrieff 25 September 1638, died 26 April 1639,

2. *Patrick*, born at Redbraes 12 January 1641.

3. *Alexander*, born at Redbraes 29 June 1644, died at Moscow 1676.

4. *Julian*, born at Polwarth Mains 23 October 1639, died at Yester 20 October 1687.

5. *Christian*, born at Redbraes 20 January 1643, died 5 February 1666.

6. *Anne*, born at Redbraes 31 October 1646, died at Edinburgh in August 1690.'

p. 19, l. 25, for 'Pettis' read 'Perris.'

p. 19, l. 28, after '*Anne*,' insert 'born 29 July 1698.'

p. 19, l. 4 from foot, after 'married,' insert 'proclamation of banns 30 January 1743 (Edin. Reg.).'

MARISCHAL

p. 38, l. 7, for '1363' read '1363-64.'

p. 44, l. 18, for 'Glenarthill' read 'Glencuthil.'

p. 45, l. 7 from foot, for 'second' read 'fourth.'

p. 49, l. 16, for '1543' read '1543-44, both parties being very young.'

p. 49, l. 16, for 'sixth' read 'seventh.'

p. 50, l. 16, after 'secondly,' insert 'banns proclaimed in Dunottar church 13 January 1571-72 (Moray Writs, box 15, No. 344).'

p. 53, l. 23, after '1598,' add note, 'The traditional circumstances of her death are curious. Having heard of the slaughter of one William Lauder, a bailie of the burgh of Lauder, by her brother Lord Home, she 'did mightily rejoice thereat, and writ it for good newes to sundry of her friends in the country. But within less than twenty-four hours after, the lady took a swelling in her throat, both without and within, after a great laughter, and could not be cured till death seized upon her with great repentance.—Pat. Anderson's *Hist. of Scotland*, cited in Chambers' *Domestic Annals*, i. 300.'

p. **53**, last l., and p. **54**, l. 1, for 'before 19 March 1623,' read 'contract 13, 21, and 22 February 1618 (*Reg. of Deeds*, cccxxxvi. 394).'

p. **54**, l. 1, delete 'Sir.'

p. **54**, ll. 14, 15, delete from 'but' to '1587' inclusive.

p. **54**, after l. 17, insert 'The Earl had a natural son *Gilbert*, legitimated 19 May 1587.[9] Another son *Robert*, probably also illegitimate, married, contract 14 March 1618, Helen, daughter of John Bruce of Graysfortrie (*Reg. of Deeds*, ccclxxxvii. 424).'

p. **59**, note 3, after 'Hay's *Gen. Coll.*' delete 'ii. 266,' and insert 'iii. 267.'

p. **62**, l. 13, after '*Mary*,' insert 'born 1695 (*Letters of James, Earl of Perth*, Camden Society, 78 *n.*).'

p. **62**, l. 21, for '1714' read '1715.'

MELFORT

p. **66**, l. 15, after 'Guards,' insert 'He was admitted a Privy Councillor 12 December 1678.'

p. **68**, l. 2 from foot, after 'married,' insert 'contract 28 February 1700 (*Reg. of Deeds*, Dalrymple, 12 January 1709).'

p. **69**, l. 13, for '1691' read '1675 (The 1691 publication was a reprint).'

p. **69**, l. 29, after 'first,' insert 'in July 1788.'

p. **70**, l. 3, for 'Royas' read 'Rozas.'

p. **70**, l. 3, delete 'Bozas of.'

p. **70**, ll. 4 and 6, for 'Castel Bianco' read 'Castel Blanco.'

p. **70**, l. 7, after 'their,' insert 'grand.'

p. **70**, l. 7, after 'daughters,' insert '*Margaret* married Don Joseph Iquaz de Vallabriga, a captain of Aragonese cavalry (*L'Art de Verifier les Dates*, fol. ed. 1821. Continuation, i. 325), and had a daughter.'

p. **70**, l. 7, after 'Theresa,' insert 'who.'

p. **70**, l. 8 from foot after 'Louis,' insert 'Jean Edward,' and for 'born' read 'baptized.'

p. **71**, before l. 1, insert

(4) '*Xavier*, baptism recorded at St. Germains 6 December 1713.'

p. **71**, l. 1, for '4' read '5.'

p. **71**, l. 5, for 'May' read 'March.'

p. **72**, l. 24, for 'subects' read 'subjects.'

LEVEN AND MELVILLE

p. **92**, after l. 23, insert

'vi. *Jean*, executrix dative to Robert, second Lord Melville, 1635 (Edin. Tests.).'

p. **94**, l. 6 from foot, after 'married,' insert 'Esther Tailor, relict of David Drummond, gentleman pensioner to James VI. (*Reg. of Deeds*, Dlvii. 23).'

p. 94, after l. 2 from foot, insert

'(4) *Margaret*, married (contract 25 March 1634), as second wife, to Mr. Thomas Maitland, minister of Garvald (*Reg. of Deeds*, DXXVII. 127); secondly, after 1637, to Mr. John Dalzell, minister of Prestonkirk (*Reg. of Deeds*, Mack., 8 February 1666).'

p. 99, l. 20, after '*Christian*,' insert 'a natural daughter.' After 'married,' insert '(contract dated 11th October 1581 (Reg. Ho. Cal., 20 November 1583).'

p. 101, l. 9, for '1613' read '1601 (*P. C. Reg.*, vi. 214).'

p. 103, l. 14, after 'Meldrum,' insert 'She was perhaps the Margaret, brother's daughter of Robert Melville of Murdocairnie, widow of Robert Ramsay, merchant, mentioned in *Fife Inhibitions*, 27 July 1602.'

p. 110, l. 20, after '1681,' insert 'in consequence of which he assumed the name and arms of Leslie (*Family of Leslie*, iii. 366).'

p. 114, l. 24, for '10 March' read '21 March (Edin. Reg.).'

p. 123, l. 2, for '17 August' read '10 August.'

GRAHAM, EARL OF MENTEITH

p. 151, l. 9, delete 'a.'

p. 151, l. 9, after 'Herries,' insert 'daughter of William Herries of Hartwood, co. Dumfries, and granddaughter of Mr. Robert Herries, minister of Dryfesdale.'

p. 151, l. 14, for 'son' read 'daughter.'

p. 151, l. 15, for 'his' read 'her (*Services of Heirs*, 1710-19, p. 2).'

p. 151, l. 15, delete from 'but' to end of sentence, and insert 'married to Michael Malcolm of Balbeadie, co. Fife, and died February 1733.'

p. 152, l. 25, delete from 'It is' down to 'Graham' on line 27, and insert 'He died about 1557, having married, first, Isobel Graham, and, secondly, Margaret, daughter of —— Shaw of Knockhill. She survived him and was described as his widow on 4 July 1558 (Protocol Book of Gilbert Grote, 52).'

p. 153, l. 25, after 'certain,' add 'but he was living on 28 February 1665 (*P. C. Reg.*, 3rd ser., ii. 630).'

p. 154, l. 15, after 'Captain,' delete to end of paragraph, and insert 'Philip Wilkieson, Balnahinch, Ireland. The marriage took place at Balnahinch in August 1714. Her husband instituted a divorce against her on 16 December 1726 (*Consistorial Processes*, Scot. Rec. Soc., No. 240), They had issue.'

p. 158, l. 28, after 'Hill,' insert 'He died before October 1595. Hill was also known as Easter Aikenhead. Helen Kincaid survived him, having issue a daughter *Agnes* Hamilton, married, before October 1595, to Alexander Hamilton of Haggs (Reg. Ho. Cal., 31 October 1595).'

p. 159, l. 23, delete '6 February 1588-89,' and insert '31 October 1595 (Reg. Ho. Cal. at date).'

p. 160, l. 6, from foot, for 'John, Lord Seton' read 'George, fourth Lord Seton.'

MIDDLETON

p. 188, l. 14, delete 'in 1705 or 1706,' and insert 'at S. Sulpice, Paris, 25 June 1702 (*Reg. of St. Germain en Laye*, i. 13).'

MONTROSE

p. 197, l 10. from foot, for 'Swinburne' read 'Symundburne.'

p. 213, note 1. Add to end of note, 'The statement in Burke is questioned by representatives of the Grahames of Auchincloich who claim, or suggest, a descent from the Dalkeith or elder branch of the Grahams. It is possible that Nisbet is right in placing the ancestors of the Grahams of Morphie a generation further back in the Montrose pedigree.'

p. 215, l. 20, for 'Robert, Duke of Albany' read 'Robert III.'

p. 220, l. 2, for 'sons' read 'children.'

p. 223, l. 2, after 'Oliver' read 'Ogilvie.'

p. 223, l. 2, after 'son,' delete comma, and add 'by her second husband James, first Lord Ogilvie of Airlie.'

p. 223, l. 19, delete from '4. *Oliver*' to end of paragraph, and alter the remaining numbers of children from '5, 6, 7' to '4, 5, 6.'

p. 224, note 7, for 'Lord Erskine' read 'Lord Graham.'

p. 225, l. 15 after 'relict,' add 'of Andrew Mowbray, burgess of Edinburgh, and.'

p. 225, l. 26, for 'Bucklyvie' read 'Buchlyvie.'

p. 227, l. 16, for 'Mathew' read 'Matthew.'

p. 230, l. 9 from foot, after 'issue,' insert 'She married, secondly, as his second wife, Sir Harie Graham of Morphie, and died in August 1587 (Edin. Tests.).'

p. 236, l. 17, delete 'Sir.'

p. 237, l. 6 from foot, for '1595' read 'March 1597-98 (Perth Reg.).'

p. 238, l. 26, for 'two' read 'three.'

p. 238, l. 27, for 'third' read 'fourth.'

p. 238, l. 27, after 'Braco,' insert '*Patrick*.'

p. 239, l. 15, after 'issue,' insert note, 'There was an assignation by John Earl of Montrose, donator to the ward and marriage of Lord Fleming to the latter himself and that in contemplation of the marriage *then contracted* between him and Lilias, dated 7 February 1582-83 (*Wigtown Inventory*, Scot. Rec. Soc., No. 127).'

p. 253, l. 8 from foot, for 'amounts appear' read 'account referred to appears.'

p. 258, ll, 3 and 4 from foot, delete 'Lord Graham.'

p. 259, l. 3 from foot, after 'troop,' insert 'He was admitted of the Privy Council, 15 November 1678.'

p. **271,** l. 9 from foot, after 'issue,' insert 'She and her sisters, Georgina and Caroline, are described as "fine, civil and cheerful-looking girls" (Miss Berry's *Journal*, ii. 391).'

p. **273,** l. 6 from foot, after '1902' add 'and also at that on 22 June 1911.'

p. **274,** after l. 8, insert

'(2) *Ronald Malise Hamilton*, born 20 September 1912.

(3) *Mary Helen Alma*, born 11 April 1909.'

DUNBAR, EARL OF MORAY

p. **301,** l. 5 from foot, after '*James*,' delete remainder of sentence, and read, 'who, in or after 1397, was presented to the Precentorship of Moray, being then fourteen years old. He resigned it in or before 1404.'

STEWART, EARL OF MORAY

p. **311,** l. 4 from foot, after '1544,' insert 'within eight days of being "schorne of the stane,"' (Moray Writs, box 15, No. 1736).'

p. **312,** l. 3, for '1525' read '1524.'

p. **312,** ll. 6, 7, 8, 9, delete from 'They' to 'issue,' and insert 'He left no legitimate issue.'

p. **312,** l. 10, for '*John*,' read '*James*.'

p. **312,** l. 15, after 'her,' insert 'She was married to John, Master of Buchan (see *ante*, *corrigenda* on vol. i. p. 269).'

STEWART, EARL OF MORAY

p. **314,** l. 28, after 'Strathearn,' add note, 'In a resignation of John Lamb, burgess of Edinburgh, 21 July 1564, he is styled Earl of Moray, Lord Pettie, Brachlie and Stratheirn (Protocol Book of Gilbert Grote, H.M. Reg. Ho., 113, 114).'

p. **316,** l. 25, for 'before November 1572,' read 'before 29 March 1571 (Moray Writs, box 15, No. 211).'

p. **316,** l. 26, after 'posthumous,' insert 'born before 18 April 1570 (*Ibid.*, box 15, No. 352).'

p. **316,** l. 28, for 'before January 1586-87,' read '3 August 1586, (*Ibid.*, No. 1694).'

p. **317,** l. 20, after '1591-92,' insert note, '(*Acts and Decreets*, ccxxxv. 5).'

p. **318,** l. 12, after '1591,' insert note '(*Acts and Decreets*, cccxxxv. 5).'

p. **318,** l. 18, after 'London,' insert 'He was a Vice-Admiral in the English Navy: he died *s.p.*, and was buried at Westminster (MS. Account of the Family, *penes* Niall Campbell, Esq.).'

p. **319,** l. 17, after 'Dunrobin,' insert 'He was retoured heir of his mother in the earldom, 22 July 1602, but the precept of clare constat was not issued till 7 May 1604, when the lands are said to have been twelve years in ward (*Responde Book*).'

p. **320,** ll. 6 and 7, delete 'to which he had succeeded on the death of his cousin James, the second holder of that title,' and insert 'which he acquired from the Earl of Morton, who had apprised the lands from Lord St. Colme (cf. vol. vii. 395).'

p, **320,** l. 22, after 'Edinburgh,' insert 'in 1638 (MS. Account of the Family *penes* Niall Campbell, Esq.).'

p. **320,** l. 23, for '*Margaret*,' read '*Mary*.'

p. **320,** l. 23, delete 'about 24,' and insert 'contract 4.'

p. **321,** l. 2, after 'buried,' insert 'at Dyke.'

p. **321,** l. 17, after 'wife,' insert 'who died after 9 March (the date of her will), and before May 1683 (Moray Writs, box 5, No. 328).'

p. **321,** l. 19, after 'unmarried,' insert 'in the twelfth year of his age (MS. History *ut sup*).'

p. **321,** l. 19, delete from '14 June' to end of sentence, and insert '1 June 1647, the date of receipt for the price of his coffin (Moray Writs, box 5, No. 971).'

p. **321,** l. 23, after 'unmarried,' add, 'and was buried in the Session-House of South Leith, 30 January 1692 (South Leith Kirk Session Minutes).'

p. **321,** l. 27, delete 'had,' and insert 'dying 2 February 1688 left.'

p. **321,** l. 28, after 'Charles,' insert 'born 16 December 1676.'

p. **321,** l. 28, after 'first,' insert 'proclamation of banns 13 February 1697 (Canongate Reg.).'

p. **321,** l. 29, after 'secondly,' insert 'proclamation of banns 24 August 1700 (*Ibid*).'

p. **321,** l. 30, for 'Dalziel,' read 'Dalzell,' and insert 'who died 10 November 1708.'

p. **321,** l. 32, after '1650,' insert '(contract 29 March 1650, tocher £36,000), (Moray Writs).'

p. **321,** l. 33, after '1668,' insert note, 'It is stated by Mr. Willcock in *A Scots Earl*, that she survived to the end of 1706, when she died at the age of eighty-five.'

p. **321,** l. 34, delete 'after March 1653,' and insert 'contract 26 August 1654 (Moray Writs).'

p. **321,** last line, delete 'in,' and insert 'contract 28 January.'

p. **322,** l. 25, after 'Revolution,' insert note, 'On his periodical visits to London as Secretary of State he used to take so much gold for his general expenses and a packet of fifty gold pieces for cards, etc. The family tradition is that he died, not at Donibristle, as stated in the text, but on his way to London, and that all his things were bundled into a box, where they remained untouched till quite recently. Whatever the facts may be, it is certain that the family have in their possession fifty new gold pieces of the period (*ex inform.* Earl of Moray).'

p. **322,** second last line, for '1700,' read '1701' (Moray Writs).

p. **322,** last line, after 'married,' insert 'before 31 January 1663 (Moray Writs).'

p. **323,** l. 2, for '20 July 1702,' read 'in 1682.'

p. **323,** l. 2, after 'issue,' insert 'besides seven children, who died *vitâ patris*, and unmarried.'

p. **323,** l. 3, after 'Doune,' insert 'born at Darnaway 1658.'

p. 323, l. 3, after '*v.p.*' insert '12 December.'

p. 323, l. 2 from foot, after 'Moray,' insert 'born 4 September 167[4] at Darnaway' (MS. Account, *ut sup.*).'

p. 324, l. 5, after 'first,' insert 'in the beginning of September 1698.'

p. 324, l. 8, after 'no,' insert 'surviving.'

p. 324, l. 8, delete 'about 1702,' and insert 'contract 26 and 30 July 1700 (Moray Writs).'

p. 324, l. 26, delete 'unmarried.'

p. 324, l. 28, after 'age,' insert 'In a letter to his brother the Earl, dated from Murrich Hof, near Breda, 17 January 1764, he says "It has pleased God to afflict me . . . by taking from me on 15th inst. my dearest wife" (Moray Writs, *ex inform.* John Macgregor, Esq., W.S.). He had decree of declarator of marriage against Sybella Barbour, daughter of the deceased John Barbour, bailie of Inverness, 19 December 1732. She at the same time raised a counter action of freedom, etc. (*Consistorial Processes*, etc., Scot. Rec. Soc., No. 281).'

p. 324, l. 7 from foot, after 'Eglintoun,' insert note, 'The marriage was considered irregular, and the parties were fined for not declaring the names of the celebrant and witnesses (Moray Writs).'

p. 325, after l. 6, insert

'6. *Hugh*, born about 1721 (*ex inform.* John Macgregor, Esq., W.S.).'

p. 325, l. 7, for '6' read '7.'

p. 325, l. 9, for '7' read '8.'

p. 325, l. 13, delete 'about,' and insert 'at his father's place, Frankfield, co. Perth, 13 May.'

p. 326, l. 1, for 'Saltarton' read 'Salterton.'

p. 328, l. 20, for 'Plowden' read 'Pounden,' and delete 'M.D.'

MORDINGTOUN

p. 332, l. 10 from foot, for 'Sir William' read 'Sir James.'

p. 333, l. 15, for 'Sir William' read 'Sir James.'

p. 334, l. 4, for 'the' read 'then.'

p. 336, l. 2, for 'in,' read 'on.'

DOUGLAS, EARL OF MORTON

p. 353, ll. 5 and 6 from foot, for 'Gifford' read 'Giffard.'

p. 358, after l. 20, insert

'2. *Mr. William*, parson of Kilbucho, styled in 1543 brother-german and heir of tailzie of the third Earl (*Harl. MS.*, 6435; *Acts and Decreets*, i. 305).'

p. 358, ll. 21, 26, 29, for '2, 3, 4' read '3, 4, 5.'

p. 358, after l. 6 from foot, insert

'6. *Helen* (*Acta Dom. Conc.*, xxxix. 48).'

p. 361, l. 18, after 'before,' delete to end of sentence with relative note, and insert 'before 17 September 1549 (*Acta Dom. Conc. et Sess.*, xxvii. 149), and possibly before December 1548 (*Treasurer's Accounts*, ix. 261).'

p. 361, l. 4 from foot, after 'Beatrice,' insert 'retoured co-heir of her father, 26 May 1551 (original retour in Advocates' Library).'

p. 363, l. 22, delete 'thrown into prison,' and insert 'was warded in Edinburgh Castle, Monday, 2 January 1580-81. Ten days after he was conveyed to Dumbarton where he remained till 27 May 1581, when he was brought back to Edinburgh (Notes in Protocol Book of John Scott, H.M. Reg. Ho.).'

p. 364, after l. 10, insert

'The Earl had also a natural daughter, *Jane*, married (contract 24 June 1579) to John Cumming of Earnside (*Reg. of Deeds*, xxi. 467).'

p. 366, l. 10, for '1488' read '1448.'

p. 368, after l. 3, insert

'4. Probably *Elizabeth*, married to Michael Balfour of Burleigh (cf. *Corrig.*, vol. i. p. 531).'

p. 372, l. 20, after '1624,' insert 'and who married (contract 15 February 1621) Katherine, daughter of Henry Forrester of Corstorphine (*Reg. of Deeds*, cccxii. 295).'

p. 372, l. 21, delete comma after 'Jean.'

p. 373, l. 12, delete 'in,' and insert 'contract 10 December (H.M. Reg. Ho. Cal.).'

p. 374, l. 4, for 'Hume' read 'Home.'

p. 378, l. 9 from foot, after 'Grandison,' insert 'She was governess to King Charles I.'s daughter, the Princess Henrietta, and after the surrender of Exeter she carried off the princess secretly to France while the King was at Newcastle (Clarendon's *Hist.*, x. 115). It is said she walked to Dover with the child on her back, attired as a beggar (*ex inform.* Hon. James Home).'

p. 379, l. 8 from foot, delete 'in 1681,' and insert 'about 1 November 1681 when a payment on account of sums due to him by the Treasury was made to his uncle, "his condition being such that without reddy money he cannot be handsomely interr'd as becomes a person of his quality" (*Treasury Papers* (*Royal Warrants*), H.M. Reg. Ho., 1 November 1681).'

p. 379, l. 8 from foot, after 'married,' insert 'first.'

p. 379, after l. 3 from foot, insert 'The Earl married, secondly, Marjory Foulis, who survived him, and married, secondly, William (Erskine), Earl of Buchan; dying before 1690 (Misc. Docs., H.M. Reg. Ho., and Edin. Tests., 19 February 1690; cf. *corr.*, vol. ii. 274).'

p. 382, l. 9 from foot, after 'Mary,' insert 'born 20 March 1737 (Canongate Reg.).'

MAXWELL, EARL OF MORTON

p. 389, l. 8 from foot, after '3rd,' insert 'Argent.'

NAIRN

p. 393, after l. 21, insert

'6. *Catherine*, eldest daughter, married, first, after 9 November 1639, when she had a charter as his future wife, to Walter Stewart, son and apparent heir of Mr. John Stewart of Cluny (*Perth Sasines*, ix. 256): secondly, about 1653, James Ogilvy of Muirtoun, afterwards of Cluny (Cortachy Writs).'

p. **393**, ll. 22, 23, for '6, 7,' read '7, 8.'

p. **399**, ll. 27, 28, delete 'two daughters, of whom only the elder married,' and insert

'1. Emily Jane, of whom after.

2. *Clementina Marie Hortense*, died, unmarried, 25 January 1836.

3. *Georgiana Gabrielle*, married, 2 Feb. 1871, the Marquis de Lavalette, and died 16 July 1907, *s.p.*

4. *Adelaide Elizabeth Josephine*, died, unmarried, 1841.

5. *Sarah Sophia Laura*, died, unmarried, 10 July 1853.'

p. **401**, l. 14. The comma after 'azure' should be deleted and placed after 'base.'

NAPIER

p. **408**, after l. 10 from foot, insert

'4. *William*, burgess of Edinburgh, who died before 1491, leaving a son and heir, *John* (Proctocol Book of James Young, 20 April 1491).'

p. **408**, ll. 9 and 5 from foot, for '4. 5.' read '5. 6.'

p. **413**, l. 26, for 'Torrie' read 'Towie.'

p. **413**, l. 10 from foot, after '1601,' insert 'Another daughter, *Bessie*, was married, contract 6 Feb. 1617, to Archibald Campbell of Glencarradale (Protocol Book of John Hay, iv. 47).'

p. **417**, l. 11, for 'of Pitcullo' read 'Balfour.'

p. **420**, l. 22, after '1616,[6]' insert 'married, contract 3 Dec. 1633, to Mr. William Cunningham of Broomhill (*Reg. of Deeds*, dxv. 298).

p. **421**, l. 2, delete 'By his wife, Anne Dunkeson,' and insert 'He married, contract 18 December 1634, Anna, daughter of Roger Duncanson of Easter Gellets, burgess of Edinburgh, and his wife, Margaret Douglas (*Gen. Reg. Sas.*, xlix. 412, xxxvii. 363). By her.'

p. **422**, after l. 3, insert

'13. *Barbara*, baptized 23 October 1606 (St. Cuthbert's Reg. Edin.).'

p. **430**, after l. 26, insert

'2. *Susanna*, married, contract 10 February 1609, to Walter Scott, younger of Whitslaid (*Reg. of Deeds*, clxxxi. 71).'

3. *Elizabeth* (perhaps by second wife), married, contract 13 and 14 August 1622, to Walter, grandson and heir of Walter Chisholm of that Ilk (*Ibid.*, cccxxix. 124).'

p. **434**, l. 2, after 'her,' insert 'who had been divorced by her first husband, Sir Thomas C. Bunbury, Bart. (cf. vol. iv. 554).'

p. **434**, l. 3, after 'had,' insert 'besides other three children (*Complete Baronetage*, iv. 118 *n.*).'

NEWARK

p. **442**, after l. 11, insert

'2. *James*, a colonel in the Army, who died in the East Indies.

3. *Charles*, died young (*Family of Leslie*, ii. 203; the order is taken from *Fife Sasines*, vii. 61, and *Gen. Reg. Inhibs.*, 5 July 1671. The same records show that Helen and Anne were the youngest daughters).'

p. **442**, ll. 12, 13, for '2, 3' read '8, 9.'

p. **442**, ll. 20, 21, for 'in or before 1676' read 'contract 22 and 26 April 1675 (*Reg. of Deeds*, Mackenzie, 31 March 1682; *Privy Seal, English Reg.* iv. 8).'

NEWBURGH

p. **448**, l. 18, after 'Livingston,' insert 'He died between 1 September and 31 October 1563, survived by his second wife, Elizabeth Douglas, (Protocol Book of Thomas Johnson, Linlithgow Town Clerk's Office).'

p. **448**, after l. 4 from foot, insert

'7. *James*, a witness, 21 April 1565 (Protocol Book *ut sup.*).'

8. *Jonet*, who was the widow of Ninian Altoun, 21 September 1578.'

p. **450**, l. 9 from foot, after 'Charles I.,' add note, 'As to his identification see *Reg. of Deeds*, ccccxxv. 154, and ccccxxix. 314).'

p. **450**, l. 6 from foot, for 'James I.' read 'James VI.'

p. **450**, note 14, for 'but actually' read 'and hers. He must have been at least forty-five, for he is a witness 2 February 1601 (Protocol Book of Andrew Ker, Linlithgow), so must have been born not later than 1587.'

p. **456**, l. 10, for 'December,' read 'September' (cf. vol. ii. 300).'

p. **456**, l. 15 from foot, for 'Chénecourt' read 'Chénencourt.'

p. **458**, l. 24, for 'Hermora' read 'Hermosa.'

p. **458**, l. 26, for 'Triorifi' read 'Trionfi.'

p. **458**, l. 30, for 'Fredericao' read 'Frederico.'

p. **459**, l. 20, for 'Marco' read 'Mario.'

NITHSDALE

p. **475**, l. 3 from foot, after 'Seton,' insert 'Lord of that Ilk.'

p. **481**, l. 23, for '1593' read '31 January 1593-94 (Edin. Tests.).'

p. **483**, l. 2 from foot, after 'Craigie,[6]' insert 'secondly, to William Stewart, younger of Dunduff (*Gen. Reg. of Inhibs.*, xxvii. 40).'

p. **484**, l. 10, after 'descended,[2]' insert 'He married (contract 5 October 1623) Marion, youngest daughter of Homer Maxwell of Speddoch (*Reg. of Deeds*, ccccii. 300).'

p. **486**, l. 3 from foot, after '*Jean*,' insert 'married (contract 13 February 1634) to John, eldest son of Robert M'Brair of Almagill (*Reg. of Deeds*, DVI. 51; *Dumfries Sasines*, 19 February 1640).'

p. 487, l. 8 from foot, after '1656,' insert 'and was dead before 3 March 1663 (*P. C. Reg.*, 3d series, i. 347).'

p. 487, l. 5 from foot, after 'Elizabeth,' insert 'widow of George Glendoning, younger of Parton (Writ *penes* Sir William Fraser's Trustees), and.'

NORTHESK

p. 496, l. 22, delete ' of Thornton,' and insert 'of Lower Tooting or Mincing Lane, London.'

p. 499, l. 18, after 'first,' insert 'contract 9 August 1671 (*Reg. of Deeds*, Durie, 28 August 1675).'

p. 503, l. 20, after 'issue,' insert 'There was a declarator of marriage raised against him in 1770 by Christian, daughter of Captain Alexander Cameron of Dungannon (*Edinburgh Consistorial Processes*, Scot. Rec. Soc., No. 567). She claimed to have been married to him at Fort William on 27 January 1767.'

p. 503, line 6 from foot, for 'Francis' read 'Frances.'

p. 508, line 12, for 'regaurdent' read 'reguardant.'

OCHILTREE

p. 512, note 3, add to end of note, 'See also Pitcairn's *Criminal Trials*, i. *335, for an account of his death by drowning in the Water of Calder.'

p. 514, l. 13, for '1586' read '7 May 1585 (*Reg. of Deeds*, xxiii. 423).'

p. 514, ll. 14 and 15, for 'whose testament was recorded 14 February 1601' read 'She died 12 December 1599 (Edin. Tests.).'

p. 514, l. 21, after '1620,' insert 'He became a minister in Ireland, and died before 13 April 1654, having married Esther Wallace, with issue (Castlewig Charter-chest).'

p. 514, l. 22, for '(4) *James*' read '(4) *Janet.*'

p. 514, l. 22, after '*Helen*,' insert

'(7) *Janet*, married to Andrew M'Dowell of Lefnoll (*Reg. of Deeds*, cccxlviii. 305).'

p. 514, after l. 22, insert

'6. *Thomas* (*Gen. Reg. of Inhibs.*, 2nd ser., iii. 104).'

p. 514, ll. 23, 25, 32 for '6, 7, 8' read '7, 8, 9.'

p. 514, l. 2 from foot, after 'father,' insert 'after 29 December 1577, the date of his will (Protocol Book of William Stewart, Junior, f. 150, Edinburgh City Chambers), and.'

p. 517, l. 10, for '1594' read '1604 (cf. vol. i. 449; *Reg. of Deeds*, cxvii. 209).'

p. 517, after l. 21. insert

'6. *Anna*, mentioned 1610 (*Reg. of Deeds*, cciii. 372).'

p. 518, l. 6, for '1639' read '1631.'

p. **518**, l. 18, for '£14' read '£4' (*Reg. Sec. Sig.*, ii. 495).'

p. **518**, l. 26, for 'William' read 'Major William (*Reg. of Deeds*, DLIX. 220).'

p. **518**, l. 31, after '*Doratie*,' insert 'She, or another daughter, was married in or before 1644 to John Livingston of Hayning (*Reg. of Deeds*, DLIX. 117).'

p. **519**, l. 2, after 'brother,' add 'She died at Edinburgh 8 February 1697, "absolutely destitute of all means whereby to be interred" (*Treasury Papers* (*Contingent Expenses*) 9 February 1697, H. M. Reg. Ho.).'

p. **519**, l. 12, delete '12,' and insert 'in.'

p. **519**, l. 13, delete 'next day,' and insert '13 of that month.'

p. **519**, l. 14, after 'Holyroodhouse,' insert note, 'His mother, Lady Ochiltree, had a grant from the Treasury on 12 February 1675 of 500 merks "for defraying the charge and expense of the funerall of the late Lord Ochiltree hir sone" (*Treasury Papers* (*Royal Warrants*), H. M. Reg. Ho.).'

OLIPHANT

p. **522**, l. 4 of notes, for 'xii.' read 'xxii.'

p. **523**, l. 5, for 'Oliferds' read 'Olifards.'

p. **523**, l. 15, after 'sons' insert note, 'It is more likely that the three sons aftermentioned were the sons of William of Lilford, but that John, Hugh and Stephen, were descendants of Hugh of Stokes. The Northamptonshire lands seem to have passed to Walter, son of David, before 26 Hen. II. (1179-80) (Pipe Roll. Soc. xxix. 85).'

p. **536**, note 10, l. 3 from foot of notes, after 'Gallery' insert 'See *Brit. Mus. Addl. MSS.*, 24276, f. 53.'

p. **539**, after third line from foot, insert

'6. *Elizabeth*, married to James Hering of Tullibole, younger of Glasclune (*Reg. Mag. Sig.*, 21 October 1501; Myln's *Vitæ Episc. Dunkelden.*, 37).'

p. **539**, second line from foot, for '6' read '7.'

p. **549**, note 13, delete 'probably.' The marriage-contract was dated 7 March 1617 (*Reg. of Deeds*, DXXXI. 30).'

p. **550**, note 12, delete bracket after 2nd ed.

p. **554**, after l. 6 insert

'2. *Isobel*, baptized 22 September 1622. At her baptism her father would not give confession of his faith (Perth Reg.),' and alter numbers of remaining children accordingly.

p. **560**, delete l. 12.

p. **560**, l. 13, before 'daughter,' insert 'a son and.'

p. **560**, after l. 13, insert

'1. *Joseph*, born at Mons 18-19 March 1684; died *v.p.* and *s.p.*'

p. **560**, l. 14, before '*Marie*,' insert '2,' and after 'Baptiste)[6]' insert 'born at Edinburgh in the Canongate 31 May 1687 (note by the ninth Lord Oliphant in an old book in the Gask Library).'

p. **560**, l. 14, for 'who' read 'She.'

p. **562**, note 10, add to note, 'and as early as 9 August 1751 (*Acts of P. C., Colonial Series*, iv. 130).'

SINCLAIR, EARL OF ORKNEY

pi. **565**, l. 28, for '1357' read '1337.'

p. **567**, l. 9 from foot, for '17 September 1358,' read 17 January 1356 (*ex inform.* Roland St. Clair, Esq.).'

p. **570**, l. 2, for 'daughter' read 'grand-daughter.'

p. **570**, l. 5 from foot, delete 'but see afterwards.'

p. **570**, l. 4 from foot, delete 'first.'

p. **571**, l. 1, for '1418' read '1422 (*Cal. of Papal Letters*, vii. 221).'

STEWART, EARL OF ORKNEY

p. **573**, l. 24, after 'had' insert 'by her, who died September 1598, (*Edin. Comm. Decreets*, 14 March 1598-99).'

p. **574**, l, 2, after '1635' insert, 'He married first, in or before 1603, Elizabeth Hamilton (*Edin. Burgh Reg. of Deeds*, 27 March 1604); secondly, in or before 1607, Margaret Lyon (*Reg. of Deeds*, ccxix. 16).'

p. **574**, l. 9, delete '1639,' and insert '22 and 24 September 1629 (*Reg. of Deeds*, cccclxi. 342).'

p. **574**, l. 12, after 'first,' add 'to Sir James Young of Seaton (*Reg. of Deeds*, ccccxxvii. 485); secondly.'

p. **574**, l. 12, for 'Abekie' read 'Arbikie.'

p. **574**, l. 13, for 'secondly' read 'thirdly.'

p. **575**, after l. 3 from foot, insert

'11. *Jean.* 12. *Katherine*, both by Marjorie Sandilands (*Acts and Decreets*, clix. 299).'

p. **576**, l. 3, after 'father,' insert 'He was of age by 25 June 1590 (*Reg. of Deeds*, xxxiv. 438).'

p. **576**, l. 8 from foot, after 'forfeited,' insert note, 'There is a Bible which is said to have belonged to the Earl, printed in London 1595, in the possession of a person in South Ronaldshay (*Old Lore Misc. of Orkney*, etc., ii. 133, January 1909).'

HAMILTON, EARL OF ORKNEY

p. **582**, l. 11 from foot, for 'Denby' read 'Danby.'

p. **583**, l. 3 from foot, after 'proper,' insert 'on a chief argent three mullets gules.'

OXFUIRD

p. **588**, l. 26, after 'married,' insert 'after 5 May 1542, when she was his affianced spouse (Andrew Brounhill's Protocol Book, Edin. City Chambers) and.'

p. **593**, l. 20, for 'in the month of' read '13.'

p. **593**, l. 21, for '1595' read '1595-96 (Court of Sess. Sederunt Book).'

p. **593**, note 4, delete 'note,' and insert '*Reg. of Deeds*, ii. 374.'

p. **594**, l. 6 from foot, after '1576,' insert 'was made Advocate-Depute to his father, 31 October 1585 (*Reg. Sec. Sig.*, liii. 59).'

p. **596**, l. 21, for 'about' read 'contract.'

p. **598**, l. 19, after 'dated,' insert '8 July (*Reg. of Deeds*, DXCIV. 332).'

p. **598**, l. 24, *Note*.—The service referred to is by Robert M. to his brother *Patrick*, not David, and is dated 1656, not 1657.

p. **598**, l. 2 from foot, after 'Galstoun,' insert 'She married, thirdly, some weeks before 6 January 1729, Henry Clark, "She might weall bee his granmother" (Letter from Lady Jean Mackenzie, relict of Sir Thomas Stewart, Lord Balcaskie, to her son Sir George Stewart of Grandtully, *Red Book of Grandtully*, ii. 324).'

p. **599**, l. 7 from foot, after 'Army,' insert 'Ensign in Scots Foot Guards, 11 January 1700.'

VOL. VII.

PANMURE

p. 1, l. 1, for title and headlines of pages, for 'Maule, Earl Panmure' read 'Maule, Earl of Panmure.'

p. 4, l. 27, for 'name' read 'surname.'

p. 4, l. 28, after 'had,' insert 'probably by his wife Godit, with whom he granted the isle at the head of Hiliuespedberne to St. Cuthbert of Carram (orig. Charter in H.M. Reg. Ho.).'

p. 8, l. 14, delete '[Stonehaven].'

p. 18, l. 18, after 'married,' insert 'contract 7 December 1562 (*Reg. of Deeds*, xv. 301).'

p. 18, l. 22, after 'married,' insert 'first (contract 30 March 1593) (*Reg. of Deeds*, xliv. 399).'

p. 18, l. 22, after 'Carmylie,' insert 'secondly, to George Strachan (*Reg. Sec. Sig.*, lxxiv. 132).'

p. 21, ll. 21, 22, for 'after November 1640' read 'contract 20 August 1641 (*Gen. Reg. Sasines*, l. 125).'

p. 22, after l. 8, insert

'1. *Patrick*, baptized 29 September 1646 (Canongate Reg.). He must have died young'; and alter numbers of remaining children accordingly.

p. 22, l. 27, for 'Fifeshire' read 'Forfarshire.'

p. 24, l. 14, for 'Bonomy' read 'Bonamy.'

p. 24, l. 7, after 'NAVAR,' insert 'He was a *connoisseur* of the highest order in all culinary matters, and when he was in London attending Parliament used to stay at the Union Hotel near Trafalgar Square for the sake of the turtle soup for which it was famous. It is said that during his whole Parliamentary career he never opened his mouth except once, when he said "What a shame," in 1815, when the mob attempted to break the windows of St. Stephen's Chapel during the discussion of the Corn Law Bill of that day (*Patrician*, iv. 522).'

p. 24, l. 6 from foot, for '6' read '26' (*Forfar Sasines*, vi. 389).'

p. 26, l. 12, after '1723,' insert 'of pleurisy, aged sixty-eight (Dunbar's *Social Life in Former Days*, i. 119).'

p. 27, l. 12, after '2nd,' insert 'argent.'

PERTH

p. 40, l. 12, after 'charter,' insert note, 'This charter is in the possession of the Earl of Kinnoull. It is dated 4 October 1486, and grants two-thirds of Ladecreif to Walter.'

p. **41**, l. 11 from foot, for 'nephew' read 'brother.'

p. **41**, l. 10 from foot, for 'Kinsale' read 'Kinnoul.'

p. **43**, l. 9, delete 'is said to have.'

p. **43**, l. 15, delete from 'Isobel' down to 'place' in line 17, and insert 'He gave a discharge of part of her tocher to her father 5 March 1478-79 (Argyll Charter-chest), and.'

p. **43**, l. 8 from foot, after 'Innerpeffray,' insert 'He was contracted to Elizabeth, daughter of Andrew, second Lord Gray, which contract was discharged in January 1501-2 (*Acta Dom. Conc.*, xii. 39).'

p. **44**, l. 20, after 'married,' insert 'Dispensation dated 20 January 1530-31 following on Papal mandate of 16 March 1529-30 (originals in possession of the Earl of Kinnoull).'

p. **45**, l. 23, for 'fourth' read 'second.'

p. **46**, l. 22, delete 'possibly on 20 October 1582,' and insert 'died at Stobhall in July 1579 (Inchaffray Papers *penes* Lord Kinnoull).'

p. **46**, last l., for 'before 1592' read '23 December 1587 (Moray Writs, box 3, No. 241).'

p. **47**, l. 3, after '*Catherine*' insert note, 'The Dunfermline Parish Register gives her name as *Margaret*.'

p. **47**, l. 16, after 'career,' insert 'he had an exemption from hostings, etc., being "diseasit in his luggis," 1 August 1587 (*Reg. Sec. Sig.*, lv. 197).'

p. **47**, after l. 27, insert

'3. *Elizabeth*, baptized 1 July 1565 (Canongate Reg.). She must have died young'; and alter numbers of remaining children accordingly.

p. **48**, l. 9, after 'first,' insert '22 June 1602 (Edin. Reg.).'

p. **48**, l. 11, after 'Muchalls, insert 'afterwards first Lord Fraser.'

p. **48**, after l. 11, insert

'9. *Sibitta* (Edinburgh Tests.).

Lord Drummond had also a son *David*, but as he is not named in Lady Drummond's testament he was probably illegitimate.'

p. **48**, l. 19, after 'record,' insert note, 'The date in text is corroborated by the *Fifth Rep. Hist. MSS. Comm.*, 644.'

p. **48**, l. 26, for 'April' read 'November.'

p. **50**, l. 20, delete 'previous to 1 February 1620, when,' and insert '(contract 10 March 1633) on 1 February 1634.'

p. **50**, l. 23, for 'second' read 'first.'

p. **50**, l. 26, for 'secondly' read 'as a third wife' (cf. vol. viii. 415).

p. **51**, l. 3, after '1639,' insert 'contract 28 and 31 October 1639 (*Reg. of Deeds*, DXXIV. 62).'

p. **52**, l. 5 from foot, for '11' read '12 (*Cal. of Stuart Papers*, ii. 145).'

p. **53**, l. 2, after 'secondly,' insert 'contract 5 October 1676 (*Perth Sasines*, vii. 44).'

p. **53**, l. 26, for '*Teresa*' read '*Francesca Teresa*, baptized 9 March 1688 (Canongate Reg.)', and delete 'born in France.'

p. 53, l. 4 from foot, for '1692' read '1693.'

p. 53, l. 3 from foot, delete 'but,' and insert 'On 2 March 1696 he was a prisoner in Stirling Castle (*P. C. Acta*). He afterwards.'

p. 56, l. 20, delete 'the daughter and heiress of Fotheringham,' and insert 'Marjory Gray the heiress of (contract 26 November 1707) (*Perth Sasines*, xvi. 227).'

POLWARTH

p. 82, second line from foot, after '1690,' insert 'Died at Edinburgh 7 May 1749, having married Lieutenant Thomas Gordon, Royal Scots Fusiliers, of the family of Buthlaw (J. M. Bulloch in *Notes and Queries*, 11th ser., ix. 326).'

p. 87, l. 16, quotation mark should follow 'tryste,' not 'horse.'

PRIMROSE

p. 110, l. 23, for '1714' read 'March 1707-8 at St. Peter's upon Cornhill, London (cf. vol. viii. 154).'

QUEENSBERRY

p. 117, after l. 4, insert

'5. *Hugh* (Protocol Book of James Young, 26 October 1497, Edin. City Chambers).'

p. 117, ll. 5, 7, 12, for '5, 6, 7' read '6, 7, 8.'

p. 117, after l. 28, insert

'3. *James* (Protocol Book *ut sup.*, 29 March 1501).'

p. 117, l. 29, for '3' read '4.'

p. 119, l. 7, after 'death,' add note, 'According to the Sheriff Roll of 1544-45 he came of age in December 1521.'

p. 125, l. 23, for '8 July' read '21 June.'

p. 126, l. 25, after '1578,' insert 'He married, first, Marion, daughter of Edward Menzies of Castlehill. There is a contract of 27 September 1549 whereby he was to divorce her and marry Elizabeth M'Clellan, widow of Alexander M'Culloch of Cardines (*Acta Dom. Conc. et Sess.*, xxvi. 76).'

p. 128, after l. 7, insert

'7. *Margaret*, presumably also illegitimate, married to William, son of Herbert Maxwell in Cavens (contract 24 May 1549) (*Acts and Decreets*, iii. 188).'

p. 135, l. 10, after 'married,' insert 'contract 28 July 1640 (*Reg. of Deeds*, DXXXI. 45).'

p. 136, l. 13, after 'secondly,' insert 'contract 26 March 1635 (*Reg. of Deeds*, Mackenzie, 6 November 1668).'

p. 140, after l. 17, insert

'4. *Margaret*, buried in Holyrood Church in March 1662 (Canongate Reg.).

5. *Henrietta*, baptized 3 January 1662 (*Ibid.*).'

p. 140, l. 18, for '4' read '6.'

p. 140, l. 19, after '1697,' insert 'and married the same day.'

p. 143, l. 13, after '*Jean*,' insert 'born at London 24 May 1701.'

p. 143, l. 19, after '*Anne*,' insert 'born at Edinburgh 12 February 1706 (*Peerage of England*, London, 1709).'

p. 143, l. 23, after 'father,' add 'having been born at Edinburgh, 24 November 1698 (*Political State of Great Britain*, 1711).'

p. 144, after l. 3 from foot, insert

'3. *Catherine*, born 21 November 1724; died 4 February 1725 (*Historical Register*).'

p. 146, l. 2, after 'original,' insert 'According to the *Privy Council Acta* the patent was stopped by the Council 30 April 1697, on the complaint of Viscount Teviot that the title Peebles had already been granted to him. But on 8 June following, a letter from the King (dated 24 May), was read, stating that it was his pleasure that the Earl should have the title Peebles, and that the Viscount's title was to be changed.'

p. 147, l. 5 from foot, after 'Queensberry,' insert 'He was infeft in Kelhead in virtue of a contract with his brother, the second Earl (*Reg. of Deeds*, DXXVI. 187).'

p. 148, l. 13, after 'Sophia,' insert 'He was baptized 9 March 1648, his mother being then dead (Canongate Reg.).'

p. 148, l. 15, after 'married,' insert 'contract 19 September 1676, Elizabeth, daughter of Thomas Ellis, merchant, Perth (*Reg. of Deeds*, Durie, 1 April 1679).'

p. 155, l. 5 from foot, after '4th,' insert 'argent.'

p. 155, last line, transfer 'for *Mar*' to the previous line, after 'or.'

REAY

p. 166, l. 19, after 'divorced,' insert 'yet he was in 1606 charged to adhere to her (*Gen. Reg. Inhibitions*, xvii. 272).'

p. 166, l. 2 from foot, for '1618' read '1619 (she had a charter as his future wife on 29 July of the latter year) (*Inverness Sasines*, i. 159).'

p. 169, after l. 23, insert 'In 1652 there is mention of Dame Rachel Mackay, relict of Donald, Lord Reay, then wife of Captain Thomas Kakyne; and of Donald Mackay, her son by Lord Reay (*Gen. Reg. Inhibitions*, 20 November 1652).'

ROLLO

p. 187, l. 16, delete comma after 'James.'

p. 187, l. 20, after 'Banks,' insert note, 'He was apparently twice married, as there is a renunciation and grant of redemption by Mr. Thomas Rollock, advocate, and his spouse, Grizel Scott, of the lands of Castlerankine and others, in the barony of Herbertshire, 26 October 1605 *Wigtown Charter-Chest*, Scot. Rec. Soc., Nos. 697, 699).'

p. 191, l. 21, after 'Balbegy, nsert 'died after 22 August 1621 and before

15 August 1622 (*Reg. of Deeds*, cccxxxix. 358; *Acts and Decreets*, ccclx. 278).'

p. **191**, after l. 24, insert

'ii. *Margaret*, married, contract 22 August 1621, to Richard Blyth, portioner of Craigie (*Reg. of Deeds*, cccxxxix. 358).

iii. *Isobel* (*Acts and Decreets*, ccclx. 278).'

p. **191**, l. 25, for 'ii.' read 'iv.'

p. **191**, l. 25, after 'married,' insert 'contract 1 March 1633 (*Perth Sasines*, vi. 222).'

p. **203**, l. 5, after 'sudenlie,' insert 'On 14 June 1696 she obtained decreet against him for aliment, he having deserted her and lived with another woman (*P. C. Decreta*).'

p. **207**, l. 15 from foot, for 'Robinson' read 'Robertson.'

p. **207**, l. 11 from foot, for 'Grey,' read 'Gray.'

ROSEBERY

p. **219**, l. 23, for 'James' read 'John.'

p. **227**, l. 7, delete comma after 'Stewart.'

p. **228**, l. 12, after '1894-95,' insert 'By Patent, dated 3 July 1911, he was created Earl of Midlothian, Viscount Mentmore of Mentmore, Bucks, and Baron Epsom of Epsom, Surrey.'

p. **229**, l. 1, after '1828,' insert semicolon, and add 'Earl of Midlothian, Viscount Mentmore of Mentmore, Bucks, and Baron Epsom of Epsom, Surrey.'

ANCIENT EARLS OF ROSS

p. **235**, l. 3 from foot, for '1316' read '1315.'

ROSS, LORD ROSS

p. **250**, after l. 11 insert

'3. Perhaps *Elizabeth*, married to Thomas Sempill, Sheriff of Renfrew (see *post*, p. 530).'

p. **252**, l. 12, after '10 May 1562,' insert 'contract dated 22 February 1561-62, at which date she had curators (*Wigtown Charter-Chest*, Scot. Rec. Soc., No. 327, where the date is erroneously given as 1571).'

p. **256**, l. 18, after 'Baronet,' add 'She was his future wife 18 March 1688 (*Gen. Reg. Sasines*, xlvii. 145).'

p. **261**, l. 11, for '10' read '21 (List of children by Lord Ross in Kelburne Family Bible).'

p. **261**, l. 15, for '18 July 1687,' read '26 December 1688 (List *ut sup.*).'

p. **261**, l. 17, for '1662' read '1692.'

p. **263**, l. 4, delete '1502,' and insert 'some time before 31 May 1499.'

ROTHES

p. 306, l. 11, for 'Earl' read 'Marquess.'
p. 308, l. 7, for 'March' read 'May.'
p. 308, l. 7, for 'Shrub Hall' read 'Shrub Hill.'
p. 311, l. 4, after 'Caskieberrie,' insert '29 May 1680.'

ROXBURGHE

p. 323, l. 25, for 'August 1484' read '3 July 1483 (*Acta Dom. Audit.*, 111*).'
p. 325, ll. 1 and 2 from foot, delete 'He is said to have been the ancestor of the Kers of Greenhead,' and accompanying note (cf. vol. v. 52, 53).
p. 326, l. 9 from foot, for '1571' read '1471.'
p. 331, l. 6, after '1551,' insert 'His will was dated 16 July 1551. He had a curious interview with his eldest son Andrew concerning it (Protocol Book of Sir William Corbet, *Scot. Rec. Soc.* Nos. 63, 64).'
p. 332, l. 8, for '1493' read '1488.'
p. 332, note 3, for '*Ibid.*' read '*Acta Dom. Conc.*'
p. 334, after l. 25, insert
'4. *Robert*, a witness, 24 January 1535-36 (Protocol Book of Thomas Kene, Adv. Lib.).'
p. 334, ll. 26, 27, for '4, 5' read '5, 6.'
p. 338, ll. 19, 20, for 'is said to have been' read 'was.'
p. 338, l. 21, after 'Douglas' insert 'of Drumlanrig,' and for '19 February 1556' read '19 February 1556-57 (*Reg. of Deeds*, ii. 79).'
p. 339, ll. 14, 15, delete from 'It does' down to 'issue and.'
p. 339, l. 17, after '1573,' add 'He had a son and heir *Andrew*, infeft in an annualrent out of Morham, 12 December 1570 (orig. instrument in H. M. Reg. Ho.).'
p. 339, l. 18, after 'married,' insert 'contract 1 December 1558 (*Reg. of Deeds*, iii. 117).'
p. 341, after l. 20, insert
'5. *Jean*, married to George Towris of Inverleith: she was his future wife 2 August 1601 (*Edin. Sasines, Secretary's Reg.*, ii. 197).'
p. 344, ll. 29 and 30, delete 'the second, third, or fourth and youngest daughters of the said Harry, Lord Ker.'
p. 345, l. 14, for 'feuar' read 'fiar.'
p. 346, l. 23, after 'first,' insert 'contract 12 and 14 October 1618 (*Reg. of Deeds*, cccxiii. 816)': and after 'Pitcur,' insert 'she was his widow in 1620 (*Ibid*).'
p. 347, l. 5, for 'step-brother' read 'half brother.'
p. 347, l. 6 from foot, after 'married,' insert 'at Glamis, 4 February 1638 (*Chronicle of Perth*, 35).'
p. 347, l. 5 from foot, after '1638,' insert reference, '*Reg. of Deeds*, DXLI. 7.'
p. 348, line 4, after 'married,' insert 'contract 5 December 1660 (*Wigtown Charter-chest*, Scot. Rec. Soc., No. 348; *Reg. of Deeds*, Mack., 3 February 1663, where 1 December is given as the date).'

p. **348**, after l. 17, insert

'The Earl had two natural daughters, *Margaret*, married, contract 30 November 1614, to John Mow, younger of that Ilk (*Gen. Reg. of Inhibs.*, 30 December 1616), and *Cecill*, who in 1636 was wife of John Ker of Gaitschaw (*Gen. Reg. of Sasines*, xlv. 24).'

p. **349**, l. 12, for '8 May' read '6 May (*The Royal Navy*, by W. Laird Clowes, 1898, ii. 457).'

p. **355**, l. 9. for 'He was dead before 1574' read 'He died in April 1565 (*Exch. Rolls*. xx. 443).'

p. **355**, l. 30, delete 'and widow of John, eighth Lord Glamis.'

p. **356**, note 3, for '356' read '536.

p. **357**, l. 5, for 'eighty-five' read 'eighty-seven.'

p. **357**, l. 11, for 'before' read 'after.'

RUTHERFORD

p. **366**, l. 1, delete entire line and accompanying reference note.

p. **366**, after line 13, insert

'William of Rutherford, son and heir of the above. William was a minor on 6 November 1363, on which dateKing Edward III. granted to John Ker the custody of his lands till his majority, and his marriage (*Cal. Doc. Scot.*, iv. 89).'

p. **366**, l. 18, delete 'was ambassador to England in 1398,' and note.

p. **366**, l, 23, delete 'was Warden of the Marches in 1400, and,' and note.

p. **366**, l. 7 from foot, for 'treaty' read 'truce.'

p. **373**, after l. 26 insert

'*f. Janet*, married, first, George Thomson, maltman, Leith; secondly, 1632, Patrick Whitelaw of that Ilk.'

p. **379**, l. 18, after '1648,' add 'She was buried in the Greyfriars, Edinburgh 24 April 1671.'

p. **380**, after l. 10, insert

'Another daughter, *Lilias*, was married, contract 25 November 1677, to Mr. William Douglas of Plewland (*Reg. of Deeds*, Durie, 22 March 1681).'

p. **381**, l. 12 from foot, for '1724' read '22 November 1720 (mourning ring *penes* Mr. Ernest Radcliffe Crump, *ex inform.* T. E. Watson, Esq.).'

p. **381**, l. 6 from foot, after 'father,' add 'being buried 14 February 1710 (Elsdon Par. Reg.).'

RUTHVEN

p. **387**, l. 8, after 'secondly,' insert '22 April 1673 (Canongate Reg.).'

p. **392**, l. 10, for 'uncle' read 'granduncle.'

ST. COLME

p. **394**, l. 16, for 'Moucastell' read 'Moncastell.'

p. **394**, l. 24, after '1581,' insert 'He was again appointed Commendator thereof on his father's resignation 20 April 1587 (*Reg. Sec. Sig.*, lv. 53).'

p. **394**, l. 26, after 'Inchmahome,' insert 'in 1592 he appears as tutor-at-law of his nephew, James, Earl of Moray (*Reg. of Deeds*, xliii. 261).'

p. **395**, l. 6, after 'issue,' insert 'besides two daughters, *Anna* and *Jean* (*Gen. Reg. of Inhibs.* (6 September 1616).'

p. **395**, l. 15, after 'ascertained,' insert 'but it was before 17 August 1643 (Moray Writs, box v. No. 1019).'

p. **395**, note 2, after '1614,' insert 'The Canongate Register, however, states that he was buried at Holyrood 27 June 1612).'

SALTOUN (ABERNETHY)

p. **405**, l. 7 from foot, after 'son,' insert 'and possibly a daughter, *Marion*, styled daughter of Sir George Abernethy of St. Andrews diocese in a Papal mandate for a dispensation for her marriage with John, son of Sir Alexander Stewart of Glasgow diocese, they being in the fourth degree of consanguinity (*Reg. Aven.*, cxcvii. 33).' She may, however, have been a sister of Sir George.

p. **406**, note 5, for '351' read 96.'

p. **412**, l. 14, for '1586' read '1566.'

p. **412**, l. 18, for 'which' read 'who.'

p. **414**, l. 8, for '21 September' read '13 July (Moray Writs, box iv, No. 480).'

p. **416**, for 'belted,' read belled.'

SALTOUN (FRASER)

p. **434**, l. 5, delete 'Sir.'

p. **440**, l. 21, for '*Margaret*' read '*Anna*.'

p. **440**, l. 22, for '31' read '14,' and at end of sentence add, 'She died in July 1663 (Slains Charters).'

p. **449**, l. 8 from foot, for 'Cambria' read 'Cambrai.'

p. **452**, l. 20, for 'Essex' read 'Sussex.'

SEAFIELD

p. **463**, l. 2 from foot, after 'issue,' insert 'She obtained decreet of divorce against him for adultery 30 July 1576 (*Hist. Records Fam. of Leslie*, iii. 73), and was married, secondly, to William Cumming of Inverallochy (*Aberdeen Hornings*, 7 May 1584).'

p. **464**, l. 20, after '1584,' insert 'In 1582 she was suing for divorce from him (*Edin. Inhibitions*, i. 134).'

p. **465**, l. 10, after 'married,' insert 'first (contract 2 December 1596), Grizel, sister of Alexander Menzies of that Ilk (*Reg. of Deeds*, lxviii. 193); secondly.'

p. **475**, l. 18, after 'Lanark,' insert 'She was his future wife 27 June 1665 (*Gen. Reg. Sasines*, xii. 235).'

p. **493**, l. 9, after '1882,' insert 'married, 9 April 1912, to the Rev. William Rice, Rector of Sympson, Bucks.'

SEAFORTH

p. 501, l. 4 from foot, for '14' read '19.'

p. 502, l. 2 from foot, after '*Murdoch*,' insert 'of Melbost and Kernsarie, and of Inverewe. Married Catherine Mackenzie and had a son *John*, said to have been killed at Auldearn, and two daughters, *Marjory*, married to Alexander Mackenzie of Cliff, and *Barbara*, married to Thomas Graham of Drynie (*Reg. of Hornings and Inhibs.*, *Inverness*, 2d series, ii. 193, 18 September 1649).'

p. 505, l. 6, for 'Margaret' read 'Isobel (Haddington Bap. Reg.).'

p. 509, l. 3, after 'Cromarty,' insert 'She had a charter as his future wife, 31 May 1655 (*Banff Sasines*, vii. 135).'

p. 509, l. 8 from foot, after '1674,' insert note, 'The date in the text is that given in Fraser's *Sutherland Book*, (i. 515), but in the *Reg. of Deeds*, Mackenzie (23 July 1709), it is stated to have been 8 September 1675.'

p. 510, l. 3, after 'Seaforth,' insert 'baptized 8 December 1661 (Kinghorn Reg.).'

p. 511, l. 17, after 'her,' insert 'Her fine complexion is said to have been ruined and to have become a lemon tint. Pope in his *Satires* mentions the incident in the line "poison from Deloraine." (See also Croker's *Lady Suffolk's Letters*).'

p. 511, last l., after 'unmarried,' add 'being drowned at Paris while skating, 8 December 1774 (*Lyon in Mourning*, Scot. Hist. Soc., iii. 348).'

p. 511, note 2, after '136,' add 'vi. 184.'

SELKIRK

p. 519, l. 6 from foot, after '1703,' insert 'Warrant to bury him in Holyrood Church, dated 23 June 1703 (*P. C. Acta*).'

SEMPILL

p. 530, ll. 4, 5, delete from 'and probably' down to 'apparent' and relative footnote 4.

p. 530, l. 17, for '1480' read '1470 (the former date is a misprint in the Commission Report).'

p. 535, l. 4, after 'On,' insert '28 August 1616 he was denounced rebel for frequenting the company of Mr. John Ogilvie, Jesuit (*Reg. of Hornings*, 12 February 1617), and on 13 May 1618 his escheat was granted to Mr. John Fentoun, comptroller-clerk to the King (*Rec. Sec. Sig.*). However, he seems quickly to have regained the royal favour, for on.'

p. 547, l. 5 from foot, for 'relieve' read 'rescue.'

p. 552, l. 12, for 'nephew' read 'cousin.'

p. 555, l. 2 from foot, delete 'and,' and insert 'was served heir to Francis, eighth Lord Sempill, 4 November 1684 (*Hist. MSS. Com.*, *Report on Stuart Papers*, iv. 81; cf. *post*, p. 559). He.'

p. 558, l. 7, after 'him,' insert 'till February 1688 (*Seafield Correspondence*, Scot. Hist. Soc., 42).'

p. 558, after l. 22, insert 'On 11 February 1705 three shillings Scots were given by the kirk-session of Innerwick "to ane called a daughter of my Lord Semple, having a testimoniall from the Tolbooth Church in Edinburgh." She was probably illegitimate.'

p. 559, ll. 20, 21, delete from 'for' to 'was,' and insert 'for Robert Sempill (son of Dykehead; see *ante*, p. 555) says he was served heir to the estate and declared Lord Sempill, but by indirect means the heir-general kept this estate and assumed the title (*Hist. MSS. Com., Rep. on Stuart Papers*, iv. 81).'

p. 564, l. 33, for 'baronetcy' read 'barony.'

SINCLAIR

p. 571, after l. 4, insert

'5. *Marjory*, married to Sir Alexander M'Culloch of Mertoun. She is called 'oo' of George, first Earl of Rothes (*Acta Dom. Conc.*, xii. 97).'

p. 572, note 1, for 'xiii.' read 'xiv.'

p. 573, l. 21, for 'Mariota' read 'Agnes'; 'after 'Bruce,' insert 'She is styled "pretended" relict of William, Lord Sinclair, 14 January 1571-72 (*Acts and Decreets*, xlix. 4).'

p. 573, l. 6 from foot, after '1575,[9]' insert 'He married, secondly, contract 29 July 1578 (original instrument in H. M. Reg. Ho.), Beatrix, daughter of Sir William Sinclair of Roslin.'

p. 574, l. 26, after 'thirty-six,' insert 'He was contracted, 21 March 1564-65, to Marion, eldest daughter of William Maitland, younger of Lethington (*Acts and Decreets*, xxxi. 391).'

p. 574, l. 28, for 'fourth' read 'fifth.'

p. 574, l. 6 from foot, after '*Catherine*,' insert 'married to Sir George Hamilton of Blackburn (*Reg. Mag. Sig.*, 21 April 1618).'

p. 574, l. 2 from foot, after 'married,' insert 'first, Catherine Nisbet (*Reg. of Deeds*, xxxvi. 109), secondly, contract 20 June 1600 (*Ibid.* ccxix. 486).'

p. 574, l. 2 from foot, for 'James' read 'Sir John.'

p. 575, l. 2, after 'Williamston,' insert 'and thirdly, John Rolland (Douglas's *Baronage*, 311).'

p. 575, l. 25, after '*Jane*,' insert 'married to George Seton of Parbroath (*Fife Inhibitions*, 6 June 1608).'

p. 580, l. 14, after 'married,' insert 'first,' and after 'Wedderburn,' insert 'and secondly, to George Ker of Samuelston (*Acta Dom. Conc.*, ix. 95).'

p. 580, l. 6 from foot, after 'Kimmerghame,' insert 'He was probably the father of

1. JOHN, who succeeded.
2. *William*, and
3. *Patrick*, both mentioned in the will of their brother John.'

p. **581**, l. 10, for '1514,' read '1514-15,' and add, 'in his will of 21 August 1513, when he was *iturus ad guerram Anglie*, he mentions, without naming, two daughters not forisfamiliated.'

p. **582**, l. 26, for 'before 12 January 1565-66,' read 'in 1563 (*Acts and Decreets*, xxxiv. 80).'

p. **582**, l. 7 from foot, after 'executors,' insert 'She was dead in May 1569 (*Acts and Decreets*, xliv. 24), and apparently before 7 March 1568-69, when her son was seised in lands which she had held in conjunct fee (*Exch. Rolls*, xx. 394).'

p. **583**, l. 11, after 'after,' insert, 'He came of age in 1566, and was seised of the estates 7 May 1567 (*Exch. Rolls*, xix. 561), except the lands which his mother had in conjunct-fee, of which he was not seised till 7 March 1568-69 (*Ibid.* xx. 394).'

p. **585**, l. 16, after 'married,' insert 'first, 13 March 1705, Margaret, daughter of John Home of Ninewells (Canongate Reg.), and secondly,'

p. **585**, l. 17, for 'Thomas' read 'Andrew (*Genealogist*, iii. 112).'

p. **587**, l. 24, before 'ultimately,' insert 'whose descendants.'

p. **587**, l. 24, for 'the heir' read 'heirs.'

p. **588**, l. 26, for 'L'Orient' read 'Lorient.'

p. **589**, note 3, for 'fraternal' read 'paternal.'

p. **592**, l. 10, for 'January' read 'July.'

VOL. VIII.

Editorial Note, l. 12, for 'second' read 'third.'

SOMERVILLE

p. **9**, l. 15, after '*Mary*,' insert 'erroneously.'

p. **9**, l. 17, after '1427,' add, 'but except the *Memorie* there is no authority for this statement (cf. *infra*, pp. 424, 425).'

p. **17**, note 10, delete '10 July to 10 August 1546, 19 March 1546-47,' and insert 'i. 24, 65.'

p. **19**, note 15, for 'xi.' read 'xv.'

p. **24**, l. 20, for 'in January' read 'between 10 February and 20 April (*Reg. of Deeds*, xli. 172, 268).'

p. **24**, l. 3 from foot, for '*Robert*,' read '*Helen*,' and insert note, 'These illegitimate children were not the children of Lord Somerville, but of his eldest son William.'

p. **26**, l. 22, for 'first' read 'seventh.'

p. **26**, note 5, for '*Ibid.*' read '*Memorie*, ii.'

p. **28**, l. 7, for 'granduncle' read 'kinsman.'

p. **32**, l. 1, for 'Foot Guards' read 'in Scotland.'

p. **32**, l. 15, after 'married,' insert 'contract 23 March 1695 (*Edin. Sas.*, lvi. 340).'

p. **34**, note 4, after 'Heirs,' add, 'Gilbert, however, was not the brother of the twelfth Lord's *atavus*, but of his *abavus*, or great-great-grandfather.'

SOUTHESK

p. **57**, note 2, for '363' read '313.'

p. **66**, l. 16, for 'Lindsay' read 'Hamilton.'

p. **66**, l. 31, after 'secondly,' insert '(contract 6 June 1643) (Inv. of Writs of Drumry at Crawford Priory).'

p. **67**, l. 7, for 'in' read '14 October,' and for 'Inchbrayock' read 'Inchbrock.'

p. **67**, l. 20, after '1654,' insert '(contract 12 December 1654, tocher 18,000 merks).'

p. **68**, l. 5, after 'contract,' insert '30.'

p. **80**, l. 3 from foot, delete from 'In 1747,' down to end of sentence.

Note.—The statement made in the *History of the Carnegies* cannot be true, as Sir John died in 1729.

p. **90**, l. 13, after 'year,' insert 'was.'

SPYNIE

p. **108,** l. 2, after 'Earl,' insert 'of.'

p. **113,** l. 15, after 'Cavalry,' insert 'Died 16 May 1911.'

STAIR

p. **124,** l. 5, after 'Cousland,' insert (*vide* p. 121).'

p. **126,** l. 11, after 'her,' insert 'who died shortly before 20 March 1708 (*Seafield Corr.*, Scot. Hist. Soc., 465).'

p. **131,** l. 8, for 'Montgomery' read 'Montgomerie.'

p. **131,** line 5 from foot, after 'of,' insert 'General.'

p. **132,** l. 31, for 'grandfather' read 'brother Hew, 26 July 1746.'

p. **133,** l. 3, after 'and,' insert 'Ensign.'

p. **133,** l. 5, delete 'lieut.-colonel Scots Fusilier Guards,' and insert 'captain and lieut.-colonel 1 April 1795.'

p. **133,** l. 12, transpose reference no. 8 to after 'there.'

p. **135,** l. 7, after 'Elphinstone,' insert '-Dalrymple.'

p. **137,** l. 5 from foot, after 'Douglas,' insert 'of St. Christopher's (cf. p. 131).'

p. **147,** ll. 19, 20, delete from 'in the lifetime' to end of sentence, and insert 'in March 1682 from a fall from his horse (*ex inform.* Capt. J. Hope, St. Mary's Isle).'

p. **147,** note 8, for 'large' read 'Large.'

p. **149,** l. 20, for 'James' read 'John.'

p. **153,** l. 16, for '1714' read '1743.'

p. **155,** l. 14, after 'surviving,' insert 'son of William.'

p. **161,** l. 7, after '1886,' insert 'married 14 January 1913 to Lieut. J. G. Ingham, R.N.'

p. **163,** l. 6 from foot, for 'eighth' read 'third.'

p. **163,** l. 6 from foot, after 'Winton' read 'of the creation of 1859.'

STIRLING

p. **169,** l. 7 from foot, insert '*Note.*—From the dates it seems doubtful that these children, *William* and *John*, were sons of William of Menstrie, though it is so stated in the Apprentice Register.'

p. **170,** l. 14, for 'Dubbiehead, co. Stirling,' read 'Dubheads, co. Perth (*Retours*, *Perth*, 473).'

p. **173,** l. 26, for 'in' read 'on.'

p. **176,** l. 4 from foot, for '1523' read '1623.'

p. **177,** l. 23, after 'married,' insert '28.'

p. **177,** l. 24, delete 'Lord Sandilands afterwards.'

p. **185,** l. 15, for 'gules' read 'azure.'

STORMONT

p. **190,** l. 15, after '1598,' insert note, 'The date in text is given in the Appendix to Lamont's *Diary* as having been copied from a journal of Moncrieff of Carnbee. But the procuratory of resignation following on the marriage-contract is dated 25 January 1598-99 (Adv. Lib. MS., 34.6.24, p. 249). And they were still only future spouses 24 April 1599 (*Reg. Mag. Sig.*).'

p. **190**, after l. 17 insert
'4. ***Christian*** (*Fife Sasines*, x. 286).'

p. **198**, l. 18, for 'before 30 July 1613' read 'six months before 7 September 1597 (*Fife Sheriff Court Books*).'

p. **198**, l. 8 from foot, for 'before 1614' read 'before 7 September 1597, when her brother David was served heir to her (*Fife Sheriff Court Books*).'

p. **200**, l. 5, before 'Drumcairn,' insert 'of.'

p. **214**, l. 15, after 'gules,' insert 'three.'

p. **214**, l. 16, after 'patée,' insert 'argent.'

STRATHALLAN

p. **217**, l. 6 from foot, after '1625,' insert 'She was buried in Holyrood Church 15 July 1668 (Canongate Register).'

p. **218**, l. 26, after 'time,' insert 'In 1658 he appears to have been incarcerated in the Edinburgh Tolbooth at the instance of his mother, but she agreed to his liberation 3 January 1659 (*Book of Old Edinburgh Club*, iv. 130).'

p. **221**, note 6, for '*Ibid.*' read '*Genealogical Memoir of the House of Drummond*, Edinburgh, 1808.'

p. **222**, l. 20, delete '(often called Elizabeth).'

p. **222**, l. 21, after '1669,' for comma put full stop, and delete remainder of sentence.

p. **222**, after l. 22, insert
'3. *Elizabeth* married, contract 20 September 1683, to Thomas, seventh Earl of Kinnoul (cf. vol. v. 231, *corrig.*).'

p. **222**, ll. 23, 24, for 'born 18, baptized 27' read 'baptized 3.'

p. **222**, l. 9 from foot, after 'married,' insert 'before 14 January 1688 (*Seafield Corr.*, Scot. Hist. Soc., 40).'

p. **223**, note 6, delete note.

p. **226**, l. 13 from foot, for 'W. P. Brigstocke' read 'William Brigstock, M.P., of Birdcombe Court, co. Somerset.'

p. **229**, ll. 5, 6, for 'died young' read 'fifth Viscount of Strathallan.'

p. **229**, l. 7, delete entry.

p. **229**, ll. 8, 9, 19, 21, 22, for '3, 4, 5, 6, 7' read '2, 3, 4, 5, 6.'

p. **229**, l. 8, after '*Charles*' insert '*Edward Louis Casimir John Silvester Mary*.'

p. **229**, l. 8, for '19' read '23.'

p. **229**, l. 22, for '13' read '12.'

p. **232**, l. 15 from foot, for '5' read '7,' and after 'London' insert 'born 7 February 1730.'

p. **233**, after l. 15 insert

'8. *Margaret*, born 24 April 1714.

9. *Anne*, born 3 June 1715.

10. *Katherine*, born 7 August 1716.

11. *Mary*, born 23 September 1717.

12. *Clementina Maria*, born 29 March 1721.

13. *Amelia Anne Sophia*, born 27 October 1727.

(All these mentioned in *The Oliphants of Gask*, 113.)'

p. **233**, l. 25, after 'Abergeldie,' insert 'for the romantic story of their marriage, see *The Oliphants of Gask*, 113.'

p. **233**, after l. 26, insert

'1 and 2. Twins, a boy and a girl, born before 6 August 1751, "in the ninth month," which seems to imply that the marriage took place in November 1750 (*The Oliphants of Gask*, 228).' And alter the numbers of children accordingly.

p. **233**, l. 9 from foot, after 'advocate' insert 'She died 1821.'

p. **233**, l. 7 from foot, after *Elizabeth*, insert 'died unmarried 1831 (*The Oliphants of Gask*, 228).'

p. **236**, l. 10, for 'Graham' read 'Graeme.'

p. **236**, l. 11 from foot, after 'issue,' insert 'and died at Edinburgh 5 November 1912.'

p. **236**, l. 7 from foot, for 'Francis' read 'Frances.'

ANCIENT EARLS OF STRATHEARN

p. **241**, note 10, for '*Ecelesia de Scion*' read '*Ecclesiæ de Scone*.'

MORAY, EARL OF STRATHEARN

p. **256**, l. 12, after 'Mary,' insert 'of.'

STEWART, EARLS OF STRATHEARN

p. **260**, l. 23, after '1425,' insert 'mandate for dispensation dated 24 February 1422-23 (*Cal. of Papal Letters*, vii. 251).'

STRATHMORE

p. **277**, l. 4, after 1492, insert reference no. '2.'

p. **280**, after l. 25, insert

'3. *Agnes* (*Acta Dom. Conc.*, xl. 120.'

p. **280**, l. 26, for '3' read '5' (see footnote 8).

p. **296**, l. 8, for 'Drumkibbo' read 'Drumkilbo.'

p. **304**, l. 2 from foot, for '1706-24' read '1706-23.'

p. **308**, l. 9, for 'Chaventon' read 'Charenton.'

p. **313**, l. 14, for 'ever' read 'never.'

p. **315**, l. 26, for 'Gordon-Rebow' read 'Gurden-Rebow.'

p. **316**, l. 21, for 'Francis' read 'Frances.'

p. **316**, l. 25, for '23' read '28.'

SUTHERLAND

p. **352**, footnote 1, for 'Canongate' read 'Haddington.'

p. **364**, l. 10 from foot, after 1888, insert 'married, 11 April 1912, Lady Eileen Gwladys Butler, elder daughter of the Earl of Lanesborough.'

LIVINGSTON, VISCOUNT TEVIOT

p. **369**, l. 6 from foot, after 'sister,' insert 'She married, before 8 June 1449, John of Kynninmond of that Ilk (Macfarlane's *Gen. Coll.*, ii. 536).'

p. **372**, ll. 22, 23, delete from 'is further said,' down to 'Somerville' and insert '(probably between the other two), Jean Somerville, who was mother of both his children (Birthbrief cited in footnote 11; *Reg. of Deeds*, ccclxiii. 157). The Birthbrief calls her Agnes, and states that she was a daughter of Lord Somerville, but she does not occur in the Somerville article. The Deed also mentions Marion Baillie, and implies that she was a daughter of Archibald Baillie of Auldston, and was previously married, contract 17 August 1575, to Robert Grahame of Westhall (*Reg. of Deeds*, xiv. 300).'

p. **374**, l. 30, after 'sergeant-major,' delete from 'of' to '1665' on l. 32, and insert 'in Buccleuch's, Kirkpatrick's, and Drummond's Regiments, becoming lieutenant-colonel 11 June 1660 (*Scots Brigade in Holland*, Scot. Hist. Soc., i. *passim*).'

TORPHICHEN

p. **378**, l. 9, after 'Lord,' insert 'of.'

p. **378**, l. 19, delete from 'He was' down to 'David II.' on l. 21.

p. **378**, l. 22, for 'in that year' read '1347.'

p. **385**, l. 15, for 'she' read 'he.'

p. **389**, l. 12, after '*Elizabeth*,' insert 'married in April 1644, as his third wife, to John Gibbeson, minister of Dalmeny (*Reg. of Deeds*, DLvii. 115), and died the same year (Scott's *Fasti Eccl. Scot.*, i. 181). There was another daughter, *Anna*: she and Elizabeth were heirs portioners of their brothers (*Reg. of Deeds*, DL. 102).'

p. **393**. l. 6 from foot, for 'Viscount Canada' read 'Lord Alexander.'

p. **398**, l. 5, for 'has' read 'had issue.'

p. **398**, l. 19, for 'gules' read 'or.'

TRAQUAIR

p. **399**. after l. 4 from foot, insert

'4. *Margaret*, who had or claimed some right to the lands of Ormiston, in Peeblesshire (*Acta Dom. Conc. et Sess.*, iv. 114).'

p. **400**, l. 5 from foot, after 'Knox,' insert 'who may have been the Lady Traquair who was buried in September 1623 (Canongate Reg.).'

TWEEDDALE

p. **417**, l. 18, for 'Militis, Domini' read 'Miles et Dominus.

p. **418**, l, 2 from foot, delete 'of Locherworth.' *Note.*—It is uncertain whether the Sir Gilbert who swore fealty to Edward I. in 1296 was Sir Gilbert of Locherworth or his contemporary Sir Gilbert of Erroll.

p. **421**, l. 10 from foot, delete '3 October 1357,' and insert '30 March 1389, but was dead before 29 August 1392 (*Laing Charters*, No. 379, (7) (8)). It is obviously he, and not his grandson William, who was Sheriff of Peebles in 1388 (*Exch. Rolls*, iii. 167).'

p. **422**, l. 24, delete from 'shortly' to 'widow,' on l. 26, and insert 'not later than 1397 as his son William witnesses a charter as William Hay of Locherworth in or before that year (*Laing Charters*, No. 379 (9)).'

p. **423**, l. 15, delete from 'He' down to 'and,' on l. 18, and insert 'He was knighted before.'

p. **424**, l. 5, after 'William,' insert 'is said to have.'

p. **424**, l. 7, for 'six' read 'four.'

p. **424**, l. 7, for 'he' read 'to have.'

p. **424**, l. 8, after 'rents,' insert 'But though he and others, the co-lords of Yester and patrons of the Kirk of Bothans, petitioned on 1 August 1420 for the erection of the Kirk into a College, it was not till 22 April 1421, by which time he was dead, that the petition was granted by the Bishop of St. Andrews (original at Yester).'

p. **424**, l. 15, for 'August' read '12 April, when his widow took instruments upon the consent of the rector of Bothans to the foundation of the college (original at Yester).'

p. **424**, l. 19, after 'Erroll,' insert note, 'It is doubtful whether this lady was a Hay at all. Her seal appended to her charter of mortification 23 February 1447-48 to the altar of the B.V.M. in the kirk of Bothans bears the arms of Hay of Yester impaling three stars or cinquefoils (original at Yester).'

p. **425**, l. 3, for '1418' read '26 January 1418-19 (Yester Writs).'

p. **425**, l. 7 from foot, delete from 'was still living 1451' down to 'Yester' in l. 3 from foot, and insert 'died in 1463 (retour of his son 12 March 1466-67, Yester Writs).'

p. **425**, last line, delete from 'If so,' down to '1517' on l. 2 of p. **426**.

p. **426**, l. 7, after 'daughter,' insert 'She married, secondly, before 2 April 1467, Patrick Dunbar of Bele, and was his widow in 1488 (Yester Writs; *Acta Dom. Aud.*, 114).'

p. **426**, after l. 10, insert

'5. *Mr. Hugh*, who appears as a witness, 1440-1447, to several charters of his brothers (Yester Writs).'

p. **426**, l. 11, for '5' read '6.'

p. **426,** l. 14, for '1425' read '3 December 1414 (original at Yester).

p. **426,** ll. 16, 19, 33, for '6, 7, 8' read '7, 8, 9.'

p. **426,** last line, delete from 'John,' down to 'Hunter,' on l. 7 of p. **427.** *Note.*—John Hay of Oliver Castle in 1475 was son and heir of Sir David Hay of Yester, and afterwards first Lord Hay of Yester.'

p. **427,** l. 14, for '1422' read '1432 (*Reg. Nig. de Aberbrothock*, No. 65).'

p. **427,** l. 2 from foot, for 'the same year, and certainly before 6 April 1434' read 'in February 1433-34.'

p. **428,** l. 5 from foot, for '1 March 1478-79' read '2 September 1478, when brieves of inquest were issued to his son (Yester Writs).'

p. **429,** after l. 11, insert

'2. *William,* who is a witness, 1470-1482, to various deeds by his father and brother (Yester Writs).'

p. **429,** l. 12, for '2' read '3.'

p. **429,** l. 13, delete 'apparently.'

p. **429,** after l. 18, insert

'4. *Robert,* who is a witness to an indenture and charter by his father in 1470 and 1474 (Yester Writs).'

p. **429,** l. 19, for '3' read '5.'

p. **429,** l. 19, delete 'married to Sir Niel Cuningham of Barns, co. Fife.'

p. **430,** l. 12 from foot, for 'before 9 November 1508' read 'in September 1508 (Retour of second Lord, Yester Writs).'

p. **430,** l. 8 from foot, after '1468,' insert 'dispensation dated 3 August 1469 (Yester Writs).'

p. **431,** l. 6 from foot, after 'age,[5]' delete 'This son,' and insert 'from a comparison of dates, however, this story is probably untrue. Sir Thomas no doubt had a son,'

p. **431,** l. 5 from foot, for '——' read 'Sir Thomas of Hoprew.'

p. **431,** l. 5 from foot, delete 'must have been born in or about 1490,' and insert 'who may have been born about 1483, as he had a precept of sasine in 1504. If so, he cannot have been the son of Elizabeth Home, who was not born before 1477, and must have been the son of a former wife.'

p. **431,** after last line, insert

'3. *William,* who had, on 9 October 1495, a charter from his father of the lands of Nether Menzeon, which had been resigned by another William Hay, styled "cousin" of the first Lord. Both these Williams witnessed the sasine of the Edinburgh and Haddington lands to John Hay, 7 October 1478 (Yester Writs).'

p. **432,** l. 1, for '3' read '4.'

p. **432,** l. 1, after 'Alexander],' insert 'of Olivercastle, of which he had a precept of infeftment in liferent from his father 21 February 1502-3 (Yester Writs), and.'

p. **432,** l. 1, after 'Menzeon,' insert 'succeeded his brother William in the latter lands.'

p. **432,** ll. 8, 11, for 'Lord John' read 'John Lord.'

p. **432**, l. 15, after '1531,' insert, 'He was alive 30 May 1552 (*Liber Act. D. Off. S. And. infra Laud.*, f. 77). He married Euphemia Wauchope: they had a charter of Nether Menzeon from the second Lord 12 July 1512 (Yester Writs).'

p. **432**, after l. 15, insert

'4. *Sir Nicholas*, prebendary of the College Kirk of Bothans, in which he founded a chaplainry at the altar of the Holy Cross 6 February 1488-89. He died in 1498 (Yester Writs).'

p. **432**, ll. 16, 19, for '4, 5' read '5, 6.'

p. **433**, last two lines, and p. **434**, first two lines, delete these entries, George and William were brothers, not sons, of the second Lord (see *supra*).'

p. **434**, l. 7, after '1521-22,' insert 'On 16 February 1538-39 he was presented to the Provostry of the College Kirk of Bothan, of which he had previously been a prebendary (Yester Writs). On 21 August 1542 he was appointed archpriest of the College Kirk of Dunbar (*Reg. Sec. Sig.*, xvi. 44).'

p. **434**, after l. 11, insert

'5. *Mr. John* of Smithfield. On 2 April 1523 he witnessed a deed by his brother, the third Lord, and on 12 August 1539 the latter chose his brother, Mr. John Hay of Smithfield, to be his arbiter in a submission (Yester Writs). On 15 February 1542-43 he,' etc., as on p. **435**, l. 20, down to end of page.

p. **434**, ll. 12, 14, 16, 23, for '5, 6, 7, 8' read '6, 7, 8, 9.'

p. **435**, l. 11, delete 'first.'

p. **435**, l. 13, delete 'secondly —— daughter and sole heiress of John Dickson of Smithfield, co. Peebles. *Note.*—Smithfield was inherited by three heiresses, Christina, Mariota, and Elizabeth Dickson, who had a precept of sasine 6 May 1501 (*Exch. Rolls*, xi. 308, 309). Smithfield appears to have been acquired by John Hay, a brother, not a son, of the third lord (see *supra*).'

p. **435**, delete ll. 17, 18, 19, and transfer remainder of entry to John Hay, son of the second Lord, as in *corrigendum* above.

p. **436**, l. 1, for '3' read '2.'

p. **436**, l. 2, after 'incorrect,' insert 'He succeeded his uncle Mr. Thomas Hay as archpriest of Dunbar (Crawfurd's MS. Baronage, f. 278, Adv. Lib.) and preceptor of S. Leonard's Hospital in 1547. He was tutor of Smithfield on 7 October 1550 (Renwick's *Peebles during Reign of Queen Mary*, 160).'

p. **436**, l. 5, after 1555-56, insert 'He died between 30 January 1557-58 and 3 May 1558 when the Provostry of Bothans was vacant through his death (Yester Writs).'

p. **436**, after l. 5, insert

'3. *John* (*secundus*), on 15 February 1540-41 John Hay of Hoprew, Master of Yester, and John Hay, his brother-german, witnessed a resignation by William Hay of Tallo at Yester (Protocol Book of Alexander Symson, Haddington, vol. 1529-1544, f. 90 b.).'

p. 436, after l. 10, insert

'John, third Lord Hay, had also a natural daughter *Elizabeth*, who had letters of legitimation under the Great Seal 18 August 1558, when she is called natural daughter of the late John, Lord Hay of Yester, grandfather of William, then Lord Hay of Yester (*Reg. Mag. Sig.*) On 22 August 1558 she was, with consent of her cousin, Thomas Hay of Smithfield, contracted to Robert Lauder of Bass (*Reg. of Deeds*, iii. 231).'

p. 437, l. 7 from foot, for '——,' read '*James*. He must have been younger than his brother Thomas, as the latter is styled Master of Yester in 1560 (Ext. Peebles Records, pp. 267-8.). When the Provostry of Bothans was vacant on 4 July 1558 both these sons were under age, and were not presented to the benefice on that account (Yester Writs).'

p. 438, l. 9, delete this entry. Elizabeth was, as mentioned above, half-sister, not natural daughter, of the fourth Lord.

p. 442, l. 19, after '*Jean*,' insert 'is said to have.'

p. 442, l. 19, after 'Barra,' insert 'A Jean Hay was the wife of Mr. William Hay of Barra, commissary of Glasgow 1613-1618, and both are mentioned in the testament of Mr. David Hay, commissary-clerk of Glasgow, confirmed on 9 May 1616 (Glasgow Tests.).'

p. 442, line 24, delete '(date not given),' and substitute 'before 23 March 1640 (*Part. Reg. of Sas., Edinburgh, etc.*, xxviii. 373).'

p. 442, l. 10 from foot, for '1561,' read '1559. In 1589 he was said to be about thirty years old, and to have a son and heir of ten years old (*John Colville's Letters*, Bannatyne Club, 330).'

p. 444, l. 22, after 'and,' insert 'was.'

p. 446, l. 9, after 'ascertained,' insert 'but it was before 18 April 1648 (see below).'

p. 446, l. 11, for 'He' read 'She.'

p. 446, l. 14, after 'Linplum,' insert 'on the Committee of War for Haddingtonshire 18 April 1648 (*Acta Parl. Scot.*, vi. pt. ii. 32): his precept of clare constat as his father's heir dated 20 July 1648 (*Edin. Sas.*, xxxvi. 186).'

p. 446, note 1, for 'will' read 'testament-dative.'

p. 447, l. 21, for '1593' read '1595-96.'

p. 449, l. 1, for '1654' read '25 May 1653 (M. I., College Kirk of Bothans).'

p. 449, l. 9, for 'will was proved' read 'testament-dative was confirmed.'

p. 449, l. 12, for 'Montgomery' read 'Montgomerie.'

p. 449, l. 21, for 'as far as is known, only two sons' read 'issue.'

p. 449, after l. 22, insert

'2. *Charles* (M. I. of first Earl in College Kirk of Bothans).

3. *Alexander*, baptized 13 March 1644 (Kirk Session Records, Yester).

4. *James*. These three sons must have died *s.p.*'

p. 449, l. 23, for '2' read '5.'

p. 450, l. 25, delete 'niece and.'

p. 450, l. 26, after 'line' insert 'daughter of William Hay of Newhall, and niece of George, who succeeded as seventh Marquess (cf. *post*, p. 460).'

p. 451, after l. 30, insert

'6. *Margaret.*

7. *Grissel.*

8. *Anne.* (These three daughters mentioned in M. I. *ut supra*.)'

p. 454, l. 1, after 'advice,' insert quotation mark.

p. 454, l. 17, for 'near Edinburgh' read 'East Lothian.'

p. 456, l. 10 from foot, for '8' read '6.'

p. 459, l. 11, after 'secondly,' insert 'after May 1695,[5]' and delete '(who was living May 1695[5]).'

p. 465, note 4, for '463' read '460.'

p. 468, l. 7, for 'Rendleshan' read 'Rendlesham.'

p. 468, l. 15, for 'Francis' read 'Frances.'

p. 469, l. 8, for 'became quarter-master general' read 'served in the quarter-master general's department.'

p. 472, l. 20, 'for 'Viceroy' read 'Governor-General.'

p. 472, after l. 2 from foot, insert

'He married, first, 18 February 1857, Helena Eleanora Augusta (lady of the bedchamber to the Princess of Wales), daughter of Count de Kielmansegge, Hanoverian minister at the Court of St. James's. She died 30 September 1871, and he married, secondly, 8 October 1873, Julia Charlotte Sophia, second daughter of Keith Stewart Mackenzie of Seaforth. She survived him, and married, secondly, 24 January 1887, the Right Hon. Sir John Rose Best, who died 24 August 1888; and thirdly, 8 February 1892, Major Sir William Evans Gordon.'

WEMYSS

p. 483, l. 12, for '1429' read '1427.'

p. 483, l. 13, for 'Elizabeth' read 'Margaret.'

p. 483, l. 29, for 'John' read 'James.'

p. 490, l. 25, after 'Henry,' insert 'Lord.'

p. 495, l. 13, for 'Margaret' read 'Elizabeth.'

p. 499, l. 1, after 'Tullibardine,' insert '(*see title* Atholl).'

p. 500, l. 4 from foot, for '1639' read '1640 (Balfour's *Annals*, ii. 427, corroborated by a letter from Lord Wemyss, Wemyss Castle Writs).'

p. 503, l. 15, after 'issue,' insert 'and was buried at Wemyss 6 May 1652 (Lamont's *Diary*, 18).'

p. 503, l. 4 from foot, for '1717' read '1715.'

p. 509, l. 7 from foot, after 'Castle,' insert reference no. '[3].'

p. 509, l. 6 from foot, delete reference no. '[3].'

p. 514, ll. 15 and 16, for 'Keek' read 'Keck.'

p. 516, l. 4, for 'Balgonie' read 'Balgone.'

p. 517, l. 14, after 'Major,' insert 'John.'

p. **517,** l. 14, after 'Blackburn,' insert 'son of John Blackburn of Killearn, co. Stirling.'

p. **518,** l. 6, for 'Yorks' read 'Yorke.'

WIGTOWN

p. **523,** l. 4, after '*Marjory*,' insert 'born 1323-24, as she was foster-sister of King David II.; ' delete 'who.'

p. **524,** l. 7 from foot, after 'arms,' insert 'He had a grant of the office of Sheriff of Peebles from David II. 8 September 1346 (copy at Yester, dated 31 December 1435).'

p. **524,** l. 3 from foot, for 'cousin' read 'uncle.'

p. **529,** l. 7 from foot, delete 'son of Alexander de Seton.'

p. **530,** l. 20, insert 'i.' before '*John*.'

p. **530,** l. 31, insert '(i)' before '*James*.'

p. **530,** l. 36, insert '(ii)' before '*William*.'

p. **531,** l. 12 from foot, after 'Albany,' insert 'Governor of Scotland.'

p. **532,** l. 3 from foot, for 'David, Lord Hay of Yester,' read 'Sir David Hay of Yester.'

p. **534,** l. 6, delete 'married to.'

p. **534,** ll. 7, 8, delete 'son to Alexander, Lord Livingstone, who.'

p. **534,** l. 9, after 'her,' insert 'but there is no evidence that this marriage was ever completed.'

p. **537,** note 9, after '*Deeds*,' insert 'iii.'

p. **547,** l. 25, after '1597,' insert 'He married Helen, daughter of Alexander Bruce of Cultmalindy, and widow of Robert Moray, younger of Abercairnie (Perthshire Sheriff Court Reg. of Deeds, 2 July 1659). She died May 1660 (Dunblane Tests).'

p. **547,** note 11, for '10 March' read '9 October.'

p. **550,** last line, after '*Helen*,' insert '9. *Margaret*, mentioned in the precept of 18 August 1669 (see p. 553).'

p. **550,** transpose notes 13 and 14.

p. **551,** l. 19, after 'afternamed,' insert '(except Jean).'

p. **551,** l. 12 from foot, delete 'person or.'

p. **553,** l. 4 from foot, for 'Earl of Panmure' read 'Earl Panmure.'

p. **555,** l. 17, after 'claimed,' insert 'in his case before the House of Lords in 1762.'

p. **558,** l. 3, for 'frases' read 'fraises.'

WINTON

p. **566,** note 6, delete reference and substitute '*Acta. Parl. Scot.*, i. 474.'

p. **570,** note 2, add at end of note, 'But if this theory is not correct, the later generations shown below were, of course, Setons in the female line only.'

p. **571**, note 3, after '*Scotichronicon*,' insert '*Ibid.*'
p. **571**, note 4, after '*Ibid.*' insert '*Orygynale Cronykil loc. cit.*'
p. **584**, l. 8, for '1557' read '1557-58.'
p. **584**, l. 9, for 'seventh' read 'sixth.'
p. **584**, l. 12, after 'adherence,' insert 'and aliment.'
p. **584**, l. 13, after 'him,' insert 'She got decree for aliment.'
p. **584**, l. 13, after '1603,' insert 'and was buried in Seton Church (cf. p. 24).'
p. **595**, l. 12, after '1673,' insert 'Christian, daughter of Lord Cranstoun, confessed to too great intimacy with him 22 May 1673 (South Leith Kirk Session Minutes).'
p. **598**, l. 10, after 'attainder of,' insert 'George, fifth Earl of Winton, and.'
p. **601**, l. 4, for 'fourth' read 'third'; and for '1688' read '1683.'
p. **602**, l, 17, after 'Cockenzie,' insert 'He went abroad at the Revolution and remained abroad till 1695. "The Earl of Winton is come home after seven years absence, and is staying at Seton" (Letter at Slains 5 December 1695).'
p. **605**, note 2, add to note, 'Doubtless identical with Magdalen M'Klear who, on 3 September 1723, made affidavit that she went to London about a fortnight after Lord Winton's committal to the Tower, and had frequent access to him during nine months thereafter (*i.e.* until his escape). She was then known as Mrs. Corsby, and in 1723 was Mrs. Jolly. She is believed to have had two children by Lord Winton, born several years before 1716, and named John Seton and Christian (Memorial for Commissioners of Forfeited Estates, respondents in appeal of Elizabeth Stevenson, Lady Pitcairn, 2 March 1724).'
p. **606**, l. 15, for 'Getre' read 'Gelre.'
p. **606**, l. 31, for 'venacular' read 'vernacular.'

INDEX

INDEX

A——, wife of Norman of Leslie, Constable of Inverurie, son of Malcolm, vii. 266.
Abbot, Charles, younger son of 1st lord Tenterden, ii. 307.
—— —— his wife Emily Frances Stuart, ii. 307.
Abdy of Albyns, Sir Thomas N., 1st bart., viii. 363.
—— Grace, wife of Albert Leveson-Gower, viii. 363.
Abel-Smith of Wilford, Henry, iv. 211.
—— —— Constance Helen, wife of Montgomerie Boyle, iv. 211.
Aberach Mackay, Ian, ancestor of the family of, vii. 160.
—— —— his wife * Mackintosh, vii. 160.
—— John, fourth chieftain, vii. 164.
—— —— his wife,* Mackay, vii. 164.
ABERCORN, HAMILTON, LORD OF, i. 46.
Abercorn, James Hamilton, eldest son of Claud, lord Paisley; lord of, i. 46; iv. 372.
—— —— his wife, Marion Boyd, i. 46; v. 167.
ABERCORN, HAMILTON, EARL OF, i. 37-74.
Abercorn, Charles, fifth earl of, i. 51 *bis*.
—— —— his wife, Katharine Hamilton, i. 49, 51.
—— Claud, fourth earl of, i. 51.
—— George, third earl of, i. 49.
—— James, first earl of, i. 40, 46; ix. 3.
—— —— his wife, Marion Boyd, i. 47; v. 167.
—— James, second earl of, i, 47, 48; v. 358.
—— —— his wife, Katharine Clifton, i. 49; v. 358.
—— James, sixth earl of, i. 57, 58.
—— —— his wife, Elizabeth Reading, i. 59.
—— James, seventh earl of, i. 59, 62.
—— —— his wife, Anne Plumer, i. 62.
—— James, eighth earl of, i. 63, 64.
—— James, tenth earl of, i. 68.
—— —— his wife, Louisa Jane Russell, i. 70.
—— James, eleventh earl of, i. 72.
—— —— his wife, Mary Anna Curzon-Howe, i. 72.
—— John James, ninth earl of, i. 63, 64, 66.
—— —— his 1st wife, Katharine Copley, i. 66.
—— —— his 2nd wife, Cecil Hamilton, i. 64, 68.
—— —— his 3rd wife, Anne Jane Gore, i. 68.

* Name unknown.

ABERCORN, HAMILTON, MARQUESS OF, i. 66-74.
Abercorn, James, second marquess of, i. 67, 68.
—— —— his wife, Louisa Jane Russell, i. 70.
—— James, third marquess of, i. 72.
—— —— his wife, Mary Anna Curzon-Howe, i. 72.
—— John James, first marquess of, i. 66, 95.
—— —— his 1st wife, Katharine Copley, i. 66.
—— —— his 2nd wife, Cecil Hamilton, i. 64, 68.
—— —— his 3rd wife, Anne Jane Gore, i. 68.
ABERCORN, HAMILTON, DUKE OF, i. 69-74.
Abercorn, James, first duke of, i. 67; ii. 247.
—— —— his wife, Louisa Jane Russell, i. 70.
—— James, second duke of, i. 70, 72.
—— —— his wife, Mary Anna Curzon-Howe, i. 72.
ABERCROMBIE, SANDILANDS, LORD, i. 75-81.
Abercrombie, James, first lord, i. 79; vi. 442; ix. 4.
—— —— his 1st wife, Jean Lichtoun, i. 79; ix. 5.
—— —— his 2nd wife, Christian Fletcher, i. 80; ix. 5.
—— James, second lord, i. 81.
Abercromby, George Ralph (Abercromby), 3rd baron, iv. 219.
ABERCROMBY, LORD GLASFOORD, iv. 179-182.
Abercromby of Abercromby, Alexander, iii. 278.
—— —— his wife, Isabella Dishington, iii. 278.
—— Alexander, i. 77.
—— —— his wife, Euphemia Kinninmont, i. 77.
—— —— Sir Thomas, vii. 8.
—— of Achquhorties, David de, vii. 269.
—— —— his wife, Margaret Leslie, vii. 269.
—— of Afforsque, John, iv. 181.
—— of Balcormo, Robert, vi. 408.
—— of Birkenbog, Sir Alexander, 1st bart., iii. 204; ix. 90.
—— —— his 2nd wife, Jane Sutherland, iii. 204.
—— —— his 3rd wife, Elizabeth Baird, ix. 90.
—— —— Alexander, iv. 19.
—— —— his wife, Jonet Ogilvie, iv. 19.

Abercromby of Birkenbog, Sir George, ii. 25.
—— his wife, Jean Ogilvy, ii. 25.
—— Sir George William, 8th bart., iv. 181.
—— James, ancestor of the family of, iv. 180.
—— Sir Robert, i. 92.
—— Sir Robert John, 5th bart., vii. 492, 566.
— of Blairdaff, David de, vii. 269.
— of Clune, George, iv. 179.
—— his 2nd wife, Margaret Gordon of Clune, iv. 179; viii. 338.
— of Fetterneir, Alexander, iv. 181.
—— his wife, Jean Seton, iv. 181.
—— Francis, iv. 181; vii. 559.
—— his 1st wife, Anne, baroness Sempill, vii. 559.
—— Hector, iv. 181.
— of Forglen, Sir Robert, i. 92.
— of Galcors, Alexander, iv. 180.
— of Kersie, Henry, ii. 67.
— of Murthly, Alexander, iii. 278.
— of Petmaquhy, James, iv. 179,
— of Pitmeddan, Alexander, 2nd laird, iv. 179.
—— Alexander, 3rd laird, iv. 179.
—— Alexander, 6th laird, iv. 179.
—— his wife, Elizabeth Leslie, iv. 180.
—— Alexander, 8th laird, iv. 180.
—— Alexander, 9th laird, iv. 180.
—— his wife, Margaret Leslie, iv. 180.
—— George, 4th laird, iv. 179.
—— his 1st wife, Christina Barclay, iv. 179.
—— his 2nd wife, Margaret Gordon, iv. 179; viii. 338.
—— James, 5th laird, iv. 179.
—— his 1st wife, Marjory Hay, iv. 179.
—— his 2nd wife, Elizabeth Gray, iv. 179.
—— James, 10th laird, iv. 180.
—— John, 7th laird, iv. 180.
— of Polton, John, bailie of Edinburgh, iii. 94.
— of Tillibody, George, i. 553.
— of Towie, Alexander, iv. 180.
— of Westballs, Hector, iv. 181.
—— William, iv. 180.
— Alexander, Mr., iv. 101,
—— his wife, Agnes Crichton, iv. 101.
— Constance Helena, wife of lieut.-col. James Ogilvie-Grant, vii. 492.
— Frances Emily, wife of 17th lord Sempill, vii. 566.
— George, 2nd son of Alexander A. of Pitmeddan, iv. 181.
— Grace, wife of Wm. Cosmo Gordon of Fyvie, i. 92.
— Helen, wife of Robert Bruce, i. 533.
Abercromby, Sir James, bart., capt. Coldstream Guards, iv. 392.
— Jean, wife of bishop Adam Bellenden, ii. 67.
— Mary, wife of Sir Thomas Maule of Panmure, vii. 8.
— Montagu, wife of 6th earl of Glasgow, iv. 219.
— Montagu, wife of William, baron Panmure, iii. 108.
— Patrick, M.D., author of *Martial Achievements of the Scottish Nation*, iv. 181.
— Robert, merchant burgess, Edinburgh, ii. 405.
ABERDEEN, GORDON, EARL OF, i. 82-99.
Aberdeen, George, first earl of, i. 88; v. 307.
—— his wife, Anna Lockhart, i. 89.
— George, third earl of, i. 90, 93.
—— his wife, Katharine Hanson, i. 93.
— George, fourth earl of, i. 67, 68, 93, 94.
—— his 1st wife, Katharine Elizabeth Hamilton, i. 68, 95.
—— his 2nd wife, Harriet Douglas, i. 67, 95; vi. 383; ix. 5.
— George, sixth earl of, i. 97, 98.
— George John James, fifth earl of, i. 95, 97.
—— his wife, Mary Baillie, i. 97; iv. 323.
— John Campbell, seventh earl of, i. 98.
—— his wife, Ishbel Maria Marjoribanks, i. 98.
— William, second earl of, i. 90.
—— his 1st wife, Mary Melville, i. 90; vi. 113.
—— his 2nd wife, Susan Murray, i. 90, 485; ix. 5.
—— his 3rd wife, Anne Gordon, i. 91; iv. 553; ix. 5 *bis*.
ABERDEEN, GORDON, VISCOUNT GORDON OF, i. 94-99.
Aberdeen, George, first Viscount Gordon of, i. 94.
Aberdein of Cairnbulg, Alexander, viii. 83, 136.
—— his wife, Helen Carnegie, viii. 83.
— Jean, wife of David Dalrymple, viii. 136.
ABERDOUR, DOUGLAS, LORD, vi. 375-387.
Aberdour, Charles, eldest son of 9th earl of Morton; styled lord, vi. 380.
— Sholto Charles, 2nd son of 13th earl of Morton; styled lord, vi. 383.
— Sholto Charles, eldest son of 18th earl of Morton; styled lord, vi. 387.
—— his wife, Minnie Christian Brenda Hay, vi. 387; viii. 471.
— William, first lord, vi. 375.
Abergavenny, George (Nevill), 11th lord, i. 60.
Aberkirdor, David, i. 110.
—— his wife, Christian Glen, i. 110.

Aberkirdor, *, wife of Wm. Arbuthnott, i. 281.
ABERNETHY, DOUGLAS, LORD OF, i. 204.
Abernethy, William, first lord of, i. 204.
ABERNETHY, STEWART, LORD, vi. 314.
Abernethy, James, first lord, vi. 314.
ABERNETHY OF ROTHIEMAY, ABERNETHY, LORD, vii. 407.
Abernethy of Rothiemay, Laurence, first lord, vii. 407.
ABERNETHY, ABERNETHY, LORD SALTOUN OF, vii. 407-416.
Abernethy, Alexander, fourth lord Saltoun of, vii. 409.
—— —— his wife, * Stewart, vii. 409.
—— Alexander, sixth lord, iv. 124, 125; vii. 411.
—— —— his 1st wife, Alison Keith, vi. 50; vii. 411.
—— —— his 2nd wife, Jean Johnstone, i. 248; vii. 412.
—— Alexander, ninth lord, vii. 414, 442.
—— George, seventh lord, vii. 413.
—— —— his wife, Margaret Stewart, i. 445; vii. 413.
—— James, third lord, vii. 408.
—— John, eighth lord, ii. 85; vii. 413, 415.
—— —— his 1st wife Magdalen Urquhart, vii. 414.
—— —— his 2nd wife, Elizabeth Stewart, vi. 318; vii. 414.
—— —— his 3rd wife, Anna Stewart, ii. 85; vii. 414.
—— Laurence, first lord, vii. 407.
—— —— his wife, Margaret *, vii. 407.
—— William, second lord, vii. 326, 408.
—— —— his 2nd wife, Isabella Borthwick vii. 408.
—— William, fifth lord, iii. 567; iv. 124; vii. 410.
—— —— his wife, Elizabeth Hay, iii. 567; vii. 411.
ABERNETHY, LORD ABERNETHY OF ROTHIEMAY, vii. 407.
ABERNETHY, LORD SALTOUN OF ABERNETHY, vii. 396-416.
Abernethy of Abernethy, Sir Alexander, iii. 10; vii. 398. 401; viii. 479.
—— —— Sir Hugh, iii. 138; iv. 11; vii. 399.
—— —— his 2nd wife Mary of Argyll, vii. 400; viii. 246.
—— Laurence of, vii. 398.
—— —— his wife, Devorguilla, vii. 398.
—— of Abernethy, Margaret, wife of John Stewart, 1st earl of Angus, i. 170; iii. 10, 13; vii. 402.
—— Orm of, vii. 397.
—— of Auchencloich, Alexander, vii. 414, 415.
—— of Balcors, John, vii. 410.
—— —— his wife, Elizabeth Lyon, vii. 410; viii. 280.

* Name unknown.

Abernethy, of Balglaly Wester, George, vi. 83.
—— of Balgounie, Sir John, vii. 405.
—— —— John, his son, vii. 405.
—— of Balmerino, Laurence, vii. 399.
—— of Balnebreich, Laurence, vii. 398.
—— of Balvenie, John, vii. 413.
—— of Barrie, James, ancestor of the family of, vii. 412.
—— —— Thomas, vii. 414.
—— of Birnes, Elizabeth, wife of James Ogilvy, ii. 9, 13.
—— —— William, ii. 9, 13; vii. 411.
—— —— his wife, Marie Ogilvie, ii. 9.
—— of Borthwickshiels, Sir Laurence, v. 391; vii. 403.
—— of Coventre, Laurence, vii. 398.
—— of Cultran, Laurence, vii. 399.
—— of Wester Dron, Laurence, vii. 398.
—— of Dumblait, Alexander, vii. 411.
—— of Dunsyre, Hugh, vii. 403.
—— —— Sir Laurence, vii. 403.
—— of Glendukie and Balmeadow, Laurence, vii. 398.
—— of Halmyre, Hugh, vii. 403.
—— —— Sir Laurence, vii. 403.
—— of Harwood, James, vii. 406.
—— —— John, vii. 406.
—— —— Oswald, vii. 406.
—— of Hawthornden, Hugh, vii. 403.
—— —— Sir Lawrence, vii. 403; ix. 64.
—— of Kincaldrum, Sir Alexander, viii. 479.
—— of Kinnaltie, John, vii. 406.
—— of Lamberton, Sir Laurence, vii. 403.
—— of Lessindrum, Alexander, vii. 411.
—— —— Alexander, 2nd son of 6th lord Saltoun, iv. 125; vii. 412.
—— —— his wife, Elizabeth Crichton, iv. 125.
—— of Lyleston, Sir Hugh, vii. 399.
—— of Maxpoffle, Sir Laurence, vii. 404.
—— of Mayen, Alexander, vii. 414.
—— —— John, ancestor of the family of, vii. 412.
—— of Oxton, Sir Hugh, vii. 399.
—— of Pitcairlie, Sir Alexander, i. 454, 455.
—— of Wester Saltoun, Alexander, 2nd son of 6th lord Saltoun, iv. 125.
—— of Saltoun, Sir George, 4th laird, vii. 404.
—— —— his wife, Alicia Wishart of Plenderleith, vii. 404.
—— —— Sir George, 5th laird, vii. 405.
—— —— Laurence, 8th laird, vii. 407.
—— —— his wife, Margaret *, vii. 407.
—— —— Sir William, 1st laird, vii. 400, 402.
—— —— his wife, Margaret *, vii. 402.
—— —— Sir William, 2nd laird, vii. 403.
—— —— Sir William, 3rd laird, vii. 403.
—— —— Sir William, 6th laird, i. 149; v. 283; vii. 405.

* Name unknown

Abernethy of Saltoun, his wife Maria Stewart, i. 149; vii. 406.
—— —— William, 7th laird, vii. 406.
—— of Teindside, James, vii. 406.
—— —— John, vii. 406.
—— —— Oswald, vii. 406.
—— Agnes, wife of William Crichton of Frendraught, iv. 124 *bis*; vii. 411.
—— Agnes, wife of William Innes of Innes, vii. 410.
—— Andrew, gend'arme, v. 464.
—— Beatrix, wife of Alex. Forbes of Pitsligo, iv. 72; vii. 410.
—— Christian, wife of Sir John Wemyss of that Ilk, vii. 408; viii. 485.
—— Elizabeth, wife of John Innes of Innes, vii. 355, 412; ix. 154.
—— Elizabeth, wife of John Gordon of Scardargue, vii. 407.
—— Elizabeth, wife of Alex. Hay of Ardendracht, vii. 409.
—— Elizabeth, wife of (1) Wm. Meldrum of Fyvie, and (2) John, lord Glamis, vii. 411; viii. 291.
—— George, 3rd son of 1st lord Saltoun, vii. 407.
—— Helen, wife of Thomas Urquhart of Fischerie, vii. 409.
—— Henry, 4th son of Laurence de A., vii. 399.
—— Isobel, wife of John Cumming of Earnside, vii. 413.
—— James, son of Thomas A., vii. 410.
—— James, advocate, clerk of Session, vii. 414.
—— Janet, wife of Alex. Ogilvy of Deskfurd, vii. 409.
—— Jean, mistress of John, duke of Albany, i. 154.
—— Jean, wife of (1) Sir John Lindsay of Kinfauns, and (2) Geo. Gordon of Gight, iii. 33; vii. 413.
—— Jean, wife of (1) Alex. Seton of Meldrum, and (2) John Urquhart, vii. 412.
—— John, Mr., iv. 54; viii. 281.
—— —— his wife, Elizabeth Lyon, iv. 54; viii. 280.
—— Jonet, wife of Alexander Ogilvy of Ogilvy, iv. 22.
—— Jonet, mistress of Thomas, master of Erskine, and wife of John Logy, v. 611.
—— Joneta, wife of Patrick Livingston, vii. 413.
—— Laurence, 2nd son of 4th lord Saltoun, vii. 410.
—— Margaret, wife of Henry Revel, vii. 397, 398.
—— Margaret, wife of John Stirling of Craigbernard, vii. 409.
—— Margaret, wife of George Meldrum of Drumbreck, vii. 412.
Abernethy, Margaret, wife of Alexander Fraser of Philorth, vii. 413, 416, 441.
—— Margaret, eldest dau. of 8th lord Saltoun, vii. 414.
—— Margaret, youngest dau. of 8th lord Saltoun, vii. 414.
—— Maria, wife of (1) A. de Leslie, and (2) Sir D. de Lindsay, iii. 10; vii. 269, 402.
—— Marion, wife of (1) Sir Robert Maitland of Thirlestane, and (2) Sir John Scrymgeour, v. 287, 289; ix. 73.
—— Marion, wife of John Stewart, ix. 155.
—— Marjory, wife of Hugh of Douglas, iii. 136, 137; vii. 399.
—— Patrick, eldest son of Laurence de A., vii. 399.
—— Sir Patrick, eldest son of Hugh de A., iv. 11; vii. 400.
—— Patrick, grandson of the Regent Albany, vii. 406.
—— Thomas, minister of Hounam, vii. 379.
—— —— his wife, Anna Rutherfurd, vii. 379.
—— Thomas, 4th son of 4th lord Saltoun, vii. 410.
—— William, elder son of Sir William A. of Saltoun, vii. 404.
—— Sir William, eldest son of Sir William A. of Saltoun, ii. 96; vi. 351; vii. 406.
—— —— his wife, Margaret Borthwick, ii. 96; vi. 351.
—— William, 4th son of 1st lord Saltoun, vii. 407.
—— William, son of 4th lord Saltoun, vii. 410.
—— William, legtd. son of 7th lord Saltoun, vii. 413.
—— *, wife of Alexander Irvine, younger of Drum, vii. 407.
—— *, wife of Walter Ogston of that Ilk, vii. 408.
ABERUTHVEN, MUGDOCK, AND FINTRY, GRAHAM, LORD, vi. 263-274.
Aberuthven, James, first lord, vi. 263.
Abingdon of Dowdeswell, John, ii. 413.
—— Katharine, wife of (1) Robert, 1st earl of Carnwath, (2) Wm. Watkins, and (3) S. Collins, ii. 413.
ABNEY-HASTINGS, EARL OF LOUDOUN, v. 515-517.
Abney-Hastiugs, Egidia Sophia Frederica Christina, v. 516.
—— Flora Paulyna Hetty Barbara, wife of 15th duke of Norfolk, v. 516.
—— Henry Cecil Plantagenet, v. 516.
ABOYNE, GORDON, LORD, i. 100.
Aboyne, John, viscount Melgum and lord, i. 100; iv. 545.
—— —— his wife, Sophia Hay, i. 100; iii. 577.

* Name unknown.

ABOYNE, GORDON, VISCOUNT OF, i. 101; iv. 546-547.
Aboyne, George, first viscount of, i. 101; iv. 546.
—— —— his wife, Anne Campbell, i. 349; iv. 546.
—— James, second viscount of, i. 101; iv. 547; vi. 58, 245, 247; vii. 200; viii. 411.
ABOYNE, GORDON, EARL OF, i. 102-105; iv. 559-562.
Aboyne, Charles, 4th son of 2nd marquess of Huntly; first earl of, i. 102; iv. 547; ix. 6.
—— —— his 1st wife, Margaret Irvine, i. 102.
—— —— his 2nd wife, Elizabeth Lyon, i. 103; viii. 299.
—— Charles, second earl of, i. 103; ix. 6.
—— —— his wife, Elizabeth Lyon, i. 103; viii. 303.
—— Charles, fourth earl of, i. 104; iv. 559.
—— —— his 1st wife, Margaret Stewart, i. 104; iv. 166.
—— —— his 2nd wife, Mary Douglas, i. 105; vi. 382; ix. 7, 141.
—— Charles, sixth earl of, iv. 560.
—— —— his 1st wife, Elizabeth Henrietta Conyngham, iv. 560.
—— —— his 2nd wife, Maria Antoinetta Pegus, iv. 560.
—— Charles, seventh earl of, iv. 562.
—— —— his wife, Amy Cunliffe Brooks, iv. 562.
—— George, fifth earl of, iv. 559; ix. 7.
—— —— his wife, Catherine Anne Cope, iv. 559.
—— John, third earl of, i. 103; ix. 6.
—— —— his wife, Grace Lockhart, i. 103.
—— Walter Biset, lord of, i. 422.
Abraham of Chapel House, Thomas, iii. 391.
—— of Crewkerne, Robert Taylor, vi. 582.
—— Louisa Mitty, wife of (1) L. G. K. Murray, (2) rev. S. J. Lott, and (3) G. W. Grove, iii. 391.
—— Mary Anne, wife of (1) commr. F. O'Bryen Fitzmaurice, and (2) lt.-col. Archibald Macintosh, vi. 582.
Abrial, Raymond Louis, Montauban, iii. 416.
—— —— his wife, Melanie Sophia Tollemache, iii. 416.
Acarsane of Glen, John, v. 106.
—— —— his wife, Isabella Vaus, v. 106.
—— Marion *or* Mariota, wife of (1) Sir R. Gordon of Lochinvar, and (2) Thos. Maclellan of Bomby, v. 105, 106, 261.
Acford, Albert Edwin, iii. 420 *n.*
—— Elizabeth, self-styled wife of William Lionel Felix, lord Huntingtower, iii. 420 *n.*
—— Henry, Bideford, iii. 420 *n.*
Acheson of Clonekearney, Sir Archibald, i. 40; ix. 2.
—— —— his wife, Margaret Hamilton, i. 40.
—— of Gosford, Alexander, vi. 8.
—— —— his wife, Helen Reid, vi. 8.
—— Helen, wife of Gavin Hume of Johnscleuch, vi. 8.
—— John, writer, Edinburgh, vi. 8.
—— —— his wife, Helen Hume, vi. 8.
—— John, Edinburgh, ii. 64.
—— John, his son, ii. 64.
—— —— his wife, Alison Bellenden, ii. 64.
Achilmere, Robert of, iii. 500.
Acklom of Wiseton, Richard, ii. 417.
—— —— Elizabeth, wife of R. Dalzell, ii. 417.
Acland-Hood, Robert, in holy orders, iv. 389.
—— —— his wife, H. A. C. C. S. Douglas-Hamilton, iv. 389.
Ada of Home, wife of (1) William de Curtenay; (2) Theobald de Lascelles, and alleged (3) William of Greenlaw, iii. 251, 254; iv. 442.
—— wife of Henry, earl of Northumberland, i. 4; viii. 560 *n.*
—— wife of Malise, son of Ferteth, earl of Strathearn, i. 4; v. 325 *n.*; viii. 241.
—— wife of Henry de Hastings, i. 4.
—— wife of Florent III., count of Holland, i. 4.
—— wife of Patrick, 5th earl of Dunbar, i. 5; iii. 253, 262.
—— dau. of Radulf, and wife of Conghal of Tullibardine, i. 453 *n.*
—— wife of (1) John Malherbe *or* Morham, and (2) Wm. Colville of Kinnaird, ii. 536.
—— wife of William de Haya, iii. 556.
—— wife of Thomas de Haya, iii. 556.
—— *probably misreading for* Ela, wife of Duncan, 5th earl of Fife, iv. 7.
—— dau. of Roland of Galloway, and wife of Walter Bisset of Aboyne, iv. 139.
—— wife of William, lord of Home, iv. 442.
Adair of Kinhilt, Ninian, v. 110.
—— —— his wife, Elizabeth Gordon, v. 110.
—— —— William, ii. 468; v. 110.
—— —— his wife, Helen Kennedy, ii. 468.
—— Christian, dau. of William A. in Altoun, iii. 278.
—— William, in Altoun, iii. 278.
Adam of Flemingstoun, son of Gilbert, iii. 557.
—— son of Angus, son of Gilbert, 1st earl of Angus, i. 162.
—— bishop of Caithness, 1222, ii. 316.
—— son of Fergus, earl of Buchan, ii. 252 *n.*; ix. 47.
—— formerly Waldeve, 2nd son of Gospatric, 2nd earl of Dunbar, iii. 247.
—— 2nd son of Duncan, 4th earl of Fife, iv. 6; v. 572.
—— —— his wife Orabilis, iv. 6; v. 572.

Adam, 3rd son of Alan of Ruthven, iv. 255.
— son of Aldan, iv. 441 *n.*
— son of Walter, son of Aldwyn, vi. 79.
— — his wife Christiana Melville, vi. 79.
— son of Gilbert, vii. 420.
— of Blairadam, William, 1st laird, iii. 549.
— of Maryburgh, William, architect, iii. 549; viii. 36.
— of Woodstoun, William, iii. 549.
Adams of Cannon Hill, Henry, vii. 393.
— Lydia Gladys, wife of P. J. L. Hore-Ruthven, vii. 393.
Adamson of Bonally, William, vi. 408.
— — his wife, Janet Napier, vi. 408.
— of Craigcrook, William, iii. 377.
— — his 1st wife, Dorothy Galloway, iii. 377.
— — William, vi. 588.
— — his wife, Janet Napier, vi. 408, 588.
— Agnes, wife of Alex. Ruthven, ix. 98.
— Elizabeth, wife of F. Ogilvy of Newgrange, i. 121.
— Henry, Perth, ix. 98.
— Janet, wife of Sir James Makgill of Rankeillor, vi. 588; ix. 146.
— Janet, wife of 2nd earl of Southesk, viii. 70.
— Katherine, wife of (1) Richard Hopper, and (2) Sir Robert Melville of Murdocairnie, i. 535; vi. 99.
— Marion, wife of Edward Little, iii. 502.
— Patrick, archbishop of St. Andrews, iv. 544; vii. 66.
— William, ii. 64.
— — his wife, Agnes Bellenden, ii. 64.
Adderley of Halstow, William, vi. 381.
— Frances, wife of 12th earl of Morton, vi. 381.
Addington, John Gellibrand (Hubbard), 1st baron, vi. 437.
— — his wife Maria Margaret Napier vi. 437.
Addinstoun of Addinstoun, Margaret, wife of George Hepburne, viii. 602.
— — Richard, vi. 7.
— — his wife, Margaret Hume, vi. 7.
— — Robert, viii. 602.
— John, merchant burgess, Edinburgh, v. 466.
Adeane, Edward Stanley, admiral, ii. 419.
— — his wife, Edith Isabella Dalzell, ii. 419.
Adeline, wife of Ansold, lord of Maule, vii. 3.
Adglay, Gilbert, ii. 571.
Aelgifu, *or* Elgiva, wife of Uchtred, earl of Northumberland, iii. 241.
Aelina, wife of Waldeve, 4th earl of Dunbar, iii. 252.
Afreka, wife of Harald Maddadsson, earl of Caithness, ii. 315; iv. 6.
Affrica of Dunscore dau. of Edgar, vi. 287.
— wife of Olaf, King of Man and the Isles, iv. 136.
Agar-Ellis, Margaret Elizabeth Diana, wife of Ivan Campbell, ii. 213.
Agnes, wife of (1) Sir Fred. Hamilton of Manor Hamilton, and (2) John Maxwell, i. 45.
— wife of Sir P. Hepburn of Hailes, ii. 137.
— dau. of Walter of Barrone, ii. 286.
— wife of Wm. Richardson, ii. 579.
— mother of Wm. Cunningham, vicar of Dundonald, iv. 231.
— wife of lord chancellor Crichton, iii. 60, 61.
— wife of Morgund, 2nd earl of Mar, v. 567, 573, 576.
— wife of Sir Wm. Ramsay of Dalhousie and Nether Liberton, iii. 90 *n.*
— wife of Thomas de Thirlestane of Abertarff, v. 277, 278.
— wife of Richard Keith, the Marischal, vi. 28.
— wife of Sir John Douglas, vi. 343.
— wife of George Maxwell of Carnsalloch, vi. 476.
— wife of Malise, 6th earl of Strathearn, viii. 249.
— wife of Galfrid de Fullarton, viii. 108.
Agnew of Ardoch, Alexander, ix. 94.
— — his wife, Barbara Gordon, ix. 94.
Agnew of Barvennan, Alexander, v. 114.
— of Creachmore, Patrick. v. 106.
— of Lochnaw, Andrew, first sheriff of Wigtoun, ii. 400.
— — Andrew, 5th laird. ii. 470.
— — Andrew, 7th laird, iv. 158; v. 264.
— — his wife, Agnes Stewart, iv. 158.
— — Sir Andrew, 2nd bart., iv. 161.
— — his wife, Anne Stewart, iv. 161.
— — Sir Andrew, 3rd bart., iii. 327.
— — Sir Andrew, 7th bart., viii. 88.
— — his wife, Madeline Carnegie, viii. 88.
— — Sir Andrew, 8th bart., v. 215.
— — Sir James, 4th bart., iii. 454.
— — his wife, Mary Montgomerie, iii. 454.
— — Patrick, 1st bart., ii. 488.
— — his wife, Margaret Kennedy, ii. 488.
— of Salchary, Patrick, v. 106.
— — his wife, Katharine Gordon, v. 106.
— — Patrick, v. 109.
— — his wife, Janet Gordon, v. 109.
— Mary Alma Victoria, wife of 11th lord Kinnaird, v. 215.
— Rosina, wife of Wm. Maclellan of Glenshinnoch, v. 264.
Aikinhead of Kilquhis Wester, Thomas, v. 403.
— — his wife, Janet Hepburn, v. 403.

Aikenhead, James, advocate, iv. 435.
—— Thomas, commissary of Edinburgh, vi. 8.
AILESBURY, BRUCE, EARL OF, iii. 466-483.
Ailesbury, Charles, third earl of, iii. 481.
—— Robert, first earl of, iii. 478.
—— Thomas, second earl of, iii. 479.
—— Thomas (Brudenell-Bruce), 1st earl of, i. 36; iii. 483.
—— Charles (Brudenell-Bruce), 1st marquess of, iii. 414.
—— —— his 2nd wife, Maria Eliza Murray, iii. 414.
AILSA OF AILSA, KENNEDY, BARON, ii. 498.
Ailsa, Archibald, first baron, ii. 497.
AILSA, KENNEDY, MARQUESS OF, ii. 497-502.
Ailsa, Archibald, first marquess of, ii. 497.
—— —— his wife, Margaret Erskine, ii. 498.
—— Archibald, second marquess of, ii. 500.
—— —— his wife, Julia Mounteney Jephson, ii. 501.
—— Archibald, third marquess of, ii. 501.
—— —— his 1st wife, Evelyn Stuart, ii. 92, 501.
—— —— his 2nd wife, Isabella MacMaster, ii. 502.
Ainslie of Blackhill, Andrew, vii. 382.
—— of Cameron, Amabilla, wife of John Wemyss, viii. 477.
—— sir John, viii. 477.
—— of Dolphingston, John, vii. 330, 331.
—— —— Marjorie, wife of Mark Ker of Maxton, vii. 330.
—— of Fala, David, vii. 376.
—— —— his wife, Mary Rutherfurd, vii. 376.
—— of Pilton, Sir Philip, iv. 293, 294; vi. 328.
—— —— his wife, Elizabeth Gray, iv. 293.
—— Charles Philip, major-general, iv. 294 *bis*.
—— —— his wife, Jane Anne Gray, iv. 294.
—— Isabel, wife of capt. John Rutherfurd, vii. 383.
—— Janet, wife of John Rutherfurd, vii. 382.
—— John, South Carolina, iii. 81.
—— —— his wife, Mary Mackenzie, iii. 81.
—— Margaret Jane, wife of 10th earl of Moray, vi. 327.
—— Mary Anne, wife of 15th lord Gray, iv. 294.
AIR, CRICHTON, VISCOUNT OF, iii. 234-238.
Air, William, first viscount of, iii. 234.
Aird, Colin of the, alleged ancestor of the earls of Ross, and of the clan Mackenzie, vii. 495.
AIRLIE, OGILVY, EARL OF, i. 106-132.
Airlie, David, third earl of, i. 126.
—— —— his wife, Grizel Lyon, i. 126; viii. 303.
—— David, fifth earl of, i. 127.
—— —— his 1st wife, Margaret Johnstone, i. 128.
—— —— his 2nd wife, Anne Stewart, i. 128.
Airlie, David, titular earl of, i. 128; ix. 8.
—— David, sixth earl of, i. 129, 130.
—— —— his 1st wife, Clementina Drummond, i. 130; ix. 8.
—— —— his 2nd wife, Margaret Bruce, i. 130; ix. 9.
—— David Graham Drummond, seventh earl of, i. 131.
—— —— his wife, Henrietta Blanche Stanley, i. 131; ix. 9.
—— David Lyulph Gore Wolseley, ninth earl of, i. 132.
—— David William Stanley, eighth earl of, i. 131.
—— —— his wife, Mabell Frances Elizabeth Gore, i. 132.
—— James, first earl of, i. 123; ix. 8.
—— —— his wife, Isobel Hamilton, i. 124; iv. 315.
—— James, second earl of, i. 125; iv. 28.
—— —— his 1st wife, Helen Ogilvy, i. 126.
—— —— his 2nd wife, Marie Grant, i. 126; iv. 548; vii. 472.
—— James, titular earl of, i. 127.
—— —— his wife, Anne Erskine, i. 127,
—— John, fourth earl of, i. 127.
—— —— his wife, Margaret Ogilvy of Cluny, i. 127.
AIRLIE, OGILVY, LORD OGILVY OF, i. 114-132.
AIRTH, GRAHAM, EARL OF, i. 133-145.
Airth, William, first earl of, i. 133, 144, 467; ii. 201; ix. 9.
—— —— his wife, Agnes Gray, i. 137; iv. 286.
—— William, second earl of, i. 140; vi. 260.
—— —— his 1st wife, Anna Hewes, i. 141; ix. 9 *bis*.
—— —— his 2nd wife, Katharine Bruce, i. 142; ix. 9.
Airth of Carnock and Plean, Elizabeth, wife of (1) *, and (2) Thomas Somerville, vii. 37; viii. 10.
—— of Plean, Sir William de, vii. 37; viii. 10.
AIRTHRIE, HOPE, VISCOUNT OF, iv. 493-505.
Airthrie, Charles, first viscount of, iv. 493.
Aislabie, John, M.P., director of South Sea Company, vii. 259.
Aitchison, Helen, wife of (1) * Fraser, (2) John Logan, (3) Wm. Berry, and (4) Archibald Stewart, provost of Edinburgh, iii. 187; ix. 68 *bis*.
—— Robert, merchant, Edinburgh, vi. 92.
Aitken of Middle Grange, James, burgess of Culross, ii. 549; vii. 213.
—— —— his wife, Agnes Primrose, vii. 213.
—— James, son of James A. of Middle Grange, ii. 549.
—— —— his wife, Katharine Colville, ii. 549.

* Name unknown.

Alais, Aglaé Elizabeth Jaqueline d'Oms d', wife of General James Louis Drummond, vi. 72.
— Marc, baron de Salindres, vicomte d', vi. 72.
Alan of Ruthven, son of Sweyn of Crawford, iv. 255.
— — his wife, Cecilia Maule, iv. 255, 256.
— of Thirlestane, son of Elsi, v. 277.
— 'Dapifer Dolensis,' or Senescal of Dol, i. 9.
— Fitz-Flaald, sheriff of Shropshire, i. 9.
— — his wife, Avelina de Hesding. i. 10.
— Fitz-jordan, of Burton, and Dol, grandson of Alan Fitz-flaald, i, 10.
— — his wife, Joan, i. 10.
— illeg. son of Thomas of Galloway, earl of Atholl, i. 421 *n*.
— elder son of Waldeve of Allerdale, iii. 244.
— Sir Henry, in Ettrick, Director of Chancery, iii. 500.
Albanie, Charles Edward Hay Allen, styled count d', iii. 585.
ALBANY, STEWART, DUKE OF, i. 146-155.
Albany, Alexander, 2nd son of King James II.; duke of, i. 20, 151, 441; ii. 334; iii. 65, 182, 222.
— — his 1st wife, Katherine Sinclair, i. 152.
— — his 2nd wife, Anne de la Tour d'Auvergne, i. 153.
— Arthur, 2nd son of King James V.; duke of, i. 155.
— Charles, 2nd son of King James VI.; duke of, i. 155.
— Charlotte, legtd. dau. of prince Charles Edward Stuart: duchess of, i. 36.
— Henry, eldest son of 4th earl of Lennox; duke of, i. 155.
— James, son of Mary, Queen of Scots; duke of, i. 155.
— James, 2nd son of King Charles II.; duke of, i. 33, 155; vi. 60.
— John, governor of Scotland, duke of, i. 154; iv. 356; v. 57; viii. 536; ix. 10.
— — his wife, Anne de la Tour d'Auvergne, i. 154.
— Louise Maximiliane-Emanuella of Stolberg-Guedern, wife of prince Charles Edward Stuart; styled countess of, i. 35.
— Murdac, governor of Scotland, second duke of, i. 17, 148, 149, 278, 328. 332, 437; ii. 174 *n*; iii. 164, 174, 430, 563; iv. 15, 48, 229; v. 340, 343.
— — his 1st wife Joanna (? Douglas), v. 342 *n*.; ix. 10.
— — his 2nd wife, Isabella, countess of Lennox, i. 150; v. 341; ix. 10.
— Robert, regent of Scotland, first duke of, i. 12, 16, 146, 436; ii. 174, 449; iii. 174, 562; iv. 14; vi. 37, 140; vii. 182, 242 *bis*, 243; ix. 9.
Albany, Robert, his 1st wife, Margaret, countess of Menteith, i. 148; vi. 138.
— — his 2nd wife, Muriella Keith, i. 148; vi. 37.
Albemarle, William de Fortibus, earl of, iv. 142.
— — his wife, Christina of Galloway, iv. 142.
— George (Keppel), 6th earl of, viii. 516.
— William Anne (Keppel), 2nd earl of, v. 364.
— — his wife, Ann Lennox, v. 364.
— Henry Fitz-james, titular duke of, vi. 70.
— — his wife, Marie Gabrielle d'Audibert, vi. 70.
Albestroff, Clementina Walkinshaw, countess of, i. 36.
Albini, Isabel de, wife of John Fitz-Alan, i. 10.
Albinus, bishop of Brechin, ii. 217 *n*.
Albus, John, Linlithgow, iii. 117.
Aldborough, John (Stratford), earl of, iii. 410.
Aldeburgh of Broxmouth, Sir Ivo de, iv. 270.
— of Kells, Sir William de, v. 256.
Aldie, Elizabeth Crichton, wife of Sir J. Ogilvy of Craig; styled lady, i. 120.
Aldiston of Cambusbarron and Blairegis, Hugh, viii. 525.
— — William, viii. 528.
Aldridge, Caroline Diana, wife of major C. J. Keith-Falconer, v. 253.
— Robert, St. Leonard's Forest, v. 253.
Aldwyn, father of Walter, vi. 79.
ALEMOOR, SCOTT, LORD, vii. 80, 81.
Alemoor, Walter, lord, ii. 237; vii. 81.
— — his wife, Mary, countess of Buccleuch, ii. 236.
Alençon, Jean II., duke of, v. 348.
Alessandro, Catalina Paulina, wife of (1) Admiral C. Elphinstone-Fleming, and (2) Commr. J. E. Katon, iii. 550.
Alexander I., King of Scots, i. 3; iii. 303; iv. 3.
— — his wife, Sybilla, i. 3.
— II., King of Scots, i. 6; v. 32, 33, 34.
— — his 1st wife, Joanna Plantagenet, i. 6; ii. 423, 430; iii. 252.
— — his 2nd wife, Marie de Coucy, i. 6.
— III., King of Scots, i. 6; vii. 400.
— — his 1st wife, Margaret Plantagenet, i. 6; iv. 9.
— — his 2nd wife, Yolande de Dreux, i. 6.
— Prince of Scotland, elder son of King Alexander III., i. 6; iv. 11.
— — his wife, Marguerite of Flanders, i. 6.
— son of Edgar the Dauntless, iii. 249.
— 8th abbot of Cupar, v. 203.
— abbot of Scone, viii. 265.
— son of Thurstan of Livingston, v. 422.
— bishop of Moray, v. 520.
— 3rd son of Donald, 6th earl of Mar, v. 578.

ALEXANDER OF TULLIBODY, ALEXANDER, LORD, viii. 173-185.
Alexander, William, first lord, viii. 173.
— William, eldest son of 1st earl of Stirling; styled lord, viii. 176; ix. 159.
— — his wife, Margaret Douglas, i. 205; viii. 177.
ALEXANDER, VISCOUNT OF STIRLING, viii. 173-174.
ALEXANDER, EARL OF STIRLING, viii. 165-185.
ALEXANDER, LORD ALEXANDER OF TULLIBODY, viii. 173-185.
ALEXANDER, VISCOUNT OF CANADA, viii. 174, 185.
Alexander of Ballochmyle, Sir Claud, 2nd bart., iii. 464.
— — his 1st wife, Diana Montgomerie, iii. 464.
— of Clow, Adam. viii. 166.
— — William, viii. 166.
— — his wife, Jonet Marshall, viii. 166.
— of Dufletter, Alexander, viii. 167.
— of Gartmore, Janet, dau. of John A., viii. 179.
— — John, 4th son of 1st earl of Stirling, vi. 159; viii. 179.
— — his wife, Agnes Graham of Gartmore, vi. 159; viii. 179.
— of Largs, Sir William, viii. 173.
— of Long Island, Sir William, viii. 174.
— of Menstrie, Alexander, 3rd laird, vi. 369; viii. 167.
— — his wife, Elizabeth Douglas, vi. 369; viii. 167.
— — Alexander, 5th laird, viii. 169.
— — his wife, Marion Graham, vi. 159; viii. 169.
— — Andrew, 2nd laird, viii. 166, 183.
— — his wife Katherine Graham, viii. 166.
— — Thomas, 1st laird, viii. 165.
— — William, 4th laird, viii. 168.
— — his wife, Elizabeth Coutts, viii. 168.
— — Sir William, the poet, i. 349; iv. 311; viii. 170, 196.
— — his wife, Janet Erskine, viii. 176.
— of Skeddaway, Thomas, ii. 572.
— — his wife, Jean Colvill, ii. 572.
— of Somerhill, James, iii. 492.
— — his wife, Charlotte Sophia Dashwood, iii. 492.
— of Tullibody, Sir William, viii. 173.
— of Turvell, William, 3rd son of 4th earl of Stirling, viii. 182.
— Archibald, bailie of Stirling, viii. 169.
— — his wife, Elizabeth Alexander, viii. 169.
— 'Mor', 2nd son of Donald, lord of the Isles; ancestor of the family of MacAlister, v. 33, 36.
— Alastair Mor, 2nd son of Donald, lord of the Isles, alleged ancestor of the family of, v. 33; viii. 165.
Alexander, Alexander, viii. 167.
— — his wife, Elizabeth Forbes, viii. 167.
— Alexander, in Menstrie, burgess of Stirling, viii. 170 *n.*
— Sir Anthony, master of works to King Charles I., viii. 174, 178.
— — his wife, Elizabeth Wardlaw, viii. 179.
— Alexander, in Milnab, viii. 183.
— Andrew, presbyter, viii. 166.
— Andrew, eldest son of Alexander A. of Menstrie, viii. 167.
— Andrew, 3rd son of William A. of Menstrie, viii. 169.
— — his wife, Janet Archibald, viii. 169.
— Charles, viii. 179.
— — his wife, Anna Drurie, viii. 179.
— Charles, graduate of Edinburgh University, viii. 179.
— Christine, wife of Patrick Kinross, viii. 170.
— David, in Muthill, viii. 183.
— Elizabeth, wife of John Leishman, viii. 168.
— Elizabeth, wife of Archibald Alexander, viii. 169.
— Elizabeth, dau. of Archibald A., viii. 169.
— Elizabeth, wife of Walter Neisch of Dubheads, viii. 170.
— Elizabeth, dau. of 1st earl of Stirling, viii. 181.
— Hannah, wife of Wm. Humphreys, viii. 184.
— James, tutor of Menstrie, viii. 168, 170.
— — his wife, Janet Gaudee, viii. 168.
— James, his son, viii. 168.
— James, burgess of Stirling, viii. 169.
— James, 2nd son of Charles A., viii. 179.
— James, lieut.-col. H.M. Foot Guards, son of 1st earl of Stirling, viii. 180; ix. 122.
— — his 1st wife, Margaret Scrimgeour, iii. 314; viii. 180; ix. 73.
— — his 2nd wife, Grizel Hay, viii. 180.
— James, father of the American claimant to earldom of Stirling, viii. 183.
— James Bruce, i. 391.
— Jane, dau. of 3rd earl of Stirling, viii. 181.
— Janet, wife of John Burn, viii. 169.
— Janet, wife of David Forrester of Logie, viii. 170.
— Janet, wife of Walter Cowan, viii. 170 *n.*
— Jean, dau. of William, lord Alexander, viii. 177.
— Jean, wife of (1) Hugh, 2nd viscount Montgomery of the Ards, and (2) major-gen. Robert Munro, viii. 180.

Alexander, John, 3rd son of Alexander A. of Menstrie, viii. 168.
— John, 2nd son of Archibald A., viii. 169.
— John, apprentice baker, viii. 169; ix. 160.
— John, in Gogar, viii. 183.
— rev. John, Belfast, viii. 184.
— Judith, wife of Sir Wm. Trumbull of Easthamstead Park, viii. 182.
— Katharine, wife of 6th lord Torphichen, viii. 177, 393; ix. 160 *bis*.
— Laurence, Kingskettle, viii. 165.
— Lucy, wife of Edward Harrington, viii. 178.
— Ludovick, 7th son of 1st earl of Stirling, viii. 180.
— Margaret, wife of John Stirling, viii. 168.
— Margaret, wife of Sir R. Sinclair of Longformacus, viii. 177, 393.
— Margaret, dau. of lt.-col. James A., viii. 180.
— Margaret, wife of Sir Wm. Murray of Dunearn viii. 180.
— Marion, wife of (1) Patrick Murray of Woodend, and (2) Jas. Muschet of Burnbank, iii. 398; viii. 168.
— Marion, wife of Duncan Paterson, viii. 170.
— Mary, wife of Robert Lee of Binfield, viii. 181.
— Mary, wife of John Philips, viii. 182.
— Peter, 6th son of 4th earl of Stirling, viii. 182.
— Robert, poet, iv. 260.
— Robert, 6th son of 1st earl of Stirling, viii. 180.
— Robert, granger in Strathdon, viii. 165.
— Robert, burgess of Stirling, viii. 169.
— Robert, 4th son of 4th earl of Stirling, viii. 182.
— Sybil Lascelles, wife of lord George G. Campbell, i. 391.
— Thomas, Kingskettle, viii. 165.
— Walter, usher in household of prince Henry, viii. 171.
— William, crown-receiver for Moray, viii. 165.
— William, Edinburgh, 1435, viii. 165.
— William, Tullibody, viii. 166.
— William, apprentice skinner, viii. 169; ix. 160.
— William, son of William A. of Menstrie, viii. 170.
— William, major-gen. American Army, viii. 183.
— — his wife Sarah Livingston, viii. 183.
Alexanderson, Laurence, Kingskettle, viii. 165.
— William, crown-receiver for Moray, viii. 165.
Algeo of Easter Walkinshaw, Robert, v. 355.
— — his wife, Margaret Stuart, v. 355.
Algitha or Ealdgith, wife of Maldred of Cumbria, iii. 241.
Alhusen of Stoke Court, Henry Christian, iii. 523.
— Mary Millard, wife of capt. E. O. Murray, iii. 523.
Alianora or Elena, of Galloway, wife of Roger de Quincy, ii. 254; iv. 142.
Alianora, wife of (1) Robert Bruce, earl of Carrick, and (2) Richard de Waleys, ii. 433.
Alianore, wife of (1) Robert de Umfraville, 3rd earl of Angus, and (2) Sir Roger Mauduit, ix. 11.
Alice, wife of (1) Sir John, 'the Red Comyn, No. 1.,' and (2) * Comyn, i. 507.
— wife of Philip de Haliburton, iv. 331.
— wife of Sir David Hume of Wedderburn, vi. 1.
— wife of Malcolm of Constabletun and Edulfistun, vii. 365.
— alleged wife of Philip Seton, iii. 252.
Alicia, wife of Sir William Lindsay of Symington; ii. 260; iii. 9.
— wife of Hugh Crauford of Loudoun, v. 490.
— wife of Sir John Campbell of Wester Loudoun, v. 492.
— wife of Murdach, 8th earl of Menteith, vi. 137.
Aline, wife of Waldeve, 4th earl of Dunbar, iii. 252.
Alison, wife of Thos. Preston of Whitehill, iii. 119.
— John, Jedburgh, v. 463.
— *, mistress of 1st Duke of Argyll, ix. 24.
Aliz of Coquetdale, wife of Edgar the Dauntless, iii. 249.
Allan, abbot of Inchaffray, viii. 245 *n.*
— John of, viii. 269.
— — his wife, Christian Brogan, viii. 269.
Allan of Faslane, 'Tosheagor,' v. 329.
— Agnes, wife of George Bruce, iii. 488.
— James, Professor of Humanity, St. Leonard's College, v. 306.
— Sarah, wife of Wm. Hamilton, ii. 50.
— Thomas, viii. 76.
— — his wife, Katharine Carnegie, viii. 76.
Allan, *, Maddox Street, viii. 408.
Allanby-Montgomerie of Garnsgate Hall, Samuel Hynman, capt., iii. 463.
— — his wife, Sophie Constance Montgomerie, iii. 463.
— Adelaide Margaret Constance, iii. 464.
— Eleanor Theresa, iii. 464.
— Sophia Egidia Gwendolen, iii. 464.

* Name unknown.

Allardice of Allardice, Alexander, i. 83.
—— his wife, Isabel Gordon, i. 83.
—— Sir George, i. 141, 142.
—— his wife, Anna Ogilvy, i. 143; iv. 37; ix. 90 *bis*.
—— James, i. 143.
—— his wife, Mary Milne, i. 143.
—— James, i. 143.
—— his wife, Ann Barclay, i. 143.
—— John, i. 281.
—— his wife, Kath. Arbuthnott, i. 281.
—— John, vi. 50.
—— his wife, Beatrix Keith, vi. 50.
—— Sir John, i. 142.
—— his wife, Mary Graham, i. 142.
—— John, i. 142.
—— his wife, Elizabeth Barclay, i. 142.
—— Robert, iv. 57.
—— his wife, Barbara Forbes, iv. 57.
—— Sarah Ann, wife of (1) Robt. Barclay of Urie, and (2) John Nudd, i. 143; ix. 9.
— Anna, wife of John Gordon of Breakly, i. 142; ix. 9 *bis*.
— Anna, dau. of Sir George A., i. 143.
— Helen, dau. of Sir John A., i. 142.
— Helen, wife of Alex. Lind of Gorgie, i. 143.
— James, ix. 10.
—— his wife, Elizabeth Keith, ix. 10.
— Jean, dau. of Sir John A., i. 142.
— John, 3rd son of Sir George A., i. 143.
— Katharine, dau. of Sir George A., i. 143.
— Margaret, dau. of Sir John A., i. 142.
— Mary, wife of Sir Alex. Ogilvy of Forglen, i. 142; ii. 23.
— Mary, wife of Andrew Hay of Mountblairy, i. 143.
— Mary, wife of James Macdonald, advocate, i. 143.
— Robert, in Petty, 1526, i. 289.
— *, wife of Irvine of Drum, i. 281.
Allardyce of Dunottar, Alexander, ii. 498.
— Eleanor, wife of Archibald, styled earl of Cassillis, ii. 498.
— James, i. 286.
—— his wife, Ann Arbuthnott, i. 286.
Allen, Anna Harriet, wife of 10th viscount of Arbuthnott, i. 316.
— Charles Edward Hay, styled count d'Albanie, alleged grandson of prince Charles Edward Stuart, iii. 585.
— Edmund, 3rd son of col. A. of Inchmartine, i. 316.
— Elizabeth, wife of 4th lord Forbes of Pitsligo, iv. 76.
— major, 12th Regt. of foot, v. 19.
— Thomas, Finchley, iv. 76.
Alleyne, Rebecca, wife of 1st earl of Radnor, iii. 391.
— John, Barbadoes, iii. 391.
Allison of Undercliffe, *, col., iii. 464.

* Name unknown.

Allison, Harold Kenneth, iii. 464.
—— his wife, Diana Montgomerie, iii. 464.
Allister, Mary, wife of John Middleton, Barbadoes, vi. 177.
Alneto, Sir Thomas de, v. 276.
Altoun, Ninian, ix. 143.
—— his wife, Jonet Livingston, ix. 143.
ALTRIE, KEITH, LORD, i. 156-159.
Altrie, George, second lord, i. 157, 159; iv. 52.
— Robert, first lord, i. 156; vi. 49, 50; ix. 10, 21.
—— his wife, Elizabeth Lundie of Benholm, i. 159; ix. 10.
Alured, a deacon, in Lindsey, iii. 2.
— of Charterhouse, Thomas, iii. 291.
—— his wife, Eleanor Constable, iii. 291.
Alva, Elizabeth, dau. of Wm. Hairstanes of Craig; wife of (1) Wm. Maxwell of Preston, and (2) Sir C. Erskine of Alva; styled lady, viii. 360.
Alvanley, Richard Pepper (Arden), 1st baron, lord chief-justice, iv. 328.
Alwin, thanc of Callendar, v. 183.
— the elder, earl of Lennox, v. 324, 326.
— Macarkell, v. 325.
— the younger, earl of Lennox, v. 327.
— son of Aulay, v. 329 *n*.
ALYTH AND LINTRATHEN, OGILVY, LORD OGILVY OF, i. 123-132.
Amabel, wife of (1) Nicholas de Fawnes, and (2) David de Graham, vi. 199, 200.
Amabilis, wife of Thomas de Colville of Oxnam, ii. 536.
Amabilla, wife of Sir Donald Campbell of Benderloch, i. 320.
— wife of Sir Adam Gordon of Gordon, justiciar of Lothian, iv. 512.
— wife of John de Wemyss of Cameron, viii. 477.
Ameland, Augusta (Murray) de, dau. of John, 4th earl of Dunmore, and wife of Prince Augustus Frederick of Great Britain, iii. 391.
Ames, Louis Eric, 2nd Life Guards, ii. 58.
—— his wife, Margaret Wilhelmina Hamilton, ii. 58.
AMESBURY, DOUGLAS, BARON DOUGLAS OF, vii. 174.
Amesbury, William, baron Douglas of, vii. 147.
— Charles (Dundas), lord, v. 312: ix. 125.
—— his wife, Margaret Maitland, v. 312.
Amicia, wife of Sir William de St. Clair, vi. 565.
AMPTHILL, BRUCE, VISCOUNT BRUCE OF, iii. 478-483.
Anabell of Stobo, dau. of Samuel, vii. 420.
Ancaster, Gilbert Henry (Heathcote) 1st earl of, iv. 561; vii. 59.
—— his wife, Evelyn Elizabeth Gordon, iv. 561.

Ancaster, Brownlow (Bertie), 5th duke of, vii. 96.
—— —— his wife, Mary Anne Layard, vii. 96.
—— Robert (Bertie), 1st duke of, ii. 304.
—— Robert (Bertie), 4th duke of, i. 490.
Ancelin, * d', iii. 382.
—— —— his wife, *, iii. 382.
ANCRAM, KER, EARL OF, v. 466-487.
Ancram, Charles, second earl of, v. 467, 468.
—— —— his wife, * v. 468.
—— Robert, first earl of, v. 71, 466.
—— —— his 1st wife, Elizabeth Murray, v. 467.
—— —— his 2nd wife, Anne Stanley, v. 466, 467.
—— Robert, third earl of, v. 78, 468, 476, 477.
—— Walter William Schomberg, eldest son of 9th marquess of Lothian; styled earl of, v. 486.
—— William, eldest son of 5th marquess of Lothian; styled earl of, v. 483.
—— —— his 1st wife, Henrietta Hobart, v. 483.
—— —— his 2nd wife, Harriet Montagu Scott, ii. 244, v. 483.
—— William Henry, elder son of 3rd marquess of Lothian; styled lord, v. 481.
—— —— his wife, Caroline D'Arcy, v. 481.
Ancrum of Craigcrook, John de, vi. 211.
Anderson of Candacraig, John, capt., 28th Regiment, iv. 557.
—— —— his wife, Catherine Gordon, iv. 557.
—— of Goland, John, self-styled lord Rutherfurd, vii. 384.
—— of Inchconnan, Grizel, v. 218.
—— of Kingask, Alexander, v. 410.
—— —— his wife, Janet Lindsay, v. 410.
—— of Monthrive, James, v. 409, 410.
—— —— his wife, Janet Lindsay, v. 409.
—— of Winterfield, John, viii. 137.
—— —— his wife, Jean Dalrymple, viii. 136.
—— Alison, wife of (1) A. Forbes of Tolquhoun, and (2) A. Forbes of Pitsligo, iv. 73.
—— Finlay, burgess of Perth, vi. 391.
—— —— his wife, Elizabeth or Isobel Davidson, vi. 391.
—— Isabel, mistress of capt. Charles Fleming, viii. 552.
—— James, maltman, Perth, ix. 8.
—— —— his wife, Janet Ogilvy, ix. 8.
Andrew, archdeacon of St. Andrews, iv. 441 *n*.
—— bishop of Caithness, v. 202; viii. 318, 319 *n*.
—— bishop of Moray, ii. 122, iii. 135: v. 277, 569; vii. 232; viii. 244, 321.
—— parson of Duffus, ii. 122; viii. 319, 320.
Andrews, Elizabeth, wife of Geo. Baillie Hamilton of Jerviswoode, iv. 322.
—— John, iv. 322.

* Name unknown.

Andr John, clerk to the Privy Council, vii. 216.
—— Katharine, wife of Archibald Primrose, viii. 215.
Anesly, Sir John of, viii. 477.
—— Amabilla, wife of John Wemyss of Cameron, viii. 477.
Anglesey, Henry William (Paget) 1st marquess of, i. 388; v. 367.
—— —— his wife, Caroline Elizabeth Villiers, i. 388.
—— James (Annesley), 3rd earl of, i. 35.
—— —— his wife, Katharine Darnley, i. 35.
Angoulême, Henry, bastard of, i. 23; viii. 540.
Angra, Sir Charles Stuart, baron Stuart de Rothesay, marquis of, ii. 304.
—— —— his wife, Elizabeth Margaret Yorke, ii. 304.
Angus, son of Gilbert, 1st earl of Angus, i. 162.
—— of the Isles, i. 321.
—— —— his wife,* Campbell, i. 321.
—— 'Og,' his son, i. 321.
—— of Garmoran, 3rd son of Somerled, v. 30.
—— MacEth, mormaer of Moray, vii. 158.
ANGUS, ANCIENT EARLS OF, i. 160-166.
Angus, Adam, second earl of, i. 161, 162.
—— Gilbert or Gillebride, fifth earl of, i. 106, 160, 416; ii. 317.
—— Gilchrist, third earl of, i. 12, 106, 161, 162; ii. 317.
—— Duffagan, perhaps an earl of, iv. 2 *n*.
—— Duncan, fourth earl of, i. 162, 165.
—— Malcolm, fifth earl of, i. 165.
—— Matilda, wife of (1) John Comyn, (2) Sir G. de Umfraville, and (3) Richard of Dover; countess of, i. 165, 167; ix. 11.
ANGUS, COMYN, EARL OF, i. 167.
Angus, John, *jure uxoris* earl of, i. 167, 506.
—— —— his wife, Matilda, countess of Angus, 166, 167.
ANGUS, UMFRAVILLE, EARL OF, i. 167-168.
Angus, Gilbert, *jure ux.* first earl of, i. 167.
—— —— his wife Matilda, countess of Angus, i. 166.
—— Gilbert, second earl of, i. 168; ii. 256; iii. 137; ix. 11.
—— —— his wife, Elizabeth Comyn, ii. 256; ix. 11.
—— Gilbert, fourth earl of, i. 168; ix. 11 *ter*.
—— —— his 1st wife, Joan Willoughby, ix. 11.
—— —— his 2nd wife, Maud de Lacy, ix. 11.
—— Robert, third earl of, i. 168; ii. 256; ix. 11.
—— —— his 1st wife, Lucy de Kyme, ix. 11.
—— —— his 2nd wife, Alianore *, ix. 11.
ANGUS, STEWART, EARL OF, i. 169-171.
Angus, John, first earl of, i. 169.
—— —— his wife, Margaret Abernethy, i. 170; iii. 10, 13; vii. 402.

* Name unknown.

Angus, Margaret, wife of Thomas, 9th earl of Mar, and mistress of 1st Earl of Douglas; countess of, i. 171, 172; iii. 153, 154; iv. 304; v. 585.
— Thomas, second earl of, i. 170; iii. 13.
— his wife, Margaret Sinclair. i. 170; vi. 567.
ANGUS, DOUGLAS, EARL OF, i. 172-213.
Angus, Archibald, fifth earl of, i. 177, 178; ii. 62, 151, 459; iii. 22, 65; iv. 31, 406; v. 103; vii. 278; ix. 12.
— — his contracted wife, Katharine Gordon, i. 182; iv. 526.
— — his 1st wife, Elizabeth Boyd, i. 183; v. 146; ix. 12.
— — his 2nd wife, Katharine Stirling, i. 183; iv. 456.
— Archibald, sixth earl of, i. 21, 187, 190; ii. 155; iii. 318, 439; iv. 261, 357; v. 56, 58, 153; vii. 41, 120, 335; viii. 17, 19, 279, 399; ix. 12 *quat.*
— — his 1st wife, Margaret Hepburn, i. 192; ii. 155; ix. 12.
— — his 2nd wife, queen Margaret Tudor, i. 21, 192; ix. 12.
— — his 3rd wife, Margaret Maxwell, i. 192; vi. 481; ix. 12.
— Archibald, eighth earl of, i. 193, 194; iv. 371, 577; vi. 228, 362; vii. 377.
— — his 1st wife, Mary Erskine, i. 196; v. 615.
— — his 2nd wife, Margaret Leslie, i. 196; vii. 294; ix. 12.
— — his 3rd wife, Jean Lyon, i. 196; viii. 291.
— Archibald, eldest son of 1st marquess of Douglas; styled earl of, i. 65, 204, 206, 544.
— — his 1st wife, Anna Stewart, i. 207.
— — his 2nd wife, Jean Wemyss, i. 206; viii. 503.
— Archibald, thirteenth earl of, i. 210; iv. 393.
— David, seventh earl of, i. 188, 193.
— — his wife, Margaret Hamilton, i. 193, 248; iv. 363.
— George, first earl of, i. 18, 171, 172; iii. 154; iv. 81; viii. 381 *bis.*
— — his wife, Mary Stewart, i. 18, 173.
— George, fourth earl of, i. 175, 176; ii. 179, 228; vii. 322.
— — his wife, Isabella Sibbald, i. 177; iii. 92.
— James, third earl of, i. 19, 175; iv. 50.
— James, twelfth earl of, i. 207.
— James, eldest son of 2nd marquess of Douglas; styled earl of, i. 208.
— William, second earl of, i. 174; iv. 48, 446; ix. 11 *bis.*
— — his wife, Margaret Hay, i. 175; ix. 165.
Angus, William, ninth earl of, i. 184, 197.
— — his wife, Egidia Graham, i. 198.
— William, tenth earl of, i. 198, 199; iii. 574.
— — his wife, Elizabeth Oliphant, i. 201; vi. 549.
— William, eleventh earl of, i. 202; v. 73 *bis.*
— — his 1st wife, Margaret Hamilton, i. 45, 204.
— — his 2nd wife, Mary Gordon, i. 204; iv. 545.
— William, 2nd son of 2nd marquess of Douglas; styled earl of, i. 209.
ANGUS, HAMILTON, EARL OF, iv. 393-397.
Angus, James George, fourteenth earl of, iv. 393.
ANGUS AND ABERNETHY, DOUGLAS, EARL OF, i. 210.
Angus, Archibald, earl of, i. 210.
ANGUS AND ORMOND, DOUGLAS, EARL OF, i. 206.
Angus, Archibald, eldest son of 1st marquess of Douglas; earl of, i. 65, 206, 544; iii. 345.
— — his 1st wife, Anna Stewart, i. 207; v. 359; ix. 13.
— — his 2nd wife, Jean Wemyss, i. 207; iv. 77; viii. 503; ix. 13.
ANGUS, DOUGLAS, MARQUESS OF, i. 210.
Angus, Archibald, marquess of, i. 210.
— master of, George, eldest son of 5th earl of Angus, i. 181, 183, 186.
— — his contracted wife, Margaret Oliphant, i. 186; vi. 542.
— — his wife, Elizabeth Drummond, i. 187; vi. 147 *n.*; vii. 45.
— master of, George D. of Pittendreich, i. 185, 187, 191; iv. 358, 360, 380; v. 60; vi. 147 *n.*, 360; vii. 120; viii. 279, 437.
— — his wife, Elizabeth Douglas, i. 188.
— master of, James, son of 6th earl of Angus, i. 192.
— Hugh de, 1250, i. 107.
Anjou, Geoffrey Plantagenet, count of. i. 2.
— — his wife, Matilda of England, i. 2.
Ankerville, David Ross, judge of the Court of Session, lord, vii. 178.
Anna, wife of Colban, 8th earl of Fife, iv. 10.
Annabel, wife of Donald Strathechin of Monycabock, viii. 530.
Annabella of Durie, dau. of Duncan, son of Duncan, earl of Fife; wife of Sir Hugh of *, viii. 245 *n.*; ix. 89.
ANNAN, MURRAY, VISCOUNT, i. 228-229.
Annan, James, second viscount, i. 228.
— — his wife, Jean Carnegie, i. 229; viii. 70.
— John, first viscount, i. 228.
— — his wife, Elizabeth Shaw, i. 228.
ANNAND, JOHNSTONE, VISCOUNT OF, i. 261.

* Name unknown.

Annand, James, first viscount of, i. 261.
—— of Kellie, David, i. 84.
—— —— Henry, i. 84.
—— of Melgum, David, iv. 273.
—— —— his wife, * Gray, iv. 273.
—— of Octerellon, Alexander, vii. 438.
—— —— his wife, Margaret Fraser, vii. 438.
—— Agnes de, alleged wife of Robert de Brus of Skelton, ii. 429.
—— Elizabeth, wife of Alex. Gordon of Braco, i. 84.
ANNANDALE, STEWART, LORD OF, i. 151.
Annandale, Alexander, lord of, i. 151.
ANNANDALE, DOUGLAS, LORD OF, iii. 270.
Annandale, George, 10th earl of Dunbar, lord of, iii. 270.
ANNANDALE, MURRAY, EARL OF, i. 214-229.
Annandale, James, second earl of, i. 228, 476; viii. 197; ix. 14.
—— —— his wife, Jean Carnegie, i. 229, viii. 70.
—— John, first earl of, i. 225, 228; v. 266; viii. 193, 197.
—— —— his wife, Elizabeth Shaw, i. 228.
ANNANDALE, JOHNSTONE, EARL OF, i. 261-271.
Annandale, George, fourth earl of, i. 269.
—— James, first earl of, i. 261; ix. 15.
—— —— his wife, Henrietta Douglas, i. 205, 263.
—— James, third earl of, i. 269.
—— William, second earl of, i. 264.
—— —— his 1st wife, Sophia Fairholm, i. 268.
—— —— his 2nd wife, Charlotte van Lore Vanden Bempde, i. 268.
ANNANDALE, JOHNSTONE, MARQUESS OF, i. 230-271.
Annandale, George Vanden Bempde, third marquess of, i. 268; iv. 500.
—— James, second marquess of, i. 268, 269; iv. 494.
—— William, first marquess of, i. 263; v. 508.
—— —— his 1st wife, Sophia Fairholm, i. 268.
—— —— his 2nd wife, Charlotte van Lore vanden Bempde, i. 268.
Anne, 1st wife of James Kennedy, 4th son of Sir Alex. K. of Craigoch and Culzean, ii. 489.
—— Constance d'Arguille, sister, ix. 23.
—— 2nd wife of Rev. Richard Aston. i. 402.
—— wife of (1) John Thursby, Madras C.S., and (2) Leveson G. K. Murray, Madras C.S., iii. 390.
Annesley, Elinor, wife of John Madan Maitland, v. 314.
—— Gilbert, v. 314.
—— Katharine, wife of 2nd earl of Arran, i. 68.

* Name unknown.

Anson, Thomas (Anson), 1st viscount, vii. 226; viii. 210.
—— Anne Frederica, wife of 8th earl of Wemyss, viii. 517.
—— Anne Margaret, wife of 4th earl of Rosebery, vii. 226.
—— Archibald H. A., col., i. 392.
—— —— his wife, Julia Susanna Ward, i. 392.
—— Frances Elizabeth, wife of (1) Charles John Murray, and (2) Ambrose Isted, viii. 210.
—— Frederica Sophia, wife of Bouverie F. Primrose, vii. 226.
Anstruther of Airdrie, Sir James, i. 477.
—— —— his wife, Katharine Skene, i. 477.
—— of Anstruther, John, iii. 20.
—— —— his wife, Elizabeth Spens, iii. 20.
—— —— Sir John, 1st bart., iv. 594; ix. 114.
—— —— his wife, Margaret Carmichael, iv. 594.
—— —— Sir John, 5th bart., iv. 594, 597.
—— —— Sir William, M.P., iv. 318.
—— —— his wife, Helen Hamilton, iv. 318.
—— of Balcaskie, Sir Philip, 2nd bart., viii. 456.
—— —— his wife, Katharine Hay, viii. 456.
—— —— Sir Robert, vi. 589.
—— —— Sir Robert, 3rd bart., iv. 388; v. 89.
—— —— his wife, Janet Erskine, v. 89.
—— of Balgarvie, Robert, general, v. 317.
—— —— his wife, Elizabeth Maitland, v. 317.
—— of Huntsmore Park, David, vi. 445.
—— —— his wife, * Donaldson, vi. 445.
—— of Pitcorthy, Cecilia, wife of John Strang, iii. 269.
—— —— Richard, iii. 269.
—— of Thirdpart, Sir Alexander, advocate-general at Madras, ii. 57.
—— Sir Alexander, 5th son of Sir Philip A. of Anstruther, v. 386.
—— —— his wife, Jane Leslie, styled lady Newark, v. 386; vi. 443.
—— Jean, wife of James Douglas, vi. 372.
—— Jean, wife of James Makgill of Rankeillor, vi. 589.
—— John, colonel, vii. 587.
—— —— his wife, Grizel Maria Thomson of Charleton, vii. 587.
—— Louisa Anne Erskine, wife of Sir F. W. Hamilton, ii. 57.
—— Robert, brigadier-general, iv. 388.
—— —— his wife, Charlotte Lucy Hamilton, iv. 388.
Anton, Christiana, wife of 9th viscount Falkland, iii. 615.
—— P., minister of Kilsyth, v. 194.
Antrim, Charlotte (McDonnell), wife of vice-admiral lord Mark R. Ker; countess of, v. 482.

* Name unknown.

Antrim, Hugh Seymour (McDonnell), 4th earl of, v. 483.
—— Mark (McDonnell), 5th earl of, v. 483.
—— Randal (McDonnell), 1st earl of, viii. 348.
—— Randal (McDonnell), marquess of, i. 48, 351; v. 563.
—— Randal William (McDonnell), 6th earl, and marquess of, v. 482.
Antrobus of Antrobus, Sir Edmund, 2nd bart., i. 528.
—— —— his wife, Anne Lindsay, i. 528.
—— of Eaton Hall, John Coutts, iii. 44.
—— —— his wife, Mary Egidia Lindsay, iii. 44.
—— Hugh Lindsay, viii. 235.
—— Katharine Mary, wife of col. Laurence George Drummond, viii. 235.
—— Margaret Freda Evelyn, wife of G. de St. C. Rollo, vii. 210.
—— Robert Craufurd, vii. 210.
Apchier, Beatrice, wife of John Stewart, lord of Aubigny and Concressault, v. 347.
—— Bérault, seigneur d', v. 347.
Apprice, Robert, iii. 294.
—— —— his wife, Anne Constable, iii. 294.
Appsley of Appsley, Cordelia, wife of capt. James Dalrymple, viii. 131.
—— —— John, viii. 131.
Apsley, Sir Alan, lieutenant of Tower of London, iii. 99.
—— Jocosa, wife of (1) Lyster Blount, and (2) 1st earl of Dalhousie, iii. 99.
Apthorp, Anna, wife of Charles H. Douglas-Hamilton, iv. 388.
Arbuckle, James, merchant burgess, Edinburgh, iii. 447.
—— Katharine, wife of (1) John Hamilton of Bardanoch, and (2) Hugh Montgomerie, iii. 447, 448; ix. 81.
ARBUTHNOTT, ARBUTHNOTT, VISCOUNT OF, i. 272-317.
Arbuthnott, David, eleventh viscount of, i. 315.
—— John, fifth viscount of, i. 310, 312.
—— —— his wife, Jean Morrison, i. 312.
—— John, sixth viscount of, i. 308, 313.
—— —— his 1st wife, Marjory Douglas, i. 313.
—— —— his 2nd wife, Jean Arbuthnott, i. 313.
—— John, seventh viscount of, i. 313.
—— —— his wife, Isabella Grahame, i. 314.
—— John, eighth viscount of, i. 314.
—— —— his wife, Margaret Ogilvy, i. 130, 314.
—— John, ninth viscount of, i. 316.
—— —— his wife, Jean Graham Drummond Ogilvy, i. 130, 316.
—— John, tenth viscount of, i. 316.
—— —— his wife, Anna Harriet Allen, i. 316.
—— Robert, first viscount of, i. 304.
—— —— his 1st wife, Marjory Carnegie, i. 304; viii. 67.
—— —— his 2nd wife, Katharine Fraser, i. 304; v. 534.
Arbuthnott, Robert, second viscount of, i. 307.
—— —— his 1st wife, Elizabeth Keith, i. 308; vi. 60.
—— —— his 2nd wife, Katharine Gordon, i. 308; viii. 78.
—— Robert, third viscount of, i. 308, 310.
—— —— his wife, Ann Sutherland Gordon, i. 316; viii. 352.
—— Robert, fourth viscount of, i. 311.
—— master of, Robert, eldest son of 6th viscount of Arbuthnott, i. 313.
ARBUTHNOTT, VISCOUNT OF ARBUTHNOTT, i. 272-317.
ARBUTHNOTT, LORD OF BERVIE, i. 305.
Arbuthnott of Achtirforfar, Alexander, i. 291.
—— —— his wife, Margaret Middleton, i. 292.
—— —— David, i. 192.
—— —— his wife, Jean Keith, i. 292.
—— —— Robert, i. 290.
—— of Arbeikie, James, tutor of Arbuthnott, 2nd son of James A. of Arrat, i. 295, 298.
—— —— his wife, Elizabeth Blair, i. 299.
—— —— Robert, i. 295, 299.
—— —— his wife, Anna Douglas, i. 299.
—— of Arbuthnott, Andrew, 15th laird, i. 290, 297.
—— —— his 1st wife, Elizabeth Carnegie, i. 297; viii. 56.
—— —— his 2nd wife, Margaret Hoppringil, i. 298.
—— —— David, 11th laird, i. 281.
—— —— his wife, Elizabeth Durham, i. 281.
—— —— Duncan de, 2nd laird, i. 274, 423.
—— —— Duncan de, 5th laird, i. 275.
—— —— Duncan de, 6th laird, i. 276.
—— —— Hugh, 9th laird, i. 278.
—— —— his wife, Margaret Keith, i. 279; vi. 39.
—— —— Hugo de Swinton, 1st laird, i. 272.
—— —— Hugo de, 3rd laird, i. 274.
—— —— Hugo, 'le Blond,' 4th laird, i. 274; v. 203.
—— —— Hugo, 7th laird, i. 276.
—— —— James, 13th laird, i. 284, 288.
—— —— his wife, Jean or Janet Stewart, i. 288, 443.
—— —— Philip de, 8th laird, i. 276.
—— —— his 1st wife, Janet Keith, i. 276; vi. 37.
—— —— his 2nd wife, Margaret Douglas, i. 276.
—— —— Robert, 10th laird, i. 279.
—— —— his wife, Giles Ogilvy, i. 112, 279.
—— —— Robert, 12th laird, i. 282; iii. 307.
—— —— his 1st wife, Margaret Wishart, i. 282; ix. 15.
—— —— his 2nd wife, Mariot Scrymgeour, i. 282.

Arbuthnott of Arbuthnott, Robert, 14th laird, i. 289; ix. 16.
—— his 1st wife, Katharine Erskine, i. 290.
—— his 2nd wife, Christian Keith, i. 290; vi. 43.
—— his 3rd wife, Helen Clephane, i. 290.
—— Sir Robert, 16th laird, i. 299.
—— his wife, Mary Keith, i. 299; vi. 50.
—— Sir Robert, 17th laird, i. 298, 301.
—— his 1st wife, Margaret Keith, i. 302; vi. 53; ix. 15.
—— his 2nd wife, Margaret Fraser, i. 302; v. 532.
—— Robert, 18th laird, i. 302, 304.
—— his 1st wife, Marjory Carnegie, i. 305; viii. 67.
—— his 2nd wife, Katharine Fraser, i. 305.
— of Arbuthnottshaugh, Thomas, M.D., i. 308.
—— his wife, Margaret Forbes, i. 308.
— of Arrat, James, 3rd son of Andrew A. of that Ilk, i. 298.
—— his wife, Margaret Livingstone, i. 298.
—— Robert, i. 298, 300, 301.
— of Balwyllo, Elizabeth, i. 304.
— of Banff, Robert, i. 284.
— of Blackstoun, Alexander, i. 296.
—— James, i. 296.
—— his wife, Margaret Rattray, i. 296.
—— William, 8th son of Robt. A. of that Ilk, i. 296.
— of Easter Brichty, Janet, i. 280.
—— John, i. 280.
—— his wife, Janet Mason, i. 280.
— of Cairnibeg and Dulladies, James, 2nd son of James A. of Arrat, i. 298, 305.
—— his wife, Elizabeth Blair, i. 299.
— of Caldhame, Robert, i. 294.
—— his wife, Margaret Grahame, i. 294.
— of Caterline, Alexander, i. 304.
—— Elizabeth, of Balwyllo, i. 304.
—— James, i. 304.
—— John, son of Simon A., i. 303, 312.
—— his wife, Magdalen Garden, i. 303.
—— John, i. 303.
—— John, 5th viscount A., i. 304, 312.
—— Robert, eldest son of David A. of Achtirforfar, i. 286, 292.
—— his wife, Margaret Arbuthnott, i. 292.
—— Mr. Robert, i. 292, 303; ix. 16.
—— Simon, i. 292, 303.
—— his wife, Magdalen Melville, i. 303.
— of Chapelton and Nether Pitforthies, Patrick, i. 299.
—— his wife, * Rait, i. 299.
— of Coschnow, John, i. 291.

* Name unknown.

Arbuthnott of Coschnow, William, i. 291.
— of Fiddes, Andrew, i. 514.
—— his wife, Helen Lindsay, i. 514.
—— Andrew, i. 286: ix. 16.
—— his 1st wife, Sara Strachan, ix. 16.
—— his 2nd wife, Janet Gordon, i. 286.
—— Andrew, 2nd son of Sir Robt. A. of that Ilk, i. 286, 302.
—— John, i. 303.
—— his wife, Helen Bruce, i. 303.
—— Robert, i. 285.
—— his wife, Isabel Burnett, i. 285.
—— Robert, i. 286.
—— his 1st wife, Margaret Barclay, i. 286.
—— his 2nd wife, Jean Burnett, i. 286.
—— his 3rd wife, Mary Arbuthnott, i. 286, 293.
— of Findowrie, Alexander, i. 295, 312.
—— his wife, Margaret Ochterlony, i. 295.
—— David, 5th son of Robt. A. of that Ilk, i. 294; iii. 322; ix. 16.
—— his 1st wife, Elizabeth Rait, i. 294.
—— his 2nd wife, * Stuart, i. 294.
—— Margaret, wife of James Carnegie, i. 295.
—— Robert. i. 294, 305.
—— his wife, Margaret Grahame, i. 294.
—— Robert, i. 294.
—— his wife, Elizabeth Rait, i. 294.
— of Finnart, James, i. 309.
—— Robert, i. 309.
— of Fordoun, John, 3rd son of 1st viscount of Arbuthnott, i. 308, 311, 312, 313.
—— his wife, Margaret Falconer, i. 308.
—— John, his son, i. 308, 313.
—— his 1st wife, Marjory Douglas, i. 313.
—— his 2nd wife, Jean Arbuthnott. i. 295, 313.
— of Kirkbraehead, Alexander, i. 307.
— Robert, son of Alex. A. of Knox, i. 307.
—— his wife, Elizabeth Riddel, i. 307.
— of Knox, Alexander, 2nd son of 1st viscount of Arbuthnott, i. 306, 311; ix. 16.
—— his 1st wife, Margaret Barclay, i. 306.
—— his 2nd wife, Jean Scott, i. 306.
—— Alexander, his son, i. 306, 307.
—— his wife, Janet Rennald, i. 307.
— of Legasland, James, i. 280.
—— John, i. 280; ix. 15 *bis*.
—— his wife, Christian Fraser, i. 280.
— of Mondynes, John, 2nd son of Robt. A. of that Ilk, i. 290.
—— his 1st wife, Katharine Pitcairn, i. 291.
—— his 2nd wife, Elizabeth Grahame, i. 291.
—— Robert, i. 291.
—— his wife, Margaret Symmer, i. 291.

* Name unknown.

Arbuthnott of Mondynes, William, i. 291.
—— —— William, vii. 18.
—— —— his wife, Isobel Maule, vii. 18.
—— of Pitcarles, Alexander, i. 291.
—— —— his wife, Margaret Middleton, i. 292.
—— —— Alexander, i. 292.
—— —— his wife, Margaret Haliburton, i. 292.
—— —— Andrew, i. 273, 285.
—— —— David, i. 286, 292.
—— —— his wife, Jean Keith, i. 292.
—— of Portertown, i. 280, 281; ix. 15 *bis*.
—— of Tortairstoun, Andrew, i. 302; ix. 16.
—— Agnes, wife of Alex. Straiton, i. 293.
—— Alexander, Principal of King's College, Aberdeen, i. 272, 285, 287.
—— Alexander, parson of Arbuthnott, i. 273, 280.
—— Alexander, 4th son of John A. of Legasland, i. 280.
—— Alexander, 4th son of David A., i. 280.
—— Mr. Alexander, 5th son of Hugh A., i. 281.
—— Alexander, 4th son of Robt. A. of that Ilk, i. 281.
—— Mr. Alexander, 2nd son of Robt. A. of Little Fiddes, i. 285.
—— Alexander, merchant, Dundee, i. 286.
—— his 1st wife, Janet Gordon, ix. 16.
—— Alexander, husband of Katharine Arbuthnott, i. 287.
—— Alexander, M.D., Dundee, i. 292.
—— Alexander, eldest son of Robt. A. of Findowrie, i. 294.
—— —— his wife, Margaret Lindsay, i. 294.
—— Alexander, in Arbeikie, i. 295.
—— Alexander, 3rd son of Andrew A. of Fiddes, i. 303.
—— Alexander, 3rd son of Sir Robt. A. of that Ilk, i. 303.
—— Alexander, Fort William, Bengal, i. 304.
—— Alexander, 9th son of 7th viscount of Arbuthnott, i. 314.
—— Alexander, son of Alex. A., Dundee, ix. 16.
—— Sir Alexander Dundas Young, admiral, i. 307.
—— —— his wife, Katharine Maria Eustace, i. 307.
—— Alexander George. i. 309.
—— Alwin de, 1241, i. 273, 274; ix. 15.
—— Ambrose, son of Robt. A. of that Ilk, i. 282.
—— Andrew, priest, i. 284.
—— Andrew, 3rd son of Robt. A. of Little Fiddes, i. 286.
—— Andrew, eldest son of John A. of Mondynes, i. 291.
—— Andrew, 3rd son of Alex. A. in Pitcarles, i. 292; ix. 16.
Arbuthnott, Andrew, 4th son of Andrew A. of Fiddes, i. 303; ix. 16.
—— Andrew, son of Robt. A., Dundee, i. 304.
—— Ann, wife of James Allardyce, i. 286.
—— Ann, dau. of Romeo A., i. 307
—— Ann, dau. of John A. of Fordoun, i. 309.
—— Ann, dau. of Thomas A., i. 310.
—— Ann, wife of Robt. Burnett, i. 310.
—— Anna, wife of Wm. Forbes, i. 307.
—— Anne, wife of John Horn, i. 310.
—— Anne Charlotte, wife of Alex. Cheape, i. 316.
—— Archibald, merchant, Edinburgh, i. 307.
—— —— his wife, Margaret Lee, i. 307.
—— Archibald, merchant in London, i. 307.
—— Archibald, son of Hugh Corsar A., i. 315.
—— Charles James Donald, i. 316.
—— —— his wife, Caroline *, i. 316.
—— Charlotte, dau. of 6th viscount of Arbuthnott, i. 313.
—— Charlotte Louisa, dau. of 8th viscount of Arbuthnott, i. 316.
—— Christian, dau. of David A. of that Ilk, i. 282.
—— Christian, wife of Alex. Fraser, i. 287.
—— Christian, wife of George Symmer, i. 293.
—— Christian, dau. of David A. of Findowrie, i. 294.
—— Christian, dau. of Romeo A., i. 307.
—— Clementina, wife of Alex. Stuart of Inchbreck, i. 316.
—— Clementina Maria, wife of Col. W. R. Campbell, i. 316.
—— David, 2nd son of Hugh A., i. 280.
—— —— his wife, Christian Rhind, i. 280.
—— David, son of John A. of Legasland, i. 280.
—— David, son of David A., i. 280.
—— David, canon of Dunkeld, i. 288.
—— David, 3rd son of Robt. A. of Caterline, i. 292.
—— David, 2nd son of David A. of Findowrie, i. 294.
—— David, 2nd son of Robt. A. of Findowrie, i. 295.
—— David, C.S.I., i. 315.
—— —— his wife, Eliza Reynolds, i. 315.
—— David, his son, i. 315.
—— David, son of Donald S. A., i. 315.
—— Donald Stuart, C.E., i. 315.
—— —— his wife, Anne Elizabeth Brand, i. 315.
—— Duncan, 5th son of 7th viscount of Arbuthnott, i. 314.
—— Edith Gertrude, i. 315.
—— Eliza Clementina, i. 315.
—— Elizabeth, wife of Patrick Barclay, i. 282.

* Name unknown.

Arbuthnott, Elizabeth, wife of (1) Thos. Fotheringham, and (2) Martin of Cardowne, i. 287.
—— Elizabeth, dau. of David A. of Findowrie, i. 294.
—— Elizabeth, dau. of Alex. A., i. 294.
—— Elizabeth, dau. of Robt. A. of Findowrie, i. 295.
—— Elizabeth, wife of Jas. Mortimer, i. 296.
—— Elizabeth, wife of Jas. Douglas, i. 299.
—— Elizabeth, wife of J. Garden, i. 299; ix. 16.
—— Elizabeth, dau. of Alex. A. of Knox, i. 307.
—— Elizabeth, wife of Wm. Forbes, i. 309.
—— Elizabeth, dau. of John A. of Fordoun, i. 309.
—— Elizabeth, dau. of Thos. A., i. 310.
—— Elizabeth, wife of Andrew Wood, i. 310.
—— Elizabeth, dau. of Alex. A., Dundee, ix. 16.
—— Elspeth, wife of Sir Jas. Young, i. 294.
—— Evander, son of Archibald A., i. 307.
—— Francis William, i. 314.
—— George, 3rd son of Robt. A. of that Ilk, i. 285.
—— George, 2nd son of Andrew A. in Pitcarles, and of Little Fiddes, i. 287.
——Mr. George, 4th son of Alex. A. of Achtirforfar, i. 292.
—— George, son of Alex. A., Arbeikie, i. 295.
—— George, in Halwestown, i. 296.
—— George, 2nd son of Andrew A. of that Ilk, i. 298.
—— George, 4th son of John A. of Caterline, i. 304.
—— Georgina Muriel, i. 315.
—— Giles, wife of (1) Cargill of Lessington, and (2) Alex. Fraser, i. 282.
—— Giles, wife of (1) Henry Grahame; (2) Andrew Strachan, and (3) Thos. Fraser, i. 287; iv. 109; ix. 16.
—— Guille, archer of Scots Guard, ix. 15.
—— Harry, 3rd son of Romeo A., i. 307.
—— Helen, wife of (1) Jas. Haliburton, and (2) George Kinnaird, i. 293.
—— Helen, wife of Alex. Fraser, i. 299.
—— Helen, wife of (1) Robt. Burnett, and (2) John Sandilands, i. 303; ix. 16.
—— Helen, wife of H. J. P. Rollo, i. 307.
—— Helen, wife of (1) John Macfarlane, and (2) John Spottiswood, i. 310.
—— Helen, dau. of 3rd viscount of Arbuthnott, i. 311.
—— Helen, wife of F. L. Scrymgeour Wedderburn, i. 316.
—— Hugh, son of Robt. A. of that Ilk, i. 279.
—— —— his wife, Janet Balmakewan, i. 279.
—— Hugh, 5th son of David A., i. 280.
—— Hugh, 3rd son of Hugh A., i. 281.
—— —— his wife, * Hay, i. 281.

* Name unknown.

Arbuthnott, Hugh, physician in France, i. 281.
—— Hugh, legtd. son of Robt. A. of that Ilk, 290.
—— Hugh, 3rd son of 6th viscount of Arbuthnott, i. 313.
—— Sir Hugh, K.C.B., M.P., i. 314.
—— Hugh, lieut.-col. 3rd Madras lt. cavalry, i. 315.
—— —— his wife, Susan Thomson Campbell, i. 315.
—— Hugh, 2nd son of Hugh Corsar A., i. 315.
—— Hugh, 3rd son of 9th viscount of Arbuthnott, i. 316.
—— Hugh Corsar, C.E., i. 315.
—— —— his wife, Marianne Gibson, i. 315.
—— Hugh Hamilton, son of John Campbell A., i. 315.
—— Isabel, dau. of Robt. A. of that Ilk, i. 287.
—— Isabel, wife of Alex. Strachan, i. 293.
—— Isabel, dau. of Alex. A. of Knox, i. 307.
—— Isabel, dau. of 3rd viscount of Arbuthnott, i. 311.
—— Isobel, wife of Sir Jas. Young, i. 294.
—— Isobel, dau. of Robert A. of Findowrie, i. 295.
—— Isobel, wife of (1) David Ochterlony of Kelly, and (2) Robert Maule of Panmure, i. 288; vii. 12.
—— Isabella Mary, dau. of 8th viscount of Arbuthnott, i. 316.
—— James, collector of Cess for Angus and Mearns, i. 280; ix. 15.
—— James, son of Robert A. of that Ilk, i. 281.
—— —— his wife, * Grahame, i. 281.
—— James, merchant burgess of Montrose, i. 286.
—— James, in Garriotsmyre, i. 296.
—— —— his wife, Katharine Stewart, i. 296.
—— James, 3rd son of Jas. A. of Arbeikie, i. 299.
—— James, shipmaster, Leith, i. 304.
—— —— his wife, Helen Arnot, i. 304.
—— James, eldest son of Romeo A., i. 307.
—— James, merchant in Edinburgh, i. 308.
—— James, captain R.N., i. 314.
—— James, son of Alex. A., Dundee, ix. 16.
—— James Gordon, i. 315.
—— Jane, dau. of 7th viscount of Arbuthnott, i. 314.
—— Janet, wife of (1) Alex. Falconer, and (2) George Auchinleck, i. 287; v. 244.
—— Janet, wife of Wm. Rait of Halgreen, i. 304.
—— Janet, dau. of Alex. A. of Knox, i. 307.
—— Janet, wife of James Lee, i. 307.
—— Jean, dau. of Robt. A. of Little Fiddes, i. 286.
—— Jean, wife of George Rait, i. 292.
—— Jean, dau. of Alex. A., Pitcarles, i. 292.

* Name unknown.

Arbuthnott, Jean, wife of James Clephane, i. 293.
—— Jean, wife of 6th viscount Arbuthnott, i. 295, 313.
—— Jean, dau. of Andrew A. of Fiddes, i. 303.
—— Jean, wife of (1) Alex. Burnett; (2) Patrick Gordon, and (3) Sir William Douglas, i. 304.
—— Jean, wife of Samuel Straton, i. 306.
—— Jean, dau. of Romeo A., i. 307.
—— Jean, wife of William Galloway, i. 307.
—— Jean, wife of Alex. Gordon, i. 309.
—— Jean, dau. of John A. of Fordun, i. 309.
—— Jean, dau. of 2nd viscount of Arbuthnott, i. 310.
—— Jean, wife of capt. Crawford of Camlurg, i. 310.
—— Jean, wife of Alex. Cavendish, i. 315.
—— Jean Ogilvy, wife of Comr. Jas. Cheape, R.N., i. 316.
—— Jeannie, wife of Nicholas Dodd Beatson-Bell, i. 315.
—— Joan, wife of Jas. Clephane, i. 293.
—— John, physician to Queen Anne, i. 273, 280.
—— John, 3rd son of John A. of Legasland, i. 280.
—— John, son of Robert A. 'in Banff,' i. 281.
—— John, 2nd son of Alex. A. of Achtirforfar, i. 292.
—— John, son of Robt. A. of Findowrie, i. 295.
—— John, 2nd son of Robt. A. of Kirkbraehead, i. 307.
—— John, eldest son of Dr. A. of Arbuthnottshaugh, i. 308.
—— John, eldest son of Hugh Corsar A., i. 315.
—— John Campbell, C.I.E., i. 315.
—— —— his wife, Jeannie Sinclair Hamilton, i. 315.
—— John Ogilvy, i. 315.
—— John Pelly, i. 315.
—— John Robert, i. 315.
—— Josette, wife of (1) capt. Hughes, and (2) Gen. Sir De Lacy Evans, i. 307.
—— Josette Eliza Jane, wife of major Wollaston, i. 307.
—— Katharine, wife of * Gorthie of that Ilk, i. 280; ix. 15.
—— Katharine, wife of John Allardice, i. 281.
—— Katharine, wife of Alex. Grahame, tutor of Morphie, i. 282.
—— Katharine, wife of Alex. Burnett, i. 285.
—— Katharine, wife of Alex. Arbuthnott, i. 287.
—— Katharine, wife of (1) David Auchinleck, and (2) Gilbert Turing, i. 287.
—— Katharine, dau. of George A., i. 287.

* Name unknown.

Arbuthnott, Katharine, wife of James Thomson, i. 292.
—— Katharine, wife of Jas. Mortimer, i. 296.
—— Katharine, wife of Francis Melville, i. 299.
—— Katharine, wife of Chas. Stirling of Kippendavie, i. 306.
—— Katharine, wife of James Moir, i. 309.
—— Katharine, wife of (1) Robt. Gordon, and (2) David Riccart, i. 310.
—— Katharine, wife of rev. D. Lyell, i. 314.
—— Kathleen Georgina, wife of lt.-col. Rait of Anniston, i. 315.
—— Lindsay George, i. 315.
—— Louise Curzon, i. 315.
—— Magdalen, dau. of Robt. A. of Findowrie, i. 295.
—— Margaret, wife of Andrew Menzies, i. 279.
—— Margaret, wife of (1) Alex. Balhirnie, and (2) John Ogilvy, i. 280.
—— Margaret, wife of (1) Robt. A. of Caterline, and (2) Sir Geo. Ogilvy, i. 286, 292.
—— Margaret, wife of Andrew Sibbald of Kair, i. 291.
—— Margaret, wife of David Guthrie, i. 292.
—— Margaret, dau. of David A. of Findowrie, i. 294.
—— Margaret, dau. of Robt. A. of Findowrie, i. 295.
—— Margaret, wife of James Ogilvy, i. 295.
—— Margaret, wife of David Ogilvie of Powrie, i. 297; ix. 16.
—— Margaret, illeg. dau. of John A., Montrose, i. 304.
—— Margaret, wife of Alex. Carnegie of Pitarrow, i. 304; viii. 75.
—— Margaret, wife of Sir John Forbes of Monymusk, i. 306.
—— Margaret, wife of Jas. Napier, Montrose, i. 305.
—— Margaret, wife of T. L. Whittier, i. 307.
—— Margaret, wife of Sir T. Burnett, i. 308.
—— Margaret, wife of William Ross, i. 309.
—— Margaret, dau. of John A. of Fordoun, i. 309.
—— Margaret, dau. of 3rd viscount of Arbuthnott, i. 311.
—— Margaret, wife of Sir Alex. Dunbar of Northfield, i. 313.
—— Margaret, dau. of Donald S. A., i. 315.
—— Margaret, wife of W. J. Lumsden, i. 316.
—— Margaret, dau. of 9th viscount of Arbuthnott, i. 316.
—— Margaret Fanny, dau. of David A., i. 315.
—— Margaret Ogilvy, i. 315.
—— Margaret *or* Marjorie, wife of Sir William Monypenny, vi. 276.

Arbuthnott, Marie, dau. of Robt. A. of Findowrie, i. 295.
— Mariot, 8th son of 7th viscount of Arbuthnott, i. 314.
— Mariota or Marion, wife of Jas. Bisset, i. 287.
— Mary, 3rd wife of Robert A. of Little Fiddes, i. 286, 293.
— Mary, dau. of Wm. A. of Mondynes, i. 291.
— Mary, wife of Alexander Hay, i. 292.
— Mary, wife of Robt. A., Deptford, i. 306, 310.
— Mary, wife of John Douglas of Tilwhilly, i. 309.
— Mary, dau. of 3rd viscount of Arbuthnott, i. 311.
— Marjory, wife of Alex. Keith of Cowtoun, i. 286.
— Marjory, wife of F. Farquharson, i. 295.
— Marjory, dau. of Jas. A. of Arbeikie, i. 299.
— Norah Gertrude, i. 315.
— Patrick, W.S., 6th son of Robt. A. of Little Fiddes, i. 286; ix. 16 *bis*.
— Patrick, canon of Dunkeld, and physician to King James v., i. 288, 289; ix. 16.
— Patrick, 2nd son of James A. of that Ilk, i. 288.
— Patrick, 3rd son of Alex. A. of Knox, i. 307.
— Mr. Peter, pedagogue to lord Thirlestane, ix. 15.
— Robert, parson of Arbuthnott, i. 273, 293.
— Robert, 2nd son of John A. of Legasland, i. 280.
— Robert, 2nd son of Robert A. of Arbuthnott, i. 284; vi. 44.
— — his wife, Marion Lundie, vi. 44.
— Robert, provost of Montrose, i. 280, 311.
— Robert, 'in Banff,' i. 281, 289.
— — his wife, * Lychtoun, i. 281.
— Robert, 4th son of Robt. A. of Little Fiddes, i. 286.
— Mr. Robert, 5th son of Alex. A. of Achtirforfar, i. 292; ix. 16.
— Robert, son of David A. of Findowrie, i. 294; iii. 322.
— — his wife, Margaret Graham, iii. 322.
— Robert, illeg. son of James A. of Arrat, i. 298.
— Robert, eldest son of Andrew A. of Fiddes, i. 302.
— Robert, merchant in Dundee, i. 304.
— Robert, illeg. son of Sir Robert A. of that Ilk, i. 304.
— Robert, 2nd son of Alex. A. of Knox, i. 306.
— — his wife, Elizabeth Malloch, i. 306.

* Name unknown.

Arbuthnott, Robert, shipwright at Deptford, i. 306.
— — his wife, Mary Arbuthnott, i. 306, 310.
— Robert, lieut-col. 31st foot, i. 307.
— — his wife, Cordelia Murray, i. 307.
— Robert, 3rd son of 7th viscount of Arbuthnott, i. 314.
— Robert, son of Hugh Corsar A., i. 315.
— Robert Keith, i. 315.
— Robin Hugh Claud, i. 315.
— Romeo, stockbroker, London, i. 307.
— — his wife, Christian Ramsay, i. 307.
— Sara, wife of Robert Stuart of Inchbreck, i. 286.
— Susanna, 5th dau. of Alex. A., Pitcarles, i. 293.
— Thomas, 2nd son of Jas. A. of Arbeikie, i. 299.
— Thomas, 2nd son of Romeo A., i. 307.
— Thomas, son of Dr. A. of Arbuthnottshaugh, i. 308.
— Thomas, 5th son of 2nd viscount of Arbuthnott, i. 309.
— — his wife, Elizabeth Falconer, i. 309.
— Walter, 2nd son of 8th vicount of Arbuthnott, i. 315.
— — his wife, Anna Maria Otley, i. 315.
— Walter Charles Warner, lt.-col., R.A., i. 315.
— — his wife, Emma Marion Parlby, i. 315.
— William, a notary, son of Hugh A., i. 281.
— William, son of Robt. A. 'in Banff,' i. 281.
— William, 6th son of Robt. A. of that Ilk, i. 281.
— — his wife, * Abirkyrdo, i. 281.
— William, General, R.A., i. 314.
— William, H.E.I.C.S., 5th son of 8th viscount of Arbuthnott, i. 315,
— — his wife, Elrington Douglas, i. 315.
— William, 4th son of 9th viscount of Arbuthnott, i. 316.
— *, wife of Straiton of Lauriston, 1300, i. 275.
— *, wife of David Rait of Drumnagair, i. 288.
— *, wife of Lindsay of Barnyards, i. 297.
Arbuthnott-Maitland of Pitrichie, Alexander, baron of Exchequer, i. 309.
— — his wife, Jean Maitland, i. 309.
— — Charles, advocate, M.P., i. 309.
— — Katharine, i. 309.
— — Margaret, i. 309.
— — Mary Ann, i. 309.
Archer-Houblon of Hallingbury Place, George, *né* Eyre, iii. 48.
— — his wife, Alice Frances Lindsay iii. 48.

* Name unknown.

Archibald, Janet, wife of Andrew Alexander, viii. 169.
Ard of Deskford, Ardach, and Skeith, Sir Christin del, iv. 44; ix. 90.
— Alexander del, vi. 568.
— John del, iv. 44.
— John del, son of Sir Christin del A., iv. 45.
— Wayland de l', ii. 320.
— — his wife, Matilda of Strathearn, ii. 320.
ARDELVE, MACKENZIE, BARON, vii. 512-513.
Ardelve, Kenneth, baron, vii. 512.
ARDMANOCH, STEWART, LORD, i. 155.
Ardmanoch, Charles, afterwards king Charles I., lord, i. 155.
ARDMANNACH, STEWART, EARL OF, vii. 246.
Ardmannach, James, 2nd son of king James III.; earl of, vii. 246.
ARDROSSAN OF ARDROSSAN, MONTGOMERIE, BARON, iii. 461-465.
Ardrossan, Hugh, first baron, iii. 460.
— — his wife, Eleonora Hamilton, iii. 461.
— Sir Fergus de, iv. 185.
Ards, Hugh (Montgomery) viscount of the Great, i. 254; viii. 547.
— — his wife, Sara Maxwell, i. 41 *n.*, 254.
Arfinn, 5th son of Thorfinn Skullsplitter, ii. 314.
Argenteau, Louis d', count of Esseneux and baron of Maelsbrock, iii. 480.
— Charlotte d', countess of Esseneux and baroness of Maelsbrock, wife of Thomas, 3rd earl of Elgin, iii. 480.
Argoult, Frances d', wife of Pierre de Forbin, iv. 43 *n.*
ARGYLL, CAMPBELL, EARL OF, i. 332-393.
Argyll, Archibald, second earl of, i. 335, 443; v. 400.
— — his wife, Elizabeth Stewart, i. 336; v. 350.
— Archibald, fourth earl of, i. 338; iv. 360, 366; v. 556; vii. 122; viii. 17, 166.
— — his 1st wife, Helen Hamilton, i. 339.
— — his 2nd wife, Margaret Graham, i. 339; vi. 159.
— — his 3rd wife, Katharine Maclean, i. 340; ix. 20 *bis*.
— Archibald, fifth earl of, i. 340; iii. 439; iv. 242; ix. 20, 21.
— — his 1st wife, Jean Stewart, i. 25, 342.
— — his 2nd wife, Jonet Cunningham, i. 343; ix. 21.
— Archibald, 'Gruamach,' seventh earl of, i. 346; v. 21; viii. 170; ix. 21 *bis*.
— — his 1st wife, Agnes Douglas, i. 349; vi. 374; ix. 21.
— — his 2nd wife, Anne Cornwallis, i. 350.
— Archibald, eighth earl of, i. 349, 351.
— — his wife, Margaret Douglas, i. 359; vi. 378.
Argyll, Archibald, ninth earl of, i. 359, 361, 520; ii. 298; iii. 208, 327, 347; v. 121, 564.
— his contr. wife Ann Hamilton, ix. 23.
— — his 1st wife, Mary Stewart, i. 366; vi. 321; ix. 24, 139 *bis*.
— — his 2nd wife, Anne *or* Jean Mackenzie, i. 368; vii. 507.
— Archibald, tenth earl of, i. 367, 368.
— — his wife, Elizabeth Talmash, i. 370.
— Archibald, twelfth earl of, i. 378.
— Colin, first earl of, i. 332; ii. 175, 177; v. 3, 4; vi. 83.
— — his wife, Elizabeth *or* Isabel Stewart, i. 332, 334.
— Colin 'Maillach,' third earl of, i. 22, 337; v. 526, 560.
— — his wife, Janet Gordon, i. 338; iv. 533; ix. 20.
— Colin, sixth earl of, i. 340, 344.
— — his 1st wife, Janet Stewart, i. 345; vi. 168; ix. 21.
— — his 2nd wife, Agnes Keith, i. 345; vi. 50; ix. 21, 134.
— George Douglas, seventeenth earl of, i. 389.
— George William, fifteenth earl of, i. 388.
— John, eleventh earl of, i. 370.
— John, thirteenth earl of, i. 383.
— John, fourteenth earl of, i. 386.
— John, Douglas Edward Henry, sixteenth earl of, i. 388.
— John George Edward Henry Douglas Sutherland, eighteenth earl of, i. 392.
ARGYLL, CAMPBELL, MARQUESS OF, i. 353.
Argyll, Archibald, marquess of, i. 351, 567; v. 120 *bis*, 477; vii. 299.
— — his wife, Margaret Douglas, i. 359; vi. 378.
ARGYLL, CAMPBELL, DUKE OF, i. 318-393.
Argyll, Archibald, first duke of, i. 368; vii. 141; ix. 24 *bis*.
— — his wife, Elizabeth Talmash, i. 370; iii. 405; ix. 24 *bis*.
— Archibald, third duke of, i. 65, 378.
— — his wife,* Whitfield, i. 380.
— George Douglas, eighth duke of, i. 389.
— — his 1st wife, Elizabeth Georgina Sutherland-Leveson-Gower, i. 390; viii. 363.
— — his 2nd wife, Maria Claughton, i. 392.
— — his 3rd wife, Ina Erskine Macneill, i. 392.
— George William, sixth duke of, i. 388.
— — his wife, Caroline Elizabeth Villiers, i. 388.
— John, second duke of, i. 370; ii. 241; iii. 354; vi. 62.
— — his 1st wife, Mary Brown, i. 376.
— — his 2nd wife, Jane Warburton, i. 376.

* Name unknown.

Argyll, John, fourth duke of, i. 381, 383.
—— —— his wife, Mary Bellenden, i. 383; ii. 74.
—— John, fifth duke of, i. 386.
—— —— his wife, Elisabeth Gunning, i. 387; ix. 25 *ter*.
—— John Douglas Edward Henry, seventh duke of, i. 388.
—— —— his 1st wife, Elizabeth Campbell, i. 388.
—— —— his 2nd wife, Joan Glassel, i. 388.
—— —— his 3rd wife, Anne Colquhoun Cunningham, i. 389.
—— John George Edward Henry Douglas Sutherland, ninth duke of, i. 392; ix. 25.
—— —— his wife, H.R.H. Princess Louise Caroline Alberta of Great Britain and Ireland, i. 393.
—— master of, Archibald, eldest son of 4th earl of Argyll, i. 339; ii. 182.
Argyll *or* Ergadia, Alexander of, i. 321.
—— —— Ewen of, viii. 246.
—— —— Isobel of, wife of Sir John Stewart of Innermeath, v. 2.
—— —— Janet of, wife of Robert Stewart of Rossyth, v. 1.
—— —— John of, vi. 203.
—— —— John of, lord of Lorn, v. 1.
—— —— Mary of, wife of (1) Magnus, King of Man; (2) Malise, earl of Strathearn; (3) Sir Hugh de Abernethy; and (4) William Fitzwaren, vii. 400; viii. 246.
—— *, wife of Sir Partick de Graham, vi. 204.
Arkell of Northumbria, v. 325.
Arkwright of Sutton Scarsdale, Robert, viii. 128.
—— Frances Elizabeth, wife of Sir Hew Dalrymple of North Berwick, viii. 128.
Arlington, Henry (Bennet), earl of, i. 31.
—— —— his wife, Isabella of Nassau, i. 31.
Armiger, Elizabeth, wife of lieut.-gen. Thomas Murray, iii. 386.
—— Robert, lieut.-general, iii. 386.
Armstrong of Kinmont, William, ii. 232; vii. 74.
—— of Gilnockie, John, vii. 371.
—— of Kirtleton, David, advocate, ii. 417.
—— of Mangerton, Christopher, vii. 371.
—— of Sark, John, vii. 99.
—— —— his wife, Katharine Graham, vii. 99.
—— Anne, wife of Robt. Dalzell of Glenae, ii. 417.
—— Christian, wife of Wm. Rutherfurd, vii. 371.
—— 'Jock o' the Side,' v. 64 *n*.
—— Simon, 'meikle Sym,' i. 242.
—— Thomas, iv. 577, 579.
Arnald, bishop of St. Andrews, i. 417; vii. 397.

* Name unknown.

Arniston, Sir James Dundas, senator of the College of Justice, lord, iii. 488.
Arnold, B. North, M.D., v. 253.
—— —— his wife, Louisa Hawkins, v. 252.
Arnot of Arnot, John, vii. 536.
—— Walter, i. 537.
—— —— his wife, Marie Balfour, i. 537.
—— of Balbarton, Walter, ii. 545, 547.
—— of Balcormo, Peter, v. 413.
—— of Berswick, Sir John, provost of Edinburgh, ii. 409; iii. 284, 285.
—— of Chapel, David, ix. 118.
—— —— his wife, Jean Gordon, ix. 118.
—— of Fernie, Sir James, i. 79.
—— —— his wife, Anne Bruce, iii. 485.
—— —— James, i. 544.
—— —— his wife, Jean Balfour, i. 544.
—— —— Sir Robert, ix. 82.
—— —— his wife, Grisel Bruce, ix. 82.
—— of Wester Fernie, James, viii. 495.
—— —— his wife, Elizabeth Wemyss, viii. 495.
—— of Frierton, John, viii. 200.
—— —— his wife, Katharine Murray, viii. 200.
—— of Mugdrum, William, v. 384.
—— of Newton, Robert, i. 542.
—— —— his wife, Margaret Averie, i. 542.
—— —— Robert, i. 542.
—— —— his wife, Margaret Balfour, i. 542.
—— of Woodmylne, James, v. 388.
—— —— *, v. 384.
—— Elizabeth, wife of R. Colville of Hiltoun, ii. 545.
—— Elizabeth, wife of 2nd lord Sempill, iii. 437; vii. 536.
—— Elizabeth, wife of Patrick Lindsay of Kilquhis, v. 403.
—— Elizabeth, wife of (1) D. Lentran, and (2) P. Lindsay, v. 413.
—— Eupham, wife of (1) Martin Corstorphine, and (2) George Lindsay, v. 414.
—— Helen, wife of (1) Isaac Morison, and (2) Sir Geo. Home of Manderston, iii. 284, 285, ix. 72 *bis*.
—— Helen, wife of James Arbuthnott, Leith, i. 304.
—— Janet, wife of John Leslie of Lumquhat, v. 388.
—— John, commissary clerk, St. Andrews, v. 414.
—— Margaret, *error for* Elizabeth, wife of R. Colville of Hiltoun and Ochiltree, ii. 545, 547.
—— Marion, wife of (1) James Nisbet, and (2) Sir Lewis Stewart, ii. 409.
Aros, Macdonell, lord Macdonell and, v. 559-565.
Aros, Angus, lord Macdonell and, v. 562.
—— —— his wife, Margaret Macdonald, v. 565.

* Name unknown.

ARRAN, STEWART, EARL OF, i. 394-398.
Arran, James, 2nd son of 2nd lord Ochiltree; earl of, i, 39, 195, 394, 445; ii. 69, 392; iv. 284, 371; v. 67, 529; vi. 513.
—— —— his wife, Elizabeth Stewart, i. 396, 445.
ARRAN, BOYD, EARL OF, v. 147-149.
Arran, Thomas, earl of, iv. 353 *n.*; v. 144, 145, 147; viii. 576.
—— —— his wife, Mary Stewart, i. 20; iv. 352.
ARRAN, HAMILTON, EARL OF, iv. 355-380.
Arran, Charles, eldest son of 1st duke of Hamilton; styled earl of, iv. 378.
—— James, first earl of, i. 288, 394; iv. 235 *n.*, 355, 358, 364; vii. 45.
—— —— his 1st wife, Elizabeth Home, iv. 358, 454; viii. 431.
—— —— his 2nd wife, Janet Beaton, iv. 358, 360; viii. 369.
—— James, second earl of, governor of Scotland, iv. 360, 366, 409; v. 353; vii. 335; viii. 16, 17; ix. 103.
—— —— his wife, Margaret Douglas, iv. 368; vi. 361; ix. 103.
—— James, third earl of, i. 38, 395; iv. 368, 371.
—— James, fifth earl of, iv. 374.
—— James, sixth earl of, iv. 376.
—— James, eldest son of Anne, duchess of Hamilton; styled earl of, iv. 383; vii. 517.
—— —— his wife, Anne Spencer, iv. 384.
—— John, fourth earl of, iv. 372.
—— William, seventh earl of, iv. 378.
ARRAN, DOUGLAS, EARL OF, iv. 381-382.
Arran, William, earl of, iv. 381.
—— —— his wife, Anne, duchess of Hamilton, iv. 381.
ARRAN AND CAMBRIDGE, HAMILTON, EARL OF, iv. 377.
Arran, James, first earl of, iv. 377.
ARRAN, LANARK, AND CAMBRIDGE, HAMILTON, EARL OF, iv. 383-397.
Arran, James, first earl of, iv. 383.
—— Richard (Butler) eldest son of James, duke of Ormonde; styled earl of, v. 360.
—— —— his wife, Mary Stewart, v. 360.
—— Arthur Saunders (Gore), 2nd earl of, i. 68; vi. 383.
—— —— his 1st wife, Katherine Annesley Gore, i. 68.
—— Arthur Saunders (Gore), 3rd earl of, i. 526.
—— Arthur Jocelyn Charles (Gore), 6th earl of, i. 132.
—— Philip Yorke Annesley (Gore), 4th earl of, vii. 392.
—— —— his wife, Elizabeth Marianne Napier, vii. 392.
ARRASE, CAMPBELL, LORD, i. 379.
Arrase, Archibald, lord, i. 378.
Arrat of Arrat, George, i. 298.
—— —— William, 1611, i. 298.
—— of Fofarty, John, viii. 599.
—— —— his wife, Mary Seton, viii. 562 *n.*, 599.
—— * * their son, and married dau., viii. 599.
Arthington of Arthington, Henry, iii. 598.
Arthur II., duke of Brittany, i. 6.
—— —— his wife, Yolande de Dreux, i. 6.
—— castellan of Lochdoon, ii. 424, 425.
—— —— his wife, * of Carrick, ii. 425.
—— Sir Frederick Leopold, 2nd bart., v. 237.
—— —— his wife, Elizabeth Hay, v. 237.
—— John, ii. 559.
—— —— his wife, Margaret Clyntoun, ii. 559.
—— John, burgess of Edinburgh, iv. 428.
—— —— his wife, Margaret Bothwell. iv. 428.
—— William, minister of Gogar, iv. 90.
Arundel, Henry Frederick (Howard), 24th earl of, v. 359.
—— —— his wife, Elizabeth Stewart, v. 359.
—— Richard Fitz Alan, earl of, i. 11.
—— William, third earl of, i. 10.
—— Isabel de, wife of John Fitz-Alan of Oswestry, i. 10.
Arundel and Surrey, Bernard Marmaduke (Howard), styled earl of, ix. 106.
Aschenbach, Henriette Maria Louise, wife of J. G. Kennedy, ii. 498.
—— Oswald, professor at Düsseldorf, ii. 499.
Ascolog *or* Magachen of Borgue, Roland, i. 321.
—— —— his wife, Katerina, i. 321.
Ash of Ashbrook, William Hamilton, vi. 383.
—— —— his wife, Emma Elizabeth Douglas, vi. 383.
Ashburnham, Bertram (Ashburnham), 4th earl of, iv. 323.
—— —— his wife, Catherine Charlotte Baillie, iv. 323.
—— John, (Ashburnham), 2nd earl of, vi. 271.
—— of Ashburnham, Sir John, ii. 578.
—— —— his wife, Elizabeth Beaumont, ii. 578.
—— —— John, ii. 578.
—— Jemima Elizabeth, wife of James, marquess of Graham, vi. 271.
Ashburton, Richard Barré (Dunning), 2nd lord, ii. 598, 601.
—— —— his wife, Anne Selby Cunningham, ii. 598.
Ashennan, Cuthbert, in Dunjop, v. 105.
Ashley, Violet, wife of Walter John Francis, earl of Mar and Kellie, v. 96.
Ashton, John, Jacobite, viii. 106.
Aske of Aughton, Robert, iii. 596.
—— Eleanora, wife of Sir Thomas Fairfax of Denton, iii. 596.

* Name unknown.

Asquith, Herbert, viii. 517.
—— his wife, Cynthia Mary Evelyn Charteris, viii. 517.
— Herbert H,, viii. 517.
Assheton of Fyfield, Christopher, iv. 531.
—— his wife, Katherine Gordon, iv. 530.
Astley of Patshull, Thomas, i. 405.
—— his wife, Margery Aston, i. 405.
ASTON OF FORFAR, ASTON, LORD, i. 399-414.
Aston, James, fifth lord, i. 413.
—— his wife, Barbara Talbot, i. 413.
—— Walter, first lord, i. 406.
—— his wife, Gertrude Sadleir, i. 408.
—— Walter, second lord, i. 409.
—— his wife, Mary Weston, i. 410.
—— Walter, third lord, i. 411.
—— his 1st wife, Eleanor Knightley, i. 411.
—— his 2nd wife, Katherine Gage, i. 411.
—— Walter, fourth lord, i. 412.
—— his wife, Mary Howard, i. 412.
ASTON, BARON ASTON OF FORFAR, i. 399-414.
Aston of Aston, Henry Hervey, 12th regt. of foot, v. 19.
—— his wife, Harriet Ingram, v. 19.
— of Bellamour, Herbert, i. 408.
—— his wife, Katherine Thimelby, i. 408.
—— John, i. 408.
— of Fole, John, i. 400.
—— his wife, Margery Walton of Fole, i. 400.
— of Louth, Alexander, i. 402.
—— his wife, Letitia Clinton, i. 402.
— of Marston, Robert, i. 400.
— of Milwich, Edward, i. 402.
—— his wife, Dorothy Eld, i. 402.
—— Walter, i. 402.
—— his wife, Ann Chetwynd, i. 402.
—— William, i. 402.
—— his wife, Elizabeth Willington, i. 402.
— of Parkhall, Frances, wife of John Whitehall, i. 400.
—— Robert, 2nd son of Sir W. Aston, i. 400.
—— his wife, Joyce Dallyson, i. 400.
—— William, i. 400.
—— his wife, Mary Rugeley, i. 400.
— of Tean, John, i. 400.
—— his wife, Margery Walton, i. 400.
— of Tixall, Walter, Sheriff of Stafford, i. 399.
—— his wife, Elizabeth Leveson, i. 400.
—— Sir Walter, baronet, i. 406.
—— his wife, Gertrude Sadleir, i. 408.
—— Sir Edward, i. 399.
—— his 2nd wife, Joane Bowles, i. 399.
—— Sir Edward, i. 400, 405.
—— his 1st wife, Mary Spencer, i. 406.
—— his 2nd wife, Anne Lucy, i. 406.
Aston of Wanlip, Devereux, 6th son of Sir Walter A., i. 405.
—— his 1st wife, Godith Skeffington, i. 405.
—— his 2nd wife, Margaret Barratt, i. 405.
— Anne, dau. of Sir Wm. A., i. 401.
— Anne, wife of John Worswick, i. 402.
— Anne, wife of Peter Yonge, i. 404.
— Anne, wife of Ralph Bayley, i. 405.
— Anne, wife of Ambrose Elton, i. 406.
— Anne, wife of Henry Somerset, i. 411.
— Barbara, wife of Thomas Clifford, i. 413.
— Charles, son of John A. of Fole, i. 401.
— Charles, 4th son of 3rd lord Aston, i. 412.
— Constance, wife of W. Fowler, i. 409.
— Dorothy, dau. of Edward A., i. 405.
— Edmund, parish of St. Paul, Covent Garden, iv. 299.
—— his wife, Elizabeth Ramsay, iv. 299.
— Edward, 4th son of Edward A. of Milwich, i. 402.
— Edward, St. Giles'-in-the-Fields, i. 403.
— Edward, of the Jewel Office, i. 406.
— Edward Walter, eldest son of 4th lord Aston of Forfar, i. 412.
— Eleanor, wife of Wm. Peyto, i. 405.
— Elizabeth, wife of N. Codington, i. 401.
— Elizabeth, dau. of Edward A., i. 404.
— Elizabeth, wife of Basil Feilding, i. 405.
— Elizabeth, wife of John Sandbach, i. 406.
— Elizabeth, wife of Sir J. Southcote, i. 401.
— Frances, wife of Sir Wm. Pershall, i. 409.
— Frances, wife of Sir Edward Gage, i. 410.
— Francis, 2nd son of 3rd lord Aston, i. 412.
— Gertrude, wife of H. Thimelby, i. 409.
— Gertrude, dau. of 2nd lord Aston, i. 410.
— Hastings, 5th son of Sir Walter A., i. 405.
— Herbert, *alias* Barrett, i. 408 *n*.
— Honoria, dau. of 1st lord Aston, i. 408.
— Jane, wife of Wm. Crompton, i. 405.
— Jane, wife of Dr. T. Elton, i. 406.
— John, son of Sir Wm. A., i. 401.
— John, 4th son of 1st lord A., i. 408.
— Joyce, wife of Sir M. Culpeper, i. 406.
— Katherine, wife of (1) Stephen Slaney, (2) Sir Wm. Chetwynd, and (3) Sir E. Cope, i. 405.
— Katherine Elizabeth, wife of Edward Weld, i. 412.
— Mabel, wife of Richard Ogden, l. 402.
— Margaret, wife of Geo. Long, i. 402.
— Margaret, dau. of 4th lord Aston, i. 413.
— Margery, wife of Thos. Astley, i. 405.
— Mary, wife of Wm. Chancey, i. 405.
— Mary, wife of C. Collier, i. 405.
— Mary, dau. of 2nd lord Aston, i. 411.
— Mary, dau. of 3rd lord Aston, i. 412.
— Mary, wife of Sir Walter Blount, i. 413.
— Philip, i. 403.

Aston, Richard, Furnival's Inn, i. 401.
—— Richard, rector of Leigh, i. 402.
—— —— his 1st wife, Julian *, i. 402.
—— —— his 2nd wife, Anne *, i. 402.
—— Richard, 5th son of Edward A., i. 404.
—— Sir Roger, vi. 516.
—— —— his wife, Marjory Stewart, vi. 516.
—— Thomas, son of Sir Wm. A., i. 401.
—— —— his wife, Margaret Sandys, i. 401.
—— Thomas, 2nd son of Wm. A. of Milwich, i. 405.
—— Thomas, of the Inner Temple, i. 406.
—— Thomas, son of 2nd lord Aston, i. 410.
—— —— his wife, Elizabeth Ogle, i. 410.
—— Thomas William Anthony, i. 412.
—— Walter, St. Giles'-in-the-Fields, i. 402.
—— —— his wife, Penelope Whitfield, i. 403.
—— Walter, cook, claimant to barony, i. 403.
—— —— his wife, Ann Wright, i. 403.
—— Walter, watchmaker, claimant to barony, i. 403.
—— —— his wife, Anne Hutchinson, i. 404.
—— Walter Hutchinson, vicar of Tardebigg, claimant to barony, i. 404.
—— —— his wife, Elizabeth Haines, i. 404.
—— Sir William, justice of King's Bench in Ireland, i. 401.
—— —— his 1st wife, Sarah Wingfield, i. 410.
—— —— his 2nd wife, Elizabeth Fellgate or Higate, i. 401.
—— —— his 3rd wife, Ursula Stockton, i. 401.
—— William, Lincoln's Inn, i. 401.
—— —— his wife, Lettice Jones, i. 401.
—— William, 3rd son of Edward A. of Milwich, i. 402.
—— —— his wife, Jane *, i. 402.
—— William, a Jesuit, i. 404.
—— William, implicated in Titus Oates' plot, i. 410.
—— William Bayley, i. 404.
Atchison *, killed accidentally by Gideon Murray of Glenpoit, iii. 504.
Atherley, Arthur, v. 483.
—— his wife, Louisa Ker, v. 483.
Athlone, Frederick William (de Ginkell), 7th earl of, iv. 496.
ATHOLL, THE CELTIC EARLS OF, i. 415-433.
Atholl, Ada, wife of John of Strathbogie; countess of, i. 424.
—— Alan (Durward), *de jure ux.* styled earl of, i. 418 *n.*, 422.
—— —— his wife, Isabella, countess of Atholl, i. 421.
—— David, eighth earl of, i. 425; vii. 496.
—— his 1st wife, Helen *, i. 425.
—— his 2nd wife, Isabella Chilham, i. 425; ix. 11.
—— David, tenth earl of, i. 428; ii. 219 *n.* 379; ix. 27.
—— —— his wife, Joan Comyn, i. 429, 509.

* Name unknown.

Atholl, David, eleventh earl of, i. 430; viii. 325.
—— —— his wife, Katharine Beaumont, i. 432.
—— David, twelfth earl of, i. 432.
—— —— his wife, Elizabeth Ferrers, i. 433.
—— David (Hasting), *de jure ux.* sixth earl of, i. 424.
—— —— his wife, Forflissa, countess of Atholl, i. 423.
—— Forflissa or Fernelith, wife of Sir David of Hasting; countess of, i. 419, 423; ix. 26.
—— Henry, third earl of, i. 418.
—— —— his wife, Margaret, i. 418.
—— Isabella, wife of (1) Thomas of Galloway, and (2) Alan Durward, i. 419.
—— John, ninth earl of, i. 425; viii. 248.
—— —— his wife, Marjory of Mar, i. 427; v. 578.
—— John of Strathbogie, *de jure ux.* seventh earl of, i. 424; iv. 8; viii. 418.
—— —— his wife, Ada, countess of Atholl, i. 424.
—— Lora, countess of, i. 422, 423.
—— Madach or Madeth, first earl of, i. 415.
—— —— his 2nd wife, Margaret of Orkney, i. 416.
—— Malcolm, second earl of, i. 416; v. 569 *n.*
—— his wife, Hextilda of Walwick, Carrow, Thornton, Henshaw and Bedrule, i. 3, 417, 504, 507, 508: ii. 252; iii. 6; vi. 288.
—— Patrick, fifth earl of, i. 419 *n.*, 422; iv. 224 *n.*; vi. 128; ix. 26.
—— —— his possible wife, Lora, i. 423.
—— Thomas of Galloway, *de jure ux.* fourth earl of, i. 420; iv. 139; vi. 530.
—— —— his wife, Isabella, countess of Atholl, i. 419.
ATHOLL, CAMPBELL, EARL OF, i. 434-435.
Atholl, John, second earl of, i. 434.
—— —— his wife, Joanna Menteith, i. 435; vi. 133; viii. 251, 257, 327.
—— Neil, first earl of, i. 323, 434.
—— —— his wife, Mary Bruce, i, 434.
ATHOLL, DOUGLAS, EARL OF, i. 435-436.
Atholl, William, earl of, i. 435, 436; vi. 340.
ATHOLL, STEWART, EARL OF, i. 436-439.
Atholl, David, duke of Rothesay, earl of, i. 17, 436; ii. 439.
—— John, eldest son of King Robert II.; earl of, ix. 27.
—— Robert (afterwards King Robert II.), earl of, i. 15, 436; ix. 27.
—— Robert, duke of Albany, earl of, i. 16, 147, 436.
—— Walter of Brechin, earl of, i. 16, 18, 436. 438; ii. 224, 321, 322; viii. 260; ix. 27.
—— —— his wife, Margaret of Brechin, i. 438; v. 581.

ATHOLL, STEWART, EARL OF, i. 440-446.
Atholl, James, the Black Knight of Lorn, earl of, i. 440.
—— his wife, Joanna Beaufort, i. 18, 440.
— John, first earl of, i. 441; iii. 570; iv. 527.
—— his 1st wife, Margaret Douglas, i. 441; iii. 170, 183.
—— his 2nd wife, Eleanor Sinclair, i. 442; ii. 334.
— John, second earl of, i. 443.
—— his wife, Janet Campbell, i. 336, 443.
— John, third earl of, i. 443.
—— his 1st wife, Grizel Rattray, i. 443.
—— his 2nd wife, Jean Forbes, i. 443; iv. 55.
— John, fourth earl of, i. 444.
—— his 1st wife, Elizabeth Gordon, i. 445; iv. 539.
—— his 2nd wife, Margaret Fleming, i. 445; viii. 540.
— John, fifth earl of, i. 445; iv. 33, 58.
—— his wife, Mary Ruthven, i. 446; iv. 265.
ATHOLL, STEWART, EARL OF, i. 447-448.
Atholl, James, seventh lord Innermeath, and earl of, i. 446, 448; v. 372; viii. 410.
—— his wife, Mary Stewart, i. 446, 448; vii. 191.
— John, sixth lord Innermeath, and earl of, i. 446, 447: iii. 29.
—— his 1st wife, Margaret Lindsay, i. 447, 512; ix. 30.
—— his 2nd wife, Mary Ruthven, i. 446, 447.
ATHOLL, MURRAY, EARL OF, i. 449-473.
Atholl, John, first earl of, i. 472; viii. 410.
—— his wife, Jean Campbell, i. 473; ii. 188.
— John, second earl of, i. 473; viii. 414.
—— his wife, Amelia Anne Sophia Stanley, i. 475.
ATHOLL, MURRAY, MARQUESS OF, i. 474-479.
Atholl, John, first marquess of, i. 474.
—— his wife, Amelia Anne Sophia Stanley, i. 475.
— John, second marquess of, i. 475, 478.
—— his 1st wife, Katharine Hamilton, i. 480.
—— his 2nd wife, Mary Ross, i. 485.
ATHOLL, MURRAY, DUKE OF, i. 449-502.
Atholl, George Augustus Frederick John, sixth duke of, i. 496, 498.
—— his wife, Anne Home-Drummond, i. 499.
— James, second duke of, i. 482, 487.
—— his 1st wife, Jane Frederick, i. 488.
—— his 2nd wife, Jean Drummond, i. 489.
Atholl, John, first duke of, i. 479; ix. 29.
—— his 1st wife, Katharine Hamilton, i. 480; iv. 382.
—— his 2nd wife, Mary Ross, i. 485; vii. 261.
— John, third duke of, i. 457, 484, 489.
—— his wife, Charlotte Murray, i. 489, 490.
— John, fourth duke of, i. 491, 495.
—— his first wife, Jean Cathcart, i. 496.
—— his 2nd wife, Margery Forbes, i. 498; iv. 65.
— John fifth duke of, i. 496, 498.
— John James Hugh Henry, seventh duke of, i. 499.
—— his wife, Louisa Moncreiffe, i. 499.
Atholl, Sir Adomar, or Aymer of; 2nd son of David, 10th earl of Atholl, i. 429, 433.
—— his wife, Maria, i. 430.
— Andrew de, i. 419.
— his supposed wife, * of Glenerrichdie and Tulloch, i. 419.
— Constantine of, son of Henry, 3rd earl of Atholl, i. 419 *n.*: ix. 26.
— Elizabeth of, wife of (1) Sir Thos. Percy and (2) Sir John le Scrope, i. 430, 433.
— Sir John of, 2nd son of John, 9th earl of Atholl, i. 427; viii. 248.
—— his wife, Matilda, i. 427.
— Isabel de, alleged wife of Edward Bruce, earl of Carrick, i. 427; ii. 436.
— Isabella of, wife of Ralph de Euer, i. 430.
— Maria de, wife of Robert de l'Isle, i. 430.
— Philippa of, wife of (1) Sir Ralph Percy, and (2) Sir John Halsham, i. 433.
Atkin, Edmond, president of Council, South Carolina, iii. 81.
—— his wife, Anne Mackenzie, iii. 81.
Atkinson of Angeston, Bradford, colonel, vi. 507.
— Anna Barbara, wife of lieut. Ian Ludovic Andrew Carnegie, vi. 507.
Atkinson, *, army contractor, ix. 31.
AUBIGNY, STEWART, LORD D', v. 356-362.
Aubigny, Esmé, first lord d', v. 356.
Aubigny, Charles (Lennox) duke of, v. 364.
— George (Stuart), seigneur d', vi. 453.
—— his wife, Katharine Howard, vi. 453.
— Jacqueline de La Queuille, wife of Robert Stuart, seigneur d', vi. 231.
— Louise Renée de Perrancoet de Keroualle, duchesse d,' i. 32; v. 363.
— Matilda d', wife of Gilbert, earl of Strathearn, viii. 242.
— William d', viii. 242, 243.
AUCHINDOUN, GORDON, LORD, iv. 549-558.
Auchindoun, George, first lord, iv. 550.

* Name unknown.

Auchinleck of Auchinleck, David, i. 287.
—— —— his wife, Katharine Arbuthnott, i. 287.
—— —— Elizabeth, wife of Sir William Douglas, i. 183, 184.
—— —— Hugh, i. 287.
—— —— Sir James, iv. 30; viii. 483; ix. 168.
—— —— his wife, Christian Douglas, viii. 483.
—— —— James, i. 183.
—— —— Sir John, i. 183; iv. 30; v. 493.
—— —— John, iv. 31.
—— of Balmanno, Anne, wife of John Ogilvy of Kinnoull, vi. 495.
—— —— Archibald, vi. 495.
—— —— George, v. 83.
—— —— his wife, Jean Erskine, v. 83.
—— —— George, i. 199; vi. 102.
—— —— his 1st wife, Isobel Melville, vi. 102.
—— —— his 2nd wife, Sarah Douglas, i. 199.
—— —— George, eldest son of Sir William A., iii. 509.
—— —— his wife, Agnes Murray, iii. 508.
—— —— Sir William, iii. 509.
—— of Barras, Sir James, iv. 30.
—— —— Sir John, iv. 30.
—— —— John, iv. 31.
—— of Fingask, George, v. 83.
—— —— his wife, Jean Erskine, v. 83.
—— of Glenbervie, Elizabeth, wife of Sir Wm. Douglas, i. 183, 184.
—— of Kemnay, James, ii. 150.
—— —— his wife, Janet Hepburne, ii. 150.
—— —— William, ii. 150.
—— of Over Kinmonth, George, i. 287; v. 244.
—— —— his wife, Janet Arbuthnott, v. 244.
—— Elizabeth, wife of Robert Gordon of Saphak, i. 85.
—— Isobel, wife of K. Mackenzie, iii. 73.
—— Sir James, ii. 540 *n.*, 541.
—— James, iii. 336.
—— —— his wife, Gelis Ross, iii. 336.
—— Marion, wife of (1) George Campbell of Loudoun, and (2) Wm. Cunningham, v. 493.
Auchmoutie of Auchmoutie, John, vii. 291.
—— —— his wife, Beatrix Leslie, vii. 290.
—— —— John, viii. 498.
—— —— his wife, Isobel Wemyss, viii. 497.
Auchmoutie, Alexander, gentleman of the King's bedchamber, vi. 417.
—— —— his wife, Elizabeth Napier, i. 122; vi. 417.
—— Andrew, burgess of Edinburgh, iii. 97.
Auchmowtie of Gosford, Sir Alexander, iii. 509.
—— —— his wife, Helen Murray, iii. 509.
AUCHMUTIE, LESLIE, LORD, vii. 301.
Auchmutie, John, lord, vii. 301.
—— of Easter Fernie, David, i. 518.
—— —— his wife, Janet Lindsay, i. 518.
Auchmuttie of Drumeldrie, vii. 372.
Auchmuttie of Drumeldrie, David, vii. 372.
—— —— his wife, Margaret Rutherfurd, vii. 372.
—— Isobel, wife of rev. John Rutherfurd, vii. 372.
Auchmuty, Henry, ix. 81.
—— *, ix. 82.
—— his wife, Elizabeth Stewart, ix. 82.
AUCHTERHOUSE, STEWART, LORD, ii. 266.
Auchterhouse, James, first lord, ii. 266.
—— —— his wife, Margaret Ogilvie, ii. 266.
Auchterlony of Kelly, William, iv. 273.
—— —— his wife, * Gray, iv. 273.
Auckland, William Morton (Eden), 1st baron, viii. 230.
—— William George (Eden), 4th baron, v. 236.
Audibert, Marie Gabrielle d', wife of (1) Henry Fitzjames, titular duke of Albemarle, and (2) John Drummond, styled viscount Forth, i. 34; vi. 70.
Audna, wife of Hlodver, son of Thorfinn Skullsplitter, ii. 314.
Aufrica, wife of William de Say, i. 5.
Aulay of Faslane and Gareloch, 5th son of Alwin, 2nd earl of Lennox, v. 329, 330, 331 *bis*, 337.
—— son of Aulay of Faslane, v. 329.
—— of Faslane, 'Tosheagor,' v. 329.
—— brother of Maldouen, earl of Lennox, v. 590.
Auld, William, burgess of Perth, iii. 559.
Auldton of Wester Softlaw, Roger de, vi. 473.
Auriol, Amelia, wife of rev. E. Auriol Drummond-Hay, v. 233.
—— Henrietta, wife of Robert Drummond-Hay of Cromlix, bp. of Salisbury, v. 232.
—— Peter, merchant, London, v. 233.
Aust, George, Chelsea, iii. 388.
—— —— his wife, Sarah Mease, iii. 388.
Austin, Adam, physician, Edinburgh, vii. 563.
—— —— his wife, Anne Sempill, vii. 563.
AVANDALE, STEWART, LORD, vi. 509-511.
Avandale, Andrew, first lord, i. 150; v. 349; vi. 509.
—— Andrew, second lord, iii. 567; vi. 510.
—— —— his wife, Margaret Kennedy, ii. 459; vi. 510.
—— Andrew, third lord, i. 511.
—— —— his wife, Margaret Hamilton, i. 511; iv. 364.
Avelina, wife of Duncan, earl of Carrick, ii. 423.
AVEN, MAUCHANSHYRE, POMOND AND DAIR, DOUGLAS, LORD, iv. 381-382.
Aven, Mauchanshyre, Pomond and Dair, William, lord, iv. 381.
AVEN, POLMONT, MACHANSHYRE, AND INNERDALE, HAMILTON, LORD, iv. 383, 397.

* Name unknown.

Aven, Polmont, Machanshyre, and Innerdale, James, first lord, iv. 383.
Avenel of Abercorn, *, wife of Sir Henry Graham of Dalkeith, vi. 194.
— of Abercorn, Roger, vi. 194.
— of Eskdale, Roger, vi. 194; vii. 424.
— of Kilbucho and Newlands, Roger, vi. 194.
— Sir Gervase, iv. 11.
— — his wife, Johanna de Clare, iv. 11.
— Robert, justiciar, i. 5; vi. 525 *n.*
— William, vi. 30 *n.*
— — his wife, Agnes Keith, vi. 30 *n.*
Averie, John, bailie of Falkland, i. 542.
— Margaret, wife of Robt. Arnot, i. 542.
AVON AND INNERDALE, HAMILTON, LORD, iv. 377-397.
Avon and Innerdale, James, first lord, iv. 377.
AVONDALE, DOUGLAS, EARL OF, iii., 173-185.
Avondale, James, first earl of, iii. 173, 567; v. 428; vii. 115.
— — his 1st wife, *, iii. 174.
— — his 2nd wife, Beatrix Sinclair, iii. 174.
Aylesbury of Edstone, Joan, wife of Thos. Somerville of Aston Somerville, viii. 1.
— — John, viii. 1.
Aylesford, Heneage (Finch), 6th earl of, iii. 393.
Aylett, Mary, wife of 9th lord Fairfax, iii. 603.
Aylmer, Charles Arthur, vii. 178.
— — his wife, Sophia Mackay, vii. 178.
Aylward, father of Dolfin, iii. 245.
Aynsley of Little Harle Tower, Alicia, wife of lord Charles Murray, i. 494.
— Gawen, i. 494.
Ayr, John, vi. 82.
— Margaret, wife of Walter Melville of Caproneston, vi. 82.
Ayre of Fastforland, Robert, iv. 333.
— of Little Carcary, Richard, viii. 48.
Aytoun of Aytoun, Sir John, iv. 490 *bis*; viii. 496.
— — Sir John, viii. 496, 501.
— — his wife, Elizabeth Wemyss, viii. 501.
— — Sir John, ii. 574.
— — his 2nd wife, Margaret Colvill, ii. 574.
— of Dynmure, John, viii. 491.
— — his wife, Agnes Wemyss, viii. 491.
— of Inchdairnie, John, vii. 205, 207.
— — his wife, Isobel Rollo, vii. 205.
— of Kinaldie, John, vii. 17; viii. 63.
— — his wife, Katharine Carnegie, viii. 63.
— of Kippo, James, v. 417.
— — John, v. 417.
— of Logie, Sir Andrew, iii. 320.

* Name unknown.

Aytoun, Andrew, senator of the College of Justice, lord Kinglassie, viii. 63.
— Elizabeth, wife of (1) Sir T. Hope of Craighall, and (2) J. Gibson of Durie, iv. 490.
— Elizabeth, wife of Sir John Wemyss of Bogie, viii. 496.
— Jane Emilia, wife of D. A. Lindsay of Wormiston, v. 417.
— Jean, wife of Patrick Maule, vii. 17.
— Margaret, wife of Sir Archibald Hope of Rankeillour, iv. 490.
— Mary, wife of P. Lindsay of Coats, v. 417.
— Mary, wife of 7th lord Rollo, vii. 207.
— Sir Robert, poet, iii. 402.
— William, goldsmith, Edinburgh, viii. 496.
— — his wife, Thomas Wemyss, viii. 496.

BABER, Sir John, iii. 399.
— — his wife, Anne, viscountess Bayning, iii. 399.
Babington, Ralph, viii. 456.
— Katharine, wife of Robt. Hay, viii. 456.
Bacon, Anthony, diplomatist, iv. 431.
— Anthony Harley, v. 238.
— Bridget, wife of (1) Edward Evers, (2) Sir C. Firebrace, and (3) Wm. Campbell, i. 382; ix. 24.
— Francis, lord Verulam, ii. 558.
— Gladys Luz, wife of Edmund Alfred Rollo George, viscount Dupplin, v. 238.
— John Joseph, i. 493.
— Katharine, wife of Col. Richard Murray, i. 493.
— Philip, Ipswich, i. 382.
Baden, Charles Louis Frederick, grand duke of, iv. 396.
— Mary, wife of 11th duke of Hamilton; princess of, iv. 396.
BADENOCH, COMYN, LORD OF, i. 503-510.
Badenoch, Sir John, 'the Red Comyn No. 1,' lord of, i. 506.
— — his wife, Alicia Lindsay, i. 507.
— Sir John 'the Black Comyn,' lord of, i. 507.
— — his wife, Alianora Baliol, i. 508; iv. 143.
— John, 'the Red Comyn No. 2,' lord of, i. 508.
— — his wife, Johanna de Valence, i. 509.
— John, lord of, i. 509.
— — his wife, Margaret Wake, i. 510.
— Walter, lord of, i. 505, 506.
— — his wife, Isabella, Countess of Menteith, i. 505.
— William, lord of, i. 505; ii. 252.
— — his wife, Marjory *or* Margaret, Countess of Buchan, ii. 252.
BADENOCH, STEWART, LORD OF, ii. 262.

Badenoch, Alexander, 4th son of King Robert II.; lord of, i. 16; ii. 262; vii. 159 *bis*.
—— —— his wife, Euphemia, Countess of Ross, ii. 261, 262; vii. 241.
—— —— his handfasted wife, Mariota Mackay, ii. 262; vii. 159.
BADENOCH, STEWART, LORD, ii. 170.
Badenoch, Francis, lord, ii. 170.
—— —— his wife, Margaret Douglas, ii. 171.
BADENOCH, GORDON, LORD, iv. 549-558.
Badenoch, George, first lord, iv. 549.
Badhame, William, dancing-master, ix. 69.
Bagenal of Newry, Sir Nicholas, iii. 479.
—— —— his wife, Anne Charlotte Bruce, iii. 479.
Bagot of the Hyde, Sir William, ix. 67.
—— —— his wife, Eleanor de Louvaine, iii. 140; ix. 67.
—— Charlotte, wife of rev. William Somerville, viii. 38.
—— Walter, rector of Blithfield, viii. 38.
Bagshot, captain, 1548, viii. 437.
Bailey, Katharine, wife of Hugh Kennedy, ii. 467.
BAILLIE, LORD FORRESTER OF CORSTORPHINE, iv. 93-96.
Baillie of Auldston, Alexander, viii. 372.
—— —— his wife, Euphame Livingston, viii. 372.
—— —— Archibald, viii. 372; ix. 163.
—— of Carphin, James, iv. 88.
—— —— his wife, Isobel Forrester, iv. 88.
—— of Corstorphine, James, iv. 91, 92.
—— —— his wife, Johanna Forrester, iv. 91, 92.
—— of Dochfour, Evan, ii. 565; iii. 494.
—— of Dunain, Alexander, vii. 456.
—— —— his wife, Katharine Grant, vii. 456.
—— of Femmeltoun, Robert, vi. 450.
—— of Hardington, William, vi. 372.
—— —— his wife, Margaret Douglas, vi. 372.
—— —— *, viii. 496.
—— of Hoprig, Sir William, viii. 331.
—— of Jerviswood, Charles, vii. 85.
—— —— his wife, Anne Hepburne-Scott, vii. 85.
—— —— George, 1st laird, viii. 373.
—— of Jerviswoode and Mellerstain, George, iv. 322; vi. 17.
—— —— his wife, Grisell Hume, vi. 15, 17.
—— —— George, 2nd son of Charles, lord Binning, iv. 322, 323.
—— —— his wife, Elizabeth Andrews, iv. 322.
—— —— George, M.P., iv. 322.
—— —— his wife, Mary Pringle, iv. 322.
—— —— George, iv. 322, 326.
—— —— his wife, Georgina Markham, iv. 327.
—— —— Grissel, wife of Sir Alex. Murray of Stanhope, iv. 322; vi. 17.

* Name unknown.

Baillie of Jerviswoode, Rachel, wife of Charles, lord Binning, iv. 322; ix. 101.
—— of Jerviswood, Robert, iv. 289.
—— of Johnskirk, John, vi. 7.
—— —— his wife, Margaret Hume, vi. 7.
—— of Lamington, Sir Samuel, ii. 40.
—— —— his wife, Margaret Hamilton, ii. 40.
—— —— Sir William, viii. 12, 331.
—— —— Sir William, v. 395, 442; vi. 4.
—— —— his wife, Marion Hume, vi. 4.
—— —— Sir William, iv. 412, 581; vi. 481.
—— —— his 1st wife, Margaret Maxwell, i. 192; vi. 481.
—— —— his 2nd wife, * Home, iv. 93.
—— —— Sir William, i. 43.
—— —— his wife, Grizel Hamilton, i. 43.
—— —— William, ii. 28; iii. 37; iv. 587.
—— —— his 1st wife, Marjory Hamilton, ii. 28.
—— —— his 2nd wife, Henrietta Lindsay, iii. 37.
—— of Lethame, James, iv. 91, 92.
—— —— his wife, Johanna Forrester, iv. 91.
—— —— William, major-general, iv. 91, 93.
—— —— his wife, Janet Bruce, iv. 93.
—— of Lochend, Gideon, viii. 66.
—— —— his wife, Magdalene Carnegie, viii. 66.
—— of Parbroath, Alexander, colonel, ii. 51.
—— —— his wife, Euphemia Hamilton, ii. 51.
—— —— Andrew, ii. 51.
—— —— his wife, Helen Hamilton, ii. 51.
—— —— Robert, ii. 51.
—— of Park, *, ii. 42.
—— —— his wife, Katharine Hamilton, ii. 42.
—— of Rosehall, William, vii. 174.
—— —— his wife, Mary Mackay, vii. 174.
—— of Saughton, James, iv. 91.
—— of Sheuglie, Alexander, vii. 456.
—— of Torwoodheid, James, eldest son of major-gen. William B. of Lethame, iv. 91.
—— —— his wife, Johanna Forrester, iv. 92.
—— Abigail, wife of Sir Hugh Carmichael of Carmichael, iv. 581.
—— Adam, 3rd son of major-gen. William B. of Lethame, iv. 91.
—— Alexander, 4th son of major-gen. William B. of Lethame, iv. 91.
—— Alexander, v. 188.
—— —— his wife, Margaret Livingston, v. 188.
—— Charles, senator of the College of Justice, lord Jerviswoode, iv. 322.
—— —— his wife, Anne Scott, iv. 322.
—— Cuthbert, rector of Sanquhar, viii. 335.
—— Elizabeth, dau. of George B. of Jerviswoode, iv. 323.
—— Elizabeth *or* Eliza, wife of John, marquess of Breadalbane, ii. 211; iv. 323.

* Name unknown.

Baillie, Evan Peter Montagu, iii. 494.
—— —— his wife, Frances Anne Bruce, iii. 494.
—— Georgiana Mary, wife of col. Sir W. J. Colville, ii. 559 *n.*, 565.
—— Georgina, wife of 7th lord Polwarth, iv. 323; vii. 85.
—— Grisell, deaconess of the Church of Scotland, iv. 323.
—— Grisell, dau. of George B. of Jerviswoode, iv. 323.
—— Helen, wife of Jas. Hamilton of Stevenston, ii. 51, 55.
—— James Pringle, 56th and 81st Regiments, iv. 323.
—— Janet, wife of Wm. Gordon of Craichlaw, v. 104.
—— John, in holy orders, canon of York Cathedral, iv. 323.
—— —— his wife, C. M. Hawkins, iv. 323.
—— John, chirurgeon, viii. 496.
—— Katharine, wife of David Wemyss, viii. 496.
—— Katharine Charlotte, wife of Bertram, 4th earl of Ashburnham, iv. 323.
—— Margaret, wife of William Murray of Spot, iii. 508.
—— Margaret, wife of (1) Edward Maxwell of Dundrennan, and (2) Sir Wm. Livingston of Culter, iv. 412; v. 442; ix. 130.
—— Margaret, wife of Sir Jas. Carmichael of Bonnytoun, iv. 587.
—— Margaret, wife of John, 7th earl of Sutherland, viii. 331.
—— Margaret, dau. of 3rd lord Forrester, ix. 92.
—— Marion, wife of (1) John, 3rd lord Lindsay of the Byres, and (2) R. Douglas of Lochleven, v. 395; vi. 367.
—— Marion, wife of (1) John, 3rd lord Somerville, and (2) Sir John Ross of Halkhead, v. 395 *n.*; vii. 250.
—— Marion, wife of (1) Robert Grahame of Westhall, and (2) Jas. Livingston of Jerviswoode, viii. 372; ix. 163.
—— Mary, wife of 5th earl of Aberdeen, i. 97; iv. 323.
—— Nellie, wife of James Hamilton, ii. 55.
—— Rachel, wife of rev. Andrew Gray, iv. 289.
—— Rachel Catherine, dau. of Geo. B. of Jerviswoode, iv. 323.
—— Robert, major 72nd Highlanders, iv. 323.
—— Robert, rev., principal of Glasgow university, v. 123; vii. 298.
—— Thomas, admiral R.N., iv. 323.
—— William, son of Wm. B. of Lamington, ii. 29.
—— William, 2nd son of major-gen. William B. of Lethame, iv. 91.
Baillie, William, eldest son of Robert B. of Femmeltoun, vi. 450.
—— —— his wife, Jean Livingston, iv. 450.
BAILLIE-HAMILTON, EARL OF HADDINGTON, iv. 326-329.
Baillie-Hamilton of Rumbletonlaw, Charles, archdeacon of Cleveland, iv. 323.
—— —— his wife, Charlotte Home, iv. 323, 481.
—— —— Amabel Georgina, wife of rev. C. J. Harland, iv. 327.
—— —— Arthur Charles, rector of Coombs, vicar of Badley, iv. 327.
—— —— his wife, Alice Ann Baird, iv. 327; ix. 101 *bis*.
—— —— Cecely, dau. of 11th earl of Haddington, iv. 329.
—— —— Charles, in holy orders, vii. 84.
—— —— Charles William, 2nd son of George, lord Binning, iv. 328.
—— —— Clifton, 3rd son of 10th earl of Haddington, iv. 327.
—— —— Eleanor Sophia, wife of rev. William Hugh Hepburne-Scott, vii. 84.
—— —— Frances, dau. of 10th earl of Haddington, iv. 327.
—— —— Gena Mary, iv. 327.
—— —— George, elder son of George, lord Binning, iv. 328.
—— —— Georgina Sophia, wife of Sir H. F. Vernon, iv. 327.
—— —— Grisell, dau. of 11th earl of Haddington, iv. 329.
—— —— Helen, dau. of George, lord Binning, iv. 328.
—— —— Helen Georgina, iv. 327.
—— —— Henry, R.N., iv. 327.
—— —— his wife, Harriet Frances Hepburne-Scott, iv. 327; vii. 85.
—— —— Katharine Ada Georgina, iv. 327.
—— —— Margaret Ellinor Georgina, iv. 327.
—— —— Mary, wife of rev. Henry Douglas, iv. 327.
—— —— Richard, 77th Regiment, and Rifle Brigade, iv. 329.
—— —— Robert, M.P., iv. 327.
—— —— his wife, Mary G. Pringle, iv. 327.
—— —— Ruth, dau. of 11th Earl of Haddington, iv. 329.
—— —— William Alexander, admiral, R.N., i. 67.
—— —— his wife, Harriet Hamilton, i. 67.
Baillie-Hamilton-Arden, George, iv. 328.
—— —— —— Henry Robert, capt. Coldstream Guards, iv. 329.
Bain of Tulloch, Alexander, v. 527.
—— —— his wife, Agnes Fraser, v. 527.
Baird of Auchmeddan, George, vii. 441.
—— —— his wife, Anna Fraser, vii. 441.
—— —— Sir James, v. 225; ix. 90.
—— —— James, the younger, v. 225.
—— —— his wife, Katharine Hay, v. 225.

Baird of Cambusnethan, i. 456 *n.*
— of Elie, William, viii. 455.
— of Glencuthill, George, vi. 44.
— — his wife, Elizabeth Keith, vi. 44.
— of Newbyth, Sir David, general, G.C.B., 1st bart., i. 93.
— — Sir David, 2nd bart., ii. 498, 500; iv. 327; viii. 236.
— — his wife, Anne Kennedy, ii. 500.
— — Sir David, 3rd bart., ii. 90.
— — his wife, Ellen Stuart, ii. 92.
— — Sir John, 2nd bart. of 1st creation, vii. 588; viii. 147.
— — his wife, Janet Dalrymple, vii. 588; viii. 147.
— — Sir John, lord of Session, viii. 447.
— — his wife, Margaret Hay, viii. 447.
— — Sir William, 1st bart. of 1st creation, ii. 47; vii. 588.
— — his second wife, Margaret St. Clair, vii. 588.
— — William, i. 93.
— of Posso, Sir Lawrence, viii. 6.
— — his alleged wife, * Somerville, viii. 6.
— of Rosemount, Jane, wife of capt. J. G. Hay of Belton, viii. 455.
— of Saughtonhall, Sir William, 5th bart., R.N., ii. 276.
— — his wife, Frances Gardiner, ii. 276.
— of Urie, Sir Alexander, 1st bart., v. 254.
— Alexander, son of Sir Wm. B. of Newbyth, ii. 47.
— — his wife, Margaret Hamilton, ii. 47.
— Alice Ann, wife of rev. A. C. Baillie-Hamilton, iv. 327; ix. 101 *bis*.
— Charles, wife of George, lord Haddo, i. 93; ix. 5.
— Christina Maria Hersey, wife of 9th viscount of Strathallan, viii. 236.
— Elizabeth, wife of (1) Sir Alex. Abercromby, and (2) col. P. Ogilvy, ix. 90.
— Janet, wife of Robert Ogilvy, ii. 13.
— Janet, wife of (1) Alan Lockhart of Lee, and (2) Wm. Livingston of Jerviswood, viii. 371.
— John, advocate, iv. 437.
— — his wife, Mary Ramsay, iv. 437.
— John Lawrence, C.M.G., v. 254.
— — his wife, Ethel Sydney Keith-Falconer, v. 254.
— Margaret, wife of Lord Gilbert Kennedy, ii. 498.
Baird-Hay of Belton and Rosemount, James George, capt., viii. 455.
— — his wife, Jane Baird, viii. 455.
Baker, Frederick, M.D., iii. 604.
— Jane Davies, wife of H. C. Fairfax, iii. 604.
— Sir John, Sissingburst, ii. 35 *n.*; ix. 99.
— — his wife, Mary Guldeford, ix. 99.

* Name unknown.

Balbirnie of Inverichte, Alexander, i. 280.
— — his wife, Margaret Arbuthnott, i. 280.
Balcanqual of Balcanqual, Alexander, viii. 198.
— — Alexander, viii. 198.
— — his wife, Margaret Murray, viii. 198.
— Archibald, vi. 367.
— Robert, vii. 187.
— — his wife, Jean Rollo, vii. 187.
— Walter, D.D., dean of Durham, i. 566; vii. 347.
BALCARRES, LINDSAY, EARL OF, i. 511-529.
Balcarres, Alexander, first earl of, i. 519.
— — his wife, Anna Mackenzie, i. 519; vii. 507.
— Alexander, fourth earl of, i. 523.
— — his wife, Elizabeth Scott, i. 523.
— Alexander, sixth earl of, i. 523; iii. 42.
— — his wife, Elizabeth Dalrymple, iii. 42; viii. 131.
— Alexander William, eighth earl of, iii. 47.
— — his wife, Margaret Lindsay, iii. 48.
— Charles, second earl of, i. 520; ix. 31.
— Colin, third earl of, i. 521.
— — his 1st wife, Mauritia de Nassau, i. 522.
— — his 2nd wife, Jean Carnegie, i. 522; vi. 499.
— — his 3rd wife, Jean Ker, i. 522; vii. 349.
— — his 4th wife, Margaret Campbell, i. 522; v. 508.
— David Alexander Edward, master of Crawford; styled lord, iii. 49.
— — his wife, Constance Lilian Pelly, iii. 49.
— James, fifth earl of, i. 523.
— — his wife, Anne Dalrymple, i. 523; viii. 132; ix. 31.
— James, seventh earl of, iii. 43.
— — his wife, M. M. F. Pennington, iii. 44.
— James Ludovic, ninth earl of, iii. 48.
— — his wife, E. F. Wilbraham, iii. 49.
BALCARRES, LINDSAY, LORD LINDSAY OF, i. 518.
Balcarres, Alexander, second lord Lindsay of, i. 519.
— David, first lord Lindsay of, i. 518.
Balcaskie of Sithboger, Thomas, viii. 522.
— Margaret of, wife of John of Greenshiels, viii. 370.
Balcormok, Walter of, vi. 170.
Bald of Kilgraston, John, v. 236.
— Mary Verena Campbell, wife of A. R. F. Hay-Drummond, v. 236.
Baldwin the Fleming, viii. 518.
— of Biggris, the King's Sheriff, viii. 519.
— of Inverkip, sheriff of Lanark, v. 549.
BALFOUR OF BURLEIGH, BALFOUR, LORD, i. 530-555.

Balfour of Burleigh, John, third lord, i. 544.
—— —— his wife, Isabel Balfour, i. 544.
—— —— Margaret, *de jure* baroness, i. 546, 553; ix. 32.
—— —— Michael, first lord, i. 537; iii. 445; vi. 98; viii. 195.
—— —— his wife, Margaret Lundin, i. 542.
—— —— Robert, *né* Arnot, second lord, i. 542, 554.
—— —— his wife, Margaret Balfour, i. 542.
—— —— Robert, fourth lord, i. 546, 552.
—— —— his wife, Margaret Melville, i. 546; vi. 110.
—— —— Robert, fifth lord, i. 547.
BALFOUR OF BURLEIGH, BRUCE, LORD, i. 554-555.
Balfour of Burleigh, Alexander Hugh, tenth lord, i. 554.
—— —— his wife, Katharine Eliza Gordon, i. 98, 555.
Balfour of Glenawley, Alexander (Balfour), 2nd lord, i. 536.
—— James, 2nd son of Sir James Balfour of Pittendreich, 1st Lord, i. 536; ix. 86.
—— —— his 1st wife, Grizel Balfour, i. 536.
—— —— his 2nd wife, Isabel *or* Elizabeth Hay, i. 536; iii. 571; ix. 86.
—— —— his 3rd wife, Anne Blaney. i. 536.
—— James, 3rd lord, i. 536.
—— —— his wife, Anne Gouldsmith, i. 536.
BALFOUR, LORD BALFOUR, i. 535.
BALFOUR, LORD BALFOUR OF BURLEIGH, i. 530-555.
BALFOUR, BARON GLENAWLEY, i. 536.
BALFOUR, LORD KILWINNING, i. 541.
Balfour of Balbuthie, Barry and Montquhannie, David, viii. 491; ix. 32.
—— —— his wife, Elizabeth Wemyss, viii. 54, 491.
—— of Balgay, Harry, iv. 282; vi. 417.
—— —— his wife, Agnes Napier, iv. 282; vi. 417.
—— of Balgarvy, John, keeper of Falkland Castle, i. 531.
—— —— Michael, i. 531.
—— —— his wife, Margaret *, i. 531.
—— —— Sir Michael, i. 539.
—— of Balledmont, David, viii. 189.
—— —— David, viii. 189.
—— —— his wife, Elizabeth Murray, viii. 189.
—— of Boghall, Alexander, ii. 184.
—— of Boquhapple, William, vi. 149.
—— of Burleigh, David, i. 532.
—— —— his wife, Agnes Forrester, i. 532.
—— —— John, i. 544.
—— —— his wife, Barbara Ross, i. 545.
—— —— Margaret, wife of Sir James Balfour of Pittendreich, i. 533, 537: vi. 98.
—— —— Margaret, wife of Robert Arnot, i. 542.

* Name unknown.

Balfour of Burleigh, Margaret, *de jure* baroness Balfour of Burleigh, i. 546, 553.
—— —— Michael, son of John B. of Balgarvy, i. 531.
—— —— his wife, Elizabeth Douglas, ix. 32.
—— —— Sir Michael, i. 531.
—— —— his wife, Margaret Muschat, i. 532.
—— —— Michael, son of David B., i. 533.
—— —— his wife, Christian Beatoun. i. 533.
—— —— Sir Michael, ambassador, i. 537; vii. 195.
—— —— his wife, Margaret Lundin, i. 542.
—— of Denmiln, Sir Michael, ii. 51; viii. 199.
—— —— Sir Michael, bart., ii. 53.
—— of Dunbog, Henry, 3rd son of 3rd lord Balfour of Burleigh, i. 545.
—— —— Henry, i. 545.
—— —— his wife, Katharine Porterfield, i. 545.
—— of Fernie, Arthur, i. 545.
—— —— his 1st wife, Dorothy Sandfoord, i. 545.
—— —— his 2nd wife, Janet Paterson, i. 545.
—— —— Francis, M.D., i. 545.
—— —— his wife, * Balfour, i. 545.
—— —— Francis, i. 545; iii. 391.
—— —— his wife, Margaret Bower, i. 545.
—— —— John, 2nd son of 3rd lord Balfour of Burleigh, i. 544, 554.
—— —— his wife, Barbara Ross, i. 545.
—— —— John, i. 545.
—— —— Sandfoord, i. 545.
—— —— Walter Francis, claimant to the barony of Balfour of Burleigh, i. 545, 554.
—— of Grange, Andrew, v. 387.
—— of New Grange, Michael, vi. 105.
—— —— his wife, Jean Melville, vi. 105.
—— of Inschery, David, ii. 571.
—— of Logie, Harie, i. 123.
—— —— his wife, Agnes Napier, i. 123.
—— of Monchaster, Sir Michael, i. 532.
—— —— his wife, Margaret Muschat, i. 532.
—— of Monimail, James, commendator of Charterhouse, vi. 98.
—— of Montquhanie, Andrew, i. 533; ix. 32 *bis*.
—— —— Sir Andrew, vi. 92.
—— —— his wife, Margaret Melville, vi. 92.
—— —— Michael, iii. 397.
—— —— Sir Michael, vii. 279.
—— of Pitcullo, Sir James, i. 536, 539, 540.
—— —— his 1st wife, Grizel Balfour, i. 536.
—— —— his 2nd wife, Elizabeth Hay, i. 536.
—— —— his 3rd wife, Anne Blaney, i. 536
—— —— Patrick, i. 536.
—— —— his wife, Katherine Ramsay, i. 536.
—— of Pittendreich, Sir James, 3rd son of Andrew B. of Montquhanny, i. 533; ix. 32.
—— —— his wife, Margaret Balfour of Burleigh, i. 533.
—— of Star, Sir Robert, ix. 32.

* Name unknown.

Balfour of Tillyochie, Henry, rector of Luncarty, vi. 368.
— of Westray, Gilbert, sheriff of Orkney, iv. 428; ix. 32.
— — his wife, Margaret Bothwell, iv. 428.
— of Whittinghame, James, v. 320.
— — his wife, Eleanor Maitland, v. 320.
— — J. M., i. 391.
— Agnes, wife of John Henderson, i. 537; ix. 32.
— Alexander, minister at Abdie, vi. 590.
— Andrew, merchant, Edinburgh, vi. 92.
— Andrew, 6th son of Andrew B. of Montquhanny, ix. 32.
— Anna, wife of David, lord Elcho, i. 543, 544; viii. 503.
— Anne, wife of Robt. Sinclair, i. 546.
— Anne, wife of Archibald Hamilton of Ballygelly, ix. 32.
— David, 8th son of Andrew B. of Montquhanny, ix. 32.
— Barbara, dau. of Arthur B. of Ferny, i. 545.
— Charles James, captain R.N., viii. 511.
— — his wife, Frances Henrietta Erskine-Wemyss, viii. 511.
— David, son of Robert B., i. 532.
— David, Netherlands army, i. 537; ix. 32.
— — his wife, Anne Bax, i. 537.
— David, M.D., ii. 51.
— — his wife, Mary Hamilton, ii. 51.
— Elizabeth, dau. of Arthur B. of Ferny, i. 545.
— Elizabeth, wife of William Murray of Drumcairn and Binn, viii. 199.
— Emelia, wife of Sir Neil Menzies, iii. 391.
— Emilia, wife of Sir John Malcolm, i. 546; ix. 33.
— Emilia, wife of 5th earl of Moray, vi. 322.
— Eustace J. A., i. 391.
— — his wife, Frances Campbell, i. 391.
— George, commendator of the charterhouse of Perth, v. 219; ix. 32.
— Gilbert, son of Sir Robt. B. of Montquhanny, i. 534.
— Grizel, wife of Sir James Balfour, i. 536.
— Helen, wife of David Barclay of Collairnie, i. 537; ix. 32.
— Henry, capt. Netherlands army, i. 537.
— — his wife, Maria van Leeuven, i. 537.
— Sir Henry, colonel, vii. 193.
— — his wife, Christian Cant, vii. 193.
— Isabel, wife of 1st lord Ruthven, i. 544.
— Isabel, wife of 3rd lord Balfour of Burleigh, i. 544.
— Isabel, dau. of 3rd lord Balfour of Burleigh, i. 546.
— Isobel, wife of Patrick Learmonth of Dairsie, vii. 546.
Balfour, Jean, wife of Jas. Arnot, i. 544.
— Jean, wife of (1) Geo. Oliphant, and (2) Sir Robt. Douglas, i. 546; ix. 33 *bis*.
— Jean, wife of James Makgill of Flasshill, vi. 590.
— John de, 1304, i. 530.
— John, in Netherlands army, i. 537.
— John, captain, vii. 193.
— — his wife, Christian Cant, vii. 193.
— John, 5th son of Andrew B. of Montquhanny, ix. 32.
— Jonet, wife of George Hume of Edrom, iv. 577.
— Jonet, wife of William, 3rd earl of Rothes, vii. 279.
— Katharine, wife of Patrick Murray of Dollerie, iii. 397.
— Margaret, wife of Sir R. Douglas of Lochleven, i. 533; vi. 368.
— Margaret, wife of Sir John Crawford, i. 544; ix. 32.
— Margaret, wife of 3rd lord Rollo, i. 546; vii. 203; ix. 152.
— Margaret, executed as a witch, ii. 440.
— Margaret, wife of (1) Andrew Leslie of Quarter, and (2) Patrick Forbes, v. 387; ix. 128.
— Margaret, *error for* Jonet, wife of William, 3rd earl of Rothes, vii. 279 *n*.
— Marie, wife of Walter Arnot, i. 537.
— Mary, wife of Gen. Bruce of Kennet, i. 547, 552; ix. 33.
— Michael, eldest son of Andrew B. of Mountquhanie, ix. 32.
— Nina, wife of Sir R. Dalrymple-Horn-Elphinstone, viii. 133.
— Pearce, i. 536.
— Robert, son of David B. of Burleigh, i. 532.
— Robert, son of Sir Robt. B. of Montquhanny, i. 534.
— Robert, 7th son of Andrew B. of Montquhanny, ix. 32.
— Robert, son of Michael B. of Burleigh, ix. 32.
— Susan, wife of Robt. Douglas, i. 546; ix. 33.
— Susan, wife of 6th lord Belhaven, ii. 53.
— Walter, son of David B. of Burleigh, i. 532.
— William, son of Margaret B. of Burleigh, i. 536.
— Sir William, lieutenant of the Tower of London, i. 544: vi. 323, 417.
— — his 1st wife, Helen Napier, vi. 417.
— *, wife of Andrew Seton of Parbroath, i. 533.
— *, wife of Dr. Francis Balfour of Fernie, i. 545.
BALGONIE, LESLIE, LORD, v. 372-381.
Balgonie, Alexander, first lord, v. 374.

* Name unknown.

Balgonie, Alexander, son of 1st earl of Leven; styled lord, v. 377, 378.
—— his wife, Margaret Leslie, v. 378; vii. 299.
— Alexander, grandson of 1st earl of Leven; styled lord. v. 377.
— Alexander, elder son of 8th earl of Leven; styled lord, vi. 119.
— David, son of George, lord Balgonie; styled lord, vi. 113 *bis*.
— David, eldest son of 5th earl of Leven; styled lord, vi. 115.
— David, eldest son of 7th earl of Leven; styled lord, vi. 118, 119.
— George, eldest son of 3rd earl of Leven; styled lord, vi. 112 *bis*, 501.
—— his wife, Margaret Carnegie, vi. 113, 501.
BALINHARD OF FARNELL, CARNEGIE, BARON, viii. 90-93.
Balinhard of Farnell, James, first baron, viii. 90.
Balinhard, Christin de, viii. 46.
— Jocelyn de, viii. 46.
— John de, father of Christin, viii. 46.
— John de, son of Christin, viii. 46.
— John de, ancestor of the family of Carnegie, viii. 46, 47.
BALIOL, LORD OF GALLOWAY, iv. 143.
Baliol of Balfour, Ingelram de, i. 530 *n*.
— of Barnard Castle, Alan, 2nd son of John de B., iv. 143.
—— Sir Alexander, lord of Baliol, iv. 143.
—— his wife, Alianora de Geneva, iv. 143.
—— Edward, King of Scotland, i. 7, 430; v. 578, 582; viii. 252.
—— Sir Hugh, iv. 142.
—— his wife, Agnes de Valence, iv. 142.
—— John, i. 4, 7; iv. 142.
—— his wife, Devorgilla of Galloway, i. 4; ii. 124; iv. 142; vi. 290.
—— John, King of Scotland, i. 7, 426; iv. 9, 143; viii. 250.
—— his wife, Isabell de Warenne, i. 7.
— of Cavers, Sir Alexander, i. 425, 426.
—— his wife, Isabella de Chilham, i. 425; ix. 11.
—— Thomas, i. 583.
— of Kilmarnock, John, v. 138.
— of Largs and Cunningham, John, King of Scotland, iv. 183.
— Ada de, wife of William de Lindsay, iii. 5; iv. 143.
— Alianora, wife of John Comyn of Badenoch and Tynedale, i. 4, 508; iv. 143.
— Cecilia, dau. of John B. and Devorgilla of Galloway, iv. 143.
— Eustace, ii. 424.
—— his wife, Helwisa Levington, ii. 424.
Baliol, Sir Henry, vii. 5.
—— his wife, Lora de Valoniis, vii. 5.
— Henry, 2nd son of King John B., i. 7; viii. 250.
— Matildis de, wife of Sir Roland de Carrick, ii. 424, 425.
— *, v. 583.
—— his wife, Isabel Stewart. v. 583.
Ballindean, *alias* Ruthven, John, iv. 102 *n*.
Ballingall of Ballingall, William, v. 398.
—— his wife, Marie Lindsay, v. 398.
—— William, v. 412.
— Agnes, wife of W. Lindsay of Pyotston, v. 412.
Balloch of the Isles, Donald, i. 439; ii. 322; iii. 180, 181.
Balloun, Jean, wife of Wm. Kellie, W.S., iii. 98.
Balmakewan of Balmakewan, George, i. 279.
— Janet, wife of Hugh Arbuthnott, i. 279.
Balmanno of Balmanno, Peter, iv. 566.
—— his wife, Euphame Carmichael, iv. 566.
BALMERINO, ELPHINSTONE, LORD, i. 556-575.
Balmerino, Arthur, sixth lord, i. 570, 571; ix. 34 *bis*.
—— his wife, Margaret Chalmers, i. 575.
— James, first lord, i. 556; ii. 83, 576; iii. 116; vii. 192; ix. 33.
—— his 1st wife, Sarah Menteith, i. 562; ix. 33.
—— his 2nd wife, Marjory Maxwell, i. 562.
— James, fifth lord, i. 570.
—— his wife, Elizabeth Carnegie, i, 571; vi. 501; ix. 34.
— John, second lord, i. 562; ii. 576.
—— his wife, Anne Ker, i. 568; v. 71.
— John, third lord, i. 568; ii. 577.
—— his wife, Ann *or* Margaret Campbell, i. 569; v. 507.
— John, fourth lord, i. 569.
—— his 1st wife, Christian Montgomerie, i. 569; iii. 452.
—— his 2nd wife, Anne Ross, i. 570.
Balmerino, master of, James, eldest son of 4th lord Balmerino, i. 569; ix. 34.
— master of, Hugh, 2nd son of 4th lord Balmerino, i. 570.
BALMORE, GORDON, LORD, iv. 549-558.
Balmore, George, first lord, iv. 550.
Balnaves of Hallhill, Henry, ii. 63; vi. 90; vii. 280.
— of Glencarse, James, viii. 202.
—— his wife, Katharine Murray, viii. 202.
— of Kirkland, James, viii. 202.
BALNEIL, LINDSAY, LORD LINDSAY OF, i. 519-523.
Balneil, Alexander, first lord Lindsay of, i. 519.

* Name unknown.

BALQUIDDER, MURRAY, LORD, i. 469; viii. 411.
Balquhidder, John, lord, i. 469.
BALQUHIDDER, MURRAY, VISCOUNT, i. 474.
Balquhidder, John, viscount, i. 474.
BALQUHIDDER, MURRAY, VISCOUNT OF, i, 479.
Balquhidder, John, first viscount of, i. 479.
Balsac, François de; seigneur d'Entraigues, v. 357.
— Guillaume de; Seigneur d'Entraigues, v. 356.
— Katharine de, wife of Esmé, 1st duke of Lennox, v. 356; ix. 126.
— de Clairmont, *, v. 357.
Baltrodi, * de, wife of Iye MacEth of Strathnaver, vii. 158.
— Walter de, bishop of Caithness, vii. 158.
BALVAIRD, MURRAY, LORD, viii. 200-214.
Balvaird, Alan David, ninth lord, viii. 213.
— Andrew, first lord, viii. 194, 199, 200.
— — his wife, Elizabeth Carnegie, viii. 68, 201; ix. 159.
— David, second lord, i. 229; viii. 199, 203.
— — his wife, Jean Carnegie, viii. 70, 197, 204.
— David, third lord, viii. 204.
— — his wife, Marjory Scot, viii. 204.
— David, fourth lord, viii. 207.
— — his wife, Anne Stewart, viii. 207.
— David, fifth lord, viii. 208.
— David William, sixth lord, viii. 210.
— William David, seventh lord, viii. 212.
— William David, eighth lord, viii. 212.
BALVANY, DOUGLAS, LORD, iii. 173-185.
Balvany, James, first lord, iii. 173.
— — his 1st wife, *, iii. 174.
— — his 2nd wife, Beatrix Sinclair, iii. 174.
BALVENIE, MURRAY, LORD, i. 474-479.
Balvenie, John, first lord, i. 474.
— — John, second lord, i. 479.
BALWEARIE, MELVILLE, LORD RAITH, MONYMAIL, AND, vi. 108-123.
Balwearie, George, first lord Raith, Monymail, and, vi. 108.
BAMBREICH, LESLIE, MARQUESS OF, vii. 301.
Bambreich, John, marquess of, vii. 301.
Bamburgh, Odard of, iv. 507 *n.*
Bampfield, Joseph, colonel, vii. 170.
Bamford-Hesketh of Gwrych Castle, R., iii. 367.
— Winifred, wife of 12th earl of Dundonald, iii. 367.
Banaster of Papenham, Sir Robert, v. 361.
— Lawrence, v. 361.
— Margaret, wife of (1) Wm. Lewes, and (2) Charles, 6th duke of Lennox, v. 361.
— Maud, wife of (1) William Comyn, and (2) William de Hasting, i. 504.
— Thurstan, i. 504.
Bandane, *alias* Ruthven, John, iv. 102 *n.*

* Name unknown.

Bandini, Charles (Bandini), 4th marquis, vi. 458.
— — his wife, Maria Cecilia, countess of Newburgh, vi. 458.
— Cristina, wife of Count Marcello Marcelli Flori, vi. 458.
— Elizabetta, wife of marquis Augustin Trionfi, vi. 458.
— Maria, wife of Cav. Frederico Pucci Boncambi, vi. 458.
— Nicoletta, wife of Charles, marquis Santa Croce of Villa Hermosa, vi. 458.
BANFF, OGILVY, LORD, ii. 1-26.
Banff, Alexander, sixth lord, ii. 22; ix. 35 *bis.*
— Alexander, seventh lord, i. 142; ii. 22, 25.
— — his wife, Jean Nisbet, ii. 25.
— George, first lord, ii. 15.
— — his 1st wife, Margaret Irvine, ii. 15, 17.
— — his 2nd wife, Janet Sutherland, ii. 18; iii. 205.
— George, second lord, ii. 18.
— — his wife, Agnes *or* Grisel Falconer, ii. 19; v. 249, ; ix. 123.
— George, third lord, ii. 20; ix. 35.
— — his wife, Jean Keith, ii. 21; v. 60; ix. 35.
— George, fourth lord, ii. 21.
— — his wife, Helen Lauder, ii. 21.
— John George, fifth lord, ii. 21.
— — his wife, Mary Ogilvie, ii. 22.
— William, eighth lord, ii. 25.
Banister, Elizabeth, wife of 7th lord Kirkcudbright, v. 273.
Bankes, Augusta Anne, wife of Edward William Douglas, vi. 385.
— George, vi. 385.
Bannatyne of Corehouse, John, iv. 365.
— — his wife, Isabella Hamilton, iv. 365.
— — John, viii. 31.
— — William, iii. 96.
— — his wife, Marion Ramsay, iii. 96.
— — William, the younger, ii. 394.
— of Kames, Hector, ii. 293.
— — Hector, son of Ninian B., ii. 297.
— — Ninian, ii. 288, 291.
— — his wife, Jonet Stewart, ii. 288.
— — Ninian, ii. 297, 298 *n.*
— — his alleged wife, Elizabeth Stewart, ii. 296.
— — his wife, Isobel Stewart, ii, 297.
— of Newhall, Sir James, lord of Session, viii. 29.
— of Newtyle, Thomas, ii. 66.
— — his wife, Marion Gilbert, ii. 66.
— Christian, dau. of Ninian B. of Kames, ii. 228.
— Elizabeth, wife of John Stewart, ii. 288, 291.
— Elizabeth, wife of James Stewart of Ardinho, ii. 293.

Bannatyne, Grizel, wife of Wm. Sandilands of Hilderstoun, viii. 391.
— James, v. 372.
— Katharine, dau. of Ninian B. of Kames, ii. 288.
— Lilias, wife of James Somerville of Drum, viii. 29.
— Martha, wife of James Somerville of Drum, viii. 30, 31.
— Richard, secretary to John Knox, iv. 157.
Bannerman of Elsick, Sir Alexander, vi. 431.
— — his wife, Margaret Scott, vi. 431.
— — Sir Alexander, bart., viii. 92.
— — Ethel Mary Elizabeth, wife of 10th earl of Southesk, viii. 92.
— of Kirkhill, Sir Alexander, bart., v. 252.
— of Wattertoun, George, i. 86.
— of Waterton, Henry, iv. 72.
— — his wife, Marjory Forbes, iv. 72.
— Elizabeth, wife of 7th lord Kirkcudbright, v. 273 *n.*
— Margaret, wife of (1) George Gordon, yr. of Haddo, and (2) Sir Wm. Keith of Ludquharn, i. 86.
— Maria, wife of 6th earl of of Kintore, v. 252; ix. 124.
Banning, Clare, wife of (1) W. S. Jones, and (2) Alex. J. Boyle, iv. 209.
— John, New South Wales, iv. 209.
Banquo, thane of Lochaber, i. 9.
Bar, David, iii. 474.
— — his wife, Bessie Bruce, iii. 474.
— Hugo, iv. 86.
Barbara, wife of Alexander Home of Hielaws and Manderston, iii. 282.
Barbour, George, i. 400.
— John, bailie of Inverness, ix. 140.
— Sybella, wife of maj.-gen. John Stewart of Pittendreich, ix. 140.
Barclay of Arngask and Fargy, Margaret, wife of Sir Andrew Murray, viii. 186.
— of Balmakewan, James, iii. 324.
— — his wife, Anna Young, iii. 324.
— — William, iii. 324.
— — William, i. 142.
— of Barclay, George, vii. 411; ix. 48.
— — his wife, Margaret Ogilvy, ii. 269; ix. 48.
— — George, vii. 412.
— of Brechin, Sir David, sheriff of Fife, ii. 222; iii. 149; vi. 343; vii. 8.
— — his wife, Margaret of Brechin, ii. 222; vii. 8.
— — Sir David, 2nd lord, ii. 223; v. 580; ix. 46.
— — his wife Jean *or* Janet Keith, ii. 224; v. 580.
— — Jean, wife of Sir David Fleming of Biggar and Cumbernauld, ii. 223; viii. 529.
Barclay of Brechin, Margaret, wife of Walter Stewart, earl of Caithness and Atholl, i. 436, 438; ii. 224; v. 581.
— of Colhill, Arthur, v. 90.
— of Collairnie, David, ii. 79.
— — David, iv. 566; v. 411; vii. 294; viii. 491.
— — his wife, Margaret Wemyss, viii. 491.
— — Sir David, v. 384; vii. 294; ix. 32.
— — his alleged wife, Helen Balfour, i. 537; ix. 32.
— — his wife, Euphemia Leslie, v. 384; vii. 291.
— — John, v. 388.
— of Drumquhendill, Jean, wife of Wm. Fraser of Faichfield, iv. 113.
— of Wester Duddingston, Margaret, wife of Sir A. Murray, viii. 186.
— of Garntully *or* Gartly, Sir Humphrey, iv. 223.
— — Patrick, i. 282.
— — his wife, Elizabeth Arbuthnott, i. 282.
— — Patrick. vii. 437.
— — *, iv. 57.
— — his wife, Katharine Forbes, iv. 57.
— of Kerkou, Alexander, vii. 405.
— — William, vii. 405.
— of Kinsleath, Hugh, ii. 223.
— of Kippo, James, viii. 186.
— — Margaret, wife of Sir Andrew Murray, viii. 186.
— of Knox, Harrie. colonel, i. 306.
— — Margaret, wife of Alex. Arbuthnott, i. 306.
— of Ladyland, David, iv. 193.
— of Lessindrum, George, vii. 411.
— of Menteith and Methlic, i. 83.
— of Monkham, Henry Ford, viii. 91.
— of Montgomerieston, James, 2nd son of David Boyle of Kelburne, iv. 197.
— — Janet, wife of James Boyle, *or* Barclay, iv. 197.
— — Robert, provost of Irvine, iv. 197.
— of Morphie, William, iii. 324.
— of Pearstoun *or* Perceton, Robert, iv. 187.
— — his wife, Katharine Wallace, iv. 187.
— — William, iv. 189, 194.
— — his wife, Jean Boyle, iv. 194.
— of Strovane, Robert, vii. 183.
— of Tolly *or* Towie, Sir Alexander, *né* Innes, ii. 32; v. 311; viii. 131.
— — Charles, *né* Maitland, v. 311.
— — his wife, Isobel Barclay, v. 311.
— — Sir David, 1281, viii. 3.
— — Isobel, wife of C. Maitland, v. 311.
— — Jean, wife of Dr. Robert Dalrymple, ii. 32; viii. 131.

* Name unknown.

Barclay of Towie, Patrick, iv. 102 *n.*, 113 *bis.*; vii. 48.
—— —— his wife, Anne Drummond, iv. 113; vii. 48.
—— —— Patrick, iii. 536.
—— —— his wife, Janet Elphinstone, iii. 536.
—— —— Walter, c. 1500, iii. 589.
—— —— Walter, vi. 413.
—— —— Walter, iv. 116.
—— —— his wife, Elizabeth Fraser, iv. 116.
—— of Urie, Alexander, vi. 35.
—— —— his wife, Katharine Keith, vi. 35.
—— —— Robert, i. 144.
—— —— his wife, Sarah Ann Allardice of Allardice, i. 144; ix. 9.
—— Alexander, 1384, ii. 539.
—— Alexander, in Banff, ix. 90.
—— Ann, wife of Jas. Allardice, i. 143.
—— Antonia, wife of John Leslie of Lumquhat, v. 388.
—— Christian, wife of Wm. Ruthven of Ballindean and Gardyne, iv. 102.
—— Christian, contracted to Alexander Abernethy, vii. 412.
—— Christian, wife of (1) James Grant of Freuchie, and (2) A. Forbes of Balfour, vii. 460.
—— Christina, mistress of King James v., i. 24.
—— Christina, wife of George Abercromby of Pitmeddan, iv. 179.
—— David, minister of Dailly, Maybole, Dumfries, Kilwinning, St. Andrews, Dairsie, vi. 103.
—— —— his wife, Alison Melville, vi. 103.
—— David, Kincardine, ix. 123.
—— Elizabeth, wife of (1) John Allardice, and (2) * Wood, i. 142.
—— Elizabeth, contr. to Robt. Maxwell of Calderwood, ii. 79.
—— Elizabeth, dau. of Patrick B. of Towie, iv. 102 *n.*
—— Elizabeth, wife of D. Lindsay of Pyotston, v. 411.
—— Mr. Gavin, burgess of Irvine, iv. 189.
—— George, merchant, Banff, ii. 21.
—— —— his wife, Isobel Ogilvy, ii. 21.
—— George, in Banff, ix. 90.
—— —— his wife, Mary Ogilvy, iv. 37; ix. 90.
—— Isabel, wife of David Carmichael of Balmedie, iv. 566.
—— Isobel, wife of Hugh Crawford of Kilbirnie, iv. 193.
—— James, banker, London, i. 143.
—— Janet, wife of (1) Wm. Stewart, yr. of Galston, and (2) Thos. Boyle, iv. 192.
—— Jean, wife of Sir David Fleming, ii. 223; viii. 529.
—— Jean, wife of Jas. Boyle of Halkishurst, iv. 189.

* Name unknown.

Barclay, John de, vi. 211; vii. 236.
—— —— his wife, Margaret Graham, vi. 211; vii. 236.
—— Katharine, wife of Alex. Fraser, 7th of Philorth, vii. 437.
—— Margaret, wife of Robt. Arbuthnott of Fiddes, i. 286.
—— Margaret, wife of David Colville, ii. 572.
—— Margaret, wife of Alex. Cunningham of Toir, iv. 188.
—— Marion Alice de Gournay, wife of Lancelot Douglas Carnegie, viii. 91.
—— Marjory, wife of James King of Barra and Bourtie, iii. 588.
—— Marjory, wife of David Rollo of Bello, vii. 183.
—— Michael, advocate, ii. 572.
—— Penelope, wife of Sir Chas. Erskine of Cambo, v. 90.
—— William, son of Walter B. of Towie, vi. 413.
—— —— his wife, Anna Napier, vi. 413.
—— *, wife of Alex. Lindsay in Haltoun, iii. 19.
Barclay-Allardice of Ury and Allardice, Margaret, wife of (1) Samuel Ritchie, and (2) Jas. Tanner, i. 144; ix. 9.
—— —— Robert, i. 144.
—— —— his wife, Mary Dalgarno, i. 144.
—— —— Robert, M.A., i. 145.
—— —— David Stuart, i. 145.
—— —— his wife, Fannie Foster Elliot, i. 145.
—— —— Mary, i. 144.
Barclay-Maitland of Towie, Charles, v. 311.
—— —— his wife, Isobel Barclay, v. 311.
Barde of Fennok, Richard de, ii. 285.
—— of Kirkwood, William le, iv. 517.
—— of Posso, Janet, wife of William Geddes, viii. 435.
—— —— John, viii. 435.
—— of Sydde and Bauchlaw, William, iv. 20 *n.*
—— Margaret, wife of Walter Murray of Tullibardine, i. 455.
BARGANY, HAMILTON, LORD, ii. 27-33.
Bargany, James, fourth lord, ii. 33.
—— John, first lord, ii. 28.
—— —— his wife, Jean Douglas, i. 205; ii. 28.
—— John, second lord, ii. 29, 483; ix. 36.
—— —— his 1st wife, Margaret Cunningham, ii. 31; iv. 249.
—— —— his 2nd wife, Alice Moore, ii. 32.
—— William, third lord, ii. 32; ix. 36.
—— —— his 1st wife, Mary Primrose, ii. 32; vii. 110.
—— —— his 2nd wife, Margaret Dundas, ii. 32.

* Name unknown.

Bargany, master of, John, elder son of 2nd lord Bargany, ii. 31.
—— —— his wife, Jean Sinclair, ii. 31; viii. 177.
Barham, Sir Charles (Middleton), bart., 1st lord, vi. 180.
—— —— his wife, Margaret Gambier, vi. 180.
—— Diana (Middleton), wife of Gerard Noel Edwards; baroness, vi. 180.
—— of Stockbridge, John Foster, M.P., iv. 97.
—— —— his wife, Katharine Grimston, iv. 97.
—— Ursula, wife of Sir Thos. Richardson, ii. 580.
Barkham of Southacre, Sir Edward, bart., ii. 583.
—— —— his wife, Frances Napier, ii. 583.
—— —— Robert, ii. 583.
—— Elizabeth, wife of 3rd lord Cramond, ii. 583.
Barlow, Elizabeth, wife of (1) Alexander, 1st lord Elphinstone, and (2) John, 6th lord Forbes, iii. 530; iv. 53, 54; ix. 84, 91.
—— Lucy, *alias* Walters, i. 30; ii. 238.
Barnard of Kinnaber, William, vi. 212.
—— Andrew, son of bishop B., i. 528.
—— —— his wife, Anne Lindsay, i. 528.
—— C. S., in holy orders, viii. 227.
—— Lucy Marion, wife of Edward Drummond, viii. 227.
—— Thomas, bishop of Limerick, i. 528.
—— *, 1st wife of William Campbell of Liston Hall, i. 382.
Barnes, Edmund Charles, v. 419.
—— —— his wife, E. M. Crosse, v. 419.
—— Katharine Frances Corbett, wife of 10th earl of Dundonald, iii. 365.
—— Thomas, Romford, iii. 365.
Barnet, Curtis, commodore R.N., v. 181.
Barnham, Benedict, alderman of London, v. 86.
—— —— his wife, Dorothy Smith, v. 86.
—— Stephen, iii. 234, 235.
—— Ursula, wife of (1) Sir R. Swift, and (2) William, 1st viscount of Air, iii. 234, 235.
Barnston, Alice Emma, wife of Major C. Napier, vi. 436.
—— Roger, vi. 436.
Barnwell, Mary Harbourne, wife of Edward Hay, v. 233.
Baron of Kinnaird, James, vii. 187; ix. 151.
—— Helen, wife of principal Robt. Rollo, vii. 187; ix. 151.
Barratt of Wymeswold, William, i. 405.
—— Margaret, wife of (1) Hugh Botham, and (2) Devereux Aston, i. 405.
BARRET OF NEWBURGH, BARRET, LORD, ii. 34-35.

* Name unknown.

Barret of Newburgh, Edward, lord, ii. 34.
—— —— his 1st wife, Jane Cary, ii. 35; ix. 36.
—— —— his 2nd wife, Katharine Fenn, ii. 35; ix. 36.
BARRET, LORD BARRET OF NEWBURGH, ii. 34-35.
Barret of Belhouse, Edward, ii. 34.
—— Sir Edward, ii. 34; ix. 36 *ter*.
—— Richard, sheriff of Essex, ii. 35.
—— Anne, wife of (1) Sir R. Harley, and (2) Sir J. Leveson, ii. 34 *n*.
—— Charles, ii. 34.
—— —— his wife, Christian Mildmay, ii. 34.
—— Dorothy, wife of 2nd lord Stanhope of Harrington, ii. 34.
—— George, ii. 35 *n*.
—— —— his wife, Elizabeth Dinely, ii. 35 *n*.
—— Walter, brother of lord Barret of Newburgh, ii. 34 *n*.
Barrett-Lennard, Sir Thomas, 1st bart., ii. 35 *n*.
Barrington, William (Barrington), 6th viscount, viii. 313.
Barrington of Barrington Hall, Sir Thomas, bart., vi. 466.
—— Charlotte Maria, wife of 12th earl of Strathmore and Kinghorne, viii. 313.
—— Lucy, wife of (1) Wm. Cheyne, and (2) Sir Toby Tyrrell, vi. 465.
—— Russell, viii. 310.
—— —— his wife, Mary Lyon, viii. 310.
BARROGILL, SINCLAIR, BARON, ii. 358.
Barrogill, George Philips Alexander, second baron, ii. 358.
—— James, first baron, ii. 358.
—— —— his 1st wife, Louisa Georgiana Philips, ii. 358.
—— —— his 2nd wife, Marie de Mariategui, duchesse de Pomar, ii. 358.
Barry of St. Leonards Hill and Keiss, Sir Francis Tress, 1st bart., iii. 396.
Barry of Witchingham Hall, William James, iii. 396.
—— —— his wife, Grace Murray, iii. 396.
—— Caroline, wife of Louis Pierre Francis Malcolm Drummond, vi. 69.
Barrymore, Richard (Barry), 6th earl of, vi. 69.
Bartoletti, Fortunata, wife of Alexander Humphreys *or* Alexander, viii. 184.
Bartolucci of Cantiano, Vincenzo, viii. 473.
—— Candida Louisa, wife of 10th marquess of Tweeddale, viii. 473.
Barton of Ballinbreich, Andrew, vii. 281.
—— of Over Barnton, Sir Robert, High Treasurer, viii. 388.
—— Elizabeth, wife of (1) William, 1st lord Panmure of Brechin and Navar, and (2) Bonamy M. Power, vii. 24; ix. 66.
—— Elizabeth, wife of (1) George Bromley, and (2) Jas. Graham of Levens, vii. 102.
—— Isaac, All Hallows, Barking, vii. 102.

Barton, John William, vii. 24.
—— Margaret, wife of John Sandilands of Calder, viii. 388.
—— Robert, the comptroller, vii. 45.
Barwick of Toulston, Frances, wife of 4th lord Fairfax, iii. 600.
—— —— Sir Robert, iii. 600.
Basset, Katharine, wife of R. Leslie, ix. 127.
—— Maud, wife of (1) William Comyn, and (2) Wm. de Hasting, i. 504.
—— Thurstan, i. 504.
Bastie, Antoine d'Arces, chevalier de la, ii. 6; iv. 356 *bis*.
Batail of Fawdon, iii. 137.
—— Custancia de, wife of Sir William of Douglas, iii. 137.
Bateman, Anne, wife of Patrick Maitland of Kilmaron, v. 313.
—— Colthurst, v. 313 *bis*.
—— Dora, wife of Admiral John Maitland, v. 313.
Bateman-Hanbury, Harriet Anne, wife of, (1) G. A. C. Dashwood, and (2) M. W. Graham, vi. 271.
Bath, Henrietta Laura (Pulteney), wife of Sir James Murray of Hillhead; countess of, iii. 517 *bis*.
—— Thomas (Thynne), 2nd marquess of, ii. 245.
Bathurst, Allen (Bathurst), 1st earl, iii. 482.
—— Henry (Bathurst), 3rd earl, v. 364.
—— —— his wife, Georgina Lennox, v. 364.
—— Benjamin, iii. 482.
—— —— his wife, Elizabeth Bruce, iii. 482.
—— Dr. Ralph, ix. 88.
Baty, Helen, wife of Alan Stewart of Threapwood, vii. 64.
Baumann, Josephine, wife of F. R. V. Douglas-Hamilton, iv. 390.
Bax, Anne, wife of David Balfour, i. 537.
—— Sir Paul, i. 537.
Baylay, Armynel Mary, wife of Canon A. H. Drummond, viii. 232.
—— Charles F. R., viii. 232.
Bayley of Normancote Grange, Ralph, i. 405.
—— —— his wife, Anne Aston, i. 405.
—— Anne, wife of Edward Aston, i. 403.
—— Nathaniel, Hanwell, v. 15.
—— —— his wife, Elizabeth Arthur Ingram, v. 15.
—— Thomas, Stafford, i. 403.
Baylie of Honingham, Richard, D.D., dean of Salisbury, ii. 584 *n*.
Bayliss, captain, vii. 382.
Bayly, John, general, C.B., R.E., ii. 529.
—— Helen Tolmie Dick, wife of C. J. C. Douglas, ii. 529.
Bayne of Tulloch, Duncan, ix. 26.
—— —— his wife, Elizabeth Stewart, i. 397; ix. 26.
Bayning of Foxley, Anne, wife of (1) Henry Murray of Berkhampstead, and (2) Sir J. Baher; viscountess, iii. 399.
Bayning of Sudbury, Paul, 1st viscount, iii. 399.
Bayntun of Spye Park, Henry, viii. 36.
—— —— his wife, Anne Wilmot, viii. 36.
—— Anne, wife of (1) Edward Rolt of Sacombe Park, and (2) James, 12th lord Somerville, viii. 36.
Beaton, Bethune, Betoun of Auchmuthie, John, viii. 95.
—— of Balfour, David, 12th laird, ii. 572.
—— —— David, 15th laird, iii. 379; iv. 492.
—— —— his wife, Rachel Hope, iv. 492.
—— —— John, 2nd laird, v. 1.
—— —— his wife, Katharine Stewart, v. 1.
—— —— John, 7th laird, iii. 317.
—— —— John, 8th laird, i. 444.
—— —— his wife, Christian Stewart, i. 444.
—— —— John, 10th laird, viii. 95.
—— —— Robert, 11th laird, v. 405.
—— of Cairntoun, James, 2nd son of David B. of Creich, iv. 337.
—— of Capuldrae, Archibald, chamberlain of Dunfermline, iii. 338; v. 556.
—— —— John, iv. 243.
—— of Easter Cochrane, James, archbishop of St. Andrews, iii. 338; ix. 75.
—— of Creich, Agnes *or* Anna, wife of (1) Sir James Chisholm of Cromlix, and (2) Sir D. Hering of Lethinty, i. 138 *n*.; vii. 290.
—— —— David, the Treasurer, 1st laird, i. 25; iv. 337, 360; v. 556.
—— —— David, 5th laird, vii. 290.
—— —— his wife, Beatrix Leslie, vii. 290.
—— —— David, 8th laird, iv. 247.
—— —— his wife, Margaret Cunningham, iv. 247.
—— —— James, viii. 196, 497.
—— —— his 2nd wife, Margaret Wemyss, viii. 497.
—— —— John, 2nd laird, i. 25, 533; ii. 230, 231; v. 5.
—— —— his wife, Janet Hay, i. 533.
—— —— Robert, 4th laird, i. 77; viii. 24.
—— of Dowald, David, i. 464.
—— of Duchal, Archibald, v. 556, 557.
—— of Kilconquhar, David, v. 416.
—— —— Thomas, v. 416.
—— of Melgund, David, cardinal, Archbishop of St. Andrews, i. 115, 339; iii. 29, 288; iv. 366, 539; vi. 88, 95; vii. 14, 280, 282, 286; viii. 16.
—— —— David, his son, i. 115, 118, 464.
—— —— James, v. 398.
—— —— his wife, Margaret Lindsay, v. 398.
—— —— James, v. 208; ix. 121.
—— —— his wife, Helen Menzies, v. 208.
—— of Skryne, Elizabeth, dau. of cardinal B., vii. 15.
—— Agnes, wife of David Colville, ii. 572.

Beaton, Agnes, wife of (1) Jas. Ochterlony, (2) George Gordon of Gight, and (3) Sir Patrick Gordon of Auchindoun; iii. 288; iv. 538; ix. 110, 111.
— Alexander, archdean of Lothian, i. 115.
— Christian, wife of (1) Michael Balfour, and (2) Patrick Kinninmont of Craighall, i. 533; ix. 32.
— Elizabeth, mistress of King James v., i. 25.
— Elizabeth, wife of James Sandilands, i. 77.
— Elizabeth, wife of John Ogilvy, i. 118.
— Elizabeth, wife of (1) John, 4th lord Innermeath, and (2) James Gray, iv. 282; v. 5.
— Elizabeth, wife of David Lindsay, v. 405.
— Elizabeth, wife of 1st viscount of Stormont, viii. 196.
— Grissel, wife of (1) Sir W. Scott of Kirkurd, and (2) A. Murray of Blackbarony, i. 251; ii. 231; iii. 503; ix. 46, 83 *bis*.
— Grizel, wife of 4th lord Lyle, v. 556.
— Isobel, mistress of J. Gray, iv. 282.
— James, archbishop of Glasgow and St. Andrews, iii. 338; v. 397, 555; viii. 487; ix. 75.
— James, archbishop of Glasgow, i. 557.
— Janet, wife of (1) Sir Robert Livingston, and (2) James (Hamilton), 1st earl of Arran, iv. 358, 360; viii. 369.
— Jonet, wife of (1) Sir Jas. Crichton, (2) Simon Preston, (3) Sir Walter Scott, and (4) James, 4th earl of Bothwell, ii. 163, 230; ix. 46.
— Katharine, wife of P. Lindsay of Wolmerston, v. 414.
— Katharine, wife of James Forbes of Kilmany, vi. 590.
— Margaret, wife of Arthur Forbes of Rires, i. 445; viii. 541.
— Margaret, wife of David, 10th earl of Crawford, iii. 29.
— Margaret, wife of John Graham of Ballargus and Claverhouse, iii. 317.
— Margaret, wife of G. Lindsay of Wormiston, v. 416.
— Mary, contracted to Hugh, master of Somerville, viii. 24.
Beatrice, prioress of Iona, dau. of Somerled, v. 31.
— wife of Sir Andrew Fraser, brother of Sir Simon F. of Oliver Castle, vii. 422.
Beatrix, dau. of Gilchrist, earl of Angus; alleged wife of Walter, 3rd lord High Steward, i. 12.
— wife of George, 11th earl of Dunbar, iii. 277.
Beauchamp, John Reginald (Lygon), 3rd earl, i. 492.
— — his 2nd wife, Katharine Otway-Cave, i. 492.
Beauchamp, Henry (Seymour), son of William, 1st marquess of Hertford; styled lord, iii. 480.
BEAUCHAMP OF BLETSHOE, GORDON, BARON, iv. 556.
Beauchamp of Bletshoe, Alexander, 12th baron, iv. 556.
— Beatrix de, wife of Hugo de Morville, v. 277.
Beauclerc, James, illeg. son of King Charles II., i. 32.
Beauclerk, Charlotte, wife of John Drummond of Stanmore, viii. 224.
— William, 2nd son of 1st duke of St. Albans, viii. 224.
Beaufort, Henry (Somerset), 2nd duke of, iii. 355.
— — his wife, Mary Osborne, iii. 355.
— Henry (Somerset), 7th duke of, v. 237.
— Henry Charles (Somerset), 6th duke of, iv. 171.
— Eleanor, wife of Sir Robert Spencer, iii. 608.
— Joan, wife of (1) King James I., and (2) Sir James Stewart of Lorn, i. 18, 450; ii. 141; iii. 564, 569; v. 2, 427.
Beaumont, Henry de, earl of Buchan and Moray, constable of Scotland, 1st lord, ii. 256, 258, 259; iii. 263; vi. 295.
— — his wife, Alicia Comyn, ii. 256, 258.
— of Stoughton Grange, Sir Thomas, ii. 578.
— — his wife, Katharine Farnham, ii. 578.
— of Vescy, Isabella de, i. 430.
— Elizabeth, wife of (1) Sir J. Ashburnham, and (2) Sir Thomas Richardson; baroness of Cramond, ii. 578.
— Elizabeth, wife of 1st earl of Nithsdale, vi. 486.
— Ermengarde de, wife of King William the Lion, i. 5.
— Sir Francis, vi. 486.
— Sir John, son of Alicia, countess of Buchan, ii. 259.
— Katharine, wife of David, 11th earl of Atholl, i. 432.
— Mary, wife of 2nd earl of Northampton, vi. 486 *n*.
— Roger de, bishop of St. Andrews, i. 418.
Becford of Altadore, ix. 55.
Bechinoe, Benjamin, capt. R.N., iii. 413.
— Mary, wife of (1) William, 4th duke of Roxburghe, and (2) John Tollemache, iii. 413; vii. 353.
Beckford of Fonthill, William, lord mayor of London, i. 60.
— — his wife, Maria Hamilton, i. 60.
— — William, author of *Vathek*, i. 60, 105; iv. 395.
— — his wife, Margaret Gordon, i. 105; iv. 395; ix. 7.

Beckford, Susan Euphemia, wife of 10th duke of Hamilton, iv. 395.
Beckman, Anne Christian, wife of David Carnegie, viii. 83.
Beckwith of Milliehope Park, Henry John, v. 370.
— Sir Thomas Sidney, K.C.B., vii. 151.
— — his wife, Mary Douglas, vii. 151.
— William Malbisse, v. 370.
— — his wife, Muriel Beatrice Gordon-Lennox, v. 370.
Bedford, John (Plantagenet), duke of, iii. 166.
— Francis (Russell), 5th duke of, viii. 40.
— John (Russell), 4th duke of, vii. 358.
— John (Russell), 6th duke of, i. 70; iv. 557.
— — his 2nd wife, Georgina Gordon, iv. 557.
Bedingfield, Elizabeth, wife of Sir Alex. Hamilton, i. 47.
Bedoch, dau. of Malcolm, 2nd earl of Atholl, i. 418.
Beecher, Anne, wife of (1) R. M. Thackeray, and (2) H. W. Carmichael-Smyth, iv. 569.
— J. H., iv. 569.
Begg, Elizabeth, wife of lieut. David Stewart, R.N., vi. 326.
Bek, Antony, bishop of Durham, ii. 538.
Belasyse of Worlaby, Henry (Belasyse), 2nd lord, v. 363.
— — his wife, Anne Brudenell, v. 363.
— — John (Belasyse), 1st lord, iii. 299.
— Barbara, wife of Sir M. Dalton, vii. 107.
— Frances, wife of Sir Thos. Ingram, v. 11.
— Henry, son of 1st viscount Fauconberg, vii. 107.
— Mary, wife of 3rd viscount Dunbar, iii. 299.
BELHAVEN, DOUGLAS, VISCOUNT OF, ii. 36-37.
Belhaven, Robert, viscount of, ii. 36.
— — his wife, Nicolas Moray, ii. 37.
BELHAVEN AND STENTON, HAMILTON, LORD, ii. 38-60.
Belhaven and Stenton, Alexander Charles, tenth lord, ii. 59.
— — his wife, Georgina Katharine Richmond, ii. 60.
— — James, fifth lord, ii. 47.
— — James, ninth lord, ii. 55, 58.
— — his wife, Georgina Watson, ii. 58.
— — John, first lord, ii. 39; v. 196.
— — his wife, Margaret Hamilton, ii. 40, 85; iv. 375.
— — John, second lord, ii. 40, 43, 44.
— — his wife, Margaret Hamilton, ii. 40, 41.
— — John, third lord, ii. 46.
— — his wife, Anne Bruce, ii. 46.
— — John, fourth lord, ii. 47.
— — Robert, sixth lord, ii. 47, 53, 54.
— — his wife, Susan Balfour, ii. 53.
Belhaven and Stenton, Robert Montgomerie, eighth lord, ii. 54.
— — his wife, Hamilton Campbell, ii. 54.
— — William, seventh lord, ii. 53.
— — his wife, Penelope Macdonald, ii. 54.
— master of, Ralph Gerard Alexander (Hamilton) ii. 60; iii. 367.
— — his wife, Grizel Winifred Louise Cochrane, ii. 60; iii. 367.
'Bell the Cat,' i. 178.
Bell of Abbeylarn, William Shirley, vi. 121.
— of Bladethouse, William, vii. 99.
— of Godsbrigg, William, vii. 99.
— of the Holmes, George, viii. 273, 274.
— of Inchture, George, viii. 274.
— of Pendell Court, William A., iv. 220.
— of Streamstown, Edward Gonne, vii. 450.
— of Whiteside, John, v. 125.
— of Woolsingham, Matthew, iii. 583.
— Anne, wife of Sir Alex. Hope of Granton, iv. 491.
— Charles, v. 635.
— — his wife, Charlotte Erskine Goodeve-Erskine, v. 635.
— Georgina, wife of Capt. Norman Leslie-Melville, vi. 121.
— Hyacinthe Mary, wife of Patrick James, lord Kelburne, iv. 220.
— James, provost of Glasgow, iv. 289.
— — his wife, Elspeth Gray, iv. 289.
— Jane, wife of William Hay, iii. 583.
— John, minister of Calder, v. 165.
— Mary Georgina, wife of gen. David M. Fraser, vii. 450.
— Sibill, wife of Fergus Graham of Plomp, vii. 99.
Bellamy, Charles, H.E.I.C.S., v. 133.
— — his wife, Louisa Gordon of Kenmure, v. 133.
Bellamy-Gordon of Kenmure, Louisa, wife of rev. Jas. Maitland, v. 133.
Bellarmine, Cardinal, i. 559.
BELLENDEN OF BROUGHTON, BELLENDEN, LORD, ii. 61-76.
Bellenden of Broughton, John, second lord, ii. 72; vii. 349; ix. 38.
— — his wife, Mary Moore, ii. 73.
— — John, third lord, ii. 74.
— — his wife, Mary Parnell, ii. 75.
— — John Ker, fifth lord, ii. 76.
— — his wife, Sarah Cumming, ii. 76.
— — Ker, fourth lord, ii. 75.
— — his wife, Elizabeth Brett, ii. 75.
— — Robert, sixth lord, ii. 75, 76.
— — William, first lord, ii. 71; ix. 38.
— — William, seventh lord, ii. 73, 76; vii. 352.
BELLENDEN, LORD BELLENDEN OF BROUGHTON, ii. 61-76.

Bellenden (Bellentyne), of Auchnoull, Sir John, justice clerk, ii. 64; iii. 278; iv. 428; ix. 137.
—— —— his 1st wife, Margaret Scott, ii. 65.
—— —— his 2nd wife, Barbara Kennedy, ii. 64, 65.
—— —— his 3rd wife, Janet Seton, ii. 66; iv. 60.
—— of Auchnoull, Sir Lewis, keeper of the Palace of Linlithgow, justice clerk, ii. 65, 68; vi. 99.
—— —— his 1st wife, Geillis Forrester, ii. 70; iv. 89.
—— —— his 2nd wife, Margaret Livingston, ii. 70; v. 443.
—— —— Patrick, parish clerk of Holyrood, ii. 62; iv. 86.
—— —— his wife, Marion Douglas, ii. 62.
—— —— Thomas, justice clerk, ii. 63.
—— —— his wife, Agnes Forrester, ii. 63.
—— —— Sir William, ii. 71; ix. 38 *bis*.
—— of Bigods, James, capt. 21st foot, ii. 73.
—— of Broughton, Sir James, ii. 70.
—— —— his wife, Elizabeth Ker, ii. 71; vii. 341.
—— —— Sir William, constable of Linlithgow Palace, ii. 71; v. 446.
—— of Castlelaw, Sir Lewis, ii. 68.
—— of Corollachill, Sir John, ii. 64.
—— of Evie, Adam, ii. 64.
—— —— Sir Patrick, ii. 63, 69.
—— —— his wife, Katharine Kennedy, ii. 63.
—— of Fawsyde, Sir Lewis, ii. 69.
—— of Horshope, Patrick, ii. 62.
—— —— his wife, Marion Douglas, ii. 62.
—— of Kilconquhar, Adam, bishop, ii. 66.
—— —— his wife, Jean Abercrombie, ii. 67.
—— —— James, ii. 66, 67.
—— —— his wife, Grisel Spens, ii. 66.
—— of Longcroft, Sir Lewis, ii. 69.
—— of Magdalens, Sir James, ii. 70.
—— of Milkburn, Thomas, ii. 63.
—— of Ochiltree, Sir Lewis, ii. 69.
—— of Pittendreich, James, ii. 68.
—— —— his wife, Agnes Bellenden, ii. 68.
—— —— John, ii. 68.
—— of St. John's Chapel, Walter, ii. 67.
—— —— his wife, Jean Hamilton, ii. 67.
—— of Spotts, Sir Lewis, ii. 68.
—— of Standenflat, Mr. Nicol, i. 446.
—— —— his wife, Jean Stewart, i. 446.
—— of Stanehouse, Adam, ii. 64.
—— —— Sir Patrick, sheriff of Orkney, ii. 63, 66, 68.
—— —— his wife, Katharine Kennedy, ii. 63.
—— —— Thomas, 'appearand,' ii. 64.
—— of Walkmylns, Sir John, ii. 64.
—— of Woodhouselee, Sir Lewis, ii. 68.
—— Adam, 5th son of bishop B., ii. 67.
—— Agnes, wife of (1) W. Adamson, and (2) Alex. Somervell, ii. 64.
Bellenden, Agnes, wife of James Bellenden of Pittendreich, ii. 65, 68.
—— Alexander, 4th son of bishop B., ii. 67.
—— Alice, dau. of 3rd lord Bellenden, ii. 75.
—— Alison, wife of John Achisoun, ii. 64.
—— Anna, dau. of Sir Lewis B., ii. 70.
—— Annabel, wife of Alex. Lauder, ii. 68; v. 296.
—— Caroline, wife of John Gawler, ii. 75.
—— Christian, wife of Matthew Forrester of Barnton, ii. 61; iv. 86.
—— David, minister of Kincardine O'Neil, ii. 67.
—— Diana, wife of John Bulteel, ii. 75.
—— Elizabeth, dau. of bishop B., ii. 67.
—— Elizabeth, wife of (1) Jas. Lawson, and (2) Sir J. Cockburn, ii. 68.
—— Elizabeth, wife of Edward Kelly, ii. 73.
—— Elizabeth, wife of John Cockburn of Ormiston, vi. 596.
—— Mr. George, precentor of Glasgow, ii. 64, 68.
—— Henrietta, dau. of 3rd lord Bellenden, ii. 75.
—— Sir Henry, governor of Hurst Castle, ii. 73.
—— Jacomina, wife of T. O. Hunter, ii. 73.
—— James, son of bishop Adam B., ii. 67.
—— James, son of 2nd lord Bellenden, ii. 73.
—— Jane, dau. of Sir John B., ii. 66.
—— Jane, wife of E. Miller, ii. 75.
—— Jean, dau. of bishop Adam B., ii. 67.
—— Jemima, dau. of James B., ii. 73.
—— John, translator of Livy and Boece, ii. 62.
—— John, 5th son of Sir John B. of Auchnoull, ii. 66.
—— John, son of bishop Adam B., ii. 67.
—— John, adventurer for Ulster, ii. 70.
—— Katharine, wife of (1) Adam Hopper, (2) Francis Bothwell, and (3) O. Sinclair of Pitcairns, ii. 62; iv. 427.
—— Katharine, dau. of John B. of Auchnoull, ii. 65; ix. 37.
—— Katharine, wife of Robert Craig, ii. 65 *n.*; ix. 38.
—— Margaret, wife of G. Forrester, ii. 61.
—— Margaret, wife of John Kincaid, ii. 63.
—— Margaret, wife of (1) Jas. Denniston, and (2) R. Hamilton, ii. 64.
—— Margaret, dau. of bishop B., ii. 67.
—— Margaret, dau. of Sir Lewis B., ii. 70.
—— Margaret, wife of Henry Erskine, styled lord Cardross, ii. 71, 72, 365; ix. 52.
—— Margaret, dau. of 3rd lord B., ii. 74.
—— Marion, wife of (1) J. Ramsay of Dalhousie, and (2) P. Murray of Falahill, ii. 65; iii. 96.
—— Mariota, wife of John Chalmer, ii. 70.
—— Mary, dau. of John B. of Auchnoull, ii. 65; ix. 37.
—— Mary, wife of Sir R. Murray, ii. 73.

Bellenden, Mary, wife of col. John Campbell (afterwards 4th duke of Argyll), i. 383; ii. 74; ix. 38.
—— Mary, wife of John Eatt, ii. 75.
—— Patrick, clerk of the Coquet, ii. 64, 69.
—— Robert, abbot of Holyrood, ii. 61; vii. 246.
—— Robert, son of bishop Adam B., ii. 67.
—— Robert, son of 2nd lord Bellenden, ii. 73.
—— Thomas, lord of Session, ii. 66.
—— —— his wife, Marion Gilbert, ii. 66.
—— Thomas, son of Mr. Wm. B., ii. 67.
—— —— his wife, Euphemia Dudingston, ii. 67.
—— Walter, canon of Holyrood, ii. 61.
—— William, son of bishop Adam B., ii. 67.
—— William, vicar of Kilconquhar, ii. 67.
—— —— his wife, Anabel Pearson, ii. 67.
—— William, adventurer for Ulster, ii. 70.
—— William, lieut.-col., ii. 73.
—— —— his wife, Jacomina Farmer, ii. 73.
—— Zachary, ii. 66.
—— *, wife of Wm, Stewart of Egilsbay, vi. 575.
—— *, wife of Henry Sinclair, iv. 428; ix. 37.
—— *, wife of Robt. Sinclair, iv. 428; ix. 37.
Bellenden-Ker, duke of Roxburghe, vii. 352-354.
Bellentyne. *See* Bellenden.
Bellew of Duleek, John (Bellew), 4th lord, vi. 490.
—— —— his 1st wife, Anne Maxwell, vi. 489.
—— —— Richard (Bellew), 3rd lord, vi. 453.
—— —— his wife, Frances Brudenel, vi. 453.
—— of Barmeath, Sir John, i. 54.
—— —— Patrick, i. 54.
—— —— his wife, Frances Hamilton, i. 54.
—— Mary Helena, wife of 18th lord Saltoun, vii. 453.
—— Thomas Arthur Grattan, vii. 453.
Bellingham, Charles, vi. 17.
—— —— his wife, Julian Hume, vi. 17.
—— John, vii. 227; ix. 152.
—— —— his wife, Alice Jane Primrose, vii. 227.
—— William Stewart, vii. 227.
Bellomont, Richard, viscount of, i. 5.
—— Ermengarde de, wife of King William the Lion, i. 5.
—— Roger de, bishop of St. Andrews, i. 418.
Belmore, Armar (Lowry-Corry), 1st earl of, v. 483.
—— —— his 2nd wife, Henrietta Hobart, v. 483.
Belshes of Tofts, John, advocate, iv. 476.
—— Helena, wife of (1) David Home of Ninewells, and (2) John Home, Chirnside, iv. 476.
Benederaloch, Campbell, lord, ii. 203.
Benederaloch, John, first lord, ii. 203.

* Name unknown.

Benette, Alexander, Northumberland, iii. 8.
—— Dyonisia, wife of Sir John de Lindsay, iii. 8.
Benham, Eda, wife of 10th lord Fairfax, iii. 605.
Benham, Joseph A. S., iii. 605.
Bennachtyne de Corrokis, John de, ii. 61.
Bennet of Chesters, Archibald, vii. 383.
—— of Grubbet, Sir William, bart., vi. 321, 498.
—— of Wallyford, John, iv. 489.
—— Cecilia, wife of John Rutherfurd of Capehope, vii. 383.
—— Christina, wife of Charles Stewart of Duncarn, vi. 321; ix. 139.
—— Elizabeth, wife of Sir Thomas Hope of Craighall, iv. 489; viii. 577 *n.*
—— Hariet Charlotte, wife of major-gen. Jas. Ramsay, iii. 104.
—— Ida Louisa, wife of 13th earl of Dalhousie, iii. 109.
—— Isabel, wife of 1st duke of Grafton, i. 31.
—— Margaret, wife of Jas. Carnegie of Finavon, vi. 498.
—— Robert, town-clerk of Musselburgh, viii. 577 *n.*
—— —— his wife, Euphame Seton, viii. 577 *n.*
—— W. H. Burlton, B.C.S., iii. 104.
Bennett of Beachampton, Sir Simon, 1st bart., v. 11.
—— —— Elizabeth Ingram, v. 11.
—— Caroline, wife of capt. Henry E. Napier, R.N., vi. 434.
Benson of Langtons, William, viii. 227.
—— Margaret Elizabeth, wife of A. H. Drummond, viii. 227.
Béranger, François de, vi. 71.
—— Marie de, wife of Louis Drummond of Lussan, vi. 71.
Berargaard, * de, viii. 208.
—— —— his wife, Henrietta Frederica Bunau, viii. 208.
Beresford, Sir George de la Poer, bart., viii. 235.
—— Marcia, wife of capt. Francis C. Drummond, viii. 235.
Beresford-Drummond, Francis Colebrooke, captain, viii. 235.
—— —— his wife, Marcia Beresford, viii. 235.
Berkeley, James (Berkeley), 3rd earl of, v. 363.
—— —— his wife, Louisa Lennox, v. 363.
—— of Kilbirny, Sir Hugh, v. 491.
—— of Garntully, Sir Humphrey, iv. 223.
—— Archibald, son of Sir Hugh B. of Kilbirny, v. 491.
—— Sir George Cranfield, G.C.B., v. 364.
—— —— his wife, Emily Charlotte Lennox, v. 364.

* Name unknown.

Berkeley, Richenda, wife of Robert, son of Wernebald, iv. 223.
— Robert de, vi. 469.
— — his wife, Cecilia of Maccustoun, vi. 469.
— Walter. viii. 319 *n.*
Berkshire, Henry Bowes (Howard), 4th earl of, vii. 103.
— — his wife, Katharine Graham, vii. 103.
— Thomas (Howard), 3rd earl of, vii. 102.
Bern, father of Gamel, ii. 370.
Bernard of Airth, v. 329.
— — his wife, Helen, v. 329.
Berner of Saskendorff, John, iv. 105.
— — his wife, Anna Dyerlink, iv. 105.
— Clara, wife of Patrick, earl of Forth and Brentford, iv. 105; ix. 93.
Bernham, David de, bishop of St. Andrews, ii. 217; viii. 476.
Berowald the Fleming, ii. 121.
Berrford, Johanna, *variant of* Joanna Beaufort, i. 450.
Berriedale, William, eldest son of 5th earl of Caithness; styled lord, ii. 343.
— — his wife, Margaret *or* Mary Sinclair, ii. 343; vii. 574.
— master of, John, eldest son of William, lord Berriedale, ii. 343.
— — his wife, Jean Mackenzie, ii. 344; vii. 507.
Bertie, Bridget, wife of 1st duke of Leeds, iii. 302.
— Louisa, wife of Sir C. Stewart, ii. 304.
— Mary Elizabeth, wife of Thomas Charles, viscount of Milsington, vii. 96.
— Vere, 3rd son of 1st duke of Ancaster, ii. 304.
Bertolf of Leslie, vii. 264.
Bertram, Robert, sheriff of Northumberland, viii. 522.
BERVIE, ARBUTHNOTT, LORD OF, i. 305.
Bervie, James, first lord of, i. 305.
Berwick, James, FitzJames, duke of, i. 34.
— — his 1st wife, Honora Bourke, i. 34.
— — his 2nd wife, Anne Bulkeley, i. 34.
— and Alba, dukes of, i. 34.
BERWICK, HOME, BARON HOME OF, iii. 287-289.
Berwick, Thomas, custumar of Edinburgh, v. 431.
Besingham, Henry de, v. 280; vi. 523 *n.*
Bessborough, John George (Ponsonby), 5th earl of, v. 368.
— — his wife, Caroline Amelia Gordon-Lennox, v. 368.
Best of Boxley, Mawdistley, iii. 603.
— Dorothy, wife of 7th lord Fairfax, iii. 603.
Beth, alleged earl of Fife, iv. 2 *n.*
Bethell, Richard, son of 3rd lord Westbury, iii. 420.
Bethoc, wife of Crinan of Dunkeld, and dau. and heir of King Malcolm II., i. 3; iii. 240.
— dau. of King Donald 'Bane,' and wife of Huctred *or* Godrith of Tynedale, i. 3, 417; vi. 288.
— dau. of Malcolm, 2nd earl of Atholl, i. 418.
— of Rowcastle, wife of Ranulf, son of Dunegal, vi. 288.
Bethune. *See also* Beaton.
— of Bandon, Robert, v. 414.
— of Blebo, John, viii. 496.
— — his wife, Margaret Wemyss, viii. 496.
Bevan of Fosbury House, Robert Cooper Lee, v. 254.
— Gwendoline, wife of (1) Ion G. N. Keith-Falconer, and (2) major F. E. Bradshaw, v. 254.
Beverley, Algernon (Percy), 1st earl of, viii. 225.
BEVERLEY, DOUGLAS, MARQUESS OF, vii. 141-144.
Beverley, James, first marquess of, vii. 141.
Beverwaerth, Louis, lord of, i. 522.
— — his wife, Elizabeth of Horn, i. 522.
Beverwest, Amelia de, wife of Thomas (Butler), styled earl of Ossory, iii. 122.
Béza, Theodore, vi. 49; viii. 289.
Bezeley, Joseph, London, vii. 103.
— — his wife, Priscilla Billingsley, vii. 103.
Bickerton, Sir John de, viii. 420.
— Richard de, viii. 420.
— — his wife, Lora de Cuningesburgh of Tullybody, viii. 420.
— Sir Walter de, iv. 149.
— — his wife, Isobel, iv. 149; ix. 93.
Biddulph of Westcombe, Sir Theophilus William, bart., viii. 44.
— — his wife, Mary Agnes Somerville, viii. 44.
— Caroline, wife of Edward Courtenay Leslie, vii. 310.
— Thomas Tregenna, vii. 310.
Bidun, Amicia de, wife of Randolph de Limesi, iii. 3.
Biggar, Ada of, viii. 519.
— Baldwin of, the King's sheriff, v. 488; viii. 519.
— Marjory of, viii. 519.
— Sir Nicholas of, viii. 519.
Bigod, Sir Hugh, chief justiciar of England, ix. 11.
— Joan, wife of Sir Philip de Kyme, ix. 11.
— Roger, earl of Norfolk, i. 5.
— — his wife, Isabella of Scotland, i. 5.
Billingsley, Case, Tottenham, vii. 103.
— Priscilla, wife of (1) rev. Charles Graham, and (2) Joseph Bezeley, vii. 103.
Billyard, Elizabeth, wife of A. W. Hamilton, ii. 58.
— W., Sydney, N.S.W., ii. 58.

Binfield, Caroline Charlotte, wife of Jas. Wemyss, viii. 510.
—— Henry, vicar of Albrighton, viii. 510.
Bingham of Castlebar, John, i. 50.
—— —— his wife, Katharine Hamilton, i. 45, 50.
—— Louisa, wife of 7th earl of Wemyss, viii. 516.
—— Rosaline Cecilia Caroline, wife of 3rd Duke of Abercorn, i. 73.
Bingley, George (Fox-Lane), baron, iii. 409.
Bingouer, Uchtred of, iv. 8.
BINNING, HAMILTON, LORD, iv. 310-329.
Binning, Charles, elder son of 6th earl of Haddington; styled lord, iv. 321, 322; ix. 101.
—— —— his wife, Rachel Baillie, iv. 322; ix. 101.
—— George, eldest son of 11th earl of Haddington; styled lord, iv. 328.
—— —— his wife, Katharine Augusta Milicent Salting, iv. 328.
—— Thomas, first lord, iii. 98: iv. 310.
Birbank, John, v. 233.
—— Maria, wife of rev. G. W. Auriol Drummond-Hay, v. 233.
Birch, *, Pinner, iii. 360.
Birch-Reynardson of Holywell Hall, C. T. S., iv. 504.
—— Etheldred Anne, wife of 6th earl of Hopetoun, iv. 504.
Birnie of Saline, Sir Andrew, senator of the College of Justice, iv. 94.
—— Margaret, wife of 4th lord Forrester of Corstorphine, iv. 94.
Bishop, Mrs, claimant to earldom of Airth, i. 144.
Bisset of Aboyne, Walter, i. 422; iv. 139.
—— —— his wife, Ada of Galloway, iv. 139.
—— of the Ard, John, v. 519.
—— of Carnbady, Thomas, vii. 32.
—— of Chirriemurelands, John, iii. 538.
—— of Craigarn, William de, vii. 232.
—— of Cuthildrayne, Sir Thomas, iv. 13.
—— of Erth, Sir Thomas, iv. 13.
—— of Glasclune, Sir Thomas, vii. 32.
—— of Easter Kinneff, James, i. 287.
—— —— his wife, Mariota Arbuthnott, i. 287.
—— of Lovat, John, v. 519.
—— of Morton and Merchamyston, William, vi. 567.
—— of Pitmuckston, Gilbert, vi. 174.
—— —— his wife, Marjorie Middleton, vi. 174.
—— of Quarrell, John, iii. 538.
—— of the Seven Glens of Antrim, Sir Hugh, v. 40.
—— —— Margery, wife of John 'Mor' Macdonald of Isla, v. 40.

* Name unknown.

Bisset, of Upsetlington, Thomas, *jure ux.* earl of Fife, iv. 13.
—— —— his wife, Isabella, countess of Fife, iv. 13.
—— —— William, i. 422.
—— John, in Ireland, i. 421 *n*.
—— John, nephew of Walter B. of Aboyne, i. 423.
—— Muriel, wife of David de Graham, v. 519; vi. 202.
—— Sir Robert, viii. 478.
—— —— his wife, Annabella Sinclair, viii. 478.
—— *, wife of Sir Andrew de Bosco, iv. 45; v. 519.
—— *, wife of Sir William Fenton, v. 519.
Blaaw, Johanna Elizabeth, wife of Dirk R. J. Mackay, vii. 173.
Blachford of Altadore, John, ii. 419.
—— —— his wife, Mary Anne Grattan, ii. 419.
Black of Gidea Hall, Adelaide, wife of Alfred Douglas Hamilton, iv. 390.
—— —— Alexander, iv. 390.
—— of Haddo, *, viii. 76.
—— —— his wife, Margaret Carnegie, viii. 76.
—— of Over Abington, ix. 15.
Blackader of Blackader, Andrew, i. 189.
—— —— Beatrix, wife of John Home, i. 189; iii. 281.
—— —— Margaret, wife of Robert Home, i. 189; iii. 281.
—— —— Robert, i. 189.
—— —— his wife, Alison Douglas, i. 189.
—— —— Robert, last laird, iii. 281.
—— of Tulliallan, Sir John, 1st bart., vi. 164.
—— —— his wife, Christian Graham, vi. 164.
—— —— Patrick, ii. 2.
—— —— his wife, Elizabeth Edmonstoun, ii. 2.
—— —— Sir Patrick, iii. 472.
—— Jean, wife of Sir David Bruce of Clackmannan, iii. 472.
—— William, M.D., i. 365.
Blackburn of Killearn, John, ix. 169.
—— —— Peter, vii. 392, 524.
—— David, in Fairlie, iv. 189.
—— Grace, wife of 8th earl of Wemyss, viii. 517.
—— Helen, wife of Alex. Bruce, i. 553.
—— Helen Agnes Smith, wife of N. G. Lampson, vii. 392.
—— Hugh, Glasgow, i. 553.
—— Hugh, wife of Alex. Bruce of Kennet, i. 553, ix. 33 *bis*.
—— John, major, viii. 517; ix. 168, 169.
—— Rebecca Marion, wife of capt. John Hope of St Mary's Isle, vii. 524.
—— Robert, in Fairlie, iv. 189.
—— —— his wife, Margaret Boyle, iv. 189.

* Name unknown.

Blackburn, Robert L., advocate, viii. 315.
—— his wife, Constance Frances Bowes-Lyon, viii. 315.
Blackdene of Altenburn and Melle, Christian, vii. 316.
— of Altonburn, William of, vii. 316.
Blackett of Matfen Hall, Sir Edward William, major-gen., C.B., bart., viii. 44.
—— his wife, Julia Frances Somerville, viii. 44.
—— Sir Hugh Douglas, bart., viii. 41.
— of Wallington, Sir William, bart., iii. 482.
— Frances, wife of Robert Bruce, M.P., iii. 482.
Blackhall of Bourtie, Alexander, iii. 591.
— Gilbert, ix. 87.
BLACKNESS, COLYEAR, LORD PORTMORE AND, vii. 92.
Blackness, David, lord Portmore and, vii. 92.
Blackwall, Adelaide, wife of capt. E. G. L. Cochrane, iii. 365.
— Samuel W., major, governor of Sierra Leone, iii. 365.
Blagrave of Calcot Park, John Henry, iv. 210; v. 253.
— Georgina, wife of capt. C. E. Keith-Falconer, v. 253.
— Kathleen Digby, wife of col. Patrick David Boyle, iv. 210.
BLAIR, MURRAY, MARQUESS OF, i. 481.
Blair, William, marquess of, i. 481.
BLAIR, MURRAY, LORD MURRAY OF, iii. 384.
Blair, James, eldest son of 1st earl of Dunmore; styled lord, iii. 385.
—— his wife, Janet Murray, iii. 385.
Blair of Adamton, David, iv. 185.
—— John, vii. 528.
— of Ardblair, James, vi. 496.
— of Auldmure, Robert, 2nd son of John B. of Blair, iii. 339.
— of Balgillo, Sir William, iv. 289.
—— his wife, Margaret Gray, iv. 289.
— of Balmyle, John, iii. 24.
—— his wife, Margaret Lindsay, iii. 24.
— of Balthayock, Alexander, vi. 539.
—— his wife, Christian Oliphant, vi. 539.
—— Alexander. iv. 275.
—— his wife, Janet Gray, iv. 275.
—— Alexander, i. 299.
—— Sir Alexander, iii. 323.
—— Neil Fergussen, i. 315.
—— his wife, Elrington Douglas, i. 315.
—— Thomas, iv. 290.
—— his wife, Margaret Gibson, iv. 290.
— of Blair, John, vii. 550.
—— his wife, Grisel Sempill, iii. 339; vii. 550.
—— John, 8th laird, ii. 289; iii. 438.
—— his wife, Helen Montgomerie, iii. 438.
Blair of Blair, John, 9th laird, ii. 513; vii. 251.
—— his wife, Helen Ross, vii. 251.
—— John, 11th laird, ii. 293: iv. 242.
—— John, 12th laird, v. 167.
—— his wife, Isabel Boyd, v. 167.
—— John, 15th laird, ii. 489: iii. 345: ix. 97.
—— his wife, Jean Cunningham, iv. 247; ix. 97.
—— William, 17th laird, iii. 354; iv. 380.
—— his wife, Margaret Hamilton, iv. 380.
— of Corbs, James, vii. 199.
—— his wife, Isobel Rolle, vii. 199.
— of Dunskey, Jane, wife of Sir Jas. Hunter, ii. 491.
—— John, ii. 491.
—— his wife, Anne Kennedy, ii. 491.
— of Kinfauns, Alexander, iv. 292; vi. 498.
—— his wife, Jean Carnegie, iv. 292; vi. 498.
—— Anna, wife of Alex. Carnegie, vi. 499; ix. 144.
—— Margaret, wife of 11th lord Gray, iv. 292; vi. 498.
—— Sir William, vi. 499.
— of Lochwood, Brice, eldest son of John B. of Blair, iii. 339.
— of Rossieochill, Andrew, vii. 194.
—— his wife, Janet Rolle, vii. 194.
— of Tarsappie, William, vi. 393.
—— his wife, Agnes Nairn, vi. 393.
— of Teasses, *, alleged wife of Norman Leslie of Leslie, vii. 267.
— Alexander, ii. 560.
—— his wife, Margaret Colville, i. 560.
— Alexander, 3rd son of John B. of Blair, iii. 339.
— his wife, Elizabeth Cochrane of Cochrane, iii. 339.
— Ann, wife of John Kennedy of Culzean, ii. 489.
— Anne, wife of * Lyon, iv. 292 *n*.
— Anna, dau. of Alex. Carnegie or Blair of Kinfauns, iv. 292 *n*.
— Arthur Kindersley, viii. 364.
—— his wife, Mary Caroline Mitchell, viii. 364.
— Egidia, wife of Jas. Kennedy of Row, ii. 454, 464.
— Elizabeth, wife of Jas. Arbuthnott of Arbeikie. i. 299.
— Elizabeth, wife of Ninian Stewart of Bute, ii. 289.
— Gavin, 5th son of Alex. B. of Blair, iii. 340.
— Giles, wife of Sir Alexander Carnegie of Balnamoon, viii. 61.
— Hugh, 4th son of John B. of Blair, iii. 339.

* Name unknown.

Blair, Jean, wife of (1) Alex. Cunningham, and (2) John Stewart of Bute, ii. 293; iv. 242; v. 166; ix. 50.
— Jean, wife of Thomas Graham of Potento, iii. 323.
— Katharine, wife of Huebeon Campbell, ii. 401; v. 492.
— Margaret, wife of Robt. Montgomerie of Giffen, iii. 430.
— Margaret, wife of Wm. Fullarton-Lindsay of Fullarton and Spynie, vi. 496.
— Thomas, iv. 71.
— — his wife, Isobel *or* Elizabeth Wemyss, iv. 71.
Blairhall, Dougal Stewart, M.P., lord, ii. 297.
Blake of Ardfry, Joseph, iii. 583.
— Elizabeth Jemima, wife of (1) George, 16th earl of Erroll, and (2) J. H. Frere, iii. 583.
Blakiston of Blakiston, Sir Thomas, 1st bart. iii. 296.
— — his wife, Mary Constable, iii. 296.
Blanchard, Eliza Maria, wife of (1) C. Ludlow, and (2) James Campbell, ii. 193, 212.
Bland of Carleton, Elizabeth, wife of Sir Philip Cary, iii. 609.
— — Richard, iii. 609.
— Dora, known as Mrs. Jordan, iii. 585.
— Francis, iii. 585.
— Humphrey, lieutenant-general, commander-in-chief in Scotland, viii. 151.
— — his wife, Elizabeth Dalrymple, viii. 151.
Blandford, George Charles (Spencer-Churchill), marquess of, i. 71.
— — his wife, Albertha Frances Anne Hamilton, i. 71.
— John (Churchill), first marquess of, ii. 532.
— — his wife, Sarah Jennings, ii. 532.
— John, styled marquess of, ii. 533.
Blandy, Mary, mistress of capt. Cranstoun, ii. 598.
BLANTYRE, STEWART, LORD, ii. 77-93.
Blantyre, Alexander, fourth lord, ii. 85, 86; ix. 38.
— — his wife, Margaret Shaw, ii. 86.
— Alexander, fifth lord, ii. 84, 86.
— — his 1st wife, Margaret Henderson, ii. 88.
— — his 2nd wife, Anne Hamilton, ii. 44, 88.
— Alexander, tenth lord, ii. 90.
— — his wife, Katharine Lindsay of Eaglescairnie, ii. 90; v. 410.
— Charles Walter, twelfth lord, ii. 92.
— — his wife, Evelyn Sutherland Leveson-Gower, ii. 92; viii. 363.
— Robert, seventh lord, ii. 88; vii. 520.
— — his 1st wife, Helen Lyon, ii. 88; viii. 305.
— — his 2nd wife, Margaret Hay, ii. 88.
Blantyre, Robert Walter, eleventh lord, ii. 91.
— — his wife, Fanny Mary Rodney, ii. 91.
— Walter, first lord, i. 517; ii. 81.
— — his wife, Nicolas Somerville, ii. 83.
— — Walter, third lord, ii. 86; ix. 38.
— — his wife, Marie Mure, ii. 86; ix. 38 *bis*.
— Walter, sixth lord, ii. 88.
— Walter, eighth lord, ii. 89.
— William, second lord, ii. 85.
— — his wife, Helen Scot, ii. 85.
— William, ninth lord, ii. 90.
— master of, James, eldest son of 1st lord Blantyre, ii. 83.
— — his wife, Dorothy Hastings, ii. 83.
— master of, Walter, only son of 12th lord Blantyre, ii. 92.
BLASONBERRIE, HUME, VISCOUNT, vi. 14-24.
Blasonberrie, Patrick, first viscount, vi. 14.
Blaw, Janet, wife of D. Primrose, vii. 214.
Blayney, Edward (Blayney), 1st lord, i. 536.
— Anne, wife of James, 1st lord Balfour. i. 536.
— Charles, i. 526.
— Helena Elizabeth, wife of P. Y. Lindsay, i. 526.
Blencowe of Bineham, John George, viii. 227.
— Florence Charlotte, wife of J. W. A. Drummond, viii. 227.
Blessington, Archibald Stewart, alleged ancestor of the family of lord, iv. 152.
Bligh, William, colonel, 3rd son of 3rd earl of Darnley, iv. 170.
— — his wife, Sophia Stewart, iv. 170.
Blinsele, John, Bute Pursuivant, Ilay Herald, v. 614 *n*.
Blood of Brickhill, Edward Magblin, i. 391.
— Gertrude Elizabeth, wife of lord Colin Campbell, i. 391; ix. 26.
Bloomfield of New Park, Fitzmaurice Gustavus, iii. 46.
— Henrietta Julia, wife of W. J. Lindsay, iii. 46.
Blount of Mapledurham, Sir Richard, iii. 99.
— of Sodington, Sir Walter, 1st bart., i. 411.
— — his wife, Elizabeth Wylde, i. 411.
— — Sir Walter, 6th bart., i. 413.
— — his wife, Mary Aston, i. 413.
— Eleanor, wife of (1) R. Knightley, and (2) Walter, 3rd lord Aston of Forfar, i. 411.
— George, i. 413.
— John, colonel, viii. 181.
— — his wife, Mary Vanlore, viii. 181.
— Lyster, son of Sir Richard B., iii. 99.
— — his wife, Jocosa Apsley, iii. 99.

Blundell of Ince Blundell, Thomas, v. 547.
— Alice Mary, wife of 13th Lord Fraser of Lovat, v. 547.
Blunt of Adderbury Manor, Charles Harris, maj.-gen., C.B., ii. 85.
— Anne Maria, wife of Charles Andrew Bruce, iii. 492.
— Sir Charles William, 3rd bart., iii. 492.
— Edward Walter, *afterwards* Mackenzie, R.A., A.D.C., iii. 85.
— — his wife, Sibell Lilian, countess of Cromartie, iii. 85.
Blyth of Craigie, Richard, portioner, ix. 152.
— — his wife, Margaret Rollo, ix. 152.
Bogle of Hamilton Farm, Patrick, iv. 177.
— — his wife, Graham Christian (Crawford) Lindsay, iv. 177.
— James, receiver-gen. of customs, ii. 51.
— — his wife, Anne Hamilton, ii. 51.
— John, Kirkcudbright, i. 140.
— — his wife, Mary Graham, i. 140.
Bohemia, Elizabeth, Queen of, i. 27.
— Frederick, King of, i. 27.
Boick, Elizabeth, wife of Robert Dalrymple of Kelloch, viii. 124.
— William, burgess of Edinburgh, viii. 124.
Bois of Biset, Sir Andrew de, iv. 45.
— — his wife, * of Biset, v. 519.
Boiswell, George, vi. 102.
— — his wife, Janet Melville, vi. 102.
Boleyne, Anne, wife of King Henry VIII. of England, iii. 608.
— Mary, wife of (1) William Cary, and (2) Wm. Stafford, iii. 608.
Bolingbroke, Frederick (St. John), 2nd lord, v. 483.
Bolton, Charles (Poulett), 2nd duke of, ii. 240.
— — his 3rd wife, Henrietta Crofts, ii. 240.
— William Henry (Orde-Powlett), first lord, ii. 529.
— John, 5th lord Scrope of, iv. 449.
BOLTON, MAITLAND, LORD THIRLESTANE AND, v. 302.
Bolton, John, first lord, v. 302.
Bomford, Robert, Rahinstown, iii. 417.
— Sarah Maria, wife of F. J. Tollemache, iii. 417.
Bonaparte, Cristine Alexandra Egypta, wife of lord Dudley C. Stuart, ii. 308.
— Lucien, prince of Canino, ii. 308.
Bonar of Grigstoun, James, iii. 401.
— — his wife, Mary Murray, iii. 401.
— of Keltic, Ninian, i. 77.
— — his wife, Isabel Strang, i. 77.
— — Ninian vi. 546.
— — his wife, Margaret Oliphant, vi. 546.
— — Walter, iii. 566; vii. 185, 187.
— — his wife, Beatrix Hay, iii. 566.

* Name unknown.

Bonar of Rossie, James, vi. 85.
— — his alleged wife, Margaret Melville, vi. 85.
— of Rossie, John, vi. 83.
— — William, vi. 85.
— — William, vi. 102.
— Janet, wife of John Melville of Raith, vi. 84, 85.
— Margaret, wife of John Melville of Raith, vi. 102.
Boncambi, Frederico Pucci, vi. 458.
— — his wife, Maria Bandini, vi. 458.
BONCLE, DOUGLAS, LORD DOUGLAS OF, i. 210.
Bonde, father of Edmund and Gillemichael, vii. 577.
Bondington, William de, bishop of Glasgow, ii. 423; vii. 419, 420.
Bonespoir, Jane, wife of Sir John Borthwick, ii. 109.
Bonkyl, Adam, vi. 404.
— Sir Alexander de, i. 13.
— Margaret of, wife of (1) Sir John Stewart, and (2) Sir David of Brechin, i. 13, 438; ii. 221.
— Randolph de, viii. 3.
Bons, Isabella Jacoba de, wife of col. Metcalfe Graham, vii. 104.
Bonsor, Sir John Winfield, ii. 565.
— — his wife, Mary Katharine Colville, ii. 565.
Bontine of Ardoch and Gartmore, William Cunningham, i. 145; iii. 550.
— — his wife, Anne Elizabeth Elphinstone Fleming, iii. 550.
Booker, Thomas, capt. 53rd regt. iv. 555.
— — his wife, Katharine Gordon, iv. 555.
Booth of Warlaby, T. C., vii. 86.
— Elizabeth, wife of Henry James Hepburne-Scott, vii. 86.
Boothroyd, Edith, wife of Lyulph G. S. Ogilvy, i. 131.
Bootle-Wilbraham, Edmund, ii. 497.
— — Edward, col. Coldstream Guards, iii. 49.
— — Emily Florence, wife of 26th earl of Crawford, iii. 49.
— — Evelyn Adela, wife of Sir J. G. Kennedy, ii. 497.
Boraille of Teviotdale, John, vii. 318.
Bord, Antoinette de, wife of Sir Wm. Livingston of Kilsyth, v. 190.
— Pierre de, v. 190.
Borland, Cecil, wife of rev. Robt. Hamilton, ii. 51.
— Francis, minister of Glassford, ii. 51.
Borselen, Wolfart van, i. 19; ii. 265 *n.*
— — his 1st wife, Mary Stewart, countess of Buchan, i. 19; ii. 265 *n.*
— — his 2nd wife, Charlotte de Bourbon-Montpensier, i. 19.

Borthwick, Borthwick, lord, ii. 94-119.
Borthwick, Archibald, *de jure* seventeenth lord, ii. 103, 116.
—— —— his wife, Margaret Nicolson Scott, ii. 103.
—— Archibald, *de jure* nineteenth lord, ii. 104, 117.
—— —— his wife, Mary Louisa Home-Home, ii. 104.
—— Archibald Patrick Thomas, twenty-first lord, ii. 119; ix. 40 *bis*.
—— —— his wife, Susanna Mary M'Taggart Stewart, ii. 119.
—— Cunninghame, twentieth lord, ii. 117.
—— —— his wife, Harriet Alice Day, ii. 118.
—— Henry, *de jure* thirteenth lord, ii. 102.
—— —— his wife, Mary Pringle, ii. 102.
—— Henry, fifteenth lord, ii. 115, 116; ix. 40.
—— —— his wife, Margaret Drummond, ii. 116.
—— James, eighth lord, ii. 112; v. 456; ix. 39 *bis*.
—— —— his wife, Margaret Hay, ii. 112; viii. 442; ix. 39.
—— John, sixth lord, ii. 109, 159; vii. 436; ix. 39.
—— —— his wife, Isobel Lindsay, ii. 109; ix. 39.
—— John, ninth lord, ii. 113; v. 457, 458.
—— —— his wife, Lilias Ker, ii. 113, 114; v. 458.
—— John, tenth lord, ii. 113; v. 474; ix. 39.
—— —— his wife, Elizabeth Ker, ii. 114; v. 474.
—— Patrick, *de jure* sixteenth lord, ii. 103, 116.
—— —— his wife, Marion Scott, ii. 103.
—— Patrick, *de jure* eighteenth lord, ii. 104, 117.
—— —— his wife, Ariana Corbett, ii. 104.
—— William, first lord, ii. 96.
—— William, second lord, ii. 97.
—— —— his wife, Mariota Hoppringle, ii. 98.
—— William, third lord, ii. 98.
—— William, fourth lord, ii. 99, 107.
—— —— his wife, Margaret Hay, ii. 107; viii. 432.
—— William, fifth lord, ii. 108.
—— William, seventh lord, ii. 110; ix. 39.
—— —— his wife, Grizel Scott, ii. 111, 230.
—— William, *de jure* eleventh lord, ii. 100.
—— —— his wife, Marion Moorehead, ii. 100.
—— William, *de jure* twelfth lord, ii. 100.
—— —— his wife, Jean Ker, ii. 101.
—— William, *de jure* fourteenth lord, ii. 102.
—— master of, Arthur *or* Thomas, elder son of 5th lord Borthwick, ii. 108; iii. 439 *n.*; viii. 581 *n.*
—— —— his wife, Mariot Seton, ii. 108; iii. 439; viii. 581; ix. 39.
Borthwick, master of, William, son of 7th lord Borthwick, ii. 112.
Borthwick, lord Borthwick, ii. 94-119.
Borthwick of Ballincrieff, Robert, master of artillery, ii. 109 *n.*
—— of Barnton, Nicholas, ii. 326.
—— of Borthwick, Thomas de, ii. 94.
—— —— Sir William, ambassador to England, ii. 95.
—— —— Sir William, captain of Edinburgh Castle, ii. 95, 328.
—— of Bourhouses, Alan, ii. 98.
—— of Catcune, Sir William, ii. 95.
—— of Cineray, Sir John, the reformer, ii. 109.
—— —— his 1st wife, Margaret Borthwick, ii. 109.
—— —— his 2nd wife, Jane Bonespoir, ii. 109.
—— —— William, ii. 109.
—— of Colylaw, Alan, ii. 98.
—— —— Sir Thomas, 3rd son of 2nd lord Borthwick, ii. 98.
—— —— his wife, Helen Rutherfurd ii. 98; vii. 369.
—— —— William, iii. 94.
—— —— his wife, * Ramsay, iii. 94.
—— —— William, their son, iii. 94, 96.
—— of Crookston, John, alleged 2nd son of 1st lord Borthwick; 1st laird, ii. 97 *n.*, 116; iii. 91, 93.
—— —— John, claimant to the peerage, ii. 116.
—— —— John, purchaser of Borthwick Castle, ii. 115 *n.*, 116.
—— —— John, 1868, ii. 118.
—— —— William, ii. 112; iii. 92.
—— of Falahill, William, ii. 101.
—— —— his wife, Barbara Borthwick, ii. 101.
—— of Fenton, Gawin, ii. 109 *n.*
—— of Glengelt, James, 2nd son of 2nd lord Borthwick, ii. 98.
—— —— James, iii. 504.
—— —— his wife, Elizabeth Murray, iii. 504.
—— of Johnstonburn, William, ii. 99.
—— —— his wife, Katharine Creighton, ii. 99.
—— —— William, ii. 99; iv. 90.
—— —— his 1st wife, Barbara Lawson, ii. 100.
—— —— his 2nd wife, Helen Preston, iv. 90.
—— —— William, colonel in Swedish service, ii. 100.
—— —— his wife, Janet Leyis, ii. 100; ix. 39.
—— —— William, major, ii. 100, 115.
—— —— his wife, Marion Moorehead, ii. 100.
—— —— William, colonel Cameronian regt., ii. 100, 115.
—— —— his wife, Jean Ker, ii. 101.

* Name unknown.

Borthwick of Lany, Nicholas, ii. 326.
— of Ligertwood, Thomas de, ii. 94.
— — Sir William, ii. 95.
— of Locherworth, Sir William, ii. 96; viii. 424.
— of Lochhill, David, king's advocate, i. 517; ii. 99 *n.*; ix. 39.
— — his wife, Marion Guthrie, i. 517.
— of Mayshiell, Henry, ii. 102.
— — William, surgeon, ii. 101.
— — his 1st wife, Marion Borthwick, ii. 102.
— — his 2nd wife, Marjorie Steuart, ii. 102.
— — his 3rd wife, Euphame Young, ii. 103.
— of Middleton, Thomas, ii. 230.
— of Nenthorn, Alexander, ii. 98, 99, 115, 116.
— — his wife, Margaret Lawson, ii. 99.
— of Newbyres, James, iv. 307, 313.
— of Pilmuir, Henry, captain, ii. 102, 115.
— — his wife, Mary Pringle, ii. 102.
— — William, surgeon, ii. 101.
— — William, son of capt. Henry B., ii. 102, 115.
— of Sauchnell, Alexander, 2nd son of Wm. B. of Soltray, ii. 103, 116.
— — Andrew, ii. 103.
— — his wife, Margaret Turnbull, ii. 103.
— — Charles, writer, ii. 103.
— of Soltray, William, son of Alex. B. of Nenthorn, ii. 99.
— — his wife, Janet Sinclair, ii. 99.
— — William, 2nd laird, ii. 99.
— — William, 3rd laird, ii. 99.
— — his wife, Katharine Creighton, ii. 99.
— — William, 4th laird, ii. 99; iv. 90.
— — his 1st wife, Barbara Lawson, ii. 100.
— — his 2nd wife, Helen Preston, iv. 90.
— — William, col., 5th laird, ii. 100.
— — his wife, Janet Leyis, ii. 100; ix. 39.
— — William, major, 6th laird, ii. 100, 115.
— — William, col., 7th laird, ii. 100, 115.
— of Stow, James, ii. 102.
— of Threeburnford, Robert, ii. 107.
— Adam, son of 3rd lord Borthwick, ii. 99.
— Adam, son of Wm. B. of Pilmuir, ii. 103.
— Agnes, wife of Sir A. Dundas, ii. 97 *n.*, 399.
— Agnes, wife of Geo. Pringle, ii. 103.
— Agnes, wife of David, lord Kennedy, ii. 107, 461.
— Agnes, wife of William, tutor of Borthwick, ii. 112.
— Alexander, 3rd son of 2nd lord Borthwick, ii. 98.
Borthwick, Alexander, son of major Wm. B., ii. 101.
— — his wife, Sibilla Cairnes, ii. 101.
— Alexander, son of Wm. B. of Pilmuir, ii. 103.
— Alexander, son of 7th lord Borthwick, ii. 112.
— Alice Rachel Anne, wife of A. C. Campbell, ii. 119.
— Anne, dau. of James B., ii. 106.
— Anne, wife of capt. R. Clephane, ii. 106.
— Archibald, minister of Greenlaw, ii. 103; ix. 39.
— — his 2nd wife, Katharine Lawson, ii. 107.
— Archibald, son of James B., ii. 106.
— Ariana, dau. of Archibald B., ii. 105.
— Ariana, dau. of Patrick B., ii. 104.
— Barbara, wife of Wm. Borthwick of Falahill, ii. 101.
— Barbara, wife of P. Hepburn, ii. 107.
— Beatrice, wife of John Lithgow, ix. 39.
— Christian, dau. of Wm. B., ii. 107.
— Cristine, dau. of 3rd lord Borthwick, ix. 39.
— David, son of col. Wm. B., ii. 101.
— David, burgess of Haddington, ix. 39.
— Elizabeth, wife of Robt. Davidson, ii. 106.
— Gabrielle Margaret Ariana, ii. 118.
— George, 1471, vii. 580.
— George, 2nd son of Wm. B., first of Soltray, ii. 107.
— Grace Laurie, ii. 106.
— Isobell, wife of (1) Thos. Davidson, and (2) Wm. Hart, ii. 110.
— Isabella, wife of 2nd lord Saltoun of Abernethy, vii. 408.
— Isolde Frances, dau. of 21st lord Borthwick, ii. 119.
— James, N. B. Insurance Co., ii. 105.
— — his wife, Sarah Finlay, ii. 105.
— James, 3rd son of Wm. B., first of Soltray, ii. 107.
— James, 2nd son of 8th lord Borthwick, ii. 113.
— James. 2nd son of 9th lord Borthwick, ii. 113.
— Jane Laurie, 'H. L. L.', ii. 106.
— Janet, wife of Alex. Lauder, ii. 108.
— Janet, wife of (1) Sir Jas. Douglas of Dalkeith, and (2) George, earl of Caithness, ii. 96, 97, 328, 330 *bis*, 401; vi. 351, 354.
— Janet, wife of Sir Adam Hepburn, lord of Hailes, ix. 39.
— Jemima, dau. of James B., ii. 106.
— John, son of 7th lord Borthwick, ii. 112.
— Jonet, wife of Peter Murray in South Bowhill, iii. 500.
— Katharine, dau. of major Wm. B. of Johnstonburn, ii. 101.

Borthwick, Katharine, wife of William, lord Kilmaurs, ii. 107; iv. 236, 238.
— Katharine, wife of Sir Jas. Crichton, ii. 108; iv. 124.
— Katharine, wife of (1) Sir Thomas Hay, master of Yester, and (2) Sir O. Sinclair of Roslin, ii. 107 *n.*, iv. 359 *n.*; viii. 431.
— Louisa Ramsay, wife of col. Wylie, ii. 105; ix. 39.
— Margaret, wife of (1) Wm. de Abernethy, and (2) Wm. de Douglas, ii. 96; vi. 351; vii. 406.
— Margaret, wife of Sir John Maxwell, ii. 97.
— Margaret, wife of John Campbell, ii. 102.
— Margaret, wife of N. G. Corbett, ii. 105.
— Margaret, dau. of James B., ii. 106.
— Margaret, wife of Prof. H. D. Hill, ii. 106.
— Margaret, dau. of Wm. B., 3rd of Soltray, ii. 107.
— Margaret, wife of Sir O. Sinclair, ii. 107.
— Margaret, wife of Sir John Borthwick of Cineray, ii. 109.
— Margaret, wife of P. Hepburn, ii. 110.
— Margaret, wife of Robt. Dundas, ii. 113.
— Margaret, wife of Thos. Hamilton of Priestfield, iii. 504; iv. 313.
— Marion, wife of Wm. Borthwick of Pilmuir, ii. 102.
— Marion, dau. of Patrick B., ii. 105.
— Mariota *or* Marion, wife of A. Hoppringle, ii. 110.
— Mary, wife of Sir Alex. Livingston, ii. 102.
— Mary, wife of Jas. Hoppringle, ii. 107.
— Mary Frances Harriet, wife of H. C. Dowdall, ii. 119.
— Mary Katharine, wife of W. G. Spens, ii. 105.
— Mary Laurie, ii. 106.
— Rachel, dau. of James B., ii. 106.
— Rachel, dau. of Archibald B., ii. 106.
— Robert, son of col. Wm. B., ii. 101.
— Sarah Laurie, wife of rev. E. J. Findlater, ii. 106.
— Sibilla, dau. of Wm. B., ii. 103.
— Thomas, son of Wm. B. of Pilmuir, ii. 103.
— Thomas Scott, ii. 105.
— Violet Dagmar Marion Olga, wife of Capt. Freeland, ii. 119; ix. 40.
— Walter, son of col. Wm. B., ii. 101.
— Walter, son of Alex. B. of Sauchnell, ii. 107.
— William, colonel, 1651, ii. 100 *n.*
— William, tutor of Borthwick, ii. 112.
— — his wife, Agnes Borthwick, ii. 112.
— William, ix. 38.
— — his wife, Beatrice Sinclair, ix. 38.
Borthwick, *, wife of Sir John Oliphant of Aberdalgy, ii. 95 *n.*
— *, *écuyer d'écurie* to Queen Mary, ii. 99 *n.*
Bosco, Sir Andrew de, iv. 45; v. 519; vi. 203.
— — his wife, * of Bisset, v. 519.
Boston, George (Irby), 3rd baron, vi. 582.
Bosvile of Craigincat and Wester Dron, David, i. 110; iv. 30.
Boswell of Auchinleck, David, iv. 365.
— — his wife, Jean Hamilton, iv. 365; ix. 103.
— — David, ii. 518.
— — his wife, Isabel Wallace, ii. 518.
— — James, iii. 487.
— — his wife, Elizabeth Bruce, iii. 487.
— — James, the author, v. 89.
— — John, ii. 404; vi. 511.
— — his 1st wife, Christian Dalzell, ii. 404.
— — his 2nd wife, Agnes Stewart, vi. 511.
— — Thomas, v. 495.
— — his wife, Annabella Campbell, v. 495.
— of Balglelly, Sir Alexander, viii. 385.
— — John, vii. 12.
— of Balglaly Wester, John, vi. 83.
— of Balgregie, David, vi. 83.
— — his wife, Elizabeth Melville, vi. 83.
— of Balmuto, Sir Alexander, viii. 385; ix. 65.
— — his 1st wife, Elizabeth Ramsay, iii. 92; ix. 65.
— — his 2nd wife, Alison Sandilands, viii. 385.
— — David, 5th laird, vi. 83, 367; viii. 485.
— — his 1st wife, Elizabeth Melville, vi. 83.
— — David, 6th laird, ii. 334.
— — his 1st wife, Grizel Wemyss, viii. 485.
— — his 2nd wife, Margaret Sinclair, ii. 334.
— — John, 2nd laird, viii. 481.
— — Sir John, 9th laird, vii. 12, 574; ix. 4, 157.
— — his wife, Isabel Sandilands, ix. 4.
— of Bowhill, John, vi. 83.
— of Glassmonth, David, vi. 83, 86; viii. 485.
— — his wife, Grizel Wemyss, viii. 485.
— of Pittedy, John, viii. 495.
— — his wife, Elizabeth Wemyss, viii. 495.
— of Tillybreak, David, viii. 485.
— — his wife, Grizel Wemyss, viii. 485.
— Robert, viii. 489.
— — his wife, Jonet Wemyss, viii. 489.

* Name unknown.

Boswell, Christine, wife of Sir Jas. Melville of Hallhill, vi. 90.
— Elizabeth, wife of Robert Douglas of Lochleven, vi. 367.
— Katharine, wife of Henry Maule of Skryne, vii. 12.
— Katharine, wife of (1) Patrick Sinclair of Balgriggie, (2) P. Murray of Williamston, and (3) John Rolland, vii. 574; ix. 157.
— Marion, wife of 6th lord Cathcart, ii. 518.
Bosworth, James Fitz James, baron of, i. 34.
Botetourt, John de, justiciar of Galloway and Annandale, i. 320; ii. 378.
Boteler, Jane, wife of John, lord Belasyse of Worlaby, iii. 299.
— Sir Robert, iii. 299.
— Sir Thomas, ix. 57.
— *, wife of Sir Thomas Hutcheson, ix. 57.
Botham, Hugh, Leicester, i. 405.
— — his wife, Margaret Barratt, i. 405.
BOTHWELL, DOUGLAS, LORD, i. 206.
Bothwell, Archibald, first lord, i. 206.
BOTHWELL, MORAY, LORD OF, ii. 120-131.
Bothwell, Sir Andrew, third lord of, ii. 127.
— — his 1st wife, *, ii. 128.
— — his 2nd wife, Christian Bruce, ii. 128, 434.
— Sir John, fourth lord of, ii. 128; vi. 139.
— — his wife, Margaret, countess of Menteith, ii. 128; vi. 138.
— Sir Thomas, fifth lord of, ii. 129.
— — his wife. Joanna Moray of Drumsargard, ii. 130: viii. 257.
— Sir Walter, first lord of, i. 449; ii. 123.
— — his supposed wife, * de Olifard, ii. 123.
— Sir William, second lord of, ii. 124.
BOTHWELL, RAMSAY, LORD, ii. 132-134.
Bothwell, John. lord, ii. 133, 151.
— — his 1st wife, Janet Kennedy, ii. 134, 459.
— — his 2nd wife, Isobel Livingston, ii. 134; iii. 93.
BOTHWELL, HEPBURN, EARL OF, ii. 135-167.
Bothwell, Adam, second earl of, ii. 153, 156; viii. 433.
— — his wife, Agnes Stewart, ii. 156, 267; iii. 94; ix. 65.
— James, fourth earl of, i. 26, 463, 465; ii. 161; iv. 154, 539, 540; v. 157, 399; vi. 48, 52; vii. 253, 540; viii. 586; ix. 39.
— — his 1st wife, Jane Gordon, ii. 165; iv. 539.
— — his 2nd wife, Mary, Queen of Scots, i. 25; ii. 166.

* Name unknown.

Bothwell, Patrick, first earl of, i. 180; ii. 143, 149, 151; vi. 83; viii. 430.
— — his 1st wife, Janet *or* Joanna Douglas, ii. 152; vi. 356.
— — his 2nd wife, Margaret Gordon, ii. 152; iv. 530.
— Patrick, third earl of, ii. 157; viii. 490; ix. 41.
— — his wife, Agnes Sinclair, ii. 159.
— mistress of, Jane Hepburn, dau. of 3rd earl of Bothwell; wife of (1) John Stewart of Coldingham, (2) John Sinclair, master of Caithness, and (3) Archibald Douglas, ii. 160, 168, 340; ix. 41 *bis*.
BOTHWELL, STEWART, EARL OF, ii. 168-178.
Bothwell, Charles, third earl of, ii. 173.
— Francis, first earl of, ii. 160, 170; iii. 572, 574; iv. 58, 464; v. 298; vii. 342, 378.
— — his wife, Margaret Douglas, i. 193; ii. 171, 231.
— Francis, second earl of, ii. 172; viii. 594 *n.*
— — his 1st wife, Isobel Seton, ii. 173; vii. 48; viii. 592.
BOTHWELL AND HARTSYDE, DOUGLAS, LORD, i. 206.
Bothwell and Hartsyde, Archibald, eldest son of 1st marquess of Douglas; first lord, i. 206.
BOTHWELL, LORD HOLYROODHOUSE, iv. 425-439.
Bothwell of Alhammer, Adam, bishop of Orkney, commendator of Holyroodhouse, i, 78; ii. 62, 166; iv. 430, 431, 434: vi. 573.
— — his wife, Margaret Murray, iv. 430.
— — John, commendator of Holyroodhouse, iv. 431.
— — his wife, Maria Carmichael, iv. 433, 580.
— of Boghead, Richard, apostolic protonotary, director of chancery, iv. 425, 427, 436.
— of Brighouse, Adam, bishop of Orkney, iv. 430.
— of Burray, Adam, bishop of Orkney, vi. 511.
— of Easton of Dunsyre, Adam, bishop of Orkney, iv. 428.
— of Glencorse, Adam, iv. 434.
— — his 1st wife, Janet Hart, iv. 434.
— — his 2nd wife, Elspeth Mowbray, iv. 435.
— — Alexander, iv. 435.
— — his wife, Mary Stewart, iv. 435; vi. 574; ix. 106, 146.
— — Alexander, claimant to title of lord Holyroodhouse, iv. 433, 436.
— — his wife, Janet Trotter, iv. 436.
— — Archibald, lieut.-col. Scots Greys, iv. 438.

Bothwell of Glencorse, Henry, iv. 433, 437, 439.
—— —— his 1st wife, Mary Ramsay, iv. 437.
—— —— his 2nd wife, Mary Campbell, iv. 437, 439.
—— —— Margaret, wife of Colin Drummond, M.D., iv. 438.
—— —— William, ancestor of the family of, iv. 426, 433.
—— of Newholme, Alexander, iv. 435.
—— of Pitoaly, Adam, i. 78.
—— —— his wife, Christian Sandilands, i. 78.
—— of Pitscottie, Adam, bailie of the Canongate, iv. 434.
—— —— his 1st wife, Janet Hart, iv. 434.
—— —— his 2nd wife, E. Mowbray, iv. 435.
—— of Quhelpsyde, Adam, bailie of the Canongate, iv. 434.
—— —— William, chamberlain of Orkney, iv. 434.
—— —— his wife, Janet Cunninghame, iv. 434.
—— of Whitekirk, Adam, bishop of Orkney, iv. 430; ix. 37.
—— —— John, commendator of Holyroodhouse, iv. 431.
—— Adam, 3rd son of Francis B., iv. 431.
—— Adam, 6th son of Adam, bishop of Orkney, iv. 431.
—— Mr. Adam, 2nd son of Adam B. of Glencorse, iv. 435; ix. 4.
—— —— his wife, Katherine Sandilands, i. 78; iv. 435; ix. 4.
—— Adam, elder son of Mr. Adam B., iv. 435.
—— Adam, 4th son of Alex. B. of Glencorse, iv. 436.
—— Adam, 8th son of Henry B. of Glencorse, iv. 438.
—— Alexander, 7th son of Francis B., iv. 431.
—— Alexander, styled master of Holyroodhouse, iv. 433, 437.
—— —— his wife, Margaret Home, iv. 438, 480.
—— Alexander, merchant, Edinburgh, iv. 436.
—— Anna, dau. of 1st lord Holyroodhouse, iv. 433; v. 621.
—— Anna, wife of rev. George Purves, iv. 436; ix. 106.
—— Anne, dau. of Henry, last lord Holyroodhouse, iv. 439; ix. 106.
—— Archibald, master of the mint in Scotland, iv. 438.
—— Arthur, 5th son of Francis B., iv. 431.
—— David, iv. 425.
—— —— his wife, Christian Lamb, iv. 425.
—— David, iv. 427.
—— —— his wife, Christian Marjoribanks, iv. 427.
Bothwell, Eleanora, dau. of Henry B. of Glencorse, iv. 439.
—— Elizabeth, wife of George Strang, iv. 431.
—— Elizabeth, dau. of Adam B. of Glencorse, iv. 435.
—— Francis, provost of Edinburgh, lord of Session, customar of Inverness, ii. 62; iv. 426.
—— —— his 1st wife, Janet Richardson, iv. 427.
—— —— his 2nd wife, Katharine Bellenden, ii. 62; iv. 427.
—— Francis, master carver to King James VI., iv. 430.
—— —— his wife, Margaret Couttis, iv. 430.
—— George, 6th son of Francis B., iv. 431.
—— George, captain, 4th son of Adam, bishop of Orkney, iv. 431.
—— George, 6th son of Alex. B. of Glencorse, iv. 437.
—— Helenor, dau. of Adam, bishop of Orkney, iv. 431.
—— Henrietta, dau. of Henry B. of Glencorse, iv. 438.
—— Henry, in holy orders in France, iv. 438.
—— Isobel, wife of Allan Couttis of Grange, iv. 428.
—— Isobel, illeg. dau. of 2nd lord Holyroodhouse, iv. 433.
—— James, 2nd son of Francis B., iv. 431.
—— Mr. James, 3rd son of Adam, bishop of Orkney, iv. 431.
—— James, iv. 436.
—— —— his wife, Margaret Johnston, iv. 436.
—— Janet, wife of Sir Archibald Napier of Merchiston, iv. 428; vi. 415.
—— Janet, wife of Wm. Calderwood, iv. 437.
—— Jean, wife of Wm. Sandilands of Cruvie, i. 78; iv. 431; ix. 4.
—— Jean, wife of Jonas Hamilton of Colquot, iv. 435.
—— Jean, illeg. dau. of 2nd lord Holyroodhouse, iv. 433.
—— John, major, iv. 431.
—— John, 4th son of Adam B. of Glencorse, iv. 435.
—— John, 2nd son of Alex. B. of Glencorse, iv. 436.
—— John, 3rd son of Alex. B. of Glencorse, iv. 436.
—— —— his 1st wife, *, iv. 436.
—— —— his 2nd wife, *, iv. 436.
—— John, apprenticed to R. Chrystie, ix. 106.
—— Katharine, wife of Alex. Sym, iv. 427.
—— Lilias, dau. of Henry B. of Glencorse, iv. 438.
—— Margaret, wife of (1) John Arthur, and (2) Gilbert Balfour of Westray, iv. 428 *bis*.

* Name unknown.

Bothwell, Margaret, wife of (1) Sir Robt. Preston, and (2) Wm. Gray, iv. 436; ix. 106.
—— Mariota, wife of Nicholas Home of Macbiehill, iv. 451.
—— Mary, illeg. dau. of 2nd lord Holyroodhouse, iv. 433.
—— Mary, wife of Jas. Aikenhead, iv. 435.
—— Mary, wife of Neil Menzies, iv. 439; ix. 106.
—— Neil, factor to South Sea Company, iv. 438.
—— Richard, elder son of Wm. B., iv. 434.
—— Robert, writer in Edinburgh, iv. 436.
—— Robert, surgeon, iv. 438.
—— —— his wife, Margaret Preston, iv. 438.
—— Vere, wife of Francis Wauchope of Cakemuir, iv. 438.
—— William, dean of Guild, Edinburgh, iv. 425, 433.
—— —— his wife, Katharine *, iv. 425.
—— William, parson of Ashkirk, iv. 427.
—— William, captain, 4th son of Francis B., iv. 431.
—— William, 5th son of the bishop of Orkney, iv. 431.
—— William, 3rd son of William B., dean of Guild, iv. 433.
—— —— his wife, Marion Somerville, iv. 433.
—— William, elder son of Wm. B. of Quhelpsyde, iv. 434.
—— —— his 1st wife, *, iv. 434.
—— —— his 2nd wife, Theodorite Daman, iv. 434.
—— —— his 3rd wife, Jane Sinclair, iv. 434.
—— William, his son, iv. 434.
—— William, eldest son of Adam B. of Glencorse, iv. 435.
—— William, 7th son of Alex. B. of Glencorse, iv. 437.
Boucard, Guillemette de, wife of Bernard Stewart, lord of Aubigny, v. 347.
Boulogne, Eustace, count of, i. 2.
—— —— his wife, Mary of Scotland, i. 2.
Boulthee, Charles, in holy orders, vii. 84.
—— —— his wife, Laura Wyndham, vii. 84.
—— Julia Frances Laura, wife of Francis Hepburne-Scott, M.P., vii. 84.
Bourbon, Jeanne de, wife of Jean de la Tour, comte d'Auvergne, i. 154.
—— Louis de, Infante of Spain, vi. 70.
—— —— his morganatic wife, Maria Teresa de Vallabriga, vi. 70; ix. 135.
Bourbon-Montpensier, Charlotte de, wife of Wolfart van Borselen, i. 19.
Bourke of Mayo, Theobald (Bourke), 6th viscount, i. 387.
—— Bridget, wife of John Gunning, i. 387.
—— Edward Roden, 6th son of 5th earl of Mayo, iii. 45.

* Name unknown.

Bothwell, Honora, wife of duke of Berwick, i. 34.
—— Norah Mary Madeline, wife of capt. H. E. A. Lindsay, iii. 45.
Bourne, Richard, Middle Temple, ii. 583.
—— —— his wife, Anna Salmon, ii. 583.
Bouverie, Bartholomew, 3rd son of 1st earl of Radnor, vii. 226.
—— Charlotte, wife of Sir H. C. St. John Mildmay, vii. 226.
—— Duncombe Pleydell, vice-admiral R.N., iii. 584.
—— Edward, 4th son of 1st earl of Radnor, iii. 391.
—— —— his wife, Katharine Murray, iii 391.
—— Harriet, wife of (1) Archibald John, 4th earl of Rosebery, and (2) Sir H. C. St. J. Mildmay, vii. 226.
—— Louisa, wife of capt. Samuel Hay, iii. 584.
—— William Henry, vi. 383.
—— —— his wife, Bridget Douglas, vi. 383.
Bowdon of Southgate, John P. B., iv. 419.
—— Helena Mary, wife of Peter Constable-Maxwell, iv. 419.
Bowen, major-general, C.B., viii. 134.
—— Mary Anne, wife of F. A. Elphinstone-Dalrymple, viii. 134.
Bower of Kincaldrum, Graham, i. 545.
—— of Scorton, John, v. 313.
—— Harriot, wife of (1) Richard Maitland, and (2) Powles Harrison, v. 313.
—— Margaret, wife of Francis Balfour, i. 545.
BOWES OF STREATLAM AND LUNEDALE, BOWES, BARON, viii. 311.
Bowes of Streatlam and Lunedale, John, baron, viii. 311.
BOWES OF STREATLAM CASTLE AND LUNEDALE, BOWES-LYON, BARON, viii. 313-317.
BOWES, BARON BOWES OF STREATLAM AND LUNEDALE, viii. 311.
BOWES, LORD GLAMIS, viii. 310-312.
BOWES, EARL OF STRATHMORE AND KINGHORNE, viii. 310-312.
Bowes of Paul's Walden, George, viii. 311, 312.
—— —— his wife, Mary Thornhill, viii. 311.
—— of Streatlam Castle and Gibside, George, viii. 310.
—— —— his 2nd wife, Mary Gilbert of Paul's Walden, viii. 310.
—— —— Mary Eleanor, wife of 9th earl of Strathmore and Kinghorne, viii. 310.
—— Anna Maria, wife of Henry James Jessop, viii. 311.
—— John, illeg. son of 10th earl of Strathmore and Kinghorne, viii. 311.
—— Mary, wife of col. Barrington Price, viii. 311.
—— Sir Robert, ambassador, i. 517 *n.*: iv. 534.

Bowes-Lyon, baron Bowes of Streatlam Castle and Lunedale, viii. 313-317.
Bowes-Lyon, lord Glamis, viii. 313-317.
Bowes-Lyon, earl of Strathmore and Kinghorne, viii. 313-317.
Bowes-Lyon of Ridley Hall, Hetton Hall, and Norton Manor, Francis, viii. 314.
—— —— his wife, Anne Katherine Sybil Lindsay, iii. 48; viii. 314.
—— of Skeynes, Patrick, viii. 315.
—— —— his wife, Alice Wiltshire, viii. 315.
—— Alexander Francis, viii. 316.
—— Angus Patrick, viii. 315.
—— Charles Lindsay Claude, viii. 314.
—— Clodagh Pamela, viii. 315.
—— Constance Frances, wife of R. L. Blackburn, viii. 315.
—— David, viii. 316.
—— Dora Cicely, viii. 314.
—— Elizabeth Angela Marguerite, viii. 316.
—— Ernest, viii. 314.
—— —— his wife, Issobel Hester Drummond, viii. 314.
—— Ernestine Hester Maud, wife of F. W. Scott, viii. 315.
—— Fergus, Black Watch, viii. 316.
—— Gavin Patrick, viii. 315.
—— Geoffrey Francis, Black Watch, viii. 314.
—— Herbert, advocate, viii. 315.
—— Jean Barbara, viii. 315.
—— Joan Issobel Margaret, wife of A. E. Parker, viii. 314.
—— John Herbert, viii. 316.
—— Kenneth, viii. 315.
—— Lilian Helen, viii. 314.
—— Malcolm, capt. 2nd Life Guards, viii. 315.
—— —— his wife, Winifred Gurden-Rebow, viii. 315.
—— Margaret Anne, viii. 315.
—— Marjorie Effie, wife of capt. D. W. Roberts, viii. 315.
—— Mary Frances, wife of 16th lord Elphinstone, viii. 316.
—— Maud Agnes, viii. 315.
—— Michael Claud Hamilton, viii. 316.
—— Mildred Marion, wife of A. E. Jessup, viii. 315.
—— Muriel Frances Margaret, viii. 314.
—— Ronald George, R.N., viii. 314.
—— Rose Constance, viii. 316.
—— Susan Frances, viii. 314.
——;Winifred Geraldine viii. 314.
Bowie of Camsiscan, William, provost of Ayr, ii. 198.
Bowie of Holehouse, James, ii. 52.
—— Anne, wife of James Hamilton, ii. 52.
—— *, wife of major Alex. Campbell, ii. 198.
Bowill, Robert de, iv. 185.

* Name unknown.

Bowlby of Gilston Park, Edward Salvin, ix. 96.
—— Katharine Isabel Salvin, wife of James Boyle, ix. 96.
Bowles of Penho Castle, Sir Thomas, i. 399.
—— J., iv. 391.
—— Joane, wife of Sir E. Aston, i. 399.
—— Lillie, wife of rev. H. A. Douglas-Hamilton, iv. 391.
Bowman of Asbgrove, John, vii. 207.
—— *olim* Lyon, viii. 307.
Bowmont, Ker, marquess of, vii. 350-360.
Bowmont, John, first marquess of, vii. 350.
—— Robert, son of 1st duke of Roxburghe; styled marquess of, vii. 351.
—— —— his wife, Essex Mostyn, vii. 351.
Bowyer of Knipersley, Sir John, bart. iii. 400.
—— —— his wife, Jane Murray, iii. 400.
—— of Leythorne, Sir Thomas, 1st bart., ix. 67.
—— —— his wife, Anne Maxwell, ix. 67.
Boyce, Nicholas, iii. 112.
—— —— his wife, Henrietta Scott, iii. 112.
Boyd, Boyd, lord, v. 136-182.
Boyd, Alexander, *de jure* third lord, v. 145, 150.
—— —— his wife, Janet Colville, v. 151; ix. 58.
—— James, second lord, iv. 186; v. 149, 153, 154.
—— James, ninth lord, v. 168, 172.
—— —— his wife, Katharine Craik, v. 173.
—— James, *de jure* fourteenth lord, v. 179, 181.
—— Robert, governor of Scotland, first lord, ii. 267, 508; v. 142, 430; vi. 354; vii. 324, 327; viii. 576.
—— —— his wife, Mariota *or* Janet Maxwell, v. 145.
—— Robert, fourth lord, v. 152.
—— —— his 1st wife, Helen Somerville, v. 155; viii. 14 *n.*
—— —— his 2nd wife, Elizabeth Napier, v. 155.
—— —— his 3rd wife, Marion Colquhoun, v. 155.
—— Robert, fifth lord, ii. 80; iv. 193, 283, 284; v. 153, 154, 155.
—— —— his wife, Margaret Colquhoun, v. 161 *bis*.
—— Robert, seventh lord, iii. 442, 443, 444; iv. 195: v. 168.
—— —— his 1st wife, Margaret Montgomerie, iii. 442; v. 170.
—— —— his 2nd wife, Christian Hamilton. iv. 315; v. 170.
—— Robert, eighth lord, v. 169, 171.
—— —— his wife, Anne Fleming, iii. 100; v. 172; viii 550; ix. 119.

Boyd, Thomas, sixth lord, v. 161, 163.
—— his 1st wife, Margaret Campbell, v. 165.
—— his 2nd wife, Jane Stockdale, v. 165.
—— his 3rd wife, Elizabeth Wallace, v. 166.
— William, tenth lord, v. 173.
—— his wife, Jean Cunningham, iv. 249; v. 174.
— William, eleventh lord, v. 175.
—— his wife, Lettice Boyd, v. 175.
— William, twelfth lord, v. 176.
—— his wife, Euphemia Ross, v. 176.
— William, thirteenth lord, v. 177.
—— his wife, Anne Livingston, v. 179.
BOYD OF KILMARNOCK, LORD, v. 136-182.
Boyd of Kilmarnock, Thomas, first lord, v. 164.
— James, eldest son of 4th earl of Kilmarnock; styled lord, iii. 581; v. 181.
— master of, Robert, eldest son of 6th lord Boyd, v. 165, 166, 168, 457.
—— his wife, Jean Ker, v. 168, 457; vii. 131.
— master of, Thomas, eldest son of 1st lord Boyd, v. 145, 147.
—— his wife, Mary Stewart, i. 20; v. 147.
BOYD, LORD BOYD, v. 136-182.
BOYD, LORD BOYD OF KILMARNOCK, v. 136-182.
BOYD, EARL OF KILMARNOCK, v. 136-182.
Boyd of Ardneil, Archibald, v. 161.
—— Sir John, v. 138.
—— Robert, 3rd son of Sir Thomas B. of Kilmarnock, v. 139.
—— Robert, 1572, v. 161.
—— Robert, 5th lord Boyd, v. 161.
— of Arran, Thomas, eldest son of 1st lord Boyd, v. 147.
—— his wife, Mary Stewart, i. 20; v. 148.
— of Auchans, Thomas, v. 165.
— of Auchintorlie, Robert, v. 155, 556.
— of Auchmarr, William, 2nd son of Sir Thomas B. of Kilmarnock, v. 139.
— of Badenheath, Margaret, wife of Robert Boyd, tutor of Eglinton, v. 139, 162.
—— Robert, 5th laird, v. 147.
—— his wife, Margaret Boyd, v. 147.
—— Robert, 8th laird, v. 139, 162.
—— Robert, 2nd son of 5th lord Boyd; tutor of Eglinton, iii. 443; v. 139, 161, 169; ix. 119.
—— his wife, Margaret Boyd of Badenheath, v. 139, 162.
—— William, ancestor of the family of, v. 139.
— William, 7th laird, v. 139, 162.
Boyd of Bedlay, Robert, v. 161.
—— his wife, Margaret Colquhoun, v. 161.
—— Thomas, v. 164.
—— Sir Thomas, 2nd son of 6th lord Boyd, v. 166.
—— his wife, Grizel Cunningham, v. 166.
— of Bolinshaw, John, v. 166.
—— Sir Thomas, v. 166.
—— his wife, Grisel Cunningham, v. 166.
— of Bondington, Sir Robert, v. 138.
— of Bonshaw, 15th cent., i. 22.
—— John, son of Robert B., v. 146.
—— Robert, ancestor of the family of, v. 146.
—— William, ix. 3.
— of Caverton, Robert, vii. 327.
—— Thomas, eldest son of 1st lord Boyd, v. 147.
— of Chapelton, Robert, v. 153.
— of Corsbie, Thomas, v. 165.
— of Meikle Cumbrae, Thomas, eldest son of 1st lord Boyd, v. 147.
— of Dalgarth and Dalswinton, Sir Robert, v. 138 *n.*
— of Dalry, Thomas, eldest son of 1st lord Boyd, v. 147.
— of Drumcol, Sir Alexander, keeper of Edinburgh Castle, ii. 384, 453, 509; v. 141, 143, 144; viii. 533, 576.
—— his wife, Janet Kennedy, v. 142.
— of Duchal, Sir Alexander, viii. 10.
—— Robert, v. 142.
— of Duncoll, Sir Alexander, ii. 509.
—— Sir Robert, v. 138 *n.*
— of Dundonald in Walters-Kyle, Robert, v. 153.
— of Dunswinton, Sir Robert, v. 138 *n.*
— of Flat, Thomas, eldest son of 1st lord Boyd, v. 147.
— of Glenkin, Sir Robert, v. 138 *n.*
— of Glens, Robert, v. 161.
—— his wife, Margaret Colquhoun, v. 161.
— of Grugar, Robert, v. 169.
— of Guaylistoun, Sir Robert, v. 138 *n.*
— of Hairschaw, John, dean of guild, Edinburgh, v. 173.
—— Thomas, v. 164.
— of Hertschaw, Sir Robert, v. 138.
— of Kilbride, Sir John, v. 138.
— of Kilmarnock, Sir Robert, 1st laird, v. 138; viii. 249.
—— Robert, 6th laird, v. 142; vi. 80.
—— his wife, Mariota *or* Janet Maxwell, v. 145.
—— Sir Thomas, 2nd laird, v. 139.
—— Sir Thomas, 3rd laird, iv. 229; v. 139, 140, 494.
—— his wife, Alice Gifford, v. 140.

Boyd of Kilmarnock, Thomas, 4th laird, v. 140, 348 *bis*.
—— —— his wife, Joanna Montgomerie, iii. 431; v. 140.
—— —— Sir Thomas, 5th laird, v. 141.
—— of Knockindon, Thomas, v. 164.
—— of Lenzie, William, viii. 524, 525.
—— of Linn, Thomas, 2nd son of Alexander, lord Boyd, v. 151.
—— —— his wife, Marion Fairlie, ii. 292; v. 151.
—— of Lyandcorse, Helen, dau. of 5th lord Boyd, v. 162.
—— of Medros, Robert, v. 169.
—— of Menfurd, Robert, v. 169.
—— of Merton Hall, Edward, ix. 119.
—— of Molany, Robert, v. 161.
—— of Munfod, Thomas, eldest son of 1st lord Boyd, v. 147.
—— of Naristoun, Archibald, 3rd son of 1st lord Boyd, v. 145.
—— —— his wife, Christian Mure, v. 146.
—— —— Thomas, eldest son of 1st lord Boyd, v. 147.
—— of Nethermains, Adam, 3rd son of 6th lord Boyd, v. 166.
—— —— his wife, Marion Galbraith, v. 166.
—— of Nodellesdale, Sir Robert, v. 138.
—— of Overtoun, Thomas, v. 164.
—— of Penkill, Adam, 1st laird, v. 151.
—— —— his wife, Helen Kennedy, ii. 460; v. 152.
—— —— Alexander, 9th laird, v. 152.
—— —— Robert, 2nd laird, v. 152.
—— —— Robert, 11th laird, v. 152.
—— —— Spencer, 12th laird, v. 152.
—— —— Thomas, vi. 106.
—— —— his wife, Anna Melville, vi. 106.
—— —— Thomas, last laird of 1st line, v. 152.
—— of Pitcon, Robert, 8th laird, v. 151.
—— —— Thomas, 1st laird, elder son of Thos. B. of Linn, v. 151.
—— —— Thomas, ix. 119.
—— —— his wife, Elizabeth Conyngham, v. 168; ix. 119.
—— of Polgavy, Thomas, eldest son of 1st lord Boyd, v. 147.
—— of Portincross, Archibald, v. 161.
—— —— Grizel, wife of A. Fullarton, v. 140.
—— —— Sir Robert, v. 138.
—— —— Robert, 3rd son of Sir Thos. B. of Kilmarnock, v. 139.
—— —— Robert, 1572, v. 161.
—— —— Robert, 5th lord Boyd, 1574, v. 161.
—— —— Robert, last laird of old line, v. 140.
—— —— William, son of Alexander Fullarton of Kilmichail, v. 140.
—— of Ralston, Alexander, chamberlain of Kilmarnock, v. 150.
—— —— his wife, Janet Colville, v. 151.
Boyd of Risedalemure, Thomas, eldest son of 1st lord Boyd, v. 147.
—— of Rysholm, Robert, iv. 185 *n*., 186.
—— of Shean, Sir Thomas, elder son of 5th lord Boyd, i. 46; v. 161.
—— of Stablegreen of Glasgow, Robert, v. 161.
—— of Stewartoun, Tarrinzean, and Tealing, Thomas, eldest son of 1st lord Boyd, v. 147.
—— of Templeton, Adam, ix. 3.
—— of Tourgill, David, colonel, v. 163, 166.
—— —— his wife, Margaret Wallace, v. 163.
—— of Trabeach, Sir Robert, v. 138 *n*.
—— of Trochrig, Adam, ancestor of the family of, v. 151.
—— —— his wife, Helen Kennedy, ii. 460; v. 152.
—— —— Ann, wife of William Boyd Robertson, v. 152.
—— —— James, archbishop of Glasgow, 1st laird, ii. 80; v. 152.
—— —— Robert, principal, 2nd laird, v. 150, 152, 168, 170.
—— —— Robert, 6th laird, v. 152.
—— of Turnberry, Thomas, eldest son of 1st lord Boyd, v. 147.
—— of Whiteside, John, 4th son of 6th lord Boyd, v. 166.
—— of Williyard, Helen, dau. of 5th lord Boyd, v. 162.
—— of Yester, Morham, Duncanlaw, and Giffordgate, Robert, v. 142; viii. 428.
—— Agnes, wife of Sir John Colquhoun, ii. 81; v. 163.
—— Agnes, wife of Sir G. Elphinstone of Blytheswood, v. 167.
—— Agnes, wife of Sir G. Morison of Dairsie, v. 171.
—— Alan, at siege of Perth, 1339, v. 139.
—— Alexander, captain, 21st regt., ii. 198.
—— Alexander, son of Sir Alex. B. of Drumcol. v. 142.
—— Alexander, chamberlain of Kilmarnock, 2nd son of 1st lord Boyd, v. 145, 150.
—— —— his wife, Janet Colville, v. 151.
—— Alexander, 5th son of 1st earl of Kilmarnock, v. 174.
—— Andrew, bishop of Argyll, ii. 517; v. 167.
—— —— his wife, Elizabeth Cunningham, v. 168.
—— Andrew, v. 205.
—— —— his wife, Marjorie Kirkaldy of Inchture, v. 205.
—— Annabella, wife of Sir John Gordon of Lochinvar, v. 102, 147.
—— Annabella, wife of (1) Edmund Hay of Talla, and (2) Patrick Dunbar of Bele, viii. 425; ix. 164 *bis*.
—— Archibald, in Bonshaw, 3rd son of 1st lord Boyd, v. 145.
—— —— his wife, Christian Mure, v. 146.

Boyd, Archibald, in Bonshaw, v. 146.
— Charles, captain Scots Dutch Brigade, v. 174.
— — his wife, Katharine Van Beest, ix. 119.
— Charles, 3rd son of 4th earl of Kilmarnock, v. 179; ix. 120 *bis*.
— — his 1st wife, *, v. 179.
— — his 2nd wife, Anne Lockhart, v. 180.
— Charles, his illeg. son, ix. 120.
— Charles, major 20th Foot, v. 179.
— — his wife, Elizabeth Halyburton, v. 180.
— Charles, son of major Charles B., v. 180 *bis*.
— Charlotte, wife of C. E. Gordon, v. 180.
— Christian, wife of A. Gray of Balgarno, iv. 273.
— Christian, wife of Sir Jas. Hamilton of Evandale, v. 163.
— Christian, wife of Sir Wm. Scott of Ardross, v. 170, 171.
— Duncan, follower of Robert the Bruce, v. 138.
— Egidia, wife of 4th earl of Eglinton, iii. 443; v. 162.
— Elizabeth, wife of Archibald, 5th earl of Angus, i. 183; v. 146; ix. 12.
— Elizabeth, wife of Thomas Douglas, v. 146; vi. 368.
— Elizabeth, wife of Sir John Cunningham of Drumquhassill, v. 163.
— Erroll, son of Wm. B., v. 174.
— Euphemia, wife of John Logie of Logie-almond, v. 152.
— Eva, dau. of 9th lord Boyd, v. 173.
— Giles, wife of 4th earl of Eglinton, iii. 443; v. 162.
— Grace, dau. of Robert B. of Trochrig, v. 152.
— Grizel, wife of Wm. Fullarton of Kilmichail, v. 140.
— Grizel, *mistake for* Margaret, wife of (1) Alex., 4th lord Forbes, and (2) David, 2nd earl of Cassillis, ii. 461 *n.*; v. 149.
— Helen, dau. of 7th lord Boyd, v. 170.
— Isabel, wife of (1) John Blair, and (2) Sir D. Campbell of Auchinbreck, v. 167.
— Isabel, wife of (1) John Sinclair, and (2) Sir John Grierson of Lag, v. 171; ix. 119.
— Isobel, wife of (1) Sir Jas. Stewart of Bute, and (2) rev. Archd. Graham or M'Ilvernock, ii. 295.
— James, archbishop of Glasgow, ii. 80; v. 152.
— James, 4th son of 3rd lord Boyd, iv. 188; v. 152.
— James, witness in 1342, v. 139.
— James, 5th son of Thomas, 6th lord Boyd, v. 167.

* Name unknown.

Boyd, James, captain Scots Dutch Brigade, v. 174.
— Janet, dau. of William B., Turriff, v. 174.
— Janet, wife of Edmund Hay of Megginch, v. 218.
— Jean, wife of Sir A. Morison of Prestongrange, v. 171.
— Jean, wife of Sir David Cunningham of Robertland, v. 173.
— John, 4th son of 1st lord Boyd, v. 146.
— Katharine, wife of David Boyle of Figgidoch, iv. 188.
— Katharine, wife of Alexander Porterfield, v. 175.
— Letitia, wife of (1) William, 2nd earl of Kilmarnock, and (2) John Gardiner, v. 175.
— Malcolm, ensign, ix. 119.
— — his wife, Mary Collins, ix. 119.
— Margaret, mistress of king James IV., and wife of John Mure of Rowallan, i. 22; v. 146.
— Margaret, wife of (1) Alexander, 4th lord Forbes, and (2) David, 2nd earl of Cassillis, ii. 460; iv. 53; v. 149.
— Margaret, wife of David Cathcart of Clolynan, ii. 509.
— Margaret, wife of 1st lord Montgomerie, iii. 432; v. 142.
— Margaret, wife of John Montgomerie of Lainshaw, iii. 436; v. 155.
— Margaret, wife of Robert Boyd of Badenheath, v. 147.
— Margaret, wife of George Colquhoun, v. 152.
— Margaret, wife of John Cunningham of Cunninghamhead, v. 162.
— Margaret, dau. of 9th lord Boyd, v. 173.
— Margaret, dau. of 1st earl of Kilmarnock, v. 175.
— Margaret, dau. of Robert B., advocate, v. 175.
— Margaret, wife of Peter Hay of Rattray v. 229.
— Marion, wife of 1st earl of Abercorn, i. 47; v. 167.
— Marion, wife of John Maxwell of Calderwood, v. 142.
— Marion, wife of Sir James Dundas of Arniston, v. 171.
— Mary, wife of Sir A. Maclean, v. 174.
— Mary, dau. of 2nd earl of Kilmarnock, v. 175.
— Patrick, 2nd son of Archibald B. of Nariston, v. 146.
— Sir Robert, witness to contract in 1205, v. 137; ix. 119.
— Robert, mentioned in charter, 1262, v. 137.
— Robert, in Ragman Roll, v. 138.
— Robert, 2nd son of Thomas B. of Linn, v. 151.

Boyd, Robert, in Kilmarnock, v. 153.
—— —— his wife, Helen Somerville, v. 153.
—— Robert, 4th son of 1st earl of Kilmarnock, v. 174.
—— Robert, glover, Kilmarnock, v. 174.
—— —— his wife, Margaret Thomson, v. 174.
—— Robert, advocate, v. 175.
—— —— his wife, Eleanora Nicolson, v. 175.
—— Sir Robert, governor of Gibraltar, vi. 502.
—— Simon Fitzalan, alleged ancestor of the family of, i. 11.
—— Thomas, merchant, Dublin, v. 175.
—— —— his wife, Mary Loftus, v. 175.
—— William, father of Sir Robert B. of Kilmarnock, v. 138 *n*.
—— William, abbot of Kilwinning, v. 141; ix. 119.
—— William, manufacturer, Turriff, v. 174.
—— William, R.N., captain 87th Foot, and 114th Foot, v. 181.
—— Zachary, minister of Glasgow, v. 172.
—— *, alleged wife of Sir John Herries of Terregles, iv. 400.
—— *, wife of (1) Hugh Mure of Polkelly, and (2) Archibald Craufurd of Craufurdland, v. 146.
—— *, wife of James Chalmers of Sauchrie, v. 152.
—— *, two sons of 3rd lord Boyd, v. 152.
Boyd-Robertson of Trochrig, v. 152.
Boyder, Henry, 76th regt., i. 131.
—— Sarah, wife of W. H. Bruce-Ogilvy, i. 131.
Boyes of Dryfesdale, iii. 56, 68.
Boyle of Kelburn, Stewartoun, Cumbrae, Finnick, Largs and Dalry, Boyle, lord, iv. 202.
Boyle of Kelburn, Stewartoun, Cumbrae, Finnick, Largs and Dalry, David, first lord, iv. 202.
Boyle of Stewartoun, Cumbraes, Fenwick, Largs and Dalry, Boyle, lord, iv. 202-221.
Boyle of Stewarton, Cumbraes, Fenwick, Largs and Dalry, David, first lord, iv. 202.
Boyle, John, eldest son of 1st earl of Glasgow; styled lord, iv. 205.
—— John, elder son of 3rd earl of Glasgow; styled lord, iv. 216.
—— John, R.N., eldest son of 4th earl of Glasgow; styled lord, iv. 217.
Boyle, lord Boyle of Kelburn, Stewartoun, Cumbrae, Finnick, Largs and Dalry, iv. 202.
Boyle, lord Boyle of Stewarton, Cumbraes, Fenwick, Largs and Dalry, iv. 202-221.
Boyle, baron Fairlie of Fairlie, iv. 220-221.

* Name unknown.

Boyle, earl of Glasgow, iv. 183-221.
Boyle, viscount Kelburn, iv. 202-221.
Boyle, baron Ross of Hawkhead, iv. 216-219.
Boyle of Ballikewin, James, iv. 206.
—— —— John, 2nd son of B. of Kelburne, iv. 187; ix. 95.
—— —— his wife, Katharine Wallace, iv. 187.
—— —— John, 2nd laird, iv. 187.
—— —— his 1st wife, Jonet Cunningham, iv. 188.
—— —— his 2nd wife, Marjorie Fraser, 188.
—— —— John, lord Boyle, iv. 206.
—— —— William, iv. 194.
—— of Ballochmartine, John, son of Wm. B. of Kelburne, iv. 187, 189.
—— —— John, iv. 190.
—— —— his wife, Marion Crawfurd, iv. 190.
—— —— John, iv. 195.
—— —— his wife, Agnes Boyle, iv. 195.
—— —— Robert, 3rd son of John B. of Kelburne, iv. 187, 189.
—— of Braidshaw, William, 4th son of John B. of Kelburne, iv. 190.
—— of Corshill, William, brother of 1st earl of Glasgow, iv. 200.
—— of Crawford Priory, Gertrude Georgina, wife of T. H. A. E. Cochrane, iv. 196, 204.
—— of Dalgarnock, John, 5th son of John B. of Kelburne, iv. 190.
—— of Downiescroft, David, iv. 194.
—— —— William, captain, iv. 193.
—— —— his 1st wife, Christian Power, iv. 194.
—— —— his 2nd wife, Elizabeth Maxwell, iv. 194.
—— —— William, iv. 194.
—— of Etal, Augusta, wife of capt. F. Fitzclarence, iv. 217.
—— of Fairlie, David, eldest son of James B. of Halkishurst, iv. 197.
—— —— his wife, Grizel Boyle, iv. 197.
—— of Figgidoch, Archibald, iv. 188, 189.
—— —— David, 2nd son of John B. of Ballikewin, iv. 188, 189.
—— —— his 1st wife, Katharine Boyd, iv. 188.
—— —— his 2nd wife, Margaret Crawfurd, iv. 189.
—— —— Robert, iv. 188.
—— —— his wife, Margaret Montgomerie, iv. 188.
—— of Halkishurst, David, iv. 189, 197.
—— —— his wife, Grizel Boyle, iv. 197.
—— —— James, iv. 188.
—— —— his 1st wife, Margaret Crawfurd, iv. 188.
—— —— his 2nd wife, Jean Barclay, iv. 189.
—— of Hareshawmuir, John, iv. 199.

Boyle of Kelburne, David, eldest son of James B. of Halkishurst, iv. 189, 190, 194, 197.

—— his wife, Grizel Boyle, iv. 197.

—— Grizel, wife of David Boyle of Halkishurst, iv. 189, 197.

—— John, maor of fee in Largs, iv. 184, 186, 192.

—— John, iv. 186.

—— John, son of Patrick B., iv. 191.

—— his wife, Agnes Fraser, iv. 192.

—— John, maor of fee in Largs, son of John B., iv. 190, 192.

—— his wife, Marion Crawfurd, iv. 193.

—— John, rector of the University of Glasgow, iv. 193, 195.

—— his wife, Agnes Maxwell, iv. 196.

—— John, sheriff of Bute, eldest son of David B., ii. 298 *n.*, iv. 198; ix. 95 *bis*.

—— his 1st wife, Marion Steuart, iv. 198.

—— his 2nd wife, Jean Mure, iv. 201.

—— Sir Patrick, iv. 186.

—— Richard, iv. 183, 184.

—— his wife, Marjory Cumin, iv. 183, 184.

—— Robert, iv. 185 *n.*, 186.

—— Robert, iv. 186.

—— William, maor of fee in Largs, iv. 186.

— of Largs, John iv. 187.

—— William, iv. 194.

— of Maldersland, John, iv. 184 *n.*, 196.

—— his wife, Agnes Maxwell, iv. 196.

—— Robert, iv. 184 *bis*.

—— his wife, Avice Mure, iv. 184.

— of Montgomerieston, James, provost of Irvine, iv. 197.

—— his wife, Janet Barclay, iv. 197.

— of Polruskane, John, iv. 190, 191.

—— his wife, Agnes Fraser, iv. 192.

—— Patrick, eldest son of John B. of Kelburne, iv. 187, 191.

—— Robert, iv. 184.

—— his possible wife, Avicia Mure, iv. 184.

— of Portry, Robert, iv. 188.

—— his wife, Margaret Montgomerie, iv. 188.

— of Rowallan, Jean, wife of col. Jas. Campbell, iv. 205; ix. 95.

— of Rysholm, Archibald, younger son of Robert B. of Kelburne, iv. 185 *n.*, 190.

—— Hugo, iv. 185 *n.*

—— John, iv. 185 *n.*, 192.

—— his wife, Agnes Fraser, iv. 192.

—— John, iv. 193.

—— his wife, Marion Crawfurd, iv. 193.

—— Katharine, wife of (1) John Johnstone, and (2) Robert Scot, i. 239; iv. 185 *n.*, ix. 14.

—— Katharine, dau. of Robert B. of Kelburne, iv. 185 *n.*

Boyle of Rysholm, Richard, ancestor of the family of, iv. 185.

— of Shewalton, David, senator of the College of Justice, lord Shewalton, iv. 207.

—— his 1st wife, Elizabeth Montgomerie, iv. 208.

—— his 2nd wife, Catherine Campbell Smythe, iv. 212.

—— John, lieut.-col. Ayrshire Militia, iv. 207.

—— Patrick, senator of the College of Justice, lord Shewalton, iv. 177, 200, 204.

—— Patrick, clerk depute of justiciary, iv. 208.

—— his wife, Mary Frances Elphinstone-Dalrymple, iv. 208; viii. 135.

—— Patrick, in holy orders, 5th son of 2nd earl of Glasgow, iv. 200, 206.

—— his 1st wife, Agnes Mure, iv. 207.

—— his 2nd wife, Elizabeth Dunlop, iv. 207.

—— William, brother of 1st earl of Glasgow, iv. 200, 204, 206.

— of Smiddieshaw, Margaret, iv. 198.

—— Patrick, burgess of Irvine, iv. 198.

—— his wife, Margaret Crawfurd, iv. 198.

— of Stewarton, William, brother of 1st earl of Glasgow, iv. 200.

— of Tullochdonnell, Thomas, 5th son of David B. of Kelburne, iv. 198.

— of Wamphray, John, iv. 185 *n.*, 186.

—— John, iv. 185 *n.*

—— Katharine, wife of (1) John Johnstone, and (2) Robert Scott, i. 239; iv. 185 *n.*, ix. 14.

— Agnes, wife of John Boyle of Ballochmartine, iv. 195.

— Agnes, dau. of rev. Patrick B. of Shewalton, iv. 214.

— Agnes Margaret, wife of F. Pratt-Barlow, iv. 210.

— Alan Reginald, iv. 221.

— Alastair Patrick, iv. 210.

— Alexander, vice-admiral R.N., iv. 209.

—— his wife, Agnes Walker, iv. 209.

— Alexander, 3rd son of vice-admiral Alexander B., iv. 210.

—— his wife, Fanny Studholme, iv. 210.

— Alexander Charles, midshipman R.N., iv. 207.

— Alexander David, R.N., iv. 210.

— Alexander James, ensign 30th regt., iv. 209; ix. 95.

—— his 1st wife, M. L. J. Hodgkinson, iv. 209.

—— his 2nd wife, Clare Banning, iv. 209.

— Alice Mary, wife of col. Sir C. Fergusson, iv. 221.

— Amelia Laura, iv. 214.

Boyle, Andrew, 8th son of John B. of Kelburne, iv. 191.
— Anna Leuisa Alexandrina, iv. 212.
— Anne, dau. of 1st earl of Glasgow, iv. 205; ix. 95 *bis*.
— Archibald, 6th son of John B. of Kelburne, iv. 190.
— Archibald Thomas, iv. 212.
— Augusta Helen Elizabeth, wife of C. L. Orr-Ewing, iv. 221.
— Caroline Elizabeth, wife of Charles Drummond, viii. 231.
— Cecil Alexander, iv. 210.
— Cecil David, iv. 214.
— Charles, captain R.N., 3rd son of 1st earl of Glasgow, iv. 204; ix. 95.
— Charles Fremoult, iv. 213.
— — his wife, Martha Trotter, iv. 213.
— Constance Antonina, iv. 214.
— David, M.P., senator of the College of Justice, lord Boyle, iv. 207.
— — his 1st wife, Elizabeth Montgomerie, iv. 208.
— — his 2nd wife, Catherine Campbell Smythe, iv. 212.
— David, 3rd son of David B. of Shewalton, iv. 211.
— David, two inf. sons of 1st earl of Glasgow, ix. 95.
— David Hugh Montgomerie, iv. 211.
— David William Maurice, ix. 96.
— Diana, wife of 2nd lord Hampton, iv. 218.
— Dorothy Montagu, wife of G. Gathorne-Hardy, iv. 221.
— Edward George, Rifle Brigade, iv. 221.
— Edward Louis Dalrymple, R.N., iv. 213.
— — his wife, Theodosia I. Ogilvie, iv. 213; ix. 96.
— Edward Patrick Ogilvie, iv. 213.
— Eleanora Charlotte, dau. of David B. of Shewalton, iv. 212.
— Elizabeth, wife of Robert Cunningham of Auchinharvie, iv. 191.
— Elizabeth, dau. of John B. of Kelburne, iv. 191.
— Elizabeth, wife of Robert Sempill of Mylnbank, iv. 195.
— Elizabeth, dau. of 1st earl of Glasgow, iv. 205.
— Elizabeth, wife of James Hope, iv. 212.
— Elizabeth, wife of rear-admiral J. Rouet-Smollett, iv. 214.
— Elizabeth, wife of Sir Geo. Douglas of Springwood Park, iv. 216.
— Elizabeth, dau. of 4th earl of Glasgow, iv. 216.
— Elizabeth Helen, dau. of vice-admiral Alexander B., iv. 210.
— Elizabeth Magdalene Graeme, iv. 209.
— Frances Minna Fremoult, iv. 213.
— Frances Montgomerie, wife of C. W. Parish, iv. 211.
Boyle, George David, dean of Salisbury, iv. 213.
— — his wife, Mary Christiana Robins, iv. 213; ix. 96.
— George Frederick, iv. 212.
— Gerard E., colonel, viii. 231.
— Gertrude G., wife of T. H. A. E. Cochrane, iii. 366; iv. 196, 204, 219.
— Godfrey Henry Patrick, iv. 210.
— Graeme Hepburn, iv. 209.
— Grissel, dau. of 2nd earl of Glasgow, ix. 96.
— Grizel, dau. of David B. of Kelburne, iv. 198; ix. 95.
— Hamilla Augusta, iv. 212.
— Helen, wife of Sir C. Dalrymple-Fergusson, iv. 212; viii. 144.
— Helen, wife of Thomas Mure, iv. 214; ix. 96.
— Helen, wife of Sir Jas. Douglas of Springwood Park, iv. 215; ix. 96.
— Helen, dau. of 3rd earl of Glasgow, iv. 216.
— Helen Graeme, iv. 209; ix. 95.
— Helen Jane, sister of 7th earl of Glasgow, iv. 209.
— Henrietta Augusta, dau. of Patrick B. of Shewalton, iv. 209.
— Henrietta Camilla, wife of col. J. S. Rothwell, iv. 211.
— Henry David, iv. 211.
— — his wife, E. C. Robinson, iv. 211.
— Henry Dundas, H.E.I.C.S., iv. 214.
— Irene Florinda Maud, iv. 214.
— Isobel, wife of Alex. Bruce of Auchenbowie, iv. 194.
— Isabella Margaret, dau. of 4th earl of Glasgow, iv. 217.
— James, merchant in Glasgow, iv. 189.
— James, procurator-fiscal, Glasgow, iv. 193.
— — his wife, Margaret Smyth, iv. 193.
— James, 5th son of John B. of Kelburne, iv. 201.
— James, captain 89th regt., H.B.M. Consul, iv. 210.
— — his wife, Blanche E. M. Pratt, iv. 210.
— James, Royal Scots Fusiliers, iv. 220.
— his wife, Katharine Isabel Salvin Bowlby, ix. 96.
— Jane, dau. of David B. of Shewalton, iv. 212.
— Jane Flora, iv. 211.
— Jane Mary, dau. of 3rd earl of Glasgow, iv. 216; ix. 96.
— Janet, wife of Jas. Stewart, iv. 189.
— Janet, wife of Jas. Jamieson of Halie Jamieson, iv. 191.
— Janet, dau. of Alex. B., New Zealand, iv. 210.
— Janet, wife of capt. W. H. Fife, iv. 210.

Boyle, Janet, dau. of 2nd earl of Glasgow, iv. 214.
— Jean, wife of Wm. Barclay of Perceton, iv. 194.
— Jean, dau. of 2nd earl of Glasgow, iv. 214.
— Jean, wife of Sir James Campbell of Lawers, v. 511; ix. 131.
— John, 4th son of David B. of Figgidoch, iv. 189.
— John, in Meikle Govane, iv. 189 *n*.
— John, 7th son of John B. of Kelburne, iv. 191.
— John, surgeon, brother of 1st earl of Glasgow, iv. 199.
— John, barrister-at-law, iv. 211; ix. 95.
— — his wife, Jane Walrond, iv. 211; ix. 96.
— John David, Rifle Brigade, iv. 220.
— Juliana, wife of 4th earl of Elgin, iii. 482.
— Katharine, wife of Dr. James MacNeill, iv. 215.
— Katharine Charlotte Anne Eliza, iv. 209.
— Katharine Minna, iv. 214.
— Louisa Laura, iv. 209.
— Margaret, wife of Robert Blakburne, iv. 189.
— Margaret, wife of John M'Gibbon, iv. 189.
— Margaret, wife of John Crawfurd of Giffordland, iv. 191.
— Margaret, dau. of John B. of Kelburne, iv. 191.
— Margaret, wife of John Cunningham of Caddell, iv. 192.
— Margaret, wife of Wm. Hamilton of Wadderhill, iv. 194.
— Margaret, *error for* Mary, wife of Wm. Wallace, iv. 198 *n*.
— Margaret, wife of Sir Alex. Cuninghame of Corshill, iv. 200.
— Margaret, dau. of 1st earl of Glasgow, iv. 205.
— Margaret, dau. of rev. Patrick B. of Shewalton, iv. 214.
— Margaret, dau. of 2nd earl of Glasgow, iv. 214.
— Marie, wife of George Makullo, iv. 193.
— Marion, wife of (1) Matthew Ross of Hayning Ross, and (2) archbishop James Law, iv. 194.
— Marion, dau. of 2nd earl of Glasgow, iv. 215.
— Marion Montgomerie, iv. 211.
— Mary, wife of (1) W. E. Hope Vere, and (2) lord David Kennedy, ii. 498.
— Mary, wife of Wm. Wallace of Shewalton, iv. 198.
— Mary, wife of James, duke of Queensberry and Dover, vii. 142.
Boyle, Mary Helen, sister of 7th earl of Glasgow, iv. 209.
— Montgomerie, captain I. Y., iv. 211.
— — his wife, Constance Helen Abel-Smith, iv. 211.
— Muriel Louisa Diana, iv. 219.
— Patrick David, colonel Grenadier Guards, iv. 209.
— — his wife, Kathleen Digby Blagrave, iv. 209.
— Patrick John Salvin, ix. 96.
— Phyllis Montgomerie, wife of Agar Williams, iv. 210; ix. 95.
— Robert, Carrickmacross, iv. 193.
— Robert, attorney, iv. 198.
— Robert, 6th son of John B. of Kelburne, iv. 201.
— Robert, captain R.A., iv. 213.
— — his wife, Frances S. Sankey, iv. 213; ix. 96.
— Robert, Glasgow diocese, 1372, ix. 95.
— Robert Elphinstone, colonel Indian army, iv. 208.
— Robert Fremoult, iv. 213.
— Sydney Herbert, lieut. Railway Pioneers, iv. 213.
— Theodosia Frances, iv. 214.
— Thomas, notary, tutor of Galston, iv. 192.
— — his wife, Janet Barclay, iv. 192.
— Walter, R.N., brother of 1st earl of Glasgow, iv. 200.
— William, in Dumbarton, iv. 190.
— William, lieut. 48th regt., iv. 207.
— William, colonel, C.B., iv. 211.
— — his wife, Louisa C. Parsons, iv. 212.
— William, 3rd son of 4th earl of Glasgow, iv. 217.
— William Henry David, iv. 212.
— — his wife, Eleanor Curzon, iv. 212.
Boyne, Gustavus (Hamilton), 1st viscount, i. 45.
— — his wife, Elizabeth Brooke, i. 45.
Boyne, Sir Patrick Ogilvie, lord, ix. 81.
Boynton, Sir Matthew, bart., v. 13.
— — his wife, Katharine Fairfax, v. 13.
Boyville del Counte de Are, Richard de, iv. 185.
— Robert de, iv. 185.
Brace of Biddenham, Francis, v. 15.
— — his wife, Eliz. Scarborough, v. 15.
Braceor, Henry, Jedworth, iv. 146.
Brachlie, James Stewart, styled lord, ix. 138.
Bradford, George Cecil Orlando (Bridgeman), 4th earl of, ii. 248.
Bradshaigh of Haigh Hall and Wigan, Sir Roger, bart., iii. 42, 400.
— his wife, Mary Murray, iii. 400.
— Elizabeth, wife of John Edwin, iii. 42.
Brady of Easter Kennet, Robert, iii. 473.

Brague, Philippe de, seigneur de Luat, v. 347.
—— —— his wife, Guyenne Stewart, v. 347.
Braidfute of Lamington, Marion, vii. 365.
Brainfoord, Edward Ruthven, styled earl of, iv. 93; ix. 92.
Bramhall, Isabella, wife of Sir Jas. Graham, i. 137.
—— John, archbishop of Armagh, i. 137; ix. 9.
Brand, Anne Elizabeth, wife of D. S. Arbuthnott, i. 315.
—— James, i. 315.
—— Thomas, major 10th Hussars, ii. 248.
—— —— his wife, Katharine Mary Montagu-Douglas-Scott, ii. 248.
BRANDON, HAMILTON, DUKE OF, iv. 384-397.
Brandon, James, first duke of, iv. 383.
Braesa, William de, ii. 423.
—— —— his wife, Matildis de Haya, ii. 423.
Brassey of Preston Hall, Henry Arthur, v. 370.
—— —— Henry Leonard Campbell, v. 370.
—— —— his wife, Violet Mary Gordon-Lennox, v. 370.
—— Hilda Madeleine, wife of Charles Henry, earl of March, v. 370.
Braye, Sarah, wife of Henry Otway; baroness, i. 492.
BREADALBANE, CAMPBELL, EARL OF, ii. 174-214.
Breadalbane, Gavin, seventh earl of, ii. 213.
—— John, first earl of, i. 360; ii. 201, 203.
—— —— his 1st wife, Mary Rich, ii. 205.
—— —— his 2nd wife, Mary Campbell, i. 361; ii. 206.
—— John, second earl of, ii. 207.
—— —— his 1st wife, Frances Cavendish, iii. 207.
—— —— his 2nd wife, Henrietta Villiers, ii. 207.
—— John, third earl of, ii. 208.
—— —— his 1st wife, Amabel Grey, ii. 208.
—— —— his 2nd wife, Arabella Pershall, ii. 209.
—— John, fourth earl of, ii. 190, 209.
—— —— his wife, Mary Turner Gavin, ii. 210.
—— John, fifth earl of, ii. 211.
—— John Alexander Gavin, sixth earl of, ii. 194, 211.
—— —— his wife, Mary Theresa Edwards, ii. 212.
BREADALBANE, CAMPBELL, MARQUESS OF, ii. 210-214.
Breadalbane, Gavin, third marquess of ii. 213; ix. 46 *bis*.
—— —— his wife, Alma Imogen Leonora Charlotta Graham, ii. 213: vi. 273; ix. 46.
—— John, first marquess of, ii. 210.
—— —— his wife, Mary Turner Gavin, ii. 210.
—— John, second marquess of, ii. 211; ix. 46.
—— —— his wife, Eliza Baillie, ii. 211; iv. 323.
BREADALBANE, CAMPBELL, VISCOUNT OF, ii. 203.
Breadalbane, John, first viscount of, ii. 203.
BREADALBANE of KENMORE, CAMPBELL, BARON, ii. 213.
Breadalbane of Kenmore, Gavin, baron, ii. 213.
BREADALBANE OF TAYMOUTH CASTLE, CAMPBELL, BARON, ii. 210.
Breadalbane of Taymouth Castle, John, first baron, ii. 210.
—— —— John, second baron, ii. 211.
Breakenridge, Mary Madeline, wife of C. C. Renny-Strachan-Carnegie, viii. 87.
—— William, vii. 87.
Breary of Scow Hall and Menston, John, iii. 597.
—— Mary, wife of Charles Fairfax, iii. 597.
Breassauch *olim* Lyon, viii. 308.
Brebner, James, Aberdeen, iv. 291.
BRECHIN, LORD OF BRECHIN, ii. 215-224.
Brechin, Henry, illeg. son of David, earl of Huntingdon, lord of, i. 4; ii. 214.
—— —— his wife, Juliana de Cornhill, i. 4; ii. 216 *bis*.
—— Sir David, lord of, i. 428: ii. 218; vi. 136.
—— —— his 1st wife, Margaret of Beokyl, i. 13; ii. 221.
—— —— his 2nd wife, Margery (de Ramsay), ii. 220, 221.
—— Margaret of, wife of Sir David Barclay, i. 438; ii. 222; ix. 27.
—— Sir William, lord of, ii. 216; viii. 245 *n*.
—— —— his wife, Elena Comyn, ii. 218, 256.
BRECHIN, STEWART, LORD OF, vii. 246.
Brechin, James, 2nd son of King James III.; lord of, vii. 246.
—— Walter, son of King Robert II.; lord of, i. 16, 438.
—— —— his wife, Margaret of Brechin, i. 438; ii. 224; ix. 27.
BRECHIN AND NAVAR, MAULE, LORD, vii. 19-27.
Brechin and Navar, Patrick, first lord, vii. 20.
Brecknell, Joseph, Chelsea, vii. 96.
—— —— his wife, Katharine Caroline Colyear, vii. 96.
Brecknock, James (Butler), 1st earl of, iii. 122.
Breese, Anne, wife of Alistair R. Innes-Ker, vii. 358.
—— W. R., New York, vii. 358.
BRENTFORD, RUTHVEN, EARL OF, iv. 104-106.
Brentford, Patrick, first earl of, iv. 104; v. 6.
—— —— his 1st wife, *, iv. 105.
—— —— his 2nd wife, Joanna Henderson, iv. 105.
—— —— his 3rd wife, Clara Berner, iv. 105.
—— Edward, son of 2nd lord Forrester; styled earl of, iv. 93.

* Name unknown.

Bressey, Benjamin, viii. 496.
—— —— his wife, Margaret Johnston, viii. 496.
—— Margaret, viii. 496.
Breton of Norton, Eliab, iv. 495.
—— Mary, wife of John Hope, iv. 495.
Brett, Elizabeth, wife of 4th lord Bellenden, ii. 75.
—— Richard, Deptford, ii. 75.
Brian Borinmha, King of Ireland, v. 567.
Brictric, father of Glassam, ii. 370.
Bridgeman, Margaret Alice, wife of John Charles Montagu Douglas Scott, lord Dalkeith, ii. 248.
Bridges, Thomas Lane Coulson, rector of Warkton, ii. 246.
—— —— his wife, Evelyn Mary Montagu-Douglas Scott, ii. 246.
Bridgewater, Francis (Egerton), 3rd duke of, viii. 361, 362.
—— John (Egerton) 1st earl of, ii. 583.
—— John (Egerton) 2nd earl of, iii. 400.
—— Scroop (Egerton), 1st duke of, ii. 533.
—— —— his wife, Elizabeth Churchill, ii. 533.
BRIENE, KER, VISCOUNT OF, v. 477-487.
Briene, Robert, first viscount of, v. 477.
Brienne, Jean de, 'dit d'Acre,' i. 6.
—— —— his wife, Marie de Coucy, i. 6.
Briggs, Amelia Mary, wife of John Kennedy, ii. 497.
—— Samuel, ii. 497.
—— William Hamilton, surgeon lieutenant-colonel, iii. 107.
—— —— his wife, Susan Georgiana Ramsay, iii. 107.
Bright of Bannercross, John, i. 486.
—— Mary, wife of Richard Dalton, i. 486.
Brigstock of Birdcombe Court, William, M.P., viii. 135, 226; ix. 161.
—— Agnes Caroline, wife of F. T. Drummond, viii. 226.
—— Georgina Anne, wife of (1) F. G. Campbell of Troup, and (2) general John H. Elphinstone Dalrymple, viii. 135.
Brinkman, Gwynnedd, wife of major-gen. C. W. Campbell, ii. 196.
—— William Edward, R.N., ii. 196.
Briot, Esther, wife of Sir John Falconer, v. 248.
Brisbane of Bishoptoun, John, vii. 554; viii. 547.
—— —— his 2nd wife Jean Sempill, vii. 554.
—— —— John, ix. 38.
—— —— his wife, Marie Mure, ix. 38.
—— —— Thomas, vii. 530 *bis*.
—— —— his wife, Mary Sempill, vii. 530.
—— of Boghall, Matthew, viii. 547 *bis*.
—— of Brisbane, Thomas, ii. 598.
—— of Rosland or Rosline, Matthew, vi. 422, 427; viii. 547 *bis*.
—— —— his wife, Helen Napier, vi. 422.
Brisbane, Elizabeth, wife of William Fleming of Boghall, viii. 530.
—— Janet, wife of James Fleming of Boghall, viii. 574.
—— John, M.D., i. 550.
—— —— his wife, Helen Bruee, i. 550.
—— John, judge-advocate R.N., vi. 427.
—— —— his wife, Margaret, baroness Napier of Merchiston, vi. 427.
—— Maria, wife of George Cranstoun, ii. 598.
—— Dr. Matthew, tutor of 3rd marquess of Montrose, vi. 259.
—— Matthew, writer, Edinburgh, vi. 427.
—— Sara, wife of Sir Wm. Mure of Rowallan, ix. 38.
—— William, parson of Erskine, v. 421.
Bristol, John (Digby) 1st earl of, i. 407.
—— Frederick William John (Hervey), 3rd marquess of, viii. 226.
Bristowe of Quickenham Hall, John, v. 541.
—— Katharine, wife of gen. Simon Fraser, *de jure* 12th lord Lovat, v. 541.
Brittany, Alan II., count of, ii. 428.
—— Arthur II., duke of, i. 6.
—— —— his wife, Yolande de Dreux, i. 6.
—— Conan IV., duke of, i. 4.
—— —— his wife, Margaret of Northumberland, i. 4.
—— Francis I., duke of, ii. 326.
—— —— his 2nd wife, Elizabeth *or* Isabella Stewart, i. 19; ii. 326.
—— John VI., duke of, ii. 326.
Britten, Richard Frederick, admiral R.N., ii. 567.
—— —— his wife, Blanch Cecile Colville, ii. 567.
Broadbent of Kirkbarrow House, John, viii. 597.
—— —— his wife, Mary Katharine Seton, viii. 597.
Brodie of Arnhall, Alexander, M.P., iv. 558; viii. 510.
—— —— his wife, Elizabeth Margaret Wemyss, vii. 510.
Brodie of Brodie, Alexander, v. 475.
—— —— James, iv. 63; v. 475.
—— —— his wife, Mary Ker, v. 475.
—— of East Grange, Alexander, vii. 469.
—— of Lethen, Alexander, vii. 469, 476.
—— —— Janet, wife of Ludovic Grant of Grant, vii. 476, 477.
—— Anne, wife of 13th lord Forbes, iv. 63.
—— Elizabeth, wife of 5th duke of Gordon, iv. 558; viii. 510.
—— Elizabeth Bogue, wife of Jas. Augustus Erskine, v. 634.
—— George, historiographer-royal for Scotland, v. 634.
Brodrick, William St. John P., viii. 518.
—— —— his 1st wife, Hilda Charteris, viii. 518.

Brogan of Auchloun, Henry, viii. 269.
— Christian, wife of John of Allan, viii. 269.
Bromhead, Sir B. P., bart., ii. 58.
— Kathleen Gonville, wife of R. E. A. Hamilton, ii. 58.
Bromley, George, Middle Temple, vii. 102.
— — his wife, Elizabeth Barton, vii. 102.
Brook of Meltham Hall, William Leigh, viii. 230.
— Charlotte Emilia, wife of C. G. A. Drummond, viii. 230.
Brooke, Francis (Greville), 1st earl, iv. 167.
— — his wife, Elizabeth Hamilton, iv. 167.
— of Brookborough, Sir Henry, i. 45.
— Elizabeth, wife of Gustavus Hamilton, 1st viscount Boyne, i. 45.
Brooks, Sir William Cunliffe, bart., iv. 562.
— Amy, wife of Charles, 11th marquess of Huntly, iv. 562.
Broomhall, Robert Bruce, senator of the College of Justice, lord, iii. 488.
BROUGHTON, BELLENDEN, LORD BELLENDEN OF, ii. 61.
Broughton, John Cam (Hobhouse), lord, vii. 468.
— — his wife, Julian Thomasina Hay, viii. 468.
Broun of Colstoun, Charles, advocate, iii. 106.
— — Christian, wife of 9th earl of Dalhousie, iii. 106.
— — Sir George, iii. 76; ix. 63.
— — his wife, Elizabeth Mackenzie, iii. 76.
— — George, lord of Session, viii. 139, 144.
— — his wife, Elizabeth Dalrymple, viii. 139.
— — Patrick, iii. 96.
— — his wife, Elizabeth Ramsay, iii. 96.
— — Robert, ii. 41.
— — William Hamilton, *né* Briggs, iii. 107.
— — his wife, Susan Georgiana Ramsay, iii. 107.
— of Froisthill, viii. 445.
— Amy, wife of Henry de Winton, iv. 81.
— Anne, wife of Sir D. Dalrymple, lord Hailes, viii. 144.
— Elizabeth, wife of John Hamilton, ii. 41.
— Gilbert, abbot of Newabbey, iv. 414.
— John, minister at Glencairn, v. 109.
— Katharine, wife of William Oliphant of Gask, vi. 549.
— *, colonel, vii. 104.
— — his wife, Jacoba Katharina Graham, vii. 104.
Broune, Robert, Kilmarnock, v. 166.
— — his wife, Marion Sellar, v. 166.
Brounfield of Greenlawdene, Stephen, vi. 587.
— — his wife, Alisone Makgill, vi. 587.

* Name unknown.

Brown of Abscourt, Jeremiah, ii. 599.
— of Finmont, David, vi. 591.
— — his wife, Jean Makgill, vi. 591.
— — Robert, vi. 591.
— — his wife, Lilias Makgill, vi. 591.
— of Glen, Thomas, iii. 128.
— — his wife, * Maxwell, iii. 128.
— of Hartree, Andrew, viii. 540.
— Richard, viii. 540.
— — his wife, Janet Fleming, viii. 540.
— of Knockduff House, Arthur, lt.-col., ii. 418.
— of Priesthill, John, iii. 329.
— of Shawmill, John, vi. 95.
— of Elliestoun, George. iv. 499.
— of Fordell, John, vi. 95.
— — his 1st wife, Katharine Melville, vi. 95.
— — John, the younger, vi. 95, 549.
— — John, i. 518.
— — his 1st wife, Katharine Lindsay, i. 518; iii. 30.
— — Sir John, viii. 200.
— — his 1st wife, Isobel Murray, viii. 200.
— of Largs, Gilbert, v. 265.
— of Mollance, Samuel, v. 125.
— — his wife, Elizabeth Gordon, v. 125; ix. 119.
— — Samuel, v. 269.
— — his wife, Margaret Maclellan, v. 269.
— Andalusia, wife of 6th earl of Carnwath, ii. 418.
— Charles, rector of Whitestone, viii. 112.
— Christian, wife of Sir John Tufton, iii. 297.
— Mr. Daniel, ix. 109.
— David, watchmaker, Edinburgh, v. 536.
— — his wife, Katharine Fraser, v. 536.
— David, minister at Belhelvie, vii. 445.
— — his wife, Isabella Fraser, vii. 445.
— Elizabeth Anne Phippen, wife of lord Esmé Stuart Gordon, iv. 561.
— Florence, wife of John M. Lindsay, viii. 112.
— George, bishop of Dunkeld, vi. 390.
— Georgina, wife of col. Alexander Hope, G.C.B., iv. 499.
— Sir Humphrey, justice of the common pleas, iii. 297.
— Isobel, wife of (1) Sir P. Murray, and (2) Sir Geo. Erskine, v. 82; viii. 189.
— John, father of 1st duchess of Argyll and Greenwich, i. 376.
— John, minister of Glencairn, iv. 486.
— — his wife, Sara Hope, iv. 486.
— Katharine, wife of Wm. Colville, ii. 573.
— Magdalen, wife of 5th lord Kinnaird of Inchture, v. 211.

* Name unknown.

Brown, Mary, wife of duke of Argyll and Greenwich, i. 376.
— Richard, half-brother of Sir Alex. Ramsay of Dalhousie, iii. 90.
— Richard, London, v. 10.
— Mr. Richard, minister of Tynron, ix. 109.
— — his wife, Katherine Hope, iv. 486.
— Sophia, wife of (1) 6th lord Cranstoun, and (2) Michael Lade, ii. 599.
— Susan, wife of Sir Arthur Ingram, v. 10.
— Thomas, vicar of Caldorclere, vii. 325.
— William, Glastonbury, iv. 561.
— William, merchant, Edinburgh, v. 211.
— W. F., captain 6th Dragoons, viii. 130.
— — his wife, Margaret Martha Dalrymple, viii. 130.
— *, 2nd wife of Sir John Ogilvy of Craigs, i. 120.
Browne of the Neale, George, i. 51.
— — John, i. 51.
— — his wife, Anne Hamilton, i. 51.
— Anne, wife of Henry Fairfax of Hurst, ii. 275; ix. 49.
— Emilia Ann, wife of C. H. Lindsay, C.B., iii. 45.
— Henry Montague, dean of Lismore, iii. 45.
— John Edward Dean, ii. 502.
— — his wife, Aline Kennedy, ii. 502.
— John Francis Archibald, ii. 502.
— Sir Richard, ambassador to Paris, v. 24.
— Sir Thomas, author of *Religio Medici*, ii. 276.
Brownlow of Lurgan, William, i. 62.
— — his wife, Elizabeth Hamilton, i. 62.
— William Vesey, major-general, viii. 162.
— — his 1st wife, Anne Henrietta Dalrymple, viii. 162.
BROXMOUTH, KER, VISCOUNT OF, vii. 350-360.
Broxmouth, John, first viscount of, vii. 350.
BRUCE, BRUCE, BARON, ii. 435.
Bruce, Robert, baron, ii. 435.
BRUCE OF AMPTHILL, BRUCE, VISCOUNT, iii. 478-483.
Bruce of Ampthill, Robert, first viscount, iii. 478.
BRUCE OF KINLOSS, BRUCE, BARON, iii. 476-483.
Bruce of Kinloss, Edward, first baron, iii. 476, 483; ix. 82 *bis*.
— — his wife, Magdalen Clerk, iii. 476.
— — Edward, second baron, iii. 476, 477.
— — Thomas, third baron, iii. 477.
— — his 1st wife, Anne Chichester, iii. 478.
— — his 2nd wife, Diana Cecil, iii. 478.
BRUCE OF SKELTON, BRUCE, BARON, iii. 478-483.
Bruce of Skelton, Robert, first lord, iii. 478.

* Name unknown.

BRUCE OF TORRY, BRUCE, BARON, iii. 486-497.
Bruce of Torry, Edward, first baron, iii. 486.
— Charles, eldest son of 2nd earl of Kincardine; styled lord, iii. 487.
— — Edward James, eldest son of 9th earl of Elgin; styled lord, iii. 496; ix. 83.
— — George Charles Constantine, eldest son of 7th earl of Elgin; styled lord, iii. 493.
BRUCE OF TOTTENHAM, BRUCE, BARON, iii. 481-483.
Bruce of Tottenham, Charles, first baron, iii. 481.
— — Thomas, second baron, iii. 481, 483.
BRUCE OF WHORLTON, BRUCE, BARON, iii. 477-483.
Bruce of Whorlton, Charles, fourth baron, iii. 481.
— — Robert, second baron, iii. 478.
— — Thomas, first baron, iii. 477.
— — Thomas, third baron, iii. 479.
BRUCE, EARL OF AILESBURY, iii. 466-483.
BRUCE, LORD BALFOUR OF BURLEIGH, i. 554.
BRUCE, BARON BRUCE, ii. 435.
BRUCE, VISCOUNT BRUCE OF AMPTHILL, iii. 478-483.
BRUCE, BARON BRUCE OF KINLOSS, iii. 476-483.
BRUCE, BARON BRUCE OF SKELTON, iii. 478-483.
BRUCE, BARON BRUCE OF TORRY, iii. 486-497.
BRUCE, BARON BRUCE OF TOTTENHAM, iii. 481-483.
BRUCE, BARON BRUCE OF WHORLTON, iii. 477-483.
BRUCE, EARL OF CARRICK, ii. 428-437.
BRUCE, BARON ELGIN OF ELGIN, iii. 495-497.
BRUCE, EARL OF ELGIN, iii. 466-497.
BRUCE, LORD OF GALLOWAY, iv. 144.
BRUCE, EARL OF KINCARDINE, iii. 484-497.
BRUCE, BARON KINLOSS, iii. 475.
Bruce of Airth, Alexander, 2nd son of Sir Robert de Brus of Clackmannan; ancestor of the family of, iii. 469.
— — Sir Alexander, v. 437.
— — his wife, Janet Livingston, v. 437.
— — Sir Alexander, captain, i. 135; iii. 542; vii. 89.
— — Sir James, iii. 433.
— — his wife, Helen Montgomerie, iii. 433.
— — Jean *or* Jessie, wife of Richard Elphinstone of Elphinstone, iii. 534, 540.
— — Sir John, v. 187 *n*.
— — Sir John, iii. 540; vii. 89.
— — his wife, Margaret Elphinstone, iii. 540.
— — Sir Robert, v. 429.
— — his wife, Janet Livingston, v. 429.
— — Sir Robert v. 187.

Bruce of Airth, Robert, iii. 473.
—— —— his wife, Marion Bruce, iii. 473.
—— —— William, viii. 545.
—— —— his wife, Jean Fleming, viii. 545.
—— of Alva, Alexander, 2nd son of Sir George B. of Carnock, iii. 485, 488.
—— of Annandale. *See* Brus of Annandale.
—— of Auchenbowie, Alexander, ancestor of the family of, iii. 469.
—— —— Alexander, iv. 194.
—— —— his wife, Isobell Boyle, iv. 194.
—— —— John, iv. 194.
—— —— Robert, viii. 384.
—— —— his wife, Margaret Sandilands, viii. 384.
—— of Balcaskie, Robert, ancestor of the family of, iii. 474.
—— —— Sir William, vi. 379.
—— of Balchristie, James Carstairs, vii. 208.
—— —— his wife, Elizabeth Cecilia Rollo, vii. 208.
—— of Bangour, Alexander, ancestor of the family of, iii. 469.
—— of Bathertshiels, Thomas, v. 403.
—— of Benburb, Alexander, ancestor of the family of, iii. 469.
—— of Bergady, Edward, iii. 473.
—— of Birgham, Sir Alexander, vi. 278.
—— of Blairhall, Edward, 2nd son of Sir David B. of Clackmannan; 1st laird, iii. 472, 473, 484, 491.
—— —— his wife, Alison Reid, iii. 474.
—— —— John, 5th laird, ii. 297; v. 385.
—— —— his wife, Jean Leslie, v. 385.
—— —— Mary, wife of Dougal Stewart, ii. 297.
—— —— Robert, 2nd laird, ii. 550: iii. 474, 491; iv. 362; vii. 547; ix. 29.
—— —— his wife, Margaret *or* Jean Hamilton, iv. 362; vii. 547.
—— —— his wife, Jean Colville, ii. 550.
—— —— Robert, 3rd laird, iii. 489.
—— —— his wife, Katharine Preston, iii. 489.
—— —— Thomas, 4th laird, i. 142.
—— of Broomhall, Sir Alexander, M.P., iii. 488.
—— —— his wife, Christian Bruce, iii. 489.
—— —— Sir Robert, 3rd son of Sir George B. of Carnock, iii. 485, 488; v. 622.
—— —— his wife, Helen Skene, iii. 488; v. 622.
—— of Bunzeon, Frederick, vii. 388.
—— —— his wife, Anne Ruthven, vii. 205, 388.
—— of Canglour, Ninian, v. 188 *n.*
—— of Carnock, Sir George, 3rd son of Edward B. of Blairhall, ii. 557; iii. 474, 484, 487, 491.
—— —— his wife, Euphame Primrose, iii. 485; vii. 216; ix. 82.
Bruce of Carnock, Sir George, 2nd laird, iii. 485, 486; ix. 82, 83.
—— —— his wife, Mary Preston, iii. 486.
—— of Carrick, Christian, illeg. dau. of King Robert I., i. 8.
—— —— Nigel, illeg. son of King Robert I., i. 8.
—— of Clackmannan, Sir David, 4th laird, iii. 469.
—— —— his wife, Jean Stewart, iii. 469.
—— —— Sir David, 6th laird, iii. 470.
—— —— his 1st wife, Janet Stirling, iii. 470.
—— —— his 2nd wife, Mariota Herries, iii. 471.
—— —— Sir David, 7th laird, iii. 471, 538; viii. 166.
—— —— his wife, Jean Blacader, iii. 472.
—— —— David, 12th laird, iii. 76.
—— —— his wife, Margaret Mackenzie, iii. 76.
—— —— Sir Henry, 11th laird, iii. 100.
—— —— his 2nd wife, Anne Ramsay, iii. 100, 315.
—— —— Henry, 15th laird, iii. 472.
—— —— John, 5th laird, iii. 469, 470.
—— —— his wife, Elizabeth Stewart, iii. 470.
—— —— Sir Robert de, 2nd laird, iii. 467.
—— —— his wife, Isabel Stewart, iii. 468.
—— —— Sir Robert de, 3rd laird, iii. 468, 470.
—— —— his wife, * Scrymgeour, iii. 469.
—— —— Sir Robert, 8th laird, i. 465; iii. 472.
—— —— his 1st wife, Janet Levingstone, iii. 472.
—— —— his 2nd wife, Margaret Murray, i. 465.
—— —— Sir Robert, 10th laird, i. 303.
—— —— Thomas de, 1st laird, iii. 466, 467.
—— —— his wife, Marjorie Charteris, iii. 467.
—— of Classingallis, Alexander, vii. 41.
—— of Cothill and Collestoune, Edward, ix. 82.
—— —— William, iii. 474, 477, 491.
—— —— his wife, Margaret Cruickshank, ix. 82.
—— of Cowden, Margaret, wife of 6th earl of Airlie, i. 130; ix. 9.
—— —— William, i. 130.
—— of Crowany, Robert, eldest son of 1st lord Bruce of Kinloss, iii. 476.
—— of Culross, Edward, iii. 475.
—— —— his wife, Magdalen Clerk, iii. 475.
—— —— Sir George, 3rd son of Edward B. of Blairhall, iii. 484.
—— —— his wife, Euphame Primrose, iii. 485; vii. 216; ix. 82.
—— of Cultmalundie, Alexander, vi. 549, ix. 169.
—— —— his wife, Jean Oliphant, vi. 549.
—— —— John, iii. 531.
—— —— his wife, Euphemia Stewart, iii. 531.

* Name unknown.

Bruce of Cultmalundie, Laurence, iv. 283.
—— his wife, Elizabeth Gray, iv. 283.
—— Laurence, the younger, v. 504.
—— Robert, ancestor of the family of, iii. 470.
— of Dirleton and Belhaven, Mary, wife of R. A. Dundas, iii. 493.
— of Downhill, Alexander, ancestor of the family of, iii. 469.
—— Sir Henry, viii. 138.
— of Earlshall, Alexander, ancestor of the family of, iii. 469.
—— Sir Alexander, 1st laird, vi. 278.
—— Alexander, vii. 281, 288.
—— his 1st wife, Euphemia Leslie, vii. 281.
—— his 2nd wife, Janet Elphinstone, vii. 288.
—— Andrew, iv. 286.
—— his wife, Helen Gray, iv. 286.
—— Peter, iii. 309.
—— his wife, Agnes Scrymgeour, iii. 309.
—— Sir William, iii. 309.
— of Escariot, Sir Alexander, vi. 278.
— of Fingask, James, iii. 471.
—— Patrick, iii. 574; iv. 262.
—— his wife, Agnes Hay, iii. 574; ix. 87.
— of Garlet, Alexander, minister of Kirkurd, i. 549.
—— his wife, Margaret Cleland, i. 549.
—— Alexander, surgeon, i. 549.
—— his 1st wife, Grizel Laffrie, i. 549.
—— his 2nd wife, Ann Stewart, i. 549.
—— Robert, i. 548.
—— his wife, Agnes Murray, i. 548.
—— William, i. 549.
— of Garioch, Christian, wife of (1) Gartnet, 7th earl of Mar, (2) Sir C. Seton, and (3) Sir Andrew Moray, i. 432; ii. 128, 434; v. 579, 583; viii. 563.
— of Graysfortrie, John, ix. 135.
— of Green, David, 3rd son of Sir David B. of Clackmannan, i. 547; iii. 472, 473.
— of Ham, Sir David, ancestor of the family of, iii. 471.
—— Walter, ii. 348.
—— his wife, Janet Sinclair, ii. 348.
— of Hill, Patrick, 2nd son of Sir David B. of Clackmannan, iii. 470.
— of Jervaux, Edward, iii. 475.
— of Kendrick, Alexander, vii. 41.
— of Kennet, Alexander, general, 7th laird, i. 547, 552.
—— his wife, Mary Balfour, i. 547, 552.
—— Alexander, 9th laird, i. 553; ix. 33.
—— his wife, Hugh Blackburn, i. 553; ix. 33 *bis*.
—— David, 4th laird, i. 550; ix. 33.
—— his wife, Marjory Young, i. 550.
—— David, 5th laird, i. 551; ix. 33.
—— James, 6th laird, i. 551.
—— his wife, Mary Swinton, i. 551.
Bruce of Kennet, Robert de, son of Thomas de Bruys, iii. 468.
—— his wife, Isabel Stewart, iii. 468.
—— Robert, 3rd laird, i. 548.
—— his wife, Elizabeth Gaw, i. 548.
—— Robert, lord Kennet, 8th laird, i. 548.
—— his wife, Helen Abercromby, i. 553.
—— Robert, the claimant, 10th laird, i. 554.
—— his 1st wife, Anne Murray, i. 554.
—— his 2nd wife, Jane Dalrymple Hamilton Fergusson, i. 554.
— of Kennet Easter, Edward, iii. 473.
—— Sir Robert, i. 548.
— of Kennet Wester, John, eldest son of David B. of Wester Kennet, iii. 472.
—— Margaret, wife of Archibald B., i. 547.
—— Peter, son of Thomas de B., i. 547; iii. 470.
—— Robert, son of David B., i, 547; iii. 472.
—— Robert, i. 548.
—— his wife, Elizabeth Gaw, i. 548.
—— Thomas, illeg. son of Sir Robert de Brus of Clackmannan, iii. 468, 469 *bis*, 470.
— of Kincavel, Alexander, ancestor of the family of, iii. 469.
— of Kinloss, Edward, 2nd son of Edward B. of Blairhall, iii. 474.
—— his wife, Magdalen Clerk, iii. 476.
— of Kinnaird, Alexander, ancestor of the family of, iii. 469.
—— David, ii. 50.
—— Elma, wife of Thomas John, 4th lord Thurlow, iii. 495.
—— Mary Elizabeth, wife of major C. L. Cumming of Dunphail, iii. 495.
—— Ninian, v. 188.
—— his wife, Margaret Livingston, v. 188.
—— Robert, iii. 539.
— of Kinross, Sir John, vii. 302.
—— his wife, Christian Leslie, vii. 301.
—— Robert, ancestor of the family of, iii. 474.
—— Sir William, vi. 261, 379.
— of Lethbertshiells, Alexander, ancestor of the family of, iii. 469.
— of Leuchars, Sir Alexander, 1st laird, vi. 278.
— of Livilands, Ninian, v. 188 *n.*
— of Longforgan, Agnes, wife of Sir Robt. de Ramsay, viii. 264.
— of Lynmylne, Robert, 4th son of Sir David B. of Clackmannan, iii. 472.
— of Muness, Robert, ancestor of the family of, iii. 470.
— of Newtoun, Alexander, ancestor of the family of, iii. 469.

Bruce of Pickering, Pagan, ancestor of the family of, ii. 429.
— of Pitkanye, Robert, eldest son of 1st lord Bruce of Kinloss, iii. 476.
— of Powfoulis, Alexander, ancestor of the family of, iii. 469.
— — Andrew, vi. 412 *bis*.
— — his wife, Janet Napier, vi. 412.
— — Archibald, vi. 413.
— — his wife, Marion Napier, vi. 413.
— — Sir James, vii. 195.
— — his wife, Marion Rollo, vii. 195.
— — James, iii. 340 *n*.
— — James, 7th laird, i. 552.
— of Rait, Sir David, 3rd laird, iii. 468, 469.
— — his wife, Jean Stewart, iii. 469.
— — Sir David, 5th laird, iii. 470 *bis*.
— — his wife, Janet Keir, iii. 470.
— — David, 7th laird, iii. 471, 472.
— — James, 8th laird, iii. 471.
— — John, 4th laird, iii. 470.
— — his wife, Elizabeth Stewart, iii. 470.
— — Sir Robert, 1st laird, iii. 468.
— — his wife, Isabel Stewart, iii. 468.
— — Sir Robert, 2nd laird, iii. 468.
— — his wife, * Scrymgeour, iii. 469.
— — Robert, 6th laird, iii. 470.
— — his wife, Elizabeth Lindsay, iii. 471.
— of Sands, Sir George, iii. 484.
— of Stanstill, Sir David, ancestor of the family of, iii. 471.
— — William, ii. 348.
— — William, ii. 348.
— — his wife, Elspeth Sinclair, ii. 348.
— of Stenhouse, Alexander, 2nd son of Sir Robert de Brus of Clackmannan, iii. 469.
— — Sir John, v. 187 *n*.
— of Symbister, William, ii. 170.
— — his wife, Margaret Stewart, ii. 169.
— of Valleyfield, Patrick, 5th son of Sir David B. of Clackmannan, iii. 473.
— of Waltoun, Alexander, ancestor of the family of, iii. 469.
— — Peter de, iii. 595.
— of Whorlton, Edward, iii. 475.
— in Sweden, Robert, ancestor of the family of, iii. 472.
— Adam, ancestor of the Comtes de Bruce, iii. 469.
— Agnes, wife of Jasper Smyth, i. 548.
— Agnes, wife of Mr. John Elphinstone, iii. 473, 532.
— Agnes, alleged wife of 4th lord Sinclair, vii. 573; ix. 157.
— Agnes, wife of John Murray of Drumphin, ix. 29.
— Alexander, son of Edward, earl of Carrick, i. 428.
— Alexander, dean of Glasgow, brother of King Robert I., ii. 433.

* Name unkoown.

Bruce, Alexander, alleged 3rd husband of Isobel Bruce, ii. 434.
— Alexander, 3rd son of Sir David B. of Clackmannan, iii. 471.
— Alexander, 2nd son of Robert B. of Rait, iii. 471.
— Alexander, 3rd son of 9th earl of Elgin, iii. 496; ix. 83.
— Alexander, inf. son of 2nd earl of Kincardine, ix. 83.
— Alison, wife of Geo. Dundas, i. 552.
— Alison, wife of Sir Jas. Colville of Ochiltree, ii. 547; iii. 473.
— Andrew, cadet of Earlshall, ii. 46.
— Annabella, wife of John Forbes, i. 552.
— Anne, dau. of Robt. B., Edinburgh, i. 550.
— Anne, wife of 3rd lord Belhaven, ii. 46; ix. 37 *bis*.
— Anne, wife of Sir Wm. Rich, iii. 479.
— Anne, wife of Sir James Arnot, iii. 485.
— Anne, wife of Sir David Murray of Stanhope, iii. 487.
— Anne Charlotte, wife of Sir Nicholas Bagenal, iii. 479.
— Arabella, dau. of 2nd earl of Elgin, iii. 479.
— Archibald, son of David B. of Green, i. 547.
— — his 1st wife, Margaret Bruce of Wester Kennet, i. 547.
— — his 2nd wife, Grizel Forrester, i. 548.
— Archibald, 2nd son of above Archibald, i. 548.
— Augusta Frederica Elizabeth, wife of dean Stanley, iii. 494.
— Augusta Mary, dau. of Thomas Charles B., iii. 494.
— Bessie, wife of David Bar, iii. 474.
— Brudenell, lieut. 3rd regiment of Guards, iii. 492.
— Burnett, son of lord Kennet, i. 553.
— Charles, lieut. in brigadier Maitland's regt., i. 551.
— Charles, 3rd son of 8th earl of Elgin, iii. 495.
— Charles, 2nd son of Frederick John B., iii. 496.
— Charles Andrew, judge in India, Governor of Prince of Wales Island, iii. 491.
— — his 1st wife, Anne Maria Blunt, iii. 492.
— — his 2nd wife, Charlotte Sophia Dashwood, iii. 492.
— Charles Dashwood, *afterwards* Preston, iii. 492.
— — his wife, Harriet Elizabeth Rivers, iii. 492.
— Charles Martha, wife of admiral Sir P. C. Durham, iii. 492.

Bruce, Charles Thomas, iii. 494.
— Charlotte Christian, wife of F. Locker, iii. 494.
— Charlotte Matilda, wife of admiral Sir P. C. Durham, iii. 492.
— Christian, wife of (1) Gratney, earl of Mar, (2) Sir Christopher Seton, and (3) Sir A. Moray of Bothwell, i. 432; ii. 128, 434; v. 579, 583; viii. 563.
— Christian, dau. of Robt. B., Edinburgh, i. 550.
— Christian, wife of (1) Robert, master of Colville, and (2) Sir Laurence Mercer of Aldie, ii. 557, 558; iii. 485; ix. 59, 82.
— Christian, alleged wife of Patrick, 7th earl of Dunbar, iii. 259.
— Christian, wife of Sir James Shaw of Sauchie, iii. 471.
— Christian, wife of (1) John Rolle, and (2) Sir Richard Gayer, iii. 479.
— Christian, wife of Alexander, 4th earl of Kincardine, iii. 489.
— Christian, dau. of 4th earl of Kincardine, iii. 489.
— Christian, dau. of 7th earl of Kincardine, iii. 490.
— Christian, wife of Jas. Erskine of Cardross, iii. 491.
— Christian, wife of James Carnegie of Balmachie, viii. 54.
— Christian Augusta, wife of H. K. Ogilvy, iii. 496.
— Christiana, wife of William, 2nd earl of Devonshire, iii. 477.
— Constance Veronica, iii. 496.
— Cornelius, two inf. sons of 2nd earl of Kincardine, ix. 83.
— David, son of Peter B., i. 547.
— David, son of Alex. B. of Garlet, i. 549.
— David, 4th son of 9th earl of Elgin, iii. 496.
— Diana, wife of (1) Sir Seymour Shirley, and (2) John, lord de Ros, iii. 479; ix. 82.
— Dorothea, wife of Jas. Sinclair, ii. 354.
— Edward de, brother of King Robert I., i. 428; ii. 433, 435; iii. 467; v. 35.
— — his alleged wife, Isabel of Atholl, i. 427; ii. 436.
— Edward, eldest son of 2nd earl of Elgin, iii. 478.
— Edward, 6th son of 7th earl of Elgin, iii. 494.
— Edward Jackson, captain R.A., viii. 138.
— — his wife, Ellen Arbuthnott Dalrymple, viii. 138.
— Elizabeth, wife of Sir W. Oliphant of Aberdalgie, i. 8; vi. 537.
— Elizabeth, wife of col. Wm. Bruce, i. 550.
— Elizabeth, wife of (1) Alex. Dundas, and (2) Robert Colless, iii. 473.
Bruce, Elizabeth, wife of Benjamin Bathurst, iii. 480.
— Elizabeth, wife of George, earl of Cardigan, iii. 480, 481.
— Elizabeth, wife of Jas. Boswell of Auchinleck, iii. 487.
— Elizabeth, wife of Simon Mackenzie of Lochslinn, vii. 505.
— Elizabeth Marjorie, wife of col. A. G. A. Durand, iii. 494.
— Elizabeth Mary, wife of H. Babington Smith, iii. 496.
— Frances Anne, wife of Evan P. M. Baillie, iii. 494.
— Francis, son of Patrick B. of Fingask, iv. 262.
— — his wife, Cecilia Ruthven, iv. 262.
— Frederick John, 4th son of 8th earl of Elgin, iii. 495.
— — his wife, Katharine Bruce Fernie, iii. 495.
— Sir Frederick William Adolphus, envoy to China, and U.S.A., G.C.B., iii. 494.
— George, major, son of Sir Robt. B. of Clackmannan, i. 303.
— George, son of Robt. B. of Kennet, i. 550.
— George, son of David B. of Kennet, i. 551.
— George, rector of Wath, iii. 488; ix. 83.
— — his wife Agnes Allan, iii. 488.
— George Abercrombie, i. 553.
— George John Gordon, i. 555.
— Grisel, wife of Sir Robt. Arnot of Fernie, ix. 82.
— Harrie, son of Robt. B. of Kennet, i. 550.
— Harriet Mary, i. 554.
— Harry, colonel, iv. 127.
— Helen, wife of John Arbuthnott of Fiddes, i. 303.
— Helen, wife of John Brisbane, i. 550.
— Helen, wife of lord Handyside, i. 554.
— Helen, wife of Alex. Cochrane of Barbachlaw, iii. 340 *n.*
— Helen, wife of Sir Geo. Weir of Blackwood, iii. 488; ix. 83.
— Helen, dau. of 4th earl of Kincardine, iii. 489.
— Helen, wife of (1) George, 7th earl of Erroll, and (2) Patrick Cheyne, iii. 569.
— Helen, wife of Robert Keith, vi. 135.
— Helen, wife of (1) Robt. Moray, and (2) Malcolm Fleming, ix. 169.
— Henrietta, wife of Thos. Ogle, iii. 479.
— Henrietta Anne, wife of Claud Hamilton, i. 554.
— Henry, Comrie, i. 550.
— — his wife, Mary Bruce, i. 550.
— Henry, son of David B. of Kennet, i. 551.

Bruce, Henry, captain R.N., viii. 138.
—— —— his wife, Mary Minchin Dalrymple, viii. 138.
—— Hugh, advocate, i. 553.
—— Isabel, wife of Eric Magnusson, King of Norway, i. 6; ii. 432, 433; vi. 290.
—— Isobel, dau. of Robert B., Edinburgh, i. 550.
—— Isobella de, wife of John Fitzmarmaduke, ii. 432 *n.*
—— Isabella, wife of James Elphinstone, iii. 528.
—— James, judge at Barbados, i. 549.
—— James, son of Robert. B., Edinburgh, i. 550.
—— James, master of the mint, i. 552.
—— —— his wife, Mary Cross, i. 552.
—— James, son of Mr. John B., i. 552.
—— James, 3rd son of Alex. B. of Kennet, i. 552.
—— James, son of lord Kennet, i. 553.
—— James, bishop of Dunkeld, and of Glasgow, chancellor of Scotland, iii. 59, 468.
—— James, in holy orders, 2nd son of 8th earl of Kincardine, iii. 490.
—— James, M.P., 5th son of 5th earl of Elgin, iii. 492.
—— James, 3rd son of F. J. B., iii. 496.
—— James, v. 403.
—— —— his wife, Margaret Lindsay, v. 403.
—— James, vii. 197.
—— —— his wife, Marion Rollo, vii. 197.
—— Jane, wife of John Edgar, i. 552.
—— Jane Hamilton, dau. of 10th lord Balfour of Burleigh, i. 555.
—— Janet, wife of Thomas Dalziel of Binns, ii. 405; iii. 477; ix. 53.
—— Janet, wife of Sir Thos. Burnett of Crimond, iii. 488, 490; ix. 83.
—— Janet, dau. of Alexander, 4th earl of Kincardine, iii. 489.
—— Janet, wife of (1) major-gen. W. Baillie of Lethame, and (2) Sir R. Nasmyth of Posso, iv. 93.
—— Janet, wife of William Livingston of Kilsyth, v. 187, 188.
—— Janet Elizabeth, dau. of F. J. B., iii. 496.
—— Jean, wife of Mr. John B., Airth, i. 552.
—— Jean, her daughter, i. 552.
—— Jean, wife of Sir Thos. Burnett, iii. 488, 490.
—— Jean, wife of John Napier of Kilmahew, iii. 490.
—— Jean, wife of major David Colyear, *alias* Robertson, vii. 89.
—— John, inf. son of King Robert I., i. 8.
—— John, minister of Airth, i. 552.
—— —— his wife, Jean Bruce, i. 552.
—— John, his 2nd son, i. 552.
—— John, eldest son of Sir David B. of Clackmannan, iii. 472.
Bruce, John Bernard, 5th son of 9th earl of Elgin, iii. 496.
—— Katharine, wife of 2nd earl of Airth and Menteith, i. 142; ix. 9.
—— Katharine, wife of William, 1st earl of Dysart, iii. 402, 404.
—— Katharine, dau. of F. J. B., iii. 496.
—— Laurence Dundas, son of lord Kennet, i. 553.
—— Laurence Dundas, R.N., i. 553; ix. 33.
—— Lewis, eldest son of F. J. B., iii. 496.
—— Louisa, wife of Sir W. R. P. Geary, iii. 492.
—— Louisa Elizabeth, dau. of 8th earl of Elgin, iii. 496.
—— Louisa Keith, wife of T. H. W. Pelham, i. 554.
—— Lucy, wife of John Grant of Kilgraston, iii. 493.
—— Lucy, dau. of 2nd earl of Kincardine, ix. 83.
—— Magdalen, wife of Sir John Erskine of Balgonie, iii. 485.
—— Magdalen, wife of Sir Jas. Nicolson of Cockburnspath, iii. 486; ix. 82, 83.
—— Margaret, wife of William, 5th earl of Sutherland, i. 8; viii. 326, 327.
—— Margaret, wife of Robert Glen, i. 8.
—— Margaret, wife of Walter Watson, i. 553; ix. 33.
—— Margaret, dau. of Alex. B. of Kennet, i. 554.
—— Margaret, dau. of Robt. B. of W. Kennet, i. 548.
—— Margaret, dau. of Alex. B. of Garlet, i. 549.
—— Margaret, dau. of Robt. B., Edinburgh, i. 550.
—— Margaret, dau. of Robt. B. of Kennet, i. 550.
—— Margaret, wife of * Nelson of Kilcathie, i. 551.
—— Margaret, wife of Sir L. Dundas, i. 552; ix. 33.
—— Margaret, wife of Sir William de Carlyle, ii. 379, 435.
—— Margaret, dau. of Sir David B. of Clackmannan, iii. 471.
—— Margaret, dau. of Edward B. of Blairhall, iii. 474.
—— Margaret, wife of Francis Nicolls, iii. 485.
—— Margaret, wife of Sir John Lumsden, iii. 486.
—— Margaret, wife of rev. Cuthbert Creighton, iii. 496.
—— Margaret, dau. of Robt. B. of Broomhall, ix. 83.
—— Marie Theresa Charlotte, wife of Maximilian, prince de Hornes, iii. 481.
—— Marion, dau. of Alex. B. of Garlet, i. 549.

* Name unknown.

Bruce, Marion, *error for* Christian, wife of Robert, master of Colville, ii. 557 *n.*
— Marion, wife of (1) John Menteith, (2) Robert Bruce, and (3) Magnus Sinclair, iii. 473; vii. 573.
— Marion, dau. of F. J. B., iii. 496.
— Marjorie, wife of Walter, 6th High Steward of Scotland, i. 8, 9, 14; v. 578; vii. 234, 526 *n.*, 527.
— Marjory, dau. of Robt. B. of W. Kennet, i. 548.
— Marjorie, dau. of 9th earl of Elgin, iii. 496.
— Mary, wife of (1) Sir Neil Campbell of Lochow, and (2) Sir Alex. Fraser of Cowie and Touch Fraser, i. 323; ii. 434; vii. 428.
— Mary, wife of 3rd duke of Richmond and Lennox, i. 385; iii. 482; v. 365.
— Mary, wife of Wm. Lumsden, i. 550.
— Mary, wife of Henry B., i. 550.
— Mary, wife of William Young, i. 551.
— Mary, dau. of James B. of Kennet, i. 552.
— Mary, dau. of lord Kennet, i. 553.
— Mary, wife of major Hope of Pinkie, i. 555.
— Mary, wife of 2nd lord Cardross, ii. 366; iii. 486; ix. 52 *bis.*
— Mary, wife of William Cochrane of Ochiltree, iii. 348, 487 *bis.*, 488.
— Mary, wife of Sir William Walter, iii. 479.
— Mary, wife of Henry, marquess of Carnarvon, iii. 482; v. 199.
— Mary, dau. of 4th earl of Kincardine, iii. 489.
— Mary, wife of Michael Elphinstone of Quarrell, iii. 539.
— Matilda, *otherwise* Margaret, dau. of King Robert I., i. 8; viii. 326 *n.*
— Matilda, wife of Thomas Isaac, i. 8.
— Matilda, wife of Hugh, earl of Ross, ii. 435; vii. 236.
— Matilda Harriet, wife of Sir John Maxwell of Pollok, iii. 493.
— Maud, wife of Hugh, 4th earl of Ross, ii. 435; vii. 236.
— Nicola, wife of (1) Sir John Morrison, and (2) John Dick of Braid, iii. 485.
— Nicholas, son of Robt. B. of Kennet, i. 550.
— Sir Nigel or Neil, brother of Robert I., ii. 433.
— Norman, son of Archd. B., i. 548.
— Norman, colonel, son of Sir Robt. B. of Clackmannan, iii. 402.
— Peter, son of Thomas B., i. 547.
— Peter, D.D., principal of St. Leonard's College, vii. 505.
— Rachel, wife of John Cleland, i. 549.
— Rachel, wife of John Milner, iii. 482.
— Rachel, dau. of Robt. B. of Broomhall, iii. 488; ix. 83.
Bruce, Rachel, wife of Jas. Drummond of Lundin, 13th lord Drummond, iii. 490; vii. 57.
— Rachel, dau. of 8th earl of Kincardine, iii. 491.
— Rachel Catherine, dau. of 9th earl of Elgin, iii. 496.
— Ralph, lieut.-col., son of lord Kennet, i. 553.
— Richard Frederick David, ix. 83.
— Sir Robert, illeg. son of King Robert I., alleged to have been created earl of Mar, i. 8; iii. 466.
— Robert, merchant, Edinburgh, i. 550.
— — his wife, Isobel Paterson, i. 550.
— Robert, their eldest son, i. 550.
— Robert, officer in the army, i. 551.
— Robert, 2nd son of lord Kennet, i. 553.
— Robert, master of Burleigh, i. 555.
— Mr. Robert, minister of Edinburgh, ii. 82; v. 456.
— Robert, major-gen., governor to Albert Edward, prince of Wales, iii. 493.
— — his wife, Katharine Mary Shaw-Stewart, iii. 493.
— Robert, 2nd son of John B. of Clackmannan, iii. 470.
— Robert, M.P., son of 4th earl of Elgin, iii. 482.
— — his wife, Frances Blackett, iii. 482.
— Robert, 2nd son of 9th earl of Elgin, iii. 496.
— Robert, vi. 412.
— — his wife, Janet Napier, vi. 412.
— Robert Arthur, iii. 494.
— Robert Dalrymple Barwick, capt. R.N., i. 550.
— Sarah, dau. of 7th earl of Kincardine, iii. 490.
— Thomas, son of Sir Robt. B., 3rd of Clackmannan, i. 547.
— Thomas, 5th son of lord Kennet, i. 553.
— — his wife, Margaret Ramsay, i. 553.
— Sir Thomas de, brother of King Robert I., ii. 433.
— — his alleged wife, Helen Erskine, v. 591.
— Thomas, in holy orders, 2nd son of 7th earl of Kincardine, iii. 490.
— Thomas, lieut.-general, A.D.C., M.P., 3rd son of 8th earl of Kincardine, iii. 490.
— Thomas, cordiner, Edinburgh, v. 462.
— Thomas Charles, M.P., 7th son of 7th earl of Elgin, iii. 494.
— — his wife, Sarah Caroline Thornhill, iii. 494.
— Veronica, wife of (1) Gustavus Hamilton, and (2) Duncan Campbell of Kames, iii. 489.
— Victor Alexander, 6th son of 9th earl of Elgin, iii. 496.

Bruce, Victoria Alexandrina Katharine, dau. of 10th lord Balfour of Burleigh, i. 555.
— William, 3rd son of Robt. B., i. 550.
— — 8th son of Robt. B. of Kennet, i. 550.
— William, lieut.-col., i. 550.
— — his wife, Elizabeth Bruce, i. 550.
— William, son of Alex. B. of Kennet, i. 553.
— — his wife, Louisa Hill, i. 553.
— William Downing, i. 547 *n.*, 550.
— William Henry, R.N., i. 552.
— *see also* Brus.
Bruce-Hope of Kinross, Sir John, iv. 490.
Bruce-Ogilvy, Donald, i. 131.
— James, lieut. R.A., i. 131.
— John, i. 131.
— William Henry, lieut. 26th Foot, i. 130.
— — his wife, Sarah Boyder, i. 130.
Brudenell, Francis (Brudenell), styled lord, i. 32; v. 363; vi. 453.
— Robert (Brudenell), 2nd baron, iii. 297, 299.
— — his 1st wife, Mary Constable, iii. 297.
— — his 2nd wife, Anne Rivers, iii. 299.
— Thomas (Brudenell), 1st baron, iii. 298.
— — his wife, Mary Tresham, iii. 298.
— of Raans, Edmund, vi. 462.
— Anne, wife of (1) Henry, 2nd lord Belasyse, and (2) Charles, 1st duke of Lennox, i. 32; v. 363.
— Dorothy, wife of (1) Charles Fane, 3rd earl of Westmoreland, and (2) Robert, 3rd viscount Dunbar, iii. 299.
— Elizabeth, wife of (1) John Cheyne of Chesham Bois, and (2) John Tyringham, vi. 462.
— Frances, wife of (1) Charles, 2nd lord Newburgh, and (2) Richard, 3rd lord Bellew of Duleek, vi. 453.
— Katharine, wife of 2nd earl of Middleton, vi. 187.
— Mary, wife of 4th earl of Kinnoull, iii. 297; v. 228.
— Mary, wife of (1) 2nd viscount Dunbar, and (2) John Dalton of Swine, iii. 298; ix. 72.
— Thomas Bruce, 4th son of George, 3rd earl of Cardigan, iii. 481, 483.
Bruhl von Martinskirk, Hans Maurice, count, vii. 84.
— — his wife, Alice Maria (Wyndham), countess of Egremont, vii. 84.
— Harriet, wife of Hugh Hepburne-Scott of Harden, vii. 84.
Brumaigne, Anne Catherine de, wife of gen. Walter Philip Colyear, vii. 91.
Brumath, Maria Anastasia von, wife of George Benedict Ogilvy von Muirton, i. 121.
Brunswick-Lüneburg, Ernest Augustus, duke of, i. 28.
— — his wife, Sophia of Great Britain, i. 28.
— George, duke of, i. 28.
Bruntfield, Adam, iv. 580.
— Stephen, iv. 580.
Brus, comte de, iii. 468 *n.*, 469.
— of Annandale, Robert, ii. 428.
— — his wife, Agnes de Paganell, ii. 429.
— Robert 'le meschin,' ii. 372, 429.
— — his wife, Euphemia, ii. 430.
— — Robert, 'the noble,' i. 231; ii. 376, 430.
— — his wife, Isabel of Huntingdon, i. 4; ii. 430.
— — Robert, the Competitor, ii. 430; iii. 466; vii. 267.
— — his 1st wife, Isabel de Clare, ii. 431; ix. 55.
— — his 2nd wife, Christiana de Ireby, ii. 373, 432.
— — Robert, earl of Carrick, ii. 426, 432.
— — his 1st wife, Marjorie of Carrick, ii. 426, 432.
— — his 2nd wife, Alianora *, ii. 433.
— — Robert, King of Scotland, i. 6, 7, 509; ii. 433; iii. 139, 145; vii. 234; viii. 248.
— — William de, i. 230, 231; ii. 374, 381, 430; iii. 253.
— — his wife, Christina, ii. 430; iii. 253.
— of Connington and Exton, Sir Bernard de, ii. 431.
— — his 1st wife, Alicia de Clare, ii. 431.
— — his 2nd wife, Constance de Morleyn, ii. 431.
— of Garioch, Christiana de, wife of (1) Gartney, earl of Mar, (2) Sir Christopher de Seton, and (3) Sir Andrew Moray, i. 432; ii. 128, 434; v. 579, 583; viii. 563.
— of Skelton and Cleveland, Adelm *or* Adam de, ii. 428.
— — his alleged wife, Emma de Ramsay, ii. 428.
— — Adam, his grandson, ii. 429.
— — Robert de, ii. 428.
— — his wife, Agnes de Paganell, ii. 429.
— Agatha de, wife of Ralph de Middleham, ii. 429.
— Agnes de, wife of William de Lancaster, iii. 4.
— Aloysia de, wife of Sir N. Graham, ii. 432 *n.*
— Beatrice de, wife of Hugo de Neville, ii. 430.
— Edward de, brother of Robert I., i. 428; ii. 433, 435; iii. 467; v. 35.
— James de, bishop of Dunkeld, chancellor of Scotland, iii. 468.
— John de, 3rd son of Wm. de Brus, ii. 430.

* Name unknown.

Brus, John, alleged son of the Competitor, ii. 432 *n.*
— John de, 4th son of Robert de B., 5th lord of Annandale, iii. 466.
— Pagan de, ii. 429.
— Peter de, iii. 4.
— — his wife, Helewise de Lancaster, iii. 4.
— Richard de, ii. 432.
— Robert de, Normandy, ii. 428.
— — his wife, Emma of Brittany, ii. 428.
— Robert de, eldest son of Robert de B., 'le meschin,' ii. 430.
— — his wife, Isabel, i. 5; ii. 430.
— William de, prior of Gisburne, ii. 428.
— William de, son of Wm. de B., ii. 430.
— William de, son of Robert the Competitor, ii. 431.
— — his wife, Elizabeth de Sully, ii. 431.
Bryant, Emily, wife of A. L. Tollemache, iii. 416.
— Sir Jeremiah, major-gen., C.B., iii. 416.
Bryante, Pierre de Clovis, seigneur de, viii. 584.
— — his wife, Marie Pieris, viii. 584.
Bryce, the procurator, vii. 30 *n.*, 34.
BRYDGES, BARON KINLOSS, v. 199-201.
Brydges, Caroline, wife of John Leigh of Addlestrop, v. 199.
Bryson of Pitcullen, Patrick, v. 220.
— — Helen, wife of (1) George, 7th earl of Erroll, and (2) Patrick Cheyne, iii. 569; ix. 86.
— — Walter, iii. 569.
— Isabel, wife of Patrick Hay of Megginch, v. 220.
BUCCLEUCH, SCOTT, EARL OF, ii. 234-249.
Buccleuch, Anna, wife of James, duke of Monmouth; countess of, i. 30; ii. 237; iii. 111; v. 379; ix. 46 *ter.*
— Francis, second earl of, ii. 233, 235; vii. 76; ix. 46.
— — his wife, Margaret Leslie, ii. 236; vii. 299.
— James, fifth earl of, ii. 237.
— — his wife, Anna, countess of Buccleugh, ii. 237.
— Mary, wife of Walter (Scott), earl of Tarras; countess of, ii. 236; v. 475; vii. 80.
— Walter, first earl of, ii. 171, 233; iii. 577.
— — his wife, Mary Hay, ii. 234.
BUCCLEUGH, SCOTT, DUKE OF, ii. 225-249.
Buccleuch, Anna, wife of (1) James, duke of Buccleuch and Monmouth, and (2) Charles, 3rd baron Cornwallis; duchess of, ii. 237, 283; iii. 111; ix. 46 *ter.*
— Charles William Henry, fourth duke of, ii. 244.
— — his wife, Harriet Katharine Townshend, ii. 244.
Buccleuch, Francis, second duke of, ii. 240.
— — his 1st wife, Jane Douglas, ii. 241; vii. 143.
— — his 2nd wife, Alice Powell, ii. 241.
— Henry, third duke of, ii. 242; vii. 143.
— — his wife, Elizabeth Montagu, ii. 243.
— James, first duke of, i. 30; ii. 237.
— — his wife, Anna, duchess of Buccleuch, ii. 237.
— Walter Frances, fifth duke of, ii. 245.
— — his wife, Charlotte Anne Thynne, ii. 245.
— William Henry Walter, sixth duke of, ii. 247.
— — his wife, Louisa Jane Hamilton, i. 71; ii. 247.
BUCCLEUCH, SCOTT, LORD SCOTT OF, ii. 233.
Buccleuch, Walter, first lord Scott of, ii. 233.
— Walter, second lord Scott of, ii. 233.
— master of, Walter, son of 1st lord Scott of Buccleuch, ii. 233; iii. 576.
BUCHAN, ANCIENT EARLS OF, ii. 250-252.
Buchan, Colban, *jure uxoris* earl of, ii. 251.
— Eva, wife of Colban; countess of, ii. 251.
— Fergus, earl of, ii. 251.
— Gartnach, mormaer and earl of, ii. 250; v. 567.
— — his wife, Ete, ii. 251; iv. 5.
— Marjory *or* Margaret, wife of William Comyn; countess of, i. 505; ii. 252, 257 *n.*
— Roger, earl of, ii. 251.
BUCHAN, COMYN, EARL OF, ii. 252-261.
Buchan, Alexander, earl of, i. 419 *n.*, 423, 451 *n.*; ii. 218, 254, 257 *n.*; iii. 263; iv. 42 *n.*; viii. 245 *n.*
— — his wife Elizabeth, Isabella, *or* Marjory de Quincy, ii. 254; iv. 142.
— Alicia, wife of Henry de Beaumont; countess of ii. 256, 258.
— Henry de Beaumont, *jure uxoris* earl of, i. 432; ii. 259; vi. 295; viii. 253, 566.
— John, earl of, ii. 256; iv. 43 *n.*; v. 99; vi. 531; viii. 250, 520.
— — his wife, Isabella of Fife, ii. 258; iv. 11.
— Margaret, wife of (1) Sir John Ross, and (2) Sir Wm. Lindsay; countess of, ii. 256, 260; iii. 9; vii. 235.
— William, *jure uxoris* earl of, i. 156, 505; ii. 252; iii. 558.
— — his wife, Marjory *or* Margaret of Buchan, ii. 252.
— William, 4th son of Alexander, earl of Buchan; self-styled earl of, ii. 256.
BUCHAN, STEWART, EARL OF, ii. 262-265.
Buchan, Alexander, 4th son of King Robert II.; first earl of, i. 16; ii. 261, 262; vi. 299; vii. 241; viii. 329, 481.
— — his wife, Euphemia, countess of Ross, ii. 262; vii. 239.

Buchan, John, Constable of France, third earl of, i. 146, 148; ii. 264; iii. 167, 168; iv. 47, 48; v. 41; vi. 38; vii. 114, 243; viii. 576.
—— —— his wife, Elizabeth Douglas, ii. 265; iii. 167.
—— Mary, dau. of King James I., wife of Wolfart van Borselen; styled countess of, i. 19; ii. 265 *n.*
—— Robert, Regent of Scotland, earl of, ii. 263.
BUCHAN, STEWART, EARL OF, ii. 266-270.
Buchan, Alexander, second earl of, ii. 267.
—— —— his 1st wife, Isobel Ogilvy, ii. 267, 268.
—— —— his 2nd wife, Margaret Ruthven, ii. 268; iv. 259.
—— Christina, wife of Robert Douglas; countess of, ii. 10, 269; vi. 316; ix. 47, 48 *bis.*
—— James, 2nd son of Black Knight of Lorn; first earl of, i. 22, 109, 441; ii. 156, 266; iii. 65; ix. 47 *bis.*
—— —— his wife, Margaret Ogilvie of Banff, i. 109; ii. 266.
—— John, third earl of, ii. 268; iv. 101; ix. 47.
—— —— his wife, Margaret Scrymgeour, ii. 268; iii. 308.
BUCHAN, DOUGLAS, EARL OF, ii. 269-272.
Buchan, James, earl of, ii. 270, 271; ix. 48.
—— —— his wife, Anne Ogilvy, ii. 271; iv. 27; ix. 48.
—— Mary, wife of James Erskine; countess of, ii. 271; ix. 48 *quat.*
—— Robert, 2nd son of Sir Robert Douglas of Lochleven; *jure uxoris* earl of, ii. 10, 269; vi. 370.
—— —— his wife, Christina Stewart, countess of Buchan. ii. 269.
BUCHAN, ERSKINE, EARL OF, ii. 271-274.
Buchan, James, 2nd son of John, earl of Mar; *jure uxoris* earl of, i. 137; ii. 271, 411; v. 621.
—— —— his 1st wife, Mary Douglas, ii. 271.
—— —— his 2nd wife, Dorothy Knyvett, ii. 272.
—— James, seventh earl of, ii. 273.
—— —— his wife, Marjory Ramsay, ii. 273; iii. 100.
—— William, eighth earl of, ii. 274, 368.
BUCHAN, ERSKINE, EARL OF, ii. 275-284.
Buchan, David, ninth earl of, ii. 275; ix. 49.
—— —— his 1st wife, Frances Fairfax, ii. 275; ix. 49.
—— —— his 2nd wife, Isabella Blacket, ii. 276.
—— David Stuart, eleventh earl of, ii. 278.
—— —— his wife, Margaret Fraser, ii. 278.
—— David Stuart, thirteenth earl of, ii. 279.
—— —— his 1st wife, Agnes Graham Smith, ii. 279.
—— —— his 2nd wife, Maria James, ii. 280.
Buchan, Henry David, tenth earl of, ii. 276.
—— —— his wife, Agnes Stewart, ii. 276; ix. 49.
—— Henry David, twelfth earl of, ii. 278.
—— —— his 1st wife, Elizabeth Cole Shipley, ii. 278.
—— —— his 2nd wife, Elizabeth Harvey, ii. 279.
—— Shipley Gordon Stuart, fourteenth earl of, ii. 280.
—— —— his wife, Rosalie Louisa Sartoris, ii. 280.
—— master of, James Erskine, ii. 269; ix. 47.
—— master of, John Erskine, ii. 269.
—— —— his 1st wife, Elizabeth Stewart, vi. 312; ix. 47, 138.
—— —— his 2nd wife, Margaret Ogilvy, ii. 269.
—— George Dunbar, 11th earl of March, alleged earl of, ii. 265 *n.*; iii. 277 *n.*
Buchan of Auchmacoy, James, iii. 590.
—— —— John, colonel, iv. 121.
—— —— Thomas, ii. 32.
—— —— his wife, Nicolas Buchan, ii. 32.
—— —— Thomas, ii. 354.
—— of Cairnbulg, John, colonel, iv. 121.
—— —— Thomas, advocate, ii. 32; iii. 544.
—— —— his 1st wife, Mary Elphinstone, iii. 544.
—— —— his 2nd wife, Grizel Hamilton, ii. 32.
—— Anne, dau. of Thos. B. of Cairnbulg, ii. 32.
—— Euphemia, wife of col. J. S. Sinclair, ii. 354.
—— George, 1661, ii. 19.
—— Margaret, wife of John King of Warbester, iii. 590.
—— Mary, dau. of Thos. B. of Cairnbulg, ii. 32.
—— Nicolas, wife of Thos. B. of Auchmacoy, ii. 32.
—— *, husband of Margaret King, iii. 590.
BUCHANAN, GRAHAM, MARQUESS OF GRAHAM AND, vi. 263-274.
Buchanan, James, first marquess of, vi. 263.
Buchanan of Ardenconnel and Craigend, James, ii. 357.
—— —— his wife, Janet Sinclair, ii. 357.
—— of Ardoch, Thomas, iii. 520.
—— of Arnprior, John, vi. 150.
—— —— his wife, Isobel Schaw, vi. 150.
—— of Auchmar, Walter, 1st laird, v. 338.
—— of Balmore, Patrick, vi. 221.
—— of Blairfad, Walter, vi. 210.
—— of Buchanan, Sir George, i. 47.
—— —— George, vi. 162 *bis*, 163.
—— —— his wife, Mary Graham, vi. 162.
—— —— George, last laird, vi. 260.
—— —— John, v. 437.
—— —— his wife, Elizabeth Livingston, v. 437.

* Name unknown.

Buchanan of Buchanan, Sir John, vii. 197; ix. 52.
—— his wife, Mary Erskine, ix. 52.
—— Maurice, v. 336; vi. 133.
—— his wife, * Menteith, vi. 133 *n.*
—— Patrick, 14th laird, vi. 221.
—— Patrick, ix. 19.
—— his wife, Margaret Campbell, ix. 19.
—— Walter, 11th laird, v. 338; vi. 35.
—— Sir Walter, 12th laird, iv. 272; ix. 109.
—— his 2nd wife, Isobel Stewart, i. 151.
—— Walter, 14th laird, vi. 152.
— of the Botown, William, major, viii. 180.
— of Cashlie, Duncan, vi. 153.
— of Corriearklet, Patrick, vi. 221.
— of Drumfad, Walter, vi. 35.
— of Drumnakil, Archibald, i. 482.
— Robert, vi. 410.
—— his wife, Katharine Napier, vi. 410.
— of Gartavertane, John, vi. 157.
— of Kirkmichael, Walter, vi. 35, 210.
— of Sallechy, Maurice, v. 336.
— of Scotscraig, Sir John, iii. 98; v. 622.
—— his wife, Margaret Hartsyde, iii. 98.
— of Torry, Archibald, collector of customs, v. 408.
—— his wife, Georgina Lindsay of Kirkforthar, v. 408.
— Sir Andrew, H.B.M. ambassador, ii. 92.
—— his wife, Georgiana Eliza Stuart, ii. 92.
— Andrew, surety for John Middleton of that Ilk, vi. 173.
— Anna, wife of Adam Napier of West Nisbet, vi. 421.
— Annabel, wife of Sir John Rollo of Bannockburn, vii. 197.
— Colin, captain 62nd Foot, viii. 139.
—— his wife, Elizabeth Pilgrim Dalrymple, viii. 139.
— Elizabeth, wife of (1) Sir Andrew Gray, and (2) Thos. Oliphant, iv. 272, 275.
— George, tutor to king James VI., ii. 468; v. 81, 297.
— Helen, wife of Alex. Colquhoun of Luss, i. 47.
— Sir John, tacksman of Orkney and Shetland, v. 222.
— Katharine, wife of John Graham of Gartur, vi. 153.
— Katharine, wife of Charles Campbell of Loragen and Lochdochart, ix. 44.
— Margaret, wife of Sir Arthur Erskine, v. 622.
— Margaret, wife of 2nd earl of Menteith, vi. 152.
— William, W.S., iii. 520.
—— his wife, Elizabeth Ann Murray, iii. 520.

* Name unknown.

Buck, Sarah, wife of baron Erskine, ii. 277; ix. 49.
Buckingham, George (Villiers), 1st duke of, iii. 122; vii. 99.
— George (Villiers), 2nd duke of, iii. 600.
Buckingham and Chandos, Richard (Grenville-Brydges-Chandos), 1st duke of, v. 200.
—— his wife, Anna Eliza Brydges, baroness Kinloss, v. 200.
—— Richard, (Grenville-Brydges Chandos), 2nd duke of, ii. 211; v. 200.
—— his wife, Mary Campbell, ii. 211.
—— Richard Plantagenet Campbell Temple-Nugent- (Brydges-Chandos-Grenville), 3rd duke of, iii. 482; v. 200.
—— his 1st wife, Caroline Hervey, v. 200.
— his 2nd wife, Alice Anne Graham-Montgomery, v. 201.
Buckingham and Normanby, John (Sheffield), duke of, i. 35; vii. 482.
—— his wife, Katharine Darnley, i. 35.
Buckinghamshire, John (Hobart), 2nd earl of, v. 483.
—— his wife, Mary Anne Drury, v. 483.
Buckland, Charles Edward, i. 525.
—— his wife, Laura Lindsay, i. 525.
Buckle, John, Wharton House, iii. 83.
—— his wife, Isabella Hay-Mackenzie, iii. 83.
Buckson, *, wife of Geo. Ramsay of Carriden, iii. 101.
Bulkeley, Thomas (Bulkeley), 1st viscount, ii. 84.
— Anne, wife of duke of Berwick, i. 34.
— Henry, master of royal household, ii. 84.
—— his wife, Sophia Stuart, ii. 84.
Buller of Morval, John. i. 66.
— of Trenant Park, Sir Edward, bart., admiral, iii. 547.
— Anna Maria, wife of Jas. D. Fullerton-Elphinstone, iii. 547.
— Mary, wife of Sir Joseph Copley, i. 66.
Buller-Fullerton-Elphinstone of Carberry, James Drummond, lieut.-col., iii. 547.
— Anna Maria, wife of capt. T. H. Montgomery, iii. 548.
— Clementina Fleming, wife of lieut.-col., Douglas Jones, iii. 547.
— Constance Lothian, iii. 553.
— Edward Charles, captain 92nd Highlanders, iii. 547.
— Elizabeth Mary, wife of dean Montgomery, iii. 548.
— George James, R.N., iii. 547.
— Gertrude, wife of James Hope, iii. 547.
— James Drummond, Bechuanaland Mounted Police, iii. 553.

* Name unknown.

Buller-Fullerton-Elphinstone, John Frederick, lieut.-colonel Scots Fusilier Guards, iii. 547.
—— Lilian, dau. of 15th lord Elphinstone, iii. 553.
—— Mountstuart William, iii. 553.
Bulleyn, *, chaplain to the earl of Lindsay, 1640, i. 350.
Bullock of Faulkbourn Hall, rev. Walter Trevolyan, i. 96.
—— Edith, wife of D. G. Hamilton-Gordon, i. 96.
—— Mary, wife of C. J. S. Douglas, Jamaica, vii. 150.
—— Richard, D.D., vii. 150.
Bullok, William, 'an ambitious churchman,' ii. 223.
Bulteel of Membland, John, ii. 75.
—— —— his wife, Diana Bellenden, ii. 75.
Bulwer of Tomard, Archibald Redfoord, v. 315.
—— —— his wife, Jean Hamilton Ramsay, v. 315.
Bunau, Henrietta Frederica, wife of (1) * de Berargaard, and (2) David, 7th viscount of Stormont, viii. 208.
—— Henry, Hanover, count, viii. 208.
Bunbury of Barton, Sir Thomas Charles, 6th bart., v. 365; ix. 111.
—— —— his wife, Sarah Lennox, iv. 554; v. 365; ix. 111.
Bunch, Elizabeth, wife of John Hay of Broganelesk, iii. 566.
Burden of Feddal, Ann, wife of Robt. Campbell of Torrie, vi. 155.
—— —— Robert, *né* Graham, vi. 155.
—— —— his wife, Agnes Campbell, vi. 155.
—— Robert, son of R. Graham of Feddal, vi. 155.
Burel of Eckford and Burellands, John, ii. 226.
Burford, Charles (Beauclerc), earl of, i. 32.
—— Anna, wife of Raymond Fairfax, iii. 604.
—— Sylvester L., Oak Lawn, iii. 604.
Burges of Greyslee and Mortimer, George, viii. 38.
—— —— his wife, Ann Wichnour Somerville, viii. 38.
—— Sir James Bland, bart., i. 529; viii. 32, 36, 39.
—— —— his 1st wife, Elizabeth Noel, ix. 31.
—— —— his 2nd wife, Anne Montolieu, ix. 31.
—— —— his 3rd wife, Margaret Janet Lindsay, i. 528; ix. 31.
Burgh, Egidia de, wife of Alexander, 5th High Steward of Scotland, i. 14, 322.
—— Elizabeth de, wife of King Robert I., i. 8; ii. 436.
—— Hubert de, i. 5.
—— —— his wife, Margaret of Scotland, i. 5.

* Name unknown.

Burgh, Richard de, earl of Ulster, i. 8, 14.
Burghersh, John (Fane), eldest son of 10th earl of Westmoreland; styled lord, ix. 25.
Burghley, William (Cecil) 1st lord, vii. 98.
Burgon, Sir Robert of, iii. 3.
Burke of Glinsk, Sir Joseph, 11th bart., iii. 418, 419.
—— —— his wife, Louisa Grace Manners, iii. 418.
—— Katharine Elizabeth Camilla, wife of William Lionel Felix, lord Huntingtower, iii. 419.
BURLEIGH, BALFOUR, LORD BALFOUR OF, i. 530-547.
BURLEIGH, BRUCE, LORD BALFOUR OF, i. 547-554.
Burlington and Cork, Charles (Boyle), 3rd earl of, iii. 482.
Burn, Elizabeth, dau. of John B., Stirling, viii. 169.
—— John, Stirling, viii. 169.
—— —— his wife, Janet Alexander, viii. 169.
—— *, captain R.N., viii. 138.
—— —— his wife, Margaret Dalrymple, viii. 138.
Burnard of Ardross and Curry, John, v. 283.
—— of Faringden, Richard, vii. 364.
—— —— Roger, vii. 364.
Burne, Sir Owen Tudor, major-general, G.C.I.E., vi. 386.
—— —— his wife, Agnes Charlotte Douglas, vi. 386.
Burnet(t of Barns, William, viii. 402.
—— —— his wife, Margaret Stewart, viii. 402.
—— of Carlops, Alexander, vi. 106.
—— —— Alexander, advocate, vii. 379.
—— —— his wife, Isobel Rutherfurd, vii. 379.
—— of Cowtown, Robert, i. 303.
—— —— his wife, Helen Arbuthnott, i. 303.
—— of Craigmyle, Alexander, v. 544.
—— —— his wife, Christian Fraser, v. 544.
—— —— James, i. 286, 305.
—— of Crimond, Robert, senator of the College of Justice, lord Crimond, iii. 488; vii. 14.
—— —— his wife, Elizabeth *or* Beatrix Maule, vii. 14.
—— —— Sir Thomas, iii. 848, 490.
—— —— his wife, Janet Bruce, iii. 488.
—— of Glenbervie, Robert, i. 311; viii. 76.
—— of Kemnay, George, viii. 80.
—— of Leys, Alexander, i. 285; ix. 91.
—— —— his 2nd wife, Marjory Forbes, iv. 54; ix. 91.
—— —— Alexander, i. 285.
—— —— his wife, Katharine Arbuthnott, i. 285.

* Name unknown.

Burnet(t of Leys, Sir Robert, 7th bart., viii. 136.
— — his wife, Margaret Dalrymple-Elphinstone, viii. 136.
— — Sir Thomas, 1st bart., i. 304; v. 531.
— — his 2nd wife, Jean Moncrieff, v. 531.
— — Sir Thomas, 3rd bart., i. 308, 311; viii. 81.
— — his wife, Margaret Arbuthnott, i. 308.
— — Sir Thomas, 8th bart., viii. 90.
— of Monboddo, James, viii. 79.
— — his wife, Elizabeth Irving, viii. 80.
— of Redhall, George, viii. 80.
— Alexander, eldest son of Sir Thomas B. of Leys, i. 304.
— — his wife, Jean Arbuthnott, i. 304.
— Alexander, archbishop of Glasgow, and of St. Andrews, iii. 72, 511, 542; iv. 248.
— Anne, wife of (1) Alexander, 7th lord Elphinstone, and (2) Patrick, 3rd lord Elibank, iii. 511, 542.
— Anne, wife of Jas. Melville of Cassingray, vi. 106.
— Elspet, wife of Alex. Middleton, vi. 177.
— Euphemia, wife of Jas. Roberton, iii. 490.
— Gilbert, bishop of Salisbury, ii. 481; viii. 80.
— — his wife, Margaret Kennedy, ii. 481.
— Isabel, wife of Robert Arbuthnott of Fiddes, i. 285.
— Jean, wife of Robt. Arbuthnott of Fiddes, i. 286.
— Jean, wife of Sir D. Carnegie of Pittarrow, viii. 79.
— John, minister at Stair, iii. 448.
— — his wife, Jean Montgomerie, iii. 448.
— John, *perhaps* son of archbishop Hamilton, iv. 362 *n*.
— Mary, wife of Roderick Mackenzie of Prestonhall, iii. 72.
— Mary, wife of Sir John Carnegie of Pittarrow, viii. 81.
— Robert, tutor of Glenbervie, i. 310.
— — his wife, Ann Arbuthnott, i. 310.
Burns of Cumbernauld, Alan, vii. 524.
— — his wife, Helen Jacqueline Hope, vii. 524.
— of Kilmahew, John William, viii. 226.
— Grace, wife of 2nd baron Napier and Ettrick, vi. 438.
— Helen Sherer, wife of A. S. Drummond, viii. 226.
— James Cleland, vi. 438.
— Robert, the poet, v. 132, 134.
BURNTISLAND, WEMYSS, LORD, ii. 281-284.
Burntisland, James, lord, ii. 282.
— — his wife, Margaret, countess of Wemyss, ii. 283; viii. 504.
Burntisland, Sir Robert Melville, lord of Session, styled lord, vi. 100.
Burrell, Elizabeth Anne, wife of (1) Douglas, 8th duke of Hamilton, and (2) Henry, marquess of Exeter, iv. 394.
— Peter, Beckenham, iv. 394.
Burrell-Drummond of Stobhall, Peter, vii. 59.
— — his wife, Clementine Sarah Drummond, vii. 59.
Burroughs, Margaret, wife of 7th lord Bellenden of Broughton, vii. 353.
Burrowes of Dangan Castle, colonel, vii. 61.
— — his wife, Susan Henrietta Sewell, vi. 73; vii. 60.
— of Stradone, Thomas, major, vii. 308.
— Honora Seward, wife of T. J. Leslie, vii. 308.
Bury, rev. Edward John, i. 388.
— — his wife, Charlotte Susan Maria Campbell, i. 387; ix. 25 *bis*, 90.
Busby, Dr., Westminster School, vii. 104.
Busson de Podolska, Elizabeth, wife of James, earl of Dirleton, iii. 130.
Bute, Angus, 3rd son of Somerled, lord of the Isles; lord of, v. 30, 31 *bis*.
— James, grandson of Somerled; lord of, i. 13; v. 31.
— Jean of, wife of Alexander, 4th High Steward, i. 13; v. 31.
BUTE, STEWART, EARL OF, ii. 299-312.
Bute, James, first earl of, ii. 298.
— — his wife, Agnes Mackenzie, ii. 298.
— James, second earl of, ii. 300.
— — his wife, Anne Campbell, i. 370; ii. 300.
— John, third earl of, ii. 301.
— — his wife, Mary Wortley Montague, ii. 302.
— John, fourth earl of, ii. 302, 305.
— — his 1st wife, Charlotte Jane Windsor, ii. 306.
— — his 2nd wife, Frances Coutts, ii. 306.
— John, fifth earl of, ii. 309.
— John, seventh earl of, ii. 311.
— John Patrick, sixth earl of, ii. 310.
BUTE, STUART, MARQUESS OF, ii. 285-309.
Bute, John, first marquess of, ii. 305.
— — his 1st wife, Charlotte Jane Windsor, ii. 306.
— — his 2nd wife, Frances Coutts, ii. 306.
BUTE, CRICHTON-STUART, MARQUESS OF, ii. 309-312.
Bute, John, second marquess of, ii. 309.
— — his 1st wife, Maria North, ii. 310.
— — his 2nd wife, Sophia Frederica Christina Hastings, ii. 310; v. 513.
— John, fourth marquess of, ii. 311.
— — his wife, Augusta Mary Monica Bellingham.

Bute, John Patrick, third marquess of, ii. 310.
— — his wife, Gwendolen Mary Anne Howard, ii. 311.
BUTLER, LORD DINGWALL, iii. 123.
Butler of Lanthony, James, 1st baron, iii. 122.
— of Tulleophelim, Theobald, viscount, iii. 121.
— of Moore Park, Francis Thomas (de Gray), lord, iii. 124.
— of Garryhundon, Sir Thomas, bart., iv. 572.
— Charles E. A. F. Somerset, i. 527.
— Delia, mistress of 1st lord Scott of Buccleuch, ii. 233.
— Eileen Gwladys, wife of George Granville (Sutherland-Leveson-Gower), styled marquess of Stafford, ix. 163.
— Elizabeth, wife of (1) Theobald, viscount Butler, and (2) Richard, 1st lord Dingwall, iii. 121.
— Elizabeth, wife of 2nd earl of Chesterfield, viii. 304.
— Evelyn Frances, wife of E. R. Drummond, viii. 237.
— Grace, wife of Sir John Cochrane of Cochrane, iii. 344, 347.
— Henrietta, wife of Henry, earl of Grantham, iii. 123.
— James Arthur, viii. 237.
— Jane, wife of (1) James, lord Villiers, and (2) 7th viscount Falkland, iii. 611, 614.
— Jane, wife of Walter Murray of Ravilly, iii. 509.
— John, student of physic, ii. 194.
— — his wife, Elizabeth Marbrough Campbell, ii. 194.
— Kathleen, wife of W. C. Lindsay, i. 527.
— Louisa Charlotte, wife of Sir J. R. Carmichael, iv. 572.
— Margaret, wife of lt.-col. R. Charteris, viii. 516.
— Mary, wife of Sir Geo. Hamilton of Greenlaw, i. 43.
— Mary, wife of Sir Geo. Hamilton of Donalong, i. 53.
— Richard, London, iii. 614.
— Thomas, captain, in Holland, ii. 233.
— William, M.D., London, vii. 151.
— — his wife, Katharine Douglas, vii. 151.
Butter of Braehouse, William, ii. 195, 196.
— of Clashbenny, George, ii. 28.
— — his wife, Mary Hay, ii. 28.
— of Gormock, John, iii. 570; viii. 337.
— — his wife, Beatrix Gordon, viii. 337.
— — Patrick, iii. 24.
— — his wife, Janet Gordon, iii. 24; iv. 279, 530.
— Elizabeth, wife of (1) John Hay of Muchalls, and (2) Hugh Maxwell, iii. 570.
Butter, Elizabeth, wife of (1) P. Stewart of Stuikis, and (2) P. Ogilvy of Inchmartine, iv. 33.
— Janet, wife of capt. John Campbell, ii. 196.
— Jean, wife of Archd. Campbell, ii. 195.
Buttergask of Buttergask, Margaret, iv. 279.
— of Cambusmichael and Collanys, Mariota de, viii. 265.
— Katharine, wife of William, master of Ruthven, iv. 259.
Butterwell, George, i. 225.
— Robert, Coalfield, i. 225.
— — his wife, Marion Murray, i. 225.
Butterworth, Jane, wife of (1) Francis Joddrell, and (2) col. George Sempill, vii. 563.
— Thomas, vii. 563.
Buxton of Dunston Hall, Geoffrey Fowell, iv. 98.
— Bernard, lieut. R.N., iv. 98.
— — his wife, Hermione Grimston, iv. 98.
Byam, Alice, wife of Samuel Eliot, iii. 583.
— William, colonel, Antigua, iii. 583.
Bygris, Hugh de, v. 488.
Byne, Charles, cornet in Bland's Dragoons, iii. 458.
— — his wife, Grace Montgomerie, iii. 458.
BYRES, LINDSAY, LORD LINDSAY OF THE, v. 392.
BYRES AND BINNING, HAMILTON, LORD, iv. 310.
Byres and Binning, Thomas, lord, iv. 310.
— of Coates, Sir John, vii. 473.
— — his wife, Lilias Grant, vii. 473.
Byron, George (Gordon), 6th lord, ii. 7; iv. 530.

CABELJAUW, Major, iii. 326.
CABERSTON, STEWART, LORD, viii. 403-409.
Caberston, John, first lord, viii. 403.
Caddell, Katharine, wife of 7th lord Gray, iv. 287.
Cadell, James, murderer of Regent Lennox, i. 38; ix. 126.
Cadogan, Sarah, wife of 2nd duke of Lennox, v. 364.
— William (Cadogan), 1st earl, v. 364.
Caesar, Sir Julius, master of the Rolls, viii. 412, 413.
— — his wife, Alice Grant, viii. 412.
Cagnioli, Timothy, banker, ii. 475.
Cainneach, father of Gartnach, mormaer and earl of Buchan, ii. 251.
Cainnech, father of Ewan, v. 566.
Cairncross of Colmslie, John, ii. 112, 230.
— — William, vii. 334.
— — his wife, Marion Pringle, vii. 334.

Cairncross, Nicol, burgess of Edinburgh, ix. 37.
—— —— his wife, Marion *, ix. 37.
—— Walter, in Lugatt, ii. 112, 230.
—— —— his wife, Grissel Scott, ii. 111, 112, 230.
Cairns of Cairns, Duncan, ix. 50.
—— —— Janet de, iv. 186.
—— —— *, wife of Stephen Crichton, ix. 50.
—— of Minniebuie, James, iii. 350.
—— of Orchardton, William, v. 259.
—— —— his wife Christian Maclellan, v. 259.
—— of Pilmuir, William, ii. 101.
—— of Whithurn, Duncan, ix. 50.
—— Elizabeth, wife of John Cochrane of Waterside, iii. 350.
—— Sibilla, wife of Alex. Borthwick, ii. 101.
Caisnet, Simon de, brother of Walter, 3rd Steward of Scotland, v. 137.
Caistron, John de, iii. 249.
CAITHNESS, ANCIENT EARLS OF, ii. 313-320.
Caithness, David, eleventh earl of, ii. 316.
—— Duncan *or* Dungad, first earl of, ii. 313.
—— —— his wife, Groa, ii. 313.
—— Erlend, sixth earl of, ii. 315.
—— Erlend ungi, tenth earl of, ii. 315, 316.
—— —— his wife, Margaret of Orkney, i. 416; ii. 315.
—— Gilbert, Gilbride *or* Gibbon, fourteenth earl of, i. 164; ii. 317.
—— Harald Maddadsson, ninth earl of, ii. 315.
—— —— his 1st wife, Afreka of Fife, ii. 315.
—— —— his 2nd wife, Gormlath *or* Hvarflod of Moray, ii. 315; vii. 231.
—— Harald Slettmali, seventh earl of, ii. 315, 316.
—— Harald ungi, joint earl of, ii. 315, 317.
—— Isabella of, wife of Wm. Sinclair of Roslin, ii. 320; vi. 567, 568; viii. 253, 254.
—— John, twelfth earl of, i. 163, 166; ii. 316.
—— John, seventeenth earl of, ii. 318.
—— Liot, second earl of, ii. 314; vi. 281.
—— —— his wife, Ragnhildis, ii. 314.
—— MacWilliam, designated 'earl of,' ii. 315 *n.*
—— Magnus, thirteenth earl of, ii. 317.
—— Magnus, fifteenth earl of, i. 162; ii. 318.
—— Magnus, sixteenth earl of, ii. 318.
—— Magnus, eighteenth earl of, ii. 319.
—— —— his wife, Katharine, ii. 319.
—— Malcolm, earl of, i. 165.
—— Malise, nineteenth earl of, i. 164; ii. 319; vi. 138; viii. 252.
—— —— his 2nd wife, Marjorie of Ross, ii. 320; vii. 236.
—— Margaret of, wife of Simon Fraser, ii. 319.
—— Matilda of, wife of Malise, 5th earl of Strathearn, ii. 318, 319; viii. 246, 252.

*Name unknown.

Caithness, Moddan, nephew of King Duncan I.; fourth earl of, ii. 314; iii. 240.
—— Paul, fifth earl of, ii. 315.
—— Rognvald, eighth earl of, ii. 315.
—— Thorfinn, third earl of, ii. 314.
—— —— his wife, Ingibiorg, i. 2; ii. 314.
CAITHNESS, STEWART, EARL OF, ii. 321-322.
Caithness, Alan, fourth earl of, i. 439; ii. 322.
—— David, son of King Robert II.; first earl of, i. 16, 437; ii. 321; viii. 259.
—— —— his wife, * Lindsay, ii. 320; iii. 14.
—— Euphemia, wife of (1) Patrick Graham, and (2) Sir P. Dunbar; countess of, i. 437; ii. 321; viii. 260.
—— Walter, third earl of, i. 437; ii. 322; viii. 260.
—— —— his wife, Elizabeth Graham, vi. 37.
CAITHNESS, CRICHTON, EARL OF, ii. 323-331.
Caithness, George, earl of, ii. 325.
—— —— his 1st wife, * Douglas, ii. 330.
—— —— his 2nd wife, Jonet Borthwick, ii. 96, 328.
CAITHNESS, SINCLAIR, EARL OF, ii. 332-359.
Caithness, Alexander, ninth earl of, ii. 341, 346.
—— —— his wife, Margaret Primrose, ii. 346; vii. 222.
—— Alexander Campbell, thirteenth earl of, ii. 357.
—— —— his wife, Frances Harriet Leigh, ii. 357.
—— George, fourth earl of, ii. 338; iii. 200; viii. 343, 346.
—— —— his wife, Elizabeth Graham, ii. 340; vi. 230.
—— George, fifth earl of, ii. 342; viii. 193.
—— —— his wife, Jean Gordon, ii. 343; iv. 541.
—— George, sixth earl of, ii. 203, 344.
—— —— his wife, Mary Campbell, i. 361; ii. 344.
—— George, seventh earl of, ii. 343, 345.
—— George Philips Alexander, fifteenth earl of, ii. 358.
—— James, twelfth earl of, ii. 342, 356; iii. 214.
—— —— his wife, Jean Campbell, ii. 356.
—— James, fourteenth earl of, ii. 358.
—— —— his 1st wife, Louisa Georgiana Philips, ii. 358.
—— —— his 2nd wife, Marie de Mariategui, duchesse de Pomar, ii. 358.
—— James Augustus, sixteenth earl of, ii. 354, 358; ix. 52.
—— —— his wife, Jessie Macleod, ii. 358.
—— John, third earl of, ii. 337; vii. 573; viii. 336.
—— —— his wife, Elizabeth Sutherland, ii. 338; iii. 197.
—— John, eighth earl of, ii. 341, 345.
—— —— his wife, Janet Carmichael, ii. 345.
—— John, eleventh earl of, ii. 350.

* Name unknown.

Caithness, John Sutherland, seventeenth earl of, ii. 359.
— William, first earl of, ii. 332; vi. 571; ix. 50.
— — his 1st wife, Elizabeth Douglas, ii. 333; iii. 167.
— — his 2nd wife, Marjory Sutherland, ii. 334.
— — his 3rd wife, Jonet Yeman, ii. 336.
— William, second earl of, ii. 337.
— — his wife, Mary Keith, ii. 337.
— William, tenth earl of, ii. 349.
— — his wife, Barbara Sinclair, ii. 350.
— master of, James Sinclair, brother of 5th earl of Caithness; styled, ii. 340.
— — his 1st wife, Elizabeth Stewart, ii. 340; vi. 574.
— — his 2nd wife, Grizel Crichton, ix. 51.
— master of, John Sinclair, eldest son of 4th earl of Caithness, ii. 340; vi. 547; ix. 51 *quat.*
— — his wife, Jane Hepburn, ii. 160, 340.
CAITHNESS, CAMPBELL, EARL OF, ii. 203.
Caithness, John, earl of, ii. 203, 344.
— — his 1st wife, Mary Cope, ii. 205.
— — his 2nd wife, Mary Douglas, ii. 206, 345.
Caldcotis of Graden, Elizabeth, wife of William Livingston of Kilsyth, v. 184.
— — William de, v. 184.
Calder of Asloun, *, iv. 71.
— — his wife, * Forbes, iv. 71.
— of Calder, Janet, elder dau. of Sir John C., i. 513.
— — Sir John, i. 336.
— — Muriella, wife of Sir John Campbell, i. 336, 513.
— — William, v. 204.
— — his wife, Janet Keith, v. 204.
— of Dun, Margaret, wife of David Sinclair, ii. 338.
— James, captain, murderer of Regent Lennox, i. 38; ix. 126.
— Fingola, wife of (1) John Munro of Foulis, and (2) John, 8th earl of Sutherland, viii. 334.
— Marjorie, contracted to Alexander Fraser, 5th of Philorth, vii. 434.
Calderwood of Pitodie, William, iv. 437.
— — his wife, Janet Bothwell, iv. 437.
— of Polton, Sir William, lord of Session, ii. 296.
— Janet, mistress of 1st lord Hamilton, iv. 353.
— Jean, wife of Sir Robert Stewart of Tillicoultry, ii. 296.
Caldwell, G. Ralston, v. 315.
— Ina Blanche, wife of Keith Maitland, v. 315.

* Name unknown.

Caledon, James Dupré (Alexander), 3rd earl of, iv. 98.
— — his wife, Jane F. H. M. Grimston, iv. 97.
Callan, George (Fielding), viscount, iii. 122.
CALLENDAR, LIVINGSTON, EARL OF, ii. 360-364.
Callendar, Alexander, second earl of, ii. 363; v. 447.
— — his wife, Mary Hamilton, ii. 363; iv. 380.
— Alexander, third earl of, ii. 363; v. 449.
— — his wife, Anne Graham, ii. 363; vi. 259.
— James, 3rd son of 1st earl of Linlithgow; first earl of, ii. 360; v. 445, 446.
— — his wife, Margaret Hay, ii. 362; iii. 372.
— James, fourth earl of, ii. 363; iii. 580; v. 449; vi. 111.
— — his wife, Margaret Hay, v. 450; viii. 447.
CALLENDAR, LIVINGSTON, LORD LIVINGSTON OF, v. 430-451.
Callendar, Alwin, thane of, v. 331.
— Duncan, thane of, v. 330.
— Malcolm, thane of, v. 330.
— — his wife, Eva, v. 330.
— of Ardkinglas, James Henry, i. 390.
— of Bordie, Walter, iv. 430.
— of Callendar, Sir John, ii. 218; v. 422.
— — Sir Patrick, v. 422, 423.
— of Craigforth, George, colonel, ii. 277.
— — James Henry, i. 390.
— of Dowradour, Robert, v. 434.
— — Robert, his grandson, v. 434.
— — his wife, Elizabeth Livingston, v. 434.
— of Kilsyth, Duncan, ancestor of the family of, v. 182.
— — Sir Patrick, v. 183.
— — Christian, wife of Sir Wm. Livingston, v. 182.
— of Manor, John, vii. 194.
— — Robert, iii. 531; v. 432; vii. 194.
— Janey Sevilla, wife of lord Archibald Campbell, i. 390.
Calverley of Eccleshill, Walter, v. 10.
— Anne, wife of John Ingram, v. 10.
CAMBRIDGE, HAMILTON, EARL OF, iv. 374.
Cambridge, James, first earl of, iv. 374.
— Charles, inf. son of King James VII.; duke of, i. 33.
— Charles, inf. son of King James VII.; duke of, i. 34.
— Edgar, son of King James VII.; duke of, i. 33.
— James, inf. son of King James VII.; duke of, i. 33.
— Charles Owen, iii. 359.
— — his wife, Katharine Pitcairn, iii. 359.

Camden, Charles (Pratt), 1st baron, ix. 13.
Camehou, Walter de, iv. 12; vi. 207.
Camera, William de, vicar of Kirkurd, iv. 85.
CAMERON, FAIRFAX, LORD FAIRFAX OF, iii. 595-606.
Cameron of Ballegarno, Jean, wife of Nicholas Erskine of Kinnoull, v. 596.
—— Sir John, iv. 333; v. 596.
—— Margaret, wife of Sir John Haliburton of Dirleton, iv. 333.
— of Brux, Sir Henry, iv. 47.
—— Katharine, wife of Alaster Forbes, iv. 47.
— of Dungannon, Alexander, capt., ix. 144.
— of Glenkindy, John, i. 60.
—— his wife, Elizabeth Hamilton, i. 60.
— of Lochiel, Allan, ii. 200; v. 562; vii. 469.
—— Donald, v. 560.
—— Donald, D.L., viii. 467.
—— Donald, M.P., ii. 247.
—— his wife, Margaret Elizabeth Scott, ii. 247.
—— Donald Walter, vi. 274.
—— his wife, Hermione Emily Graham, vi. 274.
—— Sir Ewan, iii. 357.
—— his 2nd wife, Mary Maclean, iii. 357.
—— John, the younger, ii. 200.
—— his wife, Margaret Campbell, ii. 200.
— in Fife, 1320, i. 324.
— Charles, banker, iii. 582.
— Christian, self-styled wife of lord Rosehill, ix. 144.
— Donald, father of Ewen C., v. 527.
— Ewan, son of Donald C., v. 527.
— Janet, wife of Walter Stewart of Arthurle, ii. 77.
— Jean, wife of Alastair 'Dearg' Macdonald of Strome, v. 562.
— John, bishop of Glasgow, iii. 58, 468.
— Margaret, alleged wife of Sir Nigel Cambel, i. 324.
— Mary Anne, wife of rear-admiral lord John Hay, viii. 467.
— *, wife of John Macdonald of Morar, v. 560.
Camloke, John of, iv. 49.
CAMPBELL, CAMPBELL, LORD, i. 331-393.
Campbell, Colin, second lord, i. 332.
—— his wife, Isabel Stewart of Lorne, i. 332, 334; v. 3.
— Duncan, first lord, i. 330; viii. 11.
—— his 1st wife, Marjory or Marcellina Stewart, i. 149, 331; ix. 18.
—— his 2nd wife, Margaret Stewart, i. 331.
CAMPBELL, CAMPBELL, EARL OF, i. 369.

* Name unknown.

Campbell, Archibald, first earl of, i. 369.
— George John, eldest son of 5th duke of Argyll; styled earl of, i. 387.
— John Henry, elder son of 7th duke of Argyll; styled lord, i. 389.
CAMPBELL AND LORN, CAMPBELL, LORD, i. 342.
Campbell and Lorn, Archibald, lord, i. 342.
CAMPBELL AND LORNE, CAMPBELL, LORD, i. 353.
Campbell and Lorne, Archibald, first lord, i. 353.
CAMPBELL OF LOUDOUN, CAMPBELL, LORD, v. 498-506.
Campbell of Loudoun, Hugh, first lord, v. 498.
—— his 1st wife, Margaret Gordon, v. 111, 498.
—— his 2nd wife, Elizabeth Ruthven, iv. 266; v. 114, 498.
—— his 3rd wife, Margaret Home, v. 498.
—— John, second lord, v. 499, 506.
—— his wife, Margaret, baroness of Loudoun, v. 499, 506.
CAMPBELL, EARL OF ARGYLL, i. 332-351.
CAMPBELL, MARQUESS OF ARGYLL, i. 353-393.
CAMPBELL, DUKE OF ARGYLL, i. 318-393.
CAMPBELL, LORD ARRASE, i. 379.
CAMPBELL, EARL OF ATHOLL, i. 434-435.
CAMPBELL, LORD BENEDERALOCH, ii. 203.
CAMPBELL, VISCOUNT OF BREADALBANE, ii. 203.
CAMPBELL, EARL OF BREADALBANE, ii. 203.
CAMPBELL, EARL AND MARQUESS OF BREADALBANE. ii. 174-214.
CAMPBELL, BARON BREADALBANE OF KENMORE, ii. 213.
CAMPBELL, BARON BREADALBANE OF TAYMOUTH CASTLE, ii. 210.
CAMPBELL, EARL OF CAITHNESS, ii. 203.
CAMPBELL, LORD CAMPBELL, i. 331.
CAMPBELL, EARL OF CAMPBELL, i. 369.
CAMPBELL, LORD CAMPBELL AND LORNE, i. 353.
CAMPBELL, LORD CAMPBELL OF LOUDOUN, v. 498-506.
CAMPBELL, BARON OF CHATHAM, i. 371.
CAMPBELL, EARL OF COWAL, i. 369.
CAMPBELL, LORD DUNOON, i. 379.
CAMPBELL, VISCOUNT OF GLENILA, i. 369.
CAMPBELL, LORD GLENURCHY, ii. 203.
CAMPBELL, BARONESS OF GREENWICH, i. 377.
CAMPBELL, EARL OF GREENWICH, i. 371.
CAMPBELL, DUKE OF GREENWICH, i. 374.
CAMPBELL, BARON HAMILTON OF HAMELDON, i. 388.
CAMPBELL, EARL OF HOLLAND, ii. 203, 204.
CAMPBELL, EARL AND VISCOUNT OF ILAY, i. 379.
CAMPBELL, LORD INVERARAY, i. 369.
CAMPBELL, EARL OF IRVINE, v. 21-26.

CAMPBELL, LORD KINTYRE, v. 23-26.
CAMPBELL, MARQUESS OF KINTYRE, i. 369.
CAMPBELL, VISCOUNT OF LOCHOW, i. 369.
CAMPBELL, MARQUESS OF LORNE, i. 369-393.
CAMPBELL, EARL OF LOUDOUN, v. 488-517.
CAMPBELL, LORD OF LUNDIE, i. 350.
CAMPBELL, LORD LUNDY, v. 24-26.
CAMPBELL, LORD MACHLINE, v. 506-517.
CAMPBELL, LORD MORVEN, i. 369.
CAMPBELL, LORD MULL, i. 369.
CAMPBELL, LORD ORANSAY, i. 379.
CAMPBELL, LORD ORMELIE, ii. 203, 204.
CAMPBELL, EARL OF ORMELIE, ii. 210, 213.
CAMPBELL, VISCOUNT OF PAINTLAND, ii. 203, 204.
CAMPBELL, LORD ST. CLAIR OF BERRIEDALE AND GLENURCHY, ii. 203.
CAMPBELL, BARON SUNDRIDGE OF COOMBANK, i. 386.
CAMPBELL, VISCOUNT OF TAY, ii. 203.
CAMPBELL, LORD TERRINYEAN, v. 506-517.
CAMPBELL, LORD TIRY, i. 369.
CAMPBELL, LORD WEICK, ii. 203, 204.
Campbell of Aberuchill, Colin, v. 503; ix. 43.
—— —— Sir Colin, lord of Session, iii. 73.
—— —— his wife, Katharine Mackenzie, iii. 73.
—— —— Sir Colin, bart, v. 387.
—— —— Sir James, v. 508.
—— —— his wife, Jean Campbell, v. 508.
—— —— John, ancestor of the family of, ii. 178.
—— —— his 1st wife, Agnes Moncrieff, ii. 178.
—— —— his 2nd wife, Christian Ogilvie, ii. 178.
—— —— Sir John, v. 503.
—— —— his wife, Beatrix Campbell, v. 503.
—— of Achinard, Colin, ancestor of the family of, i. 329.
—— of Achlian, Duncan, ancestor of the family of, i. 324.
—— of Airds, Alexander, ii. 203.
—— —— his wife, Jean Campbell, ii. 203.
—— —— Sir John, ancestor of the family of, i. 336.
—— of Ardbaichlorne, Colin, ii. 182.
—— of Ardcarden, Sir Archibald, commendator of Strathfillan, v. 503.
—— of Ardchattan, Sir John, ancestor of the family of, i. 336.
—— —— his wife, Muriel of Calder, i. 336.
—— —— John, ii. 202.
—— —— his wife, Susanna Campbell, ii. 202.
—— of Ardchoil, Thomas, v. 500 *n*.
—— of Ardentenie, Colin, ancestor of the family of, i. 329.
—— —— *, i. 336.
—— —— his wife, * Campbell, i. 336.

* Name unknown.

Campbell of Ardeonaig, John, 6th son of Sir John C. of Lawers, v. 504.
—— —— his 1st wife, Margaret Donaldson, ix. 131.
—— —— his 2nd wife, Margaret Menzies, v. 504.
—— of Wester Ardeonaig, Alexander, ii. 191.
—— —— his 1st wife, Jean Campbell, ii. 190.
—— of Ardkinglas, Sir Alexander, bart, viii. 313.
—— —— his wife, Marion Cheape, viii. 313.
—— —— Colin, 3rd son of Colin 'Ionganlach' C. of Lochow, i. 329.
—— —— Colin, i. 338; iii. 437.
—— —— his wife, Matilda Montgomerie, iii. 437.
—— —— Sir Colin, ii. 184, 191; vii. 550.
—— —— his wife, Mary Sempill, vii. 550.
—— —— James, ii. 183.
—— —— James, ii. 200; vii. 549.
—— —— his wife, Isobel Campbell, ii. 200.
—— —— Sir John, i. 329; ii. 183; iii. 443; iv. 373.
—— —— his 1st wife, Annas Campbell, ii. 183.
—— —— his 2nd wife, Jean Hamilton, iv. 373; ix. 104.
—— of Ardmaddie, Charles, i. 360, 381.
—— —— Colin, ii. 206.
—— —— Neil, 2nd son of marquess of Argyll, i. 358, 360; iv. 437.
—— —— his 1st wife, Vere Ker, i. 360.
—— —— his 2nd wife, Susan Menzies, i. 360.
—— of Ardnamurchan, Sir Donald, ii. 201; ix. 23.
—— —— his wife, Anna Campbell, ii. 201; ix. 23.
—— —— Sir Donald, 1st bart., dean of Lismore, i. 344.
—— —— his wife, Jean Campbell, i. 343.
—— of Ardtarua, Iver, ii. 179.
—— of Auchawillin, Colin, ancestor of the family of, i. 329.
—— of Auchendarroch, Duncan, ancestor of the family of, i. 324.
—— of Auchenreoch, Duncan, v. 502.
—— —— James, v. 501.
—— of Auchinbreck, Archibald, alleged ancestor of the family of, i. 332.
—— —— Archibald, i. 337.
—— —— his wife, Katharine Campbell, i. 337.
—— —— Dugal, ii. 293.
—— —— his wife, Finevela Macdonald, ii. 293.
—— —— Sir Dougal, 1st bart., ii. 295; vi. 238.
—— —— his 1st wife, Mary Erskine, v. 84.
—— —— his 2nd wife, Isabel Boyd, ii. 295; v. 167.
—— —— Duncan, iii. 311.

Campbell of Auchinbreck, Sir Duncan, 2nd bart., i. 47, 354.
—— his 3rd wife, Jean Colquhoun, i. 47.
—— Sir Duncan, 4th bart., M.P., i. 520.
—— his wife, Henrietta Lindsay, i. 520.
—— Sir John, ancestor of the family of, i. 336.
— of Auchindoun, John, ancestor of the family of, i. 338.
— of Auchinone, John, v. 188.
—— his wife, Isabel Livingston, v. 188.
— of Auchinroglin, Sir Hugh, v. 496.
— of Auchinryre, Alexander, ii. 186.
—— John, ii. 186.
—— his wife, Florentine Macdougall, ii. 186.
—— Patrick, ii. 186; ix. 43.
— of Auchlyne, Duncan, 8th son of Sir Robt. C. of Glenurchay, ii. 200; ix. 45.
—— his wife, Christian Dalgleish, ii. 200; ix. 45.
—— Robert, ii. 191.
— of Auchmoir, John, v. 500.
—— his wife, Marjorie Menzies, v. 500.
— of Auchnaba, Colin, ii. 202.
—— his wife, * Campbell, ii. 202.
— of Auchnacrieve, Charles, M.P., i. 381.
— of Auchreoch, John, ii. 142; v. 499.
—— his 1st wife, Margaret Moncrieff, v. 499.
—— his 2nd wife, Christian Ogilvy, ii. 142, 178; v. 499.
— of Auchtertiry, James, v. 501.
— of Balerno, John, ancestor of the family of, i. 338.
— of Ballinaby, Sir John, ancestor of the family of, i. 336.
— of Balloch, Hugh, viii. 118.
—— his wife, Janet Kennedy, viii. 118.
— of Balmuck, James, v. 501.
— of Balsalloch, Patrick, ix. 55.
— of Barbreck, Alexander, ii. 297.
—— his wife, Barbara Stewart, ii. 297.
—— Colin, illeg. son of 4th earl of Argyll, i. 340.
—— his wife, * Campbell of Barbreck, i. 340.
—— Colin, 8th laird, i. 340.
—— Donald, 1778, i. 385.
—— his wife, Mary Campbell, i. 385.
—— Donald, ii. 201.
—— his wife, Isabel Campbell, ii. 201.
—— John, ancestor of the 1st family of, i. 326.
—— his wife, Mariota of Glenurquhay, i. 326.
——of Barbreck-Lochow, Donald, dean of Lismore, i. 343.
—— his wife, Jean Campbell, i. 343.

* Name unknown.

Campbell of Barcaldine, Alexander, deputy-governor of Fort George, general, ii. 356.
—— his wife,* Sinclair, ii. 356.
—— Robert, 2nd son of Sir John C. of Glenurchy, ii. 201.
—— his wife, Anna Campbell, ii. 201.
— of Barnacarrie, John, ancestor of the family of, i. 338.
— of Barnwell, Sir Hugh, v. 498.
— of Benderloch, Sir Donald, i. 320.
—— his wife, Amabilla, i, 320.
—— Sir Duncan, i. 320; v. 490, 499.
—— his wife, Susanna Crauford, v. 490.
— of Benquhol, Sir George, v. 492.
— of Blairnarne, Colin, vi. 158, 161.
—— his wife, Janet Graham, vi. 158.
— of Blythswood, Colin, ancestor of the family of, i. 329.
— of Boghall, Colin, vi. 158.
—— his wife, Janet Graham, vi. 158.
— of Boquhan, Sir Colin, 2nd son of 4th earl of Argyll, i. 344.
—— James, 4th son of 9th earl of Argyll, i. 367.
—— his 1st wife, Mary Wharton, i. 367.
—— his 2nd wife, Margaret Leslie, i. 368; vi. 442.
—— Sir John, iv. 278.
—— his wife, Isobel Gray, iv. 277.
—— Mary, dau. of James C. of Burnbank, i. 368; ix. 24.
— of Boquhapple Wester, Archibald, vi. 157.
— of Borland, Robert, 4th son of Colin C. of Mochaster, ii. 190, 209, 212.
—— his wife, Janet Campbell, ii. 190.
— of Botuarymore, Alexander, W.S., ii. 201.
— of the Bracanrig, Hugh, ii. 401.
—— his wife, Katharine Blair, ii. 401.
—— James, ii. 401.
— of Bragleen, John, ancestor of the family of, i. 338.
— of Brownside, Hugh, ii. 401; v. 492.
—— his wife, Katharine Blair, ii. 401.
—— James, ii. 401.
— of Burnbank, Charles, i. 368; ix. 24.
—— James, 4th son of 9th earl of Argyll, i. 367; ix. 24.
—— his 1st wife, Mary Wharton, i. 367.
—— his 2nd wife, Margaret Leslie, i. 368; vi. 442.
— of Calder. *See* of Cawdor.
— of Carrick, Colin, ancestor of the family of, i. 329.
—— John, capt., i. 382.
—— his wife, Jean Campbell, i. 382; ix. 24.
—— his self-styled wife, Margaret Cochrane, ix. 24.

* Name unknown.

Campbell of Carwhin, Colin, W.S., 3rd son of Colin C. of Mochaster, ii. 190, 205.
—— —— his wife, Elizabeth Pringle, ii. 190.
—— —— Colin, eldest son of Robt. C. of Borland, ii. 190, 209.
—— —— his wife, Elizabeth Campbell, ii. 190.
—— —— Colin, brother of 4th earl of Breadalbane, ii. 190, 210.
—— of Castlehill, John, commissary of Caithness, ii. 348.
—— —— his wife, Anne Sinclair, ii. 348.
—— of Cawdor *or* Calder, Archibald, vii. 461.
—— —— his wife, Isobel Grant, vii. 461.
—— —— Sir Hugh, vi. 321.
—— —— his wife, Henriet Stewart, vi. 321.
—— —— Sir John, 3rd son of 2nd earl of Argyll, i. 336; iii. 199, 200, 201; viii. 339, 340.
—— —— his wife, Muriella of Calder, i. 336.
—— —— John, vi. 50.
—— —— his 1st wife, Mary Keith, vi. 50.
—— —— Sir John, i. 202; ii. 187; iii. 443; ix. 23.
—— —— his 1st wife, Jean Campbell, ii. 187.
—— —— his 2nd wife, Elizabeth Douglas, i. 202.
—— —— Sir John, brother of Colin C. of Ardersier, iv. 63.
—— of Cessnock, George, iii. 438.
—— —— his wife, Jonet Montgomerie, iii. 438.
—— —— Sir George, lord justice-clerk, vi. 19.
—— —— Sir Hugh, v. 499.
—— —— his wife, Elizabeth Campbell, v. 499.
—— —— John, v. 495.
—— —— his wife, Janet Campbell, v. 495.
—— —— Margaret, wife of Sir Andrew Hume, lord Cessnock, vi. 19.
—— of Clathick, John, v. 504.
—— —— his 1st wife, Margaret Donaldson, ix. 131.
—— —— his 2nd wife, Margaret Menzies, v. 504.
—— of Clonestang, Sir Hugh, v. 495.
—— of Clunes, Colin, vii. 472.
—— of Cluny, Sir John, ancestor of the family of, i. 336.
—— of Colgrain, Thomas, ancestor of the family of, v. 500 *n*.
—— of Combie, Charles, vi. 432.
—— —— his wife, Christian Graham Napier, vi. 432.
—— —— Colin, ancestor of the family of, i. 329.
—— of Corriechrombie, Sir Robert, ii. 189.
—— of Corrieleigh, John, ancestor of the family of, i. 338.
—— of Corshill, John, 2nd son of Sir George C. of Loudoun, v. 493.
Campbell of Coschambies, Sir Robert, ii. 189.
—— of Cowlath, Sir George, v. 492.
—— of Craokaig, Colin, ancestor of the family of, i. 329.
—— of Craignish, Sir Colin, i. 328.
—— —— Colin, illeg. son of 5th earl of Argyll, i. 343; ix. 21.
—— —— Cristina, 1361, i. 328.
—— —— Dugald, i. 328.
—— —— Gillespic, i. 326.
—— —— Ronald, son of Malcolm, i. 330.
—— of Crannick, John, bishop of the Isles, ii. 180.
—— of Dalnarton, Sir George, v. 492.
—— of Darvel, Sir Matthew, v. 497.
—— of Dergachie, Colin, ancestor of the family of, i. 329.
—— of Drumfad, Duncan, vi. 149.
—— —— his wife, Marjorie Campbell, vi. 149.
—— of Drumsynie, Robert, ii. 202.
—— —— his wife, Mary Campbell, ii. 202.
—— of Ducholly, Duncan, ancestor of the family of, i. 324.
—— of Duchray, Sir George, v. 492.
—— of Duneaves, Archibald, ancestor of the family of, ii. 179.
—— of Dunfallinch, Archibald, v. 500.
—— —— his wife, Elizabeth Wedderburn, v. 500.
—— of Dunloskin, Colin, ancestor of the family of, ix. 18.
—— of Dunnowell, George, v. 496.
—— of Dunoon, Colin, ancestor of the family of, i. 329.
—— of Dunstaffnage, Dugal, ancestor of the family of, i. 329.
—— —— Duncan, vii. 42.
—— of Duntroon, Duncan, 4th son of Sir Colin C. of Lochow, i. 321.
—— —— Duncan, ancestor of the family of, i. 330.
—— of Edinample, Colin, v. 505.
—— —— his wife, * Campbell, v. 505.
—— —— John, ii. 188.
—— —— Patrick, 8th son of Sir Duncan C. of Glenurchy, ii. 187, 190.
—— —— his wife, Margaret Campbell, ix. 43.
—— of Edingham, Sir George, v. 492.
—— of Edinchip, Patrick Dow More, legtd. son of Sir Duncan C. of Glenurchy, ii. 202.
—— of Edramuckie, Duncan, v. 505.
—— of Ellengreig, Neil, ancestor of the family of, i. 332.
—— of Fairfield, William, i. 388.
—— of Fern, Sir Hugh, v. 496.
—— of Finab, Alexander, colonel, i. 360.
—— —— his wife, Susan Menzies, i. 360.
—— of Finnard, James, v. 504.

* Name unknown.

Campbell of Fordew, Archibald, v. 502.
— — James, v. 501.
— of Gaolin, John, ii. 202.
— — his wife, Elspeth Campbell, ii. 202.
— of Geddes, John, prior of Ardchattan, ii. 5.
— of Glassary, Dougal, 2nd son of Sir Colin C. of Lochow, i. 325.
— — his wife, Margaret of Glassary, i. 325.
— of Glenamackrie, Colin, ancestor of the family of, i. 329.
— of Glenample, Archibald, ii. 183.
— — Colin, 2nd son of Colin C. of Glenurchy, ii. 182; ix. 43.
— — his wife, Margaret Monro, ii. 183.
— — Colin, his son, ii. 183; ix. 43 *bis*.
— — his wife, Jean Chisholm, ii. 183.
— of Glencarradale, Sir Archibald, commendator of Strathfillan, v. 503; ix. 3, 142.
— — his wife, Bessie Napier, v. 504; ix. 142.
— of Glendaruel, Archibald, ancestor of the family of, ix. 20.
— of Glenfalloch, Colin, lieut. 71st regt., ii. 192.
— — his 1st wife, * Drummond M'Gregor, ii. 192.
— — his 2nd wife, *, ii. 192.
— — James, lieut. Murray's Highland regt., ii. 191.
— — John Breadalbane, ii. 193, 194; ix. 44.
— — William, ii. 192, 198, 212.
— — his 1st wife, Effie M'Nicol, ii. 192.
— — his 2nd wife, Susanna Campbell, ii. 192.
— — William Erskine, ii. 192.
— — his wife, Susanna Campbell, ii. 192.
— of Glenfeochan, Duncan, ancestor of the family of, i. 327.
— — James, colonel, ii. 197.
— of Glenlyon, Archibald, ii. 200.
— — his wife, Jean Campbell, ii. 200.
— — Archibald, 2nd son of Sir Duncan C. of Glenurchy, ii. 179.
— — Colin, v. 504.
— — his wife, Beatrix Campbell, v. 504.
— — Duncan, v. 500.
— — his wife, Margaret Drummond, v. 500.
— — Robert, ii. 190.
— of Glensaddell, Albert Johnstone, ix. 15.
— — Dugald, iii. 39.
— — his wife, Mary Lindsay, iii. 39.
— — Dugald, claimant to the earldom of Annandale, iii. 39.
— of Glenshira, Duncan, *or* Donnochie Mor, i. 330.

* Name unknown.

Campbell of Glentarken, Alexander, ii. 186.
— — Colin, ii. 188.
— — James, v. 501.
— — Patrick, ii. 186.
— — his wife, Katharine Murray, ii. 186.
— — Patrick, 8th son of Sir Duncan C. of Glenurchy, ii. 187.
— of Glenurchy, Sir Colin, 2nd son of 1st lord C. of Lochow; 1st laird, i. 326, 331; ii. 174; ix. 18, 42.
— — his alleged wife, Mariot Stewart, ii. 176.
— — his 1st wife, Jonet Stewart, ii. 176; v. 4.
— — his 2nd wife, Margaret Stirling, ii. 178.
— — Sir Colin, 3rd laird, ii. 180.
— — his wife, Marjory Stewart, i. 442; ii. 180.
— — Colin, 6th laird, ii. 180, 182; v. 502, 503.
— — his 1st wife, Margaret Stewart, ii. 182.
— — his 2nd wife, Katharine Ruthven, ii. 182; iv. 260.
— — Sir Colin, 2nd bart., ii. 185, 188.
— — his wife, Juliana Campbell, ii. 189; v. 498.
— — Sir Duncan, 2nd laird, i. 178; ii. 175 *n.*, 178.
— — his 1st wife, Margaret Douglas, i. 178; ii. 179.
— — his 2nd wife, Margaret Moncrieff, ii. 180.
— — Sir Duncan, 4th laird, ii. 180.
— — his wife, Elizabeth Colquhoun, ii. 180.
— — Sir Duncan, 1st bart., ii. 182, 183, 184, 202; vi. 164; ix. 43.
— — his 1st wife, Janet Stewart, i. 445; ii. 185.
— — his 2nd wife, Elizabeth Sinclair, ii. 187; vii. 574, 475.
— — John 'Annam,' 3rd son of Sir Colin C. of Lochow, i. 326.
— — his wife, Mariota of Glenurquhay, i. 326.
— — Sir John, 5th laird, ii. 181.
— — his wife, Mariot Edmonstone, ii. 181.
— — Sir John, 4th bart., colonel, M.P., ii. 189, 200; ix. 45 *bis*.
— — his 1st wife, Mary Graham, i. 138; ii. 201.
— — his 2nd wife, Elizabeth Campbell, ii. 202.
— — his 3rd wife, Christian Mushet, ii. 202; ix. 45.
— — Sir John, 5th bart., ii. 201, 203.
— — his 1st wife, Mary Rich, ii. 205.
— — his 2nd wife, Mary Campbell, i. 361; ii. 205.

Campbell of Glenure, Colin, vii. 174.
—— —— his wife, Janet Mackay, vii. 174.
—— of Grougar, Sir Hugh, v. 498.
—— of Hellsglen, James, ii. 192; ix. 44.
—— —— his wife, Christian Campbell, ii. 192.
—— of the Ibert, Archibald, ii. 186.
—— —— Duncan, ii. 186.
—— —— his wife, Ann *or* Agnes Murray, ii. 186.
—— of Inchharry, Colin, v. 526.
—— of Inellan, Colin, ancestor of the family of, i. 329.
—— of Innergeldie, John, v. 504.
—— his 1st wife, Margaret Donaldson, ix. 131.
—— his 2nd wife, Margaret Menzies, v. 504.
—— of Innestore, Colin, ancestor of the family of, i. 329.
—— of Inverawe, Archibald, ii. 200.
—— —— Dugald, ii. 200.
—— —— his wife, Isobel Campbell, ii. 200.
—— —— Duncan, ancestor of the family of, i. 324.
—— —— Duncan, major Black Watch, i. 360.
—— —— his wife, Jean Campbell, i. 360.
—— of Inverliver, Alexander, ix. 23.
—— —— his wife, Anna Campbell, ix. 23.
—— of Invertschie, Archibald, v. 500.
—— —— his wife, Elizabeth Wedderburn, v. 500.
—— of Islay, Colin, ancestor of the family of, i. 329.
—— —— John, colonel, M.P., i. 387.
—— —— his wife, Charlotte Susan Maria Campbell, i. 387.
—— —— Walter, i. 387.
—— of Jura, John, ancestor of the present family of, i. 338.
—— of Kames, Duncan, iii. 489.
—— —— his wife, Veronica Bruce, iii. 489.
—— of Keithock, David, i. 512.
—— —— Donald, ancestor of the family of, i. 336.
—— of Kenmore, Neil, ancestor of the family of, i. 326.
—— of Kildalvan, Colin, ancestor of the family of, ix. 18.
—— of Kilmartin, Duncan, ancestor of the family of, i. 324.
—— of Kingart, Sir Archibald, commendator of Strathfillan, v. 503.
—— of Kinloch, John, ii. 196.
—— —— Thomas, ancestor of the family of, v. 500 *n*.
—— of Kinrotharochie, Sir John, v. 503.
—— of Kinzeancleuch, Robert, ii. 65; v. 111.
—— of Kirkton, Colin, v. 526.
—— —— Sir John, ancestor of the family of, i. 336.
—— of Kirktouchmachill, Colin, ix. 23.
—— of Kittomure, Sir George, v. 492.
Campbell of Knockamellie, Colin, ancestor of the family of, i. 329.
—— of Knockhill, Archibald, ancestor of the family of, ii. 179.
—— of Knockreoch, John, ii. 102.
—— —— his wife, Margaret Borthwick, ii. 102.
—— —— of Kylesmure, Sir Hugh, v. 498.
—— of Lagganmore, John, ancestor of the family of, i. 338.
—— of Lagvinshoch, Archibald, son of Sir Duncan C., 1st bart. of Glenurchy, ii. 186.
—— —— his 1st wife, Katharine Graham, ii. 186.
—— —— his 2nd wife, Christian Robertson, ii. 186.
—— of Lawers, Archibald, v. 502.
—— —— his wife, Agnes Ross, v. 502.
—— —— James, v. 500.
—— —— his 1st wife, Marion Forrester, v. 501.
—— —— his 2nd wife, Janet Gray, iv. 278; v. 501.
—— —— his 3rd wife, Isobel Hay, v. 501.
—— —— Sir James, ii. 557; v. 504; vi. 419.
—— —— his wife, Jean Colville, ii. 557; v. 504.
—— —— Sir James, Lyon King of Arms, v. 505.
—— —— his 1st wife, Margaret Macleod *or* Mackenzie, iii. 73; v. 505.
—— —— his 2nd wife, Ann Stewart, v. 505.
—— —— James, his eldest son, v. 505.
—— —— James, his 2nd son, v. 505.
—— —— Sir James, col. Royal Scots Greys, lieut.-gen., iv. 205, 215; v. 508, 509, 510; viii. 154.
—— —— his wife, Jean Boyle, iv. 205; v. 511.
—— —— James Mure, v. 510, 511.
—— —— his wife, Flora Macleod, v. 511.
—— —— John, 4th son of Sir Colin C. of Glenurchy, ii. 176, 178, 179; v. 499.
—— —— his 1st wife, Agnes Moncrieff, ii. 178.
—— —— his 2nd wife, Christian Ogilvie, ii. 142, 178, 182.
—— —— Sir John, v. 503.
—— —— his wife, Beatrix Campbell, ii. 182; v. 503.
—— —— Sir John, ii. 206; v. 499, 505, 506.
—— —— his wife, Margaret Campbell of Loudoun, v. 499, 506.
—— —— Sir Mungo, 4th laird, v. 505; vii. 201.
—— —— his wife, Helen Menzies, v. 505.
—— of Leix, Colin, ancestor of the family of, i. 329.
—— of Lerags, Duncan, ancestor of the 1st family of, i. 324.
—— —— John, ancestor of the 2nd family of, i. 338.
—— of Letterbean, Sir Colin, v. 4.
—— —— his wife, Jonet Stewart, v. 4.

Campbell of Letters, Dorothy, dau. of Sir John C. of Lawers, v. 504.
—— of Liston Hall, John, M.P., master in Chancery, i. 382.
—— —— his 1st wife, * Peter, i. 382.
—— —— his 2nd wife, * Hay, i. 382.
—— —— William, 4th son of John C. of Mamore, i. 382.
—— —— his 1st wife, * Barnard, i. 382.
—— —— his 2nd wife, Bridget Bacon, i. 382.
—— —— William Henry, i. 382.
—— of Lochdochart, Alexander, 7th son of Sir Robert C. of Glenurchay, ii. 199; ix. 44.
—— —— his 1st wife, Julian Robertson, ii. 199.
—— —— his 2nd wife, Magdalene Menzies, ii. 200.
—— —— Charles, ii. 192; ix. 44.
—— —— his 2nd wife, Katharine Buchanan, ix. 44.
—— —— John, eldest son of Alex. C., ix. 44.
—— —— his wife, Susanna Campbell, ii. 99.
—— —— William, ix. 44.
—— of Lochnell, Alexander, 3rd laird, ix. 23.
—— —— Alexander, 6th laird, ii. 202.
—— —— Archibald, ix. 21.
—— —— Sir Duncan, vii. 509.
—— —— his wife, Isabel Mackenzie, vii. 509.
—— —— John 'Gorm,' ancestor of the family of, i. 338.
—— —— his wife, Mary Campbell, i. 338.
—— —— Duncan, lieut.-general, vii. 447.
—— —— his wife, Eleanora Fraser, vii. 447.
—— of Lochow, Sir Colin, 'Mor,' 1st laird, i. 319; vi. 534 *n.*
—— —— Sir Colin, keeper of Dunoon Castle, 3rd laird, i. 325.
—— —— his wife, Helena of Lennox, i. 325.
—— —— Sir Colin, 'Ionganlach,' 5th laird, i. 328, 330.
—— —— his alleged wife, Margaret Drummond, i. 328.
—— —— his wife, Mariota *or* Margaret Campbell, i. 324, 328.
—— —— Colin, 7th laird, i. 332.
—— —— his wife, Isabel Stewart of Lorne, i. 332; v. 3.
—— —— Sir Duncan, 'Na-Adh,' 6th laird, i. 330.
—— —— his 1st wife, Marcellina *or* Marjory Stewart, i. 149; ii. 331.
—— —— his 2nd wife, Margaret Stewart, i. 331.
—— —— Sir Gillespic *or* Archibald, ancestor of the family of, i. 319.
—— —— his alleged wife, Margaret Somerville, i. 319; viii. 3.
—— —— his alleged wife, Effrick of Carrick, i. 319.

* Name unknown.

Campbell of Lochow, Gillespic, Archibald, *or* Celestin, 4th laird, i. 318, 326, 330.
—— —— his alleged wife, * Menteith, i. 327; vi. 133 *n.*
—— —— his wife, Isabella Lamont, i. 327.
—— —— Gillespic, Archibald, *or* Celestin, the younger, i. 332.
—— —— his wife, Elizabeth Somerville, i. 332; viii. 12.
—— —— Sir Neil, 2nd laird, i. 320, 322; viii. 565.
—— —— his 1st wife, * Crawford, i. 324; ix. 18.
—— —— his 2nd wife, Mary Bruce, i. 323; ii. 434.
—— of Lochwinnoch, Colin, ancestor of the family of, i. 329.
—— of Loragen, Charles, ix. 44.
—— —— John, ix. 44.
—— —— William, ix. 44.
—— of Loudoun, Sir Andrew, 2nd laird, v. 491.
—— —— Sir Duncan, sheriff of Ayr, 1st laird, i. 321: v. 490, 499.
—— —— his wife, Susanna Crauford of Loudoun, v. 490.
—— —— George, 3rd laird, v. 491, 494.
—— —— Sir George, 5th laird, ii. 401; v. 492.
—— —— Sir George, 6th laird, v. 492.
—— —— his wife, Elizabeth Stewart, v. 493.
—— —— George, 7th laird, v. 493.
—— —— his 1st wife, * Kennedy, v. 493.
—— —— his 2nd wife, Marion Auchinleck, v. 493.
—— —— Sir Hugh, 4th laird, v. 491.
—— —— Sir Hugh, 8th laird, v. 494.
—— —— his wife, Isobel Wallace, v. 494.
—— —— Sir Hugh, 9th laird, ii. 465, 470; v. 495.
—— —— his 1st wife, Elizabeth *or* Margaret Stewart, v. 351, 496.
—— —— his 2nd wife, Agnes Drummond, v. 496; vii. 47.
—— —— John, ancestor of the family of, ii. 178.
—— —— his 1st wife, Agnes Moncreiff, ii. 178.
—— —— his 2nd wife, Christian Ogilvie, ii. 142, 178.
—— —— Sir Hugh, 11th laird, v. 497.
—— —— his 1st wife, Margaret Gordon, v. 111, 498.
—— —— his 2nd wife, Elizabeth Ruthven, iv. 266; v. 114, 116, 498.
—— —— his 3rd wife, Margaret Home, v. 498.
—— —— Sir Matthew, 10th laird, v. 62, 496.
—— —— his wife, Isobel Drummond, v. 497.

* Name unknown.

Campbell of West Loudoun, Elizabeth, wife of (1) Wm. Wallace of Craigie, (2) Robert, 4th lord Crichton of Sanquhar, and (3) William, 3rd earl of Glencairn, iii. 226; iv. 238.
—— —— James, vii. 116, 117.
—— —— his wife, Elizabeth Crichton, ii. 513; iii. 222; vii. 116; ix. 59.
—— —— Sir John, 2nd son of Sir Hugh C. of Loudoun, v. 491.
—— —— his wife, Alicia, v. 491.
—— —— John, vii. 117.
—— —— his wife, Elizabeth Douglas, vii. 117.
—— of Lundie, Colin, 2nd son of 6th earl of Argyll, i. 345; v. 22; vi. 163, 164; ix. 21, 115.
—— —— his wife, Mary Campbell, i. 346; ii. 183; vi. 163, 164.
—— —— Sir Colin, 1st bart., i. 346; iii. 320; ix. 23.
—— —— James, 2nd son of 7th earl of Argyll, i. 350; v. 22 *bis*, 23, 24.
—— —— John, iii. 311.
—— —— his wife, Janet Hering, iii. 311.
—— —— Sir John, ii. 325; iv. 278; v. 556; vi. 173.
—— —— his wife, Isabella Gray, ii. 324; iv. 277; vi. 173.
—— —— John, ix. 73.
—— —— his wife, Elspeth Scrymgeour, ix. 73.
—— —— Thomas, ancestor of the family of, i. 334.
—— of Mamore, John, 2nd son of 9th earl of Argyll, i. 367, 381.
—— —— his wife, Elizabeth Elphinstone, i. 381; iii. 544.
—— of Martname, George, v. 493.
—— of Mauchline, Sir Matthew, v. 496.
—— of Melfort, Neil, ancestor of the family of, i. 326.
—— of Menstrie, Dougal, 3rd son of Sir Colin C. of Lochow, i. 321.
—— —— Sir Gillespic, Gillascop, *or* Archibald, i. 319.
—— —— John, i. 238.
—— —— *, his son and heir, 1364, i. 328.
—— of Mochaster, Colin, 3rd son of Sir Robert C. of Glenurchy, ii. 187, 189, 205, 210, 212.
—— —— his wife, Margaret Menzies, ii. 189.
—— —— Duncan, ii. 190.
—— —— Sir Robert, ii. 189; ix. 43.
—— —— his wife, Isabel Mackintosh, ii. 189.
—— of Monzie, Alexander, colonel, i. 360.
—— —— his wife, Susan Menzies, i. 360.
—— —— Archibald, ii. 183; ix. 43.
—— —— Duncan, ii. 186.
—— —— his wife, Ann *or* Agnes Murray, ii. 186.
—— —— Duncan, viii. 228.
—— —— his wife, Mary Drummond, viii. 228.

* Name unknown.

Campbell of Wester Morinichie, Janet, v. 502.
—— of Morven, Duncan, Jamaica, ii. 195.
—— of Moulin, John, earl of Atholl, i. 324, 434.
—— of Mugdock, Neil, 2nd son of marquess of Argyll, vi. 250, 256.
—— of Murthly, Archibald, v. 500 *n*.
—— —— John, ancestor of the family of, ii. 178.
—— —— his 1st wife, Agnes Moncrieff, ii. 178.
—— —— his 2nd wife, Christian Ogilvie, ii. 178.
—— —— John, v. 499, 502.
—— —— his 1st wife, Marjorie Menzies, v. 500.
—— —— his 2nd wife, Margaret Drummond, v. 500.
—— of Neilstoun, Neil, 2nd son of marquess of Argyll, vi. 250, 256.
—— of Newfield, Albert Johnstone, ix. 15.
—— of Newlands, John, 2nd son of Sir Geo. C. of Loudoun, v. 493.
—— of Orchard, Colin, ancestor of the family of, i. 329.
—— of Ormidale, Colin, i. 332.
—— —— Neil, 3rd son of 1st lord Campbell, i. 332.
—— of Otter, Archibald, ancestor of the family of, i. 332.
—— —— Arthur, v. 4.
—— —— his wife, Marion Stewart, v. 4.
—— of Park, Thomas, ancestor of the family of, v. 500 *n*.
—— of Peatoun, Colin, ancestor of the family of, i. 329.
—— of Pencaitland, Mary Hamilton, wife of 7th lord Ruthven, vii. 390.
—— of Possil, Thomas, ancestor of the family of, v. 500 *n*.
—— of Rachean, Colin, ancestor of the family of, i. 329.
—— of Rait, John, prior of Ardchattan, ii. 5.
—— of Redcastle, Sir Andrew, v. 491.
—— —— Sir Donald, 2nd son of Sir Colin C. of Lochow, i. 320.
—— —— his wife, Amabilla, i. 320.
—— —— Sir Duncan, i. 320.
—— —— his wife, Susanna Crauford, i. 320.
—— of Roro, Archibald, ancestor of the family of, ii. 179.
—— of Ruchill, John, 2nd son of Sir Geo. C. of Loudoun, v. 493.
—— of St. Catherine's, Colin, ancestor of the family of, i. 329.
—— of Sauchie, Sir Gillascop *or* Archibald, i. 319.
—— of Scammadale, Colin, ancestor of the family of, i. 329.
—— of Scheil, George, v. 493.
—— of Sestill, Sir James, v. 504.

Campbell of Shankston, John, col., M.P., v. 508.
— of Shawfield, Colin, ancestor of the family of, i. 329.
— — Daniel, ii. 368.
— — his wife, Katharine Erskine, ii. 368.
— — John, iv. 251; v. 509.
— — his 1st wife, Margaret Campbell, v. 509.
— — his 2nd wife, Henrietta Cunningham, iv. 251; ix. 98.
— — John, colonel, M.P., i. 387; v. 367.
— — his wife, Charlotte Susan Maria Campbell, i. 387.
— — Walter, i. 387; vii. 390; viii. 515.
— — his 1st wife, Eleanor Ker, viii. 515.
— — Walter Frederick, M.P., ii. 54; viii. 515.
— — his wife, Eleanor Charteris, viii. 515.
— of Shirvain, Duncan, ancestor of the family of, i. 324.
— of Skeldon, William, ix. 56.
— — his wife, Marion Kennedy, ix. 56.
— of Skipnish, Angus, ii. 296.
— — his wife, Jean Stewart, ii. 296.
— — Archibald, 2nd son of 2nd earl of Argyll, i. 190, 336; viii. 280.
— — his 1st wife, Jonet Stewart, ii. 288; ix. 19.
— — his 2nd wife, Jonet Douglas, i. 189, 336; viii. 279.
— — Colin, ancestor of the family of, i. 329.
— — John, ii. 293; ix. 19.
— — his wife, Marion Montgomery, ix. 19.
— — Walter, ii. 296.
— — his wife, Anne Stewart, ii. 296.
— of Sonachan, Sir John, ancestor of the family of, i. 336.
— of Sorn, Hugh, v. 497.
— — Sir John, v. 506.
— of Southhall, Duncan, ancestor of the family of, i. 324.
— of Spangok, Sir Hugh, v. 496.
— of Stobs, William, viii. 125.
— — his wife, Esther Dalrymple, viii. 125.
— of Stonefield, Alexander, ii. 202.
— — his wife, Elspet Campbell, ii. 202.
— — Archibald, ii. 24.
— — his wife, Jane Frend, ii. 24.
— — Archibald, ii. 190.
— — John, ancestor of the family of, i. 338.
— — John, lord Stonefield, ii. 301.
— — his wife, Grace Stuart, ii. 301.
— of Strachur, Colin, ii. 184.
— of Stronchormaig, Duncan, ancestor of the family of, i. 327.
Campbell of Succoth, Sir Archibald, 2nd bart., vi. 119.
— — Sir James, v. 504.
— — John, ancestor of the family of, i. 326.
— — his wife, Mariota of Glenurchay, i. 326.
— of Symontoun, Sir Colin, i. 319.
— of Tealing, Sir Colin, iii. 320.
— of Terrinzean, Sir Hugh, v. 496.
— — Hugh, eldest son of Sir Matthew C. of Loudoun, v. 357, 479.
— of Tillicoultry, Colin, i. 325 *n.*
— — Neil, i. 325 *n.*
— of Tirrefour, John, ancestor of the family of, i. 338.
— of Toranturk, John, ii. 202.
— — his wife, Elspeth Campbell, ii. 202.
— of Torrie, Colin, ancestor of the family of, i. 329.
— — Robert, vi. 154.
— — Robert, vi. 155.
— — his wife, Ann Burden of Feddal, vi. 155.
— of Torsa, Dugal, 3rd son of Sir Colin C. of Lochow, i. 321.
— of Trabeauch, Sir Hugh, v. 495.
— of Tulloch, William, 5th son of Sir John C. of Glenurchy, ii. 201; ix. 45.
— of Weasenham, Alexander Straton, ii. 119.
— — his wife, Alice Rachel Anne Borthwick, ii. 118.
— A., illeg. son of 5th earl of Argyll, i. 343.
— Adelaide Constance, wife of Arthur Lennox, v. 367.
— Agnes, dau. of 1st earl of Argyll, i. 335.
— Agnes, wife of (1) Sir James Stewart of Bute, (2) Sir James Macdonell of Antrim, and (3) Turlough Luinech O'Neill, i. 338; ii. 292; ix. 20 *ter.*, 50.
— Agnes, wife of P. Ogilvie, ii. 187.
— Agnes, wife of Colin Campbell, ii. 191.
— Agnes, wife of Dugald Campbell of Inverawe, ii. 200.
— Agnes, wife of Alex. Menzies, ii. 201.
— Agnes, wife of Sir Robert Maclellan of Bombie, v. 267, 498.
— Agnes, wife of Wm. Cunningham of Caprington, v. 497.
— Agnes, wife of Robert Graham *alias* Burden of Feddal, vi. 155.
— Alexander, father of John, Tosheachdeorac of Melphort, i. 331.
— Mr. Alexander, dean of Moray, i. 338.
— Alexander, 4th son of lord Neil C. of Ardmaddie, i. 361.
— Alexander, bishop of Brechin, i. 294; ii. 27; iii. 283; iv. 373.
— rev. Alexander, ii. 419.
— Alexander, 5th son of Colin C. of Mochaster, ii. 190.

Campbell, Alexander, officer in North British regiments, Kirktown of Strathfillan, ii. 198; ix. 44.
—— his wife, * Bowie, ii. 198.
— Alexander, 9th son of Colin C., ii. 199.
— Alexander, illeg. son of Sir Hugh C. of Loudoun, v. 496.
— Andrew, 5th son of Sir John C. of Lawers, v. 504.
— Alicia, wife of Allan Lauder of Hatton, i. 326.
— Anne, wife of 2nd marquess of Huntly, i. 349.
— Anne, wife of rev. Mr. Bulleyn, i. 350; ix. 23.
— Anne, dau. of marquess of Argyll, i. 361; ix. 23.
— Anne, wife of (1) 4th earl of Lauderdale, and (2) 7th earl of Moray, i. 368; v. 310; vi. 323.
— Ann, dau. of James C. of Burnbank, i. 368; ix. 24.
— Anne, wife of (1) 2nd earl of Bute, and (2) Alex. Fraser of Strichen, i. 370; ii. 300; v. 545; ix. 24.
— Anne, wife of William, earl of Strafford, i. 377.
— Anne, wife of Archibald Edmonstone, i. 382.
— Anne (*error for* Louisa), wife of Alex. Johnstone, i. 385; ix. 25.
— Anne, wife of Sir P. Ogilvy of Inchmartine, ii. 187; iv. 34.
— Anne, wife of Sir K. Mackenzie of Grandvale, iii. 76.
— Anne, dau. of Sir Archd. C. of Glencarradale, v. 504.
— Ann, wife of 3rd lord Balmerino, v. 507.
— Anna, wife of capt. Jas. Menzies of Comrie, i. 360.
— Anna, wife of (1) Sir Donald Campbell of Ardnamurchan, and (2) Alex. Campbell of Inverliver, ii. 201; ix. 23.
— Anna, wife of Robert MacNab of that Ilk, ii. 202; ix. 45 *bis*.
— Annabella, wife of 2nd earl of Lothian, i. 349; v. 459, 460 *bis*; ix. 21.
— Annabella, wife of (1) Alex. Napier of Merchiston, and (2) R. Fairlie of Braid, ii. 180; vi. 413; ix. 42.
— Annabella, wife of (1) Thos. Boswell of Auchinleck, and (2) John Cunningham of Caprington, v. 495.
— Annabella, wife of (1) D. Ker of Kersland, and (2) D. Dunbar of Enterkin, v. 497.
— Annas, proposed wife of 5th earl of Cassillis, i. 346; ii. 477.
— Annas, wife of John Campbell of Ardkinglas, ii. 183.

* Name unknown.

Campbell, Archibald, eldest son of Sir Duncan C. of Lochow, i. 331, 332; ix. 18.
—— his wife, Mariota of the Isles, ix. 18.
— Archibald, 5th son of 1st lord Campbell, i. 332; ii. 174.
— Archibald, captain of Skipness Castle, i. 336.
—— his 2nd wife, Janet Douglas, i. 336.
— Archibald, bishop, son of Lord Neil C., i. 360; ix. 23.
— Archibald, eldest son of 4th duke of Argyll, i. 384.
— Archibald, 2nd son of 8th duke of Argyll, i. 390.
—— his wife, Janey Sevilla Callendar, i. 390.
— Archibald, minister of Weem, i. 549.
—— his wife, Ann Stewart, i. 549.
— Archibald, 4th son of Colin C. of Glenurchy, ii. 183.
—— his wife, Margaret Toshoch, ii. 183.
— Archibald, son of John C. of Auchinryre, ii. 186.
— Archibald, writer, lieut. 74th regt., ii. 195.
—— his wife, Jean Butter, ii. 195.
— Archibald, 7th son of Colin C., ii. 198.
— Archibald, in Succoth, 3rd son of Robert C., ii. 199; ix. 44.
— Archibald, sergeant, Middlesex Militia, ii. 199.
— Sir Archibald, iv. 289.
— Archibald, his son, iv. 289.
—— his wife, Janet Gray, iv. 289.
— Archibald, only son of Sir Archd. C. of Carradale, v. 504.
— Archibald, son of Jas. C. of Hellsglen, ix. 44.
— Sir Arthur, constable of Dunstaffnage, i. 321.
— Augusta, wife of col. H. Clavering, i. 387; ix. 25.
— Barbara (Meliora), dau. of 7th earl of Argyll, i. 350; ix. 22 *bis*, 23.
— Beatrix, wife of Sir Wm. Hamilton of Manor Elieston, i. 42; v. 504; ix. 3.
— Beatrix, wife of Sir John Campbell of Lawers, ii. 182; v. 503, 504; ix. 42.
— Beatrix, dau. of Sir John C. of Glenorchy, ii. 202.
— Beatrix, wife of Colin Campbell of Glenlyon, v. 504.
— Beatrix, mother of Colin C. of Craignish, ix. 21.
— Caroline, wife of (1) Francis, earl of Dalkeith, and (2) C. Townshend; baroness of Greenwich, i. 377; ii. 241; ix. 24.
— Caroline, dau. of John C. of Liston Hall, i. 382.

Campbell, Caroline, dau. of Wm. C., governor of So. Carolina, i. 385.
— Caroline, wife of (1) Charles, 4th earl of Elgin and 3rd earl of Ailesbury, and (2) field-marshal H. Seymour Conway, i. 385; iii. 482; ix. 25, 82.
— Celestin, eldest son of 1st lord Campbell of Lochawe, i. 330, 331, 332.
— — his betrothed wife, Marion Macdonald, ix. 115.
— — his wife, Elizabeth Somerville, i. 332; viii. 12.
— — his alleged wife, * Stewart, i. 332.
— Celestin, 5th son of 1st lord Campbell of Lochow, i. 332.
— Celestin, 7th son of Sir Colin C. of Lochow, ix. 18.
— Charles, colonel, M.P., i. 367.
— — his wife, Sophia Lindsay, i. 367, 520.
— Charles, 12th son of Sir John C. of Glenurchy, ii. 202.
— Charles, inf. son of 7th earl of Argyll, i. 350; ix. 22.
— Charles, *secundus*, ix. 22.
— Charles, *tertius*, ix. 22.
— Charles, 2nd son of Dr. Charles A. C., ix. 45.
— Charles Archibald, M.D., ix. 44.
— — his wife, Marjorie M'Gillivray, ix. 45.
— Charles Colin Kinloch, ii. 197.
— Charles Hay, major Bengal Artillery, iii. 390.
— — his wife, Wemyss Jane Murray, iii. 390.
— Charles William, 39th regt., son of capt. John C., ii. 196.
— — his wife, Charlotte Olympia Cockburn Campbell, ii. 196.
— Charles William, major-general Bengal Staff Corps, claimant to earldom of Breadalbane, ii. 196, 212.
— — his wife, Gwynnedd Brinkman, ii. 196.
— Charles William, his son, ii. 196.
— Charlotte, dau. of 2nd earl of Breadalbane, ii. 207.
— Charlotte Elizabeth, wife of M. S. Vanderbyl, ii. 197.
— Charlotte Julia, wife of 13th earl of Rothes, vii. 308; ix. 153 *bis*.
— Charlotte Olympia Cockburn, wife of C. W. Campbell, ii. 196.
— Charlotte Susan Maria, wife of (1) col. John Campbell, and (2) Rev. E. J. Bury, i. 388; ix. 25 *bis*, 90.
— Christiana, wife of Duncan Macfarlane of Arrochar, i. 329.
— Christian, wife of Sir Alex. Menzies, i. 361.

* Name unknown.

Campbell, Christian, wife of Jas. Colquhoun of Garscube, ii. 181.
— Christian, wife of (1) Duncan M'Pherson, and (2) Jas. Campbell of Hellsglen, ii. 192; ix. 44.
— Christian, wife of John Ross of Galstoun, v. 508.
— Christian, dau. of Colin C., ix. 44.
— Sir Colin, 'Mor,' son of Sir Gillespic C., i. 319.
— Colin, 5th son of 8th duke of Argyll, i. 391.
— — his wife, Gertrude Elizabeth Blood, i. 391; ix. 26.
— Colin, minister of Killin and Blair-Athol, ii. 187.
— — his wife, Jean Stewart, ii. 187.
— Colin, son of Robert C., ii. 191, 212; ix. 43, 44.
— — his wife, Agnes Campbell, ii. 191.
— Colin, ensign 96th regt., ii. 198; ix. 44.
— Colin, surgeon, 39th regt., ii. 199.
— Colin, son of Archibald C., Middlesex, ii. 199.
— Colin, America, ii. 199.
— Colin, merchant in Edinburgh, ii. 202.
— Colin, commissioner of customs, v. 387.
— Colin, M.D., v. 418.
— Colin, 3rd son of George C. of Loudoun, v. 494.
— Colin, lieut.-col. in Lawers' regt., v. 505.
— Colin George Lorne, ii. 197.
— — his wife, Robina Gordon Fraser, ii. 197.
— Colin Maria Nairne, wife of Wm. Sutton, ii. 194.
— Colina Edwy, ii. 196.
— Constance, 20th child of 7th earl of Argyll, ix. 23.
— Constance Harriet, wife of Charles Emmot, i. 391.
— David, son of Sir Hugh C. of Loudoun, v. 492.
— Donald, son of Colin 'Ionganlach' C. of Lochow, i. 329.
— Donald, abbot of Coupar, and lord Privy Seal, i. 336; v. 500 *bis*.
— Douglas Walter, son of lord Walter C., i. 391.
— — his wife, Aimée Lawrence, i. 391.
— Dugal, sheriff of Dumbarton and Argyll, bailie of Atholl, i. 321.
— Dugall, dean of Argyll; styled 'of Lochow,' i. 329.
— Dugal, son of Colin 'Ionganlach' C. of Lochow, i. 329.
— Duncan, ancestor of the Maconochie or Campbells of Inverawe and their cadets, i. 324.
— Duncan 'Crosta' and 'Skeodnish,' i. 327.

Campbell, Duncan, 4th son of 1st lord Campbell, i. 332; ii. 174.
— Duncan, son of John C. of Auchinryre, ii. 186.
— Duncan, 8th son of Archibald C. of Lagvinshoch, ii. 187.
— Duncan, 2nd son of Sir Robert C. of Glenurchy, ii. 189.
— Duncan, father-in-law of Wm. C. of Glenfalloch, ii. 192.
— Duncan, 4th son of Colin C., ii. 198.
— Duncan, 5th son of Robert C., ii. 199.
— Duncan, 4th son of Sir John C. of Glenurchy, ii. 201.
— Duncan, styled Lord Ormelie, ii. 205.
— — his wife, Margaret Campbell, ii. 206.
— Duncan, elder son of Archd. C. of Lawers, v. 502.
— Duncan, 3rd son of Sir John C. of Lawers, v. 503.
— Duncan, colonel, vi. 515.
— — his wife, Katharine Stewart, vi. 515.
— Edith, wife of 7th duke of Northumberland, i. 391.
— Edward, 4th son of Jas. C. of Lawers, v. 501, 502.
— Egidia, wife of John Gordon, ii. 188.
— Egidia, wife of Sir Colin Campbell of Glenurchy, ii. 189; v. 498.
— Eleanor, wife of (1) James, 1st viscount of Primrose, and (2) John, 2nd earl of Stair, v. 508; viii. 154; ix. 131, 150.
— Elizabeth, wife of (1) James (Stewart), earl of Moray, and (2) John, 10th earl of Sutherland, i. 22, 338; vi. 312; viii. 342.
— Elizabeth, wife of John, 2nd lord Oliphant, i. 335; vi. 543.
— Elizabeth, dau. of 7th earl of Argyll, i. 350.
— Elizabeth, wife of Jas. Stuart Mackenzie, i. 377, 378; ii. 300.
— Elizabeth, dau. of John C. of Mamore, i. 383.
— Elizabeth, wife of 7th duke of Argyll, i. 388.
— Elizabeth, wife of major Clough Taylor, i. 391.
— Elizabeth, wife of D. Toshach, ii. 180.
— Elizabeth, dau. of John C. of Ardkinglas, ii. 184.
— Elizabeth, wife of Robert Irvine of Fedderat, ii. 188.
— Elizabeth, wife of Colin C. of Carwhin, ii. 190; ix. 43.
— Elizabeth, dau. of Archibald C., Succoth, ii. 199; ix. 44.
— Elizabeth, wife of Sir John C. of Glenurchy, ii. 202.
— Elizabeth, dau. of Sir John C. of Calder, iii. 201.
Campbell, Elizabeth, wife of major H. B. Lindsay, v. 418.
— Elizabeth, wife of Sir Hugh C. of Cessnock, v. 499.
— Elizabeth, dau. of Jas. C. of Lawers, v. 502.
— Elizabeth, dau. of Sir Archd. C. of Glencarradale, v. 504.
— Elizabeth, dau. of 3rd earl of Loudoun, v. 509.
— Elizabeth, wife of Robert, 4th lord Erskine, v. 494, 608.
— Elizabeth, wife of John, 5th lord Erskine, v. 610 *n.*
— Elizabeth, wife of 1st earl of Rothes, vii. 275.
— Elizabeth, dau. of 2nd earl of Argyll, contracted to George Gordon, ix. 20, 110.
— Elizabeth, dau. of 7th earl of Argyll, ix. 23.
— Elizabeth, dau. of capt. John C. of Carrick, ix. 25.
— Elizabeth, dau. of Patrick C. of Edinample, ix. 43.
— Elizabeth, wife of John Darroch, ix. 45.
— Elizabeth Anne, wife of 8th earl of Leven, vi. 119.
— Elizabeth Maitland, wife of Sir J. Pringle, ii. 211.
— Elizabeth Marbrough, wife of (1) John Butler, and (2) John Hilton, ii. 194.
— Elspeth, wife of Iain Macfarlane of Arrochar, i. 344; ix. 21.
— Elspet, wife of (1) John Campbell, and (2) Alex. Campbell of Stonefield, ii. 202.
— Elspeth Angela, dau. of lord Archibald C., i. 390.
— Emma Augusta, wife of Sir John Macneill, i. 389.
— Enid, dau. of lord Geo. Granville C., i. 391.
— Eugene, 12th son of 7th earl of Argyll, ix. 22.
— Eva, wife of J. C. Heathcote, ii. 213.
— Evelyn, wife of James Baillie Hamilton, i. 391.
— Frances, wife of Eustace J. A. Balfour, i. 391.
— Frederick, lord clerk register, i. 384, 386; vi. 269.
— — his wife, Mary Meredith, i. 384.
— Frederick, 9th son of 7th earl of Argyll, ix. 22.
— Frederic Augustus, capt., i. 71.
— Geills, dau. of Sir John C. of Glenurchy, ii. 202.
— George, 2nd son of 3rd earl of Breadalbane, ii. 209.
— George, 2nd son of Sir Mungo C. of Loudoun, v. 497.
— George, son of 1st lord Campbell of Loudoun; master of Loudoun, v. 498.
— — his wife, Jean Fleming, v. 499.

Campbell, George, 2nd son of 1st earl of Loudoun, v. 507.
— George, maltman, Leith, iv. 288*n*.
— George Andrew, son of capt. John C., ii. 197.
— — his wife, Margaret Campbell, ii. 197.
— George Augustus, H.E.I.C.S., viii. 312.
— — his wife, Sara Lyon-Bowes, viii. 312.
— George Granville, R.N., 4th son of 8th Duke of Argyll, i. 391.
— — his wife, Sybil Lascelles Alexander, i. 391.
— Gillespic, son of Sir Colin C. 'Mor,' i. 321.
— Gillespic, eldest son of 1st lord Campbell of Lochawe, i. 332.
— Grizel, wife of Sir Jas. Stewart of Ardmaleish, ii. 295; ix. 50.
— Hamilton, wife of 8th lord Belhaven, ii. 54.
— Harriot, lady of the Bedchamber, ii. 207.
— Helen, wife of (1) John, eldest son of John, lord of the Isles, and (2) Duncan, 8th earl of Lennox, i. 327; v. 39, 340; ix. 18.
— Helen, wife of first earl of Eglintoun, i. 335; iii. 435; viii. 579; ix. 19.
— Helen, wife of (1) Sir G. Kennedy, and (2) Thos. Kennedy, i. 337; ii. 463.
— Helen, wife of (1) * MacEane of Ardnamurchan, and (2) John M'Gregor, ii. 178.
— Helen, wife of John Macfarlane of Gartartan, ii. 190; ix. 43.
— Helen, wife of Alex. M'Duff, ii. 191.
— Helen, wife of Montagu Ormond Forbes, iv. 68.
— Helen, wife of Lawrence Crawfurd of Kilbirny, v. 494.
— Henrietta, lady of the Bedchamber, ii. 207.
— Henry, son of 4th duke of Argyll, i. 384.
— Henry, 6th son of Colin C., ii. 198.
— Henry, eldest son of 3rd earl of Breadalbane, ii. 208.
— Henry Tufnell, iv. 295.
— — his wife, Ethel Eveline Gray, iv. 295.
— Hugh, ii. 510, 511.
— — his wife, Margaret Cathcart of Carleton, ii. 510, 511.
— Hugh, son of John C. of Murthly, v. 500.
— Ian, rector of Kilmartin, ix. 18.
— Ian Edward Herbert, ii. 213.
— Isobel, wife of (1) James Stewart, earl of Moray, and (2) John, 10th earl of Sutherland, i. 22, 338; vi. 312; viii. 342.
— Isabel, wife of William, master of Drummond, i. 335; vii. 43; ix. 149 *bis*.

* Name unknown.

Campbell, Isabel, wife of 2nd earl of Cassillis, i. 336; ii. 465.
— Isabella, Augustinian canoness, i. 350; ix. 22.
— Isabella, dau. of marquess of Argyll, i. 361; ix. 23.
— Isabella, wife of capt. Wm. Montgomery, i. 382.
— Isobel, wife of P. MacGregor *or* Drummond, ii. 187.
— Isobel, dau. of Colin C. of Mochaster, ii. 190.
— Isobel, wife of Robt. Kirk, minister at Balquhidder, ii. 191.
— Isobel, wife of John Davies, ii. 199; ix. 44.
— Isobel, wife of James Campbell of Ardkinglass, ii. 200.
— Isabel, wife of Donald Campbell of Barbreck, ii. 201.
— Isabel, wife of John MacNaughtan, ii. 202.
— Isabella, wife of 10th earl of Carnwath, ii. 419.
— Isobel, wife of 7th earl of Crawford, iii. 25.
— Isobel, wife of Mungo Mure of Rowallan, v. 494.
— Isobel, wife of Robert, 4th lord Erskine, v. 494, 608.
— Isobel, wife of Wm. Craufurd of Lochnoris, v. 497.
— Isobel, wife of Sir John Maxwell of Pollok, v. 498.
— Isabella, wife of John Graham, Brae Leny, vi. 155.
— Isla Lorn Gavin, ii. 197.
— Ivan, 2nd son of 6th earl of Breadalbane, ii. 212.
— — his wife, Margaret Elizabeth Diana Agar Ellis, ii. 213.
— Ivar, son of lord George Granville C., i. 391.
— James, 7th son of Archibald C. of Lagvinshoch, ii. 187.
— James, lieut. Murray's Highland regt., ii. 191; ix. 44.
— James, 2nd son of William C. of Glenfalloch, and grandfather of 6th earl of Breadalbane, ii. 193, 212.
— — his wife, Eliza Maria Blanchard, ii. 193.
— James, 74th and 71st regts., ii. 199.
— James, 2nd son of Robert C., ii. 199.
— James, bookbinder to Queen Victoria, ii. 199.
— James, writer in Glasgow, ii. 199: ix. 44.
— James, 6th son of Sir John C. of Glenurchy, ii. 201.
— James, 11th son of Sir John C. of Glenurchy, ii. 202.

Campbell, James, minister of Auchterhouse, and of Lundie, ii. 273; iii. 100.
—— —— his wife, Marjory Ramsay, ii. 273.
—— James, son of John C. of Murthly, v. 500.
—— Mr. James, 3rd son of Sir Jas. C. of Lawers, v. 505.
—— James, 4th son of Patrick C. of Edinample, ix. 43.
—— James, Montreal, ix. 45.
—— —— his wife, Louise V. Phillips, ix. 45.
—— Jane, dau. of duke of Argyll and Greenwich, i. 377.
—— Jane, wife of Geo. H. Johnston, i. 385; ix. 25.
—— Jane, wife of Francis Sempill of Beltries, vii. 549.
—— Janet, wife of (1) Jas. Maitland, and (2) Patrick Murray, i. 222.
—— Janet, wife of John Stewart, 2nd earl of Atholl, i. 336, 443; ix. 28.
—— Janet, wife of Hector Maclean of Dowart, i. 340.
—— Janet, wife of Robert Campbell of Borland, ii. 190; ix. 43.
—— Janet, wife of Alex. Maitland, v. 308.
—— Janet, wife of John Campbell of Cessnock, v. 495.
—— Janet, dau. of James C. of Lawers, v. 502.
—— Janet, dau. of Sir Archd. C. of Glencarradale, v. 504.
—— Janet, wife of (1) Alexander, 4th lord Fraser of Lovat, and (2) Donald Gorm Macdonald of Slait, v. 527.
—— Janet, alleged wife of Andrew Drummond of Ballyclone, vii. 44.
—— Jean, wife of Sir John Lamont of Inveryne, i. 336 *n.*; ix. 19 *bis*.
—— Jean, wife of (1) Angus Mackintosh, and (2) Sir Donald Campbell, i. 343.
—— Jean, wife of (1) John, 1st viscount Kenmure, and (2) Sir Harry Montgomery, i. 349; iii. 446; v. 118, 120; ix. 22 *bis*.
—— Jean, wife of George Maxwell of Dalswinton, i. 360; ix. 23.
—— Jean, wife of Duncan Campbell of Inverawe, i. 360.
—— Jean, wife of 1st marquess of Lothian, i. 361; v. 477.
—— Jean, wife of 2nd marquess of Lothian, i. 368; v. 479.
—— Jean, wife of capt. John Campbell of Carrick, i. 382; ix. 24.
—— Jean, wife of John Murray, 1st earl of Atholl, i. 473; ii. 188.
—— Jean, wife of Sir John Hamilton of Lettrick, ii. 27; iv. 373.
—— Jean, wife of Robert Fleming, ii. 186.
—— Jean, wife of Sir John Campbell of Cawdor, ii. 187.
—— Jean, wife of Alex. Campbell of Ardeonaig, ii. 190.
Campbell, Jean, wife of Wm. Campbell, ii. 191.
—— Jean, wife of (1) * Ogilvie, and (2) Colin Campbell of Glenfalloch, ii. 193.
—— Jean, annuitant on Compassionate List, ii. 199.
—— Jean, wife of (1) Archd. Campbell of Glenlyon, (2) P. Roy MacGregor, and (3) D. Stewart of Appin, ii. 200.
—— Jean, wife of John Stewart of Tullynadies, ii. 201.
—— Jean, wife of Alex. Campbell of Airds, ii. 203.
—— Jean, wife of John Stewart of Ardmaleish, ii. 293; ix. 50.
—— Jean, wife of James, 12th earl of Caithness, ii. 356.
—— Jean, wife of (1) Robert Montgomerie of Giffen, and (2) Ludovic, 2nd duke of Lennox, iii. 442; v. 357, 497.
—— Jean, wife of 12th lord Forbes, iv. 63.
—— Jean, wife of 6th lord Lindores, v. 387.
—— Jean, wife of D. Crawford of Kerse, v. 498.
—— Jean, wife of 2nd earl of Panmure, v. 507; vii. 22.
—— Jean, wife of Sir Jas. Campbell of Aberuchill, v. 508.
—— Jean, dau. of 6th earl of Argyll, ix. 21.
—— Jean, dau. of capt. John C. of Carrick, ix. 25.
—— Jean, dau. of Colin C., ix. 44.
—— Jemima, marchioness Grey, and baroness Lucas of Crudwell, wife of 2nd earl of Hardwicke, ii. 208.
—— Joan, dau. of lord Geo. G. C., i. 391.
—— John, father-in-law of lieut.-col. Hugh Arbuthnott, i. 315.
—— John 'M'Cwill,' son of Dougal, son of Sir Neil C., i. 324, 328, 330.
—— John, rector of Kilmartin, 2nd son of Colin 'Ionganlach' C. of Lochow, i. 329; ix. 18.
—— John, Toscheachdeorac of Melphort, i. 331.
—— John, prior of Ardchattane, ii. 5.
—— John, bishop of the Isles, ii. 177; ix. 21, 42.
—— John, 4th son of Archibald C. of Lagvinshoch, ii. 187.
—— John, 9th son of Sir Duncan C. of Glenurchy, ii. 188.
—— John, 2nd son of Colin C. of Mochaster, ii. 190.
—— John, Kylettormore, ii. 195.
—— —— his wife, Janet Butter, ii. 195.
—— John, 43rd regt., ii. 198; ix. 44.
—— John, 74th and 82nd regts., ii. 199.
—— John, Fort William, claimant to Breadalbane earldom, ii. 206.
—— John, major 74th Foot, v. 419.

* Name unknown.

Campbell, John, son of John C. of Murthly, v. 500.
— John, in Carse Grange, v. 500.
— John, illeg. son of Sir John C. of Lawers, v. 504.
— John, colonel, Dunoon, vii. 308.
— John, provost of Collegiate Church of Kilmun, ix. 20.
— John, 2nd son of James C. of Burnbank, ix. 24.
— John, son of Patrick C. of Balsalloch, ix. 55.
— — his wife, Jean Stewart, ix. 55.
— John Breadalbane, Florida, ii. 197.
— — his wife, Katharine M'Donald, ii. 198.
— John Erskine, Cape Mounted Police, ii. 197.
— John Thomas, v. 419.
— — his wife, Anne Catherine Lindsay, iv. 295; v. 419.
— Julian, wife of Murdoch Maclean of Lochbuy, ii. 200; ix. 45.
— Juliana, wife of John Gordon, ii. 188.
— Juliana, wife of Sir Colin Campbell of Glenurchy, ii. 189; v. 498.
— Katharine, wife of (1) James, master of Ogilvy, and (2) David, 9th earl of Crawford, i. 118, 511; iii. 28; ix. 8.
— Katharine, wife of Torquil Macleod, i. 335.
— Katharine, contr. to Geo. Gordon; wife of (1) Maclean of Duart, and (2) A. Campbell of Auchinbreck, i. 337; ix. 20, 110.
— Katharine, wife of Sir William Murray of Tullibardine, i. 462; ii. 180; ix. 28.
— Katharine, wife of Walter Stewart of Balquhidder, ii. 177 *n.*
— Katharine, wife of Alex. MacDougall, ii. 188; ix. 43.
— Katharine, wife of Andrew Toshach, ii. 200.
— Katharine, wife of Alex. Robertson of Lude, ii. 201.
— Katharine, contracted to James Haldane, ix. 19.
— Katharine, dau. of 10th earl of Argyll, ix. 24.
— Katharine Black, illeg. dau. of 6th duke of Argyll, ix. 25.
— Lilah Olive, i. 391.
— Lilias, dau. of Archibald C., Succoth, ii. 199; ix. 44.
— Louisa, wife of Alexander Johnstone, i. 385; ix. 25.
— Lucie, dau. of Colin C., ix. 44.
— M., probably dau. of principal Neil C. of Glasgow University, vii. 520.
— Margaret, wife of 5th lord Erskine, i. 336; v. 610.
— Margaret, wife of James, lord Doune and St. Colme, i. 340; iii. 188.
Campbell, Margaret, wife of 3rd lord Balmerino, i. 569.
— Margaret, wife of Sir W. Lindsay of Balgawies, i. 512.
— Margaret, wife of Colin Campbell of Lochow, i. 324, 328, 330.
— Margaret, wife of Thomas, 6th lord Boyd, i. 47; v. 165.
— Margaret, wife of 3rd earl of Balcarres, i. 522; v. 508.
— Margaret, wife of (1) A. Napier, and (2) J. Dickson, ii. 177; vi. 410, 411.
— Margaret, wife of John MacDougall of Raray, ii. 181.
— Margaret, wife of Allan MacDougall of Raray, ii. 182; ix. 42.
— Margaret, wife of 6th earl of Glencairn, ii. 183; iv. 244.
— Margaret, wife of John Toshoch, ii. 186.
— Margaret, wife of Sir Alex. Menzies, ii. 187.
— Margaret, dau. of Colin C. of Mochaster, ii. 191.
— Margaret, wife of George A. Campbell, ii. 197.
— Margaret, wife of John Cameron, ii. 200; ix. 45.
— Margaret, wife of Duncan M'Corquodale, ii. 202.
— Margaret, alleged wife of lord Ormelie, ii. 206.
— Margaret, wife of Angus 'Og' Macdonald of Troternish, v. 47.
— Margaret, wife of Sir Alan Lockhart of Lee, v. 494.
— Margaret, wife of Thomas Kennedy of Bargany, v. 495.
— Margaret, wife of Alex. Nisbet of Bankhead, v. 496.
— Margaret, wife of Sir John Wallace of Craigie, v. 497.
— Margaret, wife of John Kennedy of Blairquhan, v. 498.
— Margaret, wife of Sir W. Cunningham of Cunninghamhead, v. 498.
— Margaret, wife of Sir Wm. Edmonstone of Duntreath, v. 502.
— Margaret, dau. of Sir Archd. C. of Glencarradale, v. 504.
— Margaret, wife of John Campbell of Shawfield, v. 509; ix. 131.
— Margaret, sister of 5th earl of Loudoun, v. 511.
— Margaret, wife of Sir John Graham of Braco, vi. 238.
— Margaret, wife of 6th earl of Wemyss, viii. 515.
— Margaret, wife of Patrick Buchanan of Buchanan, ix. 19.
— Margaret, dau. of 9th earl of Argyll, ix. 24.
— Margaret, dau. of 1st duke of Argyll, ix. 24.

Campbell, Margaret, wife of Patrick Campbell of Edinample, ix. 43.
— Margaret Alice, ii. 197.
— Margaret Lillias, wife of Duncan M'Callum, the Foxhunter, ii. 209.
— Marie, dau. of Sir John C. of Lawers, v. 504.
— Marion, wife of 2nd lord Seton, i. 334; viii. 579; ix. 18 *bis*.
— Marion, wife of Sir Robert Menzies, i. 337.
— Marion, dau. of James C. of Lawers, v. 502.
— Marion, dau. of James C., ix. 45.
— Mariot, wife of Wm. Stewart of Baldorran, ii. 178.
— Mariot, wife of Archibald Campbell of Glenlyon, ii. 179.
— Mariot, wife of Alex. Hume, ii. 181.
— Mariota, wife of Colin Campbell of Lochow, i. 324, 328, 330.
— Marjory, wife of Thomas Graham of Duchray, ii. 190.
— Marjory, wife of Archd. Stirling of Coldoch, ii. 200; ix. 45.
— Marjory, dau. of Sir John C. of Glenurchy, ii. 202.
— Marjory, wife of Edward Toshach of Monzievaird, v. 504.
— Marjorie, wife of (1) Walter Graham of Loch Chon, and (2) Duncan Campbell of Drumfad, vi. 149.
— Mary, wife of Angus Macdonald, i. 335.
— Mary, wife of John 'Gorm' Campbell, i. 338.
— Mary, wife of (1) John, 6th earl of Menteith, and (2) Colin Campbell of Lundie, i. 346; ii. 183; vi. 163, 164; ix. 43.
— Mary, wife of Sir Robt. Montgomery, i. 349.
— Mary, wife of 2nd lord Rollo, i. 350; vii. 202; ix. 22.
— Mary, wife of Henry, lord Holyroodhouse, i. 360; iv. 437.
— Mary, wife of (1) 6th earl of Caithness, and (2) 1st earl of Breadalbane, i. 361; ii. 206, 344, 345.
— Mary, dau. of 9th earl of Argyll, i. 368; ix. 24.
— Mary, wife of Edward, viscount Coke, i. 377.
— Mary, wife of 2nd earl of Rosebery, i. 382; vii. 223; ix. 24 *bis*.
— Mary, wife of Donald Campbell of Barbreck, i. 384; ix. 25.
— Mary, wife of R. Robertson of Fascally, ii. 200.
— Mary, wife of Robert Campbell of Drumsynie, ii. 202.
— Mary, wife of Archd. Cockburn of Langton, ii. 206 *n*., 207; ix. 45.
Campbell, Mary, wife of 2nd duke of Buckingham, ii. 211; v. 200.
— Mary, wife of Thos. Grant of Balmacaan, vii. 472.
— Mary, wife of George Middleton of Erroll, viii. 157.
— Mary, dau. of Colin C., ix. 44.
— Mary Emma, wife of rev. E. Carr Glyn, i. 391.
— Mary Gwynnedd, ii. 197.
— Matthew, 2nd son of George C. of Loudoun, v. 494.
— Matthew, Livonia, v. 497 *n*.
— Moir, wife of Sir John Lamont of Inveryne, i. 336 *n*.; ix. 19 *bis*.
— Mor, wife of Hector Macgilleoin, ix. 18.
— Mungo, exciseman, iii. 459.
— Niall Diarmid, son of lord Archibald C., i. 390.
— Sir Neil, Nicholas *or* Nigel, king's bailie for Lochow, i. 320, 322.
— — his 2nd wife, Mary Bruce, i. 323; ii. 434.
— Neil, advocate, 3rd son of lord Neil C. of Ardmaddie, i. 360 *n*., 361; ix. 23.
— — his 1st wife, Vere Ker, i. 360; v. 475.
— — his 2nd wife, Susan Menzies, i. 360.
— Neil, 3rd son of John C. of Mamore, i. 381.
— Neil, maltman, Leith, iv. 288 *n*.
— Neil, principal of Glasgow University, viii. 84.
— Norman, ix. 45.
— Pamela Louisa Augusta Ambrose, wife of lord E. W. Hamilton, i. 71.
— Patrick, 2nd son of Sir Colin C. of Glenurchy, ii. 176, 179.
— Patrick, 3rd son of Sir Duncan C. of Glenurchy, ii. 179.
— Patrick, surgeon, R.N., ii. 202.
— Patrick, vicar of Kilmartin, ix. 18.
— Patrick, 3rd son of Patrick C. of Edinample, ix. 43.
— Primrose, wife of Simon, 11th lord Fraser of Lovat, i. 382; v. 540; ix. 25 *bis*, 132.
— Robert, minister of Moulin, ii. 187.
— — his wife, Jean Menzies, ii. 187.
— Robert, grandson of Sir Robt. C. of Glenurchy, ii. 191, 212.
— — his wife, Susanna Menzies, ii. 191.
— Robert, grandson of above, ii. 191; ix. 43.
— Robert, captain, H.E.I.C.S., ii. 195.
— — his wife, Jean Campbell, ii. 195.
— Robert, lieut.-capt. 99th regt., ii. 198.
— — his wife, Jean Sinclair, ii. 198.
— Robert, lieut. 42nd regt., ii. 199.
— Robert, merchant in Edinburgh, ii. 202.

Campbell, Robert, 4th son of Sir George C. of Loudoun, v. 493.
— Robert, 3rd son of Dr. Charles A. C., ix. 45.
— Rosslyn, ix. 45.
— Susan, wife of John Stewart of Urrard, i. 361.
— Susan Thomson, wife of col. Hugh Arbuthnott, i. 315.
— Susanna, wife of William Campbell of Glenfalloch, ii. 192.
— Susanna, wife of (1) William Erskine Campbell of Glenfalloch, and (2) capt. Macfarlane, ii. 192; ix. 44.
— Susanna, dau. of Archibald C., Succoth, ii. 199; ix. 44.
— Susanna, wife of John Campbell of Lochdochart, ii. 199.
— Susanna, wife of John Campbell of Ardchattan, ii. 202.
— Susanna, dau. of Colin C., ix. 44.
— Susanna Sophie, dau. of James C., ii. 194.
— Thomas, 3rd son of Sir Geo. C. of Loudoun, v. 493.
— Thomas, commendator of Holywood, v. 496.
— Thomas, 3rd son of Sir James C. of Lawers, v. 505.
— Victoria, dau. of 7th earl of Argyll, i. 350; ix. 22 *bis*.
— Victoria, dau. of 8th duke of Argyll, i. 391; ix. 26.
— Walter, 3rd son of 8th duke of Argyll, i. 390.
— — his wife, Olivia Rowlandson Miln, i. 390.
— Walter, 10th son of Sir John C. of Glenurchy, ii. 202.
— Walter, 5th son of James C. of Lawers, v. 501, 502.
— William, governor of Nova Scotia, and of South Carolina, i. 385; ix. 25.
— — his wife, Sarah Izard, i. 385.
— William, R.N., S. Carolina, i. 385, 386.
— William, 5th son of Sir Robt. C. of Glenurchy, ii. 191, 212.
— — his wife, Jean Campbell, ii. 191.
— William, Hanover, Jamaica, ii. 195.
— William, 4th son of Robert C., ii. 199.
— William, adventurer in African Company, ii. 202; ix. 45.
— William, 7th son of Sir John C. of Lawers, v. 504.
— William, 4th son of Sir James C. of Lawers, v. 505.
— William, illeg. son of Sir Jas. C. of Lawers, v. 506.
— — his wife, Janet M'Gruder, v. 506.
— William Henry, London, iv. 68.
— William John Lamb, R.N., father of 6th earl of Breadalbane, ii. 193, 212.
— — his wife, Rosanna Doughty, ii. 194.
Campbell, *, wife of Angus Mor, lord of the Isles, i. 321; v. 34.
— *, wife of Campbell of Ardentinny, i. 336.
— *, wife of Mr. Colin Campbell of Auchnaba, ii. 202.
— *, wife of Ninian Stewart of Bute, ii. 289.
— *, wife of John Scrymgeour, Constable of Dundee, iii. 311.
— *, alleged wife of John Campbell of Murthly, v. 500 *n*.
— *, wife of Colin Campbell of Edinample, v. 505.
— *, wife of D. Dunbar of Enterkin, v. 505.
— *, wife of Iain 'Brayach' M'Iain of Ardnamurchan, ix. 20.
CAMPCASTELL, SCOTT, LORD, ii. 237; vii. 80-81.
Campcastell, Walter, lord, ii. 237; vii. 81.
Camperdown, Adam (Duncan), 1st viscount Duncan of, i. 554; viii. 127.
— Robert (Duncan), 1st earl of, viii. 130.
— — his wife, Janet Dalrymple, viii. 130.
CAMPSIE, LIVINGSTON, LORD, v. 191-194.
Campsie, James, first lord, v. 192.
CANADA, ALEXANDER, VISCOUNT OF, viii. 174-185.
Canada, William, first viscount of, viii. 174.
Canaries, James, D.D., ii. 273.
— — his wife, Anne Erskine, ii. 273.
Candler of Callan, Morton Pinckney, Dun Edin and Belwood, Edward, vii. 565.
— — his wife, Maria Janet, baroness Sempill, vii. 566.
Canham, Katharine, wife of rev. Alex. Gough, and bigamous wife of John, lord Dalmeny, vii. 223.
Canning, Charles John (Canning) earl of, ii. 304.
— — his wife, Charlotte Stuart, ii. 304.
Cant of Over Liberton, Henry, iv. 305.
— of Morton, John, vi. 393.
— of Priestfield, Adam, iv. 305.
— — Henry, iv. 305.
— Barbara, wife of John Nairn of Mukkersy, vi. 393.
— Christian, wife of (1) Col. Sir Henry Balfour, (2) Capt. John Balfour, and (3) Peter Rollock of Pilton, vii. 193.
— David, captain, vii. 193.
— Elizabeth *or* Isobel, wife of John Ramsay, ii. 132.
— Margaret, wife of Thomas Hamilton of Orchardfield and Priestfield, iv. 305.
Cantantilly, Elena, wife of Sir Jas. Cunningham of Hassendean, iv. 225 *n*.
Cantelupe, William de, iii. 7.
Cantes, Mary, wife of (1) Sholto Henry, 8th lord Kirkcudbright, and (2) Robert Davies, v. 273.

* Name unknown.

Capel, Adela Caroline Hariet, wife of 13th earl of Eglinton, iii. 463.
—— Arthur Risden, viii. 63.
—— —— his wife, Mary Anne Jemima Carnegie-Arbuthnott, viii. 63.
Capel-Carnegie-Arbuthnott of Balnamoon, James Carnegie, viii. 63.
—— —— his wife, Ethel Lydia Hill, viii. 63.
—— Arthur Risden, viii. 63.
—— —— his wife, Mary Anne Jemima Carnegie-Arbuthnott of Balnamoon, viii. 63.
—— Edith Alice, wife of Malcolm Galloway, viii. 63.
—— Elizabeth, viii. 63.
—— Enid, viii. 63.
—— Evelyn Frederica, wife of Constantine A. Ionides, viii. 63.
—— Harold, viii. 63.
—— Helen Mary, viii. 63.
—— Margaret, wife of Arthur Layard, viii. 63.
—— Mary Anne, viii. 63.
Capell, Adolphus, vii. 61.
—— Harriet Mary, wife of (1) George, viscount Forth, and (2) E. C. Dering, vi. 73; vii. 61.
Capella, William de, iii. 118.
Car, Thomas, abbot of Kelso, 3rd son of Thos. Ker of Ferniehurst, v. 54.
Caramiceley, Robert of, iv. 563.
CARDIFF OF CARDIFF CASTLE, STUART, BARON, ii. 305-312.
Cardiff, John, first baron, ii. 305.
Cardigan, George, (Brudenell), 3rd earl of, iii. 480.
—— —— his wife, Elizabeth Bruce, iii. 480.
—— George (Brudenell-Bruce), 4th earl of, ii. 243.
—— —— his wife, Mary Montagu, ii. 243.
—— Robert (Brudenell), 2nd earl of, i. 32; iii. 297, 299; v. 228; vi. 187.
—— Thomas, 1st earl of, iii. 298.
CARDROSS, ERSKINE, LORD, ii. 365-368; v. 618-621.
Cardross, David, second lord, ii. 365; ix. 52 *ter*.
—— —— his 1st wife, Anne Hope, ii. 366; iv. 491; ix. 109.
—— —— his 2nd wife, Mary Bruce, ii. 366; ix. 52.
—— David, fourth lord, ii. 274, 368.
—— Henry, 3rd son of 1st lord Cardross; styled lord, ii. 365; v. 621.
—— —— his wife, Margaret Bellenden, ii. 71, 365.
—— Henry, third lord, ii. 367; ix. 52.
—— —— his wife, Katharine Stewart, ii. 367; ix. 52.
—— John, 7th earl of Mar, first lord, ii. 365; v. 618.
Carew of Beddington Park, Sir Benjamin Hallowell, G.C.B., iv. 390.
—— Henrietta Charlotte, wife of rev. Adolphus Douglas-Hamilton, iv. 390.
Carey, Sir Robert, warden of the Marches, iv. 473; vii. 342.
—— Martha, wife of 1st earl of Middleton, vi. 185.
Cargill of Leesington, i. 282.
—— —— his wife, Giles Arbuthnott, i. 282.
Carkettill, John of, iii. 95.
CARLAVEROCK CASTLE, CONSTABLE-MAXWELL, LORD HERRIES OF, iv. 423-424.
Carleton of Carleton, Sir Thomas, v. 262.
Carlingford, Edward Barnham (Swift), viscount of, iii. 235.
—— —— his wife, Mary Crichton, iii. 235.
Carlisle, Sir James (Hay), elder son of Sir Jas. Hay of Kingask; earl of, v. 218, 228.
—— —— his 1st wife, Honora Denny, v. 219.
—— —— his 2nd wife, Lucy Percy, v. 219.
—— Charles (Howard), 1st earl of, vii. 106.
—— —— his wife, Anne Howard, vii. 106.
—— Charles (Howard), 3rd earl of, v. 16.
—— George (Howard), 6th earl of, viii. 362.
—— Septimus E., vii. 566.
—— —— his wife, Caroline L. Forbes, vii. 566.
Carlton of Carlton, Edward Montagu Stuart Granville (Montagu-Stuart-Wortley-Mackenzie), 1st viscount, ii. 303.
CARLYLE, MAXWELL, LORD, vi. 482-487.
Carlyle, John, first lord, ii. 394 *n.*; vi. 482.
CARLYLE OF TORTHORWALD, CARLYLE, LORD, ii. 369-394.
Carlyle of Torthorwald, Elizabeth, wife of (1) Sir Jas. Douglas, and (2) Wm. Sinclair; lady; i. 248; ii. 389, 391.
—— —— James, third lord, ii. 388.
—— —— his wife, Janet Scrimgeour, ii. 388; iii. 308.
—— —— James (Douglas), *de jure ux.* lord, i. 248; ii. 392, 507.
—— —— John, first lord, i. 238; ii. 382; iv. 403, 404, 405.
—— —— his 1st wife, Elizabeth Kirkpatrick, ii. 380, 385.
—— —— his 2nd wife, Janet *, ii. 385.
—— —— his 3rd wife, Margaret Douglas, ii. 385.
—— —— Michael, fourth lord, i. 248; ii. 382, 388.
—— —— his 1st wife, Janet Charteris, ii. 389.
—— —— his 2nd wife, Mariota Maxwell, ii. 389.
—— —— William, second lord, ii. 386.
—— —— his wife, Janet Maxwell, ii. 387; vi. 478.
CARLYLE, LORD CARLYLE OF TORTHORWALD, ii. 369-394.

* Name unknown.

Carlyle of Blairboy, John, ii. 386.
— of Boytath, James, 2nd laird, ii. 390.
— — his wife, Margaret Carlyle, ii. 390.
— — James, 3rd laird, ii. 390.
— — his 1st wife, Janet Carruthers, ii. 390.
— — his 2nd wife, Marion Johnstone, ii. 390.
— — John, 4th son of 4th lord C., ii. 390.
— — Thomas, 4th laird, ii. 390.
— — his wife, Margaret Menzies, ii. 390.
— of Brackenquhat, William, ii. 390.
— of Brydekirk, Adam, ancestor of the family of, ii. 382, 385.
— — his wife, Ellen Carruthers, ii. 382.
— — Alexander, ii. 382 *n.*
— — Alexander, D.D., minister of Inveresk, ii. 382; vi. 115; vii. 520.
— — Herbert, ix. 53.
— — *, vii. 99.
— of Cargow, William de, ii. 377.
— — his wife, Sapientia, ii. 377.
— — Sir William, ii. 377.
— — his wife, Margaret Bruce, ii. 379, 435.
— of Carlyle, Eudo, ii. 375.
— — Hildred, ii. 370.
— — Odard, ii. 371, 372, 377 *n.*
— — Roger, ii. 376, 377.
— — Robert, ii. 372.
— — Sir William, ii. 376.
— — William, the younger, ii. 377.
— — his wife, Sapientia, ii. 377.
— — William, ii. 377; iv. 399.
— of Crunzanstoun, Sir William, ii. 379.
— — his wife, Margaret Bruce, ii. 379, 435.
— of Cumquinten, Eudo de, ii. 375.
— — Hildred de, ii. 371.
— — Sir William, ii. 376.
— of Gamelsby and Glassanby, Christian, wife of William Ireby, ii. 373.
— — Eva, wife of (1) Robert Lovell, and (2) Alan de Chartres, ii. 373.
— — Hildred, ii. 370.
— — Odard, son of Robert C., ii. 373.
— of Hodelme, Odard de, ii. 371.
— — Robert de, ii. 372.
— of Kinmount, Adam, ii. 373, 381.
— — William, ii. 378; iv. 399.
— of Limekilns, Adam, ii. 382 *n.*
— — Edward, ix. 53.
— of Locharthur, John, 2nd laird, ii. 390, 392.
— — Michael, 3rd son of 4th lord C., ii. 339.
— — his wife, Grizel Maxwell, ii. 389; vi. 484 *n.*; ix. 153.
— — Michael, d. 1763, ii. 390.
— — William, ii. 390.
— of Lockerbie, Robert, ii. 372, 374.

* Name unknown.

Carlyle of Luce, Sir John, ii. 383.
— — William, ii. 379.
— of Minnigap, Sir William, ii. 379.
— of Mowe and Shielhauch, George, ii. 386.
— of Ormesby, Adam, ii. 375.
— — Eudo, ii. 375.
— of Pittenain, Robert, ii. 386.
— — his wife, Margaret Weir, ii. 386.
— of Robiequhat *or* Searigs, Alexander, ii. 391.
— of Torthorwald, Sir John, 2nd laird, ii. 381, 382.
— — William, 1st laird, ii. 380.
— — his wife, Elizabeth Kirkpatrick, ii. 381.
— Adam, son of Roger of C., ii. 376, 377.
— Adam, 2nd son of Sir John C., ii. 382.
— Agnes, dau. of Thomas C. of Boytath, ii. 390.
— Agnes, wife of James Veitch, ii. 391.
— Agnes, wife of Wm. Graham of Plomp, vii. 99.
— Alexander, son of Robert C., ii. 391.
— Alexander, D.D., minster of Inveresk, ii. 382; vi. 115; vii. 520.
— Alice, wife of Wm. Graham of Plomp, vii. 99.
— Ansketil de, ii. 371 *n.*
— Edward, ii. 391 *n.*
— Elizabeth, dau. of 2nd lord Carlyle, ii. 388.
— Elizabeth, wife of John Thomson, ii. 391.
— Elizabeth, wife of 3rd lord Sempill, vii. 548 *n.*
— Elizabeth, wife of Robert Herries, ix. 53.
— Esota, wife of Arthur Graham, ii. 391.
— Eudo, grandson of Eudo of C., ii. 377.
— Eufamia, contracted to Sir S. Carruthers, ii. 386.
— George, merchant, Dumfries, ii. 390.
— — his wife, Elizabeth Nisbet, ii. 391.
— George, the successful litigant in 1770, ii. 391.
— Gilbert de, ii. 377 *n.*
— Ivo, ii. 378 *n.*
— James, rector of Kirkpatrick-cro, ii. 385, 386.
— James, Scots Greys, ii. 390.
— James, eldest son of George C., ii. 391.
— James, son of Patrick C., ii. 391.
— James, merchant in Dumfries, ii. 391.
— James, son of Jas. C., of Boytath, ii. 391.
— John, grandson of Ivo C., ii. 378 *n.*
— John, 2nd son of Sir William C., ii. 379.
— Sir John, conservator of truce with England, ii. 380.
— John, eldest son of 1st lord C., ii. 386.
— John, major, Virginia, iii. 601.

Carlyle, Joseph, ii. 391.
— Katharine, wife of S. Carruthers, ii. 388.
— Margaret, wife of James Carlyle of Boytath, ii. 390.
— Margaret, dau. of George C., ii. 391.
— Mariot, wife of 1st lord Herries of Terregles, ii. 386; iv. 404.
— Mary, wife of Herbert Cunningham, ii. 390.
— Patrick, 2nd son of James C., of Boytath, ii. 391.
— — his wife, Isabel Carruthers, ii. 391.
— Peter, 5th son of 4th lord C., ii. 391.
— Richard de, son of Odard of C., ii. 371.
— Robert, son of Richard de C., ii. 371.
— Robert, grandson of 1st lord C., ii. 386.
— Robert, son of Jas. C., of Boytath, ii. 391.
— — his wife, * Wright, ii. 391.
— Robert, murderer of * Turner, iii. 231; ix. 70.
— Samuel, ii. 391.
— Sarah, wife of W. Herbert, iii. 601, 604.
— Thomas, Travalah, co. Denbigh, ii. 391.
— Sir William, son of Eudo, ii. 376.
— William, son of Ivo C., ii. 378 *n*.
— William, grandson of Sir Wm. C., ii. 380.
— William, killed at Dettingen, ii. 390.
— William, brother of Robert C., iii. 231.
— *, wife of Sir Adam Murray of Drumcreiff, ii. 386.
Carmarthen, Thomas, 1st marquess of, iii. 302.
CARMICHAEL, CARMICHAEL, LORD, iv. 585-597.
Carmichael, Andrew, seventh lord, iv. 592, 596.
— James, first lord, iv. 585; ix. 114.
— — his wife, Agnes Wilkie, iv. 585.
— James, third lord, iv. 593.
— — his wife, Elizabeth Maitland, iv. 593.
— John, second lord, iv. 589.
— — his wife, Beatrix Drummond, iv. 591; viii. 219.
— John, fourth lord, iv. 594.
— — his 1st wife, Elizabeth Shovel, iv. 595.
— — his 2nd wife, Jean Vigor, iv. 596.
— John, fifth lord, iv. 591, 596.
— — his wife, Janet Grant, iv. 596.
— Thomas, sixth lord, iv. 592.
— master of, Sir William, eldest son of 1st lord Carmichael, iv. 585, 588.
— — his wife, Grizel Douglas, iv. 588.
CARMICHAEL OF CARMICHAEL, CARMICHAEL, LORD, iv. 590-597.
Carmichael of Carmichael, John, first lord, iv. 590.

* Name unknown.

CARMICHAEL, LORD CARMICHAEL, iv. 585-597.
CARMICHAEL, LORD CARMICHAEL OF CARMICHAEL, iv. 590-597.
CARMICHAEL, EARL OF HYNDFORD, iv. 563-597.
CARMICHAEL, VISCOUNT OF INGLISBERRY, iv. 590-597.
CARMICHAEL, VISCOUNT OF NEMPHLAR, iv. 590-597.
Carmichael of Abernethy, David, iv. 568.
— — Peter, iv. 564.
— of Aithernie, James, iv. 568.
— of Annatshill, Sir Hugh, iv. 581.
— of Balmblae, James, 1st laird, iv. 566.
— — his wife, Euphan Myrton, ii. 573; iv. 567.
— — James, 3rd laird, iv. 567.
— — Robert, M.D., 2nd laird, iv. 567; viii. 202.
— — his wife, Jean Murray, iv. 567; viii. 202.
— — Robert, captain, v. 408.
— — his wife, Katharine Lindsay, v. 408.
— of Balmedie, David, 5th laird, iv. 566; ix. 112.
— — his wife, Isabel Barclay, iv. 566.
— — David, 7th laird, iv. 566; ix. 112 *bis*.
— — his 1st wife, Margaret *or* Jean Oliphant, iv. 566.
— — his 2nd wife, Margaret Myrton, iv. 566.
— — Sir David, 8th laird, iv. 567.
— — his 1st wife, Anne Carmichael, iv. 567, 588.
— — his 2nd wife, Cecilia Fotheringham, iv. 567.
— — David, the younger, iv. 567.
— — his wife, Euphemia Dempster, iv. 567.
— — David, 9th laird, iv. 568; ix. 112.
— — his wife, Anna Graham, iv. 568; ix. 112.
— — David, 10th laird, iv. 568.
— — his wife, Janet Coutts, iv. 568; ix. 112.
— — David, the younger, iv. 568; ix. 112.
— — his wife, Mary Tatham, iv. 568.
— — James, 2nd laird, iv. 564, 565.
— — his wife, Elizabeth Folkart, iv. 565.
— — James, 3rd laird, iv. 565.
— — his wife, Margaret Kincraigie, iv. 565.
— — James, 6th laird, iv. 566; viii. 63.
— — his wife, Jane Carnegie, viii. 63.
— — John, 1st laird, iv. 564.
— — his wife, Isobel Sibbald, iv. 564.
— — Peter, 4th laird, iv. 565; ix. 112.
— of Bonningley, Sir Hugh, iv. 581.
— of Bonnytoun, Henrietta, wife of Robert Dundas of Arniston, iv. 587.

Carmichael of Bonnytoun, Sir James, iv. 587, 588 *n.*; ix. 114.
—— —— his wife, Margaret Grier, iv. 587.
—— —— Sir James, iv. 587.
—— —— Sir James, iv. 587.
—— —— his wife, Margaret Baillie, iv. 587.
—— —— Sir John, iv. 587.
—— —— his wife, Henrietta Johnstone, i. 264; iv. 587.
—— —— Sir William, iv. 587.
—— of Cairncross, Sir John, iv. 581.
—— of Carmichael, Sir Hugh, 8th laird, iv. 580.
—— —— his wife, Abigail Baillie, iv. 581.
—— —— Sir James, iv. 584.
—— —— his wife, Agnes Wilkie, iv. 585.
—— —— Sir John, 1st laird, ii. 396; iv. 563 *bis*, 573.
—— —— his wife, * Wardlaw, iv. 564.
—— —— John, 3rd laird, iv. 573, 574.
—— —— John, 6th laird, iv. 576, 583; viii. 19; ix. 113.
—— —— his wife, Elizabeth Somerville, iv. 577; viii. 19.
—— —— Sir John, 7th laird, warden of the West Marches, iv. 576, 578; ix. 113 *bis*.
—— —— his wife, Margaret Douglas, iv. 580.
—— —— Sir John, 9th laird, iv. 581.
—— —— his wife, Elizabeth Hume, vi. 11; ix. 113.
—— —— William, 2nd laird, iv. 564, 573 *bis*.
—— —— William, 4th laird, iv. 575; ix. 113.
—— —— William, 5th laird, iv. 576.
—— —— Sir William, the yr., i. 205; iv. 588.
—— —— his wife, Grizel Douglas, i. 205; iv. 589.
—— of Chingillis, James, iv. 566.
—— of Craigpottie, Sir David, iv. 567.
—— —— James, iv. 566.
—— —— Peter, iv. 564, 566.
—— of Crosfoord, David, iv. 592.
—— of Currie, Sir Hugh, iv. 581.
—— —— Sir John, iv. 579.
—— of Dron, James, i. 177; iv. 564.
—— —— Peter, sheriff of Forfar, i. 177; iv. 564, 565.
—— —— his wife, Euphame Wemyss, iv. 565.
—— of Edrom, Archibald, iv. 576, 577; ix. 113.
—— —— Henry, iv. 577.
—— of Eglismagirdle, David, iv. 566.
—— —— Sir David, iv. 567.
—— of Fentoun, Sir John, iv. 579.
—— of Folkarton, James, i. 177; iv. 564, 565.
—— —— his wife, Elizabeth Folkart, iv. 565.
—— of Little Galway, Sir John, iv. 563.
—— of Grange, William, ii. 413.
—— of Greenhill, John, constable of St. Andrews, iv. 564.

* Name unknown.

Carmichael of Hailes, James, iv. 591.
—— —— his wife, Janet Clerk, iv. 591.
—— of Hiefleld, James, iv. 580.
—— of Hyndford, Sir Daniel, 1st laird, iv. 585, 587, 588 *n.*
—— —— his wife, Anna Scot, iv. 586.
—— of Kildowny, James, iv. 566.
—— of Kirkdrum *or* Kirkdroyne, James, iv. 566.
—— —— Peter, iv. 564, 566.
—— of Lag, Sir James, iv. 587.
—— of Langherdmanstoun, Sir Hugh, iv. 581.
—— —— James, iv. 578, 580.
—— —— John, iv. 578.
—— of Luthrie, David, iv. 568.
—— of Mauldslie, Sir Daniel, 1st laird, iv. 585, 592.
—— —— Daniel, 2nd laird, iv. 592.
—— —— his wife, Barbara Lockhart, iv. 592.
—— —— Daniel, 3rd laird, iv. 592, 596.
—— —— his wife, Emilia Hepburn, iv. 592; ix. 114.
—— —— Thomas, iv. 592, 596.
—— of Meadowflat, Grizel, wife of Walter Carmichael of Park, iv. 583.
—— —— John, constable of St. Andrews, iv. 564, 574.
—— —— John, iv. 576; ix. 12.
—— —— John, the younger, viii. 371; ix. 14.
—— —— his wife, Janet Johnston, i. 246; viii. 371, 372; ix. 14.
—— —— John, bailie of the barony of Crawford Muir, ii. 231; iv. 564, 583; vi. 449.
—— —— his wife, Elizabeth Scott, ii. 231.
—— —— Sir John, iv. 564.
—— —— Margaret, wife of David, 5th earl of Crawford and Duke of Montrose, iii. 23, 25.
—— —— Margaret, dau. of John C., iv. 564.
—— —— Robert *error for* John, iv. 564 *n.*
—— —— William, heritable captain of the Castle of Crawford, iv. 564.
—— of Mosmyning, Sir James, iv. 587.
—— of Park, Charles, iv. 582; ix. 113.
—— —— his wife, * Crichton, iv. 582.
—— —— Gavin, iv. 576, 582.
—— —— his wife, Geils Craufurd, iv. 582.
—— —— John, iv. 576, 582.
—— —— Walter, iv. 583.
—— —— his wife, Grizel Carmichael, iv. 583.
—— of Ponfeigh, Walter, iv. 583.
—— of Redmyre, William, iv. 575.
—— of Skirling, Sir Thomas Gibson, 7th bart., vi. 436.
—— —— his wife, Anne Napier, vi. 436.
—— —— William, King's solicitor, M.P., iv. 591.
—— —— his 1st wife, Helen Craig, iv. 591.
—— —— his 2nd wife, Margaret Menzies, ii. 43; iv. 591.

* Name unknown.

Carmichael of Westraw, Sir James, 1st bart., iv. 584.
—— —— his wife, Agnes Wilkie, iv. 585.
—— of Whelphill, James, iv. 565.
—— —— his wife, Elizabeth Folkart, iv. 565.
—— —— James, iv. 565.
—— —— his wife, Margaret Kincraigie, iv. 565.
—— —— Peter, iv. 565.
—— of Wiston, Sir Hugh, iv. 581.
—— —— Sir John, iv. 563.
—— —— John, iv. 574.
—— —— John, iv. 582.
—— of Wray, Archibald, iv. 577.
—— —— John, iv. 577.
—— Abigail, wife of (1) *, and (2) Hugh Weir of Clowburn, iv. 580; ix. 113.
—— Agnes, wife of John Dundas of Duddingston, iv. 568, 588.
—— Anna, wife of bishop Walter Whiteford, iv. 581, 582; ix. 113.
—— Anne, wife of lt.-col. John Montgomerie, iii. 452.
—— Anne, wife of Sir David Carmichael of Balmedie, iv. 567, 588.
—— Anne, wife of John Dundas of Duddingston, iv. 568.
—— Anne, wife of Sir Jas. Stewart of Burray, iv. 568.
—— Anne, dau. of Dr. Thos. C., iv. 568.
—— Anne, wife of John Maxwell of Blawarthill, iv. 593.
—— Anne, wife of Gerald Dusign, iv. 594.
—— Anne Theophila, wife of J. W. F. Dumergue, iv. 571.
—— Archibald, capt. Royal Marines, iv. 594.
—— Barbara, dau. of Daniel C. of Mauldsley, iv. 592.
—— Barbara, wife of John Cockburn of Ormiston, ix. 114.
—— Barré Grace, dau. of Claude D. J. C., iv. 573.
—— Bartholomew, eldest son of Wm. C. of Carmichael, iv. 576.
—— Beatrix, wife of John Cockburn of Ormiston, iv. 593; ix. 114 *ter*.
—— Cecilia, wife of * Barns, ii. 573.
—— Cecilia, dau. of David C. of Balmedie, v. 568.
—— Charles, H.E.I.C.S., Bombay, iv. 594.
—— Charles, 6th son of 1st earl of Hyndford, iv. 592.
—— Charles Henry Edward, iv. 569.
—— —— his wife, Harriet Morley, iv. 569.
—— Charles Montauban, gen. Indian Army, iv. 569.
—— —— his wife, M. E. Graham, iv. 569.
—— Charles Paget, C.S.I., iv. 570.
—— —— his 1st wife, Georgina Judge, iv. 570.
—— —— his 2nd wife, A. V. Crofton, iv. 570.

* Name unknown.

Carmichael, Claude Dundas James, Madras Police, iv. 570, 573.
—— —— his wife, Mary Glencairn Shaw, iv. 573.
—— Constance Barré, wife of rev. E. Jermyn, iv. 570.
—— Daniel, eldest son of Daniel C. of Mauldslie, iv. 592.
—— David, 3rd son of John de C., ix. 113.
—— David Fremantle, iv. 570.
—— —— his 1st wife, Jane T. Gee, iv. 570.
—— —— his 2nd wife, S. M. Truelock, iv. 571.
—— Elizabeth, mistress of King James v.; wife of Sir John Somerville, i. 24; ii. 160, 168; iv. 565; viii. 14.
—— Elizabeth, wife of Sir W. Scott of Buccleuch, ii. 230.
—— Elizabeth, wife of David Home, younger of Wedderburn, iii. 280; vi. 1.
—— Elizabeth, dau. of David C. of Balmedie, iv. 568.
—— Elizabeth, dau. of Dr. Thomas C., iv. 568.
—— Elizabeth, dau. of Bartholomew C., iv. 576 *bis*.
—— Elizabeth, wife of John Home of Huttonhall, iv. 580.
—— Elizabeth, wife of (1) rev. John Chiesley, and (2) John Muir of Annestoun, iv. 583; ix. 114.
—— Elizabeth, dau. of Wm. C. of Skirling, iv. 591; ix. 114.
—— Elizabeth, wife of Sir John Livingston of Abercorn, vi. 449.
—— Elizabeth, wife of John Fleming, ix. 114.
—— Euphame, wife of (1) Peter Balmanno, and (2) John Ramsay, iv. 566.
—— Euphame, wife of David Tullie, iv. 566.
—— Euphame, wife of William Dick, iv. 568.
—— Eupham, dau. of David C. of Balmedie, iv. 568.
—— Evelyn George Massey, iv. 571.
—— Florence Graham, iv. 569.
—— Frederick, son of Mr. John C., iv. 566.
—— Frederick, only son of 3rd earl of Hyndford, iv. 595.
—— Gawin, 3rd son of Charles C. of Park, ix. 114.
—— Gawin, only son of above, ix. 114.
—— George, rector of Tynynghame, treasurer of Glasgow, iv. 575; viii. 370.
—— George, 2nd son of Daniel C. of Mauldsley, iv. 592.
—— George Gawler Irving, I.S.C., iv. 570.
—— George Lynedoch, lieut.-col. 95th regt., iv. 571.
—— —— his wife, Eva Maria Saunders, iv. 571.
—— Gertrude Wilson, iv. 570.

Carmichael, Grizel, wife of Stephen Lockhart, iv. 583.
— Grizel, wife of Archibald Nisbet of Carfin, iv. 592.
— Grizel, dau. of Daniel C. of Mauldsley, iv. 592.
— Grizel, wife of Jas. Livingston of Jerviswood, viii. 372.
— Helen, dau. of Robert C. of Balmblae, iv. 567.
— Helen, wife of John Gibson of Durie, iv. 591, 596; ix. 114.
— Helen, dau. of Sir John C., ix. 113.
— James, M.P.; 3rd son of 2nd earl of Hyndford, iv. 594.
— James, illeg. son of Archibald C. of Edrom, iv. 578.
— James Barré Hood, iv. 570.
— James Dodington, C.B., colonel 32nd regt., iv. 570.
— — his 1st wife, Barré Latter, iv. 570.
— — his 2nd wife, Teresa Ann Morris, iv. 570.
— James Forrest Halkett, major R.E., iv. 570.
— Sir James Morse, 3rd bart., iv. 573.
— Sir James Robert, 2nd bart, iv. 572.
— — his wife, Louisa Charlotte Butler, iv. 572.
— Jane Trevelyan, wife of H. G. Wedderburn, iv. 571.
— Janet, wife of John, 8th earl of Caithness, ii. 345.
— Janet, dau. of John C. of Meadowflat, viii. 372.
— Jean, wife of James Lockhart, iv. 581, 582.
— Jean, dau. of David C. of Balmedie, ix. 112.
— Jean, dau. of William C. of that Ilk, ix. 113.
— John, tailor burgess of Edinburgh, iv. 126.
— Mr. John, minister of Kilconquhar, iv. 566; ix. 112 *quat.*
— John, 5th son of David C. of Balmedie, iv. 567.
— John, 4th son of David C. of Balmedie, iv. 568.
— John, capt. 60th troop of horse, iv. 586 *bis.*
— John, 2nd son of Daniel C. of Mauldsley, iv. 592.
— John, 3rd son of Daniel C. of Mauldsley, iv. 592.
— John, 5th son of 1st earl of Hyndford, iv. 592.
— John, in Blairsroar, vii. 206.
— — his wife, Joanna Rollo, vii. 206.
— John, captain of Crawford, ix. 12.
— — his wife, Katharine Douglas, i. 185; ix. 12.
Carmichael John, illeg. son of Hugh C. of Carmichael, ix. 113.
— John, illeg. son of Gavin C. of Park, ix. 113.
— John, 2nd son of Charles C. of Park, ix. 114.
— John, commisser of Lanark, ix. 114.
— Katharine, wife of Wm. Crichton, tutor of Sanquhar, iii. 227.
— Katharine, mistress of King James v.; wife of Sir John Somerville, ii. 160, 168; iv. 565; viii. 14.
— Katharine, wife of (1) William Weir, and (2) Hugh Robert Lockhart, iv. 583.
— Katrine, dau. of David C. of Balmedie, ix. 112.
— Katharine Georgiana, wife of Sir W. H. Curzon Wyllie, iv. 571.
— Louisa, dau. of Sir J. R. C., iv. 573.
— Louisa Maria, wife of Edward Wylly, iv. 571.
— Magdalene, dau. of Robert C., iv. 567 *bis.*
— Margaret, dau. of David C. of Balmedie, iv. 566.
— Margaret, dau. of Sir Hugh C. of Carmichael, iv. 581, 582.
— Margaret, wife of Wm. Telfer of Haircleugh, iv. 583.
— Margaret, wife of Sir John Anstruther of Anstruther, iv. 594.
— Margaret, wife of Archd. Douglas of Glenbervie, ix. 12.
— Margaret, wife of Robt. Wardlaw of Kilbaberton, ix. 113.
— Margaret, dau. of Gawin C., ix. 114.
— Maria, wife of 1st lord Holyroodhouse, iv. 433, 580.
— Marion, wife of (1) James Stewart of Allanton, and (2) Robt. Denholm of West Shields, iv. 583; ix. 114.
— Marion, dau. of John C. of Meadowflat, viii. 372.
— Marion, dau. of 1st lord Carmichael, ix. 114.
— Martha, wife of John Kennedy of Kirkmichael, iv. 588.
— Mary, wife of John Hamilton, iv. 578.
— Mary, wife of (1) Sir Wm. Lockhart, and (2) Sir William Weir, iv. 588.
— Mary, wife of Sir Archibald Stewart of Castlemilk, iv. 589.
— Mary, wife of John Montgomerie of Giffen, iv. 593.
— Mary, wife of Charles O'Hara, iv. 594.
— Mary Adelaide, iv. 570.
— May, wife of rev. E. R. Hollings, iv. 573.
— Mungo, 4th son of David C. of Balmedie, iv. 567.
— Rachel, wife of Archibald Hamilton, iv. 583.

Carmichael, Rachel, wife of Sir John Wilkie of Foulden, iv. 588 ; ix. 114 *bis*.
— Rachel, wife of Jas. Weir of Stonebyres, iv. 589.
— Robert, in Ethybetoun, iv. 566.
— Robert, iv. 567.
— — his wife, Katharine Lindsay of Kirkforthar, iv. 567 ; ix. 112.
— Robert, 5th son of David C. of Balmedie, iv. 568.
— Rose Gordon, wife of commander Oswald Niven, R.N., iv. 569.
— Samuel, 5th son of 1st lord Carmichael, v. 588.
— Stewart, Jamaica, iv. 567.
— Thomas, M.D., iv. 568.
— — his wife, Margaret Smyth of Aithernie, iv. 568.
— William, illeg. son of David C. of Balmedie, iv. 566.
— William, writer to the Signet, iv. 568.
— William, illeg. son of Archibald C. of Edrom, iv. 578.
— William, Calcutta, iv. 592.
— William, 4th son of Daniel C .of Mauldsley, iv. 592.
— William, LL.D., archbishop of Dublin, iv. 593.
— — his wife, * Godshall, iv. 594.
— William, 2nd son of John C., minister of Kilconquhar, ix. 112.
— William, eldest son of David C. of Balmedie, ix. 112.
— William, 6th son of David C. of Balmedie, ix. 112.
— *, dau. of James C. of Balmedie and Craigpottie, iv. 566.
Carmichael-Anstruther of Carmichael, Sir John, 5th bart., iv. 594, 597.
— — Sir Windham Frederick, 10th bart., iv. 563, 597.
Carmichael-Smyth of Aithernie. James, censor of the Royal College of Physicians, London, iv. 568.
— — his wife, Mary Holyland, iv. 569.
— Charles Montauban, general Indian Army, iv. 569.
— — his wife, M. E. Graham, iv. 569.
— David Edward Paget, R.N., iv. 572.
— David Scott, iv. 569.
— — his 1st wife, Anne Sherwood, iv. 569.
— — his 2nd wife, Isabella F. Oakes, iv. 569.
— Eleanor Elton, iv. 571.
— George Henry Edward Hyndford, iv. 572.
— George James Graham, iv. 572.
— — his wife, J. T. S. Holder, iv. 572.

* Name unknown.

Carmichael-Smyth, George Monro, major-general Bengal Army, iv. 571.
— — his 1st wife, Jane Ross, iv. 572.
— — his 2nd wife, C. B. Hamilton, iv. 572.
— Georgina Christina, wife of lieut-col.-Wm. Forrest, iv. 572.
— Harriet Olivia, iv. 571.
— Henry William, major Bengal Engineers, iv. 569.
— — his wife, Anne Beecher, iv. 569.
— Sir James. major-general, 1st bart., iv. 569, 572.
— — his wife. Harriet Morse, iv. 572.
— James Dodington, col. 32nd regt., iv. 570.
— Sir James Robert, 2nd bart., iv. 572.
— Maria, iv. 571.
— Maria Agnes, wife of Dr. Alex. Monro, iv. 572.
— Mark Wood, capt. Madras Cavalry. iv. 571.
— — his wife, Marianne Hutton, iv. 571.
— Methven W. A., iv. 572.
— Robert Hervey, iv. 571.
— Robert Stewart, major 93rd Highlanders, iv. 571.
— — his 1st wife, A. R. Hervey, iv. 571.
— — his 2nd wife, D. S. Tudor, iv. 571.
— William Henry, Bengal C. S., iv. 569.
Carnaby of Halton, Reginald, vii. 101.
— — his wife, Susanna Graham, vii. 101.
Carnarvon, Henry John George (Herbert), 3rd earl of, iii. 124.
— John (Brydges), eldest son of James, duke of Chandos ; styled marquess of, iii. 406.
— — his wife, Katharine Tollemache, iii. 406.
CARNEGIE OF KINNAIRD, CARNEGIE, LORD, viii. 65-93.
CARNEGIE OF LEUCHARS, CARNEGIE, LORD, viii. 65-93.
— Charles Alexander, eldest son of 10th earl of Southesk ; styled lord, viii. 92.
— Sir David, first lord, i. 514 ; iv. 127 ; viii. 54, 64.
— — his wife, Margaret Lindsay, i. 514 ; viii. 66.
— David, eldest son of 1st earl of Southesk ; styled lord, ii. 414 ; iv. 315 ; viii. 66.
— — his wife, Margaret Hamilton, i. 258 ; iv. 315 ; viii. 66.
— James, only son of 5th earl of Southesk ; styled lord, viii. 74.
— master of, David Carnegie, eldest son of 1st lord Carnegie, ii. 414 ; viii. 66.
— — his wife, Margaret Hamilton, iv. 315 : viii. 66.
CARNEGIE, BARON BALINHARD OF FARNELL, viii. 90-93.

Carnegie, lord Carnegie of Kinnaird, viii. 65-93.
Carnegie, lord Carnegie of Leuchars, viii. 65-93.
Carnegie, lord Eglismaldie, vi. 494-508.
Carnegie, earl of Ethie, vi. 494-495.
Carnegie, lord Lour, vi. 494-495.
Carnegie, earl of Northesk, vi. 493-508.
Carnegie, lord Rosehill, vi. 495-508.
Carnegie, earl of Southesk, viii. 46-93.
Carnegie of Ananie and Arnhall, Sir David, viii. 86.
— of Auchmithie, Sir John, vi. 494.
— of Auchquhandlen, Sir Robert, viii. 51.
— of Balbardie, Sir John, viii. 58.
— of Baldovie, Sir James, viii. 89.
— of Balglassie, David, viii. 54.
— — his wife, Margaret Livingstone, viii. 54.
— of Ballindarg, Robert, vi. 495.
— — Robert, vi. 495.
— — his wife, Anne Carnegie of Kinnoull, vi. 495.
— of Balmachie, David, viii. 54.
— — his wife, Margaret Livingstone, viii. 54.
— — David, viii. 57.
— — James, viii. 54, 60.
— — his wife, Christian Bruce, viii. 54.
— — James, last laird, viii. 55.
— of Balmedesyde and Pittaquhop, Elizabeth, wife of John Inglis of Inglistarvit, viii. 60.
— — Margaret, wife of William Dundas, viii. 60.
— of Balnabreich, Robert, viii. 58.
— — his wife, Margaret Ogilvy, viii. 58.
— of Balnamoon, Sir Alexander, 1st laird, viii. 61.
— — his wife, Giles Blair, viii. 61.
— — Alexander, 5th laird, viii. 62.
— — his wife, Margaret Graham, viii. 62.
— — James, 3rd laird, viii. 62.
— — his 1st wife, Margaret Carnegie, viii. 62.
— — his 2nd wife, Jean Fothringham, viii. 62.
— — James, 4th laird, viii. 62.
— — Sir John, 2nd laird, i. 125; viii. 61; ix. 49.
— — his 1st wife, Elizabeth Ogilvy, i. 125; viii. 61; ix. 8.
— — his 2nd wife, * Graham, viii. 61.
— — James, 6th laird, i. 295; viii. 62.
— — his wife, Margaret Arbuthnott of Findowrie, i. 295; viii. 62.
— — Sir Robert, viii. 51.
— — his wife, Margaret Guthrie, viii. 53.
— of Balveny, David, viii. 54.
— — his wife, Margaret Livingstone, viii. 54.

* Name unknown.

Carnegie of Banquhry, Sir John, viii. 58.
— of Birkhill, Mungo, sheriff-clerk of Haddington, viii. 76, 77.
— — his wife, Janet Dick, viii. 76.
— of Boysack, James, 4th laird, vi. 496.
— — John, 1st laird, vi. 495.
— his wife, Margaret Erskine, vi. 495.
— — John, 2nd laird, vi. 495.
— — his wife, Jean Fothringham, vi. 495; viii. 62.
— — John, 3rd laird, vi. 495, 496.
— — his wife, Margaret Skene, vi. 496.
— of Braikie, James, vi. 495.
— — his wife, Anne Ogilvy, vi. 495.
— — John, vi. 495.
— — his wife, Anne Auchinleck, vi. 495.
— of Caraldston, Sir John, vi. 494.
— — Sir Robert, vi. 494.
— of Carcary, Duthac de, viii. 48.
— — his wife, Mariota of Kinnaird, viii. 48.
— of Little Carcary, George, viii. 56.
— — Katharine, viii. 56.
— of Careston, Sir Alexander, viii. 61.
— — Sir John, viii. 61.
— of Nether Careston, John, viii. 61.
— — Sir Robert, viii. 61.
— of Carnegie, James, viii. 47.
— — his wife, Isobel Liddell, viii. 47.
— — Sir James, 3rd bart. of Pittarrow, viii. 85.
— — John, 1st laird, viii. 46, 47.
— — John, 2nd laird, viii. 47.
— — John, 3rd laird, viii. 47.
— — John, illeg. son of Sir Robert C. of of Kinnaird, iv. 281, 284; viii. 54, 57, 60; ix. 35.
— — his wife, Katharine Fotheringhame, viii. 58.
— of Charleton, George viii. 82.
— — his wife, Susan Scott, viii. 82.
— — George, viii. 82.
— — his wife, Madeline Connel, viii. 82.
— — John, viii. 82.
— — his wife, Mary Fullerton, viii. 82.
— of Colluthie, David, iii. 278; viii. 53, 59.
— — his 1st wife, Elizabeth Ramsay, viii. 53, 60.
— — his 2nd wife, Eupheme Wemyss, iii. 278; viii. 61, 491.
— — his 3rd wife, Janet Henrison, viii. 64.
— — Sir David, viii. 61, 64.
— — his wife, Margaret Lindsay, i. 514!; viii. 66.
— of Cookstoun, Alexander, viii. 55.
— — his wife, Margaret Livingstone, viii. 55.
— — David, son of Hercules C., viii. 55.
— — David, last laird, viii. 55.
— — John, viii. 51.
— — his wife, Eupheme Strachan, viii. 51.

Carnegie of Craig, David, viii. 67.
—— —— his wife, Katharine Wemyss, viii. 67, 501; ix. 159.
—— —— Sir John, 3rd son of 1st earl of Southesk, viii. 66.
—— —— his wife, Jane Scrymgeour, iii. 314; viii. 67.
—— of Craigo, David, dean of Brechin, viii. 55.
—— —— his wife, Helen Lindsay, viii. 55.
—— —— David, the younger, viii. 55.
—— —— his wife, * Stewart, viii. 55.
—— —— Elizabeth, viii. 55.
—— of Crechie, John viii. 57.
—— of Cruikston, David, vii. 14.
—— of Deischland, David, viii. 57.
—— —— John, viii. 57.
—— of Dunlappie, Sir John, vi. 494.
—— of Dunnichen, David, viii. 61.
—— —— John, viii. 57.
—— —— Sir Robert, vi. 494; viii. 58, 61.
—— —— his wife, Isobel Gray, iv. 286; viii. 61.
—— of Erlesfield, Sir John, viii. 58.
—— of Ethie, David, vi. 492.
—— —— Sir Robert, 1st laird, viii. 51.
—— of Fair Oak, John Jervis, vi. 505.
—— —— his 1st wife, Charlotte Stevenson, vi. 505.
—— —— his 2nd wife, Georgina Marjoribanks, vi. 505.
—— of Fethies, Sir Robert, viii. 51.
—— of Finavon, Barbara, wife of Sir Robert Douglas of Glenbervie, vi. 498.
—— —— James, 1st laird, vi. 497.
—— —— his wife, Anna Lundin, v. 303; vi. 498.
—— —— James, 2nd laird, vi. 498; viii. 295, 308.
—— —— his 1st wife, Margaret Bennet, vi. 498.
—— —— his 2nd wife, Violet Nasmith, vi. 498.
—— —— James, 3rd laird, vi. 498.
—— of Little Fithie, Sir James, viii. 89.
—— of Framedrum, Sir David, viii. 86.
—— of Fullerton, Sir David, viii. 86.
—— of Gartnafuaran, David, viii. 83.
—— —— James, viii. 83.
—— of Glenhuckie, David, viii. 83.
—— —— James, viii. 83.
—— of Glendye, Sir James, viii. 90.
—— of Idvy, Sir Robert, viii. 51.
—— of Inglismaldie, Sir John, vi. 494.
—— of Kinblethmont, Sir John, vi. 424.
—— —— John, vi. 495.
—— —— his wife, Jean Fothringham, vi. 495.
—— of Kinfauns, Alexander, vi. 499.
—— —— his 1st wife, Anna Blair, vi. 499; ix. 144.
—— —— his 2nd wife, Margaret Nairne, vi. 393, 499.

* Name unknown.

Carnegie of Kinfauns, Alexander, vi. 499.
—— —— his wife, Jean Carnegie, vi. 499.
—— —— Margaret, wife of John, lord Gray of Gray, vi. 498.
—— of Kinnaber, George, viii. 82.
—— —— his wife, Madeline Connel, viii. 82.
—— —— John, viii. 82.
—— —— his wife, Mary Fullerton, viii. 82.
—— of Kinnaird, David, 7th laird, iii. 278; viii. 53, 59.
—— —— his 1st wife, Elizabeth Ramsay of Leuchars and Colluthie, viii. 53 60.
—— —— his 2nd wife, Euphame Wemyss, iii. 278; viii. 61, 491.
—— —— his 3rd wife, Janet Henrison, viii. 64.
—— —— Sir David, 8th laird, viii. 61, 64.
—— —— his wife, Margaret Lindsay, i. 514; viii. 66.
—— —— Duthac de, 1st laird, viii. 48.
—— —— his wife, Mariota of Kinnaird, viii. 48.
—— —— John, 3rd laird, viii. 50.
—— —— his wife, * Waus, viii. 51.
—— —— John, 4th laird, viii. 51.
—— —— his wife, Euphame Strachan, viii. 51.
—— —— Sir John, 6th laird, v. 205; viii. 56, 58, 60.
—— —— his 1st wife, Agnes Wood, viii. 58.
—— —— his 2nd wife, Margaret Keith, vi. 49; viii. 59.
—— —— Sir Robert, 5th laird, vi. 189, 493; viii. 51.
—— —— his wife, Margaret Guthrie, viii. 53.
—— —— Walter, 2nd laird, viii. 49.
—— —— his probable wife, * Lindsay, viii. 49.
—— of Kinnaldie, Sir John, vi. 494.
—— of Kinnoull, Anne, wife of Robt. Carnegie, vi. 495.
—— —— James, vi. 495.
—— —— his wife, Anne Ogilvy, vi. 495.
—— —— John, vi. 495.
—— —— his wife, Anne Auchinleck, vi. 495.
—— —— Robert, vi. 495.
—— —— his wife, Anne Carnegie, vi. 495.
—— of Leuchars, David, viii. 60.
—— —— his wife, Elizabeth Ramsay, viii. 53, 60.
—— —— Sir David, viii. 86.
—— —— Elizabeth, viii. 60.
—— —— Margaret, viii. 60.
—— of Leuchland, Robert, viii. 55.
—— —— his wife, Marjorie Wedderburn, viii. 56.
—— —— William, viii. 55.
—— of Lour, Patrick, 4th laird, vi. 499.
—— —— his wife, Margaret Bower, vi. 499.
—— —— Patrick, 5th laird, vi. 499.
—— —— his wife, Rachel Anne Forbes, vi. 499.

* Name unknown.

Carnegie of Lour, Patrick, 3rd laird, vi. 498.
— — his 1st wife, Elizabeth Graham, vi. 498.
— — his 2nd wife, Margaret Graham, vi. 498.
— — Patrick, 2nd laird, vi. 498.
— — his wife, Alison Watson, vi. 498.
— — Patrick, 3rd son of 2nd earl of Northesk; 1st laird, vi. 498.
— — his 1st wife, Marjory Threipland, vi. 498.
— — his 2nd wife, Margaret Stewart, vi. 498.
— of Lunan, Sir John, vi. 494.
— of Many, John, viii. 53.
— — his wife, Margaret Waus, viii. 53.
— of Marytoun, Sir David, viii. 86.
— of Mondyncs, Sir Alexander, viii. 74.
— of Old Montrose, Sir David, viii. 86.
— of Murdocairnie, Robert, vi. 89.
— of Ochterlony, John, viii. 57.
— of Odmeston, Sir Alexander, viii. 74.
— — James, sheriff-depute of Forfarshire, viii. 75.
— of Panbride, David, 2nd son of Sir Robert C. of Kinnaird, viii. 53, 59.
— — his 1st wife, Elizabeth Ramsay, viii. 53, 60.
— of Pitkennedy, Sir David, viii. 86.
— of Pittarrow, Sir Alexander, 4th son of 1st earl of Southesk, i. 304; vi. 497; viii. 67, 74.
— — his wife, Margaret Arbuthnott, i. 304; viii. 75.
— — Sir David, 1st bart., vii. 220; viii. 67, 76.
— — his 1st wife, Katharine Primrose, vii. 220; viii. 77.
— — his 2nd wife, Katharine Gordon, i. 308; viii. 78.
— — his 3rd wife, Jean Burnett, viii. 79.
— — Sir David, 4th bart., viii. 86.
— — his wife, Agnes Murray Elliot, viii. 86.
— — George, 6th son of Sir John C. of Pittarrow, viii. 81.
— — his wife, Susan Scott, viii. 82.
— — George, viii. 82.
— — his wife, Madeline Connel, viii. 82.
— — Sir James, 3rd bart., viii. 81, 83.
— — his wife, Christian Doig of Cookston and Balzeordie, viii. 85.
— — Sir James, 5th bart., viii. 88.
— — his wife, Charlotte Lysons, viii. 89.
— — Sir James, 6th bart., viii. 90.
— — his 1st wife, Katharine Hamilton Noel, viii. 90.
— — his 2nd wife, Susan Katharine Mary Murray, iii. 394; viii. 91.
Carnegie of Pittarrow, Sir John, 3rd son of 1st earl of Southesk, viii. 66, 74.
— — his wife, Jane Scrymegeour, iii. 314; viii. 67.
— — Sir John, 2nd bart., viii. 78, 80.
— — his wife, Mary Bnrnett, viii. 81.
— — John, eldest son of George C., viii. 82.
— — his wife, Mary Fullerton of Kinnaber, viii. 82.
— of Punderlaw, David, viii. 57.
— — James, viii. 54.
— — John, viii. 54, 57.
— of Redcastle, Sir John, vi. 494.
— of Seaton, Sir John, 2nd son of David C. of Colluthie, vi. 494; viii. 61.
— — John, illeg. son of Sir Robert C. of Kinnaird, viii. 57.
— of Seggieden, Sir John, viii. 58.
— of Southesk, Sir James, viii. 84.
— of Strachan, Sir James, 1st laird, viii. 89.
— — Sir James, 2nd laird, viii. 90.
— of Stronvar, David, vii. 524; viii. 83.
— — his 1st wife, Julie Boletta Zeuthen, viii. 83.
— — his 2nd wife, Susan Mary Anne Carnegie, viii. 83 *bis*.
— — James, viii. 83.
— — his wife, Mary Bethune Gillespie, viii. 83.
— of Tulibirnis, John, viii. 50 *bis*.
— of Vayne, Sir Alexander, viii. 61.
— — his wife, Giles Blair, viii. 61.
— Agnes, wife of Sir Jas. Sandilands, i. 78; viii. 67; ix. 5.
— Agnes, wife of Patrick Livingstone, viii. 54.
— Agnes, wife of principal Robert Paterson, viii. 55.
— Agnes, wife of Sir Alex. Falconer of Halkerston, v. 246; viii. 64.
— Agnes, dau. of Sir David C. of Southesk, viii. 88.
— Agnes, dau. of Sir James C. of Southesk, viii. 90.
— Alexander, captain, sheriff of Angus, viii. 61; ix. 49.
— — his wife, Jean Erskine, ii. 274; viii. 62; ix. 49.
— Alexander, accountant, London, viii. 75.
— Alexander, merchant, London, viii. 76.
— Alexander, Jamaica, viii. 81.
— Alexander Bannerman, viii. 92.
— Andrew, 7th son of Sir Alexander C. of Pittarrow, viii. 76.
— Anna, wife of Patrick Wood of Bonnington, vi. 497.
— Anna, dau. of 3rd earl of Northesk, vi. 500.
— Anna, wife of Sir Alex. Hope of Kerse, vi. 501.

Carnegie, Anne, wife of Sir John Ogilvy of Inverquharity, vi. 498.
— Anne, wife of James Knox, viii. 62.
— Anne, wife of rear-admiral Robert Wauchope, viii. 87.
— Anne Letitia, wife of Jas. Cruickshank of Langley Park, vi. 506.
— Arabella Charlotte, wife of Samuel H. Romilly, viii. 91.
— Archibald, 2nd son of David C. of Pittarrow, viii. 77.
— Beatrice Diana Cecilia, wife of rev. H. H. Stewart, viii. 91.
— Cecil, dau. of Sir John C. of Balnamoon, viii. 62.
— Charles, elder son of James C. of Finavon, vi. 498.
— Charles, dean of Brechin, viii. 75, 79.
— — his wife Barbara Martin, viii. 75.
— Charles, M.P., inspector of constabulary, viii. 89.
— Charlotte, wife of (1) Thomas F. Scrymseoure Fothringham, and (2) F. B. Elliot, viii. 89.
— Christian, wife of 1st duke of Montrose, vi. 265, 500.
— Christian, dau. of 4th earl of Northesk, vi. 502.
— Christian, dau. of Sir Robert C. of Kinnaird, viii. 57.
— Christina Mary, viii. 87.
— Clementina, dau. of 5th earl of Southesk, viii. 74.
— Constance Mary, C.I., wife of 9th earl of Elgin, iii. 496; viii. 91.
— David, 2nd son of John C. of Boysack, vi. 496.
— David, elder son of Sir Alexander C. of Balnamoon, viii. 61.
— David, son of Mungo C. of Birkhill, viii. 76.
— David, merchant, West Indies, viii. 79.
— David, 3rd son of Sir John C. of Pittarrow, viii. 81.
— David, Gottenburg, viii. 83.
— — his wife, Anne Christian Beckman, viii. 83.
— David Alexander, vi. 507.
— David Wynford, explorer and author, viii. 91.
— Dora Susan, wife of Ernest von Rodakowski, viii. 92.
— Dorothea Helena, viii. 91.
— Duthac de, 2nd son of John de Balinhard, viii. 47, 48.
— Edward Hugo, viii. 82.
— — his wife, Emilie Prange, viii. 82.
— Eleanor, wife of James Evans, viii. 88.
— Elizabeth, wife of Andrew Arbuthnott of that Ilk, i. 297; viii. 56.
— Elizabeth, wife of 5th lord Balmerino, i. 571; vi. 501; ix. 34.
Carnegie, Elizabeth, wife of 3rd earl of Hopetoun, iv. 500; vi. 503.
— Elizabeth, wife of John Guthrie of that Ilk, viii. 62.
— Elizabeth, wife of John Graham of Balgowan, viii. 62.
— Elizabeth, dau. of Alexander C. of Balnamoon, viii. 62.
— Elizabeth, wife of 1st lord Balvaird, viii. 63, 201; ix. 159.
— Elizabeth, dau. of Sir David C. of Pittarrow, viii. 78.
— Elizabeth, wife of Alex. Strachan of Tarrie, viii. 80, 87.
— Elizabeth, dau. of Sir John C. of Pittarrow, viii. 83.
— Elizabeth, dau. of Sir James C. of Pittarrow, viii. 86.
— Elizabeth, dau. of Sir David C. of Southesk, viii. 87.
— Elizabeth Erica, viii. 92.
— Elizabeth Margaret, wife of gen. F. R. Thackeray, vi. 506.
— Emma, wife of James Douglas of Cavers, viii. 88.
— Euphame, wife of Robert Graham of Morphie, viii. 64.
— Frances, dau. of 2nd earl of Northesk, vi. 499.
— George, lieut.-col., vi. 503.
— — his wife, Elizabeth Swinton, vi. 503.
— George, major-general, viii. 82.
— — his wife, Maria Priscilla Wakefield. viii. 82.
— George, advocate, viii. 86.
— George David Howard, viii. 82.
— George James, iii. 365; vi. 503.
— — his wife, Frances Jacobina Nicholson, iii. 365; vi. 503.
— Georgina Henrietta, dau. of 7th earl of Northesk, vi. 506.
— Gilbert, 2nd son of Duthac de C., viii. 48.
— Grisel, dau. of Sir David C. of Pittarrow, viii. 78.
— Helen, wife of (1) Wm. Lundie of Benholm, (2) Robert Turing of Foveran, and (3) John Gordon of Glenbucket, viii. 56.
— Helen, wife of Alex. Aberdein of Cairnbulg, viii. 83.
— Helen Alice, wife of Francis Eden Lacy, vi. 507.
— Helena Mariota, viii. 92.
— Henrietta, dau. of 4th earl of Northesk, vi. 502.
— Henry, midshipman H.E.I.C.S., viii. 81.
— Hercules, viii. 55.
— Ian Ludovic Andrew, R.N., vi. 507.
— — his wife, Anna Barbara Atkinson, vi. 507.

Carnegie, Isabel, wife of Gordon of Glenbucket, viii. 57.
— James, minister at Redgorton and at Barrie, viii. 55.
— — his wife, Ann Gardyne, viii. 55.
— James, legtd. son of Robert C. of Balnahreich, viii. 58.
— James, Charleston, So. Carolina, viii. 75.
— James, merchant, Montrose, viii. 79, 81.
— James, H.E.I.C.S., viii. 83.
— — his wife, Margaret Gillespie, viii. 83.
— James, his son, viii. 83.
— James, 2nd son of Sir James C. of Pittarrow, viii. 85.
— James, vicar of Seaford, viii. 86.
— James, son of Lancelot Douglas C., viii. 91.
— James Duthac, viii. 92.
— James Edward, viii. 82.
— Jane, dau. of Sir David C. of Southesk, viii. 87.
— Jane Christian, wife of Wm. Fullarton Lindsay-Carnegie, vi. 496, 506; viii. 112.
— Janet, wife of Wm. Maule of Auchrinnie, vii. 9; viii. 51.
— Janet, dau. of Mungo C. of Birkhill, viii. 76.
— Janet, wife of capt. W. Keith, viii. 76.
— Janet, dau. of Sir David C. of Pittarrow, viii. 80.
— Jean, wife of (1) James Murray, 2nd earl of Annandale, and (2) David, 4th viscount Stormont, i. 229; viii. 70, 197, 204.
— Jean, wife of (1) Alexander Lindsay, master of Spynie, and (2) John Lindsay of Edzell, i. 515; vi. 497; viii. 104, 107.
— Jean, wife of 3rd earl of Balcarres, i. 522; vi. 499.
— Jean, wife of Alex. Blair of Kinfauns, iv. 292; vi. 498.
— Jean, wife of (1) James Carmichael of Balmedie, and (2) A. Dundas of Fingask, iv. 566; viii. 63.
— Jean, dau. of 3rd earl of Northesk, vi. 500.
— Jean, wife of Gilbert Reid of Collieston, viii. 57.
— Jean, dau. of Sir David C. of Pittarrow, viii. 80.
— Jean, wife of Robert Taylor of Kirktonhill, viii. 83.
— Jean Douglas, dau. of capt. John Douglas C., vi. 507.
— John, 2nd son of James C. of Balmachie, viii. 54.
— John, 2nd son of Sir John C. of Pittarrow, viii. 81.
— John, lieut.-colonel, viii. 85.
— — his wife, Katharine Tireman, viii. 85.
Carnegie, John, captain 9th lancers, viii. 87.
— — his wife, Elizabeth Susan Grey, viii. 87.
— John, post-captain R.N., viii. 89.
— John Douglas, vi. 507.
— — his wife, Margaret Jean Johnstone-Douglas, vi. 507.
— John Douglas, eldest son of above, vi. 507.
— Julie Isabella, wife of col. Charles Hope of Cowdenknowes, vii. 524; viii. 83.
— Katharine, wife of 11th earl of Erroll, iii. 579; viii. 70.
— Katharine, wife of Sir John Hamilton of Lettrick, iv. 214; viii. 58; ix. 35, 104.
— Katharine, dau. of William C. of Leuchland, viii. 56.
— Katharine, dau. George of C. of Little Carcary, viii. 56.
— Katharine, wife of David Ramsay of Balmain, viii. 56.
— Katharine, wife of John Aytoun of Kinnaldie, viii. 63.
— Katharine, wife of 1st earl of Traquair, viii. 67, 405.
— Katharine, wife of Thomas Allan, viii. 76.
— Katharine, wife of David Watson, viii. 78.
— Katharine Agnes Blanche, wife of col. C. C. E. Morgan, viii. 92.
— Katharine Ethel, viii. 92.
— Katharine Jane Elizabeth, dau. of 10th earl of Northesk, vi. 507.
— Lancelot Douglas, M.V.O., viii. 91.
— — his wife, Marion Alice de Gournay Barclay, viii. 91.
— Madeline, wife of Sir A. Agnew of Lochnaw, viii. 88.
— Magdalene, wife of James, marquess of Montrose, i. 126; vi. 250, 253; viii. 68.
— Magdalene, wife of William Graham of Claverhouse, iii. 324, 325; vi. 497.
— Magdalene, wife of John Moodie of Ardbikie, vi. 499.
— Magdalene, wife of (1) Gideon Baillie of Lochend, and (2) Sir J. Crawford of Kilbirnie, viii. 66; ix. 159.
— Margaret, wife of 2nd earl of Carnwath, ii. 414; viii. 66.
— Margaret, wife of 1st earl of Dalhousie, iii. 99; viii. 67.
— Margaret, wife of Sir Jas. Scrimgeour of Dudhope, iii. 311, 313; viii. 57.
— Margaret, wife of Patrick Kinnaird of Kinnaird, v. 205; viii. 58.
— Margaret, wife of George, lord Balgonie and Raith, vi. 113, 501.
— Margaret, dau. of 1st earl of Northesk, vi. 497.
— Margaret, wife of P. Lyon of Auchterhouse, vi. 498; viii. 303.

Carnegie, Margaret, wife of Sir C. Ramsay of Balmain, vi. 495.
—— Margaret, wife of John Fullarton of Fullarton, vi. 496; viii. 109.
—— Margaret, wife of (1) John Foulis, and (2) Charles Lewis, vi. 498.
—— Margaret, dau. of 3rd earl of Northesk, vi. 500.
—— Margaret, wife of Chas. Watson of Saughton, vi. 503.
—— Margaret, dau. of capt. J. Douglas C., vi. 507.
—— Margaret, wife of Patrick Falconer, viii. 54.
—— Margaret, legtd. dau. of Sir John C. of Kinnaird, viii. 59.
—— Margaret, wife of James Carnegie of Balnamoon, viii. 62, 76.
—— Margaret, dau. of Alexander C. of Balnamoon, viii. 62.
—— Margaret, wife of George Dunbar of Inchbrock, viii. 67.
—— Margaret, wife of Black of Haddo, viii. 76.
—— Margaret, wife of Henry Fletcher of Saltoun, viii. 78.
—— Margaret, dau. of Sir John C. of Pittarrow, viii. 83.
—— Margaret Mary Adeliza, vi. 506.
—— Marion, wife of Gilbert Gray of Bandirran, vi. 281; viii. 58.
—— Mariota Susan, viii. 91.
—— Marjory, wife of (1) William Halyburton, and (2) 1st viscount Arbuthnott, i. 305; viii. 67.
—— Marjorie, wife of (1) James Scott, and (2) John Prestoune, vi. 497.
—— Mary, dau. of 4th earl of Northesk, vi. 502.
—— Mary, wife of Walter Long of Preshaw, vi. 506.
—— Mary, wife of Strachan of Carmyle, viii. 57.
—— Mary, wife of (1) col. John Scott, and (2) * Forbes, viii. 83.
—— Mary, dau. of Sir James C. of Pittarrow, viii. 86.
—— Mary, wife of Thomas Henry Graham of Edmond Castle, viii. 88.
—— Mary Anne, wife of rev. Dr John Kemp, vi. 504.
—— Mary Anne, dau. of Sir David C. of Southesk, viii. 88.
—— Mary Elizabeth, viii. 92.
—— Mary Georgina, vi. 505.
—— Robert, 3rd son of 1st earl of Northesk, vi. 496.
—— Robert, 5th son of 2nd earl of Northesk, vi. 499.
—— Robert, parson of Kinnoull, viii. 54.
—— —— his wife, Elizabeth Wemyss, viii. 54, 491.

* Name unknown.

Carnegie, Robert, minister expectant, viii. 55.
—— Robert, 4th son of Sir Alexander C. of Pittarrow, viii. 75.
—— Robert, M.D., viii. 75.
—— Robert, 6th son of Sir David C. of Pittarrow, viii. 79.
—— Robert Francis, major Gordon Highlanders, viii. 91.
—— Stewart, wife of Wm. Fullarton of Fullarton, *afterwards* Lindsay of Spynie, vi. 496; viii. 111.
—— Susan Mary Anne, wife of David Carnegie of Stronvar, viii. 83 *bis*.
—— Swynfen Thomas, rear-admiral R.N., vi. 505.
—— —— his wife, Louisa Albertina Hope, vi. 506.
—— Sylvester, Arbroath, vi. 502.
—— Walter de, 2nd son of John de C. of Carnegie, viii. 47.
—— Walter, 2nd son of Walter C. of Kinnaird, viii. 50.
—— William, 2nd son of 3rd earl of Southesk, iii. 405; viii. 71.
—— William, 5th son of Sir David C. of Pittarrow, viii. 78.
Carnegie-Arbuthnott of Balnamoon, Anne, viii. 63.
—— —— Helen, viii. 63.
—— —— James, 6th laird, i. 295; viii. 62, 82.
—— —— his wife, Margaret Arbuthnott, i. 295; viii. 62.
—— —— James, 7th laird, viii. 62, 63.
—— —— James, 8th laird, viii. 63.
—— —— his wife, Anne Hunter, viii. 63.
—— —— Mary Anne Jemima, wife of Arthur Risden Capel, viii. 63.
—— Alexander, viii. 62.
—— Anne, viii. 62.
—— Charles, viii. 62.
—— Elizabeth, viii. 62.
—— Helen, wife of A. Knox of Keithock, viii. 63.
—— Jean, viii. 62.
—— John, viii. 62.
—— Margaret, viii. 62.
Carnegie-Knox, James, viii. 63 *bis*.
Carnoto, Thomas de, vii. 236.
CARNWATH, DALZELL, EARL OF, ii. 395-420.
Carnwath, Alexander, eldest son of 6th earl of Carnwath; titular earl of, ii. 416.
—— —— his wife, Elizabeth Jackson, ii. 416.
—— Arthur Alexander, ninth earl of, ii. 419; ix. 55.
—— Gavin, second earl of, ii. 413; viii. 25 *n.*; ix. 54 *bis*.
—— —— his 1st wife, Margaret Carnegy, ii. 414.
—— —— his 2nd wife, Margaret Erskine, ii. 414; v. 86.

Carnwath, Harry Burrard, tenth earl of, ii. 419; ix. 55.
—— —— his wife, Isabella Campbell, ii. 419.
—— Henry Arthur Hew, eighth earl of, ii. 419; ix. 55.
—— James, third earl of, ii. 414; ix. 54 *ter*.
—— —— his wife, Mary Seton, ii. 414; viii. 601; ix. 54, 55.
—— John, fourth earl of, ii. 415; ix. 54 *bis*, 55.
—— Robert, first earl of, ii. 408, 411; ix. 54 *bis*.
—— —— his 1st wife, Christian Douglas, ii. 413; vii. 129.
—— —— his 2nd wife, Katharine Abingdon, ii. 413.
—— Robert, fifth earl of, ii. 415; v. 127; ix. 54, 55.
—— —— his 1st wife, Grace Montgomery, ii. 416; iii. 457.
—— —— his 2nd wife, Grizel Urquhart, ii. 416.
—— —— his 3rd wife, Margaret Hamilton, ii. 416.
—— —— his 4th wife, Margaret Vincent, ii. 416.
—— Robert Alexander, sixth earl of, ii. 417; ix. 55.
—— —— his 1st wife, Jane Parkes, ii. 417.
—— —— his 2nd wife, Andalusia Brown, ii. 418.
—— Robert Harris Carnwath, eleventh earl of, ii. 420; ix. 55 *bis*.
—— —— his wife, Emily Sulivan Hippisley, ii. 420.
—— Thomas Henry, seventh earl of, ii. 419; ix. 55.
—— —— his 1st wife, Mary Anne Grattan, ii. 419.
—— —— his 2nd wife, Isabella Eliza Eardley Wilmot, ii. 419.
Carpentar, William, *temp.* David II., v. 139.
Carpenter of Eddlewood, Oliver, iv. 341.
—— of Ingleston, Adam, v. 590.
—— of Redbourn, George, viii. 312.
—— —— Mary Elizabeth Louisa Rodney, wife of 11th earl of Strathmore and Kinghorne, viii. 312.
—— Almeria, ix. 109.
—— George, lt.-general, M.P., v. 127.
Carr of Cocken, Ralph, iii. 601.
—— of Etal, Charlotte Hay, wife of rev. Wm. Holwell, iii. 582.
—— —— Sir William, bart., iii. 581, 583; iv. 217; vii. 175.
—— —— William Hay, 2nd son of 15th earl of Erroll, iii. 583.
—— of Sleaford, Sir Robert, v. 71.
—— Isabella, wife of 15th earl of Erroll, iii. 581.
—— Margaret, wife of (1) Alexander Mackay, and (2) Jas. Farquharson of Invercauld, vii. 175.
Carr, Richard Fitzwilliam, vii. 315.
—— William, killed at Flodden, vii. 332.
—— William Holwell, vicar of Menheoiot, iii. 582.
CARR-BOYLE, EARL OF GLASGOW, iv. 218.
Carre of Cavers, Sir Andrew, v. 53; vii. 585; ix. 158.
—— of Nisbet, Margaret, wife of Matthew St. Clair, vii. 53, 585.
—— Anne, wife of William, 1st duke of Bedford, v. 71.
CARRICK, ANCIENT EARLS OF, ii. 421-427.
Carrick, Adam de Kilconcath, *de jure ux.* earl of, ii. 426, 432; viii. 245 *n*.
—— Alexander, alleged earl of, iii. 137.
—— Duncan, first earl of, ii. 422; iv. 138.
—— —— his wife, Avelina Fitzalan, ii. 423; ix. 1.
—— Gilbert of Galloway, ancestor of the earls of, ii. 421: iv. 136, 137.
—— Margaret, Marjorie *or* Martha, wife of (1) Adam de Kilconcath, and (2) Robert Bruce; countess of, ii. 426, 432.
—— Neil, second earl of, i. 12; ii. 426, 445.
—— —— his wife, Margaret Stewart, i. 12; ii. 426.
CARRICK, BRUCE, EARL OF, ii. 428-437.
Carrick, Alexander, earl of, ii. 436.
—— —— his wife, Eleonora Douglas, ii. 137, 437; iii. 142; iv. 227.
—— David, earl of, ii. 436.
—— Edward, earl of, ii. 435; vii. 235 *bis*.
—— —— his alleged wife, Isabel of Atholl, i. 427; ii. 436.
—— Robert, *de jure ux.* earl of, ii. 426, 432.
—— —— his 1st wife, Margaret, countess of Carrick, ii. 426, 432.
—— —— his 2nd wife, Alianora, ii. 433.
—— Robert, guardian of Scotland, earl of, i. 7; ii. 218, 433, 435.
CARRICK, STEWART, EARL OF, ii. 438-439.
Carrick, David, duke of Rothesay, earl of, ii. 438; iii. 279 *n*.
—— James, prince *or* steward of Scotland, earl of, ii. 439.
—— John, eldest son of King Robert II.; earl of, i. 15, 17, 147; ii. 438; viii. 265.
—— —— his wife, Annabella Drummond, ii. 438; vii. 37.
CARRICK, STEWART, EARL OF, ii. 440-442.
Carrick, John, 3rd son of Robert, earl of Orkney; earl of, ii. 440; vi. 573, 576.
—— —— his wife, Elizabeth Howard, ii. 442.
CARRICK, CUNNINGHAM, EARL OF, iv. 227.
Carrick, William, earl of, iv. 227.
Carrick, Charles Henry (Somerset) 6th earl of, i. 527.
—— of Straiton, Sir John de, ii. 423.
—— Alan, parson of Kirkemanen and Straiton, ii. 425.
—— Alexander, son of Duncan, earl of Carrick, ii. 425.

Carrick, Elena de, prioress of North Berwick, ii. 506.
—— Gilbert, son of Sir Gilbert de C., ii. 425, 445; v. 336.
—— Gilbert Fitz-Roland de, ii. 424.
—— Malcolm, illeg. son of Gilbert of C., ii. 421; iv. 137.
—— Malcolm, son of Roland of C., ii. 425, 445.
—— Mary de, alleged wife of John Kennedy of Dunure, ii. 447.
—— Sir Roland de, 'Ceanncinneal,' ii. 423, 426, 443, 445.
—— —— his wife, Mathildis de Baliol, ii. 424.
—— Roland de, heir of Matilda de C., ii. 424, 425, 445.
—— * de, wife of Arthur, the Castellan of Lochdoon, ii. 425.
Carrideby, Elena, wife of Sir Jas. Cunningham of Hassendean, iv. 225 *n.*
CARRINGTON, RAMSAY, LORD RAMSAY OF, iii. 99-110.
Carrington, Robert John (Carrington), 2nd lord, ii. 566.
Carrington, Sir Archibald Primrose, lord clerk register, justice-general, lord, vii. 218.
—— Cecile Katherine Mary, wife of 1st viscount Colville, ii. 566.
Carron, Alexander, *alias* Scrymgeour, iii. 303.
Carruthers of Holmains, John, i. 222.
—— —— his wife, Blanche Murray, i. 222.
—— —— John, ii. 390.
—— —— *, in 1570, i. 224.
—— of Mouswald, Archibald, i. 220, 238, 239.
—— —— his 1st wife, * Johnstone, i. 238.
—— —— his 2nd wife, Marion Scott, i. 239.
—— —— John, captain of Lochmaben, i. 235.
—— —— Sir Simon, ii. 228, 382, 386, 387.
—— —— his contr. wife, Eufamia Carlyle, ii. 386.
—— —— his wife, Isabella Scott, ii. 228.
—— —— Simon, ii. 388.
—— —— his wife, Katharine Carlyle, ii. 388.
—— —— Simon, last laird, i. 223, 242.
—— —— his 1st wife, Agnes Murray, i. 223.
—— —— his 2nd wife, Mariota Johnstone, i. 242.
—— Ellen, wife of Adam Carlyle of Bridekirk, ii. 382.
—— Isabel, wife of Patrick Carlyle, ii. 391.
—— Janet, wife of Jas. Carlyle, ii. 390.
—— John de, 1361, iii. 55.
Carsewell, William, v. 583.
—— —— his wife, Isabel Stewart, v. 583.
Carson, Aglionby Ross, LL.D., ii. 117.
Carstairs of Kilconquhar, Sir John, 1st laird, iii. 510.
—— James, ix. 4.
—— —— his wife, * Sandilands, ix. 4.

* Name unknown.

Carstairs, William, captain, 4th son of Sir John C. of Kilconquhar, iii. 510.
—— —— his wife, Helen Murray, iii. 509.
Carstares, William, Principal of Edinburgh University, secretary to King William III., ii. 20; v. 91.
Carter, John Money, lieut-col. 1st Royals, iii. 522.
—— —— his wife, Janet Ferguson Murray, iii. 522.
Carter-Campbell of Ardpatrick, James, captain R.N., iii. 416.
—— Susan Eleanor, wife of A. F. C. Tollemache, iii. 416.
Carteret, Grace, wife of Lionel, 4th earl of Dysart, iii. 408.
—— Frances, wife of 4th marquess of Tweeddale, viii. 464.
Carthorpe of Carthorpe, Eustachia, wife of Richard Fairfax, iii. 595.
—— —— John, iii. 595.
Cartwright of Aynhoe, Thomas Robert Brook, vi. 120.
—— —— his wife, Elizabeth Jane Leslie-Melville of Melville, vi. 119, 120.
—— —— William, iii. 599.
—— Stephen Ralph, rector of Aynhoe, iii. 584.
Carun of Cupar, iii. 304.
Carwood of Carwood, Janet, wife of John Fleming, viii. 541.
—— —— Margaret, waiting-woman to Queen Mary, v. 438; viii. 541.
CARY, VISCOUNT FALKLAND, iii. 607-617.
CARY, BARON HUNSDON OF SKUTTERSKELFE, iii. 616-617.
Cary of Aldenham and Great Berkhamstead, Sir Edward, ii. 35; iii. 609.
—— —— his wife, Katharine Knyvett, iii. 609.
—— of Great Berkhamstead, Sir Adolphus, iii. 609.
—— —— his wife, Anne Corbet, iii. 609.
—— of Caddington, Sir Philip, iii. 609.
—— —— his wife, Elizabeth Bland, iii. 609.
—— of Carysbrooke, Wilson Jefferson, iii. 604.
—— of Ceelys, Wilson, colonel, iii. 600, 603.
—— —— Wilson Miles, colonel, iii. 603.
—— of Chilton Foliot, Thomas, iii. 608.
—— —— his wife, Margaret Spencer, iii. 608.
—— of Clovelly, Robert, ancestor of the family of, iii. 608.
—— of Cockington, Robert, iii. 608.
—— —— Sir William, iii. 607.
—— —— his 1st wife, Elizabeth Paulet, iii. 608.
—— —— his 2nd wife, Alice Fulford, iii. 608.
—— of Leven Grove and Skutterskelfe, George, general, iii. 613.
—— —— his wife, Isabella Ingram, iii. 613.

Cary of Plashey and Thremhall Priory, Sir John, iii. 608.
— — his wife, Joyce Denny, iii. 608.
— of St. James's, Edward, iii. 610; ix. 88.
— — his wife, Anne Lucas, iii. 610; ix. 88.
— of Snettisham, Sir Wymond, iii. 608.
— — his wife, Katharine Jernegan, iii. 608.
— of Torr Abbey, Robert, ancestor of the family of, iii. 608.
— Almeria Augusta, wife of rev. Wm. Digby, iii. 615.
— Ann, dau. of Thomas C., iii. 608.
— Anne, a Benedictine nun, iii. 611.
— Anne Christiana, wife of capt. S. Morland, iii. 616.
— Archibald, U.S.A., iii. 605.
— — his wife, Monimia Fairfax, iii. 605.
— Byron Charles Ferdinand Plantagenet, captain R.N., iii. 615.
— — his wife, Selina Mary Fox, iii. 615.
— Byron Plantagenet, R.N., iii. 617.
— Charles Lucius, iii. 615.
— Charlotte, wife of Bryan Fairfax, iii. 597.
— Charlotte, wife of Anthony Chapman, iii. 614; ix. 88.
— Charlotte Maria, wife of Samuel Charters, iii. 615.
— Dorothy, dau. of 6th viscount Falkland, iii. 614; ix. 88.
— Sir Edmund, iii. 597.
— Elizabeth, wife of 8th lord Fairfax, iii. 603.
— Elizabeth, in religion 'sister Clementina,' iii. 611.
— Elizabeth Blair, wife of F. Fairfax, iii. 603.
— Emelia Sophia, wife of Major C. T. Grant of Grant, iii. 615.
— Emma Christiana, dau. of 9th viscount Falkland, iii. 616.
— Emma Emelia, wife of Thomas B. Ferguson, iii. 615.
— Frances, wife of 1st earl of Grandison, iii. 611.
— Frances, dau. of 7th viscount Falkland, iii. 614.
— Sir Henry, baron Hunsdon, iii. 608.
— — his wife, Ann Morgan, iii. 608.
— Henry John, 4th son of 6th viscount Falkland, iii. 614.
— Jane, wife of lord Barret of Newburgh, ii. 35; ix. 36.
— Jane, dau. of 7th viscount Falkland, iii. 614.
— John, son of Patrick C., iii. 610.
— Katharine, wife of Sir F. Knollys, iii. 608.
— Katharine, wife of 2nd earl of Home, iii. 611; iv. 467.
Cary, Katharine Mary, dau. of 12th viscount Falkland, iii. 617.
— Lavinia Matilda, dau. of Lucius Ferdinand, Master of Falkland, iii. 615.
— Leeke, 3rd son of 6th viscount Falkland, iii. 614.
— Lettice, dau. of 12th viscount Falkland, iii. 617.
— Sir Lorenzo, iii. 610; ix. 88.
— Lucia, wife of major John Grattan, iii. 615
— Lucius William Charles Augustus Frederick, iii. 616.
— — his wife, Sarah Christiana Keighley, iii. 616.
— Lucy, in religion 'Sister Magdalena,' iii. 611.
— Lucy, wife of lieut.-gen. Comte de Rothe, iii. 614; ix. 88.
— Margaret, dau. of Thomas C., iii. 608.
— Mary, wife of Sir John Delaval, iii. 608.
— Mary, a Benedictine nun, iii. 611.
— Mary, dau. of 7th viscount Falkland, iii. 614.
— Mary Elizabeth, wife of John Law, D.D., iii. 614.
— Mary Randolph, wife of Orlando Fairfax, iii. 604.
— Mary Selina, dau. of 12th viscount Falkland, iii. 617.
— Offley H., rector of Trusham, iii. 607 *n.*
— Patrick, poet, iii. 610; ix. 88.
— — his wife, Susan Uvedale, iii. 610; ix. 88.
— Patricia, dau. of Patrick C., ix. 88.
— Philip Plantagenet, iii. 617.
— Sarah, wife of G. W. Fairfax, iii. 600.
— Selina Catherine, wife of C. E. Fox, iii. 615.
— Susanna Patricia, ix. 88.
— Victoria, wife of (1) Sir W. Uvedale, and (2) B. Price, iii. 611.
— William, gentleman of the bedchamber to King Henry VIII., iii. 608.
— — his wife, Mary Boleyne, iii. 608.
— *, in religion 'Father Placid,' iii. 610.
Caryll, John, vii. 511.
— — his wife, Mary Mackenzie, vii. 511.
Carysfort, Granville Leveson (Proby), 3rd earl of, i. 67.
Cas of Fordell, Richard, v. 457.
CASKIEBERRIE, LESLIE, LORD, vii. 301.
Caskieberrie, John, lord, vii. 301.
Cassidy of Monastereven, Edward, iv. 422.
— — his wife, A. M. J. Constable-Maxwell-Scott, iv. 422.
CASSILLIS, KENNEDY, EARL OF, ii. 443-502.
Cassillis, Archibald, eleventh earl of, ii. 492, 494.
— — his 1st wife, Katharine Schuyler, ii. 495.
— — his 2nd wife, Ann Watts, ii. 495.

* Name unknown.

Cassillis, Archibald, twelfth earl of, ii. 497; ix. 58.
—— —— his wife, Margaret Erskine of Dun, ii. 498.
—— Archibald, styled earl of, ii. 498.
—— —— his wife, Eleanor Allardyce of Dunottar, ii. 498.
—— Archibald, fourteenth earl of, ii. 501.
—— Archibald, styled earl of, ii. 501.
—— —— his wife, Frances Emily Stewart, ii. 502.
—— David, first earl of, ii. 107, 460.
—— —— his 1st wife, Agnes Borthwick, ii. 107, 461.
—— —— his 2nd wife, Grizel *or* Margaret Boyd, ii. 461; v. 149.
—— David, tenth earl of, ii. 462.
—— Gilbert, second earl of, ii. 461, 464; v. 149, 495.
—— —— his wife, Isabella Campbell, i. 336; ii. 465.
—— Gilbert, third earl of, ii. 468; v. 107; ix. 56 *ter*.
—— —— his wife, Margaret Kennedy, ii. 471.
—— Gilbert, fourth earl of, i. 24; ii. 471; viii. 289; ix. 56.
—— his contr. wife, Jean Hamilton, iv. 370; ix. 104.
—— —— his wife, Margaret Lyon, ii. 473; viii. 288.
—— John, fifth earl of, ii. 475, 515; iv. 245; ix. 56 *ter*.
—— —— his contracted wife, Jean Cunningham, iv. 245; ix. 57.
—— —— his proposed wife, Annas Campbell, i. 346; ii. 477.
—— —— his wife, Jean Fleming, ii. 477; viii. 542, 545, 547.
—— John, sixth earl of, i. 567; ii. 474, 477.
—— —— his 1st wife, Jean Hamilton, ii. 481; iv. 315.
—— —— his 2nd wife, Margaret Hay, ii. 481; vii. 348.
—— John, seventh earl of, ii. 482; ix. 57.
—— —— his 1st wife, Susan Hamilton, ii. 484; ix. 57.
—— —— his 2nd wife, Mary Fox, ii. 484; ix. 57.
—— John, eighth earl of, ii. 485; ix. 57.
—— —— his wife, Susan Hamilton, ii. 485; ix. 57.
—— Thomas, ninth earl of, ii. 443, 485, 492; iii. 388.
—— master of, Hew Kennedy, 2nd son of 4th earl of Cassillis, ii. 474, 476; ix. 56.
—— —— his wife, Katharine M'Dowall, ii. 474.
—— master of, Sir Thomas Kennedy, 2nd son of 3rd earl of Cassillis, ii. 471, 486.
—— —— his wife, Elizabeth M'Gill, ii. 486.
Castel Bianco, José de Royas, count of, vi. 70.
—— —— his 1st wife, Mary Drummond, vi. 70.
—— —— his 2nd wife, Frances Drummond, vi. 70.
CASTLEFIELD, PRIMROSE, LORD PRIMROSE AND, vii. 109-111.
Castlefield, James, first lord Primrose and, vii. 110.
CASTLEHAVEN, MACKENZIE, LORD, iii. 74-80.
Castlehaven, George, first lord, iii. 74, 75.
CASTLEHAVEN OF CASTLEHAVEN, HAY-MACKENZIE, BARON, iii. 84-86.
Castlehaven of Castlehaven, Anne, first baroness, iii. 84.
Castlemaine of Horsley, Paul, captain, ii. 562.
—— —— his wife, Margaret Colville, ii. 562.
Castlestewart, Andrew (Stewart), first baron, vi. 516.
—— —— his wife, Margaret Kennedy, vi. 516.
—— Andrew (Stewart), second lord, vi. 517.
—— —— his wife, Anne Stewart, i. 446; vi. 517.
—— John (Stewart), fifth lord, vi. 517.
—— Andrew Thomas (Stewart), 1st earl, vi. 519.
—— Walter Stewart, ancestor of the earls of, i. 150.
Castletown, John W. (Fitzpatrick), 1st lord, iii. 394.
Catesby, Dorothy, wife of Sir William Dormer, iii. 295.
Catford, Ella Louise, wife of Lucius Plantagenet Cary, master of Falkland, iii. 617.
—— E. W., iii. 617.
CATHCART, CATHCART, LORD, ii. 503-531.
Cathcart, Alan, first lord, ii. 507; v. 607.
—— —— his wife, Janet Maxwell, ii. 509.
—— Alan, third lord, ii. 510, 512.
—— —— his wife, Helen Sempill, ii. 513; vii. 538.
—— Alan, fourth lord, ii. 514; iii. 228.
—— —— his contracted wife, Elizabeth Crichton, ii. 514; vii. 539.
—— —— his 1st wife, Margaret Wallace, ii. 516.
—— —— his 2nd wife, Florence M'Dougal, ii. 516.
—— Alan, fifth lord, ii. 516.
—— —— his 1st wife, Margaret Stewart, ii. 172, 517.
—— —— his 2nd wife, Jean Colquhoun, i. 47; ii. 517.
—— Alan, sixth lord, ii. 517.
—— —— his wife, Marion Boswell, ii. 518.
—— Alan, seventh lord, ii. 518.
—— —— his wife, Elizabeth Dalrymple, ii. 518; viii. 147.

Cathcart, Alan Frederick, twelfth lord, ii. 530.
—— his wife, Isabella Sophia Cathcart, ii. 531.
— Charles, eighth lord, ii. 518.
—— his 1st wife, Marion Schaw, ii. 519.
—— his 2nd wife, Elizabeth Malyn, ii. 520.
— Charles Murray, eleventh lord, ii. 527.
—— his wife, Henrietta Mather, ii. 529.
— Charles Schaw, ninth lord, i. 496; ii. 520; ix. 58.
—— his wife, Jean Hamilton, ii. 521.
— John, second lord, ii. 509.
—— his 1st wife, Margaret Kennedy, ii. 510.
—— his 2nd wife, Margaret Douglas, ii. 510; vii. 117.
— William Schaw, tenth lord, ii. 524.
—— his wife, Elizabeth Elliot, ii. 526.
CATHCART, CATHCART, EARL, ii. 503-531.
Cathcart, Alan, fourth earl, ii. 531; ix. 58.
— Alan Frederick, third earl, ii. 530; ix. 58.
—— his wife, Isabella Sophia Cathcart, ii. 523, 531.
— Charles Murray, second earl, ii. 527.
—— his wife, Henrietta Mather, ii. 529.
— George, fifth earl, ii. 531; ix. 58.
— William Schaw, first earl, ii. 524.
—— his wife, Elizabeth Elliot, ii. 526.
CATHCART OF CATHCART, CATHCART, VISCOUNT, ii. 525-531.
Cathcart of Cathcart, Alan Frederick, third viscount, ii. 530.
—— Charles Murray, second viscount, ii. 527.
—— William Schaw, first viscount, ii. 524.
— master of, Alan, eldest son of 2nd lord Cathcart, ii. 510; v. 555.
—— his wife, Agnes Lyle, ii. 510; v. 554.
— master of, Alan, grandson of 2nd lord Cathcart, ii. 510, 512.
— master of, Alan, elder son of 4th lord Cathcart, ii. 516; ix. 58.
—— his wife, Isobel Kennedy, ii. 516.
— master of, Alan, elder son of 7th lord Cathcart, ii. 518.
CATHCART, LORD CATHCART, ii. 503-531.
CATHCART, EARL CATHCART, ii. 503-531.
CATHCART, VISCOUNT CATHCART OF CATHCART, ii. 525-531.
CATHCART, BARON GREENOCK OF GREENOCK, ii. 525-531.
Cathcart of Arvy, Hugh, 5th son of 2nd lord Cathcart, ii. 512 *bis*.
—— his wife, Egidia Crawfurd, ii. 512.
— of Bardarroch, William, ii. 513; ix. 58.
— of Carbiston, Janet, wife of David Cathcart of Duchray, ii. 511.
—— Robert, ii. 512.
—— William, ii. 512 *bis*.
Cathcart of Carleton, Alan, ii. 510.
—— Sir Hew, 1st bart., ii. 511.
—— John, ii. 516.
—— Sir John, 2nd bart., ii. 491.
—— his 2nd wife, Elizabeth Kennedy, ii. 491.
—— Sir John Andrew, 5th bart., ii. 498.
—— his wife, Hannah Eleanor Kennedy, ii. 498.
—— Margaret, wife of (1) Robert Cathcart of Killochan, and (2) Hugh Campbell, ii. 510.
—— Sir Reginald Archibald Edward, 6th bart., ii. 511.
—— Robert, grandson of 2nd lord Cathcart, ii. 511.
—— Sibyll, wife of John Cathcart of Glendowis, ii. 510, 511.
— of Cathcart, Alan de, Constable of Ayr, ii. 504.
—— Sir Alan, ii. 505.
—— his wife, * Wallace, ii. 505.
—— Sir Alan, ii. 506.
—— Sir Alan, ii. 506.
—— Alan, ii. 506.
—— Sir Alan, ii. 507.
—— his wife, Janet Maxwell, ii. 509.
—— Rainaldus, Ranulfus *or* Reginald de, ii. 503.
—— William de, ii. 504.
—— William de, ii. 504.
—— Sir William de, ii. 504.
— of Clavannis, Alan, ii. 511.
—— his wife, Janet Cathcart, ii. 511.
—— David, 4th son of 2nd lord Cathcart, ii. 511.
—— his wife, Agnes Crawfurd, ii. 511.
— of Clolynan and Pennyfodzach, Alan, ii. 509.
—— David, ii. 509.
—— his wife, Margaret Boyd, ii. 509.
— of Drumjowan, James, ii. 513.
— of Drumsmoden, William, ii. 513.
— of Nether Drumsmoden, Hugh, ii. 513.
— of Duchray, Alan, ii. 511.
—— David, 4th son of 2nd lord Cathcart, ii. 511, 512.
—— his wife, Agnes Crawfurd, ii. 511.
— of Galryne, John, ii. 509.
— of Genoch, John, i. 92.
—— his wife, Anne Gordon, i. 92.
—— Robert, ancestor of the family of, ii. 511.
— of Glendowis, John, 3rd son of 2nd lord Cathcart, ii. 511, 512.
—— his wife, Sibill Cathcart, ii. 510, 511.
—— Jonet, wife of R. Crawfurd, ii. 511.
—— Marion, wife of G. Graham, ii. 511.
— of Killochan, Sir Hew, 1st bart., ii. 511.
—— Sir Reginald Archibald Edward, 6th bart., ii. 511.

* Name unknown.

Cathcart of Killochan, Robert, 2nd son of 2nd lord Cathcart, ii. 510.
— — his wife, Margaret Cathcart, ii. 510.
— — Robert, his son, ii. 511.
— of Knockskaith, Hugh, 5th son of 2nd lord Cathcart, ii. 512.
— — his wife, Egidia Crawfurd, ii. 512.
— of Pitcairlie, Robert, ii. 512.
— of Trogwein *or* Trevor *or* Troweir, Alan, ii. 512.
— — Hugh, 3rd son of 1st lord Cathcart, ii. 509.
— of Waterside, Alan, viii. 117.
— Adelaide, wife of J. R. de Trafford, ii. 529.
— Adolphus Frederick, lieut.-col., ii. 527.
— — his wife, Margaret Home, ii. 527.
— Alan, eldest son of 1st lord Cathcart, ii. 509.
— Allan, illeg. son of 3rd lord Cathcart, ii. 513.
— Alan, illeg. son of Alan, master of Cathcart, ii. 516.
— Alice, dau. of Sir George C., ii. 527.
— Anne, dau. of Sir George C., ii. 527.
— Archibald Hamilton, rector of Methby, ii. 522.
— — his wife, Frances Henrietta Fremantle, ii. 522.
— Archibald Hamilton, 5th son of 3rd earl Cathcart, ii. 531; ix. 58 *bis*.
— Archibald William, ii. 522.
— Augusta Sophia, dau. of 1st earl Cathcart, ii. 527; ix. 58.
— Augustus Ernest, King's Royal Rifle Corps, ii. 529.
— Augustus Murray, lieut.-col. Grenadier Guards, ii. 529.
— — his wife, Jean Mary Orde-Powlett, ii. 529.
— Cecilia, wife of John de Perthic, ii. 504.
— Cecilia, wife of capt. E. T. Rose, ii. 531.
— Charles, lieut. 79th regt., ii. 531.
— Charles Allan, quarter-master-general to the Forces in India, M.P., ambassador to China, ii. 522.
— Charlotte, dau. of Archibald H. C., ii. 523.
— Charlotte Catherine, maid-of-honour, ii. 524.
— Christian, wife of Alex. Hamilton of Brentwood, ii. 509.
— Constance, wife of W. H. Ferrand, ii. 529.
— David, 3rd son of 6th lord Cathcart, ii. 518.
— Eleonora, wife of Sir John Houston, ii. 520.
— Elizabeth, dau. of 8th lord Cathcart, ii. 520.
Cathcart, Elizabeth, wife of gen. Sir J. Douglas of Glenfinart, ii. 529.
— Elizabeth Sarah, wife of major Robt. Stuart, ii. 523.
— Emily, dau. of 3rd earl Cathcart, ii. 531.
— Emily Sarah, Woman of the Bedchamber, ii. 527.
— Eva, dau. of 3rd earl Cathcart, ii. 531.
— Frances Louisa, ii. 522.
— Frederica, wife of John Lodge, ii. 523.
— Frederick, col., minister plenipotentiary, ii. 526.
— — his wife, Jane M'Adam of Craigengillan, ii. 526.
— Frederick Adrian, York and Lancaster regt., ii. 529.
— Sir George, K.C.B., adjutant-gen., ii. 526.
— — his wife, Georgina Greville, ii. 527.
— George, lieut. 4th batt. Princess of Wales' Own, ii. 531.
— George Greville, ii. 527.
— Georgiana Mary, ii. 527.
— Gilbert, 2nd son of 4th lord Cathcart, ii. 516 *bis*.
— Helenor, wife of David Stewart, ii. 509.
— Henrietta Louisa Frances, ii. 529.
— Ida, wife of T. L. Hare, ii. 530.
— Isobella Sophia, wife of Sir S. Crompton, ii. 523, 531.
— James, 2nd son of 6th lord Cathcart, ii. 518.
— James, major, 3rd son of 7th lord Cathcart, ii. 518.
— Jane, wife of 4th duke of Atholl, i. 496; ii. 523.
— Jane, dau. of Sir George C., ii. 527.
— Jean, wife of John Shaw of Haily, ii. 512.
— Jean, wife of (1) Thos. Cathcart, and (2) Archibald Dunbar, ix. 58.
— John, illeg. son of 4th lord Cathcart, ii. 516.
— Jonet, wife of John Crawfurd of Drongane, ii. 512.
— Katharine Selina, wife of Robert Smith, ii. 523.
— Leta Adine, ii. 529.
— Louisa, wife of (1) David, 7th viscount Stormont, and (2) Robert Fulke Greville; countess of Mansfield, ii. 523; viii. 206, 209.
— Louisa, dau. of 1st earl Cathcart, ii. 527.
— Louisa, dau. of Sir George C. ii. 527.
— Louisa Margaret, ii. 527.
— Margaret *or* Marion, wife of Sir Wm. Sempill of Eliotstoun, ii. 509; vii. 530, 531.
— Margaret, wife of John Hunter, ii. 512.
— Margaret, illeg. dau. of 4th lord C., ii. 516.
— Margaret, wife of Sir A. Whitefoord, ii. 518.
— Margaret, dau. of 8th lord C., ii. 520.

Cathcart, Marianne Elizabeth, ii. 523.
— Marion, dau. of 3rd earl Cathcart, ii. 531.
— Marjory, wife of James Dalrymple of Stair, viii. 117.
— Mary, wife of Thos. Graham of Balgowan, ii. 523.
— Mary Anne, wife of 7th lord Napier of Merchiston, ii. 520; vi. 435.
— Mary Elizabeth, dau. of 1st earl Cathcart, ii. 527.
— Mary Mildred, dau. of col. Augustus M. C., ii. 529.
— Reginald, King's Royal Rifle Corps, ii. 531.
— Robert, illeg. son of 4th lord C., ii. 516.
— Schaw, ensign 3rd regt., ii. 519.
— Sibella, wife of John Wallace of Craigie, ii. 512.
— Thomas, ix. 58.
— — his wife, Jean Cathcart, ix. 58.
— Vera, ii. 529.
— William Harold, Worcester regt., ii. 529.
Cathe, *see* Keith.
Catlett, Charles, iii, 603.
Caulfield of Raheenduff, Wade Toby, capt. 3rd Dragoon Guards, vii. 389.
— — his wife, Janet Ruthven, vii. 389.
Cauz, Matilda de, ii. 215.
Cavendish, Elizabeth, wife of 6th earl of Lennox, v. 354; ix. 126.
— Fanny, wife of F. J. Howard, ii. 499.
— Frances, wife of 2nd earl of Breadalbane, ii. 207.
— Henrietta, wife of Lionel, lord Huntingtower, iii. 407.
— Jane, wife of Charles Cheyne of Chelsea, vi. 466.
— Philip, illeg. son of 2nd duke of Devonshire, iii. 407 *n.*
— Victor Christian William, P.C., M.P., vi. 400.
— — his wife, Evelyn Emily Mary Fitzmaurice, vi. 400.
— Sir William, v. 354.
Cavendish-Bentinck, Charles William Frederick, rev., viii. 316.
— Nina Cecilia, wife of 14th earl of Strathmore and Kinghorne, viii. 316.
Cavendish-Harley, Margaret, wife of 2nd duke of Portland, vi. 189 *n.*
CAVERTON, KER, LORD KER OF, vii. 343.
Cawdor, Donald, thane of, 1419, vi. 302.
— William, thane of, iv. 18; v. 204; vii. 434.
— — his 2nd wife, Janet Keith, v. 204.
— James, murderer of Regent Lennox, ix. 126.
— *see also* Calder.
Cazenove, Reginald F., 6th Dragoon Guards, iii. 85.
— — his wife, Lilian Janet Macdonald, iii. 85.
Cecil, Diana, wife of (1) Henry, 18th earl of Oxford, and (2) Thomas, 1st earl of Elgin, iii. 478.
— Katharine, wife of 4th earl of Kinnoull, v. 228.
— Lucy, wife of William, 4th marquess of Winchester, i. 350.
— Mary Arabella Arthur, wife of 10th earl of Galloway, iv. 172.
— Thomas, 2nd son of 1st marquess of Exeter, v. 367.
— — his wife, Sophia Georgiana Lennox, v. 367.
— William, secretary to Queen Elizabeth, i. 559, 561.
Cecilia, princess, dau. of Edward IV. of England, i. 333; iii. 22; iv. 449.
— of Kelour, dau. of Malise, earl of Strathearn, viii. 247.
— of Maccustoun, wife of Robert de Berkeley, vi. 469.
— 'daughter of John'; wife of Patrick, 7th earl of Dunbar, iii. 259, 262.
— wife of Sir Walter of Ruthven, iv. 255.
— wife of Sir R. Crauford of Loudoun, v. 490.
CESSFORD, KER, LORD KER OF, vii. 343.
CESSFORD, KER, MARQUESS OF, vii. 350-360.
Cessford, John, first marquess of, vii. 350.
Cessnock, Sir Alexander Hume, lord of Session, styled lord, vi. 18.
— — his wife, Margaret Campbell, vi. 19.
— Sir George Campbell, lord of Session, styled lord, vi. 19.
Chalmer of Newton and Strathavin, John, viii. 430.
— — his wife, Mariota Hay, viii. 430.
— Christian, wife of Humphrey Rollo, vii. 194.
— Elena, wife of Wm. Wallace of Craigo, ii. 510 *n.*
— John, Troquhan, ii. 70.
— — his wife, Mariota Bellenden, ii. 70.
— Margaret, wife of (1) Sir Jas. Ogilvy of Deskford and Findlater, and (2) Alex. Irvine of Drum, iv. 18; ix. 89.
— Thomas, assassin of King James I., v. 501.
Chalmers of Corraith, James, vi. 514.
— — his wife, Janet Stewart, vi. 514.
— of Cults, Sir George, viii. 360.
— of Gadgirth, James, vii. 64.
— — his wife, Margaret Stewart, vii. 64.
— — James, v. 496.
— — Sir John, vii. 63; viii. 115.
— — John, iii. 447.
— — his wife, Margaret Montgomerie, iii. 447.

Chalmers of Corraith, *, iv. 349.
—— —— his wife, Elizabeth Hamilton, iv. 349.
—— of Methlic, i. 83, 84.
—— of Raderny, John, D.D., minister of Kilconquhar, vi. 443.
—— of Sauchrie, James, v. 152.
—— —— his wife, * Boyd, v. 152.
—— of Strichen, Andrew, vii. 435.
—— —— his wife, Christina Fraser, vii. 435.
—— —— William, v. 543.
—— —— his wife, Isobel or Elizabeth Forbes, v. 543.
—— Alexander, minister of Cairnie, iv. 555.
—— —— his wife, Anne Gordon, iv. 555.
—— Annie Harriet Curzon, wife of Andrew Rollo of Ashgrove, vii. 207.
—— George, vii. 535.
—— —— his wife, Isobel Sempill, vii. 535.
—— Isobel, dau. of James C., Edinburgh, iii. 319.
—— Isobel, wife of Geo. Crichton of Beildiston and Crichie, ix. 93.
—— James, merchant-burgess of Edinburgh, iii. 319.
—— John, captain, i. 575.
—— John, lieut.-col., vii. 207.
—— Margaret, wife of 6th lord Balmerino, i. 575.
—— Marion, wife of Wm. Dalrymple of Stair, viii. 115, 116.
—— Thomas, 1455, iii. 277 *n*.
—— William, vicar of Kirkurd, iv. 85.
Chambelle, Sir Nicholas de, *alias* Sir Neil Campbell, i. 322.
Chamberlayne of Maugersbury, Edmund, i. 58.
—— Cassandra Agnes, wife of Sir John Hamilton, i. 58.
Chambord, Henry v., count of, iii. 6.
Champneys, Francis Henry, M.D., viii. 129.
—— —— his wife, Virginia Julian Dalrymple, viii. 129.
Chancey of Sutton Coldfield, William, i. 405.
—— —— his wife, Mary Aston, i. 405.
Chandler, Daniel, ii. 581.
—— *, ii. 581.
—— —— his wife, Abigail *, ii. 581.
Chandos, Henry (Brydges), 2nd duke of, iii. 482; v. 199.
—— —— his wife, Mary Bruce, iii. 482.
—— James, 1st duke of, iii. 406.
—— James, 3rd duke of, iii. 483; v. 199.
Chandos-Pole of Radborne Hall, Edward Sacheverell, i. 70.
—— Carolina, wife of lord C. J. Hamilton, i. 70.
Chantry, Maria, wife of Archibald Montgomerie, iii. 449.
Chaplin, Henry, M.P., viii. 364.
—— —— his wife, Florence Sutherland-Leveson-Gower, iii. 85; viii. 364.

* Name unknown.

Chapman of Tarrant Gunville, Anthony, iii. 614; ix. 88.
—— —— his wife, Charlotte Cary, iii. 614.
—— Frederick, ii. 56.
—— —— his wife, Mary Nisbet Hamilton, ii. 56.
—— Henry, Thirsk, iii. 601.
—— —— his wife, Dorothy Fairfax, iii. 601.
—— Rhoda, wife of (1) Thomas Hussey, and (2) Ferdinando, 2nd lord Fairfax, iii. 598.
—— Symon, Lanark, viii. 368.
—— Thomas, London, iii. 598.
Charles I., King of Scots, i. 28; iii. 370; vii. 99; viii. 594; ix. 99.
—— —— his wife, Henrietta Maria of Bourbon, i. 28.
Charles II., King of Scots, i. 29; viii. 594.
—— —— his wife, Katharine of Braganza, i. 30.
Charles Louis zu Simmern, elector palatine of the Rhine, i. 27; v. 481.
Charlotte of Mecklenburgh-Strelitz, wife of King George III., vii. 352.
—— Princess, dau. of King George IV., iii. 491.
Charlwood of Windlesham, Benjamin, vii. 357.
—— Harriet, wife of (1) James, 5th duke of Roxburghe, and (2) lt.-col. W. F. O'Reilly, vii. 357.
CHARTERIS, EARL OF WEMYSS, viii. 513-518.
Charteris of Amisfield, Francis, colonel, viii. 509, 513.
—— —— Janet, wife of James, 4th earl of Wemyss, viii. 509.
—— —— Sir John, vii. 125, 130.
—— —— his 1st wife, Janet Douglas, vii. 125; ix. 150.
—— —— his 2nd wife, Agnes Maxwell, iv. 412; vi. 479.
—— —— Sir John, viii. 548.
—— —— his wife, Margaret Fleming, viii. 548.
—— —— Sir John, iii. 235.
—— —— his wife, Katharine Crichton, iii. 235.
—— of Cagnore, Thomas, vii. 368.
—— of Cahir Lodge, Richard, lieut.-colonel, viii. 516.
—— —— his wife, Margaret Butler, viii. 516.
—— of Charteris, Alan de, ii. 373.
—— —— his wife, Eva de Carlyle, ii. 373.
—— of Cuthelgurdie, John, iv. 278.
—— —— his wife, Janet Gray, iv. 278.
—— —— John, vi. 369.
—— —— Patrick, viii. 279.
—— of Grubet, Thomas, vii. 368.
—— of Hornby and Cockran, Francis, colonel, viii. 513.
—— of Kelwood, James, v. 270.
—— —— his wife, Florence M'Ghie, v. 270.
—— of Kilmichael, Sir John, viii. 548.

Charteris of Kinfauns, John, iii. 27.
—— his wife, Euphemia Lindsay, iii. 27.
—— John, iii. 32.
—— his wife, Janet Chisholm, iii. 32.
—— Sir Henry, *né* Lindsay, 2nd son of 10th earl of Crawford, iii. 29, 32.
—— his 1st wife, Helen Chisholm, iii. 32.
—— his 2nd wife, Margaret Shaw, iii. 33.
—— Thomas, ix. 10.
—— his wife, Janet Stewart, ix. 10.
—— Sir William, v. 186 *n*.
—— his wife, Christina Erskine, v. 186, 605; vi. 221.
— of Neidpath, Francis Wemyss, viii. 515.
— of Newmills, Francis, colonel, viii. 509.
— of Prestonpatrick and Holm, Francis, colonel, viii. 513.
— Alan Dudley, viii. 517.
— Alfred Walter, lieut. 71st Foot, viii. 517.
— Anne, dau. of 5th earl of Wemyss, viii. 514.
— Anne, wife of 4th earl of Warwick, viii. 516.
— Augusta, wife of 2nd lord Rossmore, viii. 514.
— Caroline, dau. of 6th earl of Wemyss, viii. 516.
— Charlotte, wife of Andrew Fletcher of Saltoun, viii. 515.
— Cynthia Mary Evelyn, wife of Herbert Asquith, viii. 517.
— Eleanor, wife of W. F. Campbell of Shawfield, viii. 515.
— Evan Edward, viii. 517.
— Evelyn, wife of 4th viscount de Vesci, viii. 517.
— Frances, wife of Wm. Trail, D.D., viii. 513.
— Francis, eldest son of 8th earl of Wemyss, viii. 517.
— Frederick William, captain R.N., viii. 516.
—— his wife, Louisa Keppel, viii. 516.
— Guy Laurence, viii. 517.
— Harriet, wife of Sir G. Grant Suttie, viii. 516.
— Henrietta, dau. of 5th earl of Wemyss, viii. 513.
— Henrietta Charlotte Elizabeth, wife of 6th earl of Stamford, viii. 514.
— Hilda, wife of W. St. John P. Brodrick, viii. 518.
— Hugo Francis, viii. 517.
— Irene Corona, viii. 517.
— Ivo Alan, viii. 517.
— Jane, wife of lt.-col. Philip Dundas, viii. 516.
— Janet, wife of 4th lord Carlyle, ii. 389, 391.
Charteris, Janet, dau. of 5th earl of Wemyss, viii. 513.
— Jean, wife of James Maclellan of Balmangan, v. 271.
— Katharine, wife of brigade-major E. R. Stewart, iv. 169; viii. 514.
— Katharine, dau. of 5th earl of Wemyss, viii. 513.
— Katharine, wife of George Harry, lord Grey of Groby, viii. 515.
— Lilian Harriet, wife of (1) Sir H. C. Pelly, and (2) Sir H. F. R. Yorke, iii. 49; viii. 518.
— Louisa, wife of Wm. Wells, viii. 517.
— Louisa Antoinetta, wife of Wm. Forbes of Callendar, viii. 515.
— Margaret, wife of Nicol Rutherfurd of Grubet, vii. 368.
— Margaret, wife of col. John Wildman, viii. 515.
— Marjorie, wife of Thomas de Bruys of Clackmannan, iii. 467.
— Mary, viii. 517.
— Susan, wife of Sir H. Clinton, viii. 514.
— Susan, dau. of 6th earl of Wemyss, viii. 515.
— Walter, 2nd son of 6th earl of Wemyss, viii. 515.
— Walter, captain 92nd Highlanders, viii. 516.
Charters, Katharine, wife of Alex. Hay of Spott, viii. 456.
— Laurence, advocate, viii. 456.
— Samuel, iii. 615.
—— his wife, Charlotte Maria Cary, iii. 615.
Chastel, Louis de, sieur de la Barthe, viii. 512.
—— his wife, Walpole Wemyss, viii. 512.
Chatelherault, Hamilton, duke of, iv. 367-372.
Chatelherault, James, first duke of, iv. 367, 540; viii. 439.
— James, 6th earl of Abercorn, claimant to the dukedom of, i. 59.
— James, 2nd marquess of Abercorn; duke of, i. 69.
— William Alexander Louis Stephen, duke of, iv. 396.
CHATHAM, CAMPBELL, BARON OF, i. 371.
Chatham, John, baron of, i. 371.
Chatto of Chatto, Thomas, vii. 369.
— of Mainhouse, Alexander, vii. 590.
— Isabella Mary, wife of 14th lord Sinclair, vii. 590.
Cheam, John de, bishop of Glasgow, iii. 137.
Cheap(e of Kilquhis, James, v. 403.
— of Rossie, James, v. 403; viii. 202.
— of Sauchie, George, viii. 313.

Cheap(e of Strathtyrum, Alexander, i. 316.
—— —— his wife, Anne Charlotte Arbuthnott, i. 316.
—— —— James, i. 131.
—— —— his wife, Griselda Johanna Helen Ogilvy, i. 131.
—— Alison, wife of Wm. Murray of Inchmurray, viii. 202.
—— James, commr. R.N., i. 316.
—— —— his wife, Jean Ogilvy, i. 316.
—— Marion, wife of (1) Sir Alex. Campbell of Ardkinglas, and (2) Thomas, 11th earl of Strathmore and Kinghorne, viii. 313.
—— Rebecca, wife of Sir Andrew Murray of Inchmurray, viii. 202.
Chen, Henry le, bishop of Aberdeen, ii. 257; viii. 251.
Chénencourt, Thérèse Josephine, wife of James Eyre, vi. 456.
Cherrières, Eudoxie Saulnier de, wife of Louis Edward Geneviève Drummond, vi. 69.
Cherry, James Frederick, vii. 310.
—— —— his wife, Emily Louisa Leslie, vii. 310.
Chesham, Charles Compton (Cavendish), 1st lord, iv. 560.
—— —— his wife, Catherine Susan Gordon, iv. 560.
—— of Chesham Bois, Sir John, vi. 462.
—— Eleanor, wife of (1) Sir John Penyston, and (2) Sir Thos. Cheyne, vi. 462.
Chester, Hugh Kevilioc, earl of, i. 4.
—— Isabel, wife of Robert de Brus of Annandale; countess of, ii. 430.
—— John le Scot, earl of, i. 4; ii. 430.
—— Ranulf, the younger, earl of, vi. 286.
—— of Chicheley, Charles, viii. 225.
—— Barbara, wife of John Drummond, viii. 225.
Chesterfield, Philip (Stanhope), 2nd earl of, viii. 304.
—— —— his 2nd wife, Elizabeth Butler, viii. 304.
hetwode of Woodbrooke, Edward Wilmot, v. 635.
—— —— his wife, Jane Janetta Erskine, v. 635.
Chetwynd of Grendon Hall, Sir George, 4th bart., v. 515.
—— —— his wife, Florence Cecilia Paget, v. 515.
—— of Ingestrie, Sir William, i. 405.
—— —— his 2nd wife, Katharine Aston, i. 405.
—— of Rudge, John, i. 402.
—— Ann, wife of Walter Aston, i. 402.
—— Cecil, wife of 7th marquess of Lothian, v. 485.
Chetwynd-Talbot, Constance Harriet Mahonesa, wife of 8th marquess of Lothian, v. 485.
CHEYNE, CHEYNE, LORD, vi. 466-468.
Cheyne, Charles, first lord, vi. 466.
—— —— his 1st wife, Jane Cavendish, vi. 466.
CHEYNE, LORD CHEYNE, vi. 466-468.
CHEYNE, VISCOUNT OF NEWHAVEN, vi. 461-468.
Cheyne of Chendith, Francis, vi. 465.
—— —— his 1st wife, Elizabeth Wright, vi. 465.
—— —— his 2nd wife, Anne Fleetwood, vi. 465.
—— —— John, vi. 464.
—— —— his wife, Margaret Skipwith, vi. 464.
—— —— John, vi. 465.
—— of Chesham Bois, Francis, vi. 465.
—— —— his 1st wife, Elizabeth Wright, vi. 465.
—— —— his 2nd wife, Anne Fleetwood, vi. 465.
—— —— John, vi. 462.
—— —— his wife, Perina Whitney, vi. 462.
—— —— John, vi. 462.
—— —— his wife, Elizabeth Brudenell, vi. 462.
—— —— John, vi. 462, 463.
—— —— his wife, Margaret Ingleton, vi. 463.
—— —— Sir Thomas, vi. 461.
—— —— his wife, Eleanor Chesham, vi. 462.
—— of Cogenhoe, Sir John, vi. 462.
—— —— John, vi. 463.
—— of Drayton Beauchamp, Sir Francis, vi. 464.
—— —— his wife, Mary Powle, vi. 464.
—— —— Sir John, vi. 461, 462.
—— —— his 1st wife, Joan Fitz Marmaduke, vi. 462.
—— —— his 2nd wife, Agnes Lexham, vi. 462.
—— —— John, vi. 463.
—— —— his wife, Margaret Ingleton, vi. 463.
—— —— John, vi. 463.
—— —— his 1st wife, Winifred Mordaunt, vi. 463.
—— —— his 2nd wife, Joyce Lee, vi. 464.
—— —— Robert, vi. 463.
—— —— his 1st wife, Eliz. Webbe, vi. 463.
—— —— Roger, vi. 461.
—— —— Thomas, vi. 461.
—— —— William, vi. 461.
—— —— his wife, Joan *, vi. 461.
—— of Duffus, Mary, wife of Nicholas Sutherland, iii. 191.
—— —— Reginald, iii. 190.
—— —— his wife, Mary of Duffus, iii. 190; vi. 34, 37 *n.*; vii. 160.
—— of Durie, Reginald le, viii. 245.

* Name unknown.

Cheyne of Essilmont, Patrick, i. 84; ii. 14; iii. 569, 571, 573; v. 220.
—— —— his 2nd wife, Helen Bryson, iii. 569.
—— —— Patrick, iii. 571.
—— —— his contracted wife, Isobel *or* Elizabeth Hay, iii. 571.
—— —— his wife, Magdalen Fraser, vii. 440.
—— —— Thomas, i. 84.
—— —— his wife, Elizabeth Gordon, i. 84.
—— of Inverugie, Jean, wife of N. Sutherland of Duffus, vi. 34; vii. 160.
—— —— Mariota *or* Mary, wife of (1) John Douglas of Strabrock, and (2) John Keith, vi. 34, 343, 354 *n*.
—— —— Reginald, vi. 34, 343.
—— —— his wife, Mary of Duffus, ii. 122; iii. 190; vi. 34, 37 *n*.; vii. 160.
—— —— Reginald, vi. 37 *n*.
—— —— his proposed wife, Muriella Keith, vi. 37.
—— of Ranieston and Pitfichie, Thomas, iv. 112.
—— —— his wife, Katharine Fraser, iv. 112.
—— of Straloch, viii. 568.
—— —— John, 1499, i. 84.
—— —— John, iv. 73.
—— —— his wife, Margaret Forbes, iv. 73.
—— Christian, wife of Sir Alex. Seton of Seton, viii. 568.
—— Edmond, 3rd son of John C. of Chendith, vi. 465.
—— Elizabeth, wife of (1) Patrick Hay of Megginch, and (2) George Hay of Keillour, iii. 573; v. 220.
—— Elizabeth, wife of Sir Henry Monson, vi. 467.
—— Elizabeth, wife of (1) Peter Hay of Megginch, and (2) Patrick, 6th lord Oliphant, v. 220; vi. 553.
—— Francis, Lincoln's Inn, vi. 466.
—— Henry, 4th son of John C. of Drayton Beauchamp, vi. 464.
—— Isabel, wife of (1) Patrick Hay of Megginch, and (2) George Hay of Keillour, iii. 573; v. 220.
—— Katharine, dau. of John C., vi. 464.
—— John, 2nd son of John C. of Drayton Beauchamp, vi. 463.
—— John, youngest son of Francis C. of Chendith, vi. 466.
—— Reginald le, High Chamberlain, ii. 537; vi. 289.
—— —— his 2nd wife, Eustacia Colville of Ochiltree, ii. 537.
—— Thomas, 3rd son of John C. of Drayton Beauchamp, vi. 464.
—— William, son of Francis C. of Chesham Bois, vi. 465.
—— —— his wife, Lucy Barrington, vi. 465.
—— *, wife of Sir Andrew Fraser, vii. 425.

* Name unknown.

Chichester, Henry Thomas (Pelham), 3rd earl of, i. 554.
—— Thomas (Pelham), 1st earl of, vii. 308.
—— of Raleigh, Sir Robert, K.B., iii. 478.
—— Anne, wife of 1st earl of Elgin, iii. 478.
—— Francis Algernon James, capt., iv. 172.
—— —— his wife, Emily Octavia Stewart, iv. 172.
—— Spencer Stanley, iv. 169.
—— —— his wife, Anne Harriet Stewart, iv. 169.
Chiesley of Dalry, John, v. 628.
—— —— Walter, major, v. 628.
—— John, minister of Quothquan, iv. 583.
—— —— his wife, Elizabeth Carmichael, iv. 583; ix. 114.
—— John, his 3rd son, ix. 114.
—— Walter, eldest son of the minister of Quothquan, ix. 114.
—— William, his 2nd son, ix. 114.
—— Rachel, wife of James Erskine, lord Grange, v. 628.
Child of Berthwaite Hall, Mary Charlotte, wife of Hamilton Fleming, viii. 557.
—— —— William, viii. 557.
Chilham of Chilham, Isabella de, wife of (1) David, 8th earl of Atholl, and (2) Alex. Baliol, i. 425; ix. 11, 27.
—— —— Richard de, i. 425.
—— —— his wife, Roesia of Dover, i. 425.
—— —— Richard de, ix. 11.
—— —— his wife, Matilda, countess of Angus, i. 167; ix. 11.
—— —— Richard, brother of Isabella C., ix. 11.
Chinnery-Haldane, James Brodrick, v. 342.
Chirnside, Ninian, iv. 453.
Chisholm of Aldencraw, Muriel, wife of Alex. Sutherland, iii. 193.
—— of Ard, Alexander, v. 520.
—— of Chisholm, Alexander, vii. 500.
—— —— his wife, Janet *or* Mary Mackenzie, v. 561; vii. 500.
—— —— John, iii. 193.
—— —— Walter, ix. 142.
—— —— his wife, Elizabeth Scott, ix. 142.
—— —— William, vii. 590.
—— of Comar, v. 525.
—— —— his wife, * Fraser, v. 525.
—— —— Alexander, vii. 500.
—— —— his wife, Mary Mackenzie, v. 561; vii. 500.
—— —— Alexander, vii. 505.
—— —— his wife, * Mackenzie, vii. 505.
—— of Crombie, Sir James, iii. 32.
—— of Cromlix, Sir James, i. 117; vi. 418; viii. 216.
—— —— his wife, Jean Drummond of Innerpeffray, viii. 216.

* Name unknown.

Chisholm of Cromlix, Sir James, vii. 290.
—— his wife, Anna *or* Agnes Beaton, vii. 290.
—— Edmund, vi. 412.
—— John, i. 138.
—— his wife, Jean Graham, i. 138.
—— John, iv. 247; ix. 97.
—— his wife, Margaret Cunningham, iv. 247.
— of Gask, Alexander, iv. 334.
—— Katharine, wife of Walter Haliburton, iv. 334.
— of Kiltarlity, Alexander, v. 520.
— of Paxton, Quarrelwood and Greeshope, Muriel, wife of Alex. Sutherland, iii. 193.
— of Strathglass, iv. 516.
—— Alexander, iv. 46.
— Anne, wife of (1) John Napier of Merchiston, and (2) Wm. Cunningham of Craigends, vi. 420.
— Beatrix, bigamous wife of Thos. Ogilvy of Westercraig, i. 117.
— Helen, wife of Sir Henry Charteris of Kinfauns and Caraldston, iii. 32.
— James, bishop of Dunblane, ii. 134; iii. 570.
— Janet, wife of John Charteris of Kinfauns, iii. 32.
— Janet, wife of (1) Sir Alex. Napier, (2) Sir Ninian Seton, and (3) Sir James Towers, vi. 412.
— Jean, wife of C. Campbell of Glenample, ii. 183.
— Jean, wife of Sir Jas. Stirling of Keir, vi. 226.
— Jean, wife of James Drummond of Innerpeffray, viii. 216.
— Mary Agnes, wife of 14th lord Sinclair, vii. 590.
— William, bishop of Dunblane, vi. 226.
— William, his nephew, bishop of Dunblane, vi. 227, 232.
— William, bishop of Vaison, cardinal, i. 558.
— *, wife of Thomas Gordon of Ruthven, iv. 516.
Chival, Robert, iv. 43.
Choisy, Jean de l'Hopital, comte de, i. 154.
—— his wife, Eleonora Stewart, i. 154.
Cholmley of Roxby, Sir Henry, iii. 597.
— Mary, wife of rev. Henry Fairfax, iii. 597.
Cholmondeley of Vale Royal, Thomas, viii. 225.
— Hester, wife of John Drummond, viii. 225.
Christabella, wife of (1) Sir Giles Eyre, and (2) Francis, lord Glassfoord, iv. 182; vii. 56.
Christian, first bishop of Galloway, iv. 136.
Christian of Strogeith, wife of Walter Olifard, vi. 527; viii. 241.

* Name unknown.

Christiana of Bassenthwaite and Bolton, wife of Duncan Lascelles, iii. 245.
Christian, wife of Reginald More, Great Chamberlain of Scotland, i. 454.
Christian, wife of (1) Walter de Lindsay, lord of Lamberton, and (2) Walter de Percy of Kildale, iii. 5.
Christian, 1st wife of Sir Alex. Ramsay of Dalhousie, iii. 91, 93.
Christian, wife of John de Home, iv. 443.
Christian, wife of Sir John Maxwell of Caerlaverock, vi. 473.
Christiana, dau. of Adam, son of Gilbert, vii. 420.
Christian, wife of Sir Gilbert Fraser, sheriff of Peebles, vii. 421.
Christie of Durie, Charles Maitland, i. 525.
—— his wife, Mary Butler Lindsay, i. 525.
—— James, v. 312.
—— his wife, Mary Turner Maitland, v. 312.
— Alexander, writer, Edinburgh, v. 309; vi. 589.
—— his wife, Katharine Makgill, vi. 589, 600.
— James, W.S., vii. 215.
—— his wife, Jean Primrose, vii. 215.
— James, his son, vii. 215.
— Jane, wife of 4th duke of Gordon, iv. 556.
— Janet, wife of Robert Maitland Macgill, v. 309.
Christin, father of Dungal, dempster of Lennox, ii. 504.
Christin, 7th son of Alwin, 2nd earl of Lennox, v. 330; ix. 125.
Christin, judge of Lennox, v. 330 *n.*; ix. 125.
Christina, wife of (1) Sir David de Lindsay of Luffness and Crawford, and (2) Sir Robt. de Pinkeney, iii. 7.
Christina, wife of Angus Sutherland of Torboll, iii. 194.
Christina, wife of Olaf, 5th King of Man and the Isles, vii. 233.
Christina, wife of (1) Wm. de Brus, and (2) Patrick, 5th earl of Dunbar, ii. 430; iii. 253, 259.
Christina, Queen of Denmark, iv. 355.
Christina, dau. of Malcolm, 2nd earl of Atholl, and possible wife of Thomas of Lundin, i. 418.
Christison, John, burgess of Dysart, viii. 188.
—— his wife, Helen Murray, viii. 188.
— Margaret, wife of Wm. Lindsay of Mungo's Wells, v. 393.
— William, burgess of Cupar, v. 398.
— his wife, Isobel Lindsay, v. 398.
Christopher of Dirleton and Belhaven, Robert Adam, M.P., P.C., iii. 493.
—— his wife, Mary Bruce, iii. 493.

Chrystie, James, in holy orders, vi. 180.
—— —— his wife, Mary *, vi. 180.
—— John, barber, ix. 106.
Chubbe, Jane, wife of Alexander Livingston, vi. 450.
—— Matthew, Dorchester, vi. 450.
Chudleigh, Sir John, bart., i. 404.
—— Susan, wife of rev. Dr. Haines, i. 404.
Church, John, ii. 357.
—— Maria Petronella, wife of John Sinclair, ii. 357.
CHURCHILL OF EYEMOUTH, CHURCHILL, LORD, ii. 532-533.
Churchill of Eyemouth, John, lord, ii. 532.
—— —— his wife, Sarah Jennings, ii. 532.
—— —— John, styled lord, ii. 533.
—— of Sandridge, John (Churchill), lord, ii. 532.
CHURCHILL, LORD CHURCHILL OF EYEMOUTH, ii. 533.
Churchill, Anne, wife of 4th earl of Sutherland, ii. 533.
—— Anne Emily, wife of 7th duke of Roxburghe, vii. 358.
—— Arabella, mistress of King James VII., i. 34.
—— Elizabeth, wife of 1st duke of Bridgewater, ii. 533.
—— Henrietta, *suo jure* duchess of Marlborough, wife of 2nd earl of Godolphin, ii. 533.
—— Mary, wife of 2nd duke of Montagu, ii. 533.
—— Sir Winston, ii. 532.
—— —— his wife, Elizabeth Drake, ii. 532.
Cissoris of Longforgan, Roger, iv. 271.
Clanbrassil, Henry (Hamilton), 2nd earl of, ii. 32.
—— —— his wife, Alice Moore, ii. 32.
Clanricarde, William (Bourke), 7th earl of, i. 34.
Clanwilliam, Richard (Meade), 3rd earl of, iv. 561.
—— Richard James (Meade), 4th earl of, ii. 567; iv. 483.
Claphame, Margaret, in Bordland of Longforgan, iv. 271.
CLAIRMONT AND FETTERCAIRN, MIDDLETON, LORD OF, vi. 184.
Clairmont and Fettercairn, John, 1st lord, vi. 183.
—— John, elder son of 2nd earl of Middleton; styled lord, vi. 188.
Clare, Alicia de, wife of Sir Bernard de Brus, ii. 431.
—— Isobel de, wife of Robert de Brus, the Competitor, ii. 431; ix. 55.
—— Johanna de, wife of (1) Duncan, 9th earl of Fife, and (2) Sir Gervase Avenel, iv. 11.
Clarence, George (Plantagenet), brother of King Edward IV. of England; duke of, i. 20.

* Name unknown.

Clarendon, Edward (Hyde), 1st earl of, i. 33, 362.
—— Edward (Hyde), 3rd earl of, v. 359.
—— —— his wife, Katharine O'Brien, v. 359.
—— Henry (Hyde), 4th earl of, vii. 144.
—— George William Frederick (Villiers), 4th earl of, iv. 97.
—— —— his wife, Katharine Grimston, iv. 97.
Claricia, dau. of King David I., i. 4.
Clark of Clochindarg, Andrew, v. 206.
—— —— his wife, Margaret Kinnaird, v. 206.
—— —— Andrew, v. 207.
—— of Rupertswood, Sir William T., bart., iii. 50.
—— Henry, ix. 147.
—— —— his wife, Christian Makgill, ix. 147.
—— Jabez, capt. H.E.I.C.S., iii. 81.
—— John, major-general, K.H., viii. 129.
—— —— his wife, Charlotte Sophia Dalrymple, viii. 129.
—— May Janet, wife of capt. R. H. Lindsay, iii. 50.
—— *, captain, husband of Mary Mackenzie, dau. of 3rd earl of Cromartie, iii. 81.
Clarke, Charles John, iii. 413.
—— —— his wife, Gertrude Florinda Gardiner, iii. 413.
—— Francis, Massachusetts, iii. 600.
—— May, wife of Arch. Hamilton, ii. 56.
Claughton, Maria, wife of (1) col. Anson, and (2) 8th duke of Argyll, i. 392.
—— Thomas Legh, bishop of St. Albans, i. 392.
—— —— his wife, Julia Susanna Ward, i. 392.
CLAVERHOUSE, GRAHAM, LORD GRAHAM OF, iii. 324-333.
Claverhouse, David, third lord Graham of, iii. 331.
—— James, second lord Graham of, iii. 331.
—— John, first lord Graham of, iii. 324.
—— —— his wife, Jean Cochrane, iii. 330, 352.
Clavering, Alice, wife of Herbert, viscount Windsor, ii. 306.
—— Charles John, iii. 547.
—— Diana Maria, wife of J. D. Fullerton-Elphinstone, iii. 547.
—— Henry, colonel, i. 387.
—— —— his wife, Augusta Campbell, i. 387.
—— Sir James John, K.B., i. 387; vi. 436.
—— —— his wife, Diana West, i. 387.
—— Sir John, bart., ii. 306.
—— Maria Margaret, wife of 8th lord Napier of Merchiston, vi. 436.
Clayhills of Baldovie, Robert, iii. 320; vi. 590.
—— —— his wife, Katharine Makgill, vi. 590.
—— of Craigie, Robert, iii. 320.

* Name unknown.

Clayhills, Andrew, minister of Monifieth, vii. 216.
—— his wife, Katharine Primrose, vii. 216.
— Jean, wife of Adam Primrose, vii. 215.
Clayton of Marsden Park, Sir William Robert, 5th bart., vii. 153.
— Caroline Margaret, wife of 7th Marquess of Queensberry, vii. 153.
Cleland of Cleland, Alexander, ii. 27.
—— his wife, Mary Hamilton, ii. 27.
—— James, viii. 11.
—— his wife, Janet Somerville, viii. 11.
—— ii. 41.
—— ii. 49.
—— his wife, Margaret Hamilton, ii. 49.
—— William, viii. 11.
—— William, ii. 81.
—— his wife, Marion Stewart, ii. 81.
— of Faskin, James, iii. 342.
—— Margaret, wife of Gavin Cochrane of Craigmure, iii. 342.
—— William, iii. 342.
— of Gartness, George, ii. 48.
—— his wife, Margaret Hamilton, ii. 48.
— of Stonepath, James, i. 549.
— John, Edinburgh, i. 549.
—— his wife, Rachel Bruce, i. 549.
— Margaret, wife of Alex. Bruce, i. 549.
— Margaret, wife of John Hamilton of Udston, ii. 41.
Clement, bishop of Dunblane, viii. 243.
Clements, Dorothy, iii. 411.
Clepburn, *, alleged wife of 3rd lord Lindores, v. 385.
Clephane of Carslogie, Douglas Maclean, maj.-gen., ii. 106.
—— George, i. 459; iv. 273.
—— his wife, Margaret Gray, iv. 273.
—— George, i. 290, 293; vii. 410.
—— George, vi. 589.
—— his wife, Katharine Orme, vi. 589.
—— Thomas, the younger, viii. 489.
—— his wife, Jonet Wemyss, viii. 489.
— of Hillcairnie, James, i. 293; vi. 546.
—— his 1st wife, Jean Arbuthnott, i. 293.
—— his 2nd wife, Margaret Oliphant, vi. 546.
— of Quhelplaw, George, vii. 410.
— Anna, wife of James Makgill of Rankeillor, vi. 589.
— Helen, wife of (1) Robt. Arbuthnott of that Ilk, and (2) Alex. Campbell, bishop of Brechin, i. 290, 293; ix. 16.
— R., capt. R.N., ii. 106.
—— his wife, Anne Borthwick, ii. 106.
Clerk of Balbirnie, Sir Alexander, iii. 476.
— of Lonyanys, John, viii. 6.
—— his wife, Margaret Hay, viii. 6.

* Name unknown.

Clerk of Penicuik, Sir George, 7th bart, iii. 547.
—— John, iv. 289; vii. 506.
—— his wife, Mary Gray, iv. 289.
—— Sir John, 2nd bart., baron of the Court of Exchequer, iv. 163, 591.
—— his wife, Margaret Stewart, iv. 163.
— of Pittencrieff, Sir Alexander, provost of Edinburgh, iii. 318; vii. 213.
—— his wife, Marion Primrose, iii. 317; vii. 213.
—— James, iii. 509.
—— his wife, Elizabeth Erskine, iii. 509.
— Alexander, minister of Inverness, ii. 172 *n.*
—— his wife, * Elliot, ii. 172 *n.*
— Elizabeth Harriet, wife of captain E. C. Buller-Fullerton Elphinstone, iii. 547.
— Guy le, Jedworth, iv. 146.
— Helen, wife of Simon Mackenzie, vii. 506.
— Janet, wife of James Carmichael of Hailes, iv. 591.
— Magdalen, wife of (1) Edward, 1st lord Bruce of Kinloss, and (2) Sir Jas. Fullerton, iii. 476.
Clerk-Maxwell of Middlebie, James, professor, iv. 78 *n.*
Clerkson, Robert, Master of the Hospital of St. Leonard, iii. 275.
Clermont, *see* Clairmont.
Cleveland, Barbara (Villiers), duchess of, i. 31; iv. 391.
— Charles (Villiers), 1st duke of, i. 31.
— Henry George (Powlett), 4th duke of, vii. 227.
—— his wife, Katharine L. W. Stanhope, vii. 227.
Cliffe of Belle Vue, Anthony John, iv. 173.
— Amy Mary Pauline, wife of 11th earl of Galloway, iv. 173.
— Edward, v. 417.
—— his wife, Elizabeth Lindsay, v. 417.
Clifford, Henry (de Clifford), 10th baron, iii. 293.
— Thomas (de Clifford), 6th baron, iii. 164.
— Margaret (Tufton), wife of Thomas, earl of Leicester; baroness, i. 378.
— of Chudleigh, Charles (Clifford), 6th baron, iv. 420.
—— Hugh (Clifford), 2nd baron, iii. 299; vi. 454.
—— Hugh (Clifford), 3rd baron, i. 413.
— of Douglas, Sir Robert, iii. 140.
— of Tixall, Sir Thomas, i. 406 *n.*
—— Thomas, i. 409 *n.*
— Alice Mary, wife of Sir Walter H. Dalrymple, viii. 129.
— Anne, wife of (1) Richard, 7th earl of Dorset, and (2) Philip, 4th earl of Pembroke, v. 71.

* Name unknown.

Clifford, Anne, wife of (1) gen. John Joseph Mahony, and (2) Don Carlo Severino, vi. 454.
— Charles, 2nd son of 6th lord Clifford of Chudleigh, iv. 420.
— Eleanor, wife of (1) Sir Ninian Markenfield, and (2) Sir John Constable, iii. 293.
— Elizabeth, wife of (1) William, 4th viscount Dunbar, and (2) Charles Gregory Fairfax, iii. 299.
— Frances, wife of Wm. Middleton, vi. 455.
— Sir Henry, V.C., K.C.M.G., C.B., viii. 129.
— Margaret, wife of (1) Sir Ninian Markenfield, and (2) Sir John Constable, iii. 293.
— Thomas, eldest son of 2nd lord Clifford of Chudleigh, vi. 454.
— — his wife, Charlotte Maria, countess of Newburgh, vi. 454.
Clifford - Constable of Tixall, Sir Thomas Hugh, 1st bart., i. 414 *n.*
CLIFTON OF LEIGHTON - BROMSWOLD, STEWART, LORD, v. 358-362.
Clifton of Leighton-Bromswold, Esmé, first lord, v. 358.
— — his wife, Catherine Clifton, v. 358.
— — Katharine, wife of (1) Henry (O'Brien), lord Ibrican, and (2) Sir J. Williamson; baroness, v. 359.
— — Gervase (Clifton), 1st baron, i. 49; v. 358.
— — his wife, Katharine Darcy of Leighton, i. 49.
— — Theodosia (Hyde), wife of John Bligh; baroness, v. 359.
— of Donington Park, Charles Frederick, v. 515.
— — his wife, Edith Maud, countess of Loudoun, v. 515.
— of Lytham, Thomas, v. 514, 515.
— — Thomas Henry, v, 215.
— of Warton Hall, Augustus Wykeham, v. 514.
— — his wife, Bertha Lelgarde (Hastings), baroness Grey de Ruthyn, v. 514.
— Eleanor, wife of Ralph Constable, iii. 291.
— Ezekias, iii. 291.
— Frances Victoria, wife of K. F. Kinnaird, v. 215.
— Katharine, wife of (1) Esmé, 3rd duke of Lennox, and (2) James, 2nd earl of Abercorn, i. 49; v. 358.
Clifton-Hastings-Campbell, Edith Winifred Lelgarde, v. 516.
— — Gilbert Theophilus Clifton, v. 516.
— — his wife, Maud Kemble Hamilton, v. 516.
— — Irene Mary Egidia, v. 516.
— — Margaret Selina Flora Maud, v. 516.
Clinton, Charles Randolph (Trefusis), 19th baron, ii. 247; vi. 386.
— — his wife, Elizabeth Georgiana Kerr, v. 484.
— Frederick, lt.-col., ii. 243.
— — his wife, Mary Margaret Montagu, ii. 243.
— Sir Henry, lieut.-general, G.C.B., viii. 514.
— — his wife, Susan Charteris, viii. 514.
— Sir John, vii. 30, 31 *n.*
— Margaret, wife of (1) 2nd lord Colville of Culross, (2) John Arthur, and (3) N. Hooper, ii. 559.
Clive, Robert (Clive), 1st lord, vii. 563.
— of Styche, Richard, vii. 563.
— — his wife, Rebecca Gaskell, vii. 563.
— Anne, wife of col. G. Sempill, vii. 563.
Cloncurry, Valentine Browne (Lawless), 2nd lord, v. 367.
Close, F. B., iv. 561.
— — his wife, M. Humble, iv. 561.
Clugny, Amelia Constance Gertrude Etiennette de, wife of (1) * Godet, and (2) A. J. Cochrane-Johnstone, iii. 360.
— baron de, governor of Guadaloupe, iii. 360.
Clunes of Neilston, Hugh, iii. 202.
— — John, iii. 202.
— — his wife, Janet Sutherland, iii. 202.
— Anne, wife of Duncan Sutherland, iii. 202.
— Magdalene, wife of Hugh Sutherland, iii. 202, 207.
Clutterbuck of Warkworth, John, viii. 310.
— — his wife, Mary Anne Lyon, viii. 310.
— Thomas, lord of the Admiralty, treasurer of the Navy, iii. 407.
— — his wife, Henrietta Tollemache, iii. 407.
Clutton, William, i. 92.
— — his wife, Elizabeth *, i. 92.
CLYDESDALE, DOUGLAS, MARQUESS OF, iv. 381-382.
Clydesdale, William, marquess of, iv. 381.
CLYDESDALE, HAMILTON, MARQUESS OF, iv. 377-397.
Clydesdale, James, first marquess, iv. 377.
— James, eldest son of 5th duke of Hamilton; styled marquess of, iii. 356; iv. 392.
Cobbett, Sir Ralph, governor of Dundee, vi. 256.
Cobbold of Holy Wells, John Dupuis, iii. 395.
— — his wife, Evelyn Murray, iii. 395.
COCHRANE OF DUNDONALD, COCHRANE, LORD, iii. 344-368.
Cochrane of Dundonald, John, styled lord, iii. 351, 352.

* Name unknown.

Cochrane, Thomas, eldest son of 9th earl of Dundonald; captain R.N., styled lord, iii. 362; ix. 77.
— Thomas Hesketh Douglas Blair, son of 12th earl of Dundonald; styled lord, iii. 367.
— William, first lord, ii. 297; iii. 344.
— — his wife, Eupheme Scott, ii. 346.
— William, elder son of 1st earl of Dundonald; styled lord, iii. 346, 350.
— — his wife, Katharine Kennedy, ii. 482; iii. 350.
COCHRANE OF PAISLEY AND OCHILTREE, COCHRANE, LORD, iii. 346-368.
Cochrane of Paisley and Ochiltree, William, first lord, iii. 346.
— master of, John, eldest son of William, lord Cochrane, iii. 351.
COCHRANE, LORD COCHRANE OF DUNDONALD, iii. 344-368.
COCHRANE, LORD COCHRANE OF PAISLEY AND OCHILTREE, iii. 346-368.
COCHRANE, EARL OF DUNDONALD, iii. 334-368.
Cochrane of Ascog, Charles, iii. 335 *n.*
— — David, iii. 335 *n.*
— — Edward, iii. 335 *n.*
— — John, iii. 335 *n.*
— — Ninian, iii. 335 *n.*
— of Ashkirk, Charles Home, captain R.N., iii. 340 *n.*
— of Auchincreugh, Alexander, iii. 341.
— — his wife, Elizabeth Cochrane, iii. 339.
— — Alexander, colonel, iii. 341.
— — his wife, Agnes Richiesson, iii. 341.
— — James, iii. 341.
— — his 1st wife, Marion Peebles, iii. 341.
— — his 2nd wife, Ursula Hamilton, iii. 342.
— of Barbachlaw, Alexander, 4th laird, 2nd son of George C. of Barbachlaw, iii. 340 *n.*
— — Alexander, 8th laird, grandson of James C. of Barbachlaw, iii. 340 *n.*
— — Alexander, 9th laird, commissioner of supply, iii. 340 *n.*
— — his 1st wife, Helen Bruce, iii. 340 *n.*
— — his 2nd wife, Margaret Maule, iii. 340 *n.*; vii. 21.
— — Alexander, 10th laird, commissioner of supply, iii. 340 *n.*
— — Alexander, 11th laird, iii. 340 *n.*
— — George, 2nd laird, iii. 340.
— — Henry, 12th laird, iii. 340 *n.*
— — James, 5th laird, 3rd son of George C. of Barbachlaw, iii. 340 *n.*
— — James, 6th laird, legtd. son of Jas. C. of Barbachlaw, iii. 340 *n.*
— — James, 7th laird, commissioner to Parliament for Linlithgow, iii. 340 *n.*
— — his wife, Margaret Hamilton, iii. 340 *n.*
Cochrane of Barbachlaw, John, 1st laird, iii. 340 *n.*
— — Michael, 3rd laird, iii. 340 *n.*
— of Bollinshaw *or* Bonshaw, Alexander, 4th son of William, lord Cochrane, ii. 491; iii. 352.
— — Alexander, his son, iii. 352.
— of Cabbage Hall, Archibald, iii. 340 *n.*
— — John, iii. 340 *n.*
— — Thomas, bailie in Musselburgh, iii. 340 *n.*
— of Cochrane, Alexander, 3rd son of Alexander Blair of Blair, iii. 339.
— — his wife, Elizabeth Cochrane, iii. 339.
— — Allan, son of Robert of C., iii. 336; ix. 74 *ter.*
— — Cosmo de, iii. 334.
— — Elizabeth, wife of A. Blair, iii. 339.
— — Goscelin *or* Glosmus de, iii. 334.
— — James, iii. 336.
— — John de, 1346, iii. 334.
— — John de, 1370, iii. 335 *n.*
— — John, iii. 336.
— — John, ix. 75.
— — his wife, Elizabeth Semple, ix. 75.
— — John, ix. 75.
— — his wife, Marion Stewart, ix. 75.
— — John, ix. 76.
— — his 1st wife, Mary Lindsay, ix. 76.
— — his 2nd wife, Elizabeth Semple, ix. 76.
— — Sir John, British Envoy to Denmark and Holland, iii. 341, 343.
— — his wife, Grace Butler, iii. 344.
— — Robert, 1368, v. 203.
— — Robert, son of William C. of Cochrane, iii. 335.
— — Robert, father of Allan C., ix. 74.
— — Robert, 2nd son of Allan C., iii. 336, 337; ix. 75.
— — Waldeve de, iii. 334.
— — William de, 1296, iii. 335.
— — William, son of Goslin of C., iii. 335.
— — his wife, Mary, ii. 397; iii. 335.
— — William, son of John C., iii. 338, 340 *n. bis.*
— — his wife, Elizabeth Montgomerie, iii. 339.
— — Sir William, 2nd son of Alexander and Elizabeth C. of Cochrane, iii. 341, 344.
— — his wife, Euphame Scott, iii. 346.
— of Easter Cochrane, John, iii. 336 *n.*, 338; ix. 75.
— — Michael, iii. 336 *n.*
— — his wife, Eupheme Erskine, iii. 336 *n.*
— — Peter, iii. 336 *n.*; ix. 75.
— — his wife, Isobel Spreull, ix. 75.
— of Corsefoord, John, iii. 337.
— — his wife, Margaret Morton, iii. 338.

Cochrane of Corsefoord, John, ix. 75.
—— his wife, Elizabeth Semple, ix. 75.
—— Robert, iii. 337.
— of Cowdoun, Alexander, iii. 341.
—— Sir William, iii. 341, 344; v. 172.
— of Craigmure, Gavin, iii. 342.
—— his wife, Margaret Cleland, iii. 342.
— of Craigton, John, ix. 76.
—— his wife, Elizabeth Semple, iii. 338; ix. 76.
— of Culross, Charles, iii. 348.
—— James, lieut.-colonel, iii. 349.
—— his wife, Margaret Hawkison, iii. 349.
—— Thomas, major, M.P., iii. 349, 358.
—— his 1st wife, Elizabeth Ker, iii. 359.
—— his 2nd wife, Jean Stuart, iii. 359.
— of Ferguslie, Hugh, colonel, iii. 342.
—— his wife, Joan Savage, iii. 342.
—— John, iii. 351.
—— his wife, Grizel Cochrane, iii. 351.
—— William, iii. 358.
— of Grange, James, judge-advocate, iii. 350.
—— his wife, Cecilia Oliphant, iii. 350.
— of Kilmaronock, Thomas, iii. 356 *ter*.
—— William, joint-keeper of the Signet, iii. 351, 356; vi. 259; ix. 77.
—— his wife, Grizell Graham, vi. 259.
— of Langnewton, Robert, iii. 335.
—— William, iii. 335.
—— his wife, Mary, iii. 335.
— of Lee, Alice, iii. 335 *n*.
—— Charles, iii. 335 *n*.
—— David, iii. 335 *n*.
—— Edward, iii. 335 *n*.
—— John, iii. 335 *n*.
—— Ninian, iii. 335 *n*.
— of Lincliff, John, iii. 336; ix. 74.
—— John, iii. 337; ix. 74.
—— his wife, Margaret Morton, iii. 338; ix. 74.
— of Linkfield, Charles Home, captain, R.N., iii. 340.
— of Lonbank and Quarrelton, Michael, iii. 336 *n*.
—— his wife, Euphame Erskine, iii. 336 *n*.
—— Peter, iii. 336 *n*.
— of Ochiltree, Charles, iii. 348.
—— James, lieut.-col., iii. 349.
—— his wife, M. Hawkison, iii. 349.
—— Sir John, 2nd son of 1st earl of Dundonald, iii. 339, 346, 358.
—— his wife, Margaret Strickland, iii. 348.
—— Thomas, major, M.P., iii. 349, 358.
—— his 1st wife, Elizabeth Ker, iii. 359.
—— his 2nd wife, Jean Stuart, iii. 359.
—— William, commissioner of supply, iii. 348.
—— his wife, Mary Bruce, iii. 348, 487.
—— William, the younger, iii. 348.
Cochrane of Paisley, Sir William, iii. 345.
— of Pitfour, David, iii. 337 *n*.; ix. 75.
—— Francis iii. 337 *n*.; ix. 75.
—— John, iii. 337.
—— his wife, Margaret Morton, iii. 338.
—— John, iii. 337 *n*.
—— Peter, iii. 337 *n*.; ix. 75.
—— Robert *or* Roger, ix. 75.
— of Polkellie, Thomas, 3rd son of William, lord Cochrane, iii. 351.
—— his wife, Diana Cuninghame, iii. 351.
—— William, ix. 77.
— of Rochsoles, Patrick, ix. 76.
— of Waterside, John, 2nd son of Sir John C. of Ochiltree, iii. 347, 348, 350.
—— his wife, Hannah de Werth, iii. 350.
—— John, iii. 350.
—— his wife, Elizabeth Cairns, iii. 350.
— Alexander, cornet in Lord Stair's dragoons, iii. 349.
— Alexander Charles Purves, capt. 40th Pathans, ix. 76.
— Alexander Forrester Inglis, admiral, G.C.B., iii. 360, 362.
—— his wife, Maria Shaw, iii. 360.
— Alice Laura Sophia, wife of G. O. Newton, iii. 366.
— Andrew, governor of Dominica, iv. 501.
—— his wife, Georgina Johnston-Hope, iv. 501.
— Anne, wife of Sir George Preston of Valleyfield, iii. 349.
— Anne, dau. of William C. of Kilmaronock, iii. 351.
— Anne, dau. of 2nd earl of Dundonald, iii. 353.
— Anne, wife of James, 5th duke of Hamilton, iii. 355, 356 *bis*.; iv. 165, 392; ix. 77.
— Anne, dau. of 9th earl of Dundonald, iii. 362.
— Archibald, captain R.N., iii. 362.
—— his wife, Hannah Jane Mowbray, iii. 362.
— Sir Arthur Auckland Leopold Pedro, K.C.B., admiral R.N., iii. 365.
— Basil, captain, deputy-governor of the Isle of Man, iii. 349.
— Basil, R.N., 2nd son of 6th earl of Dundonald, iii. 357.
— Basil, Madras Civil Service, 7th son of 8th earl of Dundonald, iii. 359, 360.
—— his wife, Caroline Gosling, iii. 360.
— Basil, lieut.-col. 36th Foot, iii. 362.
— Sir Bryce, colonel, iii. 342.
—— his wife, Elizabeth Napier, iii. 342.
— Charles, 3rd son of John C. of Waterside, iii. 350.
— Charles, A.D.C. to Lord Cornwallis, iii. 359.
—— his wife, Katharine Pitcairn, iii. 359.

Cochrane, Charles, 4th son of Sir John C. of Ochiltree, ix. 76.
—— Charlotte, dau. of 6th earl of Dundonald, iii. 357.
—— Christian, dau. of William of Kilmaronock, iii, 351.
—— David, 3rd son of Robert C. of Cochrane, iii. 337.
—— David, 3rd son of John C. of Cochrane, ix. 75.
—— Dorothy, dau. of William C. of Cochrane, iii, 339.
—— Dorothy, dau. of 9th earl of Dundonald, iii. 362.
—— Douglas Robert Hesketh Roger, iii. 367.
—— Elizabeth, wife of capt. John Lennox of Woodhead, iii. 342.
—— Elizabeth, dau. of William C. of Ochiltree, iii. 349.
—— Elizabeth, wife of Patrick Heron, iii. 360.
—— Elizabeth, wife of Robert Sempill of Beltries, vii. 549.
—— Elizabeth Mary Harriet, dau. of 11th earl of Dundonald, iii. 366.
—— Ernest Grey Lambton, captain R.N., iii. 365.
—— —— his 1st wife, Adelaide Blackwall, iii. 365.
—— —— his 2nd wife, Elizabeth Frances Maria Katharine Doherty, iii. 365.
—— Esther Rose Georgina, dau. of 11th earl of Dundonald, iii. 366.
—— Euphemia, wife of col. John Erskine, iii. 349.
—— Euphemia, dau. of John C. of Waterside, iii. 350.
—— Eupheme, dau. of Sir John C. of Ochiltree, ix. 76.
—— George, captain in the army, iii. 349.
—— George Augustus Frederick, lieut.-colonel, M.P., iii. 360.
—— Gilbert, son of Michael C. of Barbachlaw, iii. 340 *n*.
—— Grizel, dau. of 8th earl of Dundonald, iii. 360.
—— Grizel, wife of Thos. Dunlop of Househill, iii. 343.
—— Grizel, wife of John Ker of Morieston, iii. 350, 359; ix. 76 *bis*.
—— Grizel, wife of 11th lord Ross of Halkhead, iii. 350; vii. 258.
—— Grizel, wife of John Cochrane of Ferguslie, iii. 351.
—— Grizel Winifred Louise, wife of R. G. A. Hamilton, Master of Belhaven, ii. 60; iii. 367.
—— Helen, dau. of Michael C. of Barbachlaw, iii. 340 *n*.
—— Helen, wife of John, 15th earl of Sutherland, iii. 352; viii. 354.
Cochrane, Henriette, dau. of William C. of Ochiltree, iii. 349.
—— Horatio Barnardo William, 92nd Highlanders, iii. 365.
—— —— his wife, Frances Jacobina Nicholson, iii. 365.
—— Isabella, wife of John Ogilvy of Balbegno, iii. 351.
—— James, son of James C. of Barbachlaw, iii. 340 *n*.
—— James, illeg. son of James C. of Barbachlaw, iii. 340 *n*.
—— James, 3rd son of 1st earl of Dundonald, ix. 77.
—— James Atholl, vicar of Mansfield, iii. 360.
—— —— his wife, Mary Smithson, iii. 360.
—— Janet, dau. of John C. of Cochrane, and perhaps wife of * Maxwell, iii. 338.
—— Janet, wife of (1) Major T. Woodhall, and (2) Sir G. Tuite, iii. 362.
—— Jean, wife of (1) John, 1st viscount of Dundee, and (2) Wm. 3rd viscount of Kilsyth, iii. 328, 330, 352; v. 193, 194.
—— Jean Alice Elaine, iii. 368.
—— John, illeg. son of Alex. C. of Barbachlaw, iii. 340 *n*.
—— John, lieut. R.N., iii. 349.
—— John deputy-commissary to the forces in North Britain, iii. 359.
—— —— his wife, * Birch, iii. 359.
—— Katharine, wife of David Smythe of Methven, iii. 351.
—— Katharine, wife of 6th earl of Galloway, iii. 356; iv. 165; ix. 38, 95.
—— Katharine, wife of Wm. Wood, iii. 357; ix. 77.
—— Katharine Elizabeth, wife of John W. Fleming, iii. 366.
—— Louisa Katharine Emma, wife of 2nd baron O'Neill, iii. 366.
—— Magdalen, wife of Lewis Kennedy, ii. 491.
—— Margaret, dau. of William C. of Cochrane, iii. 339.
—— Margaret, wife of 9th earl of Eglinton, iii. 352, 455; ix. 77.
—— Margaret, wife of Lewis Kennedy, ix. 24.
—— Marjorie Gwendolen Elsie, iii. 368.
—— Mary, dau. of Wm. C. of Ochiltree, iii. 349.
—— Mary, dau. of 6th earl of Dundonald, iii. 357.
—— Robert, 8th son of Wm. C. of Ochiltree, iii. 349.
—— Susan, wife of (1) Charles, 6th earl of Strathmore and Kinghorne, and (2) George Forbes, iii. 355; iv. 165; viii. 308.
—— Thomas, son of James C. of Cochrane, iii. 336 *n*., 337; ix. 75.

* Name unknown.

Cochrane, Thomas, 3rd son of Sir John C. of Ochiltree, ix. 76.
— Thomas Horatio Arthur Ernest, iii. 366.
— — his wife, Gertrude Boyle, iii. 366.
— Uchtred, captain R.N., iii. 342 ; ix. 76.
— William, 2nd son of Robert C. of Cochrane, iii. 337.
— William, 2nd son of col. Alex. C. of Auchincreugh, iii. 342.
— William, Rutherglen, iii. 335 *n.*
— William, eldest son of Wm. C. of Ochiltree, iii. 348.
— William, judge-advocate, iii. 350.
— — his wife, * Turnbull, ix. 76.
— William, 2nd son of John C. of Cochrane, ix. 75.
— William Erskine, major 15th Dragoons, iii. 362.
— — his wife, Mary Ann Manson, iii. 362.
— *, wife of gen. Alex. Hamilton, iv. 309.
Cochrane-Johnstone, Andrew James, 12th son of 8th earl of Dundonald, iii. 360.
— Elizabeth, wife of 9th lord Napier, iii. 360.
Cockayne of Rushton, Sir William, iv. 301.
— Martha, wife of (1) John, viscount of Haddington, earl of Holdernesse, and (2) Montagu Bertie, lord Willoughby d'Eresby, 2nd earl of Lindsay, iv. 301.
COCKBURN, BARONESS FORRESTER OF CORSTORPHINE, iv. 96-97.
Cockburn of Cessford, William, vii. 328.
— of Choicelee, Christopher, vi. 11.
— — his wife, Jean Hume, vi. 11.
— of Clerkington, John, v. 298 ; vii. 583.
— — his 1st wife, Helen Maitland, v. 298.
— — his 2nd wife, Sibyl Cockburn, vii. 583.
— — Patrick, ii. 594.
— — his wife, Margaret Cranston, ii. 594.
— — Sir Richard, lord privy seal, i. 517 ; v. 296, 298, 300.
— of Cockburn, Sir James, vii. 586.
— — John de, iii. 88.
— — William, iii. 281.
— — his wife, Isobel Home, iii. 281.
— of Henderland, William, vii. 71.
— — William, vii. 369.
— — his wife, Katharine Rutherfurd, vii. 369.
— — William, viii. 537, 539.
— of Langton, Sir Alexander de Lindsay, ancestor of the family of, iii. 9.
— — Sir Archibald, iii. 76 ; v. 544.
— — his wife, Elizabeth Mackenzie, iii. 76.
— — Sir Archibald, their elder son, ii. 207, 300.
— — Archibald, advocate, ii. 206 *n.*, 207.
— — his wife, Mary Campbell, ii. 207.

* Name unknown.

Cockburn of Langton, Sir James, ii. 142.
— — Sir William, iii. 540.
— — his wife, Helen Elphinstone, iii. 540.
— — Sir William, joint principal Usher to King Charles I., iv. 246 ; vii. 197.
— of Newbigging, James, v. 289.
— — Patrick, v. 289.
— — Thomas, v. 291.
— of Ormiston, Adam, lord justice-clerk, iv. 318.
— — his wife, Susanna Hamilton, iv. 318.
— — George, iv. 96.
— — his wife, Caroline, baroness Forrester of Corstorphine, iv. 96.
— — John, the younger, ii. 156.
— — his wife, Margaret Hepburne, ii. 155.
— — John, viii. 386.
— — his wife, Alison Sandilands, viii. 386.
— — Sir John, lord justice-clerk, ii. 68 ; iii. 286 ; vi. 596 ; vii. 386 ; viii. 390.
— — his 1st wife, Alison Home, iii. 286.
— — his 2nd wife, Elizabeth Bellenden, ii. 68.
— — John, v. 474.
— — John, M.P., lord of the Admiralty, iv. 96, 593.
— — his 1st wife, Beatrix *or* Barbara Carmichael, iv. 593 ; ix. 114 *ter.*
— — his 2nd wife, Isabella Rowe, iv. 96.
— of Nether Pitforthies, Alexander, i. 297.
— of Skirling, Sir James, iv. 409.
— — his wife, Janet *or* Jean Herries, iv. 409 ; ix. 105.
— — William, vi. 570.
— — his wife, Christian Sinclair, vi. 570.
— of Strivlyne, William, vii. 328.
— of Sunderland Hall, William, vii. 369.
— — his wife, Katharine Rutherfurd, vii. 369.
— of Sunderland, William, viii. 537, 539.
— of Temple, Samuel, viii. 401.
— Agnes, wife of Sir Wm. Ker of Halden, v. 474.
— Alice, wife of Sir Robt. Stewart of Shillinglaw and Hopcailzie, viii. 401.
— Anne, wife of P. Hume of Hutton Bell, vi. 9.
— Barbara, wife of Henry, 10th lord Sinclair, vii. 586.
— Christian, wife of John Home of Slegden, ix. 72.
— Elizabeth, wife of Alex. Fraser of Strichen, v. 544.
— Elizabeth, wife of Alex. Hume of North Berwick, vi. 7.
— Graham, wife of rev. Robt. Stewart, ii. 90.
— Helen, wife of Wm. Hay of Linplum, viii. 446 *n.*
— Isabella, wife of Sir John Rollo of Bannockburn, vii. 196, 197.

Cockburn, Jean, wife of David Scrymgeour, iii. 313.
—— Jean, wife of (1) Alex. Dunbar of Grange, and (2) Thos. Mackenzie of Pluscardine and Auchmadies, vii. 505.
—— Katharine, wife of 1st viscount of Oxfuird, vi. 596; ix. 147.
—— Margaret, wife of P. Hepburn, ii. 142.
—— Margaret, wife of Sir Walter Scott of Buccleuch, ii. 227.
—— Margaret, wife of (1) Gavin Crichton, and (2) John Wardlaw, iii. 64.
—— Margaret, wife of (1) Alex. Home, and (2) Sir Wm. Graham, iii. 282.
—— Margaret, wife of 8th lord Sinclair, vii. 576.
—— Marion, wife of John St. Clair of Herdmanston, vii. 581.
—— Marjorie, wife of Walter Scott of Sinton, vii. 71.
—— Mary, wife of rev. Chas. Shuttleworth, iv. 96.
—— Sibyl, wife of (1) Sir Wm. St. Clair of Herdmanston, and (2) John Cockburn of Clerkington, vi. 595; vii. 583.
—— William, tutor of Langton, iv. 453.
Cockerell, Richard Howe, capt. R.N., iii. 463.
—— —— his wife, Theresa Newcomen, iii. 463.
Codington of Holm Patrick, Nicholas, i. 401.
—— —— his wife, Elizabeth Aston, i. 401.
Cogenhoe of Cogenhoe, Agnes, vi. 462 *n.*
—— —— William, vi. 462 *n.*
Coigny, Augustin Louis Joseph Casimir Gustave de Franquetot, 3rd duc de, viii. 127.
—— —— his wife, Henrietta Dundas Dalrymple-Hamilton of Bargany, viii. 127, 161.
Coke, Edward, son of 1st earl of Leicester; styled viscount, i. 377.
—— —— his wife, Mary Campbell, i. 377.
—— of Stoke Pogis, Sir Edward, i. 407, 408 *n.*
—— Anne, wife of Ralph Sadleir, i. 408 *n.*
—— Gertrude, wife of 7th earl of Dunmore, iii. 395.
—— Marjorie, wife of North Victor Cecil Dalrymple-Hamilton, viii. 162.
Colban, mormaer of Buchan, vii. 157.
Coldingham, Home, lord, iv. 465-484.
Coldingham, Alexander, first lord, iv. 465.
Coldstream, John, schoolmaster of Fowlis, vi. 555.
Cole, Edward Maule, vicar of Wetwang, v. 635.
—— —— his wife, Eliza Philadelphia Erskine Goodeve-Erskine, v. 635.
Cole-Hamilton of Beltrim, William Hamilton, ancestor of the family of, i. 42.
Coleman, William Peagum, surgeon R.N., v. 312.
—— —— his wife, Isabella Maitland, v. 312.
Colepeper of Thoresway, John (Colepeper), 1st lord, i. 57.
—— —— his wife, Judith Colepeper, i. 57.
—— —— John, 3rd lord, i. 57.
—— —— his wife, Frances Colepeper, i. 57.
—— —— Thomas, 2nd lord, i. 57; ii. 209; iii. 602.
—— of Hollingbourne, Sir Thomas, i. 57.
—— of Leeds Castle, Katharine, wife of 5th lord Fairfax, iii. 602.
—— Charlotte, wife of Sir John Pershall, ii. 209.
—— Elizabeth, wife of col. Jas. Hamilton, i. 57.
—— Frances, wife of John, 3rd lord Colepeper, i. 57.
—— Judith, wife of John, 1st lord Colepeper of Thoresway, i. 57.
—— Margaret, wife of William Hamilton of Chilston Park, i. 57.
Coligny, Gaspard de, lord of Chatillon, iv. 317.
—— —— his wife, Anne de Polignac, iv. 317.
—— Albertine von Rothberg, wife of (1) gen. Comte Rapp, and (2) George, duc de Melfort, vii. 60.
—— Henrietta de, wife of (1) Thomas, 3rd earl of Haddington, and (2) Gaspard de Champagne, Comte de la Suze, iv. 317; ix. 101.
Colin of the Aird, alleged ancestor of the earls of Ross, and of the Clan Mackenzie, vii. 495.
—— son of Carun of Cupar, iii. 304.
Colla Uais, high King of Ireland, v. 27, 28.
Collace, John de, viii. 49.
—— of Balnamoon, *, iv. 276.
—— —— his wife, * Gray, iv. 276; ix. 99.
—— —— John, viii. 60.
—— —— Robert, iii. 473; vii. 195.
—— —— his wife, Elizabeth Bruce, iii. 473.
—— Agnes, wife of (1) James Rollok of Duncrub, and (2) Peter Oliphant of Turings, vi. 545; vii. 195.
Collas, John Jervoise, Jersey, ii. 280.
—— —— his wife, Maria James, ii. 280.
Colleville, Gilbert de, ii. 535.
Colley of Castle Carbery, Sir Henry, i. 40 *n.*
—— —— Henry, i. 62.
—— —— his wife, Mary Hamilton, i. 62.
—— Anne, wife of Sir Claud Hamilton of Castle Toome, i. 40 *n.*
Collier of Yarlet, Christopher, i. 405.
—— —— his wife, Mary Aston, i. 405.
—— *, wife of gen. James Murray of Beauport, iii. 516; ix. 84.
—— John, Hastings, ix. 84.
Collingwood, Luke, iv. 299.
—— —— his wife, Margaret Ramsay, v. 299.
Collins of Baddow, Anthony, iii. 602.

* Name unknown.

Collins of Belmont, John Gunn, capt. 13th Light Dragoons, iii. 391.
— — his wife, Augusta Murray, iii. 391.
— Ælitia, wife of James Maxwell, ix. 105.
— Martha, wife of 7th lord Fairfax, iii. 602.
— Mary, wife of Malcolm Boyd, ix. 119.
— Samuel, M.D., ii. 413; ix. 66.
— — his 2nd wife, Katharine Abingdon, ii. 413.
— William Fellowes, major Royal Scots Greys, vii. 359.
Collinson, Anna Mary, wife of 15th earl of Moray, vi. 329.
— George J., vicar of St. James's, Clapham, vi. 329.
Collom, Harriet Phillips, wife of P. O. Murray, iii. 521.
— James, Stratton, iii. 521.
Colly, Andrew, London, viii. 124.
— — his wife, Jean Dalrymple, viii. 124.
Colquhoun of Balvie, Sir Humphrey, viii. 26.
— — his wife, Margaret Somerville, viii. 26.
— of Bedlay, George, v. 161.
— of Benheath, George, v. 161.
— — his wife, Margaret Boyd, v. 161.
— of Camstradden, Alexander, vi. 161.
— — his wife, Anna Graham, vi. 161.
— of Colquhoun, *see* of Luss.
— of Craance, Sir John, vi. 152.
— of Craiguchty, Sir John, vi. 152.
— of Drumskeath, Patrick, ix. 59.
— of Garscadden, William, captain, ii. 89.
— — his 1st wife, Elizabeth Stewart, ii. 89.
— of Garscube, James, ii. 181.
— — his wife, Christian Campbell, ii. 181.
— of Glens, George, 4th laird, v. 152, 161; ix. 119.
— — his wife, Margaret Boyd, v. 152, 161.
— — Margaret, wife of 5th lord Boyd, v. 152, 161 *bis*.
— of Luss, v. 328.
— — Alexander, i. 47; v. 161, 165.
— — his wife, Helen Buchanan, i. 47.
— — Anne, wife of James Grant of Pluscardine, vii. 480.
— — Humphrey, v. 606; viii. 12 *n*., 15 *bis*.
— — his wife, Helen Erskine, v. 606.
— — his contracted wife, Alison Somerville, viii. 15.
— — Humphrey, ii. 181; vi. 225.
— — his 1st wife, Helen Graham, vi. 225.
— — his 2nd wife, Elizabeth Napier, v. 155.
— — Sir Humphrey, i. 343; iv. 242, 373.
— — his 1st wife, Janet Cunningham, i. 343; iv. 242.
— — his 2nd wife, Jean Hamilton, iv. 373; ix. 104.
Colquhoun of Luss, Sir Humphrey, 5th bart., vii. 480.
— — Sir Ian, bart., vii. 482.
— — Sir James, *né* Grant, 6th bart., vii. 481.
— — his wife, Ann Colquhoun of Luss, vii. 480.
— — Sir James, 1st bart. of Gt. Britain, vi. 269; vii. 481 *n*., 482, 484; viii. 357.
— — his wife, Helen Sutherland, vii. 482; viii. 356.
— — John, v. 342.
— — Sir John, lord high chamberlain, i. 456 *n*.; ii. 454; iv. 528.
— — his 2nd wife, Elizabeth, countess of Moray, iv. 528; vi. 306, 310.
— — Sir John, ii. 181; v. 155, 350, 607; vi. 152.
— — his 1st wife, Elizabeth Stewart, v. 350.
— — Sir John, ii. 81; v. 163.
— — his 2nd wife, Agnes Boyd, ii. 81; v. 163.
— — Sir John, 1st bart., vi. 241.
— — his wife, Lilias Graham, vi. 241.
— — Sir John, v. 308.
— — Sir Ludovick, *né* Grant, vii. 481, 482, 483.
— — his 1st wife, Marion Dalrymple, vii. 484; viii. 142.
— of Pemont and Drumskeath, Patrick, ii. 543.
— — his wife, Elizabeth Colville, ii. 543.
— of Smythfield, George, viii. 526.
— of Stahlegreen of Glasgow, George, v. 161.
— — his wife, Margaret Boyd, v. 161.
— Adam, rector of Stobo, ii. 462.
— Agnes, wife of 3rd Lord Somerville, viii. 15.
— Alison, wife of Sir Thomas Home of Langshaw, iv. 451.
— Elizabeth, wife of (1) Sir D. Campbell, (2) J. Maxwell, and (3) P. Fleming, ii. 180.
— Francesca, wife of (1) Robt. Colville of Cleish, and (2) G. Mercer, ii. 543, 569, 570.
— Jean, wife of (1) Alan, 5th lord Cathcart, (2) Sir Duncan Campbell of Auchinbreck, and (3) Sir Wm. Hamilton, i. 47; ii. 517.
— Jean, wife of Sir Matthew Stewart, ii. 81.
— John, goldsmith in Edinburgh, i. 140.
— — his wife, Margaret Graham, i. 140.
— Lilias, wife of (1) Sir J. Stirling, and (2) Charles Maitland, v. 308.
— Margaret, probable wife of Sir David Murray of Tullibardine, i. 456.
— Marion, wife of (1) Robert, 4th lord Boyd, and (2) Thos. Crawfurd of Jordanhill, v. 155 *bis*.

Colquhoun, Marjory, wife of (1) Sir D. Campbell, (2) J. Maxwell, and (3) P. Fleming, ii. 181 *n*.
—— Peter, burgess of Glasgow, iii. 529.
—— —— his wife, Isabella or Elizabeth Elphinstone, iii. 529.
—— Peter, his son, iii. 530.
Colt of Auldhame, Oliver, ii. 89.
—— —— his wife, Helen Stewart, ii. 89.
—— —— Robert, advocate, ii, 89.
—— —— his wife, Grizel Dundas, ii. 89.
—— Elizabeth, wife of James Willis, ii. 89.
—— Helen, wife of Sir David Rae, ii. 89.
—— Margaret, dau. of Oliver C., ii. 89.
—— Mary, wife of major C. Pye, ii. 89.
—— Oliver, son of Oliver C. of Auldhame, ii. 89.
Columba, Saint, i. 156, 158.
COLVILLE OF CULROSS, COLVILLE, LORD, ii. 535-568.
Colville of Culross, Alexander, *de jure* fifth lord, ii. 552, 559.
—— —— his wife, Mary Erskine, ii. 559; v. 91.
—— —— Alexander, seventh lord, ii. 562.
—— —— his wife, Elizabeth Erskine, ii. 563; v. 89.
—— —— Charles John, tenth lord, ii. 564, 566.
—— —— his wife, Cecile Katharine Mary Carrington, ii. 566.
—— —— Charles Robert William, eleventh lord, ii. 567.
—— —— his wife, Ruby Streatfield, ii. 567.
—— —— James, first lord, ii. 548, 553.
—— —— his 1st wife, Isabel Ruthven, ii. 556; iv. 262.
—— —— his 2nd wife, Helen Schaw, ii. 557.
—— —— James, second lord, ii. 557; viii. 500.
—— —— his 1st wife, Magdalen Young, ii. 558.
—— —— his 2nd wife, *, ii. 559.
—— —— his 3rd wife, Margaret Clyntoun, ii. 559.
—— —— John, fourth lord, ii. 559.
—— —— John, sixth lord, ii. 560.
—— —— his wife, Elizabeth Johnston, ii. 561.
—— —— John, eighth lord, ii. 563.
—— —— his wife, Amelia Webber, ii. 563.
—— —— John, ninth lord, ii. 563, 565.
—— —— his 1st wife, Elizabeth Ford, ii. 566.
—— —— his 2nd wife, Anne Law, ii. 566.
COLVILLE OF CULROSS, COLVILLE, VISCOUNT, ii. 535-568.
Colville of Culross, Charles John, first viscount, ii. 566.
—— —— his wife, Cecile Katharine Mary Carrington, ii. 566.
—— —— Charles Robert William, second viscount, ii. 567.
—— —— his wife, Ruby Streatfield, ii. 567.

* Name unknown.

COLVILLE OF OCHILTREE, COLVILLE, LORD, ii. 569-575.
Colville of Ochiltree, David, self-styled lord, ii. 574.
—— —— Robert, first lord, ii. 573.
—— —— his 1st wife, Janet Wemyss, ii. 573; viii. 499.
—— —— his 2nd wife, Euphan Myrton, ii. 573.
—— —— Robert, second lord, ii. 572, 573.
—— —— his wife, Margaret Wemyss, ii. 573.
—— —— Robert, third lord, ii. 574.
—— —— Robert, self-styled lord, ii. 574.
—— master of, Charles Alexander, R.N., ii. 567.
—— —— James John, 3rd son of 8th lord Colville of Culross, ii. 563.
—— —— Robert, 2nd son of 1st lord Colville of Culross, ii. 557.
—— —— his contr. wife, Elizabeth Wemyss, viii. 497.
—— —— his wife, Christian Bruce, ii. 557.
COLVILLE, LORD COLVILLE OF CULROSS, ii. 535-568.
COLVILLE, VISCOUNT COLVILLE OF CULROSS, ii. 535-568.
COLVILLE, LORD COLVILLE OF OCHILTREE, ii. 569-575.
Colville of Balbedie, James, v. 404.
—— —— his wife, Helen Lindsay, v. 404.
—— of Bally M'Laughlin, James, ii. 558.
—— —— William, ii. 559.
—— of Barnwell, Sir Robert, ii. 540.
—— —— Sir William, ii. 542; iv. 401.
—— of Blair, Alexander, justiciar-depute, ii. 549.
—— —— his wife, Agnes Wardlaw, ii. 549.
—— of Cleish, Robert, son of Sir James C. of East Wemyss, ii. 552, 554, 569.
—— —— his wife, Francisca Colquhoun, ii. 570.
—— —— Robert, 2nd laird, ii. 553, 554, 571.
—— —— his wife, Margaret Lindsay, ii. 571.
—— —— Robert, 3rd laird, ii. 572.
—— —— his wife, Beatrix Haldane, ii. 572.
—— —— Sir Robert, 4th laird, ii. 573.
—— —— his 1st wife, Janet Wemyss, ii. 573.
—— —— his 2nd wife, Euphan Myrton, ii. 573.
—— of West Comrie, Alexander, principal of New College, St. Andrews, ii. 550; v. 304.
—— —— his wife, Anne le Blanc, ii. 551.
—— —— John, commendator of Culross, ii. 549, 550.
—— —— his wife, Elizabeth Melville, ii. 550.
—— of Condie, Matthew, ii. 570.
—— —— William, ii. 570.
—— of Craigflower, Andrew, ancestor of the family of, ii. 574.

Colville of Crombie, James, illeg. son of Sir Jas. C. of Easter Wemyss, ii. 552.
— of Culross, Alexander, commendator, ii. 548, 554, 571.
— — his wife, Nicolas Dundas, ii. 549.
— — John, commendator, ii. 169, 550.
— — his wife, Elizabeth Melville, ii. 550; vi. 92.
— — William, commendator, ii. 545; v. 609.
— — his wife, Euphame Dundas, ii. 545.
— of Dale, Robert, ii. 539.
— of Drumcross, Cuthbert, ii. 540, 544 *n.*
— of Feuallroul, Robert, ii. 55.
— of Gosford, Sir Thomas, ii. 538.
— of Heitoun, Margaret, v. 56.
— — Philip de, ii. 535.
— — Sir Robert, ii. 540.
— — his wife, Christian Crichton, ii. 541.
— of Hiltoun, Robert, King's chamberlain, ii. 542, 543.
— — his wife, Margaret Logan, ii. 544.
— — Robert, director of Chancery, ii. 543 *bis*, 544.
— — his wife, Elizabeth Arnot, ii. 545.
— of Huip, James, ii. 571.
— of Kincardine, Alexander, *de jure* fifth lord Colville of Culross, ii. 552, 559.
— — his wife, Mary Erskine, ii. 559.
— — John, commendator of Culross, ii. 550.
— — his wife, Elizabeth Melville, ii. 550.
— — John, minister of Midcalder, ii. 551.
— — his wife, Mary Preston, ii. 551.
— of Kinnaird, William, 2nd son of Thomas C. of Oxnam, ii. 536.
— — his wife, Ada *, ii. 536.
— of Nether Kinneddar, James, 549.
— — Robert, minister of Culross, ii. 549.
— — his wife, Katharine Melville, ii. 549.
— — Mr. Robert, his son, ii. 549.
— of North Lathamis, Robert, ii. 571.
— — his wife, Margaret Lindsay, ii. 571.
— of Lurg, John, commendator of Culross, ii. 550.
— — John, minister of Midcalder, ii. 551.
— of Maxton, Margaret, v. 56.
— — Sir Robert, ii. 540.
— — his wife, Christian Crichton, ii. 541.
— — Sir Robert, ii. 541.
— — his wife, Euphame Wallace, ii. 541.
— of Ochiltree, Elizabeth, wife of (1) Robert Colville of Ravenscraig, and (2) P. Colquhoun of Pemont, ii. 459, 543, 544.
— — Eustacia, wife of Reginald le Cheyne, ii, 537 *bis*.
— — Sir James, director of Chancery, ii. 546.
— — his 1st wife, Alison Bruce, ii. 547.
— — his 2nd wife, Margaret Forrester, ii. 547.

* Name unknown.

Colville of Ochiltree, Sir John, ii. 536, 537.
— — Margaret, ii. 543; v. 56.
— — Sir Robert, 2nd son of Sir Thomas C., ii. 538.
— — his wife, Katharine *, ii. 539.
— — Sir Robert, ii. 539.
— — Robert, ii. 540.
— — his wife, Margaret Colville, ii. 540.
— — Sir Robert, ii. 541.
— — his wife, Christian Crichton, ii. 541; iii. 222.
— — Sir Robert, ii. 541; v. 55, 151.
— — his wife, Euphame Wallace, ii. 541.
— — Robert, director of Chancery, ii. 544; vii. 330.
— — his wife, Elizabeth Arnot, ii. 545.
— — Robert, *né* Ayton, ii. 574.
— — his wife, Janet Wedderburn, ii. 574.
— — Thomas, 3rd son of Thomas C. of Oxnam, ii. 536.
— — Sir Thomas, ii. 537.
— — William, ii. 537.
— — his wife, * de Normanville, ii. 537.
— — Sir William, ii. 542; v. 56; vii. 370; ix. 51 *n.*
— — his 1st wife, Elizabeth Kennedy, ii. 459, 542.
— — his 2nd wife, Margaret Ker, ii. 543.
— — his 3rd wife, Elizabeth Crichton, ii. 543.
— of Oxnam, Sir John, ii. 537.
— — Margaret, ii. 543; v. 56.
— — Philip de, ii. 535.
— — Sir Robert, 2nd son of Sir Thomas C., ii. 538.
— — his wife, Katerina *, ii. 539.
— — Sir Robert, his son, ii. 539.
— — Robert, son of Sir Thos. C., ii. 540.
— — his wife, Margaret Colville, ii. 540.
— — Sir Robert, ii. 540; vii. 322.
— — his wife, Christian Crichton, ii. 541.
— — Sir Robert, ii. 541.
— — his wife, Eupham Wallace, ii. 541.
— — Robert, director of Chancery, ii. 544; v. 55.
— — his wife, Elizabeth Arnot, ii. 545.
— — Thomas de, son of Philip C., 536.
— — his wife, Amabilis, ii. 536.
— — Sir Thomas, son of Wm. C., ii. 537.
— — Sir Thomas, son of Sir Robert de C., ii. 539.
— — his wife, Margaret Lindsay, ii. 540; iii. 12.
— — William, ii. 537.
— — his wife, * de Normanville, ii. 537.
— of Pitkany, Robert, illeg. son of Robt. C. of Hiltoun, ii. 546.
— — his wife, Margaret Scougall, ii. 546.
— of Ravenscraig, Robert, ii. 543.
— — his wife, Elizabeth Colville, ii. 543.

* Name unknown.

Colville of Ravenscraig, William, ii. 543.
— of Spindleston, Philip, ii. 538.
— — his wife, Agnes Mordington, ii. 538.
— — Robert, ii. 538.
— — William, ii. 537.
— — William, ii. 538.
— of Swyneside, Sir Robert de, ii. 539.
— of Symington, Sir Robert, ii. 540.
— — Sir William, ii. 542.
— of Tillicoultrie, Sir James, ii. 552.
— — his wife, Janet Douglas, ii. 553.
— — Sir James, ambassador, ii. 553.
— of East Wemyss, Sir James, director of Chancery, ii. 546, 569.
— — his 1st wife, Alison Bruce, ii. 547.
— — his 2nd wife, Margaret Forrester, ii. 547.
— — Sir James, 2nd laird, ii. 548, 552; v. 153, 495.
— — his wife, Janet Douglas, ii. 553; vi. 371.
— — Sir James, ambassador to France, 3rd laird, ii. 553.
— — his 1st wife, Isabel Ruthven, ii. 556.
— — his 2nd wife, Helen Schaw, ii. 557.
— — Robert, illeg. son of Robert C. of Hiltoun, ii. 546.
— — his wife, Margaret Scougall, ii. 546.
— of Whitsome, John, ii. 539.
— — Sir Thomas, ii. 538.
— — William de, ii. 539.
— Abraham, professor at Sedan, ii. 551.
— Alexander, collector of customs, ii. 559.
— — his wife, Mary Erskine, ii. 559.
— Alexander, collector of customs, his son, ii. 560.
— Alexander, 4th son of Robert C. of Cleish, ii. 571.
— Alison, dau. of Sir James C. of Ochiltree, ii. 552.
— Andrew, apprenticed to John Rig, ii. 572.
— Anna, dau. of Mr. John C., ii. 552.
— Anne, dau. of 5th lord C. of Culross, ii. 560.
— Anne, wife of James Forsyth, ii. 565.
— Anne Amelia, wife of viscount Newry, ii. 565.
— Arthur, Pitmillie, ii. 575.
— Arthur Edward William, C.B., ii. 565.
— — his wife, Olivia Spencer-Churchill, ii. 565.
— Blanch Cecile, wife of adm. R. F. Britten, ii. 567.
— Charles, lieut.-gen., ii. 560, 562.
— Charles, capt. 21st N.B. Fusiliers, ii. 562.
— Sir Charles, governor of Mauritius, ii. 564.
— — his wife, Jane Mure, ii. 564.
— Cicill, wife of L. Mercer of Meikleour, ii. 548, 557.
Colville, David, 2nd son of Sir Robert C., ii. 541, 543, 546.
— David, 5th son of Robt. C. of Cleish, ii. 572.
— David, 2nd son of Robt. C. of Cleish, ii. 572.
— — his wife, Agnes Betoun, ii. 572.
— David, 2nd son of David C., ii. 572.
— — his wife, Margaret Barclay, ii. 572.
— David, self-styled lord Colville of Ochiltree, ii. 574.
— Elizabeth, wife of Robert Petrie, ii. 562.
— Elizabeth, wife of A. Dundas of Fingask. ii. 571.
— Elizabeth, wife of Jas. Lindsay of Dowhill, ii. 572; ix. 59.
— Elizabeth, wife of Sir Wm. Dalgleish, ii. 573.
— Euphan, wife of Jas. Monypenny, ii. 571.
— George, 2nd son of rev. John C., ii. 552.
— George, physician, Dundee, ii. 560.
— George, lieut. in col. Gooch's regt., ii. 562.
— George, 41st regt., ii. 565.
— George Cecil, ii. 567.
— George Charles, barrister, ii. 567.
— Georgiana Clementina, wife of J. Ridgway, ii. 565.
— Grizel, wife of J. Preston of Valleyfield, ii. 550.
— Grizel, wife of H. Echlin of Pittadro, ii. 571.
— Grizel, wife of James Mitchell of Bandeath, ii. 573.
— Helen, wife of John Moncrieff of Balcaskie, ii. 557; ix. 59.
— Henry, minister of Orphir, ii. 570.
— — his wife, Katharine Douglas, ix. 59.
— Isabel, wife of Mr. G. Johnston, ii. 560.
— Ivo de, ii. 538.
— James, 4th son of Sir Robert C., ii. 542, 546.
— James, eldest son of 1st lord Colville of Culross, ii. 557.
— — his contr. wife, Elizabeth Wemyss, ii. 557; viii. 497.
— James, 2nd son of John C. of West Comrie, ii. 550.
— James, captain R.N., ii. 562.
— James, 3rd son of Robt. C. of Cleish, ii. 571.
— James, 4th son of Robt. C. of Cleish, ii. 573.
— James, in Nether Kinlochie, ii. 574.
— — his wife, Margaret Wallace, ii. 574.
— Janet, wife of Robt. Douglas, ii. 572; ix. 59.
— Janet, wife of Alexander, *de jure* 3rd lord Boyd, v. 151; ix. 58.
— Jean, wife of Sir James Campbell of Lawers, ii. 548, 557; v. 504, 505.
— Jean, wife of Mr. John Duncan, ii. 549.

Colville, Jean, wife of Robt. Bruce of Blairhall, ii. 550.
— Jean, wife of Thos. Alexander, ii. 572.
— John, abbot of Culross, ii. 546.
— John, minister of Kilbride, master of Requests, ii. 570.
— — his wife, Janet Russell, ii. 570.
— John, son of Mr. John C. ii. 570.
— John, 2nd son of Robt. C. of Cleish, ii. 571.
— John, wright, Elie, ii. 574.
— Katharine, wife of Geo. Home of Spott, ii. 546, 548.
— Katharine, wife of Jas. Aitken, ii. 549.
— Katharine, wife of James Melville of Hallhill and Nethergrange, ii. 550; vi. 91.
— Katharine, dau. of 5th lord Colville of Culross, ii. 560.
— Katharine, wife of rev. R. Frankland, ii. 565.
— Katharine, alleged wife of Thomas Ker of Kershaugh and Fernieburst, v. 51 *n.*, 79 *n.*
— Katharine Dorothea, wife of Sir J. Simeon, ii. 565.
— Margaret, wife of P. Murray of Pardewis, i. 464, 548; ii. 549.
— Margaret, wife of Robert de Colville, ii. 540.
— Margaret, alleged wife of A. Ker of Fernyhirst, ii. 543.
— Margaret, wife of (1) Wm. Menteith, (2) P. Home, and (3) Jas. Cunningham, ii. 552.
— Margaret, dau. of 1st lord Colville of Culross, ii. 548, 557.
— Margaret, wife of Alex. Blair, ii. 560.
— Margaret, wife of capt. P. Castlemaine, ii. 562.
— Margaret, dau. of 2nd viscount Colville, ii. 567.
— Margaret, wife of Sir Jerome Lindsay, ii. 570.
— Margaret, wife of A. Sinclair of Aith, ii. 571.
— Margaret, dau. of Robt. C. of Cleish, ii. 572.
— Margaret, dau. of David C., ii. 572.
— Margaret, wife of D. Wemyss of Fingask, ii. 573.
— Margaret, wife of Sir John Ayton, ii. 574.
— Margaret, wife of 1st lord Sempill, vii. 533.
— Marion, dau. of Mr. John C., ii. 552.
— Marjorie, dau. of Isaac Dobson, ii. 559.
— Mary, dau. of 5th lord Colville of Culross, ii. 560.
— Mary, wife of rev. Allan Logan, ii. 574.
— Mary, wife of Duncan Campbell of Glenlyon, ix. 59.
— Mary Catharine, wife of Sir J. W. Bonsor, ii. 565.
Colville, Matthew, son of Matthew C. o Condie, ii. 570.
— Penelope, dau. of 5th lord Colville of Culross, ii. 560.
— Philip de, iv. 331.
— — his wife, Agnes de Mordington, iv. 331.
— Philip, 3rd son of Sir Robert C., ii. 542.
— Richard, 1449, ii. 540 *n.*
— Robert, son of Mr. John C., ii. 580.
— Robert, self-styled lord Colville of Ochiltree, ii. 574.
— Robert Alfred, ii. 565.
— Samuel, author of *Scots Hudibras*, ii. 550.
— Sara, dau. of the commendator of Culross, ii. 545.
— Sarah, dau. of principal Alex. C., ii. 551.
— Stanley Cecil James, C.V.O., C.B., R.N., ii. 566.
— — his wife, Adelaide Jane Meade, ii. 567.
— Susanna, wife of (1) J. Monypenny, and (2) D. Preston, ii. 549; iii. 120.
— Sybil Marion, dau. of 2nd viscount Colville, ii. 567.
— Sir Thomas, attendant on princess Margaret, ii. 540, 544 *n.*
— Thomas, 2nd son of Robert, master of Colville, ii. 557.
— Thomas, son of Mr. John C., ii. 570.
— Thomas, 5th son of Robt. C. of Cleish, ii. 570.
— William, son of James C., ii. 542.
— William, 4th son of Robt. C. of Cleish, ii. 570.
— William, minister in Edinburgh, ii. 572; ix. 59.
— — his wife, Katharine Brown, ii. 572.
— William, Balcormie Mill, ii. 574.
— Sir William James, K.C.V.O., C.B., ii. 564.
— — his wife, Georgiana M. Baillie, ii. 559 *n.*, 565.
— *, wife of * Marshall, ii. 537.
— *, wife of * Maitland, ii. 537.
— *, wife of * Heron, ii. 537.
— *, wife of Henry Stewart of Whitelaw, ii. 570.
COLYEAR, COLYEAR, LORD, vii. 92-97.
Colyear, David, first lord, vii. 92.
COLYEAR, LORD COLYEAR, vii. 92-97.
COLYEAR, VISCOUNT OF MILSINGTON, vii. 92-97.
COLYEAR, LORD PORTMORE AND BLACKNESS, vii. 92.
COLYEAR, EARL OF PORTMORE, vii. 88-97.
Colyear, Caroline, wife of 1st lord Scarsdale, vii. 94.
— Charles, M.P., 'Beau Colyear,' vii. 94.
— Sir David, 2nd bart., vii. 91.
— — his wife, Katharine Sedley, vii. 91.

* Name unknown.

Colyear, Elizabeth, wife of Lionel Cranfield (Sackville), 1st duke of Dorset, vii. 91.
— Sir James, lieut.-col. in service of States-General, vii. 91.
— John David, 1st regt. Foot Guards, vii. 95.
— Julia, dau. of 3rd earl of Portmore, vii. 96.
— Juliana, wife of Henry Dawkins of Standlynch, vii. 94.
— Katharine Caroline, wife of Joseph Brecknell, vii. 96.
— Mary, dau. of 3rd earl of Portmore, vii. 95.
— Mary Anne, wife of (1) Veitch of Dawick, and (2) Sir George Nicolson of Carnock, vii. 91.
— Walter Philip, general, governor of Bonn and Namur, v. 174; vii. 90.
— — his wife, Anne Catherine de Brumaigne, vii. 91.
— William, lieut.-col., equerry to the duke of Cumberland, vii. 95.
— *alias* Robertson, Sir Alexander, 1st bart., vii. 89.
— — his wife, Jean Murray, vii. 90.
— — David, major, vii. 88.
— — his wife, Jean Bruce, vii. 89.
— — David Alexander, vii. 89.
— — Jean, vii. 89.
— — Sabina *or* Martha, wife of Sir John Nicolson of Tillicoultry, vii. 89.
— — *, wife of T. Dunbar of Grange, vii. 89.
Colyear-Dawkins of Over Norton, James, vii. 95.
Compton, Anne, wife of 1st marquess of Clanricarde, vi. 486 *n.*
— Charles, M.P., viii. 232.
— Elizabeth, wife of Henry Drummond, viii. 232.
— James, cadet of earls of Northampton, iii. 44.
— Katrine Cecilia, wife of 10th lord Dingwall, iii. 124.
— Penelope, wife of John, 1st baron Muncaster, iii. 44.
Comyn, earl of Angus, i. 167.
Comyn, lord of Badenoch, i. 503-510.
Comyn, earl of Buchan, ii. 252-261.
Comyn of Badenoch, Sir John, 'the Red Comyn No. 1,' i. 419 *n.*, 423, 425, 506; ii. 126, 254.
— — his wife, Alicia Lindsay, i. 507; iii. 5.
— — Sir John, 'the Black Comyn,' i. 4, 507; ii. 218; iii. 5 *n.*, 9; vi. 129.
— — his wife, Alianora Baliol, i. 508.
— — Sir John, 'the Red Comyn No. 2,' i. 429, 508; iv. 256; v. 334.
— — his wife, Johanna de Valence, i. 509.

* Name unknown.

Comyn of Badenoch, John i. 509.
— — his wife, Margaret Wake, i. 510.
— of Cumbernauld, Sir John, viii. 520.
— of Fonthill, William, i. 504.
— — his wife, Maud Banaster, i. 504.
— — William, his son, i. 504.
— of Gorgie, Sir Fergus, viii. 562.
— of Inverallochy, Alexander, vii. 438.
— — his wife, Margaret Fraser, vii. 438.
— of Kilbride, David, ancestor of the family of, i. 505.
— — his wife, Isabella de Valloniis, i. 505.
— — John, ii. 126 *n.*
— — William, ii. 126 *n.*
— of Kirkintilloch, Sir John, viii. 520.
— — William, i. 507; vi. 129 *n.*, 131.
— — his wife, Isabella Russell, i. 507; vi. 129.
— of Lenzie, Sir John, viii. 520.
— of Leuchars, Roger, viii. 419.
— of Machan, John, iv. 341.
— of Muckrath, William, vi. 198.
— of Northallerton, Richard, i. 504; ii. 252; viii. 319 *n.*; ix. 30.
— — his wife, Hextilda of Walwick, Carrow, Thornton, Henshaw and Bedrule, i. 3, 417, 504, 507, 508; ii. 252; iii. 6; vi. 288; ix. 30.
— of Rowallan, *, iv. 183.
— — Sir Walter, iv. 184.
— Adomar *or* Aymer, i. 510.
— Agnes, wife of Philip Meldrum, ii. 254.
— Agnes, wife of Maliee, 6th earl of Strathearn, ii. 256; viii. 249; ix. 47.
— Sir Alexander, sheriff of Wigtownshire and Aberdeenshire, keeper of Urquhart and Tarwedale Castles, ii. 255.
— Alexander, 4th son of Sir John, 'the Red Comyn No. 1.' ix. 30.
— Alice, wife of Sir Henry Beaumont, iii. 263.
— Bertold, inf. son of John, earl of Angus, i. 167.
— Bigla, *alias* Matilda of Glencarnie, vii. 455 *n.*
— Dornagilla, alleged wife of Sir Archibald Douglas, iii. 141.
— Edoyna, wife of Gilbert de Haya of Erroll, iii. 558 *n.*
— Elena, wife of Sir William of Brechin, ii. 218, 256.
— Elizabeth, wife of Richard Talbot, i. 429 *n.*, 509, 510.
— Elizabeth, wife of William, 5th earl of Mar, ii. 254; v. 576.
— Elizabeth, wife of Sir G. Umfraville, 2nd earl of Angus, ii. 256; ix. 11.
— Fergus, son of William, 1st earl of Buchan, ii. 253.

* Name unknown.

Comyn, Henry, son of Walter, earl of Menteith, vi. 130.
— Idonea, wife of Sir Adam Fitz Gilbert, ii. 253; ix. 30.
— Idonea, wife of Sir Gilbert Hay, ii. 253; iii. 558.
— Jean, wife of William, 2nd earl of Ross, i. 505; vii. 233.
— Joan, wife of David de Strathbogie, 10th earl of Atholl, i. 429, 509, 510; ix. 27.
— John, earl of Angus, i. 167, 506 *n.*
— John, eldest son of Alexander, 1st earl of Buchan, i. 256; iv. 43 *n.*; vi. 531.
— John, son of Robert de C., i. 503.
— — his wife, * Giffard, i. 504.
— John, son of Richard C., i. 505.
— John, 'le jeon,' i. 507.
— Margaret, countess of Buchan, wife of (1) Sir John Ross, and (2) Sir Wm. Lindsay, ii. 256, 260; iii. 9; vii. 235.
— Margaret, wife of Sir Nicholas Soulis, ii. 256; viii. 250; ix. 47.
— Margaret, wife of Sir John Keith of Keith-Marischal, vi. 29.
— Marjorie, wife of Patrick, 8th earl of Dunbar, ii. 256; iii. 263.
— Marjorie, wife of Richard Boyle of Kelburne, iv. 183.
— Odinell *or* Odo, son of Richard C., i. 505.
— Richard, son of William, earl of Buchan, i. 505.
— Sir Richard, son of Richard C., i. 506.
— Richard, justiciary, i. 506 *n.*
— Robert de, earl of Northumberland, i. 503; iii. 242.
— Robert, slain at Dumfries, ix. 30.
— Roger, son of Alexander, earl of Buchan, ii. 255.
— Simon, son of Richard C., i. 505.
— Walter, son of William C. of Fonthill, i. 504.
— Walter, 2nd son of William C., i. 419 *n.*, 421, 505; ii. 254.
— — his wife, Isabella, countess of Menteith, i. 505; vi. 127.
— Walter, lord clerk register, vi. 127 *n.*
— William de, bishop of Durham, chancellor, i. 503; ix. 30.
— William, slain at Durham, i. 503, 504; ix. 30.
— William, son-in-law of Robt. Fitzhugh, i. 505 *n.*
— William, son of Richard C., i. 506.
— Sir William, son of William, 1st earl of Buchan, ii. 253.
— William, provost of St. Mary's Church, St. Andrews, self-styled earl of Buchan, ii. 256; iv. 43; vii. 421, 422.
— *, 2nd husband of Alicia, widow of Sir John 'the Red Comyn No. 1,' i. 507.

* Name unknown.

Comyn, *, wife of Alexander of Argyll, i. 507.
— *, wife of Sir Wm. Galbraith of Dalserf, i. 507; vi. 29.
— *, wife of Sir Andrew Moray of Bothwell, i. 507; ii. 126.
— *, wife of Godfrey Moubray, i. 507.
— *, wife of Richard Siward, i. 507.
Con of Auchrie, Patrick, iii. 575.
Conall, Magdalene, wife of Patrick Murray, iii. 401; ix. 79.
Conan IV., duke of Brittany, earl of Richmond, i. 4.
— — his wife, Margaret of Huntingdon, i. 4.
— illeg. son of Henry, 3rd earl of Atholl, i. 418, 419.
Coneway, James, Leith, vii. 213.
— — his wife, Margaret Primrose, vii. 213.
Congalton of Congalton, John, ix. 102 *bis.*
— — William, viii. 442.
— — his 1st wife, Beatrix Hay, viii. 442; ix. 167.
— of West Fenton, Edward, iv. 335; viii. 575; ix. 102.
— — his wife, Janet Seton, iv. 335; viii. 575.
— Johanna, wife of Wm. Haliburton, ix. 102.
Congasb, James of, 2nd son of Morgund, 2nd earl of Mar, v. 569.
Conghal of Tullibardine, i. 453 *n.*
— — his wife, Ada, dau. of Radulf, i. 453 *n.*
Coningsburg of Stapilgorton, William de, vi. 471; vii. 424.
— of Tullybody, Lora, wife of (1) Richard de Bickerton, and (2) Sir Thomas Hay of Locherworth, viii. 420.
— — Sir William de, viii. 420.
— Alicia de, wife of John Fraser of Rig, vii. 424.
— Galfrid de, iv. 222 *n.*, 225 *n.*
Conn of the Hundred Fights, high King of Ireland, v. 27.
Connel, Sir John, viii. 82.
— Madeline, wife of George Carnegie, viii. 82.
Connemara, Robert (Bourke), baron, iii. 107.
— — his wife, Susan Georgiana Ramsay, iii. 107.
Connor of Ballybricken, Daniel, v. 316.
— Katharine, wife of Sir F. L. Maitland of Lindores, v. 316.
Conolly of Castletown, Thomas, v. 365.
— — his wife, Louisa Augusta Lennox, v. 365.
CONSTABLE, CONSTABLE, LORD, iii. 296-300.
Constable, Henry, first lord, iii. 296.
CONSTABLE, LORD CONSTABLE, iii. 296-300.

* Name unknown.

CONSTABLE, VISCOUNT DUNBAR, iii. 290-300.
Constable of Benningholme, Matthew, iii. 297.
—— of Bentley, Sir Ralph, iii. 292.
—— —— his wife, Jane Radcliffe, iii. 292.
—— of Burton Constable, Sir Henry, sheriff of Yorkshire, iii. 294, 295.
—— —— his wife, Margaret Dormer, iii. 295.
—— —— Sir Henry, iii. 296.
—— —— his wife, Mary Tufton, iii. 297.
—— —— Sir John, sheriff of Yorkshire, iii. 290.
—— —— his 1st wife, Agnes Metham, iii. 290.
—— —— his 2nd wife, Anne Strickland, iii. 291.
—— —— Sir John, iii. 290, 293.
—— —— his wife, Joan Neville, iii. 293.
—— —— Sir John, iii. 293, 294.
—— —— his 1st wife, Margaret Scrope, iii. 294.
—— —— his 2nd wife, Katharine Nevill, iii. 295.
—— —— Ralph, iii. 290.
—— —— his 1st wife, Anne Eure, iii. 290.
—— of Charterhouse, Ralph, iii. 291.
—— of Easington, Kilnsea and Bentley, Sir Ralph, iii. 292.
—— —— Robert, iii. 292.
—— —— Robert, iii. 292.
—— —— William, iii. 292.
—— of Everingham, Sir Marmaduke, 4th bart., iv. 418.
—— —— Sir Robert, iii. 294.
—— of Flamborough, Sir Robert, iii. 290.
—— —— Sir William, bart., iii. 597.
—— of Halsham, Sir Henry, iii. 294, 295.
—— of Holderness, Sir John, iii. 290.
—— of Keyingham, Gabriel, iii. 292.
—— of Kirkby Knowle, Sir John, iii. 294.
—— —— his wife, Elizabeth *or* Margaret Cresswell, iii. 294.
—— of Manor House, Otley, Thomas Angus, iv. 418; ix. 106.
—— —— his wife, Elizabeth Ducarel, iv. 418.
—— of Newbuilding, John, iii. 294.
—— of Newton Garth, Michael, iii. 291.
—— —— his wife, Jane Throckmorton, iii. 291.
—— of North Park, Elizabeth, wife of Robert Dalton, iii. 293.
—— —— Frances, dau. of Ralph C., iii. 293.
—— —— Joan, wife of John Eastoft, iii. 293.
—— —— Ralph, iii. 293.
—— of St. Sepulchre's, George, iii. 291.
—— —— Henry, iii. 291.
—— —— Michael, son of Ralph C., iii. 291, 292.
—— —— Michael, son of Henry C., iii. 291.
—— —— Michael, son of Michael C., iii. 291.
—— —— Ralph, iii. 290.
Constable of Upsall, Joseph, chief-steward of Holderness, iii. 294.
—— of Wallace Craigie, William Browne, ii. 279.
—— —— his wife, Mary Margaret Erskine, ii. 279.
—— of Woodhouse Grange, Ralph, iii. 291.
—— Anne, wife of William Haggerston, iv. 418.
—— Anne, dau. of Michael C., iii. 291.
—— Anne, wife of Matthew Parker, iii. 292.
—— Anne, wife of John Lounde, iii. 292.
—— Anne, wife of Brian Palmes, iii. 293.
—— Anne, wife of Robert Apprice, iii. 294.
—— Anne, wife of Simon Scrope of Danby, iii. 297.
—— Averilla, wife of Thos. Smith, iii. 294.
—— Brian, 6th son of Sir John C., iii. 292.
—— Cicely, wife of Francis Tunstall, iii. 298.
—— Dorothy, wife of Roger Lawson, iii. 296.
—— Eleanor, wife of Thos. Alured, iii. 291.
—— Elizabeth, wife of Sir Thos. Metham, iii. 290.
—— Elizabeth, wife of * Foster, iii. 292.
—— Elizabeth, wife of Christopher Frothingham, iii. 293.
—— Elizabeth, wife of Gabriel Dayles, iii. 294.
—— Everilda, wife of Thomas Crathorne, iii. 294.
—— Everilda, wife of Thos. Smith, iii. 294.
—— Everilda, dau. of John C., iii. 294 *n.*
—— Frances, wife of Sir C. Hildyard, iii. 293.
—— Francis, 5th son of Sir John C., iii. 292.
—— George, the Minories, iii. 295 *n.*
—— Henry, 3rd son of 1st viscount Dunbar, iii. 297.
—— Jane, wife of Thos. Thornton, iii. 291.
—— Jane, dau. of Sir John C., iii. 292.
—— John, 3rd son of Sir John C., iii. 294.
—— John, eldest son of 2nd viscount Dunbar, iii. 298.
—— Joseph, officer in service of Charles I., iii. 294.
—— Joseph, alleged son of John C. of Newbuilding, iii. 294 *n.*
—— Katharine, abbess of Benedictine abbey, Teignmouth, iv. 418.
—— Katharine, dau. of Michael C., iii. 292.
—— Katharine, wife of Henry Stevenson, iii. 292.
—— Katharine, wife of Sir Ralph Ellerker, iii. 292.
—— Katharine, wife of Francis Hunt, iii. 294.
—— Katharine, wife of Sir Thomas Fairfax, iii. 295.

* Name unknown.

Constable, Katharine, wife of William Middleton, iii. 297.
— Katharine, wife of John More, iii. 298.
— Margaret, dau. of Ralph C., iii. 293.
— Margaret, wife of Sir Edward Stanhope, iii. 296.
— Margaret, dau. of Sir Henry C., iii. 297.
— Margery, wife of Brian Stapleton, iii. 292.
— Mary, dau. of Charles Stanley-C., iv. 418.
— Mary, wife of 24th lord Mowbray and Stourton, iv. 418.
— Mary, wife of Leonard Robinson, iii. 291.
— Mary, wife of William Tocketts, iii. 294.
— Mary, wife of Sir Thos. Blakiston, iii. 296.
— Mary, wife of Robert, lord Brudenell, iii. 296.
— Mary, dau. of 2nd viscount Dunbar, iii. 298.
— Mrs., wife of (1) * Constable, and (2) Colin Campbell of Glenfalloch, ii. 192.
— Ralph, son of Gabriel C. of Keyingham, iii. 292.
— Ralph, 4th son of Sir John C., iii. 294.
— Robert, an English spy, v. 64.
— William, 3rd son of Sir John C., iii. 292.
CONSTABLE-MAXWELL, LORD HERRIES OF TERREGLES, iv. 420-424.
CONSTABLE-MAXWELL, LORD HERRIES OF CARLAVEROCK CASTLE, AND EVERINGHAM, iv. 423-424.
Constable-Maxwell of Everingham, Marmaduke, iv. 419.
— — his wife, Theresa Apollonia Wakeman, iv. 419.
— of Scarthingwell, Henry, iv. 420.
— — his wife, Juliana Middleton, iv. 420.
— of Terregles, Alfred, iv. 419.
— — Frederick, iv. 419.
— — Marmaduke, iv. 419.
— — his wife, Mary Marsden, iv. 419.
— Agatha Mary, wife of Edward Pilkington, iv. 419.
— Alice Clare, wife of P. J. C. Howard, iv. 419.
— Angela Mary, wife of James Eric Drummond, iv. 423; viii. 237.
— Bernard, iv. 422.
— — his 1st wife, Mathilda Jessup, iv. 422.
— — his 2nd wife, Alice Mary Charlotte Fraser, iv. 422; v. 548.

* Name unknown.

Constable-Maxwell, Charles, 3rd son of Wm. Haggerston-Maxwell-Constable, iv. 418.
— — his 1st wife, Elizabeth Stanley, iv. 418.
— — his 2nd wife, Mary Macdonald, iv. 418.
— David Philip, iv. 422.
— Eleanor Mary, iv. 423.
— Emily Josephine, iv. 423.
— Everilda, iv. 423.
— Gerald Joseph, iv. 422.
— Gwendoline, iv. 423.
— Gwendoline Mary, wife of 15th duke of Norfolk, iv. 423.
— Helena Mary Teresa, iv. 419.
— Ian Simon Joseph, iv. 422.
— Joan, iv. 422.
— John, 6th son of 10th lord Herries of Terregles, iv. 423.
— Joseph, in holy orders, iv. 420.
— Marcia, iv. 423.
— Margaret Mary Ethelreda, iv. 422.
— Mary, wife of Charles Langdale of Houghton, iv. 420.
— Mary Agnes, iv. 423.
— Mary Philomena, iv. 422.
— Peter, iv. 419.
— — his wife, Helena M. Bowdon, iv. 419.
— Peter, iv. 423.
— Robert, iv. 419.
— Ronald Joseph Tarlagan, iv. 422.
— Teresa, iv. 423.
— Theresa, wife of Charles Clifford, iv. 420.
— Walter, 5th son of 10th lord Herries of Terregles, iv. 422.
— his wife, H. M. A. Herbert, iv. 423.
— Wilfrid, iv. 419.
— William, 2nd son of 10th lord Herries of Terregles, iv. 422.
— Winifred, iv. 423.
— Winifrede Mary, iv. 422.
Constable-Maxwell-Scott of Abbotsford, Joseph, iv. 422.
— Alice Mary Josephine, wife of E. Cassidy, iv. 422.
— Herbert Francis Joseph, iv. 422.
— Joseph Michael, R.N., iv. 422.
— Malcolm Joseph, R.N., iv. 422.
— Margaret Mary Lucy, iv. 422.
— Mary Josephine, wife of A. A. Dalgleish, iv. 422.
— — Walter Joseph, captain, iv. 422.
Constable-Maxwell-Stuart of Terregles and Traquair, Henry, iv. 420.
— — his wife, Juliana Middleton, iv. 420.
— — Herbert, iv. 420.
— Edmund, iv. 420.
— — his wife, Mary Anne Constable-Maxwell, iv. 420, 422.

Constantia, wife of Adam Fraser of Hailes, vii. 419.
Constantine of Goswyck, i. 421 *n.*
—— nephew of Henry, 3rd earl of Atholl, i. 418, 419 *n.*
—— abbot of Newbattle, iii. 88.
—— 2nd son of Waldeve, 4th earl of Dunbar, iii. 252.
Convall, son of Duncan of Tullibardine, i. 419.
Conway, Edward (Conway), 1st earl, i. 137.
—— and Killultagh, Edward (Conway), 2nd viscount, iii. 296 *n.*
—— Anne Seymour, wife of George Damer, i. 386; ix. 25.
—— Henry Seymour, field-marshal, i. 385.
Conyers of Horden, Sir Baldwyn, bart., viii. 408.
—— Theresa, wife of 5th earl of Traquair, viii. 408.
Conyngham, Henry (Conyngham), 1st marquess, iv. 560.
—— of Auchenharvie, Adam, v. 168; ix. 119.
—— Elizabeth, wife of (1) Thos. Boyd of Pitcon, and (2) Mr. Andrew Boyd, v. 168; ix. 119.
—— *See also* Cunningham.
Cook, Edwin Adolphus, major 11th Hussars, v. 368.
—— —— his wife, M. A. Palmer, v. 368.
—— James, Rampore, iii. 105.
—— Rachel, wife of Andrew Ramsay, iii. 105.
—— *, lieut. R.N., vi. 396.
—— —— his wife, Mary Nairn, vi. 396.
Cooke, Charles Edward Stephen, major, iv. 172.
—— —— his wife, Mary Louisa Stewart, iv. 172.
—— Thomas Ivie, major, i. 494.
—— —— his wife, Amelia Murray, i. 494.
Cooksey, John, v. 634.
—— Mary Anne, wife of Henry David Erskine, v. 634.
Cooper, Sir Alfred, F.R.C.S., v. 237.
—— —— his wife, A. C. E. Duff, v. 237.
—— Amelia Charlotte, dau. of Thomas C., i. 478 *n.*
—— Henrietta Maria, dau. of Thomas C., i. 478 *n.*
—— Margaret, wife of Alex. Maitland, v. 312.
—— Thomas, London, i. 477.
—— —— his wife, Charlotte Murray, i. 477.
Cope of Brewerne, Sir Charles, 2nd bart., iv. 559.
—— —— Katharine Anne, wife of 9th marquess of Huntly, iv. 559.
—— of Canon's Ashby, Sir Edward, i. 405.
—— —— his wife, Katharine Aston, i. 405.
—— Isabel, wife of Henry (Rich), 1st earl of Holland, ii. 205.

* Name unknown.

Cope, Sir John, general, v. 509.
—— Sir Walter, Kensington, ii. 205.
Copley of Sprotborough, Sir Joseph, bart., i. 66.
—— —— his wife, Mary Buller, i. 66.
—— —— Sir Joseph, colonel, bart., i. 64.
—— —— his wife, Cecil Hamilton, i. 64.
—— Katharine, wife of 1st marquess of Abercorn, i. 66.
Corbet of Fogo, Patrick, iii. 254; vii. 365.
—— of Hardgray, John, ii. 381.
—— of Langton, Nicholas, iii. 254.
—— of Makerston, Cristina, wife of William, son of Patrick, 5th earl of Dunbar, i. 274; iii. 254; iv. 7.
—— —— Nicholas, iii. 254.
—— —— Patrick, iii. 254.
—— —— Walter, i. 274; iii. 254; iv. 8.
—— of Moreton Corbet, Sir Robert, iii. 607.
—— of Tolcross, James, vii. 80.
—— —— his wife, Margaret Scott. vii. 80.
—— —— John, ii. 104.
—— Aliz, wife of Duncan, son of Duncan, 5th earl of Fife, iv. 8.
—— Andrew, captain, ii. 305.
—— —— his wife, Augusta Stuart, ii. 305.
—— Anne, wife of Sir A. Cary, iii. 609.
—— Ariana, wife of P. Borthwick, ii. 104.
—— Matilda, wife of Philip de Seton, viii. 561.
—— Sybilla, mistress of King Henry I. of England, i. 3.
—— Walter, 3rd son of William and Christina C. of Makerstoun, iii. 254.
Corbett, Cunningham, Glasgow, ii. 104.
—— Nathaniel Gordon, R.N., ii. 105.
—— —— his wife, Margaret Borthwick, ii. 105.
Core, 9th son of Alwin, 2nd earl of Lennox, v. 330.
Corehouse, George Cranstoun, advocate, lord, ii. 598.
Cormac, abbot of Turriff, ii. 251.
Cornell of Correnden and Hazel Hall, John, ii. 419.
—— Jane, wife of (1) Major A. Morrison, and (2) col. R. A. G. Dalzell, ii. 419.
Cornewall, rev. F. H. W., bishop of Worcester, i. 64.
—— —— his wife, Anne Hamilton, i. 64.
Cornhill, Juliana de, wife of Henry of Brechin, ii. 216.
—— Ralf de, ii. 216.
Cornwall, Charles, inf. son of King Charles I.; duke of, i. 28.
—— of Bonhard, John, 3rd laird, vi. 156.
—— —— his 2nd wife, Margaret Moubray, vi. 157.
—— —— John, colonel, 8th laird, vi. 591; ix. 121.
—— —— his wife, Margaret Houston, ix. 120
—— —— Nicholas, vii. 74.

Cornwall of Moccas Court, Sir George, i. 92.
— of Printadocis, Nicholas, vii. 74.
— Caroline, wife of Sir Wm. Duff-Gordon, M.P., i. 92.
— Margaret, wife of Hugh Makgill of Grange, vi. 591.
Cornwallis, Charles (Cornwallis), 3rd baron, ii. 239.
— — his wife, Anna, duchess of Buccleuch, ii. 237.
— Charles (Cornwallis) 2nd marquess, iv. 557.
— — his wife, Louisa Gordon, iv. 557.
— of Brome, Sir William, i. 350.
— — his wife, Lucy Nevill, i. 350.
— Anne, wife of 7th earl of Argyll, i. 350; v. 22; ix. 22.
Corona, Teresa, wife of Jacobo Errico de Bove Stuardo, i. 30*n*.
Corrie, Joseph, Dumfries, iv. 495.
— Sophia, wife of William Hope-Weir, iv. 495.
Corry, Hugh of, i. 231.
— of Newbie, Herbert, i. 222.
— — his wife, Esota Murray, i. 222.
Corsby of Ulcottis, Robert, ii. 387.
Corse-Scott of Synton, Francis, ancestor of the family of, vii. 75.
Corser of the Hyde, Haden, vii. 310.
— of New Place, William Blacklock Haden, vii. 310.
— — his wife, Georgina Leslie, vii. 310.
CORSTORPHINE, FORRESTER, LORD FORRESTER OF, iv. 80-100.
Corstorphine of Balcaithly, James, v. 414.
— of Nydie, James, v. 414.
— — his wife, Elizabeth Lindsay, v. 414.
— Martin, v. 414.
— — his wife, Eupham Arnot, v. 414.
— William, Kingsbarns, v. 405.
— — his wife, Margaret Lindsay, v. 405.
Cospatric, 'brother of Dolfin'; second earl of Dunbar, iii. 241, 246.
Cossins of Cossins, Thomas, viii. 276.
Costelloe of Lackeen Castle, vii. 226.
— Jessie Katharine, wife of G. E. Primrose, vii. 226.
Cotes of Cotes and Woodcote, John, viii. 37.
— Mary, wife of Wriothesley Digby of Meriden, viii. 37.
Cotterell of Garnons, Sir John Richard Geers, 4th bart., v. 370.
— — his wife, Evelyn Amy Gordon-Lennox, v. 370.
Cotton, Sir Robert Salusbury, bart., M.P., iii. 406.
— — his wife, Elizabeth Tollemache, iii. 406.
Coucy, Alice de, wife of Arnold III., count of Guignes, iii. 5.
— Marie de, wife of King Alexander II., i. 6.
Coucy, Iolande de, wife of Robert, Comte de Dreux, vi. 564.
— Enguerrand III., sire de, iii. 5.
— Ingelram de Guignes, sire de, iii. 5.
— — his wife, Christian de Lindsay, iii. 5.
COUPAR, ELPHINSTONE, LORD, ii. 576-577.
Coupar, Arthur, fifth lord, i. 570, 571.
— James, first lord, i. 122, 562; ii. 576.
— — his 1st wife, Margaret Haliburton, ii. 577.
— — his 2nd wife, Marion Ogilvy, i. 126; ii. 577.
— James, fourth lord, i. 570; iv. 116.
— John, second lord, i. 568.
— John, third lord, i. 569.
— Margaret, wife of (1) John Maclellan of Borgue, and (2) John MacCulloch of Ardwall, v. 264, 266.
— William, bishop of Galloway, i. 471; v. 264.
Coupland, Harriet, wife of admiral J. A. Murray, i. 493.
— John de, v. 596; vii. 316.
— William, Shrewsbury, i. 493.
Courtenay, Anthony Lefroy, D.D., i. 525.
— — his wife, Elizabeth Pringle Lindsay, i. 525.
— Sir Piers, ii. 397.
— William, ii. 301.
— — his wife, Jean Stuart, ii. 301.
Courtown, James George (Stopford), 3rd earl of, ii. 243.
— — his wife, Mary Scott, ii. 243.
— James Thomas, 4th earl of, ii. 244.
— — his wife, Charlotte Albinia Scott, ii. 244.
COUSLAND, MAKGILL, LORD MAKGILL OF, vi. 596-601.
COUSLAND, DALRYMPLE, BARON OXENFOORD OF, viii. 159-164.
Cousland, Beatrix (Ruthven), widow of Sir John Home of Cowdenknowes; styled lady, iv. 266.
Coussmaker of Dane Court, Evert George, i. 526.
— Katharine Eliza, wife of bishop Lindsay, i. 526.
Coustoun, Alexander, burgess of Culross, vii. 214.
— — his wife, Katharine Primrose, vii. 214.
— Robert, Culross, vii. 214, 215.
— — his wife, Marion *or* Marjory Primrose, vii. 215.
Coutts of Bowhill, Alan, iii. 119.
— of Grange, Allan, iv. 428, 430.
— — his wife, Isobel Bothwell, iv. 428.
— of Rossyth, Alan, iii. 120.
— Alan, chamberlain of Dumfermline, viii. 168.
— — his wife, Marjory Walwood, viii. 168.

Coutts, Elizabeth, wife of Wm. Alexander Menstrie, viii. 168.
— Frances, wife of 1st marquess of Bute, ii. 306.
— George, saddler, Maybole, vi. 411.
— — his wife, Katharine Napier, vi. 411.
— Helen, wife of Richard Preston of Whitehill, iii. 119.
— Janet, wife of David Carmichael of Balmedie, iv. 568.
— Margaret, wife of Francis Bothwell, iv. 430.
— Peter, merchant, Edinburgh, iv. 568.
— Thomas, banker, ii. 306.
Coventry of Greenlands, Thomas Darby, iv. 389.
— Emma Catherine Frances, wife of col. F. S. Douglas-Hamilton, iv. 389.
Covington, Alexander Lockhart, senator of the College of Justice, lord, iii. 581.
COWAL, CAMPBELL, EARL OF, i. 369-393.
Cowal, Archibald, first earl of, i. 369.
Cowal, Maurice, viii. 379.
Cowane of Tailzartoun, John, provost of Stirling, vi. 238.
— Marie, wife of Sir William Graham of Braco, vi. 238.
— Walter, Stirling, viii. 170 *n.*
— — his wife, Janet Alexander, viii. 170 *n.*
Coward, Bridget, wife of George Hamilton, M.P., i. 60.
— William, col., i. 60.
Cowley, William (Cowley), 2nd earl, viii. 512.
— Eva Cecelia, wife of R. G. Erskine-Wemyss, viii. 512.
COWPER, LORD DINGWALL, iii. 123-124.
Cowper, Francis Thomas de Gray, (Cowper), 7th earl, iii. 124.
— George Augustus, 4th earl, iii. 123.
— George Augustus Frederick, 6th earl, iii. 124; v. 485.
— George Nassau, 3rd earl, iii. 123.
— Peter Leopold Louis Francis Nassau, 5th earl, iii. 123.
— — his wife, Emily Mary Lambe, iii. 123.
— William, 2nd earl, iii. 123.
— — his 1st wife, Henrietta de Nassau, iii. 123.
— Adine Eliza Anne, wife of J. H. C. Fane, iii. 124.
— Amabell, wife of lord W. T. Kerr, iii. 124.
— Florence Amabell, wife of A. E. W. M. Herbert, iii. 124.
— Henrietta Emily Mary, iii. 124.
— Henry Frederick, M.P., iii. 124.
Cowran, Cosmus de, iii. 335.
Cowse, Kenton, i. 61.
— — his wife, * Hamilton, i. 61.
* Name unknown.

Cox of Castletown, Katharine, wife of capt. W. Villiers-Stuart, ii. 307.
— Michael, ii. 307.
— of Stanford Vale, Joseph, vii. 482.
— — his wife, Katharine Sophia Sheffield, vii. 482.
— of the Wings, Henry Hill, viii. 467.
— Anne, wife of 3rd viscount of Preston, vii. 108.
— Charlotte, wife of A. R. Hamilton, ii. 57.
— John, merchant, London, vii. 108.
— Katharine Sophia, wife of lieut.-gen. Francis Grant, vii. 482.
— Mary, wife of 3rd earl of Peterborough, vii. 108.
— Mary Catharine, wife of (1) James Gordon Hay, and (2) Edward Magee, viii. 467.
— Thomas, Aldersgate St., London, vii. 108.
— *, v. 629.
— — his wife, Jean Erskine, v. 629.
Crackenthorp, Christopher, Westmoreland, i. 545.
— — his wife, Dorothy Sandfoord, i. 545.
Cradock of Swansea, Sir Matthew, iv. 531.
— — his wife, Katharine Gordon, iv. 530.
Craggs, Harriet, wife of (1) R. Eliot of Port Eliot, and (2) John Hamilton, capt. R.N., i. 63; ix. 3.
— James, secretary of state, i. 63.
Craggs-Eliot, Edward, i. 63.
Craig of Balnely, John, iv. 54; viii. 280.
— — Thomas, iv. 54; viii. 280.
— — his wife, Elizabeth Lyon, iv. 54.
— of Craig Fintray *or* Craigston, Alexander, iv. 54.
— of Riccarton, James, advocate, professor of Civil Law, v. 545.
— — his wife, Marion Fraser, v. 544.
— — Thomas, ii. 594.
— — his wife, Elizabeth Cranstoun, ii. 594.
— — Thomas, iv. 591.
— Alexander, ix. 21.
— Helen, wife of William Carmichael of Skirling, iv. 591.
— Janet, wife of John Sandilands, i. 75.
— Janet, wife of David Makgill of Rankeillor, vi. 589.
— John, advocate, vi. 589.
— — his wife, Jean Heriot of Ramornie, vi. 589.
— Mariota de, wife of * Watson, v. 282.
— Robert, i. 75; ix. 38.
— — his wife, Katharine Bellenden, ii. 65 *n.*; ix. 38.
— Sir Thomas, the jurist, i. 75; ii. 65.
* Name unknown.

Craigengelt of Craigengelt, John, provost of Stirling, vi. 447.
Craighall, Sir John Hope of Craighall, 2nd bart., lord of Session, lord, iv. 489.
Craigie of Dunbarnie, John, v. 415.
—— —— his wife, Mary Lindsay, v. 415.
—— of Gairsay, Sir William, ii. 40.
—— —— his wife, Anne Hamilton, ii. 40.
—— —— William, ii. 442.
—— —— his wife, * Stewart, ii. 442.
—— of Hawhill, Charles Hackett, v. 410.
—— of Hupe, James, vi. 569.
—— —— his wife, Margaret Sinclair, vi. 569.
—— of Merchamstoun, John de, iii. 55; vi. 474.
—— Emily Jeanette, wife of (1) J. W. M. Lyte, and (2) F. C. Maitland, v. 314.
—— John, colonel, v. 314.
—— Margaret, wife of (1) John Stewart, and (2) Sir Herbert Maxwell, vi. 474.
—— Margaret Maria, wife of lieut.-col. John Lindsay, v. 410.
—— Thomas de, iv. 340 *n.*
—— Thomas, professor at St. Andrews, ix. 132.
Craik, William, iii. 94.
—— —— his wife, Janet Fleming, iii. 94.
Craill of Stewartoun, John, vii. 148.
—— —— his wife, Sophia Douglas, vii. 148.
Cral, J. D., viii. 139.
—— —— his wife, Elizabeth Rosina Dalrymple, viii. 139.
CRAMOND, BEAUMONT, BARONESS OF, ii. 578.
Cramond, Elizabeth, wife of (1) Sir J. Ashburnham, and (2) Sir T. Richardson; baroness of, ii. 578.
CRAMOND, RICHARDSON, LORD, ii. 578-584.
Cramond, Henry, third lord, ii. 583.
—— —— his wife, Frances Napier, ii. 583.
—— Thomas, second lord, ii. 581, 582, 584 *n.*
—— —— his wife, Anne Gurney, ii. 582.
—— William, fourth lord, ii. 583.
—— —— his 1st wife, Elizabeth Barkham, ii. 583.
—— —— his 2nd wife, Elizabeth Daniel, ii. 583.
—— William, fifth lord, ii. 584.
—— master of, Sir Thomas Richardson, ii. 580.
—— —— his 1st wife, Elizabeth Hewett, ii. 581.
—— —— his 2nd wife, Mary Hanbury, ii. 581.
—— of Aldbar, William, viii. 48.
—— —— his wife, * de Kinnaird, viii. 48.
—— —— vii. 9.
—— Katharine, wife of (1) Sir Thos. Maule of Panmure, and (2) Robert Keith, vii. 9.
Cranach, John de, bishop of Brechin, viii. 49.

* Name unknown.

Cranborne, Charles (Cecil), son of 2nd earl of Salisbury; styled viscount, iii. 129, 130; v. 228.
—— —— his wife, Diana Maxwell, iii. 130.
Cranbrook, Gathorne (Gathorne-Hardy), 1st earl, iv. 221.
Crane, Henry, iii. 609.
CRANSTOUN, CRANSTOUN, LORD, ii. 585-602.
Cranstoun, Charles Frederick, eleventh lord, ii. 602.
—— James, fourth lord, ii. 597.
—— —— his wife, Anne Don, ii. 597.
—— James, sixth lord, ii. 597, 599.
—— —— his wife, Sophia Brown, ii. 599.
—— James, eighth lord, ii. 599, 600.
—— —— his wife, Elizabeth Montolieu, ii. 600.
—— James Edmund, ninth lord, ii. 599, 600.
—— —— his wife, Anne Linnington Macnamara, ii. 601.
—— James Edward, tenth lord, ii. 601.
—— —— his wife, Elizabeth Scale, ii. 601.
—— John, second lord, ii. 594.
—— —— his 1st wife, Elizabeth Scott, ii. 233, 595.
—— —— his 2nd wife, Helen Lindsay, ii. 595; v. 401.
—— William, first lord, ii. 593.
—— —— his wife, Sarah Cranstoun, ii. 592.
—— William, third lord, ii. 595; iii. 314; v. 533.
—— —— his wife, Mary Leslie, ii. 596; v 379.
—— William, fifth lord, ii. 597.
—— —— his wife, Jean Ker, ii. 597; v. 479.
—— William, seventh lord, ii. 600.
—— master of, James, 2nd son of 1st lord C., ii. 593.
—— —— his 1st wife, Elizabeth Makgill, ii. 593; vi. 595.
—— —— his 2nd wife, Elizabeth Stewart, ii. 172, 594.
CRANSTOUN, LORD CRANSTOUN, ii. 585-602.
Cranston of Corsbie, George, iv. 471.
—— —— his wife, Isobel Home, iv. 471.
—— —— John, iv. 471.
—— —— Patrick, iv. 477.
—— —— his wife, Marion Home, iv. 477.
—— —— Thomas, vi. 9.
—— —— his wife, Elizabeth Hume, vi. 9.
—— of Crailing, William, ii. 588.
—— of Cranston, Andrew de, ii. 585.
—— —— Elfric de, ii. 585.
—— —— John de, son of Ralph de C., ii. 586.
—— —— John de, nephew of Sir Thomas de C., ii. 589; iii. 501.
—— —— John, ii. 590.
—— —— his wife, Janet Scott, ii. 230, 590.
—— —— Sir John, ii. 591.
—— —— his wife, Margaret Ramsay, ii. 591; iii. 96.

Cranston of Cranston, Ralph de, ii. 586.
—— —— Sarah, wife of William, 1st lord Cranstoun, ii. 592.
—— —— Thomas de, ii. 586.
—— —— Sir Thomas, ii. 587 ; iv. 257.
—— —— Sir William, son of Thos. de C., ii. 587 ; ix. 60.
—— —— Sir William, ii. 589.
—— —— his wife, Margaret Hume, ii. 590.
—— —— Sir William, ii. 590.
—— —— his wife, * Johnston, ii. 590.
—— of Cranstoundaw, William, ix. 60.
—— of Denholm, John, ii. 589.
—— —— John, ii. 590.
—— —— his wife, Janet Scott, ii. 230, 590.
—— —— Sir John, ii. 591.
—— —— his wife, Margaret Ramsay, ii. 592 ; iii. 96.
—— —— Thomas, ii. 586 ; ix. 59.
—— —— Sir Thomas, ii. 587.
—— —— Sir William, ii. 587.
—— —— William, eldest son of Sir Thomas C., ii. 588.
—— of Elburne, Thomas, ii. 590 ; vi. 592.
—— —— his wife, Helen Makgill, vi. 592.
—— of Glenraith, Alexander, ii. 591.
—— of Howford, John, ii. 589.
—— —— his wife, Agnes Quhitlaw, ii. 589.
—— of Kirkhope, Sir John, vii. 74.
—— of Lyleston, William, ii. 592.
—— of Morriestoun, John, ii. 592.
—— —— Sir John, iv. 285.
—— —— his wife, Barbara Gray, iv. 285.
—— of Newcranston, Andrew de, iii. 54.
—— —— Radulph de, iii. 54.
—— —— Thomas, ii. 586 ; ix. 59.
—— —— William, ix. 60.
—— of Smailholm, John, ii. 589.
—— —— John, ii. 592.
—— —— his wife, Margaret Ramsay, ii. 593.
—— —— Sir John, vii. 74.
—— of Sprouston, John, ii. 586.
—— —— Sir John, ii. 591.
—— of Thirlestanemains, Cuthbert, ii. 592.
—— of Whitehope, William, ix. 60.
—— of Woolie, William, ii. 592.
—— Agnes, dau. of 1st lord Cranstoun, ii. 594.
—— Agnes, dau. of 3rd lord Cranstoun, ii. 597.
—— Alexander, 2nd son of 3rd lord Cranstoun, ii. 597.
—— Alexander, 2nd son of 4th lord Cranstoun, ii. 597.
—— Alexander, in Leith, iv. 125.
—— —— his wife, Elizabeth Crichton, iv. 125.
—— Andrew, 5th son of Sir Wm. C., ii. 591.
—— Anna Caroline, ii. 601.
—— Anne, wife of Gabriel Selby, ii. 598.

* Name unknown.

Cranston, Barbara, wife of John Seton of Touch, ii. 594.
—— Barbara, dau. of 3rd lord Cranstoun, ii. 597.
—— Brown, 2nd son of 6th lord Cranstoun, ii. 599.
—— Charles, 6th son of 5th lord Cranstoun, ii. 598.
—— Charles, 4th son of 6th lord Cranstoun, ii. 599.
—— —— his wife, Elizabeth Turner, ii. 599.
—— Charlotte, dau. of 6th lord Cranstoun, ii. 600.
—— Christian, dau. of 3rd lord Cranstoun, ii. 597 ; ix. 170.
—— Eliza Linnington, wife of R. Ford, ii. 601.
—— Elizabeth, wife of Wm. Douglas, ii. 592.
—— Elizabeth, wife of Thos. Craig of Riccarton, ii. 594 ; ix. 60.
—— Elizabeth, wife of John Edgar, ii. 594.
—— Elizabeth, dau. of 3rd lord Cranstoun, ii. 597.
—— Elizabeth, dau. of 5th lord Cranstoun, ii. 599.
—— Elizabeth, dau. of 6th lord Cranstoun, ii. 600.
—— George, 6th son of Sir Wm. C., ii. 591.
—— George, 7th son of 5th lord Cranstoun, ii. 598.
—— —— his wife, Maria Brisbane, ii. 598.
—— George, advocate, lord Corehouse, ii. 598.
—— George, colonel, 5th son of 6th lord Cranstoun, ii. 599.
—— Harie, factor to 3rd lord C., ii. 595.
—— Helen, wife of Mungo Rig, ii. 592.
—— Helen, dau. of 3rd lord Cranstoun, ii. 597.
—— Helen d'Arcy, wife of Prof. Dugald Stewart, ii. 598.
—— Henry, colonel of horse, ii. 594, 595.
—— —— his wife, Margaret Wauchope, ii. 594.
—— Henry Kerr, Navy Pay Office, ii. 598.
—— —— his 1st wife, Christina Smart, ii. 598.
—— —— his 2nd wife, Mary Ann Whitefoord, ii. 598.
—— Isobel, wife of Sir G. Elliot of Stobs, ii. 594.
—— James, 2nd son of Sir Thomas de C., ii. 588.
—— James, 2nd son of Sir Wm. C., ii. 590.
—— Jane Anne, wife of Wenceslaus, Gottfried, count of Purgstall, ii. 598.
—— Janet, wife of John Knowis, ii. 590.
—— Janet, wife of John Seton of Touch, ii. 594.
—— Jean, wife of Thomas Rutherford of Hunthill, ii. 592 ; vii. 378.
—— Jean, dau. of 5th lord Cranstoun, ii. 599.

Cranston, John, illeg. son of John C. of that Ilk, ii. 590.
—— John, eldest son of Sir John C. of that Ilk, ii. 592.
—— John, factor to 3rd lord Cranstoun, ii. 595.
—— Katharine, wife of W. Sandilands, ix. 4.
—— Margaret, wife of Sir R. Scott of Thirlestane, ii. 591; vi. 430.
—— Margaret, wife of * Douglas, ii. 592.
—— Margaret, wife of * Cockburn of Clerkington, ii. 594.
—— Margaret, dau. of 3rd lord Cranstoun, ii. 597.
—— Margaret Nicolson, wife of Wm. Cunningham, ii. 598.
—— Marion, wife of (1) R. Scott, and (2) John Hume, ii. 591.
—— Mary, dau. of 3rd lord Cranstoun, ii. 597.
—— Mary, wife of Archibald Megget, ii. 599.
—— Pauline Emily, dau. of 10th lord Cranstoun, ii. 601.
—— Peter, in Legertwood, iv. 298.
—— Peter, priest, vi. 429; vii. 73.
—— Robert, in Legertwood, iv. 298.
—— —— his wife, Elizabeth *or* Alison Ramsay, iv. 298.
—— Sara, wife of Sir R. Dobie of Stanyhill, ii. 594.
—— Thomas de, ii. 585.
—— Thomas de, Constable of Edinburgh Castle, ii. 588 *n.*; iii. 57.
—— Thomas, in Gowrie conspiracy, ii. 590.
—— Thomas, 4th son of 1st lord Cranston, ii. 594, 595.
—— William, illeg. son of Sir Thomas de C., ii. 589.
—— William Henry, capt., ii. 597; ix. 60.
—— —— his wife, Anne Murray, ii. 597.
—— *, dau. of capt. Wm. Henry C., ii. 597.
—— *, wife of Sir Patrick Ruthven of that Ilk, ii. 589; iv. 257.
—— *, wife of Nicol Rutherfurd of Grubet, vii. 368.
Crathorne of Crathorne, Thomas, iii. 294.
—— Mary, wife of Joseph Constable, iii. 294.
Craven, William (Craven), 2nd earl of, iv. 97.
—— —— his wife, Emily Mary Grimston, iv. 97.
—— of Lenchwick, Sir William, iii. 598.
—— —— his wife, Elizabeth Fairfax, iii. 598.
—— Anne, wife of rev. R. A. Johnson, viii. 159.
—— Isabel Sophie, wife of 7th duke of Lennox, v. 370.
—— William George, v. 370.

* Name unknown.

Craw of Falabank, William, ii. 169.
—— John, tutor to the sons of Alexander, duke of Albany, i. 152.
CRAWFORD, LINDSAY, EARL OF, iii. 1-51.
Crawford, Alexander, second earl of, iii. 17; iv. 271; vii. 7.
—— —— his wife, Marjory, iii. 18.
—— Alexander, fourth earl of, iii. 18, 21, 177; iv. 48, 348; v. 45; viii. 47, 49.
—— —— his wife, Margaret Dunbar, iii. 21.
—— Alexander, seventh earl of, iii. 21, 24.
—— —— his wife, Isobel Campbell, iii. 25.
—— Alexander, fifteenth earl of, iii. 34.
—— Alexander, twenty-third earl of, i. 523; iii. 42.
—— —— his wife, Elizabeth Dalrymple, iii. 42; viii. 131.
—— Alexander William, twenty-fifth earl of, iii. 47.
—— —— his wife, Margaret Lindsay, iii. 48.
—— David, first earl of, i. 108; iii. 13, 15; v. 601, 604.
—— —— his wife, Elizabeth Stewart, i. 16; iii. 15; ix. 61.
—— David, third earl of, iii. 18, 192.
—— —— his wife, Marjory Ogilvy, iii. 18.
—— David, fifth earl of, i. 280; ii. 324; iii. 22; iv. 18, 48, 276, 348.
—— —— his 1st wife, Elizabeth Hamilton, iii. 23; iv. 351, 353.
—— —— his 2nd wife, Margaret Carmichael, iii. 23, 25.
—— David, eighth earl of, iii. 25.
—— —— his 1st wife, Elizabeth Hay, iii. 26, 567.
—— —— his 2nd wife, Katharine Stirling, iii. 27.
—— —— his 3rd wife, Isobel Lundy, iii. 27.
—— David, ninth earl of, iii. 19, 25, 27.
—— —— his 1st wife, Jonet Gray, iii. 28; iv. 275.
—— —— his 2nd wife, Katharine Campbell, i. 118; iii. 28.
—— David, tenth earl of, iii. 29.
—— —— his wife, Margaret Beaton, iii. 29.
—— David, eleventh earl of, i. 85; iii. 30, 594; viii. 290; ix. 32.
—— —— his 1st wife, Lilias Drummond, iii. 31; vii. 47.
—— —— his 2nd wife, Grizel Stewart, i. 445; iii. 31.
—— David, twelfth earl of, iii. 31; viii. 102; ix. 61.
—— —— his wife, Jean Ker, iii. 32; v. 457.
—— George, fourteenth earl of, iii. 33; viii. 103.
—— —— his wife, Elizabeth Sinclair, iii. 34.
—— George, twenty-first earl of, iii. 40.
—— —— his wife, Jean Hamilton, iii. 40.
—— George, twenty-second earl of, iii. 41; v. 402, 407.

Crawford, Henry, thirteenth earl of, iii. 29, 32; ix. 62.
—— his 1st wife, Helen Chisholm, iii. 32.
—— his 2nd wife, Margaret Shaw, iii. 33.
— James, twenty-fourth earl of, iii. 43; viii. 108.
—— his wife, Margaret Maria Frances Pennington, iii. 44.
— James Ludovic, twenty-sixth earl of, iii. 48.
—— his wife, Emily Florence Wilbraham, iii. 49.
— John, sixth earl of, iii. 24, 567.
—— his wife, Mariota Home, iii. 24.
— John, seventeenth earl of, i. 355 *n.*; iii. 35; iv. 174; v. 402.
—— his wife, Margaret Hamilton, iii. 36; iv. 375.
— John, nineteenth earl of, iii. 38.
—— his wife, Emilia Stewart, iii. 38; vi. 323.
— John, twentieth earl of, iii. 39; vii. 111; ix. 62.
—— his wife, Jean Murray, i. 489; iii. 39.
— Ludovic, sixteenth earl of, iii. 34; viii. 107; ix. 61.
—— his alleged wife, Margaret Graham, i. 138; iii. 34.
— William, eighteenth earl of, iii. 37; ix. 62.
—— his 1st wife, Mary Johnstone, i. 264; iii. 37.
—— his 2nd wife, Henrietta Seton, iii. 37, 374.
— master of, Alexander, elder son of 5th earl of Crawford, iii. 23; viii. 273.
—— his wife, Janet Gordon, iii. 23; iv. 279, 530.
— master of, Alexander, eldest son of 8th earl of Crawford; 'the wicked,' iii. 26; ix. 61.
—— his wife, Janet or Jean Sinclair, iii. 26; vii. 572.
— master of, David, eldest son of 11th earl of Crawford, iii. 31; vii. 131; viii. 101.
— master of, David Alexander Edward, eldest son of 26th earl of Crawford, iii. 49.
—— his wife, Constance Lilian Pelly, iii. 49.
— master of, John, 2nd son of 5th earl of Crawford, iii. 24; iv. 279.
CRAWFURD, VISCOUNT GARNOCK, iv. 174-178.
CRAWFURD (LINDSAY), VISCOUNT OF MOUNT CRAWFORD, iv. 175.
Crawford, Crawfurd of Allantown, David, ii. 297.
— of Auchenames, *, ancestor of the family of, v. 490.
—— James, iv. 243.
—— his wife, Elizabeth Cunningham, iv. 243.

* Name unknown.

Crawford of Auchenames, Patrick, iv. 192.
—— his wife, Agnes Fraser, iv. 192.
—— Patrick, M.P., vii. 563.
—— his 2nd wife, Sarah Sempill, vii. 563.
—— William, ii. 493.
— of Auchencross, George, ii. 411.
—— his wife, * Dalzell, ii. 411.
— of Bastehelm, John, ii. 288 *n.*
— of Bedland, John, the yr., iv. 189.
— of Beircrofts, Robert, vi. 158.
—— his wife, Helen Kincaid, vi. 158.
— of Bothkennar, John, iv. 305.
— of Braidshaw, Elizabeth, iv. 190.
— of Cairnie, David, iii. 567.
— of Camlurg, *, captain, i. 310.
—— his wife, Jean Arbuthnott, i. 310.
— of Carse, Alexander, vi. 598.
—— his wife, Christian Makgill, vi. 598.
—— Bartholomew, vi. 511.
—— his wife, Anne Stewart, vi. 511.
— of Cartsburn, Patrick, iv. 189.
— of Clolynane, Robert, ii. 511.
—— his wife, Janet Cathcart, ii. 511.
—— William, ii. 511.
— of Cousland, Hugh, v. 489.
— of Craufordjohn, John, 1st laird, v. 488.
—— John, son of Sir Reginald C. of Loudoun, iii. 136; v. 489 *ter.*
— of Craufurdland, Archibald, v. 146.
—— his 2nd wife, * Boyd, v. 146.
—— John, v. 175.
—— his wife, Eleanora Nicolson, v. 175.
— of Creychtie, John, vii. 437.
— of Crosby, Hugh, 1st laird, v. 489.
— of Daleglis, Roger de, ii. 506.
— of Dalgarnock, Edward de, ii. 400.
— of Draffen, Hugh, v. 490.
—— his wife, Alicia, v. 490.
— of Drongane, John, ii. 512 *bis.*
—— his wife, Jonet Cathcart, ii. 512.
—— Robert, ii. 542.
— of Fedderat, John, vii. 437.
—— William, iv. 19; vii. 456, 457.
—— his wife, Katharine Ogilvy, iv. 19.
—— William, vii. 438.
—— his wife, Christiana Fraser, vii. 438.
— of Ferme, James, ii. 81.
—— his wife, * Stewart, ii. 81.
— of Giffordland, Elizabeth, iv. 190.
—— John, iv. 190, 191.
—— his 1st wife, Margaret Boyle, iv. 191.
—— Isabella, v. 161.
—— Margaret, v. 161.
— of Glendowis, Robert, ii. 511.
—— William, ii. 511.
— of Greenock, Malcolm, vii. 535.
— of Haining, Agnes, wife of Thos. Livingston, v. 437.

* Name unknown.

Crawford of Haining, William, v. 437.
— of Hillhouse and Holmes, Robert, ii. 511.
— — William, ii. 511.
— of Inverallan, William, vii. 456.
— of Johnshill, Dr., vii. 531.
— of Jordanhill, Thomas, captain, provost of Glasgow, v. 155, 161 *n.*; viii. 544.
— — his wife, Marion Colquhoun, v. 155.
— of Kerse, Bartholomew, ii. 511.
— — David, viii. 540.
— — his wife, Janet Fleming, v. 437; viii. 540.
— — David, v. 498; vi. 237.
— — his wife, Jean Campbell, v. 498.
— — Reginald, v. 489.
— of Kilbirnie, Hugh, iv. 193.
— — his 2nd wife, Isobel Barclay, iv. 193.
— — Sir John, iv. 174, 238, 246.
— — his wife, Mary Cunningham, iv. 246.
— — Sir John, i. 544; viii. 66.
— — his 1st wife, Margaret Balfour, i. 544.
— — his 2nd wife, Magdalene Carnegie, viii. 66; ix. 159.
— — Lawrence, v. 494.
— — his wife, Helen Campbell, v. 494.
— — Malcolm, iii. 224.
— — his wife, Mariota Crichton, iii. 224.
— — Patrick, *né* Lindsay, iii. 36; iv. 174; ix. 95.
— — his wife, Margaret Crawfurd, iv. 174; ix. 95.
— — Robert, vii. 531.
— — his wife, Margaret Sempill, vii. 531.
— of Leiffnoris, Lochnoris, George, vi. 517.
— — his wife, Margaret Stewart, vi. 517.
— — Sir George, ii. 511.
— — William, v. 494.
— — William, vii. 126.
— — his wife, Agnes Craufurd, vii. 126.
— — William, v. 497.
— — his wife, Isobel Campbell, v. 497.
— of Over Lochrig, Bute Lindsay, capt. 92nd Foot, iii. 40.
— — Robert Lindsay Hamilton, capt. 92nd Foot, iii. 40.
— of Loudoun, Hugh, 2nd laird, v. 489.
— — Hugh, 3rd laird, v. 489.
— — his wife, Alicia, v. 490.
— — Sir Reginald, Sheriff of Ayr, 1st laird, v. 488.
— — his wife, Margaret de Loudoun, v. 488.
— — Sir Reginald, 4th laird, v. 490.
— — his wife, Cecilia, v. 490.
— — Sir Reginald, 5th laird, v. 490.
— — Susanna, wife of Sir Duncan Campbell, i. 321; v. 490, 491.
— of Newark, Alexander, ii. 492.
Crawford of Previk, John, vii. 536 *bis*.
— — *, his son, vii. 536.
— of Rathen, Alexander, vii. 444.
— — Margaret, vii. 444.
— of Restalrig, Ronald, ii. 308; iii. 237.
— of Skeldon, Alexander, ii. 489.
— — his wife, Margaret Kennedy, ii. 489.
— of Smiddieshaw, Margaret, wife of Patrick Boyle, iv. 198.
— — William, iv. 198.
— of Stevenston, Hugh, iv. 224; v. 489.
— of Tramprane, John, vi. 346.
— of Tredonell, capt. Patrick, i. 40.
— — his wife, Johanna Everard, i. 40.
— Adam, son of Sir Reginald C. of Loudoun, v. 489.
— Agnes, wife of David Cathcart of Duchray, ii. 511.
— Agnes, wife of William Craufurd of Lochnorris, vii. 126.
— Andrew, father-in-law of Sir Neil Campbell, i. 322; ix. 18.
— Anna, wife of Alex. Kennedy of Kilhenzie, ii. 493.
— Anna, wife of Archibald Stewart of Blackhall, iv. 174.
— Anna, wife of Alexander Cunningham of Corsehill, iv. 238.
— (Lindsay), Anne, wife of H. Maule of Kelly, iv. 175.
— (Lindsay), Anne, dau. of 1st viscount Garnock, iv. 176.
— Anne, wife of Sir Wm. Dalrymple of Cousland, viii. 121.
— (Lindsay), Archibald, 3rd son of Patrick Lindsay Crawfurd of Kilbirnie, iv. 175.
— (Lindsay), Charles, captain R. N., 5th son of 1st viscount Garnock, iv. 176.
— Christian, wife of Walter Stewart, ii. 81.
— Christina, wife of John Dalrymple, younger of Stair, viii. 116.
— (Lindsay), David, 4th son of 1st viscount Garnock, iv. 176.
— Egidia, wife of Hugh Cathcart, ii. 512.
— Geils, wife of Gavin Carmichael of Park, iv. 582.
— George, son of Wm. C. of Lefnoris, v. 494.
— George, Glasgow, viii. 121.
— (Lindsay), Graham Christian, wife of Patrick Boyle, iv. 177.
— (Lindsay), James, surveyor of customs, 3rd son of 1st viscount Garnock, iv. 175, 176, 178 *n.*
— James, land steward at Castle Dawson, iv. 178 *n.*
— (Lindsay), Janet, dau. of 2nd viscount Garnock, iv. 177.
— Janet, alleged wife of Thos. Hamilton of Priestfield, iv. 305.

* Name unknown.

Crawford, Jean, wife of Sir James Sandilands of Slamannan, viii. 389.
— (Lindsay), John, advocate, 2nd son of 1st viscount Garnock, iv. 176.
— John, in Shaw, ix. 103.
— — his wife, Jean Hamilton, ix. 103.
— Katharine, wife of Robert Crichton of Ryhill, iii. 226.
— Katharine, wife of Patrick Douglas, vii. 126.
— (Lindsay), Magdalen, wife of Geo. Dundas of Duddingston, iv. 175.
— (Lindsay), Magdalen, dau. of 1st viscount Garnock, iv. 176.
— Marabella, wife of Jas. Stewart, ii. 288.
— Margaret, wife of 5th earl of Dumfries, ii. 308; iii. 237.
— Margaret, wife of Sir Archibald of Douglas, iii. 136.
— Margaret, wife of James Boyle of Halkishurst, iv. 188 *bis*.
— Margaret, wife of (1) John Park, and (2) David Boyle of Figgidoch, iv. 189.
— (Lindsay), Margaret, wife of David Boyle of Kelburne, iv. 175, 203.
— (Lindsay), Margaret, wife of Neil M'Neil of Ugadale, iv. 176, 178 *n*.
— Margaret, alleged wife of Sir Malcolm Wallace of Elderslie, v. 490.
— Marion, wife of (1) Jas. Oswell, and (2) Jas. Dalzell, ii. 411.
— Marion, wife of John Boyle of Kelburne, iv. 193.
— Marion, wife of John Boyle of Ballochmartine, iv. 190.
— Marion, wife of John Fleming of Easter Glen, viii. 530.
— Martha, wife of James Dalrymple of Harvieston, viii. 125.
— Mary, wife of Jas. Stewart of Blairhall, ii. 297.
— Mary, wife of (1) Sir A. Napier of Lauriston, and (2) Robert M'Alexander of Crossclays, vi. 416.
— Mary Lindsay, dau. of 21st earl of Crawford, iii. 41.
— Nicol, Nether Liberton, iv. 90.
— (Lindsay), Patrick, 2nd son of Patrick Lindsay Crawfurd of Kilbirnie, iv. 174, 203.
— Reginald, parson of Strathaven, v. 489.
— Reginald, servant of King Robert Bruce, vi. 338.
— Robert, eldest son of Malcolm C. of Greenock, vii. 535.
— — his contracted wife, Isabel Sempill, vii. 535.
— William, son of Sir Reginald C. of Loudoun, v. 489.
— * *, daus. of Sir Andrew C., i. 322.

* Name unknown.

Crawford, *, 1st wife of Sir Neil Campbell of Lochow, ix. 18.
Crayke of Marton, Ralph, v. 173.
— John, York, v. 173.
— Katharine, wife of 9th lord Boyd, v. 173.
Crebarrin, Adam de, vi. 198.
— John de, vi. 198.
Crectune, Turstan de, iii. 53.
Creighton of Haltoun and Luncartie, Alison, wife of David Drummond, master of Maderty, viii. 219.
— — Isabella, viii. 219.
— — John, viii. 219.
— Katharine, wife of (1) Wm. Borthwick, and (2) Jas. Lawson, ii. 99.
Cressingham, Hugh, treasurer of King Edward I. of England, iii. 88; viii. 4.
Cresswell of Nunkeeling, Ralph, iii. 294.
— Elizabeth *or* Margaret, wife of John Constable, iii. 294.
— of Roberton, William, vi. 343.
— Margaret, vi. 343.
Cressy of Birkin, Everingham, vii. 222.
— Dorothea, wife of 1st earl of Rosebery, vii. 222.
Crewe, Robert (Crewe-Milnes), 1st earl of, vii. 228.
— — his wife, Margaret E. H. Primrose, vii. 228.
— of Steyne, Thomas (Crewe), baron, ii. 208.
— Jemima, wife of Henry Grey, duke of Kent, ii. 208.
CRICHTON, CRICHTON, LORD, iii. 52-68.
Crichton, James, second lord, ii. 327, 330; iii. 61.
— — his wife, Janet Dunbar, iii. 63 *bis*, 66; iv. 123; vi. 306.
— William, first lord, i. 175; ii. 325, 588; iii. 56, 57, 167, 171, 176, 177, 220; iv. 129, v. 426.
— — his wife, Agnes, iii. 61.
— William, third lord, i. 20; iii. 64; iv. 123.
— — his wife, Marion Livingston, iii. 64; v. 431.
CRICHTON OF FRENDRAUGHT, CRICHTON, LORD, iv. 129-134.
Crichton, James, first lord, iv. 129.
— — his 1st wife, Janet *or* Margaret Leslie, iv. 130; v. 378.
— — his 2nd wife, Marion Irving, iv. 130.
— — his 3rd wife, J. *, iv. 130.
CRICHTON OF SANQUHAR, CRICHTON, LORD, iii. 219-238.
Crichton of Sanquhar, Charles, 2nd son of William, 2nd earl of Dumfries; styled lord, iii. 235; viii. 147, 150.
— — his wife, Sarah Dalrymple, iii. 235; viii. 147.

* Name unknown.

Crichton of Sanquhar, Edward, seventh lord, iii. 227, 229.
—— his wife, Margaret Douglas, iii. 229; vii. 125.
—— Penelope, wife of William Dalrymple of Glenmure; baroness, iii. 236.
—— Robert, first lord, iii. 222; vi. 5.
—— his 1st wife, Margaret Hay, iii. 223.
—— his 2nd wife, Christian Erskine, iii. 223; v. 432, 596.
—— Robert, second lord, iii. 224; iv. 403, 405.
—— his wife, Marion Maxwell, iii. 225.
—— Robert, third lord, iii. 225; vii. 119.
—— his wife, Elizabeth Murray, i. 222; iii. 225.
—— Robert, fourth lord, iii. 226.
—— his wife, Elizabeth Campbell, iii. 226.
—— Robert, sixth lord, iii. 227, 229.
—— his wife, Margaret Cunningham, iii. 229.
—— Robert, eighth lord, iii. 230; vii. 130; ix. 71 *ter*.
—— his wife, Anne Farmer, iii. 231; ix. 71.
—— Robert, eldest son of William, 2nd earl of Dumfries; styled lord, iii. 235.
—— William, fifth lord, ii. 514; iii. 225, 226; vii. 539, 546.
—— his wife, Elizabeth Fleming, iii. 227; viii. 541.
—— William, self-styled lord, iii. 232.
—— William, ninth lord, ii. 393; iii. 128, 227, 232; v. 222; vii. 133.
—— his 1st wife, Euphemia Seton, iii. 234.
—— his 2nd wife, Ursula Barnham, iii. 234.
—— William, tenth lord, iii. 235.
—— his wife, Penelope Swift, iii. 235.
—— William, eleventh lord, iii. 236.
CRICHTON OF SANQUHAR, CRICHTON-DALRYMPLE, LORD, iii. 236-237.
Crichton, William (Dalrymple), son of William, earl of Dumfries and Stair; styled lord, viii. 156.
CRICHTON OF SANQUHAR, MACDOWALL-CRICHTON, LORD, iii. 236-238.
Crichton of Sanquhar, Elizabeth Penelope, wife of John, viscount Mountstuart; baroness, ii. 308; iii. 237.
—— Patrick, fourteenth lord, iii. 237.
—— his wife, Margaret Crauford, iii. 237.
—— William, thirteenth lord, iii. 237.
—— his 1st wife, Anne Gordon, i. 90; iii. 237.
—— his 2nd wife, Anne Duff, iii. 237.
—— William, son of 4th earl of Dumfries; styled lord, iii. 237.
CRICHTON OF SANQUHAR, CRICHTON-STUART, LORD, ii. 309-312.
Crichton of Sanquhar, John, sixteenth lord, ii. 309.
CRICHTON, VISCOUNT OF AIR, iii. 234-238.
CRICHTON, EARL OF CAITHNESS, ii. 323-331.
CRICHTON, LORD CRICHTON, iii. 52-68.
CRICHTON, LORD CRICHTON OF FRENDRAUGHT, iv. 129-134.
CRICHTON, LORD CRICHTON OF SANQUHAR, iii. 219-238.
CRICHTON, EARL OF DUMFRIES, iii. 219-238.
CRICHTON, VISCOUNT FRENDRAUGHT, iv. 123-134.
CRICHTON, EARL OF MORAY, iii. 63; vi. 309.
Crichton of Abercrombie, James, i. 79; iii. 227.
— of Airlywicht, Sir Robert, vii. 190.
— of Wester Aldie, James, vii. 198.
—— his wife, Helen Mercer, vii. 198.
— of Arbeikie, George, major, vi. 574.
—— his wife, Jean Stewart, vi. 574; viii. 296.
— of Auchingoul, George, 3rd son of James C. of Frendraught and Kinnairdie, iv. 128, 129, 132.
—— his wife, Jean Irvine, iv. 133.
—— James, eldest son of Sir James C. of Frendraught, iv. 126.
—— his wife, Elizabeth Gordon, iv. 128; viii. 348.
—— James, 2nd son of 5th viscount Frendraught, iv. 133; ix. 93.
—— his wife, Margaret Gordon, iv. 133.
— of Bagthrop, Humphrey, iii. 57, 220.
— of Barmuckity, Laurence, 3rd son of Sir Robert C. of Sanquhar, iii. 221.
—— Sir Robert, sheriff of Dumfries, iii. 221.
—— his wife, Elizabeth, iii. 221.
— of Bedlieston, George, 2nd son of Sir James C. of Frendraught, iv. 125.
—— his wife, Isobel Chalmers, ix. 93.
— of Benchellis, James, 2nd son of William C., tutor of Sanquhar, iii. 227.
—— William, son of 8th lord Crichton of Sanquhar, iii. 232.
— of Berriedale, William de, iii. 54.
— of Blacadye, Margaret, dau. of 7th lord Crichton of Sanquhar, iii. 230.
— of Blackhouse, James, 2nd son of Stephen C. of Cairns, ii. 324.
—— his wife, Agnes Hepburn, ii. 324.
— of Blackness, Sir George, ii. 323, 325; vii. 319, 320.
— of Bognie, Sir James, iv. 125.
— of Borthwickshiels, George, vii. 319, 320.
— of Bradewood, William de, iii. 55, 56.
— of Brawl, Sir George, admiral, iii. 62.
— of Brunstane, James, iii. 120.
—— John, ii. 469; iii. 120 *bis*.
—— William de, iii. 55, 56.

Crichton of the Byres, Humphrey, iii. 57, 220.
— of Cairns, Sir James, son of George C., earl of Caithness, ii. 329, 330.
— — Stephen, ii. 323; iii. 56; vii. 319.
— — his wife, * Cairns of Cairns and Whitburn, ix. 50.
— of Castlemains, James, iii. 228; ix. 70.
— — his wife, Mary Douglas, iii. 228.
— of Cluny, George, ii. 324.
— — Robert, king's advocate, ii. 407.
— — Robert, his 2nd son, ii. 407.
— — Sir Robert, ii. 411; v. 7, 221; vi. 319; vii. 188, 190.
— — his wife, Margaret Stewart, v. 7.
— of Comisties, George, iv. 125.
— — Sir James, iv. 125.
— — Janet, wife of Sir Jas. Macgill of Rankeillour, iv. 130.
— of Conzie, George, iv. 123, 124 *bis*; vii. 410.
— — Sir James, iv. 123.
— — James, iv. 126.
— of Craigs, James, eldest son of Adam C. of Ruthven, ii. 323.
— — his wife, Agnes Hepburn, ii. 324.
— of Crailing, John de, iii. 55.
— of Cranstonriddell, Sir James, iv. 124, 155.
— — his wife, Janet Betoun, ii. 230; ix. 46.
— — James, ix. 46.
— — Sir Patrick, iii. 226 *n*.
— of New Cranston, Thomas de, burgess of Berwick, iii. 54.
— — his 1st wife, Eda, iii. 54.
— — his 2nd wife, Isabella, iii. 54.
— — William de, iii. 54.
— of Crawfordstoun, Agnes, iii. 221.
— — Alexander, 2nd son of Sir Robert C. of Sanquhar, iii. 221.
— — James, iii. 128.
— — his wife, * Maxwell, iii. 128.
— — John, iii. 221, 234.
— of Crichie, George, 2nd son of Sir Jas. C. of Frendraught, iv. 125.
— — his wife, Isobel Chalmers, ix. 93.
— of Crichton, Sir John de, iii. 54, 56.
— — sir John, iii. 56, 57, 220.
— — his wife, Christian de Gremislaw, iii. 57.
— — William de, ii. 323; iii. 54, 55 *ter*, 56.
— — his wife, Margaret Preston, iii. 57; ix. 62.
— — Sir William de, chancellor of Scotland, i. 175; ii. 325, 588; iii. 56, 57, 167, 171, 176, 177, 220; iv. 129; v. 426; ix. 62.
— — his wife, Agnes, iii. 61.
— of Crunan, Patrick, chirurgeon in Dundee, iii. 380.
— — his wife, Grisell Galloway, iii. 380.
— of Culreoch and Grobdale, Margaret, wife of James Gordon of Lochinvar, v. 108 *bis*.

* Name unknown.

Crichton of Cumnock, James, 2nd son of William C., tutor of Sanquhar, iii. 227.
— of Darlay, Sir James, iv. 125.
— of Darnhaunch, William, eldest son of Wm. C., tutor of Sanquhar, iii. 226, 232.
— of Drumerocemuir, William, ix. 130.
— of Drummalie, Robert, lord advocate, iv. 279.
— of Dryfesdale, William de, iii. 55, 56.
— of Dunbeath, Sir George, admiral, iii. 62.
— of Eliok, Sir Robert, sheriff of Dumfries, iii. 221.
— — Robert, senator of the College of Justice, iii. 187; iv. 279; vi. 592; vii. 188.
— — his wife, Elizabeth Stewart, iii. 187.
— — Robert, ix. 51.
— of Ferniflat, James, i. 79.
— of Little Forg, George, iv. 124, 125.
— of Forgandenny, Sir James, iv. 123.
— — Sir Robert, son of Robert C. of Kinnoull, iii. 224.
— — his wife, Marion Maxwell, iii. 225.
— of Frendraught, George, iv. 125, 126.
— — his wife, Isobel Chalmers, ix. 93.
— — Sir James, lord great chamberlain of Scotland, ii. 327; iii. 62.
— — his wife, Jonet Dunbar, iii. 62, 63 *bis*; iv. 123; vi. 306.
— — Sir James, son of 3rd lord Crichton iii. 63, 66, 224; iv. 123.
— — his wife, Katharine Borthwick, ii. 108; iv. 124.
— — Sir James, iv. 124.
— — his wife, Johanna *or* Joneta Keith, iv. 125; vi. 50.
— — Sir James, i. 100; ii. 16; iv. 126; v. 222.
— — his wife, Elizabeth Gordon, iv. 128; viii. 348.
— — William, iv. 124; vii. 411.
— — his wife, Agnes Abernethy, iv. 124; vii. 411.
— of Gardin, Sir Robert, vii. 190.
— of Gilberton, William de, iii. 57.
— — his wife, Margaret Preston, iii. 57; ix. 62.
— of Grameslaw, William de, iii. 57, 58.
— of Hownam, John de, iii. 55.
— of Inverkeithing, Sir James, iv. 123.
— of Invernyte, John, iv. 124.
— of Kinblethmont, William de, iii. 54.
— of Kinnairdie, James, iv. 126.
— — his wife, Elizabeth Gordon, iv. 126.
— of Kinnoull, Robert, eldest son of Sir Robert C. of Sanquhar, iii. 221, 222.
— — his 1st wife, Margaret Hay, iii. 223.
— — his 2nd wife, Christian Erskine, iii. 223.

Crichton of Kinnouil, Robert, son of 1st lord Crichton of Sanquhar, iii. 223.
—— —— his wife, Marion Stewart, iii. 223; v. 350.
—— of Kippendavy, Adam, ii. 324.
—— —— his 1st wife, Elizabeth Stirling, ii. 324.
—— —— his 2nd wife, Isobel Gray, ii. 324.
—— of Kirkpatrick-Irongray, Alexander, 2nd son of Sir Robert C. of Sanquhar, iii. 221.
—— —— Edward, 6th son of Sir Robert C. of Sanquhar, iii. 221.
—— —— Sir James, son of 3rd lord Crichton, iii. 66; iv. 123.
—— —— John, son of Robert C., iii. 222.
—— —— Sir Robert, son of Edward C., iii. 220.
—— —— Robert, son of Edward C., iii. 222.
—— —— Robert, son of Robert C., iii. 222; v. 108; vii. 118.
—— —— Robert, 2nd lord Crichton, iii. 224; iv. 123.
—— of Kretilhouse, Edward de, ii. 325.
—— of Logyaldtoun, Sir James, iv. 125.
—— of Longniddry, Sir Robert, sheriff of Dumfries, iii. 221.
—— of Lugton, Sir David, iv. 309.
—— —— Patrick, vii. 291.
—— —— his wife, Elizabeth Leslie, vii. 291.
—— of Malar, Sir James, iv. 123.
—— of Merchamstoun, John de, iii. 55.
—— of Molyne, Gavin, 2nd son of 2nd lord Crichton, iii. 64; iv. 124.
—— —— his wife, Margaret Cockburn, iii. 64.
—— of Monkshill, James, iv. 126.
—— of Naughton, David, vii. 289.
—— —— his wife, Janet Leslie, iii. 533; vii. 289.
—— —— Sir Peter, vii. 289.
—— of Panbride, Robert, iii. 310.
—— of Petlandy, Patrick, ix. 70.
—— —— his wife, Margaret Sinclair, ix. 70.
—— —— Robert, ix. 70.
—— of Pitquhenzie, James, iv. 126.
—— of Rachills, Gavin, 2nd son of 2nd lord Crichton, iii. 64; iv. 124.
—— —— his wife, Margaret Cockburn, iii. 64.
—— of Riccarton, Henry, vii. 44.
—— —— Janet, wife of Henry Drummond, vii. 44.
—— —— Robert, son of 1st lord Crichton of Sanquhar, iii. 223.
—— of Rossie, John, ix. 70.
—— —— his wife, Katharine Ross, ix. 70.
—— —— Laurence, ix. 70.
—— —— Margaret, wife of Andrew Stewart of Calzebrochan, ix. 70.
—— of Rossieochill, William, son of 8th lord Crichton of Sanquhar, iii. 232.
Crichton of Ruthven, Sir Adam, v. 83.
—— —— his wife Margaret Erskine, v. 83.
—— —— Adam, ii. 324.
—— —— his 1st wife, Elizabeth Stirling, ii. 324.
—— —— his 2nd wife, Isobel Gray, ii. 324; iv. 277; vi. 172.
—— —— James, 2nd son of Stephen C. of Cairns, ii. 323.
—— —— his wife, Agnes Hepburn, ii. 324.
—— —— James, v. 525.
—— —— his wife, Janet Ogston, v. 525.
—— —— John, v. 218, 525.
—— —— his wife, Janet Fraser, i. 117; v. 525.
—— —— John, iii. 26.
—— —— his wife, Isobel Lindsay, iii. 26.
—— —— Patrick, chirurgeon in Dundee, iii. 380.
—— —— his wife, Grisell Galloway, iii. 380.
—— —— Thomas, iii. 380.
—— of Ruthvendenny, Sir Adam, vii. 543.
—— —— James, vii. 533.
—— of Ryhill, John, tutor of Sanquhar, ii. 404; iii. 225; viii. 541.
—— —— his wife, Christian Dalzell, ii. 403.
—— —— Robert, ii. 404; iii. 226.
—— —— his wife, Katharine Crawford, iii. 226.
—— —— Robert, 3rd son of Wm. C., tutor of Sanquhar, i. 229; iii. 228.
—— —— his wife, Agnes Macbrair, iii. 228.
—— —— William, eldest son of Wm. C., tutor of Sanquhar, iii. 226, 227, 233.
—— of St. Leonard's, James, sheriff of Dumfries, iii. 234.
—— —— John, iii. 221, 234.
—— of Sanquhar, Edward, iii. 220.
—— —— Sir Robert, sheriff of Dumfries, coroner of Nithsdale, iii. 58, 192, 220.
—— —— his wife, Elizabeth *, iii. 221.
—— —— Robert, sheriff of Dumfries, iii. 222.
—— —— his wife, Christian Erskine, iii. 223.
—— —— William de, iii. 53, 56, 219.
—— —— his wife, Isabella de Ros of Sanquhar, iii. 53, 219.
—— of Sheepcotleys, Humphrey, iii. 220.
—— of Strathurd, James, iv. 275.
—— —— his wife, Christian Gray, iv. 275.
—— —— Sir John, iv. 101, 124, 261.
—— —— his wife, Janet Ruthven, iv. 261.
—— —— John, i. 120.
—— of Townhead, William, iii. 227, 232.
—— of Uras, Patrick, vi. 42.
—— of Vogrie, William de, iii. 58.
—— of Welchtoun, Thomas de, iii. 55, 57.
—— —— William de, iii. 55, 56.
—— —— his 2nd wife, Margaret, iii. 57.
—— of Whitburn, Stephen, ix. 50.
—— of Winterhope, Humphrey, iii. 220.
—— of Winton, Sir William, viii. 576.

* Name unknown.

Crichton, Abraham, provost of Dunglas, lord of Session, ii. 324; ix. 61.
—— his wife, Matilda Luvell, iii. 20; ix. 61.
— Adam, 2nd son of Adam C. of Ruthven, ii. 324.
— Agnes, wife of Alexander, 2nd lord Glamis, iii. 61; viii. 274.
— Agnes, wife of (1) George Sinclair, and (2) Sir A. Ker of Cessford, iii. 226 *n.*; v. 453; vii. 331, 332; viii. 274.
— Agnes, wife of (1) Wm. Ruthven of Ballindean, and (2) A. Abercromby, iv. 101.
— Agnes, wife of John Leslie of Weittis, iv. 125.
— Alisaundre de, del counte de Edneburk, iii. 53, 219.
— Alexander de, in garrison at Edinburgh Castle, iii. 54.
— Alexander, preceptor of Hospital of St. Mary Magdalene, iii. 120.
— Alexander, son of Jas. C. of Auchingoul, ix. 93.
— Anna, wife of Robt. Spens of Tulloch, iv. 125.
— Anna, dau. of Jas. C. of Auchingoul, ix. 93.
— Anne, wife of (1) Wm. Seton of Meldrum, and (2) Gilbert Ogilvy of Craig, iv. 126; ix. 93.
— Barbara, dau. of Alex. C. of Crawfordstoun, iii. 221.
— Charles, 3rd son of 6th viscount Frendraught, iv. 133.
— Christian, wife of (1) Sir R. Colville of Ochiltree, and (2) Alexander, 3rd lord Erskine, ii. 508; iii. 222, 541; v. 607.
— David, 2nd son of James C. of St. Leonard's, iii. 234.
— Douglas, ix. 93.
— Edward de, 5th son of William de C., iii. 55, 57.
— Elizabeth, lady Aldie, wife of Sir J. Ogilvy of Craig, i. 120.
— Elizabeth, wife of (1) Sir John Murray, and (2) Sir Simon Preston, i. 460.
— Elizabeth, contracted to 4th lord Cathcart, ii. 514; iii. 228; vii. 539.
— Elizabeth, wife of (1) William Douglas of Drumlanrig, (2) Jas. Campbell of West Loudoun, and (3) Sir Wm. Colville, ii. 543; iii. 222; vii. 116; ix. 59.
— Elizabeth, wife of 1st earl of Huntly, iii. 61; iv. 524.
— Elizabeth, dau. of Alex. C. of Crawfordstoun, iii. 221.
— Elizabeth, dau. of Robert C. of Ryhill, iii. 228.
— Elizabeth, dau. of Charles, lord Crichton, iii. 235, 236.
— Elizabeth, wife of 8th earl of Eglinton, iii. 236, 453; ix. 81 *bis*.
Crichton, Elizabeth, wife of 2nd lord Fraser, iv. 115, 116, 128.
— Elizabeth, wife of (1) A. Abernethy of Lessindrum, and (2) A. Cranstoun, iv. 125; vii. 412.
— Elizabeth, wife of Robt. Irving of Corniehaugh, iv. 133.
— Elizabeth, wife of gen. Alexander Hamilton, iv. 309; ix. 100.
— Elizabeth, wife of Archibald Napier of Merchiston, vi. 410.
— Elizabeth, wife of 2nd lord Hay of Yester, viii. 433.
— Elizabeth, wife of Andrew, master of Rothes, ix. 50.
— Elspet, dau. of Jas. C. of Auchingoul, ix. 93.
— Francis, 4th son of James C. of Kinnairdie, iv. 128, 129.
— Francis, 2nd son of 5th viscount Frendraught, iv. 133.
— George, 3rd son of 2nd lord Crichton, iii. 64.
— George, in holy orders, 7th son of Sir Robert C. of Sanquhar, iii. 222.
— George, 4th son of 6th viscount Frendraught, iv. 132; ix. 93.
— George, son of Geo. C. of Bedliestoun and Crichie, ix. 125.
— Grisel, wife of (1) dean Thos. Dunbar, and (2) Sir Jas. Sinclair of Murchil, ix. 51.
— Helen, wife of William Crichton, sheriff-depute of Ayr, iii. 228.
— Helen, wife of Wm. Hay of Muldavit, iv. 129.
— Helen, wife of D. Lindsay of Kirkforthar, v. 404.
— Henry, abbot of Dunfermline, vi. 83.
— Herbert, 4th son of 3rd lord Crichton of Sanquhar, iii. 226.
— Isobel, dau. of Robert C. of Ryhill, iii. 228.
— Isabel, wife of Robt. Dunbar of Burgie, iv. 129; ix. 93.
— James, son of Gavin C., iii. 64, 66.
— James, 'the Admirable,' iii. 187.
— James, 2nd son of Robert C. of Ryhill, iii. 228.
— James, 6th son of 5th lord Crichton of Sanquhar, iii. 228.
— James, 3rd son of James C. of St. Leonard's, iii. 234.
— James, 2nd son of Sir John C. of Strathurd, iv. 124.
— James, son of John C. of Invernyte, iv. 124.
— James, legtd. son of Sir Jas. C. of Frendraught, iv. 126.
— James, slain about 1542, vii. 410.
— Jane, wife of J. Preston of Whitehill, iii. 120.
— Janet, wife of John, 3rd lord Maxwell, ii. 328, 330; vi. 477.

Crichton, Janet, wife of 2nd earl of Morton, vi. 358.
— Janet, wife of Sir Jas. Makgill of Rankeillor, vi. 589.
— Janet, wife of Wm. Fleming of Bord, viii. 527.
— Janet, dau. of Jas. C. of Auchingoul, ix. 93.
— Jean, dau. of Alexander C. of Crawfordland, iii. 221.
— Jean, illeg. dau. of Sir Jas. C. of Frendraught, iv. 126.
— Jean, wife of W. Stewart of Outlaw, iv. 131.
— Jean, wife of Andrew Ker, v. 51 *n.*
— Jean, wife of Laurence Makgill, vi. 593.
— Johan de, in garrison at Edinburgh Castle, iii. 54.
— Sir John de, d. bef. 1338, iii. 54.
— John de, sheriff of Kinross, keeper of Lochleven Castle, iii. 55, 56.
— John, 2nd son of John C. of Brunstane, iii. 120.
— John, in entail of Crawfordstoun, son of Robert C., iii. 221.
— John, eldest son of James C. of St. Leonard's, iii. 221, 234.
— John, iii. 223; v. 596.
— — his wife, Christian Erskine of Kinnoull, v. 432, 596.
— John, eldest son of 5th lord Crichton of Sanquhar, iii. 227.
— John, 4th son of Robert C. of Ryhill, iii. 228.
— John, colonel, 3rd son of 1st earl of Dumfries, iii. 235.
— John, vicar of Dalkeith, vi. 359.
— John, 2nd son of Jas. C. of Abercrombie and Bencheillis, ix. 70.
— Katharine, dau. of Robert C. of Ryhill iii. 228.
— Katharine, wife of Sir John Charteris iii. 235.
— Katharine, wife of Sir Alex. Stewart of Garlies, iv. 155.
— Magdalen, wife of Laurence Oliphant iv. 130; vi. 554.
— Magdalen, wife of Alex. Stewart of Lesmurdie, iv. 133.
— Margaret, wife of (1) Wm. Todrik, (2) George Halkerstoun, and (3) George, 4th earl of Rothes, i. 20; iii. 66, 67; vii. 284, 287 *n.*
— Margaret, wife of (1) Sir A. Murray of Balvaird, and (2) Sir Mungo Murray of Claremont, i. 467; viii. 190.
— Margaret, wife of (1) Sir Wm. Stirling, and (2) John, 1st lord Sempill, ii. 325; vii. 533.
— Margaret, wife of Robert, 1st lord Dalzell, ii. 408; ix. 53.
Crichton, Margaret, dau. of Alex. C. of Crawfordstoun, iii. 221.
— Margaret, wife of David Herries of Terregles, iii. 222; iv. 403 *bis.*
— Margaret, wife of Alexander Hume of Polwarth, iii. 224; vi. 5.
— Margaret, dau. of Robert C. of Ryhill, iii. 228.
— Margaret, dau. of 5th lord Crichton of Sanquhar, contr. to Andrew Sempill, iii. 228; vii. 539, 544.
— Margaret, dau. of Charles, lord Crichton, iii. 235, 236.
— Margaret, dau. of Wm. C. of Frendraught, iv. 124.
— Margaret, dau. of Jas. C. of Kinnairdie, iv. 129.
— Margaret, wife of Peter Hay of Megginch, v. 218.
— Margaret, wife of Sir Geo. Livingston of Ogilface. v. 442; ix. 130.
— Margaret, contr. to Robert, master of Sempill, vii. 543.
— Margaret, dau. of Jas. C. of Auchingoul, ix. 93.
— Marion, abducted by Gavin Dalzell, ii. 406; vii. 188.
— Mariota, wife of Malcolm Crawford of Kilbirnie, iii. 224.
— Marjory, wife of Andrew, master of Rothes, ix. 50.
— Martin, brother of Sir James C. of Cranston Riddell, iv. 124.
— Mary, wife of Edward, viscount of Carlingford, iii. 235.
— Mary, dau. of Charles, lord Crichton, iii. 235, 236.
— Mary, dau. of 2nd earl of Dumfries, iii. 236.
— Mary, wife of 6th lord Oliphant, iv. 129; vi. 554.
— Nicholas de, iii. 53.
— Patrick, 5th son of Sir Robert C. of Sanquhar, iii. 221.
— Penelope, dau. of 2nd earl of Dumfries, iii. 236.
— Sir Robert, eldest son of Robert C. of Ryhill, i. 229; iii. 228.
— — his wife, Margaret Drummond, viii. 218.
— Robert, bishop of Dunkeld, ii. 62.
— Robert, chaplain of Hospital of St. Mary Magdalene, iii. 120.
— Robert, brother of John C. of Crawfordstoun, iii. 221.
— Robert, son of Robert C. of Ryhill, iii. 226.
— Robert, 3rd son of Sir John C. of Strathurd, iv. 124; vii. 410.
— Thomas de, rector of Hailes, iii. 53 *bis.*
— Thomas de, del counte de Bercwyke, iii. 53.

Crichton, Thomas, burgess of Berwick, iii. 54.
—— —— his 1st wife, Eda, iii. 54.
—— —— his 2nd wife, Isabella, iii. 54.
—— Thomas de, son of William de C., iii. 55, 57.
—— Thomas, 4th son of Sir Robert C. of Sanquhar, iii. 221.
—— Turstan de, iii. 53.
—— William de, rector of Crichton, iii. 54.
—— Sir William, *perhaps error for* Airth, iii. 53.
—— William, son of Gavin C., iii. 64, 66.
—— William, illeg. son of 3rd lord Crichton of Sanquhar, iii. 226.
—— William, tutor of Sanquhar, ii. 406; iii. 227.
—— —— his wife, Katharine Carmichael, iii. 227.
—— William, eldest son of James C. of Abercrombie, iii. 228; ix. 70.
—— William, sheriff-depute of Ayr, iii. 228.
—— —— his wife, Helen Crichton, iii. 228.
—— William, 3rd son of Robert C. of Ryhill, iii. 228.
—— William, 2nd son of James C. of Kinnairdie, iv. 128, 129.
—— William, wounded by Flemings, 1542, viii. 541.
—— William, son of Jas. C. of Auchingoul, ix. 93.
—— *, eldest son of 6th viscount Frendraught, iv. 133.
—— *, wife of Sir James Dunbar of Blackcraig, iii. 224.
—— *, wife of David Macbrair, iii. 228.
—— *, *perhaps* wife of Thos. Kilpatrick of Closeburn, ix. 70.
Crichton or Murray of Glenmuir and Castle Murray, Sir Robert, i. 229; iii. 228; viii. 218.
—— —— his wife, Margaret Drummond, viii. 218.
—— —— Anna, wife of lord James Murray of Dowally, i. 229; iii. 228.
—— —— Jean, wife of George Stirling of Auchyll, iii. 228.
CRICHTON-DALRYMPLE, LORD CRICHTON OF SANQUHAR, iii. 236, 237.
CRICHTON-DALRYMPLE, EARL OF DUMFRIES, iii. 236-237.
Crichton-Dalrymple, Elizabeth, wife of John Macdowall of French, iii. 236.
CRICHTON-STUART, LORD CRICHTON OF SANQUHAR, ii. 310-312; iii. 237-238.
CRICHTON-STUART, EARL OF DUMFRIES, ii. 310-312; iii. 237-238.
Crichton-Stuart of Falkland Palace, Ninian Edward, ii. 311.
—— —— his wife, Ismay Lucretia Mary Preston.

* Name unknown.

Crichton-Stuart, Audrey, ii. 309.
—— Cecilia, ii. 309.
—— Colum Edmund, ii. 311.
—— Constance, ii. 309.
—— Dudley, ii. 309.
—— Herbert, ii. 309.
—— —— his wife, Fanny Adelaide Labouchere, ii. 309.
—— James Frederick Dudley, M.P., ii. 309.
—— —— his wife, Gertrude Frances Seymour, ii. 309.
Crichton-Stuart, Margaret, wife of capt. Colin William Macrae of Ascog, ii. 311.
—— Mary Anne Frances, ii. 309.
—— Patrick James, lieut. Grenadier Guards, ii. 309.
—— —— his 1st wife, Cecil Kirk, ii. 309.
—— —— his 2nd wife, Ellen Kate Phillips, ii. 309.
—— Patrick James Herbert, M.P., ii. 308.
—— —— his wife, Hannah Tighe, ii. 309.
Crimond, Robert Burnett, senator of the College of Justice, lord, iii. 488.
Crinan the Thane, hereditary lay-abbot of Dunkeld and seneschal of the Isles, i. 1; ii. 314; iii. 239; iv. 3.
—— —— his wife, Bethoc of Scotland, i. 1; iii. 240.
Cristinus, 7th son of Alwin, 2nd earl of Lennox, v. 330; ix. 125.
—— judex de Levenax, v. 330 *n.*; ix. 125.
Croc of Kilbride, Robert, ii. 504; v. 549.
—— Robert de, i. 11.
—— —— his wife, Eschina de Molle, i. 11.
Crofton of Mote, Sir Edward, 3rd bart. iv. 169.
—— —— his wife, Charlotte Stewart, iv. 169.
—— Annabella Violet, wife of C. P. Carmichael, iv. 570.
—— John, iv. 570.
Crofts of West Stow, Edmond, ii. 580.
—— Henrietta, wife of 2nd duke of Bolton, ii. 240.
—— Henry, R.N., commr. H.M.S. *Gosport*, ii. 240.
—— James, major-gen.. illeg. son of James, duke of Monmouth, ii. 240.
—— Margaret, wife of John Southwell, ii. 580.
CROMARTIE, MACKENZIE, EARL OF, iii. 69-86.
Cromartie, George, first earl of, iii. 73; vii. 260, 495.
—— —— his 1st wife, Anna Sinclair, iii. 75.
—— —— his 2nd wife, Margaret, countess of Wemyss, ii. 283; iii. 77; viii. 504.
—— George, third earl of, i. 572; iii. 78.
—— —— his wife, Isabella Gordon, iii. 80.
—— John, second earl of, iii. 75, 77; v. 535.
—— —— his 1st wife, Elizabeth Gordon, i. 103; iii. 77; ix. 6.
—— —— his 2nd wife, Mary Murray, iii. 77 512.
—— —— his 3rd wife, Anne Fraser, iii. 78; v. 535.

CROMARTIE, HAY-MACKENZIE, EARL OF, iii. 84-86.
Cromartie, Anne, wife of 3rd duke of Sutherland; countess of, iii. 84, 520; viii. 364.
— Francis, second earl of, iii. 84, 85; viii. 364.
— Sibell Lilian, wife of major E. W. Blunt; countess of, iii. 85.
Cromarty, John Mackenzie, eldest son of 3rd earl of Cromartie, commander of the Order of the Sword in Sweden, count, iii. 82.
— — his wife, Margery Forbes, iii. 82.
Cromlex and Erne, John (Hay), lord, v. 231.
CROMLIX, DRUMMOND, LORD DRUMMOND OF, viii. 220-238.
Crommenane of Balfron, Thomas de, vii. 30 *n.*
Crompton of Stone, William, i. 405.
— — his wife, Jane Aston, i. 405.
— of Woodend, Sir Samuel, 1st bart., M.P., ii. 523, 530.
— — his wife, Isabella Sophia Cathcart, ii. 523.
— Elizabeth Mary, wife of 3rd earl Cathcart, ii. 523, 530.
— Elizabeth, wife of 3rd earl of Marchmont, vi. 22.
— Windmill, merchant, London, vi. 22.
Cromwell, Oliver, ii. 235; v. 121.
Crook, Elsie Ida, wife of G. P. Fairfax, iii. 604.
Crosbie, Maria, wife of B. Drummond, viii. 231.
— William Arthur, viii. 231.
Crosby of Corby, Adam, ix. 53.
— Robert, ix. 53.
— of Ormesby, Matilda, wife of Adam de Carlyle, ii. 375; ix. 53.
Cross of Bank, John, iii. 464.
— — his wife, Theresa Montgomerie, iii. 464.
— Mary, wife of James Bruce, i. 552.
Crossar, Andrew, murderer of Robert Scott, vii. 71.
Crosse, Emily Marian, wife of (1) capt. E. C. Barnes, and (2) David, 11th earl of Lindsay, v. 419.
— Robert, Doctors' Commons, v. 419.
Crouly, Sir Miles, iv. 549.
— — his wife, Anne Gordon, iv. 549; ix. 111.
Crousar of Manuel, Christian, viii. 6.
Cruger, Samuel Peach, i. 494.
Cruickshank of Langley Park, James, vi. 506.
— — his wife, Anne Letitia Carnegie, vi. 506.
— of Stracathro, Alexander, vi. 496; viii. 111.
— Amy, wife of capt. Alexander Lindsay, vi. 496; viii. 111.
Cruickshank, Elizabeth, wife of Andrew Gray of Balgownie, iv. 288.
— Margaret, wife of Wm. Bruce of Cothill, ix. 82.
Cruickshanks of Aswanley, iv. 515.
— Elizabeth, mother of Jock and Tam Gordon, iv. 515.
Crump, Elizabeth, wife of Charles Beauchamp Ker, v. 482.
— Ernest Radcliffe, ix. 154.
— William, Farnham, v. 482.
Cuillane, Katharine, wife of Jas. Halyburton of Essie, v. 230.
Culane, Margaret, wife of James Innes of Innes, vii. 354.
Cullace, Andrew, burgess of Aberdeen, v. 602.
CULLEN, OGILVY, LORD OGILVY OF, iv. 37-41.
Cullen, Charles (Cockayne), 1st viscount, iv. 301.
Culpeper of Deane, Sir Martin, i. 406.
— — his wife, Joyce Aston, i. 406.
Culpeper, *see also* Colepeper.
CULROSS, COLVILLE, LORD COLVILLE OF, ii. 535-568.
CULROSS, COLVILLE, VISCOUNT COLVILLE OF, 535-568.
Cumberland, Francis (Clifford), 4th earl of, vii. 100.
CUMBERNAULD, FLEMING, LORD, viii. 546 558.
Cumbernauld, John, first lord, viii. 546.
Cumming of Altyre, Alexander, ancestor of the family of, vi. 301.
— — his wife, Euphemia Dunbar, vi. 301.
— — Alexander, iv. 179; vii. 286, 461.
— — his wife, Margaret Gordon, iv. 178.
— — James, v. 529.
— — his wife, Mary Fraser, v. 529.
— — Thomas, vii. 461.
— — his wife, Margaret Grant, vii. 461.
— of Denend, William, vii. 437.
— of Drummine, William, ii. 41.
— of Earnside, Alexander, vii. 276.
— — his wife, Margaret Leslie, vii. 276.
— — John, vii. 458.
— — John, ix. 141.
— — his wife, Jane Douglas, ix. 141.
— — John, vii. 413, 461.
— — his wife, Isobel Abernethy, vii. 413.
— — Thomas, vii. 458, 461.
— — his wife, Margaret Grant, vii. 458.
— — William, iv. 59.
— — his wife, Jean Forbes, iv. 59.
— of Inverallochy, v. 531.
— — Sir William, Lyon King of Arms, vii. 41.
— — William, vii. 437.
— — his wife, Elizabeth Grant, ix. 155.
— of Kinchirdie, David, vii. 471.
— of Kindrocht, William, vii. 437.

Cumming of Kininmont, Charles, iv. 64.
—— —— his wife, Sophia Forbes, iv. 64.
—— Elizabeth, wife of Alex. Hamilton, ii. 41.
—— Elizabeth, wife of John Hope, *probably mistake for* Eumont, iv. 485.
—— Isabella, wife of Archibald Grant of Dalfour, vii. 461.
—— Jane, wife of gen. John Leslie, vi. 117.
—— John Melville, general, vi. 117.
—— —— his wife, Jane Cumming, vi. 117.
—— Sarah, wife of 5th lord Bellenden, ii. 76.
—— Thomas, banker, Edinburgh, vi. 117.
—— *, 'the Fair Maid of Moray,' iv. 526.
—— *, a surgeon, v. 532 *n.*
Cumming Bruce of Dunphail, Roseisle and Kinnaird, Charles Lennox, major, iii. 495.
—— —— his wife, Mary Elizabeth Bruce, i. 506 *n.*; iii. 495.
—— —— Elizabeth Mary, wife of 8th earl of Elgin, iii. 495.
Cumming Gordon of Altyre and Gordonstoun, Sir Alexander Penrose, 1st bart., vii. 485.
—— —— his wife, Helen Grant, vii. 485.
CUMRA, STUART, LORD, ii. 299-312.
Cumra, James, first lord, ii. 299.
Cuningsburg, *see* Coningsburg.
Cunliffe, Henry, vicar of Shifnal, iii. 394.
—— —— his 2nd wife, Alexandrina Victoria Murray, iii. 394.
—— Sir Robert Henry, 4th bart., general, iii. 395.
CUNNINGHAM, EARL OF CARRICK, iv. 227.
CUNNINGHAM, EARL OF GLENCAIRN, iv. 222-252.
CUNNINGHAM, LORD KILMAURS, iv. 232-252.
Cunningham of Achinbowy, Robert, i. 112.
—— —— his wife, Isobel Glen, i. 112.
—— of Adintoun, Cuthbert, iv. 235.
—— of Aiket, John, iv. 238.
—— of Auchenharvie, Adam, v. 168; ix. 119.
—— —— Sir David, 1st bart., v. 166.
—— —— Edward, iii. 435; iv. 191.
—— —— Robert, iv. 191.
—— —— Robert, his son, iv. 191.
—— —— his wife, Elizabeth Boyle, iv. 191.
—— —— William, alleged ancestor of the family of, iv. 234.
—— of Auchinyards, William, alleged ancestor of the family of, iv. 234.
—— of Badlane, Thomas, iv. 227, 228, 229, 231.
—— of Ballindalloch, Andrew, iv. 226.
—— of Barns, Sir Neil, *or* Nigel, iv. 226, 229; ix. 96.
—— —— his wife, Joanna Douglas, ix. 96.
—— of Wester Barns, John, viii. 433.
—— —— John, vii. 290.
—— —— his wife, Euphemia Leslie, vii. 290.
—— of Bedlaw, 1676, ii. 29.

* Name unknown.

Cunningham of Bedlaw, William, alleged ancestor of the family of, iv. 234.
—— of Belton, Elizabeth, wife of 1st lord Hay of Yester, viii. 430; ix. 165.
—— —— George, viii. 430.
—— —— Sir William, viii. 430.
—— of Birkshaw, Andrew, vii. 119.
—— —— his wife, Agnes Douglas, vii. 119.
—— of Bonaly, Adam, advocate, iv. 246.
—— —— Robert, iv. 231.
—— —— his wife, Marion Lockhart, iv. 231.
—— —— Sir William, iv. 230; ix. 96.
—— —— William, ix. 96.
—— of Bonnington, William, viii. 371.
—— of Boquhan, William, ii. 366.
—— —— his wife, Margaret Erskine, ii. 366.
—— of Broomhill, Sir John, v. 384.
—— —— his wife, Janet Leslie, v. 384.
—— —— William, ix. 142.
—— —— his wife, Anna Napier, vi. 420; ix. 142.
—— of Brownhill, John, ii. 348.
—— —— his wife, Elizabeth Sinclair, ii. 348.
—— —— William, ii. 42, 55.
—— —— his wife, Elizabeth Hamilton, ii. 42.
—— of Caddell, John, son of John C. of Glengarnock, iv. 192.
—— —— his wife, Margaret Boyle, iv. 192.
—— of Cagan, Robert, captain, viii. 141.
—— of Cambuskeith, John, 2nd son of 6th earl of Glencairn, iv. 244.
—— —— his wife, Margaret Knox, iv. 245.
—— —— John, his son, iv. 245.
—— of Caprington, Sir Adam, vi. 587.
—— —— John, iii. 229; iv. 239, 241; v. 495.
—— —— his 1st wife, Annabella Campbell, v. 495.
—— —— his 2nd wife, Elizabeth Cunningham, iv. 239.
—— —— Sir John, 1st bart., iv. 230.
—— —— Sir John, 3rd bart., iii. 457.
—— —— his wife, Elizabeth Montgomerie, iii. 457.
—— —— Thomas, ancestor of the family of, iv. 228.
—— —— Sir William, superior, 1399, iv. 229.
—— —— Sir William, i. 48.
—— —— his wife, Margaret Hamilton, i. 48.
—— —— Sir William, v. 497; vii. 133.
—— —— his wife, Agnes Campbell, v. 497.
—— —— Sir William, vii. 295.
—— —— his 1st wife, Margaret Leslie, vii. 295.
—— —— Sir William, 2nd bart., viii. 131.
—— of Carlung, Hugh, ancestor of the family of, iv. 239.
—— of Carncurin, William, alleged ancestor of the family of, iv. 234.
—— of Cockilbie, Mr. Cuthbert, iv. 238.

Cunningham of Corsehill, Alexander, 4th laird, iv. 238, 246.
—— —— his wife, Marion Porterfield, iv. 238.
—— —— Alexander, 5th laird, iv. 238.
—— —— his wife, Mary Houstoun, iv. 238.
—— —— Alexander, the younger, iv. 238.
—— —— his wife, Anna Crawford, iv. 238.
—— —— Sir Alexander, 1st bart., iv. 238.
—— —— his wife, Mary Stewart, iv. 238.
—— —— Sir Alexander, 2nd bart., iv. 200 *bis*; ix. 95.
—— —— his wife, Margaret Boyle, iv. 200; ix. 95.
—— —— Andrew, 2nd son of 3rd earl of Glencairn, iv. 238, 252.
—— —— his wife, Margaret Cunningham, iv. 238.
—— —— Cuthbert, 2nd laird, iv. 238, 239.
—— —— his wife, Maud Cunningham, iv. 238.
—— —— Patrick, 3rd laird, iv. 238.
—— —— Sir Thomas A. A. Montgomery-, 10th bart., iv. 238.
—— of Craigbait, Alexander, iv. 239.
—— of Craigends, Alexander, iv. 243.
—— —— his wife, Elizabeth Cunningham, iv. 243.
—— —— Alexander, ii. 520.
—— —— his wife, Anne Houston, ii. 520.
—— —— Gabriel, v. 188.
—— —— his wife, Elizabeth Livingston, v. 188.
—— —— John, i. 389; iii. 464.
—— —— William, 1st laird, iv. 234.
—— —— William, vii. 533, 536.
—— —— William, vi. 420, 421.
—— —— his wife, Anne Chisholm, vi. 420.
—— —— William, vii. 387.
—— —— his wife, Anne Ruthven, vii. 387.
—— of Crosby, Alexander, iv. 239.
—— —— his wife, Janet Hamilton, iv. 239.
—— of Cunninghamhead, John, v. 162.
—— —— his wife, Margaret Boyd, v. 162.
—— —— John, vi. 238.
—— —— his wife, Mary Edmonstoue, vi. 238.
—— —— Robert, 1st laird, iv. 231.
—— —— his wife, Marion Lockhart, iv. 231.
—— —— William, alleged ancestor of the family of, iv. 230.
—— —— Sir William, 1st bart., v. 498.
—— —— his 2nd wife, Margaret Campbell, v. 498.
—— —— Sir William, 2nd bart., vii. 387.
—— —— his wife, Anne Ruthven, vii. 387.
—— —— Sir William, 3rd bart., vii. 387.
—— of Cutteswray, Alexander, iv. 238.
—— —— Andrew, 2nd son of 3rd earl of Glencairn, iv. 238.
—— of Dankeith, *, vi. 372.
—— —— his wife, Jean Douglas, vi. 372.

* Name unknown.

Cunningham of Davidstoun, Robert, 4th son of 3rd earl of Glencairn, iv. 239.
—— of Drips, Sir Alexander, iv. 233.
—— of Drumalin, Cuthbert, iv. 235.
—— of Drummond, Sir Alexander, iv. 234.
—— of Drummore, Sir William, iv. 229.
—— of Drumquhassil, Andrew, alleged ancestor of the family of, iv. 226.
—— —— John, viii. 541.
—— —— Sir John, ii. 552; v. 163.
—— —— his 2nd wife, Elizabeth Boyd, v. 163.
—— —— John, iii. 536.
—— —— his wife, Margaret Elphinstone, iii. 536.
—— of Duchray, Sir Alexander, iv. 234.
—— of Enterkine, John, W.S., viii. 125.
—— —— William, ii. 29; vi. 178.
—— —— his wife, Katharine Hamilton, ii. 29.
—— of Eschend, Andrew, iv. 226.
—— —— his wife, Margaret *, iv. 226.
—— of Finlaystoun, Sir Alexander, iv. 232, 233.
—— of Garvard, Robert, eldest son of Sir Wm. C. of Kilmaurs, iv. 227.
—— of Geise, John, ii. 348.
—— —— his wife, Elizabeth Sinclair, ii. 348.
—— of Gilbertland, ii. 41.
—— —— his wife, * Hamilton, ii. 41.
—— of Glencairn, Sir Alexander, iv. 233.
—— of Glengarnock, Sir James, iv. 245.
—— —— his wife, Katharine Cunningham, iv. 245.
—— —— John, ii. 146; iv. 192.
—— —— John, viii. 537.
—— —— his wife, Margaret Fleming, viii. 537; ix. 169.
—— —— Reginald, alleged ancestor of the family of, iv. 225.
—— —— William, iii. 433.
—— —— his wife, Agnes Montgomerie, iii. 433.
—— of Grange, Edward, iv. 224.
—— of Grugar, Robert, iv. 225.
—— of Hassendean, Sir James, iv. 225 *n.*
—— —— his wife, Elena Quarentely, iv. 225 *n.*
—— —— James, iv. 225 *n.*
—— —— Sir William, iv. 229.
—— of Hassendean Bank, Christal, iv. 229.
—— —— James, iv. 229.
—— of Hilton, Sir Alexander, iv. 233.
—— of Innerleithen, James, 3rd son of 4th earl of Glencairn, iv. 241; v. 63.
—— of Kerilaw, James, 3rd son of 6th earl of Glencairn, iv. 245.
—— of Kilbride, Sir Alexander, iv. 233.
—— —— Sir William, iv. 227.
—— of Kildinnie, Andrew, iv. 226.
—— —— his wife, Margaret *, iv. 226.

* Name unknown.

Cunningham of Kilfassane, Andrew, iv. 226.
—— —— Sir Humphrey, iv. 226, 229, 231.
—— of Kilmaronock, Sir Alexander, iv. 233.
—— —— John, 2nd son of 6th earl of Glencairn, iv. 244, 246.
—— —— his wife, Margaret Knox, iv. 245.
—— of Kilmaurs, Sir Alexander, ii. 328; iii. 63; iv. 232.
—— —— his wife, Margaret Hepburn, iv. 234.
—— —— Edward, iv. 224.
—— —— his wife, * Stewart, iv. 224.
—— —— Hervey de, iv. 224.
—— —— Hugh, iv. 225.
—— —— Richard de, iv. 223.
—— —— Sir Robert, bailie of Cunningham, iii. 431 *bis*; iv. 231; vi. 366.
—— —— his wife, Agnes Montgomerie, iii. 431; iv. 232.
—— —— Robert, son of Edward C., iv. 225.
—— —— Sir William, lord of Carrick, iv. 226.
—— —— his wife, Margaret *, iv. 227.
—— —— Sir William, iv. 224, 227, 228.
—— —— his 1st wife, Margaret Danielston, iv. 230; ix. 96.
—— —— his 2nd wife, Marjory *or* Mary Stewart, i. 18; iv. 230; ix. 2.
—— of Kincleven, Sir William, iv. 227.
—— of Kirktonholm, Sir Walter Montgomery, iv. 252.
—— of Lainshaw, Alexander Montgomerie; self-styled lord Lyle, v. 557.
—— —— his wife, Elizabeth Montgomerie, v. 557.
—— —— William, ii. 598.
—— —— his wife, Margaret Nicolson Cranstoun, ii. 598.
—— of Lambroughton, Hugh, iv. 225.
—— —— Robert, iv. 225.
—— —— Sir William, iv. 227.
—— of Langlands, Sir William, iv. 236.
—— of Wester Loudoun, William, v. 493, 495.
—— —— his wife, Marion Auchinleck, v. 493.
—— of Milncraig, Sir David, 1st bart., M.P., viii. 147.
—— —— his 1st wife, Margaret Dalrymple, viii. 147.
—— of Milncraig and Livingstone, Sir David ii. 303; iii. 457.
—— —— his wife, Mary Montgomerie, iii. 457.
—— of Montgrenane, Alexander, commendator of Kilwinning, iv. 240, 241, 243.
—— —— his wife, Jean Blair, iv. 242.
—— —— Hugh, 3rd son of 3rd earl of Glencairn, iv. 238, 242.
—— —— James, iv. 242, 246.

* Name unknown.

Cunningham of Montgrenane, Robert, 4th son of 3rd earl of Glencairn, iv. 239.
—— —— his wife, Mariota *, iv. 239.
—— —— Thomas, ii. 30.
—— of Netherton, Robert, v. 164.
—— of Neve, Sir William, iv. 229.
—— of Overtoun, Robert, v. 164.
—— of Pearston, Sir William, iv. 229.
—— of Pennymore, Agnes, wife of 2nd lord Ochiltree, vi. 512.
—— of Polmaise, iii. 527; iv. 238.
—— of Polquhairn, Hugh de, iv. 225.
—— —— Sir William, iv. 227.
—— of Powton, Alexander, viii. 117.
—— —— his wife, Isabel Dunbar, viii. 117.
—— of Ranfurly, Robert, iv. 225 *n.*
—— of Redhall, Robert, eldest son of 1st earl of Glencairn, iv. 234.
—— —— Sir William, iv. 229.
—— —— Sir William, iv. 236; ix. 97.
—— of Robertland, Sir Alexander, iv. 245.
—— —— his wife, Margaret Cunningham, ix. 97.
—— —— David, iv. 240; vii. 547.
—— —— Sir David, 2nd bart., v. 173.
—— —— his wife, Jean *or* Eva Boyd, v. 173.
—— —— Sir David, 4th bart., iii. 351; iv. 249.
—— —— his wife, Elizabeth Hamilton, iv. 249, 380.
—— —— Diana, wife of Thomas Cochrane of Polkellie, iii. 351.
—— —— William, alleged ancestor of the family of, iv. 234.
—— of Ross, James, iv. 242, 246.
—— —— John, 2nd son of 5th earl of Glencairn, iv. 242; ix. 97.
—— —— John, 2nd son of 6th earl of Glencairn, iv. 243, 244; ix. 97.
—— —— his wife, Margaret Knox, ix. 97 *bis*.
—— —— John, his son, iv. 245; ix. 97.
—— of Scoulock, Thomas, ii. 290.
—— of Skelmorlie, Sir William, iv. 227.
—— of Snaid, John, viii. 433.
—— of Stevenston, Alexander, commendator of Kilwinning, iv. 241, 243.
—— —— James, 3rd son of 6th earl of Glencairn, iv. 245.
—— of Stewarton, Sir Alexander, 2nd bart., iv. 200.
—— —— his wife, Margaret Cunningham, iv. 200.
—— of Syid, Andrew, 2nd son of 4th earl of Glencairn, iv. 241.
—— of Toir, Alexander, iv. 188.
—— —— his wife, Margaret Barclay, iv. 188.
—— of Walterstoun, Hugh, vii. 537.
—— of Warrix, Sir William, iv. 229.
—— of Warwickhill, Sir William, iv. 229.
—— of Waterstoun, Alexander, iv. 246.

* Name unknown.

Cunningham of Waterstoun, Archibald, brother of 1st earl of Glencairn, iv. 232.
—— —— Hugh, 3rd son of 3rd earl of Glencairn, iv. 238, 239, 242.
—— —— Ninian, iv. 239.
—— —— William, iv. 234.
—— of Woodhall, Adam, advocate, iv. 246.
—— —— William, iv. 230, 231; ix. 96.
—— Alexander, commendator of Kilwinning, ii. 293; iv. 240, 241, 243.
—— Alexander, iii. 437 *n.*
—— —— his wife, Elizabeth Montgomerie, iii. 437 *n.*
—— Alexander, 4th son of Sir Wm. C. of Kilmaurs, iv. 228, 229, 231.
—— Alexander, 3rd son of 1st earl of Glencairn, iv. 234.
—— Alexander, elder son of Alex. C. of Corsehill, iv. 238.
—— —— his wife, Anna Crawford, iv. 238.
—— Alexander, 3rd son of 7th earl of Glencairn, iv. 246.
—— Alexander, 6th son of 11th earl of Glencairn, iv. 250.
—— Alexander, 4th son of 12th earl of Glencairn, iv. 251.
—— Anna, wife of bishop Robert Wallace, ix. 97.
—— Anne, wife of Sir Robt. Dalrymple of Castleton, i. 523; viii. 131.
—— Anne, wife of 2nd marquess of Hamilton, iv. 245, 375.
—— Anne, dau. of 7th earl of Glencairn, iv. 247.
—— Anne, dau. of 8th earl of Glencairn, iv. 249.
—— Ann, dau. of John C. of Ross, ix. 97.
—— Anne Colquhoun, wife of (1) Dr. G. C. Monteath, and (2) 7th duke of Argyll, i. 389.
—— Anne Selby, wife of 2nd lord Ashburton ii. 598.
—— Archibald, 2nd son of Andrew C. of Kilfassane, iv. 226, 229, 231.
—— Sir Archibald, son of Sir Nigel C., iv. 226, 229, 231 *bis.*
—— Archibald, 2nd son of 2nd lord Kilmaurs, ix. 97.
—— Boyd Alexander, iii. 464.
—— Charles, 7th son of 11th earl of Glencairn, iv. 250.
—— Edward, 4th son of 1st earl of Glencairn, iv. 234.
—— Elizabeth, wife of Jas. Hamilton, ii. 55.
—— Elizabeth, wife of (1) Laurence, 1st lord Oliphant, and (2) Sir John Elphinstone of Airth, iii. 529; vi. 543.
—— Elizabeth, wife of Sir John Cunningham of Caprington, iv. 239.
—— Elizabeth, wife (1) of Jas. Craufurd of Auchenames, and (2) Alex. Cunningham of Craigends, iv. 243.
Cunningham, Elizabeth, wife of Sir Ludovic Stewart of Minto, iv. 247; ix. 97 *bis.*
—— Elizabeth, wife of Wm. Hamilton of Orbistoun, iv. 249; ix. 98.
—— Elizabeth, dau. of 12th earl of Glencairn, iv. 251.
—— Elizabeth, wife of (1) Thos. Boyd of Pitcon, and (2) bishop Andrew Boyd, v. 168; ix. 119.
—— Elizabeth, wife of brigadier-general John Middleton of Seaton, vi. 178.
—— Elizabeth, wife of Sir James Makgill, vi. 587.
—— Elizabeth, wife of Wm. Wallace of Helenton, ix. 97.
—— Esther, wife of (1) William Fletcher of New Cranstoun, and (2) Sir Jas. Dalrymple of Cousland, viii. 120, 125.
—— Galfrid de, *error for* Cunigsburg, iv. 222 *n.*
—— Sir George, colonel in Swedish service, iv. 193; viii. 391.
—— —— his wife Elizabeth *, viii. 391.
—— George, in Rawis of Grugair, v. 167.
—— Gilbert de, *error for* Cuningsburg, iv. 225 *n.*
—— Grizel, wife of Sir Thomas Boyd of Bedlay and Bolinshaw, v. 166.
—— Harriet, wife of Sir A. Don, iv. 251, 252.
—— Helen, wife of (1) John Stewart, and (2) Sir W. Stewart of Monkton, vi. 513.
—— Henrietta, wife of John Campbell of Shawfield, iv. 251; ix. 98.
—— Henrietta, wife of Sir Alex. Don of Newton Don, iv. 251, 252.
—— Herbert, writer, Dumfries, ii. 390.
—— —— his wife, Mary Carlyle, ii. 390.
—— Isobell, wife of James Stewart of Ambrismore, ii. 290.
—— Isobel, wife of John Scrymgeour, Constable of Dundee, iii. 311.
—— Isobel, wife of (1) David Makgill of Cranston Riddell, and (2) James Wardlaw, vi. 593.
—— Isobel, wife of (1) Jas. Livingston, and (2) Wm. Weir, viii. 371.
—— Isobel, wife of Peter Sandilands of North Pittedie, ix. 4.
—— James, brother of John C. of Drumquhassill, ii. 552.
—— —— his wife Margaret Colville, ii. 552.
—— James, prior of Lesmahagow, iv. 241.
—— —— his wife Jean Blair, iv. 242.
—— James, 8th son of 11th earl of Glencairn, iv. 250.
—— James, 4th son of 6th earl of Glencairn, ix. 97.
—— Jane *or* Janet, wife of (1) Archibald, 5th earl of Argyll, and (2) H. Colquhoun, i. 343; iv. 242; vii. 552.
—— Janet, wife of Sir A. Hepburn, ii. 146.

* Name unknown.

Cunningham, Janet, wife of John Boyle of Ballikewin, iv. 188.
— Janet, wife of Wm. Bothwell of Quhelpsyde, iv. 434.
— Janet, wife of 4th earl of Glencairn, iv. 240, 241.
— Janet Lucretia, wife of 15th earl of Eglinton, iii. 464.
— Jean, wife of (1) Alex. Sinclair of Latheron, and (2) Wm. Sinclair of Ratter, ii. 348; ix. 52.
— Jean, wife of Henry Elphinstone of Pittendreich, iii. 527.
— Jean, wife of Robt. Fergusson of Craigdarroch, iv. 239.
— Jean, wife of (1) Geo. Haldane, and (2) Thos. Kirkpatrick, iv. 243; ix. 97.
— Jean, contracted to 5th earl of Cassillis, iv. 245; vii. 552; ix. 57.
— Jean, wife of John Blair of that Ilk, iv. 247; ix. 97.
— Jean, wife of 1st earl of Kilmarnock, iv. 249; v. 174.
— John, 5th son of Sir Wm. C. of Kilmaurs, iv. 228, 229, 231.
— John, illeg. son of Sir Wm. C. of Kilmaurs, iv. 231.
— John, 3rd son of 11th earl of Glencairn, iv. 250.
— John A. E., Balgownie, Culross, v. 565.
— Katharine, wife of Robt. Fergusson of Craigdarroch, iv. 243.
— Katharine, wife of Sir Jas. Cunningham of Glengarnock, iv. 245.
— Katharine, dau. of 11th earl of Glencairn, iv. 251.
— Lilias, dau. of 7th earl of Glencairn, iv. 247.
— Malcolm Fleming, 5th son of 11th earl of Glencairn, iv. 250.
— Margaret, wife of 2nd lord Bargany, ii. 31; iv. 249; ix. 36.
— Margaret, wife of J. A. Stuart-Wortley-Mackenzie, ii. 303.
— Margaret, wife of (1) Gilbert Kennedy, and (2) Robert, 6th lord Crichton of Sanquhar, iii. 229.
— Margaret, wife of (1) James Cochrane, and (2) James Murehead, iii. 340 *n*.
— Margaret, wife of (1) John Wallace of Craigie, and (2) Andrew, 2nd lord Ochiltree, iv. 241; vi. 513; ix. 97.
— Margaret, wife of Fergus Macdowall, iv. 228.
— Margaret, wife of Andrew Cunningham of Corsehill and Cuttiswray, iv. 238.
— Margaret, wife of Sir L. M. Maclean of Duart, iv. 243; ix. 97.
— Margaret, wife of Sir Alex. Cunningham of Robertland, iv. 245.
— Margaret, wife of (1) Jas. Hamilton of Evandale, and (2) Sir Jas. Maxwell of Calderwood, iv. 245.
Cunningham, Margaret, wife of (1) David and (2) John Chisholm of Cromlix, iv. 247.
— Margaret, wife of 5th earl of Lauderdale, iv. 249, 252; v. 310.
— Margaret, wife of Nicol Graham of Gartmore, iv. 250, 252; ix. 98.
— Margaret, wife of James, master of Lyle, v. 557.
— Margaret, wife of Wm. Napier of Ardmore, vi. 421.
— Margaret, wife of Jas. Dalrymple of Nunraw, viii. 141.
— Marion, wife of Wm. Montgomerie, iii. 440.
— Marion, wife of (1) James, 1st earl of Findlater, and (2) Alexander, master of Saltoun, iv. 29, 247; vii. 444; ix. 98.
— Marion, dau. of Andrew C. of Birkshaw, vii. 119 *n*.
— Marion, dau. of John C. of Ross, ix. 97.
— Mariot, wife of 1st lord Herries of Terregles, iv. 404.
— Mary, wife of John Crawford of Kilbirnie, iv. 246; ix. 97.
— Mary, dau. of 11th earl of Glencairn, iv. 251.
— Maud, wife of Cuthbert Cunningham of Aiket, iv. 238.
— Ninian, executor of Bishop of Argyll, 1562; iv. 239.
— Richard, brigadier-general, vii. 221.
— — his wife Grisel Primrose, vii. 221.
— Robert de, constable of Carlaverock Castle, iv. 225.
— Robert, son and heir of Robert de C., iv. 225 *n*.
— Robert, minister of the priory of Fail, Provincial of the Order of the Holy Trinity, iv. 239.
— his wife, Mariota *, iv. 239.
— Robert, colonel, joint Principal Usher to King Charles I., iv. 246.
— — his wife, Anne Scot, iv. 246.
— Susanna, wife of John Napier of Kilmahew, iv. 243; vii. 552.
— Susanna, wife of Alex. Lauder of Hatton, iv. 246.
— Susanna, wife of Hew Dalrymple of Nunraw, viii. 141.
— William, in Dolphinton, ii. 392, 394.
— William, son of Sir Archibald C., iv. 226, 231 *bis*.
— William, vicar of Dundonald, canon of Glasgow, iv. 231; vii. 529.
— William, dean of Brechin, bishop of Argyll, iv. 239.
— William, 2nd son of the commendator of Kilwinning, iv. 242, 246.

* Name unknown.

Cunningham, William, rector of Inchcailleoch, prebendary of Bonhill and Fluris, iv. 243.
— William, eldest son of William C. of Craigends, vi. 421.
— — his wife, Elizabeth Napier, vi. 421.
— William de, sheriff of Ayr, v. 491; vii. 529.
Cunningham-Ruthven of Cunninghamhead, Sir William, 3rd bart., vii. 387.
Curgenven, Peter, viii. 37.
— — his wife, Frances Rotherham, viii. 37.
Currie, Archibald, vii. 207.
— — his wife, Jessie Rollo, vii. 207.
— Simon, vi. 592.
— — his wife, Helen Makgill, vi. 592.
Curriehill, Sir James Skene, lord president of the College of Justice, lord, iii. 488.
Curerour, James, ii. 4.
Cursham of Hartwell, Curzon, in holy orders, iii. 417.
— Alice Elizabeth, wife of A. E. Tollemache, iii. 417.
Curtenay, William de, iii. 254, 440.
— — his wife, Ada of Dunbar, lady of Home and Pullys, iii. 254, 440, 442.
Curzon of Kedleston, Sir Nathaniel, 4th bart., vii. 94.
— Eleanor, wife of W. H. D. Boyle, iv. 212.
— Henry Dugdale, iv. 212.
Curzon-Howe, Mary Anna, wife of 2nd duke of Abercorn, i. 72.
Cust, Perigrine Francis, ii. 245.
— — his wife, Isabella Mary Scott, ii. 244.
Custance, Frederick Hambledon, col., C.B., vii. 154.
— Olive Eleanor, wife of Alfred Bruce Douglas, vii. 154.
Custancia, wife of Sir William of Douglas, 'Longleg,' iii. 137.
Cuthbert of Castlehill, v. 561.
— — his wife, Margaret Macdonald, v. 561.
— of Drakies, James, v. 565.
— John, town-clerk of Inverness, iii. 212.
— — his wife, Katharine Sutherland, iii. 212.
Cutlar of Orroland, John, v. 261.
— — his wife, Nicolas Maxwell, v. 261.
Cyprian, master, vi. 198.

DACRE, RICHARD (Lennard), 12th baron, ii. 35.
— — his wife, Dorothy North, ii. 35.
— Thomas (Barrett-Lennard), 17th lord, ii. 35 *n.*
— of Gillesland, Thomas, 2nd baron, warden of the Middle Marches, v. 54, 57: vii. 333.
Dacre, Hugh, vi. 342.
— — his wife, Elizabeth Maxwell, vi. 342 *n.*
— Sir William, vi. 342; vii. 578.
Dacres, captain R.N., viii. 141.
— — his wife, Arabella Boyd Dalrymple, viii. 141.
DAER, DOUGLAS, LORD, iv. 381; vii. 516-525.
Daer, Basil William, 2nd son of 4th earl of Selkirk; styled lord, vii. 521.
— John, 3rd son of 4th earl of Selkirk; styled lord, vii. 522.
— William, 3rd son of 1st marquess of Douglas; first lord, i. 205; iv. 381; vii. 516.
— — his wife, Anne, duchess of Hamilton, iv. 381.
— William, son of John, earl of Selkirk and Ruglen; styled lord, vii. 362.
Daes, Beatrix, wife of P. Lindsay, v. 408, 409.
— William, merchant burgess, St. Andrews, v. 408.
Dagmore, Edward Ernest, vicar of Parkstone, v. 237.
— — his wife, Elizabeth Hay, v. 237.
D'Aguilar, Georgina Isabella, wife of vice-admiral Keith Stewart of Glasserton, iv. 166.
— Simha, iv. 166.
Dakins of Brandsburton, John, iii. 292.
— Marjory, wife of M. Constable, iii. 292.
Dalbiac, Sir Charles, lieut.-gen., vii. 357.
— Susanna Stephanie, wife of 6th duke of Roxburghe, vii. 357.
Dale, Dorothy, wife of 14th lord Forbes, iv. 64; ix. 91.
— William, Covent Garden, iv. 64.
Dalgarno, Alexander, Aberdeen, i. 144.
— Mary, wife of Robt. Barclay-Allardice, i. 144.
Dalgleish of Errol, Sir William Ogilvy, 1st bart., iv. 36.
— of Scotscraig, William, v. 316.
— Christian, wife of D. Campbell, ii. 200; ix. 45.
— Margaret, wife of Jas. Heriot-Maitland of Ramornie, v. 316.
— Walter, ii. 200.
— Sir William, ii. 573.
— — his wife, Elizabeth Colvill, ii. 573.
Dalglish, Alexander Augustus, iv. 422.
— — his wife, M. J. Constable-Maxwell-Scott, iv. 422.
DALHOUSIE, RAMSAY, EARL OF, iii. 87-110.
Dalhousie, Arthur George Maule, fourteenth earl of, iii. 109.
— — his wife, Mary Adelaide Heathcote Drummond Willoughby, iii. 109.
— Charles, seventh earl of, iii. 103; vii. 23; ix. 66.

Dalhousie, Fox Maule, eleventh earl of, iii. 104, 107; vii. 1, 24.
—— —— his wife, Montagu Abercromby, iii. 108.
—— George, second earl of, iii. 100.
—— —— his wife, Anne Fleming, iii. 100; v. 172; viii. 550.
—— George, fourth earl of, iii. 102.
—— George, eighth earl of, iii. 103; vii. 23 *ter*.
—— —— his wife, Elizabeth Glen, iii. 103.
—— George, ninth earl of, iii. 103, 105: ix. 66.
—— —— his wife, Christian Broun, iii. 106.
—— George, twelfth earl of, iii. 104, 108.
—— —— his wife, Sarah Frances Robertson, iii. 108.
—— James Andrew, tenth earl of, iii. 106; ix. 67.
—— —— his wife, Susan Georgiana Hay, iii. 107; viii. 471; ix. 67.
—— John William, thirteenth earl of, iii. 109.
—— —— his wife, Ida Louisa Bennet, iii. 109.
—— William, first earl of, iii. 99.
—— —— his 1st wife, Margaret Carnegie, iii. 99; viii. 67.
—— —— his 2nd wife, Jocosa Apsley, iii. 99.
—— William, third earl of, ii. 73; iii. 101.
—— —— his wife, Mary Moore, iii. 101.
—— William, fifth earl of, iii. 102.
—— William, sixth earl of, iii. 102; ix. 66 *bis*.
—— —— his 1st wife, Jean Ross, iii. 102: vii. 259.
—— —— his 2nd wife, Janet Martin, iii. 102.
DALHOUSIE OF DALHOUSIE CASTLE, RAMSAY, BARON, iii. 106-107.
Dalhousie, George, first baron, iii. 106.
—— James Andrew, second baron, iii. 106.
DALHOUSIE, RAMSAY, MARQUESS OF, iii. 106-107.
Dalhousie, James Andrew, marquess of, iii. 106.
—— —— his wife, Susan Georgiana Hay, iii. 107; viii. 471.
DALHOUSIE, RAMSAY, LORD RAMSAY OF, iii. 98.
Daliel, *see* Dalzell.
DALKEITH, DOUGLAS, LORD, vi. 369-379.
Dalkeith, Robert, eldest son of 6th earl of Morton; styled lord, vi. 378.
—— William, last lord, vi. 379.
DALKEITH, SCOTT, EARL OF, ii. 237.
Dalkeith, Francis, elder son of 2nd duke of Buccleuch; styled earl of, ii. 241.
—— —— his wife, Caroline Campbell, i. 377; ii. 241.
—— George, eldest son of 3rd duke of Buccleuch; styled earl of, ii. 243; ix. 46.
—— James, first earl of, ii. 237; vi. 379.
—— —— his wife, Anna, duchess of Buccleuch, ii. 237.
Dalkeith, James, 2nd son of above; styled earl of, ii. 240.
—— —— his wife, Henrietta Hyde, ii. 240.
—— John Charles, 2nd son of 6th duke of Buccleuch; styled earl of, ii. 247.
—— —— his wife, Margaret Alice Bridgeman, ii. 240.
DALKEITH, STEWART, LORD, v. 356-362.
Dalkeith, Esmé, first lord, v. 356.
Dallas, Margaret, wife of William Oliphant, collector of excise, vi. 562.
Dallyson, Joyce, wife of Robert Aston, i. 400.
—— William, judge of King's Bench, i. 400.
Dalmahoy of Dalmahoy, Alexander *or* William, iv. 362; ix. 103.
—— —— his wife, Agnes Hamilton, iv. 362.
—— —— Sir John, iii. 130.
—— of the Priory, Thomas, M.P., master of Buckhounds, iii. 130.
—— —— his wife, Elizabeth Maxwell, iii. 130.
—— of Ravelrig, Sir William, iii. 282.
—— —— William, vii. 445.
—— —— his wife, Mary Fraser, vii. 445.
—— Jean, wife of Sir Patrick Home of Lumsden, iii. 282.
DALMENY, PRIMROSE, LORD, vii. 221-229.
Dalmeny, Albert Edward Harry Meyer Archibald, styled lord, vii. 228.
—— —— his wife, Dorothy Alice Margaret Augusta Grosvenor, vii. 228.
—— Archibald, first lord, vii. 221.
—— John, eldest son of 2nd earl of Rosebery; styled lord, vii. 223.
—— —— his wife, Katherine Canham, vii. 223.
—— Archibald, elder son of 4th earl of Rosebery; styled lord, vii. 227.
—— —— his wife, Katharine Lucy Wilhelmina Stanhope, vii. 227.
Dalreoch, Andrew of, i. 452.
DALRYMPLE, DALRYMPLE, VISCOUNT, viii. 149-164.
Dalrymple, John, first viscount, viii. 149.
—— John, son of 5th earl of Stair; styled viscount, viii. 157.
—— John James, son of 11th earl of Stair; styled viscount, viii. 163.
—— —— his wife, Violet Harford, viii. 163.
DALRYMPLE, VISCOUNT DALRYMPLE, viii. 149-164.
DALRYMPLE, LORD GLENLUCE, viii. 149-164.
DALRYMPLE, LORD NEWLISTON, viii. 149-164.
DALRYMPLE, BARON OXENFOORD OF COUSLAND, viii. 159-164.
DALRYMPLE, VISCOUNT OF STAIR, viii. 118-164.
DALRYMPLE, EARL OF STAIR, viii. 114-164.
DALRYMPLE, LORD STRANRAER, viii. 149-164.
Dalrymple of Annaston, John, vi. 407.
—— of Balkissock, Alexander, viii. 116.
—— of Bolton, James, viii. 115.

Dalrymple of Bolton, John, iv. 336.
— of Borthwick, Sir James, 1st bart., ii. 115 *n.*, 317; viii. 120.
— of Camraggan, James de, ancestor of the family of, viii. 114, 115.
— — John, viii. 115.
— — John, viii. 115.
— — his wife, Elizabeth Dalrymple, viii. 115.
— — Robert, viii. 115.
— of Carriden, Campbell, lieut.-col. 3rd Dragoons, governor of Guadeloupe, viii. 137.
— — his wife, Margaret Douglas, viii. 131, 137.
— of Castleton, Sir Robert, ii. 31; v. 539. viii. 126.
— — his 1st wife, Johanna Hamilton of Bargany, ii. 31; viii. 126.
— — his 2nd wife, Anne Cunninghame, viii. 131.
— of Cleland, William, viii. 122.
— of Cousland, Sir James, 1st bart., viii. 120.
— — Sir John, 2nd bart., viii. 120.
— — his 1st wife, Elizabeth Fletcher, viii. 120.
— — his 2nd wife, Sidney Sinclair, viii. 124.
— — Sir John, 4th bart., vi. 597; viii. 121.
— — his wife, Elizabeth Hamilton-Makgill, vi. 597: viii. 121.
— — Sir William, 3rd bart., viii. 120.
— — his 1st wife, Agnes Crawford, viii. 121.
— — his 2nd wife, Ann Philp, viii. 123.
— of Dalbane, Robert, viii. 115.
— of Dalmahoy, George, advocate, M.P., viii. 150.
— — his wife, Euphame Myrton, viii. 150.
— of Dalrymple, Adam de, ii. 445; viii. 116.
— — Gilchrist, son of Adam de D., ii. 445; viii. 114.
— — Hew, son of Roland de D., ii. 445; viii. 114.
— — Malcolm, son of Gilchrist de D., ii. 445; viii. 114.
— — Roland de, ii. 445; viii. 114.
— of Drummore, Hew, lord of Justiciary, viii. 132.
— — his wife, Anne Horn, viii. 132.
— of Drummurchie, James, 2nd son of James D. of Stair, viii. 117 *bis*, 118.
— — his wife, Janet Kennedy, viii. 118.
— of Fordel, Hew, 5th son of Sir John D. of Cousland, viii. 124.
— — his wife, Helen Wemyss, viii. 124, 512.
— — Marton, viii. 122.
— — his wife, Frances Ingram Spence, viii. 122.
Dalrymple of Fordel, William, viii. 122.
— — his wife, Diana Molyneux, viii. 122.
— of Glenmure, William, 5th son of 1st earl of Stair, colonel, M.P., iii. 236; viii. 149, 154.
— — his wife, Penelope, countess of Dumfries, iii. 236; viii. 150.
— of Hailes, Christian, dau. of lord Hailes, viii. 144.
— — Sir David, 1st bart., lord advocate, viii. 143.
— — his wife, Janet Rochead, viii. 143.
— — Sir David, 3rd bart., lord of Justiciary, lord Hailes, viii. 143.
— — his 1st wife, Anne Broun, viii. 144.
— — his 2nd wife, Helen Fergusson, viii. 144.
— — Sir James, 2nd bart., viii. 143.
— — his wife, Christian Hamilton, iv. 321; viii. 143.
— — Sir James, 4th bart., viii. 146.
— — Sir John Pringle, 5th bart., viii. 146.
— — his wife, Mary Rushworth, viii. 146.
— of Harvieston, James, viii. 125.
— — his wife, Martha Crawford, viii. 125.
— of High Mark, Adolphus John, 2nd bart., viii. 140.
— — his wife, Anne Graham, viii. 140.
— — Hew Whitefoord, 1st bart., viii. 140.
— — his wife, Frances Leighton, viii. 140.
— of Inglesfield, James, viii. 115.
— of Inglistoun, John, vi. 407.
— of Kelloch, Sir James, 1st bart., ii. 317; viii. 120.
— — his 1st wife, Katharine Dundas, viii. 120.
— — his 2nd wife, Esther Cunningham, viii. 125.
— — his 3rd wife, Jean Halket, viii. 125.
— — Sir William, 3rd bart., viii. 120.
— — Robert, W.S., viii. 124.
— — his wife, Elizabeth Boick, viii. 124.
— of Laucht, James, ancestor of the family of, viii. 114, 115.
— — John, vi. 407.
— — Robert, viii. 115.
— of Newhailes, Sir Charles, 1st bart., M.P., viii. 144.
— — his wife, Alice Mary Hunter Blair, viii. 145.
— of North Berwick, Sir John, 5th bart., viii. 128.
— — his wife, Charlotte Warrender, viii. 128.
— — Sir John Warrender, 7th bart., viii. 128.
— — his wife, Sophia Pattle, viii. 128.

Dalrymple of North Berwick, Sir Hew, 1st bart., lord president of the Court of Session, i. 478; ii. 31; viii. 125.
—— —— his 1st wife, Marion Hamilton, ii. 44; viii. 126; ix. 37.
—— —— his 2nd wife, Elizabeth Hamilton of Bangour, viii. 142.
—— —— Sir Hew, 2nd bart., i. 211; ii. 31.
—— —— his 1st wife, Margaret Sainthill, ii. 31; viii. 126.
—— —— his 2nd wife, Martha Edwin, ii. 31; viii. 130.
—— —— Sir Hew, 3rd bart., viii. 126.
—— —— his wife, Janet Duff, viii. 126.
—— —— Sir Hew, 4th bart., viii. 127.
—— —— his wife, Jane Duncan, viii. 127.
—— —— Sir Hew, 6th bart., viii. 128.
—— —— his wife, Frances Elizabeth Arkwright, viii. 128.
—— —— Sir Walter Hamilton, 8th bart., viii. 129.
—— —— his wife, Alice Mary Clifford, viii. 129.
—— of Nunraw, Hew, viii. 141.
—— —— his 1st wife, Susanna Cunningham, viii. 141.
—— —— his 2nd wife, Dorothea MacCormick, viii. 141.
—— —— James, viii. 141.
—— —— his wife, Margaret Cunningham, viii. 141.
—— of Pilmuir, James, viii. 115.
—— of Polbuth, James, viii. 115.
—— of Stair, James, 4th laird, viii. 117.
—— —— his wife, Isabel Kennedy, viii. 117.
—— —— James, 6th laird, viii. 117.
—— —— his wife, Marjory Cathcart, viii. 117.
—— —— James, 7th laird, viii. 118.
—— —— his wife, Janet Kennedy, viii. 118.
—— —— Sir James, president of the Court of Session, 8th laird, viii. 118.
—— —— his wife, Margaret Ross, viii. 119.
—— —— John, 5th laird, viii. 117.
—— —— his wife, Margaret Dunbar, viii. 117.
—— —— Sir John, the younger, ii. 483; viii. 120, 147.
—— —— William, 1st laird, viii. 115 *bis*.
—— —— his wife, Agnes Kennedy of Stair, viii. 115.
—— —— William, 2nd laird, viii. 115.
—— —— his wife, Marion Chalmers, viii. 115.
—— —— William, 3rd laird, viii. 116.
—— —— his wife, Margaret Wallace, viii. 116.
—— Agnes, wife of Sir Gilbert Elliot of Minto, viii. 146.
—— Agnes, dau. of Sir William D. of Kelloch, viii. 123.
—— Agnes, dau. of 1st earl of Stair, viii. 151.
Dalrymple, Agnes, wife of John More Nisbet of Cairnhill, viii. 160.
—— Agnes Mary, viii. 129.
—— Alexander, 2nd son of lord Westhall, viii. 137.
—— Alexander, 6th son of Sir Hew D. of North Berwick, viii. 141.
—— Alexander, hydrographer to Board of Admiralty, viii. 146.
—— Alexander Duncan, viii. 138.
—— Alice Mary, dau. of Sir Charles D. of Newhailes, viii. 145.
—— Ann, dau. of lord Westhall, viii. 137.
—— Anne, wife of 5th earl of Balcarres, i. 523; viii. 132; ix. 31.
—— Anne, wife of Sir Jas. Stewart of Goodtrees, ii. 276; viii. 142.
—— Anne, wife of T. Pritchard, viii. 124.
—— Anne, wife of Alex. Oswald, viii. 130.
—— Anne, wife of Sir John Dick Lauder, viii. 160.
—— Anne Henrietta, wife of major-gen. W. V. Brownlow, viii. 162.
—— Anne Walton, viii. 139.
—— Arabella Boyd, wife of capt. Dacres, viii. 141.
—— Argyle, captain 68th Foot, viii. 151.
—— Basil Walter, viii. 161.
—— Beatrice Susan, wife of Archibald Seton, lord Montgomerie, viii. 163.
—— Campbell James, commissioner at Havana, viii. 139.
—— —— his wife, Rosina Walton, viii. 139.
—— Caroline, wife of James Morgan Strahan, viii. 122.
—— Charles, 7th son of Sir Robt. D. of Castleton, iii. 42; viii. 131.
—— —— his 1st wife, Elizabeth Edwin, iii. 42; viii. 131.
—— —— his 2nd wife, Margaret Douglas, viii. 131, 137.
—— Charles, surgeon 4th Dragoon Guards, viii. 137.
—— Charles, student of medicine, viii. 145.
—— Charles, 4th son of col. Wm. D., viii. 150.
—— Charlotte, dau. of Robert D. of Kelloch, viii. 124.
—— Charlotte Douglas, wife of Wm. Gordon of Campbeltown, viii. 138.
—— Charlotte Elizabeth, wife of vice-admiral Sir John C. White, viii. 140.
—— Charlotte Sophia, wife of major-gen. John Clark, viii. 129.
—— Christian, wife of Hugh Stewart, viii. 123.
—— Christian, dau. of Sir John D. of Cousland, viii. 124.
—— Christian, dau. of Sir James D. of Borthwick, viii. 125.
—— Christian Elizabeth Louisa, wife of commr. John S. Dumaresq, viii. 145.

Dalrymple, David, 8th son of Sir James D. of Borthwick, viii. 125.
— David, lord of Session, lord Westhall, viii. 136.
— — his wife, Jean Aberdein, viii. 136.
— David Charles Herbert, R.N., viii. 145.
— — his wife, Margaret Anna Stewart, viii. 145.
— Donald Francis Napier, viii. 161.
— Dorothea, wife of William Grant of Congalton, viii. 142.
— Eleanor, wife of Sir Thomas Hay of Alderston, viii. 142.
— Eleanor, wife of Jas. Fergusson of Craigdarroch, viii. 151.
— Eleonora, dau. of lord provost John D., viii. 146.
— Eleanora Jean, wife of James Rannie, viii. 139.
— Elizabeth, wife of Wm. Duff, ii. 32; viii. 131.
— Elizabeth, wife of 7th lord Cathcart, ii. 518; viii. 147.
— Elizabeth, wife of 23rd earl of Crawford, 6th earl of Balcarres, iii. 42; viii. 131.
— Elizabeth, wife of Thos. Hamilton, Makgill, vi. 597; viii. 124.
— Elizabeth, wife of John Dalrymple of Camraggan, viii. 115.
— Elizabeth, wife of Wm. Hamilton of Bangour, viii. 123.
— Elizabeth, dau. of Robert D. of Kelloch, viii. 124.
— Elizabeth, wife of George Gray, viii. 124.
— Elizabeth, wife of George Broun of Colstoun, viii. 139.
— Elizabeth, wife of Sir Jeffrey Prendergast, viii. 142.
— Elizabeth, wife of Sir James Suttie of Balgone, viii. 142.
— Elizabeth, wife of John M'Douall of Freuch, viii. 150.
— Elizabeth, wife of lieut.-gen. Humphrey Bland, viii. 151.
— Elizabeth, dau. of 1st earl of Stair, viii. 151.
— Elizabeth Hamilton, dau. of 9th earl of Stair, viii. 160.
— Elizabeth Pilgrim, wife of capt. Colin Buchanan, viii. 139.
— Elizabeth Rosina, wife of J. D. Cral, viii. 139.
— Elizabeth Warrender, viii. 130.
— Ellen Arbuthnott, wife of capt. E. J. Bruce, viii. 138.
— Emily Ellen, dau. of 10th earl of Stair, viii. 163.
— Esther, wife of William Campbell of Stobs, viii. 125.
— Esther, dau. of Sir James D. of Borthwick, viii. 125.
Dalrymple, Euphemia, dau. of George D. of Dalmahoy, viii. 151.
— Frances Ellen, wife of rev. George Roberts, viii. 122.
— Frances Mary, wife of lieut.-gen. Edward Fanshaw, viii. 140.
— George, colonel, viii. 138.
— — his wife, Martha Willet Miller, viii. 138.
— George, ensign in col. Handysyd's Regiment, viii. 150.
— George Grey, Scots Fusilier Guards, viii. 160.
— — his wife, Ellinor Alice Napier, vi. 437; viii. 160.
— George North, viii. 160.
— — his wife, Jane Margaret Vannet, viii. 160.
— George William Francis, viii. 160.
— Georgina Hacking, wife of Sir W. H. Sewell, viii. 129.
— Gustavus, 4th son of Sir John D. of Cousland, viii. 124.
— Harriet Fane, viii. 139.
— Hew, lieut. R.N., viii. 122.
— Hew, 6th son of Sir William D. of Cousland, viii. 122.
— Hew, 5th son of Robert D. of Kelloch, viii. 124.
— Hew, 5th son of Sir James D. of Borthwick, viii. 125.
— Hew, 2nd son of Hew D. of Drummore, viii. 132.
— — his wife, Ann Inglis, viii. 132.
— Hew, eldest son of lord Westhall, viii. 137.
— Hew, major, viii. 138.
— — his wife, Marianne Straker, viii. 139.
— Hew, 19th regiment, viii. 142.
— Hew, R.N., captain H.M.S. *Canada*, viii. 145.
— Hew Clifford, viii. 129.
— Hew Hamilton, brigadier Royal Company of Archers, viii. 162.
— Hew Manners, viii. 139.
— — his wife, Agnes Macrae Elliot, viii. 139.
— Hew North, viii. 163.
— Helen Jane, wife of Alexander M'Lean of Ardgour, viii. 129.
— Helena, dau. of Hew D. of Nunraw, viii. 142.
— Hugh, cornet in Lord Cadogan's Dragoons, viii. 150.
— Isobel, dau. of 1st viscount of Stair, viii. 147.
— James, lt.-col. Royal Regiment, vii. 589; viii. 145.
— — his wife, Elizabeth St. Clair, vii. 589; viii. 145.
— James, son of James D. of Stair, viii. 117.

Dalrymple, James, lt.-col., 3rd son of Sir William D. of Kelloch, viii. 123.
—— James, 3rd son of Sir John D. of Cousland, viii. 124.
—— James, eldest son of Robert D. of Kelloch, viii. 124.
—— James, son of James D. of Harvieston, viii. 125.
—— James, 6th son of Sir Hew H. D. of North Berwick, viii. 130.
—— —— his wife, Mary Naesmyth, viii. 130.
—— James, captain of Dragoons, viii. 131.
—— —— his wife, Cordelia Appsley, viii. 131.
—— James, 6th son of Hew D. of Drummore, viii. 137.
—— James, captain, viii. 138.
—— —— his wife, Anne Gascoigne, iv. 324; viii. 138.
—— James, son of Hew D. of Nunraw, viii. 141.
—— James, eldest son of Sir John D., advocate, viii. 149.
—— James Pilgrim, lieut.-col., viii. 139.
—— Jane, wife of major-gen. Roberts, viii. 123.
—— Jane Georgina, wife of Sir A. P. Vivian, viii. 162.
—— Janet, 'the Bride of Lammermoor,' wife of David Dunbar, younger of Baldoon, vii. 381; viii. 147.
—— Janet, wife of 1st earl of Camperdown, viii. 130.
—— Janet, dau. of Sir James D. of Hailes, viii. 146.
—— Janet, wife of (1) Sir John Baird of Newbyth, and (2) gen. James St. Clair of Dysart, viii. 147.
—— Janet Jemima, wife of rev. James George Fussell, viii. 129.
—— Jean, wife of George Reid, viii. 124.
—— Jean, wife of Andrew Colly, viii. 124.
—— Jean, dau. of Sir James D. of Borthwick, viii. 125.
—— Jean, wife of John Anderson of Winterfield, viii. 137.
—— Jean, wife of Sir James Fergusson of Kilkerran, viii. 144.
—— Jean Margaret Florence, viii. 163.
—— Johanna, dau. of Sir Hew D. of North Berwick, viii. 143.
—— Sir John, lord advocate, joint-secretary of State for Scotland, ii. 30; iii. 328; v. 193; vi. 108; viii. 147.
—— —— his wife, Elizabeth Dundas of Newliston, viii. 149.
—— John, elder son of William D. of Stair, viii. 116.
—— —— his 1st wife, Christina Crawfurd, viii. 116.
—— —— his 2nd wife, Elizabeth *, viii. 116.

* Name unknown.

Dalrymple, John, major, 40th regt. of foot, viii. 122.
—— John, admiral R.N., viii. 124.
—— —— his wife, Elenore Howard, viii. 124.
—— John, 2nd son of Sir Walter H. D. of North Berwick, viii. 129.
—— John, advocate, eldest son of Hew D. of Drummore, viii. 132.
—— John, lieut.-col., 30th regiment of foot, viii. 137.
—— John, captain 6th Dragoons, viii. 140.
—— —— his 1st wife, Jean Whitefoord, viii. 140.
—— —— his 2nd wife, Mary Ross, viii. 140.
—— John, lord provost of Edinburgh, viii. 145.
—— —— his wife, Ann Young Pringle, viii. 145.
—— John, captain Inniskilling Dragoons M.P., viii. 150.
—— John Aymer, viii. 163.
—— John Hamilton, Montego Bay, viii. 142.
—— John Henry Manners Rutland, viii. 139.
—— Katharine, wife of capt. Hugh Moodie, viii. 124.
—— Katharine, dau. of Robert D. of Kelloch, viii. 124.
—— Kirby, captain 74th regiment, viii. 141.
—— —— his wife, Ann M'Cormick, viii. 141.
—— Leighton Cathcart, lieut.-col. 15th Hussars, viii. 140.
—— Magdalen, dau. of Sir James D. of Hailes, viii. 146.
—— Margaret, wife of Sir John Schaw, ii. 519; viii. 142.
—— Margaret, wife of 3rd earl of Loudoun, v. 509; viii. 151; ix. 131 *ter*.
—— Margaret, wife of John Sinclair of Freswick, viii. 124.
—— Margaret, wife of Adam Hepburn of Humbie, viii. 124.
—— Margaret, wife of (1) capt. Burn, R.N., and (2) Dr. James Wardrop, viii. 138.
—— Margaret, wife of * M'Alpin, viii. 139.
—— Margaret, wife of capt. Alex. Duncan of St. Fort, viii. 139.
—— Margaret, dau. of Hew D. of Nunraw, viii. 142.
—— Margaret, wife of Sir D. Cunninghame of Milncraig, viii. 147.
—— Margaret, dau. of George D. of Dalmahoy, viii. 151.
—— Margaret Martha, wife of capt. W. F. Brown, viii. 130.
—— Margaret Penny, wife of Alan Maconochie Welwood, viii. 160.
—— Marion, wife of 4th lord Reay, ii. 32; v. 539; vii. 176; viii. 131.
—— Marion, wife of Ludovick Colquhoun of Luss, *afterwards* Sir L. Grant, vii. 484; viii. 142.

* Name unknown.

Dalrymple, Marion, dau. of lord Westhall, viii. 137.
— Marion, wife of Archibald Hamilton of Dalzell, viii. 139.
— Marion, dau. of Sir Hew D. of North Berwick, viii. 142.
— Marion Violet, viii. 163.
— Marjorie, dau. of Sir Walter H. D. of North Berwick, viii. 129.
— Marjorie Louise, viii. 163.
— Martha, dau. of James D. of Harvieston, viii. 125.
— Martha Willet, wife of 9th earl of Stair, viii. 138, 160.
— Mary Adelaide Wilhelmina Elizabeth, viii. 161.
— Mary Evelyn, dau. of 10th earl of Stair, viii. 162.
— Mary Martha, wife of Thos. Eustace Smith, viii. 138.
— Mary Minchin, wife of capt. Henry Bruce, R.N., viii. 138.
— Matthew Martin, viii. 123.
— Patricia, viii. 130.
— Penelope Crichton, viii. 150.
— Peter, viii. 130.
— Rachel, dau. of Sir James D. of Hailes, viii. 146.
— Robert, M.D., 3rd son of Sir Robt. D. of Castleton, ii. 31; viii. 131.
— — his wife, Jean Barclay of Towie, ii. 32.
— Robert, 2nd son of William D. of Stair, viii. 116.
— Robert, 3rd son of Robert D. of Kelloch, viii. 124.
— Robert, 3rd son of Sir Hew Hamilton D. of Bargany, viii. 128.
— Sir Robert, bart., capt. and lieut.-col. Scots Fusilier Guards, viii. 133; ix. 160 *bis*.
— — his wife, Graeme Hepburn, viii. 133; ix. 160.
— Robert, 3rd son of lord Westhall, viii. 137.
— Robert Makgill, vicar of Sneinton, viii. 162.
— Robert Stair, captain 11th Dragoons, viii. 126.
— Robert Stair, H.E.I.C.S., viii. 130.
— Romney Beckford, viii. 123.
— Samuel, general, governor of Berbice, viii. 123.
— — his 1st wife, Hannah Tweddell, viii. 123.
— — his 2nd wife, Mary Amelia Head, viii. 123.
— Samuel, lieut.-col., Madras Artillery, C.B., viii. 141.
— — his wife, Margaret Mackenzie, viii. 142.
— Sarah, wife of Charles, lord Crichton, iii. 235; viii. 147.
Dalrymple, Sidney, wife of * Lester, viii. 124.
— Simon, lieut.-col. 14th regiment, viii. 123.
— Stair, 8th son of Sir Robert D. of Castleton, viii. 132.
— Sybil, viii. 129.
— Thomas, 3rd son of James D. of Stair, viii. 117.
— Thomas, 7th son of Sir James D. of Borthwick, viii. 125.
— Thomas, M.D., physician to the King in Scotland, viii. 143.
— Thomas, 2nd son of Sir James D. of Hailes, viii. 145.
— Virginia Julian, wife of F. H. Champneys, viii. 129.
— Walter Francis, viii. 161.
— — his wife, Agnes Raney Owen, viii. 161.
— Walter Grey North Hamilton, viii. 160.
— Wemyss, wife of Leveson Keith Granville Murray, iii. 390; viii. 123.
— Wilhelmina, viii. 122.
— William, 3rd son of William D. of Stair, viii. 116.
— William, 5th son of Robert D. of Kelloch, viii. 124.
— William, 6th son of Sir James D. of Borthwick, viii. 125.
— William, 4th son of Sir Hew Hamilton D. of Bargany, viii. 128.
— William, merchant, Cadiz, viii. 131.
— William, 4th son of Lord Westhall, viii. 137.
— William, captain, viii. 141.
— — his wife, Elizabeth Hamilton, viii. 141.
— William, 9th son of Sir James D. of Hailes, viii. 146.
— William, major-gen., M.P., lieut.-governor of Chelsea Hospital, viii. 150.
— — his wife, Marianne Dorothy Harland, viii. 150.
— William Henry Clarence, captain, H.E.I.C.S., viii. 138.
— his wife, Margaret Werge, viii. 138.
— Zelda Raney, wife of lt. J. G. P. Ingham, R.N., viii. 161; ix. 160.
Dalrymple-Elphinstone, Ann, viii. 136.
— Eleonora, wife of Wm. Wemyss of Cuttlehill, viii. 136.
— Elizabeth, wife of George Leith of Overhall, viii. 136.
— James, viii. 132.
— — his wife, Margaret Davidson of Midmar, viii. 132.
— Jean, wife of capt. Alex. Davidson of Newton, viii. 136.
— Margaret, wife of Sir R. Burnett of Leys, viii. 136.

* Name unknown.

Dalrymple-Elphinstone, Marion, wife of James Mansfield of Midmar, viii. 136.
— Mary, wife of Ernest Gordon of Park, viii. 136.
Dalrymple-Fergusson of Kilkerran, Sir Charles, 5th bart., iv. 212; viii. 144.
— — his wife, Helen Boyle, iv. 212; viii. 144.
Dalrymple-Hamilton of Bargany, Henrietta Dundas, wife of Augustin Louis Joseph Casimir Gustave de Franquetot, duc de Coigny, viii. 127, 161.
— — Sir Hew, 4th bart. of North Berwick, viii. 127.
— — his wife, Jane Duncan, viii. 127.
— — John, ii. 31; viii. 130.
— — his 1st wife, Anne Wemyss, ii. 31; viii. 131, 512.
— — his 2nd wife, Margaret Montgomery, ii. 31; iii. 449; viii. 131.
— — North de Coigny, Scots Guards, viii. 161.
— — his wife, Marcia Kathleen Anne Liddell, viii. 162.
— — North Victor Cecil, viii. 162.
— — his wife, Marjorie Coke, viii. 162.
— Frederick Hew George, R.N., viii. 162.
— Victoria Alexandra, viii. 162.
Dalrymple-Hay of Park Place, Sir John Charles, 3rd bart., admiral R.N., G.C.B., vi. 437.
— — his wife, Eliza Napier, vi. 437.
Dalrymple-Horn-Elphinstone of Horn and Logie Elphinstone, Sir Graeme, 4th bart., viii. 133.
— — his wife, Margaret Anne Alice Fairlie, viii. 133.
— — Sir James, 2nd bart., viii. 133.
— — his wife, Mary Maxwell, viii. 133.
— — Robert, lieut.-gen., viii. 132; ix. 160.
— — his wife, Mary Elphinstone of Logie Elphinstone, viii. 132.
— — Sir Robert, 1st bart., viii. 133; ix. 160 *bis*.
— — his wife, Graeme Hepburn, viii. 133; ix. 160.
— — Sir Robert, 3rd bart., viii. 133.
— — his wife, Nina Balfour, viii. 133.
Dalrymple-Murray-Kynnynmond of Melgund and Kynnynmond, Hew, 3rd son of Sir David D. of Hailes, viii. 146.
— — his wife, Isabella Somerville, viii. 146.
Dalton of Hawkswell, Sir Marmaduke, vii. 107.
— — his wife, Barbara Belasyse, vii. 107.
— — Mary, wife of 2nd viscount of Preston, vii. 107.
— of Myton, Robert, iii. 293.
— — his wife, Elizabeth Constable, iii. 293.
Dalton of Swine, John, ix. 72.
— — his wife, Mary Brudenell, ix. 72.
— Bright, son of Richard D., i. 486 *n*.
— Mary, wife of lord John Murray of Pitnacree, i. 486.
— Richard, Sheffield, i. 486.
DALVEEN, DOUGLAS, LORD DOUGLAS OF, vii. 143-144.
DALZELL, DALZELL, LORD, ii. 407.
Dalzell, Richard, son of Alex., titular lord Carnwath; styled lord, ii. 416.
— Robert, first lord, i. 407; ix. 53 *bis*.
— — his wife, Margaret Crichton, i. 408.
— Robert Hippisley, elder son of 12th earl of Carnwath; styled lord, ii. 420.
DALZELL, DALZELL, BARON, ii. 408.
Dalzell, Robert, first baron, i. 408.
— — his wife, Margaret Crichton, i. 408.
— master of, Robert, eldest son of 1st lord Dalzell, viii. 25 *n*.
DALZELL, EARL OF CARNWATH, ii. 395-420.
DALZELL, LORD DALZELL, ii. 407.
DALZELL, BARON DALZELL, ii. 408.
DALZELL, BARON LIBERTON, ii. 408.
Dalzell of Amisfield, Sir John, ii. 408.
— — his wife, Marion Arnot, ii. 409.
— — Sir Robert, ii. 409.
— of Balybucht, Robert, ii. 400.
— of Barncrosh, James, captain, v. 129.
— — John, chamberlain of Kenmure, v. 129.
— — his wife, Henrietta Gordon, v. 129.
— of Binns, Thomas, ii. 405; ix. 53.
— — his wife, Jonet Bruce, ii. 405; iii. 477; ix. 53.
— — Thomas, general, ii. 405; iii. 383, 477; viii. 220.
— of Botheax, Adam, ii. 399.
— — Sir John, ii. 398.
— — Robert, ii. 400.
— — Thomas, ii. 400.
— of the Bracanrig, Sir John, ii. 397, 399.
— — John, ii. 401.
— — Robert de, ii. 400, 401.
— — his wife, Agnes Hamilton, ii. 401.
— of Brownside, John, ii. 401.
— — Robert, ii. 400.
— of Budhouse, Robert, ii. 400.
— of Carlowrie, David, ii. 399.
— — Peter, ii. 399.
— — Walter, ii. 399.
— of Chisholm, William, ii. 411; ix. 54.
— — his wife, Margaret Stirling, ix. 54.
— of Dalzell, George de, 1st laird, ii. 398, 400; viii. 380.
— — his wife, * Sandilands, ii. 398.
— — George, *probably error for* 'Robert,' 1446, ii. 400.
— — Sir John de, 3rd laird, ii. 398.
— — Robert, 4th laird, ii. 400.
— — his wife, Agnes Hamilton, ii. 401.

* Name unknown.

Dalzell of Dalzell, Robert, 6th laird, ii. 403.
— —his wife, Margaret Hamilton, ii. 403.
— — Robert, 7th laird, ii. 404; viii. 14 *n*.
— — his 1st wife, Elizabeth Somerville, ii. 404; viii. 14 *n*.
— — his 2nd wife Cristine Dundas, ii. 404 *bis*.
— — Robert, 8th laird, ii. 405; ix. 53.
— — his wife, Janet Hamilton, ii. 406.
— — Sir Robert, 9th laird, ii. 407.
— — his wife, Margaret Crichton, ii. 408.
— — Sir William de, sergeant of Lanark, 2nd laird, ii. 396.
— — his 2nd wife, Mary *, ii. 397.
— — William, 5th laird, ii. 402; vi. 478.
— — his wife, Gelis *or* Elizabeth Hamilton, ii. 402.
— of Dalzell Mill, Nicol, ii. 406.
— of Eliock, Margaret, dau. of Robert, 5th earl of Carnwath, ii. 416.
— — Robert, ii. 401, 404, 405, 407.
— — Sir William, ii. 397, 401.
— — William, ii. 401.
— of Elliotstown, Adam, ii. 399.
— of Gashogill, Gavin, ii. 413; ix. 54 *bis*.
— of Glenae, Sir John, ii. 408.
— — his wife, Marion Arnot, ii. 409.
— — Sir John, 2nd bart., ii. 409, 410; ix. 54.
— — his wife, Henrietta Murray, ii. 410.
— — John, R.N., ii. 417.
— — Margaret, wife of Capt. D. S. Dalzell, ii. 417.
— — Sir Robert, 1st bart., ii. 409; ix. 53 *bis*.
— — his 1st wife, Katharine Sandilands, i. 79; ii. 409; ix. 4, 53.
— — his 2nd wife, Margaret Johnstone, i. 259; ii. 409.
— — his 3rd wife, Violet Riddell, ii. 409.
— — Sir Robert, 3rd bart., ii. 410, 415.
— — Robert, advocate, ii. 417.
— — his wife, Anne Armstrong, ii. 417.
— — Robert Brainerd, ii. 417.
— of Home, Gavin, ii. 413.
— of Johnston, Thomas, ii. 411.
— of Newton, Sir John, ii. 408.
— of Sandyholme, John, ii. 401.
— — Robert, ii. 400.
— — Robert, ii. 401.
— Agnes, dau. of lt.-col. Thomas D., ii. 410.
— Agnes, dau. of Sir Robt. D. of Glenae, ii. 410.
— Alexander, surgeon, H.E.I.C.S., ii. 417.
— Andrew, 2nd son of Robert D. of that Ilk, ii. 404.
— Anna, wife of John Hamilton, ii. 413.

* Name unknown.

Dalzell, Archibald, 3rd son of Robt. D. of that Ilk, ii. 406.
— — his wife, Jean Dalzell, ii. 406.
— Arthur Edward, C.B., ii. 418.
— — his wife, Muriel Windham Knatchbull, ii. 418.
— Arthur John, elder son of 10th earl of Carnwath, ii. 419.
— Charlotte Augusta, ii. 418.
— Charlotte Emma Maud, wife of col. L. Rolleston, ii. 418.
— Christian, wife of (1) J. Somervill; (2) John Lindsay; and (3) John Crichton of Ryhill, ii. 403; iii. 225.
— Christian, wife of John Boswell, ii. 404.
— Christian, wife of John Hamilton, ii. 407.
— Christian, dau. of 2nd earl of Carnwath, ii. 414.
— Claud, 5th son of Robt. D. of that Ilk, ii. 407.
— David, merchant, Glasgow, ii. 410.
— Dougall Stewart, capt., ii. 417.
— — his wife, Margaret Dalzell, ii. 417.
— Edith Isabella, wife of admiral E. S. Adeane, ii. 419.
— Eleanor Carnwath, ii. 419.
— Eleanor Jane Elizabeth, ii. 418.
— Eliza Jane, wife of J. M. Leake, ii. 417.
— Elizabeth, dau. of Robt. D. of that Ilk, ii. 407.
— Elizabeth, wife of major John Hay, ii. 415; viii. 459; ix. 55.
— Elizabeth, wife of Sir A. G. Grierson, ii. 417.
— Elizabeth, dau. of Alex., titular earl of Carnwath, ii. 417.
— Elizabeth, wife of H. A. Douglas, ii. 417; vii. 151.
— Elizabeth, dau. of 5th earl of Carnwath, ii. 417.
— Elizabeth, dau. of Robert D., ii. 417.
— Emma Maria, dau. of 6th earl of Carnwath, ii. 418.
— Euphemia, dau. of 5th earl of Carnwath, ii. 416.
— Frances, wife of gen. Alex. Hamilton, ii. 50; iv. 309.
— Gavin, son of Robt. D. of that Ilk, ii. 406.
— George, M.A., Glasgow Univ., ii. 403.
— Helen, wife of John Stirling, ii. 405.
— Henrietta, dau. of Sir Robt. D. of Glenae, ii. 409, 410.
— Henrietta, dau. of lt.-col. Thomas D., ii. 410.
— Hugh de, sheriff of Lanark, ii. 395.
— Ida Elizabeth, dau. of 11th earl of Carnwath, ii. 420.
— James, merchant in Edinburgh, ii. 402.
— James, apprentice in Edinburgh, ii. 405.
— James, 4th son of Robert D., 8th laird of that Ilk, ii. 407.

Dalzell, James, capt., 2nd son of Sir Robt. D. of Glenae, ii. 409; ix. 53.
—— —— his wife, * Graham, v. 129; ix. 54.
—— James, educated at Douai, ii. 410; ix. 54 *bis*.
—— James, 3rd son of 1st lord Dalzell, ii. 411; ix. 54.
—— —— his wife, Marion Craufurd, ii. 411.
—— James, R.N., ii. 417.
—— Janet, dau. of Robt. D. of that Ilk, ii. 407.
—— Jean, wife of Arch. Dalzell, ii. 406.
—— Jean, wife of Thomas Gibson, ii. 410.
—— Jean, wife of Claud Muirhead, ii. 414.
—— John, 3rd son of Robert D. of that Ilk, ii. 402.
—— John, in Knowhubill, ii. 402.
—— John, 5th son of Wm. D. of that Ilk, ii. 403.
—— John, 4th son of Robert D. of that Ilk, ii. 403.
—— John, merchant in Edinburgh, ii. 405.
—— Sir John, 2nd son of Sir John D. of Glenae, ii. 410.
—— John, 4th son of Alexander, titular earl of Carnwath, ii. 417.
—— John, minister of Prestonkirk, ix. 136.
—— —— his wife, Margaret Melville, ix. 136.
—— Katharine, wife of John Roberton, ii. 405.
—— Margaret, wife of John Hamilton, ii. 404.
—— Margaret, wife of Robt. Nisbet, ii. 407.
—— Margaret, wife of John Wilson, ii. 411.
—— Margaret, dau. of 2nd earl of Carnwath, ii. 414.
—— Margaret, wife of Sir Robt. Grierson, ii. 417.
—— Margaret, wife of John Hamilton of Udston, ii. 38, 41; iv. 354.
—— Marion, wife of (1) John Montgomery, and (2) M. Lindsay, ii. 403.
—— Marion, dau. of Robt. D. of that Ilk, ii. 407.
—— Mary, wife of Alexander, 3rd earl of Kellie, ii. 409; v. 87.
—— Mary, wife of Robert Lawrie of Maxwelton, ii. 409, 410; ix. 54.
—— Mary, dau. of Sir John D., 2nd bart. of Glenae, ii. 410.
—— Mary, wife of (1) 6th viscount Kenmure, and (2) Sir John Lumisden, ii. 410; v. 127; ix. 54, 119.
—— Mary, wife of Sir Jas. Muirhead, ii. 411.
—— Mary, dau. of 2nd earl of Carnwath, ii. 414.
—— Mary Isabella, wife of Major T. Leith, ii. 418.
—— Muriel Marjorie, ii. 418.
—— Ninian, ii. 403.

* Name unknown.

Dalzell, Patrick, 3rd son of Wm. D. of that Ilk, ii. 403.
—— Paul, 3rd son of Robert D. of that Ilk, ii. 403.
—— Sir Ralph, iii. 16.
—— Robert de, ii. 396.
—— Sir Robert de, sergeant of Lanark, ii. 396.
—— Robert, eldest son of Wm. D. of that Ilk, ii. 402.
—— Robert, 3rd son of 2nd earl of Carnwath, ii. 414.
—— Robert, 2nd son of Alexander, titular earl of Carnwath, ii. 417.
—— Robert, 2nd son of 5th earl of Carnwath, ii. 417.
—— —— his wife, Elizabeth Acklom, ii. 417.
—— Robert, 2nd son of brigadier Thos. D., ix. 54.
—— Robert Alexander George, col., C.B., ii. 418.
—— —— his wife, Sarah Bushby Harris, ii. 418.
—— Robert Augustus, capt. Scots Fusilier Guards, ii. 419.
—— Ronald Arthur, younger son of 11th earl of Carnwath, ii. 420.
—— Thomas de, ii. 394.
—— Thomas, son of Wm. D. of that Ilk, ii. 402.
—— Thomas, 6th son of Robt. D. of that Ilk, ii. 407.
—— Thomas, lieut.-col. Scots Guards, ii. 409.
—— —— his wife, Isabel Fergusson, ii. 410.
—— Thomas, 4th son of David D., ii. 411.
—— Violet, dau. of Sir Robt. D. of Glenae, ii. 409, 410.
—— Violet Charlotte, wife of H. G. Henderson, ii. 420.
—— William, son of Sir Wm. de D., ii. 397, 398.
—— William, 2nd son of Robt. D. of that Ilk, ii. 403.
—— William, 2nd son of 1st earl of Carnwath, ii. 413.
—— * wife of Geo. Crawford, yr. of Auchencross, ii. 411.
—— * younger dau. of Sir John D. of Glenae and Newton, ii. 409.
—— * wife of Wm. Drummond of Riccarton, ix. 53.
Damaan of Birtewelte, Adrian, professor at Leyden, Dutch agent at Scottish Court, ii. 269; iv. 434; ix. 48.
—— —— his wife, Margaret Stewart, ii. 269.
—— Theodorite, wife of William Bothwell, iv. 434.
Damancell of Newbattle, Charles, v. 473.
—— Charles, in Strathmiglo, v. 473.

* Name unknown.

Damer, John, eldest son of Joseph, lord Milton, i. 386; ix. 25 *bis*.
— — his wife, Anne Seymour Conway, i. 386.
Dana, Edward, in holy orders, v. 212.
— — his wife, Helen Kinnaird, v. 212.
Danby, Thomas (Osborne), 1st earl of, iii. 301.
Daniel, Elizabeth, wife of 3rd lord Cramond, ii. 583.
— James, Norwich, ii. 583.
Danielston of Danielston, Elizabeth, wife of Sir R. Maxwell of Calderwood, iv. 230 *n*.
— — Sir John, viii. 522.
— — his wife, * Fleming, viii. 522.
— — Margaret, wife of Sir Wm. Cunningham of Kilmaurs, iv. 229 *n*., 230.
— — Sir Robert, iv. 230.
— of Inchcailloch, Sir John, viii. 523.
— of Kilmaronock, Sir John, viii. 523.
— Hew, vii. 35.
— Robert, conservator of the privileges, Middleburg, iii. 575; iv. 430.
— Walter de, bishop of St. Andrews, v. 392.
D'Arces, Antoine, chevalier de la Bastie, ii. 6; iv. 356 *bis*.
D'Arcy, Caroline, wife of 4th marquess of Lothian, v. 481.
Darcy, Katherine, wife of Gervase, lord Clifton, i. 49.
Darell, Edward Tierney Gilchrist, v. 238.
— Florence Mary, wife of 13th earl of Kinnoull, v. 238.
Darlington, Henry (Vane), 1st earl of, iv. 494.
— Katharine, illeg. dau. of King James VII.; baroness of, i. 35.
DARNLEY, STEWART, LORD, v. 348-361.
Darnley, John, first lord, ii. 288; v. 348, 430.
— — his wife, Margaret Montgomerie, v. 349.
— Henry, eldest son of Matthew, 4th earl of Lennox; styled lord, i. 22, 26, 155, 192; ii. 459; iv. 157; v. 352, 354, 440; viii. 490.
— — his wife, Mary, Queen of Scots, i. 25; v. 354.
DARNLEY, STEWART, LORD, ii. 168.
Darnley, Francis, second lord, ii. 170.
— — his wife, Margaret Douglas, ii. 170.
— John, prior of Coldingham, first lord, i. 24; ii. 168.
— — his wife, Jean Hepburn, ii. 160, 169; ix. 41 *bis*.
DARNLEY, STEWART, LORD, v. 355.
Darnley, Robert, lord, v. 355.
DARNLEY, STEWART, EARL OF, v. 356-362.
Darnley, Esmé, first earl of, v. 356.
DARNLEY, LENNOX, EARL OF, v. 363-371.
Darnley, Charles, illeg. son of King Charles II.; earl of, i. 32; v. 363-371.

* Name unknown.

Darnley, John (Bligh), 1st earl of, v. 359.
— — his wife, Theodosia, baroness Clifton, v. 359.
— John (Bligh), 3rd earl of, iv. 170.
— James, vii. 93 *n*.
— Katharine, wife of (1) 3rd earl of Anglesey, and (2) 1st duke of Buckingham and Normanby, i. 35; vii. 93 *n*.
Darroch, John, minister of Craignish, ix. 45.
— — his wife, Elizabeth Campbell, ix. 45.
Dashwood of Kirtlington, Sir James, 2nd bart., i. 492; iv. 167.
— Anne, wife of 7th earl of Galloway, iv. 167.
— Anne Amelia, wife of (1) Charles Murray, and (2) Geo. Warde, i. 492.
— Charlotte Sophia, wife of (1) Charles Andrew Bruce, and (2) Jas. Alexander, iii. 492.
— Francis, v. 318.
— — his wife, Isabel Anne Maitland, v. 318.
— George Astley Charles, vi. 271.
— — his wife, Harriet Anne Bateman-Hanbury, vi. 271.
— Thomas, H.E.I.C.S., i. 492; iii. 492.
D'AUBIGNY, STEWART, LORD, v. 356-362.
D'Aubigny, Esmé, first lord, v. 356.
Davenport of Ballynacourty, Thomas E., iii. 390.
— Martha Frances Vincent, wife of col. Alex. H. Murray, iii. 390.
David I., King of Scots, i. 2, 3; iii. 244; iv. 2 *n*., 3 *bis*.; viii. 240.
— — his wife, Matilda of Huntingdon, i. 3.
David II., King of Scots, i. 8; iii. 145; iv. 398; vii. 238.
— — his 1st wife, Joan Plantagenet, i. 9; iii. 145; iv. 141; ix. 1.
— — his 2nd wife, Margaret Drummond, i. 9; ii. 262, 445; vi. 348; vii. 32.
— earl of Huntingdon, i. 4.
— — his wife, Maud of Chester, i. 4.
— son of David, earl of Huntingdon, i. 4 *n*.
— younger son of King Alexander III., i. 6.
— son of Morgund, 2nd earl of Mar, v. 570.
— of Haliburton, son of Truite, iv. 330, 331.
— of Inchesyreth, iii. 558.
— Michael, possessor of the bell of St. Medan, i. 113.
Davidson of Hedderwick, Thomas, ii. 110.
— — his wife, Isobel Borthwick, ii. 110.
— of Marchcleuch, Robert, ii. 107.
— — his wife, Elizabeth Borthwick, ii. 107.
— of Midmar, James, viii. 132.
— — Margaret, wife of James Dalrymple-Elphinstone, viii. 132.

Davidson of Newton, Alexandor, captain, viii. 136.
—— —— his wife, Jean Dalrymple-Elphinstone, viii. 136.
—— of Tulloch, Duncan, vi. 499.
—— Elizabeth, wife of (1) Adam Ramsay, (2) Finlay Anderson, and (3) G. Nairn, vi. 391.
—— Elizabeth Caroline, wife of P. A. Watson Carnegie, vi. 499.
—— John, minister of Liberton, and of Prestonpans, ii. 466; v. 111.
—— John, servant to John Crichton, viii. 541.
—— Isobel, wife of (1) Adam Ramsay, (2) F. Anderson, and (3) George Nairn, vi. 391.
—— Margaret, wife of David Leslie of Leslie, vii. 270.
—— Sir Robert, provost of Aberdeen, vii. 270.
—— Thomas, commissary clerk of Aberdeen, i. 86.
—— —— his wife, Janet Gordon, i. 86.
Davies, Daniel, v. 132.
—— Deborah Duff, the 'lovely Davies' of Burns, v. 132.
—— Francis Henry, registrar of the Court of Chancery, vi. 71.
—— George, Wilmington, iii. 605.
—— Harriet, wife of capt. Adam Gordon, v. 132.
—— John, surgeon, Glassary, ii. 199.
—— —— his wife, Isobel Campbell, ii. 199.
—— Robert, R.N., v. 273.
—— —— his wife, Mary Cantes, v. 273.
—— Mary, mistress of King Charles II., i. 32.
Davson, Harry Miller, major R.A., vii. 592.
—— —— his wife, Georgina Violet St. Clair, vii. 592.
Davy-Davies, Oscar, ii. 246.
—— —— his wife, Alice *, ii. 246.
Dawes of Rockspring, James, vii. 150.
—— Basilia, wife of (1) R. Quarrell, and (2) C. J. S. Douglas, vii. 150.
Dawkins of Over-Norton, James, vii. 95.
—— of Standlynch and Over-Norton, Henry, M.P., vii. 94.
—— —— his wife, Juliana Colyear, vii. 94.
Dawkins-Pennant of Penrhyn Castle, George Hay, vi. 383.
—— Juliana Isabella Mary, wife of Edward Gordon Douglas, vi. 383.
Dawson, George, iv. 390.
—— —— his wife, Bertha Douglas-Hamilton, iv. 390.
Day of Frindsbury, Thomas Hermitage, ii. 118.
—— Harriet Alice, wife of 20th lord Borthwick, ii. 118.
Dayles, Gabriel, iii. 294.
—— —— his wife, Elizabeth Constable, iii. 294.

* Name unknown.

Deas, Thomas, cook at Leuchars House, viii. 72 *n.*
de Blacquière, Anna Maria, wife of John, viscount Kirkwall, vi. 581.
de Blois, Cecilia Sarah Jane, wife of lord Wm. Kennedy, ii. 499.
—— William N., Halifax, ii. 499.
de Burgh, Elizabeth, wife of King Robert I., i. 8.
DECHMONT, HAMILTON, BARON, vi. 578-584.
Dechmont, George, first baron, vi. 579.
Decies, John (Horsley-Beresford), 2nd lord, vi. 272.
Dedem, Maria Johana Bertha Christina de, wife of baron Eric Mackay, vii. 172.
Delacombe, Fanny, wife of James Augustus Erskine, v. 634.
—— Henry Ivatt, general, C.B., v. 634.
Delamere, Hugh (Cholmondeley), 2nd lord, v. 237.
—— —— his 1st wife, Sarah Hay, v. 237.
de Lancey, James, lt.-governor of New York, ii. 495.
—— *, wife of John Watts, New York, ii. 495.
De la Pole, Anna, dau. of John, duke of Suffolk, i. 334; vi. 540.
De la Perte, Jeanne Elizabeth, wife of Louis Drummond of Yvoy-le-Pré, vi. 69.
Del Ard of Ardach, Deskford and Skeith, Sir Christin, iv. 44.
—— —— Colin, vii. 495.
—— —— John, iv. 44.
—— —— John, son of Sir Christin, iv. 45.
Delaval of Dissington, William, iv. 299.
—— —— his wife, Mary Widdrington, iv. 299.
—— of Seaton Delaval, Sir John, iii. 608.
—— —— Ralph, v. 376, 378.
—— —— his wife, Anne Leslie, v. 378.
De la Vale of Dalzell, Sir Robert, ii. 395.
Delawarr, John (West), 1st earl of, vi. 436.
Delisle, Mary, wife of lt.-gen. John Ramsay, iii. 104.
—— Philip, Calcutta, iii. 104.
D'Ellemeet, Cornelius de Jonge, receiver-general of the United Provinces, iii. 519.
—— Maria Margaritta, wife of (1) William lord North and Grey, and (2) Patrick, 5th lord Elibank, iii. 519.
Delmé of Cams Hall, John, i. 493.
—— Julia, wife of admiral J. A. Murray, i. 493.
DELORAINE, SCOTT, EARL OF, iii. 111-114.
Deloraine, Francis, second earl of, iii. 112.
—— —— his 1st wife, Mary Lister, iii. 112.
—— —— his 2nd wife, Mary Scrope, iii. 113.
—— Henry, first earl of, ii. 239; iii. 111.
—— —— his 1st wife, Anne Duncombe, iii. 112.
—— —— his 2nd wife, Mary Howard, iii. 112 vii. 511.

* Name unknown.

Deloraine, Henry, third earl of, iii. 113.
—— —— his wife, Elizabeth Fenwick, iii. 113.
—— Henry, fourth earl of, iii. 113.
—— —— his wife, Frances Heath, iii. 113.
de Mauley of Canford, Charles Frederick Ashley Cooper (Ponsonby), 2nd baron, vi. 386.
—— —— William Francis (Spencer-Ponsonby), 1st baron, v. 214.
De Moleyns, Hersey Alice Eveleigh, wife of John Adrian Louis, 7th earl of Hopetoun and 1st marquess of Linlithgow, iv. 504.
de Montalt, Cornwallis (Maude) 1st earl, iii. 550.
Dempster of Auchterless, James, iii. 201.
—— —— his wife, Janet Grant, iii. 201; vii. 461.
—— —— Robert, representative of the family of, iv. 567.
—— of Balbougie, James, iv. 567.
—— of Luthrie, Euphemia, wife of David Carmichael, iv. 567, 568.
—— of Morehous *or* Muiresk, James, vii. 438.
—— —— Robert, representative of the family of, iv. 567.
—— —— *, ix. 48.
—— —— his wife, Elenor Stewart, ix. 48.
—— of Pitliver, Robert, iv. 567.
—— Margaret, contr. to Simon Fraser, vii. 438.
—— Walter, iii. 14.
—— —— his wife, Katharine *, iii. 14.
Denbigh, William (Feilding), 1st earl of, i. 405; iii. 122; iv. 378.
—— William Basil Percy (Feilding), 7th earl of, viii. 211.
Denham of Coltness and Westshiel, Sir James Steuart, bart., viii. 512.
—— —— his wife, Frances Wemyss, viii. 512.
Denholm of Muirhouse, John, ii. 43.
—— of Westshiels, James, ii. 43.
—— —— Robert, iv. 583.
—— —— his 2nd wife, Marion Carmichael, iv. 583.
—— —— Sir William, ii. 368.
—— —— his wife, Katharine Erskine, ii. 368.
—— Katharine, wife of James Hamilton of Pencaitland, ii. 43.
—— Marion, wife of Sir R. Hamilton of Presmennan, ii. 43; ix. 36.
Denmark, Frederick III., King of, i. 33.
—— George, (husband of Queen Anne); prince of, i. 33.
—— Waldemar, King of, vi. 569.
Denney, Honora, wife of baron Hay of Sawley, v. 219.
Dennison, Jenny, wife of 8th lord Fairfax, iii. 603.
Denoiston, James, Linlithgow, ii. 64.
—— —— his wife, Margaret Bellenden, ii. 64.

* Name unknown

Denniston, Robert, conservator of privileges in Low Countries, iii. 575; iv. 430.
Denny, Sir Edmund, iii. 608.
—— James, viii. 413.
—— —— his wife, Diana Murray, viii. 413.
—— Joyce, wife of (1) W. Walsingham, and (2) Sir John Cary, iii. 608.
Dent, Elizabeth, wife of (1) Sir Francis Vere, and (2) Patrick, 3rd earl of Tullibardine, viii. 412.
—— John, citizen of London, viii. 412.
—— —— his 2nd wife, Alice Grant, viii. 412.
De Quincy, Elena, wife of A. de la Zouche, iv. 142.
—— Elizabeth, Isabella *or* Marjorie, wife of Alex. Comyn, earl of Buchan, ii. 254; iv. 142.
—— Margaret *or* Agnes, wife of William, earl of Ferrars and Derby, ii. 254; iv. 142.
—— Sir Robert, iv. 6; v. 572.
—— —— his wife, Orabilis, iv. 6.
—— Roger, constable of Scotland, ii. 585; iv. 142; viii. 562.
—— —— his wife, Elena of Galloway, iv. 142.
Derby, William (Ferrars), 7th earl of, iv. 142.
—— —— his wife, Agnes *or* Margaret de Quincy, ii. 254; iv. 142.
—— Edward (Stanley), 12th earl of, iv. 393.
—— James (Stanley), 7th earl of, i. 475; iii. 383.
—— —— his wife, Charlotte de la Tremouille, i. 475.
—— James (Stanley), 10th earl of, i. 488.
—— William (Stanley), 6th earl of, v. 467.
—— —— his wife, Elizabeth Vere, v. 467.
Derby of Horton, Cobbett, v. 236.
—— Katharine Louisa, wife of Arthur Hay-Drummond, v. 236.
Derder, wife of Gospatric, earl of Lothian, 3rd earl of Dunbar, iii. 250.
Dering, Edward Cholmondeley, vi. 73; vii. 61.
—— —— his wife, Harriet Mary Capell, vi. 73.
Derwentwater, Francis (Ratcliff), 2nd earl of, i. 32; vi. 454.
—— —— his wife, Mary Tudor, i. 32; vi. 454.
DESKFORD, OGILVY, LORD OGILVY OF, iv. 26-41.
DESKFORD, OGILVY, LORD, iv. 28.
Deskford, James, lord, iv. 28.
—— Walter, eldest son of 3rd earl of Findlater; styled lord, iv. 36; ix. 90.
DESKFORD AND INCHMARTIN, OGILVY, LORD OGILVY OF, iv. 28-41.
Deskford and Inchmartin, James, first lord, iv. 28.
—— Sir Patrick, styled lord, iv. 28, 35, 36.
Desmond, George (Feilding), 1st earl of, i. 401; iii. 122.
DESMOND, PRESTON, EARL OF, iii. 122.

Desmond, Richard, earl of, iii. 122.
Dessé, lieutenant of the King of France, 1548, vii. 283.
D'Este, Augusta Emma, wife of Sir Thos. Wilde, baron Truro of Bowes, iii. 392.
— Sir Augustus Frederick, colonel, K.G.H., son of Prince Augustus Frederick, duke of Sussex, iii. 392.
De Trafford of Croston Hall, John Randolphus, ii. 529.
— — his wife, Adelaide Cathcart, ii. 529.
— — Sigismund Cathcart, ii. 530.
— Charles Alan, ii. 530.
— — his wife, Victoria Seymour, ii. 530.
— Daphne Elizabeth Adelaide Mary, ii. 530.
— Elfrida Adelaide, ii. 530.
— Ermyntrude Frances, ii. 530.
— Galfrid Aloysius Cathcart, ii. 530.
— — his wife, Cecile Elizabeth Margaret de Stacpoole, ii. 530.
— Geoffrey Edmond, ii. 530.
— Henrietta, wife of H. R. Orde-Powlett, ii. 530.
— Joan Agnes Seymour, ii. 530.
— Mary Adelaide. ii. 530.
— Ralph Eric, ii. 530.
— Randolphus Cathcart, ii. 530.
— Reginald Francis, ii. 530.
— Sicell Noel, ii. 530.
Deuchar, Maukyne, mistress of 6th earl of Crawford, iii. 24.
de Vall of Kilsyth, Robert, v. 182.
Devaux, Mrs., mistress of 4th viscount Dunbar, iii. 299 *n.*
de Vesci, John (Vesey), 4th viscount. viii. 518.
— — his wife, Evelyn Charteris, viii. 517.
Devisme, Emily, wife of Sir Henry Murray, viii. 210.
— Gerard, Lisbon, viii. 210.
Devon, Henry Hugh (Courtenay), 14th earl of, vii. 309.
— — his wife, Anne Maria Leslie, vii. 308.
Devonshire, William (Cavendish), 1st earl of, v. 354.
— William (Cavendish), 2nd earl of, iii. 477.
— — his wife, Christiana Bruce, iii. 477.
— William (Cavendish), 2nd duke of, iii. 407.
Devorgilla of Galloway, wife of John Baliol of Barnard Castle, i. 4, 7; ii. 431; iii. 5, 161; iv. 142, 183.
— wife of David Olifard, ii. 124.
— wife of Laurence de Abernethy, vii. 398.
Dewar of Laverocklaw, William, v. 93.
— — his wife, Anne Erskine, v. 93.
— Christian, wife of Adam Hume, vi. 7.
Deyncourt, William, vi. 344.
Dick of Braid, John, iii. 485.
— — his wife, Nicola Bruce, iii. 485.
— — William, vi. 244; viii. 287.
— of Colluthie, James, v. 316.
— — his wife, Isabella Makgill of Rankeillour, v. 316.
— of Corbie, Anna, dau. of Wm. D. of Grange, v. 386.
— of Craighouse, Sir Andrew, v. 387; vi. 379.
— — his wife, Jean Leslie, v. 387.
— of Grange, William, v. 388.
— — William, v. 386; viii. 76.
— — his 1st wife, Elizabeth Leslie, v. 386; ix. 128 *bis.*
— of Holland, Andrew, sheriff of Orkney, v. 387.
— — his wife, Jean Leslie, v. 387.
— of North Berwick, William, vi. 8.
— of Prestonfield, Sir Alexander, i. 524.
— — Sir James, viii. 221.
— — Sir William, 2nd bart., iii. 76.
— — his wife, Anne Mackenzie. iii. 76.
— of Rankeillour, Margaret, wife of Frederick Lewis Maitland, v. 316.
— Andrew, advocate, iv. 94.
— — his wife, Clara Ruthven, iv. 94.
— Elizabeth, wife of Robert Lindsay, i. 524.
— Gilbert, burgess of Edinburgh, iii. 377.
— — his wife, Katherine Lawson, iii. 377.
— Janet, dau. of Wm. D. of Grange, v. 387.
— Janet, wife of Jas. Leslie of Lumquhat, v. 388.
— Janet, wife of Mungo Carnegie of Birkhill, viii. 76.
— William, iv. 568,
— — his wife, Eupheme Carmichael, iv. 568.
— Sir William, provost of Edinburgh, iii. 485.
— William, minister of Cupar, vi. 590.
— — his 2nd wife, Isabel Makgill of Rankeillor, vi. 589.
Dick-Conyngham of Prestonfield, Sir William Stewart, 10th bart., iv. 228.
— Margaret Alice, wife of A. M. Forbes of Brux, iv. 67.
— — Sir William Hanmer, 8th bart., iv. 67.
Dick Lauder of Fountainhall and Grange, Sir John, 8th bart., viii. 160.
— — his wife, Anne Dalrymple, viii. 160.
Dickenson, Edward, attorney, v. 15 *n.*
Dickson of Belchester, iv. 476.
— his wife, Katharine Nisbet, iv. 475.
— of Buchtrig, Robert, iv. 298.
— of Glencotho, John, viii. 538.
— of Hartree, John, senator of the College of Justice, vii. 505.

Dickson of Hucheonfield, Robert, v. 282.
—— —— his wife, Marion, v. 282.
—— of Ormiston, John, viii. 538.
—— —— Robert, v. 282.
—— of Peill, Robert, iv. 298.
—— —— his wife, Isobel Ramsay, iv. 298.
—— of Rachan, John, viii. 538.
—— of Smithfield, Christina, ix. 166.
—— —— Elizabeth, ix. 166.
—— —— John, viii. 435.
—— —— Mariota, ix. 166.
—— —— *, wife of John Hay of Yester, viii. 435; ix. 166.
—— of Stanefauld, Robert, iii. 286.
—— his wife, Nicolas Home, iii. 286.
—— Elizabeth, wife of Sir Geo. Mackenzie of Rosehaugh, vii. 505.
—— Isobel, wife of Robert Ramsay, iv. 298.
—— James, lieut.-general H.E.I.C.S., v. 416.
—— —— his wife. Rachel Lindsay, v. 416.
—— John, Ross Herald, ii. 177.
—— —— his wife, Margaret Campbell, ii. 177.
—— Robert, *or* Hobbe, page, ii. 112.
Digby of Geashill, William (Digby), 5th baron, viii. 37.
—— of Meriden, Wriothesley, iii. 584; viii. 37.
—— —— his wife, Mary Cotes, viii. 37.
—— Charles, canon of Windsor, viii. 38.
—— —— his wife, Mary Somerville, viii. 38.
—— Everard C., colonel Grenadier Guards, vi. 400.
—— —— his wife, Emily Louisa Anne Fitzmaurice, vi. 400.
—— Mary, wife of Major Hugh Somerville, iii. 584; viii. 37.
—— rev. William, iii. 615.
—— William Henry, Twickenham, ii. 497.
—— —— his wife, Anne Kennedy, ii. 497.
Dillon, Charles (Dillon), 1st viscount, iii. 613.
—— Henry (Dillon), 2nd viscount, iii. 613.
—— Henry (Dillon), 8th viscount, i. 54.
—— —— his wife Frances Hamilton, i. 54.
—— Henry Augustus (Lee-Dillon), 13th viscount, ii. 58.
—— Arthur, lieut.-gen., governor of Toulon, iii. 613.
—— Arthur Richard, archbishop of Narbonne, ix. 88.
—— Gerald, recorder of Dublin, i. 51.
—— —— his wife, Mary Hamilton, i. 51.
—— Laura, wife of 6th viscount Falkland, iii. 613.
—— Margaret Frances Florence, wife of W. J. Hamilton, ii. 58.
Dinely, Elizabeth, wife of (1) Geo. Barret, and (2) Sir J. Baker, ii. 35 *n.*
—— Thomas, ii. 35 *n.*
DINGWALL, KEITH, LORD, iii. 115-116.

* Name unknown.

Dingwall, Andrew, lord, iii. 115, 312; vi. 43, 512; vii. 66, 501.
DINGWALL, PRESTON, LORD, iii. 117-125.
Dingwall, Richard, first lord, iii. 121.
—— —— his wife, Elizabeth Butler, iii. 121.
—— Elizabeth, wife of James, 1st duke of Ormonde; baroness, iii. 122.
DINGWALL, BUTLER, LORD, iii. 123.
Dingwall, Charles, *de jure* fourth lord, iii. 123.
—— James, third lord, iii. 123.
DINGWALL, NASSAU D'AUVERQUERQUE, BARONESS, iii. 123.
—— Frances, wife of lieut.-col. Elliot; baroness, iii. 123.
DINGWALL, COWPER, LORD, iii. 123-124.
Dingwall, George Augustus, *de jure* seventh lord, iii. 123.
—— George Augustus Frederick, *de jure* ninth lord, iii. 124.
—— —— his wife Anne Florence, baroness Lucas, iii. 124.
—— George Nassau, *de jure* sixth lord, iii. 123.
—— —— his wife, Hannah Anne Gore, iii. 123.
—— Peter Leopold Louis Francis Nassau, *de jure* eighth lord, iii. 123.
—— —— his wife Emily Mary Lambe, iii. 123.
—— Francis Thomas de Gray, tenth lord, iii. 124.
—— —— his wife, Katrine Cecilia Compton, iii. 124.
DINGWALL, HERBERT, LORD, iii. 125.
Dingwall, Auberon Thomas, eleventh lord, iii. 124, 125.
Dingwall of Kildun, v. 44.
—— —— his wife, Janet Macdonald, v. 44.
—— —— Thomas, vii. 499.
—— of Lochalsh, Thomas, vii. 499.
Diodati, Sarah Lydia, wife of D. H. Verelst, i. 91.
DIRLETON, MAXWELL, EARL OF, iii. 126-131.
—— James, earl of, iii. 128.
—— —— his wife, Elizabeth Busson de Podolska, iii. 130.
DIRLETON, HALIBURTON, LORD HALIBURTON OF, iv. 330-338.
Dirleton, Janet, wife of William, 2nd lord Ruthven; baroness, iv. 259, 337.
—— James, ninth lord, iv. 267, 338.
—— John, first lord Haliburton of, iv. 335.
—— John, tenth lord, iv. 267, 338.
—— Patrick, seventh lord, iv. 261, 337.
—— William, eighth lord, iv. 263, 337.
Dirleton, John Nisbet, senator of the College of Justice, lord, i. 259.
DIRLTOUN, ERSKINE, LORD, ix. 116, 117.
Dirltoun, Thomas, first lord, v. 84; ix. 116.
Disbrowe, Sir Edward Cromwell, G.C.H., ii. 497.
—— —— his wife, Anne Kennedy, ii. 497.

Dishington of Ardross, George, viii. 384.
—— —— Paul, viii. 385.
—— —— Thomas, vii. 372.
—— —— his wife, Barbara Sandilands, vii. 372.
—— —— William, v. 283.
—— —— William, viii. 384.
—— —— his 1st wife, * Sandilands, viii. 384.
—— of Curry, William. v. 283.
—— of Pittenweem, Sir Thomas, vii. 69.
—— —— his wife, Elizabeth Scott, vii. 69.
—— Elizabeth, wife of John Wemyss of Pittencrieff, iv. 71 *n.*
—— Isabella, wife of (1) Alex. Abercromby, and (2) Patrick Dunbar, iii. 278.
Dispensa of Longniddry, Nicholas de, vii. 526.
Dixie, Sir Alexander Beaumont Churchill, 11th bart., vii. 154.
—— —— his wife, Florence Caroline Douglas, vii. 154.
Dixon, Henrietta Maria, wife of rev. E. C. Tollemache, iii. 416.
—— *, lieut.-col. 81st regt., iii. 416.
Dobie of Stanyhill, Sir Robert, ii. 594.
—— —— his wife, Sara Cranstoun, ii. 594.
Dobson, Isaac, ii. 559.
—— —— his wife, Marjorie Colville, ii. 559.
Doherty of Red Castle, Richard, iii. 365.
—— Elizabeth Frances Maria Katharine, wife of capt. E. G. L. Cochrane, iii. 365.
Doig of Balzeordie, Christian, wife of Sir James Carnegie, viii. 85.
—— of Cookston, Christian, wife of Sir Jas. Carnegie of Pittarrow and Southesk, viii. 85.
—— —— David, viii. 85.
—— —— his wife, Magdalen Symmer of Balzeordie, viii. 85.
—— of Dunrobin, Paul, vi. 319.
Dolas of Cantray, Rothiemurchus, and Urquhart, Alexander, vii. 460.
Dolfin of Cumbria, iii. 243.
—— son of Aylward, iii. 245.
DOLPHINSTOUN, KER, LORD KERR OF, v. 466-487.
Dolphinstoun, Robert, first lord Kerr of, v. 466.
DOLPHINGSTONE, KER, LORD KERR OF, v. 477-487.
Dolphingstone, Robert, first lord Kerr of, v. 477.
Domnagart, elder son of Fergus of Dalriada, v. 28.
Domville of Santry House, Sir Compton P. T., 1st bart., i. 526.
—— —— his 1st wife, Elizabeth Frances Lindsay, i. 526.
Don of Newton, Sir Alexander, 1st bart., ii. 597.
—— —— Sir Alexander, 4th bart., vii. 83.
* Name unknown.

Don of Newton, Sir Alexander, 5th bart., iv. 251.
—— —— his wife, Henrietta Cunningham, iv. 251.
—— Anne, wife of 4th lord Cranstoun, ii. 597.
—— Mary, wife of Francis Scott of Beechwood, vii. 83.
Donada, wife of Finlay, earl of Moray, vi. 281.
Donald 'Bane,' 2nd son of Malcolm 'Ceannmor'; King of Scots, i. 2 *bis*, 3; iii. 240.
—— son of Emhin; mormaor of Mar, v. 566.
—— son of Malcolm MacEth, earl of Ross, iv. 136; vii. 231.
—— son of Alastair 'Mor,' ancestor of the MacAlastairs, v. 36.
—— Sir, of Mar, 4th son of Morgund, 2nd earl of Mar, v. 569.
—— Bane MacWilliam, iii. 132, 133; iv. 139.
Donaldson of Drumbowie, James, ii. 406.
—— James, advocate, ix. 130.
—— Jean, wife of (1) Wm. Eigge, and (2) Sir Wm. Ker of Blackhope, ix. 130.
—— Michael, prior of St. Serf's, vi. 371.
—— *, wife of David Leslie *or* Anstruther of Huntsmore Park, vi. 445.
Doncaster, Sir James (Hay), elder son of Sir Jas. Hay of Kingask; viscount, v. 218.
—— —— his 1st wife, Honora Denny, v. 219.
—— —— his 2nd wife, Lucy Percy, v. 219.
DONCASTER, SCOTT, EARL OF, ii. 237-241.
Doncaster, Charles, eldest son of 1st duke of Buccleuch; styled earl of, ii. 239.
—— James, duke of Monmouth, illeg. son of King Charles II.; 1st earl of, ii. 237.
—— Francis, 2nd duke of Buccleuch; 2nd earl of, ii. 241.
Dodsworth, Anna Harriet, wife of canon A. H. Drummond, viii. 232.
—— William, viii. 232.
Dondovan, Gilbert of, i. 452.
Donegal, Arthur (Chichester), 1st marquess of, iv. 169.
Donington of Donington, Charles Frederick (Clifton), 1st baron, v. 515.
Donoughmore, Richard John (Hely-Hutchinson), fourth earl of, i. 67.
Doone of Exmoor, Sir Ensor, vi. 316 *n.*
Dorchester, Joseph (Milton), earl of, i. 386.
—— Katharine (Sedley), mistress of King James II. and VII., and wife of 1st earl of Portmore; countess of, i. 35; vii. 93.
Dormer, John (Dormer), 10th lord, v. 483.
—— —— his wife, Elizabeth Ker, v. 483.
—— of Eythorpe, Sir William, iii. 295.
—— —— his 2nd wife, Dorothy Catesby, iii. 295.
—— Margaret, wife of Sir Henry Constable, iii. 295.
Dörr, Charles Edouard Napoleon, vii. 208.
—— —— his wife, Margaret Bowman Rollo, vii. 208.
* Name unknown.

Dorset, Edward (Sackville), 4th earl of, iii. 477.
—— Lionel Cranfield (Sackville), 1st duke of, vii. 91.
—— —— his wife, Elizabeth Colyear, vii. 91.
—— Richard (Sackville), 5th earl of, iv. 479.
Dougalson of Troquhain, John, v. 102.
—— Janet, wife of George Gordon, v. 102.
Doughty, John, Shropshire, ii. 194, 212.
—— Rosanna, wife of W. J. L. Campbell, ii. 194, 212.
DOUGLAS, DOUGLAS, LORD, i. 206.
Douglas, Archibald, eldest son of 1st marquess of Douglas; styled lord, i. 206.
—— —— his 1st wife, Anna Stewart, i. 207.
—— —— his 2nd wife, Jean Wemyss, i. 207.
DOUGLAS, DOUGLAS, EARL OF, iii. 132-185.
Douglas, Archibald, 'the Grim,' third earl of, ii. 130; iii. 10, 146, 147, 153 *n.*, 157; iv. 147, 148, 514, 515.
—— —— his wife, Joanna Moray, ii. 130; iii. 161; vi. 133; viii. 257.
—— Archibald, fourth earl of, i. 18, 217, 219, 235; ii. 586; iii. 163, 165, 429; iv. 444 *ter.*; v. 100, 285; vii. 431; viii. 7, 528, 573.
—— —— his wife, Margaret Stewart, i. 18, 235; iii. 166; iv. 402.
—— Archibald, fifth earl of, ii. 449, 587, 588; iii. 168; iv. 445; vii. 320; ix. 56.
—— —— his wife, Euphemia Graham, iii. 170; viii. 260; ix. 162.
—— James, second earl of, iii. 153, 155; v. 586; vii. 432.
—— —— his wife, Isabel Stewart, i. 16; iii. 157.
—— James, seventh earl of, iii. 60, 163, 171, 172, 567; iv. 428.
—— —— his 1st wife, *, iii. 174.
—— —— his 2nd wife, Beatrix Sinclair, iii. 174; vi. 571.
—— James, ninth earl of, i. 441; iii. 174, 178, 222; iv. 233, 350, 447.
—— —— his 1st wife, Margaret Douglas, iii. 170, 183.
—— —— his 2nd wife, Anne Holland, iii. 183.
—— William, first earl of, i. 146, 147, 171, 172; ii. 586; iii. 148, 427; iv. 563; v. 281, 285, 584, 594; viii. 265.
—— —— his wife, Margaret of Mar, ii. 539; iii. 153; v. 585.
—— William, sixth earl of, iii. 59, 170; v. 428; viii. 532.
—— —— his wife, Jean *or* Janet Lindsay, iii. 20, 172.
—— William, eighth earl of, i. 175, 219, 441; ii. 99 *n.*, 326, 507, 540 *n.*, 587; iii. 21, 167, 175; iv. 350, 446; v. 45, 46, 257, 428, 429; vii. 321 *bis.*
—— —— his wife, Margaret Douglas, iii. 170, 178.

* Name unknown.

DOUGLAS, DOUGLAS, MARQUESS OF, i. 204-211.
—— Archibald, third marquess of, i. 209, 210.
—— —— his wife, Margaret Douglas, i. 211.
—— James, second marquess of, i. 207; iii. 325; iv. 77, 586; ix. 13.
—— —— his 1st wife, Barbara Erskine, i. 208; v. 626.
—— —— his 2nd wife, Mary Ker, i. 208; v. 478.
—— William, first marquess of, i. 202, 204, 263; ii. 28; iv. 588, 589.
—— —— his 1st wife, Margaret Hamilton, i. 45, 204; ix. 13.
—— —— his 2nd wife, Mary Gordon, i. 204; iv. 545.
—— James George, fourth marquess of, iv. 393.
DOUGLAS, DOUGLAS, DUKE OF, i. 210.
Douglas, Archibald, duke of, i. 210; iv. 393; ix. 13 *bis.*
—— —— his wife, Margaret Douglas, i. 211; ix. 13.
—— master of, Archibald, elder son of 3rd earl of Douglas, iii. 165; v. 286.
—— master of, Archibald, elder son of 4th earl of Douglas, iii. 168.
—— master of, Sir James, twin brother of 8th earl of Douglas, iii. 178, 279.
DOUGLAS OF AMESBURY, DOUGLAS, BARON, vii. 147.
Douglas of Amesbury, William, baron, vii. 147.
DOUGLAS OF BONCLE, DOUGLAS, LORD, i. 210.
Douglas of Boncle, Archibald, lord, i. 210.
DOUGLAS OF DALVEEN, DOUGLAS, LORD, vii. 143-144.
Douglas of Dalveen, Charles, lord, vii. 143.
DOUGLAS OF DORNOCK, DOUGLAS, LORD, vii. 138-156.
Douglas of Dornock, William, first lord, vii. 138.
DOUGLAS OF DOUGLAS, DOUGLAS, LORD, i. 212.
Douglas of Douglas, Archibald James Edward Stewart, first lord, i. 212; iv. 482.
—— —— his 1st wife, Lucy Graham, i. 213; vi. 268.
—— —— his 2nd wife, Frances Scott, i. 213; ii. 242.
DOUGLAS OF DOUGLAS, HOME, BARON, iv. 482-484.
Douglas of Douglas, Cospatrick Alexander, first baron, iv. 482; ix. 109.
DOUGLAS OF ETTRICK, DOUGLAS, LORD, iii. 216-218.
Douglas of Ettrick, George, first lord, iii. 217.
DOUGLAS OF HAWICK AND TIBBERIS, DOUGLAS, LORD, vii. 134-156.

Douglas, Archibald, eldest son of 1st marquess of Douglas; styled lord, i. 206.
—— —— his 1st wife, Anna Stewart, i. 207.
—— —— his 2nd wife, Jean Wemyss, i. 206, 207.
—— Francis Archibald Kelhead, elder son of 9th marquess of Queensberry; styled lord, vii. 155.
—— William, first lord, vii. 134.
DOUGLAS OF KINMONTH, DOUGLAS, LORD, vii. 138-156.
Douglas of Kinmonth, William, first lord, vii. 138.
DOUGLAS OF LOCHLEVEN, DOUGLAS, BARON, vi. 384-385.
Douglas of Lochleven, George, baron, vi. 384.
—— —— his wife, Susan Elizabeth Yarde-Buller, vi. 385.
DOUGLAS OF LOCKERBIE, DOUGLAS, LORD, vii. 143-144.
Douglas of Lockerbie, Charles, lord, vii. 143.
DOUGLAS OF LYNE, DOUGLAS, LORD, vii. 145-147.
Douglas of Lyne, William, first lord, vii. 145.
DOUGLAS OF MIDLEBIE, DOUGLAS, LORD, vii. 138-156.
Douglas of Midlebie, William, first lord, vii. 138.
DOUGLAS OF MUNARD, DOUGLAS, LORD, vii. 145-147.
Douglas of Munard, William, first lord, vii. 145.
DOUGLAS OF NEIDPATH, DOUGLAS, LORD, vii. 145-147.
Douglas of Neidpath, William, first lord, vii. 145.
DOUGLAS OF PRESTON, DOUGLAS, LORD, i. 210.
Douglas of Preston, Archibald, lord, i. 210.
DOUGLAS OF ROBERTON, DOUGLAS, LORD, i. 210.
Douglas of Roberton, Archibald, lord, i. 210.
DOUGLAS OF THORNHILL, DOUGLAS, LORD, vii. 143-144.
Douglas of Thornhill, Charles, lord, vii. 143.
DOUGLAS, LORD ABERDOUR, vi. 375-389.
DOUGLAS, LORD OF ABERNETHY, i. 204.
DOUGLAS, EARL OF ANGUS, i. 172-213.
DOUGLAS, MARQUESS OF ANGUS, i. 210.
DOUGLAS, EARL OF ANGUS AND ABERNETHY, i. 210.
DOUGLAS, EARL OF ANGUS AND ORMOND, i. 206.
DOUGLAS, EARL OF ARRAN, LANARK AND SELKIRK, iv. 381-382.
DOUGLAS, EARL OF ATHOLL, i. 435-436.
DOUGLAS, LORD AVEN, MAUCHANSHYRE, POMOND, AND DAIR, iv. 381-382.
DOUGLAS, EARL OF AVONDALE, iii. 173-185.
DOUGLAS, LORD BALVANY, iii. 173-185.
DOUGLAS, VISCOUNT OF BELHAVEN, ii. 36-37.
DOUGLAS, MARQUESS OF BEVERLEY, vii. 141-144.
DOUGLAS, LORD BOTHWELL, i. 206.
DOUGLAS, EARL OF BUCHAN, ii. 269-272.
DOUGLAS, MARQUESS OF CLYDESDALE, iv. 381-382.
DOUGLAS, LORD DAER, iv. 381; vii. 516.
DOUGLAS, LORD DOUGLAS, i. 206.
DOUGLAS, EARL OF DOUGLAS, iii. 132-185.
DOUGLAS, MARQUESS OF DOUGLAS, i. 204.
DOUGLAS, DUKE OF DOUGLAS, i. 210.
DOUGLAS, BARON DOUGLAS OF AMESBURY, vii. 147.
DOUGLAS, LORD DOUGLAS OF BONCLE, i. 210.
DOUGLAS, LORD DOUGLAS OF DALVEEN, vii. 143-144.
DOUGLAS, LORD DOUGLAS OF DORNOCK, vii. 138-156.
DOUGLAS, LORD DOUGLAS OF DOUGLAS, i. 212.
DOUGLAS, LORD DOUGLAS OF ETTRICK, iii. 216-218.
DOUGLAS, LORD DOUGLAS OF HAWICK AND TIBBERIS, vii. 134-156.
DOUGLAS, LORD DOUGLAS OF KINMONTH, vii. 138-156.
DOUGLAS, BARON DOUGLAS OF LOCHLEVEN, vi. 384-385.
DOUGLAS, LORD DOUGLAS OF LOCKERBIE, vii. 143-144.
DOUGLAS, LORD DOUGLAS OF LYNE, vii. 145-147.
DOUGLAS, LORD DOUGLAS OF MIDLEBIE, vii. 138-156.
DOUGLAS, LORD DOUGLAS OF MUNARD, vii. 145-147.
DOUGLAS, LORD DOUGLAS OF NEIDPATH, vii. 145-147.
DOUGLAS, LORD DOUGLAS OF PRESTON, i. 210.
DOUGLAS, LORD DOUGLAS OF ROBERTON, i. 210.
DOUGLAS, LORD DOUGLAS OF THORNHILL, vii. 143-144.
DOUGLAS, DUKE OF DOVER, vii. 141-144.
DOUGLAS, VISCOUNT OF DRUMLANRIG, vii. 134-156.
DOUGLAS, EARL OF DRUMLANRIG, vii. 138-156.
DOUGLAS, EARL OF DUMBARTON, iii. 216-218.
DOUGLAS, EARL OF FORFAR, iv. 77-79.
DOUGLAS, LORD OF GALLOWAY, iv. 144.
DOUGLAS, LORD GLENBERVIE OF KINCARDINE, i. 184.
DOUGLAS, DUKE OF HAMILTON, i. 205; iv. 381.
DOUGLAS, LORD HARTSYDE, i. 206; iv. 77-79.
DOUGLAS, LORD HILLHOUSE, vii. 146-147.
DOUGLAS, LORD OF JEDBURGH FOREST, i. 204.

DOUGLAS, VISCOUNT OF JEDBURGH FOREST, i. 210.
DOUGLAS, BARON KELHEAD OF KELHEAD, vii. 154.
DOUGLAS, EARL OF MAR, v. 585-586.
DOUGLAS, EARL OF MARCH, vii. 145-147.
DOUGLAS, EARL OF MORAY, vi. 308-310.
DOUGLAS, LORD MORDINGTOUN, i. 202; vi. 331-336.
DOUGLAS, EARL OF MORTON, vi. 337-389.
DOUGLAS, VISCOUNT OF NITH, vii. 138-156.
DOUGLAS, EARL OF ORKNEY, vi. 377.
DOUGLAS, EARL OF ORMOND, vi. 585-586.
DOUGLAS, EARL OF PEEBLES, vii. 145-147.
DOUGLAS, EARL OF QUEENSBERRY, vii. 134-156.
DOUGLAS, MARQUESS OF QUEENSBERRY, vii. 138-156.
DOUGLAS, DUKE OF QUEENSBERRY, vii. 112-156.
DOUGLAS, VISCOUNT OF RICCARTOUN, vii. 146-147.
DOUGLAS, BARON RIPPON, vii. 141-144.
DOUGLAS, VISCOUNT OF ROSS, vii. 138-156.
DOUGLAS, EARL OF RUGLEN, vii. 146-147.
DOUGLAS, EARL OF SALLWAY, vii. 143-144.
DOUGLAS, BARON SOLWAY OF KINMOUNT, vii. 152.
DOUGLAS, VISCOUNT OF TIBBERIS, vii. 143-144.
DOUGLAS, LORD TORTHORWALD, ii. 393.
DOUGLAS, VISCOUNT OF TORTHORWALD, vii. 138-156.
DOUGLAS, DUKE OF TOURAINE, iii. 166-176.
DOUGLAS, EARL OF SELKIRK, vii. 516-525.
DOUGLAS, LORD SHORTCLEUCH, iv. 381; vii. 516.
DOUGLAS, LORD WANDELL, iv. 77-79.
DOUGLAS, EARL OF WIGTOWN, iii. 168.
Douglas of Abercorn, James, iii. 173.
—— —— his 1st wife, * Stewart, iii. 174.
—— —— his 2nd wife, Beatrix Sinclair, iii. 174.
—— —— William, iii. 175.
—— —— his wife, Margaret Douglas, iii. 170, 176, 178.
—— of Aberdalgy, William, vi. 375.
—— of Aberdour, James, afterwards 7th earl of Douglas, iii. 173.
—— —— Sir James, vi. 344.
—— —— his 1st wife, Agnes Dunbar, vi. 348.
—— —— his 2nd wife, Egidia Stewart, vi. 348.
—— —— Sir James, illeg. son of Sir James D. of Dalkeith, vi. 349.
—— —— John, illeg. son of Sir Jas. D. of Dalkeith, vi. 347, 349.
—— —— Robert, vi. 360.
—— of Adeston, James, iv. 337.
—— of Altoun, Sir James, vii. 124.
—— of Annacroich, Robert, vi. 93.

* Name unknown.

Douglas of Archland, John, vi. 595.
—— —— his wife, Marion Menzies, vi. 595.
—— of Ardit, Sir Robert, 4th bart., iv. 103.
—— —— his wife, Mary Ruthven, iv. 103.
—— of Ardoch, Sir James, vii. 124.
—— of Arkland, John, i. 226, 229.
—— —— his wife, Marie Grierson, i. 226, 229.
—— of Aschescheillis, Sir George, vi. 370.
—— of Auchincassill, James, vii. 116.
—— of Avoch, James, 2nd son of 3rd earl of Douglas, iii. 173.
—— of Avondale, James, v. 343 *n.*
—— of Baky, Henry, viii. 274.
—— of Balbartanes, James, vi. 354.
—— of Baldwinsgill, Sir James, vi. 349.
—— of Ballibocht, Sir William, ii. 400, 401.
—— of Balneathill, Archibald, iv. 57, 372.
—— —— his wife, Barbara Forbes, iv. 57.
—— of Balvany, James, 2nd son of 3rd earl of Douglas, iii. 172; iv. 69; vi. 309; viii. 529.
—— —— John, 5th son of 7th earl of Douglas, iii. 174, 181, 183.
—— of Barns, Sir William, vi. 339.
—— of Barras, Mr. Gavin, i. 198.
—— —— his 1st wife, Jean Menzies, ix. 13.
—— —— his 2nd wife, Elizabeth Keith, i. 198.
—— of Beaufort, Henry, v. 524.
—— of Bedrule, Hugh, iii. 147.
—— —— Sir James, i. 509; iii. 144.
—— —— William, iii. 147.
—— of Blackerstone, Sir Robert, ii. 37 *bis.*
—— —— his 1st wife, * Douglas of Blackerstone, ii. 37.
—— —— his 2nd wife, Susanna Douglas, ii. 37.
—— of Blackness, Sir James, vi. 338.
—— —— Sir William, vi. 339.
—— of Blackpule, William, vii. 326.
—— of Blairforth, William, vi. 375.
—— of Boharm, James, iii. 173.
—— of Bondingston, William, vi. 138.
—— of Bonjedward, vii. 371.
—— —— George, v. 462; viii. 400.
—— —— his 1st wife, Isobel Ker, v. 462.
—— —— his 2nd wife, Margaret Stewart, viii. 400.
—— —— George, iii. 508.
—— —— his wife, Christian Murray, iii. 508.
—— —— Isabella, Countess of Mar and Garioch, iii. 155.
—— —— Sir James, 'the Good,' iii. 144.
—— —— Margaret, wife of Thos. Johnson, iii. 155.
—— of Bonnington, Sir William, vi. 339.
—— of Borg, Henry, iii. 175; vi. 351, 353.
—— —— his wife, Margaret Douglas, iii. 175; vi. 351.
—— —— Hugh, vi. 351, 355; viii. 577.
—— —— his wife, Christian Seton, viii. 577.
—— —— Hugh, viii. 583.
—— —— Sir William, brother of Sir James D. of Dalkeith, vi. 343.

* Name unknown.

Douglas of Bothwell, Archibald, iv. 77.
— of Brachly, James, iii. 173.
— of Braidwood, Sir William, i. 183, 197.
— — his wife, Elizabeth Auchinleck of Glenbervie, i. 184.
— of Breconwbat, Charles, H.E.I.C.S., vii. 149.
— of Bridgeford, Gavin, ancestor of the family of, i. 198; ix. 13.
— — Isobel, i. 313.
— — Marjory, wife of 6th viscount of Arbuthnott, i. 313.
— — Robert, i. 313.
— of Broughton, John, M.P., vii. 146.
— of Buittle, Isabella, wife (1) of Sir M. Drummond, and (2) Alex. Stewart; countess of Mar and Garioch, iii. 154.
— — Hugh, iii. 147.
— — Sir James, 'the Good,' iii. 145.
— — William, iii. 147.
— of Caldor-Clere, Sir James, vi. 338.
— of Callendar, Sir James, vi. 332.
— of Carmichael, Sir Archibald, iii. 147, 157.
— — Hugh, iii. 147.
— — Sir James, iii. 144; iv. 563.
— — William, iii. 147.
— of Carnalloway and Outragh, Archibald Edward, rector of Drumgoon, iii. 391.
— — his wife, Susan Murray, iii. 391.
— of Carnglass, Sir Archibald, regent of Scotland, iii. 141.
— of Carr, Sir Arthur Percy, 5th bart., vi. 373.
— of Cashogil, Archibald, ancestor of the family of, vii. 116.
— — Sir Robert, vii. 132 *bis*.
— — William, vii. 125.
— — his wife, Janet Douglas, vii. 125.
— of Cavers, Sir Archibald, regent of Scotland, youngest son of Sir William D., 'le Hardi,' iii. 141, 146, 265.
— — Sir Archibald, illeg. son of 2nd earl of Douglas, ii. 587 *bis*; iii. 157; vii. 112.
— — Sir Archibald, sheriff of Teviotdale, ii. 588; iv. 151.
— — George, vi. 327.
— — his wife, Grace Stewart, vi. 327.
— — Isabella, countess of Mar, wife of (1) Sir Malcolm Drummond, and (2) Alex. Stewart; i. 173; iii. 152, 153, 157; iv. 47.
— — James, 1529, vii. 119.
— — Sir James, v. 59, 60.
— — his wife, Christian Ker, v. 59.
— — Sir James, ii. 592.
— — his 1st wife, Margaret Cranstoun, ii. 592.
— — James, viii. 88.
— — his wife, Emma Carnegie, viii. 88.
— — Sir William, 1450, vii. 323, 326.
— — William, the yr., i. 189.
— — his contr. wife, Alison Douglas, i. 189.
Douglas of Cavers, Sir William, ii. 591, 592.
— — William, v. 75.
— — Sir William, vi. 17.
— — his wife, Elizabeth Douglas, vi. 16.
— of Chanlofute, James, viii. 545.
— — his wife, Mary Fleming, viii. 545.
— of Chapelerne, Sir William, vii. 128.
— of Classiedeuglie, Robert, vi. 375.
— of Clattie, Robert, vi. 370.
— of Cluny, William, 3rd son of 2nd earl of Angus, i. 175, 178.
— of Cockburnspath, David, i. 248.
— — his wife, Margaret Hamilton, i. 248
— of Colquhair, Sir William, vi. 372.
— — William, vi. 375.
— of Comlodden, James, advocate, lieut.-gen., 2nd son of 2nd earl of Queensberry, vii. 136.
— — his wife, Anna Hamilton, vii. 136.
— — James, elder son of above, vii. 137.
— — Margaret, vii. 137.
— — William, vii. 137.
— of Corsbatt and Wester Barras, Mr. John, i. 198.
— — his wife, Jean Fraser, i. 198.
— of Cragmuie, John, captain, 3rd son of 2nd earl of Queensberry, vii. 137.
— of Craigincune, John, vii. 118.
— of Crarie, Sir James, vii. 124.
— of Creswell, Andrew, vi. 338.
— of Culbirney, Henry, vi. 366.
— of Cullendrane, William, vi. 375.
— of Cumnock, William, vii. 134.
— of Cuthilgurdy, Sir Robert, vi. 369.
— — his wife, Margaret Erskine, vi. 369.
— of Dalkeith, Henry, vi. 351, 353.
— — his wife, Margaret Douglas, vi. 351.
— — Sir James, 1st laird, ii, 397, 447; iii. 55, 56, 152; iv. 80, 346; v. 520, 597; vi. 342, 344.
— — his 1st wife, Agnes Dunbar, iii. 153 *n*, 261; vi. 346, 348.
— — his 2nd wife, Egidia Stewart, i. 15; iii. 428; vi. 348.
— — Sir James, 2nd laird, iii. 55; vi. 350; ix. 84.
— — his 1st wife, Elizabeth Stewart, i. 18; vi. 350.
— — his 2nd wife, Janet Borthwick, ii. 96; vi. 350.
— — Sir James, 3rd laird, iii. 175; vi. 352.
— — his wife, Elizabeth Gifford, vi. 353.
— — Mary, wife of Sir Thos. Erskine of Erskine, iii. 151; v. 597, 598.
— — Sir William, 'the Flower of Chivalry,' vi. 196, 340.
— of Dalqueich, Sir Robert, vi. 367.
— of Dalvene, Hugh, vii. 128.
— — Hugh, vii. 132.
— of Davidstoun, Andrew, vi. 338.
— of Dirleton, Sir James, vi. 332.
— of Dornock, Archibald, 1st laird, vii. 135.

Douglas of Dornock, William, in entail to Neidpath, vii. 145.
— of Douglas, Archibald, iii. 135.
— — his wife, Margaret Crawford, iii. 136.
— — Archibald James Edward Steuart or, i. 209; iv. 393.
— — Hugh, 'the Dull,' seventh lord of, iii. 140, 147.
— — Sir James, 'the Good,' fifth lord of, i. 13: iii. 140, 142, 499, 526.
— — Jane Margaret, wife of Henry James (Montagu), lord Montagu of Boughton, ii. 243; iv. 482.
— — William, first lord of, iii. 132.
— — Sir William, 'Longleg,' third lord of, iii. 136.
— — his wife, Custancia de Batail, iii. 137.
— — Sir William, 'le Hardi,' fourth lord of, iii. 138; vii. 424.
— — his 1st wife, Elizabeth Stewart, i. 13; iii. 140.
— — his 2nd wife, Eleanor de Lovain, iii. 139, 140.
— — William, sixth lord of, iii. 146.
— — William, seventh lord of, iii. 148; vi. 341; viii. 378.
— of Douglasdale, Hugh, eldest son of 'Longleg,' iii. 137; vii. 399.
— — his wife, Marjory Abernethy, iii. 137; vii. 399.
— of Douglas-Support, Archibald, ix. 13.
— of Drumcors, Sir James, iv. 345.
— of Drumgarland, Robert, vi. 368.
— — his wife, Janet Ramsay, vi. 368.
— of Drumlanrig, Sir Archibald, regent of Scotland, iii. 141, 146, 265.
— — Isabella, countess of Mar, iii. 154.
— — James, 4th laird, vii. 117.
— — his wife, Janet Scott, ii. 228; vii. 117.
— — Sir James, warden of the West Marches, 6th laird, vii. 119; ix. 150.
— — his 1st wife, Margaret Douglas, i. 190; vii. 125.
— — his 2nd wife, Christian Montgomerie, iii. 436; vii. 125.
— — James, 7th laird, vii. 129; viii. 545.
— — his wife, Mary Fleming, vii. 132; viii. 545.
— — Sir William, 1st laird, i. 217; iii. 157; vii. 112.
— — his alleged wife, Elizabeth Stewart, vii. 112.
— — his 1st wife, Jean Murray, vi. 349; vii. 114.
— — his 2nd wife, Jacoba Douglas, vi. 349; vii. 114.
— — William, 2nd laird, vii. 114.
— — his wife, Janet Maxwell, vi. 475; vii. 114.
Douglas of Drumlanrig, William, 3rd laird, vii. 115.
— — his wife, Elizabeth Crichton, iii. 222; vii. 116.
— — Sir William, 5th laird, ii. 402; v. 288, 291; vii. 117.
— — his wife, Elizabeth Gordon, v. 105; vii. 118.
— — Sir William, 8th laird, ii. 394; iii. 233; v. 109; vii. 133.
— — his wife, Isobel Ker, v. 458; vii. 134.
— of Duffus, James, iii. 173.
— of Dumcrieff, George, 4th son of 2nd duke of Queensberry, vii. 143.
— of Dunbar, Archibald, iii. 165.
— of Dunfedling, William, vi. 375.
— of Dupplin, William, vi. 375.
— of Earl's Gift, Charles, rector of Donagheady, vi. 383.
— — his 1st wife, Isabella Gore, vi. 383.
— — his 2nd wife, Agnes Julia Rich, vi. 383.
— of Edderdor, James, iii. 173.
— of Edrington, George, ancestor of the family of, i. 188.
— of Ersmortoun, James (?), vii. 127.
— — John, ii. 403; vii. 126.
— of Eskdale, Hugh, iii. 147.
— — William, iii. 147.
— of Esperton, Sir Henry, vi. 364; vii. 527.
— of Ettrick Forest, Sir James, iii. 144.
— of Fawdon, Sir James, iii. 145.
— — Sir William, iii. 137.
— of Fawsyde, James, vi. 332.
— of Fewroull, William, v. 75.
— of Fossoway, Robert, vi. 369.
— of Freertown, Robert, vi. 371.
— of Galloway, Sir Archibald, iii. 159; iv. 144.
— of Garransoun, Sir William, vii. 128.
— of Garvald, vii. 72.
— of Gask, William, vi. 375.
— of Glenbervie, [Sir Alexander, 7th bart.], vi. 498.
— — his wife, Barbara Carnegie, vi. 498.
— — Archibald, i. 184.
— — his 1st wife, Agnes Keith, i. 184; vi. 45.
— — his 2nd wife, Margaret Carmichael, ix. 12.
— — his 3rd wife, Elizabeth Irvine, i. 184; ix. 12.
— — Sir Robert, 4th son of 9th earl of Angus, i. 198.
— — Sir Robert, 6th bart., i. 198.
— — Robert, only son of Sir Alex. D. of Glenbervie, vi. 498.
— — Sir William, 2nd son of 5th earl of Angus, i. 183.
— — his wife, Elizabeth Auchinleck, i. 183, 184.
— — William, i. 184, 197; ix. 91.
— — his wife, Egidia Graham, i. 198.

Douglas of Glenbervie, Sir William, i. 304.
—— —— his wife, Jean Arbuthnott, i. 304.
—— of Glenfinart, Charles John Cathcart, ii. 529.
—— —— his wife, Helen Tolmie Dick Bayley, ii. 529.
—— —— sir John, general, K.C.B., ii. 529.
—— —— his wife, Elizabeth Cathcart, ii. 529.
—— —— Neil Cecil Frederick, ii. 529.
—— of Glenmaid, Sir James, vii. 124.
—— of Gorbals, Sir Robert, ii. 37.
—— —— his wife, Susanna Douglas, ii. 37.
—— of Greenlaw, William, vi. 484.
—— —— his wife, Agnes Maxwell, vi. 484.
—— of Hailes, Archibald, iii. 135.
—— of Halbertshire, William, illeg. son of 3rd earl of Douglas, iii. 163.
—— of Halkerton, Sir Henry, vi. 364; vii. 527.
—— of Haltoun, William, vi. 375.
—— of Hawick, Sir James, vii. 124.
—— —— Sir William, 1st laird, vii. 113.
—— —— Sir William, 2nd laird, vii. 114.
—— —— Sir William, 7th laird, vii. 129.
—— —— his wife, Margaret Gordon, v. 109; vii. 129.
—— of Hawthornden, Sir William, 1st laird, vi. 343 *n.*, 354 *n.*; vii. 319.
—— of Hawthornsyke, John, vi. 357.
—— of Hedderwick, Robert, vi. 375.
—— —— William, vi. 375.
—— of Helenhill, Sir George, vi. 370.
—— —— his 1st wife, Jonet Lindsay, vi. 370.
—— —— his 2nd wife, Margaret Durie, vi. 370.
—— of Hermiston, Sir Andrew, ancestor of the earls of Morton, iii. 136; vi. 337.
—— —— Archibald, iii. 135; v. 570; vi. 337.
—— —— Sir James, vi. 338.
—— —— his wife, Joan *, vi. 339.
—— —— William, iii. 136; vi. 338.
—— of Howpasley, Sir James, vii. 132.
—— of Inchmarlo, Archibald, ancestor of the family of, vi. 352.
—— of Jedburgh, Sir James, iii. 144.
—— of Jedburgh Forest, Isabella, countess of Mar, wife of (1) Sir M. Drummond, and (2) Alex. Stewart, i. 173; iii. 154.
—— of Jerviswood, George, viii. 373.
—— of Keillour, Sir Archibald, iv. 57; vi. 372; ix. 23.
—— —— his wife, Barbara Forbes, iv. 57; vi. 372.
—— —— Sir Henry, vi. 366.
—— of Kelhead, Sir Charles, 5th bart., vii. 151.
—— —— his wife, Caroline Scott Montagu, ii. 243; vii. 152.

* Name unknown.

Douglas of Kelhead, Sir James, 1st bart., vii. 137, 145, 155.
—— —— his wife, Katharine Douglas, vii. 137, 149.
—— —— Sir John, 3rd bart., vii. 150.
—— —— his wife, Christian Cunningham, vii. 150.
—— —— Sir William, 2nd son of 1st earl of Queensberry, vii. 135, 147.
—— —— his 1st wife, Agnes Fawsyde, vii. 147.
—— —— his 2nd wife, Jean Stuart, vii. 148.
—— —— Sir William, 2nd bart., vii. 149.
—— —— his wife, Helen Erskine, vii. 149.
—— —— Sir William, 4th bart., vii. 149, 151, 155.
—— —— his wife, Grace Johnstone of Lockerby, vii. 151.
—— of Kilbirny, Henry, v. 524; vi. 366.
—— —— Sir James, v. 524.
—— —— his wife, Janet Fenteun, v. 524.
—— of Kilbucho, William, vi. 340.
—— of Killennoquhye, William, vi. 375.
—— of Killyvarran, John, illeg. son of Sir James D. of Drumlanrig, vii. 133.
—— of Kilspindie, Archibald, 'Graysteel,' i. 185, 191.
—— —— his wife, Isabel Hoppar, i. 185; iii. 502.
—— —— Archibald, i. 185; iii. 26; viii. 385.
—— —— his wife, * Lindsay, iii. 26.
—— —— Patrick, iv. 283.
—— —— his wife, Agnes *or* Anne Gray, iv. 283.
—— of Kincavil, Sir James, vi. 338.
—— —— Sir William, the Knight of Liddesdale, iv. 345; vi. 339.
—— of Kinnesswood, Archibald, 3rd son of 5th earl of Merton, vi. 372.
—— —— his wife, Barbara Ferbes, vi. 372.
—— —— Sir William, vi. 371.
—— of Kinross, Sir Robert, vi. 369.
—— of Kintore, Archibald, 3rd son of 7th earl of Douglas, iii. 174; vi. 308.
—— —— his wife, Elizabeth Dunbar, vi. 306, 308.
—— of Kirkandrews, Sir Archibald, regent of Scotland, iii. 141.
—— of Kirkhope, Sir James, vii. 124.
—— of Kirkness, Sir George, vi. 373.
—— —— his wife, Margaret Forrester, vi. 373; ix. 141.
—— —— Sir Robert, i. 546.
—— —— his wife, Jean Balfour, i. 546.
—— —— Sir William, vi. 371.
—— —— William, general, vi. 373.
—— —— William, his uncle, vi. 373.
—— of Knocktown, Sir James, vii. 124.
—— of Laidgreen, Margaret, wife of (1) Sir D. Stewart of Rossyth, and (2) H. Mercer of Meiklour, vi. 368.

* Name unknown.

Douglas of Langhope, James, commendator of Melrose, vii. 74.
— of Langnewton, Sir Henry de, iii. 14, 335.
— — his wife, Marjory Stewart, iii. 14.
— of Lauderdale, Hugh, iii. 147.
— — Sir James, 'the Good,' iii. 144.
— — William, iii. 147.
— of Laudonia, Sir James, vi. 338.
— — Sir William, vi. 196, 339.
— of Leswalt, William, vii. 115.
— of Liddesdale, Sir Archibald, regent of Scotland, iii. 140, 146; vi. 340.
— — his wife, Beatrice Lindsay, iii. 141.
— — George, earl of Angus, i. 173; iii. 154.
— — Isabella, countess of Mar, wife of (1) Sir M. Drummond, and (2) Alex. Stewart, iii. 154.
— — Sir James, eldest son of 1st earl of Douglas, iii. 155.
— — Sir William, i. 432; ii. 435; iii. 89, 90, 147, 148 *ter*; vi. 339, 347; viii. 257, 569.
— — his wife, Elizabeth Maxwell, vi. 342, 473.
— — William, afterwards 1st earl of Douglas, iii. 149.
— of Lincluden, William, vi. 484.
— — his wife, Agnes Maxwell, vi. 484.
— of Livingston, Sir Andrew, vi. 337.
— — Archibald, iii. 135; v. 570; vi. 337.
— of Locharben, Sir James, vii. 125.
— of Lochleven, Sir Henry, 1st laird, vi. 343, 364.
— — his wife, Margery Stewart, vi. 364.
— — Sir Henry, 3rd laird, vi. 366; vii. 273.
— — his wife, Elizabeth Erskine, vi. 367.
— — Sir Robert, 4th laird, vi. 367.
— — his 1st wife, Elizabeth Boswell, vi. 367.
— — his 2nd wife, Isobel Sibbald, i. 177; iv. 564; vi. 567.
— — his 3rd wife, Marion Baillie, v. 395; vi. 367.
— — Sir Robert, 5th laird, vi. 368.
— — his 1st wife, Margaret Balfour, vi. 368.
— — his 2nd wife, Margaret Hay, iii. 565; vi. 368.
— — Sir Robert, 6th laird, vi. 360, 369.
— — his wife, Margaret Erskine, ii. 269; v. 612; vi. 361, 369.
— — Robert, the younger, i. 196; vi. 374, 550.
— — his wife, Jean Lyon, vi. 375; viii. 291.
— — Sir William, 2nd laird, vi. 365.
— — his wife, Elizabeth *or* Marjorie Lindsay, iii. 17; vi. 365; viii. 483.
— — his possible 2nd wife, Christian *, viii. 483.
Douglas of Lochleven, Sir William, 7th laird, ii. 553; vi. 363, 371.
— — his wife, Agnes Leslie, vi. 372.
— of Lochnaw, William, vii. 115.
— of Logyachry, Sir William, vi. 339.
— of Longniddry, vi. 84.
— — Francis, vi. 371.
— of Lothian, Sir James, vi. 338.
— — his wife, Joan *, vi. 339.
— — Sir William, iii. 147; vi. 196.
— of Lugtoun, Sir Henry, iii. 335; vi. 343, 364.
— — his wife, Margery Stewart, i. 14; vi. 364.
— — Sir Henry, vi. 366.
— — his wife, Elizabeth Erskine, vi. 367.
— — Sir James, 2nd son of Sir Wm. D. of Lochleven, vi. 365.
— of Mains, Alexander, v. 351.
— — his wife, Margaret Stewart, v. 351.
— — Andrew, captain, ii. 491.
— — Sir Archibald, ii. 37.
— — James, i. 211.
— — Malcolm, ii. 36.
— — Nicholas, ancestor of the family of, vi. 343.
— — his wife, Janet Galbraith, vi. 344.
— of Maw, William, vi. 375.
— of Mondynes, James, viii. 74.
— of Montgreenan, James, advocate, lieut.-gen., vii. 136.
— — his wife, Anna Hamilton, vii. 136.
— — James, vii. 137.
— — Margaret, vii. 137.
— — William, vii. 137.
— of Mordington, Sir George, ii. 392; v. 463.
— — his wife, Margaret Dundas, v. 463.
— — Sir James, vi. 346.
— — Sir James, ii. 360; vi. 332.
— — his wife, Ann Oliphant, vi. 332.
— — William, 2nd son of Sir Jas. D. of Dalkeith, vi. 348.
— of Morebattle, Sir Archibald, regent of Scotland, iii. 141.
— of Morton, Sir James, 1st laird, vi. 346.
— — his 1st wife, Agnes Dunbar, iii. 261; vi. 346, 348.
— — his 2nd wife, Egidia Stewart, i. 15; vi. 348.
— — James, 1634, viii. 372, 373.
— — William, 4th son of Sir James D. of Dalkeith, ii. 400, 401; vi. 352, 354, 355; vii. 116.
— of Mortonwoods, Sir Robert, iii. 128.
— of Mosshouses, William, vi. 364.
— of Mouswald, Sir James, vii. 124.
— — Sir James, 2nd son of Sir James D. of Drumlanrig, vii. 132, 133.
— — his 1st wife, *, vii. 133.
— — his 2nd wife, Helena Grierson, vii. 133.

* Name unknown.

Douglas of Muldarge, Robert, vii. 506.
—— —— his wife, Jean Mackenzie, vii. 506.
—— of Neidpath, William, 2nd son of 1st duke of Queensberry, vii. 145.
—— —— his wife, Jane Hay, vii. 145.
—— of Netherdale, Archibald, ancestor of the family of, vi. 352.
—— of Newlands, William, vi. 340.
—— of Nithsdale, Sir William, illeg. son of Archibald, 3rd earl of Douglas, iii. 163.
—— —— his wife, Egidia Stewart, i. 16; iii. 164.
—— —— Sir William, son of above, iii. 164.
—— —— Egidia, wife of (1) Henry St. Clair, earl of Orkney, and (2) Alex. Stewart, iii. 164; vi. 570.
—— of Orkney, William, vi. 377.
—— —— William, vi. 379.
—— of Panlathie, George, i. 198.
—— —— Thomas, viii. 48.
—— —— his wife, Isobel Liddell, viii. 47.
—— of Parkhead, Sir George, illeg. son of Sir Geo. D. of Pittendreich, i. 188; ii. 392.
—— —— Sir James, i. 396; ii. 392.
—— —— his wife, Elizabeth Carlyle, i. 248; ii. 392.
—— —— James, provost of Abernethy, 2nd son of 10th earl of Angus, vi. 331.
—— of Peinyeric, George, viii. 373.
—— —— William, vi. 484.
—— —— his wife, Agnes Maxwell, vi. 484.
—— of Petty, James, afterwards 7th earl of Douglas, iii. 173.
—— of Pharington, Sir William, vi. 371.
—— of Pitdriechie, James, vi. 332.
—— of Pittendreich, Archibald, illeg. son of Regent Morton, iii. 203; vi. 363.
—— —— his wife, Elizabeth Sutherland, vi. 364.
—— —— David, i. 188.
—— —— Sir George, master of Angus, i. 185, 187, 191; iv. 358, 360; v. 60; vi. 147 *n.*, 360; vii. 120; viii. 279, 437.
—— —— his wife, Elizabeth *or* Isabella Douglas of Pittendreich, i. 188; ix. 12.
—— of Plewland, William, ix. 154.
—— —— his wife, Lilias Rutherfurd, ix. 154.
—— of Polmoody, Sir James, iii. 144.
—— —— Sir William vi. 341.
—— of Ponfeigh, William, iv. 573.
—— of Preston, Sir James, vi. 346.
—— of Pumpherston, James, iv. 337.
—— —— Joseph, viii. 389.
—— —— his wife, Mary Sandilands, viii. 389.
—— —— William, viii. 26.
—— —— his 1st wife, Mary Somerville, viii. 26.
—— of Ralston, Sir James, v. 524; vi. 365; vii. 248.
—— —— his wife, Jonet Fenton of Drumblate and Towie, v. 524; vi. 366.
Douglas of Raquarrell, Gavin, ix. 13.
—— of Rattray, James, iii. 193.
—— of Rattray Crimond, Sir Archibald, regent of Scotland, iii. 141.
—— of Reidhaw, Sir James, vii. 124.
—— of Reidsyde, James, vi. 332.
—— of Roberton, Sir James, vi. 349.
—— —— Sir John, elder son of 1st earl of Morton, vi. 356.
—— —— his wife, Janet Crichton, vi. 358.
—— of Romanno, Sir Archibald, 'the Grim,' iii. 147.
—— —— Hugh, iii. 147.
—— —— William, iii. 147.
—— of Ross, Sir James, vii. 124.
—— of Rumgally, Sir George, vi. 370.
—— of Rutherglen, Sir Archibald, 'the Grim,' iii. 147.
—— —— Hugh, iii. 147.
—— —— William, iii. 147.
—— of St. Christopher's, John, general, viii. 131, 137; ix. 160.
—— of St. Olla, Robert, M.P., colonel, vi. 381.
—— of St. Saens, Isabella, countess of Mar, iii. 154.
—— —— William, earl of Douglas and Mar, iii. 154.
—— of Sandilands, Sir Francis, i. 202.
—— —— his wife, * Fleming, i. 202.
—— of Sanquhar, William, vii. 134.
—— of Schireffhall, William, vi. 375.
—— of Segy, William, vi. 375.
—— of Forest of Selkirk, Sir Archibald, 'the Grim,' iii. 141, 160.
—— —— Hugh, iii. 147.
—— —— William, iii. 147.
—— of Selkirk, Isabella, countess of Mar, wife of (1) Sir M. Drummond, and (2) Alex. Stewart, iii. 154.
—— baron of Skälby, vi. 352.
—— count Skenning, vi. 352.
—— of Skirling, James, advocate, lieut.-gen., vii. 136, 137.
—— —— his wife, Anna Hamilton, vii. 136.
—— —— James, elder son of above, vii. 137.
—— —— Margaret, vii. 137.
—— —— William, vii. 137.
—— of Smithfield, Sir James, vi. 379.
—— —— his wife, Ann Hay, vi. 380.
—— of Spot, Patrick, vii. 21.
—— —— Sir Robert, ii. 36, 393.
—— —— his wife, Nicolas Moray, ii. 37.
—— of Springwood Park, Sir George, 2nd bart., iv. 216.
—— —— his wife, Elizabeth Boyle, iv. 216.
—— —— Sir James, admiral of the White, iv. 215.
—— —— his 2nd wife, Helen Boyle, iv. 215.
—— of Spynie, George, bishop of Moray, i. 192, 194; viii. 57, 95.

* Name unknown.

Douglas of Stabilgorton, Hugh, iii. 147.
— — Sir James, 'the Good,' iii. 144.
— — William, iii. 147.
— — Sir William, vi. 341.
— of Stanhouse, John, iv. 159; vii. 133.
— — his wife, Helen Stewart, iv. 159.
— of Stobs, James, sheriff of Teviotdale, ii. 589.
— of Stonypath, Sir James, vi. 349.
— — James, viii. 74.
— — Sir William, vi. 373.
— of Stow, James, 3rd son of 1st earl of March, vii. 146.
— of Strabrock, Sir James, vi. 343 *n.*, 354 *n.*
— — John, vi. 343, 354 *n.*
— — his wife, Mariota *or* Mary Cheyne, vi. 34, 343, 354 *n.*
— — Sir William, ii. 325, 330; vi. 354 *n.*
— of Strathendry, Robert, i. 546.
— — his wife, Susan Balfour, i. 546; ix. 33.
— of Strathern, James, 2nd son of 3rd earl of Douglas, iii. 173.
— of Tannachy, Henry, i. 199.
— of Tarres, Robert, hippocomus to prince Henry, iii. 128.
— of Templand, Sir James, vii. 124.
— of Terregles, Sir Archibald, regent of Scotland, iii. 141.
— — Janet, wife of Andrew, 2nd lord Herries of Terregles, iv. 406.
— of Tibbers, Sir William, vii. 118.
— of Tibbersmote, Sir William, v. 288.
— of Tillyochie, Sir Robert, vi. 368.
— of Tilquhilly, Archibald, alleged ancestor of the family of, vi. 352.
— — John, alleged ancestor of the family of, vi. 354 *n.*
— — John, i. 309.
— — his wife, Mary Arbuthnott, i. 309.
— of Tofts, William, v. 460.
— of Torthorwald, Sir James, ii. 392; vi. 513, 517.
— — his wife, Elizabeth Carlyle, ii. 391.
— — William, vii. 134.
— of West Calder, Sir Archibald, iii. 141, 146.
— — John, iii. 142.
— of Westerkirk, Sir James, iii. 144.
— — Sir William, vi. 341.
— of Whitecamp, Sir James, vii. 124.
— of Whitehope, James, ii. 228.
— of Whittinghame, Sir Archibald, v. 196; vi. 373.
— — Archibald, v. 196; vi. 352.
— — Arthur, eldest son of Sir A. D. of Kellour, vi. 372.
— — his wife, Isobel Douglas, vi. 372.
— — Elizabeth, wife of 1st viscount of Kingston, v. 196, 197; vi. 352.
— — Isobel, wife of Arthur Douglas, vi. 373.
Douglas of Whittinghame, Sir James, vi. 346.
— — his wife, Agnes Dunbar, vi. 346.
— — William, 4th son of Sir Jas. D. of Dalkeith, vi. 352, 354, 410.
— — William, ii. 161, 270; v. 298; vi. 371; vii. 72.
— — his wife, Elizabeth Maitland, v. 298; ix. 124.
— — William, ix. 40.
— of Whytrigs, James, ancestor of the family of, i. 184.
— of Woodfield, James, vi. 354.
— of Zetland, William, vi. 377.
— — William, vi. 379.
— Agnes, wife of 7th earl of Argyll, i. 349; vi. 374.
— Agnes, wife of Wm. Hay of Urie, i. 184; ix. 12.
— Agnes, wife of (1) Sir J. Livingston of Callendar, and (2) John Gordon of Gordon, iv. 518; v. 184; vi. 349.
— Agnes, wife of 5th lord Livingston, v. 436; vi. 358.
— Agnes, wife of Thos. Hamilton of Raploch, vi. 367.
— Agnes, illeg. dau. of Sir James D. of Drumlanrig, vii. 128.
— Agnes, wife of Roger Grierson of Lag, vii. 117.
— Agnes, wife of Andrew Cunningham of Birkshaw, vii. 119.
— Agnes Charlotte, wife of Sir Owen Tudor Burne, vi. 386.
— Alexander, canon of Spynie, vicar of Elgin, iii. 135.
— Alexander, bishop of Moray, viii. 100.
— Alexander, 3rd son of Sir Wm. D. of Lochleven, vi. 366; ix. 141.
— Alexander, macer of the Court of Session, vi. 368, 411.
— — his wife, Isabella Little, vi. 411.
— Alexander, captain 38th Foot, 5th son of 4th earl of Selkirk, vii. 522.
— Alfred Bruce, vii. 154.
— — his wife, Olive Eleanor Custance, vii. 154.
— Alice, wife of Alex. Guthrie, i. 184.
— Alice Louisa, wife of bishop Alexander Ewing, vi. 386.
— Alison, dau. of 4th earl of Angus, i. 178.
— Alison, wife of (1) Robt. Blackadder, and (2) Sir D. Hume, i. 189.
— Alison, illeg. dau. of Sir James D. of Drumlanrig, vii. 128.
— Anne, alleged wife of 2nd lord Graham, i. 178; ix. 12.
— Ann, wife of 2nd earl of Kinnoull, v. 224; vi. 378.
— Anne, wife of 7th earl Marischal, vi. 59, 378.

Douglas, Anne, wife of 7th lord Sempill, vi. 333, 335; vii. 558; ix. 156.
— Anne, wife of William Finch, vii. 143; ix. 151.
— Ann, dau. of earl of Angus and Ormond, ix. 13.
— Anne Georgina, wife of C. S. H. Drummond Moray, vii. 153.
— Anna, dau. of 1st marquess of Douglas, i. 205.
— Anna, wife of (1) Jas. Sibbald, and (2) R. Arbuthnott, i. 299.
— Anna, wife of Patrick Porterfield of Comiston, vi. 334.
— Anna, wife of David, lord Elcho, vii. 140, 145; viii. 507, 515; ix. 151.
— Annas, dau. of James D., vi. 372.
— Archibald, supp. illeg. son of 2nd earl of Angus, i. 175 *n*.
— Archibald, 4th son of Arch. D. of Glenbervie, i. 184.
— Mr. Archibald, parson of Glenbervie, i. 198.
— Archibald, colonel of the Scottish Regiment in France, eldest son of 1st marquess of Douglas, i. 206; iii. 216.
— Archibald, 2nd son of James, 1st lord Torthorwald, ii. 393.
— Archibald, rector of Douglas, senator of the College of Justice, ii. 161, 169.
— — his wife, Jane Hepburne, Mistress of Bothwell, ii. 160.
— Archibald, elder son of James, commendator of Melrose, vi. 372.
— Archibald, colonel, 4th son of Sir William D. of Kelhead, vii. 148.
— — his wife, Elizabeth Ellis, ix. 151.
— Archibald, 5th son of Sir William D., 2nd bart. of Kelhead, vii. 149.
— Archibald, captain, ix. 100.
— his wife, Frances Gray, iv. 287; ix. 100.
— Archibald Edward, canon of Galloway, vii. 153.
— Archibald Johnston, 18th regiment of foot, vii. 151.
— Archibald Roderick Sholto, vi. 387.
— — his wife, Winona Constance de Maraisville Peake, vi. 387.
— Arthur Gascoigne, bishop of Aberdeen and Orkney, vi. 386.
— — his wife, Anna Maria Harriet Richards, vi. 386.
— Arthur James, capt. R.N., vi. 383.
— Barbara, wife of Charles Gray, iv. 290.
— Barbara, wife of Sir Robert Keith of Keith-Marischal, vi. 33.
— Barbara Elrington, wife of (1) James Vaughan Allen of Inchmartine, (2) N. F. Blair, and (3) Wm. Arbuthnott, i. 315.
— Beatrice, wife of Robert, lord Keith, vi. 43, 358.
Douglas, Beatrice, wife of 6th lord Maxwell, vi. 361, 482; ix. 141.
— Beatrix, wife of (1) William, 1st earl of Erroll, and (2) Arthur Forbes, iii. 175, 564; iv. 70; vi. 353 *n*.
— saint Brice, bishop of Moray, iii. 134, 135, 252; v. 571.
— Bridget, wife of W. H. Bouverie, vi. 383.
— Bruce Francis Sholto, vii. 154.
— Campbellina, dau. of 4th lord Mordingtoun, vi. 335.
— Caroline, wife of W. A. Fox Lane, vi. 383.
— Cecil Charles, 2nd son of 9th marquess of Queensberry, vii. 155.
— Charles, *de jure* 5th lord Mordingtoun, vi. 335.
— Charles, only child of 8th earl of Morton, vi. 379.
— Charles, M.P., 2nd son of 3rd duke of Queensberry, vii. 144.
— Charles, 2nd son of Archibald, earl of Angus and Ormond, ix. 13.
— Charles James Sholto, barrister-at-law, collector of customs, Jamaica, vii. 150, 153.
— — his 1st wife, Basilia Dawes, vii. 150.
— — his 2nd wife, Mary Bullock, vii. 150.
— Charles William Sholto, 2nd son of 18th earl of Morton, vi. 387.
— Charlotte, sister of 16th earl of Morton, vi. 383.
— Christian, wife of Alex. Irvine, i. 184.
— Christian, wife of Richard Douglas, ii. 270.
— Christian, wife of 1st earl of Carnwath, ii. 413; vii. 129.
— Christian, wife of Sir Alex. Stewart of Garlies, iv. 159; vii. 126; ix. 94 *bis*.
— Christian, wife of (1) Laurence, master of Oliphant, and (2) Alexander, 1st earl of Home, iv. 465; vi. 373, 550.
— Christian, dau. of Sir W. D. of Kelhead, vii. 151.
— Christian, wife of (1) Sir Wm. Douglas, (2) David Wemyss, and (3) Sir Jas. Auchinleck, viii. 483.
— David, 2nd son of 5th earl of Douglas, iii. 59, 170, 171.
— David, brother of Sir George D. of Pittendreich, vi. 361.
— Mr. David, 2nd son of Sir Henry D. of Lochleven, vi. 367.
— David, 9th son of Sir William D. of Kelhead, vii. 149.
— — his wife, * Thomson, vii. 149.
— Dorothy Madeline, dau. of 9th marquess of Queensberry, vii. 155.
— Dunbar, commander R.N., vii. 522.

* Name unknown.

Douglas, Mr. Duncan, parson of Glenbervie, i. 198.
— Edith Gertrude, wife of St. George Lane Fox Pitt, vii. 155.
— Edward William, vi. 385.
— — his 1st wife, Augusta Anne Bankes, vi. 385.
— — his 2nd wife, Evelyn Anne Trefusis, vi. 385.
— Egidia, dau. of 4th earl of Angus, i. 178.
— Egidia, wife of (1) Henry, 2nd earl of Orkney, and (2) Alexander Stewart, iii. 164; vi. 570.
— Eleanor, wife of (1) Alexander Bruce, earl of Carrick, (2) Sir Jas. Sandilands, (3) Sir Wm. Towers, (4) Sir D. Wallace, and (5) Sir P. Hepburn, ii. 137, 437, 506; iii. 142; viii. 379, 380 *bis*; ix. 55.
— Eleanor, wife of Sir Wm. Fraser of Philorth, iii. 157, 163 *n.*; vii. 432.
— Eleanor or Elene, wife of (1) William, 2nd lord Graham, and (2) James, 1st lord Ogilvy of Airlie, i. 114; v. 186 *n.*; vi. 223; ix. 7, 12, 137.
— Elene, wife of John Fairlie of Braid, vi. 365.
— Eliza, wife of Sir John Drummond of Innerpeffray, vii. 44.
— Elizabeth, wife of (1) Alexander, 1st lord Forbes, and (2) David, 1st lord Yester, i. 174; iv. 48, 49, 50; viii. 429.
— Elizabeth, wife of Robert Graham of Fintry, i. 178; iii. 316.
— Elizabeth, wife of Sir Alex. Falconer of Halkerton, i. 184; v. 245.
— Elizabeth, wife of Robert, 3rd lord Lyle, i. 186; v. 555.
— Elizabeth, wife of 3rd lord Hay of Yester, i. 189; viii. 435.
— Elizabeth, dau. of 6th earl of Angus, i. 193.
— Elizabeth, wife of (1) John, 8th lord Maxwell, earl of Morton, (2) Alex. Stewart of Garlies, and (3) John Wallace of Craigie; styled countess of Nithsdale, i. 194; iii. 175; iv. 151, 159; vi. 483.
— Elizabeth, wife of Thos. Gordon, i. 199; iv. 583.
— Elizabeth, wife of John Campbell, i. 202.
— Elizabeth, wife of (1) John Stewart, earl of Buchan, (2) Sir Thomas Stewart, and (3) Wm. Sinclair, earl of Orkney and Caithness, ii. 265, 333; iii. 167.
— Elizabeth, wife of Alex. Ramsay of Dalhousie, iii. 92; ix. 65.
— Elizabeth, wife of John Innes of Leuchars, iii. 203.
— Elizabeth, wife of 9th earl of Erroll, iii. 375; vi. 374.
— Elizabeth, wife of Andrew Fraser of Stoneywood and Muchalls, iv. 113.
Douglas, Elizabeth, wife of (1) Sir Wm. Douglas of Cavers and (2) Andrew Hume, lord Kimmerghame, vi. 16.
— Elizabeth wife of Robert, lord Keith, vi. 43, 358.
— Elizabeth, sister of Sir James D. of Dalkeith, vi. 344.
— Elizabeth, wife of Sir Thos. Somerville of Carnwath, vi. 344; viii. 5.
— Elizabeth, dau. of 1st earl of Morton, vi. 356.
— Elizabeth, wife of James, 4th earl of Morton, vi. 360, 362.
— Elizabeth, wife of Richard Lovel of Ballumby, vi. 366.
— Elizabeth, wife of Alex. Alexander of Menstrie, vi. 369; viii. 167.
— Elizabeth, wife of George, 1st lord Ramsay of Dalhousie, vi. 370.
— Elizabeth, wife of John Campbell of Wester Loudoun, vii. 117.
— Elizabeth, contr. to Andrew Ker, yr. of Cessford, vii. 125, 338; ix. 153 *bis*.
— Elizabeth, wife of Sir James Montgomery of Stobo, vii. 522.
— Elizabeth, wife of Michael Balfour of Burleigh, ix. 32, 141.
— Elizabeth, wife of Alex. Livingston of West Quarter, ix. 143.
— Elizabeth Christian, dau. of Sir William D. of Kelhead, vii. 151.
— Elizabeth Katinka, wife of H. St. G. Foote, viii. 152.
— Ellen, sister of Sir James D. of Dalkeith, vi. 344.
— Ellen Susan Anne, V.A., wife of rev. Douglas Hamilton Gordon, i. 196; vi. 386.
— Emily, dau. of lt.-col. John D., vi. 383.
— Emma Elizabeth, wife of Wm. Hamilton Ash, vi. 383.
— Erskine, M.D., Hexham, vii. 149.
— — his wife, Mrs. Wetters, vii. 149.
— Euphame, dau. of James D., vi. 372.
— Euphemia, wife of 6th lord Lindsay of the Byres, v. 400; vi. 370.
— Euphemia, wife of Sir Thomas Lyon of Baldukie, vi. 374; viii. 287.
— Florence Caroline, wife of Sir A. B. C. Dixie, vii. 154.
— Frances, wife of Sir Wm. Stewart of Cumloden, iv. 168; vi. 383.
— Frances, dau. of 13th earl of Morton, vi. 382.
— Frances Caroline, dau. of 5th marquess of Queensberry, vii. 152.
— Frances Harriet, wife of 6th earl Fitzwilliam, vi. 386.
— Francis, 8th son of 9th earl of Angus, i. 199; ix. 13.
— Francis, 3rd son of 2nd lord Mordingtoun, vi. 334.
— Francis, son of 5th earl of Morton, vi. 373.

Douglas, Francis, son of Hugh D. of Borg, viii. 583.
—— —— his contr. wife, Helenor Seton, viii. 24, 583.
—— Francis Edward, 8th son of Sir William D. of Kelhead, vii. 149.
—— —— his wife, Mrs. Hunter, vii. 149.
—— Francis William Bouverie, 2nd son of 7th marquess of Queensberry, vii. 153.
—— Freskin, parson of Douglas, dean of Moray, iii. 135.
—— Freskin, alleged son of Sir Andrew D. of Hermiston, vi. 338.
—— Gavin, bishop of Dunkeld, i. 185; ii. 455; vii. 571; ix. 12.
—— Gavin, university of Glasgow, 1489, vii. 117.
—— George, eldest son of 5th earl of Douglas; master of Angus, i. 181, 183, 186; iv. 564 *n.*
—— —— his wife, Elizabeth Drummond, i. 187; vi. 147 *n.*
—— George, commendator of Arbroath, bishop of Moray, i. 192, 194; iv. 235, 371, 539; viii. 57, 95.
—— Mr. George, chaplain of Drumlithie, i. 198.
—— George, colonel of the Scottish Regiment in France, 5th son of 1st marquess of Douglas, i. 258; iii. 216.
—— George, 4th son of 1st lord Torthorwald, ii. 393.
—— George, *called by Godscroft*, youngest son of 7th earl of Douglas, iii. 175.
—— George, captain, 5th son of Sir William D. of Kelhead, iii. 450; vii. 148.
—— —— his wife, Elizabeth Livingstone, iii. 450; ix. 81.
—— George, 5th son of 1st marquess of Douglas, i. 126, 205; iii. 216.
—— George, 3rd son of 1st duke of Queensberry, vii. 140.
—— George, parson of Kirkmichael, iv. 577.
—— George, pensioner of priory of St. Andrews, vi. 364.
—— George, captain in Friesland Infantry, vi. 378.
—— George, 4th son of 13th earl of Morton, vi. 382.
—— George, brother of 1st viscount of Drumlanrig, vii. 133.
—— George, 4th son of 1st earl of Queensberry, vii. 135.
—— George Henry, admiral R.N., vi. 385.
—— —— his wife, Charlotte Martha Parker, vi. 385.
—— Georgina, dau. of 6th marquess of Queensberry, vii. 153.
—— Gertrude Georgina, wife of Thomas Stock, vii. 153.
—— Gertrude Jane, wife of Mark G. K. Rolle, vi. 386.
—— Giles, dau. of 4th earl of Angus, i. 178.
Douglas, Grizel, wife of William, master of Carmichael, i. 205; iv. 589.
—— Harriet, wife of (1) James, viscount Hamilton, and (2) George, 4th earl of Aberdeen, i. 67, 95; vi. 383; ix. 5.
—— Harriet Bridget Emily, vi. 386.
—— Harriet Christian, wife of rev. A. Duncombe, vii. 152.
—— Helen, dau. of 2nd earl of Angus, and wife of (1) William, 2nd lord Graham, and (2) James, 1st lord Ogilvie of Airlie, i. 114; v. 186 *n.*; vi. 222; ix. 7, 12, 137.
—— Helen, wife of Roger Grierson of Lag, vii. 126.
—— Helen, dau. of Patrick D., vii. 126.
—— Helen, dau. of Sir Wm. D. of Hawick, vii. 129.
—— Helen, wife of John Menzies of Castlehill, vii. 133.
—— Helen, wife of capt. John Erskine, vii. 150.
—— Helen, dau. of Sir John D. of Kelhead, vii. 150.
—— Helen, wife of Sir Jas. Hall of Dunglass, vii. 522.
—— Helen, dau. of 2nd earl of Morton, ix. 140.
—— Henrietta, wife of 1st earl of Annandale, i. 205, 263.
—— Henrietta, wife of Sir Robt. Grierson of Lag, vii. 137 *bis*, 145.
—— Henry, canon of Spynie, iii. 135.
—— Henry, 6th son of 7th earl of Douglas, iii. 175.
—— Henry, prisoner in England, 1338, vi. 344 *n.*
—— Henry, 2nd son of Sir Robt. D. of Lochleven, vi. 368.
—— Henry, 3rd son of Thomas D., vi. 368.
—— Henry, rector of Hanbury, vi. 385.
—— —— his wife, Mary Baillie-Hamilton, iv. 327; vi. 385.
—— Henry Alexander, vii. 151.
—— —— his wife, Elizabeth Dalzell, ii. 417; vii. 151.
—— Hugh, son of Hugh, earl of Ormond; dean of Brechin, i. 114; vi. 586.
—— Hugh, canon of Spynie, archdeacon of Moray, iii. 135.
—— Hugh, eldest son of Sir William of D., iii. 136, 137.
—— —— his wife, Marjory Abernethy, iii. 137; vi. 338.
—— Hugh, incumbent of Old Roxburgh, iii. 140, 148.
—— Hugh, 3rd son of Patrick D., vii. 126.
—— Hugh, archdeacon of St. Andrews, ix. 11.
—— Hugh, 5th son of William D. of Drumlanrig, ix. 150.
—— Isabella, wife of (1) Sir A. Ramsay, and (2) Thos. Livingston, i. 178; iii. 192; ix. 65 *bis*.

Douglas, Isabel, wife of Jas. Melville, i. 184.
— Isabel, wife of 1st duke of Queensberry, i. 205; vii. 140; ix. 13.
— Isobel, wife of William Murray of Spot, iii. 508.
— Isobel, wife of Alex. Home of Home, iv. 453.
— Isabella, wife of (1) Robert, 1st earl of Roxburghe, and (2) James, 2nd marquess of Montrose, vi. 258, 378; vii. 348.
— Isobel, dau. of James D., vi. 372.
— Isobel, wife of Walter Scott of Synton, vii. 72.
— Isobel, wife of Sir Wm. Lockhart of Carstairs, vii. 137.
— Isabel, dau. of 2nd duke of Queensberry, vii. 143.
— Isobel, dau. of 1st earl of March, vii. 146.
— Isobel, dau. of Sir William D. of Kelhead, vii. 148.
— Isabella Helen, wife of Charles Hope, iv. 503; vii. 523.
— Isabella Margaret, dau. of 4th earl of Selkirk, vii. 522.
— J., vii. 512.
— — his wife, Agnes Mackenzie, vii. 512.
— Jacoba, wife of (1) Sir John Hamilton of Cadzow, and (2) Sir W. Douglas of Drumlanrig, iv. 346; vi. 349; vii. 114; ix. 103.
— James, 2nd son of Archd. D. of Glenbervie, i. 184.
— James, son of 6th earl of Angus; master of Angus, i. 192.
— James, parson of Glenbervie, i. 198.
— James, col. of Scots Regt. in France, 3rd son of 1st marquess of Douglas, i. 204; iii. 216.
— James, colonel of the Scottish Regiment in France, 6th son of 1st marquess of Douglas, i. 205.
— James, minister of Aboyne, and Arbuthnott, i. 299.
— James, son of 2nd lord Torthorwald, ii. 394.
— Sir James, 2nd son of 3rd earl of Douglas, iii. 166, 167.
— James, 2nd son of 7th earl of Douglas, iii. 174; vii. 248.
— James, in holy orders, iii. 516.
— — his wife, William-Mina Murray, iii. 516.
— James, commendator of Pluscarden, iii. 283; vi. 363.
— — his wife, Anna Home, iii. 283; vi. 363.
— James, lieut.-general, 1688, iv. 132.
— James, only son of Archibald, earl of Moray, vi. 310.
Douglas, James, 2nd son of 1st lord Mordingtoun, vi. 333.
— James, 3rd son of Sir James D. of Lothian, vi. 344.
— Mr. James, 2nd son of Henry D. of Borg, vi. 351.
— James, 2nd son of 1st earl of Morton, vi. 356.
— James, grandson of 2nd earl of Morton, vi. 358.
— James, commendator of the abbey of Melrose, vi. 372.
— — his 1st wife, Mary Ker, v. 68; vi. 372; ix. 116 *bis*.
— — his 2nd wife, Helen Scott, vi. 372.
— — his 3rd wife, Jean Anstruther, vi. 372.
— James, 3rd son of 13th earl of Morton, vi. 382.
— James, eldest son of Patrick D., vii. 126.
— James, M.D., Carlisle, vii. 149.
— — his wife, Mary Maxwell, vii. 149.
— James, 3rd son of Jas. D. of Drumlanrig, ix. 150.
— James Edward Sholto, vii. 153.
— — his wife, Martha Lucy *, vii. 153.
— James Sholto, grandson of Sir John D. of Kelhead, vii. 153.
— Jane, wife of col. John Steuart, i. 209; ii. 89.
— Jane, wife of 4th earl of Perth, i. 205; vii. 53.
— Jane, wife of 2nd duke of Buccleuch, ii. 241; vii. 143.
— Jane, wife of John Cumming of Earnside, ix. 141.
— Jane Margaret, wife of baron Montagu of Boughton, ii. 243.
— Jane Margaret Mary, wife of R. Johnstone Douglas, vii. 152.
— Janet, wife of (1) David Scott, and (2) George, 2nd earl of Rothes, i. 178; ii. 228; vii. 278.
— Janet, wife of 2nd lord Herries, i. 186; iv. 406; ix. 105.
— Janet, wife of (1) John, 6th lord Glamis, and (2) Archibald Campbell of Skipness, i. 189, 336; viii. 279.
— Janet, wife of 3rd lord Ruthven, i. 193; iv. 261; viii. 399.
— Janet, wife of Sir Jas. Murray of Cockpool, i. 226; vii. 129.
— Janet, wife of Sir P. Hepburn of Dunsyre, 1st earl of Bothwell, ii. 152; vi. 356.
— Janet, wife of Sir Jas. Colville of East Wemyss, ii. 553; vi. 371.
— Janet, wife of 1st lord Fleming, iii. 175; viii. 533.
— Janet, wife of Alex. King, iii. 589.
— Janet, wife of (1) William, master of

* Name unknown.

Somerville, and (2) Sir Alex. Gordon of Kenmure, v. 104; vii. 117; viii. 12.
Douglas, Jonet, wife of 2nd lord Kirkcudbright, v. 268; vii. 135; ix. 124, 150.
—— Janet, dau. of Archibald, earl of Moray, v. 523 *n.*; vi. 310.
—— Janet, wife of 5th lord Maxwell, vi. 480; vii. 118.
—— Janet, wife of Roger Grierson of Lag, vii. 117.
—— Janet, wife of (1) Wm. Douglas of Cashogill, and (2) John Charteris of Amisfield, vii. 125; ix. 125.
—— Janet, wife of (1) James Tweedie of Drumelzier, and (2) William Ker of Cessford, vii. 126, 341.
—— Janet, illeg. dau. of Sir James D. of Drumlanrig, vii. 128.
—— Janet, wife of Wm. Livingstone of Jerviswood, vii. 133.
—— Janet, wife of William Irving of Bonshaw, vii. 150.
—— Jean, wife of John Wishart, i. 199.
—— Jean, wife of 1st lord Bargany, i. 205; ii. 28.
—— Jean, wife of Francis, earl of Dalkeith, ii. 241; vii. 143; ix. 151.
—— Jean, wife of Sir John Kennedy of Culzean, ii. 491.
—— Jean, wife of 3rd earl of Home, iv. 478; vi. 378; ix. 108.
—— Jean, wife of (1) P. Edmonston of Woolmet, (2) Porterfield of Hapland, and (3) Cunningham of Dankeith, vi. 372.
—— Jean, dau. of 5th earl of Morton, vi. 374.
—— Jean, 'oy' of the provost of Lincluden, vii. 127.
—— Jean, dau. of Sir William D. of Hawick, vii. 129.
—— Jean, dau. of 1st earl of March, vii. 146.
—— Jean, wife of Hugh Maxwell of Dalswinton, vii. 150.
—— Jean, wife of Sir Richard Rutherfurd, vii. 366.
—— Jean, wife of Wm. Livingston of Jerviswood, viii. 373.
—— Joan, wife of Jas. Skene, i. 184.
—— Joanna, wife of 1st earl of Bothwell, ii. 152; vi. 356.
—— Joanna, 1st wife of Murdac, duke of Albany, earl of Fife and Menteith, v. 342 *n.*; ix. 10.
—— Joanna, alleged wife of 2nd lord Spynie, viii. 104 *n.*
—— Joanna, wife of Sir Nigel Cunningham, ix. 96.
—— John, admiral R.N., i. 92.
—— John, son of 4th earl of Angus, i. 178.
—— John, 3rd son of Arch. D. of Glenbervie, i. 184.
Douglas, John, in Lintalee, i. 202.
—— —— his wife, Margaret Douglas, i. 202.
—— John, archbishop of St. Andrews, i. 340.
—— John, legtd. son of viscount Belhaven, ii. 37.
—— Sir John, 2nd son of Sir Jas. D. of Lothian, ii. 223; vi. 342.
—— —— his wife, Agnes Munfode, vi. 343.
—— John, 3rd son of 1st lord Torthorwald, ii. 393.
—— John, illeg. son of James D. of Drumlanrig, ii. 403; vii. 126.
—— John, parson of Longformacus, iv. 430.
—— John, D.D., minister of Crail, v. 413.
—— —— his wife, Katharine Lindsay, v. 413.
—— John, Newcastle, vi. 16.
—— John, 3rd son of Henry D. of Borg, vi. 351.
—— John, parson of Newlands, vi. 368.
—— John, 4th son of 6th earl of Morton, vi. 377.
—— John, lieut.-col. 1st Foot Guards, vi. 382.
—— —— his wife, Frances Lascelles, vi. 382.
—— John, vi. 353 *n.*
—— —— his alleged wife, * Abernethy of Hawthornden, vi. 353 *n.*
—— John, 'oy' of the provost of Lincluden, vii. 127.
—— John, Madras, 4th son of Sir John D. of Kelhead, vii. 150.
—— John, vicar of Kirkconnell, dean, vii. 117.
—— John, 2nd son of Sir William D. of Drumlanrig, vii. 118.
—— John, advocate, 3rd son of 4th earl of Selkirk, vii. 522.
—— Joseph, Edrington, v. 413.
—— —— his wife, Alison Lindsay, v. 413.
—— Katharine, wife of A. H. Gordon, i. 92.
—— Katharine, wife of John Carmichael, i. 185; ix. 12.
—— Katharine, dau. of 10th earl of Angus, i. 202.
—— Katharine, wife of Sir Wm. Ruthven of Dunglass, i. 205; iv. 103.
—— Katharine, wife of Alex. Hope of Greenbraes, iv. 486.
—— Katharine, wife of Menzies of Stenhouse, vii. 148.
—— Katharine, wife of Sir Wm. Maxwell of Springkell, vii. 149.
—— Katharine, wife of Wm. Butler, M.D., vii. 151.
—— Katharine, wife of Sir James Douglas of Kelhead, vii. 137, 145, 149.
—— Katharine, wife of David Durie of that Ilk, vi. 371.
—— Katharine, wife of Archibald Napier of Merchiston, vi. 409, 410.

* Name unknown.

Douglas, Katharine, wife of John Halkett, vii. 523.
— Katharine, wife of (1) Henry Colville, and (2) Wm. Stewart of Egilshay, ix. 59.
— Katharine Heron, vii. 151.
— Katharine Jean, wife of Loftus Wigram, vii. 524.
— Lewis, 4th son of 2nd lord Mordingtoun, vi. 334.
— Louisa Anne, wife of T. C. Whitmere of Apley Park, vii. 152.
— Lucy, wife of 4th earl of Nithsdale, i. 206; vi. 488; ix. 13.
— Margaret, wife of 4th earl of Lennox, i. 22, 26, 191, 192; vi. 353; vi. 311.
— Margaret, wife of Sir D. Campbell of Glenurchy, i. 178; ii. 179.
— Margaret, wife of John Erskine, i. 184.
— Margaret, wife of Semple of Fulwood, i. 185.
— Margaret, wife of Sir Jas. Douglas of Drumlanrig, i. 190; vii. 125.
— Margaret, wife of (1) Sir Walter Scott, and (2) Francis Stuart, earl of Bothwell, i. 193; ii. 171, 231; ix. 12, 46.
— Margaret, only child of 8th earl of Angus, i. 197, 518; ix. 13.
— Margaret, wife of William Forbes of Menymusk, ii. 199; ix. 13.
— Margaret, wife of John Douglas in Lintalee, i. 202.
— Margaret, wife of William, lord Alexander, i. 205; viii. 177.
— Margaret, wife of 1st viscount of Kingsten, i. 207; v. 196.
— Margaret, wife of Archibald, duke of Douglas, i. 211; ix. 13.
— Margaret, wife of 1st earl of Hartfell, i. 258; vii. 135.
— Margaret, wife of (1) Philip de Arbuthnott, and (2) Fairlie of Braid, i. 276, 278; vi. 350.
— Margaret, wife of Archibald, marquess of Argyll, i. 359; vi. 378.
— Margaret, the 'Fair Maid of Galloway,' wife of (1) William, 8th earl of Douglas, (2) James, 9th earl of Douglas, and (3) John, earl of Atholl, i. 441; iii. 176, 178.
— Margaret, wife of (1) Herbert Maxwell, and (2) William, lord Carlyle, ii. 385, 386.
— Margaret, wife of 2nd lord Cathcart, ii. 510; vii. 117.
— Margaret, wife of 1st lord Ramsay of Dalhousie, iii. 97; ix. 66.
— Margaret, wife of William Maxwell of Cavens, iii. 126.
— Margaret, alleged wife of Hervey le Marescal, iii. 135.
— Margaret, alleged wife of Hervey of Keith-Hervey, iii. 135; vi. 26.
— Margaret, wife of Henry Douglas of Borg, iii. 175; vi. 351.
Douglas, Margaret, wife of (1) Edward, 7th lord Crichton of Sanquhar, (2) William, earl of Menteith, and (3) Robert Wauchope of Niddrie, iii. 229; vi. 163; vii. 126.
— Margaret, wife of 5th lord Haliburton iv. 337.
— Margaret, wife of James, 2nd earl of Arran, iv. 368; vi. 361; ix. 103.
— Margaret, alleged wife of Sir Herbert Herries of Terregles, but perhaps wife of his grandfather Sir John, iv. 402.
— Margaret, wife of Sir John Carmichael, iv. 580; ix. 113 *bis*.
— Margaret, alleged wife of William Melville of Raith, vi. 84.
— Margaret, wife of Wm. Melville of Pitconmark, vi. 90, 369.
— Margaret, wife of David Melville of Newmills and Prinlaws, vi. 93.
— Margaret, sister of Sir James D. of Dalkeith, vi. 344.
— Margaret, wife of Sir John Wallace of Craigie, vi. 365.
— Margaret, wife of Henry Stewart of Rossyth, vi. 368.
— Margaret, wife of Wm. Baillie of Hardington, vi. 372.
— Margaret, wife of John Wemyss of Methil, vi. 373; viii. 498.
— Margaret, wife of Sir Donald Macdonald of Slate, vi. 379.
— Margaret, wife of H. Maule of Balmakellie, vii. 21.
— Margaret, wife of John Jardine of Applegirth, vii. 125.
— Margaret, wife of Sir Robt. Montgomerie of Skelmerlie, vii. 129.
— Margaret, wife of (1) Sir Alex. Jardine of Applegirth, and (2) Sir David Theirs, vii. 137, 145.
— Margaret, dau. of Sir William D. of Kelhead, vii. 148.
— Margaret, wife of (1) col. Campbell Dalrymple of Carriden, and (2) Charles Dalrymple, viii. 131, 137.
— Margaret, wife of John Hepburne of Beinstoun, ix. 40.
— Margaret, wife of Rogor Duncanson, ix. 142.
— Margaret, wife of Wm. Maxwell, ix. 150.
— Marion, dau. of Arch. D. of Glenbervie, i. 184.
— Marion, wife of Cuthbert, 2nd earl of Glencairn, i. 186; iv. 236 *ter*.
— Marion, wife of P. Bellentyne, ii. 62.
— Marion, wife of John Lindsay of Dowhill, vi. 369.
— Marion, wife of John Scott of Thirlestane, vi. 429.
— Marjory or Mary, wife of (1) David

duke of Rothesay, and (2) Sir Walter Haliburton, i. 18; ii. 439; iii. 161, 163; iv. 334.
Douglas, Marjory, wife of Andrew Keith, i. 184.
— Marjory, wife of 6th viscount of Arbuthnott, i. 313.
— Mary, wife of 4th earl of Aboyne, i. 105; vi. 382; ix. 7, 141.
— Mary, alleged 2nd wife of 1st lord Ogilvy of Airlie, i. 114, 186.
— Mary, wife of (1) Alex., 1st lord Forbes, and (2) Sir D. Hay of Locherworth, i. 174; iv. 49; viii. 429.
— Mary, wife of 2nd earl of Linlithgow, i. 202; v. 447.
— Mary, 10th dau. of 1st marquess of Douglas, i. 206.
— Mary, alleged wife of John Kennedy of Dunure, ii. 447.
— Mary, wife of (1) John Johnstone of Wamphray, and (2) Jas. Crichton of Castlemains, iii. 228; vii. 148.
— Mary, wife of 2nd earl of Dunfermline, iii. 374; vi. 378.
— Mary, wife of 1st lord Ogilvy of Deskford, iv. 26; vi. 374.
— Mary, wife of 3rd earl of Galloway, iv. 163; vii. 137, 145.
— Mary, wife of Sir Thos. Ker of Redden, v. 464.
— Mary, wife of (1) Reginald More, and (2) Thomas Erskine, vi. 342.
— Mary, dau. of James D., vi. 372.
— Mary, dau. of Sir William D. of Kelhead, vii. 150.
— Mary, wife of major-gen. Sir T. S. Beckwith, vii. 151.
— Mary, dau. of 1st earl of March, vii. 146.
— Mary, dau. of 4th earl of Selkirk, vii. 522.
— Mary Elizabeth, wife of rev. T. W. Gage, vii. 152.
— Sir Neil, lieut.-general, i. 315.
— Nicola(s, wife of James Johnstone, i. 245, 247; vii. 125; ix. 14.
— Patrick, illeg. son of Sir James D. of Drumlanrig, vii. 126, 128.
— — his 1st wife, Marion Menzies, ix. 150.
— — his 2nd wife, Katharine Craufurd, vii. 126.
— Peggy, wife of Archibald, duke of Douglas, i. 211; ix. 13.
— Raymond Wilfrid Sholto, vii. 154.
— Richard, 3rd son of Wm. D. of Whittinghame, ii. 270.
— — his wife, Christian Douglas, ii. 270.
— Richard, 2nd son of 2nd earl of Morton, vi. 358.
— Richard, macer of the Court of Session, vi. 368.
Douglas, Robert, provost of Lincluden, iv. 159; vii. 127, 128.
— Robert, merchant, Edinburgh, iv. 289.
— — his wife, Barbara Gray, iv. 289.
— Robert, son of John D., parson of Longformacus, iv. 430.
— Robert, minister of Edinburgh, vi. 370.
— Robert, 2nd son of James D., commendator of Melrose, vi. 372; ix. 92.
— — his wife, Katharine Forrester, ix. 92, 141.
— Robert, eldest son of 5th earl of Morton, vi. 374.
— — his wife, Jean Lyon, vi. 374.
— Robert, master of horse to Henrietta, duchess of Orleans, vi. 378.
— Robert, 5th son of 13th earl of Morton, vi. 382.
— Robert, only son of Sir R. D. of Glenbervie, vi. 498.
— Robert, 3rd son of William D. of Drumlanrig, vii. 117.
— Robert, 4th son of 2nd earl of Queensberry, vii. 137.
— Robert, 3rd son of Sir William D. of Kelhead, vii. 148; ix. 151.
— Robert, ix. 59.
— — his wife, Janet Colville, ii. 572; ix. 59.
— Roderick Walter Sholto, vi. 387.
— Ronald John Sholto, 5th son of 18th earl of Morton, vi. 387.
— Sara, dau. of Arch. D. of Glenbervie, i. 185.
— Sarah, wife of (1) Robert Strachan, and (2) George Auchinleck, i. 199.
— Sarah, dau. of Sir William D. of Kelhead, vii. 148.
— Sarah, wife of 6th marquess of Queensberry, vii. 150, 153.
— Sholto Augustus, vii. 154.
— Sholto Charles John Hay, vi. 387.
— Sholto George, vii. 154.
— — his wife, Loretta Mooney, vii. 154.
— Sophia, wife of John Craill of Stewartoun, vii. 148.
— Stair, captain R.N., iii. 361; vii. 150.
— Stewart, lieut.-general, vii. 149.
— Susanna, wife of Sir Robt. Douglas of Blackerston, ii. 37.
— Thomas, brother of Sir Jas. D. of Dalkeith, vi. 343.
— Thomas, 3rd son of Sir Henry D. of Lochleven, vi. 367.
— Thomas, eldest son of Sir R. D. of Lochleven, vi. 368.
— — his wife, Elizabeth Boyd, v. 146; vi. 368.
— Thomas, R.N., 10th son of Sir William D. of Kelhead, vii. 149.
— Triamor, 2nd son of Patrick D., vii. 126.

Douglas, Willelma, wife of William of Galbraith, iii. 138.
— William, abbot of Holyrood, i. 188.
— William, 2nd son of 1st marquess of Douglas, i. 204.
— William, 4th son of earl of Angus and Ormond, i. 207; ix. 13.
— William, alleged son of James, 2nd lord Torthorwald, ii. 394 *n*.
— William, ii. 592.
— — his wife, Elizabeth Cranstoun, ii. 592.
— William, brigadier-general, v. 16.
— — his wife, Anne Howard, v. 16.
— William, father of Archibald D. of Livingston and Herdmanston, v. 570.
— William, 2nd son of 2nd lord Mordingtoun, vi. 334.
— Sir William, the elder; illeg. son of Sir Jas. D. of Laudonia, vi. 344.
— William, eldest son of Sir Jas. D. of Dalkeith, vi. 349, 351.
— — his wife, Margaret Borthwick, ii. 96; vi. 351.
— William, grandson of 2nd earl of Morton, vi. 358.
— William, in Linton, vi. 371.
— William, 3rd son of 6th earl of Morton, vi. 377.
— William, 4th son of 9th earl of Morton, vi. 380.
— William, 2nd son of 12th earl of Morton, vi. 381.
— William, illeg. son of Sir William D. of Hawick, vii. 129.
— William, eldest son of Sir Wm. D. of Kelhead, vii. 148.
— William, 2nd son of Sir Wm. D., 2nd bart. of Kelhead, vii. 149.
— Mr. William, parson of Kilbucho, ix. 140.
— William Sholto, 4th son of 18th earl of Morton, vi. 387.
— William Robert Keith, M.P., vii. 151.
— — his wife, Elizabeth Irvine, vii. 151.
— *, husband of Grace Ogilvy, dau. of 7th lord Banff, ii. 25.
— *, wife of Geo. Scott of Bunraw, vii. 72.
— *, wife of Andrew Ker of Altonburn and Cessford, vii. 323.
— *, wife of A. Rutherfurd, canon of Jedburgh, vii. 371.
— *, alleged wife of Sir Wm. Hay of Locherworth, viii. 421.
Douglas-Halyburton of Pitcur, Hamilton, R.N., vi. 384.
DOUGLAS-HAMILTON, DUKE OF HAMILTON, iv. 381-397.
Douglas-Hamilton of Arran, Mary Louise, wife of James, marquess of Graham, iv. 396.

* Name unknown.

Douglas-Hamilton of Gidea Hall, Alfred, iv. 390.
— — his 1st wife, Adelaide Black, iv. 390.
— — his 2nd wife, H. A. Blackburne Peters, iv. 390.
— Adolphus, M.A., in holy orders, iv. 390.
— — his wife, H. C. Carew, iv. 390.
— Alexander, iv. 390.
— Alfred Hamilton Douglas, barrister-at-law, iv. 390.
— Algernon Percy, iv. 389.
— — his wife, Idonia Douglas-Hamilton, iv. 389, 390.
— Angus Falconar, major Q. O. Cameron Highlanders, iv. 391.
— — his wife, A. W. Mackenzie, iv. 391.
— Anne, wife of Arthur, 1st marquess of Donegal, iv. 393.
— Anne, dau. of 9th duke of Hamilton, iv. 395.
— Anne, iv. 395; ix. 104.
— Archibald, M.P., iv. 394.
— Archibald Barrington Seymour, iv. 389.
— Archibald Douglas Schomberg, iv. 390.
— Aubrey Reginald, 57th regt., iv. 389.
— — his wife, Lucy FitzGerald, iv. 389.
— Augustus Barrington Price Anne Powell, lieut. R.N., iv. 388.
— — his wife, M. C. Hyde, iv. 388.
— Augustus John, iv. 388.
— Augustus Maitland Ronald, R.N., iv. 390.
— — his wife, Thérèse M. St. C. Wentworth, iv. 391.
— Augustus Maynard, iv. 391.
— Basil Sholto Anne, capt. Army Service Corps, iv. 391.
— Bertha, wife of George Dawson, iv. 390.
— Charles George Archibald, lieut. 11th Hussars, iv. 396.
— Charles Henry, capt. R.N., iv. 388.
— — his 1st wife, Anna Apthorp, iv. 388.
— — his 2nd wife, E. A. Hill, iv. 389.
— — his 3rd wife, S. J. Spence, iv. 389.
— Charles Powell, admiral R.N., iv. 388.
— — his wife, Lucretia Prosser, iv. 388.
— Charles Reginald Sydney, capt. Gordon Highlanders, iv. 391.
— — his wife, M. I. H. Whitla, iv. 391.
— Charlotte, wife of Charles Edwin of Dunraven, iv. 391.
— Charlotte, wife of 11th duke of Somerset, iv. 395.
— Claud Archibald Aubrey, iv. 389.
— Douglas Rynes, capt., iv. 390.
— — his wife, F. Graves, iv. 390.
— Elizabeth, dau. of 4th duke of Hamilton, iv. 391.
— Elizabeth, wife of 12th earl of Derby, iv. 393.

Douglas-Hamilton, Flora Mary Ida, wife of major R. M. Poore, iv. 389.
—— Francis Seymour, col. R.A., iv. 389.
—— —— his wife, E. C. F. Coventry, iv. 389.
—— Frederic, consul general, Ecuador, iv. 390.
—— —— his wife, Marina Norton, iv. 390.
—— Frederick, iv. 390.
—— Frederick Robert Vere, iv. 390.
—— —— his wife, Josephine Baumann, iv. 390.
—— Hamilton Anne, archdeacon of Kimberley, iv. 391.
—— —— his wife, Lillie Bowles, iv. 391.
—— Hamilton Charles James, envoy extraordinary at Brazil, iv. 388.
—— —— his wife, M. S. Robinson, iv. 388.
—— Helena Augusta Charlotte Constance Sidney, wife of rev. R. Fuller Acland-Hood, iv. 389.
—— Herbert Eustace Seymour, iv. 389.
—— Isabel Frances Ulrica Iris, wife of capt. Cyril J. Ryder, iv. 389.
—— James Angus, iv. 391.
—— Jean, dau. of 13th duke of Hamilton, iv. 397.
—— Katharine, dau. of 4th duke of Hamilton, iv. 391; ix. 104.
—— Kenneth Aubrey FitzGerald Seymour, Royal Fusiliers, iv. 389.
—— Lesley Reginald Coventry, Q. O. Cameron Highlanders, iv. 389.
—— Lucy Charlotte, wife of brigadier-gen. R. Anstruther, iv. 388.
—— Mary Victoria, wife of (1) prince Albert of Monaco, and (2) count Tassilo Festetics, iv. 396.
—— Nina Susannah, wife of Sir William C. Dunbar, iv. 390.
—— Octavius, major-general, iv. 391.
—— —— his wife, K. A. W. Macleod, iv. 391.
—— Patrick, iv. 390.
—— Percy Seymour, iv. 389.
—— —— his wife, Edith H. Wills, iv. 389.
—— Spencer, colonel, iv. 392.
—— Susan, wife of A. T. Keck, iv. 391; ix. 104.
—— Susan, wife of 5th earl of Dunmore, iv. 394.
—— Susan Harriet Catherine, wife of (1) Henry, 5th duke of Newcastle, and (2) * Opdebeck, iv. 395.
—— William Arthur, curate of Waldren, iv. 390.
DOUGLAS-HOME, EARL OF HOME, iv. 482-484.
Douglas-Home, Alexander Frederick, grandson of 12th earl of Home, iv. 483.
—— Beatrix Lucy, wife of capt. H. H. P. Dundas, iv. 483.
—— Bridget, iv. 483.
—— Issobel Charlotte, iv. 483.
—— Margaret Jane, iv. 483.
Douglas-Home, Mary Elizabeth Margaret, wife of R. C. Meade, lord Gillford, iv. 483.
Douglas-Pennant, Edward Gordon, vi. 383.
—— —— his 1st wife, Juliana Isabella Mary Dawkins-Pennant, vi. 383.
—— —— his 2nd wife, Mary Louisa Fitzroy, vi. 383.
DOUGLAS-SCOTT, DUKE OF QUEENSBERRY, ii. 242-244.
DOUGLAS AND CLYDESDALE, DOUGLAS-HAMILTON, MARQUESS OF, iv. 396.
Douglas and Clydesdale, Douglas, son of 13th duke of Hamilton; styled marquess of, iv. 396.
DOUGLAS OF DOUGLAS, HOME, BARON, iv. 482-483.
Douglas of Douglas, Cospatrick Alexander, first baron, iv. 482.
—— —— his wife, Lucy Elizabeth Montagu of Douglas, ii. 243; iv. 482.
Doull of Thuster, John, writer, vii. 175.
—— Mary, wife of 3rd lord Reay, vii. 175.
DOUNE, STEWART, LORD, iii. 186-190; vi. 316-330.
—— Francis Douglas, eldest son of 17th earl of Moray; styled lord, vi. 327.
—— James, first lord, iii. 187; vi. 316, 319; ix. 68 *bis*.
—— —— his wife, Margaret Campbell, i. 340; iii. 188; ix. 68 *bis*.
—— James, second lord, iii. 189; vi. 316.
—— —— his wife, Elizabeth, countess of Moray, iii. 189; vi. 316.
—— James, elder son of 3rd earl of Moray; styled lord, vi. 320.
—— —— his wife, Margaret Home, vi. 321.
—— James, eldest son of 4th earl of Moray; styled lord, vi. 321; ix. 139 *bis*.
—— James, eldest son of 5th earl of Moray; styled lord, iii. 406; vi. 323; ix. 140 *bis*.
—— —— his wife, Katharine Tollemache, iii. 406; vi. 323.
—— James, eldest son of 9th earl of Moray; styled lord, vi. 326.
—— John, 2nd son of 9th earl of Moray; styled lord, vi. 326.
—— master of, James, iii. 189.
—— —— his wife, Elizabeth Stewart, iii. 189; vi. 316.
Dovedale, Sir John de, i. 322.
Dovenald of Galloway, iv. 135.
DOVER, DOUGLAS, DUKE OF, vii. 141.
Dover, Charles, second duke of, vii. 143.
—— —— his wife, Katharine Hyde, vii. 143.
—— James, first duke of, vii. 141.
—— —— his wife, Mary Boyle, vii. 142.
Dowdall, Harold Challoner, barrister, ii. 119.
—— —— his wife, Mary Frances Harriet Borthwick, ii. 119.
Dowell of Skibo, Patrick, vii. 175.
—— of Winterfield, Patrick, vii. 175.

Downshire, Arthur W. J. W. B. Trumbull (Hill), 6th marquess of, viii. 182.
Downy, John, Fife, ix. 127.
Drake of Ashe, Sir John, ii. 532.
—— —— Sir John, 1st bart., ii. 532.
—— captain, husband of Anne Mackenzie, dau. of 3rd lord Cromartie, iii. 81.
—— Elizabeth, wife of Sir W. Churchill, ii. 532.
Drayton, Michael, i. 407.
—— Thomas, South Carolina, iii. 81.
—— —— his wife, Mary Mackenzie, iii. 81.
—— Thomas, his son, iii. 81.
Drelincourt, Anne, wife of 3rd viscount of Primrose, vii. 111.
—— Charles, minister of Reformed Church in Paris, vii. 111 *n.*
—— Peter, dean of Armagh, vii. 111.
Dreux, Robert, 2nd comte de, vi. 564.
—— —— his wife, Iolande de Coucy, vi. 564.
—— Eleanor de, wife of (1) Hugh de Chateauneuf, and (2) Robert de Saint-clair, vi. 564.
—— Yolande de, wife of King Alexander III., i. 6.
Drever, John, I.M.S., vii. 178.
—— —— his wife, Charlotte Mackay, vii. 178.
Drew, John, iii. 391.
—— —— his wife, Susan Murray, iii. 391.
Driver, Elma, wife of C. F. Hepburne-Scott, vii. 86.
—— Johnson, Edinburgh, vii. 86.
Drogheda, Henry (Moore), 1st earl of, ii. 32, 73; iii. 101.
Drumcairn, James (Murray), Jacobite creation, viscount of, viii. 205.
—— Sir John Hamilton, lord clerk register, lord, iv. 310.
—— Thomas Hamilton, senator of the College of Justice, lord, iv. 309.
DRUMLANRIG, DOUGLAS, VISCOUNT OF, vii. 134-156.
Drumlanrig, Francis Archibald, eldest son of 8th marquess of Queensberry; styled viscount of, vii. 154.
—— William, first viscount of, vii. 134.
—— —— his wife, Isobel Ker, vii. 134.
DRUMLANRIG, DOUGLAS, EARL OF, vii. 138-156.
Drumlanrig, Charles, 2nd son of 3rd duke of Queensberry; styled earl of, vii. 144.
—— Henry, elder son of 3rd duke of Queensberry; styled earl of, vii. 144.
—— —— his wife, Elizabeth Hope, iv. 498; vii. 144.
—— James, elder son of 1st duke of Queensberry; styled earl of, vii. 140, 145.
—— James, 2nd son of 2nd duke of Queensberry; styled earl of, vii. 142.
—— William, first earl of, vii. 138.
Drumlanrig, master of, James, eldest son of 1st earl of Queensberry, vii. 135.
—— —— his 1st wife, Mary Hamilton, iv. 375; vii. 136.
DRUMMOND, DRUMMOND, LORD, vii. 41-62.
Drummond, Charles Edward, sixteenth lord, vii. 60.
—— David, second lord, i. 335 *n.*, 459 *n.*; vii. 45; viii. 215.
—— —— his 1st wife, Margaret Stewart, vii. 45, 46.
—— —— his 2nd wife, Lilias Ruthven, iv. 260; vii. 46.
—— Edward, twelfth lord, vii. 53, 56.
—— —— his wife, Elizabeth Middleton, vi. 188; vii. 57.
—— George, seventeenth lord, vii. 60.
—— —— his 1st wife, Albertine von Rothberg Coligny, vii. 60.
—— —— his 2nd wife, Susan Henrietta Sewell, vii. 60.
—— George Essex Montifex, only son of viscount Forth; styled lord, vii. 61.
—— James, fourth lord, vii. 48; ix. 149.
—— —— his wife, Isabella Seton, vii. 48; ix. 149.
—— James, sixth lord, vii. 50.
—— —— his wife, Anne Gordon, vii. 51.
—— James, seventh lord, vii. 51.
—— —— his 1st wife, Jane Douglas, vii. 53.
—— —— his 2nd wife, Lilias Drummond, vii. 50, 53; viii. 223, 415.
—— —— his 3rd wife, Mary Gordon, vii. 53.
—— James, eighth lord, vii. 53.
—— —— his wife, Jean Gordon, vii. 54.
—— James, ninth lord, vii. 54.
—— James, thirteenth lord, vii. 57.
—— —— his wife, Rachel Bruce, iii. 490; vii. 57.
—— James, fourteenth lord, vii. 58.
—— —— his wife, Clementina Elphinstone, iii. 549; vii. 59.
—— James Louis, fifteenth lord, vi. 72; vii. 59.
—— John, first lord, i. 457; ii. 179; iii. 22; vii. 40, 187.
—— —— his wife Elizabeth Lindsay, iii. 22; vii. 42.
—— John, fifth lord, vii. 48.
—— —— his wife, Jean Ker, vii. 49.
—— John, tenth lord, vii. 55.
—— John, eleventh lord, vii. 53, 56.
—— —— his 1st wife, * Fotheringham, vii. 56.
—— —— his 2nd wife, Mary Stuart, vii. 56.
—— Patrick, third lord, iii. 29; vii. 47; viii. 216; ix. 149.
—— —— his 1st wife, Elizabeth Lindsay, i. 512; vii. 47.
—— —— his 2nd wife, Agnes Drummond, vii. 47.

* Name unknown.

Drummond, Thomas, 2nd son of James Lundin *or* Drummond; styled lord, vii. 58.
DRUMMOND OF CROMLIX, DRUMMOND, LORD, viii. 220-238.
Drummond of Cromlix, William, first lord, viii. 220.
DRUMMOND OF GILESTOUN, DRUMMOND, LORD, vi. 66-74.
Drummond of Gilestoun, John, first lord, vi. 66.
DRUMMOND OF RICCARTOUN, CASTLEMAINS, AND GILSTOUN, DRUMMOND, LORD, vi. 66-74.
Drummond of Riccartoun, Castlemains, and Gilston, George, lord, vii. 60.
—— —— John, first lord, vi. 67.
—— George Essex Montifex, grandson of George, earl of Melfort; styled lord, vi. 73.
DRUMMOND OF STOBHALL, DRUMMOND, BARON, vii. 58-59.
Drummond of Stobhall, James, baron, vii. 58.
—— master of, Walter, grandson of 1st lord Drummond, vii. 43; viii. 572.
—— —— his wife, Elizabeth Graham, vi. 225; vii. 43.
—— master of, Sir William, 2nd son of 1st lord Drummond, vii. 42; ix. 19.
—— —— his 1st wife, Isobel Campbell, i. 335; vii. 43; ix. 149.
—— —— his 2nd wife, Mariota *or* Marjorie Forrester, iv. 87; vii. 43.
DRUMMOND, LORD DRUMMOND, vii. 41-62.
DRUMMOND, LORD DRUMMOND OF CASTLEMAINS, vi. 66-74.
DRUMMOND, LORD DRUMMOND OF CROMLIX, viii. 220-238.
DRUMMOND, LORD DRUMMOND OF GILESTOUN, vi. 66-74.
DRUMMOND, LORD DRUMMOND OF RICCARTOUN, vi. 66-74.
DRUMMOND, BARON DRUMMOND OF STOBHALL, vii. 58-59.
DRUMMOND, VISCOUNT OF FORTH, vi. 66-74.
DRUMMOND, LORD MADERTIE, viii. 216-238.
DRUMMOND, VISCOUNT OF MELFORT, vi. 66-74.
DRUMMOND, EARL OF MELFORT, vi. 66-74.
DRUMMOND, LORD PERTH, iii. 549; vii. 58-59.
DRUMMOND, EARL OF PERTH, vii. 28-62.
DRUMMOND, VISCOUNT OF STRATHALLAN, viii. 215-238.
Drummond, duke of Perth (Jacobite creation), vii. 52-57.
—— of Achyndonan, Malcolm, viii. 520.
—— of Albury Park, Henry, viii. 232.
—— —— his wife, Henrietta Hay-Drummond, viii. 233.
—— of Annat, James, viii. 215.
—— of Ardenalochreth, Margaret, vii. 29.
—— of Ardeureane, Christian, vii. 29.
Drummond of Argeth, Sir John, vii. 41.
—— of Auchenchelloch, Robert, 3rd son of 2nd earl of Perth, vii. 50.
—— of Auchincloich, James, viii. 216.
—— of Auchindonan. Malcolm, vii. 31.
—— of Auchleskin, James, viii. 216.
—— of Auchterarder, James, viii. 216.
—— —— John, vii. 35.
—— —— Sir John, vii. 41.
—— of Balloch, George, vii. 47.
—— —— George, vi. 421.
—— —— his wife, Agnes Napier, vi. 421.
—— —— James, 1st laird, vi. 539.
—— —— his wife, * Oliphant, vi. 539.
—— —— William, v. 500.
—— of Balliclone, Andrew, vii. 43, 46.
—— —— his alleged wife, Janet Campbell, vii. 44.
—— —— William, vii. 194.
—— —— his wife, Margaret Rollo, vii. 194.
—— of Balmaclone, James, viii. 216.
—— of Balnaguard, i. 495.
—— of Blair, George, iii. 399; v. 219.
—— —— his wife, Katharine Hay, v. 219.
—— —— Walter, ancestor of the family of, vii. 40.
—— of Blair Drummond, James, vii. 585.
—— of Boquhapple, Gilbert, vi. 134, 137; vii 30.
—— —— his wife, Matilda, vi. 31.
—— of Broich, George, ii. 116.
—— of Cadland, Andrew Berkeley, banker, viii. 229.
—— —— his wife, Mary Perceval, viii. 229.
—— —— Andrew Cecil, viii. 230.
—— —— Andrew Robert, viii. 229.
—— —— his wife, Elizabeth Frederica Manners, viii. 229.
—— —— Edgar Atheling, viii. 230.
—— —— his wife, Louisa Theodosia Pennington, viii. 230.
—— —— Robert, banker, viii. 229; ix. 161.
—— —— his wife, Winifred Thomson, viii. 229.
—— of Calyequhat, James, viii. 215.
—— of Cargill, James, 2nd son of 2nd lord Drummond, viii. 216.
—— —— John, 1st laird, vii. 35.
—— —— his wife, Mary de Montefichet, vii. 35.
—— —— Sir John, Justiciar of Scotland; 3rd laird, iv. 82; vi. 569; vii. 39.
—— —— his wife, Elizabeth St. Clair, vi. 569; vii. 39.
—— —— Sir John, 6th laird, vi. 224; vii. 40.
—— —— his wife, Elizabeth Lindsay, iii. 22; vii. 42.
—— —— Sir Malcolm, 2nd laird, iii. 159; iv. 515; vii. 37, 113; viii. 381.
—— —— his wife, Isabella Douglas of Mar, iii. 154; vii. 39.

* Name unknown.

Drummond of Cargill, Sir Malcolm, 5th laird, vii. 40.
—— his wife, Marion Murray, i. 458; vii. 40.
—— Sir Walter, 4th laird, vii. 39.
—— his alleged wife, Margaret Ruthven, vii. 40.
— of Carnbady, Maurice, vii. 32.
—— his wife, Mariota Erskine, vii. 32.
— of Carnock, David, vii. 37.
—— Sir John, vii. 200.
—— his wife, Margaret Rollo, vii. 200.
—— Robert, iii. 534, 535.
—— his wife, Marjory Elphinstone, iii. 534.
—— William, alleged ancestor of the family of, vii. 37.
—— his alleged wife, Elizabeth Airth, vii. 37.
— of Cesnock, John, vi. 66.
— of Classingallis, Sir John, vii. 41.
— of Coldoch, James, 3rd son of Sir Malcolm D. of Stobhall, vii. 40, 44.
— of Colquhalzie, John, vi. 153.
— of Concraig, John, vi. 139; vii. 32 *n.*, 36.
—— his wife, Margaret, countess of Menteith, vi. 138; vii. 32 *n.*
—— Sir John, vi. 214.
—— his wife, Matilda Graham, vi. 214.
—— Maurice, steward of Strathearn, 1st laird, vii. 31.
—— his wife, Mariota Erskine, v. 596; vii. 32.
—— Maurice, steward of Strathearn, 2nd laird, vii. 32.
—— Maurice, steward of Strathearn, i. 457; vii. 40.
—— his wife, Isabel Murray, i. 458.
— of Corryvauchter, James, ancestor of the family of, vii. 40.
— of Corskeply, Thomas, viii. 592.
— of East Craigton, James, viii. 216.
— of Cultechaldich, John, vii. 44.
—— his wife, Isabella, vii. 44.
— of Cultmalundie, David, viii. 394.
—— his wife, Katharine Sandilands, viii. 394.
— of Deanston, Walter, dean of Dunblane, clerk register, vii. 40.
— of Drongy, John, vi. 148.
— of Drumlanrig, Sir Malcolm, vii. 113.
— of Drummond, David, vii. 46.
—— James, 2nd son of 2nd lord Drummond, viii. 216.
—— John, 4th laird, vii. 34.
—— his wife, Mary de Montefichet, vii. 35, 36.
—— Malcolm 'Beg,' seneschal to Malduin, earl of Lennox; lord of, vii. 28.
—— Sir Malcolm, 2nd laird, vii. 29.
—— his wife, * Graham, vi. 208; vii. 30.

* Name unknown.

Drummond of Drummond, Sir Malcolm, 3rd laird, vii. 31.
—— Sir Malcolm, 5th laird, vii. 37.
—— his wife, Isabella Douglas of Mar, v. 586; vii. 39.
— of Drummonderinoch, Thomas, 4th son of Sir Malcolm D. of Stobhall, vii. 40.
—— his wife, * Scot, vii. 40.
— of Drymen, David, vii. 46.
—— James, viii. 216.
— of Duchal, John, vi. 66.
— of Enderby Hall, Cecil George Assheton, viii. 230.
—— his wife, Charlotte Emilia Brook, viii. 230.
— of Fordew, John, vii. 44.
— of the Grange, Henry, v. 235.
—— his wife, Henrietta Hay, v. 235.
—— Henry, viii. 232; ix. 161.
—— his wife, Elizabeth Compton, viii. 232.
—— William, vi. 17.
— of Hawthornden, William, the poet, v. 467; vii. 48, 172, 178.
— of Inchaffray, James, commendator, i. 469; viii. 215.
— of Innerpeffray, Agnes, wife of (1) Sir Hugh Campbell of Loudoun, (2) Hugh, 3rd earl of Eglinton, and (3) Patrick, 3rd lord Drummond; iii. 441; v. 496, 497; vii. 44, 47.
—— James, 2nd son of 2nd lord Drummond, viii. 215.
—— his wife, Jean Chisholm, viii. 216.
—— Jean, wife of Sir James Chisholm of Cromlix, viii. 216.
—— Sir John, 4th son of 1st lord Drummond, vii. 44.
—— his 1st wife, * Drummond, vii. 44.
—— his 2nd wife, Eliza Douglas, vii. 44.
—— John, vii. 44, 45, 46; viii. 279.
—— his wife, Margaret Stewart, i. 22; vii. 44; ix. 149.
— of Invermay, David, vii. 197.
—— his wife, Annabella Rollo, vii. 197.
— of Iping, Harvey, viii. 314.
— of Keltie, Clementina, wife of 6th earl of Airlie, i. 130; ix. 8.
—— Gavin, i. 130.
—— his wife, Clementina Graham of Duntrune, i. 130.
— of Kildees, James, ancestor of the family of, vii. 40.
— of Kilvallach, Jean, wife of John, 13th earl of Sutherland, vii. 48.
— of Kincardine, James, viii. 216.
— of Kinloch, Sir Malcolm, vii. 38.
— of Ladecrief, Walter, 3rd son of Sir Walter D. of Stobhall, vii. 40; ix. 148.
— of Lentibbert, John, vii. 49.

* Name unknown.

Drummond of Logiealmond, Sir John, 4th son of 2nd earl of Perth, vii. 50, 346.
—— —— his wife, Grizel Steuart, vii. 50.
—— —— John, iii. 388.
—— —— his wife, Katharine Murray, iii. 388.
—— —— Thomas, v. 210.
—— —— his 1st wife, Anne Kinnaird, v. 210.
—— —— his 2nd wife, Grizel Leslie, vi. 443.
—— —— Sir William, vii. 346, 353.
—— of Luncarty, David, master of Maderty, viii. 219.
—— —— his wife, Alison Creightoun, viii. 219.
—— —— Margaret, dau. of David, master of Maderty, viii. 219.
—— of Lundin, James, iii. 490; vii. 57.
—— —— his wife, Rachel Bruce, iii. 490.
—— —— Robert, 3rd son of 1st earl of Melfort, vi. 68; vii. 57.
—— —— his wife, Anne Inglis, vii. 57.
—— of Lussan, James, captain of cavalry in French service, vi. 71.
—— —— his wife, Marie de Béranger, vi. 71.
—— —— James Louis, general in French service, vi. 72.
—— his wife, Aglaé G. J. d'Oms Alais, vi. 72.
—— of Machany, Sir James, 1st laird, viii. 216.
—— —— his 2nd wife, Katharine Hamilton, ii. 27; viii. 216.
—— —— Sir James, 2nd laird, viii. 217, 223.
—— —— his 1st wife, Mary Haliburton, viii. 223.
—— —— his 2nd wife. Anna Hay, iii. 573; viii. 223.
—— —— his 3rd wife, Lilias Muirhead, viii. 223.
—— —— Sir John, viii. 223.
—— —— his wife, Margaret Stewart, viii. 223.
—— —— William, viii. 224, 228.
—— —— his wife, Margaret Murray, vi. 396; viii. 228.
—— of Mar, Sir Malcolm, vii. 37, 113.
—— of Medhope, Alexander, iii. 535.
—— —— Sir Alexander, i. 561, 562.
—— of Megginch, Sir Adam, admiral R.N., K.C.H., i. 497.
—— —— his wife, Charlotte Murray, i. 497.
—— —— John, i. 489; iv. 553.
—— of Megour, Alexander, vi. 146 *n.*
—— —— Malcolm, vi. 146.
—— —— his wife, * Graham, vi. 146.
—— —— William, vii. 47.
—— of Meiklour, Maurice, vii. 32.
—— of Muirhall, John, vi. 66.
—— of Ochtertyre, Sir John, iv. 82; vii. 39.
—— of Pitcairns, major, vii. 200.
—— —— his wife, Anna Rollo, vii. 200.

* Name unknown.

Drummond of Pitkellonie, David, vii. 205.
—— —— his wife, Mary Rollo, vii. 205.
—— —— John, vii. 200.
—— —— his wife, Jean Rollo, vii. 200.
—— of Port, William, vii. 47.
—— of Redenham, John, viii. 225.
—— —— his wife, Georgina Augusta Harvey, viii. 225.
—— of Riccartoun, John, vi. 66.
—— —— Henry, vii. 44, 46, 47.
—— —— his wife, Janet Crichton, vii. 44.
—— —— Henry, viii. 388.
—— —— his wife, Margaret Sandilands, viii. 388.
—— —— William, ix. 53.
—— —— his wife, * Dalzell, ix. 53.
—— —— Sir William, 3rd bart., vi. 420.
—— of Roseneath, John, vii. 34.
—— of Smithston, Andrew, 5th son of Sir Malcolm D. of Cargill, vii. 40.
—— —— Sir John, vii. 41.
—— —— William, vii. 46.
—— of Stanmore, Andrew, banker, viii. 224.
—— —— his wife, Isabella Strachan, viii. 224.
—— —— George, viii. 224.
—— —— his wife, Martha Harley, viii. 224.
—— —— George, viii. 224.
—— —— his wife, Marianne Portman, viii. 224.
—— —— George Harley, viii. 224.
—— —— his wife, Margaret Munro, viii. 224.
—— —— John, M.P., viii. 224.
—— —— his wife, Charlotte Beauclerk, viii. 224.
—— of Stobhall, Clementina Sarah, wife of Peter, 2nd lord Gwydyr, vii. 59.
—— —— Sir John, justiciar of Scotland, vii. 39.
—— —— his wife, Elizabeth St. Clair, vi. 569; vii. 39.
—— —— John, i. 333.
—— of Strageith, James, viii. 216.
—— of Strathallan, Andrew John, general, i. 495; viii. 233.
—— of Strathurd, Sir Malcolm, v. 587, 597, vii. 38.
—— —— his wife, Isabel, countess of Mar, v. 586; vii. 39.
—— of Swaylands, George James, viii. 224, 237.
—— —— his wife, Elizabeth Cecile Sophia Norman, viii. 224.
—— of Torwoodlee, Sir William, viii. 220.
—— of Tullibardine, i. 495.
—— of Uchtermachin, James, viii. 216.
—— of Uchtermuthill, James, viii. 216.
—— of Yvoy-le-Pré, Louis, styled comte de Melfort, vi. 69.
—— —— his wife, Jeanne Elizabeth de la Porte, vi. 69.
—— Agnes, wife of (1) Sir Hugh Campbell of

Loudoun, (2) Hugh, 3rd earl of Eglinton, and (3) Patrick, lord Drummond, iii. 441; v. 496, 497; vii. 44, 47.
Drummond, Agnes, wife of John, earl of Mar, v. 621; ix. 133.
— Agnes, wife of Sir Thos. Seton of Olivestob, viii. 592.
— Alfred Manners, capt. Rifle Brigade, viii. 230.
— — his wife, Augusta Verscboyle, viii. 230.
— Algernon Heneage, viii. 227.
— — his wife, Margaret Elizabeth Benson, viii. 227.
— Algernon Cecil Heneage, viii. 227.
— Allan Harvey, viii. 225.
— — his wife, Katharine Adine Geraldine Hervey, viii. 226.
— Amelia Anne, wife of lieut.-col. Charles Greenhill-Gardyne, viii. 236; ix. 162.
— Amelia Anne Sophia, dau. of 4th viscount of Strathallan, ix. 162.
— Amelia Felicia, dau. of James, Comte de Lussan, vi. 71.
— Andrew, iv. 438.
— — his wife, Margaret Drummond, iv. 438.
— Andrew, colonel of horse in French service, vi. 69.
— — his wife, Magdalene Silvie de Ste. Hermione, vi. 69.
— Andrew, colonel in Royalist army, viii. 217, 223.
— Andrew, 6th son of 4th viscount of Strathallan, viii. 229.
— Andrew John, eldest son of Andrew R. D. of Cadland, viii. 229.
— Andrew John, general, governor of Dumbarton Castle, viii. 233.
— Andrew Mortimer, viii. 225, 227.
— — his wife, Emily Charlotte Percy viii. 225.
— Anna, wife of John, earl of Mar, v. 621; vii. 46; ix. 133, 149.
— Anna, wife of R. Napier of Boquhopple, vi. 420.
— Anna, wife of Sir Thos. Seton of Olivestob, viii. 592.
— Annabella, wife of King Robert II., i. 17; ii. 438; vii. 37; ix. 2.
— Annabella, wife of William, 1st earl of Montrose, vi. 225; vii. 45.
— Annabella, dau. of Gilbert D. of Boquhapple, vii. 31.
— Annabella Henriette, wife of comte de Marguerie, vi. 69.
— Annas, mistress of 1st earl of Buccleuch, ii. 235.
— Anne, wife of 12th earl of Erroll, iii. 579; vii. 51; ix. 87.
— Anne, wife of (1) Patrick Barclay of Towie, and (2) Andrew, 1st lord Fraser, iv. 113; vii. 48; ix. 149 *bis*.
Drummond, Anne, wife of Sir John Houston of Houston, vi. 68.
— Anne, dau. of 4th earl of Perth, vii. 53.
— Anne, wife of Patrick Rattray of Craighall, viii. 218.
— Anne, wife of Thos. Graeme of Balgowan, viii. 223.
— Anne, dau. of Sir John D. of Machany, viii. 228.
— Anne, dau. of 4th viscount of Strathallan, ix. 162.
— Archibald, M.D., Bristol, iv. 438.
— Archibald Spencer, Scots Guards, viii. 226.
— — his wife, Helen Sherer Burns, viii. 226.
— Arthur, rector of Charlton, viii. 231.
— — his 1st wife, Margaretta Maria Wilson, viii. 232.
— — his 2nd wife, Caroline Eliza Moring Grey, viii. 232.
— Arthur Berkeley, viii. 232.
— — his wife, Edith Charlotte Lambert, viii. 232.
— Arthur David, viii. 236.
— Arthur Hislop, canon, viii. 232.
— — his 1st wife, Armynel Mary Baylay, viii. 232.
— — his 2nd wife, Anna Harriet Dodsworth, viii. 232.
— Beatrix, wife of 1st earl of Hyndford, iv. 591; viii. 219.
— Beatrix, mistress of James (Hamilton), 1st earl of Arran, iv. 358, 364; vii. 45.
— Berkeley, viii. 231.
— — his wife, Maria Crosbie, viii. 231.
— Cecil Elizabeth, wife of rev. Heneage Drummond, viii. 227.
— Charles, a Jesuit, 3rd son of 4th earl of Perth, vii. 53.
— Charles, banker, viii. 230.
— — his wife, Frances Dorothy Lockwood, viii. 230.
— Charles, viii. 230.
— — his wife, Mary Dulcibella Eden, viii. 230.
— Charles, viii. 231.
— — his wife, Caroline Elizabeth Boyle, viii. 231.
— Charles Edward, prelate in Papal Household, vi. 72.
— Charles Edward Louis Casimir John Silvester Mary, viii. 229; ix. 161 *bis*.
— Charles Spencer, viii. 232.
— — his wife, Mary Innes, viii. 232.
— Clementina Maria, dau. of 4th viscount of Strathallan, ix. 162.
— Clementina Sarah, wife of 21st baron Willoughby de Eresby, iii. 549.

Drummond, Colin, M.D., iv. 438.
— — his wife, Margaret Bothwell of Glencorse, iv. 438.
— Cyril Augustus, viii. 230.
— — his wife, Edith Belle Wilkins, viii. 230.
— David, 3rd son of 1st lord Drummond, vii. 43, 44.
— David, 6th son of Sir James D. of Machany, viii. 217.
— David, Leyden University, viii. 223.
— David, gentleman pensioner, ix. 135.
— — his wife, Esther Tailor, ix. 135.
— David, illeg. son of 3rd lord Drummond, ix. 149.
— David Robert, viii. 225.
— — his wife, Hilda Margaret Harris, viii. 225.
— Sir Edmund, K.C.I.E., viii. 235.
— — his wife, Julia Mary Sutherland, viii. 235.
— Edmund Berkeley, viii. 227.
— — his wife, Mabel Tuke, viii. 227.
— Edmund Charles, admiral R.N., viii. 235.
— — his wife, Dora Naylor, viii. 235.
— Edmund Rupert, R.N., viii. 237.
— — his wife, Evelyn Frances Butler, viii. 237.
— Edmund Traherne, viii. 231.
— — his wife, Isabel Henrietta Knights, viii. 231.
— Sir Edward, i. 558.
— Edward, 5th son of 4th earl of Perth, vii. 53, 56.
— — his wife, Elizabeth Middleton, vi. 188; vii. 57.
— Edward, viii. 227.
— — his wife, Lucy Marion Barnard, viii. 227.
— Edward, secretary to Sir R. Peel, viii. 231.
— Elizabeth, wife of (1) Sir David Fleming, and (2) George, master of Angus, i. 187; vi. 147 *n.*; vii. 45; viii. 534.
— Elizabeth, wife of 5th lord Elphinstone, iii. 541; vii. 48.
— Elizabeth, wife of Thos. Kinnaird of Kinnaird, v. 204; vii. 39.
— Elizabeth, wife of Thos. Hay of Balhousie, v. 231; viii. 222; ix. 161.
— Elizabeth, wife of 2nd viscount of Strathallan, vi. 68; viii. 222; ix. 161.
— Elizabeth, dau. of Gilbert D. of Boquhapple, vii. 31.
— Elizabeth, wife of Dr. Andrew St. Clair, vii. 585.
— Elizabeth, dau. of 5th viscount of Strathallan, viii. 233; ix. 162.
— Ellen, dau. of Gilbert D. of Boquhapple, vii. 31.
Drummond, Eric Roderick Brook, viii. 230.
— — his wife, Frederica Lilian Norris, viii. 230.
— Ernest George, in holy orders, viii. 236.
— Eupheme, wife of 2nd lord Fleming, vii. 44, 45; viii. 536.
— Eustace Harvey, viii. 227.
— Frances, wife of José de Rozas, count of Castel Blanco, vi. 70.
— Frances Mary, viii. 236.
— Frances Teresa, dau. of 4th earl of Perth, vii. 53.
— Francis Berkeley, viii. 226.
— — his wife, Ellen Urquhart, viii. 226.
— Francis Charles, viii. 235.
— — his wife, Charlotte Mary Atholl Oakeley, viii. 235.
— Francis Colebrooke, captain, viii. 235.
— — his wife, Marcia Beresford, viii. 235.
— Francis William, viii. 227.
— Frederick, H.E.I.C.S., viii. 236.
— Frederick Boyd Heneage, viii. 227.
— Frederick Harvey John, viii. 226.
— Frederick John, viii. 227.
— Frederick Thomas, viii. 226.
— — his wife, Agnes Caroline Brigstock, viii. 226.
— Geoffrey Heneage, viii. 227.
— Gerald Morton, viii, 231.
— — his wife, Alice Edith Marshall, viii. 231.
— Sir George, lord provost of Edinburgh, iv. 289, 438.
— — his wife, Helen Gray, iv. 289.
— George, 2nd son of Andrew D., iv. 438.
— George, younger son of Geo. D. of Blair, v. 219.
— George, son of D. of Balloch, v. 226.
— George, 5th son of Sir James D. of Machany, viii. 217.
— George Henry, viii. 224.
— Grisel, possible wife of lieut.-gen. Sir William Drummond, viii. 222.
— Harvey, viii. 225.
— — his wife, Susan Caroline Drummond, viii. 225.
— Harvey Gerald Burns, viii. 226.
— Heneage, in holy orders, viii. 227.
— — his wife, Cecil Elizabeth Drummond, viii. 227.
— Henrietta, dau. of 1st earl of Melfort, vi. 70.
— Henrietta, dau. of 2nd titular duke of Perth, vii. 54.
— Henrietta Maria, viii. 224.
— Henry, elder son of Geo. D. of Blair, v. 219.
— Henry, grandson of 1st lord Drummond, vii. 44.
— — his wife, Janet Crichton of Riccarton, vii. 44.

Drummond, Henry, eldest son of 2nd earl of Perth, vii. 50.
—— Henry, banker, viii. 232.
—— —— his wife, Anne Dundas, viii. 232.
—— Henry Benedict, captain in French navy, vi. 71.
—— Henry Dundas, viii. 225.
—— —— his wife, Sophia Jane Mackinnon, viii. 225.
—— Henry Ludovic, R.N., viii. 230.
—— Henry Murray, rector of Byford, viii. 235.
—— —— his wife, Katharine Gamand Gwillim, viii. 235.
—— Henry Roger, rector of Fawley, viii. 232.
—— —— his wife, Susannah Wells, viii. 232.
—— Henry Walter, viii. 231.
—— —— his wife, Mary Louisa Margaret Levett, viii. 231.
—— Herbert Charles, viii. 236.
—— Hersey Annabella, viii. 236.
—— Hugh Fitzhardinge, viii. 227.
—— Hugh Frederick, viii. 226.
—— Isabel, wife of Sir Matthew Campbell of Loudoun, iii. 442; v. 497.
—— Isabella, wife of John Graham of Gartur, vi. 153.
—— Isabel, dau. of Andrew D. of Stanmore, viii. 224.
—— Issobel Hester, wife of Ernest Bowes-Lyon, viii. 314.
—— Ida Mary, wife of M. C. A. Drummond, viii. 237.
—— James, depute clerk of petitions, viii. 31.
—— —— his wife, Margaret Jamieson, viii. 31.
—— James, only son of James, lord Perth, vii. 59.
—— James, 2nd son of 2nd lord Maderty, viii. 217.
—— James, R.N., eldest son of 5th viscount of Strathallan, viii. 233.
—— James, viii. 386.
—— —— his wife, Agnes Sandilands, viii. 386.
—— James, captain, ix. 127.
—— —— his wife, Anna Leslie, ix. 127.
—— James Andrew John Laurence Charles, M.P., viii. 229, 234.
—— —— his wife, Amelia Sophia Murray, i. 498; viii. 234.
—— James Arthur Laurence, viii. 235.
—— James Eric, viii. 237.
—— —— his wife, Angela Mary Constable-Maxwell, iv. 423; viii. 237.
—— Sir James Robert, admiral R.N., viii. 234.
—— —— his wife, Katharine Elliot, viii. 234.
—— James Sutherland, viii. 235.
—— Jane, wife of (1) James, 2nd duke of Atholl, and (2) lord Adam Gordon, i. 489; iv. 553.
Drummond, Jane, wife of Thos. Murray of Berkhampstead, iii. 399.
—— Jean, wife of 3rd earl of Montrose, vi. 237; vii. 46; ix. 137.
—— Jean, governess to the children of King James VI.; wife of Robert, lord Roxburghe, vii. 47, 346.
—— Jean, wife of John, 3rd earl of Wigtoun, vii. 50, 344, 346; viii. 551; ix. 149.
—— Jean, wife of Andrew Wood of Largo, viii. 217.
—— Jean, wife of Patrick Graeme of Inchbrakie, viii. 218.
—— Jean, wife of John, 13th earl of Sutherland, viii. 350.
—— Jocelyn Heneage, viii. 227.
—— Johanna, dau. of Gilbert D. of Boquhapple, vii. 31.
—— John, ensign in Sir William Lockhart's regiment of foot, vi. 66.
—— John, lieut.-gen., secretary of state for Scotland, vi. 66; vii. 51; ix. 135.
—— —— his 1st wife, Sophia Lundin of Lundin, v. 303.
—— John, lieutenant of the Guard of the King of Poland, major-general, vi. 70.
—— John, vi. 144.
—— —— his wife, Marion *, vi. 144.
—— John, 2nd son of Malcolm Beg, vii. 29.
—— —— his wife, Elena (Stewart), vii. 29.
—— John, dean of Dunblane, vii. 40.
—— John, styled viscount Forth, vi. 70.
—— —— his wife, Marie Gabrielle d'Audibert, vi. 70.
—— John, captain, killed at Newcastle, viii. 217.
—— John, 3rd son of 2nd lord Maderty, viii. 217.
—— John, ennobled in Sweden, viii. 217.
—— John, viii. 225.
—— —— his 1st wife, Hester Cholmondeley, viii. 225.
—— —— his 2nd wife, Barbara Chester, viii. 225.
—— John, 5th son of 4th viscount of Strathallan, viii. 229.
—— John David, viii. 237.
—— John Edmond, captain R.N., viii. 235.
—— —— his wife, Olive Munro, viii. 235.
—— John William, viii. 226.
—— John William Ainslie, Scots Guards viii. 226.
—— —— his wife, Florence Charlotte Blencowe, viii. 227.
—— Katharine, wife of 1st earl of Tullibardine, i. 469; vii. 47; ix. 29.
—— Katharine, wife of James, master of Rothes, vii. 47, 296, 297.

* Name unknown.

Drummond, Katharine, wife of 1st lord Rollo of Duncrub, vii. 196; viii. 217.
—— Katharine, wife of Alex. Robertson of Strowan, viii. 217.
—— Katharine, dau. of 4th viscount of Strathallan, ix. 162.
—— Kenneth Mackenzie, viii. 231.
—— Laurence George, colonel, viii. 235.
—— —— his wife, Katharine Mary Antrobus, viii. 235.
—— Léon Maurice, vi. 71, 72.
—— —— his wife, Lucie Marie de Longuemare, vi. 71.
—— Léontine, dau. of Léon Maurice D., vi. 71.
—— Lilias, wife of 1st earl of Dunfermline, i. 518; iii. 372; vii. 47.
—— Lilias, wife of 11th earl of Crawford, iii. 31; vii. 47.
—— Lilias, wife of 5th lord Oliphant, vi. 551; viii. 217.
—— Lilias, 1st wife of James, lord Murray of Gask, vii. 50, 346; viii. 414; ix. 149 *bis*.
—— Lilias, 3rd wife of James, 2nd earl of Tullibardine, and (2) James, 4th earl of Perth, vii. 50, 53; viii. 223, 415; ix. 149 *bis*.
—— Lilias, dau. of Sir John D. of Machany, viii. 228.
—— Lindsay, viii. 235.
—— Lister Maurice, viii. 231.
—— Louis Jean Edward, colonel in French service, vi. 70; ix. 135.
—— Louis Edward Geneviève, colonel on French staff, vi. 69.
—— —— his wife, Eudoxie Saulnier de Cherrières, vi. 69.
—— Louis Pierre Francis Malcolm, vi. 69.
—— —— his 1st wife, Caroline Barry, vi. 69.
—— —— his alleged 2nd wife, Caroline Mackenzie, vi. 69.
—— Louisa, dau. of 1st earl of Melfort, vi 70.
—— Lucie Clementine, wife of Francis Henry Davies, vi. 71; vii. 60.
—— Ludovic, 4th son of 2nd lord Maderty, viii. 218.
—— Malcolm, eldest son of 1st lord Drummond, vii. 42.
—— Malcolm, son of Gilbert D., vii. 30 *n*.
—— Malcolm, son of Robert A. J. D., viii. 235.
—— Malcolm Cyril, viii. 232.
—— —— his wife, Zina Lilias Ogilvie, viii. 232.
—— Malcolm David George, viii. 226.
—— Malcolm Hugh, R.N., viii. 226.
—— —— his wife, Mabel Jeannie Otway Mayne, viii. 226.
—— Maldwin, viii. 230.
—— his wife, Albertine Louise Huck, vii. 230.
—— Margaret, wife of (1) John Logie of that Ilk, and (2) King David II., i. 9; ii. 262, 445; vi. 348; vii. 32.
Drummond, Margaret, dau. of 1st lord Drummond; mistress of King James IV., i. 22; vii. 44.
—— Margaret, alleged wife of Colin Campbell of Lochow, dau. of Sir John D. of Stobhall, i. 328.
—— Margaret, wife of 15th lord Borthwick, ii. 116.
—— Margaret, wife of Robert, 3rd lord Elphinstone, iii. 535.
—— Margaret, wife of 5th lord Elphinstone, iii. 541; vii. 48.
—— Margaret, wife of (1) John Campbell of Murthly, (2) D. Campbell of Glenlyon, and (3) John Lyon of Cossins, v. 500.
—— Margaret, wife of (1) John Home, and (2) Alex. Hepburn, vi. 17.
—— Margaret, wife of Thos. Hay of Balhousie, v. 231.
—— Margaret, wife of Andrew Drummond, iv. 438.
—— Margaret, dau. of 1st earl of Melfort, vi. 70.
—— Margaret, wife of Jas. Muirhead of Bredisholm, viii. 217.
—— Margaret, wife of Sir Robert Crichton or Murray of Cockpool, viii. 218.
—— Margaret, wife of John Graeme of Inchbrakie, viii. 219.
—— Margaret, dau. of 1st viscount of Strathallan, viii. 222; ix. 161.
—— Margaret, dau. of Sir John D. of Machany, viii. 228.
—— Margaret, wife of George Haldane of Gleneagles, viii. 233; ix. 162.
—— Margaret, wife of 1st earl of Tullibardine, ix. 29.
—— Margaret, dau. of 2nd lord Drummond, ix. 149.
—— Margaret, dau. of 4th viscount of Strathallan, ix. 162.
—— Margaret Alice, viii. 236.
—— Margaret Cicely, viii. 237.
—— Margaret Gwendolen Mary, viii. 237.
—— Marianne Jane, wife of G. D. Graeme of Inchbrakie, viii. 236.
—— Marie Augusta Gabrielle Berengère Blanche, wife of col. Mackenzie Fraser, vi. 73; vii. 61.
—— Marie Cecile Henriette, dau. of James, comte de Lussan, vi. 72.
—— Marie Louise Susan Edith Grace, comtesse de Lussan, baroness de Valrose, vi. 73; vii. 61.
—— Mary, wife of (1) Gideon Scott of Highchester, and (2) Sir Jas. Sharp of Scotscraig, vi. 68; vii. 82; ix. 135.
—— Mary, wife of Josè de Rozas, count of Castel Blanco, vi. 70: ix. 135.

Drummond, Mary, dau. of James, 2nd titular duke of Perth, vii. 54.
— Mary, wife of 9th earl Marischal, vi. 61, 561; vii. 53.
— Mary, wife of Sir Archibald Stirling of Keir, vii. 47.
— Mary, wife of John Haldane of Gleneagles, viii. 219.
— Mary, wife of Duncan Campbell of Monzie, viii. 228.
— Mary, dau. of 4th viscount of Strathallan, ix. 162.
— Maurice, C.B., viii. 231.
— — his wife, Adelaide Lister, viii. 231.
— Maurice Charles Andrew, viii. 237.
— — his wife, Ida Mary Drummond, viii. 237.
— Maurice James David, viii. 237.
— Maurice John Heneage, viii. 227.
— Mortimer Heneage, viii. 227.
— Mortimer Percy, viii. 225.
— — his 1st wife, Jane Nairne, viii. 225.
— — his 2nd wife, Emmeline Fanny Rawlins, viii. 225.
— Mortimer Percy George Douglas, viii. 225.
— — his wife, Alice Ward, viii. 225.
— Morton, rector of Wanstead, viii. 231.
— — his wife, Caroline Traherne, viii. 231.
— Myra, viii. 237.
— Patrick, 4th son of Sir James D. of Machany, viii. 217.
— Philip, in French service, vi. 69.
— Rachel, dau. of 13th lord Drummond, vii. 58.
— Robert, 3rd son of 1st earl of Melfort, vi. 68: vii. 57.
— Robert, 2nd son of Sir John D. of Cargill and Stobhall, vii. 39.
— Robert, eldest son of James Lundin *or* Drummond of Lundin, vii. 57.
— Robert, viii. 231.
— — his wife, Augusta Charlotte Fraser, viii. 231.
— Robert Andrew John, viii. 235.
— — his wife, Anna Maria Reade, viii. 235.
— Robert Charles, captain Seaforth Highlanders, viii. 236.
— Robert Hugh, viii. 236.
— Sibylla, dau. of 1st lord Drummond, vii. 45 *bis*.
— Sibylla, wife of Gilbert Ogilvy of Ogilvy, vii. 46.
— Sibilla, dau. of 3rd lord Drummond, ix. 149.
— Spencer, viii. 227.
— Spencer Heneage, viii. 227.
— Susan Caroline, wife of Harvey Drummond, viii. 225.
— Sybil Frances, viii. 237.
Drummond, Teresa Margarita, dau. of 1st earl of Melfort, vi. 70.
— Thomas, in service of Charles VII., emperor of Germany, vi. 69.
— Thomas, 8th son of Sir James D. of Machany, viii. 217.
— Thomas, 6th son of Sir John D. of Machany, viii. 228.
— Sir Victor Arthur Wellington, K.C.M.G., viii. 230.
— — his wife, Elizabeth Lamson, viii. 230.
— Walter, eldest son of Sir William, master of Drummond, iv. 278; vii. 43; ix. 149.
— — his contracted wife, Elizabeth Gray, iv. 278; ix. 149.
— — his wife, Elizabeth Graham, vi. 225; vii. 43.
— Walter, dean of Dunblane, vii. 40, 41.
— Walter, viii. 231.
— — his wife, Isabella Mary Hervey, viii. 231.
— Walter John, viii. 236.
— William, abbé at Liége, vi. 69.
— Sir William, 5th son of 2nd earl of Perth, vii. 50, 344, 346, 348.
— William, 7th son of Sir James D. of Machany, viii. 217.
— Sir William, lieutenant-general of the Forces, viii. 218 *ter*., 219.
— — his wife, Elizabeth Johnston, viii. 222.
— — his possible 2nd wife, Grizel Drummond, viii. 222.
— William, 4th son of 4th viscount of Strathallan, viii. 229.
— — his wife, Anne Nairne, viii. 229.
— William Charles, viii. 230.
— William Charles, his son, viii. 230.
— William Henry, lieut.-col. 27th regt., viii. 229.
— William Henry, in Zulu war, viii. 236.
— William Percy, viii. 226.
— Wingfield Fraser, viii. 231.
— Xavier, ix. 135.
— *, self-styled son of 6th titular duke of Perth, vii. 58.
— *or* M'Gregor, *, wife of Colin Campbell of Glenfalloch, ii. 192.
Drummond-Hay of Cromlix, Francis John, 2nd son of 10th earl of Kinnoull, v. 235.
— — Robert, archbishop of York, 2nd son of 8th earl of Kinnoull, v. 232.
— — his wife, Henrietta Auriol, v. 232.
— Abigail, v. 233.
— Edward Auriol, D.D., rector of Hadleigh, v. 233.
— — his 1st wife, Elizabeth de Vismes, v. 233.
— — his 2nd wife, Amelia Auriol, v. 233.

* Name unknown.

Drummond, George William Auriol, rector of Bawmarsh, v. 233.
—— —— his 1st wife, Elizabeth Margaret Marshall, v. 233.
—— —— his 2nd wife, Maria Birbank, v. 233.
—— John Auriol, commander R.N., v. 233.
—— Peter Auriol, lieut.-col. 5th W. Yorkshire Militia, v. 233.
—— —— his wife, Mary Bridget Miles, v. 233.
—— Robert Auriol, v. 233, 234.
—— —— his 1st wife, Julia Eyre, v. 235.
—— —— his 2nd wife, Sarah Harley, v. 235.
—— Thomas Auriol, v. 233.
Drummond-Willoughby, Mary Adelaide Heathcote, wife of 14th earl of Dalhousie, iii. 109.
DRUMRY, CRAWFORD (LINDSAY), LORD, iv. 175-178.
Drurie, Anna, wife of Charles Alexander, viii. 179.
Drury, Mary Anne, wife of 2nd earl of Buckinghamshire, v. 483.
—— Sir Thomas, bart., v. 483.
—— Sir William, v. 52, 65.
Dubourgay, raised a regiment in British service, iii. 217.
Ducarel, Elizabeth, wife of T. A. Constable, iv. 418.
Du Croc, French ambassador, ii. 165.
Dudgeon, Robert Ellis, M.D., ii. 354.
—— —— his wife, Amelia Anne Sinclair, ii. 354.
DUDHOPE, SCRYMGEOUR, VISCOUNT, iii. 313-315.
Dudhope, James, second viscount, iii. 314, 321, 322.
—— —— his wife, Isabella Ker, iii. 314; vii. 346.
—— John, first viscount, iii. 313; ix. 73.
—— —— his wife, Margaret Seton, iii. 313.
—— John, third viscount, iii. 313, 315.
—— —— his wife, Anna Ramsay, iii. 100, 315.
DUDHOPE, SCRYMGEOUR, VISCOUNT OF, iii. 315.
Dudhope, John, viscount of, iii. 315.
Dudingston of Sandford, Stephen, ii. 67.
—— Euphemia, wife of Thos. Bellenden, ii. 67.
Dudley, Edward (Sutton), 9th lord, iv. 465.
Duff of Braco, William, vii. 483.
—— —— his 1st wife, Janet Ogilvy, iv. 38.
—— —— his 2nd wife, Jean Grant, vii. 482.
—— of Crombie, Sir James, bart., i. 92.
—— —— William, sheriff-depute of Ayrshire, viii. 126, 131.
—— —— his wife, Elizabeth Dalrymple, ii. 32; viii. 131.
—— of Dipple, William, iii. 211.
—— of Findachyfield, iv. 18.
—— of Hatton, Alexander, vii. 486.
—— —— his wife, Anne Duff, vii. 486.
Duff of Hatton, Garden, iii. 214.
—— —— his wife, Louisa Sutherland Dunbar, iii. 214.
—— —— Jane, wife of Sir James Grant of Grant, vii. 486.
—— of Maldavit, Andrew, viii. 420 *n.*
—— —— his wife, Helen Hay, viii. 420 *n.*
—— Agnes Cecil Emmeline, wife of (1) George Robert, viscount Dupplin, (2) Herbert Flower, and (3) Sir A. Cooper, v. 237.
—— Anne, wife of (1) William, 4th earl of Stair, and (2) Alexander Gordon, lord Rockville, i. 91; iii. 237; viii. 156; ix. 71.
—— Anne, wife of Alex. Duff of Hatton, vii. 486.
—— Helen, wife of Wm. Sutherland of Roscommon, iii. 211.
—— Janet, wife of Sir Hew Hamilton Dalrymple of Bargany, viii. 126.
Duff-Gordon of Crombie, Sir William, 2nd son of lord Rockville, i. 92.
—— of Fyvie, Sir Alexander Cornwall, i. 92.
—— —— Sir Maurice, i. 92.
—— of Maryculter, Sir Cosmo Edmund, i. 92.
—— Cosmo, i. 92.
Duffagan, *perhaps* earl of Angus, *or* Fife, iv. 2 *n.*
Dufferin and Clandeboye, Price (Blackwood), 4th lord, viii. 470.
—— —— his wife, Helen Selina Sheridan, viii. 470.
DUFFUS, SUTHERLAND, LORD, iii. 191-215.
Duffus, Alexander, first lord, iii. 207.
—— —— his 1st wife, Jean Mackenzie, iii. 209; vii. 507.
—— —— his 2nd wife, Jean Innes, iii. 209.
—— —— his 3rd wife, Margaret Stewart, iii. 209; vi. 321.
—— —— his 4th wife, Margaret Forbes, iii. 209; iv. 63.
—— Benjamin, sixth lord, iii. 211, 214.
—— —— his wife, Janet Mackay, iii. 214.
—— Eric, titular lord, iii. 211, 213.
—— —— his wife, Elizabeth Dunbar, iii. 213.
—— George, seventh lord, iii. 215.
—— James, second lord, iii. 209.
—— —— his wife, Margaret Mackenzie, iii. 210; vii. 509; ix. 156.
—— James, fifth lord, iii. 214; ix. 70.
—— Kenneth, third lord, iii. 210, 212.
—— —— his wife, Charlotte Christina Sioblade, iii. 212.
—— Mary of, wife of Reginald le Cheyne, iii. 191; vi. 34.
—— Sir Walter de Moravia, lord of, ii. 122; vii. 232; viii. 321.
—— —— his wife, Euphemia de Ross, ii. 122; 32; viii. 321.

Dugald, rector of Kilpatrick, v. 328, 329, 333.
Dugall of Skipnish, son of Swein, iii. 335.
— of Lorn, Mull and Jura, 2nd son of Somerled, v. 29, 30, 31.
— Scrag, eldest son of Dugall of Lorn, v. 30.
— ancestor of Clan Dugall, 3rd son of Reginald, lord of the Isles, v. 32.
— of Stranith, vi. 286.
Dugdale, Stephen, conspirator, i. 411.
Duguid of Auchinhove, William, iv. 73.
— — his wife, Jonet Forbes, iv. 73.
Duibhne *or* O'Duin, Clan, i. 318.
Dukenfield of Dukenfield, Robert, iii. 596.
— Katharine, wife of (1) John Tempest, and (2) rev. Henry Fairfax, iii. 596.
Dumaresq, John Saumarez, commander R.N., viii. 145.
— — his wife, Christian Elizabeth Louisa Dalrymple, viii. 145.
— Susan Frances Sophia, wife of capt. Louis Hope, iv. 503.
— William John, captain, iv. 503.
DUMBARTON, DOUGLAS, EARL OF, iii. 216-218.
Dumbarton, George, first earl of, i. 205; iii. 216; ix. 70.
— — his wife, Anne Wheatley, iii. 217.
— George, second earl of, iii. 217.
— of Hallys and Lecbernard, Robert, viii. 522.
Dumergue, J. W. F., I.C.S., iv. 571.
— — his wife, Anne T. Carmichael, iv. 571.
DUMFRIES, CRICHTON, EARL OF, iii. 219-238.
Dumfries, William, first earl of, i. 135; iii. 221, 232; vii. 134; ix. 71.
— — his 1st wife, Euphemia Seton, iii. 234.
— — his 2nd wife, Ursula Barnham, iii. 234.
— William, second earl of, iii. 235; ix. 71.
— — his wife, Penelope Swift, iii. 235.
— William, third earl of, iii. 235, 236.
— Penelope, wife of William Dalrymple of Glenmure; countess of, iii. 235, 236; viii. 150.
DUMFRIES, CRICHTON-DALRYMPLE, EARL OF, iii. 236-237.
Dumfries, William, fourth earl of, iii. 237; viii. 155.
— — his 1st wife, Anne Gordon, i. 90; iii. 237; viii. 156.
— — his 2nd wife, Anne Duff, i. 92; iii. 237; viii. 156.
DUMFRIES, MACDOWALL-CRICHTON, EARL OF, iii. 236-238.
Dumfries, Elizabeth Penelope, wife of John, viscount Mountstuart; countess of, ii. 308; iii. 237.
Dumfries, Patrick, fifth earl of, ii. 308; iii. 237; v. 512.
— — his wife, Margaret Crauford, iii. 237.
DUMFRIES, CRICHTON-STUART, EARL OF, ii. 309-312; iii. 237-238.
Dumfries, John, sixth earl of, ii. 309.
— — his 1st wife, Maria North, ii. 310.
— — his 2nd wife, Sophia Frederica Christina Hastings, ii. 310.
— John, eighth earl of, ii. 311.
— John Patrick, seventh earl of, ii. 310.
DUMORE, PRESTON, BARON, iii. 122.
Dumore, Richard, baron, iii. 122.
Dun, David Erskine, lord of Session, lord, v. 632.
— of Ratee, Ardwne, and Bothquhanstoun, Nicholas, iv. 19.
— David, vi. 79.
— Malcolm, son of David D. vi. 79.
— — his wife, Eva Melville, vi. 79.
DUNBAR, DUNBAR, EARL OF, iii. 239-279.
Dunbar, George, tenth earl of, iii. 220, 259, 260, 261, 270; iv. 444.
— — his wife, Christiana de Seton, iii. 273; ix. 71.
— George, eleventh earl of, iii. 273, 276.
— — his 1st wife, Janet Seton, iii. 275 *n.*; viii. 573.
— — his 2nd wife, Beatrix *, iii. 277.
— — his possible 3rd wife, Alicia Hay, iii. 277; viii. 426.
— Gospatric, first earl of, iii. 3, 241.
— Gospatric, second earl of, iii. 245, 246; iv. 440, 507 *n.*
— Gospatric, third earl of, iii. 247, 249; iv. 440, 441.
— — his wife, Derdere, iii. 250.
— Patrick, fifth earl of, i. 417 *n.*, 422; iii. 252; iv. 442; v. 569 *n.*; viii. 562.
— — his 1st wife, Ada, i. 5; iii. 253.
— — his 2nd wife, Christina, i. 232; ii. 430; iii. 253.
— Patrick, sixth earl of, i. 12; iii. 253, 255.
— — his wife, Euphemia Stewart, i. 12; iii. 256.
— Patrick, seventh earl of, iii. 257, 425; iv. 509.
— — his wife, Cecilia, iii. 259.
— Patrick, the Competitor, eighth earl of, i. 5; iii. 259, 262.
— — his wife, * Comyn, iii. 264.
— Patrick, ninth earl of, iii. 264; vi. 296, 298; viii. 255.
— — his 1st wife, Ermegarde *, iii. 268.
— — his 2nd wife, Agnes Randolph, iii. 266, 268; vi. 294, 296 *bis*.
— Waldeve, fourth earl of, iii. 251; iv. 441; viii. 319 *n.*
— — his wife, Aelina, iii. 252.

* Name unknown.

DUNBAR, HOME, EARL OF, iii. 280-289.
Dunbar, George, earl of, i. 559; iii. 286, 371.
—— —— his wife, Elizabeth Gordon, iii. 288.
DUNBAR, CONSTABLE, VISCOUNT, iii. 290-300.
—— Henry, first viscount, iii. 296.
—— —— his wife, Mary Tufton, iii. 297.
—— John, second viscount, iii. 297.
—— —— his wife, Mary Brudenell, iii. 298.
—— Robert, third viscount, iii. 298.
—— —— his 1st wife, Mary Belasyse, iii. 299.
—— —— his 2nd wife, Dorothy Brudenell, iii. 299.
—— William, fourth viscount, iii. 298, 299.
—— —— his wife, Elizabeth Clifford, iii. 298.
Dunbar, James (Murray), created by Prince James Edward Stuart, earl of, viii. 205.
DUNBAR, LORD OF ANNANDALE, iii. 270.
DUNBAR, EARL OF DUNBAR, iii. 239-279.
DUNBAR, LORD OF MAN, iii. 270.
DUNBAR, EARL OF MARCH, iii. 262-279.
DUNBAR, EARL of MORAY, vi. 298-307.
Dunbar of Altcash, Alexander, viii. 331 *n.*, 332.
—— —— his wife, Janet Sutherland, viii. 332.
—— of Asleisk, Alexander, ancestor of the family of, viii. 332.
—— —— George, viii. 67.
—— of Auchtermonzie, Sir David, iii. 21.
—— of Balbuthie, Archibald, 3rd son of 11th earl of Dunbar, iii. 279.
—— of Baldoon, Sir David, bart., iii. 452; iv. 162; viii. 147.
—— —— his 1st wife, Janet Dalrymple, viii. 147; ix. 160.
—— —— his 2nd wife Helenor Montgomerie, iii. 452.
—— —— Mary, wife of lord Basil Hamilton, vii. 519, 520.
—— —— Sir Robert, iv. 162.
—— of Bennagefield, vii. 471.
—— of Biel, Sir Patrick, iii. 260, 274; viii. 8, 260.
—— —— his wife, Euphemia, countess Palatine of Strathearn, ii. 322; iii. 260; viii. 260.
—— —— Patrick, ix. 164.
—— —— his wife, Annabella Boyd, viii. 425; ix. 164 *bis*.
—— of Birkenside. Sir John, iii. 259.
—— —— John, his son, iii. 259.
—— of Blackcraig, Sir James, iii. 224.
—— —— his wife, * Crichton, iii. 224.
—— of Blantyre, Cuthbert, 2nd son of Sir John D. of Cumnock and Mochrum, iii. 261.
—— —— Sir David, iii. 261.
—— —— William, v. 497; viii. 117.
—— of Bogsmoray, v. 245.
—— of Brawl, Janet, wife of 2nd lord Crichton, iii. 62, 64.

* Name unknown.

Dunbar of Brigham, Sir David, iii. 275, 276.
—— of Burgie, Robert, iv. 129.
—— —— his wife, Isobel Crichton, iv. 129.
—— of Carnousie, Sir Alexander, vi. 306.
—— of Chirnside, George, 2nd son of 11th earl of Dunbar, iii. 278.
—— of Clugstone, Margaret, wife of Sir Alex. Stewart of Garlies, iv. 155.
—— —— Sir Patrick, iv. 155.
—— of Cluny, Sir Alexander, vi. 306.
—— of Cockburn, Sir David, iii. 21.
—— —— Sir David, 6th son of 10th earl of Dunbar, iii. 275, 276.
—— —— Margaret, wife of (1) Alexander, 4th earl of Crawford, and (2) Sir W. Wallace, iii. 21, 275.
—— of Conzie, James, iv. 123; viii. 332, 333.
—— of Crethmond, Beatrix, wife of Gilbert Hay of Urie, iii. 563, 564.
—— —— Sir John, iii. 564.
—— of Cumnock, Sir Alexander, ancestor of the family of, vi. 306.
—— —— Sir Alexander, vii. 281; ix. 110.
—— —— his wife, Joan Leslie, vii. 281; ix. 110.
—— —— Sir David, iii. 261.
—— —— George, alleged ancestor of the family of, iii. 261, 263.
—— —— Sir James, ii. 5; vii. 355; viii. 332, 333.
—— —— Sir John, iii. 261.
—— —— Sir Patrick, iii. 261.
—— —— Patrick, iii. 261.
—— —— Sir Patrick, viii. 339.
—— —— his wife, Janet Gordon, viii. 339.
—— of Duffus, Sir Alexander, ancestor of the family of, vi. 306.
—— of Dunbeath, Janet, wife of 2nd lord Crichton, iii. 62, 64.
—— of Durn, Sir William, iv. 38.
—— —— Sir William, 3rd bart., vii. 483.
—— —— his 1st wife, Clementina Grant, vii. 483.
—— of Enterkin, David, v. 497, 505; ix. 58.
—— —— his wife, Annabella Campbell, v. 497, 505.
—— of Frendraught, Jonet, wife of (1) James, 2nd lord Crichton, and (2) John Sutherland, ii. 327; iii. 62, 63, 66; iv. 123, 528; vi. 306, 308, 310.
—— of Grange, Alexander, vii. 505.
—— —— his wife, Jean Cockburn, vii. 505.
—— —— Thomas, vii. 89.
—— —— his wife, * Colyear *alias* Robertson, vii. 89.
—— of Grangehill, viii. 343.
—— —— Ninian, ii. 15.
—— —— his wife, Mary Ogilvy, ii. 15.
—— —— Thomas, iii. 211.
—— —— his wife, Janet Dunbar of Westfield, iii. 211.

* Name unknown.

Dunbar of Hempriggs, Benjamin, the younger, vii. 174.
—— Janet Sinclair, vii. 174.
—— Sir Benjamin Sutherland, 3rd bart., iii. 211, 214.
—— his wife, Janet Mackay, iii. 214.
—— Elizabeth, wife of (1) Sir Robt. Gordon, and (2) James Sutherland, iii. 210.
—— Garden Duff, iii. 215.
—— Sir George Duff Sutherland, 6th bart., iii. 214.
—— Sir James, 1st bart., iii. 210.
—— his wife, Elizabeth Dunbar of Hempriggs, iii. 210.
—— Sir William, last bart. of old creation, iii. 210.
—— Sir William, 2nd bart., iii. 211.
—— his 1st wife, Elizabeth Dunbar of Westfield, iii. 211.
—— his 2nd wife, Jean Sinclair, ii. 346; iii. 211.
—— his 3rd wife, Henrietta Rose, iii. 211.
— of Incbbrock, George, viii. 67; ix. 159.
—— his wife, Margaret Carnegie, viii. 67.
— of Kilbuiac, Alexander, ancestor of the family of, viii. 332.
— of Kilboyack, Alexander, iv. 126.
— of Kilcolmkill, Alexander, viii. 332, 333.
—— his wife, Janet Sutherland, viii. 332.
—— James, viii. 333.
— of Kilconquhar, Alison, wife of David M'Culloch, iii. 278.
—— Andrew, 7th laird, iii. 278; viii. 491.
—— his wife, Eupheme Wemyss, iii. 278.
—— Elizabeth, dau. of Patrick D., 6th laird, iii. 278.
—— Sir George, *olim* 11th earl of Dunbar, iii. 277.
—— his wife, Beatrix *, iii. 277.
—— Janet, wife of (1) William Mundall, and (2) William Adair, iii. 278.
—— Margaret, wife of (1) Wm. Macdowal, (2) John Vaus, (3) John Wemyss, and (4) John Giffart, iii. 278.
—— Patrick, 2nd laird, iii. 277.
—— his wife, Elizabeth Sinclair, iii. 277.
—— Patrick, 3rd laird, iii. 277.
—— his wife, Christian Home, iii. 277.
—— Patrick, 4th laird, iii. 278.
—— his 1st wife, Jonet Dunbar, iii. 261, 278.
—— his 2nd wife, Isabella Dishington, iii. 278.
—— Patrick, 5th laird, iii. 278.
—— his wife, Christian M'Dowell, iii. 278.

* Name unknown.

Dunbar of Kilconquhar, Patrick, 6th laird, iii. 278.
—— his wife, Margaret Gordon, iii. 278.
— of Kintore, John, vi. 299.
— of Leuchold, George, iv. 494.
— of Loch, Andrew, ii. 64.
—— Margaret, ii. 64.
— of Machermore, Nugent, capt., iii. 261.
—— *, iii. 447.
—— his wife, Elizabeth Montgomerie, iii. 447.
— of Mochrum, Sir Alexander, ancestor of the family of, vi. 306; viii. 332.
—— Sir James, v. 259.
—— Sir James, 3rd bart., ii. 49.
—— his wife, Jacobina Hamilton, ii. 49.
—— Sir John, son of Sir Patrick D. of Cumnock, iii. 261.
—— Sir John, iii. 261.
—— his wife, Margaret Dunbar of Mochrum, iii. 261.
—— Sir John, steward of Kirkcudbright, iv. 152 *bis.*
—— his 2nd wife, Janet Stewart, iv. 152.
—— Sir John, v. 259 *bis.*
—— his wife, Katharine Maclellan, v. 259.
—— Sir John, 1576, iii. 278.
—— Sir William Cospatrick, 9th bart., C.B., iii. 261; iv. 390.
— of Morton, George, iii. 270.
— of Mordington, Agnes, wife of Sir Jas. Douglas of Dalkeith, iii. 261.
—— Elizabeth, wife of David, duke of Rothesay, i. 17; iii. 161, 271, 275, 279 *n.*
— of Newburn, Sir Gavin, 2nd son of 10th earl of Dunbar, iii. 273, 276 *bis.*; vii. 113.
— of Northfield, Alexander, ancestor of the family of, viii. 332.
—— Sir Alexander, 5th bart., i. 313.
—— his wife, Margaret Arbuthnott, i. 313.
—— Sir Archibald Hamilton, 7th bart., iii. 269 *n.*
—— Sir Patrick, 3rd bart., ii. 353.
— of Pankill, Alexander, iv. 159.
—— his wife, Nicolas Stewart, iv. 159.
— of Sanchar, Patrick, ii. 5.
—— his wife, Elspet Ogilvy, ii. 5.
—— Walter, ii. 5.
— of Sorn, William, v. 497.
— of Spot, Archibald, 3rd son of 11th earl of Dunbar, iii. 278.
— of Thunderton, Archibald, iii. 210.
— of Tibbers, George, iii. 270.
— of Westfield, Sir Alexander, iii. 63, 195; vi. 306; vii. 268.
—— his wife, Isobel Sutherland, iii. 195; vi. 306.
—— his alleged wife, Ann Leslie, vii. 268.

Dunbar of Westfield, Alexander, iii. 211.
—— —— Elizabeth, wife of Sir William Dunbar, iii. 211.
—— —— Sir James, iii. 261.
—— —— his wife, Euphemia Dunbar, iii. 261.
—— —— Sir James, sheriff of Moray, iv. 20.
—— —— his wife, Elizabeth Ogilvy, iv. 20.
—— —— Janet, wife of Thomas Dunbar of Grangehill, iii. 211.
—— —— Thomas, iii. 211.
—— —— his wife, Janet Dunbar, iii. 211.
—— —— Sir Patrick, viii. 339.
—— —— his wife, Janet Gordon, viii. 339.
—— of Whittinghame, Agnes, wife of Sir Jas. Douglas of Dalkeith, iii. 261.
—— Ada, lady of Pullys, wife of (1) William de Courtenay, and (2) Theobald de Lascelles, iv. 440.
—— Æthelreda of, wife of King Duncan II., i. 3; iii. 245.
—— Agnes, wife of John Maitland of Thirlestane, v. 284.
—— Agnes, wife of Thomas Maclellan of Bombie, v. 259.
—— Agnes, wife of Archibald (Douglas), earl of Moray, vi. 306.
—— Agnes, wife of Sir James Douglas of Dalkeith, vi. 346, 348.
—— Agnes of, alleged wife of Sir Wm. Sinclair of Roslin, vi. 565.
—— Agnes, wife of Sir Jas. Douglas of Dalkeith, iii. 153 *n.*
—— Sir Alexander, 3rd son of Patrick, 7th earl of Dunbar, iii. 259; viii. 565 *n.*
—— Alexander, 2nd son of 1st earl of Moray, vi. 301.
—— —— his wife, Matilda Fraser, vi. 301.
—— Alexandrina, dau. of Sir William D. of Hempriggs, iii. 211.
—— Alice, alleged wife of Philip de Seton, iii. 252; viii. 561.
—— Anne, wife of 1st earl of Seafield, iv. 38.
—— Archibald, ix. 58.
—— —— his wife, Jean Cathcart, ix. 58.
—— Beatrix, wife of Wm. Falconer of Dinduff, v. 245.
—— Charlotte, wife of Wm. Sinclair, iii. 211.
—— Christian, dau. of Sir William D. of Hempriggs, iii. 211.
—— Cristina, wife of Alex. Innes of Innes, vii. 354.
—— Colin *or* Columba, dean of Dunbar, bishop of Moray, iii. 274, 276 *bis.*
—— Constantine, 2nd son of 4th earl of Dunbar, iii. 252.
—— David, tutor of Kilconquhar, iii. 278 *n.*
—— David, in Clonstang, viii. 118.
—— Elizabeth, wife of David, duke of Rothesay, i. 17; iii. 161, 271, 275, 279 *n.*
—— Elizabeth, wife of John Ogilvy, ii. 5.
Dunbar, Elizabeth, wife of Jas. Sinclair of Durran, ii. 353.
—— Elizabeth, wife of (1) Archibald (Douglas), earl of Moray, and (2) Sir John Colquhoun of Luss, iii. 62; vi. 306, 308, 310.
—— Elizabeth, dau. of Sir Benjamin S. D., iii. 214.
—— Elizabeth, dau. of Sir William D. of Hempriggs, iii. 211.
—— Elizabeth, wife of Eric, titular lord Duffus, iii. 211, 213.
—— Elizabeth, *really* Agnes, wife of John Maitland of Thirlestane, iii. 261.
—— Elizabeth, wife of Robt. Stewart of Ravenstone, iv. 162.
—— Euphemia, wife of Uchtred M'Dowall, ii. 474.
—— Euphemia, wife of Sir James Dunbar of Westfield, iii. 261.
—— Euphemia, wife of George Graham, iii. 279.
—— Euphemia, wife of Alexander Cumming, vi. 301.
—— Gavin, the poet, archbishop of Glasgow, chancellor of Scotland, first president of the Court of Session, ii. 461, 462; iv. 152; v. 244; viii. 16.
—— George, son of Sir Patrick D. of Biel, iii. 260.
—— Grizel, dau. of Sir Wm. D. of Hempriggs, iii. 211.
—— Helen, wife of Charles Hope-Vere of Craigiehall and Blackwood, iv. 494.
—— Helen, alleged wife of Philip de Seton, iii. 252; viii. 561.
—— Helen, wife of (1) Alex. Melvill, (2) Sir John Wemyss, and (3) Andrew Moncur, viii. 484.
—— Henrietta, wife of Wm. Sinclair Wemyss, iii. 215.
—— James, 2nd son of Sir James D. of Hempriggs, iii. 211.
—— James, precentor of Moray, vi. 301; ix. 138.
—— Janet, wife of (1) William Seton, and (2) Adam Johnstone of Johnstone, i. 236; iii. 275 *n.*; viii. 574.
—— Janet, wife of (1) John Sinclair, and (2) H. Innes, iii. 211.
—— Janet, wife of Sir William Keith of Inverugie, vi. 34.
—— Janet, wife of * Fraser of Lovat, vi. 304.
—— Sir John, 2nd son of Sir Alex. D. of Westfield, iii. 261.
—— —— his wife, Margaret Dunbar, iii. 261.
—— Sir John, son of Patrick, 9th earl of Dunbar, iii. 269.
—— John, 5th son of 10th earl of Dunbar, iii. 274, 276 *bis.*
—— John, *de jure ux.* earl of Fife, iv. 13.
—— —— his wife, Isabella, countess of Fife, iv. 13.

* Name unknown.

Dunbar, John, sheriff of Moray, v. 530; vi. 317.
— — his wife, Elizabeth Fraser, v. 530.
— John, 'vallet' to Sir Robert Erskine, vi. 298.
— Jonet, wife of Patrick Dunbar of Kilconquhar, iii. 261, 278.
— Kenneth, eldest son of Sir Wm. D. of Hempriggs, iii. 211.
— Mabilla, alleged wife of Robert, 6th earl of Sutherland, viii. 330 *n.*
— Margaret, wife of (1) Alexander, 4th earl of Crawford, and (2) Sir Wm. Wallace, iii. 21, 275.
— Margaret, *mistakenly said to be* wife of 1st earl of Douglas, iii. 153.
— Margaret, dau. of Sir William D. of Hempriggs, iii. 211.
— Margaret, wife of Sir John Dunbar, iii. 261.
— Margaret, wife of Alex. Mackenzie of Kilcoy, vii. 502.
— Margaret, wife of (1) John Dalrymple of Stair, and (2) Alex. Cunningham of Powton, viii. 117.
— Mariot, wife of David Falconer of Halkerton, v. 244.
— Marjorie, wife of (1) Sir John Swinton, and (2) Lucas Stirling, iii. 279.
— Mary, wife of Archibald (Douglas), earl of Moray, vi. 306.
— Nicholas, illeg. son of 10th earl of Dunbar, iii. 276.
— Mr. Patrick, chancellor of Aberdeen, 'oy' of Janet Grant, wife of Alex. Sutherland and Jas. Dempster, iii. 201.
— Patrick, son of Sir Patrick D. of Biel, iii. 260.
— Sir Patrick, father of George, 10th earl of Dunbar, and of John, earl of Moray, iii. 260, 266, 269, 270; vi. 298.
— — his 2nd wife, Isabella Randolph, iii. 260; vi. 295, 296.
— Rachel, wife of Jas. Sutherland, iii. 211.
— Sir Robert, seneschal of Dunbar, iii. 254, 257.
— Robert Sutherland, iii. 211.
— Thomas, dean of Moray, ix. 51.
— — his wife, Grisel Crichton, ix. 51.
— Sir Wawan *or* Gavin, 2nd son of 10th earl of Dunbar, iii. 273, 276 *bis*; vii. 113.
— William, 2nd son of Patrick, 5th earl of Dunbar, iii. 254, 257; vii. 398; viii. 3.
— — his wife, Christiana Corbet, iii. 254; iv. 7.
— William, the poet, ii. 455; iii. 260.
— Williamina, dau. of Sir Wm. D. of Hempriggs, iii. 211.
— *, wife of Robert Grant in Milton of Muckcrach, vii. 471.

* Name unknown.

DUNBLANE, OSBORNE, VISCOUNT, iii. 301-302.
Dunblane, Perigrine, first viscount, iii. 302.
— — his wife, Bridget Hyde, iii. 302.
Duncan I., King of Scots, i. 1; ii. 314; iii. 240 *bis*; vi. 282.
— II., King of Scots, i. 2; iii. 245.
— — his wife, Æthelreda, iii. 245.
— the 'Judex,' i. 107.
— 3rd son of Malcolm, 2nd earl of Atholl, i. 418.
— son of Malise, i. 453 *n.*
— lay-abbot of Dunkeld, iii. 240 *n.*
— 2nd son of Duncan, 5th earl of Fife, iv. 7; viii. 246 *n.*
— — his wife, Aliz Corbet, iv. 8.
— of Lorn, 2nd son of Dugall of Lorn, v. 30.
— 6th son of Alwin, 2nd earl of Lennox, v. 328, 330 *bis*.
— 2nd son of Maldwin, 3rd earl of Lennox, v. 333.
— son of Gilchrist of Arrochar, v. 333.
— son of Walter Macalan of Faslane, v. 341.
— — his wife, Helen Campbell, v. 341.
— of Luss, v. 139.
— Sir, of Faslane, son of Aulay, v. 329.
— 2nd son of Donald, 6th earl of Mar, v. 578.
— tosheach of Clan Morgan, vii. 157.
— 2nd son of Michael of Wemyss, viii. 476.
Duncan of Camperdown, Adam, first viscount, viii. 159.
— — his wife, Henrietta Dundas, viii. 159.
— of St. Fort, Alexander, capt. H.E.I.C.S., viii. 139.
— — his wife, Margaret Dalrymple, viii. 139.
— Adamina, wife of 8th earl of Stair, viii. 159.
— Gavin, sheriff's officer, vii. 17.
— Henrietta, wife of Sir Jas. Fergusson, i. 554.
— Jane, wife of Sir Hew Dalrymple Hamilton of North Berwick and Bargany, viii. 127.
— John, minister of Culross, ii. 549.
— — his wife, Jean Colville, ii. 549.
— William, chirurgeon in Dundee, iii. 572.
Duncanson of Fingask, Henry, i. 111.
— of Fynnech, Robert, i. 455.
— of Easter Gellets, Roger, ix. 142.
— — his wife, Margaret Douglas, ix. 142.
— Anna, wife of Alex. Napier of Torrie-Easter, vi. 421; ix. 142.
— John, dean of the Chapel Royal, Stirling, vi. 8.
— Marion, wife of Mr. Alex. Hume, vi. 8.

Dunch, *, major, vii. 261.
—— —— his wife, Margaret Wharton, vii. 261.
Duncombe of Battlesden, Anne, wife of 1st lord Deloraine, iii. 112.
—— —— William, lord justice of Ireland, iii. 112.
—— Augustus, dean of York, vii. 152.
—— —— his wife, Harriet Christian Douglas, vii. 152.
—— Sir Charles, lord mayor of London, i. 376.
DUNCRUB, ROLLO, LORD ROLLO OF, vii. 195-211.
Duncurry, Thomas of, i. 215.
DUNDAFF, GRAHAM, VISCOUNT OF, vi. 263-274.
Dundaff, James, first viscount of, vi. 263.
Dundas of Arniston, Sir James, 1st laird, ii. 113; iii. 508; vi. 546.
—— —— Sir James, senator of the College of Justice, iii. 488; v. 171, 622; viii. 120.
—— —— his 1st wife, Marion Boyd, v. 171.
—— —— his 3rd wife, Helen Skene, iii. 488; v. 622.
—— —— Robert, lord of Session, ii. 32.
—— —— Robert, lord president of the Court of Session, i. 212; ii. 89; iv. 588.
—— —— his wife, Henrietta Carmichael, iv. 587.
—— —— Sir Robert, 1st bart., iv. 483.
—— of Ballinbreich, Sir Lawrence, 1st laird, vii. 306.
—— of Blair, William, iii. 544.
—— —— his wife, Elizabeth Elphinstone, iii. 544.
—— of Bloxholm Hall, Robert Adam, M.P., iii. 493.
—— —— his wife, Mary Bruce, iii. 493.
—— of Cottis, Alexander, iii. 473.
—— —— his wife, Elizabeth Bruce, iii. 473.
—— of Carronhall, Thomas, v. 317.
—— of Duddingston, George, iv. 175.
—— —— his wife, Magdalen Lindsay, iv. 175.
—— —— James, vii. 14.
—— —— his wife, Isobel Maule, vii. 14.
—— —— John, iv. 496.
—— —— his wife, Margaret Hope, iv. 496.
—— —— John, iv. 568, 588.
—— —— his wife, Anne *or* Agnes Carmichael, iv. 568, 588.
—— of Dundas, Sir Archibald, sheriff of Linlithgow, ii. 97 *n.*, 399, 400; vii. 249.
—— —— his wife, Agnes Borthwick, ii. 97 *n.*
—— —— Duncan, v. 290.
—— —— George, vi. 546; viii. 390.
—— —— his wife, Katharine Oliphant, vi. 545.
—— —— George, i. 552.
—— —— his wife, Alison Bruce, i. 552.

* Name unknown.

Dundas of Dundas, Sir James, v. 2, 429; viii. 383.
—— —— his 2nd wife, Christian Stewart, v. 2.
—— —— Sir James, viii. 386.
—— —— his wife, Margaret Sandilands, viii. 386.
—— —— James, colonel, M.P., iv. 64.
—— —— his wife, Jean Forbes, iv. 64.
—— —— John, iv. 81.
—— —— Sir Walter, viii. 392; ix. 51.
—— —— Walter, v. 376, 378; vi. 109; vii. 477.
—— —— his wife, Christian Leslie, v. 378.
—— of Eckling, Archibald, ii. 400.
—— —— James, ii. 399.
—— of Fingask, Alexander, ii. 549; iii. 473.
—— —— his wife, Elizabeth Bruce, iii. 473.
—— —— Archibald, ii. 545, 571; v. 463; viii. 60.
—— —— his wife, Elizabeth Colvill, ii. 571.
—— —— Archibald, iv. 566.
—— —— his wife, Jean Carnegie, iv. 566.
—— —— Thomas, M.P., v. 317.
—— —— his wife, Janet Maitland, v. 317.
—— —— Thomas, major-general, M.P., iv. 481.
—— —— his wife, Eleonora Home, iv. 481.
—— of Harvieston, John, ii. 113, 115.
—— —— Robert, 2nd son of Sir Jas. D. of Arniston, ii. 113.
—— —— his wife, Margaret Borthwick, ii. 113.
—— of Kerse, Sir Laurence, i. 552.
—— —— his wife, Margaret Bruce, i. 552.
—— of Kincavil, William, ii. 299, 366.
—— of Newliston, Elizabeth, wife of 1st earl of Stair, viii. 149.
—— —— James, ii. 404.
—— —— Sir John, vii. 219; viii. 149; ix. 152, 160.
—— —— his wife, Agnes Gray, iv. 289; vii. 219.
—— of Zetland, Sir Laurence, vi. 381.
—— Agnes, wife of Sir Adam Forrester of Corstorphine, iv. 81.
—— Alison, wife of D. Lindsay of Pyotston, v. 411.
—— Anna, wife of John Erskine of Carnock, ii. 366.
—— Anne, wife of (1) H. Drummond, and (2) Jas. Strange, viii. 232.
—— Barbara, wife of Alexander Melville, master of Melville and lord Raith, vi. 109.
—— Charles, v. 312.
—— —— his wife, Margaret Maitland, v. 312.
—— Charles, captain, 4th son of Sir Jas. D. of Arniston, vi. 178.
—— Christian, wife of 1st earl of Bute, ii. 299.
—— Christian, wife of Sir John Sandilands of Calder, viii. 382.

Dundas, Cristine, wife of (1) Robt. Dalzell, and (2) Jas. Roberton, ii. 405, 407.
— Elizabeth, wife of Sir P. Murray of Elibank, iii. 509.
— Eufame, wife of Wm. Colville, ii. 545.
— George, preceptor of Torphichen, v. 393 *n.*
— Grizel, wife of Robt. Colt, ii. 89.
— Helen, wife of Robert Middleton, vi. 178.
— Henrietta, wife of Adam, 1st viscount Duncan of Camperdown, viii. 159.
— Henry Herbert Philip, captain 15th Hussars, iv. 483.
— — his wife, Beatrix Lucy Douglas-Home, iv. 483.
— Isabel, wife of 4th lord Torphichen, viii. 392.
— John, Edinburgh, vii. 451.
— Katharine, wife of Sir. Jas. Dalrymple of Borthwick and Kelloch, viii. 120.
— Lilias, wife of Alex. Hume of Rollandstoun, vi. 9.
— Margaret, wife of 3rd lord Bargany, ii. 32.
— Margaret, wife of (1) Sir W. Sharp of Ballindoch, and (2) Sir James Sinclair of Murchil, ii. 340; ix. 51.
— Margaret, wife of (1) David Home of Fischwick, (2) Wm. Ker of Ancrum, and (3) Sir Geo. Douglas of Mordington, v. 463.
— Marion Stirling, wife of col. James Hay Fraser, vii. 451.
— Nicolas, wife of Alex. Colvill, i. 464; ii. 549.
— Philip, lieut.-colonel, viii. 516.
— — his wife, Jane Charteris, viii. 516.
— Richard, ambassador to King Edward IV., v. 144 *n.*
— Walter, 2nd son of Walter D., vii. 477.
— — his wife, Jean Houstoun, vii. 477.
— William, M.P., ii. 303.
— — his wife, Mary Stuart, ii. 303.
— William, son of Archibald D. of Fingask, viii. 60.
— — his wife, Margaret Carnegie, viii. 60.
— *, probable wife of John Maitland, younger of Thirlestane, v. 290.
— *, wife of Sir Alex. Livingston of Callendar, v. 429.
— *, wife of * Lindsay, v. 393 *n.*
DUNDEE, SCRYMGEOUR, EARL OF, iii. 303-315.
Dundee, John, earl of, iii. 315; v. 306, 379.
— — his wife, Anna Ramsay, iii. 100, 315.
DUNDEE, GRAHAM, VISCOUNT OF, iii. 316-333.
Dundee, David, third viscount of, iii. 324, 331.
— David, fourth titular viscount of, iii. 332.
— James, second viscount of, iii. 331.

* Name unknown.

Dundee, James, sixth titular viscount of, iii. 332.
— John, first viscount of, i. 208, 521; iii. 324; v. 124, 307; vii. 259.
— — his wife, Jean Cochrane, iii. 330, 352; v. 193.
— William, fifth titular viscount of, iii. 332.
— Randulph of, v. 242.
DUNDONALD, COCHRANE, LORD COCHRANE OF, iii. 344-368.
DUNDONALD, COCHRANE, EARL OF, iii. 334-368.
Dundonald, Archibald, ninth earl of, iii. 359, 360.
— — his 1st wife, Anne Gilchrist, iii. 361.
— — his 2nd wife, Isabella Raymond, iii. 362.
— — his 3rd wife, Anna Maria Plowden, iii. 362.
— Douglas Mackinnon Baillie-Hamilton, twelfth earl of, iii. 367.
— — his wife, Winifred Bamford-Hesketh, iii. 367.
— John, second earl of, iii. 346, 351, 352.
— — his wife, Susanna Hamilton, iii. 353; iv. 382.
— John, fourth earl of, iii. 348, 352, 354; ix. 77 *bis.*
— — his 1st wife, Anne Murray, iii. 354, 386.
— — his 2nd wife, Mary Osborne, iii. 355.
— Thomas, sixth earl of; iii. 351, 356.
— — his wife, Katharine Hamilton, iii. 357; vii. 519.
— Thomas, eighth earl of, i. 65; iii. 349, 358; ix. 77.
— — his 1st wife, Elizabeth Ker, iii. 359.
— — his 2nd wife, Jean Stuart, iii. 359.
— Thomas, tenth earl of. iii. 362; ix. 77.
— — his wife, Katharine Frances Corbett Barnes, iii. 365.
— Thomas Barnes, eleventh earl of, iii. 366.
— — his wife, Louisa Harriet Mackinnon, iii. 366.
— William, first earl of, i. 65; iii. 341, 343, 344.
— — his wife, Euphame Scott, iii. 346; ix. 76.
— William, third earl of, iii. 353.
— William, fifth earl of, iii. 356.
— William, seventh earl of, iii. 357.
Dundrennan, Thomas Maitland, senator of the College of Justice, lord, viii. 397.
DUNFERMLINE, SETON, EARL OF, iii. 369-375.
Dunfermline, Alexander, first earl of, i. 540; iii. 369; viii. 589, 593.
— — his 1st wife, Lilias Drummond, iii. 372; vii. 47.
— — his 2nd wife, Grizel Leslie, iii. 372; vii. 296.
— — his 3rd wife, Margaret Hay, iii. 372; viii. 447.

Dunfermline, Alexander, third earl of, iii. 374; ix. 78 *bis*.
— Charles, second earl of, iii. 373; viii. 451; ix. 77, 78 *bis*.
— — his wife, Mary Douglas, iii. 374; vi. 378; ix. 78.
— James, fourth earl of, i. 91; iii. 374; viii. 454.
— — his wife, Jean Gordon, iii. 375; iv. 549; ix. 78.
Dungal, son of Udard, i. 231.
— son of Christin, dempster of Lennox, ii. 504.
— of Stranith, vi. 286.
Dungarvan, Charles (Boyle), styled viscount, vii. 142.
— — his wife, Jane Seymour, vii. 142.
DUNGLAS, HOME, LORD, iv. 464-484.
Dunglas, Alexander, first lord, iv. 464.
— Charles, eldest son of 7th earl of Home; styled lord, iv. 480.
— Charles Cospatrick Archibald, son of 12th earl of Home; styled lord, iv. 483.
— — his wife, Lilian Lambton, iv. 483.
— William, eldest son of 9th earl of Home; styled lord, iv. 481.
DUNKELD, GALLOWAY, LORD, iii. 376-382.
Dunkeld, James, first lord, iii. 377.
— — his wife, * Norter, iii. 378.
— James, third lord, iii. 380; ix. 78.
— — his wife, Eleanor Sale, iii. 381.
— Thomas, second lord, iii. 378.
— — his wife, Margaret Thomson, iii. 379.
— James Galloway, comte de, ii. 381.
— — his 1st wife, Marie Marguerite Angelique Le Rat, iii. 382.
— — his 2nd wife, *, iii. 382.
Dunlop of Bishoptoun, Hugh, vii. 564.
— — Janet, wife of 13th lord Sempill, vii. 564.
— of Househill, Thomas, iii. 343.
— — his wife, Grizel Cochrane, iii. 343.
— Alexander, professor of Greek, Glasgow University, iv. 207.
— Elizabeth, wife of rev. Patrick Boyle of Shewalton, iv. 207.
— Sir John, bart., vii. 227.
— — his 2nd wife, Harriet Primrose, vii. 227.
— Jonet, wife of Ninian Stewart of Bute, ii. 289.
— Jonet, wife of Alex. Montgomerie of Giffen, iii. 430.
DUNMORE, MURRAY, EARL OF, iii. 383-396.
Dunmore, Alexander Edward, sixth earl of, iii. 394, 553.
— — his wife, Katharine Herbert, iii. 394.

* Name unknown.

Dunmore, Alexander Edward, eighth earl of, iii. 395.
— — his wife, Lucinda Dorothea Kemble, iii. 395.
— Charles, first earl of, i. 475; iii. 383; v. 192.
— — his wife, Katharine Watts, iii. 384.
— Charles Adolphus, seventh earl of, iii. 395.
— — his wife, Gertrude Coke, iii. 395.
— George, fifth earl of, iii. 389, 392.
— — his wife, Susan Douglas-Hamilton, iii. 392; iv. 395.
— John, second earl of, iii. 385, 386, 545.
— John, fourth earl of, iii. 388.
— — his wife, Charlotte Stewart, iii. 389; iv. 166.
— William, third earl of, iii. 385, 387.
— — his wife, Katharine Nairne, iii. 387; vi. 396.
DUNMORE OF DUNMORE, MURRAY, BARON, iii. 392-396.
Dunmore, George, first baron, iii. 392.
— John, notary, Dundee, i. 563.
Dunn of Higham House, John Charles, vii. 489.
— Mary Anne, wife of lieut.-col. Francis William Grant, vii. 489.
Dunne, Abbé, 1737, i. 481.
DUNNING OF DUNNING AND PITCAIRNS, ROLLO, LORD, vii. 209-210.
Dunning, John Rogerson, first lord, vii. 209.
— Patrick, ix. 75.
— — his wife, Isobel Spreull, ix. 75.
DUNOON, CAMPBELL, LORD, i. 379.
Dunoon, Archibald, first lord, i. 378.
Dunsany, Edward Wadding (Plunkett), 14th lord, v. 213.
— — his 2nd wife, Eliza Kinnaird, v. 213.
Dunsmure, David, viii. 295.
— Cecilia, wife of (1) John Lyon of Brigton, and (2) James Stewart, viii. 295.
DUPPLIN, HAY, VISCOUNT OF, v. 231.
Dupplin, Thomas, first viscount of, v. 229 231.
DUPPLIN, HAY, VISCOUNT, v. 222-239.
Dupplin, Edmund Alfred Rollo George, styled viscount, v. 238.
— — his wife, Gladys Luz Bacon, v. 238.
— George, first viscount, v. 222.
— — his wife, Margaret Haliburton, v. 223.
— George Robert, lieut. 1st Life Guards; styled viscount, v. 237.
— — his wife, A. C. E. Duff, v. 237.
Durand, Algernon George Arnold, colonel C.B., C.I.E., iii. 494.
— — his wife, Elizabeth Marjorie Bruce, iii. 494.
Durandus the Justiciar, iii. 3.

Durham, George Frederick D'Arcy (Lambton), 2nd earl of, i. 71.
—— his wife, Beatrix Frances Hamilton, i. 71.
— John George (Lambton), 1st earl of, iii. 495; vi. 386.
— of Duntarvy, James, silversmith, ii. 161.
—— his wife, Margaret Hepburn, ii. 161.
— of Grange, Robert, vii. 18.
— of Largo, Sir Alexander, Lyon King of Arms, vi. 185.
—— Alexander, vii. 380.
—— his wife, Margaret Rutherford, vii. 380.
— of Piltoun and Luffness, John Cunningham, vii. 585.
— of Pitkerro, James, vi. 185; vii. 13.
— of Easter Powrie, Alexander, vi. 185.
— Alexander, silversmith, ii. 161.
— Elizabeth, wife of David Arbuthnott, i. 281.
— Grizel, wife of 1st earl of Middleton, vi. 185.
— Henry, vii. 18.
—— his wife, Isobel Maule, vii. 18.
— Isabella, wife of George St. Clair, vii. 585.
— James, viii. 21.
— Margaret, wife of Andrew Maule of Gourdie, vii. 13.
— Sir Philip Charles, admiral, G.C.B., iii. 492.
—— his 1st wife, Charles Martha *or* Charlotte Matilda Bruce, iii. 492.
—— his 2nd wife, Ann Henderson of Fordel, ix. 83.
— *, wife of Henry Maule of Melgund, vii. 13.
Durie of Belnollo, viii. 245.
— of Durie, David, vi. 371; vii. 294; viii. 494.
—— his wife, Katharine Douglas, vi. 371.
— Duncan of, son of Duncan, earl of Fife, viii. 245 *n*.
—— Gilbert, ancestor of the family of, viii. 245.
— of Grange, David, vii. 374.
—— George, vii. 373, 383 *bis*, 384.
—— his wife, Margaret Ogilvy, vii. 373.
—— John, vii. 373.
—— John, vii. 373.
—— Robert, vii. 373.
—— his wife, Christine Rutherfurd, vii. 373.
—— William, vii. 373.
— of East Newton, Robert, viii. 495.
—— his wife, Margaret *or* Magdalene Durie, viii. 495.
— Agatha, dau. of George D. of Grange, vii. 374.

* Name unknown.

Durie, Christian, dau. of Robert D. of Grange, vii. 373.
— Elizabeth, wife of Sir Jas. Wemyss of Bogie, viii. 494; ix. 168.
— Isabella, wife of (1) D. Pitcairn, and (2) John Lindsay, v. 404.
— Janet, wife of (1) David Martin, and (2) Jas. Wemyss, ii. 281.
— Janet, wife of 5th earl of Rothes, vii. 294.
— John, minister of Montrose, vii. 19.
— Margaret, wife of (1) Wm. Scott of Abbotshall, and (2) Sir Geo. Douglas of Helenhill, vi. 370.
— Margaret, wife of Henry Wemyss, viii. 495.
— Margaret *or* Magdalene, wife of R. Durie of East Newton, viii. 495.
— Simeon, minister of Arbroath, vii. 19.
—— his wife, Christian Maule, vii. 19.
— *, wife of * Anderson of Goland, vii. 384.
Durward of Lintrathen, Isabel, alleged 1st wife of Sir Walter Ogilvy of Carcary, i. 111.
— of Lundin, Sir Alan, a regent of Scotland, i. 6, 418; ii. 218, 255; iv. 11; v. 575.
—— his 1st wife, Marjory, i. 6.
—— his possible 2nd wife, Isabella, countess of Atholl, i. 422.
—— Malcolm, i. 11; v. 572.
—— his wife, * of Mar, v. 572.
—— Thomas, i. 418; v. 572 *bis*, 573.
—— his wife, Christina *or* Margaret of Atholl, i. 418.
— Anna, probable wife of Colban, 8th earl of Fife, iv. 10.
— Ermengarde, wife of William Soulis, viii. 250 *n*.
Dusign, Gerald, Bath, iv. 594.
—— his wife, Anne Carmichael, iv. 594.
DUTTON, HAMILTON, BARON, iv. 384-397.
Dutton, Alexander, seventh baron, iv. 395.
— James, first baron, iv. 384.
Duval, Jacques Victor, Bordeaux, v. 419.
— Jeanne Eudoxie Marie, wife of 10th earl of Lindsay, v. 419.
Duvenald of Dunscore, 2nd son of Dougal of Nithsdale, vi. 286.
Dyce, William, schoolmaster, Selkirk, iii. 515.
Dyer, James Hardwicke, vicar of Great Waltham, v. 312.
Dyerlink, Anna, wife of John Berner of Saskendorff, iv. 105.
DYSART, MURRAY, EARL OF, iii. 397-420.
Dysart, Elizabeth, wife of (1) Sir Lionel Tollemache, and (2) John, duke of Lauderdale; countess of, i. 370; iii. 402 *n*., 403; v. 304, 308; vii. 300.
— William, first earl of, iii. 399, 401; ix. 79.
—— his wife, Katharine Bruce, iii. 402.

* Name unknown.

DYSART, TOLLEMACHE, EARL OF, iii. 406-420.
Dysart, Lionel, third earl of, iii. 404, 406.
—— —— his wife, Grace Wilbraham, iii. 406.
—— Lionel, fourth earl of, iii. 407.
—— —— his wife, Grace Leveson-Gower, iii. 408.
—— Lionel, fifth earl of, iii. 408, 410.
—— —— his 1st wife, Charlotte Walpole, iii. 411.
—— his 2nd wife, Magdalene Lewis, iii. 411.
—— Lionel William John, seventh earl of, iii. 415, 418.
—— —— his wife, Maria Elizabeth Toone, iii. 418.
—— Louisa, wife of John Manners; countess of, iii. 412; viii. 158.
—— Wilbraham, sixth earl of, iii. 408, 409, 411.
—— —— his wife, Anna Maria Lewis, iii. 412.
—— William John Manners, eighth earl of, iii. 419, 420.
—— —— his wife, Cecilia Florence Newton, iii. 420.

EADMUND, son of King Harold II. of England, iii. 243 *n.*
Ealdgith, *or* Algitha, wife of Maldred of Cumbria, iii. 241.
Eardley Wilmot, col., ii. 419.
—— Isabella Eliza, wife of (1) J. H. Lecky, and (2) 7th earl of Carnwath, ii. 419.
Early, Annie Ridge, wife of R. R. Fairfax, iii. 604.
—— Charles, Washington, U.S.A., iii. 604.
Eastoft, John, iii. 293.
—— —— his wife, Jean Constable, iii. 293.
Easton, Euphame, wife of Alex. Nairn of Greenyards, vi. 393.
Eatt, John, Cambridge, ii. 75.
—— —— his wife, Mary Bellenden, ii. 75.
Eccles of Eccles, James, ii. 460.
—— —— his wife, Janet Graham, ii. 460.
—— —— James, viii. 373.
—— —— Mungo, viii. 373.
—— Margaret, wife of Henry Lindsay-Bethune, v. 416.
—— Martin, M.D., Edinburgh, v. 416.
Echlin of Pittadro, Harry, ii. 571.
—— —— his wife, Grizel Colville, ii. 571.
Ed, the earl, iv. 2 *n.*; vi. 284.
—— his wife, *, vi. 285.
Eda, 1st wife of Thomas de Crichton, burgess of Berwick, iii. 54.
Eddleston, Edulph of, iii. 86.
Edelrad, earl of Fife, i. 2; ii. 2; vi. 284.
Eden of West Auckland, Sir John, 4th bart., iv. 496.
—— George, 2nd son of 4th baron Auckland, v. 236.
—— —— his wife, Amy V. P. Hay, v. 236.

* Name unknown.

Eden, Maria, wife of (1) 7th earl of Athlone, and (2) Admiral William Johnstone Hope, iv. 496.
—— Mary Dulcibella, wife of C. Drummond, viii. 230.
EDERDALE, STEWART, EARL OF, vii. 246.
Ederdale, James, earl of, vii. 246.
Edgar, King of Scots, i. 3; iv. 3 *bis.*
—— the Ætheling, iii. 241; vii. 28.
—— father of Walter of Cultmalundie, vi. 531.
—— of Bewick, Caistron, etc., 'Unnithing *or* 'the Dauntless,' 4th son of Gospatric, 2nd earl of Dunbar, iii. 247, 248.
—— of Dunscore and Dalgarnock, son of Donald, vi. 287.
—— of Cultmalundie, Walter, iv. 255, 256.
—— of Sanquhar, Richard, iii. 53, 219.
—— —— his wife, * de Ros of Sanquhar, iii. 53, 219.
—— of Wedderlie, John, vii. 74.
—— —— John, ii. 594.
—— —— his wife, Elizabeth Cranstoun, ii. 594.
—— John, advocate, i. 552.
—— —— his wife, Jane Bruce, i. 552.
—— Margaret, wife of (1) Wm. Spottiswood of Spottiswood, and (2) Walter Scott of Harden, vii. 74.
—— Sir Patrick, iv. 255, 443.
—— —— his wife, Marjota Ruthven, iv. 255, 443.
—— Thomas, major 25th Foot, vii. 176.
—— —— his wife, Mary Mackay, vii. 176.
Edington of Clarybald, David, iii. 93.
—— of Edington, Thomas, iii. 95, 97.
—— —— his wife, Elizabeth Ramsay, iii. 95.
—— —— William, iii. 95, 96.
Edith *or* Matilda, wife of Henry I. of England, i. 2.
Edmestoun of Edmestoun, John, iv. 471.
—— Helen, wife of (1) Henry Haitlie, and (2) Wm. Home of Bellitaw, iv. 471: ix. 108.
—— *, wife of Andrew Ker, cupbearer to King Robert III. v. 51 *n.*
Edmond, colonel, Stirling, viii. 374.
—— *, wife of Sir Thos. Livingston, viii. 374.
Edmonds, John, Cambridge, v. 9.
—— Katharine, wife of Sir Wm. Ingram, D.C.L., v. 9.
Edmonston(e of Culloden, Sir William, i. 18.
—— —— his wife, Mary Stewart, i. 18.
—— of Duntreath, Sir Archibald, 3rd laird, iii. 435; vi. 225; vii. 251.
—— —— Archibald, 9th laird, i. 382.
—— —— his 1st wife, Anne Erskine, ii. 368.
—— —— his 2nd wife, Anne Campbell, i. 382.
—— —— Sir James, 6th laird, vi. 238.

* Name unknown.

Edmonston(e, Sir John, ancestor of the family of, i. 16.
—— —— his wife, Isabella Stewart, i. 16; iii. 157.
—— —— Sir William, 1st laird, vi. 217.
—— —— his wife, Mary Stewart, i. 18; vi. 217.
—— —— Sir William, 4th laird, vi. 224; vii. 276.
—— —— his wife, Elizabeth Leslie, vii. 276.
—— —— William, 5th laird, ii. 181; iii. 186; v. 351, 395.
—— —— his 1st wife, Agnes Stewart, v. 351.
—— —— his 2nd wife, Margaret Campbell, v. 502.
—— of Edmonston, Andrew, iv. 476.
—— —— David, vii. 579.
—— —— Sir David, ii. 144.
—— —— his wife, Jonet Napier, ii. 144.
—— —— Elizabeth, wife of P. Blacatir, ii. 2.
—— —— Sir James, ii. 2; iv. 85, 451; vi. 407.
—— —— his 1st wife, Isobel Forrester, iv. 85.
—— —— his 2nd wife, Janet Napier, vi. 407.
—— —— Sir John, i. 16.
—— —— his wife, Isobel Stewart, i. 16; iii. 157.
—— —— Sir John, ii. 68.
—— —— his wife, Janet Lawson, ii. 68.
—— —— John, v. 290.
—— —— his wife, Margaret Maitland, v. 290 *bis*.
—— —— John, vii. 339.
—— —— his wife, Agnes Ker, vii. 339.
—— —— Margaret, wife of Sir Walter Ogilvy, ii. 2.
—— of Ednam, David, v. 290.
—— —— James, iii. 281; v. 290.
—— —— his wife, Katharine Home, iii. 281.
—— —— John, v. 290.
—— —— his wife, Margaret Maitland, v. 290.
—— —— John, vii. 72.
—— —— William, v. 290.
—— of Newton, James, vii. 203.
—— of Tulliallan, Jonet, *error for* Margaret, wife of Sir Walter Ogilvy, ii. 1.
—— of Woolmet, David, vi. 10.
—— —— his wife, Alison Hume, vi. 10; vii. 378.
—— —— Patrick, vi. 372.
—— —— his wife, Jean Douglas, vi. 372.
—— Alison, wife of Archibald Napier of Woolmet, vi. 416.
—— Christian, wife of (1) 2nd lord Ross of Halkhead, and (2) George Knollis, vii. 251.
—— Elizabeth, wife of John Montgomerie, master of Eglintoun, iii. 435.
—— Janet, wife of Adam Home, iv. 451.
—— Janet, wife of 1st earl of Montrose, vi. 225.
—— Katharine, wife of David Murray of Alich, i. 461.
Edmonston(e, Margaret, wife of Sir Alex. Home of Halyburton, iv. 476.
—— Margaret, wife of George Scott of Synton, vii. 72.
—— Margaret, wife of John Somerville, viii. 6 *n*.
—— Mariot, wife of Sir J. Campbell of Glenurchy, ii. 181.
—— Marjorie, wife of (1) Mungo Graham of Orchill, and (2) Sir John Maxwell of Pollok, vi. 229.
—— Mary, alleged wife of Patrick Hume, vi. 3 *n*.
—— Mary, wife of (1) John Cunningham of Cunninghamhead, and (2) Sir W. Graham of Braco, vi. 238.
Edmund, prince of Cumbria, son of Malcolm 'Ceannmor,' i. 2.
—— of Beanley, uncle of Gospatric, 2nd earl of Dunbar, iii. 243, 246.
—— son of Bonde, vii. 577.
Ednam of Murraythwaite, Elizabeth, wife of John Murray, i. 217.
Edulph of Gillemmorestun *or* Eddleston, son of Uthred, iii. 87.
Edward I., King of England, i. 7; iv. 9, 12, 509; v. 578; viii. 562 *n*.
Edward II., i. 9; iv. 12; viii. 562 *n*.
Edward III., i. 7.
Edward the Ætheling, i. 2.
—— son of Malcolm 'Ceannmor,' i. 2.
—— of Edlingham and Belton, 3rd son of Gospatric, 2nd earl of Dunbar, iii. 248.
—— —— his wife, Sibilla, iii. 248.
—— the constable of David I., vi. 285.
Edwardes of Prinknash Park, Thomas Dyer, vii. 310.
—— Sir Herbert Benjamin, major-general K.C.B., K.C.S.I., iii. 413.
—— —— his wife, Emma Sidney, iii. 413.
—— Noëlle Lucy Martha Dyer, wife of 19th earl of Rothes, vii. 310.
Edwards of Welham Grove, Francis, iv. 385.
—— —— his wife, Anna Margaret Vernatti, iv. 385.
—— Elizabeth, wife of (1) Charles Graydon, (2) Alex. Sutherland of Kinminitie, and (3) Sir K. Mackenzie of Grandvale, iii. 204; ix. 63, 69.
—— Gerard Anne, iv. 386.
—— —— his wife, Jane Noel, iv. 387.
—— Gerard Noel, iv. 388.
—— —— his wife, Diana Middleton, baroness Barham, vi. 180.
—— John, Dublin, ii. 212.
—— Mary Theresa, wife of sixth earl of Breadalbane, ii. 212.
Edwards-Hamilton, Anne, 3rd son of 4th duke of Hamilton, iv. 386.
Edwards-Noel, Gerard Noel, iv. 388.
Edwin, earl of Mercia, iii. 241.

Edwin of Dunraven and Llanvihangel, Charles, iv. 391.
—— —— his wife, Charlotte Hamilton, iv. 391.
—— Elizabeth, wife of Chas. Dalrymple, iii. 42.
—— John, husband of Elizabeth Bradshaigh, iii. 42.
—— Martha, wife of Sir Hew Dalrymple, ii. 31; viii. 130.
Edzell, Sir David Lindsay, senator of the College of Justice; lord, i. 513.
Effingham, Francis (Howard), 1st earl of, vii. 512.
—— Kenneth Alexander (Howard), 1st earl of, vii. 225.
—— —— his wife, Charlotte Primrose, vii. 225.
Effrick, alleged wife of Sir Gillespie Cambel, i. 319.
Egerton of Betley, Randolph, major-general, iii. 399.
—— —— his wife, Elizabeth Murray, iii. 399.
—— of Ellesmere, Francis Leveson Gore, viii. 361.
—— of Newborough, Charles, iii. 399.
—— —— his wife, Elizabeth Murray, iii. 399.
—— Cecely Louisa, wife of 6th earl of Selkirk, vii. 524.
—— Penelope, wife of Sir R. Napier of Luton Hoo, ii. 583.
Eggilvyn, Patrick de, i. 107.
Egius of Markinch, iv. 5; viii. 475.
EGLINTON, MONTGOMERIE, EARL OF, iii. 421-465.
Eglinton, Alexander, sixth earl of, iii. 442, 445; viii. 591.
—— —— his 1st wife, Anna Livingstone, iii. 446; v. 446; ix. 81.
—— —— his 2nd wife, Margaret Scott, ii. 233; iii. 446; vii. 255, 257.
—— Alexander, eighth earl of, iii. 451, 452.
—— —— his 1st wife, Elizabeth Crichton, iii. 236, 453; ix. 71.
—— —— his 2nd wife, Grace Popeley, iii. 453.
—— —— his 3rd wife, Katharine St. Quintin, iii. 454.
—— Alexander, ninth earl of, iii. 353, 354, 454.
—— —— his 1st wife, Margaret Cochrane, iii. 352, 455; ix. 77.
—— —— his 2nd wife, Anne Gordon, i. 89; iii. 456; ix. 5.
—— —— his 3rd wife, Susanna Kennedy, ii. 491; iii. 456.
—— Alexander, tenth earl of, iii. 456, 458.
—— Archibald, eleventh earl of, iii. 456, 459.
—— —— his 1st wife, Jean Lindsay, iii. 41, 460.
—— —— his 2nd wife, Frances Twisden, iii. 460; ix. 81 *bis*.
Eglinton, Archibald William, thirteenth earl of, iii. 462; viii. 560 *n.*, 605.
—— —— his 1st wife, Theresa Newcomen, iii. 463.
—— —— his 2nd wife, Adela Caroline Hariet Capel, iii. 463.
—— Archibald William, fourteenth earl of, iii. 463.
—— —— his wife, Sophia Adelaide Theodosia Worsley, iii. 463.
—— George Arnulf, fifteenth earl of, iii. 463, 464; viii. 592.
—— —— his wife, Janet Lucretia Cuninghame, iii. 464.
—— Hugh, first earl of, ii. 511 *n.*; iii. 432, 434; ix. 19.
—— —— his wife, Helen Campbell, i. 335; iii. 435.
—— Hugh, second earl of, iii. 436, 438; v. 153.
—— —— his wife, Marion Seton, ii. 108; iii. 439; v. 154; viii. 581.
—— Hugh, third earl of, iii. 439, 440; v. 156.
—— —— his 1st wife, Jane Hamilton, iii. 441; iv. 370.
—— —— his 2nd wife, Agnes Drummond, iii. 441; vii. 44.
—— Hugh, fourth earl of, iii. 441, 442; iv. 241; v. 162.
—— —— his 1st wife, Egidia Boyd, iii. 443; v. 162.
—— —— his 2nd wife, Helen Kennedy, iii. 443.
—— Hugh, fifth earl of, i. 541; iii. 443; iv. 244; v. 162, 167, 356, 454; ix. 80.
—— —— his wife, Margaret Montgomerie, iii. 442, 444; ix. 81.
—— Hugh, seventh earl of, i. 567, 569; iii. 446, 450; vii. 298.
—— —— his 1st wife, Anne Hamilton, iii. 451; iv. 375.
—— —— his 2nd wife, Mary Leslie, iii. 451; vii. 299.
—— Hugh, twelfth earl of, iii. 449, 460.
—— —— his wife, Eleonora Hamilton, iii. 461.
—— master of, Archibald, eldest son of John, master of Eglinton, iii. 435.
—— master of, John, eldest son of 2nd lord Montgomerie, iii. 435.
—— —— his wife, Elizabeth Edmonstoun, iii. 435.
Eglinton of Ardrossan and Eglinton, Elizabeth, wife of John Montgomerie of Eaglesham, iii. 428 *bis*.
—— of Eglinton, Bryce de, v. 137.
—— —— Sir Hugh, iii. 428 *bis*., 432; vii. 528.
—— —— his 1st wife, Agnes More, iii. 428 *n.*
—— —— his 2nd wife, Egidia Stewart, i. 15; iii. 428 *n.*; ix. 80.
EGLISMALDIE, CARNEGIE, LORD, vi. 494-508.
Eglismaldie, John, first lord, vi. 494.

Egmont, John (Perceval), 2nd earl of, viii. 229.
Egremont, Alice Maria (Wyndham), wife of Hans Maurice, count Bruhl von Martinskirk; countess of, vii. 84.
— George (Wyndham), 4th earl of, vii. 84.
— William, the 'Boy of,' iii. 245.
Eigge, William, Edinburgh, ix. 130.
— — his wife, Jean Donaldson, ix. 130.
Ela, wife of Duncan, 5th earl of Fife. iv. 7.
ELBOTLE, MAXWELL, LORD, iii. 126-131.
Elbotle, James, lord, iii. 129.
Elchies, Patrick Grant, senator of the college of Justice, lord, vii. 484.
ELCHO, WEMYSS, LORD, viii. 500-518.
Elcho, David, eldest son of 1st earl of Wemyss; styled lord, viii. 502.
— — his 1st wife, Anna Balfour, i. 544; viii. 503.
— David, son of 2nd earl of Wemyss; styled lord, viii. 504.
— David, son of Margaret, countess of Wemyss; styled lord, viii. 506.
— — his 1st wife, Anna Douglas, vii. 140; viii. 507.
— David, eldest son of 3rd earl of Wemyss; styled lord, viii. 508 *bis*.
— David, eldest son of 4th earl of Wemyss; author of the *Journal*; styled lord, viii. 509, 513; ix. 168.
— Francis, son of 5th earl of Wemyss; styled lord, viii. 514.
— — his wife, Susan Tracy Keck, viii. 514.
— Francis, son of above; styled lord, viii. 515.
— — his wife, Margaret Campbell, viii. 515.
— Francis, M.P., col. London Scottish Rifles, styled lord, viii. 517.
— — his wife, Anne Frederica Anson, viii. 517.
— John, first lord, viii. 500.
— Hugo Richard, M.P., styled lord, viii. 217.
— — his wife, Mary Constance Wyndham, viii. 517.
ELCHO, WEMYSS, LORD WEMYSS OF, viii. 499-518.
Eld of Seighford, Richard, i. 402.
— Dorothy, wife of Edward Aston, i. 402.
Elen, wife of (1) Malcolm, earl of Fife, and (2) Donald, 6th earl of Mar, v. 578.
Elena, wife of Sir Andrew Livingston, sheriff of Lanark, v. 422, 423.
ELGIN, BRUCE, EARL OF, iii. 466-497.
Elgin, Charles, fourth earl of, iii. 481, 491; v. 199.
— — his 1st wife, Anne Saville, iii. 482.
— — his 2nd wife, Juliana Boyle, iii. 482.
— — his 3rd wife, Caroline Campbell, i. 385; iii. 482.
Elgin, Charles, fifth earl of, iii. 491.
— — his wife, Martha White, iii. 491.
— James, eighth earl of, iii. 494.
— — his 1st wife, Elizabeth Mary Cumming-Bruce, iii. 495.
— — his 2nd wife, Mary Louisa Lambton, iii. 495.
— Robert, second earl of, iii. 478, 486.
— — his wife, Diana Grey, iii. 478.
— Thomas, first earl of, iii. 477.
— — his 1st wife, Anne Chichester, iii. 478.
— — his 2nd wife, Diana Cecil, iii. 478.
— Thomas, third earl of, iii. 479.
— — his 1st wife, Elizabeth Seymour, iii. 480.
— — his 2nd wife, Charlotte d'Argenteau, iii. 480.
— Thomas, seventh earl of, iii. 491, 492.
— — his 1st wife, Mary Hamilton Nisbet, iii. 493.
— — his 2nd wife, Elizabeth Oswald, iii. 493.
— Victor Alexander, ninth earl of, iii. 495, 496.
— — his 1st wife, Constance Mary Carnegie, iii. 496; viii. 91.
— William Robert, sixth earl of, iii. 492.
ELGIN OF ELGIN, BRUCE, BARON, iii. 495-497.
Elgin of Elgin, James, first baron, iii. 495.
— — Victor Alexander, second baron, iii. 496.
Elgiva, *or* Aelgifu, wife of Uchtred, earl of Northumberland, iii. 241.
ELIBANK, MURRAY, LORD, iii. 498-524.
Elibank, Alexander, fourth lord, iii. 512.
— — his wife, Elizabeth Stirling, iii. 512.
— Alexander, seventh lord, iii. 513, 520.
— — his wife, Mary Clara Montolieu, iii. 520.
— Alexander, eighth lord, iii. 521.
— — his wife, Janet Oliphant, iii. 521; vi. 562.
— Alexander Oliphant, ninth lord, iii. 522.
— his wife, Emily Maria Montgomery, iii. 522.
— George, sixth lord, iii. 512, 514, 519.
— — his wife, Isabel Mackenzie, iii. 83, 519.
— Montolieu Fox Oliphant, tenth lord, iii. 523.
— — his wife, Blanche Alice Scott, iii. 523.
— Patrick, first lord, iii. 507.
— — his 1st wife, Margaret Hamilton, iii. 508.
— — his 2nd wife, Elizabeth Dundas, iii. 508.
— — his 3rd wife, Helen Lindsay, iii. 509.
— — his 4th wife, Agnes Nicolson, iii. 510.
— — his 5th wife, Katharine Weir, iii. 510; ix. 84.

Elibank, Patrick, second lord, iii. 510.
—— —— his wife, Elizabeth Stewart, iii. 510; viii. 405.
—— Patrick, third lord, iii. 511.
—— —— his wife, Anna Burnet, iii. 511, 542.
—— Patrick, fifth lord, iii. 512, 514, 518; vi. 561 *n*.
—— —— his wife, Maria Margaritta de Jonge d'Ellemeet, iii. 519.
ELIBANK OF ELIBANK, MURRAY, VISCOUNT, ix. 84.
Elibank, Montolieu Fox Oliphant, first viscount, iii. 523.
ELIBANK, MURRAY, BARON MURRAY OF, ix. 84.
Elibank, master of, Alexander William Charles Oliphant Murray, iii. 523.
—— —— his wife, Hilda Louisa Janey Wolfe-Murray, iii. 523.
Elinga of Zuydelynde, Pieter Emmanuel, vi. 560.
—— Marie Magdeleine, wife of (1) Louis François de l'Église, and (2) William, 9th lord Oliphant, vi. 559.
Eliot of Port Eliot, Richard, i. 63.
—— —— his wife, Harriet Craggs, i. 63.
—— Alicia, wife of 17th earl of Erroll, iii. 583.
—— Edward Craggs-Eliot, lord, i. 63.
—— Samuel, Antigua, iii. 583.
Elizabeth, wife of (1) Wm. Clutton, and (2) Charles Gordon of Fyvie, i. 92.
—— wife of Sir Robert Crichton of Sanquhar, iii. 221.
—— illeg. dau. of King Henry I. of England, and alleged wife of Fergus, prince of Galloway, iv. 136.
—— wife of Sir Wm. Stewart, 2nd of Garlies, iv. 150.
—— wife of James Hamilton of Schawfield, Whitecamp and Kirkhope, iv. 348.
—— wife of (1) * Forrester of Haining, and (2) Thos. Livingston of Haining, v. 437.
—— wife of (1) John Gordon, and (2) Sir Robert Livingston, iv. 514.
—— wife of (1) Sir Wm. Douglas of Liddesdale, and (2) Hugh Dacre, vi. 342.
—— wife of Reginald Graham of Pickhill, vii. 104.
—— wife of Robert Maitland of Queensberry vii. 116.
—— wife of Sir Robert Sempill of Eliotstoun and Southannan, vii. 529.
—— 2nd wife of John Dalrymple, younger of Stair, viii. 116.
—— wife of (1) col. Sir Geo. Cunningham, and (2) Wm. Sandilands of Hilderstoun, viii. 391.
Ellem of Renton, David, iii. 282.
—— —— Janet, wife of Patrick Home, iii. 282.

* Name unknown.

Ellenborough, Edward (Law), 1st earl of, ii. 566.
Ellerker of Risby, Sir Ralph, iii. 292.
—— —— his wife, Katharine Constable, iii. 292.
—— Ralph, iii. 293.
—— —— his wife, Frances Skipwith, iii. 293.
Ellesmere, Thomas (Egerton), 1st baron, ii. 558.
—— Francis (Egerton), 1st earl of, viii. 362.
—— —— his wife, Harriet Katharine Greville, viii. 362.
Elletson, Roger Hope, v. 200.
—— —— his wife, Anne Eliza Gammon, v. 199.
Elliot of Braidley, Martin, vii. 74.
—— of Dinlayhyre, William, vii. 379.
—— —— his wife, Margaret Rutherfurd, vii. 379.
—— of Falnash, *, vii. 75.
—— —— his wife, Esther Scott, vii. 75.
—— of Greenwells, Andrew, ii. 526; viii. 86.
—— —— his wife, Elizabeth Plumstead, ii. 526.
—— —— Elizabeth, wife of 1st earl Cathcart, ii. 526.
—— of Horsliehill, Gilbert, vii. 74.
—— of Lariston, William, ii. 232.
—— —— his wife, Mary Scott, ii. 232.
—— of Minto, Sir Gilbert, viii. 146.
—— —— his wife, Agnes Dalrymple, viii. 146.
—— of Redheugh, Robert, ii. 172.
—— —— his 2nd wife, Jean Stewart, ii. 172.
—— of Stobs, Sir Gilbert, 'with the gowden gartins,' vii. 75.
—— —— his wife, Margaret Scott, vii. 75.
—— —— Sir Gilbert. 1st bart., ii. 594.
—— —— his 1st wife, Isobel Cranstoun, ii. 594.
—— —— Sir William, 2nd bart., iii. 511.
—— of Wolflee *or* Woollie, Cornelius, iii. 551.
—— —— Sir Gilbert, ii. 595.
—— —— James, W.S., iii. 81.
—— —— his wife, Caroline Hunter, iii. 81.
—— Agnes Macrae, wife of Hew Manners Dalrymple, viii. 139.
—— Agnes Murray, wife of Sir David Carnegie of Southesk, viii. 86.
—— Edwin Day, Vermont, U.S.A., i. 145.
—— Elizabeth, wife of 9th earl of Northesk, vi. 507.
—— Fannie Foster, wife of David S. Barclay Allardice, i. 145.
—— Frederick Boilleau, viii. 90.
—— —— his wife, Charlotte Carnegie, viii. 89.
—— Sir George, admiral R.N., K.C.B., vi. 506; viii. 90, 235.
—— George, rear-admiral R.N., vi. 507.
—— George, H.M. commissariot department, viii. 139.

* Name unknown.

Elliot, Georgina Maria, wife of 8th earl of Northesk, vi. 506.
— Hester, wife of rev. A. Clerk, ii. 172 *n.*
— Katharine, wife of admiral Sir J. R. Drummond, viii. 234.
— *, lieut.-colonel, iii. 123.
— — his wife, Frances Nassau d'Auverquerque, iii. 123.
Elliott, Edmund, Jacobite, vii. 106.
— Janet Hyndford, wife of (1) Sir J. Gibson Carmichael, and (2) John, 12th lord Elphinstone, iii. 551.
Ellis, Elizabeth, wife of col. Archd. Douglas, ix. 151.
— Thomas, Perth, ix. 151.
Ellison of Hebburn, Cuthbert, viii. 212.
— Louisa, wife of 4th earl of Mansfield, viii. 212.
ELPHINSTONE, ELPHINSTONE, LORD, iii. 525-554.
Elphinstone, Alexander, first lord, iii. 530.
— — his wife, Elizabeth Barlow, iii. 531.
— Alexander, second lord, iii. 531.
— — his wife, Katharine Erskine, iii. 532; v. 612.
— Alexander, fourth lord, iii. 536.
— — his wife, Jane Livingston, iii. 537; v. 443.
— Alexander, fifth lord, iii. 538, 540; v. 619.
— — his wife, Elizabeth *or* Margaret Drummond, iii. 541; vii. 48.
— Alexander, sixth lord, iii. 538, 541.
— — his wife, Lilias Elphinstone, iii. 541, 542.
— Alexander, seventh lord, iii. 542.
— — his wife, Anne Burnet, iii. 542.
— Charles, ninth lord, iii. 544.
— — his wife, Elizabeth Primrose, iii. 545; vii. 110.
— Charles, tenth lord, iii. 388, 545.
— — his wife, Clementina Fleming of Biggar and Cumbernauld, iii. 545; viii. 555.
— John, eighth lord, iii. 542.
— — his wife, Isabel Maitland, iii. 543; v. 309.
— John, eleventh lord, iii. 546, 549; vi. 64.
— — his wife, Anne Ruthven, iii. 550; vii. 389.
— John, twelfth lord, iii. 551.
— — his wife, Janet Hyndford Elliott, iii. 551.
— John, thirteenth lord, iii. 551.
— John, fourteenth lord, iii. 550, 552.
— Robert, third lord, iii. 532, 534.
— — his wife, Margaret Drummond, iii. 535.
— Sidney Herbert, sixteenth lord, iii. 553.
— — his wife, Mary Frances Bowes-Lyon, viii. 316.

* Name unknown.

Elphinstone, William, fifteenth lord, iii. 547, 552.
— — his wife, Constance Euphemia Woronzow Murray, iii. 394, 553.
— master of, Alexander, eldest son of 3rd lord Elphinstone, ii. 392; iii. 535, 537; ix. 130.
— master of, James Drummond, eldest son of 15th lord Elphinstone, iii. 553.
ELPHINSTONE OF ELPHINSTONE, ELPHINSTONE, BARON, iii. 552.
Elphinstone of Elphinstone, John, first baron, iii. 552.
ELPHINSTONE OF ELPHINSTONE, ELPHINSTONE, BARON, iii. 553.
Elphinstone of Elphinstone, Sidney Herbert, second baron, iii. 553.
— — William, first baron, iii. 552.
ELPHINSTONE, LORD BALMERINOCH *or* BALMERINO, i. 556-575.
ELPHINSTONE, LORD COUPAR, ii. 576-577.
ELPHINSTONE, LORD ELPHINSTONE, iii. 525-554.
ELPHINSTONE, BARON ELPHINSTONE OF ELPHINSTONE, iii. 552-554.
ELPHINSTONE, VISCOUNT KEITH, iii. 548-549.
ELPHINSTONE, BARON KEITH OF BANHEATH, iii. 548-549.
ELPHINSTONE, BARON KEITH OF STONEHAVEN, MARISCHAL, iii. 548-549.
Elphinstone of Airth, Elizabeth, wife of William Dundas of Blair, iii. 544.
— — Sir John, iii. 529; vi. 543.
— — his 2nd wife, Margaret Oliphant, iii. 529; vi. 542.
— — his 3rd wife, Elizabeth Cuninghame, iii. 529; vi. 543.
— of Baberton, Sir John, 2nd son of 3rd lord Elphinstone, iii. 534.
— of Balnaborth, James, 2nd son of 4th lord Elphinstone, iii. 538.
— — his 1st wife, Katharine Gordon, iii. 538.
— — his 2nd wife, Helen Forbes, iii. 538.
— of Bannockburn, John, 7th son of 4th lord Elphinstone, iii. 539.
— — his wife, Barbara Gordon, iii. 539.
— of Barnes, James, 2nd son of 4th lord Elphinstone, iii. 538, 541.
— of Blythswood, George, vii. 549.
— — Sir George, provost of Glasgow, lord justice-clerk, ii. 36; iv. 584; v. 167, 170.
— — his wife, Agnes Boyd, v. 167.
— of Calderhall, Richard, iii. 540, 543.
— — his wife, Jean Bruce, iii. 540.
— — William, ancestor of the family of, iii. 533.
— — his wife, Janet Henderson, iii. 533.
— of Carberry, John Fullerton, H.E.I.C.S., iii. 546, 547.

lphinstone of Carberry, Wm., H.E.I.C.S., 3rd son of 10th lord Elphinstone, iii. 546.
—— —— his wife, Elizabeth Fullerton of Carberry, iii. 546.
—— of Carnock, Alexander, iii. 531.
—— —— his wife, Elizabeth Barlow, iii. 530.
—— of Chapelton, Isabella or Elizabeth, wife of (1) David Lindsay, (2) Peter Colquhoun, (3) Robert Maxwell, and (4) David Stewart, iii. 530; ix. 84.
—— of Chirriemurelands, James, iii. 538.
—— of Congarth, Robert, iii. 534.
—— —— his wife, Margaret Drummond, iii. 534.
—— of Cragorth, Robert, iii. 534.
—— of Craigrossy, Sir John, iii. 529.
—— of Dunlugas, Alexander, iii. 531.
—— —— Alexander, ix. 85.
—— —— his wife, Jean Elphinstone, iii. 538; ix. 85.
—— of Elieston, James, 3rd son of 2nd lord Elphinstone, iii. 533.
—— —— his 1st wife, Janet Leslie, iii. 533; vii. 289.
—— —— his second wife, Agnes Ramsay, iii. 533.
—— of Elphinstone, Agnes, wife of Sir Gilbert Johnstone, i. 236; iii. 527.
—— —— Alexander, 2nd laird, iii. 526.
—— —— Alexander, 3rd laird, iii. 526.
—— —— Sir Alexander, 6th laird, iii. 527.
—— —— Alexander, elder son of Sir John E., iii. 530; v. 609.
—— —— John de, 1st laird, iii. 525, 526.
—— —— his wife, Marjorie Erth, iii. 526.
—— —— Sir John, vi. 54.
—— —— his wife, Margaret Keith, vi. 54.
—— —— Richard, iii. 540, 543.
—— —— his wife, Jean Bruce, iii. 540.
—— —— Sir William, 4th laird, iii. 526.
—— —— his wife, Mary Leslie, iii. 526.
—— —— William de, 5th laird, iii. 527.
—— —— his wife, Margaret Hepburne, ix. 84.
—— of Erthbeg, Alexander de, iii. 526.
—— —— Henry, iii. 528.
—— —— Sir John, iii. 528.
—— of Fordel, Alexander, iii. 531.
—— of Gargunnock, Alexander, iii. 528.
—— —— Alexander, iii. 531.
—— —— his wife, Elizabeth Barlow, iii. 530.
—— of Gorbals, Sir George, ii. 36.
—— of Inverdovat, James, 3rd son of 2nd lord Elphinstone, iii. 533.
—— —— his 1st wife, Jean Leslie, iii. 533; vii. 289.
—— —— his 2nd wife, Agnes Ramsay. iii. 533.
—— of Invernochty, Alexander, iii. 530.
—— —— James, 3rd son of 3rd lord Elphinstone, iii. 535.
Elphinstone of Kildrummy, Alexander, iii. 530; v. 619.
—— of Logie, Sir James, receiver-general, ii. 23.
—— of Logie Elphinstone, Sir James, last bart., viii. 132.
—— —— Mary, wife of lieut.-gen. Robert Dalrymple-Horn of Horn, viii. 132.
—— of Pettinain, Alexander, grandson of 3rd lord Elphinstone, ii. 392; iii. 540.
—— of Pittendreich, Henry, 2nd laird, iii. 527.
—— —— his wife, Jean Cuninghame, iii. 527.
—— —— Sir John, 3rd laird, iii. 528; v. 393, 395; vi. 543.
—— —— his 1st wife, Euphemia * of Stirkshaw, iii. 529.
—— —— his 2nd wife, Margaret Oliphant, iii. 529.
—— —— his 3rd wife, Elizabeth Cuninghame, iii. 529.
—— —— William, 1st laird, iii. 527; v. 392.
—— of Plean, Alexander, iii. 531.
—— of Quarrell, Alexander, iii. 531.
—— —— his wife, Elizabeth Barlow, iii. 531.
—— —— James, 2nd son of 4th lord Elphinstone, iii. 538.
—— —— his 1st wife, Katharine Gordon, iii. 538; ix. 85.
—— —— his 2nd wife, Helen Forbes, iii. 538.
—— —— Michael, 9th son of 4th lord Elphinstone, iii. 539.
—— —— his wife, Mary Bruce, iii. 539.
—— —— Sir Robert, iii. 539, 542.
—— of Quhytlaw, Sir John, 2nd son of 3rd lord Elphinstone, iii. 535.
—— of Schank, John, ii. 571.
—— of Rossie, Alexander, eldest son of 4th lord Elphinstone, iii. 540.
—— —— his wife, Elizabeth Drummond, iii. 541.
—— of Easter Rossy, Robert, iii. 534.
—— of Scotstoun, Alexander, iii. 528.
—— of Selmes, Sir John, 2nd son of 3rd lord Elphinstone, iii. 535.
—— —— his wife, Giles Elphinstone of Selmes, iii. 536.
—— —— Lawrence, ancestor of the family of, iii. 527, 535.
—— —— William, iii. 535, 536.
—— of Stirkfield and Stirkshaws, Alexander, iii. 530.
—— of Stirkshaw, Sir John, iii. 528, 529.
—— —— his wife, Euphemia *, iii. 529.
—— of Trosness, William, sheriff-depute of Orkney, iii. 533; ix. 84.
—— —— his wife, Janet Henderson, iii. 533.
—— of Warthill, Alexander, iii. 542.
—— —— John, iii. 539.
—— —— his wife, Barbara Gordon, iii. 539.

* Name unknown.

Elphinstone, of Woodside, v. 165.
— Agnes, wife of 1st lord Ogilvie of Deskford, iii. 536; iv. 26.
— Agnes, wife of John, 12th earl of Sutherland, iii. 539; viii. 347.
— Alexander. 5th son of 4th lord Balmerino, i. 570.
— Alexander, 2nd son of Sir Wm. E. of Elphinstone, iii. 527.
— Alexander, 4th son of 2nd lord Elphinstone, iii. 533.
— Alexander, inf. son of 1st lord Balmerino, ix. 33.
— Anna, contr. to Thos. Kinnaird of Culbin, iii. 538; ix. 85.
— Anna, wife of Walter, 6th lord Torphichen, iii. 542; viii. 393.
— Anna, dau. of 8th lord Elphinstone, iii. 544.
— Annas, wife of John, 12th earl of Sutherland, iii. 539; viii. 347.
— Anne, dau. of 4th lord Balmerino, i. 570.
— Anne Stuart, dau. of 11th lord Elphinstone, iii. 551.
— Archibald, 5th son of 9th lord Elphinstone, iii. 545.
— Barbara, wife of John Hamilton, i. 562.
— Charles, 2nd son of 10th lord Elphinstone, iii. 546.
— Charles, captain H.M.S. *Greyhound*, iii. 546.
— Charles, admiral R.N., M.P., governor of Greenwich Hospital, iii. 550.
— — his wife, Catalina Paulina Alessandro, iii. 550.
— Christian, wife of Sir Thos. Urquhart, iii. 540.
— Clementina, wife of James, lord Perth, iii. 549; vii. 59.
— Clementina Fleming, dau. of 11th lord Elphinstone, iii. 551.
— Egidia, wife of Sir James Sempill of Beltries, vii. 549.
— Eleanor, dau. of 9th lord Elphinstone, iii. 545; ix. 25.
— Eleanora, wife of William Adam of Woodstoun and Blairadam, iii. 549.
— Elizabeth, wife of John Campbell of Mamore, i. 381; iii. 544.
— Elizabeth, wife of Heliseus of Kinninmonth, iii. 527; vii. 272.
— Elizabeth, wife of Sir David Somerville, iii. 531.
— Elizabeth, dau. of 2nd lord Elphinstone, iii. 534.
— Elizabeth, wife of Robert Innes, iii. 536; vii. 356.
— Elizabeth, dau. of 5th lord Elphinstone, iii. 540.
— Elizabeth, mistress of Sir James Hamilton of Finnart, iv. 362.
Elphinstone, Elizabeth Mackenzie, dau. of 11th lord Elphinstone, iii. 551.
— Ellonas, dau. of 9th lord Elphinstone, iii. 545.
— Euphemia, mistress of King James v., and wife of John Bruce of Cultmalundie, i. 24; iii. 531.
— George, rector of Scots College at Rome, and Douai, iii. 536; ix. 85.
— George Keith, admiral, C.B., iii. 548; vi. 64, 269.
— Grizel, wife of capt. Woodgrave Gascoigne, iii. 545.
— Helen, wife of (1) Sir W. Cockburn, and (2) Mr. Henry Rollok, iii. 540; vii. 187.
— Hugh, master of Balmerino, i. 570.
— Innes, 6th son of 4th lord Elphinstone, iii. 538.
— Isobel, wife of James Hamilton of Haggs, iii. 534.
— James, commendator of Balmerino *or* Coupar, i. 557; iii. 536; v. 6.
— James, 4th son of Sir Wm. E. of Elphinstone, iii. 527.
— James, eldest son of Henry E. of Pittendreich, iii. 527.
— — his wife, Isabella Bruce, iii. 528.
— James, 2nd son of 1st lord Elphinstone, iii. 531.
— James, 4th son of 8th lord Elphinstone, iii. 543.
— James, R.N., 3rd son of 9th lord Elphinstone, iii. 545.
— James, eldest son of 4th lord Balmerino; master of Balmerino, i. 569; ix. 34.
— James Drummond Buller-Fullerton, H.E.I.C.S., lieut.-colonel, iii. 547.
— — his 1st wife, Diana Maria Clavering, iii. 547.
— — his 2nd wife, Anna Maria Buller, iii. 547.
— James Ruthven, H.E.I.C.S., iii. 550.
— Janet, wife of (1) Robert Leslie of Rosmarkie, and (2) Alex. Bruce of Earlshall, iii. 534; vii. 288.
— Janet, wife of (1) P. Barclay of Tolly, and (2) Jas. Stewart of Ryland, iii. 536; ix. 85.
— Jean, wife of 7th earl of Moray, i. 570; vi. 324.
— Jean, contr. to John Kinross, iii. 530; ix. 84.
— Jean, contr. to Alex. Elphinstone of Dunlugus, iii. 538; ix. 85.
— Jean, wife of Arthur, 10th lord Forbes, iii. 540; iv. 60 *bis*.
— Jean, dau. of 5th lord Elphinstone, iii. 541.
—[1]Jean, wife of Sir Robt. Milne, ix. 85.
— John, bailie of Glasgow, iii. 527.

Elphinstone, John, canon of Aberdeen, rector of Innernochty, iii. 473, 532.
—— —— his wife, Agnes Bruce, iii. 473, 532.
—— John, legtd. son of James E. of Elieston and Inverdovat, iii. 533.
—— John, 4th son of 3rd lord Elphinstone, iii. 535, 536.
—— John, 6th son of 8th lord Elphinstone, iii. 543, 544.
—— John, 2nd son of 9th lord Elphinstone, iii. 545.
—— —— his wife, Marjory Fleming, iii. 545.
—— John, keeper of Kildrummy Castle, vii. 185.
—— Keith, wife of David Erskine of Cardross, iii. 551.
—— Lilias, wife of 6th lord Elphinstone, iii. 541, 542.
—— Lockhart, 4th son of 10th lord Elphinstone, iii. 548.
—— Margaret, wife of Andrew, 2nd lord Fraser, i. 562; iv. 115.
—— Margaret, wife of Sir John Preston, i. 570; ix. 34.
—— Margaret, wife of John Livingston of Dunipace, iii. 534.
—— Margaret, wife of John Cuninghame of Drumquhassell, iii. 536.
—— Margaret, wife of Sir John Bruce of Airth, iii. 540.
—— Margaret, wife of (1) Geo. Leslie of Balquhain, (2) Sir Jas. Gordon of Park, and (3) John Fullerton of Dudwick, iii. 544.
—— Margaret, wife of Auguste Charles Joseph, Count de Flahault, iii. 549.
—— Margaret, wife of Sir Jas. Gordon of Park, iv. 65.
—— Margaret, wife of Robert Lindsay, ix. 31.
—— Marie, ix. 31.
—— Marion, wife of Geo. Norvell of Boghall, ix. 85.
—— Marjorie, wife of Francis Fraser of Kinmundy, i. 562; iv. 113.
—— Marjory, wife of Robert Drummond of Carnock, iii. 534.
—— Mary, dau. of 1st lord Elphinstone, iii. 531.
—— Mary, wife of Thos. Buchan of Cairnbulg, iii. 544.
—— Mary, dau. of 10th lord Elphinstone, iii. 549.
—— Sir Michael, master of the household of King James VI., iii. 533.
—— Michael, ix. 31.
—— Mountstuart, D.C.L., governor of Bombay, iii. 550.
—— Norman, 3rd son of Sir Wm. E. of Elphinstone, iii. 527.
—— Primrose, dau. of 10th lord Elphinstone, iii. 549.
Elphinstone, Primrose, wife of Alexander, 9th earl of Home, iii. 545; iv. 481.
—— Robert, rector of Kincardine, iii. 528, 531, 532.
—— Robert, illeg. son of 1st lord Balmerino, ix. 34.
—— Thomas, brother of 1st lord Elphinstone, iii. 528, 529, 532.
—— William, bishop of Aberdeen, ii. 6; iii. 527; v. 395, 638.
—— William, canon of Glasgow, archdeacon of Teviotdale, iii. 527.
—— William, rector of Clatt, canon of Aberdeen, iii. 528, 532.
—— William, 5th son of 3rd lord Elphinstone, iii. 536.
—— William, 3rd son of 4th lord Elphinstone, iii. 538.
—— William, ensign in col. Prestoun's regiment, iii. 544.
—— William, H.E.I.C.S., iii. 546; vi. 64.
—— —— his wife, Elizabeth Fullerton of Carberry, iii. 546.
—— William George Keith, C.B., major-general, iii. 546.
Elphinstone-Dalrymple of Horn and Logie Elphinstone, Sir Edward Arthur, 6th bart., viii. 134.
—— —— his wife, Jane Muriel Hawkes, viii. 134.
—— —— Sir Robert Graeme, 5th bart., viii. 134.
—— —— his wife, Flora Loudoun Macleod, viii. 134.
—— Anne Alexandrina, viii. 135.
—— Ann Graeme, viii. 136.
—— Charles, viii. 134; ix. 160.
—— —— his 1st wife, Harriet Albinia Louisa Gordon, viii. 134.
—— —— his 2nd wife, Christian Skene, viii. 135.
—— David Riccart, 2nd son of Sir Robert Dalrymple-Horn-Elphinstone, viii. 133.
—— Elizabeth Magdalene, viii. 135.
—— Ernest George Beck, viii. 135.
—— Francis Anstruther, viii. 134.
—— —— his wife, Mary Anne Bowen, viii. 134.
—— George Augustus Frederick, viii. 135.
—— Henrietta Marion, wife of Thomas Coats Leslie, viii. 136.
—— Hew Drummond, viii. 134.
—— —— his wife, Helenora Katharine Heron-Maxwell, viii. 134.
—— John Hamilton, general, viii. 135.
—— —— his wife, Georgina Anne Brigstock, viii. 135.
—— John Maxwell, commander R.N., viii. 133.
—— Louisa Sarah, viii. 136.
—— Margaret Burnett, wife of rev. J. M. Warren, viii. 134.

Elphinstone-Dalrymple, Mary Frances, wife of Patrick Boyle of Shewalton, iv. 208; viii. 135.
—— Stair, viii. 134.
—— William Robert, viii. 135.
Elphinstone-Fleming of Cumbernauld and Biggar, Charles, admiral R.N., M.P., governor of Greenwich Hospital, iii. 550; viii. 555.
—— —— Clementina, wife of 4th viscount Hawarden, iii. 550.
—— Anne Elizabeth, wife of W. Cunninghame Bontine, iii. 550.
—— Mary Keith, wife of (1) Alex. Macalister, and (2) Morgan Lloyd, iii. 550.
Elsi of Thirlestane and Newington, son of Winter, v. 277.
Elsmore, captain, 1654, i. 473.
Elton of Hazel, Ambrose, i. 406.
—— —— his wife, Anne Aston, i. 406.
—— of the Nether Hall, George, iv. 569.
—— Mary, wife of Thos. Holyland, iv. 569.
—— Thomas, M.D., i. 406.
—— —— his wife, Jane Aston, i. 406.
Elyne of Mar, wife of (1) Sir John Menteith, lord of Arran, and *perhaps* (2) Sir James Garioch, v. 579; vi. 132.
Emhin *or* Evan, son of Kenneth, v. 566.
Emma, wife of (1) Ethelred II. of England, and (2) Canute, ii. 428.
—— wife of Robert de Brus, ii. 428.
—— wife of Malise, 5th earl of Strathearn, viii. 246.
Emmot of Brookfield, Thomas, i. 391.
—— Charles, i. 391.
—— —— his wife, Constance Harriet Campbell, i. 391.
Encombe, John (Scott), eldest son of 3rd earl of Eldon; styled viscount, v. 548.
—— —— his wife, Mary Laura Fraser, v. 548.
Engaine of Crailing, Berengar, vi. 525 *n.*
Engelvaart, Nicoline, wife of Willem Karel Mackay, vii. 173.
England, Kings of—
—— Edward I., i. 7; iv. 9, 12, 509; v. 578; viii. 562 *n.*
—— Edward II., i. 9; iv. 12; viii. 562 *n.*
—— Edward III., i. 7.
—— Ethelred II., ii. 426.
—— Harold II., ii. 243 *n.*
—— Henry I., i. 3; iv. 136.
—— Henry II., i. 2.
—— Henry III., i. 6.
—— Henry IV., iii. 165, 263.
—— Henry VII., i. 21, 27.
—— Henry VIII., i. 21; iii. 608; vii. 121.
—— John, i. 6; ix. 11.
—— Richard II., i. 147.
—— Stephen, i. 2.
—— Matilda, 'the] Empress Maud,' queen of, i. 2.
ENZIE, GORDON, EARL OF, v. 543-562.
Enzie, George, first earl of iv. 543; v. 459.
—— George, eldest son of 1st marquess of Huntly; styled earl of, iv. 545.
EPSOM OF EPSOM, PRIMROSE, BARON, ix. 152.
Epsom of Epsom, Archibald Philip, first baron, ix. 152.
Erc, v. 27.
Erchebaudesson, Malcolm, Peeblesshire, iii. 499.
Ergadia, *or* Argyll, Alexander of, i. 321.
—— Ewen of, v. 2, 130; viii. 246.
—— Isobel of, wife of Sir John Stewart of Innermeath, v. 2.
—— Janet of, wife of Robert Stewart of Rossyth, v. 1, 2.
—— John of, vi. 203.
—— John of, lord of Lorn, v. 1, 2.
—— Mary of, wife of (1) Magnus, King of Man, (2) Malise, earl of Strathearn, (3) Sir Hugh de Abernethy, and (4) William Fitzwarin, vii. 401; viii. 246.
—— *, wife of Sir Patrick de Graham, vi. 204.
Eric Magnusson, King of Norway, i. 6.
—— —— his 1st wife, Margaret of Scotland, i. 6.
—— —— his 2nd wife, Isabel Bruce, i. 6.
—— Bloodyaxe, ii. 314.
—— Slagbrellir, ii. 315.
—— —— his wife, Ingigerd, ii. 315.
Erica, wife of (1) count de Manderscheidt, and (2) Sir Wm. Stewart of Houstoun and Pittenweem, vii. 68.
Ermigarda, 1st wife of Patrick, 9th earl of Dunbar, iii. 268, 269.
Ernald, bishop of St. Andrews, iii. 422 *n.*; vii. 397.
Erne, John Henry (Crichton), 4th earl of, iii. 57.
ERROLL, HAY, EARL OF, iii. 555-587.
Erroll, Andrew, eighth earl of, iii. 569, 571.
—— —— his 1st wife, Jean Hay, iii. 568, 571.
—— —— his 2nd wife, Agnes Sinclair, ii. 342; iii. 571.
—— Charles, thirteenth earl of, iii. 579; ix. 87.
—— Charles Gore, twentieth earl of, iii. 586; v. 181.
—— —— his wife, Mary Caroline L'Estrange, iii. 587.
—— Francis, ninth earl of, iii. 572, 574; iv. 58; ix. 86, 87 *ter.*
—— —— his 1st wife, Margaret Stewart, iii. 576; vi. 316.
—— —— his 2nd wife, Mary Stewart, i. 445; iii. 576.
—— —— his 3rd wife, Elizabeth Douglas, iii. 576; vi. 374.

* Name unknown.

Erroll, George, seventh earl of, iii. 566, 568.
—— —— his 1st wife, Margaret Robertson, iii. 569.
—— —— his 2nd wife, Helen Bryson, iii. 569.
—— George, sixteenth earl of, iii. 582.
—— —— his wife, Elizabeth Jemima Blake, iii. 582.
—— Gilbert, eleventh earl of, iii. 378; viii. 70.
—— —— his wife, Katharine Carnegie, iii. 379; viii. 70.
—— James, fifteenth earl of, iii. 581; v. 181.
—— —— his 1st wife, Rebecca Lockhart, iii. 581.
—— —— his 2nd wife, Isabella Carr, iii. 581.
—— John, twelfth earl of, i. 88; iii. 573, 579.
—— —— his wife, Anne Drummond, iii. 579; vii. 51; ix. 87.
—— Mary, wife of Alexander Falconer of Dalgaty; countess of, iii. 579, 580; v. 247; vii. 351.
—— Nicholas, second earl of, iii. 565 *bis.*; iv. 525 *bis.*
—— —— his contracted wife, Margaret Gordon, iv. 525.
—— —— his wife, Elizabeth Gordon, iii. 565; iv. 525.
—— William, first earl of, ii. 327; iii. 563 *bis.*, 564; iv. 276; vii. 431.
—— —— his wife, Beatrix Douglas, iii. 175, 564.
—— William, third earl of, iii. 565; iv. 52; vii. 279, 434.
—— —— his 1st wife, Isabel Gordon, iii. 565; iv. 530.
—— —— his 2nd wife, Elizabeth Leslie, iii. 566; vii. 276.
—— William, fourth earl of, iii. 24, 25, 26, 567; vii. 435, 436.
—— —— his 1st wife, Christian Lyon, iii. 567; viii. 277; ix. 162.
—— —— his 2nd wife, Margaret Ker, iii. 567; vii. 326; viii. 384, 385.
—— William, fifth earl of, iii. 568.
—— —— his wife, Elizabeth Ruthven, iii. 568; iv. 259; vii. 252.
—— William, sixth earl of, iii. 567, 568: iv. 260; v. 218.
—— —— his wife, Helenor Stewart, iii. 568; v. 353.
—— William, tenth earl of, iii. 576, 577; ix. 87.
—— —— his wife, Anne Lyon, iii. 578; viii. 296.
—— William, seventeenth earl of, iii. 581, 583.
—— —— his 1st wife, Jane Bell, iii. 583.
—— —— his 2nd wife, Alicia Eliot, iii. 583.
—— —— his 3rd wife, Harriet Somerville, iii. 584; viii. 38.
Erroll, William George, eighteenth earl of, iii. 585.
—— —— his wife, Elizabeth Fitzclarence, iii. 585.
—— William Henry, nineteenth earl of, iii. 585.
—— —— his wife, Eliza Amelia Gore, iii. 586.
ERSKINE, ERSKINE, LORD, v. 601-636.
Erskine, Alexander, third lord, v. 607.
—— —— his 1st wife, Christian Crichton, ii. 508, 541; iii. 222; v. 607.
—— —— his 2nd wife, Elyne Home, iv. 448; v. 608.
—— Charles, tenth lord, v. 626.
—— —— his wife, Mary Maule, v. 627; vii. 24.
—— Frances, wife of James Erskine, knight-marshal of Scotland; baroness, v. 633.
—— John, fifth lord, iii. 535; v. 557, 609.
—— —— his wife, Margaret *or* Elizabeth Campbell, i. 336; v. 609.
—— John, sixth lord, v. 81, 612.
—— —— his wife, Annabella Murray, i. 464; v. 615.
—— John, seventh lord, v. 615.
—— —— his 1st wife, Agnes *or* Anna Drummond, v. 621; vii. 46.
—— —— his 2nd wife, Marie Stewart, v. 356, 620.
—— John, eighth lord, v. 623.
—— —— his wife, Jean Hay, iii. 577; v. 623.
—— John, ninth lord, v. 623, 625.
—— —— his 1st wife, Elizabeth Scott, ii. 234; v. 625.
—— —— his 2nd wife, Jean *or* Mary Mackenzie, v. 626; vii. 508.
—— John, eleventh lord, v. 629.
—— —— his 1st wife, Margaret Hay, v. 232, 631.
—— —— his 2nd wife, Frances Pierrepont, v. 632.
—— John Francis, thirteenth lord, v. 633.
—— —— his wife, Frances Floyer, v. 634.
—— John Francis Ashley, styled lord, v. 96.
—— John Francis Erskine, sixteenth lord, v. 635.
—— —— his wife, Alice Mary Sinclair Hamilton, v. 636.
—— John Francis Miller, fifteenth lord, v. 635.
—— —— his wife, Philadelphia Stuart-Menteath, v. 635.
—— John Thomas, fourteenth lord, v. 633.
—— —— his wife, Janet Miller, v. 635.
—— Robert, first lord, v. 551, 601.
—— —— his alleged wife, * Stewart, v. 3, 604; ix. 115.
—— —— his wife, Elizabeth Lindsay, iii. 17; v. 604.

* Name unknown.

Erskine, Robert, fourth lord, v. 81, 608.
—— —— his wife, Elizabeth *or* Isobel Campbell, v. 494, 608.
—— Thomas, second lord, v. 185, 186, 605; vi. 223.
—— —— his wife, Janet Douglas, v. 606.
—— Thomas, elder son of John, earl of Mar; styled lord, v. 632.
—— —— his wife, Charlotte Hope, iv. 497; v. 632.
ERSKINE OF RESTORMEL CASTLE, ERSKINE, BARON, ii. 277.
Erskine, Thomas, son of Henry David, 10th earl of Buchan; baron, ii. 277.
—— —— his 1st wife, Frances Moore, ii. 277.
—— —— his 2nd wife, Sarah Buck, ii. 277.
—— master of, Alexander, son of 2nd lord Erskine, v. 606.
—— —— his wife, Christian Crichton, ii. 508; iii. 222; v. 608.
—— master of, Robert, eldest son of 4th lord Erskine, v. 608.
—— master of, Robert, eldest son of 5th lord Erskine, v. 610.
—— —— his wife, Margaret Graham, v. 611; vi. 230.
—— master of, Thomas, 2nd son of 5th lord Erskine, v. 611.
—— —— his wife, Margaret Fleming, v. 611; viii. 540.
ERSKINE, EARL OF BUCHAN, ii. 272-280.
ERSKINE, LORD CARDROSS, ii. 365-368; v. 618-621.
ERSKINE, LORD DIRLTOUN, ix. 116, 117.
ERSKINE, LORD ERSKINE, v. 601-636.
ERSKINE, BARON ERSKINE OF RESTORMEL CASTLE, ii. 277.
ERSKINE, BARON ERSKINE OF DIRLETOWNE, v. 85-97.
ERSKINE, VISCOUNT OF FENTOUN, v. 85-97.
ERSKINE, EARL OF KELLIE, v. 81-97.
ERSKINE, EARL OF MAR, v. 589-635.
Erskine of Aberdona, Isabella, wife of James Murray, iii. 521.
—— —— James, iii. 521.
—— of Abernyte, Sir Thomas, v. 85.
—— of Alloa, Sir Robert, 1st laird, v. 593.
—— —— Thomas, elder son of John, earl of Mar, v. 632.
—— —— his wife, Charlotte Hope, v. 632.
—— of Alva, Sir Charles, 1st bart., ii. 49; v. 622, 627; ix. 133.
—— —— his 1st wife, Mary Hope, iv. 491; v. 622.
—— —— his 2nd wife, Helen Skene, iii. 488; v. 622.
—— —— Sir Henry, 5th bart., vii. 587.
—— —— his wife, Janet Wedderburn, vii. 587.
—— —— Sir James, 6th bart., vii. 588.
Erskine of Alva, Sir John, 3rd bart., vii. 587.
—— —— his wife, Katharine St. Clair, vii. 587.
—— of Arnprior, Alexander, 2nd son of 4th lord Erskine, v. 81.
—— of Balgarno, Sir Thomas, v. 85.
—— of Balgonie, James, v. 608.
—— —— his wife, Christian Stirling, v. 609.
—— —— Sir John, iii. 485.
—— —— his wife, Magdalen Bruce, iii. 485.
—— of Balhagartie, Alexander, son of 2nd lord Erskine, v. 607, 608.
—— —— John, i. 184.
—— of Banchory, Sir Allan, v. 592.
—— of Bandeath, Charles, iv. 491.
—— of Barns, Sir Robert, iv. 344.
—— of Blackgrange, Arthur, 5th son of 5th lord Erskine, v. 438, 400, 440, 611.
—— —— his wife, Magdalen Livingston, v. 84, 438, 611.
—— of Boquhan, Sir George, senator of the College of Justice, v. 82.
—— —— his wife, Isobel Brown, v. 82.
—— of Brechin, Sir Thomas, ambassador to France, iv. 87; v. 610.
—— —— his wife, Agnes Ogilvy, i. 118.
—— of Brewhaugh, Sir Robert, v. 594.
—— of Brotherstanes, Sir Thomas, v. 611.
—— —— his wife, Margaret Fleming, v. 611.
—— of Cadzow, Sir Robert, iv. 344.
—— of Cambo, Sir Alexander, 2nd bart., Lyon King of Arms, v. 91.
—— —— his wife, Anne Erskine, v. 87, 91.
—— —— Sir Charles, 1st bart., Lyon King of Arms, v. 86, 90.
—— —— his wife, Penelope Barclay, v. 90.
—— —— Sir Charles, 3rd bart., Lyon King of Arms, v. 92, 93.
—— —— Sir Charles, 6th bart., v. 93.
—— —— his wife, Margaret Chiene, v. 93.
—— —— Sir Charles, 8th bart., v. 93.
—— —— David, Lyon Clerk, v. 92.
—— —— his 1st wife, * Grant, v. 93.
—— —— his 2nd wife, * Young, v. 93.
—— —— Sir John, 4th bart., Albany Herald, v. 92.
—— —— Sir William, 5th bart., Unicorn Pursuivant, v. 92.
—— —— Sir William, 7th bart., v. 93.
—— of Cambusbarron and Cangnoir, Alexander, 2nd son of 4th lord Erskine, v. 81.
—— of Cambuskenneth, Alexander, captain, v. 621; ix. 133 *bis*.
—— —— his wife, * Croft, v. 621; ix. 133.
—— of Cardross, David, iii. 551.
—— —— James, vi. 154.
—— —— John, v. 617.

* Name unknown.

Erskine of Carnock, John, lieut.-col., M.P., ii. 366, 367; iii. 487; vi. 114; vii. 176.
—— —— his 1st wife, Jane Mure of Caldwell, ii. 366.
—— —— his 2nd wife, Anna Dundas of Kincavil, ii. 366.
—— —— his 3rd wife, Lilias Stirling, ii. 366.
—— —— his 4th wife, Mary Stuart, ii. 366.
—— of Craig, Sir James, 4th son of Alex. E. of Gogar, v. 83.
—— —— his wife, Mary Erskine, v. 83.
—— of Crambeth, Sir Allan, v. 592.
—— of Culheg and Culmoir, Alexander, v. 82.
—— of Dirleton, Sir Thomas, 2nd son of Alex. E. of Gogar, v. 85.
—— of Dryburgh and Holmes, Joan Berry, wife of rev. G. E. B. Erskine, ii. 278.
—— of Dun, Sir Alexander, vi. 495; viii. 101.
—— —— his wife, Margaret Lindsay, viii. 101.
—— —— Augustus John Kennedy, v. 600.
—— —— David, lord Dun, i. 127; v. 632, 633.
—— —— John, 1st laird, v. 600.
—— —— John, 3rd laird, v. 186 *n.*
—— —— John, 4th laird, i. 290; v. 244.
—— —— Sir John, 5th laird, iv. 259.
—— —— his wife, Margaret Ruthven, ii. 268; iv. 259.
—— —— John, 6th laird, iii. 27.
—— —— his 1st wife, Elizabeth Lindsay, iii. 27.
—— —— John, 8th laird, i. 119, 159.
—— —— his wife, Agnes Ogilvy, i. 119.
—— —— John, 9th laird, i. 159, 298; iii. 30; ix. 11.
—— —— his wife, Margaret Keith, i. 519; iii. 30; ix. 11 *bis.*
—— —— John, 10th laird, i. 159.
—— —— John, 11th laird, vi. 495.
—— —— his wife, Magdalen Haliburton, vi. 495.
—— —— John, the yr., son of Sir Alexander E., viii. 101.
—— —— John, 17th laird, ii. 498; v. 600.
—— —— his wife, Mary Baird, v. 600.
—— —— Margaret, wife of 1st marquess of Ailsa, ii. 498; v. 600.
—— —— Robert, 7th laird, v. 5.
—— —— Sir Thomas, ancestor of the family of, v. 597.
—— of Over Dunnotter, Walter, 2nd son of 3rd lord Erskine, v. 608.
—— of Edenshead, Charles, advocate, ii. 367.
—— —— his wife, Ann Scott of Edenshead, ii. 367.
—— of Ednam, Sir Robert, v. 594, 600.
—— of Elhotle, Sir Thomas, v. 85.
—— of Erskine, Henry de, 1st laird, v. 590.
—— —— Sir John, 2nd laird, v. 590.
Erskine of Erskine, Sir John, 3rd laird, i. 14; v. 423 *n.*, 591.
—— —— Sir Robert, 5th laird, i. 328, 435; iii. 10, 467; v. 467, 592, 600; vi. 298.
—— —— his 1st wife, Beatrice Lindsay, iii. 10; v. 595.
—— —— his 2nd wife, Christian Menteith, iv. 14; v. 580, 595.
—— —— Sir Robert, 7th laird, v. 601, 620, 623.
—— —— his wife, Elizabeth Lindsay, v. 604.
—— —— Sir Thomas, 6th laird, v. 596; ix. 133.
—— —— his 1st wife, Mary Douglas, v. 597, 598; vi. 342, 345.
—— his 2nd wife, Janet Keith, ii. 223, 224; v. 581, 597, 604.
—— —— Sir William, 4th laird, v. 591.
—— of Favour Royall, Sir James, v. 83.
—— of Fentonbarns, Sir Thomas, v. 85.
—— of Ferrytoun, Sir Robert, v. 594.
—— of Forgandenny, Sir Thomas, v. 85.
—— of Gaherston, Sir Robert, v. 594.
—— of Gogar, Sir Alexander, joint-governor to King James VI., i. 466; iii. 284; v. 81, 611; vii. 65.
—— —— his wife, Margaret Home, iv. 460; v. 82.
—— of Glenshinnoch, Sir Robert, iv. 344.
—— of Grange, James, lord justice-clerk; lord Grange, v. 627, 632, 633.
—— —— his wife, Rachel Chiesley, v. 627.
—— of Haliburton, Sir Thomas, v. 85.
—— of Halkhill, Sir John, v. 137.
—— —— John, his son, 1262; v. 137.
—— of Halkishurst, John, iv. 188.
—— of Hassindean, Sir Thomas, v. 85.
—— of Inchmartine and Inchture, Sir Allan, v. 592; viii. 368, 480.
—— —— his wife, Isabel Inchmartine, v. 592; viii. 480.
—— of Innerteil, Sir George, senator of the College of Justice, iii. 72; v. 82.
—— —— his wife, Isobel Brown, v. 82.
—— of Kellie, Alexander, son of 2nd lord Erskine, v. 607.
—— —— Sir Thomas, 2nd son of Alex. E. of Gogar, v. 85.
—— of Kildrummy, v. 619.
—— of Kinnoull, Christian, wife of (1) John Crichton, and (2) Robert, 1st lord Crichton of Sanquhar, iii. 223; v. 432, 596.
—— —— Sir John, iii. 223; v. 432, 596.
—— —— Sir Nicholas, iv. 517.
—— —— his wife, Elizabeth Keith, iv. 517.
—— —— Sir Robert, v. 595.
—— —— his wife, Christian Menteith, iv. 14; v. 595.
—— —— Sir Thomas, 2nd son of Sir Robert E., v. 596.
—— —— his 1st wife, Jean Cameron, v. 596.
—— —— his 2nd wife, Elizabeth Keith, v. 596.

Erskine of Kinnoull, William, v. 596.
— of Kintulach, Sir Robert, v. 595; viii. 252 *n*.
—of Largs, John, 2nd son of John E. of Erskine, v. 591 *bis*.
— of Lenzie, Sir Robert, viii. 525.
— of Logy, John, i. 159.
— of the Malers, Sir Robert, v. 595.
— of Michellis, Sir Thomas, v. 84.
— of Nisbet, Sir John, eldest son of 4th lord Erskine, v. 609.
— — Sir Robert, v. 594.
— of Otterstoun, Sir John, iii. 509; v. 622; ix. 133.
— — his wife, Margaret Inglis, v. 622.
— of the Park of Clackmannan, Sir Robert, v. 594.
— of Pittarrow, Alexander, v. 607.
— of Pittenweem, Thomas, vii. 69.
— of Pittodrie, Henry Knight, colonel, iv. 65.
— — his wife, Mary Erskine of Pittodrie, iv. 65.
— — Henry William Knight, v. 600.
— — John, ancestor of the family of. v. 600.
— — John, i. 184.
— — his wife, Margaret Douglas, i. 184.
— — Mary, wife of col. Henry Knight, iv. 65.
— — Thomas, iv. 65.
— — his wife, Anne Forbes, iv. 65.
— of Pow of Alloa, Sir Robert, v. 594.
— of Raploch, Andrew, v. 592.
— of Roscobie, Sir James, 4th son of Alex. E. of Gogar, v. 83.
— of Restenneth, Alexander, v. 82.
— of Easter Row, Sir Thomas, v. 85.
— of Little Sauchie, James, v. 608; viii. 176.
— — his wife, Christine Stirling, v. 609.
— of Seggie, Sir Thomas, v. 85.
— of Sheirgarten, Robert, v. 609.
— of Syntoun, vii. 71 *n*.
— — Alexander, v. 607.
— of Somerville, John, viii. 25.
— of Torry, William, M.P., ii. 366; ix. 52.
— — his wife, Magdalen Lumsdain, ii. 366.
— — Sir William, 1st bart., viii. 510.
— of Tulchgorne, Robert, eldest son of 4th lord Erskine, v. 607, 608.
— of Tullibody, Sir James, 4th son of Alex. E. of Gogar, v. 83.
— of Venlaw, Archibald, major. v. 312.
— — his wife, Margaret Maitland, v. 312.
— of Wemyss, Sir Alan, viii. 481.
— — Margaret, wife of Sir John Glen of Inchmartin, iv. 16, 29; viii. 480.
— of Windingtoun and Wingtounhall, Sir Thomas, v. 84.
Erskine, Adam, commendator of Cambuskenneth, v. 81, 83, 443, 611.
— Adam, 3rd son of Jas. E. of Little Sauchie, v. 609.
— Agnes, dau. of Sir Charles E. of Cambo, v. 93.
— Agnes, wife of William Menteith of Kerse, v. 608.
— Agnes Helen, v. 95.
— Albany Stuart Mar, ii. 280.
— — his wife, Alice Helen Keyser, ii. 280.
— Alexander, parson of Moniabroch *or* Kilsyth, v. 609.
— Alexander, captain, commendator of Cambuskenneth, iv. 316, 433; v. 621; ix. 133.
— Alexander, his illeg. son, iv. 433; v. 621.
— Alexander, eldest son of Alex. E. of Gogar, v. 82.
— Alexander, joint Lyon King of Arms, v. 91, 92.
— Alexander, elder son of capt. Alex. E. of Cambuskenneth, ix. 133.
— Alexander, 2nd son of Alexander E. of Dun, viii. 101.
— Alexander Penrose Forbes, in holy orders, v. 96.
— Alice, alleged 1st wife of Walter, 6th lord High Stewart, i. 14.
— Alicia Diana, wife of (1) rev. Somerville Hay, and (2) capt. Jas. Young, ii. 279; iii. 584.
— Alice Maud Mary, dau. of Walter Henry, earl of Mar and Kellie, v. 96.
— Andrew, lieut. 71st Foot, and 24th Foot, v. 89.
— Anna, wife of 12th lord Forbes, iv. 63; v. 86; ix. 91.
— Anna, wife of Sir Robt. Mowbray of Barnbougle, v. 86.
— Anna, dau. of Sir Alex. E. of Cambo, v. 92.
— Anna, wife of 6th earl of Rothes, v. 622; vii. 299.
— Anna, dau. of Mary, countess of Buchan, ix. 48.
— Annabella, 4th dau. of John, earl of Mar, v. 622.
— Annabella, wife of Robt. Stewart of Culbeg, v. 625.
— Anne, wife of (1) James, lord Ogilvy, and (2) Sir Alex. MacDonald, i. 127.
— Anne, wife of Jas. Canaries, D.D., ii. 273.
— Anne, wife of Archibald Edmonstone, ii. 368.
— Anne, wife of John, 3rd lord Melville of Monymail. v. 83; vi. 106.
— Anne, wife of Sir A. Erskine of Cambo, v. 87, 91.
— Anne, dau. of 5th earl of Kellie, v. 89.

Erskine, Anne, wife of William Dewar of Laverocklaw, v. 93; ix. 133.
—— Anne Agnes, dau. of Henry David, 10th earl of Buchan, ii. 277.
—— Anne Caroline, wife of rev. Joseph Haskell, v. 634.
—— Archibald, 5th son of Alex. E. of Gogar, v. 83.
—— Archibald, alleged 4th son of Sir Wm. E. of Erskine, v. 592.
—— Sir Arthur, 5th son of John, earl of Mar, v. 621: ix. 133.
—— —— his wife, Margaret Buchanan, v. 622.
—— Arthur, 3rd son of Sir John E. of Dun, vii. 18.
—— —— his wife, Margaret Maule, vii. 18.
—— Augustus William, 17th Lancers, v. 95.
—— —— his wife, Harriet Susannah Forbes, v. 95.
—— Barbara, wife of James, 2nd marquess of Douglas, i. 208; v. 626.
—— Charles, capt. Edinburgh regt., ii. 367.
—— Charles, 2nd son of Sir Chas. E. of Cambo, v. 91.
—— Charles, cardinal, v. 92; ix. 117 *ter*.
—— Charles, lieut.-col.; eldest son of lord Grange, v. 628, 633.
—— —— his wife, Agnes Syme, v. 628.
—— Charles Herbert Stewart, major, v. 95.
—— Charles Thomas, in holy orders. v. 634.
—— Charlotte, dau. of John Francis, earl of Mar, v. 634.
—— Charlotte Frances, dau. of John Francis earl of Mar, v. 634.
—— Christian, wife of Sir Alex. Home of Manderston, iii. 284; v. 84.
—— Christian, wife of David Stewart, yr. of Rossyth, v. 608.
—— Christian Isabella, wife of John Gordon, ii. 279.
—— Christina, wife of (1) Patrick, 1st lord Graham, and (2) Sir Wm. Charteris of Kinfauns, v. 186, 605; vi. 221.
—— Colin, 8th son of Sir Alex. E. of Cambo, v. 92.
—— —— his wife, Agatha Gigli, ix. 117.
—— Constance Elise, v. 96.
—— David, 4th son of David E. of Cambo, v. 93.
—— David, abbot of Inchmahome and Dryburgh, v. 611.
—— David, 2nd son of Sir John E. of Dun, vii. 18.
—— —— his wife, Jane Maule, vii. 18.
—— Dorothy, wife of * Walker, ix. 48.
—— Dorothy Christian, v. 95.
—— Elizabeth, wife of Wm. Urie, i. 397.
—— Elizabeth, dau. of James, 1st earl of Buchan, ii. 272.

* Name unknown.

Erskine, Elizabeth, wife of Duncan Wemyss of Rires, ii. 223; iv. 519; v. 600; viii. 482.
—— Elizabeth, wife of Henry Lee-Harvey, ii. 279.
—— Elizabeth, wife of (1) Walter Macfarlan, and (2) Alexander, 7th lord Colville of Culross, ii. 563; v. 89.
—— Elizabeth, dau. of col. John E., iii. 349 *n*.
—— Elizabeth, wife of (1) Jas. Clerk of Pittencreiff, and (2) col. George Murray, iii. 509; ix. 84.
—— Elizabeth, wife of John Hay, iii. 573.
—— Elizabeth, dau. of Alexander, viscount of Fentoun, v. 86.
—— Elizabeth, wife of Alex. Fraser of Inverallochy, v. 87.
—— Elizabeth, wife of Sir George Falconer of Halkerton, v. 244.
—— Elizabeth, wife of Sir Alex. Seton of Touch, v. 607.
—— Elizabeth, wife of Robert Graham of Gartmore, v. 611; vi. 158.
—— Elizabeth, wife of Walter Seton of Touch, v. 612.
—— Elizabeth, wife of 2nd lord Napier of Merchiston, v. 624; vi. 426.
—— Elizabeth Crompton, wife of col. G. Callander, ii. 277.
—— Elyne Mary, v. 96.
—— Eupheme, wife of Michael Cochrane, iii. 336 *n*.
—— Evelyn Hilda Stuart, wife of W. E. Guinness, ii. 280.
—— Evelyn Mary Elise, wife of major H. Lowther, v. 95.
—— Fairfax, 4th son of David, earl of Buchan, ii. 276.
—— —— his wife, Annabella Manning, ii. 276.
—— Frances, wife of col. Jas. Gardiner, ii. 276.
—— Frances, wife of major-gen. W. Wemyss of Wemyss, viii. 510.
—— Frances Elizabeth, wife of rev. F. Tufnell, v. 96.
—— Frances Jemima, wife of William James Goodeve, v. 635.
—— Sir Francis, 2nd son of John, earl of Mar, v. 624.
—— Francis Walter, 2nd son of Walter John Francis, earl of Mar and Kellie, iv. 96.
—— George, 4th son of Alexander, viscount of Fentoun, v. 86.
—— George, 2nd son of David E., v. 93.
—— George, 2nd son of John, earl of Mar, v. 626 *bis*.
—— George, bailie of the regality of Alloa, v. 580 *n*., 591, 599.
—— George Eden Biber, clk., ii. 278.
—— —— his wife, Joan Berry Erskine of Dryburgh, ii. 278.

Erskine, George Francis, captain, ii. 277.
—— George Francis Albany, ii. 278.
—— —— his wife, Agnes Maria Mason, ii. 278.
—— George Lewis, son of David, earl of Buchan, ii. 276.
—— Harry, lieut.-col.; 3rd son of Charles, earl of Mar, v. 629.
—— Helen, alleged wife of Sir Thomas Bruce, v. 591.
—— Helen, wife of Humphrey Colquhoun of Luss, v. 606.
—— Henrietta, wife of Thos. Forbes of Auchry, ii. 273; ix. 49.
—— Henrietta, wife of Peter Smith, M.D., ii. 277.
—— Henry, lord advocate and dean of the faculty, ii. 277.
—— —— his 1st wife, Christian Fullerton, ii. 277.
—— —— his 2nd wife, Erskine Monro, ii. 277.
—— Henry David, 7th son of Henry David, 12th earl of Buchan, ii. 279.
—— Henry David, 3rd son of John Francis, earl of Mar, v. 634.
—— —— his wife, Mary Anne Cooksey, v. 634.
—— Henry David, capt. R.M., v. 634.
—— —— his wife, Eliza Ingle, v. 634.
—— Henry Walter Coningsby, v. 95.
—— Isabella, wife of (1) W. L. Hamilton, and (2) John, 14th earl of Glencairn, ii. 278; iv. 252.
—— Isabella, wife of Sir John Wemyss, v. 592; viii. 480, 482.
—— Isobel, wife of Patrick Graham of Kilpont, v. 607; vi. 145.
—— James, master of Buchan, ii. 269.
—— —— his wife, Christian Strang, ii. 269.
—— James, senator of the College of Justice, lord Grange, v. 241.
—— James, vicar of Falkirk, v. 609.
—— James, advocate, knight-marshal of Scotland, v. 628, 633.
—— —— his wife, Frances Erskine, v. 633.
—— James Augustus, assistant commissary-general, v. 634.
—— —— his 1st wife, Fanny Delacombe, v. 634.
—— —— his 2nd wife, Elizabeth B. Brodie, v. 634.
—— James Floyer, capt. 26th regt., v. 634.
—— —— his wife, Susan Sharpe, v. 634.
—— James Francis, colonel; 2nd son of Frances, baroness Erskine, v. 633.
—— James, *error for* John, colonel, depute governor of Stirling Castle, v. 627 *n.*
—— Jane, dau. of John Francis, earl of Mar, v. 634.
—— Jane Janetta, wife of E. W. Chetwode, v. 635.
Erskine, Janet, *perhaps* wife of Walter Stewart of Lennox, i. 150; v. 605.
—— Janet, wife of 1st earl of Stirling, ii. 235; viii. 171, 176.
—— Janet, alleged wife of John Montgomerie of Stair, iii. 426.
—— Janet, wife of Sir Robt. Anstruther of Balcaskie, v. 89.
—— Janet, dau. of 4th lord Erskine, v. 609.
—— Janet, wife of John Murray of Touchadam, v. 612.
—— Janet, wife of Robert Hay of Drumelzier, viii.
—— Jean, wife of (1) Geo. Gray of Halkerton, and (2) capt. Alex. Carnegie, ii. 274; viii. 62; ix. 49.
—— Jean, wife of (1) Geo. Auchinleck, and (2) John Leslie. v. 83.
—— Jean, wife of John Scott of Harden, v. 88; vii. 82; ix. 117.
—— Jean, wife of James Preston of Valleyfield, v. 609.
—— Jean, wife of * Cox, v. 629.
—— Jean, wife of Sir Hugh Paterson of Bannockburn, v. 629.
—— John, master of Buchan, ii. 269.
—— —— his 1st wife, Elizabeth Stewart, vi. 312; ix. 47.
—— —— his 2nd wife, Margaret Ogilvy, ii. 269.
—— John, 2nd son of James, 1st earl of Buchan, ii. 272.
—— John, colonel, depute-governor of Stirling Castle, iii. 349; v. 627.
—— —— his 1st wife, Mary Maule, v. 627; vii. 24.
—— —— his 2nd wife, Euphemia Cochrane, iii. 349.
—— John, 3rd son of David E., v. 93.
—— John, 4th son of Sir Charles E. of Cambo, v. 93.
—— John, son of Adam E., v. 609.
—— John, abbot of Dryburgh, commendator of Inchmahome and Cambuskenneth, v. 612.
—— John, elder son of Sir Arthur E., v. 622.
——Sir John, 6th son of John, earl of Mar, v. 622.
—— —— his wife, Margaret Inglis, v. 622.
—— John, dean of Cork. v. 629.
—— John, capt. American regiment, vii. 150.
—— —— his wife, Helen Douglas, vii. 150.
—— John, D.D., Edinburgh, vii. 176.
—— —— his wife, Christina Mackay, vii. 176.
—— John, vicar of Aberlemno, viii. 51.
—— John Francis, captain, v. 634.
—— John M'Loughlin Fraser, ii. 279.
—— —— his wife, Ann Thorne, ii. 279.

* Name unknown.

Erskine, Katharine, wife of Robert Arbuthnott of that Ilk, i. 290.
— Katharine, wife of (1) Sir W. Denholm, and (2) Daniel Campbell, ii. 368.
— Katharine, wife of Alexander, 1st lord Elphinstone, iii. 532; v. 612.
— Katharine, wife of 2nd earl of Haddington, iv. 316; v. 622.
— Katharine Anne, wife of Wm. Fraser of Fraserfield, ii. 276; vii. 445.
— Louisa Frances, dau. of Walter Henry, earl of Mar and Kellie, v. 96.
— Magdalen, wife of Alex. Monypenny, ii. 367.
— Margaret, wife of Sir Robert Douglas of Lochleven, and mistress of King James v., i. 24; ii. 269, 553; vi. 369, 612.
— Margaret, wife of Sir J. Glen of Inchmartin, i. 110, 112; v. 592; viii. 480.
— Margaret, wife of Sir Jas. Graham, i. 137; ii. 272.
— Margaret, dau. of John E., 9th of Dun, i. 159; iii. 30.
— Margaret, wife of Sir Wm. Vincent, ii. 279.
— Margaret, wife of Wm. Cunningham, ii. 366.
— Margaret, wife of William E., ii. 367.
— Margaret, wife of 2nd earl of Carnwath, ii. 414; v. 86.
— Margaret, wife of Geo. Home of Lundeis, ii. 552; v. 612.
— Margaret, wife of (1) Sir John Mackenzie of Tarbat, and (2) Sir Jas. Foulis of Colinton, iii. 71; v. 83; ix. 63.
— Margaret, wife of (1) Sir Adam Crichton, and (2) Jas. Reid, v. 83.
— Margaret, wife of Sir W. Sharp of Scotscraig, v. 91.
— Margaret, dau. of Sir Charles E. of Cambo, v. 93.
— Margaret, wife of James Haldane of Gleneagles, v. 609.
— Margaret, wife of 2nd earl of Kinghorne, v. 622; viii. 298.
— Margaret, wife of John Carnegie of Boysack, vi. 495.
— Margaret, wife of Patrick Maule of Panmure, vii. 18; ix. 148.
— Margaret, wife of James Rutherfurd of Rutherfurd, vii. 367.
— Margaret, wife of Wm. Gray of Innereichty, ix. 49.
— Maria, dau. of 2nd lord Cardross, ii. 367.
— Mariann Craig, wife of J. H. Gordon, ii. 279.
— Marion *or* Mariota, wife of Maurice Drummond of Concraig, v. 596; vii. 32.
— Mariota, wife of 2nd earl Marischal, v. 607; vi. 41.
— Marjory, wife of (1) Simon Fraser of Inverlochy, and (2) Charles, 4th lord Fraser, ii. 273; iv. 119.
Erskine, Marjorie Gladys Stuart, ii. 280.
— Mary, wife of Archibald, 8th earl of Angus, i. 196; v. 615.
— Mary, wife of Wm. Hamilton of Wishaw, ii. 49.
— Mary, wife of 2nd lord Forbes of Pitsligo, ii. 272; iv. 75.
— Mary, wife of (1) S. Fraser of Inverlochy, and (2) Charles, 4th lord Fraser, ii. 273; iv. 119; ix. 49.
— Mary, wife of Jas. Nimmo, ii. 368.
— Mary, wife of Alexander, *de jure* lord Colville of Culross, ii. 559; v. 91.
— Mary, wife of Alexander Webster, D.D., iii. 349 *n*.
— Mary, wife of 10th earl of Glencairn, iv. 250; v. 626.
— Mary, wife of Sir James Erskine of Tullibody, v. 83.
— Mary, alleged wife of Sir Dugald Campbell of Auchinbreck, v. 84.
— Mary, alleged wife of William Livingston of Kilsyth, v. 186, 607 *n*.
— Mary, wife of 3rd earl of Kintore, v. 241, 629; ix. 123.
— Mary, wife of (1) William, 6th ear Marischal, and (2) Patrick, 1st earl of Panmure, v. 622; vi. 56, 59; vii. 20; ix. 133.
— Mary, dau. of John, earl of Mar, v. 625.
— Mary, wife of capt. Alexander Leslie, advocate, vi. 114.
— Mary, wife of John Buchanan of that Ilk, ix. 52.
— Mary Anne, dau. of John Francis, earl of Mar, v. 634.
— Mary Margaret, wife of W. B. Constable, ii. 279.
— Matilda, wife of John Graham of Gartur, vi. 154.
— Metalane, dau. of Sir Chas. E. of Cambo, v. 91.
— Muriel Agnes Stuart, wife of major C. S. H. D. Willoughby, ii. 280.
— Penelope, wife of Macdonald of Clanranald, v. 91.
— Penelope, dau. of Sir Alex. E. of Cambo, v. 92.
— Penelope, wife of Jas. Stewart of Balado, v. 93.
— Penelope, dau. of Sir Charles E. of Cambo, v. 93.
— Rachel, dau. of lord Grange, v. 629.
— Robert, eldest son of James E. of Little Sauchie, v. 609.
— Sophia, wife of 3rd lord Forbes of Pitsligo, iv. 75; v. 626.
— Sophia, wife of Alexander, master of Saltoun, v. 86; vii. 444.
— Sophia, wife of Sir Wm. Sharp, v. 92.

Erskine, Thomas, advocate, ii. 367.
—— —— his wife, Rachel Libberton, ii. 367.
—— Thomas, 7th son of Sir Alex. E. of Cambo, v. 92.
—— —— his wife, Jean Rue, v. 92.
—— Sir Thomas, son of 1st lord Erskine, v. 603, 604.
—— Thomas, captain; 5th son of Jas. E. of Little Sauchie, v. 609.
—— Thomas, vicar of Beighton, v. 634.
—— —— his wife, Charlotte Watson, v. 634.
—— Thomas, 2nd son of capt. Alex. E. of Cambuskenneth, ix. 133.
—— Veronica, wife of Walter Lockhart, ii. 367.
—— Walter Augustus, lieut. R.G.A., v. 95.
—— Walter Coningsby, v. 634.
—— William, deputy-governor of Blackness Castle, ii. 367.
—— —— his wife, Margaret Erskine, ii. 367.
—— William, 2nd son of Sir John E. of Erskine, v. 591.
—— William, parson of Campsie, v. 609; viii. 171, 176.
—— William, 5th son of 4th lord Erskine, v. 609.
—— William, master of the Charterhouse, v. 622.
—— William, younger son of Sir Arthur E., v. 622.
—— William Augustus Forbes, M.V.O., v. 96.
—— *, wife of Walter Lindsay, iii. 19.
—— *, dau. of capt. Alex. E. of Cambuskenneth, ix. 133.
Erskine-Murray of Aberdona, Alexander Erskine, iii. 521.
Erskine-Wemyss of Wemyss, James Hay, viii. 511.
—— —— his wife, Augusta Millicent Anne Mary Kennedy Erskine, ii. 500; viii. 511.
—— —— Michael John, viii. 512.
—— —— Randolph Gordon, viii. 512.
—— —— his 1st wife, Lilian Mary Paulet, viii. 512.
—— —— his 2nd wife, Eva Cecelia Cowley, viii. 512.
—— Dora Mina Kittina, wife of Henry George Grosvenor, viii. 512.
—— Edward Pellew, viii. 511.
—— Frances Henrietta, wife of capt. C. J. Balfour, R.N., viii. 511.
—— Hugo, viii. 511.
—— Mary Frances, wife of Cecil Stratford Paget, viii. 512.
—— Mary Millicent, viii. 512.
—— Rosslyn, captain R.N., viii. 512.
—— —— his wife, Victoria Morier, viii. 512.
Erth of Drem and Walchton, Johanna de, wife of * Gourlay, v. 391.

* Name unknown.

Erth of Erthbeg, Marjorie, wife of John de Elphinstone, iii. 526.
—— Alice of, lady of Craigbernard, vi. 216.
—— Thomas of, lord of Waughton, iii. 526.
Erwin. *See* CAMPBELL, EARL OF IRVINE, v. 25.
ESKDAILL, SCOTT, LORD SCOTT OF QUHITCHESTER AND, ii. 234.
Eskdaill, Walter, first lord Scott of Quhitchester and, ii. 234.
ESKDAILL, SCOTT, LORD SCOTT OF WHITCHESTER AND, ii. 237.
Eskdaill, James, first lord Scott of Whitchester and, ii. 237.
—— Walter Henry, eldest son of 6th duke of Buccleuch; styled lord, ii. 247.
ESKDAILL, MAXWELL, LORD, vi. 482-487.
Eskdaill, John, first lord, vi. 482.
Eskgrove, Sir David Rae, senator of the College of Justice, lord, ii. 89.
Espec, William, Yorkshire, vii. 315.
Essé, d', vii. 283.
Esseby, Clarebald de, vi. 528.
—— *or* Esseville, William de, iii. 245.
—— —— his wife, Hectreda *or* Octruda, iii. 245.
Esseneux, Louis d'Argenteau, count of, iii. 480.
—— Charlotte d'Argenteau, wife of Thomas, 3rd earl of Elgin; countess of, iii. 480.
Essex, Arthur (Capel), 6th earl of, iii. 463.
—— Christian de Valloniis, countess of, i. 505.
Este, Augusta Emma D', wife of Sir T. Wilde, baron Truro of Bowes, iii. 392.
—— Sir Augustus Frederick D', col., K.G.H., son of H.R.H. the duke of Sussex, iii. 392.
Ete, wife of Gartnait, earl of Buchan, ii. 251; iv. 5.
Eth, the earl, iv. 2 *n.*; vi. 284.
Eth, 2nd son of Alwin, 1st earl of Lennox, v. 327.
Etheldreda of Dunbar, wife of Randolph de Lindsay, iii. 3, 245.
Ethelred, earl of Fife, son of Malcolm 'Ceannmor,' i. 2; ii. 2; vi. 284.
Ethelred II., King of England, ii. 426.
Etherington of Newton Garth, Richard, iii. 291.
—— —— his wife, Jane Throckmorton, iii. 291.
ETHIE, CARNEGIE, EARL OF, vi. 494-495.
Ethie, John, earl of, vi. 494.
—— —— his 1st wife, Magdalen Haliburton, vi. 495.
—— —— his 2nd wife, Marjory Maule, vi. 495.
Ethna, wife of David de Haya of Erroll, iii. 556.
Ethne, wife of Ferteth, earl of Strathearn, iii. 557; viii. 241.

Ethreda, wife of Waldeve, son of Gillemin, iii. 245.
ETTRICK, DOUGLAS, LORD DOUGLAS OF, iii. 216-218.
ETTRICK, RUTHVEN, LORD RUTHVEN OF, iv. 104-106.
Ettrick, Alexander, eldest son of Patrick, lord Ruthven of Ettrick; styled lord, iv. 105.
—— —— his wife, *, iv. 105.
ETTRICK OF ETTRICK, NAPIER, BARON, vi. 437-439.
Ettrick of Ettrick, Francis, first baron, vi. 437.
—— —— his wife, Anne Jane Charlotte Lockwood, vi. 438.
Eugenius *or* Ewen of Glenerrichdie and Tulloch, i. 419.
—— —— his wife, Mary, i. 419.
Eugene of Stobo, grandson of Samuel, vii. 420.
Eumont, Elizabeth, wife of John Hope, iv. 486.
Euphemia, wife of Patrick MacCalzean of Cliftonhall, i. 120.
—— wife of Sir Walter de Moravia, lord of Duffus, ii. 122; vii. 232.
—— wife of (1) Wm. Comyn of Kilbride, and (2) Sir Andrew Moray, ii. 126.
—— wife of Robert de Brus of Annandale, ii. 430.
—— wife of Sir John Elphinstone of Pittendreich and Stirches, iii. 529.
Eure, Anne, wife of Ralph Constable, iii. 290.
—— Ralph de, i. 430.
—— —— his wife, Isabella of Atholl, i. 430.
—— Robert, iii. 290.
—— Sir William, commissioner for England, ii. 63.
Eustace, count of Boulogne, i. 2.
—— —— his wife, Mary of Scotland, i. 2.
—— Katharine Maria, wife of admiral Arbuthnott, i. 307.
Euston, Henry (Fitzroy), 1st earl of, i. 31.
—— —— his wife, Isabel Bennet, i. 31.
Eva, dau. of Swan, lord of Tippermuir, and wife of Alan, son of Walter Ruthven, i. 12.
—— countess of Buchan, wife of Colban, ii. 251.
—— wife of William de Haya, 1st laird of Erroll, iii. 555, 556 *ter*.
—— wife of David de Haya of Erroll, iii. 557.
—— wife of Alwin, 2nd earl of Lennox, v. 328.
—— wife of Malcolm, thane of Callendar, v. 183, 330.
EVAN, HAMILTON, LORD, iv. 372-397.
Evan, James, first lord, iv. 372.

* Name unknown.

Evan, James, eldest son of 1st marquess of Hamilton; styled lord, iv. 373.
Evans of Ash Hill Towers, Eyre, vii. 492.
—— of Tuddenham, John Arthur, captain, vii. 451.
—— —— his wife, Margaret Eleanora Georgina Fraser, vii. 451.
—— Ann Trevor Corry, wife of 10th earl of Seafield, vii. 492.
—— Caroline Louisa, wife of James Ogilvie-Grant, vii. 492.
—— Cecilia, maid to Winifred, countess of Nithsdale, vi. 488.
—— Charlotte, wife of 17th lord Saltoun, vii. 452.
—— De Lacy, general, G.C.B., M.P., i. 307.
—— George Thomas, major, vii. 492.
—— James, Norwood, viii. 88.
—— —— his wife, Eleanor Carnegie, viii. 88.
—— Thomas Brown, Oxford, vii. 452.
Evelyn, Elizabeth, wife of R. Pierrepont, vi. 468.
Everard, Johanna, wife of (1) Sir John Hamilton, (2) 4th lord Sempill, (3) Patrick Craffurd, and (4) Sir Geo. Marbury, i. 40; vii. 553.
—— Levimus, councillor of state to king of Spain, i. 40.
EVERINGHAM, CONSTABLE-MAXWELL, LORD HERRIES OF, iv. 423-424.
Evers, Edward, Ipswich, i. 382; ix. 24.
—— —— his wife, Bridget Bacon, i. 382.
—— Sir Ralph, v. 398.
Ewart, David, colonel Bengal Artillery, iii. 105.
—— —— his wife, Ann Finlay Anderson Ramsay, iii. 105.
—— Giles, mistress of John Johnston of that Ilk, i. 247.
Ewen of Lorn, v. 2, 30; viii. 246.
—— *or* Eugenius, son of Conan, illeg. son of Henry, 3rd earl of Atholl, i. 419.
—— —— his wife, Mary, dau. of Convall, i. 419.
Ewing, Alexander, D.C.L., bishop of Argyll and the Isles, vi. 386.
—— —— his wife, Alice Louisa Douglas, vi. 386.
—— Janet, wife of David Sinclair of Broynach, ii. 341.
Exeter, John (Holland), duke of, iii. 183.
—— William (Cecil), 2nd earl of, iii. 478.
—— Henry (Cecil), 1st marquess of, iv. 394.
—— —— his wife, Elizabeth Burrell, iv. 394.
Extilda *or* Hextilda, wife of, (1) Richard Comyn, and (2) Malcolm, earl of Atholl, i. 3, 417, 504, 507, 508; ii. 252; iii. 6; vi. 288.
Eyre of Grove, Anthony, v. 235.
—— of Hassop, Dorothea, self-styled countess of Newburgh, wife of col. C. Leslie of Balquhain, vi. 456.

Eyre of Hassop, Francis, self-styled earl of Newburgh, vi. 455.
—— —— his wife, Dorothy Gladwin, vi. 455.
—— —— Francis, self-styled earl of Newburgh, vi. 456.
—— —— Thomas, self-styled earl of Newburgh, vi. 456.
—— —— his wife, Margaret Kennedy, ii. 500; vi. 456.
—— of Warkworth, Francis, vi. 455.
—— —— his wife, Mary Frances Guillelma Radcliffe, vi. 455.
—— of Welford Park, George, iii. 48.
—— —— his wife, Alice Frances Lindsay, iii. 48.
—— Barbara, vi. 456.
—— Caroline, vi. 456.
—— Charles, vi. 456.
—— Charlotte, vi. 456.
—— Sir Giles, judge of the King's Bench, iv. 182.
—— —— his wife, Christabella *, iv. 182.
—— James, Metz, vi. 456.
—— —— his wife, Thérèse Joséphine de Chénencourt, vi. 456.
—— Julia, wife of Robert Auriol Drummond-Hay, v. 235.
—— Mary, wife of Arthur Onslow, vi. 456.
—— Radcliffe, dau. of F. E. of Hassop, vi. 456.
EYTHIN, KING, LORD, iii. 588-594.
Eythin, James, lord, iii. 592.

FAA, SIR JOHN, ii. 481.
Fagan of Feltrim, Christopher, i. 51.
—— Elizabeth, wife of 4th lord Strabane, i. 51.
Fagel, James, baron, vii. 178.
—— Mary Katharine Anna Jacoba, wife of 10th lord Reay, vii. 178.
Fagniani, Maria, wife of 3rd marquess of Hertford, vii. 147 *n*.
FAILFORD, STEWART, LORD OCHILTREE, AND, vi. 511.
Failford, Andrew, lord, vi. 511.
FAIRFAX OF CAMERON, FAIRFAX, LORD, iii. 595-606.
Fairfax of Cameron, Albert Kirby, twelfth lord, iii. 606; ix. 87.
—— —— Bryan, eighth lord, iii. 601, 603.
—— —— his 1st wife, Elizabeth Cary, iii. 603.
—— —— his 2nd wife, Jenny Dennison, iii. 603.
—— —— Charles Snowden, tenth lord, iii. 605.
—— —— his wife, Eda Benham, iii. 605.
—— —— Ferdinando, second lord, iii. 598.
—— —— his 1st wife, Mary Sheffield, iii. 598.
—— —— his 2nd wife, Rhoda Chapman, iii. 598.

* Name unknown.

Fairfax of Cameron, Henry, fourth lord, iii. 597, 600.
—— —— his wife, Frances Barwick, iii. 600.
—— —— John Contée, eleventh lord, iii. 604, 605.
—— —— his wife, Mary Kirby, iii. 605.
—— —— Robert, seventh lord, iii. 602.
—— —— his 1st wife, Martha Collins, iii. 602.
—— —— his 2nd wife, Dorothy Best, iii. 603.
—— —— Thomas, first lord, iii. 596.
—— —— his wife, Eleanora Aske, iii. 596.
—— —— Thomas, third lord, iii. 599.
—— —— his wife, Anne Vere, iii. 599.
—— —— Thomas, fifth lord, iii. 601.
—— —— his wife, Katharine Culpeper, iii. 602.
—— —— Thomas, sixth lord, iii. 602.
—— —— Thomas, ninth lord, iii. 603.
—— —— his 1st wife, Mary Aylett, iii. 603.
—— —— his 2nd wife, Louisa Washington, iii. 603.
—— —— his 3rd wife, Margaret Herbert, iii. 603.
FAIRFAX, LORD FAIRFAX OF CAMERON, iii. 595-606.
Fairfax of Elmley, Charles Gregory (Fairfax), 10th viscount, iii. 300.
—— —— his wife, Elizabeth Clifford, iii. 299.
—— —— Thomas (Fairfax), 1st viscount, iii. 296; v. 10, 12, 13.
—— —— his wife, Katharine Constable, iii. 296.
—— of Ashgrove, Henry, iii. 604.
—— —— his wife, Anne Caroline Herbert, iii. 604.
—— of Askham, Richard, iii. 595.
—— of Belvoir, George William, iii. 600, 603.
—— —— his wife, Sarah Cary, iii. 600.
—— —— William, governor of the Bahamas, president of the King's Council, Virginia, iii. 600.
—— —— his 1st wife, Sarah Walker, iii. 600.
—— —— his 2nd wife, Deborah Gedney, iii. 600.
—— of Denton and Nunappleton, Sir Thomas, iii. 596.
—— —— his wife, Dorothy Gale, iii. 596.
—— —— Sir Thomas, iii. 596.
—— —— his wife, Eleanora Aske, iii. 596.
—— of Gilling, Sir Thomas, iii. 296.
—— —— his wife, Katharine Constable, iii. 296.
—— —— Charles Gregory, iii. 300.
—— —— his wife, Elizabeth Clifford, iii. 299.
—— of Hurst, Henry, ii. 275.
—— —— his wife, * Browne, ii. 275.
—— of Oglethorpe, Henry, in holy orders, iii. 596.
—— —— his 1st wife, Katharine Dukenfield, iii. 596.
—— —— his 2nd wife, Mary Cholmley, iii. 597.

* Name unknown.

Fairfax of Scow Hall, Charles, governor of Hull, author of *Analecta Fairfaxiana*, iii. 597.
—— —— his wife, Mary Breary, iii. 597.
—— of Shannon Hill, Ferdinando, iii. 603.
—— —— his wife, Elizabeth Blair Cary, iii. 603.
—— of Steeton, Sir Guy, iii. 595.
—— —— his wife, Isabella Ryther, iii. 595.
—— —— Sir William, iii. 595.
—— —— his wife, Elizabeth Manners, iii. 596.
—— —— Sir William, iii. 596.
—— —— his wife, Isabel Thwaites, iii. 596.
—— of Toulston, Henry, sheriff of Yorkshire, iii. 600.
—— —— his wife, Anne Harrison, iii. 600.
—— —— Henry, his eldest son, iii. 600.
—— of Vaucluse, Albert, iii. 604.
—— of Walton, Richard, iii. 595.
—— —— his wife, Eustachia Carthorpe, iii. 595.
—— —— Sir Thomas. iii. 296.
—— —— William, bailiff of York, iii. 594.
—— Ada Raymond, iii. 604.
—— Albert, surgeon, iii. 604.
—— Anne, wife of George Wentworth, iii. 597.
—— Anne, wife of Charles Catlett, iii. 603.
—— Anne, wife of (1) Lawrence Washington, and (2) George Lee, iii. 600.
—— Anne, dau. of Henry F. of Toulston, iii. 601.
—— Anne, wife of Ralph Carr, iii. 601.
—— Aurelia, wife of col. J. W. Irwin, iii. 605.
—— Barwick, Tadcaster, iii. 601.
—— Brian, Wetherby, iii. 601.
—— Bryan, LL.D., iii. 597.
—— —— his wife, Charlotte Cary, iii. 597.
—— Caroline Snowden, iii. 605.
—— Charles, killed at Marston Moor, iii. 598.
—— Charles Edmund, iii. 605.
—— Dorothy, wife of Sir Wm. Constable, iii. 597.
—— Dorothy, wife of Richard Hutton, iii. 599.
—— Dorothy, wife of Henry Chapman, iii. 601.
—— Dorothy, wife of (1) R. Stapleton, and (2) B. Sherard, iii. 601.
—— Dorothy, wife of (1) John Ingram, and (2) Sir Thos. Norcliffe, v. 10.
—— Elizabeth, wife of Sir William Craven, iii. 598.
—— Elizabeth, wife of rev. D. Griffith, iii. 603.
—— Ellen, wife of Sir William Selby, iii. 598.
—— Ethelbert, son of Orlando F., iii. 605.
—— Ethelbert, 5th son of 9th lord Fairfax, iii. 605.
—— Eugenia, wife of (1) E. Mason, and (2) C. K. Hyde, iii. 605.
Fairfax, Frances, wife of David Erskine, earl of Buchan, ii. 275.
—— Frances, wife of Thos. Widdrington, iii. 598.
—— Frances. wife of rev. N. Rymer, iii. 601.
—— Frances, wife of Denny Martin, iii. 602.
—— Frances Marvin, wife of E. L. Rhett, iii. 606.
—— Guy Percy, iii. 604.
—— —— his wife, Elsie Ida Crook, iii. 604.
—— Hannah, wife of Warner Washington, iii. 601.
—— Henry Culpepper, F.R.S., iii. 602.
—— Henry Malcolm, iii. 604.
—— Henry Reginald, iii. 604.
—— Herbert Carlyle, iii. 604.
—— —— his wife, Jane Davies Baker, iii. 604.
—— Isabella Christian, iii. 604.
—— John, 8th son of 1st lord Fairfax, iii. 597.
—— Jane Cary, iii. 605.
—— Josephine, wife of Tunstall Smith, iii. 605.
—— Katharine, wife of (1) Sir M. Boynton, (2) R. Stapleton, (3) Sir A. Ingram, and (4) W. Wickham, v. 13.
—— Lavinia, iii. 605.
—— Margaret, wife of rev. David Wilkins, iii. 602.
—— Margaret, wife of Watkinson Payler of Thoraldby, v. 12.
—— Mary, wife of Henry Arthington, iii. 598.
—— Mary, wife of 2nd duke of Buckingham, iii. 599.
—— Mary, dau. of 4th lord Fairfax, iii. 601.
—— Mary, dau. of 5th lord Fairfax, iii. 602.
—— Mary Cecilia, iii. 606.
—— Mary Edith, wife of Dr. J. J. Moncure, iii. 605.
—— Mary Isabel, iii. 604.
—— Monimia, wife of Geo. Davies, iii. 605.
—— Monimia, wife of Arch. Cary, iii. 605.
—— Orlando, M.D., Virginia, iii. 604.
—— —— his wife, Mary Randolph Cary, iii. 604.
—— Orlando Cary, iii. 604.
—— Peregrine, 9th son of 1st lord Fairfax, iii. 597.
—— Randolph, iii. 604.
—— Raymond, iii. 604.
—— —— his wife, Anna Burford, iii. 604.
—— Raymond, 4th son of 9th lord Fairfax, iii. 605.
—— Reginald, commander U.S. and Confederate States Navy, iii. 605.
—— Ronald Randolph, iii. 604.
—— —— his wife, Anne Ridge Early, iii. 604.
—— Ronald Randolph, his son, iii. 604.
—— Sarah, wife of major John Carlyle, iii. 601, 603.
—— Thomas, eldest son of rev. Henry F. of Oglethorpe, iii. 597.

Fairfax, Thomas, Scandaroon, iii. 597.
— Thomas, R.N., iii. 600.
— Thomas, Virginia, iii. 605.
— Ursula, dau. of 2nd lord Fairfax, iii. 598.
— Ursula, wife of Wm. Cartwright, iii. 599.
— William, captain, iii. 597.
— William Henry, 28th regiment of foot, iii. 601.
Fairholm of Craigiehall, John, i. 268.
— — Sophia, wife of 1st marquess of Annandale, i. 268.
— of Greenknowe, George, i. 497; iv. 66.
— — his wife, Caroline Elizabeth Forbes, iv. 66.
— Andrew, iv. 578.
— Elizabeth Marjory, wife of J. C. P. Murray, i. 497.
Fairley, Elizabeth, wife of 5th lord Reay, vii. 176.
— John, collector of customs, Ayr, vii. 176.
FAIRLIE OF FAIRLIE, BOYLE, BARON, iv. 220-221.
Fairlie of Fairlie, David, first baron, iv. 220.
— of Braid, i. 278 *n.*
— — John, vi. 365.
— — his wife, Elene Douglas, vi. 365.
— — John, iv. 84.
— — Robert, viii. 489.
— — his wife, Mariota Wemyss, viii. 489.
— — Robert, ix. 42.
— — his wife, Annabella Campbell, ix. 42.
— — Sir William, viii. 6.
— — his wife, Giles Herring, viii. 6.
— of Bruntsfield, John, vii. 193.
— — his wife, Elizabeth Weston, vii. 193.
— — William, iv. 205.
— — his wife, Jean Mure, iv. 205.
— of Coodham, James Ogilvie, viii. 133.
— of Fairlie, John, ii. 292; v. 151.
— — Sir Robert, iv. 192 *n.*
— of Plewlands, Robert, viii. 489.
— Helen, wife of Henry Forrester of Niddry, iv. 84.
— Margaret Anne Alice, wife of Sir G. Dalrymple-Horn-Elphinstone, viii. 133.
— Marion, wife of (1) Thomas Boyd of Linn, and (2) Sir Jas. Stewart of Bute, ii. 292; v. 151.
Fairweather, Robert, minister of Crail, v. 415.
— — his wife, Ann Lindsay, v. 415.
FALCONER OF HALKERTON, FALCONER, LORD, v. 242-255.
Falconer of Halkerton, Alexander, first lord v. 246, 248.
— — his wife, Anne Lindsay, v. 249, 401.
— — Alexander, second lord, v. 249.
— — his wife, Margaret Ogilvy, i. 126; v. 249.
Falconer of Halkerton, Alexander, fifth lord, v. 251.
— — his wife, Frances Mackworth, v. 251.
— — Algernon Hawkins Thomond, eleventh lord, v. 254.
— — his wife, Sydney Charlotte Montagu, v. 254.
— — Anthony Adrian, seventh lord, v. 242, 251; vi. 64.
— — his wife, Christina Elizabeth Sighterman, v. 251.
— — Anthony Adrian, ninth lord, v. 252.
— — his 1st wife, Julia Renny, v. 252.
— — his 2nd wife, Louisa Hawkins, v. 252.
— — Arthur George, eldest surviving son of 9th earl of Kintore; styled lord, v. 254.
— — David, third lord, v. 249; ix. 123.
— — David, fourth lord, v. 241, 247, 250; ix. 123.
— — his wife, Catherine Margaret Keith, v. 241, 250.
— — Francis Alexander, tenth lord, v. 253.
— — his wife, Louisa Madeleine Hawkins, v. 253.
— — William, sixth lord, v. 251.
— — his wife, *, v. 251.
— — William, eighth lord, v. 252.
— — his wife, Maria Bannerman, v. 252.
FALCONER, LORD FALCONER OF HALKERTON, v. 242-255.
— of Ballandro, Elizabeth, dau. of David F. of Halkerton, v. 244.
— — Robert, grandson of Alex. F. of Lethens, v. 243, 244.
— of Balmashanner, David, v. 407.
— of Balnakettle, James, v. 251.
— — his wife, Jean Falconer, v. 251.
— of Carlowrie, George, ancestor of the family of, v. 247.
— — his wife, Janet Marjoribanks, v. 247.
— of Dinduff, William, v. 245.
— — his wife, Beatrix Dunbar, v. 245.
— of Diracroft, Sir Alexander, v. 248.
— of Drimmie, Robert, v. 246.
— — his wife, Isobel Rossie, v. 246.
— of Fernychtie, Sir Alexander, v. 245.
— of Glenfarquhar, Sir Alexander, 1st bart., v. 247.
— — his 1st wife, Marjory Irvine, ix. 123.
— — his 2nd wife, Helen Grahame, ix. 123.
— — Sir Alexander, 2nd bart., v. 247, 250.
— — Sir David, M.P., v. 246.
— — his wife, Margaret Hepburn, v. 247.
— of Halkerton, Alexander, 2nd laird, v. 243; ix. 123.
— — Sir Alexander, 7th laird, v. 246.
— — his wife, Agnes Carnegie, v. 246; viii. 64.

* Name unknown.

Falconer of Halkerton, Alexander, 6th laird, v. 246.
—— —— his wife, Isabel Gray, iv. 283; v. 246.
—— —— Sir Alexander, 5th laird, v. 245.
—— —— his wife, Elizabeth Douglas, i. 184; v. 245.
—— —— David, 1st laird, i. 278; v. 243.
—— —— David, 4th laird, v. 244; vi. 173, 174.
—— —— his wife, Mariot Dunbar, v. 244 *bis*.
—— —— Sir George, 3rd laird, v. 243.
—— —— his wife, Elizabeth Erskine, v. 244.
—— of Innerlochtie, Hew, v. 245.
—— of Kincorth, Samuel, v. 245.
—— of Kingoven, Ranulph, v. 242.
—— of Kinguthin, Henry, v. 242.
—— of Lethen, Alexander, v. 243; ix. 123.
—— —— Sir Alexander, v. 245.
—— —— his wife, Elizabeth Douglas, v. 245.
—— —— Alexander, v. 246.
—— —— his wife, Isobel Gray, v. 246.
—— —— Sir Alexander, v. 246.
—— —— his wife, Agnes Carnegie, v. 246.
—— —— David, v. 244.
—— —— Sir George, v. 244; ix. 123.
—— of Lethenbar, Andrew, v. 243.
—— of Middleton, David, v. 244; vi. 173.
—— of Monkton, James, v. 251.
—— —— his wife, Jean Falconer, v. 251.
—— of Newton, Alexander, v. 243.
—— —— Sir David, lord president of College of Justice, iii. 580; v. 247.
—— —— his 1st wife, Elizabeth Nairn, v. 247; vi. 393.
—— —— his 2nd wife, Mary Norvell, v. 247.
—— —— David, v. 250.
—— —— his wife, Katharine Margaret Keith, v. 250.
—— —— Patrick, v. 246.
—— of Phesdo, Archibald, ancestor of the family of, v. 245.
—— —— George, captain R.N., v. 245, 250.
—— —— his wife, Hannah Ivie, v. 250.
—— —— George, v. 250.
—— —— Sir James, i. 308, 309.
—— —— John, advocate, v. 245.
—— Agnes, wife of 2nd lord Banff, ii. 19; v. 249; ix. 35 *bis*, 123.
—— Agnes, wife of (1) Alex. Keith of Benholm, and (2) John, master of Forrester, iv. 92; v. 248.
—— Agnes, wife of Alex. Guthrie of that Ilk, v. 245.
—— Alexander, v. 244.
—— —— his wife, Janet Arbuthnott, i. 287; v. 244.
—— Alexander, advocate, v. 247.
—— —— his wife, Mary, countess of Erroll, v. 247.
—— Alexander, 2nd son of 2nd lord Falconer, v. 249.
—— Andrew, 8th son of Sir John F., v. 248.
Falconer, Charles, 6th son of Sir John F., v. 248.
—— Charles, 3rd son of 7th lord Falconer of Halkerton, v. 251.
—— Colin, bishop of Argyll, and of Moray, v. 245.
—— —— his wife, Lillas Rose, v. 245.
—— David, godson of King David II., v. 243.
—— David, 3rd son of Sir John F., v. 248; ix. 123.
—— David, insurance broker, v. 250.
—— —— * his wife, Lamplugh, v. 250.
—— Elizabeth, wife of Thos. Arbuthnott, i. 309.
—— Elizabeth, wife of Alex. Lindsay of Broadland, v. 244.
—— Elizabeth, dau. of Sir D. F. of Newton, v. 248.
—— Elizabeth, dau. of 2nd lord Falconer, v. 249.
—— Elizabeth, wife of Sir C. Ramsay of Balmain, ix. 123 *bis*, 124.
—— Esther, dau. of Sir John F., v. 248.
—— Euphame, wife of John Row of Bandeath, v. 249; ix. 123.
—— Gervase, v. 243.
—— Grizel, *error for* Agnes, wife of 2nd lord Banff, ii. 19 *n.*; ix. 123.
—— Helen, dau. of 2nd lord Falconer, v. 249.
—— Isobel, wife of Dr. Francis, v. 246.
—— Isobel, wife of John Middleton of Kilhill, vi. 173; ix. 123.
—— James, 2nd son of Sir John F., v. 248.
—— James, 3rd son of 2nd lord Falconer, v. 249.
—— Jane, wife of (1) James Forbes of Thornton, and (2) James Auchterlony, v. 249.
—— Janet, *error for* Marjorie, wife of A. Wishart of Carnbeg, v. 244; ix. 123.
—— Jean, wife of John Fullarton of Kinnaber, v. 246; ix. 124.
—— Jean, wife of John Grant of Moyness, v. 248.
—— Jean, wife of Jas. Falconer of Monkton and Balnakettle, v. 251.
—— John, bishop of Dundee, iii. 380.
—— Sir John, deputy treasurer-depute, v. 307.
—— Sir John, master of the Mint to King Charles I., v. 248.
—— —— his 1st wife, Sibil Ogilvy, v. 248.
—— —— his 2nd wife, Esther Briot, v. 248.
—— John, eldest son of Sir John F., v. 248.
—— John, v. 250.
—— —— his wife, * Nairn, v. 250.
—— Katharine, wife of Hugh Rose of Kilravock, v. 244.
—— Katharine, wife of Joseph Hume of Ninewells, v. 248.
—— Katharine, dau. of 5th lord Falconer, v. 250.

* Name unknown.

Falconer, Magdalen, wife of capt. G. Lindsay of Kirkforthar, v. 407.
— Margaret, wife of John Arbuthnott of Fordoun, i. 308.
— Margaret, wife of Patrick Bruce of Valleyfield, iii. 472.
— Margaret, dau. of Sir David F. of Newton, v. 247.
— Margaret, dau. of Sir John F., v. 248.
— Margaret, dau. of Sir Alex. F. of Halkerton, v. 248 *bis*.
— Marjory, wife of Geo. Norvell of Boghall, v. 251.
— Marjorie, wife of A. Wishart of Carnbeg, ix. 123.
— Marjorie, wife of Angus Macintosh, *or* Williamson, of Termett, ix. 123.
— Mary, wife of * Fullerton of Dudwick, v. 248.
— Mary, dau. of 5th lord Falconer, v. 251.
— Patrick, 4th son of Sir John F., v. 248.
— Sir Patrick, advocate, v. 248.
— Patrick, viii. 54.
— — his wife, Margaret Carnegie, viii. 54.
— Peter, *clericus regis*, v. 242.
— Ranulf, v. 243.
— — his wife, Muriella, v. 243.
— Robert, son of Henry F., v. 242.
— Robert, 5th son of Sir John F., v. 248.
— Thomas, 2nd son of 1st lord Falconer of Halkerton, ix. 123.
— William, 7th son of Sir John F., v. 248.
— William, 2nd son of 7th lord Falconer of Halkerton, v. 251.
Falconer-Hay of Dalgaty, Alexander, advocate, iii. 580; ix. 87.
— — his wife, Mary, countess of Erroll, iii. 580.
Falconer-Stewart of Binny, George, ancestor of the family of, v. 247.
Falkiner, Sir Leslie, 7th bart., ii. 530.
— — his 2nd wife, Kathleen Mary Orde Powlett, ii. 530.
FALKLAND, CARY, VISCOUNT, iii. 607-617.
Falkland, Anthony, fifth viscount, iii. 612.
— — his wife, Rebecca Lytton, iii. 613.
— Byron Plantagenet, twelfth viscount, iii. 615, 616.
— — his wife, Mary Reade, iii. 617.
— Charles John, ninth viscount, iii. 615.
— — his wife, Christiana Anton, iii. 615.
— Henry, first viscount, iii. 609; ix. 88 *bis*.
— — his wife, Elizabeth Tanfield, iii. 610.
— Henry, fourth viscount, iii. 612.
— — his wife, Rachel Hungerford, iii. 612.
— Henry Thomas, eighth viscount, iii. 615.
— Lucius, second viscount, iii. 611; ix. 88.
— — his wife, Lettice Morison, iii. 612.

* Name unknown.

Falkland, Lucius, third viscount, iii. 612.
— Lucius Bentinck, tenth viscount, iii. 615, 616.
— — his 1st wife, Amelia Fitzclarence, iii. 616.
— — his 2nd wife, Elizabeth Katharine Gubbins, iii. 616.
— Lucius Charles, seventh viscount, iii. 614.
— — his 1st wife, Jane Butler, iii. 614.
— — his 2nd wife, Sarah Inwen, iii. 614.
— Lucius Henry, sixth viscount, iii. 611, 613.
— — his 1st wife, Dorothy Molineux, iii. 613.
— — his 2nd wife, Laura Dillon, iii. 613.
— Plantagenet Pierrepoint, eleventh viscount, iii. 615, 616.
— — his wife, Mary Anne Maubert, iii. 616.
— Lucius Henry, styled earl of, iii. 617.
— master of, Lucius Ferdinand, son of 7th viscount Falkland, iii. 614.
— — his wife, Anne Leith, iii. 615.
— master of, Lucius Plantagenet, eldest son of 12th viscount Falkland, iii. 617.
— — his wife, Ella Louise Catford, iii. 617.
— master of, Lucius William Charles Augustus Frederick, son of 10th viscount Falkland, iii. 616.
— — his wife, Sarah Christiana Keighley, iii. 616.
Fane, Grace, wife of 2nd earl of Home, iv. 467; ix. 108.
— Julian Henry Charles, iii. 124.
— — his wife, Adine Eliza Anne Cowper, iii. 124.
Fanshaw(e, Anne, ix. 93.
— Edward, lieut.-general, C.B., viii. 141.
— — his wife, Frances Mary Dalrymple, viii. 141.
— William, master of Requests, i. 30.
— — his wife, Mary Walters, i. 30.
Fareham, Louise Renée Perranooet de Kerouaille, countess of, v. 362.
Farmer of Easton, Sir George, iii. 231.
— Anne, wife of (1) Robert, 8th lord Crichton of Sanquhar, (2) * Sands, and (3) Barnaby, 6th earl of Thomond, iii. 231.
— Sir Henry, i. 376 *n*.
— Jacomina, wife of lt.-col. W. Bellenden, ii. 73.
FARNELL, CARNEGIE, BARON BALINHARD OF, viii. 90-93.
Farnham of Bedworth, Katharine, wife of Sir Thos. Beaumont, ii. 578.
— — Thomas, ii. 578.
— John Maxwell, ancestor of the lords, vi. 471.

* Name unknown.

Farquhar, Charity Graeme, wife of rev. A. Hamilton, ii. 56.
—— Margaret, wife of Sir James Melville of Hallhill and Burntisland, vi. 92.
—— Sir Walter, 1st bart., ii. 56.
—— Sir Walter Minto Townsend, 2nd bart., vii. 177.
—— —— his wife, Erica Mackay, vii. 177.
Farquharson of Finzean, Francis, i. 295.
—— —— his wife, Marjorie Arbuthnott, i. 295.
—— of Invercauld, James, vii. 175.
—— —— his wife, Margaret Carr, vii. 175.
—— —— James, i. 485.
—— —— his wife, Amelia Murray, i. 485.
—— —— John, i. 476.
—— —— his 3rd wife, Margaret Murray, i. 476.
Farwell of the Lowlands, Frederick Cooper, iv. 68.
—— Eveline Louisa Michell, wife of capt. W. R. D. Forbes, iv. 68.
Fauconberg, Thomas (Belasyse), 1st viscount, v. 11; vii. 107.
Fawkes, Lionel Grimston, col. R.A., ii. 501.
—— Lois, ii. 501.
—— Monica, ii. 501.
Fawnys, Adam de, iv. 331.
—— Christian de, wife of William de Haliburton, iv. 331.
—— Richard de, iv. 331.
Fawsyde of Fawsyde, George, vii. 148.
—— —— James, ii. 68.
—— —— his wife, Janet Lawson, ii. 68.
—— —— Robert, v. 295.
—— —— his wife, Marion Maitland, v. 295.
—— —— William, viii. 523.
—— —— his wife, Marjory Fleming, styled countess of Wigtown, viii. 522, 523.
—— of Lathame, Malcolm, v. 551.
—— Agnes, wife of Sir Wm. Douglas of Kelhead, vii. 148.
Fay, Comte de, i. 60.
—— —— his wife, Elizabeth Hamilton, i. 60.
Fearn, David, writer, Edinburgh, vi. 597.
—— —— his wife, Anna Hamilton, vi. 597.
Fearnside, J., London, ii. 198.
—— Sarah Priscilla, wife of W. B. S. Campbell, ii. 198.
Federeth, William de, constable of Roxburgh Castle, ii. 122.
—— —— his wife, Christian Moray, ii. 122.
Feilden, William Leyland, canon, vii. 590.
—— —— his wife, Jane Elizabeth St. Clair, vii. 590.
Feilding, Adelaide Emily, wife of Charles Archibald Murray, viii. 211.
—— Basil, father of 1st earl of Denbigh, i. 405.
—— —— his wife, Elizabeth Aston, i. 405.
Feilding, Sir Charles, i. 401.
—— —— his wife, Ursula Stockton, i. 401.
Felicia, wife of John Maitland of Thirlestane, v. 284.
Felix, bishop of Moray, viii. 319 *n*.
Fellgate, Elizabeth, wife of (1) Cotton Gill, and (2) Sir Wm. Aston, i. 401.
—— William, London, i. 401.
Fell, Dr. John, dean of Christ Church, Oxford, vii. 105.
Felton, Robert de, castellan of Lochmaben, iv. 225; vi. 203.
—— William de, constable of Roxburgh Castle, ii. 396.
Fellowes of Shottisham, John, in holy orders, viii. 310.
—— —— his wife, Susan Lyon, viii. 310.
Fénélon, François de Salignac de la Mothe, v. 159.
Fenn, Hugh, Wotton-under-Edge, ii. 35.
—— Katharine, wife of (1) H. Perry, (2) lord Barret of Newburgh, and (3) Wm. Morgan, ii. 35; ix. 36.
FENTOUN, ERSKINE, VISCOUNT OF, v. 85-97.
Fentoun, Alexander, son of 1st earl of Kellie; styled viscount of, v. 86.
—— —— his wife, Anne Seton, iii. 372; v. 86.
—— Thomas, first viscount of, v. 85; vii. 69.
—— of the Ard, Sir William, v. 519; vi. 203.
—— —— his wife, Cecilia Bisset, v. 519.
—— of Baky, Isabella, wife of Alexander Nairn, viii. 277.
—— —— Jonet, wife of (1) Robert Halyburton, and (2) Sir Jas. Douglas of Ralston, v. 394, 524; vi. 366.
—— —— Margaret, wife of Walter Ogilvy of Oures, and mistress of David Lindsay of Lethnot, i. 110; iii. 18; viii. 277.
—— —— Walter, v. 394; vi. 366.
—— of Beaufort, Margaret, i. 110.
—— —— Walter, i. 110.
—— of Beauly, William de, v. 520.
—— of Buttergask, Collace, and Strathfentoun, Janet, junior, wife of (1) Robert Stewart, and (2) William Halkett, viii. 274 *bis*.
—— of Coulas, viii. 264.
—— of Drumblate and Towie, Jonet, wife of Sir James Douglas of Ralston, v. 524; vi. 366.
—— of Fentoun, Sir John, iii. 561.
—— —— William, v. 522.
—— of Fentounbarns, John, viii. 27.
—— of Gutters, John, viii. 27.
—— of Kilbirny, Jonet, wife of Sir Jas. Douglas, v. 524.
—— of Kiltarlity, Sir William, v. 519; vi. 203 *bis*.
—— —— William de, v. 425, 520.
—— of Wester Ogil, v. 206.
—— Alice de, wife of Sir H. St. Clair of Roslin, vi. 566.

Fentoun, Felicia, wife of Oliver Ogilvy, ix. 7.
— Janet, wife of Hugh Fraser of Lovat, v. 522.
— John, comptroller-clerk to King James VI., ix. 156.
Fenwick, Elizabeth, wife of 3rd lord Deloraine, iii. 113.
— John, iii. 113.
— *, vii. 104.
— — his wife, Margaret Graham, vii. 104.
Ferchar, 10th son of Alwin, 2nd earl of Lennox, v. 330.
Fergus Mor, King of Dalriada, v. 27.
— of Carrick, iii. 426.
— of Oughtermachany, 5th son of Gilbert, earl of Strathearn, viii. 243.
— uncle of Hugo de Arbuthnott, i. 275.
— 'son of the earl,' iii. 254.
Fergushill of Cunninghamhead, William de, iv. 231.
— of Fergushill, William de, iv. 231 *bis*.
Ferguson of Pitfour, James, lord of Session, and Justiciary, iii. 517; vi. 64.
— — his wife, Anne Murray, iii. 517.
— of Raith, James, vi. 112.
— — William, vi. 112.
— Thomas, chaplain of Largo, v. 395.
— Thomas Benyon, barrister-at-law, iii. 615.
Ferguson-Davie of Creedy, Sir Henry R., general, 1st bart., vii. 209.
— Harriet Anne, wife of gen. R. Rollo, vii. 209.
Fergusson of Craigdarroch, James, viii. 151.
— — his wife, Eleanor Dalrymple, viii. 151.
— — Robert, iv. 243.
— — his wife, Katharine Cunningham, iv. 243.
— — Robert, iv. 239.
— — his wife, Jean Cunningham, iv. 239.
— — Robert, ii. 410.
— — his 2nd wife, Elizabeth Grier, iii. 410.
— of Kilkerran, Sir Adam, 3rd bart., iv. 234, 249, 252.
— — Sir Charles, 7th bart., D.S.O., M.V.O., col. Grenadier Guards, iv. 221.
— — his wife, Alice Mary Boyle, iv. 221.
— — Sir Charles Dalrymple, 5th bart., viii. 144.
— — his wife, Helen Boyle, iv. 212; viii. 144.
— — Sir James, 2nd bart., lord of Session and Justiciary, iv. 249; v. 311; viii. 144.
— — his wife, Jean Maitland, iv. 249; v. 311.

* Name unknown.

Fergusson of Kilkerran, Sir James, 4th bart., i. 554; viii. 144.
— — his 1st wife, Jean Dalrymple, viii. 144.
— — his 2nd wife, Henrietta Duncan, i. 554.
— — Sir James, 6th bart., G.C.S.I., K.C.M.G., C.I.E., iii. 107; iv. 221; viii. 144.
— — his wife, Edith Christian Ramsay, iii. 107.
— — Sir John, ii. 488.
— — his wife, Helen Kennedy, ii. 488.
— Finlay, London, v. 273.
— — his wife, Elizabeth Maclellan. v. 273.
— Helen, wife of Sir D. Dalrymple, lord Hailes, viii. 144.
— Isabel, wife of col. Thomas Dalzell, ii. 410.
— Jane Dalrymple Hamilton, wife of Robert Bruce, i. 554.
— Lucy Jane, wife of (1) capt. A. D. Hay Fraser, and (2) F. J. Stewart Hay Newton, vii. 452.
— Robert, major, Ayr, vii. 452.
Fernboys, John de, iv. 43.
Ferne of Muklaree, David de, vi. 215.
Fernie, E. W., High Field, Great Berkhampstead, iii. 495.
— Catherine Bruce, wife of (1) W. Raeburn, and (2) F. J. Bruce, iii. 495.
— Martha, wife of (1) Norman Lindsay, and (2) Robert Wardlaw, v. 402.
Ferquhard Macintagart of Applecross, vii. 231.
Ferrand of Birstarth Hall, William Harris ii. 529.
— — his wife, Constance Cathcart, ii. 529.
— of Harden Grange, William Busfield, ii. 92.
— — his 2nd wife, Fanny Mary Stewart, ii. 92.
— of St. Ives, William, ii. 529.
— Geofrey William, ii. 529.
Ferrers, Laurence (Shirley), 4th earl, i. 384.
— — his wife, Mary Meredith, i. 384; ix. 25.
Ferrers of Groby, Henry (Ferrers), 3rd baron, i. 433.
— — William, 2nd son of William, 7th earl of Derby; 1st baron, iv. 142.
— — William de, iv. 142.
— — his wife, Margaret *or* Agnes de Quincy, iv. 142.
— — William de, iii. 139.
— — his wife, Eleanor de Lovain, iii. 139; ix. 67.
— — Sir William, vi. 135.
— — his wife, Elena, vi. 135.
— of Grugar, William, iv. 225.
— of Lambroughton, William, iv. 225.

Ferrers of Rothiemay, Sir William, vi. 136.
— of Tamworth, Sir John, v. 377.
— of Tranent, William, viii. 566.
— Alice, wife of (1) John Halliday, and (2) Sir A. Ingram, v. 11.
— Elizabeth, wife of David, 12th earl of Atholl, i. 433.
— Frances, wife of Sir John Packington, v. 377.
— William, mercer, London, v. 11.
Ferry, David George, apothecary, Bath, iii. 410.
— — his wife, Jane Murray, iii. 410.
Ferteth, 3rd son of Gilbert, earl of Strathearn, viii. 242.
Festetics, Count Tassilo, Austrian Imperial Guard, iv. 396.
— — his wife, M. V. Douglas Hamilton, iv. 396.
FETTERCAIRN, MIDDLETON, LORD CLAIRMONT AND, vi. 184.
Feversham, William (Duncombe), 2nd baron, iv. 171.
— — his wife, Louisa Stewart, iv. 171.
Fiddes, Andrew de, iv. 49.
— Fergus de, iv. 43 *n.*
— John de, iv. 42 *n.*; viii. 528.
Field, Marshall, Chicago, viii. 230.
— — his wife, A. L. Huck, viii. 230.
Fielding of Lecagh, George, baron, iii. 122.
— Margaret, wife of 1st duke of Hamilton, iv. 378.
— Sir Robert, iii. 235.
— — his wife, Mary Swift, iii. 235.
FIFE, THE ANCIENT EARLS OF, iv. 1-15.
Fife, Beth, alleged earl of, iv. 2 *n.*
— Colban, eighth earl of, i. 427 *n.*; iv. 9, 10.
— — his wife, Anna, iv. 12.
— Constantine, second earl of, iv. 2, 3.
— Duffagan, alleged earl of, iv. 2 *n.*
— Duncan, fourth earl of, i. 416; iv. 5.
— Duncan, fifth earl of, ii. 315; iv. 6; vii. 397; viii. 319 *n.*
— — his wife, Ela, iv. 7.
— Duncan, ninth earl of, iii. 138 *n.*; iv. 9, 11; vii. 400.
— — his wife, Johanna de Clare, iv. 11.
— Duncan, tenth earl of, ii. 258; iii. 142, 263; iv. 11, 14; vi. 134.
— — his wife, Mary de Monthermer, iv. 12.
— Edelrad, *or* Ethelred, 3rd son of King Malcolm Canmore; first earl of Fife, i. 2; iv. 2; vi. 284.
— Gillemichael, third earl of, iv. 4.
— Isabella, wife of (1) Sir William Ramsay of Colluthie, (2) Walter Stewart, (3) Sir Thomas Bisset of Upsetlington, and (4) John Dunbar; countess of, i. 15, 146; iv. 13; vi. 134; viii. 368.
Fife, John (Dunbar), *de jure ux.* earl of, iv. 13.
— Macduff, alleged earl of, iv. 1, 2 *n.*
— Malcolm, sixth earl of, iv. 8; v. 570.
— — his wife, Matilda of Strathearn, iv. 8; viii. 244.
— Malcolm, seventh earl of, ii. 123; iv. 8, 9.
— — his wife, Helen of Wales, iv. 9; v. 578.
— Thomas (Bisset), *de jure ux.* earl of, iv. 13.
— Walter (Stewart), *de jure ux.* earl of, iv. 13, 14.
— William (Ramsay), *de jure ux.* earl of, iv. 13; ix. 46.
FIFE, STEWART, EARL OF, iv. 14-15.
Fife, Murdach, thirteenth earl of, i. 149; iv. 15; v. 340, 342.
— — his 1st wife, Johanna Douglas (?), v. 342 *n.*
— — his 2nd wife, Isabella, countess of Lennox, v. 341.
— Robert, twelfth earl of, i. 146; iv. 14, 229 *n.*; v. 340, 594; viii. 265, 267; ix. 121.
— master of, Robert (Stewart), 2nd son of Murdach, duke of Albany, i. 150.
Fife, James (Duff), 4th earl, iii. 414; v. 237.
— — his wife, Maria Caroline Manners, iii. 414.
— James (Duff), 5th earl, iii. 585.
— — his wife, Agnes Georgiana Elizabeth Hay, iii. 585.
— William (Duff), 1st earl, iv. 38; vii. 483.
— — his 1st wife, Janet Ogilvy, iv. 38.
— — his 2nd wife, Jean Grant, vii. 482.
— Annabella of, wife of Sir Hugh de *, viii. 245 *n.*; ix. 89.
— Marion of, alleged wife of 8th earl of Dunbar, iii. 263.
— of Langton Hall, William Henry, capt. 9th Lancers, iv. 210.
— — his wife, Janet Boyle, iv. 210.
FINCASTLE, MURRAY, VISCOUNT OF, iii. 384.
Fincastle, James, eldest son of 1st earl of Dunmore; styled viscount, iii. 385.
— — his wife, Janet Murray, iii. 385.
Finch, Anna Francesca Wilhelmine, wife of C. J. Murray of Loch Carron, iii. 393.
— Elizabeth, wife of William, 1st earl of Mansfield, viii. 206.
— Mary, wife of (1) William, marquess of Halifax, and (2) John, 1st duke of Roxburghe, vii. 351.
— William, vii. 143.
— — his wife, Anne Douglas, vii. 143.
Finch-Hatton of Eastwell Park, George, viii. 209.
— — his wife, Elizabeth Mary Murray, viii. 209.
FINDLATER, OGILVY, EARL OF, iv. 16-41.

* Name unknown.

Findlater, James, first earl of, iv. 26.
— — his 1st wife, Elizabeth Leslie, iv. 29; vii. 295.
— — his 2nd wife, Marion Cunningham, iv. 29, 247.
— James, third earl of, iv. 35.
— — his 1st wife, Anne Montgomery, iv. 36; ix. 89 *bis*.
— — his 2nd wife, Mary Hamilton, iii. 363; iv. 36, 380; ix. 89.
— James, fourth earl of, iv. 37.
— — his wife, Anne Dunbar, iv. 38.
— James, fifth earl of, iv. 39.
— — his 1st wife, Elizabeth Hay, iv. 39; v. 232.
— — his 2nd wife, Sophia Hope, iv. 39, 496.
— James, sixth earl of, ii. 22; iv. 39.
— — his wife, Mary Murray, i. 487; iv. 40; ix. 90.
— James, seventh earl of, iv. 40.
— — his wife, Cristina Teresa Murray, iv. 40; ix. 90.
— Patrick, second earl of, iv. 28, 29, 35; ix. 89.
— — his wife, Elizabeth Ogilvy, iv. 29, 35.
— Eric J., F. C. minister of Balquhidder, ii. 106.
— — his wife, Sarah Laurie Borthwick, ii. 106.
Finlay de Campsy, son of Robert of Reidheugh, v. 329.
— — his wife, *, v. 329.
— father of Roger of Drumelzier, vii. 420.
— Agnes, 1427, vi. 276.
— Sarah, wife of Jas. Borthwick, ii. 105.
— William, minister of Polmont, ii. 106.
Finlayson of Killeith, John, vi. 513; ix. 26.
— — his wife, Marie Stewart, vi. 513; ix. 26.
— — Matthew, vii. 193.
— Mariota, wife of Josias Stewart of Bonnington, vi. 515.
Finn Arnasson, jarl, i. 2; ii. 314.
Finney, rev. Thomas, i. 60.
— — his wife, Bridget Hamilton, i. 60.
Firebrace, Sir Cordell, i. 382.
— — his wife, Bridget Bacon, i. 382.
Fisher of Springdale, Edward, v. 418.
— — Sharples, v. 418.
— — his wife, C. M. H. Lindsay, v. 418.
— Jane Edith, wife of Henry George Lindsay, v. 418.
Fitz-Alan of Oswestry, John, i. 10.
— — his wife, Isabel de Albini, i. 10.
— — William, son of the senescal of Dol, i. 10, 11.
— of Sharrington, Olive, dau. of Alan Fitzjordan, i. 10.
— Alicia, wife of William Spina, i. 10.

* Name unkoown.

Fitz-Alan, Avelina, wife of Duncan, son of Gilbert, *afterwards* earl of Carrick, ii. 423; ix. 1.
— David, son of 2nd High Steward, i. 12.
— Jordan, eldest son of Alan Fitz-Flaad, i. 10.
— — his wife, Mary, i. 10.
— Jordan, son of Alan Fitz-Jordan, i. 10.
— Leonard, 3rd son of 2nd High Steward, ix. 1.
— Richard, earl of Arundel, i. 11.
— Simon, supposed ancestor of Boyds, i. 11.
— Walter, 1st High Steward of Scotland, i. 10; iii. 133, 422; v. 548.
— — his wife, Eschyna de Molle, i. 11.
— Walter, 3rd High Steward, i. 12; iii. 423, 424 *n.*; v. 550.
Fitzalan-Howard, Anne, wife of general Ralph Drury Ker, v. 485.
Fitzcharles, Catherine, Charlotte *or* Cecilia, illeg. dau. of King Charles II., i. 31.
— Charles, earl of Plymouth, illeg. son of King Charles II., i. 30.
Fitzclarence, Amelia, wife of 10th viscount Falkland, iii. 616.
— Augusta, wife of (1) lord John Kennedy-Erskine of Dun, and (2) lord John F. Gordon Halyburton, ii. 499; iv. 559.
— Augusta Georgiana Frederica, iv. 217.
— Elizabeth, wife of 18th earl of Erroll, iii. 585.
— Frederick, lieut.-gen., G.C.H., commander-in-chief at Bombay, iv. 217.
— — his wife, Augusta Boyle, iv. 217.
Fitz-Flaald, Alan, i. 9.
— — his wife, Avelina de Hesding, i. 10.
FitzGerald of Kintail, Colin, alleged ancestor of Mackenzie clan, vii. 495.
— Caroline, wife of 1st lord Fitzmaurice of Leigh, vi. 400.
— Helen Maria, wife of J. C. S. Macdowall, ix. 71.
— Sir John Forster, field-marshal, i. 129.
— — his wife, Jean Ogilvy, i. 129.
— Lucy, wife of A. R. Douglas-Hamilton, iv. 389.
— Nora, wife of Wm. Fitzherbert, v. 322.
— R. A., ix. 71.
— Robert, M.L.C., Sydney, N.S.W., iv. 389.
— W. J., Lichfield, Connecticut, vi. 400.
FitzGilbert of Anstruther, Walter, iv. 341.
— of Cadzow, Sir David FitzWalter, iv. 342.
— — Sir Walter, iv. 340.
— — his 1st wife, Helen *, iv. 341.
— — his 2nd wife, Mary Gordon, iv. 341, 513.
— of Hamilton, Sir Walter, ancestor of Hamilton family, iv. 303.

* Name unknown.

FitzGilbert of Kinneil, Sir Walter, iv. 341, 342.
—— of Machan, Sir Walter, iv. 341, 342.
—— Sir Adam, ii. 253.
—— —— his wife, Idonea Comyn, ii. 253; ix. 30.
—— Christian, ii. 253; ix. 30.
Fitzhardinge, Maurice Frederick Fitzhardinge (Berkeley), 1st baron, v. 367.
—— —— his wife, Charlotte Lennox, v. 367.
Fitzherbert of Tissington, Sir Richard, 5th bart., v. 322.
—— William, v. 322.
—— —— his wife, Nora Fitzgerald, v. 322.
Fitzhugh, Robert, i. 505 *n.*
—— Sara, wife of William Comyn, i. 505 *n.*
FitzJames, Henrietta, wife of lord Waldegrave, i. 34.
—— Henry, admiral of the French galleys, i. 34.
—— Ignatia, i. 35.
—— James, duke of Berwick, i. 34.
Fitzjohn, Eustace, Northumberland, vii. 3.
Fitz-Jordan, Alan, i. 10.
—— —— his wife, Joan, i. 10.
—— Jordan, i. 10.
Fitz-Maldred of Raby, Robert, iii. 241.
Fitz Marmaduke, Joan, wife of Sir John Cheyne, vi. 462.
—— Sir Robert, vi. 462.
FITZMAURICE, EARL OF ORKNEY, vi. 581-584.
Fitzmaurice of Leigh, Edmond George Petty (Fitzmaurice), 1st lord, vi. 400.
—— —— his wife, Caroline Fitzgerald, vi. 400.
—— of Llewenny Hall, Thomas, vi. 581.
—— —— his wife, Mary, countess of Orkney, vi. 581.
—— of Tregof, Henry George Hamilton, vi. 582.
—— —— Henry Warrender, vi. 582.
—— —— his wife, Sarah Jane Roose, vi. 582.
—— Alexander Edward, brother of 7th earl of Orkney, vi. 582.
—— Alexander Temple, lieut. 72nd regt., vi. 582.
—— —— his wife, Adela Mary Scrope, vi. 582.
—— Beatrix Frances, wife of 6th marquess of Waterford, vi. 400.
—— Charles George Francis, captain 1st Dragoons, vi. 400.
—— Emily Charlotte, dau. of 5th earl of Orkney, vi. 583.
—— Emily Louisa Anne, wife of col. Everard C. Digby, vi. 400.
—— Evelyn Emily Mary, wife of V. C. W. Cavendish, vi. 400.
—— Frederick O'Bryen, commander R.N., vi. 582.
—— —— his wife, Mary Ann Abraham, vi. 582.
Fitzmaurice, Isabella Emily, wife of John Burnham Garrett, vi. 582.
—— Isabella Emma Elizabeth, wife of (1) S. L. Schuster, and (2) lieut.-gen. H. F. Keane, vi. 582.
—— James Terence, captain R.N., vi. 582.
—— —— his wife, Frances Rhoda Ouseley, vi. 582.
—— Mary Constance Hamilton, dau. of 7th earl of Orkney, vi. 583.
—— Mary Louisa, wife of Edward R. Spearman, vi. 583.
—— William Edward, major 2nd Life Guards, M.P., vi. 581.
—— —— his 1st wife, Hester Herford, vi. 581.
—— —— his 2nd wife, Anne Louisa Hatton, vi. 581.
Fitzpatrick, Edith Susan Esther, wife of Sir C. A. Murray, iii. 394.
Fitz-Roger, Robert, iv. 142.
Fitz-Roy, Barbara, mistress of 4th duke of Hamilton, i. 31; iv. 391.
—— Blanche, wife of Sir Coutts Lindsay, i. 524.
—— Sir Charles Augustus, K.C.B., iv. 171; v. 367.
—— —— his wife, Mary Lennox, v. 367.
—— Charlota, wife of 1st earl of Litchfield, i. 31.
—— Charlotta Jemima Henrietta Boyle, wife of (1) Jas. Howard, and (2) Wm., earl of Yarmouth, i. 30.
—— Henry, i. 524.
—— Mary Caroline, wife of vice-admiral Keith Stewart, iv. 171.
—— Mary Louisa, wife of 1st baron Penrhyn, vi. 383.
—— Richard, son of King John of England, ix. 11, 27.
Fitz-Truite, Richard, ii. 372.
—— Richard, his son, ii. 372.
Fitz-Walter of Cadzow, Sir David, iv. 301, 342.
—— of Eddlewood, Sir David, iv. 343.
—— Alan, 2nd High Steward, i. 12; iii. 424; v. 549.
—— —— his wife, Eva, i. 12; ix. 1.
—— Christian de, countess of Essex, i. 505; vii. 5.
—— John, iv. 301, 342.
—— —— his wife, Elizabeth Stewart, iv. 342.
—— Margaret, dau. of Walter, 1st High Steward, ix. 1.
Fitzwarin, William, constable of Urquhart Castle, iv. 44; viii. 247.
—— —— his wife, Mary of Argyll, ii. 505; viii. 246.
Fitz-William, Thomas (Fitz-William), 4th viscount, i. 413.

Fitz-William, William Thomas Spencer (Fitz-William), 6th earl, vi. 386.
—— —— his wife, Frances Harriet Douglas, vi. 386.
—— Mary, wife of Geo. Talbot, i. 413.
Fitzwilliams, Charles, illeg. son of 4th viscount Dunbar, iii. 299 *n.*
Flaald, senescal of Dol, i. 9.
Flack, James Medlicott, viii. 557.
—— —— his wife, Jane Sarah Fleming, viii. 557.
Flahault de la Billardrie, Auguste Charles Joseph, comte de, iii. 549; vi. 399.
—— —— his wife, Margaret, baroness Keith and baroness Nairn, vi. 398.
—— Adelaide Elizabeth Joseph de. ix. 142.
—— Clementina Marie Hortense de, ix. 142.
—— Georgiana Gabrielle de, wife of the marquis de Lavalette, ix. 142.
—— Sarah Sophia Laura de, ix. 142.
Flambard, Ralph, bishop of Durham. iv. 444.
Flanders, Guy, count of, i. 6.
Fledaldus, senescal of Dol, i. 9.
Fleet of Tewin, James, ii. 520.
—— —— his wife, Elizabeth Malyn, ii. 520.
Fleetwood of Missenden, Sir William, vi. 465.
—— Sir William, i. 224.
—— Anne, wife of Francis Cheyne, vi. 465.
—— Bridget, wife of Sir Geo. Murray, i. 224.
FLEMING, FLEMING, LORD, viii. 532-558.
Fleming, Charles, twelfth lord, viii. 555.
—— James, fourth lord, vi. 88; viii. 542.
—— —— his wife, Barbara Hamilton, iv. 370; viii. 542.
—— John, second lord, ii. 454.
—— —— his 1st wife, Euphame Drummond, vii. 44, 45; viii. 536.
—— —— his 2nd wife, Margaret Stewart, v. 351; viii. 530, 536 *bis.*
—— —— his 3rd wife, Agnes Somerville, viii. 537.
—— John, fifth lord, viii. 540, 543.
—— —— his wife, Elizabeth Ross, vii. 252; viii. 544.
—— John, sixth lord, v. 443; viii. 545.
—— —— his 1st wife, Lilias Graham, vi. 239; viii. 546.
—— —— his 2nd wife, Sarah Maxwell, iv. 413; viii. 546.
—— John, seventh lord, viii. 549.
—— John, eighth lord, viii. 551.
—— John, ninth lord, viii. 552.
—— John, eleventh lord, viii. 554.
—— Malcolm, third lord, iii. 226; viii. 537.
—— —— his wife, Janet Stewart, i. 22; viii. 540; ix. 2.
Fleming, Robert, first lord, ii. 453; viii. 10 429 *bis*, 526, 532.
—— —— his 1st wife, Janet Douglas, iii. 175; viii. 533.
—— —— his 2nd wife, Margaret Lindsay, viii. 533.
—— William, tenth lord, viii. 552.
FLEMING, LORD CUMBERNAULD, viii. 546-558.
FLEMING, LORD FLEMING, viii. 532-558.
FLEMING, EARL OF WIGTOWN, viii. 519-558.
Fleming of Achmoir, Sir Malcolm, viii. 524; ix. 169.
—— of Altermony, Sir Robert, viii. 533.
—— of Ardrie, Patrick, viii. 525.
—— of Arretshole, James, viii. 547.
—— —— his wife, Janet Brisbane, viii. 547.
—— —— John, viii. 531, 545.
—— of Auchloun, Sir David, viii. 269, 528.
—— of Auchindonan, Sir Malcolm, vii. 31; viii. 520.
—— of Nether Auchinreoch, James, viii. 527.
—— —— William, viii. 526.
—— of Auchtermony, Sir David, viii. 535.
—— —— Sir John, viii. 535.
—— —— Malcolm, viii. 539.
—— of Balbardy, Sir Robert, viii. 533.
—— of Ballinkeir, Sir John, viii. 535.
—— of Balloch, John, viii, 527.
—— —— Patrick, viii. 525.
—— of Barbeth, Sir David, viii. 528.
—— of Barbreck, Sir Malcolm, viii. 531.
—— of Barrochan, Alexander, viii. 545.
—— of Biggar, Clementina, wife of 10th lord Elphinstone, iii. 545; viii. 555.
—— —— Sir David, ii. 397, 399; iii. 173; iv. 347, 519; viii. 269, 527.
—— —— his 1st wife, Jean Barclay, viii. 529.
—— —— his 2nd wife, Isabel of Monycabock, viii. 530.
—— —— Sir David, grandson of 1st lord Fleming, viii. 534.
—— —— his wife, Elizabeth Drummond, i. 187; vii. 45; viii. 534.
—— —— Janet *or* Jean, wife of (1) John, 1st lord Thirlestane, and (2) John, 5th earl of Cassillis, ii. 477; v. 300, 301; viii. 542, 545, 547.
—— —— John, legtd. son of 3rd lord Fleming, viii. 541.
—— —— his wife, Janet Carwood, viii. 541.
—— —— Sir Malcolm, ii. 447; v. 139; viii. 524.
—— —— his wife, Christian *, v. 139; viii. 525.
—— —— Sir Malcolm, iii. 171; iv. 275; v. 141; viii. 531.
—— —— his wife, Elizabeth Stewart, i. 149; viii. 531, 532.

* Name unknown.

Fleming of Biggar, Sir Patrick, viii. 520, 524; ix. 169.
—— —— his wife, Joanna Fraser of Oliver Castle, vii. 422; viii. 524.
—— —— Sir Robert, viii. 532.
—— —— his 1st wife, Janet Douglas, iii. 175; viii. 533.
—— —— his 2nd wife, Margaret Lindsay, viii. 533.
—— of Blairegis, Sir David, viii. 528.
—— of Boghall, David, ancestor of the family of, viii. 530, 531.
—— —— James, parish-clerk of Biggar, viii. 530.
—— of Boghall, James, 2nd son of 1st earl of Wigtown, viii. 547.
—— —— his wife, Janet Brisbane, viii. 547.
—— —— John, viii. 530.
—— —— his wife, Marion Crawford, viii. 530.
—— —— John, viii. 531, 545.
—— —— John, last laird, viii. 547.
—— —— Malcolm, viii. 530.
—— —— his wife, Elizabeth Houston, viii. 530.
—— —— William, viii. 530, 538.
—— —— his wife, Elizabeth Brisbane, viii. 530.
—— of Bord, Agnes, wife of John Lindsay of Covington, viii. 527.
—— —— George, viii. 526.
—— —— his wife, Elizabeth Fleming, viii. 526, 535.
—— —— James, viii. 525, 530.
—— —— James, viii. 526.
—— —— James, viii. 527.
—— —— John, viii. 527.
—— —— Patrick, viii. 525.
—— —— Robert, viii. 527.
—— —— William, v. 431; viii. 526, 534.
—— —— his 1st wife, *, viii. 526.
—— —— his 2nd wife, Euphemia Livingston, v. 431; viii. 526, 534.
—— —— William, viii. 526.
—— —— his wife, Agnes Livingston of Manerstoun, viii. 527.
—— —— William, viii. 527.
—— —— his wife, Janet Crichton, viii. 527.
—— of Bracanrig, David, ii. 399.
—— —— Malcolm, ii. 401.
—— of Brackenleys, John, viii. 541.
—— of Cambusbarron, Sir David, viii. 528.
—— of Cardoness, Sir Malcolm, viii. 521.
—— of Cardrona, Malcolm, viii. 538.
—— of Carmnole, Sir Malcolm, viii. 522.
—— of Carwood, John, viii. 541.
—— —— his wife, Margaret Carwood, viii. 541.
—— of Cassillis, Sir David, viii. 528.
—— of Castle Rankine, Sir John, viii. 535.
—— of Catscleuch, John, viii. 549.
—— of Cavers, Sir David, sheriff of Roxburgh, viii. 528.

* Name unknown.

Fleming of Clifton, Malcolm, viii. 538.
—— of Covintoun, Malcolm, viii. 538.
—— of Cowshirway, Sir Robert, viii. 534.
—— of Cramond, Marjorie, *perhaps* sister of Thomas, earl of Wigtown, viii. 525.
—— of Croy, Patrick, viii. 525.
—— of Culwenny, Sir Robert, viii. 533.
—— of Cumbernauld, Clementina, wife of 10th lord Elphinstone, iii. 545; viii. 555.
—— —— Sir David, ii. 397, 399; iii. 173; iv. 519; viii. 269, 527.
—— —— his 1st wife, Jean Barclay, viii. 329.
—— —— his 2nd wife, Isabel of Monycabock, viii. 530.
—— —— Sir David, brother of 2nd lord Fleming, viii. 534.
—— —— Sir Malcolm, iii. 171; iv. 275; v. 141; viii. 531.
—— —— his wife, Elizabeth Stewart, i. 149; viii. 531, 532.
—— —— Sir Malcolm, sheriff of Dumbarton, viii. 520.
—— —— his wife, Marjorie *, viii. 522.
—— —— Robert, viii. 520.
—— —— Sir Robert, viii. 532.
—— —— his 1st wife, Janet Douglas, iii. 175; viii. 533.
—— —— his 2nd wife, Margaret Lindsay, viii. 533.
—— of Dalnotrie, Patrick, viii. 525.
—— of Dalzell, Sir Malcolm, ii. 395; viii. 522.
—— of Drumelzier, Malcolm, viii. 538.
—— of Drumgryne, John, viii. 549.
—— of Drumtablay, Sir David, viii. 528.
—— of Dunbulls, Sir David, viii. 534.
—— —— Sir John, viii. 535.
—— of Edmonstoun, *, illeg. son of 1st earl of Wigtown, viii. 549.
—— of Eliston, Malcolm, viii. 538.
—— of Farm, Sir Gilbert, 5th bart., iii. 545.
—— of Fulwood, Sir Malcolm, viii. 520.
—— —— Thomas, *olim* earl of Wigtown, iii. 159; v. 139; viii. 524, 525.
—— of Galnethe, Sir David, viii. 528.
—— of Garscadden, Patrick, viii. 525.
—— of Gilmerton, Jean, wife of 5th earl of Cassillis, viii. 547.
—— of Easter Glen, John, viii. 530.
—— of Nether Glen, William, viii. 530.
—— of Glencotho, Malcolm, viii. 538.
—— of Glentall, Sir David, viii. 528.
—— of Glenrusco, James, viii. 525.
—— —— Malcolm, viii. 525, 531.
—— —— Patrick, viii. 525.
—— of Grantully, Mariota, iv. 227.
—— of Haddockston, Malcolm, viii. 530.
—— of Hallmyre, Malcolm, viii. 538.
—— of Halls, Sir Malcolm, viii. 522.
—— of Henderland, James, viii. 537.
—— of Hopcastle, Malcolm, viii. 538.
—— of Kerse, Malcolm, viii. 539.

* Name unknown.

Fleming of Kilbotho, Malcolm, viii. 539.
—— of Kilmaronock, Sir Malcolm, viii. 522.
—— of Kingledores, Malcolm, viii. 539.
—— of Kirkintilloch, Sir Malcolm, i. 510; viii. 520.
—— —— Malcolm, viii. 539.
—— —— Thomas, ii. 447; viii. 523.
—— of Knoclucbirvan, Sir Malcolm, viii. 522.
—— of Kyllinsith, Sir Malcolm, viii. 522.
—— of Leckbernard, Sir Malcolm, viii. 522.
—— of Lenzie, Sir David, grandson of 1st lord Fleming, viii. 534.
—— —— his wife, Elizabeth Drummond, i. 187; vii. 45; viii. 534.
—— —— Sir Malcolm, viii. 524 *bis*.
—— —— Robert, viii. 520.
—— —— Thomas, viii. 524.
—— of Lindmill, Marjory, wife of William of Fawsyde, viii. 522, 523; ix. 169.
—— of Lour, Sir David, viii. 534.
—— of Meiklegall, Sir David, viii. 528.
—— of Over Menzean, James, viii. 525.
—— —— Malcolm, viii. 525, 531.
—— —— Patrick, viii. 525.
—— —— William, viii. 526.
—— of Milntown, James, viii. 547.
—— —— his wife, Janet Brisbane, viii. 547.
—— —— John, viii. 531, 545.
—— of Mochrum, Sir Malcolm, viii. 521.
—— of Moness, Robert, ii. 186.
—— —— his wife, Jean Campbell, ii. 186.
—— of Monycabock, Malcolm, viii. 533, 534.
—— —— his wife, Euphemia Livingston, v. 431; viii. 526, 534.
—— of Mosfennan, Malcolm, viii. 539.
—— of Mureton, Sir David, viii. 528.
—— of Olivercastle, Sir Malcolm, viii. 525.
—— —— Patrick, viii. 525.
—— —— Sir Robert, viii. 533.
—— of Petkeny, Sir Robert, viii. 533.
—— of Poltoun, Sir Malcolm, viii. 520.
—— of Quarter Chapel, James, viii. 542.
—— of Rachan, Malcolm, viii. 538.
—— of Seymores, Sir John, viii. 535.
—— of Sithboger, Sir Malcolm, viii. 522.
—— of Smithston, Patrick, viii. 525.
—— of Stoneham Park, John Willis, iii. 366.
—— —— his wife, Katharine Elizabeth Cochrane, iii. 366.
—— of Straiton, Sir David, viii. 528.
—— of Sunderland, James, viii. 537.
—— —— Malcolm, viii. 539.
—— of Thankerton, Sir David, viii. 534.
—— —— Jean, wife of (1) John, 1st lord Thirlestane, and (2) John, 5th earl of Cassillis, ii. 477; v. 300, 301; viii. 542, 545, 547.
—— of Torwood, Sir Malcolm, viii. 531.
—— of Tullygart, Marjory, wife of William of Fawsyde, viii. 522, 523; ix. 169.
—— of Tweoures, Patrick, viii. 525.
—— of Urisland, Malcolm, viii. 538.
Fleming of Wigtown, Clementina, wife of 10th lord Elphinstone, iii. 545; viii. 555.
—— —— Sir Malcolm, viii. 521.
—— of Woodland, Sir David, viii. 528.
—— Agnes, wife of 6th lord Livingston, v. 439, 442; viii. 540; ix. 129.
—— Alexander, 4th son of 1st earl of Wigtown, viii. 548, 555.
—— Alexander, 2nd son of 2nd earl of Wigtown, viii. 550.
—— Anna, wife of (1) Sir Wm. Livingston of Darnchester, and (2) Sir J. Seton of Barns, v. 190; viii. 548.
—— Anna, dau. of James F. of Boghall, viii. 547.
—— Anne, wife of (1) Robert, 8th lord Boyd, and (2) George, 2nd earl of Dalhousie, iii. 100; v. 172; viii. 550; ix. 119.
—— Arabella, viii. 556.
—— Baldwin the, viii. 519.
—— Charles, captain in earl of Mar's regiment of foot, viii. 551.
—— Charles Ross, M.D., claimant to earldom of Wigtown, viii. 548, 555, 556; ix. 169.
—— —— his wife, Ann Hamilton, viii. 557.
—— Duncan, viii. 522.
—— Eleanor, wife of 2nd earl of Wemyss, viii. 503, 550.
—— Elizabeth, wife of 5th lord Crichton of Sanquhar, iii. 227; viii. 541.
—— Elizabeth, wife of George Fleming of Bord, viii. 526, 535.
—— Elizabeth, contr. to James Livingston, viii. 534; ix. 129, 169.
—— Elizabeth, dau. of 5th lord Fleming, viii. 544.
—— Elizabeth, wife of John Stewart of Dhucarrick, viii. 555.
—— Elizabeth, dau. of rev. James F., viii. 556.
—— Elizabeth, wife of John Livingston, ix. 120.
—— Elspeth, illeg. dau. of capt. Charles F., viii. 552.
—— Eustace, dau. of rev. James F., viii. 556.
—— Evota, wife of John of Ramsay, viii. 523.
—— Francis, 3rd son of James F. of Boghall, viii. 547.
—— George, parish clerk of Biggar, viii. 530.
—— Hamilton, lieut. 13th regiment, viii. 557.
—— —— his wife, Mary Charlotte Child, viii. 557.
—— Harriet Jane Laura, wife of capt. Wm. Gyll, viii. 557.
—— Harry, 4th son of 3rd earl of Wigtown, viii. 551.
—— Helen, dau. of Malcolm F., viii. 547.

Fleming, Helen, dau. of 2nd earl of Wigtown, viii. 550.
— Helenor, wife of 2nd earl of Wemyss, viii. 503, 550; ix. 168.
— Henrietta, dau. of 5th earl of Wigtown, viii. 553.
— Isobel, contr. to John Tervait, viii. 535.
— James, 2nd son of John F. of Carwood, viii. 542.
— James, 2nd son of James F. of Boghall, viii. 547.
— James, student at Glasgow University, viii. 551.
— James, reverend, viii. 555.
— — his wife, Janet Forsyth, viii. 555.
— James, rector of Castlane, viii. 555.
— — his wife, Magdalen Way, viii. 556.
— Jane, dau. of 1st earl of Wigtown, contracted to James Grant of Freuchie, vii. 474; viii. 548.
— Jane Sarah, wife of J. M. Flack, viii. 557.
— Janet, wife of Sir John Stewart of Minto, ii. 78.
— Janet, wife of (1) Wm. Craik, and (2) Cuthbert Ramsay, ii. 157; iii. 94.
— Jonet, wife of Sir William Seton of Seton, ii. 223; iv. 519; viii. 529, 572; ix. 46.
— Janet, wife of (1) John, master of Livingston, (2) John Sandilands of Calder, and (3) D. Craufurd of Kerse, v. 437; viii. 388, 540.
— Janet, dau. of William F. of Bord, viii. 526.
— Janet, wife of Richard Brown of Hartree, viii. 540.
— Jean, wife of George, master of Loudoun, v. 498; viii. 548.
— Jean, wife of 2nd earl of Panmure, vii. 24; viii. 550, 552, 553; ix. 148.
— Jean, wife of Wm. Bruce of Airth, viii. 545.
— Jean, dau. of James F. of Boghall, viii. 547.
— Jean, wife of Adam Murray of Carden, viii. 547.
— Jean, wife of Sir John Grierson of Lag, viii. 550; ix. 169.
— Jean, dau. of 3rd earl of Wigtown, viii. 552.
— Jeffray, vii. 580.
— Johanna, wife of (1) John Livingston, (2) John Sandilands, and (3) D. Crawfurd, viii. 540.
— John, prebendary, viii. 526.
— John, viii. 530, 536.
— — his wife, Margaret Hamilton, viii. 530.
— John, 3rd son of John F. of Carwood, viii. 542.
Fleming, John, lieut.-col., tutor to Boghall, viii. 547 *bis*, 552, 553; ix. 169.
— John, attorney, viii. 556.
— John, schoolmaster, ix. 114.
— — his wife, Elizabeth Carmichael, ix. 114.
— Katharine, wife of 1st earl of Bothwell, ii. 153.
— Lucrece, wife of Robt. Graham of the Fauld, viii. 545.
— Lilias, wife of Sir D. Murray of Stanhope, viii. 548.
— Lilias, dau. of 2nd earl of Wigtown, viii. 550.
— Lilias, wife of Richard Story, viii. 552.
— Sir Malcolm the, viii. 519.
— Malcolm, elder son of Malcolm F. of Cumbernauld, ii. 506; iv. 273; viii. 532.
— Malcolm, eldest son of Patrick F., viii. 531.
— Malcolm, 3rd son of Patrick F., viii. 531.
— Malcolm, prior of Whithorn, viii. 537, 538.
— Malcolm, 3rd son of 1st earl of Wigtown, viii. 547.
— — his wife, Helen Bruce, ix. 169.
— Margaret, wife of (1) Robert, master of Graham, (2) Thomas, master of Erskine, and (3) John (Stewart), 4th earl of Atholl, i. 445; ii. 185; v. 611; vi. 231; viii. 540; ix. 28.
— Margaret, wife of Patrick, master of Gray, iv. 275; viii. 532.
— Margaret, wife of Geo. Home of Broxmouth, viii. 526.
— Margaret, wife of John Cunningham of Glengarnock, viii. 537; ix. 169.
— Margaret, wife of Sir Jas. Forrester of Carden, viii. 544.
— Margaret, wife of Sir John Charteris of Amisfield, viii. 548.
— Margaret, dau. of 3rd earl of Wigtown, viii. 552.
— Margaret, wife of Sir Archibald Foulis Primrose of Dunipace, viii. 554.
— Margaret, dau. of 2nd earl of Wigtown, ix. 169.
— Marion, wife of Wm. Maule of Panmure, ii. 223; vii. 7, 8; viii. 529.
— Mariota, wife of Wm. Veitch of Dawick, viii. 531.
— Mariota, wife of R. Stirling, viii. 531.
— Mariota, wife of Sir Wm. Stirling of Keir, viii. 534.
— Marjory, wife of John Elphinstone, iii. 545.
— Marjorie, foster-sister of King David II., viii. 522, 523; ix. 169.
— Mary, wife of (1) William Maitland of Lethington, and (2) George Meldrum of Fyvie, v. 295; viii. 541.

Fleming, Mary, wife of Harry Maule of Kellie, vii. 22; viii. 553.
— Mary, wife of Jas. Douglas of Drumlanrig, vii. 132; viii. 545.
— Mary, dau. of Malcolm F., viii. 547.
— Mary, wife of Archibald Stewart, yr. of Castlemilk, viii. 548.
— Mary, dau. of rev. Jas. F., viii. 556.
— Matthew, minister at Culross, iii. 454.
— Matthew, 3rd son of rev. James F., viii. 555.
— Patrick, ii. 181.
— — his wife, Elizabeth Colquhoun, ii. 181.
— Patrick, 3rd son of William F. of Boghall, viii. 531 *bis*.
— Rachel, wife of Geo. Lindsay of Covington, viii. 548.
— Robert, 2nd son of 1st lord Fleming, viii. 534.
— Sir Robert, cornet of Life Guards, viii. 551; ix. 169.
— Sarah, dau. of 1st earl of Wigtown, viii. 548.
— Theobald the, Lesmahagow, iii. 133 *n*.
— Thomas, bailie of barony of Monypenny, vi. 276.
— Thomas, 2nd son of William F. of Boghall, viii. 531.
— Thomas, illeg. son of 4th lord Fleming, viii. 543.
— Thomas, in the army, viii. 555.
— Thomas, rector of St. John's, Jamaica, viii. 556.
— W. Alexander, Bishopthorpe Vicarage, Leeds, viii. 548.
— Waldeve the, viii. 519.
— Walter, viii. 522.
— William the, viii. 519.
— William, provost of Biggar, viii. 531.
— William, 2nd son of Patrick F., viii. 531.
— William, illeg. son of 3rd lord Fleming, viii. 541.
— William, provost of Collegiate Church of Biggar, viii. 541.
— William, bailie of Perth, viii. 543.
— William, brother of lieut.-col. John F., viii. 547.
— Sir William, chamberlain of household to King Charles II., viii. 550, 552, 553.
— William, merchant, Glasgow, viii. 555.
— *, wife of Sir Francis Douglas of Sandilands, i. 202.
— *, father of Thomas, 2nd earl of Wigtown, viii. 521, 522.
— *, wife of Sir John Danielston, viii. 522.
— *, contracted to James Tweedie of Drumelzier, viii. 537.
— *, dau. of 2nd lord Fleming, viii. 537.
Fletcher of Aberlady, John, i. 552.
— — his wife, Mary Swinton, i. 551.

* Name unknown.

Fletcher of Balmirmer, Robert, ix. 62.
— — his wife, Elizabeth Lindsay, iii. 33; ix. 62.
— of New Cranstoun, Sir John, King's advocate, ii. 595.
— — William, viii. 120, 125.
— — his wife, Esther Cunningham, viii. 120, 125.
— of Boquhan, Henry, general, i. 368.
— of Huttonhill, Sir George, i. 258; vii. 101.
— — his wife, Mary Johnstone, i. 258.
— of Innerpeffer, Andrew, senator of the College of Justice, v. 230: ix. 121.
— — his wife, * Hay, v. 230.
— of Saltoun, Sir Andrew, 1st laird, iii. 217; vii. 442; viii. 31.
— — Andrew, viii. 515.
— — his wife, Charlotte Charteris, viii. 515.
— — Henry, viii. 78.
— — his wife, Margaret Carnegie, viii. 78.
— — Henry, general, i. 368.
— — Sir Robert, viii. 78.
— Andrew, lord of Session, lord Milton, viii. 78.
— Christian, wife of (1) rev. Jas. Grainger, and (2) James, 1st lord Abercrombie, i. 80; ix. 5.
— Christian, wife of Henry Home of Lauder, iii. 283.
— David, bishop of Argyll, iii. 283.
— Elizabeth, wife of Sir John Dalrymple of Kelloch, viii. 120.
— Jean, wife of 1st viscount of Kingston, v. 196; ix. 121.
Florence III., count of Holland, i. 4.
— — his wife, Ada of Scotland, i. 4.
Florence V., count of Holland, i. 4.
Flori, Marcello Marcelli, count, vi. 458.
— — his wife, Cristina Bandini, vi. 458.
Flower, Herbert, v. 237.
— — his wife, A. C. E. Duff, v. 237.
— Mary, wife of Edward Hay, v. 233.
— Peter, merchant, London, v. 233.
Floyer, Charles, governor of Madras, v. 634.
— Frances, wife of John Francis, earl of Mar, v. 634.
Foley of Stoke Edith Park, Edward Thomas, vi. 271.
— — his wife, Emily Graham, vi. 271.
Folkart of Folkarton, *, iv. 565.
— — Elizabeth, wife of James Carmichael of Balmedie, iv. 565.
— — Solph, ancestor of the family of, iv. 565.
— Beatrice, wife of John Sinclair, viii. 370.
— Richard, son of Solph of, iv. 565.

* Name unknown.

Follett, Gilbert, Coldstream Guards, iii. 396.
—— his wife, Mildred Murray, iii. 396.
— John Skirrow, iii. 396.
— Sir William, ii. 501.
Folliard, Eleanor, wife of G. M'Can, ix. 3.
— William, ix. 3.
Fonia, wife of Reginald, lord of the Isles, v. 31.
Foote of Rosehill, Alexander Leith Ross, D.D., ii. 500.
— Alice Marjorie Cunningham, wife of (1) C. Day, and (2) A. J. W. H. Kennedy-Erskine, ii. 500.
— Henry St. George, vii. 153.
—— his wife, Elizabeth Katinka Douglas, vii. 152.
FORBES, FORBES, LORD, iv. 42-68.
Forbes, Alexander, first lord, iv. 49, 69, 70.
—— his wife, Elizabeth Douglas, i. 174; iv. 48, 49.
— Alexander, fourth lord, iv. 52; vii. 324.
—— his wife, Grizel *or* Margaret Boyd, iv. 53; v. 149.
— Alexander, eleventh lord, iv. 62.
—— his 1st wife, Anne Forbes, iv. 62.
—— his 2nd wife, Elizabeth Forbes, iv. 62.
— Arthur, fifth lord, iv. 53.
—— his wife, Agnes Lyon, i. 189; iv. 53; viii. 277.
— Arthur, tenth lord, iv. 60.
—— his wife, Jean Elphinstone, iii. 539; iv. 61.
— Francis, fifteenth lord, iv. 64.
— Horace Courtenay Gammell, twentieth lord, iv. 67, 68.
— James, second lord, iv. 50.
—— his wife, Egidia Keith, iv. 50; vi. 41.
— James, sixteenth lord, iii. 82; iv. 63, 64.
—— his 1st wife, Mary Forbes, iv. 64, 75.
—— his 2nd wife, Elizabeth Gordon, iv. 65.
— James, seventeenth lord, iv. 65.
—— his wife, Katharine Innes, iv. 65.
— James Ochoncar, eighteenth lord, iv. 66.
—— his wife, Elizabeth Hunter, iii. 81; iv. 66.
— John, sixth lord, iv. 53; viii. 277.
—— his 1st wife, Katharine Stewart, i. 442; iv. 53.
—— his 2nd wife, Christian Lundin, iv. 53, 54.
—— his 3rd wife, Elizabeth Barlay, iii. 531; iv. 53, 54.
— John, eighth lord, iv. 57, 537, 539.
—— his 1st wife, Margaret Gordon, iv. 58, 59, 539; ix. 91.
—— his 2nd wife, Jonet Seton, ii. 66; iv. 60.
Forbes, John, ninth lord, iv. 59, 60.
— Walter, nineteenth lord, iv. 67.
—— his 1st wife, Horatia Shaw, iv. 67.
—— his 2nd wife, Louisa Ormond, iv. 68.
— William, third lord, iv. 51.
—— his wife, Christian Gordon, iv. 51, 525.
— William, seventh lord, iv. 55, 61; vi. 46; ix. 91.
—— his wife, Elizabeth Keith, iv. 55.
— William, twelfth lord, iv. 62.
—— his 1st wife, Jean Campbell, iv. 63.
—— his 2nd wife, Anna Erskine, iv. 63; v. 86; ix. 91.
—— his 3rd wife, Barbara Forbes, iv. 63.
— William, thirteenth lord, iv. 63.
—— his wife, Anne Brodie, iv. 63.
— William, fourteenth lord, iv. 43, 64.
—— his wife, Dorothy Dale, iv. 64; ix. 91.
— master of, Arthur, 3rd son of 8th lord Forbes, iii. 540; iv. 60.
—— his wife, Jean Elphinstone, iii. 539.
— master of, James, eldest son of 18th lord Forbes, iv. 66.
— master of, John, 2nd son of 6th lord Forbes, iii. 589; iv. 54; viii. 280.
—— his wife, Elizabeth Lyon, i. 189; iv. 54.
— master of, John, 2nd son of 7th lord Forbes, iv. 56, 57, 537, 539.
—— his wife, Margaret Gordon, iv. 58, 59, 539.
— master of, Jonathan Barrington, 2nd son of 19th lord Forbes, iv. 67.
— master of, William, eldest son of 12th lord Forbes, iv. 63: ix. 49.
FORBES OF PITSLIGO, FORBES, LORD, iv. 69-76.
Forbes of Pitsligo, Alexander, first lord, iv. 75.
—— his wife, Jean Keith, iv. 75; vi. 57.
—— Alexander, second lord, ii. 577; iv. 75.
—— his wife, Mary Douglas, ii. 272; iv. 75.
—— Alexander, third lord, iv. 64, 75.
—— his wife, Sophia Erskine, iv. 75; v. 626.
—— Alexander, fourth lord, iv. 75.
—— his 1st wife, Rebecca Norton, iv. 76.
—— his 2nd wife, Elizabeth Allen, iv. 76.
FORBES, LORD FORBES, iv. 42-68.
FORBES, LORD FORBES OF PITSLIGO, iv. 69-76.
Forbes, earl of Granard, Patrick, ancestor of the family of, iv. 51.
— of Aberdour, Alexander, iv. 75.
— of Abergardene, William, iv. 52.
— of Alford, Sir Alexander, iv. 47.

Forbes of Ardache, Sir Christian[de, iv. 44.
— of Asloun, John, iv. 63.
— of Auchannasse, George, iv. 72.
— — his wife, Marion Ogilvy, iv. 73.
— of Auchindoir, Sir Alexander, iv. 48.
— of Auchintoul, Duncan, ancestor of the family of, iv. 47.
— — James, i. 85.
— of Auchry, Thomas, 2nd son of Walter F. of Tolquhon, ii. 273.
— — his wife, Henrietta Erskine, ii. 273.
— of Balfluig, John, ii. 19.
— — his wife, Mary Ogilvy, ii. 19.
— — John, iv. 62.
— — his wife, Christian Forbes, iv. 62.
— of Balfour, Arthur, i. 444, 513.
— — his wife, * Stewart, i. 444.
— — Arthur, 'Black,' iv. 55.
— — Arthur, vii. 460.
— — his wife, Christian Barclay, vii. 460.
— of Balvenie, Arthur, 1st laird, vii. 442.
— of Blacktoun, Abraham, 8th son of 7th lord Forbes, iv. 56.
— — James, vii. 441.
— — his wife, Magdalen Fraser, vii. 441.
— of Bothron, Sir William, iv. 70.
— of Boyndlie, John, 3rd son of Alex. F. of Pitsligo, iv. 72.
— — his wife, Agnes Gray, iv. 72.
— of Brako, Alexander, iv. 75.
— of Brux, Alaster 'Cam,' iv. 47.
— — his wife, Katharine Cameron of Brux, iv. 47.
— — Alexander, iv. 54.
— — his wife, Marjory Forbes, iv. 54.
— — Atholl Monson, iv. 67.
— — his wife, Margaret Alice Dick-Cunyngham, iv. 67.
— — Charles Murray Hay, 95th regt., iv. 67.
— — his wife, C. L. E. Spencer, iv. 67.
— — James Hunter, iv. 67.
— — John, 'with the strik hair white,' iv. 51.
— — John, 'the gleyed,' iv. 71.
— — John, 6th laird, iv. 73.
— — his wife, Janet Forbes, iv. 73.
— — John, 8th laird, iii. 538; iv. 74.
— — his wife, Marjory Forbes, iv. 74.
— of Callendar, William, 1st laird, v. 450.
— — William, viii. 516.
— — his wife, Louisa Antoinetta Charteris, viii. 515.
— of Carreston, viii. 103.
— of Castleforbes, Patrick, ancestor of the family of, iv. 51.
— of Cluny, Sir Alexander, iv. 49.
— of Corse, James Ochoncar, vii. 564.
— — his wife, Harriet Hall, vii. 564.
— — John Walter, vii. 564.
— — Patrick, 1st laird, iv. 51.

* Name unknown.

Forbes of Corse, Patrick, bishop of Aberdeen, iv. 28.
— — William, v. 619.
— of Corsindae, Duncan, iv. 51.
— — his wife, Christian Mercer, iv. 51.
— — James, 1st laird, iv. 50.
— — James, vi. 175.
— — his wife, Katharine Mortimer, vi. 175.
— — John, v. 543.
— — John, ix. 132.
— — his wife, Margaret Fraser, ix. 132.
— — William, iv. 55.
— — his wife, Elizabeth Keith, iv. 55.
— — William, iv. 56.
— — his wife, Janet Forbes, iv. 56.
— of Coul, Patrick, 1st laird, iv. 51.
— of Cowburtibeg, John, iv. 74.
— of Craigievar, Sir Arthur, 6th bart., vii. 564.
— — Sir John, 7th bart., iv. 66; vii. 564.
— — his wife, Charlotte Elizabeth Forbes, iv. 66; vii. 564.
— — Sir William, 5th bart., vii. 564.
— — his wife, Sarah Sempill, vii. 564.
— — Sir William, 8th bart., vii. 564, 566.
— — his 1st wife, Caroline Louisa Forbes, vii. 566.
— — his 2nd wife, Frances Emily Abercromby, vii. 566.
— — his 3rd wife, Mary Beresford Sherbrooke, vii. 567.
— — Sir William, 1st bart., iv. 51; viii. 103.
— — Sir William, 3rd bart., iv. 38.
— of Craiglogy, Sir Alexander, iv. 47.
— — John, iv. 45.
— of Culloden, Duncan, 3rd laird, vii. 354, 356.
— — Duncan, lord president of the Court of Session, iii. 79.
— — Sir John, ancestor of the family of, iv. 46.
— of Culquhary, Duncan, ancestor of the family of, iv. 47.
— of Daach, William, iv. 71.
— — his wife, Elizabeth Forbes, iv. 71.
— of Druminnor, Sir Alexander, iv. 49.
— — Sir John, ii. 447.
— — his wife, Margaret Kennedy, ii. 447.
— of Echt, Alexander *or* Arthur, ix. 90.
— — his wife, Elizabeth Lyon, ix. 90.
— — Arthur, iv. 62, 63; vii. 442.
— — his 1st wife, Anna Forbes, iv. 62.
— — his 2nd wife, Barbara Forbes, iv. 63.
— — James, vi. 499.
— of Edinbancbory, Sir Alexander, iv. 47.
— — John, iv. 45.
— of Faithly, John, iv. 72.
— of Fiddes, Sir Alexander, iv. 49.
— of Fingask, Alexander, iv. 112.
— — his wife, Christina Fraser, iv. 112.

Forbes of Meikle Fintray, Sir Alexander, iv. 47, 48, 53.
—— of Fodderbirse, William, 3rd son of 7th lord Forbes, iv. 56.
—— —— his wife, Marjory Forbes, iv. 56.
—— of Forbes, Sir Alexander, iv. 46 *n.*, 47, 271, 518; vii. 431.
—— —— his wife, Elizabeth Douglas, i. 174; iv. 48, 49.
—— —— Sir Christin de, iv. 44; ix. 90.
—— —— Duncan, 1st laird, iv. 43.
—— —— James, iv. 50, 522.
—— —— John, *circ.* 1306, iv. 43.
—— —— John, sheriff of Aberdeen, iv. 45.
—— —— his wife, Margaret, iv. 46.
—— —— Sir John, iv. 46, 108, 271.
—— —— his wife, Elizabeth *or* Margaret Kennedy, iv. 46.
—— of Fordyce, Patrick, bishop of Aberdeen, iv. 28.
—— of Formartin, Sir John, iv. 46.
—— —— his wife, Mariota Preston of Formartin, iv. 46.
—— of Fotherbirs, Sir Alexander, iv. 47.
—— of Foveran, Sir John, ancestor of the family of, iv. 46.
—— of Fynrossie, John, iv. 46.
—— of Glasloch, Sir William, iv. 69.
—— of Glencarve, Alaster, iv. 47.
—— of Groddie, Alexander, i. 85.
—— —— his 2nd wife, Janet Gordon, i. 85.
—— of Invereman, Alaster, ancestor of the family of, iv. 46.
—— of Kearn, Sir Alexander, iv. 48.
—— of Kilmany, James, 3rd son of Arthur F. of Rires, iv. 74; vi. 590.
—— —— his wife, Katharine Bethune, vi. 590.
—— of Kilmuck, Duncan, ancestor of the family of, iv. 51.
—— of Kincraigy, Patrick, 1st laird, iv. 51.
—— of Kinedward, John, iv. 53.
—— of Kindrocht, John, iv. 74.
—— of Kinnaldie, Sir William, iv. 46, 69, 523; vii. 432.
—— —— his wife, Agnes Fraser of Glaslath, iv. 70; vii. 432.
—— of Knocksowle, Alexander, iv. 72.
—— of Kungsgård, Arthold, major-general, governor of Pomerania, baron, iv. 52 *n.*
—— of Kyninmond, Sir William, iv. 70.
—— of Lare, William, 3rd son of 6th lord Forbes, iv. 55.
—— of Leslie, Duncan, ancestor of the family of, iv. 51.
—— —— John, 1st laird, v. 384 *bis.*
—— —— his wife, Jean Leslie, v. 384.
—— —— William, iv. 43, 55.
—— of Lethenty, George, ancestor of the family of, iv. 71.
Forbes of Lethenty, James, 5th son of 7th lord Forbes, iv. 56.
—— —— his wife, Margaret Forbes, iv. 56, 73.
—— —— John, iv. 73.
—— —— William, iv. 73.
—— of Logie, Arthur, 4th son of 7th lord Forbes, iv. 56, 538.
—— of Logy Fintray, William, 3rd son of 7th lord Forbes, iv. 56.
—— —— his wife, Marjory Forbes, iv. 56.
—— of Ludquhairn, Robert, tutor of Craigievar, i. 307; iv. 117.
—— —— William, i. 307.
—— —— his wife, Anna Arbuthnott, i. 307.
—— of Many, William, 1st laird, viii. 54.
—— of Medwyn, John Houblon, vii. 452.
—— —— his wife, Alexandra C. M. Fraser, vii. 452.
—— —— William, v. 95.
—— of Melgum, William, iv. 73.
—— of Monymusk, Duncan, 1st laird, iv. 51, 111.
—— —— Sir John, 3rd bart., i. 306.
—— —— his wife, Margaret Arbuthnott, i. 306.
—— —— John, the younger, iv. 64, 75.
—— —— his wife, Mary Forbes, iv. 75.
—— —— William, 2nd laird, i. 199.
—— —— his wife, Margaret Douglas, i. 199; ix. 13.
—— —— Sir William, 4th bart., v. 241.
—— —— his wife, Jean Keith, v. 241.
—— of Newhall, John, advocate, i. 552.
—— —— his wife, Annabella Bruce, i. 552.
—— of Newton, Robert, vii. 475.
—— of Oneil, v. 619.
—— of Pettallochy, John, iv. 72.
—— of Pitsligo, Alexander, 2nd laird, iv. 51, 70.
—— —— his wife, Maria Hay, iv. 70.
—— —— Alexander, 3rd laird, iv. 71.
—— —— his wife, Isobel *or* Elizabeth Wemyss, iv. 71.
—— —— Alexander, the 'Red,' 5th laird, iv. 72.
—— —— his wife, Beatrix Abernethy, iv. 72; vii. 410.
—— —— Alexander, 7th laird, iv. 72, 73.
—— —— his 1st wife, Alison Anderson, iv. 73.
—— —— his 2nd wife, Barbara Keith, iv. 73; vi. 51.
—— —— his 3rd wife, Margaret Mackintosh, iii. 204; iv. 74.
—— —— John, 4th laird, iv. 72; v. 526; vii. 437.
—— —— his 1st wife, Jean Keith, iv. 72.
—— —— his 2nd wife, Isabel *or* Elizabeth Innes, iv. 72.
—— —— Sir John, 8th laird, iv. 62, 74.
—— —— his wife, Christian Ogilvy, i. 113; v. 26, 74.

Forbes of Pitsligo, Sir John Stuart, 8th bart., v. 484.
—— his wife, Harriet Louisa Anne Ker, v. 484.
—— Margaret, wife of James Forbes of Lethinty, iv. 56, 73.
—— Sir William, 1st laird, iv. 46, 69.
—— his wife, Agnes Fraser, iv. 69.
—— William, 6th laird, iv. 56, 72, 73.
—— his wife, Catharine Gordon, iv. 73.
—— Sir William, 7th bart., vi. 117.
—— his wife, Williamina Stuart, vi. 117.
— of Putachie, Archibald, 3rd son of 12th lord Forbes, iv. 63.
—— his wife, Elizabeth Forbes, iv. 63.
—— Arthur, 'black,' son of 6th lord Forbes, iv. 55.
— of Quhitfield, Sir Alexander, iv. 49.
— of Rires, Arthur, ancestor of the family of, iv. 71.
—— his wife, Elizabeth Wemyss, iv. 71.
—— Arthur, 4th laird, i. 445.
—— his wife, Margaret Beaton, i. 445; viii. 541.
—— Arthur, 5th laird, i. 467.
—— John, i. 76.
—— his wife, Barbara Sandilands, i. 76.
—— Robert, 6th laird, iv. 62, 74; vii. 17.
— of Seton, Elizabeth, wife of gen. James Hay, viii. 466.
—— James, viii. 466.
— of Skeith, Sir Christian de, iv. 44.
— of Skellatur, Alaster, ancestor of the family of, iv. 47.
— of Strathdee, Sir Alexander, iv. 49 *bis*; v. 551.
— of Thornton, James, i. 308; v. 249.
—— his wife, Jane Falconer, v. 249.
— of Tolquhoun, Alexander, iv. 56.
—— Alexander, iv. 73.
—— his wife, Alison Anderson, iv. 73.
—— Sir Alexander, ii. 23.
—— Sir John, iv. 46.
—— his wife, Mariota Preston, iv. 46.
—— Malcolm, iv. 51.
—— his wife, Egidia Forbes, iv. 51.
—— Walter, 10th laird, ii. 13, 273; iv. 74.
—— his wife, Jean Forbes, iv. 74.
—— William, 1504, i. 84.
—— William, iii. 568.
—— his wife, Isabel Hay, iii. 568.
—— William, 9th laird, ii. 13; v. 543.
—— his wife, Janet Ogilvy, ii. 13.
—— William, i. 87; vii. 441, 443.
—— William, son of Thomas F. of Auchry, ii. 273.
— of Towie, Alexander, i. 85.
—— his 2nd wife, Janet Gordon, i. 85.
—— [Alexander], iv. 537.
—— his wife, Margaret Campbell, iv. 537.
— of Tullireoth, James, iv. 50.
Forbes of Meikle Wardis, John, iv. 72.
—— Malcolm, iv. 70 *bis*.
—— Sir William, iv. 69.
— of Watertoun, Sir John, ancestor of the family of, iv. 46.
—— his wife, Mariota Preston, iv. 46.
—— John, i. 87.
—— his wife, Jean Gordon, i. 87.
—— Thomas, iii. 204; vi. 182.
— traditional ancestor of the family of Morgan or Mackay, vii. 157.
— Alexander, alleged Governor of Urquhart Castle, iv. 43 *n.*, 46 *n.*
— Mr. Alexander, 4th son of 2nd lord Forbes, iv. 51.
— Alexander, 4th son of 6th lord Forbes, ix. 91.
— Andrew, Chief Registrar of the Isle of Man, iv. 65.
— Anna, wife of (1) Sir John Seton Barns, and (2) John Hamilton, iv. 57; viii. 589.
— Anna, wife of Arthur Forbes of Echt, iv. 62.
— Anna, wife of Andrew Middleton of Balbegno, vi. 182.
— Annabella, wife of Patrick, master of Gray, iv. 50, 275.
— Annabella, wife of Matthew Lumsden of Tullicarn, iv. 55.
— Anne, wife of 11th lord Forbes, iv. 62, 74.
— Anne, dau. of 11th lord Forbes, iv. 62.
— Anne, wife of Thos. Erskine of Pittodrie, iv. 65.
— Archangel, in the Order of Capuchins; William, eldest son of 8th lord Forbes, iv. 58.
— Archangel, in the Order of Capuchins; John, 9th lord Forbes, iv. 60.
— Archibald, 3rd son of 13th lord Forbes, iv. 63.
— Arthur, illeg. son of 8th lord Forbes, iv. 60.
— Arthur, captain, 5th son of 10th lord Forbes, iv. 62.
— Arthur, colonel, 3rd son of 11th lord Forbes, iv. 62.
— Arthur, Breda, iv. 63.
— Arthur, 3rd son of Sir Wm. F. of Pitsligo, iv. 70.
—— his wife, Beatrix Douglas, iii. 175, 564; iv. 70.
— Arthur, 2nd son of John F. of Pitsligo, iv. 72.
— Arthur, 4th son of the 'Red Laird' of Pitsligo, iv. 72.
—— his wife, Margaret Leslie, iv. 72.
— Atholl Laurence Cunyngham, iv. 67.
— Barbara, wife of (1) Robert Allardyce, (2) Alex. Hay of Delgatie, and (3) Sir

Archibald Douglas of Balneathill, iv. 57; vi. 372.
Forbes, Barbara, wife of 2nd earl of Seaforth, iv. 62; vii. 508; ix. 91.
— Barbara, wife of (1) Arthur Forbes of Echt, and (2) William, 12th lord Forbes, iv. 63.
— Caroline Ann, wife of rev. F. W. Robberds, vii. 565.
— Caroline Elizabeth, wife of Geo. Fairholme, iv. 66.
— Caroline Louisa, wife of (1) Sir Wm. Forbes of Craigievar, and (2) S. E. Carlisle, vii. 566.
— Charlotte Elizabeth, wife of Sir John Forbes of Craigievar, iv. 66; vii. 564.
— Charlotte Frances, vii. 565.
— Christian, wife of 1st lord Ruthven, iv. 52, 101, 258.
— Christian, wife of George Johnston of Caskieben, iv. 56.
— Christian, wife of John Forbes of Balfluig, iv. 62.
— Christian, wife of G. Straton of Lauriston, iv. 72.
— Christian, wife of Thomas Fraser of Strichen, iv. 74; v. 543, 544.
— Christian, wife of Patrick Maule, vii. 17.
— David, 4th son of 8th lord Forbes, iv. 60, 61.
— Duncan, J.P., Aberdeen, vii. 564.
— — his wife, Sarah Forbes, vii. 564.
— Egidia, wife of Malcolm Forbes of Tolquhoun, iv. 51.
— Elizabeth, wife of Alexander Irvine of Drum, iv. 50.
— Elizabeth, wife of James Grant of Freuchie, iv. 54; vii. 460; ix. 90.
— Elizabeth, wife of (1) Gilbert Keith, and (2) Alexander Innes, iv. 54; vi. 44; vii. 355.
— Elizabeth, wife of Henry, 5th lord Sinclair, iv. 56; vii. 574.
— Elizabeth, wife of James Skene of Skene, iv. 62.
— Elizabeth, wife of 11th lord Forbes, iv. 62.
— Elizabeth, wife of John Leith of Whitehaugh, iv. 63.
— Elizabeth, wife of Professor John Gregory, iv. 64.
— Elizabeth, wife of William Forbes of Daach, iv. 71.
— Elizabeth, wife of Gilbert Johnston of Caskieben, iv. 71.
— Elizabeth, wife of (1) Michael Fraser of Stoneywood, and (2) W. Wood of Balbegno, iv. 111.
— Elizabeth, wife of (1) Wm. Chalmer of Strichen, (2) Thos. Fraser of Strichen, and (3) Thos. Fraser of Knockie and Strichen, v. 543.
Forbes, Elizabeth, wife of Robert Grant of Druminnor, vii. 564.
— Elizabeth, wife of (1) Henry Spittal of Blairlogie, and (2) Alex. Alexander, viii. 167.
— Elizabeth Jane, dau. of 18th lord Forbes, iv. 67.
— Emily, dau. of 19th lord Forbes, iv. 68.
— Frederick, 3rd son of 18th lord Forbes, iv. 66.
— George, master of the Horse to the Chevalier St. George, iii. 355.
— — his wife, Susan Cochrane, iii. 355; viii. 308.
— Gordon, Ham Common, iii. 417.
— Granville Hamilton, rector of Broughton, v. 485.
— — his wife, Georgiana Augusta Ker, v. 485.
— Hamilton, major-general, Bengal Staff Corps, vii. 451.
— — his wife, Elizabeth Fraser, vii. 451.
— Harriet Susannah, wife of Augustus Wm. Erskine, v. 95.
— Hector, 6th son of the 'Red Laird' of Pitsligo, iv. 73.
— Helen, wife of (1) James Elphinstone of Balnaboth, and (2) Kinnaird of Culbin, iii. 538.
— Helen, wife of John Makgill of Kemback, vi. 590.
— Hugh, eldest son of Sir Wm. F. of Craigievar, iv. 38.
— — his wife, Janet Ogilvy, iv. 38.
— Isabel, wife of John Gordon of Pitlurg, iv. 57.
— Isobel, dau. of 8th lord Forbes, iv. 59.
— Isabel, wife of William Urquhart, iv. 71.
— Isobel, wife of (1) Michael Fraser of Stoneywood, and (2) W. Wood of Balbegno, iv. 111.
— Isobel, wife of (1) Wm. Chalmer, (2) Thos. Fraser, and (3) Thos. Fraser, v. 543.
— Isabel, wife of (1) Alex. Innes, and (2) Sir D. Lindsay of Edzell, i. 513; vii. 356.
— Isobel, wife of Sir John Ogilvy of Lintrathen, ix. 7.
— Isabella Anne, wife of F. J. Tollemache, iii. 417.
— Isabella Drummond, wife of Baron Ernest de Poelnitz, iv. 67.
— Ivan Courtenay, iv. 68.
— James, son of Wm. F. of Fodderbirse, iv. 56.
— James, illeg. son of 8th lord Forbes, iv. 60.
— James, captain, 6th son of 10th lord Forbes, iv. 62.
— James, colonel, 2nd son of 11th lord Forbes, iv. 62.

Forbes, James, lieut.-col. Coldstream Guards, iv. 66.
— James, 3rd son of A. Forbes of Rires, iv. 74.
— James, parson and prebendary of Forbes, ix. 91.
— James Ochoncar, major 3rd batt. Gordon Highlanders, vii. 564.
— Janet, wife of Sir John Gordon of Haddo, i. 87.
— Janet, wife of (1) John, earl of Atholl, (2) Alex. Hay of Delgaty, and (3) Wm. Leslie of Balqnhain, i. 443; iv. 55.
— Janet, wife of William Forbes of Corsindae, iv. 56.
— Janet, wife of John Forbes of Brux, iv. 73.
— Jonet, wife of William Duguid of Auchinhove, iv. 73.
— Janet, wife of lt-col. P. Grant of Wester Elchies, vii. 475.
— Janet Marjory, vii. 565.
— Jean, wife of 5th lord Ogilvie of Airlie, i. 119; iv. 56.
— Jean, wife of (1) John, 3rd earl of Atholl, (2) Alex. Hay, and (3) W. Leslie, i. 443; iv. 55.
— Jean, wife of Alex. Sutherland of Kinminitie, iii. 204.
— Jean, wife of col. James Dundas of Dundas, iv. 64.
— Jean, wife of William Cumyn of Earnside, iv. 59.
— Jean, wife of Walter Forbes of Tolquhon, iv. 74.
— Jean, wife of Sir Harry Innes of Innes, vii. 356.
— John, brigadier, col. 17th foot, iii. 358.
— John, illeg. son of Sir John F. of Forbes, iv. 47.
— John, colonel, 3rd son of 10th lord Forbes, iv. 61.
— John, lieut. 79th Cameron Highlanders, iv. 66.
— John, 3rd son of John F. of Pitsligo, iv. 72.
— John, master of Pitsligo, iv. 76.
— — his wife, Rebecca Ogilvy, iv. 76.
— Katharine, wife of Sir Wm. Murray of Blebo, i. 467.
— Katharine, wife of Barclay of Gartly, iv. 57.
— Katharine, wife of Wm. Gordon of Rothiemay, iv. 60.
— Margaret, wife of Dr. Arbuthnott of Arbuthnottshaugh, i. 308.
— Margaret, wife of Geo. Sinclair of Mey, ii. 351; iv. 57; ix. 52.
— Margaret, wife of (1) Alexander, 1st lord Duffus, and (2) Sir Robt. Gordon, iii. 209; iv. 63; ix. 91.
Forbes, Margaret, wife of Alex. Meldrum of Fyvie, iv. 50.
— Margaret, wife of Andrew Fraser of Muchalls and Kinmundy, iv. 54, 110.
— Margaret, wife of (1) George Sinclair of Dunbeath, and (2) Claud Hamilton, iv. 59.
— Margaret, wife of John Cheyne of Straloch, iv. 73.
— Margaret, wife of Thomas Fraser of Cairnbulg, iv. 117.
— Mariota, wife of Alex. Gordon of Lesmoir, iv. 73.
— Marjory, wife of (1) John, lord Macleod, and (2) John, 4th duke of Atholl, i. 498; iii. 82; iv. 65.
— Marjory, wife of (1) Alex. Forbes of Brux, and (2) Alex. Burnett of Leys, iv. 54; ix. 91.
— Marjory, wife of William Forbes of Fodderbirse, iv. 56.
— Marjory, wife of (1) H. Bannerman, and (2) Alex. Menzies, iv. 72.
— Marjory, wife of John Forbes of Brux, iv. 74.
— Marjory Winifred, iv. 68.
— Mary, wife of Sir John Gordon of Haddo, i. 88; iv. 75.
— Mary, wife of (1) H. Rose of Kilravock, and (2) Kinnaird of Culbin, iv. 62.
— Mary, wife of John Ogilvie of Balbegno, iv. 64.
— Mary, wife of (1) John Forbes, yr. of Monymusk, and (2) James, 16th lord Forbes, iv. 64, 75; ix. 91.
— Mary, wife of Jas. Gordon of Cobairdy, iv. 65.
— Mary, wife of James Irvine of Kingcaussie, vi. 266.
— Mary Anne, wife of Walter Henry, earl of Mar and Kellie, v. 95.
— Mary Elizabeth, wife of Sir John Hay of Haystoun, iv. 65.
— Mary Stuart, wife of C. B. Lee-Mainwaring, iv. 67.
— Montagu Ormond, 9th son of 19th lord Forbes, iv. 68.
— — his wife, Helen Campbell, iv. 68.
— Peter de, founder of the French family of Forbin, iv. 43 *n.*
— Richard, archdeacon of Ross, iv. 50.
— Rachel Anne, wife of P. Watson-Carnegie, vi. 499.
— Robert, prior of Monymusk, iv. 56.
— Robert, H.E.I.C.S., Bengal, iv. 66.
— Robert, 4th son of 11th lord Forbes, ix. 91.
— Robert Alaster Cam, captain R.N., iv. 65.
— Robert Shaw Brook, Queensland, iv. 67.
— Sarah, wife of Duncan Forbes, vii. 564.
— Sophia, wife of Chas. Cumine of Kininmont, iv. 64.

Forbes, Susan Janet Emilia, iii. 355.
—— Susanna, wife of Sir W. Urquhart, iv. 50.
—— Violet, wife of Gilbert Menzies of Pitfoddels, iv. 73.
—— Violet, wife of Walter Ogilvy of Boyne, iv. 74; ix. 91.
—— Walter Robert Drummond, captain Gordon Highlanders, iv. 68.
—— —— his wife, E. L. M. Farwell, iv. 68.
—— William, merchant, Aberdeen, i. 309.
—— —— his wife, Elizabeth Arbuthnott, i. 309.
—— Sir William, 2nd son of Sir John F. of Forbes, iv. 46.
—— William, provost of the church of St. Giles, iv. 50.
—— William, 'brother Archangel of the Capuchin Order, iv. 58.
—— William, colonel, Governor of Stadt, iv. 61.
—— William, lieut. R.N., 4th son of 17th lord Forbes, iv. 65.
—— William, eldest son of Alexander F. of Pitsligo, iv. 70.
—— —— his wife, Mariota Ogilvy, iv. 71.
—— William, 4th son of John F. of Pitsligo, iv. 72.
—— William, son of the laird of Echt, viii. 277.
—— —— his wife, Elizabeth Lyon, viii. 277.
—— *, captain in French regiment of Ogilby, iii. 514.
—— *, wife of James Menzies of Lashgoune, iv. 70.
—— *, wife of William Lawson, iv. 71.
—— *, wife of William White, iv. 71.
—— *, wife of William Woodman of Fenzies, iv. 71.
—— *, wife of Calder of Asloun, iv. 71.
—— *, wife of Mowat of Balquholly, iv. 71.
—— *, wife of Alex. Tulloch of Montcoffer, iv. 71.
—— *, wife of John Gordon of Botary, iv. 71.
—— *, wife of Alex. Keith of Pittendrum, iv. 72.
—— *, wife of Sir Alex. Fraser, 10th of Philorth, vii. 443.
—— *, viii. 83.
—— —— his wife, Mary Carnegie, viii. 83.
FORBES-SEMPILL, LORD SEMPILL, vii. 566-568.
Forbes-Sempill, Arthur Lionel Ochoncar, R.N., vii. 567.
—— —— his wife, Muriel Emily Spencer, vii. 567.
—— Douglas, major Seaforth Highlanders, vii. 566.
—— Evelyn Courtenay, wife of Capt. Duncan Vernon Pirie, vii. 567.
—— Gertrude Emily, vii. 567.

* Name unknown.

Forbes, Gwendolin Janet, vii. 567.
—— Katharine Charlotte Elizabeth Stewart, wife of George Muirhead, vii. 566.
—— Margaret, dau. of 18th lord Sempill, vii. 567.
—— Robert Abercromby, vii. 567.
Forbin d'Oppède, marquis de, iv. 43 *n*.
—— Palamède de, Governor of Provence, iv. 43 *n*.
—— Pierre de, iv. 43 *n*.
—— —— his wife, Françoise d'Argoult, iv. 43 *n*.
Force, Maréchal de la, iv. 546.
Ford of Coolgreeny, Matthew, i. 56.
—— —— his wife, Margaret Hamilton, i. 56.
—— of Heavitree, Richard, ii. 601.
—— —— his wife, Eliza Linnington Cranstoun, ii. 601.
—— of the Lea, Francis, ii. 566.
—— —— his wife, Elizabeth Hothersall, ii. 566.
—— Elizabeth, wife of 9th lord Colville of Culross, ii. 566.
Fordyce of Ayton, John, receiver-gen. of the land-tax in Scotland, iv. 556.
—— Alexander, Roehampton, i. 528; ix. 31.
—— —— his wife, Margaret J. Lindsay, i. 528; ix. 31 *bis*.
—— George, provost of Aberdeen, ix. 31.
Forest, Alison, wife of * Hepburn, v. 434 *n*., ix. 129.
Foresta of Duncanlaw, Isobel de, viii. 425.
Forestar, Walter, bishop of Brechin, viii. 49.
Forester of Willey Park, Cecil (Weld), 1st baron, ii. 566; vii. 451.
—— Henry William, vii. 451.
—— —— his wife, Eleanora Alexandrina Fraser, vii. 451.
Forestier-Walker, Sir Edward Walter, major-gen., K.C.B., vii. 490.
—— —— his wife, Jane Ogilvie-Grant, vii. 490.
—— Sir Frederick W. E., general, K.C.B., vii. 490.
FORFAR, ASTON, LORD ASTON, BARON OF, i. 399-414.
FORFAR, ASTON, BARON ASTON OF, i. 407-414.
Forfar, James, fifth lord Aston of, i. 413.
—— Walter, first lord Aston of, i. 406.
—— Walter, second lord Aston of, i. 409.
—— Walter, third lord Aston of, i. 411.
—— Walter, fourth lord Aston of, i. 412.
FORFAR, DOUGLAS, EARL OF, iv. 76-79.
Forfar, Archibald, first earl of, i. 207; iv. 77.
—— —— his wife, Robina Lockhart, iv. 78.
—— Archibald, second earl of, iv. 78.
Forman of Dawane, Sir John, vii. 367.
—— —— his wife, Helen Rutherford, vii. 367, 371.

* Name unknown.

Forman, Andrew, bishop of Moray, i. 182.
— Isobel, wife of Sir Patrick Home of Fastcastle and Balwoolsey, iv. 451.
FORMARTYNE, GORDON, VISCOUNT OF, i. 88-99.
Formartyne, George, first viscount of, i. 88.
Forne, father of Ivo of Coquetdale, iii. 249.
Forrest, Robert, minister at Abbotshall, vii. 197.
— — his wife, Marion Rollo, vii. 197.
— William, lieut.-col. Bengal Army, iv. 572.
— — his wife, Georgina C. Carmichael-Smyth, iv. 572.
FORRESTER OF CORSTORPHINE, FORRESTER, LORD, iv. 80-100.
Forrester of Corstorphine, George, first lord, iv. 90; ix. 92.
— — his wife, Christian Livingston, iv. 92; v. 190.
FORRESTER OF CORSTORPHINE, BAILLIE, LORD, iv. 93-96.
Forrester of Corstorphine, Caroline, wife of George Cockburn of Ormiston; baroness, iv. 95, 96.
— — James, second lord, iv. 91, 92 *bis*, 93, 106.
— — his 1st wife, Johanna or Jean Forrester, iv. 92.
— — his 2nd wife, Janet Ruthven, iv. 93.
— — George, fifth lord, iv. 95.
— — his wife, Charlotte Rowe, iv. 95.
— — George, sixth lord, iv. 96.
— — William, third lord, iv. 94.
— — his wife, Lilias Forrester, iv. 92.
— — William, fourth lord, iv. 94.
— — his wife, Margaret Birnie, iv. 94.
FORRESTER OF CORSTORPHINE, COCKBURN, BARONESS, iv. 96-97.
Forrester of Corstorphine, Anna Maria, baroness, iv. 97.
FORRESTER OF CORSTORPHINE, GRIMSTON, LORD, iv. 97-100.
Forrester of Corstorphine, James Walter, tenth lord, iv. 97.
— — his wife, Charlotte Jenkinson, iv. 97.
— — James Walter, eleventh lord, iv. 98.
— — his wife, Elizabeth Joanna Weyland, iv. 98.
— — James Walter, twelfth lord, iv. 98.
— — his wife, Margaret Frances Graham, iv. 98.
— master of, John, son of 1st lord Forrester, iv. 92.
— — his wife, Agnes Falconer, iv. 92; v. 248.
FORRESTER, LORD FORRESTER OF CORSTORPHINE, iv. 80-100.
— of Airth, Sir George, iv. 91.
Forrester of Arngibbon, Thomas, v. 187 *n.*
— of Auchindenny, Henry, 2nd son of Sir John F. of Corstorphine, iv. 84.
— of Badlormie, Sir John, iv. 83.
— of Barnton, John, iv. 86.
— — Matthew, ii. 61; iv. 86.
— — his wife, Christian Bellenden, ii. 61.
— of Nether Barnton, James, ix. 92.
— of Bavelaw, Henry, iv. 84.
— — his wife, Helen Fairlie, iv. 84.
— of Blackburne, Sir John, iv. 85.
— of Calziemuck, Robert, provost of Stirling, vi. 447.
— of Carden, David, i. 75; ii. 547; ix. 4.
— — Sir Duncan, Comptroller of the Household of James IV., iv. 87; v. 188.
— — Sir James, vi. 392; vii. 385; viii. 544.
— — his wife, Margaret Fleming, viii. 544.
— — Sir Walter, vi. 223.
— — his wife, Agnes Graham, vi. 223.
— of Castlecary, Sir Adam, iv. 80.
— of Clerkington, Sir Adam, iv. 81.
— — Alexander, iv. 87.
— — Sir George, iv. 91.
— of Corstorphine, Sir Adam, Provost of Edinburgh, 1st laird, iv. 80, 99.
— — his 1st wife, Agnes Dundas, iv. 81.
— — his 2nd wife, Margaret *, iv. 81.
— — Sir Alexander, 4th laird, iv. 85; v. 289; ix. 92 *bis*.
— — Alexander, 6th laird, iv. 87.
— — his wife, Margaret Forrester, iv. 87.
— — Sir Archibald, 5th laird, iv. 86, 99; ix. 92.
— — his 1st wife, Margaret Hepburne, ii. 148; iv. 86.
— — his 2nd wife, Agnes Tod, iv. 86.
— — George, 10th laird, ii. 71; iv. 90.
— — his wife, Christian Livingston, iv. 90, 92; v. 190.
— — Henry, 9th laird, iv. 88, 89 *bis*; ix. 141.
— — his wife, Helen Preston, iv. 90.
— — James, 7th laird, iv. 87, 99.
— — his wife, Agnes Forrester, iv. 87, 88.
— — Sir James, 8th laird, iv. 88; ix. 92.
— — his wife, Jonet Lauder, i. 5, 7; iv. 89.
— — Sir John, 2nd laird, iv. 82, 150 *bis*; vii. 39.
— — his 1st wife, Margaret *, iv. 82, 83, 84.
— — his 2nd wife, Jean St. Clair, iv. 84; vi. 570.
— — his 3rd wife, Marion Stewart, iv. 84.
— — Sir John, 3rd laird, ii. 326; iv. 85.
— — his wife, * Wigmore, iv. 85; ix. 92.
— of Currie, Sir James, iv. 89.
— of Dechmont, John, iv. 84.
— — his wife, Elizabeth Murray, iv. 84.

* Name unknown.

Forrester of Drylaw, Elizabeth, wife of David MacGill of Nisbet and Cranstoun Riddell, iv. 88; vi. 593.
—— —— Gilbert, iv. 85.
—— —— Gilbert, ii. 61.
—— —— his wife, Margaret Bellenden, ii. 61.
—— —— Thomas, iv. 82, 83.
—— of Drymen, Sir George, iv. 91.
—— of Fairliehope, Sir Adam, iv. 80.
—— —— Alexander, iv. 88.
—— —— James, iv. 88.
—— of Freirtoune, James, iv. 88.
—— of Garden, David, i. 75; ii. 547; ix. 4.
—— —— his wife, Elizabeth Sandilands, i. 75; ix. 3.
—— of Gartness, Duncan, vi. 414.
—— of Grange, Sir George, iv. 91.
—— of Hayning, *, v. 437.
—— —— his wife, Elizabeth *, v. 437.
—— —— Sir George, iv. 91.
—— of Incherathnyne, John, iv. 84.
—— of Kilbaberton, Henry, iv. 84.
—— of Langniddry, James, ix. 92.
—— of Lauriston, Henry, iv. 89.
—— —— Sir James, iv. 89.
—— of Liberton, Sir John, iv. 83 *bis*.
—— of Nether Liberton, Adam, ix. 64.
—— of Logie, David, viii. 170.
—— —— his wife, Janet Alexander, viii. 170.
—— of Longhermiston, Sir James, iv. 89.
—— of Meadowfield, James, iv. 88.
—— —— James, iv. 87 *quat.*, 88.
—— —— his wife, Agnes Forrester, iv. 87, 88.
—— —— Sir John, iv. 83.
—— of Niddry, Sir Adam, iv. 80.
—— —— Henry, iv. 84, 85.
—— —— his wife, Helen Fairlie, iv. 84.
—— —— John, iv. 84.
—— —— his wife, Elizabeth Murray, iv. 84.
—— —— John, ix. 103.
—— —— his wife, Elizabeth Hamilton, ix. 103.
—— of Ochtertyre, Sir John, iv. 82.
—— —— his wife, Margaret *, iv. 82.
—— of Oxgangs, Henry, iv. 83, 84.
—— of Philipston, Sir George, iv. 91.
—— of Saughton, Sir George, iv. 91.
—— —— his wife, Christian Livingston, iv. 91.
—— of Strathendry, Thomas, vi. 373.
—— of Thirlestane, Alexander, iv. 86, 87.
—— —— Sir Archibald, iv. 86.
—— —— James, iv. 88.
—— of Torwood, Sir James, vi. 448.
—— —— Sir Walter, v. 501.
—— of Torwoodheid, Margaret, wife of Sir Wm. Ross of Murieston, iv. 91.
—— —— Sir George, iv. 91.
—— —— Sir James, iv. 91; vii. 257.
—— of Whitburn, Sir Adam, iv. 80; ix. 191.

* Name unknown.

Forrester, Agnes, wife of (1) David Balfour, and (2) Jas. Pringle of the Tynnes, i. 532; ix. 32.
—— Agnes, wife of Thos. Bellenden, ii. 63.
—— Agnes, wife of (1) James Forrester of Corstorphine and Meadowfield, and (2) Simon Preston of Preston, iv. 87, 88 *bis*.
—— Agnes, dau. of Henry F. of Corstorphine, iv. 90.
—— Andrew, major, Horse Guards; 4th son of 4th lord Forrester of Corstorphine, iv. 95.
—— Annabel, wife of (1) Jas. Sinclair of Banks, and (2) Thos. Rollo, vii. 187.
—— Archibald, 2nd son of Henry F. of Oxgangs and Niddry, iv. 84.
—— Christian, wife of (1) Jas. Hamilton of Grange, and (2) rev. John Wauch, iv. 92.
—— David, 2nd son of Henry F. of Corstorphine, iv. 90.
—— David, bailie of Stirling, viii. 373.
—— Elizabeth, wife of Sir Alex. Lauder of Halton, iv. 84.
—— Euphame, dau. of Henry F. of Corstorphine, iv. 90.
—— Geilis, wife of Sir L. Bellenden, ii. 70; iv. 89.
—— Grizel, wife of Archd. Bruce, i. 548.
—— Harriet, wife of Edward Walter, iv. 95.
—— Harry, illeg. son of Sir James F., iv. 89.
—— Hector, 2nd son of Sir Archd. F. of Corstorphine, iv. 86.
—— Helen, dau. of 2nd lord Forrester, iv. 92; vii. 257 *n.*; ix. 92.
—— Henry, 3rd son of Henry F. of Corstorphine, iv. 90.
—— Isobel, wife of Sir James Edmonstone, iv. 85.
—— Isobel, wife of James Baillie of Carphin, iv. 88.
—— J——, wife of Wm. Napier of Wrightshouses, ix. 91.
—— James, illeg. son of James F. of Corstorphine, iv. 88.
—— James, lieut. R.N., iv. 95.
—— James, son of Sir Jas. F. of Corstorphine, ix. 92.
—— Janet, wife of 2nd lord Maxwell, iv. 84; vi. 476, 477.
—— Janet, wife of William Touris, iv. 86.
—— Janet, dau. of Sir Walter F., iv. 87.
—— Janet, dau. of 4th lord Forrester of Corstorphine, iv. 95.
—— Jean, Johanna *or* Jonet, wife of James Baillie of Letham, 2nd lord Forrester of Corstorphine, iv. 91, 92, 93.
—— John, 3rd son of Sir John F. of Corstorphine, iv. 83.
—— John, 3rd son of Sir Archibald F. of Corstorphine, iv. 87.
—— John, 4th son of Henry F. of Corstorphine, iv. 90.

Forrester, John, capt. R.N., iv. 95, 96.
—— —— his wife, Elizabeth Tyrrel, iv. 95.
—— John, 3rd son of Henry F. of Niddry, ix. 91.
—— Katharine, wife of Thos. Lauriston of Lauriston, iv. 89.
—— Katharine, wife of Robt. Douglas, iv. 90; ix. 92, 141.
—— Lilias, wife of Wm. Baillie of Corstorphine, iv. 92, 93 *n.*, 94.
—— Lilias, wife of W. Stirling of Herbertshire, iv. 95.
—— Margaret, wife of Sir Jas. Colville, ii. 547.
—— Margaret, wife of (1) John Stewart, and (2) Robt. Ramsay of Cockpen, iv. 86.
—— Margaret, wife of Alex. Forrester of Corstorphine, iv. 87.
—— Margaret, wife of (1) Alexander Telfer, and (2) John Schaw, iv. 92.
—— Margaret, wife of P. Haldane of Gleneagles, iv. 95.
—— Margaret, wife of Sir Geo. Douglas of Kirkness, vi. 373; ix. 141.
—— Margaret, wife of (1) *, and (2) Henry Livingston of Falkirk, vi. 448.
—— Margaret, wife of David Primrose, vii. 215.
—— Margaret, wife of 10th lord Ross of Halkhead, vii. 257.
—— Marion, wife of Andrew Leper, iv. 82.
—— Marion, wife of Wm. Livingston, v. 187.
—— Marion, wife of (1) Sir H. Shaw of Cambusmore, and (2) Jas. Campbell of Lawers, v. 501.
—— Marion *or* Marjorie, wife of (1) Sir William, master of Drummond, and (2) Sir James Sandilands of Calder, iv. 87; vii. 43; viii. 385; ix. 92.
—— Martha, wife of Thos. Maule of Pitlevie, vii. 17 *bis.*
—— Matthew, a soldier, vi. 173.
—— Sara, wife of John Inglis, iv. 90.
—— Sir Walter, son of Alexander F, of Corstorphine, iv. 87.
—— William, esquire, Linlithgow, iv. 80.
Forret, Janet, wife of Walter Arnot, ii. 547.
Forrett, William, pedagogue to 1st marquess of Montrose, vi. 242.
Forster of Forrest, Forster Hill, v. 417.
—— (*or* Foster), Sir John, Warden of the English Marches, v. 65, 67.
—— Robert Carnaby, iv. 396.
—— —— his wife, Mary Montagu, iv. 396.
—— Thomas, general, M.P., v. 126, 127.
—— *, wife of brigade-major Geo. Lindsay, v. 417.
Forsyth of Garvell, James, vii. 197.
—— —— his wife, Marion Rollo, vii. 197.

* Name unknown.

Forsyth, Alexander, D.D., rector of Letterkenny, viii. 555.
—— Christian, wife of Professor John Rutherfurd, vii. 371.
—— Helen, mistress of 4th earl of Rothes, vii. 291.
—— James, capt. 1st Dragoon Guards, ii. 565.
—— —— his wife, Anne Colville, ii. 565.
—— Janet, wife of rev. Jas. Fleming, viii. 555.
Fortescue of Dromiskin, Chichester, v. 482.
—— —— his wife, Elizabeth Wellesley, v. 482.
—— —— Sir Faithful, vii. 101.
—— Chichester, colonel, vii. 101.
—— Elizabeth, wife of 5th marquess of Lothian, v. 482.
—— Elizabeth, wife of Sir R. Graham of Norton Conyers, vii. 101.
FORTH, DRUMMOND, VISCOUNT OF, vi. 66-74.
Forth, George, sixth viscount of, vi. 71, 72; vii. 60.
—— George Henry Charles Francis Malcolm; styled viscount, vi. 73; vii. 61.
—— —— his wife, Harriet Mary Capell, vi. 73.
—— John, first viscount of, vi. 66.
—— John, 4th son of 1st earl of Melfort; styled viscount, vi. 67, 69, 70, 74.
—— —— his wife, Marie Gabrielle d'Audibert, vi. 70.
FORTH, RUTHVEN, EARL OF, iv. 101-106.
Forth, Patrick, earl of, iv. 102, 103, 258; v. 6; ix. 93.
—— —— his 1st wife, *, iv. 105.
—— —— his 2nd wife, Joanna Henderson, iv. 105.
—— —— his 3rd wife, Clara Berner, iv. 105; ix. 93.
Forth of Redwood, James, i. 61.
—— Dorothy, wife of rev. Francis Hamilton, i. 61.
Fortibus *or* Forz, William de, earl of Albemarle, iv. 142.
—— —— his wife, Christina of Galloway, iv. 142.
FORTROSE, MACKENZIE, VISCOUNT, vii. 512-513.
Fortrose, Kenneth, lord, vii. 510.
—— Kenneth, son of 5th earl of Seafield; styled lord, vii. 512.
—— —— his wife, Mary Stewart, iv. 165; vii. 512.
—— Kenneth, viscount, vii. 512.
Forveleth, wife of Norin of Monorgund, v. 329.
—— dau. of Kerald, ix. 26.
Fossart, Richard, Jedworth, iv. 146.
Foster of Jardinefield, Anthony, viii. 461.

* Name unknown.

Foster, Alicia, wife of Wm. Hay-Newton, viii. 461.
—— James, D.D., presbyterian minister, v. 178.
—— *, husband of Elizabeth Constable, iii. 293.
Fotheringham of Ballathrone, Thomas, v. 398.
—— —— his wife, Helen Lindsay, v. 398.
—— of Caverton, John, vii. 326.
—— of Laurencetown, Henry de, iv. 270.
—— of Fothringham, Thomas Frederick Scrymseoure, viii. 90.
—— of Powrie, David, vi. 495.
—— —— Peter, v. 535.
—— —— his wife, Anne Fraser, v. 535.
—— —— Thomas, i. 280; iii. 19.
—— —— Thomas, i. 287.
—— —— his wife, Elizabeth Arbuthnott, i. 287.
—— —— Thomas, v. 398.
—— —— his wife, Helen Lindsay, v. 398.
—— —— Thomas, iv. 290, 567.
—— —— his wife, Margaret Gibson, iv. 290.
—— —— Thomas, v. 536.
—— —— Thomas Frederick Scrymseoure, viii. 90.
—— —— his wife, Charlotte Carnegie, viii. 89.
—— Amelia, wife of Hugh Fraser, self-styled lord Lovat, v. 536.
—— Cecilia, wife of Sir D. Carmichael of Balmedie, iv. 567.
—— Isabella, wife of Wm. Ruthven of Freeland, iv. 260.
—— Jean, wife of (1) John Carnegie of Boysack, and (2) James Carnegie of Balnamoon, vi. 495; viii. 62.
—— Katharine, wife of Sir D. Lindsay of Beaufort and Edzell, iii. 19.
—— Katharine, wife of John Carnegie of that Ilk and Seaton, viii. 58.
—— Mariot, wife of George Graham of Claverhouse, iii. 323.
Fothes, Fergus de, iv. 43 *n.*
—— John de, iv. 42 *n.*
Foulis of Colinton, Sir Alexander, ii. 294; vi. 450.
—— —— his wife, Elizabeth Hepburn, ii. 294.
—— —— James, iv. 313.
—— —— Sir James, vi. 420.
—— —— Sir James, iii. 72; v. 83.
—— —— his wife, Margaret Erskine, iii. 72; v. 83.
—— of Dunipace, Archibald, vii. 220.
—— —— George, vii. 220.
—— —— his wife, Margaret Cunninghame, vii. 220.
—— of Leadhills, Anna, wife of Sir James Hope, iv. 492.

* Name unknown.

Foulis of Leadhills, Robert, iv. 492.
—— of Ravelston, George, vii. 216.
—— —— Sir John, 1st bart., vii. 220; viii. 446.
—— —— his 1st wife, Margaret Primrose, 220.
—— of Woodhall, John, vi. 498.
—— —— his wife, Margaret Carnegie, vi. 498.
—— Janet, wife of Gilbert Primrose, vii. 216.
—— Janet, wife of Thos. Hamilton of Parkley, ix. 101.
—— Jean, wife of John Hay, viii. 446.
—— John, apothecary, Edinburgh, vi. 92.
—— John, *error for* Soulis, vi. 206.
—— Margaret, wife of Thomas Hamilton, lord advocate, iv. 312, 313.
—— Marjorie, wife of (1) William, 8th earl of Morton, and (2) William (Erskine), 2nd earl of Buchan, ix. 49, 141.
—— Mary, wife of John Napier of Shanbothy, vi. 420.
—— Mary, wife of major Jas. Livingston, vi. 450.
—— Thomas, goldsmith, Edinburgh, viii. 171.
—— William, keeper of the Privy Seal, ii. 588 *n.*; vi. 403.
—— William de, prevost of collegiate church of Bothwell, iii. 57.
Foulis-Primrose of Dunipace, Sir Archibald, vii. 220.
—— —— his 1st wife, Margaret Fleming, vii. 220; viii. 554.
—— —— his 2nd wife, Mary Primrose, vii. 220, 222.
Fountain of Southacre, Sir Andrew, ii. 584 *n.*
Fourbuire *or* Fourbour, Marion, wife of Adam Hepburn of Hailes, ix. 40.
Fowell Buxton, Sir Thomas, bart., G.C.M.G., vii. 86.
—— —— Edith Frances, wife of Walter George Hepburne-Scott, master of Polwarth, vii. 86.
Fowler of St. Thomas' Priory, Walter, i. 409.
—— —— his wife, Constance Aston, i. 409.
—— Ethel Mary, wife of (1) S. Watson, and (2) lord T. F. A. Kennedy, ii. 499.
—— Robert, ii. 499.
—— William, Edinburgh, iv. 411.
Fownes of Kittery Court, Thomas, prebendary of Wells, viii. 33.
—— —— his 2nd wife, Anne Vannam Somerville, viii. 33.
Fox of Fox Hall, Francis, rev., iii. 615.
—— Anne, wife of 6th earl of Nithsdale, vi. 490.
—— Caroline Amelia, wife of Sir W. F. P. Napier, vi. 434.

Fox, Charles Edward, Master of Equity, Bombay, iii. 615.
—— Henry Edward, general, vi. 434.
—— John, Lincoln's Inn Fields, ii. 484.
—— Mary, wife of 7th earl of Cassillis, ii. 484.
—— Selina Mary, wife of B. C. F. P. Cary, iii. 615.
Fox-Lane, Robert, son of George, lord Bingley, iii. 409.
—— —— his wife, Bridget Henley, iii. 408.
—— William Augustus, vi. 383.
—— —— his wife, Caroline Douglas, vi. 383.
Foxlowe of Staveley Hall, William, lieut.-gen., i. 486.
—— —— his wife, Mary Murray, i. 486.
France, king of, Charles VII., iii. 166.
—— —— Henry II., i. 23, 26.
—— —— Henry IV., i. 28.
—— —— Francis I., i. 23.
—— —— Francis II., i. 26.
—— —— John, iii. 149.
—— —— Louis XI., i. 19.
—— —— his wife, Margaret of Scotland, i. 19.
—— —— Louis XIV., i. 29; vii. 52.
—— queen of, Marie Antoinette, viii. 361.
Francis of Blair, Hew, iv. 185.
—— —— James, iv. 185.
—— of Stane, Elizabeth, wife of William Montgomerie of Greenfield, iii. 436, 437.
—— —— Robert, iii. 436, 437.
—— Dr., 'Apparisiis,' v. 246.
—— —— his wife, Isobel Falconer, v. 246.
Frankland, Roger, rector of Yarlington, ii. 565.
—— —— his wife, Katharine Colville, ii. 565.
Frankland-Russell of Great Thirkleby, Sir Robert, bart., i. 492.
—— —— his wife, Louisa Anne Murray, i. 492.
Franquetot, Evelyn de, viii. 128.
—— Louis Robert Henri François de, viii. 127.
—— Georgine Elizabeth Fanny de, wife of 3rd earl Manvers, viii. 127.
—— Louisa Jane Henrietta Emily de, wife of 10th earl of Stair, viii. 127, 161.
—— Marie de, viii. 128.
FRASER, FRASER, LORD, iv. 107-122.
Fraser, Andrew, first lord, iv. 111, 112.
—— —— his 1st wife, Elizabeth Douglas, ii. 270; iv. 113.
—— —— his 2nd wife, Anne Drummond, iv. 113; vii. 48.
—— Andrew, second lord, iv. 113, 114; vi. 58.
—— —— his 1st wife, Margaret Elphinstone, i. 562; iv. 115.
—— —— his 2nd wife, Anna Haldane, iv. 115 *bis*.
—— —— his 3rd wife, Elizabeth Crichton, iv. 115, 116, 123.
Fraser, Andrew, third lord, iv. 117; ix. 93.
—— —— his 1st wife, Katharine Fraser, i. 305; iv. 118; v. 534.
—— —— his 2nd wife, Jean *or* Mary Mackenzie, iv. 118; v. 626.
—— Charles, fourth lord, iv. 118.
—— —— his wife, Margaret *or* Marjory Erskine, ii. 273; iv. 119.
FRASER OF LOVAT, FRASER, LORD, v. 518-548.
Fraser of Lovat, Amelia, wife of Alexander Mackenzie *or* Fraser; baroness, iv. 119; v. 535, 538; vii. 446.
—— —— Alexander, fourth lord, v. 527.
—— —— his wife, Janet Campbell, v. 527.
—— —— Archibald Campbell, *de jure* thirteenth lord, v. 541.
—— —— his wife, Jane Fraser, v. 542.
—— —— Hugh, first lord, v. 523; vii. 433.
—— —— his wife, Violetta Lyon, v. 523; viii. 276.
—— —— Hugh, third lord, iv. 23; v. 526, 530.
—— —— his 1st wife, Anna Grant, v. 526.
—— —— his 2nd wife, Janet Ross, v. 526.
—— —— Hugh, fifth lord, v. 528.
—— —— his wife, Elizabeth Stuart, i. 445 v. 528, 529.
—— —— Hugh, seventh lord, v. 532.
—— —— his wife, Isobel Wemyss, v. 532; viii. 499.
—— —— Hugh, eighth lord, v. 534.
—— —— his wife, Anne Mackenzie, v. 534.
—— —— Hugh, ninth lord, v. 534, 537.
—— —— his wife, Amelia Murray, v. 534.
—— —— Hugh, son of Amelia, baroness Fraser of Lovat; self-styled lord, v. 536.
—— —— his wife, Amelia Fothringham, v. 536.
—— —— Simon, sixth lord, v. 529; vii. 439, 441.
—— —— his 1st wife, Katharine Mackenzie, v. 530.
—— —— his 2nd wife, Jean Stewart, iii. 189; v. 530.
—— —— his 3rd wife, Katharine Rose, v. 530; vii. 465.
—— —— Simon, eleventh lord, v. 534, 535, 537, 545; vii. 141, 446.
—— —— his 1st wife, Margaret Grant, v. 539.
—— —— his 2nd wife, Primrose Campbell, i. 382; v. 540.
—— —— Simon, *de jure* twelfth lord, v. 540; ix. 132.
—— —— his wife, Katharine Bristowe, v. 541.
—— —— Simon, thirteenth lord, v. 542, 547.
—— —— his wife, Alice Mary Blundell, v. 547.
—— —— Simon Joseph, fourteenth lord, v 548.

Fraser of Lovat, Thomas, second lord, v. 524; viii. 278.
—— —— his 1st wife, Janet Gordon, v. 525.
—— —— his 2nd wife, Janet Gray; iv. 275; v. 525.
—— —— Thomas, tenth lord, v. 536.
—— —— his wife, Sybilla Macleod, v. 536.
—— master of, William, 2nd son of 2nd lord Fraser, iv. 115, 116.
FRASER, LORD FRASER, iv. 107-122.
FRASER, LORD FRASER OF LOVAT, v. 518-548.
FRASER, BARON LOVAT OF LOVAT, v. 546-548.
FRASER, LORD SALTOUN, vii. 417-453.
Fraser of Aberdour, Andrew, vii. 437.
—— —— John, vii. 437, 441.
—— of Aberluthnot, John, i. 277.
—— of Abertarff, Archibald Campbell, colonel, v. 541.
—— —— Archibald Thos. Frederick, v. 542.
—— —— his wife, Janet Macpherson, v. 542.
—— —— Hugh, v. 521.
—— of Aboyne, Sir Alexander, iv. 517; vii. 427.
—— —— Sir John, iv. 517.
—— —— Margaret, wife of Sir Wm. Keith of Keith-Marischal and Dunottar, iv. 517, 518, 521; vi. 36.
—— of Abriachan, Alexander, vii. 476.
—— of Agaes, Hugh, v. 526.
—— of Alathy, Thomas, iv. 109.
—— of Arcles, Hugh, v. 526.
—— of the Ard, Hugh, v. 520.
—— of Ardachie, James, 3rd son of 4th lord Lovat, v. 528.
—— of Ardendracht, Sir John, 2nd son of Sir William F. of Cowie, vii. 429, 433 *n*.
—— —— Marjory *or* Margaret, wife of Alexander Hay of Dronlaw, iii. 562.
—— of Ardglassie, John, vii. 434 *bis*.
—— of Ardlaw, Alexander, vii. 436.
—— —— Sir William, vii. 431.
—— of Ardranich, Thomas, v. 524.
—— of Auchincross, Sir Alexander, vii. 427.
—— of Auchinschogill, John, vii. 429, 431, 435.
—— of Balgownie, William, advocate, M.P., ii. 276; vii. 444.
—— —— his wife, Katharine Anne Erskine, ii. 276; vii. 445.
—— of Balhelvie, John, vii. 430.
—— —— his wife, Marjory of Monymusk, vii. 430.
—— —— John, his son, vii. 430.
—— of Ballebrochy, Sir Alexander, vii. 427.
—— of Ballecaranach, Thomas, v. 524.
—— of Beaufort, Hugh, v. 526.
—— —— Thomas, v. 524.
—— —— Thomas, 4th son of 7th lord Fraser of Lovat, v. 533, 535, 536.
—— —— his wife, Sybilla Macleod, v. 536.
Fraser of Beauly, Hugh, v. 528.
—— of Blairmormond, Alexander, vii. 437.
—— of Bodichail, Alexander, vii. 436.
—— of Brackla, Robert, ii. 197.
—— of Brea, Sir James, Governor of Inverness, v. 531 *bis*, 534.
—— —— his wife, Beatrice Wemyss, v. 531.
—— —— James, 2nd laird, v. 531.
—— —— James, minister of Culross, iv. 289.
—— —— his wife, Isobel Gray, iv. 289.
—— of Brotherton, Sir Simon, sheriff of Kincardine, vii. 425, 433 *n*.
—— —— his wife, Margaret of Caithness, ii. 319; vii. 426.
—— of Broxmouth, Sir Alexander, iv. 270.
—— of Byth, Sir Alexander, vii. 433.
—— of Cairnbulg, Sir Alexander, vii. 440.
—— —— Alexander, iv. 112; vii. 440.
—— —— Andrew, iv. 112.
—— —— Charles, iv. 121.
—— —— Robert, vii. 440.
—— —— Thomas, 4th son of 2nd lord Fraser, iv. 115, 116, 117, 121.
—— —— his 1st wife, Margaret Forbes, iv. 117.
—— —— his 2nd wife, Margaret Seton, iv. 117.
—— of Castle Fraser, Charles, iv. 121.
—— —— C. Mackenzie, colonel, viii. 231.
—— of Little Clintertie, John, 3rd son of Michael F. of Stoneywood, iv. 112.
—— of Cluny, Sir Alexander, vii. 428.
—— —— Margaret, wife of Sir Wm. Keith, iv. 517, 518, 521; vi. 36.
—— of Colly, Alexander, vii. 431.
—— of Cornton, Sir Alexander, brother of Sir Richard F. of Touch Fraser, iv. 107; vii. 424.
—— —— Thomas, iv. 108; vi. 35.
—— —— Thomas, his grandson, iv. 108.
—— of Wester Corse, Thomas, iv. 109.
—— of Cowie, Sir Alexander, chamberlain of Scotland, vii. 426.
—— —— his wife, Mary Bruce, i. 277; ii. 434; vii. 428.
—— —— Sir Alexander, sheriff of Aberdeen, ii. 261; vii. 430.
—— —— Sir Alexander, vi. 171: vii. 432.
—— —— his wife, Marjory Menzies, vii. 433.
—— —— John, vii. 429.
—— —— Margaret, wife of Sir Wm. Keith of Keith-Marischal, vi. 36; vii. 429.
—— —— Sir William, 2nd son of Sir Alexander F. of Touch, vii. 429.
—— —— his wife, Margaret Moray, vii. 429.
—— —— Sir William, iii. 562; vii. 431.
—— —— his wife, Eleanor Douglas, iii. 157; vii. 432.
—— of Crechie, Walter, vii. 437.
—— of Park of Creichmond and Crychtie, Alexander, vii. 437.

Fraser of Culburtie, Elizabeth, dau. of Francis F. of Kinmundy, iv. 113, 116.
— — Sir William, vii. 431.
— of Culbokie, James, 3rd son of 2nd lord Lovat, v. 525.
— — William, vii. 505.
— of Culpressache, Sir Alexander, vii. 427.
— of Dalcross, John, v. 528.
— — his wife, Anna Fraser, v. 528.
— — Thomas, v. 524.
— of Dalgaty, Margaret *or* Marjorie, wife of Alexander Hay of Dronlaw, iii. 562.
— of Denend, Alexander, vii. 437.
— — Sir Alexander, vii. 439.
— — Thomas, vii. 439.
— of Denis, Thomas, iv. 112.
— — his wife, Katharine Hill, iv. 112.
— of Drem, Sir Bernard, vii. 418.
— — his wife, *, sister of Nes of Lundin, vii. 419.
— of Drip, Sir Alexander, vii. 427.
— of Drumelzier, Sir Laurence, v. 519; vii. 420.
— of Drumquhendill, William, 3rd son of 1st lord Fraser, iv. 113.
— — his wife, Jean Barclay, iv. 113.
— of Duffus, Alexander, vii. 428.
— — Hugh, v. 526.
— of Durris, Sir Alexander, sheriff of Aberdeen, vii. 430.
— — his 1st wife, Joanna *or* Janet Ross, ii. 261; vii. 239 *bis*, 431.
— — his 2nd wife, Elizabeth Hamilton, iv. 346; vii. 431.
— — Alexander, illeg. son of Sir Alexander F., sheriff of Aberdeen, vii. 431.
— — Alexander, i. 282.
— — his wife, Giles Arbuthnott, i. 282.
— — Alexander, i. 83.
— — his wife, Margaret Gordon, i. 83.
— — Alexander, i. 287.
— — his wife, Christian Arbuthnott, i. 287.
— — Alexander, i. 299; iv. 112, 113; vii. 440.
— — his wife, Helen Arbuthnott, i. 299.
— — Sir Alexander, physician to King Charles II., iv. 113.
— — Andrew, iv. 113.
— — Robert, vii. 440.
— — Thomas, i. 299.
— — Sir William, 2nd son of Sir Alexander F. of Cowie, vii. 429.
— — his wife, Margaret Moray, vii. 429.
— — William, master of Fraser, iv. 116.
— of Esse, Hugh, v. 520.
— of Essintuly Wester, John, vii. 430.
— — his wife, Marjory of Monymusk, vii. 430.

* Name unknown.

Fraser of Essuly, Sir Alexander, vii. 427.
— of Faichfield, William, burgess of Aberdeen, iv. 113.
— — his wife, Jean Barclay, iv. 113.
— — William, iv. 113.
— — his wife, Christian Garioch, iv. 113.
— of Fairliehope, Hugh, v. 520.
— of Faithlie, Sir Alexander, vii. 439.
— — Sir William, vii. 435.
— of Fanellan, Thomas, v. 543.
— of Fetteresso, Margaret, wife of Sir W. Keith, vi. 36.
— of Forglen, Sir John, iv. 108; v. 519; vii. 430, 433 *n*.
— of Foulis, Simon, v. 530.
— of Foyness, Alexander, governor of Lovat, v. 533.
— — James, 3rd son of 2nd lord Lovat, v. 525.
— of Fraserburgh, Sir Alexander, vii. 439.
— of Fraserdale, Alexander, son of Roderick Mackenzie of Prestonhall, v. 536.
— — his wife, Amelia, baroness Fraser of Lovat, v. 535.
— of Fraserfield, Alexander, vii. 445.
— — Margaret, wife of Henry David Mitchell, vii. 445 *bis*.
— — William, M.P., ii. 276; vii. 444.
— — his wife, Katharine Anne Erskine, ii. 276; vii. 445.
— — William, ii. 278; vii. 445.
— — William, vii. 445.
— of Frendraught, v. 519.
— — James, 4th son of Sir Andrew F. of Uchtredstruther, vii. 426.
— — his wife, Mariozita *or* Margaret of Frendraught, vii. 426.
— — Sir James, vii. 426.
— — James, vi. 301; vii. 426.
— — Matilda, wife of Alexander Dunbar, vi. 301; vii. 426.
— of Fruid, v. 519.
— — Katharine, betrothed to Malcolm Fleming, and wife of James Tweedie of Drumelzier, viii. 537 *bis*.
— of Garvocks, Sir Alexander, vii. 427.
— of Glasloch, William, iv. 69.
— of Greencastle, Gilbert, iv. 110.
— — Thomas, iv. 110.
— of Guisachan, Hugh, vii. 501.
— of Hailes, Adam, vii. 418, 419.
— — his wife, Constantia, vii. 419.
— — Sir Bernard, vii. 419, 420.
— — Sir Laurence, vii. 420.
— of Inchany, Thomas, v. 543.
— of Inchbarry and Ingliston, Hugh, v. 526.
— of Inverallochy, Sir Alexander, vii. 439 *bis*.
— — Alexander, v. 87.
— — his wife, Elizabeth Erskine, v. 87.

Fraser of Inverallochy, Alexander Mackenzie, general, vii. 511.
—— —— his wife, Helen Mackenzie, vii. 511.
—— —— Charles, iv. 121.
—— —— Sir Simon, v. 531.
—— —— his wife, Jean Moncrieff, v. 531.
—— —— Simon, ix. 29.
—— —— his wife, Elizabeth Murray, ix. 29.
—— —— Simon, ii. 273; ix. 29.
—— —— his wife, Margaret Erskine, ii. 273; iv. 119.
—— —— William, ii. 274; iv. 120, 121.
—— of Invernorth, Sir Alexander, vii. 440.
—— —— Alexander. iv. 112; vii. 440.
—— —— Andrew, iv. 112.
—— —— Robert, vii. 440.
—— —— William, iv. 114.
—— of Keith-Hundeby, Eda, wife of Hugh Lorens, vi. 28; vii. 418.
—— of Keith-Simon, Simon, v. 518; vi. 26, 28; vii. 418.
—— of Kilbirny, Thomas, v. 524.
—— of Kilmyles, Hugh, v. 526, 530.
—— —— Sir James, v. 534.
—— of Kilray, Thomas, v. 524.
—— of Kiltarlity, Hugh, v. 520.
—— of Kindrocht, Alexander, vii. 437.
—— —— Sir Alexander, vii. 439.
—— —— Thomas, vii. 439.
—— of Kinkell, James, v. 525.
—— —— Sir Simon, v. 531.
—— of Kinlyn, Agnes, wife of K. Mackenzie of Kintail, vii. 498.
—— of Kinmundy, Andrew, iv. 110.
—— —— his 1st wife, Margaret Forbes, iv. 110.
—— —— his 2nd wife, Marjory Hay, iv. 110.
—— —— Andrew, sheriff-depute of Aberdeen, iv. 111.
—— —— Francis, 2nd son of 1st lord Fraser, iv. 113, 115.
—— —— his wife, Marjory Elphinstone, i. 562; iv. 113.
—— —— John, son of Gilbert F. of Watertoun, iv. 111 *bis*.
—— —— Thomas, iv. 108; vi. 35.
—— —— Thomas, iv. 109.
—— —— his 1st wife, *, iv. 109.
—— —— his 2nd wife, Giles Arbuthnott, i. 287; iv. 109.
—— of Kinmylie, Simon, eldest son of 7th lord Lovat; master of Lovat, v. 532.
—— of Kinnaird, Sir Alexander, vii. 428.
—— of Kinnell, Alexander, vi. 39, 40.
—— —— his wife, Marion Keith, vi. 39.
—— —— Hugh, v. 519.
—— —— Robert, 4th son of 2nd lord Lovat; ancestor of the family of, v. 525.
—— —— his wife, Janet Gelly, v. 525.
—— of Kinneries, Alexander, vii. 476.
—— —— Alexander, colonel, vii. 506.

* Name unknown.

Fraser of Kinneries, Sir James, v. 534.
—— of Kinnowdie, Hugh, v. 528.
—— of Kirktoun, Hugh, v. 526.
—— of Knock, John, iv. 192.
—— —— his wife. Margaret Stuart, iv. 192.
—— of Knockie, Thomas, 2nd son of 4th lord Fraser of Lovat, v. 528, 529, 543.
—— —— his wife, Isobel *or* Elizabeth Forbes, v. 543; vii. 438.
—— of Lathindie, Andrew, iv. 110.
—— of Leadclune, William, v. 542.
—— —— Sir William, F.R.S., 1st bart., v. 542.
—— of Lentran, Alexander, v. 545.
—— —— Thomas, major, v. 546.
—— of Lonmay, James, vii. 445.
—— —— his wife, Eleanor Lindsay, i. 523; vii. 445.
—— —— William, cornet of dragoons, vii. 445.
—— of Lovat, Alexander, 2nd laird, v. 521.
—— —— his 1st wife, Elizabeth Keith, v. 521.
—— —— his 2nd wife, Marion Keith, v. 521.
—— —— Amelia, betrothed to Alexander, master of Saltoun, and wife of Alexander Mackenzie, iv. 119; v. 535, 538; vii. 446.
—— —— Archibald Campbell, colonel, M.P., v. 541, 546.
—— —— his wife, Jane Fraser, v. 542.
—— —— Hugh, 1st laird, v. 519.
—— —— Hugh, 3rd laird, v. 521; vi. 303, 304.
—— —— his 1st wife, Janet Fentoun, v. 522.
—— —— his 2nd wife, Isabella Wemyss, v. 522; viii. 483.
—— —— Sir Simon, 1254, v. 519.
—— —— Sir Simon, possible ancestor of the family of, v. 519; vii. 425.
—— —— his wife, Margaret of Caithness, ii. 319; vii. 426.
—— —— Simon, brigadier-general, M.P., v. 540.
—— —— his wife, Katharine Bristowe, v. 541.
—— —— Thomas, 4th laird, v. 522.
—— —— Thomas Alexander, v. 546.
—— —— his wife, Charlotte Georgina Dorothea Jerningham, v. 546.
—— of Mayne, David, v. 531.
—— —— Simon, v. 531.
—— of Memzie, James, ancestor of the family of, vii. 433.
—— —— James, vii. 434.
—— —— John, vii. 444.
—— —— William, 3rd son of Michael F. in Techmuiry, vii. 433.
—— of Mongewell Park, Alexander Caspar, vii. 592.
—— of Easter Moniack, Thomas, v. 543.
—— of Morvin, Sir Simon, v. 519.
—— of Moy, Thomas, v. 524.

Fraser of Muchalls, Sir Andrew, 2nd laird, iv. 109.
—— his wife, Muriel Sutherland, iv. 109.
—— Andrew, iv. 54.
—— his wife, Margaret Forbes, iv. 54.
—— Andrew, ii. 270.
—— his wife, Elizabeth Douglas, ii. 270.
—— Andrew, vii. 48.
—— his wife, Anne Drummond, vii. 48.
—— Charles, iv. 121.
—— Thomas, 1st laird, iv. 108.
— of New Muircroft, Alexander, vii. 436.
— of Ness Castle, Marjory, wife of 15th lord Saltoun, vii. 448.
—— Simon, vii. 440, 448 *bis*.
— of Newton, Thomas, major, v. 546.
— of Norham, Thomas, iv. 109.
— of Oliver Castle, iv. 107; v. 519.
—— Joanna, wife of Sir Patrick Fleming of Biggar, vii. 422; viii. 524.
—— Margaret *or* Mary, wife of Sir Gilbert de Haya of Locherwart, vii. 422; viii. 419.
—— Sir Simon, sheriff of Traquair and Peebles, vii. 421.
—— Sir Simon, Keeper of the Forests of Traquair and Selkirk, vii. 421.
—— his wife Mary [? Oliphant], vi. 533 *n*.; vii. 421.
—— Sir Simon, Keeper of the Forest of Traquair, ii. 218; vii. 422; viii. 4, 418, 524.
—— his wife, Maria, vii. 422.
— of Panbride, Sir Alexander, vii. 427.
— of Philorth, Sir Alexander, 1st laird; ii. 261; iv. 45, 108, 346; vii. 239, 430.
—— his 1st wife, Janet Ross, ii. 261; vii. 239 *bis*, 431.
—— his 2nd wife, Elizabeth Hamilton, iv. 346; vii. 431.
—— Sir Alexander, 3rd laird, v. 430, 519, 523; vii. 433, 435.
—— his wife, Marjorie Menzies, vii. 433.
—— Alexander, 4th laird, iii. 565; vii. 433, 435.
—— his wife, Margaret Hay, iii. 565.
—— Alexander, 5th laird, vii. 434.
—— his contracted wife, Marjerie Calder, vii. 434.
—— Alexander, 7th laird, vii. 436.
—— his 1st wife, Katharine Barclay, vii. 437.
—— his 2nd wife, Katharine Menzies, vii. 437.
—— Sir Alexander, 8th laird, ii. 9, 14; iv. 112, 412; v. 112; vii. 438.
—— his 1st wife, Magdalen Ogilvy, ii. 9; vii. 440.
—— his 2nd wife, Elizabeth Maxwell, iv. 412; v. 112, 412; vii. 440.
Fraser of Philorth, Alexander, 9th laird, vii. 440.
—— his 1st wife, Margaret Abernethy, vii. 413, 416, 440.
—— his 2nd wife, Isabel Gordon, v. 116; vii. 441.
—— Sir Alexander, 10th laird, iv. 114; vii. 441.
—— his 1st wife, * Forbes, vii. 443.
—— his 2nd wife, Elizabeth Seton, vii. 413, 443.
—— Sir Gilbert, sheriff of Traquair and Peebles, ancestor of the family of, vii. 418, 420.
—— his wife, Christian, vii. 421.
—— Sir William, 2nd laird, iii. 157, 562; iv. 47, 69, 515; vii. 431.
—— his wife, Eleanor Douglas, iii. 157; vii. 432.
—— Sir William, 6th laird, vii. 434.
—— his wife, Elizabeth Keith, vii. 435.
— of Pheppachy, Hugh, v. 527.
— of Pitallochy, Alexander, vii. 437.
— of Pitsligach, Sir William, vii. 431.
— of Pittendreich, Thomas, iv. 108; vi. 35.
— of Pittulie, Alexander, vii. 440.
—— his 1st wife, Margaret Abernethy, vii. 441.
—— Sir William, vii. 431.
— of Quarrelbuss, Andrew, vii. 437.
—— John, vii. 437.
— of Querelwood, Hugh, v. 526.
— of Rathillock, Andrew, vii. 437.
—— Walter, vii. 437.
— of Rig, John, vii. 421, 423.
—— his wife, Alicia de Conigburg, vii. 424.
—— Sir Richard, vii. 424.
— of Sauchek, Michael, iv. 112.
—— Thomas, 2nd son of Michael F. of Stoneywood, iv. 112.
—— his wife, Katharine Hill, iv. 112.
— of Scatterty, Sir Alexander, vii. 433.
—— James, vii. 438.
— of Stoneywood, Sir Andrew, 2nd laird, iv. 109.
—— his wife, Muriel Sutherland, iv. 109; ix. 69, 93.
—— Andrew, 4th laird, iv. 109 *bis*, 110.
—— his 1st wife, Margaret Forbes, iv. 54, 110.
—— his 2nd wife, Marjery Hay, iv. 110.
—— Andrew, 5th laird, iv. 110.
—— his wife, Margaret Irvine, iv. 110.
—— Andrew, 7th laird, i. 562; iv. 111, 112.
—— Michael, 6th laird, iv. 111.
—— his wife, Isobel *or* Elizabeth Forbes, iv. 111.
—— Thomas, 1st laird, iv. 108.

* Name unknown.

Fraser of Stoneywood, Thomas, 3rd laird, iv. 109, 110.
—— —— his 1st wife, * Stewart, ix. 93.
—— —— his 2nd wife, Giles Arbuthnott, i. 287; iv. 109.
—— of Strachan, Sir Alexander, vii. 427.
—— —— John, vii. 429.
—— —— Margaret, wife of Sir Wm. Keith, vi. 36; vii. 429.
—— of Strichen, Alexander, 5th laird, v. 544; vi. 323; ix. 132.
—— —— his 1st wife, Elizabeth Cockburn, v. 544.
—— —— his 2nd wife, Emilia Stewart, iii. 38; v. 544; vi. 323.
—— —— Alexander, 7th laird, judge of the Court of Session, general of the mint, ii. 300 *n.*; v. 545.
—— —— his wife, Ann Campbell, i. 370; ii. 300; v. 545.
—— —— Alexander, 8th laird, ii. 300 *n.*; v. 545.
—— —— his wife, Jean Menzies, v. 545.
—— —— Alexander, 9th laird, v. 546.
—— —— his wife, Emilia Leslie, v. 546.
—— —— James, 6th laird, v. 545.
—— —— Katharine, wife of William Forbes of Corsindae, v. 543; vii. 438.
—— —— Thomas, 3rd son of Alex. F. of Philorth; v. 543; vii. 438.
—— —— his wife Isobel *or* Elizabeth Forbes, v. 543; vii. 438.
—— —— Thomas, 1st laird of 2nd line, 2nd son of 4th lord Fraser of Lovat, v. 528, 542, 543; vii. 438, 439.
—— —— his wife, Elizabeth *or* Isobel Forbes, v. 543; vii. 438.
—— —— Thomas, 2nd laird, v. 543; ix. 132.
—— —— his 1st wife, Christian Forbes, v. 543.
—— —— his 2nd wife, Margaret Macleod, iii. 71; v. 543; vii. 502.
—— —— Thomas, 3rd laird, v. 544; ix. 132 *bis.*
—— —— his wife, Christian Forbes, iv. 74; v. 544.
—— —— Thomas, 4th laird, v. 544.
—— —— his wife, Marion Irvine, v. 544.
—— —— Thomas Alexander, 10th laird, v. 546.
—— —— his wife, Charlotte Georgina Dorothea Jerningham, v. 546.
—— —— Violet, wife of James Sutherland of Kinstearie, iii. 202; v. 543; vii. 438.
—— of Struy, William, tutor of Lovat, v. 527, 528 *bis*, 529; vii. 463.
—— —— his wife, Elizabeth, Isobel *or* Janet Grant, v. 527; vii. 461 *n.*
—— —— William, vii. 173.
—— —— his wife, Joanna Mackay, vii. 173.

* Name unknown.

Fraser of Teachers, William, 2nd son of 2nd lord Lovat, v. 525.
—— of Techmuiry, Alexander, vii. 438.
—— —— his wife, Janet Fraser, vii. 443.
—— —— Jane, wife of Jas. Gordon, vii. 438.
—— —— Michael, vii. 433.
—— —— William, vii. 438.
—— of Teniechiel, v. 535.
—— of Torbreck, Robert, v. 319; ix. 125.
—— —— his wife, Anne Maitland, v. 319.
—— of Torhendry, Thomas, 4th son of 2nd lord Fraser, iv. 116, 117.
—— —— his 1st wife, Margaret Forbes, iv. 117.
—— —— his 2nd wife, Margaret Seton, iv. 117.
—— of Touch Fraser, Sir Alexander, chamberlain of Scotland, iv. 107; vii. 426.
—— —— his wife, Mary Bruce, i. 277; ii. 434; vii. 428.
—— —— Sir Gilbert, vii. 420, 424.
—— —— his wife, Christiana, vii. 421, 424.
—— —— John, vii. 429.
—— —— Margaret, wife of William de Keith, vi. 36; vii. 429.
—— —— Sir Richard, iv. 107; vii. 424.
—— of Tulykeraw, Alexander, vii. 437.
—— of Tyrie, Alexander, vii. 440.
—— —— Andrew, vii. 437.
—— —— James, vii. 440.
—— —— Thomas, vii. 439.
—— —— Sir William, vii. 435.
—— of Easter Tyrie, Hugh, v. 544.
—— of Uchtredstruther, Sir Alexander, sheriff of Stirling, vii. 427.
—— —— Sir Andrew, sheriff of Stirling, vii. 425.
—— —— his probable wife, * Cheyne of Duffus, vii. 425.
—— of Uddell, Sir James, tutor of Lovat, v. 531.
—— of Waterton, Francis, 3rd laird, iv. 111.
—— —— Gilbert, 3rd son of Andrew F. of Stoneywood, iv. 111.
—— —— John, 2nd laird, iv. 111.
—— Agnes, wife of Sir Wm. Forbes of Kynnaldy and Pitsligo, iv. 69, 70; vii. 432.
—— Agnes, wife of (1) John Boyle of Kelburne, and (2) P. Crawfurd of Auchinames, iv. 192.
—— Agnes, wife of (1) Lachlan Macintosh, and (2) Sir Walter Innes, v. 520.
—— Agnes, wife of John Grant of Culcabok, v. 521 *n.*, 523; vii. 459.
—— Agnes, wife of (1) John Grassich Mackenzie of Gairloch, and (2) Thos. Chisholm of Comer, v. 525.
—— Agnes, wife of (1) William Macleod of Dunvegan, and (2) Alex. Bain of Tulloch, v. 527.

* Name unknown.

Fraser, Agnes, wife of (1) K. Mackenzie of Inverlawl, (2) Alex. Mackenzie of Ballone, and (3) Simon Mackenzie of Lochslinn, iii. 71; vii. 505.
— Alastair, 2nd son of Simon, 11th lord Fraser of Lovat, v. 540.
— Alastair Edward, lieut.-col. Scots Fusilier Guards, v. 547.
— — his wife, Georgina Mary Heneage, v. 547.
— Alastair Joseph, 4th son of 13th lord Fraser of Lovat, v. 548.
— Alexander, *né* Mackenzie, iii. 72; v. 536.
— — his wife, Amelia, baroness Fraser of Lovat, iii. 72; v. 535.
— Alexander, 2nd son of Sir Andrew F. of Stoneywood and Muchalls, iv. 109.
— Alexander, 3rd son of Andrew F. of Kinmundy, iv. 110.
— Alexander, 3rd son of John F. of Watertoun, iv. 111.
— Alexander, 2nd son of Sir Simon F., sheriff of Kincardine, v. 519; vii. 426.
— Alexander, eldest son of Thos. F. of Beaufort, v. 536.
— Alexander, 3rd son of 7th lord Fraser of Lovat; tutor of Lovat, v. 533, 534.
— — his wife, Sybilla Mackenzie, v. 533.
— Alexander, 2nd son of Simon, 11th lord Fraser of Lovat, v. 540.
— Alexander, eldest son of Alexander F. of Philorth, vii. 437.
— — his wife, Beatrice *or* Alice Keith, vi. 43; vii. 437.
— Alexander, 2nd son of Walter F. of Rathillock and Crechie, vii. 437.
— Alexander, elder son of Alexander, master of Saltoun, vii. 443.
— Alexander David, captain 92nd Highlanders, vii. 450.
— Alexander Gordon, in holy orders; claimant to the Lovat title, v. 537 *n.*
— Alexandra Katharine May, wife of J. H. Forbes of Medwyn, vii. 452.
— Alice Mary Charlotte, wife of Bernard Constable-Maxwell, iv. 422; v. 548.
— Alick Christian, vii. 592.
— — his wife, Margaret Helen St. Clair, vii. 592.
— Amelia, grand-daughter of Amelia, baroness Lovat, v. 536.
— Amelia Charlotte, wife of C. R. S. Murray, v. 547; ix. 132.
— Andrew, eldest son of 2nd lord Fraser, iv. 114, 116.
— Andrew, 5th son of 2nd lord Lovat, v. 525.
— — his alleged wife, Morella Grant, v. 525; vii. 458 *n.*
Fraser, Sir Andrew, brother of Sir Simon F. of Oliver Castle, vii. 422.
— — his wife, Beatrice *, vii. 422.
— Andrew, 2nd son of Sir Andrew F., sheriff of Stirling, vii. 425.
— Andrew, illeg. son of John F. of Forglen, vii. 430.
— Andrew, 5th son of Sir Alexander F. of Philorth, vii. 430.
— Anna, wife of John Fraser of Dalcros, v. 528.
— Anna, wife of Hector Monro of Foulis, v. 529; ix. 132.
— Anna, wife of John, 13th earl of Sutherland, v. 533; viii. 350.
— Anna, wife of William Hay of Urie, vii. 440; ix. 155 *bis.*
— Anna, wife of George Baird of Auchmeddan, vii. 441.
— Anne, wife of (1) Norman Macleod, (2) Peter Fothringham, and (3) John, earl of Cromartie, iii. 78; v. 535.
— Anne, wife of 2nd lord Kinnaird, v. 210, 534; ix. 121, 132.
— Anne, dau. of Alex. F. of Strichen, v. 546.
— Anne, dau. of 12th lord Saltoun, vii. 446.
— Annie Mary Eleanor, wife of (1) 15th lord Zouche of Haryngworth, and (2) Arthur William, 2nd lord Trevor, vii. 452.
— Archibald, 2nd son of col. Archibald Campbell F. of Lovat, v. 542; ix. 25.
— Arthur David Hay, capt. Scots Guards, vii. 452.
— — his wife, Lucy Jane Fergusson, vii. 452.
— Augusta Charlotte, wife of Robert Drummond, viii. 231.
— Barbara, wife of Geo. Ogilvy, ii. 11; vii. 440.
— Bernard, probably son of Udard F., vii. 418.
— Brenda Margaret, vii. 592; ix. 158.
— Cecilia, wife of Patrick of Greenlaw and the Hirsel, iii. 251.
— Charlotte Elizabeth Eleanor, wife of (1) W. H. A. Keppel, and (2) admiral Sir H. F. Stephenson, vii. 452.
— Charlotte Henrietta, wife of Sir Matthew Sausse, v. 547.
— Christian, wife of Patrick Gordon, younger of Methlic, i. 85, 86; iv. 111.
— Christian, wife of John Arbuthnott of Legasland, i. 280.
— Christian, wife of Alex. Burnett of Craigmill, v. 544.
— Christiana, wife of Wm. Crawford of Fedderat, vii. 438.
— Christina, wife of (1) Alex. Seton, and (2) Alex. Forbes, iv. 112.

* Name unknown.

Fraser, Christina, wife of Andrew Chalmers of Strichen, vii. 435.
— David Macdowall, general, vii. 450.
— — his wife, Mary Georgina Bell, vii. 450.
— David Macdowall, Cape Mounted Rifles, vii. 450.
— Edward Hay, vii. 450.
— Egidia, wife of Ferquhard Mackintosh of Mackintosh, v. 524.
— Eleanor Katharine, vii. 451.
— Eleanora, wife of (1) Sir George Ramsay of Bamff, and (2) lieut.-gen. Duncan Campbell of Lochnell, vii. 447.
— Eleanora, wife of Wm. Macdowall Grant of Arndilly, vii. 448.
— Eleanora Alexandrina, wife of Henry W. Forester, vii. 451.
— Elizabeth, wife of Francis Sinclair of Keiss, ii. 343.
— Elizabeth, dau. of Andrew F. of Kinmundy, iv. 110.
— Elizabeth, dau. of William F. of Faichfield, iv. 114.
— Elizabeth, wife of Walter Barclay of Towie, iv. 116.
— Elizabeth, dau. of 2nd lord Fraser, iv. 117.
— Elizabeth, wife of Sir Wm. Leslie of Balquhain, v. 522.
— Elizabeth, wife of John Dunbar, v. 530.
— Elizabeth, wife of Wm. Gordon of Awdiale, vii. 438.
— Elizabeth, wife of Sir Robt. Keith of Ackergill, vii. 440.
— Elizabeth, wife of maj.-gen. Hamilton Forbes, vii. 451.
— Etheldreda Mary, wife of Francis Oswald Lindley, v. 548.
— Euphemia, wife of (1) Lachlan Mackintosh, and (2) Sir Walter Innes, v. 520, 521 *n*.
— Frances Georgina, wife of Sir Pyers Mostyn, v. 547.
— Frances Jean, dau. of Alexander F. of Strichen, v. 546.
— George, 6th son of Sir Alexander F. of Philorth, vii. 433.
— George, 3rd son of Alexander F. of Philorth, vii. 434 *bis*.
— George, 42nd, 60th, and 59th regiments, vii. 447.
— George, R.N., 2nd son of 18th lord Saltoun, vii. 453.
— George, uncle of Thomas F. of Strichen, ix. 132.
— George Edward Stafford, v. 547.
— Hector, 5th son of Alexander F., younger of Philorth, vii. 437.
— Helen, wife of James Gordon of Park, vii. 445.
— Helen Charlotte Isabel, D.Sc., vii. 452.
Fraser, Henrietta, wife of John Gordon of Kinellar, vii. 445.
— Henrietta, dau. of 14th lord Saltoun, vii. 447.
— Henry Emo, v. 542.
— Henry Thomas, lieut.-col. Scots Fusilier Guards, v. 547.
— Hugh, 4th son of 3rd lord Lovat, v. 527.
— Hugh, 3rd son of Thomas F. of Beaufort, v. 537.
— Hugh, 2nd son of Sir Simon F., sheriff of Kincardine, vii. 426.
— Hugh Joseph, captain Scots Guards, v. 547.
— Isobel, dau. of Michael F. of Stoneywood, iv. 112.
— Isobel, dau. of 2nd lord Lovat, v. 525.
— Isabel, wife of Alex. Macdonell o Glengarry, v. 534; ix. 132 *bis*.
— Isabel, dau. of Thomas F. of Beaufort, v. 537.
— Isabel, wife of Gilbert Menzies, vii. 432.
— Isabella, wife of Mr. David Brown, vii. 445.
— Isabella, wife of lieut. Æneas Mackay, ix. 132.
— James, member of the Council of Nova Scotia, iii. 586.
— James, 5th son of Andrew F. of Muchalls, iv. 114.
— James, 7th son of 2nd lord Fraser, iv. 117.
— James, 6th son of Alexander F., yr. of Philorth, vii. 437.
— James, 6th son of 6th lord Lovat, v. 532.
— James, captain in Polish service, v. 533.
— James, 2nd son of Thos. F. of Strichen, v. 544.
— James, 4th son of 2nd lord Fraser, ix. 93.
— James Hay, colonel Bengal Staff Corps, vii. 451.
— — his 1st wife, Marion Stirling Dundas, vii. 451.
— — his 2nd wife, Emily Caroline Vandeleur, vii. 451.
— Jane, wife of John Morrison of Auchintoul, v. 546.
— Janet, wife of (1) John Crichton of Ruthven, and (2) Thos. Ogilvy of Westercraig, i. 117; v. 525; ix. 8.
— Janet, wife of Ewen Macpherson of Cluny, v. 540; ix. 132.
— Janet, wife of Alex. Fraser of Techmuiry, vii. 443.
— Jean, wife of Mr. John Douglas of Corsbatt, i. 198.
— Jean, dau. of Thos. F. of Cairnbulg, iv. 117.
— Jean, wife of (1) Sir Jas. Stuart of Newton and Kilcoy, and (2) Alex. Mackenzie, v. 543; vii. 502.
— Jean, dau. of Jas. F. of Tyrie, vii. 440.

Fraser, Mr. John, 2nd son of Thos. F. of Stoneywood, iv. 110.
—— John, eldest son of Andrew F. of Stoneywood, iv. 111.
—— John, 4th son of Thomas F. of Beaufort; 'le Chevalier Fraser,' v. 537.
—— John, Carnarvon, claimant to the Lovat title, v. 537 *n.*
—— John, 4th son of Sir Alexander F. of Philorth, vii. 433.
—— John, rector of the University of Paris, vii. 438.
—— John, brother of 1st lord Saltoun, vii. 441.
—— John, half-brother of Hugh, master of Lovat, vii. 458 *n.*
—— —— his wife, Morella Grant, vii. 458 *n.*
—— John Simon Frederick, colonel, M.P., v. 542.
—— Katharine, wife of (1) Sir Hugh Sinclair, (2) 1st viscount of Arbuthnott, and (3) 3rd lord Fraser, i. 305; iv. 118; v. 533, 536.
—— Katharine, wife of Thos. Cheyne of Ranieston and Pitfichie, iv. 112.
—— Katharine, wife of Sir Wm. Murray of Ochtertyre, v. 535.
—— Katharine, wife of David Brown, v. 536.
—— Katharine, dau of Thos. F. of Beaufort, v. 537.
—— Katharine, dau. of Archibald T. F. F. of Abertarff, v. 542.
—— Katharine Anne, wife of D. F. Mitchell of Thainston, vii. 445.
—— Katharine Frances Graham, vii. 450.
—— Katharine Thurlow, wife of John Stewart Menzies of Chesthill, vii. 451.
—— Laura Violet Jemima, vii. 451.
—— Laurence, Peebles, vii. 420.
—— Magdalen, wife of Hugh Rose of Kilravock, v. 543.
—— Magdalen, wife of Patrick Cheyne of Essilmont, vii. 440.
—— Magdalen, wife of James Forbes of Blackton, vii. 441.
—— Margaret, *error for* Marjorie, wife of Sir William Keith, i. 276; v. 521.
—— Margaret, wife of (1) Sir Robt. Arbuthnott, and (2) Sir J. Haldane of Gleneagles, i. 302; v. 532.
—— Margaret, wife of Jas. Murray, i. 457.
—— Margaret, wife of David Stuart, 11th earl of Buchan, ii. 278.
—— Margaret, wife of Sir Jas. Innes of Orton, iv. 117.
—— Margaret, wife of Thos. Gordon of Newark, iv. 117.
—— Margaret, wife of John Hamilton of Buthernock and Baldowie, iv. 345.
—— Margaret, wife of Hector de Kilmalew, v. 523.
—— Margaret, wife of John Mackay of Strathnaver, v. 525; vii. 163; ix. 131.
Fraser, Margaret, wife of Allan M'Ranald of Leyis, v. 527; ix. 131.
—— Margaret, wife of Jas. Cuming of Altyre, v. 529; ix. 131.
—— Margaret, wife of col. Andrew Monro, v. 534.
—— Margaret, dau. of 9th lord Lovat, v. 535.
—— Margaret, wife of (1) Alex. Cumyn of Inverallochy, and (2) Alex. Annand of Octerellon, vii. 438.
—— Margaret, dau. of 15th lord Saltoun, vii. 448.
—— Margaret, wife of John Forbes of Corsindae, ix. 132.
—— Margaret Eleanora Georgina, wife of capt. J. A. Evans, vii. 451.
—— Margaret Mary, wife of capt. Archibald Stirling of Keir, v. 548.
—— Maria Elizabeth Florence, vii. 450.
—— Marion, wife of (1) John Montgomerie, and (2) John Boyle, iv. 188.
—— Marion, wife of Jas. Craig of Riccarton, v. 544.
—— Marjorie, wife of (1) John Montgomerie of Flatt, and (2) John Boyle of Ballikewin, iv. 188.
—— Marjorie, wife of 1st earl Marischal, v. 521; vi. 40.
—— Marjory, wife of Ferquherd Macintosh of Mackintosh, v. 524.
—— Marjorie, sister of 17th lord Saltoun, vii. 451.
—— Marjory, illeg. dau. of 3rd lord Fraser, ix. 93.
—— Marjorie Alexandrina Louisa, vii. 452.
—— Marjory Lucy Kathleen, wife of Edward Pratt-Barlow, vii. 452.
—— Mary, wife of D. Ross of Balnagown, v. 533.
—— Mary, wife of Wm. Dalmahoy of Ravelrig, vii. 445.
—— Mary, dau. of 14th lord Saltoun, vii. 447.
—— Mary Alexander, dau. of 18th lord Saltoun, vii. 453.
—— Mary Eleanor, dau. of William F., vii. 451.
—— Mary Laura, wife of viscount Encombe, v. 548.
—— Muriel Mary Rose, v. 548.
—— Nes, Peebles, vii. 420.
—— Sir Radulph, of the household of King Henry II. of England, v. 518; vii. 417.
—— Robina Gordon, wife of C. G. L. Campbell, ii. 197.
—— Sarah Rachel, wife of Sir Charles Gore, iii. 586.
—— Sheila Helen, vii. 592.
—— Simon, captain, iv. 119; v. 537.
—— Sir Simon, 2nd son of Sir Andrew F. of Touch-Fraser, v. 519.

Fraser, Simon, master of Lovat, eldest son of 3rd lord Lovat, v. 527.
— Simon, son of David F. of Mayne, v. 531.
— Simon, High Sheriff of Tweeddale, vii. 419 *n*.
— Simon, elder son of Sir Simon F., sheriff of Kincardine, vii. 426.
— Simon, contracted to Margaret Dempster, vii. 438.
— Simon, 4th son of Sir Alexander F. of Philorth, vii. 440.
— Simon, 2nd son of 15th lord Saltoun, vii. 448.
— Simon, lieut. Madras Cavalry, vii. 451.
— Simon, 3rd son of 18th lord Saltoun, vii. 453.
— Sophia, dau. of Thos. F. of Cairnbulg, iv. 117.
— Sophia, dau. of 12th lord Saltoun, vii. 446.
— Stewart Mackenzie, 2nd son of Alex. F. of Strichen, v. 545.
— Susanna, wife of Simon Mackenzie of Allangrange, vii. 506.
— Sybilla, dau. of Thos. F. of Beaufort, v. 537.
— Sybilla, dau. of Simon, 11th lord Fraser of Lovat, v. 540.
— Thomas, Murthockstoun, ii. 226.
— Thomas, 4th son of Andrew F. of Muchalls, iv. 114.
— Thomas, 6th son of 2nd lord Lovat, v. 525.
— — his alleged wife, Anna Macleod, v. 525.
— Thomas, prior of Beauly, v. 529.
— Thomas, 5th son of 6th lord Lovat, v. 532.
— Thomas, 5th son of Thos. F. of Beaufort, v. 537.
— Thomas, 4th son of Alex. F. of Strichen, v. 544.
— Thomas, 3rd son of Alex. F. of Strichen, v. 545.
— Thomas, end of 12th cent., vii. 418.
— Thomas, 2nd son of Sir Simon F. of Oliver Castle, vii. 422.
— Thomas, 5th son of Sir Alex. F. of Philorth, vii. 440.
— Udard, vii. 418.
— — his wife, *, dau. of Kylvert, vii. 418.
— Violet, wife of James Sutherland, iii. 202.
— Walter, uncle of Thos. F. of Strichen, ix. 132.
— William, 2nd son of Andrew F. of Kinmundy, iv. 110.
— William, 4th son of Michael F. of Stoneywood, iv. 112.

* Name unknown.

Fraser, William, son of Wm. F. of Faichfield and Invernorth, iv. 114.
— William, Dundee, v. 520.
— — his wife, * Scrymgeour, v. 520.
— William, 2nd son of Thos. F. of Lovat, v. 521 *n*., 523.
— William, 4th son of Alex. F. of Strichen, v. 546.
— William, dean of Glasgow, bishop of St. Andrews, Chancellor and Regent of Scotland, vii. 421, 423.
— William, illeg. son of John F. of Forglen, vii. 430.
— William, 3rd son of Sir Alexander F. of Philorth, vii. 433.
— William, 7th son of Alexander F., yr. of Philorth, vii. 437.
— William, 2nd son of Sir Alexander F. of Philorth, vii. 440.
— William, advocate, 2nd son of 12th lord Saltoun, vii. 446.
— William, 3rd son of 15th lord Saltoun vii. 448, 450.
— — his wife, Elizabeth Graham Grant, vii. 450.
— William, son of col. James Hay F., vii. 451.
— William, 3rd son of 18th lord Saltoun, vii. 453.
— William, uncle of Thos. F. of Strichen, ix. 132.
— William Henry, 5th son of col. Archibald C. F. of Lovat, v. 542.
— William Murray, major Bengal Staff Corps, vii. 451.
— *, wife of Donald, progenitor of the family of Macdonald of Glengarry, v. 559.
Frederick II., the Great, king of Prussia, vi. 62, 63, 64.
— Jane, wife of (1) James Lannoy, and (2) 2nd duke of Atholl, i. 488.
— Sir John, bart., i. 488.
— Thomas, Westminster, i. 488.
Freebairn, James, author of *L'Éloge d'Écosse et des Dames Écossaises*, iii. 355.
FREELAND, RUTHVEN, LORD RUTHVEN OF, vii. 385-393.
Freeland, Lewis Grey, capt., ii. 119.
— — his wife, Violet Dagmar Marion Olga Borthwick, ii. 119.
Freemantle of Abbots-Aston, John, ii. 522.
— Frances Henrietta, wife of rev. A. H. Cathcart, ii. 522.
French of Battle, Richard, vii. 103.
— — his wife, Susanna Reeve, vii. 103.
Frenche of Thornydikes, Robert, iv. 472.
— — his wife, Margaret Turnbull, iv. 472.
— — Robert, vi. 7.
— — his wife, Anne Hume, vi. 7.

* Name unknown.

Frend of Ballyrehy, Benjamin, ii. 24.
— Jane, wife of (1) Alex. Ogilvy, and (2) Archd. Campbell, ii. 24.
FRENDRAUGHT, CRICHTON, VISCOUNT, iv. 123-134.
Frendraught, George, fifth viscount, iv. 128, 132.
— — his wife, Jean Irving, iv. 133.
— James, first viscount, iv. 125, 126, 129.
— — his 1st wife, Janet *or* Margaret Leslie, iv. 130; v. 378.
— — his 2nd wife, Marion Irving, iv. 130.
— — his 3rd wife, J. *, iv. 130.
— James, second viscount, iv. 131, 133.
— — his wife, Christian Urquhart, iv. 131 *bis*.
— James, sixth viscount, iv. 133.
— — his wife, Margaret Gordon, iv. 133.
— Lewis, fourth viscount, iv. 130, 131 *bis*.
— — his wife, Marjory Seaton, iv. 132.
— William, third viscount, iv. 131.
— of Auchinfitheach, Sir Duncan, viii. 419.
— of Frendraught, Margaret *or* Mariozita, wife of James Fraser, vii. 426.
Frere of Royden, John Hookham, iii. 583.
Freeale, Margaret, wife of James Murray, i. 457.
Frisall, Katharine, wife of William Stewart of Ambrismore, ii. 290.
Freskin of Kerdal, iii. 134.
— de Moravia, i. 449, 450; ii. 120; vii. 268 *n*. viii. 319.
— Hugh, ancestor of the earls of Sutherland, ii. 121; viii. 320.
Freslay of Arngask and Fargy, Henry de, viii. 186.
Froissart, the chronicler, iii. 152.
Frothingham, Christopher, iii. 293.
— — his wife, Elizabeth Constable, iii. 293.
— Edmond, iii. 292.
— Jane, wife of Robert Constable, iii. 292.
Fulford of Dunsford, Sir Baldwin, iii. 608.
— Alice, wife of Sir Wm. Cary, iii. 608.
Fullarton of Carleton, John, author of *The Turtle Dove*, v. 120.
— of Crosby, Adam, vii. 527, 528.
— — Rankin, v. 492.
— of Dudwick, John, iii. 544.
— — his wife, Margaret Elphinstone, iii. 544.
— — John, colonel, viii. 108.
— — his wife, Elizabeth Preston, viii. 108.
— — *, v. 248.
— — his wife, Mary Falconer, v. 248.
— of Fullarton, Adam de, v. 492; vii. 529.
— — Galfridus de, King's Fowler, viii. 108.
— — his wife, Agnes, viii. 108.

* Name unknown.

Fullarton of Fullarton, John, vi. 496; viii. 109.
— — his 1st wife, Margaret Carnegie, vi. 496; viii. 109.
— — his 2nd wife, Rebecca Nairne, viii. 109.
— — Ranken, vii. 529.
— — William de, vii. 529.
— — William, M.P., vii. 177.
— — his wife, Marianne Mackay, vii. 177.
— — William, viii. 108.
— — his wife, Margaret Lindsay of Spynie, viii. 105, 108.
— — William, iv. 249; viii. 108.
— — his contracted wife, Elizabeth Cunningham, iv. 249.
— — his wife, Susanna Fullarton, viii. 108.
— — William, viii. 109.
— — his wife, Susanna Ogilvy, viii. 109.
— — William, claimant to the barony of Spynie, vi. 496.; viii. 109.
— — his 1st wife, Stewart Carnegie, vi. 496; viii. 111.
— — his 2nd wife, Margaret Blair, vi. 496; viii. 111.
— of Glenquoich, William, vi. 496.
— of Haddo, William, i. 83.
— of Kilmichail, Alexander, v. 140.
— of Kinnaber, Charles, viii. 82.
— — John, v. 246.
— — his wife, Jean Falconer, v. 246.
— — Mary, wife of John Carnegie of Pittarrow and Charleton, viii. 82.
— of Methlic, William, i. 83.
— of Portincross, William, grandson of Robt. Boyd of Portincross, v. 140.
— of Spynie, William, i. 129; viii. 109.
— Elizabeth, dau. of William F. of Fullarton, viii. 108, 109.
— Elizabeth, wife of D. Ogilvy of Cluny, viii. 109.
— Jean, wife of Sir John Wedderburn of Blackness, viii. 109.
— Margaret, wife of Walter Ogilvy of Clova. i. 129; viii. 109; ix. 8.
— Margaret, dau. of William F. of Fullarton, viii. 108, 109.
— Marion, wife of William Gray, iv. 278.
— Susannah, dau. of John F. of Fullarton, viii. 109.
— William, son of Rankin F. of Corsby, v. 492.
Fuller-Acland-Hood, Sir Alexander B. P., 3rd bart., iv. 389.
Fullerton of Ardo, William, i. 512.
— of Broughtonhall, George, ii. 277.
— of Carberry, Elizabeth, wife of William Elphinstone, H.E.I.C.S., iii. 546.
— — John, iii. 546.
— of Carstairs, William, iii. 546.

Fullerton of Denoon, George, viii. 293.
—— —— his wife, Matilda Nevey, viii. 293.
—— Christian, wife of Henry Erskine, M.P., ii. 277.
—— Sir James, iii. 476.
—— —— his wife, Magdalen Clerk, iii. 476.
—— Jean, wife of (1) * Navoy, and (2) David Lindsay, i. 515.
—— *, wife of Robert Lindsay of Balhall, i. 512.
Fullerton-Elphinstone of Carberry, John, iii. 546.
—— —— William, iii. 546.
—— Anne, iii. 548.
—— Clementina, wife of admiral Sir Pulteney Malcolm, iii. 548.
—— Elizabeth, iii. 548.
Fulton of Fulton, Sir William, vii. 366.
Funnell, Edward, ii. 499.
—— Susan, wife of (1) Wm. Kennedy, and (2) G. A. Trevor, ii. 499.
Fussell, James George, in holy orders, viii. 129.
—— —— his wife, Janet Jemima Dalrymple, viii. 129.
Futhes, Alan of, viii. 528.
—— Andrew of, iv. 49.
—— John of, viii. 528.
Fyfe, John, minister of Gask, vi. 552.
Fyvie, Seton, lord, iii. 368-375.
—— Alexander, first lord, iii. 369.
—— —— his 1st wife, Lilias Drummond, i. 518; iii. 372; vii. 47.
—— —— his 2nd wife, Grizel Leslie, iii. 372; vii. 296.
—— —— his 3rd wife, Margaret Hay, iii. 372; viii. 447.
—— Charles, eldest son of 2nd earl of Dunfermline; styled lord, iii. 374; ix. 78.
Fydell, Elizabeth, wife of bishop C. D. Lindsay, i. 526.
—— Thomas, Boston, i. 526.

G., A., piper to the Lyons in Aboyne, viii. 307.
Gaderar of Auldcash, Alexander, vii. 458.
Gage of Firle, Sir Thomas, i. 411.
—— of Hengrave, Sir Edward, bart., i. 410.
—— —— his 2nd wife, Frances Aston, i. 410.
—— of Raunds, Robert, v. 267.
—— Katharine, wife of 3rd lord Aston of Forfar, i. 411; ix. 26.
—— Mary, wife of (1) John Rowley, (2) Sir Geo. Trevelyan, and (3) Robert, 1st lord Kirkcudbright, v. 267.
—— Thomas Wentworth, vicar of Higham Ferrers, vii. 152.
—— —— his wife, Mary Elizabeth Douglas, vii. 152.

* Name unknown.

Gainsborough, Baptist (Noel), 4th earl of iv. 388.
—— Charles (Noel), 1st earl of, viii. 90.
—— Charles George (Noel), 2nd earl of, iii. 585.
—— Charles William Francis (Noel), 3rd earl of, iv. 388.
—— Henry (Noel), 6th earl of, iv. 388.
Gaisford of Offington, Thomas, v. 485.
—— —— his wife, Alice Mary Ker, v. 485.
Galbraith of Dalserf, Joanna, wife of * Keith, iii. 138; vi. 29.
—— —— William, vi. 29.
—— of Galbraith, Sir William, vi. 29.
—— —— his wife, * Comyn, vi. 29.
—— of Gartconnell, Janet, wife of Nicholas Douglas, vi. 344.
—— of Kilcroich, Robert, v. 166.
—— Andrew de, a relative of 1st lord Lyle, v. 552.
—— Gillescop, ancestor of the family of, v. 327.
—— Isabella, wife of George Maxwell of Carnsalloch, vi. 476.
—— James, in remainder to the barony of Lyle, v. 555.
—— Marion, wife of Adam Boyd of Nethermains, v. 166.
—— Maurice, v. 330.
—— Robert, parson of Spott, vii. 582 *bis*.
—— William, iii. 138.
—— —— his wife, Willelma Douglas, iii. 138.
Gale, Dorothy, wife of (1) John Rokeby, and (2) Sir Thos. Fairfax, iii. 596.
—— George, goldsmith, York, iii. 596.
Galfrid, Steward of Kinghorn, v. 202.
—— bishop of Dunkeld, v. 203.
—— son of Gunnild, vi. 79.
Galichtlie of Ebrux, Christina, wife of David Ogilvy of Templehall, ix. 89.
Galiena, wife of Philip de Moubray, iii. 245; vi. 529.
Galightly, Henry, illeg. son of King William the Lion, i. 5.
—— Patrick, the Competitor, i. 5.
Gall of Maw, Alexander, i. 548.
—— Macsgillin, progenitor of the clan Gall of the Glens, v. 31.
—— Elizabeth, wife of Robt. Bruce, i. 548.
—— Marion, wife of (1) David Ross, and (2) Alexander, 8th lord Reay, vii. 177.
—— *see also* Gaw.
Galloway, The Ancient Lords of, iv. 135-144.
Galloway, Alan, constable of Scotland, fourth lord of, i. 420; iv. 139, 224; v. 277.
—— —— his 1st wife, *, iv. 141.
—— —— his 2nd wife, Margaret of Huntingdon, i. 4; iv. 141.
—— —— his 3rd wife, * de Lacy, iv. 141.

* Name unknown.

Galloway, Christina of, wife of William de Fortibus, earl of Albemarle, iv. 142; v. 277.
—— Devorgilla of, wife of John de Baliol of Barnard Castle, i. 4, 7; ii. 431; iii. 5, 161; iv. 141, 142, 183; v. 277.
—— Elena of, wife of Roger de Quincy, iv. 142; v. 277.
—— Fergus, first lord of, ii. 421; iii. 245; iv. 135; v. 32.
—— —— his alleged wife, Elizabeth, illeg. dau. of King Henry I. of England, iv. 136.
—— Gilbert, joint-lord of, ii. 421; iv. 136, 137.
—— Roland, constable of Scotland, third lord of, i. 420; ii. 422; iii. 133; iv. 137, 138, 140; v. 277.
—— —— his wife, Elena de Morville, iv. 137.
—— Uchtred, second lord of, ii. 421; iii. 245; iv. 136, 138.
—— —— his wife, Gunhild, iv. 137.
Galloway, Neil of, 2nd earl of Carrick, i. 12; ii. 426.
—— —— his wife, Margaret Stewart, i. 12.
—— Thomas of, 2nd son of Roland, the Constable, i. 420; iv. 139.
—— —— his wife, Isabella, countess of Atholl, i. 419.
—— Thomas of, son of Alan, lord of Galloway, iv. 141.
—— Thomas of, illeg. son of Alan of Galloway, iv. 143.
GALLOWAY, BALIOL, LORD OF, iv. 143.
Galloway, John, fifth lord of, i. 7; iv. 143.
—— —— his wife, Isabella de Warenne, i. 7.
GALLOWAY, BRUCE, LORD OF, iv. 144.
Galloway, Edward, sixth lord of, iv. 144.
GALLOWAY, DOUGLAS, LORD OF, iv. 144.
Galloway, Sir Archibald, seventh lord of, i. 147, 277; iii. 159; iv. 144; viii. 523.
—— Margaret Douglas, wife of 8th and 9th earls of Douglas, 'the Fair Maid of,' iii. 170, 171.
GALLOWAY, STEWART, EARL OF, iv. 145-173.
Galloway, Alan Plantagenet, tenth earl of, iv. 172.
—— —— his wife, Mary Arabella Arthur Cecil, iv. 172.
—— Alexander, first earl of, iv. 160.
—— —— his wife, Grizel Gordon, iv. 160; v. 113.
—— Alexander, third earl of, iv. 161, 162.
—— —— his wife, Mary Douglas, iv. 163; vii. 137.
—— Alexander, fourth earl of, iv. 163.
—— Alexander, sixth earl of, iv. 164.
—— —— his 1st wife, Anne Keith, iv. 165; vi. 62.
—— —— his 2nd wife, Katharine Cochrane, iii. 356; iv. 165.
Galloway, George, eighth earl of, iv. 167, 170.
—— —— his wife, Jane Paget, iv. 170.
—— James, second earl of, iv. 161.
—— his 1st wife, Catherine Houghton, iv. 161.
—— —— his 2nd wife, Nicolas Grierson, iv. 161.
—— James, fifth earl of, iv. 163; v. 477.
—— —— his wife, Katharine Montgomerie, iii. 456; iv. 164.
—— John, seventh earl of, iv. 165, 166.
—— —— his 1st wife, Charlotte Mary Greville, iv. 167.
—— —— his 2nd wife, Anne Dashwood, iv. 167.
—— Randolph, ninth earl of, iv. 171.
—— —— his wife, Harriet Blanche Somerset, iv. 171.
—— Randolph Henry, eleventh earl of, iv. 172.
—— —— his wife, Amy Mary Pauline Cliffe, iv. 173.
GALLOWAY, LORD DUNKELD, iii. 376-382.
Galloway of Baldovie, John, 4th son of 3rd lord Dunkeld, iii. 379.
—— —— his wife, Elizabeth Hay, iii. 379.
—— of Cheshunt, William, viii. 63.
—— Andrew, 5th son of 2nd lord Dunkeld, iii. 379.
—— Christian, dau. of Mr. Patrick G., iii. 377.
—— Claude, illeg. son of 3rd lord Dunkeld, ix. 78.
—— Dorothy, wife of Wm. Adamson of Craigerook, iii. 377.
—— Elizabeth, wife of John Falconer, bishop of Dundee, iii. 380.
—— Grisell, wife of Patrick Crichton, iii. 380.
—— Sir James, Master of Requests, iii. 377.
—— —— his wife, * Norter, iii. 378.
—— James, 'Comte de Dunkeld,' eldest son of 3rd lord Dunkeld, iii. 381.
—— Jean, dau. of 2nd lord Dunkeld, iii. 380.
—— Katharine, wife of Thos. Forbes of Waterton, iii. 380.
—— Malcolm, viii. 63.
—— —— his wife, Edith Alice Capel-Carnegie-Arbuthnott, viii. 63.
—— Margaret, wife of Thos. Rattray, bishop of Dunkeld, iii. 380.
—— Mary, dau. of 3rd lord Dunkeld, iii. 381; ix. 78.
—— Patrick, minister of the King's House, Moderator of the General Assembly, iii. 376.
—— —— his 1st wife, Matillo Guthrie, iii. 377.
—— —— his 2nd wife, Katharine Lawson, iii. 377.
—— Thomas, baxter, burgess of Dundee, iii. 376.
—— —— his wife, Christian Nicoll, iii. 376.

* Name unknown.

Galloway, Mr. Thomas, 3rd son of 2nd lord Dunkeld, iii. 379.
— William, i. 307.
— — his wife, Jean Arbuthnott, i. 307.
— William, elder son of Mr. Patrick Galloway, iii. 377.
— Mr. William, 2nd son of 2nd lord Dunkeld, iii. 379.
Galmoye, Edward (Butler), 2nd viscount, iii. 509.
Galston of Galston, John, v. 138 *n*.
Galway, Robert (Monckton-Arundell), 4th viscount, v. 233.
— — his 2nd wife, Mary B. Milnes, v. 233; ix. 122.
Gambier, James (Gambier), admiral R.N., lord, ii. 525; iii. 363; vi. 180.
— Margaret, wife of Charles, lord Barham, vi. 180.
Gamble, John, M.D., ii. 353.
— Marianne, wife of Col. J. S. Sinclair, ii. 353.
Gamel, son of Bern, ii. 370.
Gamelin, bishop of St. Andrews, viii. 476.
Gamon of Minchenden, Richard, v. 199.
— — Sir Richard, bart., i. 494.
— — his 2nd wife, Amelia Murray, i. 494.
— Anne Eliza, wife of (1) Roger Hope Elletson, and (2) James, 3rd duke of Chandos, vi. 199.
Garden of Durlathers, George, vi. 44.
— of Lawton, David, i. 299.
— — John, i. 299, 303.
— — his wife, Elizabeth Arbuthnott, i. 299.
— of Leys, *, i. 117.
— — his wife, Beatrix Ogilvy, i. 117.
— — David, v. 6.
— — his wife, Jean Stewart, v. 6.
— of Gardin, David, i. 121; v. 7.
— — his 2nd wife, Elizabeth Stewart, v. 7.
— of Newgrange, Francis, *alias* Ogilvy, i. 121.
— — his 1st wife, Helen Gardin, i. 121.
— — his 2nd wife, Elizabeth Adamson, i. 121.
— Alexander, in Drumgeich, iv. 280.
— — his wife, Geilis Gray, iv. 280.
— Helen, wife of F. Ogilvy of Newgrange, i. 121.
— Magdalen, wife of John Arbuthnott of Caterline, i. 303.
Garden-Campbell of Troup and Glenlyon, Francis, viii. 135.
— — his wife, Georgina Anne Brigstock, viii. 135.
Gardiner, Charlotte, dau. of John G., v. 175.
— David, elder son of col. James G., ii. 276.

* Name unknown.

Gardiner, Frances, wife of Sir W. Baird of Saughtonhall, ii. 276.
— Gertrude Florinda, wife of (1) C. J. Clarke, and (2) Charles Tollemache, iii. 413.
— James, colonel, ii. 276.
— — his wife, Frances Erskine, ii. 276.
— James, 2nd son of above, ii. 276.
— John, v. 175.
— — his wife, Lettice Boyd, v. 175.
— Richmond, wife of Lawrence Inglis, ii. 276.
— William, general, iii. 413.
Gardyne of Buchrowye and Half-Clunie, David, ii. 397.
— Ann, wife of James Carnegie, viii. 55.
— George, captain, Aberdeen, v. 6.
— *, husband of a dau. of 7th earl of Crawford, iii. 25.
GARIOCH, THE ANCIENT LORDS OF, v. 581-589.
Garioch, Alexander Stewart, *de jure ux.* earl of Mar and, ii. 263; v. 588.
— — his wife, Isabella, countess of Mar and Garioch, v. 587.
— Christian Bruce, wife of Gartnet, earl of Mar; lady of, v. 579, 583.
— Margaret, wife of (1) Sir Wm. Douglas, and (2) Sir John Swinton; lady of, v. 585.
— Isabella, countess of Mar and, v. 587.
— Thomas, earl of Mar and lord of, v. 583.
GARIOCH, STEWART, EARL OF, v. 637.
Garioch, Alexander, 2nd son of king James II.; earl of, i. 152; v. 638.
— John, 4th son of king James II.; earl of, v. 637.
— John, 3rd son of king James III.; earl of, v. 639.
GARIOCH, GOODEVE-ERSKINE, LORD, v. 635-636.
Garioch, John Francis Erskine, lord, v. 635.
— — his wife, Alice Mary Sinclair Hamilton, v. 636.
— John Francis Hamilton Sinclair Cunliffe Brookes Forbes, styled lord, v. 636.
— — his wife, Sibyl Mary Dominica Heathcote, v. 636.
— *or* Garvyauch, Andrew del, iii. 260.
— Christian, wife of Wm. Fraser of Faichfield, iv. 113.
— Sir James, v. 580.
— — his alleged wife, Elyne of Mar, v. 580.
— William, tutor to Alexander, master of Saltoun, vii. 446.
GARLIES, STEWART, LORD, iv. 160-173.
Garlies, Alexander, first lord, iv. 159.
— — his wife, Grizel Gordon, iv. 160; v. 113.
— Alexander, elder son of 1st earl of Galloway; styled lord, iv. 160.
— — his 1st wife, Anne Howard, iv. 160.
— — his 2nd wife, Margaret Graham, i. 138; iv. 161.

* Name unknown.

Garlies, Alexander, eldest grandson of 1st earl of Galloway ; styled lord, iv. 161.
— George, R.N., eldest surviving son of 7th earl of Galloway ; styled lord, iv. 170.
— John, M.P., eldest surviving son of 6th earl of Galloway ; styled lord, iv. 167.
— — his wife, C. M. Greville, iv. 167.
— Randolph, M.P., eldest son of 8th earl of Galloway ; styled lord, iv. 171.
— Randolph Algernon Ronald, Scots Guards, styled lord, iv. 173.
GARLIES, STEWART, BARON STEWART OF, iv. 167-173.
Garlies, John, first baron Stewart of, iv. 167.
— master of, Alexander, eldest son of 6th earl of Galloway, iv. 165.
— Alexander, eldest son of 7th earl of Galloway, iv. 167.
Garmoran, Alan of, fourth lord of, v. 32.
— Amy, *or* Euphemia, of ; wife of John, 7th lord of the Isles, v. 32, 39.
— Angus of, 3rd son of Somerled, v. 30.
— Dugall of, third lord of, v. 32.
— Reginald of, sixth lord of, v. 32.
— Roderick of, ancestor of Clan Ruari, v. 32.
— Roderick of, second lord of, v. 32.
— Roderick of, fifth lord of, v. 32, 39.
GARNOCK, CRAWFURD, VISCOUNT, iv. 174-178.
GARNOCK, LINDSAY, VISCOUNT, iv. 174-178.
Garnock, George, fourth viscount, iii. 40 ; iv. 177.
— John, first viscount, iv. 175, 203.
— — his wife, Margaret Stewart, ii. 299 ; iv. 175.
— John, third viscount, iv. 177.
— Patrick, second viscount, iii. 40 ; iv. 176.
— — his wife, Mary Home, iv. 177.
— Reginald Bethune, elder son of 11th earl of Lindsay ; styled viscount, v. 419.
— — his wife, Beatrice Mary Shaw, v. 420.
Garrard, George, iii. 296 *n.*
— Jane, wife of Sir Thos. Spencer, viii. 366.
— Sir John, viii. 366.
Garrett, John Burnham, vi. 582.
— — his wife, Isabella Emily Fitzmaurice, vi. 582.
Garrison, Martha Estelle, wife of C. M. Ramsay, iii. 109.
— William R., New York, iii. 109.
Garstin, John Bradstreet, viii. 450.
— Mary, wife of Wm. Hay of Duns Castle, viii. 450.
GARTHIE, GORDON, LORD, iv. 549-558.
Garthie, George, first lord, iv. 550.
Garthshore of Garthshore, James, D.D., ii. 49.
— — Alexander, ii. 51.
— Jean, wife of John Hamilton, ii. 49.
Gartnach, mormaer of Buchan, ii. 250.
Garvine of Camusescan, Thomas, provost of Ayr, iii. 448.
— — his wife, Helenor Montgomerie, iii. 448.
Gascoigne, Anne, wife of (1) Thomas, 7th earl of Haddington, and (2) James Dalrymple, iv. 324 ; viii. 138 ; ix. 107.
— Sir Charles, iv. 324.
— Woodgrave, captain, iii. 545.
— — his wife, Grizel Elphinstone, iii. 545.
GASK, MURRAY, LORD, i. 468-474 ; viii. 411.
Gask, John, lord, i. 469.
— John, lord (*second creation*), i. 474.
— Galfrid of, viii. 242.
— Geoffrey of, i. 452 *n.*
— Gilbert of, i. 452.
— Isenda of, wife of Gilbert, earl of Strathearn, i. 452 *n.*
— Sir Richard of, viii. 242.
Gason, Wills Crofts, colonel, vi. 383.
— — his wife, Agnes Julia Rich, vi. 383.
Gass, *, assassin of John, 3rd lord Maxwell, vi. 477.
Gaskell, Nathaniel, Manchester, vii. 562.
— Sarah, wife of 12th lord Sempill, vii. 562.
— Rebecca, wife of Richard Clive of Styche, vii. 563.
Gatacre of Gatacre, Edward, vi. 436.
— Annabella Jane, wife of major C. Napier, vi. 436.
Gathorne-Hardy, Gathorne, iv. 221.
— — his wife, Dorothy Montagu Boyle, iv. 221.
Gaudee, Janet, wife of James Alexander, viii. 168.
Gauden, Euphemia, wife of rev. Wm. Macdowal, ix. 71.
Gavin of Langton, David, ii. 210 ; v. 318 ; ix. 45.
— — his 1st wife, * Hearsey, ix. 45.
— — his 2nd wife, Elizabeth Maitland, v. 318 ; ix. 45.
— — Mary Turner, wife of 1st marquess of Breadalbane, ii. 210.
Gaw of Maw, iii. 318 *n.*
— — Alexander, i. 548.
— — John, vi. 421.
— — his wife, Jean Napier, vi. 421.
— Egidia, *or* Geillis, wife of William Graham of Claverhouse, iii. 318.
— Elizabeth, wife of Robert Bruce of Wester Kennet, i. 548.
— *see also* Gall.
Gawler of Bishopsgate, John Bellenden, 2nd Life Guards, ii. 75.

* Name unknown.

Gawler of Rainbridge Cottage, Henry, ii. 75.
—— —— John, ii. 75.
—— —— his wife, Caroline Bellenden, ii. 75.
Gayer of Stoke Poges, Sir Richard, K.B., iii. 479.
—— —— his wife, Christian Bruce, iii. 479.
Geary, Sir William Richard Powlett, bart., iii. 492.
—— —— his wife, Louisa Bruce, iii. 492.
Geddes of Kirkurd, vii. 75.
—— —— his wife, * Scott, vii. 75.
—— Bessie, wife of Henry Murray, i. 225.
—— William, viii. 435.
—— —— his wife, Janet Barde of Posso, viii. 435.
Gedy, John, abbot of Arbroath, viii. 264 *n.*
Gee, Jane Theophila, wife of David F. Carmichael, iv. 570.
—— Robert, iv. 570.
Gedney, Bartholomew, colonel, iii. 600.
—— Deborah, wife of (1) F. Clarke, and (2) William Fairfax, iii. 600.
Gelly, Janet, wife of Robert Fraser, v. 525.
Geneva, Alianora de, wife of Sir Alexander de Baliol, iv. 143.
—— Louis, count of, i. 19.
—— —— his wife, Annabella Stewart, i. 19.
Geoffrey, bishop of Dunkeld, v. 203.
—— son of King Henry II.; bishop of Lincoln, vi. 524.
George of Kynnell, Patrick, i. 121.
—— —— his wife, Jean Ogilvy, i. 121.
Gerard of Abbots Bromley, Thomas (Gerard), 1st baron, iv. 265.
—— —— his wife, Elizabeth Woodford, iv. 265.
—— of Gerard's Bromley, Digby, 5th lord, iv. 384.
—— —— Elizabeth, wife of 4th duke of Hamilton, iv. 384.
Gerod, Nathaniel, London, viii. 101.
Germany, Maximilian I., emperor of, i. 19.
Gesemuth, Adam de, ii. 373, 432.
—— —— his wife, Cristiana de Ireby, ii. 432.
Gevane, Jonet, wife of Jas. Hay of Smithfield, viii. 435.
Gib, Elizabeth, wife of Gilbert Gray, Dundee, iv. 284.
Gibb, John, in Over Lassodie, iii. 189.
—— Mary, wife of (1) * Ormeston, and (2) capt. John Leslie, v. 388.
Gibbons of Stanwell, Sir John, 1st bart., iii. 386 *n.*
—— of Vere, Elizabeth, wife of (1) Jas. Lawes, and (2) William, 8th earl of Home, iv. 481; ix. 109.
—— —— William, iv. 481.
Gibbs, Sir Henry, bart., i. 536 *n.*
—— Sir Vicary, chief justice of the Common Pleas, vii. 510.
—— —— his wife, Frances Cerjat Mackenzie, vii. 510.

* Name unknown.

Gibson of Clatto, Sir Alexander, iii. 97.
—— of Cliftonhall and Kersie, Sir Alexander, v. 314.
—— —— Helen, wife of Sir Alex. C. Maitland, v. 314.
—— of Durie, Sir Alexander, 1st bart., lord president of the Court of Session, iii. 97, 121; iv. 290.
—— —— Sir Alexander, viii. 203.
—— —— his wife, Marjory Murray, viii. 203.
—— —— John, iv. 490.
—— —— his wife, Elizabeth Aytoun, iv. 490.
—— —— John, iv. 591.
—— —— his wife, Helen Carmichael, iv. 591.
—— of Wester Granton, Alexander, clerk of parliament, iv. 90.
—— of Nether Liberton, Alexander, iv. 90.
—— Alexander, vi. 597.
—— —— his wife, Elizabeth Steuart, vi. 597.
—— Alexander, minister of Canisbay, ii. 349.
—— —— his wife, Margaret Sinclair, ii. 349.
—— Andrew, Culross, vii. 214.
—— —— his wife, Mause Primrose, vii. 214.
—— Archibald, i. 315.
—— Frances, wife of Charles, 9th viscount Irvine, v. 18.
—— Jean, wife of G. Preston of that Ilk, iii. 121.
—— Jean, wife of major John Montgomerie, iii. 454.
—— Jean, wife of (1) Sir H. MacCulloch, and (2) John, 4th lord Lindores, v. 385.
—— John, iii. 94.
—— —— his wife, * Ramsay, iii. 94.
—— John, nephew of George Ramsay of Dalhousie, iii. 94.
—— John, ix. 75.
—— —— his wife, Marion Stewart, ix. 75.
—— Mr. John, minister of Dalmeny, ix. 163.
—— —— his 3rd wife, Elizabeth Sandilands, ix. 163.
—— Malcolm, clerk of Session, vi. 598.
—— —— his wife, Elizabeth Hamilton, vi. 598.
—— Margaret, wife of (1) Thos. Fotheringham, (2) Sir Thomas Blair, and (3) William, master of Gray, iv. 290.
—— Marianne, wife of H. C. Arbuthnott, i. 315.
—— Thomas, ii. 410.
—— —— his wife, Jean Dalzell, ii. 410.
—— *, wife of Charles Lyon, viii. 310.
Gibson-Carmichael of Skirling, Sir John, 6th bart., iii. 551; iv. 591, 596.
—— —— Sir Thomas David, 11th bart., iv. 591.
Gibson-Craig of Riccarton, James, 1st bart., iii. 84.

* Name unknown.

Gibson-Craig, Annie, wife of John Hay Mackenzie, iii. 83, 520.
Gibson-Maitland of Clifton Hall, Sir Alexander Charles, 2nd bart. v. 314.
—— —— his wife, Helen Gibson, v. 314.
Giffard of Fonthill, Adam, i. 504.
—— —— *, wife of John Comyn, i. 504.
—— of Sheriffhall, James. vi. 353.
—— —— James, his son, vi. 352, 355.
—— David, son of William G., vi. 355, 357.
—— Elizabeth, wife of Sir James Douglas of Dalkeith, vi. 353.
—— John, in Gorme, iii. 278.
—— —— his wife, Margaret Dunbar, iii. 278.
—— William, vi. 355.
GIFFORD, HAY, EARL OF, viii. 453-474.
Gifford, George, son of 4th marquess of Tweeddale; styled earl of, viii. 465.
—— George, eldest son of 7th marquess of Tweeddale; styled earl of viii. 468.
—— George, eldest son of 8th marquess of Tweeddale; styled earl of, viii. 470.
—— —— his wife, Helen Selina Sheridan, viii. 470.
—— John, first earl of, viii. 453.
—— William George Montagu; styled earl of, viii. 473.
Gifford of Burstall, Sir John, vi. 188.
—— —— his wife, Katharine Middleton, vi. 188; ix. 137.
—— of Lethington, Hugh, v. 281.
—— of Longforgan, Hugh, iv. 270.
—— of Yester, Alice, wife of Thos. Boyd of Kilmarnock, v. 140; viii. 428.
—— —— Sir Hugh, the necromancer, viii. 434.
—— —— Sir Hugh, v. 140, 281; viii. 422.
—— —— Joanna, wife of Sir Thomas Hay of Locherwart, viii. 422, 424.
—— Ada, wife of Sir Andrew Gray of Broxmouth, iv. 270.
—— Mary Anne, dau. of Sir John G. of Burstall, vi. 188.
Gigli, Agatha, wife of Colin Erskine, ix. 117.
Gilbert, earl of Pembroke, i. 15.
—— —— his wife, Marjory of Scotland, i. 5.
—— Sir, of Belnollo, viii. 245.
—— of Dalgarnock, vi. 287.
—— Sir, of Durie, 3rd son of Robert, earl of Strathearn, viii. 245.
—— of Fochabers, vi. 302.
—— of Glencairnie, 7th son of Gilbert, earl of Strathearn, vi. 302; vii. 455 *n.*, 456; viii. 243.
—— father of Walter of Machan, i. 510.
—— father of Roger, iii. 244.
—— father of Adam of Flemingstoun, iii. 557; vii. 420.
—— abbot of Cambuskenneth, v. 425.
—— prior of St. Andrews, vi. 125.
—— son of Richerius, viii. 319 *n.*

* Name unknown.

Gilbert of Paul's Walden, Edward, viii. 310.
—— —— Mary, wife of (1) Geo. Bowes of Streatlam Castle, and (2) A. R. Stoney, viii. 310.
—— Edmund, in holy orders, v. 483.
—— Marion, wife of (1) Thos. Bannatyne, and (2) Thos. Bellenden, ii. 66.
—— Mary, wife of major-gen. Robert Ker, v. 483.
Gilchrist of Kinveachy and Glencairnie, eldest son of Gilbert, earl of Strathearn, viii. 242.
—— judge of Lennox, v. 330 *n.*
—— of Arrochar, 7th son of Alwin, 2nd earl of Lennox, v. 330 *bis*, 331, 333.
—— of Amisfield, *, captain, R.N., iii. 361.
—— Anne, wife of Archibald, 9th earl of Dundonald, iii. 361; ix. 77.
—— Constance Macdonald, wife of 7th earl of Orkney, vi. 583.
GILESTOUN, DRUMMOND, LORD DRUMMOND OF, vi. 66.
Gill Rewach Vickhimi, illeg. son of Alex. Fraser of Lovat, v. 521.
—— Charlotte, wife of capt. John Kennedy, ii. 496.
—— Cotton, London, i. 401.
—— —— his wife, Elizabeth Fellgate *or* Filgate, i. 401.
—— Lawrence, ii. 496.
Gillebride, ancestor of Clan Donald, v. 28 *bis.*
Gillecallum, son of Somerled, v. 31.
Gillecolm Mareschal, iv. 138.
Gilledomnan, ancestor of Clan Donald, v. 28.
Gillemichel, father-in-law of Gartnach, mormaer of Buchan, ii. 251.
—— son of Boude, vii. 577.
Gillemin, father of Waldeve, iii. 245.
Gillemor Scolgo, Tarland, v. 569.
Gillepatrick of Glenham, 3rd son of Dougal of Stranith, vi. 287.
—— Roy, son of Rory, v. 44.
Gillescop, v. 278.
—— Galbard, ancestor of the family of Galbraith, v. 327.
Gillespie of Chirriebelly, Hugh, vii. 204.
—— —— his wife, Susanna Rollo, vii. 204.
—— of Kirkton, John, viii. 83.
—— of Mountquhanie, David, viii. 83.
—— Christian, wife of Archibald Primrose, vii. 215.
—— George, v. 119.
—— George, minister in Edinburgh, iii. 401.
—— —— his wife, Margaret Murray, iii. 401.
—— Margaret, wife of James Carnegie, viii. 83.
—— Mary Bethune, wife of Jas. Carnegie of Stronvar, viii. 83.
—— Patrick, principal of Glasgow College, vii. 577.

* Name unknown.

Gillford, Richard Charles (Meade), eldest son of the 4th earl of Clanwilliam; styled lord, iv. 483.
—— —— his wife, M. E. M. Douglas-Home, iv. 483.
Gillies, John, D.D., minister of Blackfriars Church, Glasgow, vi. 117.
—— Rebecca, wife of gen. David Leslie, vi. 117.
Gillocher, father of Morgund, 2nd earl of Mar, v. 567.
Gillokonel Manthac, brother of Duncan, earl of Carrick, ii. 422 *n*.
Gilmour of Craigmillar, Sir Alexander, vii. 258.
—— —— his wife, Grizel Ross, vii. 258.
—— —— Sir Andrew, 1st laird, iii. 121.
—— Sir John, lord president of the Court of Session, i. 358.
Gilronan, father-in-law of Sir John Erskine of Halkhill, v. 137, 591 *n*.
Gilton, Grizel Sempill, divorced wife of Jas. Hamilton of Stanehouse, and mistress of Archbishop Hamilton; styled lady, vii. 546.
Girace, Bernard Stewart, marchese de, v. 347.
Giustiniani, Benedict, prince, vi. 454.
—— —— his wife, Cecilia Carlotta Francisca Anna, countess Mahony, vi. 454.
GIUSTINIANI, EARL OF NEWBURGH, vi. 457-458.
Giustiniani, Laurence James Angelo Philip Dominic Louis Ignatius John Joseph Vincent, vi. 455.
—— James Thomas Joseph Vincent, cardinal bishop of Albano, vi. 455, 458.
GIUSTINIANI-BANDINI, EARL OF NEWBURGH, vi. 458-460.
Giustiniani-Bandini, Carolina, wife of count de Solza, vi. 459.
—— Elena, wife of prince C. Rospigliosi, vi. 459.
—— Giuseppe Maria, 3rd son of 9th earl of Newburgh, vi. 459.
—— Lorenzo Maria, 2nd son of 9th earl of Newburgh, vi. 459.
—— Maria Cecilia, dau. of 8th earl of Newburgh, vi. 459.
—— Maria Cristina, dau. of 8th earl of Newburgh, vi. 459.
—— Maria Giuseppina, dau. of 9th earl of Newburgh, vi. 459.
—— Maria Isabella, wife of Esmé William Howard, vi. 459.
—— Nicoletta Maria, wife of Mario, duca Grazioli, vi. 459.
Gladstone of Glendye, Sir Thomas, viii. 90.
—— of Fasque, Sir Thomas, bart., viii. 90.
—— of Hawarden, William Henry, ii. 92.
—— —— his wife, Gertrude Stuart, ii. 92.
—— *see also* Gledstanes.
Gladwin, John, Mansfield, vi. 455.
—— Dorothy, wife of Francis Eyre of Hassop, vi. 455.
GLAMIS, LYON, LORD, viii. 270-317.
Glamis, Alexander, second lord, iii. 61; viii. 273.
—— —— his wife, Agnes Crichton, iii. 61; viii. 274.
—— Charles, fourteenth lord, viii. 307.
—— George, fifth lord, v. 524; viii. 278.
—— James, fifteenth lord, viii. 305, 308.
—— John, third lord, iii. 567; iv. 53, 277; viii. 274.
—— —— his wife, Elizabeth Scrymgeour, viii. 276.
—— John, fourth lord, viii. 272, 277.
—— —— his wife, Elizabeth Gray, iv. 277; viii. 277.
—— John, sixth lord, viii. 278.
—— —— his wife, Jonet Douglas, i. 189; viii. 279.
—— John, seventh lord, vi. 87; viii. 281.
—— —— his wife, Jean or Janet Keith, vi. 43; viii. 284.
—— John, the Chancellor, eighth lord, ii. 473; viii. 58, 288.
—— —— his wife, Elizabeth Abernethy, vii. 411; viii. 291.
—— John, tenth lord, viii. 296.
—— John, twelfth lord, viii. 303.
—— John, thirteenth lord, viii. 305.
—— Patrick, first lord, viii. 270, 533.
—— —— his wife, Isobel Ogilvy, ii. 454; viii. 271.
—— Patrick, ninth lord, viii. 100, 291.
—— —— his wife, Anne Murray, i. 470; viii. 294.
—— Patrick, eleventh lord, viii. 297, 299.
—— Patrick, eldest son of 4th earl of Strathmore; styled lord, viii. 305.
—— Philip, 2nd son of 4th earl of Strathmore; styled lord, viii. 305.
—— Thomas, sixteenth lord, viii. 305, 308.
—— master of, Sir Thomas Lyon, brother of 8th lord Glamis, viii. 284.
—— —— master of, Patrick John, viii. 316.
GLAMIS, BOWES, LORD, viii. 310-312.
Glamis, John, seventeenth lord, viii. 310.
—— —— his wife, Mary Eleanor Bowes, viii. 310.
—— John, eighteenth lord, viii. 311.
—— —— his wife, Mary Millner, viii. 311.
GLAMIS, LYON-BOWES, LORD, viii. 312-313.
Glamis, Thomas, nineteenth lord, viii. 312.
—— Thomas George, son of 11th earl of Strathmore and Kinghorne; styled lord, viii. 312.
—— —— his wife, Charlotte Grimstead, viii. 312.
—— Thomas George, twentieth lord, viii. 312.
GLAMIS, BOWES-LYON, LORD, viii. 313-317.

Glamis, Claude, twenty-first lord, viii. 313.
— Claude George, twenty-second lord, viii. 315.
— Patrick, eldest son of 14th earl of Strathmore and Kinghorne; styled lord, viii. 316.
— — his wife, Dorothea Beatrice Godolphin-Osborne, viii. 316.
Glanville of St. Clere, William Evelyn, vii. 307.
— George Raymond Evelyn, vii. 307.
— — his wife, Jane Elizabeth Leslie, vii. 307.
GLASFOORD, ABERCROMBY, LORD, iv. 179-182.
Glasfoord, Francis, lord, iv. 181.
— — his 1st wife, Anne, baroness Sempill, iv. 181; vii. 559.
— — his 2nd wife, Christabella *, iv. 182.
GLASGOW, BOYLE, EARL OF, iv. 183-221.
Glasgow, David, first earl of, iv. 175, 199, 200; vi. 61.
— — his 1st wife, Margaret Lindsay, iv. 175, 203.
— — his 2nd wife, Jean Mure, iv. 205.
— David, seventh earl of, iv. 208, 219.
— — his wife, Dorothea Elizabeth Thomasina Hunter-Blair, iv. 220.
— George, fourth earl of, iii. 41; iv. 178 *n.*, 216.
— — his 1st wife, Augusta Hay, iii. 582; iv. 217.
— — his 2nd wife, Julia Sinclair, iv. 218.
— George Frederick, sixth earl of, iv. 218.
— — his wife, Montagu Abercromby, iv. 219.
— James, fifth earl of, iv. 217, 218.
— — his wife, Georgina Ann Hay-Mackenzie, iii. 83; iv. 218.
— John, second earl of, iv. 206.
— — his wife, Helenor Morison, iv. 206.
— John, third earl of, iv. 206, 215.
— — his wife, Elizabeth Ross, iv. 215 vii. 262.
Glasreth of Glassary, John, i. 325; vii. 235.
— John de, son of Radulph of Dundee, vii. 6.
— Margaret, wife of Dougal Campbell, i. 325.
Glass, Alexander Grant, v. 315.
— Georgina Harriet, wife of Col. Keith Ramsay Maitland, v. 315.
Glassam, son of Brictric, ii. 370.
Glassary, Gilbert of, iii. 305.
— John of, i. 325; vii. 235.
— *or* Glasreth, Agnes of, wife of Alexander Scrymgeour, Constable of Dundee, iii. 305.

* Name unknown.

Glassel of Longniddry, John, i. 389.
— Joan, 2nd wife of 7th duke of Argyll, i. 388.
Glassford of Dougalstoun, James, advocate, iii. 81.
— — John, iii. 81.
— — his wife, Margaret Mackenzie, iii. 81.
— Euphemia, dau. of John G., iii. 81.
— Isabella, her sister, iii. 81.
Gledstanes, Gladstanes of Cocklaw, James, vii. 377, 382.
— of Dod, *, vii. 72.
— — William, vii. 382.
— of Gledstanes, James de, i. 147.
— — James of, vii. 115.
— — his wife, Jonet Murray, vii. 115.
— — James, vii. 377, 382.
— — *, ii. 41.
— — his wife, * Hamilton, ii. 41.
— — *, wife of James Somerville, viii. 9.
— of Whitelaw, captain, vii. 72.
— — his wife, Ann Scott, vii. 72.
— Barbara, wife of John Rutherford of Hyndhousefield, vii. 377.
— Euphan, wife of John Rutherford of Capehope, vii. 382.
— Eupham, wife of John Lyon of Auldbar, viii. 287.
— George, archbishop of St. Andrews, viii. 287, 293.
— Lilias, wife of Richard Rutherford of Littleheuch, vii. 382.
— Mary, wife of George Scott of Synton, vii. 72.
Glen of Auchlevin, Isabel, wife of (1) Sir W. Ogilvy of Lintrathan, and (2) Robert Conynghame of Auchinbowy, i. 112; iv. 16, 29.
— of Balmuto, Sir John, i. 110, 112: iv. 16, 29.
— — his wife, Margaret Erskine, iv. 16, 29; v. 592; viii. 480, 483; ix. 168.
— of the Bar, James, vii. 540.
— of Glen, Sir John, v. 592.
— — his wife, Margaret Erskine, v. 592.
— of Glensland, Christian, wife of (1) David Ogilvy, (2) David Aberkirdor, and (3) David Stewart of the Gloom, i. 110; vii. 370.
— of Inchmartin, Sir John, i. 110, 112.
— — Mariote *or* Marjory, wife of Sir A. Ogilvy, i. 110; iv. 16, 29, 30, 31.
— of Longcroft, Andrew, iii. 103.
— Elizabeth, wife of 8th earl of Dalhousie. iii. 103.
— Margaret, wife of Edward Maxwell of Lawston, iv. 416.
— Richard de, vii. 424.
— Robert, i. 8.
— — his wife, Margaret Bruce, i. 8.

* Name unknown.

GLENALMOND, MURRAY, VISCOUNT, i. 478.
Glenalmond, John, viscount, i. 478.
GLENALMOND, MURRAY, VISCOUNT OF, i. 479.
Glenalmond, John, first viscount of, i. 479.
Glenawley, Alexander (Balfour), 2nd baron, i. 536.
—— James, 1st baron, i. 536, 539; ix. 86.
—— —— his 1st wife, Grizel Balfour, i. 536.
—— —— his 2nd wife, Elizabeth *or* Isobel Hay, i. 536; iii. 571; ix. 86.
—— —— his 3rd wife, Anne Blaney, i. 536.
—— James, 3rd baron, i. 536.
—— —— his wife, Anne Gouldsmith, i. 536.
Glenbervie of Kincardine, Sylvester (Douglas), lord, i. 184.
GLENCAIRN, CUNNINGHAM, EARL OF, iv. 222-252.
Glencairn, Alexander, first earl of, iv. 232.
—— —— his wife, Margaret Hepburn, iv. 234.
—— Alexander, fourth earl of, iv. 239, 244; v. 556; vii. 537, 540.
—— —— his 1st wife, Janet Hamilton, iv. 239, 241, 364.
—— —— his 2nd wife, Janet Cunningham, iv. 241.
—— Alexander, ninth earl of, iv. 246, 249; v. 310.
—— —— his wife, Nicolas Stewart, iv. 249; v. 311.
—— Cuthbert, second earl of, iv. 235.
—— —— his wife, Marion Douglas, i. 186; iv. 236.
—— James, sixth earl of, iv. 243; v. 454; vii. 551.
—— —— his 1st wife, Margaret Campbell, ii. 183; iv. 243, 244.
—— —— —— his 2nd wife, Agnes Hay, iv. 244.
—— James, thirteenth earl of, iv. 251.
—— John, tenth earl of, iv. 249.
—— —— his 1st wife, Jean Erskine, iv. 250; v. 626.
—— —— his 2nd wife, Margaret Napier, iv. 250.
—— John, fourteenth earl of, iv. 234, 251.
—— —— his wife, Isabella Erskine, ii. 278; iv. 252.
—— William, third earl of, iv. 236, 240, 244; ix. 97.
—— —— his 1st wife, Katharine Borthwick, ii. 107; iv. 238.
—— —— his 2nd wife, Elizabeth Campbell, iv. 238.
—— William, fifth earl of, iv. 242, 244; ix. 97 *bis*.
—— —— his wife, Janet Gordon, iv. 242; v. 109.
Glencairn, William, seventh earl of, iv. 246.
—— —— his wife, Janet Ker, iv. 246; v. 457; ix. 97.
—— William, eighth earl of, i. 362; iv. 242, 247; v. 563.
—— —— his 1st wife, Anne Ogilvy, iv. 29, 248.
—— —— his 2nd wife, Margaret Montgomery, iii. 450; iv. 248; ix. 98.
—— William, eleventh earl of, iv. 250.
—— —— his wife, Henrietta Stewart, iv. 163, 250.
—— William, twelfth earl of, iv. 234, 251.
—— —— his wife, Elizabeth Macguire, iv. 251; ix. 98 *bis*.
—— master of, William, son of Cuthbert, 2nd earl of Glencairn, iv. 236; v. 351.
—— master of, William, eldest son of 4th earl of Glencairn, ii. 146; iv. 241; v. 154.
—— —— his wife, Janet Hamilton, iv. 239, 241, 364.
—— master of, William, eldest son of 7th earl of Glencairn, iv. 243.
—— master of, William, eldest son of 8th earl of Glencairn, iv. 246.
Glendonwyn, Glendinning of Drumrash, George, v. 265.
—— —— John, ix. 117.
—— —— John, v. 109.
—— —— his wife, Helen Stewart, v. 109.
—— —— John, v. 112.
—— —— his wife, Margaret Vans, v. 112.
—— of Gelston, Elizabeth, wife of (1) George Glendoning, (2) John Maxwell, and (3) Thos. Maxwell, vi. 487; ix. 144.
—— —— William, vi. 487.
—— of Glencorse, Bertilmo, v. 105.
—— —— his wife, Margaret Gordon, v. 105; ix. 117.
—— of Glendonwyn, Bertilmo, v. 105.
—— —— John, v. 105.
—— —— Ninian, vii. 375.
—— —— Sir Simon, vii. 370.
—— of Parton, Alexander, vi. 479.
—— —— his contracted wife, Agnes Maxwell, vi. 479.
—— —— George, the younger, ix. 144.
—— —— his wife, Elizabeth Glendoning, ix. 144.
—— —— John, vi. 476.
—— —— his wife, Agnes Maxwell, vi. 476.
—— —— John, v. 264; vi. 479.
—— —— his wife, Marion Maclellan, v. 264.
—— —— Ninian, vi. 479.
—— —— his 1st wife, Katharine Maxwell, vi. 479.
—— —— Robert, iv. 415.
—— —— his wife, Margaret Maxwell, iv. 415; ix. 105.
—— Jean, wife of John Gordon of Penninghame and Muirfad, v. 108; ix. 117.

Glendonwyn, John, vii. 571.
—— —— his 2nd wife, Elizabeth Sinclair, vii. 571.
—— Margaret, wife of Robert Rutherford of Chatto, vii. 370.
—— Robert, Kirkcudbright, v. 108 *n*.
—— Robert, minister of Kirkcudbright, v. 265.
—— *, wife of David Maxwell of Newark, v. 265.
Glengall, Richard (Butler), 2nd earl of, viii. 516.
GLENILA, CAMPBELL, VISCOUNT OF, i. 369-393.
Glenila, Archibald, first viscount of, i. 369.
GLENLIVET, GORDON, LORD OF, i. 102.
Glenlivet, Charles, first lord of, i. 102.
GLENLUCE, DALRYMPLE, LORD, viii. 119-164.
Glenluce, James, first lord, viii. 119.
GLENLUCE, DALRYMPLE, LORD, viii. 149-164.
Glenluce, John, first lord, viii. 149.
GLENLYON, MURRAY, VISCOUNT OF, i. 479-502.
Glenlyon, John, first viscount of, i. 479.
GLENLYON OF GLENLYON, MURRAY, BARON, i. 496-502.
Glenlyon, George Augustus Frederick John, second lord, i. 496.
—— James, first lord, i. 496.
—— John James Hugh Henry, third lord, i. 499.
GLENORCHY, CAMPBELL, LORD, ii. 203-214.
Glenorchy, John, first lord, ii. 203.
—— John, 2nd son of 1st earl of Breadalbane; styled lord. ii. 207 *n*.
—— John, son of 2nd earl of Breadalbane; styled lord, ii. 208.
—— John, 2nd son of 3rd earl of Breadalbane; styled lord, ii. 209.
—— —— his wife, Willielma Maxwell, ii. 209.
GLENSHIE, MURRAY, VISCOUNT OF, i. 481.
Glenshie, William, viscount of, i. 481.
GLENTILT, MURRAY, EARL OF, i. 481.
Glentilt, William, earl of, i. 481.
GLENURCHY, CAMPBELL, LORD, ii. 203.
Glenurquhay, Mariota of, wife of John Cambell, i. 326.
Glerawley, William (Annesley), 1st viscount, i. 68.
Gloucester, Henry, 4th son of King Charles I.; duke of, i. 29.
—— William, son of Queen Anne; duke of, i. 33.
—— William Henry, 3rd son of Frederick, prince of Wales; duke of, iii. 411: ix. 109.
—— —— his wife, Maria Walpole, iii. 411.
—— Ralph (de Monthermer), earl of, i. 428.
—— and Hertford, Gilbert (de Clare), 1st earl of, ii. 431.

* Name unknown.

Gloucester and Hertford, Gilbert (de Clare), 3rd earl of, iv. 11.
Glover, John, vicar of Brading, iii. 390.
—— —— his wife, Susan Emma Murray, iii. 390.
Glynn, Edward Carr, lord bishop of Peterborough, i. 391.
—— —— his wife, Mary Emma Campbell, i. 391.
Godet, *, Martinique, iii. 360.
—— —— his wife, Amelia C. G. E. de Clugny, iii. 360.
Godfrey, toshach of the Isles, ancestor of Clan Donald, v. 28.
—— of Old Hall, Edward, vi. 385.
—— —— his wife, Susan Elizabeth Yarde-Buller, vi. 385.
Godith, wife of (1) Richard Skeffington, and (2) Devereux Aston, i. 405.
Godit, wife of Roger de Maule, ix. 148.
Godolphin, Francis (Godolphin), 2nd earl of, ii. 533.
—— —— his wife, Henrietta (Churchill), duchess of Marlborough, ii. 533.
Godolphin-Osborne, Dorothea Beatrix, wife of Patrick, lord Glamis, viii. 316.
—— William, ix. 85.
—— —— his wife, Georgiana Augusta Henrietta Keith-Elphinstone, ix. 85.
Godred, King of Man and the Isles, v. 29.
Godrith, son of Waldeve of Tynedale, i. 417.
—— —— his wife, Bethoc of Scotland, i. 3, 417.
Godschall, *, wife of (1) *, and (2) archbishop William Carmichael, iv. 594.
—— Sir Thomas, lord mayor of London, iv. 594.
Goelet, May, wife of 8th duke of Roxburghe, vii. 359.
—— Ogden, New York, vii. 359.
Gofton of Stockwell, John, ii. 581.
—— —— his wife, Mary Hanbury, ii. 581.
GOLDILANDS, SCOTT, LORD, iii. 111-114.
—— Henry, first lord, ii. 239; iii. 111.
Goldman, Margaret, wife of James Rollo of Monkisholm, vii. 191.
—— William, bailie of Dundee, vii. 191.
Goldthorpe, Anne, wife of Hugh Ingram, v. 9.
—— Richard, M.P., lord mayor of York, v. 9.
Gonzaga, Anne de, wife of Edward, 4th son of Frederick V., elector palatine, v. 27.
—— Marie Louise de, wife of Ladislas VII., king of Poland, iv. 548.
Goodenough, Florence Selina, wife of Sir T. V. Lister, ii. 58.
—— James Graham, C.B., C.M.G., capt. R.N., ii. 58.
Goodeve, William James, v. 635.
—— his wife, Frances Jemima Erskine, v. 635.

* Name unknown.

GOODEVE-ERSKINE, LORD GARIOCH, v. 635-636.
GOODEVE-ERSKINE, EARL OF MAR, v. 635-636.
Goodeve-Erskine, Charlotte Erskine, wife of Charles Bell, v. 635.
— Eliza Philadelphia Erskine, wife of rev. Edward Maule Cole, v. 635.
— Frances Jemima Erskine, wife of lieut.-gen. James Nowell Young, v. 635.
— Madeline Erskine, v. 635.
GORDON, GORDON, LORD, iv. 522-543.
Gordon, Alexander, eldest son of 2nd earl of Huntly; styled lord, iv. 529; vii. 457; ix. 20.
— Alexander, eldest son of 4th earl of Huntly; styled lord, iv. 370, 536.
— — his wife, Barbara Hamilton, iv. 370, 536; ix. 104, 110.
— George, 2nd son of 1st earl of Huntly; styled lord, iv. 52, 525, 526.
— George, 2d son of 4th earl of Huntly; styled lord, i. 85; iv. 539.
— — his contr. wife, Jean Hamilton, iv. 370.
— — his wife, Anne Hamilton, iv. 370, 541.
— John, eldest son of 3rd earl of Huntly; styled lord, iv. 532.
— — his wife, Margaret Stewart, i. 22; iv. 532; vii. 44.
GORDON, GORDON, DUKE OF, iv. 253, 506-558.
Gordon, Alexander, second duke of, i. 91; iv. 551.
— — his wife, Henrietta Mordaunt, iv. 551.
— Alexander, fourth duke of, i. 70; iv. 555.
— — his 1st wife, Jane Maxwell, iv. 556.
— — his 2nd wife, Jane Christie, iv. 556, 557.
— Cosmo George, 3rd duke of, i. 103; iv. 553.
— — his wife, Catharine Gordon, i. 91; iv. 553; ix. 111.
— George, first duke of, iv. 549; viii. 353; ix. 111.
— — his wife, Elizabeth Howard, iv. 550.
— George, fifth duke of, i. 105; iv. 253, 557; v. 134, 367.
— — his wife, Elizabeth Brodie, iv. 558; viii. 510.
GORDON AND BADENOCH, GORDON, LORD, iv. 543-549.
Gordon and Badenoch, George, first lord, iv. 543.
— George, eldest son of 1st marquess of Huntly; styled lord, iv. 286, 545.
— George, eldest son of 2nd marquess of Huntly; styled lord, iv. 546, 548.
GORDON OF ABERDEEN, GORDON, VISCOUNT, i. 94.
Gordon of Aberdeen, George, first viscount, i. 94.
GORDON OF HUNTLY, GORDON, BARON, iv. 556-558.
Gordon of Huntly, Alexander, first baron, iv. 556.
— George, second baron, iv. 557.
GORDON, GORDON-LENNOX, DUKE OF, v. 369-371.
Gordon, Charles Henry, first duke of, iv. 253; v. 369.
— — his wife, Frances Harriett Greville, v. 369.
— Charles Henry, second duke of, v. 369.
— — his 1st wife, Amy Mary Ricardo, v. 370.
— — his 2nd wife, Isabel Sophie Craven, v. 370.
— master of, Sir Alexander Seton, styled iv. 520, 521.
GORDON, EARL OF ABERDEEN, i. 82-99.
GORDON, LORD ABOYNE, i. 100.
GORDON, VISCOUNT ABOYNE, iv. 546.
GORDON, VISCOUNT OF ABOYNE, i. 101.
GORDON, EARL OF ABOYNE, i. 102-105; iv. 547.
GORDON, LORD AUCHINDOUN, iv. 549-558.
GORDON, LORD BADENOCH, iv. 549-558.
GORDON, LORD BALMORE, iv. 549-558.
GORDON, BARON BEAUCHAMP OF BLETSHOE, iv. 556.
GORDON, EARL OF ENZIE, iv. 543-558.
GORDON, VISCOUNT FORMARTYNE, i. 88-99.
GORDON, LORD GARTHIE, iv. 549-558.
GORDON, LORD OF GLENLIVET, i. 102.
GORDON, LORD GORDON, iv. 522-543.
GORDON, DUKE OF GORDON, iv. 253, 506-558.
GORDON, LORD GORDON AND BADENOCH, iv. 543-549.
GORDON, VISCOUNT GORDON OF ABERDEEN, i. 94.
GORDON, BARON GORDON OF HUNTLY, iv. 556-558.
GORDON, LORD HADDO, i. 88-99.
GORDON, EARL OF HUNTLY, iv, 523-562.
GORDON, EARL OF HUNTLY AND ENZIE, iv. 549-558.
GORDON, MARQUESS OF HUNTLY, iv. 506-562.
GORDON, VISCOUNT OF INVERNESS, v. 549-558.
GORDON, LORD KELLIE, i. 88-99.
GORDON, VISCOUNT OF KENMURE, v. 98-135.
GORDON, LORD KINCARDINE, iv. 549-558.
GORDON, LORD LOCHABER, iv. 549-558.
GORDON, LORD OF LOCHINVAR, v. 98-135.
GORDON, BARON MELDRUM OF MORVEN, iv. 559-562.
GORDON, VISCOUNT MELGUM, i. 100.
GORDON, LORD METHLIC, i. 88-99.
GORDON, BARON MORDAUNT OF TURVEY, iv. 556-558.

GORDON, EARL OF NORWICH, iv. 556-558.
GORDON, LORD OF STRATHAVEN, i. 102-105.
GORDON, LORD STRATHAVEN, iv. 549-558.
GORDON, EARL OF SUTHERLAND, viii. 337-361.
GORDON, LORD TARVES, i. 88-99.
Gordon of Abergeldie, Sir Alexander, iv. 523, 525.
—— —— his wife, Beatrice Hay, iv. 525.
—— —— Sir Alexander, v. 525.
—— —— Alexander, iii. 204.
—— —— his wife, Margaret Mackintosh, iii. 204.
—— —— Peter, viii. 233.
—— of Aboyne, Adam, 2nd son of 2nd earl of Huntly, iv. 529.
—— —— his wife, Elizabeth, countess of Sutherland, iv. 530; viii. 334, 336.
—— —— Adam, 3rd son of 1st marquess of Huntly, iv. 544.
—— —— William, iv. 530.
—— —— his wife. Janet Ogilvy, iv. 530.
—— of Acarsane, Sir Robert, 2nd son of Sir John G. of Lochinvar, v. 105.
—— —— his wife, Mariota Acarsane of Glen, iv. 106.
—— of Achanachie, Charles, vi. 182.
—— —— his wife, Elizabeth Middleton, vi. 182.
—— of Aikenhead, John, ii. 279.
—— —— his wife, Christian Isabella Erskine, ii. 279.
—— —— John Henry, ii. 279.
—— —— his 1st wife, Mariann Craig Erskine, ii. 279.
—— —— his 2nd wife, Margaret Elizabeth Grierson, ii. 279.
—— —— William, ancestor of the family of, v. 104.
—— —— his wife, Janet Baillie, v. 104.
—— of Airds, Alexander, ix. 118.
—— —— his wife, Elizabeth Gordon, ix. 118.
—— —— John, v. 270.
—— of Airds of Crossmichael, William, v. 109.
—— —— his wife, Mary M'Ghie, v. 109.
—— of Airds of Kells, Alexander, ancestor of the family of, v. 102.
—— of Archadlie, Patrick, i, 84.
—— —— William, portioner, 2nd son of Jas. G. of Haddo, i. 86.
—— of Ardlach, John, iv. 516.
—— —— his wife, Elizabeth Maitland, iv. 516.
—— of Ardoch, Adam, ancestor of the family of, iv. 525.
—— —— 1716, ii. 518.
—— —— Adam, v. 94.
—— of Assynt, William, M.P., viii. 357.
—— of Auchentoul, Alexander, senator of the College of Justice, iv. 133.
—— of Auchindoun, Adam, 6th son of 4th earl of Huntly, iv. 24, 57, 58, 537, 540.
Gordon of Auchindoun, Adam, 3rd son of 1st marquess of Huntly, iv. 544; viii. 347.
—— —— Sir Alexander, v. 525.
—— —— James, 5th son of 4th earl of Huntly, iv. 537, 538.
—— —— Sir Patrick, iv. 537, 538; vii. 281; viii. 286.
—— —— his 1st wife, Joan Leslie, vii. 281; ix. 110.
—— —— his 2nd wife, Agnes Beaton, iv. 538; ix. 111.
—— of Auchingilbert, William, v. 104.
—— of Auchinreoch, Alexander, 2nd son of William G. of Lochinvar, v. 101.
—— —— John, iv. 411.
—— of Auchlane, Alexander, admiral-depute of South-west coast, v. 109.
—— —— John, v. 124.
—— of Auchterarne, Laurence, 4th son of 1st marquess of Huntly, iv. 545.
—— of Auchterhouse, George, 4th son of Jas. G. of Methlic, i. 83.
—— of Awdiale, William, vii. 438.
—— —— his wife, Elizabeth Fraser, vii. 438.
—— of Avachie, John, vi. 575.
—— of Badinscoth, ii. 18.
—— —— his wife, Jean Ogilvy, ii. 18.
—— of Balmaclellan, John, v. 104.
—— of Balmeg, William, ancestor of the family of, v. 104.
—— —— his wife, Janet Baillie, v. 104.
—— of Balmonth, Alexander, v. 100.
—— —— John, v. 100.
—— —— Thomas, v. 100.
—— —— William de, v. 99.
—— of Bar, John, v. 117.
—— —— his wife, Rosina Gordon, v. 117.
—— of Nether Barcaple, Sir John, v. 117.
—— of Barnbarroch, Agnes, wife of (1) John Grierson of Bargatton, and (2) Robert Maclellan of Nunton, v. 261.
—— —— Alexander, v. 106.
—— —— James, v. 261.
—— —— John, v. 106.
—— of Barncrosh, James, 4th son of Sir John G. of Lochinvar, v. 112, 120.
—— —— his wife, Margaret Vans, iv. 112; ix. 118 *bis*.
—— of Barquhill, Alexander, son of Wm. G. of Craiglaw, iv. 156.
—— of Barrallmad, John, ii. 18.
—— of Barvoranby, George, v. 102.
—— of Beldorny, Adam, ancestor of the family of, iv. 525.
—— —— Alexander, vii. 464.
—— —— his wife, Margaret Grant, vii. 464.
—— —— George, vii. 464.
—— of Benholm, John, vi. 49, 53.
—— of Beoch, John, v. 117.
—— of Birkenburn, James, ii. 9.
—— —— his wife, Janet Gordon, ii. 9.

Gordon of Blairshinnoch, George, iv. 28.
—— of Bordland, Sir George, iv. 535.
—— of Botary, John, iv. 71.
—— —— his wife, * Forbes, iv. 71.
—— of Braco, Alexander, 2nd son of Patrick G. of Methlic and Haddo, i. 84.
—— —— his wife, Elizabeth Annand, i. 84.
—— —— Patrick, i. 84.
—— —— his wife, Janet Seton, i. 85.
—— of Braes of Mar, Sir George, iv. 535.
—— of Breakly, John, i. 142.
—— —— his wife, Anna Graham, i. 142; ix. 9 *bis*.
—— of Buckie, John, i. 564; ii. 9.
—— —— his wife, Agnes Gordon, ii. 9.
—— —— John, ii. 188.
—— —— his wife, Juliana *or* Egidia Campbell, ii. 188.
—— of Buittle, James, 4th son of Sir John G. of Lochinvar, v. 112, 120.
—— —— his wife, Margaret Vans, v. 112; ix. 118 *bis*.
—— —— James, master of Kenmure, v. 112.
—— —— John, v. 112.
—— of the Burn, Adam, commander of the Forces, M.P., iv. 552; viii. 514.
—— —— his wife, Jane Drummond, iv. 553.
—— of Cairnburrow, John, vi. 49.
—— of Campbelton, v. 131.
—— —— William, viii. 138.
—— —— his wife, Charlotte Douglas Dalrymple, viii. 138.
—— of Cardoness, John, iv. 162.
—— —— his wife, Elizabeth Stewart, iv. 162.
—— of Carleton, Alexander, ancestor of the family of, v. 102.
—— of Carroll, Adam, ancestor of the family of, iv. 525.
—— of Castle-Stewart, Elizabeth, wife of William Stewart, iv. 162.
—— of Castramine, David, v. 106.
—— —— his wife, Isabel Muirhead, v. 106.
—— of Charles Island, Sir Robert, 1st bart., v. 115.
—— —— his wife, Elizabeth Ruthven, v. 116.
—— of Clubsgovil, Mary, wife of col. James King, iii. 591.
—— of Clune, Margaret, wife of (1) George Abercromby of Leys, and (2) Alex. Cumming, iv. 179; viii. 338.
—— of Cluny, Alexander, ancestor of the family of, iv. 533; vii. 461.
—— —— his wife, Janet Grant, iv. 533.
—— —— Alexander, ii. 9.
—— —— his wife, * Ogilvy, ii. 9.
—— —— Charles, viii. 158.
—— —— John, ii. 9.
—— —— Kenneth, i. 306.
—— —— his wife, Elizabeth Malloch, i. 306.

* Name unknown.

Gordon of Cluny, Robert, i. 310.
—— —— his wife, Katharine Arbuthnott, i. 310.
—— —— Robert, son of Kenneth G., i. 306.
—— —— Sir Thomas, i. 199; ii. 12.
—— —— his wife, Elizabeth Douglas, i. 199.
—— of Cobairdy, James, iv. 65.
—— —— his wife, Mary Forbes, iv. 65.
—— of Cocklarachie, Sir George, iv. 536.
—— —— George, viii. 337.
—— —— his wife, * Gordon, viii. 337.
—— of Coldstone, James, iv. 22.
—— —— his wife, Margaret Ogilvy, iv. 22.
—— of Wester Corse, John, iv. 109.
—— of Craig, George, 3rd son of Wm. G. of Lochinvar, v. 102.
—— —— his wife, Janet Maclellan *or* Dougalson, v. 102.
—— —— George, viii. 338.
—— —— his wife, Helenor Gordon, viii, 338.
—— —— Robert, v. 100.
—— —— William, ancestor of the family of, iv. 516.
—— of Craig of Auchindoir, Francis, ii. 19.
—— —— his wife, Agnes Ogilvy, ii. 19.
—— of Craiglaw, Alexander, iv. 156.
—— —— William, iv. 155, 156; v. 104.
—— —— his wife, Janet Baillie, v. 104.
—— of Crathlet, William, legtd. son of Sir John G. of Lochinvar, v. 105.
—— of Crogo, Roger, ancestor of the family of, v. 102.
—— —— his wife, Geylles Macnaught of Crogo, v. 102.
—— of Cromar, Sir George, iv. 535.
—— of Crossmichael, Sir Robert, v. 113.
—— of Cuckney, George T., ii. 501.
—— of Cuil, Alexander, v. 108, 123.
—— —— William, v. 108.
—— —— his wife, Ann Kennedy, v. 108.
—— of Culreoch, William, v. 108.
—— —— his wife, Helen Stewart, v. 108.
—— of Culvennan, D. A., v. 124 *n*.
—— —— William, ancestor of the family of, v. 104.
—— —— William, ix. 119.
—— of Over Culwha, John, v. 261.
—— of Dalpholly, Sir Adam, viii. 125.
—— —— his wife, Jean Halket, viii. 125.
—— of Dawach, Sir George, iv. 535.
—— of Denend, George, vii. 439.
—— of Deskford, John, 3rd son of 4th earl of Huntly, i. 119; iv. 21, 536.
—— —— his wife, Elizabeth Gordon, iv. 21, 536.
—— of Drumnakeith, Agnes, wife of James Ogilvy, iv. 19.
—— of Drumrash, William, v. 131; ix. 119.
—— of Duchray, James, i. 85.
—— of Earlsfield, James, iv. 22.

* Name unknown.

Gordon of Earlston, Alexander, ancestor of the family of, v. 102.
—— —— Sir Alexander, v. 125.
—— —— his 2nd wife, Marion Gordon, v. 125.
—— —— Sir John, v. 132.
—— of Ellon, Alexander, viii. 135.
—— —— Arthur John Lewis, C.M.G., i. 96.
—— —— his wife, Caroline Augusta Hamilton-Gordon, i. 96.
—— —— William, 2nd son of 3rd earl of Aberdeen, i. 94.
—— of Embo, Adam, ancestor of the family of, iv. 525.
—— —— John, iii. 206.
—— —— Sir John, 4th bart., vii. 176 *n.*
—— —— his 1st wife, Elizabeth Sutherland, iii. 212; ix. 69.
—— —— his 2nd wife, Margaret Sutherland, vii. 176 *n.*
—— —— Sir William, vii. 176 *n.*
—— of Endrig, Alexander, 5th son of Sir John G. of Lochinvar, v. 112.
—— —— Sir John, v. 117.
—— of Essie, John, 2nd son of Sir John G. of Gordon, i. 82; iv. 515.
—— —— his wife, Elizabeth *or* Margaret Maitland, iv. 516.
—— of Farr, vii. 165.
—— of Fawnes, Sir Adam, iv. 510.
—— —— his wife, Alicia de Gordon, iv. 508.
—— of Fetterletter, Robert, i. 83.
—— of Findlater, John, 3rd son of 4th earl of Huntly, ii. 10; iii. 570; iv. 536.
—— of Fyvie, Charles, eldest son of lord Rockville, i. 92.
—— —— his wife, Elizabeth Clutton, i. 92.
—— —— William Cosmo, i. 92.
—— —— his wife, Grace Abercromby, i. 92.
—— of Fyvie Castle, William, general, M.P., 3rd son of 2nd earl of Aberdeen, i. 91.
—— —— William, his son, i. 91.
—— of Galloway, Nova Scotia, Sir Robert, 1st bart., v. 115.
—— —— Robert, v. 116.
—— of Garrocher, William, v. 112.
—— of Garty, Alexander, viii. 338.
—— —— Gilbert, viii. 337.
—— —— his wife, Isabel Sinclair, viii. 337.
—— —— John, viii. 337.
—— —— Patrick, viii. 337.
—— of Gategill, Alexander, 3rd son of Sir Robt. G. of Lochinvar, v. 106.
—— —— James, v. 106.
—— of Gelston, Robert, 2nd son of Sir Robt. G. of Lochinvar, v. 116.
—— of Gight, Alexander, ancestor of the family of, viii. 573.
—— —— George, son of Wm. G. of Schivas, ii. 7.
—— —— George, 3rd laird, iii. 288; iv. 539.
—— —— his wife, Agnes Betoun, iv. 539.
Gordon of Gight, George, 6th laird, iii. 33, 573.
—— —— his 2nd wife, Jean Abernethy, iii. 33; vii. 413.
—— —— George, 7th laird, i. 123.
—— —— his wife, Elizabeth Ogilvy, i. 123.
—— —— John, v. 543.
—— —— William, ancestor of the family of, iv. 530.
—— of Glasgow, William, ancestor of the family of, v. 104.
—— of Glastyrim, George, iii. 204.
—— —— his wife, Violet Strachan, iii. 204.
—— of Glen, Sir Robert, 2nd son of Sir John G. of Lochinvar, v. 105.
—— —— his wife, Mariota Acarsane of Glen, v. 106.
—— —— Sir Robert, 1st bart., v. 108, 112, 113.
—— of Glenbucket, viii. 57.
—— —— his wife, Isabel Carnegie, viii. 57.
—— —— John, viii. 56.
—— —— his wife, Helen Carnegie, viii. 56.
—— —— Patrick, i. 304.
—— —— his wife, Jean Arbuthnott. i. 304.
—— of Glendaveney, Alexander, i. 309.
—— —— his wife, Jean Arbuthnott, i. 309.
—— of Glengerrack, Alexander, ii. 21.
—— —— his wife, Helen Lauder, ii. 21.
—— of Glenkens, Sir Adam de, v. 99.
—— —— William de, v. 99; ix. 117.
—— of Glenloy, Alexander, iv. 536.
—— of Glenluce, James, styled 'titular,' ix. 118.
—— of Glenquicken, William, v. 112.
—— of Glenskyreburn, Sir Robert, v. 105.
—— of Glentanner, John, 2nd son of 3rd earl of Aboyne, i. 104; ix. 6.
—— —— his wife, Clementina Lockhart, i. 104; ix. 6.
—— of Golspie Kirkton, Adam, viii. 337.
—— of Gordon, Sir Adam, husband of Alicia of Gordon, iv. 508.
—— —— Adam, 5th laird, iv. 510.
—— —— his wife, Marjorie, iv. 510.
—— —— Sir Adam, 6th laird, justiciar of Lothian, iii. 264; iv. 510; vi. 471; vii. 423.
—— —— his wife, Amabilla, iv. 512.
—— —— Sir Adam, 7th laird, iv. 513.
—— —— Sir Adam, lord of Gordon, iv. 516.
—— —— his wife, Elizabeth Keith, iv. 517, 518 *bis.*
—— —— Alicia, wife of Sir Adam Gordon, iv. 508.
—— —— Elizabeth, wife of Sir Alexander Seton, i. 82; ii. 223; iv. 518, 519; viii. 572; ix. 109.
—— —— John, 8th laird, ii. 94; iv. 514.
—— —— his wife, Elizabeth, iv. 514.
—— —— Sir John, 9th laird, iv. 515.
—— —— John, lord of Gordon, iv. 518; vi. 349.
—— —— his wife, Agnes Douglas, iv. 518; vi. 348.

Gordon of Gordon, Richard *or* Richer, 1st laird, iv. 507.
—— —— Sir Thomas, 2nd laird, iv. 508.
—— —— Sir Thomas, 3rd laird, iv. 508.
—— —— his wife, Marjorie, iv. 508.
—— of Gordonstoun, Sir John, eldest son of Wm. G. of Lochinvar, v. 102.
—— —— Sir Robert, 1st bart., ix. 110.
—— —— his wife, Louise Gordon, ix. 110.
—— —— Sir Robert, 3rd bart., iii. 211; iv. 63.
—— —— his 1st wife, Margaret Forbes, iii. 209; iv. 63.
—— —— his 2nd wife, Elizabeth Dunbar, iii. 210.
—— —— Sir Robert, claimant to earldom of Sutherland, viii. 359.
—— of Grandoun, Thomas, iv. 126.
—— —— his wife, Janet Gordon, iv. 126.
—— of Grange, Hugh, v. 109.
—— —— his wife, Margaret Gordon, v. 109.
—— —— William, ancestor of the family of, v. 104.
—— —— William, v. 126.
—— of Greenlaw, Sir John, v. 119.
—— —— John, 2nd son of 5th viscount of Kenmure, v. 125; ix. 119.
—— —— his wife, Nicolas Stewart, v. 125.
—— —— Sir Robert, eldest son of Sir John G. of Lochinvar, v. 113.
—— —— William, W.S., 4th son of Sir Alex. G. of Earlston, v. 131.
—— of Grobdale, William, v. 108.
—— of Haddo, James, presumed ancestor of the family of, i. 83; iv. 516.
—— —— James, 2nd laird, i. 85.
—— —— his wife, Marjory Menzies, i. 85.
—— —— James, 3rd laird, i. 86.
—— —— his 1st wife, Jean Keith, i. 86; vi. 49.
—— —— his 2nd wife, Agnes Gordon, i. 86.
—— —— Sir George, 3rd bart., president of the College of Justice, lord Haddo, i. 87, 88 *bis*.
—— —— his wife, Anna Lockhart, i. 89.
—— —— Sir John, 1st bart., i. 86, 353; ii. 16.
—— —— his wife, Janet Forbes, i. 87.
—— —— Sir John, 2nd bart., i. 87.
—— —— his wife, Mary Forbes, i. 88; iv. 75.
—— —— Patrick, 1st laird, i. 83.
—— —— his wife, Marion Ogilvy, i. 84; iv. 19.
—— of Halleaths, Gilbert, vii. 24.
—— of Hallhead, George, vi. 432.
—— —— his wife, Henrietta Hope Napier, vi. 432.
—— —— Robert, i. 93.
—— —— his wife, Henrietta Gordon, i. 93.
—— of Hardlands, James, v. 109; ix. 118 *bis*.
—— —— John, v. 104.
—— of Haslefield, John, v. 117.
—— of Hills, Alexander, admiral-depute of south-west coast, v. 109.
Gordon of Hilton, John, ii. 188.
—— —— his wife, Juliana Campbell, ii. 188.
—— of Hiltown of Inverboyndlie, George, iv. 28.
—— of Holm, Adam, 2nd son of Sir Alex. G. of Stitchill, v. 100.
—— —— Quintin, v. 100.
—— of Huntly, Alexander, alleged son of Adam de G., iv. 509.
—— of Invergordon, Adam, ancestor of the family of, iv. 525.
—— —— Sir William, 1st bart., iii. 80.
—— of Invermarkie, Sir George, iv. 535.
—— of Kelly, James, i. 83.
—— —— Patrick, i. 83.
—— of Keithmore, Adam, iv. 537.
—— —— James, iv. 538.
—— —— Sir Patrick, iv. 537, 538.
—— of Kenmure, Sir Alexander, eldest son of Sir John G. of Lochinvar, v. 102.
—— —— his 1st wife, Janet Kennedy, ii. 459; v. 103.
—— —— his 2nd wife, Janet Douglas, v. 104; vii. 117.
—— —— his 3rd wife, Elizabeth Stewart, v. 103, 104.
—— —— Janet, wife of (1) Lachlan Mackintosh, and (2) Jas. Ogilvy, v. 103, 105; ix. 56.
—— —— Louisa, wife of Charles Bellamy, v. 133.
—— of Kethock's Mill, Thomas, vi. 176.
—— of Kildrummie, Charles Edward, v. 180.
—— of Kindrocht, George, vii. 439.
—— of Kinellar, John, vii. 445, 447.
—— —— his wife, Henrietta Fraser, vii. 445.
—— of Kintessock, Alexander, viii. 339.
—— of Kirkconnell, Alexander, ancestor of the family of, ix. 117.
—— of Kirkdale, George, v. 108.
—— of Kirkland of Balmaclellan, William, v. 113.
—— of Knockblewis, Patrick, i. 84.
—— of Larglegastell and Markleif, William, v. 104.
—— of Law, Arthur, vii. 562.
—— —— Katharine, wife of col. George Sempill, vii. 562.
—— of Lesmoir, Alexander, iv. 73, 126.
—— —— his wife, Mariota Forbes, iv. 73.
—— —— James, iv. 22.
—— —— his 2nd wife, Margaret Ogilvy, iv. 22.
—— —— James, iii. 538.
—— —— Sir James, vii. 445.
—— —— Sir John, i. 88.
—— —— his wife, Janet Gordon, i. 88.
—— —— William, ancestor of the family of, i. 82; iv. 516.
—— of Letterfourie, Alexander, ancestor of the family of, viii. 573.
—— of Littlehass, William, v. 113.

Gordon of Locheil, Sir George, iv. 536.
—— of Lochinvar, Sir Adam de, 1st laird, v. 99.
—— —— Sir Alexander, 4th laird, v. 100.
—— —— James, 9th laird, v. 106, 261; vii. 119.
—— —— his wife, Margaret Crichton, v. 108.
—— —— Sir John, 7th laird, v. 101, 102, 147.
—— —— his alleged 1st wife, Annabella Boyd, v. 102, 147; viii. 426.
—— —— his 2nd wife, Elizabeth Lindsay, v. 104.
—— —— Sir John, 10th laird, justiciar of Galloway, ii. 472; v. 108, 110; ix. 118.
—— —— his 1st wife, Juliana Home, v. 111.
—— —— his 2nd wife, Elizabeth Maxwell, iv. 412; v. 112; ix. 118.
—— —— Sir John, 2nd bart., v. 109, 117.
—— —— his wife, Jean Campbell, v. 118.
—— —— Sir Robert, 8th laird, iv. 153 *bis*; v. 104, 105.
—— —— his wife, Mariota Acarsane, v. 106.
—— —— Sir Robert, 1st bart., v. 112, 113.
—— —— his wife, Elizabeth Ruthven, iv. 266; v. 116; ix. 118 *bis*.
—— —— Roger, 3rd laird, v. 99.
—— —— Roger, 5th laird, v. 100.
—— —— William de, 2nd laird, v. 98.
—— —— William, 6th laird, v. 100.
—— of Lochinver, John, iv. 109.
—— of Longormes, John, dean of Salisbury, viii. 345; ix. 110.
—— —— his wife, Geneviève Petaw, ix. 110.
—— of Lothmore, Alexander, viii. 338.
—— of Marle, George, viii. 337.
—— of Melgund, Laurence, 4th son of 1st marquess of Huntly, iv. 545.
—— of Mellerstaines, George, iv. 550.
—— of Methlic, James, 1st laird, i. 83.
—— —— James, 3rd laird, i. 83.
—— —— James, 5th laird, i. 85.
—— —— James, 6th laird, i. 86.
—— —— Patrick, 2nd laird, i. 83.
—— —— Patrick, 4th laird, i. 83.
—— of Midmar, Sir Alexander, 3rd son of 1st earl of Huntly, iv. 523, 525.
—— —— his wife, Beatrice Hay, iv. 525.
—— —— Alexander, i. 115.
—— —— his contr. wife, Janet Ogilvy, i. 115.
—— —— George, i. 115.
—— of Muirfad, John, v. 108.
—— —— Robert, 3rd son of James G. of Lochinvar, v. 109.
—— —— William, v. 108.
—— of Mundork in Crosherie, William, ancestor of the family of, v. 104; ix. 117.
—— of Navidale, Alexander, viii. 338.
—— —— Sir Alexander, 5th son of 11th earl of Sutherland, viii. 346.
—— —— his wife, Margaret Macleod, viii. 346.
Gordon of Nethermuir, David, supposed ancestor of the family of, i. 85.
—— of Newark, Thomas, M.D., iv. 117.
—— —— his wife, Margaret Fraser, iv. 117.
—— of New Galloway, Sir John, v. 119.
—— of Norham, John, iv. 109.
—— of Park, Ernest, viii. 136.
—— —— his wife, Mary Dalrymple-Elphinstone, viii. 136.
—— —— Sir James, iii. 544; iv. 65; vii. 445.
—— —— his 1st wife, Helen Fraser, vii. 445.
—— —— his 2nd wife, Margaret Elphinstone, iii. 544.
—— —— Sir John, iii. 323.
—— —— John, his eldest son, iii. 323.
—— —— his wife, Elizabeth Graham, iii. 323.
—— —— Sir John, i. 126.
—— —— his wife, Helen Ogilvy, i. 126.
—— —— Sir John, vii. 445.
—— of Penninghame, Alexander, v. 108, 123.
—— —— John, v. 108.
—— —— his wife, Jean Glendonwyn, v. 108.
—— —— John, v. 108.
—— —— William, 2nd son of James G. of Lochinvar, v. 108, 123; ix. 94.
—— —— his wife, Helen Stewart, iv. 156; v. 108.
—— —— William, son of John G., v. 108.
—— —— his wife, Ann Kennedy, v. 108; ix. 118.
—— of Boreland of Penninghame, Sir John, v. 109.
—— of Mains of Penninghame, William ancestor of the family of, v. 104.
—— of Pitlurg, John, ancestor of the family of, i. 82; iv. 516; vii. 407.
—— —— his wife, Elizabeth Abernetby, vii. 407.
—— —— John, iii. 539; iv. 57.
—— —— his wife, Isabel Forbes, iv. 57.
—— —— Sir Robert, i. 442.
—— —— his wife, Jean Stewart, i. 442.
—— of Prestonhall, Adam, commander of the Forces in Scotland, iv. 552; viii. 514.
—— —— his wife, Jane Drummond, i. 489; iv. 553.
—— of Rothiemay, John, iv. 127.
—— —— William, ii. 16; iv. 60, 126.
—— —— his wife, Katharine Forbes, iv. 60.
—— —— purchaser from lord Saltoun, vii. 442.
—— of Rusco, Sir Robert, 2nd son of Sir John G. of Lochinvar, v. 105.
—— —— William, 2nd son of John G. of Muirfad, v. 108.
—— —— his wife, Margaret Gordon, v. 108.
—— of Ruthven, Patrick, i. 158.
—— —— Thomas, i. 82; iv. 516 *bis*.
—— —— his 1st wife, * Hay, iv. 516.
—— —— his 2nd wife, * Innes, iv. 516.
—— —— his 3rd wife, * Chisholm, iv. 516.

* Name unknown.

Gordon of Sallagh, v. 226, 227.
— of Sallachy, vii. 169.
— of Saphak, James, i. 85.
— — Robert, i. 87.
— — his wife, Elizabeth Auchinleck, i. 85.
— of Scardargue, John, i. 82; iv. 515; vii. 407.
— — his wife, Elizabeth *or* Margaret Maitland, iv. 516.
— of Schivas, Adam, 2nd son of 2nd earl of Huntly, iv. 529.
— — William, iv. 275, 530.
— — his wife, Janet Ogilvy, ii. 7; iv. 530.
— of Seaton, James, vi. 177.
— of Seggieden, James, iv. 22.
— — his wife, Margaret Ogilvy, iv. 22.
— of Shirmers, Sir Alexander, v. 100.
— — William, v. 125.
— — his wife, Jean Gordon, v. 125.
— of Slagnaw, Alexander, v. 109.
— — his wife, Janet Kennedy, v. 109.
— of Stitchill, Sir Adam de, 1st laird, iv. 511, 512; v. 98; vi. 291.
— — Sir Alexander, 4th laird, v. 100; ix. 117.
— — James, 9th laird, v. 106.
— — Sir John, 7th laird, v. 101, 102.
— — Sir John, 10th laird, v. 108, 110.
— — Sir John, 12th laird, v. 117.
— — Sir Robert, 8th laird, v. 103, 104, 105.
— — Sir Robert, 11th laird, v. 112, 113.
— — Roger, 3rd laird, v. 99, 100.
— — Roger, 5th laird, v. 100.
— — William de, 2nd laird, iv. 512, 513; v. 98.
— — William, 6th laird, v. 100.
— of Straloch, Sir Robert, i. 308.
— of Strathavon, Alexander, vii. 461.
— — his wife, Janet Grant, iv. 533; vii. 461.
— — Alexander, 2nd son of 5th earl of Huntly, iv. 541.
— — his wife, Agnes Sinclair, ii. 342; iii. 571; iv. 541; ix. 51.
— of Strathbogie, Sir Adam, iv. 512.
— — his wife, Amabilla, iv. 512.
— — John de, i. 82.
— of Strathdee, Sir George, iv. 535.
— of Strathdon, Alexander, 2nd son of 5th earl of Huntly, iii. 571, 572; iv. 73, 541.
— — Alexander, his son, iii. 572.
— of Strathoun, Alexander, 2nd son of 3rd earl of Huntly, iv. 533.
— of Strome, Sir George, iv. 535.
— of Tarpersie, George, iv. 28.
— of Tarves, James, i. 85.
— of Techmuiry, James, vii. 438.
— — his wife, Jane Fraser of Techmuiry, vii. 438.
Gordon of Tilliehilt, John, 4th son of Jas. G. of Methlic and Haddo, i. 85, 86.
— of Tillichaudie, George, viii. 338 *n.*
— — his wife, Helenor Gordon, viii. 338.
— — John, viii. 337.
— of Tochir, Sir George, iv. 536.
— of Torscrachane, Sir John, v. 102.
— — Sir Robert, v. 105.
— of Troquhain, George, 3rd son of William G. of Lochinvar, v. 102.
— of Wardhouse, Adam, ancestor of the family of, iv. 525.
— — Arthur, vii. 562.
— — Charles Edward, v. 180.
— — his wife, Charlotte Boyd, v. 180.
— — Katharine, vii. 562.
— of Whitehill, William, ancestor of the family of, v. 104.
— of Whytepark, Roger, v. 270.
— — his wife, Florence M'Ghie, v. 270.
— Adam, son of Patrick G. of Glenbucket, i. 304.
— Adam, dean of Caithness, iv. 22, 525.
— Adam, supposed brother of Richer G. of Gordon, iv. 508, 509.
— Adam, father of Adam G., 1232, iv. 509.
— Adam, his son, iv. 509.
— Adam, illeg. son of John G. of Essie, iv. 516 *bis*.
— Adam, 2nd son of 2nd earl of Huntly, iv. 529; viii. 336, 360.
— — his wife, Elizabeth, countess of Sutherland, iv. 530; viii. 334, 336.
— Adam, commander of the Forces, iv. 552; viii. 514.
— Adam, captain 81st regt., collector of customs, Portpatrick, v. 132.
— — his wife, Harriet Davies, v. 132.
— Adam, brother of John G. of Avachie, vi. 575.
— — his wife, Marjorie Sandilands, vi. 575.
— Adam, Ferrar, viii. 337.
— Adam, lieut.-col. in Swedish service viii. 348.
— Agnes, wife of James Gordon of Haddo, i. 86.
— Agnes, wife of (1) Jas. Ogilvy, and (2) John Gordon, ii. 9.
— Agnes, wife of Sir Gilbert Hay of Kilmalamak, iv. 531.
— Agnes, wife of James Ogilvy of Findlater, iv. 531.
— Agnes, wife of (1) Wm. Maxwell of Kelton and Buittle, and (2) John Lindsay of Wauchope, v. 125; vi. 488.
— Agnes, wife of Thomas Maclellan of Auchlane, v. 259.
— Alexander, rector of Fetteresso, precentor of Moray, bishop of Aberdeen, i. 83: ii. 6.

Gordon, Alexander, 6th son of Jas. G. of Methlic and Haddo, i. 85.
— Alexander, senator of the College of Justice, lord Rockville, i. 91; iii. 237.
— — his wife, Anne Duff, i. 92; iii. 237; viii. 156.
— Alexander, lieut.-col., 3rd son of lord Rockville, i. 92.
— Sir Alexander, lieut.-col., K.C.B., i. 93.
— Alexander, bishop of Glasgow, of Galloway, and of the Isles, titular archbp. of Athens, iv. 154, 155, 156, 533; viii. 215 *bis*; ix. 110.
— — his wife, Barbara Logie of Ennis, iv. 533.
— Alexander, illeg. son of John G. of Essie, iv. 516 *bis*.
— Alexander, legtd. son of 2nd earl of Huntly, iv. 531.
— Alexander, 35th regt. of Foot, 2nd Life Guards, iv. 557.
— Alexander, 'Picture Gordon,' v. 104 *n*.
— Alexander, 3rd son of John G. of Muirfad, v. 108.
— Alexander, in Penninghame, v. 109.
— Alexander, master of Sutherland, viii. 338.
— — his wife, Janet Stewart, i. 443; viii. 338.
— Alexander Henry, i. 92.
— — his wife, Katharine Douglas, i. 92.
— Alexander Stuart, ii. 279.
— Allan, i. 391.
— — his wife, Olivia Rowlandson Miln, i. 390.
— Alice, dau. of 4th earl of Aberdeen, i. 95.
— Alicia, dau. of George, Lord Haddo, i. 93.
— Anna, wife of 9th earl of Eglinton, i. 89; iii. 456; ix. 5.
— Annabel, wife of Cuthbert Macdowell of Spotts, ix. 117.
— Anne, wife of 4th earl of Dumfries, i. 90; iii. 237; viii. 156.
— Anne, wife of 2d earl of Aberdeen, i. 91; iv. 553; ix. 5 *bis*.
— Anne, wife of John Cathcart of Genock, i. 92.
— Anne. wife of Edward Place of Skelton Grange, i. 94.
— Ann, dau. of 1st earl of Aboyne, i. 103.
— Ann, wife of 3rd viscount of Arbuthnott, i. 310; viii. 352.
— Ann, wife of 3rd earl of Moray, iv. 545; vi. 320.
— Ann, wife of 3rd earl of Perth, iv. 547; vii. 51; ix. 111, 149.
— Anne, wife of Sir Miles Crouly, iv. 549; ix. 111.
— Anne, wife of Mr. Alexander Chalmers, iv. 555.
Gordon, Anne, wife of 9th earl of Kellie, v. 94.
— Anne, wife of George Kinnaird, v. 211; ix. 121.
— Armyne Evelyn, iv. 561.
— Arthur, v. 413.
— — his wife, Alison Lindsay, v. 413.
— Barbara, wife of (1) *, (2), Gilbert Keith of Troup, and (3), John Elphinstone, iii. 539.
— Barbara, wife of (1) Mr. Anthony Stewart, and (2) Alex. Agnew of Ardoch, iv. 155; ix, 94.
— Beatrice, wife of lord Alex. Kennedy, ii. 501.
— Beatrix, wife of John Butter of Gormack, viii. 337.
— Beatrice, wife of Wm. Sinclair of Dunbeath, viii. 339.
— Beatrice Mary, wife of Francis Henry Meade, iv. 561.
— Bertrand, 3rd son of 10th marquess of Huntly, iv. 560.
— Caroline, dau. of lieut.-col. Lockhart G., ix. 7.
— Caroline Katharine, dau. of 4th earl of Aberdeen, i. 95.
— Cecil James, capt. 42nd Highlanders, iv. 560; ix. 112.
— — his wife, Emily Moore, iv. 560; ix. 112.
— Charles, apprenticed to G. Reid, i. 87; ix. 5.
— Charles, capt. 56th regt., 6th son of 2nd earl of Aberdeen, i. 92.
— Sir Charles, K.C.B., colonel 42nd Highlanders, i. 93.
— Charles, 4th son of 2nd marquess of Huntly, iv. 547.
— Charles, capt. 54th regt., lieut. 89th regt., iv. 552.
— Charles, 5th son of William, lord Strathnaver, viii. 356.
— Charles Edward Park, lieut.-gen., C.B., viii. 398.
— Charles Henry Granville, lieut. 3rd batt. Gordon Highlanders, v. 561.
— Charles Shipley, ii. 279.
— — his wife, Katharine Stirling-Stuart, ii. 279.
— Charles William, M.P., i. 92.
— Charlotte, dau. of 2nd duke of Gordon, iv. 553.
— Charlotte, wife of Charles, 4th duke of Richmond and Lennox, iv. 557, 558; v. 366; ix. 111.
— Charlotte Sophia, dau. of 9th marquess of Huntly, iv. 560.
— Christian, wife of 3rd lord Forbes, iv. 52, 525.
— Christian, wife of Sir Robert Menzies, iv. 533; ix. 110.

* Name unknown.

Gordon, Christian Frederick, iv. 561.
—— —— his wife, Margaret Humble, iv. 561.
—— Clementina, dau. of John G. of Glentanner, i. 104; ix. 6 *bis*.
—— Cosmo, col. of 3rd regt. of Foot Guards, 4th son of 2nd earl of Aberdeen, i. 91.
—— Cosmo, general, 4th son of lord Rockville, i. 92.
—— Cosmo, son of general Cosmo G. i. 92.
—— David, 5th son of Sir John G. of Lochinvar, v. 105.
—— David, 2nd son of 14th earl of Sutherland, viii. 352.
—— Douglas, 2nd son of 4th earl of Aboyne, i. 105; ix. 7.
—— —— his wife, Louisa Leslie, i. 105.
—— Douglas William Cope, M.P., lieut. Coldstream Guards, iv. 560.
—— Dudley Gladstone, 2nd son of 7th earl of Aberdeen, i. 99.
—— Edom o', iv. 537.
—— Edward Maxwell, lieut. 22nd Foot, v. 132.
—— Eleanor, 6th dau. of 2nd earl of Huntly, iv. 531; ix. 110.
—— Eleanor, wife of 14th lord Saltoun, vii. 447.
—— Eleanor, contracted to R. Monro of Foulis, viii. 343.
—— Elena Mary, wife of major G. L. Wickham, iv. 561.
—— Elizabeth, wife of Thos. Chene of Essilmont, i. 84.
—— Elizabeth, dau. of lord Rockville, i. 92.
—— Elizabeth. dau. of 2nd earl of Aberdeen, i. 93.
—— Elizabeth, dau. of 2nd earl of Aboyne, i. 103.
—— Elizabeth, wife of John Mackenzie, 2nd son of 1st earl of Cromarty, i. 103; iii. 77; ix. 6.
—— Elizabeth, wife of 4th earl of Atholl, i. 445; iv. 539.
—— Elizabeth, wife of 2nd lord Torthorwald, ii. 394; v. 113.
—— Elizabeth, wife of, (1) Nicholas, 2nd earl of Erroll, and (2) John, lord Kennedy, ii. 457; iii. 565; iv. 525.
—— Elizabeth, wife of George (Home), earl of Dunbar, iii. 288.
—— Elizabeth, wife of (1) Alexander Ogilvy of Deskford, and (2) John Gordon of Deskford, iv. 22, 23, 27, 525, 536.
—— Elizabeth, wife of 16th lord Forbes, iv. 65.
—— Elizabeth, wife of Jas. Crichton of Frendraught and Kinnairdie, iv. 128.
—— Elizabeth, wife of (1) Alex. Maclellan of Gelston, and (2) Sir Robert Maxwell of Spottes, iv. 411.
—— Elizabeth, wife of John, 7th lord Herries of Terregles, lord Maxwell, 3rd earl of Nithsdale, iv. 417; v. 116; vi. 487; ix. 144.
Gordon, Elizabeth, wife of Alexander Livingston, iv. 545; v. 447.
—— Elizabeth, wife of rev. John Skelly, iv. 553.
—— Elizabeth, wife of Sir Wm. Douglas of Drumlanrig, v. 105; vii. 118.
—— Elizabeth, wife of (1) Uchtred Macdowall, and (2) Alex. Livingstone of Little Airds, v. 106.
—— Elizabeth, wife of (1) William Grierson of Brocloch, and (2) Ninian Adair of Kinhilt, v. 110; ix. 118.
—— Elizabeth, wife of (1) Wm. Maxwell, and (2) Samuel Brown, v. 125; ix. 119.
—— Elizabeth, wife of 3rd earl Marischal, iv. 530; vi. 43.
—— Elizabeth, wife of [Forbes] of Lethintie, viii. 338.
—— Elizabeth, wife of James Wemyss of Wemyss, viii. 358, 510.
—— Elizabeth, wife of Alex. Gordon of Airds, ix. 118.
—— Elizabeth, dau. of Jas. G. of Barncrosh, ix. 118.
—— Ellen Frances, wife of 12th lord Torphichen, viii. 398.
—— Esmé Stuart, iv. 561; ix. 112.
—— —— his wife, Elizabeth A. P. Brown, iv. 561.
—— Ethelreda Caroline, wife of lieut.-col. Henry Wickham, iv. 561.
—— Euphemia, wife of 5th viscount of Strathallan, viii. 233; ix. 162 *bis*.
—— Evelyn Elizabeth, wife of 1st earl of Ancaster, iv. 561.
—— Frances, dau. of John, *de jure* viscount of Kenmure, v. 133.
—— Frances Isabella Ker, dau. of lord William G., iv. 554; v. 19; ix. 111.
—— Francis, 2nd son of 1st marquess of Huntly, iv. 544.
—— Francis Arthur, lieut.-col. 1st Life Guards, iv. 560, 561; ix. 112.
—— —— his wife, Isabel Grant, iv. 560.
—— Francis Mackenzie, lieut. 20th Madras Native Infantry, v. 132.
—— George, eldest son of Patrick G. of Methlic and Haddo, i. 84.
—— —— his wife, * Hay, i. 84.
—— George, elder son of James G. of Haddo, i. 86.
—— —— his wife, Margaret Bannerman, i. 86.
—— George, 2nd son of 1st earl of Aboyne, i. 103; ix. 6.
—— George, R.N., 2nd son of John G. of Glentanner, i. 104; ix. 6.
—— George, R.N., M.P.; of the 'No Popery' riots, i. 484; iv. 554.

* Name unknown.

Gordon, George, 3rd son of Alex. G. of Lesmoir, iv. 127.
— George, son of bishop Alexander G., iv. 533.
— George, rector of Chesterton, iv. 559.
— — his wife, Charlotte Anne Vaughan, iv. 559.
— George, Tobago, v. 102.
— George, 4th son of Sir Robt. G. of Lochinvar, v. 106.
— George, 6th son of 12th earl of Sutherland, viii. 348.
— — his wife, Rose Macdonell, viii. 348.
— George, 6th son of William, lord Strathnaver, viii. 356.
— George, major Indian Army, viii. 113.
— — his wife, Mary Elizabeth Lindsay Carnegie, viii. 113.
— George, captain in col. de Vilage's regt., viii. 374.
— — his wife, Isabel Livingston, viii. 374.
— George, eldest son of Alexander, lord Gordon, ix. 20.
— George, eldest son of 3rd earl of Huntly, ix. 110.
— — his contracted wife, Katharine or Elizabeth Campbell, ix. 110.
— George, elder son of 4th marquess of Huntly, ix. 111.
— George, M.D., Banff, ix. 121.
— Georgina, wife of 6th duke of Bedford, i. 70; iv. 557.
— Grace Cicelie, wife of 5th earl of Lonsdale, iv. 561.
— Grace Margaret, wife of Wm. Graham of Mossknow, i. 104; ix. 6.
— Granville Armyne, iv. 561; ix. 112 *bis*.
— — his 1st wife, Charlotte D'Olier Roe, iv. 561.
— — his 2nd wife, Margaret Humble, iv. 561.
— Granville Cecil Douglas, Scots Guards, iv. 561.
— Grizel, wife of Jas. Grant of Knockando, i. 103.
— Grizel, wife of 1st earl of Galloway, iv. 160; v. 113.
— Grissell, dau. of John G. of Greenlaw, v. 125.
— Grizel, wife of James Gordon, v. 126.
— Grizel, wife of Mr. Robert Gordon, v. 124, 126.
— Hamilton, ii. 279.
— Harriet, wife of W. A. Lindsay of Deerpark, i. 98; iii. 46.
— Harriet Albinia Louisa, wife of Charles Elphinstone-Dalrymple, viii. 134.
— Harry Wolrige, captain 79th Cameron Highlanders, iii. 586.
— Helen, wife of George Kinnaird, i. 103; v. 211; ix. 6, 121.
Gordon, Helen, wife of (1) Sir Wm. Sinclair of Westray, and (2) David Hepburn, iv. 531.
— Helen, wife of Sir Thos. Maclellan of Bombie, v. 110, 264.
— Helen, wife of Sir Jas. Colquhoun of Luss, viii. 356.
— Helen, wife of Sir Wm. Sinclair of Warsetter, iv. 531; vii. 570.
— Helen, dau. of John, 15th earl of Sutherland, viii. 355.
— Helenor, wife of G. Gordon of Tilliwhoudie, viii. 338.
— Henrietta, wife of Robert Gordon of Hallhead, i. 93.
— Henrietta, dau. of John, viscount Melgum, i. 100; ix. 6.
— Henrietta, wife of (1) George, lord Seton, and (2) John, lord Linton, iv. 547; viii. 406, 595; ix. 111.
— Henrietta, dau. of 2nd duke of Gordon, iv. 553.
— Henrietta, wife of John Dalzell of Barncrosh, v. 129.
— Henrietta Ellen, wife of R. M. Middleton, vi. 179.
— Henry, 2nd son of John G. of Aikenhead, ii. 279.
— Henry, in the Polish service, iv. 547.
— Henry, major H.E.I.C.S., iv. 559.
— — his wife, Louisa Payne, iv. 559.
— Ian Archibald, 3rd son of 7th earl of Aberdeen, i. 99.
— Isabel, wife of Alex. Allardice of that Ilk, i. 83.
— Isabella, wife of 3rd lord Cromartie, iii. 80.
— Isabel, wife of 3rd earl of Erroll, iii. 566; iv. 530.
— Isobel, wife of (1) Uchtred Macdowall, and (2) Alex. Livingstone, v. 106.
— Isabel, wife of Alex. Fraser of Philorth, v. 116; vii. 441.
— Isabel, wife of John M'Ghie of Balmaghie, v. 126.
— Isabella, wife of rev. C. Douglas of Earl's Gift, vi. 383.
— James, rector of Lonmay, i. 83.
— James, 5th son of Jas. G. of Methlie and Haddo, i. 85.
— James, 3rd son of 1st earl of Aberdeen, i. 89.
— James, 3rd son of lieut.-col. John G. of Glentanner, i. 104; ix. 6.
— James, 2nd son of Geo. G. of Midmar, i. 115.
— James, Jesuit, professor of Hebrew and Divinity, 5th son of 4th earl of Huntly, iv. 21, 537.
— James, 4th son of 2nd earl of Huntly, iv. 530.
— James, chancellor of Moray, iv. 533.

Gordon, James, 2nd son of 2nd marquess of Huntly, iv. 547.
— James, of the Lesmoir family, vi. 554.
— — his wife, Margaret Menzies, vi. 554.
— James, page to Sir Robert G. of Lochinvar, v. 114.
— James, son of John G. of Beoch, v. 117.
— — his wife, Rosina Gordon, v. 117.
— James, Coatbridge, v. 125 *n*.
— James, Welsh Fusiliers, v. 125.
— — his wife, Grizel Gordon, v. 126.
— James, 3rd son of 6th viscount of Kenmure, v. 129.
— James, 100th regt. of Foot, v. 133.
— James Chisholm, vi. 179.
— James Henry, 2nd son of 5th earl of Aberdeen, i. 97.
— Jane, wife of Hugh Primrose Lindsay, i. 92, 528.
— Jane, dau. of 4th earl of Aberdeen, i. 95.
— Jane, wife of Huistean Mackay of Farr, vii. 166; viii. 346.
— Janet, wife of Alex. Forbes of Groddic and Towie, i. 85.
— Janet, wife of Thos. Davidson, i. 86.
— Janet, wife of Sir John Gordon of Lesmoir, i. 88.
— Janet, wife of Andrew Arbuthnott of Fiddes, i. 286; ix. 16.
— Janet, wife of 3rd earl of Argyll, i. 338; iv. 533.
— Janet, wife of James Gordon, ii. 9.
— Janet, wife of (1) Alexander, master of Crawford, (2) Patrick, master of Gray, (3) Patrick Butter, and (4) Jas. Halkerston, iii. 24, 25; iv. 279, 530; ix. 61.
— Janet, wife of (1) Jas. Crichton of Auchingoul, and (2) Thos. Gordon of Grandoun, iv. 126.
— Janet, wife of 5th earl of Glencairn, iv. 242; v. 109.
— Janet, wife of George Herries of Maidenpaup, iv. 405.
— Janet, wife of James Innes of Innes, iv. 526; vii. 354.
— Janet, wife of (1) Alex. Innes, and (2) Thomas Gordon, iv. 539; viii. 343.
— Janet, wife of (1) Alex. Stewart of Garlies, and (2) Sir Wm. Keith of Inverugie, v. 105; ix. 94.
— Janet, dau. of Wm. G. of Penninghame, v. 109.
— Janet, wife of Patrick Agnew of Salchary, v. 109.
— Janet, wife of John Macdowall of Garthland, v. 113.
— Janet, wife of 2nd lord Fraser of Lovat, v. 524, 525.
— Janet, wife of principal George Middleton, vi. 177.
Gordon, Janet, wife of Sir P. Dunbar of Westfield, viii. 339.
— Janet, wife of G. Sinclair of Ulbster, viii. 357.
— Janet, contracted to Archd. Mure of Torhousmure, ix. 118.
— Jean, wife of (1) Claud, lord Strabane, and (2) Sir Phelim O'Neile, i. 50; iv. 545.
— Jean, wife of John Forbes of Waterton, i. 87.
— Jean, dau. of 1st earl of Aberdeen, i. 89.
— Jean, wife of Sir Geo. Ogilvy, ii. 12.
— Jean, wife of (1) James, 4th earl of Bothwell, (2) Alexander, 11th earl of Sutherland, and (3) Alexander Ogilvy of Boyne, ii. 166; iv. 539; viii. 345; ix. 41.
— Jean, wife of George, 5th earl of Caithness, ii. 343; iv. 541; ix. 51.
— Jean, wife of 4th earl of Dunfermline, iii. 375; iv. 549; ix. 78.
— Jean, wife of 2nd earl of Haddington, iv. 316, 547.
— Jean, wife of (1) Alex. Innes, and (2) Thos. Gordon, iv. 539; vii. 355; viii. 343; ix. 52.
— Jean, wife of 2nd titular duke of Perth, iv. 551; vii. 54.
— Jean, dau. of 2nd duke of Gordon, iv. 553.
— Jean, wife of Wm. Gordon of Shirmers, v. 125.
— Jean, wife of Patrick Grant of Rothiemurchus, vii. 463.
— Jean, wife of capt. R. Stewart of Eday, viii. 351.
— Jean, wife of James, lord Maitland, v. 311; viii. 355.
— Jean, wife of David Arnot of Chapel, ix. 118.
— Joanna, wife of 10th earl of Kellie, v. 94.
— Johanna, wife of 7th earl of Stair, viii. 158.
— John, 3rd son of Sir Adam G. of Gordon, i. 82; iv. 513.
— John, 2nd son of 2nd earl of Aberdeen, i. 90.
— John, admiral R.N., i. 93.
— John, 5th son of 1st marquess of Huntly, i. 100; iv. 545.
— John, 5th son of 1st earl of Aboyne, i. 103; ix. 6.
— John, lt.-col. H.E.I.C.S., i. 104; ix. 6.
— John, son of Patrick G. of Glenbucket, i. 304.
— Sir John, M.D., i. 468.
— — his wife, Anna Murray, i. 467.
— John, master of Huntly, iv. 155.
— — his wife, Jean Stewart, iv. 155.
— John, v. 260.
— — his wife, Isobel McDowall, v. 260.

Gordon, John, at Keirshill, v. 125 *n*.
—— —— his wife, Christian McBurnie, v. 125 *n*.
—— John, lieut. R.N., v. 132.
—— John, vii. 512.
—— —— his wife, Frances Mackenzie, vii. 512.
—— John, dean of Salisbury, viii. 345; ix. 110.
—— —— his wife, Geneviève Petaw, ix. 110.
—— John Frederick, admiral R.N., iv. 559.
—— —— his wife, Augusta Fitzclarence, iv. 559.
—— Jonet, contracted to Geo. Morrison of Barrak, i. 87.
—— Jonet, wife of James Ogilvy of that Ilk and Findlater, iv. 25.
—— Katharine, wife of (1) Cosmo, 3rd duke of Gordon, and (2) Gen. Staats Long Morris, i. 90; iv. 554; ix. 111.
—— Katharine, wife of Robt. Hepburn of Clerkington, i. 92.
—— Katharine, dau. of 3rd earl of Aberdeen, i. 94.
—— Katharine, wife of * Williams, i. 104; ix. 6.
—— Katharine, dau. of 4th earl of Aboyne, i. 104; ix. 7.
—— Katharine, contr. to Archibald, eldest son of George, 4th earl of Angus, i. 182; iv. 526.
—— Katharine, wife of (1) 2nd viscount of Arbuthnott, and (2) Sir David Carnegie, i. 308; viii. 78; ix. 16.
—— Katharine, wife of James Elphinstone of Barnes, iii. 538; ix. 85.
—— Katharine, wife of W. Forbes of Pitsligo, iv. 73.
—— Katharine, wife of (1) Perkin Warbeck, (2) James Strangeways of Fyfield, (3) Sir Matthew Cradock, and (4) Christopher Assheton, iv. 530.
—— Katharine, wife of John Andrew, count Morsztyn, iv. 548.
—— Katharine, wife of Francis, 7th earl of Wemyss, iv. 553; viii. 513.
—— Katharine, wife of capt. Thos. Booker, iv. 555.
—— Katharine, wife of capt. John Anderson, iv. 557.
—— Katharine, wife of Patrick Agnew of Salchary, v. 106.
—— Katharine, dau. of Wm. G. of Penninghame, v. 109.
—— Katharine, wife of Thos. McCulloch of Cardoness, v. 110; ix. 118.
—— Katharine, wife of James Innes of Rothmackenzie and Cromie, vii. 355.
—— Katharine Eliza, wife of 10th lord Balfour of Burleigh, i. 98, 555.

* Name unknown.

Gordon, Katharine Susan, wife of 1st lord Chesham, iv. 560.
—— Laurence, commendator of Glenluce, iv. 155.
—— Lewis, 4th son of 2nd duke of Gordon, iv. 552.
—— Lewis, R.N., 2nd son of 10th marquess of Huntly, iv. 560.
—— Lilias, wife of Wm. Hay of Fetterletter, iii. 573.
—— Lockhart, judge-advocate-general of Bengal, i. 104; ix. 6.
—— —— his 1st wife, Isabella Levi, i. 104; ix. 6 *bis*.
—— —— his 2nd wife, Catharine Wallop, i. 104; ix. 6 *bis*.
—— Lockhart, rev., i. 104; ix. 7 *bis*.
—— London Harcourt, i. 104; ix. 7.
—— Louisa, wife of Charles, 2nd marquess Cornwallis, iv. 557.
—— Louise, wife of Sir Robert Gordon of Gordonstoun, viii. 345; ix. 110.
—— Madelina, wife of (1) Sir Robert Sinclair of Stevenston, and (2) C. F. Palmer of Luckley Park, iv. 557.
—— Margaret, wife of Alex. Fraser of Durris, i. 83.
—— Margaret, dau. of 1st earl of Aberdeen, i. 89.
—— Margaret, wife of Sir B. A. Coutts Trotter, i. 92, 524.
—— Margaret, wife of Wm. Beckford of Fonthill-Gifford, i. 105; ix. 7.
—— Margaret, dau. of Kenneth G. of Cluny, i. 306.
—— Margaret, wife of Patrick (Hepburn) 1st earl of Bothwell, ii. 152, 165; iv. 530.
—— Margaret, wife of P. Dunbar of Kilconquhar, iii. 278.
—— Margaret, contr. to 2nd earl of Erroll, iii. 565; iv. 525.
—— Margaret, wife of John, master of Forbes, iv. 58, 59, 539; ix. 91.
—— Margaret, wife of 6th viscount Frendraught, iv. 133 *bis*.
—— Margaret, wife of (1) Geo. Abercromby of Leys and Birkenbog, and (2) Alexander Cumming, iv. 179; viii. 338.
—— Margaret, wife of Hew Rose of Kilravock, iv. 526.
—— Margaret, *error for* Jean, wife of (1) A. Innes, and (2) T. Gordon, iv. 539; viii. 343 *n*.
—— Margaret, wife of Thos. Maclellan of Bomby, v. 102, 259.
—— Margaret, wife of (1) Bertilmo Glendonwyn of Glencorse, and (2) Patrick Sinclair of Spotts, v. 105; ix. 117.
—— Margaret, wife of John Gordon of Rusco, v. 108.
—— Margaret, wife of Hugh Gordon of Grange, v. 109.

Gordon, Margaret, wife of Hugh Campbell of Terrinzean, v. 111, 498.
— Margaret, wife of Alex. Kennedy of Bargany, v. 112; ix. 118.
— Margaret, wife of John M'Naught of Kilquhanatie, v. 116.
— Margaret, wife of Wm. Maclellan of Balmangan, v. 270.
— Margaret, wife of Sir Wm. Douglas of Hawick, v. 109; vii. 129.
— Margaret, wife of principal Alexander Middleton, vi. 176.
— Margaret, wife of Mungo Grant of Duthil, vii. 472.
— Margaret, dau. of 10th earl of Sutherland, viii. 343.
— Margaret, dau. of 3rd earl of Huntly, ix. 110.
— Margaret, illeg. dau. of Sir Robt. G. of Lochinvar, ix. 118.
— Margaret Ethel, wife of 3rd baron Harlech, iv. 561.
— Marion, wife of Sir Alex. Gordon of Earlston, v. 125, 131.
— Marion, wife of Alex. Lennox of Callie, ix. 118.
— Marjorie Adeline, wife of 1st baron Pentland, i. 99.
— Martha, wife of John Udny of Udny, i. 89.
— Mary, dau. of James G. of Haddo, i. 86.
— Mary, wife of 12th lord Saltoun, i. 89; vii. 446.
— Mary, wife of Thos. Horton of Howroyde Hall, i. 94.
— Mary, wife of 8th lord Polwarth, i. 97; vii. 86.
— Mary, wife of 1st marquess of Douglas, i. 204; iii. 216; iv. 545, 546.
— Mary, wife of Sir Walter Fitzgilbert of Cadzow, iv. 341, 513.
— Mary, alleged wife of Sir David Fitz Walter, iv. 343 *n*.
— Mary, wife of Alexander Irvine of Drum, iv. 548.
— Mary, wife of (1) Adam Urquhart of Meldrum, and (2) James, 4th earl of Perth, iv. 549; vii. 53.
— Mary, dau. of 2nd duke of Gordon, iv. 553.
— Mary, wife of F. C. W. Seymour, iv. 560.
— Mary, wife of Wm. Maclellan of Barscobe, v. 117.
— Mary, wife of Sir P. Maxwell of Springkell, v. 126.
— Mary, wife of David Ross of Balnagown, viii. 346.
— Mary Katharine, wife of Edmund Turnor, iv. 561.
— Patricia Heron, wife of Wm. Ramsay Maule of Panmure, vii. 24; ix. 66.
Gordon, Patrick, eldest son of James G. of Methlic and Haddo. i. 85, 86.
— — his wife, Christian Fraser, i. 85, 86; iv. 111.
— Patrick, 2nd son of Sir John G. of Haddo, i. 87.
— Patrick, general, the diarist, iii. 454.
— Patrick, bishop of Aberdeen, iv. 127.
— Patrick, 4th son of 1st earl of Aboyne, ix. 6.
— Peter, Abergeldie, iv. 292.
— — his wife, Elizabeth Gray, iv. 292.
— Sir Robert, G.C.B., G.C.H., i. 93.
— Robert, rector of Barley, i. 526.
— — his wife, Elizabeth Frances Lindsay, i. 526.
— Robert, 8th son of 4th earl of Huntly, iv. 538.
— Robert, 4th son of Wm. G. of Penninghame, v. 109.
— Robert, minister of Crossmichael, v. 126.
— — his wife, Grizel Gordon, v. 126.
— Robert, 78th regt. of foot, v. 133.
— Sir Robert, 1st bart., author of *Genealogie of the Earls of Sutherland*, iii. 206; viii. 345, 359.
— — his wife, Louisa Gordon, viii. 345.
— Robert, commissioner to parliament, viii. 350, 351.
— — his wife, Jane Mackay, vii. 170; viii. 350.
— Robert G., Kingston-on-Thames, v. 104 *n*.
— Roger, legtd. son of Sir Alex. G. of Kenmure, v. 104.
— Roger, 5th son of Sir Robert G. of Lochinvar, v. 106.
— Rosina, wife of (1) John Gordon of Bar, and (2) James Gordon, v. 117.
— Susan, dau. of 3rd earl of Aberdeen, i. 94.
— Susan, wife of (1) John, 9th earl of Westmoreland, and (2) lieut.-col Woodford, iv. 555.
— Susan, wife of 5th duke of Manchester, iv. 557.
— Susanne, wife of George Kinnaird, v. 211; ix. 121.
— Thomas, rector of Linton, canon of Moray, iv. 512, 513.
— Thomas, 9th son of 4th earl of Huntly, iv. 539.
— — his wife, Janet Gordon, iv. 539; viii. 343.
— Thomas, in Mill of Dess, viii. 338.
— Thomas, lieut. Scots Fusiliers, ix. 150.
— — his wife, Margaret Scott, ix. 150.
— William, chancellor of Moray, bishop of Aberdeen, ii. 5; iv. 533.
— William, M.P., vice-admiral for Scotland, i. 93; iv. 554; v. 19.
— — his wife, Frances Ingram Shepherd, iv. 554.

Gordon, William, 4th son of 4th earl of Huntly, iv. 21, 537.
— William, alleged son of Alex. G., iv. 509.
— William, crusader, iv. 510 *bis*.
— William, 5th son of 1st earl of Huntly, iv. 523, 525.
— William, 3rd son of 5th earl of Huntly, iv. 541.
— William, 7th son of Sir Robert G. of Lochinvar, v. 106.
— William, in Penninghame, v. 109.
— — his wife, Mary M'Ghie, v. 109.
— William, commendator of Glenluce, v. 112.
— William, 3rd son of Alexander, master of Sutherland, viii. 339.
— William, 4th son of James G. of Barncrosh, ix. 118.
— William Henry Pelham, v. 132.
— *, alleged wife of 2nd lord Innermeath, iv. 533.
— *, wife of * Walker, Westminster, v. 124 *n*.
— *, wife of Geo. Gordon of Cochlarachie, viii. 337.
— *, wife of John Robson, viii. 338.
Gordon-Cumming of Altyre, Sir William Gordon, 2nd bart., vii. 490.
— Eleanora, wife of capt. George H. E. Ogilvie-Grant, vii. 490.
Gordon-Halyburton of Pitcur, Douglas, 2nd son of 4th earl of Aboyne, i. 105; iv. 559.
— — his wife, Louisa Leslie, i. 105.
— John Frederick, admiral R.N., ii. 500; iv. 559.
— — his wife, Augusta Fitzclarence, ii. 499.
GORDON-LENNOX, EARL of KINRARA, v. 369-371.
GORDON-LENNOX, DUKE of GORDON, v. 369-371.
GORDON-LENNOX, DUKE OF LENNOX, v. 367-371.
Gordon-Lennox, Alexander Francis Charles, M.P., capt. Royal Horse Guards, v. 368.
— — his wife, Emily Frances Towneley, v. 368.
— Algernon Charles, col. Grenadier Guards, v. 369.
— — his wife, Blanche Maynard, v. 369.
— Amelia Frederica, v. 368.
— Amy Gwendoline, v. 370.
— Augusta Katharine, wife of prince Edward of Saxe-Weimar, v. 368.
— Bernard Charles, capt. Grenadier Guards, v. 370.
— Caroline Amelia, wife of 5th earl of Bessborough, v. 368.
— Caroline Elizabeth, v. 369.
— Cecilia Catherine, wife of 4th earl of Lucan, i. 73; v. 369.

* Name unknown.

Gordon-Lennox, Doris Hilda, v. 370.
— Esme Charles, capt. Scots Guards, v. 370.
— Evelyn Amy, wife of Sir J. R. G. Cotterell, v. 370.
— Fitzroy George Charles, v. 368.
— Florence Augusta, v. 369.
— Francis Charles, capt. Scots Guards, v. 369.
— Frederick Charles, v. 370.
— George Charles, M.P., v. 368.
— — his wife, M. A. Palmer, v. 368.
— Helen Magdalen, v. 370.
— Henry Charles George, M.P., v. 368.
— — his wife, Amelia Susannah *, v. 368.
— Lucy Frances, v. 368.
— Muriel Beatrice, wife of W. M. Beckwith, v. 370.
— Sarah Georgiana, v. 368.
— Violet Mary, wife of H. L. C. Brassey, v. 370.
— Walter Charles, M.P., v. 369.
— — his wife, Alice Elizabeth Ogilvie-Grant, v. 369; vii. 490.
Gordon-Moore, Cecil James, capt. 42nd Highlanders, iv. 560.
Gore of Barrowmount, Ralph, colonel, vii. 225.
— of Hookestowe, Charles, iii. 123.
— of Manor Gore, Sir William, bart., i. 45.
— — his wife, Hannah Hamilton, i. 45.
— Anne, wife of 1st earl Howe, i. 72.
— Anne Jane, wife of (1) Henry Hatton, and (2) 9th earl of Abercorn, i. 68; ix. 4.
— Caroline Annesley, wife of 9th lord Ruthven, vii. 392.
— Sir Charles, G.C.B., K.H., iii. 586.
— Eliza Amelia, V.A., wife of 19th earl of Erroll, iii. 586.
— Hannah Anne, wife of 3rd earl Cowper, iii. 123.
— Sir John, K.C.B., admiral, i. 72.
— Mahell Frances Elizabeth, wife of 8th earl of Airlie, i. 132.
— Mary Katharine, wife of G. H. Lindsay, i. 526.
— Percy, wife of Francis Ward Primrose, vii. 225.
Gore-Browne, Harold, col. King's Royal Rifle Corps, iii. 396.
— — his wife, Muriel Murray, iii. 396.
— Robert Melvill, in holy orders, vii. 210.
— — his wife, Agnes Katharine Rollo, vii. 210.
— Sir Thomas, K.C.M.G., C.B., iii. 396.
Gore-Langton of Newton Park, William Henry Powell, M.P., v. 200.
— — his wife, Anne Eliza Mary Grenville, v. 200.
— — William Stephen, v. 201.

* Name unknown.

Gore-Langton, Edward Grenville, iii. 522.
—— —— his wife, Florence Emily Murray, iii. 522.
Gorges, Edward (Gorges), 1st lord, vi. 452.
—— —— his wife, Jane Sproxtoune, vi. 452.
—— Sarah, wife of 9th lord Kirkcudbright, v. 273.
—— Thomas, colonel, v. 273.
Goring, colonel, v. 472.
Gormlath or Hvarflod, wife of Harald Maddadsson, earl of Caithness, ii. 315; vii. 231.
Gorthie of Gorthie, *, i. 280; ix. 15.
—— —— his wife, Katharine Arbuthnott, i. 280.
Gosford, Sir A. Acheson, ancestor of the earl of, i. 40.
Gosling of Hassobury, Robert, v. 487.
—— Caroline, wife of (1) rev. S. Lawry, and (2) Basil Cochrane, iii. 360.
—— George, iii. 360.
—— William Sullivan, capt. Scots Guards, v. 487.
—— —— his wife, Victoria Alexandrina Alberta Ker, v. 486.
Gospatric, son of Uchtred, earl of Northumberland, iii. 241.
—— 'brother of Dolfin,' iii. 241, 246.
—— of Dundas, and Derwentwater, 2nd son of Waldeve of Allerdale, iii. 244.
—— 2nd son of Duncan II. and Æthelreda, iii. 245.
Goswyck, Constantine of, i. 421.
Gothred MacWilliam, i. 420.
Gough, Alexander, vicar of Thorpe-le-Soken, vii. 223.
—— —— his wife, Katharine Canham, vii. 223.
Gouldsmith of Crayford, Sir Francis, i. 536.
—— Anne, wife of (1) Wm. Warren, and (2) James, 2nd lord Balfour, i. 536.
Gourlay of Ballindean, Thomas, iv. 32.
—— —— his wife, Agnes Ogilvy, iv. 32.
—— of Dargo, Gilbert, iv. 281.
—— of Kincraig, William, vi. 591.
—— —— his wife, Jean Makgill, vi. 591.
—— of Lamlethan, John, vi. 84.
—— —— his wife, Elizabeth Melville, vi. 84, 85.
—— Alison, wife of Alex. Livingston of Dunipace, ix. 129.
—— David, burgess of Edinburgh, iii. 317; vii. 213, 217.
—— —— his wife, Marion Primrose, iii. 317; vii. 213.
—— David, his 3rd son, iii. 318.
—— Euphan, mistress of 21st earl of Crawford, iii. 40.
—— Gilbert, eldest son of David G., iii. 318; vii. 217.
—— —— his wife, Janet Primrose, vii. 217.

* Name unknown.

Gourlay, Hugo de, vii. 420.
—— Jean, wife of Thomas Melville, vi. 104.
—— Robert, iii. 318.
—— William, son of Johanna de Erth of Drem and Wauchton, v. 391.
Gourton, Edward de, vi. 566.
Govan of Cardrona, William, viii. 538.
—— of Ponfeigh, Lawrence, iv. 573, 583.
—— Mr. James, minister of Blackford, vi. 549.
—— —— his wife, Janet Oliphant, vi. 549.
GOWER, LEVESON-GOWER, BARON, viii. 362-365.
Gower, George Granville, first baron, iii. 84; viii. 362.
—— Granville (Leveson Gower), 2nd earl, viii. 360.
GOWRIE, RUTHVEN, EARL OF, iv. 254-268.
Gowrie, James, second earl of, iv. 264, 267, 337; vi. 234.
—— John, third earl of, i. 470; iv. 264, 267, 337, 338; v. 222.
—— William, first earl of, i. 27, 195, 395; ii. 342, 553; iv. 263, 283, 337, 338, 465; viii. 401.
—— —— his contracted wife, Mary Gray, iv. 263, 282.
—— —— his wife, Dorothea Stewart, iv. 263, 267; vi. 168.
—— master of, Alexander, 3rd son of 1st earl of Gowrie; styled, iv. 264, 267; ix. 99.
Grace, Clara Louisa, wife of William Middelton of Stockeld, iv. 418.
—— William, iv. 418.
Graeme of Balgowan, Thomas, viii. 223 *bis*.
—— —— his wife, Anne Drummond, viii. 223.
—— of Garvock, James, vii. 205.
—— of Gorthie, David, vi. 262 *n*.
—— —— Mungo, vi. 262.
—— of Inchbrakie, George, vii. 194.
—— —— his wife, Marjorie Rollo, vii. 194.
—— —— George Drummond, K.H., viii. 236.
—— —— his wife, Marianne Jane Drummond, viii. 236.
—— —— John, ii. 186.
—— —— John, postmaster-general, viii. 219.
—— —— his 1st wife, Margaret Drummond, viii. 219.
—— —— Patrick, ancestor of the family of, ii. 182; vi. 225, 230.
—— —— his wife, Margaret Stewart, ii. 182.
—— —— Patrick, vi. 248; viii. 218.
—— —— his wife, Jean Drummond, viii. 218.
—— —— Patrick, vi. 394.
—— —— Patrick, vii. 203.
—— —— William, vi. 224.
—— Mary, wife of capt. Robert Rollo, vii. 205.
—— Henry, alleged illeg. son of 16th earl of Crawford, iii. 35.
—— *see also* Graham.
Grafton, Henry (Fitzroy), 1st duke of, i. 31.
GRAHAM, GRAHAM, EARL, vi. 265-274.

Graham, David, first earl, vi. 265.
GRAHAM AND BUCHANAN, GRAHAM, MARQUESS OF, vi. 263-274.
Graham, David, 2nd son of 1st duke of Montrose; styled marquess of, vi. 265.
—— James, son of 2nd duke of Montrose; styled marquess of, vi. 270.
—— —— his 1st wife, J. E. Ashburnham, vi. 271.
—— James, captain 1st Life Guards; styled marquess of, vi. 273.
—— James, eldest son of 5th duke of Montrose; styled marquess of, vi. 273.
—— —— his wife, Mary Louise Douglas-Hamilton of Arran, iv. 396; vi. 274.
GRAHAM AND MONTDIEU, GRAHAM, LORD, vi. 247-274.
Graham and Montdieu, James, first lord, vi. 247.
GRAHAM OF BELFORD, GRAHAM, BARON, vi. 265-274.
Graham of Belford, David, first baron, vi. 265.
GRAHAM OF CLAVERHOUSE, GRAHAM, LORD, iii. 324-332.
Graham of Claverhouse, David, third lord, iii. 331.
—— James, second lord, iii. 331.
—— John, first lord, iii. 324.
GRAHAM OF ESK, GRAHAM, LORD, vii. 98-108.
Graham of Esk, Richard, first lord, vii. 105.
GRAHAM OF KINCARDINE, GRAHAM, LORD vi. 221-274.
Graham, James, 2nd son of 1st marquess of Montrose; styled lord, iii. 99; vi. 255.
—— John, eldest son of 1st marquess of Montrose; styled lord, vi. 253.
—— Patrick, first lord, vi. 220.
—— —— his wife, Christian Erskine, v. 605; vi. 221, 222.
—— William, second lord, vi. 222.
—— —— his wife, Eleanor or Anne Douglas, i. 178; vi. 222; ix. 12 *bis*.
—— William, third lord, vi. 223.
—— —— his 1st wife, Annabel Drummond, vi. 225; vii. 45.
—— —— his 2nd wife, Janet Edmonstone, vi. 225.
—— —— his 3rd wife, Christian Wawane, vi. 225.
GRAHAM OF KINPONT, GRAHAM, LORD, i. 136.
Graham of Kinpont, John, lord, i. 136, 137.
—— master of, John, grandson of 2nd earl of Montrose. vi. 232.
—— —— his wife, Jean Drummond, vi. 232.
—— master of, Robert, eldest son of 2nd earl of Montrose, vi. 230.
—— —— his wife, Margaret Fleming, vi. 231; viii. 540.
GRAHAM, LORD ABERUTHVEN, MUGDOCK AND FINTRY, vi. 263.
GRAHAM, EARL OF AIRTH, i. 133-145.
GRAHAM, VISCOUNT OF DUNDAFF, vi. 263-274.
GRAHAM, VISCOUNT OF DUNDEE, iii. 316-333.
GRAHAM, EARL GRAHAM, vi. 265-274.
GRAHAM, MARQUESS OF GRAHAM AND BUCHANAN, vi. 263-274.
GRAHAM, LORD GRAHAM AND MONTDIEU, vi. 247-274.
GRAHAM, LORD GRAHAM AND MUGDOCK, vi. 235.
GRAHAM, BARON GRAHAM OF BELFORD, vi. 265-274.
GRAHAM, LORD GRAHAM OF CLAVERHOUSE, iii. 324-333.
GRAHAM, LORD GRAHAM OF ESK, vii. 98-108.
GRAHAM, LORD GRAHAM OF KINCARDINE, vi. 220-274.
GRAHAM, LORD KILBRYDE, i. 135.
GRAHAM, LORD KINPONT, i. 135-145.
GRAHAM, EARL OF KINCARDINE, vi. 247-274.
GRAHAM, EARL OF MENTEITH, vi. 138.
GRAHAM, EARL OF MENTEITH, vi. 142-165.
GRAHAM, EARL OF MONTROSE. vi. 224-274.
GRAHAM, MARQUESS OF MONTROSE, vi. 247-274.
GRAHAM, DUKE OF MONTROSE, vi. 191-274.
GRAHAM, VISCOUNT OF PRESTON, vii. 98-108.
GRAHAM, EARL OF STRATHERN, i. 135.
Graham(e of Abercorn, Sir John, vi. 195.
—— —— Sir John, only son of above, vi. 138 *n.*; 196.
—— —— Sir Nicholas, vi. 194.
—— —— Sybilla, wife of Sir William More, vi. 196.
—— of Aberfoyle, Walter, 5th son of 1st earl of Menteith, vi. 149.
—— of Aberruthven, John, iii. 324.
—— —— William, iii. 324.
—— —— William, vi. 224.
—— of Achincross. Sir Patrick, vi. 213.
—— of Airth, Sir James. vi. 153.
—— —— James, judge-admiral of Scotland, ii. 363.
—— —— his wife, Mary Livingston, ii. 363.
—— —— Patrick, ancestor of the family of, vi. 225.
—— of Airthray, Sir William, 1st bart., vi. 238, 243.
—— —— his 1st wife, Margaret Keith, vi. 49, 238.
—— —— his 2nd wife, Mary Edmonstone, vi. 238.
—— of the Ard, Patrick, v. 520.
—— of Ardoch, Robert Bontine Cunninghame, vi. 149.

Graham of Ardoch, Thomas, ancestor of the family of, vi. 147.
— of Ardochmore, Sir Patrick, vi. 213.
— — Walter, vi. 219.
— of Arthuret, Sir Richard, vii. 100.
— of Auchincass, Thomas, ii. 381, 382.
— — his wife, Jonet Kirkpatrick, ii. 381, 382.
— of Auchincloich, John, alleged ancestor of the family of, vi. 213; ix. 137.
— — Robert, vi. 240.
— — Walter, vi. 219.
— of Auchinhowie, Robert, vi. 240.
— — Walter, ancestor of the family of, vi. 219.
— of Auchmar, Patrick, 2nd son of 1st earl of Menteith, vi. 144.
— of Balgowan, John, vii. 194, 195.
— — his wife, Marjorie Rollo, vii. 194.
— — John, viii. 62.
— — his wife, Elizabeth Carnegie, viii. 62.
— — Thomas, iv. 497, 568.
— — his 1st wife, Christian Hope, iv. 497.
— — his 2nd wife, Christian Leslie, vi. 443.
— — Thomas, M.P., ii. 523.
— — his wife, Mary Cathcart, ii. 523.
— — William, ancestor of the family of, vi. 219.
— of Balgownie, John, 1668, iii. 324.
— of Balkello, George, iii. 321, 322.
— — Sir William, iii. 320, 321.
— of Ballagan, Walter, ancestor of the family of, vi. 148.
— of Ballancleroch, Sir William, vi. 217.
— of Ballargus, John, 1st laird, 2nd son of Robert G. of Strathcarron and Fintry, iii. 316.
— — Sir Robert, ancestor of the family of, vi. 219.
— of Ballochallan, Walter, ancestor of the family of, vi. 151.
— of Balluny, George, iii. 322.
— — his wife, Mariot Fotheringham, iii. 323.
— of Balmakewan, William Barclay, i. 314; iii. 324.
— of Balmullo, Sir William, iii. 320; ix. 74.
— of Beircrofts, Gilbert, 4th son of 3rd earl of Menteith, vi. 158.
— of Blairccsnock, George, vi. 152.
— — John, vi. 153; ix. 136.
— of Blawatwood, Arthur, ii. 391.
— — his wife, Esota Carlyle, ii. 391.
— of Bofreslie, John, vi. 159; ix. 136.
— of Boquhapple, Andrew, 5th son of 3rd earl of Menteith, vi. 159.
— — George, 3rd laird, vi. 150.
— — his wife, Marjoric Graham, vi. 150.
— — Thomas, custumar of Inverness, etc., 2nd laird, vi. 149 *bis*.
— — his wife, Christine Oliphant, vi. 150.
Graham of Boquhapple, Thomas, 4th laird, vi. 150, 419.
— — his 2nd wife, Isobel Schaw, vi. 150.
— — Walter, 1st laird, vi. 149.
— — his wife, Marjorie Campbell, vi. 149.
— — Walter, 6th laird, iv. 150.
— — his wife, Jean Graham, iii. 323; vi. 150.
— — William, 5th laird, vi. 150.
— — his wife, Margaret Stirling, vi. 150.
— — William, 7th laird, colonel, vi. 150.
— — his 1st wife, Janet Herries, vi. 151.
— — his 2nd wife, Katharine Lythgow, vi. 151.
— of Boquhapple Wester, Robert, 3rd son of 3rd earl of Menteith, vi. 157.
— — his wife, Elizabeth Erskine, vi. 158.
— of Braco, Sir James, 4th bart., vi. 238, 262.
— — Sir John, 2nd bart., vi. 238, 253.
— — his wife, Margaret Campbell, vi. 238.
— — Sir William, iii. 282.
— — his wife, Margaret Cockburn, iii. 282.
— — Sir William, 1st bart., vi. 238, 243.
— — his 1st wife, Margaret Keith, vi. 49, 238.
— — his 2nd wife, Mary Edmonstone, vi. 238.
— — Sir William, 3rd bart., vi. 238, 254.
— — his wife, Marie Cowane, vi. 238.
— of Easter Brigton, John, iii. 235 *bis*, *n.*
— — William, iii. 325.
— of Buchanan, James, vi. 260.
— of Buchlyvie, Patrick, ancestor of the family of, vi. 225.
— of Cairnie, Walter, ancestor of the family of, vi. 225.
— of Callander, Alexander, vi. 217, 219.
— — George, ancestor of the family of, vii. 223, 224.
— of Calziemuck, Thomas, vi. 150.
— of Canonbie, Arthur, vii. 98.
— of Carlisle, William, vii. 98.
— of Nether Carlowrie, Sir David de, vi. 211.
— of Cessfurd, Sir Robert, vi. 215, 538.
— of Claverhouse, George, 6th laird, iii. 321, 322; vi. 150.
— — his wife, Mariot Fotheringham, iii. 323.
— — John, 1st laird, iii. 316.
— — John, 2nd laird, iii. 317.
— — his wife, Margaret Beton, iii. 317.
— — John, 3rd laird, iii. 318.
— — John, 8th laird, iii. 324.
— — his wife, Jean Cochrane, iii. 330, 352; v. 193.
— — Sir Robert, ancestor of the family of, vi. 219.

Graham of Claverhouse, William, 4th laird, iii. 317, 318.
—— his wife, Egidia Gaw, iii. 318.
—— Sir William, 5th laird, iii. 319.
—— his 1st wife, Agnes Lundie, iii. 321.
—— his 2nd wife, Margaret Murray, iii. 321; ix. 74.
—— William, 7th laird, iii. 324; vi. 250, 253, 256.
—— his wife, Magdalen Carnegie, iii. 324; vi. 497.
— of Claypotts, David, iii. 320, 323.
—— Sir William, iii. 320, 323.
— of Clifton, Henry de, vi. 197, 201.
— of Coldene, John de, iii. 54.
—— his wife, Isabella, iii. 54.
— of Courance, Robert, 1562, i. 247.
— of Cousland, Radulph de, vi. 194, 198.
— of Craigcrook, Sir David de, vi. 211.
— of Craigie, George, iii. 322.
—— Sir William, iii. 320.
— of Craiguchty, Patrick, 2nd son of 1st earl of Menteith, vi. 144.
— of Crichton, John de, iii. 54.
— of Crigie, John, ix. 123.
— of Daldouran, Walter, ancester of the family of, vi. 151.
— of Dalkeith, Sir Henry, eldest son of Sir Peter G., vi. 194.
—— Sir Henry, eldest son of above, vi. 194.
—— Sir Henry, his elder son, vi. 194.
—— his wife, * Avenel, vi. 194.
—— Sir John, vi. 195.
—— his wife, Isabella *, iii. 54; vi. 196.
—— Sir John, only son of above, vi. 138 *n.*, 196, 340, 342.
—— Sir Nicholas, vi. 194.
—— his wife, Maria of Strathearn, v. 577; vi. 195; viii. 247.
—— Sir Peter de, vi. 194.
—— his wife, Geva, vi. 194.
—— William de, vi. 193.
— of Dougalston, Walter, ancestor of the family of, vi. 219.
— of Downans, John, 2nd laird, vi. 148.
—— Thomas, 1st laird, vi. 147, 148.
—— Thomas, eldest son of John G. of Downans and Duchray, vi. 148.
— of Drongy, Walter, vi. 149.
— of Drumlean, Walter, ancestor of the family of, vi. 151.
— of Duchray, John, 1st laird, vi. 148.
—— his 1st wife, *, vi. 148.
—— his 2nd wife, Christine Graham, vi. 148.
—— John, 3rd laird, vi. 148.
—— his wife, Katharine Stewart, vi. 148.
—— John, 'Highland Hector,' 5th laird, vi. 148, 161.
—— his wife, Marion Graham, vi. 148 *n.*, 161.

* Name unknown.

Graham of Duchray, Thomas, 4th laird, vi 148.
—— Thomas, ii. 190.
—— his wife, Marjory Campbell, ii. 190.
—— William, 2nd laird, vi. 148.
—— his wife, Christine Macfarlane, vi. 148.
— of Dudhope, John, Constable of Dundee, iii. 328.
— of Dundaff, Sir David de, vi. 208, 211.
—— Sir David de, vi. 211 *bis*.
—— Sir John, vi. 204.
—— his wife, Marjory *, vi. 205.
—— Sir John, the younger, vi. 205.
—— Sir Patrick, vi. 213.
—— his 1st wife, Matilda *, vi. 214.
—— his 2nd wife, Euphemia *or* Egidia Stewart, i. 15; vi. 214.
—— Sir William de, vi. 215.
—— his 1st wife, *, vi. 217.
—— his 2nd wife, Mary Stewart, i. 18; vi. 217; ix. 11.
— of Dundaffmuir, Sir David de, sheriff of Berwick, v. 332; vi. 200.
—— his wife, Agnes Noble, vi. 202.
— of Dundee, John, iii. 328.
— of Dundurn, Walter, ancestor of the family of, vi. 151.
— of Duntrune, Alexander, 5th laird, iii. 332.
—— Alexander, last laird, i. 130.
—— Clementina, wife of Gavin Drummond of Keltie, i. 130.
—— David, 2nd laird, iii. 332.
—— James, 4th laird, iii. 332.
—— Sir Robert, ancestor of the family of, vi. 219.
—— Walter, 1st laird, 3rd son of Sir William G. of Claverhouse, iii. 321, 332.
—— his wife, Elizabeth Guthrie, iii. 322.
—— William, 3rd laird, iii. 332.
—— his wife, Christian Graham, iii. 332.
— of Edmond Castle, Thomas Henry, viii. 88.
—— his wife, Mary Carnegie, viii. 88.
— of Elvingston, David de, vi. 198.
—— John de, vi. 198.
—— Peter, ancestor of the family of, vi. 198.
— of Esk, Fergus, vii. 99.
—— Sir Richard, 1st bart., vii. 99.
— of Eskbank, William, ancestor of the family of, vi. 219.
— of Eskdale, Sir John, vi. 195.
—— Sir John, only son of above, vi. 196.
—— Sir Nicholas, vi. 194.
— of Ewisdale, Sir Robert, vi. 218.
— of the Fauld, George, vii. 98.

* Name unknown.

Graham of the Fauld, Robert, viii. 545.
—— —— his wife, Lucrece Fleming, viii. 545.
—— of Feddal, Robert, elder son of Robert G. in Shannochill, vi. 155.
—— —— his wife, Agnes Campbell, vi. 155.
—— of Fintry, David, son of Robt. G., ix. 74.
—— —— David, vi. 225, 358.
—— —— his wife, J—— Graham, vi. 225.
—— —— Sir David, i. 118.
—— —— his wife, Margaret Ogilvy, i. 118.
—— —— David, vi. 256.
—— —— John, vi. 163, 164.
—— —— John, iii. 315; vi. 256.
—— —— his wife, Jean Scrymgeour, iii. 315.
—— —— David, 1711, viii. 62.
—— —— Sir Robert, ancestor of the family of, iii. 307, 316; vi. 218, 220.
—— —— his 1st wife, Janet Lovel, iii. 316; vi. 218.
—— —— his 2nd wife, Matilda Scrimgeour, iii. 307; vi. 218.
—— —— Robert, 2nd laird, son of Robert G. of Strathcarron, iii. 316.
—— —— his wife, Elizabeth Douglas, i. 178; iii. 316.
—— —— William, ix. 61.
—— of West Fordoun, Alexander, vi. 229.
—— —— Mungo, vi. 229.
—— of Forest of Nicholl, Sir Richard, vii. 100.
—— of French, John, iii. 327.
—— of Gallingad, John, 1st laird, vi. 148.
—— —— Robert, 3rd laird, vi. 149.
—— —— Walter, 2nd laird, i. 139; vi. 148.
—— of Gardrany, Henry, 2nd son of Patrick G. of Kilpont, vi. 145, 152.
—— of Gargunnock, David, vi. 222.
—— of Gartavertane, Andrew, 5th son of 3rd earl of Menteith, vi. 159.
—— —— Gilbert, 4th son of 3rd earl of Menteith, vi. 157, 158.
—— —— his wife, Helen Kincaid, vi. 158.
—— —— Ninian, vi. 158.
—— —— Robert, vi. 159.
—— —— Walter, 2nd son of 3rd earl of Menteith, vi. 157.
—— —— William, vi. 158.
—— of Gartmore, Agnes, wife of John Alexander, vi. 159; viii. 179.
—— —— Gilbert, viii. 179.
—— —— Sir John, 2nd bart., i. 139, 141; vi. 149.
—— —— Nicol, iv. 250.
—— —— his wife, Margaret Cunningham, iv. 250, 252.
—— —— Robert, 3rd son of 3rd earl of Menteith; 1st laird, v. 189 *n.*; vi. 157, 158.
—— —— his wife, Elizabeth Erskine, v. 611; vi. 158.
—— —— Robert, 3rd laird, vi. 159.
—— —— Robert, 6th laird, vi. 149.
Graham of Gartmore, Robert, 2nd son of Nicol G., iv. 252.
—— —— Robert Bontine Cunninghame, vi. 149.
—— —— Thomas, ancestor of the family of, vi. 147.
—— —— William *or* Ninian, 2nd laird, vi. 158.
—— —— his wife, Janet Graham, vi. 158.
—— —— Sir William, 1st bart., vi. 149, 159.
—— —— his wife, Elizabeth Graham, i. 139; vi. 149.
—— of Gartur, George, 2nd laird, vi. 152.
—— —— his wife, Isobel Kinross, vi. 153.
—— —— James, 6th laird, vi. 153, 154.
—— —— his wife, Anna Graham, vi. 154.
—— —— James, 7th laird, vi. 154.
—— —— his wife, Elizabeth Wilkieson, vi. 154; ix. 136.
—— —— Jasper, 3rd laird, vi. 153.
—— —— his wife, Agnes Graham, vi. 153.
—— —— John, 4th laird, vi. 153; ix. 136.
—— —— his 1st wife, Katharine Buchanan, vi. 153.
—— —— his 2nd wife, Isabella Drummond, vi. 153.
—— —— John, 9th laird, vi. 154, 155.
—— —— his wife, Matilda Erskine, vi. 154.
—— —— Walter, 1st laird; 2nd son of 2nd earl of Menteith, vi. 152.
—— —— his 1st wife, Isobel Graham, vi. 152; ix. 136.
—— —— his 2nd wife, Margaret Shaw, vi. 152; ix. 136.
—— —— Walter, 5th laird, vi. 153.
—— —— his wife, Marion Graham, i. 137; vi. 153.
—— —— William, 8th laird, vi. 154.
—— —— his wife, Christian Somerville, vi. 154.
—— of Garvock, William, 5th son of Sir Wm. G. of Dundaff, vi. 219.
—— of Glassford, Thomas, vi. 149 *bis*.
—— of Glenny, John, vi. 148.
—— —— Walter, ancestor of the family of, vi. 148 *bis*.
—— of Gotterstone, John, iii. 326.
—— —— Sir William, iii. 320.
—— of Graemeshall, Patrick, ancestor of the family of, vi. 225.
—— of Graham, Sir William, vi. 217.
—— —— his 1st wife, *, vi. 217.
—— —— his 2nd wife, Marjorie *or* Mary Stewart, i. 18; iv. 230; vi. 217.
—— of Gretquerquer, David de, vi. 201.
—— of Grugar, Walter, ancestor of the family of, vi. 219.
—— of Gogar, Radulph de, vi. 194, 198.
—— of Gorthie, Mungo, vi. 262.
—— —— Patrick, ancestor of the family of, vi. 225.

* Name unknown.

Graham of Hallyards, John, senator of the College of Justice, vi. 236; viii. 387.
—— —— his wife, Janet Murray, viii. 387.
—— of Illaston, Sir Patrick, vi. 210.
—— of Inchbrakie, *see* Graeme.
—— of Innermay, Sir Robert, vi. 238, 240; vii. 394; viii. 101.
—— —— his wife, Anne Lindsay, vi. 239; viii. 101.
—— of Kerdale, Sir Patrick de, vi. 203.
—— —— his wife, *, of Ergadia, *or* Argyll, vi. 204.
—— —— William de, vi. 204.
—— —— his wife, * Hay, vi. 204.
—— of Kilbride, John, 3rd son of 1st earl of Menteith, vi. 145.
—— —— his wife, Margaret Muschet, vi. 146.
—— —— Walter, vi. 149, 156.
—— of Bowton of Kilbride, Walter, ancestor of the family of, vi. 151.
—— of Kilbucho, John, vi. 340.
—— of Killearn, John, ancestor of the family of, vi. 229.
—— —— Robert, last laird, vi. 229.
—— —— William, canon, rector of Killearn, vi. 229.
—— of Kincardine, David, ancestor of the family of, vi. 202.
—— —— Euphemia, wife of (1) 5th earl of Douglas, and (2) 1st lord Hamilton, iii. 170; vi. 143.
—— —— Sir Patrick, vi. 205; viii. 245.
—— —— his wife, Annabella de Strathearn, vi. 207; viii. 245.
—— —— Sir Patrick, vi. 143, 213, 538.
—— —— his 1st wife, Matilda *, vi. 214.
—— —— his 2nd wife, Eufamia Stewart, countess of Strathearn, ii. 322; vi. 143, 211; viii. 260.
—— —— Sir William de, vi. 216.
—— —— his 1st wife, *, vi. 217.
—— —— his 2nd wife, Mary Stewart, i. 18; vi. 217.
—— of Kinnaber, Sir David, vi. 212.
—— of Kinpunt, Malise, vi. 142.
—— —— his 1st wife, Jane de Rochford, vi. 144.
—— —— his 2nd wife, Marion *, vi. 144.
—— —— Sir Patrick de, 2nd son of Sir David de G., vi. 196, 210.
—— —— Patrick, 2nd son of Sir Patrick G. of Dundaff, vi. 143, 214.
—— —— Patrick, 2nd son of 1st earl of Menteith, vi. 144 *bis*, 151.
—— —— his wife, Isobel Erskine, v. 607; vi. 145.
—— —— Sir Robert, 3rd son of Sir Patrick G. of Dundaff, v. 426; vi. 214.
—— —— his wife, Marion Oliphant, vi. 215, 537.

* Name unknown.

Graham of Kirkandrews, Thomas, vii. 98.
—— of Kirkstall, Sir James, bart., viii. 140.
—— of Knockdolian, Andrew, ii. 455.
—— —— Gilbert, ii. 511.
—— —— his wife, Marion Cathcart, ii. 511.
—— —— Robert, ii. 460; vi. 226 *n.*, 229.
—— —— his wife, Helen Kennedy, ii. 460; iii. 443.
—— —— Robert, vi. 230.
—— —— his wife, Christian Graham, vi. 230.
—— —— Robert, i. 512; iii. 318 *n.*
—— —— his contracted wife, Egidia Gaw, iii. 318.
—— —— his wife, Elizabeth Sempill, i. 512; iii. 318 *n.*; vii. 550.
—— —— Walter, ancestor of the family of, vi. 219.
—— of Levens, Henry, groom of the Bedchamber, M.P., vii. 102.
—— —— his wife, Mary Tndor, i. 32; vii. 102.
—— —— James, M.P., vii. 102.
—— —— his 1st wife, Dorothy Howard, vii. 102.
—— —— his 2nd wife, Elizabeth Barton, vii. 102.
—— of Liddell, Sir Richard, vii. 100.
—— of Loch Chon, Walter, 5th son of 1st earl of Menteith, vi. 149, 152, 156.
—— of Logyachray, Sir William, vi. 216.
—— of Lundie, Sir William, iii. 320.
—— of M'Keanston, John, vi. 155.
—— —— Robert, 3rd son of John G. of Gartur, vi. 153, 154.
—— —— his 1st wife, Jean Menteith, vi. 155.
—— —— his 2nd wife, Mary Stirling, vi. 155.
—— of Meathie, James, vi. 498.
—— of Medhope, John, vii. 98.
—— of Meiklewood, David, supposed ancestor of the family of, vi. 222.
—— of Merton, Sir David, v. 519; vi. 202.
—— —— his wife, Muriel Bisset, vi. 202.
—— of Mondowie, John, vi. 161.
—— —— his wife, Jean Kinross, vi. 161.
—— of Monorgund, Agnes, wife of D. Lindsay of Edzell, i. 515.
—— —— James, i. 515.
—— of Montrose, Sir Nigel, ii. 432 *n.*
—— —— his alleged wife, Aloysia Bruce, ii. 432 *n.*
—— of Old Montrose, Sir David, son of Sir Patrick G. of Mugdock, vi. 208; vii. 236.
—— —— Sir Robert, vi. 218.
—— of Monvrachy, John, 4th son of 1st earl of Menteith, vi. 147, 149.
—— of Monzie, George, vii. 197.
—— —— his wife, Anna Rollo, vii. 197.
—— of Morphie, David, i. 281, 282; v. 186 *n.*
—— —— Francis, captain, iii. 324 *bis*.
—— —— Sir Harie, ix. 137.
—— —— his 2nd wife, Janet Graham, vi. 230; ix. 137.

Graham of Morphie, Henry, i. 287; ix. 16.
—— —— his wife, Giles Arbuthnott, i. 287.
—— —— John, alleged ancestor of the family of, vi. 213.
—— —— Robert, i. 198.
—— —— Robert, vi. 244; viii. 64.
—— —— his wife, Euphame Carnegie, viii. 64.
—— —— Sir Robert, vi. 256; ix. 74.
—— —— Robert, son of Sir Robt. G. of Morphie, ix. 74.
—— —— his wife, Margaret Graham, iii. 324; ix. 74 *bis*.
—— —— William Barclay, i. 314.
—— of Morton, Alan, vi. 346 *n*.
—— —— Sir John, vi. 346 *n*.
—— of Mossknow, William, i. 104.
—— —— his wife, Grace Margaret Gordon, i. 104; ix. 6.
—— of the Mote, Fergus, ancestor of the family of, vii. 98.
—— of Muckersie, Sir Robert, vi. 239.
—— of Mucklaree, David, vi. 215.
—— of Mugdock, David, ancestor of the family of, vi. 202.
—— —— Sir Patrick de, vi. 205.
—— of Netherby, Sir Frederick Ulric, 3rd bart., iv. 273.
—— —— Sir George, 2nd bart., vii. 101.
—— —— his wife, Mary Johnstone, i. 258; vii. 101.
—— —— Sir James, 1st bart., iv. 169; vii. 104.
—— —— his wife, Katharine Stewart, iv. 169.
—— —— Sir Richard, 1st bart., vii. 99.
—— —— his wife, Katharine Musgrave, vii. 100.
—— —— Sir Richard, 3rd bart., vii. 104.
—— —— his wife, Anne Howard, vii. 106.
—— —— Sir Richard James, 4th bart., vii. 104.
—— —— Robert, rector of Arthuret, vii. 104, 107, 108.
—— —— his wife, Frances Graham, vii. 104.
—— —— Walter, grandson of Richard G., vii. 98.
—— of Newlands, John, vi. 340.
—— of Norton Conyers, Sir Reginald, 4th bart., vii. 104 *bis*.
—— —— his wife, Jacoba Katharina Graham, vii. 104.
—— —— Sir Reginald Henry, 8th bart., vii. 101.
—— —— Sir Richard, vii. 100.
—— —— Sir Richard, 1st bart., vii. 101.
—— —— his wife, Elizabeth Fortescue, vii. 101.
—— of Nunnington, Reginald, vii. 99, 101.
—— —— his wife, Susanna Washington, vii. 99.
—— of Nunnery, William, probable ancestor of the family of, vii. 98.
—— of Glen of Ogilvie, John, iii. 327.
Graham of Glen of Ogilvie, Sir William, iii. 321.
—— of Orchill, David, M.P., vi. 230.
—— —— David, vi. 397.
—— —— his wife, Louisa Nairn, vi. 397.
—— —— James, vi. 154, 262.
—— —— Sir John, 2nd laird, vi. 230.
—— —— his wife, * Maxwell, iv. 415.
—— —— Mungo, 1st laird, vi. 229.
—— —— his wife, Marjorie Edmonstone, vi. 229.
—— of Panholes, William, v. 189 *n*.
—— of Pentland, Radulph de, vi. 194, 198.
—— of Pickhill, Metcalfe, col., adjutant-general, vii. 104.
—— —— his 1st wife, Isabella Jacoba de Bons, vii. 104.
—— —— his 2nd wife, Elizabeth Nevill, vii. 104.
—— —— Reginald, vii. 104.
—— —— his wife, Elizabeth *, vii. 104.
—— of Pitcairns, George, vii. 197.
—— —— his wife, Anna Rollo, vii. 197.
—— of Plomp, Fergus, vii. 99.
—— —— his wife, Sibill Bell, vii. 99.
—— —— William, vii. 99.
—— —— his wife, Alice *or* Agnes Carlyle, vii. 99.
—— of Polder, John, vi. 148.
—— —— Sir William, 1st bart., vi. 149, 159.
—— —— his wife, Elizabeth Graham, vi. 149.
—— of Port, John, 4th son of 1st earl of Menteith, vi. 147, 149.
—— —— his wife, * Campbell, vi. 147.
—— of Potento, Thomas, 2nd son of George G. of Claverhouse, iii. 323.
—— —— his wife, Jean Blair, iii. 323.
—— of Randelington, Sir Richard, vii. 100.
—— of Rathernes, Mungo, vi. 229.
—— of Redgorton, William, ancestor of the family of, vi. 219.
—— of Rednock, George, tutor of Menteith, vi. 160, 163.
—— —— his wife, Agnes Macdougall, vi. 161.
—— —— John, 3rd son of Geo. G., vi. 161.
—— —— James, vi. 161.
—— of Rosetrees, William, ancestor of the family of, vii. 98.
—— of Scatraig, Sir Patrick de, vi. 204.
—— of Scotston, Sir Robert, vi. 238, 240; vii. 394.
—— —— his wife, Anne Lindsay, vi. 239.
—— of Simundburn, Sir Henry, vi. 194.
—— —— Henry, 2nd son of Sir Henry G. of Dalkeith, vi. 197, 201.
—— of Soyoch, Patrick, ancestor of the family of, vi. 151.
—— of Strabracken, Andrew, ii. 455.
—— of Strathcarron, David de, vi. 201.
—— —— Sir Robert, iii. 307, 316; vi. 218.

* Name unknown.

Graham of Strowan, Patrick, ancestor of the family of, vi. 225.
— of Succoth, Sir David, vi. 209.
— of Tarbolton, Sir Henry, vi. 194.
— — Sir John, vi. 198.
— — Sir Nicholas, 2nd son of Sir Henry G. of Dalkeith, vi. 197.
— of Tealing, Sir William, iii. 320.
— of Thornick, Ninian, i. 247.
— — his wife, Margaret Johnstone, i. 247.
— — Robert, i. 247.
— — Walter, ancestor of the 2nd family of, vi. 225.
— of Torrie, William, vi. 154.
— of Wester Torrie, Walter, vi. 150 *n*.
— of Tullibelton, Patrick, vi. 248.
— of Wallastown, Alexander, 2nd son of 2nd earl of Montrose, iii. 439; vi. 229.
— — his wife, Marion Seton, iii. 439; vi. 229; viii. 581.
— — Sir Nicholas, ancestor of the family of, vi. 197.
— — Walter le, ii. 400; v. 492; vi. 219.
— of Wardropton, Sir Robert, vi. 238.
— of Wariston, George, iii. 323.
— — Sir William, iii. 323.
— of Westhall, Robert, viii. 371.
— — his wife, Margaret Livingston, viii. 371.
— — Robert, ix. 163.
— — his wife, Marion Baillie, ix. 163.
— of Woodend, John, vi. 154.
— — his wife, Matilda Erskine, vi. 154.
— Agnes, wife of Sir Wm. Murray of Tullibardine, i. 466; vi. 230.
— Agnes, dau. of Walter G. of Gartur, vi. 152.
— Agnes, wife of Jasper Graham of Gartur, vi. 153.
— Agnes, dau. of John G. of Brae Leny, vi. 155.
— Agnes, wife of Sir Walter Forrester of Carden, vi. 223.
— Agnes Caroline, wife of lt.-col. John Murray of Touchadam, vi. 273.
— Alan de, 2nd son of William de G. of Dalkeith, vi. 199.
— Alexander, tutor of Morphie, i. 282.
— — his wife, Katharine Arbuthnott, i. 282.
— Alexander, 2nd son of William G. of Claverhouse, iii. 319.
— Alexander, eldest son of Maliso, 1st earl of Menteith, vi. 144.
— Alexander, probable son of Peter de G. of Dalkeith, vi. 198.
— Alexander, 5th son of Sir Patrick de G. of Dundaff, vi. 215.
— Alexander, 2nd son of Alexander G. of Callander, vi. 220.
Graham, Alexander, pensioner of Cambuskenneth, vi. 229.
— Alison, wife of Gilbert Primrose, iii. 317; vii. 213.
— Alistair Mungo, R.N., vi. 274.
— Allan, capt. Bengal Artillery, iv. 569.
— Alma Imogen Leonora Carlotta, wife of marquess of Breadalbane, ii. 213; vi. 273; ix. 46.
— Andrew, 3rd son of 1st earl of Airth and Menteith, i. 137.
— Andrew Gray *or*, (*alias* Henry Lindsay), i. 138.
— Andrew, 3rd son of John G. of Downans and Duchray, vi. 148.
— Andrew, 2nd son of Wm. G. of Duchray, vi. 148.
— Andrew, 4th son of Gilbert G. of Gartavertane, vi. 150.
— Andrew, bishop of Dunblane, vi. 226, 233.
— Anna, wife of 3rd earl of Callender, ii. 363; vi. 259.
— Anna, wife of David Carmichael of Balmedie, iv. 568; ix. 112.
— Anna, married dau. of John G. of Duchray, vi. 148.
— Anna, wife of Jas. Graham of Gartur, vi. 154.
— Anna, wife of Alex. Colquhoun of Camstradden, vi. 161.
— Anna, wife of Sir John Lyon of Glamis, viii. 260, 270.
— Anne, wife of Sir Mungo Murray of Blebo, i. 138, 467.
— Anne, wife of Robert Young of Auldbar, iii. 324.
— Anne, dau. of 2nd viscount of Preston, vii. 107.
— Anne, wife of Sir Adolphus John Dalrymple, viii. 140.
— Archibald, 7th son of 1st earl of Airth and Menteith, i. 138; ix. 9.
— — his wife, Janet Johnston, i. 138.
— Archibald, bishop of the Isles, ii. 295 *n*.
— Archibald, 5th son of Geo. G. of Rednock, vi. 161.
— Barbara, dau. of Geo. G. of Boquhapple, vi. 150.
— Beatrice Violet, wife of 2nd lord Greville, vi. 273.
— Beatrix, wife of 3rd lord Madderty, vi. 241; viii. 219.
— Caroline, dau. of 3rd duke of Montrose, vi. 271; ix. 138.
— Charles, 6th son of 1st earl of Airth, i. 138.
— Charles, 2nd son of 2nd marquess of Montrose, vi. 258.
— Charles, rector of Southchurch, vii. 103.
— — his wife, Priscilla Billingsley, vii. 103.

Graham, Charles, eldest son of 1st viscount of Preston, vii. 106.
—— Christian, wife of William Graham of Duntrune, 5th titular viscount of Dundee, iii. 332.
—— Christian, a Glasgow witch, v. 169.
—— Christian, wife of Sir Wm. Livingston of Kilsyth, v. 189; vi. 159.
—— Christian, wife of John Graham of of Downans and Duchray, vi. 148.
—— Christian, dau. of Jasper G. of Gartur, vi. 153.
—— Christian, illeg. dau. of Robert G. of Gartmore, vi. 158.
—— Christian, wife of Sir John Blackadder of Tulliallan, vi. 164.
—— Christian, wife, of (1) Jas. Haldane of Gleneagles, and (2) Sir Thomas Maule of Panmure, vi. 223: vii. 10.
—— Christian, wife of Robert Graham of Knockdolian, vi. 230.
—— David, 3rd son of Robert G. of Strathcarron and Fintry, iii. 316.
—— David, elder son of James G. of Gartur, vi. 154.
—— David de, killed at Corbridge, vi. 197.
—— David de, Berwickshire, vi. 199.
—— —— his wife, Amabel, vi. 199, 200.
—— Sir David de, v. 332; vi. 200.
—— —— his wife, Agnes Noble, vi. 202.
—— Sir David de, v. 519; vi. 202.
—— —— his wife, Muriel Bisset, v. 519; vi. 202.
—— Sir David de, vi. 196, 209.
—— David, 2nd son of Sir David G. of Old Montrose, vi. 212.
—— David, 3rd son of 1st marquess of Montrose, vi. 254.
—— Dorothea, wife of 2nd lord Rollo of Duncrub, vi. 241; vii. 201.
—— Dougall, 2nd son of Geo. G. of Rednock, vi. 161.
—— Douglas Malise, R.F.A., vi. 274.
—— Duncan, 4th son of Thos. G. of Downans, vi. 148.
—— Duncan, in Gartlonan, vi. 148.
—— —— his wife, Margaret Graham, vi. 148.
—— Egidia, wife of William, 9th earl of Angus, i. 198.
—— Eleanor, wife of Sir Arthur Rawdon, i. 137, 141; iii. 327; vi. 260: ix. 9 *bis*.
—— Elizabeth, wife of John Arbuthnott of Mondynes, i. 291.
—— Elizabeth, wife of Sir Wm. Graham of Gartmore, i. 139, 142, 144; vi. 149.
—— Elizabeth, wife of 4th earl of Caithness, ii. 338; vi. 230.
—— Elizabeth, wife of John Gordon of Park, iii. 323.
—— Elizabeth, wife of Wm. Livingston of Kilsyth, v. 187; vi. 222.
Graham, Elizabeth, wife of Sir John Stewart of Dundonald, vi. 37, 218; ix. 27.
—— Elizabeth, wife of Andrew M'Lachlan of Drumlean, vi. 150.
—— Elizabeth, dau. of Jasper G. of Gartur, vi. 153.
—— Elizabeth, wife of John Macfarlane, vi. 161.
—— Elizabeth, wife of Walter, master of Drummond, vi. 225; vii. 43.
—— Elizabeth, dau. of David G. of Fintry, vi. 354, 358.
—— Elizabeth, wife of P. Carnegie of Lour, vi. 498.
—— Elizabeth, wife of Sir Cuthbert Heron, vii. 101.
—— Elizabeth, wife of James Somerville, viii. 31.
—— Elizabeth, wife of Sir John Lyon of Glamis, viii. 260, 270.
—— Elizabeth, dau. of Sir Wm. G. of Kincardine, ix. 27.
—— Elspeth, niece of 6th earl of Menteith, vi. 163.
—— Emily, wife of E. T. Foley of Stoke Edith Park, vi. 271.
—— Euphemia, wife of (1) Archibald, 5th earl of Douglas, and (2) James, 1st lord Hamilton, iii. 23, 170; iv. 351, 352; viii. 260; ix. 162.
—— Euphame, wife of (1) Robert Vaus of Barnbarroch, and (2) Sir Wm. Stewart of Garlies, iv. 150; vi. 151; ix. 94 *bis*.
—— Fergus, 3rd son of Sir George G. of Netherby, vii. 103.
—— Frances, wife of rev. Robert G. of Netherby, vii. 104.
—— Francis, Queen's College, Oxford, vii. 99.
—— Francis Charles, 2nd son of rev. Charles G., vii. 104.
—— George, husband of Euphemia Dunbar, iii. 279.
—— Mr. George, vicar and provost of Hamilton, iv. 350.
—— George, 6th son of Wm. G. of Duchray, vi. 148.
—— George, 2nd son of Geo. G. of Boquhapple, vi. 150.
—— George, 4th son of Jasper G. of Gartur, vi. 153.
—— George, 5th son of Robt. G. of M'Keanston, vi. 155.
—— George, 2nd son of 5th earl of Menteith, vi. 163.
—— —— his wife, Grisel Stirling, vi. 163.
—— George, R.N., governor of Newfoundland, M.P., vi. 266, 267 *bis*.
—— George, merchant, Edinburgh, viii. 31.
—— Georgina Charlotte, wife of 10th earl of Winchilsea, vi. 271; ix. 138.

Graham, Gilbert, 5th son of Wm. G. of Duchray, vi. 148.
— Gilbert, in Rednock, vi. 153.
— — his wife, Mary Graham, vi. 153.
— Giles, wife of William, 9th earl of Angus, i. 198.
— Grizel, dau. of Wm. G., i. 140.
— Grizel, wife of William Cochrane of Kilmaronock, iii. 351; vi. 259.
— Grizel, wife of Sir James Keith of Powburn, vi. 238 *bis*.
— Sir Harry, illeg. son of 4th earl of Montrose, vi. 241.
— Harry, colonel in Dutch service, vi. 255, 256 *n*.
— Helen, wife of Sir Arthur Rawdon, i. 137, 141; iii. 327; vi. 260; ix. 9 *bis*.
— Helen, wife of George Lundie, iii. 322.
— Helen, dau. of Geo. G. of Boquhapple, vi. 150.
— Helen, dau. of 5th earl of Menteith, vi. 163.
— Helen, wife of Humphrey Colquhoun of Luss, vi. 225.
— Helen, wife of Sir Alex. Falconer of Glenfarquhar, ix. 123.
— Helen Violet, dau. of 5th earl of Montrose, vi. 274.
— Henrietta Maria, dau. of Sir Richard G. of Netherby, vii. 101.
— Henry, vi. 153.
— — his wife, Margaret Menteith, vi. 153.
— Henry, 6th son of Sir Wm. G. of Dundaff, vi. 219.
— Hermione Emily, wife of Donald Cameron of Lochiel, vi. 274.
— Herries, wife of M. Malcolm of Balbeadie, vi. 151; ix. 136.
— Hew, illeg. son of Geo. G. of Rednock, vi. 161 *bis*.
— Hutcheon, illeg. son of 'Long Will' G., vii. 98.
— Idonea, wife of Sir Adam of Swinburne, vi. 197; ix. 137.
— Isabel, wife of Walter, 6th lord High Stewart, i. 14; vi. 197.
— Isabella, *error for* Helen, dau. of Sir Jas. G., and wife of capt. Rawdon, i. 173, 141; iii. 327; vi. 260.
— Isabella, wife of 7th viscount of Arbuthnott, i. 314.
— Isobel, wife of Walter Stirling of Auchyll, vi. 148.
— Isobel, wife of Walter Graham of Gartur, vi. 152.
— Isobel, wife of Alexander Middleton, vi. 172.
— J—, wife of David Graham, 3rd of Fintry, vi. 225.
— Jacoba Katharina, wife of (1) Sir Reginald Graham, and (2) col. Brown, vii. 104.
Graham, Sir James, 2nd son of 1st earl of Airth and Menteith, i. 137, 141; ix. 9.
— — his 1st wife, Margaret Erskine, i. 137; ii. 272.
— — his 2nd wife, Isabella Bramhall, i. 137.
— James, son of William G., i. 139.
— James, merchant, Dundee, iii. 332.
— James, 2nd son of Thomas G. of Boquhapple, vi. 150.
— James, 3rd son of Wm. G. of Gartur, vi. 154.
— James, 2nd son of Robt. G. of M'Keanston, vi. 155.
— James, 3rd son of Gilbert G. of Gartavertane, vi. 159.
— Mr. James, 3rd son of 1st lord Graham, vi. 222.
— James, 2nd son of John G. of Braco, vi. 238.
— Janet, wife of James Eccles of Eccles, ii. 460.
— Janet, dau. of Geo. G. of Boquhapple, vi. 150.
— Janet, wife of John Stewart of Annat, vi. 153.
— Janet, dau. of Wm. G. of Gartur, vi. 154.
— Janet, wife of (1) William Graham of Gartavertane, and Gartmore, and (2) Colin Campbell of Blairnarne, vi. 158.
— Janet, wife of Gilbert Keith of Inverugie, vi. 222.
— Janet, wife of (1) Sir A. Murray of Balvaird, and (2) Sir H. Graham of Morphie, vi. 230; viii. 188; ix. 137.
— Jean, wife of 2nd Lord Ogilvy of Airlie, i. 116; vi. 223.
— Jean, wife of John Chisholm of Cromlix, i. 138.
— Jean, wife of Walter Graham of Boquhapple, iii. 323; vi. 150.
— Jean, mistress of William Chisholm, bishop of Dunblane, vi. 226.
— Jean, dau. of 1st marquess of Montrose, vi. 254.
— Jean, wife of Jonathan Urquhart of Cromarty, vi. 259.
— John, son of Archibald G., i. 138.
— John, 3rd son of William G. of Claverhouse, iii. 319.
— John, lieutenant in Sir Wm. Lockhart's regiment, iii. 326.
— John, notary, Stirling, v. 187 *n*.
— Sir John de, vi. 137, 208.
— — his wife, Mary, countess of Menteith, vi. 137, 208.
— John, illeg. son of 1st earl of Menteith, vi. 146.
— Sir John 'of the bright sword,' vi. 146 *n*.
— John, 4th son of John G. of Downans and Duchray, vi. 148.

Graham, John, 3rd son of John G. of Gallingad, vi. 148.
— John, 3rd son of Geo. G. of Boquhapple, vi. 150.
— John, illeg. son of Gaspard G. of Gartur, vi. 153 *bis*.
— John, captain, 2nd son of John G. of Gartur, vi. 153.
— John, 2nd son of James G. of Gartur, vi. 154.
— John, younger son of James G. of Gartur, vi. 154.
— John, in Brae Leny, vi. 155.
— — his wife, Isabella Campbell, vi. 155.
— John, illeg. son of Robt. G. of Gartmore, vi. 158.
— John, nephew of 6th earl of Menteith, vi. 163.
— John, perhaps son of Peter de G. of Dalkeith, vi. 198.
— John, 3rd son of Sir David G. of Old Montrose, vi. 213.
— John, 2nd son of Sir William G. of Dundaff, vi. 217.
— John, younger son of Sir James G. of Braco, vi. 238.
— John, 2nd son of 4th earl of Montrose, vi. 241 *n*.
— John, son of Sir Robert G. of Morphie, vi. 244.
— John, 3rd son of 1st duke of Montrose, vi. 266.
— John, merchant in Dundee, vi. 498.
— Jonet, wife of Humphrey Rollo, vii. 186.
— Jonet, wife of Robert Rollo of Duncrub, vii. 186, 187.
— Katharine, wife of * Sellick, i. 140.
— Katharine, wife of A. Campbell of Lagvinshoch, ii. 186.
— Katrine, dau. of Geo. G. of Boquhapple, vi. 150.
— Katharine, wife of Humphrey Moray of Ogilvy and Abercairny, vi. 220.
— Katharine, dau. of 4th earl of Montrose, vi. 241.
— Katharine, wife of John Armstrong of Sark, vii. 99.
— Katharine, dau. of Sir Richard G. of Netherby, vii. 101.
— Katharine, wife of 11th earl of Suffolk, vii. 103.
— Katharine, wife of 4th lord Widdrington, vii. 104, 107.
— Katharine, wife of Andrew Alexander of Menstrie, viii. 166.
— Lilias, wife of John, lord Fleming, 1st earl of Wigtown, vi. 239; viii. 546; ix. 137.
— Lilias, wife of Sir John Colquhoun of Luss, vi. 241.

* Name unknown.

Graham, Lucy, wife of Archibald, lord Douglas of Douglas, i. 213; vi. 268.
— Lucy, wife of 2nd earl Powis, vi. 271; ix. 138.
— Magdalene, wife of Robert Graham, iii. 324; ix. 74.
— Malise, in Kirkland of Aberfoyle, vi. 148.
— Margaret, wife of (1) Alexander, lord Garlies, and (2) Ludovic, 16th earl of Crawford, i. 138; iii. 34; iv. 161.
— Margaret, wife of John Colquhoun, i. 140.
— Margaret, wife of Alex. Stirling of Auchyll, i. 141.
— Margaret, wife of (1) Geo. Symmer, and (2) Robert Arbuthnott of Findowrie, i. 294; iii. 322.
— Margaret, wife of 4th earl of Argyll, i. 339; vi. 159.
— Margaret, dau. of Robt. G. of Knockdolian, ii. 460.
— Margaret, wife of (1) Alex. Ogilvie, and (2) John Inglis, iii. 319; ix. 74.
— Margaret, wife of Alexander Strachan, iii. 323.
— Margaret, dau. of 1st earl of Montrose, v. 351.
— Margaret, dau. of Robert G. of Gartmore, v. 189 *n*.
— Margaret, wife of Thomas, 9th earl of Mar, v. 584; vi. 139.
— Margaret, wife of Robert, master of Erskine, v. 611; vi. 230.
— Margaret, wife of (1) Hugh, 4th earl of Ross, and (2) John de Barclay, vi. 211; vii. 236.
— Margaret, wife of Sir John Somerville of Cambusnethan, vi. 226; viii. 14.
— Margaret, wife of 1st lord Napier of Merchiston, vi. 241, 424.
— Margaret, wife of Duncan Graham, vi. 148.
— Margaret, dau. of George G. of Boquhapple, vi. 150.
— Margaret, wife of Thos. Stewart of Ballymoran, vi. 154.
— Margaret, dau. of Robt. G. of Gartmore, vi. 158.
— Margaret, alleged wife of Sir William Douglas, vi. 197, 342.
— Margaret, dau. of 1st duke of Montrose, vi. 266.
— Margaret, wife of 1st lord Nairn, vi. 394.
— Margaret, wife of P. Carnegie of Lour, vi. 498.
— Margaret, wife of * Fenwick, vii. 104.
— Margaret, wife of Alexander Carnegie of Balnamoon, viii. 62.
— Margaret Frances, wife of (1) A. Æ.

* Name unknown.

Mackintosh, and (2) James W. (Grimston), 3rd earl of Verulam, iv. 98.
Graham, Marion, wife of Walter Graham of Gartur, i. 137; vi. 153.
— Marion, wife of Wm. Schaw of Knockhill, vi. 150.
— Marion, dau. of Geo. G. of Boquhapple, vi. 150.
— Marion, dau. of Walter G. of Boquhapple, vi. 150.
— Marion, dau. of James G. of Gartur, vi. 154.
— Marion, wife of Alex. Alexander of Menstrie, vi. 159; viii. 169.
— Marion, wife of 2nd lord Ogilvy of Airlie, i. 116; vi. 223.
— Mariot, wife of Alexander Guthrie of Kincaldrum, iii. 322.
— Marjorie, wife of George Graham of Boquhapple, vi. 150.
— Marjorie, dau. of Geo. G. of Boquhapple, vi. 150.
— Martha, dau. of 3rd duke of Montrose, vi. 271.
— Mary, wife of Sir John Campbell of Glenorchy, i. 138; ii. 201.
— Mary, wife of James Hodge of Gladsmuir, i. 139.
— Mary, elder dau. of lord Kinpont, wife of Sir John Allardice of Allardice, i. 139, 142.
— Mary, wife of John Bogle, i. 140.
— Mary, married dau. of John G. of Duchray, vi. 148.
— Mary, wife of Gilbert Graham in Rednock, vi. 153.
— Mary, dau. of Walter G. of Gartur, vi. 153.
— Mary, dau. of John G. of Rednock, vi. 161.
— Mary, wife of George Buchanan of Buchanan, vi. 162.
— Mary, wife of Sir E. Musgrave of Scaleby, vii. 101.
— Mary, wife of John Michell, vii. 103.
— Mary, dau. of Reginald G. of Pickhill, vii. 104.
— Mary, dau. of 1st viscount of Preston, vii. 107.
— Mary Eliot, wife of gen. C. M. Carmichael, iv. 569.
— Mary Helen Alma, ix. 138.
— Mathias, vii. 99 *n.*
— Matilda, wife of Sir John Drummond of Concraig, vi. 214.
— Matilda, wife of Alex. Lindsay, ix. 61.
— Montagu William, capt. Coldstream Guards, M.P., vi. 271.
— — his wife, Harriet Anne Bateman-Hanbury, vi. 271.
— Mungo, 3rd son of Walter G. of Boquhapple, vi. 150.
Graham, Mungo, 3rd son of Robt. G. of M'Keanston, vi. 155.
— Nicolas, wife of John Moray of Abercairny, vi. 230.
— Patrick, 5th son of 1st earl of Airth, i. 138.
— Patrick, sheriff depute of Stirlingshire, vi. 150, 151.
— Patrick, 2nd son of Walter G. of Boquhapple, v. 150.
— Patrick, rector of Kilmore, vi. 151.
— Patrick, 3rd son of William de G., vi. 199.
— Patrick, 2nd son of Sir Patrick G. of Mugdock, vi. 208.
— Patrick, 4th son of Sir Robt. G. of Kinpunt, vi. 215.
— Patrick, archbishop of St. Andrews, vi. 219, 354, 358.
— Patrick, brother of Sir Robt. G. of Fintry, vi. 219.
— Patrick, canon, rector of Glasgow University, vi. 223.
— Patrick, 2nd son of Sir Wm. G. of Braco, ix. 137.
— Peter *or* Peres, 'del counte de Dunfres,' vi. 197.
— Richard, the sorcerer, ii. 70.
— Richard, in Netherby, vii. 98.
— Richard, University College, Oxford, vii. 102.
— Robert, 4th son of 1st earl of Airth, i. 138.
— Robert, 3rd son of Gaspard G. of Gartur, vi. 153.
— Robert, in Shannochill, 3rd son of John G. of Gartur, vi. 153, 154.
— — his 1st wife, Jean Menteith, vi. 155.
— — his 2nd wife, Mary Stirling, vi. 155.
— Robert, 3rd son of Walter G. of Gartur, vi. 153.
— Robert, in Shannochill, 4th son of Robt. G. of M'Keanston, vi. 155.
— — his wife, Katharine Menteith, vi. 155.
— Robert, 3rd son of Sir Henry G. of Dalkeith, vi. 198.
— Robert, 4th son of 1st lord Graham, vi. 222.
— Robert, 3rd son of Sir John G. of Braco, vi. 238, 259.
— Robert, 4th son of 1st marquess of Montrose, vi. 254.
— Robert James Stuart, Brooklyn, vii. 104.
— Susanna, dau. of 1st viscount of Preston, vii. 107.
— Susanna, wife of Reginald Carnaby, vii. 101.
— Thomas, writer, Glasgow, v. 180.
— Thomas, 3rd son of Patrick G. of Kilpont, vi. 145.

Graham, Thomas, in Inchrie, 4th son of Wm. G. of Duchray, vi. 148 *bis*, 161.
— Thomas, 3rd son of Wm. G. of Boquhapple, vi. 150.
— Thomas, eldest son of Sir Robt. G. of Kinpunt, vi. 215.
— Umfrid, 5th son of Sir Robt. G. of Kinpunt, vi. 215.
— Violet Hermione, wife of 5th duke of Montrose, vi. 273; ix. 138.
— Walter, 2nd son of Walter G. of Gartur, vi. 152.
— Walter, eldest son of Geo. G. of Gartur, vi. 153 *bis*.
— Walter, 2nd son of Jasper G. of Gartur, vi. 153 *bis*.
— Walter, eldest son of Wm. G. of Gartur, vi. 154.
— Walter, 4th son of Geo. G. of Rednock, vi. 161.
— Walter, 3rd son of Sir Robt. G. of Kinpunt, vi. 215.
— William, self-styled earl of Menteith, i. 139, 142.
— William, lieut. in earl of Airlie's troop, 1686, ii. 490 *n*.
— William, tutor of Fintry, iii. 319 *n*.
— William, eldest son of Sir Wm. G. of Claverhouse, iii. 321.
— William, 3rd son of Thos. G. of Downans, vi. 148.
— William, senior, merchant, Edinburgh, vi. 151.
— William, 3rd son of Walter G. of Gartur, vi. 152.
— William, 2nd son of 3rd duke of Montrose, vi. 154.
— William, 6th son of Sir Henry G. of Dalkeith, vi. 197.
— William, 2nd son of Peter de G. of Dalkeith, vi. 198.
— William de, son of Alan de G., vi. 199.
— William, 2nd son of above, vi. 199.
— William de, keeper of Lochleven Castle, vi. 211.
— William, 'Long Will,' vii. 98.
— William, capt. R.N., 2nd son of James G. of Levens, vii. 102.
— William, dean of Carlisle and Wells, vii. 103.
— — his 1st wife, Mary Offley, vii. 103.
— — his 2nd wife, Alice *, vii. 103.
— William, in holy orders, vii. 103, 105, 108.
— — his wife, Susanna Reeve, vii. 103.
— *, wife of James Arbuthnott, i. 281.
— *, 2nd wife of John Hamilton, 5th son of Wm. H. of Wishaw, ii. 52.
— *, wife of Malcolm Drummond of Megour, vi. 146.

* Name unknown.

Graham, *, dau. of John G. of Downans and Duchray, vi. 148.
— *, wife of Sir Malcolm Drummond, vi. 208.
— *, 1st wife of William, 3rd earl of Ross, vi. 204.
— *, 2nd wife of Sir John Carnegie of Balnamoon. viii. 61.
— *, wife of capt. Jas. Dalzell, ix. 54.
Graham-Montgomery of Stanhope, Sir Graham, 3rd bart., v. 201.
— Alice Anne, wife of (1) Richard, 3rd duke of Buckingham and Chandos, and (2) Wilbraham, 1st earl Egerton of Tatton, v. 201.
Graham-Stirling of Craigbarnet, Charles Campbell, major, vi. 154.
— — Caroline Frances, wife of commr. G. H. Miller, R.N., vi. 156.
Grahamslaw of Newton, John, v. 461, 462.
— Helen, wife of Robert Ker of Newton, v. 462.
Graimes, Jehan de, Provence, vi. 191 *n*.
Grainger, James, minister of Kinneff, i. 80, 308; vi. 59.
— — his wife, Christian Fletcher, i. 80.
Gramont, Philibert, comte de, i. 55 *bis*.
— — his wife, Elizabeth Hamilton, i. 55.
— Claude Charlotte de, wife of Henry Howard, earl of Stafford, i. 56.
— Marie Elizabeth de, Abbess of Poussay, i. 56; ix. 3.
Granard, Patrick Forbes, ancestor of the family of Forbes, earl of, iv. 51.
Grandison, George Mason (Villiers), 2nd earl, ii. 306.
— John (Fitzgerald), 1st earl, iii. 611.
— William (Villiers), 2nd viscount. i. 31; vi. 378.
— John (Villiers), 3d viscount, vi. 379.
Grange, James Erskine, 2nd son of Charles, earl of Mar; lord justice-clerk, styled lord, v. 241, 627, 632.
— — his wife, Rachel Chiesley, v. 628.
Grant, master of, Francis William, 2nd son of 6th earl of Seafield, vii. 489.
— master of, John Charles, 3rd son of 6th earl of Seafield, vii. 489.
— of Abernethy, John, vii. 467.
— of Abriachan, Ludovic, vii. 476.
— of Achmonie, Ludovic, vii. 476.
— of Aonach, Duncan, v. 562.
— — his wife, Katharine Macdonald. v. 562.
— of Ardneillie, James, v. 530; vii. 465.
— — his 1st wife, Grizel Menzies, ix. 155.
— — his 2nd wife, Katharine Rose, v. 530; vii. 465.
— of Arndilly, David, vii. 450.
— — William Macdowall, vii. 448.
— — his wife Eleanora Fraser, vii. 448.

* Name unknown.

Grant of Auchatemrach, John, vii. 476.
—— —— Ludovic, vii. 476.
—— of Auchernak, James, vii. 466.
—— of Auchnarrows, James, vii. 466.
—— —— John, vii. 466.
—— of Auchnastank, Ludovick, vii. 472.
—— of Nether Auchroisk, John, vii. 458.
—— of Auldcash, John, vii. 458.
—— of Avielochan, Mungo, vii. 471.
—— of Ballindalloch, Alexander, captain, vii. 483.
—— —— his wife, Penuel Grant, vii. 483.
—— —— Sir George, bart., viii. 55.
—— —— John, vii. 461.
—— —— John, last laird of 1st line, vii. 478.
—— —— John, ix. 128.
—— —— his wife, Margaret Leslie, ix. 128.
—— —— Patrick, ancestor of the 1st family of, vii. 457.
—— —— Patrick, vii, 464.
—— —— his wife, Grissel Grant, vii. 463.
—— —— William, lieut.-col., ancestor of the 2nd family of, vii. 478.
—— —— his wife, Anne Grant, vii. 478.
—— —— William, major, vii. 483.
—— of Balmacaan, Thomas, 'dubh,' vii. 472.
—— —— his wife, Mary Campbell, vii. 472.
—— of Blairfindy, William, ancestor of the family of, vii. 457.
—— of Cantraydown, Patrick, vii. 457.
—— of Cardeny, Charles Cathcart, capt. R.N., vii. 482.
—— of Carnoch, John, vii. 476.
—— —— Ludovick, vii. 476.
—— of Cluniebeg, Patrick, tutor of Grant, vii. 470, 474.
—— —— his 1st wife, Anna Sutherland, iii. 207; vii. 470.
—— —— his 2nd wife, Sibyl Mackenzie, vii. 470.
—— of Cluniemore, John, vii. 476.
—— —— Ludovick, vii. 476.
—— —— Patrick, tutor of Grant, vii. 207; vii. 470.
—— of Clurie, Duncan, vii. 468.
—— of Congalton, William, viii. 142.
—— —— his wife, Dorothea Dalrymple, viii. 142.
—— of Corriemony, Duncan, vii. 464.
—— —— John, ancestor of the family of, vii. 458.
—— —— his wife, * Strachan, vii. 458.
—— —— John, vii. 464.
—— —— John, grandson of John G. of Grant, vii. 466.
—— —— John, vii. 476.
—— of Craigo, Sir George, bart., viii. 55.
—— of Culbin, George, major, governor of Fort George, vii. 478.
—— —— Sir Ludovick, vii. 478.

* Name unknown.

Grant of Culcabok, John, ii. 179; v. 521 *n.*, 523; vii. 459.
—— of Culnakirk, John, vii. 476.
—— —— Ludovick, vii. 476.
—— of Culvullin, Patrick, vii. 472.
—— of Dalfour, Archibald, vii. 460.
—— —— his wife, Isabella Cumming, vii. 461.
—— of Dalvey, Sir James, 1st bart., vii. 80.
—— —— his wife, Agnes Scott, vii. 80.
—— of Dandaleith, Duncan, vii. 465.
—— —— John, vii. 465.
—— of Delnahaitnich, Mungo, vii. 471.
—— of Dovelly, John, keeper of Tarnaway Castle, vi. 296.
—— of Druminnor, Robert, vii. 564.
—— —— his wife, Elizabeth Forbes, vii. 564.
—— of Dunphail, Francis, lieut.-gen., M.P., i. 491; vii. 482.
—— —— his wife, Katharine Sophia Cox, vii. 482.
—— —— Lewis, colonel, vii. 478.
—— —— Sir Ludovick, vii. 478.
—— of Duthil, Mungo, vii. 471.
—— —— his 1st wife, Margaret Gordon, vii. 472.
—— —— his 2nd wife, Elspeth Grant, vii. 472.
—— of Edinvillie, James, vii. 465.
—— of Elchies, John, vii. 303.
—— of Easter Elchies, Duncan, ancestor of the 1st family of, vii. 460.
—— —— his wife, Marjory Leslie, vii. 460.
—— —— Patrick 'Og,' ancestor of the 2nd family of, vii. 465.
—— —— his wife, Margaret Innes, vii. 465.
—— of Wester Elchies, Patrick, lieut.-col., ancestor of the 2nd family of, vii. 475.
—— —— his wife, Janet Forbes, vii. 475.
—— of Finlarg, William, vii. 460.
—— of Freuchie, Sir Duncan, 1st laird, vii. 455, 497.
—— —— Duncan, the younger, vii. 464.
—— —— his wife, Margaret Mackintosh, iii. 204; vii. 464.
—— —— James, 3rd laird, iv. 20; vii. 459; ix. 90.
—— —— his 1st wife, Elizabeth Forbes, iv. 20, 54; vii. 460.
—— —— his 2nd wife, Christian Barclay, vii. 459.
—— —— James, 7th laird, iii. 204; vii. 468, 472, 473.
—— —— his contracted wife, Jean Fleming, vii. 474; viii. 549.
—— —— his wife, Mary Stewart, vi. 320; vii. 474; ix. 139 *bis*.
—— —— John, the younger, vii. 456.
—— —— his wife, Muriel Mackintosh, vii. 456 *bis*.
—— —— John, 2nd laird, i. 84; iv. 19; vii. 457.
—— —— his wife, Margaret Ogilvy, iv. 19; vii. 458; ix. 89.

Grant of Freuchie, John, 4th laird, vii. 280, 289, 461.
—— —— his 1st wife, Margaret Stewart, i. 444; vii. 463.
—— —— his 2nd wife, Janet *or* Jean Leslie, iii. 533; vii. 289, 463.
—— —— John, 5th laird, i. 470; vii. 466.
—— —— his wife, Lilias Murray, i. 470; vii. 467.
—— —— Sir John, 6th laird, vii. 469.
—— —— his wife, Mary Ogilvy, iv. 27; vii. 470.
—— —— Ludovick, 8th laird, vii. 476.
—— of Gartenbeg, Mungo, ancestor of the family of, vii. 472.
—— of Gartenmore, John, vii. 472.
—— of Gellovie, Mungo, ancestor of the family of, vii. 471.
—— of Glencarnie, John, sheriff of Inverness, vii. 454.
—— —— his wife, Matilda of Glencarnie, vii. 454.
—— —— John, vii. 458.
—— of Glenmoriston, Ian Robert James Murray, vii. 459.
—— —— John, 1st laird, vii. 459.
—— —— his 1st wife, Elizabeth *or* Isabella Innes, vii. 459.
—— —— his 2nd wife, Agnes Fraser, v. 521 *n*., 523; vii. 459.
—— —— John, vii. 476.
—— of Grant, Alexander, brigadier-general, vi. 323; vii. 477, 479.
—— —— his 1st wife, Elizabeth Stewart, vi. 323; vii. 480.
—— —— his 2nd wife, Anne Smith, vii. 480.
—— —— Charles Thomas, major, iii. 615.
—— —— his wife, Emelia Sophia Cary, iii. 615.
—— —— Sir James, bart., vii. 356, 477, 480.
—— —— his wife, Anne Colquhoun of Luss, vii. 480.
—— —— Sir James, bart., vii. 485.
—— —— his wife, Jane Duff of Hatton, vii. 485.
—— —— John, vii. 462.
—— —— his 1st wife, Margaret Stewart, i. 444; vii. 463.
—— —— his 2nd wife, Janet Leslie, vii. 289.
—— —— Sir Lewis Alexander, vii. 486, 487.
—— —— Ludovick, vii. 476.
—— —— his 1st wife, Janet Brodie of Lethen, vii. 477.
—— —— his 2nd wife, Jean Houstoun, vii. 477.
—— —— Sir Ludovick, bart., iv. 39; vii. 478, 483.
—— —— his 1st wife, Marion Dalrymple, vii. 484; viii. 142.
—— —— his 2nd wife, Margaret Ogilvy, iv. 39; vii. 484.
Grant of Grantsfield, Alexander, i. 103.
—— —— his wife, Elizabeth Lyon, i. 103; viii. 303.
—— of Hempriggs, Patrick, vii. 463.
—— —— his wife, Jean Gordon, vii. 463.
—— of Inverallan, John le, vii. 454.
—— —— John, vii. 466.
—— of Kilgraston, Francis, i. 524.
—— —— John, iv. 294.
—— —— his wife, Margaret Gray, iv. 294.
—— —— John, iii. 493.
—— —— his wife, Lucy Bruce, iii. 493.
—— of Kinchirdie, Mungo, vii. 471.
—— of Kinminitie, James, iii. 204.
—— —— John, vii. 467.
—— of Kinveachie, John, vii. 466.
—— of Knockando, James, i. 103.
—— —— his wife, Grizel Gordon, i. 103.
—— —— Mungo, ancestor of the family of, vii. 472.
—— of Lethen, John, vii. 467.
—— of Lurg, Robert, ancestor of the family of, vii. 465.
—— —— his wife, Katharine Stewart, vii. 465.
—— of Muckerach, Patrick, vii. 463.
—— —— his wife, Jean Gordon, vii. 463.
—— of Muckrath, William, vii. 460.
—— of Monymusk, Archibald, ancestor of the family of, vii. 460.
—— —— his wife, Isabella Cumming, vii. 461.
—— —— Sir Arthur Henry, 9th bart., vii. 461.
—— of Moyness, James, ancestor of the family of, vii. 465.
—— —— his 2nd wife, Katharine Rose, vii. 465.
—— —— John, v. 248.
—— —— his wife, Jean Falconer, v. 248.
—— of Mulben, John, eldest son of James G. of Freuchie, vii. 461.
—— —— Sir John, vii. 469.
—— —— his wife, Mary Ogilvy, iv. 27; vii. 470.
—— of Mullochard, Mungo, vii. 472.
—— —— his wife, Mary Grant, vii. 472.
—— of Parkhill, John, vii. 280, 462.
—— of Prestongrange, William, lord of Session, iv. 596.
—— of Pitcherrell Croy, John, vii. 476.
—— —— Ludovick, vii. 476.
—— of Pluscardine, James, vii. 480.
—— —— his wife, Anne Colquhoun of Luss, vii. 480.
—— —— Ludovick, vii. 476.
—— of Rothes, John, 1st laird, vii. 303.
—— of Rothiemurchus, Duncan, vii. 469.
—— —— his wife, Muriel Ross, vii. 468.
—— —— James, 1st laird, vii. 460.
—— —— his 1st wife, Elizabeth Forbes, iv. 20, 54; vii. 460.
—— —— his 2nd wife, Christian Barclay, vii. 460.

Grant of Rothiemurchus, John Peter, sheriff-substitute of Inverness-shire, vii. 463.
— — Patrick, 2nd son of John G. of Grant, vii. 463, 466.
— — his wife, Jean Gordon, vii. 463.
— — Patrick MacAlpine, vii. 470.
— — his wife, Mary Grant, vii. 470.
— of Sheuglie, John, ancestor of the family of, vii. 458.
— of Stratherrick, vii. 454.
— of Strome, Patrick, vii. 465.
— of Tullochcarron, John, vii. 478.
— — William, vii. 478.
— of Urquhart, John, vii. 457.
— — Patrick, vii. 457.
— of Windmill Hill, Francis, lieut.-gen., vii. 482.
— Agnes, wife of Donald Cameron of Cameron, vii. 459.
— Agnes, wife of David Rose, vii. 461.
— Agnes, *or* Annas, wife of (1) Sir L. Mackintosh of Dunachton, and (2) L. Mackintosh of Borlum, vii. 468.
— Alexander, in Mains of Mulben, vii. 470.
— — his wife, Isobel Nairn, vii. 471.
— Alice, wife of (1) John Dent, and (2) Sir Julius Cæsar, viii. 412.
— Anna, wife of 3rd lord Lovat, v. 526; vii. 458.
— Anna, wife of Sir P. Ogilvy of Boyne, vii. 475.
— Anne, wife of K. Mackenzie of Gairloch, vii. 473.
— Anne, wife of P. Grant, minister of Logie Easter, vii. 478.
— Anne, wife of Wm. Grant of Ballindalloch, vii. 478.
— Ann, dau. of Sir Ludovick G. of Grant, vii. 484.
— Anne Charlotte, wife of lord Geo. Murray, bishop of St. Davids, i. 491.
— Anne Drummond, wife of Sir Harry Innes of Innes, vii. 356, 483.
— Anne Margaret, sister of the 5th and 6th earls of Seafield, vii. 486.
— Barbara, wife of Colin Mackenzie of Kintail, iii. 69; vii. 464, 501.
— Charles John Cecil, captain, vii. 228.
— — his wife, Sibyl Myra Caroline Primrose, vii. 228.
— Christiana, dau. of John G. of Freuchie, vii. 459.
— Christopher, Lancashire, viii. 412.
— Clementina, wife of Sir Wm. Dunbar of Durn, vii. 483.
— David, 6th son of Ludovick G. of Grant, vii. 478.
— Elizabeth, wife of John Mackenzie of Kintail, vii. 459, 499.
— Elizabeth, contracted to Wm. Fraser of Struy, wife of (1) John Leslie of Balquhain, and (2) Wm. Cumming of Inverallochy, vii. 463; ix. 155.
Grant, Elizabeth, wife of Alexander Cumming of Altyre, vii. 466.
— Elizabeth, wife of Mungo Grant of Kinchirdie, vii. 472.
— Elizabeth, wife of Hugh Rose of Kilravock, vii. 478.
— Elizabeth, dau. of Sir Ludovick G. of Grant, vii. 485.
— Elizabeth Graham, wife of William Fraser, vii. 450.
— Sir Francis William, lieut.-col., M.P., vii. 486, 487.
— — his 1st wife, Mary Anne Dunn, vii. 489.
— — his 2nd wife, Louisa Emma Maunsell, vii. 489.
— George, captain, governor of Dumbarton Castle, vii. 471.
— Grissel, wife of Patrick Grant of Ballindalloch, vii. 463.
— Helen, mistress of Donald Macdonald of Glengarry, v. 561, 562; vii. 464.
— Helen, wife of Sir Alex. P. Cumming Gordon of Altyre, vii. 485.
— Henry, Congalton, v. 253.
— — his wife, Isabella Catherine Keith-Falconer, v. 253.
— Humphrey, eldest son of Sir James G. of Grant, vii. 481.
— Isabel, wife of A. Campbell of Glenlyon, ii. 179; vii. 461.
— Isabel, wife of lieut.-col. F. A. Gordon, iv. 560.
— Isobel, contracted to W. Fraser of Strowie, and wife of (1) John Leslie, and (2) Wm. Cumming, vii. 463; ix. 155.
— James, 2nd son of Duncan G. of Dandaleith, vii. 465.
— James Thomas, registrar of the Provincial Court of Benares, vii. 486.
— Jane, dau. of Sir James G. of Grant, vii. 487.
— Janet, wife of (1) Alex. Sutherland, and (2) Jas. Dempster, iii. 201; vii. 461.
— Janet, wife of John, 4th earl of Hyndford, iv. 596.
— Janet, alleged 1st wife of William Fraser of Struy, v. 527; vii. 461 *n*.
— Janet, wife of Alex. Gordon of Strathavon, vii. 461.
— Janet, wife of Sir R. Mackenzie of Scatwell, vii. 479.
— Jean, wife of (1) Wm. Sutherland, and (2) Thos. Mackenzie, iii. 206; vii. 468, 504.
— Jean, wife of Wm. (Duff), baron Braco of Kilbride, 1st earl Fife, vii. 482.
— Sir John, 'Ian Ruadh,' sheriff of Inverness, vii. 454.
— — his wife, Matilda of Glencarnie, vii. 454.

Grant, John, illeg. son of John G. of Grant, vii. 464.
— John, eldest son of Ludovick G. of Grant, vii. 477.
— Katharine, wife of Alexander Ogilvy of Kempcairn, iv. 27; vii. 468.
— Katharine, wife of (1) Lachlan Macintosh, and (2) A. Baillie of Dunain, vii. 456.
— Katharine, wife of John Haliburton, vii. 458 *n.*
— Katharine, dau. of John G. of Grant, vii. 464.
— Sir Laurence, sheriff of Inverness, vii. 454.
— Lilias, wife of Sir W. Innes of Balveny, vii. 468.
— Lilias, wife of John Byres of Coates, vii. 473.
— Louisa, wife of Captain Wm. Keith-Falconer, v. 252.
— Magdalen, dau. of Sir James G. of Grant, vii. 487.
— Margaret, baroness Gray, wife of D. H. Murray, iv. 295.
— Margaret, wife of Simon, 11th lord Fraser of Lovat, v. 539; vii. 479.
— Margaret, wife of Thomas Cumming of Erneside, vii. 458.
— Margaret, wife of Thomas Cumming of Altyre, vii. 461.
— Margaret, wife of Alex. Gordon of Beldornie, vii. 464.
— Margaret, wife of Roderick Mackenzie of Redcastle, vii. 475.
— Margaret, dau. of Sir Ludovick G. of Grant, vii. 485.
— Margaret, wife of major-gen. Francis Stuart of Lesmurdie, vii. 497.
— Mariana, dau. of Sir Ludovick G. of Grant, vii. 485.
— Marjory, dau. of John G. of Grant, vii. 464.
— Mary, wife of (1) Lewis, 3d marquess of Huntly, and (2) James, 2nd earl of Airlie, i. 126; iv. 548; vii. 472.
— Mary, wife of Patrick MacAlpine Grant of Rothiemurchus, vii. 470.
— Mary, wife of Mungo Grant of Mullochard, vii. 472.
— Mary, wife of Sir Alex. Hamilton of Haggs, vii. 475; ix. 155.
— Mary, dau. of Sir Ludovick G. of Grant, vii. 485.
— Mary Ann, wife of lieut.-gen. James Lindsay, i. 524.
— Morella, wife of Andrew *or* John Fraser, v. 525; vii. 458 *n.*
— Muriel, wife of Patrick Leslie of Balquhain, vii. 456.
— Patrick, son of Marjory Lude *or* Grant, vii. 455.
Grant, Patrick MacIan Roy, vii. 455.
— — his wife, Janet Mackintosh, vii. 455.
— Patrick, minister of Logie Easter, vii. 478.
— — his wife, Anne Grant, vii. 478.
— Patrick, senator of the College of Justice, lord Elchies, vii. 484.
— Penuel, wife of capt. Alex. Grant of Ballindalloch, vii. 483.
— Penuel, wife of Henry Mackenzie, vii. 485.
— Penuel, dau. of Sir James G. of Grant, vii. 487.
— Robert, illeg. son of Patrick G. of Cluniemore, vii. 470.
— Robert 'Og,' in Milton of Muckerach, vii. 471.
— Robert, 5th son of Sir John G. of Freuchie, vii. 471.
— — his wife, * Dunbar, vii. 471.
— Robert Henry, brother of 5th and 6th earls of Seafield, v. 486.
— Sophia, dau. of Sir James G. of Grant, vii. 483.
— Sweyne, in Ballintomb, vii. 475.
— — his wife, * Grant, vii. 475.
— William, Congalton, v. 252.
— Sir William Kerr, lieut.-gen., K.C.B., iv. 560.
— *, wife of David Erskine, Rothesay Herald, v. 93.
— *, alleged wife of Hector Mackintosh of Mackintosh, vii. 459.
— *, dau. of Duncan G., younger of Freuchie, vii. 466.
— *, Father, a seminary priest, vii. 471.
— *, wife of Sweyne Grant in Ballintomb, vii. 475.
— *, contracted wife of Hector Mackenzie, vii. 497.
Grant-Suttie of Balgone, Sir George, 5th bart., viii. 516.
— — his wife, Harriet Charteris, viii. 516.
— — Sir James, 6th bart., vii. 358; viii. 163.
— — his wife, Susan Harriet Innes-Ker, vii. 358.
— — Susan Harriet, wife of (1) 11th earl of Stair, and (2) Sir Neil Menzies, viii. 163.
Grantham, Henry (de Nassau), earl of, iii. 123.
— — his wife, Henrietta Butler, iii. 123.
Granville, John (Carteret), 1st earl, iii. 408; viii. 464.
— Court d'Ewes, incumbent of Alnwick, i. 497.
— — his wife, Charlotte Augusta Leopoldina Murray, i. 497.
Grattan of Tinnehinch, James, iii. 418.
— — his wife, Laura Maria Murray, iii. 418.

* Name unknown.

Grattan, Mary Anne, wife of (1) J. Blachford, and (2) 7th earl of Carnwath, ii. 419.
— Henry, ii. 419.
— John, major, adjutant-general, India, iii. 615.
Graves, Frances, wife of capt. D. R. Douglas-Hamilton, iv. 390.
— Hugh Ryves, Limerick, iv. 390.
GRAY, GRAY, LORD, iv. 269-296.
Gray, Andrew, first lord, i. 459 *n.*; iv. 273.
— — his wife, Elizabeth Wemyss, iv. 273, 274; viii. 482.
— Andrew, second lord, iii. 23, 65, 565: iv. 275, 276; vii. 323.
— — his 1st wife, Janet Keith, iv. 41, 276.
— — his 2nd wife, Elizabeth Stewart, i. 442: iv. 276.
— — his 3rd wife, Margaret Houstoun, iv. 277; v. 554.
— — his 4th wife, Elizabeth Hay, iii. 565; iv. 276; ix. 86, 99 *bis*, 110.
— Andrew, seventh lord, iv. 286.
— — his 1st wife, Anne Ogilvy, iv. 27, 286, 287; ix. 48 *bis*.
— — his 2nd wife, Mary Guldeford, iv. 287; ix. 99, 100.
— — his 3rd wife, Catherine Caddell, iv. 287.
— Charles, twelfth lord, iv. 293.
— Evelyn Pounden, wife of J. M. Smith; baroness, iv. 293, 295; vi. 328.
— Francis, fifteenth lord, iv. 294.
— — his wife, Mary Ann Johnstone, iv. 294.
— George Philip Murray, 14th earl of Moray, eighteenth lord, iv. 293, 295; vi. 329.
— John, ninth lord, iv. 291.
— — his wife, Marjorie Gray, iv. 291; viii. 203.
— John, tenth lord, iv. 292.
— — his wife, Helen Stuart, ii. 88; iv. 292.
— John, eleventh lord, iv. 292.
— — his wife, Margaret Blair-Carnegie of Kinfauns, iv. 292; vi. 498.
— John, fifteenth lord, iv. 294.
— — his wife, Mary Anne Ainslie, iv. 294.
— Madelina, dau. of 14th lord Gray; baroness, iv. 295.
— Margaret (Grant), wife of D. H. Murray; baroness, iv. 295; viii. 211.
— Patrick, third lord, iv. 279, 280.
— — his wife, Janet Gordon, iv. 279, 530.
— Patrick, fourth lord, iv. 280; viii. 293.
— — his wife, Mariota Ogilvy, i. 118; iv. 281.
— Patrick, fifth lord, iv. 283.
— — his wife, Barbara Ruthven, iv. 261, 284.
Gray, Patrick, sixth lord, iv. 285; ix. 99.
— — his 1st wife, Elizabeth Lyon, iv. 285; viii. 291.
— — his 2nd wife, Mary Stewart, iv. 286; vi. 574.
— Patrick, eighth lord, iv. 290.
— — his wife, Barbara Murray, iv. 290; viii. 203.
— William John, thirteenth lord, iv. 294.
— master of, James Maclaren Stuart, iv. 295.
— master of, Patrick, eldest son of 1st lord Gray, iv. 275, 278.
— — his 1st wife, Margaret Fleming, iv. 275; viii. 532.
— — his 2nd wife, Annabella Forbes, iv. 50, 275.
— master of, Patrick, eldest son of 5th lord Gray, i. 395, 558; ii. 69; iv. 285, 464.
— master of, Patrick, only son of 7th lord Gray, iv. 287.
— master of, Patrick, only son of 8th lord Gray, iv. 291; ix. 100.
— master of, William, eldest son of Sir Wm. Gray of Pittendrum, iv. 287, 288, 290; viii. 69.
— — his 1st wife, Anne Gray, mistress of Gray, iv. 287, 290.
— — his 2nd wife, Margaret Gibson, iv. 290.
— mistress of, Anne, wife of William Gray of Pittendrum, iv. 287 *bis*, 290.
GRAY, LORD GRAY, iv. 269-296.
Gray of Balgarno, Andrew, iv. 272 *bis*, 273.
— — his wife, Christian Boyd, iv. 273.
— — Andrew, iv. 220.
— — his wife, Janet Hay, v. 220.
— — Marjory, wife of John, 5th titular duke of Perth, ix. 149.
— — Patrick, iii. 310; v. 208.
— — his wife, Margaret Scrimgeour, iii. 310.
— — William, iv. 292.
— — his wife, Anne Gray, iv. 292.
— of Balgillo, Sir Andrew, iv. 276.
— — Patrick, iv. 277.
— of Balgownie, Andrew, iv. 288.
— — his wife, Elizabeth Cruikshank, iv. 288.
— of Balgray, Margaret, dau. of Robert G. of Drummalie, iv. 280.
— of Ballumbie, Gilbert, iv. 281.
— of Bandirran, Euphan, wife of Sir P. Kinnaird of Inchture, iv. 282.
— — Gilbert, iv. 281; v. 209.
— — his 1st wife, Marion Carnegie, iv. 281; viii. 58.
— — his 2nd wife, Elizabeth Hay, iv. 281; v. 220; vii. 191.
— — William, 4th son of 5th lord Gray, iv. 284.
— — his wife, Elizabeth Gray, iv. 284.

Gray of Brighouse, Thomas, burgess of Aberdeen, iv. 288.
— of Broxmouth, Sir Andrew, iv. 269.
— — Sir Andrew, iv. 272; ix. 99.
— — his 1st wife, Janet Mortimer, iv. 272.
— — his 2nd wife, Elizabeth Buchanan, iv. 272.
— — Sir John, iv. 270.
— — Sir Patrick, iv. 271.
— — his wife, Margaret *, iv. 271.
— of Bruchty, Sir Andrew, iv. 276.
— of Bullion, Andrew, burgess of Dundee, iv. 285; ix. 99.
— — his wife, Margaret Reid, iv. 285.
— of Buttergask, Gilbert, 3rd son of 2nd lord Gray, iv. 277, 278, 279.
— — his wife, Egidia Mercer, iv. 279.
— — James, brother of 4th lord Gray, iv. 280, 281.
— — his wife, Margaret Scott, iv. 280.
— — Patrick, iv. 280; ix. 99.
— — his wife, Marion Ogilvy, iv. 281.
— of Carse, William, viii. 300.
— of Castle Huntly, Patrick, iv. 278.
— of Cluny, Andrew, 'scutifer regis,' iv. 274.
— — Sir Andrew, eldest son of Patrick, master of Gray, iv. 274, 275.
— of Cowstoun, Gilbert, iv. 281.
— of Craigie, Sir Andrew, iv. 270.
— — Sir John, iv. 270.
— of Mylnetoune of Craigie, John, portioner, iii. 322.
— of Cranslie, Robert, i. 517; iv. 285.
— of Crichie, John, 3rd son of Sir Wm. G. of Pittendrum, iv. 288.
— — his wife, Alison Troup, iv. 288.
— — John, iv. 288, 290, 291.
— — his wife, Marjorie Gray, iv. 291.
— of Davidstoun, Gilbert, iv. 281.
— — James, 3rd son of 5th lord Gray, iv. 284.
— of Drummalie, Robert, brother of 4th lord Gray, iv. 279, 280 *bis*, 281.
— — his wife, Marjorie Strachan, iv. 279.
— — Robert, 2nd laird, iv. 279.
— of Dunninald, Andrew, v. 5, 6.
— of Flisk, Sir Andrew, iv. 276.
— of Fofarty, William, viii. 300.
— of Forester Seat, Patrick, iv. 283.
— of Foulis, Sir Andrew, iv. 272, 274; vii. 7, 8.
— — Andrew, iv. 273.
— — his wife, Elizabeth Wemyss, iv. 273.
— — Gilbert, ix. 28.
— of Gothrastown, Sir Andrew, iv. 276.
— of Halkerton, George, ii. 274.
— — his wife, Jean Erskine, ii. 274.
— of Hayston, Andrew, iii. 33.
— — his wife, Margaret Lindsay, iii. 33.
— — William, viii. 300.

* Name unknown.

Gray of Heton, Sir Thomas, compiler of *Scalacronica*, vi. 191.
— of Huntly, Elizabeth, wife of (1) John, 4th lord Glamis, (2) Alexander, 3rd earl of Huntly, and (3) George, 4th earl of Rothes, iv. 277, 532; vii. 285; viii. 283.
— of Inchyra, Edward, rector of Lundy, iv. 277.
— of Invereightie, William, viii. 295, 296, 300.
— — his wife, Helen Lyon, viii. 296.
— — William, ix. 49.
— — his wife, Margaret Erskine, ix. 49.
— of Invergowrie, Sir Patrick, iv. 282.
— — his 1st wife, Euphemia Murray, i. 464; iv. 282.
— — his 2nd wife, Agnes Napier, i. 123; iv. 282; vi. 417.
— — Patrick, iv. 282.
— of Kilmalamok, Patrick, iv. 283.
— of Kingudy, Patrick, iii. 310.
— of Kinneff, Sir Andrew, son of Patrick, master of Gray, iv. 274, 275.
— — Andrew, 2nd son of 1st lord Gray, iv. 274.
— — Patrick, iv. 274, 275.
— of Kinnell, Patrick, iv. 282.
— of Knap, William, viii. 300.
— of Laurencetoun, Sir John, iv. 270.
— of Legertlaw, Gilbert, iv. 279.
— of Leitfie, Sir Andrew, iv. 276.
— — Robert, iv. 277.
— of Longforgan, Sir Andrew, iv. 269.
— — his wife, Ada Gifford, iv. 270.
— of Lundy, Sir Andrew, iv. 276.
— of Lynedoch, William, portioner, vi. 392.
— — his wife, Margaret Nairn, vi. 392.
— of Middle Mawis, Robert, iv. 279.
— of Mylnhill, Gilbert, burgess of Dundee, iv. 284.
— — his wife, Elizabeth Gib, iv. 284.
— — Robert, iv. 285.
— — his wife, Jean Lauder, i. 517; iv. 285.
— of Mombenis, Patrick, iv. 283.
— of Muirtown, Andrew, 4th son of 2nd lord Gray, iv. 277, 288.
— of Nevay, William, viii. 300.
— of Newton of Schives, Andrew, iv. 274.
— — Sir Andrew, iv. 276.
— of Pitscandlie, William, iv. 284.
— of Pittendrum, Andrew, alleged ancestor of the family of, iv. 277 *n. bis*, 288.
— — Sir William, iv. 277 *n.*, 287, 288.
— — his wife, Egidia Smith, iv. 288.
— — William, styled master of Gray, iv. 287, 288, 290.
— of Pokemill, Gilbert, iv. 279.
— of Reidcastle, James, 4th son of 4th lord Gray, iv. 282.
— — his wife, Elizabeth Beaton, iv. 282.
— of Scheves, Andrew, iv. 277 *n.*, 288.

Gray of Scheves, George, iv. 277 *n*.
— — Gilbert, iv. 179.
— — James, iii. 589.
— — Robert, iv. 72, 277 *n*.
— of Skethin, Andrew, vii. 8.
— of Skibo, Andrew, alleged ancestor of the family of, iv. 275.
— Agnes, wife of William, 1st earl of Airth and Menteith, i. 137; ix. 9.
— Agnes, wife of John Forbes of Boyndlie, iv. 72.
— Agnes, dau. of Gilbert G. of Bandirran, iv. 281.
— Agnes, dau. of Sir Patrick G. of Invergowrie, iv. 282.
— Agnes, wife of P. Douglas of Kilspindie, iv. 283.
— Agnes, wife of (1) Robert Logan of Restalrig, (2) Alexander, 5th lord Home, and (3) Sir Thos. Lyon of Balducky, iv. 283, 462; viii. 287.
— Agnes, wife of (1) Sir John Dundas, and (2) Sir Archibald Primrose, iv. 289; vii. 219; ix. 152, 160.
— Agnes, wife of Henry Livingston, vi. 448.
— Alexander, 2nd son of Sir Patrick G. of Broxmouth, iv. 271, 272.
— Alexander, merchant in Aberdeen, iv. 274.
— — his wife, Elizabeth Hay, iv. 274.
— Alexander, 4th son of Sir Wm. G. of Pittendrum, iv. 289.
— Alexander, captain in Dutch service, iv. 291.
— Alexander, vi. 448.
— — his wife, Helen Little, vi. 448.
— Andrew, i. 117.
— — his wife, Margaret Ogilvy, i. 117.
— Andrew Graham or, (*alias* Henry Lindsay), i. 138.
— Andrew, grandfather of Sir Wm. G. of Pittendrum, iv. 277 *n*., 288.
— Andrew, captain; 2nd son of 4th lord Gray, iv. 281.
— Andrew, 2nd son of Sir Patrick G. of Invergowrie, iv. 282.
— Andrew, minister of Outer High Kirk, Glasgow, iv. 289.
— — his wife, Rachel Baillie, iv. 289.
— Andrew, in Peterhead, iv. 288 *n*.
— Andrew, eldest son of 11th lord Gray, iv. 292.
— Anne, wife of P. Douglas of Kilspindie, iv. 283.
— Ann, wife of Mr. Wm. Gray, iv. 289.
— Anne, wife of Wm. Gray of Ballegarno, iv. 292.
— Anne, wife of George Paterson of Castle Huntly, iv. 293.
— Anne Florence de, baroness Lucas, wife of 6th earl Cowper, iii. 124.
Gray, Barbara, wife of Sir John Cranstoun of Morristoun, iv. 285.
— Barbara, wife of Robt. Douglas, iv. 289.
— Barbara, dau. of 9th lord Gray, iv. 292.
— Barbara, dau. of 11th lord Gray, iv. 293.
— Charles, advocate, iv. 290 *bis*.
— — his wife, Barbara Douglas, iv. 290.
— Charles, 2nd son of 10th lord Gray, iv. 292.
— Charlotte, dau. of 11th lord Gray, iv. 293.
— Christian, wife of James Crichton of Strathurd, iv. 275.
— Sir David, son of Sir Andrew G. of Broxmouth, iv. 270.
— David, 3rd son of 1st lord Gray, iv. 275.
— David, killed at Tangier, iv. 289.
— David, 5th son of 9th lord Gray, iv. 292.
— Elizabeth, wife of Sir Thomas Maule, i. 459 *n*.; iv. 272.
— Elizabeth, wife of James King of Barra, iii. 589.
— Elizabeth, wife of Jas. Abercromby of Pitmeddan, iv. 179.
— Elizabeth, wife of Andrew Moncur of that Ilk, iv. 271.
— Elizabeth, wife of D. Rollock of Ballachie, iv. 275; vii. 183.
— Elizabeth, wife of (1) John, 4th lord Glamis, (2) Alexander, 3rd earl of Huntly, and (3) George, 4th earl of Rothes; contr. to Walter Drummond, iv. 277, 278, 532; vii. 285; viii. 278; ix. 99.
— Elizabeth, dau. of Sir Patrick G. of Invergowrie, iv. 282.
— Elizabeth, wife of Laurence Bruce, iv. 283.
— Elizabeth, wife of (1) Patrick Kinnaird of Inchture, and (2) Wm. Gray of Bandirran, iv. 284; v. 208.
— Elizabeth, wife of Sir John Leslie of Newton, iv. 286; v. 386; vii. 295; ix. 127.
— Elizabeth, wife of Peter Gordon, iv. 292.
— Elizabeth, wife of Sir Philip Ainslie, iv. 293.
— Elizabeth, wife of Patrick Lyon of Brigton, viii. 295.
— Elspeth, wife of James Bell, iv. 289.
— Ethel Eveline, wife of H. T. Campbell, iv. 295.
— Euphan, dau. of Sir Patrick G. of Invergowrie, iv. 282.
— Euphemia, wife of Patrick Kinnaird of Inchture, v. 209.
— Frances, wife of (1) captain Jas. Mackenzie, and (2), capt. Archd. Douglas, iv. 287; ix. 100.
— Geilis, wife of (1) Alexander Whitelaw, and (2) Alexander Gardin, iv. 280.
— Geils, dau. of Sir Wm. G. of Pittendrum, iv. 289.

Gray, George, 4th son of Sir Patrick G. of Broxmouth, iv. 271, 272.
— George, viii. 125.
— — his 2nd wife, Elizabeth Dalrymple, viii. 125.
— Gilbert, son of Gilbert G. of Bandirran, iv. 281.
— Helen, wife of Sir D. Maxwell of Tealing, iv. 283.
— Helen, wife of A. Bruce of Earlshall, iv. 286.
— Helen, wife of Sir Geo. Drummond, iv. 289.
— Helen, wife of Wm. Stirling of Keir, iv. 293.
— Henry, alleged illeg. son of 16th earl of Crawford, iii. 34.
— Henry de, Fife, iv. 269.
— Sir Hugh de, county of Berwick, iv. 269.
— Hugo de, bef. 1248, iv. 269.
— Isobel, wife of (1) Sir Jas. Scrimgeour, (2) Adam Crichton, and (3) Sir John Campbell of Lundy, ii. 324; iii. 308; iv. 277.
— Isobel, wife of James King of Barra, iii. 589.
— Isobel, wife of Alexander Stratoun of Lauriston, iv. 277.
— Isobel, wife of (1) D. Strachan of Carmylie, and (2) Sir A. Falconer of Halkerton, iv. 283; v. 246.
— Isobel, wife of Sir R. Carnegie of Dunnichen, iv. 286; viii. 61.
— Isobel, wife of (1) Walter Hamilton, and (2) Mr. James Fraser, iv. 289.
— James, notary, iii. 341.
— James, 3rd son of John G. of Crichie, iv. 288.
— James, 3rd son of 9th lord Gray, iv. 291.
— James, 4th son of 4th lord Gray, iv. 282; v. 5; viii. 58, 339.
— — his alleged wife, Janet Stewart, i. 443; viii. 339; ix. 28.
— — his wife, Elizabeth Betoun, v. 5.
— Jane Anne, wife of major-gen. C. P. Ainslie, iv. 294.
— Janet, wife of (1) Wm. Ogilvy of Inchmartin, and (2) Jas. Sandilands of Cruvy, i. 76; iv. 33, 279.
— Janet, wife of (1) Alex. Blair of Balthayock, (2) Thomas, 3rd lord Lovat, and (3) David, 9th earl of Crawford, iii. 28; iv. 275; v. 524, 525; ix. 61.
— Janet, wife of Sir Alex. Ogilvy of Auchterhouse, iv. 272.
— Janet, wife of (1) John Charteris, (2) Sir D. Wemyss, (3) Wm. Keith, and (4) Jas. Campbell, iv. 278; v. 501; vi. 34 *bis*; viii. 487; ix. 99.
— Janet, wife of Geo. Campbell, Leith, iv. 288 *n.*
— Janet, wife of Arcbibald Campbell, iv. 289.
Gray, Janet, wife of John Ballantine Rollo, vii. 207.
— Jean, wife of 1st earl of Wemyss, iv 286; viii. 500.
— Jean, dau. of William, master of Gray, iv. 290.
— Jean, wife of 9th earl of Moray, iv. 293; vi. 326.
— John, elder son of Sir John G. of Broxmouth, iv. 270.
— John, 6th son of Sir Andrew G. of Broxmouth, iv. 272, 273.
— John, prior of Strathfillan, v. 501.
— John, Kilmarnock, vii. 207.
— John, dean of Caithness, viii. 348.
— Katharine, alleged wife of Sir Wm. Murray of Tullibardine, i. 460 *n.*
— Katharine, wife of Alex. Inglis of Murdistoun, iv. 289.
— Katharine, wife of Jas. Paterson of Kirktoun, iv. 292.
— Katharine, wife of John Stewart of Redcastle and Laitheris, v. 5.
— Kathleen Eileen Moray, iv. 295.
— Lilias, wife of (1) David Tyrie of Drumkilho, and (2) John Oliphant of Newtyle, iv. 283; vi. 548.
— Lonsdale Richard Douglas, capt. 6th Dragoons, iv. 295.
— Margaret, wife of (1) Wm. Murray of Tullibardine, and (2) Geo. Clephane of Carslogie, i. 459; iv. 273, 275.
— Margaret, wife of Sir Wm. Hay of Errol, iii. 563; iv. 271.
— Margaret, wife of 1st lord Lyle, iv. 275; v. 553.
— Margaret, wife of Jas. Ogilvy of Balfour, iv. 283.
— Margaret, wife of Sir Wm. Blair of Balgillo, iv. 289.
— Margaret, dau. of 11th lord Gray, iv. 293.
— Margaret, wife of John Grant of Kilgraston, iv. 294.
— Marie, dau. of Gilbert G., iv. 282.
— Marion, wife of * Lindsay, iv. 271.
— Marion, dau. of Sir Patrick G. of Invergowrie, iv. 282.
— Marion *or* Marjorie, wife of (1) Patrick, master of Ruthven, and (2) P. Ogilvie of Inchmartin, iv. 33, 262.
— Marjory, wife of (1) * Kinninmont of that Ilk, and (2) Silvester Rattray of Craighall, iv. 278.
— Marjorie, wife of 9th lord Gray, iv. 291; viii. 203.
— Marjorie, dau. of 9th lord Gray, iv. 292.
— Mary, wife of David Seton of Parbroath, iv. 263.
— Mary, wife of 3rd lord Lindores, iv. 286; v. 385.

* Name unknown.

Gray, Mary, wife of John Clerk of Penicuik, iv. 289.
— Patrick, 3rd son of Sir Patrick G. of Broxmouth, iv. 271, 272.
— Patrick, 4th son of Sir Andrew G. of Broxmouth, iv. 272, 273, 275; v. 257.
— Patrick, student at Douai College, iv. 286.
— Patrick, perpetual vicar of Rossie, ix. 99.
— Rachel, dau. of Mr. Andrew G., Glasgow, iv. 289.
— Robert, 2nd son of James G. of Buttergask, iv. 280.
— Robert, 5th son of 4th lord Gray, iv. 282.
— Robert, 4th son of John G. of Crichie, iv. 288.
— Robert, 2nd son of Sir Wm. G. of Pittendrum, iv. 288.
— Robert, 2nd son of Mr. Andrew G., iv. 289.
— Thomas, son of Sir Andrew G. of Longforgan and Broxmouth, iv. 270.
— Thomas, 2nd son of Sir Andrew G. of Broxmouth and Foulis, iv. 272.
— Thomas, in Dundee, grandson of Sir Andrew G. of Broxmouth, iv. 272 *bis*.
— Thomas, son of James G. of Buttergask, iv. 280.
— — his wife, Margaret Kinnaird, iv. 280.
— Thomas de, vii. 422, 427 *bis*.
— Thora Zelma Grace, iv. 295.
— William, ii. 12.
— — his wife, Helen Ogilvy, ii. 12.
— William, 5th son of Sir Andrew G. of Broxmouth, iv. 272, 273.
— William, grandson of Sir Andrew G. of Broxmouth, iv. 272.
— William, son of 2nd lord Gray, iv. 278.
— — his wife, Marion Fullarton, iv. 278.
— William, in Inchture, sheriff-depute of Forfar, burgess of Dundee, iv. 284.
— — his wife, Elizabeth Gray, iv. 284.
— William, apprentice in Edinburgh, iv. 288 *n*.
— William, merchant, Edinburgh, iv. 288 *n*.
— William, son of Mr. Andrew G., iv. 289.
— William, minister of Duns, iv. 289.
— — his wife, Ann Gray, iv. 289.
— William, 2nd son of William, master of Gray, iv. 290.
— William, 2nd son of 9th lord Gray, iv. 291.
— William, ix. 106.
— — his wife, Margaret Bothwell, iv. 436; ix. 106.
— *, wife of John Ross of Kinfauns, iv. 272.
— *, wife of Herring of Glasclune, iv. 272.

* Name unknown.

Gray, *, wife of Wm. Auchterlony of Kelly, iv. 273.
— *, wife of David Annand of Melgum, iv. 273.
— *, wife of Maclellan of Bombie, iv. 273.
— *, wife of * Parker, iv. 273.
— *, wife of Andrew Monorgund of that Ilk, iv. 275.
— *, wife of * Collace of Balnamoon, iv. 276; ix. 99.
Graydon, Charles, receiver-general of Customs, ix. 63, 69.
— — his wife, Elizabeth Edwards, ix. 63, 69 *bis*.
— Charles, his son, ix. 69.
Grayme of Scatterty and Byth, Thomas, vii. 433.
— Elizabeth, *error for* Gray, wife of (1) John, 4th lord Glamis, (2) Alex., 3rd earl of Huntly, and (3) George, 4th earl of Rothes, iv. 277 *n*.; vii. 285 *n*.
'Graysteel,' Douglas, i. 185.
— Eglinton, iii. 445.
Grazioli, Mario, duke, vi. 459.
— — his wife, Nicoletta Giustiniani-Bandini, vi. 459.
Great Britain, James I., king of, i. 27; v. 354; vii. 549; viii. 95, 216.
— James II., king of, i. 29, 32; vii. 136, 138.
— Charles I., king of, i. 28; iii. 370; vii. 99; viii. 594: ix. 99.
— Charles II., king of, i. 29; viii. 594.
— George III., king of, vii. 144.
— George IV., king of, vii. 487.
— William III., king of, i. 29, 33; vii. 140.
— Anne, queen of, i. 33.
— Mary II., queen of, i. 33.
— Victoria, queen of, i. 393.
'Green Abbot,' the, v. 44.
Greenaway, Eliza, wife of lt.-col. Francis Napier, vi. 432.
— John, keeper of stores, Portsmouth Dockyard, vi. 432.
Greenhill-Gardyne of Finavon and Glen Forsa, Charles, lieut.-colonel, vi. 498; viii. 236.
— — his wife, Amelia Anne Drummond, viii. 236; ix. 162.
Greenlaw, Sir William of, iv. 331.
Greenshiels, John of, viii. 370.
— — his wife, Margaret of Balcaskie, viii. 370.
GREENOCK OF GREENOCK, CATHCART, BARON, ii. 525-531.
Greenock of Greenock, Alan Frederick, third baron, ii. 530.
— Charles Murray, second baron, ii. 527.
— William Schaw, first baron, ii. 524.
— Alan, eldest son of 3rd earl of Cathcart; styled lord, ii. 531.

* Name unknown.

GREENWICH, CAMPBELL, BARONESS OF, i. 377.
Greenwich, Caroline, wife of (1) Francis, earl of Dalkeith, and (2) George, 1st marquess of Townshend; baroness of, i. 377; ii. 242.
GREENWICH, CAMPBELL, EARL OF, i. 371.
Greenwich, John, earl of, i. 370.
GREENWICH, CAMPBELL, DUKE OF, i. 374.
Greenwich, John, duke of, i. 370.
Gregory, bishop of Brechin, vii. 398.
— of Frendraught, John, minister of Drumoak, iv. 128, 130.
— Alexander, iv. 128.
— John, M.D., F.R.S., professor at Edinburgh, iv. 64.
— — his wife, Elizabeth Forbes, iv. 64.
Greig, Agnes, wife of 8th lord Rollo, vii. 208.
— William, Gayfield Place, Edinburgh, vii. 208.
Grelod *or* Grelauga, wife of Thorfinn Skull-splitter, ii. 314.
Gremislaw of Gremislaw, Christian de, wife of Sir John de Crichton, iii. 57, 60, 62.
Grenolias de Cournou, Louis, vi. 560.
— — his wife, Marie Jeanne Oliphant, vi. 560.
GRENVILLE, BARON KINLOSS, v. 199-201.
Grenville, Anne, wife of lt.-col. G. R. Hardaway, v. 200.
— Anne Eliza Mary, wife of W. H. P. Gore-Langton, v. 200.
— Caroline Jemima Elizabeth, dau. of 3rd duke of Buckingham and Chandos, v. 200.
Greswolde of Solihull, Marshall, in holy orders, iii. 411.
— — Mary, wife of David Lewis of Malvern Hall, iii. 411, 412.
Greville, Algernon William (Greville), 2nd baron, v. 238; vi. 273.
— — his wife, Beatrice Violet Graham, vi. 273.
— of Milcote, Sir Edward, v. 11.
— Algernon Frederick, Bath King of Arms, v. 369.
— Camilla Dagmar Violet, wife of capt. A. G. Hay, v. 238.
— Charles, viii. 362.
— Charlotte Mary, wife of 7th earl of Galloway, iv. 167.
— Frances Harriett, wife of 6th duke of Lennox, v. 369.
— Georgina, wife of Sir Geo. Cathcart, ii. 527.
— Harriet Katharine, wife of 1st earl of Ellesmere, viii. 362.
— Mary, wife of Sir Arthur Ingram, v. 11.
— Robert Fulke, ii. 524.
— — his wife, Louisa Cathcart, countess of Mansfield, ii. 523; viii, 206, 209.
Grey, Annabella, wife of Alexander, baron Hume of Berwick; countess de, vi. 23.
Grey, Jemima, wife of 2nd earl of Hardwicke; marchioness de, ii. 208; vi. 23.
— Thomas Philip (de Grey), earl de, iii. 124.
Grey of Groby, George Harry (Grey), lord, viii. 515.
— — his wife, Katharine Charteris, viii. 515.
Grey de Ruthyn, Barbara (Yelverton), wife of (1) 7th earl of Loudoun, and (2) Sir Hastings R. Yelverton; baroness, v. 514.
— Bertha Lelgarde (Hastings), wife of Augustus W. Clifton; baroness, v. 514.
Grey of Wilton, William (Grey), 14th lord, viii. 436.
Grey of Backworth, John, colonel, viii. 87.
— of Barnfield, Robert T. Moring, viii. 232.
— of Ballincor, James, iii. 415.
— of Lehena, Francis, iii. 415, 418.
— Amabel, wife of 3rd earl of Breadalbane, ii. 208.
— Caroline Eliza Moring, wife of rev. A. Drummond, viii. 232.
— Charles C., captain R.N., iv. 483.
— Diana, wife of Robert, 2nd earl of Elgin, iii. 478.
— Diana, wife of George Middleton of Seaton, vi. 178.
— Elizabeth Susan, wife of capt. John Renny-Strachan-Carnegie, viii. 87.
— John de, bishop of Norwich, iv. 140.
— Katharine Rebecca, wife of William, lord Huntingtower, iii. 415.
— Maria, wife of 12th earl of Home, iv. 483.
— Sir Robert de, ii. 396.
— Sarah, wife of F. T. Tollemache, iii. 415.
— William Booth, viii. 38.
— — his wife, Frances Somerville, viii. 38.
Grey-Egerton of Oulton Park, Sir Philip de Malpas, 10th bart., vii. 525.
— Cecely Louisa, wife of 6th earl of Selkirk, vii. 524.
'Greysteel,' Archibald Douglas of Kilspindie, called, i. 185.
— Alexander Seton, 6th earl of Eglinton, called, iii. 445.
Greystock, Ralph, 5th baron of, iii. 271.
Grier of Lag, *see* Grierson of Lag.
— Elizabeth, wife of Robt. Fergusson, ii. 410.
— Jean, dau. of Sir Wm. G. of Lag, iv. 587.
— Janet, wife of William King of Barra and Bourtie, iii. 589.
— Margaret, wife of Sir Jas. Carmichael of Bonnytoun, iv. 587.
Grierson of Bardannoch, William, lieut.-col., ii. 279.
— of Bargatton, John, v. 261.
— — his wife, Agnes Gordon, v. 261.

Grierson of Bargatton, William, i. 226, 229.
—— —— his wife, Elizabeth Murray, i. 226.
—— —— William, viii. 373.
—— —— his wife, Janet Livingston, viii. 373.
—— of Brocloch, William, v. 110; ix. 118.
—— —— his wife, Elizabeth Gordon, v. 110; ix. 118.
—— of Capenoch, John, i. 226.
—— —— his wife, Elizabeth Murray, i. 226.
—— of Dalgoner, James, i. 246.
—— —— his wife, Elizabeth Johnstone, i. 246.
—— of Lag, Sir Alexander Gilbert, 6th bart., ii. 417.
—— —— his wife, Elizabeth Dalzell, ii. 417.
—— —— Gilbert, ii. 382; iii. 220.
—— —— his wife, Isabella Kirkpatrick, ii. 382; iii. 220.
—— —— Sir John, iv. 587; v. 171; viii. 550.
—— —— his 1st wife, Jean Fleming, viii. 550; ix. 169.
—— —— his 2nd wife, Isabel Boyd, v. 171.
—— —— Robert, vii. 126.
—— —— his wife, Helen Douglas, vii. 126.
—— —— Sir Robert, iv. 161; viii. 204.
—— —— his wife, Margaret Murray of Cockpool, i. 226; viii. 204.
—— —— Robert, son of Sir John G., i. 229.
—— —— Sir Robert, 1st bart., v. 125; vii. 137.
—— —— his wife, Henrietta Douglas, vii. 137.
—— —— Sir Robert, 5th bart., ii. 417.
—— —— his wife, Margaret Dalzell, ii. 417.
—— —— Roger, vii. 117.
—— —— his wife, Agnes *or* Janet Douglas, vii. 117.
—— —— Sir William, iv. 413; vi. 163; vii. 133.
—— —— his wife, Nicolas Maxwell, iv. 413.
—— Helena, wife of Sir James Douglas of Mouswald, vii. 133.
—— Margaret Elizabeth, wife of (1) D. B. Hope Johnstone, and (2) John Henry Gordon, ii. 279.
—— Marie, wife of John Douglas, i. 226, 229.
—— Nicolas, wife of David Scot of Scotstarvet, i. 226; viii. 204.
—— Nicolas, wife of 2nd earl of Galloway, iv. 161.
—— Robert, murderer of John M'Brair, vii. 118.
Griffin, Cyrus, viii. 408.
—— —— his wife, Christiana Stewart, viii. 408.
Griffith, Charles Bodval, rector of Bishopstone, vii. 391.
—— —— his wife, Wilhelmina Dells Owena Hore-Ruthven, vii. 391.
Grillo di Mondragone, Maria Nicoletta Giuseppa Francesca Raffaela Cornelia Melchiora Gaspara Baldassara Angela Giovanna Luisa Guidetta, wife of 6th earl of Newburgh, vi. 458.
Grim, son of Guy; waggoner of Roxburgh, viii. 2.
Grimes of Eske, Sir Richard, vii. 100.
Grimstead, Charlotte, wife of Thomas George, lord Glamis, viii. 312.
—— Joseph Valentine, viii. 312.
Grimston, James Bucknall (Grimston), 3rd viscount, iv. 96.
—— —— his wife, Harriet Walter, iv. 96.
—— James Walter (Grimston), styled viscount, iv. 98.
GRIMSTON, LORD FORRESTER OF CORSTORPHINE, iv. 97-100.
Grimston, Aline, iv. 98.
—— Charles, capt. Coldstream Guards, iv. 97.
—— Charlotte, dau. of 1st baron Verulam, iv. 96.
—— Edward Harbottle, rector of Pebmarsh, iv. 97.
—— —— his wife, Frances Horatia Morier, iv. 97.
—— Elizabeth, iv. 98.
—— Emily Mary, wife of 2nd earl of Craven, iv. 97.
—— Francis Sylvester, rector of Wakes Colne, iv. 97.
—— —— his wife, C. G. Morier, iv. 97.
—— Harriet, dau. of 1st baron Verulam, iv. 96.
—— Harriot Elizabeth, wife of major F. H. Poore, iv. 98.
—— Helen, dau. of 3rd earl of Verulam, iv. 98.
—— Hermione, wife of lieut. Bernard Buxton, R.N., iv. 98.
—— Jane, wife of Sir Alfred Jodrell, iv. 98.
—— Jane Frederica Harriet Mary, wife of 3rd earl of Caledon, iv. 97.
—— Katharine, wife of (1) John Foster Barham, and (2) George W. F. (Villiers), 4th earl of Clarendon, iv. 97.
—— Mary Augusta Frederica, wife of 4th earl of Radnor, iv. 97.
—— Maud, wife of major Paulyn F. C. Rawdon-Hastings, iv. 98; v. 515.
—— Robert, 3rd son of 1st earl of Verulam, iv. 97.
—— Robert, in holy orders, iv. 98.
—— —— his wife, G. M. A. Villiers, iv. 98.
—— Sybil, iv. 98.
—— Vera, iv. 98.
—— William, commander R.N., iv. 98.
Groa, wife of Duncan, 1st earl of Caithness, ii. 313.
Grosvenor, Dorothy Alice Margaret Augusta, wife of Albert Edward H. M. A., lord Dalmeny, vii. 228.
—— Henry George, vii. 228; viii. 512.
—— —— his wife, Dora Mina Kittina Erskine-Wemyss, viii. 512.

Grosvenor, Jane Louisa Octavia, wife of (1) Gamel, lord Muncaster, and (2) H. B. Lindsay, iii. 43.
Grove, George Wilson, iii. 391.
—— —— his wife, Louisa Mitty Abraham, iii. 391.
Gruoch, wife of (1) Gillecomgan, earl of Moray, and (2) Macbeth, earl of Moray, vi. 282, 283.
Guaylistoun of Guaylistoun, John, v. 138 *n.*
Gubbins of Kilrush and Stoneham, Joseph, general, iii. 616.
—— Elizabeth Catherine, wife of (1) William Aubrey de Vere, 9th duke of St. Albans, and (2) Lucius Bentinck, 10th viscount Falkland, iii. 616.
Gudin, Theodore, viii. 467.
—— —— his wife, Margaret Louis Gordon Hay, viii. 467.
Gudland, Thomas, iii. 336.
Guignes, Arnold III., count of, iii. 5.
—— —— his wife, Alice de Coucy, iii. 5.
—— Ingelram de, sire de Coucy, iii. 5.
—— —— his wife, Christian de Lindsay, iii. 5.
Guelders, Arnold, duke of, i. 20.
—— Renaud I., count of, i. 6.
—— —— his wife, Margaret of Flanders, i. 6.
GUILFORD, MAITLAND, EARL OF, v. 305.
Guilford, John, earl of, v. 305.
Guilford, Frederic (North), 2nd earl of, i. 528.
—— George Augustus (North), 3rd lord, ii. 310.
Guindesmoth, wife of Peter, lord of Maule, vii. 2.
Guinness, Walter E., ii. 280.
—— —— his wife, Evelyn Hilda Stuart Erskine, ii. 280.
Guise, Claude, duke of, i. 23.
Guldeford of Hemsted in Cranbrook, Sir Thomas, ix. 99.
—— Mary, wife of (1) John Baker, (2) Sir John Sydenham, and (3) Andrew, 7th lord Gray, iv. 287; ix. 99.
Gulstone, Allan James, iv. 265.
Gunhild, mother of Galfrid, vi. 79.
—— wife of Kol, ii. 315.
Gunhilda, wife of Uchtred of Galloway, iii. 245; iv. 137.
—— wife of Orm, son of Ketel, iii. 245.
Gunn of Killearnan, Alexander, vii. 167, 168.
—— —— his wife, Mary Mackay, vii. 167.
—— —— Alexander, vii. 169.
—— —— his wife, Christina Mackay, vii. 169.
—— —— Alexander MacDavid, vii. 165.
—— —— his wife, Barbara Mackay, vii. 165.
—— —— William MacAlister, vii. 165.
—— John Robson, chieftain of clan, viii. 338.
—— —— his wife, * Gordon, viii. 338.

* Name unknown.

Gunn, Katharine, wife of lieut.-col. Angus Mackay, vii. 168.
GUNNING, BARONESS HAMILTON OF HAMELDON, i. 387.
Gunning of Castle Coote, John, i. 387; iv. 393.
—— —— his wife, Bridget Bourke, i. 387.
—— Elizabeth, baroness Hamilton of Hameldon; wife of (1) 6th duke of Hamilton and Brandon, and (2) 5th earl of Argyll, i. 387; iv. 393; ix. 25 *ter.*
Guppyld, Norman, vii. 271.
—— William, vii. 271.
Gurden-Rebow of Wyvenhoe Park, Hector John, viii. 315.
—— Winifred, wife of capt. Malcolm Bowes-Lyon, viii. 315.
Gurdon, Sir Adam, iv. 509.
—— —— his wife, Constance Vernuz, iv. 510.
Gurney of North Runcton, Daniel, iii. 584.
—— Anne, wife of 1st lord Cramond, ii. 582.
—— Sir Richard, bart., ii. 582.
—— —— his 1st wife, Elizabeth Sandford, ii. 582.
Guthred, rebel in Moray, ii. 253.
Guthrie of Collieston, Henry, vii. 13.
—— —— his wife, Janet Lyon, vii. 12.
—— —— Sir Henry, vii. 373.
—— —— John, vii. 13.
—— of Cruikston, John, vii. 13.
—— of Guthrie, Alexander, v. 245.
—— —— his wife, Agnes Falconer, v. 245.
—— —— Sir David, vii. 8 *bis*, 9.
—— —— his wife, * Maule, vii. 8.
—— —— David, iii. 322.
—— —— John, viii. 62.
—— —— his wife, Elizabeth Carnegie, viii. 62.
—— of Kair and Castletown, David, i. 292.
—— —— his wife, Margaret Arbuthnott, i. 292.
—— of Kinblethmont, Robert, i. 118.
—— —— his 1st wife, Isabel Ogilvy, i. 118.
—— of Kincaldrum, Alexander, i. 184.
—— —— his wife, Alice Douglas, i. 184.
—— —— Alexander, son of David G. of Guthrie, iii. 322 *bis.*
—— —— his wife, Mariot Graham, iii. 322.
—— of Kingedward, Sir Henry, ix. 69.
—— of Kingenny, Andrew, vii. 14.
—— —— his wife, Marjorie Maule, vii. 14.
—— of Lunan, *, viii. 53.
—— —— Robert, iv. 283.
—— of Pitmowis, Patrick, i. 120.
—— Alexander, Common Clerk of Edinburgh, i. 517; iii. 377; vii. 14; viii. 64.
—— —— his wife, Janet Henrison, viii. 64.
—— Alexander, merchant burgess, Edinburgh, vii. 373.
—— Barbara, wife of (1) Wm. Lindsay of Culsh, and (2) Alex. Sutherland of Mosstowie, ix. 69.

* Name unknown.

Guthrie, Bethia, wife of Wm. Maule of Cruikston, vii. 14.
— Elizabeth, wife of Walter Graham of Duntrune, iii. 322.
— Elizabeth, wife of Alexander Maule, vii. 9.
— Euphame, wife of Robt. Montgomerie, ix. 8.
— James, minister of Stirling, viii. 452.
— John, bishop of Moray, iv. 127.
— Mr. John, minister of Perth, ix. 71.
— John, captain of Castle Campbell, vi. 159.
— — his wife, Helen Short, vi. 159.
— Margaret, wife of Sir James Ogilvy of Newgrange, i. 121.
— Margaret, wife of Wm. Rutherfurd of Quarrelholes, vii. 373.
— Margaret, wife of Sir Robert Carnegie of Kinnaird, viii. 53.
— Marion, wife of (1) David Borthwick, and (2) lord Menmuir, i. 517.
— Matillo, wife of Mr. Patrick Galloway, iii. 377.
— Nicolas, wife of David Ogilvy, i. 120.
Guttorm Sperra, ii. 320.
Guy, father of Grim of Berwick, viii. 2.
Gwillim, James, viii. 235.
— Katharine Gamand, wife of rev. H. M. Drummond, viii. 235.
Gwydyr, Peter, 1st lord, vii. 59.
— — his wife, Priscilla, baroness Willoughby de Eresby, vii. 59.
— Peter, 2nd lord, vii. 59.
— — his wife, Clementina Sarah Drummond of Stobhall, vii. 59.
Gwyn, Nell, i. 32.
Gwynne, John, captain, v. 226.
Gwyther, George, vii. 308.
— — his wife, Henrietta Anne, countess of Rothes, vii. 308.
Gylconell, son of Edgar of Dunscore, vi. 287.
Gyll, William, captain 2nd Life Guards, viii. 557.
— — his wife, Harriet Jane Laura Fleming, viii. 557.
Gyloclery, father of Morgund, 2nd earl of Mar, v. 567.

H. L. L., the hymn-writer, ii. 106; ix. 39.
Haakon, king of Norway, v. 33, 34.
— son of Paul, 5th earl of Caithness, ii. 315.
HADDINGTON, HAMILTON, EARL OF, iv. 303-329.
Haddington, Charles, fifth earl of, iv. 319.
— — his wife, Margaret, countess of Rothes, iv. 319; vii. 302.
— Charles, eighth earl of, iv. 324.
— — his wife, Sophia Hope, iv. 325, 498.
Haddington, George, tenth earl of, iv. 322, 326.
— — his wife, Georgina Markham, iv. 327.
— George, eleventh earl of, iv. 328.
— — his wife, Helen Catherine Warrender, iv. 328.
— John, fourth earl of, iv. 317; vii. 76, 219.
— — his wife, Christian Lindsay, iii. 37; iv. 318; ix. 101.
— Thomas, first earl of, iii. 98; iv. 310; v. 471, 617 *n.*
— — his 1st wife, Margaret Borthwick, iv. 313.
— — his 2nd wife, Margaret Foulis, iv. 312, 313.
— — his 3rd wife, Julian Ker, iv. 313; v. 68.
— Thomas, second earl of, iv. 315; v. 622.
— — his 1st wife, Katharine Erskine, iv. 316; v. 622.
— — his 2nd wife, Jean Gordon, iv. 316, 547.
— Thomas, third earl of, iv. 317.
— — his wife, Henriette de Coligny, iv. 317.
— Thomas, sixth earl of, iv. 320; v. 477; vii. 303.
— — his wife, Helen Hope, iv. 320, 493.
— Thomas, seventh earl of, iv. 323; vi. 21.
— — his 1st wife, Mary Holt, iv. 324.
— — his 2nd wife, Anne Gascoigne, iv. 324; ix. 101.
— Thomas, ninth earl of, iv. 325.
— — his wife, Maria Parker, iv. 326.
HADDINGTON, RAMSAY, VISCOUNT OF, iv. 297-302.
Haddington, John, viscount, iii. 97 *n.*; iv. 300, 311.
— — his 1st wife, Elizabeth Ratcliffe, iv. 301.
— — his 2nd wife, Martha Cockayne, iv. 301.
— David de, rector of Lilford, iii. 525; vi. 528.
— John de, prior of St. Andrews, vi. 275.
HADDO, GORDON, LORD, i. 88-99.
Haddo, George, president of the College of Justice; first lord, i. 88.
— — his wife, Anna Lockhart, i. 89.
— George, 2nd son of 1st earl of Aberdeen; styled lord, i. 89; ix. 5.
— George, eldest son of 3rd earl of Aberdeen; styled lord, i. 93.
— — his wife, Charles Baird, i. 93; ix. 5.
— George, eldest son of 7th earl of Aberdeen; styled lord, i. 98.
Hadow, Walter Henry, v. 238.
— — his wife, Constance Blanche Louisa Hay, v. 238.
Hadykes, James (Murray), Jacobite creation, lord, viii. 205.

Haggerston of Haggerston, Sir Carnaby 3rd bart., iv. 418.
—— —— his wife, Elizabeth Middelton, iv. 418.
—— William, 2nd son of Sir Thomas H., iv. 418.
—— —— his wife, Anne Constable, iv. 418.
Haggerston-Constable of Everingham, William, iv. 418.
—— —— his wife, Winifred Maxwell of Terregles, iv. 418; vi. 490.
Haig of Bemersyde, James, 12th laird, ii. 228.
—— —— his wife, Margaret Scott, ii. 228.
—— —— John, 8th laird, v. 286.
—— —— his wife, Mary Maitland, v. 286.
—— —— Petrus de Haga *or*, 2nd laird, vii. 577.
—— —— his wife, Ada St. Clair, vii. 577.
—— —— William, 13th laird, iv. 469.
—— —— his wife, Isebel Home, iv. 469.
—— —— William, king's solicitor, 19th laird, i. 563.
—— —— Zerubbabel, 22nd laird, iv. 479.
—— Elizabeth *or* Janet, wife of James Home of Ayton, iv. 479.
HAILES, HEPBURN, LORD, ii. 135-167.
Hailes, Patrick, first lord, ii. 141.
—— —— his wife, Elyne Wallace, ii. 142.
—— Patrick, second lord, ii. 149, 151; iv. 452.
—— —— his 1st wife, Janet Douglas, ii. 152.
—— —— his 2nd wife, Margaret Gordon, ii. 152.
—— master of, Adam, eldest son of 1st lord Hailes, ii. 142, 148; iv. 448.
—— —— his wife, Elyne Home, ii. 148; iv. 447, 448; v. 608.
—— master of, Patrick, 2nd son of 1st earl of Bothwell; styled, ii. 153.
—— —— his 1st wife, Nicolas Home, ii. 153.
—— —— his 2nd wife, Katharine Fleming, ii. 153.
—— Sir David Dalrymple, senator of the College of Justice, lord, iv. 321.
Haines, Elizabeth, wife of rev. W. H. Aston, i. 404.
—— Nathan, D.D., i. 404.
Haining, Margaret Wallace, wife of * Ross; styled lady, v. 163; vi. 514.
Haitlie of Mellerstain, Henry, vi. 1.
—— —— his wife, Sibilla Home, vi. 1.
—— —— Henry, iv. 471 *bis*.
—— —— his contr. wife, Margaret Home, iv. 471.
—— —— his wife, Helen Edmestoun, iv. 471.
—— —— John, iv. 471.
—— —— John, son of Henry H., ix. 108.
—— Alexander, illeg. son of John H. of Mellerstain, iv. 471.
Halcro of Halcro, Harry *or* Hugh, vi. 574.
—— —— his wife, Barbara Stewart, vi. 574.

* Name unknown.

Haloro of Halcre, Hugh, i. 397.
—— —— his wife, Jean Stewart, i. 397.
Haldane of Ardonnen, James, v. 504.
—— of Gleneagles, George, iv. 243.
—— —— his wife, Jean Cunningham, iv. 243.
—— —— George, *né* Cockburn, viii. 233.
—— —— his wife, Margaret Drummond, viii. 233; ix. 162.
—— —— James, vi. 223.
—— —— his contr. wife, Katharine Campbell, ix. 19.
—— —— his wife, Christian Graham, vi. 223.
—— —— James, v. 609.
—— —— his wife, Margaret Erskine, v. 609.
—— —— James, i. 470, 514; iv. 115; v. 504.
—— —— his wife, Margaret Murray, i. 470.
—— —— Sir James, v. 532.
—— —— his wife, Margaret Fraser, v. 532.
—— —— John, v. 341; vi. 407.
—— —— his wife, Agnes Menteith, vi. 407.
—— —— [John], his wife, Marjory Lawson, ii. 99 *n*.
—— —— John, ii. 572.
—— —— Sir John, viii. 499.
—— —— his wife, Katharine Wemyss, viii. 499.
—— —— John, viii. 219.
—— —— his 1st wife, Mary Drummond, viii. 219.
—— —— Patrick, advocate, iv. 95; v. 312.
—— —— his wife, Margaret Forrester, iv. 95.
—— of Haldane, William, vii. 329.
—— Anna, wife of Andrew, 2nd lord Fraser, iv. 115 *bis*.
—— Beatrice, wife of R. Colville of Cleish, ii. 572.
—— George, governor of Jamaica, iv. 95.
—— Helen, wife of Sir D. Lindsay of Edzell, i. 514.
—— *, 2nd wife of Charles Barclay-Maitland of Towie, v. 312.
Hale of King's Walden, William, i. 62.
—— Mary, wife of col. Plumer of Blakesware, i. 62.
—— *, sergeant, viii. 460.
—— —— his wife, Dorothy Hayhurst, viii. 460.
Hales, Maria de, dau. of Kylvert, vii. 419.
HALIBURTON OF DIRLETON, HALIBURTON, LORD, iv. 330-338.
Haliburton of Dirleton, George, third lord, iii. 307; iv. 273, 336.
—— —— his wife, Mariota, iv. 336.
—— —— James, fourth lord, iv. 337.
—— —— Janet, wife of William, 2nd lord Ruthven; baroness, iv. 337.
—— —— John, first lord, iv. 335, 446.
—— —— his wife, Janet Seton, iv. 335; viii. 575.

* Name unknown.

Haliburton of Dirleton, Patrick, second lord, iv. 335; ix. 102.
— — his wife, Margaret Hepburn, ii. 148; iv. 335; ix. 102.
— — Patrick, fifth lord, iv. 337; ix. 102.
— — his 1st wife, Margaret Douglas, iv. 337.
— — his 2nd wife, Christian Wawane, iv. 337; ix. 102.
HALIBURTON, LORD HALIBURTON OF DIRLETON, iv. 330-338.
Halyburton of Arcles, George, v. 526.
— of Ballegarno, Sir John, iv. 333.
— of Balmablare, John, iv. 335.
— of Denhead, George, bishop of Aberdeen, v. 415.
— of Dirleton, Sir John, iv. 333.
— — Sir Walter, ii. 537; iv. 257, 333, 518; vii. 275; viii. 572.
— — his 1st wife, *, iv. 334.
— — his 2nd wife, Isobel Stewart, i. 149; iv. 334; vii. 275.
— — Walter, lord high treasurer, iii. 163; iv. 334.
— — his wife, Mary *or* Marjory Douglas, i. 18; iii. 163; iv. 334.
— of Elbothel, Walter, v. 392.
— of Essie, James, v. 230.
— — his wife, Katharine Cuillane, v. 230.
— of Gask, George, v. 526.
— — Sir Walter, iv. 334 *bis*.
— — his wife, Katharine Chisholm of Gask, iv. 334.
— — William, the yr., vii. 183.
— — his wife, Elizabeth Ogilvy, vii. 183.
— of Gogar, George, iv. 333.
— of Haliburton, Sir Adam, iv. 332.
— — his wife, Isabella, iv. 332.
— — David de, son of Truite, iv. 330, 331.
— — Sir Henry de, iv. 331; vii. 365.
— — his wife, Agnes de Mordington, iv. 331.
— — Sir John de, iv. 332, 333; ix. 102.
— — his 1st wife, Christian Vaus of Dirleton, ix. 102.
— — his 2nd wife, Margaret Cameron of Ballegarno, iv. 333; ix. 102.
— — Philip, iv. 331.
— — his wife, Alice, iv. 331.
— — Walter de, grandson of Truite, iv. 330.
— — Sir Walter, high sheriff of Berwick, iv. 332, 443; ix. 102 *ter*.
— — Sir Walter, iv. 333.
— — his wife, Isabel Stewart, iv. 334; vii. 242, 275.
— — Sir Walter, iv. 334; viii. 8.
— — his wife, Mary Douglas, iv. 334.
— — William, iv. 331.
— — his wife, Christian de Fawnys, iv. 331.

* Name unknown.

Haliburton of Kirkton of Essie, James, vii. 190.
— of Mertoun, Henry, v. 462.
— — his wife, Katharine Ker, v. 462.
— — John, last laird, vii. 76.
— of Molle, Sir Henry, iv. 330; viii. 3.
— — Johanna, wife of (1) * Wyschard, and (2) Adam de Roule, iv. 330.
— of Muirhouselaw, George, ii. 542; vii. 370.
— of Pitcur, Agatha, wife of 13th earl of Morton, vi. 382.
— — Andrew, vii. 12.
— — his 1st wife Margaret Maule, vii. 12,
— — David, iii. 73.
— — Douglas Gordon *or*, i. 105: iv. 559; ix. 7.
— — his wife, Louisa Leslie, i. 105.
— — George, vii. 16.
— — Sir George, iii. 313.
— — Sir James, ii. 577; vi. 495.
— — his wife, Margaret Scrymgeour, iii. 313.
— — Sir James, vii. 346.
— — his wife, Mary Ker, vii. 346; viii. 70; ix. 153.
— — James, M.P., vi. 382.
— — James, colonel, vi. 384.
— — Walter, 2nd son of Sir Walter H. of Dirleton, iv. 334.
— — his wife, Katharine Chisholm of Pitcur, iv. 334.
— — William, viii. 67.
— — his wife, Marjorie Carnegie, i. 305; viii. 67.
— of Saline, John, vii. 407.
— of Seggie, Patrick, iv. 337.
— of Thorngreen, James, iii. 313.
— Adam, son of Walter de H., iv. 331.
— Sir Alexander, 3rd son of Sir Adam de H., iv. 332, 333 *bis*; ix. 102 *bis*.
— Alexander, 1409, iv. 333.
— Alexander, merchant, Edinburgh. viii. 105.
— Andrew, 3rd son of 3rd lord Haliburton of Dirleton, iv. 336.
— Archibald, eldest son of George, 3rd lord Haliburton of Dirleton, iv. 336.
— — his wife, Helen Shaw, iv. 336.
— Christina, wife of George, 1st earl of Rothes, iv. 335; vii. 275.
— David, legtd. son of 5th lord Haliburton of Dirleton, iv. 337.
— Elizabeth, wife of major Charles Boyd, v. 180.
— Elizabeth, wife of Peter Rollo of Pilton. vii. 190.
— George, bishop of Dunkeld, i. 126.
— George, ii. 542; vii. 370.
— Henry, ii. 538.
— — his wife, Agnes Mordington, ii. 538.

* Name unknown.

Haliburton, James, captain, i. 293.
—— —— his wife, Helen Arbuthnott, i. 293; ix. 16.
—— James, tutor of Pitcur, provost of Dundee; i. 534; viii. 58.
—— Jean, wife of Henry (St. Clair), 1st earl of Orkney, iv. 333; vi. 569; ix. 102.
—— Sir John, 2nd son of Sir Adam H., iv. 332, 333: ix. 101 *bis*.
—— John, 1409, iv. 333.
—— John, vicar of Greenlaw, iv. 335.
—— John, Edinburgh and Dunkirk, v. 180.
—— John, vii. 458 *n*.
—— —— his wife, Katharine Grant, vii. 458 *n*.
—— John, 4th son of 1st lord Haliburton, ix. 102.
—— John Frederick Gordon-, admiral R.N., M.P., iv. 559.
—— —— his wife, Augusta Fitzclarence, iv. 559.
—— Jonet, wife of Francis Hay of Balhousie, v. 230.
—— Jonet, wife of 2nd lord Ruthven, iv. 259.
—— Magdalen, wife of (1) John Erskine of Dun, and (2) John, 1st earl of Northesk, vi. 495.
—— Margaret, wife of Alex. Arbuthnott, i. 292.
—— Margaret, wife of P. Lindsay, ii. 90.
—— Margaret, wife of lord Coupar, ii. 577.
—— Margaret, wife of (1) Sir G. Mackenzie of Rosehaugh, and (2) R. Mackenzie of Prestonhall, iii. 73; vii. 505.
—— Margaret, wife of George Ker of Fawdonside, iv. 337; v. 58; vii. 330.
—— Margaret, wife of (1) Patrick Ogilvie, younger of Inchmartine, and (2) George, 1st viscount Dupplin, iv. 34; v. 221, 223.
—— Margaret, wife of John Lindsay of Wormiston, v. 415.
—— Margaret, wife of Thos. Maule of Panmure, vii. 16.
—— Marion, wife of Ralph Ker of Primsydeloch, v. 53 *n*.
—— Mariota, wife of 4th lord Home, iv. 337, 460.
—— Marion *or* Mary, wife of Sir James Drummond of Machany, viii. 223.
—— Robert, 3rd son of Sir Walter H., iv. 334.
—— Robert, v. 394.
—— —— his wife, Jonet Fenton of Baky, etc., v. 394.
—— Truite, ancestor of the family of, iv. 330.
—— Walter, 1409, iv. 333.
—— Walter, 3rd son of 1st lord Haliburton, ix. 102.
—— William, 4th son of Sir Walter H. of Dirleton, iv. 335.
—— —— his wife, Johanna Congalton, ix. 102.
Haliburton, William, 2nd son of Geo. H. of Pitcur, vii. 12, 15.
—— —— his wife, Elizabeth Maule, vii. 12.
Halifax, George (Savile), 1st viscount, iii. 48.
—— William (Savile), marquess of, iii. 482; vii. 351.
—— —— his wife, Mary Finch, vii. 351.
Halkerston of Southwood, James, iv. 279.
—— —— his wife, Janet Gordon, iii. 24; iv. 279, 530.
Halkerstoun, George, custumar of Edinburgh, iii. 67; vii. 284 *n*.
—— —— his wife, Margaret Crichton, iii. 66; vii. 284.
—— James, son of George H., iii. 67; vii. 287.
HALKERTON, FALCONER, LORD FALCONER OF, v. 242-255.
Halkett of Petconochy, William, iv. 30.
—— of Gosford and Pitfirrane, Sir Peter, 2nd bart., vi. 325.
—— —— his wife, Amelia Stewart, vi. 325.
—— of Pitfirrane, Sir Charles, ix. 78.
—— —— George, vii. 68.
—— —— his wife, Isobel Hepburn, vii. 68.
—— —— Sir Robert, ii. 573; vii. 68 *bis*.
—— —— William, iv. 30.
—— Anne, wife of (1) Sir R. Henderson of Fordel, and (2) Sir Thomas Myrton of Cambo, ii. 573.
—— Grizell, wife of Sir Thos. Ker of Cavers, vi. 15.
—— James, brother of Robert H. of Pitfirrane, vii. 68.
—— Jean, wife of (1) Sir Adam Gordon of Dalpholly, and (2) Sir James Dalrymple of Borthwick, viii. 125.
—— John, vii. 523.
—— —— his wife, Katharine Douglas, vii. 523.
—— Mary, wife of brig.-gen. Robt. Murray, ix. 78.
Hall of Dunglass, Sir James, 2nd bart., vi. 17.
—— —— his 1st wife, Anne Hume, vi. 17.
—— —— Sir James, 4th bart., vii. 522.
—— —— his wife, Isabella Margaret Douglas, vii. 522.
—— Augusta, wife of J. A. Herbert, iv. 423.
—— Sir Charles, vice-chancellor of England, vii. 564.
—— Elizabeth Mary, wife of Charles Maitland, v. 312.
—— Harriet, wife of James O. Forbes of Corse, vii. 564.
—— Herbert Goodenough King, captain R.N., D.S.O., viii. 213.
—— —— his wife, Mabel Emily Murray, viii. 213.
—— captain, 1650, v. 226.
Halliday of the Leasowes, and of Castlemains, John Delap, major, iii. 410.
—— —— his wife, Jane Murray, iii. 410.

Halliday of Moffat, Katharine, wife of Sir Wm. Somerville, viii. 6.
— of Portnellan, *, vi. 533 *n.*
— — his wife, * Oliphant, vi. 533 *n.*
— of Tullibole, John, vi, 549 *n.*
— — William, vii. 200.
— — his 2nd wife, Isabel Rollo, vii. 200.
— John, eldest son of Sir Leonard H., v. 11.
— — his wife, Alice Ferrers, v. 11.
— Katharine, wife of Wm. Oliphant of Gask, vi. 549; ix. 145.
— Sir Leonard, lord mayor of London, v. 11.
Hallewes, Elizabeth Boyle, wife of 10th earl of Northesk, vi. 507.
— George Skene, general, vi. 507.
Halsham, Sir John, i. 433.
— — his wife, Philippa of Atholl, i. 433.
Halton, Charles Maitland; lord of Session, lord, v. 306; ix. 124, 125.
Halwis, wife of Adam Olifard, vi. 530.
Hamel, Emir de, Order of Observantines, i. 283.
HAMELDON, GUNNINO, BARONESS HAMILTON OF, i. 387.
Hameldon, Elizabeth, baroness Hamilton of, i. 387.
HAMELDON, HAMILTON, BARON HAMILTON OF, i. 387.
Hameldon, Douglas, baron Hamilton of, i. 387, 388.
HAMELDON, CAMPBELL, BARON HAMILTON OF, i. 388.
Hameldon, George William, first baron Hamilton of, i. 388.
Hameldun, Gilbert de, clericus, iv. 340 *n.*
HAMILTON, HAMILTON, BARON OF, i. 46.
Hamilton, James, eldest son of Claud, lord Paisley; baron of, i. 46.
HAMILTON, HAMILTON, LORD, iv. 349-397.
Hamilton, James, first lord, ii. 38; iii. 22, 23, 179, 181; iv. 350, 431, 522; vi. 143, 475, 538*n.*
— — his 1st wife, Euphemia Graham, iii. 170; iv. 351, 352; vi. 143: viii. 260.
— — his 2nd wife, Mary Stewart, i. 20; iv. 352; v. 149.
— James, second lord, i. 20; iv. 355.
— — his 1st wife, Elizabeth Home, iv. 358, 454.
— — his 2nd wife, Janet Beaton, iv. 358, 360.
— James, third lord, iv. 360, 366.
— — his wife, Margaret Douglas, iv. 368.
— James, fourth lord, iv. 368.
— John, 3rd son of 2nd earl of Arran; styled lord, iv. 369, 370, 409; vii. 254.
— — his wife, Margaret Lyon, iv. 372; viii. 288.
HAMILTON, HAMILTON, MARQUESS OF, iv. 372-380.

* Name unknown.

Hamilton, James, second marquess of, ii. 40, 85, 477; iv. 369.
— — his wife, Anna Cunningham, iv. 245, 375.
— James, third marquess of, iv. 376; vi. 244, 246; vii. 347; viii. 57.
— — his wife, Margaret Fielding, iv. 378.
— John, first marquess of, ii. 27, 474; iv. 370.
— — his wife, Margaret Lyon, iv. 372; viii. 288.
— William, fourth marquess of, iv. 378.
— — his wife, Elizabeth Maxwell, iii. 130; iv. 380.
HAMILTON, HAMILTON, DUKE OF, iv. 339-381.
Hamilton, Anne, wife of William, earl of Selkirk; duchess of, i. 49; iv. 378, 381; viii. 302; ix. 23.
— James, first duke of, ii. 28; iv. 377; ix. 104.
— — his wife, Margaret Fielding, iv. 378.
— William, second duke of, i. 49; iii. 129; iv. 378.
— — his wife, Elizabeth Maxwell, iii. 130; iv. 380.
HAMILTON, DOUGLAS-HAMILTON, DUKE OF, iv. 381-397.
Hamilton, Alexander, tenth duke of, iv. 395.
— — his wife, Susan Euphemia Beckford, iv. 395.
— Alfred Douglas, thirteenth duke of, iv. 389, 396.
— — his wife, Nina M. B. Poore, iv. 396.
— Archibald, ninth duke of, iv. 392, 394.
— — his wife, Harriet Stewart, iv. 166, 394.
— Douglas, eighth duke of, i. 211; iv. 393; ix. 13, 81.
— — his wife, E. A. Burrell, iv. 394.
— James, fourth duke of, i. 31; ii. 49; iii. 353; iv. 383.
— — his 1st wife, Anne Spencer, iv. 384.
— — his 2nd wife, Elizabeth Gerard, iv. 384.
— James, fifth duke of, iv. 384, 392.
— — his 1st wife, Anne Cochrane, iii. 355; iv. 392; ix. 77.
— — his 2nd wife, Elizabeth Strangways, iv. 392.
— — his 3rd wife, Anne Spenser, iv. 392.
— James, sixth duke of, iv. 393; ix. 104.
— — his wife, Elizabeth Gunning, i. 387; iv. 393.
— James George, seventh duke of, i. 211; iv. 393.

Hamilton, William, third duke of, i. 205, 480; iii. 347; iv. 381; vii. 139.
—— —— his wife, Anne, *suo jure* duchess of Hamilton, iv. 381.
—— William Alexander Anthony Archibald, eleventh duke of, iv. 395; ix. 105.
—— —— his wife, princess Mary of Baden, iv. 396.
—— William Alexander Louis Stephen, twelfth duke of, iv. 396.
—— —— his wife, Mary Montagu, iv. 396.
Hamilton of Dalzell, John Glencairn Carter, first lord, vi. 120.
—— —— his wife, Emily Eleanor Leslie-Melville, vi. 120.
HAMILTON OF HAMELDON, HAMILTON, BARON, iv. 394.
Hamilton of Hameldon, Douglas, baron, i. 387, 388; iv. 393.
HAMILTON OF HAMILTON, HAMILTON, VISCOUNT, i. 65-74.
Hamilton of Hamilton, James, 8th earl of Abercorn, first viscount, i. 65.
—— —— James, eldest son of 1st marquess of Abercorn; styled viscount, i. 66.
—— —— his wife, Harriet Douglas, i. 67; vi. 383.
—— —— James, third viscount, i. 68.
—— —— John James, second viscount, i. 66.
Hamilton of Stackallan, Gustavus, 1st baron, i. 45.
—— —— his wife, Elizabeth Brooke, i. 45.
HAMILTON, BARON OF STRABANE, HAMILTON, LORD, i. 48-74.
Hamilton, James, first lord, i. 48.
HAMILTON OF STRABANE, HAMILTON, MARQUESS OF, i. 69.
Hamilton, James, first marquess of, i. 69.
—— James, second marquess of, i. 72.
—— James Albert Edward, eldest son of 2nd duke of Abercorn; styled marquess of, i. 72.
—— —— his wife, Rosaline Cecilia Caroline Bingham, i. 73.
HAMILTON OF WISHAW, HAMILTON, BARON, ii. 54.
Hamilton of Wishaw, Robert Montgomerie, first baron, ii. 54.
—— —— his wife, Hamilton Campbell, ii. 54.
HAMILTON OF HAMELDON, CAMPBELL, BARON, i. 387-393.
Hamilton of Hameldon, George William, first baron, i. 388.
HAMILTON OF HAMELDON, GUNNING, BARONESS, i. 387.
Hamilton of Hameldon, Elizabeth, wife of (1) James, 6th duke of Hamilton and Brandon, and (2) John, 5th duke of Argyll; baroness, i. 387.
HAMILTON, LORD OF ABERCORN, i. 46.
HAMILTON, EARL OF ABERCORN, i. 37-74.
HAMILTON, MARQUESS OF ABERCORN, i. 66-74.
HAMILTON, DUKE OF ABERCORN, i. 69-74.
HAMILTON, EARL OF ARRAN, iv. 355-377.
HAMILTON, EARL OF ARRAN AND CAMBRIDGE, iv. 377-383.
HAMILTON, EARL OF ARRAN, LANARK, AND CAMBRIDGE, iv. 383-397.
HAMILTON, EARL OF ANGUS, iv. 393-397.
HAMILTON, LORD AVON AND INNERDALE, iv. 377-397.
HAMILTON, LORD AVEN, POLMONT, MACHANSHYRE, AND INNERDALE, iv. 383-397.
HAMILTON, LORD BARGANY, ii. 27-33.
HAMILTON, LORD BELHAVEN, ii. 38-60.
HAMILTON, LORD BINNING, iv. 310-329.
HAMILTON, DUKE OF BRANDON, iv. 384-397.
HAMILTON, LORD BYRES AND BINNING, iv. 310.
HAMILTON, EARL OF CAMBRIDGE, iv. 374.
HAMILTON, DUKE OF CHATELHERAULT, iv. 367.
HAMILTON, MARQUESS OF CLYDESDALE, iv. 377-397.
HAMILTON, LORD DAER, vii. 516-525.
HAMILTON, BARON DECHMONT, vi. 578-584.
HAMILTON, MARQUESS OF DOUGLAS, iv. 396.
HAMILTON, BARON DUTTON, iv. 384-397.
HAMILTON, LORD EVAN, iv. 372-397.
HAMILTON, BARON OF HAMILTON, i. 46.
HAMILTON, LORD HAMILTON, iv. 349-397.
HAMILTON, VISCOUNT HAMILTON OF HAMILTON, i. 65-74.
HAMILTON, MARQUESS OF HAMILTON, iv. 372-380.
HAMILTON, DUKE OF HAMILTON, iv. 339-381.
HAMILTON, BARON HAMILTON OF HAMELDON, iv. 394.
HAMILTON, LORD HAMILTON, BARON OF STRABANE, i. 48-74.
HAMILTON, MARQUESS OF HAMILTON OF STRABANE, i. 69-74.
HAMILTON, BARON HAMILTON OF WISHAW, ii. 54.
HAMILTON, EARL OF HADDINGTON, iv. 303-329.
HAMILTON, LORD HILLHOUSE, vii. 361-363.
HAMILTON, LORD INNERDALE, iv. 374-381.
HAMILTON, BARON OF KILPATRICK, i. 46.
HAMILTON, VISCOUNT OF KIRKWALL, vi. 578-584.
HAMILTON, EARL OF LANARK, iv. 378-380.
HAMILTON, LORD MACHANESCHYRE, iv. 378-380.
HAMILTON, EARL OF MELROSE, iv. 310-311.
HAMILTON, LORD MELROS OF TYNNINGHAM, iv. 325-326.
HAMILTON, BARON OF MOUNTCASTELL, i. 46.
HAMILTON, BARON OF MOUNTCASTLE, i. 58-74.

HAMILTON, EARL OF ORKNEY, vi. 578-584.
HAMILTON, LORD PAISLEY, i. 39-74.
HAMILTON, BARON OF PAISLEY, i. 46.
HAMILTON, LORD POLMONT, iv. 378-380.
HAMILTON, VISCOUNT OF RICCARTOUN, vii. 361-363.
HAMILTON, EARL OF RUGLEN, vii. 361-363.
HAMILTON, EARL OF SELKIRK, vii. 516-525.
HAMILTON, LORD SHORTCLEUCH, vi. 516-525.
HAMILTON, BARON OF STRABANE, i. 48-74.
HAMILTON, VISCOUNT OF STRABANE, i. 58-74.
Hamilton of Abercorn, James, master of Paisley, i. 46.
—— of Aitkenhead Easter, Gavin, ix. 136.
—— —— his wife, Helen Kincaid, vi. 158; ix. 136.
—— of Alanshaw, Robert, ii. 38.
—— of Arran, Mary Louise, wife of James, marquess of Graham, iv. 396; vi. 274.
—— of Auchingemmill, John, iv. 365.
—— —— his wife, Jean Hamilton, iv. 365.
—— of Avandale, Sir James, vi. 511.
—— of Balbyne, James, iv. 305.
—— —— Thomas, iv. 305.
—— —— Thomas, senator of the College of Justice, iv. 312.
—— of Baldernock, John, iv. 345.
—— —— his wife, Margaret Fraser, iv. 345.
—— of Baldony, Sir Claud, 3rd son of 1st lord Paisley, i. 40.
—— of Baldoon, Basil, 6th son of 3rd duke of Hamilton, vii. 518.
—— —— his wife, Mary Dunbar of Baldoon, vii. 519.
—— —— Basil, vii. 519.
—— —— his wife, Isabella Mackenzie, vii. 511, 519.
—— —— Dunbar, vii. 361, 520.
—— —— his wife, Helen Hamilton, vii. 521.
—— —— William, vii. 519; ix. 156.
—— of Ballencrieff, Sir Alexander, iv. 304.
—— —— his wife, Elizabeth Stewart, iv. 304.
—— —— Alexander, iv. 305.
—— —— his wife, Isobel Schaw, iv. 305.
—— —— Sir Alexander, vi. 12.
—— —— Alexander, M.P., v. 480.
—— —— his wife, Mary Ker, v. 480.
—— —— Sir Archibald, iv. 304.
—— —— James, iv. 305.
—— —— John, son of Sir Walter Fitzgilbert of Hamilton, iv. 303; v. 344.
—— —— his wife, Elizabeth Stewart, iv. 303; v. 344.
—— —— Thomas, burgess of Edinburgh, iv. 305.
—— —— Thomas, senator of the College of Justice, iv. 313.
—— of Ballygelly, Archibald, ix. 32.
—— —— his wife, Anne Balfour, ix. 32.
—— of Bangour, Elizabeth, wife of (1) James Hamilton of Hedderwick, and (2) Sir Hew Dalrymple of North Berwick, viii. 142.
Hamilton of Bangour, John, ii. 407.
—— —— his wife, Marion Hamilton, ii. 407.
—— —— John, ii. 416; viii. 142.
—— —— William, the poet, ii. 33; iii. 355; viii. 123.
—— —— his 2nd wife, Elizabeth Dalrymple, viii. 123.
—— of Bardanoch, John, keeper of the Palace of Holyrood House, iii. 447, 448.
—— —— his wife, Katharine Arbuckle, iii. 447.
—— of Bardowie, John, iv. 345, 346.
—— —— his wife, Margaret Fraser, iv. 345.
—— of Bargany, Sir John, legtd. son of 1st marquess of Hamilton, ii. 27, 488; iv. 374.
—— ——his wife, Jean Campbell, ii. 27.
—— —— John, ii. 31; iii. 450.
—— ——his 1st wife, Anne Wemyss, ii. 31; viii. 512.
—— —— his 2nd wife, Margaret Montgomerie, ii. 31; iii. 449.
—— of Barncleugh, James, ii. 41, 42.
—— —— his wife, Margaret Hamilton, ii. 42.
—— —— John, ii. 42.
—— —— Margaret, ii. 42.
—— —— Quintin, ii. 42.
—— —— Robert, ii. 42.
—— —— Mary, wife of Wm. Nisbet of Dirleton, ii. 44.
—— of Barns, David, iv. 344.
—— of Barnton, John, vii. 361.
—— of Barr, *, ii. 41.
—— —— his wife, * Hamilton, ii. 41.
—— of Bathgate, Robert, ix. 100.
—— —— his wife, Elizabeth Hamilton, ix. 100.
—— —— Sir William, iv. 345, 346.
—— of Bearcrofts, Sir John, ix. 36.
—— —— his wife, Margaret Hamilton, ix. 36.
—— of Beltrim, William, elder son of Claud H. of Montalony, i. 42.
—— of Biel, John, 2nd lord Belhaven, ii. 44.
—— —— his wife, Margaret Hamilton, ii. 44.
—— —— Mary, wife of Wm. Nisbet, ii. 44, 47.
—— of Binning, Thomas, iv. 313.
—— of Wester Binning, Robert, iv. 315, 316.
—— of Blackburn, Sir George, vii. 576; ix. 157.
—— —— his wife, Katharine Sinclair, vii. 574; ix. 157.
—— of Blair, John, ancestor of the family of, iv. 362; vii. 547.
—— —— John, iv. 194.
—— —— John, i. 562.
—— —— his wife, Barbara Elphinstone, i. 562.
—— of Boggs, James, ii. 407, 408, 413.
—— of Bogwood, Bernard, viii, 485.
—— —— his wife, Mariota Towers, viii. 448.
—— of Borland, George, alleged ancestor of the family of, iv. 346.

* Name unknown.

Hamilton of Bothwellhaugh, James, assassin of Regent Moray, i. 24; ii. 41; vi. 316.
— of Bourtreehill, Robert, iii. 40, 443, 461.
— of Braidwood, James, iv. 469.
— — his wife, Helen Home, iv. 469.
— of Brentwood, Alexander, ii. 509.
— — his wife, Christian Cathcart, ii. 509.
— — Sir James, vii. 64.
— of Wester Brichty, John, iv. 348.
— of Broomhill, David, vii. 547.
— — his wife, Margaret Sempill, vii. 547.
— — Sir James, sheriff of Lanark, ii. 39.
— — his wife, Margaret Hamilton, ii. 39, 41.
— — John, illeg. son of 1st lord Hamilton, ii. 38; iv. 353, 361.
— — his wife, Janet *or* Elizabeth Hamilton, ii. 38; iv. 354.
— — his alleged wife, Margaret Dalzell, ii. 38, 404; iv. 354.
— — John, ii. 38; iv. 354.
— — his wife, Anne Hamilton, ii. 39.
— — Sir John, ii. 39.
— — his wife, Margaret Hamilton, ii. 40.
— — Margaret, wife of Gavin Hamilton, ii. 406.
— of Brownmuir, Robert, ii. 51.
— — William, iii. 342.
— of Byres, Sir Thomas, iv. 313; v. 401.
— of Cadogan Square, Sir Charles Edward, 1st bart., v. 516.
— of Cadzow, Sir David, iv. 343, 344; v. 345.
— — his wife, Janet Keith of Galston. iv. 145, 345; v. 345; vi. 29.
— — James, iv. 347; ix. 129.
— — his wife, Janet Livingston, iv. 348; v. 429; ix. 129.
— — Sir James, iv. 349; vi. 40, 215.
— — his 1st wife, Euphemia Graham, iv. 351, 352; viii. 260.
— — his 2nd wife, Mary Stewart, iv. 352.
— — Sir John, iv. 345, 346; v. 346; ix. 102.
— — his wife, Jacoba Douglas, iv. 346; vi. 349; ix. 103.
— of Cambuskeith, John, vii. 534.
— — his wife, Janet Montgomery, vii. 534.
— — Walter, ancestor of the family of, iv. 343.
— of Carcluie, Archibald, iii. 462.
— — his wife, Jane Montgomerie, iii. 462.
— of Carriden, Sir John, ii. 28.
— — his wife, Jean Douglas, ii. 28.
— of Castle Confey, Archibald, iv. 382.
— of Castle Damph, John, 2nd son of Sir James H. of Manor Elieston, i. 42.
— of Castle Hamilton, Sir Francis, 1st bart., i. 40 *n*.
Hamilton of Castle Toome, Sir Claud, eldest son of Sir Claude H. of Cocknogh, i. 40 *n*.
— — his 2nd wife, Anne Colley, i. 40 *n*.
— of Charters, Edward William Terrick, ii. 56.
— — his wife, Anne Thacker, ii. 56.
— of Chilston Park, John, i. 57.
— — his wife, Mary Wright, i. 57.
— — William, i. 57.
— — his wife, Margaret Colepeper, i. 57.
— of Clinton Clare, James, capt., ii. 489.
— — his wife, Agnes Kennedy, ii. 489.
— of Clonyn, Sir Claud, 2nd son of Sir Alex. H. of Innerwick, i. 40 *n*.
— — his wife, Jane Lauder, i. 40 *n*.
— of Clydesdale, John, iv. 363.
— — his wife, Janet Home, iv. 363.
— of Coats, Paul, ancestor of the family of, ix. 103.
— of Cobham, Charles, 9th son of 6th lord Abercorn, i. 61.
— of Cocknogh, Sir Claud, i. 40 *n*.
— of Coldstream, Sir John, iv. 311.
— — Thomas, iv. 313.
— of Coltness, John, ii. 41.
— — his wife, Helen Whiteford, ii. 41.
— of Colquot, Jonas, iv. 435.
— — his wife, Jean Bothwell, iv. 435.
— of Columbie, Sir James, viii. 370.
— of Corshill, James, ix. 41.
— of Court Nichola, Archibald, iv. 382.
— of Cowbelhauch, James, viii. 372.
— of Cowdenknowes, Thomas, iv. 313.
— of Crawfordjohn, Charles, vii. 361.
— — Dunbar, vii. 361.
— — James, v. 163.
— — John, vii. 361.
— of Dalserf, David, 2nd son of Sir John H. of Cadzow, iv. 347.
— — *, wife of Archibald Hamilton, ii. 49.
— of Dalzell, Sir Alexander, vi. 321.
— — Archibald, ii. 43.
— — Archibald, viii. 139.
— — his wife, Marion Dalrymple, viii. 139.
— — Gavin, ancestor of the family of, iv. 349.
— — James, 1st laird, ii. 407, 408, 413.
— — James, ii. 42.
— — his wife, Margaret Hamilton, ii. 42.
— of Darngaber, Thomas, iv. 347.
— of Dechmont, Alexander, W.S., ii. 43.
— — his wife, Mary Kinloch, ii. 44.
— — Mary, wife of Wm. Nisbet of Dirleton, ii. 43, 47.
— of Donalong, Sir George, 4th son of 1st earl of Abercorn, i. 47, 52; vii. 554.
— — his wife, Mary Butler, i. 53.
— — James, master of Paisley, i. 46.
— — James, i. 58.
— — his wife, Elizabeth Reading, i. 59.
— of Drem, Thomas, iv. 313.

* Name unknown.

Hamilton of Drumcairn, James, iv. 305.
— — Thomas, iv. 305.
— — Thomas, senator of the College of Justice, iv. 310, 312.
— of Drumcors, David, iv. 345.
— of Drumry, William, son of archbishop H., iv. 362; vii. 546, 547.
— of Dublin, Sir Alexander, vii. 555.
— of Dulata, John, i. 42.
— — his wife, Sarah Hamilton, i. 42.
— of Dunamana, Sir John Stewart, 1st bart., i. 42.
— of Ecclesmachan, Robert, ii. 61.
— — his wife, Margaret Bellenden, ii. 64.
— of Ellieston, Sir James, iv. 350.
— of Evandale, Sir James, v. 163.
— — his wife, Christian Boyd, v. 163.
— — James, eldest son of Jas. H. of Liberton, iv. 245.
— — his wife, Margaret Cunningham, iv. 245.
— of Falahill, James, eldest son of Patrick H. of Little Preston, vi. 597, 601.
— of Ferguslie, Allan, ii. 169.
— of Fingaltoun, Sir John, iv. 343, 346 *ter*.
— — his 1st wife, Jane Lyddell, iv. 343.
— — his 2nd wife, Anna Seton, iv. 343.
— of Finnart, Sir James, 1st lord Hamilton, iv. 351.
— — Sir James, legtd. son of 1st earl of Arran, ii. 547, 569; iv. 360, 365, 366; v. 56, 352, 556; vii. 333; vii. 14, 16, 370; ix. 103.
— — his wife, Margaret Livingston, iv. 361; viii. 369.
— of Gairen, James, viii. 372.
— of Galston, Andrew, ii. 397.
— of Gilkerscleugh, James, ancestor of the family of, iv. 361.
— — John, ii. 42.
— — his wife, Jean Hamilton, ii. 42.
— of Gilmerton, Sir James, viii. 370.
— of Glenawley, Archibald, ancestor of the family of, ix. 32.
— of Glenshinnoch, David, iv. 344.
— of Grange, Ayrshire, John, ii. 41.
— — his wife, Margaret Hamilton, ii. 41; v. 173.
— — Fife, David, 4th son of 2nd earl of Arran, iv. 369, 409.
— of Grange-Breich, James, iv. 92.
— — his wife, Christian Forrester, iv. 92.
— — Sir John, ix. 36.
— of Greenlaw, Sir George, i. 42, 43, 52; vii. 554; ix. 3.
— — his 1st wife, Isobel Leslie, i. 42.
— — his 2nd wife, Mary Butler, i. 42.
— of Easter Greenlees, Sir Robert, i. 41.
— of Haggs, Sir Alexander, v. 189 *n.*; ix. 136.
— — his wife, Agnes Hamilton, ix. 136.
Hamilton of Haggs, Sir Alexander, vii. 475.
— — his wife, Mary Grant, vii. 475.
— — James, iii. 534, 535.
— — his wife, Isobel Elphinstone, iii. 534.
— of Hallcraig, Archibald, ii. 489; iv. 583.
— — his wife, Rachel Carmichael, iv. 583.
— of Hedderwick, James, viii. 142.
— — his wife, Elizabeth Hamilton, viii. 142.
— of Herries. John, illeg. son of 1st earl of Arran, iv. 363, 408, 409, 410 *bis*.
— of Hill, Gavin, vi. 158.
— — his wife, Helen Kincaid, vi. 158.
— of Hilston Park, John, v. 636.
— of Humbie, Thomas, iv. 313.
— of Inchmachan, Robert, ii. 64.
— — his wife, Margaret Bellenden, ii. 64.
— of Innerwick, Sir Alexander, 1st laird, iv. 304.
— — his wife, Elizabeth Stewart, i. 170; iv. 304.
— — Alexander, 3rd laird, iv. 305.
— — his wife, Isobel Schaw, iv. 305.
— — Sir Alexander, last laird, i. 40 *n.*; iii. 128, 286, 508; iv. 309, 316; v. 458; vi. 12.
— — his 1st wife, Alison Home, iii. 286.
— — his 2nd wife, Christian Hamilton, iv. 309.
— — his 3rd wife, Elizabeth Ker, v. 458.
— — Sir Archibald, 2nd laird, iv. 304.
— — his alleged wife, Margaret Montgomerie, iv. 304.
— — Hugh, 4th laird, iv. 305.
— — James, iv. 305, 469.
— — his wife, Helen Home, iv. 469.
— — John Fitzwalter, ancestor of the family of, iv. 301, 342.
— of Inverdovat, Gavin, ix. 37.
— of Inverkeithing, David, iv. 369, 409.
— of Kilbrachmont, ii. 39.
— — James, vii. 69.
— — Philip, viii. 496.
— — his wife, Margaret Wemyss, viii. 496.
— of Killagh, Sir Francis, 1st bart., i. 40 *n.*
— of Killishandra, Sir Charles, vii. 554.
— — his wife, Francelina Sempill, vii. 554.
— of Killyleagh, William, viii. 557.
— of Kinbraxmont, George, vi. 421.
— — his wife, Jean Napier, vi. 421.
— — John, vi. 421.
— of Kincavil, James, sheriff of Linlithgow, vii. 550; ix. 103.
— — his wife, Isobel Sempill, vii. 550.
— — Sir Patrick, iv. 354, 361; ix. 10, 103.
— — his wife, Margaret *or* Katharine Stewart, i. 153; iv. 354; ix. 10.
— of Kinglass, John, ix. 120.
— — his wife, Lilias Livingston, ix. 120.
— of Kings Cramond, John, vii. 361.

Hamilton of Kinnell, James, bishop of Argyll, iv. 363; vii. 546; ix. 103.
—— —— his wife, Janet Murray, ix. 103.
—— of Kirkhope, James, iv. 348.
—— —— John, iv. 348.
—— of Ladyflat, David, viii. 583.
—— —— his wife, Margaret Seton, viii. 583.
—— of Larbert, Alan, iv. 344.
—— of Leat, William, 2nd son of Sir Wm. H. of Manor Elieston, i. 42.
—— —— his wife, Mary Walkingshaw, i. 42.
—— of Leckprevick, Sir Robert, i. 41.
—— of Letham, William, iii. 448; ix. 81.
—— —— his wife, Mary Montgomerie, iii. 448.
—— of Lettrick, Sir John, legtd. son of 1st marquess of Hamilton, ii. 27, 488; iv. 284, 373.
—— —— his 1st wife, Katharine Carnegie, iv. 284; viii. 58; ix. 35, 104.
—— —— his 2nd wife, Jean Campbell, ii. 27; iv. 373.
—— of Liberton, Sir James, legtd. son of 1st earl of Arran, iv. 360; viii. 16.
—— —— Sir James, iv. 245; v. 163.
—— —— his wife, Christian Boyd, v. 163.
—— of Peel of Livingston, Patrick, iii. 234.
—— —— his wife, Euphemia Seton, iii. 234.
—— of Loughmuck, William, iv. 195.
—— —— his wife, Margaret Boyle, iv. 194.
—— of Luffness, Thomas, iv. 313.
—— of Machanmuir, John, legtd. son of 1st lord Hamilton, iv. 353, 361.
—— —— his 1st wife, Janet Hamilton, iv. 354.
—— —— his alleged 2nd wife, Margaret Dalzell, iv. 354.
—— of Magdalens, Sir John, lord clerk Register, iv. 307.
—— —— his wife, Agnes Hamilton, iv. 308; ix. 100.
—— of Manor Elieston, Sir James, i. 41; ix. 3.
—— —— his 1st wife, Mary Jacob, i. 42.
—— —— his 2nd wife, Eleanor Innes, i. 42.
—— —— Sir William, eldest son of Sir Claud H. of Shawfield, i. 41, 42.
—— —— his 1st wife, Elizabeth Johnston, i. 41.
—— —— his 2nd wife, Beatrix Campbell, i. 42; v. 504; ix. 3.
—— —— William, i. 42.
—— —— his wife, Deborah *, i. 42.
—— of Manor Hamilton, Sir Frederick, i. 43; ix. 3.
—— —— his 1st wife, Sidney Vaughan, i. 44.
—— —— his 2nd wife, Agnes *, i. 45.
—— —— James, i. 45; vi. 9.
—— —— his wife, Katharine Hamilton, i. 45, 50.

* Name unknown.

Hamilton of Marlborough House, Sir John, 1st bart., capt. R.N., i. 58.
—— —— his wife, Cassandra Agnes Chamberlayne, i. 58.
—— of Melrose, Thomas, iv. 313.
—— of Monkland, Thomas, iv. 313.
—— of Montalony, Claud, high sheriff of Tyrone, i. 42.
—— —— his wife, Isabella *, i. 42.
—— of Neuburg, Alexander, count of the Holy Roman Empire, i. 47.
—— —— Julius, count of the Empire, i. 48.
—— —— his wife, Maria Ernestina von Staremberg, i. 48.
—— of Newton, John, W.S., ii. 49.
—— —— his wife, Jean Garthshore, ii. 49.
—— —— John, viii. 14.
—— —— his wife, * Somerville, viii. 14.
—— of Nielsland, John, ii. 40.
—— —— his wife, Elizabeth Hamilton, ii. 38, 40.
—— of Orbistoun, Mr. Gavin, provost of the Collegiate Church of Bothwell, iv. 348; ix. 103.
—— —— James, vi. 600.
—— —— his wife, Henrietta Makgill of Oxfuird, vi. 600.
—— —— John, illeg. son of Gavin H., iv. 349.
—— —— John, 4th laird, ii. 407.
—— —— his wife, Christian Dalzell, ii. 407.
—— —— Sir John, lord Justice Clerk, ii. 407; iv. 584.
—— —— Mr. Robert, canon of Glasgow, iv. 349.
—— —— William, iv. 249; ix. 98.
—— —— his wife, Elizabeth Cunningham, iv. 249.
—— of Orchardfield, Thomas, burgess of Edinburgh, iv. 305.
—— —— his wife, Margaret Cant, iv. 305.
—— of Painshill, Charles, i. 61.
—— of Paisley Abbey, Claud, i. 37; vii. 541.
—— of Pardovan, Archibald, R.N., iv. 382.
—— of Parkhill, James, ix. 103.
—— of Parklie, James, vii. 14.
—— —— his wife, Isobel Maule, vii. 14.
—— —— Thomas, ii. 85; ix. 101.
—— —— his 1st wife, Helen Stewart, ii. 85; ix. 101.
—— —— his 2nd wife, Janet Foulis, ix. 101.
—— of Peill, James, ix. 41.
—— of Pencaitland, Alexander, W.S., ii. 43.
—— —— his wife, Mary Kinloch, ii. 44.
—— —— James, lord Pencaitland, ii. 43; ix. 36.
—— —— his wife, Katharine Denholm, ii. 43.
—— —— John, ii. 43; iv. 591.
—— —— his wife, Margaret Menzies, ii. 43.
—— —— Mary, wife of Wm. Nisbet of Dirleton, ii. 43, 44, 47.

* Name unknown.

Hamilton, of Pettincraig, John, vii. 546.
— of Pitconmark, David, 3rd son of Regent Arran, vi. 89.
— of Presmennan, Mary, wife of Wm. Nisbet, ii. 44.
— — Sir Robert, lord Presmennan, ii. 42, 43, 296; viii. 126.
— — his wife, Marion Denholm, ii. 43.
— — Thomas, master of the king's wardrobe, ii. 44.
— of Preston, Gelis or Elizabeth, wife of Wm. Dalzell, ii. 402.
— — Sir John, ancestor of the family of, iv. 343.
— — John, ii. 413.
— — his wife, Anna Dalzell, ii. 413.
— — Sir Patrick, vii. 80.
— — Sir Robert, viii. 583.
— — Sir William, iv. 349.
— — his wife, Agnes Hamilton, iv. 349.
— of Little Preston, Sir Patrick, iv. 308; ix. 100 *ter*.
— — his wife, Elizabeth Macmorran, iv. 308.
— — Patrick, vi. 597.
— — his wife, Elizabeth Makgill, vi. 597.
— of Priestfield, Sir Alexander, general of artillery, iv. 309, 314.
— — his 1st wife, * Dalziel, iv. 309.
— — his 2nd wife, * Cochrane, iv. 309.
— — his 3rd wife, Elizabeth Crichton, iv. 309.
— — Sir James, iv. 314.
— — his wife, Anna Hepburn, iv. 314.
— — Thomas, burgess of Edinburgh, iv. 305.
— — his alleged wife, Janet Crawford, iv. 305.
— — his wife, Elizabeth Leslie, iv. 305.
— — Thomas, senator of the College of Justice, lord Priestfield, iv. 306.
— — his 1st wife, Elizabeth Heriot, iv. 307.
— — his 2nd wife, Elizabeth Murray, iii. 504; iv. 307; ix. 83, 84, 100.
— — Thomas, senator of the College of Justice, lord Drumcairn, iv. 309.
— — his 1st wife, Margaret Borthwick, iii. 504; iv. 313.
— — his 2nd wife, Margaret Foulis, iv. 312, 313.
— — his 3rd wife, Julian Ker, iv. 313.
— of Raith, David, 3rd son of Regent Arran, iv. 369; vi. 89 *bis*, 95, 101; ix. 103 *bis*.
— of Raploch, Gavin, viii. 24, 27.
— — Gavin, v. 241.
— — his wife, Margaret Keith, v. 241.
— — James, son of Walter H., ii. 40; iv. 347.
— — James, vii. 545.

* Name unknown.

Hamilton of Raploch, Thomas, vi. 367.
— — his wife, Agnes Douglas, vi. 367.
— — Walter, ancestor of the family of, iv. 347.
— of Redhouse, Sir John, iv. 316.
— — Thomas, viii. 405.
— — his wife, Magdalene Stewart, viii. 405.
— of Riccarton, Archibald, R.N., ii. 521; iii. 610: iv. 382; vii. 361.
— — his 1st wife, Anne Lucas, iii. 610; iv. 382.
— — his 2nd wife, Jane Hamilton, i. 62; iv. 382.
— — John, master of the mint, vii. 361.
— of Roberton, Thomas, iii. 32; v. 168, 457.
— — his wife, Jean Ker, iii. 32; v. 168, 457.
— of Roscrea, Sir George, i. 42.
— of Rosehall, Sir Archibald, 1st bart., ii. 42, 296.
— — Archibald, 4th laird, ii. 43.
— — Sir Hugh, 3rd bart., ii. 42.
— — his wife, Margaret Stirling, ii. 42.
— — Sir James, 2nd bart., ii. 42, 88.
— — his wife, Frances Stewart, ii. 88.
— of Saddell, David, bishop of Lismore, abbot of Dryburgh, iv. 354.
— of St. John's Chapel, Jean, wife of Walter Bellenden, ii. 67.
— — James, ii. 154; iv. 363.
— — his wife, Marie Hepburn, iv. 363.
— — John, iv. 363.
— of St. Mary's Isle, Basil, vii. 520.
— of Saltcoats, Alexander, W.S., ii. 43.
— — John, ii. 43.
— — Mary, wife of Wm. Nisbet, ii. 44, 47.
— of Samuelston, James, iv. 363; vii. 289.
— — his 2nd wife, Janet Seton, vii. 289.
— — Sir John, illeg. son of 1st earl of Arran, i. 193, 248; iv. 363, 456; ix. 103.
— — his wife, Janet Home of Samuelston, iv. 456.
— — William, iii. 286.
— — his wife, Jean Home of Quhytlaw, iii. 286.
— of Sanquhar, Walter, ancestor of the family of, iv. 343.
— — William, ii. 463; iv. 365 *n.*; vii. 543.
— — his wife, Katharine Kennedy, ii. 463.
— of Schawfield, Alexander, iv. 348, 351.
— — Sir Claud, 3rd son of 1st lord Paisley, i. 40.
— — his wife, Janet Hamilton, i. 41.
— — James, iv. 348 *bis*.
— — his wife, Elizabeth *, iv. 348.
— of Shean, James, master of Paisley, i. 46.

* Name unknown

Hamilton of Shiels of Kilbride, Sir James, v. 556.
—— of Silvertonhill, Alexander, alleged ancestor of the family of, iv. 348.
—— —— Francis, v. 167.
—— —— Sir Frederick Harding Anson, 7th bart., viii. 14.
—— —— John, son of 1st lord Hamilton, iv. 353, 361.
—— —— Sir Robert, 1st bart., ii. 40, 44; vi. 450.
—— —— his wife, Anne Hamilton, ii. 40.
—— —— Sir Robert, 2nd bart., ii. 40.
—— of Sorn, William, ii. 463.
—— —— his wife, Katharine Kennedy, ii. 463.
—— of Sprouston, James, ii. 154; iv. 363.
—— —— his wife, Marie Hepburne, ii. 154.
—— of Stanehouse, James. iv. 362; vii. 545.
—— —— his 1st wife, Margaret Mowat of Stanehouse, vii. 545.
—— —— his 2nd wife, Grisel Sempill, iv. 362; vii. 545.
—— of Stevenston, James, 5th son of Robert H. of Wishaw, ii. 52, 55.
—— —— his wife, Helen Baillie, ii. 55.
—— —— James, ii. 55.
—— —— his wife, Mary Nisbet, ii. 55.
—— of Stoneypath, Robert, viii. 24.
—— —— his wife, Jean Somerville, viii. 24.
—— of Strabane, Claud, younger son of Claud H. of Montalony, i. 42.
—— —— James, master of Paisley, i. 46.
—— of Sundrum, Claude, ii. 521.
—— —— John, ii. 521; iii. 449.
—— —— his wife, Lilias Montgomerie, iii. 449.
—— of Swanston, James, ix. 37.
—— of Torbain, David, 3rd son of Regent Arran, vi. 89.
—— of Torry, William, son of archbishop H., iv. 362.
—— of Trabroun, Sir John, iv. 314.
—— —— his wife, Catherine Peebles, iv. 314.
—— of Trebinshun, Sir Edward Archibald, 2nd bart., i. 58.
—— —— Sir Edward Joseph, 1st bart., admiral R.N., i. 58.
—— of Tweedie, John, viii. 14.
—— —— his wife, * Somerville, viii. 14.
—— of Tynninghame, John Fitzwalter, ancestor of the family of, iv. 301, 342.
—— —— Thomas, iv. 313.
—— of Udston, Alexander, ii. 41.
—— —— his wife, Elizabeth Cumming, ii. 41.
—— —— Andrew, alleged ancestor of the family of, iv. 345, 346.
—— —— Elizabeth, wife of John Hamilton of Nielsland, ii. 38, 40; iv. 354.

* Name unknown.

Hamilton of Udston, John, ii. 41.
—— —— his wife, * Dalzell, ii. 41.
—— —— John, ii. 41.
—— —— his wife, Margaret Muirhead, ii. 41.
—— —— John, commissioner of Supply, ii. 41.
—— —— his wife, * Stewart, ii. 41.
—— —— John, sheriff of Clydesdale, ii. 41.
—— —— his wife, Margaret Cleland, ii. 41.
—— —— John, collector of customs, ii. 41.
—— —— his wife, Elizabeth Brown, ii. 41.
—— —— Patrick, ii. 38, 40.
—— —— William, 'Willie Wisehead,' ii. 39, 41.
—— —— William, major, ii. 41, 47.
—— of Wadderhill, William, son of John H. of Blair, iv. 194.
—— —— his wife, Margaret Boyle, iv. 194.
—— of Wishaw, Charles, ii. 52.
—— —— James, ii. 48.
—— —— Robert, ii. 52, 53.
—— —— his wife, Susan Balfour, ii. 53.
—— —— Robert, the younger, ii. 49, 51.
—— —— his wife, Jean Hamilton of Brownmuir, ii. 51.
—— —— William, 3rd son of John H. of Udston, ii. 41, 47, 48.
—— —— his wife, Beatrix Douglas, ii. 48.
—— —— William, the antiquary, ii. 41, 48; iv. 344.
—— —— his 1st wife, Anne Hamilton, ii. 49.
—— —— his 2nd wife, Mary Erskine, ii. 49.
—— —— William, son of Robert H., ii. 51, 52.
—— —— his wife, Bethia Hamilton, ii. 49, 52.
—— of Weatherley, Charles, ii. 49.
—— —— his wife, Euphemia Hamilton, ii. 43, 49.
—— of Westburn, Gabriel, vi. 432.
—— of Westport, Walter, *né* Sandilands, viii. 391.
—— of Whitecamp, James, iv. 348.
—— —— his wife, Elizabeth *, iv. 348.
—— —— John, iv. 348, 351.
—— —— Robert, iv. 348, 351.
—— —— William, iv. 348, 351.
—— of Whitelaw, Sir William, i. 478.
—— of Woodbrook, Sir John, 1st bart., i. 42.
—— Agnes, wife of Robert Dalzell, ii. 401.
—— Agnes, wife of Sir John Hamilton of Magdalens, iv. 308; ix. 100.
—— Agnes, wife of George Winram, iv. 308; ix. 100.
—— Agnes, wife of Sir Jas. Hamilton of Preston, iv. 349.
—— Agnes, wife of James, 5th lord Somerville, iv. 361, 365; viii. 21.
—— Agnes, wife of Alex. *or* Wm. Dalmahoy of that Ilk, iv. 362; ix. 103.
—— Agnes, wife of Sir Alex. Hamilton of Haggs, ix. 136.

* Name unknown.

Hamilton, Albertha Frances Anne, wife of George Charles, marquess of Blandford, i. 71.
— Alexander, 2nd son of Sir Claud H. of Shawfield, i. 42.
— Alexander, 2nd son of Robert H., i. 42.
— Sir Alexander, 5th son of 1st earl of Abercorn, i. 47.
— — his wife, Elizabeth Bedingfield, i. 47.
— Alexander, son of Sir Arch. H. of Rosehall, ii. 42.
— Alexander, 11th son of William H. of Wishaw, ii. 50.
— — his 1st wife, Frances Dalzell, ii. 50.
— — his 2nd wife, Barbara Lilley, ii. 50.
— Alexander, 3rd son of John H., ii. 52.
— Alexander, in Preston, ii. 140.
— — his wife, Agnes Hepburne, ii. 140.
— Alexander, Dumbarton, iii. 338.
— Alexander, 3rd son of Alex. H. of Innerwick, iv. 305.
— Alexander, general of Artillery, iv. 309.
— — his 1st wife, * Dalziel, iv. 309.
— — his 2nd wife, * Cochrane, iv. 309.
— — his 3rd wife, Elizabeth Crichton, iv. 309; ix. 100.
— Alexander, son of Sir Alex. H. of Innerwick, iv. 316.
— Alexander, illeg. son of Sir Jas. H. of Finnart, iv. 361.
— Alexander, 4th son of John H. of Samuelston, iv. 363.
— Alexander, eldest son of Jas. H. of St. John's Chapel, iv. 363.
— Alexander, 4th son of Sir John H. of Lettrick, ix. 36.
— Alexander Edmund, ii. 57.
— Alexandra Phyllis, dau. of 2nd duke of Abercorn, i. 73.
— Alice Mary Sinclair, wife of John Francis Erskine, earl of Mar, v. 636.
— Alison, wife of Geo. Hepburne of Rollanstoun, ii. 140.
— Alison, wife of John Montgomerie of Thornton, iv. 304.
— Alison, dau. of Alex. H. of Innerwick, iv. 305.
— Andrew, officer in the army, ii. 46.
— Andrew, senator of the College of Justice, lord Redhouse, iv. 307.
— — his wife, Jean Laing, iv. 307.
— Andrew, illeg. son of Sir James H. of Finnart, iv. 361.
— Andrew, 5th son of Jas. H. of St. John's Chapel, iv. 363.
— Anna, wife of Sir P. Houston, ii. 28; ix. 36.
— Anna, dau. of Sir Archibald H., ii. 43.
— Anna, dau. of lord Pencaitland, ii. 44.

* Name unknown.

Hamilton, Anna, dau. of 5th earl of Haddington, iv. 320.
— Anna, wife of 4th lord Somerville, iv. 364; viii. 18.
— Anna, wife of 5th earl of Huntly, iv. 370, 541.
— Anna, wife of David Fearn, vi. 597.
— Anna, wife of lieut.-gen. James Douglas of Comlodden, Montgreenan and Skirling, vii. 136.
— Anna, dau. of 5th earl of Haddington, vii. 303.
— Anne, wife of 5th lord Sempill, i. 48; vii. 555.
— Anne, wife of Geo. Browne of the Neale, i. 51.
— Anne, dau. of capt. John H., i. 63.
— Anne, wife of rev. F. H. W. Cornewall, i. 64.
— Anne, wife of Sir H. Mackworth, i. 64.
— Anne, wife of John Hamilton of Broomhill, ii. 39.
— Anne, wife of Sir Robt. Hamilton of Silvertonhill, ii. 40, 45.
— Anne, wife of Sir Wm. Craigie, ii. 40.
— Anne, wife of Wm. Hamilton of Wishaw, ii. 41, 49.
— Anne, wife of 5th lord Blantyre, ii. 44, 88.
— Anne, wife of Jas. Bogle, ii. 51.
— Anne, dau. of Mr. Robert Hamilton, ii. 51.
— Anne, wife of Hugh, lord Montgomerie, iii. 451; iv. 375.
— Anne, dau. of 1st earl of Haddington, iv. 315.
— Anne, wife of 3rd earl of Southesk, iv. 380; viii. 71.
— Anne, 3rd son of 4th duke of Hamilton, iv. 385.
— — his 1st wife, Mary Edwards, iv. 385.
— — his 2nd wife, Anna Charlotte Maria Powell, iv. 388.
— Anne, wife of Dr. Charles Ross Fleming, viii. 557.
— Count Anthony, author of the *Mémoires de Gramont*, i. 55.
— Anthony, D.D., archdeacon of Colchester, ii. 50, 56.
— — his wife, Anne Terrick, ii. 50.
— Anthony, archdeacon of Taunton, ii. 56.
— — his wife, Charity Graeme Farquhar, ii. 56.
— Anthony George, 2nd son of lord George F. H., i. 71.
— Archibald, archbishop of Casbel, i. 40 *n*.
— Archibald, 4th son of Sir Wm. H. of Manor Elieston, i. 42.
— Archibald, son of Sir Archd. H. of Rosehall, ii. 42.

Hamilton, Archibald, son of lord Presmennan, ii. 44.
— Archibald, 6th son of Wm. H. of Wishaw, ii. 52.
— Archibald, surgeon, 92nd Foot, ii. 56.
— — his wife, May Clarke, ii. 56.
— Archibald, his son, ii. 56.
— Archibald, illeg. son of Gavin H. of Orbiston, iv. 349.
— Archibald, v. 412.
— — his wife, Margaret Traill, v. 412.
— Archibald, colonel, vi. 433.
— Archibald, 4th son of James H. of Stanehouse, vii. 547.
— Archibald William, R.N., ii. 58.
— — his wife, Elizabeth Billyard, ii. 58.
— Arthur John, 5th son of 2nd duke of Abercorn, i. 73.
— Arthur Richard, ii. 57.
— — his 1st wife, Charlotte Cox, ii. 57.
— — his 2nd wife, Annie Steele, ii. 57.
— Augustus Terrick, capt. 71st regt., ii. 57.
— Barbara, wife of * Ralston of Ralston, ii. 41.
— Barbara, wife of (1) Alexander, lord Gordon, and (2) James, 4th lord Fleming, iv. 370, 536; viii. 527, 542; ix. 101 *bis*, 110.
— Beatrix Frances, wife of 2nd earl of Durham, i. 71.
— Bethia, wife of Wm. Hamilton of Wishaw, ii. 49, 52.
— Bethia, dau. of 7th lord Belhaven, ii. 54.
— Betty, wife of Wm. Ramsay, ii. 53.
— Betty Alice Adeline, i. 67.
— Bridget, wife of rev. T. Finney, i. 60.
— Cecil, wife of (1) John James, 1st marquess of Abercorn, and (2) Sir Joseph Copley, i. 64, 68; ix. 3.
— Cecil, wife of Sir Robt. Stewart, lord Tillicoultry, ii. 44, 296.
— Cecil Frances, wife of 4th earl of Wicklow, i. 68; iii. 46.
— Cecilia, wife of R. Perkins of Lifford, i. 50.
— Cecilia Black, wife of major-gen. G. M. Carmichael-Smyth, iv. 572.
— Charles, 'Comte de Arran,' i. 32.
— Charles, author of *Transactions during the Reign of Queen Anne*, iv. 391.
— Charles, his only child, iv. 392.
— Charles, his only child, iv. 392.
— Charles, 3rd son of Charles, 5th earl of Haddington, and Margaret, countess of Rothes, vii. 303.
— Charles, lieut.-colonel, governor of Blackness Castle, ix. 101.
— Charles Anthony, deputy-clerk of the Council, ii. 57.
— Charlotte, grand-dau. of 6th lord Abercorn, i. 60.

* Name unknown.

Hamilton, Charlotte, dau. of Charles H. of Weatherley, ii. 49.
— Christian, wife of Sir Mungo Murray of Blebo, i. 467; vi. 597.
— Christian, wife of James Nimmo, iv. 92, 93.
— Christian, wife of Sir Alex. Hamilton of Innerwick, iv. 309.
— Christian, wife of (1) Robert, 9th lord Lindsay of the Byres, and (2) Robert, 7th lord Boyd, iv. 315; v. 170, 402.
— Christian, dau. of 4th earl of Haddington, iv. 319.
— Christian, wife of Sir James Dalrymple of Hailes, iv. 321; viii. 143.
— Christian, wife of (1) Sir P. Home of Polwarth, and (2) Robert, 2nd lord Jedburgh, v. 78; vi. 12.
— Christian, wife of captain Charles Napier, R.N., vi. 432.
— Christian, wife of John Shairp of Houstoun, ix. 100.
— Christiana, wife of Sir Geo. Monroe of Newmore, i. 45.
— Clarice Jessie Evelyn, wife of 12th lord Napier and Ettrick, ii. 59; vi. 438.
— Claud, commendator of Paisley, 5th son of 2nd earl of Arran, i. 37, 196; ii. 475; iv. 369, 371; v. 160, 353; ix. 2 *bis*, 103, 104.
— Claud, elder son of Robert H., i. 42.
— Claud, 4th son of Sir Claud H. of Shawfield, i. 43.
— Claud, 2nd son of 1st marquess of Abercorn, i. 67.
— — his wife, Elizabeth Emma Proby, i. 67.
— Claud, iv. 59.
— — his wife, Margaret Forbes, iv. 59.
— Claud John, colonel, M.P., i. 70.
— — his wife, Carolina Chandos Pole, i. 70.
— Claud Nigel, 7th son of 2nd duke of Abercorn, i. 73.
— Claud Richard, R.N., i. 67.
— Constantine Henry, lieut.-col. R.A., ii. 58.
— Cuthbert, son of Sir Jas. H. of Finnart, ix. 103.
— Cynthia Elinor Beatrix, i. 73.
— Daniel, clerk of the Admiralty Court; brother of 2nd lord Belhaven, ii. 44; ix. 37.
— Daniel, writer, Edinburgh, ix. 37.
— — his wife, Mary Hamilton, ix. 37.
— Mr. David, rector of Carstairs, iv. 349.
— David, son of John H. of Broomhill, iv. 354.
— David, son of archbishop H., iv. 362.
— Diana, dau. of 2nd duke of Hamilton, iv. 380.
— Dorothy Henrietta, ii. 59.

Hamilton, Douglas James, major Irish Guards, i. 67.
—— —— his wife, Margaret Frances Hely-Hutchinson, i. 67.
—— Edith Lilian, wife of N. A. Sinclair, ii. 59.
—— Eleanor, wife of John Murray of Philiphaugh, vii. 519.
—— Eleonora, wife of Hugh, 12th earl of Eglinton, iii. 461.
—— Elizabeth, wife of Matthew, 2nd earl of Lennox, i. 20; iv. 351, 353; v. 351.
—— Elizabeth, dau. of Sir William H. of Manor Elieston, i. 42.
—— Elizabeth, dau. of 5th earl of Abercorn, i. 52.
—— Elizabeth, wife of 1st viscount Rosse, i. 54.
—— Elizabeth, wife of Philibert, comte de Gramont, i. 55.
—— Elizabeth, wife of E. Stede of Stedehill, i. 58.
—— Elizabeth, wife of (1) John Cameron of Glenkindy, and (2) comte de Fay, i. 60.
—— Elizabeth, wife of (1) Wm. Brownlow, and (2) Martin, comte de Kearnie, i. 62.
—— Elizabeth, wife of Glynn Wynn, i. 64.
—— Elizabeth, wife of capt. J. Livingston, ii. 40; vi. 450.
—— Elizabeth, wife of Wm. Cunningham, ii. 42.
—— Elizabeth, wife of (1) 5th earl of Crawford, and (2) John Forrester of Niddrie, iii. 23; iv. 353; ix. 103.
—— Elizabeth, wife of Sir Wm. Stewart, iii. 447 *n.*
—— Elizabeth, wife of Francis, 1st earl Brooke and earl of Warwick, iv. 167.
—— Elizabeth, wife of (1) James, lord Kilmaurs, and (2) Sir D. Cunningham, iv. 249, 330.
—— Elizabeth, wife of Sir Wm. Scott of Ardross, iv. 309.
—— Elizabeth, dau. of 4th earl of Haddington, iv. 319.
—— Elizabeth, wife of Sir Alex. Fraser of Cowie, iv. 346.
—— Elizabeth, wife of Chalmers of Gadgirth, iv. 349.
—— Elizabeth, wife of Robert, master of Sempill, iv. 365; vii. 543.
—— Elizabeth, alleged wife of Robert, master of Sempill, iv. 365 *n.*
—— Elizabeth, wife of 1st viscount of Kingston, v. 196; ix. 36.
—— Elizabeth, wife of Sir Andrew Melville of Garvock, vi. 94.
—— Elizabeth, wife of Malcolm Gibson, vi. 598.
—— Elizabeth, wife of lt.-col. George Makgill, vi. 598.
—— Elizabeth, wife of Roger Kirkpatrick, vii. 547.
Hamilton, Elizabeth, wife of capt. William Dalrymple, viii. 141.
—— Elizabeth, wife of Sir James Stewart of Eday and Tullos, ix. 146.
—— Elizabeth, wife of Wm. Hamilton of Bathgate, ix. 100.
—— Emma Frances, i. 67.
—— Ernest William, M.P., 7th son of 1st duke of Abercorn, i. 71.
—— —— his wife, Louisa Augusta Ambrose Campbell, i. 71.
—— Euphame, dau. of 6th lord Belhaven, ii. 53.
—— Euphemia, wife of Chas. Hamilton of Weatherley, ii. 43, 49.
—— Euphemia, wife of col. A. Baillie, ii. 51; ix. 37.
—— Eupham, illeg. dau. of provost Gavin H., ix. 103.
—— Frances, wife of (1) Henry, 8th viscount Dillon, and (2) Patrick Bellew, i. 54.
—— Frances, wife of W. Tooker of Chilcompton, i. 60.
—— Frances, dau of rev. Francis H., i. 61.
—— Frances, wife of 3rd earl of Scarborough, vi. 580.
—— Francis, rector of Dunleer, etc., i. 60.
—— —— his wife, Dorothy Forth, i. 61.
—— Francis, son of Mr. Robert H., ii. 51.
—— Francis, son of James H. of Stevenston, ii. 56.
—— Frederick, eldest son of Sir F. H. of Manor Hamilton, i. 45.
—— Frederick Spencer, M.P., 6th son of 1st duke of Abercorn, i. 71.
—— Sir Frederick William, K.C.B., ii. 57.
—— —— his wife, Louisa Anne Erskine Anstruther, ii. 57.
—— Gavin, commendator of Kilwinning, ii. 38, 406; v. 497.
—— Gavin, his illeg. son, ii. 38.
—— Gavin, 3rd son of John H. of Orbiston, ii. 407.
—— Gavin, illeg. son of Gavin H. of Orbistoun, iv. 349 *bis.*
—— Gavin, 2nd son of 1st earl of Arran, iv. 360.
—— Gavin, his legtd. son, iv. 360.
—— Gavin, 2nd son of John H. of Samuelston, iv. 363.
—— Gavin, 2nd son of James, 2nd earl of Arran, iv. 369, 409.
—— Gawyne, 1531, viii. 279.
—— George, 6th son of Sir Claud H. of Shawfield, i. 43.
—— Sir George, of the Regiment de Hamilton, i. 53; iv. 381.
—— —— his wife, Frances Jennings, i. 54.
—— George, colonel in the Foot Guards, i. 57.

Hamilton, George, 2nd son of John H. of Chilston, i. 58.
—— —— his wife, * Vasserot, i. 58.
—— George, cornet of Horse, M.P., i. 60.
—— —— his wife, Bridget Coward, i. 60.
—— George, R.N., grandson of 6th earl of Abercorn, i. 60.
—— George, rector of Taughboyne and Donagheady, canon of Windsor, i. 63; ix. 3.
—— —— his wife, Elizabeth Onslow, i. 63.
—— George, eldest son of canon H., i. 64.
—— George, in Preston, ii. 140.
—— George, 2nd son of Thomas H. of Priestfield, iv. 305.
—— George Francis, M.P., i. 70.
—— —— his wife, Maud Caroline Lascelles, i. 70.
—— Georgiana Susan, wife of 5th earl of Winterton, i. 71.
—— Georgina Violet, wife of James Cowie Simpson, ii. 59.
—— Gilbert, ancestor of the family of, iv. 340.
—— Gilbert de, clericus, iv. 340 *n*.
—— Gilbert Claud, Grenadier Guards, i. 70.
—— Gladys Mary, wife of 7th earl of Wicklow, i. 73.
—— Granville, eldest son of major Douglas James H., i. 67.
—— Grizel, wife of Sir William Baillie of Lamington, i. 43.
—— Grizel, dau. of 1st lord Bargany, ii. 28; ix. 36.
—— Grizel, wife of Thos. Buchan, ii. 32.
—— Grizel, wife of 5th earl of Rothes, vii. 293; ix. 103.
—— Grizel, dau. of James H. of Stanehouse, vii. 547.
—— Grisell, wife of 2nd earl Stanhope, ix. 101.
—— Gustavus, merchant, Edinburgh, iii. 489.
—— —— his wife, Veronica Bruce, iii. 489.
—— Guy Ernest Frederic, i. 71.
—— Hannah, wife of Sir Wm. Gore of Manor Gore, i. 45.
—— Harriot, wife of rev. Wm. Peter, i. 60.
—— Harriot, dau. of canon H., i. 64.
—— Harriet, wife of admiral W. A. Baillie Hamilton, i. 67.
—— Harriet, wife of George (Boyle), earl of Orrery, vi. 580.
—— Harriet Georgina Louisa, wife of 2nd earl of Lichfield, i. 71.
—— Harriot Margaret, dau. of 1st marquess of Abercorn, i. 68.
—— Harry, president of the College of Surgeons, son of lord Presmennan, ii. 44; ix. 37 *ter*.
—— —— his wife, Katharine Ross, ii. 44.

* Name unknown.

Hamilton, Helen, wife of 4th earl of Argyll, i. 339; iv. 360.
—— Helen, wife of Sir J. Somervile, ii. 27; ix. 36.
—— Helen, wife of Mr. James Hamilton, ii. 41, 42.
—— Helen, wife of Sir P. Murray, ii. 49.
—— Helen, wife of Andrew Baillie, ii. 51.
—— Helen, dau. of 1st earl of Haddington, iv. 315; ix. 101.
—— Helen, wife of William Anstruther, iv. 318.
—— Helen, wife of James Livingston of Abercorn, vi. 449.
—— Helen, wife of 4th earl of Selkirk, vii. 521.
—— Helen Violet., ii. 59.
—— Henrietta, dau. of 4th duke of Hamilton, ix. 104.
—— Henry, Jamaica, 71st regt., ii. 52.
—— Henry George, R.N., ii. 57.
—— —— his wife, Fanny Elizabeth Tower, ii. 57.
—— Hugh, alleged brother of Walter Fitz Gilbert, iv. 340 *n*.
—— Ida, dau. of lord Claud John H., i. 70.
—— Isabel, wife of 5th lord Seton, i. 39; iii. 369; viii. 588.
—— Isobel, dau. of 1st earl of Abercorn, i. 48.
—— Isabella, wife of lord Geo. Seymour, i. 64.
—— Isobel, wife of 1st earl of Airlie, i. 124; iv. 315.
—— Isabella, wife of John Bannatyne of Corehouse, iv. 365.
—— Isabel, wife of 3rd lord Sempill, vii. 543.
—— Jacobina, wife of Sir James Dunbar, ii. 49; ix. 37.
—— James, 5th son of Sir Claud H. of Shawfield, i. 43.
—— James, son of Sir Geo. H. of Greenlaw, i. 43.
—— James, master of Paisley, eldest son of Claud, lord Paisley, i. 40, 46.
—— James, colonel, eldest son of Sir Geo. H. of Donalong, i. 53, 56.
—— —— his wife, Elizabeth Colepeper, i. 57.
—— James, equerry to Frederick, prince of Wales, i. 60.
—— James, i. 201.
—— —— his wife, Elizabeth Oliphant, i. 201; vi. 549.
—— James, minister of Eaglesham, ii. 41, 42.
—— —— his wife, Helen Hamilton, ii. 42.
—— James, advocate, ii. 46.
—— —— his wife, Anne Walkinshaw, ii. 46.
—— James, 3rd son of Wm. H. of Wishaw, ii. 49.
—— James, minister of Paisley, ii. 51.
—— —— his wife, Elizabeth Millar, ii. 51.

Hamilton, James, 4th son of Wm. H. of Wishaw, ii. 52.
—— —— his wife, Anne Bowie, ii. 52.
—— James, eldest son of Jas. H. of Stevenston, ii. 56.
—— Sir James, keeper of the Park of Holyrood House, iv. 314.
—— James, illeg. son of 1st or 2nd earl of Haddington, iv. 315.
—— James, illeg. son of 1st lord Hamilton, iv. 351, 353.
—— James, illeg. son of Sir Jas. Hamilton of Finnart, iv. 361.
—— James, another illeg. son of the same, iv. 362.
—— James, illeg. son of archbp. H., iv. 362; vii. 547.
—— James, sub-dean of Glasgow, bishop of Lismore, iv. 363; ix. 103.
—— James, 4th son of Jas. H. of St. John's Chapel, iv. 363.
—— James, 2nd son of 1st duke of Hamilton, iv. 378.
—— James, lieut.-col. Coldstream Guards, iv. 388.
—— —— his wife, Lucy Lloyd, iv. 388.
—— James, grandson of lord Anne H., iv. 388.
—— James, eldest son of James H. of Stanehouse, vii. 545, 547.
—— James, son of Sir Patrick H. of Kincavil, ix. 10.
—— James, illeg. son of provost Gavin H., ix. 103.
—— James Martin, iv. 572.
—— Jane, wife of Edward Moore, i. 61.
—— Jane, wife of lord Archibald Hamilton of Riccarton, i. 62; iv. 382.
—— Jane, wife of (1) Wm. Plumer, (2) R. J. Lewin, and (3) R. Plumer-Ward, i. 64.
—— Jane, dau. of Jas. H. of St. John's Chapel, iv. 363.
—— Jane *or* Janet, wife of William Stewart, iv. 365.
—— Janet, wife of Sir Claud Hamilton of Shawfield, i. 41.
—— Janet, dau. of Sir Claud H. of Shawfield, i. 43.
—— Janet, wife of Jas Muirhead, ii. 41.
—— Janet, wife of Alex. Garthshore, ii. 51.
—— Janet, wife of Alexander, master of Glencairn, iv. 239, 241, 364.
—— Janet, wife of John Hamilton of Broombill, iv. 354.
—— Janet, wife of Alexander Home of Graden and Darnchester, iv. 471.
—— Jean, wife of John Hamilton of Gilkerscleugh, ii. 42.
—— Jean, wife of Robt. Hamilton, yr. of Wishaw. ii. 51.
—— Jean, wife of Geo. Ramsay of Barnton, ii. 53.
Hamilton, Jean, wife of rear-admiral C. Sotheby, ii. 54.
—— Jean, wife of Sir Alex. Livingston of Dalderse, ii. 362.
—— Jean, contr. to George, lord Gordon; wife of Hugh, 3rd earl of Eglinton, ii. 473; iii. 441; iv. 370.
—— Jean, wife of 6th earl of Cassillis, ii. 481; iii. 351; iv. 315.
—— Jean, wife of 9th lord Cathcart, ii. 521.
—— Jean, wife of 21st earl of Crawford, 3rd viscount Garnock, iii. 41.
—— Jean, wife of Alexander, master of Glencairn, iv. 241, 364.
—— Jean, wife of Sir Jas. Maxwell of Calderwood, iv. 245.
—— Jean, wife of Robt. Bruce of Blairball, iv. 362.
—— Jean, dau. of John H. of St. John's Chapel, iv. 363.
—— Jean, wife of (1) David Boswell of Auchinleck, (2) John Hamilton of Auchingemmill, and (3) John Crawford, iv. 365; ix. 103 *bis*.
—— Jean, wife of James, master of Somerville, iv. 365; viii. 21; ix. 103.
—— Jean, wife of (1) Robert, 5th lord Ross of Halkhead, and (2) Robert, 2nd lord Melville, iv. 317 *n.*; vi. 101; vii. 255; ix. 136.
—— Jean, wife of (1) Sir H. Colquhoun, and (2) Sir J. Campbell of Ardkinglas, iv. 373; ix. 104.
—— Jean, wife of Charles Stewart of Duncarn, vi. 321; ix. 139 *bis*.
—— Jean, wife of Thos. Hay of Park, ix. 36.
—— Jean, wife of John Home, ix. 100.
—— Jean Barbara Bertha Elizabeth, i. 71.
—— Jeannie Sinclair, wife of J. C. Arbuthnott, i. 315.
—— Jessie, dau. of Archibald H., ii. 56.
—— Joanna, alleged wife of Robert, master of Sempill, vii. 543 *n.*
—— Jocelyn Campbell Patrick, i. 67.
—— Johanna, wife of Sir Robt. Dalrymple, ii. 31.
—— John, commendator and abbot of Paisley, bishop of Dunkeld, archbishop of St. Andrews, papal legate, i. 37, 38, 248; ii. 154, 165, 388, 441; iv. 362, 367 *bis*; v. 163, 439; vii. 537, 539, 545, 546.
—— John, 3rd son of 2nd earl of Arran, i. 38, 196; ii. 475; iv. 369; v. 160.
——Sir John, 2nd son of 1st lord Paisley, i. 40.
—— —— his wife, Johanna Everard, i. 40.
—— John, major-general, i. 55; ix. 3.
—— —— his wife, Elizabeth McCan, ix. 3.
—— John, 4th son of 6th earl of Abercorn, i. 59.
—— John, archdeacon of Raphoe, i. 60.

Hamilton, John, R.N., 2nd son of 7th earl of Abercorn, i. 63.
—— —— his wife, Harriet Craggs, i. 63; ix. 3.
—— John, elder son of 2nd lord Bargany; master of Bargany, ii. 31.
—— —— his wife, Jean Sinclair, ii. 31; viii. 177.
—— John, 2nd son of Alex. H. of Udston, ii. 41.
—— John, son of Sir Archd. H. of Rosehall, ii. 42.
—— John, 5th son of Jas. H. of Barncleugh, ii. 43.
—— John, Gartness, ii. 48.
—— John, 5th son of Wm. H. of Wishaw, ii. 49.
—— John, 4th son of Robt. H. of Wishaw, ii. 52.
—— John, 5th son of Wm. H. of Wishaw, ii. 52.
—— —— his 1st wife, Isabella Stirling, ii. 52.
—— —— his 2nd wife, * Graham, ii. 52.
—— John, eldest son of James H. of Stevenston, ii. 55.
—— John, son of Allan H. of Ferguslie, ii. 169; ix. 41.
—— —— his wife, Margaret Stewart, ii. 169.
—— John, merchant, Jamaica, iii. 448.
—— —— his wife, Margaret Montgomerie, iii. 448.
—— John, iv. 57.
—— —— his wife, Anna Forbes, iv. 57.
—— John, 2nd son of Alex. H. of Innerwick, iv. 305.
—— John, rector of the University of Paris, iv. 306.
—— John, 3rd son of 4th earl of Haddington, iv. 318.
—— John, advocate, cashier to Board of Police, iv. 321; vi. 384; vii. 521.
—— —— his wife, Margaret Home, iv. 321.
—— Mr. John, rector of Dunbar, iv. 363.
—— John, Jesuit, iv. 414.
—— John, iv. 578.
—— —— his wife, Mary Carmichael, v. 578.
—— John, lieut.-col. Scots Guards, vi. 597, 601.
—— John, vicar of Eastwood, vii. 542.
—— John, 2nd son of James H. of Stanehouse, vii. 547.
—— John, 7th son of James H. of Stanehouse, vii. 547.
—— John, son of Jas. H. of Corshill, ix. 41.
—— —— his wife, Margaret Stewart of Whitelaw, ii. 169; ix. 41.
—— John George Peter, i. 71.
—— Julia, dau. of R. E. A. H., ii. 58.
—— Katharine, wife of (1) Jas. Hamilton of Manor Hamilton, (2) Owen Wynne, and (3) John Bingham, i. 45, 50.
—— Katharine, wife of (1) Wm. Lenthall of Burford, and (2) Charles, 5th earl of Abercorn, i. 49, 52.

* Name unknown.

Hamilton, Katharine, dau. of canon H., i. 64.
—— Katharine, dau. of 3rd duke of Abercorn, i. 73.
—— Katharine, wife of 1st duke of Atholl, i. 480; iv. 382; ix. 29.
—— Katharine, wife of Sir Jas. Drummond, ii. 27; viii. 216; ix. 36.
—— Katharine, wife of Wm. Cuningham, ii. 29; ix. 36.
—— Katharine, wife of * Baillie of Park, ii. 42.
—— Katharine, dau. of lord Presmennan, ii. 44.
—— Katharine, wife of Mr. D. Pitcairn, ii. 51.
—— Katharine, wife of Thomas, 6th earl of Dundonald, iii. 357; vii. 519.
—— Katharine, wife of 14th earl of Morton, vi. 384.
—— Katharine Elizabeth, wife of 4th earl of Aberdeen, i. 68, 95.
—— Katharine Elizabeth, wife of 4th earl of Mount Edgcumbe, i. 71.
—— Leonore Agnes Watson Nisbet, wife of R. B. Whiteside, ii. 58.
—— Louisa Charlotte, wife of prof. John Tyndall, i. 67.
—— Louisa Jane, wife of 6th duke of Buccleuch, i. 71; ii. 247.
—— Lucia, wife of Sir Donough O'Brien of Lemineagh, i. 56.
—— Lucrece *or* Lucy, dau. of 1st earl of Abercorn, i. 48; ix. 3.
—— Margaret, mistress of Gavin Hamilton, commendator of Kilwinning, ii. 38, 406; iv. 354.
—— Margaret, wife of Sir Archibald Acheson of Clonkearney, i. 40; ix. 2.
—— Margaret, wife of Walter Innes of Ortoun, i. 42.
—— Margaret, wife of (1) Sir J. Stewart of Methven, and (2) Sir J. Seton of Gargunnock, i. 43; ix. 126.
—— Margaret, wife of 11th earl of Angus, i. 45, 204; ix. 13.
—— Margaret, wife of Sir W. Cunningham, i. 48.
—— Margaret, wife of Matthew Ford of Coolgreeny, i. 56.
—— Margaret, wife of (1) John Kennedy, and (2) Sir D. Ogilvy, i. 124; ii. 28, 489.
—— Margaret, wife of (1) Jas. Johnstone, (2) David, 7th earl of Angus, and (3) Sir P. Whitelaw, i. 193, 241, 248: iv. 363; ix. 14, 103.
—— Margaret, wife of (1) David, lord Carnegie, and (2) James, 1st earl of Hartfell, i. 258; iv. 315; viii. 66; ix. 15 *bis*, 159.
—— Margaret, wife of 1st lord Ochiltree, i. 394; iv. 364; vi. 511.

* Name unknown.

Hamilton, Margaret, wife of Sir James Hamilton of Broomhill, ii. 39, 41.
— Margaret, wife of 1st lord Belhaven, ii. 40, 85; iv. 375.
— Margaret, wife of Sir S. Baillie, ii. 40.
— Margaret, wife of 2nd lord Belhaven, ii. 40, 44.
— Margaret, dau. of John H. of Udston, ii. 41.
— Margaret, wife of * Hamilton of Airdrie, ii. 41.
— Margaret, wife of Jas. Hamilton of Dalzell, ii. 42.
— Margaret, dau. of lord Presmennan, ii. 44.
— Margaret, wife of Alex. Baird, ii. 47.
— Margaret, wife of Geo. Cleland of Gartness, ii. 48.
— Margaret, wife of Cleland of Cleland, ii. 49.
— Margaret, wife of Robt. Dalzell of Dalzell, ii. 403.
— Margaret, wife of J. Walkinshaw, ii. 407.
— Margaret, wife of 5th earl of Carnwath, ii. 416.
— Margaret, wife of John, 17th earl of Crawford, iii. 36; iv. 375, 381.
— Margaret, wife of James Cochrane of Barbachlaw, iii. 340 *n.*
— Margaret, wife of Patrick Murray of Elibank, iii. 508.
— Margaret, wife of Wm. Kirkcaldy of Grange, iv. 309.
— Margaret, wife of 1st earl of Kintore, iv. 317; v. 241.
— Margaret, wife of John Hope of Hopetoun, iv. 318, 493.
— Margaret, dau. of 6th earl of Haddington, iv. 321.
— Margaret, *error for* Mary Stewart, wife of 1st lord Hamilton, iv. 353 *n.*
— Margaret, dau. of James H. of St. John's Chapel, iv. 363.
— Margaret, dau. of John H. of St. John's Chapel, iv. 363.
— Margaret, wife of 9th lord Maxwell, iv. 373; vi. 485.
— Margaret, wife of William Blair of that Ilk, iv. 380.
— Margaret, wife of 4th earl of Panmure, iv. 383; vii. 26; ix. 104.
— Margaret, wife of Sir Gideon Scott of Highchester, vii. 79.
— Margaret, wife of Robert Bruce of Blairhall, vii. 547.
— Margaret, wife of Hugh Somerville of Drum, 8th lord Somerville, viii. 27.
— Margaret, wife of John Fleming, viii. 530.
— Margaret, wife of (1) Pierre, comte de Réance, and (2) François Philippe, comte de Marmier, ix. 3.
Hamilton, Margaret, wife of Sir John Hamilton of Bearcrofts, ix. 36.
— Margaret, dau. of Sir John H. of Magdalens, ix. 100.
— Margaret Elizabeth, dau. of Archd. Wm. H., ii. 58.
— Margaret Wilhelmina, wife of L. E. Ames, ii. 58.
— Maria, wife of (1) Francis Marsh, and (2) William Beckford of Fonthill, i. 60.
— Maria, dau. of 1st marquess of Abercorn, i. 68.
— Marie, dau. of John H. of St. John's Chapel, iv. 363.
— Marion, dau. of Sir Hugh H. of Rosehall, ii. 42.
— Marion, dau. of lord Pencaitland, ii. 44.
— Marion, wife of Sir Hew Dalrymple of North Berwick, ii. 44; viii. 126; ix. 37, 160.
— Marion, wife of John Hamilton of Bangour, ii. 407.
— Marion, wife of James Makcartney, iv. 306.
— Marion, dau. of Jas. H. of St. John's Chapel, iv. 363.
— Marion, wife of Jas. Ross, ix. 101.
— Marjory, wife of Wm. Baillie, ii. 28.
— Mary, wife of Gerald Dillon, i. 51.
— Mary, wife of 3rd viscount Kingsland, i. 54; ix. 3.
— Mary, wife of H. Colley of Castle Carbery, i. 61.
— Mary, dau. of canon H., i. 64.
— Mary, wife of Alex. Cleland, ii. 27.
— Mary, dau. of Sir Robert H. of Silverton, ii. 40.
— Mary, wife of Dr. D. Balfour, ii. 51.
— Mary, dau. of 6th lord Belhaven, ii. 53.
— Mary, wife of (1) Alexander, 2nd earl of Callendar, (2) Sir Jas. Livingston, and (3) James, 3rd earl of Findlater, ii. 363; iv. 36, 380; ix. 104.
— Mary, dau. of 4th earl of Haddington, iv. 319.
— Mary, wife of James, master of Drumlanrig, iv. 375; vii. 136.
— Mary, dau. of 1st duke of Hamilton, iv. 378.
— Mary, dau. of Anne, duchess of Hamilton, iv. 382.
— Mary, wife of rev. Henry Douglas, vi. 385.
— Mary, wife of R. Macdonald of Clanranald, vii. 520.
— Mary, wife of Daniel Hamilton, ix. 37.
— Mary, dau. of 2nd earl of Haddington, ix. 101.
— Mary Brenda, i. 71.
— Mary Cecilia Rhodesia, i. 73.

* Name unknown.

Hamilton, Mary Clarke Mary Nisbet, ii. 59.
— Mary Elizabeth Jane Douglas, wife of Francis Napier. vi. 433.
— Mary Geraldine, wife of H. A. Newton, ii. 59.
— Mary Nisbet, wife of F. Chapman, ii. 56.
— Mary Stuart, wife of 2nd lord Tollemache, i. 67.
— Maude Evelyn, C.I., V.A., wife of 5th marquess of Lansdowne, i. 72; vi. 400.
— Maud Kemble, wife of G. T. C. Clifton-Hastings-Campbell, v. 516.
— Muriel Louise, wife of W. M. J. Martin, ii. 59; ix. 37.
— Nicolas, wife of Sir Alex. Hope, ii. 32.
— Nicolas, dau. of Jas. H. of St. John's Chapel, iv. 363.
— Oliver, burgess of Hamilton, iv. 306.
— Patrick, abbot of Ferne, ii. 468.
— Patrick, legtd. son of 1st earl of Haddington, iv. 315, 316.
— Patrick, 3rd son of Jas. H. of St. John's Chapel, iv. 363.
— Patrick, W.S., ix. 100.
— Patrick *or* Peter Douglas, lieut. 12th Light Dragoons, ii. 53.
— Paul, captain of Arran, ix. 103.
— Penelope, dau. of 7th lord Belhaven, ii. 54.
— Philippa, wife of (1) Benjamin Pratt, and (2) Michael O'Connell, i. 62; ix. 3.
— Quentin, son of lord Presmennan, ii. 44.
— Quintin, son of Wm. H. of Wishaw, ii. 48.
— Rachel, wife of rev. Neville Walter, i. 60.
— Rachel, dau. of canon H., i. 64.
— Rachel, dau. of lord Presmennan, ii. 44.
— Rachel, dau. of Mr. Robert H., ii. 51.
— Rachel, wife of Sir Wm. Weir of Blackwood, ix. 37.
— Rachel, dau. of Charles, lord Binning, ix. 101.
— Ralph Gerard Alexander, master of Belhaven, ii. 60.
— — his wife, Grizel Winifred Louise Cochrane, ii. 60; iii. 367.
— Rebecca, ix. 100.
— Richard, brigadier-general, 5th son of Sir G. H. of Donalong, i. 55.
— Richard George, son of major Douglas J. H., i. 67.
— Robert, 3rd son of Sir Claud H. of Shawfield, i. 42.
— Robert, i. 315.
— Robert, writer, Edinburgh, ii. 41.
— Robert, son of Sir Arch. H. of Rosehall, ii. 42.
— Robert, son of lord Pencaitland, ii. 44.
Hamilton, Robert, 10th son of lord Presmennan, ii. 44.
— Robert, 4th son of 3rd lord Belhaven, ii. 46.
— Robert, son of William H., ii. 50.
— Robert, minister of Hamilton, ii. 51.
— — his wife, Cecil Borland, ii. 51.
— Robert, son of above, ii. 51.
— Robert, col., 2nd son of 6th lord Belhaven, ii. 53.
— Robert, son of James H. of Stevenston, ii. 55.
— Robert, Sanquhar, ii. 240.
— Robert, 3rd son of James H. of Stanehouse, vii. 547.
— Robert, 6th son of James H. of Stanehouse, vii. 547.
— Robert Cecil, R.N., i. 71.
— Robert Edward Archibald, I.S.C., ii. 58.
— — his wife, Kathleen Gonville Bromhead, ii. 58.
— Robert William, lieut.-col. Grenadier Guards, ii. 55, 56. 57, 59.
— — his wife, Charlotte Maria Palmer, ii. 59.
— Ronald Douglas, 4th son of 1st duke of Abercorn, i. 71.
— Ronald James, eldest son of lord Geo. F. H., i. 71.
— Sarah, wife of John Hamilton of Dulata, i. 42.
— Sarah, dau. of P. H. of Little Preston, vi. 597.
— Susan, wife of John, 7th earl of Cassillis, ii. 479, 483, 484; iv. 378.
— Susan, wife of John, 8th earl of Cassillis, ii. 485; vii. 362.
— Susan Mary, wife of Peter Ramsay, ii. 54.
— Susannah, dau. of 6th lord Belhaven, ii. 53.
— Susanna, wife of Adam Cockburn of Ormiston, iv. 318.
— Susannah, wife of (1) John, 2nd earl of Dundonald, and (2) Charles, 3rd marquess of Tweeddale, iii. 353; iv. 382; viii. 462.
— Sidney, wife of Sir John Hume of Castle Hume, i. 45; vi. 9.
— Sybil Jean, ii. 58.
— Thomas, R.N., 4th son of Sir Geo. H. of Donalong, i. 55.
— Thomas, 3rd son of John H. of Chilston, i. 58.
— Thomas, 3rd son of Sir John H. of Lettrick, ii. 27.
— Thomas, 2nd son of Sir Robt. H. of Silverton, ii. 40.
— Thomas, 10th son of Wm. H. of Wishaw, ii. 50.
— Thomas, 2nd son of 4th earl of Haddington, iv. 318.

Hamilton, Thomas, 2nd son of 7th earl of Haddington, iv. 324.
— Mr. Thomas, canon of Dunkeld, iv. 349, 351.
— Thomas, 6th son of James H. of St. John's Chapel, iv. 363.
— Thomas, king's advocate, vi. 593.
— Thomas, burgess of Glasgow, vi. 597.
— — his wife, Elizabeth Dalrymple, vi. 597.
— Thomas, colonel, Scots Guards, vi. 597, 601.
— — his wife, Elizabeth Steuart, vi. 597.
— Thomas, 5th son of James H. of Stanehouse, vii. 547.
— Ursula, wife of James Peebles of Auchincreugh and Mainshill, iii. 342.
— Violet, wife of Robert Stewart of Tillicoultry, ii. 296.
— Victoria Henrietta, wife of capt. J. G. Goodenough, R.N., ii. 58.
— Walter, merchant, iv. 289.
— — his wife, Isobel Gray, iv. 289.
— Sir Walter Fitz Gilbert, ancestor of the family of, iv. 340.
— Walter of, son of Gilbert, iv. 340, 342.
— Walter, 2nd son of Patrick H. of Little Preston, vi. 597.
— Walter Kerr, bishop of Salisbury, ii. 56.
— — his wife, Isabel Lear, ii. 56.
— Sir William, 1st bart., 3rd son of 1st earl of Abercorn, i. 47; ix. 3.
— — his wife, Jean Colquhoun, i. 47.
— William, 2nd son of 2nd earl of Abercorn, i. 49.
— William, page to Frederick, prince of Wales, i. 57.
— William, colonel, grandson of 6th earl of Abercorn, i. 60.
— William, R.N., 8th son of 6th earl of Abercorn, i. 61.
— William, R.N., 6th son of 7th earl of Abercorn, i. 64.
— William, 2nd son of Sir John H. of Lettrick, ii. 27.
— William, major, ii. 28.
— — his wife, Mary Hay, ii. 28.
— William, 2nd son of John H. of Udston, ii. 41.
— William, capt. 22nd Foot, ii, 41, 47.
— William, 2nd son of John H. of Coltness, ii. 41.
— William, 4th son of Sir A. H. of Rosehall, ii. 42.
— William, 6th son of Jas. H. of Barncleugh, ii. 43.
— William, W.S., son of lord Presmennan, ii. 44.
— William, 3rd son of Wm. H. of Wishaw, ii. 49.
Hamilton, William, of both Scottish and English bars, ii. 49.
— — his wife, Helen Hay, ii. 50.
— William, Lincoln's Inn, ii. 50.
— — his wife, Sarah Allan, ii. 50.
— William, 2nd son of Wm. H. of Wishaw, ii. 52.
— William, Jamaica, ii. 52.
— William, capt. Bengal N. I., ii. 54.
— — his wife, Marcellina Antonia Mendes, ii. 54.
— William, Jamaica, ii. 55.
— — his wife, Elizabeth Nisbet, ii. 55.
— William, merchant burgess, Edinburgh, iv. 308.
— William, 4th son of 4th earl of Haddington, iv. 318.
— William, burgess of Canongate, iv. 364; ix. 103.
— William, 3rd son of 1st duke of Hamilton, iv. 378.
— William, 2nd son of Anne, duchess of Hamilton, iv. 382.
— William, M.P.; 2nd son of 4th duke of Hamilton, iv. 384.
— William, eldest son of col. Thomas H., vi. 597.
— William Gerard, M.P., ii. 50.
— William John, M.P., ii. 57.
— — his 1st wife, Martin Trotter, ii. 57.
— — his 2nd wife, Margaret Frances Florence Dillon, ii. 58.
— William Leslie, ii. 278; iv. 252.
— — his wife, Isabella Erskine, ii. 278.
— William Richard, under-sec. Foreign Affairs, ii. 56, 57.
— — his wife, Juliana Udny, ii. 57.
— Winifred Maude, ii. 59.
— *, wife of Kenton Cowse, i. 61.
— *, wife of Sir Wm. Vere of Stonebyres, ii. 27.
— *, wife of Cunningham of Gilbertland, ii. 41.
— *, wife of Gladstanes of Gladstanes, ii. 41.
— *, wife of Hamilton of Barr, ii. 41.
— *, wife of Hamilton of Grange, ii. 41.
— *, wife of Learmont of Newholm, ii. 41.
— *, said to have killed George, 4th earl of Dalhousie, iii. 102.
— *, father of Sir Alexander H. of Dublin, vii. 555.
— — his wife, Anne Sempill, vii. 555.
— *, wife of James Livingston of Jerviswood, viii. 371.
— *, wife of John Wemyss, ix. 103.
Hamilton-Buchanan of Spittal and Leny, John, iv. 346.
Hamilton-Campbell of Pencaitland, Mary, wife of 7th lord Ruthven, vii. 390.
HAMILTON-DALRYMPLE, EARL OF STAIR, viii. 158-164.

* Name unknown.

Hamilton-Dalrymple of Bargany, Sir Hew, 3rd bart. of North Berwick, viii. 126.
—— —— his wife, Janet Duff, viii. 126.
—— of Cleland and Fordell, Sir North, viii. 121, 159.
—— —— his 1st wife, Margaret Penny, viii. 159.
—— —— his 2nd wife, Martha Willet Dalrymple, viii. 138, 160.
—— of Cousland, Sir John, 5th bart., vi. 598; viii. 121, 158.
—— —— his 1st wife, Harriet Johnson, viii. 159.
—— —— his 2nd wife, Adamina Duncan, viii. 159.
—— Agnes, viii. 122.
—— Elizabeth, wife of Myles Sandys, viii. 121.
—— James, midshipman R.N. viii. 121.
—— Jane, wife of William Horsman, viii. 122.
—— Martha, wife of lieut. Thos. Sampson, viii. 122.
—— Robert, capt. 3rd Guards, viii. 121.
—— William, midshipman, R.N. viii. 121.
Hamilton-Gordon, Sir Alexander, K.C.B., 2nd son of 4th earl of Aberdeen, i. 95.
—— —— his wife, Caroline Herschel, i. 96.
—— Alexander, lieut.-col. R.A., i. 96.
—— —— his wife, Isabel Newmarch, i. 96.
—— Caroline Augusta, wife of A. J. L. Gordon of Ellon, i. 96.
—— Douglas, canon of Salisbury, i. 196.
—— —— his wife, Ellen Susan Anne Douglas, i. 96; vi. 386.
—— Douglas George, i. 96.
—— —— his wife, Edith Bullock, i. 96.
—— Ellen Louisa, i. 97.
—— Ernest Arthur. i, 96.
—— Frances, i. 97.
—— Francis Henry, i. 96.
—— George Arthur Maurice, eldest son of 1st baron Stanmore, i. 97.
—— George Herschel, i. 96.
—— George William, i. 96.
—— Katharine Ellen, i. 97.
—— Kathleen Isabella, i. 96.
—— Louisa, i. 96.
—— Rachel Nevil, i. 97.
—— Victoria Alberta Alexandrina, wife of V. A. E. Garth Marshall, i. 96.
—— William Hugh, i. 96.
—— —— his wife, Florence Evelyn Vickers, i. 97.
—— William Reginald, i. 96.
Hamilton-Makgill of Fala and Oxfuird, Elizabeth, wife of Sir John Dalrymple, vi. 597; viii. 121, 124.
—— of Oxfuird, Thomas, vi. 597; viii. 124.
—— —— his wife, Elizabeth Dalrymple, vi. 597.
Hamilton-Nisbet of Dirleton, Biel, Pencaitland, etc., Mary, wife of Wm. Nisbet, ii. 43, 47.
—— of Dirleton and Belhaven, Mary, wife of Thomas, 7th earl of Elgin, iii. 493.
—— —— William, iii. 493.
Hammersley, Cecilia, wife of Henry Stuart, ii. 307.
—— Charles, ii. 307.
Hammond of St. Alban's Court, Anthony, vi. 181.
—— Phoebe, wife of (1) Thos. Thomson, and (2) rev. Alex. Middleton, vi. 181.
Hampden, Henry Robert (Brand), 2nd viscount, ii. 248.
Hampton, John Slaney (Pakington), 2nd lord, iv. 218.
—— —— his wife, Diana Boyle, iv. 218.
Hanbury of Kelmarsh, Sir John, ii. 581.
—— —— his wife, Mary Whetle, ii. 581.
—— Mary, wife of (1) Sir M. Sandys, (2) Sir T. Richardson, and (3) John Gofton, ii. 581.
Handyside, Robert Handyside, lord, i. 554.
—— —— his wife, Helen Bruce, i. 554.
Hanef, quæstor of Magnus IV. of Norway, ii. 316.
Hanmer, Charlotte Emma, wife of col. Charles Lennox Ker, v. 484.
Hannah, wife of William, 7th lord Forrester of Corstorphine, iv. 96.
Hannay of Mochrum, Sir Robert, i. 59.
—— George, minister of Alves, iv. 548 *n*.
—— Jane, wife of (1) Charles, 1st earl of Mountrath, and (2) Sir Robt. Reading, i. 59.
Hanover, Ernest Augustus, elector of, i. 28.
—— —— his wife, Sophia von Simmern, i. 28.
—— George, elector of, i. 28.
Hanson, Katharine, wife of 3rd earl of Aberdeen, i. 93.
—— Oswald, Wakefield, i. 93.
Harald Maddadsson, i. 163.
—— —— his wife, Hvarflod *or* Gormlath, ii. 315; vii. 231.
Harborough, Philip (Sherard), earl of, iii. 601.
Harcarse, Adam de, abbot of Melrose, iii. 253.
Hardaway, George Rowley, lt.-colonel R.A., v. 200.
—— —— his wife, Anne Grenville, v. 200.
Hardie, William, minister of Crail, and St. Andrews, v. 415.
—— —— his wife, Katharine Lindsay, v. 415.
Hardwicke, Philip (Yorke), 2nd earl of, vi. 23.
—— —— his wife, Jemima, marchioness de Grey, baroness Lucas of Crudwell, ii. 208; vi. 23.

Hardwicke, Philip (Yorke), 3rd earl of, i. 526, 529; ii. 304.
—— —— his wife, Elizabeth Scot Lindsay, i. 529.
Hardy, * lieut. R.N., v. 250.
—— —— his wife, Hannah Ivie, v. 250.
Hardy-Johnston, Alice Louisa, wife of Trevor Ogilvie-Grant, vii. 493.
—— Thomas Masterman, M.I.C.E., vii. 493.
Hare of Stow Hall, Thomas Leigh, M.P., ii. 531.
—— —— his wife, Ida Cathcart, ii. 531.
Harewood, Henry (Lascelles), 3rd earl of, i. 70; viii. 213.
Harford of Down Place, Frederick Henry, colonel, viii. 163.
—— —— Henry, vi. 581.
—— Violet, wife of John James, viscount Dalrymple, viii. 163.
Harland of Sproughton Hall, Sir Robert, viii. 151.
—— Frances, wife of lord Edward Murray, i. 487.
—— Marianne Dorothy, wife of major-gen. Wm. Dalrymple, viii. 150.
Harlech, George Ralph Charles (Ormsby-Gore), 3rd baron, iv. 561.
—— —— his wife, Margaret Ethel Gordon, iv. 561.
Harley, Abigail, wife of 8th earl of Kinnoull, v. 232.
—— Elizabeth, wife of David Murray of South Warnborough, iii. 513.
—— Martha, wife of G. Drummond of Stanmore, viii. 224.
—— Sir Robert, K.B., ii. 34 *n.*
—— —— his wife, Anne Barret, ii. 34 *n.*
—— Sarah, wife of 10th earl of Kinnoull, v. 235.
—— Thomas, 4th son of 3rd earl of Oxford, iii. 513; viii. 224.
—— Thomas, lord mayor of London, v. 235.
Harman, Edward, rector of Pickwell, ii. 359.
—— Marianne, wife of rev. C. A. Sinclair, ii. 359.
Harold II., king of England, iii. 243 *n.*
Harper of Cambusnethan, Sir John, sheriff-depute of Lanarkshire, viii. 29.
Harriman of Tivoli, Joseph, vii. 208.
—— —— his wife, Margaret Bowman Rollo, vii. 208.
Harrington, William (Stanhope), 2nd earl of, vii. 513.
—— Edward, page of honour to the prince of Orange, viii. 178.
—— —— his wife, Lucy Alexander, viii. 178.
Harris of Donnington, Alfred, viii. 225.
—— Helen, wife of Clement A. Middleton, vi. 180.
—— Hilda Margaret, wife of D. R. Drummond, viii. 225.
—— John, Canada, ii. 418.

* Name unknown.

Harris, Sarah Bushby, wife of R. A. G. Dalzell, ii. 418.
—— Thomas Noel, vi. 180.
Harrison of South Cave, Richard, iii. 600.
—— Anne, wife of Henry Fairfax, iii. 600.
—— Helen, wife of D. Lindsay, bishop of Ross, iii. 19.
—— John, iii. 294 *n.*
—— Powles, v. 313.
—— —— his wife, Harriot Bower, v. 313.
—— Rachel, alleged wife of 1st lord Reay, vii. 169.
Harrowby, Dudley (Ryder), 2nd earl of, ii. 308.
—— —— his wife, Frances Stuart, ii. 308.
—— Dudley Francis Stuart, 3rd earl of, ii. 308.
—— Henry Dudley, 4th earl of, ii. 308.
—— John Herbert Dudley, 5th earl of, ii. 308.
Harrup, Robert, surgeon, Dumfries, ix. 64.
Hart, James, burgess of the Canongate, iv. 434.
—— Janet, wife of Adam Bothwell, iv. 434.
—— William, advocate, ii. 110, 112.
—— —— his wife, Isobell Borthwick, ii. 110.
HARTFELL, JOHNSTONE, EARL OF, i. 256-271.
Hartfell, George, fifth earl of, i. 269.
—— James, first earl of, i. 256; ix. 15 *bis.*
—— —— his 1st wife, Margaret Douglas, i. 258; vii. 135.
—— —— his 2nd wife, Elizabeth Johnstone, i. 258.
—— —— his 3rd wife, Margaret Hamilton, i. 258; iv. 315; ix. 15 *bis.*
—— James, second earl of, i. 261.
—— —— his wife, Henrietta Douglas, i. 263.
—— James, fourth earl of, i. 269.
—— William, third earl of, i. 264.
—— —— his 1st wife, Sophia Fairholm, i. 268.
—— —— his 2nd wife, Charlotte van Lore vanden Bempde, i. 268.
Hartigan, Edward, in holy orders, ix. 71.
—— Susan Mary, wife of J. C. S. Macdowall, ix. 71.
Hartopp, Anna Maria, wife of capt. W. C. Montagu Douglas Scott, ii. 246.
—— Sir William Edmund Cradock, 3rd bart., ii. 246.
HARTSYDE, DOUGLAS, LORD, i. 206; iv. 77-79.
Hartsyde, Archibald, first lord, i. 206; iv. 77.
—— Margaret, wife of John Buchanan of Scotscraig, iii. 98.
Harvard-Arsael, 2nd son of Thorfinn Skull-splitter, ii. 314.

Harvey of Castle Semple, John, ii. 279.
— of Langley Park, Sir Robert Grenville, 2nd bart., iii. 524.
— — his wife, Emily Blanche Murray, iii. 524.
— Sir Eliab, G.C.B., viii. 225.
— Elizabeth, wife of Henry David, 12th earl of Buchan, ii. 279.
— Georgina Augusta, wife of John Drummond, viii. 225.
— John, monk of Newbattle, iii. 93.
Haselwood, Hester, wife of John Middleton, vi. 177.
Hasill, Anna Maria Susanna, wife of John Somerville, viii. 31.
Haskoll, Joseph, in holy orders, v. 634.
— — his wife, Anne Caroline Erskine, v. 634.
Hasler, Fanny Georgina Jane, C.I., wife of 11th lord Reay, vii. 179.
— Richard, Aldingbourne, vii. 179.
HASTANG *or* HASTING, EARL OF ATHOLL, i. 424.
Hasting of Cockpen, Robert, iii. 89.
— of Dun, John de, sheriff and forester of the Mearns, i. 423; vi. 525 *n.*
— of Keith, Sir Robert, vi. 31; viii. 4, 419.
— of Legerwood, Sir Robert, ii. 219.
— of Longforgan, Sir Edmund de, iv. 269.
— Sir David de, i. 423.
— — his wife, Fernelith of Atholl, i. 423.
— Sir Edward, *de jure ux.* earl of Menteith, vi. 130.
— — his wife, Isabella Russell, vi. 129.
— Henry de, i. 4.
— — his wife, Ada of Huntingdon, i. 4.
— John, the Competitor, styled earl of Menteith, i. 4; vi. 130, 135.
Hastings, Francis (Rawdon Hastings), 1st marquess of, ii. 310; v. 512; ix. 131.
— — his wife, Flora, countess of Loudoun, v. 511.
— Adelaide Augusta Lavinia, wife of Sir W. K. Murray of Ochtertyre, v. 513.
— Bertha Lelgarde, wife of Augustus Wykeham Clifton, v. 514.
— Sir Charles Abney, bart., v. 515.
— Dorothy, wife of (1) Sir Jas. Stewart, and (2) 2nd earl of Roscommon, ii. 83.
— Flora Elizabeth, dau. of 1st marquess of Hastings, v. 513.
— Frances Augusta Constance, wife of 4th earl of Romney, v. 514.
— Sir Richard, constable of Knaresborough, viii. 382.
— Selina Constantia, wife of Charles John Henry, v. 513.
— Sophia Frederica Christina, wife of 2nd marquess of Bute, ii. 310; v. 513.
— Victoria Maria Louisa, wife of J. F. S. Kirwan, v. 514.
Haswell, James, abbot of Newbattle, v. 453.
— John, Dirleton, iv. 335.
Hath, son of Gilbrid, c. 1220, i. 419.
Hatton of Eastwell, George Touch, iv. 498.
— of Great Clonard, Henry, M.P., i. 68.
— — his wife, Anne Jane Gore, i. 68.
— Anne Louisa, wife of major W. E. Fitzmaurice, vi. 581.
— John, Deal, vi. 581.
— Louisa Anne, wife of major-gen. Charles Hope of Waughton, iv. 498.
Havewood, Rogor de, vi. 566.
Hawarden, Cornwallis (Maude), 1st viscount, ii. 307.
— Cornwallis, 4th viscount, iii. 550.
Hawden, Bernard de, iii. 253, 255.
Hawes of Purley Hall, Frances, wife of (1) lord Wm. Hamilton, and (2) William, 2nd viscount Vane, iv. 384.
— Francis, iv. 384.
Hawincross of Hawincross, Angus, vi. 214.
Hawke, John M., v. 238.
— Josephine Maria, wife of 13th earl of Kinnoull, v. 238.
Hawkes, Jane Muriel, wife of Sir E. A. Elphinstone-Dalrymple, viii. 134.
— John Gibbons, Dunlavin, viii. 134.
HAWKHEAD, BOYLE, BARON ROSS OF, iv. 216-219.
Hawkins, Cecilia Mary, wife of canon John Baillie, iv. 323.
— Charles, canon of York, iv. 323.
— Francis, v. 252.
— Francis, v. 253.
— Louisa, wife of (1) Anthony Adrian, 7th earl of Kintore, and (2) Dr. B. N. Arnold, v. 253.
— Louisa Madeleine, wife of 8th earl of Kintore, v. 253.
Hawkison, Margaret, wife of lieut.-col. James Cochrane, iii. 349.
Hawley, Francis (Hawley), 2nd baron, iii. 102.
— — his wife, Elizabeth Ramsay, iii. 101.
— Henry, lieut.-general, v. 179.
Haworth, Martin E., 60th Rifles, vii. 309.
— — his wife, Mary Elizabeth, countess of Rothes, vii. 309.
HAY OF KINFAUNS, HAY, LORD, v. 222-239.
Hay of Kinfauns, George, first lord, v. 222.
HAY OF PEDWARDINE, HAY, BARON, v. 232-239.
Hay of Pedwardine, George Henry, first baron, v. 232; ix. 122.
HAY OF YESTER, HAY, LORD, viii. 430-474.
Hay of Yester, James, seventh lord, viii. 444.
— — his wife, Margaret Ker, v. 485; viii. 444.

Hay of Yester, John, first lord, viii. 429; ix. 165.
— — his 1st wife, Mary Lindsay, v. 394; viii. 430.
— — his 2nd wife, Elizabeth Cunningham of Belton, viii. 430; ix. 165.
— — John, second lord, viii. 432.
— — his wife, Elizabeth Crichton, viii. 433.
— — John, third lord, viii. 434; ix. 166.
— — his wife, Elizabeth Douglas, i. 189; viii. 435.
— — John, fourth lord, viii. 436.
— — his wife, Margaret Livingston, v. 435; viii. 436.
— — John, eighth lord, viii. 447; ix. 167.
— — his 1st wife, Jean Seton, iii. 373; viii. 448.
— — his 2nd wife, Margaret Montgomery, iii. 450; viii. 449.
— — John, eldest son of 2nd earl of Tweeddale; styled lord, v. 304, 308; viii. 456.
— — his wife, Mary Maitland, v. 306; viii. 458.
— — William, fifth lord, viii. 438.
— — his wife, Margaret Ker, v. 63; viii. 442.
— — William, sixth lord, viii. 442; ix. 167.
— — his wife, Mary Maxwell, iv. 413; viii. 443.
Hay, James, eldest son of 17th earl of Erroll; styled lord, iii. 584.
— William, eldest son of 9th earl of Erroll; styled lord, iii. 576.
— John (Hay), baron, v. 231.
— of Sawley, Sir James, elder son of Sir Jas. H. of Kingask; baron, v. 218.
— — his 1st wife, Honora Denny, v. 219.
— — his 2nd wife, Lucy Percy, v. 219.
Hay, viscount Dupplin, v. 222-239.
Hay, viscount of Dupplin, v. 231-239.
Hay, earl of Erroll, iii. 555-587.
Hay, earl of Gifford, viii. 453-474.
Hay, lord Hay of Kinfauns, v. 222-239.
Hay, baron Hay of Pedwardine, v. 232-239.
Hay, lord Hay of Yester, viii. 430-474.
Hay, baron Kilmarnock of Kilmarnock, iii. 585-587.
Hay, earl of Kinnoull, v. 217-239.
Hay, earl of Tweeddale, viii. 448-474.
Hay, marquess of Tweeddale, viii. 416-474.
Hay of Aberdalgie, Sir George, v. 222.
— of Achmore, Sir David, iii. 561; viii. 428.
— — William, iii. 564.
— of Adenauthan, John, iii. 558.
— of Alderstown, Edmund, ancestor of the family of, viii. 426.
Hay of Alderstown, Sir Thomas, bart., viii. 142.
— — his wife, Eleanor Dalrymple, viii. 142.
— of Ardendraught, Alexander, 1st laird, iii. 562.
— — his wife, Marjory or Margaret Fraser, iii. 562.
— — Alexander, vii. 409.
— — his wife, Elizabeth Abernethy, vii. 409.
— — 1440, vii. 432.
— — Sir William, vii. 435.
— of Ardgeath, Francis, iii. 574.
— — Nicholas, iii. 565.
— — Sophia, wife of John, viscount Melgum, iii. 577.
— of Ardit, Alexander, viii. 189.
— of Ardlethen, Francis, iii. 570.
— — George, 4th son of 7th earl of Erroll, iii. 570.
— — his wife, Marjory Keith, iii. 570.
— of Meikle Arnage, William, iii. 564.
— of Auchinfitheach, Sir Gilbert de, viii. 419.
— of Auchens, Sir Gilbert de, viii. 419.
— of Auchinshogill, Sir William, vii. 435.
— of Auchtercool, Gilbert de, iii. 558.
— — his wife, Idonea Comyn, ii. 253; iii. 558.
— of Auchtermuir, Sir Thomas, viii. 427.
— of Auldhamstocks, Alexander, viii. 455.
— of Awne in Boyne, Sir Gilbert de, viii. 419.
— — John de, viii. 420.
— of Baldovie, Elizabeth, wife of (1) Jas. Rattray, and (2) John Galloway, iii. 379.
— of Balhousie, Francis, W.S., v. 230.
— — his 1st wife, Jonet Haliburton, v. 230.
— — his 2nd wife, Elspet Oliphant, v. 230.
— — Francis, eldest son of Geo. H. of Balhousie, v. 230.
— — George, v. 230; ix. 122.
— — his wife, Marion Nicolson, v. 230.
— — Thomas, v. 231.
— — his wife, Margaret or Elizabeth Drummond, v. 231.
— of Bandirran, John de, viii. 263.
— of Barra, Edmund, ancestor of the family of, viii. 426.
— — Sir James, viii. 442.
— — his alleged wife, Jean Hay, viii. 442; ix. 167.
— — Sir John, provost of Edinburgh, lord clerk Register, i. 566.
— — Sir William, viii. 446.
— — William, commissary of Glasgow, ix. 167.
— — his wife, Jean Hay, ix. 167.
— of Baune, John, viii. 459.

Hay of Belton, David, 3rd son of 1st marquess of Tweeddale, viii. 454.
—— —— his wife, Rachel Hayes, viii. 454.
—— —— David, 91st regt., viii. 455.
—— —— George, viii. 432.
—— —— James, major, viii. 454.
—— —— his wife, Dorothea Hay, viii. 454, 461.
—— —— James, rear-admiral R.N., viii. 455.
—— —— his wife, Mary Hathorn Stewart, viii. 455.
—— —— James George, capt. 92nd Highlanders, viii. 455.
—— —— his wife, Jane Baird, viii. 455.
—— —— John, viii. 454.
—— of Blairmormond, William, vii. 437.
—— of Blankes, John, viii. 430.
—— of Blebo, Peter, son of Peter H. of Naughton, i. 467, 468.
—— —— his wife, Margaret Murray, i. 468.
—— of Boyne, John de, viii. 420.
—— —— his wife, Margaret, viii. 420.
—— —— Sir John, i. 15; viii. 421.
—— —— his wife, Margaret Stewart, i. 15; viii. 421.
—— of Brechin, Sir Gilbert de, viii. 419.
—— of Broganelesk, John, 4th son of 3rd earl of Erroll, iii. 566.
—— —— his wife, Elizabeth Bunch, iii. 566.
—— of Brunthill, Alexander, iii. 573.
—— of Campsie, George, 4th son of 8th earl of Erroll, iii. 572.
—— of Carmuck, Gilbert, 2nd son of Sir Gilbert H. of Dronlaw, iii. 562.
—— of Caputh, Sir Thomas, iii. 561.
—— of Cassingray, Nicholas, iii. 559.
—— of Cocklaw, Edmund, ancestor of the family of, viii. 426.
—— of Corsbie, John, viii. 459.
—— —— Sir William, viii. 459.
—— of Cowie, Sir William, iii. 335 *n.*, 562.
—— —— his wife, Margaret Gray, iii. 563.
—— of Craigtoun, Sir George, lord chancellor, and keeper of the Great Seal, v. 222.
—— of Crawgaston, Gilbert, viii. 277.
—— —— his wife, Janet Lyon, viii. 277.
—— of Crethmond, William, iii. 563.
—— of Park of Creichmond, William, vii. 437.
—— of Cribbs, John, viii. 459.
—— of Crimond, Francis, iii. 575.
—— of Cromlix, John, colonel, v. 231; vii. 204; viii. 207.
—— —— his wife, Marjory Murray, v. 231; viii. 207.
—— of Crugilton Castle, Francis, v. 230.
—— of Dalgety, i. 84.
—— —— Alexander, 1st laird, iii. 562.
—— —— his wife, Marjory *or* Margaret Fraser of Ardendraught and Dalgaty, iii. 562.
Hay of Dalgety, Alexander, i. 443; iv. 55.
—— —— his wife, Janet *or* Jean Forbes, i. 443; iv. 55.
—— —— Alexander, i. 159.
—— —— his wife, Elizabeth Keith, i. 159.
—— —— Alexander, iv. 57.
—— —— his wife, Barbara Forbes, iv. 57.
—— —— Alexander, 3rd son of Sir David Falconer of Newton, iii. 580; v. 247; ix. 87.
—— —— his wife, Mary, countess of Erroll, iii. 580; v. 247.
—— —— William, iii. 562.
—— —— William, iii. 571.
—— —— his wife, Beatrix Hay, iii. 571.
—— of the Forest of Doune, Sir Gilbert de, viii. 419.
—— of Dronlaw, Alexander, iii. 562.
—— —— his wife, Marjory *or* Margaret Fraser, iii. 562.
—— —— Sir Gilbert, 2nd son of Sir Thomas H. of Erroll, iii. 562.
—— —— his wife, Elizabeth Reid, iii. 562; ix. 85.
—— —— Nicholas, iii. 558.
—— —— his wife, Johanna, iii. 559.
—— of Drum, James, iii. 105.
—— —— his wife, Mary Ramsay, iii. 105.
—— of Drumboote, Richard Augustin, viii. 115.
—— of Drumelzier, Alexander, viii. 449.
—— —— his 1st wife, Anne Stuart, ii. 88; viii. 450.
—— —— his 2nd wife, Jean Hay, viii. 450 455.
—— —— Robert, H.E.I.C.S., viii. 450.
—— —— his wife, Janet Erskine, viii. 450.
—— —— William, 2nd son of 1st earl of Tweeddale, vi. 261; viii. 449.
—— —— his wife, Elizabeth Seton, v. 197; viii. 449.
—— of Duncanlaw, Edmund, viii. 425.
—— —— Sir John, viii. 433.
—— —— Sir Thomas, viii. 423.
—— of Duninald, Peter, elder son of Sir Geo. H. of Netherliff, v. 223.
—— of Duns Castle, William, viii. 450.
—— —— his wife, Mary Garstin, viii. 450.
—— of Dupplin, Francis, W.S., v. 230.
—— —— Sir George, v. 222.
—— —— his wife, Margaret Haliburton, v. 223.
—— of Ederpolls, Sir Gilbert de, iii. 560.
—— —— William, iii. 556.
—— of Enzie, Sir John, i. 15.
—— —— Sir Thomas, iv. 516.
—— of Erroll, David de, 2nd laird, iii. 556.
—— his 1st wife, Ethna of Strathearn, iii. 557; viii. 244.
—— —— his 2nd wife, Eva, iii. 557.

Hay of Erroll, Sir David de, 6th laird, iii. 560.
—— —— his 1st wife, * Keith of Innerpeffer, iii. 561.
—— —— his 2nd wife, Margaret *, iii. 561.
—— —— Sir George, 5th son of Peter H. of Megginch, v. 220; ix. 122.
—— —— Gilbert de, 3rd laird, iii. 557.
—— —— his wife, Idonea Comyn, ii. 253; iii. 558.
—— —— Sir Gilbert de, constable of Scotland, 5th laird, iii. 559; vi. 33; viii. 565; ix. 85, 164.
—— —— Gilbert, 9th laird, iii. 563; vi. 220.
—— —— his wife, Alicia Hay, iii. 563; viii. 426.
—— —— Nicholas de, 4th laird, iii. 557, 558; viii. 417; ix. 85.
—— —— his wife, Johanna, iii. 559.
—— —— Sir Thomas, constable of Scotland, 7th laird, ii. 94; iii. 561; iv. 271.
—— —— his wife, Elizabeth Stewart, i. 16; iii. 561.
—— —— William de, pincerna, 1st laird, iii. 555, 557 *bis*, *n.*; viii. 319 *n.*, 416.
—— —— his wife, Eva, iii. 556.
—— —— Sir William, constable of Scotland, 8th laird, iii. 562; ix. 85 *bis*.
—— —— his wife, Margaret Gray, iii. 563.
—— of Eskindy, Finlay de, viii. 6.
—— of Essendy, Laurence, vi. 212; viii. 6.
—— of Esslemont, Francis, iii. 575.
—— of Etal, Augusta, wife of 4th earl of Glasgow, iii. 582; iv. 216.
—— of Faichfleld, Edmund, ancestor of the family of, viii. 426.
—— of Easter Fenton, Sir Thomas de, viii. 419.
—— of Fetterletter, William, 5th son of 8th earl of Erroll, iii. 573.
—— —— his wife, Lilias Gordon, iii. 573.
—— of Findlaiston, Alexander, i. 292.
—— —— his wife, Mary Arbuthnott, i. 292.
—— of Flemingstoun, David de, iii. 557.
—— of Forthar, Christian, viii. 480.
—— of Fossoway, Nicholas, iii. 559.
—— of Galbrydstain, Sir Thomas, iii. 561.
—— of Gammilstoun, George, viii. 432.
—— —— John, viii. 432, 435.
—— of Garvock, Sir Thomas de, viii. 419.
—— of Giffordsgate, Sir Thomas, viii. 422.
—— —— his wife, Joanna Gifford, viii. 422.
—— of Glaswell, Sir John, viii. 433.
—— —— Thomas de, viii. 422.
—— of Glenelg, Sir George, v. 221.
—— of Glendovok, William, iii. 565.
—— of Glengavill, John, viii. 430.
—— of Glenrusk, Sir John, viii. 433.
—— of Gourdie, William, viii. 445.
—— of Haystoun, Sir Duncan Edwyn, 10th bart., viii. 435.

* Name unknown.

Hay of Haystoun, John, vii. 75.
—— —— Sir John, 6th bart., iv. 66.
—— —— his wife, Mary Elizabeth Forbes, iv. 65.
—— of Hedderwick, Sir George, v. 222.
—— of Hoprew, Sir John, viii. 434.
—— —— his wife, Elizabeth Douglas, viii. 435.
—— —— John, master of Yester, viii. 436; ix. 166.
—— —— Sir Thomas, master of Yester, viii. 431; ix. 165.
—— of Inchconnan, Peter, v. 218.
—— —— his wife, Margaret Crichton, v. 218.
—— of Inchmichael, Francis, iii. 574.
—— of Inchtuthill, Elizabeth, wife of (1) 5th lord Sempill, and (2) 1st lord Mordington, iii. 577; vi. 333; vii. 555.
—— —— Sir Thomas, constable of Scotland, iii. 561.
—— —— William, iii. 567.
—— of Inchyra, Nicholas, iii. 558.
—— —— William, iii. 561.
—— —— his wife. Beatrix Douglas, iii. 564.
—— of Innernyte, Sir George, lord Clerk Register, iv. 308; v. 221; vi. 391.
—— —— George, v. 223.
—— —— his wife, Ann Douglas, v. 223, 224.
—— —— Peter, v. 223.
—— of Innerpeffer, Sir Thomas, iii. 561.
—— of Jedworthfield, John, viii. 430.
—— of Easter Kennet, Alexander, lord Clerk Register, vii. 466.
—— of Kerdale, vi. 204.
—— of Killour, Sir Andrew, 2nd laird, iii. 573; ix. 86, 121.
—— —— his wife, Margaret Kinnaird, iii. 573; v. 209; ix. 121.
—— —— George, 4th son of 8th earl of Erroll, iii. 572; ix. 86.
—— —— his wife, Isabel Cheyne, iii. 573.
—— —— Sir John, 3rd laird, iii. 573, 579.
—— of Kilmalamak, Sir Gilbert, iv. 531.
—— —— his wife, Agnes Gordon, iv. 531.
—— of Kilspindie, Nicholas, iii. 559.
—— of Kinfauns, Sir George, lord Clerk Register, v. 221.
—— —— his wife, Margaret Haliburton, v. 223.
—— of Kingask, Sir James, comptroller of Scotland, iv. 241; v. 218, 220; viii. 193.
—— —— his wife, Margaret Murray, v. 218.
—— of Kingildores, Edmund, viii. 425.
—— of Kingsmeadows, Sir James, M.D., 5th bart., viii. 435.
—— —— John, 3rd son of John H. of Smithfield, viii. 435.
—— of Kinnowdie, John, v. 528.
—— of Kinross, George, v. 224.
—— of Kirkland, George, v. 229.
—— —— his wife, Isobel Rollok, v. 229.
—— of Kirklands of Cross Kirk, John, viii. 448.

Hay of Kirklands of Erroll, Peter, elder son of Sir Geo. H. of Netherliff, iv. 223.
—— of Kirkland of Megginch, Peter, v. 229.
—— —— his wife Margaret Boyd, v. 229.
—— of Ladyside, Sir Thomas de, viii. 419.
—— of Latham, Francis, W. S., v. 230.
—— of Lawfield, John, viii. 456.
—— —— Robert, viii. 456.
—— —— his wife, Katherine Babington, viii. 456.
—— —— William, viii. 456.
—— —— his wife, Elizabeth Sinclair, viii. 456.
—— of Lesbany, Nicholas, iii. 565.
—— of Lesk, William, 5th son of 3rd earl of Erroll, iii. 566.
—— —— his wife, Barbara Gordon, iii. 567.
—— of Nether Lesk, Barbara, iii. 567.
—— of Lethington, William, viii. 441.
—— of Leuchars, Thomas, vi. 275; viii. 419.
—— of Lewis, Sir George, 2nd son of P. H. of Megginch, v. 221.
—— of Leys, Edmund, v. 217.
—— —— Edmund, his elder son, v. 217.
—— —— Peter, v. 217, 218.
—— —— William, ancestor of the family of, iii. 557; v. 217.
—— of Linplum, Charles, major-general, viii. 446, 462.
—— —— Edmund, v. 102 *n.*, 147 *n.*; viii. 425 *bis.*
—— —— his wife, Annabella Boyd, v. 102, 147; viii. 425; ix. 164 *bis.*
—— —— George, viii. 465.
—— —— Sir James, 1st bart., viii. 446; ix. 167.
—— —— his 1st wife, Jean Scott, vi. 431; viii. 446.
—— —— his 2nd wife, Anna Livingston, viii. 446.
—— —— James, viii. 450.
—— —— John, viii. 446.
—— —— his wife, Jean Foulis, viii. 446.
—— —— Robert, viii. 450.
—— —— his wife, Janet Erskine, viii. 450.
—— —— Sir Robert, 2nd bart., viii. 446, 462.
—— —— Sir William, viii. 428.
—— —— William, viii. 443, 446.
—— —— his wife, Helen Cockburn, viii. 446 *n.*
—— —— Sir William, viii. 446; ix. 167.
—— —— his wife, Anna Murray, viii. 446; ix. 167.
—— of Locherworth, Sir David, viii. 427; ix. 86, 165.
—— —— his wife, Mary Douglas, i. 174; viii. 429.
—— —— Sir Gilbert de, viii. 418; ix. 164.
—— —— his wife, Mary *or* Margaret Fraser of Oliver Castle, vii. 422; viii. 419.
—— —— Sir John de, viii. 417.
—— —— his wife, * de Lyne of Locherworth, viii. 417.
—— —— John, viii. 430.

* Name unknown.

Hay of Locherworth, Sir Thomas de, viii. 419.
—— —— his wife, Lora de Cuningesburgh of Tullibody, viii. 420.
—— —— Sir Thomas de, sheriff of Peebles, viii. 421; ix. 164.
—— —— his wife, Joanna Gifford of Yester, v. 285; viii. 422.
—— —— Sir Thomas, viii. 427; ix. 165 *bis.*
—— —— Sir William de, viii. 417.
—— —— Sir William, sheriff of Peebles, viii. 421; ix. 164.
—— —— his wife, * Douglas, viii. 421.
—— —— Sir William, i. 174; viii. 423; ix. 164 *sext.*
—— —— his wife, Alicia *, viii. 424; ix. 164 *bis.*
—— —— William, the younger, viii. 425; ix. 164.
—— of Lochloy, John, vi. 204, 303.
—— —— John, v. 528.
—— —— William, alleged ancestor of the family of, v. 218.
—— of Logie, Thomas, 2nd son of 3rd earl of Erroll, iii. 566.
—— —— his wife, Margaret Logie, iii. 566.
—— of Lonyanys, Laurence de, viii. 6.
—— of Lorny, William, 5th son of 3rd earl of Erroll, iii. 567.
—— —— his wife, Barbara Gordon, iii. 567.
—— of Lyne, Sir John, viii. 433.
—— of Mains, John, viii. 459.
—— of Mayne, William, vii. 466.
—— of Megginch, Edmund, 2nd laird, v. 218.
—— —— his wife, Janet Boyd, v. 218.
—— —— George, v. 230.
—— —— his wife, Beatrix Hay, v. 230.
—— —— Patrick, 5th laird, v. 220.
—— —— his 1st wife, Isabel Bryson, v. 220.
—— —— his 2nd wife, Elizabeth *or* Isabel Cheyne, iii. 573; v. 220; vi. 553.
—— —— Peter, 1st laird, v. 217.
—— —— Peter, 3rd laird, v. 218.
—— —— his wife, Margaret Crichton, v. 218.
—— —— Peter, 4th laird, v. 219.
—— —— his wife, Margaret Ogilvy, iv. 33; v. 220.
—— —— Peter, v. 223 *bis.*
—— —— Sir Peter, vi. 549.
—— of Menzeon, George, 4th son of 1st lord Hay of Yester, viii. 432; ix. 166.
—— —— his wife, Euphemia Wauchope, ix. 166.
—— —— William, *perhaps* grandson of Edmund H. of Talla, viii. 430; ix. 165.
—— of Nether Menzeon, William, 3rd son of 1st lord Hay of Yester, ix. 165 *bis.*
—— of Mochrum, Francis, W.S., v. 230.
—— of Monktoun, George, viii. 434.
—— —— Gilbert, viii. 443.
—— —— William, 3rd son of 1st lord Hay of Yester, viii. 433; ix. 165, 166.

* Name unknown.

Hay of Mordington, Edmund, ancestor of the family of, viii. 426.
— of Morham, Sir Thomas, viii. 423.
— — Sir William, viii. 428.
— of Mountblairy, Andrew, W.S., i. 143.
— — his 1st wife, Ann Ogilvy, ii. 24.
— — his 2nd wife, Mary Allardice, i. 143.
— — Edmund, ancestor of the family of, viii. 426.
— of Muchalls, Alexander, ix. 85, 86.
— — George, iii. 570.
— — John, 2nd son of 7th earl of Erroll, iii. 570.
— — his wife, Elizabeth Butter, iii. 570.
— of Muiresk, George, 2nd son of 9th earl of Erroll, iii. 576.
— of Muldavit, William, iv. 129.
— — his wife, Helen Crichton, iv. 129.
— of Murage, Peter, v. 219.
— — his wife, Margaret Ogilvy, v. 220.
— of Naughton, George, v. 386.
— — George, iv. 260.
— — his wife, Maria Ruthven, iv. 260.
— — John, iii. 558.
— — Peter, i. 467, 563.
— of Netherliff, Sir George, i. 561; v. 220; ix. 122.
— — his wife, Margaret Haliburton, v. 221; ix. 89.
— of Nethertoun, John, viii. 430.
— of Newhall, George, viii. 465.
— — Edward, iii. 83, 519; viii. 460.
— — his wife, Maria Murray Mackenzie, iii. 83, 519.
— — John, advocate, viii. 459.
— — his wife, Dorothy Hayhurst, viii. 459.
— — John, *afterwards* Hay-Mackenzie, iii. 83; viii. 461.
— — his wife, Anne Gibson-Craig, iii. 83.
— — Sir William, lieut.-col., viii. 459.
— — his wife, Margaret Hay, viii. 446, 459.
— — William, major, viii. 460.
— — his 1st wife, Katharine Hay, viii. 460, 465.
— — his 2nd wife, Mary Nisbet of Dirleton, viii. 460.
— of Newraw, George, 4th son of 7th earl of Erroll, iii. 570.
— — his wife, Marjory Keith, iii. 570.
— of Newton, John, viii. 430.
— — William, viii. 430.
— of Nunraw, Alexander, viii. 450.
— — Charles Erskine, viii. 451.
— — James, viii. 451.
— — Robert, viii. 450.
— — his wife, Kalitza Psaraki, viii. 451.
— of Oliver Castle, Mr. George, ix. 165.
— — John de, viii. 426; ix. 165.
— — John, viii. 429.
— — Sir John, viii. 433.
Hay of Park, Thomas, ix. 36.
— — his wife, Jean Hamilton, ix. 36.
— of Peel, Francis, W.S., v. 230.
— of Philipston, Sir Thomas de, viii. 419.
— of Pitcullen, Sir George, iii. 379.
— of Pitfour, James, iii. 573.
— — his wife, Jean Hay, iii. 573.
— — Sir Patrick, ii. 28.
— of Pitsindie, Sir George, lord Clerk Register, v. 221.
— of Petgowny, Gilbert, iii. 563.
— — his wife, Beatrix Dunbar, iii. 564.
— of Pethponti, Nicholas, iii. 559.
— of Petmulin, William de, iii. 555.
— — his wife, Eva, iii. 555.
— of Polgavy, viii. 430.
— of Posso, James, viii. 435.
— — John, viii. 435.
— of Raeshaw, Sir Thomas de, viii. 419.
— of Ranfield, Edmund, ancestor of the family of, viii. 426.
— of Rannes, Charles, ii. 22.
— — Edmund, ancestor of the family of, viii. 426.
— — James, ii. 21.
— of Rattray, Francis, W.S., v. 230.
— — Patrick, M.D., v. 229.
— — his wife, Jean Ogilvy, v. 229.
— — Peter, 3rd son of Peter H. of Megginch, v. 220, 229; ix. 122.
— — his wife, Margaret Boyd, v. 229.
— of Redsheil, George, viii. 432.
— — John, viii. 432, 435.
— of Rossieclerach, Sir Gilbert de, iii. 559.
— of Scroggis, John, viii. 443.
— of Seggie, George, v. 224.
— of Seton, James, general, 2nd son of 7th marquess of Tweeddale, viii. 466.
— — his wife, Elizabeth Forbes of Seton, viii. 466.
— — James Gordon, viii. 467.
— — his wife, Mary Katharine Cox, viii. 467.
— of Seyfield, George, 4th son of 7th earl of Erroll, iii. 570.
— of Slains, George, 4th son of 8th earl of Erroll, iii. 572.
— — Sir Gilbert de, 1st laird, iii. 560, 561.
— of Smithfield, *, v. 60.
— — his wife, Margaret Ker, v. 59.
— — Sir Duncan Edwyn, 10th bart. viii. 435.
— — James, viii. 435.
— — his wife, Jonet Gevane, viii. 435.
— — Sir James, 1st bart., viii. 435.
— — Sir James, 3rd bart., vi. 380.
— — John, 5th son of 2nd lord Hay of Yester, ix. 166.
— — his 1st wife, * Dickson of Smithfield, ix. 166.
— — his 2nd wife, Janet Scott, viii. 435.

* Name unknown.

Hay of Smithfield, John, his son, viii. 443.
—— —— Sir John, 6th bart., iv. 66.
—— —— his wife, Mary E. Forbes, iv. 65.
—— —— Thomas, viii. 435; ix. 167.
—— of Snaid, Sir John, 2nd son of 1st lord Hay of Yester, viii. 431, 432.
—— —— his wife, Elizabeth Crichton, viii. 433.
—— of Spott, Alexander, 3rd son of 1st marquess of Tweeddale, viii. 455.
—— —— his wife, Katharine Charters, viii. 456.
—— —— Robert, viii. 456.
—— —— his wife, Katharine Babington, viii. 456.
—— —— William, viii. 456.
—— —— his wife, Elizabeth Sinclair, viii. 456.
—— of Spynie, Sir George, v. 222.
—— of Mill of Strathavin, John, viii. 430.
—— —— William, viii. 430.
—— of Swynhope, James, viii. 435.
—— —— John, viii. 435.
—— of Talla, Edmund, viii. 416, 425; ix. 86, 164.
—— —— his wife, Annabella Boyd, v. 102, 147; viii. 425; ix. 164 *bis*.
—— —— John, ii. 154.
—— —— his wife, Jean Hepburn, ii. 154.
—— —— Sir William, viii. 425, 428.
—— —— William, ix. 166.
—— of Templeton, Gilbert, viii. 277.
—— —— his wife, Janet Lyon, viii. 277.
—— of Thankerton, John, viii. 430.
—— —— Sir John, viii. 433.
—— of Todrig, Sir John, viii. 433.
—— of Torburne, Thomas de, viii. 422.
—— of Touch, Sir John, i. 15; viii. 421.
—— of Tullibody, Egidia, wife of Sir Alexander Seton of Gordon, iv. 524; viii. 421.
—— —— John de, vi. 38; viii. 263, 420.
—— —— his wife, Margaret, viii. 420.
—— —— Sir John, i. 15; viii. 421.
—— —— his wife, Margaret Stewart, i. 15; viii. 421.
—— of Tullibothwell, John de, viii. 263, 420.
—— of Tullyhow, George, v. 223.
—— —— his wife, Ann Douglas, v. 223, 224.
—— of Tullykeraw, William, vii. 437.
—— of Tullynachton, John de, viii. 264.
—— of Turnaluif, Francis, iii. 575.
—— of Turriff, Francis, 3rd son of 9th earl of Erroll, iii. 576.
—— of Tyrie, George, v. 224.
—— of Ugstoun, John, viii. 430.
—— —— Sir John, viii. 434.
—— of Urie, Gilbert, iii. 563, 565; ix. 86.
—— —— his wife, Beatrix Dunbar, iii. 564.
—— —— William, iii. 562, 563.
Hay of Urie, William, vii. 437; ix. 12.
—— —— his wife, Agnes Douglas, i. 184; ix. 12.
—— —— William, vii. 440.
—— —— his wife, Margaret Fraser, vii. 440.
—— of Whittinghame, Alexander, viii. 449.
—— —— his 1st wife, Anne Stuart, ii. 88; viii. 450.
—— —— his 2nd wife, Jean Hay, viii. 450, 455.
—— —— Robert, H.E.I.C.S., viii. 450.
—— —— his wife, Janet Erskine, viii. 450.
—— of Woodcockdale, David, ii. 50.
—— of Yester, Sir David, iii. 564; vi. 80, 540; viii. 416, 424, 425, 427 *bis*, 532, 533; ix. 86, 165.
—— —— his wife, Mary Douglas, i. 174; viii. 429.
—— —— John, viii. 429.
—— —— his 1st wife, Mary Lindsay, v. 394; viii. 430.
—— —— his 2nd wife, Elizabeth Cunningham of Belton, viii. 430.
—— —— Sir Thomas, viii. 422.
—— —— his wife, Joanna Gifford of Yester, v. 285; viii. 422.
—— —— Sir Thomas, viii. 427.
—— —— Sir William, viii. 423.
—— —— his wife, Alicia *, viii. 424; ix. 164 *bis*.
—— Abigail, dau. of 8th earl of Kinnoull, v. 234.
—— Adelaide Harriet Augusta, wife of 2nd earl of Gainsborough, iii. 585.
—— Agnes, wife of P. Bruce of Fingask, iii. 574; ix. 87.
—— Agnes, wife of (1) Sir Geo. Preston, and (2) James, 6th earl of Glencairn, iv. 244.
—— Agnes, wife of David Rattray of Craighall, v. 230.
—— Agnes, dau. of 6th lord Hay of Yester, viii. 444 *bis*.
—— Agnes Blanche Marie, wife of baron Herbert von Hindenburg, v. 237.
—— Agnes Georgiana Elizabeth, wife of James, earl Fife, iii. 585.
—— Alexander, 6th son of 7th earl of Erroll, iii. 570.
—— Alexander, eldest son of 8th earl of Erroll, iii. 572.
—— Sir Alexander, lord Clerk Register, iv. 310.
—— Alexander, H.E.I.C.S. Navy, viii. 450.
—— Alexander, 6th son of Sir Wm. H. of Newhall, viii. 461.
—— Alexander, 3rd son of Nicholas H., ix. 85, 86.
—— Alexander, 3rd son of 1st earl of Tweeddale, ix. 167.
—— Alicia, wife of *perhaps* (1) George, earl of March, and (2) Gilbert Hay of Erroll, iii. 277, 563; viii. 426.

* Name unknown.

Hay, Alice Mary Emily, wife of Charles Edward Hay Allen, iii. 585.
— Alistair George, capt. 3rd batt. Black Watch, v. 237.
— — his wife, Camilla Dagmar Violet Greville, v. 238.
— Amy Violet Powlett, wife of George Eden, v. 236.
— Andrew, alleged son of Sir William H. of Yester, viii. 427.
— Andrew, rector of Biggar, provost of Bothans, viii. 429; ix. 165.
— Anna, wife of (1) Wm. Murray of Abercairny, and (2) Sir Jas. Drummond of Machany, iii. 573; viii. 223.
— Anna, dau. of 2nd earl of Kinnoull, v. 224.
— Anna, dau. of Sir William H. of Linplum, viii. 447.
— Anne, wife of 3rd earl of Winton, iii. 577; viii. 594.
— Anne, dau. of 8th earl of Kinnoull, v. 234.
— Ann, wife of 9th earl of Morton, vi. 380.
— Anne, wife of 12th lord Ross of Halkhead, vii. 261; viii. 462.
— Anne, dau. of Robert H. of Drumelzier, viii. 451.
— Anne, wife of (1) Sir P. Hepburn-Murray of Balmanno, and (2) Archibald Stirling of Keir, viii. 451.
— Anne, dau. of 3rd marquess of Tweeddale, viii. 463.
— Anne, dau. of 1st earl of Tweeddale, ix. 168.
— Archibald, 3rd son of 2nd earl of Kinnoull, ix. 122.
— Arthur, major 3rd batt. Q. O. Cameron Highlanders, iii. 586.
— Arthur, colonel, F.R.S., viii. 472.
— Arthur Vincent, Irish Guards, viii. 473.
— Arthur William Henry, v. 236.
— — his wife, Mary Scott, v. 236.
— Augusta, wife of 4th earl of Glasgow, iii. 582; iv. 216.
— Augusta Sophia, wife of 14th lord Saye and Sele, v. 237.
— Auriol Camilla Sharlie Blanche, v. 238.
— Beatrix, wife of William Hay of Delgaty, iii. 571.
— Beatrix, wife of George Hay of Megginch, v. 230.
— Beatrix, wife of Wm. Wauchope of Niddrie, viii. 436.
— Beatrix, wife of Wm. Congalton of Congalton, viii. 442; ix. 167.
— Beatrix, wife of Walter Bonar of Keltie, iii. 566.
— Beatrix, contr. to Alex. Keith, and *perhaps* wife of Sir Alexander Gordon of Midmar, iii. 566; iv. 525.
Hay, Caroline Augusta, wife of John Morant, iii. 584.
— Cecilia Leila, wife of capt. G. A. Webbe, iii. 586.
— Charles, next of kin to 6th lord Banff, ii. 22.
— Charles, glass manufacturer, v. 224; ix. 122.
— Charles, 2nd son of 1st earl of Tweeddale, ix. 167.
— Charles Edward, captain 2nd Foot, viii. 471.
— Charlotte, wife of rev. Wm. Holwell, iii. 582.
— Charlotte Georgiana, viii. 467.
— Christian, *error for* Jean, wife of John, earl of Mar, v. 624 *n.*
— Christian, wife of Wm. Stewart of Traquair, viii. 400, 434.
— Christian, wife of Thos. Hay, sheriff-depute of Peebles, viii. 429.
— Christian, wife of Henry Lauder, viii. 438.
— Christian, wife of Archibald Newton of Newton, viii. 444 *bis.*
— Christian, dau. of Robert H. of Drumelzier, viii. 451.
— Claude George, M.P., v. 238.
— Constance Blanche Louisa, wife of W. H. Hadow, v. 238.
— Cuthbert Joseph, viii. 467.
— David de, parson of Erroll, iii. 557, 558; v. 217.
— Mr. David, 4th son of Gilbert H., yr. of Erroll, iii. 363; ix. 85, 86 *bis.*
— David, 2nd son of David H. of Belton, viii. 454.
— David, in Indian Army, viii. 455.
— David, 5th son of Sir Wm. H. of Newhall, viii. 461.
— David, commissary-clerk of Glasgow, ix. 167.
— Diana Hungerford, viii. 455.
— Dorothea, wife of major Jas. Hay of Belton, viii. 454.
— Dorothea Frances, wife of John Henry Ley, viii. 468.
— Dulcibella Jane, wife of ven. C. N. Wodehouse, iii. 584.
— Edmund, rector of the Scots College, Pont-à-Musson, iv. 306; v. 219, 220.
— Edward, governor of Barbadoes, v. 233.
— — his 1st wife, Mary Flower, v. 233.
— — his 2nd wife, Mary Harbourne Barnwell, v. 233.
— Edward, commander R.N., viii. 455.
— Edward Douglas John, viii. 473.
— Edward George, colonel, viii. 468.
— Egidia, wife of 1st earl of Huntly, i. 15; iv. 524; viii. 421.

Hay, Eleanor, wife of 1st earl of Linlithgow, iii. 572; v. 444, 445.
—— Elizabeth, wife of (1) Sir John Leslie, and (2) James, 1st lord Balfour, i. 536; iii. 571; ix. 32 *bis*.
—— Elizabeth, wife of 8th earl of Crawford, iii. 26, 567.
—— Elizabeth, wife of Sir Geo. Leslie of Rothes, iii. 562; vii. 273.
—— Elizabeth, wife of (1) George, 2nd earl of Huntly, and (2) Andrew, 2nd lord Gray, iii. 565; iv. 276, 528, 529, 531; ix. 86, 99 *bis*, 110.
—— Elizabeth, wife of 5th lord Saltoun, iii. 567; vii. 411; ix. 86.
—— Elizabeth, wife of William, master of Marischal, iii. 570; vi. 49; ix. 134.
—— Elizabeth, dau. of John H., iii. 573.
—— Elizabeth, wife of (1) Hugh, 5th lord Sempill, and (2) James, 1st lord Mordingtoun, iii. 577; vi. 333; vii. 555; ix. 87.
—— Elizabeth, wife of James, earl of Findlater and Seafield, iv. 39; v. 232.
—— Elizabeth, wife of Alex. Gray, iv. 274.
—— Elizabeth, wife of (1) Gilbert Gray of Bandirran, and (2) Wm. Rollock of Balbegie, iv. 281; v. 220; vii. 191; ix. 122.
—— Elizabeth, dau. of 2nd earl of Kinnoull, v. 225; ix. 122.
—— Elizabeth, dau. of 8th earl of Kinnoull, v. 234.
—— Elizabeth, wife of (1) Sir F. L. Arthur, and (2) rev. E. E. Dagmore, v. 237.
—— Elizabeth, wife of Duncan Macdowal of Makerstoun, viii. 426.
—— Elizabeth, wife of Jas. Tweedie of Drumelzier, viii. 434.
—— Elizabeth, wife of 4th lord Seton, viii. 436, 583.
—— Elizabeth, legtd. dau. of 4th lord Hay of Yester, viii. 438.
—— Elizabeth, wife of Robert Swinton of Swinton, viii. 442.
—— Elizabeth, wife of Wm. Ker of Broomland, viii. 442.
—— Elizabeth, wife of James Tweedie of Drumelzier, viii. 444 *bis*.
—— Elizabeth, dau. of David H. of Belton, viii. 455.
—— Elizabeth, dau. of Sir Wm. H. of Newhall, viii. 461.
—— Elizabeth, wife of James Joseph Hope-Vere, viii. 468.
—— Elizabeth, wife of 2nd duke of Wellington, viii. 471.
—— Elizabeth, wife of Robt. Lauder of the Bass, ix. 167 *bis*.
—— Elizabeth Blanche Mary, v. 238.
—— Elizabeth Seton, viii. 451.
—— Elspeth, wife of Walter Scott in Essinside, vii. 75.
—— Emily, wife of Sir Robert Peel, viii. 472.
Hay, Emma, wife of rear-admiral James Erskine-Wemyss, iii. 584; viii. 511.
—— Eupham, dau. of 7th earl of Erroll, iii. 571.
—— Evelyn Elizabeth Vane, wife of Sir R. D. Moncreiffe, v. 236.
—— Evolyn Vane, v. 236.
—— Fanny, wife of rev. S. R. Cartwright, iii. 584.
—— Flaminia, wife of capt. George James, iii. 582.
—— Florence Agnes Adelaide, wife of capt. H. Wolrige Gordon, iii. 586.
—— Frances, wife of Charles Manners or Tollemache of Market Overton, iii. 413; viii. 450, 460; ix. 168 *bis*.
—— Frances, dau. of 15th earl of Erroll, iii. 582.
—— Frances, wife of col. R. T. Lloyd, v. 237.
—— Francis, page of honour to queen Victoria, iii. 586.
—— Francis, 2nd son of Francis H. of Balhousie, v. 230.
—— Francis, 5th son of David H. of Belton, viii. 455.
—— Francis George, 2nd son of 12th earl of Kinnoull, v. 237.
—— Frederick, Bengal C. S., viii. 471.
—— George, 2nd son of George H. of Ardlethen, iii. 570.
—— George, son of Alexander H. of Brunthill, iii. 573.
—— George, son of John H., burgess of Edinburgh, iii. 573.
—— Sir George, tacksman of Orkney and Shetland, v. 222.
—— George, 3rd son of George H. of Balhousie, v. 231.
—— George, in Murie, vi. 549.
—— —— his wife, Helen Oliphant, vi. 549.
—— George, son of Peter H. of Rattray, vii. 191.
—— —— his wife, Isobel Rollo, vii. 191.
—— George, 2nd son of major James H. of Belton, viii. 455.
—— George, son of major William H. of Newhall, viii. 460.
—— George, 2nd son of general James H., viii. 467.
—— George Harley, grandson of 13th earl of Kinnoull, v. 238.
—— George Lewis, viii. 461.
—— Gilbert, 3rd son of 1st earl of Erroll, iii. 564.
—— Gilbert de, St. Andrews, viii. 423.
—— Gilbert, 6th son of 1st marquess of Tweeddale, viii. 456.
—— Gilbert, eldest son of Nicholas H., ix. 85, 86.
—— Gilbert Allan Rowland, iii. 587.
—— Giles, wife of 1st earl of Huntly, viii. 421.

Hay, Grace, dau. of 4th marquess of Tweeddale, viii. 465.
— Grizel, contracted to Robert Home of Heuch, viii. 442.
— Grizel, wife of lt.-col. James Alexander, viii. 180; ix. 122.
— Grizel, wife of George Hepburn of Alderston, viii. 444 *bis*.
— Grissel, dau. of 1st earl of Tweeddale, ix. 168.
— Gwendoline Vane, v. 236.
— Hannah Charlotte, wife of John Sharp, viii. 468.
— Hannah Charlotte, wife of Simon Watson-Taylor, viii. 471.
— Harriet Jane, dau. of 15th earl of Erroll, iii. 582.
— Harriet Jemima, wife of Daniel Gurney, iii. 584.
— Helen, wife of Wm. Hamilton, ii. 50.
— Helen *or* Helenor, wife of Alexander, 1st earl of Linlithgow, iii. 572; v. 444, 445.
— Helen, dau. of 9th earl of Erroll, iii. 577; ix. 87.
— Helen, wife of Andrew Duff of Maldavit, viii. 420 *n*.
— Henrietta, wife of Robert Roper of Muffets, v. 234.
— Henrietta, wife of Henry Drummond of Albury Park, v. 235; viii. 233.
— Henrietta, wife of Charles Alexander Moir of Leckie, viii. 451.
— Henry, alleged son of Sir William H. of Yester, viii. 427.
— Henry Claude Frederick, v. 236.
— — his wife, Harriet Lepel Dorothea Sayer, v. 236.
— Hugh de, 4th son of Nicolas de H. of Erroll, iii. 559.
— Hugh, vi. 549.
— — his wife, Katharine Oliphant, vi. 549.
— Mr. Hugh, 5th son of Sir Wm. H. of Locherworth, ix. 164.
— Ida Agnes Vane, wife of Reginald West, v. 236.
— Isobel, wife of 1st lord Oliphant, iii. 565; vi. 541.
— Isobel, wife of William Forbes of Tolquhon, iii. 568.
— Isabel, wife of (1) John Leslie of Balquhain, and (2) James, lord Balfour, iii. 571; ix. 86 *bis*.
— Isabel, dau. of 9th earl of Erroll, iii. 577; v. 146, 152; ix. 87 *bis*.
— Isabella, wife of lieut.-gen. W. Wemyss, iii. 584; viii. 511.
— Isobel, wife of (1) Alex. Robertson of Fascally, and (2) Jas. Campbell of Lawers. v. 501.
— Isabel, wife of Robert Lauder of the Bass, viii. 432.
Hay, Isobel, dau. of Sir James H. of Linplum, viii. 447.
— Isobel, dau. of Peter H. of Megginch, ix. 122.
— Isobel, illeg. dau. of Francis H. of Balhousie, ix. 122.
— Isabella Anne, dau. of 15th earl of Erroll, iii. 582.
— Ivan Josslyn Lumley, iii. 587.
— James, merchant, Banff, ii. 21.
— — his wife, Helen Lauder, ii. 21.
— James, next of kin to 6th lord Banff, ii. 22.
— James, colonel, 3rd son of Geo. H. of Killour, iii. 573.
— James, 2nd son of 12th earl of Erroll, iii. 579; ix. 87.
— James, H.E.I.C.S., 3rd son of 15th earl of Erroll, iii. 581; ix. 87.
— James, captain in earl of Morton's regiment, v. 224; ix. 122 *bis*.
— James, 3rd son of 2nd earl of Kinnoull, v. 224; viii. 180.
— James, 3rd son of 4th lord Hay of Yester, viii. 437; ix. 167.
— James, son of Wm. H. of Gourdie, viii. 445.
— James, W.S., warden of the mint, viii. 461.
— — his wife, Jane Henderson, viii. 461.
— James, 4th son of 1st earl of Tweeddale, ix. 167.
— Jane, wife of P. Murray of Ochtertyre, v. 219.
— Jane, wife of Archibald Murray of Murrayfield, viii. 461.
— Jane, dau. of 7th marquess of Tweeddale, viii. 468.
— Jane, wife of Sir R. C. H. Taylor, viii. 472.
— Janet, wife of John Beatoun, i. 533.
— Janet, wife of Sir Alex. Home of Home, iv. 445.
— Janet, wife of Andrew Gray of Balledgarno, v. 220; ix. 122.
— Janet, dau. of Francis H. of Balhousie, v. 230.
— Jean, wife of Andrew, 8th earl of Erroll, ii. 568, 569, 571.
— Jean, wife of James Hay of Pitfour, iii. 573.
— Jean, dau. of John H., Edinburgh, iii. 573.
— Jean, wife of John, earl of Mar, iii. 577; v. 624.
— Jean, wife of Sir Alex. Home of Home, iv. 445; viii. 426.
— Jean, dau. of 2nd earl of Kinnoull, v. 225.
— Jean, wife of William, 1st earl of March, vii. 146; viii. 456.
— Jean, wife of 8th earl of Rothes, vii. 304; viii. 462.

Hay, Jean, alleged wife of Sir James Hay of Barra, viii. 442; ix. 167 *bis*.
— Jean, wife of Alex. Horsburgh of Horsburgh, viii. 444.
— Jean, dau. of Sir James H. of Linplum, viii. 447.
— Jean, wife of Alex. Hay of Drumelzier, viii. 450, 455.
— Jean, wife of Wm. Hay of Barra, ix. 167.
— Jemima, dau. of 15th earl of Erroll, iii. 582.
— John, provost of Dundee, i. 533.
— John, iii. 101.
— — his wife, Euphame Ramsay, iii. 101.
— John de, 3rd son of William, 1st laird of Erroll, iii. 556.
— — his wife, Juliana, iii. 556.
— John de, parson of Erroll, iii. 559.
— John, in holy orders, 3rd son of 3rd earl of Erroll, iii. 566.
— John, burgess of Linlithgow, Stirling, Perth, Edinburgh, and Banff, iii. 573.
— — his wife, Elizabeth Erskine, iii. 573.
— John, son of John H., iii. 573.
— John, eldest son of Peter H. of Rattray, v. 229.
— John, rector of Eppsworth, v. 233.
— John, son of John H. of Tullibody, vi. 38.
— — his wife, Christian Keith, vi. 38.
— Sir John, admiral R.N., vi. 387.
— John, Scottish Observantines, Cologne, vi. 540 *n*.
— John, preceptor of St. Leonard's, viii. 445.
— John, 2nd son of Sir Wm. H. of Linplum, viii. 447.
— John, 5th son of Alex. H. of Drumelzier, viii. 450.
— John, 3rd son of William H. of Spott, viii. 456.
— John, brigadier-general, viii. 458.
— — his 1st wife, Elizabeth Dalzell, ii. 414; viii. 459.
— — his 2nd wife, Elizabeth Orby, viii. 459; ix. 168.
— John, rear-admiral R.N., 3rd son of 7th marquess of Tweeddale, viii. 467.
— — his wife, Mary Anne Cameron, viii. 467.
— Sir John, G.C.B., admiral of the Fleet, viii. 470.
— — his wife, Annie Christina Lambert, viii. 471.
— John, 3rd son of Sir Gilbert H. of Dronlaw, ix. 85.
— John, 3rd son of 3rd lord Hay of Yester, ix. 166.
— John Arthur Lambert, R.N., viii. 471.
— Jonet, wife of Sir John Leslie, v. 386; ix. 128.
— Josslyn Victor, iii. 587.
Hay, Julia, dau. of 8th marquess of Tweeddale, viii. 472.
— Julian Thomasina, wife of Sir John Cam Hobhouse, viii. 468.
— Katharine, wife of (1) R. Moncur of Balluny, and (2) G. Drummond of Blair, v. 219.
— Katharine, wife of Wm. Kynman of Hill, v. 220; ix. 122.
— Katharine, wife of Jas. Baird, yr. of Auchmeddan, v. 225.
— Katharine, dau. of Francis H. of Balhousie, v. 230.
— Katharine, wife of Sir Philip Anstruther of Balcaskie, viii. 456.
— Katharine, wife of capt. William Hay of Newhall, viii. 460, 465.
— Katharine, dau. of 3rd marquess of Tweeddale, viii. 463.
— Lauderdale, viii. 455.
— Laurence, 3rd son of 7th earl of Erroll, iii. 570.
— Lewis, 5th son of 9th earl of Erroll, iii. 576.
— Louisa, wife of Sir Thomas Moncreiffe, v. 236.
— Louisa Jane, wife of R. B. Wardlaw-Ramsay, viii. 471.
— Malcolm de, parson of Erroll, iii. 556, 557.
— Malcolm Vivian, viii. 467.
— Margaret, wife of William, 2nd earl of Angus, i. 175; viii. 426; ix. 165.
— Margaret, wife of 7th lord Blantyre, ii. 89; viii. 451.
— Margaret, wife of 4th lord Borthwick, ii. 107; viii. 432, 438.
— Margaret, wife of 8th lord Borthwick, ii. 112; viii. 442; ix. 39.
— Margaret, wife of (1) Alexander, 1st earl of Dunfermline, and (2) James, 1st earl of Callander, ii. 362; iii. 372; viii. 447.
— Margaret, wife of (1) Henry, lord Ker, and (2) John, 6th earl of Cassillis, ii. 481; iii. 578; vii. 347; ix. 153.
— Margaret, wife of Robert Crichton, afterwards 1st lord Crichton of Sanquhar, iii. 223.
— Margaret, probably wife of Norman Leslie, iii. 562; vii. 269.
— Margaret, wife of (1) Alexander Fraser, (2) Sir Gilbert Keith, and (3) Robert Douglas, iii. 565; vi. 368; vii. 434.
— Margaret, wife of 4th lord Oliphant, iii. 570; vi. 548.
— Margaret, dau. of 8th earl of Erroll, iii. 573.
— Margaret, wife of Sir John Seton of Barns, iii. 577; ix. 87.
— Margaret, wife of James, earl of Linlithgow and Callendar, iii. 579, 580; v. 450.

Hay, Margaret, wife of Chas. Cameron, iii. 582.
— Margaret, contr. to John Gordon, iv. 536.
— Margaret, wife of Alexander, lord Spynie, v. 222; viii. 104.
— Margaret, dau. of 2nd earl of Kinnoull, v. 224.
— Margaret, dau. of 8th earl of Kinnoull, v. 233.
— Margaret, wife of Robert de Keith, vi. 33.
— Margaret, wife of Sir Henry de Maule of Panmure, vii. 6; viii. 418.
— Margaret, wife of 3rd earl of Roxburghe, vii. 349; viii. 456.
— Margaret, wife of John, earl of Mar, v. 232, 631.
— Margaret, wife of John Clark of Lonyanys, viii. 6.
— Margaret, dau. of Sir David H. of Locherworth, viii. 429; ix. 165.
— Margaret, wife of Sir Robert Lauder of Poppill, viii. 438.
— Margaret, dau. of 6th lord Hay of Yester, viii. 444 *bis*.
— Margaret, wife of William Hay of Newhall, viii. 446, 459.
— Margaret, dau. of Sir James H. of Linplum, viii. 447.
— Margaret, wife of Sir John Baird of Newbyth, viii. 447.
— Margaret, wife of Sir Henry Seton of Culbeg, viii. 451.
— Margaret, dau. of David H. of Belton, viii. 455.
— Margaret, wife of Allan MacDougall of Gallanach, viii. 461.
— Margaret, dau. of Peter H. of Megginch, ix. 122.
— Margaret, dau. of 1st earl of Tweeddale, ix. 168.
— Margaret Florence, v. 238.
— Margaret Julia, wife of F. A. Lushington, iii. 585.
— Margaret Louis Gordon, wife of Theodore Gudin, viii. 567.
— Maria, alleged wife of Alexander Forbes of Pitsligo, iv. 70.
— Maria Elizabeth, wife of rev. George Moore, iii. 582.
— Mariana, *error for* Elizabeth, wife of David, earl of Crawford, iii. 567.
— Marion, possible wife of Sir Alex. Hepburn of Whitsome, ii. 145; ix. 41.
— Marion, wife of George Broun of Colstoun, viii. 434.
— Mariota, wife of Sir David Ogilvy of Inchmartin, iv. 31.
— Mariota, wife of John Chalmer of Strathavin, viii. 430.
— Marjorie, wife of Andrew Fraser of Kinmundy, iv. 110.
Hay, Marjory, wife of Jas. Abercromby of Pitmeddan, iv. 179.
— Marjory, dau. of Peter H. of Megginch, ix. 122.
— Mary, wife of (1) G. Butler, and (2) Wm. Hamilton, ii. 28.
— Mary, wife of 1st earl of Buccleuch, ii. 234; iii. 577.
— Mary, wife of gen. John Scott of Balcomie, iii. 581; ix. 70, 87.
— Mary, wife of 8th earl Marischal, v. 224; vi. 60.
— Mary, wife of John Hume, bishop of Oxford, and Salisbury, v. 234.
— Mary, dau. of Sir Wm. H. of Newhall, viii. 461.
— Mary Turner, viii. 468.
— Matillidis, wife of William de Braosa, ii. 423.
— Minnie Christina Brenda, wife of Sholto Charles, lord Aberdour, vi. 387; viii. 471.
— Muriel Henrietta Constance, wife of count A. Munster, v. 238.
— Nicholas de, parson of Fossoway, dean of Dunkeld, iii. 559.
— Nicholas de, father of Sir David de H. of Erroll, iii. 560.
— Nicholas, prebendary of Bothans, viii. 427; ix. 165.
— Nicholas, 3rd son of Sir Wm. H. of Erroll, ix. 85, 86.
— Nicholas, his 2nd son, ix. 85, 86,
— Nicholas, 5th son of Gilbert H., yr. of Erroll, ix. 86 *bis*.
— Patrick, son of Alexander H. of Brunthill, iii. 573.
— Patrick, lieut.-col., v. 228 *n*.
— Peter, 5th son of 2nd earl of Kinnoull, v. 224; ix. 122.
— Peter, 2nd son of Peter H. of Megginch, ix. 122.
— Rachel, dau. of David H. of Belton, viii. 455.
— Rebecca, wife of George Oliphant, v. 230.
— Robert de, parson of Erroll, iii. 556, 557; viii. 416.
— Robert, 3rd son of 7th lord Hay of Yester, viii. 447.
— Robert, master of robes to king James VI., v. 219.
— Robert, 4th son of 2nd earl of Kinnoull, v. 224; ix. 122.
— Sir Robert John, lieut.-gen., K.C.B., viii. 455.
— — his wife, Georgina Harvey Ramsay, viii. 455.
— Rosemary Constance Ferelith, iii. 587.
— Samuel, captain, 4th son of 17th earl of Erroll, iii. 584.
— — his wife, Louisa Pleydell Bouverie, iii. 584.

Hay, Sarah Maria, wife of George Murray, bishop of Rochester, v. 235.
— Sarah, wife of 2nd lord Delamere, v. 237.
— Sereld Mordaunt Alan Josslyn, R.N., iii. 587.
— Somerville, 4th son of 17th earl of Erroll, iii. 584.
— — his wife, Alicia Diana Erskine, ii. 279; iii. 584.
— Sophia, wife of John, viscount Melgum and lord Aboyne, i. 100.
— Susan, wife of John Scott of Malleny, viii. 461.
— Susan, dau. of 3rd marquess of Tweeddale, viii. 463.
— Susan Elizabeth Clementine, wife of capt. W. Waring, viii. 473.
— Susan Georgiana, wife of 1st marquess of Dalhousie, iii. 107; viii. 471.
— Susanna, dau. of David H. of Belton, viii. 455.
— Sir Thomas, master of Yester, iv. 359; viii. 430 *bis*.
— — his contr. wife, Elizabeth Home, iv. 358, 454; viii. 431: ix. 165.
— — his wife, (?) Katharine Borthwick, ii. 107 *n.*; iv. 359; viii. 431.
— Thomas, abbot of Glenluce, ii. 472.
— Thomas de, 4th son of William, 1st laird of Erroll, iii. 556.
— — his wife, Ada, iii. 556.
— Mr. Thomas, 6th son of Gilbert H., yr. of Erroll, iii. 563; ix. 85, 86 *bis*.
— Thomas, parson of Turriff, iii. 570.
— Thomas, 2nd son of 8th earl of Erroll, iii. 572; ix. 86.
— Thomas, 4th son of 9th earl of Erroll, iii. 576.
— Thomas, 3rd son of 12th earl of Erroll, iii. 579.
— Thomas, 4th son of Peter H. of Rattray, v. 229.
— Thomas, minister of Cross Kirk, Peebles, viii. 401, 437, 444; ix. 167.
— Thomas, clerk of Glasgow diocese, viii. 427.
— Thomas, sheriff-depute of Peebles, viii. 429.
— — his wife, Christian Hay, viii. 429.
— Thomas, preceptor of St. Leonard's, viii. 434; ix. 166 *bis*.
— Thomas, provost of Bothans, tutor of Yester and Smithfield, viii. 436, 438; ix. 166 *bis*.
— Thomas, rector of Rendlesham, viii. 468.
— — his wife, Harriet Kinloch, viii. 468.
— Thomas William, viii. 471.
— Violet Vane, v. 236.
— Walter, 2nd son of Gilbert H., yr. of Erroll, iii. 563; ix. 85, 86.
Hay, William, half-brother to 6th lord Banff, ii. 22.
— William de, 2nd son of William, 1st laird of Erroll, iii. 556.
— — his wife, Ada, iii. 556.
— William de, 2nd son of David de H. of Erroll, iii. 557.
— William de, fell at Dupplin, iii. 560.
— William, 2nd son of Peter H. of Megginch, v. 218.
— William, 4th son of Peter H. of Megginch, v. 220.
— William, captain in earl of Morton's regiment, v. 224; ix. 122.
— William, 2nd son of 7th earl of Kinnoull, v. 231.
— William de, slain at Neville's Cross, viii. 421.
— Sir William de, commissioner to Rome, viii. 424 *n.*
— William, eldest son of Sir William H. Locherworth and Yester, viii. 425; ix. 164.
— William, son of John H., preceptor of St. Leonard's, viii. 445.
— William, eldest son of Alex. H. of Drumelzier, viii. 450.
— William, 2nd son of Wm. H. of Drumelzier, viii. 451.
— William, 3rd son of David H. of Belton, viii. 454.
— William, captain 83rd regt., viii. 456.
— William, 7th son of 1st marquess of Tweeddale, viii. 456.
— William, 2nd son of Sir David H. of Locherworth, ix. 165.
— *, 2nd wife of John Campbell of Liston Hall, i. 382.
— *, wife of Thos. Gordon of Ruthven, iv. 516.
— *, wife of Sir Andrew Fletcher of Innerpeffer, v. 230.
— *, wife of * Robertson, vii. 88.
Hay-Drummond of Cromlix, Arthur, v. 236.
— — his wife, Katharine Louisa Derby, v. 236.
— — Charles Rowley, col. Scots Fusilier Guards, v. 236.
— — his wife, Arabella Augusta Meyrick, v. 236.
— — Robert, capt. Coldstream Guards, v. 236.
— Sarah Maria, wife of Geo. Murray, bishop of Rochester, i. 491.
HAY-MACKENZIE, BARON CASTLEHAVEN OF CASTLEHAVEN, iii. 84-86.
HAY-MACKENZIE, EARL OF CROMARTIE, iii. 84-86.
HAY-MACKENZIE, BARON MACLEOD OF CASTLE LEOD, iii. 84.
HAY-MACKENZIE, VISCOUNT TARBAT OF TARBAT, iii. 84-86.

* Name unknown.

Hay-Mackenzie of Cromartie, Anne, wife of 3rd duke of Sutherland; countess of Cromartie, iii. 84; viii. 363, 461.
—— —— John, iii. 83, 520; viii. 461.
—— —— his wife, Annie Gibson-Craig, iii. 83, 520.
—— of Newhall, Edward, iii. 83, 519; viii. 460.
—— —— his wife, Maria Murray Hay-Mackenzie of Cromartie, iii. 83.
—— Constance, wife of Sir E. A. Stewart-Richardson, iii. 85.
—— Dorothea, wife of Sir D. Hunter Blair, 3rd bart., iii. 83.
—— Georgina Ann, wife of 5th earl of Glasgow, iii. 83; iv. 218; ix. 64.
—— Isabella, wife of John Buckle, iii. 83.
—— Janet Frances Isobel, iii. 86.
—— Roderick Grant, son of Sibell Lilian, countess of Cromartie; styled lord Tarbat, iii. 85.
Hay-Newton of Newton, John, viii. 461.
—— —— Richard, viii. 461.
—— —— his wife, Anne Stuart, viii. 461.
—— —— Richard, viii. 461.
—— —— William, viii. 461.
—— —— his wife, Alicia Foster, viii. 461.
—— Francis John Stuart, vii. 452.
—— —— his wife, Lucy Jane Fergusson, vii. 452.
—— Jean, wife of Jas. Walker of Dalry, viii. 461.
Hayes of Great Bedgbury, Sir James, iii. 612; viii. 454.
—— —— his wife, Rachel Hungerford, iii. 612.
—— Rachel, wife of David Hay of Belton, viii. 454.
Hayhurst, Dorothy, wife of (1) sergeant Hale, and (2) John Hay of Newhall, viii. 459.
—— Hesketh France, vicar of Middlewich, v. 253.
—— John, Quernmore, viii. 460.
Hayman, Frances Louisa, wife of 16th lord Somerville, viii. 42.
—— John, viii. 42.
Head the earl, witness to a charter, c. 1128, iv. 2 *n*.
—— of Ashfield, Roper, viii. 123.
—— Elizabeth Lindsay, wife of Sir N. A. Staples, i. 525.
—— Sir Francis Bond, 1st bart., lt.-governor of Upper Canada, viii. 38.
—— —— his wife, Julia Valenza Somerville, viii. 38.
—— James, commr. H.E.I.C. Navy, i. 525.
—— —— his wife, Cecilia Martha Harvey Lindsay, i. 525.
—— Mary Amelia, wife of gen. Samuel Dalrymple, viii. 123.
—— Sarah, wife of Patrick Ruthven, iv. 265.
Headlam, Elizabeth, wife of (1) Sir John Hotham, and (2) Sir John Constable, iii. 293.
Heardson of Claythorpe, Thomas, iii. 113.
—— —— his wife, Mary Lister, iii. 112.
Hearsey, * Middelburg, ix. 45.
—— *, 1st wife of David Gavin of Langton, ix. 45.
Heart of Chappell, Joseph, vi. 598.
—— —— his wife, Helen Makgill, vi. 598.
Heath of Stanstead, Thomas, iii. 113.
—— Frances, wife of (1) Henry Knight, and (2) 4th lord Deloraine, iii. 113.
Heathcote of Longton Hall, Robert Edensor, iii. 43.
—— —— his wife, Elizabeth Keith Lindsay, iii. 43.
—— of Normanton, Sir John, 2nd bart., vi. 382.
—— Bridget, wife of 13th earl of Morton, vi. 382.
—— Sir Gilbert, 4th bart., M.P., iii. 414.
—— —— his wife, Katharine Sophia Manners, iii. 414.
—— Sir Gilbert John, 5th bart., vii. 59.
—— —— his wife, Clementina, baroness Willoughby de Eresby, vii. 59.
—— John Cuthbert, ii. 213.
—— —— his wife, Eva Campbell, ii. 213.
—— S. J., vicar of Williton, ii. 213.
Heatley of Bairfoot, vii. 505.
—— Isobel, wife of Colin Mackenzie of Pluscardine, vii. 505; ix. 156.
Hectreda of Allerdale, wife of (1) Randulf de Lindesay, and (2) William de Esseville, iii. 3, 245.
Helbert, Charles Helbert, ii. 498.
—— —— his wife, Evelyn Mary Kennedy, ii. 498.
Hele of Halwell, Roger, vii. 94.
—— —— his wife, Julian Prestwood, vii. 94.
—— Julian, wife of (1) 3rd duke of Leeds, and (2) Charles, 2nd earl of Portmore, vii. 94.
Helen, 1st wife of David, 8th earl of Atholl, i. 425.
Helen, wife of (1) Malcolm, 7th earl of Fife, and (2) Donald, 6th earl of Mar, i. 427; iv. 9; v. 578.
Helen, alleged wife of Philip Seton, iii. 252; viii. 561.
Helen, alleged wife of David de Haya of Erroll, iii. 557 *n*.
Helen, wife of Sir Walter Fitzgilbert of Cadzow, iv. 341.
Helen, wife of Bernard of Airth, v. 329.
Helen, wife of (1) John Ker of Hilltoune, and (2) Lawrence Makgill, vi. 593.
Helias Fitz Huctred of Dundas, iii. 245.
Helias, brother of Jocelyn, bishop of Glasgow, iii. 423.

* Name unknown.

Hely-Hutchinson, Margaret Frances, wife of major D. J. Hamilton, i. 67.
Heming of Weddington, George, viii. 37.
— Amicia, wife of Hugh Somerville, viii. 37.
Henderson of Buscot Park, Sir Alexander, 1st bart., ii. 420.
— — Harold Greenwood, ii. 420.
— — his wife, Violet Charlotte Dalzell, ii. 420.
— of Fordel, Ann, wife of adm. Sir P. C. Durham, ix. 83.
— — James, justice-clerk, vii. 64.
— — James, i. 465; iii. 533.
— — his wife, Jean *or* Jonet Murray, i. 465.
— — Sir John, i. 537.
— — his 1st wife, Agnes Balfour, i. 537; ix. 32.
— — Sir John, vi. 321.
— — Sir John, 1st bart., ii. 88.
— of Latoun, Andrew, viii. 193.
— of Liston, John, viii. 461.
— Anna, wife of Archibald Stewart of Dunearn, vi. 321.
— Frances, wife of Robt. Lindsay, i. 525.
— Helen, wife of Wm. Murray of Romanno, viii. 19.
— Isaac, Rome, iii. 50.
— Isobel, wife of Thos. Stewart of Galston, vii. 64.
— James, ix. 92.
— — his wife, Margaret Ruthven, ix. 92.
— Jane, wife of James Hay, viii. 461.
— Janet, wife of (1) Wm. Elphinstone of Trosness, and (2) Thomas Livingston of Hayning, iii. 533; ix. 84.
— Joanna, wife of Patrick Ruthven, iv. 105.
— John, colonel, governor of Dumbarton Castle, iv. 105.
— Margaret, wife of 5th lord Blantyre, ii. 88.
— Matthew, murderer of Mrs. William Dalrymple, viii. 141.
— Ruth, wife of W. P. Lindsay, iii. 50.
Heneage of Hainton Hall, George, v. 547.
— Georgina Mary, wife of lieut.-col. Alastair E. Fraser, v. 547.
— Henrietta, wife of Lionel, lord Huntingtower, iii. 407.
Henley, Bridget, wife of (1) Robert Fox-Lane, and (2) John Tollemache, iii. 408; ix. 79.
Hennessy, R., vii. 153.
— — his wife, Martha Lucy *, vii. 153.
Henred of Barton, Richard de, vi. 524.
Henrison, Janet, wife of (1) Alex. Guthrie, and (2) David Carnegie of Kinnaird, viii. 64.

* Name unknown.

Henry, king of Scots, i. 26; vi. 354.
— — his wife, Mary, queen of Scots, i. 25.
Henry I., king of England, i. 3; iv. 136.
Henry II., king of England, i. 2.
Henry III., king of England, i. 6.
Henry IV., king of England, iii. 165, 263.
Henry VII., king of England, i. 21, 27.
Henry VIII., king of England, i. 21; iii. 608; vii. 121.
Henry IV., king of France, v. 617.
Henry V., emperor of Germany, i. 2.
— — his wife, Matilda of England, i. 2.
Henry, earl of Northumberland and Huntingdon, son of king David I., i. 4; iv. 5, 7.
— — his wife, Ada de Warenne, i. 4.
Henry, inf. son of David, earl of Huntingdon, i. 4.
Henry of Brechin, illeg. son of David, earl of Huntingdon, i. 4; ii. 214; iii. 6.
— — his wife, Julian, i. 4.
Henry of Stirling, illeg. son of David, earl of Huntingdon, i. 4; ii. 215; iii. 6.
Henry, abbot of Arbroath, 1198, i. 418.
Henry, son of Fergus of Carrick, iii. 426.
Henry, 2nd son of Alan of Ruthven, iv. 255.
Henry, abbot of Kelso, iv. 565.
Henry, 8th son of Alwin, 2nd earl of Lennox, v. 330.
Henry Frederick, duke of Rothesay and prince of Wales, eldest son of king James VI., i. 27; iii. 370; iv. 432; v. 617; vii. 213.
Henry of Straffan, John Joseph, v. 513.
— Charles John, v. 513.
— — his wife, Selina Constantia Hastings, v. 513.
— Charles Stewart, colonel Royal Horse Artillery, viii. 42.
— — his wife, Louisa Harriet Somerville, viii. 42.
— George, minister of Corstorphine, v 415.
HEPBURN, EARL OF BOTHWELL, ii. 135-167.
HEPBURN(E, LORD HAILES, ii. 135-167.
HEPBURN, DUKE OF ORKNEY, ii. 161-167.
Hepburn of Addinstoun, Christian, wife of 4th earl of Winton, viii. 602.
— — George, viii. 602.
— — his wife, Margaret Addinstoun, viii. 602.
— of Alderston, George, viii. 444.
— — his wife, Grizel Hay, viii. 444.
— of Auldhamstocks, Sir Alexander, ii. 146.
— — his wife, Jonet Cunynghame, ii. 146.
— — Thomas, ii. 145.
— of Ballinghard *or* Bonhard, Adam, legtd. son of Patrick H., bishop of Moray, ii. 143.
— — Patrick, illeg. son of bishop of Moray, ii. 143.

Hepburn(e of Bearford, Sir Robert, v. 247.
— of Beinston, John, ii. 142, 150, 178.
— — his wife, Margaret Douglas, ix. 40.
— — Patrick, 2nd son of 1st lord Hailes, ii. 142.
— — his wife, Christian Ogilvie, ii. 142, 178.
— — Sir Patrick, legtd. son of John H., ii. 142.
— — his wife, Margaret Cockburn, ii. 142.
— of Birkinsyde, James, ii. 154 *n.*
— — Patrick, ii. 154.
— — his wife, Agnes Hoppringle, ii. 154.
— — Patrick, ii. 154 *n.*
— — Robert, ii. 154 *n.*
— of Bolton, Patrick, styled master of Hailes, ii. 153, 163; iv. 454.
— — his 1st wife, Nicola Home, ii. 153; iv. 454.
— — his 2nd wife, Katharine Fleming, ii. 153.
— of Borthwick, ii. 115 *n.*
— of Cleishbeny, Patrick, bishop of Moray, ii. 143.
— of Clerkington, Robert, i. 92.
— — his wife, Katharine Gordon, i. 92.
— of Colbrandspath, Adam, ii. 135.
— of the Craigs, Sir Adam, ii. 136, 149, 155, 156, 163; vii. 408; ix. 129.
— — his wife, Elizabeth Ogstoun, ii. 136; vii. 408.
— — Adam, vi. 6.
— — his wife, Isabella Hume, vi. 6.
— — John, ii. 149.
— of Crashaws *or* Cracho, William, ii. 162.
— — his wife, Margaret Home, ii. 162.
— of Duntarvy, Robert, parson of Hauche, ii. 145.
— of East Craig, John, viii. 602.
— — Patrick, vi. 7.
— — his wife, Margaret Hume, vi. 7.
— — William, vi. 7.
— of Fairnington, Marie *or* Marioun, wife of James Hamilton, ii. 154.
— — Patrick, ii. 154; iv. 363.
— of Foorde, Elizabeth, wife of (1) Sir John Stewart of Bute, and (2) Sir Alex. Foulis of Colinton, ii. 294.
— — James, burgess of Perth, ii. 154.
— — his wife, Jonet Oliphant, ii. 155.
— — Robert, ii. 145, 294.
— of Fortoun, Henry, ii. 162.
— of Gilmerton, William, ii. 162.
— of Hailes, Adam, ii. 135.
— — his wife, Marion Fourbour, ix. 40.
— — Sir Adam, ii. 138; iv. 234; vii. 580; ix. 39, 40.
— — his wife, Janet Borthwick, vi. 351; ix. 39, 40.
Hepburn(e of Hailes, Sir Patrick, ii. 136.
— — his 1st wife, Agnes *, ii. 137.
— — his 2nd wife, Eleanor Douglas, ii. 137; iii. 142.
— — Patrick, the younger, ii. 137.
— — his wife, * de Vaux, ii. 138.
— — Sir Patrick, ii. 141; iii. 279; iv. 335.
— — his 2nd wife, Elene Wallace, ii. 142.
— of Humbie, Adam, viii. 124.
— — his wife, Margaret Dalrymple, viii. 124.
— — James, last laird, vii. 84.
— — Thomas, ii. 237; vii. 82; viii. 222.
— — his wife, Elizabeth Johnston, viii. 222.
— of Kirklandhill, John, ii. 163.
— — Patrick, ii. 163.
— of Luffness, Sir Patrick, vii. 67.
— of Magdalens, James, ii. 154.
— — Robert, ii. 145.
— of Malcolmston, Alexander, son of Patrick H. of Whitsome, ii. 147.
— of Merkill, John, ii. 136.
— of Nunraw, Sir Patrick, ii. 142.
— — his wife, Margaret Cockburn, ii. 142.
— of Pannywell, George, ii. 154.
— — his wife, Janet *or* Jayne Hepburn, ii. 154.
— of Pettyntoskane, Patrick, son of 1st lord Hailes, v. 434.
— of Prendergest, Sir Patrick, ii. 141.
— of Quhytcastell, Patrick, ii. 142.
— of Riccarton (*see* of Whitsome).
— of Rollandston, Agnes, wife of Wm. Hamilton, ii. 140.
— — George, son of Sir Adam H. ii. 139.
— — his wife, Jonet Malvyn, ii. 139.
— — George, custumar of Haddington, ii. 140.
— — his wife, Alison Hamilton, ii. 140.
— — James, son of Wm. H., ii. 154, 162, 163.
— — his wife, Jonet Oliphant, ii. 155.
— — John, custumar of Haddington, ii. 139.
— — his wife, Margaret Wricht, ii. 140.
— — Patrick, grandson of George H., ii. 140.
— — Patrick, son of George H. of Pannywell, ii. 154 *n.*, 155.
— — William, 3rd son of 1st earl of Bothwell, ii. 154.
— — his wife, Marion Maxwell, ii. 154.
— of St John's Chapel, Marie or Marion, wife of James Hamilton, ii. 154; iv. 363.
— of Sherefbygyn, Sir Patrick, sheriff of Berwick, ii. 141.
— of Smeaton, Patrick, iii. 121.
— of Southalls, Adam, ii. 135.

* Name unknown.

Hepburn(e of Traprain, Adam, ii. 135.
— of Tullibole, Laurenee, ix. 65.
— — his wife, Elizabeth Ramsay, iii. 95; ix. 65.
— of Waughton, David, viii. 384.
— — his wife, Christian Sandilands, viii. 384.
— — John, vii. 256.
— — his wife Mary Ross, vii. 256.
— — his alleged 2nd wife, Barbara Leslie, iv. 103.
— — Kentigern, vi. 5.
— — his wife, Margaret Lauder, vi. 5.
— — Patrick, 1423, iv. 445.
— — Sir Patrick, ii. 136, 149, 163; vi. 6.
— — his wife Helen Hepburn, ii. 149.
— — Sir Patrick, ii. 150; vii. 68.
— — Sir Patrick, i. 470; iv. 314.
— — his wife, Jean Murray, i. 470.
— of Whitsome and Riccarton, Alexander, 3rd son of 1st lord Hailes, ii. 143; v. 435.
— — his wife, Jonet Napier, ii. 144; vi. 407.
— — Sir Alexander, the younger, ii. 144.
— — his wife, Isobel Wardlaw, ii. 144; iii. 309.
— of Whitsome, Sir Alexander, admiral-depute, ii. 145.
— — his 1st wife, Elene Sinclair, ii. 145.
— — his 2nd wife, Marion Hay, ii. 145; ix. 41.
— — his 3rd wife, Marion Wardlaw, ii. 145.
— — Sir Alexander, of Darnley's household, ii. 145, 146, 162.
— — his wife, Jonet Cunynghame, ii. 146.
— — George, 3rd son of Sir Adam H., ii. 139.
— — his wife, Jonet Malvyn, ii. 139.
— — Patrick, ii. 145, 146.
— — his wife, Susanna Napier, ii. 147; vi. 416.
— of Newton of Whitsome, William, ancestor of the family of, ii. 162, 163.
— of Winterfield, John, vii. 256.
— — his wife, Mary Ross, vii. 256.
— Adam, dean of Dunbar, ii. 140.
— Adam, master of Hailes, ii. 142, 148; iv. 447, 448.
— — his wife, Elyne Home, ii. 148; iv. 448.
— Agnes, wife of 4th lord Livingston, ii. 144; v. 434.
— Agnes, dau. of Sir Alex. H., ii. 146.
— Agnes, dau. of Patrick H. of Whitsome, ii. 147.
— Agnes, wife of James Crichton of Ruthven, ii. 324.
— Agnes, wife of Alexander, master of Home, ii. 141; iv. 450; ix. 40, 107.
— Alexander, eldest son of Sir Alex. H. of Whitsome, ii. 146.
Hepburn(e, Alexander, vi. 17.
— — his wife, Margaret Drummond, vi. 17.
— Anna, wife of Sir Jas. Hamilton of Priestfield, iv. 314.
— Annabella, wife of George Soutar, ii. 154 *n.*
— Archibald, son of Patrick H., yr. of Hailes, ii. 138.
— Archibald, burgess of Haddington, ii. 138.
— Archibald, eldest son of Patrick H. of Whitsome, ii. 147.
— David, iv. 531.
— — his wife, Helen Gordon, iv. 531.
— David, lieut.-colonel, viii. 133.
— Elizabeth, wife of Alex., master of Montgomerie, ii. 141; iii. 432.
— Elizabeth, wife of John Lundy, ii. 145.
— Elizabeth, dau. of Sir Alex. H. of Whitsome, ii. 146.
— Elizabeth, wife of Wm. Lundin, ii. 148.
— Elizabeth, wife of (1) Sir Wm. Preston of Preston, and (2) Alex. Livingston of Dunipace, ii. 149; v. 429; ix. 41, 129.
— Elizabeth, wife of Geo. Ramsay of Dalhousie, iii. 95.
— Elizabeth, wife of P. Hume of Polwarth, vi. 6.
— Elizabeth, wife of William Innes of Innes and Forresterseat, vii. 355.
— Emilia, wife of Daniel Carmichael, iv. 592; ix. 114.
— Francis, 2nd son of Patrick H. of Smeaton, iii. 121.
— — his wife, Agnes Preston, iii. 121.
— Graeme, wife of Sir Robert Dalrymple Horn-Elphinstone, viii. 133.
— Euphemia, wife of A. Makdowell, ii. 148.
— George, son of Patrick H., bishop of Moray, ii. 143.
— George, dean of Dunkeld, ii. 147, 155.
— George, bishop of the Isles, ii. 147, 150, 155.
— George, alleged son of 1st earl of Bothwell, ii. 155.
— Gregory, ii. 139.
— Helen, wife of 2nd lord Somerville, ii. 141; viii. 12.
— Helen, dau. of Sir Alex. H., ii. 146.
— Helen, wife of Patrick Hepburn, yr. of Wauchton, ii. 136, 149, 163.
— Helen, wife of Walter, earl of Tarras, ii. 237; vii. 82.
— Isobel, dau. of Sir Alex. H., ii. 146.
— Isobel, wife of (1) Geo. Halkett of Pitfirrane, and (2) Sir Wm. Stewart of Pittenweem, vii. 68.
— James, bishop of Moray, ii. 144; v. 435; ix. 41.
— James, 4th son of Sir Alex. H., ii. 146.
— Jane, Janet, *or* Joanna, Mistress of

Bothwell; handfasted to Robert Lauder, and wife of (1) John Stewart, lord Darnley, (2) John Sinclair, master of Caithness, and (3) Archibald Douglas, i. 24; ii. 160, 168, 340; ix. 2, 41 *bis*.
Hepburn(e, Jane, Janet *or* Joanna, wife of 3rd lord Seton, ii. 140, 152; viii. 580.
— Jane, dau. of Sir Alex. H., ii. 146.
— Janet, wife of (1) J. Somerville, and (2) J. Auchinleck, ii. 150; viii. 14.
— Janet *or* Jayne, wife of Geo. Hepburn of Pannywell, ii. 154.
— Jean, wife of John Hay of Talla, ii. 154.
— Jean, wife of William, master of Ruthven, iv. 259; ix. 41.
— Jean, wife of (1) Thos. Ross of Craigie, and (2) Peter Oliphant of Turin, vi. 545.
— Joanna, wife of Sir John Stewart of Minto, ii. 80.
— John, bishop of Dunblane, ii. 140.
— John, prior of St. Andrews, founder of St. Leonard's College, ii. 147, 151, 155, 156; ix. 41 *bis*.
— John, parson of Dalry, ii. 150.
— John, bishop of Brechin, ii. 155.
— Sir John, colonel of the Scottish Regiment in France, iii. 216 *n*.
— John, minister of Old Greyfriars, Edinburgh, iv. 592.
— John, servant of the lord treasurer, vi. 422.
— Katharine, dau. of Sir Alex. H., ii. 146.
— Margaret, wife of 6th earl of Angus, i. 192; ii. 155; ix. 12.
— Margaret, wife of John Murray, i. 457.
— Margaret, dau. of Sir Alex. H. of Whitsome, ii. 146.
— Margaret, wife of (1) 2nd lord Haliburton, (2) Andrew Ker, and (3) A. Forrester of Corstorphine, ii. 148; iv. 86, 87, 335; vii. 324 *bis*; ix. 102.
— Margaret, wife of 1st lord Sinclair, ii. 150, 159, 336; v. 435.
— Margaret, wife of (1) J. Cockburn, and (2) J. Murray, ii. 155.
— Margaret, wife of Jas. Durhame, ii. 161.
— Margaret, wife of 1st earl of Glencairn, iv. 234.
— Margaret, wife of Sir D. Falconer of Glenfarquhar, v. 247 *bis*.
— Margaret, wife of Sir Wm. Elphinstone of Elphinstone, ix. 84.
— Maria, dau. of Sir Alex. H., ii. 146.
— Marion, wife of P. Livingston, ii. 144.
— Marion, dau. of Sir Alex. H., ii. 146.
— Marion, wife of Robert Hume of Heuch, vi. 6.
— Mariota, wife of P. Kinnaird of Inchture, v. 207.
— Patrick, writer, ii. 107.
— — his wife, Barbara Borthwick, ii. 107.
Hepburn(e, Patrick, bishop of Moray, ii. 142, 158, 162; iv. 58, 59 *n*.; viii. 94.
— Patrick, parson of Kinoir, ii. 110, 143; iv. 59.
— — his wife, Margaret Borthwick, ii. 110.
— Patrick, rector of Linton, ii. 148.
— Patrick, master of Hailes, ii. 153, 158.
— — his 1st wife, Nicolas Home, ii. 153.
— — his 2nd wife, Katharine Fleming, ii. 153.
— Patrick, slain 1501, vii. 368.
— Thomas, 3rd son of Sir Alex. H., ii. 146.
— William, 2nd son of Patrick H., yr. of Hailes, ii. 138.
— William, son of Sir Adam H., ii. 139.
— — his wife, Elizabeth Touris, ii. 139.
— William, illeg. son of 4th earl of Bothwell, ii. 167.
Hepburn-Murray of Balmanno, Sir Patrick, viii. 451.
— — his wife, Anne Hay, viii. 451.
Hepburne-Scott of Harden and Humbie, Hugh, vii. 84.
— — his wife, Harriet Bruhl, vii. 84.
— Alexander Noel, vii. 86.
— Anne, wife of Charles Baillie of Jerviswood, vii. 85.
— Charles Francis, vii. 86.
— — his wife, Elma Driver, vii. 86.
— Edith Christian, vii. 86.
— Elizabeth Ann, wife of col. C. Wyndham of Rogate, vii. 85.
— Francis, barrister-at-law, M.P., vii. 84.
— — his wife, Julia Frances Laura Boultbee, vii. 84.
— George, M.D., 3rd son of 8th lord Polwarth, vii. 86.
— — his wife, Anne Mary Smith, vii. 86.
— George William, rector of Kentisbeare, vii. 84.
— Georgina Mary, dau. of 8th lord Polwarth, vii. 86.
— Grizel Frances Katharine, vii. 86.
— Grizel Katharine, dau. of 8th lord Polwarth, vii. 86.
— Harriet Diana, dau. of 6th lord Polwarth, vii. 85.
— Harriet Frances, wife of Henry Baillie-Hamilton, iv. 327; vii. 85.
— Helen Georgina, dau. of 7th lord Polwarth, vii. 85.
— Helen Victoria, vii. 86.
— Henry Francis, 2nd son of 6th lord Polwarth, vii. 85.
— — his wife, Georgina Baillie, vii. 85.
— Henry James, 2nd son of 8th lord Polwarth, vii. 86.
— — his wife, Elizabeth Booth, vii. 86.
— Henry Robert, barrister-at-law, vii. 85.
— — his wife, Ada Home, iv. 483; vii. 85.

Hepburne-Scott, Katharine, dau. of 7th lord Polwarth, vii. 85.
— Katharine Grace, dau. of 8th lord Polwarth, vii. 86.
— Lilias, dau. of 8th lord Polwarth, vii. 86.
— Margaret Mary, vii. 86.
— Maria Annabell, wife of maj.-gen. G. C. D. Lewis, vii. 85.
— Mary Harriet, dau. of 8th lord Polwarth, vii. 86.
— Patrick John, vii. 86.
— Robert, 4th son of 8th lord Polwarth, vii. 86.
— Walter George, eldest son of 8th lord Polwarth; master of Polwarth, vii. 86.
— — his wife, Edith Frances Fowell Buxton, vii. 86.
— Walter Thomas, eldest son of Walter George H.-S., master of Polwarth, vii. 86.
— William Hugh, prebendary of Sarum, vii. 84.
— — his wife, Eleanor Sophia Baillie-Hamilton, vii. 84.
Herbert, Charles (Somerset), styled lord, v. 360.
— — his wife, Mary Villiers, v. 360.
HERBERT, LORD DINGWALL, iii. 125.
Herbert, the Chancellor, abbot of Kelso, iii. 424; iv. 4.
Herbert of Llanarth, John Arthur, iv. 423.
— — his wife, Augusta Hall, iv. 423.
— Anne Caroline, wife of Henry Fairfax, iii. 604.
— Auberon Edward William Molyneux, D.C.L., iii. 124.
— Frances, wife of 4th earl of Seaforth, vii. 510.
— Henrietta Maria Arienwen, wife of Walter Constable-Maxwell, iv. 423.
— John Carlyle, Maryland, iii. 604.
— Katharine, wife of 6th earl of Dunmore, iii. 394.
— Margaret, wife of 9th lord Fairfax, iii. 603.
— William, Virginia, iii. 603.
— Winifred, wife of 5th earl of Nithsdale, iv. 417; vi. 489.
Hereford, Humphrey de Bohun, earl of, i. 4.
— — his wife, Margaret of Scotland, i. 4.
— Humphrey de Bohun, last earl of, iii. 158.
Herford of Down Place, Henry, vi. 581.
— Hester, wife of major W. E. Fitzmaurice, vi. 581.
Hering, Herring of Gilmerton, Sir John, viii. 6.
— of Glasclune, James, ix. 145.
— — his wife, Elizabeth Oliphant, ix. 145.
— — *, iv. 272.
— — his wife, * Gray, iv. 272.

* Name unknown.

Hering of Lethendy, David, iii. 307.
— — his wife, Margaret Maitland, iii. 307.
— — James, i. 443.
— — his wife, Isabel Stewart, i. 443.
— — *, viii. 338.
— — his wife, Elizabeth Gordon, viii. 338.
— of Tullibole, James, ix. 145.
— Giles, wife of (1) Sir Wm. Somerville, and (2) Sir Wm. Fairlie, viii. 6.
— Janet, wife of John Campbell of Lundy, iii. 311.
Heriot of Burnturk, Walter, vii. 281.
— — his wife, Grisel Leslie, vii. 281.
— of Ramornie, Jean, wife of John Craige vi. 589.
— — William, captain, v. 316.
— of Trabroun, James, iv. 307; v. 298.
— — James, iv. 314; v. 298; viii. 390.
— — his wife, Isobella Maitland, v. 298; viii. 390.
— David, advocate, vi. 594.
— — his wife, Margaret Makgill, vi. 594.
— Elizabeth, wife of Thos. Hamilton of Priestfield, iv. 307.
— Elizabeth, wife of Wm. Livingston of Newbigging, viii. 373.
— Elizabeth, wife of 2nd lord Torphichen, viii. 390.
— George, goldsmith, vii. 217; viii. 373.
— — his 2nd wife, Alison Primrose, vii. 217.
— James, brother of George H., viii. 373.
— Margaret, wife of Thomas Ogilvie of Ogilvie, iii. 321.
— Ralouka, wife of W. G. L. Montagu Douglas Scott, ii. 246.
— Warner, col., ii. 246.
Heriot-Maitland of Ramornie, James, W.S., v. 316.
— — his wife, Margaret Dalgleish, v. 316.
Heriz family in Derbyshire and Nottinghamshire, iv. 398.
— of Elstaneford, Richard de, iv. 400.
— of Nithsdale, Robert de, iv. 400.
— of Westerkirk, Richard de, iv. 400.
— Gilbert de, iv. 399.
— Henry de, iv. 399.
— Ivon de, iv. 399.
— Nigel de, forester to Alexander II., iv. 399.
— Ralph de, iv. 399.
— Sir Robert de, seneschal of Annandale, iv. 399.
— Sir Robert, iv. 400.
— Roger de, iv. 399.
— Thomas de, iv. 399.
— William de, i. 231; iv. 399 *bis*.

* Name unknown.

Heriz, Sir William de, ii. 378; iv. 399 *bis*.
HERMITAGE, SCOTT, VISCOUNT OF, iii. 111-114.
Hermitage, Henry, first viscount of, ii. 239; iii. 111.
Heron of Chipchase, Sir Cuthbert, 1st bart., vii. 101.
—— —— his wife, Elizabeth Graham, vii. 101.
—— of Heron, Patrick, vii. 520.
—— —— Patrick, iii. 360.
—— —— his wife, Elizabeth Cochrane, iii. 360.
—— of Marieton, *, vi. 570.
—— —— his wife, * Sinclair, vi. 570.
—— of St. Mary's Isle, Patrick, vii. 520.
—— John the bastard, vii. 329.
—— *, husband of * Colville, ii. 537.
Heron-Maxwell of Springkell, Sir John Shaw, 4th bart., viii. 133, 134.
—— Helenora Katharine, wife of Hew D. Elphinstone-Dalrymple, viii. 134.
—— Mary, wife of Sir James Dalrymple-Horn-Elphinstone, viii. 133.
HERRIES OF CARLAVEROCK CASTLE AND EVERINGHAM, CONSTABLE - MAXWELL, LORD, iv. 423-424.
Herries of Carlaverock Castle, Marmaduke, lord, iv. 423.
HERRIES OF TERREGLES, HERRIES, LORD, iv. 393-413.
Herries of Terregles, Agnes, wife of John Maxwell; lady, iv. 409, 420.
—— —— Andrew, second lord, iv. 403, 404, 405; ix. 105 *bis*.
—— —— his 1st wife, Beatrix Herries, vi. 405.
—— —— his 2nd wife, Janet Douglas, i. 186; iv. 406; ix. 105.
—— —— his 3rd wife, Nicolas Home, iv. 407, 454.
—— —— Herbert, first lord, iii. 224; iv. 403.
—— —— his 1st wife, Mariot Carlyle, ii. 386; iv. 404.
—— —— his 2nd wife, Mariot Cunyngham, iv. 404.
—— —— William, third lord, iv. 369, 406, 407.
—— —— his wife, Katharine Kennedy, iv. 408.
HERRIES OF TERREGLES, MAXWELL, LORD, iv. 409-418.
Herries of Terregles, John, fourth lord, iv. 410.
—— —— his wife, Agnes, lady Herries of Terregles, iv. 409.
—— —— John, sixth lord, iv. 415, 421.
—— —— his wife, Elizabeth Maxwell, iv. 415.
—— —— John, seventh lord, iv. 416; ix. 106.
—— —— his wife, Elizabeth Gordon, iv. 417; vi. 487.

* Name unknown.

Herries of Terregles, Robert, eighth lord, iv. 417.
—— —— his wife, Lucy Douglas, i. 206; iv. 417.
—— —— William, fifth lord, iv. 413.
—— —— his wife, Katharine Ker, iv. 414; v. 455.
—— —— William, ninth lord, iv. 417.
—— —— his wife, Winifred Herbert, iv. 417.
HERRIES OF TERREGLES, CONSTABLE-MAXWELL, LORD, iv. 420-424.
Herries of Terregles, Gwendoline Mary, wife of 15th duke of Norfolk; baroness, iv. 423; ix. 106.
—— —— Marmaduke, eleventh lord, iv. 423; ix. 106.
—— —— his wife, Angela Mary Charlotte Howard, iv. 423.
—— William, tenth lord, iv. 419, 420.
—— —— his wife, Marcia Vavasour, iv. 422.
—— master of, Robert, eldest son of 7th lord Herries, v. 123; ix. 119 *bis*.
HERRIES, LORD HERRIES OF TERREGLES, iv. 398-413.
Herries of Bernwell, Andrew, iv. 401, 405.
—— —— Sir David, iv. 403.
—— of Hartwood, William, ix. 136.
—— of Kirkpatrick-Irongray, Robert, iv. 402.
—— of Mabie, George, iv. 402.
—— —— his wife, Mariot Murray, iv. 402.
—— —— Robert, 4th son of Sir Herbert H. of Terregles, iv. 402.
—— —— Robert, son of George H., iv. 402.
—— —— Robert, iv. 402.
—— of Maidenpaup, Archibald, iv. 404, 421.
—— —— George, iv. 405.
—— —— his wife, Janet Gordon, iv. 405.
—— —— John, ix. 124.
—— —— John, his son, iv. 405; ix. 124.
—— —— his wife, Elizabeth Maclellan, ix. 124.
—— —— Roger, 4th son of 1st lord Herries of Terregles, iv. 404, 406, 407.
—— —— William, iv. 405.
—— of Myrtoun, Robert, iv. 401, 402.
—— of Redcastle, Archibald, iv. 404.
—— of Terrauchty, George, iv. 402, 403; ix. 53, 105.
—— —— Robert, iv. 402; ix. 53.
—— —— his wife, Elizabeth Carlyle, ix. 53.
—— of Terregles, Sir David, 5th laird, iv. 403.
—— —— his wife, Margaret Crichton, iii. 222; iv. 403 *bis*.
—— —— Sir Henry, *error for* Sir Herbert, iv. 401 *n*.
—— —— Sir Herbert, 3rd laird, ii. 401; iv. 401.
—— —— his alleged wife, Margaret Douglas, iv. 402.

Herries of Terregles, Sir John, 1st laird, iv. 400.
— — his wife, Margaret [Douglas], iv. 400.
— — Sir John, 2nd laird, iv. 400, 402.
— — his wife, Euphemia Lindsay, iii. 12; iv. 400, 401.
— — John, 4th laird, iv. 402.
— Andrew, 2nd son of 2nd lord Herries of Terregles, iv. 406; ix. 105.
— Beatrix, wife of 2nd lord Herries of Terregles, iv. 406.
— David, 3rd son of Robt. H. of Mabie, iv. 402.
— Elizabeth, dau. of 2nd lord Herries of Terregles, iv. 406, 407.
— Herbert, curator to John H., and to Sir David H. of Terregles, iv. 402, 403 *bis*.
— James, 2nd son of Sir John H. of Terregles, iv. 401.
— Janet, 2nd wife of John Johnstone of that Ilk, i. 238.
— Janet, wife of col. William Graham of Boquhapple, vi. 151.
— Janet *or* Jean, wife of Sir James Cockburn of Skirling, iv. 409; ix. 105.
— Sir John, alleged 5th son of Sir John H. of Terregles, iv. 401.
— John, 4th son of Robt. H. of Mabie, iv. 402.
— John, 3rd son of 1st lord Herries of Terregles, iv. 404, 406; ix. 105.
— Katharine, wife of Alex. Stewart, yr. of Garlies, iv. 158, 408.
— Margaret, wife of Gilbert Maclellan, iv. 407; v. 269.
— Mariota, wife of (1) Sir David Stewart, and (2) Sir David Bruce, iii. 471.
— Mary, wife of Andrew Ker, v. 51 *n*.
— Mungo *or* Kentigern, 2nd son of 1st lord Herries of Terregles, iv. 404, 406.
— Richard, 2nd son of Robert H. of Mabie, iv. 402.
— Sir Robert, *perhaps* son of Sir John H., and his wife, Margaret Douglas, iv. 402.
— Robert, minister of Dryfesdale, ix. 136.
— William, 4th son of Sir John H. of Terregles, iv. 401.
— William, rector of Kirkpatrick, rector of Glasgow University, iv. 402.
— *, wife of Herbert, 1st lord Maxwell, iv. 402; vi. 475.
— *, wife of Sir John Macfarlane of that Ilk, iv. 405.
Herring, *see* Hering.
Herschel, Sir John, bart., i. 96.
— Caroline, wife of Sir Alex. Hamilton-Gordon, i. 96.
Herteshеved, Alan de, viii. 567.
Hertford, Edward (Seymour), 1st earl of, v. 355; vii. 120.

* Name unknown.

Hertford, Edward (Seymour), earl of, v. 357.
— — his wife, Frances Howard, v. 357.
— Francis (Seymour-Conway), 2nd marquess of, v. 18.
— — his wife, Isabella Anne Ingram, v. 18.
— Francis Charles, 3rd marquess of, v. 19.
— Francis Hugh George, 5th marquess of, viii. 212.
— — his wife, Emily Mary Murray, viii. 211.
— Hugh, 6th marquess of, ii. 530.
Hervey, son of Warin, vi. 25 *n*.
— of Bodvel, William, vii. 225.
— — his wife, Dorothea Arabella Primrose, vii. 225.
— of Langley Park, Robert, v. 200.
— — Sir Robert Bateson, bart., v. 200.
— Agnes Rosina, wife of major R. S. Carmichael-Smyth, iv. 571.
— Caroline, wife of 3rd duke of Buckingham and Chandos, v. 200.
— Henry, capt. R.N., iv. 571.
— Isabella Mary, wife of W. Drummond, viii. 231.
— Katharine Adine Geraldine, wife of A. H. Drummond, viii. 226.
— Lionel Charles, viii. 231.
Hesding, Avelina de, wife of Alan Fitz-Flaald, i. 10.
Heth, earl of Moray, vi. 284.
— — his wife, *, vi. 284.
Heton of Heton, Sir Henry, vii. 368.
— Joan, wife of Robert Rutherfurd, vii. 368.
Hewan, *, capt. 4th Dragoon Guards, v. 388.
— — his wife, Elizabeth Leslie, v. 388.
Hewes, Anna, wife of 2nd earl of Airth and Menteith, i. 141; ix. 9 *bis*.
Hewetson, Lydia, wife of rev. John Middleton, vi. 180.
— Nathaniel, in holy orders, vi. 180.
Hewett of Pishiobury, Sir William, ii. 581.
— — his wife, Elizabeth Wiseman, ii. 581.
— Elizabeth, wife of Thos. Richardson, master of Cramond, ii. 581.
Hextilda of Walwick, Carrow, Thornton, Henshaw and Bedrule, wife of (1) Richard Comyn, and (2) Malcolm, 2nd earl of Atholl, i. 3, 417, 504, 507, 508; ii. 252; iii. 6; vi. 288.
Hickes of Combe, Robert, viii. 32.
— of Dinder, Elizabeth, wife of capt. George Somerville, viii. 32.
Higford of Hartsfield, Higford, ii. 358.
— Lilian, wife of N. M. Sinclair, ii. 359.
Higgins, H. V., vii. 358.
Sir Hildred, in Cumberland, ii. 370.

* Name unknown.

Hildyard of Winestead, Sir Christopher, iii. 293.
—— his wife, Frances Constable, iii. 293.
Hill of Cathcart, James, ii. 513 *n.*
— Arthur Gibson, viii. 63.
— Elizabeth Ann, wife of C. H. Douglas-Hamilton, iv. 389.
— Ethel Lydia, wife of James C. Capel-Carnegie-Arbuthnott, viii. 63.
— H. D., rev. professor, ii. 196.
—— his wife, Margaret Borthwick, ii. 196.
— John, burgess of Edinburgh, vi. 591.
—— his wife, Agnes Makgill, vi. 591.
— Justly, archdeacon of Bucks, iv. 389.
— Katharine, wife of Thomas Fraser of Sauchok and Denis, iv. 112.
— Louisa, wife of Wm. Bruce, i. 553.
— Thomas, i. 553.
HILLHOUSE, DOUGLAS, LORD, vii. 146-147.
Hillhouse, William, lord, vii. 146.
HILLHOUSE, HAMILTON, LORD, vii. 361-363.
Hillhouse, John, first lord, vii. 361.
Hilton, John, ii. 194.
—— his wife, Elizabeth Marbrough Campbell, ii. 194.
— Sybil, wife of Michael Constable, iii. 291.
— William, iii. 291.
Hindenburg, baron Herbert von, v. 237.
—— his wife, Agnes Blanche Marie Hay, v. 237.
Hippisley of Lamborne Place, Henry, ii. 420.
— Emily Sulivan, wife of 11th earl of Carnwath, ii. 420.
Hislop, John, Dalkeith, v. 406.
—— his wife, Jane Lindsay, v. 406.
Histilla, *see* Hextilda.
Hlodver, eldest son of Thorfinn Skull-splitter, ii. 314.
Hoare of Mitcham Grove, William Henry, v. 215.
— Mary Jane, wife of 10th lord Kinnaird of Inchture, v. 215.
Hobart, Henrietta, wife of (1) 1st earl of Belmore, and (2) William, earl of Ancram, v. 483.
Hobhouse, Sir John Cam, 2nd bart., viii. 468.
—— his wife, Julian Thomasina Hay, viii. 468.
Hoby of Bisham, Sir Edward, 1st bart., viii. 183.
— Elizabeth, wife of (1) John Hoby, and (2) Henry, 5th earl of Stirling, viii. 183.
— John, M.P., husband of Elizabeth Hoby, viii. 183.
Hodelme *or* Hoddom, Odard of, i. 231; ii. 371, 377 *n.*
— Robert of, ii. 372.
Hoeufft, Petronella, wife of Constantyn W. F. Mackay, vii. 172.
Hodge of Gladsmuir, James, i. 139.
— Mary, wife of William Graham, i. 139.
— Robert, collector to the lords of Session, vi. 595.
—— his wife, Marie Makgill, vi. 595.
Hodges of Hemstead, Thomas Law, iii. 516; iv. 66.
— Frances Dorothea, wife of Robert Forbes, iv. 66.
— Henry, in holy orders, iii. 516.
—— his wife, Cordelia Murray, iii. 516.
— James, Masulipatam, i. 493.
— Mary Anne, wife of lord Wm. Murray, i. 493; ix. 29.
Hodgson, J. Crawford, Alnwick, iv. 299 *n.*
Hodgkinson, Mary Louisa Jane, wife of Alex. J. Boyle, iv. 209.
— William, New South Wales, iv. 209.
Hodierna, dau. of king David I., i. 4.
Hog of Newliston, Roger, viii. 157.
—— Thomas, v. 318.
—— his wife, Mary Julian Maitland, v. 138.
Hogg, James, the 'Ettrick Shepherd,' ii. 244.
Hohler of Fawkham Manor, Henry Booth, vii. 210.
— Constance Maud, wife of Eric N. Rollo, vii. 210.
Holder, Jeanie Theresa Sarah, wife of G. J. G. Carmichael-Smyth, iv. 572.
HOLDERNESSE, RAMSAY, EARL OF, iv. 301-302.
Holdernesse, John, earl of, iii. 96 *n.*; iv. 301, 312.
Holdernesse, Robert (D'Arcy), earl of, v. 481.
Holford of Westonbirt, George, i. 525.
—— Robert Stayner, i. 524.
—— his wife, Mary Anne Lindsay, i. 524.
— Alice, wife of 4th earl Grey, i. 525.
— Evelyn, wife of * Benson, i. 525.
— Margaret, wife of 3rd earl of Morley, i. 525.
Holland, Florent III., count of, i. 4; vii. 231.
—— his wife, Ada of Scotland, i. 4.
— Florent V., the Competitor, count of, i. 4; v. 577; vii. 231.
— Henry (Rich), 1st earl of, ii. 205.
HOLLAND, CAMPBELL, EARL OF, ii. 203, 204.
Holland, John, first earl of, ii. 203.
Holland of Holland, Georgina Carolina (Lennox); wife of Henry Fox; baroness, v. 365.
— Henry (Fox), lord, v. 365.
— Anne, wife of (1) John Nevill, (2) John Nevill, and (3) James, 9th earl of Douglas, iii. 183.
— Harriet, mistress of 2nd viscount Newcomen, ix. 82.

* Name unknown.

Holland, Philemon, ix. 88.
— Richard, precentor of Moray, iv. 528; vi. 310.
Hollings, Edmund Raven, vicar of St. John's, Bethnal Green, iv. 573.
— — his wife, Mary Carmichael, iv. 573.
Holmes, Leonard, lord, iii. 516.
— Edward, iii. 291.
— — his wife, Anne Strickland, iii. 291.
— Katharine, wife of Edward Rushworth, iii. 516; viii. 146.
— Thomas, vii. 225.
— — his wife, Charlotte Primrose, vii. 225.
Holt of Redgrave, Rowland, iv. 324.
— Mary, wife of (1) Gresham Lloyd, and (2) Thomas, 7th earl of Haddington, iv. 324; vii. 306.
Holwell, William, vicar of Menheniot, iii. 582.
Holyland, Mary, wife of Dr. Jas. Carmichael-Smyth, iv. 569.
— Thomas, Bromley, iv. 569.
— — his wife, Mary Elton, iv. 569.
HOLYROODHOUSE, BOTHWELL, LORD, iv. 425-439.
Holyroodhouse, Henry Bothwell of Glencorse, styled lord, iv. 433, 437.
— — his 1st wife, Mary Ramsay, iv. 437.
— — his 2nd wife, Mary Campbell, iv. 437, 439.
— John, first lord, iv. 431.
— — his wife, Maria Carmichael, iv. 433.
— John, second lord, iv. 431, 433; viii. 27; ix. 106.
— Alexander Bothwell, styled master of, iv, 433, 437.
Homan, Sir William Jackson, bart., ii. 307.
— — his wife, Charlotte Stuart, ii. 307.
HOME, HOME, LORD, iv. 440-484.
— Alexander, first lord, ii. 148; iv. 448; vi. 83; ix. 107.
— his 1st wife, Marion Lauder, iv. 449; vii. 319, 320; ix. 107.
— his 2nd wife, Margaret Montgomerie, iii. 433; iv. 449, 451.
— Alexander, second lord, i. 183; iii. 501; iv. 358, 359, 449 *bis*, 451; v. 50, 51, 149, 639.
— — his 1st wife, Isobel Douglas, iv. 359 *n.*, 453.
— — his 2nd wife, Nicola Ker, iv. 359 *n.*, 453.
— Alexander, third lord, iii. 282; iv. 454; vii. 330; ix. 107.
— — his wife, Agnes Stewart, ii. 157; iv. 456.
— Alexander, fifth lord, iv. 460, 473; v. 61; ix. 108.
— — his 1st wife, Margaret Ker, iv. 462; vii. 339.
— — his 2nd wife, Agnes Gray, iv. 283, 462.
Home, Alexander, sixth lord, ii. 171; iii. 283; iv. 266, 463, 474; v. 73, 462 *bis*.
— George, fourth lord, iv. 360, 453, 456, 458.
— — his wife, Mariota Haliburton, iv. 458, 460.
HOME, HOME, EARL OF, iv. 440-484.
Home, Alexander, first earl of, iv. 464; ix. 108.
— — his 1st wife, Christian Douglas, iv. 465; vi. 373.
— — his 2nd wife, Mary Sutton, iv. 465.
— Alexander, fourth earl of, iv. 479; ix. 108.
— — his wife, Anne Sackville, iv. 479.
— Alexander, seventh earl of, iv. 480; vi. 15.
— — his wife, Anne Ker, iv. 480; v. 479.
— Alexander, ninth earl of, iv. 481.
— — his 1st wife, Primrose Elphinstone, iii. 545; iv. 481.
— — his 2nd wife, Marion Home, iv. 481.
— — his 3rd wife, Abigail B. Ramey, iv. 481.
— Alexander, tenth earl of, iv. 482.
— — his wife, Elizabeth Scott, ii. 243; iv. 482.
— Charles, sixth earl of, iv. 479; ix. 109.
— — his wife, Anne Purves, iv. 479; ix. 109.
— Charles Alexander Douglas, twelfth earl of, iv. 483.
— — his wife, Maria Grey, iv. 483.
— Cospatrick Alexander, eleventh earl of, iv. 482.
— — his wife, Lucy Elizabeth Montagu, ii. 243; iv. 482.
— James, second earl of, iii. 611; iv. 466, 477.
— — his 1st wife, Katharine Cary, iii. 611; iv. 467.
— — his 2nd wife, Grace Fane, iv. 467; ix. 108.
— James, third earl of, ii. 413; iv. 475, 477.
— — his wife, Jean Douglas, iv. 478; vi. 378; ix. 108.
— James, fifth earl of, iv. 479.
— — his wife, Anne Ramsay, iii. 101; iv. 479.
— William, eighth earl of, iv. 480; ix. 109.
— — his wife, Elizabeth Gibbons, iv. 481.
HOME, DOUGLAS-HOME, EARL OF, iv. 482-484.
HOME OF BERWICK, HOME, BARON, iii. 287-289.
Home of Berwick, George, baron, iii. 286.
— master of, Alexander, eldest son of 1st lord Home, iv. 449.
— — his wife, Elizabeth Hepburne, ii. 150; iv. 450.
— master of, Alexander, eldest son of 2nd lord Home, iv. 454.
— master of, Alexander, elder son of 4th lord Home, i. 25; iv. 458, 459.
HOME, LORD COLDINGHAM, iv. 465-484.

HOME, LORD DUNGLAS, iv. 464-484.
HOME, EARL OF DUNBAR, iii. 280-289.
HOME, LORD HOME, iv. 440-484.
HOME, EARL OF HOME, iv. 440-484.
HOME, BARON HOME OF BERWICK, iii. 287-289.
HOME, LORD JEDBURGH, iv. 465-484.
Home of Ayton, Alexander, ix. 108.
—— —— his wife, Margaret Home, ix. 108.
—— —— George, 3rd son of 1st lord Home, iv. 449, 450 *bis*, 468; ix. 107.
—— —— James, 2nd son of 6th earl of Home, iv. 479, 481.
—— —— his wife, Elizabeth *or* Janet Haig, iv. 479.
—— —— Jean, wife of George Home, iv. 479 *bis*.
—— —— William, vi. 591.
—— of Balwoolsy, Sir Patrick, iv. 450.
—— of Bardstoun, Alexander, iv. 452.
—— of Bassendean, William, iv. 471, 473; ix. 108.
—— —— his wife, Marion Pringle, iv. 471.
—— of Bedrule, Harie, 3rd son of Sir Jas. H. of Cowdenknowes, iv. 473 *bis*.
—— —— his wife, Margaret Sinclair, iv. 473.
—— of Bedshiel, Alexander, iv. 453.
—— of Bellitaw, William, 5th son of Sir John H. of Cowdenknowes, ix. 108 *bis*.
—— —— his wife, Helen Edmestoun, iv. 471.
—— of Blackader, David, portioner, vi. 9.
—— —— John, 4th son of Sir David H. of Wedderhurn, iii. 281.
—— —— his wife, Beatrix Blackader, i. 189; iii. 281.
—— —— John, iv. 473.
—— —— Sir John, iv. 476.
—— —— his wife, Katharine Home, iv. 476.
—— —— Sir John, 3rd bart., iv. 321.
—— of Blackader Wester, Robert, 5th son of Sir David H. of Wedderburn. iii. 281.
—— —— his wife, Margaret Blackader, i. 189; iii. 281.
—— of Blaissinhraid, Sir Alexander, iv. 476.
—— of Blyth, Sir James, iv. 472.
—— of Bondynghame, Sir Patrick, iv. 450.
—— of Brigham, Sir Alexander, iv. 446.
—— of Brighamschelis, Sir David, iii. 281.
—— of Bromehill, Sir Alexander, iv. 476.
—— of Broomhouse, Patrick, vii. 367.
—— —— his wife, Helen Rutherfurd, vii. 367, 371.
—— of Brotherstanes, John, iv. 468.
—— of Broxfield, Alexander, iv. 455.
—— —— Margaret, wife of George, 5th earl Marischal, i. 158; iv. 462; vi. 53.
—— of Broxmouth, George, viii. 526.
—— —— his wife, Margaret Fleming, viii. 526.
—— —— George, iii. 285.
—— —— his wife, Katharine Lauder, iii. 285.
Home of Broxmouth, Sir George, iii. 287.
—— —— his wife, Elizabeth Gordon, iii. 288.
—— of Chirnside, Sir Alexander, iv. 448.
—— of Colhrandpeth, Sir Patrick, iv. 450.
—— of Coldingham, Alexander, iv. 464.
—— of Cowdenknowes, Sir James, iv. 472; ix. 108.
—— —— his wife, Katharine Home, iv. 473 *bis*.
—— —— Sir James, iii. 288.
—— —— his wife, Anne Home, iii. 288; iv. 475.
—— —— Sir James, eldest son of Sir James H. of Whitrig, iv. 475, 477.
—— —— his wife, Jean Douglas, iv. 478.
—— —— Sir John, iv. 469; v. 453.
—— —— his wife, Margaret Ker, iv. 470; vii. 334.
—— —— Sir John, iv. 474.
—— —— his 1st wife, Marie Sinclair, ii. 342; iv. 474; ix. 51, 108.
—— —— his 2nd wife, Beatrice Ruthven, iv. 266, 474.
—— —— Mungo, iv. 468.
—— —— his wife, Elizabeth Stewart, iv. 469.
—— of Crailing, John, iv. 467; v. 50.
—— —— Thomas, vii. 367.
—— of Cranshaws, David, ii. 342; iii. 285.
—— —— his wife, Katharine Lauder, iii. 285.
—— —— John, iii. 285.
—— of Crossrig, David, iv. 578.
—— of Crowde, Thomas, vii. 367.
—— of Crukisfeylde, Sir Alexander, iv. 446.
—— of Crumstane, Sir John, 3rd son of Sir Geo. H. of Manderston, ii. 591; iii. 285.
—— —— his wife, Marion Cranstoun, ii. 591.
—— of Darnchester, Alexander, iv. 470.
—— —— his wife, Janet Hamilton, iv. 471.
—— —— William, 2nd laird, iv. 471.
—— of Dunglas, Sir Alexander, iv. 444.
—— —— his wife, Jean Hay, iv. 445; viii. 426.
—— of Duns, George, 3d son of 1st lord Home, iv. 450.
—— —— Sir John, master of the Wardrobe to king James IV., iv. 450.
—— —— Sir John, iv. 476.
—— —— his wife, Katharine Home, iv. 476.
—— of Eccles, Sir George, iv. 473.
—— —— his wife, Jean Home, iv. 473.
—— —— Sir James, iv. 472.
—— —— his wife, Katherine Home, iv. 473.
—— —— Sir James, commendator of the Priory of Eccles, iv. 473, 477.
—— —— his wife, Isobel Home, iv. 463, 473.
—— of Edrom, David, iv. 578.
—— —— George, iv. 577.
—— —— his wife, Jonet Balfour, iv. 577.
—— —— Jonet, wife of Archibald Carmichael, iv. 577.
—— of Ersiltoun, John, iv. 450, 452, 467; vi. 144.
—— —— his wife, Margaret Ker, ii. 543; iv. 468; vii. 324.

Home of Ersiltoun, Sir John, iv. 469.
—— —— his wife, Margaret Ker, iv. 470; vii. 334.
—— —— Sir John, 5th laird, iv. 474.
—— —— his 1st wife, Marie Sinclair, iv. 474.
—— —— his 2nd wife, Beatrice Ruthven, iv. 266, 475.
—— —— Mungo, iv. 468.
—— —— his wife, Elizabeth Stewart, iv. 469; ix. 47.
—— of Ewisdale, Alexander, iv. 455.
—— of Fast Castle, Cuthbert, ii. 8; iii. 437; iv. 451.
—— —— his wife, Elizabeth Mairtene, ii. 8; iv. 451; ix. 107.
—— —— Sir Patrick, 4th son of 1st lord Home, ii. 8 *n.*; iv. 449, 450, 452, 468.
—— —— his 1st wife, *, iv. 450.
—— —— his 2nd wife, Isohel Forman, iv. 451.
—— of Fischwick, David, v. 463.
—— —— his wife, Margaret Dundas, v. 463.
—— of Forest of Dye, David, iii. 285.
—— of Friarness, Elizabeth, wife of (1) Sir Thos. Hay, and (2) James, lord Hamilton, earl of Arran, iv. 358, 454 *bis*; vii. 581 *bis*; viii. 431; ix. 165.
—— of Gartsherrie, Alexander, iv. 470.
—— of Godscroft, David, the historian, i. 189, 201; v. 111.
—— of Gordonshall, Sir Patrick, iv. 450.
—— of Graden, Alexander, iv. 470.
—— —— his wife, Janet Hamilton, iv. 471.
—— —— William, iv. 471.
—— of Greenlaw, Alexander, iv. 452.
—— —— Sir Alexander, 4th son of Sir John H. of Cowdenknowes, iv. 476.
—— —— Anna, wife of Sir Jas. Home of Whitrig, iv. 475.
—— —— William, iii. 251 *n.*, 254, 256.
—— —— his wife, M. the countess, iii. 251.
—— of Greenwood, Alexander, iv. 452.
—— of Halyburton, Sir Alexander, iv. 476.
—— —— his wife, Margaret Edmonston, iv. 476.
—— of Hassingdean, Alexander, iv. 455.
—— of Hassington, Sir Alexander, iv. 446.
—— of Herdrig, Sir Henry, iv. 475.
—— —— his wife, Katharine Nisbet, iv. 475.
—— of Hielaws, Alexander, 3rd son of Sir David H. of Wedderburn, iii. 282.
—— of Hogistoun, Sir Alexander, iv. 446.
—— of Home, Adaccus de, iv. 441 *n.*
—— —— Adam 'the Long' de, iv. 441 *n.*
—— —— Aldan de, *possibly* steward to the earls of Dunbar, iv. 441.
—— —— Sir Alexander, deputy keeper of Coldingham Priory, iv. 444, 446.
—— —— his wife, Janet Hay, iv. 445, 446; viii. 426.

* Name unknown.

Home of Home, Sir Alexander, sheriff-depute of Berwick, iv. 446; vi. 2; ix. 107.
—— —— his 1st wife, Marion Lauder, iv. 447; vii. 319, 320; ix. 107 *bis*.
—— —— his 2nd wife, Margaret Montgomerie, iii. 433; iv. 449, 551.
—— —— Alexander, eldest grandson of 1st lord Home, iv. 452.
—— —— his 1st wife, Isobel Douglas, iv. 453.
—— —— his 2nd wife, Nicola Ker, iv. 453.
—— —— Anna, wife of 2nd earl of Lauderdale, iii. 97; iv. 465, 467, 477; v. 303, 304; vi. 321; ix. 108.
—— —— Galfrid de, iv. 443.
—— —— Geoffrey, lord of, iv. 443.
—— —— Gilbert de, son of Aldin; steward of the earls of Dunbar, iv. 441.
—— —— Gregory de, iv. 443.
—— —— John, iv. 443.
—— —— his wife, Christian, iv. 443.
—— —— Sir John, their son, iv. 443, 446.
—— —— John de, father of Sir William de H., iv. 442.
—— —— Margaret, wife of 5th earl of Moray, iv. 465, 466, 477; vi. 321; ix. 139.
—— —— Robert de, son of Adam the Long, iv. 441 *n.*
—— —— Roger de, iv. 441 *n.*
—— —— Sir Thomas, iv. 443, 446.
—— —— his wife, Nicola Pepdie of Dunglas, iv. 444, 446.
—— —— William, son of Patrick, alleged ancestor of the family of, iv. 440.
—— —— his alleged wife, Ada, iv. 440, 442.
—— —— Sir William de, iv. 442.
—— —— William de, iv. 441, 442.
—— —— his 1st wife, Ada, iv. 443.
—— —— his 2nd wife, Mariota Ruthven, iv. 255, 443.
—— of Hordean, Sir Patrick, iv. 450.
—— of Horsley, Sir George, iii. 287.
—— of Hoscote, George, vii. 73.
—— of Howlaws, Sir Alexander, iv. 447.
—— of Hownam, John, v. 50.
—— of Huttonhall, Elizabeth, illeg. dau. of 3rd lord Home, iv. 458 *bis*.
—— —— Sir Alexander, iv. 449.
—— —— Alexander, illeg. son of John H., iv. 457, 580.
—— —— John, illeg. son of 3rd lord Home, iv. 457.
—— —— John, iv. 580.
—— —— his wife, Elizabeth Carmichael, iv. 580.
—— of Hyndlawhill, George, 2nd son of Sir Geo. H. of Manderston, iii. 284.
—— of Inverallon, Alexander, iv. 452.
—— —— Alexander, illeg. son of John H., iv. 457.
—— —— John, illeg. son of 3rd lord Home, i. 183; iv. 457.
—— of Jardinefield, Sir David, iii. 281.

Home of Jedburgh, Alexander, iv. 464.
— of Kames, George, iii. 283.
— — his wife, Margaret Home, iii. 283.
— — Henry, commissary of Lauder, iii. 283.
— — his wife, Christian Fletcher, iii. 283.
— of Kellie, George, iv. 177.
— of Lambden, Sir Alexander, iv. 446.
— of Langshaws, Sir Alexander, iv. 447.
— — Sir Thomas, 5th son of 1st lord Home, iv. 451, 468.
— — his 1st wife, Janet Rynd, iv. 451.
— — his 2nd wife, Alison Colquhoun, iv. 451.
— of Letham Hoippis, Alexander, parson of Spott and Dunbar, iv. 470.
— of Lintlaws, Sir Alexander, iv. 446.
— of Lumsden, Sir Patrick, 1st bart., iii. 282.
— of Machiehill, Nicholas, iv. 451.
— — his wife, Mariota Bothwell, iv. 451.
— of Manderston, Alexander, 2nd laird, iii. 282.
— — his wife, Barbara *, iii. 282.
— — Alexander, 3rd laird, iii. 283.
— — his wife, Jean Home, iii. 284.
— — Sir Alexander, 4th laird, ii. 168; iii. 284.
— — his wife, Christian Erskine, iii. 284; v. 84.
— — Sir Alexander, master of the Household to the princess of Orange, 6th laird, i. 285; iii. 284.
— — his wife, Margaret Moricson, iii. 284.
— — Alexander, 7th laird, iii. 284.
— — Sir David, 1st laird, iii. 282.
— — his wife, Isobel Hoppringil, iii. 281.
— — Sir George, 5th laird, i. 285; iii. 282, 284.
— — his 1st wife, Elizabeth *or* Isobel Home, iii. 284.
— — his 2nd wife, Helen Arnot, iii. 285; ix. 72.
— — John, vi. 12.
— of Maw, Alexander, iv. 452.
— of Mellerstain, John, iv. 458.
— of Mersington, Sir James, iv. 472.
— of Merton, Alexander, iv. 469.
— of Montgrenan, Sir Patrick, iv. 450.
— of East Morieston, Sir George, iv. 473.
— — Harie, iv. 473.
— — Mark, iv. 473.
— of Nesbitslee, Sir Patrick, iv. 450.
— of Ninewells, John, v. 247; ix. 158.
— of Paxton, William Forman, vii. 590.
— of Pincartoun, Sir George, iv. 473.
— — Sir George, commendator of Eccles, iv. 473.
— — Jean, wife of Sir Geo. Home, iv. 473.

* Name unknown.

Home of Polwarth, Sir David, iii. 281.
— of Preston, Sir Alexander, iv. 446.
— of Primroknow *or* Prymbroke-knolls, Sir George, iii. 286; viii. 97.
— of Quhytlaw, Jean, wife of Wm. Hamilton of Samuelston, iii. 286.
— — Sir William, iii. 286.
— — his wife, Mary Quhytlaw, iii. 286.
— of Rathburn, Patrick, 3rd son of Sir Thos. H. of Home, iv. 444, 445, 446.
— of Raufburn, Sir Patrick, iv. 451.
— of Reidpath, Anna, wife of Sir Jas. Home of Whitrig, iv. 475.
— of Renton, Alexander, iii. 282; ix. 72.
— — his wife, Margaret Cockburn, iii. 282.
— — Sir Alexander, 1st bart., iii. 282; viii. 596 *n*.
— — his wife, Margaret Scott, iii. 282.
— — Sir John, lord of Session and lord Justice-Clerk, iii. 282; viii. 596; ix. 72.
— — his 1st wife, Janet Home, iii. 282.
— — his 2nd wife, Margaret Stewart, ii. 172; iii. 282.
— — Patrick, 2nd son of Alex. H. of Manderston, iii. 282.
— of Restennet, Alexander, iv. 464.
— of Easter Rossy, George, iv. 450.
— of St. Leonard's, David, iii. 285.
— of Samuelston, Alexander, iv. 453.
— — his wife, Nicola Ker, iv. 453.
— — Janet, wife of Sir John Hamilton, iv. 363, 456.
— of Simprin, Bartholomew, 7th son of Sir David H. of Wedderburn, iii. 281.
— of Slegden, John, iii. 286.
— — his wife, Christian Cockburn, ix. 72.
— — Nicolas, wife of Robert Dickson of Stanefauld, iii. 286.
— of Smailholm, Harie, iv. 473.
— — John, iv. 468; v. 50.
— — Mungo, iv. 468.
— of Snuke, Sir Alexander, iii. 284.
— of Spott, Anna, wife of James Stewart, iii. 283; vi. 363.
— — George, ancestor of the family of, iv. 445, 446; ix. 106.
— — George, ii. 546; iii. 284.
— — his 2nd wife, Katharine Colville, ii. 546, 548.
— — George, ii. 546, 548; iii. 284; vi. 363.
— — Sir George, 3rd son of Sir Alex. H. of Manderston, iii. 287; v. 454.
— — his wife, Elizabeth Gordon, iii. 288.
— — Jean, wife of Alex. Home of Manderston, iii. 284.
— of Easter Spott, Alexander, iii. 283.
— of Steill, James, iii. 286.
— — John, iii. 286.
— of Stracathro, Alexander, iii. 283.

Home of Synlawis, Sir James, eldest son of Sir John H. of Cowdenknowes, iv. 472.
—— —— John, iv. 468, 469.
—— —— Sir John, vii. 334.
—— —— his wife, Margaret Ker, vii. 334.
—— of Thornton, Alexander, iv. 452.
—— of Tonchadam, Alexander, iv. 452.
—— of Tynnes, Alexander, iv. 455.
—— —— John, 'the king's Master Hunter,' iii. 283.
—— of Ulston, Alexander, iv. 463.
—— of Wedderburn, Sir David, 2nd son of Sir Thomas H. of Home, ii. 587; iii. 280; iv. 444, 445, 446 *bis*; vi. 1; vii. 319, 369.
—— —— his wife, Alicia, iii. 280; vi. 1 *bis*.
—— —— David, the younger, iii. 280; vi. 1.
—— —— his wife, Elizabeth Carmichael, iii. 280; vi. 1.
—— —— Sir David, father of 'the Seven Spears,' iii. 281, 282; vi. 2.
—— —— his wife, Isobel Hoppringle, iii. 281.
—— —— Sir David, 'a Spear,' i. 189; iii. 281.
—— —— his wife, Alison Douglas, i. 189.
—— —— Sir David, ii. 168; iv. 471 *n.*; v. 110, 111, 498.
—— —— David, ii. 592; iv. 476; vi. 12.
—— —— his wife, Margaret Home, iv. 476.
—— —— George, comptroller, iii. 280; iv. 473, 476; vi. 1. 23; vii. 580 *bis*; viii. 192.
—— —— his wife, Mariota St. Clair of Kimmerghame, iii. 280; iv. 448; vi. 2; vii. 580.
—— —— William Foreman, ii. 527.
—— of Whitrig, Sir James, eldest son of Sir John H. of Cowdenknowes, iv. 475.
—— —— John, iv. 450, 467; v. 50.
—— of Whitsome, Alexander, iii. 283.
—— of Whitsomelaws, Sir Patrick, iv. 450.
—— of Wolfflee, Sir David, ii. 587; vi. 1.
—— Ada, wife of H. R. H. Scott, iv. 483; vii. 85.
—— Adam, 2nd son of Sir Patrick H. of Fast Castle, iv. 451.
—— —— his wife, Janet Edmonstone, iv. 451.
—— Agnes, wife of P. Hume of Polwarth, iii. 283; vi. 7.
—— Albert, 3rd son of George H. of Hyndlawhill, iii. 285.
—— Alexander, eldest son of 1st lord Home, iv. 449; ix. 107.
—— —— his wife, Annes Hepburn, iv. 450; ix. 40, 107.
—— Alexander, illeg. son of John H., abbot of Jedburgh, iv. 453.
—— Alexander, parson of Spott and Dunbar, chanter of Ross, iv. 470; ix. 108.
—— Alexander, in holy orders, iv. 481.
—— —— his 1st wife, Primrose Elphinstone, iii. 545; iv. 481.
—— Alexander, younger son of Sir David H. of Wedderburn, vi. 1.
Home, Alexander, chamberlain of North Berwick, vi. 6, 10 *n.*
—— Alexander, son of John H. of Manderston, vi. 12.
—— —— his wife, Anne Hume, vi. 12.
—— Alexander, 4th son of Alex. H. of Renton, ix. 72.
—— Alexander H., captain R.N., vi. 2, 23.
—— Alicia, dau. of Sir Alex. H. of Home, iv. 445.
—— Alison, wife of A. Hamilton of Innerwick, iii. 286.
—— Alison, wife of Thos. Ramsay of Wyliecleuch, iv. 298.
—— Alison, wife of Sir Walter Ogilvy of Dunlugus, ii. 8; iv. 451.
—— Alison, wife of Sir Wm. Sinclair of Roslin, iv. 451.
—— Alison, wife of Henry Wardlaw of Torrie, iv. 457.
—— Andrew, parson and pensioner of Lauder, iii. 281.
—— Andrew, 6th son of 2nd lord Home, iv. 453.
—— Andrew, abbot and commendator of Jedburgh and Restennet, tutor of Home, iv. 461, 463; viii. 287; ix. 107.
—— Anna, dau. of Sir Geo. H. of Manderston, iii. 285.
—— Anna, wife of James Douglas, prior of Pluscardine, vi. 363.
—— Anna, wife of John Stewart of Coldingham, ix. 72.
—— Anna, dau. of 3rd earl of Home, ix. 108.
—— Anne, wife of Sir Jas. Home of Coldingknowes, iii. 288; iv. 475.
—— Anne, dau. of Alex. H. of Renton, ix. 72.
—— Barbara, wife of Robt. Cairncross of Colmslie, ix. 108.
—— Caroline, dau. of 9th earl of Home, iv. 481.
—— Charles, 3rd son of Sir John H. of Renton, iii. 282.
—— Charlotte, wife of ven. Charles Baillie Hamilton, iv. 323, 481.
—— Charlotte Lucy, dau. of 11th earl of Home, iv. 483.
—— Christian, wife of Patrick Dunbar of Kilconquhar, iii. 277.
—— Christiana, dau. of Sir Alex. H. of Home, iv. 445.
—— Cospatrick, lieut.-col. 3rd batt. Royal Scots, iv. 483.
—— David, 4th son of Sir Geo. H. of Manderston, iii. 285.
—— David, 7th son of 1st lord Home, iv. 451.
—— David, prior of Coldingham, iv. 453.
—— Edward, younger son of Adam H., iv. 451.
—— Elene, wife of Alex. Ramsay of Dalhousie, ix. 65.

Home, Eleonora, wife of major-gen. Thomas Dundas, iv. 481.
— Elizabeth, wife of Sir Geo. Home of Manderston, iii. 284.
— Elizabeth, wife of Theophilus, lord Howard de Walden, 2nd earl of Suffolk, iii. 288; iv. 475.
— Elizabeth, wife of (1) Sir Thos. Hay, master of Yester, and (2) James, lord Hamilton, 1st earl of Arran, iv. 358, 454 *bis*; vii. 581 *bis*; viii. 431; ix. 165.
— Elizabeth, wife of Thos. Ker of Kershaugh, iv. 444; v. 51 *n.*
— Elizabeth, wife of Sir Robt. Logan of Restalrig, iv. 451.
— Elizabeth, wife of David Hume of Rollandstoun, vi. 9.
— Elizabeth, wife of John Makgill, vi. 591.
— Elizabeth, dau. of 3rd earl of Home, ix. 108.
— Elizabeth Eleanora, dau. of 11th earl of Home, iv. 483.
— Elspeth, dau. of Alex. H. of Renton, ix. 72.
— Elyne, wife of (1) Sir Adam Hepburn, master of Hailes, and (2) Alexander, 3rd lord Erskine, ii. 148; iv. 447, 448; v. 608: ix. 107, 133.
— Francis Douglas, capt., claimant to the title of Marchmont, vi. 23.
— George, eldest of 'the Seven Spears of Wedderburn,' iii. 281.
— George, 4th son of Alex. H. of Manderston, iii. 283.
— George, 2nd son of Geo. H. of Hyndlawhill, iii. 285.
— George, son of Wm. H. of Kirklands of Bassendean, iv. 471.
— George, 3rd son of 6th earl of Home, iv. 479.
— — his wife, *, iv. 479.
— George, son of Andrew H., abbot of Jedburgh, ix. 107.
— George Douglas, 7th son of 11th earl of Home, iv. 483.
— Grisel, wife of John Rutherfurd, 'the Cock of Hunthill,' vii. 377.
— Helen, wife of (1) Sir Adam Hepburn, master of Hailes, and (2) Alexander, 3rd lord Erskine, ii. 148; iv. 448; v. 608; ix. 107, 133.
— Helen, dau. of Sir Patrick H. of Fast Castle, iv. 451.
— Helen, wife of James Hamilton of Innerwick, iv. 469.
— Helen, dau. of Alex. H. of Renton, ix. 72.
— Isabella, dau. of George H. of Wedderburn, iii. 280; ix. 72.
— Isobel, wife of William Cockburn of Cockburn, iii. 281.

* Name unknown.

Home, Isobel, wife of Sir Geo. Home of Manderston, iii. 284.
— Isobel, illeg. dau. of 3rd lord Home, iv. 457.
— Isobel, wife of Sir James Home of Eccles, iv. 463, 473.
— Isobel, wife of William Haig of Bemersyde, iv. 469.
— Isobel, wife of (1) George (?) Cranston of Corsbie, and (2) James Home, rector of Hilton, iv. 471.
— Isabel, dau. of 3rd earl of Home, iv. 478.
— Isabel, wife of Robert Ker of Ancrum and Woodheid, v. 461.
— Isabella, prioress of North Berwick, vi. 5.
— Isobel, dau. of Sir John H. of Renton, ix. 72.
— Isabella Jane, wife of commr. Charles St. Clair, vii. 590.
— James, rector of Hilton, iv. 471 *n.*
— — his wife, Isobel Home, iv. 471.
— James, vi. 10.
— — his wife, Elizabeth Hume, vi. 9.
— James Archibald, barrister-at-law, iv. 482.
— Jane, wife of (1) Patrick, lord Polwarth, and (2) capt. Bruce, iv. 479; vi. 16.
— Jane, dau. of 7th earl of Home, iv. 480.
— Janet, wife of Alex. Home of Renton, iii. 282, 285.
— Janet, wife of J. Cockburn of Ormiston, iii. 286.
— Jean, mistress of Robert, master of Erskine, v. 611.
— Jean, dau. of 3rd earl of Home, ix. 108.
— John, 2nd son of George H. of Wedderburn and Mariota St. Clair, iii. 280.
— John, prior of Coldingham, dean of the Chapel Royal, iv. 450.
— John, 3rd son of Sir Patrick H. of Fast Castle, iv. 451.
— John, abbot of Jedburgh, iv. 453, 454; v. 461.
— John, his illeg. son, iv. 453.
— John, another illeg. son, iv. 453.
— John, provost of Dunglas, iv. 463.
— John, legtd. son of Sir James H. of Cowdenknowes, iv. 474.
— John, Chirnside, iv. 407, 476.
— — his wife, Helena Belshes, iv. 476.
— John, ix. 100.
— — his wife, Jean Hamilton, ix. 100.
— John, 2nd son of Alex. H. of Darnchester, ix. 108.
— Jonet, dau. of Sir Alex. H. of Home, iv. 445.
— Jonet, dau. of Alex. H. of Renton, ix. 72.
— Juliana, wife of Sir John Gordon of Lochinvar, v. 111.

Home, Katharine, wife of James Edmondstoun of Ednam, iii. 281.
— Katharine, wife of (1) John Sinclair of Herdmanston, and (2) Archibald Douglas, iv. 448; vii. 580; ix. 107.
— Katharine, dau. of Cuthbert H., iv. 451.
— Katharine, wife of Sir Jas. Home of Cowdenknowes, iv. 473 *bis*.
— Katharine, wife of (1) Sir John Home of Duns, and (2) Sir John Home of Blacater, iv. 476.
— Machtilla, dau. of Geo. H. of Hyndlawhill, iii. 285.
— Marcia, dau. of Geo. H. of Hyndlawhill, iii. 285.
— Margaret, wife of George, 5th earl Marischal, i. 158; iv. 462; vi. 53; ix. 108, 134.
— Margaret, wife of John Stewart, ii. 171; ix. 41.
— Margaret, wife of lieut.-col. A. F. Cathcart, ii. 527.
— Margaret, wife of John Swinton of Swinton, iii. 281.
— Margaret, wife of George Home of Kames, iii. 283.
— Margaret, wife of John Hamilton, advocate, iv. 321.
— Margaret, wife of Alex. Bothwell, styled master of Holyroodhouse, iv. 438, 480.
— Margaret, wife of Sir Alex. Erskine of Gogar, iv. 460; v. 82.
— Margaret, wife of 5th earl of Moray, iv. 465, 466, 477; vi. 321; ix. 108, 139.
— Margaret, wife of Wm. Turnbull of Bedrule, iv. 471.
— Margaret, wife of (1) Sir Mark Ker of Littledean, and (2) David Home, iv. 476.
— Margaret, wife of (1) Hugh, 1st lord Campbell of Loudoun, and (2) Archibald Stewart of Ardgowan, v. 498.
— Margaret, wife of Matthew Sinclair, ix. 158.
— Margaret, dau. of Alex. H. of Renton, ix. 72.
— Margaret, wife of Alex. Home of Ayton, ix. 108.
— Marie, dau. of Sir John H. of Cowdenknowes, iv. 476.
— Marion, wife of Patrick Cranston of Corsbie, iv. 477.
— Marion *or* Mariota, wife of John, 6th earl of Crawford, iii. 24; iv. 454 *bis*.
— Mariota, wife of Jas. Towers of Inverleith, iii. 282.
— Marjory, dau. of 6th earl of Home, iv. 480.
— Mark, 3rd son of Sir John H. of Cowdenknowes, iv. 471.
— Mark, 5th son of Sir John H. of Cowdenknowes, iv. 476.
Home, Mary, wife of 1st viscount Garnock, iv. 177.
— Mary Louisa, wife of Archibald Borthwick, ii. 104.
— Matthew, illeg. son of John H., abbot of Jedburgh, iv. 453.
— Montagu Cospatrick, iv. 483.
— Nicholas, 6th son of 1st lord Home, iv. 451.
— Nicol, vi. 587.
— — his wife, Alisone Makgill, vi. 587.
— Nicola, wife of (1) Andrew, 2nd lord Herries, and (2) Patrick Hepburn of Bolton, ii. 153; iv. 406, 407, 454.
— Nicolas, dau. of Sir Alex. H. of Home, iv. 448.
— Patrick, 8th son of Sir David H. of Wedderburn, iii. 281.
— Patrick, 4th son of 2nd lord Home, iv. 453.
— Patrick, 2nd son of Alex. H. of Renton, ix. 72.
— Sibilla, wife of Henry Haitley of Mellerstaines, vi. 1.
— Thomas, in Tyninghame, iv. 445, 446.
— Thomas, elder son of Adam H., iv. 451.
— Thomas, illeg. son of Sir John H. of Cowdenknowes, iv. 476.
— William, stabler to king James VI., ii. 169.
— — his wife, Mary Whitelaw, ii. 169.
— William, 5th son of Sir Geo. H. of Manderston, iii. 285.
— William, 5th son of 2nd lord Home, iv. 453, 456.
— William, 2nd son of 1st earl of Home, iv. 465.
— William, provost of Dunglas, iv. 465.
— William, sheriff-depute of Berwickshire, iv. 478.
— William Montagu Douglas, iv. 482.
— William Sholto, major-general, iv. 483.
— *, wife of Sir W. Baillie of Lamington, iv. 93.
— *, wife of Sir John Oliphant of Aberdalgy, iv. 444.
Home, *see also* Hume.
Home-Drummond of Blair Drummond, Henry, i. 499.
— Anne, wife of 6th duke of Atholl, i. 499.
Home-Home of Longformacus, John, ii. 104.
Hommel, Helene, wife of Daniel Mackay, vii. 173.
Honeyman of Graemsay, Patrick, ii. 354; iv. 168.
— — his wife, Margaret Sinclair, ii. 354.
— Katharine, wife of M. G. J. Stewart, iv. 168.
Hood, Andrew, in Balgay, v. 208.

* Name unknown.

Hood, Sir Samuel, bart., admiral R.N., vii. 514.
— — his wife, Mary Frederica Elizabeth Mackenzie, iv. 166; vii. 514.
Hooper, Nicholas, ii. 559.
— — his wife, Margaret Clyntoun, ii. 559.
Hoorne of Duffel, Marie van, wife of (1) Thierry de Lienden, and (2) Sir Alex. Stewart, earl of Mar and Garioch, v. 588.
— — William van, v. 588.
— — his wife, Marie van Randerode, v. 588.
HOPE, HOPE, LORD, iv. 493-505.
Hope, Charles, first lord, iv. 493.
— Charles, eldest son of 2nd lord Hopetoun; styled lord, iv. 497, 500.
HOPE, VISCOUNT OF AIRTHRIE, iv. 493-505.
HOPE, LORD HOPE, iv. 453-505.
HOPE, EARL OF HOPETOUN, iv. 485-505.
HOPE, BARON HOPETOUN OF HOPETOUN, iv. 500-505.
HOPE, MARQUESS OF LINLITHGOW, iv. 485-505.
HOPE, BARON NIDDRY OF NIDDRY, iv. 502-505.
Hope of Abercorn, John, iv. 493.
— of Airthrey, Sir James, vi. 238.
— of Balcomie, Sir William, 1st bart., iv. 492.
— of Belmont, James, W.S., iii. 547.
— — his wife, Gertrude Buller-Fullerton-Elphinstone, iii. 547.
— of Bridge Castle, Thomas, vii. 524.
— of Byres, Charles, iv. 320, 493.
— of Caldecottes, Thomas, iv. 488.
— of Cowdenknowes, Charles, vii. 524; viii. 83.
— — his wife, Isabella Julie Carnegie, vii. 524.
— of Craighall, Sir John, 2nd bart., lord of Session, lord Craighall, iv. 489.
— — his wife, Margaret Murray, iv. 489.
— — Sir Thomas, 1st bart., king's advocate, i. 133; ii. 441; iv. 487; viii. 572 *n.*
— — his wife, Elizabeth Bennet, iv. 489; viii. 577 *n.*
— — Sir Thomas, 3rd bart., iv. 490.
— — his wife, Elizabeth Aytoun, iv. 490.
— of Craigiehall, Charles, 3rd son of 1st earl of Hopetoun, iv. 494.
— — his 1st wife, Catherine Weir, iv. 494.
— — his 2nd wife, Anne Vane, iv. 494.
— — his 3rd wife, Helen Dunbar, iv. 494.
— of Easter Drylaw, Edward, iv. 486.
— — his 1st wife, Katharine Paterson, iv. 486.
— — his 2nd wife, Janet Watson, iv. 486.
— of Edmonston, Thomas, iv. 488.
— of Feathorstone Castle, James, iv. 502.
Hope of Granton, Sir Alexander, cupbearer to king Charles I., iv. 490.
— — his wife, Anne Bell, iv. 491.
— — Charles, lord president of the Court of Session, iv. 212, 495.
— — his wife, Charlotte Hope, iv. 495, 499.
— — William, 9th son of Sir James H. of Hopetoun, iv. 492.
— — his wife, Elizabeth Clerk, iv. 493.
— of Western Granton, Thomas, iv. 488.
— — Sir Thomas, lord Justice-General, iv. 490.
— of Greenbraes, Alexander, iv. 486.
— — his wife, Katharine Douglas, iv. 486.
— of Hopetoun, Charles, iv. 320, 493.
— — his wife, Henrietta Johnstone, iv. 493.
— — Sir James, lord of Session, iv. 491.
— — his 1st wife, Anna Foulis, iv. 492.
— — his 2nd wife, Mary Keith, iv. 492; vi. 60.
— — John, iv. 318, 493; ix. 109.
— — his wife, Margaret Hamilton, iv. 318, 493.
— of Kerse, Sir Alexander, 1st bart., iv. 490.
— — his wife, Louisa Hunter, iv. 490.
— — Sir Alexander, 2nd bart., ii. 32.
— — his wife, Nicolas Hamilton, ii. 32.
— — Sir Alexander, 3rd bart., vi. 501.
— — his wife, Anna Carnegie, vi. 501.
— — Sir Thomas, lord Justice-General, iv. 490.
— — his wife, Helen Rae, iv. 490.
— of Kininmounth, Thomas, iv. 488.
— of Kirkliston, Sir William, iv. 492.
— of Luffness, George William, ii. 243.
— — his wife, Caroline Georgina Montagu, ii. 243.
— — Henry Walter, vii. 227.
— — his wife, Mary Katharine Constance Primrose, vii. 227.
— of Prestongrange, Thomas, iv. 488.
— of Rankeillour, Sir Archibald, lord of Session, iv. 490.
— — his wife, Margaret Aytoun, iv. 490.
— — Sir John, general, 6th son of 2nd earl of Hopetoun, iv. 498, 501.
— — his 1st wife, Elizabeth Hope, iv. 496.
— — his 2nd wife, Louisa D. Wedderburn, iv. 502.
— of St. Mary's Isle, John, captain R.N., vii. 524.
— — his wife, Rebecca Marion Blackburn, vii. 524.
— of Waughton, Charles, major-general, M.P., iv. 498.
— — his wife, Louisa Anne Hatton, iv. 498.

Hope, Adrian, C.B., colonel 93rd Highlanders, iv. 503.
— Sir Alexander, col., G.C.B., lieut.-governor of Edinburgh Castle, M.P., iv. 499; v. 484.
— — his wife, Georgina Brown, iv. 499.
— Alicia, dau. of 4th earl of Hopetoun, iv. 504.
— Anne, wife of 2nd lord Cardross, ii. 366; iv. 491; ix. 109.
— Anne, dau. of Sir Jas. H. of Hopetoun, iv. 492.
— Anne, dau. of 1st earl of Hopetoun, iv. 497.
— Anne, dau. of 2nd earl of Hopetoun, iv. 498.
— Charles, R.N., commissioner at Chatham dockyard, iv. 496.
— — his wife, Susan Anne Sawyer, iv. 496.
— Charles, advocate, lieut.-governor of Isle of Man, iv. 503.
— — his wife, Isabella Helen Douglas, iv. 503; vii. 523.
— Charles Archibald, 2nd son of 6th earl of Hopetoun, iv. 504.
— Charles Dunbar, capt. R.F.A., vii. 524.
— — his wife, Edythe Mary Ramsden, vii. 524.
— Charles Melbourne, 2nd son of 1st marquess of Linlithgow, iv. 504.
— Charlotte, wife of Charles Hope of Granton, iv. 495, 499.
— Charlotte, wife of Thomas, lord Erskine, iv. 497; v. 632.
— Christian, wife of Thos. Graham of Balgowan, ii. 523; iv. 497.
— David, goldsmith, iv. 487.
— Dorothea Louisa, iv. 504.
— Edward Stanley, C.B., vi. 400.
— Elizabeth, wife of Ninian Lowis, iv. 486; ix. 109.
— Elizabeth, wife of Hugh Wycht, iv. 486.
— Elizabeth, dau. of Sir Thos. H. of Craighall, iv. 491.
— Elizabeth, dau. of Sir James H. of Hopetoun, iv. 492.
— Elizabeth, wife of Sir John Hope of Rankeillour, iv. 496, 502.
— Elizabeth, wife of Henry, earl of Drumlanrig, iv. 498; vii. 144.
— Elizabeth, wife of rev. Dr. John Kemp, iv. 499.
— Elizabeth, wife of Patrick Rig, ix. 109.
— Elizabeth Caroline, wife of Henry William Edmond (Fitzmaurice), earl of Kerry, vi. 400.
— Estella Mary, iv. 504.
Hope, Sir George, admiral R.N., iv. 496.
— — his 1st wife, Jemina Johnstone-Hope, iv. 496, 501.
— — his 2nd wife, Georgina Mary Anne Kinnaird, iv. 496; v. 213.
— George, captain R.N., iv. 503.
— — his wife, Anne Carmichael Napier, iv. 503; vi. 437.
— George, St. Albans, eldest son of Sir Thos. H., ix. 109.
— Helen, wife of 6th earl of Haddington, iv. 318, 321, 493.
— Helen, wife of James Watson of Saughton, iv. 497.
— Helen, wife of rev. John Sandilands, viii. 397.
— Hele Charlotte, wife of John Knight, iv. 496.
— Helen Jacqueline, wife of Alan Burns of Cumbernauld, vii. 524.
— Henrietta, dau. of John H., M.P., iv. 496.
— Henrietta, wife of 6th lord Napier of Merchiston, iv. 496; vi. 432.
— Henrietta, dau. of 2nd earl of Hopetoun, iv. 498.
— Henry, burgess of Edinburgh, iv. 487.
— — his wife, Jaqueline de Tott *or* Joanna Juvitot, iv. 487.
— Henry, burgess of Edinburgh, eldest son of Henry H., iv. 487; ix. 109.
— Henry, lieut.-governor of Canada, iv. 496.
— — his wife, Sarah Jones, iv. 496.
— Henry, 5th son of 2nd earl of Hopetoun, iv. 498.
— Henry, 5th son of 4th earl of Hopetoun, iv. 503.
— James, writer, iv. 487 *ter*.
— James, W.S., Keeper of the Signet, iv. 212; viii. 397.
— — his wife, Elizabeth Boyle, iv. 212.
— Sir James, admiral, K.C.B., v. 214.
— — his 1st wife, Frederica Eliza Kinnaird, v. 214.
— Jane, dau. of 4th earl of Hopetoun, iv. 504.
— Jean, wife of (1) Henry, viscount Melville, and (2) Thomas, 1st lord Wallace, iv. 498, 503.
— Jean Elizabeth, iv. 500.
— John, of the county of Peebles, 1296, iv. 485.
— John de, alleged ancestor of the Hopetoun family, iv. 485.
— — his wife, Elizabeth Cumming, iv. 485.
— John, *alias* 'Petit John, trumpet,' iv. 485.
— John, burgess of Edinburgh, iv. 485.
— — his wife, Elizabeth Eumont, iv. 486.

Hope, Sir John, G.C.H., lieut.-general, iv. 495.
— — his 1st wife, Mary Scott, iv. 495.
— — his 2nd wife, Jane Hester Macdougall, iv. 495.
— John, M.P., iv. 495.
— — his wife, Mary Breton, iv. 495.
— John, 3rd son of 2nd earl of Hopetoun, iv. 498.
— John, partner with Geo. Wemyss, viii. 497.
— Jonet, dau. of Edward H., iv. 486.
— Katharine, wife of Richard Brown, iv. 486; ix. 109.
— Katharine Marion, vii. 524.
— Louis, capt. Coldstream Guards, iv. 503.
— — his wife, S. F. S. Dumaresq, iv. 503.
— Louisa Albertina, wife of rear-admiral Swynfen Thomas Carnegie, vi. 506.
— Louisa Dorothea, wife of rev. Henry Francis Charles Ker, v. 484.
— Louisa Margaret, wife of Lionel A. A. Tollemache, ix. 80.
— Magdalene, dau. of Edward H., iv. 486.
— Margaret, dau. of Charles Hope-Vere, iv. 496.
— Margaret, wife of John Dundas of Duddingston, iv. 496.
— Margaret, wife of Alex. Maclean of Ardgour, iv. 499.
— Mary, wife of Sir Charles Erskine of Bandeath, iv. 491; v. 622.
— Mary Anne, wife of Sir P. Murray of Ochtertyre, iv. 499.
— Mary Dorothea, dau. of 1st marquess of Linlithgow, iv. 504.
— Rachel, wife of D. Betoun of Balfour, iv. 492.
— Sara, wife of Mr. John Brown, iv. 486.
— Sophia, wife of 5th earl of Findlater, iv. 39, 496.
— Sophia, wife of 8th earl of Haddington, iv. 325, 498.
— Thomas, Leith, iv. 485.
— Thomas, 8th son of 4th earl of Hopetoun, iv. 503.
— William, 6th son of 4th earl of Hopetoun, iv. 503.
— Sir William, admiral R.N., i. 270; iv. 495.
— — his wife, Anne Johnstone Hope, i. 270; iv. 496, 500.
Hope-Johnstone of Annandale, John James, claimant of Annandale peerages, 1820, i. 270.
— John James, claimant in 1876, i. 271.
— Mary, dau. of adm. Sir Wm. Hope, i. 270.
Hope-Scott of Abbotsford, James Robert, iv. 422.
— — his wife, Charlotte Lockhart, iv. 422.
Hope-Scott, Mary Monica, wife of Joseph Constable-Maxwell, iv. 422.
Hope-Vere of Blackwood, Charles, iv. 494.
— — James Joseph, viii. 468.
— — his wife, Elizabeth Hay, viii. 468.
Hope-Weir of Blackwood, William, 1st Dragoon Guards, iv. 494; ix. 109.
— — his wife, Sophia Corrie, iv. 495.
— of Craigiehall, Charles, iv. 494.
— — William Edward, ii. 498.
— — his wife, Mary Boyle, ii. 498.
Hope-Wallace of Featherstone Castle, James, iv. 502.
— — his wife, Mary Frances Nugent, iv. 503.
HOPETOUN, HOPE, EARL OF, iv. 485-505.
Hopetoun, Charles, first earl of, iv. 318, 320, 493.
— — his wife, Henrietta Johnstone, i. 269; iv. 494.
— James, third earl of, i. 269; iv. 500.
— — his wife, Elizabeth Carnegie, iv. 500; vi. 503.
— John, second earl of, iv. 497.
— — his 1st wife, Anne Ogilvy, iv. 39, 497.
— — his 2nd wife, Jean Oliphant, iv. 497.
— — his 3rd wife, Elizabeth Leslie, iv. 497; vi. 115.
— John, fonrth earl of, i. 270; iv. 498, 501.
— — his 1st wife, Elizabeth Hope, iv. 496, 502.
— — his 2nd wife, Louisa Dorothea Wedderburn, iv. 502.
— John, fifth earl of, iv. 504.
— — his wife, Louisa Macdonald, iv. 504.
— John Adrian Louis, seventh earl of, iv. 504.
— — his wife, Hersey Alice Eveleigh de Moleyns, iv. 504.
— John Alexander, sixth earl of, iv. 504.
— — his wife, Etheldred Anne Birch Reynardson, iv. 504.
— Victor Alexander John, eighth earl of, vi. 504.
HOPETOUN OF HOPETOUN, HOPE, BARON, iv. 500-505.
Hopetoun of Hopetoun, James, first baron, iv. 500.
Hoppar, Adam, provost of Edinburgh, custumar of Inverness, iv. 427 *bis*.
— — his wife, Katharine Bellenden, ii. 62; iv. 427.
— Isobel, wife of (1) John Murray of Blackbarony, and (2) Sir A. Douglas of Kilspindie, i. 185; iii. 501, 502; ix. 83 *bis*.
— Richard, burgess of Edinburgh, vi. 99.
— — his wife, Katharine Adamson, vi. 99.
Hoppringle of Hoppringle, James, ii. 103.
— — Mariota, alleged wife of 2nd lord Borthwick, ii. 98.

Hoppringle of Galashiels, Andrew, ii. 110.
—— his wife, Mariota or Marion Borthwick, ii. 110.
—— James, ii. 107.
—— his wife, Mary Borthwick, ii. 107.
— of St. John's Chapel, George, ii. 154.
—— his wife, Elizabeth Ker, ii. 154.
— of Smailholm, David, iii. 281.
— Agnes, wife of P. Hepburn, ii. 154.
— Alexander, in Coldstream, iv. 298.
—— his wife, Margaret Ramsay, iv. 298.
— Christine, wife of John Rutherfurd of Hunthill, vii. 376.
— Elizabeth, prioress of Coldingham, iii. 283.
— Isobel, wife of Sir David Home of Wedderburn, and mother of 'the Seven Spears,' iii. 281.
— Jonet, in Coldstream, iv. 298.
— Margaret, wife of Andrew Arbuthnott of that Ilk, i. 298.
— Robert, vi. 6.
—— his wife, Katharine Hume, vi. 6.
Hore of Cragyn, Walter, v. 549.
— of Harperstown, Walter, vii. 391.
—— his wife, Mary Elizabeth Thornton, baroness Ruthven, vii. 391.
— James Ruthven, in holy orders, vii. 391.
HORE-RUTHVEN, LORD RUTHVEN OF FREELAND, vii. 391-393.
Hore-Ruthven, Alexander Gore Arkwright, capt. 1st Dragoon Guards, vii. 392.
—— his wife, Zara Eileen Pollok, vii. 392.
— Alexander Leslie Melville, vii. 391.
— Alison Mary, vii. 392.
— Anne, vii. 391.
— Beatrix Mary Leslie, wife of (1) C. L. Orr-Ewing, and (2) C. E. Malcolm, vii. 393.
— Bridget Helen, vii. 392.
— Cavendish Bradstreet, lieut. R.N., vii. 391.
— Charles Edward Stewart, 51st regt., vii. 391.
—— his wife, Marianne Wood, vii. 391.
— Christian Malise, captain 42nd Highlanders, Black Watch, vii. 393.
— Georgina Jocelyn, vii. 392.
— Jane Stewart, wife of George O'Grady, vii. 392.
— Jean Elizabeth St. Loe, vii. 392.
— Margaret Leslie, vii. 392.
— Maria Frederica, vii. 391.
— Mary Elizabeth, vii. 391.
— Mary Lowen, wife of rev. W. H. Sutton, vii. 391.
— Philip James Leslie, vii. 393.
—— his wife, Lydia Gladys Adams, vii. 393.
— Walter, major H.E.I.C.S., vii. 391.
— Wilhelmina, vii. 391.
Hore-Ruthven, Wilhelmina Dells Owena wife of rev. C. B. Griffith, vii. 391.
— William, vii. 391.
—— his wife, Dells Honoria Lowen, vii. 391.
Horn, Elizabeth, wife of Louis, lord of Beverwaerth; countess, i. 522.
— of Horn, Anne, wife of Hew Dalrymple of Drummore, viii. 132.
—— John, advocate, viii. 132.
— of Westhall, John, advocate, i. 310, 312.
—— his wife, Anne Arbuthnott, i. 310.
Horndon of Pencrebar, William, viii. 87.
— David, viii. 87.
—— his wife, Dorothy Olivia Renny-Strachan-Carnegie, viii. 87.
Hornes, Elizabeth Philippina, wife of prince Gustavus Adolphus of Stolberg-Guedern, and princess of, iii. 481.
— Maximilian, prince de, iii. 480.
—— his wife, Marie Theresa Charlotte Bruce, iii. 480.
Horrie, Margaret, wife of Henry Stewart of Killinnan, i. 397.
Horsburgh of Horsburgh, Alexander, viii. 444.
—— his wife, Jean Hay, viii. 444.
—— Alexander, viii. 444.
Horsley-Beresford, Caroline Agnes, wife of (1) James, 4th duke of Montrose, (2) W. S. Stirling Crawfurd, and (3) Marcus H. Milner, vi. 272.
Horsman, William, viii. 122.
—— his wife, Jane Hamilton-Dalrymple, viii. 122.
Horton of Howroyde Hall, Thomas, i. 94.
—— his wife, Mary Gordon, i. 94.
Hotham, Beaumont Williams, vii. 209.
— Sir John, iii. 293.
—— his wife, Elizabeth Headlam, iii. 293.
— Mary Eleanor, wife of William C. W., master of Rollo, vii. 209.
Hothersall, Elizabeth, wife of Francis Ford, ii. 566.
— John, ii. 566.
Houghton, Katharine, wife of 2nd earl of Galloway, iv. 161.
— Sir Richard, bart., iv. 161.
Houston of Coilsfield, Patrick, iii. 447.
— of Cottreoch, William, ix. 116.
—— his wife, Katharine McCulloch, ix. 116.
—— William, their son, ix. 116.
— of Houstoun, John, v. 434; vii. 531.
—— his wife, Margaret Sempill, vii. 531.
—— John, iv. 433; vii. 531.
—— his wife, Elizabeth Sinclair, ii. 334.
—— Sir John, 1615, v. 190.
—— Sir John, vi. 68.
—— his wife, Anne Drummond, vi. 68.
—— Sir John, ii. 520; ix. 81.
—— his wife, Eleonora Cathcart, ii. 520; ix. 58, 81.

Houston of Houston, Sir Patrick, vii. 257.
— — Sir Patrick, 1st bart., ii. 28; iii. 417; vii. 477.
— — his wife, Anna Hamilton, ii. 28.
— Agnes, wife of James, 3rd lord Livingston, v. 433, 434.
— Anne, wife of Alex. Cunninghame of of Craigends, ii. 520.
— Elizabeth, wife of (1) John Whitefoord, and (2) Sir Wm. Ross of Muriston, vii. 257.
— Elizabeth, wife of M. Fleming of Beghall, viii. 530.
— Helen, wife of John Shaw, ii. 86.
— James, sub-dean of Glasgow, iii. 439.
— Janet, wife of Sir Wm. Montgomerie of Giffen, iii. 430.
— Jean, wife of (1) Walter Dundas, (2) Richard Lockhart of Lee, and (3) Ludovic Graut of Grant, vii. 477 *bis*.
— Margaret, wife of (1) Robert, 2nd lord Lyle, and (2) Andrew, 2nd lord Gray, iv. 277; v. 554.
— Margaret, wife of (1) Sir W. Livingston of Kilsyth, and (2) John Cornwall of Bonhard, v. 190; ix. 120.
— Peter, v. 554, 555.
— — his wife, Mariota Lyle, v. 554.
— Sir William, general, G.C.B., v. 318.
— — his wife, Jane Maitland, v. 318.
Howard of Bindon, Thomas (Howard), viscount, v. 357.
— of Escrick, Edward (Howard), baron, vii. 106.
— of Glossop, Edward (Howard), 1st lord, iv. 423; v. 516.
— de Walden, Theophilus (Howard), 2nd baron, iv. 475.
— — his wife, Elizabeth Home, iii. 288; iv. 475.
— of Corby, Philip J. C., iv. 419.
— — his wife, A. C. Constable-Maxwell, iv. 419.
— of Worksop, Thomas, i. 412.
— — his wife, Mary Elizabeth Savile, i. 412.
— Alfred John, ii. 499.
— — his wife, Mary Alice Kennedy, ii. 499.
— Alice Mary Elizabeth Fitzalan, wife of 10th earl of Loudoun, v. 516.
— Angela Mary Charlotte, wife of 11th lord Herries of Terregles, iv. 423.
— Anne, wife of Alexander, lord Garlies, iv. 160.
— Anne, wife of (1) Rich, 5th viscount Irvine, and (2) brigadier-general William Douglas, v. 16.
— Anne, wife of Richard, 1st viscount of Preston, vii. 106.
— Anne, wife of 1st earl of Carlisle, vii. 106.
Houston, Charles, grandson of 1st earl of Berkshire, iii. 112.
— Sir Charles, K.B., viii. 124.
— Dorothy, wife of col. James Graham of Levens, vii. 102.
— Edward George Fitzalan, ii. 311.
— Elenore, wife of admiral John Dalrymple, viii. 124.
— Elizabeth, wife of (1) Sir Robt. Southwell, and (2) John, earl of Carrick, ii. 442.
— Elizabeth, wife of George, 1st duke of Gordon, iv. 550; ix. 111.
— Esmé William, C.V.O., C.M.G., vi. 459.
— — his wife, Maria Isabella Giustiniani-Bandini, vi. 459.
— Frances, wife of Sir Edw. Villiers, ii. 207.
— Frances, wife of Colin Lindsay of Deerpark, iii. 46.
— Frances, wife of (1) Robert, earl of Essex, and (2) Robert, earl of Somerset, v. 71.
— Frances, wife of (1) Henry Prannell, (2) Edward, 1st earl of Hertford, and (3) Ludovick, 2nd duke of Lennox, v. 357; ix. 126.
— Frederick John, M.P., ii. 499.
— — his wife, Fanny Cavendish, ii. 499.
— Gwendolen Mary Anne, wife of 3rd marquess of Bute, ii. 311.
— Hannah, wife of 10th earl of Rothes, vii. 306.
— Harriet Elizabeth Georgiana, wife of 2nd duke of Sutherland, viii. 362.
— Henry, father of 1st earl of Effingham, vii. 512.
— — his wife, Mary Mackenzie, vii. 512.
— James, grandson of Theophilus, earl of Suffolk, i. 30.
— — his wife, Charlotte Jemima Henrietta Boyle *or* Fitzroy, i. 30.
— Katharine, wife of (1) George, Seigneur d'Aubigny, and (2) James, 1st viscount of Newburgh, v. 358; vi. 453.
— Margaret, wife of 2nd earl of Leven, v. 379.
— Mary, wife of 4th lord Aston of Forfar, i. 412; ix. 26.
— Mary, wife of (1) 1st lord Deloraine, and (2) W. Wyndham, iii. 112.
— Mary Rachel, dau. of 15th duke of Norfolk, iv. 423.
— Matthew, Hackney, vii. 306.
— Thomas, colonel, v. 360.
— — his wife, Mary Villiers, v. 360.
— William, 4th son of 1st earl of Berkshire, vii. 102.
Howburn, *see* Hepburn.
Howden, James C., M.D., vii. 207.
— — his wife, Eliza Rollo, vii. 207.
Howe, Richard William (Penn), 1st earl, i. 72.
— — his 2nd wife, Anne Gore, i. 72.

Howe, Sir William, vi. 115.
Howie *or* Howieson, John, minister of Cambuslang, ii. 80.
Hownam, William de, v. 277.
Hoya, James Spens, Swedish ambassador, count of, ix. 100.
Hozier, Henry Montagu, colonel, C.B., i. 131.
—— —— his wife, Henrietta Blanche Ogilvy, i. 131.
Huck, Albertine Louise, wife of (1) Marshall Field, and (2) Maldwin Drummond, viii. 230.
—— Louis C., Chicago, viii. 230.
Huctred of Tynedale, i. 3, 504.
Huddleston, Thomas, i. 64.
—— —— his wife, Elizabeth Mackworth, i. 64.
Hugh Kevilioc, earl of Chester, i. 4.
Hugh, son of Duncan, 4th earl of Angus, i. 165.
Hugh, son of Freskin; ancestor of the earls of Sutherland, ii. 121; viii. 320.
Hugh, abbot of Newbotle, iii. 423 *n*.
Hugh, 2nd son of Gillemichael, 3rd earl of Fife, iv. 5; viii. 475.
Hugh, bishop of St. Andrews, iv. 441 *n*.
Hugh, son of Leving of Levingston, v. 422 *n*.
Hugh of Kinmonth, son of William, vi. 529.
Hugh, abbot of Abernethy, vii. 396.
Hugh, son of Orm of Pitgrunzie, vii. 398.
Hugh, prior of Inchaffray, viii. 244, 245 *n*.
Hugh of Markinch, grandson of Gillemichael, earl of Fife, viii. 475.
Hughes of Berryhall, John, viii. 597.
—— Mary, wife of John Seton, viii. 597.
—— capt., i. 307.
—— —— his wife, Josette Arbuthnott, i. 307.
Humberston of Humberston, May, wife of major Wm. Mackenzie, vii. 510, 513.
—— —— Matthew, vii. 510.
—— —— Thomas Frederick Mackenzie, vii. 510, 513.
Humberston-Mackenzie of Humberston, Francis, M.P., vii. 510, 513.
Humble, Margaret, wife of (1) F. B. Close, (2) C. F. Gordon, and (3) Granville A. Gordon, iv. 561.
—— W. F., Chester, iv. 561.
HUME OF BERWICK, HUME, BARON, vi. 22-23.
Hume of Berwick, Alexander, lord, vi. 22.
—— —— his wife, Annabella Yorke, vi. 23.
HUME, VISCOUNT BLASONBERRIE, vi. 14-24.
HUME, BARON HUME OF BERWICK, vi. 22-23.
HUME, EARL OF MARCHMONT, vi. 1-24.
HUME, LORD POLWARTH, vi. 14-24.
HUME, LORD POLWARTH OF POLWARTH, REDBRAES, AND GREINLAW, vi. 14-24.
Hume of Argaty, Alexander, 3rd laird, vi. 4.
—— —— George, 2nd laird, vi. 4, 157.
—— —— his wife, Margaret Erskine, vi. 4.
Hume of Argaty, George, last laird, vi. 4.
—— —— Margaret, vi. 4.
—— —— Patrick, 1st laird, vi. 3.
—— of Auchinvald, Patrick, vi. 3.
—— of Bedshiel, George, vi. 11.
—— —— his wife, Isabel Hume, vi. 11.
—— of Belshele, Patrick, vi. 6.
—— of Brighamshiels, Patrick, vi. 2.
—— of Byrecleuch, Alexander, vi. 5.
—— of Carculanrig, Sir Patrick, vi. 10.
—— of Castellaw, Patrick, vi. 3.
—— of Castle Hume, Sir John, bart., i. 45.
—— —— his wife, Sidney Hamilton, i. 45.
—— of Channaybank, Alexander, vi. 5.
—— of Coldstream, Thomas, vi. 11.
—— of Correquhormbie, Sir Patrick, 2nd son of Geo. H. of Argaty, vi. 4.
—— of Drumchose, George, 7th son of Patrick H. of Polwarth, vi. 9 *bis*.
—— of Estraw, Patrick, vi. 3.
—— of Fishwick, Sir Patrick, vi. 10.
—— of Glenshee, Patrick, vi. 3.
—— of Hawkslaw, Robert, 6th son of Sir Patrick H. of Polwarth, vi. 11.
—— of Hetschawe, Patrick, vi. 3.
—— of Heuch, Alexander, 2nd son of Alex. H. of Polwarth, vi. 5.
—— —— Alexander, provost of Edinburgh, vi. 6, 8.
—— —— Robert, vi. 5.
—— —— his wife, Marion Hepburn, vi. 6.
—— —— Robert, 3rd laird, vi. 6; viii. 442.
—— —— his contracted wife, Grizel Hay, viii. 442.
—— of Hutton Bell, Patrick, vi. 9.
—— —— his 1st wife, Elizabeth Hume of Hutton Bell, vi. 9.
—— —— his 2nd wife, Anne Cockburn, vi. 9.
—— —— William, vi. 9.
—— of Inchanach, Patrick, vi. 3.
—— of Johnscleugh, Alexander, 2nd son of Patrick H. of Polwarth, vi. 6, 8.
—— —— Alexander, 3rd laird, vi. 8.
—— —— Archibald, vi. 8.
—— —— Gavin, vi. 8.
—— —— his wife, Helen Acheson, vi. 8.
—— of Kimmerghame, Alexander, vi. 5.
—— —— Andrew, lord of Session, lord Kimmerghame, v. 545; vi. 16.
—— —— his wife, Elizabeth Douglas, vi. 16.
—— —— Sir David, iii. 281.
—— —— George, 5th son of Sir Patrick H. of Polwarth, vi. 11.
—— —— his wife, Isabel Hume, vi. 11.
—— —— George, vi. 11; vii. 219.
—— —— his wife, Margaret Primrose, vi. 11; vii. 219.
—— —— George, iv. 479.
—— —— his wife, Jean Home of Ayton, iv. 479.
—— —— Robert, vi. 11.
—— —— his wife, Katharine Hume, vi. 11.

Hume of Kimmerghame, Robert, vi. 11.
— of Kingsrig, Sir Patrick, vi. 10.
— of Law, Patrick, vi. 4.
— — his wife, Margaret Wemyss, vi. 4.
— — Patrick, his son, vi. 4.
— — Patrick, vi. 10.
— — his wife, Jean *or* Janet Hume, vi. 10.
— of Lundies, Alexander, ii. 181.
— — his wife, Mariot Campbell, ii. 181.
— — George, ii. 181, 552; vi. 4, 157.
— — his wife, Margaret Erskine, vi. 4.
— — Patrick, vi. 3.
— of Miltoun, Patrick, vi. 3.
— of Murehouse, Patrick, vi. 3.
— of Ninewells, David, iv. 476.
— — his wife, Helena Belshes, iv. 476.
— — David, the philosopher, v. 248.
— — John, v. 247; ix. 158.
— — his wife, Mary Norvell, v. 247.
— — Joseph, v. 248.
— — his wife, Katharine Falconer, v. 247.
— of North Berwick, Alexander, vi. 5.
— — Alexander, provost of Edinburgh, iv. 93; vi. 6, 7, 8, 10 *n*.
— — Alexander, son of Adam H., vi. 7.
— — his wife, Elizabeth Cockburn, vi. 7.
— — Sir John, vi. 8.
— — his wife, Margaret *, vi. 8.
— of Northfield of Coldingham, Sir Patrick, vi. 10.
— of Polwarth, Alexander, 2nd laird, vi. 3, 4.
— — his 1st wife, Elizabeth Wardlaw, vi. 5.
— — his 2nd wife, Margaret Crichton, iii. 224; vi. 5.
— — his 3rd wife, Margaret Lauder, vi. 5.
— — David, eldest son of Geo. H. of Wedderburn, vi. 2.
— — Patrick, 1st laird, vi. 1.
— — his 1st wife, Margaret Sinclair of Polwarth, iv. 443; vi. 2; vii. 580.
— — his 2nd wife, Ellen Schaw, vi. 3.
— — Patrick, alleged 2nd laird, vi. 3 *n*.
— — his alleged wife, Mary Edmonston, vi. 3 *n*.
— — Patrick, 3rd laird, vi. 6.
— — his wife, Elizabeth Hepburn, vi. 6.
— — Patrick, 4th laird, vi. 7.
— — his wife, Agnes Home, iii. 283; vi. 7.
— — Sir Patrick, 5th laird, vi. 10.
— — his wife, Julian Ker, v. 68; vi. 11.
— — Sir Patrick, 1st bart., vi. 11.
— — his wife, Christian Hamilton, vi. 12.
— — Sir Patrick, 2nd bart., vi. 12; ix. 42.
— — his wife, Grisell Ker, vi. 14, 15.
— of Redbraes, Alexander, vi. 4.
— — Patrick, vi. 7.
— of Reddane, Sir Patrick, vi. 10.

* Name unknown.

Hume of Rednach, Patrick, vi. 3.
— of Rollandstoun, Alexander, vi. 9.
— — his 2nd wife, Lilias Dundas, vi. 9.
— — David, vi. 9.
— — his wife, Elizabeth Home, vi. 9.
— of Strathbran, Patrick, vi. 3.
— of Trottenshaw, Alexander, vi. 5.
— of Tully Castle, Sir Charles, 4th bart., vi. 9.
— — Sir George, 1st bart., vi. 8.
— — his wife, Mary Maynard, vi. 9.
— — Sir Gustavus, 3rd bart., vi. 9.
— — Sir John, 4th son of Patrick H. of Polwarth, vi. 8.
— — his wife, Margaret *, vi. 8.
— — Sir John, 2nd bart., vi. 9.
— — his wife, Sidney Hamilton, vi. 9.
— of Vigornshalch, Patrick, vi. 3.
— of Easter Lawis of Whitsome, Sir Patrick, vi. 10.
— of Wodehousleye, Patrick, vi. 3.
— Adam, vi. 407.
— — his wife, Janet Napier, vi. 407.
— Adam, parson of Polwarth, v. 404; vi. 7, 10 *n*.
— — his wife, Christian Dewar, vi. 7.
— Alexander, the poet, minister of Logie, vi. 7.
— — his wife, Marion Duncanson, vi. 8.
— Alexander, eldest son of Sir John H. of North Berwick, vi. 8.
— Alexander, colonel in Russian service, vi. 12.
— Sir Alexander, lord of Session, styled lord Cessnock, vi. 18.
— — his wife, Margaret Campbell, vi. 19.
— Alison, wife of Sir Jas. Schaw of Sauchie, vi. 4.
— Alison, wife of (1) David Edmonstone of Woolmet, and (2) Thomas Rutherfurd of Hunthill, vi. 10; vii. 378.
— Andrew, legtd. son of Gavin H., vi. 6.
— Anne, wife of Robert French of Thornydikes, vi. 7.
— Anne, wife of Thomas Aikenhead, vi. 8.
— Anna, wife of Sir John Seton of Barns, vi. 9.
— Anne, wife of Alexander Home, vi. 12.
— Anne, wife of Sir Jas. Hall of Dunglas, vi. 17.
— Caleb, son of Mr. Alex. H., vi. 8.
— Christian, dau. of 1st earl of Marchmont, vi. 17.
— Christian, wife of Sir John Seton of Garleton, viii. 596.
— Christian, dau. of Sir Patrick H. of Polwarth, ix. 134.
— David, 2nd son of Geo. H. of Argaty, vi. 4.
— Dina, dau. of Mr. Alex. H., vi. 8.
— Elizabeth, wife of P. Hume of Hutton Bell, vi. 9.

* Name unknown.

Hume, Elizabeth, wife of (1) Thos. Cranston, and (2) James Home, vi. 9; ix. 34.
— Elizabeth, wife of Patrick, lord Polwarth, vi. 9, 16.
— Elizabeth, wife of (1) Sir Jas. Carmichael, and (2) John Maxwell of Knock, vi. 11.
— Elizabeth, wife of Charles Sinclair of Hermiston, vi. 17, 21; vii. 589.
— Gavin, 3rd son of Alex. H. of Polwarth, vi. 6.
— George, 4th son of Alex. H. of Polwarth, vi. 6.
— George, rector of Innismacsaint, vi. 9.
— Grisell, wife of George Baillie of Jerviswood, vi. 15, 17, 21.
— Helen, dau. of Adam H., vi. 7.
— Helen, wife of John Acheson, vi. 8.
— Helen, wife of A. Wauchope of Niddrie, vi. 17, 21.
— Isabella, wife of Adam Hepburn of Craig, vi. 6.
— Isabel, wife of Geo. Hume of Bedshiel and Kimmerghame, vi. 11.
— James, 5th son of Patrick H. of Polwarth, vi. 9.
— James, 4th son of Sir Patrick H. of Polwarth, vi. 11.
— Janet, wife of Sir Andrew Ker of Ferniehirst, v. 58, 59 *bis*; vi. 4.
— Janet or Jean, wife of Patrick Home of Law, vi. 10.
— Jean, wife of Christopher Cockburn of Choicelee, vi. 11.
— Jean, wife of 7th lord Torphichen, vi. 17; viii. 394.
— John, D.D., bishop of Oxford, and of Salisbury, v. 234.
— — his wife, Mary Hay, v. 234.
— John, 3rd son of Gavin H. of Johnscleuch, vi. 8.
— John, 3rd son of Sir Patrick H. of Polwarth, vi. 11.
— John, elder son of Andrew H., lord Kimmerghame, vi. 17.
— — his wife, Margaret Drummond, vi. 17.
— Joseph, Notting Hill, iii. 416.
— Julian, wife of Richard Newton of that Ilk, vi. 12.
— Julian, wife of Charles Bellingham, vi. 17.
— Katharine, wife of John Lindsay of Drem and Dirleton, v. 404.
— Katharine, wife of Robert Hoppringle, vi. 6.
— Katharine, wife of Robert Hume of Kimmerghame, vi. 11.
— Margaret, wife of (1) Sir W. Cranstoun, and (2) James Murray, ii. 590; ix. 60.
— Margaret, prioress of North Berwick, dau. of Alex. H. of Polwarth, v. 461; vi. 5, 6 *bis*.
Hume, Margaret, contr. to Sir John Stirling of Keir, iv. 4.
— Margaret, wife of (1) Patrick Hepburn, and (2) Richard Addinstoun, vi. 7.
— Margaret, wife of John Baillie of Johnskirk, vi. 7.
— Margaret, prioress of North Berwick, dau. of Patrick H. of Polwarth, vi. 10.
— Marion, wife of Sir Wm. Baillie of Lamington, vi. 4.
— Matilda, wife of rev. H. F. Tollemache, iii. 416.
— Naomi, dau. of Mr. Alex. H., vi. 8.
— Patrick, son of Geo. H. of Lundies, ii. 552.
— — his contracted wife, Margaret Colville, ii. 552.
— Patrick, 2nd son of Adam H., vi. 7.
— — his wife, Margaret Wauchope, vi. 7.
— Patrick, 2nd son of Andrew H., lord Kimmerghame, vi. 17.
— Patrick, 2nd son of 2nd earl of Marchmont, vi. 19.
— Robert, 2nd son of 1st earl of Marchmont, vi. 16.
— Sophia, wife of Joseph Johnston of Hilton, vi. 11.
— Thomas, legtd. son of Andrew H., vi. 6.
— * wife of [Raguel Bennet] of Chesters, vi. 8.
Hume Campbell of Marchmont, Sir Hugh, 7th bart., vi. 23.
— Alexander, lord Clerk Register, M.P., vi. 19.
— — his wife, Elizabeth Perris, vi. 19.
— Anne, wife of Sir Wm. Purves of Purveshall, vi. 19; ix. 134.
— Anne, wife of Sir John Paterson of Eccles, vi. 21.
— Diana, wife of Walter Scott of Harden, vi. 21, 22.
— Grisell, dau. of 2nd earl of Marchmont, vi. 19.
— Jean, wife of James Nimmo, vi. 19; ix. 134.
— Margaret dau. of 2nd earl of Marchmont, vi. 19.
— Margaret, wife of major-gen. Jas Stuart, vi. 21.
Hume-Dick of Humewood, William Wentworth Fitzwilliam, v. 253.
— Williamina Emily, wife of C. A. Keith-Falconer, v. 253.
Humphreys of the Larches, William, viii. 184.
— — his wife, Hannah Alexander, viii. 184.
— Alexander, claimant to the earldom of Stirling, viii. 184.
— — his wife, Fortunata Bartoletti, viii. 184.

* Name unknown.

Hundolee of Caverton, John, vii. 328.
Hungerford of Blackbourton, Anthony, iii. 612.
—— Rachael, wife of (1) Henry, 4th viscount Falkland, and (2) Sir Jas. Hayes, iii. 612.
Hunsdon, Henry (Cary), 1st lord, i. 396; v. 64.
HUNSDON OF SKUTTERSKELFE, CARY, BARON, iii. 616-617.
Hunsdon, Henry, 1st baron, iii. 608.
—— Lucius Bentinck, baron, iii. 616.
Hunt of Pittencrieff, James, v. 315.
—— —— James Alexander, v. 315.
—— —— his wife, Helen Maitland, v. 315.
—— Deborah, wife of lieut.-col. Alex. Murray of Frimley, iii. 389.
—— Eliza, wife of Roger Rollo, vii. 207.
—— Francis, iii. 294.
—— —— his wife, Katherine Constable, iii. 294.
—— Robert, commissioner-in-chief of the Bahama Islands, iii. 389.
—— Thomasina Agnes, wife of Sir Alex. C. Ramsay Gibson Maitland, v. 315.
—— captain, 6th regt. of Foot, vii. 207.
—— —— his wife, * Bowman, vii. 207.
Hunter of Balcarres, Patrick, i. 76.
—— of Blackness, David, viii. 63.
—— of Crailing, Walter, iii. 81.
—— of Hunterston, John, ii. 512.
—— —— his wife, Margaret Cathcart, ii. 512.
—— of Polmood, Edward, viii. 427.
—— —— Walter, iii. 81.
—— —— his wife Caroline Mackenzie, iii. 81; iv. 66.
—— of Waverley Abbey, Thomas Orby, M.P., ii. 73.
—— —— his wife, Jacomina Bellenden, ii. 73.
—— Andrew, D.D., professor of divinity, vi. 435.
—— —— his wife, Mary Schaw Napier, vi. 435.
—— Anne, wife of James Carnegie Arbuthnott of Balnamoon, viii. 63.
—— Caroline, wife of Jas. Elliot, W.S., iii. 81.
—— Elizabeth, wife of 18th lord Forbes, iii. 81; iv. 66.
—— Louisa, wife of Sir Alex. Hope of Kerse, iv. 490.
—— Patrick, capt. Bengal Infantry, vii. 208.
—— —— his wife, Jane Rollo, vii. 208.
—— Robert, major-general, governor of Jamaica, viii. 459; ix. 55.
—— —— his wife, Elizabeth Orby, viii. 459.
—— William, minister at Banff, ii. 20. 21.
—— —— his 2nd wife, Mary Ogilvy, ii. 21.
Hunter-Blair of Blairquhan, Sir David, 3rd bart., iii. 83.
—— —— his wife, Dorothea Hay-Mackenzie, iii. 83.

* Name unknown.

Hunter-Blair of Blairquhan, Sir David Oswald, 5th bart., O.S.B., ii. 492.
—— —— Sir Edward, 4th bart., iv. 220; viii. 145.
—— Alice Mary, wife of Sir Charles Dalrymple of Newhailes, viii. 145.
—— Dorothea Elizabeth Thomasina, wife of 7th earl of Glasgow, iv. 220.
Hunter-Weston of Hunterston, Jane, wife of lieut.-col. Gould Read Weston, ii. 512.
Huntingdon, David, 4th son of King David I.; earl of, i. 4, 7; ii. 215, 216; v. 326; vii. 266.
—— —— his wife, Maud of Chester, i. 4.
—— Henry, earl of, i. 4, 7; iv. 254.
—— —— his wife, Ada de Warenne, i. 4.
—— John le Scot, earl of, i. 4; ii. 215; vii. 266.
—— Margaret of, wife of Alan of Galloway, i. 4; iv. 141.
—— Matilda, *or* Maud of, wife of (1) Simon de St. Liz, and (2) King David I., i. 3.
—— Waltheof, earl of, i. 3.
—— George (Hastings), 4th earl of, ii. 83.
HUNTINGTOWER, MURRAY, LORD OF, iii. 402-406.
Huntingtower, Elizabeth, wife of (1) Sir L. Tollemache, and (2) John, duke of Lauderdale; lady of, iii. 403.
—— William, first lord of, iii. 402.
—— —— his wife, Katharine Bruce, iii. 402.
HUNTINGTOWER, TOLLEMACHE, LORD OF, iii. 406-420.
Huntingtower, Lionel, son of 3rd earl of Dysart; styled lord, iii. 407.
—— —— his wife, Henrietta Cavendish *or* Heneage, iii. 407.
—— William, eldest son of John Manners, and Louisa, countess of Dysart; styled lord, iii. 412, 415.
—— —— his wife, Katharine Rebecca Grey, iii. 415.
—— William Lionel Felix, son of 8th earl of Dysart; styled lord, iii. 418, 420 *n*.
—— —— his wife, Katherine Elizabeth Camilla Burke, iii. 419.
HUNTLY, SETON, EARL OF, iv. 521-523.
Huntly, Alexander, first earl of, iii. 193, 565; iv. 17, 50, 52, 70, 253, 521.
—— —— his 1st wife, Egidia Hay, i. 15; iv. 524; viii. 421.
—— —— his 2nd wife, Elizabeth Crichton, iv. 524.
—— —— his alleged 3rd wife, Elizabeth Lindsay, iii. 61.
—— —— his alleged 4th wife, * Cumming, the Fair Maid of Moray, iv. 526.
HUNTLY, GORDON, EARL OF, iv. 523-562.
Huntly, Alexander, third earl of, iv. 19 *n*., 277, 529, 531; ix. 110.
—— —— his 1st wife, Jean Stewart, i. 442; iv. 532.
—— —— his 2nd wife, Elizabeth Gray, iv. 532.

* Name unknown.

Huntly, George, second earl of, i. 84; ii. 1, 165; iii. 565; iv. 449, 526; vii. 570 *n.*, viii. 534, 535.
—— —— his 1st wife, Elizabeth Dunbar, countess of Moray, iv. 527; vi. 306, 310.
—— —— his 2nd wife, princess Annabella Stewart, i. 19; iv. 528.
—— —— his 3rd wife, Elizabeth Hay, iii. 565; iv. 528, 531.
—— George, fourth earl of, ii. 339; iii. 25; iv. 21, 54, 366, 533, 534; vii. 122, 292, 366; viii. 339.
—— —— his wife, Elizabeth Keith, ii. 165; iv. 536; vi. 43.
—— George, fifth earl of, i. 38, 39; ii. 165; iv. 58, 536, 539; v. 353; vii. 165; ix. 111.
—— —— his wife, Anna Hamilton, iv. 370, 539, 541.
—— George, sixth earl of, iii. 574; iv. 58, 539, 541; vi. 317; vii. 165.
—— —— his wife, Henrietta Stewart, iv. 541, 544.
HUNTLY, GORDON, MARQUESS OF, iv. 506-562.
Huntly, Alexander, fifth marquess of, iv. 551.
—— —— his wife, Henrietta Mordaunt, iv. 551.
—— Alexander, seventh marquess of, iv. 555.
—— —— his 1st wife, Jane Maxwell, iv. 556.
—— —— his 2nd wife, Jane Christie, iv. 556.
—— Charles, tenth marquess of Huntly, iv. 560.
—— —— his 1st wife, Elizabeth Henrietta Conyngham, iv. 560.
—— —— his 2nd wife, Maria Antoinetta Pegus, iv. 560.
—— Charles, eleventh marquess of, iv. 562.
—— —— his wife, Amy Cunliffe Brooks, iv. 562.
—— Cosmo George, sixth marquess of, iv. 553.
—— —— his wife, Catherine Gordon, i. 90; iv. 554.
—— George, first marquess of, iv. 543.
—— —— his wife, Henrietta Stewart, iv. 541. 544; v. 356.
—— George, second marquess of, i. 353; iv. 127, 545; vii. 169.
—— —— his wife, Anne Campbell, i. 349; iv. 546.
—— George, fourth marqess of, i. 102; iv. 253, 549; viii. 69; ix. 111.
—— —— his wife, Elizabeth Howard, iv. 550.
—— George, eighth marquess of, iv. 253, 557.
—— —— his wife, Elizabeth Brodie, iv. 558.
—— George, ninth marquess of, i. 105; iv. 559; ix. 111.
—— —— his wife, Catherine Anne Cope, iv. 559.
—— Lewis, third marquess of, iv. 584, 558.
—— —— his wife, Mary Grant, i. 126; iv. 548; vii. 472.
—— master of, Alexander, eldest son of 2nd earl of Huntly, iv. 531.
Huntly, master of, Sir George Seton, eldest son of 1st earl of Huntly, iv. 526.
HUNTLY AND ENZIE, GORDON, EARL OF, iv. 549-558.
Huntly and Enzie, George, first earl of, iv. 549.
Huntly Gordon, the marquis, iv. 547 *n.*
Huse, Christian, wife of Walter de Lindsay, iii. 6.
Hussey, Sir Edward, bart., iii. 598.
—— Thomas, iii. 598.
—— —— his wife, Rhoda Chapman, iii. 598.
Hutcheson, Sir Thomas, ix. 57.
—— —— his wife, * Boteler, ix. 57.
Hutchinson of Gales, Peter, i. 404.
—— of Owthorpe, Charles, ii. 484.
—— Anne, wife of Walter Aston, i. 404.
—— Isabella *or* Elizabeth, wife of (1) John, lord Kennedy, and (2) John, earl of Selkirk, ii. 484; vii. 362; ix. 57.
Hutchison, *, Princes Gate, London, iv. 597 *n.*
Hutson, William, iv. 306.
—— —— his wife, Elizabeth Leslie, iv. 305.
Hutt, Sir William, K.C.B., viii. 311.
—— —— his wife, Mary Millner, viii. 311.
Hutton of Nether Poppleton, Sir Thomas, iii. 599.
—— Henry, iv. 571.
—— Marianne, wife of capt. M. W. Carmichael-Smyth, iv. 571.
—— Richard, iii. 599.
—— —— his wife, Dorothy Fairfax, iii. 599.
Hvarflod *or* Gormlath, wife of Harald Maddadsson, earl of Caithness, ii. 315; vii. 231.
Hyde of Allruy, Bridget, wife of 2nd duke of Leeds, iii. 302.
—— —— Sir Thomas, bart., iii. 302.
—— Anne, wife of King James VII., i. 33.
—— Charles Kelth, iii. 605.
—— Henrietta, wife of James, earl of Dalkeith, ii. 240.
—— John, judge of the Supreme Court, Calcutta, iv. 388.
—— Katharine, wife of 3rd duke of Queensberry, vii. 144.
—— Maria Catherine, wife of A. B. P. A. P. Douglas-Hamilton, iv. 388.
—— Theodosia, wife of John Bligh, v. 359.
Hynd, Christian, wife of Walter Kennedy of Glentig, ii. 456.
HYNDFORD, CARMICHAEL, EARL OF, iv. 563-597.
Hyndford, Andrew, sixth earl of, iv. 592, 596.
—— James, second earl of, iv. 593.
—— —— his wife, Elizabeth Maitland, iv. 593; v. 311.
—— John, first earl of, iv. 589.
—— —— his wife, Beatrix Drummond, iv. 591; viii. 219.

* Name unknown.

Hyndford, John, third earl of, iv. 594.
— — his 1st wife, Elizabeth Shovel, iv. 595.
— — his 2nd wife, Jean Vigor, iv. 596.
— John, fourth earl of, iv. 591, 596.
— — his wife, Janet Grant, iv. 596.
— Thomas, fifth earl of, iv. 592, 596.
Hythus, Adam de, i. 5.

Iain Sprangach, 3rd son of Angus 'Mor,' lord of the Isles; ancestor of Macdonald of Ardnamurchan, v. 35.
Ibracan, Henry (O'Brien), styled lord, v. 359.
— — his wife, Katharine Stewart, v. 359.
Ichmare, king in Scotland, v. 28.
Idingtown, *see* Edington.
Ikerrin, Charles Ernest Alfred French Somerset Butler, styled viscount, i. 527.
— — his wife, Ellen Rosamund Mary Lindsay, i. 527.
Ilay, Campbell, earl and viscount of, i. 379.
Ilay, Archibald, earl and viscount of, i. 371, 375, 378.
Ilchester, Henry Stephen (Fox), 3rd earl of, i. 492.
— — his wife, Caroline Leonora Murray, i. 492.
Ile, John de, *alias* Lyle, v. 550, 581.
Imergi, ancestor of Clan Donald, v. 28.
Inchiquin, Murrough (O'Brien), 5th earl of, vi. 581.
— — his wife, Mary, countess of Orkney, vi. 580.
— William (O'Brien), 4th earl of, vi. 580.
— — his wife, Anne, countess of Orkney, vi. 580.
Inchmarnock, Stuart, lord, ii. 299-312.
Inchmarnock, James, first lord, ii. 299.
Inchmartin, Ogilvy, lord Ogilvy of Deskford and, iv. 28-41.
Inchmartin of Inchmartin, Sir John, i. 426; v. 592.
— — his wife, Margaret Wemyss, v. 592; viii. 480.
— Isabel, wife of Sir Alan Erskine, v. 592; viii. 480.
Inchsyreth, David de, iii. 558; ix. 304.
— John de, iii. 558.
— Tiphanie de, wife of Alexander Scrymgeour of Dundee, ix. 72.
Inchture, Kinnaird, lord Kinnaird of, v. 202-216.
Inge of Thorpe Constantine, William Phillips, iv. 169.
— — his wife, Elizabeth Euphemia Stewart, iv. 169.
Ingebiorg, wife of John Sinclair, Foud of Zetland, vi. 569.
Ingibiorg, wife of Thorfinn, 3rd earl of Caithness, ii. 314.
Ingibiorg, wife of king Malcolm III., i. 2.
Ingigerd, wife of Eric Slagbrellir, ii. 315.
Ingle, Eliza, wife of capt. Henry David Erskine, v. 634.
— John, v. 634.
Ingleton of Thornton, Robert, vi. 463.
— Margaret, wife of John Cheyne, vi. 463.
Inglis of Ardit, David, vii. 372.
— — John, iii. 319.
— — his wife, Margaret Graham, iii. 319.
— of Cramond, Sir John, 2nd bart., viii. 132.
— — Sir John, 4th bart., viii. 396.
— of Hinschelwood, Mungo, viii. 371.
— — his wife, Isobel *or* Jonat Livingston, viii. 371.
— of Lochend, George, iii. 273.
— of Manor, Thomas, ii. 226.
— of Murdistoun, Alexander, iv. 289.
— — his wife, Catherine Gray, iv. 289.
— of Otterstoun, Margaret, wife of Sir John Erskine, v. 622; ix. 133.
— — William, v. 622.
— of Tarvet, v. 393.
— — Alexander, v. 398; viii. 60 *n.*
— — John, viii. 60.
— — his wife, Elizabeth Carnegie, viii. 60.
— Ann, wife of Hew Dalrymple, viii. 132.
— Anne, wife of 9th lord Torphichen, viii. 396.
— Eupham, wife of John Makgill, vi. 591.
— Janet, wife of Mr. John Rutherfurd, vii. 372.
— John, son of Thos. I., Auldliston, iv. 90.
— — his wife, Sara Forrester, iv. 90.
— John, v. 279.
— Katharine, ancestress of Geo. Martine of Clermont, viii. 60.
— Lawrence, ii. 276.
— — his wife, Richmond Gardiner, ii. 276.
— Thomas, in Auldliston, iv. 90.
— *, wife of George Lindsay, v. 393.
Inglisberry, Carmichael, viscount of, iv. 590-597.
Inglisberry, John, first viscount of, iv. 590.
Ingram, Ingram, lord, v. 13-20.
Ingram, Henry, first lord, v. 13.
Ingram, lord Ingram, v. 13-20.
Ingram, viscount Irvine, v. 9-20.
Ingram of Barrowby, Arthur, iii. 613.
— — Isabella, wife of general Geo. Cary, iii. 613.
— — Arthur, v. 12.
— — his wife, Jane Mallory, v. 12.
— of Cattal and Thorpe, Sir William, D.C.L., ancestor of the family of, v. 9.
— — his wife, Katharine Edmonds, v. 9.
— of Sheriff Hutton, Sir Thomas, M.P., P.C., v. 11; ix. 115.
— — his wife, Frances Belasyse, v. 11.

* Name unknown.

Ingram of Temple Newsam, Sir Arthur, M.P., sheriff of Yorkshire, v. 10.
—— —— his 1st wife, Susan Brown, v. 10.
—— —— his 2nd wife, Alice Ferrars, v. 11.
—— —— Sir Arthur, sheriff of Yorkshire, v. 12.
—— —— his 1st wife, Eleanor Slingsby, v. 12.
—— —— his 2nd wife, Katharine Fairfax, v. 12.
—— —— Thomas, v. 12.
—— —— his wife, Mary Payler, v. 12.
—— Anne, dau. of John I., v. 10.
—— Anne, wife of James Trott, v. 10.
—— Ann, wife of Henry Stapleton, v. 13.
—— Barbara, dau. of Sir Arthur I., v. 13.
—— Benjamin, 4th son of Sir Arthur I., v. 11.
—— Charles, 3rd son of Sir Arthur I., v. 11.
—— Charles, M.P., adjutant-general, v. 15.
—— —— his wife, Elizabeth Scarborough, v. 15.
—— Elizabeth, dau. of John I., v. 10.
—— Elizabeth, wife of Sir Simon Bennett, v. 11.
—— Elizabeth, wife of Robert, lord Rich, 5th earl of Warwick, v. 12.
—— Elizabeth, wife of Hugo Meynell, v. 19.
—— Elizabeth Arthur, wife of Nathaniel Bayley, v. 15, 17 *n*.
—— Frances, wife of lord William Gordon, iv. 554; v. 19.
—— Harriet, wife of col. H. H. Aston, v. 19.
—— Hugh, tallow-chandler, London, v. 9.
—— —— his wife, Anne Goldthorpe, v. 9.
—— Hugh, 2nd son of John I., v. 10.
—— Isabella, wife of lt.-col. F. Ramsden, v. 15.
—— Isabella Anne, wife of 2nd marquis of Hertford, v. 18.
—— John, 3rd son of Hugh I., v. 10.
—— John, 3rd son of John I., v. 10.
—— John, 2nd son of Sir Arthur I., v. 10.
—— —— his 1st wife, Anne Calverley, v. 10.
—— —— his 2nd wife, Dorothy Fairfax, v. 10.
—— John, 5th son of 3rd viscount Irvine, v. 15.
—— Katharine, wife of Sir Christopher Nevill, v. 13.
—— Louisa Susannah, wife of Sir John Ramsden, v. 19.
—— Sir William, D.C.L., Secretary to the Council in the North, v. 9.
—— William, eldest son of John I., v. 10.
—— William, merchant in Holland, v. 16.
Ingram-Meynell of Temple-Newsam, Hugo Charles, v. 19.
INNERDALE, HAMILTON, LORD, iv. 374-381.
Innerdale, James, first lord, iv. 374.
Innerkip, William of, iv. 49.
INNERMEATH, STEWART, LORD, v. 1-8.
Innermeath, James, fifth lord, v. 6.
—— —— his wife, Helen Ogilvy, i. 118; v. 6.
—— John, fourth lord, v. 5.
—— —— his wife, Elizabeth Betoun, iv. 282; v. 5.
—— Richard, third lord, v. 4; ix. 110.
—— —— his wife, Margaret Lindsay, v. 4, 395.
—— Thomas, second lord, v. 4.
—— —— his alleged wife, * Gordon, iv. 533.
—— —— his wife, Janet Keith, v. 4; vi. 41; vii. 277.
—— Walter, first lord, v. 3 *bis*, 4.
—— —— his wife, Margaret Lindsay, v. 4, 394.
—— John, sixth lord, i. 447; v. 7.
—— —— his 1st wife, Margaret Lindsay, i. 447, 512.
—— —— his 2nd wife, Mary Ruthven, i. 447.
Innerpaphrie, John (Hay), viscount of, v. 231.
INNES, INNES-KER, EARL, vii. 357-360.
Innes, James Robert, first earl, vii. 357.
—— of Aberchirder, Robert, vii. 354.
—— of Auchluncart, Walter, ii. 18.
—— —— his wife, Mary Ogilvy, ii. 18.
—— of Balnagall, Walter, vii. 500.
—— —— his wife, Margaret Mackenzie, vii. 500.
—— of Balveny, Sir Robert, bart., iv. 65.
—— —— Sir Walter, vii. 468.
—— —— his wife, Lilias Grant, vii. 468.
—— of Borlum, Harry, iii. 211.
—— —— his wife, Janet Sutherland, iii. 211.
—— of Cockstoun, Sir Alexander, vii. 198.
—— —— his wife, Joanna Rollo, vii. 198.
—— of Coitts, Alexander, ancestor of the family of, vii. 355.
—— of Cromie, Alexander, 3rd laird, i. 513; iii. 590; vii. 355, 356.
—— —— his 1st wife, Elizabeth Dunbar, vii. 356.
—— —— his 2nd wife, Isabel Forbes, i. 513; iv. 55; vii. 356.
—— —— James, 2nd laird, vii. 355.
—— —— his 1st wife, Katharine Gordon, vii. 355.
—— —— his 2nd wife, Margaret Innes, vii. 355.
—— —— Robert, 1st laird, vii. 354, 355.
—— —— his wife, * Meldrum, vii. 355.
—— of Corskie, John, vii. 575.
—— of Elrick, Thomas, iii. 569.
—— of Forresterseat, William, vii. 355.
—— —— his 1st wife, Agnes Abernethy, vii. 410.
—— —— his 2nd wife, Elizabeth Hepburne, vii. 355.
—— of Innes, Alexander, 13th laird, ii. 337; iii. 197; vii. 354, 355.
—— —— his wife, Cristina Dunbar, vii. 354.

* Name unknown.

Innes of Innes, Alexander, 14th laird, ii. 337; vi. 44; vii. 355, 410.
—— his wife, Elizabeth Forbes, iv. 54; vi. 44; vii. 355.
—— Alexander, 16th laird, ii. 342; vii. 355.
—— his alleged wife, Barbara *or* Beatrix Sinclair, ii. 342; ix. 51.
—— his wife, Janet *or* Jean Gordon, iv. 539; vii. 355; viii. 343.
—— Sir Harry, 4th bart., vii. 356.
—— his wife, Jean Forbes, vii. 356.
—— Sir Harry, 5th bart., vii. 356.
—— his wife, Anne Drummond Grant, vii. 356, 483.
—— James, 12th laird, iv. 72; vii. 354.
—— his 1st wife, Janet Gordon, iv. 526; vii. 354.
—— his 2nd wife, Margaret Culane, vii. 354.
—— Sir James, 3rd bart., vii. 348, 356.
—— his wife, Margaret Ker, vii. 348.
—— Sir James Norcliffe, 6th bart., vii. 331, 353.
—— his 1st wife, Mary Wray of Langton, vii. 357.
—— his 2nd wife, Harriet Charlwood, vii. 357.
—— John, 17th laird, vii. 355, 412.
—— his wife, Elizabeth Abernethy, vii. 355, 412.
—— Robert, 11th laird, vii. 354.
—— Robert, 18th laird, ii. 351; iii. 536; vii. 356.
—— his wife, Elizabeth Elphinstone, iii. 536.
—— Sir Robert, 1st bart., vii. 356.
—— his wife, Grizel Stewart, vi. 318; vii. 356.
—— Sir Robert, 2nd bart., iii. 209; vii. 256, 356.
—— his wife, Jean Ross, vii. 256, 356.
—— Sir Walter, 10th laird, v. 520; vii. 354.
—— his wife, Euphemia *or* Agnes Fraser, v. 520.
—— William, 9th laird, vii. 354.
—— William, 15th laird, vii. 355; ix. 154.
—— his 2nd wife, Elizabeth Hepburne, vii. 355.
— of Inverbrakye, John, vii. 500.
—— Walter, vii. 500.
—— his wife, Margaret Mackenzie, vii. 500.
— of Invermarky, Robert, i. 442; vii. 356.
—— his wife, Elspeth Stewart, i. 442.
— of Kinkell, Robert, vii. 439.
— of Kinnermonie, William, iii. 202.
— of Leuchars, John, v. 398; vii. 575.
—— his wife, Isobel Lindsay, v. 398.
Innes of Leuchars, John, iii. 203.
—— his wife, Elizabeth Douglas, iii. 203.
— of Lichnet, James, iii. 207.
—— his wife, Isabella Ross, iii. 207.
— of Orton, Sir James, bart., iv. 117.
—— his wife, Margaret Fraser, iv. 117.
—— Sir Robert, bart., iv. 65.
—— Walter, i. 42.
—— his wife, Margaret Hamilton, i. 42.
— of Pethnik, vii. 355.
— of Rothmackenzie, James, vii. 355.
—— his 1st wife, Katherine Gordon, vii. 355.
—— his 2nd wife, Margaret Innes, vii. 355.
—— Robert, vii. 354, 355.
—— his wife, * Meldrum, vii. 355.
— of Sandside, Harry, iii. 211.
— of Thurston, Sir James, i. 42.
— of Towie, Sir Alexander, *alias* Barclay, ii. 32.
— Beatrix, wife of Alexander Urquhart of Cromarty, vii. 412.
— Eleanor, wife of Sir Jas. Hamilton of Manor Elieston, i. 42.
— Elizabeth, wife of Alex. Sinclair of Stamster, ii. 337.
— Elizabeth, wife of (1) Geo. Meldrum of Fyvie, and (2) J. Forbes of Pitsligo, iv. 72.
— Elizabeth, wife of John Grant of Culcabok and Glenmoriston, vii. 459.
— Elspet, wife of William King of Barra, iii. 590.
— Isabel, wife of (1) George Meldrum, and (2) John Forbes, iv. 72.
— Isobel, alleged wife of Thomas (Dunbar), 3rd earl of Moray, v. 521; vi. 304, 305 *n*.
— Isobel, handfasted wife of James (Dunbar), 4th earl of Moray, vi. 305, 306.
— Isabella, wife of John Grant of Culcabok and Glenmoriston, vii. 459.
— Janet, lady Greeshop, wife of (1) William Sutherland of Duffus, and (2) Hugh Rose, iii. 196.
— Janet, wife of William Sutherland, 8th laird of Duffus, iii. 197.
— Jean, wife of 1st lord Duffus, iii. 209.
— Sir John, vii. 268.
—— his alleged wife, Margaret Leslie, vii. 268.
— John Stuart, Grafton, viii. 232.
— Katharine, wife of 17th lord Forbes, iv. 65.
— Margaret, wife of William Sutherland, iii. 202.
— Margaret, wife of Sir James Ogilvy of Deskford and Findlater, iv. 18.
— Margaret, wife of James Innes of Rothmackenzie and Cromie, vii. 355.
— Mary, wife of C. S. Drummond, viii. 232.

* Name unknown.

Innes, *, wife of Thomas Gordon of Ruthven, iv. 516.
INNES-KER, EARL INNES, vii. 357-360.
INNES-KER, DUKE OF ROXBURGHE, vii. 356-360.
Innes-Ker of Innes, Sir James, ii. 72 *n.*; vii. 356.
—— Alistair Robert, Royal Horse Guards, vii. 358.
—— —— his wife, Anne Breese, vii. 358.
—— Bertram, vii. 358.
—— Charles James, Gentleman Usher, vii. 358.
—— Charles John, lt.-col. Scots Guards, vii. 357.
—— —— his wife, Blanche Mary Williams, vii. 357.
—— Charlotte Isabella, wife of George Russell, vii. 358.
—— Evelyn Anne, wife of major W. F. Collins, vii. 359.
—— Isabel, wife of Guy G. Wilson, vii. 359.
—— Margaret Frances Susan, wife of major J. A. Orr-Ewing, iii. 359.
—— Robert Edward, Irish Guards, vii. 358.
—— Susan Harriet, wife of Sir James Grant Suttie, vii. 358.
—— Victoria Alexandrina, wife of major C. H. Villiers, vii. 359.
Insula of Whitsome, John de, v. 550.
—— —— Walter de, v. 550.
—— of Woodford, John de, v. 550.
—— Alanus de, v. 550.
—— Christian de, Perth, vi. 531.
—— Petrus de, v. 550.
—— Radulphus de, ancestor of the Lyle family, v. 549.
—— William de, v. 550.
INVERARAY, CAMPBELL, LORD, i. 369.
Inveraray, Archibald, first lord, i. 369.
Inverbervie, Robert, 1st viscount Arbuthnott and lord Bervie, styled lord, i. 305.
INVERKEITHING, SCRYMGEOUR, LORD, iii. 315.
Inverkeithing, John, lord Scrymgeour and, iii. 315.
INVERKEITHING, PRIMROSE, VISCOUNT of, vii. 221-229.
Inverkeithing, Archibald, first viscount of, vii. 221.
INVERNESS, GORDON, VISCOUNT OF, iv. 549-558.
Inverness, George, first viscount of, iv. 549.
—— John (Hay), earl of, v. 231.
—— John (Hay), duke of, v. 231.
Invernochty, James Elphinstone, senator of the College of Justice, lord, i. 557; iii. 535.
Inverpeffer, John de, iv. 332.
—— —— his wife, Margaret Sinclair, iv. 332.

* Name unknown.

Inverpeffer, Sir Malcolm de, iv. 332.
—— Nicolaus de, viii. 46.
—— Patrick de, iii. 305.
INVERUGIE AND KEITH HALL, KEITH, LORD KEITH OF, v. 240-255.
Inverugie, Ian Douglas Montagu, eldest son of 9th earl of Kintore; styled lord, v. 254.
—— William Adrian, eldest son of 7th earl of Kintore; styled lord, v. 253.
Inwen, John, Southwark, iii. 614.
—— Sarah, wife of (1) Henry, 10th earl of Suffolk, and (2) Lucius Charles, 7th viscount Falkland, iii. 614.
Ionides, Constantine Albert, viii. 63.
—— —— his wife, Evelyn Frederica Capel-Carnegie-Arbuthnott, viii. 63.
Ipswich, Henry (Fitz-Roy), 1st viscount, i. 31.
Irby, Charlotte Isabella, wife of 5th earl of Orkney, vi. 582.
Ireby of Gamelsby and Glassanby, Christian, wife of (1) Thomas de Lascelles, (2) A. de Gesemuthe, and (3) Robert Bruce, ii. 373, 432.
—— Eva, dau. of Christian de Carlyle, ii. 373.
—— William, ii. 373.
—— —— his wife, Christian Carlyle of Gamelsby and Glassanby, ii. 373.
Ireland of Drimmie, Gilbert, v. 207.
—— —— his wife, Janet Kinnaird, v. 207.
—— of Kinclevin, Alexander, burgess of Perth, vi. 391.
—— —— his wife, Isabella Scott, vi. 391.
IRVINE, CAMPBELL, EARL OF, i. 350; v. 21-26.
Irvine, James, 2nd son of 7th earl of Argyll; earl of, i. 347, 350; v. 24; ix. 22 *ter.*
IRVINE, INGRAM, VISCOUNT, v. 9-20.
Irvine, Arthur, third viscount, v. 13, 14.
—— —— his wife, Isabella Machell, v. 14.
—— Arthur, sixth viscount, v. 15, 16.
—— Charles, ninth viscount, v. 15, 18.
—— —— his wife, Frances Gibson *or* Shepheard, v. 18.
—— Edward, second viscount, v. 13, 14.
—— —— his wife, Elizabeth Sherard, v. 14.
—— Edward Machell, fourth viscount, v. 15, 16.
—— George, eighth viscount, v. 15, 17.
—— Henry, first viscount, v. 13.
—— —— his wife, Essex Montagu, v. 13.
—— Henry, seventh viscount, v. 15, 17.
—— —— his wife, Anne Scarborough, v. 17.
—— Rich, fifth viscount, v. 15, 16.
—— —— his wife, Anne Howard, v. 16.
Irvine of Artamford, John, vi. 554.
—— of Beltie, Alexander, i. 184.
—— —— his wife, Christian Douglas, i. 184.
—— of Cairnfield, Richard, vi. 554.
—— —— his wife, Margaret Oliphant, vi. 554.
—— of Drum, Sir Alexander, 5th laird, iv. 70; vi. 39.
—— —— his wife, Elizabeth Keith, vi. 39.

Irvine of Drum, Alexander, the younger, vii. 407.
—— his wife, * Abernethy, vii. 407.
—— Alexander, 6th laird, iv. 50.
—— his 1st wife, Elizabeth *or* Marion Forbes, iv. 50.
—— Alexander, 7th laird, vi. 172; vii. 435; ix. 89.
—— his 2nd wife, Margaret Chaumer, iv. 18; ix. 89.
—— Alexander, 8th laird, i. 184, 281; iv. 110.
—— his wife, Janet Allardyce, i. 281.
—— Alexander, the younger, ix. 89.
—— his wife, Elizabeth Ogilvy, ix. 89.
—— Alexander, 9th laird, vi. 50.
—— his wife, Elizabeth Keith, iv. 50.
—— Alexander, 10th laird, ii. 17, 188, 270.
—— his wife, Mariota Douglas, ii. 270.
—— Alexander, 11th laird, i. 103; iii. 314; iv. 130, 133; vii. 442; ix. 74.
—— his wife, Magdalene Scrymgeour, iii. 314.
—— Alexander, 12th laird, iv. 133 *n.*, 548.
—— his 1st wife, Mary Gordon, iv. 548.
—— William, 2nd laird, i. 233.
— of Fedderate, Alexander, iv. 35.
—— his wife, Elizabeth Ogilvy, iv. 35.
—— Robert, 2nd son of Alex. I. of Drum, ii. 188; v. 544.
—— his wife, Elizabeth Campbell, ii. 188.
— of Kellie, Alexander, vii. 22.
— of Luddington House, Walter, vii. 151.
— of Watertoun and Welltoun, Margaret, wife of Andrew Fraser of Stoneywood, iv. 110.
— Alexander, son of Richard I. of Cairnfield, vi. 554.
— Elizabeth, wife of Arch. Douglas of Glenbervie, i. 184; ix. 12.
— Elizabeth, wife of W. R. K. Douglas, vii. 151.
— James, in Artomford, iii. 204.
—— his wife, Margaret Sutherland, iii. 204.
— Jean, wife of 5th viscount Frendraught, iv. 133.
— Jean, wife of Patrick Makgill, vi. 591.
— Margaret, wife of 1st earl of Aboyne, i. 102.
— Margaret, wife of George, 1st lord Banff, ii. 15, 17.
— Marion, wife of 1st viscount Frendraught, vi. 130.
— Marion, wife of Thomas Fraser of Strichen, v. 544.
— Marjory, wife of Sir Alex. Falconer of Glenfarquhar, ix. 123.

* Name unknown.

Irving of Bonshaw, Christopher, i. 247.
—— his wife, Margaret Johnstone, i. 247.
—— Edward, i. 247.
—— John, vii. 205.
—— William, vii. 150.
—— his wife, Janet Douglas, vii. 150.
—— William, vii. 203.
—— his wife, Emilia Rollo, vii. 203.
— of Corniehaugh, Robert, iv. 133.
—— his wife, Elizabeth Crichton, iv. 133.
— of Kirkpatrick, Thomas, vii. 99.
— of Knockhill, John, 'the duke of Hoddom,' i. 218.
— of Tulloch, James, iv. 124.
— Amelia Maria, wife of Clement Sobieski Rollo, vii. 205.
— Blanche, wife of John Murray of Muraythwaite, i. 218.
— Herbert, i. 223.
—— his wife, Margaret Murray, i. 223.
— James, murderer of Turner, ix. 70.
— Marion, wife of John Murray of Muraythwaite, i. 218.
Irwin, Ingram, lord, *see* IRVINE, v. 13 *n.*
— James W., colonel, iii. 605.
Isaac, Joanna, wife of John, lord of Lorn, i. 8.
— Katharine, grand-dau. of king Robert I., i. 8.
— Thomas, i. 8.
—— his wife, Matilda Bruce, i. 8.
— MacElibarn, i. 453.
Isabella of Huntingdon, wife of Robert de Brus, lord of Annandale, i. 4; vii. 267.
Isabel of Mar, wife of king Robert the Bruce, i. 8; v. 578.
Isabella, wife of Roger Bigod, earl of Norfolk, i. 5.
Isabel, wife of (1) Robert de Brus, and (2) Robert de Ros, i. 5; ii. 430.
Isabella, wife of Claud Hamilton of Montalony, i. 42.
Isabel, dau. of John, 9th earl of Atholl; alleged wife of Edward Bruce, i. 427; iii. 436.
Isabel, dau. of Duncan, 9th earl of Fife, and wife of John Comyn, 2nd earl of Buchan, ii. 258; iv. 11.
Isabella, 2nd wife of Thomas de Crichton, burgess of Berwick, iii. 54.
Isabel, wife of (1) Sir Richard Oliver, (2) Sir Wm. Stewart of Jedworth, and (3) Sir Walter de Bickerton, iv. 149; v. 346; ix. 93.
Isabella, wife of Sir Adam Haliburton, iv. 332.
Isabella, wife of Sir John Graham of Dalkeith and Abercorn, vi. 196.
Isabella, wife of John Drummond of Fordew and Cultechaldich, vii. 44.

Isobel, wife of Sir John St. Clair of Herdmanston, vii. 580.
Isabella, wife of (1) John de Lindsay, and (2) Patrick Sandilands, viii. 380.
Isabelle Claire d'Arguille, sister, ix. 22.
Isla, 'Good' John of, 7th lord of the Isles, v. 39.
Isles, Olaf, 5th king of Man and the, vii. 233.
—— —— his wife, Cristina de Ross, vii. 233.
Isles, Macdonald, lord of the, iv. 27-48.
Isles, Alexander, fifth lord of the, v. 30, 33, 34, 35.
—— —— his wife, Juliana of Lorn, v. 30, 35.
—— Alexander, ninth lord of the, v. 43, 48.
—— —— his 1st wife, Elizabeth Seton, v. 44.
—— —— his 2nd wife, * Macphee, v. 44.
—— Angus 'Mor,' fourth lord of the, v. 33, 48.
—— —— his wife, * Campbell, i. 321; v. 34.
—— Angus 'Og,' sixth lord of the, v. 35, 36.
—— —— his wife, Agnes O'Cathan, v. 37.
—— Donald, third lord of the, v. 32.
—— —— his wife, * Stewart, v. 33; ix. 1.
—— Donald, eighth lord of the, ii. 264, 265; v. 40, 48; vii. 159, 242; ix. 18.
—— —— his wife, Mary Leslie, v. 42; vii. 243.
—— Donald, son of Angus Macdonald of Troternish, self-styled lord of the, v. 47.
—— John, seventh lord of the, i. 432; v. 37.
—— —— his 1st wife, Amy or Euphemia MacRuari, v. 39; ix. 115 *bis*.
—— —— his 2nd wife, Margaret Stewart, i. 16; v. 40.
—— John, tenth lord of the, i. 441; ii. 266; v. 45, 48; vii. 498.
—— —— his wife, Elizabeth Livingstone, v. 47, 431; ix. 115.
—— Reginald, second lord of the, iv. 141; v. 30, 31; vi. 288.
—— —— his wife, Fonia, v. 31.
—— Somerled, first lord of the, v. 28; vii. 230.
—— —— his wife, Ragnhildis of the Isles, v. 30.
Isles, Agnes of the, wife of Sir John Montgomerie of Eaglesham and Ardrossan, iii. 430.
—— Angus of the, son of John, v. 39, 340.
—— John of the, eldest son of John, 7th lord of the Isles, v. 39, 340.
—— —— his wife, Helen Campbell, i. 327; v. 340.
—— Mariota of the, wife of (1) Archibald Campbell, yr. of Lochow, and (2) Alexander Sutherland of Dunbeath, ix. 18.
—— of Lochalsh, Alexander of the, v. 44.
—— —— Celestine of the, v. 44, 561, 564.
—— —— Sir Donald of the, v. 44.

* Name unknown.

Isles of Lochalsh, Margaret, wife of Alastair Macdonell of Glengarry, v. 44, 559.
Isoun, *, vi. 542.
—— —— his wife, Katharine Oliphant, vi. 542.
Isted of Ecton, Ambrose, viii. 210.
—— —— his wife, Frances Elizabeth Anson, viii. 210.
Ivie, Hannah, wife of (1) lieut. Hardy, R.N., (2) capt. Geo. Falconer of Phesdo, and (3) John Mill of Fearn, v. 250.
Ivo of Coquetdale, son of Forne, iii. 249.
Izard, Ralph, So. Carolina, i. 385.
—— Sarah, wife of Wm. Campbell, i. 385.

J——, 3rd wife of 1st viscount Frendraught, iv. 130.
Jack, Thomas, vicar of Eastwood, vii. 542.
—— *, taverner, Perth, ix. 13.
—— *, engaged to 2nd marquess of Douglas, ix. 13.
Jackson, Caroline Edith, wife of G. G. Kennedy, ii. 497.
—— Colville Coverly, B.C.S., ii. 497.
—— Elizabeth, wife of Alex. Dalzell, titular lord Carnwath, ii. 416.
—— Elizabeth, wife of rev. Edmund Luttrell Stuart, vi. 327.
—— Harriet Elizabeth, wife of lt.-col. James Montgomerie, iii. 449.
—— J. L., rector of Swanage, vi. 327.
—— Thomas, Westbury, iii. 449.
Jacob, Arthur Otway, lieut. 20th Hussars, ii. 500.
—— —— his wife, Violet Augusta Mary Frederica Kennedy Erskine, ii. 500.
—— Mary, wife of Sir James Hamilton of Manor Elieston, i. 42.
—— Sir Robert, Sol. Gen. for Ireland, i. 42.
Jaffrey, John, Episcopalian minister, Kirkcudbright, v. 268.
—— Katharine, heroine of the old ballad of Lochinvar, v. 101 *n*.
Jaik, Margaret, wife of James King, iii. 589.
James I., king of Scots, i. 18; iii. 166, 169; viii. 381.
—— —— his wife, Joan Beaufort, i. 18, 450; ii. 141; iii. 564, 569; v. 2.
James II., king of Scots, i. 19.
—— —— his wife, Marie of Gueldres, i. 20; iii. 60; v. 604, 637.
James III., king of Scots, i. 20.
—— —— his wife, Margaret of Denmark, i. 20; v. 144, 147, 638.
James IV., king of Scots, i. 21; vii. 44, 250; viii. 13, 580.
—— —— his wife, Margaret Tudor, i. 21, 26, 27; iv. 261; v. 150; vi. 166, 167.

* Name unknown.

James v., king of Scots, i. 23; vii. 120; viii. 488.
—— —— his 1st wife, Madeleine de Valois, i. 23.
—— —— his 2nd wife, Marie de Guise Lorraine, i. 23; iv. 23; v. 527; vii. 122; viii. 283, 585.
James vi., king of Scots, i. 26; v. 354; vii. 549; viii. 95, 216.
—— —— his wife, Anne of Denmark, i. 27; iv. 264, 433, 580; ix. 99.
James vii., king of Scots, i. 29, 32; vii. 136, 138.
—— —— his 1st wife, Anne Hyde, i. 33.
—— —— his 2nd wife, Mary Beatrice Eleanor d'Este, i. 33.
James viii., king of Scots, i. 35; viii. 73, 307.
—— —— his wife, Clementina Sobieska, i. 35.
Sir James, 2nd son of Morgund, 2nd earl of Mar, v. 569, 573.
James, George, captain Royal Scots Greys, iii. 582.
—— Maria, wife of (1) John J. Collas, and (2) David Stuart, 13th earl of Buchan, ii. 280.
—— William, ii. 280.
Jamesone of Cookstown, Alexander, viii. 51.
Jameson, David, ix. 30.
—— —— his wife, Jonet Lindsay, iii. 29; ix. 30.
Jamieson of Halie Jamieson, James, iv. 191.
—— —— his wife, Janet Boyle, iv. 191.
—— Gavin, in the Waulkmyln of Calder, viii. 31.
—— John, D.D., author of *Scottish Dict.*, i. 549.
—— Margaret, wife of (1) James Somerville of Drum, and (2) James Drummond, viii. 31.
Jane, wife of (1) * Macdonnell, and (2) Patrick Ruthven, iv. 265.
Janet, 2nd wife of William, 1st lord Carlyle of Torthorwald, ii. 385.
Janet, wife of Robert Rutherford, 3rd of Chatto, vii. 370.
Jardine of Applegirth, Sir Alexander, 5th laird, vi. 479.
—— —— his wife, Elizabeth Maxwell, vi. 479.
—— —— Sir Alexander, vi. 430; viii. 22.
—— —— his contr. wife, Margaret Somerville, viii. 22.
—— —— Sir Alexander, i. 251.
—— —— his 1st wife, Elizabeth Johnstone, i. 251.
—— —— his 2nd wife, Jean Stewart, v. 7; ix. 115.
—— —— Alexander, father of 1st bart., ii. 42.
—— —— Sir Alexander, 1st bart., vii. 137.
—— —— his wife, Margaret Douglas, vii. 137.
—— —— Sir John, 4th laird, viii. 12.
—— —— his wife, Helen Somerville, viii. 12.
—— —— John, 6th laird, vii. 125.
—— —— his wife, Margaret Douglas, vii. 125.

* Name unknown.

Jardine, Elizabeth, wife of Jas. Johnstone of that Ilk, i. 245.
—— Elizabeth, wife of A. Hamilton of Rosehall, ii. 42.
—— Janet, wife of Cuthbert Murray of Cockpool, i. 223.
—— Katharine, wife of Sir R. Scott of Thirlestane, vi. 430.
Jeanne, wife of Guy de Maumont, Seigneur de St. Quentin, v. 348.
Jedburgh, Home, lord, iv. 465-484.
Jedburgh, Alexander, first lord, iv. 465.
Jedburgh, Ker, lord, v. 49-80.
Jedburgh, Andrew, first lord, v. 63 *bis*, 66, 67, 68 *bis*, 69, 70, 72; ix. 116 *quat*.
—— —— his 1st wife, Anna Stewart, v. 75; vi. 516.
—— —— his 2nd wife, Katharine McCulloch, ix. 116.
—— Robert, second lord, v. 70, 76, 452, 476.
—— —— his wife, Christian Hamilton, v. 78.
—— William, third lord, v. 479.
—— —— his wife, Jean Campbell, v. 479.
—— William Henry, elder son of 3rd marquess of Lothian; styled lord, v. 481.
—— master of, Sir Andrew, only son of 1st lord Jedburgh; senator of the College of Justice, v. 68, 73, 74, 75.
—— —— his wife, Margaret Ker, v. 76, 458.
Jedburgh, Ker, lord Kerr of, v. 477-487.
Jedburgh, Robert, first lord Kerr of, v. 477.
Jedburgh Forest, Douglas, lord of, i. 204.
Jedburgh Forest, William, first lord of, i. 204.
Jedburgh Forest, Douglas, viscount of, i. 210.
Jedburgh Forest, Archibald, viscount of, i. 210.
Jenkinson, Charlotte, wife of 1st earl of Verulam, iv. 97.
Jennings of Sandridge, Richard, i. 54; ii. 532.
—— —— his wife, Frances Thornhurst, ii. 532.
—— —— Sarah, wife of John, lord Churchill of Eyemouth, ii. 532.
—— Frances, wife of (1) Sir Geo. Hamilton, and (2) R. Talbot, duke of Tyrconnell, i. 54; ix. 3.
Jephson, Sir Richard Mounteney, 1st bart., ii. 501.
—— Julia, wife of 2nd marquess of Ailsa, ii. 501.
Jermy of Bayfield, John, ii. 584.
—— —— William, ii. 584.
—— —— his wife, Elizabeth Richardson, ii. 583.
Jermyn of Edmundsbury, Thomas (Jermyn), 2nd baron, i. 55.
—— E., in holy orders, iv. 570.
—— —— his wife, Constance Barré Carmichael, iv. 570.
Jernegan of Somerleyton, John, iii. 609.

Jernegan, Catherine, wife of (1) H. Crane, and (2) Sir Wymond Cary, iii. 608.
Jerningham of Cossy Hall, Sir George William, 7th bart., v. 546.
—— Charlotte Georgina Dorothea, wife of Thomas Alexander, 12th lord Fraser of Lovat, v. 546.
Jersey, Edward (Villiers) 1st earl of, ii. 207.
—— George, 4th earl of, i. 388.
Jerusalem, John, king of, i. 6.
Jervis, Mary, wife of W. H. Ricketts of Longwood, vi. 505.
Jerviswoode, Charles Baillie, senator of the College of Justice, lord, iv. 322.
Jessop, Henry James, viii. 311.
—— —— his wife, Anna Maria Bowes, viii. 311.
Jessup, Alfred Dupont, Philadelphia, iv. 422.
—— Alfred E., viii. 315.
—— —— his wife, Mildred Marion Bowes-Lyon, viii. 315.
—— Mathilda, wife of Bernard Constable-Maxwell, iv. 422.
Joan, wife of Alan Fitz-jordan of Burton, senescal of Dol, i. 10.
Joanna, lady of Strathnaver, wife of Freskin de Moravia of Duffus, ii. 122, 316.
Joanna, wife of Nicolas de Haya of Erroll, iii. 559.
Joanna, wife of William Ruthven of Ruthven, 1363, iv. 256.
Joan, wife of Sir James Douglas of Lothian, vi. 339.
Joan, wife of William Cheyne of Drayton Beauchamp, vi. 461.
Joass of Colleonard, John, ii. 21.
—— —— his wife, Mary Ogilvy, ii. 21.
Jocelyn, bishop of Glasgow, iii. 134, 423; v. 328; vi. 26.
Jodrell of Bayfield, Sir Alfred, bart., iv. 98.
—— —— his wife, Jane Grimston, iv. 98.
—— of Yeardsley, Francis, vii. 563.
—— —— his wife, Jane Butterworth, vii. 563.
—— Sir Paul, ii. 601.
—— Paulina Elizabeth, wife of Sir J. H. Seale, ii. 601.
John, king of England, i. 6; ix. 11.
John, king of Jerusalem, i. 6.
John of Brienne and Acre, i. 6.
—— ——his wife Marie de Coucy, i. 6.
John of Allincrum, vii. 366.
John of Derby, chamberlain of Berwick, iv. 443.
John of Dunort and Invertuyl, son of Richard of Invertuyl, v. 202, 203.
—— —— his wife, Isabella de Kinnaird, v. 202.
John of Edlingham, son of Waldeve, iii. 248.
John of Inchesyreth, iii. 558.
John of Inverness, chancellor of Moray, ii. 129.
John of Lorn, son of Duncan, v. 30.
John of Mamylcroft, son of Matthew, iii. 90.
Sir John of Methil, viii. 475, 476.
John of Penshiell, viii. 476.
John le Scot, earl of Chester and Huntingdon, i. 4.
John, son of Uchtred, ii. 251, 252; vii. 267.
John, bishop of Caithness, 1200, ii. 316.
John Fitzmarmaduke, ii. 432 *n.*
—— —— his wife, Isobella Bruce, ii. 432 *n.*
John, father of Cecilia, wife of Patrick, 7th earl of Dunbar, iii. 259, 262.
John, *called* Albe, rural dean of Fife and Fothrif, iii. 304.
John 'Gilbuy,' burgess of Cupar, iii. 304.
John, son of Duncan, son of Lagman, v. 42.
John, 'son of the earl of Mar,' v. 570.
John, son of Gilchrist, 3rd earl of Mar, v. 573.
John, abbot of Scone, viii. 273.
John, son of Michael the Clerk, viii. 475.
Johnson of Bonjedward, Thomas, iii. 155.
—— —— his wife, Margaret Douglas, iii. 155.
—— Harriet, wife of Sir John Hamilton Dalrymple of Cousland, viii. 159.
—— Robert Augustus, in holy orders, viii. 159.
—— —— his wife, Anne Craven, viii. 159.
—— Dr. Samuel, i. 382.
Johnston of Caskieben, George, iv. 56.
—— —— his wife, Christian Forbes, iv. 56.
—— —— Sir George, v. 580.
—— —— Gilbert, iv. 71.
—— —— his wife, Elizabeth Forbes, iv. 71.
—— —— Sir John, i. 367.
—— of Hilton, Joseph, vi. 11.
—— —— his wife, Sophia Hume, vi. 11.
—— —— *, 1683, iv. 478.
—— of Kedlock, George, v. 408.
—— of Lathrisk, David, v. 316.
—— of Warriston, Sir Archibald, i. 568; viii. 222, 412, 496.
—— Arthur, physician to king Charles I., ii. 11; iv. 56; ix. 15.
—— Christina, wife of James King, iii. 589.
—— Elizabeth, wife of Richard, lord Dalzell, ii. 417.
—— Elizabeth, wife of 6th lord Colville of Culross, ii. 561.
—— Elizabeth, wife of (1) Thos. Hepburn of Humbie, and (2) major-gen. Sir Wm. Drummond, viii. 222.
—— George, notary public, v. 407.
—— —— his wife, Helen Lindsay, v. 407.
—— George, Dublin, vi. 432.
—— George Henry, i. 385.
—— —— his wife, Jane Campbell, i. 385.
—— Henrietta Maria, wife of Francis, 6th lord Napier of Merchiston, vi. 432.
—— James, secretary of State, iv. 37.
—— Janet, wife of Archibald Graham, i. 138.
—— Margaret, wife of (1) Sir John Wemyss of Bogie, and (2) B. Bressey, viii. 496.

* Name unknown.

Johnston, Mary, wife of Charles Maitland of Rankeillour, v. 316.
— Sir Robert, the historian, v. 116.
— Sophie, self-styled wife of 2nd lord Bargany, ix. 36.
JOHNSTONE OF EVANDALE, JOHNSTONE, LORD, i. 256.
Johnstone of Evandale, James, first lord, i. 256.
— — James, second lord, i. 261.
JOHNSTONE OF LOCHMABEN, JOHNSTONE, LORD, i. 261.
Johnstone of Lochmaben, James, first lord, i. 261.
JOHNSTONE OF LOCHWOOD, JOHNSTONE, LORD, i. 255-269.
Johnstone of Lochwood, James, first lord, i. 255, 256.
— — James, second lord, i. 261.
JOHNSTONE OF MOFFATDALE, JOHNSTONE, LORD, i. 256-261.
Johnstone of Moffatdale, James, first lord, i. 256.
— — James, second lord, i. 261.
— master of, William, 2nd son of 1st earl of Hartfell, i. 258.
JOHNSTONE, VISCOUNT OF ANNAND, i. 261.
JOHNSTONE, EARL OF ANNANDALE, i. 261-271.
JOHNSTONE, MARQUESS OF ANNANDALE, i. 230-271.
JOHNSTONE, EARL OF HARTFELL, i. 256-261.
JOHNSTONE, LORD JOHNSTONE OF EVANDALE, i. 256, 261.
JOHNSTONE, LORD JOHNSTONE OF LOCHMABEN, i. 261.
JOHNSTONE, LORD JOHNSTONE OF LOCHWOOD, i. 255-269.
JOHNSTONE, LORD JOHNSTONE OF MOFFATDALE, i. 256-261.
Johnstone of Blacklaws, James, i. 258.
— — William, lieut.-col. in the Douglas regt., i. 258.
— of Brackenthwaite, Gilbert, i. 233.
— of Carnsalloch, Alexander, vi. 434.
— — his wife, Hester Napier, vi. 434.
— of Corhead, James, i. 258.
— of Corrie, Adam, son of James J. of that Ilk, i. 241, 243.
— — George, i. 241.
— — James, i. 241.
— of Dunskellie, Sir James, iii. 128; vii. 76, 130.
— — Sir John, i. 250.
— of Elchieshields, ii. 390.
— of Elphinstone, Andrew, ii. 590.
— — Sir Gilbert, 2nd son of Adam J. of that Ilk, i. 236.
— — his wife, Agnes Elphinstone, i. 236; iii. 527.
— — James, iv. 261.
— — his wife, Margaret Ruthven, iv. 261.
Johnstone of Elphinstone, James, vi. 95.
— — his wife, Jonet Melville, vi. 95.
— — Sir John, iv. 436.
— — Sir Samuel, i. 258.
— of Eremynie, Robert, i. 246.
— — his wife, Marion Maxwell, i. 246.
— — Simon, i. 241, 243, 246.
— of Girthhead, George, son of J. of Corrie, i. 241.
— of Graitney, James, colonel, vii. 388.
— — his wife, Isabel, baroness Ruthven of Freeland, vii. 388.
— — William, vii. 388.
— of Hardgraif, James, i. 247.
— of Howcleuch, John, illeg. son of John J. of that Ilk, i. 247.
— — Mungo, son of Robt. J. of Raecleuch, i. 246.
— — Robert, i. 246.
— of Johnstone, Adam, *temp.* David II., i. 234.
— — Adam, i. 234.
— — his 2nd wife, Janet Dunbar, i. 236; viii. 574.
— — Sir Adam, i. 239.
— — his wife, Marion Scott, i. 239 *bis*.
— — Sir Gilbert, 'son of John,' i. 230, 231.
— — Gilbert, 3rd laird, i. 232.
— — Gilbert, 1296, i. 233.
— — Gilbert, 1347, i. 233.
— — James, son of Sir Adam J., i. 240.
— — his supposed wife, Mary Maxwell, i. 240; vi. 479.
— — James, the younger, i. 245, 247.
— — his wife, Margaret Hamilton, i. 193, 248; iv. 363; ix. 14, 103.
— — Sir James, captain of Lochmaben, i. 252; vi. 484.
— — his wife, Sara Maxwell, i. 254; iv. 413.
— — Sir James, i. 254; vii. 99.
— — his 1st wife, Margaret Douglas, i. 258.
— — his 2nd wife, Elizabeth Johnstone, i. 258.
— — his 3rd wife, Margaret Hamilton, i. 258.
— — John, i. 231.
— — Sir John, i. 232; viii. 245.
— — his wife, Mary de Strathearn of Strathy, viii. 245.
— — John, *c.* 1315-1332, i. 233.
— — Sir John, 1377, i. 233.
— — John, son of Adam J., 237.
— — John, son of James J., i. 242.
— — his 1st wife, Elizabeth Jardine, i. 245.
— — his 2nd wife, Nicola Douglas, i. 245; vii. 125; ix. 14.
— — Sir John, i. 248; vii. 99 *n.*
— — his wife, Margaret Scott, i. 251; ii. 231.

Johnstone of Lochhouse, James, i. 246.
—— —— John, i. 246.
—— of Lockerby, Grace, wife of Sir Wm. Douglas of Kelhead, vii. 151.
—— —— William, vii. 151.
—— of Myrehead, Archibald, vii. 99 *n*.
—— of Neiss, James, i. 246.
—— of Newbie, John, iv. 158.
—— —— his wife, Elizabeth Stewart, iv. 158, 415.
—— of Pettinain, Matthew, i. 237.
—— of Raecleuch, John, i. 247.
—— —— Robert, i. 245.
—— —— his wife, Marion Maxwell, i. 245.
—— —— Robert, tutor of Johnstone, i. 246.
—— of Rachill, Adam, *temp.* David II., i. 234.
—— of Sheens, Samuel, i. 241.
—— —— William, i. 241.
—— —— his wife, Janet Johnstone, i. 241.
—— of Stapleton, John, 3rd son of 1st earl of Annandale and Hartfell, i. 263.
—— —— his wife, Mary Maclean, i. 264.
—— —— Mary, wife of Robert Young, i. 246
—— —— Robert, son of Robt. J. of Raecleuch, i. 246.
—— of Wamphray, James, 6th son of James J. of that Ilk, i. 241.
—— —— his wife, Margaret M'Lellan, i. 241; v. 262.
—— —— Janet, wife of William Johnstone, i. 241.
—— —— John, ancestor of the family of, i. 239.
—— —— John, i. 239; iv. 185 *n*.
—— —— his wife, Katharine Boyle of Wamphray and Rysholm, iv. 185 *n*.; ix. 14.
—— —— John, i. 241; vii. 148.
—— —— his wife, Mary Douglas, iii. 228; vii. 148.
—— —— Robert, vii. 203.
—— —— his wife, Isabella Rollo, vii. 203.
—— —— Robert, captain, vii. 205.
—— —— his wife, Jean Rollo, vii. 205.
—— —— William, son of Samuel J. of Sheens, i. 241.
—— —— his wife, Janet Johnstone, i. 241.
—— of Westerhall, Sir Frederic John William, 8th bart., i. 271.
—— —— James, ii. 393; vi. 549.
—— —— his 1st wife, Euphame Oliphant, vi. 549.
—— —— his 2nd wife, Margaret Johnstone, i. 251.
—— —— Sir James, 3rd bart., i. 128; iii. 516; v. 212.
—— —— his wife, Barbara Murray, iii. 516.
—— —— Sir James, 4th bart., i. 270.
—— —— Sir William, 5th bart., iii. 517.
—— of Whitriggs and Redmyre, Gilbert, i. 233.
Johnstone, Agnes, dau. of Sir James J. of that Ilk, i. 254; ix. 15.
—— Agnes, wife of Jas. Kennedy, ii. 467.
—— Agnes, wife of William Maclellan of Nunton, v. 260.
—— Alexander, son of Robt. J. of Raecleuch, i. 246.
—— Andrew James Cochrane, vi. 437.
—— Archibald, son of Adam J. of that Ilk i. 236.
—— Barbara, wife of 6th lord Kinnaird, v. 212.
—— Bethia, 4th dau. of 1st earl of Hartfell, i. 259.
—— Cecilia, wife of 6th lord Rollo, vii. 206.
—— Christian, wife of James Willison, ix. 15.
—— David, legtd. son of James J. of that Ilk, i. 242.
—— David, illeg. son of John J. of that Ilk, i. 247.
—— Dorothea, wife of John Maitland of Auchengassel, i. 247; ix. 14.
—— Elizabeth, wife of James Grierson, i. 246.
—— Elizabeth, dau. of John J. of that Ilk, i. 247.
—— Elizabeth, wife of Alex. Jardine, i. 251.
—— Elizabeth, wife of Sir Wm. Hamilton, i. 41, 251.
—— Elizabeth, wife of 1st earl of Hartfell, i. 258.
—— Elizabeth, wife of Sir W. Cranstoun, ii. 590.
—— Elizabeth, wife of 9th lord Napier of Merchiston, vi. 437.
—— George, 4th son of 1st earl of Annandale and Hartfell, i. 264.
—— George, minister of Monikie, ii. 560.
—— —— his wife, Isabel Colville, ii. 560.
—— Grizel, wife of (1) Sir Robt. Maxwell, and (2) Patrick Vans, i. 252; iv. 411.
—— Henrietta, wife of Sir John Carmichael, i. 264; iv. 587.
—— Henrietta, wife of 1st earl of Hopetoun, i. 269; iv. 494.
—— Herbert, captain of Lochmaben, i. 235, 237.
—— James, eldest son of John J. of that Ilk, 1478, i. 238.
—— James, abbot of Soulseat, i. 242.
—— James, eldest son of John J. of that Ilk, i. 247.
—— —— his wife, Margaret Hamilton, i. 193, 248; iv. 363; ix. 14, 103.
—— James, major 61st Foot, iv. 294.
—— James, son of James J. of Elphinstone, vi. 95.
—— James, merchant, Edinburgh, vii. 206.
—— James, the Chevalier, vii. 206.
—— Jane, wife of Alex. Macdonald of Camiscross, i. 264.

Johnstone, Janet, wife of Cuthbert Murray of Drumcreiff, i. 219.
— Janet, wife of (1) John Carmichael, (2) Wm. Weir, and (3) Wm. Livingston of Jerviswood, i. 246; viii. 371; ix. 14.
— Janet, wife of Sir Wm. Murray of Stanhope, i. 258.
— Jean, wife of (1) William, master of Carlyle, (2) Alexander, 6th lord Saltoun, and (3) Wm. Kerr, i. 248; ii. 388; vii. 412.
— John, fiar of Johnstone, 1484, i. 238.
— John, 4th son of James J. of that Ilk, i. 241, 243.
— John, abbot of Soulseat, i. 242.
— John, legtd. son of James J. of that Ilk, i. 242.
— John, colonel, i. 268; ix. 15.
— — his wife, Charlotte van Lore vanden Bempde, i. 268.
— John, 5th son of 1st marquess of Annandale, i. 269.
— Jonet, dau. of John J. of Wamphray, vii. 148.
— Margaret, wife of 5th earl of Airlie, i. 128.
— Margaret, wife of Christopher Irving, i. 247.
— Margaret, wife of Ninian Graham, i. 247.
— Margaret, wife of Jas. Johnstone of Westerhall, i. 251.
— Margaret, wife of Sir Robt. Dalzell, i. 259; ii. 409.
— Margaret, wife of Sir Jas. Montgomerie, i. 264.
— Margaret, wife of James Bothwell, iv. 436.
— Marion, wife of Jas. Carlyle, ii. 390.
— Mariota, wife of Simon Carruthers, i. 242.
— Mary, wife of (1) Sir Geo. Graham, and (2) Sir Geo. Fletcher, i. 258; vii. 101.
— Mary, wife of 18th earl of Crawford, i. 264; iii. 37, 39; ix. 15.
— Mary Ann, wife of 15th lord Gray, iv. 294.
— Patrick, son of Adam J. of that Ilk, i. 236.
— Robert, son of Jas. J. of Elphinstone, vi. 95.
— Sara, wife of Sir Robert Maxwell of Spottes, iv. 411.
— Simon, illeg. son of Sir John J. of that Ilk, i. 252.
— Thomas, father of Gilbert J. of Whytriggs, i. 233.
— William, son of Adam J. of that Ilk, i. 236.
— William, 1519, son of Sir Adam J., i. 240.
— William, son of James J. of that Ilk, i. 241, 243.
Johnstone, William, son of Robt. J. of Raecleuch, i. 246.
— William, 2nd son of 1st earl of Hartfell, i. 258.
— William, 3rd son of 1st marquess of Annandale, i. 268.
Johnstone-Douglas of Comlongan Castle, A. H., vi. 507.
— of Lockerby, Robert, vii. 152.
— — his wife, Jane Margaret Mary Douglas, vii. 152.
— Margaret Jean, wife of capt. J. D. Carnegie, vi. 507.
Johnstone-Hope of Annandale, Anne, wife of admiral Sir Wm. Hope, i. 270; iv. 496, 500.
— Sir George, admiral, K.C.B., iv. 496; v. 213.
— — his 1st wife, Jemima Johnstone-Hope, iv. 496, 501.
— — his 2nd wife, Georgina Mary Anne Kinnaird, v. 213; ix. 121.
— Georgina, wife of Andrew J. Cochrane, iii. 360; iv. 501.
— Jemima, wife of admiral G. Hope, iv. 496, 501.
— Lucinda, dau. of 3rd earl of Hopetoun, iv. 501.
— Sir William, admiral R.N., i. 270; iv. 495.
— — his 1st wife, Anne Johnstone-Hope, iv. 496, 500.
— — his 2nd wife, Maria Eden, iv. 496.
Joisel, Pierre de, seigneur de St. Remy-en-Bouzemont et de Betoncourt, v. 439.
— — his wife, Jeanne de Pedefer, v. 439.
Jones of Henllys, John, ii. 500.
— Douglas, lieut.-colonel, iii. 547.
— — his wife, Clementina Fleming Buller-Fullerton-Elphinstone, iii. 547.
— Emily, wife of Mark F. Napier, vi. 438.
— Harriet Loyd, wife of lord Wantage, i. 524.
— John, LL.D., prebendary of Mullaghbrack, iv. 496.
— Katharine, wife of W. H. Kennedy Erskine of Dun, ii. 500.
— Lettice, wife of Wm. Aston, i. 401.
— Richard Prankerd, Charfield, ii. 499.
— — his wife, Elizabeth Charlotte Neeld, ii. 499.
— Sarah, wife of Henry Hope, lieut.-governor of Canada, iv. 496.
— William Sydney, iv. 209.
— — his wife, Clare Banning, iv. 209.
Jordan Fitz-Alan, senescal of Dol, i. 10.
— — his wife, Mary, i. 10.
— son of Alan Fitz-Jordan, i. 10.
Jordan-Fitzjordan of Burton, grandson of Alan Fitz-flaad, i. 10.
Jordan, Dora Bland, styled Mrs., ii. 499; iii. 585.

Joussey, Robert, merchant, Edinburgh, iv. 284.
Judge, Georgina, wife of C. P. Carmichael, iv. 570.
Juliana of Lorn, wife of Alexander, lord of the Isles. v. 30, 35.
Juliana of Witton, Wyndgates, etc., wife of Ranulf de Merlay, iii. 249.
Julian, wife of Henry of Brechin, i. 4.
Juliana, wife of John de Haya, iii. 556.
Justice, Cristina, wife of John Rollo of Pitmeadie and Pilton, vii. 190.
—— William, merchant burgess, Edinburgh, vii. 190.
Juvitot, Joanna, wife of Henry Hope, iv. 487.

Kaas, Kirstine, wife of Sir Andrew Sinclair, vii. 575.
Kakyne, Thomas, captain, ix. 151.
—— —— his wife, Rachel Winterfield *or* Harrison, ix. 151.
Kali Hundasson, *supposed* Norse name for Duncan i., king of Scotland, ii. 314.
—— Kolsson, *alias* Rognvald, earl of Orkney, and Caithness, ii. 315.
Kari the Icelander, vii. 314.
—— Robertus de, vii. 315.
Kateson, *pseudonym of* William Murray, duke of Rannoch, i. 481.
Katerina, wife of Roland Ascolog *or* Magachen, i. 321.
Katharine of York, 3rd dau. of king Edward iv. of England, vii. 245.
Katharine, wife of Magnus, 18th earl of Caithness, ii. 319.
Katharine, wife of Sir Robert Colville of Oxnam and Ochiltree, ii. 539.
Katharine, wife of (1) Sir Walter Lindsay of Kinneff, and (2) Walter Dempster, iii. 14.
Katharine, wife of Sir Alex. Ramsay of Dalhousie, iii. 90.
Katharine, wife of William Bothwell, burgess of Edinburgh, iv. 425.
Katharine, wife of Sir John Menteith of Rusky, lord of Arran and Knapdale, v. 580; vi. 132.
Katharine, 3rd wife of John, 8th earl of Sutherland, viii. 334.
Katon, James Edward, commander R.N., iii. 550.
Kaye of Woodsome, Sir John, 1st bart., iii. 454.
—— —— his wife, Katharine St. Quintin, iii. 454.
Keane, Hussey Fane, lieut.-gen., K.C.B., vi. 583.
—— —— his wife, Isabella E. E. Fitzmaurice, vi. 582.
Kearnie, Martin, comte de, i. 62.
—— —— his wife, Elizabeth Hamilton, i. 62.
Keck of Great Tew, Anthony Tracy, iv. 391; viii. 514.
—— —— his wife, Susan Hamilton, iv. 391.
—— Susan Tracy, wife of Francis, lord Elcho, viii. 514.
Keighley of Idlicote, Henry Peach, major, iii. 616.
—— Sarah Christiana, wife of (1) capt. Lucius W. C. A. F. Cary, and (2) col. Boyle Vandeleur, iii. 616.
Keir of Forgandenny, Laurence, viii. 296.
Keirie of Gogar, John, iv. 120, 121.
Keith, Keith, lord, vi. 39-65.
Keith, Robert, eldest son of 3rd earl Marischal; styled lord, vi. 43.
—— —— his wife, Elizabeth *or* Beatrice Douglas, vi. 43, 358.
—— William, first lord, vi. 39.
—— William, eldest son of 4th earl Marischal; styled lord, vi. 49.
—— —— his wife, Elizabeth Hay, iii. 570; vi. 49.
Keith, Elphinstone, viscount, iii. 548-549.
Keith, George, first viscount, iii. 362, 548.
—— —— his 1st wife, Jean Mercer of Aldie, iii. 548; vi. 395.
—— —— his 2nd wife, Hester Maria Thrale, iii. 548; ix. 85.
Keith and Altrie, Keith, lord, vi. 51.
Keith and Altrie, George, lord, i. 159; vi. 51.
Keith of Banheath, Elphinstone, baron, iii. 548-549.
Keith of Banheath, George, first baron, iii. 548.
—— —— Margaret, wife of comte de Flahault; baroness, iii. 549.
Keith of Inverugie and Keith Hall, Keith, lord, v. 240-255.
Keith of Inverugie and Keith Hall, John, first lord, v. 240.
Keith of Stonehaven-Marischal, Elphinstone, baron, iii. 548-549.
Keith of Stonehaven-Marischal, George, first baron, iii. 548.
—— —— Margaret, wife of comte de Flahault; baroness, iii. 549; vi. 395, 398.
—— master of, William Keith, eldest son of 2nd earl Marischal, vi. 41, 42.
Keith, lord Altrie, i. 156-159; vi. 51.
Keith, lord Dingwall, iii. 115-116.
Keith, lord Keith, vi. 39-65.
Keith, lord Keith of Inverugie and Keith Hall, v. 240-255.
Keith, earl of Kintore, v. 240-255.
Keith, earl Marischal, vi. 25-65.
Keith of Aboyne, Elizabeth, wife of (1) Sir Adam Gordon of Huntly, (2) Sir Nicholas Erskine of Kinnoull, and (3) Thomas Somerville of Carnwath, iv. 517, 518 *bis*; v. 596; vi. 37; viii. 9; ix. 109.
—— —— Sir William, vi. 36.

Keith of Ackergill, Sir Robert, vii. 440.
— — his wife, Elizabeth Fraser, vii. 440.
— — William, vi. 46.
— — his wife, Margaret Keith, vi. 46.
— of Alnedan, Sir Robert, vi. 31.
— of Altrie, George, vi. 52.
— of Auchincloich, Robert, vi. 43.
— of Auchinhamper, William, vi. 46.
— of Auchtidonald, Sir Robert, vi. 31.
— of Auquhorsk, Alexander, ancestor of the family of, vi. 41.
— — Robert, vi. 43, 46.
— — his wife, Beatrice Douglas, vi. 43, 46.
— of Benholm, Sir Alexander, iv. 92; v. 248.
— — his wife, Agnes Falconer, iv. 92; v. 248.
— — Elizabeth, wife of Sir Archibald Primrose of Carrington, vi. 54; vii. 219.
— — George, vi. 53.
— — his wife, Margaret Ogilvy, vi. 53.
— — Sir James, 2nd son of 5th earl Marischal, i. 122; vi. 53, 55; vii. 219; ix. 31, 135.
— — his wife, Margaret Lindsay, vi. 54; ix. 31.
— — John, 4th son of 5th earl Marischal, vi. 54.
— — Robert, 3rd son of William, master of Marischal, vi. 44 *n.*, 49.
— — Sir Robert, vi. 51.
— — William, vi. 55.
— of Buthlaw, David, vi. 45.
— of Cantray, Robert, vi. 48.
— of Carlogy, William, vi. 46.
— of Caskieben, Sir John, knight marischal of Scotland, v. 240.
— — his wife, Margaret Hamilton, v. 241.
— of Cluny, Elizabeth, wife of (1) Sir Adam Gordon, (2) Sir Nicholas Erskine, and (3) Thomas Somerville, iv. 517, 518 *bis*; v. 596; vi. 37; viii. 9; ix. 109.
— of Cocklaw, Nathaniel, vi. 55.
— of Cowtoun, Alexander, i. 286.
— — his wife, Marjory Arbuthnott, i. 286.
— — John, i. 292.
— of Craibstone, Sir Alexander, vi. 37.
— of Craig, James, vi. 55.
— — John, ancestor of the family of, vi. 41.
— of Culpresso, William, vi. 46.
— of Dalserf, Sir Bernard de, iii. 138; vi. 29.
— of Deer, William, vi. 57.
— of Delny, Sir William, master of the king's wardrobe, iii. 116.
— of Dingwall, Sir Andrew, iii. 115; vii. 66.
— — John, iii. 116.
— — Sir William, iii. 116.
Keith of Doun, Sir Alexander, vi. 37.
— of Drumfad, Sir William, vi. 35.
— of Duffus, John, vi. 34.
— — his wife, Mary Cheyne, vi. 34.
— of Dunottar, Sir Alexander, knight marischal of Scotland, vi. 44.
— — Alexander, vi. 64.
— — Sir William, vi. 36.
— of Durne, Gideon, portioner, ii. 5.
— — William, vi. 46.
— of Fetteresso, Sir William, vi. 36.
— — William, vi. 46.
— of Forest of Cowie, Sir William, vi. 36.
— of Forsa, Andrew, iii. 115.
— of Fortheres, William, vi. 46.
— of Galston, Janet *or* Joanna, wife of (1) D. Hamilton of Cadzow, and (2) Sir Alex. Stewart of Darnley, ii. 397; v. 345, 346 *bis*, 491; vi. 29.
— — Robert (?), ancestor of the family of, vi. 29.
— — Sir William, ambassador to England, v. 345; vi. 29.
— of Galvail, Sir William, vi. 34.
— of Garvals, William, vi. 41.
— of Garvock, William, vi. 46.
— of Glackreoch, Alexander, i. 156.
— of Glendowachy, Sir Alexander, vi. 37.
— of Grandon, Sir Alexander, i. 108, 109; vi. 37.
— — his wife, Marjorie Stewart, vi. 37.
— — Christian, wife of Sir P. Ogilvy of Auchterhouse, i. 109; vi. 37, 301.
— of Harvieston, James, vi. 56.
— of Hythe, Sir William, vi. 34.
— of Innerpeffer, Sir John, iii. 561 *bis*.
— — *, wife of Sir David de Haya of Erroll, iii. 561.
— of Innerpeffin, Sir Robert, vi. 32.
— of Inverugie, Andrew, v. 599.
— — Gilbert, vi. 222.
— — his wife, Janet Graham, vi. 222.
— — Sir Gilbert, iii. 565; vii. 434; ix. 50.
— — his wife, Margaret Hay, iii. 565.
— — John, 2nd son of Sir Edward K. of Keith-Marischal, iii. 220; vi. 33.
— — his wife, Mary de Cheyne of Inverugie, vi. 34.
— — Sir Patrick, i. 114.
— — his wife, Elizabeth Ogilvy, i. 114.
— — Sir William, iv. 72; v. 105; vi. 34, 49; ix. 69, 94.
— — his 1st wife, Janet Dunbar, vi. 34.
— — his 2nd wife, Janet Gordon, v. 105; ix. 94.
— — his 3rd wife, Christine Sutherland of Duffus, iii. 193; ix. 69.
— — William, the younger, iv. 278; vi. 34; ix. 99.
— — his wife, Janet Gray, iv. 278.
— of Jackston, viii. 76.

* Name unknown.

Keith of Keith-Hervey, Hervey de, king's marischal, vi. 25.
—— —— his alleged wife, Margaret Douglas, vi. 26.
—— —— Malcolm, vi. 26.
—— of Keith-Hundeby, Philip, vi. 28.
—— —— his wife, Eda Lorens, vi. 28.
—— of Keith-Marischal, Sir Edward, marischal of Scotland, vi. 30, 32, 33.
—— —— his 1st wife, Isabella Sinton of Sinton, vi. 33.
—— —— his 2nd wife, Christian Menteith, v. 580, 595, 599; vi. 33, 132.
—— —— Hervey, marischal of Scotland, vi. 28.
—— —— Sir John de, marischal of Scotland, vi. 28.
—— —— his wife, Margaret Cumyn, vi. 28.
—— —— Philip, joint-marischal of Scotland, vi. 26, 28.
—— —— his wife, Eda Lorens of Hundeby, vi. 28.
—— —— Sir Robert, marischal of Scotland, iii. 53; iv. 514 *n.*; v. 281, 284; vi. 27, 30.
—— —— his wife, Barbara Douglas, vi. 33.
—— —— Sir Robert, marischal of Scotland, v. 521; vi, 38.
—— —— his wife, *, of Troup, vi. 39.
—— —— his alleged 2nd wife, Elizabeth Lindsay, iii. 17; vi. 39.
—— —— Sir Robert, marischal of Scotland, eldest son of 1st earl Marischal, vi. 39, 40; viii. 574.
—— —— his wife, Janet Seton, vi. 40; viii. 574.
—— —— Sir William de, vi. 29.
—— —— his wife, Barbara Seton, vi. 30.
—— —— Sir William, marischal of Scotland, iv. 108, 521; v. 584; vi. 33, 35.
—— —— his wife, Margaret Fraser, vi. 36.
—— —— Sir William, marischal of Scotland, iv. 522; vi. 39.
—— —— his wife, Mary *or* Marjorie Fraser, vi. 40.
—— —— Nova Scotia, William, vi. 54.
—— of Kincardine, William, vi. 46.
—— of Kinellar, James, vi. 55.
—— of Kininmonth, Bouchtains, and Half-Clunie, Alexander, ii. 399.
—— of Kinmundy, Sir William, vi. 35.
—— of Kintore, Sir Robert, vi. 31.
—— of Kirkmichael, Sir William, vi. 35.
—— of Kirktoun of Longley, George, vi. 51.
—— of Ladiesfurd, Barbara, wife of Alex. Forbes of Pitsligo, iv. 73.
—— of Laidacht, Robert, vi. 43.
—— of Longforgund, Alexander, vi. 30 *n.*
—— of Ludquhairn, Janet, wife of (1) Sir Thos. Barclay, and (2) Sir Thos. Erskine, v. 599.

* Name unknown.

Keith of Ludquhairn, John, ancestor of the family of, vi. 35.
—— —— William, ii. 171.
—— —— William, the younger, vi. 49, 51.
—— —— his wife, Margaret Keith, vi. 49.
—— —— Sir William, i. 86; iv. 114; vi. 55.
—— —— his wife, Margaret Bannerman, i. 86.
—— of Wester Markinch, Sir William, vi. 36.
—— of Mulboy, Robert, vi. 43, 46.
—— of Northfield, James, last laird, vi. 39.
—— —— John, ancestor of the family of, vi. 39.
—— of Ochterotherstruther, Sir William, v. 391; vi. 36.
—— of Pirchock, Janet, wife of (1) Sir D. Barclay, and (2) Sir Thos. Erskine, v. 580, 586, 597, 599.
—— of Pittendreich, William, v. 392; vi. 35, 36.
—— —— his wife, Margaret Fraser, vi. 36.
—— of Pittendrum, Alexander, 4th son of 3rd earl Marischal, vi. 44.
—— —— his wife, Marion Lundie, i. 284; vi. 44.
—— —— [Alexander], iv. 72.
—— —— his wife, * Forbes, iv. 72.
—— —— Alexander, vi. 44, 55.
—— —— Gilbert, vi. 44.
—— —— his wife, Elizabeth Forbes, iv. 54; vi. 44.
—— —— John, vi. 44.
—— —— his wife, * Barclay, vi. 44.
—— —— William, vi. 44.
—— —— his wife, Barbara Keith, vi. 44.
—— of Powburn, Sir James, vi. 238.
—— —— his wife, Grizel Graham, vi. 238 *bis.*
—— of Ravelston, Sir Alexander, knight marischal of Scotland, vi. 45.
—— —— Alexander, vi. 64.
—— —— Helen Margaret Oliphant, wife of Sir Wm. Murray of Ochtertyre, vi. 45.
—— of Ravenscraig, Andrew, i. 184.
—— —— his wife, Marjory Douglas, i. 184.
—— —— John, 4th son of Sir Wm. K. of Inverugie, vi. 34.
—— —— John, iii. 116.
—— of Sinton, Sir Edward, vi. 33.
—— —— his 1st wife, Isabella Sinton, vi. 33.
—— —— his 2nd wife, Christian Menteith, v. 580, 595, 599; vi. 132.
—— of Easter Skene, William, vi. 46.
—— of Strabrock, John, iii. 220; vi. 33.
—— —— his wife, Mariota Cheyne, vi. 34.
—— of Strachan, Sir William, vi. 36.
—— of Straloch, Sir William, vi. 34.
—— of Strathauchin, William, vi. 46.
—— of Strathekin, Sir William, vi. 36.
—— of Tertowie, Robert, vi. 46.
—— of Torterston, David, vi. 45.

* Name unknown.

Keith of Traquair, Edward, v. 281.
— of Troup, Alexander, vi. 44, 49.
— — George, son of Gilbert K., vi. 44.
— — Gilbert, 3rd son of 3rd earl Marischal, iv. 54; vi. 44, 46.
— — his wife, Elizabeth Forbes, iv. 54; vi. 44.
— — Gilbert, iii. 539; vi. 54.
— — his wife, Barbara Gordon, iii. 539.
— — John, vi. 39.
— — Sir Robert, marischal of Scotland, vi. 38.
— — his wife, * of Troup, vi. 39.
— — William, 2nd son of 3rd earl Marischal, vi. 44.
— of Uchterutherstruther, Sir William, v. 391; vi. 36.
— of Uras, Alexander, vi. 44.
— — William, vi. 42.
— of Whiterig, Robert, vi. 55.
— — Robert, deputy-sheriff of the Mearns, vi. 59.
— of Whithorn Priory, Agnes, wife of (1) James, earl of Moray, and (2) Colin, 6th earl of Argyll, i. 345; iv. 158; vi. 50, 316; ix. 21, 134.
— Adam, rector of Keith-Marischal, vi. 29, 30.
— Agnes, wife of Sir A. Douglas of Glenbervie, i. 184; vi. 45.
— Agnes, wife of William Avenel, vi. 30 *n.*
— Agnes, alleged wife of * Douglas, vi. 354 *n.*
— Alexander, in Redbych, ii. 5.
— — his wife, Marjorie Ogilvy, ii. 5.
— Alexander, his son, ii. 5.
— Sir Alexander, eldest son of Sir Wm. K. of Inverugie, iii. 566; vi. 34.
— Alexander de, parson of Hoddom, vi. 28 *n.*
— Alexander, brother of John K. of Troup, vi. 39.
— Alexander, 4th son of 1st earl Marischal, vi. 41.
— Alice, wife of Alexander Fraser, vi. 43 *n.*
— Alice *or* Alison, wife of 6th lord Saltoun, vi. 50; vii. 411.
— Andrew, 3rd son of Sir Wm. K. of Inverugie, vi. 34.
— Anna, wife of Patrick Smith of Braco, vi. 54.
— Annas, wife of (1) James, the regent Moray, and (2) Colin, 6th earl of Argyll, i. 345; iv. 158; vi. 50, 316; ix. 134.
— Anne, wife of 6th earl of Galloway, iv. 165; vi. 62.
— Anne, illeg. dau. of William, master of Marischal, vi. 50.
— Ann, wife of 6th earl of Morton, vi. 53; 377.

* Name unknown.

Keith, Anne, dau. of 6th earl Marischal, vi. 57.
— Anthony, 2nd son of 2nd earl Marischal, vi. 41.
— Barbara, wife of Wm. Keith of Pittendrum, vi. 44.
— Barbara, dau. of William, master of Marischal, vi. 50.
— Barbara, wife of Alex. Forbes of Pitsligo, vi. 51.
— Beatrice, wife of Alexander Fraser, vi. 43; vii. 437.
— Beatrix, wife of John Allardyce of Allardyce, vi. 50.
— Charles, 4th son of 1st earl of Kintore, v. 241.
— Christian, wife of Robert Arbuthnott, i. 290; vi. 43.
— Christian, dau. of Alex. K. in Redhych, ii. 5.
— Christian, wife of Sir Robert Erskine of Kinnonll, iv. 14.
— Christiana, wife of Robert Maitland of Thirlestane, v. 280, 281; vi. 33.
— Christian, wife of (1) John Hay, and (2) Sir Wm. Lindsay, v. 392; vi. 38.
— Christian, wife of Thos. Monypenny of Pitmillie and Leuchars, vi. 39, 276.
— Christian, wife of Walter Ogilvy of Craigboyne, vi. 45.
— David, joint king's-marischal to Alexander II., vi. 27.
— David, marischal, vi. 27.
— David, king's-marischal, vi. 27.
— Edmund, 3rd son of John de K., vi. 33.
— Sir Edward, 2nd son of John de K., vi. 33.
— Egidia, wife of 2nd lord Forbes, iv. 51; vi. 41.
— Elizabeth, wife of Robert Lumisdane, i. 156.
— Elizabeth, wife of (1) Alex. Hay of Delgaty, and (2) James Allardes, i. 159; ix. 10.
— Elizabeth, wife of 2nd viscount of Arbuthnott, i. 308; vi. 60.
— Elizabeth, wife of 7th lord Forbes, iv. 55, 58; vi. 34.
— Elizabeth, wife of 4th earl of Huntly, iv. 536; vi. 43.
— Elizabeth, wife of Alexander Fraser of Lovat, v. 521.
— Elizabeth, wife of Alex. Irvine, 5th of Drum, vi. 39.
— Elizabeth, wife of Geo. Baird of Glencuthil, vi. 44.
— Elizabeth, wife of (1) Colin, master of Oliphant, and (2) William, 4th lord Sinclair, vi. 45, 543; vii. 573.
— Elizabeth, wife of John Keith, vi. 49.
— Elizabeth, wife of Alex. Irvine, 9th of Drum, vi. 50.

Keith, Elizabeth, wife of Sir Wm. Fraser of Philorth, vii. 435.
—— Sir George, 2nd son of 6th earl Marischal, i. 301; vi. 56, 60.
—— George, 3rd son of 1st earl of Kintore, v. 241.
—— George, rector of Keith, vi. 45.
—— Gilbert, marischal, vi. 27.
—— Gilbert, legtd. son of 5th earl Marischal, vi. 54; ix. 135.
—— Gilbert, vi. 172.
—— —— his wife, Janet Middleton, vi. 172.
—— Hervey, *probably error for* H. le Marescal, iii. 135.
—— Isobel, wife of Alexander Strachan of Thornton, vi. 51.
—— Isabel, wife of Sir Edward Turnour, vi. 60.
—— James, governor of the Ukraine, field-marshal, governor of Berlin, vi. 61, 62, 63.
—— Janet, wife of Philip de Arbuthnott, i. 276; vi. 37.
—— Janet, wife of (1) Sir David Barclay of Brechin, and (2) Sir Thomas Erskine of Erskine, ii. 223, 224; v. 580, 586, 597, 599, 604; vi. 35.
—— Janet, wife of (1) Sir D. Hamilton of Cadzow, and (2) Sir Alex. Stewart of Darnley, iv. 145, 345.
—— Janet, wife of (1) John, master of Rothes, and (2) Thomas, 2nd lord Innermeath, v. 4; vi. 41; vii. 277.
—— Janet, wife of (1) Alan Kinnaird, and (2) William, thane of Cawdor, v. 204.
—— Janet, wife of 2nd lord Gray, iv. 276; vi. 41.
—— Janet, wife of 7th lord Glamis, vi. 43; viii. 284.
—— Janet, wife of 2nd earl of Montrose, vi. 45, 228.
—— Jean, wife of Jas. Gordon of Haddo, i. 86; vi. 49.
—— Jean, wife of David Arbuthnott, i. 292.
—— Jean, wife of George, 3rd lord Banff, ii. 21; vi. 60; ix. 35.
—— Jean, wife of (1) Sir David Barclay of Brechin, and (2) Sir Thomas Erskine, ii. 223, 224; v. 580, 586, 597, 599, 604; vi. 35.
—— Jean, wife of John Forbes of Pitsligo, iv. 72.
—— Jean, wife of 1st lord Forbes of Pitsligo, iv. 75; vi. 57.
—— Jean, alleged 1st wife of Sir Alex. Seton of Gordon, the younger, iv. 524 *n.*
—— Jean, wife of Sir W. Forbes of Monymusk, v. 241.
—— Jean, dau. of 2nd earl of Kintore, v. 241.
—— Jean, wife of 7th lord Glamis, vi. 43; viii. 284.
—— Johanna *or* Joneta, wife of Sir James Crichton of Frendraught, iv. 125 *bis*; vi. 50.
Keith, John de, rector of Crichton, iii. 53.
—— John, elder son of Sir Robert K., marischal of Scotland, vi. 30, 33.
—— —— his wife, * de Soulis, vi. 33.
—— John, eldest son of Sir Wm. K. of Keith-Marischal, vi. 36; viii. 268.
—— —— his wife, Jean *or* Joanna Stewart, i. 16; vi. 36; viii. 268.
—— John, 3rd son of 1st earl Marischal, vi. 41.
—— John, 4th son of William, master of Marischal, vi. 49.
—— —— his wife, Elizabeth Keith, vi. 49.
—— John, rector of Duffus, vi. 50, 51.
—— John, youngest son of 6th ear Marischal, v. 240; vi. 56, 57.
—— Katharine, wife of Alexander Barclay of Urie, vi. 35.
—— Katharine Margaret, wife of 5th lord Falconer, v. 241, 250.
—— Margaret, wife of (1) J. Erskine of Dun, and (2) 10th earl of Crawford, i. 159; iii. 30; ix. 11 *bis*.
—— Margaret, wife of Hugh Arbuthnott of that Ilk, i. 279; vi. 39.
—— Margaret, wife of Sir Robert Arbuthnott of that Ilk, i. 302; vi. 53.
—— Margaret, dau. of Alex. K. in Redhych, ii. 5.
—— Margaret, wife of William, 2nd earl of Caithness, ii. 337; ix. 50.
—— Margaret, wife of Sir James de Lindsay of Crawford, ii. 540; iii. 12; vi. 37.
—— Margaret, wife of Gavin Hamilton of Raploch, v. 241.
—— Margaret, wife of 4th earl Marischal, vi. 34, 43, 48.
—— Margaret, wife of (1) Wm. Keith, yr. of Ludquharn, (2) Sir John Carnegie of Kinnaird, and (3) Sir Wm. Graham of Braco, vi. 49, 234; viii. 59.
—— Margaret, wife of John Kennedy of Blairquhan, vi. 50.
—— Margaret, wife of Sir John Elphinstone of Elphinstone, vi. 54.
—— Marion, wife of Alex. Fraser of Kinnell and Lovat, v. 521; vi. 39.
—— Marjory, wife of George Hay of Ardlethen, iii. 570.
—— Mary, wife of John, lord Kilpont, i. 139; vi. 57; ix. 9.
—— Mary, wife of Sir Robt. Arbuthnott, i. 299; vi. 50; ix. 16.
—— Mary, alleged wife of Sir Wm. Murray of Tullibardine, i. 460 *n.*
—— Mary, wife of (1) Sir Jas. Hope of Hopetoun, and (2) Sir A. Murray of Blackbarony, iv. 492; vi. 60.
—— Mary, wife of John Campbell of Calder, vi. 50.
—— Mary, wife of 6th earl of Wigtoun, vi. 62; viii. 554; ix. 135.

* Name unknown.

Keith, Muriella, wife of Robert, duke of Albany, i. 148; ii. 264; iv. 517; vi. 37.
— Philip, rector of Biggar, vi. 30 *bis*.
— Richard, son of David the marischal, vi. 27.
— — his wife, Agnes, vi. 28.
— Sir Richard, 2nd son of Sir Wm. K. of Keith-Marischal, vi. 30 *bis*.
— Robert, 2nd son of Robert, master of Marischal; commendator of Deer, i. 156; iii. 115; vi. 43, 50, 52.
— Robert, 2nd son of 4th earl Marischal; commendator of Deer, i. 156; vi. 50.
— Robert, bishop of Fife, i. 286.
— Robert, grandson of Sir Robert K., king's marischal, vi. 33.
— — his wife, Margaret Hay, vi. 33.
— Robert, grandson of Sir Wm. K. of Keith-Marischal and Dunottar, vi. 37.
— Robert, 3rd son of 2nd earl marischal, vi. 41.
— Sir Robert, 3rd son of 6th earl Marischal, vi. 56.
— Robert, vii. 9 *n*.
— — his wife, Katharine Cramond, vii. 9.
— Robert, illeg. son of 5th earl Marischal, ix. 135.
— — his wife, Helen Bruce, ix. 135.
— Walter, captain, Montrose, viii. 76.
— — his wife, Janet Carnegie, viii. 76.
— Sir William, governor of Berwick, vi. 33; viii. 567.
— William, 2nd son of Sir Wm. K. of Inverugie, vi. 34; ix. 99.
— — his wife, Janet Gray, iv. 278; vi. 34.
— William, 2nd son of Wm. K. of Pittendrum, vi. 44.
— William, student at Geneva, vi. 49, 51.
— *, iii. 138; vi. 29.
— — his wife, Joanna de Galbraith of Dalserf, vi. 29.
Keith-Elphinstone, Georgiana Augusta Henrietta, wife of (1) Augustus John Villiers, and (2) lord Wm. Godolphin Osborne, ix. 85.
KEITH-FALCONER, EARL OF KINTORE, v. 251-255.
KEITH-FALCONER, BARON KINTORE OF KINTORE, v. 252-255.
Keith-Falconer, Alexander, 2nd son of 6th earl of Kintore, v. 252.
— Arthur, 4th son of 8th earl of Kintore, v. 254.
— Blanche Catherine, wife of G. R. F. Smith, v. 254.
— Cecil Edwards, capt. Northumberland Fusiliers, v. 253.
— — his wife, Georgina Blagrave, v. 253.

* Name unknown.

Keith-Falconer, Charles Adrian, v. 253.
— — his wife, Williamina Hume Dick, v. 253.
— Charles James, major 4th Light Dragoons, v. 253.
— — his wife, Caroline Diana Aldridge, v. 253.
— Christian Elizabeth, v. 252.
— Diana Mary, v. 253.
— Dudley Metcalfe Courtenay, v. 254.
— Ethel Sydney, wife of John L. Baird, v. 254.
— Evelyn Millicent, v. 253.
— Florence, wife of rev. H. F. Hayhurst, v. 253.
— Francina Constantia, v. 252.
— Hilda Madeleine, v. 254.
— Ida Madeleine, v. 253.
— Ion Grant Neville, v. 254.
— — his wife, Gwendoline Bevan, v. 254.
— Isabella Katharine, wife of Henry Grant, v. 253.
— Katharine Margaret, v. 252.
— Madeleine Dora, wife of capt. F. H. Tonge, v. 254.
— Maria Remembertina, v. 252.
— Mary, dau. of 6th earl of Kintore, v. 252.
— Maude, dau. of 8th earl of Kintore, v. 254.
— Sibella, dau. of 5th earl of Kintore, v. 252.
— Sybil Blanch, v. 253.
— Victor Francis Alexander, capt. Somerset Light Infantry, v. 253.
— Violet Katharine, v. 253.
— William, capt. R.N., v. 252.
— — his wife, Louisa Grant, v. 252.
Keith-Murray of Ochtertyre, Sir William, 7th bart., vi. 45.
— — his wife, Helen Margaret Oliphant Keith, vi. 45.
KELBURNE, BOYLE, VISCOUNT, iv. 202-221.
Kelburne, James, R.N., eldest surviving son of 4th earl of Glasgow; styled lord, iv. 217, 218.
— Patrick James, R.N., eldest son of 7th earl of Glasgow; styled lord, iv. 220; ix. 96.
Kelehathonin, grandson of Malcolm, 2nd earl of Atholl, i. 418.
KELHEAD OF KELHEAD, DOUGLAS, BARON, vii. 154.
Kelhead of Kelhead, Francis Archibald, baron, vii. 154.
KELLIE, GORDON, LORD, i. 88-99.
Kellie, George, first lord, i. 88.
KELLIE, ERSKINE, EARL OF, v. 81-97.
Kellie, Alexander, third earl of, v. 87.
— — his 1st wife, Anna Kirkpatrick, v. 87.
— — his 2nd wife, Mar Dalzell, ii. 409; v. 87.

Kellie, Alexander, fourth earl of, v. 88, 477.
—— —— his wife, Anne Lindsay, i. 522; v. 88.
—— Alexander, fifth earl of, v. 88.
—— —— his 1st wife, Louisa Moray, v. 89.
—— —— his 2nd wife, Janet Pitcairn, v. 89.
—— Archibald, seventh earl of, v. 89, 90.
—— Charles, eighth earl of, v. 93.
—— John Francis Miller, eleventh earl of, v. 94, 635.
—— Methven, tenth earl of, v. 94, 95.
—— —— his wife, Joanna Gordon, v. 94.
—— Thomas, first earl of, v. 82, 84.
—— —— his 1st wife, Anne Ogilvy, v. 86; ix. 116.
—— —— his 2nd wife, Elizabeth Pierrepont, v. 86.
—— —— his 3rd wife, Dorothy Smith, v. 86.
—— Thomas, second earl of, v. 87.
—— Thomas, ninth earl of, v. 93.
—— —— his wife, Anne Gordon, v. 94.
—— Thomas Alexander, sixth earl of, v. 89.
—— Walter Coningsby, twelfth earl of, v. 59, 634, 635.
—— —— his wife, Elise Youngson, v. 95.
—— Walter Henry, thirteenth earl of, v. 95.
—— —— his wife, Mary Anne Forbes, v. 95.
—— Walter John Francis, fourteenth earl of, v. 96.
—— —— his wife, Violet Ashley, v. 96.
—— Egidia *or* Geills, wife of J. Ramsay of Edington, iii. 98.
—— Margaret, wife of Sir John Seton of St. Germains, viii. 592.
—— William, W.S., iii. 98; viii. 592.
—— —— his wife, Jean Balloun, iii. 98.
Kelly, Edward, Dublin, ii. 73.
—— —— his wife, Elizabeth Bellenden, ii. 73.
KELSO, KER, EARL OF, vii. 350-360.
Kelso, John, first earl of, vii. 350.
Kemble of Knock, Horace William, iii. 395.
—— Lucinda Dorothea, wife of 8th earl of Dunmore, iii. 395.
Kemp of Slindon, Anthony, vi. 457.
—— Anne, wife of 4th earl of Newburgh, vi. 457.
—— John, D.D., minister of the Tolbooth, Edinburgh, vi. 504.
—— —— his 2nd wife, Margaret Carnegie, vi. 504.
—— —— his 3rd wife, Elizabeth Hope, iv. 490.
—— Thomas, D.D., London, ii. 22.
—— —— his wife, Mary Ogilvie, ii. 22.
Kench, John de, vii. 404.
Kendal, Charles, infant son of king James VII.; duke of, i. 33.
KENMURE, GORDON, VISCOUNT OF, v. 98-135.
Kenmure, Adam, eighth viscount of, v. 132, 135.
—— —— his wife, Mary Anne Wildey, v. 135.
—— Alexander, fifth viscount of, iii. 328; v. 108, 123; ix. 119 *bis*.
—— —— his 1st wife, Agnes Gordon, v. 124.
—— —— his 2nd wife, Marion M'Culloch, v. 125.
—— —— his 3rd wife, Grizel *or* Isabella Stewart, iv. 162; v. 125.
—— John, first viscount of, v. 117.
—— —— his wife, Jean Campbell, i. 349; v. 118, 120.
—— John, second viscount of, v. 120; ix. 118.
—— John, third viscount of, v. 112, 120.
—— John, *de jure* viscount of, v. 129, 131.
—— —— his wife, Frances Mackenzie, v. 132; vii. 512.
—— John, seventh viscount of, v. 132, 133.
—— —— his wife, Sarah Ann Morgan, v. 134.
—— Robert, fourth viscount of, v. 112, 120; ix. 118 *bis*.
—— —— his wife, Martha Norton, v. 126.
—— Robert, *de jure* viscount of, v. 129 *bis*, 130.
—— William, sixth viscount of, v. 126.
—— —— his wife, Mary Dalzell, ii. 410; v. 129; ix. 119.
—— William, *de jure* viscount of, v. 132, 133.
—— master of, James, 3rd son of James Gordon of Barncrosh; styled, v. 112.
—— master of, Robert, eldest son of Alexander, 6th viscount of Kenmure; styled, v. 129.
Kenne, Christopher, vi. 574.
—— Elizabeth, vi. 574.
KENNEDY, KENNEDY, LORD, ii. 453.
Kennedy, David, third lord, ii. 457, 460.
—— Gilbert, first lord, ii. 449, 452; v. 493; viii. 10, 533, 534; ix. 113.
—— —— his 1st wife, Katharine Maxwell, ii. 454; vi. 475.
—— —— his 2nd wife, Isabel Ogilvie, i. 112; ii. 454; viii. 271.
—— James, eldest son of 6th earl of Cassillis; styled lord, ii. 479, 481.
—— John, second lord, ii. 454, 456.
—— —— his 1st wife, Elizabeth Montgomerie, ii. 457; iii. 433.
—— —— his 2nd wife, Elizabeth Gordon, ii. 457; iv. 525.
—— —— his 3rd wife, Elizabeth Kennedy, ii. 457.
—— John, eldest son of 7th earl of Cassillis; styled lord, ii. 484.
—— —— his wife, Isabella *or* Elizabeth Hutcheson *or* Hutchinson, ii. 484; ix. 57.
KENNEDY, MARQUESS OF AILSA, ii. 497-502.
KENNEDY, EARL OF CASSILLIS, ii. 443-502.
KENNEDY, LORD KENNEDY, ii. 453.

Kennedy of Ardmillan, Hugh, ii. 489.
—— —— his wife, Jean Kennedy, ii. 489.
—— —— Thomas, ii. 488; v. 108; vi. 97.
—— —— Thomas, ii. 489.
—— of Ardstinchar, Alexander, 'Dalgour,' ii. 450.
—— —— Hugh, 'venez avec le sou,' ii. 450.
—— —— Thomas, ii. 451.
—— of Baltersane, Sir Alexander, ii. 488.
—— —— James, ii. 454.
—— —— his wife, Egidia Blair, ii. 454.
—— —— John, ii. 516.
—— —— his wife, Florence M'Dougal, ii. 516.
—— —— Thomas, major, ii. 489.
—— of Bardrochat, Thomas, ancestor of the family of, ii. 452.
—— —— of Bargany, Alexander, 4th laird, ii. 468, 471.
—— —— Alexander, v. 112.
—— —— his wife, Margaret Gordon, v. 112; ix. 118.
—— —— Sir Alexander, ii. 488.
—— —— his wife, Agnes Kennedy, ii. 488.
—— —— Gilbert, 2nd laird, ii. 458.
—— —— Gilbert, 7th laird, ii. 476; v. 113.
—— —— his wife, Jean or Anna Stewart, vi. 516.
—— —— Hugh, 6th son of 2nd earl of Cassillis, ii. 467.
—— —— his wife, Katharine Bailey, ii. 467.
—— —— Thomas, 1st laird, 5th son of Sir Gilbert K. of Dunure, ii. 452.
—— —— Sir Thomas, 3rd laird, ii. 458.
—— —— his wife, Katharine Kennedy, ii. 458.
—— —— Thomas, 5th laird, ii. 468.
—— —— his wife, Margaret Campbell, v. 495.
—— —— his contr. wife, * Kennedy, ii. 468.
—— —— Thomas, 6th laird, ii. 473; viii. 117.
—— —— his 1st wife, Agnes Montgomerie, iii. 440.
—— —— his 2nd wife, Isobel Stewart, vi. 514.
—— —— Thomas, 8th laird, ii. 488; vi. 515.
—— —— his wife, Margaret Stewart, vi. 515.
—— of Bennan, Thomas, ancestor of the family of, ii. 452.
—— of Beoch, Gilbert, illeg. son. of Alex. K of Ardstinchar, ii. 450.
—— of Blairquhan, Sir Gavin, ii. 463.
—— —— his wife, Helen Campbell, i. 337; ii. 463.
—— —— Gilbert, the younger, iii. 229.
—— —— his wife, Margaret Cunningham, iii. 229.
—— —— James, ii. 462, 468.
—— —— James, i. 223; iv. 152, 158, 408 *bis*.
—— —— his wife, Agnes Murray, i. 223; iv. 408.

* Name unknown.

Kennedy of Blairquhan, James, 2nd son of Sir Thos. K. of Culzean, ii. 451, 487.
—— —— his wife, Anne Stewart, ii. 487.
—— —— James, his son, ii. 487.
—— —— Sir John, 4th son of Sir Gilbert K. of Dunure, ii. 451.
—— —— John, his son, ii. 451, 510; v. 142.
—— —— John, vi. 50, 516.
—— —— his wife, Margaret Keith, v. 263; vi. 50.
—— —— John, v. 498.
—— —— his wife, Margaret Campbell, v. 498.
—— —— John, vi. 517.
—— —— his wife, Marie Stewart, ii. 517.
—— —— Roland, ii. 445.
—— —— William, ii. 487.
—— of Brunston, James, 3rd son of 1st earl of Cassillis, ii. 463, 468.
—— of Buchmonyn, Fergus, ii. 450.
—— —— John, ii. 425, 449 *n*.
—— of Carloch, John, vi. 515.
—— of Carrick, Sir John, eldest son of James K. of Dunure, ii. 449, 452.
—— of Cassillis, John, 1st laird, ii. 444.
—— —— his alleged wife, Marjory Montgomerie, ii. 444, 446.
—— —— his wife, Mary *, ii. 447.
—— —— Sir John, ii. 449 *n*., 453; iii. 169.
—— of Coif, Gilbert, ii. 457.
—— —— John, ancestor of the first family of, ii. 452, 507.
—— —— John, ii. 457.
—— —— Thomas, 4th son of 1st earl of Cassillis, ii. 463, 468.
—— —— his 1st wife, Helen Campbell, i. 337; ii. 463.
—— —— his 2nd wife, Katharine Corry, ii. 463.
—— of Craig, John, iii. 437.
—— —— his wife, Barbara Rule, iii. 437.
—— of Craigoch, Sir Alexander, 3rd son of Sir Thomas K., ii. 488.
—— —— his wife, Agnes Kennedy, ii. 488.
—— —— Alexander, 2nd son of Sir Alex. K., ii. 489, 493.
—— —— his 1st wife, *, ii. 493.
—— —— his 2nd wife, Anna Crawford, ii. 493.
—— of Crochba, Gilbert, provost of church of Maybole, ii. 454; ix. 56.
—— of Culzean, Sir Alexander, 3rd son of Sir Thos. K., ii. 488; ix. 57.
—— —— his wife, Agnes Kennedy, ii. 488.
—— —— Sir Archibald, 1st bart., ii. 490.
—— —— his wife, Elizabeth Leslie, ii. 490; vi. 442.
—— —— David, 3rd son of 2nd earl of Cassillis, ii. 465.
—— —— his wife, Janet Kennedy, ii. 466.
—— —— James, ii. 487.
—— —— his wife, Anne or Janet Stewart, ii. 487; iv. 159.

Kennedy of Culzean, John, v. 261.
—— —— his wife, Katharine Maclellan, v. 261.
—— —— John, ii. 28, 489.
—— —— his 1st wife, Anne Blair, ii. 489.
—— —— his 2nd wife, Margaret Hamilton, i. 124; ii. 489.
—— —— Sir John, 2nd bart., ii. 491.
—— —— his wife, Jean Douglas, ii. 491.
—— —— Sir John, 3rd bart., ii. 492.
—— —— Sir Thomas, 3rd son of 3rd earl of Cassillis, ii. 471, 474, 475, 486.
—— —— his wife, Elizabeth M'Gill, ii. 486; vi. 594.
—— —— Sir Thomas, 4th bart., ii. 443, 485, 492.
—— —— Thomas, eldest son of Sir Thos. K. of Culzean, ii. 487.
—— of Cundry *or* Konrey, Thomas, ii. 445 *n.*
—— of Daljedburgh, Duncan, ii. 466.
—— of Dalmerton, Sir Thomas, ii. 445 *n.*
—— of Dalrymple, Sir James, viii. 114.
—— —— John, viii. 114.
—— of Drumellan, David, ii. 493.
—— —— his wife, * Kennedy, ii. 493.
—— of Drummurchie, Thomas, ii. 476.
—— of Drumnellan, Gilbert, vi. 411.
—— of Dunure, Sir Gilbert, ii. 425, 444, 447, 506.
—— —— his wife, Agnes Maxwell, ii. 448.
—— Gilbert, ii. 452.
—— —— his 1st wife, Katharine Maxwell, ii. 454.
—— —— his 2nd wife, Isabel Ogilvie, ii. 454.
—— —— Sir James, ii. 448; iv. 230; ix. 56.
—— —— his wife, Marjory *or* Mary Stewart, i. 18; ii. 448 *bis*; iv. 230; ix. 32.
—— —— John, ii. 424 *n.*, 425, 444.
—— —— his wife, Mary *, ii. 446.
—— of Dunymuick, Alexander, ii. 490.
—— of Garrihorn, David, ii. 488.
—— —— his wife, Margaret Kennedy of Garriborn, ix. 57.
—— —— Hew, ix. 57.
—— of Girvanmains, Alexander, 2nd son of John, lord Kennedy, ii. 457.
—— —— Gilbert, ii. 489; ix. 57.
—— —— his wife, Marion Kennedy, ii. 489.
—— —— Sir Gilbert, ii. 491.
—— —— his wife, Jean Kennedy, ii. 491.
—— —— Sir Hew, ii. 65, 458, 465, 467, 468; vii. 164; viii. 339 *n.*, 341.
—— —— his wife, Janet Stewart, i. 443; viii. 338.
—— of Glentig, Alexander, ii. 456.
—— —— his wife, Janet Wallace, ii. 456.
—— —— Walter, parson of Douglas, ii. 454.
—— —— his wife, Christian Hynd, ii. 456.
—— —— William, ii. 468.
—— of Grenare, John, ii. 471.
—— of Guiltree, John, ii. 464.
—— —— his wife, Christian Kennedy, ii. 464.

* Name unknown.

Kennedy of Guiltree, John, ii. 464.
—— —— Sir Thomas, ii. 415.
—— of Kilhenzie, Alexander, ii. 493.
—— —— his 2nd wife, Anna Crawford, ii. 493.
—— —— Alexander, captain in Duram's regt., ii. 493.
—— —— Helen, wife of John Shaw of Dalton, ii. 493.
—— —— John, advocate, ii. 493.
—— —— his wife, Helen Monteith, ii. 493.
—— of Kirkintulloch, Sir Gilbert, viii. 524.
—— —— Sir Hugh, ii. 444, 448.
—— of Kirkcryst, John, v. 263.
—— —— his wife, Margaret Keith, v. 263.
—— of Kirkhill, Thomas, ancestor of the family of, ii. 452.
—— of Kirkmichael, David, 6th son of Sir Gilbert K. of Dunure, ii. 452.
—— —— David, iii. 447.
—— —— his wife, Mary Montgomerie, iii. 447.
—— —— John, iv. 588.
—— —— his wife, Martha Carmichael, iv. 588.
—— —— John Shaw, ii. 493.
—— —— Thomas, ii. 452.
—— of Kirkoswald, Thomas, ii. 452.
—— of Knockdaw, Fergus, viii. 118.
—— —— Fergus, viii. 119.
—— —— his wife, Margaret Ross, viii. 119.
—— of Knockdolian, Gilbert, ii. 445 *n.*
—— of Leffnol, Gilbert, ii. 452.
—— —— Roland, ii. 452.
—— of Lenzie, Fergus, ii. 449 *n.*
—— —— John, 1357, viii. 524.
—— —— John, 1405, ii. 449 *n.*
—— of Lochland, Martin, ii. 464.
—— of Monunshion, Alexander, ancestor of the family of, ii. 458.
—— of Pavonia, Archibald, collector of customs, New York, ii. 494.
—— —— his 1st wife, * Massam, ii. 494.
—— —— his 2nd wife, Maria Walter, ii. 494.
—— of Pinwherry, Alexander, ancestor of the family of, ii. 458.
—— —— Thomas, v. 76.
—— —— his wife, Jean Ker, v. 76.
—— of Row, James, ii. 454.
—— —— his wife, Egidia Blair, ii. 454, 464.
—— of Skeldon, John, iii. 436.
—— —— his wife, Margaret Mure, ii. 463; iii. 436.
—— of Stair, Agnes, wife of William Dalrymple, iii. 427 *n.*; viii. 115.
—— of Uchtrelure, James, ii. 467.
—— —— his wife, Agnes Johnstone, ii. 467.
—— Adolphus Archibald, ii. 499.
—— Agnes, wife of Sir Alex. Kennedy of Culzean, ii. 488.
—— Agnes, wife of James Hamilton of Clinton-Clare, ii. 489, ix. 57.

* Name unknown.

Kennedy, Alexander, canon of Glasgow Cathedral, ii. 444 *n.*
— Alexander, 3rd son of 1st lord Kennedy, ii. 454.
— Alexander, legtd. son of Alex. K. of Girvanmains, ii. 458.
— Alexander, 4th son of Alex. K. of Craigoch, ii. 494.
— Alexander, 2nd son of Archibald, styled earl of Cassillis, ii. 498.
— Alexander, Black Watch, ii. 591.
— — his wife, Beatrice Gordon, ii. 501.
— Alexander, son of Hugh K. in Craigneill, iii. 443.
— — his wife, Helen Kennedy, iii. 443.
— Alice Emily, dau. of adm. Sir William Robt. K., ii. 497.
— Alice Jane, wife of lt.-gen. Jonathan Peel, ii. 500.
— Aline, wife of 5th baron Kilmaine, ii. 502.
— Angus, 3rd son of 3rd marquess of Ailsa, ii. 502.
— Anna, dau. of James K., ii. 489.
— Anne, wife of John, earl of Selkirk and Ruglen, ii. 485 *bis*; vii. 362; ix. 57.
— Anne, wife of John Blair of Dunskey, ii. 491.
— Anne, wife of Sir E. C. Disbrowe, ii. 497.
— Anne, wife of William H. Digby, ii. 497.
— Anne, wife of Sir David Baird, ii. 500.
— Ann, wife of William Gordon of Penninghame and Muirfad, v. 108; ix. 118.
— Archibald, 5th son of 2nd earl of Cassillis, ii. 467.
— Barbara, wife of Sir J. Bellenden, ii. 64, 65.
— Barbara, wife of James Montgomerie of Lainshaw, iii. 437.
— Charles, colonel, ii. 484.
— Charles, 2nd son of 3rd marquess of Ailsa, ii. 502.
— Christian, wife of John Kennedy of Guiltree, ii. 464.
— Clementina, wife of G. Watson of Bilton Park, ii. 492.
— Constance Eleanor, wife of col. L. G. Fawkes, ii. 501.
— David, son of Walter K. of Glentig, ii. 456.
— David, advocate, ii. 485, 490.
— David, J.P. and D.L., Ayrshire, ii. 498; ix. 58.
— — his wife, Mary Boyle, ii. 498.
— Edward Briggs, ii. 497.
— — his wife, Caroline Edith Jackson, ii. 497.
— Egidia, dau. of David K. of Culzean, ii. 466.
Kennedy, Elizabeth, alleged 1st wife of 1st lord Ogilvy of Airlie, i. 114.
— Elizabeth, wife of Sir John Forbes of Druminnor, ii. 447 *n.*; iv. 46.
— Elizabeth, wife of (1) John, lord Kennedy, and (2) Wm. Power, ii. 457.
— Elizabeth, wife of Sir Wm. Colville, ii. 459, 542.
— Elizabeth, dau. of 6th earl of Cassillis, ii. 482; ix. 57.
— Elizabeth, dau. of 7th earl of Cassillis, ii. 485.
— Elizabeth, wife of Sir John Cathcart of Carleton, ii. 491.
— Elizabeth, wife of Alexander Stewart of Garlies and the Grenan, iv. 152.
— Emma Andalusia, wife of (1) George 5th earl of Portarlington, and (2) H. B. Portman, ii. 499.
— Evelyn, dau. of 3rd marquess of Ailsa, ii. 502.
— Evelyn Anne, wife of A. Young, ii. 501.
— Evelyn Mary, wife of C. H. Helbert, ii. 498.
— Fergus, H.E.I.C.S., ii. 499.
— Fergus de Carrick Frere, ii. 499.
— Frances, wife of baron de Weiller, ii. 497.
— George, legtd. son of Alex. K. of Girvanmains, ii. 458.
— Gilbert, illeg. son of Sir Gilbert K. of Dunure, ii. 447, 451, 452.
— Gilbert, son of Hew, master of Cassillis, ii. 474.
— Gilbert, alleged 3rd son of 4th earl of Cassillis, ii. 474 *n.*
— — his wife, Katharine M'Dowall, ii. 474 *n.*
— Gilbert, R.N., 5th son of Archibald, styled lord Cassillis, ii. 498.
— — his wife, Margaret Baird, ii. 498.
— Gilbert George, police magistrate, ii. 497.
— — his wife, Alice Lyon, ii. 497.
— Hannah Eleanor, wife of Sir J. A. Cathcart, ii. 498.
— Helen, wife of (1) Robert Graham, and (2) Adam Boyd, ii. 460.
— Helen, wife of Wm. Adair of Kinhilt, ii. 468.
— Helen, dau. of 6th earl of Cassillis, ii. 482.
— Helen, wife of (1) James Mure, and (2) John Fergusson, ii. 488; ix. 57.
— Helen, wife of (1) Hugh, 4th earl of Eglinton, (2) John Graham, and (3) Alexander Kennedy, iii. 443.
— Hew, master of Cassillis, ii. 474, 476.
— — his wife, Katharine M'Dowall, ii. 474.
— Henry (*alias* MacKenede), ii. 444.
— Hermione Julia, ii. 501.

Kennedy, Hugh, 4th son of 3rd marquess of Ailsa, ii. 502.
—— Hugh, in Craigneill, iii. 443.
—— Irene Clare, wife of John Bell, ii. 501.
—— Isobel, wife of Alan, master of Cathcart, ii. 516.
—— Isabel, wife of Jas. Dalrymple of Stair, viii. 117.
—— Isabella Matilda, wife of H. Montgomery-Campbell, ii. 497.
—— James, bishop of Dunkeld, and St. Andrews, ii. 449, 453, 478; iii. 18, 177; iv. 445; v. 393; viii. 115.
—— James, son of Walter K. of Glentig, ii. 456.
—— James, chamberlain to 3rd earl of Cassillis, ii. 463.
—— James, 3rd son of 7th earl of Cassillis, ii. 484.
—— James, 4th son of Sir Alex. K. of Culzean, ii. 489.
—— —— his 1st wife, Anne *, ii. 489.
—— —— his 2nd wife, Katharine Mure, ii. 489.
—— James, son of Archibald K. of Pavonia, ii. 494.
—— James Archibald Frere, ii. 499.
—— Jane, dau. of Robert K., ii. 497.
—— Jane, wife of Sir Andrew Melville of Garvock, vi. 94.
—— Janet, contracted to Arcbibald, 5th earl of Angus; wife of (1) Sir Alex. Gordon of Kenmure, and (2) Sir John Ramsay, lord Bothwell; and mistress of king James IV., i. 22, 183; ii. 134, 269, 459; v. 103; ix. 56.
—— Janet, wife of David Kennedy of Culzean, ii. 466.
—— Janet, wife of Fergus M'Dowall, ii. 468.
—— Janet, wife of (1) John Kennedy, and (2) Alexander Gordon, v. 109.
—— Janet, wife of Sir Alex. Boyd of Drumcol, v. 142.
—— Janet, wife of (1) James Dalrymple of Stair, and (2) Hugh Campbell of Balloch, viii. 118.
—— Jean, wife of Robert (Stewart), 1st earl of Orkney, i. 24; ii. 471; vi. 573; ix. 146.
—— Jean, wife of Hugh Kennedy of Ardmillan, ii. 489.
—— Jean, dau. of John K. of Culzean, ii. 490.
—— Jean, wife of Sir Gilbert Kennedy of Girvanmains, ii. 491.
—— Jean, wife of Wm. Stewart of Carragan, ix. 56.
—— John, 3rd son of John, lord Kennedy, ii. 458; ix. 56.
—— John, son of James K., ii. 489.
—— John, eldest son of John K. of Culzean, ii. 489.

* Name unknown.

Kennedy, John, lieut. R.N., son of Lewis K., ii. 491.
—— John, 2nd son of 11th earl of Cassillis, ii. 496.
—— —— his wife, Charlotte Gill, ii. 496.
—— John, secretary of Legation, ii. 496.
—— —— his wife, Amelia Mary Briggs, ii. 497.
—— John, 3rd son of Archibald, styled earl of Cassillis, ii. 498.
—— John, lieut. 4th Royal Scots Fusiliers, ii. 501.
—— —— his wife, Mary Adelaide Learmonth, ii. 501.
—— John, Largs, v. 109.
—— —— his wife, Janet Kennedy, v. 109.
—— John, in Chapel at Lochhead of Lochryan, v. 113.
—— John, provost of the chapel royal, St. Andrews, v. 394.
—— John, minister of Peterculter, vii. 206.
—— John Gilbert, ii. 498.
—— —— his wife, Henriette Marie Louise Aschenbach, ii. 499.
—— Sir John Gordon, K.C.M.G., ii. 497.
—— —— his wife, Evelyn Adela Bootle-Wilbraham, ii. 497.
—— Julia Alice, wife of col. R. W. B. Follett, ii. 501.
—— Katharine, wife of Alexander, styled lord Montgomerie, ii. 456; iii. 432.
—— Katharine, wife of Thomas Kennedy of Bargany, ii. 458.
—— Katharine, wife of (1) William, 3rd lord Herries of Terregles, and (2) John Wallace, ii. 458 *n.*; iv. 408.
—— Katharine, wife of (1) Quintin Mure, and (2) Wm. Hamilton, ii. 463.
—— Katharine, dau. of David K. of Culzean, ii. 466.
—— Katharine, wife of (1) Sir P. Vaus of Barnbarroch, and (2) Wm. Maclellan of Auchlane, ii. 471; v. 259.
—— Katharine, wife of William, lord Cochrane, ii. 482, 483; iii. 350, 352; ix. 77.
—— Katharine, dau. of John K. of Culzean, ii. 490.
—— Katharine, wife of capt. Lawrence Nugent, ii. 491.
—— Katharine, wife of Dr. Joseph Mallet, ii. 494.
—— Lewis, collector of customs, Irvine, ii. 491; ix. 24.
—— —— his wife, Magdalen *or* Margaret Cochrane, ii. 491.
—— Margaret, wife of Sir John Forbes of Druminnor, ii. 447; iv. 46.
—— Margaret, wife of Andrew, 2nd lord Avandale, ii. 460; vi. 510.
—— Margaret, dau. of David K. of Culzean, ii. 466.
—— Margaret, wife of (1) William Wallace,

and (2) Gilbert, 3rd earl of Cassillis, ii. 471.
Kennedy, Margaret, wife of Gilbert Burnet, bishop of Salisbury, ii. 481.
— Margaret, wife of Sir P. Agnew, ii. 488.
— Margaret, wife of Alex. Craufurd of Skeldon, ii. 489.
— Margaret, dau. of Robert K., ii. 497.
— Margaret, wife of Thomas Eyre of Hassop, ii. 500; vi. 456; ix. 58, 143.
— Margaret, wife of John, 2nd lord Cathcart, ii. 510.
— Margaret, wife of Andrew, 3rd lord Ochiltree and 1st baron Castle-Stuart, vi. 516.
— Marian, wife of Gilbert Kennedy of Girvanmains, ii. 489; ix. 57.
— Marion, contracted to (1) John Wallace, and (2) James Boyd, ii. 456; v. 148.
— Marion, wife of (1) Thos. Maclellan of Bombie, and (2) William Campbell of Skeldon, ii. 467; v. 262; ix. 56.
— Marjory, dau. of 3rd marquess of Ailsa, ii. 502.
— Mary, dau. of 6th earl of Cassillis, ii. 482.
— Mary, dau. of 7th earl of Cassillis, ii. 485.
— Mary, dau. of major Thos. K. of Baltersan, ii. 489.
— Mary, dau. of Sir Archibald K. of Culzean, ii. 491.
— Mary, wife of Richard Oswald, ii. 500.
— Mary, wife of 6th lord Rollo, vii. 206.
— Mary Alice, wife of A. J. Howard, ii. 499.
— Mary Oswald, ii. 499.
— Nigel, 9th son of Archibald, styled earl of Cassillis, ii. 499.
— — his 1st wife, Katharine Anne Frere May, ii. 499.
— — his 2nd wife, Elizabeth Charlotte Neeld, ii. 499.
— Quintin, abbot of Crossraguel, ii. 462, 465.
— Robert, 5th son of 1st lord Kennedy, ii. 454.
— Robert, 3rd son of 11th earl of Cassillis, ii. 496.
— — his wife, Jane Macomb, ii. 496.
— Robert, son, of Archibald K. of Pavonia, ii. 494.
— Robert, vi. 411.
— — his wife, Marion Napier, vi. 411.
— Sophia Eliza, wife of John Levett, ii. 497.
— Susanna, wife of Sir P. McKie of Larg, ii. 488.
— Susanna, wife of 9th earl of Eglinton, ii. 491; iii. 456.
— Thomas, 2nd son of 2nd earl of Cassillis, ii. 465.
Kennedy, Thomas, 4th son of John K. of Culzean, ii. 490; ix. 57.
— Thomas, 6th son of Alex. K. of Craigoch, ii. 494.
— Thomas, barrister, New Jersey, ii. 494.
— Thomas Francis Archibald, lieut.-col., ii. 499.
— — his wife, Ethel Mary Fowler, ii. 499.
— Walter, parson of Douglas, ii. 456.
— — his wife, Christian Hynd, ii. 456.
— William, 4th son of John, lord Kennedy, ii. 458.
— William, abbot of Crossraguel, ii. 461; ix. 56 *bis*.
— William, 5th son of Alex. K. of Craigoch, ii. 491.
— William, capt. R.A., ii. 499.
— — his wife, Cecilia Sarah Jane de Blois, ii. 499.
— William, 30th regt., ii. 499.
— — his wife, Susan Funnell, ii. 499.
— Sir William Robert, K.C.B., admiral, ii. 497.
— — his wife, Edith Louisa Stopford, ii. 497.
— * contracted to Thomas Kennedy, Bargany, ii. 468.
— * wife of David Kennedy of Drumellan, ii. 493.
— * wife of George Campbell of Loudoun, v. 493.
Kennedy-Erskine of Dun, Augustus John William Henry, ii. 500.
— — his wife, Alice Marjorie Cunninghame Foote, ii. 500.
— — John, 2nd son of 1st marquess of Ailsa, ii. 499.
— — his wife, Augusta Fitzclarence, ii. 499.
— — William Henry, ii. 500.
— — his wife, Katharine Jones, ii. 500.
— Augusta Millicent Anne Mary, wife of J. H. Erskine-Wemyss, ii. 500; viii. 511.
— Millicent Augusta Vivian, ii. 500.
— Violet Augusta Mary Frederica, wife of A. O. Jacob, ii. 500.
— Wilhelmina, wife of 2nd earl of Munster, ii. 500.
Kennet, Robert Bruce, senator of the College of Justice, lord, i. 553.
— of Coxhow, Mary, wife of 5th earl of Seaforth, vii. 511.
— — Nicholas, vii. 511.
Kenneth Macalpine, king of Scots, v. 28; viii. 264 *n*.
— of Kintail, eponymous ancestor of the clan Mackenzie, vii. 495, 496.
— — his wife, Morna Macdougal, vii. 496.
Kenneth, father of Gartnach, mormaer of Buchan, ii. 251.

* Name unknown.

Kenneth, grandfather of Donald, mormaer of Mar, v. 566.
Kenneth, father of Malcolm of Middleton, vi. 170.
Kenny, Mary Cecilia Violet, wife of vice-admiral G. A. Primrose, vii. 226.
—— Thomas, M.P., vii. 226.
Kent, Edmund (Holland), 4th earl of, v. 588.
—— Henry (Grey), duke of, ii. 208; vi. 23.
—— —— his 1st wife, Jemima Crewe, ii. 208.
—— of Innerwick, Robert, iii. 424.
—— —— Helen, wife of John Montgomerie, iii. 424.
—— Elizabeth, wife of lord Henry Murray, i. 493.
—— Richard, Liverpool, i. 493.
Keogh, Mary Anne, wife of major James Rollo, vii. 207.
Keppel, Louisa, wife of capt. F. W. Charteris, viii. 516.
—— William H. A., vii. 452.
—— —— his wife, Charlotte Elizabeth Eleanor Fraser, vii. 452.
KER OF CESSFORD AND CAVERTON, KER, LORD, vii. 343-350.
Ker, Harry, 2nd son of 1st earl of Roxburghe; styled lord, v. 457, 475, 476; vii. 344, 347.
—— —— his wife, Margaret Hay, iii. 578; vii. 347; ix. 153 *bis*.
—— Robert, first lord, vii. 343.
—— William, elder son of 1st earl of Roxburghe; styled lord, vii. 345.
KER OF CESSFORD AND CAVERTON, KER, LORD, vii. 350-360.
Ker of Cessford and Caverton, John, first lord, vii. 350.
KERR OF DOLPHINSTOUN, KER, LORD, v. 466-487.
Kerr of Dolphinstoun, Robert, first lord, v. 466.
KER OF KERSHAUGH, KER, BARON, v. 483-487.
Ker of Kershaugh, William, first baron, v. 483; ix. 131.
KERR OF LANGNEWTOUNE, KER, LORD, v. 466-487.
Kerr of Langnewtoune, Robert, first lord, v. 466.
KER OF NEWBATTLE, KER, LORD, v. 469-487.
Ker of Newbattle, William, first lord, v. 469.
KERR OF NEWBOTTLE, OXNAM, JEDBURGH, DOLPHINGSTONE, AND NISBITTS, KER, LORD, v. 477-487.
Kerr of Newbottle, Oxnam, Jedburgh, Dolphingstone, and Nisbitts, Robert, first lord, v. 76, 77, 477.
KERR OF NISBET, KER, LORD, v. 466-487.
Kerr of Nisbet, Robert, first lord, v. 466.
KER OF WAKEFIELD, KER, BARON, vii. 351-352.
Ker of Wakefield, Robert, first baron, vii. 351.
KER OF WAKEFIELD, KER, EARL, vii. 351-352.
Ker of Wakefield, Robert, first earl, vii. 351.
KER, EARL OF ANCRAM, v. 466-487.
KER, MARQUESS of BOWMONT, vii. 350-360.
KER, VISCOUNT OF BRIENE, v. 477-487.
KER, VISCOUNT OF BROXMOUTH, vii. 350-360.
KER, MARQUESS OF CESSFORD, vii. 350-360.
KER, LORD JEDBURGH, v. 49-80.
KER, EARL OF KELSO, vii. 350-360.
KER, LORD KER of CESSFORD and CAVERTON, vii. 343-350.
KER, LORD KER OF CESSFORD AND CAVERTON, vii. 350-360.
KER, BARON KER OF KERSHAUGH, v. 483, 487.
KER, LORD KER OF NEWBATTLE, v. 469-487.
KER, LORD KERR OF NEWBOTTLE, OXNAM, JEDBURGH, DOLPHINSTONE, AND NISBITTS, v. 477.
KER, LORD KERR OF NISBET, LANGNEWTOUNE, AND DOLPHINSTOUN, v. 466-487.
KER, BARON KER OF WAKEFIELD, vii. 351-352.
KER, EARL KER OF WAKEFIELD, vii. 351-352.
KER, EARL OF LOTHIAN, v. 456-487.
KER, MARQUESS OF LOTHIAN, v. 452-487.
KER, LORD NEWBOTLE, v. 456.
KER, LORD ROXBURGHE, vii. 341-360.
KER, EARL OF ROXBURGHE, vii. 343-360.
KER, DUKE OF ROXBURGHE, vii. 344-360.
Ker of Abbotrule, Charles, 1st laird, v. 474.
—— —— his wife, Cecily Scott, v. 474.
—— of Altonburn, Andrew, 2nd son of Robert K., ii. 323; vii. 318, 319.
—— —— Andrew, ii. 541; v. 49, 50; vii. 321.
—— —— his 1st wife, * Douglas, vii. 323.
—— —— his 2nd wife, Margaret Tweedie, vii. 323.
—— —— Henry, vii. 317.
—— —— John, 1st laird, vii. 316.
—— —— his wife, Mariota *, vii. 316.
—— —— John, 3rd laird, vii. 318.
—— —— Richard, vii. 318.
—— —— Robert, vii. 318.
—— —— Sir Robert, vii. 341.
—— —— Walter, v. 49, 50 *bis*, 51; vii. 326.
—— of Ancrum, Robert, 3rd son of Sir Andrew K. of Ferniebirst, v. 57, 58, 59 *bis*, 63 *ter*, 77, 460.
—— —— his wife, Isabel Home, v. 460.
—— —— Sir Robert, provost of Jedburgh, iii. 371; v. 56, 459, 460, 462, 464; viii. 194.
—— —— his 1st wife, Elizabeth Murray v. 466, 467.
—— —— his 2nd wife, Anne Stanley, v. 466, 467.

* Name unknown.

Ker of Ancrum, William, v. 72, 454, 462; vii. 342.
— — hi wife, Margaret Dundas, v. 463.
— — Sir William, v. 452, 460, 468.
— — his wife, Anne Ker, v. 459, 460, 470.
— of Ashiesteil, Sir Andrew, v. 74.
— of Bedrule, Andrew, v. 58, 59.
— of Blackhope, Sir William, 2nd son of 1st earl of Lothian, v. 457.
— — his wife, Jean Donaldson, ix. 130.
— of Boithill, William, vii. 325.
— of Bonnington, James, 2nd son of Andrew K. of Altonburn, vii. 321.
— of Borthwickshiels, Andrew, ii. 323; vii. 319, 320.
— of Boydislands, Robert, vii. 341.
— of Broomland, William, viii. 442.
— — his wife, Elizabeth Hay, viii. 442.
— of Broxfield, Mark, vii. 330.
— of Buchtrig, Sir Thomas, ancestor of the family of, v. 464.
— of Carrosheuch, Andrew, v. 58.
— — Sir Andrew, v. 72.
— of Cattiscleuch, Andrew, vii. 321.
— of Cavers, John, son of John K. of West Nisbet, v. 70, 78.
— — Thomas, ancestor of the family of, v. 53.
— — Sir Thomas, vi. 15.
— — his wife, Grisell Halket, vi. 15.
— of Caverton, Sir Andrew, vii. 330, 332.
— — his wife, Agnes Crichton, vii. 332.
— — Sir Andrew, eldest son of Sir Walter K. of Cessford, vii. 337.
— — his contracted wife, Elizabeth Douglas, vii. 125, 338; ix. 153.
— — Sir Robert, warden of the Middle Marches, vii. 325, 328, 329.
— — his wife, Christian Rutherfurd, vii. 329.
— — Walter, v. 50; vii. 324 *bis*, 326.
— — his 1st wife, *, vii. 329.
— — his 2nd wife, Agnes Crichton, iii. 61; vii. 329.
— of Cessford, Andrew, 1st laird, v. 49, 50 *bis*; vii. 321, 323; ix. 153.
— — his 1st wife, * Douglas, vii. 323.
— — his 2nd wife, Margaret Tweedie, vii. 323.
— — Andrew, the younger, eldest son of Andrew K. of Altonburn, vii. 322, 323.
— — his wife, Margaret Hephurn, ii. 148; vii. 324.
— — Sir Andrew, 3rd laird, iv. 470; v. 57, 58; vii. 330, 332.
— — his wife, Agnes Crichton, iii. 226 *n.*; vii. 333.
— — Sir Andrew, the younger, son of Walter K. of Cessford, vii. 125, 337.
— — his contracted wife, Elizabeth Douglas, vii. 125, 338; ix. 153.

* Name unknown.

Ker of Cessford, Margaret, dau. of Andrew K., iv. 52; vii. 324.
— — Sir Robert, the younger, vii. 329.
— — his wife, Christian Rutherfurd, vii. 329.
— — Sir Robert, 6th laird, v. 72; vii. 341.
— — his 1st wife, Margaret Maitland, v. 296; vii. 345.
— — Walter, 2nd laird, iv. 468; v. 49, 50 *bis*, 55; vii. 323, 325, 326, 332, 367; ix. 153 *bis*.
— — his 1st wife, *, vii. 329.
— — his 2nd wife, Agnes Crichton, iii. 61; vii. 329; viii. 274.
— — Sir Walter, 4th laird, v. 59, 452; vii. 334.
— — his wife, Isabella Ker, v. 59; vii. 337.
— — William, 5th laird, ii. 171; vii. 339.
— — his wife, Janet Douglas, v. 72; vii. 126, 341.
— of Chatto, James, v. 464; vii. 377, 379.
— — William, vii. 78.
— — his wife, Christian Scott, vii. 78.
— — of Clarilaw, Sir Robert, vii. 343.
— of Cockpen, Sir William, 2nd son of 1st earl of Lothian, v. 457.
— of Coitlaw, Mark, v. 455.
— of Corbet, John, v. 464.
— — his wife, Isabel Ker, v. 464.
— of Crailing, Sir Andrew, v. 51.
— — Sir James, 4th son of Sir Thos. K. of Ferniehurst, v. 53, 69, 73.
— — his wife, Mary Rutherford of Hundalie, v. 70.
— — Thomas, v. 50, 51.
— — Walter, iv. 468.
— of Over Crailing, Thomas, 3rd son of Sir Thos. K. of Ferniehirst, v. 69, 73.
— of Dirleton, *, iv. 52.
— — his wife, Margaret *, iv. 52.
— — Andrew, v. 58.
— — his wife, Janet Home, v. 58.
— of Dolphingston, Andrew, eldest son of Mark K., ix. 153.
— — Mark, ii. 542; v. 55; vii. 330, 335, 354; ix. 153.
— — his wife, Marjorie Ainslie of Dolphingston, vii. 331.
— of Dryburgh Abbey, William, v. 55.
— of Erneheuch, William, vii. 340.
— of Eshtries, John, v. 70.
— of Ewinstoun, William, v. 455.
— — his wife, Jean Johnstone, i. 248; v. 455.
— of Fawdonside, Andrew, vi. 514; vii. 337.
— — his 2nd wife, Margaret Stewart, vi. 514.
— — George, tutor of Cessford, vii. 330, 334, 335.
— — his wife, Margaret Haliburton, vii. 330.

* Name unknown.

Ker of Fawdonside, George, iii. 120.
—— —— his contr. wife, Janet Scott, ii. 230.
—— —— Sir Walter, v. 459; vii. 330, 348.
—— of Fentoun, Andrew, Iconimus of Kelso, v. 454.
—— —— his wife, Isabella Whitlaw, v. 454.
—— of West Fenton, Sir Andrew, v. 58.
—— of Ferniehurst, Sir Andrew, warden of the Middle Marches, ii. 543, 545; v. 51, 52, 55, 60, 72, 77; vii. 333.
—— —— his alleged wife, Margaret Colville ii. 543; v. 56.
—— —— his wife, Janet Hume, v. 59 *bis*; vi. 4.
—— —— Sir Andrew, provost of Jedburgh, v. 72; ix. 116.
—— —— his wife, Anna Stewart, v. 72, 73, 75; vi. 516.
—— —— Sir Andrew, master of Jedburgh, i. 202; v. 75; vi. 331.
—— —— Sir John, warden of the Middle Marches, v. 59 *bis*, 60, 72, 77, 461.
—— —— his wife, Katharine Ker, v. 61; vii. 334.
—— —— Margaret, wife of Thomas K. of Smailholm, v. 50, 51, 52, 55.
—— —— Ralph, ancestor of the family of, v. 49, 51 *n*.
—— —— Robert, son of Sir James K. of Crailing, v. 70, 76.
—— —— Thomas, 3rd son of Andrew K. of Altenburn and Cessford, v. 49, 50, 51 *n*., 452; vii. 324.
—— —— his wife, Margaret Ker, v. 51 *bis*, 52.
—— —— Sir Thomas, provost of Jedburgh, warden of the Middle Marches, iv. 471; v. 52, 62, 72; ix. 116.
—— —— his 1st wife, Janet Kirkaldy, v. 67, 68.
—— —— his 2nd wife, Janet Scott, ii. 231; v. 69.
—— of Fernielee, vii. 73.
—— —— Sir Thomas, colonel, iv. 105.
—— —— his wife, Christiana Ruthven, i. 124; iv. 105.
—— —— Sir Thomas, vii. 78.
—— of Feuelrule, Sir Andrew, v. 55, 60.
—— —— Sir Andrew, v. 74, 75.
—— —— Andrew, v. 74.
—— —— Janet, dau. of Sir Thomas K. of Ferniehurst, v. 62, 63.
—— —— Sir John, v. 60.
—— —— Sir Thomas, v. 62.
—— of the Forest of Ettrick, John, vii. 315, 316.
—— —— his wife, Marieta, vii. 316.
—— of the Forest of Selkirk, John, vii. 315, 316.
—— of Friarness, George, vii. 581.
—— of Frogdean, Henry, vii. 83.
—— of Gateshaw, George, vii. 338.
Ker of Gateshaw, James, iv. 468; vii. 324.
—— —— John, ix. 154.
—— —— his wife, Cecill Ker, ix. 154.
—— —— Lancelot, vii. 335.
—— —— Thomas, ancestor of the family of, vii. 321.
—— of Gillistengues, William, v. 55.
—— of Gledhouse, Mark, v. 455.
—— of Nether Gogar, Andrew, 2nd son of Sir John K. of Ferniehirst, v. 60, 61.
—— of Graden, Henry, vii. 379.
—— —— his wife, Lilias Rutherfurd, vii. 379.
—— of Grange, William, 2nd son of Sir Thos. K. of Ferniehirst, v. 67.
—— —— his wife, Elizabeth Lyon, v. 68.
—— of Greenhead, Andrew, eldest son of Ralph K. of Primsideloch, v. 53, 80.
—— —— Sir Andrew, 1st bart., vii. 79.
—— —— his 1st wife, Elizabeth Scott, vii. 79.
—— —— his 2nd wife, Katharine Wemyss, viii. 501.
—— of Grubet, Sir James, v. 69.
—— of Halden, Sir William, v. 474.
—— —— his wife, Agnes Cockburn, v. 474.
—— of Halyden, Sir Robert, vii. 343.
—— of Hardenwede, Walter, vii. 326.
—— of Heriotmure, Sir Mark, v. 457.
—— of Hieton, Robert, ancestor of the family of, v. 53.
—— of Hilltoune, John, vi. 593.
—— —— his wife, Helen *, vi. 593.
—— of Hindhope, Andrew, vii. 326.
—— —— Walter, vii. 326.
—— of Hirsell, Sir Andrew, son of Mark K. of Littledean (?) v. 64; vii. 331, 337.
—— —— Sir John, iv. 476.
—— —— Walter, vii. 342.
—— of Hownam, Sir Andrew, v. 51.
—— —— Thomas, v. 50, 51.
—— of Hundalie, Sir James, M.P., v. 70.
—— —— his wife, Mary Rutherford, v. 70.
—— of Huntleisland, Andrew, v. 50.
—— —— Walter, v. 50.
—— of Huttenhall, George, iv. 449.
—— of Jedburgh, Sir John, v. 75, 471; vii. 377.
—— of Jedburgh Forest, Andrew, v. 59.
—— —— Sir John, v. 59.
—— —— John, v. 70.
—— of Jedwardsfield, Sir Robert, v. 466.
—— of Kelso, Sir Robert, vii. 343.
—— of Kershaugh, Andrew, cupbearer to king Robert III., v. 51 *n*.
—— —— his wife, * Edmistoun, v. 51 *n*.
—— —— Andrew, v. 51 *n*.
—— —— his wife, Jean Crichton, v. 51 *n*.
—— —— Andrew, v. 51 *n*.
—— —— his wife, Mary Herries, v. 51 *n*.

* Name unknown.

Ker of Kershaugh, Ralph, v. 51 *n*.
— — his wife, Mary Towers, v. 51 *n*.
— — Sir Thomas, v. 51 *n*.; viii. 9 *n*.
— — his alleged wife, Margaret Somerville, v. 51 *n*.; viii. 9.
— — Thomas, iv. 444.
— — his wife, Elizabeth Home, iv. 444.
— — Thomas, v. 51 *n*.
— — his wife, Katharine Colville, v. 51 *n*.
— — Thomas, v. 50, 51 *n*.
— — his wife, Margaret Ker of Ferniehirst, v. 51.
— of Kersland, David, v. 497.
— — his wife, Annabella Campbell, v. 497.
— — John, iii. 438.
— — his wife, Agnes Montgomerie, iii. 438.
— — Robert, ii. 101.
— — William, ancestor of the family of, vii. 316.
— of King's Cramond, Charles, director of Chancery, v. 477, 480.
— — his wife, Janet Murray, v. 478.
— of Langlie, William, 5th son of Thos. K. of Ferniehirst, v. 55, 59.
— of Langnewton, Sir Robert, v. 466.
— of Langsland, Andrew, vii. 321.
— of Langton, John, 2nd son of Sir Andrew K. of Ferniehirst, v. 60.
— of Lintalee, James, v. 73.
— of Linton, George, vii. 335, 337, 342; viii. 15.
— — James, ancestor of the family of, vii. 321.
— — Walter, viii. 15, 25.
— — William, v. 463 *bis*; vii. 77.
— of Littledean, John Strother, iii. 103; vii. 23.
— — his wife, Jean Maule, iii. 103; vii. 23.
— — Sir Mark, eldest son of Sir John K. of Hirsel, iv. 476.
— — his wife, Margaret Home, iv. 476.
— — Mark, 2nd son of Walter K. of Caverton, vii. 330, 354.
— — his wife, Marjorie Ainslie, vii. 331.
— — Walter, viii. 15, 25.
— — Walter, brigadier-general, vii. 331, 353; ix. 130.
— — Walter Foster, brigade-major 9th Foot, vii. 331.
— of Lochtour, Sir John, v. 464.
— — his 2nd wife, Jean Ker, v. 464.
— of Lusaney, v. 80.
— of Mauldslie, Sir Mark, 3rd son of 1st earl of Lothian, v. 457; vii. 330, 334.
— of Maxton, Mark, vii. 330.
— — his wife, Marjorie Ainslie of Dolphingston, vii. 330.
— of Maxwellhaugh, Andrew, v. 59.
Ker of Maxwellhaugh, Sir Andrew, v. 74.
— — Gilbert, v. 62.
— — Sir James, 4th son of Sir Thos. K. of Ferniehirst, v. 69.
— — his wife, Mary Rutherford, v. 69, 70.
— of Mersington, James, vii. 335, 337.
— — Sir Thomas, vii. 367.
— — his wife, Helen Rutherfurd, vii. 367, 371.
— — Thomas, vii. 342.
— — Thomas, vii. 79.
— — his wife, Margaret Scott, vii. 79.
— of Mertoun, William, vii. 325.
— of Morieston, James *or* John, iii. 350, 359; ix. 76.
— — his wife, Grizel Cochrane, iii. 350; ix. 76 *bis*.
— of Newbattle, Anne, wife of Sir Wm. Ker of Ancrum, v. 452, 459, 460.
— — Mark, commendator of Newbattle, iii. 95; v. 453; vii. 334, 337, 342.
— — his wife, Helen Leslie, v. 454; vii. 289.
— of Newfield, Robert, viii. 515.
— of Newton, Robert, v. 461.
— — his wife, Isabel Home, v. 461.
— — Robert, v. 461.
— — his wife, Helen Grahamslaw, v. 462.
— — Robert, v. 462.
— — his wife, Euphemia Douglas, v. 462.
— of Nisbet, Andrew, v. 72.
— — John, vii. 318.
— of West Nisbet, John, v. 70.
— — his wife, Jean Ker, v. 70; ix. 116.
— of Ormiston, Sir Mark, vii. 341.
— — William, vii. 340.
— of Overtoun, William, 2nd son of Wm. K. of Ancrum, v. 463.
— — William, v. 463 *bis*.
— of Oxnam, Sir Andrew, v. 52, 55, 57.
— — Sir Andrew, v. 72.
— — Sir Andrew, only son of 1st lord Jedburgh, v. 68, 73, 74, 75.
— — Sir James, 4th son of Sir Thos. K. of Ferniehurst, v. 69.
— — Sir Thomas, v. 63, 67.
— — Thomas, 3rd son of Sir Thos. K. of Ferniehirst, v. 69.
— of Prestongrange, Mark, commendator of Newbattle, Master of Requests, v. 455.
— — his wife, Margaret Maxwell, v. 456.
— of Primside, Andrew, 1st laird, vii. 320.
— — Andrew, 2nd laird, v. 50; vii. 321.
— — James, vii. 320.
— — Thomas, vii. 321.
— — Walter, v. 50.
— of Primsideloch, Andrew, v. 53.
— — Gilbert, vii. 335, 337, 342.

Ker of Primsideloch, Ralph, 2nd son of Thos. K. of Ferniehurst, v. 52, 57, 80.
—— —— his 1st wife, Margaret Murray, v. 52.
—— —— his 2nd wife, Margaret Rutherford, v. 53.
—— —— his 3rd wife, Marion Halliburton, v. 53 *n*.
—— of Quitebankdene, Richard, vii. 320.
—— of Reddcn, Sir Thomas, 3rd son of Wm. K. of Ancrum, v. 463.
—— —— his 1st wife, Jean Ker, v. 464.
—— —— his 2nd wife, Mary Douglas, v. 464.
—— of Rickiltoun, Sir Robert. 5th son of Sir Thos. K. of Ferniehirst, v. 70, 73.
—— of Roxburghe, William, 1st laird, vii. 340.
—— of Old Roxburgh, Andrew, vii. 322.
—— of Romanno Grange, Andrew, Iconimus of Kelso, v. 454.
—— of St. Thomas's Chapel, Sir Andrew, v. 60.
—— —— Sir John, v. 60.
—— of Samuelston, George, iv. 449.
—— —— George, iii. 92, 280; vii. 580; ix. 157.
—— —— his wife, Mariota St. Clair of Kimmerghame, iii. 280; iv. 453; vii. 580.
—— —— Nicola, wife of (1) Alexander, 2nd lord Home, and (2) Sir Alex. Ramsay of Dalhousie, iii. 92; iv. 453 *bis*.
—— of Selkirk, William, vii. 325.
—— of Smailholm, Andrew, v. 50.
—— —— Robert, vii. 318.
—— —— Thomas, 3rd son of Andrew K. of Altonburn and Cessford, v. 49, 50, 80.
—— —— Walter, iv. 468; v. 50; vii. 327.
—— of Sprouston, Sir Robert, vii. 342, 343.
—— of Spynie, James, iv. 474.
—— of Swinside, Sir Andrew, v. 74.
—— of Syndlaws, James, iv. 474.
—— of Trearne, Stephen, iii. 429.
—— of Wawtyswelys, Richard, vii. 320.
—— of Wellis, and Welshawhed, Sir Andrew, v. 74.
—— —— Sir Thomas, v. 74.
—— of Woodheid, Robert, 3rd son of Sir Andrew K. of Ferniehurst, v. 57, 58, 59 *bis*, 63 *ter*, 77, 460.
—— —— William, v. 462.
—— of Yair, William, 5th son of Andrew K. of Cessford and Altonburn, v. 50 *bis*, vii. 325.
—— Agnes, wife of John Edmonstone of Edmonstone, vii. 339; ix. 153.
—— Alexander, younger son of William K., *alias* Kirkaldy of Grange, v. 68.
—— Alice Mary, wife of Thos. Gaisford of Offington, v. 485.
—— Alison, wife of John Rutherford of Hunthill, v. 76; vii. 379; ix. 116 *ter*, 154.
Ker, Andrew, eldest son of Andrew K. of Auldtonburn and Cessford, ii. 148; vii. 322, 323.
—— —— his wife, Margaret Hepburne, ii. 148.
—— Andrew, in Ashysteil and Bowerhope, v. 51.
—— Andrew, 4th son of Wm. K. of Ancrum, v. 464.
—— Sir Andrew, master of Jedburgh, v. 75, 458.
—— —— his wife, Margaret Ker, v. 458; xi. 130.
—— Andrew del, of the county of Stirling, vii. 316.
—— Andrew, 3rd son of Sir Andrew K. of Cessford, vii. 334, 337.
—— —— his wife, Marion Pringle, vii. 334.
—— Andrew, son of Thomas K., Morham, ix. 153.
—— Anna, dau. of 1st earl of Ancram, ix. 131.
—— Anne, wife of 2nd lord Balmerino, i. 568; v. 71.
—— Anne, wife of (1) Alexander, 7th lord Home, and (2) Henry Ogle, iv. 480; v. 479.
—— Anne, dau. of 1st lord Jedburgh, v. 76; ix. 116.
—— Anne, wife of Alexander, master of Saltoun, v. 474; vii. 443.
—— Anne, wife of 4th earl of Wigtown, vii. 348, 353; ix. 153 *bis*.
—— Anne Katharine, dau. of 6th marquess of Lothian, v. 484.
—— Archibald, slain by Ogilvies and Kinnairds, v. 208.
—— Bessie, dau. of Sir Andrew K. of Caverton, vii. 338.
—— Caroline Sidney, dau. of 5th marquess of Lothian, v. 483.
—— Cecill, wife of John Ker of Gaitschaw, ix. 154.
—— Cecil Elizabeth, dau. of 7th marquess of Lothian, v. 485.
—— Cecil Victoria Constance, wife of John Walter Edward, 2nd lord Montagu of Beaulieu, ii. 246; v. 486.
—— Charles, 2nd son of 1st earl of Ancram, v. 71. 467.
—— Charles, son of 2nd earl of Lothian, v. 459, 460.
—— Charles Beauchamp, 10th Dragoons, v. 482.
—— —— his wife, Elizabeth Crump, v. 482.
—— Charles Lennox, lieut.-col. 3rd batt. Black Watch, v. 484.
—— —— his wife, Charlotte Emma Hanmer, v. 484.
—— Christian, wife of Sir James Douglas of Cavers, v. 59.
—— Christian, wife of Walter Scott of Whitefield and Harden, vii. 83.

Ker, Christine, wife of col. Oswald R. Middleton, vi. 180.
— Eleanor, wife of Walter Campbell of Shawfield, viii. 515.
— Elizabeth, wife of Sir Jas. Bellenden, ii. 71; vii. 341.
— Elizabeth, wife of 10th lord Borthwick, ii. 114; v. 474.
— Elizabeth, wife of G. Hoppringle, ii. 154.
— Elizabeth, wife of (1) Philip Rutherford, and (2) Sir Walter Scott of Buccleuch, ii. 228; vii. 331, 334, 367.
— Elizabeth, wife of Thomas, 8th earl of Dundonald, iii. 359; ix. 77.
— Elizabeth, wife of Andrew Lundin, v. 62.
— Elizabeth, wife of Sir Alex. Hamilton of Innerwick, v. 458.
— Elizabeth, wife of col. Nathaniel Rich, v. 458.
— Elizabeth, wife of George, 13th lord Ross of Halkhead, v. 480; vii. 262.
— Elizabeth, wife of 10th lord Dormer, v. 483.
— Elizabeth Georgiana, wife of 17th lord Clinton, v. 484.
— Essex, bridesmaid to queen Charlotte, vii. 351, 353.
— Frances, wife of Geo. Livingston of Bedlormie, v. 474.
— Frances, wife of George Wade, v. 484.
— Frederic Herbert, admiral R.N., v. 484.
— — his wife, Emily Sophia Maitland, v. 484.
— Frederic Walter, major, D.S.O., v. 486.
— — his wife, Helen Victoria Lilian Ker, v. 486.
— Gene, younger dau. of 2nd earl of Lothian, v. 459.
— George, 2nd son of Ralph K. of Primsideloch. v. 53, 58.
— — his wife, * Shaw, v. 53.
— George, 4th son of Thomas K. of Ferniehurst, v. 54.
— George, son of Andrew K. of Fentoun, v. 454.
— George, 3rd *or* 4th son of Mark K. of Newbattle, v. 455.
— George, 5th son of Sir Wm. K. of Ancrum, v. 464.
— Georgiana Augusta, wife of rev. G. H. Forbes, v. 485.
— Gilbert, elder son of Andrew K. of Greenhead and Primsideloch, v. 53.
— Grisell, wife of 1st earl of Marchmont, vi. 15.
— Grisel, dau. of Sir Andrew K. of Caverton, vii. 338.

* Name unknown.

Ker, Harriet Louisa Anne, wife of Sir John Stuart Forbes, v. 484.
— Harry, 2nd son of 2nd earl of Roxburghe, vii. 349.
— Helen Victoria Lilian, wife of major F. W. Ker, v. 486.
— Henrietta, wife of Sir Francis Scott of Thirlestane, v. 475; vi. 431.
— Henrietta Maria, dau. of 1st earl of Ancram, ix. 130.
— Henry, of the county of Edinburgh, vii. 316.
— Henry, sheriff of Roxburgh, vii. 317, 318.
— Henry Francis Charles, rector of Dittisham, v. 484.
— — his wife, Louisa Dorothea Hope, v. 484.
— Hugh, in Ersilton, vii. 316.
— Isobel, wife of 2nd viscount Dudhope, iii. 314; vii. 346.
— Isobel, wife of Sir Walter Ker of Cessford, v. 59; vii. 337.
— Isobel, dau. of William K., *alias* Kirkaldy of Grange, v. 68.
— Isobel, wife of Geo. Douglas of Bonjedward, v. 462.
— Isabel, wife of John Ker of Corbet, v. 464.
— Isobel, wife of Sir Wm. Douglas of Drumlanrig, v. 458; vii. 134.
— Isobel, wife of John Rutherford of Hunthill, vii. 339, 376.
— Isobel Alice Adelaide, wife of Jas. Cospatrick Scott, v. 487.
— James, 4th son of 1st earl of Lothian, v. 457, 459.
— James, 5th son of 1st marquess of Lothian, v. 478.
— Janet, wife of (1) Geo. Turnbull, and (2) Sir Walter Scott, ii. 230; v. 59; ix. 115.
— Janet, wife of 7th earl of Glencairn, iv. 246 *bis*; ix. 97.
— Jean, wife of 2nd earl of Roxburghe, i. 522; vii. 347, 348 *bis*, 353.
— Jean, wife of 3rd earl of Balcarres, i. 522; vii. 349.
— Jean, wife of col. Wm. Borthwick of Johnstonburn, ii. 101.
— Jean, wife of 5th lord Cranstoun, ii. 597; v. 479.
— Jean, wife of (1) Robert, master of Boyd, (2) David, 12th earl of Crawford, and (3) Mr. Thos. Hamilton of Robertoun, iii. 32; v. 166, 168, 457; vii. 131.
— Jean, dau. of William K., *alias* Kirkaldy of Grange, v. 68 *bis*.
— Jean, wife of John Ker of West Nisbet, v. 70 ix. 116.
— Jean, wife of Thos. Kennedy of Pinwhirrie, v. 76.

Ker, Jean, younger dau. of 2nd earl of Lothian, v. 460, 466, 470.
—— Jean, wife of (1) Sir John Ker of Lochtour, and (2) Sir John Wauchope of Niddrie, v. 464.
—— Jean, wife of 2nd earl of Perth, vii. 49, 345.
—— Jean, wife of Robert Scott of Iliston and Harden, vii. 78.
—— Jean, wife of Sir Geo. Towers of Inverleith, viii. 501; ix. 153.
—— Jean Janet, wife of 3rd marquess of Lothian, v. 480.
—— Joanna, younger dau. of 2nd earl of Lothian, v. 460, 466.
—— John, 4th son of 2nd earl of Roxburghe, ii. 72; vii. 349.
—— John, 4th son of Ralph K. of Primsideloch, v. 53, 58.
—— Sir John, in Ashysteil, v. 61.
—— —— his wife, Katharine Ker, v. 61.
—— John, 4th son of Sir John K. of Ferniehirst, v. 62 *bis*.
—— John, grandson of William K., *alias* Kirkaldy of Grange, v. 68.
—— John, illeg. son of Sir Mark K. of Mauldslie, v. 457.
—— John, 5th son of 1st earl of Lothian, v. 457, 476.
—— John, captain, 5th son of 3rd earl of Lothian, v. 474.
——John, colonel 31st regt., v. 478.
—— John, 'the hunter of Swhynhope,' vii. 315.
—— John, 2nd son of John K. of the Forest of Ettrick, vii. 317.
—— John Montagu Hobart, v. 485.
—— Julian, wife of (1) Sir P. Hume of Polwarth, and (2) Thomas, 1st earl of Haddington, iv. 313; v. 68; vi. 11; ix. 116.
—— Katharine, wife of 5th lord Herries of Terregles, iv. 414; v. 455.
—— Katharine, wife of Sir John Ker of Ferniehirst, v. 61, 62; vii. 334.
—— Katharine, wife of Henry Haliburton of Mertoun, v. 462.
—— Katharine, wife of James Stewart of Traquair, viii. 401.
—— Katharine, dau. of 1st earl of Ancram, ix. 131.
—— Lilias, wife of 9th lord Borthwick, ii. 113; v. 457, 458.
—— Lilias, wife of Nicholas Lewin, v. 76; ix. 116.
—— Lilias, dau. of 3rd earl of Lothian, v. 475; ix. 131.
—— Louisa, wife of gen. George Henry Lennox, v. 364, 481.
—— Louisa, wife of Arthur Atherley, v. 483.
—— Margaret, wife of (1) Sir Jas. Sandilands, and (2) William, 4th earl of Erroll, i. 75; iii. 567; vii. 326; viii. 383, 385; ix. 86.
Ker, Margaret, wife of (1) John Home of Ersilton, (2) Sir Wm. Colville, and (3) Robert Rynde, ii. 543; iv. 468; ix. 59 *bis*, 108.
—— Margaret, wife of D. Preston of Whitehill, iii. 120.
—— Margaret, wife of Sir G. Ramsay of Wyliecleuch, iii. 99 *n.*; iv. 299.
—— Margaret, wife of 5th lord Home, iv. 462; vii. 339.
—— Margaret, wife of Sir John Home of Cowdenknowes, iv. 470, 475: vii. 334.
—— Margaret, in Ashysteil, v. 51.
—— Margaret, wife of (1) James Menzies of Culdares, and (2) Hay of Smithfield, v. 59.
—— Margaret, wife of 5th lord Hay of Yester, v. 62; viii. 442.
—— Margaret, wife of (1) James, 7th lord Hay of Yester, and (2) Sir A. Ker, master of Jedburgh, v. 76, 458; viii. 445; ix. 130.
—— Margaret, wife of Sir Robt. Melville of Burntisland, v. 69; vi. 101.
—— Margaret, wife of Sir John Macdowall of Garthland, v. 76; ix. 116.
—— Margaret, wife of Jas. Richardson of Smeatoun, v. 475.
—— Margaret, wife of 1st lord Scott of Buccleuch, ii. 233; vii. 341.
—— Margaret, wife of Sir Wm. Scott of Harden, vii. 77.
—— Margaret, wife of George Roule of Primside, vii. 321.
—— Margaret, contr. to Andrew Macdougal, Makerstoun, vii. 332.
—— Margaret, wife of Sir James Innes of Innes, vii. 348, 353; ix. 153.
—— Margaret, dau. of 1st earl of Ancram, ix. 130.
—— Margaret, wife of John Mow of Mow, ix. 154.
—— Margaret Isobel, dau. of 9th marquess of Lothian, v. 486.
—— Mark, abbot and commendator of Newbottle, iii. 95; v. 453; vii. 334, 337, 342.
—— Mark, general, governor of Edinburgh Castle, v. 478.
—— Mark Ralph George, general, v. 484.
—— Mark Robert, vice-admiral R.N., v. 482.
—— —— his wife, Charlotte Macdonnell, countess of Antrim, v. 482.
—— Mary, wife of 2nd marquess of Douglas, i. 208; v. 478.
—— Mary, wife of (1) Jas. Halyburton of Pitcur, and (2) James, 2nd earl of Southesk, ii. 412; vii. 346; viii. 70; ix. 154.
—— Mary, wife of James Douglas, commendator of Melrose, v. 68; vi. 372; ix. 116 *bis*.

Ker, Mary, dau. of 1st lord Jedburgh, v. 76; ix. 116.
— Mary, wife of Sir Jas. Richardson of Smeatoun, v. 458.
— Mary, wife of Sir Thomas Ker of Redden, v. 464.
— Mary, wife of James Brodie of Brodie, v. 475.
— Mary, wife of Alex. Hamilton of Ballincrieff, v. 480.
— Mary, wife of col. Frederick St. John, v. 483.
— Mary, wife of Henry Kidd of Lowood, v. 486.
— Mary, bridesmaid to queen Charlotte, vii. 351.
— Mary, inf. dau. of 2nd lord Jedburgh, ix. 116.
— Nicol, of the county of Peebles, vii. 316.
— Ralph, 6th son of Andrew K. of Cessford and Altonburn, v. 50 *bis*.
— Ralph, 1330, vii. 315.
— Ralph, 3rd son of Walter K. of Cessford, v. 55; vii. 331.
— Ralph Drury, general, C.B., v. 485.
— — his wife, Anne Howard, v. 485.
— Richard, in Eliston, vii. 315.
— Robert, abbot of Kelso, 4th son of Andrew K. of Cessford and Altonburn, v. 50; vii. 324, 327.
— Robert, illeg. son of Robt. K. of Woodheid and Ancrum, v. 462.
— Robert, director of Chancery, son of Chas. K. of King's Cramond, v. 478.
— Robert, captain of Grenadiers, v. 480.
— Robert, major-general, K.H., v. 483.
— — his wife, Mary Gilbert, v. 483.
— Robert, admiral, vi. 180.
— Robert, Newcastle-on-Tyne, 1231, vii. 314.
— Robert, servitor of William, earl of Douglas, vii. 317.
— Robert, lieut.-colonel 6th Inniskillen Dragoons, vii. 351.
— Robert, 6th son of 1st earl of Ancram, ix. 130.
— Robert, 4th son of Sir Andrew K. of Cessford, ix. 153.
— Schomberg Robert, 2nd son of 6th marquess of Lothian, v. 483.
— Sophia, dau. of Harry, Lord Ker, vii. 348; ix. 153.
— Stanley, 4th son of 1st earl of Ancram, v. 71. 467; ix. 130.
— Thomas, contracted to Elizabeth Scott, ii. 231; vii. 339; ix. 153 *bis*.
— Thomas, abbot of Kelso, 3rd son of Thos. K. of Ferniehurst, v. 50, 53, 57.
— Thomas, in Ashysteil, v. 51.
— — his wife, Margaret Ker, v. 51.
— Thomas, rector of Yetholm, v. 54.
Ker, Thomas, eldest son of Sir Andrew K. of Ferniehirst, v. 57, 59.
— Thomas, apprentice to Thos. Bruce, cordiner, v. 462.
— Vere, wife of lord Neil Campbell of Ardmaddie, i. 360; v. 475.
— Vere, wife of Dr. Wilkinson, v. 468.
— Victoria Alexandrina Alberta, wife of capt. W. S. Gosling, v. 486.
— Sir Walter Talbot, admiral R.N., K.C.B., v. 485.
— — his wife, Amabel Cowper, iii. 124; v. 485.
— Wilhelmina Emilia, wife of col. John M'Leod, v. 481.
— William, commendator of Kelso, v. 53, 56, 58, 63.
— William, 3rd son of Sir John K. of Ferniehirst, v. 60, 62.
— William, elder son of William K., *alias* Kirkaldy of Grange, v. 68.
— William, illeg. son of Robt. K. of Woodheid and Ancrum, v. 462.
— William, son of Sir Wm. K. of Halden, v. 474.
— William, lieut.-general, colonel 7th Dragoons, M.P., viii, 349.
— William, sheriff of Tweeddale, 3rd son of 2nd earl of Roxburghe, vii. 349.
— William D., Glasgow, ix. 130.
— * captain, who burnt Towie House, iv. 537.
— *, wife of William Scott of Harden, vii. 73.
Ker-Bellenden, John Bellenden, ii. 75.
Kerdal, Freskin of, iii. 134.
KERSHAUGH, KER, BARON KER OF, v. 483-487.
Keroualle, Louise Renée de Perrancoet de; duchess of Portsmouth, i. 32; v. 363.
Kerry, Henry William Edmond, elder son of 5th marquess of Lansdowne; styled earl of, vi. 400.
— — his wife, Elizabeth Caroline Hope, vi. 400.
Kestern, John de, iii. 249.
Ketel, father of Orm, iii. 245.
Keth MacFadoill, Loch Lomond, vi. 25 *n.*
Ketkert, see Cathcart.
Kettins, Sir Simon of, vi. 213.
Keudell *, baron von, iii. 523.
— — his wife, Blanche Emmeline Murray, iii. 523.
Keyser of Cross Oak, Alfred, ii. 280.
— Alice Ellen, wife of A. S. M. Erskine, ii. 280.
Kiarval, king of Ireland, ii. 314.
Kid, James, minister of Holyrood, viii. 222.
Kidd of Longforgan, Christian, dau. of Roger Cissoris, iv. 271.

* Name unknown.

Kidd of Lowood, Henry, v. 486.
—— —— his wife, Mary Ker, v. 486.
Kielmansegge, count de, Hanoverian minister, ix. 168.
—— Helena Eleanora Augusta de, wife of Arthur Hay, viscount Walden, ix. 168.
KILBIRNIE, CRAWFORD (LINDSAY), LORD, iv. 175-178.
KILBRYDE, GRAHAM, LORD, i. 133-145.
Kilbryde, William, president of the Privy Council and Great Justiciary of Scotland, lord, i. 135.
Kilconcath, Adam de, ii. 426.
—— —— his wife, Margaret, countess of Carrick, ii. 246; viii. 245 *n.*
Kildrummy, Alexander, eldest son of 4th lord Elphinstone; styled lord, iii. 537, 541.
—— James, 2nd son of 4th lord Elphinstone; styled lord, iii. 537, 538.
Kilmaine, Francis William (Browne), 4th baron, ii. 502.
Kilmalew, Alexander de, v. 524.
—— Eugene de, v. 524.
—— Hector de, v. 523.
—— —— his wife, Margaret Fraser, v. 523.
KILMARNOCK, BOYD, EARL OF, v. 136-182.
Kilmarnock, James, *de jure* fifth earl of, v. 181.
—— William, first earl of, v. 173.
—— —— his wife, Jean Cunningham, iv. 249; v. 174.
—— William, second earl of, v. 175.
—— —— his wife, Letitia Boyd, v. 175.
—— William, third earl of, v. 176.
—— —— his wife, Euphemia Ross, v. 176; vii. 261.
—— William, fourth earl of, i. 572; iii. 580; v. 131, 177; ix. 120 *ter.*
—— —— his wife, Anne Livingston, v. 179, 450.
KILMARNOCK, BOYD, LORD BOYD OF, v. 136-182.
KILMARNOCK OF KILMARNOCK, HAY, BARON, iii. 585-587.
Kilmarnock of Kilmarnock, Charles Gore, third baron, iii. 586.
—— —— Victor Alexander Sereld, eldest son of 20th earl of Erroll; styled lord, iii. 587.
—— —— William George, first baron, iii. 585.
—— —— William Henry, second baron, iii. 585.
Kilmaron, Thomas of, iii. 304.
KILMAURS, CUNNINGHAM, LORD, iv. 232-252.
Kilmaurs, Alexander, first lord, iv. 232.
—— —— his wife, Margaret Hepburn, iv. 234.
—— Alexander, fifth lord, iv. 239.
—— Alexander, tenth lord, iv. 249.
—— Cuthbert, third lord, iv. 235; v. 145.
—— James, seventh lord, iv. 243.
Kilmaurs, James, eldest surviving son of 8th earl of Glencairn; styled lord, iv. 249.
—— —— his wife, Elizabeth Hamilton, iv. 249, 380.
—— James, fourteenth lord, iv. 251.
—— John, eleventh lord, iv. 249.
—— John, eldest son of 11th earl of Glencairn; styled lord, iv. 250.
—— John, fifteenth lord, iv. 251.
—— Robert, second lord, iv, 234; ix. 128.
—— —— his wife, Christian Lindsay, iv. 235; v. 394; viii. 577.
—— William, fourth lord, iv. 236.
—— William, sixth lord, iv. 242.
—— William, eighth lord, iv. 244, 246.
—— William, ninth lord, iv. 247.
—— William, eldest son of 8th earl of Glencairn; styled lord, iv. 249; vii. 133.
—— William, twelfth lord, iv. 250.
—— William, thirteenth lord, iv. 251.
—— William, eldest son of 12th earl of Glencairn; styled lord, iv. 251.
—— master of, Robert, eldest son of 1st lord Kilmaurs, iv. 234.
—— —— his wife, Christian Lindsay, iv. 235.
—— Robert, son of Wernebald, lord of, iv. 222.
—— Robert, son of Robert, lord of, iv. 223.
Kilmore, Malcolm of, husband of Marjorie Montgomerie, iii. 426.
Kilmorey, John (Needham), 1st viscount, v. 86.
—— —— his wife, Dorothy Smith, v. 86.
—— Francis Jack (Needham), 2nd earl of, ii. 565.
KILPATRICK, HAMILTON, BARON OF, i. 46-74.
Kilpatrick, James, eldest son of Claud, lord Paisley; first baron of, i. 46.
—— of Colquhoun, Humphrey, v. 331.
Kilpont, *see* Kinpont.
KILSYTH, LIVINGSTON, VISCOUNT OF, v. 183-194.
Kilsyth, James, first viscount of, v. 191.
—— —— his wife, Euphame Cunningham, v. 192.
—— James, second viscount of, v. 192.
—— William, third viscount of, iii. 330, 352; v. 192.
—— —— his 1st wife, Jean Cochrane, iii. 352; v. 193.
—— —— his 2nd wife, Barbara Macdougall, v. 194.
Kilvington of Hatfield, Orfeur William, vicar of Brignall, vi. 436.
—— —— his wife, Maria Margaret Napier, vi. 436.
Kilwinning, Michael (Balfour), lord, i. 541, 554; iii. 445.
—— Hugh (Montgomerie), lord, i. 541; iii. 444.

Kilwinning, Alexander (Seton), lord, i. 541; iii. 445; viii. 591.
Kimmerghame, Andrew Hume, lord of Session, lord, vi. 16.
Kinardley, Stephen of, vi. 170.
Kinbuck of Meiklour, Alan, vii. 32.
Kincaid of Kincaid, James, vii. 292.
—— —— his wife, Christian Leslie, vii. 291.
—— of Warriston, John, ii. 63; vi. 158.
—— —— his wife, Margaret Bellenden, ii. 63.
—— —— John, iii. 96.
—— —— his wife, Jean Ramsay, iii. 96.
—— Helen, wife of (1) R. Crauford of Beircrofts, (2) Gilbert Graham of Gartavertanc, and (3) Gavin Hamilton of Hill, vi. 158.
KINCARDINE, GORDON, LORD, iv. 549-558.
Kincardine, George, first lord, iv. 550.
KINCARDINE, BRUCE, EARL OF, iii. 484-497.
Kincardine, Alexander, second earl of, iii. 486; viii. 452.
—— —— his wife, Veronica van Arsen van Somelsdyke, iii. 487.
—— Alexander, third earl of, iii. 487; ix. 83.
—— Alexander, fourth earl of, iii. 488.
—— —— his wife, Christian Bruce, iii. 489.
—— Alexander, sixth earl of, iii. 489.
—— —— his wife, Jean [Nisbet], iii. 489 *n.*
—— Charles, ninth earl of, iii. 481, 491.
—— —— his wife, Martha White, iii. 491.
—— Edward, first earl of, iii. 486.
—— James, twelfth earl of, iii. 494.
—— —— his 1st wife, Elizabeth Mary Cumming-Bruce, iii. 495.
—— —— his 2nd wife, Mary Louisa Lambton, iii. 495.
—— Robert, fifth earl of, iii. 489.
—— Thomas, seventh earl of, iii. 490.
—— —— his wife, Rachel Paunceford, iii. 490.
—— Thomas, eleventh earl of, iii. 492.
—— —— his 1st wife, Mary Hamilton Nisbet, iii. 493.
—— —— his 2nd wife, Elizabeth Oswald, iii. 493.
—— Victor Alexander, thirteenth earl of, iii. 495, 496.
—— —— his wife, Constance Carnegie, iii. 496.
—— William, eighth earl of, iii. 490.
—— —— his wife, Janet Roberton, iii. 490.
—— William Robert, tenth earl of, iii. 492.
KINCARDINE, GRAHAM, EARL OF, vi. 247-274.
Kincardine, James, first earl of, vi. 247.
—— James, second earl of, vi. 257.
—— James, eldest son of 3rd duke of Montrose; styled earl of, vi. 271.
—— James Angus, grandson of 5th duke of Montrose; styled earl of, vi. 274.
KINCLAVEN, STEWART, LORD, ii. 441.
Kinclaven, John, lord, ii. 440; vi. 573, 576.
Kincraigie of Kincraigie, David, iv. 565.
—— James, provost of St. Mary's Church, St. Andrews, v. 397.
—— Margaret, wife of James Carmichael of Balmedie, iv. 565.
KINFAUNS, HAY, LORD HAY OF, v. 222-239.
KING OF SCOTS—
—— —— Alexander I., i. 3; iii. 303; iv. 3.
—— —— his wife, Sybilla, i. 3.
—— —— Alexander II., i. 6; v. 32, 33, 34.
—— —— his 1st wife, Joanna Plantagenet, i. 6; ii. 423, 430; iii. 252.
—— —— his 2nd wife, Marie de Coucy, i. 6.
—— —— Alexander III., i. 6; vii. 400.
—— —— his 1st wife, Margaret Plantagenet, i. 6; iv. 9; vii. 400.
—— —— his 2nd wife, Yolande de Dreux, i. 6.
—— —— Charles I., i. 28; iii. 370; vii. 99; ix. 99.
—— —— his wife, Henrietta Maria de Bourbon, i. 28.
—— —— Charles II., i. 29.
—— —— his wife, Katharine of Braganza, i. 30.
—— —— David I., i. 2, 3; iii. 244; iv. 2 *n.*, 3 *bis*; viii. 240.
—— —— his wife, Matilda of Huntingdon, i. 3.
—— —— David II., i. 8; iii. 145; iv. 398; vii. 238.
—— —— his 1st wife, Joanna Plantagenet, i. 9; iii. 145; iv. 141; ix. 1.
—— —— his 2nd wife, Margaret Drummond, i. 9; ii. 262, 445; vi. 348; vii. 32.
—— —— Donald Bane, i. 2, 3; iii. 240.
—— —— Duncan I., i. 1; ii. 314; iii. 240 *bis*; vi. 282.
—— —— Duncan II., i. 2; iii. 245.
—— —— his wife, Æthelreda of Dunbar, iii. 245.
—— —— Edgar, son of Malcolm 'Ceannmor, i. 3; iv. 3 *bis*.
—— —— Edward Baliol, i. 7, 430; v. 578, 582; viii. 252.
—— —— Henry, i. 26; vi. 354.
—— —— his wife, Mary, queen of Scots, i. 25.
—— —— James I., i. 18; iii. 166, 169; viii. 381.
—— —— his wife, Joan Beaufort, i. 18, 450; ii. 141; iii. 564, 569; v. 2, 427.
—— —— James II., i. 19.
—— —— his wife, Marie of Gueldres, i. 20; iii. 60; v. 604, 637.
—— —— James III., i. 20.
—— —— his wife, Margaret of Denmark, i. 20; v. 144, 147, 638.
—— —— James IV., i. 21; vii. 44, 250; viii. 13, 580.
—— —— his wife, Margaret Tudor, i. 21, 26, 27; iv. 261; v. 150; vi. 166, 167.

King of Scots, James v., i. 23; vii. 120; viii. 488.
—— —— his 1st wife, Madeleine de Valois, i. 23.
—— —— his 2nd wife, Marie de Guise Lorraine, i. 23; iv. 23; v. 527; vii. 122; viii. 283, 585.
—— —— James vi., i. 26; v. 354; vii. 549; viii. 95, 216.
—— —— his wife, Anne of Denmark, i. 27; iv. 264, 433, 580; ix. 99.
—— —— James vii., i. 32; vii. 136, 138.
—— —— his 1st wife, Anne Hyde, i. 33.
—— —— his 2nd wife, Mary Beatrice Eleanor d'Este, i. 33.
—— —— James viii., i. 35; viii. 73, 307.
—— —— his wife, Clementina Sobieska, i. 35.
—— —— John Baliol, i. 4, 7, 426; iv. 9, 143; viii. 250.
—— —— his wife, Isabella de Warenne, i. 7.
—— —— Kenneth Macalpin, v. 28; viii. 264 *n.*
—— —— Macbeth, iii. 240; iv. 1.
—— —— Malcolm ii., i. 1; ii. 314; iii. 240 *bis*; viii. 266.
—— —— Malcolm iii., 'Ceannmor,' i. 1; ii. 314; iii. 240 *bis*; iv. 1; vi. 283, 284.
—— —— his 1st wife, Ingibiorg of Orkney, i. 2; ii. 314.
—— —— his 2nd wife, Margaret of England, i. 2; viii. 476.
—— —— Malcolm iv., 'the Maiden,' i. 4, 5; iv. 5, 6; v. 30; vii. 158.
—— —— Robert i., i. 7, 426; ii. 433, 435; iii. 139, 145; v. 35, 577, 579; vii. 234; viii. 248.
—— —— his 1st wife, Isabel of Mar, i. 8; v. 578.
—— —— his 2nd wife, Elizabeth de Burgh, i. 8; vii. 234.
—— —— Robert ii., i. 9, 15; iii. 467.
—— —— his 1st wife, Elizabeth Mure, i. 16, 135; ix. 2.
—— —— his 2nd wife, Euphemia of Ross, i. 16, 134, 436; vi. 297; vii. 181 *n.*, 236; viii. 263.
—— —— Robert iii., i. 17.
—— —— his wife, Annabella Drummond, i. 17; vii. 37.
—— —— William, 'the Lion,' i. 4, 5; v. 325.
—— —— his wife, Ermengarde de Bellomont, i. 5.
King, Thomas (King), 5th lord, i. 485.
KING, LORD EYTHIN, iii. 588-594.
King of Barra and Bourtie, James, iii. 588.
—— —— his wife, Marjory Barclay, iii. 588.
—— —— James, iii. 589.
—— —— his wife, Isobel *or* Elizabeth Gray, iii. 589.
—— —— James, iii. 591.
—— —— his wife, Beatrice Lumsden, iii. 591.
—— —— William, iii. 588.
—— —— William, iii. 588, 589.
—— —— his wife, Janet Grier, iii. 589.
King of Barra and Bourtie, William, iii. 590.
—— —— his 1st wife, Elspet Innes, iii. 590.
—— —— his 2nd wife, Isobel Panton, iii. 590.
—— —— his 3rd wife, Elizabeth Menzies, iii. 590.
—— of Birness and Dudwick, James, lieut. gen. in Swedish and in British service, iii. 592.
—— —— his 1st wife, Diliana van der Borchens, iii. 593.
—— of Corrard, Sir Charles Simeon, 3rd bart., iii. 589 *n.*
—— of Warbester, David, 4th son of James K. of Barra, iii. 590.
—— —— his wife, Mary Stewart, iii. 590.
—— —— John, iii. 590.
—— —— his wife, Margaret Buchan, iii. 590.
—— of Westerhouse, James, iii. 588.
—— —— William, iii. 589.
—— Alexander, advocate, 3rd son of James K. of Barra, iii. 589.
—— —— his wife, Janet Douglas, iii. 589.
—— Alexander, 2nd son of William K. of Barra, iii. 591.
—— David, major in Sir John Ruthven's regiment, iii. 590.
—— George, Waratah, vii. 226.
—— Goda, niece of Robert K., Aberdeen, iii. 588.
—— Hans Jacob, son of col. James K., iii. 591.
—— Henry, in Swedish service, iii. 590.
—— Isobel, dau. of Wm. K. of Barra, iii. 590.
—— James, burgess of Aberdeen, iii. 589.
—— —— his 1st wife, Margaret Jaik, iii. 589.
—— —— his 2nd wife, Christina Johnston, iii. 589.
—— James, in Swedish service, iii. 590.
—— James, colonel in Swedish service, iii. 591.
—— —— his wife, Mary Gordon, iii. 591.
—— Jane, wife of Alexander Blackhall of Bourtie, iii. 591.
—— Jane, wife of F. A. Primrose, vii. 226.
—— John, eldest son of William K. of Barra and Bourtie, iii. 589.
—— Margaret, wife of * Buchan, iii. 590.
—— Matthew, Stafford, i. 402.
—— Prudence, wife of Edward Aston, i. 402.
—— Robert, Aberdeen, iii. 588.
—— Wilhelmina, wife of admiral Murray of Pitcaithly, i. 485.
—— William, elder son of James K. of Barra, iii. 591.
—— *, 3rd son of David K. of Warbester; in in the Swedish service, iii. 590.
KINGARTH, STUART, VISCOUNT, ii. 299-312.

* Name unknown.

Kingarth, James, first viscount, ii. 299.
KINGHORNE, LYON, EARL OF, viii. 293-310.
Kinghorne, Charles, sixth earl of, viii. 307.
— James, seventh earl of, viii. 305, 308.
— John, second earl of, v. 222, 224; viii. 296.
— — his 1st wife, Margaret Erskine, v. 622; viii. 298.
— — his 2nd wife, Elizabeth Maule, vii. 21; viii. 299.
— John, fourth earl of, viii. 303.
— John, fifth earl of, viii. 305.
— Patrick, first earl of, iii. 578; viii. 293.
— — his wife, Anne Murray, i. 470; viii. 294.
— Patrick, third earl of, viii. 299.
— — his wife, Helen Middleton, vi. 185; viii. 302.
— Thomas, eighth earl of, viii. 305, 308.
KINGHORNE, BOWES, EARL OF, viii. 310-312.
Kinghorne, John, ninth earl of, viii. 310.
— — his wife, Mary Eleanor Bowes, viii. 310.
— John, tenth earl of, viii. 311.
— — his wife, Mary Millner, viii. 311.
KINGHORNE, LYON-BOWES, EARL OF, viii. 312-313.
Kinghorne, Thomas, eleventh earl of, viii. 312.
— Thomas George, twelfth earl of, viii. 313.
KINGHORNE, BOWES-LYON, EARL OF, viii. 313-317.
Kinghorne, Claude, thirteenth earl of, viii. 313.
— Claude George, fourteenth earl of, viii. 315.
Kinglassie, Andrew Aytoun, senator of the College of Justice, lord, viii. 63.
KINGSBURNE, CRAWFORD (LINDSAY), LORD, iv. 175-178.
Kingsland, Nicholas (Barnewall), 3rd viscount, i. 54.
— — his wife, Mary Hamilton, i. 54; ix. 54.
KINGSTON, MAXWELL, LORD, iii. 126-131.
Kingston, James, lord, iii. 129.
KINGSTON, SETON, VISCOUNT OF, v. 195-198.
Kingston, Alexander, first viscount of, v. 195; viii. 560 *n.*, 594, 595, 601.
— — his 1st wife, Jean Fletcher, v. 196; ix. 121.
— — his 2nd wife, Elizabeth Douglas, v. 196; vi. 352.
— — his 3rd wife, Elizabeth Hamilton, v. 196; ix. 36, 121.
— — his 4th wife, Margaret Douglas, i. 207; v. 196.
— Archibald, second viscount of, v. 197; viii. 603.
— James, third viscount of, v. 88, 197.
— — his wife, Anne Lindsay, i. 522; v. 197.
Kingston, master of, Charles, eldest son of 1st viscount of Kingston, v. 196.
Kingston-upon-Hull, Evelyn (Pierrepont), 1st duke of, ii. 302.
— Robert (Pierrepont), 1st earl of, v. 632.
KINGSTON-UPON-THAMES, RAMSAY, BARON OF, iv. 301-302.
Kingston-upon-Thames, John, baron, iv. 301, 312.
Kinloch of Cruvie, John, viii. 383.
— of Gilmerton, Sir Alexander, 8th bart., viii. 468.
— — Sir Francis, 2nd bart., ii. 24; vi. 442; vii. 82.
— — his wife, Mary Leslie, vi. 442; ix. 143.
— — Sir Francis, 3rd bart., ii. 44; v. 407.
— Anna, wife of Gideon Scott of Highchester, vii. 82.
— Harriet, wife of rev. lord Thomas Hay, viii. 468.
— Margaret, wife of Sir Jas. Sandilands of Calder, viii. 383.
— Mary, wife of Alex. Hamilton, ii. 44.
KINLOSS, BRUCE, LORD, iii. 475.
Kinloss, Edward, first lord, iii. 475.
— — his wife, Magdalen Clerk, iii. 476.
— Edward, second lord, iii. 477.
— Thomas, third lord, iii. 477.
KINLOSS, BRYDGES, BARON, v. 199-201.
Kinloss, Charles, sixth baron, v. 199.
KINLOSS, GRENVILLE, BARON, v. 199-200.
Kinloss, James, seventh baron, v. 199.
— — his 1st wife, Margaret Nicol, v. 199.
— — his 2nd wife, Anne Eliza Gammon, v. 199.
KINLOSS, MORGAN-GRENVILLE, BARON, v. 199-201.
Kinloss, Richard Plantagenet, ninth baron, v. 200.
— — his wife, Mary Campbell, ii. 211; v. 200.
— Richard Plantagenet Campbell Temple Nugent Brydges Chandos, tenth baron, iii. 482; v. 200.
— — his 1st wife, Caroline Hervey, v. 200.
— — his 2nd wife, Alice Anne Graham-Montgomery, v. 200.
— Anna Eliza, wife of Richard, duke of Buckingham and Chandos; baroness, v. 200.
— Mary, wife of L. F. H. C. Morgan; baroness, iii. 482; v. 201.
— master of, Richard George, v. 201.
KINLOSS, BRUCE, BARON BRUCE OF, iii. 476-483.
KINMOUNT, DOUGLAS, BARON SOLWAY OF, vii. 152.
Kinmount, Charles, baron Solway of, vii. 152.
KINNAIRD, LIVINGSTON, LORD OF, vi. 452.
Kinnaird, James, first lord of, vi 452.

KINNAIRD OF INCHTURE, KINNAIRD, LORD, v. 202-216.
Kinnaird of Inchture, Arthur Fitzgerald, tenth lord, v. 215.
—— —— his wife, Mary Jane Hoare, v. 215.
—— —— Arthur Fitzgerald, eleventh lord, v. 215.
—— —— his wife, Mary Alina Victoria Agnew, v. 215.
—— —— Charles, fifth lord, v. 211; ix. 121.
—— —— his wife, Magdalen Brown, v. 211.
—— —— Charles, sixth lord, v. 212.
—— —— his wife, Barbara Johnstone, v. 212.
—— —— Charles, seventh lord, v. 212.
—— —— his wife, Elizabeth Ransom, v. 212.
—— —— Charles, eighth lord, v. 213.
—— —— his wife, Olivia Laetitia Catherine Fitzgerald, v. 213.
—— —— George, first lord, v. 209.
—— —— his wife, Margaret Crichton, v. 209.
—— —— George William Fox, ninth lord, v. 214.
—— —— his wife, Frances Anna Georgiana Spencer-Ponsonby, v. 214; ix. 122.
—— —— Patrick, second lord, v. 210.
—— —— his wife, Anne Fraser, v. 210, 534; ix. 121.
—— —— Patrick, third lord, v. 210.
—— —— his 1st wife, Henrietta Maria Murray, iii. 386; v. 210.
—— —— his 2nd wife, Elizabeth Lyon, v. 210; viii. 300.
—— —— Patrick, fourth lord, v. 210.
KINNAIRD OF ROSSIE, KINNAIRD, BARON, v. 214-216.
Kinnaird of Rossie, George William Fox, first baron, v. 214.
—— master of, Charles Fox, v. 214.
—— master of, Douglas Arthur, lieut. Scots Guards, v. 215.
—— master of, George, eldest son of 2nd lord Kinnaird, v. 210.
—— master of, Victor Alexander, v. 214.
KINNAIRD, CARNEGIE, LORD CARNEGIE OF, viii. 65-93.
Kinnaird, Sir Robert Carnegie, senator of the College of Justice, lord, viii. 51.
KINNAIRD, LORD KINNAIRD OF INCHTURE, v. 202-216.
KINNAIRD, BARON KINNAIRD OF ROSSIE, v. 214-216.
KINNAIRD, BARON ROSSIE OF ROSSIE, v. 214.
Kinnaird of Balgavy, Balgally, George, v. 206.
—— —— John, v. 206.
—— of Balgerno, Patrick, v. 209.
—— of Byreflats, Patrick, viii. 296.
—— of Chethynrawoch, Sir Richard, v. 204.
—— of Clochindarg, George, v. 208.
—— —— Patrick, v. 208.
—— —— Patrick, v. 209.
Kinnaird of Couston, George, i. 293.
—— —— his wife, Helen Arbuthnott, i. 293.
—— of Culbin [Alexander], iv. 62.
—— —— his wife, Mary Forbes, iv. 62.
—— —— Thomas, v. 204.
—— —— his wife, Egidia Moray of Culbin, v. 204; viii. 325.
—— —— Thomas, ix. 85.
—— —— his wife, Anna Elphinstone, iii. 538; ix. 85.
—— —— Walter, ix. 85.
—— —— his wife, Helen Forbes, iii. 538.
—— of Drimmie, Sir George, viii. 300.
—— —— Patrick, iv. 32; v. 206.
—— —— Patrick, v. 209.
—— of Dunnoir, Allan, ix. 121.
—— of Hill, Alan de, iii. 470.
—— of Inchmichaell, Patrick, v. 209.
—— of Inchture, Andrew, iv. 32.
—— —— George, 4th laird, v. 206.
—— —— his wife, Janet Ogilvy, v. 206.
—— —— Sir George, 10th laird, v. 209.
—— —— his wife, Margaret Crichton, v. 209.
—— —— John, 3rd laird, v. 206.
—— —— John, 5th laird, v. 206.
—— —— John, 9th laird, v. 209.
—— —— Patrick, 6th laird, v. 207.
—— —— his 1st wife, Mariota Hepburn, v. 207.
—— —— his 2nd wife, Margaret Moncur, v. 207.
—— —— Patrick, 7th laird, v. 207.
—— —— his wife, Elizabeth Gray, iv. 284; v. 207.
—— —— Patrick, 8th laird, v. 208; viii. 296.
—— —— his wife, Euphemia Gray, iv. 282; v. 209.
—— —— Reginald, 1st laird; 2nd son of Sir Richard K. of Kinnaird, v. 205.
—— —— his wife, Marjorie Kirkaldy of Inchture, v. 205.
—— —— Walter, 2nd laird, v. 205.
—— —— his wife, Margaret *, ix. 121.
—— of Kinbrichour, Allan, ix. 121.
—— of Kinnaird, Alan, 7th laird, v. 204.
—— —— his wife, Mary Murray, v. 204.
—— —— Alan, 9th laird, iii. 563; v. 204.
—— —— his wife, Janet Keith, v. 204.
—— —— Andrew, 11th laird, iii. 194, 310; iv. 32; v. 204, 206.
—— —— John, 12th laird, iii. 194 197; v. 205.
—— —— his wife, Janet Ogilvy, iv. 32; v. 205.
—— —— John, 15th laird, v. 205.
—— —— his wife, Margaret Ogilvy, v. 205; vi. 451.
—— —— John, the younger, v. 205; vi. 451.
—— —— Patrick, 13th laird, iv. 32; v. 205.
—— —— his wife, Elizabeth Scot, v. 205.

* Name unknown.

Kinnaird of Kinnaird, Patrick, 14th laird, v. 205.
— — his wife, Margaret Carnegie, v. 205; viii. 58.
— — Radulphus *or* Ruffus, 1st laird, v. 202.
— — Radulphus, 3rd laird, v. 203.
— — Richard, 2nd laird, v. 202.
— — Sir Richard, 4th laird, v. 203.
— — Richard, 5th laird, v. 203; ix. 121.
— — Sir Richard, 6th laird, v. 204; ix. 121 *bis*.
— — Thomas, 8th laird, v. 204.
— — his wife, Egidia Murray, v. 204.
— — Thomas, 10th laird, v. 204.
— — his wife, Elizabeth Drummond, v. 204; vii. 39.
— of Kinnynmond, Sir Richard, v. 204.
— of Meadowacre, George, v. 208.
— — Patrick, v. 208.
— of Mergitlands, George, v. 207.
— of Polgavy, Patrick, v. 209.
— of Rossie, Sir George, v. 209; viii. 300.
— — his wife, Margaret Crichton, v. 209.
— of Skelbo, Andrew, iii. 194; viii. 333.
— — John, iii. 194, 197.
— — Thomas, 2nd son of Thos. K. of Kinnaird, v. 204 *bis*.
— of Unthank, Patrick, v. 209.
— Alan, 2nd son of Richard de K., ix. 121 *bis*.
— Alexander, 4th son of 1st lord Kinnaird, v. 209.
— Andrew, 2nd son of Patrick K. of Inchture, v. 208.
— — his wife, Helen Menzies, v. 208.
— Andrew, illeg. son of Patrick K. of Inchture, v. 208.
— Anne, wife of Thos. Drummond of Logiealmond, v. 210.
— Arthur Middleton, v. 216.
— Augusta Olivia, wife of Roland Yorke-Bevan, v. 215.
— Barbara, dau. of Patrick K. of Inchture, v. 208.
— Charles, 5th son of 1st lord Kinnaird, v. 209.
— David, 7th son of Richard de K., ix. 121.
— Douglas James William, M.P., v. 212.
— Edward Griffin, v. 212.
— Eliza, wife of 14th lord Dunsany, v. 213.
— Elizabeth, wife of Patrick Ogilvy of Inchmartine, iv. 32; v. 207.
— Elizabeth, dau. of 6th lord Kinnaird, v. 212.
— Emily Cecilia, v. 215.
— Frederica Eliza, wife of admiral Sir James Hope, v. 214.
— Frederica Georgiana, wife of Dr. Alfred Orlando Jones, v. 215.
— Frederick John Hay, v. 213; ix. 121.
Kinnaird, George, 6th son of 1st lord Kinnaird, v. 210, 211.
— — his wife, Margaret Maitland, v. 211.
— George, v. 211; ix. 121.
— — his 1st wife, Helen Gordon, i. 103; v. 211; ix. 6 *bis*.
— — his 2nd wife, Anne *or* Susanne Gordon, v. 211; ix. 121.
— George, his eldest son, v. 211.
— George, his 3rd son, v. 211.
— George, nephew of Patrick K. of Inchture, v. 207.
— George, 2nd son of Patrick K. of Inchture, v. 207.
— — his wife, Elizabeth Moncur, v. 207.
— George William Ransom, eldest son of 7th lord Kinnaird, v. 212; ix. 121.
— Georgina Mary Anne, wife of admiral Sir G. Johnstone Hope, v. 213; ix. 121.
— Gertrude Mary, v. 215.
— Gilbert, son of Andrew K. of Kinnaird, v. 204.
— Graham Hay St. Vincent de Ros, R.N., v. 214.
— Helen, wife of rev. Edward Dana, v. 212.
— Hugh, 4th son of Richard de K., ix. 121.
— Isabella, wife of John, son of Richard of Invertuyl, v. 202.
— James, 3rd son of 1st lord Kinnaird, v. 209.
— Janet, wife of Gilbert Ireland, v. 207.
— Janet, dau. of Patrick K. of Inchture, v. 208.
— John, 3rd son of Thomas K. of Kinnaird, v. 204.
— — his wife, Margaret Mowat, v. 204.
— John, 2nd son of Patrick K. of Kinnaird, v. 205.
— John, eldest son of John, last laird of Kinnaird, v. 205.
— John, 2nd son of 1st lord Kinnaird, v. 209.
— Kenneth Fitzgerald, v. 215.
— — his wife, Frances Victoria Clifton, v. 215.
— Laura Margaretta, v. 213.
— Louisa Elizabeth, dau. of 10th lord Kinnaird, v. 215.
— Margaret, wife of Sir A. Hay of Killour, iii. 573; v. 209; ix. 121.
— Margaret, wife of Thos. Gray, iv. 280.
— Margaret, wife of Andrew Clark, v. 206.
— Margaret, dau. of George K., v. 211.
— Margaret, wife of Thos. Wiggons, v. 212.
— Margaret Alma, v. 216.
— Mariota, wife of Alex. Skene, v. 204.
— Mariota de, wife of Duthac de Carnegie, viii. 48.

Kinnaird, Marjory, wife of Andrew Kinnaird, v. 207 *n*.
—— Olivia Barbara, wife of Sir R. H. A. Ogilvy, v. 214.
—— Olivia Cecilia Laura, v. 214.
—— Patrick, 3rd son of Patrick K. of Kinnaird, v. 205.
—— Patrick, H.E.I.C.S., Bengal, v. 212.
—— Patrick Charles, v. 216.
—— Ralph, eldest son of Sir Richard de K., v. 203.
—— Reginald, 3rd son of Richard de K., ix. 121.
—— Thomas, 2nd son of Radulphus de K., v. 203.
—— Thomas de, Aberdeenshire, vii. 428.
—— Thomas, 6th son of Richard de K., ix. 121.
—— William, eldest son of Walter K. of Inchture, v. 206.
—— —— his wife, Margaret Levington, v. 206.
—— William, 5th son of Richard de K., ix. 121.
—— *, wife of David Panter of Newmanswalls, viii. 48.
—— *, wife of William Cramond of Aldbar, viii. 48.
Kinnear of Kinnear, David, v. 399.
—— —— his wife, Elizabeth Lindsay, v. 399.
—— —— David, ix. 63.
—— Mary, wife of Sir Kenneth Mackenzie of Grandvale, ix. 63.
Kinninmond of Cassendilly, James, v. 392.
—— of Craighall, Andrew, v. 397.
—— —— Andrew, viii. 494.
—— —— Patrick, ix. 32.
—— —— his wife, Christian Beaton, i. 533; ix. 32.
—— of Kinninmond, Alexander, vii. 272.
—— —— Andrew, viii. 486.
—— —— his wife, Agnes Wemyss, viii. 486.
—— —— Andrew, v. 397.
—— —— his wife, Janet Lindsay, v. 397.
—— —— Andrew, viii. 489.
—— —— his wife, Grizel Wemyss, viii. 489.
—— —— Andrew, vii. 575; viii. 494, 497.
—— —— his 1st wife, Helen Sinclair, vii. 575.
—— —— his 2nd wife, Cecilia Wemyss, viii. 494, 497.
—— —— Heliseus de, iii. 527.
—— —— his wife, Elizabeth Elphinstone, iii. 527; vii. 272.
—— —— John, ix. 163.
—— —— his wife, Isobel Livingston, viii. 369; ix. 163.
—— —— *, iv. 278.
—— —— his wife, Marjory Gray, iv. 278.
—— Euphemia, wife of (1) Alex. Abercrombie, and (2) Andrew Sandilands, i. 77.

* Name unknown.

Kinninmond, Margaret, wife of Jas. Wemyss, viii. 494.
—— Matthew, archdeacon of St. Andrews, and bishop of Aberdeen, ii. 251; iv. 6; v. 569, 572; vii. 265; viii. 319 *n*.
KINNOULL, HAY, EARL OF, v. 217-239.
Kinnoull, Archibald Fitzroy George, thirteenth earl of, v. 238.
—— —— his 1st wife, J. M. Hawke, v. 238.
—— —— his 2nd wife, F. M. Darell, v. 238.
—— George, first earl of, iii. 321 *n*.; v. 220; ix. 122.
—— —— his wife, Margaret Haliburton, iv. 34; v. 223.
—— George, second earl of, v. 223.
—— —— his wife, Ann Douglas, v. 224; vi. 378.
—— George, third earl of, v. 225.
—— George, fifth earl of, v. 228.
—— George, twelfth earl of, v. 237.
—— —— his wife, Emily Blanch Charlotte Somerset, v. 237.
—— George Henry, eighth earl of, v. 232.
—— —— his wife, Abigail Harley, v. 232.
—— Robert Auriol, tenth earl of, v. 234.
—— —— his 1st wife, Julia Eyre, v. 235.
—— —— his 2nd wife, Sarah Harley, v. 235.
—— Thomas, seventh earl of, v. 231.
—— —— his wife, Elizabeth Drummond, v. 231; viii. 222; ix. 161.
—— Thomas, ninth earl of, v. 234.
—— —— his wife, Constantia Kyrle-Ernlie, v. 234.
—— Thomas Robert, eleventh earl of, v. 235.
—— —— his wife, Louisa Burton Rowley, v. 235.
—— William, fourth earl of, v. 226.
—— —— his 1st wife, Mary Brudenell, iii. 297; v. 228.
—— —— his 2nd wife, Katharine Cecil, v. 228.
—— William, sixth earl of, v. 229.
KINPONT, GRAHAM, LORD, i. 133-145.
Kinpont, John, eldest son of William, earl of Airth and Menteith; styled lord, i. 136, 137, 138; vi. 249.
—— —— his wife, Mary Keith, i. 136, 139; vi. 57; ix. 9.
—— William, president of the Privy Council, and Great Justiciary of Scotland, first lord, i. 135.
—— William, grandson of William, earl of Airth and Menteith; styled lord, i. 140.
—— —— his 1st wife, Anna Hewes, i. 141.
—— —— his 2nd wife, Katharine Bruce, i. 142.
KINRARA, GORDON-LENNOX, EARL OF, v. 369-371.
Kinrara, Charles Henry, first earl of, v. 369.
—— Charles Henry, styled earl of, v. 370.

Kinross, Henry, portioner of Cambushinnie, viii. 198.
—— —— his wife, Christian Murray, viii. 198.
—— Isobel, wife of George Graham of Gartur, vi. 153 *bis*.
—— Jean, wife of John Graham of Rednock, vi. 161.
—— Patrick, viii. 170.
—— —— his wife, Cristine Alexander, viii. 170.
KINTAIL, MACKENZIE, LORD MACKENZIE OF, vii. 504-512.
KINTAIL, MACKENZIE, BARON MACKENZIE OF, vii. 513-514.
Kintail, Sir Roderick Mackenzie, tutor of, iii. 69.
KINTORE, KEITH, EARL OF, v. 240-255.
Kintore, George, *de jure* earl of, v. 242; vi. 64.
—— John, first earl of, v. 240; vi. 57.
—— —— his wife, Margaret Hamilton, iv. 317; v. 241.
—— John, third earl of, v. 241.
—— —— his wife, Mary Erskine, v. 241, 629.
—— William, second earl of, v. 241.
—— —— his wife, Katharine Murray, v. 241; viii. 204.
—— William, fourth earl of. v. 242.
KINTORE, KEITH-FALCONER, EARL OF, v. 251-255.
Kintore, Algernon Hawkins Thomond, ninth earl of, v. 254.
—— —— his wife, Sydney Charlotte Montagu, v. 254.
—— Anthony Adrian, fifth earl of, v. 242, 251; vi. 9.
—— —— his wife, Christina Elisabeth Sighterman, v. 251.
—— Anthony Adrian, seventh earl of, v. 252.
—— —— his 1st wife, Julia Renny, v. 252.
—— —— his 2nd wife, Louisa Hawkins, v. 252.
—— Francis Alexander, eighth earl of, v. 253.
—— —— his wife, Louisa Madaleine Hawkins, v. 253.
—— William, sixth earl of, v. 252.
—— —— his wife, Maria Bannerman, v. 252.
KINTORE OF KINTORE, KEITH-FALCONER, BARON, v. 252-255.
Kintore of Kintore, Anthony Adrian, first baron, v. 252.
KINTYRE, CAMPBELL, LORD, v. 23-26.
Kintyre, Archibald, second lord, i. 350; v. 25.
—— James, 2nd son of 7th earl of Argyll; first lord, i. 350; v. 23; ix. 22 *ter*.
KINTYRE, CAMPBELL, MARQUESS OF, i. 369-393.
Kintyre, Archibald, first marquess of, i. 369.
Kir, Johannes, Durham, vii. 315.
Kirby, Edmund, colonel U.S. army, iii. 605.
—— Mary, wife of 11th lord Fairfax, iii. 605.
Kirk of Annevale, John, ii. 309.
—— Cecil, wife of P. J. Crichton-Stuart, ii. 309.
—— Colin, W.S., ii. 191 *n*.
—— Robert, minister at Balquhidder, ii. 191.
—— —— his 1st wife, Isabel Campbell, ii. 191.
—— William, son of Mr. Robert K., ii. 191 *n*.
KIRKCALDY, MELVILLE, VISCOUNT OF, vi. 108-123.
Kirkcaldy, George, first viscount of, vi. 108.
—— of Grange, James, iv. 369; vi. 87, 88; viii. 282.
—— —— his wife, Janet Melville, vi. 95.
—— —— Janet, wife of Sir Thos. Ker of Ferniehirst, v. 63, 67.
—— —— Sir John, viii. 495.
—— —— Sir Robert, viii. 300; ix. 128.
—— —— his wife, Anna Leslie, ix. 128.
—— —— Sir William, iv. 157; v. 65, 67, 294, 399; viii. 283.
—— —— William, *alias* Ker, 2nd son of Sir Thos. Ker of Ferniehirst, v. 67.
—— —— his wife, Elizabeth Lyon, v. 68; viii. 291.
—— —— William, iv. 309; v. 68.
—— —— his wife, Margaret Hamilton, iv. 309.
—— of Inchture, John de, v. 205.
—— —— Marjorie, wife of (1) Andrew Boyd, and (2) Reginald Kinnaird, v. 205.
—— of Kinghorne, James, viii. 282.
—— —— Sir Robert, viii. 300.
—— —— William, viii. 283.
—— Isabel, wife of Henry Wemyss, viii. 495.
—— James, vii. 80.
—— Jean, wife of William Scott, vii. 80.
—— Margaret, wife of David Murray of Little Ardit, viii. 187.
—— Marion, wife of Wm. Sempill of Craigbait, vii. 533.
Kirkconnel, Janet de, wife of Aymer Maxwell, vi. 474.
KIRKCUDBRIGHT, MACLELLAN, LORD, v. 256-274.
Kirkcudbright, Camden Gray, ninth lord, v. 273.
—— —— his wife, Sarah Gorges, v. 273.
—— James, fifth lord, v. 269.
—— —— his wife, Margaret Drummond, v. 269.
—— John, third lord, v. 264, 268.
—— —— his wife, Ann Maxwell, v. 268.
—— John, seventh lord, v. 272.
—— —— his wife, Elizabeth Banister *or* Bannerman, v. 273.
—— Robert, first lord, v. 264.
—— —— his 1st wife, Agnes Campbell, v. 267, 498.
—— —— his 2nd wife, Mary Montgomery v. 267.
—— —— his 3rd wife, Mary Gage, v. 267.

Kirkcudbright, Sholto Henry, eighth lord, v. 273.
—— —— his wife, Mary Cantes, v. 273.
—— Thomas, second lord, v. 264, 267; ix. 124.
—— —— his wife, Jonet Douglas, v. 268; vii. 135; ix. 150.
—— William, fourth lord, v. 269.
—— William, sixth lord, v. 271.
—— —— his wife Margaret Murray, v. 272.
Kirkland, John, vii. 422.
—— John, his son, vii. 422.
—— William, vii. 422.
Kirkpatrick of Auchenleck, Thomas, iv. 243.
—— of Closeburn, Roger, iv. 243.
—— —— Sir Thomas, ii. 380, 382.
—— —— his wife, Margaret *, ii. 382.
—— —— Thomas, i. 222.
—— —— his wife, Marion Murray, i. 222.
—— —— Sir Thomas, iv. 158, 243; vii. 130.
—— —— his wife, Jean Cunningham, iv. 243; ix. 97.
—— —— Sir Thomas, M.P., iv. 413.
—— —— Sir Thomas, 1st bart., viii. 392.
—— —— his wife, Isabel Sandilands, viii. 392.
—— —— Sir Thomas, 3rd bart., viii. 395.
—— of Dalgarnock, Adam, vii. 117.
—— of Kirkmichael, Alexander, iii. 182.
—— of Kirkpatrick, Sir Duncan, ii. 382.
—— —— his wife, Isabel *, ii. 382.
—— —— Elizabeth, wife of Wm. Carlyle of Torthorwald, ii. 381, 382.
—— —— Isabella, wife of Gilbert Grierson of Lag, ii. 382.
—— —— Ivo of, i. 231.
—— —— Jonet, wife of Thomas Graham of Auchincass, ii. 381, 382.
—— —— Roger, v. 289.
—— of Molyne and Raehills, Alexander, iii. 64.
—— of Pennersax, Adam, vii. 117.
—— of Torthorwald, Isabella, wife of Gilbert Grierson of Lag, iii. 220.
—— Anna, wife of 3rd earl of Kellie, v. 87.
—— Elizabeth, wife of John, 1st lord Carlyle of Torthorwald, ii. 380, 382, 385.
—— Grizel, wife of capt. Robert Sandilands, viii. 395.
—— John, governor of Bois-le-duc, v. 87.
—— Margaret, wife of John MacHenry, ix. 80.
—— Roger, vii. 547.
—— —— his wife, Elizabeth Hamilton, vii. 547.
—— Samuel, iv. 158.
—— —— his wife, Elizabeth Stewart, iv. 158.
—— Sir Thomas de, 1394, ix. 80.
Kirktoun of Bonjedburgh and Stuartfield, Adam, vii. 378.
—— —— his wife, Grisel Rutherfurd, vii. 378.
—— Adam, v. 55.

* Name unknown.

Kirktoun, Agnes, wife of John Rutherfurd, 'the Cock of Hunthill,' vii. 376.
KIRKWALL, HAMILTON, VISCOUNT OF, vi. 578-584.
Kirkwall, George, first viscount of, vi. 578.
—— John, son of Mary, countess of Orkney; styled viscount, vi. 581.
—— —— his wife, Anna Maria de Blacquière, vi. 581.
—— Murrough, son of Anne, countess of Orkney; styled viscount, vi. 580.
Kirwan of Mayne, John Forbes Stratford, v. 514.
—— —— his wife, Victoria Maria Louisa Hastings, v. 514.
Knatchbull, Muriel Windham, wife of A. E. Dalzell, ii. 418.
—— Norton, col., ii. 418.
Knight of Lea Castle, John, iv. 496.
—— —— his wife, Helen Charlotte Hope, iv. 496.
—— Henry, eldest son of Robert, lord Luxborough, iii. 113.
—— —— his wife, Frances Heath, iii. 113.
—— Henry, colonel, iv. 65.
—— —— his wife, Mary Erskine, iv. 65.
—— William, rector of Steventon, iv. 495.
—— —— his wife, J. H. Macdougall, iv. 495.
Knightley of Offchurch, Robert, i. 411.
—— —— his wife, Eleanor Blount, i. 411.
Knights of Nethercote, William, viii. 231.
—— Isabel Henrietta, wife of E. T. Drummond, viii. 231.
Knollis, George, vii. 251.
—— —— his 1st wife, Grizel Rattray, vii. 251.
—— —— his 2nd wife, Christian Edmonstone, vii. 251.
Knollys, Sir Francis, K.G., iii. 608.
—— —— his wife, Katharine Cary, iii. 608.
—— William, lord of St. John's, prior of Torphichen, v. 639.
Knott of Stockland, Thomas, v. 312.
—— Anne, wife of rev. C. Maitland, v. 312.
Knowis, John, burgess of Linlithgow, ii. 590.
—— John, his son, ii. 590.
—— —— his wife, Janet Cranstoun, ii. 590.
—— William, ii. 590.
—— —— his wife, Helen Makgill, ii. 590; vi. 592.
Knox of Keithock, Andrew, viii. 62, 63.
—— —— his wife, Helen Carnegie-Arbuthnott, viii. 63.
—— Andrew, bishop of the Isles, ix. 97.
—— James, viii. 62.
—— —— his wife, Anne Carnegie, viii. 62.
—— Janet, wife of Sir John Stewart of Traquair, viii. 400; ix. 164.
—— Mr. John, i. 194; iv. 245, 565; v. 297; vi. 514; vii. 540.
—— —— his 2nd wife, Margaret Stewart, vi. 514.

Knox, Margaret, wife of John Cunningham of Kilmaronock and Cambuskeith, iv. 245; ix. 97 *bis*.
—— Margaret, wife of Mr. John Somerville, viii. 22.
Knyvett of Buckenham, Sir Henry, iii. 609.
—— —— Sir Philip, bart., ii. 272.
—— Dorothy, wife of James Erskine, earl of Buchan, ii. 272.
—— Katharine, wife of (1) 2nd baron Paget of Beaudesert, and (2) Sir Edward Cary, iii. 609.
Kol, father of Kali *or* Rognvald, earl of Orkney and Caithness, ii. 315.
Kyd, Elizabeth, wife of Henry Lindsay of Wormiston, v. 416.
—— Thomas, merchant, v. 416.
Kylvert, father of Oliver of Olivercastle, vii. 418.
Kynman of Hill, William, v. 220.
—— —— his wife, Katharine Hay, v. 220.
Kyrle-Ernlie of Whetham, Constantia, wife of Thomas, lord Hay of Kinfauns, v. 234.
—— —— John, v. 234.
Kyle, Adam, burgess of Edinburgh, vi. 413.
—— Janet, wife of Andrew Napier, vi. 413.
Kyme of Kyme, Sir Philip, ix. 11.
—— —— his wife, Joan de Bigod, ix. 11.
—— Lucy, wife of Robert de Umfraville, 3rd earl of Angus, ix. 11.

Laballot, ix. 6.
La Bastie, Antoine d'Arces, chevalier de, ii. 6; iv. 356 *bis*.
—— defender of Glamis, v. 399.
Labouchere of Broomhall, John, ii. 309.
—— Fanny Adelaide, wife of Herbert Crichton-Stuart, ii. 309.
La Chambre, Louis, comte de, i. 153.
—— —— his wife, Anne de la Tour d'Auvergne, i. 153.
—— Philippe, cardinal, i. 153.
La Coast, Louise Maria, wife of 3rd lord Macdonald of Sleat, ix. 109.
Lacy of Cockermouth, Sir Thomas, ix. 11.
—— Francis Eden, vi. 507.
—— —— his wife, Helen Alice Carnegie, vi. 507.
—— Hugh de, i. 420; iv. 141 *bis*.
—— Maud de, wife of (1) Gilbert (de Umfraville), 4th earl of Angus, and (2) Henry (Percy), 1st earl of Northumberland, ix. 11.
—— * de, wife of Alan of Galloway, iv. 141.
Lade, Michael, councillor of law, ii. 599.
—— —— his wife, Sophia Brown, ii. 599.
Laffrie *or* Lafriese, Grizel, wife of Alex. Bruce, i. 549.
—— James, writer, i. 549.
Laing of Caverton, Alexander, vii. 321.

* Name unknown.

Laing of Spittals and Redhouse, Jean, wife of Andrew Hamilton, iv. 307.
—— —— John, keeper of the Signet, iv. 307.
—— David, Thurso, iii. 104.
—— David (*alias* Montgomerie), v. 557.
—— —— his wife, Jean Montgomerie of Lainshaw, v. 557.
—— Kate Sinclair, wife of lt.-col John Ramsay, iii. 104.
Lamb of Beauport, Sir Charles Montolieu, bart., iii. 461.
—— —— his wife, Mary Montgomerie, iii. 460, 461.
—— of Burville, Sir Archibald, 3rd bart., viii. 36, 39.
—— of Helstone, Sir James Bland, 1st bart., viii. 39.
—— Andrew, bishop of Galloway, v. 109.
—— Christian, wife of David Bothwell, iv. 425.
—— Edward, iv. 425.
—— John, burgess of Edinburgh, ix. 138.
Lambart of Beau Park, Charles, v. 485.
—— Frances Thomasine, wife of 2nd earl Talbot, v. 485.
Lambe, Emily Mary, wife of (1) 5th earl Cowper, and (2) lord Palmerston, iii. 123.
Lambeden, Henry de, abbot of Kelso, v. 490.
Lambert of Denham Court, Nathaniel G., viii. 471.
—— Annie Christina, wife of admiral Sir John Hay, viii. 471.
—— Edith Charlotte, wife of A. B. Drummond, viii. 232.
—— Sir Henry E. F., bart., viii. 232.
Lamberton, Sir Alexander, vii. 271.
—— William, bishop of St. Andrews, iii. 143.
Lambinus, father of James of Loudoun, v. 488.
Lambton of Harraton Hall, John, general, viii. 310.
—— —— his wife, Susan Lyon, viii. 310.
—— Alice Anne Caroline, wife of 17th earl of Morton, vi. 386.
—— Lilian, wife of Charles Cospatrick Archibald Home, styled lord Dunglas, iv. 483.
—— Mary Louisa, C.I., wife of James, 8th earl of Elgin, iii. 495.
—— William Frederick, M.P., iv. 483.
Lamington, Charles Wallace Alexander Napier Ross (Cochrane-Baillie), 2nd baron, iii. 360.
Lammie of Dunkenny, George, viii. 293.
—— of Kinnalty, viii. 293.
Lamond, John, ii. 288.
—— *, wife of Robert Stewart in Bute, ii. 288.
Lamont of Inveryne, Sir Coll, vii. 553.
—— —— his wife, Barbara Sempill, vii. 553.

* Name unknown.

Lamont of Inveryne, Sir John, i. 336.
—— his wife, Jean or Moir Campbell, i. 336; ix. 19.
— of Lamont, Archibald, iii. 78.
—— his wife, Amelia Mackenzie, iii. 78.
—— Dougal, son of Archibald L. of Steillag, ii. 297.
—— Sir John, 3rd laird, i. 327.
— of Steillag, Archibald, ii. 297.
—— Dougal, ii. 297.
—— his wife, Margaret Stuart, ii. 297.
— Mary or Isabella, wife of Sir Gillespie Campbell of Lochow, i. 327, 330.
Lamplugh, *, wife of David Falconer, v. 250.
Lampson, Jean Leslie, wife of major Walter Patrick Hore-Ruthven, vii. 392.
— Norman George, vii. 392.
—— his wife, Helen Agnes Smith Blackburn, vii. 392.
Lamson, Charles, New York, viii. 230.
— Elizabeth, wife of Sir V. A. W. Drummond, viii. 230.
Lamy, John, minister of Maryton, vi. 244.
LANARK, HAMILTON, EARL OF, iv. 378-380.
Lanark, William, earl of, iii. 130, 378; iv. 378.
—— his wife, Elizabeth Maxwell, iii. 129, 130.
Lancaster, Henry (Plantagenet), 1st duke of, iii. 150, 153.
— Alicia de, wife of Sir William de Lindsay, iii. 4.
— Avicia de, wife of Richard de Morville, v. 277.
— Heloise de, wife of Peter de Brus, iii. 4.
— William de, lord of Kendal, iii. 4.
—— his wife, Agnes de Brus, iii. 4.
Landell, William de, bishop of St. Andrews, iii. 55; viii. 264 *n.*
Landells of Brunecnolleflat, John, viii. 3.
—— William, viii. 3.
— of Landells, John de, 1227, v. 276.
—— John, vii. 364.
—— William de, vii. 364; ix. 107.
—— his wife, Jonet, ix. 107.
— of Swynset, Katharine, wife of John Lauder, ix. 107.
Lane-Fox-Pitt, St. George, vii. 155.
—— his wife, Edith Gertrude Douglas, vii. 155.
Lanesborough, John Vansittart Danvers (Butler), 6th earl of, ix. 163.
Lang, Alexander, minister of Donaghadee, iii. 436, 437 *n.*
—— his wife, Jean Montgomerie, iii. 436.
Langdale of Houghton, Charles, iv. 420.
—— his wife, Mary Constable-Maxwell, iv. 420.

* Name unknown.

Langeton, Sir John, warden of York Castle, vi. 38.
Langlands of Brydestoun, Patrick, viii. 296.
— of Collace, Patrick, portioner, viii. 296.
— of Langlands, George, vii. 75.
—— his wife, Esther Scott, vii. 75.
— William, St. Andrews, ii. 109.
LANGNEWTOUNE, KER, LORD KERR OF, v. 466-487.
Langnewtoune, Robert, first lord Kerr of, v. 466.
Langton of Langton, Bennet, vii. 306.
—— his wife, Mary Lloyd, vii. 306.
Lannoy, James, Hammersmith, i. 488.
—— his wife, Jane Frederick, i. 488.
— Leonora, i. 488 *n.*
Lansdowne, Henry (Fitzmaurice), 4th marquess of, vi. 399.
—— his wife, Emily Jane, baroness Nairn, vi. 399.
— Henry Charles Keith Petty (Fitzmaurice), 5th marquess of, vi. 400.
—— his wife, Maude Evelyn Hamilton, vi. 400.
Lapasture, Henri Pierre (Ducarel), comte de, iv. 418.
Laper, James, mason, iv. 112.
La Queuille, Jacqueline de, wife of Robert Stuart, seigneur d'Aubigny, vi. 231.
La Roche, Elias Poiret, sieur de, iii. 77.
Lascelles of Bassenthwaite and Bolton, Duncan, iii. 245.
—— his wife, Christiana, iii. 245.
— of Harewood, Edward, vi. 382.
— of Sion Hill, George Edwin, viii. 213.
—— his wife, Louisa Nina Murray, viii. 213.
— Frances, wife of lt.-col. John Douglas, i. 67; vi. 382.
— Maud Caroline, wife of lord George F. Hamilton, i. 70.
— Sir Roger, viii. 437.
— Theobald de, iii. 254; iv. 440.
—— his wife, Ada Dunbar, lady of Pullys, iv. 440.
— Thomas de, ii. 373, 432.
—— his wife, Cristiana de Ireby, ii. 373, 432.
Lask, Thomas of, viii. 528.
Lastic St. Jal, Albert, comte de, iii. 416.
—— his wife, Laura Tollemache, iii. 416.
La Suche of Fausyde, Nodref and Travernent, Alan, viii. 566, 567.
Latimer of Danby, Thomas, 1st viscount, iii. 301.
— of Whitby Strand, William le, viii. 564.
— Johanna, wife of Sir Alexander Comyn, ii. 256.
— John (Nevill), lord, i. 350.
Latter, Barré, wife of col. Jas. Dodington Carmichael, iv. 570.
Latoun, Sir Brian, v. 398.

La Tour, Anne de, wife of (1) Alexander, duke of Albany, and (2) Louis, comte de la Chambre, i. 153.
— Anne de, wife of John, duke of Albany, i. 154; ix. 10.
— Bertrand de, comte d'Auvergne et de Bouillon, i. 153.
— Jean de, comte d'Auvergne, i. 154.
— — his wife, Jeanne de Bourbon, i. 154.
Lauder of Aldcathy, John, iv. 447.
— of the Bass, Sir Robert, 'with the Boreit Whynger,' iv. 447.
— — Robert, viii. 432.
— — his wife, Isabel Hay, viii. 432.
— — Robert, ii. 160; iii 285; ix. 167.
— — his handfasted wife, Jane Hepburne, ii. 160.
— — his wife, Elizabeth Hay, ix. 167.
— of Bielmouth, Sir Robert, Clerk of Exchequer, ii. 19.
— — his wife, Helen Ogilvy, ii. 19.
— of Dunbar, Maurice, ix. 2.
— of Fountainhall, Sir John, lord of Session, ii. 21; ix. 35.
— of Gogar, Sir Ludovick, sheriff of Edinburgh, vi. 596.
— of Halton, Sir Alexander, iv. 84.
— — his wife, Elizabeth Forrester, iv. 84.
— — Alexander, ii. 108.
— — his wife, Janet Borthwick, ii. 108.
— — Alexander, ii. 68; iv. 246; v. 298.
— — his 1st wife, Mary Maitland, v. 298.
— — his 2nd wife, Annabel Bellenden, ii. 68.
— — Alexander, iv. 246.
— — his wife, Susanna Cunningham, iv. 246.
— — Allan, i. 326.
— — his wife, Alicia Campbell, i. 326.
— — Elizabeth, wife of Charles Maitland, lord Halton, 3rd earl of Lauderdale, iii. 543: v. 306.
— — George, viii. 12.
— — his wife, Katharine Somerville, viii. 12.
— — John, *alias* Maitland, 2nd son of 3rd earl of Lauderdale, v. 310.
— — Richard, v. 306.
— — Sir William, v. 298.
— of Hownam and Swynset, Elizabeth, vii. 319.
— — Katharine, vii. 319.
— — Marion, wife of Sir Alex. Home, iv. 447; vii. 319, 320.
— of North Raw, Sir Alexander, iv. 84.
— of Pitscandlie, George, viii. 81.
— of Poppill, Sir Robert, viii. 438.
— — his wife, Margaret Hay, viii. 438.
— of Quarrelwood, Robert, v. 281.
— of Ratho, Alan, iii. 428.
Lauder of Westhall, Sir Alexander, iv. 84.
— Alan de, v. 550.
— Agnes, wife of Gilbert Middleton of Middleton, vi. 172.
— Alexander, provost of Edinburgh, v. 291.
— Duncan, son of Gilbert of, iii. 88.
— Elizabeth, wife of Sir Alex. Napier of Merchiston, vi. 406.
— George, 2nd son of Sir Robt. L. of Bielmouth, ii. 19.
— Gilbert of, 1204, iii. 88.
— Gilbert of, 1428, v. 492.
— Helen, wife of (1) George, 4th lord Banff, (2) Alex. Gordon, and (3) Jas. Hay, ii. 21; ix. 35 *bis*.
— Henry, viii. 438.
— — his wife, Christian Hay, viii. 438.
— Jane, wife of Sir C. Hamilton of Clonyn, i. 40 *n*.
— Jean *or* Jonet, wife of (1) James Forrester of Corstorphine, (2) Sir John Campbell of Cawdor, (3) Mr. John Lindsay, and (4) Patrick Gray of Cransley, *or* Robert Gray of Milhill, i. 517; iv. 88, 89, 285.
— John, iv. 447; ix. 107.
— — his wife, Katharine Landells of Swynset, iv. 447; ix. 107.
— Katharine, wife of (1) John Swinton, (2) David Home, and (3) George Home, iii. 285.
— Margaret, lady of Wauchton, wife of Alex. Hume of Polwarth, vi. 5.
— Marion, wife of Sir Alexander Home, 1st lord Home, ix. 107 *bis*.
— Robert, son of Sir Robt. L. of Bielmouth, ii. 19.
— William, bailie of Lauder, ix. 134.
LAUDERDALE, MAITLAND, EARL OF, v. 276-323.
Lauderdale, Anthony, tenth earl of, v. 320.
— Charles, third earl of, iii. 328; iv. 249; v. 306.
— — his wife, Elizabeth Lauder of Halton, v. 306, 308.
— Charles, sixth earl of, iv. 38; v. 311.
— — his wife, Elizabeth Ogilvy, v. 311.
— Charles, twelfth earl of, v. 312, 321.
— Frederick Henry, thirteenth earl of, v. 313, 321; ix. 125 *bis*.
— — his 1st wife, Charlotte Sarah Sleigh, v. 321.
— — his 2nd wife, Ada Twyford Simpson, v. 322.
— James, seventh earl of, v. 311, 317.
— — his wife, Mary Turner Lombe, v. 317.
— James, eighth earl of, iii. 583; v. 318, 322; ix. 125.
— — his wife, Eleanor Todd, v. 319.
— James, ninth earl of, v. 320.

Lauderdale, John, first earl of, iii. 321 *n.*; v. 276, 302.
—— —— his wife, Isobel Seton, iii. 372; v. 301.
—— John, second earl of, v. 303.
—— John, fifth earl of, v. 310.
—— —— his wife, Margaret Cunningham, iv. 249; v. 310.
—— Richard, fourth earl of, v. 309, 477.
—— —— his wife, Anne Campbell, i. 368; v. 310.
—— Thomas, eleventh earl of, v. 318, 320.
—— —— his wife, Amelia Young, v. 320.
LAUDERDALE, MAITLAND, VISCOUNT OF, v. 302-323.
Lauderdale, John, first viscount of, v. 302.
LAUDERDALE, MAITLAND, DUKE OF, v. 305-306.
Lauderdale, John, duke of, i. 521; ii. 29; iii. 404; v. 305; viii. 458; ix. 108 *bis*.
—— —— his 1st wife, Anna Home, iv. 465; v. 303; ix. 108.
—— —— his 2nd wife, Elizabeth Murray, countess of Dysart, i. 370, 378, 380; iii. 403; v. 304; vii. 480; viii. 221.
LAUDERDALE OF THIRLESTANE CASTLE, MAITLAND, LORD, v. 319-320.
Lauderdale of Thirlestane Castle, Anthony, third lord, v. 319.
—— —— James, first lord, v. 318.
—— —— James, second lord, v. 319.
Launder, Katharine, wife of George, 4th lord Mordingtoun, vi. 335.
—— Robert, rector of Shenley, vi. 335.
Lauragais, Anne de la Tour, wife of John, duke of Albany; comtesse d'Auvergne et de, i. 154.
Laurence of Coventre, son of Orm, vi. 530.
—— of Dunlappie, son of Orm, v. 573.
—— of Govan, iv. 573.
—— Aimée, wife of Douglas Walter Campbell, i. 391.
—— John, New York, i. 391.
Laurie of Maxwelton, Robert, ii. 410.
—— —— his wife, Mary Dalzell, ii. 410.
—— —— Sir Robert, 5th bart., vii. 389.
—— —— his wife, Elizabeth Maria Ruthven, vii. 389.
—— Bethia, wife of David Rollo, vii. 198.
—— Jean, wife of Colin Mackenzie, vii. 508.
—— Robert, dean of Edinburgh, bishop of Brechin, vii. 197 *n.*, 198, 508.
Lauriston of Lauriston, Thomas, iv. 89.
—— —— his wife, Katharine Forrester, iv. 89.
Lautour of Hexton House, Joseph Andrew, iii. 518 *n.*
—— —— his wife, Caroline Young, iii. 518 *n.*
Lavalette, marquis de, ix. 142.
—— —— his wife, Georgiana Gabrielle de Flahault, ix. 142.
La Vall of Kilsyth, Robert de, v. 424; viii. 522.
Lavelette, ix. 6.
Law, Anne, wife of 9th lord Colville of Culross, ii. 566.
—— Elizabeth, wife of major Charles Murray, viii. 209.
—— James, archbishop of Glasgow, i. 201; iv. 194.
—— —— his 3rd wife, Marion Boyle, iv. 194.
—— John, professor of philosophy, Glasgow, iii. 544.
—— John, D.D., archdeacon of Rochester, iii. 614.
—— —— his wife, Mary Elizabeth Cary, iii. 614.
—— John, D.D., viii. 209.
—— Margaret, wife of R. Wemyss of Earl's Seat, viii. 492.
Lawford of Winton, Ernest Bruce Acland, iii. 464.
—— —— his wife, Gertrude Montgomerie, iii. 464.
Lawless, Mary Margaret, wife of (1) baron de Robeck, and (2) Sussex Lennox, v. 366.
Lawry, S., in holy orders, iii. 360.
—— —— his wife, Caroline Gosling, iii. 360.
Lawson of Burgh, Sir Ralph, iii. 296.
—— of Cairnmuir, James, ii. 107.
—— of Humbie, ii. 99.
—— —— James, ii. 68.
—— —— his wife, Elizabeth Bellenden, ii. 68.
—— Barbara, wife of Wm. Borthwick, ii. 100.
—— James, ii. 99.
—— —— his wife, Katharine Creighton, ii. 99.
—— James, minister of Edinburgh, iii. 377.
—— Janet, wife of (1) Jas. Fawside, and (2) Sir J. Edmonstone, ii. 68.
—— Katharine, wife of Mr. Archibald Borthwick, ii. 107.
—— Katharine, wife of (1) Gilbert Dick, and (2) Mr. P. Galloway, iii. 377.
—— Katharine, wife of James Primrose, vii. 216.
—— Margaret, wife of Alex. Borthwick, ii. 99.
—— Marjory, wife of (1) Sir John Haldane of Gleneagles, and (2) William Meldrum of Cleish, ii. 99 *n.*
—— Richard, bookseller, Edinburgh, vii. 216.
—— Roger, eldest son of Sir Ralph L. of Burgh, iii. 296.
—— —— his wife, Dorothy Constable, iii. 296.
—— William, merchant, Edinburgh, iii. 377.
—— William, Dysart, iv. 71.
—— —— his wife, * Forbes, iv. 71.
Layard, Arthur, vii. 63.
—— —— his wife, Margaret Capel-Carnegie-Arbuthnott, viii. 63.
—— Mary Anne, wife of 5th duke of Ancaster, vii. 96.
—— Peter, major, vii. 96.
—— W. T., general, viii. 63.

* Name unknown.

Leader of Ashgrove, Thomas Leonard, captain 79th Highlanders, iii. 521.
—— —— his wife, Janet Oliphant Murray, iii. 521.
Leake of Thorpe Hall, John Martin, vi. 179.
—— Jonas M., M.D., ii. 417.
—— —— his wife, Eliza Jane Dalzell, ii. 417.
—— Susanna Maria, wife of rear-admiral R. G. Middleton, vi. 179.
Lear, Francis, dean of Salisbury, ii. 56.
—— Isabel, wife of rev. W. K. Hamilton, ii. 56.
Learmonth of Balcomie, George, vii. 290.
—— —— his wife, Euphemia Leslie, vii. 290.
—— —— Sir James, lord of Session, i. 78.
—— —— his wife, Margaret Sandilands, i. 78.
—— —— Sir John, vi. 591.
—— —— his wife, Cecile Makgill, vi. 591.
—— of Clatto, William, viii. 497.
—— —— his wife, Cecilia Wemyss, viii. 497.
—— of Dairsie, James, i. 77.
—— —— his wife, Janet Sandilands, i. 77.
—— —— Patrick, vii. 546.
—— —— his wife, Isobel Balfour, vii. 546.
—— of Dean, Alexander, col., M.P., ii. 501.
—— of Newholm, ii. 41.
—— —— his wife, * Hamilton, ii. 41.
—— James, provost of St. Mary's Church, St. Andrews, v. 399.
—— Katharine, wife of Jas. Melville of Hallhill and Nethergrange, vi. 91.
—— Mary Adelaide, wife of lord John Kennedy, ii. 501.
—— Robert, advocate, St. Andrews, ii. 235.
—— Thomas, advocate, viii. 31.
—— Thomas, his son, viii. 31.
Le Blanc, Anne, wife of Alex. Colville, D.D., ii. 551.
—— Catharine, wife of Sir Alex. Purves, vi. 19.
Le Blanche, Maria, wife of major Hamilton Maxwell, v. 133.
Lechmere, Sir Edmund Hungerford, 2nd bart., iii. 513.
—— —— his wife, Maria Clara Murray, iii. 513.
Leckie, Core, ancestor of the family of, v. 330.
—— R. G. Edwards, major, v. 330 *n.*
—— John Hartpole, ii. 419.
—— —— his wife, Isabella Eliza Eardley Wilmot, ii. 419.
Leconfield, Henry (Wyndham), 2nd lord, vii. 227.
—— —— his wife, Constance Evelyn Primrose, vii. 227.
Ledesma, Juan de, vii. 551.
—— Maria de, wife of col. Wm. Sempill, vii. 551.
Le Despencer, Sir Francis (Dashwood), lord, v. 318.

* Name unknown.

Le Despenser, Hugh, vi. 292.
Lee of Binfield, Robert, viii. 181, 182.
—— —— his wife, Mary Alexander, viii. 181.
—— of Burston, Sir Anthony, vi. 464.
—— Abbie, wife of commander Augustus Charles Murray, R.N., iii. 389.
—— Charles, illeg. son of 4th viscount Dunbar, iii. 299 *n.*
—— David, New York, iii. 389.
—— George, Virginia, iii. 601.
—— Joyce, wife of John Cheyne, vi. 464.
—— Judith, wife of 4th earl of Stirling, viii. 182.
—— Margaret, wife of Archibald Arbuthnott, i. 307.
—— Mrs.; Rachel Fanny Antonia (Dashwood), wife of Matthew Allen Lee, ix. 7.
—— Robert Edward, Confederate general, iii. 601.
—— Sophia Francis, wife of James Seton-Broadbent, viii. 598.
Lee-Harvey of Castle-Semple, Henry, ii. 279.
—— —— his wife, Elizabeth Erskine, ii. 279.
Lee-Mainwaring of Knaresborough Abbey, Charles Benjamin, iv. 67.
—— —— his wife, Mary Stuart Forbes, iv. 67.
Leech, Stephen, iii. 524.
—— —— his wife, Alice Florence Murray, iii. 524.
Leeds, George (Godolphin Osborne), 10th duke of, viii. 316.
—— Peregrine (Osborne), 2nd duke of, iii. 302, 355.
—— Peregrine Hyde (Osborne), 3rd duke of, vii. 94.
—— —— his wife, Julian Hele, vii. 94.
—— Thomas (Osborne), 1st duke of, i. 30; iii. 301.
Leeke, Penelope, wife of 2nd baron Lucas of Shenfield, iii. 614.
Lees, Andrew, ii. 296.
—— —— his wife, Helen Stuart, ii. 296.
L'Église, Louis François de, vi. 560.
—— —— his wife, Marie Magdeleine Elinga, vi. 559.
Leicester, Edward (Coke), earl of, i. 377.
—— —— his wife, Margaret (Tufton), baroness Clifford, i. 378.
—— of Holkham, Thomas (Coke), 2nd earl of, iii. 395; viii. 162.
—— —— his 1st wife, Juliana Whitbread, iii. 395.
Leigh of Addlestrop, John, v. 199.
—— —— his wife, Caroline Brydges, v. 199.
—— of Rushall Hall, William, dean of Hereford, ii. 357.
—— Frances Harriet, wife of 13th earl of Caithness, ii. 357.
—— Thomas Gerard, rector of Walton-on-the Hill, i. 493.
—— —— his wife, Henriana Matilda Murray, i. 493.

Leighton of Duninald, Robert, v. 223.
—— —— Patrick, i. 79.
—— of Ulishaven, Robert, vii. 17.
—— —— Robert, 1613, v. 223.
—— —— Walter, i. 116.
—— —— his wife, Marjorie, i. 116.
—— Frances, wife of Sir Hew Whitefoord Dalrymple of High Mark, viii. 140.
—— Francis, general, viii. 140.
—— Jean, wife of 1st lord Abercrombie, i. 79; ix. 5.
—— Margaret, wife of Thos. Maule of Pitlevie, vii. 17.
—— Sir Walter of, i. 108.
—— *, wife of Robert Arbuthnott, i. 281.
Leinster, Charles William (FitzGerald), 4th duke of, viii. 363.
—— —— his wife, Caroline Sutherland-Leveson-Gower, viii. 363.
—— James (Fitzgerald), 1st duke of, v. 365.
—— —— his wife, Emily Mary Lennox, v. 365.
Leishman, John, Stirling, viii. 168.
—— —— his wife, Elizabeth Alexander, viii. 168.
Leitch, *, alleged mother of the 'Black' Stewart of Bute, ii. 286.
Leith of Fyvie, Alexander John (Forbes-Leith), lord, iv. 64.
—— of Courtastoune, John, viii. 296.
—— of Drumgowan, John, viii. 296, 297.
—— of Edengarioch, Elizabeth, alleged wife of Sir Norman Leslie, vii. 268.
—— of Harthill, Patrick, i. 290.
—— of Leithhall, John, ii. 20.
—— —— his wife, Janet Ogilvy, ii. 19.
—— of Petmathen and Palmerscross, Thomas, major, ii. 418.
—— —— his wife, Mary Isabella Dalzell, ii. 418.
—— of Overhall, George, viii. 136.
—— —— his wife, Elizabeth Dalrymple-Elphinstone, viii. 136.
—— of Whitehaugh, John, viii. 297.
—— —— John, iv. 63.
—— —— his wife, Elizabeth Forbes, iv. 63.
—— Anne, wife of Lucius Ferdinand Cary, master of Falkland, iii. 615.
—— Charles, colonel, iii. 615.
—— James, major, V.C., vi. 438.
—— —— his wife, Isabella Shaw, vi. 438.
Lekprevick of Polcarn, James, iv. 227.
L'Enclos, Ninon de, ix. 101.
Lennard of Horsford, Richard, ii. 35.
Lennie, Symon de, burgess of Perth, vi. 531.
LENNOX, THE CELTIC EARLS OF, v. 324-343.
Lennox, Alwin, first earl of, v. 324, 326.
—— Alwin, second earl of, v. 327, 331.
—— —— his wife, Eva, v. 328; vi. 125.
—— Donald, sixth earl of, v. 336, 425.

* Name unknown.

Lennox, Sir Duncan, eighth earl of, i. 149, 150; ii. 176; iv. 345; v. 339, 426; vi. 216, 217, 408.
—— —— his wife, Helena Campbell, i. 327; v. 340; ix. 18.
—— Isabella, wife of Murdach, duke of Albany; countess of, i. 149, 150; v. 339, 343; vi. 409.
—— Sir John Menteith, styled earl of, v. 335.
—— Malcolm, fourth earl of, v. 333, 550.
—— —— his wife, Margaret, v. 334.
—— Malcolm, fifth earl of, ii. 425; v. 334.
—— Maldouen, third earl of, iii. 136; v. 328-331 *passim*.
—— —— his wife, Elizabeth *or* Beatrix Stewart, i. 12; v. 332.
—— Margaret, wife of Walter of Faslane; countess of, v. 330, 337.
—— Walter, *de jure uxoris* seventh earl of, v. 337.
—— —— his wife, Margaret, countess of Lennox, v. 337.
LENNOX, STEWART, EARL OF, v. 348-355.
Lennox, Charles, sixth earl of, v. 354.
—— —— his wife, Elizabeth Cavendish, i. 22; v. 354.
—— Esme, eighth earl of, i. 195; v. 352, 356; vi. 388.
—— James, fifth earl of, v. 354.
—— John, first earl of, v. 348; vii. 532.
—— —— his wife, Margaret Montgomerie, iii. 433; v. 348.
—— John, third earl of, iv. 358; v. 351.
—— —— his wife, Elizabeth Stewart, i. 442; v. 352.
—— Matthew, second earl of, v. 351, 554, 555; vii. 532, 539.
—— —— his alleged 1st wife, Margaret Lyle, v. 351, 554.
—— —— his 2nd wife, Elizabeth Hamilton, i. 20; iv. 353; v. 351.
—— Matthew, fourth earl of, i. 27, 38; ii. 168; iii. 436; iv. 147, 153, 237; v. 188, 353; vii. 122: ix. 126 *ter*.
—— —— his wife, Margaret Douglas, i. 192; v. 353; vi. 228.
—— Robert, seventh earl of, i. 396; v. 82, 352, 355.
—— —— his wife, Elizabeth Stewart, i. 396, 445; v. 355.
LENNOX, STEWART, DUKE OF, v. 344-362.
Lennox, Charles, sixth duke of, v. 360.
—— —— his 1st wife, Elizabeth Rogers, v. 361.
—— —— his 2nd wife, Margaret Banaster, v. 361.
—— —— his 3rd wife, Frances Stewart, ii. 84; v. 361.
—— Esme, first duke of, v. 352, 356, 443; viii. 344.
—— —— his wife, Katharine de Balsac, v. 356.

Lennox, Esme, third duke of, v. 358.
—— his wife, Katharine Clifton, i. 49; v. 358.
— Esme, fifth duke of, v. 360.
— James, fourth duke of, v. 360.
—— his wife, Mary Villiers, v. 360.
— Ludovick, second duke of, iv. 160; v. 10, 356; vi. 576; viii. 403.
—— his 1st wife, Sophia Ruthven, iv. 266; v. 357.
—— his 2nd wife, Jean Campbell, v. 357, 497; ix. 81.
—— his 3rd wife, Frances Howard, v. 357.
LENNOX, LENNOX, DUKE OF, v. 363-371.
Lennox, Charles, first duke of, i. 32; v. 363.
—— his wife, Anne Brudenell, v. 363.
— Charles, second duke of, v. 364.
—— his wife, Sarah Cadogan, v. 364.
— Charles, third duke of, v. 365.
—— his wife, Mary Bruce, v. 365.
— Charles, fourth duke of, v. 364, 366.
—— his wife, Charlotte Gordon, iv. 557; v. 366.
— Charles, fifth duke of, v. 367.
—— his wife, Caroline Paget, v. 367.
— Charles Henry, sixth duke of, v. 369.
—— his wife, Frances Harriett Greville, v. 369.
— Charles Henry, seventh duke of, v. 369.
—— his 1st wife, Amy Mary Ricardo, v. 370.
—— his 2nd wife, Isabel Sophie Craven, v. 370.
— master of, John, son of Matthew, earl of Lennox, vi. 226.
LENNOX, EARL OF DARNLEY, v. 363-371.
LENNOX, DUKE OF LENNOX, v. 363-371.
LENNOX, EARL OF MARCH, v. 363-371.
LENNOX, DUKE OF RICHMOND, v. 363-371.
LENNOX, BARON OF SETTRINGTON, v. 363-371.
LENNOX, BARON TARBOLTON, v. 363-371.
Lennox of Cally, Alexander, i. 221; ix. 118.
—— his wife, Marion Gordon, ix. 118.
—— Anna, wife of Richard Murray of Broughton, i. 221.
—— John, v. 270.
—— his wife, Agnes Maclellan, v. 270.
—— William, vi. 278 *bis*.
— of Woodhead, ii. 296.
—— his wife, Margaret Stewart, ii. 296.
—— John, captain, iii. 342.
—— his wife, Elizabeth Cochrane, iii. 342.
—— Margaret, dau. of Wm. L., v. 342.
—— William, v. 342.
— Alexander, 2nd son of Walter, 7th earl of Lennox, v. 339.
— Alexander Alan, claimant to title of Lennox, v. 339.
— Alan, 3rd son of Walter, 7th earl of Lennox, v. 339.
Lennox, Ann, wife of 2nd earl of Albemarle, v. 364.
— Arthur, master of the Ordnance, lord of the Treasury, v. 367.
—— his wife, Adelaide Constance Campbell, v. 367.
— Cecilia, dau. of 2nd duke of Lennox, v. 365.
— Charlotte, wife of 1st lord Fitzhardinge, v. 367.
— Donald, legtd. son of Duncan, 8th earl of Lennox, v. 342.
—— his wife, Elizabeth Stewart, v. 342.
— Frederick, capt. 7th Foot, v. 366.
— Georgina, wife of Henry, 3rd earl Bathurst, v. 364.
— Georgina Carolina, baroness Holland of Holland, wife of Henry (Fox), lord Holland, v. 365.
— Elizabeth, wife of (1) Alexander *, and (2) Sir John Stewart of Darnley, v. 341, 343, 347.
— Emily Charlotte, wife of Sir G. C. Berkeley, v. 364.
— Emily Mary, wife of (1) James, 1st duke of Leinster, and (2) William Ogilvie, v. 365.
— George Henry, general, Constable of the Tower of London, v. 364.
—— his wife, Louisa Ker, v. 364.
— Helena of, alleged wife of Sir C. Campbell of Lochow, i. 325.
— Henry Adam, 3rd son of 4th duke of Lennox, v. 366.
— Jane, wife of Lawrence Peel of Kemptown, v. 367.
— Sir John 'Mor,' alleged son of an earl of Lennox, i. 325.
— John George, lieut.-col., M.P., v. 366.
—— his wife, Louisa Frederica Rodney, v. 366.
— Louisa, wife of James, 3rd earl of Berkeley, v. 363.
— Louisa Augusta, wife of Thomas Conolly, v. 365.
— Louisa Maddelena, wife of W. F. F. Tighe, v. 367.
— Louisa Margaret, dau. of 2nd duke of Lennox, v. 365.
— Malcolm of, elder son of Maldouen, 3rd earl of Lennox, v. 332.
— Malcolm, illeg. son of Duncan, 8th earl of Lennox, v. 342.
— Margaret, wife of Robert Menteith of Rusky, v. 341, 343.
— Mary, alleged wife of Sir C. Campbell of Glenurchy, ii. 175.
— Mary, wife of Sir C. A. Fitzroy, v. 367.
— Mary Louisa, dau. of 2nd duke of Lennox, v. 364.
— Sarah, wife of Sir Peregrine Maitland, v. 367.

* Name unknown.

Lennox, Sarah, wife of (1) Sir T. C. Bunbury, and (2) col. Geo. Napier, v. 365; vi. 433; ix. 111.
— Sophia Georgiana, wife of lord Thomas Cecil, v. 367.
— Sussex, postmaster of Jamaica, v. 366.
— — his wife, Mary Margaret Lawless, v. 366.
— Thomas, illeg. son of Duncan, 8th earl of Lennox, v. 342.
— Walter, 4th son of Walter, 7th earl of Lennox, v. 339.
— Mr. William, illeg. son of 8th earl of Lennox, v. 342.
— William Pitt, M.P., v. 366.
— — his 1st wife, Mary Anne Paton, v. 366.
— — his 2nd wife, Ellen Smith, v. 366.
— — his 3rd wife, Maria Jane Molyneux, v. 366.
Le Normand, Mlle., fortune-teller, viii. 184.
Lenthall of Burford, William, i. 49.
— — his wife, Katharine Hamilton, i. 49.
— Sir John, marshal of the King's Bench, ix. 3.
— — his wife, Hester Temple, ix. 3.
— Katharine, wife of James, lord Paisley, i. 49.
Lentran of Newgrange, David, v. 413, 414.
— — his wife, Elizabeth Arnot, v. 413.
— Elizabeth, wife of John Lindsay of Wolmerston, v. 414.
Leny of Leny and Buchanan, John, ii. 425.
Leon and Granada, Alphonso, king of, iii. 145.
— Maria de, wife of Henry Balfour, i. 537.
Leper, Andrew, burgess of Edinburgh, iv. 82.
— — his wife, Marion Forrester, iv. 82.
Le Rat, Marie Marguerite Angelique, wife of James Galloway, 'comte de Dunkeld,' iii. 382.
Lermont, *see* Learmonth.
LESLIE, LESLIE, LORD, vii. 274-311.
Leslie, George, first lord, vii. 273.
— — his 1st wife, Margaret Lundin, vii. 275.
— — his 2nd wife, Christian Haliburton, vii. 275.
— — his 3rd wife, Elizabeth Campbell, vii. 275.
— John, eldest son of Margaret, countess of Rothes; styled lord, vii. 302.
— Malcolm George Dyer-Edwardes, styled lord, vii. 310.
LESLIE, LESLIE, EARL OF, vii. 301.
Leslie, John, earl of, vii. 301.
LESLIE UPON LEVEN, LESLIE, LORD, vii. 274.
Leslie upon Leven, George, lord, vii. 274.
LESLIE, LORD AUCHMUTIE, vii. 301.
LESLIE, LORD BALGONIE, v. 372-381.
LESLIE, MARQUESS OF BAMBREICH, vii. 301.
LESLIE, LORD CASKIEBERRIE, vii. 301.
LESLIE, LORD LESLIE, vii. 273-311.
LESLIE, EARL OF LESLIE, vii. 301.
LESLIE, LORD LESLIE UPON LEVEN, vii. 274.
LESLIE, EARL OF LEVEN, v. 372-381.
LESLIE, LORD LINDORES, v. 382-390.
LESLIE, VISCOUNT OF LUGTOUN, vii. 301.
LESLIE, EARL OF MELVILLE, vi. 110-118.
LESLIE, LORD NEWARK, vi. 440-445.
LESLIE, EARL OF ROSS, vii. 241-244.
LESLIE, EARL OF ROTHES, vii. 264-311.
LESLIE, DUKE OF ROTHES, vii. 301.
Leslie of Abercrombie, David, vi. 442.
— of Aikinway, George, i. 85; iv. 536.
— — William, vii. 460.
— of Ardersier, Robert, 3rd son of 4th earl of Rothes, vii. 286, 287.
— — his wife, Janet Elphinstone, iii. 534; vii. 288.
— of Auchingoul, William, iv. 133.
— of Auldcraig, Robert, ix. 115.
— of Balcomie, Alexander, vi. 366.
— of Balgonie, Sir Alexander, v. 376.
— — his wife, Anna Renton, v. 377.
— — Alexander, colonel, v. 378; vii. 299.
— — his wife, Margaret Leslie, vii. 299.
— of Ballinbreich, James, elder son of James, master of Rothes, vii. 296.
— — Norman, son of Sir Andrew L., vii. 272.
— — Norman, son of Sir George L., vii. 272.
— — William, vii. 279.
— of Ballybay, James, ancestor of the family of, vii. 290.
— of Balmain, John, eldest son of Andrew, master of Rothes, vii. 276.
— — his wife, Janet Keith, vi. 41; vii. 277.
— of Balmuto, George, vii. 277.
— of Balquhain, Sir Andrew, 3rd laird, vii. 269, 270.
— — Charles, col., K.H., vi. 456.
— — his wife, Dorothea Eyre of Hassop, vi. 456.
— — George, ancestor of the family of, vii. 271.
— — George, count, iii. 544.
— — his wife, Margaret Elphinstone, iii. 544.
— — John, sheriff of Aberdeen, ii. 7; iv. 55.
— — John, iii. 571, 590; vii. 439.
— — his 1st wife, Elizabeth *or* Isobel Grant, vii. 463; ix. 155.
— — his 2nd wife, Elizabeth *or* Isobel Hay, i. 536; iii. 571.
— — his 3rd wife, Jean Erskine, v. 84.
— — John, 3rd son of Patrick L. Duguid, v. 546.
— — Patrick, vii. 456.
— — his wife, Muriel Grant, vii. 456.

Leslie of Balquhain, Sir William, v. 372, 522.
—— —— his 1st wife, Elizabeth Fraser, v. 522.
—— —— William, ii. 7.
—— —— his 1st wife, Elizabeth Ogilvy, ii. 7.
—— —— William, iv. 55, 180.
—— —— his 1st wife, Jean *or* Janet Forbes, i. 414; iv. 55.
—— of Boglillie, Sir Alexander, v. 376.
—— of Burdsbank, George, vii. 288.
—— —— George, ix. 90.
—— of Cairnie, Andrew, vii. 269.
—— —— George, vii. 269.
—— —— William, 2nd son of 4th earl of Rothes, vii. 286, 293.
—— of Cocklarachie, George, iv. 536.
—— of Corbie, Sir John, eldest son of Sir John L. of Newton, v. 386, 387; ix. 128.
—— —— his wife, Jonet Hay, v. 386; ix. 128.
—— of Cowcairnie, Walter, vii. 291.
—— —— his wife, Elizabeth Wardlaw, vii. 291.
—— of Crukitstak, John, iv. 125.
—— of Cushnie, James, vii. 297.
—— —— Norman, vii. 272.
—— of Darkland, William, clk., ii. 356.
—— —— his wife, Margaret Sinclair, ii. 356.
—— of Drummuir, George, 1st laird, v. 372.
—— of Duffus, Patrick, v. 382.
—— of Duglie, Robert, vii. 287.
—— of Dunbog, George, vii. 274.
—— of Dunlappie, Norman, vii. 272.
—— of Edingarioch, George, vi. 172.
—— of Edrom, John, v. 377.
—— of Fettercairn, George, vii. 274.
—— of Fetterneir, iv. 181.
—— of Findrassie, Robert, 3rd son of 4th earl of Rothes, vii. 286, 287.
—— —— his wife, Janet Elphinstone, iii. 534; vii. 288.
—— —— Robert, 2nd laird, vii. 288.
—— of Easter Fithie, William, vii. 279.
—— of Fithkill, Alexander, vii. 241, 273.
—— —— Sir George, vii. 241, 270, 272.
—— of Foulis-Mowat, John, vii. 273, 274.
—— of Hilteasses, George, vii. 286.
—— of Iden, vii. 440.
—— of Inchmartin, Sir Alexander, iv. 35; v. 377; ix. 89.
—— of Innergellie, George, vii. 273.
—— —— Norman, vii. 273.
—— of Innerpeffer, Robert, iv. 305.
—— of Insch-Leslie, Sir Alexander, iv. 35; v. 377.
—— of Kilmany, Andrew, 4th son of 4th earl of Rothes, vii. 286, 287, 290, 292.
—— —— his 1st wife, Grisel Hamilton, vii. 293.
—— —— Sir Andrew, 3rd son of 5th earl of Rothes, vii. 294.
—— of Kingedward, Euphemia, countess of Ross, ii. 263, 264.
Leslie of Kingedward, Mary, wife of Donald, lord of the Isles, ii. 264.
—— of Kininvie, Alexander, 1st laird, v. 372.
—— of Kirklands of Lathrisk, Patrick, v. 382.
—— of Leslie, Alexander, earl of Ross, vii. 241.
—— —— Alexander, 2nd son of Sir Andrew L. of Balquhain, vii. 270, 276.
—— —— his wife, Joanna Leslie, vii. 270.
—— —— Sir Andrew, iii. 10; vii. 268.
—— —— his wife, Mary Abernethy, iii. 10; vii. 269, 402.
—— —— Sir Andrew, their son, vii. 269.
—— —— Sir Andrew, his son, iii. 562; iv. 515; vii. 269.
—— —— Sir David, iii. 562; iv. 335; v. 269; vii. 269, 273; viii. 270.
—— —— his wife, Margaret Davidson, vii. 270.
—— —— George, vi. 172; vii. 276 *bis*.
—— —— his alleged 1st wife, Christian Leslie, vii. 276.
—— —— his 2nd wife, Violet Middleton, vi. 172.
—— —— Sir George, of Rothes, vii. 241.
—— —— Joanna, wife of Alexander Leslie, vii. 270.
—— —— Malcolm of, son of Bertolf, vii. 265.
—— —— Norman of, son of Malcolm, vii. 266.
—— —— his wife, A., vii. 266.
—— —— Norman, son of Norman the Constable, vii. 267.
—— —— Sir Norman, vii. 268.
—— —— his alleged wife, Elizabeth Leith of Edengarioch, vii. 268.
—— —— his alleged wife, * of Rothes, vii. 268.
—— —— Norman, the yr., son of Andrew, vii. 269, 272.
—— —— his alleged wife, Margaret Hay, iii. 562; vii. 269.
—— —— Sir Norman, son of Sir Geo. L. of Rothes, iii. 273; v. 270.
—— —— Sir Walter, ii. 260, 261; iii. 239, 271.
—— —— his wife, Euphemia Comyn, countess of Ross, ii. 261; iii. 239, 272.
—— of New Leslie, George, 1st laird, v. 372.
—— of Lochmylne, Sir John, v. 386.
—— of Lour, Norman, vii. 272.
—— of Lumbany, Sir Andrew, v. 382, 384; vii. 294.
—— —— Patrick, v. 384; vii. 294.
—— of Lumquhat, James, 3rd son of Sir John L. of Newton, v. 386, 388.
—— —— his wife, Janet Dick, v. 388.
—— —— John, captain, v. 388.
—— —— his wife, Mary Gibb, v. 388.
—— —— John, v. 388.
—— —— his wife, Janet Arnot, v. 388.

* Name unknown.

Leslie of Lumquhat, John, v. 388.
—— —— his wife, Antonia Barclay, v. 388.
—— —— John, v. 389.
—— —— his wife, Jane Reeve, v. 389.
—— of Melrose, William, iv. 133.
—— of Milndeans, James, sheriff-depute of Fife, vii. 304.
—— —— Katharine, vii. 304, 307.
—— of Moircleuch, Walter, i. 447; v. 372.
—— of Monorgan, Sir Walter, viii. 264.
—— of Mugdrum, Ludovick, governor of Berwick, v. 384; ix. 127 *bis*.
—— of Myres, John, v. 386.
—— of Newton, George, v. 382, 386; vii. 295.
—— —— Sir John, 5th son of 5th earl of Rothes, v. 382, 386; vii. 295.
—— —— his wife, Elizabeth Gray, iv. 286; v. 386; vii. 295, 301.
—— of East Nisbet, Sir Alexander, v. 377.
—— of Otterstoun, James, ix. 127.
—— —— his wife, Anna Leslie, ix. 127.
—— —— Walter, vii. 291.
—— of Parkhill, John, rector of Kinnoir, iii. 31; vii. 279, 282, 462; ix. 110.
—— —— his wife, Euphemia Moncrieff, vii. 280.
—— of Philorth, Sir Walter, viii. 264.
—— of Pitcairlie, Patrick, commendator of Lindores, v. 382; vii. 294.
—— —— his wife, Jean Stewart, v. 383.
—— —— Patrick, his son, v. 384.
—— of Pitcaple, Alexander, iv. 180.
—— —— David, iv. 72.
—— —— James, i. 448.
—— —— John, iv. 127.
—— of Pitnamoon, Alexander, vii. 241.
—— —— Sir George, vii. 241.
—— of Pittendreich House, Patrick, v. 382.
—— of Pokmylne, Patrick, v. 382.
—— of Quarter, Alexander, 1st laird, v. 386, 387.
—— —— his wife, Margaret Balfour, v. 387.
—— —— Alexander, 3rd laird, v. 387.
—— —— his wife, Jean Campbell, v. 387.
—— —— John, 2nd laird, v. 387.
—— —— his wife, * Spital, v. 387.
—— of Rosmarkie, Robert, iii. 534; vii. 286, 287.
—— of Rothes, Sir George, iii. 526; vii. 241, 269 *bis*, 270, 271.
—— —— his wife, Elizabeth Hay, iii. 562; vii. 273.
—— —— George, vii. 273.
—— —— his 1st wife, Margaret Lundin, vii. 275.
—— —— his 2nd wife, Christian Haliburton, vii. 275.
—— —— his 3rd wife, Elizabeth Campbell, vii. 275.
—— —— Sir Norman, ii. 128 *n.*; vii. 268.

* Name unknown.

Leslie of Rothes, Norman, vii. 270, 273; viii. 574.
—— —— his wife, Christian Seton, vii. 273; viii. 574.
—— of Rothienorman, James, vii. 297.
—— —— Norman, vii. 272.
—— of Stenton, Katharine, vii. 304 *bis*, 307.
—— —— Thomas, captain, M.P., vii. 304.
—— of Tarbert, Sir Edward, i. 105.
—— —— Louisa, wife of major Douglas Gordon-Halyburton of Pitcur, i. 105.
—— of Tochir, George, iv. 536.
—— of Tulliefurie, William, iv. 125.
—— of Tyrie, vii. 440.
—— of Wardis, Alexander, 3rd laird, iv. 124.
—— —— William, 4th laird, ii. 13; iv. 125.
—— of Weittis, John, iv. 125.
—— —— his wife, Agnes Crichton, iv. 125.
—— of Woidraiff, Patrick, v. 382.
—— of Woodfield, Alexander, vii. 241.
—— —— Sir George, vii. 241.
—— Agnes, dau. of James, master of Rothes; wife of Andrew Wardlaw of Torrie, i. 43; vii. 296.
—— Agnes, wife of 5th earl of Morton, vi. 372; vii. 290.
—— Agnes, wife of Meldrum of Seggie, vii. 288.
—— Sir Alexander, field-marshal in the Swedish service; lord general of all the Scottish forces, v. 373.
—— Alexander, major-general, vi. 114, 116.
—— —— his wife, Mary Margaret Tullideph, vi. 115.
—— Alexander, illeg. son of 5th earl of Rothes, ix. 127.
—— Alice Julia, vii. 310.
—— Amelia, dau. of 13th earl of Rothes, vii. 308.
—— Sir Andrew, 1253, vii. 267.
—— Andrew, equerry to dowager princess of Wales, vii. 305, 307.
—— Anna, dau. of 2nd earl of Leven, v. 380.
—— Anna, wife of John Forbes of Leslie, v. 384; ix. 127.
—— Anna, dau. of 1st lord Newark, vi. 442.
—— Anna, wife of Jas. Leslie of Otterstoun, ix. 127.
—— Anna, wife of capt. Jas. Drummond, ix. 127.
—— Anna, wife of Robert Kirkaldy of Grange, ix. 128.
—— Anne, wife of (1) Hugh, master of Lovat, and (2) Sir Ralph Delaval, v. 378, 533.
—— Anne, wife of 6th earl of Northesk, vi. 115, 503.
—— Ann, wife of Sir Alex. Dunbar of Westfield, vii. 268.
—— Anne Maria, wife of 14th earl of Devon, vii. 309.

Leslie, Barbara, wife of (1) Sir J. Ruthven of Dunglass, and (2) Hepburn of Waughton, ii. 297; iv. 103; v. 378.
— Beatrix, wife of (1) David Beaton of Creich, and (2) John Auchmoutie of that Ilk, vii. 290.
— Charles, brother of the master of Newark, vi. 443.
— Charles, col. in Dutch service, vii. 304.
— Charles, 2nd son of 10th earl of Rothes, vii. 306.
— Charlotte, dau. of 6th earl of Leven, vi. 117.
— Christian, wife of Walter Dundas, v. 378; ix. 127.
— Christian, wife of (1) James, 3rd marquess of Montrose, and (2) Sir John Bruce of Kinross, vi. 261; vii. 301.
— Christian, wife of Thos. Graham of Balgowan, vi. 443.
— Christian, dau. of baroness Newark, vi. 443.
— Christian, alleged wife of George Leslie of Leslie, vii. 276.
— Christian, wife of James Kincaid of that Ilk, vii. 291.
— Cristina, wife of William, 2nd lord Sinclair, ii. 334; vii. 276, 570.
— David, 2nd son of John L. of Lumquhat, v. 388.
— David, 2nd son of baroness Newark, vi. 443.
— David, lieut.-general, v. 384, 624, 625; vi. 440.
— David, general, 3rd son of 6th earl of Leven, vi. 116.
— — his wife, Rebecca Gillies, vi. 117.
— Edward Courtenay, vii. 310.
— — his wife, Caroline Biddulph, vii. 310.
— Elizabeth, wife of Sir Jas. Sinclair of Moy, ii. 352; v. 384.
— Elizabeth, wife of Sir Archibald Kennedy of Culzean; ii. 490; vi. 442.
— Elizabeth, wife of (1) William, 3rd earl of Erroll, and (2) Sir W. Edmonstone of Duntreath, iii. 566; vii. 276.
— Elizabeth, wife of (1) David Wemyss, and (2) James, 2nd lord Ogilvy of Deskford, iv. 29; vii. 295; viii. 498.
— Elizabeth, wife of Alex. Abercromby of Pitmeddan, iv. 180.
— Elizabeth, wife of (1) Thos. Hamilton of Priestfield, and (2) William Hutson, iv. 305.
— Elizabeth, wife of 2nd earl of Hopetoun, iv. 497; vi. 115.
— Elizabeth, wife of Wm. Dick of Grange, v. 386; ix. 128 *bis*.
— Elizabeth, wife of capt. Hewan, v. 388.
— Elizabeth, dau. of 2nd lord Newark, vi. 443.
— Elizabeth, wife of * Magnus, vi. 445.

* Name unknown.

Leslie, Elizabeth, wife of Patrick Crichton of Lugton, vii. 291.
— Elizabeth Jane, wife of major A. Wathen, vii. 308.
— Emilia, wife of Alex. Fraser of Strichen, v. 546.
— Emily Louisa, wife of James F. Cherry, vii. 310.
— Euphemia, wife of Sir. D. Barclay, v. 384.
— Euphemia, wife of 7th lord Lindsay of the Byres, v. 400; vii. 294.
— Euphemia, abbess of Elcho, vii. 241 *n*.
— Euphemia, wife of Alex. Bruce of Earlshall, vii. 281.
— Euphemia, wife of (1) G. Learmonth of Balcomie, and (2) John Cunningham of West Barns, vii. 290.
— Euphemia, dau. of James, master of Rothes, vii. 296.
— Francis, H.E.I.C.S., vi. 445.
— Francis, 7th son of 9th earl of Rothes, vii. 305.
— Francis, Wemyss, ix. 127.
— George, captain of the Castle of Blair in Atholl, v. 372.
— George, bailie of Atholl, captain of Blair Athol, v. 372.
— George, colonel; son of George L., v. 373.
— George, 2nd son of Alexander, 5th earl of Leven and 4th earl of Melville, vi. 114.
— George, H.E.I.C.S., vi. 117.
— — his wife, Jacomina Gertrude Vander-Graaff, vi. 117.
— George, murdered by 2nd earl of Rothes, vii. 277.
— George, 2nd son of James, master of Rothes, vii. 296.
— George, 6th son of 1st lord Lindores, ix. 127.
— Georgiana, dau. of 13th earl of Rothes, vii. 308.
— Georgina, wife of W. B. Haden Corser, vii. 310.
— Grace, wife of John Bazley White, vii. 310.
— Grizel, wife of (1) Walter Heriot of Burnturk, and (2) Henry Wardlaw of Torrie, vii. 281.
— Grizel, wife of 1st earl of Dunfermline, iii. 372; vii. 296.
— Grizel, wife of Thos. Drummond of Logiealmond, vi. 443.
— Helen, dau. of 1st lord Newark, vi. 442.
— Helen, wife of (1) Gilbert Seton of Parbroath, and (2) Mark Ker, commendator of Newbattle, v. 454, 455; vii. 289.
— Helen, wife of Dr. John Chalmers of Raderny, vi. 443.
— Helen, wife (1) Alex. Gray, and (2) Thos. Livingston, vi. 448.

Leslie, Henrietta Anne, wife of C. K. Murray, vii. 308.
—— Henry, 3rd son of Mary Elizabeth, countess of Rothes, vii. 310.
—— Henry, 7th son of 1st lord Lindores, ix. 127.
—— Hughina, dau. of John L. of Lumquhat, v. 389.
—— Isobel, wife of (1) Robert Lundie of Newhall, and (2) Sir G. Hamilton of Greenlaw, i. 43; vii. 296.
—— Isabella, wife of James, master of Sinclair, vii. 294, 574.
—— James, capt. in Spanish service, iii. 33.
—— —— his wife, Jean Lindsay, iii. 33.
—— James, son of John L. of Pitcaple, iv. 127.
—— James, 3rd son of 2nd earl of Melville, vi. 113.
—— James, brother of the master of Newark, vi. 443.
—— James, illeg. son of John L. of Parkhill, vii. 281.
—— James, rector of Aberdour, and of Rothes, vii. 281.
—— James, lieut. in Army, ix. 127.
—— James, colonel, 2nd son of 1st lord Newark, ix. 143.
—— Jane, wife of Sir J. W. B. Stuart of Fettercairn, vi. 117.
—— Jane, wife of John Sanford of Minehead, vi. 445.
—— Jane, dau. of 9th earl of Rothes, vi. 305.
—— Janet, wife of 1st viscount Frendraught, iv. 130; v. 378; ix. 127.
—— Janet, wife of Sir John Cunningham, v. 384.
—— Janet, alleged wife of Robert, 3rd lord Sempill, vii. 551.
—— Janet, wife of Robert Stewart, ix. 115.
—— Janet *or* Jean, wife of (1) D. Crichton of Nauchton, (2) John Grant of Freuchie, and (3) James Elphinstone of Ellieston, iii. 533; vii. 289, 463; ix. 84.
—— Jean, wife of Andrew Dick of Holland and Craighouse, v. 387.
—— Jean, dau. of John L. of Quarter, v. 387.
—— Jean, wife of (1) John Stewart of Innernytie, and (2) John Bruce of Blairhall, v. 385; ix. 127.
—— Jean, dau. of baroness Newark, vi. 444.
—— Jean, wife of Duncan Menzies of Weem, vii. 297.
—— Joanna, dau. of 1st lord Newark, vi. 442.
—— Joanna, dau. of baroness Newark, vi. 444.
—— Joan *or* Jane, wife of (1) Sir Alex. Dunbar of Cumnock, and (2) Sir P. Gordon of Auchindoun, vii. 281; ix. 110.
—— Joanna, wife of Durham of Grange, vii. 288.
Leslie, John, bishop of Ross, v. 157, 158 *ter*, 441; vii. 501.
—— —— his wife, Christian Scrymgeour, vii. 501.
—— John, son of John L. of Corbie, v. 386.
—— John, general, vi. 117.
—— —— his wife, Jane Cuming, vi. 117.
—— John, lt.-col. 3rd Foot, vi. 444.
—— John, brother of Norman L. of Leslie, vii. 267.
—— John, bishop of Ross, vii. 287.
—— John, legtd. son of Norman L., master of Rothes, vii. 286.
—— John, 3rd son of Robert L. of Findrassie, vii. 288.
—— Katharine, wife of 1st earl of Melville, i. 546; v. 378, 381; vi. 109.
—— Katharine, wife of Geo. Crichton of Little Forg, iv. 125.
—— Katharine, dau. of baroness Newark, vi. 444.
—— Katharine, wife of Sir John Oliphant of Kellie, vii. 291.
—— Katharine Caroline, wife of capt. John Parker, vii. 309.
—— Leonard, commendator of Coupar, v. 373.
—— Leonard, alleged son of Norman L. of Leslie, vii. 268.
—— Ludovic, Barbados, ix. 127.
—— Lydston Horton, vii. 310.
—— —— his wife, Elizabeth Anne Reece, vii. 310.
—— Margaret, contracted to David Barclay, and wife of 8th earl of Angus, i. 196; vii. 294; ix. 12.
—— Margaret, wife of Jas. Campbell of Burnbank, i. 368; vi. 442.
—— Margaret, wife of 4th lord Balfour of Burleigh, i. 546; vi. 110.
—— Margaret, wife of (1) Alexander, lord Balgony, (2) Francis, 2nd earl of Buccleuch, and (3) David, 2nd earl of Wemyss, ii. 236; v. 378, 379; vii. 81, 299, 301; viii. 503.
—— Margaret, wife of Alex. Abercromby of Pitmeddan, iv. 180.
—— Margaret, wife of Arthur Forbes, iv. 72.
—— Margaret, wife of 2nd lord Madderty, v. 384; viii. 217; ix. 127, 161.
—— Margaret, half-sister of 1st earl of Leven, v. 373.
—— Margaret, wife of William Leslie, v. 386.
—— Margaret, dau. of 3rd earl of Leven, vi. 113.
—— Margaret, dau. of baroness Newark, vi. 444.
—— Margaret, wife of Donald, lord of the Isles, vii. 243.
—— Margaret, wife of Sir John Innes of Innes, vii. 268.

Leslie, Margaret, wife of David de Abercromby, vii. 269.
—— Margaret, wife of Alexander Cumming of Earnside, vii. 276.
—— Margaret, wife of Sir Wm. Cunninghame of Caprington, vii. 295.
—— Margaret, wife of John Moray, vii. 296.
—— Margaret, dau. of 9th earl of Rothes, vii. 305.
—— Margaret, wife of John Grant of Ballindalloch, ix. 128.
—— Marjory, wife of Duncan Grant of Easter Elchies, vii. 460.
—— Martin Leslie, vii. 309.
—— —— his wife, Georgina Frances Studdy, vii. 309.
—— Mary, wife of William, lord Haddo, i. 90; vi. 113.
—— Mary, wife of (1) Sir F. Kinloch of Gilmerton, and (2) Sir Alex. Ogilvie of Forglen, ii. 24; vi. 442; ix. 143.
—— Mary, wife of Donald, lord of the Isles, ii. 264; vii. 243.
—— Mary, wife of 3rd lord Cranstoun, ii. 596; v. 379.
—— Mary, wife of Hugh, 7th earl of Eglinton, iii. 451; vii. 299, 301.
—— Mary, wife of Sir Wm. Elphinstone of Elphinstone, iii. 526.
—— Mary, wife of Sir Robert Melville of Murdocairnie, vi. 99; vii. 295.
—— Mary, wife of Dr. Jas. Walker of Innerdovat, vi. 115.
—— Mary, dau. of 2nd lord Newark, vi. 443.
—— Mary, wife of 3rd earl of Portmore, vii. 95, 306.
—— Mary, dau. of 13th earl of Rothes, vii. 308.
—— Mary Anne, wife of John Rutherford of Edgerston, vi. 115.
—— Mary Christiana, vi. 117.
—— Mary Eleanor, vii. 310.
—— Mary Elizabeth, wife of 6th lord Ruthven, vi. 117; vii. 390.
—— Mary Euphrasia, vii. 310.
—— Mildred Emily, vii. 310.
—— Norman, eldest son of Andrew L. of Leslie, iii. 562.
—— Norman, master of Rothes, eldest son of 4th earl of Rothes, iv. 565; vii. 286.
—— —— his wife, Isobel Lindsay, v. 398; vii. 286.
—— Norman, deputy chamberlain, vii. 240, 270.
—— —— his wife, Margaret *, vii. 270, 271.
—— Norman, canon of Moray, vii. 270 *n.*
—— Peter, parson of Rothes, vii. 290.
—— Philip, Boulogne, vi. 445.
—— —— his wife, Frances Manners, vi. 445.
—— Raymond Evelyn, vii. 310.
—— Robert, 6th son of 5th earl of Rothes, v. 382.

* Name unknown.

Leslie, Robert, lessee of the revenues of the bishopric of Orkney, v. 383.
—— —— his 2nd wife, Katharine Basset, ix. 127.
—— Robert, legtd. son of Norman L., master of Rothes, vii. 286.
—— Robert, legtd. son of 4th earl of Rothes, vii. 291.
—— Robert, 6th son of 5th lord Rothes, vii. 295.
—— Robert, 5th son of William L. of Aikenway, vii. 460.
—— Robert, Barbados, ix. 127.
—— Simon de, 1278, vii. 268.
—— Thomas Coats, viii. 136.
—— —— his wife, Henrietta Marion Elphinstone-Dalrymple, viii. 136.
—— Thomas Jenkins, vii. 308.
—— —— his wife, Honora Seward Burrowes, vii. 308.
—— Walter, parson of Menmore, i. 448.
—— —— his wife, Elizabeth Stewart, i. 448.
—— Sir Walter, 3rd son of Sir Andrew L. of Leslie, vii. 239, 269, 271 *bis*; viii. 327.
—— —— his wife, Euphemia, countess of Ross, vii. 238, 239.
—— William, 3rd son of William L. of Wardis, ii. 13.
—— —— his wife, Elizabeth Ogilvy, ii. 13.
—— William, v. 386.
—— —— his wife, Margaret Leslie, v. 386.
—— William, ensign, 42nd regt., captain 17th regt., vi. 116.
—— William, 5th son of Alexander L., styled lord Newark, vi. 445.
—— —— his wife, * Senior, vi. 445.
—— William, eldest son of Alexander L. of Leslie, vii. 276.
—— William, major commandant of invalids, vii. 305.
—— *, alleged wife of Sir Andrew Moray, ii. 128 *n.*
—— *, married dau. of col. Geo. Leslie, v. 373.
—— * alleged 1st wife of Henry, 1st lord Methven, vi. 167 *bis.*
—— *, son of Geo. L. of Burdsbank, ix. 90.
—— —— his wife, Mary Ogilvy, iv. 37; ix. 90.
LESLIE-MELVILLE, EARL OF LEVEN, vi. 118-123.
LESLIE-MELVILLE, EARL OF MELVILLE, vi. 118-123.
Leslie-Melville of Branston Hall, Alexander, advocate, vi. 118.
—— —— his wife, Charlotte Smith, vi. 118.
—— of Melville and Monimail, Elizabeth Jane, wife of T. R. B. Cartwright, vi. 119, 120 *bis.*
—— Adelaide Harriet, vi. 121.
—— Alfred John, H.E.I.C.S., vi. 121.

* Name unknown.

Leslie-Melville, Anna Maria, wife of Sir Wm. Stirling-Maxwell, vi. 120.
—— Anna Maria, dau. of John Thornton L.-M., vi. 121.
—— Archibald Alexander, vi. 122.
—— Clara Sophia, vi. 121.
—— Constance Betty, vi. 122.
—— David Archibald, vi. 119.
—— David William, vi. 122.
—— Emily Eleanor, wife of John, 1st lord Hamilton of Dalzell, vi. 120.
—— Emily Maria, wife of Robt. Williams of Beidehead, vi. 121.
—— Ernest, vi. 121.
—— Florence Lucy, vi. 121.
—— Harriet Rosa, vi. 121.
—— Ian, 4th son of 11th earl of Leven, vi. 122.
—— Jane Elizabeth, wife of Francis Pym, vi. 118.
—— Julia Louisa, wife of lieut.-gen. R. Robertson, vi. 121.
—— Lucy, wife of Henry Smith, vi. 118.
—— Marianne, wife of Abel Smith, M.P., vi. 119.
—— Norman, capt. Grenadier Guards, vi. 121.
—— —— his wife, Georgina Bell, vi. 121.
—— Robert Samuel, in holy orders, vi. 118.
—— Susan Lucy, vi. 120.
—— William Henry, H.E.I.C.S., vi. 118.
Lesouris, *see* Lysurs.
Lestalrig, John de, vi. 207.
—— —— his wife, Annabella de Strathearn, vi. 207; viii. 245.
—— Simon de, vi. 207.
Lester, *, viii. 124.
—— —— his wife, Sidney Dalrymple, viii. 124.
Le Stevenon van Birkenrode, Matthew, viii. 375.
—— —— his wife, Katharine Elizabeth Livingston, viii. 375.
—— Matthew, his son, viii. 375.
L'Estrange of Tynte Lodge, Edmund, iii. 587.
—— —— Mary Caroline, wife of 20th earl of Erroll, iii. 587.
Lethbridge of Sandhill, Sir Thomas Buckler, 2nd bart., viii. 41.
—— of Westaway, Sir Christopher, bart., viii. 37.
—— Elizabeth Cannon, wife of Major Hugh Somerville, viii. 37.
Leven, Leslie, earl of, v. 372-381; vi. 110-118.
Leven, Alexander, first earl of, iv. 35, 36; v. 374; vii. 298, 299; viii. 28.
—— —— his wife, Anna Renton, v. 377.
—— Alexander, second earl of, v. 378.
—— —— his wife, Margaret Howard, v. 378.

* Name unknown.

Leven, Alexander, fifth earl of, vi. 113.
—— —— his 1st wife, Mary Erskine, iv. 114.
—— —— his 2nd wife, Elizabeth Monypenny, vi. 114; ix. 136.
—— Alexander, seventh earl of, vi. 117.
—— —— his wife, Jane Thornton, vi. 118.
—— Alexander, tenth earl of, vi. 122.
—— David, third earl of, v. 381; vi. 106, 109, 110.
—— his wife, Anna Wemyss, ii. 283; vi. 112; viii. 506.
—— David, fourth earl of, vi. 113.
—— David, sixth earl of, vi. 115.
—— —— his wife, Wilhelmina Nisbet, vi. 116.
—— Katharine, countess of, v. 380.
—— Margaret, wife of Francis Montgomerie; countess of, iii. 451; v. 380.
Leven, Leslie-Melville, earl of, vi. 118-123.
Leven, David, eighth earl of, vi. 119.
—— —— his wife, Elizabeth Anne Campbell, vi. 119.
—— John David, twelfth earl of, vi. 122.
—— John Thornton, ninth earl of, vi. 118, 120.
—— —— his 1st wife, Harriet Thornton, vi. 121.
—— —— his 2nd wife, Sophia Thornton, vi. 121.
—— Ronald Ruthven, eleventh earl of, vi. 122.
—— —— his wife, Emma Selina Portman, vi. 122.
Leveson of Halling, Sir John, ii. 34 *n.*
—— —— his wife, Christian Mildmay, ii. 34.
—— Elizabeth, wife of Sir W. Aston, i. 400.
—— James, London and Calais, i. 400.
Leveson-Gower, baron Gower, viii. 362.
Leveson-Gower, duke of Sutherland, viii. 361-365.
Leveson-Gower, Charlotte Sophia, wife of Henry Charles, duke of Norfolk, viii. 362.
—— Elizabeth Mary, wife of 2nd marquess of Westminster, viii. 362.
—— Francis, 3rd son of 1st duke of Sutherland, viii. 361.
Levett of Wichnor Park, John, ii. 497.
—— —— his wife, Sophia Eliza Kennedy, ii. 497.
—— —— Theophilus John, viii. 231.
—— Mary Louisa Margaret, wife of H. W. Drummond, viii. 231.
Levi, Isabella, wife of col. Lockhart Gordon, and dau. of Elias L., i. 104; ix. 6 *bis*.
Leving of Levinglands, v. 421.
Levington of Saltcoats, iv. 258.
—— —— Isabel, wife of (1) Walter Lindsay of Beaufort, and (2) William, 1st lord Ruthven, iii. 19; iv. 258 *bis*.
—— Edward of, ii. 589.
—— Helwisa, wife of Eustace Baliol, ii. 424.

Levington, James, bishop of Dunkeld, v. 206.
—— Margaret, wife of William Kinnaird, v. 206.
—— Matildis, wife of Roland de Carrick, ii. 424, 425.
—— Thomas, burgess of Edinburgh, v. 206.
Lewes of the Vann, William, v. 361.
—— —— his wife, Margaret Bannaster, v. 361.
Lewin of Amble, Thomas, vii. 379.
—— —— his wife, Helen Rutherfurd, vii. 379; ix. 116.
—— of Warkworth, Thomas, ix. 116.
—— Nicholas, ix. 116.
—— —— his wife, Lilias Ker, v. 76; ix. 116.
—— Richard John, R.N., i. 64.
—— —— his wife, Jane Hamilton, i. 64.
Lewis of Malvern Hall, David, iii. 411, 412.
—— —— his wife, Mary Greswolde, iii. 411, 412.
—— Charles, vi. 498.
—— —— his wife, Margaret Carnegie, vi. 498.
—— George Charles Degen, major-general, R.E., vii. 85.
—— —— his wife, Maria Annabell Hepburne-Scott, vii. 85.
—— Magdalene, wife of Lionel, 5th earl of Dysart, iii. 411.
—— *, Carmarthen, vii. 103.
Lexham of Houghton-in-the-Dale, William, vi. 462.
—— —— his wife, Margaret *, vi. 462 *n.*
—— Agnes, wife of (1) Sir John Cheyne, and (2) Edmond Molyneux, vi. 462.
Ley, John Henry, viii. 468.
—— —— his wife, Dorothea Frances Hay, viii. 468.
Leyden of Vlaerdingen, Diederick de, vii. 91 *n.*
Leyis of Bothans, John of, iii. 93.
—— —— his wife, Margaret, iii. 93.
—— Janet, wife of col. Wm. Borthwick, ii. 100; ix. 39.
—— William, merchant burgess, Edinburgh, ix. 39.
Libberton of Nether Barnton, James, iv. 91.
—— of Leyden, James, iv. 91.
—— John, burgess of Edinburgh, ii. 368.
—— Rachel, wife of Thos. Erskine, ii. 367.
LIBERTON, DALZELL, BARON, ii. 408.
Liberton, Robert, first baron, ii. 408.
Lichfield, Thomas George (Anson), 2nd earl of, i. 71.
—— —— his wife, Harriet Georgiana Louisa Hamilton, i. 71.
—— Thomas William (Anson), 1st earl of, i. 393; viii. 517.
Lichtoun, *see* Leighton.
Liddale of Halkerston, Sir James, iii. 65.
—— George, rector of the Forest of Ettrick, iii. 500.

* Name unknown.

Liddel, Sir Adolphus, K.C.B., viii. 162.
—— Marcia Kathleen Anne, wife of col. North de C. Dalrymple-Hamilton, viii. 162.
Liddell of Cumberland, Richard (Graham), baron, vii. 105.
Liddel(l of Balhanein and Panlathyn, John de, vii. 6.
—— —— John, vii. 10.
—— —— his wife, * Maule, vii. 10.
—— —— Thomas de, vii. 6.
—— of Panlathie, Robert, viii. 47.
—— rev. Henry George, viii. 310.
—— —— his wife, Charlotte Lyon, viii. 310.
—— Isobel, wife of (1) Jas. Carnegie of Carnegie, and (2) Thos. Douglas of Panlathie, viii. 47.
Lienden, Thierry de, v. 588 *n.*
—— —— his wife, Marie van Hoorne. v. 588.
Lilbourne, William, v. 302.
Lilburn, Sir John, iv. 515.
—— companion of the Bastard Heron, 1500, vii. 329.
Lilburne, Robert, colonel, v. 121.
Lilley, Barbara, wife of Alex. Hamilton, ii. 50.
Limesi, Alienora de, wife of William de Lindsay, iii. 3.
—— Gerard de, iii. 3.
—— —— his wife, Amicia de Bidun, iii. 3.
—— Randolph de, iii. 3.
—— Walter de, 3rd son of Sir David de Lindsay, iii. 6.
—— —— his wife, Christian Huse, iii. 6.
Lincoln, Henry (de Lacy), earl of, vi. 533.
—— Richard of, 1250, iv. 330.
Lind of Gorgie, Alexander, i. 143.
—— —— his wife, Helen Graham, i. 143.
Lindesay of Fordington in Lindsey, Sir Walter de, iii. 1.
—— Walter de, son of Wiliam de L., iii. 2.
—— Walter de, justiciar, iii. 3.
—— William de, iii. 2.
—— Baldric de, iii. 1.
—— Randulf de, iii. 3 *bis.*
—— —— his wife, Etheldreda, Hectreda *or* Octreda of Allerdale, iii. 3, 245.
Lindesay, *see also* Lindsay.
Lindley, Francis Oswald, v. 548.
—— —— his wife, Etheldreda Mary Fraser, v. 548.
LINDORES, LESLIE, LORD, v. 382-390.
Lindores, Alexander, sixth lord, v. 385, 387.
—— —— his wife, Jean Campbell, v. 387.
—— Francis John, seventh lord, v. 387.
—— James, third lord, v. 383, 385.
—— —— his 1st wife, * Ormiston, v. 385.
—— —— his 2nd wife, Mary Gray, iv. 286; v. 385.
—— —— his 3rd wife, * Clepburn, v. 385.

* Name unknown.

Lindores, John, fourth lord, v. 385; vii. 302.
—— —— his 1st wife, Marion Ogilvy, i. 126; v. 385.
—— —— his 2nd wife, Jean Gibson, v. 385.
—— David, fifth lord, v. 385 *bis*.
—— —— his wife, Margaret Stewart, v. 386.
—— John, eighth lord, v. 389.
—— —— his wife, Jane Reeve, v. 389.
—— Patrick, first lord, v. 382; ix. 127.
—— —— his wife, Jean Stewart, v. 383; vi. 574.
—— Patrick, second lord, v. 384; ix. 127.
Lindores, John of, vii. 398.
—— —— his wife, Margaret of Pitgrunzie, vii. 398.
LINDSAY, LINDSAY, EARL OF, iii. 35-51; v. 391-402.
Lindsay, David, *de jure* seventh earl of, v. 407.
—— David Clark Bethune, eleventh earl of, v. 419.
—— —— his wife, Emily Marian Crosse, v. 419.
—— George, fifth earl of, iii. 40.
—— —— his wife, Jean Hamilton, iii. 40.
—— George, sixth earl of, iii. 41; v. 402, 407.
—— Henry, *de jure* ninth earl of, v. 416, 418.
—— —— his wife, Coutts Trotter, v. 419.
—— John, first earl of, iii. 35; iv. 174; v. 402; ix. 62 *bis*.
—— —— his wife, Margaret Hamilton, iii. 36.
—— John, third earl of, iii. 38.
—— —— his wife, Amelia Stewart, iii. 38.
—— John, fourth earl of, iii. 39.
—— —— his wife, Jean Murray, iii. 39.
—— John Trotter, tenth earl of, v. 419.
—— —— his wife, Jeanne Eudoxie Marie Duval, v. 419.
—— Sir Patrick, *de jure* eighth earl of, v. 410.
—— William, second earl of, iii. 37.
—— —— his wife, Mary Johnstone, iii. 37.
LINDSAY, LINDSAY, LORD, iii. 51.
Lindsay, Alexander, elder son of 5th earl of Crawford; styled lord, iii. 23.
—— —— his wife, Janet Gordon, iii. 23.
—— Alexander, son of 5th earl of Balcarres; *de jure* lord, i. 523; iii. 42.
—— George, *de jure* lord, iii. 35; viii. 107.
—— James, lord, i. 516, 523; iii. 35.
—— John, i. 515; iii. 35.
LINDSAY OF BALCARRES, LINDSAY, LORD, i. 518-519.
Lindsay of Balcarres, Alexander, second lord, i. 519; ix. 31.
—— —— his wife, Anna Mackenzie, i. 519.
—— —— David, first lord, i. 518; ix. 31.
—— —— his wife, Sophia Seton, i. 518; iii. 372.
LINDSAY OF BALNEIL, LINDSAY, LORD, i. 519-523.
Lindsay of Balneil, Alexander, first lord, i. 519.
—— —— his wife, Sophia Mackenzie, i. 519.
LINDSAY OF THE BYRES, LINDSAY, LORD, v. 392-420.
Lindsay of the Byres, David, second lord, v. 394, 396.
—— —— his wife, Janet Ramsay of Pitcruvie, v. 394, 395.
—— —— David, sixteenth lord, v. 407.
—— —— David Clark Bethune, twentieth lord, v. 419.
—— —— his wife, Emily Marian Crosse, v. 419.
—— —— Sir Henry, *de jure* eighteenth lord, v. 416, 418.
—— —— his wife, Coutts Trotter, v. 419.
—— —— James, seventh lord, v. 400.
—— —— his wife, Euphemia Leslie, v. 400.
—— —— John, first lord, v. 392.
—— —— his wife, * Stewart, v. 3, 393.
—— —— John, 'out with the sword,' third lord, ii. 134; iii. 528; v. 4, 357, 393, 395.
—— —— his wife, Marion Baillie, v. 395.
—— —— John, fifth lord, v. 397.
—— —— his contr. wife, Marjory Lindsay, ix. 128.
—— —— his wife, Helen Stewart, i. 443; v. 398.
—— —— John, eighth lord, iii. 32, 97; v. 401.
—— —— his wife, Anna Oliphant, v. 401.
—— —— John, tenth lord, iii. 35; v. 402.
—— —— John Trotter, nineteenth lord, v. 419.
—— —— his wife, Jeanne Eudoxie Marie Duval, v. 419.
—— —— Patrick, fourth lord, v. 393, 396.
—— —— his wife, Isabella Pitcairn, v. 396.
—— —— Patrick, sixth lord, i. 443; v. 399, 404; vii. 293.
—— —— his wife, Euphemia Douglas, v. 400; vi. 370.
—— —— Sir Patrick, *de jure* seventeenth lord, v. 410.
—— —— Robert, ninth lord, iii. 35; v. 401, 407.
—— —— his wife, Christian Hamilton, iv. 315; v. 402.
—— master of, James, son of 17th earl of Crawford, iii. 36.
—— master of, James, son of 6th lord Lindsay of the Byres, v. 400; vii. 293.
—— —— his wife, Euphemia Leslie, v. 400; vii. 294.
—— master of, James Ludovic, son of 25th earl of Crawford; styled, iii. 49.
—— —— his wife, Constance Lilian Pelly, iii. 49.
—— master of, Robert Alexander David, styled, iii. 49.
LINDSAY, EARL OF BALCARRES, i. 511-529.
LINDSAY, EARL OF CRAWFORD, iii. 1-51.
LINDSAY, VISCOUNT GARNOCK, iv. 174-178.
LINDSAY, BARON OF GLENESK, i. 511-515.
LINDSAY, EARL OF LINDSAY, iii. 35-51; v. 391-420.

* Name unknown.

LINDSAY, LORD LINDSAY, iii. 51.
LINDSAY, LORD LINDSAY OF BALCARRES, i. 518-519.
LINDSAY, LORD LINDSAY OF BALNEIL, i. 519-523.
LINDSAY, LORD LINDSAY OF THE BYRES, v. 392-420.
LINDSAY, DUKE OF MONTROSE, iii. 22-23.
LINDSAY, LORD PARBROATH, iii. 35-51; v. 402-420.
LINDSAY, LORD SPYNIE, viii. 94.
LINDSAY, BARON WIGAN OF HAIGH HALL, iii. 43-51.
Lindsay of Aberchirdir, David, v. 395.
— of Abercorn, Sir William, v. 391.
— — his wife, Christiana Mure, v. 391.
— of Annatland, Sir Jerome, Lyon King of Arms, ii. 570; iii. 19.
— — his 1st wife, Margaret Colvill, ii. 570.
— — his second wife, * Lindsay, iii. 19.
— of the Ard, Sir David, iii. 19.
— — Walter, iii. 18.
— of Ardargie, Donald, viii. 112.
— of Auchmuthie, Alexander, viii. 95.
— of Auchtermonzie, Alexander, 2nd son of 4th earl of Crawford, iii. 21, 24.
— — his wife, Isabel Campbell, iii. 25.
— of Balcarres, Charles Robert, iii. 42.
— — his wife, Elizabeth Thompson, iii. 42.
— — Sir Coutts, iii. 49.
— — Sir David, i. 517, 518.
— — his wife, Sophia Seton, i. 518.
— — Hugh Barlow, iii. 43.
— — his wife, Jane Louisa Octavia Grosvenor, iii. 43.
— — James, lieut.-gen., i. 524.
— — his 1st wife, Mary Anne Grant, i. 524.
— — his 2nd wife, Anne Trotter, i. 524.
— — John, lord Menmuir, i. 5, 6.
— — his 1st wife, Marion Guthrie, i. 517.
— — his 2nd wife, Jane Lauder, i. 517.
— — John, eldest son of Lord Menmuir, i. 517, 518.
— — Robert, 2nd son of 5th earl of Balcarres, i. 524.
— — his wife, Elizabeth Dick, i. 524.
— of Balgawies, David, i. 512.
— — Sir Walter, i. 511; iii. 29.
— — his wife, Margaret Campbell, i. 512.
— — William, i. 512.
— of Balhall, David, i. 512.
— — John, i. 512.
— — Katharine, wife of Duncan Robertson of Destraven, i. 512.
— — Robert, 5th son of 9th earl of Crawford, i. 512; iii. 29.
— — his 1st wife, * Fullerton, i. 512.
— — his 2nd wife, Elizabeth Sempill, i. 512; iii. 318 *n.*; vii. 550.

* Name unknown.

Lindsay of Ballinscho, Sir John, 3rd son of 10th earl of Crawford, iii. 29.
— — his 1st wife, Margaret Keith, i. 159; iii. 30; ix. 10.
— — his 2nd wife, Katharine Lindsay, i. 518; iii. 30.
— of Balmain, David, v. 394.
— of Baltrody, Sir Alexander, iii. 13.
— of Barcloy, Sir Philip de, ancestor of the family of, iii. 8.
— of Barnwell, Margaret, wife of Sir Thomas de Colville, ii. 540.
— of Barnyards, i. 297.
— — his wife, * Arbuthnott, i. 297.
— of Beaufort, David, iii. 18.
— — Sir David, iii. 19.
— — his 1st wife, Katharine Fotheringham, iii. 19.
— — his 2nd wife, Elizabeth Spens, iii. 20.
— — his contr. wife, Agnes Ogilvy, iii. 20.
— — Walter, 2nd son of 3rd earl of Crawford, iii. 18.
— — his wife, Isobel Levington, iii. 18; iv. 258.
— of Bonhill, Patrick, 'Tosheagor,' v. 330.
— of Borthwickshiels, Sir William, v. 391.
— of Botheax, Sir, James, ii. 398.
— of Breneville, Sir David de, elder son of William de L., iii. 8.
— of Broadland, Alexander, v. 244.
— — his wife, Elizabeth Falconer, v. 244.
— of Boysack, Alexander, viii. 102.
— of the Byres, Sir David, justiciar of the Lothians, iii. 8, 255 *n.*; v. 488; vi. 288.
— — Sir David de, son of Sir Alex. de L., iii. 10.
— — his wife, Maria Abernethy, iii. 10.
— — Sir John, v. 392; vii. 320.
— — his wife, * Stewart, v. 393.
— — Sir William, 4th son of Sir David L. of Crawford, iii. 11; v. 391.
— — his wife, Christiana Mure, v. 391.
— — Sir William, iii. 526, 527; iv. 521; v. 391; vi. 35, 36; viii. 531.
— — his wife, Christian Keith, v. 392; vi. 35, 38.
— of Canterland, Alexander, son of Sir David L. of Edzell, i. 513.
— — his 1st wife, Jean Murray, i. 514.
— — his 2nd wife, Helen Haldane, i. 514.
— — John, baron of Glenesk, i. 514, 515.
— of Caraldston, Sir Henry, 2nd son of 10th earl of Crawford, iii. 29, 32.
— — his 1st wife, Helen Chisholm, iii. 32.
— — his 2nd wife, Margaret Shaw, iii. 33.
— of Careston, Alexander, viii. 103.
— of Carnock, John, v. 401.
— of Cassendilly, Sir John, v. 392.
— of Chawmelayne-Newtown, vii. 320.
— of Coats, Patrick, v. 417.
— — his wife, Mary Ayton, v. 417.

* Name unknown.

Lindsay of Covington, James, viii. 537.
—— —— George, viii. 548.
—— —— his wife, Rachel Fleming, viii. 548.
—— —— Sir John, iv. 564.
—— —— John, ii. 227; viii. 533.
—— —— John, i. 240; ii. 228.
—— —— his wife, * Scott, ii. 228.
—— —— John, ii. 403; viii. 21, 539.
—— —— his wife, Christian Dalzell, ii. 403.
—— —— John, viii. 18, 21, 373.
—— —— John, viii. 527.
—— —— his wife, Agnes Fleming of Bord, viii. 527.
—— of Craigie, William, ancestor of the family of, iii. 8.
—— of Craigsanquhar, Norman, v. 402.
—— of Crawford, Sir Alexander, iii. 5 *n.*, 9.
—— —— his wife, * Stewart, iii. 9.
—— —— Alicia de, wife of Sir H. de Pinkeney, iii. 6, 7.
—— —— David, 2nd son of justiciar William de L., iii. 3, 6.
—— —— his wife, Marjory of Scotland, iii. 6.
—— —— Sir David, justiciar, iii. 7.
—— —— his wife, Christina, iii. 7.
—— —— Sir David, son of Sir Alexander L., iii. 10, 35.
—— —— his wife, Maria Abernethy, iii. 10; vii. 269, 402.
—— —— Sir Gerard de, iii. 7, 10.
—— —— Sir James de, iii. 11, 266.
—— —— his wife, Egidia Stewart, i. 15; iii. 11.
—— —— Sir James, justiciar, ii. 398; iii. 12, 428; viii. 267.
—— —— his wife, Margaret Keith, iii. 12; vi. 37.
—— —— William de, justiciar, iii. 2; iv. 255.
—— —— his 1st wife, *, iii. 3.
—— —— his 2nd wife, Alienora de Limesi, iii. 3.
—— of Culsh, William, ix. 69.
—— —— his wife, Barbara Guthrie, ix. 69.
—— of Deerpark, Colin, 4th son of 24th earl of Crawford, iii. 45.
—— —— his wife, Frances Howard, iii. 45.
—— —— William Alexander, Windsor Herald, K.C., iii. 46.
—— —— his wife, Harriet Gordon, i. 98; iii. 46.
—— of Dirleton, John, v. 403.
—— of Dowhill, James, ix. 59.
—— —— his wife, Elizabeth Colville, ii. 572; ix. 59.
—— —— John, ii. 571; iii. 187; vi. 369, 370.
—— —— his 1st wife, Marion Douglas, vi. 369.
—— —— his 2nd wife, Marjory Stewart, iii. 187; v. 5.
—— —— Sir William, ancestor of the family of, iii. 14.
—— —— his wife, Matilda Stewart, iii. 14.
—— of Drem, John, 2nd son of 5th lord Lindsay of the Byres, v. 398.

* Name unknown.

Lindsay of Drem, John, v. 403.
—— —— his wife, Katharine Hume, v. 404.
—— —— Sir William, v. 391.
—— of Dunkenny, David, bishop of Brechin, and of Edinburgh, iii. 72; vii. 198; viii. 55.
—— of Dunnottar, Sir William, v. 391.
—— —— his wife, Christian Keith, v. 391.
—— of Dunrod, v. 555.
—— —— David, iii. 529; ix. 84.
—— —— his wife, Isabella *or* Elizabeth Elphinstone, iii. 529.
—— —— John, iii. 335.
—— —— *, iii. 338.
—— of Eaglescairnie, James, ancestor of the family of, v. 405, 408.
—— —— Katharine, wife of 10th lord Blantyre, ii. 90.
—— —— Patrick, deputy secretary for War, ii. 90; v. 409.
—— —— his wife, Margaret Haliburton of Eaglescairnie, v. 410.
—— —— Sir Patrick, major-gen., K.G.H., K.C.B., iii. 38; v. 408, 410.
—— of Earlscairnie, John, 6th son of 8th earl of Crawford, iii. 27.
—— of Edindony, David, v. 394.
—— of Edzell, Sir David, eldest son of Walter L. of the Ard, iii. 19; iv. 21.
—— —— David, afterwards 9th earl of Crawford, i. 511; iii. 19, 25, 27.
—— —— his 1st wife, Jonet Gray, iii. 28.
—— —— his 2nd wife, Katharine Campbell, i. 511; iii. 28.
—— —— Sir David, eldest son of 9th earl of Crawford, iii. 29.
—— —— his wife, Margaret Beaton, iii. 29.
—— —— Sir David, i. 511, 513; vii. 47, 131; viii. 193.
—— —— his 1st wife, Helen Lindsay, i. 513.
—— —— his 2nd wife, Isabel Forbes, i. 513.
—— —— David, justiciary in Glenesk, i. 514; viii. 101, 102.
—— —— his wife, Margaret Wishart, i. 514.
—— —— David, claimant to earldom of Crawford, i. 515.
—— —— his 1st wife, Agnes Graham, i. 515.
—— —— his 2nd wife, Jean Fullerton, i. 515.
—— —— David, last holder of barony, i. 516; iv. 568.
—— —— John, i. 303, 515.
—— —— his wife, Jean Carnegie, i. 515; vi. 497; viii. 104, 107.
—— —— Walter, 2nd son of 3rd earl of Crawford, iii. 18.
—— —— his wife, Isabel Levington, iii. 19.
—— of Elhothel, Sir John, v. 392.
—— of Elmthorpe, Walter James, lieut.-col., iii. 46.
—— —— his wife, Henrietta Julia Bloomfield, iii. 46.
—— of Esperston, Andrew, 1st laird, v. 393 *n.*

* Name unknown.

Lindsay of Evelick, Sir Alexander, i. 294.
— — Sir Alexander, viii. 207.
— — his wife, Amelia Murray, viii. 207.
— — David, ancestor of the family of, iii. 20.
— of Feddinch, William, 2nd son of Patrick L. of Wolmerston, v. 414.
— — his wife, Margaret Wemyss, v. 414.
— — William, their son, v. 414.
— of Finavon, Alexander, viii. 103.
— — George, viii. 103.
— — Sir Robert, v. 401.
— of Garlobank, Alexander, viii. 102.
— — John, viii. 102.
— of Garmylton, Andrew, v. 392.
— of Glaslie, David, v. 396.
— of Glasnevin, George Hayward, i. 526.
— — his wife, Mary Katharine Gore, i. 526.
— — Henry Gore, lieut.-col., i. 527.
— — his wife, Ellen Sarah Morgan, i. 527.
— of Glenesk, Sir Alexander, iii. 11, 12; v. 391.
— — his 1st wife, Katharine Stirling of Glenesk, iii. 13.
— — his 2nd wife, Marjory Stewart, i. 14; iii. 14.
— — Sir David, ii. 438; iii. 12, 14, 15.
— — his wife, Jean, Kathrina or Elizabeth Stewart, i. 16; iii. 15.
— — Sir David, eldest son of Walter L. of Beaufort, iii. 19.
— — his 1st wife, Katharine Fotheringham, iii. 19.
— — his 2nd wife, Elizabeth Spens, iii. 20.
— — his contr. wife, Agnes Ogilvy, iii. 20.
— — David, i. 511; iii. 19, 27.
— — his 1st wife, Jonet Gray, iii. 28; iv. 275.
— — his 2nd wife, Katharine Campbell, i. 511; iii. 28.
— — Sir David, i. 513.
— — his 1st wife, Helen Lindsay, i. 513.
— — his 2nd wife, Isabel Forbes, i. 513.
— — David, i. 514.
— — his wife, Margaret Wishart, i. 514.
— — David, i. 515.
— — his 1st wife, Agnes Graham, i. 515.
— — his 2nd wife, Jean Fullerton, i. 515.
— — David, last laird, i. 516.
— — John, i. 515.
— — his wife, Jean Carnegie, i. 515.
— of Kilbirnie, Patrick, 5th son of 1st earl of Lindsay, iv. 174.
— — his wife, Margaret Crawfurd, iv. 174.
— of Kilquhis, James, v. 403.
— — his wife, Margaret Paterson, v. 403.
— — James, v. 403.
— — his wife, Marie Monteith, v. 403.
Lindsay of Kilquhis, Norman, 3rd son of 5th lord Lindsay of the Byres, v. 398, 402.
— — his 1st wife, Isobel Lundie, v. 402.
— — his 2nd wife, Martha Fernie, v. 402.
— — Patrick, v. 403.
— — his wife, Elizabeth Arnot, v. 403.
— — Sir Robert, v. 401.
— of Kinblethmont, Alexander, viii. 102.
— — Walter, 2nd son of 3rd earl of Crawford, iii. 18.
— of Kinfauns, Sir John, vii. 413.
— — his wife, Jean Abernethy, vii. 413.
— of Kinneff, Sir Walter, iii. 14.
— — his wife, Katharine *, iii. 14.
— — Walter, iii. 14.
— of Kirkforthar, Christopher, 10th laird, v. 406, 407.
— — his wife, Amelia Malcolm, v. 407.
— — Christopher, 11th laird, v. 407.
— — David, 2nd laird, v. 396.
— — David, 4th laird, v. 397, 404.
— — his wife, Helen Crichton, v. 404.
— — David, eldest son of Patrick L., v. 405.
— — his wife, Elizabeth Bethune, v. 405.
— — David, 7th laird, v. 405.
— — his wife, Jean Pitcairn, v. 405.
— — David, 8th laird, v. 405.
— — his 1st wife, Elizabeth Pearson, v. 406.
— — his 2nd wife, Bethia Ramsay, v. 406.
— — David, 13th laird, v. 407.
— — George, 12th laird, v. 407.
— — his 1st wife, Elizabeth Seton, v. 407.
— — his 2nd wife, Magdalen Falconer, v. 407.
— — Georgina, wife of A. Buchanan of Torry, v. 408.
— — John, 5th laird, v. 404.
— — his 1st wife, Marjory Pitcairn, v. 404.
— — his 2nd wife, Isabella Durie, v. 404.
— — John, 9th laird, v. 406.
— — his wife, Katharine Seton, v. 406.
— — Katharine, wife of Robert Carmichael, iv. 567.
— — Patrick, advocate, 1st laird, v. 393, 396.
— — his wife, Isabella Pitcairn, v. 396.
— — Patrick, 3rd laird, v. 397.
— — Patrick, 6th laird, v. 404.
— — his wife, Helen Orme, v. 405.
— of Kirkmichael, Sir James de, iii. 11.
— of Kirktoun in Ferne, Robert, iii. 20; ix. 61.
— — his wife, Matilda Luvell, iii. 20.
— of Kittedie, Norman, v. 402.
— of Lamberton, Walter de, justiciar, iii. 3.
— — Walter de, justiciar, iii. 4.
— — his wife, Christian *, iii. 4.

* Name unknown.

Lindsay of Lamberton, Sir William de, ambassador to England, iii. 4.
—— —— his wife, Alicia de Lancaster, iii. 4.
—— —— William de, bailiff for king of Scotland, iii. 5.
—— —— his wife, Ada de Baliol, iii. 5; iv. 143.
—— of Lamberton Parva, Walter, iii. 5.
—— of Latham, Sir John, v. 393.
—— of Leith, Patrick, ancestor of the family of, v. 415.
—— of Lekoquhy, David, iii. 25.
—— —— Patrick, iii. 20.
—— —— William, 3rd son of 3rd earl of Crawford, iii. 20.
—— of Lethnot, David, iii. 18.
—— of Leuchars, Sir Coutts, i. 92, 524.
—— —— his wife, Blanche Fitzroy, i. 524.
—— of Leuchland, David, viii. 55.
—— of Leys, Alexander, viii. 103.
—— of Lochbill, Bernard, iii. 509.
—— of Luffness, Alicia de, wife of Sir H. de Pinckney, iii. 6, 7.
—— —— David, iii. 3, 6.
—— —— Sir David, iii. 7.
—— —— Sir Gerard de, iii. 7, 10.
—— —— Sir William de, iii. 2.
—— of Manerstoun, John, viii. 369.
—— of Wester Markinch, Sir William, vi. 36.
—— of Molesworth, Gilbert de, iii. 5.
—— of Montago, David, grandson of 3rd earl of Crawford, iii. 20.
—— of Month, Sir Robert, v. 401.
—— of the Mount, Sir David, senior, Lyon King of Arms, v. 392.
—— of Mungo's Wells, William, v. 393.
—— —— his wife, Margaret Christison, v. 393.
—— of Newdosk, David, 2nd son of 1st earl of Crawford, iii. 17.
—— of Newton of Nydie, John, v. 409.
—— of Ochterotherstruther, Sir William, v. 392; vi. 36.
—— of Orkie, Sir Robert, v. 400, 401.
—— of Ormiston, Sir Alexander, ancestor of the family of, iii. 9.
—— —— Alexander de, iii. 55.
—— of Pitairlie, Sir John, ancestor of the family of, iii. 20.
—— —— his wife, * Somerville, viii. 20.
—— of Pitcruvie, Sir John, v. 396.
—— —— his wife, Elizabeth Lundie, v. 396.
—— of Pittardie, Sir James, viii. 20.
—— of Pittendreich, Sir William, v. 392; vi. 36.
—— of Pittorlie, David, bishop of Ross, iii. 19.
—— —— his 1st wife, Jonet Ramsay, iii. 19.
—— —— his 2nd wife, Helen Harieson, iii. 19.
—— of Pitroddie, Sir James, 5th son of 10th earl of Crawford, iii. 30; viii. 107.

* Name unknown.

Lindsay of Plowlands, George, v. 406.
—— —— his wife, Christian Tytler, v. 406.
—— of Pyotston, David, 3rd son of 4th lord Lindsay of the Byres, v. 396, 411.
—— —— David, v. 411.
—— —— his 1st wife, Elizabeth Barclay, v. 411.
—— —— his 2nd wife, Alison Dundas, v. 411.
—— —— his 3rd wife, Grizell Melville, v. 412.
—— —— Patrick, the younger, v. 412.
—— —— his wife, Margaret Traill, v. 412.
—— —— William, 2nd son of 4th lord Lindsay of the Byres, v. 396, 411.
—— —— his wife, Isobel Logan, v. 411.
—— —— William, v. 412.
—— —— his wife, Agnes Ballingall, v. 412.
—— —— William, v. 412, 415, 416.
—— —— his wife, Margaret Seton, v. 412.
—— of Rascaroll, *, i. 225.
—— —— his wife, Agnes Murray, i. 225.
—— —— Henry, i. 225, 229.
—— —— his wife, Bessie Geddes, i. 225.
—— of Rathillet, Sir David, Lyon King of Arms, iii. 19.
—— of Ravelgreen, Elizabeth, wife of Robert Fletcher of Balmirmer, iii. 33; ix. 62.
—— of Rossie, Sir William, iii. 14.
—— of Sandefurde, Alexander, viii. 95.
—— of Skryne, Walter, 4th son of William L. of Lekoquhy, iii. 20.
—— of Spynie, Alexander, 4th son of 10th earl of Crawford, viii. 95.
—— —— his wife, Jean Lyon, viii. 97.
—— —— William, claimant to the barony of Spynie, vi. 496; viii. 109.
—— —— his 1st wife, Stewart Carnegie, vi. 496; viii. 109.
—— —— his 2nd wife, Margaret Blair, vi. 496.
—— of Straiton, Robert, i. 525.
—— —— his wife, Frances Henderson, i. 525.
—— of Symington, Sir James, iii. 9.
—— —— Margaret, wife of Sir Thomas de Colville, ii. 540.
—— —— Sir William, i. 319; ii. 260; iii. 9.
—— —— his 1st wife, Alicia *, iii. 9.
—— —— his 2nd wife, Margaret Comyn, countess of Buchan, ii. 260; iii. 9.
—— of Thurston, Sir John, vi. 212.
—— —— Walter, probable ancestor of the family of, iii. 5.
—— of Touchfraser, Sir William, v. 391; vi. 35.
—— of Torwood, William, viii. 531.
—— of Tynedale, Sir Alexander, iii. 5 *n.*, 9.
—— of Uchterutherstruther, Sir William, v. 392; vi. 36.
—— of Vayne, Alexander, 5th son of Sir David L. of Beaufort, iii. 20.
—— —— David, v. 6.
—— —— his wife, Marjory Stewart, v. 6.

* Name unknown.

Lindsay of Virginia, U.S.A., Sir Jerome, ancestor of the family of, iii. 19 *n.*
— of Wauchope, John, v. 125.
— — his wife, Agnes Gordon, v. 124.
— of Wauchopdale, Sir Simon de, ancestor of the family of, iii. 8.
— of Westville, Sir Coutts, i. 92, 524.
— of Wigtown, Sir James, viii. 523.
— of Wormiston or Wolmerston, David Ayton, 9th laird, v. 417.
— — his wife, Jane Emilia Ayton, v. 417.
— — George, 5th laird, v. 415.
— — his wife, Margaret Bethune, v. 416.
— — Henry, 7th laird, v. 416.
— — his 1st wife, Elizabeth Kyd, v. 416.
— — his 2nd wife, Margaret Eccles, v. 416.
— — John, 2nd laird, v. 413.
— — his wife, Elizabeth Lentran, v. 414.
— — John, 4th laird, v. 415.
— — his wife, Margaret Haliburton, v. 415.
— — John, 6th laird, v. 416.
— — Patrick, v. 399.
— — his wife, Euphemia Douglas, v. 399.
— — Patrick, 1st laird, v. 413.
— — his 1st wife, Margaret Lundie, v. 413.
— — his 2nd wife, Elizabeth Arnot, v. 413.
— — Patrick, 3rd laird, v. 414.
— — his wife, Katharine Bethune, v. 414.
— — Patrick, 8th laird, v. 417.
— — his wife, Mary Ayton, v. 417.
— of Woodwray, Henry, lieut.-col. under Gustavus Adolphus, iii. 30, 33, 34.
— — Sir John, 3rd son of 10th earl of Crawford, iii. 29; viii. 95, 100, 102.
— — John, lieut.-col. under Gustavus Adolphus, iii. 30.
— Agnes, dau. of Sir Walter L. of Balgawies, i. 512.
— Agnes, wife of (1) James Murray, and (2) Wm. Melville, i. 464.
— Agnes, dau. of Walter L. of Beaufort, iii. 20.
— Agnes, wife of John Preston of Gorton, v. 406, 408.
— Agnes, wife of John Macgill of Kemback, v. 415.
— Alexander, only child of David L. of Edzell, i. 514.
— — his wife, Anna Wemyss, i. 514; viii. 501.
— Alexander, 3rd son of lord Menmuir, i. 517.
— Alexander, Madras Staff Corps, i. 525.
— Alexander, in Haltoun, iii. 19.
— — his wife, * Barclay, iii. 19.
— Alexander, 3rd son of Wm. L. of Lekoquhy, iii. 20.

* Name unknown.

Lindsay, Alexander, rector of Belhelvie, canon of Aberdeen, iii. 22.
— Alexander, elder son of 5th earl of Crawford; styled master of Crawford and lord Lindsay, iii. 23.
— — his wife, Janet Gordon, iii. 23.
— Alexander, 2nd son of 7th earl of Crawford, iii. 25.
— — his wife, Matilda Graham, ix. 61.
— Alexander, eldest son of 8th earl of Crawford; the 'wicked master' of Crawford, i. 511; iii. 26.
— — his wife, Janet Sinclair, iii. 26.
— Alexander, lt.-col. under Gustavus Adolphus, iii. 30.
— Alexander, vice-chamberlain to king James VI., iii. 30; viii. 95.
— Alexander, 3rd son of Sir Wm. L. of the Byres, v. 392.
— Alexander, brother of Andrew L. of Esperston, v. 393 *n.*
— Alexander, 3rd son of David L. of Kirkforthar, v. 405.
— Alexander, 5th son of Wm. L. of Pyotston, v. 411.
— Alexander, 8th son of Patrick L. of Wolmerston, v. 414.
— Alexander, lieut., H.E.I.C.S., v. 416.
— Alexander, H.E.I.C.S., vi. 496; viii. 111.
— — his wife, Amy Cruickshank, viii. 111.
— Alexander, capt. 8th Hussars, vi. 496; viii. 111.
— — his wife, Jane Lindsay Carnegie, vi. 496 *bis*; viii. 113.
— Alexander, eldest son of 2nd lord Spynie, vi. 497.
— — his wife, Jean Carnegie, vi. 497.
— Alexander, apprenticed to Alex. Haliburton, viii. 105.
— Alexander, son of 'the wicked master of Crawford,' ix. 61.
— Alexander Dick, Bengal C.S., i. 525.
— Alexander Monypenny, advocate, v. 417.
— — his wife, Mary Sprott, v. 417.
— Alexina, wife of Thos. H. Sandford, iii. 43.
— Alexina Frances, wife of E. J. T. Ross of Bladensburg, iii. 47.
— Alfred, Coonoor, iii. 46.
— — his wife, Isabel Katharine Northcote, iii. 46.
— Alice Frances, wife of George (Eyre) Archer-Houblon, iii. 48.
— Alice Margaret, i. 527.
— Alicia, wife of (1) Sir John Comyn of Badenoch, and (2) * Comyn, i. 507; iii. 5, 9.
— Alicia de, a nun, iii. 10.
— Alison, dau. of Sir John L. of Pitcruvie, v. 397.

* Name unknown.

Lindsay, Alison, wife of (1) David Lindsay, and (2) Arthur Gordon, v. 404, 413.
— Alison, wife of Joseph Douglas, v. 413.
— Alison, dau. of George L. of Wormiston, v. 418.
— Amy, dau. of Alex. L., vi. 496.
— Anna, dau. of 1st earl of Balcarres, i. 520.
— Anna, wife of 7th earl of Rothes, iii. 37; vii. 301; ix. 62 *bis*.
— Anna, wife of (1) Jas. Murray of Pardewis, and (2) Wm. Melville of Tongland, vi. 95.
— Anna, wife of Harry Maule of Kellie, vii. 22.
— Anna, dau. of 2nd lord Spynie, viii. 105, 108.
— Annas, dau. of 13th earl of Crawford, ix. 62.
— Anne, wife of Wm. Moncrieff, i. 516.
— Anne, wife of (1) 4th earl of Kellie, and (2) 3rd viscount Kingston, i. 522; v. 88, 197.
— Anne, wife of Sir E. Antrobus, i. 528.
— Anne, the poetess, wife of A. Barnard, i. 528; ix. 31 *bis*.
— Anne, dau. of 18th earl of Crawford, iii. 38.
— Anne, wife of R. Wardlaw Ramsay, iii. 43.
— Anne, wife of 1st lord Falconer of Halkerton, v. 249, 401.
— Ann, wife of Mr. R. Fairweather, v. 415.
— Anne, dau. of lt.-col. John L., v. 410.
— Anne, dau. of Geo. L. of Wormiston, v. 418.
— Anne, wife of Sir Robert Graham of Scotston, vi. 239; viii. 101.
— Anne Alice, v. 418.
— Ann Craigie, v. 416.
— Ann Katharine, wife of John T. Campbell, iv. 295; v. 419.
— Anne Katherine Sybil, wife of F. Bowes-Lyon, iii. 48; viii. 314.
— Anne Keith Yorke, i. 525.
— Archibald, chantor of Aberdeen, v. 393.
— Archibald Lionel, v. 420.
— — his wife, Ethel Tucker, v. 420.
— Arosinus de, iii. 2.
— Arthur Alexander, i. 527.
— Beatrix, wife of (1) Sir A. Douglas, and (2) Sir Robt. Erskine, iii. 10, 141, 142; v. 595 *bis*.
— Beatrix, dau. of Patrick L., v. 408.
— Beatrix, grand-dau. of Beatrix Daes, v. 409.
— Bethune, major, v. 418.
— Caroline Felicie, dau. of Sir H. Lindsay Bethune, v. 419.
— Caroline Frances, wife of G. D. Rowley, i. 526.
Lindsay, Cecilia Martha Harvey, wife of James Head, i. 525.
— Charles, archdeacon of Kildare, i. 526.
— — his wife, Anne Rowley, i. 526.
— Charles Bazil, i. 525.
— — his wife, Anna M'Donnell, i. 525.
— Charles Dalrymple, bishop of Kildare, i. 526.
— — his 1st wife, Elizabeth Fydell, i. 526.
— — his 2nd wife, Katharine Eliza Coussmaker, i. 526.
— Charles Hugh, C.B., M.P., iii. 45.
— — his wife, Emilia Ann Browne, iii. 45.
— Charles Ludovic, capt. Grenadier Guards, iii. 45.
— Charles Robert, i. 525.
— Charlotte Jane, dau. of Sir H. Lindsay-Bethune, v. 419.
— Christian de, wife of Ingelram de Guignes, sire de Coucy, iii. 5.
— Christian, wife of 4th earl of Haddington, iii. 37; iv. 318; vi. 500; ix. 62, 101.
— Christian, dau. of 18th earl of Crawford, iii. 38.
— Christian, wife of (1) John Seton, and (2) Robert, 2nd lord Kilmaurs, iv. 235; v. 394; viii. 578; ix. 128.
— Christian, dau. of Robt. L. in Kirkton of Ferne, ix. 61.
— Claud, 3rd son of 11th earl of Crawford, iii. 31.
— Claud George, R.N., i. 527.
— Claud Reginald, Monsignore, iii. 47.
— Colin, 3rd son of 3rd earl of Balcarres; styled lord Cummerland, i. 522.
— Colin, Bengal C. S., i. 525.
— Colin, brigadier-general, i. 525.
— Constance Madelene Helen, wife of Sharples Fisher, v. 418.
— Constance Norah Edith, v. 418.
— Cynthia Anne, dau. of 27th earl of Crawford, iii. 50.
— David, 3rd son of 1st lord Lindsay of Balcarres, i. 519.
— Sir David de, regent of Scotland, High Chamberlain, iii. 5, 8.
— — his wife, Margaret de Lindsay, iii. 5, 8.
— David de, diocese of Glasgow, iii. 10.
— David, eldest son of Sir David de L. of Crawford, iii. 11.
— David, 3rd son of Sir David L. of Beaufort and Edzell, iii. 19.
— rev. David, Southwark, iii. 19.
— David, supposed illeg. son of 'the wicked master' of Crawford, iii. 26.
— David, parson of Lethnot, iii. 27.
— David, in Cupar, v. 404, 405.
— — his wife, Alison Lindsay, v. 404, 413.
— David, minister of Cockpen, v. 406, 408.
— — his wife, Euphemia Wilson, v. 406.

Lindsay, David, sergeant, Perthshire Militia, v. 407, 410.
— David, 2nd son of W. L. of Pyotston, v. 412.
— David, 3rd son of John L. of Wolmerston, v. 414.
— David, 7th son of Patrick L. of Wolmerston, v. 414.
— David, 4th son of George L. of Wormiston, v. 416.
— David, son of Alex. L., vi. 496.
— David, hatmaker, Edinburgh, viii. 24.
— — his wife, Jean Somerville, viii. 24.
— David, in Kirkton of Ferne, ix. 61.
— David Alexander Edward, styled lord Balcarres, iii. 49.
— — his wife, Constance Lilian Pelly, iii. 49.
— David Balcarres, i. 527.
— — his wife, Maud Grace Miller, i. 527.
— David Bethune, capt. 4th N. I. Bengal, v. 417.
— David Ludovic Peter, iii. 45.
— Sir Duncan, iii. 9.
— Edith, dau. of Charles Hugh L., iii. 45.
— Edward Campbell, v. 418.
— Edward Reginald, barrister, in holy orders, iii. 50.
— Edwin, H.E.I.C.S., Madras, iii. 43.
— Eleanor, wife of Jas. Fraser, i. 523; vii. 445.
— Elizabeth, wife of 3rd lord Drummond, i. 512; iii. 29; vii. 47; ix. 29.
— Elizabeth, dau. of 3rd lord Balcarres, i. 523.
— Elizabeth, wife of Ninian Stewart of Largobroughton, ii. 290.
— Elizabeth, wife of J. Erskine of Dun, ii. 302; iii. 27; vii. 16.
— Elizabeth, wife of Sir Henry de Prestoun, iii. 11.
— Elizabeth, wife of Robert, 1st lord Erskine, iii. 17; v. 604.
— Elizabeth, alleged 2nd wife of Sir Robert Keith of Keith-Marischal, iii. 17; vi. 39; ix. 62.
— Elizabeth, wife of Sir Thomas Maule of Panmure, iii. 21; vii. 8.
— Elizabeth, wife of John, 1st lord Drummond, iii. 22; vii. 42.
— Elizabeth, wife of D. Lyon of Baky, iii. 24.
— Elizabeth, contr. to Thos. Maule, iii. 27 *n.*; vii. 16.
— Elizabeth, wife of 3rd earl of Northesk, iii. 37; vi. 499.
— Elizabeth, dau. of C. Robert L. of Balcarres, iii. 43.
— Elizabeth, wife of (1) Robert Bruce of Rait, and (2) Alexander Scott, iii. 470, 471.
— Elizabeth, mistress of James (Hamilton), 1st earl of Arran, iv. 363.
Lindsay, Elizabeth, wife of Sir John Gordon of Lochinvar, v. 104.
— Elizabeth, wife of John Lundin, v. 394.
— Elizabeth, wife of Walter Lundie of that Ilk, v. 397.
— Elizabeth, wife of D. Kinnear of Kinnear, v. 399.
— Elizabeth, wife of Jas. Corstorphine of Nydie, v. 414.
— Elizabeth, wife of G. Seton of Careston, v. 414.
— Elizabeth, wife of Edward Cliffe, v. 417.
— Elizabeth, dau. of D. A. L., v. 418.
— Elizabeth, dau. of Geo. L. of Wormiston, v. 418.
— Elizabeth, wife of Sir W. Douglas of Lochleven, vi. 365.
— Elizabeth Balcarres, v. 417.
— Elizabeth Frances, wife of rev. R. Gordon, i. 526.
— Elizabeth Frances, wife of Sir C. P. T. Domville, i. 526.
— Elizabeth Janet, v. 416.
— Elizabeth Keith, wife of R. E. Heathcote, iii. 43.
— Elizabeth Pringle, wife of rev. A. L. Courtenay, i. 525.
— Elizabeth Scot, wife of 3rd earl of Hardwicke, i. 529.
— Ellen Rosamund Mary, wife of viscount Ikerrin, i. 527.
— Emilia, wife of Eric Rudd, v. 417.
— Emily Florence Henrietta, v. 418.
— Emily Rose, wife of col. Duncan Stewart, viii. 112.
— Euphemia, affianced to David, duke of Rothesay, i. 17; iii. 15.
— Eufemia, wife of Sir John Herries, iii. 12; iv. 400, 401.
— Eufemia, wife of John Charteris of Kinfauns, iii. 27.
— Euphan, dau. of Patrick L. of Wolmerston, v. 415.
— Evelyn Margaret, wife of J. F. Mason, iii. 50.
— Flora, iii. 43.
— Frances Ruby Vera, iii. 46.
— Francis Howard, Scotch Education Dept., iii. 46.
— George, 2nd son of Sir David L. of Beaufort and Edzell, iii. 19.
— George, 3rd son of 1st lord Lindsay of the Byres, v. 393.
— — his wife, * Inglis, v. 393.
— George, 4th son of J. L. of Wolmerston, v. 414.
— — his wife, Eupham Arnot, v. 414.
— George, 5th son of P. L. of Wolmerston, v. 414.
— George, elder son of Wm. L. of Pyotston, v. 412, 415.

* Name unknown.

Lindsay, George, lieut. R.N., v. 417.
—— George, brigade-major, v. 417.
—— —— his wife, * Forster, v. 417.
—— George, 7th son of Geo. L. of Wormiston, v. 417.
—— George, eldest son of Patrick L. of Coats, v. 417.
—— George, ix. 128.
—— George Humphrey Maurice, iii. 46.
—— George Macintosh, Rifle Brigade, i. 527.
—— Georgina Kathleen, wife of W. O'C. Morris, i. 527.
—— Gerard, 3rd son of 1st earl of Crawford, iii. 17.
—— Harriet, wife of Warren Hastings Sands, v. 416.
—— Harriet Maria, in religion 'sister Mary Raphael,' iii. 47.
—— Harry, 3rd son of Wm. L. of Pyotston, v. 411.
—— Helen, wife of (1) Richard Melville of Baldovie, and (2) Andrew Arbuthnott of Fiddes, i. 302, 514; ix. 16.
—— Helen, wife of Sir David Lindsay of Edzell, baron of Glenesk, i. 513; iii. 30.
—— Helen, wife of 2nd lord Cranstoun, ii. 595: v. 401; ix. 60.
—— Helen, dau. of 13th earl of Crawford, iii. 33.
—— Helen, wife of Sir R. Sinclair of Stevenston, iii. 37.
—— Helen, dau. of 18th earl of Crawford, iii. 38.
—— Helen, wife of 1st lord Elibank, iii. 509.
—— Helen, wife of Thos. Fotheringham of Powrie, v. 398.
—— Helen, wife of Sir William Scott of Ardross, v. 402.
—— Helen, wife of Jas. Colvill of Balbedie, v. 404.
—— Helen, wife of George Johnston, v. 407.
—— Helen, wife of Mr. John Wood, v. 414.
—— Helen, wife of David Carnegie of Craigo, dean of Brechin, viii. 55.
—— Henrietta, wife of Sir D. Campbell, i. 520.
—— Henrietta, wife of Wm. Baillie of Lamington, iii. 37.
—— Henry, *alias* Andrew Gray or Graham, i. 138.
—— Henry, 7th son of bishop L., i. 527.
—— Henry, 4th son of 13th earl of Crawford, iii. 33; ix. 61.
—— Henry Bethune, major 3rd Bengal Cavalry, v. 418.
—— —— his wife, Elizabeth Campbell, v. 418.
—— Henry Edith Arthur, capt. Gordon Highlanders, iii. 45.
—— —— his wife, Norah Mary Madeline Bourke, iii. 45.

* Name unknown.

Lindsay, Henry Edzell Morgan, R.E., i. 527.
—— —— his wife, Ellen Katharine Thomas, i. 527.
—— Henry George, v. 418.
—— —— his wife, Jane Edith Fisher, v. 418.
—— Henry James Hamilton, v. 419.
—— Hugh Barlow, Bombay Civil Service, iii. 43.
—— —— his wife, Jane Louisa Octavia Grosvenor, iii. 43.
—— Hugh Primrose, i. 528.
—— —— his wife, Jane Gordon, i. 92, 528.
—— Ingelram de, bishop of Aberdeen, iii. 17, 18.
—— Ingelram, 4th son of Walter L. of Beaufort, iii. 20.
—— Isobel, wife of 3nd lord Ogilvy of Airlie, i. 116; iii. 25.
—— Isobel, dau. of 1st lord Lindsay of Balcarres, i. 519.
—— Isobell, wife of (1) 6th lord Borthwick, and (2) George Preston, ii. 109, 110; iii. 27; ix. 39.
—— Isabel, wife of Sir John Maxwell of Pollok, iii. 11; ix. 61.
—— Isabel, dau. of Alex. L., iii. 19.
—— Isobel, wife of J. Crichton of Ruthven, iii. 26.
—— Isabella, wife of F. B. Montgomerie, iii. 47.
—— Isabel, wife of Sir Wm. Scott of Balweary, v. 396.
—— Isabel, wife of (1) Norman Leslie, master of Rothes, (2) Wm. Christison, and (3) John Innes, v. 398; vii. 286.
—— Isobel, dau. of David L., yr. of Kirkforthar, v. 405.
—— Isobel, wife of Henry Makgill, vi. 591.
—— Isabella, wife of Mr. Andrew Rollo, vii. 198.
—— Mr. James, parson of Fettercairn, i. 512.
—— James, son of David L. of Edzell, i. 516.
—— James, rector of St. Brioc, canon of Aberdeen, iii. 15.
—— Mr. James, 4th son of Sir David L. of Beaufort, iii. 19.
—— James, 5th son of 3rd earl of Crawford, iii. 20.
—— James, 2nd son of 8th earl of Crawford, iii. 26.
—— Mr. James, parson of Fettercairn, iii. 29.
—— James, 2nd son of 11th earl of Crawford, iii. 31.
—— James, col., 2nd son of 18th earl of Crawford, iii. 37.
—— Sir James, K.C.M.G., M.P., iii. 44.
—— —— his wife, Sarah Savile, iii. 44.
—— James, vicar-general of the friars minor, iii. 564.
—— James, rector of Benhame, v. 393.
—— James, 4th son of Ninian L. of Kilquhis, v. 404; ix. 128.

Lindsay, James, 2nd son of P. L. of Kirkforthar, v. 405, 408.
— James, 2nd son of D. L. of Kirkforthar, v. 405.
— James, 3rd son of P. L., St. Andrews, v. 408.
— James, H.E.I.C.S., v. 409.
— James, 2nd son of David L. of Pyotston, v. 411, 412.
— James, 5th son of John L. of Wolmerston, v. 414.
— James, 3rd son of P. L. of Wolmerston, v. 414.
— James, 2nd son of Patrick L. of Coats, v. 417.
— James, *tertius*, 6th son of 17th earl of Crawford, ix. 62.
— James Howard, barrister-at-law, iii. 46.
— James Stair, capt. 14th Foot, i. 525.
— Jane, wife of R. Lundin of Balgonie, v. 400.
— Jane, wife of John Hislop, v. 406.
— Jane, dau. of Henry L. of Wormiston, v. 417.
— Jane, wife of capt. Reeve, v. 417.
— Jane Coutts, wife of lieut. Jas. S. Trotter, R.N., v. 419.
— Jane Evelyn, dau. of 25th earl of Crawford, iii. 48.
— Jane Kathleen Mary, v. 418.
— Janet, wife of Edward Whitmore, i. 516.
— Janet, wife of D. Auchmutie, i. 518.
— Janet, wife of * Ramsay of Balnabreich, iii. 20.
— Janet, wife of 6th earl of Douglas, iii. 20, 172.
— Janet, wife of Andrew Kinninmond, v. 397.
— Janet, wife of Henry, master of Sinclair, v. 398; vii. 574.
— Janet, wife of P. Lindsay, St. Andrews, iv. 409.
— Janet, wife of Jas. Anderson of Mounthrive, v. 409.
— Janet, wife of Alex. Anderson of Kingask, v. 410.
— Janet, dau. of John L., Cupar, v. 413.
— Jean, wife of 6th lord Torphichen, i. 514; viii. 393.
— Jean, wife of William, 6th earl of Douglas, iii. 20, 172.
— Jean, dau. of 12th earl of Crawford, iii. 32; v. 457.
— Jean, wife of capt. Jas. Leslie, iii. 33.
— Jean, wife of 11th earl of Eglinton, iii. 41, 460.
— Jean, dau. of Patrick L. of Eaglescairnie, v. 410.
— Jean, wife of John Melville of Carnbee, v. 411.

* Name unknown.

Lindsay, Jean, wife of Mungo Livingston, viii. 373.
— Jessie Frances, v. 418.
— John, rector of Lethnot, i. 511, 516; iii. 29.
— — his 1st wife, Marion Guthrie, i. 517.
— — his 2nd wife, Jane Lauder, i. 517.
— John, son of Sir David L. of Edzell, i. 513.
— John, capt., son of John L. of Edzell, i. 515.
— John, 2nd son of David L. of Edzell, i. 516.
— John, 2nd son of 1st lord Lindsay of Balcarres, i. 519.
— John, lieut.-col. 71st Highlanders, i. 528.
— — his wife, Charlotte North, i. 528.
— Sir John de, chamberlain of Scotland, iii. 8.
— — his wife, Dyonisia Bene, iii. 8.
— John, illeg. son of Sir Alex. L. of Glenesk, iii. 15.
— Sir John, 4th son of 3rd earl of Crawford, iii. 20.
— John, in Clochy, iii. 20.
— — his wife, Katharine Strachan, iii. 20.
— John, 2nd son of 1st lord Ruthven, iii. 20; iv. 258.
— — his wife, Libra Livingston, iv. 258.
— John, in Downy, iii. 21.
— Sir John, K.B., eldest son of Sir Henry Charteris of Kinfauns, iii. 32.
— — his wife, Jean Abernethy, iii. 32.
— John, 3rd son of 17th earl of Crawford, iii. 36; ix. 62.
— John, lieutenant R.N., iii. 46.
— Mr. John, minister of Lethnot, v. 84.
— John, brother of Sir Walter L., preceptor of Torphichen, v. 393 *n.*
— John, 2nd son of P. L. of Kilquhis, v. 403.
— John, burgess of Cupar, v. 404, 411, 412.
— — his wife, Janet Williamson, v. 412.
— John, 3rd son of P. L. of Kirkforthar, v. 405.
— John, 4th son of John L. of Kirkforthar, v. 407.
— John, lieut.-col. 53rd Foot, v. 409, 410.
— — his wife, Margaret Maria Craigie, v. 410.
— John, 2nd son of J. L. of Wolmerston, v. 414.
— John, merchant, Crail, v. 415.
— John, illeg. son of L. of Covington, viii. 19.
— John de, viii. 380.
— — his wife, Isabella *, viii. 380.
— John Mackenzie, W.S., viii. 112.
— — his wife, Florence Brown, viii. 112.
— John Scott, v. 416.
— John Scott, W.S., v. 417.
— Jonet, wife of (1) Wm. Marshall, and (2) David Jameson, iii. 29; ix. 30.

* Name unknown.

Lindsay, Jonet, wife of Sir D. Murray of Balvaird, v. 396; viii. 187.
—— Jonet, wife of (1) Andrew Lundie, (2) Sir Wm. Scott, and (3) Sir George Douglas, vi. 370.
—— Jonet, dau. of 5th earl of Crawford, ix. 61.
—— Jonet, dau. of Robt. L. in Kirkton of Ferne, ix. 61.
—— Joyce Emily, iii. 50.
—— Juda, wife of *, v. 412.
—— Katharine, wife of (1) 10th earl of Crawford, and (2) John Brown of Fordell, i. 518; iii. 30.
—— Katharine, wife of 10th lord Blantyre, ii. 90; v. 410.
—— Katharine, contr. to Walter Scott, ii. 227.
—— Katharine, dau. of 13th earl of Crawford, iii. 33.
—— Katharine, wife of Patrick L., lord provost of Edinburgh, governor of Isle of Man, iii. 38; v. 409.
—— Katharine, wife of John Wemyss, iii. 38.
—— Katharine, wife of Alex. Seton, v. 394.
—— Katharine, wife of Thos. Myreton of Cambo, v. 398.
—— Katharine, wife of James Lundie of that Ilk, v. 401.
—— Katharine, wife of (1) capt. R. Carmichael, and (2) major C. Seton, v. 408.
—— Katharine, wife of John Douglas, D.D., v. 413.
—— Katharine, wife of Mr. Wm. Hardie, v. 415.
—— Katharine, dau. of John L. of Wormiston, v. 415.
—— Katharine Hepburne, iii. 43.
—— Kenneth Andrew, iii. 50.
—— Laura, wife of C. E. Buckland, i. 525.
—— Leonard Cecil Colin, iii. 47.
—— —— his wife, Clare Vaughan, iii. 47.
—— Lilias, dau. of 1st lord Lindsay of Balcarres, i. 519.
—— Lilias, dau. of 13th earl of Crawford, ix. 62.
—— Lionel, 6th son of 26th earl of Crawford, iii. 50.
—— Lionel Arthur, i. 527.
—— Mabel, wife of lt.-col. W. J. F. Ramsden, iii. 44.
—— Mabel Marion, dau. of 25th earl of Crawford, iii. 48.
—— Magdalen, wife of L. M'Intosh, i. 515.
—— Margaret, wife of Adam Menzies, i. 512.
—— Margaret, wife of Sir D. Carnegie of Kinnaird, i. 514; viii. 66.
—— Margaret, wife of Alex. Watson, i. 516; iv. 568 *bis*.

* Name unknown.

Lindsay, Margaret, wife of Sir Alexander Strachan, i. 518; ix. 31.
—— Margaret, dau. of 1st lord Lindsay of Balcarres, i. 519.
—— Margaret, wife of 6th earl of Wigtown, i. 522; viii. 554; ix. 31.
—— Margaret, wife of (1) Alex. Arbuthnott, and (2) Jas. Pearson, i. 294, 295.
—— Margaret, wife of John, 6th lord Innermeath and earl of Atholl, i. 447, 512; iii. 29; ix. 28, 61.
—— Margaret, wife of Alexander, 25th earl of Crawford, i. 524; iii. 48.
—— Margaret, wife of (1) A. Fordyce, and (2) Sir J. B. Burges, i. 528.
—— Margaret, wife of Sir Thos. Colville of Oxnam, ii. 540; iii. 12.
—— Margaret, wife of R. Colville of Cleish, ii. 571.
—— Margaret, wife of Sir David de Lindsay, iii. 5, 9.
—— Margaret, wife of John Blair of Balmyle, iii. 24.
—— Margaret, dau. of Sir John L. of Woodwray, iii. 30.
—— Margaret, wife of Thos. Murray, iii. 33.
—— Margaret, wife of A. Gray of Hayston, iii. 33.
—— Margaret, dau. of 14th earl of Crawford, iii. 34.
—— Margaret, dau. of 17th earl of Crawford, iii. 37.
—— Margaret, dau. of 18th earl of Crawford, iii. 37, 38.
—— Margaret, wife of Sir G. Douglas of Helenhill, iii. 97.
—— Margaret, wife of Walter, 1st lord Innermeath, v. 4, 394.
—— Margaret, wife of (1) Richard, 3rd lord Innermeath, and (2) Sir Jas. Stewart of Beath, iii. 186; v. 4, 395.
—— Margaret, alleged wife of James, lord Innermeath, v. 396.
—— Margaret, wife of Jas. Beaton of Melgund, v. 398.
—— Margaret, wife of James, master of Rothes, v. 400; vii. 296.
—— Margaret, dau. of 7th lord Lindsay of the Byres, v. 400.
—— Margaret, dau. of 9th lord Lindsay of the Byres, v. 402.
—— Margaret, wife of James Bruce, v. 403.
—— Margaret, wife of Patrick Traill, v. 404; ix. 128.
—— Margaret, dau. of David L., yr. of Kirkforthar, v. 405.
—— Margaret, wife of Wm. Corstorphine, v. 405.
—— Margaret, dau. of Patrick L. of Wolmerston, v. 414.
—— Margaret, dau. of Henry L. of Wormiston, v. 417.

Lindsay, Margaret, wife of A. R. Hogg, v. 418.
—— Margaret, wife of J. M. Melville, v. 418.
—— Margaret, wife of Sir Jas. Keith of Benholm, vi. 54; ix. 31.
—— Margaret, wife of Gabriel Sempill of Craigbait, vii. 534.
—— Margaret, wife of Alexander Erskine of Dun, viii. 101.
—— Margaret, wife of 1st lord Fleming, viii. 533.
—— Margaret Caroline, wife of P. Orr, v. 416.
—— Margaret Catherine Frances, iii. 47.
—— Margaret Cynthia, dau. of 27th earl of Crawford, iii. 50.
—— Margaret Elizabeth, wife of L. A. Majendie, iii. 48.
—— Margaret Janet, wife of (1) Alex. Fordyce, and (2) Sir J. B. Burges, i. 528; ix. 31 *bis*.
—— Margaret Louisa, iii. 46.
—— Margaret Northesk, viii. 112.
—— Marie, wife of Wm. Ballingall of that Ilk, v. 398.
—— Marion, wife of (1) 3rd lord Lyle, and (2) Wm. Menzies of Roro, v. 555; ix. 133.
—— Marion Margaret Violet, wife of marquess of Granby, iii. 45.
—— Mariot, wife of John Sempill of Cathcart, vii. 534.
—— Marjory, wife of Sir Wm. Douglas of Lochleven, iii. 17.
—— Marjory, wife of Andrew Stewart of Beith, v. 393.
—— Marjorie, contr. to John, 5th lord Lindsay of the Byres, ix. 128.
—— Martin Eccles, major, v. 416.
—— —— his wife, Margaret Augusta Tovey, v. 416.
—— Martin William, v. 419.
—— Mary, dau. of 11th earl of Crawford, iii. 31.
—— Mary, wife of D. Campbell of Glensaddell, iii. 39.
—— Mary, dau. of Wm. Alex. L., iii. 46; ix. 62.
—— Mary, wife of John Cochrane of Cochrane, iii. 338.
—— Mary, wife of John Hay of Yester, v. 394; viii. 430.
—— Mary, dau. of Patrick L., lord provost of Edinburgh, v. 409.
—— Mary, wife of John Craigie, v. 415.
—— Mary, dau. of David Ayton L. of Wormiston, v. 417.
—— Mary, mistress of 1st lord Reay, vii. 169.
—— Mary Anne, wife of R. S. Holford, i. 524.
—— Mary Ann Leslie, v. 418.
—— Mary Augusta, wife of Sir R. Temple, i. 525.
Lindsay, Mary Butler, wife of C. M. Christie, i. 525.
—— Mary Catharine Caroline, wife of T. S. Lindsay, i. 527.
—— Mary Egidia, wife of J. C. Antrobus, iii. 44.
—— Mary Susan Felicia, wife of F. G. L. Meynell, iii. 48.
—— Maud Isabella, iii. 44.
—— Michael, ii. 403.
—— —— his wife, Marion Dalzell, ii. 403.
—— Michael William Howard, Seaforth Highlanders, iii. 46.
—— Muriel Maud Stewart, wife of W. J. Y. S. Watkins, v. 420.
—— Nancy Winifred Robina, iii. 45.
—— Norman, 3rd son of Jas. L. of Kilquhis, v. 403.
—— Norman, 3rd son of Norman L. of Kilquhis, v. 404.
—— Mr. Patrick, 2nd son of David L. of Balgawies, i. 512.
—— Patrick, archbishop of Glasgow, ii. 85; iii. 321 *n*.
—— Patrick, 3rd son of 8th earl of Crawford, iii. 26.
—— Patrick, 5th son of 17th earl of Crawford, iii. 36; iv. 174.
—— —— his wife, Margaret Crawfurd of Kilbirnie, iv. 174.
—— Patrick, 3rd son of 18th earl of Crawford, iii. 37.
—— Patrick, eldest son of James L. of Kilquhis, v. 403.
—— Patrick, 3rd son of David L., yr. of Kirkforthar, v. 405.
—— Patrick, deacon of the wrights, St. Andrews, v. 408.
—— —— his wife, Beatrix Daes, v. 408.
—— Patrick, rector of grammar school, St. Andrews, v. 408.
—— —— his wife, Janet Lindsay, v. 409.
—— Patrick, lord provost of Edinburgh; governor of Man, v. 409.
—— —— his 1st wife, Margaret Monteir, v. 409.
—— —— his 2nd wife, Janet Murray, v. 409.
—— —— his 3rd wife, Katharine Lindsay, iii. 38; v. 409.
—— Patrick, burgess of Crail, v. 411, 412.
—— Mr. Patrick, Cupar, v. 412.
—— Patrick, 6th son of Patrick L. of Wolmerston, v. 414.
—— Patrick, 3rd son of Patrick L. of Coats, v. 417.
—— Patrick, son of 'the wicked master of Crawford,' ix. 61.
—— Philip Yorke, H.E.I.C.S., i. 526.
—— —— his wife, Helena Elizabeth Blaney, i. 526.
—— Rachel, wife of archbp. Spottiswoode, iii. 20.

Lindsay, Rachel, wife of lieut.-gen. Jas. Dickson, v. 416.
— Reginald, 3rd son of Sir Alex. de L. of Crawford, iii. 9.
— Rhoda, wife of Carl von Schubort, i. 525.
— Richard, cornet 20th Dragoons, iii. 43.
— Robert, 4th son of lord Menmuir, i. 517.
— — his wife, Margaret Elphinstone, ix. 31.
— Sir Robert, V.C., K.C.B., i. 524.
— — his wife, Harriet Loyd Jones, i. 524.
— Robert, 2nd son of David L., yr. of Kirkforthar, v. 405.
— Robert, 4th son of Patrick L. of Kirkforthar, v. 405.
— Robert, 2nd son of P. L. of Wolmerston, v. 413 *bis*.
— Robert, 4th son of P. L. of Wolmerston, v. 414.
— Robert Hamilton, capt. 2nd Royal Dragoons, iii. 50.
— — his wife, May Janet Clark, iii. 50.
— Roger, 1553, vii. 127.
— Ronald Charles, secretary of Legation, iii. 50.
— Samuel, v. 406.
— Sophia, wife of col. Chas. Campbell, i. 365, 367, 520; ix. 31.
— Sophia, wife of Sir Robert Moray, i. 519; iii. 403.
— Stewart Lindsay, wife of 3rd earl of Norbury, v. 419.
— Stuart, 6th son of P. L. of Wormiston, v. 418.
— Susan, wife of Thomas Tod, viii. 112.
— Susanna, dau. of 18th earl of Crawford, iii. 38.
— Thomas, illeg. son of Sir David L. of Edzell, i. 531.
— Thomas, lieut. 33rd Foot, i. 526.
— Thomas, 5th son of Walter L. of Beaufort, iii. 20.
— Thomas, 4th son of 18th earl of Crawford, iii. 38; ix. 62.
— Violet Harriet Isobel, iii. 47.
— Sir Walter de, iii. 1.
— Walter de, iii. 2.
— Walter, 3rd son of Sir David de L. of Luffness, iii. 6.
— — his wife, Christian Huse, iii. 6.
— Walter, eldest son of Sir David L. of Beaufort and Edzell, iii. 19, 25.
— Walter, 3rd son of Walter L. of Beaufort, iii. 20.
— Sir Walter, preceptor of Torphichen, v. 393 *n*.
— Walter, brigadier-general, R.H.A., vi. 496.
— Walter Charles, i. 527.
— — his wife, Kathleen Butler, i. 527.
Lindsay, Walter Patrick, 2nd son of 26th earl of Crawford, iii. 50.
— — his wife, Ruth Henderson, iii. 50.
— William, 5th son of 5th earl of Balcarres, i. 525.
— William do, 1134, iii. 2.
— William de, iii. 2; viii. 319 *n*.
— — his 2nd wife, Alicnora de Limesey, iii. 3.
— William de, 3rd son of the justiciar, seneschal to the steward of Scotland, iii. 3, 7.
— William de, chancellor of Scotland, iii. 6.
— William, rector of Ayr, chamberlain of Scotland, iii. 10; vi. 211.
— William, 5th son of 8th earl of Crawford, iii. 27.
— William, capt. R.N., iii. 38.
— William, son of 1st lord Ruthven, iv. 258.
— William, 2nd son of Sir Wm. L. of the Byres, v. 392.
— William, 5th son of P. L. of Kirkforthar, v. 405.
— William, 7th son of Mr. David L., v. 406.
— William, 6th son of J. L. of Wolmerston, v. 414.
— William, H.E.I.C.S., v. 416.
— William, provost of Innerpeffray, viii. 215.
— William Duff, R.N., i. 525.
— William John Coussmaker, rev., i. 527.
— — his wife, Rosamond Emily Mundy, i. 527.
— William Tucker, v. 420.
— *, son of Patrick L., archbishop of Glasgow, ii. 85.
— *, wife of David Stewart, earl palatine of Strathern, ii. 321: iii. 14; viii. 259.
— *, *probably* wife of (1) Alexander Ramsay of Carnock, and (2) * Brun, iii. 11, 90.
— *, 1st wife of Sir Jerome Lindsay of Annatland, iii. 19.
— *, wife of * Gardyne, iii. 25.
— *, wife of * Douglas of Kilspindie, iii. 26.
— *, *probable* wife of Walter Carnegie of Kinnaird, viii. 50.
Lindsay-Bethune of Kilconquhar, Henry, v. 416.
— — his 1st wife, Elizabeth Kyd, v. 416.
— — his 2nd wife, Margaret Eccles, v. 416.
— — John, v. 416.
— — Sir John, 1st bart., v. 416, 418.
— — his wife, Coutts Trotter, v. 419.
Lindsay-Carnegie of Boysack, Donald Christian Strachan, major Bengal Cavalry, vi. 496; viii. 113; ix. 160.
— — Henry Alexander, vi. 496; viii. 113.
— — his wife, Agnes Rait of Anniston, viii. 113.
— — James, commander R.N., vi. 496; viii. 111, 112.

* Name unknown.

Lindsay-Carnegie of Boysack, James Fullarton, advocate, vi. 496; viii. 111.
—— —— his wife, Mary Elizabeth Strachan, viii. 111.
—— —— William Fullarton, R.A., vi. 496; viii. 111, 112.
—— —— his wife, Jane Christian Carnegie, vi. 496, 506; viii. 112.
—— of Kinblethmont, William Fullarton, vi. 496.
—— Helen, vi. 496.
—— Jane, wife of capt. Alexander Lindsay, vi. 496 *bis*; viii. 111, 113.
—— Mary Elizabeth, wife of major Geo. Gordon, viii. 113.
—— Susan, wife of Robert Ramsay, vi. 496; viii. 113.
—— William, viii. 112.
Lindsay-Crawfurd of Kilbirnie, Patrick, iii. 36; iv. 174; ix. 95.
—— —— his wife, Margaret Crawfurd, iv. 174; ix. 95.
—— Bute, capt. 92nd Foot, iii. 40.
—— Mary, dau. of 21st earl of Crawford, iii. 41.
—— John, claimant to the viscountcy of Garnock, iv. 178 *n.*
Lindsay-Hamilton-Crawford, Robert, capt. 92nd Highlanders, iii. 40; ix. 62.
Lindsey, Montagu (Bertie), 2nd earl of, iii. 302; iv. 301.
—— —— his wife, Martha Cockayne, iv. 301.
Linley, Mary, wife of Francis, 10th lord Oliphant, vi. 561.
LINLITHGOW, LIVINGSTON, EARL OF, v. 421-451.
Linlithgow, Alexander, first earl of, v. 190, 445.
—— —— his wife, Helenor Hay, iii. 572; v. 445.
—— Alexander, second earl of, i. 135; ii. 360; v. 446; vi. 55.
—— —— his 1st wife, Elizabeth Gordon, iv. 545; v. 447.
—— —— his 2nd wife, Mary Douglas, i. 202; v. 447.
—— George, third earl of, ii. 362, 363; v. 447; ix. 130 *ter.*
—— —— his 1st wife, Elizabeth Maule, v. 448; vii. 21.
—— —— his 2nd wife, Agnes Wauchope, v. 449.
—— George, fourth earl of, ii. 363; v. 449.
—— —— his wife, Henrietta Sutherland, iii. 209; v. 449.
—— James, fifth earl of, ii. 363; v. 178, 449.
—— —— his wife, Margaret Hay, iii. 579, 580; v. 450.
LINLITHGOW, HOPE, MARQUESS OF, iv. 485-505.
Linlithgow, John Adrian Louis, first marquess of, iv. 504.
—— —— his wife, Hersey Alice Eveleigh de Moleyns, iv. 504.
Linlithgow, Victor Alexander John, second marquess of, i. 270; iv. 504.
LINTON, STEWART, LORD, viii. 403-409.
Linton, Charles, son of 6th earl of Traquair; styled lord, viii. 408.
—— —— his wife, Mary Ravenscroft, viii. 408.
—— Charles, son of 7th earl of Traquair; styled lord, viii. 409.
—— John, first lord, viii. 403.
—— John, son of 1st earl of Traquair; styled lord, viii. 404.
—— —— his 1st wife, Henrietta Gordon, iv. 547; viii. 406, 595.
—— —— his 2nd wife, Anne Seton, viii. 406, 600.
—— Robert, chaplain, Edinburgh, vi. 405.
LINTRATHEN, OGILVY, LORD OGILVY OF ALYTH AND, i. 123-132.
Lisle, John (Dudley), 7th viscount, iv. 358.
—— of Woodford, John, v. 550.
—— *, captain in col. Rich's regiment, v. 228.
—— in Northumberland, v. 549.
Lister of Burwell, Matthew, iii. 113.
—— Adelaide, wife of M. Drummond, viii. 231.
—— Mary, wife of (1) Thos. Heardson, and (2) 2nd earl of Deloraine, iii. 112.
—— Thomas Villiers, K.C.M.G., ii. 58.
—— —— his wife, Florence Selina Goodenough, ii. 58.
Lister-Kaye of Manor House, Arthur, captain, viii. 315.
LITCHFIELD, STEWART, EARL OF, v. 360-361.
Litchfield, Bernard, earl of, v. 359.
—— Charles, earl of, v. 360.
Litchfield, Edward Henry (Lee), 1st earl of, i. 31.
—— —— his wife, Charlota Fitz Roy, i. 31.
Lithgow of Drygrange, James, vi. 151.
—— —— William, ix. 39.
—— John, ix. 39.
—— —— his wife, Beatrice Borthwick, ix. 39.
—— Katharine, wife of (1) James Thomson of Colmslie, and (2) col. William Graham, vi. 151.
Litster, John, order of Observantines, i. 283.
Little of Shabden Park, Archibald, vii. 591.
—— Clement, burgess of Edinburgh, vi. 411.
—— Edward, burgess of Edinburgh, iii. 502.
—— —— his wife, Marion Adamson, iii. 502.
—— Isabella, wife of (1) Alex. Napier of Inglistoun, and (2) Alex. Douglas, vi. 411.
—— Jane, wife of 15th lord Sinclair, vii. 591.
—— Jeva, mistress of Waldemar, king of Denmark, vi. 569.
—— Katharine, wife of Alex. Napier, vi. 411.
—— William, iii. 502.
—— —— his wife, Margaret Murray, iii. 502.
—— *, wife of John Seton, viii. 577 *n.*

* Name unknown.

Littlejohn, Ewpham, alleged wife of 2nd earl of Tullibardine, i. 472 *n.*
— John, stewart clerk of Fife, viii. 197 *n.*
— — his wife, Anna Murray, viii. 197 *n.*
Littler, Mildred, mistress of 1st earl of Breadalbane, ii. 206.
Liulph of Maccustoun, son of Maecus, vi. 469.
Liverpool, Charles (Jenkinson), 1st earl of, iv. 97.
LIVINGSTON OF CALLENDAR, LIVINGSTON, LORD, v. 430-451.
Livingston, Alexander, fifth lord, ii. 144; v. 435; ix. 129 *bis.*
— — his 1st wife, Janet Stewart, v. 435; ix. 129.
— — his 2nd wife, Agnes Douglas, v. 436; vi. 358.
— — his 3rd wife, Jeanne de Pedefer, v. 439.
— Alexander, seventh lord, v. 443.
— — his wife, Helen Hay, iii. 572; v. 445.
— Alexander, eighth lord, v. 446.
— — his 1st wife, Elizabeth Gordon, iv. 545; v. 447.
— — his 2nd wife, Mary Douglas, i. 202; v. 447.
— George, ninth lord, v. 447.
— — his 1st wife, Elizabeth Maule, v. 448; vii. 21.
— — his 2nd wife, Agnes Wauchope, v. 449.
— George, tenth lord, v. 449.
— — his wife, Henrietta Sutherland, iii. 209; v. 449.
— of Callendar, James, first lord, iv. 351; v. 430, 603 *n.*
— — his wife, Marian *, v. 430; vi. 537 *n.*, 538 *n.*
— — James, second lord, iii. 223; v. 431, 596.
— Sir James, third lord, v. 185, 433; viii. 534, 577 *n.*; ix. 129 *ter.*
— — his 1st wife, Elizabeth Fleming, viii. 534; ix. 129.
— — his 2nd wife, Agnes Houston, v. 433.
— James, eleventh lord, v. 449.
— — his wife, Margaret Hay, iii. 579, 580; v. 450.
— James, only son of earl of Linlithgow and Callendar; styled lord, iii. 580; v. 450.
— William, fourth lord, v. 434.
— — his wife, Agnes Hepburn, ii. 144; v. 435.
— William, sixth lord, v. 437, 439; vi. 447.
— — his wife, Agnes *or* Janet Fleming, v. 439, 442; viii. 540; ix. 129.
— master of, Alexander, eldest son of 4th lord Livingston, v. 185, 435.

* Name unknown.

Livingston, master of, John, eldest son of 5th lord Livingston, v. 436.
— — his wife, Janet Fleming, v. 436; viii. 388, 540.
— master of, John, eldest son of 1st earl of Linlithgow, v. 445.
LIVINGSTON OF ALMOND, LIVINGSTON, LORD, ii. 360-364.
Livingston of Almond, Alexander, second lord, ii. 363.
— — Alexander, third lord, ii. 363.
— — James, 3rd son of 1st earl of Linlithgow, first lord, ii. 360; viii. 549.
— — his wife, Margaret Hay, ii. 362; viii. 447.
— — James, fourth lord, ii. 363.
LIVINGSTON OF FLACRAIG, LIVINGSTON, LORD, vi. 453-460.
Livingston of Flacraig, James, first lord, vi. 453.
— Sigismondo Maria Bandino Giuseppe, eldest son of 9th earl of Newburgh; styled lord, vi. 459.
LIVINGSTON OF HYNDFORD, LIVINGSTON, LORD, viii. 376.
Livingston of Hyndford, Thomas, lord, viii. 376.
LIVINGSTON OF PEEBLES, LIVINGSTON, LORD, viii. 376.
Livingston of Peebles, Thomas, lord, viii. 376.
LIVINGSTON, EARL OF CALLENDAR, ii. 360-364.
LIVINGSTON, LORD CAMPSIE, v. 192-194.
LIVINGSTON, VISCOUNT OF KILSYTH, v. 183-194.
LIVINGSTON, LORD OF KINNAIRD, vi. 452.
LIVINGSTON, VISCOUNT OF KINNAIRD, vi. 453-460.
LIVINGSTON, EARL OF LINLITHGOW, v. 421-451.
LIVINGSTON, LORD LIVINGSTON OF ALMOND, ii. 360-364.
LIVINGSTON, LORD LIVINGSTON OF CALLENDAR, v. 430-451.
LIVINGSTON, LORD LIVINGSTON OF FLACRAIG, vi. 453-460.
LIVINGSTON, LORD LIVINGSTON OF HYNDFORD, viii. 376.
LIVINGSTON, LORD LIVINGSTON OF PEEBLES, viii. 376.
LIVINGSTON, VISCOUNT OF NEWBURGH, vi. 452-453.
LIVINGSTON, EARL OF NEWBURGH, vi. 446-460.
LIVINGSTON, VISCOUNT TEVIOT, viii. 368-377.
Livingston(e of Abbotshall, Sir Alexander, viii. 375.
— — Sir Thomas, viii. 375.
— of Abercorn, James, vi. 449.
— — his wife, Helen Hamilton, vi. 449.

Livingston(e of Abercorn, Sir John, vi. 447, 448, 451.
—— —— his wife, Elizabeth Carmichael, vi. 449.
—— of Little Airds, Alexander, v. 106.
—— —— his wife, Elizabeth *or* Isobelle Gordon, v. 106.
—— of Hill of Auchenfure, Sir Robert, viii. 369.
—— of Auchengenis, James, v. 431.
—— of Baitford, William, viii. 373.
—— of Balcastell, Edward, v. 185.
—— —— William, 5th son of Sir John L. of Callendar, v. 184.
—— —— William, son of Edward L., v. 185, 432.
—— —— his wife, Elizabeth Graham, v. 186.
—— of Baldoran, James, v. 430.
—— —— Robert, v. 188.
—— —— William, v. 187.
—— —— his wife, Jonet Bruce, v. 187.
—— of Baloralloch, James, v. 434.
—— —— William, v. 185.
—— of Banks, John, viii. 368.
—— of Bantaskine, David, ix. 129.
—— —— his wife, Elizabeth Shaw, ix. 129.
—— of Banton, John, ancestor of the family of, v. 426.
—— of Barncloich, Sir James, v. 190, 191.
—— —— his wife, Euphame Cunningham, v. 192.
—— of Bedlormie, Sir George, ancestor of the family of, v. 442.
—— —— his wife, Margaret Crichton, v. 442; ix. 130.
—— —— George, v. 474.
—— —— his wife, Frances Ker, v. 474.
—— of Beldstane, John, viii. 370.
—— of Benquhol, Alexander, v. 492.
—— of Biel, James, groom of the bedchamber to Charles I., vi. 450, 451; ix. 143.
—— —— his wife, Anne Naesmith, vi. 450; ix. 143.
—— of Broriebanks, John, viii. 368.
—— of Brighouse, Sir James, 3rd son of 1st earl of Linlithgow, ii. 360; v. 445, 446.
—— of Broominch, Sir Alexander, v. 429.
—— of Brownlie, James, viii. 370.
—— of Caldhame, James, i. 294.
—— of Callendar, Sir Alexander, justiciary of Scotland, 4th laird, iii. 58, 171; v. 257, 426.
—— —— his wife, * Dundas, v. 429.
—— —— James, 5th laird, captain of Stirling Castle, v. 184, 429.
—— —— his wife, Marian *, v. 429.
—— —— Sir John, 3rd laird, iv. 518; v. 184, 425; vi. 446.
—— —— his 1st wife, * Menteith, v. 426.
—— —— his 2nd wife, Agnes Douglas, iv. 518; v. 426; vi. 348.

* Name unknown.

Livingston(e of Callendar, Sir William, 1st laird, v. 423.
—— —— his wife, Christian of Callendar, v. 183, 423.
—— —— William, 2nd laird, v. 424.
—— of Carmuirs, James, v. 431.
—— of Castlecary, Patrick, ii. 144.
—— —— his wife, Marion Hepburne, ii. 144.
—— of Castletoun, James, v. 434.
—— —— William, v. 185.
—— of Catscleuch, Sir Alexander, v. 429; vii. 321.
—— —— James, ix. 129.
—— of Columbie, James, viii. 370.
—— of Colzium, James, v. 192.
—— of Cowhellhauch, James, viii. 372.
—— of Cowlath, Alexander, v. 492.
—— of Culter, James, captain of Stirling Castle, v. 429.
—— —— James, his son, v. 431.
—— —— Sir William, 5th son of 6th lord Livingston, v. 442.
—— —— his wife, Margaret Baillie, v. 442; ix. 130.
—— —— William, son of Sir Wm. L., ix. 130.
—— —— his wife, Margaret Baillie, ix. 130.
—— —— William, v. 442.
—— —— his wife, Helen Livingston of West Quarter, v. 442; vi. 448.
—— of Dalderse, Sir Alexander, illeg. son of 1st earl of Callendar, ii. 362.
—— —— his wife, Jean Hamilton, ii. 362.
—— —— Alexander, his son, ii. 362.
—— of Dalnarton, Alexander, v. 492.
—— of Darnchester, William, v. 187.
—— —— Sir William, v. 189.
—— —— Sir William, iv. 470; v. 189.
—— —— Sir William, v. 190.
—— —— his wife, Anna Fleming, v. 190; viii. 548.
—— of Dolders, Patrick, vii. 413.
—— —— his wife, Joneta Abernethy, vii. 413.
—— of Drumry, John, v. 423 *n.*; viii. 368.
—— —— his wife, * Wemyss of East Wemyss, viii. 368, 480.
—— —— Robert, viii. 368, 481.
—— —— Sir Robert, viii. 368.
—— —— his wife, Margaret, viii. 369.
—— —— Sir Robert, son of William L., iii. 93; viii. 369, 485.
—— —— Sir Robert, viii. 369.
—— —— his wife, Jonet Betoun, iv. 360; viii. 369.
—— —— William, v. 422; viii. 368.
—— —— his wife, Margaret, v. 423.
—— —— William, viii. 369.
—— —— his contracted wife, Euphemia Wemyss, viii. 369, 483.
—— of Duchray, Alexander, v. 492.
—— of Dunipace, Alexander, ancestor of the family of, v. 429.

* Name unknown.

Livingston(e of Dunipace, Alexander, v. 435; ix. 128.
—— —— his wife, Alison Gourlay, ix. 129.
—— —— Alexander, ii. 149; v. 437, 439; vi. 446, 447; ix. 129.
—— —— his wife, Elizabeth Hepburn, ii. 149; ix. 129.
—— —— John, iii. 534.
—— —— his wife, Margaret Elphinstone, iii. 534.
—— —— John, i. 298.
—— of Dunloppie, Alan, viii. 372.
—— of Edingham, Alexander, v. 492.
—— of Falkirk, Henry, vi. 446.
—— —— his 2nd wife, Margaret Forrester, vi. 448.
—— —— James, v. 431.
—— of Fennochthaucht and Middilthrid, William, v. 188.
—— of Fildes, Alexander, v. 429; vi. 404; ix. 128.
—— —— Alexander, ix. 129.
—— of Gairdoch, George, vi. 519.
—— —— William, vi. 518.
—— of Gartsherrie, Sir William, iv. 471.
—— of Over Garwalis, William, v. 187 *n.*, 188.
—— of Glassinwell, Edward, v. 185.
—— —— William, v. 185.
—— of Glen, James, v. 431.
—— of Glentirran, Sir Alexander, 1st bart., ii. 102, 363.
—— —— his wife, Mary Borthwick, ii. 102.
—— of Gilmerton, James, viii. 370.
—— of Gorgie, William, v. 422; viii. 368, 563.
—— —— Sir William, sheriff of Haddington, v. 423.
—— of Graden, William, v. 184.
—— of Haining, John, ix. 145.
—— —— his wife, * Stewart, ix. 145.
—— —— Thomas, 3rd son of 5th lord Livingston, v. 436, 437; vi. 446.
—— —— his 1st wife, Agnes Crawfurd of Haining, v. 437.
—— —— his 2nd wife, Elizabeth Forrester, v. 437.
—— —— Thomas, iii. 534.
—— —— his wife, Janet Henderson, iii. 534.
—— of Inches, Alexander, v. 186 *n.*
—— —— James, v. 187 *n.*
—— of Inchmawchane, Alexander, v. 185.
—— of Jaw, James, v. 431.
—— of Jerviswood, Hugh, viii. 372.
—— —— his wife, Bessie Wilkie, viii. 372.
—— —— James, 1st laird, viii. 370.
—— —— James, 2nd laird, viii. 370.
—— —— his 1st wife, * Lockhart, viii. 371.
—— —— his 2nd wife, * Hamilton, viii. 371.
—— —— James, 3rd laird, viii. 371.
—— —— his wife, Isobel Cunningham, viii. 371.

* Name unknown.

Livingston(e of Jerviswood, James, 4th laird, viii. 372.
—— —— his 1st wife, Grizel Carmichael, viii. 372.
—— —— his 2nd wife, Marion Baillie, viii. 372; ix. 163.
—— —— his 3rd wife, Agnes *or* Jean Somerville, viii. 372; ix. 163.
—— —— William, viii. 371.
—— —— his 1st wife, Janet Baird, viii. 371.
—— —— his 2nd wife, Janet Johnstone, i. 246; viii. 371.
—— —— William, vii. 133; viii. 372, 373.
—— —— his wife, Janet Douglas, vii. 133; viii. 373.
—— —— William, son of Hugh L., viii. 372.
—— —— his wife, Bethia Livingston, viii. 373.
—— of West Kerse, William, v. 191.
—— of Kilhill, James, vi. 175.
—— of Kilsyth, Edward, 2nd laird, v. 185.
—— —— Sir James, 9th laird, v. 190, 191.
—— —— his wife, Euphame Cunningham, v. 192.
—— —— Sir William, ancestor of the family of, v. 183.
—— —— his wife, Christian of Callendar, v. 183, 424.
—— —— William, 1st laird, v. 184, 426.
—— —— his wife, Elizabeth Caldcotes, v. 184.
—— —— Sir William, 3rd laird, v. 185, 435.
—— —— his wife, Elizabeth Graham, v. 186; vi. 222.
—— —— William, 4th laird, v. 186, 187, 435.
—— —— his wife, Jonet Bruce, v. 187.
—— —— Sir William, 5th laird, iv. 470; v. 188; ix. 120 *bis*.
—— —— his wife, Christian Graham, v. 189; vi. 159.
—— —— Sir William, 6th laird, v. 189.
—— —— his 1st wife, Antoinette de Bord, v. 190.
—— —— his 2nd wife, Margaret Houston, v. 190.
—— —— William, 7th laird, v. 190, 191.
—— —— his wife, Margaret Ramsay, iii. 98; v. 191.
—— —— William, 8th laird, v. 191.
—— of Kinnaird, Sir James, vi. 452.
—— —— his 1st wife, Katharine Howard, vi. 453.
—— —— his 2nd wife, Anne Poole, vi. 453.
—— —— Sir John, v. 205; vi. 446, 451.
—— —— his wife, Jane Sproxtoune, vi. 451.
—— —— Robert, alleged ancestor of the family of, v. 426; vi. 446.
—— of Kippen, Sir Alexander, v. 429.
—— of Kirkland, John, viii. 373.
—— of Kittomure, Alexander, v. 492.
—— of Lenturk, James, v. 429.
—— of Lethbert, James, v. 431.

Livingston(e of Lethington, Sir Alexander, 3rd bart., viii. 374, 376.
—— —— his wife, Sara Tyllings, viii. 375.
—— —— Sir Thomas, 2nd bart., viii. 376; ix. 29.
—— —— his wife, Macktellina Walrave, viii. 376.
—— of Livingston, Alexander, ancestor of the family of, v. 106.
—— —— his wife, Elizabeth *or* Isobelle Gordon, v. 106.
—— —— Gavin, iii. 501; viii. 382.
—— of Livingston Manor, Philip, viii. 184.
—— —— Robert, ancestor of the family of, ix. 129.
—— of Manerstoun, Agnes, wife of Wm. Fleming of Bord, viii. 527.
—— —— Henry, vi. 446. 449.
—— —— James, vi. 449.
—— —— John, vi. 449.
—— of Manuel, Alexander, v. 436.
—— —— William, v. 436.
—— of Middlebinning, vi. 446.
—— of Muirhousehill, Gavin, iii. 501; viii. 382.
—— of Musbrig, William, viii. 368.
—— of Newbigging, Alexander, major, viii. 374.
—— —— his wife, Mary Livingston, viii. 374.
—— —— Alexander, Scots Guards, viii. 374.
—— —— his 1st wife, Marion Monteith, viii. 374.
—— —— his 2nd wife, Ann Livingston, viii. 374.
—— —— Alexander, writer, viii. 374.
—— —— his wife, Ann Nairn, viii. 374.
—— —— James, 2nd laird, viii. 369.
—— —— James, 3rd laird, viii. 11, 370.
—— —— James 4th laird, viii. 370.
—— —— Mungo, viii. 372, 373.
—— —— his wife, Jean Lindsay, viii. 373.
—— —— Quentigern, viii. 374.
—— —— Sir Robert, 1st laird, viii. 10, 369.
—— —— his wife, Margaret (?) Somerville, viii. 10, 369.
—— —— William, viii. 373.
—— —— his wife, Elizabeth Heriot, viii. 373.
—— of Nova Scotia, Sir Thomas, 1st bart., viii. 374; ix. 163.
—— —— his wife, * Edmond, viii. 374.
—— of Ogilface, Sir George, 4th son of 6th lord Livingston, v. 442.
—— —— his wife, Margaret Crichton, v. 442; ix. 130.
—— of Phildes, Alexander, captain of Methven Castle, v. 429; vi. 404; ix. 128.
—— —— Alexander, ii. 149; ix. 129.
—— —— his wife, Elizabeth Hepburn, ii. 149.
—— of West Quarter, Alexander, vi. 448.
—— —— his 1st wife, Elizabeth Wedderspoon, vi. 448.
—— —— his 2nd wife, Elizabeth Douglas, ix. 143.

* Name unknown.

Livingston(e of West Quarter, Sir George, ancestor of the 2nd family of, v. 442.
—— —— Helen, wife of William Livingston, v. 442.
—— —— Sir James, iv. 380.
—— —— his wife, Mary Hamilton, ii. 363; iv. 380.
—— —— Robert, alleged ancestor of the family of, v. 426; vi. 446.
—— of Skirling, James, vi. 450, 451.
—— of Slamannan, James, v. 431.
—— of Strath, James, v. 431.
—— of Terrinterran, Sir Alexander, v. 429.
—— —— Alexander, v. 432, 434 *n.*
—— —— Alexander, vi. 150.
—— —— his wife, Christine Oliphant, vi. 150.
—— of Tortrevan, George, v. 448.
—— of Wauchton, Sir Alexander, viii. 375.
—— —— Sir Thomas, viii. 376.
—— of East Wemyss, John, v. 423 *n.*
—— —— Sir Robert, son of William L., ii. 134; viii. 369.
—— —— Sir Robert, viii. 369.
—— —— his wife, Jonet Betoun, iv. 360; viii. 369.
—— —— Sir William, v. 423 *n.*
—— —— his wife, * Erskine, v. 423 *n.*
—— of Winchelhaugh, Sir John, vi. 448.
—— Adam, 3rd son of James L. of Jerviswood, viii. 371.
—— Agnes, dau. of Sir Wm. L. of Kilsyth, v. 189.
—— Agnes, dau. of Jas. L. of Jerviswood, viii. 373.
—— Alexander, 2nd son of 3rd earl of Linlithgow, ii. 362, 363; v. 449.
—— —— his wife, Mary Hamilton, ii. 363.
—— Alexander, 3rd son of William L. of Balcastell, v. 184.
—— Alexander, 2nd son of William L. of Kilsyth, v. 188.
—— Alexander, 2nd son of 1st lord Livingston of Callendar, v. 431, 433.
—— Alexander, illeg. son of Jas. L., rector of Culter, v. 437.
—— Alexander, commendator of Cambuskenneth, v. 443.
—— Alexander, major, v. 447.
—— —— his wife, Mary Livingston, v. 447.
—— Alexander, 3rd son of Sir Henry L., vi. 450.
—— Alexander, 4th son of Sir John L., vi. 450.
—— —— his wife, Jane Chubbe, vi. 450.
—— Mr. Alexander, minister of Monyabrock, ix. 129.
—— Allan, 3rd son of Wm. L. of Jerviswood, viii. 373.
—— Sir Andrew, sheriff of Lanark, v. 422.
—— —— his wife, Elena, v. 422.
—— Anna, wife of 6th earl of Eglinton, iii. 446; v. 446; ix. 81.

* Name unknown.

Livingston(e, Anna, dau. of William L. of Kilsyth, v. 191.
— Anna, wife of Sir James Hay of Linplum, viii. 446.
— Anne, wife of 4th earl of Kilmarnock, iii. 580; v. 178, 179, 450.
— Anne, dau. of 1st viscount of Kilsyth, v. 192.
— Anne, wife of Alex. Livingston, viii. 374.
— Sir Archibald, sheriff of Linlithgow, and Stirling, v. 422.
— Bethia, wife of Wm. Livingston of Jerviswood, viii. 373.
— Charles, illeg. son of 2nd earl of Newburgh, vi. 453 *n.*
— Christian, wife of 1st lord Forrester of Corstorphine, iv. 92; v. 190.
— Christian, wife of John Lawson of Boghall, v. 189.
— Christian, wife of 1st viscount of Oxfuird, v. 191; vi. 598; ix. 147.
— David, the missionary, v. 421 *n.*
— David, rector of Ayr, provost of Lincluden, v. 431, 432.
— David, 5th son of Henry L. of Falkirk, vi. 448.
— Dorothy, wife of Lord Stanhope of Harrington, vi. 452.
— E. B., F.S.A.Scot., v. 185 *n.*, 424.
— Eleanor, dau. of 2nd earl of Linlithgow, v. 447.
— Elizabeth, wife of (1) maj.-gen. Robert Montgomerie, and (2) capt. George Douglas, iii. 450; v. 192; ix. 81.
— Elizabeth, wife of John, earl of Ross, lord of the Isles, iv. 525 *n.*; v. 47, 431; ix. 115.
— Elizabeth, wife of Gabriel Cunningham of Craigends, v. 188.
— Elizabeth, dau. of Sir Wm. L. of Kilsyth, v. 189.
— Elizabeth, dau. of Sir Alex. L. of Callendar, v. 429.
— Elizabeth, wife of Robert Callander of Dowradour, v. 434.
— Elizabeth, wife of John Buchanan of that Ilk, v. 437.
— Euphemia, wife of (1) Malcolm Fleming, and (2) Wm. Fleming of Bord, v. 431: viii. 526.
— Euphame, wife of Alex. Baillie of Auldston, viii. 372.
— George, in Falkirk, 7th son of William L. of Kilsyth, ix. 120.
— Helen, wife of Jas. Wetherspune of Brighouse, v. 439.
— Helen, wife of Wm. Livingston of Culter, v. 442; vi. 448.
— Helena, wife of John Stirling of Herbertshire, ii. 362; ix. 52.
— Harriet, dau. of 3rd earl of Callendar, ii. 363.
Livingston(e, Henriet, wife of 2nd viscount of Oxfuird, v. 449; vi. 599.
— Sir Henry, preceptor of Torphichen, v. 184; ix. 128.
— Henry, in Falkirk, v. 437.
— Henry, 3rd son of 6th lord Livingston, v. 442.
— Mr. Henry, minister of St. Ninians, vi. 448.
— — his wife, Agnes Gray, vi. 448.
— Sir Henry, Scots Brigade in Holland, vi. 449, 451.
— — his wife, Johanna Turck, vi. 449.
— Hugh, 2nd son of Wm. L. of Jerviswood, viii. 372 *bis.*
— Isabel, wife of (1) John Ramsay, lord Bothwell, and (2) N. Ramsay of Dalhousie, ii. 134; iii. 93.
— Isabel, wife of John Campbell of Auchinone, v. 188.
— Isobel, contr. to Sir John of Wemyss, and wife of John Kinninmond of that Ilk, viii. 369; ix. 163.
— Isobel, wife of Mungo Inglis, viii. 371.
— Isobel, wife of capt. Geo. Gordon, viii. 374.
— James, 5th son of William L. of Kilsyth, v. 188.
— James, 4th son of Sir John L. of Callendar, v. 426.
— James, son-in-law of Thomas Berwick, v. 431.
— Mr. James, rector of Culter, v. 435, 437; ix. 129.
— James, major, vi. 450.
— — his wife, Mary Foulis, vi. 450.
— James, brother of William L. of Jerviswood, viii. 371.
— James, 2nd son of William L. of Jerviswood, viii. 373.
— James, 2nd son of Mungo L. of Newbigging, viii. 374 *bis.*
— James, 7th son of Henry L. of Falkirk, ix. 143.
— Janet, wife of Robert Bruce of Clackmannan, iii. 472.
— Janet, wife of Jas. Hamilton of Cadzow, iv. 348; v. 429; ix. 129.
— Janet, wife of Sir Alex. Bruce of Airth, v. 437.
— Janet, dau. of Wm. L. of Jerviswood, viii. 373.
— Janet, wife of Wm. Grierson of Bargattan, viii. 373.
— Janet, dau. of Sir Alex. L., viii. 375.
— Jean, wife of 4th lord Elphinstone, iii. 537; v. 443.
— Jean, wife of William Baillie, vi. 450.
— John, captain, ii. 40; vi. 450.
— — his wife, Elizabeth Hamilton, ii. 40.
— Mr. John, author, minister of Stranraer, v. 117, 170.

Livingston(e, John, 2nd son of Wm. L. of Kilsyth, v. 187.
— John, in Falkirk, v. 188; ix. 120.
— — his wife, Elizabeth Fleming, ix. 120.
— John, burgess of Stirling, v. 432.
— John, burgess of Stirling, his grandfather, v. 433.
— John, 2nd son of 6th lord Livingston, v. 442.
— John, lt.-col. Scots Brigade in Holland, vi. 449.
— John, merchant, Edinburgh, vi. 450.
— John, king's esquire and usher, viii. 369.
— John, merchant, Edinburgh, viii. 374.
— John, 3rd son of Wm. L. of Jerviswood, viii. 372 *bis*.
— Jonat, wife of Mungo Inglis, viii. 371 *n*.
— Jonet, wife of Ninian Altoun, ix. 143.
— Katharine Elizabeth, wife of Matthew Le Stevenon van Birkenrode, viii. 375.
— Libra, wife of John Ruthven, iv. 258.
— Lilias, wife of John Hamilton of Kinglass, ix. 120.
— Magdalen, maid-of-honour to queen Mary; wife of (1) Sir A. Erskine, and (2) Sir Jas. Scrymgeour, iii. 313: v. 84, 438.
— Margaret, wife of (1) Jas. Arbuthnott of Arrat, and (2) David Carnegie of Balmachie, i. 298; viii. 54.
— Margaret, wife of (1) Sir L. Bellenden, and (2) Patrick (Stewart), 2nd earl of Orkney, ii. 70; v. 443; vi. 576.
— Margaret, wife of (1) Sir Jas. Hamilton of Finnart, and (2) John Wemyss, iv. 361, 362; viii. 369, 484.
— Margaret, wife of (1) Ninian Bruce, and (2) Alexander Baillie, v. 188; ix. 120.
— Margaret, wife of Robt. Montgomery of Haslehead, v. 190.
— Margaret, wife of Andrew Rutherford of Hunthill, and (2) William Pearson, v. 191; vii. 380; ix. 121.
— Margaret, wife of 4th lord Hay of Yester, v. 435; viii. 437.
— Margaret, wife of 2nd earl of Wigtown, v. 446; viii. 549.
— Margaret, wife of (1) Sir Thos. Nicolson of Carnock, (2) Sir G. Stirling of Keir, and (3) Sir J. Stirling of Keir, v. 447; ix. 130.
— Margaret, wife of Alexander Carnegie of Cookstoun, viii. 55.
— Margaret, wife of Robert Graham of Westhall, and (2) John Tailzicfeir, viii. 371.
— Margaret, dau. of Wm. L. of Jerviswood, viii. 373.
— Marion, wife of 3rd lord Crichton, iii. 64; v. 431.
— Marion, wife of Jas. Ogilvy of Findlater, iv. 25; v. 439.
Livingston(e, Marion, wife of David Rollo of Kincledie and Powis, vii. 186.
— Martha, viii. 373.
— Mary, wife of James Graham, ii. 363.
— Mary, one of 'the queen's Maries,' wife of John Sempill, v. 437; vii. 538, 548.
— Mary, wife of Major Alex. Livingston, v. 447; viii. 374.
— Mary, wife of William Sinclair of Galwaldmoir, vi. 450.
— Mary, wife of 4th lord Ochiltree, vi. 518; ix. 145.
— Mary, dau. of Alex. L. of Newbigging, viii. 374.
— Maws, ix. 130.
— Patrick, 3rd son of Edward L. of Kilsyth, v. 185.
— Patrick, eldest son of Sir Wm. L. of Callendar, v. 424.
— Patrick, brother of John L. of Dunipace, viii. 54.
— — his wife, Agnes Carnegie, viii. 54.
— Patrick, 4th son of William L. of Kilsyth, ix. 120.
— Sir Robert, 1360, iv. 514.
— — his contr. wife, Elizabeth, iv. 514.
— Robert, 4th son of Edward L. of Kilsyth, v. 185.
— Robert, comptroller, 1450, v. 428 *bis*; vi. 446.
— Robert, killed at Pinkie, v. 435 *n*.
— Robert, 6th son of Sir John L. of Abercorn, vi. 450.
— Robert, baker, Edinburgh, viii. 169.
— Robert, 4th son of Sir Robert L. of Drumry, viii. 369.
— Sarah, wife of major-gen. William Alexander, viii. 184.
— Mr. Thomas, rector of Carnock, treasurer of Glasgow, vi. 447, 448 *bis*.
— — his wife, Helen Little, vi. 448.
— Sir Thomas, lt.-col. in Dutch Service, viii. 374; ix. 163.
— Sir Thomas, colonel of Royal Scots Dragoons, v. 193; viii. 375.
— Thomas, ix. 65.
— — his wife, Isobel Douglas, i. 178; ix. 65.
— Thurstan de, son of Leving, iii. 87.
— Walter, 4th son of Sir Wm. L. of Callendar and Kilsyth, v. 424.
— William, infant son of 3rd viscount of Kilsyth, iii. 330; v. 193, 194.
— William, 2nd son of Wm. L. of Balcastell, v. 184.
— William, 3rd son of Wm. L. of Kilsyth, v. 187.
— William, eldest son of Wm. L. of Kilsyth, v. 187.
— — his wife, Marion Forrester, v. 187.
— William, in Inchmahane, v. 188.
— William, 5th son of Sir Wm. L. of Callendar and Kilsyth, v. 424, 425 *n*.

Livingston(e, William, captain of Kirkwall Castle, v. 435; ix. 129.
—— —— his wife, Margaret Strang, ix. 129.
—— William, son of Henry L. in Falkirk, v. 437.
—— William, brother of Alex. L. of Dunipace, vi. 447, 448.
—— William, captain, eldest son of Wm. L. of Jerviswood, viii. 373.
—— *, wife of Walter Macfarlane of that Ilk, v. 432 *n*.
—— *, wife of Archibald Seton, viii. 577 *n*.
Llanover, Benjamin (Hall), lord, iv. 423.
Llewellyn, prince of North Wales, iii. 5; iv. 9; v. 578.
Lloyd of Aston Hall, Richard Thomas, col., v. 237.
—— —— his wife, Frances Hay, v. 237.
—— of Hindlesham, Sir Richard, iv. 388.
—— Gresham, iv. 324; vii. 306.
—— —— his wife, Mary Holt, vii. 306.
—— John Horatio, Q.C., vi. 437.
—— Louisa Mary, wife of Wm. Napier, vi. 437.
—— Lucy, wife of capt. James Hamilton, iv. 388.
—— Mary, wife of (1) John, 10th earl of Rothes, and (2) Bennet Langton, iv. 324; vii. 306.
—— Morgan, iii. 550.
Lluyd, *, 1703, vii. 446.
Loccard, *see* Lockhart.
Lochaber, Alexander of the Isles, lord of, vi. 302.
LOCHABER, GORDON, LORD, iv. 549-558.
Lochaber, George, first lord, iv. 549.
LOCHINVAR, GORDON, LORD OF, v. 98-135.
Lochinvar, John, first lord of, v. 119.
Lochlan, eldest son of Uchtred of Galloway, iv. 137.
LOCHMABEN, MURRAY, LORD MURRAY OF, i. 228.
Lochore, Constantine of, iii. 304.
—— Sir David de, viii. 478 *bis*.
—— *, wife of Sir Michael Wemyss of Wemyss, viii. 478, 479.
—— Hugh of, sheriff of Fife, iii. 304.
LOCHOW, CAMPBELL, VISCOUNT OF, i. 369-393.
Lochow, Archibald, first viscount of, i. 369.
—— Dougall de, dean of Argyll, i. 329.
Locker, Edward Hawke, F.R.S., commissioner of Greenwich Hospital, iii. 494.
—— Frederick, iii. 494.
—— —— his wife, Charlotte Christian Bruce, iii. 494.
LOCKERBIE, DOUGLAS, LORD DOUGLAS OF, vii. 143-144.
Lockerbie, Charles, lord Douglas of, vii. 143.
Lockhart of Abbotsford, Charlotte, wife of James Robert Hope, iv. 422.

* Name unknown.

Lockhart of Cambusnethan, viii. 29.
—— of Carnwath, Sir George, lord president, i. 364; ii. 414; iv. 592; v. 628.
—— —— George, i. 103; viii. 554.
—— —— his wife, Euphemia Montgomerie, i. 104; iii. 457.
—— —— George, i. 104.
—— —— his wife, Fergusia Wishart, i. 104.
—— of Carstairs, Sir James, vii. 261.
—— —— his wife, Grizel Ross, vii. 261.
—— —— Sir William, iv. 588.
—— —— his wife, Mary Carmichael, iv. 588.
—— —— Sir William, vii. 137.
—— —— his wife, Isabel Douglas, vii. 137.
—— of Castlehill, viii. 29.
—— —— James, the younger, iv. 592.
—— —— his wife, Barbara Lockhart, iv. 592.
—— of Cleghorn, Allan, iv. 581; vii. 254.
—— —— his wife, Elizabeth Ross, vii. 254.
—— —— Quintigern *or* Mungo, vii. 254.
—— —— Sir Stephen, iv. 31, 403.
—— of Covington and Craighouse, Alexander, senator of the College of Justice, lord Covington, iii. 581; v. 180.
—— of Kirktown, Walter, ii. 367.
—— —— his wife, Veronica Erskine, ii. 367.
—— of Lee, viii. 8.
—— —— Sir Alan, v. 494.
—— —— his wife, Margaret Campbell, v. 494.
—— —— Alan, viii. 371.
—— —— his wife, Janet Baird, viii. 371.
—— —— Sir James, son of Sir Mungo L., vi. 357; viii. 371.
—— —— James, viii. 25.
—— —— Sir James, lord Justice-Clerk, lord Lee, i. 89; iv. 588.
—— —— Richard, vii. 477.
—— —— his wife, Jean Houstoun, vii. 477.
—— —— Simon, vi. 211.
—— —— Sir William, colonel, ii. 413; iii. 326; iv. 78; vi. 66.
—— of Stevenston, Adam, iv. 224; v. 489.
—— —— Margaret, iv. 224; v. 489.
—— of Tarbrax, George, i. 89.
—— —— William, i. 89.
—— of Wicketshaw, Hugh Robert, iv. 583.
—— —— his wife, Katharine Carmichael, iv. 583.
—— —— Stephen, iv. 583.
—— —— his wife, Grizel Carmichael, iv. 583.
—— Allan, son of Sir Stephen L. of Cleghorn, viii. 15.
—— —— his 2nd wife, Marion Somerville, viii. 15.
—— Anna, wife of 1st earl of Aberdeen, i. 89.
—— Anne, wife of C. Boyd, v. 180.
—— Anne, wife of Sir John Wemyss of Bogie, viii. 496.
—— Barbara, wife of (1) James Lockhart, and (2) Daniel Carmichael, iv. 592

Lockhart, Clementina, wife of John Gordon of Glentanner, i. 104 ; ix. 6.
— Elizabeth, wife of Andrew Murray of Blackbarony, iii. 503.
— Euphame, wife of (1) John, 6th earl of Wigtown, and (2) major-gen. P. MacElligot, viii. 554.
— Gavin, burgess of Lanark, viii. 372.
— — his wife, Bessie Wilkie, viii. 372.
— Grace, wife of (1) John, 3rd earl of Aboyne, and (2) James, 8th earl of Moray, i. 103; vi. 325 ; ix. 6.
— James, iv. 581.
— — his wife, Jean Carmichael, iv. 581.
— John, 1440, vi. 475.
— John, v. 496.
— — his wife, Mariota Nisbet, v. 496.
— John Gibson, iv. 422.
— Marion, wife of Robert Cunningham of Cunninghamhead, iv. 231.
— Rebecca, wife of 15th earl of Erroll, iii. 581.
— Robina, wife of 1st earl of Forfar, iv. 78.
— William, burgess of Edinburgh, iii. 503.
— Sir William, advocate, viii. 496.
— *, wife of Jas. Livingston of Jerviswood, viii. 371.
Lockwood of Dew's Hall, Edward, viii. 230.
— Anne Jane Charlotte, wife of 1st baron Napier and Ettrick, vi. 437.
— Frances Dorothy, wife of C. Drummond, viii. 230.
— Robert Manners, vi. 438.
Loder of Whittlebury, Sir Robert, 1st bart., M.P., iv. 171.
— Adela Maria, wife of (1) major-gen. Alex. Stewart, and (2) col. Basil Lloyd-Anstruther, iv. 171.
Lodge, John, ii. 523.
— — his wife, Frederica Cathcart, ii. 523.
Loen, Sir Bartholomew de, i. 149.
— — his wife, Philippa Mowbray of Barnbougle, i. 149.
— David de, i. 149; vi. 140.
— — his wife, Janet Stewart, i. 149.
Loftus of Rathfarnham, Sir Adam, v. 175.
— Henry, 5th son of 2nd marquess of Ely, vii. 489.
— — his wife, Louisa Emma Maunsell, vii. 489.
— Mary, wife of Thos. Boyd, v. 175.
Logan of Coatfield and Greenlaw, Andrew, vii. 215.
— of Fastcastle, Robert, iv. 462.
— of Logan, Mr. Allan, minister of Torryburn and Culross, ii. 574.
— — his wife, Mary Colvill, ii. 574.
— of Raiss, John, vii. 554.
— — his wife, Grissel Sempill, vii. 554.
— of Restalrig, Sir Robert, i. 16 *n.*
— — his wife, Katharine Stewart, i. 16 *n.*

* Name unknown.

Logan of Restalrig, Sir Robert, viii. 9.
— — his wife, Giles Somerville, viii. 9.
— — Sir Robert, iv. 451.
— — his wife, Elizabeth Home, iv. 451.
— — Robert, iv. 283 ; viii. 582, 583.
— — his 1st wife, Margaret Seton, viii. 583.
— — his 2nd wife, Agnes Gray, iv. 283, 462.
— — Robert, ii. 486 ; iv. 462 *bis*.
— — his wife, Elizabeth M'Gill, ii. 486.
— Alison, wife of David Primrose, vii. 215.
— Isobel, wife of Wm. Lindsay of Pyotstoun, v. 411.
— Margaret, wife of R. Colville of Hiltoun, ii. 544, 547.
Logie of Ennis, Barbara, wife of bishop Alexander Gordon, iv. 533.
— of Glenalmond, Sir Malise de, vi. 531.
— of Logie, Herman de, iii. 305.
— — John, vii. 33.
— — his wife, Margaret Drummond, i. 9 ; vii. 32.
— — John, their son, ii. 445 ; iii. 267 *n.* ; vii. 33 ; viii. 420.
— — Sir Malise de, i. 451.
— of Logiealmond, John, v. 152.
— — his wife, Euphemia Boyd, v. 152.
— — Margaret, wife of (1) Thomas Hay, and (2) Robert Murray, iii. 566, 568 ; v. 152.
— of Strathgartney, Sir John, v. 579, 593.
— John, v. 611 *n.*
— — his wife, Jonet Abernethy, v. 611.
— Robert, 1325, vi. 137.
Lombe, Mary Turner, wife of 7th earl of Lauderdale, v. 317.
— Sir Thomas, alderman of London, v. 317.
London, John of, son of Nes, i. 450.
— Robert of, illeg. son of king William the Lion, i. 5.
— *or* Lundin, Malcolm de, i. 11.
— Thomas de, i. 11, 418, 421 *n.*
Londonderry, Thomas (Ridgway), 1st earl of, v. 83.
— William Vane (Stewart), 3rd marquess of, vii. 358.
Long of Preshaw, Walter, vi. 506.
— — his wife, Mary Carnegie, vi. 506.
— George, Clerkenwell, i. 402.
— — his wife, Margaret Aston, i. 402.
— Samuel, London, v. 318.
— — his wife, Jane Maitland, v. 318.
Longavile, William (Douglas), earl of, iii. 172.
Longuemare, Lucie Marie de, wife of Léon Maurice Drummond, vi. 71.
Longueville, Louis of Orleans, duke of, i. 23.
— — his wife, Marie de Lorraine, i. 23.
— Archibald (Douglas), earl of, iii. 168 ; viii. 7.
Loraine, de, *see* Deloraine, iii. 112.

Lorens of Keith-Hundeby, Eda, wife of Philip de Keith, vi. 28; vii. 418.
—— Hugh, vi. 28; vii. 418.
—— —— his wife, Eda Fraser of Keith-Hundeby, vi. 28.
Lonsdale, Hugh Cecil (Lowther), 5th earl of, iv. 561.
—— —— his wife, Grace Cicelie Gordon, iv. 561.
Lorn, Dugall of, 2nd son of Somerled, v. 30.
—— Duncan of, son of Dugall, v. 30.
—— Eugene of, v. 2.
—— Ewen of, v. 30, 33.
—— Isobel of, wife of Sir John Stewart of Innermeath, v. 2.
—— Janet of, wife of Robert Stewart of Rosyth, v. 1.
—— John of, son of Duncan, v. 30.
—— John of, v. 1, 2.
—— —— his wife, Joanna de Isak, i. 8; v. 2.
—— Juliana of, wife of Alexander, lord of the Isles, v. 30, 35.
—— Sir Patrick of, 1402, i. 330.
—— * of, wife of the king of Norway, v. 30.
—— James Stewart, the Black Knight of, i. 440; v. 2.
—— John Stewart, lord of, v. 2.
—— —— his wife, Isobel of Lorn, v. 2.
—— John Stewart, lord of, i. 332; ii. 176, 177; v. 3.
—— Robert Stewart, lord of, v. 1.
—— —— his wife, Janet of Lorn, v. 1.
—— Robert Stewart, lord of, v. 3.
—— —— his wife, Margaret *or* Johanna Stewart, i. 149; v. 3.
—— Walter Stewart, lord of, i. 133; ii. 177; v. 4.
—— Colin Campbell, lord of, i. 333; v. 4.
—— —— his wife, Isabel *or* Elizabeth Stewart of Lorn, i. 332; v. 3.
LORNE, CAMPBELL, LORD, i. 353-393.
Lorne, Archibald, first lord, i. 353.
—— Archibald, elder son of marquess of Argyll; styled lord, i. 361.
—— —— his 1st wife, Mary Stewart, i. 366.
LORNE, CAMPBELL, MARQUESS OF, i. 369-393.
Lorne, Archibald, first marquess of, i. 369.
—— John George Edward Henry Douglas Sutherland, styled marquess of, i. 392.
—— —— his wife, H.R.H. princess Louise of Great Britain and Ireland, i. 393.
Lorraine of Homylknoll, Patrick, vii. 369.
—— —— Robert, vii. 369.
Lothian, Gospatrick, 3rd earl of Dunbar, styled earl of, iii. 250.
—— Patrick, 5th earl of Dunbar, styled earl of, iii. 252.
LOTHIAN, KER, EARL OF, v. 456-487.
Lothian, Mark, first earl of, v. 456.
—— —— his wife, Margaret Maxwell, iv. 412; v. 456.

* Name unknown.

Lothian, Robert, second earl of, v. 80, 458.
—— —— his wife, Annabella Campbell, i. 349; v. 459, 460 *bis*; ix. 21.
—— Robert, fourth earl of, v. 475; viii. 299.
—— William, third earl of, v. 76, 77, 460, 467, 468.
—— —— his wife, Anne Ker, v. 459, 460, 466, 469.
LOTHIAN, KER, MARQUESS OF, v. 452-487.
Lothian, John William Robert, seventh marquess of, v. 485.
—— —— his wife, Cecil Chetwynd, v. 485.
—— Robert, first marquess of, v. 473, 475.
—— —— his wife, Jean Campbell, i. 361; v. 477.
—— Robert Schomberg, tenth marquess of, v. 487.
—— Schomberg Henry, ninth marquess of, v. 486.
—— —— his wife, Victoria Alexandrina Montagu-Douglas-Scott, ii. 247; v. 486.
—— William, second marquess of, v. 478.
—— —— his wife, Jean Campbell, i. 368; v. 479.
—— William, third marquess of, v. 480.
—— —— his 1st wife, Margaret Nicolson, v. 480; ix. 119.
—— —— his 2nd wife, Jean Janet Ker, v. 480.
—— William, sixth marquess of, v. 483.
—— —— his 1st wife, Henrietta Hobart, v. 483.
—— —— his 2nd wife, Harriet Montagu Scott, ii. 244; v. 483.
—— William Henry, fourth marquess of, v. 480.
—— —— his wife, Caroline D'Arcy, v. 481.
—— William John, fifth marquess of, v. 481.
—— —— his wife, Elizabeth Fortescue, v. 482.
—— William Schomberg Henry, eighth marquess of, v. 485.
—— —— his wife, Constance Harriet Mahonesa Chetwynd, v. 485.
Lott, S. Jordan, in holy orders, iii. 391.
—— —— his wife, Louisa Mitty Abraham, iii. 391.
LOUDOUN, CAMPBELL, LORD CAMPBELL OF, v. 498-506.
Loudoun, Hugh, first lord, v. 498; ix. 81.
—— —— his 1st wife, Margaret Gordon, v. 111, 498.
—— —— his 2nd wife, Elizabeth Ruthven, iv. 266; v. 114, 498.
—— —— his 3rd wife, Margaret Home, v. 498.
—— John, second lord, v. 506.
—— —— his wife, Margaret, baroness of Loudoun, v. 499, 506.
—— Margaret, wife of Sir John Campbell of Lawers; baroness of, v. 499, 506.
LOUDOUN, CAMPBELL, EARL OF, v. 488-517.

Loudoun, Flora Mure, wife of Francis (Rawdon Hastings), 1st marquess of Hastings; countess of, ii. 310; v. 511.
— Hugh, third earl of, v. 508.
— — his wife, Margaret Dalrymple, v. 509; viii. 151.
— James, second earl of, v. 507; viii. 69.
— — his wife, Margaret Montgomerie, iii. 452; v. 507.
— James Mure, fifth earl of, iv. 205; v. 511; viii. 463.
— — his wife, Flora Macleod, v. 511.
— John, first earl of, v. 506.
— — his wife, Margaret Campbell, v. 499, 506.
— John, fourth earl of, v. 509.
LOUDOUN, RAWDON-HASTINGS, EARL OF, v. 512-515.
Loudoun, George Augustus Francis, seventh earl of, v. 513.
— — his wife, Barbara (Yelverton), baroness Grey de Ruthyn, v. 514.
— Henry Weysford Charles Plantagenet, ninth earl of, v. 514.
— — his wife, Florence Cecilia Paget, v. 515.
— Paulyn Reginald Serlo, eighth earl of, v. 514.
LOUDOUN, ABNEY-HASTINOS, EARL OF, v. 515-517.
Loudoun, Charles Edward Hastings, tenth earl of, v. 516.
— — his wife, Alice Mary Elizabeth Fitzalan Howard, v. 516.
— Edith Maud, wife of Charles Frederick Clifton; countess of, v. 515.
LOUDOUN, RAWDON-HASTINOS, VISCOUNT, v. 512-515.
Loudoun, Francis, first viscount, v. 512.
— master of, George, son of 1st lord Campbell of Loudoun, v. 498.
— — his wife, Jean Fleming, v. 499; viii. 548.
Loudoun, Gideon Ernest, field-marshal in Imperial Army, baron, v. 497 *n.*
— James de, son of Lambin, iv. 223; v. 488.
— Margaret de, wife of Sir Reginald Crauford, v. 488.
— Matthew, Livonia, v. 497 *n.*
Louis XI., king of France, i. 19.
— — his wife, Margaret of Scotland, i. 19.
Louise Caroline Alberta, princess of Great Britain, wife of 9th duke of Argyll, i. 393.
Lounde, John, Naburn, iii. 292.
— — his wife, Anne Constable, iii. 292.
LOUR, CARNEGIE, LORD, vi. 494-495.
Lour, David, eldest son of 1st earl of Northesk; styled lord, iii. 325; vi. 495.
— John, lord, vi. 494.
Lourestoun, John, in Gorgie, vi. 413.
— — his wife, Marion Napier, vi. 413.
Lovaine, Eleanor de, wife of (1) Wm. de Ferrers, (2) Sir Wm. Douglas, and (3) Sir Wm. Bagot of the Hyde, iii. 139, 140, 147; ix. 67.
LOVAT, FRASER, LORD FRASER OF, v. 518-548.
Lovat, Amelia, wife of Alexander Mackenzie of Prestonhall; baroness Fraser of, v. 536, 538.
— Alexander, fourth lord Fraser of, v. 527.
— — his wife, Janet Campbell, v. 527.
— Archibald Campbell, *de jure* thirteenth lord Fraser of, v. 541.
— — his wife, Jane Fraser, v. 542.
— Hugh, first lord Fraser of, v. 523; vii. 433.
— — his wife, Violetta Lyon, v. 523; viii. 276.
— Hugh, third lord Fraser of, v. 526, 530.
— — his 1st wife, Anna Grant, v. 526; vii. 458.
— — his 2nd wife, Janet Ross, v. 526.
— Hugh, fifth lord Fraser of, v. 528.
— — his wife, Elizabeth Stuart, i. 3[illegible], 445; v. 628, 529.
— Hugh, seventh lord Fraser of, v. 532.
— — his wife, Isabel Wemyss, v. 532; viii. 499.
— Hugh, eighth lord Fraser of, v. 534.
— — his wife, Anna Mackenzie, iii. 73; v. 534.
— Hugh, ninth lord Fraser of, iii. 384; v. 534, 537.
— — his wife, Amelia Murray, i. 478; v. 534.
— Hugh, son of Amelia, baroness Fraser of Lovat; self-styled lord Fraser of, iii. 72; v. 536.
— — his wife, Amelia Fothringham, v. 536.
— Simon, sixth lord Fraser of, v. 529; vii. 439, 441.
— — his 1st wife, Katharine Mackenzie, v. 530; vii. 502.
— — his 2nd wife, Jean Stewart, iii. 189; v. 530.
— — his 3rd wife, Katharine Rose, v. 530.
— Simon, eleventh lord Fraser of, iii. 78; v. 534, 535, 537, 545; vii. 141, 446.
— — his 1st wife, Margaret Grant, v. 539; vii. 479.
— — his 2nd wife, Primrose Campbell, i. 382; v. 540.
— Simon, *de jure* twelfth lord Fraser of, v. 540.
— — his wife, Katharine Bristowe, v. 541.
— Simon, thirteenth lord Fraser of, v. 542, 547.
— — his wife, Alice Mary Blundell, v. 547.

Lovat, Simon Joseph, fourteenth lord Fraser of, v. 548.
— Thomas, second lord Fraser of, v. 524.
— — his 1st wife, Janet Gordon, v. 525.
— — his 2nd wife, Janet Gray, iv. 275; v. 525.
— Thomas, tenth lord Fraser of, v. 536.
— — his wife, Sybilla Macleod, v. 536.
— Thomas Alexander, twelfth Lord Fraser of, v. 546.
— — his wife, Charlotte Georgina Dorothea Jerningham, v. 546.
— master of, Alexander, 3rd son of 7th lord Fraser of Lovat, v. 533.
— — his wife, Sybilla Mackenzie, v. 533.
— master of, Hugh, 2nd son of 7th lord Fraser of Lovat, v. 532.
— — his wife, Anna Leslie, v. 378, 532.
— master of, Simon, eldest son of 3rd lord Fraser of Lovat, v. 527.
— master of, Simon, eldest son of 7th lord Fraser of Lovat, v. 532.
— master of, Simon, eldest son of Simon, 11th lord Fraser of Lovat, v. 510, 539.
LOVAT OF LOVAT, FRASER, BARON, v. 546-548.
Lovat of Lovat, Thomas Alexander, first baron, v. 546.
Lovell of Ballumbie, Sir Richard, iii. 192, 316; vi. 366.
— — his wife, Elizabeth Douglas, vi. 366.
— of Giffen, James, vi. 534 *n.*
— of Hazelhead, James, vi. 534 *n.*
— of Muirhouse, Richard, vi. 366.
— Janet, wife of Robert Graham of Strathcarron and Fintry, iii. 316; vi. 218.
— John, iv. 299.
— — his wife, Jane Ramsay, iv. 299.
— Robert, ii. 373.
— — his wife, Eva de Carlyle, ii. 373.
Lowe of Oxton Hall, Henry Porter, vii. 567.
Lowen, Dells Honoria, wife of William Hore, vii. 391.
— Sir Pierce, lieut.-colonel, vii. 391.
Lowis, Ninian, merchant, Edinburgh, iv. 486.
— — his wife, Elizabeth Hope, iv. 486.
Lowry, James, burgess, Edinburgh, i. 539.
Lowther, Henry, major Indian army, v. 95.
— — his wife, Evelyn Mary Elise Erskine, v. 95.
Loyd-Lindsay, Sir Robert, V.C., K.C.B., i. 524.
— — his wife, Harriet Loyd-Jones, i. 524.
Luc, John de, iv. 107.
Lucan, George (Bingham), 4th earl of, v. 369.
— — his wife, Cecilia Catherine Gordon-Lennox, i. 73; v. 369.
— Richard (Bingham), 2nd earl of, viii. 516.
Lucas of Crudwell, Anne Florence, wife of 6th earl Cowper; baroness, iii. 124.
Lucas of Crudwell, Auberon Thomas, baron, iii. 125.
— — Francis Thomas de Gray, baron, iii. 124.
— — Jemima, wife of 2nd earl of Hardwicke; baroness, ii. 208; vi. 23.
— of Shenfield, Charles (Lucas), 2nd baron, iii. 610.
— — his wife, [Penelope] Leeke, iii. 614.
— Ann, wife of (1) Edward Cary, and (2) Archibald Hamilton, iii. 610, 613, 614; ix. 88.
Lucy of Charlecote, Sir Thomas, i. 406.
— of Drumsargard, Sir Anthony de, viii. 256.
— Anne, wife of Sir Edward Aston, i. 406.
Lude, Marjory, wife of * Grant, vii. 455.
Ludlow, Christopher, Chipping-Sudbury, ii. 193.
— — his wife, Eliza Maria Blanchard, ii. 193.
Ludovic, eldest son of Thorfinn Skull-splitter, ii. 314.
Luffness, William de Lindsay, baron of, iii. 3.
LUGTOUN, LESLIE, VISCOUNT OF, vii. 301.
Lugtoun, John, viscount of, vii. 301.
Lumb of Wallington Lodge, Edward, vi. 438.
— Harriet Blake Armstrong, wife of 2nd baron Napier and Ettrick, vi. 438.
Lumley, Henrietta Susan Beresford, wife of Edmund L'Estrange, iii. 587.
Lumsdain, Sir James, ii. 366.
— Magdalen, wife of Wm. Erskine of Torry, ii. 366.
Lumsden of Auchrady, Robert, i. 156.
— of Balmedie, W. J., i. 316.
— — his wife, Margaret Arbuthnott, i. 316.
— of Clova, John, iii. 591 *bis.*
— of Innergelly, Sir John, iii. 486.
— — his wife, Margaret Bruce, iii. 486.
— of Tulliearn, Matthew, iv. 55.
— — his wife, Annabella Forbes, iv. 55.
— Andrew, secretary to prince Charles Edward, i. 550.
— Andrew, bishop of Edinburgh, v. 130.
— Beatrice, wife of James King of Barra, iii. 591.
— Isobel, wife of Sir Jas. Sinclair, ii. 199.
— Jean, wife of Jas. Skene of Wester Corse and Northam, iv. 110.
— John, eldest son of the bishop of Edinburgh, v. 130.
— — his wife, Mary Dalzell, iii. 410; v. 130.
— William, writer, i. 550.
— — his wife, Mary Bruce, i 550.
Lundie, Lundin, Lundy of Balgonie, David, vi. 546.
— — his wife, Lilias Oliphant vi. 546.

* Name unknown.

Lundie, Lundin, Lundy of Balgonie, John, viii. 495.
—— Sir Robert, lord High Treasurer, v. 395, 397; vi. 84.
—— Robert, iii. 321; v. 400.
—— his wife, Jane Lindsay, v. 400.
— of Benholm, Elizabeth, wife of lord Altrie, i. 159; ix. 10.
—— Robert, i. 159, 284; vi. 44.
—— William, viii. 56.
—— his wife, Helen Carnegie, viii. 56.
— of Easter Conland, John, viii. 495.
—— his wife, Janet Wemyss, viii. 495.
— of Wester Denhead, George, iii. 322.
—— his wife, Helen Graham, iii. 322.
— of Feddinch, Euphemia, wife of William Melville of Raith, vi. 84, 85, 86.
— of Gorthie, viii. 190.
— of Inchmeddan, William, viii. 56.
— of Lundin, James, v. 401.
—— his wife, Catherine Lindsay, v. 401.
—— Sir James, iv. 102.
—— his 1st wife, Christian Ruthven, iv. 102.
—— James, 2nd son of John Drummond, 1st earl of Melfort, vi. 68.
—— James, vii. 57.
—— his wife, Rachel Bruce, vii. 57.
—— John, iv. 54; v. 394, 395; vii. 275.
—— his 1st wife, Isobel Wemyss, v. 395.
—— Sir John, keeper of Stirling Castle, v. 394, 395; vii. 44; viii. 487.
—— his contr. wife, Elizabeth Lindsay, v. 394.
—— his wife [Isabella Forrester], vii. 44.
—— John, the younger, ii. 145.
—— his wife, Elizabeth Hepburne, ii. 145.
—— John, i. 469.
—— John, last laird, v. 302.
—— John, son of Robert Maitland and Margaret L., v. 303.
—— Malcolm, i. 11; v. 572.
—— his alleged wife, * of Mar, v. 572.
—— Margaret, wife of Robert Maitland, v. 302.
—— Robert, 2nd son of 1st earl of Lauderdale, v. 302.
—— his wife, Margaret Lundin, v. 303.
—— Robert, vii. 57.
—— his wife, Anne Inglis, vii. 57.
—— Sophia, wife of John Drummond, v. 303; vi. 67, 68.
—— Thomas, 'Ostiarius,' i. 11, 418, 421 *n.*; v. 572.
—— his wife, Christina *or* Margaret of Athell, i. 418.
—— Walter of, iv. 269; vi. 170.
—— Walter, ii. 145; v. 62, 397; vi. 102.
—— his wife, Elizabeth Lindsay, v. 397.

* Name unknown.

Lundie of Lundin, William, ii. 148; iv. 102.
—— his wife, Elizabeth Hepburne, ii. 148.
—— William, i. 542; iv. 261; ix. 32.
—— his 1st wife, Christian Ruthven, iv. 261.
—— William, iv. 105.
—— his wife, Elspeth Ruthven, iv. 105.
— of Newhall, Robert, i. 539.
— of Pitlochy, Andrew, v. 395.
— of Pratis, Sir Thomas, vi. 541; ix. 68.
—— his wife, Christian Sutherland of Duffus, iii. 193; vi. 541; ix. 68.
— of Tullo, William, viii. 56.
— Agnes, wife of Sir Wm. Graham of Claverhouse, iii. 321.
— Andrew, younger son of Walter L. of that Ilk, v. 62.
—— his wife, Elizabeth Ker, v. 62.
— Anna, wife of Jas. Carnegie of Finavon, v. 303; vi. 498.
— Christian, wife of 6th lord Forbes, iv. 53.
— Sir Colin de, i. 418.
— David, v. 397.
—— his wife, Elizabeth Lundie, v. 397.
— David, brother of L. of Gorthy, viii. 190.
— Elizabeth, wife of (1) Sir John Lindsay of Pitcruvie, and (2) D. Lundie, v. 396, 397.
— Euphemia, wife of Sir D. Wemyss of Wemyss, viii. 486.
— Isobel, wife of (1) David, 8th earl of Crawford, and (2) George, 4th earl of Rothes, iii. 27; vii. 285.
— Isobel, wife of Norman Lindsay of Kilquhis, v. 402.
— Isobel, wife of John Melville of Raith, vi. 102.
— Magdalene, wife of principal George Wemyss, viii. 495.
— Margaret, wife of 1st lord Balfour of Burleigh, i. 542; ix. 32.
— Margaret, wife of P. Lindsay of Wolmerston, v. 413.
— Margaret, wife of George Leslie of Fythkill and Rothes, vii. 275.
— Marion, wife of (1) Alex. Keith of Pittendrum, and (2) Robt. Arbuthnott, i. 284; vi. 44.
Lundy, Campbell, lord, v. 24-26.
Lundy, James, 2nd son of 7th earl of Argyll; lord, i. 350; v. 24.
Lushington of Rosière, Frederick Astell, Bengal C.S., iii. 585.
— Sir Henry, 3rd bart., iii. 104.
— Laura, wife of Sir H. Ramsay, iii. 104.
Luss of Auchmar, Duncan de, v. 139.
Lussan, George Drummond, comte de, vi. 72; vii. 60.
— James Drummond, comte de, vi. 71.
— James Louis Drummond, comte de, vi. 72.

Lussan, Jean d'Audibert, comte de, vi. 70.
— Marie Louise Susan Edith Grace Drummond, comtesse de, vi. 73; vii. 61.
Luttrell, Francis Fownes, vi. 327.
— Marcia, wife of Douglas Wynne Stuart, vi. 327.
Luvel, Henry, viii. 319 *n.*
— Matilda, wife of (1) Robert Lindsay, and (2) Abraham Crichton, iii. 20; ix. 61.
Luxborough, Robert (Knight), lord, iii. 113.
Lyall, Mr. David, minister of Banchory-Deveniek, Aberdeen and Montrose, ix. 5.
— — his wife, Mary Sandilands, ix. 5.
— Patrick, i. 126.
— — his wife, Margaret Ogilvy, i. 126.
Lycklama a Nyeholt, Ina Petronella, wife of Edward Mackay, vii. 173.
Lyddell of Preston, Sir James, iv. 343.
— Jane, wife of Sir John Hamilton of Fingaltoun, iv. 343.
— Isabell, mistress of Patrick Hepburn, bishop of Moray, ii. 143.
Lyell, David, minister of Careston, i. 314.
— — his wife, Katharine Arbuthnott, i. 314.
LYLE, LYLE, LORD, v. 549-558.
Lyle, Alexander Montgomerie Cunninghame; self-styled lord, v. 557.
— — his wife, Elizabeth Montgomerie of Lainshaw, v. 557.
— James Montgomerie of Lainshaw; self-styled lord, iii. 436; v. 556.
— John, fourth lord, iii. 436; iv. 239; v. 555; vii. 536.
— — his wife, Grizel Beaton, v. 556.
— Robert, first lord, v. 552.
— — his 1st wife, Margaret Gray, iv. 275; v. 553.
— — his 2nd wife, Margaret Wallace, v. 553.
— Robert, second lord, ii. 508; iv. 276; v. 433, 552, 553.
— — his 1st wife, Margaret Seton, v. 554; viii. 578; ix. 132.
— — his 2nd wife, Margaret Houstoun, iv. 277; v. 554.
— Robert, third lord, v. 555.
— — his contr. wife, Elizabeth Douglas, i. 186.
— — his wife, Marion Lindsay, v. 555.
— master of, James, son of 4th lord Lyle, v. 555, 557.
— — his wife, Margaret Cunningham, v. 557.
LYLE, LORD LYLE, v. 549-558.
Lyle of Ardardane, John, v. 553.
— of Auchentorlie, John, v. 556.
— of Boquhan, Sir John, v. 551, 556; ix. 132 *bis*, 133.
— of Castlehill, Sir Robert, v. 553.
— of Cragbate, Alan, v. 552 *bis*.
Lyle of Cragbate, Alexander, v. 552; ix. 132.
— — his wife, Elizabeth Lyle, v. 552 *bis*.
— of Duchal, Sir John de, v. 550.
— — his wife, Margaret de Vaus, v. 551.
— — Sir John, 2nd laird, v. 551.
— — Sir Robert, iv. 49; v. 551.
— — his wife, Elizabeth Stewart, v. 552.
— of Shiels of Kilbride, Robert, v. 555.
— of Kilmacolm, John, v. 556.
— of Kindrocht, Sir Robert, v. 551.
— of Lathhame, Sir John, v. 551.
— of Lundy, Sir John de, v. 550, 581.
— — John, v. 556.
— of Lyle, Sir Robert, v. 552.
— of Newark, Agnes, wife of (1) Alan Cathcart, and (2) John Maxwell of Stanelie, v. 554.
— — Robert, v. 554.
— of Stanypeth, George, v. 552.
— of Strathdee, Sir Robert, v. 551, 581.
— Alexander, 2nd son of Sir John L. of Duchal, v. 551.
— Agnes, wife of (1) Alan, master of Cathcart, and (2) John Maxwell, ii. 510.
— Elizabeth, wife of Alex. Lyle of Cragbate, v. 552 *bis*.
— Elizabeth, wife of John Stewart of Blackhall, v. 553.
— George, eldest son of 2nd lord Lyle, viii. 578; ix. 132.
— George, 3rd son of 2nd lord Lyle, v. 554, 556.
— Jean, wife of Sir Neil Montgomerie of Lainshaw, iii. 436; v. 556; ix. 133.
— John, 4th son of 2nd lord Lyle, v. 554, 555.
— Jonet, wife of 1st lord Ogilvy of Airlie, i. 114.
— Katharine, wife of Archibald Maclachlan of that Ilk, v. 555.
— Margaret, alleged wife of (1) Matthew, 2nd earl of Lennox, and (2) Jas. Stewart of Blackhall, v. 351, 554.
— Mariota, wife of Peter Houstoun, v. 554.
— Nicholas, 5th son of 2nd lord Lyle, v. 554, 555.
— Radulf del, v. 549.
— William, 3rd son of Sir John L. of Duchal, v. 551, 552.
LYNE, DOUGLAS, LORD DOUGLAS OF, vii. 145-147.
Lyne, William, lord Douglas of, vii. 145.
— of Locherworth, David de, viii. 417.
— — Robert de, vi. 198, 199; viii. 417.
— — *, wife of Sir John de Haya, viii. 417.
— of Lyne, *, Ayrshire, iv. 227.
Lynedoch of Balgowan, Thomas (Graham), lord, ii. 523; iv. 497; vi. 219.
LYON, LYON, LORD, viii. 293-317.

* Name unknown.

Lyon, Patrick, first lord, viii. 293.
LYON, LYON, VISCOUNT, viii. 299-317.
Lyon, Patrick, first viscount, viii. 299.
LYON, LORD GLAMIS, viii. 270-317.
LYON, EARL OF KINGHORNE, viii. 293-317.
LYON, LORD LYON, viii. 293-317.
LYON, VISCOUNT LYON, viii. 299-317.
LYON, LORD SIDLAW, viii. 299-317.
LYON, LORD STRADICHTIE, viii. 299-317.
LYON, EARL OF STRATHMORE, viii. 261-317.
LYON, LORD TANNADYCE, viii. 299-317.
Lyon of Auchterhouse, Patrick, M.P., vi. 498; viii. 303, 307.
—— —— his wife, Margaret Carnegie, vi. 498; viii. 303.
—— of Auchtermunny, Alexander, viii. 274, 533.
—— —— his wife, Agnes Crichton, viii. 274.
—— of Auldbar, James, 2nd son of 1st earl of Kinghorne, viii. 294, 297.
—— —— John, vi. 373; viii. 287, 293, 296.
—— —— his wife, Eupham Gledstanes, viii. 287.
—— —— Sir Thomas, tutor of Glamis, vii. 189; viii. 284, 291.
—— —— his 1st wife, Agnes Gray, iv. 283, 463; viii. 287.
—— —— his 2nd wife, Eupham Douglas, vi. 374; viii. 287.
—— of Baky, David, lay rector of Forbes, tutor of Glamis, iii. 24; viii. 276, 277.
—— —— his wife, Elizabeth Lindsay, iii. 24.
—— —— John, viii. 274.
—— —— John, writer, viii. 300.
—— —— Patrick, viii. 300.
—— of Aikers of Baky, John, viii. 296.
—— of Baldukie, Sir Thomas, master of Glamis, viii. 284.
—— of Balgillo, John, viii. 272.
—— of Balmedie, David, v. 524.
—— of Ballinchore, Sir John, viii. 265.
—— of Balmuckatie, George, viii. 276.
—— —— Sir John, viii. 265.
—— of Balnavis, George, v. 524.
—— of Balumbie, Sir Thomas, viii. 284.
—— of Banchory, Alexander, viii. 274.
—— of Bandirran, John, viii. 263.
—— of Belhelvies, Alexander, chantor of Moray, viii. 278.
—— —— Patrick, viii. 300.
—— of Nether Blackhall, Patrick, viii. 300.
—— of Bondington, Sir John, viii. 266.
—— of Brakeless, John, viii. 264.
—— of Wester Braky, David, v. 524.
—— of Brigton, Charles, viii. 295.
—— —— David, viii. 295.
—— —— Frederick, vi. 574; viii. 294.
—— —— John, viii. 295.
—— —— his wife, Cecilia Dunsmure, viii. 295.
—— John, viii. 295.
—— —— his wife, Euphemia Young, viii. 295.
Lyon of Brigton, Patrick, viii. 295.
—— —— his wife, Elizabeth Gray, viii. 295.
—— of Brydestoun, John, viii. 296.
—— of Little Buttergask, John, viii. 274.
—— of Byreflats, John, viii. 296.
—— —— Patrick, viii. 300.
—— of Cambusmichael, Sir John, viii. 265.
—— of Cardani-Berclay, Patrick, viii. 271.
—— of Castle Lyon, Patrick, viii. 300.
—— of Collace, John, viii. 274.
—— of Collanys, Sir John, viii. 265.
—— of Cossins, David, ancestor of the family of, iii. 24; viii. 276.
—— —— his wife, Elizabeth Lindsay, iii. 24.
—— —— David, i. 116.
—— —— his alleged wife, Mary Ogilvy, i. 116.
—— —— John, 2nd laird, viii. 276.
—— —— John, 3rd laird, viii. 276.
—— —— John, v. 500.
—— —— his wife, Margaret Drummond, v. 500.
—— of Courtastonne, Alexander, chantor of Moray, viii. 278.
—— —— Sir John, clerk of the privy seal, viii. 263, 265.
—— —— John, vi. 224; viii. 273, 274.
—— —— his wife, Elizabeth Scrymgeour, viii. 276.
—— of Craichie, John, viii. 296.
—— of Culmalegy, John, viii. 288.
—— of Wester Denoon, Patrick, viii. 293.
—— of Drumgley and Drumgeith, Sir Patrick, viii. 271.
—— of Drumgowan, John, viii. 296.
—— of Drumtochty, Frederick, viii. 294.
—— of Eassie, Patrick, viii. 300.
—— of Haltoun of Eassie, John, i. 116; viii. 276, 288.
—— —— his wife, Marjory Ogilvy, i. 116.
—— of Fofarty, Patrick, viii. 300.
—— of Fordell, Sir John, chamberlain of Scotland, viii. 263.
—— of the Loch of Forfar, Sir John, viii. 266.
—— of Forteviot, John, viii. 264.
—— of Fothros, Patrick, eldest son of Sir John L. of Glamis, viii. 269, 270.
—— —— Patrick, viii. 300.
—— of the Garth, Patrick, viii. 293.
—— of Glamis, Sir John, chamberlain of Scotland, viii. 264, 265.
—— —— his wife, Jean *or* Johanna Stewart, i. 16; viii. 266, 268.
—— —— Sir John, viii. 269.
—— —— his wife, Elizabeth *or* Anna Graham, viii. 260, 270.
—— —— Sir Patrick, viii. 270.
—— —— his wife, Isobel Ogilvy, i. 112; viii. 271.
—— of Westhill of Glamis, David, captain, viii. 300.
—— —— John, viii. 296.

Lyon of Westhill of Glamis, Patrick, viii. 300.
— of Glendowachy, Sir John, viii. 266.
— of Haystoun, Patrick, viii. 300.
— of Hetton House, John, viii. 310.
— — his wife, Anne Price, viii. 310.
— — Thomas, M.P., viii. 309.
— — his wife, Mary Elizabeth Wren, viii. 309.
— of Holms, Patrick, viii. 300.
— of Mains of Huntly, Patrick, viii. 293.
— of Inchkeith, Sir John, viii. 265.
— — Patrick, viii. 300.
— of Inchture, John, viii. 274.
— — Patrick, viii. 300.
— of Inglistoun, Patrick, viii. 295.
— — Frederick, tutor of Kinghorne, viii. 294.
— of Innerarity, Patrick, captain, viii. 308.
— of Johnson Hall, Edward, ii. 497.
— of Kindongwane, Sir John, viii. 265.
— of Kinghorne, Sir John, 1st laird, viii. 266.
— — his wife, Johanna Stewart, i. 16; viii. 266, 268.
— — Sir Patrick, viii. 271.
— of Kinnaird, Patrick, viii. 300.
— of Kinnalty, Patrick, viii. 293.
— of Haltoun of Kinnell, David, v. 524.
— — George, v. 524.
— of Kippocleft, Sir John, viii. 265.
— of Kirktoun of Kinnettles, Patrick, viii. 295.
— of Lenros, John, viii. 296.
— of Letham, David, viii. 270.
— — his wife, Marjory Strachan, viii. 270.
— of Longforgan, Sir John, viii. 264.
— — Patrick, viii. 293.
— of Melgund, Sir Thomas, viii. 284.
— of Muiresk, John, ii. 18.
— — his wife, Margaret Ogilvy, ii. 18.
— of Mylnehill, John, viii. 296.
— of Newton, Patrick, viii. 300.
— of Easter Ogil, John, viii. 288.
— — John, viii. 272.
— — William, ancestor of the family of, viii. 272.
— — William, v. 206.
— — William, last laird, viii. 272.
— of Wester Ogil, Andrew Thomson, viii. 276.
— — David, ancestor of the family of, iii. 24.
— — George, viii. 276.
— of Petedy, Alexander, viii. 274.
— of Pettanys, William, viii. 272.
— of Puresk, John, viii. 274.
— of Redeplowland, David, viii. 270.
— — Sir John, viii. 266.
— of Reidie, Patrick, viii. 300.
— of St. Margaret's Inch, Patrick, viii. 293.
Lyon of Schenevale, Patrick, viii. 269, 270.
— — Patrick, viii. 300.
— of Scrogerfield, Frederick, M.P., viii. 294.
— — his 1st wife, Margaret Ogilvie, viii. 295.
— — his 2nd wife, Jean Stewart, vi. 574; viii. 296.
— — Patrick, viii. 295.
— — his wife, Elizabeth Gray, viii. 295.
— — Sir Thomas, viii. 284.
— of Strathfentoun, John, viii. 274.
— of Tannadice, Sir John, the Chamberlain, viii. 266.
— — John, son of the Treasurer, viii. 293.
— — Patrick, viii. 292, 293.
— — Sir Thomas, the Treasurer, viii. 292.
— of Tentsmuir, Patrick, viii. 300.
— of Thornton, Patrick, viii. 300.
— of Thuriston, Sir John, viii. 266.
— of Tullos, John, viii. 296.
— of Tullynachton, John, viii. 264.
— of Woodhall and Wodoley, Sir John, viii. 266.
— Agnes, wife of (1) Arthur, 5th lord Forbes, and (2) John Ross of Craigy, i. 189; iv. 53; viii. 277.
— Agnes, dau. of John L. of Brigton, viii. 296.
— Agnes, dau. of 6th lord Glamis, ix. 162.
— Alexander, 1392, viii. 266 *n.*
— Anna, dau. of Sir Thomas L. of Auldbar, viii. 287.
— Anna, wife of David Nevay, viii. 296.
— Anne, wife of 10th earl of Erroll, iii. 578; viii. 296.
— Anne, dau. of Thomas L., viii. 310.
— Anne, wife of John Simpson, viii. 310.
— Alice, wife of G. G. Kennedy, ii. 497.
— Cecilia, dau. of John L. of Brigton, viii. 296.
— Charles, 3rd son of 1st earl of Strathmore, viii. 303.
— Charles, viii. 310.
— — his wife, * Gibson, viii. 310.
— Charlotte, wife of rev. H. G. Liddell, viii. 310.
— Christian, wife of 4th earl of Erroll, iii. 567; viii. 277; ix. 162.
— Elizabeth, wife of 1st earl of Aboyne, i. 103; viii. 299.
— Elizabeth, wife of (1) Charles, 2nd earl of Aboyne, (2) Patrick, 3rd lord Kinnaird, and (3) capt. Alex. Grant, i. 103; viii. 303.
— Elizabeth, wife of (1) John, master of Forbes, (2) Thos. Craig of Balnely, (3) John Tulloch, (4) John Abernethy, and (5) A. Forbes of Echt, i. 189; iv. 54; vii. 410; viii. 280; ix. 90.
— Elizabeth, wife of (1) Patrick, 6th lord Gray, and (2) Wm. Ker *or* Kirkaldy of Grange, iv. 285; v. 68; viii. 291.

* Name unknown.

Lyon, Elizabeth, wife of Sir Alex. Erskine of Gogar, v. 84.
— Elizabeth, wife of Alex. Robertson of Strowan, viii. 273.
— Elizabeth, wife of Wm. Forbes, viii. 277.
— Euphan, dau. of John L. of Brigton, viii. 296.
— Frances, wife of rev. T. Thurlow, viii. 310.
— George, slain at Flodden, viii. 276.
— George, 2nd son of 6th lord Glamis, i. 189; viii. 280, 281.
— Grizel, wife of 3rd earl of Airlie, i. 127; viii. 303.
— Helen, wife of 7th lord Blantyre, ii. 88; viii. 305.
— Helen, wife of Wm. Gray of Invereightie, viii. 296.
— James de, canon of Aberdeen, viii. 266 *n.*
— James, illeg. son of Sir Thos. L. of Auldbar, viii. 288.
— James Philip, H.E.I.C.S., viii. 309.
— Jane, dau. of Thomas, 8th earl of Strathmore, viii. 310.
— Jean, wife of (1) Robert Douglas, (2) Archibald, 8th earl of Angus, and (3) Alex. Lindsay, lord Spynie, i. 196; vi. 375; viii. 97, 291.
— Jean, dau. of 1st earl of Kinghorne, viii. 296.
— Janet, wife of (1) Henry Guthrie of Collieston, and (2) Henry Maule of Skryne, vii. 12.
— Janet, wife of Gilbert Hay of Templeton, viii. 277.
— Joan, dau. of 2nd earl of Kinghorne, viii. 299.
— John, son of David L. of Letham, viii. 270.
— John, servitor to 9th lord Glamis, viii. 293.
— John, bailie of Edinburgh, viii. 295.
— — his wife, Margaret Nevay, viii. 295.
— John, 2nd son of John L. of Brigton, viii. 295.
— Jonet, wife of James Serymgeour, iii. 307.
— Joseph, 3rd son of John L. of Brigton, viii. 296.
— Margaret, wife of (1) Gilbert, 4th earl of Cassillis, and (2) John, 1st marquess of Hamilton, ii. 474; iv. 372; viii. 288.
— Margaret, wife of Sir Jas. Stewart of Eday and Tullos, vi. 574; viii. 288.
— Margaret, wife of Jas. Rynd of Broxmouth, viii. 277.
— Margaret, dau. of 6th lord Glamis, viii. 280.
— Michael, nephew of the chamberlain of Scotland, viii. 266.
— Michael, brother of 1st lord Glamis, viii. 270.
Lyon, Mariota, wife of William Ochterlony, viii. 277.
— Mary, wife of (1) Sir R. Scott of Cruikston, and (2) R. Sempill of Beltrees, vi. 430; vii. 549; viii. 287.
— Marie, dau. of 2nd earl of Kinghorne, viii. 298.
— Mary, dau. of 4th earl of Strathmore, viii. 305.
— Mary, wife of Russell Barrington, viii. 310.
— Mary, wife of Thos. Wilkinson, viii. 310.
— Mary, dau. of 8th earl of Strathmore, viii. 310.
— Mary Anne, wife of John Clutterbuck, viii. 310.
— Patrick, v. 500.
— — his wife, Elizabeth Wedderburn, v. 500.
— Patrick, nephew of the chamberlain of Scotland, viii. 266.
— Patrick, 4th son of 1st lord Glamis, viii. 272.
— Patrick, advocate, viii. 295.
— — his wife, Elizabeth Gray, viii. 295.
— Sibilla, dau. of 8th lord Glamis, viii. 291.
— Susan, wife of rev. J. Fellowes, viii. 310.
— Susan, wife of gen. J. Lambton, viii. 310.
— Susanna, wife of David Nairne of Drumkilbo, viii. 296.
— Thomas, chaplain of St John at Baky, viii. 284.
— Thomas, 2nd son of Sir Thomas L. of Auldbar, viii. 287, 293.
— Thomas, son of Thos. L. of Hetton House, viii. 310.
— Violetta, wife of 1st lord Fraser of Lovat, v. 523; viii. 276.
— William, slain at Flodden, viii. 276.
LYON-BOWES, LORD GLAMIS, viii. 312-313.
LYON-BOWES, EARL OF STRATHMORE AND KINGHORNE, viii. 312-313.
Lyon-Bowes of Paul's Walden, Thomas, viii. 312.
— Charlotte, dau. of Thomas George, lord Glamis, viii. 312.
— Frances, wife of Hugh Charles Trevanion, viii. 312.
— Mary Isabella, wife of J. W. Willis, viii. 312.
— Sarah, wife of (1) G. A. Campbell, and (2) major C. P. Ainslie, viii. 312.
Lysons of Hempsted Court, Daniel, in holy orders, viii. 89.
— Charlotte, wife of Sir James Carnegie of Southesk, viii. 89.
Lysurs of Gorton, William, vi. 81.
— Christiana, wife of Thos. Melville of Haddington, vi. 79.

Lysurs, David de, c. 1233-36, iii. 88.
—— Gregory, chaplain, vi. 79.
—— Patrick, rector of Newton, iv. 85.
Lyte, J. W. Maxwell, v. 314.
—— —— his wife, E. J. Craigie, v. 314.
Lytton of Knebworth, Sir Roland, iii. 613.
—— Rebecca, wife of 5th viscount Falkland, iii. 613.
Lyttelton, Charles George (Lyttelton), 5th baron, v. 201.

M., the Countess, wife of William of Greenlaw, iii. 251.
M'Adam of Craigengillan, Frederick, 4th son of 1st earl Cathcart, ii. 526.
—— —— his wife, Jane M'Adam of Craigengillan, ii. 526.
—— —— Quentin, ii. 526.
—— Janet, mistress of Sir R. Gordon of Lochinvar, v. 115.
—— Mary, wife of Richard Maitland, v. 313.
M'Alexander of Crossclays, Robert, vi. 416.
—— —— his wife, Mary Craufurd, vi. 416.
—— Marion, wife of Wm. Stewart, vi. 515.
MacAlister, Alexander 'mor,' 2nd son of Donald, lord of the Isles; ancestor of the family of, v. 33.
—— The Clan, not connected with the Alexander family, viii. 165.
—— of Loup, Glenbarr, Strathaird, and Torrisdale, Ancestor of the family of, v. 33.
—— of Torrisdale, Alexander, iii. 550.
—— Abbot, i. 329.
—— * mistress of Colin 'Ionganlach' Campbell of Lochow, i. 329.
Macallan of Faslane, Walter, v. 341.
M'Alpin, *, viii. 139.
—— —— his wife, Margaret Dalrymple, viii. 139.
M'Anemoir, John, vii. 501.
M'Arthur-Moir of Hillfoot, James, v. 417.
—— Jessie Forrester, wife of E. de S. S. Rudd, v. 417.
Macartney, George (Macartney), earl, ii. 305.
—— —— his wife, Jane Stuart, ii. 305.
M'Athair, Patrick, ix. 42.
Macaulay of Lochbroom, Isabel, wife of Murdoch Mackenzie of Kintail, vii. 496.
—— —— Murdoch, vii. 496.
M'Awlay of Gartmore, Walter, vi. 157.
Macbeth, king of Scots, iii. 240; iv. 1; vi. 282.
—— —— his wife, Gruoch, vi. 282, 283.
M'Brair of Almagill, John, ix. 144.
—— —— his wife, Jean Maxwell, vi. 486; ix. 144.
—— —— Robert, i. 225; iii. 228; ix. 144.
—— —— his wife, Margaret Murray, i. 225.

* Name unknown.

M'Brair, Agnes, wife of Robert Crichton of Ryhill, iii. 228.
—— David, iii. 228.
—— —— his wife, * Crichton, iii. 228.
—— John, chaplain, Dumfries, vii. 118.
M'Burnie, Christian, wife of John Gordon, Keirshill, v. 125 *n*.
MacCairbre, an Irish harper, i. 335.
M'Callum, Duncan, the Foxhunter, ii. 209.
—— —— his wife, Margaret Lillias Campbell, ii. 209.
—— John, claimant to earldom of Breadalbane, ii. 209.
M'Carthy, Charlotte, wife of John, 1st earl Delawarr, i. 387.
MacClellan, *see* Maclellan.
Macclesfield, George (Parker), 4th earl of, iv. 326.
MacCormick, Ann, wife of capt. Kirby Dalrymple, viii. 141.
—— Dorothea, wife of Hew Dalrymple of Nunraw, viii. 141.
—— Joseph, D.D., viii. 141.
—— Samuel, general examiner of excise, viii. 141.
MacCalzean of Cliftonhall, Martha, wife of David Ogilvy, i. 120.
—— —— Patrick, i. 120.
—— —— his wife, Euphemia MacCalzean, i. 120.
M'Can, Elizabeth, wife of maj.-gen. John Hamilton, ix. 3.
—— Glesney, ix. 3.
—— —— his wife, Eleanor Folliard, ix. 3.
M'Corquodale of Phantilands, Archibald, ii. 202.
—— —— Duncan, ii. 202.
—— —— his wife, Margaret Campbell, ii. 202.
M'Coull of Morir, vii. 497.
—— Alan, assassin of John Stewart, lord of Lorn, v. 3.
—— Margaret, wife of Alex. Mackenzie of Kintail, vii. 497.
MacCulloch of Ardwall, John, v. 125, 264, 266.
—— —— his wife, Margaret Coupar, v. 264, 266.
—— of Auchenglour, William, v. 263.
—— of Cardoness, Alexander, ix. 150.
—— —— his wife, Elizabeth M'Clellan, ix. 150.
—— —— Ninian, i. 223.
—— —— his wife, Agnes Murray, i. 223.
—— —— Thomas, v. 110.
—— —— his wife, Katharine Gordon, v. 110; ix. 118.
—— of Drouchtag, David, iii. 278.
—— —— his wife, Alison Dunbar, iii. 278.
—— of Mertoun, Sir Alexander, ix. 157.
—— —— his wife, Marjory Sinclair, ix. 157.

* Name unknown.

MacCulloch of Myretoun, William, v. 263.
— of Piltoun, Sir Hugh, v. 385.
— — his wife, Jean Gibson, v. 385.
— of Whiteside, Marion, wife of (1) * Bell, and (2) Alexander, 5th viscount of Kenmure, v. 125.
— Alexander, Ross-shire, v. 44.
— Ebenezer, merchant, Glasgow, iii. 236.
— Ebenezer, merchant, Edinburgh, iii. 236.
— — his wife, Penelope Macdowall, iii. 236.
— George, iv. 193.
— — his wife, Marie Boyle, iv. 193.
— Katharine, wife of (1) Wm. Houston of Cottreoch, and (2) Andrew, 1st lord Jedburgh, ix. 116.
— Mary Isabel, wife of John Macdowall, iii. 236.
Maccus, son of Undwain, vi. 469.
Maccusville, Hugo de, *probably error for* Moreville, vi. 469 *n.*
M'Dermeit, John, minister at Ayr, iii. 448.
— — his wife, Jean Montgomerie, iii. 448.
M'Donachy of Melness and Hope, Donald, vii. 162.
Macdonald of Sleat, Alexander (Macdonald), 1st baron, v. 45.
— — Godfrey (Macdonald), 3rd baron, iv. 504.
— — his wife, Louise Maria La Coast, ix. 109.
— — Ronald Archibald (Macdonald), 6th baron, v. 45.
MACDONALD, LORD OF THE ISLES, v. 27-48.
MACDONALD, EARL OF ROSS, v. 41-47.
Macdonald of Aberchalder, Alastair 'Mor,' ancestor of the family of, v. 562.
— of Achuilt, Donald, v. 561.
— of Ardnabie, John 'Mor,' ancestor of the family of, v. 562.
— of Ardnamurchan, vii. 507.
— — John, *or* Iain Sprangach, 3rd son of Angus, lord of the Isles; progenitor of the family of, v. 35.
— of Camiscross, Alexander, i. 264.
— — his wife, Jane Johnstone, i. 264.
— — Roderic, i. 264.
— of Benbecula, Angus 'riabhach,' v. 39.
— — Hugh, 3rd son of Alexander, earl of Ross, v. 44.
— of Clanranald, Allan, 2nd chieftain, v. 39.
— — Allan, 14th chieftain, v. 91.
— — his wife, Penelope Erskine, v. 91.
— — Allan Douglas, capt. R.A., 22nd chieftain, v. 39.
— — Ranald, 18th chieftain, ii. 54; vii. 520.
— — his 1st wife, Mary Hamilton, vii. 520.

* Name unknown.

Macdonald of Clanranald, Reginald, 2nd son of John, 7th lord of the Isles; ancestor of the family of, v. 39, 40.
— of Cnocancluith, Marcus, 9th son of John, 7th lord of the Isles, v. 40.
— of Culachie, Alastair 'Mor,' ancestor of the family of, v. 562.
— of Dunyveg and the Glens, Iain Mor Tainisteir, 5th son of John, 7th lord of the Isles, v. 40, 41.
— — his wife, Margery Bisset, v. 40.
— — Sir James, ii. 291, 293.
— of Easter Drakies, Angus, v. 565.
— of Garmoran, Reginald, 2nd son of John, 7th lord of the Isles, v. 39.
— of Glencoe, Alexander, 12th chieftain, v. 37.
— — John 'Fraoch,' ancestor of the family of, v. 37.
— of Glengarry, Æneas Ranald, i. 525.
— — Alastair, v. 560.
— — his wife, Margaret Macdonald of Lochalsh, v. 44, 560.
— — Alexander, vii. 509.
— — his 1st wife, Isabel Fraser, v. 534; ix. 132.
— — his 2nd wife, Mary Mackenzie, vii. 509.
— — Alexander, v. 565.
— — Angus, v. 560.
— — his 1st wife, Janet Maclean, v. 561.
— — his 2nd wife, Margaret Macleod, v. 561.
— — his 3rd wife, Janet *or* Mary Mackenzie, v. 561; vii. 500.
— — Angus, v. 562.
— — his wife, Margaret Macdonald, v. 565.
— — Donald, ancestor of the family of, v. 39, 559.
— — his 1st wife, Laleve M'Iver, v. 559.
— — his 2nd wife, * Fraser, v. 559.
— — Donald M'Angus M'Alastair, v. 529, 561; vii. 464, 501.
— — his 1st wife, Margaret Macdonald, v. 562.
— — his 2nd wife, Katharine Mackintosh, v. 562.
— — Donald, vii. 464.
— — his wife, Helen Grant, vii. 464; ix. 155.
— of Glentilt, Hugh, 8th son of John, 7th lord of the Isles, v. 40.
— of Isla, John 'Mor,' 5th son of John, 7th lord of the Isles, v. 40.
— of Keppoch, Alexander, 'Alastair Carrach,' ancestor of the family of, v. 40; vii. 160.
— — Chichester, 20th chieftain, v. 40.
— of Kingedward, *, son of Donald, lord of the Isles, ii. 265.

* Name unknown.

Macdonald of Kintyre, John 'Mor,' 5th son of John, 7th lord of the Isles, v. 40, 41.
—— of Leek, John 'Og,' ancestor of the family of, v. 562.
—— of the Isles of Lochalsh, Sir Alexander, v. 44, 47, 560.
—— —— Sir Donald, v. 44, 458.
—— of Lochalsh, Lochcarron and Lochbroom, Celestine, sheriff of Inverness, 2nd son of Alexander, 9th lord of the Isles, v. 44.
—— —— his wife, Finvola Maclean, v. 44.
—— —— Margaret, wife of Alastair Macdonald, of Morar and Glengarry, v. 44, 560, 561.
—— of Lundie, Allan, ancestor of the family of, v. 560.
—— of Macdonald, Sir Alexander, iii. 457.
—— of Morar, Alexander, v. 559, 560.
—— —— his wife, Mary Maclean, v. 560.
—— —— Alexander, v. 560.
—— —— his wife, Margaret Macdonald of Lochalsh, v. 44, 560.
—— —— Angus 'riabhach,' v. 39.
—— —— Donald, v. 561.
—— —— his 1st wife, Margaret Macdonald, v. 562.
—— —— his 2nd wife, Katharine Mackintosh, v. 562.
—— —— John, v. 559.
—— —— his wife, * Macleod, v. 559.
—— —— John, v. 560.
—— —— his wife, * Cameron, v. 560.
—— of Moydart, Allan, captain of Clanranald, v. 562.
—— of Sana, Alexander, ii. 296.
—— —— his wife, Anne Stewart, ii. 296.
—— of Scotus, Donald 'Gorm,' ancestor of the family of, v. 562.
—— of Shian, Angus 'Mor,' ancestor of the family of, v. 560.
—— of Skirhough, Hugh, v. 45.
—— of Sleat, Sir Alexander, 7th bart., i. 127.
—— —— his 1st wife, Anne Erskine, i. 127.
—— —— his 2nd wife, Margaret Montgomerie, iii. 457.
—— —— Sir Alexander, 9th bart., v. 45.
—— —— Donald 'Gorm,' v. 528.
—— —— his wife, Janet Campbell, v. 528.
—— —— Donald, 'Gorm Mor,' vii. 503.
—— —— his 2nd wife, Mary Mackenzie, vii. 503.
—— —— Sir Donald, 1st bart., v. 45, 565; vii. 504.
—— —— his wife, Janet Mackenzie, vii. 504.
—— —— Sir Donald, 3rd bart., vi. 379.
—— —— his wife, Margaret Douglas, vi. 379.
—— —— Hugh, 3rd son of Alexander, 9th lord of the Isles, v. 44.
—— —— Sir James, 2nd bart., iii. 71; vii. 169.
—— —— his 1st wife, Margaret Mackenzie, iii. 71.

* Name unknown.

Macdonald of Strome, Alastair, v. 560.
—— —— his wife, Margaret Macdonald *or* Ylis, v. 560.
—— —— Alastair 'Dearg,' eldest son of Donald M. of Glengarry, v. 562.
—— —— his wife, Jean Cameron, v. 562.
—— of Sunart, Dougall, 5th son of Reginald of Clanranald, v. 39.
—— of Torrurdane, Donald, v. 561.
—— of Troternish, Angus 'Og,' master of the Isles, v. 47 *bis*.
—— —— his wife, Margaret Campbell, v. 47.
—— of North Uist, Godfrey, 3rd son of John, 7th lord of the Isles, v. 40, 41.
—— —— Hugh, 3rd son of Alexander, 9th lord of the Isles, v. 45.
—— Alexander, 2nd son of 3rd lord of the Isles, v. 32; viii. 165.
—— Alexander, brother of Sir James M. of Sleat, vii. 169.
—— —— his wife, Ann Mackay, vii. 169.
—— Alexander, legtd. son of 9th lord of the Isles, ix. 115.
—— Angus, 4th son of Alexander, 5th lord of the Isles, v. 35.
—— Angus, son of John of the Isles, v. 39, 341.
—— Angus, 6th son of John, 7th lord of the Isles, v. 40.
—— Angus, bishop of the Isles; 2nd son of Donald, 8th lord of the Isles, v. 42.
—— Angus, legtd. son of John, lord of the Isles, v. 47.
—— —— his wife, Margaret *or* Mary Campbell, i. 335; v. 47.
—— Angus, 3rd son of John M. of Morar, v. 560.
—— Angus, 3rd son of Angus M. of Glengarry, v. 561.
—— Angus, legtd. son of Donald M. of Glengarry, v. 562; vii. 464.
—— Anna, wife of Robert, son of Duncan Maclagmayn, v. 42.
—— Charles, 6th son of Alexander, 5th lord of the Isles, v. 36.
—— Donald 'Balloch,' v. 43, 46.
—— Donald 'Dubh,' son of Angus 'Og' of Troternish, v. 47.
—— Donald, 2nd son of John M. of Morar, v. 560.
—— Donald, 2nd son of Alastair 'Dearg' M. of Strome, v. 562.
—— Donald 'Donn,' vii. 475.
—— Donald, legtd. son of 9th lord of the Isles, ix. 115.
—— Elizabeth, wife of Angus 'Dubh' Mackay of Strathnaver, v. 40; vii. 159, 160.
—— Elizabeth, wife of John Roy Mackenzie of Gairloch, v. 561.
—— Finegella *or* Finevole, wife of (1) D. Campbell, and (2) John Stewart, ii. 293; v. 37.

Macdonald, Godfrey, 5th son of Alexander, 5th lord of the Isles, v. 35.
— Godfrey, 3rd son of Alastair M. of Morar and Glengarry, v. 560.
— Hugh, historian of the lords of the Isles, v. 28.
— Hugh, legtd. son of 9th lord of the Isles, ix. 115.
— Isabella, wife of Sir Rory Macleod of Dunvegan, v. 562.
— James, at siege of Rothesay, ii. 291.
— James, sheriff-substitute of Kincardineshire, i. 143.
— — his wife, Mary Allardice, i. 143.
— Janet, wife of Dingwell of Kildun, v. 44.
— Janet, wife of Malcolm Mackintosh, v. 562.
— Jean, dau. of James, lord of Bute, and wife of Alexander, 4th High Steward, i. 13.
— John, Kintyre, iii. 447.
— — his wife, Elizabeth Stewart, iii. 447.
— John 'Dubh,' eldest son of Alexander, 5th lord of the Isles, v. 35.
— John, eldest son of John, 7th lord of the Isles, v. 39, 340; ix. 18.
— — his wife, Helen Campbell, i. 327; v. 39.
— John 'Dall,' 3rd son of Reginald of Clanranald, v. 39.
— John, son of John 'Dall,' v. 39.
— John, legtd. son of John, 10th lord of the Isles, v. 47.
— John 'Odhar,' v. 560.
— John, 2nd son of Angus M. of Glengarry, v. 561.
— Katharine, wife of John Breadalbane Campbell, ii. 198.
— Katharine, wife of Duncan Grant, v. 562.
— Lilian Janet, wife of (1) Francis, 2nd earl of Cromartie, and (2) R. F. Cazenove, iii. 85.
— Louisa, wife of 5th earl of Hopetoun, iv. 504.
— Margaret, wife of James Montgomerie of Coilsfield, iii. 447.
— Marion, betrothed to Celestine Campbell; wife of Alexander Sutherland, ix. 115.
— Mary, wife of William, 5th earl of Ross, v. 37; vii. 239.
— Mary, wife of Lachlan Maclean of Duart, v. 40.
— Margaret, 2nd wife of Angus Mackay of Strathnaver, v. 40 *n.*; vii. 160.
— Margaret, wife of * Cuthbert of Castlehill, v. 561.
— Margaret, wife of Donald Macdonald of Glengarry, v. 562.
— Margaret, wife of Torquil Macleod, v. 562.
Macdonald, Margaret, wife of Angus, lord Macdonell and Aros, v. 565.
— Margaret, wife of Kenneth Mackenzie of Kintail, vii. 498.
— Mary, wife of Charles Constable-Maxwell, iv. 418.
— Penelope, wife of 7th lord Belhaven, ii. 53.
— Ranald, 4th son of Alastair M. of Morar and Glengarry, v. 560.
— Reginald, 2nd son of Alexander, 5th lord of the Isles, v. 35.
— Roderick, 5th son of Alastair M. of Morar and Glengarry, v. 560.
— Somerled, 3rd son of Alexander, 5th lord of the Isles, v. 35.
— Thomas, iv. 418.
— *, a monk, 3rd son of Donald, 8th lord of the Isles, v. 42.
— *, son of Donald 'Dubh,' v. 47.
— *, 1st wife of John, 8th earl of Sutherland, viii. 334.
MACDONELL AND AROS, MACDONELL, LORD, v. 559-565.
Macdonell and Aros, Angus, lord, v. 562.
— — his wife, Margaret Macdonald, v. 565.
MACDONELL, LORD MACDONELL AND AROS, v. 559-565.
Macdonell of Antrim, Sir James, i. 338.
— — his wife, Agnes Campbell, i. 338.
— of Dunyveg, Alexander, chief of Clan Donnel, i. 338.
— — Iain Mor Tainisteir, v. 40, 41.
— — Sir James, ii. 291, 293.
— Anna, wife of (1) C. B. Lindsay, and (2) H. H. Lindsay, i. 525, 528.
— Rose, wife of George Gordon, viii. 348.
— *see also* Macdonald.
Macdougall of Ardintrive, John, iv. 495.
— of Dunollie, Alexander, ii. 188.
— — his wife, Katharine Campbell, ii. 188.
— — Duncan, ii. 186.
— — John, vii. 497.
— — Sir John, ii. 188.
— of Gallanach, Allan, viii. 461.
— — his wife, Margaret Hay, viii. 461.
— of Lorn, Alexander, v. 35, 36; vii. 496.
— of Macdougall, John, captain, vii. 389.
— — his wife, Anne Ruthven, vii. 389.
— of Makerston, Andrew, ii. 148.
— — his wife, Euphemia Hepburne, ii. 148.
— — Dougal, vii. 529; viii. 424.
— — Dougal, ii. 148; viii. 425.
— — Dougal, vii. 332; ix. 153.
— — Duncan, viii. 426, 428.
— — his wife, Elizabeth Hay, viii. 426.
— — Fergus, iv. 228.
— — his wife, Margaret Cunningham, iv. 228.

* Name unknown.

Macdougall of Makerston, Henry, v. 194.
—— —— Sir William, vii. 75, 79.
—— —— his wife, Margaret Scott, vii. 75.
—— of Raray, Allan, ii. 182.
—— —— his wife, Margaret Campbell, ii. 182.
—— —— John, ii. 181.
—— —— his wife, Margaret Campbell, ii. 181.
—— Alexander, bailie of the Canongate, viii. 605.
—— Andrew, son of Dougal M. of Makerstoun, vii. 332.
—— Anna, wife of Alex. Mackenzie of Kintail, vii. 497.
—— Anne Isabel, wife of Walter Scott of Raeburn, vii. 79.
—— Barbara, wife of 3rd viscount of Kilsyth, v. 194.
—— Dougall, 5th son of Reginald Macdonald of Clanranald; eponymous ancestor of the family of, v. 39.
—— Florence, wife of (1) J. Kennedy, and (2) 4th lord Cathcart, ii. 516.
—— Florentine, wife of John Campbell, ii. 186.
—— Jane Hester, wife of (1) Sir John Hope, and (2) rev. W. Knight, iv. 495.
—— Morna, wife of Kenneth of Kintail, vii. 496.
M'Dowal, M'Dowell, M'Doual of French, Fergus, ii. 468.
—— —— his wife, Janet Kennedy, ii. 468.
—— —— John, son of Wm. M., iii. 278.
—— —— John, iii. 236; viii. 150.
—— —— his wife, Elizabeth Crichton Dalrymple, viii. 150.
—— —— Patrick, iii. 327.
—— —— William, iii. 278.
—— —— his wife, Margaret Dunbar, iii. 278.
—— of New Freuch, John Crichton Stuart, ix. 71.
—— —— his 1st wife, Helen Maria FitzGerald, ix. 71.
—— —— his 2nd wife, Susan Mary Hartigan, ix. 71.
—— of Garthland, Christian, wife of Patrick Dunbar of Kilconquhar, iii. 278.
—— —— John, v. 113.
—— —— his wife, Janet Gordon, v. 113.
—— —— Sir John, v. 76.
—— —— his wife, Margaret Ker, v. 76.
—— —— John, ii. 474.
—— —— Uchtred, ii. 474.
—— —— his wife, Euphemia Dunbar, ii. 474.
—— —— Uchtred, vi. 168.
—— —— his wife, Margaret Stewart, vi. 168.
—— of Lefnoll, Andrew, ix. 144.
—— —— his wife, Janet Stewart, ix. 144.
—— of Linplum, Dugal, viii. 425.
—— of Machermore, Uchtred, v. 106.
—— —— his wife, Elizabeth *or* Isobelle Gordon, v. 106.
—— of Quarterland, John, ii. 450.
M'Dowal of Spotts, Andrew, ix. 117.
—— —— Cuthbert, ix. 117.
—— —— his wife, Annabel Gordon, ix. 117.
—— Sir Dougal, 1306, ii. 433.
—— Dungal, ii. 454.
—— Eleanora, wife of Wm. Macghie of Balmaghie, iii. 237.
—— Fergus, son of Dungal M., ii. 454.
—— Isabel, dau. of Dungal M., ii. 454.
—— Isobel, wife of (1) Jas. Maclellan of Nunton, and (2) John Gordon, v. 260.
—— John, merchant, Glasgow, iii. 236.
—— —— his wife, Mary Isabell Macculloch, iii. 236.
—— Katharine, wife of (1) John Kennedy, master of Cassillis, and (2) James, lord Ochiltree, ii. 474; vi. 518.
—— Penelope, wife of Ebenezer Macculloch, iii. 236.
—— William, H.E.I.C.S., 2nd son of John M. of Freuch, iii. 236.
—— William, prebendary of Peterborough, ix. 71.
—— —— his wife, Euphamia Gauden, ix. 71.
—— William Sutherland, rector of Owsden, ix. 71.
—— *see also* Macdougal.
MACDOWALL-CRICHTON, LORD CRICHTON OF SANQUHAR, iii. 236-238.
MACDOWALL-CRICHTON, EARL OF DUMFRIES, 236-238.
Macduff, alleged thane of Fife, i. 279; iv. 1, 2 *n*.
—— of Reres and Croy, 2nd son of Malcolm, 7th earl of Fife, iv. 9; viii. 248.
McDuff of Cambusurich, Alexander, ii. 191.
—— —— his wife, Helen Campbell, ii. 191.
M'Duine of Lochow, Duncan, i. 318.
MacEane of Ardnamurchan, *, husband of Helen Campbell, ii. 178.
MacElligot, Peter, major-general in Austrian service, viii. 554.
—— —— his wife, Euphame Lockhart, viii. 554.
MacEth of Moray, ii. 316.
—— of Strathnaver, Iye, vii. 158.
—— —— his wife, * de Baltrodi, vii. 158.
Macfarlane, Gilchrist of Arrochar, ancestor of the clan, v. 330.
—— of Gartartan, Andrew, ix. 43.
—— of Macfarlane and Arrochar, Duncan, 1st laird, i. 329.
—— —— his wife, Christian Campbell, i. 329.
—— —— Duncan, 8th laird, vi. 512.
—— —— his 1st wife, Isobel Stewart, vi. 512.
—— —— Sir John, 6th laird, i. 444; iv. 405.
—— —— his 2nd wife, * Herries, iv. 405.
—— —— his 3rd wife, Helen Stewart, i. 444.
—— —— John, 10th laird, ii. 172.
—— —— his 2nd wife, Helen Stewart, ii. 172.
—— —— his 3rd wife, Elspeth Campbell, i. 344; ix. 21.

* Name unknown.

Macfarlane of Macfarlane, John, 14th laird, i. 310.
—— his 2nd wife, Helen Arbuthnott, i. 310.
—— Walter, 4th laird, v. 432 *n.*
—— his wife, * Livingston, v. 432 *n.*
—— Walter, the antiquary, i. 310; v. 89.
—— his wife, Elizabeth Erskine, ii. 563; v. 89.
— Christine, wife of Wm. Graham of Duchray, vi. 148.
— John, 2nd son of Andrew M. of Gartartan, ii. 190; ix. 43.
—— his wife, Helen Campbell, ii. 190.
— John, vi. 161.
—— his wife, Elizabeth Graham, vi. 161.
— *, capt., Callander, ii. 193.
MacFirbis, alleged ancestor of the family of Forbes, iv. 42.
M'Gauchen, Mary, wife of Aymer de Maccuswell, vi. 470.
M'Ghee of Pluntoun, James, v. 259.
M'Ghie of Balmaghie, Alexander, v. 109.
—— his wife, Helen Stewart, v. 109.
—— John, v. 126.
—— his wife, Isabel Gordon, v. 126.
—— William, iii. 237.
—— his wife, Eleanor Macdowall, iii. 237.
— Florence, wife of (1) Jas. Charteris, (2) Roger Gordon, and (3) Thos. Maclellan, v. 270.
— Mary, wife of William Gordon of Airds of Crossmichael, v. 109.
M'Gibbon, Duncan, in Kelburnefoot, iv. 189.
— John, in Kelburnefoot, iv. 189.
—— his wife, Margaret Boyle, iv. 189.
MacGill, *see* Makgill.
M'Gillilan of Redcastle, Ingeram, v. 257.
— John, ii. 450.
M'Gillivray, Marjorie, wife of Dr. C. A. Campbell, ix. 45.
Macgilleoin, Hector, ix. 18.
—— his wife, Mor Campbell, ix. 18.
Macgregor of Glenstrae, Alister, i. 347; vi. 236.
— of Inverardran, Gregor, ii. 192.
— of Macgregor, John 'MacEwin MacAlester,' ii. 178.
—— his wife, Helen Campbell, ii. 178.
—— Sir John Atholl Bannatyne, 3rd bart., viii. 212.
—— Sir Malcolm, 4th bart., viii. 214.
— Alexander Murray, major-gen., ii. 357.
—— his 2nd wife, Charlotte Ann Sinclair, ii. 357.
— Allaster M'Allaster, vii. 467.
— Emily Louisa, wife of William David Murray, styled viscount Stormont, viii. 212.
— Isabella, wife of Patrick C. Sinclair, ii. 357.
— James, dean of Lismore, vii. 456.

* Name unknown.

Macgregor, Margaret Helen Mary, wife of 6th earl of Mansfield, viii. 214.
— Patrick Roy, Kenmore, ii. 200.
—— his wife, Jean Campbell, ii. 200.
— *or* Drummond of Culcrieff, Patrick, the younger, ii. 187.
—— his wife, Isobel Campbell, ii. 187.
— *, 1st wife of Colin Campbell of Glenfalloch, ii. 192.
M'Gruder, Janet, wife of Wm. Campbell, v. 505.
Macguire of Castle Nugent, Hugh, lt.-col., ii. 520.
—— his wife, Elizabeth Malyn, ii. 520.
— of Drumdow, Elizabeth, wife of 12th earl of Glencairn, iv. 251; ix. 98 *bis*.
—— Hugh, iv. 251.
MACHANESCHYRE, HAMILTON, LORD, iv. 378-380.
Machaneschyre, William, lord, iv. 378.
MacHenry, Dougall, Glencoe, v. 37.
— John, son of Malcolm, ix. 80.
—— his wife, Margt. Kirkpatrick, ix. 80.
Macheth of Moray, ii. 316.
Machico, Sir Charles Stuart, baron Stuart de Rothesay, count, ii. 304.
MACHLINE, CAMPBELL, LORD, v. 506-517.
Machline, James, elder son of 1st earl of Loudoun; styled lord, v. 506.
— John, first lord, v. 506.
M'Iain of Ardnamurchan, Iain, ix. 20.
—— his wife, * Campbell, ix. 20.
—— Mariota, ix. 20.
MacIldhui, *, mistress of Sir Colin Campbell of Lochow, i. 326.
M'Ilvernock, *alias* Graham, Archibald, bishop of the Isles, ii. 295 *n*.
Macintagart of Applecross, Ferquhard, vii. 231.
M'Intosh, not descended from Duncan, 4th earl of Fife, iv. 6.
— *see* Mackintosh.
Macintyre, Anne, wife of (1) G. J. Buller-Fullerton-Elphinstone, and (2) rev. Hugh M'Lachlan, iii. 547.
— John, LL.D., minister of Kilmonivaig, iii. 547.
MacIver, Laleve, wife of Donald, progenitor of the family of Macdonald of Glengarry, v. 559.
Mackay, Eth, ancestor of the clan, vi. 285.
MACKAY, LORD REAY, vii. 157-179.
MACKAY, BARON REAY OF DURNESS, vii. 178-179.
Mackay of Achmonie, Gillies, vii. 476.
— of Bighouse, George, iii. 214.
—— Hugh, major, vii. 174, 176.
—— his 1st wife, Margaret Mackay of Bighouse, vii. 174.
—— his 2nd wife, Isabella Mackenzie, vii. 174.

* Name unknown.

Mackay of Bighouse, Margaret, wife of major Hugh Mackay, vii. 174.
—— —— William, 1st laird, vii. 165.
—— —— his wife, Isabella Mackenzie, vii. 165.
—— of Blackcastle, Alexander, F.S.A., vii. 157 *n.*
—— of Borley, Hugh, captain, vii. 173.
—— —— his 1st wife, Anna Mackay, vii. 173.
—— —— William, captain, vii. 169.
—— of Braegaul, John, vii. 166.
—— of Creich, Thomas, vii. 161.
—— of Croystoun, John, vii. 161.
—— of Dirlot, John, ii. 340.
—— —— Iye 'Roy,' vii. 161.
—— of Durness, Iye Mor, vii. 158.
—— of Farr, Donald, iii. 198, 199; vii. 163; viii. 340.
—— —— his wife, Helen Sinclair, vii. 164.
—— —— Sir Donald, 1st bart., vii. 167.
—— —— his 1st wife, Barbara Mackenzie, vii. 168, 504.
—— —— his 2nd wife, Elizabeth Thompson, vii. 169.
—— —— his 3rd wife, Marjory Sinclair, vii. 169.
—— —— Hugh *or* Huistean 'Dhu,' iii. 202; vii. 165.
—— —— his 1st wife, Elizabeth Sinclair, ii. 342; vii. 166; ix. 51, 151.
—— —— his 2nd wife, Jane Gordon, vii. 166; viii. 346.
—— —— Iye 'Dhu,' ii. 339; vii. 164; viii. 340, 344 *bis.*
—— —— his 1st wife, Helen Macleod, vii. 162, 165.
—— —— his 2nd wife, Christina Sinclair, vii. 165.
—— of Ferancostgraig, Angus 'Dhu,' vii. 159.
—— of Hope, Iye 'Roy,' vii. 162.
—— of Kinloch, George, vii. 169.
—— —— William, vii. 169.
—— —— his wife, Ann Mackay, vii. 169.
—— of Little Isles of Strathnaver, Farquhar, physician, vii. 159.
—— of Melness, Angus, ancestor of the family of, vii. 168.
—— —— Farquhar, physician to king Robert II., vii. 159.
—— —— Iye 'Roy,' vii. 162.
—— of Ophemert, Barthold Johan Christian, baron of the Netherlands, vii. 171.
—— —— his wife, Anna Magdalena Frederica Henriette van Renesse, vii. 171.
—— of Polgowan, John, advocate, M.P., vii. 262.
—— —— his wife, Jane Ross of Hawkhead, vii. 262.
—— of Rhenorea, Æneas, lieutenant, ix. 132.
—— —— his wife, Isabella Fraser, ix. 132.
—— of Sandwood, Charles, vii. 169.
—— —— his wife, Elizabeth Mackay, vii. 169.
Mackay of Skerray, James, vii. 177.
—— —— John, captain, vii. 177 *n.*
—— of Skibo, George, advocate, vii. 175.
—— —— his wife, Anne Sutherland, iii. 214; vii. 175.
—— —— George, vii. 175.
—— of Scourie, Donald 'Balloch,' 1st laird, vii. 165.
—— —— his wife, Euphemia Munro, vii. 165.
—— —— Hugh, colonel, 2nd laird, vii. 169, 170.
—— —— Hugh, lieut.-general, vii. 174.
—— of Strathhalladale, Angus 'Dhu,' vii. 159.
—— of Strathnaver, Angus, vii. 159.
—— —— his wife, * Macleod, vii. 159.
—— —— Angus 'Dhu,' vii. 159.
—— —— his 1st wife, Elizabeth Macdonald, v. 40; vii. 159, 160.
—— —— his 2nd wife, Margaret Macdonald, v. 40; vii. 160.
—— —— Angus 'Roy,' vii. 160, 161.
—— —— his wife, * Mackenzie, vii. 161.
—— —— Donald, vii. 158.
—— —— his wife, * MacNeill, vii. 158.
—— —— Donald, iii. 198; vii. 163.
—— —— his wife, Helen Sinclair, vii. 164.
—— —— Sir Donald, 1st bart., vii. 167.
—— —— his 1st wife, Barbara Mackenzie, vii. 168, 504.
—— —— his 2nd wife, Elizabeth Thompson, vii. 169.
—— —— his 3rd wife, Marjory Sinclair, vii. 169.
—— —— Hugh *or* Huistean 'Dhu,' vii. 165.
—— —— his 1st wife, Elizabeth Sinclair, ii. 342.
—— —— his 2nd wife, Jane Gordon, viii. 346.
—— —— Iye 'Mor,' vii. 158.
—— —— Iye, vii. 158; viii. 327.
—— —— Iye 'Roy,' vii. 161; viii. 336.
—— —— his wife, * O'Beolan, vii. 162.
—— —— Iye 'Dhu,' vii. 164; viii. 340.
—— —— his 1st wife, Helen Macleod, vii. 162, 165.
—— —— his 2nd wife, Christina Sinclair, vii. 165.
—— —— John, vii. 162; viii. 336; ix. 131.
—— —— his wife, Margaret Fraser, vii. 163; ix. 131.
—— —— Neil 'Vass,' v. 40 *n.*; vii. 160.
—— —— his wife, * Munro, vii. 160.
—— of Strathy, Hugh, 2nd laird, vii. 170.
—— —— his wife, Jane Mackay, vii. 170.
—— —— Iye 'Roy,' vii. 161.
—— —— John, vii. 166.
—— —— his wife, Agnes Sinclair, ii. 340; vii. 166; ix. 151.
—— Æneas, brigadier-general, 3rd son of 2nd lord Reay, vii. 170.
—— —— his wife, Margaret von Puckler, vii. 171.

* Name unknown.

Mackay, Æneas, col. of Mackay's Scots regiment, vii. 171.
—— his wife, Ursulina Philippina van Haeften, vii. 171.
— Æneas, prime minister of the Netherlands, baron, vii. 172.
—— his wife, Elizabeth Wilhelmina van Lynden, vii. 172.
— Æneas, 3rd son of Theodoor Philip M., vii. 172.
—— his wife, Hermina Clasina den Beer Poortugael, vii. 172.
— Æneas Alexander, son of baron Eric M., vii. 172.
— Alexander, M.P., commander-in-chief of the Forces in Scotland, vii. 175.
—— his wife, Margaret Carr, vii. 175.
— Alexander Willem Rynhard, vii. 172.
— Angus, son of Angus 'Dhu' of Strathnaver, vii. 160.
— Angus, 3rd son of Iye 'Roy' of Strathnaver, vii. 162.
— Angus, lieut.-col. in Danish service, vii. 168.
—— his wife, Katharine Gunn, vii. 168.
— Ann, wife of Alexander Macdonald, vii. 169.
— Ann, wife of William Mackay of Kinloch, vii. 169.
— Ann, wife of John Watson of Muirhouse, vii. 175.
— Anne, dau. of George M. of Skibo, vii. 175.
— Anne Marion Erskine, vii. 178.
— Anna, wife of capt. Hugh Mackay of Borley, vii. 173.
— Annas, wife of John Sinclair of Brims, vii. 167.
— Arnolda, dau. of col. Æneas M., vii. 171.
— Barbara, wife of Alexander MacDavid Gunn of Killearnan, vii. 165.
— Barbara, wife of 2nd lord Reay, vii. 170.
— Barthold, vii. 173.
—— his wife, Alpheda Louise van der Wyck, vii. 173.
— Charlotte, wife of John Drever, vii. 178.
— Christina, wife of John Mackintosh of Dalziel, vii. 166.
— Christina, wife of Alex. Gunn of Killearnan, vii. 169.
— Christina, wife of Dr. John Erskine, vii. 176.
— Clara, dau. of 8th lord Reay, vii. 178.
— Constantyn Willem Ferdinand, vii. 172.
—— his wife, Petronella Hoeufft, vii. 172.
— Cornelis Anne, baron of the Netherlands, vii. 171.
— Daniel, elder son of baron Æneas M., vii. 172.
Mackay, Daniel, 6th son of Theodoor Philip M., vii. 173.
—— his wife, Helene Hommel, vii. 173.
— Dirk Rynhard Jehan, vii. 173.
—— his wife, Johanna Elizabeth Blaaw, vii. 173.
— Donald, eldest son of Iye M. of Strathnaver, vii. 159; viii. 327.
— Donald, 2nd son of 2nd lord Reay, vii. 170.
—— his wife, Anne Munro, vii. 170.
— Donald, colonel, vii. 171.
—— his wife, Arnolda Margaret van den Steen, vii. 171.
— Donald, major, vii. 171.
—— his wife, Isabella Constantia de Geer van Rynhuyzen, vii. 171.
— Donald, captain, Mackay's Scots regiment, vii. 171.
— Donald, vice-admiral R.N., vii. 175.
—— his wife, Helen Martha Twinning, vii. 175.
— Donald, son of 1st lord Reay, ix. 151.
— Edward, vii. 173.
—— his wife, Ina Petronella Lycklama a Nyeholt, vii. 173.
— Eleanor, wife of Donald Macleod of Assynt, vii. 165.
— Elizabeth, wife of John Mac-gill-eoin of Lochbuy, vii. 161.
— Elizabeth, wife of Charles Mackay of Sandwood, vii. 169.
— Elizabeth, dau. of George M. of Skibo, vii. 175.
— Elizabeth Granville, dau. of 8th lord Reay, vii. 178.
— Eric, baron, vii. 172.
—— his wife, Maria Johana Bertha Christina de Dedem, vii. 172.
— Erica, wife of Sir Walter M. T. Farquhar, vii. 177.
— Florence, wife of Neil Macleod of Assynt, vii. 164.
— Frances Jacoba, wife of baron Vygh of the Snor and Appelenburg, vii. 171.
— Frans, major-general, vii. 171.
—— his wife, Maria Adelheid van Heeckeren van Enghuizen, vii. 171.
— Frans, ensign, vii. 171.
— George, eldest son of 2nd lord Reay, vii. 170.
— Georgina, dau. of 5th lord Reay, vii. 177.
— Harriet, dau. of 3rd lord Reay, vii. 176.
— Hew, 3rd son of 1st lord Reay, vii. 168.
— Hugh, general, iii. 330; v. 124; vii. 510.
— Hugh, ensign in earl of Sutherland's regiment, vii. 174.
— Huistean 'Dhu,' tutor to Angus 'Dhu' M. of Strathnaver, vii. 159.
— Ian 'Aberach,' son of Angus 'Dhu' of Strathnaver, vii. 160.
—— his wife, * Macintosh, vii. 160.

* Name unknown.

Mackay, Jane, wife of Alex. Sutherland of Berriedale, vii. 165.
— Jane, dau. of 1st lord Reay, vii. 168.
— Jane, wife of (1) Robert Gordon, and (2) Hugh Mackay, vii. 170; viii. 350.
— Janet, wife of 6th lord Duffus, iii. 214.
— Janet, wife of Colin Campbell of Glenure, vii. 174.
— Joanna, wife of Wm. Fraser of Struy, vii. 173.
— Johan François Hendrik Jacobus Ernestus, vii. 172.
— — his wife, Margaretha Clara Françoise van Lynden, vii. 172.
— Johan Jacob, vii. 172.
— John 'Roy,' 2nd son of Angus 'Dhu' of Strathnaver, vii. 160.
— John 'Riavach,' vii. 161, 162.
— John 'Mor,' cousin of Iye 'Dhu,' vii. 164 *n.*; viii. 340.
— John 'Beg,' son of Iye 'Dhu' of Farr, vii. 165.
— John, captain, 4th son of col. Donald M., vii. 171.
— John, Ben Reay, vii. 177 *n.*
— John Jacob, 2nd son of 10th lord Reay, vii. 178.
— Katharina Wilhelmina, vii. 173.
— Louisa Wilhelmina Elizabeth Amarantha, vii. 173.
— M., rev., LL.D., vii. 178 *n.*
— Margaret, wife of David Sinclair, ii. 341.
— Margaret, wife of Walter Murray of Polrossie, vii. 163.
— Margaret, dau. of 1st lord Reay, vii. 169.
— Margaret, dau. of col. Æneas M., vii. 171.
— Margaret, wife of 3rd lord Reay, vii. 174.
— Margaret, dau. of 4th lord Reay, vii. 176.
— Margaretha Clara Françoise, vii. 173.
— Maria Christina Elizabeth, vii. 172.
— Maria Jacoba, vii. 173.
— Marianne, wife of Wm. Fullarton of Fullarton, vii. 177.
— Marion, dau. of 3rd lord Reay, vii. 176.
— Marion, wife of 5th lord Reay, vii. 176.
— Mariota, alleged handfasted wife of Alexander Stewart, lord of Badenoch, vii. 159.
— Martin, Galloway, vii. 159.
— Mary, wife of (1) Sir Hector Munro of Foulis, and (2) Alex. Gunn of Killearnan, vii. 167.
— Mary, wife of Sir Roderick Macleod of Talisker, vii. 168.
— Mary, wife of Wm. Baillie of Rosehall, vii. 174.
— Mary, dau. of Geo. M. of Skibo, vii. 175.
— Mary, dau. of 3rd lord Reay, vii. 175.
Mackay, Mary, wife of major Thomas Edgar, vii. 176.
— Mary, dau. of 8th lord Reay, vii. 178.
— Neil, grandson of Iye M. of Strathnaver, vii. 159.
— Neil, his son, vii. 159.
— Neil 'Naverach,' vii. 161.
— — his wife, * Sutherland of Croystoun, vii. 161.
— Norman, 7th son of Theodoor Philip M., vii. 173.
— Paul, progenitor of the Polson Mackays, vii. 159.
— Reinera, vii. 171.
— Reinhard Alexander, vii. 172.
— Robert, colonel, 5th son of 2nd lord Reay, i. 476; vii. 173.
— Robina, dau. of Hugh M. of Bighouse, vii. 174.
— Roderick, son of Angus 'Dhu' of Strathnaver, vii. 160.
— Rorie Gald, vii. 159.
— Rupert, 7th son of 1st lord Reay, vii. 169.
— Sophia, wife of Charles A. Aylmer, vii. 178.
— Sibylla, wife of (1) L. Mackintosh of Aberardor, and (2) Alex. Rose, vii. 174.
— Theodoor Philip, vii. 172.
— — his wife, Juliana Anna van Lynden, vii. 172.
— Theodora, vii. 171.
— Willem Karel, vii. 173.
— — his wife, Nicoline Engelvaart, vii. 173.
— William, son of Angus 'Dhu' of Strathnaver, vii. 160.
— William 'Roy' *or* 'Red,' vii. 160.
— *, wife of Hector Mackenzie of Auchterneed, vii. 161.
— *, wife of A. Sutherland of Dirlot, vii. 161.
— *, wife of Hugh Macleod of Assynt, vii. 162.
— *, wife of Alexander Sutherland, vii. 162; viii. 335.
— *, wife of Hugh Moray of Aberscross, vii. 163.
— *, wife of John, 4th chieftain of the Aberach Mackays, vii. 164.
Mackay-Forbes of Farr, Huistean, vii. 166.
M'Kelly of Inchkeith, John, viii. 265.
MacKennedy, Henry, ii. 444.
— John, ii. 444, 445 *n.*
— Sir Gilbert, ii. 447.
MACKENZIE OF KINTAIL, MACKENZIE, LORD, vii. 504-515.
Mackenzie of Kintail, Colin, second lord, iii. 69; vii. 506.
— — his wife Margaret Seton, iii, 372; vii. 507.

* Name unknown.

Mackenzie of Kintail, George, third lord, vii. 507.
—— Kenneth, first lord, iii. 69; vii. 504.
—— his first wife, Jean Ross, vii. 504.
—— his 2nd wife, Isabel Ogilvy, vii. 504.
—— Kenneth, fourth lord, vii. 509.
—— Kenneth, fifth lord, vii. 510.
—— William, sixth lord, vii. 511.
MACKENZIE OF KINTAIL, MACKENZIE, BARON, vii. 513-514.
Mackenzie of Kintail, Francis Humberston, baron, vii. 513.
MACKENZIE, BARON ARDELVE, vii. 512-513.
MACKENZIE, LORD CASTLEHAVEN, iii. 75-80.
MACKENZIE, EARL OF CROMARTIE, iii. 69-86.
MACKENZIE, VISCOUNT FORTROSE, vii. 512-513.
MACKENZIE, LORD MACKENZIE OF KINTAIL, vii. 504-512.
MACKENZIE, LORD MACLEOD, iii. 75-82.
MACKENZIE, LORD SEAFORTH, vii. 513-514.
MACKENZIE, EARL OF SEAFORTH, vii. 495-515.
MACKENZIE, VISCOUNT OF TARBAT, iii. 75-80.
Mackenzie of Achilty, Roderick, ancestor of the family of, vii. 498.
—— his 1st wife, * Maclean, vii. 498.
—— his 2nd wife, * Macleod, vii. 498.
—— his 3rd wife, * Ross, vii. 498.
— of Allan, Isobel, wife of Simon Mackenzie, vii. 505.
— of Allangrange, Colin, vii. 500.
—— George Falconer, vii. 506.
—— James, vii. 506.
—— John, vii. 506.
—— Simon, advocate, vii. 505.
—— his 1st wife, Isobel Mackenzie of Allan, vii. 505.
—— his 2nd wife, Susanna Fraser, vii. 506.
— of Applecross, Alexander, ancestor of the family of, vii. 503.
—— his 1st wife, Annabella Mackenzie, vii. 503.
—— his 2nd wife, Christian Munro, vii. 503.
—— Alexander, vii. 509.
—— Colin, vii. 501.
— of Ardfaillie, Roderick, vii. 165, 500, 503.
—— his wife, Finguella Munro, vii. 500.
— of Ardloch and Kinellan, Alexander, 4th son of Sir John M. of Tarbat, iii. 73.
— of Arisaig, Colin, vii. 507.
— of Assynt, Colin, vii. 501.
—— John, M.P., vii. 509.
—— his wife, Sibyl Mackenzie, vii. 509.
—— Kenneth, vii. 509.
—— his wife, Frances Mackenzie, vii. 509.
— of Auchmadies, Colin, vii. 505.
—— his wife, Isobel Heatley, vii. 505; ix. 156.

* Name unknown.

Mackenzie of Auchmadies, Thomas, vii. 504.
—— his 1st wife, Jean Grant, iii. 206; vii. 468, 504.
—— his 2nd wife, Jean Cockburn, vii. 505.
— of Auchterneed, Hector, vii. 161.
—— his wife, * Mackay, vii. 161.
— of Avoch, George, vii. 507.
— of Ballone, Alexander, iii. 71; vii. 505 *bis*.
—— his wife, Agnes Fraser, vii. 505.
— of Balmungie, George, vii. 507.
— of Breda, Alexander, vii. 511.
—— his wife, Maria Rebecca Mackenzie, vii. 511.
— of Carbaransby, v. 560.
— of Chanonrie, Roderick, vii. 502.
— of Coigeach, Sir Roderick, 2nd son of Colin M. of Kintail, iii. 69; vii. 502.
—— his wife, Margaret Macleod, iii. 69; v. 543.
— of Cromartie, Sir George, 2nd bart., iii. 76.
—— his wife, Elizabeth Reid, iii. 76.
—— Isabella, wife of 6th lord Elibank, iii. 80, 83, 519.
—— Sir Kenneth, 1st bart., iii. 75.
—— Sir Kenneth, 3rd bart., iii. 76.
—— Kenneth, grandson of 2nd earl of Cromartie, iii. 78, 83, 519; ix. 64.
—— his 2nd wife, Jane Petley, iii. 83.
—— Maria, wife of Edward Hay of Newhall, iii. 83.
— of Cullicudden, Kenneth, constable of the bishopric of Ross, vii. 503.
— of Culloden, Colin, 3rd son of Sir Roric M. of Tarbat, iii. 71.
—— his wife, * Mackenzie, iii. 71.
— of Culteleod, Colin, vii. 500.
—— Sir Roderick, 2nd son of Colin M. of Kintail, iii. 69.
—— his wife, Margaret Macleod, iii. 69.
— of Davochmaluag, Alexander, ancestor of the family of, vii. 498.
—— Roderick, vii. 503.
— of Davochpolls, Isobel, wife of Colin Mackenzie of Killin, vii. 502.
— of Eileandonan, John, vii. 499.
— of Fairburn, Murdoch, vii. 503.
— of Farnese, George, son of Sir James M. of Royston, iii. 76.
—— his wife, Isabella Stewart, iii. 76.
— of Findon, Sir Roderick, vii. 506.
— of Fotherty, John, vii. 499.
— of Gairloch, Alexander, iii. 71; vii. 504.
—— Alexander, iii. 73.
—— his wife, Barbara Mackenzie, iii. 73.
—— Hector, ancestor of the family of, vii. 497, 498.
—— his contracted wife, * Grant, vii. 497.
—— his wife, * MacRanald, vii. 497.
—— John, the younger, vii. 502.

* Name unknown.

Mackenzie of Gairloch, John 'Grassich,' v. 525.
—— —— his wife, Agnes Fraser, v. 525.
—— —— John 'Roy,' v. 561.
—— —— his wife, Elizabeth Macdonald, v. 561.
—— —— Kenneth, vii. 473.
—— —— his wife, Anne Grant, vii. 473.
—— —— Sir Kenneth John, 7th bart., viii. 213.
—— —— his wife, Marjorie Louisa Murray, viii. 213.
—— of Garve, Alexander, vii. 497.
—— of Glenelg, Kenneth, vii. 503.
—— of Glen Muick, Sir Allan Russell, 2nd bart., iii. 587.
—— of Grandvale, Sir George, 2nd bart., iii. 76.
—— —— his wife, Elizabeth Reid, iii. 76.
—— —— Sir Kenneth, 1st bart., iii. 75.
—— —— his 1st wife, Mary Kinnear, ix. 63.
—— —— his 2nd wife, Anne Campbell, iii. 76.
—— —— his 3rd wife, Elizabeth Edwards, ix. 63, 69 *bis*.
—— —— Sir Kenneth, 3rd bart., iii. 76.
—— of Hilton, Duncan, ancestor of the family of, vii. 497.
—— of Inchkeith, Sir George, viii. 300.
—— of Inscherorie, Kenneth, vii. 503.
—— of Inverlawl, Kenneth, iii. 71.
—— —— his wife, Agnes Fraser, iii. 71; vii. 505.
—— of Kilcoy, Alexander, 4th son of Colin M. of Kintail, vii. 502.
—— —— his 1st wife, Jean Fraser, v. 543; vii. 502.
—— —— his 2nd wife, Margt. Dunbar, vii. 502.
—— of Killin, Alexander, vii. 497.
—— —— John, 2nd son of Kenneth M. of Kintail, vii. 498.
—— —— Colin, vii. 502.
—— —— his 1st wife, Katharine Macleod, vii. 502.
—— —— his 2nd wife, Isobel Mackenzie, vii. 502.
—— of Kincardine and Kintowdie, George, 2nd son of 2nd earl of Seaforth, vii. 508.
—— —— his wife, Mary Skene, vii. 508.
—— of Kingwalledrum, Roderick, 4th son of 2nd earl of Seaforth, vii. 508.
—— of Kinlochluichart, Alexander, vii. 497.
—— of Kintail, Alexander, 'Ionraic,' vii. 161, 495, 497.
—— —— his 1st wife, Anna Macdougall, vii. 497.
—— —— his 2nd wife, Margaret M'Coull, vii. 497.
—— —— his alleged wife, Agnes Campbell, i. 335.
—— —— Colin 'Cam,' iii. 69; v. 530, 560; vii. 500; ix. 156.
—— —— his wife, Barbara Grant, iii. 69; vii. 464, 501.
Mackenzie of Kintail, John, son of the eponymous Kenneth, vii. 496.
—— —— his alleged wife, Margaret de Strathbogie, vii. 496.
—— —— John, vii. 498.
—— —— his wife, Elizabeth Grant, vii. 459, 499.
—— —— Kenneth, 'na sroine,' vii. 496.
—— —— his wife, Finvola Macleod, vii. 496.
—— —— Kenneth, 'a' bhlair,' vii. 497.
—— —— his 1st wife, Margaret Macdonald, vii. 497.
—— —— his 2nd wife, Agnes Fraser, vii. 498.
—— —— Kenneth, 'na cuirc,' i. 443; vii. 499; ix. 28.
—— —— his wife, Elizabeth Stewart, i. 443; vii. 500.
—— —— Kenneth, v. 562; vii. 503.
—— —— his 1st wife, Jean Ross, vii. 504.
—— —— his 2nd wife, Isabel Ogilvy, vii. 504.
—— —— Murdoch 'na h'uagh,' vii. 496.
—— —— his wife, Isabel Macaulay of Lochbroom, vii. 496.
—— —— Murdoch, 'na drochaid,' vii. 496.
—— —— his wife, Finvola Macleod, vii. 496.
—— of Lentran, Alexander, vii. 174.
—— of Lewis, George, vii. 507.
—— of Lochalsh, Kenneth, 1st laird, vii. 499.
—— —— Kenneth, vii. 503.
—— of Lochbroyne, John, vii. 499.
—— of Lochslinn, John, vii. 504.
—— —— his wife, Isobel Mackenzie, iii. 71; vii. 504.
—— —— Simon, M.P., vii. 505.
—— —— his 1st wife, Eliz. Bruce, vii. 505.
—— —— his 2nd wife, Agnes Fraser, iii. 71; vii. 505.
—— of Loganshauch, Alexander, vii. 504.
—— —— George, vii. 504.
—— of Logie, Donald, vii. 506.
—— of Meyne, Kenneth, vii. 497.
—— —— his 1st wife, Margaret Macdonald, vii. 497.
—— of Moidart, Colin, vii. 507.
—— of Ord, Alexander Watson, capt. 91st Highlanders, iv. 391.
—— —— Thomas, vii. 503.
—— —— his wife, Annabella Mackenzie, vii. 503.
—— of Pittendre, Isobel, wife of Colin Maccenzie of Killin, vii. 502.
—— of Pluscardine, Colin, vii. 505.
—— —— Kenneth, vii. 503.
—— —— Thomas, 6th son of 1st lord Mackenzie of Kintail, vii. 169, 504.
—— of Prestonhall, Alexander, v. 536, 538.
—— —— his wife, Amelia, baroness Fraser of Lovat, v. 535.
—— —— Roderick, lord Justice-Clerk, iii. 72.
—— —— his 1st wife, Mary Burnet, iii. 72.
—— —— his 2nd wife, Margaret Halyburton, iii. 73.

Mackenzie of Rasay, George, vii. 507.
— of Redcastle, Roderick, ancestor of the family of, vii. 500, 501, 503.
— — his wife, Finguella Monro, vii. 500.
— — Roderick, vii. 475.
— — his wife, Margaret Grant, vii. 475.
— of Rosehaugh, Sir George, king's advocate, i. 366; ii. 298, 300; iii. 73, 76; vii. 505.
— — his 1st wife, Elizabeth Dickson, vii. 505.
— — his 2nd wife, Margaret Halyburton, iii. 72; vii. 505.
— — George, ii. 300; vii. 505.
— of Rosmarkie, Roderick, vii. 502.
— of Royston, Sir James, 1st bart., iii. 72, 76.
— — his wife, Elizabeth Mackenzie, iii. 76.
— of Little Scattoll, Kenneth, vii. 503.
— of Scatwell, Kenneth, 2nd son of Sir Rorie M. of Tarbat, iii. 71.
— — his 1st wife, Margaret Munro, iii. 71.
— — his 2nd wife, Janet Ross, iii. 71.
— — Sir Roderick, vii. 479.
— — his wife, Janet Grant, vii. 479.
— of Seaforth, Francis Humberston, vii. 510, 513.
— — his wife, Mary Proby, vii. 514.
— — Jean, wife of (1) John Sinclair, and (2) Alexander, 1st lord Duffus, iii. 209.
— — Mary Frederica Elizabeth, wife of (1) admiral Sir S. Hood, and (2) J. A. Stewart of Glasserton, iv. 166; vii. 514.
— of Strathbraan, Strathgarve, and Strathconan, Alexander, vii. 497.
— of Strome, Kenneth, vii. 503.
— — Kenneth, 1st laird, v. 562.
— of Suddie, Kenneth, ancestor of the family of, vii. 498.
— of Tarbat, Sir George, lord Justice-General, 2nd bart., iii. 73; vii. 219.
— — his 1st wife, Anna Sinclair, iii. 75.
— — his 2nd wife, Margaret, countess of Wemyss, iii. 77; viii. 504.
— — Sir John, 1st bart., iii. 71.
— — his wife, Margaret Erskine, iii. 72; v. 83.
— — Sir Roderick, tutor of Kintail, vii. 502.
— — his wife, Margaret Macleod, iii. 69, 71; vii. 502.
— of Tarvey, Colin, 3rd son of Sir Rorie M. of Tarbat, iii. 71.
— — his wife, * Mackenzie, iii. 71.
— of Torosay, Sir Rorie, iii. 70.
— Agnes, wife of 1st earl of Bute, ii. 298; ix. 50.
— Agnes, wife of Roderick Macleod of the Lews, vii. 498.
— Agnes, wife of L. Mackintosh of Mackintosh, vii. 500.

* Name unknown.

Mackenzie, Agnes, dau. of Colin M. of Kintail, vii. 503.
— Agnes, wife of J. Douglas, vii. 512.
— Alexander, *afterwards* Fraser, iii. 72.
— — his wife, Amelia Fraser, iii. 72.
— Alexander, 5th son of Simon M. of Lochslinn, vii. 506.
— Alexander, colonel, vii. 510.
— — his wife, Elizabeth Paterson, vii. 510.
— Dr. Alexander, vii. 511.
— — his wife, Jane Mackenzie, vii. 511.
— Amelia, wife of Archibald Lamont, iii. 78.
— Amelia, dau. of 3rd earl of Cromartie, ix. 64.
— Anna Watson, wife of major A. F. Douglas-Hamilton, iv. 391.
— Annabella, wife of (1) Thos. Mackenzie of Ord, and (2) Alex. Mackenzie of Applecross, vii. 503.
— Annabella, wife of Thos. Mackenzie, vii. 506.
— Anne, wife of (1) 1st earl of Balcarres, and (2) 9th earl of Argyll, i. 368, 519; vii. 507.
— Anne, wife of John Sinclair of Murkle, ii. 346; iii. 76.
— Anne, wife of 8th lord Lovat, iii. 73; v. 534.
— Anne, wife of Sir Wm. Dick, iii. 76.
— Anna, dau. of John, 2nd earl of Cromartie, iii. 78.
— Anne, wife of (1) Edmond Atkin, and (2) John Murray, M.D., iii. 81.
— Anne, dau. of 3rd earl of Seaforth, vii. 509.
— Augusta, wife of Sir W. Murray of Ochtertyre, iii. 81; ix. 64.
— Augusta Ann, dau. of Kenneth, lord Seaforth, vii. 514.
— Barbara, wife of Alex. Mackenzie of Gairloch, iii. 73; ix. 63.
— Barbara, wife of 1st lord Reay, vii. 168, 504.
— Barbara, wife of John Urquhart of Cromarty, vii. 509; ix. 156.
— Campbell, 4th son of Sir Kenneth M. of Grandvale, iii. 76.
— Caroline, wife of (1) capt. Drake, and (2) W. Hunter of Crailing, iii. 81; iv. 66.
— Caroline, wife of Louis Pierre Francis Malcolm Drummond, vi. 69; vii. 513.
— Caroline, dau. of Kenneth, lord Seaforth, vii. 514.
— Charles, 6th son of Sir Rorie M. of Tarbat, iii. 71; ix. 63.
— Charlotte Elizabeth, dau. of Kenneth, lord Seaforth, vii. 514.
— Colin, 2nd son of Sir Kenneth M. of Grandvale, iii. 76.
— Colin, 2nd son of Colin M. of Killin, vii. 502.

Mackenzie, Colin, 3rd son of 2nd earl of Seaforth, vii. 508.
—— —— his wife, Jean Laurie, vii. 508.
—— Dugald, 4th son of Kenneth M. of Kintail, vii. 500, 501.
—— Edward Walter, *né* Blunt; R.A., A.D.C., iii. 85.
—— —— his wife, Sibell Lilian, countess of Cromartie, iii. 85.
—— Elizabeth, dau. of Roderick M. of Prestonhall, iii. 72.
—— Elizabeth, wife of col. J. Stewart of Grandtully, iii. 76.
—— Elizabeth, wife of Sir G. Broun of Coalstoun, iii. 76; ix. 63.
—— Elizabeth, wife of (1) Sir A. Cockburn, and (2) Sir James Mackenzie of Royston, iii. 76.
—— Elizabeth, wife of W. Urquhart of Cromarty, vii. 500.
—— Elizabeth, dau. of major William M., vii. 511.
—— Elizabeth, dau. of col. Alexander M., vii. 511.
—— Euphemia, wife of Wm. Stewart of Castle Stewart, vii. 512.
—— Frances, wife of John, *de jure* viscount of Kenmure, v. 132; vii. 512.
—— Frances, wife of Kenneth Mackenzie of Assynt, vii. 509.
—— Frances, wife of Joseph Wall, vii. 512.
—— Frances Cerjat, wife of Sir Vicary Gibbs, vii. 510.
—— Frances Katharine, dau. of Kenneth, lord Seaforth, vii. 514.
—— Francis John, R.N., vii. 514.
—— George, 3rd son of Roderick M. of Prestonhall, iii. 72.
—— George, lt.-col. 71st regt., iii. 80.
—— George, 2nd son of Thomas M. of Pluscardine, vii. 505.
—— George, M.D., author of *Eminent Writers of the Scots Nation*, vii. 508.
—— Gerard, 5th son of Sir Kenneth M. of Grandvale, iii. 76.
—— Gideon, 5th son of 2nd earl of Cromartie, iii. 78.
—— Hector, grandson of Alexander M. of Kintail, vii. 497.
—— Helen, wife of gen. Alex. Mackenzie Fraser, vii. 511.
—— Helen, wife of Joshua Henry Mackenzie, vii. 514.
—— Henry, author of *The Man of Feeling*, vii. 485.
—— —— his wife, Penuel Grant, vii. 485.
—— Hugh, Scots Dutch Brigade, and Montgomerie's Highlanders, iii. 78.
—— Hugh, son of Amelia, baroness Fraser of Lovat, v. 536, 538.
—— Isobel, wife of (1) John Mackenzie of Lochslin, and (2) Colin Mackenzie of Tarvey, iii. 71; vii. 504.
Mackenzie, Isabel, wife of 3rd earl of Seaforth, iii. 73, 210; vii. 509.
—— Isabella, wife of William Mackay of Bighouse, vii. 165.
—— Isabella, wife of Major Hugh Mackay of Bighouse, vii. 174.
—— Isabel, wife of (1) R. Macleod of Macleod, and (2) Sir D. Campbell of Lochnell, vii. 509.
—— Isabella, wife of B. Hamilton of Baldoon, vii. 511, 520.
—— James, 7th son of Sir Rorie M. of Tarbat, iii. 71; ix. 63.
—— James, M.D., Rheims, iii. 73; ix. 63.
—— James, 3rd son of Sir Kenneth M. of Grandvale, iii. 76.
—— James, captain, Dragoons, iv. 288.
—— Jane, dau. of 3rd earl of Cromartie, iii. 81.
—— Jane, wife of Simon Mackenzie, vii. 505.
—— Jane, wife of Dr. Alex. Mackenzie, vii. 511.
—— Janet, wife of (1) Angus Macdonald of Glengarry, and (2) Alex. Chisholm of Chisholm, vii. 500.
—— Janet, wife of Lachlan Maclean of Duart, vii. 503.
—— Janet, wife of Sir Donald Macdonald of Sleat, vii. 504.
—— Jean, wife of (1) John Sinclair, master of Berriedale, and (2) Alexander, 1st lord Duffus, ii. 344; iii. 209; vii. 507; ix. 52.
—— Jean, wife of Sir Thos. Stewart of Balcaskie, iii. 76; ix. 147.
—— Jean, wife of (1) John, earl of Mar, and (2) Andrew, 3rd lord Fraser, iv. 118; v. 626; vii. 508.
—— Jean, wife of Robert Douglas of Muldarge, vii. 506.
—— John, archdeacon of Ross, iii. 71.
—— John, 2nd son of Sir John M. of Tarbat, iii. 72.
—— John, 2nd son of Roderick M. of Prestonhall, iii. 72.
—— Joshua Henry, senator of the College of Justice, lord Mackenzie, vii. 514.
—— —— his wife, Helen Mackenzie, vii. 514.
—— Katharine, wife of Sir C. Campbell of Aberuchill, iii. 73; ix. 63.
—— Katharine, wife of Dr. Adam Murray, iii. 76.
—— Katharine, wife of 6th lord Lovat, v. 530; vii. 502.
—— Katharine, wife of Hector Munro of Foulis, vii. 498.
—— Katharine, wife of Alex. Ross of Balnagowan, vii. 500.
—— Katharine, wife of Thos. Griffin Tarpley, vii. 512.

Mackenzie, Kenneth, 6th son of Sir John M. of Tarbat, iii. 73; ix. 63 *bis*.
—— —— his wife, Isobel Auchinleck, iii. 73.
—— Kenneth, his son, iii. 73.
—— Sir Kenneth, eldest son of Kenneth M. of Kintail, vii. 498.
—— Kenneth, elder son of Colin M. of Killin, vii. 502.
—— Kenneth, 3rd son of 1st lord Mackenzie of Kintail, vii. 504.
—— Kenneth, general, viii. 142.
—— Lucy Victoria, wife of Victor Alexander Sereld, lord Kilmarnock, iii. 587.
—— Margaret, wife of Sir Wm. Sinclair of Mey, ii. 355; vii. 509.
—— Margaret, wife of Sir Jas. Macdonald of Sleat, iii. 71; ix. 63.
—— Margaret, wife of (1) Roderick Macleod, and (2) Sir Jas. Campbell, iii. 73.
—— Margaret, dau. of Sir Kenneth M. of Grandvale, iii. 76.
—— Margaret, wife of D. Bruce of Clackmannan, iii. 76; ix. 63 *bis*.
—— Margaret, wife of John Glassford, iii. 81.
—— Margaret, wife of 2nd lord Duffus, iii. 210; vii. 509; ix. 156.
—— Margaret, wife of Walter Innes of Inverbrakye and Balnagall, vii. 500.
—— Margaret, dau. of Colin M. of Kintail, vii. 503.
—— Margaret, wife of Wm. Webb, vii. 512.
—— Margaret, wife of lieut.-col. Samuel Dalrymple, viii. 141.
—— Maria, wife of Nicholas Price of Saintfield, vii. 511; ix. 156 *bis*.
—— Maria Rebecca, wife of Alex. Mackenzie, vii. 511.
—— Marjory, wife of Robert Monro of Foulis, vii. 500.
—— Mary, dau. of 2nd earl of Cromartie, iii. 78; ix. 64.
—— Mary, wife of (1) capt. Clark, (2) Thos. Drayton, (3) John Ainslie, and (4) * Middleton, So. Carolina, iii. 81.
—— Mary, wife of Alex. Macdonell of Glengarry, vii. 509.
—— Mary, wife of (1) Angus Macdonald of Glengarry, and (2) Alex. Chisholm of Comar, v. 561; vii. 500.
—— Mary, wife of (1) John, earl of Mar, and (2) Andrew, 3rd lord Fraser, iv. 118; v. 626.
—— Mary, wife of Donald 'Gorm Mor' Macdonald of Sleat, vii. 503.
—— Mary, dau. of Roderick M. of Davochmaluag, vii. 503.
—— Mary, wife of capt. Dougal Stewart, vii. 511.
—— Mary, wife of (1) John Caryll, and (2) Francis Sempill, vii. 511, 556.
—— Mary, wife of Henry Howard, vii. 512.

* Name unknown.

Mackenzie, Mary Ann, dau. of Kenneth M. of Cromartie, iii. 83; ix. 64.
—— Murdoch, bishop of Moray and Orkney, iv. 288.
—— Murdoch, 5th son of Colin M. of Kintail, vii. 502.
—— Nicol, 3rd son of 5th earl of Seaforth, vii. 511; ix. 156.
—— Norman, Scots Dutch Brigade, iii. 78.
—— Patrick, 4th son of 2nd earl of Cromartie, iii. 78.
—— Robert, captain in the earl of Mar's regiment, 1688, vii. 508.
—— Roderick, eldest son of 1st earl of Cromartie, iii. 75.
—— Roderick, 2nd son of 2nd earl of Cromartie, iii. 78, 83.
—— Ronald, 2nd son of 5th earl of Seaforth, vii. 511.
—— Simon, 2nd son of Simon M. of Lochslinn, vii. 505.
—— —— his wife, Jane Mackenzie, vii. 505.
—— Simon, advocate, vii. 506.
—— —— his wife, Helen Clerk, vii. 506.
—— Sibyl, wife of John Mackenzie of Assynt, vii. 509.
—— Sibylla, wife of (1) John Macleod of Macleod, (2) Alexander Fraser, master of Lovat, and (3) P. Grant of Cluniemore, v. 533; vii. 470, 506.
—— Sophia, dau. of 1st earl of Cromartie, ix. 64.
—— Thomas, 4th son of Simon M. of Lochslinn, vii. 506.
—— —— his wife, Annabella Mackenzie, vii. 506.
—— Torquil, son of Sir Rorie M. of Tarbat, ix. 63.
—— Torquil, 5th son of Sir John M. of Tarbat, ix. 63.
—— William, capt. Scots Brigade in Holland, H.E.I.C.S., iii. 78.
—— William, prior of Scots monastery at Würzburg, vii. 509.
—— William, major, vii. 510.
—— —— his wife, May Humberston, vii. 510.
—— William Frederick, M.P., vii. 514.
—— *, wife of Angus 'Roy' Mackay of Strathnaver, vii. 161.
—— *, wife of Allan Macleod of Gairloch, vii. 497.
—— *, superior of Beauly Priory, vii. 497.
—— *, wife of Alex. Chisholm of Comer, vii. 505.
Mackenzie-Fraser of Castle Fraser and Inverallochy, Frederick, lt.-col., vi. 73; vii. 61.
—— —— his 1st wife, Marie Augusta Gabrielle Bérengère Blanche Drummond, vi. 73; vii. 61.

* Name unknown.

Mackenzie-Humberston of Seaforth, Thomas Frederick, vii. 510, 513.
M'Kie of Lurg, Patrick, iv. 155.
—— —— his wife, Margaret Stewart, iv. 155.
—— —— Sir Patrick, ii. 488.
—— —— his wife, Susanna Kennedy, ii. 488.
—— Nathaniel, minister of Crossmichael, v. 132.
M'Kilrevich, Gill Rewach Vickhimi, ancestor of the family of, v. 521.
MacKinnon of MacKinnon, William, iii. 366.
—— Louisa Harriet, wife of 11th earl of Dundonald, iii. 366.
—— Sophia Jane, wife of H. D. Drummond, viii. 225.
Mackintosh of Aberardor, Lauchlin, vii. 174.
—— —— his wife, Sibylla Mackay, vii. 173.
—— of Borlum, Lachlan, vii. 468.
—— —— his wife, Agnes Grant, vii. 468.
—— of Dalziel, John, vii. 166.
—— —— his wife, Christina Mackay, vii. 166.
—— of Glenloy, iv. 536.
—— of Dunnachtan, *see* of Mackintosh.
—— of Mackintosh and Dunnachton, Alexander Æneas, 27th captain of Clan Chattan, iv. 98.
—— —— his wife, Margaret Frances Graham, iv. 98.
—— —— Duncan, 11th captain, iv. 51.
—— —— Ferquherd, 12th captain, v. 524.
—— —— his wife, Egidia *or* Marjory Fraser, v. 524.
—— —— Hector, vii. 459.
—— —— his alleged wife, * Grant, vii. 459.
—— —— Lachlan, 8th captain, v. 520.
—— —— his wife, Euphemia *or* Agnes Fraser, v. 520.
—— —— Lachlan, 14th captain, v. 104.
—— —— his wife, Janet Gordon, v. 103.
—— —— Lachlan 'Mor,' 16th captain, ii. 189; v. 562; vii. 166, 466, 500.
—— —— his wife, Agnes Mackenzie, vii. 500.
—— —— Sir Lachlan, 17th captain, i. 343; vii. 468.
—— —— his wife, Annas *or* Agnes Grant, vii. 468.
—— —— Malcolm, 10th captain, vii. 160, 455, 456.
—— —— William, 15th captain, iii. 204; iv. 535, 536.
—— of Tereynie, Angus, i. 472.
—— —— his wife, Jean Murray, i. 472.
—— of Termett, Angus, ix. 123.
—— —— his wife, Marjorie Falconer, ix. 123.
—— of Torcastle, Angus, i. 343.
—— —— his wife, Jean Campbell, i. 343.
—— —— Lachlan, i. 515.
—— —— his wife, Magdalen Lindsay, i. 515.
—— Archibald, lieut.-col. R.M.L.I., vi. 582.
—— —— his wife, Mary Anne Abraham, vi. 582.

* Name unknown.

Mackintosh, Isabel, dau. of Angus M. of Torcastle, i. 343.
—— Isabel, wife of Sir Robert Campbell, ii. 189; ix. 43.
—— Janet, wife of Patrick MacIan Roy Grant, vii. 455.
—— Katharine, wife of Donald Macdonald of Glengarry, v. 562.
—— Lachlan, 'Badenoch,' vii. 456.
—— —— his 3rd wife, Katharine Grant, vii. 456.
—— Malcolm, v. 562.
—— —— his wife, Janet Macdonald, v. 562.
—— Margaret, wife of (1) Duncan Grant, (2) Alex. Forbes, (3) Alex. Gordon, and (4) Wm. Sutherland, iii. 204; iv. 74; vii. 464; ix. 69.
—— Margaret, dau. of Lachlan M. of Dunnachton, v. 562.
—— Muriel, wife of John Grant, younger of Freuchie, vii. 456 *bis*.
—— *, wife of Ian Aberach Mackay, vii. 160.
M'Klear, Margaret *or* Magdalen, *alias* Mrs. Corsby, Mrs. Jolly; alleged wife of 5th earl of Winton, viii. 605; ix. 170.
—— *, physician, Edinburgh, viii. 605.
Mackworth of the Gnoll, Herbert, v. 251.
—— Elizabeth, wife of Thos. Huddleston, i. 64.
—— Frances, wife of (1) 6th lord Falconer of Halkerton, and (2) 7th viscount Montagu, v. 251.
—— Sir Henry, bart., i. 64.
—— —— his wife, Anne Hamilton, i. 64.
Macky, John, the author, i. 371; ix. 24.
M'Kye, John Ross, iv. 215.
—— —— his wife, Jean Ross, iv. 215.
M'Kynnestre, Elizabeth, mother of Wm. Maclellan of Sennick, v. 266.
Maclachlan of Drumlean, Andrew, vi. 150.
—— —— his wife, Elizabeth Graham, vi. 150.
—— of Duchal, Archibald, v. 555.
—— of Maclachlan, Archibald, v. 555.
—— —— his wife, Katharine Lyle, v. 555.
—— Hugh, minister of Tarbert, iii. 547.
—— —— his wife, Anne Macintyre, iii. 547.
Maclagman, Duncan, v. 42.
Maclaine of Lochbuy, Hector, ii. 200.
—— —— John Mac-gill-eoin, vii. 161.
—— —— his wife, Elizabeth Mackay, vii. 161.
—— —— Murdoch, ii. 200.
—— —— his wife, Julian Campbell, ii. 200.
Maclean of Ardgour, Alexander, viii. 129.
—— —— his wife, Helen Jane Dalrymple, viii. 129.
—— —— Charles, iv. 499.
—— —— his wife, Margaret Hope, iv. 499.
—— of Duart, Hector 'Roy,' v. 560.
—— —— Hector 'Mor,' v. 561; ix. 20.

* Name unknown.

Maclean of Duart, Hector 'Og,' i. 340.
—— his wife, Janet Campbell, i. 340.
—— Hector 'Og,' vii. 503.
—— his 1st wife, Janet Mackenzie, vii. 503.
—— Hector 'Mor,' iii. 70.
—— Lachlan, 'Lubanach,' v. 40.
—— his wife, Mary Macdonald, v. 40.
—— Lachlan 'Bronnach,' v. 54, 589.
—— his 2nd wife, Janet Stewart, v. 589.
—— Lachlan 'Og,' i. 335.
—— his wife, Katharine Campbell, i. 335.
—— Lachlan 'Cattanach,' i. 337.
—— his 2nd wife, Katharine Campbell, i. 337.
—— Sir Lachlan 'Mor,' iv. 243.
—— his wife, Margaret Cunningham, iv. 243.
— Alaster, at siege of Rothesay, ii. 291.
— Sir Alexander, v. 174.
—— his wife, Mary Boyd, v. 174.
— Farquhar MacHeachen, vii. 498.
— Finvola, wife of Celestine Macdonald of Lochalsh, v. 44.
— Janet, wife of Angus Macdonald of Glengarry, v. 561.
— Katharine, wife of (1) Archibald, 4th earl of Argyll, (2) Callough O'Donell of Tyrconnell, and (3) John Stewart of Appin, i. 340; ix. 20 *bis*.
— Mary, wife of James Johnstone of Stapleton, i. 264.
— Mary, wife of Alexander Macdonald of Morar, v. 560.
— *, wife of Roderick Mackenzie of Achilty, vii. 498.
MACLELLAN, LORD KIRKCUDBRIGHT, v. 256-274.
Maclellan of Auchenglour, Thomas, v. 263.
— of Auchinha, James, tutor of Nunton, v. 260.
—— his wife, Katharine Broun, v. 260.
—— Robert, v. 260, 261.
— of Auchlane, Elizabeth, wife of John Maclellan of Borgue, v. 264.
—— John, tutor of Gelston, v. 259.
—— Thomas, tutor of Bombie, v. 259, 262.
—— his wife, Agnes Gordon, v. 259.
—— Sir William, tutor of Bombie, v. 259, 264 *bis*, 265, 270.
—— his wife, Katharine Kennedy, v. 259.
—— William, 2nd son of John M. of Borgue, v. 264, 269.
— of Balgreddane, Robert, v. 263.
—— Thomas, v. 263.
— of Balmangan, James, v. 271.
—— his wife, Jean Charteris, v. 271.
—— Robert, v. 271.
—— his wife, *, v. 271.

* Name unknown.

Maclellan of Balmangan, Robert, last owner, v. 271.
—— Thomas, v. 266, 270.
—— his 1st wife, Janet Maclellan, v. 270.
—— his 2nd wife, Florence M'Ghie, v. 270.
—— William, v. 259, 270.
—— his wife, Margaret Gordon, v. 270.
— of Bardrochwood, Thomas, v. 258.
— of Barmagachan, Thomas, v. 269.
—— William, v. 259.
—— his wife, Elizabeth Mure, v. 260.
— of Barscobe, William, v. 117.
—— his wife, Mary Gordon, v. 117.
— of Bombie, *, iv. 273; v. 257.
—— his wife, * Gray, iv. 273; v. 257.
—— Sir Robert, 7th laird, v. 264.
—— his 1st wife, Agnes Campbell, v. 267.
—— his 2nd wife, Mary Montgomery, v. 267.
—— his 3rd wife, Mary Gage, v. 267.
—— Thomas, 2nd laird, ii. 385; v. 258; ix. 104.
—— his 1st wife, Margaret Gordon, v. 102, 259.
—— his 2nd wife, Agnes Dunbar, v. 259.
—— Thomas, 4th laird, v. 107, 261; vii. 118, 119.
—— his 2nd wife, Marion Accarsane, v. 261.
—— Thomas, 5th laird, v. 262.
—— his wife, Marion Kennedy, ii. 467; v. 262.
—— Thomas, 6th laird, v. 262.
—— his 1st wife, Helen Gordon, v. 110, 264.
—— his 2nd wife, Grizel Maxwell, iv. 412; v. 264.
—— William, 1st laird, v. 258.
—— his wife, Marion Carlyle, v. 258.
—— William, 3rd laird, v. 259.
—— his wife, Elizabeth Mure of Bardrochwood, v. 260.
— of Borgue, John, v. 264.
—— his 1st wife, Elizabeth Maclellan, v. 264.
—— his 2nd wife, Margaret Coupar, v. 264.
— of Borness, Robert, v. 271.
—— William, v. 271.
—— his wife, Agnes MacCulloch, v. 271.
—— William, v. 271.
—— his wife, Margaret Murray, v. 272.
— of Cors, Sir Robert, v. 266.
— of Croftis, William, v. 259, 270.
— of Culcaigreis, Thomas, v. 263.
— of Drumrukalzie, William, v. 270.

* Name unknown.

Maclellan of Galtway, Gilbert, v. 259, 270.
—— —— his wife, Margaret Maclellan, v. 259, 270.
—— of Garcrego, Thomas, v. 258.
—— of Gelston, 1578, vii. 129.
—— —— Alexander, iv. 411.
—— —— his wife, Elizabeth Gordon, iv. 411.
—— —— William, v. 264.
—— —— his wife, Margaret Maclellan, v. 264.
—— of Glenshinnoch, William, provost of Kirkcudbright, v. 264.
—— —— his wife, Rosina Agnew, v. 264.
—— of Glenturk, Thomas, v. 258.
—— —— William, v. 258.
—— of Kirkcarsell, Thomas, v. 260.
—— of Kirkcaswell, William, v. 260.
—— —— his wife, Agnes Johnstone, v. 260.
—— of Kirkchrist, Thomas, v. 260.
—— —— Thomas, v. 263.
—— of Lessens, Sir Robert, v. 266.
—— —— Thomas, v. 266.
—— of Nunton, James, v. 260.
—— —— his wife, Isobel M'Dowall, v. 260.
—— —— Robert, v. 261.
—— —— his wife, Agnes Gordon, v. 261.
—— —— Robert, v. 261.
—— —— Thomas, v. 260, 264.
—— —— his wife, Marion Maclellan, v. 261, 264.
—— —— William, tutor of Bombie, iv. 153; v. 260, 261.
—— —— his wife, Agnes Johnstone, v. 260.
—— of Overlaw, Thomas, v. 263.
—— of Plumtoun, Thomas, v. 261.
—— of Polmaddy, William, v. 259.
—— of Rosses, Sir Robert, v. 266.
—— of Sennick, James, v. 270.
—— —— his *possible* wife, Elizabeth M'Kynnestre, v. 266.
—— —— William, *perhaps* son of James M. of Sennick, v. 266.
—— of Grange of Sennick, William, v. 270.
—— of Skelrie, Thomas, v. 263.
—— of Troquhain, John, v. 102.
—— of Twynam, Sir Robert, v. 266.
—— of Wigtoun, Patrick, sheriff of Galloway, v. 257.
—— Agnes, wife of John Lennox of Cally, v. 270.
—— Agnes, dau. of Thos. M. of Balmangan, v. 271.
—— Ann, wife of Sir Robert Maxwell of Spottis, v. 267.
—— Christian, wife of Wm. Cairns of Orchardton, v. 259.
—— David, v. 256 *n.*
—— Elizabeth, wife of Finlay Fergusson, v. 273.
—— Elizabeth, wife of John Herries of Maidenpaup, ix. 124.
—— Elizabeth, wife of Alex. M'Culloch of Cardoness, ix. 150.
Maclellan, Elspeth, dau. of Thos. M. of Balmangan, v. 271.
—— Esota, ix. 80.
—— Gilbert de, v. 256.
—— Gilbert, in Balmangan, 3rd son of Thos. M. of Bombie, v. 259.
—— —— his wife, Margaret Herries, iv. 407; v. 269.
—— Gilbert, 3rd son of Thos. M. of Balmangan, v. 270.
—— Grizel, dau. of Thos. M. of Balmangan, v. 271.
—— Helen, wife of Alex. Mure of Cassencary, v. 270.
—— James, 3rd son of Wm. M. of Balmangan, v. 270.
—— James, eldest son of Sir Samuel M., v. 271.
—— Janet, wife of George Gordon, v. 102.
—— Janet, wife of Wm. Maxwell of Milton, v. 269.
—— Janet, wife of Thos. Maclellan of Balmangan, v. 270.
—— Janet, their dau., v. 271.
—— John, custumar of Kirkcudbright, v. 257.
—— John, 2nd son of Wm. M. of Nunton, v. 260.
—— John, elder son of Wm. M. of Auchlane, v. 269.
—— Katharine, wife of Sir John Dunbar of Mochrum, v. 259.
—— Katharine, wife of John Kennedy of Culzean, v. 261.
—— Margaret, wife of Jas. Johnstone of Wamphray, i. 241; v. 262.
—— Margaret, wife of Gilbert Maclellan of Galtway, v. 259.
—— Margaret, dau. of John M. of Borgue, v. 264.
—— Margaret, wife of (1) Wm. Maclellan of Gelston, and (2) Patrick Vaus of Librack, v. 264.
—— Margaret, wife of Samuel Brown of Mellance, v. 269.
—— Margaret, dau. of Thos. M. of Balmangan, v. 271.
—— Marion, wife of (1) Sir David Murray, and (2) John Reddik, i. 225.
—— Marion, wife of (1) Thos. Maclellan of Nunton, and (2) John Glendonwyn, yr. of Parton, v. 261, 264.
—— Mary, wife of Sir Robert Maxwell of Spottis, v. 267.
—— Mary, dau. of 5th lord Kirkcudbright, v. 269.
—— Sir Samuel, provost of Edinburgh, v. 271.
—— Thomas, 2nd son of Thos. M. of Auchlane, v. 259.
—— Thomas, 4th son of Thos. M. of Bombie, v. 259.

Maclellan, Thomas, 3rd son of William M. of Nunton, v. 260.
— Thomas, 2nd son of Thos. M. of Nunton, v. 261.
— — his wife, Nicolas Maxwell, v. 261.
— Thomas, 4th son of Thos. M. of Balmangan, v. 270.
— William, elder son of Wm. M. of Glenshinnoch, v. 264.
— William, 2nd son of Thos. M. of Balmangan, v. 270.
— *, elder son of 6th lord Kirkcudbright, v. 272.
MACLEOD, MACKENZIE, LORD, iii. 74-82.
Macleod, George, first lord, iii. 74.
— John, 2nd son of 1st earl of Cromartie; styled lord, iii. 75, 78.
— — his 1st wife, Elizabeth Gordon, i. 100; iii. 77; ix. 6.
— John, eldest son of 3rd earl of Cromartie; styled lord, iii. 80, 82.
— — his wife, Marjory Forbes, iii. 82; iv. 65.
— master of, George, grandson of George, 1st earl of Cromartie; styled, iii. 78.
MACLEOD OF CASTLE LEOD, HAY-MACKENZIE, BARON, iii. 84-86.
Macleod of Castle Leod, Anne, baroness, iii. 84.
MacLeod of Assynt, Donald 'Bane,' vii. 165.
— — his wife, Eleanor Mackay, vii. 165.
— — Hugh, vii. 162.
— — his wife, * Mackay, vii. 162.
— — Neil, vii. 162, 164.
— — his wife, Florence Mackay, vii. 164.
— — Neil, vi. 252.
— — Torquil, vii. 501.
— of Cadboll, Roderick, ii. 601.
— of Dunvegan, Roderick, v. 561.
— — Sir Rory, v. 562.
— — his wife, Isabella Macdonald, v. 562.
— — Rorie, v. 505.
— — William, v. 527.
— — his wife, Agnes Fraser, v. 527.
— of Gairloch, Allan, vii. 497.
— — his wife, * Mackenzie, vii. 497.
— of Geanies, Donald, advocate, iii. 83.
— — his wife, Jane Petley, iii. 83.
— of Harris, Malcolm, vii. 496.
— — William, vii. 499.
— of Lewis, Katharine, wife of Colin Mackenzie of Killin, vii. 502.
— — Margaret, wife of (1) Sir Roderick Mackenzie of Tarbat, and (2) Thos. Fraser of Strichen, iii. 69, 71; v. 543; vii. 502.
— — Roderick, vii. 498.
— — his wife, Agnes Mackenzie, vii. 498.
— — Torquil, 2nd, vii. 235, 496.
— — his wife, Dorothea of Ross, vii. 235.

* Name unknown.

MacLeod of Lewis, Torquil, 4th, vii. 159.
— — Torquil, 8th, i. 335.
— — his wife, Katharine Campbell, i. 335.
— — Torquil, 'Conanach,' v. 562; vii. 502; ix. 63.
— — his wife, Margaret Macdonald, v. 562.
— of Macleod, John, v. 536.
— — his wife, Sybilla Mackenzie, v. 533.
— — Norman, ii. 353; iv. 552; v. 535.
— — his wife, Anne Fraser, v. 535.
— — Roderick, vi. 511.
— — his wife, Margaret Stewart, iii. 187; vi. 511.
— — Roderick, iii. 73.
— — his wife, Margaret Mackenzie. iii. 73.
— — Roderick, vii. 509.
— — his wife, Isabel Mackenzie, vii. 509.
— of Raasay, John, v. 511.
— of Talisker, Sir Roderick, vii. 168.
— — his 1st wife, Mary Mackay, vii. 168.
— Agnes, wife of Hugh Sutherland, iii. 194.
— Anna, wife of Thomas Fraser, v. 525.
— Barbara, wife of Jas. Stewart of Burray, iii. 187; ix. 68.
— Donald, capt. R.N., C.B., iv. 391.
— Finvola, wife of Kenneth Mackenzie of Kintail, vii. 496.
— Finvola, wife of Murdoch Mackenzie of Kintail, vii. 496.
— Flora, wife of James Mure Campbell of Rowallan and Lawers, v. 511.
— Flora Loudoun, wife of Sir R. G. Elphinstone-Dalrymple, viii. 134.
— Helen, wife of Iye 'Dhu' Mackay of Farr, vii. 162, 165.
— James William, viii. 134.
— Jessie, wife of James, 16th earl of Caithness, ii. 358.
— John, colonel R.A., v. 481.
— — his wife, Wilhelmina Emilia Ker, v. 481.
— Katharine Augusta Westenra, wife of major-gen. O. Douglas-Hamilton, iv. 391.
— Malcolm M'Rorie, vii. 506.
— Margaret, wife of baron de Virte, ii. 601.
— Margaret, wife of Sir Jas. Campbell of Lawers, v. 505.
— Margaret, wife of Angus Macdonald of Glengarry, v. 561.
— Margaret, wife of Sir Alex. Gordon of Navidale, viii. 346.
— Mary, wife of capt. D. Ramsay, R.N., ii. 353.
— Mary, dau. of William M. of Harris, vii. 499.
— Neil, executed at Glasgow, 1612, iii. 70.
— Roderick, M.D., ii. 358.

MacLeod, Sibylla, wife of Thos. Fraser of Beaufort, v. 536.
—— William 'Dhu,' vii. 498.
—— *, wife of Roderick Mackenzie of Achilty, vii. 498.
—— *, wife of Angus Mackay of Strathnaver, vii. 159.
M'Locherry of the Isles, Loughlan, vi. 203.
M'Lolan, Gilbert, v. 256.
—— Gilbert, his son, v. 256 *bis*.
—— John, son of Sir Matthew M'L., v. 256.
—— Sir Matthew, v. 256.
—— Patrick, son of Gilbert M'L., v. 256.
Macmartin of Letterfinlay, v. 564.
MacMaster, Hugh, Kausani, N.W.P., ii. 502.
—— Isabella, wife of 3rd marquess of Ailsa, ii. 502.
M'Math, Helen, wife of (1) John Naesmyth, and (2) Patrick Murray, iii. 400.
M'Micking of Miltonise, Gilbert, vii. 226.
—— Helen Mary, wife of Sir H. W. Primrose, vii. 226.
Macmillar, Finlay, v. 501.
Macmorran of Euarlands, Ninian, merchant burgess of Edinburgh, iv. 308.
—— Elizabeth, wife of Sir Patrick Hamilton of Little Preston, iv. 308.
—— George, vii. 217.
—— —— his wife, Elizabeth Primrose, vii. 217.
—— John, bailie of Edinburgh, ii. 351.
MacNab of Bovain, Finlay, ii. 182.
—— of MacNab, Robert, ii. 202.
—— —— his 3rd wife, Anna Campbell, ii. 202; ix. 45.
Macnamara, Anne Linnington, wife of 9th lord Cranstoun, ii. 601.
—— John, St. Christopher, W.I., ii. 601.
Macnaught of Crogo, Andrew, v. 102.
—— —— Geylles, wife of Roger Gordon, v. 102.
—— of Kilquhanatie, John, v. 116.
—— —— his wife, Margaret Gordon, v. 116.
—— Marion, v. 117.
Macnaughton of Macnaughton, v. 121.
—— —— John, ii. 202.
—— —— his wife, Isabel Campbell, ii. 202.
M'Neal of Ugadale, Neil, iv. 176.
—— —— his wife, Margaret Crawford (Lindsay), iv. 176.
Macneill of Colonsay, Archibald, i. 392.
—— —— Sir John, G.C.B., i. 389.
—— —— his 3rd wife, Emma Augusta Campbell, i. 389.
—— of Gigha, Iye, vii. 158.
—— of Illandrow, Robert, ix. 50.
—— —— his wife, Elizabeth Ruthven, ix. 50.
—— of Kilmory, John, ii. 298 *n*.
—— of Neilhall, Dr. James, iv. 215.
—— —— his wife, Catharine Boyle, iv. 215.

* Name unknown.

Macneill, Ina Erskine, 3rd wife of 8th duke of Argyll, i. 392.
—— *, wife of Donald Mackay of Strathnaver, vii. 158.
M'Nicol, Effie, wife of Wm. Campbell, ii. 192.
Macomb, Alexander, gen., U.S.A., ii. 496.
—— Jane, wife of Robert Kennedy, ii. 496.
Maconochie of Inverawe, Duncan, ancestor of the family of, i. 324.
Maconochie-Welwood of Meadowbank, Alan, viii. 160.
—— —— his wife, Margaret Penny Dalrymple, viii. 160.
Macowall, Margaret, wife of Ninian Bannatyne, ii. 288.
Macphee of Lochaber, v. 44.
—— *, wife of Alexander, 9th lord of the Isles, v. 44.
Macpherson of Cluny, Duncan, colonel, v. 542.
—— —— Ewen, v. 540.
—— —— his wife, Janet Fraser, v. 540.
—— Duncan, in Cult, ii. 192; ix. 44 *bis*.
—— —— his wife, Christian Campbell, ii. 192.
—— Janetta, wife of A. T. F. Fraser of Abertarff, v. 542.
—— Sir John, diplomat, ii. 522.
—— William, general, vii. 207.
—— —— his wife, Mary Isabella Rollo, vii. 207.
Macpherson-Grant of Ballindalloch and Invereshie, Sir John, 4th bart., vii. 463, 478.
Macqueen of Braxfield, Robert Dundas, iii. 462.
—— —— his wife, Lilias Montgomerie, iii. 462.
—— Fitzherbert, viii. 130.
—— —— his wife, Mary Naesmyth, viii. 130.
Macrae of Pitcon, George, v. 151.
MacRanald of Moydart, Ranald, vii. 497.
—— *, wife of Hector Mackenzie, ancestor of Gairloch, vii. 497.
MacRuari of Garmoran, v. 32, 36.
—— of Kintail, Reginald *or* Ronald, vii. 237.
MacSwein of Killislate, Dougall, vi. 130.
Mactaggart of Ardwell, Sir John, bart., ii. 502.
—— —— Susanna, wife of J. O. Ommancy, ii. 502.
MacTaggart-Stewart of Southwick and Ardwell, Sir Mark John, 1st bart., ii. 119, 502; viii. 145.
—— —— his wife, Marian Ommaney, ii. 502.
—— Frances Emily, wife of Archibald, styled earl of Cassillis, ii. 502.
—— Susanna Mary, wife of 21st lord Borthwick, ii. 119.
Mactyre of Gerloch, Paul, vii. 238.

* Name unknown.

MacVurich, historians of the family of Macdonald of the Isles, v. 27, 28.
M'Ward, Mr. Robert, v. 120.
M'William of Badenoch, Gillescop, vi. 127.
— designated 'earl of Caithness,' ii. 315 *n*.
Madan, Henrietta Anne, wife of lieut.-col. J. H. Keith Stewart, iv. 169.
— Martin, colonel, v. 314.
— Penelope, wife of Sir Alex. Maitland, v. 314.
— Spencer, D.D., iv. 169.
MADERTIE, DRUMMOND, LORD, viii. 216-238.
Madertie, David, third lord, viii. 218; ix. 161.
— — his 1st wife, Alison Creightoun, viii. 219.
— — his 2nd wife, Beatrix Graham, vi. 241; viii. 219.
— James, first lord, vii. 46; viii. 216.
— — his wife, Jean Chisholm, viii. 216.
— James Andrew John Laurence Charles, tenth lord, viii. 234.
— John, second lord, viii. 217.
— — his wife, Margaret Leslie, v. 384; viii. 217; ix. 161 *bis*.
— William, fourth lord, viii. 218, 219.
— — his wife, Elizabeth Johnston, viii. 222.
— William, fifth lord, viii. 222.
— — his wife, Elizabeth Drummond, viii. 222.
— master of, David, son of 2nd lord Madertie, viii. 217.
— — his 1st wife, Alison Creightoun of Luncarty, viii. 219.
Magachen, Roland Ascolog *or*, i. 321.
— — his wife, Katerina, i. 321.
Magbiadr, jarl in Caithness and Moray, ii. 314; vi. 281.
Magee, Edward, viii. 467.
— — his wife, Mary Catherine Cox, viii. 467.
Magnus IV., king of Norway, v. 34.
Magnus, son of Colban, earl of Buchan, ix. 47.
Magnus, *, vi. 445.
— — his wife, Elizabeth Leslie, vi. 445.
Mahony, Cecilia Carlotta Francisca Anna, wife of Benedict, prince Giustiniani; countess, vi. 454.
— John Joseph, count, vi. 454.
— — his wife, Anne Clifford, vi. 454.
Main, Christian, wife of Thos. Wemyss, viii. 496.
— David, writer, viii. 496.
— — his wife, Grisel Weir, viii. 496.
Maistertoun, Margaret, wife of James Primrose of Barhill, vii. 213.
MAITLAND, MAITLAND, VISCOUNT, v. 302-323.

* Name unknown.

Maitland, Frederick Colin, eldest son of 13th earl of Lauderdale; styled viscount, v. 321.
— — his wife, Gwendoline Lucy Williams, v. 322.
— James, eldest son of 5th earl of Lauderdale; styled viscount, v. 311.
— — his wife, Jean Sutherland *or* Gordon, iv. 249; v. 311; viii. 355.
— John, first viscount, ii. 477; v. 302.
— John, eldest son of 1st earl of Lauderdale; styled lord, i. 567; v. 303.
— Richard, eldest son of 3rd earl of Lauderdale; styled lord, iii. 328; v. 309.
MAITLAND, EARL OF GUILFORD, v. 305.
MAITLAND, EARL OF LAUDERDALE, v. 276-323.
MAITLAND, VISCOUNT OF LAUDERDALE, v. 302-323.
MAITLAND, DUKE OF LAUDERDALE, v. 305-306.
MAITLAND, LORD LAUDERDALE OF THIRLESTANE CASTLE, v. 319-320.
MAITLAND, VISCOUNT MAITLAND, v. 302-323.
MAITLAND, MARQUESS OF MARCH, v. 305.
MAITLAND, BARON PETERSHAM, v. 305.
MAITLAND, LORD THIRLESTANE, v. 299-323.
MAITLAND, LORD THIRLESTANE AND BOLTON, v. 302, 323.
MAITLAND, LORD THIRLESTANE, MUSSELBURGH AND BOLTOUN, v. 305.
Maitland of Ardross, Alexander, v. 283.
— of Auchinhreck, James, iii. 306; v. 287.
— — his wife, Egidia Scrymgeour, iii. 306; v. 287.
— of Auchencreiff, Robert, ancestor of the family of, v. 283.
— — Robert, v. 300.
— of Auchingassil, James, ancestor of the family of, v. 287.
— — James, i. 222; v. 288.
— — his wife, Janet Campbell, i. 222.
— — John, v. 288, 299.
— — John, i. 247; v. 288, 299, 300; vii. 131.
— — his wife, Dorothea Johnstone, i. 247.
— — Robert, son of James M. of Bagraw, v. 288.
— of Bagbie, James, v. 302.
— — John, v. 302.
— — Robert, v. 280.
— of Bagraw, James, v. 287.
— of Balbreggan, John, v. 316.
— — Patrick, v. 316.
— of Blyth, Sir John, v. 299.
— — Sir Richard, v. 299.
— — William, v. 278.
— — William, v. 289.
— of Bolton, James, son of William M. of Lethington, v. 295, 299, 302.
— — his wife, Agnes Maxwell, iv. 415; v. 296.

Maitland of Bolton, Robert, v. 280.
— of Braidwood, Sir John, i. 197.
— of Burnscleuch, William, v. 289.
— of Clifton Hall, Sir Alexander Charles, 2nd bart., v. 314.
— — his wife, Helen Gibson of Clifton Hall, v. 314.
— of Covington, John, v. 284.
— of Cowanstone, John, v. 284.
— of Craigieburn, Charles, lieut.-colonel, vi. 433.
— — his wife, Isabella Napier, vi. 433.
— of Currie, Alexander, v. 283.
— of Dudhope, Charles, v. 306.
— of Dunbar, Sir John, v. 300.
— of Dundrennan, Thomas, viii. 397.
— of Eccles, James, ancestor of the family of, v. 287.
— of Egrope, William, v. 290.
— of Fairgirth, James, D.D., minister of Kells, v. 133.
— — his 2nd wife, Louisa Bellamy-Gordon, v. 133.
— of Farnington, William, v. 289.
— of Forest of Lauder, Charles, v. 306.
— of Freugh, John, v. 316.
— — his wife, Jane Maxwell, v. 316.
— — Patrick, v. 316.
— — his wife, Jane Maitland, v. 316; vii. 307.
— of Over Gogar, Richard, lord Justice-Clerk, v. 309.
— — his wife, Anne Campbell, i. 368; v. 310.
— of Garvet, Richard, grandson of Secretary Lethington, v. 296.
— of Gight, Sir Richard, i. 82.
— — Robert, ancestor of the family of, v. 283.
— of Gilbertoun, John, v. 301.
— — his wife, Isobel Seton, iii. 372; v. 301.
— of Gilmerton, Charles, v. 306.
— of Glassary, Charles, v. 306.
— of Haddington Abbey, William, v. 295.
— of Halsington, Thomas, v. 282.
— of Halton, Charles, 3rd son of 1st earl of Lauderdale, ii. 30; iii. 304 *n.*; v. 303, 305, 306.
— — his wife, Elizabeth Lauder of Halton, v. 306.
— of Hedderwick, Sir Richard, v. 278.
— — William, v. 278.
— — William, v. 289.
— of Innerleithen, William, v. 281.
— of Inverkeithing, Charles, v. 306.
— of Kilmaron, Patrick, v. 313.
— — his wife, Anne Bateman, v. 313.
— of Ladystoun, Robert, v. 280.
— of Lethington, John, 2nd laird, v. 285; viii. 422.
— — his 1st wife, Felicia, v. 284.
— — his 2nd wife, Agnes Dunbar, iii. 261; v. 284.
Maitland of Lethington, Sir John, keeper of the great seal, chancellor, 7th laird, v. 299.
— — his wife, Jean Fleming, v. 300; viii. 512.
— — Sir Richard, 6th laird, v. 279, 289, 291; viii. 559, 579.
— — his wife, Mariota Cranston, v. 293.
— — Robert, 1st laird, v. 280.
— — his wife, Christiana Keith, v. 280, 281; vi. 33.
— — Sir Robert, 3rd laird, iii. 306; v. 285, 286.
— — his wife, Marion Abernethy, iii. 306; v. 287.
— — William, 4th laird, v. 289.
— — his wife, Margaret Wardlaw, v. 289.
— — William, 5th laird, v. 290; vii. 118.
— — his wife, Martha *or* Margaret Seton, v. 291; viii. 579.
— — William, the younger, secretary of State, lord of Session, v. 293, 298.
— — his 1st wife, Jonet Menteith, iv. 537; v. 295.
— — his 2nd wife, Mary Fleming, v. 295; viii. 541.
— of Lindores, Sir Frederick Lewis, rear-admiral, R.N., K.C.B., v. 316.
— — his wife, Catharine Connor, v. 316.
— of Lundin, Robert, 2nd son of 1st earl of Lauderdale, v. 302.
— — his wife, Margaret Lundin of Lundin, v. 302.
— of Musselburgh, Sir John, v. 300.
— of Netherdale, Robert, iv. 516.
— of Ormiston, Thomas, v. 282.
— — William, v. 281.
— of Pencaitland, Alexander, v. 283; vi. 473.
— of Pitrichie, Alexander, *né* Arbuthnott, i. 309, 312.
— — his wife, Jean Maitland, i. 309.
— — Sir Charles, i. 309.
— — Charles, i. 309.
— — Jean, wife of A. Arbuthnott, i. 309.
— — Richard, lord of Session, 1st bart., v. 283.
— of Queensberry, James, v. 287.
— — Robert, vii. 116.
— — his wife, Elspeth, vii. 116.
— of Rankeillour, Charles, 17th Light Dragoons, v. 316.
— — his wife, Mary Johnston, v. 316.
— — Frederick Lewis, capt. R.N., v. 315.
— — his wife, Margaret Dick, v. 316.
— of Ravelrig, Sir John, advocate, v. 310.
— — his wife, Margaret Cunningham, v. 310.
— of Schivas, Robert, v. 282.
— — his wife, * Schivas, v. 283.
— of Shillinglaw, William, v. 282.
— — his wife, Elizabeth Watson, v. 282.

* Name unknown.

Maitland of Thankerton, Sir John, v. 300.
—— —— his wife, Janet Fleming, v. 300.
—— of Thirlestane, John, 4th laird, v. 284; vi. 474.
—— —— his 1st wife, Felicia, v. 284.
—— —— his 2nd wife, Agnes Dunbar, iii. 261; v. 284.
—— —— Sir John, commendator of Coldingham, 9th laird, ii. 69; v. 295 *bis*, 297.
—— —— his wife, Jean Fleming, v. 300; viii. 542.
—— —— Sir Richard, 1st laird, v. 278.
—— —— his wife, Avice of Thirlestane, v. 278.
—— —— Sir Richard, 8th laird, v. 279, 289, 291, 298.
—— —— his wife, Mariota Cranston, v. 293.
—— —— Robert, 3rd laird, v. 280.
—— —— his wife, Christiana Keith, v. 280, 281; vi. 33.
—— —— Sir Robert, 5th laird, v. 286.
—— —— his wife, Marion Abernethy, iii. 306; v. 287.
—— —— William, 2nd laird, v. 278, 279.
—— —— William, 6th laird, v. 287, 289.
—— —— his wife, Margaret Wardlaw, v. 289.
—— —— William, 7th laird, v. 290.
—— —— his wife, Martha *or* Margaret Seton, v. 291; viii. 579.
—— of Tibbers, John, v. 284.
—— —— Sir Robert, iii. 262; v. 286.
—— —— William, v. 291; vii. 118.
—— of Tibbers Mote, James, v. 288.
—— —— Robert, v. 288.
—— of Tillicoultry, Charles, v. 311.
—— —— his 1st wife, Isobel Barclay, v. 311.
—— —— his 2nd wife, * Haldane, v. 312.
—— —— his 3rd wife, Janet Moncreiffe, v. 312.
—— —— Charles, 2nd Dragoon Guards, 22nd Dragoons, v. 312.
—— —— his wife, Elizabeth Mary Hall, v. 312.
—— of Traquair, Thomas, v. 282.
—— —— his wife, Margaret, v. 282.
—— —— William, bailie of Lauderdale, v. 281.
—— —— his wife, Isabella, v. 282.
—— —— William, v. 282.
—— —— his wife, Elizabeth Watson, v. 282.
—— of Tullous, Sir Robert, v. 285.
—— Ada Marian, wife of Sir Ralph H. S. Wilmot, v. 322.
—— Agnes Maud, v. 315.
—— Alexander, 5th son of 3rd earl of Lauderdale, v. 308.
—— —— his wife, Janet Campbell, v. 308.
—— Alexander, v. 312.
—— —— his wife, Margaret Cooper, v. 312.
—— Sir Alexander, general, 1st bart., v. 314.
—— —— his wife, Penelope Madan, v. 314.

* Name unknown.

Maitland, Alexander Gibson, advocate, v 314, 315.
—— —— his wife, Susan Ramsay of Barnton, v. 315.
—— Alfred Henry, capt. Cameron Highlanders, v. 322.
—— —— his wife, Edith Scobell, v. 322.
—— Anna, wife of Robert, master of Winton, v. 301; viii. 592.
—— Anne, wife of R. Fraser of Torbreck, v. 319; ix. 125.
—— Augustus, lieut.-col. of the Guards, v. 314.
—— Augustus, W.S., v. 314.
—— —— his wife, Eliza Jane Richards, v. 314.
—— Barbara, wife of (3) Helenus Halkerston of Rathillet, v. 309.
—— Charles, 3rd son of 3rd earl of Lauderdale, v. 308.
—— —— his wife, Lilias Colquhoun, v. 308.
—— Charles, son of Alexander M., v. 308.
—— Charles, rector of Little Langford, v. 312.
—— —— his wife, Anne Knott, v. 312.
—— Charles, R.N., v. 312.
—— Charles, midshipman R.N., v. 314.
—— Charles James Fox, 4th son of 8th earl of Lauderdale, v. 319.
—— Charlotte, dau. of Patrick John M., v. 313.
—— Charlotte, dau. of 8th earl of Lauderdale, v. 320.
—— Eleanor, wife of James Balfour of Whittinghame, v. 320.
—— Elizabeth, wife of D. Gavin of Langton, ii. 210; v. 318.
—— Elizabeth, wife of John Gordon of Essie, iv. 516 *bis*.
—— Elizabeth, wife of 2nd earl of Hyndford, iv. 593; v. 311.
—— Elizabeth, wife of Wm. Douglas of Whittinghame, v. 298; ix. 124.
—— Elizabeth, dau. of Chas. M. of Tillicoultry, v. 312.
—— Elizabeth, wife of (1) Jas. Ogilvy of Inchmartine, and (2) gen. Robt. Anstruther, v. 317; ix. 125.
—— Ellen, dau. of major-gen. F. C. M., v. 313.
—— Emily Sophia, wife of admiral F. H. Ker, v. 484.
—— Frederick, son of Patrick John M., v. 313.
—— Frederick, general, v. 314.
—— —— his wife, Katharine Prettyjohn, v. 314.
—— Frederick Charles, v. 314.
—— —— his wife, Emily Jeanette Craigie, v. 314.
—— Frederick Colthurst, major-general, H.E.I.C.S., v. 313.
—— —— his wife, Anna D. Williams, v. 313.

Maitland, Frederick Thomas, lieut.-col., v. 314.
—— his wife, Emily Augusta Mary Newlands, v. 314.
— George, archdeacon of Larne, v. 312.
— George, lieut.-col. Bengal Staff Corps, v. 313.
— George Ramsay, W.S., v. 315.
—— his wife, Alice Anne Nisbet, v. 315.
— Hannah Charlotte, wife of 7th marquess of Tweeddale, v. 318; viii. 466.
— Helen, wife of John Cockburn of Clerkington, v. 298.
— Helen, wife of Jas. A. Hunt of Pittencrieff, v. 315.
— Helen, wife of 11th lord Torphichen, viii. 397.
— Ian Colin, son of viscount Maitland, v. 322.
— Isabel, wife of 8th lord Elphinstone, iii. 543; v. 309; ix. 125.
— Isabel, dau. of Charles M., v. 309.
— Isobella, wife of James Heriot of Traboun, v. 298.
— Isabella, wife of W. P. Colcman, v. 312.
— Isabella, wife of Wm. Roy of Nenthorn, v. 316.
— Isabella, wife of 2nd lord Torphichen, viii. 390.
— Isobel, younger dau. of duke of Lauderdale, ix. 124.
— Isabel Anne, wife of Francis Dashwood, v. 318.
— James, lieut.-col. 75th Foot, v. 313.
— James, 2nd son of Sir A. C. M., v. 314.
— James, brigadier, vi. 112.
— Jane, wife of Sir Jas. Fergusson of Kilkerran, iv. 249; v. 311.
— Jane, wife of Sir Archibald Ogilvy of Inchmartine, v. 312.
— Jane, wife of (1) John, 11th earl of Rothes, and (2) Patrick Maitland of Freugh, v. 316; vii. 307.
— Jane, wife of (1) Samuel Long, and (2) Sir Wm. Houston, v. 318.
— Janet, wife of Thomas Dundas of Fingask, v. 317.
— Janet, wife of Hugh, 4th lord Somerville, v. 291; viii. 18.
— Jean, dau. of 1st earl of Lauderdale, v. 303.
— Jean Hamilton, wife of A. R. Bulwer, v. 315.
— John, Longniddry, ii. 586.
— John, only son of William M. of Thirlestane, v. 289 *bis*.
—— his wife, * Dundas, v. 290.
— John, colonel; 3rd son of 5th earl of Lauderdale, v. 311.

* Name unknown.

Maitland, John, rear-admiral, R.N., v. 313.
—— his 1st wife, Elizabeth Ogilvy, v. 313.
—— his 2nd wife, Dora Batcman, v. 313.
— John, accountant to the Court of Session, v. 314.
—— his wife, Mary Isabella Wood, v. 314.
— John, M.P., lieut.-col. 71st Foot, v. 317.
— John, col. 32nd Foot; 3rd son of 8th earl of Lauderdale, v. 319.
— John Madan, v. 314.
—— his 1st wife, Elinor Annesley, v. 314.
—— his 2nd wife, Harriet Pratt, v. 314.
— Julian Jane, wife of Sir John Warrender, v. 320.
— Katharine, dau. of Alex. M. of Pitrichie, i. 309.
— Keith, barrister-at-law, v. 315.
—— his wife, Ina Blanche Caldwell, v. 315.
— Keith Ramsay, col. 79th Highlanders, v. 315.
—— his wife, Georgine Harriet Glass, v. 315.
— Laura, wife of C. Ross, v. 313.
— Margaret, wife of John Gordon of Essie, i. 82; iv. 516.
— Margaret, dau. of Alex. M. of Pitrichie, i. 309.
— Margaret, wife of (1) James Scrymgeour, and (2) David Hering, iii. 307.
— Margaret, wife of John Edmonstone, v. 290.
— Margaret, wife of Robert Ker of Cessford, v. 297; vii. 345.
— Margaret, wife of (1) C. Ogilvy, (2) Major A. Erskine, and (3) Charles Dundas, lord Amesbury, v. 312.
— Margaret, dau. of Sir A. C. Ramsay-Gibson-M., v. 315.
— Maria Anne, wife of rev. J. H. Dyer, v. 312.
— Marion, contr. to James Sinclair; wife of Robert Fawsyde, v. 295; ix. 157.
— Mary, wife of John Haig of Bemersyde, v. 286.
— Mary, wife of Alexander Lauder of Hatton, v. 298.
— Mary, wife of 2nd marquess of Tweeddale, v. 304, 305; viii. 458; ix. 108.
— Mary, wife of John Melville of Cairnie, v. 309.
— Mary, wife of 4th earl of Southesk, v. 309; viii. 72; ix. 125.
— Mary, wife of Edward Stanley, v. 319.
— Mary, wife of John Rollo, vii. 208.
— Mary, dau. of Sir Richard M. of Lethington, vii. 583.
— Mary Ann, dau. of Alex. M. of Pitrichie, i. 309.
— Mary Jane, wife of 12th earl of Meath, v. 320.

Maitland, Mary Julian, wife of Thos. Hog of Newliston, v. 318.
—— Mary Turner, wife of Jas. Christie of Durie, v. 312.
—— Mary Turner, wife of H. Scrymgeour Wedderburn, v. 316.
—— Mary Turner, dau. of Patrick M. of Freugh, v. 316.
—— Nora, wife of Wm. Fitzherbert, v. 322.
—— Patrick John, v. 313.
—— —— his wife, Laura Roberts, v. 313.
—— Sir Peregrine, G.C.B., v. 484.
—— —— his wife, Sarah Lennox, v. 367, 484.
—— Richard, deputy-adjutant-gen., v. 312.
—— —— his wife, Mary MacAdam, v. 312.
—— Richard, R.N., 86th Foot, etc., v. 313.
—— —— his wife, Harriot Bower, v. 313.
—— Robert, eldest son of Sir Robert M. of Thirlestane, v. 287.
—— Robert, 2nd son of Wm. M. of Lethington, v. 291, 298.
—— Robert, midshipman, R.N., v. 316.
—— Sophia, dau. of 1st earl of Lauderdale, v. 303.
—— Susan Jean, v. 315.
—— Sydney George William, in holy orders; 3rd batt. Royal Scots Fusiliers, v. 322.
—— —— his wife, Ella Frances Richards, v. 322.
—— Thomas, brother of Secretary Lethington, v. 297, 298.
—— Thomas, 4th son of 3rd earl of Lauderdale, v. 308; ix. 125.
—— Sir Thomas, M.P., lieut.-gen., governor of Malta, v. 317.
—— Thomas, minister of Garvald, ix. 136.
—— —— his wife, Margaret Melville, ix. 136.
—— Valdave Charles Lauder, v. 317.
—— William, 'Burd-alane,' v. 280.
—— William, v. 309.
—— —— his 1st wife, Christian MacGill, v. 309; vi. 599.
—— —— his 2nd wife, Margaret Walker, v. 309.
—— William, 2nd son of gen. Sir Alex. M., v. 314.
—— William Forbes, v. 315.
—— William Mordaunt, lieut.-gen., v. 318.
—— —— his 1st wife, Mary Orpen, v. 318.
—— —— his 2nd wife, Jane Walker, v. 318.
—— William Ramsay, v. 315.
—— *, 2nd son of William M. of Thirlestane, v. 281.
—— *, husband of * Colville, ii. 537.
—— colonel, 72nd Bengal N.I., vii. 208.
Maitland-Gordon of Kenmure, James Charles, v. 133.
Maitland-Makgill of Oxfuird, Robert, grandson of 2nd viscount of Oxfuird, v. 309; vi. 600.
—— —— his wife, Janet Christie, vi. 600.

* Name unknown.

Maitland-Makgill of Rankeillour, David, iv. 130.
Majendie of Castle Hedingham, Lewis Ashurst, iii. 48.
—— —— his wife, Margaret Elizabeth Lindsay, iii. 48.
Makcartney, James, Edinburgh, iv. 306.
—— —— his wife, Marion Hamilton, iv. 306.
MAKGILL OF COUSLAND, MAKGILL, LORD, vi. 596-601.
Makgill of Cousland, James, first lord, vi. 595.
MAKGILL, VISCOUNT OF OXFUIRD, vi. 587-601.
Makgill of Balvormy, David, vi. 592.
—— of Cranston Makgill, George, vi. 599.
—— —— Patrick, vi. 597, 599; ix. 147.
—— of Cranstoun Riddell, David, king's advocate, 1st laird, ii. 486; vi. 591, 592.
—— —— his 1st wife, Elizabeth Forrester, iv. 88; vi. 593.
—— —— his 2nd wife, Isobel Cuninghame, vi. 593.
—— —— David, 2nd laird, vi. 594; ix. 147.
—— —— his wife, Marie Sinclair, vi. 595; vii. 583.
—— —— David, 3rd laird, vi. 595.
—— —— Sir James, 1st bart., vi. 595.
—— —— his 1st wife, Katharine Cockburn, vi. 596.
—— —— his 2nd wife, Christian Livingston, vi. 598.
—— of Drylaw, David, iv. 88.
—— —— his 1st wife, Elizabeth Forrester of Drylaw, iv. 88; vi. 593.
—— of Fingask, James, vi. 590.
—— —— John, vi. 591.
—— —— Robert, 1st laird, vi. 591.
—— of Flasshill, James, vi. 590.
—— —— his wife, Jean Balfour, vi. 590.
—— of Grange, Hew, vi. 591.
—— —— his wife, Margaret Cornwall, vi. 591.
—— of Kemback, Sir George, 11th bart., vi. 590.
—— —— John, M.D., 1st laird, vi. 590.
—— —— his 1st wife, Helen Forbes, vi. 590.
—— —— his 2nd wife, Euphame Paterson, vi. 590.
—— —— John, v. 415.
—— —— his wife, Agnes Lindsay, v. 415.
—— of Lindores, David, v. 316.
—— of Lochcotes, David, ii. 486.
—— of Nisbet, David, king's advocate, 1st laird, ii. 486; vi. 592; ix. 147 *bis*.
—— —— David, lord of Session, 2nd laird, vi. 594.
—— of Oxfuird, Christian, wife of Wm. Maitland, v. 309; vi. 599; ix. 125.
—— —— Henrietta, wife of Jas. Hamilton of Orbiston, vi. 600.
—— of Quhytebanks, David, vi. 592.

Makgill of Rankeillor, David, 4th laird, vi. 589.
—— —— his wife, Elizabeth Ruthven, iv. 260; vi. 589.
—— —— David, 6th laird, vi. 589, 600.
—— —— his wife, Janet Craige, vi. 589.
—— —— Isabella, wife of Mr. William Dick, and mother of James Dick of Colluthie, v. 316; vi. 589.
—— —— Sir James, clerk-register, v. 65; vi. 588.
—— —— his wife, Janet Adamson, vi. 588; ix. 146.
—— —— James, 2nd laird, vi. 588.
—— —— his wife, Jean Wemyss, vi. 588; viii. 497.
—— —— James, 3rd laird, vi. 589.
—— —— his wife, Anna Clephanc, vi. 589.
—— —— Sir James, 5th laird, vi. 589.
—— —— his 1st wife, Janet Crichton, iv. 130; vi. 589.
—— —— his 2nd wife, Isabel Preston, vi. 589.
—— —— James. 7th laird, v. 316; vi. 589, 600.
—— —— his wife, Jean Anstruther, vi. 589.
—— —— Katharine, wife of Alexander Christie, vi. 589.
—— of Ransburn, David, vi. 592.
—— Agnes, wife of John Hill, vi. 591.
—— Alexander, surgeon, vi. 589.
—— Alexander, 3rd son of James M. of Rankeillor, vi. 591.
—— Alexander, 2nd son of David M. of Cranston Riddell, vi. 593.
—— Alexander, provost of Corstorphine, vi. 594.
—— Alexander, 6th son of David M. of Cranston Riddell, vi. 595.
—— Alison, wife of (1) Stephen Brounfield, and (2) Nicoll Home, vi. 587.
—— Andrew, 2nd son of 1st viscount of Oxfuird, vi. 597.
—— Anna, wife of John Ross of Millanderdale, vi. 595.
—— Anna, wife of Sir Jas. Richardson of Smeaton, vi. 598.
—— Cecile, wife of Sir John Learmonth of Balcomie, vi. 591.
—— Christian, wife of (1) Alex. Crawford of Carse, (2) Geo. Ross of Galston, and (3) Henry Clark, vi. 598; ix. 147.
—— David, professor at Montpelier, vi. 591.
—— David, advocate, canon of Dunkeld, vi. 591.
—— David, eldest son of Lawrence M., vi. 593.
—— David, 5th son of 1st viscount of Oxfuird, vi. 598; ix. 147.
—— Elizabeth, wife of (1) Robert Logan of Restalrig, (2) Thos. Kennedy of Culzean, and (3) Wm. Mure of Rowallan, ii. 487; vi. 594; ix. 57 *bis*.
Makgill, Elizabeth, wife of James, master of Cranstoun, ii. 593; vi. 595.
—— Elizabeth, wife of David Wod of Dunone, vi. 591.
—— Elizabeth, wife of Patrick Hamilton of Little Preston, vi. 597.
—— Elizabeth, dau. of 1st viscount of Oxfuird, vi. 598.
—— Elizabeth, dau. of 2nd viscount of Oxfuird, vi. 600.
—— George, captain, 9th son of Jas. M. of Rankeillor, vi. 591.
—— George, 5th son of David M. of Cranston Riddell, vi. 594.
—— George, lieut.-col. Scots Guards, vi. 598, 600.
—— —— his wife, Elizabeth Hamilton, vi. 598.
—— George, master of Oxfuird, vi. 599; ix. 147.
—— Helen, wife of (1) Thomas Cranston, (2) William Knowis, and (3) Simon Currie, ii. 590; vi. 592; ix. 60.
—— Helen, wife of Joseph Heart of Chappell, vi. 598.
—— Henry, minister of Dunfermline, vi. 591.
—— —— his 1st wife, Isobel Lindsay, vi. 591.
—— —— his 2nd wife, Margaret Wardlaw, vi. 591.
—— Sir James, provost of Edinburgh, vi. 587.
—— —— his 1st wife, Elizabeth Cunyngham, vi. 587.
—— —— his 2nd wife, Helen Wardlaw, vi. 587.
—— James, son of Laurence M., vi. 594.
—— James, eldest son of 1st viscount of Oxfuird, vi. 596.
—— Janet, dau. of Laurence M., vi. 594.
—— Jean, wife of John Scrymgeour of Kirktown, vi. 590.
—— Jean, wife of (1) Wm. Gourlay of Kincraig, and (2) David Brown of Finmont, vi. 591.
—— Jean, dau. of David M. of Cranston Riddell, vi. 594.
—— John, eldest son of Sir Jas. M., vi. 587.
—— —— his wife, Margaret Preston, vi. 587.
—— John, minister of Flisk, vi. 591.
—— —— his wife, Euphame Inglis, vi. 591.
—— John, collegiate church of Dunbar, vi. 591.
—— —— his wife, Elizabeth Home, vi. 591.
—— John, writer to the signet, vi. 594.
—— —— his 2nd wife, Maria Sandilands, vi. 594.
—— John, 5th son of David M., vi. 595.
—— —— his wife, Marion Menzies, vi. 595.
—— Katharine, wife of Robert Clayhills of Baldovie, vi. 590.
—— Katharine, wife of capt. John Ruthven, vi. 598.

Makgill, Katharine, wife of Alexander Christie, vi. 600.
— Laurence, advocate, vi. 593.
— — his 1st wife, Jean Crichton, vi. 593.
— — his 2nd wife, Helen *, vi. 593.
— Laurence, his 2nd son, vi. 593.
— Lilias, wife of Henry Pitcairn of Pitlour, vi. 590.
— Lilias, wife of Robert Brown of Kinmount, vi. 591.
— Margaret, wife of William Redpath, vi. 587.
— Margaret, wife of John Skene, vi. 590.
— Margaret, wife of David Heriot, vi. 594 *bis*.
— Margaret, dau. of 1st viscount of Oxfuird, vi. 598.
— Marie, wife of Robert Hodge, vi. 595.
— Marie, dau. of 1st viscount of Oxfuird, vi. 599.
— Marie, dau. of 2nd viscount of Oxfuird, vi. 600.
— Patrick, 3rd son of Sir Jas. M. of Rankeillor, vi. 590.
— Patrick, minister of Barrie, and Monikie, vi. 591.
— — his wife, Jean Irwine, vi. 591.
— Patrick, 3rd son of David M. of Cranstoun Riddell, vi. 595.
— Rachel, wife of (1) George Stewart, and (2) Archibald Wauchope, vi. 591.
— Robert, lord of Session, lord Foord, vi. 590.
— — his wife, Margaret Purves, vi. 590.
— Robert Maitland; self-styled viscount of Oxfuird, v. 309; vi. 600.
— — his wife, Janet Christie, v. 309.
— Samuel, Ulster, vi. 591.
— Thomas, 3rd son of Laurence M., vi. 593.
— Thomas, 4th son of David M., vi. 595.
— William, M.D., one of the founders of the Edinburgh College of Physicians, vi. 591.
— Zachary, 5th son of Sir Jas. M. of Rankeillor, vi. 591.
Makullo, George, iv. 193.
— — his wife, Marie Boyle, iv. 193.
Malbeth Bere of Liberton and Lecbernard, vi. 76.
Malcolm II., king of Scots, i. 1; ii. 314; iii. 240 *bis*; viii. 266.
Malcolm III., 'Ceannmor,' king of Scots, i. 1; ii. 314; iii. 240 *bis*; iv. 1; vi. 283, 284.
— — his 1st wife, Ingibiorg, i. 2; ii. 314.
— — his 2nd wife, Margaret of England, i. 2; viii. 476.
Malcolm IV., 'the Maiden,' king of Scots, i. 4, 5; iv. 5, 6; v. 30; vii. 158.
Malcolm of Achnagart, vii. 265.
Malcolm of Constabletun, vii. 365.
— — his wife, Alice, vii. 365.

* Name unknown.

Malcolm of Craigarn, son of Ferquhard, earl of Ross, vii. 232.
Malcolm of Cumbria, son of Crinan, iii. 240, 242.
Malcolm of Middleton, son of Kenneth, vi. 170.
Malcolm, alleged 3rd son of king Malcolm 'Ceannmor,' i. 2.
Malcolm, elder son of king David I., i. 3.
Malcolm, illeg. son of king Alexander I., i. 3.
Malcolm, son of Malcolm, 4th earl of Atholl, i. 418.
Malcolm, son of Gilbert, lord of Galloway, ii. 421.
Malcolm Fitz-Roland, Kirkmichael, ii. 425.
Malcolm, son of Henry, son of Fergus of Carrick, iii. 426.
Malcolm Macheth, claimant to the earldom of Moray, v. 29; vii. 158.
Malcolm, son of Duncan, v. 183.
— — his wife, Eva of Lennox, v. 183.
Malcolm, 4th son of Alwin, 2nd earl of Lennox, v. 328, 329.
Malcolm, 3rd son of Malcolm, 5th earl of Lennox, v. 336.
Malcolm, eldest son of Morgund, 2nd earl of Mar, v. 569, 573.
Malcolm, son of Gilchrist, 3rd earl of Mar, v. 572, 573.
Malcolm Beg, seneschal to Malduin, earl of Lennox, vii. 28.
Malcolm, brother of Norman, constable of Inverurie, vii. 266.
Malcolm of Balbeadie, Michael, v. 407; ix. 136.
— — his wife, Herries Graham, vi. 151; ix. 136.
— of Lochore and Innertiel, Sir John, i. 546.
— — his wife, Emilia Balfour, i. 546.
— of Maxtoke Castle, Charles Edward, vii. 393.
— — his wife, Beatrix Mary Leslie Hore-Ruthven, vii. 393.
— Amelia, wife of Christopher Lindsay, v. 407.
— Andrew, burgess of Edinburgh, vi. 174.
— Ann, wife of Geo. Oliphant, i. 546.
— rev. David, ix. 161.
— Sir Pulteney, admiral, G.C.B., iii. 548.
— — his wife, Clementina Fullerton-Elphinstone, iii. 548.
Maldouen, grandfather of Alwin, 1st earl of Lennox, v. 326.
Maldouen, dean of Lennox, v. 328.
Maldred of Cumbria, son of Crinan, iii. 240, 242.
Maldred, 2nd son of Maldred of Cumbria iii. 241.
Maleville, Normandy, vi. 75.
Malherbe, Gilbert, vi. 135 *n*.

Malherbe, John, ii. 536.
—— —— his wife, Ada, ii. 536.
—— Matilda, wife of Galfrid Melville of Melville, vi. 77.
Maling, Christopher Simpson, lieut.-col. Bengal Native Infantry, iii. 390.
—— —— his wife, Wemyss Jane Murray, iii. 390.
Malise, son of Malcolm, 2nd earl of Atholl, i. 418.
Malise, seneschal of Strathearn, i. 453; v. 325 *n.*; viii. 241, 242.
—— —— his wife, Ada, i. 4; v. 325 *n.*; viii. 241.
Malise of Rossie, 6th son of Gilbert, earl of Strathearn, viii. 243.
—— —— his son, viii. 243.
Mallet, Dr. Joseph, ii. 494.
—— —— his wife, Katharine Kennedy, ii. 494.
—— William, the poet, vi. 267.
Malleverer, Hugh, i. 231.
Malleville, Guillaume de, vi. 75.
Malloch of Multriesbill, Alexander, i. 306.
—— Elizabeth, wife of (1) Robt. Arbuthnott, and (2) Kenneth Gordon, i. 306.
—— Robert, merchant in Edinburgh, i. 306.
Mallory of Studley, Sir John, v. 12.
—— Jane, wife of Arthur Ingram, v. 12.
Malvoisin, Ralph, vii. 3.
—— William, bishop of Glasgow, and St. Andrews, i. 423; ii. 536; viii. 476.
Malvyn, Jonet, wife of Geo. Hepburne, ii. 139.
Malyn, Elizabeth, wife of (1) Jas. Fleet, (2) Capt. Sabine, (3) 8th lord Cathcart, and (4) lt.-col. Maguire, ii. 520; ix. 58.
—— Thomas, Southwark and Battersea, ii. 520.
—— William, private secretary to Cromwell, v. 467 *n.*
Man, Olaf, 5th king of, iv. 143; vii. 233.
—— —— his wife, Christina de Ross, vii. 233.
—— George, 10th earl of Dunbar, lord of, iii. 270.
—— Alexander Stewart, lord of, i. 152.
—— Murray, duke of Atholl, sovereign of Isle of, i. 488, 490.
—— Stanley, earl of Derby, sovereign of Isle of, i. 488.
Manchester, George (Montagu), 4th duke of, vi. 271.
—— George (Montagu), 6th duke of, v. 254.
—— William (Montagu), 5th duke of, iv. 557; viii. 470.
—— —— his wife, Susan Gordon, iv. 557.
Manderscheidt, count de, vii. 68.
—— —— his wife, Erica *, vii 68.
Mandeville, Roger de, a Competitor, i. 5.

* Name unknown.

Mann, lieut.-col., 1656, v. 228 *n.*
Manners of Haddon, Henry John Brinsley (Manners), baron, iii. 45.
—— of Grantham Grange, John, iii. 412; viii. 158.
—— —— his wife, Louisa, countess of Dysart, iii. 412; viii. 158.
—— of Market Overton, Charles, iii. 413.
—— —— his 1st wife, Frances Hay, viii. 450, 460.
—— Elizabeth, wife of Sir Wm. Fairfax, iii. 596.
—— Elizabeth Emily, wife of G. W. Montagu Douglas Scott, ii. 248.
—— Elizabeth Frederica, wife of A. R. Drummond, viii. 229.
—— Frances, wife of (1) George (Carpenter), earl of Tyrconnel, and (2) Philip Leslie, vi. 445.
—— Katharine Sophia, wife of Sir Gilbert Heathcote, 4th bart., iii. 414.
—— Laura, wife of 7th earl of Stair, viii. 158.
—— Louisa Grace, wife of 6th duke of St. Albans, iii. 414.
—— Lucy, wife of 2nd duke of Montrose, vi. 268.
—— Maria Carolina, wife of James, viscount Macduff, iii. 414.
—— Sir Robert, iii. 596.
—— William, 2nd son of 2nd duke of Rutland, iii. 412.
Manners, *alias* Tollemache, Charles, 3rd son of John Manners and Louisa, countess of Dysart, iii. 413.
—— John, 2nd son of John Manners and Louisa, countess of Dysart, iii. 412.
—— Laura, wife of John William Henry Dalrymple, iii. 414.
Manning, Annabella, wife of Fairfax Erskine, ii. 276.
Mansel *or* Mansfeild, Richard, West Leek, ii. 582.
—— —— his wife, Elizabeth Richardson, ii. 582.
MANSFIELD, MURRAY, EARL OF, viii. 206-214.
Mansfield, Alan David, sixth earl of, i. 226; viii. 213.
—— —— his wife, Margaret Helen Mary MacGregor, viii. 214.
—— William David, fourth earl of, iii. 394; viii. 212.
—— —— his wife, Louisa Ellison, viii. 212.
—— William David, fifth earl of, viii. 213.
—— David William, third earl of, viii. 210.
—— —— his wife, Frederica Markham, viii. 210.
—— Louisa (Cathcart), wife of (1) David, 7th viscount of Stormont, and (2) Robert Fulke Greville; countess of, ii. 523; viii. 206, 209.

Mansfield, David, second earl of, viii. 206, 208.
—— his 1st wife, Henrietta Frederica Bunau, viii. 208.
—— his 2nd wife, Louisa Cathcart, countess of Mansfield, ii. 523; viii. 206, 209.
— William, first earl of, viii. 206.
—— his wife, Elizabeth Finch, viii. 206.
MANSFIELD, MURRAY, BARON OF, viii. 205-214.
Mansfield, William, first baron of, viii. 205; ix. 14.
Mansfield, Charles (Cavendish), eldest son of William, duke of Newcastle; styled lord, v. 361.
—— his wife, Elizabeth Rogers, v. 361.
— of Midmar, James, viii. 136.
—— his wife, Marion Dalrymple-Elphinstone, viii. 136.
Manson of Bridgend, George, ii. 349.
—— his wife, Katharine Sinclair, ii. 349.
— Alexander, iii. 362.
— Mary Ann, wife of major W. E. Cochrane, iii. 362.
Manvers, Sydney William Herbert (Pierrepont), 3rd earl, viii. 127.
—— his wife, Georgine Elizabeth Fanny de Franquetot, viii. 127.
MAR, THE ANCIENT EARLS OF, v. 566-589.
Mar, Donald, sixth earl of, iv. 9; v. 577.
—— his wife, Helen of North Wales, v. 578.
— Donald, eighth earl of, i. 427; iii. 191 *n.*; v. 581; vi. 137.
—— his wife, Isabel Stewart, v. 583.
— Duncan, fourth earl of, v. 569, 573.
— Gartnet *or* Gratney, seventh earl of, ii. 257; iii. 191 *n.*; v. 578.
—— his wife, Christian Bruce, ii. 434; v. 579.
— Gilchrist, third earl of, v. 570, 574.
—— his wife, Orabilis, iv. 6; v. 571.
— Isabella, wife of (1) Sir Malcolm Drummond of Strathurd, and (2) Sir Alexander Stewart; countess of, i. 173; iii. 152, 153, 157, 537; iv. 47; v. 587, 597, 602; vi. 37; vii. 39, 432; viii. 528.
— Margaret, wife of (1) William, 1st earl of Douglas, and (2) Sir John Swinton of Swinton; countess of, iii. 152, 153; iv. 333 *bis*; v. 585; vii. 112, 113, 579.
— Morgund, second earl of, v. 567.
—— his wife, Agnes, v. 567, 573.
— Ruadri *or* Rotheri, first earl of, ii. 250; v. 567.
— Thomas, ninth earl of, ii. 586; iii. 152; iv. 45; v. 580, 583, 593; vi. 139.
—— his 1st wife, Margaret Graham, v. 584; vi. 138.
—— his 2nd wife, Margaret Stewart, i. 171; v. 584.
Mar, William, fifth earl of, ii. 255; v. 574; viii. 245 *n.*
—— his 1st wife, Elizabeth Comyn, ii. 254; v. 576.
—— his 2nd wife, Muriel of Strathearn, v. 576; viii. 247.
MAR, DOUGLAS, EARL OF, v. 585-586.
Mar, James, son of 1st earl of Douglas; styled earl of, iii. 155; v. 585, 586.
— William, 1st earl of Douglas; *de jure ux.* earl of, iii. 152; v. 585.
—— his wife, Margaret, countess of Mar, v. 585.
STEWART, EARL OF MAR, v. 587-589.
Mar, Alexander, illeg. son of the Wolf of Badenoch; earl of, ii. 263; iii. 154; iv. 46, 47, 69, 519; v. 42, 551, 587, 601, 619, 623; viii. 529; ix. 133.
—— his 1st wife, Isabella, countess of Mar, v. 586.
—— his 2nd wife, Marie van Hoorn of Duffel, v. 588.
MAR, STEWART, EARL OF, v. 637-639.
Mar, Alexander, 2nd son of king James II.; earl of, i. 152; v. 638.
— James, legtd. son of king James V.; earl of, i. 24; v. 639; vi. 314.
— John, 4th son of king James II.; earl of, i. 20, 151; v. 637.
— John, 3rd son of king James III.; earl of, i. 21; iii. 588; v. 639.
MAR, ERSKINE, EARL OF, v. 589-635.
Mar, Charles, earl of, iv. 120; v. 626.
—— his wife, Mary Maule, v. 627; vii. 24.
— John, the Regent, earl of, v. 613.
—— his wife, Annabella Murray, i. 464; v. 613.
— John, earl of, ii. 411; iii. 537, 591; v. 165, 356, 615; vi. 547; viii. 25.
—— his 1st wife, Anne Drummond, v. 621; vii. 46.
—— his 2nd wife, Marie Stewart, v. 356, 620.
— John, earl of, v. 623.
—— his wife, Jean Hay, iii. 577; v. 623.
— John, earl of, v. 625.
—— his 1st wife, Elizabeth Scott, ii. 234; v. 625.
—— his 2nd wife, Jean *or* Mary Mackenzie, v. 626.
— John, earl of, i. 373; v. 126, 508, 629.
—— his 1st wife, Margaret Hay, v. 232, 631.
—— his 2nd wife, Frances Pierrepont, v. 632.
— John Francis, earl of, v. 633.
—— his wife, Frances Floyer, v. 634.
— John Francis Miller, earl of, v. 635.
—— his wife, Philadelphia Stuart-Menteath, v. 635.
— John Thomas, earl of, v. 635.
—— his wife, Janet Miller, v. 635.

Mar, Robert, earl of, iv. 48, 49; v. 602, 604, 613.
—— —— his wife, Elizabeth Lindsay, iii. 17; v. 604.
MAR, GOODEVE-ERSKINE, EARL OF, v. 635-636.
Mar, John Francis Erskine, earl of, v. 635.
—— —— his wife, Alice Mary Sinclair Hamilton, v. 636.
Mar, John (Erskine), duke of, v. 231, 631.
—— master of, Thomas, son of 1st lord Erskine; styled, v. 602, 605.
—— Donald, son of Evan; mormaor of, v. 566.
—— Sir Donald of, 4th son of Morgund, 2nd earl of Mar, v. 569.
—— Ellen of, wife of Sir John Menteith of Rusky, v. 579; vi. 132.
—— Sir John Swinton; lord of, v. 585; vii. 113.
—— —— his wife, Margaret, countess of Mar, v. 585.
—— Marjorie of, wife of John of Strathbogie, earl of Atholl, i. 427; iii. 191 *n.*; v. 578; viii. 325.
—— Mary of, wife of Kenneth, 4th earl of Sutherland, iii. 191; v. 578; viii. 325.
—— of Achtirforfar, John, i. 290.
Maranham, Thomas Cochrane, Grand Cross of the Cruzero of Brazil, marquis of, iii. 364.
Marbury, Sir George, i. 40.
—— —— his wife, Johanna Everard, i. 40.
MARCH, DUNBAR, EARL OF, iii. 262-279.
March, George, fifth earl of, iii. 161, 165, 260, 261, 270, 275; iv. 332, 333; v. 284, 286.
—— —— his wife, Christiana de Seton, iii. 273; viii. 571.
—— George, sixth earl of, ii. 142; iii. 276 *bis.*
—— —— his 1st wife, Janet Seton, iii. 275 *n.*; viii. 573.
—— —— his 2nd wife, Beatrix *, iii. 277.
—— —— his *possible* 3rd wife, Alicia Hay, iii. 277; viii. 426.
—— Patrick, 5th earl of Dunbar, earl of, iii. 252; viii. 562.
—— Patrick, first earl of, iii. 255.
—— —— his wife, Euphemia Stewart, iii. 255.
—— Patrick, second earl of, iii. 257.
—— —— his wife, Cecilia, iii. 259.
—— Patrick, third earl of, iii. 262.
—— —— his wife, Marjorie Comyn, ii. 256; iii. 264.
—— Patrick, fourth earl of, ii. 136; iii. 264; viii. 567.
—— —— his 1st wife, Ermegarde *, iii. 268.
—— —— his 2nd wife, Agnes Randolph, iii. 266, 268; vi. 294.
MARCH, STEWART, EARL OF, i. 20.
March, Alexander, 2nd son of king James II.; earl of, i. 20, 151.

* Name unknown.

MARCH, STEWART, EARL OF, v. 355.
March, Robert, earl of, v. 352, 355; ix. 126.
—— —— his wife, Elizabeth Stewart, i. 445; v. 355.
MARCH, STEWART, EARL OF, v. 358-362.
March, Esme, first earl of, v. 358.
—— —— his wife, Catherine Clifton, v. 358.
MARCH, LENNOX, EARL OF, v. 363-371.
March, Charles, first earl of, i. 32; v. 363.
—— Charles, 2nd son of 2nd duke of Lennox; styled earl of, ii. 479; v. 364.
—— Charles Henry, eldest son of 7th duke of Lennox; styled earl of, v. 370.
—— —— his wife, Hilda Madeleine Brassey, v. 370.
MARCH, DOUGLAS, EARL OF, vii. 145-147.
March, William, 2nd son of 1st duke of Queensberry; first earl of, vii. 140, 144.
—— —— his wife, Jean Hay, vii. 145, 146; viii. 456.
—— William, second earl of, vii. 146.
—— —— his wife, Anne Hamilton, countess of Ruglen, vii. 146, 362.
—— William, third earl of, vii. 146.
MARCH, MAITLAND, MARQUESS OF, v. 305.
March, John, marquess of, v. 305.
Marchal, William, viii. 420.
Marchand, William, chaplain, vii. 531.
MARCHMONT, HUME, EARL OF, vi. 1-24.
Marchmont, Alexander, second earl of, vi. 17.
—— —— his wife, Margaret Campbell, vi. 19.
—— Hugh, third earl of, vi. 20.
—— —— his 1st wife, Anne Western, vi. 21.
—— —— his 2nd wife, Elizabeth Crompton, vi. 22.
—— Patrick, first earl of, vi. 12; vii. 70, 146.
—— —— his wife, Grisell Ker, vi. 15.
Marescal, Hervey le, iii. 135.
—— —— his wife, Margaret Douglas, iii. 135.
Margaret of Caithness, wife of Sir Simon Fraser, ii. 319; vii. 426.
Margaret of Flanders, wife of (1) Alexander, prince of Scotland, and (2) Renaud, count of Gueldres, i. 6.
Margaret of Huntingdon, wife of Alan, lord of Galloway, i. 4, 7.
Margaret of Huntingdon, wife of (1) Conan IV., duke of Brittany, and (2) Humphrey de Bohun, earl of Hereford, i. 4.
Margaret of Scotland, wife of Hubert de Burgh, i. 5.
Margaret of Scotland, wife of Eric Magnusson, king of Norway, i. 6; iii. 258.
Margaret, the maid of Norway, i. 6, 7; iii. 258; v. 34.
Margaret of Orkney, wife of (1) Madach, 1st earl of Atholl, and (2) Erlend Ungi, earl of Orkney and Caithness, i. 416; ii. 315, 316.
Margaret, wife of Eustace de Vesci, i. 5.
Margaret, *possible* 1st wife of Sir Nigel Cambel, i. 324.

Margaret, dau. of Malcolm, 2nd earl of Atholl, and *possible* wife of Thomas of Lundin, i. 418.
Margaret, wife of Henry, 3rd earl of Atholl, i. 418, 421.
Margaret, wife of Michael Balfour of Burleigh, i. 531.
Margaret, wife of Neil, earl of Carrick, ii. 426.
Margaret, wife of Sir Patrick Ramsay of Dalhousie, iii. 90.
Margaret, 2nd wife of Sir Alex. Ramsay of Dalhousie, 6th laird, iii. 21.
Margaret, wife of John of Leyis of Bothans, iii. 93.
Margaret, wife of Sir David de Haya of Erroll, iii. 561.
Margaret, wife of John Forbes of Forbes, iv. 46.
Margaret, wife of Ker of Dirleton, iv. 52.
Margaret, wife of Sir Adam Forrester of Corstorphine, iv. 81.
Margaret, wife of Sir John Forrester of Corstorphine, iv. 83.
Margaret, wife of William Cunningham of Kildinnie and Kilfassane, iv. 226.
Margaret, wife of Sir William Cunningham of Kilmaurs, lord of Carrick, iv. 227.
Margaret, wife of Sir Patrick Gray of Broxmouth and Craigie, iv. 271.
Margaret, wife of Sir John Herries of Terregles, iv. 400.
Margaret, wife of Malcolm, 4th earl of Lennox, v. 334.
Margaret, wife of William Livingston of Gorgie, v. 423.
Margaret, wife of Sir Geo. Livingston of Ogilface, v. 412.
Margaret, wife of Sir John Hume of North Berwick and Tully Castle, vi. 8.
Margaret, wife of (1) Thomas (Dunbar), 2nd earl of Moray, and (2) Sir John Ogilvy of Lintrathen and Airlie, i. 113; vi. 303.
Margaret, wife of Norman Leslie, vii. 270, 271.
Margaret, wife of Laurence, 1st lord Abernethy of Saltoun, vii. 407.
Margaret, wife of Sir Wm. St Clair of Herdmanston, vii. 579.
Margaret, wife of John de Hay of Tullibody, viii. 420.
Margaret, wife of Walter Kinnaird, ix. 121.
Marguerie, comte de, vi. 69.
—— his wife, Annabella Henriette Drummond, vi. 69.
Maria, wife of David, 10th earl of Atholl, i. 430.
Maria, wife of (1) Sir Simon Fraser, and (2) Richard Siward, vi. 533 *n.*; vii. 421.
Maria, wife of Sir Simon Fraser of Oliver Castle, vii. 422.
Mariategui, José de, ii. 358.
Mariategui, Marie, duchesse de Pomar, wife of (1) the Condé de Medina Pomar, and (2) James, 14th earl of Caithness, ii. 358.
Marion, wife of (1) * Scott, and (2) Geo. Henderson of Fordel, ii. 65.
Marion, wife of (1) Sir Wm. Oliphant of Aberdalgie and Hasilhead, and (2) James, 1st lord Livingston, v. 430, 431; vi. 537 *n.*, 538 *n.*
Marion, wife of (1) Malise, 1st earl of Menteith, and (2) John Drummond, vi. 144.
Mariota of Glenurquhay, wife of John Cambell, 'Annam,' i. 326.
Mariota of Stobo, dau. of Samuel, vii. 420.
Mariota, mistress of Sir Alexander Stewart, earl of Buchan, ii. 262; vii. 159.
Mariota, wife of Robert Cunningham of Davidstoun and Montgrenane, iv. 239.
Mariota, *consanguinea regis*, wife of George, 3rd lord Haliburton of Dirleton, iv. 336.
Mariota, wife of (1) William, lord of Home, and (2) Patrick Edgar, iv. 443.
Mariota, wife of John Ker of the Forest of Ettrick and Altonburn, vii. 316.
MARISCHAL, KEITH, EARL, vi. 25-65.
Marischal, George, fifth earl, i. 157, 159; iii. 312; vi. 49, 51; ix. 21.
—— his 1st wife, Margaret Home, iv. 462; vi. 53; ix. 108, 135.
—— his 2nd wife, Margaret Ogilvy, i. 122; vi. 53.
— George, eighth earl, v. 240; vi. 60.
—— his wife, Mary Hay, v. 88, 224; vi. 60.
— George, tenth earl, i. 308; iii. 546; v. 241; vi. 62; ix. 135.
— William, first earl, vi. 39.
—— his wife, Mary *or* Marjorie Fraser, v. 521; vi. 40.
— William, second earl, ii. 3; vi. 41.
—— his wife, Mariota *or* Muriella Erskine, v. 607; vi. 41.
— William, third earl, vi. 42.
—— his wife, Elizabeth Gordon, iv. 530; vi. 43.
— William, fourth earl, i. 156; vi. 43, 46.
—— his wife, Margaret Keith, iv. 55; vi. 31, 48.
— William, sixth earl, i. 122; iv. 127; vi. 54.
—— his wife, Mary Erskine, v. 622; vi. 56.
— William, seventh earl, vi. 57.
—— his 1st wife, Elizabeth Seton, vi. 59; viii. 595.
—— his 2nd wife, Anne Douglas, vi. 59, 378.
— William, ninth earl, vi. 61.
—— his wife, Mary Drummond, vi. 61; vii. 53.

* Name unknown.

Marischal, master of, Robert, eldest son of 3rd earl Marischal, vi. 43.
— — his wife, Elizabeth *or* Beatrice Douglas, vi. 43, 358.
— master of, William, eldest son of 4th earl Marischal, vi. 49.
— — his wife, Elizabeth Hay, iii. 570; vi. 49; ix. 134.
Marjoribanks of Balbardie, Thomas, viii. 393.
— of Calder, Thomas, viii. 393.
— of Leuchie, John, v. 247.
— of Marjoribanks, Thomas, viii. 393.
— — his wife, Margaret Sandilands, viii. 393.
— of Ratho, Thomas, lord clerk register, iv. 224 *n.*; vi. 588.
— Christian, wife of David Bothwell, iv. 427.
— Edward, vi. 505.
— general, v. 247.
— Georgina, wife of J. J. Carnegie, vi. 505.
— Ishbel Maria, wife of 7th earl of Aberdeen, i. 98.
— Janet, wife of George Falconer, v. 247.
— William, burgess of Edinburgh, vii. 214.
— — his wife, Marion Purdie, vii. 214.
Marjory, *possible* dau. of Henry, earl of Northumberland, i. 5.
Marjory, wife of Gilbert, earl of Pembroke, i. 5; iii. 8.
Marjory, wife of Alan Durward, i. 6.
Marjory, wife of Patrick of Ogilvy, i. 108.
Marjorie, wife of Henry Stewart of Rosyth, 1458, i. 114.
Marjorie, wife of Walter Lichtoun of Ulyshaven, i. 116.
Marjory, wife of John, 9th earl of Atholl, i. 427; v. 578.
Marjory, wife of Sir David de Lindsay of Luffness and Crawford, iii. 6.
Marjory, wife of Alexander, 2nd earl of Crawford, iii. 18.
Marjorie, wife of Sir Thomas of Gordon, iv. 508.
Marjorie, wife of Adam of Gordon, iv. 510.
Marjory, wife of Sir William, master of Drummond, vii. 42, 43.
Marjorie, wife of Sir Nicol Rutherfurd of Rutherfurd, vii. 365.
Markenfield, Sir Ninian, iii. 293.
— — his wife, Eleanor *or* Margaret Clifford, iii. 293.
Markham of Cotham, Robert, i. 408.
— Frederica, wife of 3rd earl of Mansfield, viii. 210.
— Georgina, wife of 10th earl of Haddington, iv. 327.
— Gertrude, wife of Sir Thomas Sadleir, i. 408.
— Robert, archdeacon of York, iv. 327.
Markham, William, archbishop of York, viii. 210.
Marlborough, George (Spencer-Churchill), 5th duke of, iv. 169.
— — his wife, Susan Stewart, iv. 169.
— George, 6th duke of, iv. 171.
— — his wife, Jane Stewart, iv. 171.
— George Charles, 8th duke of, i. 71.
— — his wife, Albertha Frances Anne Hamilton, i. 71.
— Henrietta (Churchill), wife of 2nd earl of Godolphin; duchess of, ii. 533.
— John (Churchill), 1st duke of, i. 521, 522; ii. 532.
— — his wife, Sarah Jennings, ii. 532; vi. 20.
— John Winston (Churchill), 7th duke of, vii. 358.
— — his wife, Frances Anne Emily Stewart, vii. 358.
Marmier, François Philippe, comte de, ix. 3.
— — his wife, Margaret Hamilton, ix. 3.
— Philippe François, marquis de, ix. 3.
Marsden, Anthony, vicar of Gargrave, iv. 419.
— Mary, wife of Marmaduke Constable-Maxwell, iv. 419.
Marsh, Elizabeth, wife of col. T. Hervey, i. 60.
— Francis, i. 60.
Marshall of Auchnacree, George, iii. 29; ix. 30.
— — William, iii. 29; ix. 30.
— — — his wife, Janet Lindsay, iii. 29.
— of Berry House, Sir Samuel, v. 233.
— of Cessford, Edmond, vii. 578.
— of Gidea Hall, W. T., colonel, viii. 231.
— of Monk Coniston, Victor Alexander Ernest Garth, i. 96.
— — his wife, Victoria Alberta Alexandrina Gordon, i. 96.
— Alice Edith, wife of G. M. Drummond, viii. 231.
— Elizabeth Margaret, wife of rev. G. W. Auriol Drummond-Hay, v. 233.
— James, major, H.E.I.C.S., vii. 208.
— Jane, wife of John Rollo, vii. 208.
— Sir John, K.C.B., rear-admiral, vi. 179.
— Jonet, wife of Wm. Alexander of Clow viii. 166.
— Mary Woolston, wife of Geo. Middleton, vi. 179.
— *, husband of * Colville, ii. 537.
— lieut.-colonel, 1654, v. 228 *n.*
Martacus, alleged earl of Mar, v. 567 *n.*
Martin of Carden, David, ii. 281.
— — his wife, Janet Durie, ii. 281.
— of Cardowne, i. 287.
— — his wife, Elizabeth Arbuthnott, i. 287.

* Name unknown.

Martin of Medhope, Elizabeth, wife of Cuthbert Home, ii. 8; iv. 451; vi. 357.
— Barbara, wife of Charles Carnegie, dean of Brechin, viii. 75.
— Denny, iii. 602.
— George, vicar of Great Ness, i. 495.
— — his wife, Mary Murray, i. 495.
— George, notar in Dailly, ii. 29.
— George, minister of Dundee, viii. 75.
— Janet, wife of 6th earl of Dalhousie, iii. 102.
— William Michael Jamieson, R.A., ix. 37.
— — his wife, Muriel Louise Hamilton, ii. 59; ix. 37.
Martine of Clermont, George, viii. 60.
Martinozzi, Laura, wife of Alphonso, duke of Modena, i. 33.
Marwood, William, vi. 451.
— — his wife, Jane Sproxtoune, vi. 451.
Mary, queen of Scots, i. 24, 25, 400; ii. 164, 166, 167; v. 157, 353, 354, 436, 437, 440, 528; vi. 370; vii. 122, 124, 283, 293, 411, 541; viii. 490, 585, 586.
Mary, queen of Great Britain, dau. of king James II., and wife of king William III., i. 33; ii. 238.
Mary of Argyll, wife of (1) Malise, 5th earl of Strathearn, and (2) Sir Hugh Abernethy, viii. 246.
Mary of Mar, alleged wife of Kenneth, earl of Sutherland, i. 427 *n.*; v. 578; viii. 325.
Mary, dau. of Malcolm 'Ceannmor,' and wife of Eustace, count of Boulogne, i. 2.
Mary, wife of Jordan Fitz-Alan of Burton, senescal of Dol, i. 10.
Mary, dau. of Convall, and wife of Ewen of Glenerrichdie and Tulloch, i. 419.
Mary, wife of (1) William de Cochrane, and (2) Sir William de Dalzell, ii. 397.
Mary, wife of John de Wardrope, v. 329.
Mary, wife of John Kennedy of Dunure, ii. 446.
Mary, wife of (1) * Oliphant, and (2) Sir Richard Siward, vi. 533 *n.*
Mason of Eynsham Hall, James Francis, count of Pomarão, iii. 50.
— — his wife, Evelyn Margaret Lindsay, iii. 50.
— of Rosebank, John, iv. 437.
— — his wife, Mary Ramsay, iv. 437.
— Agnes Maria, wife of G. F. A. Erskine, ii. 279.
— Edgar, Maryland, iii. 605.
— Humphrey, captain, vi. 59.
— J. M., vicar of Marriche, ii. 279.
— Janet, wife of John Arbuthnott, i. 280.
Massam, *, wife of Archibald Kennedy, New York, ii. 494.
Massani, Giuseppe Maria, vi. 459.
— Maria Sophia Angelica, wife of 8th earl of Newburgh, vi. 459.

* Name unknown.

Massey, Godfrey Hugh, major 19th Foot, vii. 489.
— — his wife, Louisa Emma Maunsell, vii. 489.
Masson, John de, vii. 423, 424.
— Katharine, alleged wife of a lord Sempill, vii. 561 *n.*
— Marion, dau. of Robert M., vii. 561 *n.*
— Robert, bailie of Culross, vii. 561 *n.*
Massy-Dawson, Francis Dennis, vii. 590.
— — his wife, Susan St. Clair, vii. 590.
Matalent, William, v. 276.
Mather, Henrietta, wife of 2nd earl Cathcart, ii. 529.
— Thomas, ii. 529.
Mathetema, Cornelius de, vii. 537.
Mathow, Bessie, wife of Harrie Ruthven, ix. 98.
Matilda of Caithness, wife of Malise, 5th earl of Strathearn, i. 164; ii. 318, 319; viii. 246, 252.
Matilda of Glencarnie, wife of John Grant of Freuchie, vii. 454; viii. 244.
Matilda of Mar, wife of king Robert the Bruce, v. 578.
Matilda of Strathearn, wife of Malcolm, 6th earl of Fife, iv. 8; viii. 244.
Matilda, 'good queen Maud,' dau. of Malcolm 'Ceannmor,' and wife of Henry I. of England, i. 2.
Matilda, wife of (1) the emperor Henry V., and (2) Geoffrey Plantagenet; grand-dau. of Malcolm 'Ceannmor,' i. 2.
Matilda, grand-dau. of Malcolm 'Ceannmor,' and wife of Stephen, king of England, i. 2.
Matilda, wife of John of Atholl, i. 427.
Matilda, wife of Adam de Carlyle, ii. 375.
Matilda, wife of Dolfin, son of Aylward, iii. 245.
Matilda, wife of Alexander, earl of Menteith, vi. 134.
Matilda, 1st wife of Sir Patrick Graham of Dundaff, vi. 214.
Matilda, wife of Gilbert de Drummond of Wester Boquhapple, vii. 31.
Matthæus Tortus, *alias* Cardinal Bellarmine, i. 559.
Matthew, father of John of Mamylcroft, iii. 90.
Maubert, John Francis, Norwood, iii. 616.
— Mary Anne, wife of 11th viscount Falkland, iii. 616.
Maud of Huntingdon, wife of (1) Simon de St. Liz, and (2) king David I., i. 3.
Maud, 'the Empress,' i. 2.
Maud, 'good queen,' i. 2.
Maud, wife of David, earl of Huntingdon, i. 4.
Maude, Cornwallis, elder son of 1st earl de Montalt, iii. 550.
— Georgiana, wife of lord Wm. Stuart, ii. 307.

Maudit of Eshot and Bockenfield, Sir Roger, ix. 11.
—— —— his wife, Alianore, ix. 11.
Mauld of Cookstoun, William, viii. 55.
—— Patrick, St. Andrews, v. 413.
MAULE OF WHITECHURCH, MAULE, VISCOUNT, vii. 23.
Maule of Whitechurch, William, viscount, vii. 23.
MAULE, LORD BRECHIN AND NAVAR, vii. 20.
MAULE, VISCOUNT MAULE OF WHITECHURCH, vii. 23.
MAULE, EARL OF PANMURE, vii. 1-27.
MAULE, LORD PANMURE OF BRECHIN AND NAVAR, vii. 24.
MAULE, EARL OF PANMURE OF FORTH, vii. 23.
Maule of Arbirlot, Harry, vii. 22.
—— of Ardowny, Thomas, vii. 17.
—— —— his 1st wife, Margaret Lychtoun, vii. 17.
—— —— his 2nd wife, Martha Forrester, vii. 17.
—— of Auchrinnie, William, vii. 9.
—— —— his wife, Janet Carnegy, vii. 9; viii. 51.
—— of Balgreggie, Henry, vii. 12.
—— of Balishan, Sir Thomas, vii. 8.
—— of Ballumbie, James, 2nd son of 2nd earl of Panmure, vii. 25.
—— of Balmakellie, Henry, vii. 19, 20.
—— —— his 1st wife, Jean Wemyss, vii. 21; viii. 501.
—— —— his 2nd wife, Margaret Douglas, vii. 21.
—— —— Patrick, vii. 19.
—— of Balruddery and Banvy, Sir Thomas, iii. 306.
—— of Belhelvie, James, vii. 25.
—— of Brechin, Patrick, vii. 19.
—— of Camiston, John, 2nd son of Robt. M. of Panmure, vii. 12.
—— of Carmyle, Christina, wife of Alexander, son of John of Strathechin, vii. 6.
—— of Carnegie, Robert, viii. 48, 57.
—— —— Thomas, viii. 57.
—— of Cathlie, Harry, vii. 22.
—— of Colleweston, Patrick, vii. 19.
—— of Cruikston, William, vii. 13.
—— —— his wife, Bethia Guthrie, vii. 14.
—— of Downy, Patrick, vii. 19.
—— of Edzell, James, vii. 25.
—— of Foulis, Cecilia, wife of Alan, son of Swan, iv. 255, 256.
—— —— Christian de, wife of Roger de Mortimer, vii. 4.
—— —— Sir William de, iv. 255; vii. 3.
—— of Glaslettir, Henry, vii. 7.
—— of Glenesk, James, vii. 25.
—— of Gourdie *or* Guildie, Andrew, vii. 13.
—— —— his wife, Margaret Durham, vii. 13.
—— of Easter Innerpeffer, Henry, vii. 12.
Maule of Inverkeillor, John, baron of the Court of Exchequer, vii. 23, 24.
—— of Kellie, Harry, 3rd son of 2nd earl of Panmure, vii. 1, 22, 25.
—— —— his 1st wife, Mary Fleming, vii. 22; viii. 553.
—— —— his 2nd wife, Anna Lindsay, iv. 175; vii. 22.
—— —— William, general, iv. 177; vii. 23.
—— of Lethnot, James, vii. 25.
—— of Maule, Ansold, lord of, vii. 2.
—— —— his wife, Rectrude, vii. 2.
—— —— Ansold, son of Guarin; lord of, vii. 2.
—— —— Ansold, son of Peter; lord of, vii. 2.
—— —— his wife, Adeline, vii. 3.
—— —— Guarin, lord of, vii. 2.
—— —— his wife, Hersende, vii. 2.
—— —— Guarin, son of Peter, vii. 2.
—— —— Peter, lord of, vii. 2.
—— —— his wife, Guindesmoth, vii. 2.
—— —— Peter, 6th lord of, vii. 3.
—— —— Peter, 3rd son of Sir Henry de M. of Panmure, vii. 6.
—— of Melgund, Henry, vii. 13.
—— —— his wife, * Durham, vii. 13.
—— —— James, of diving-bell fame, vii. 13.
—— of Navar, Patrick, vii. 19.
—— of Panmure, Sir Henry de, 3rd laird, vii. 6, 235.
—— —— his wife, Margaret Hay, vii. 6; viii. 418.
—— —— Patrick, 12th laird, vii. 13, 18.
—— —— his wife, Margaret Erskine, vii. 18; ix. 148.
—— —— Patrick, 13th laird, vii. 19.
—— —— his 1st wife, Frances Stanhope, vii. 20.
—— —— his 2nd wife, Mary Waldrum, vii. 20.
—— —— his 3rd wife, Mary Erskine, v. 622; vii. 20.
—— —— Sir Peter de, 1st laird, vii. 5, 26.
—— —— his wife, Christian de Valoniis, ii. 218; vii. 5.
—— —— Robert 10th laird, vii. 10.
—— —— his 1st wife, Isobel Mercer, vii. 11.
—— —— his 2nd wife, Isobel Arbuthnott, i. 288; vii. 12.
—— —— Thomas, 6th laird, vii. 7.
—— —— his wife, Elizabeth Gray, i. 459; iv. 272; vii. 7.
—— —— Sir Thomas, 7th laird, i. 438; ii. 223, 224; vii. 7.
—— —— his wife, Mary Abercrombie, vii. 8.
—— —— Sir Thomas, 8th laird, iii. 307; vii. 8.
—— —— his 1st wife, Elizabeth Lindsay, iii. 17 *n.*, 21; vii. 8.
—— —— his 2nd wife, Katharine Cramond, vii. 9.

* Name unknown.

Maule of Panmure, Sir Thomas, 9th laird, vii. 9.
—— his 1st wife, Elizabeth Rollok, vii. 10, 184.
—— his 2nd wife, Christian Graham, vi. 223; vii. 10.
—— Thomas, 11th laird, iii. 311; vii. 14; viii. 57, 289.
—— his contracted wife, Elizabeth Lindsay, iii. 27; vii. 16.
—— his wife, Margaret Halyburton, vii. 16.
—— Walter, 4th laird, vi. 275; vii. 7; viii. 46.
—— William de, 2nd laird, vii. 6.
—— his wife, Ethana de Vaux, vii. 6.
—— William, 5th laird, vii. 7.
—— his wife, Marion Fleming, ii. 223; vii. 7; viii. 529.
—— William, general; 3rd son of Harry M. of Kellie, vii. 23.
—— William Ramsay, 2nd son of 8th earl of Dalhousie, vii. 24.
—— his 1st wife, Patricia Heron Gordon, vii. 24.
—— his 2nd wife, Elizabeth Barton, vii. 24.
— of Pitlevy, Robert, vii. 12.
—— Thomas, vii. 17.
— of Skethin, Sir Thomas, vii. 8.
— of Skryne, Andrew, portioner, vii. 13.
—— Henry, vii. 12.
—— his 1st wife, Katharine Boswell, vii. 12.
—— his 2nd wife, Janet Lyon, vii. 12.
—— William, vii. 7, 8; viii. 529.
— Agnes, wife of * Strachan of Carmylie, vii. 12.
— Alexander, elder son of Sir Thos. M. of Panmure, vii, 9.
—— his wife, Elizabeth Guthrie, vii. 9.
— Alexander, son of Jas. M., Eyemouth, vii. 17.
— Barbara, wife of Thos. Wishart of Bondarge, vii. 13.
— Beatrix, wife of R. Burnet of Crimond, vii. 14.
— Bethia, wife of Jas. Murray of Skirling, vii. 14.
— Cecilia de, wife of Walter de Ruthven, vii. 4.
— Christian, wife of Simeon Durie, vii. 19.
— David, 3rd son of Andrew M. of Gourdie, vii. 13.
— David, 3rd son of Thos. M. of Panmure, vii. 14.
— Eleanor, wife of Alex. Morrison of Prestongrange, vii. 14.
— Elizabeth, wife of Alexander Strachan of Carmylie, vii. 10.

* Name unknown.

Maule, Elizabeth, wife of William Haliburton, vii. 12.
— Elizabeth, wife of Thos. Pearson, vii. 13.
— Elizabeth, wife of Robt. Burnet of Crimond, vii. 14.
— Elizabeth, wife of (1) John, 2nd earl of Kinghorn, and (2) George, 3rd earl of Linlithgow, v. 448; vii. 21; viii. 299; ix. 148.
— Elizabeth, wife of (1) Jas. Strachan of Carmylie, and (2) Geo. Strachan, vii. 18; ix. 148.
— Eremburga, dau. of Peter, lord of Maule, vii. 2.
— Euphemia, wife of P. Ochterlony of Bonhard and Knox, vii. 18.
— Geils, dau. of Robt. M. of Panmure, vii. 12.
— George, mariner, England, vii. 17.
— Grisel, wife of Gilbert Wishart, vii. 13.
— Hersende de, vii. 2.
— Hubeline de, vii. 2.
— Isabel, wife of * Ramsay of Panbride, vii. 9.
— Isabel, wife of Henry Ramsay of Panbride, vii. 10.
— Isobel, dau. of Robt. M. of Panmure, vii. 12.
— Isobel, wife of (1) Jas. Dundas of Duddingston, and (2) Jas. Hamilton of Parklie, vii. 14.
— Isobel, wife of William Arbuthnott of Mondynes, i. 291; vii. 18.
— Isobel, wife of Henry Durham, vii. 18.
— James, Eyemouth, vii. 17.
— James, 2nd son of Harry M. of Kellie, vii. 1, 23.
— Jane, wife of David Erskine, vii. 18.
— Janet, wife of Alexander Ochterlony of Kelly, vii. 7.
— Janet, wife of James Strachan of Balvousie, vii. 12.
— Janet, wife of Wm. Oliphant of Kirkhill, vii. 14.
— Jean, dau. of Robt. M. of Panmure, vii. 12.
— Jean, wife of (1) George, lord Ramsay, and (2) John S. Kerr of Littledean, iii. 103; vii. 23.
— Jean, wife of 2nd earl of Northesk, vi. 497; vii. 21.
— John, in holy orders, 2nd son of Roger de M., vii. 4.
— Katharine, dau. of Robt. M. of Panmure, vii. 12.
— Katharine, wife of John Ochterlony of the Guynd, vii. 17.
— Katharine, dau. of Thos. M. of Pitlevie, vii. 17.
— Margaret, wife of Alex. Cochrane of Barbachlaw, iii. 340 *n.*; vii. 21.

* Name unknown.

Maule, Margaret, alleged wife of James Stewart, son of 5th lord Innermeath, v. 7 *n.*; vii. 18.
— Margaret, wife of Andrew Haliburton of Pitcur, vii. 12.
— Margaret, wife of Sir Archibald Murray of Blackbarony, vii. 14.
— Margaret, dau. of Thos. M. of Pitlevie, vii. 17.
— Margaret, wife of Arthur Erskine, vii. 18.
— Marion, wife of Sir Alex. Seaton of Kilcroich, vii. 14.
— Marjory, wife of (1) Wm. Nairn, and (2) John, 1st earl of Northesk, vi. 495; vii. 13.
— Marjory, wife of Andrew Guthrie of Kingenny, vii. 14.
— Mary, wife of (1) Charles, earl of Mar, and (2) col. John Erskine, v. 627; vii. 24.
— Michael de, vii. 4.
— Odeline de, vii. 2.
— Patrick, son of Robert M., St. Andrews, vii. 17.
— — his 1st wife, Christian Forbes, vii. 17.
— — his 2nd wife, Jean Ayton, vii. 17.
— Ralph, 2nd son of Ansold, lord of Maule, vii. 3.
— Richard de, eldest son of Roger, vii. 4, 5.
— Robert, eldest son of Andrew M. of Gourdie, vii. 13.
— Robert, commissary of St. Andrews, vii. 16, 20.
— — his wife, Katharine Myretoun, vii. 17.
— Robert, 2nd son of Thos. M. of Pitlevie, vii. 17.
— Robert de, Yorkshire, vii. 3.
— Roger de, brother of William, vii. 3, 4.
— — his wife, Godit, ix. 148.
— Stephen de, Yorkshire, vii. 3.
— Theobald de, vii. 2.
— Thomas, eldest son of Thos. M. of Pitlevie and Ardowny, vii. 17.
— Thomas, rector of Foulis, vii. 4 *bis*.
— Thomas, governor of Brechin Castle, vii. 6.
— William de, son of Peter, lord of Maule, vii. 2.
— William, 2nd son of Sir Henry de M. of Panmure, vii. 6.
— William, 2nd son of Sir Thos. M. of Panmure, vii. 9.
— William, 2nd son of Andrew M. of Gourdie, vii. 13.
— William, in Sweden, vii. 16.
— William, son of George M., vii. 17.
— William, archdeacon of Lothian, vii. 5.
— *, wife of Sir David Guthrie, vii. 8.
— *, wife of John Liddel of Panlathyne, vii. 10.

* Name unknown.

Maumont, Anne de, wife of Bernard Stewart of Aubigny, v. 348.
— Guy de; seigneur de St. Quentin, v. 348.
— — his wife, Jeanne, v. 348.
Maunsell of Thorpe Malsor, George Edmond, in holy orders, iii. 417.
— — his 2nd wife, Matilda Anne Frances Tollemache, iii. 417.
— Georgina, wife of Lewis Alexander Grant, vii. 489.
— Louisa Emma, wife of (1) Francis William, 6th earl of Seafield, (2) major G. H. Massey, and (3) lord Henry Loftus, vii. 489.
— Richard, ii. 376, 377 *n.*
— Robert George, Limerick, vii. 489 *bis*.
Maurice, prince, son of Frederick v., count palatine, count von Simmern, i. 27; vi. 247.
— the Hungarian, commander of the dromond, vii. 28.
Mautalent, John, v. 280.
— Robert, v. 280.
— — his wife, Christiana, v. 280.
— Sir Thomas, v. 276.
— William, v. 276.
Maxton, Christian, wife of Anthony Murray of Dollerie and Raith, iii. 397.
MAXWELL, MAXWELL, LORD, vi. 475-492.
Maxwell, Herbert, first lord, ii. 381; vi. 475.
— — his 1st wife, * Herries, iv. 402; vi. 475.
— — his 2nd wife, Katharine Seton, v. 348; vi. 475; viii. 575.
— John, third lord, vi. 477.
— — his wife, Janet Crichton, ii. 330; vi. 477.
— John, fourth lord, ii. 402; vi. 478; vii. 581.
— — his wife, Agnes Stewart, iv. 152; vi. 478.
— John, eighth lord, ii. 389; vi. 361, 376, 482; viii. 542.
— — his wife, Elizabeth Douglas, i. 194; vi. 483.
— John, ninth lord, iii. 128; v. 69; vi. 484; vii. 131; viii. 193.
— — his wife, Margaret Hamilton, iv. 373; vi. 485.
— John, twelfth lord, iv. 416; vi. 487.
— — his wife, Elizabeth Gordon, v. 116; vi. 487.
— Robert, second lord, vi. 476.
— — his wife, Janet Forrester, iv. 84; vi. 476.
— Robert, fifth lord, ii. 404; iv. 153, 409; vi. 479; vii. 122, 335.
— — his 1st wife, Janet Douglas, vi. 480; vii. 118.
— — his 2nd wife, Agnes Stewart, ii. 157 vi. 480.

* Name unknown.

Maxwell, Robert, sixth lord, vi. 47, 481.
—— —— his wife, Beatrix Douglas, vi. 361, 482.
—— Robert, seventh lord, vi. 482.
—— Robert, tenth lord, v. 69; vi. 483, 485.
—— —— his wife, Elizabeth Beaumont, vi. 486.
—— Robert, eleventh lord, iv. 416; vi. 487.
—— Robert, thirteenth lord, iv. 417; vi. 488.
—— —— his wife, Lucy Douglas, vi. 488; ix. 13.
—— William, fourteenth lord, iv. 417; vi. 488.
—— —— his wife, Winifred Herbert, vi. 488.
—— William, son of 5th earl of Nithsdale; styled lord, iv. 417; vi. 490.
—— —— his 1st wife, Katharine Stuart, vi. 490; viii. 407.
—— —— his 2nd wife, Anne Fox, vi. 490.
—— master of, James, brother of 1st earl of Nithsdale; styled, vi. 483.
—— master of, John, eldest son of 2nd lord Maxwell, ii. 328, 331; vi. 477.
—— —— his wife, Janet Crichton, ii. 328, 330; vi. 477.
—— master of, John, 2nd son of 5th lord Maxwell; styled, iv. 409 *bis*; vi. 481.
—— —— his wife, Agnes, lady Herries of Terregles, iv. 409; vi. 481.
—— master of, Robert, elder son of 6th lord Maxwell, v. 107; vi. 481; vii. 123 *bis*.
Maxwell, lord Carlyle, vi. 482-487.
Maxwell, earl of Dirleton, iii. 126-131.
Maxwell, lord Elbotle, iii. 126-131.
Maxwell, lord Eskdaill, vi. 482-487.
Maxwell, lord Herries of Terregles, iv. 409-418.
Maxwell, lord Kingston, iii. 126-131.
Maxwell, lord Maxwell, vi. 475-492.
Maxwell, earl of Morton, vi. 388-389, 482-487.
Maxwell, earl of Nithsdale, vi. 469-492.
Maxwell, lord Farnham, John, ancestor of the family of, vi. 471.
—— of Aikenhead, John, ancestor of the family of, vi. 470.
—— —— William, ii. 399.
—— of Auchincloich, John, vi. 219.
—— of Auldhouse, John, ancestor of the family of, vi. 470.
—— of Ballegerno, James, iii. 128.
—— of Balmaugan, Edward, v. 261.
—— of Bernetoun, George, 2nd son of 3rd lord Maxwell, ii. 331; vi. 477.
—— of Blawarthill, John, iv. 593.
—— —— his wife, Anne Carmichael, iv. 593.
—— —— Zacharias, iv. 593.
—— of Breconside, James, iv. 416; v. 112.
—— —— his wife, Margaret Vans, iv. 416; v. 112.
—— of Breoch, Edward, ancestor of the family of, iv. 412.
—— of Broomholm, Robert, ancestor of the family of, vi. 477.
Maxwell of Buittle, William, 3rd son of 3rd earl of Nithsdale, v. 124; vi. 488.
—— —— his wife, Agnes Gordon, v. 124.
—— of Calderwood, Sir John, 2nd laird, ii. 97; v. 145, 492; vi. 219.
—— —— his 1st wife, Margaret Borthwick, ii. 97.
—— —— Sir John, 3rd laird, v. 142; vii. 63.
—— —— his wife, Marion Boyd, v. 142.
—— —— Sir John, 8th laird, ii. 79.
—— —— his 2nd wife, Elizabeth Stewart, ii. 79.
—— —— Sir Robert, 1st laird, iv. 230 *n*.
—— —— his wife, Elizabeth Danielston of Mauldslie, iv. 230 *n*.
—— —— Robert, 6th laird, iii. 530.
—— —— his wife, Isabella *or* Elizabeth Elphinstone, iii. 529.
—— —— Robert, 7th laird, ii. 79 *n*.
—— —— his wife, (?) Elizabeth Barclay, ii. 79.
—— —— Sir James, iv. 245.
—— —— his wife, Margaret Cunningham, iv. 245.
—— —— Sir James, 1st bart., iv. 245.
—— —— his wife, Jean Hamilton, iv. 245.
—— —— John, ancestor of the family of, vi. 470.
—— of Cardoness, John, ancestor of the family of, vi. 470.
—— of Carlaverock, Aymer de, chamberlain of Scotland, vi. 470.
—— —— his wife, Mary M'Gauchen, vi. 470.
—— —— Sir Eustace, vi. 472.
—— —— his wife, Agnes Maxwell, vi. 472.
—— —— Sir Herbert, auditor for Baliol, iv. 340; vi. 471.
—— —— Herbert, vi. 473.
—— —— Sir Herbert, vi. 474.
—— —— his wife, Katharine Stewart, vi. 474.
—— —— his *possible* 2nd wife, Margaret de Cragy, vi. 474.
—— —— Sir Herbert, ii. 399; iv. 84; vi. 475.
—— —— his 1st wife, * Herries, vi. 475.
—— —— his 2nd wife, Katharine Seton, v. 348; vi. 475; viii. 575.
—— —— John de, sheriff of Teviotdale, vi. 470.
—— —— Sir John, son of Herbert of M., vi. 471.
—— —— Sir John, son of Sir John M., v. 280; vi. 472.
—— —— Sir John, v. 283; vi. 473.
—— —— his wife, Christian *, vi. 473.
—— —— Sir Robert, vi. 473.
—— —— Robert, eldest son of 1st lord Maxwell, vi. 475; viii. 8.
—— of Carlyle, John, ii. 389; vi. 482.
—— of Carnsalloch, George, 4th son of 1st lord Maxwell, vi. 476.
—— —— his 1st wife, Agnes *, vi. 476.
—— —— his 2nd wife, Isabella Galbraith, vi. 476.

* Name unknown.

Maxwell of Carnsalloch, Sir Herbert, vi. 474.
—— —— Sir Herbert, iv. 84, 150; vi. 475.
—— —— William, iv. 158.
—— —— his wife, Elizabeth Stewart, iv. 158.
—— of Carruchan, James, ancestor of the family of, iv. 416.
—— —— William, claimant to Herries Peerage, iv. 416, 421.
—— —— William, iv. 421; vi. 490.
—— of Castlemilk, Robert, illeg. son of 6th lord Maxwell, vi. 482.
—— of Cavens, Herbert, iii. 126.
—— —— Herbert, son of William M. of Cavens, iii. 126.
—— —— James, ancestor of the family of, iii. 126; vi. 477.
—— —— William, iii. 127.
—— —— his wife, Katharine Weir, iii. 127.
—— —— William, his son, iii. 127, 129.
—— of Clowden, Herbert, ancestor of the family of, vi. 478, 480.
—— of Conheath, Sir Herbert, vi. 474.
—— —— his alleged wife, Margaret Cragy, vi. 474.
—— of Cowglen, George, ii. 79; iii. 338.
—— —— John, ancestor of the family of, vi. 470.
—— —— John, son of George M., iii. 338.
—— of Cowhill, Archibald, iii. 127.
—— —— John, vi. 480.
—— —— Robert, ancestor of the family of, vi. 477 *n.*
—— —— William, iii. 127, 128.
—— of Crustanes, Robert, i. 225; iii. 127.
—— —— his wife, Nicolas Murray, iii. 127.
—— of Culcreuch, James, iii. 128.
—— of Dalswinton, George, ix. 23.
—— —— his wife, Jean Campbell, i. 360; ix. 23.
—— —— Hugh, vii. 150.
—— —— his wife, Jean Douglas, vii. 150.
—— —— John, ancestor of the family of, vi. 471.
—— of Dargavel, John, ii. 181.
—— —— his wife, Elizabeth Colquhoun, ii. 181.
—— of Dicbar, John, vii. 532.
—— of Dinwiddie, Robert, ancestor of the family of, vi. 477.
—— of Dirleton, James, ancestor of the family of, iii. 126; vi. 477.
—— of Meikle Dripps, Sir Herbert, iii. 336; vi. 475.
—— of Drumcoltran, Edward, vi. 479.
—— —— Herbert, ancestor of the family of, vi. 478, 479.
—— of Drumpark, Robert, ancestor of the family of, vi. 477.
—— of Dundrennan, Edward, v. 442.
—— —— his wife, Margaret Baillie, iv. 412; v. 442; ix. 130 *bis.*
—— of Feualroull, John, v. 62.
Maxwell of Garrarie, John, vi. 11.
—— his wife, Elizabeth Hume, vi. 11.
—— of Gelston, John, 2nd son of 3rd earl of Nithsdale, vi. 487.
—— —— his wife, Elizabeth Glendoning, vi. 487.
—— of Gleneslin, Thomas, ancestor of the family of, vi. 478.
—— of Glenkens, John de, v. 99.
—— of Gribton, James, iv. 415.
—— —— John, 2nd laird, iv. 415.
—— —— Sir William, 2nd son of 5th lord Herries of Terregles, iv. 415.
—— —— his wife, Barbara Johnstone, iv. 415.
—— —— William, the younger, iv. 415.
—— of Herries, John, ancestor of the family of, vi. 481 *bis.*
—— of Hillis, Edward, vi. 479; ix. 53.
—— —— Herbert, ancestor of the family of, vi. 478, 479.
—— of Innerwick, James, iii. 128.
—— —— his wife, Elizabeth Busson de Podolska, iii. 130.
—— of Kelton, William, 3rd son of 3rd earl of Nithsdale, v. 125; vi. 488.
—— of Killilung, Robert, ancestor of the family of, vi. 477.
—— of Kilmacolm, Patrick, v. 556.
—— of Kirkconnel, Agnes, wife of Thos. Maxwell, vi. 476.
—— —— Aymer, vi. 474.
—— —— his wife, Janet de Kirkconnel, vi. 474.
—— —— James, 3rd son of 8th lord Maxwell, vi. 483.
—— —— John, i. 225.
—— —— his wife, Marion Murray, i. 225.
—— —— Thomas, 2nd son of 2nd lord Maxwell, vi. 476.
—— —— his wife, Agnes Maxwell of Kirkconnell, vi. 476.
—— of Kirkhouse, James, iii. 128.
—— —— Robert, 2nd son of William M., Cavens, iii. 127.
—— —— his wife, Nicolas Murray, i. 225; iii. 127.
—— —— Robert, 3rd son of Herbert M. of Cavens, iii. 127.
—— —— Robert, vi. 487.
—— —— his wife, Elizabeth Maxwell, vi. 487.
—— —— William, grandson of William M., iii. 127.
—— —— William, grandson of Herbert M., iii. 127, 129.
—— of Kirklands of Kirkbean, Robert, iii. 127.
—— —— William, iii. 127, 129.
—— of Knock, John, vi. 11.
—— of Lawston, Edward, iv. 416.
—— —— his wife, Margaret Glen, iv. 416.
—— of Libbertoun, John, viii. 15.
—— —— Robert, iv. 84.
—— of Lochmaben, James, iii. 128.

Maxwell of Lochrutonn, Edward, vi. 480.
—— Herbert, ancestor of the family of, vi. 478.
— of Logan, Alexander, iii. 127.
—— John, ancestor of the family of, vi. 481 *bis*.
— of Maxwell, Sir Herbert, vi. 471; viii. 3.
— of the Mearns, Sir John, vi. 473.
— of Middlebie, John, ancestor of the family of, vi. 484.
—— his wife, Marion Maxwell, ix. 143.
— of Milton, William, v. 269.
—— his wife, Janet Maclellan, v. 269.
— of Monreith, Sir Alexander, 2nd bart., iii. 457.
—— his wife, Jean Montgomerie, iii. 457.
—— Edward, ancestor of the family of, vi. 475.
—— Sir William, 3rd bart., iv. 556.
—— Sir William, 4th bart., v. 316.
— of Mortonwoods, James, iii. 128.
— of Munches, James, ancestor of the family of, iv. 416.
— of Newark, David, v. 265.
—— his wife, * Glendinning, v. 265.
—— Sir George, vii. 550.
—— his wife, Elizabeth Sempill, vii. 550.
—— John, ancestor of the family of, vi. 471.
—— Patrick, v. 554.
—— Patrick, vii. 535.
—— Patrick, v. 556.
—— Patrick, iv. 250.
—— his wife, Margaret Napier, iv. 250.
— of Newbellie, James, 3rd son of Robt. M. of Kirkhouse, iii. 128.
— of Newlaw, Edward, commendator of Dundrennan, iv. 412.
—— John, provost of Dumfries, iv. 412, 414.
—— William, v. 125.
—— his wife, Elizabeth Gordon, v. 125.
— of Orchardton, Sir Robert, i. 252.
—— his wife, Grisel Johnstone, i. 252.
—— Sir Robert, 1st bart., iv. 411; v. 267, 268; vi. 487.
—— his wife, Mary *or* Ann Maclellan, v. 267, 268.
— of Pencaitland, Sir Herbert de, vi. 471.
—— Sir John, v. 592; vi. 473.
—— his wife, Christian *, vi. 473.
— of Polgavy, David, viii. 430.
— of Pollok, *or* Nether Pollok, John, ancestor of the family of, vi. 470.
—— Sir John, 4th laird, ii. 448; iii. 11.
—— his 1st wife, Isabel Lindsay, iii. 11.
—— Sir John de, 7th laird, ii. 400.
—— John, 8th laird, vii. 532.
—— John, *de jure ux.* 11th laird, ii. 404.

* Name unknown.

Maxwell of Pollok, *or* Nether Pollok, Sir John, 12th laird, iv. 196; vi. 230.
—— his 2nd wife, Marjorie Edmonstone, vi. 229.
—— Sir John, 13th laird, iv. 196; v. 498.
—— his 1st wife, Isobel Campbell, v. 498.
—— Sir John, senator of the College of Justice, lord Pollok; 15th laird, iv. 593.
—— Sir John, 9th bart., iii. 493.
—— his wife, Matilda Harriet Bruce, iii. 493.
— of Nether Pollok, John (4th lord Maxwell), superior of, iii. 337.
— of Portrack, Homer, ancestor of the family of, vi. 477.
— of Preston, Mary, wife of 17th earl of Sutherland, viii. 359.
—— William, ii. 209; viii. 359.
—— Willielma, wife of lord Glenorchy, ii. 209.
— of Redcastle, Sir J., iv. 405.
—— his wife, Agnes, iv. 405.
— of Southbar, Adam, vi. 476.
—— his wife, Marion Stewart, ii. 78; vi. 476.
— of Speddoch, Homer, iv. 158 *n.*; ix. 143.
— of Spottis, Sir Robert, iv. 411; vi. 484.
—— his 1st wife, Elizabeth Gordon, iv. 411.
—— his 2nd wife, Sara Johnstone, iv. 411.
—— Sir Robert, 1st bart., v. 267.
— of Springkell, John, ancestor of the family of, vi. 471.
—— Sir Patrick, 1st bart., v. 126, 127; vii. 149; viii. 30.
—— his 2nd wife, Mary Gordon, v. 126.
—— Sir William, 2nd bart., vii. 149.
—— his wife, Katharine Douglas, vii. 149.
— of Stanelie, Gabriel, vii. 538.
—— John, ancestor of the family of, vi. 471.
—— John, v. 555.
—— his wife, Agnes Lyle, ii. 510; v. 555.
— of Sweetheart, Sir Robert, iv. 415.
— of Tarres, James, iii. 128.
— of Tealing, Sir David, iv. 283.
—— his wife, Helen Gray, iv. 283.
—— Eustace, vi. 475 *n.*
—— Hugh, i. 562.
—— Hugh, iii. 570.
—— his wife, Elizabeth Butter, iii. 570.
—— William, iii. 307; viii. 425.
— of Terrauchtie, James, ancestor of the family of, iv. 416.
— of Terregles, Sir John, iv. 410; v. 62, 110, 481; vii. 123, 128.
—— his wife, Agnes Herries, iv. 409; v. 481.
—— Winifred, wife of William Haggerston-Constable, iv. 418.

Maxwell of Threave, Robert, ancestor of the family of, vi. 477.
—— of Tinwald, Edward, ancestor of the family of, vi. 475.
—— —— Edward, ii. 385, 386 *bis*.
—— —— Herbert, ii. 385.
—— —— his wife, Margaret Douglas, ii. 385.
—— of Tuppendean, James Primrose, ii. 279.
—— of Tyndwell, Edward, vi. 480.
—— of Woodhead, Robert, i. 225.
—— —— his wife, Agnes Lindsay, i. 225.
—— Agnes, wife of Sir G. Kennedy of Dunure, ii. 447, 448.
—— Agnes, wife of John Boyle of Kelburne, iv. 196.
—— Agnes, wife of Sir John Charteris of Amisfield, iv. 412; vi. 479.
—— Agnes, wife of Jas. Maitland of Bolton, iv. 415; v. 296.
—— Agnes, wife of Sir Eustace Maxwell of Carlaverock, vi. 472.
—— Agnes, wife of Robert de Pollok, vi. 473.
—— Agnes, wife of John Glendoning of Parton, vi. 476.
—— Agnes, betrothed to Alex. Glendoning of Parton, vi. 479.
—— Agnes, wife of Wm. Douglas of Greenlaw, vi. 484.
—— Alexander, illeg. son of 4th lord Herries of Terregles, iv. 413.
—— Alexander, 3rd son of Sir Wm. M. of Gribton, iv. 415.
—— Alexander, captain in France, iv. 416.
—— Alexander, alleged father-in-law of the Knight of Liddesdale, vi. 473.
—— Alice, dau. of Jas. M., ix. 105.
—— Ann, wife of 3rd lord Kirkcudbright, v. 268.
—— Anne, dau. of 4th earl of Nithsdale, vi. 488.
—— Anne, wife of John, 4th lord Bellew of Duleek, vi. 489.
—— Anne, wife of Sir Thos. Bowyer, ix. 67.
—— Annabella, wife of Thos. Wemyss, viii. 496.
—— Aymer, alleged 2nd son of Sir Robert M. of Carlaverock, vi. 474.
—— Bessie, granddau. of Herbert M. of Cavens, iii. 127.
—— Caroline Rose, wife of David Henry, 12th earl of Buchan, ii. 279.
—— Charles, 2nd son of Robt. M. of Kirkhouse, iii. 128; v. 465.
—— Christian, dau. of 2nd lord Maxwell, iv. 477.
—— Christian, dau. of 3rd lord Maxwell, iv. 478.
—— David, brother of John M., bishop of Ross, iii. 127.
—— David, 5th son of Robt. M. of Kirkhouse, iii. 128.
Maxwell, David, 5th son of 1st lord Maxwell, iv. 476.
—— David, 3rd son of 2nd lord Maxwell, vi. 476.
—— Diana, wife of Charles Cecil, styled viscount Cranborne, iii. 129, 130.
—— Edmund of, vi. 469.
—— Edward, 4th son of 5th lord Maxwell of Terregles, iv. 415.
—— Edward, 2nd son of Sir Wm. M. of Gribton, iv. 415.
—— Edward, crusader in 1246, vi. 471.
—— Edward, 4th son of 4th lord Maxwell, vi. 479, 480.
—— Egidia, wife of James Scrymgeour, constable of Dundee, iii. 305, 306.
—— Elizabeth, wife of (1) William, 2nd duke of Hamilton, and (2) Thos. Dalmahoy, iii. 129, 130; iv. 380; ix. 104.
—— Elizabeth, wife of capt. W. Boyle of Downiescroft, iv. 194.
—— Elizabeth, wife of (1) Sir John Gordon of Lochinvar, and (2) Sir Alex. Fraser of Philorth, iv. 412; v. 112; vii. 440; ix. 118.
—— Elizabeth, wife of 6th lord Herries of Terregles, iv. 416; vi. 483.
—— Elizabeth, wife of 3rd earl of Wintoun, iv. 416; viii. 595; ix. 106.
—— Elizabeth, wife of (1) Sir Wm. Douglas, and (2) Hugh, 4th lord Dacre, vi. 342 *n.*, 473.
—— Elizabeth, alleged wife of Jardine of Applegirth, vi. 479.
—— Elizabeth, wife of Robert Maxwell of Kirkhouse, vi. 487.
—— Frederick, rector of Scots seminary, Madrid, iv. 416; ix. 106.
—— Gavin, 3rd son of 1st lord Maxwell, vi. 475.
—— George, son of Patrick M. of Newark, vii. 535.
—— —— his wife, Marian Sempill, vii. 535.
—— Grissel, wife of Michael Carlyle, ii. 389; vi. 484 *n.*; ix. 53.
—— Grisel, dau. of William M. of Carnsalloch, iv. 158 *n.*
—— Grissel, wife of Sir Thos. Maclellan of Bombie, iv. 412; v. 264.
—— Grissel, dau. of 5th lord Herries of Terregles, iv. 415.
—— Hamilton, major, v. 133.
—— —— his wife, Maria le Blanche, v. 133.
—— Henry, illeg. son of 4th lord Maxwell, vi. 479.
—— Herbert, i. 222.
—— —— his wife, Elizabeth Murray, i. 222; iii. 225.
—— Herbert, vicar of Carlaverock, iv. 410; vi. 478 *n.*
—— Herbert de, sheriff, vi. 469.
—— Herbert, in Cavens, ix. 150.
—— Hew, highwayman, iv. 412.

Maxwell, Isaac, vi. 536.
—— his wife, Helen Siward of Kellie, vi. 533, 536.
— James, *né* Cecil, grandson of earl of Dirleton, iii. 129.
—— his wife, Diana Maxwell, iii. 130.
— James, 4th son of 4th lord Herries of Terregles, iv. 412.
— James, illeg. son of 4th lord Herries of Terregles, iv. 413.
— James, 5th son of 5th lord Herries of Terregles, iv. 415.
—— his wife, Ælitia Collins, ix. 105.
— Jane, dau. of John M. of Newlaw, iv. 412.
— Jane, wife of 4th duke of Gordon, iv. 556.
— Jane, wife of John Maitland of Freugh, v. 316.
— Jane, wife of * Wharwood, ix. 67.
— Janet, wife of 2nd lord Carlyle, ii. 387; vi. 478.
— Janet, wife of Robert, 1st lord Boyd, v. 145.
— Janet, wife of Sir Wm. Douglas of Drumlanrig, vi. 475; vii. 115.
— Janet, dau. of 1st lord Maxwell, vi. 476.
— Jean, dau. of James M. of Kirkconnel, vi. 483.
— Jean, dau. of 8th lord Maxwell, vi. 483.
— Jean, wife of John M'Brair, vi. 486; ix. 144.
— Jock, grandson of Herbert M. of Cavens, iii. 126.
— John, slain by Murray of Cockpool, i. 220; vi. 477; ix. 13.
— John de, sheriff of Teviotdale, vi. 470.
— John, 3rd son of sheriff Herbert de Maccuswell, vi. 470.
— John, 1296, vi. 471 *n.*
— John, minister of Mortlach, bishop of Ross, iii. 72, 127.
— John, 2nd son of Herbert M. of Cavens, iii. 126.
— John, son of above, iii. 126.
— John, 6th son of 1st lord Maxwell, vi. 476.
— John, abbot of Holywood, vi. 478 *bis*.
— John, abbot of Dundrennan, vi. 479.
— John, illeg. son of 4th lord Maxwell, vi. 479.
— Katharine, wife of Gilbert, lord Kennedy, ii. 454; vi. 475.
— Katharine, wife of Ninian Glendoning of Parton, vi. 479.
— Katharine, 3rd dau. of Sir Alex. M. of Monreith, ix. 81.
— Margaret, wife of (1) Archibald, 6th earl of Angus, and (2) Sir Wm. Baillie of Lamington, i. 192; vi. 481; ix. 143.

* Name unknown.

Maxwell, Margaret, dau. of Geo. M. of Cowglen, ii. 79.
— Margaret, granddau. of Herbert M. of Cavens, iii. 127.
— Margaret, wife of Sir John Montgomerie of Eaglesham and Ardrossan, iii. 430; v. 140; vi. 474.
— Margaret, wife of 1st earl of Lothian, iv. 412; v. 456.
— Margaret, wife of Robt. Glendinning of Parton, iv. 415: ix. 105.
— Margaret, wife of (1) John Wallace of Craigie, and (2) Wm. Stewart of Dunduff, vi. 483; ix. 143.
— Margaret, wife of William Sempill, vii. 538.
— Maria, wife of capt. Adam Gordon, v. 133.
— Marion, wife of Robt. Johnstone of Raecleuch, i. 246.
— Marion, wife of Wm. Hepburne, ii. 154.
— Marion, wife of 2nd lord Crichton of Sanquhar, iii. 225.
— Marion, wife of John Maxwell, ix. 143.
— Mariota, wife of 4th lord Carlyle, ii. 389.
— Mariot, dau. of 1st lord Maxwell, vi. 476.
— Mariota, wife of 1st lord Boyd, v. 145.
— Marjory, wife of 1st lord Balmerinoch, i. 562.
— Marrietta *or* Mary, wife of (1) William Cochrane, and (2) Sir William Dalzell, ii. 397; iii. 335.
— Mary, wife of James Johnstone of that Ilk, i. 240; vi. 479.
— Mary, wife of Robert Maxwell, iii. 127.
— Mary, wife of 6th lord Hay of Yester, iv. 113; viii. 443.
— Mary, wife of 4th earl of Traquair, vi. 488; viii. 406.
— Mary, dau. of 6th earl of Nithsdale, vi. 490.
— Mary, wife of Dr. Jas. Douglas, Carlisle, vii. 149.
— Michael, 8th son of 6th lord Herries of Terregles, iv. 416.
— Niccol, son of 2nd lord Maxwell, vi. 477.
— Nicolas, wife of Sir William Grierson of Lag, iv. 413.
— Nicolas, wife of (1) John Cutlar, and (2) Thomas Maclellan, v. 261.
— Richard, servitor to 8th lord Maxwell, iii. 127.
— Robert, son of Alexander M. of Logan, iii. 127.
— Robert, 4th son of Robt. M. of Kirkhouse, iii. 128.
— Robert, captain in France, iv. 416.
— Robert, Glasgow, vii. 535.
—— his wife, Margaret Sempill, vii. 535.
— Robert, son of James M., ix. 105.

Maxwell, Sara, wife of (1) Sir Jas. Johnstone of that Ilk, (2) John, 1st earl of Wigtoun, and (3) Hugh, 1st viscount Montgomery of Ards, i. 41, 254; iv. 407, 413; vi. 478 *n.*; viii. 546.
— Thomas, 3rd son of Sir Robert M. of Orchardton, vi. 487.
— — his wife, Elizabeth Glendoning, vi. 487.
— William, elder son of Herbert M. of Cavens, iii. 126; ix. 150.
— — his wife, Margaret Douglas, iii. 126.
— William, grandson of Wm. Cochrane of Cochrane, iii. 338.
— William, legtd. son of Sir John M. of Terregles, iv. 413.
— William, captain in France, iv. 416.
— William, 8th son of 1st lord Maxwell, vi. 476.
— William, 8th son of 3rd lord Maxwell, vi. 478.
— Winifred, wife of Wm. Haggerston-Constable, vi. 490.
— *, wife of Jas. Crichton of Crawfordston, iii. 128.
— *, wife of Thos. Brown of Glen, iii. 128.
— *, husband of Janet Cochrane, iii. 338.
— *, wife of Sir John Graham, 2nd of Orchell, iv. 415; vi. 230.
Maxwell-Constable, Clementina, iv. 419.
— Katharine, iv. 419.
— Mary, wife of J. Webb-Weston, iv. 419.
— Theresa, iv. 419.
Maxwell-Stuart of Terregles and Traquair, Henry, iv. 420.
— — his wife, Juliana Middleton, iv. 420.
— Herbert, iv. 420.
— Agnes, iv. 420.
— Arthur, iv. 420.
— Blanche, iv. 420.
— Charles, iv. 420.
— Edmund, iv. 420.
— — his wife, Mary Anne Constable-Maxwell, iv. 420, 422.
— George, iv. 420.
— Henry, iv. 420.
— Juliana, iv. 420.
— Laura, iv. 420.
— Louisa Mary Josephine, iv. 420.
— Philip, iv. 420.
May, James Frere, major, ii. 499.
— Katharine Anne, wife of lord Nigel Kennedy, ii. 499.
Mayerne, Dr., vi. 451 *n.*
Maynard of Estaines ad Turrim, William, 2nd lord, iii. 402.
— — his 2nd wife, Margaret Murray, iii. 402.
— Henry (Maynard), viscount, i. 497; v. 369.

* Name unknown.

Maynard of Curriglasse, Sir William, vi. 9.
— Blanche, wife of col. Algernon Charles Gordon-Lennox, v. 369.
— Charles Henry, colonel Royal Horse Guards, i. 497; v. 369.
— — his wife, Frances Julia Murray, i. 497.
— Mary, wife of Sir Geo. Hume of Tully Castle, vi. 9.
Mayne of Teffont Evias, John, iii. 362.
— — his wife, Isabella Raymond, iii. 362.
— Henry Otway, major, viii. 226.
— Mabel Jeannie Otway, wife of M. H. Drummond, viii. 226.
Mayo, Richard (Bourke), 5th earl of, iii. 45.
Meade, Adelaide Jane, wife of S. C. J. Colville, ii. 567.
— Francis, Henry, iv. 561.
— — his wife, Beatrice Mary Gordon, iv. 561.
Mearns, Roland de, vi. 470.
Mease, Sarah, wife of (1) capt. Wm. Murray, R.N., and (2) George Aust, iii. 388.
Meath, Reginald (Brabazon), 12th earl of, v. 320.
— — his wife, Mary Jane Maitland, v. 320.
Medicis, Catherine de, queen consort of France, i. 25.
Medici, Cosmo III. de, grand duke of Tuscany, iv. 553.
Medina Pomar, general, condé de, ii. 358.
— — his wife, Marie de Mariategui, ii. 358.
Medway, John Stewart (Gathorne-Hardy), styled lord, iv. 221.
Megget, Archibald, writer, Edinburgh, ii. 599.
— — his wife, Mary Cranstoun, ii. 599.
Megott, Mary, Southwark, ix. 78.
Meigle, Michael de, i. 107.
Meiklejohn, Robert, skinner, Edinburgh, viii. 169.
Melbourne, Peniston (Lambe), 1st viscount, iii. 123.
MELDRUM OF MORVEN, GORDON, BARON, iv. 559-562.
Meldrum of Morven, George, first baron, iv. 559.
— of Altermony, William, viii. 264.
— of Haltoun of Auchterles, George, ii. 12.
— — his wife, Elizabeth Ogilvy, ii. 12.
— of Cleish and Binns, William, ii. 99 *n.*, 570.
— — his wife, Marjory Lawson, ii. 99 *n.*
— of Dalrevach, William, viii. 264.
— of Drumbreck, George, vii. 412.
— — his wife, Margaret Abernethy, vii. 412.
— of Fyvie, Alexander, iv. 50.
— — his wife, Margaret Forbes, iv. 50.

Moldrum of Fyvie, Andrew, iv. 125.
— — Sir George, iv. 72, 124.
— — his wife, Isobel *or* Elizabeth Innes, iv. 72.
— — George, viii. 541.
— — his wife, Mary Fleming, viii. 541.
— — William, ancestor of the family of, viii. 254, 568.
— — William, vii. 355.
— — William, vii. 411.
— — his wife, Elizabeth Abernethy, vii. 411.
— of Leathers, Patrick, ii. 24.
— — Peter, vi. 556.
— — his wife, Mary Ogilvy, vi. 556.
— of Meldrum, Elizabeth, wife of William Seton, iv. 521.
— — Philip, ii. 254; vi. 170.
— — his wife, Agnes Comyn, ii. 254.
— — William, iv. 521.
— of Methlic, i. 83.
— of Montcoffer, William, ii. 10.
— of Ord, John, portioner, vii. 464.
— Elizabeth, wife of James Sandilands of Cruvy, i. 76.
— George, Crail, v. 413 *bis*.
— — his wife, Janet Williamson, v. 412.
— Grissel, wife of John Melville of Raith, vi. 102; vii. 575.
— Jean, wife of (1) Sir A. Innes, and (2) Geo. Ogilvy, ii. 24.
— John, 1630, ii. 16; iv. 127 *bis*.
— *, wife of Robert Innes of Cromie and Rothmackenzie, vii. 355.
MELFORT, DRUMMOND, VISCOUNT OF, vi. 66-74.
Melfort, John, first viscount of, vi. 66.
MELFORT, DRUMMOND, EARL OF, vi. 66-74.
Melfort, Charles Edward, *de jure* fifth earl of, vi. 71, 72.
— George, sixth earl of, vi. 72.
— — his 1st wife, Albertine de Rotberg, vi. 73.
— — his 2nd wife, Susan Henrietta Sewell, vi. 73.
— James, *de jure* third earl of, vi. 71; ix. 135.
— — his wife, Marie de Béranger, vi. 71.
— James Louis, *de jure* fourth earl of, vi. 72; vii. 58.
— — his wife, Aglaé Elizabeth Jaqueline d'Oms Alais, vi. 72.
— John, first earl of, vi. 66; vii. 51, 139.
— — his 1st wife, Sophia Maitland-Lundin of Lundin, v. 303; vi. 68.
— — his 2nd wife, Euphemia Wallace, vi. 69.
— John, *de jure* second earl of, vi. 70.
— — his wife, Marie Gabrielle d'Audibert, i. 34; vi. 70.

* Name unknown.

Melfort, Louis (Drummond) comte de, vi. 69.
— — his wife, Jeanne Elizabeth de la Porte, vi. 69.
— Louis Pierre François Malcolm (Drummond), comte de, vi. 59.
— — his 1st wife, Caroline Barry, vi. 69.
— — his 2nd wife, Caroline Mackenzie, vi. 69; vii. 513.
— George (Drummond), duc de, vi. 72; vii. 60.
— James Louis (Drummond), duc de, vii. 61.
— John (Drummond), 1st duke of, (Jacobite creation), vi. 67.
— John (Drummond), 2nd duc de, i. 34.
— — his wife, Marie Gabrielle d'Audibert, comtesse de Lussan, i. 34; vi. 70.
MELGUM, GORDON, VISCOUNT, i. 100.
Melgum, John, viscount, i. 100; iv. 127, 545.
— — his wife, Sophia Hay, i. 100; iii. 577.
Melgund, Mariota Ogilvy, styled lady, i. 115.
Melkofr *or* Melmare, 3rd son of king Duncan I., i. 415.
Mellish of Ragnal, Charles, vii. 565.
— Maria, wife of 14th lord Sempill, vii. 565.
Mellor, colonel, M.P., iv. 172.
— Walter Clifford, iv. 172.
— — his wife, Helen Blanche Stewart, iv. 172.
MELROS OF TYNNINGHAM, HAMILTON, LORD, iv. 325-326.
Melros of Tynningham, Thomas, lord, iv. 325.
MELROSE, RAMSAY, LORD, iv. 300.
Melrose, John, lord, iv. 300, 312, 313.
MELROSE, RAMSAY, LORD RAMSAY OF, iii. 98.
MELROSE, HAMILTON, EARL OF, iv. 310-311.
Melrose, Thomas, earl of, iii. 591; iv. 195, 310.
— William, minister at Findo-Gask, iii. 570.
Melville, Henry (Dundas), 1st viscount, iv. 498; vii. 58; viii. 232.
— — his 2nd wife, Jean Hope, iv. 498.
MELVILLE, LESLIE, EARL OF, vi. 110-118.
Melville, Alexander, fourth earl of, vi. 113 *bis*.
— — his 1st wife, Mary Erskine, vi. 114.
— — his 2nd wife, Elizabeth Monypenny, vi. 114; ix. 136.
— Alexander, sixth earl of, vi. 117.
— — his wife, Jane Thornton, vi. 118.
— Alexander, ninth earl of, vi. 121, 122.
— David, second earl of, vi. 110.
— — his wife, Anna Wemyss, vi. 112.
— David, third earl of, vi. 113.
— David, fifth earl of, vi. 115.
— — his wife, Wilhelmina Nisbet, vi. 116.
— David, seventh earl of, vi. 119.
— — his wife, Elizabeth Anne Campbell, vi. 119.

Melville, George, first earl of, v. 381; vi. 107; viii. 76.
—— —— his wife, Katharine Leslie, v. 378, 379; vi. 109.
—— John David, eleventh earl of, vi. 122.
—— John Thornton, eighth earl of, vi. 118, 120.
—— —— his 1st wife, Harriet Thornton, vi. 121.
—— —— his 2nd wife, Sophia Thornton, vi. 121.
—— Ronald Ruthven, tenth earl of, vi. 121, 122.
—— —— his wife, Emma Selina Portman, vi. 122.
—— master of, Alexander, eldest son of 1st earl of Melville, vi. 109.
—— —— his wife, Barbara Dundas, vi. 109.
MELVILLE OF MONIMAIL, MELVILLE, LORD, vi. 96-123.
Melville of Monimail, George, fourth lord, vi. 92, 106.
—— —— John, third lord, vi. 105.
—— —— his wife, Anne Erskine, v. 83; vi. 106.
—— —— Robert, first lord, vi. 96.
—— —— his 1st wife, Katharine Adamson, vi. 99.
—— —— his 2nd wife, Mary Leslie, vi. 99; vii. 295.
—— —— his 3rd wife, Jean Stewart, vi. 99, 574.
—— —— Robert, second lord, vi. 91, 99, 101.
—— —— his 1st wife, Margaret Ker, vi. 101.
—— —— his 2nd wife, Jean Hamilton, vi. 101; vii. 255; ix. 136.
MELVILLE, VISCOUNT OF KIRKCALDY, vi. 108-123.
MELVILLE, EARL OF LEVEN, vi. 75-123.
MELVILLE, EARL OF MELVILLE, vi. 75-123.
MELVILLE, LORD MELVILLE OF MONIMAIL, vi. 96-123.
MELVILLE, LORD RAITH, MONIMAIL, AND BALWEARIE, vi. 108-123.
Melville of Abbotshall, Sir Robert, vi. 97, 99.
—— of Abden, John, 2nd son of Sir John M. of Raith, vi. 89.
—— of Allegevin, James, i. 184.
—— of Ardmure, James, vi. 104.
—— —— his wife, Jean Sinclair, vi. 104.
—— of Baldovie, Richard, i. 302, 303, 514; ix. 16.
—— —— his wife, Helen Lindsay, i. 302, 514.
—— of Balgarvie, James, 5th son of 1st earl of Melville, vi. 110.
—— —— his wife, Elizabeth Moncreiff, vi. 110.
—— of Burntisland, James, vi. 91.
—— —— Sir James, vi. 91.
—— —— Sir Robert, son of 1st lord Melville of Monimail, vi. 97, 98, 99.
Melville of Cairnie, John, v. 309.
—— —— his wife, Mary Maitland, v. 309.
—— —— Thomas, ancestor of the family of, vi. 104.
—— of Callange, John, vi. 82.
—— of Caproneston, John, vi. 82.
—— —— Walter, vi. 82.
—— —— his wife, Margaret Ayr, vi. 82.
—— of Carnbee, Galfrid, ancestor of the family of, vi. 77.
—— —— John, vi. 80.
—— —— John, v. 411.
—— —— his wife, Jean Lindsay, v. 411.
—— —— Sir John, vii. 254.
—— —— his wife, Alison, Alice, or Helen Ross, vii. 254.
—— of Cassingray, James, i. 546; vi. 106.
—— —— his wife, Anne Burnett, vi. 106.
—— of Mills of Dairsie, David, vi. 93.
—— of East Mains of Dalhousie, David, burgess of Edinburgh, iii. 92.
—— —— his wife, Elizabeth Wardlaw, iii. 92.
—— of Drumeorse, Sir James, vi. 90.
—— of Dura, William, vi. 84.
—— of Durachmore, John, vi. 82.
—— of Dysart, James, i. 184.
—— —— his wife, Isabel Douglas, i. 184.
—— of Ednam, Gregory, vi. 78.
—— of Feddinch, James, vi. 103.
—— of Garvock, Sir Andrew, master of the Household to queen Mary, vi. 93.
—— —— his 1st wife, Jane Kennedy, vi. 94.
—— —— his 2nd wife, Elizabeth Hamilton, vi. 94.
—— —— Sir George, under-master of the Household to king Charles II., vi. 94, 107; ix. 135.
—— —— his wife, Esther Tailor, ix. 135.
—— —— Sir Robert, vi. 99.
—— of Glenbervie, John, sheriff of the Mearns, i. 278.
—— of Moss of Grangemyre, Sir Robert, vi. 97.
—— of Granton, John, son of John M. of Carnbee, vi. 80.
—— of Grendon, Galfrid, vi. 77.
—— of Grieston, Thomas, vi. 80.
—— of Haddington, Thomas, vi. 79, 81.
—— —— his wife, Christiana Lysurs, vi. 79.
—— of Hallhill, Sir James, 4th son of Sir John M. of Raith, vi. 90, 93.
—— —— his wife, Christine Boswell, vi. 90.
—— —— James, 2nd laird, ii. 550; vi. 91, 105.
—— —— his 1st wife, Katharine Colville, ii. 549; vi. 91.
—— —— his 2nd wife, Katharine Learmonth, vi. 91.
—— —— Sir James, 3rd laird, ii. 550; vi. 91.
—— —— his wife, Margaret Farquhar, vi. 91.
—— —— James, 4th laird, vi. 92.

Melville of Hallhill, James, 5th son of 1st earl of Melville, i. 546; vi. 110.
— of Halsynton, Thomas, v. 282.
— of Hanley, James Moncrieff, W.S., v. 418.
— — his wife, Margaret Lindsay, v. 418.
— of Harviestoun, John, v. 604.
— of Kilwinning, William, commendator, iii. 443; vi. 94.
— of Easter Kinghorn, John, vi. 89.
— of Wester Kinghorn, Gilbert, minister of Arngask and Glendevon, vi. 92.
— — Robert, vi. 92.
— of Leebernard, Galfrid, vi. 76.
— of Liberton, Galfrid, sheriff of Edinburgh Castle, vi. 75.
— of Melville, Agnes, wife of Robert Ross, ii. 399; vi. 80; vii. 249, 250.
— — Galfrid, sheriff of Edinburgh Castle, 1st laird, vi. 75.
— — his 1st wife, *, vi. 77.
— — his 2nd wife, Matilda Malherbe, vi. 77.
— — Gregory, 2nd laird, vi. 78.
— — Sir Gregory, sheriff of Aberdeen, 5th laird, vi. 79.
— — John, 7th laird, vi. 79.
— — John, 9th laird, vi. 80.
— — John, 11th laird, vi. 80.
— — Sir Richard, sheriff of Linlithgow, 3rd laird, vi. 78, 81.
— — his wife, Margaret Prat, vi. 78.
— — Thomas, 8th laird, vi. 79.
— — Thomas, 10th laird, vi. 80.
— — Thomas, 12th laird, vi. 80.
— — Thomas, last laird, vii. 249, 250.
— — William, 4th laird, vi. 78, 81.
— — William, 6th laird, vi. 79.
— of Monimail, Sir Robert, treasurer-depute, vi. 98.
— of Mosshouse, Thomas, vi. 80.
— of Muiravonside, Sir Richard, vi. 78.
— of Murdocairnie, Sir Robert, secretary of state, i. 535, 537; ii. 69; iv. 473; vi. 90, 96.
— — his 1st wife, Katharine Adamson, i. 535; vi. 99.
— — his 2nd wife, Mary Leslie, vi. 99.
— — his 3rd wife, Jean Stewart, vi. 99.
— — his alleged wife, Margaret Balfour, i. 535.
— of Nethergrange, James, vi. 91.
— of Newmill, David, 5th son of Sir John M. of Raith, vi. 92.
— — his wife, Margaret Douglas, vi. 93.
— of Pitconmark, John, vi. 82.
— — Sir John, vi. 89.
— — William, eldest son of Sir John M. of Raith, vi. 89.
— — his wife, Margaret Douglas, vi. 90, 369.

* Name unknown.

Melville of Pitdovie, Andrew, i. 303.
— — his wife, Helen Lindsay, i. 302.
— of Pitgarvie, David, vi. 182.
— of Pitnamoon, David, vi. 182.
— of Pitscottie, John, vi. 82.
— — William, 2nd son of Wm. M. of Raith, vi. 84 *bis*.
— of Ferry of Portincraig, Sir Robert, vi. 100.
— of Prinlaws, David, vi. 93.
— — James, vi. 91.
— — Sir James, vi. 93.
— — John, vi. 93, 101.
— of Raith, Alexander, vi. 197.
— — John, 1st laird, vi. 82.
— — his alleged wife, * Stewart, vi. 82.
— — Sir John, 2nd laird, vi. 83.
— — his wife, Marjory Scott, vi. 82, 83.
— — John, the younger, vi. 83, 85.
— — his wife, Janet Bonar, vi. 84, 85.
— — Sir John, 4th laird, vi. 86.
— — his 1st wife, Margaret Wemyss, vi. 89; viii. 486.
— — his 2nd wife, Helen Napier, vi. 89; 412.
— — John, 5th laird, iv. 369; vi. 90, 101, 369.
— — his 1st wife, Isobel Lundie, vi. 102.
— — his 2nd wife, Margaret Bonar, vi. 102.
— — his 3rd wife, Grizell Meldrum, vi. 102; vii. 575.
— — John, 6th laird, vi. 103.
— — his wife, Margaret Scott, vi. 103, 104.
— — John, 7th laird, vi. 105.
— — his wife, Anne Erskine, vi. 106.
— — William, 3rd laird, vi. 83.
— — his alleged 1st wife, Margaret Douglas, vi. 83.
— — his 2nd wife, Euphemia Lundie, vi. 83, 86.
— of Shawmill, Katharine, wife of (1) Robert White of Maw, and (2) John Brown of Fordell, vi. 95.
— of Stanehouse, Galfrid, vi. 77.
— of Stenhouse, John, son of John M. of Carnbee, vi. 80.
— of Tartraven, Sir Gregory, vi. 79.
— — John, vi. 79.
— of Temple, Thomas, vi. 79, 81.
— of Tongland, Frederick, vi. 95.
— — William, senator of the College of Justice, i. 464; vi. 94.
— — his wife, Agnes *or* Anna Lindsay, i. 464; vi. 95.
— of Torbain, Sir John, vi. 89.
— of Westhall, John, v. 604.
— of Woodfield, Sir Robert, vi. 97.
— Agnes, wife of John Ramsay of Priorletham, vi. 102.

* Name unknown.

Melville, Alexander, master of Melville, vi. 109.
—— —— his wife, Barbara Dundas, vi. 109.
—— Alicia, wife of Richard, son of Galfrid, vi. 79, 81.
—— Alison, wife of Mr. David Barclay, vi. 103.
—— Mr. Andrew, moderator of the General Assembly, iii. 540; viii. 290.
—— Andrew, 3rd son of Wm. M. of Raith, vi. 84, 85.
—— Andrew, burgess of Kirkcaldy, viii. 484.
—— —— his wife, Helen Dunbar, viii. 484.
—— Anna, dau. of James M. of Halhill, ii. 550; vi. 92.
—— Anna, wife of Thos. Boyd of Penkill, vi. 106.
—— Christiana, wife of Adam, son of Walter, vi. 79, 81.
—— Christian, wife of Thos. Oliphant, vi. 99; ix. 136.
—— Christian, dau. of John M. of Raith, vi. 103.
—— David, 2nd son of Wm. M. of Melville, vi. 79.
—— David, 4th son of Wm. M. of Raith, vi. 84, 85.
—— David, burgess of Edinburgh, vi. 86.
—— David, 3rd son of John M. of Raith, v. 104.
—— Edith, wife of Clement A. Middleton, vi. 180.
—— Elizabeth, wife of John Colville, ii. 550; vi. 92.
—— Elizabeth, wife of Mr. Robert Murray, iii. 401; vi. 105.
—— Elizabeth, wife of David Boswell of Balgregie and Balmuto, vi. 83.
—— Elizabeth, wife of John Gourlay of Lamlethan, vi. 84, 85.
—— Euphame, dau. of John M. of Raith, vi. 105.
—— Eva, wife of Malcolm Dun, vi. 79, 81.
—— Mr. Francis, minister of Arbuthnott, i. 299.
—— —— his wife, Katharine Arbuthnott, i. 299.
—— Gelis, wife of Henry Pitcairn of Drongy, vi. 85.
—— Mr. Gilbert, minister of Arngask and Glendevon, vi. 92.
—— Grizell, wife of D. Lindsay of Pyotston, v. 412.
—— Henry, 3rd son of Sir Andrew M. of Garvock, vi. 94.
—— Hugh, 5th son of Galfrid M. of Melville, vi. 77.
—— Isobel, wife of Geo. Auchinleck, vi. 102.
—— Isabel, dau. of 3rd lord Melville of Monimail, vi. 106.
—— Janet, wife of James Kirkaldy of Grange, vi. 95.
—— Janet, wife of George Boiswell, vi. 102.
Melville, Jean, wife of Michael Balfour of New Grange, vi. 105.
—— Jean, dau. of 3rd lord Melville of Monimail, vi. 106.
—— Jean, dau. of James M. of Hallhill, ix. 135.
—— John, illeg. son of Sir John M. of Raith, vi. 88, 95.
—— John, 3rd son of Jas. M. of Hallhill, vi. 92.
—— John, son of Mr. Robert M., Simprin, vi. 92.
—— John, 2nd son of 3rd lord Melville of Monimail, vi. 106.
—— Jonet, wife of Geo. Hepburne, ii. 139.
—— Jonet, wife of James Johnstone of Elphinstone, vi. 95.
—— Katharine, wife of Mr. Robert Colville, ii. 549.
—— Katharine, wife of Mr. Robert Melville vi. 92.
—— Katharine, dau. of John M. of Raith, vi. 103.
—— Katharine, dau. of 3rd lord Melville of Monimail, vi. 106.
—— Magdalen, wife of Simon Arbuthnott, i. 303.
—— Margaret, alleged wife of James Bonar of Rossie, vi. 85.
—— Margaret, dau. of Mr. Robert M., Simprin, vi. 92.
—— Margaret, wife of Sir A. Balfour of Mountquhany, vi. 92.
—— Margaret, wife of Sir James Wemyss of Bogie, vi. 102; viii. 494.
—— Margaret, dau. of John M. of Raith, vi. 103.
—— Margaret, wife of James Scrimgeour of Wester Cartmore, vi. 105.
—— Margaret, wife of Robert Ramsay, ix. 136.
—— Margaret, wife of (1) Thos. Maitland, and (2) John Dalzell, ix. 136.
—— Richard, 6th son of Galfrid M. of Melville, vi. 78.
—— Sir Robert, 4th son of Galfrid M. of Melville, vi. 77.
—— Mr. Robert, minister of Simprin, vi. 92.
—— —— his wife, Katharine Melville, vi. 92.
—— Stephen, *perhaps* son of Sir Richard M. of Melville, vi. 81.
—— Susanna, wife of Andrew, earl of Teviot, vii. 374.
—— Mr. Thomas, minister of Terregles, iv. 416.
—— Thomas, 3rd son of Galfrid M. of Melville, vi. 77.
—— Thomas, 2nd son of John M. of Raith, vi. 102.
—— Mr. Thomas, minister of Kinglassie, vi. 104.
—— —— his wife, Jean Gourlay, vi. 104.

Melville, Thomas, 1406, vii. 529.
— Walter, 7th son of Galfrid M. of Melville, vi. 78.
— Walter, son of Stephen M., vi. 82.
— Walter, son of David M., burgess of Edinburgh, vi. 86.
— Walter, 6th son of Sir John M. of Raith, vi. 93.
— William, merchant, Edinburgh, vi. 92.
— William, 2nd son of Sir Andrew M. of Garvock, vi. 94.
— *, 5th dau. of John M. of Raith, vi. 102.
— *, rev. canon, rector of Barnes, vi. 180.
Mendes, P., Calcutta, ii. 54.
— — his wife, Marcellina Antonia *, ii. 54.
Menmuir, John Lindsay, 2nd son of 9th earl of Crawford; senator of the College of Justice, lord, i. 511, 516; iii. 29.
Mennes, Sir Matthew, ii. 442; ix. 55.
— — his wife, Margaret Stewart, ii. 442.
MENTEITH, THE ANCIENT EARLS OF, vi. 124-141.
Menteith, Alan, seventh earl of, iv. 14; vi. 134.
— — his wife, Marjory *, vi. 134.
— Alexander, sixth earl of, i. 12; vi. 133.
— — his wife, Matilda *, vi. 134.
— Gilchrist, first earl of, v. 328; vi. 125.
— Isabella, wife of (1) Walter Comyn, and (2) Sir John Russell; countess of, vi. 127.
— Sir John (Graham), *jure ux.* earl of, vi. 138.
— — his wife, Mary, countess of Menteith, i. 326; vi. 137.
— Margaret, wife of (1) John Moray of Bothwell, (2) Thomas, earl of Mar, (3) John Drummond of Concraig, and (4) Robert Stewart; countess of, i. 146, 148; ii. 128; iv. 14; v. 584; vi. 138.
— Mary, wife of Walter Stewart; countess of, vi. 127, 130.
— Mary, wife of Sir John Graham; countess of, i. 326; vi. 135, 137, 208.
— Maurice or Muredach, second earl of, vi. 125.
— Maurice, third earl of, vi. 126.
— Murdach, eighth earl of, vi. 135.
— — his wife, Alicia *, vi. 137.
— Robert (Stewart); *jure ux.* earl of, i. 146; iv. 14; vi. 140.
— — his wife, Margaret, countess of Menteith, i. 148; vi. 138.
— Walter (Comyn); *jure ux.* earl of, i. 505; iii. 558; iv. 221 *n.*; vi. 127; vii. 232.
— Walter (Stewart); 3rd son of 3rd High Stewart; *jure ux.* earl of, i. 12; iii. 331; vi. 130; ix. 1.
— — his wife, Mary, countess of Menteith, vi. 130.
MENTEITH, HASTINGS, EARL OF, vi. 135.

* Name unknown.

Menteith, John, earl of, vi. 135.
MENTEITH, GRAHAM, EARL OF, vi. 142-165.
Menteith, Alexander, second earl of, vi. 145, 151.
— — his wife, Margaret Buchanan, vi. 152.
— John, fourth earl of, vi. 160.
— — his wife, Marion Seton. vi. 160.
— John, sixth earl of, vi. 163.
— — his wife, Mary Campbell, ii. 183; vi. 164.
— Malise, first earl of, i. 133; iv. 355; v. 601; vi. 142; viii. 260.
— — his 1st wife, Jane de Rochford, vi. 144.
— — his 2nd wife, Marion *, vi. 144.
— William, third earl of, vi. 152, 156.
— — his wife, Margaret Moubray, vi. 157.
— William, fifth earl of, vi. 162.
— — his wife, Margaret Douglas, vi. 162; vii. 125.
— William, seventh earl of, i. 133, 144, 467; ii. 201; vi. 164.
— — his wife, Agnes Gray, i. 137; iv. 286.
— William, eighth earl of, i. 140.
Menteith of Aldcathie, James, vi. 153, 155.
— of Alva, William, ii. 180.
— of Arran, Sir John, v. 579, 599, 600; vi. 132.
— — his wife, Elyne of Mar, v. 579.
— — Sir John, i. 326; v. 580; vi. 132.
— — his wife, Katharine *, v. 580; vi. 132.
— of Caverkay, John, iii. 473.
— — his wife, Marion Bruce, iii. 473.
— of Kerse, Sir John, ancestor of the family of, i. 12; vi. 132.
— — John, v. 426.
— — Sir John, i. 562.
— — Walter, vi. 132.
— — William, ii. 180; v. 608.
— — his 1st wife, Agnes Erskine, v. 608.
— — his 2nd wife, Margaret Moncrieff, ii. 180.
— — William, v. 295.
— — Sir William, viii. 191.
— of Knapdale, Sir John, i. 326; vi. 132.
— of Ludquhairn, Christian, *see* of Pirchock.
— — Sir John, v. 599.
— of Menteith, Eva, wife of Alwin, 2nd earl of Lennox, vi. 125.
— — Joanna, wife of (1) Malise, earl of Strathearn, (2) John (Campbell), earl of Atholl, (3) Sir Maurice Murray, and (4) William, 5th earl of Sutherland, i. 435; ii. 130; iii. 162; v. 581; vi. 132; viii. 251, 257, 327; ix. 27.

* Name unknown.

Menteith of Pirehock, Christian, wife of (1) Sir Edward Keith of Sinton, and (2) Sir Robert Erskine of that Ilk, ii. 224; v. 580, 595, 599; vi. 33, 132.
— of Randyford, William, ii. 552.
— — his wife, Margaret Colville, ii. 552.
— of Roseneath, Alexander, vii. 34, 35.
— of Rusky, Agnes, wife of John Haldane of Gleneagles, v. 341; vi. 407.
— — Elizabeth, wife of John Napier of Merchiston, i. 335; v. 341; vi. 407, 408.
— — Sir John, 2nd son of Walter Stewart, earl of Menteith, i. 12; iii. 263; v. 335, 580, 581; vi. 132, 137.
— — Sir John, vi. 132.
— — his wife, Ellen of Mar, v. 579; vi. 132.
— — Sir John, vi. 132.
— — his wife, Katharine *, vi. 132.
— — Sir Murdac, i. 458; vi. 407.
— — his wife, Christian Murray, i. 458.
— — Patrick, vi. 407.
— — Robert, v. 341.
— — his wife, Margaret of Lennox, v. 341; vi. 407.
— — Walter, ancestor of the family of, vi. 132, 137.
— — Walter, his son, v. 595.
— of Strathgartney, Sir John, v. 579, 593.
— Alexander de, 4th son of Alexander, earl of Menteith, iv. 272; vi. 134; vii. 401.
— Alexander, vii. 217.
— — his wife, Agnes Primrose, vii. 217.
— Anna, wife of Sir Andrew Murray of Murrayshall, viii. 201.
— James, provost of Stirling, vi. 410.
— — his wife, Isabella Napier, vi. 410.
— Jean, wife of R. Graham of M'Keanston, vi. 155.
— John, sheriff of Clackmannan, i. 454; iii. 467; vii. 34.
— Jonet, wife of William Maitland of Lethington, v. 295.
— Katharine, wife of R. Graham in Shannochill, vi. 155.
— Katharine, wife of (1) Sir A. Murray of Balvaird, and (2) Sir G. Auchinleck of Balmanno, viii. 191.
— Margaret, wife of Sir Roger de Mortimer, iv. 272.
— Margaret, wife of Henry Graham, vi. 153.
— Maurice, *circa* 1293, 1309, vi. 134 *n*.
— Peter, 2nd son of Alexander, earl of Menteith, vi. 134.
— Robert, warden clerk of the Middle Marches, vii. 340.
— Sarah, wife of 1st lord Balmerinoch, i. 562; ix. 33.
— Walter, son of Walter M. of Kerse, v. 595.

* Name unknown.

Menteith, *, wife of Sir John Livingston of Callendar, v. 426.
— *, wife of Maurice Buchanan of Buchanan, vi. 133 *n*.
— *, alleged 1st wife of Archibald Campbell of Lochow, i. 327; vi. 133 *n*.
MENTMORE OF MENTMORE, PRIMROSE, VISCOUNT, ix. 152.
Mentmore of Mentmore, Archibald Philip, first viscount, ix. 152.
Menzies of Auldquhat, Gilbert, ix. 13.
— — his wife, Jean Menzies, ix. 13.
— of Balgownie, Francis, vi. 554.
— — his wife, Margaret Oliphant, vi. 554.
— of Boltoquhane, Adam, i. 512.
— — his wife, Margaret Lindsay, i. 512.
— of Carse, William, ii. 200.
— of Castlehill, Edward, ix. 150.
— — John, vii. 133.
— — his wife, Helen Douglas, vii. 133.
— of Chesthill, John Stewart, vii. 451.
— — his wife, Katharine Thurlow Fraser, vii. 451.
— of Comrie, James, tutor of Menzies, i. 360.
— — his wife, Anna Campbell, i. 360.
— of Culdares, James, 1st laird, v. 59.
— — his wife, Margaret Ker, v. 59.
— — James, col., ii. 191.
— of Culteraliers, Alexander, iv. 591.
— of Dumblait, Patrick, vii. 411.
— of Durne, Thomas, provost of Aberdeen, ii. 13.
— — his wife, Margaret Ogilvy, ii. 5.
— — Thomas, ii. 5, 13.
— — his wife, Elizabeth Ogilvy, ii. 13.
— of Ferryhill, Patrick, vii. 411.
— of Findon, Gilbert, vii. 433.
— — Gilbert, provost of Aberdeen, vii. 437 *bis*.
— of Hangingshaw, John, ii. 390.
— of Kinmundy, Sir Paul, ii. 5.
— of Lashgoune, James, iv. 70.
— — his wife, * Forbes, iv. 70.
— of Menzies, Alexander de, i. 14.
— — his wife, Egidia Stewart, i. 14.
— — Alexander, ii. 185, 189; ix. 155.
— — his 1st wife, Margaret Campbell, ii. 187.
— — James, i. 444; v. 500.
— — his wife, Barbara Stewart, i. 444.
— — Sir John, v. 500.
— — Sir John, 4th bart., i. 497.
— — his wife, Charlotte Murray, i. 497.
— — Sir Neil, 6th bart., iii. 391.
— — Sir Robert, ii. 179.
— — Sir Robert, i. 337; iv. 533; v. 502.
— — his 1st wife, Christian Gordon, iv. 533; ix. 110.
— — his 2nd wife, Marion Campbell, i. 337.

* Name unknown.

Menzies of Menzies, Robert, the younger, viii. 394.
— — — his wife, Anne Sandilands, viii. 394.
— — — Sir Robert, 3rd bart., ii. 300.
— — — his wife, Mary Stuart, ii. 300.
— of Morinichie, Robert, v. 502.
— of Pitfoddels, Gilbert, provost of Aberdeen, iv. 73.
— — his wife, Violet Forbes, iv. 73.
— — Gilbert, vi. 554.
— — Thomas, 1st laird, provost of Aberdeen, ii. 5; iii. 589.
— — Thomas, provost of Aberdeen, ii. 5 *bis*.
— — William, vii. 557.
— — his 2nd wife, Jean Sempill, vii. 557.
— of Rannoch, Alexander, v. 499.
— of Redhall, iv. 229 *n*.
— of Roro, William, ix. 133.
— — his wife, Marion Lindsay, ix. 133.
— of Saltcoats, Alexander, ii. 43.
— — Margaret, wife of (1) John Hamilton, and (2) Wm. Carmichael, ii. 43.
— of Stenhouse, vii. 148.
— — his wife, Katharine Douglas, vii. 148.
— of Tiggermark, Thomas, iii. 401.
— — his wife, Elizabeth Murray, iii. 401.
— of Weem, Alexander de, vi. 532.
— — Sir Alexander, v. 505; vii. 297.
— — Sir Alexander, 1st bart., i. 360 *bis*.; ii. 201.
— — his wife, Agnes Campbell, ii. 201.
— — Sir Alexander, 2nd bart., i. 361.
— — his wife, Christian Campbell, i. 361.
— — Sir David, vi. 570.
— — his wife, Marjory Sinclair, vi. 570.
— — Duncan, vii. 297.
— — his wife, Jean Leslie, vii. 297.
— Alexander, iv. 72.
— — his wife, Marjory Forbes, iv. 72.
— Andrew, provost of Aberdeen, i. 279.
— — his wife, Margaret Arbuthnott, i. 279.
— Elizabeth, wife of (1) John Lumsden, and (2) William King, iii. 590 *bis*.
— Gilbert, vii. 432.
— — his wife, Isabel Fraser, vii. 432.
— Grizel, wife of James Grant of Ardneidlie, ix. 155.
— Helen, wife of (1) Jas. Betoun, and (2) Andrew Kinnaird, v. 208; ix. 121.
— Helen, wife of Sir Mungo Campbell of Lawers, v. 505.
— James, Comrie, ix. 106.
— Jean, wife of Alex. Fraser of Strichen, v. 545.
— Jean, wife of Mr. Robt. Campbell, ii. 187.
— Jean, wife of (1) Gilbert Menzies of Auldquhat, and (2) Gavin Douglas of Raquarrall, ix. 13.
Menzies, Katharine, wife of James Gray of Schivas, iii. 589.
— Katharine, wife of rear-admiral Jack H. Murray, iii. 390.
— Katharine, wife of (1) Alex. Straton of that Ilk, and (2) Alex. Fraser of Philorth, vii. 437.
— Magdalene, wife of Alex. Campbell, ii. 200.
— Margaret, wife of (1) John Hamilton, and (2) Wm. Carmichael of Skirling, iv. 591.
— Margaret, wife of C. Campbell of Mochaster, ii. 189; ix. 43.
— Margaret, wife of (1) James Gordon, and (2) Patrick, 6th lord Oliphant, vi. 554.
— Margaret, wife of John Campbell of Ardeonaig, v. 504.
— Margaret, wife of Thos. Carlyle of Boytath, ii. 390.
— Marion, wife of (1) John Douglas of Archland, and (2) John Makgill, vi. 595.
— Marion, wife of Patrick Douglas, ix. 150.
— Mariota, dau. of Thos. M. of Durne, ii. 5.
— Marjory, wife of Jas. Gordon of Methlic and Haddo, i. 85.
— Marjory, wife of Cuthbert Murray of Cockpool, i. 220.
— Marjorie, dau. of Thos. M. of Durne, ii. 5.
— Marjorie, wife of John Campbell of Murthly, v. 500.
— Marjory, wife of Sir Alex. Fraser of Philorth, vii. 433.
— Neil, son of Jas. M., Comrie, ix. 106.
— — his wife, Mary Bothwell, iv. 439; ix. 106.
— Robert, burgess of Aberdeen, ix. 13.
— Susan, wife of (1) lord Neil Campbell, and (2) col. Alex. Campbell, i. 360.
— Susanna, wife of Robt. Campbell, ii. 191.
— William, St. Ann's, Jamaica, v. 545.
— colonel, 1646, iv. 546.
Mercer of Aldie, Sir James, vii. 217.
— — Jean, wife of captain George Keith Elphinstone, R.N., iii. 548; vi. 395.
— — Jean, wife of Robert Murray, or Nairn, 2nd son of 2nd lord Nairn, vi. 395.
— — John, burgess of Perth, i. 454.
— — Laurence, iv. 279; vii. 436.
— — Sir Laurence, iii. 485.
— — his wife, Christian Bruce, ii. 557; iii. 485; ix. 59, 82.
— — Sir Laurence, last laird, vi. 395.
— — William, colonel, vi. 395.
— — his wife, Margaret Murray of Pitcaithly, iii. 548; vi. 395.
— of Ballief, * provost of Perth, iv. 51.
— of Clavage, Laurence, iv. 260; ix. 98.
— — his wife, Jean Ruthven, iv. 260.
— — William, vii. 200.
— — his wife, Anna Rollo, vii. 200.

* Name unknown.

Mercer of Clavage, *, vii. 203.
— of Faithlie, Sir Henry, vii. 435.
— — Laurence, vii. 436.
— of Meiklour, Henry, vi. 368.
— — his wife, Margaret Douglas, vi. 367.
— — John, burgess of Perth, vi. 213, 536; vii. 32.
— — Laurence, iv. 261.
— — his wife, Janet Ruthven, iv. 261.
— — Laurence, ii. 557.
— — his wife, Cicill Colville, ii. 557.
— of Newton, James, ix. 98.
— of Saline, Gilbert, ii. 570.
— — his wife, Francisca Colquhoun, ii. 570.
— of Tyrie, Sir Henry, vii. 435.
— — Laurence, vii. 436.
— Christian, wife of (1) Gilbert Skene, and (2) D. Forbes of Corsindae, iv. 51.
— Cochrane, dau. of col. William M. of Aldie, vi. 396.
— Egidia, wife of Gilbert Gray of Buttergask, iv. 279.
— Helen, wife of (1) James Crichton of Wester Aldie, and (2) Mr. Andrew Rollo, vii. 198.
— Isobel, wife of Robert Maule of Panmure, vii. 11.
— James, elder son of Robert M. of Aldie, vi. 395.
— Katharine, dau. of col. William M. of Aldie, vi. 369.
— Margaret, wife of James Robertson of Lude, vi. 396.
— Nicolas, wife of James Primrose, vii. 217.
Mercer-Elphinstone, Margaret, baroness Keith and baroness Nairn; wife of count de Flahault, vi. 398.
Mercer-Henderson of Fordel, George William, vii. 227.
— — his wife, Alice Jane Primrose, vii. 227.
Meredith of Henbury, Amos, i. 384.
— — Sir William, i. 384.
— Mary, wife of (1) 4th earl Ferrers, and (2) Frederick Campbell, i. 384; ix. 25 *ter*.
Meriadec, Hervé, lord of Longueville, iii. 178.
Merlay, Ranulf de, lord of Morpeth, iii. 249.
— — his wife, Juliana of Dunbar, iii. 249.
— Roger de, iv. 8.
— * de, iv. 8.
— — his wife, *, dau. of Duncan, 5th earl of Fife, iv. 8.
Merschell, Elizabeth, wife of Edward Primrose, vii. 213.
— George, provost of Lincluden, vii. 127.
Metham of Metham, Sir Thomas, iii. 290.
— Agnes, wife of Sir John Constable, iii. 290.
METHIL, WEMYSS, LORD, viii. 500-518.

* Name unknown.

Methil, John, first lord, viii. 500.
METHLIC, GORDON, LORD, i. 88-99.
Methlic, George, first lord, i. 88.
METHVEN, STEWART, LORD, vi. 166-169.
Methven, Henry, first lord, 2nd son of 2nd lord Avandale, iii. 186; v. 153; vi. 166, 510.
— — his 1st wife, * Leslie, vi. 167.
— — his 2nd wife, queen Margaret Tudor, i. 21; vi. 166, 167.
— — his 3rd wife, Janet Stewart, i. 443; vi. 167; viii. 339.
— Henry, second lord, vi. 168.
— — his wife, Jean Ruthven, iv. 262; vi. 168.
— Henry, third lord, vi. 169.
— — his wife, * Stewart, vi. 169.
— master of, John, eldest son of 1st lord Methven, vi. 167.
Methven, Charles (Lennox), 1st baron, i. 32.
Methven, David Smythe of Methven, senator of the College of Justice, lord, iii. 517; iv. 212.
Mexborough, John (Savile), 3rd earl of, iii. 44.
Meynell of Hoar Cross, Hugo, v. 19.
— — his wife, Elizabeth Ingram, v. 19.
— — Charles, v. 19.
— Frederick George Lindley, *né* Wood, iii. 48.
— — his wife, Mary Susan Felicia Lindsay, iii. 48.
Meyners, *see* Menzies.
Meyrick, Arabella Augusta, wife of lieut.-col. C. R. Hay-Drummond, v. 236.
— William Henry, colonel, v. 236.
Michael of Methil, viii. 471.
Michael of Penshiel or Mayshiel, viii. 476.
Michael 'Redhood,' burgess of Cupar, iii. 304.
Michael, son of Orm of Abernethy, vii. 397.
Michael the Clerk, father of John, viii. 475.
Michel, servant to the Venetian ambassador, vi. 489.
Michell, John, Richmond, vii. 103.
— — his wife, Mary Graham, vii. 103.
Middelton of Stockeld, Peter, iv. 418.
— — Peter, iv. 420.
— — William, iii. 297.
— — his wife, Katharine Constable, iii. 297.
— — William, 2nd son of William Haggerston-Maxwell-Constable, iv. 418.
— — his wife, Clara Louisa Grace, iv. 418.
— Elizabeth, wife of Sir Carnaby Haggerston, iv. 418.
— Juliana, wife of Henry Constable-Maxwell-Stuart, iv. 420.
Middleham, Ralph, ii. 429.
— — his wife, Agatha de Brus, ii. 429.
— Ribald, lord of, ii. 429.
Middlemast, John, v. 73.

* Name unknown.

Middlemore, agent of queen Elizabeth, v. 111.
Middleton, Henry (Willoughby), 8th baron, iii. 393.
MIDDLETON, MIDDLETON, EARL OF, vi. 170-190.
Middleton, John, first earl of, i. 358, 362; v. 122, 563; vi. 183; vii. 219.
— — his 1st wife, Grizel Durham, vi. 185.
— — his 2nd wife, Martha Carey, vi. 185.
— Charles, second earl of, iii. 347; vi. 186.
— — his wife, Katharine Brudenal, vi. 187.
MIDDLETON, LORD OF CLAIRMONT AND FETTERCAIRN, vi. 184.
MIDDLETON, EARL OF MIDDLETON, vi. 170-190.
Middleton of Balbegno, Andrew, vi. 182.
— — his 1st wife, Elizabeth Ramsay, vi. 182.
— — his 2nd wife, Anna Forbes, vi. 182.
— — Robert, vi. 182.
— — his wife, Anne Ogilvy, vi. 182.
— of Berrihill, Alexander, vi. 174.
— — his wife, Margaret Robertson, vi. 174.
— of Caldhame, John, vi. 175.
— — Robert, vi. 175, 176.
— — his wife, Katharine Strachan, vi. 176.
— of Clerkhill, Henry, vi. 172.
— of Courthill, James, vi. 174.
— of Cramondgorth, Henry, vi. 173.
— of Davidstoun, John, vi. 173.
— of Erroll, George, banker, viii. 157.
— — his wife, Mary Campbell, viii. 157.
— of Futtaburgh, Laurence, capt., vi. 173.
— — his 2nd wife, Grisel Mowat, vi. 173.
— of Halkerton, John, v. 244.
— of Kilhill, Gilbert, vi. 172.
— — John, vi. 173.
— — his 1st wife, Isabella Falconer, vi. 173; ix. 123.
— — his 2nd wife, Katharine Strachan, vi. 174.
— — John, vi. 174.
— — his 1st wife, Elizabeth Ramsay, vi. 175.
— — his 2nd wife, Katharine Mortimer, vi. 175.
— — John, vi. 175.
— — his wife, Euphemia Mortimer, vi. 176.
— of Kincardine O'Neil, William, vi. 181.
— — his wife, Madeline Sinclair, vi. 181.
— of Lethamdolls, George, vi. 178.
— — his wife, Elizabeth Wilson, vi. 178.
— of Middleton, Gilbert, father of Laurence M., vi. 171.
Middleton of Middleton, Gilbert, son of Laurence M., vi. 171, 172.
— — his 1st wife, Marjorie Wishart, vi. 172.
— — his 2nd wife, Agnes Lauder, vi. 172.
— — Humphrey, vi. 170.
— — Humphrey, vi. 171.
— — John, v. 244; vi. 173.
— — Laurence, vi. 171.
— — his wife, Nicolas Straton, vi. 171.
— — Walter, in Invercany, vi. 171.
— of Mosshall, George, vi. 178.
— — his wife, Elizabeth Wilson, vi. 178.
— of Muirton, John, vi. 175,
— of Newtibber, John, vi. 173.
— of Netherseat of Halkerton, John, vi. 173.
— — John, vi. 174.
— of Pitgarvie, Andrew, vi. 182.
— — his 1st wife, Elizabeth Ramsay, vi. 182.
— — his 2nd wife, Anna Forbes, vi. 182.
— of Seaton, George, advocate, vi. 178.
— — his wife, Diana Grey, vi. 178.
— — John, brigadier-general, M.P., vi. 177.
— — his wife, Elizabeth Cuninghame, vi. 178.
— Alexander, 4th son of Laurence M. of Middleton, vi. 171.
— Alexander, eldest son of Gilbert M. of Middleton, vi. 172.
— — his wife, Isabel Grahame, vi. 172.
— Mr. Alexander, 4th son of John M. of Kilhill, vi. 175.
— Alexander, principal of King's College, Aberdeen, vi. 176.
— — his wife, Margaret Gordon, vi. 176.
— Alexander, comptroller of customs, Aberdeen, vi. 177.
— — his wife, Elspet Burnet, vi. 177.
— Alexander, elder son of John M., Barbados, vi. 177.
— Alexander, Boston, U.S.A., vi. 177.
— — his wife, Ann Todd, vi. 177.
— Alexander, vi. 179.
— — his wife, Elizabeth Neave, vi. 179.
— Alexander, curate of St. Alphage, Canterbury, vi. 181.
— — his wife, Phœbe Hammond, vi. 181.
— Andrew, 3rd son of Andrew M. of Pitgarvie, vi. 182.
— Charles, 4th son of principal George M. vi. 178.
— Sir Charles, 1st bart., R.N., vi. 180.
— — his wife, Margaret Gambier, vi. 180.
— Charles, 2nd son of Andrew M. of Pitgarvie, vi. 182.
— Charles, chevalier of the order of St. Louis, vi. 188.

Middleton, Charles John, principal registrar H.M. Court of Probate, vi. 179.
—— —— his wife, Katharine Anne Strong, vi. 179.
—— Clement Alexander, judge at Karachi, vi. 179.
—— —— his 1st wife, Edith Melville, vi. 180.
—— —— his 2nd wife, Helen Harris, vi. 180.
—— David, 2nd son of Laurence M. of Middleton, vi. 171.
—— David, factor to the duke of Bedford, vi. 182.
—— Elizabeth, dau. of John M. of Kilhill, vi. 175.
—— Elizabeth, wife of Charles Gordon of Achanachie, vi. 182.
—— Elizabeth, wife of Wm. Spelman of Wickmer, vi. 186.
—— Elizabeth, wife of Edward Drummond, 6th titular duke of Perth, vi. 188; vii. 57, 58.
—— Emily Augusta, dau. of Charles John M., vi. 180.
—— Francis, 6th son of John M. of Kilhill, vi. 175.
—— Francis, 5th son of Robt. M. of Caldhame, vi. 181.
—— Francis, illeg. son of Sir James M., vi. 182.
—— George, son of Laurence M. of Futtaburgh, vi. 173.
—— George, heir to Berrihill, vi. 174.
—— George, 4th son of John M. of Middleton, vi. 174.
—— George, principal of King's College, Aberdeen, vi. 177.
—— —— his wife, Janet Gordon, vi. 177.
—— George, eldest son of Alex. M., Aberdeen, vi. 177.
—— George, 5th son of principal George M., vi. 178.
—— George, Cheshire, vi. 179.
—— —— his wife, Mary Woolston Marshall, vi. 179.
—— Dr. George, 6th son of Robt. M. of Caldhame, vi. 181.
—— Gilbert, Jesuit in Paris, vi. 181.
—— Grizel, wife of 8th earl of Morton, vi. 185, 379.
—— Helen, wife of 1st earl of Strathmore and Kinghorne, vi. 185; viii. 302.
—— Sir James, 'tribunus militaris,' vi. 182.
—— James, 3rd son of John M. of Kilhill, vi. 175.
—— Janet, wife of Gilbert Keith, vi. 172.
—— Janet Mary Woolston, vi. 179.
—— John, legtd. son of John M. of Middleton, vi. 174.
—— John, Barbados, vi. 177.
—— —— his wife, Mary Allister, vi. 177.
—— John, 2nd son of above, vi. 177.
—— —— his wife, Hester Haselwood, vi. 177.
Middleton, John, their elder son, vi. 177.
—— John, vicar of Burnham-on-Crouch, vi. 180.
—— —— his 1st wife, Lydia Hewetson, vi. 180.
—— —— his 2nd wife, Mary *, vi. 180.
—— John, 2nd son of 1st earl of Middleton, vi. 186.
—— Katharine, wife of (1) Sir John Gifford, and (2) lieut.-gen. Michael Rothe, vi. 188; ix. 137.
—— Margaret, wife of Robert Strachan in Kinkell, vi. 175.
—— Margaret, wife of 5th earl of Stair, viii. 157.
—— Marjorie, wife of Gilbert Bisset of Pitmuckston, vi. 174.
—— Oswald Robert, colonel K.O. Royal Lancaster regt., vi. 180.
—— —— his wife, Christine Kerr, vi. 180.
—— Patrick, 5th son of John M. of Kilhill, vi. 175.
—— Patrick, Cracow, vi. 178.
—— —— his wife, Susannah Moer, vi. 178.
—— Patrick, major-general in Polish service, vi. 178.
—— —— his wife, Janet de Seher, vi. 178.
—— Richard, 2nd son of John M., vi. 177.
—— Robert, collector of customs, vi. 178.
—— —— his wife, Helen Dundas, vi. 178.
—— Robert, 3rd son of above, vi. 180.
—— Robert, 3rd son of Robt. M. of Caldhame, vi. 181.
—— Robert Gambier, rear-admiral, vi. 178.
—— —— his wife, Susanna Maria Leake, vi. 179.
—— Robert Marshall, vi. 179.
—— —— his wife, Henrietta Ellen Gooden, vi. 179.
—— Thomas, 5th son of principal Alex. M., vi. 181.
—— Violet, wife of (1) * of Thainstoun, and (2) Geo. Leslie of Leslie, vi. 172.
—— Walter, 3rd son of Laurence M. of Middleton, vi. 171.
—— William, 6th son of principal George M., vi. 178.
—— William, col. 17th Madras N.I., vi. 179.
—— —— his wife, Harriet Theophila Sterling, vi. 179.
—— William, 3rd son of principal Alex. Middleton, vi. 181.
—— William, colonel, burgess of Aberdeen, vi. 181.
—— William, vi. 455.
—— —— his wife, Frances Clifford, vi. 455.
—— William Gambier, vi. 179.
—— —— his wife, Sophia Margaret Mouat, vi. 179.
—— *, 4th husband of Mary Mackenzie, dau. of 3rd earl of Cromartie, iii. 81.

* Name unknown.

Middleton, *, wife of Mr. Robert Ogilvie, minister of Methlick, vi. 183.
Midford, George, Morpeth, i. 494.
Midleton, William St. John P. (Brodrick), 9th viscount, viii. 518.
—— his 1st wife, Hilda Charteris, viii. 518.
MIDLOTHIAN, PRIMROSE, EARL OF, ix. 152.
Midlothian, Archibald Philip, first earl of, ix. 152.
Miggel, Michael de, i. 107.
Mildmay of Apethorpe, Sir Walter, ii. 34.
— Christian, wife of Charles Barret, ii. 34.
Mill of Fearn, John, v. 250.
—— his wife, Hannah Ivie, v. 250.
— Dorothy, wife of Wm. Stockdale, v. 165.
— Thomas, Yorkshire, v. 165.
Millar, Elizabeth, wife of Mr. Jas. Hamilton, ii. 51.
— Mr. Robert, ii. 51.
Miller of Dalswinton, Patrick, v. 635.
— of Muirshiels, James Brook, vi. 156.
— Andrew, South Queensferry, vi. 545 *n.*
—— his wife, Katharine Oliphant, vi. 545 *n.*
— Ephraim, Hertingfordbury, ii. 75.
—— his wife, Caroline Bellenden, ii. 75.
— George, i. 527.
— George Harry, commr. R.N., vi. 156.
—— his wife, Caroline Frances Graham Stirling of Craigbarnet, vi. 156.
— James, advocate, vii. 255.
—— his wife, Elspeth Ross, vii. 255.
— Janet, wife of John Thomas, earl of Mar, v. 635.
— Martha Willet, wife of col. George Dalrymple, viii. 138.
— Maud Grace, wife of D. B. Lindsay, i. 527.
— Sibylla, wife of James Primrose, vii. 216.
Millner of Staindrop, J., viii. 311.
— Mary, wife of (1) John, 10th earl of Strathmore and Kinghorne, and (2) Sir Wm. Hutt, viii. 311.
Mills, Mrs., London, vi. 489.
Miln, John Clarkson, Bute, i. 390.
— Olivia Rowlandson, wife of (1) lord Walter Campbell, and (2) Allan Gordon, i. 390.
Milne of Balwyllie, Robert, provost of Montrose, i. 143.
— Mary, wife of James Allardice, i. 143.
Milner, John, Wakefield, iii. 482.
—— his wife, Rachel Bruce, iii. 482.
— Marcus Henry, D.S.O., vi. 272.
—— his wife, Caroline Agnes Horsley-Beresford, vi. 272.
Milnes of Bawtry Hall, Pemberton, v. 233.
— Mary Bridget, wife of (1) lieut.-col. P. Auriol Drummond-Hay, and (2) Robert, viscount Galway, v. 233.

* Name unknown.

MILSINGTON, COLYEAR, VISCOUNT OF, vii. 92-97.
Milsington, Brownlow Charles, only son of 4th earl of Portmore; styled viscount of, vii. 96.
— David, elder son of 1st earl of Portmore; styled viscount of, vii. 93.
—— his wife, Bridget Noel, vii. 93.
— David, elder son of 2nd earl of Portmore; styled viscount of, vii. 94.
— Thomas Charles, eldest son of 3rd earl of Portmore; styled viscount of, vii. 95.
—— his wife, Mary Elizabeth Bertie, vii. 96.
Milton, Joseph (Damer), lord, i. 386.
— Andrew Fletcher, lord of Session, lord, viii. 78, 81, 84 *bis.*
Mir Cossim, nabob of Bengal, viii. 309.
Mitchell of Bandeath, James, ii. 573.
—— his wife, Grizel Colvill, ii. 573.
— of Fraserfield, Henry David, vii. 445.
—— his wife, Margaret Fraser, vii. 445.
— of Stow, Alexander, M.P., vii. 179.
—— his wife, Fanny G. J. Hasler, vii. 179.
— of Thainston, Duncan Forbes, vii. 445.
—— his wife, Katharine Anne Fraser, vii. 445.
— Mary Caroline, wife of (1) A. K. Blair, (2) George, 3rd duke of Sutherland, and (3) Sir A. K. Rollit, viii. 364.
— Richard, D.D., viii. 363.
Mitchelson of Middleton, purchaser of Borthwick Castle, ii. 115 *n.*
Mitton of Weston-under-Lyziard, Edward, iii. 406.
—— Elizabeth, wife of Sir Thomas Wilbraham, iii. 406.
Moddan, titular earl of Caithness, grandson of Crinan, iii. 240.
Modena, Alphonso IV. (d'Este), duke of, i. 33.
—— his wife, Laura Martinozzi, i. 33.
Moer, Susannah, wife of Patrick Middleton, vi. 178.
Mohun, Charles (Mohun), 5th lord, iv. 384.
Moigne, Sir Walter de, v. 584.
Moir of Invernettie, James, i. 309.
—— his wife, Katharine Arbuthnott, i. 309.
— of Leckie, Charles Alexander, viii. 451.
—— his wife, Henrietta Hay, viii. 451.
— of Lonmay, William, vii. 445.
— of Stoneywood, James, iv. 120.
— of Whitehills, William, vii. 445.
Moira, Francis (Rawdon Hastings), 2nd earl of, v. 512.
—— his wife, Flora, countess of Loudoun, v. 511.
Molesworth, Gilbert de, *perhaps* 2nd son of Walter de Lindsay, lord of Lamberton, iii. 5.

Molineux, Dorothy, wife of 6th viscount Falkland, iii. 613.
—— Francis, London, iii. 613.
Molle, Eschina de, wife of (1) Robert de Croc, and (2) Walter Fitz-alan, 1st High Steward of Scotland, i. 11.
Mollison, Helen, dau. of Wm. M., vii. 585.
—— William, London, vii. 585.
—— —— his wife, * St. Clair, vii. 585.
Molyneux, Caryll (Molyneux), 3rd viscount, i. 411.
—— Capel, in holy orders, v. 366.
—— Diana, wife of capt. William Dalrymple of Cleland and Fordel, viii. 122.
—— Edmond, London, vi. 462.
—— —— his wife, Agnes Lexham, vi. 462.
—— Maria Jane, wife of W. P. Lennox, v. 366.
—— *, Preston, viii. 122.
Monaco, Albert, duke of Valentinois, prince of, iv. 396.
—— —— his wife, M. V. Douglas-Hamilton, iv. 396.
Monck, George, general, i. 259, 362; ii. 236; v. 121, 228 *n.*; vii. 81.
Moncreiff, Moncrieff, Moncrieffe of Balcaskie, Sir Alexander, i. 468.
—— —— John, i. 468.
—— —— his wife, Katharine Murray, i. 468.
—— —— John, ix. 59.
—— —— his wife, Helen Colville, ii. 557; ix. 59.
—— of Methven, Gilbert, vi. 169.
—— of Moncrieffe, Sir John, iv. 31.
—— —— John, ii. 180; iv. 32; vii. 280.
—— —— his alleged 1st wife, Egidia Ogilvy, iv. 32.
—— —— Sir John, 1st bart., v. 531.
—— —— Sir John, 2nd bart., iii. 509.
—— —— Sir Robert Drummond, 8th bart., v. 236.
—— —— his wife, Evelyn E. V. Hay, v. 236.
—— —— Sir Thomas, 5th bart., iii. 105; v. 312.
—— —— his wife, Elizabeth Ramsay, iii. 105.
—— —— Sir Thomas, 7th bart., i. 499; v. 236; viii. 211.
—— —— his wife, Louisa Hay, v. 236.
—— —— Sir William, v. 502; vii. 195.
—— —— William, the younger, vi. 546.
—— —— his wife, Jean Oliphant, vi. 546.
—— —— William, ii. 184; iv. 260; viii. 189.
—— of Sauchope, James, v. 414.
—— —— his wife, Margaret Wemyss, v. 414.
—— Agnes, wife of John Campbell of Lawers, ii. 178.
—— Agnes, wife of (1) Thos. Scott of Abbotshall, and (2) Robert, master of Ross, vii. 252.
—— Alexander, minister at Scoonie, iii. 401.
—— —— his wife, Anna Murray, iii. 401.

* Name unknown.

Moncreiff, Andrew, brother of Sir Alex. M. of Balcaskie, i. 468.
—— Andrew, burgess of Perth, ii. 155.
—— —— his wife, Jonet Oliphant, ii. 155.
—— Andrew, minister of Crail, viii. 187.
—— —— his wife, Janet Moncrieff, viii. 187.
—— Blanche, wife of Charles Archibald Murray, viii. 211.
—— Elizabeth, wife of Wm. Murray, i. 463.
—— Elizabeth, wife of Alex. Ruthven of Freeland, iv. 260; ix. 98.
—— Elizabeth, wife of Jas. Melville of Hall hill and Balgarvie, vi. 110.
—— Euphemia, wife of John Leslie of Parkhill, vii. 280.
—— Gilbert, physician to king James VI., i. 463.
—— Isobella, wife of George Rollo of Duncrub, vii. 194.
—— Janet, wife of Charles Barclay-Maitland, v. 312.
—— Janet, wife of (1) Andrew Moncrieff, and (2) Wm. Murray of Little Ardit, both ministers of Crail, viii. 187.
—— Jean, wife of (1) Sir S. Fraser of Inverallochy, and (2) Sir Thos. Burnett of Leys, v. 531.
—— John, prior of Blantyre, i. 463.
—— Louisa, wife of 7th duke of Atholl, i. 499.
—— Margaret, dau. of John M. of Balcaskie, i. 468.
—— Margaret, wife of (1) Sir D. Campbell, and (2) Wm. Menteith, ii. 180.
—— Margaret, wife of G. Sinclair, ii. 355.
—— Margaret, wife of captain Geo. Murray, Royal Scots, iii. 509.
—— Margaret, wife of John Campbell of Auchreoch, v. 499.
—— William, minister of Largo, i. 516.
—— —— his wife, Anne Lindsay, i. 516.
Moncur of Balluny, Robert, v. 219.
—— —— his wife, Katharine Hay, v. 219.
—— of Moncur, Andrew, iv. 271; v. 205.
—— —— his wife, Elizabeth Gray, iv. 271.
—— —— Andrew, viii. 484.
—— —— his wife, Helen Dunbar, viii. 484.
—— —— Andrew, v. 207.
—— Andrew, in Rawis, v. 207.
—— Elizabeth, wife of George Moncur, v. 207.
—— James, iv. 32.
—— —— his wife, Christian Ogilvy, iv. 32.
—— Katharine, v. 207.
—— Margaret, wife of P. Kinnaird of Inchture, v. 207.
—— Thomas, i. 443; v. 398.
—— —— his wife, Helen Stewart, i. 443; v. 398; ix. 128.
Moncure, Dr. John Jaqueline, iii. 605.
Mondragone, Dominico (Grillo), duke of, vi. 458.

Monmouth, Henry (Carey), 2nd earl of, vi. 185.
— James, illeg. son of king Charles II.; duke of, i. 30; ii. 237; v. 379, 381.
— — his wife, Anna, countess of Buccleuch, ii. 237; vi. 107.
Monorgund of Monorgund, Andrew, iv. 275.
— — his wife, * Gray, iv. 275.
Monro of Craiglockhart, Alexander, M.D., iv. 572.
— — his wife, Maria Agnes Carmichael-Smyth, iv. 572.
— of Meikle Findon, Robert, vii. 500.
— — his wife, Marjory Mackenzie, vii. 500.
— Alexander, Glasgow, ii. 277.
— Andrew, colonel, v. 534.
— — his wife, Margaret Fraser, v. 534.
— Erskine, wife of (1) Jas. Turnbull, and (2) Henry Erskine, M.P., ii. 277.
— Finguella, wife of Roderick Mackenzie of Redcastle, vii. 500.
— Margaret, wife of C. Campbell of Glenample, ii. 183.
— *see also* Munro.
Monson, John (Monson), 1st lord, iv. 494.
Monson of Castlemaine, William (Monson) lord, vi. 318.
— — his wife, Margaret Stewart, vi. 318.
— of Burton, Sir Henry, 3rd bart., vi. 467.
— — his wife, Elizabeth Cheyne, vi. 467.
— George, colonel, iv. 494.
— — his wife, Anne Vane, iv. 494.
Montacute, William de, ii. 379.
Montagu, George (Montagu), 3rd duke of, ii. 243.
— — his wife, Mary Montagu, ii. 243.
— John (Montagu) 2nd duke of, ii. 243, 533.
— — his wife, Mary Churchill, ii. 533.
— Anthony Joseph (Montagu), 7th viscount, v. 251.
— — his wife, Frances Mackworth, v. 251.
Montagu of Beaulieu, Henry John (Montagu Douglas Scott Montagu), 2nd son of 5th duke of Buccleuch; 1st baron, ii. 246.
— — his wife, Cicely Susan Stuart-Wortley-Mackenzie, ii. 246.
— — John Walter Edward, 2nd baron, v. 486.
— — his wife, Cecil Victoria Constance Ker, v. 486.
Montagu of Boughton, Henry James (Montagu), 7th lord, iv. 482.
— — his wife, Jane Margaret Douglas, ii. 243; iv. 482.
— Caroline Georgina, wife of G. W. Hope of Luffness, ii. 243.
— Caroline Maria, wife of 3rd duke of Montrose, vi. 271.
— Elizabeth, wife of 3rd duke of Buccleuch, ii. 242.

* Name unknown.

Montagu, Jane Caroline, dau. of lord Montagu of Boughton, ii. 243.
— Lucy Elizabeth, wife of 11th earl of Home, ii. 243; iv. 482.
— Mary, wife of George, duke of Montagu, ii. 243.
— Mary, wife of (1) 12th duke of Hamilton, and (2) R. C. Forster, iv. 396.
— Mary Margaret, wife of lt.-col. F. Clinton, ii. 243.
— Susan, wife of 8th marquess of Tweeddale, viii. 470.
— Sydney Charlotte, wife of 9th earl of Kintore, v. 254.
MONTAGU - DOUGLAS - SCOTT, DUKE OF QUEENSBERRY, ii. 244-249.
Montagu-Douglas-Scott, Alice Christina, ii. 248.
— Charles Henry, ii. 246.
— Charles Thomas, G.C.B., admiral R.N., ii. 246.
— — his wife, Ada Mary Ryan, ii. 247.
— Charles William, ii. 247.
— Constance Anne, wife of Douglas Halyburton Cairns, ii. 248.
— David John, ii. 247.
— Evelyn Mary, wife of rev. T. L. C. Bridges, ii. 246.
— Francis George, Grenadier Guards, ii. 248.
— Francis Walter, ii. 246.
— George William, capt. 10th Hussars, ii. 248.
— — his wife, Elizabeth Emily Manners, ii. 248.
— — Henry Francis, major 3rd batt. Royal Scots, ii. 248.
— Herbert Andrew, capt. Irish Guards, ii. 248.
— John Charles, styled lord Dalkeith, ii. 247.
— — his wife, Margaret Alice Bridgeman, ii. 248.
— Katharine Mary, wife of major Thos. Brand, ii. 248.
— Margaret Elizabeth, wife of Cameron of Lochiel, ii. 247.
— Margaret Harriet, wife of 3rd earl of Romney, ii. 245.
— Margaret Ida, ii. 248.
— Mary Charlotte, wife of col. W. R. Trefusis, ii. 247.
— Mary Theresa, ii. 248.
— Phyllis Anne, ii. 248.
— Sybil Anne, ii. 248.
— Victoria Alexandrina, wife of (1) 9th marquess of Lothian, and (2) Bertram Talbot, ii. 247; v. 486.
— Walter Charles, 3rd son of 5th duke of Buccleuch, ii. 246.
— — his wife, Anna Maria Hartopp, ii. 246.

Montagu-Douglas-Scott, Walter George Leon, ii. 246.
—— —— his wife, Ralouka Warner Heriot ii. 246.
—— Walter Henry, styled lord Eskdaill, eldest son of 6th duke of Buccleuch, ii. 247.
—— Walter John, styled lord Whitchester, ii. 248.
—— William Walter, ii. 248.
Montagu-Stuart-Wortley, Francis Dudley, 2nd son of 2nd baron Wharncliffe, ii. 303.
Montalt of Brechin and Kinblethmont, William de, viii. 419.
MONTDIEU, GRAHAM, LORD GRAHAM AND, vi. 247-274.
Montdieu, James, first lord Graham and, vi. 247, 248.
Monteath, George Cunningham, i. 389.
—— —— his wife, Anne Colquhoun Cunningham, i. 389.
Montefichet of Auchterarder, Cargill, and Kincardine, Mary, wife of John Drummond, vii. 35.
—— —— Sir William de, vii. 35.
—— of Cargill, Devorgilla, vii. 35.
—— —— Richard de, vii. 36 *n.*
—— —— William de, vi. 529; vii. 427.
—— Dervorgilla de, wife of David de Olifard, vi. 529.
—— Laurence de, vi. 529.
—— Margaret, vii. 35.
—— Sir Walter de, vi. 529.
Monteir, David, Edinburgh, v. 409.
—— Margaret, wife of Patrick Lindsay, v. 409.
Monteith, Alexander, surgeon-apothecary, ii. 493.
—— George, Edinburgh, viii. 374.
—— Helen, wife of John Kennedy of Kilhenzie, ii. 493.
—— Marie, wife of Jas. Lindsay of Kilquhis, v. 403.
—— Marion, wife of Alex. Livingston, viii. 374.
Montferrand, Jean de, v. 350.
—— —— his wife, Anne Monypenny, v. 350; vi. 278 *n.*
Montfort, Simon de, earl of Leicester, i. 168.
Monthermer, Mary de, wife of Duncan, 10th earl of Fife, iv. 12, 14.
MONTGOMERIE, MONTGOMERIE, LORD, iii. 431-465.
Montgomerie, Alexander, first lord, iii. 431.
—— —— his wife, Margaret Boyd, iii. 432; v. 142.
—— Alexander, styled lord, iii. 432; ix. 80 *bis.*
—— —— his wife, Katharine Kennedy, ii. 456; iii. 432; ix. 80.
Montgomerie, Archibald, eldest son of 12th earl of Eglinton; styled lord, iii. 460, 461.
—— —— his wife, Mary Montgomerie, iii. 460, 461.
—— Archibald Seton, eldest son of 15th earl of Eglinton; styled lord, iii. 464.
—— —— his wife, Beatrice Susan Dalrymple, viii. 163.
—— Hugh, second lord, iii. 432, 434; ix. 80.
—— —— his wife, Helen Campbell, i. 335; iii. 435.
—— Hugh, grandson of 1st earl of Eglinton; styled lord, iii. 436, 438.
—— —— his wife, Marion Seton, iii. 439; viii. 581.
—— Hugh, eldest son of 6th earl of Eglinton; styled lord, iii. 450.
—— —— his 1st wife, Anne Hamilton, iv. 375.
—— —— his 2nd wife, Mary Leslie, iii. 451.
—— Hugh, 3rd son of Archibald, lord Montgomerie; styled lord, iii. 462.
—— James, 4th son of 9th earl of Eglinton; styled lord, iii. 456.
MONTGOMERIE OF THE GREAT ARDS, MONTGOMERIE, VISCOUNT, iii. 433.
Montgomery of the Great Ards, Hugh (Montgomery), 1st viscount, i. 41 *n.*; iii. 433.
—— —— his wife, Sarah Maxwell, iv. 413; viii. 546.
—— —— Hugh, 2nd viscount, viii. 180.
—— —— his wife, Jean Alexander, viii. 180.
—— —— Hugh, 3rd viscount, iii. 433.
—— master of, Alexander, eldest son of 1st lord Montgomerie, ii. 141; iii. 432.
—— —— his wife, Elizabeth Hepburn, ii. 141; iii. 432.
—— master of, Hugh, eldest son of 9th earl of Eglinton, iii. 456; ix. 81.
—— earl of, *probably error for* Alexander (eldest son of 8th earl of Eglinton), styled lord M., iii. 354.
MONTGOMERIE, BARON ARDROSSAN OF ARDROSSAN, iii. 461-465.
MONTGOMERIE, EARL OF EGLINTON, iii. 421-465.
MONTGOMERIE, LORD MONTGOMERIE, iii. 431-465.
MONTGOMERIE, VISCOUNT MONTGOMERIE OF THE GREAT ARDS, iii. 433.
MONTGOMERIE, EARL OF MOUNT ALEXANDER, iii. 433.
MONTGOMERIE, EARL OF WINTON, iii. 462-465.
Montgomerie, Montgomery, of Annick Lodge, Alexander, R.N., H.E.I.C.S., iii. 449; iv. 208.
—— —— his wife, Elizabeth Taylor, iii. 449.
—— of Ardrossan, Sir Alexander, iii. 430; iv. 232; vii. 529.

Montgomerie, Montgomery of Ardrossan, Sir John, iii. 429; iv. 232, 257.
— — his 1st wife, Agnes of the Isles, iii. 430.
— — his 2nd wife, Margaret Maxwell, iii. 430; v. 140; vi. 474.
— of Auchinhude, Hugh, iii. 436.
— of Bondyngton, Alexander, 2nd son of John M. of Eaglesham, iii. 428.
— of Bowhouse, John, bailie-depute of Cunningham, iii. 432.
— — his wife, * Ramsay, iii. 432.
— of Braidstane, Robert, iii. 433.
— of Carny, John, iii. 428.
— of Cassillis, Christian, dau. of Sir Neil M., ii. 444; iii. 426.
— — Marjorie, wife of Malcolm, ii. 444; iii. 426.
— — Marjorie, dau. of John M., constable of Ayr, ii. 444; iii. 427.
— — Sir Neil, iii. 426.
— of Coilsfield, Alexander, 2nd laird, iii. 447.
— Alexander, 4th laird, iii. 448, 460.
— — his wife, Lilias Montgomerie of Skelmorlie, iii. 448.
— — Hugh, 3rd laird, iii. 447.
— — his 1st wife, Jean Primrose, iii. 447; vii. 110.
— — his 2nd wife, Katharine Arbuckle, iii. 447, 448.
— — Hugh, 5th laird, iii. 449, 460 *bis*.
— — James, 4th son of 6th earl of Eglinton, iii. 447, 453, 455.
— — his wife, Margaret Macdonald, iii. 447.
— of Corscraig, John, vii. 533.
— of Corsehill, Sir Walter, bart., v. 557.
— of Dreghorn, Arthur, iii. 436.
— — William, 2nd son of 1st earl of Eglinton, iii. 436.
— of Dunbulg, John, iii. 428.
— of Eaglesham, John, ii. 452 *n.*; iii. 428; vii. 528.
— of Eastwood, Sir John, iii. 425.
— of Eglinton, Hugh, iii. 434; v. 150.
— — John, iii. 428.
— — his wife, Elizabeth of Eglinton, iii. 428.
— of Figgidoch, Alexander, iv. 188.
— of Flatt, John, iv. 188.
— — his wife, Marjorie *or* Marion Fraser, iv. 188.
— of Garboldisham, Frederick Butler, iii. 47.
— — his wife, Isabella Lindsay, iii. 47.
— of Giffen, Alexander, 5th laird, iii. 430.
— — his wife, Jonet Dunlop, iii. 430.
— — Daniel, 11th laird, iii. 431.

* Name unknown.

Montgomerie, Montgomery, of Giffen, Francis, M.P., 2nd son of 7th earl of Eglinton, iii. 451, 453; v. 380; vii. 303.
— — his 1st wife, Margaret, countess of Leven, iii. 451; v. 380.
— — his 2nd wife, Elizabeth Sinclair, iii. 451.
— — Sir Henry, 2nd son of 6th earl of Eglinton, iii. 446.
— — his wife, Jean Campbell, i. 349; iii. 446.
— — Hugh, 8th laird, iii. 430.
— — Hugh, 9th laird, iii. 431.
— — Sir John, 1st laird, iii. 429.
— — his 1st wife, Agnes of the Isles, iii. 430.
— — his 2nd wife, Margaret Maxwell, iii. 430.
— — John, 10th laird, iii. 431.
— — John, iv. 593.
— — his wife, Mary Carmichael, iv. 593.
— — Margaret, wife of (1) Hugh, 5th earl of Eglinton, and (2) Robert, 7th lord Boyd, iii. 442, 444; v. 170; ix. 81.
— — Mary, wife of (1) Archibald, lord Montgomerie, and (2) Sir C. M. Lamb, iii. 460.
— — Patrick, 6th laird, iii. 430; vii. 534.
— — Robert, 2nd laird, 2nd son of Sir John M. of Eaglesham, iii. 429, 430.
— — Robert, 4th laird, iii. 430.
— — his wife, Margaret Blair, iii. 430.
— — Robert, 7th laird, iii. 430, 437.
— — Robert, master of Eglinton, 12th laird, iii. 431, 442.
— — his wife, Jean Campbell, iii. 442; v. 497.
— — Sir William, 3rd laird, iii. 430.
— — his wife, Janet Houston, iii. 430.
— of Greenfield, William, 2nd son of 1st earl of Eglinton, iii. 436.
— of the Hall, Sir Henry Conyngham, 1st bart., vii. 154.
— of Hesilhead, Hugh, 3rd son of Alexander, master of Montgomerie, iii. 433.
— — Hugh, v. 162.
— — his wife, Helen Boyd, v. 162.
— — Hugh, vii. 550.
— — his wife, Marian Sempill, vii. 550.
— — John, vii. 534.
— — Marion, wife of (1) Craufurd of Auchenames, (2) William, 2nd lord Sempill, and (3) John Campbell of Skipnish, iii. 437 *n.*; vii. 536; ix. 19.
— — Robert, v. 190.
— — his wife, Margaret Livingston, v. 190.
— — *, wife of * Macaulay of Ardincaple, iii. 433.
— of Innerwick, John, son of Alan M., iii. 424.
— — his wife, Helen Kent, iii. 424.

* Name unknown.

Montgomerie, Montgomery, of Irvine, Patrick, v. 153.
— of Kilmore, Marjorie, wife of Malcolm, son of Henry, iii. 426.
— of Kilwinning, Hugh, iii. 443.
— of Lainshaw, David, iii. 437 *n.*
— — Elizabeth, wife of capt. Alexander Montgomerie Cunninghame, v. 557.
— — James, self-styled lord Lyle, iii. 436; v. 556.
— — his wife, Barbara Kennedy, iii. 437.
— — Jean, wife of David Laing, v. 557.
— — John, vi. 14.
— — Sir Neil, 3rd son of 1st earl of Eglinton, iii. 436, 439; iv. 190, 191; v. 154 *bis*.
— — his wife, Margaret Mure, ii. 463; iii. 436.
— — Neil, 2nd laird, iii. 436.
— — his wife, Jean Lyle, iii. 436; v. 556.
— of Lochhouse, Robert, 2nd son of Sir John M. of Eaglesham, iii. 430.
— of Polnoon, John, iii. 428.
— — Sir John, iii. 429.
— of Milnestaneflat, Sir Neil, ix. 80.
— — Robert, ix. 80.
— of Portry, Hugh, iv. 188 *bis*.
— of Rosemount, William, capt., i. 382.
— — his wife, Isabella Campbell, i. 382.
— of Skelmorlie, Cuthbert, iii. 438.
— — George, 2nd son of 1st lord Montgomerie, ii. 403; iii. 433.
— — George, iii. 438.
— — his wife, Katharine Montgomerie, iii. 438.
— — Sir Hugh, 11th bart., iii. 448.
— — Sir James, 10th bart., the plotter, i. 264, 266; v. 448; vii. 259, 260.
— — his wife, Margaret Johnstone, i. 264.
— — John, ii. 403.
— — his wife, Marion Dalzell, ii. 403.
— — Lilias, wife of Alexander Montgomerie of Coilsfield, iii. 433, 448.
— — Sir Robert, i. 350.
— — his wife, Mary Campbell, i. 349.
— — Robert, 6th laird, iv. 241; vii. 550.
— — his wife, Dorothea Sempill, vii. 550.
— — Sir Robert, vii. 129.
— — his wife, Margaret Douglas, vii. 129.
— — Sir Robert, 5th bart., iii. 448; ix. 81.
— of Southennan, Sophie Constance, wife of S. H. Allanby, iii. 463.
— of Stair, Alan, 2nd son of John M., iii. 426.
— — John, constable of Ayr, iii. 426.
— — his wife, Janet Erskine, iii. 426.
— — John, father of Marjorie of Stair and Kilmore, iii. 426.
— — Marjorie, wife of Malcolm, son of Henry, iii. 426.
— of Stane, Arthur, iii. 436.
Montgomerie, Montgomery of Stane, Hugh, iii. 440.
— — his wife, Margaret Montgomerie, iii. 440.
— — William, iii. 436.
— — his wife, Elizabeth Francis, iii. 436.
— of Stanhope, Sir James, bart., iii. 522.
— of Stobo, Sir James, bart., vii. 522.
— — his wife, Elizabeth Douglas, vii. 522.
— of Thornton, John, iv. 304.
— — John, his son, iv. 304.
— — his wife, Alison Hamilton, iv. 304.
— of Whim, Archibald, judge of Rungpore, B.C.S., iii. 522.
— Agnes, wife of Sir R. Cunningham of Kilmaurs, iii. 431.
— Agnes, wife of W. Cunningham of Glengarnock, iii. 433.
— Agnes, wife of John Ker of Kersland, iii. 438.
— Agnes, wife of Thomas Kennedy of Bargany, iii. 440.
— Agnes, wife of 4th lord Sempill, iii. 442; vii. 552.
— Agnes, dau. of Robert M. of Giffen, iii. 442.
— Agnes, *perhaps* wife of Sir Wm. Sempill of Eliotstoun, vii. 530.
— Sir Alan, iii. 423.
— Alan, 4th son of Sir Alan M., iii. 425.
— Alan, *perhaps* grandson of Sir John M. of Eastwood, iii. 425.
— Alexander, elder son of John M. of Stair, iii. 426, 427.
— Alexander, alleged eldest son of 2nd lord Montgomerie, iii. 435 *n.*
— Sir Alexander, colonel, 3rd son of 6th earl of Eglinton, iii. 446.
— Alexander, son of major-gen. Robert M., iii. 450.
— Alexander, colonel, 2nd son of Francis M. of Giffen, iii. 452.
— Alfred, commissioner of Inland Revenue, vii. 154.
— Anna, dau. of James M. of Coilsfield, iii. 447.
— Anna, dau. of 6th earl of Eglinton, iii. 450.
— Anne, dau. of Alex. M. of Coilsfield, iii. 450.
— Anne, wife of (1) Robert Seton, and (2) James, 3rd earl of Findlater, iii. 452; iv. 36; ix. 89.
— Anne, wife of Sir Andrew Ramsay of Waughton, and (2) Sir P. Ogilvy of Boyne, iii. 452; ix. 81.
— Anne, wife of Sir Robt. Cunningham of Kilmaurs, iv. 232.
— Archibald, 1690, i. 367.
— Archibald, H.E.I.C.S., iii. 449.
— — his wife, Maria Chantry, iii. 449.

Montgomerie, Montgomery, Arnulf de, castellan of Pembroke Castle, iii. 421.
— Charlotte, dau. of 9th earl of Eglinton, iii. 458.
— Christian, wife of 4th lord Balmerino, i. 569; iii. 452; ix. 34.
— Christian, contracted to Matthew Stewart; wife of Sir Jas. Douglas of Drumlanrig, iii. 436; v. 353; vii. 125.
— Christian, alleged wife of a Colquhoun of Luss, iii. 437.
— Christian, alleged wife of James Pringle, iii. 448 *n*.
— Christian, wife of James Moray of Abercairney, iii. 458; ix. 81.
— Constantine, 3rd son of Robert M. of Giffen, iii. 430.
— Diana, wife of (1) Sir C. Alexander, and (2) H. K. Allison, iii. 464.
— Edith Mary, wife of capt. A. R. Trotter, iii. 464.
— Egidia, wife of 5th lord Rendlesham, iii. 463.
— Eleonora, wife of Francis Stuart of Pittendreich, iii. 457.
— Elizabeth, wife of John, 2nd lord Kennedy, ii. 457; iii. 433.
— Elizabeth, wife of William Cochrane of Cochrane, iii. 338, 339.
— Elizabeth, dau. of Sir Neil M. of Lainshaw, iii. 437.
— Elizabeth, wife of Alex. Cunningham, iii. 437 *n*.
— Elizabeth, wife of * Dunbar of Machirmore, iii. 447.
— Elizabeth, wife of col. P. Ogilvy of Lonmay and Inchmartin, iii. 452; iv. 36.
— Elizabeth, wife of Sir John Cunningham of Caprington, iii. 457.
— Elizabeth, wife of David Boyle, lord Boyle, iv. 208.
— Elspet, wife of G. Ogilvy of Friock, i. 122; ix. 8.
— Emily Maria, wife of 9th lord Elibank, iii. 522.
— Euphemia, wife of George Lockhart of Carnwath, iii. 457.
— Ezekiel, in entail of Giffen, iii. 431.
— Frances, wife of James Ritchie of Busbie, iii. 449.
— Frances, dau. of 9th earl of Eglinton, iii. 458.
— Francis Cuninghame, 3rd son of 15th earl of Eglinton, iii. 464.
— George, lieut.-col., v. 228 *n*.
— Georgina Theresa, wife of W. Mure of Caldwell, iii. 464.
— Gertrude, wife of E. B. A. Lawford, iii. 464.
— Gilbert de, Normandy, iii. 421.

* Name unknown.

Montgomerie, Montgomery, Grace, wife of 5th earl of Carnwath, ii. 416; iii. 457.
— Grace, wife of cornet Charles Byne, iii. 457.
— Grissel, wife of Robert Sempill of Craigbait, vii. 534.
— Helen, wife of Sir J. Bruce of Airth, iii. 433.
— Helen, dau. of Sir Neil M. of Lainshaw, iii. 437.
— Helen, wife of John Blair of Blair, iii. 438.
— Helen, wife of Francis Stuart of Pittendreich, iii. 457; vi. 324; ix. 81, 140.
— Helenor, wife of Thomas Garvine, iii. 448.
— Helenor, wife of David Dunbar, iii. 452.
— Henry, 3rd son of Sir Alan M., iii. 424.
— Hew, 4th son of 1st earl of Eglinton, iii. 437.
— Hew, legtd. son of Robert, bishop of Argyll, iii. 437.
— Hilda Rose, wife of T. Mosley, iii. 463.
— Hugh de, Normandy, iii. 421.
— Hugh de, son of Roger, earl of Shrewsbury, iii. 421.
— Hugh, killed at Otterburn, iii. 429.
— Hugh, son of James M., iii. 439.
— Hugh, major, 2nd son of 8th earl of Eglinton, iii. 454.
— Isobel, wife of John Mure of Caldwell, iii. 437.
— Isabel, dau. of Robert M. of Giffen, iii. 440.
— Isabella, wife of Archibald Mure of Rowallan, iii. 431.
— James, grandson of Alexander, master of Montgomerie, iii. 432, 433, 439.
— James, lieut-general, iii. 449.
— — his wife, Harriet Elizabeth Jackson, iii. 449.
— James, son of maj.-gen. Robert M., iii. 450.
— James Francis, dean of Edinburgh, iii. 548.
— — his wife, Elizabeth Mary Buller-Fullerton-Elphinstone, iii. 548.
— Jane, wife of Archibald Hamilton of Carcluie, iii. 462.
— Janet, wife of (1) John Hamilton of Cambuskeith, and (2) Wm. Sempill of Cathcart, vii. 534.
— Janet, wife of 3rd lord Ross of Halkhead, vii. 252.
— Jean, wife of Matthew Stewart, iii. 440.
— Jean, wife of Mr. Alexander Lang, iii. 436, 437 *n*.
— Jean, wife of (1) Mr. John Burnet, and (2) Mr. John M'Dermeit, iii. 448.
— Jean, wife of Sir Alex. Maxwell, iii. 457.
— Joanna, wife of Sir Thos. Boyd of Kilmarnock, iii. 431; v. 140.

Montgomerie, Montgomery, John, *perhaps* ancestor of the comtes de Montgomery, iii. 430.
— John, nephew of Hugh, 2nd earl of Eglinton, iii. 436.
— John, elder son of Sir Neil M. of Lainshaw, iii. 436.
— — his wife, Margaret Boyd, iii. 436; v. 155.
— John, M.P., lieut.-col., governor of New York, iii. 452, 455; ix. 81.
— — his wife, Mary Carmichael, iii. 452.
— John, major, 3rd son of 8th earl of Eglinton, iii. 454.
— — his wife, Jean Gibson, iii. 454.
— Jonet, wife of Geo. Campbell of Cessnock, iii. 438.
— Jonet, illeg. dau. of 1st earl of Eglinton, iii. 438.
— Katharine, wife of George Montgomerie of Skelmorlie, iii. 438.
— Katharine, illeg. dau. of col. Sir Alex. M., iii. 447.
— Katharine, dau. of Hugh M. of Coilsfield, iii. 448.
— Katharine, dau. of Alex. M. of Coilsfield, iii. 449.
— Katharine, wife of 5th earl of Galloway, iii. 456; iv. 164.
— Lilias, wife of John Hamilton of Sundrum, iii. 449.
— Lilias, wife of (1) R. D. Macqueen, and (2) R. A. Oswald, iii. 462.
— Margaret, wife of John Hamilton of Bargany, ii. 31; iii. 450; viii. 131.
— Margaret, wife of (1) John, 1st earl of Tweeddale, and (2) William, 8th earl of Glencairn, iii. 450; iv. 248; viii. 449; ix. 98.
— Margaret, wife of Sir Archibald Mure of Rowallan, iii. 425.
— Margaret, wife of Alexander, 1st lord Home, iii. 433; iv. 451 *bis*.
— Margaret, wife of John Stewart, lord Darnley, earl of Lennox, iii. 433; v. 348, 349.
— Margaret, wife of William, 2nd lord Sempill, iii. 437; vii. 536.
— Margaret, wife of Hugh Montgomerie of Stane, iii. 440.
— Margaret, wife of Robert, 1st earl of Winton, iii. 442, 450; viii. 591; ix. 80.
— Margaret, wife of (1) Hugh, 5th earl of Eglinton, and (2) Robert, 7th lord Boyd, iii. 444; v. 170; ix. 81.
— Margaret, wife of John Chalmers of Gadgirth, iii. 447.
— Margaret, wife of John Hamilton, Jamaica, iii. 448.
— Margaret, wife of 2nd earl of Loudoun, iii. 452; v. 507; ix. 131.
Montgomerie, Montgomery, Margaret, dau. of 8th earl of Eglinton, iii. 454; ix. 81.
— Margaret, wife of Sir Alexander Macdonald of Macdonald, iii. 457; ix. 81.
— Margaret, wife of Robert Boyle of Figgidoch, iv. 188.
— Margaret, alleged wife of Sir Archibald Hamilton of Innerwick, iv. 304.
— Marjory, wife of William, master of Somerville, iii. 433; viii. 12.
— Mary, wife of D. Kennedy of Kirkmichael, iii. 447.
— Mary, wife of William Hamilton of Letham, iii. 448.
— Mary, wife of Sir James Agnew, iii. 454.
— Mary, wife of Sir David Cunningham of Milncraig, iii. 457.
— Mary, dau. of Francis M. of Giffen, iii. 452.
— Mary, wife of George, 4th earl of Winton, iii. 452; viii. 602.
— Mary, wife of 1st lord Kirkcudbright, v. 267.
— Matilda, wife of Colin Campbell of Ardkinglas, iii. 437.
— Michael, legtd. son of Robert, bishop of Argyll, iii. 437.
— Murthaueh de, Homage Roll, iii. 425.
— Nigel, *alias* Sir Neil M. of Lainshaw, iii. 436; iv. 191.
— Philip de, son of Roger, earl of Shrewsbury, iii. 421.
— Robert, archbishop of Glasgow, ii. 80.
— Robert de, Normandy, iii. 421.
— Robert, son of Roger, earl of Shrewsbury, iii. 421.
— Robert, first to settle in Scotland, iii. 422.
— Sir Robert, eldest son of Alan M., iii. 424, 425.
— Robert, rector of Kirkmichael, bishop of Argyll, iii. 437; ix. 80.
— Robert, legtd. son of Robert, bishop of Argyll, iii. 437.
— Robert, major-general, gentleman of the bed-chamber to king Charles II., iii. 450, 453; v. 228 *n*.
— — his wife, Elizabeth Livingstone, iii. 450; v. 192.
— Robert, in Haltoun, ix. 8.
— — his wife, Euphame Guthrie, ix. 8.
— Roger de, *c*. 1050; iii. 421.
— Roger de, governor of Normandy, earl of Shrewsbury, iii. 421.
— Roger de, son of Roger, earl of Shrewsbury, iii. 421.
— Roger, lieut. R.N., 2nd son of 12th earl of Eglinton, iii. 462.
— Seton Montolieu, lieut. Scots Fusilier Guards, iii. 463.
— — his wife, Nina Janet Williams, iii. 463.

Montgomerie, Montgomery, Susanna, wife of John Renton of Lambertoun, iii. 457.
— Susanna, dau. of Archibald, 11th earl of Eglinton, iii. 460.
— Sibyl, wife of 8th marquess of Queensberry, vii. 154.
— Sybil Amelia Adela, dau. of 13th earl of Eglinton, iii. 463.
— Theresa, wife of John Cross, iii. 464.
— Thomas de, Homage Roll, iii. 425.
— Thomas, 4th son of Robt. M. of Giffen, iii. 430.
— Thomas, parson of Eaglesham, rector of Glasgow University, iii. 433.
— Thomas, Dumfries, Virginia, iii. 449.
— Thomas Henry, captain 42nd Highlanders, iii. 548.
— — his wife, Anna Maria Buller-Fullerton-Elphinstone, iii. 547.
— William de, Normandy, iii. 421.
— William, in holy orders, 1175, iii. 423.
— William, 2nd son of 2nd earl of Eglinton, iii. 439.
— William, his illeg. son, iii. 440.
— — his wife, Marion Cunyngham, iii. 440.
— William Alexander, lieut. 2nd Dragoons, iii. 464.
— *, 3rd son of John, master of Eglintoun, iii. 436.
— comtes de, in France, iii. 430.
Montgomery-Campbell of Bennington Park, Arthur William, ii. 497.
— — Hugh, ii. 497.
Montgomery-Cuninghame of Corsehill, Sir Thomas Andrew Alexander, 10th bart., iv. 238.
— — Sir Walter, 4th bart., iii. 437 *n.*
Monthermer, Sir Ralph de, i. 428; ii. 379; iv. 12.
— — his wife, Joan Plantagenet, countess of Gloucester, iv. 12.
Mont Louis, comtesse de, vii. 208.
Montolieu, Anne, wife of Sir J. B. Burges, ix. 31.
— David, baron de St. Hypolite, iii. 512.
— Elizabeth, wife of 8th lord Cranstoun, ii. 600.
— Elizabeth, wife of rev. Gideon Murray, iii. 512.
— Lewis Charles, lt.-col., baron de St. Hypolite, ii. 600; iii. 520.
— Mary Clara, wife of 7th lord Elibank, iii. 520.
MONTROSE, GRAHAM, EARL OF, vi. 224-274.
Montrose, James, fifth earl of, vi. 242; vii. 199.
— — his wife, Magdalen Carnegie, vi. 253.
— John, third earl of, vi. 231.
— — his wife, Jean Drummond, vi. 237; vii. 46; ix. 137.

* Name unknown.

Montrose, John, fourth earl of, iv. 266; v. 443; vi. 239; vii. 294.
— — his wife, Margaret Ruthven, iv. 266; vi. 241; ix. 99.
— William, first earl of, iv. 235 *n.*; vi. 224.
— — his 1st wife, Annabel Drummond, vi. 225; vii. 45.
— — his 2nd wife, Janet Edmonstone, vi. 225.
— — his 3rd wife, Christian Wawane, iv. 337; vi. 225; ix. 102, 137.
— William, second earl of, vi. 45, 226.
— — his wife, Janet Keith, vi. 45, 228.
— — his contr. wife, Mary Somerville, vi. 228; viii. 14.
MONTROSE, GRAHAM, MARQUESS OF, vi. 247-274.
Montrose, James, first marquess of, i. 125, 126, 352; iii. 323, 324 *bis*; iv. 129. 547; v. 225; 227; vi. 58, 242; vii. 201; viii. 297, 298, 349.
— — his wife, Magdalen Carnegie, i. 126; vi. 250, 253; viii. 68.
— James, second marquess of, iii. 99, 323; v. 228; vi. 255.
— — his wife, Isabella Douglas, vi. 255, 378; vii. 348.
— James, third marquess of, i. 141; iii. 326, 327; vi. 259; ix. 137.
— — his wife, Christian Leslie, vi. 261; vii. 301, 302.
— James, fourth marquess of, vi. 261; viii. 68.
— — his wife, Christian Carnegie, vi. 265; viii. 68.
MONTROSE, GRAHAM, DUKE OF, vi. 191-274.
Montrose, Douglas Beresford Malise Ronald, fifth duke of, vi. 273.
— — his wife, Violet Hermione Graham, vi. 273; ix. 138.
— James, first duke of, vi. 263.
— — his wife, Christian Carnegie, vi. 265, 500.
— James, third duke of, v. 541; vi. 268.
— — his 1st wife, Jemima Elizabeth Ashburnham, vi. 271.
— — his 2nd wife, Caroline Maria Montagu, vi. 271.
— James, fourth duke of, vi. 271.
— — his wife, Caroline Agnes Horsley-Beresford, vi. 272.
— William, second duke of, vi. 266.
— — his wife, Lucy Manners, vi. 268.
MONTROSE, LINDSAY, DUKE OF, iii. 22-23.
Montrose, David, duke of, iii. 22; viii. 50.
— — his 1st wife, Elizabeth Hamilton, iii. 23; iv. 351, 353.
— — his 2nd wife, Margaret Carmichael of Meadowflat, iii. 23.
Monymusk of Monymusk, Sir John, vii. 237, 430.
— — his wife, Janet de Ross, vii. 237.

Monymusk of Monymusk, Marjery de, wife of John Fraser of Balhelvie, vii. 430.
—— *, elder dau. of M. of Monymusk, vii. 237.
MONYPENNY, MONYPENNY, LORD, vi. 275-279.
Monypenny, Alexander, second lord, vi. 278.
—— William, first lord, vi. 276.
—— —— his wife, Katharine Stewart, vi. 278.
MONYPENNY, LORD MONYPENNY, vi. 275-279.
Monypenny of Ardweny, Alexander, vi. 278.
—— —— Sir William, vi. 277.
—— —— William, vi. 277 *n.*
—— of Balbot, Thomas, vi. 276.
—— of Balgradane and Bordland of Rattray, Sir William, vi. 277.
—— of Butteleis, Sir William, vi. 277, 278.
—— of Concressault, Alexander, v. 350.
—— —— Anne, wife of (1) John Stewart of Henriestoun and Oizon, (2) Jean de Montferrand, and (3) Antoine de la Roche Chandre, v. 350; vi. 278 *n.*
—— —— Sir William, vi. 277.
—— —— his wife, Katharine Stewart, vi. 277, 278.
—— of Drumavet, John, vi. 275.
—— of Erth, William, vi. 276.
—— of Escariot, Alexander, vi. 278.
—— of Feldy, Alexander, vi. 278.
—— —— Sir William, vi. 278.
—— of Kirkandrews and Kirkinnon, Sir William, vi. 278.
—— of Easter Lecky, Sir William, vi. 278.
—— of Lethbertscheiles, Sir William, vi. 277.
—— of Leuchars, Alexander, vi. 278.
—— —— Janet, vi. 275.
—— —— Thomas, vi. 275; viii. 419.
—— —— Thomas, vi. 276.
—— —— his wife, Christian Keith, vi. 276.
—— —— William, vi. 277.
—— —— Sir William, vi. 278.
—— of Monypenny, Sir William, vi. 276, 277.
—— of Pitmilly, Alexander, ii. 367; vi. 114.
—— —— his wife, Magdalen Erskine, ii. 367.
—— —— James, ii. 571.
—— —— his wife, Euphan Colvill, ii. 571.
—— —— John de, vi. 275.
—— —— John, *temp.* David II., vi. 275.
—— —— John, 1336, vi. 275.
—— —— John, elder son of Thos. M. of Pitmillie and Leuchars, vi. 276.
—— —— John, ii. 549.
—— —— his wife, Susanna Colville, ii. 549.
—— —— Thomas, vi. 275; viii. 419.
—— —— Thomas, vi. 276.
—— —— his wife, Christian Keith, vi. 39, 276.

* Name unknown.

Monypenny of Pitmilly, Thomas, son of John M., vi. 276.
—— —— William, vi. 277.
—— of Seryne, John, vi. 275.
—— of Torseraehan, Alexander, vi. 278.
—— —— Sir William, vi. 278.
—— Mr. David, brother of Thos. M. of Pitmillie, vi. 277 *bis.*
—— Elizabeth, wife of Alexander, 5th earl of Leven, and 4th earl of Melville, vi. 114; ix. 136.
—— Mr. George, son of Thos. M. of Pitmillie, vi. 277 *bis.*
—— James, son of Thos. M. of Pitmillie, vi. 277 *bis.*
—— Margaret, wife of (1) D. Ogilvy of that Ilk, and (2) Alex. Ogilvy, i. 118.
—— Thomas, 2nd son of Thos. M. of Pitmillie, vi. 277 *bis.*
—— Sir William, vi. 276.
—— —— his wife, Margaret *or* Marjorie Arbuthnott, ii. 278; vi. 276.
Moodie of Arbeikie, James, i. 295, 299.
—— John, vi. 499.
—— —— his wife, Magdalene Carnegie, vi. 499.
—— Hugh, captain, viii. 124.
—— —— his wife, Katharine Dalrymple, viii. 124.
—— *see also* Mudie.
Mooney, Loretta, wife of Sholto George Douglas, vii. 154.
Moore of Mooresfort, Maurice Crosbie, iv. 560.
—— Alice, wife of (1) 2nd earl of Clanbrassil, and (2) 2nd lord Bargany, ii. 32.
—— Edward, i. 61.
—— —— his wife, Jane Hamilton, i. 61.
—— Edward, vicar of Frittenden, ii. 245.
—— —— his wife, Harriet Janet Sarah Scott, ii. 245.
—— Emily, wife of Cecil James Gordon, iv. 560.
—— Frances, wife of Thomas Erskine, attorney-general, ii. 277.
—— Francis, brother of general Sir John M., iii. 460.
—— —— his wife, Frances Twisden, iii. 460.
—— George, rector of Wrotham, iii. 582.
—— James, the Greek scholar, vii. 520.
—— John, archbishop of Canterbury, iii. 582.
—— John, M.D., author of *Zeluco*, iv. 393.
—— Sir John, general, iii. 460; iv. 394.
—— Mary, wife of (1) 3rd earl of Dalhousie, and (2) 2nd lord Bellenden, ii. 73; iii. 101; ix. 66.
—— William, M.P., ii. 277.
Moorehead, Marion, wife of major Wm. Borthwick of Johnstonburn, ii. 100.
Mora, mistress of king Robert II., and alleged ancestress of the Stewarts of Bute, ii. 286.

Mera of Dalry, William de, v. 138.
Merant of Brockenhurst, John, iii. 584.
Meravia, *see* Moray.
MORAY, THE ANCIENT LORDS *or* EARLS OF, vi. 280-285.
Moray, Angus, earl of, vi. 285.
— Ed *or* Eth, earl of, iv. 2 *n.*; vi. 284.
— — his wife, *, vi. 284.
— Finlay, earl of, vi. 281.
— — his wife, Donada, vi. 281.
— Gillecomgan, earl of, vi. 282.
— — his wife, Gruoch, vi. 282.
— Lulach, earl of, vi. 282, 283.
— Macbeth, earl of, iii. 240; iv. 1; vi. 282.
— — his wife, Gruoch, vi. 282, 283.
— Maelbrighde Mac Ruaidhri, earl of, vi. 281, 282.
— Malcolm, earl of, vi. 282.
— Melsnechtai, earl of, vi. 284.
— Ruadri, earl of, vi. 281 *n.*
— Sigurd Eysteinssen, earl of, vi. 280.
— Thorfinn Sigurdssen, earl of, vi. 280, 282.
— William Fitz Duncan, earl of, i. 3; iii. 245.
MORAY, RANDOLPH, EARL OF, vi. 286-295.
Moray, John, third earl of, i. 431; iii. 89, 260; vi. 295.
— — his wife, Euphemia Ross, i. 134, 436; vi. 297; vii. 236.
— Thomas, first earl of, i. 169, 215; ii. 433; iii. 144, 260; iv. 270; vi. 291.
— — his wife, Isobel Stewart, i. 13; vi. 294.
— Thomas, second earl of, iv. 583 *n.*; vi. 295.
MORAY, BEAUMONT, EARL OF, vi. 295.
Moray, Henry (de Beaumont), constable of Scotland; styled earl of Buchan and, vi. 295.
MORAY, PLANTAGENET, EARL OF, iii. 150.
Moray, Henry (Plantagenet), duke of Lancaster; earl of, iii. 150, 267.
MORAY, DUNBAR, EARL OF, vi. 298-307.
Moray, Elizabeth, Mary *or* Agnes, wife of (1) Archibald Douglas, earl of Moray, (2) George, master of Huntly, and (3) Sir John Colquhoun of Luss; countess of, iii. 193; iv. 527; vi. 306, 308.
— James, fourth earl of, vi. 301, 304.
— — his wife, Katharine *or* Janet Seton, vi. 305.
— John, first earl of, iii. 260; vi. 298.
— — his wife, Marjorie Stewart, i. 16; vi. 298, 301.
— Patrick (4th earl of Dunbar), styled earl of, ii. 136; iii. 266; vi. 295, 296.
— — his wife, Agnes Randolph, vi. 294.
— Thomas, second earl of, vi. 302.
— — his wife, Margaret *, i. 113; vi. 303.

* Name unknown.

Moray, Thomas, third earl of, v. 522; vi. 303; vii. 242.
— — his wife (?), Isobel Innes, v. 521; vi. 304.
MORAY, DOUGLAS, EARL OF, vi. 308-310.
Moray, Archibald, earl of, iii. 62, 63, 174, 178, 193; v. 522; vi. 308.
— — his wife, Elizabeth Dunbar, iii. 193; iv. 527; vi. 306, 308.
MORAY, CRICHTON, EARL OF, iii. 63; vi. 309.
Moray, James, earl of, ii. 327; iii. 63; vi. 309.
— — his wife, Janet Dunbar of Brawl, ii. 327; iii. 62.
MORAY, STEWART, EARL OF, vi. 311-312.
Moray, David, 3rd son of king James II.; earl of, i. 20; vi. 311.
— James, illeg. son of king James IV.; earl of, i. 22; ii. 459; iv. 366; v. 103; vi. 311; vii. 122.
— — his wife, Elizabeth *or* Isobel Campbell, i. 338; vi. 312; ix. 155.
MORAY, STEWART, EARL OF, vi. 313-330.
Moray, Alexander, fifth earl of, vi. 322; ix. 139 *bis*.
— — his wife, Emilia Balfour, vi. 322; ix. 139 *bis*.
— Archibald George, thirteenth earl of, vi. 329.
— Charles, sixth earl of, vi. 323.
— — his wife, Anne Campbell, i. 368; vi. 323.
— Edmund Archibald, fifteenth earl of, vi. 327, 329.
— — his wife, Anna Mary Collinson, vi. 329.
— Elizabeth, wife of James Stewart; countess of, iii. 189; vi. 316.
— Francis, seventh earl of, vi. 323; ix. 140.
— — his 1st wife, Elizabeth Murray, vi. 324; viii. 202; ix. 140 *bis*.
— — his 2nd wife, Jean Elphinstone, i. 570; vi. 324; ix. 140.
— Francis, ninth earl of, iv. 293; vi. 326.
— — his wife, Jean Gray, iv. 293; vi. 326.
— Francis, tenth earl of, iv. 293; vi. 327.
— — his 1st wife, Lucy Scott, vi. 327.
— — his 2nd wife, Margaret J. Ainslie, vi. 327.
— Francis, eleventh earl of, vi. 328.
— Francis James, sixteenth earl of, vi. 329.
— — his wife, Gertrude Floyer Smith, vi. 329.
— George, fourteenth earl of, iv. 293; vi. 329.
— James, legtd. son of king James V.; Regent of Scotland; first earl of, i. 24, 26, 183; ii. 269; vi. 312; vii. 284; ix. 138, 139 *bis*.
— — his wife, Agnes *or* Annas Keith, vi. 50, 316.

Moray, James, 'the bonnie earl,' *jure ux.* second earl of, iv. 538, 542; v. 301; vi. 316.
—— —— his wife, Elizabeth, countess of Moray, iii. 189; vi. 316.
—— James, third earl of, vi. 319; vii. 395, 467; ix. 138 *bis*.
—— —— his wife, Anne Gordon, iv. 545; vi. 320.
—— James, fourth earl of, iii. 209; vi. 320; ix. 139.
—— —— his wife, Margaret Home, iv. 465; vi. 321; ix. 108, 139.
—— James, eighth earl of, vi. 325; ix. 140.
—— —— his 1st wife, Grace Lockhart, vi. 325.
—— —— his 2nd wife, Margaret Wemyss, vi. 325; viii. 508.
—— John, twelfth earl of, vi. 328.
MORAY, LORD OF BOTHWELL, ii. 120-131.
MORAY, EARL OF STRATHEARN, viii. 255-258.
Moray of Abercairny, Humphrey, vi. 220.
—— —— his wife, Katharine Graham, vi. 220.
—— —— James, ii. 492; iii. 458; vii. 206.
—— —— his wife, Christian Montgomerie, iii. 458.
—— —— Sir John, viii. 252, 255.
—— —— his wife, Mary de Strathearn, viii. 252.
—— —— John, vi. 230.
—— —— his wife, Nicolas Graham, vi. 230.
—— —— Robert, i. 465, 468; ii. 37; v. 503; vii. 296.
—— —— his wife, Katharine Murray, i. 465.
—— —— Sir Robert, i. 361.
—— —— Robert, the younger, ix. 169.
—— —— his wife, Helen Bruce, ix. 169.
—— —— William, vi. 546.
—— —— his wife, Margaret Oliphant, vi. 546.
—— —— William, iii. 573.
—— —— his wife, Anna Hay, iii. 573.
—— —— William, v. 89.
—— of Aberscross, Hugh, vii. 163.
—— —— his wife, * Mackay, vii. 163.
—— —— Hugh, his son, vii. 163.
—— of Airthrey, Maurice, viii. 257.
—— of Aldie, John, i. 450, 452.
—— of Avondale, Maurice, sheriff of Clydesdale, viii. 256, 257.
—— of Beharm, William, ii. 122.
—— of Bothwell, Sir Andrew, 2nd son of 1st lord of Bothwell, ii. 125; iv. 11.
—— —— his 1st wife, * Comyn, ii. 126.
—— —— his 2nd wife, Euphemia *, ii. 126.
—— —— Sir Andrew, companion of Sir Wm. Wallace, ii. 126; v. 579.
—— —— Sir Andrew, Guardian of Scotland, i. 432; ii. 127, 259, 435; viii. 255; ix. 40.
—— —— his 2nd wife, Christian Bruce, ii. 128, 434.

* Name unknown.

Moray of Bothwell, Joanna, wife of (1) Sir Thomas Moray, and (2) 3rd earl of Douglas, ii. 130; iii. 162.
—— —— John, ii. 128; vi. 139.
—— —— his wife, Margaret of Menteith, ii. 128; vi. 138.
—— —— Sir Thomas, ii. 129; iii. 161, 162; viii. 257.
—— —— his wife, Joanna Moray of Drumsargard, iii. 161; vi. 133; viii. 257.
—— —— Sir Walter, i. 451; ii. 123; iii. 137; vi. 528 *n.*
—— —— his wife, * Olifard of Bothwell, ii. 123; vi. 529.
—— —— Sir William, *panetarius Scotiæ*, ii. 124; iii. 425 *n.*; viii. 4 *n.*
—— of Brachlie, William, ii. 122; viii. 320.
—— of Cortachy, Walter, brother of Maurice M., earl of Strathearn, ii. 130; iii. 162; vii. 34 *n.*; viii. 257.
—— of Culbin, Sir Alexander, i. 451.
—— —— Alexander, iii. 305.
—— —— Angus, vii. 160.
—— —— Egidia, wife of Thos. Kinnaird, v. 204: viii. 325.
—— —— Gilbert, viii. 325.
—— —— his wife, Eustachia Sutherland, viii. 325.
—— —— Reginald, viii. 325.
—— of Culnacloich, John, i. 452.
—— of Drumsargard, Sir Alexander, iii. 162; vi. 215; vii. 237.
—— —— his wife, Janet de Ross, vii. 237.
—— —— Joanna, wife of (1) Sir Thos. Moray of Bothwell, and (2) Sir Archibald, 3rd earl of Douglas, ii. 130; iii. 161, 162; vi. 133: viii. 257.
—— —— John, 1331, i. 322.
—— —— Sir John, viii. 252, 255.
—— —— his 1st wife, *, viii. 256.
—— —— his 2nd wife, Mary of Strathearn, viii. 252, 255.
—— —— Sir Maurice, i. 435; ii. 130, 320 *n.*; viii. 327; ix. 27.
—— —— his wife, Joanna of Menteith, i. 435; iii. 162; viii. 327.
—— —— Walter, viii. 422.
—— —— Sir William, i. 452 *n.*; ii. 131; viii. 255.
—— of Duffus, Freskin de, ii. 120; vii. 268 *n.*; viii. 319.
—— —— Freskin, son of Walter, i. 450; ii. 122.
—— —— his wife, Johanna of Strathnaver, ii. 122, 316.
—— —— Hugh, canonized as Saint Hugh, i. 449, 450; ii. 122, 316; viii. 320.
—— —— Mary, wife of Reginald le Cheyne of Inverugie, iii. 191; vi. 34.
—— —— Walter de, ii. 122; viii. 321.
—— —— his wife, Euphemia de Ross, ii. 122; vii. 232; viii. 321.

* Name unknown.

Moray of Drumsargard, William, son of Freskin, i. 449, 450; ii. 121; viii. 320.
— of Durdie-Inglis, Patrick, bishop of Moray, commendator of Scone, iv. 32.
— of Fala, Roger, iii. 499, 526.
— of Gask, Sir Malcolm, sheriff of Perth, i. 449, 450, 451.
— — his wife, *, of Gask, i. 451.
— — William, sheriff of Perth, iv. 257.
— of Glaswell, Walter, viii. 422.
— of Glenservy, Sir John, viii. 255.
— — his wife, Maria de Strathearn, viii. 252, 255.
— of Hawick, Maurice, viii. 257.
— of Kildun, Richard de, ii. 121.
— of Kinrotharochie, Robert, v. 503.
— of Llanbryde, Sir Malcolm, sheriff of of Perth, i. 451.
— of Lilford, Walter de, vi. 529 *n.*
— of Ogilvy, Humphrey, vi. 220.
— — his wife, Katharine Graham, vi. 220.
— — Sir John, viii. 255.
— of Pettyn, Sir Walter de, ii. 122.
— — William de, sheriff of Invernaryn, i. 449; ii. 122; viii. 320.
— — Sir William de, ii. 123.
— — his alleged wife, * of Fife, i. 451 *n.*; ii. 123.
— of Ruthtrelan, John, i. 452.
— of Skelbo, Gilbert, archdeacon of Moray, ii. 121; viii. 321.
— — Hugh, viii. 321.
— — Richard, ii. 121; viii. 321.
— of Sproustoa, Maurice, viii. 257.
— of Strabrock, Freskin, ii. 120.
— — Hugh, ii. 122; viii. 320.
— — William, ii. 121.
— of Strathavon, Maurice, viii. 257.
— of Sutherland, Sir William de, viii. 321, 322.
— of Torburne, Walter, viii. 422.
— Alexander de, grandfather of Richard M. of Kildun, ii. 122.
— Alexander de, 1281, iii. 558.
— Andrew, son of Freskin; bishop of Moray, ii. 121.
— Sir Andrew, 1211, ii. 122 *n.*
— Andrew, son of St. Hugh; bishop of Moray, i. 452; ii. 122.
— Andrew, parson of Duffus, ii. 122.
— Archibald, bishop of Moray, i. 452.
— Christian, wife of Wm. de Federeth, ii. 122.
— David de, bishop of Moray, ii. 124.
— Elizabeth de, wife of John Forrester of Niddry and Dechmont, iv. 84.
— Elizabeth, wife of 5th lord Rollo, vii. 206.
— St. Gilbert, bishop of Caithness, i. 449, 450; ii. 121; iii. 199; viii. 321.
— John, sheriff of Perth, i. 449, 450.

* Name unknown.

Moray, John, son of John of London, son of Nes, i. 450.
— John, brother of Gilbert, bishop of Caithness, i. 450; ii. 121.
— Mr. John, minister at Dunfermline, vii. 296.
— — his wife, Margaret Leslie, vii. 296.
— Louisa, wife of 5th earl of Kellie, v. 89; ix. 117.
— Macheth of, ii. 316; vi. 285.
— Margaret, wife of Sir Wm. Fraser of Cowie and Durris, vii. 429, 430.
— Mariot, wife of Geo. Herries of Mabie and Terrauchtie, iv. 402.
— Mary, wife of Sir Reginald le Chen, ii. 122.
— Maurice, *perhaps* 3rd son of Sir Andrew M., ix. 40.
— Murdoch de, son of Alexander, ii. 121.
— Nicolas, wife of Sir Robt. Douglas of Spott, ii. 37.
— Richard, brother of Gilbert, bishop of Caithness, ii. 121; viii. 321.
— Sir Richard, viii. 322.
— Sir Robert, founder of the Royal Society, iii. 403.
— — his wife, Sophia Lindsay, iii. 403.
— Thomas de, 1336, ii. 128 *n.*; ix. 40.
— Thomas, 2nd son of Sir Andrew M. of Bothwell, ii. 128, 129.
— William, canon of Moray, ii. 122.
— William de, illeg. son of William, earl of Sutherland, viii. 329.
— *, brother of Maurice, earl of Strathearn, viii. 256.
Mordaunt, John (Mordaunt), lord, vi. 463.
MORDAUNT OF TURVEY, GORDON, BARON, iv. 556.
Mordaunt of Turvey, Alexander, 17th baron, iv. 556, 558.
— Henrietta, wife of Alexander, 2nd duke of Gordon, iv. 551, 556.
— Winifred, wife of John Cheyne, vi. 463.
MORDINGTOUN, DOUGLAS, LORD, vi. 331-336.
Mordingtoun, Charles, *de jure* fifth lord, vi. 335.
— George, fourth lord, vi. 334.
— — his wife, Katharine Launder, vi. 335.
— James, first lord, i. 202; iii. 577; vi. 333.
— — his 1st wife, Ann Oliphant, vi. 332, 552.
— — his 2nd wife, Elizabeth Hay, vi. 333; ix. 87.
— James, third lord, vi. 334.
— — his wife, Agnes, Ann *or* Jean Seton, v. 196; vi. 334.
— Mary, wife of Wm. Weaver; *suo jure* baroness, vi. 335.
— William, second lord, vi. 333.
— — his wife, Elizabeth Sempill, vi. 334; vii. 557.

* Name unknown.

Mordingtoun, Agnes de, wife of (1) Philip de Colville, and (2) Sir H. do Haliburton, ii. 538; iv. 331.
— Peter de, ii. 538; iv. 332.
More of Abercorn, Reginald, great chamberlain of Scotland, ancestor of the family of, i. 454.
— — his wife, Christian * of Aldie, i. 454.
— — Reginald, vi. 342.
— — his wife, Mary Douglas, vi. 342.
— — Sir William, i. 454; vi. 196.
— — his wife, Sybilla Graham of Abercorn, vi. 196.
— — William, iv. 80.
— of Berriedale, Reginald, viii. 253.
— of Kirklington, John, iii. 298.
— — his wife, Katharine Constable, iii. 298.
— — John, his son, iii. 298.
— of Kittymure, Alexander, iii. 526.
— of Tullibardine, Sir William, i. 454.
— Agnes, wife of Sir Hugh Eglinton, iii. 428 *n*.
— John, vicar-general of the Dominicans, viii. 272.
— Margaret, wife of D. Sinclair, ii. 341.
— Robert, ix. 100.
— — his wife, Jane Ramsay, ix. 100.
— Winifred, dau. of John M. of Kirklington, iii. 298.
— *olim* Lyon, viii. 307.
Moreson of Plewlands and Broomhouse, John, iv. 89.
— of Whitehouse, John, iv. 90.
Moreville, *see* Morville.
Morgan, *or* Mackay, Clan, vii. 157.
— of Arkesden, Sir Thomas, iii. 608.
— of Biddlesdon Park, George Manners, captain 4th Dragoon Guards, v. 201.
— — Luis Ferdinand Harry Courthope, v. 201.
— — his wife, Mary Grenville, baroness Kinloss, v. 200, 201.
— of Ruperra, Sir Lewis, vi. 468.
— — his wife, Anna *, vi. 468.
— — Mary, wife of Edmond Thomas of Wenvoe, vi. 468.
— Ann, wife of 1st baron Hunsdon, iii. 608.
— Courtenay Charles Evan, col., viii. 92.
— — his wife, Katharine Agnes Blanche Carnegie, viii. 92.
— Ellen Sarah, wife of lieut.-col. H. Lindsay, i. 527.
— Frederick C., viii. 92.
— Sarah Ann, wife of John, 7th viscount of Kenmure, v. 134.
— William, steward, ii. 35.
— — his wife, Katharine Fenn, ii. 35.
— Mrs., London, iv. 489.
MORGAN-GRENVILLE, BARON KINLOSS, v. 199-201.

* Name unknown.

Morgan-Grenville, Caroline Mary Elizabeth Grenville, v. 201.
— Harry Nugent, v. 201.
— Luis Chandos Francis Temple, v. 201.
— Robert William, v. 201.
— Thomas George Breadalbane, v. 201.
Morham, Adam de, iii. 525.
— John, *alias* Malherbe, ii. 536.
— — his wife, Ada, ii. 536.
— John, his son, ii. 536.
Morier, Frances Horatia, wife of rev. E. H. Grimston, iv. 97.
— John Philip, iv. 97 *bis*.
— Katharine Georgina, wife of rev. Francis S. Grimston, iv. 97.
— Sir Robert Barnet David, G.C.B., viii. 512.
— Victoria, wife of commr. Rosslyn Erskine-Wemyss, viii. 512.
Morison of Dairsie, Sir George, v. 170.
— — his wife, Agnes Boyd, v. 170.
— — Sir John, iii. 485.
— — his wife, Nicola Bruce, iii. 485.
— of Prestongrange, Alexander, v. 469; vii. 14.
— — his wife, Eleanor Maule, vii. 14.
— — Sir Alexander, v. 171.
— — his wife, Jean Boyd, v. 171.
— — William, i. 312; iv. 206.
— of Tooley Park, Sir Richard, iii. 612.
— Helenor, wife of 2nd earl of Glasgow, iv. 206.
— Isaac, bailie of Edinburgh, iii. 284; ix. 72.
— — his wife, Helen Arnot, ix. 72.
— Jean, wife of 5th viscount Arbuthnott, i. 312.
— John, ii. 406.
— Katharine, wife of William, lord Strathnaver, viii. 356.
— Lettice, wife of 2nd viscount Falkland, iii. 612.
— Margaret, wife of Sir Alex. Home of Manderston, iii. 284.
— V., parson of Benholm, i. 273.
Morker, earl of the Northumbrians, iii. 241.
Morland, Servante, captain, iii. 616.
Morley, James, i. 129.
— Harriet, wife of C. H. E. Carmichael, iv. 569.
— Maria, wife of D. Ogilvy of Clova, i. 129.
— William, iv. 569.
Morleyn, Constance de, wife of Sir Bernard de Brus, ii. 431.
Mornington, Richard (Wellesley) 1st lord, v. 482.
Morref, Erchebaud de, Peeblesshire, iii. 489.
Morris of Crome Hall, Thomas, iv. 570.
— of Gartnamona, William O'Connor, i. 527.
— — his wife, Georgina Kathleen Lindsay, i. 527.

Morris, Staats Long, general, M.P., i. 91; iv. 554, 556.
—— —— his wife, Katharine Gordon, i. 90.
—— Teresa Ann, wife of (1) capt. Scott, and (2) col. J. D. Carmichael, iv. 570.
—— *, vii. 369 *n.*
—— —— his wife, Katharine Selc, vii. 369 *n.*
Morrison of Auchingoul, George, iv. 131.
—— —— Theodore, iv. 131.
—— of Auchintoul, John, v. 546.
—— —— his wife, Jane Fraser, v. 546.
—— of Barrak, George, i. 87.
—— —— his wife, Jonet Gordon, i. 87.
—— of Bognie and Frendraught, George, iv. 131.
—— Theodore, iv. 131.
—— of Gunnersbury Park, Alexander, major, ii. 419.
—— —— his wife, Jane Cornell, ii. 419.
—— Janet, wife of Francis Sinclair, ii. 346.
Mosman of Longhermiston and Currie, John, iv. 89.
—— James, goldsmith, iv. 89.
Morse, Harriet, wife of major-gen. Sir James Carmichael-Smyth, iv. 572.
—— Robert, general R.E., iv. 572.
Morshead, Anderson, colonel-commandant of Engineers, vii. 309.
—— Louisa, wife of 15th earl of Rothes, vii. 309.
Morsztyn, John Andrew, grand treasurer of Poland; count, iv. 547, 548.
—— —— his wife, Katharine Gordon, iv. 548.
Mortimer of Ballandro and Inverbervie, Sir Roger, i. 324, 434.
—— of Craigievar, James, i. 296.
—— —— his wife, Elizabeth Arbuthnott, i. 296.
—— —— John, i. 296; vi. 175; ix. 47.
—— of Dunmore, Roger, ii. 223.
—— of Flemington, John, vi. 176.
—— of Foulis, Roger de, vii. 4.
—— —— his wife, Christian de Maule, vii. 4.
—— —— Sir Roger de, iv. 272.
—— —— his wife, Margaret Menteith, iv. 272.
—— Edmund de, 1302, iv. 12.
—— Euphemia, wife of John Middleton of Caldhame, vi. 176.
—— Janet, wife of Sir A. Gray of Broxmouth, iv. 272.
—— Katharine, mistress of king David II., i. 170.
—— Katharine, wife of (1) James Forbes of Corsindae, and (2) John Middleton of Kilhill, vi. 175.
MORTON, DOUGLAS, EARL OF, vi. 337-389.
Morton, George, twelfth earl of, vi. 380.
—— —— his 1st wife, * Muirhead, vi. 381.
—— —— his 2nd wife, Frances Adderley, vi. 381.

* Name unknown.

Morton, George, fifteenth earl of, vi. 384.
—— —— his wife, Susan Elizabeth Yarde-Buller, vi. 385.
—— George Sholto, sixteenth earl of, vi. 383, 385.
—— —— his wife, Frances Theodora Rose, vi. 385.
—— James, first earl of, ii. 97; v. 606; vi. 354.
—— —— his wife, Joanna Stewart, i. 19; vi. 356.
—— James, third earl of, ii. 63; vi. 358, 369; viii. 539; ix. 140.
—— —— his wife, Katharine Stewart, i. 22; vi. 359, 361.
—— James, the Regent, fourth earl of, i. 27, 38, 188, 250, 444; iv. 540; v. 158 *ter*; vi. 360, 362, 482; vii. 542, 548; viii. 23, 289 *bis*, 291; ix. 141.
—— —— his wife, Elizabeth Douglas, vi. 361, 362.
—— James, ninth earl of, vi. 377, 379.
—— —— his wife, Ann Hay of Smithfield, vi. 380.
—— James, tenth earl of, vi. 380.
—— James, thirteenth earl of, vi. 381.
—— —— his 1st wife, Agatha Halyburton, vi. 382.
—— —— his 2nd wife, Bridget Heathcote, vi. 382.
—— John, second earl of, ii. 62; vi. 356.
—— —— his wife, Janet Crichton, vi. 358.
—— Robert, seventh earl of, vi. 378.
—— —— his wife, Elizabeth Villiers, vi. 378; ix. 141.
—— Robert, eleventh earl of, vi. 380.
—— Sholto Charles, fourteenth earl of, vi. 383.
—— —— his wife, Katharine Hamilton, vi. 384.
—— Sholto George Watson, eighteenth earl of, vi. 386.
—— —— his wife, Helen Geraldine Maria Ponsonby, vi. 386.
—— Sholto John, seventeenth earl of, vi. 386.
—— —— his 1st wife, Helen Watson, vi. 386.
—— —— his 2nd wife, Alice Anne Caroline Lambton, vi. 386.
—— William, fifth earl of, vi. 363, 371.
—— —— his wife, Agnes Leslie, vi. 372; vii. 290.
—— William, sixth earl of, ii. 235; v. 120, 224 *ter*, 225; vi. 375; vii. 395; viii. 296; ix. 23.
—— —— his wife, Ann Keith, vi. 53, 377.
—— William, eighth earl of, vi. 379; ix. 141 *quat.*
—— —— his 1st wife, Grizel Middleton, vi. 185, 379.
—— —— his 2nd wife, Marjorie Foulis, ix. 49, 141.

Morton, master of, James Douglas, son-in-law of 3rd earl of Morton; styled, vi. 361.
—— —— his wife, Elizabeth Douglas, i. 194; vi. 360, 362, 483.
—— master of, John Douglas, elder son of 1st earl of Morton, vi. 356.
MORTON, MAXWELL, EARL OF, vi. 388-389, 482-487.
Morton, John, *de jure* second earl of, vi. 484.
—— —— his wife, Margaret Hamilton, vi. 485.
—— John, first earl of, i. 250; vi. 361, 375, 388, 482.
—— —— his wife, Elizabeth Douglas, i. 194; vi. 483.
—— of Jedburgh, Andrew, v. 70.
—— Margaret, wife of John Cochrane of Cochrane, iii. 338; ix. 336.
—— *, tutor to David, lord Balgonie, vi. 115.
MORVEN, CAMPBELL, LORD, i. 369-393.
Morven, Archibald, first lord, i. 369.
Morvic, Hugh de, v. 278.
Morville, Elena, Eva *or* Hellaria de, wife of Roland of Galloway, iv. 139, 140; v. 277.
—— Hugh de, constable of Scotland, ii. 375; iv. 4, 222; v. 276, 277; vii. 577.
—— —— his wife, Beatrice de Beauchamp, v. 277.
—— Richard de, constable of Scotland, iv. 138, 139, 140, 223 *bis*; v. 277, 488; vii. 577; viii. 319 *n*.
—— —— his wife, Avicia of Lancaster, v. 277 *bis*.
—— William de, constable of Scotland, iii. 87; iv. 139, 223; v. 100, 277, 488; vii. 577.
—— *, wife of Hugh de Arbuthnott, i. 275.
Moscrop, George, provost of Jedburgh, v. 74.
Mosley of Bangors Park, Tonman, iii. 463.
—— —— his wife, Hilda Rosa Montgomerie, iii. 463.
—— Sir Tonman, 3rd bart., iii. 463.
Mostyn of Mostyn, Sir Roger, 3rd bart., vii. 351.
—— of Talacre, Sir Pyers, 8th bart., ii. 530; v. 547.
—— —— his wife, Frances Georgina Fraser, v. 547.
—— Clementina Frances, wife of S. C. de Trafford, ii. 530.
—— Essex, wife of 2nd duke of Roxburghe, vii. 351.
Mouat of Hougaland, John, vi. 575.
—— —— his wife, Christian Stewart, vi. 575.
—— Sophia Margaret, wife of Wm. G. Middleton, vi. 179.
MOULIN, MURRAY, LORD MURRAY OF, iii. 384.
Moultray of Markinch, John, vi. 86, 87.
Mounsey, James, i. 221.
Mount Alexander, earls of, i. 382.
—— Hugh (Montgomerie), earl of, iii. 433.

* Name unknown.

MOUNTCASTELL, HAMILTON, BARON OF, i. 46.
Mountcastell, James, eldest son of Claud, lord Paisley; first baron of, i. 46.
MOUNTCASTLE, HAMILTON, BARON OF, i. 58-74.
Mountcastle, James, first baron of, i. 58.
—— James, eldest son of 7th earl of Abercorn; baron, i. 65.
MOUNT CRAWFORD, CRAWFORD (LINDSAY), VISCOUNT OF, iv. 175.
Mount Edgcumbe, William Henry (Edgcumbe), 4th earl of, i. 71.
—— —— his wife, Katharine Elizabeth Hamilton, i. 71.
MOUNTJOY IN THE ISLE OF WIGHT, STUART, VISCOUNT, ii. 306-312.
Mountjoy, John, first viscount, ii. 305.
Mountjoy, Herbert Hickman (Windsor), baron, ii. 306.
—— —— his wife, Alice Clavering, ii. 306.
—— Luke (Gardiner), viscount, iii. 413.
Mountrath, Charles (Coote), 1st earl of, i. 59.
—— —— his wife, Jane Hannay, i. 59.
MOUNT STUART, STUART, LORD, ii. 299-312.
Mount Stuart, James, first lord, ii. 299.
MOUNT STUART OF WORTLEY, STUART, BARON, ii. 302-312.
Mount Stuart of Wortley, John, 2nd baron, ii. 306.
—— —— Mary, wife of 3rd earl of Bute; baroness, ii. 302.
Mountstuart, John, eldest son of 3rd earl of Bute; styled viscount, ii. 305.
—— John, eldest son of 4th earl of Bute; styled viscount, ii. 306, 308.
—— —— his wife, Elizabeth Penelope Crichton, countess of Dumfries, ii. 308; iii. 237.
Moutray of Seafield, viii. 488.
Mow of Mow, John, ix. 154.
—— —— his wife, Margaret Ker, ix. 154.
—— Robert, vii. 322.
Mowat of Balquholly, *, iv. 71.
—— —— his wife, * Forbes, iv. 71.
—— —— James, ii. 342.
—— —— *, ii. 348.
—— of Bogside and Busbie, James, v. 165.
—— of Freswick, ii. 348.
—— of Garth, Thomas, vi. 173.
—— of Knockintibber, Charles, iii. 439.
—— of Stenhouse, Sir John, viii. 10.
—— Grisel, wife of capt. L. Middleton of Futtaburgh, vi. 173.
—— Janet, wife of 1st lord Somerville, viii. 10.
—— Margaret, mistress of Wm. Sinclair of Mey, ii. 342.
—— Margaret, wife of John Kinnaird, v. 204.
Mowbray and Stourton, Charles (Stourton), 24th lord, iv. 418.
—— —— his wife, Mary Constable, iv. 418.

* Name unknown.

Mowbray of Barnbougle and Dalmeny, Sir John, ii. 145; vi. 157.
—— —— his wife, Elene Sinclair, ii. 145.
—— —— John, viii. 390.
—— —— Philip, iii. 245; vi. 529.
—— —— his wife, Galiena, iii. 245.
—— —— Philip, i. 431.
—— —— Philip, ii. 400.
—— —— Philippa, wife of Sir Bartholomew de Loen, i. 149.
—— —— Robert, vi. 415.
—— —— Robert, the younger, ii. 557.
—— —— his wife, Helen Schaw, ii. 557.
—— —— Sir Robert. v. 86.
—— —— his wife, Anna Erskine, v. 86.
—— —— Roger, son of Philip, iii. 245.
—— —— Roger, vi. 136; vii. 402.
—— of Hilfield, South Bordland, and Marisfield, Robert, iii. 305.
—— of Kinmonth, Philip de, vi. 529.
—— —— his wife, Galiena, iii. 245; vi. 529.
—— of Pitliver, James, vi. 415.
—— of Sherburn Hall, Arthur, iii. 362.
—— Sir Alexander de, 2nd son of Roger M. of Barnbougle, i. 431, 432; ii. 259.
—— Andrew, burgess of Edinburgh, ix. 102, 137.
—— —— his wife, Christian Wawane, iv. 337; ix. 137.
—— Elizabeth, wife of Charles Murray, iii. 500.
—— Elizabeth, wife of Sir Archibald Napier of Merchiston, ii. 147; iv. 89; vi. 414, 415, 418.
—— Elspeth, wife of Adam Bothwell, iv. 435; ix. 106.
—— Geoffrey, v. 583; vi. 566.
—— —— his wife, Isabel Stewart, v. 583.
—— Hannah Jane, wife of capt. Archibald Cochrane, R.N., iii. 362.
—— John de, i. 509; viii. 565.
—— John, viii. 390.
—— —— his wife, Elizabeth Sandilands, viii. 389.
—— Margaret, wife of (1) John Cornwall of Bonhard, and (2) William, 3rd earl of Menteith, vi. 157.
—— Margaret, wife of (1) Francis Napier, and (2) Wm. Mowbray, vi. 415.
—— William, vi. 415.
—— —— his wife, Margaret Mowbray, vi. 415.
Moyness, Jane Leslie, wife of (1) Sir Alex. Dunbar of Cumnock, and (2) Sir P. Gordon of Auchindoun; styled lady, ix. 110.
Moysie, David, officer in household of king James VI., viii. 97.
Muir of Annestoun, John, ix. 114.
—— —— his wife, Elizabeth Carmichael, iv. 583; ix. 114.
—— —— John, ix. 114.
Muirhead of Balgreddane, James, v. 263.
Muirhead of Billies, John, v. 106.
—— of Bredisholme, James, ii. 86.
—— —— his wife, Helen Stewart, ii. 86.
—— —— James, viii. 217.
—— —— his wife, Margaret Drummond, viii. 217.
—— —— John Grosset, i. 495.
—— —— his wife, Jean Murray, i. 494.
—— of Castramine, Isabel, wife of David Gordon, v. 106.
—— —— John, v. 106.
—— of Linhouse, Alexander, vi. 381.
—— of Lauchop, Claud, ii. 414.
—— —— his wife, Jean Dalzell, ii. 414.
—— —— James, ii. 41.
—— —— his 1st wife, Janet Hamilton, ii. 41.
—— —— his 2nd wife, Margaret Cunynghame, iii. 340 *n*.
—— —— Sir James, v. 263; viii. 26.
—— —— his 2nd wife, Margaret Somerville, viii. 26.
—— —— Sir James, ii. 411.
—— —— his wife, Mary Dalzell, ii. 411.
—— George, Fochabers, vii. 566.
—— —— his wife, Katharine C. E. S. Forbes-Sempill, vii. 566.
—— Lilias, wife of (1) Sir W. Stewart of Minto, and (2) Sir Jas. Drummond of Machany, viii. 223; ix. 161.
—— Margaret, wife of John Hamilton, ii. 41.
—— *, wife of George Douglas, *afterwards* 12th earl of Morton, vi. 381.
Mulgrave, Edmund (Sheffield), 1st earl of, iii. 598.
MULL, CAMPBELL, LORD, i. 369-393.
Mull, Archibald, first lord, i. 369.
Multon, Sir Hubert de, i. 322.
—— Margaret de, widow of Sir Hubert, and *possibly* 1st wife of Sir Neil Campbell, i. 322, 324.
MUNARD, DOUGLAS, LORD DOUGLAS OF, vii. 145-147.
Munard, William, first lord Douglas of, vii. 145.
Muncaster, Gamel Augustus (Pennington), 4th baron, iii. 43.
—— John (Pennington), 1st baron, iii. 44.
—— Lowther Augustus John (Pennington), 3rd baron, viii. 230.
Mundale, William, husband of Janet Dunbar, iii. 278.
Mundy, Frederic Clinton, i. 527.
—— Rosamond Emily, wife of Rev. W. J. C. Lindsay, i. 527.
Munfichet, *see* Montefichet.
Munfode, Agnes, wife of (1) John Munfode, and (2) Sir John Douglas, vi. 343.
Munro of Assynt, Hector, vii. 503.
—— —— Hugh, vii. 165.

* Name unknown.

Munro of Auchenbowie, Alexander, ii. 296.
—— his wife, Anne Stewart, ii. 296.
— of Culrain, Sir George, vii. 170.
— of Foulis, George, vii. 160.
—— his 1st wife, Isobel Ross, vii. 160.
—— Hector, 13th laird, vii. 498.
—— his 1st wife, Katharine Mackenzie, vii. 498.
—— Hector, 19th laird. v. 529.
—— his 1st wife, Anna Fraser, v. 529.
—— Sir Hector, 1st bart., vii. 167.
—— his wife, Mary Mackay, vii. 167.
—— John, viii. 334.
—— his wife, Fingola of Calder, viii. 334.
—— Robert, 14th laird, vii. 165.
—— Robert, 15th laird, ii. 183; iv. 25.
—— his 1st wife, Margaret Ogilvy, iv. 25.
—— Robert, 16th laird, vii. 464, 500; viii. 343.
—— his contr. wife, Barbara Grant, vii. 464.
—— his 1st wife, Marjory Mackenzie, vii. 500.
—— his 2nd wife, Eleanor Gordon, viii. 343.
—— Sir Robert, the Black Baron, iii. 71, 205; v. 530.
—— his 1st wife, Margaret Sutherland, iii. 205.
— of Lindertis, Sir Campbell, bart., viii. 235.
— of Newmoir, Andrew, vii. 503.
—— Sir George, i. 45; vii. 170.
—— his 2nd wife, Christiana Hamilton, i. 45.
— of Obsdale, George, viii. 180.
— of Tarbat, George, iii. 70.
— Alexander, viii. 224.
— Alexander, Edinburgh, iii. 413; ix. 80.
— Ann, wife of Donald Mackay, vii. 170.
— Christian, wife of Alex. Mackenzie of Applecross, vii. 503.
— Elizabeth, wife of commander W. F. Tollemache, iii. 413.
— Euphemia, wife of Donald Mackay of Scourie, vii. 165.
— Sir George, major-general, commander-in-chief, iv. 248; v. 448.
— Margaret, wife of G. H. Drummond of Stanmore, viii. 224.
— Olive, wife of capt. J. E. Drummond, viii. 235.
— Robert, general, ii. 17.
— Robert, major-general, viii. 180.
—— his 2nd wife, Jean Alexander, viii. 180.
— Robert, half-brother of Alexander Sutherland, viii. 334, 335.
— Margaret, wife of Kenneth Mackenzie of Scatwell, iii. 71.
Munro, *, wife of Neil Mackay of Strathnaver, vii. 160.
Munster, George (Fitzclarence), 1st earl of, ii. 499; iii. 585.
— William George (Fitzclarence), 2nd earl of, ii. 500.
—— his wife, Wilhelmina Kennedy Erskine, ii. 500.
— count Alexander, v. 238.
—— his wife, Muriel H. C. Hay, v. 238.
Murdach of Croy, son of Corc, v. 330.
Murdach of Duntreath, 2nd son of Malcolm, 5th earl of Lennox, v. 336.
Murdach, father of Alwin, 1st earl of Lennox, v. 326.
Murdach Albanach, the bard, v. 326 *n.*, 327.
Murdach, 2nd son of Alwin, 2nd earl of Lennox, v. 328.
Murdoch of Comlodden, Patrick, vii. 136.
— John, apothecary, Edinburgh, vi. 519.
—— his wife, Anna Stewart, vi. 519.
Mure of Aird, Margaret, wife of (1) Sir Neil Montgomerie of Lainshaw, and (2) John Kennedy of Skeldon, ii. 463; iii. 436.
—— Quintin, ii. 463.
—— his wife, Katharine Kennedy of Kilmore, ii. 463.
— of Auchindrane, James, ii. 488.
—— his wife, Helen Kennedy, ii. 488.
—— John, ii. 474, 476, 487, 488.
—— Sir John, ii. 489.
— of Bardrochwood, Alexander, v. 260.
—— Elizabeth, wife of William Maclellan of Bombie, v. 259, 260 *bis*.
— of Barmagachan, Peter, v. 259.
— of Caldwell, Sir Adam, vii. 531.
—— his wife, Elizabeth Sempill, vii. 531.
—— John, vii. 250.
—— John, vii. 538.
—— John, vii. 252, 539.
—— his 1st wife, Isobel Montgomerie, iii. 437.
—— his 2nd wife, Christian Ross, iii. 93; vii. 252.
—— Sir John, iii. 442.
—— Robert, vii. 543, 551.
—— his wife, Barbara Preston, vii. 543.
—— William, ii. 366.
—— William, iv. 214.
—— William, advocate, iv. 207.
—— William, ii. 564.
—— William, iii. 464.
—— his wife, Georgina Theresa Montgomerie, iii. 464.
— of Cassencary, Alexander, v. 270.
—— his wife, Helen Maclellan, v. 270.
—— John, v. 270.
— of Polkellie, Hugh, v. 146.
—— his wife, * Boyd, v. 146.
— of Polruskane, Avicia, dau. of Gilchrist

* Name unknown.

Mor of Rowallan, and *possibly* wife of Robert Boyle of Kelburne, iv. 183, 184.
Mure of Rowallan, Sir Adam, i. 15.
—— Adam, iv. 342.
—— Sir Arcbibald, iii. 425.
—— his wife, Margaret Montgomerie, iii. 425.
—— Archibald, iii. 431.
—— his wife, Isabella Montgomerie, iii. 431.
—— Gilchrist Mor, iv. 183.
—— Jean, wife of (1) Wm. Fairlie, and (2) David, 1st earl of Glasgow, iv. 205.
—— John, v. 146.
—— his wife, Margaret Boyd, v. 146.
—— John, v. 161.
—— Mungo, iv. 191; v. 494.
—— his wife, Isobel Campbell, v. 494.
—— William, vi. 594.
—— his 2nd wife, Elizabeth Makgill, ii. 487; vi. 594.
—— Sir William, ii. 86; iv. 183, 201.
—— his wife, Sara Brisbane, ix. 38.
—— William, last laird, iv. 205.
—— William, 4th son of 1st earl of Glasgow and Jean Mure, iv. 205.
— of Skeldon, Quintin. iii. 436.
— of Torhousmure, Archibald, ix. 118.
—— his contr. wife, Janet Gordon, v. 109; ix. 118.
— of Warriston House, Thomas, iv. 214.
—— his wife, Helen Boyle, iv. 214.
— Agnes, wife of rev. Patrick Boyle of Shewalton, iv. 207.
— Agnes, two daus. of Sir Wm. M. of Rowallan, ix. 57.
— Christian, wife of Archibald Boyd of Nariston, v. 146.
— Christiana, wife of Sir William Lindsay of the Byres, v. 391.
— Elizabeth, wife of king Robert II., i. 15, 135.
— George, lieut.-col., iv. 214.
— Jane, wife of Sir C. Colville, ii. 564.
— Jane, wife of John Erskine of Carnock, ii. 366.
— Jean, wife of (1) Gavin Ralston, and (2) John Boyle of Kelburne, iv. 201.
— Katharine, wife of Jas. Kennedy, ii. 489.
— Margaret, *error for* M. Fraser, wife of Sir Wm. Keith of Pittendreich, v. 392.
— Marie, wife of (1) 3rd lord Blantyre, and (2) John Brisbane of Bishoptoun, ii. 86; ix. 38 *bis*.
— Marjory, wife of Sir John Ross of Halkhead, vii. 250.
Muriella, wife of Ranulf the Falconer, v. 243.
Muriel, mother of Thos. Olifard, vi. 524.
Murkle, John Sinclair, senator of the College of Justice, lord, ii. 345.
MURRAY, MURRAY, LORD, i. 469-479; viii. 411.
Murray, John, lord (*1st creation*), i. 469.
— John, lord (*2nd creation*), i. 474.
— John, lord (*3rd creation*), i. 478.
— John, lord (*4th creation*), i. 479.
— John, son of 1st marquess of Atholl; styled lord, i. 480.
MURRAY OF BLAIR, MURRAY, LORD, iii. 384.
Murray of Blair, Charles, first lord, iii. 384.
MURRAY OF ELIBANK, MURRAY, BARON, ix. 84.
Murray of Elibank, Alexander William Charles Oliphant, first baron, iii. 523.
—— his wife, Hilda J. Wolfe-Murray, iii. 523.
MURRAY OF GASK, MURRAY, LORD, viii. 412.
Murray of Gask, James, eldest son of 3rd earl of Tullibardine; styled lord, viii. 412.
MURRAY OF LOCHMABEN, MURRAY, LORD, i. 228.
Murray of Lochmaben, James, second lord, i. 228.
—— John, first lord, i. 228.
—— his wife, Elizabeth Shaw, i. 228.
MURRAY OF MOULIN, MURRAY, LORD, iii. 384.
Murray of Moulin, Charles, first lord, iii. 384.
MURRAY OF STANLEY, MURRAY, BARON, i. 495-502.
Murray of Stanley, John, first baron, i. 495.
MURRAY OF TILLIMET, MURRAY, LORD, iii. 384.
Murray of Tillimet, Charles, first lord, iii. 384.
MURRAY OF TULLIBARDINE, MURRAY, LORD, i. 469-501.
Murray of Tullibardine. John, first lord, i. 468.
—— his wife, Katharine Drummond, i. 469.
MURRAY OF TYNNINGHAM, MURRAY, LORD, i. 228.
Murray of Tynningham, James, second lord, i. 228.
—— John, first lord, i. 228.
—— his wife, Elizabeth Shaw, i. 228.
Murray, William, eldest son of 1st lord Murray of Tullibardine; master of, i. 469.
Murray, Alexander, 26th regt., styled count, iii. 514.
— of Melgum, Sir Joseph, count, iv. 40.
MURRAY, VISCOUNT ANNAN, i. 228.
MURRAY, EARL OF ANNANDALE, i. 214-229.
MURRAY, EARL OF ATHOLL, i. 449-473.
MURRAY, MARQUESS OF ATHOLL, i. 474-479.
MURRAY, DUKE OF ATHOLL, i. 449-502.
MURRAY, LORD BALQUIDDER, i. 469; viii. 411.
MURRAY, VISCOUNT BALQUHIDDER, i. 474.
MURRAY, VISCOUNT OF BALQUIDDER, i. 479.
MURRAY, LORD BALVAIRD, viii. 200-214.

MURRAY, LORD BALVENIE, i. 474, 479.
MURRAY, MARQUESS OF BLAIR, i. 481.
MURRAY, EARL OF DUNMORE, iii. 383-396.
MURRAY, BARON DUNMORE OF DUNMORE, iii. 392-396.
MURRAY, EARL OF DYSART, iii. 397-420.
MURRAY, LORD ELIBANK, iii. 498-524.
MURRAY, VISCOUNT ELIBANK OF ELIBANK, ix. 84.
MURRAY, VISCOUNT OF FINCASTLE, iii. 384.
MURRAY, LORD GASK, i. 469, 474, 479; viii. 411.
MURRAY, VISCOUNT GLENALMOND, i. 478.
MURRAY, VISCOUNT OF GLENALMOND, i. 479.
MURRAY, VISCOUNT OF GLENLYON, i. 479-502.
MURRAY, BARON GLENLYON OF GLENLYON, i. 496-502.
MURRAY, VISCOUNT OF GLENSHIE, i. 481.
MURRAY, EARL OF GLEN TILT, i. 481.
MURRAY, LORD OF HUNTINGTOWER, iii. 402-420.
MURRAY, SOVEREIGN OF THE ISLE OF MAN, i. 488.
MURRAY, BARON OF MANSFIELD, viii. 205.
MURRAY, EARL OF MANSFIELD, viii. 206-214.
MURRAY, LORD MURRAY, i. 469-479; viii. 411.
MURRAY, LORD MURRAY OF BLAIR, iii. 384.
MURRAY, BARON MURRAY OF ELIBANK, ix. 84.
MURRAY, LORD MURRAY OF LOCHMABEN, i. 228.
MURRAY, LORD MURRAY OF MOULIN, iii. 384.
MURRAY, BARON MURRAY OF STANLEY, i. 495.
MURRAY, LORD MURRAY OF TILLIMET, iii. 384.
MURRAY, LORD MURRAY OF TULLIBARDINE, i. 469.
MURRAY, LORD MURRAY OF TYNNINGHAM, i. 228.
MURRAY, BARON PERCY, i. 499.
MURRAY, DUKE OF RANNOCH, i. 481.
MURRAY, LORD SCONE, viii. 192-214.
MURRAY, LORD OF SCONE, viii. 193-214.
MURRAY, VISCOUNT STORMONT, viii. 186-214.
MURRAY, LORD STRANGE, i. 488.
MURRAY, EARL STRANGE, i. 495-502.
MURRAY, EARL OF STRATHARDLE, i. 479-502.
MURRAY, LORD STRATHBRAN, i. 481.
MURRAY, EARL OF STRATHTAY, i. 479-502.
MURRAY, EARL OF TULLIBARDINE, i. 469, 474, 478; viii. 410-415.
MURRAY, MARQUESS OF TULLIBARDINE, i. 479.
MURRAY, EARL OF WESTMINSTER, iii. 514.
Murray of Aberlednoch Wester, Alexander, i. 462; ix. 28 *bis*.
—— —— his wife, Isobel Reidheucb, i. 462.
—— —— William, i. 463.
—— —— his wife, Elizabeth Moncreiff, i. 463.
—— of Aberscors, John, iii. 204.
Murray of Aikwood, Sir Walter, iii. 507.
—— of Aliburn, Sir Gideon, iii. 504.
—— of Alich, *or* Alichmore, David, 3rd son of Sir Wm. M. of Tullibardine, i. 461.
—— —— his wife, Katharine Edmonstone, i. 461.
—— —— William, i. 461, 462.
—— of Annandale, Sir William, i. 215.
—— —— his wife, Isabel Randolph, i. 215; vi. 291.
—— of Arbenie, *, iii. 398.
—— of Little Ardit, David, parish clerk of Abernethy, viii. 187, 189.
—— —— his wife, Margaret Kirkaldy, viii. 187.
—— —— William, minister of Crail, parson of Eassie and Nevay, viii. 187.
—— —— his 1st wife, Janet Moncrieff, viii. 187.
—— —— his 2nd wife, Helen Wood, viii. 187.
—— of Ardormy, Andrew, iii. 310.
—— of Arngask, Sir Andrew, viii. 188.
—— —— Sir Andrew, viii. 189.
—— —— Sir Andrew, viii. 190.
—— —— Andrew, minister of Abdie, viii. 200.
—— —— Sir David, viii. 186, 187.
—— of Auchtermuchty, Sir David, viii. 191.
—— of Aytoun, Alexander, ii. 25.
—— —— his wife, Mary Ogilvy, ii. 25.
—— of Badlormie, John, iv. 83.
—— of Middletoun of Balhagies, David, viii. 188.
—— of Balgony, David, viii. 199.
—— of Ballencrieff, Sir Archibald, iii. 504.
—— —— Andrew, iii. 503.
—— —— Sir Gideon, iii. 504.
—— —— John, iii. 502.
—— of Balmblae, Sir David, viii. 192, 194.
—— of Balquhidder, Sir David, viii. 195.
—— —— Sir Mungo, viii. 195.
—— of Balvaird, Sir Andrew, i. 459; viii. 186.
—— —— his wife, Margaret Barclay of Arngask and Kippo, viii. 186.
—— —— Sir Andrew, viii. 188.
—— —— his 1st wife, Margaret Ross, vii. 252; viii. 188.
—— —— his 2nd wife, Jonet Graham, vi. 230; viii. 188.
—— —— Sir Andrew, viii. 189.
—— —— his wife, Margaret Crichton, i. 466; viii. 190.
—— —— Sir Andrew, viii. 190, 193 *ter*.
—— —— his wife, Katharine Menteith, viii. 191.
—— —— Sir Andrew, minister of Abdie, viii. 196, 199, 200.
—— —— his wife, Elizabeth Carnegie, viii. 68, 201.
—— —— Sir David, viii. 187.
—— —— his wife, Jonet Lindsay, v. 396; viii. 187.

* Name unknown.

Murray of Bambreich, Sir Mungo, viii. 196.
— of Banuercross, John, i. 485.
— — Mary, i. 486.
— of Beaupert House, James, general, governor of Quebec, of Minorca, and of Hull, iii. 514, 515.
— — his 1st wife, * Collier, iii. 516; ix. 84.
— — his 2nd wife, Anne Whitham. iii. 516.
— of Berkhampstead, Henry, groom of the bedchamber to Charles I., iii. 399.
— — his wife, Anne Bayning, iii. 399.
— — Thomas, provost of Eton, iii. 399, 401.
— — his wife, Jane Drummond, iii. 399.
— of Bernaglis, Sir David, i. 455.
— of Binn, Andrew, viii. 199.
— — Sir David, viii. 193.
— — David, viii. 199.
— — his wife, Agnes Moncreiffe, viii. 199.
— — Gilbert, viii. 194, 199.
— — Sir John, viii. 202.
— — John, viii. 202, 207.
— — Sir Patrick, componitor of the Treasury, viii. 188.
— — his wife, Isobel Brown, viii. 189.
— — William, viii. 199.
— — his wife, Elizabeth Balfour, viii. 199.
— of Blackbarony, Sir Alexander, 4th bart., iii. 520.
— — Andrew, sheriff of Edinburgh, iii. 502; ix. 83 *bis*.
— — his 1st wife, Elizabeth Lockhart, iii. 503.
— — his 2nd wife, Grizel Betoun, ii. 231; iii. 503; ix. 83 *bis*.
— — Sir Archibald, 1st bart., iii. 503, 504; iv. 489.
— — his wife, Margaret Maule, vii. 14.
— — Sir Archibald, 3rd bart., iv. 492.
— — his wife, Mary Keith, iv. 492; vi. 60.
— — Sir Digby, 11th bart., iii. 503.
— — John, elder son of Wm. M., iii. 501.
— — John, depute Clerk Register, iii. 498, 500, 501; ix. 83.
— — his wife, Isobel Hoppar, iii. 502; ix. 83 *bis*.
— — Sir John, eldest son of Andrew M., iii. 503; v. 467; vii. 90.
— — his 2nd wife, Margaret Wauchope, ix. 60.
— of Blebo, Charles, i. 467.
— — Sir John, i. 467.
— — Sir Mungo, 2nd bart., i. 467.
— — his 1st wife, Anna Graham, i. 138, 467.
— — his 2nd wife, Christian Hamilton, i. 467; vi. 597.
— — Sir William, 1st bart., i. 467.
— — his 1st wife, Katharine Forbes, i. 467.
— — his 2nd wife, Eupham Ogilvy, i. 467.

* Name unknown.

Murray of Bowhill, John, ancestor of the family of, iii. 499.
— of Broughton, John, secretary to prince Charles, v. 130, 131.
— — in Kirkcudbright, Alexander, M.P., i. 221.
— — his wife, Euphame Stewart, i. 221.
— — Alexander, M.P., i. 221.
— — David, i. 221.
— — George, i. 221.
— — his wife, Isabel Vans, i. 221.
— — James, M.P., i. 221.
— — his wife, Katharine Stewart, i. 221; iv. 166.
— — John, M.P., i. 221.
— — Mungo, son of Cuthbert M. of Cockpool, i. 221.
— — Richard, M.P., i. 221.
— — his wife, Anna Lennox, i. 221.
— of Cambusavie, John, iii. 199.
— of Camsyny, Sir David, i. 455.
— — his wife, Isobel Stewart, i. 455.
— of Carden, Adam, viii. 547.
— — his wife, Jean Fleming, viii. 547.
— of Castleton, Sir William, i. 460.
— — his wife, Margaret Stewart, i. 442, 460.
— of Carsehead, David, iii. 398.
— of Cavens, Sir James, iii. 509.
— — his wife, Isobel Murray, iii. 509.
— of Clairden, David, ii. 353.
— of Claremont, Sir Mungo, 4th son of Sir Wm. M. of Tullibardine, i. 466, 469.
— — his wife, Margaret Crichton, i. 467.
— — Sir William, i. 467; viii. 194, 200.
— — his 1st wife, Katharine Forbes, i. 467.
— — his 2nd wife, Eupham Ogilvy, i. 467.
— of Clonyaird, Sir David, son of Sir Charles M. of Cockpool, i. 224.
— — his wife, Marion Maclellan. i. 225.
— of Cockpool, ii. 126.
— — i. 214.
— — Sir Adam, 1st laird, i. 216.
— — Sir Charles, 4th laird, i. 218.
— — Sir Charles, 8th laird, i. 223; iii. 127.
— — his wife, Margaret Somerville, i. 224; viii. 19; ix. 13.
— — Cuthbert, 5th laird, i. 219; iii. 225; vi. 477.
— — his wife, Marjory Menzies, i. 220.
— — Cuthbert, 7th laird, i. 223.
— — his wife, Janet Jardine, i. 223.
— — Sir James, 9th laird, i. 224, 226; iii. 128.
— — his wife, Janet Douglas, i. 226; vii. 129.
— — Sir John, 6th laird, i. 220, 222.
— — Sir John, 2nd bart., i. 225, 227.
— — his wife, Elizabeth Shaw, i. 228.
— — Margaret, wife of Sir Robt. Grierson of Lag, i. 226; viii. 204.

Murray of Cockpool, Patrick, 2nd laird, i. 216.
—— —— Sir Richard, 1st bart., dean of Manchester, i. 225, 226.
—— —— Sir Robert, i. 229, 476; viii. 218, 452.
—— —— Sir Thomas, 3rd laird, i. 216, 217, 222.
—— —— Sir William, ancestor of the family of, i. 215.
—— —— his wife, Isabel Randolph, i. 215; vi. 291.
—— of Collenows, Sir David, viii. 191.
—— of Colmieslichill, Sir Walter, iii. 507.
—— —— his wife, Elizabeth Pringle, iii. 507.
—— of Comlongan, George, i. 216.
—— —— William, i. 215, 233.
—— of Conland, John, 2nd son of Sir Andrew M. of Balvaird, viii. 186.
—— of Cringletie, Alexander, viii. 461.
—— —— Alexander, ii. 296.
—— —— his wife, Katharine Stuart, ii. 296.
—— of Culbardie, James, iii. 199.
—— —— his wife, Elizabeth Stewart, iii. 199.
—— of Cumnock, Sir John, viii. 202.
—— of Cushete, David, i. 461.
—— of Danesfield, Charles Robert Scott, v. 547.
—— —— his wife, Amelia Charlotte Fraser, v. 547.
—— of Denork, Sir Mungo, i. 466.
—— of Deuchar, John, ancestor of the family of, iii. 499.
—— —— Sir Patrick, ii. 42; viii. 32.
—— of Dollerie, Anthony, 4th laird, iii, 397.
—— —— his wife, Christian Maxton, iii. 397.
—— —— David, 2nd laird, iii. 397.
—— —— his wife, Margaret Pitcairn, iii. 397.
—— —— David, 5th laird, iii. 397.
—— —— Patrick, 1st laird, 5th son of Sir David M. of Tullibardine, i. 457; iii. 397.
—— —— his wife, Katharine Balfour, iii. 397.
—— —— Patrick, 3rd laird, iii. 397.
—— of Dolphinston, Archibald, vii. 90.
—— —— Walter, lieut.-col., vii. 90.
—— —— his wife, Jean Balfour, vii. 90.
—— of Dorney House, Frances Maria, ii. 386.
—— —— Thomas, lieut.-general, 7th son of 1st earl of Dunmore, iii. 385.
—— —— his wife, Elizabeth Armiger, iii. 386.
—— of Dowally, James, capt. Royal Scots, M.P., i. 475; iii. 228.
—— —— his wife, Ann Murray *or* Crichton, i. 476; iii. 228.
—— of Drumcairn, Gilbert, viii. 199, 200.
—— —— Sir John, tutor of Stormont, lord of Justiciary, viii. 202.
—— —— his wife, Katharine Murray, viii. 200, 202.
—— —— John, viii. 202, 207.
—— —— Sir Mungo, i. 470; viii. 193, 196.
—— —— his 1st wife, Anna Murray, viii. 190, 197.
Murray of Drumcairn, William, viii. 199, 200.
—— —— his wife, Elizabeth Balfour, vii. 199.
—— of Drumcreiff, Sir Adam, 2nd son of Sir Charles M. of Cockpool, i. 218, 219.
—— —— his wife, * Carlyle, ii. 386.
—— —— Adam, i. 219.
—— —— Cuthbert, i. 219.
—— —— his wife, Janet Johnstone, i. 219.
—— of Drumdewan, Alexander, colonel, i. 466.
—— of Drumduff, Andrew, minister of Abdie, viii. 200.
—— —— Sir David, viii. 194.
—— —— William, viii. 199.
—— of Drumphin, Alexander, i. 462.
—— —— his wife, Isobel Reidheuch, i. 462.
—— —— John, i. 463; ix. 29.
—— —— his wife, Agnes Bruce, ix. 29.
—— —— William, i. 463.
—— —— his wife, Elizabeth Moncreiff, i. 463.
—— of Drumstinchall, Adam, i. 223, 229.
—— —— Alexander, i. 223.
—— —— David, son of Sir John M. of Cockpool, i. 223.
—— —— Florence, son of Sir Thos. M. of Cockpool, i. 217.
—— —— John, i. 223.
—— of Wester Duddingston, Sir David, viii. 187.
—— of Dunearn, William, 4th son of Andrew M. of Blackbarony, iii. 504, 517; viii. 446.
—— —— Sir William, 1st bart., iii. 504; viii. 180.
—— —— his wife, Margaret Alexander, viii. 180.
—— —— Sir William, 2nd bart., iii. 509.
—— —— his wife, Jean Murray, iii. 509.
—— of Dunipace, William, 3rd son of 1st lord Elibank, iii. 508.
—— of Eddleston, Sir John, viii. 445.
—— of Elcho, Sir David, viii. 194.
—— —— Sir Gideon, 1st laird, ii. 593; iii. 503, 504; vii. 74, 77.
—— —— his wife, Margaret Pentland, iii. 506.
—— —— Sir Patrick, 1st bart., ii. 593; iii. 507.
—— —— his 1st wife, Margaret Hamilton, iii. 508.
—— —— his 2nd wife, Elizabeth Dundas, iii. 508.
—— —— his 4th wife, Helen Lindsay, iii. 509.
—— of Fala, Archibald, vii. 90.
—— —— Roger de, son of Archibald de Moravia, iii. 499, 526.
—— —— Walter, lieut.-col., vii. 90.
—— —— his wife, Jean Balfour, vii. 90.
—— of Falahill, James, ii. 590.
—— —— his wife, Margaret Hume, ii. 590.
—— —— James, viii. 400.
—— —— his wife, Margaret Stewart, viii. 400.

* Name unknown.

Murray of Falahill, John, keeper of Newark Castle, ii. 228; iii. 499.
— — his wife, Isabella Scott, ii. 228.
— — John, son of Patrick M., ii. 155; iii. 499.
— — his wife, Margaret Hepburne, ii. 155.
— — Patrick, iii. 499 *bis*.
— — Patrick, ii. 65; iii. 503 *n*., 504.
— — his 1st wife, Agnes Murray, iii. 504.
— — his 2nd wife, Marion Bellenden, ii. 65; iii. 96.
— of Feddal, Sir Mungo, i. 466.
— of Frimley, Alexander, lieut.-col., 3rd son of 4th earl of Dunmore, iii. 389.
— — his wife, Deborah Hunt, iii. 389.
— of Gallowhill, i. 214.
— of Garth, Sir Mungo, son of 1st earl of Atholl, i. 473.
— of Geanies, Sir Patrick, iv. 487; v. 82; viii. 188.
— — his wife, Isobel Brown, viii. 189.
— of Glencarse, Dr. James, i. 457, 484.
— — his wife, Emilia Murray of Strowan, i. 457.
— of Glendoick, Sir Andrew, viii. 196, 200.
— — Sir David, viii. 192.
— — Sir Thomas, 1st bart., iii. 398.
— of Glenfinart, John, 4th earl of Dunmore, iii. 388.
— of Glenpoit, Gideon, iii. 504.
— — John, iii. 502.
— of Gospertie, Sir David, master of the king's stable, tutor of Balvaird, viii. 188, 191.
— — his wife, Elizabeth Betoun, viii. 196.
— of Haltoun, Andrew, sheriff of Edinburgh, iii. 503.
— of Hawick, Jonet, wife of James of Gledstanes, vii. 115.
— of Hillhead, Sir James, 7th bart., lieut.-general, iii. 517.
— — his wife, Henrietta Laura, countess of Bath, iii. 517.
— — Sir Robert, 6th bart., iii. 517.
— — his wife, Janet Murray, iii. 517.
— of Inchmurray, Sir Andrew, 1st laird, viii. 201.
— — James, viii. 202.
— — William, viii. 202.
— — his wife, Alison Cheape, viii. 202.
— of Kelach, James, son of Sir David M. of Tullibardine, i. 457.
— — his wife, Margaret Fresale, i. 457.
— — John, i. 457.
— — his wife, Margaret Hepburn, i. 457.
— of Forest of Kershope, James, iii. 500.
— of Kilbaberton, Sir James, keeper of munition, Edinburgh Castle, iii. 127, 509, 510; viii. 178.
— — his wife, Katharine Weir, iii. 509.
— — Sir James, iii. 509, 510.
— — his wife, Isobel Murray, iii. 509.
Murray of Castlerigs of Kinghorn, John, iii. 502.
— of Kippo, Andrew, minister of Abdie, viii. 200.
— — Sir David, viii. 186, 187.
— — his wife, Jonet Lindsay, viii. 187.
— — David, viii. 199.
— of Langhermiston, John, iii. 507, 508.
— — William, 2nd son of Sir Gideon M. of Elibank, iii. 507, 511.
— — his wife, Katharine Skene, iii. 507; ix. 84 *bis*.
— — William, 3rd son of 1st lord Elibank, iii. 508.
— — his 1st wife, Isobel Douglas, iii. 508.
— — his 2nd wife, Margaret Baillie, iii. 508.
— of Langshaw, Sir Gideon, iii. 505.
— — Patrick, iii. 507.
— of Lethindy, Alexander David, viii. 213.
— of Letter Bannachty, Sir Andrew, i. 459; viii. 186.
— — his wife, Margaret Barclay of Kippo and Arngask, viii. 186.
— — Sir Andrew, viii. 190.
— — his wife, Katharine Menteith, viii. 190.
— — David, viii. 190, 199.
— — his wife, Agnes Moncreiffe, viii. 199.
— — William, viii. 187, 198.
— — his wife, Barbara Pitcairn, viii. 198; ix. 161.
— of Liberton, John, iii. 502.
— of Livingstone, John, iii. 502.
— — Patrick, iii. 507.
— — Patrick, iii. 385, 507.
— — Sir Walter, 3rd son of Sir Gideon M. of Elibank, iii. 507.
— — his wife, Elizabeth Pringle, iii. 507.
— of Loch Carron, Charles James, M.P., iii. 393.
— — his wife, Anna Francesca Wilhelmina Finch, iii. 393.
— of Lochmaben, Sir John, i. 225, 226, 227.
— of Lochmiln, David, iii. 398.
— of Logiealmond, Sir Patrick, viii. 411.
— of Lundy, Robert, merchant, Paris, v. 25.
— of Manuel, Andrew, i. 214, 217.
— — Robert, i. 214, 217.
— of Melgum, John, ancestor of the family of, iii. 499.
— — Sir Joseph, bart., iv. 40.
— of Melgund, Alexander, viii. 143.
— — his wife, Janet Rochead, viii. 143.
— of Mount Lothian, Patrick, captain, viii. 32.
— of Murrayfield, Archibald, viii. 461.
— — his wife, Jane Hay, viii. 461.

Murray of Murrayshall, Sir Andrew, 1st laird, viii. 201.
—— —— his 1st wife, Anna Menteith, viii. 201.
—— —— his 2nd wife, Rebecca Cheape, viii. 202.
—— —— Andrew, 2nd laird, viii. 201.
—— of Murraythwaite, Andrew, 4th laird, i. 218.
—— —— Andrew, 9th laird, i. 218, 224.
—— —— his wife, Janet Murray, i. 224.
—— —— Gavin, 3rd laird, i. 218.
—— —— John, 6th son of Sir Thos. M. of Cockpool; 1st laird, i. 217.
—— —— his wife, Elizabeth de Ednam of Murraythwaite, i. 217.
—— —— John, i. 218.
—— —— his wife, Marion Irving, i. 218.
—— —— John, i. 218.
—— —— his wife, Blanche Irving, i. 218.
—— —— John, vice-lieut. of Dumfries, i. 218.
—— —— John Dalrymple, i. 218.
—— —— Patrick, 2nd laird, i. 217.
—— —— William, i. 218, 228.
—— of Naughton, Egidia, wife of Thos. Kinnaird of that Ilk, v. 204.
—— of Newraw, Patrick, 2nd son of Anthony M. of Dollerie, iii. 398.
—— —— his wife, Elizabeth Murray, iii. 398.
—— of Newton, David, captain of Douglas Castle, i. 216.
—— —— William, iii. 504, 517.
—— —— Sir William, 1st bart., iii. 504.
—— of Northfield of Coldingham, Patrick, 'dapifer regis,' vi. 10.
—— of Ochtertyre, Sir David, ancestor of the family of, iii. 397.
—— —— David, 2nd laird, iii. 397.
—— —— his wife, Margaret Pitcairn, iii. 397.
—— —— David, 4th laird, i. 462.
—— —— Patrick, 5th son of Sir David M. of Tullibardine, i. 457; iii. 397.
—— —— Patrick, 3rd laird, iii. 397.
—— —— Patrick, 5th laird, v. 219.
—— —— his wife, Jane Hay, v. 219.
—— —— Patrick, 7th laird, ii. 186 *bis*.
—— —— Sir Patrick, 4th bart., ii. 49.
—— —— his wife, Helen Hamilton, ii. 49.
—— —— Sir Patrick, M.P., 6th bart., iii. 81; iv. 499.
—— —— his wife, Mary Anne Hope, iv. 499.
—— —— William, 6th laird, viii. 198.
—— —— his wife, Bethia Murray, viii. 198.
—— —— Sir William 1st bart., iv. 291.
—— —— Sir William, 3rd bart., v. 535.
—— —— his wife, Katharine Fraser, v. 353.
—— —— Sir William, 5th bart., iv. 499.
—— —— his wife, Augusta Mackenzie, iii. 81.
—— —— Sir William, 7th bart., v. 513; vi. 45.
—— —— his 1st wife, Helen Margaret Oliphant Keith, vi. 45.
—— —— his 2nd wife, Adelaide Louisa Lavinia Hastings, v. 513.
Murray of Ogleface, John, iv. 83.
—— of Orchardfield, John, iii. 502.
—— of Overmenzean, John, iii. 502.
—— of Pardewis, Anthony, i. 464.
—— —— James, 3rd son of Sir Wm. M. of Tullibardine, i. 463, 465.
—— —— his 1st wife, Marion Preston, i. 464.
—— —— his 2nd wife, Agnes *or* Anna Lindsay, i. 464; vi. 95.
—— —— John, i. 464.
—— —— Patrick, i. 464, 548; ii. 549.
—— —— his wife, Margaret Colvill, i. 464; ii. 548.
—— of the Park, Sir Andrew, viii. 189.
—— of Philiphaugh, John, keeper of Newark Castle, 1st laird, iii. 499.
—— —— John, 3rd laird, iii. 499.
—— —— his wife, Margaret Hepburn, ii. 155.
—— —— Sir John, vii. 79.
—— —— John, M.P., vii. 519.
—— —— his wife, Eleanor Hamilton, vii. 519.
—— —— Patrick, 2nd laird, iii. 499.
—— —— Patrick, 9th laird, ii. 83.
—— of Pilmuir, John, colonel, iii. 401.
—— of Pitcairly, William, captain, i. 466, 469; ix. 29.
—— —— his wife, Katharine Preston, ix. 29.
—— of Pitkaithly, George, vice-admiral, i. 484.
—— —— his wife, Wilhelmina King, i. 485.
—— —— Margaret, wife of col. Wm. Mercer of Aldie, vi. 395.
—— —— William, vi. 395.
—— of Pitlochie, Sir Andrew, 1st laird, viii. 201.
—— —— Sir Andrew, 2nd laird, viii. 201.
—— of Pitnacree, John, iv. 33.
—— —— John, general, i. 485.
—— —— his wife, Mary Dalton, i. 486.
—— —— Mary, wife of lieut.-gen. Wm. Foxlowe, i. 486.
—— of Pittencreiff, George, capt. Royal Scots, lieut.-col. Horse Guards, iii. 509, 511; ix. 84.
—— —— his 1st wife, Margaret Moncreiffe, iii. 509.
—— —— his 2nd wife, Elizabeth Erskine, iii. 509; ix. 84.
—— —— George, son of col. Geo. M., iii. 509.
—— of Pittillock, John, 2nd son of Sir Andrew M. of Balvaird, viii. 186.
—— of Ploro, Gideon, iii. 504.
—— —— John, iii. 502.
—— of Polgour, Sir John, i. 460, 462.
—— —— his wife, Elizabeth Crichton, i. 460.
—— of Polmaise, John, v. 612.
—— —— his wife, Janet Erskine, v. 612.
—— —— Sir John, i. 468; v. 218.
—— —— John, ii. 366.
—— —— his wife, Lilias Stirling, ii. 366.
—— —— John, i. 554.

Murray of Polmaise, William, ancestor of the family of, viii. 387.
—— —— William, i. 554.
—— of Polrossie, Walter, vii. 163.
—— —— his wife, Margaret Mackay, vii. 163.
—— of Polton, James, iii. 352; v. 409.
—— of Priestfield, Sir Andrew, viii. 189.
—— of Priesthope, Gideon, iii. 504.
—— —— John, iii. 502.
—— of Raith, Anthony, iii. 397.
—— —— his wife, Christian Maxton, iii. 397.
—— of Ravilly, Oliver, iii. 509.
—— —— Richard, iii. 509.
—— —— Walter, 4th son of 1st lord Elibank, iii. 509.
—— —— his wife, Jane Butler, iii. 509.
—— —— William, iii. 509.
—— of Redcastle, Sir Patrick, 3rd earl of Tullibardine, i. 470, 501; viii. 411.
—— of Reidkirk, John, viii. 193, 197.
—— of Romanno, William, viii. 19.
—— —— his 2nd wife, Agnes Somerville, viii. 19.
—— —— his 3rd wife, Helen Henderson, viii. 19; ix. 159.
—— of Rosses, John, v. 266.
—— of Ryvale, ii. 126.
—— —— Sir Thomas, i. 214, 217.
—— —— William, i. 215, 233.
—— of Segy, Sir David, viii. 192, 193.
—— of Simprim, Patrick, ix. 84 *bis*.
—— of Skirling, James, vii. 14.
—— —— his wife, Bethia Maule, vii. 14.
—— —— Sir James, iii. 511.
—— —— John, ancestor of the family of, iii. 499.
—— of Slaithwaite, David, i. 216.
—— —— Ninian, i. 216.
—— of Smyddiehill, James, i. 121.
—— —— his wife, Isabella Quhytlaw, i. 121.
—— of Spot, *, iv. 94.
—— —— his wife, Clara Forrester, iv. 94.
—— —— William, 3rd son of 1st lord Elibank, iii. 508.
—— of Stanhope [Sir Alexander, 3rd bart.].
—— —— his wife, Grisell Baillie of Jerviswoode and Mellerstain, iv. 322.
—— —— Sir David, viii. 548.
—— —— his wife, Lilias Fleming, viii. 548.
—— —— Sir David, 2nd bart., v. 478.
—— —— his wife, Anne Bruce, iii. 487; v. 478.
—— —— Sir William, i. 258; ii. 410.
—— —— his wife, Janet Johnstone, i. 258.
—— of Stanwell, John, iii. 386.
—— of Stewartown, Patrick, i. 215.
—— of Strowan, Alexander, i. 462.
—— —— Amelia, wife of lord George Murray, i. 457, 484.

* Name unknown.

Murray of Strowan, Emilia, wife of Dr. James Murray of Glencarse, i. 457.
—— —— James, major-gen., M.P., i. 484.
—— —— John, ancestor of the family of, i. 457.
—— John, afterwards 3rd duke of Atholl, i. 484, 489.
—— of Taymount, William, 5th son of 1st earl of Dunmore, iii. 385, 387.
—— —— his wife, Katharine Nairne, iii. 387.
—— of Tibbermore, Alexander, ancester of the family of, i. 458.
—— —— John, iv. 259.
—— —— his wife, Isobel Ruthven, iv. 259.
—— —— John, iii. 398.
—— —— Patrick, viii. 189.
—— of Touchadam, Andrew, ancestor of the family of, i. 214; iv. 346.
—— —— Sir John, vi. 357.
—— —— John, iv. 430; v. 612.
—— —— his contr. wife, Katharine Erskine, v. 612.
—— —— his wife, Janet Erskine, v. 612.
—— —— John, ii. 366.
—— —— his wife, Lilias Stirling, ii. 366.
—— —— John, lieut.-col., vi. 273.
—— —— his wife, Agnes Caroline Graham, vi. 273.
—— —— Sir William, vii. 576.
—— —— William, i. 554.
—— of Traquair, William, ii. 267.
—— —— his wife, Margaret Murray, ii. 267, 399.
—— of Trewin, John, chamberlain of Strathearn, i. 456.
—— —— his wife, Margaret Ruthven, i. 457.
—— of Tullibancher, William, 2nd son of Alex. M. of Aberlednoch, i. 463.
—— —— his wife, Elizabeth Moncreiff, i. 463.
—— of Tullibardine, Andrew, 2nd laird, i. 454.
—— —— Sir David, 6th laird, i. 455.
—— —— his wife, Isobel Stewart, i. 455.
—— —— Sir David, 7th laird, i. 455; iii. 455; v. 603 *n*.
—— —— his wife, Margaret [Colquhoun], i. 456.
—— —— Sir John, 4th laird, i. 454.
—— —— Sir John, 12th laird, i. 466, 468; viii. 292.
—— —— his wife, Katharine Drummond, i. 469.
—— —— Sir Patrick, 3rd son of 1st earl of Tullibardine, i. 470; viii. 410, 411.
—— —— Walter, 5th laird, i. 454.
—— —— his wife, Margaret le Barde, i. 455.
—— —— Sir William, 1st laird, i. 450, 452.
—— —— his wife, Ada of Tullibardine, i. 453.
—— —— Sir William, 3rd laird, i. 454.
—— —— William, sheriff of Perth and Banff, 8th laird, i. 456, 458.
—— —— his wife, Margaret Gray, i. 456 *n*., 459; iv. 273.

Murray of Tullibardine, Sir William, 9th laird, i. 459.
—— —— Sir William, 10th laird, i. 461 *bis*; viii. 166.
—— —— his wife, Katharine Campbell, i. 462; ii. 180; ix. 28.
—— —— Sir William, comptroller of Scotland, 11th laird, i. 462, 465.
—— —— his wife, Agnes Graham, i. 466; vi. 230.
—— of Wallaceton, John, i. 462; iv. 259.
—— of South Warnborough, David, M.P., iii. 513.
—— —— his wife, Elizabeth Harley, iii. 513.
—— of Whitehouse, John, v. 177.
—— —— his wife, Euphemia Ross, v. 177.
—— of Williamston, Patrick, vii. 575.
—— —— his wife, Katharine Boswell, vii. 575.
—— of Woodend, Alexander, iii. 398; ix. 78.
—— —— his 1st wife, Marion Alexander, iii. 398; viii. 168; ix. 78.
—— —— his 2nd wife, Barbara Murray, iii. 398; ix. 78.
—— —— his 3rd wife, Agnes Nairn, iii. 398; ix. 79.
—— —— Anthony, 5th laird, iii. 398.
—— —— Patrick, 1st laird, iii. 398.
—— —— his wife, Elizabeth Murray, iii. 398.
—— —— Patrick, 3rd laird, iii. 398; vii. 198.
—— —— his 1st wife, Giles Murray, iii. 398; ix. 79.
—— —— his 2nd wife, Helen Oliphant, vii. 198.
—— —— Thomas, 4th laird, iii. 398.
—— —— his wife, Jean Murray, ix. 79.
—— of Yrhartmoir, John, iv. 33.
—— Adam, vicar of Troqueer, i. 224.
—— Dr. Adam, Stirling, iii. 76.
—— —— his wife, Katharine Mackenzie, iii. 76.
—— Agnes, wife of (1) Ninian Maculloch, and (2) Jas. Kennedy, i. 223.
—— Agnes, wife of Simon Carruthers, i. 223.
—— Agnes, wife of Lindsay of Rascarroll, i. 225.
—— Agnes, wife of Robt. Maxwell, i. 225.
—— Agnes, wife of Thos. Steuart of Grandtully, i. 459.
—— Agnes, dau. of Alex. M. of Aberlednoch, i. 463.
—— Agnes, wife of Robert Bruce of Kennet, i. 548.
—— Agnes, wife of Duncan Campbell of Monzie, ii. 186.
—— Agnes, dau. of Alex. M. of Woodend, iii. 398.
—— Agnes, contr. to Alex. Napier of Merchiston, iii. 502; vi. 412; ix. 83.
—— Agnes, wife of Patrick Murray of Falahill, iii. 504.
Murray, Agnes, 'muckle-mouthed Meg'; wife of Sir Wm. Scott of Harden, iii. 507 *n.*; vii. 77.
—— Agnes, wife of George Auchinleck, iii. 508.
—— Alastair Heneage, lieut. Grenadier Guards, iii. 393.
—— Alexander, 3rd son of Alex. M. of Aberlednoch, i. 463.
—— ? Alexander, eldest son of L. G. K. Murray, iii. 390.
—— Alexander, dean, 3rd son of Anthony M. of Dollerie, iii. 398.
—— —— his wife, Elizabeth Oliphant, iii. 398.
—— Alexander, canon of Moray, rector of Hawick, and Forest of Ettrick, iii. 499, 500 *bis*; ix. 83.
—— Alexander, 26th regt., author of the 'Elibank Plot,' iii. 514.
—— Alexander, canon of Inchaffray, ix. 78.
—— Alexander Henry, brigadier-general, iii. 390.
—— —— his wife, Martha Frances Vincent Davenport, iii. 390.
—— Alexander William Charles Oliphant, M.P.; styled master of Elibank, iii. 523.
—— —— his wife, Hilda Louisa Janey Wolfe-Murray, iii. 523.
—— Alexander William Oliphant, rector of Chignal Smealy, iii. 521.
—— Alexandrina Amelia, iii. 390.
—— Alexandrina Victoria, wife of rev. Henry Cunliffe, iii. 394.
—— Alice Florence, wife of Stephen Leech, iii. 524.
—— Amelia, wife of (1) John, master of Sinclair, and (2) Jas. Farquharson, i. 485; vii. 587.
—— Amelia, wife of (1) Major T. I. Cooke, and (2) Sir Richard Gamon, i. 494.
—— Amelia, wife of (1) Hugh, 9th lord Fraser of Lovat, and (2) Simon, 11th lord Fraser of Lovat, i. 478; v. 534, 536, 538.
—— Amelia, dau. of 4th viscount of Stormont, viii. 204.
—— Amelia, wife of Sir Alex. Lindsay of Evelick, viii. 207.
—— Amelia Matilda, maid of honour to queen Victoria, i. 492.
—— Amelia Sophia, wife of 8th viscount of Strathallan, i. 498; viii. 234.
—— Mr. Andrew, 1457, i. 456.
—— Sir Andrew, ancestor of viscounts of Stormont, i. 459.
—— Andrew, 2nd son of Sir Wm. M. of Castleton, i. 461, 462.
—— Andrew, 4th son of Sir Wm. M. of Tullibardine, i. 464.
—— Andrew, exchanged for Sir J. Segrave, ii. 127.
—— Andrew, in Warmwood, iii. 501.

Murray, Andrew, 2nd son of Andrew M. of Blackbarony, iii. 503.
— Andrew, 2nd son of William M. of Letter Bannachty, viii. 198.
— Andrew David, major Cameron Highlanders, viii. 213.
— Angus David, lieut. R.N., viii. 213.
— Anna, wife of (1) Sir John Gordon, and (2) col. Patrick Robertson, i. 467 ; ix. 29.
— Anna, wife of 1st earl of Kinghorn, i. 470 ; viii. 294.
— Anna, dau. of col. James M., iii. 401.
— Anna, wife of Mr. Alexander Moncrieffe, iii. 401.
— Anna, wife of 2nd viscount Stormont, viii. 190, 197.
— Anna, wife of John Littlejohn, viii. 197 *n.*
— Anna, wife of Sir Wm. Hay of Linplum, viii. 446 ; ix. 167.
— Annabella, wife of John, earl of Mar, i. 464 ; v. 615.
— Annabella, wife of David Ross, i. 470 ; ix. 29.
— Anne, wife of 4th earl of Tullibardine, i. 473 ; viii. 415.
— Anne, wife of capt. James Murray of Dowally, i. 476.
— Anne, dau. of capt. Jas. M., i. 476.
— Anne, wife of Robt. Bruce of Kennet, i. 554.
— Ann, wife of Duncan Campbell of Monzie, ii. 186.
— Anne, wife of capt. W. H. Cranstoun, ii. 597.
— Anne, wife of John, 4th earl of Dundonald, iii. 354, 386.
— Anne, dau. of 4th earl of Dunmore, iii. 392.
— Anne, wife of Robert Pierrepoint, iii. 400.
— Anne, dau. of Thos. M. of Berkhampstead, iii. 400.
— Anne, dau. of 1st earl of Dysart, iii. 402 ; ix. 79.
— Anne, wife of James Ferguson of Pitfour, iii. 517.
— Anne, dau. of 6th viscount of Stormont, viii. 207.
— Anne Harriet, dau. of gen. James M., iii. 516.
— Anthony, son of Sir David M. of Tullibardine, i. 458.
— Anthony, parson of Utricton, ix. 79 *bis.*
— Archibald, son of Sir Chas. M. of Cockpool, i. 225.
— Arthur Cecil, lieut. 5th Gurkhas, iii. 523.
— Arthur Charles, 5th son of capt. Virginius M., iii. 389.
— Augusta, wife of Louis Stanislas Kostka, prince de la Trimouille, iii. 390.
— Augusta, wife of H.R.H. prince Augustus Frederick of Great Britain; *afterwards* styled de Ameland, iii. 391.
Murray, Augusta, wife of capt. John Gunn Collins, iii. 391.
— Augustus Charles, commander R.N., iii. 389.
— — his wife, Abbie Lee, iii. 389.
— Barbara, wife of Alex. Murray of Woodend, iii. 398 ; ix. 78.
— Barbara, wife of Sir Jas. Johnstone of Westerhall, iii. 516.
— Barbara, wife of 8th lord Gray, iv. 290 ; viii. 203.
— Barbara, dau. of Sir Andrew M. of Inchmurray, viii. 202.
— Bessie, dau. of Alex. M. of Aberlednoch, i. 463.
— Bethia, wife of Sir Arch. Hamilton, ii. 42.
— Bethia, wife of William Murray of Ochtertyre, viii. 198.
— Blanche, wife of John Carruthers of Holmains, i. 222.
— Blanche Emmeline, wife of baron von Keudell, iii. 523.
— Caroline, dau. of 2nd earl of Mansfield, viii. 210.
— Caroline, dau. of 3rd earl of Mansfield, viii. 211.
— Caroline Leonora, wife of 3rd earl of Ilchester, i. 492.
— Cecil Henry Alexander, iii. 394.
— Cecilia Sarah, viii. 211.
— Charles, son of Cuthbert M. of Drumcreiff, i. 219.
— Charles, son of Sir Charles M. of Cockpool, i. 219.
— Charles, 3rd son of Cuthbert M. of Cockpool, i. 221.
— Charles, illeg. son of Sir David M. of Clonyaird, i. 225.
— Charles, 6th son of Sir Chas. M. of Cockpool, i. 225.
— — his wife, Giles *, i. 225.
— Sir Charles, major Royal Regt. of Horse, i. 467 *n.*
— Charles, 4th son of 1st duke of Atholl, i. 482.
— Charles, H.E.I.C.S., i. 492.
— — his wife, Anne Amelia Dashwood, i. 492.
— Charles, 7th son of 4th duke of Atholl, i. 498.
— Charles, 2nd son of 1st marquess of Atholl, iii. 383.
— — his wife, Katharine Watts, iii. 383.
— Charles, 4th son of 1st earl of Dunmore, iii. 385.
— Charles, 2nd son of 3rd earl of Dunmore, iii. 387.
— Charles, eldest son of Henry M. of Berkhampstead, iii. 399.

* Name unknown.

Murray, Charles, 2nd son of Thos. M. of Berkhampstead, iii. 400.
— Charles, burgess of Edinburgh, 4th son of John M. of Falahill, iii. 500.
— — his wife, Elizaboth Mowbray, iii. 500.
— Charles, viii. 146.
— — his wife, Isabella Somerville, viii. 146.
— Charles, 5th son of 5th viscount of Stormont, viii. 206.
— Charles, captain 28th Dragoons, viii. 209.
— — his wife, Elizabeth Law, viii. 209.
— Charles, colonel in army of the Parliament, viii. 412.
— Charles Archibald, viii. 210.
— — his 1st wife, Adelaide Emily Feilding, viii. 211.
— — his 2nd wife, Blanche Moncreiffe, viii. 211.
— Sir Charles Augustus, K.C.B., P.C., British minister to Swiss Confederation, Persia, Saxony, Denmark, and Portugal, iii. 392.
— — his 1st wife, Elise Wadsworth, iii. 393.
— — his 2nd wife, Edith Susan Esther Fitzpatrick, iii. 394.
— Charles Gideon, 3rd son of 10th lord Elibank, iii. 523.
— Charles Henry, 5th son of 7th lord Elibank, iii. 521; ix. 84.
— Charles John, barrister-at-law, viii. 210.
— — his wife, Frances Elizabeth Anson, viii. 210.
— Charles Knight, barrister, vii. 308.
— — his wife, Henrietta Anne Leslie, vii. 308.
— Charles Wadsworth, iii. 393.
— Charlotte, wife of Thos. Cooper, i. 477.
— Charlotte, dau. of lord George M., i. 485.
— Charlotte, wife of 3rd duke of Atholl, i. 489, 490.
— Charlotte, dau. of 3rd duke of Atholl, i. 494.
— Charlotte, wife of (1) Sir John Menzies, and (2) Sir Adam Drummond, i. 497.
— Charlotte, wife of W. H. Oliphant, iii. 522.
— Charlotte Augusta Leopoldina, wife of rev. C. d'E. Granville, i. 497.
— Charlotte Sophia, wife of rev. Townshend Selwyn, i. 492.
— Charlotte Wilhelmina, wife of (1) Wm. Scott, and (2) S. H. Ware, M.D., i. 493.
— Christian, wife of Sir Murdac Menteith of Rusky, i. 458.
— Christian, wife of 1st lord Seton, i. 461; viii. 576.
— Christian, wife of Geo. Douglas of Bonjedward, iii. 508.
Murray, Christian, wife of Henry Kinross, viii. 198.
— Christian, dau. of David M. of Letter Bannachty, viii. 200.
— Christian, dau. of Sir Andrew M. of Balvaird, ix. 161.
— Christina, dau. of Patrick M. of Woodend, iii. 398, 401.
— Cristina Teresa, wife of James, 7th earl of Findlater, iv. 40; ix. 90.
— Clara Isabel, wife of Oswald Partington, iii. 524.
— Clara Mary, dau. of 8th lord Elibank, iii. 522.
— Clara Melville, dau. of 7th lord Elibank, iii. 521.
— Constance Euphemia Woronzow, wife of 15th lord Elphinstone, iii. 394, 553.
— Cordelia, wife of lieut.-col. Robt. Arbuthnott, i. 307.
— Cordelia, wife of rev. Henry Hodges, iii. 516.
— Cuthbert, son of Cuthbert M. of Cockpool, i. 221.
— Cuthbert, eldest son of Sir Chas. M. of Cockpool, i. 224.
— David, 3rd son of Sir Wm. M. of Castleton, i. 461, 462.
— David, illeg. son of 2nd earl of Tullibardine, i. 472.
— David, merchant, Leith, ii. 597.
— Mr. David, 6th son of Patrick M. of Woodend, iii. 401; ix. 79.
— David, Lanarkshire, vi. 473.
— David, 4th son of David M. of Letter Bannachty, viii. 200 *bis*.
— David Henry, major Scots Fusilier Guards, iv. 295; viii. 211.
— — his wife, Margaret, baroness Gray, iv. 295; viii. 211.
— David Rodney, rector of Cusop and Brampton Brian, iii. 513.
— — his wife, Frances Portal, iii. 513.
— Diana, wife of James Denny, viii. 413 *bis*.
— Dudley Oliphant, barrister-at-law, iii. 522.
— Edward, capt., 6th son of 1st marquess of Atholl, i. 476; iii. 384 *bis*.
— — his wife, Katharine Skene, i. 477.
— Edward, 10th son of 4th duke of Atholl, i. 486.
— — his wife, Frances Harland, i. 487.
— Edward, vicar of Northolt, i. 492.
— — his wife, Ruperta Catherine Wright, i. 492.
— Edward, 3rd son of 4th duke of Atholl, i. 497.
— Edward Oliphant, capt. Queen's Own Cameron Highlanders, iii. 523.
— — his wife, Mary Millard Albusen, iii. 523.

Murray, Elizabeth, dau. of Cuthbert M. of Cockpool, i. 222.
— Elizabeth, wife of (1) Robert, 3rd lord Crichton, and (2) Herbert Maxwell, i. 222; iii. 225.
— Elizabeth, wife of (1) John Grierson, and (2) Wm. Grierson, i. 226, 229.
— Elizabeth, wife of Thos. Moncur of Month, i. 465.
— Elizabeth, wife of major John Murray, i. 487.
— Elizabeth, wife of Sir E. J. Murray-MacGregor, i. 498.
— Elizabeth, wife of Geo. Sinclair, ii. 353.
— Elisabeth, wife of rev. John Murray, dean of Killaloe, iii. 388.
— Elizabeth, wife of Patrick Murray of Woodend, iii. 398.
— Elizabeth, wife of (1) maj.-gen. R. Egerton, and (2) Chas. Egerton, iii. 399.
— Elizabeth, wife of Sir Henry Newton, *alias* Puckering, iii. 400.
— Elizabeth, wife of (1) Thos. Menzies, and (2) col. Jas. Murray, iii. 401.
— Elizabeth, wife of (1) Jas. Borthwick of Newbyres, and (2) Thos. Hamilton of Priestfield, iii. 504; iv. 307; ix. 83, 84, 100.
— Elizabeth, wife of Arch. Stirling, iii. 508.
— Elizabeth, dau. of 2nd lord Elibank, iii. 511.
— Elisabeth, dau. of 3rd lord Elibank, iii. 512.
— Elizabeth, dau. of 4th lord Elibank, iii. 517.
— Elizabeth, wife of David Smythe of Methven, iii. 517.
— Elizabeth, mistress of Sir James Hamilton of Finnart, iv. 362.
— Elizabeth, wife of Sir Robert Ker of Ancrum, v. 466, 467.
— Elizabeth, wife of Francis Stewart, vi. 323; viii. 202.
— Elizabeth, wife of David Balfour of Balledmont, viii. 189.
— Elizabeth, wife of Alex. Tosheach of Monzievaird, viii. 198; ix. 161.
— Elizabeth, dau. of 5th viscount of Stormont, viii. 207.
— Elizabeth, dau. of 3rd earl of Tullibardine, viii. 413.
— Elizabeth, dau. of 4th earl of Tullibardine, viii. 415.
— Elizabeth, wife of Simon Fraser of Inverallochy, ix. 29.
— Elizabeth Ann, wife of rear-admiral W. H. Shirreff, iii. 513.
— Elizabeth Ann, wife of William Buchanan, iii. 520.
— Elizabeth Anne, dau. of 3rd earl of Mansfield, viii. 211.
— Elizabeth Mary, wife of George Finch Hatton, viii. 209.
Murray, Elspeth, wife of Thos. Moncur, i. 465.
— Emilia, wife of (1) Hugh, 9th lord Lovat, and (2) Simon, 11th lord Lovat, i. 478; v. 534, 536, 538.
— Emilia, wife of Alexander Cochrane of Bollinshaw, iii. 351.
— Emilia, dau. of col. Geo. M. of Pittencreiff, iii. 509.
— Emily Blanche, wife of Sir R. G. Harvey, iii. 524.
— Emily Jane, wife of Sir John Oswald, i. 493.
— Emily Mary, wife of 5th marquess of Hertford, viii. 211.
— Esota, wife of Herbert Corry, i. 222.
— Eupheme, wife of (1) Robt. Stewart of Rosyth, (2) Robert Pitcairn, and (3) Sir Patrick Gray, i. 464; iv. 282.
— Evan John MacGregor, major-general, C.B., 2nd bart., i. 498.
— — his wife, Elizabeth Murray, i. 498.
— Evelyn, wife of J. D. Cobbold, iii. 395.
— Evelyn Izme, dau. of 10th lord Elibank, iii. 524.
— Florence Emily, wife of E. G. Gore-Langton, iii. 522.
— Frances Julia, wife of C. H. Maynard, i. 497.
— Francis, 2nd son of the commendator of Inchaffray, iii. 401.
— Frederica Louisa, wife of lieut.-col. J. H. Stanhope, viii. 211.
— Frederick, R.N., 11th son of 1st duke of Atholl, i. 487.
— Frederick John George, colonel, 3rd Dragoon Guards, viii. 211.
— Gavin, son of Sir Thos. M. of Cockpool, i. 217.
— Gavin, 5th son of Cuthbert M. of Cockpool, i. 221.
— George, 6th son of Cuthbert M. of Cockpool, i. 222.
— Sir George, groom of the bedchamber, i. 224.
— — his wife, Bridget Fleetwood, i. 224.
— George, 8th son of 1st marquess of Atholl, i. 477; vi. 394.
— George, lieut.-gen. to prince Charles Edward, i. 457, 482.
— — his wife, Amelia Murray, i. 484.
— George, bishop of St. David's, i. 491.
— — his wife, Anne Charlotte Grant, i. 491.
— George, bishop of Rochester, i. 491.
— — his wife, Sarah Maria Hay-Drummond, i. 491; v. 235.
— George, auditor of the Exchequer, iii. 520.
— George, 4th son of 8th lord Elibank, iii. 521.

Murray, George, lieut.-general, auditor of the Exchequer, viii. 209.
— George Earn, 4th son of capt. Virginius M., iii. 389.
— Georgiana Katharine, viii. 211.
— Gideon, chaplain-general to the Army, prebendary of Durham, iii. 512, 514.
— — his wife, Elizabeth Montolieu, iii. 512.
— Gideon, 2nd son of 7th lord Elibank, iii. 520.
— Giles, wife of Patrick Murray of Woodend, iii. 398.
— Grace, wife of W. J. Barry of Witchingham Hall, iii. 396.
— Harriet Buccleuch, dau. of 7th lord Elibank, iii. 521.
— Helen, wife of Alex. Seton of Parbroath, i. 461.
— Helen, wife of (1) Sir Alex. Auchmowtie, and (2) capt. Wm. Carstairs, iii. 509.
— Helen, wife of Patrick Murray, Edinburgh, iii. 511.
— Helen, wife of Sir John Mackenzie of Coul, iii. 512.
— Helen, wife of Sir John Stewart of Grandtully, iii. 517.
— Helen, dau. of 8th lord Elibank, iii. 522.
— Helen, wife of John Chrystison, viii. 188.
— Helen Anne, dau. of 7th lord Elibank, iii. 521.
— Helen Nicolas, 'Nicky,' dau. of 5th viscount of Stormont, viii. 207.
— Henriana Matilda, wife of rev. T. G. Leigh, i. 493.
— Henrietta, wife of Francis Cockburn, i. 468.
— Henrietta, wife of Sir John Dalzell, ii. 410.
— Henrietta, dau. of 2nd lord Elibank, iii. 511.
— Henrietta Maria, wife of (1) Charles, 2nd earl of Aboyne, and (2) Patrick, 3rd lord Kinnaird, iii. 386; v. 210.
— Henry, grandnephew of Sir Richard M. of Cockpool, i. 225.
— — his wife, Bessie Geddes, i. 225.
— Henry, ensign Coldstream Guards, i. 492.
— — his wife, Katharine Otway-Cave, i. 492.
— Henry, lieut.-col. Manx Fencibles, i. 493.
— — his wife, Elizabeth Kent, i. 493.
— Sir Henry, lieut.-general, K.C.B., viii. 209.
— — his wife, Emily Devisme, viii. 210.
— Henry Alexander, iii. 390.
— — his wife, Fannie Morris Babcock, iii. 390.
— Honry Anthony, rear-admiral R.N., iii. 394.
Murray, Herbert, 5th son of Sir Thos. M. of Cockpool, i. 217.
— Hilda Louisa Janey Wolfe, wife of lord Murray of Elibank, iii. 523.
— Humphrey, 4th son of Alex. M. of Aberlednoch, i. 463.
— Isabella, wife of Patrick Ogilvy of Muirton, i. 121.
— Isabel, wife of M. Drummond of Cencraig, i. 458.
— Isobel, wife of Sir James Murray of Baberton and Cavens, iii. 509, 510.
— Isabel, wife of John Brown of Fordell, viii. 200.
— Jack Charles, eldest son of lt.-col. Alex. M. of Frimley, iii. 389.
— Jack Henry, rear-admiral R.N., iii. 390.
— — his wife, Katharine Menzies, iii. 390.
— James, illeg. son of Sir James M. of Cockpool, i. 226.
— James, H.E.I.C.S., i. 484 *n.*
— James, 2nd son of 3rd duke of Atholl, i. 491.
— Sir James, 2nd son of 4th duke of Atholl; lieut.-gen., K.C.H., i. 496.
— — his wife, Emily Frances Percy, i. 496.
— James, 4th son of Thos. M. of Berkhampstead, iii. 400.
— James, colonel, governor of Edinburgh Castle, iii. 401.
— — his wife, Elizabeth Murray, iii. 401.
— James, in South Bowhill, iii. 500.
— James, in Sundhope, iii. 500.
— James, general, governor of Quebec, and Minorca, iii. 515.
— — his 1st wife, * Collier, iii. 516; ix. 84.
— — his 2nd wife, Anne Whitham, iii. 516.
— James, advocate, 4th son of 7th lord Elibank, iii. 521.
— — his wife, Isabella Erskine of Aberdona, iii. 521.
— James, M.D., Perth, iv. 567; viii. 202; ix. 112.
— — his wife, Helen Stewart, viii. 202.
— James, Bryanston Sq., vii. 591.
— James, advocate, M.P., Jacobite plenipotentiary, viii. 205.
— James, 2nd son of 6th viscount of Stormont, viii. 207.
— James, younger son of 4th earl of Tullibardine, viii. 415.
— James Arthur, vice-admiral, R.N., i. 493.
— — his 1st wife, Harriet Coupland, i. 493.
— — his 2nd wife, Julia Delmé, i. 493.
— James Charles Plantagenet, 3rd son of 1st lord Glenlyon, i. 497.
— — his wife, Elizabeth Marjory Fairholme, i. 497.

* Name unknown.

Murray, James Patrick, 44th regt., M.P., iii. 516.
—— his wife, Elizabeth Rushworth, iii. 516.
— Jane, dau. of Henry M. of Berkhampstead, iii. 400.
— Jane, wife of Sir John Bowyer, iii. 400 *ter*.
— Janet, wife of Andrew M. of Murraythwaite, i. 224.
— Janet, illeg. dau. of Sir Jas. M. of Cockpool, i. 226.
— Janet, wife of Sir Robt. Stewart of Minto, ii. 79.
— Janet, wife of James, lord Blair and viscount Fincastle, iii. 385.
— Janet, wife of Sir Robert Murray of Hillhead, iii. 517.
— Janet, wife of Patrick Lindsay, v. 409.
— Janet, wife of Charles Ker of King's Cramond, v. 478.
— Janet, wife of James Somerville of Drum, viii. 32; ix. 159.
— Janet, dau. of William M. of Little Ardit, viii. 187.
— Janet, wife of John Stretton, viii. 187.
— Janet, wife of (1) James, 1st lord Torphichen, (2) John Graham of Hallyards, and (3) Sir Peter Young, viii. 387.
— Janet, dau. of Alex. M. of Woodend, ix. 79.
— Janet, wife of Archd. Napier, ix. 79.
— Janet, wife of Jas. Hamilton of Kinnell, ix. 103.
— Janet Ferguson, wife of lt.-col. J. M. Carter, iii. 522.
— Janet Oliphant, wife of T. L. Leader, iii. 521.
— Janet Oliphant, wife of John Steuart of Dalguise, iii. 522.
— Jean, wife of James Henderson, i. 465.
— Jean, dau. of Sir Mungo M., i. 468.
— Jean, wife of Sir Patrick Hepburn, i. 470; ix. 29.
— Jean, wife of Angus M'Intosh, i. 472.
— Jean, dau. of 1st earl of Atholl, i. 473.
— Jean, wife of 20th earl of Crawford, i. 489; iii. 39.
— Jean, wife of J. G. Muirhead, i. 494.
— Jean, wife of Alex. Lindsay of Canterland, i. 514.
— Jean, dau. of 3rd earl of Dunmore, iii. 388.
— Jean, dau. of Mr. Wm. M., Dysart, iii. 399.
— Jean, wife of Sir Wm. Murray of Duncarne, iii. 509.
— Jean, dau. of lieut.-col. George M. of Pittencreiff, iii. 509.
— Jean, wife of Dr. R. Carmichael of Balmblae, iv. 567; viii. 202.
— Jean, wife of Sir Alexander Colyear *alias* Robertson, vii. 90.
Murray, Jean, wife of Sir Wm. Douglas of Drumlanrig, vii. 114.
— Jean, wife of Sir Andrew Myrton of Gogar, viii. 150.
— Jean, wife of John Rigge, viii. 200.
— Jean, dau. of 5th viscount of Stormont, viii. 207.
— Jean, wife of Thos. Murray of Woodend, ix. 79.
— John, capt., 2nd son of 1st earl of Tullibardine, i. 469.
— John, minister at Trinity Gask, i. 472.
— John, son of capt. Edward M., i. 477, 485.
—— his wife, Euphame Ross, i. 477; vii. 261.
— John, major, dean of Killaloe, i. 487.
—— his wife, Elisabeth Murray, i. 487; iii. 388.
— John, capt. H.M.S. *Port Mahon*, i. 491; ix. 29.
— John, M.D., South Carolina, iii. 81.
—— his wife, Anne Mackenzie, iii. 81.
— John, capt. R.N., 4th son of 4th earl of Dunmore, iii. 390.
— John, 3rd son of Alexander M. of Woodend, iii. 398.
— John, 3rd son of Thos. M. of Berkhampstead, iii. 400.
— John, minister at Methven, iii. 401.
—— his wife, Elizabeth Scrymgeour, iii. 401.
— John, in Sundhope, iii. 500.
— John, capt., 3rd son of 2nd lord Elibank, iii. 510.
— John, 5th son of 4th lord Elibank, iii. 513.
— John, in Eschiesteill, vii. 79.
—— his wife, Janet Scott, vii. 79.
— John, slain by David Lundie, viii. 190.
— John, master cook and browstar, viii. 293.
— John, foreman baxter, viii. 293.
— John, 2nd son of Sir Wm. M. of Claremont, ix. 29.
— John Oliphant, chamberlain to king of Bavaria, iii. 521.
— John Stevens, lieut. R.N., i. 484 *n*.
— Jonet, wife of James Henderson, i. 465.
— Juliana, wife of John Newport of Scupholm, viii. 413.
— Katharine, dau. of Alex. M. of Aberlednoch, i. 463.
— Katharine, wife of Robert Moray, i. 465.
— Katharine, wife of John Moncreiff, i. 468.
— Katharine, wife of 5th lord Rollo, i. 476; vii. 206.
— Katharine, dau. of 1st marquess of Atholl, i. 478.
— Katharine, wife of J. Somerville, ii. 83.

Murray, Katharine, wife of P. Campbell of Glentarken, ii. 186.
— Katharine, wife of Walter Scrimgeour of Glaswell and Torbirnis, iii. 310.
— Katharine, wife of 3rd lord Nairne, iii. 386; vi. 397.
— Katharine, wife of John Drummond of Logie Almond, iii. 388.
— Katharine, wife of Edward Bouverie, iii. 391.
— Katharine, dau. of 1st earl of Dysart, iii. 402.
— Katharine, dau. of 2nd lord Elibank, iii. 511.
— Katharine, dau. of 7th lord Elibank, iii. 521.
— Katharine, wife of 2nd earl of Kintore, v. 241; viii. 204.
— Katharine, wife of Sir John Murray of Drumcairn, viii. 200, 202.
— Katharine, wife of John Arnot of Freirton, viii. 200.
— Katharine, wife of James Balnavis of Glencarse, viii. 202.
— Katharine, dau. of Sir John M. of Drumcairn, viii. 202.
— Katharine, dau. of 1st lord Balvaird, viii. 203.
— Katharine, dau. of 5th viscount of Stormont, viii. 207.
— Katharine, dau. of brig.-gen. Robt. M., ix. 78.
— Katharine Maria, dau. of lord Henry M., i. 493.
— Lancelot, 3rd son of Sir Thos. M. of Cockpool, i. 217.
— Laurence, 5th son of Sir Wm. M. of Tullibardine, i. 464.
— Lilias, wife of John Grant, i. 470; vii. 467, 469.
— Leveson Granville Keith, Madras Civil Service, iii. 390.
— — his 1st wife, Wemyss Dalrymple, iii. 390; viii. 123.
— — his 2nd wife, Ann Thursby, iii. 390.
— Louisa, wife of Sir J. C. Reade, iii. 513.
— Louisa Anne, wife of Sir Robert Frankland, i. 492.
— Louisa Nina, wife of George Edwin Lascelles, viii. 213.
— Mabel Emily, wife of capt. Herbert Goodenough King Hall, viii. 213.
— Margaret, wife of Herbert Irving, i. 223.
— Margaret, illeg. dau. of Charles M., i. 225.
— Margaret, wife of Robert Macbrair, i. 225.
— Margaret, wife of Robert Grierson, i. 226.
— Margaret, wife of Thos. Stewart of Grandtully, i. 461.
Murray, Margaret, dau. of Alex. M. of Aberlednoch, i. 463.
— Margaret, wife of Robt. Bruce of Clackmannan, i. 465.
— Margaret, wife of Peter Hay of Blebo, i. 468.
— Margaret, dau. of Sir Mungo M. of Claremont, i. 468.
— Margaret, wife of James Haldane, i. 470.
— Margaret, wife of John Farquharson, i. 476.
— Margaret, dau. of Patrick M. of Falahill, wife of Wm. Murray of Traquair, and mistress of James Stewart, earl of Buchan, ii. 267; viii. 399.
— Margaret, wife of Henry Sutherland of Torboll, iii. 192.
— Margaret, wife of (1) archdeacon George Young, and (2) Sir Wm. Graham, iii. 321; ix. 74.
— Margaret, dau. of 3rd earl of Dunmore, iii. 388.
— Margaret, wife of Mr. Wm. Murray, Dysart, iii. 398.
— Margaret, dau. of above, iii. 398.
— Margaret, wife of Mr. George Gillespie, iii. 401.
— Margaret, wife of William, 2nd lord Maynard of Estaines ad Turrim, iii. 402.
— Margaret, contr. to Henry Wardlaw of Torry, and wife of William Little, iii. 502; ix. 83.
— Margaret, dau. of 2nd lord Elibank, iii. 511.
— Margaret, wife of William Mercer *or* Nairne of Aldie, iii. 548.
— Margaret, wife of Adam Bothwell, bishop of Orkney, commendator of Holyroodhouse, iv. 430.
— Margaret, wife of Sir John Hope of Craighall, iv. 489.
— Margaret, wife of Ralph Ker of Primsideloch, v. 52.
— Margaret, wife of Sir James Hay of Kingask, v. 218.
— Margaret, dau. of Sir John M. of Blackbarony, vi. 412.
— Margaret, wife of Arthur Myretoun of Pitollie, viii. 187.
— Margaret, wife of William Spens, viii. 189.
— Margaret, wife of William Myretoun of Cambo, viii. 190; ix. 160.
— Margaret, wife of Alex. Balcanqual of Balcanqual, viii. 198.
— Margaret, dau. of 5th viscount of Stormont, viii. 207.
— Margaret, alleged wife of Sir Alexander Seton, viii. 569 *n*.
— Margaret, 2nd dau. of Alex. M. of Woodend, ix. 79.

Murray, Margaret, 3rd dau. of Alex. M. of Woodend, ix. 79.
— Margaret Jane, wife of 16th lord Sinclair, vii. 591.
— Maria, dau. of 8th lord Elibank, iii. 522.
— Maria Clara, wife of Sir E. H. Lechmere, iii. 513.
— Marianne Oliphant, wife of P. H. Paterson, iii. 522.
— Marie, dau. of 1st earl of Annandale, i. 228.
— Marion, wife of Thos. Kirkpatrick of Closeburn, i. 222.
— Marion, wife of Robt. Butterwell, i. 225.
— Marion, wife of John Maxwell, i. 225.
— Marion, wife of John Murray of Broughton, i. 226, 229.
— Marion, wife of Sir M. Drummond of Cargill, i. 458.
— Marion, wife of Jas. Pringle of Whitebank, iii. 503.
— Mariota, dau. of Sir Thomas M. of Cockpool and Ryvel, i. 218.
— Marjory, dau. of 8th earl of Dunmore, iii. 395.
— Marjory, wife of col. J. Hay of Cromlix, v. 231; viii. 207.
— Marjory, dau. of William M. of Drumcairn, viii. 200.
— Marjory, wife of Sir Alex. Gibson of Durie, viii. 203.
— Marjory, dau. of 6th viscount of Stormont, viii. 208.
— Marjory Louisa, wife of Sir Kenneth John Mackenzie of Gairloch, viii. 213.
— Mary, dau. of Sir Mungo M., i. 468.
— Mary, 2nd wife of Sir John Moncreiffe, i. 472.
— Mary, dau. of lord Edward M., i. 487.
— Mary, wife of 6th earl of Findlater, i. 487; iv. 40; ix. 90.
— Mary, wife of rev. George Martin, i. 495.
— Mary, wife of 2nd earl of Cromartie, iii. 77.
— Mary, wife of Sir Roger Bradshaigh, iii. 400.
— Mary, wife of James Bonar, iii. 401.
— Mary, wife of John, master of Tarbet, iii. 512.
— Mary, dau. of 4th lord Elibank, iii. 517.
— Mary, wife of A. F. Lindley, iii. 520.
— Mary, dau. of 8th lord Elibank, iii. 522.
— Mary, wife of (1) *, and (2), Alan Kinnaird of Kinnaird, v. 204.
— Mary, dau. of 5th viscount of Stormont, viii. 207.
— Mary Alice Oliphant, iii. 523.
— Mary Anne, dau. of lord William M., i. 493.
— Maurice, wright, Glasgow, v. 180.

* Name unknown.

Murray, Mildred, wife of Gilbert Follett, iii. 396.
— Mona Elizabeth, i. 493.
— 'Muckle-mouthed Meg,' iii. 507 *n.*; vii. 77.
— Mungo, 5th son of 1st marquess of Atholl, i. 476.
— Mungo, 5th son of Alex. M. of Woodend, iii. 402; ix. 79.
— Mungo, 2nd son of 2nd earl of Tullibardine, ix. 29.
— Muriel, wife of col. H. Gore-Browne iii. 396.
— Nicolas, wife of Robt. Maxwell of Kirkhouse, i. 225; iii. 127.
— Nicolas, dau. of Sir Mungo M., i. 468.
— Nicolas Helen, 'Nicky,' dau. of 5th viscount of Stormont, viii. 207.
— Nina Charlotte, wife of Hylton Philipson, iii. 524.
— Patrick, illeg. son of Patrick M. of Cockpool, i. 216.
— Patrick, tutor of Cockpool, i. 222.
— — his wife, Janet Campbell, i. 222.
— Patrick, commendator of Inchaffray, iii. 400.
— — his 1st wife, Helen M'Math, iii. 400.
— — his 2nd wife, Magdalene Conall, iii. 401; ix. 79.
— Patrick, 3rd son of above, iii. 401.
— Patrick, son of Sir Jas. M. of Skirling, iii. 511.
— — his wife, Helen Murray, iii. 511.
— Patrick, elder son of 4th earl of Tullibardine, viii. 415.
— Patrick Oliphant, captain Madras M.S., iii. 521.
— — his wife, Harriet Phillips Collom, iii. 521.
— Peter, in South Bowhill, iii. 500.
— — his wife, Jonet Borthwick, iii. 500.
— Rebecca, wife of George Shaw, viii. 202.
— Reginald Augustus Frederick, iii. 389.
— — his wife, Louisa Ford, iii. 389.
— Richard, lieut.-col., son of lord Henry M., i. 493.
— — his 1st wife, Katharine Bacon, i. 493.
— — his 2nd wife, Margaret Tennison, i. 493.
— Sir Richard, bart., ii. 73.
— — his wife, Mary Bellenden, ii. 73.
— Richard, 6th son of 1st earl of Dunmore, iii. 385.
— Robert, vicar of Anwoth, i. 225.
— Robert, 4th son of Sir David M. of Tullibardine, i. 457.
— Robert, 5th son of 1st earl of Tullibardine, i. 470; ix. 29.
— Robert, 4th son of 4th duke of Atholl, i. 497.
— Sir Robert, Justice-Clerk, i. 519.
— — his wife, Sophia Lindsay, i. 519.

Murray, Robert, brigadier-general, M.P., 3rd son of 1st earl of Dunmore, iii. 385; ix. 78.
—— —— his wife, Mary Halket, ix. 78.
—— Robert, 4th son of Henry M. of Berkhampstead, iii. 399.
—— Robert, minister at Strathmiglo, and Methven, iii. 401; vi. 105.
—— —— his wife, Elizabeth Melville, iii. 401; vi. 105.
—— Robert, iii. 566.
—— —— his wife, Margaret Logie of Logiealmond, iii. 566.
—— Robert, archdeacon of Dunkeld, viii. 188.
—— Robert, 6th son of 5th viscount of Stormont, viii. 206.
—— Robert Dundas, 6th son of 7th lord Elibank, iii. 521.
—— Roger, in Sundhope, burgess of Edinburgh, iii. 500, 501.
—— Ronald, 3rd son of capt. Virginius M., iii. 389.
—— Samuel Hood, lieut.-col., iii. 391.
—— —— his wife, Susan Sempill, iii. 391.
—— Sophia, dau. of 1st earl of Annandale, i. 228; vi. 487.
—— Susan, wife of 2nd earl of Aberdeen, i. 90, 485; ix. 5.
—— Susan, wife of (1) J. Tharp, (2) John Drew, and (3) rev. A. E. Douglas, iii. 391.
—— Susan Catharine Mary, wife of 9th earl of Southesk, iii. 394; viii. 91.
—— Susan Emma, wife of rev. John Glover, iii. 390.
—— Sybil Louisa, wife of lt.-col. C. H. C. Willoughby, iii. 393.
—— Thomas, 10th son of Sir David M. of Tullibardine, i. 458.
—— Thomas, iii. 33.
—— —— his wife, Margaret Lindsay, iii. 33.
—— Thomas, 3rd son of Henry M. of Berkhampstead, iii. 399.
—— Thomas, 6th son of 1st lord Elibank, iii. 510.
—— Thomas Montolieu, 3rd son of 8th lord Elibank, iii. 521.
—— Verah, dau. of 3rd earl of Tullibardine, viii. 413.
—— Victoria Alexandrina, dau. of 7th earl of Dunmore, iii. 396.
—— Virginia, dau. of Henry Alexander M., iii. 390.
—— Virginia, a canoness, iii. 390.
—— Virginia, dau. of 4th earl of Dunmore, iii. 392.
—— Virginius, capt. 94th regt., commissioner of goldfields, iii. 389.
—— —— his wife, Elizabeth Alicia Poitiers, iii. 389.
—— Walter, 7th son of Sir David M. of Tullibardine, i. 458.
Murray, Walter, brother of Sir Alexander M. of Drumsergarth, vii. 237.
—— Walter, servant of James, earl of Bothwell, vii. 583 *bis*.
—— Wemyss Jane, wife of (1) major C. H. Campbell, and (2) lt.-col. C. S. Maling, iii. 390.
—— William, 4th son of 1st marquess of Atholl, i. 476; vi. 394.
—— —— his wife, Margaret Nairne, vi. 394.
—— William, 42nd, 77th, and 73rd regts., i. 492; ix. 29.
—— —— his wife, Mary Anne Hodges, i. 493.
—— William, post-captain R.N., iii. 387.
—— —— his wife, Sarah Mease, iii. 388.
—— William, 3rd son of 4th earl of Dunmore, iii. 389.
—— William, 4th son of Alexander M. of Woodend, iii. 398.
—— William, minister and parson of Dysart, iii. 398, 401; ix. 79 *bis*.
—— —— his wife, Margaret Murray, iii. 398.
—— William, 5th son of Thos. M. of Berkhampstead, iii. 400.
—— William, St. Mary le Savoy, iii. 402 *n*.
—— William, in Sundhope, iii. 499, 500, 501 *bis*.
—— William, in Warmwood, iii. 500.
—— William, his majesty's troop of Guards, iii. 510.
—— William, advocate, viii. 202.
—— William, M.P., lord Chief-Justice of the King's Bench, viii. 205.
—— —— his wife, Elizabeth Finch, viii. 206.
—— William, musicianer to 1st earl of Kinghorne, viii. 293.
—— William, brother of 4th earl of Tullibardine, viii. 412.
—— William, captain of Edinburgh Castle, viii. 569 *n*., 570.
—— William-Mina, wife of rev. Jas. Douglas, iii. 516.
—— *see also* Moray.
—— *see also* Stewart-Murray, i. 500.
Murray *or* Crichton of Glenmuir and Castle Murray, Sir Robert, i. 229, 476; viii. 218, 452.
—— —— his wife, Margaret Drummond, viii. 218.
—— Anna, wife of lord Jas. Murray, i. 475; iii. 228.
—— Jean, wife of George Stirling of Auchyll, iii. 228.
Murray *or* Robertson, John, lieut. 42nd regt., i. 486 *n*.
Murray-Aynsley, Athole Keturah, wife of rev. Sir Herbert Oakeley, i. 494.
—— Charles, dean of Bocking, 7th son of 3rd duke of Atholl, i. 494.
—— —— his wife, Alicia Midford Aynsley, i. 494.
—— Charlotte, wife of Sir J. Oswald, i. 494.
—— Elizabeth Anne, i. 494.

Murray-Aynsley, John, of Little Harle Tower, i. 494.
—— his wife, Emma Sarah Peach, i. 494.
Murray-Graham of Murrayshall, Henry Stewart, lieut.-col., viii. 201.
Murray-Kennedy of Knocknalling, John, M.V.O., vii. 591.
— Violet Frances, wife of capt. Archibald James Murray St. Clair, vii. 591.
Murray-Keith, Sir Robert, vi. 62.
Murray-MacGregor, Sir Evan John, major-general, C.B., 2nd bart., i. 498.
—— his wife, Elizabeth Murray, i. 498.
Murray-Mackenzie of Cromarty, Maria, wife of Edward Hay of Newhall, iii. 83, 519.
—— Isabella, dau. of 6th lord Elibank, iii. 83, 520.
Murray-Stewart of Broughton and Cally, Horatio Granville, i. 221.
Murref, Thomas de, 1336, ii. 128 *n.*; ix. 40.
Murrells, Frances, 2nd wife of 4th earl of Portmore, vii. 96.
— William, vii. 96.
Murthockston of that Ilk, *, wife of Richard le Scot, ii. 225.
Musbrig, Hugh of, viii. 368.
Muscamp of Wooler, Robert de, vi. 194.
Muschamp, Sir Robert de, iv. 331; v. 577; viii. 246.
— Marjory de, wife of Malise, 5th earl of Strathearn, viii. 246, 247.
Muschet of Burnbank, James, viii. 168.
—— his wife, Marion Alexander, viii. 168.
— of Craighead, Robert, ii. 202.
— of Finlarig, James, ii. 179.
— of Tolgarth, James, vi. 146.
—— James, ii. 179.
— Christian, wife of Sir John Campbell, ii. 202.
— Janet, wife of John Rutherfurd, vii. 372.
— Margaret, wife of Sir Michael Balfour, i. 532.
— Margaret, wife of John Graham of Kilbride, vi. 146.
Musgrave of Cumcatch, Thomas, vii. 100.
— of Norton Conyers, Sir Thomas, vii. 100.
— of Scaleby and Hayton Castle, Sir Edward, vii. 101.
—— his wife, Mary Graham, vii. 101.
— Henry, illeg. son of 4th viscount Dunbar, iii. 299 *n.*
— Katharine, wife of Sir R. Graham of Esk and Netherby, vii. 100.
— Sir Thomas, warden of Berwick, iv. 515.

* Name unknown.

MUSSELBURGH, MAITLAND, LORD THIRLESTANE AND, v. 305.
Musters, Robert de, ii. 373.
Musurus Pasha, ii. 246.
Mylne, Sir Robert, provost of Linlithgow, ix. 85.
—— his wife, Jean Elphinstone, ix. 85.
— rev. R. S., ix. 85.
Myreton of Cambo, Thomas, v. 398.
—— his wife, Katharine Lindsay, v. 398.
—— Sir Thomas, ii. 573; iv. 566.
—— his wife, * Halket, ii. 573.
—— William, vii. 17; viii. 190.
—— his wife, Margaret Murray, viii. 190; ix. 160.
— of Gogar, Sir Andrew, bart., viii. 150.
—— his wife, Jean Murray, viii. 150.
— of Pitollie, Arthur, viii. 187.
—— his wife, Margaret Murray, viii. 187.
— Euphan, wife of (1) Robert, 1st lord Colvill of Ochiltree, and (2) James Carmichael of Balmblae, ii. 573; iv. 567; ix. 59.
— Euphame, wife of Geo. Dalrymple of Dalmahoy, viii. 150.
— Katharine, wife of Robert Maule, commissary of St. Andrews, vii. 17.
— Margaret, wife of David Carmichael of Balmedie, iv. 566.

NAESMYTH of Ersiltoun, John, iv. 474.
— of Posso, Sir James, 1st bart., vi. 498.
—— Sir James, 3rd bart., viii. 130.
—— Sir Richard, iv. 93.
—— his wife, Janet Bruce, iv. 93.
— Anne, wife of Jas. Livingston of Biel and Skirling, vi. 450; ix. 143.
— John, Prestonpans, iii. 94.
—— his wife, Margaret Ramsay, iii. 94.
— John, chirurgeon to king James VI., iii. 400; vi. 450.
—— his wife, Helen M'Math, iii. 400.
— Mary, wife of (1) James Dalrymple, and (2) Fitzherbert Macqueen, viii. 130.
— Violet, wife of Jas. Carnegie of Finavon, vi. 498.
NAIRN, NAIRN, LORD, vi. 390-401.
Nairn, Emily Jane, wife of Henry, 4th marquess of Lansdowne; baroness, vi. 399.
— Henry Charles Keith Petty, eighth baron, vi. 400.
—— his wife, Maude Evelyn Hamilton, vi. 400.
— John, third lord, vi. 397.
—— his wife, Katharine Murray, iii. 386; vi. 397.
— Margaret, wife of count de Flahault de la Billardrie; baroness, vi. 398.
— Robert, first lord, vi. 393.
—— his wife, Margaret Graham, vi. 394.

* Name unknown.

Nairn, William, second lord, i. 476; vi. 394.
—— —— his wife, Margaret Nairn, i. 477; vi. 394, 395.
—— William, fourth lord, vi. 398.
—— —— his wife, Caroline Oliphant, vi. 398.
—— William, fifth lord, vi. 398.
—— William (Murray), earl of, vi. 395.
NAIRN, LORD NAIRN, vi. 390-401.
Nairn(e of Aldie, William, iii. 548.
—— —— his wife, Margaret Murray, iii. 548.
—— of Auchroisk, John, vii. 458.
—— of Baky, David, viii. 277.
—— of Bannockburn, Robert, advocate, vi. 392.
—— of Benchills, Jean, dau. of John N. of Mukkersy, vi. 393.
—— —— Margaret, wife of Alex. Carnegie of Kinfauns, vi. 393.
—— of Cromdale, John, vii. 458.
—— of Drumkilbo, David, viii. 296.
—— —— his wife, Susanna Lyon, viii. 296.
—— of Dunsinnan, Sir Thomas, viii. 109.
—— of Garden, Robert, vi. 392.
—— of Greenyards, Alexander, advocate, vi. 393.
—— —— his wife, Euphame Easton, vi. 393.
—— —— Alexander, vi. 393.
—— of Easter Greenyards, Robert, advocate, vi. 392.
—— of Kinclevin, John, vi. 391.
—— of Morenge, vii. 471.
—— of Mukkersy, George, 2nd laird, vi. 390.
—— —— George, 3rd laird, vi. 390.
—— —— his 2nd wife, Elizabeth *or* Isobel Davidson, vi. 391.
—— —— John, 1st laird, vi. 390.
—— —— his wife, Margaret Oliphant, vi. 390.
—— —— John, 4th laird, vi. 391.
—— —— John, sheriff-depute of Perth, vi. 392.
—— —— his wife, Barbara Cant, vi. 393.
—— —— Robert, advocate, vi. 392.
—— —— his wife, Katharine Preston, vi. 392.
—— —— Thomas, 5th laird, vi. 391, 392.
—— —— his wife, Elizabeth Fyfe, vi. 392.
—— of Ochtergavin, Thomas, vi. 392.
—— of Sandford, *, vi. 390.
—— —— David, vi. 495; vii. 13.
—— of Strathurd, *, iii. 398.
—— —— Robert, advocate, i. 121; vi. 392.
—— —— Sir Robert, vi. 392, 393.
—— —— his wife, Margaret Graham, vi. 394.
—— Agnes, wife of Patrick Murray of Woodend, iii. 398; ix. 79.
—— Agnes, wife of Wm. Blair of Tarsappie, vi. 393.
—— Amelia Ann Sophia, wife of Laurence Oliphant of Gask, vi. 396.

* Name unknown.

Nairn(e, Alexander, 5th son of George N. of Mukkersy, vi. 391.
—— Alexander, 4th son of John N. of Mukkersy, vi. 391.
—— Anne, wife of Wm. Drummond, viii. 229.
—— Ann, wife of Alex. Livingston, viii. 374.
—— Archibald, vi. 391.
—— —— his wife, Katharine Ramsay, vi. 391.
—— Brabazon, dau. of lieut.-col. John N., vi. 398.
—— Charles, officer in the Dutch service, vi. 397.
—— Charlotte, wife of John Robertson of Lude, vi. 396.
—— Clementina, dau. of 3rd lord Nairn, vi. 398.
—— David, major in French service, viii. 229.
—— Edward, 6th son of 3rd lord Nairn, vi. 397.
—— Elizabeth, wife of Sir David Falconer of Newton, v. 247; vi. 393.
—— George, eldest son of John N. of Mukkersy, vi. 391.
—— George, 2nd son of Geo. N. of Mukkersy, vi. 391.
—— George, elder son of Thomas N. of Mukkersy, vi. 392.
—— Helen, dau. of John N. of Mukkersy, vi. 391.
—— Henrietta, dau. of 2nd lord Nairn, vi. 397.
—— Henry, officer in the French service, vi. 398.
—— Isobel, dau. of George N. of Mukkersy, vi. 391.
—— Isobel, wife of Alex. Grant, vii. 470.
—— James, 6th son of George N. of Mukkersy, vi. 391.
—— James, 4th son of Robert N. of Mukkersy, vi. 393.
—— James, 4th son of 2nd lord Nairn, vi. 396.
—— James, eldest son of 3rd lord Nairn, vi. 397.
—— James Drummond, viii. 225.
—— Jane, wife of M. P. Drummond, viii. 225.
—— John of, deputy-bailie, iv. 48.
—— John, lieut.-colonel 1st Royals, vi. 398.
—— —— his wife, Brabazon Wheeler, vi. 398.
—— John, captain-lieutenant in Fraser's 71st regt., vi. 398.
—— John, merchant, Edinburgh, viii. 374.
—— Katharine, wife of (1) Walter Stewart, and (2) James Ogilvy of Muirton, i. 121.
—— Katharine, wife of 3rd earl of Dunmore, iii. 387; vi. 396.

Nairn(e, Louisa, wife of David Graham of Orchil, vi. 397.
—— Margaret, wife of William Murray, lord Nairn, i. 477; iv. 394, 395.
—— Margaret, wife of William Gray, vi. 392.
—— Margaret, wife of 4th viscount of Strathallan, vi. 396; viii. 228.
—— Margaret, dau. of 3rd lord Nairn, vi. 398.
—— Margaret, wife of Alex. Carnegie of Kinfauns, vi. 499.
—— Marjory, wife of Duncan Robertson of Drumachin, vi. 396.
—— Mary, dau. of 2nd lord Nairn, vi. 396.
—— Mary, wife of lieut. Cook, R.N., vi. 396.
—— Rebecca, wife of John Fullarton of Fullarton, viii. 109.
—— Robert, 3rd son of George N. of Mukkersy, vi. 391.
—— Robert, 5th son of 3rd lord Nairn, vi. 397.
—— Thomas, 7th son of George N. of Mukkersy, vi. 391.
—— Thomas, 7th son of 3rd lord Nairn, vi. 398.
—— William, burgess of Dunkeld, vi. 391 *bis*.
—— William, captain in the service of king Charles II., vi. 393.
—— William, captain of the *Calmar*, vi. 396.
—— William, 2nd son of 3rd lord Nairn, vi. 397.
—— William, son of David N. of Sandford, vii. 13.
—— —— his wife, Marjory Maule, vi. 495; vii. 13.
—— *, wife of John Falconer, v. 250.
Namur, Guy, comte de, iii. 89; vi. 296.
Naper of Kilmahew, John, vi. 403 *bis*.
—— of Merchiston, Alexander, provost of Edinburgh, vi. 403.
—— John le, king's hunter, Essex, vi. 402.
—— John le, first mention in Scotland, vi. 402, 403.
—— John le, Dumbartonshire, vi. 402.
—— John le, Peeblesshire, vi. 402.
—— Matthew le, Forfarshire, vi. 402.
—— Meingot, Essex, vi. 402.
—— Robert, Lincolnshire, vi. 402.
—— Thomas le, forester of Shotover, vi. 402.
—— William le, Waltham, vi. 402.
—— *see also* Napier.
Napier and Ettrick, Archibald, ancestor of the family of, iv. 428.
NAPIER OF MERCHISTON, NAPIER, LORD, vi. 402-439.
Napier of Merchiston, Archibald, first lord, vi. 420, 422.
—— —— his wife, Margaret Graham, vi. 241, 424.
—— —— Archibald, second lord, vi. 425.
—— —— his wife, Elizabeth Erskine, v. 624; vi. 252, 425.

* Name unknown.

Napier of Merchiston, Archibald, third lord, vi. 426.
—— —— Francis, sixth lord, vi, 428, 432.
—— —— his 1st wife, Henrietta Hope, iv. 496; vi. 432.
—— —— his 2nd wife, Henrietta Maria Johnston, vi. 432.
—— —— Francis, eighth lord, vi. 435.
—— —— his wife, Maria Margaret Clavering, vi. 436.
—— —— Francis, tenth lord, vi. 437.
—— —— his wife, Anne Jane Charlotte Lockwood, vi. 438.
—— —— Margaret, wife of John Brisbane; baroness, vi. 419, 427.
—— —— Thomas, fourth lord, vi. 427.
—— —— William, seventh lord, vi. 434.
—— —— his wife, Mary Anne Cathcart, vi. 435.
—— —— William John, ninth lord, vi. 436.
—— —— his wife, Elizabeth Cochrane Johnstone, iii. 360; vi. 437.
—— —— William John George, eleventh baron, vi. 438.
—— —— his 1st wife, Harriet B. A. Lumb, vi. 438.
—— —— his 2nd wife, Grace Burns, vi. 438.
—— master of, Francis Edward Basil, eldest son of 2nd baron Napier and Ettrick, vi. 438.
—— —— his wife, Clarice Jessie Evelyn Hamilton, ii. 59; vi. 438.
—— master of, John, only son of Margaret, baroness Napier of Merchiston, vi. 428.
—— mistress of, Elizabeth, wife of Sir William Scott of Thirlestane, vi. 428.
NAPIER, BARON ETTRICK OF ETTRICK, vi. 437-439.
NAPIER, LORD NAPIER OF MERCHISTON, vi. 402-439.
Napier of Abden, Helen, wife of Sir John Melville of Raith, vi. 89 *bis*, 101.
—— of Annaston, John, vi. 407.
—— of Ardmore, William, vi. 421.
—— —— his wife, Margaret Cuningham, vi. 421.
—— of Auchterarder, Cargill, etc., Duncan, vii. 35.
—— —— William, vii. 35.
—— of Balbertane, Alexander, vi. 405.
—— of Balcormo, John, vi. 408.
—— —— his wife, Margaret Preston, vi. 408.
—— of Ballacharne, Robert, vi. 418, 420.
—— of Ballikinrain, vi. 403.
—— —— Robert Dunmore, vi. 156.
—— of Barnisdale, Archibald, vi. 410.
—— of Blackstoun, Adam, ancestor of the family of, vi. 421.
—— —— his wife, Anna Buchanan, vi. 421.
—— of Boquhopple, Alexander, vi. 420.

Napier of Boquhopple, Robert, vi. 420.
—— —— his 1st wife, *, vi. 420.
—— —— his 2nd wife, Anna Drummond, vi. 420.
—— of Calziemuck, George, vi. 407, 408.
—— of Corstorphine, Sir Archibald, vi. 416.
—— of Craigannet, William, ancestor of the family of, vi. 421.
—— of Croftangrie, Francis, vi. 415.
—— —— his wife, Margaret Mowbray, vi. 415.
—— of Culcreuch, Alexander, vi. 420.
—— —— Robert, vi. 420, 425.
—— —— William, vi. 420.
—— of Edinbellie, Sir Alexander, vi. 411.
—— —— his wife, Janet Chisholm, vi. 411.
—— —— Archibald, vi. 410.
—— —— Sir Archibald, vi. 413.
—— of Gargunnock, Alexander, vi. 411, 412.
—— of Gartness, Sir Alexander, vi. 411.
—— —— Archibald, vi. 409.
—— of Inchemone, John, vi. 419.
—— —— his wife, Anne Chisholm, vi. 419.
—— of Inglistoun, Alexander, vi. 411, 412.
—— —— his wife, Isabel *or* Katharine Little, vi. 411.
—— —— John, vi. 407.
—— —— Mungo, vi. 411.
—— of Kilmahew, John, vi. 403 *bis*.
—— —— John, iv. 243.
—— —— his wife, Susanna Cunningham, iv. 243.
—— —— John, iv. 250.
—— —— John, iii. 490.
—— —— his wife, Jean Bruce, iii. 490.
—— —— Margaret, wife of (1) P. Maxwell of Newark, and (2) John, 10th earl of Glencairn, iv. 250.
—— of Lauriston, Sir Alexander, senator of the College of Justice, vi. 414, 416, 421, 422.
—— —— his wife, Mary Craufurd, vi. 416.
—— —— Alexander, his son, vi. 416.
—— —— Sir Archibald, iv. 89; vi. 414; vii. 192.
—— —— his 2nd wife, Elizabeth Moubray, vi. 414.
—— of Leslie, Henry, joint-admiral-depute, ii. 143; vi. 406.
—— —— his wife, Janet Ramsay, vi. 406.
—— of Luton Hoo, Alexander, ancestor of the family of, vi. 413.
—— —— Sir Robert, bart., ii. 583.
—— —— his 2nd wife, Penelope Egerton, ii. 583.
—— of Merchiston, Alexander, 1st laird, vi. 403.
—— —— Sir Alexander, 2nd laird, vi. 404.
—— —— his wife, Elizabeth Lauder, vi. 406.

* Name unknown.

Napier of Merchiston, Alexander, 5th laird, ii. 180; vi. 412; ix. 83.
—— —— his contr. wife, Agnes Murray, iii. 502; vi. 412.
—— —— his wife, Annabella Campbell, ii. 180; vi. 413.
—— —— Sir Alexander, 8th laird, vi. 422.
—— —— his wife, Margaret Graham, vi. 424.
—— —— Archibald, 4th laird, i.; 335 vi. 408.
—— —— his 1st wife, Katharine Douglas, vi. 409, 410.
—— —— his 2nd wife, Elizabeth Crichton, vi. 410.
—— —— his 3rd wife, Margaret Campbell, ii. 177; vi. 410, 412; ix. 42.
—— —— Sir Archibald, 6th laird, vi. 413.
—— —— his 1st wife, Janet Bothwell, iv. 428; vi. 415.
—— —— his 2nd wife, Elizabeth Moubray, iv. 89; vi. 415.
—— —— John, 3rd laird, vi. 407.
—— —— his wife, Elizabeth Menteith of Rusky, v. 341; vi. 407.
—— —— John, 7th laird, inventor of logarithms, iv. 428; vi. 413, 417.
—— —— his 1st wife, Elizabeth Stirling, vi. 418.
—— —— his 2nd wife, Anne Chisholm, vi. 420.
—— of Merchiston Hall, Charles, captain, R.N., vi. 432.
—— —— his 1st wife, Grizel Warrender, vi. 432.
—— —— his 2nd wife, Christian Hamilton, vi. 432.
—— of Napier, Sir Archibald Lennox Milliken, 10th bart., vi. 420.
—— of West Nisbet, Adam, vi. 421.
—— —— his wife, Anna Buchanan, vi. 421.
—— —— Archibald, vi. 421.
—— of Phildes, Alexander, v. 429; vi. 404.
—— of Pitliver, Francis, vi. 415.
—— of the Pultrielands, Sir Alexander, vi. 405.
—— —— John, vi. 407.
—— of Rusky, John, vi. 407.
—— —— his wife, Elizabeth Menteith, vi. 407.
—— of Schanbodie, John, vi. 420.
—— —— his wife, Mary Foulis, vi. 420.
—— of Tomdarroch, Robert, vi. 418, 420.
—— of Torrie-Easter, Alexander, vi. 421.
—— —— his wife, Anne Duncanson, vi. 421; ix. 142.
—— —— Anne, vi. 421.
—— —— John, vi. 420.
—— —— his wife, Mary Foulis, vi. 420.
—— —— William, vi. 421.
—— —— his wife, Margaret Cunningham, vi. 421.
—— of Woolmet, Archibald, vi. 414, 416.
—— —— his wife, Alison Edmonston, vi. 416.
—— of Wrightshouses, vi. 403.

Napier of Wrightshouses, Robert, vi. 410.
—— —— his wife, Margaret Napier, vi. 410.
—— —— William, ix. 91.
—— —— his wife, J. Forrester, ix. 91.
—— Abellina, wife of William Wardlaw of Riccarton, vi. 417.
—— Agnes, wife of (1) Sir P. Gray, (2) Henry Balfour, and (3) John Ogilvy, i. 123; iv. 282; vi. 417.
—— Agnes, wife of George Drummond of Balloch, vi. 421.
—— Agnes Dundas, vi. 432.
—— Alexander, 3rd son of Sir Alexander N. of Merchiston, vi. 406.
—— Alexander, 3rd son of maj.-gen. Mark N., vi. 433.
—— Andrew, burgess of Edinburgh, vi. 413.
—— —— his wife, Janet Kyle, vi. 413.
—— Anna, wife of William Berclay, vi. 413.
—— Anna, wife of Wm. Cunningham of Broomhill, vi. 420; ix. 142.
—— Anna, dau. of Adam N. of West Nisbet, vi. 421.
—— Anne, wife of Sir Thomas Gibson Carmichael, vi. 436.
—— Anne Carmichael, wife of capt. G. Hope, iv. 503; vi. 437.
—— Archibald, son of Andrew N., Edinburgh, vi. 413.
—— Archibald, eldest son of Robert N. of Boquhopple, vi. 420.
—— Archibald, ix. 79.
—— —— his wife, Janet Murray, ix. 79.
—— Archibald Lennox Colquhoun William John George, vi. 439.
—— Augusta Caroline Harriet Georgina, ii. 59; vi. 438.
—— Barbara, wife of Sir James Calder of Slamannan, viii. 389.
—— Barbara, dau. of John N. of Merchiston, ix. 142.
—— Basil, lieut. R.N., vi. 438.
—— Basil, Imperial Yeomanry, vi. 438.
—— Bessie, wife of Sir Archd. Campbell of Glencarradale, v. 504; ix. 142.
—— Caroline, wife of Neville Reid, vi. 436.
—— Sir Charles, K.C.B., admiral of the Blue, vi. 432.
—— Charles, major, vi. 436.
—— —— his 1st wife, Alice Emma Barnston, vi. 436.
—— —— his 2nd wife, Annabella Jane Gatacre, vi. 436.
—— Sir Charles James, lieut.-general, commander-in-chief in India, vi. 434.
—— Christian Graham, wife of Chas. Campbell of Combie, vi. 432.
—— Claude Inverness, vi. 438.
—— Eliza, wife of admiral Sir J. C. Dalrymple Hay, vi. 437.
Napier, Elizabeth, wife of (1) James, 6th lord Ogilvy of Airlie, and (2) Alexander Auchmoutie, i. 122; vi. 417.
—— Elizabeth, wife of (1) col. Walter Scott of Harlawood, and (2) col. Sir Bryce Cochrane, iii. 342; ix. 75.
—— Elizabeth, wife of (1) H. Colquhoun of Luss, and (2) Robert, 3rd lord Boyd, v. 155.
—— Elizabeth, a nun at Sciennes, vi. 410.
—— Elizabeth, dau. of Sir Alexander N. of Lauriston, vi. 416.
—— Elizabeth, wife of Wm. Cunningham, vi. 421.
—— Elizabeth Agnes, wife of major C. C. Graham Stirling of Craigbarnet, vi. 156.
—— Elizabeth Marianne, wife of Philip (Gore), 4th earl of Arran, vii. 392.
—— Ellinor Alice, wife of G. Grey Dalrymple, vi. 437; viii. 160.
—— Frances, wife of (1) Sir E. Barkham, and (2) 2nd lord Cramond, ii. 583.
—— Francis, lieut.-col. of Marines, vi. 432.
—— —— his wife, Eliza Greenaway, vi. 432.
—— Francis, H.E.I.C.S., vi. 432.
—— Francis, W.S., vi. 433.
—— —— his wife, Mary Elizabeth Jane Douglas Hamilton, vi. 433.
—— Francis, R.N., vi. 436.
—— Frederick William Scott, vi. 438.
—— Gabriel Hamilton, vi. 432.
—— George, colonel, comptroller of Army accounts, vi. 433.
—— —— his 1st wife, Elizabeth Pollock, vi. 433.
—— —— his 2nd wife, Sarah Lennox, v. 365; vi. 433.
—— Sir George Thomas, general, vi. 434.
—— Georgina, vi. 438.
—— Helen, wife of Sir John Melville of Raith, vi. 412.
—— Helen, dau. of Archibald N. of Woolmet, vi. 416.
—— Helen, wife of Sir William Balfour, vi. 417; ix. 142.
—— Helen, wife of Matthew Brisbane, vi. 422.
—— Henrietta, dau. of 7th lord Napier of Merchiston, vi. 435.
—— Henrietta Hope, wife of Geo. Gordon of Hallhead, vi. 432.
—— Henry, joint admiral-depute, ii. 143; vi. 406.
—— Henry Alfred, rector of Swyncombe, vi. 436.
—— Henry Edward, capt. R.N., vi. 434.
—— —— his wife, Caroline Bennett, vi. 434.
—— Hester, wife of Alex. Johnstone of Carnsalloch, vi. 434.
—— Hope, lieut. R.N., vi. 433.
—— Isabella, wife of Jas. Menteith, provost of Stirling, vi. 410.

Napier, Isabella, wife of lieut.-col. Chas. Maitland of Craigieburn, vi. 433.
—— James, postmaster of Montrose, i. 306.
—— —— his wife, Margaret Arbuthnott, i. 306.
—— James, 7th son of 7th lord Napier of Merchiston, vi. 434.
—— James John, lieut. of Marines, vi. 434.
—— Janet, wife of (1) * Ramsay, and (2) John Wilson, ii. 134.
—— Janet, wife of (1) Sir Jas. Edmondston, (2) Alex. Hepburn, and (3) Adam Hume, ii. 144; vi. 407.
—— Janet, wife of Wm. Adamson of Bonally, vi. 408.
—— Janet, dau. of Archibald N. of Merchiston, vi. 410.
—— Janet, wife of (1) A. Bruce of Powfoulis, and (2) R. Bruce, vi. 412.
—— Janet, dau. of Sir Archibald N. of Edinbellie, vi. 416.
—— Jean, wife of (1) John Gaw of Maw, and (2) George Hamilton, vi. 421.
—— Jean, wife of Sir Thos. Nicolson of Carnock, vi. 426.
—— Joan, dau. of John N. of Merchiston, vi. 420.
—— John, 2nd son of Archibald N. of Merchiston, vi. 411.
—— John, son of John N. of Shanbothy, vi. 420.
—— John, 2nd son of Robert N. of Boquhopple, vi. 420.
—— John, R.N., vi. 426.
—— John, 25th regt., vi. 433.
—— John, son of William N., ix. 142.
—— John George, H.E.I.C.S., vi. 433.
—— John Scott, col. Gordon Highlanders, vi. 438.
—— —— his wife, Isabella Shaw, vi. 438.
—— Katharine, wife of R. Buchanan of Drumnakil, vi. 410.
—— Katharine, wife of Geo. Coutts, vi. 411.
—— Katharine, wife of (1) Walter Stewart, and (2) Jas. Ogilvy, ix. 141.
—— Katharine Douglas, vi. 433.
—— Louisa Mary, vi. 433.
—— Lucy Matilda, dau. of 9th lord Napier of Merchiston, vi. 437.
—— Lilias, dau. of 1st lord Napier of Merchiston, vi. 424 *bis*.
—— Marcia Anne Symson, wife of Alex. Ogilvy, vi. 433.
—— Margaret, dau. of John N. of Merchiston, vi. 408.
—— Margaret, wife of (1) Robert Napier of Wrightshouses, and (2) Thos. Corry of Kelwood, vi. 410.
—— Margaret, dau. of Alexander N. of Merchiston, vi. 412.

* Name unknown.

Napier, Margaret, dau. of Sir Alexander N. of Lauriston, vi. 416.
—— Margaret, wife of James Stewart of Rosyth, vi. 421.
—— Margaret, wife of Sir George Stirling of Keir, vi. 424.
—— Marion, dau. of Archibald N. of Merchiston, vi. 410.
—— Marion, wife of Robert Kennedy, vi. 411.
—— Marion, wife of (1) John Lourestoun, and (2) Archibald Bruce of Powfoulis, vi. 413.
—— Marion, dau. of Sir Archibald N. of Merchiston, vi. 417.
—— Maria, wife of rev. T. H. Yorke, vi. 433.
—— Maria Margaret, wife of rev. O. W. Kilvington, vi. 436.
—— Maria Margaret, wife of 1st baron Addington, vi. 437.
—— Mark, major-general, vi. 433.
—— —— his 1st wife, Anne Neilson, vi. 433.
—— —— his 2nd wife, Margaret Symson, vi. 433.
—— Mark, sheriff, vi. 433.
—— Mark, lieut.-general, vi. 433.
—— Mark Francis, barrister, M.P., vi. 438.
—— —— his wife, Emily Jones, vi. 438.
—— Mary Elizabeth, dau. of 7th lord Napier of Merchiston, vi. 435.
—— Mary Schaw, wife of prof. A. Hunter, D.D., vi. 435.
—— Patrick, lieut. R.N., vi. 434.
—— Philip Henry, vi. 438.
—— Richard, barrister, vi. 434.
—— —— his wife, Anna Louisa Stewart, vi. 434.
—— Robert, 2nd son of Alexander N. of Merchiston, vi. 404.
—— Susanna, wife of P. Hepburn of Whitsome, ii. 147; vi. 416.
—— Sophia, dau. of 8th lord Napier of Merchiston, vi. 436.
—— Stewart, lieut. of Marines, vi. 434.
—— Sir Thomas Erskine, K.C.B., governor of Edinburgh Castle, vi. 432.
—— Walter, 5th son of Sir Archibald N. of Merchiston, vi. 416.
—— William, 3rd son of Archibald N. of Merchiston, vi. 411.
—— William, 6th son of Sir Archibald N. of Merchiston, vi. 416.
—— William, clerk of the works, Hong-Kong, vi. 437.
—— —— his wife, Louisa Mary Lloyd, vi. 437.
—— William, burgess of Edinburgh, ix. 142.
—— William Charles, lieut. R.A., vi. 433.
—— William Francis Cyril James, ii. 59; vi. 438.
—— Sir William Francis Patrick, general, K.C.B., vi. 434; vii. 392.
—— —— his wife, Caroline Amelia Fox, vi. 434.

Nasmyth, *see* Naesmyth.
Nassau, Amelia de, wife of Thomas, styled earl of Ossory, iii. 122.
— Henry de, lord of Auverquerque, iii. 122.
— Isabella of, wife of Henry, earl of Arlington, i. 31.
— Mauritia de, wife of 3rd earl of Balcarres, i. 522.
— Richard Savage, son of 3rd earl of Rochford, iv. 392.
— — his wife, Anne Spenser, iv. 392.
NASSAU D'ALBUQUERQUE, BARONESS DINGWALL, iii. 123.
Nassau d'Auverquerque, Henrietta de, wife of 2nd earl Cowper, iii. 123.
NAVAR, MAULE, LORD BRECHIN AND, vii. 19-27.
Navar, Patrick, first lord Brechin and, vii. 20.
Navoy, Elizabeth, wife of Sir Jas. Kinloch, i. 516.
Naylor of Leighton Hall, John, viii. 235.
— Dora, wife of admiral E. C. Drummond, viii. 235.
Neale of Plessey and Codnor Castle, Sir Richard, viii. 596.
— Frances, wife of John Seton, viii. 596.
Neall, James, Fordyce & Downe, Messrs., ix. 31.
Neave, Elizabeth, wife of Alex. Middleton, vi. 179.
— Richard, secretary to Chelsea Hospital, vi. 179.
Needham of Lambeth, Sir Robert, ii. 239.
— Elinor, mistress of James, duke of Monmouth, ii. 239.
Neeld, Elizabeth Charlotte, wife of (1) capt. White, R.N., (2) rev. R. P. Jones, and (3) lord Nigel Kennedy, ii. 499.
— Sir John, 1st bart., ii. 499.
NEIDPATH, DOUGLAS, LORD DOUGLAS OF, vii. 145-147.
Neidpath, William, first lord Douglas of, vii. 145.
Neilson of Craigcaffie, John, vi. 433.
— of Dalrymple, v. 140.
— of Kilcathie, i. 551.
— — his wife, Margaret Bruce, i. 551.
— Anne, wife of major-gen. Mark Napier, vi. 433.
— Thomas, perpetual vicar of Stanehouse, ii. 38.
Neish of Dubheads, Walter, viii. 170; ix. 160.
— — his wife, Elizabeth Alexander, viii. 170.
NEMPHLAR, CARMICHAEL, VISCOUNT OF, iv. 590-597.
Nemphlar, John, first viscount of, iv. 590.
Nes of Banff, v. 569.
Nes of London, i. 450; vii. 419, 420.
Nes, son of William, v. 571; viii. 319 *n*.
Nesbitt of Dene, William, vi. 419.
— of the Pultrielands, William, vi. 419.
NEVARE, STEWART, LORD OF, vii. 246.
Nevare, James, lord of, vii. 246.
Nevay of Nevay, David, viii. 296.
— — his wife, Anna Lyon, viii. 296.
— — John, viii. 295.
— of Reidie, Sir David, viii. 300.
— Margaret, wife of John Lyon, viii. 295.
Nevers, Charles de Gonzaga, duke of, iv. 548.
Nevill(e of Auborn, Sir Christopher, v. 13.
— — his wife, Katharine Ingram, v. 13.
— of Lessuden, Sir John, vii. 317.
— of Raby, Ralph, vii. 317.
— of Thornton Bridge, Joan, wife of Sir John Constable, iii. 293.
— — Ralph, iii. 293.
— Adeline, dau. of 5th earl of Westmoreland, iii. 295.
— Elizabeth, wife of col. Metcalfe Graham, vii. 104.
— Hugo de, ii. 430.
— — his wife, Beatrice de Brus, ii. 430.
— John, senior, iii. 183.
— — his wife, Anne Holland, iii. 183.
— John, junior, iii. 183.
— — his wife, Anne Holland, iii. 183.
— Ralph, 3rd earl of Westmoreland, iii. 183.
— Katharine, wife of Sir John Constable, iii. 295.
— Lucy, wife of Sir Wm. Cornwallis, i. 350.
— Ralph, bishop of Chichester, i. 420.
— Ralph de, 1391, iii. 13.
NEWARK, LESLIE, LORD, vi. 440-445.
Newark, Alexander, styled lord, vi. 443, 444.
— — his wife, Elizabeth Price, vi. 444.
— David, first lord, i. 79; v. 375, 376, 384; vi. 440.
— — his wife, Anna Yorke, vi. 442.
— David, second lord, vi. 442.
— — his wife, Elizabeth Stewart, vi. 443.
— Jean, wife of Sir Alexander Anstruther; styled baroness, v. 385; vi. 443.
— John, styled lord, vi. 444.
— William, styled lord, vi. 444.
NEWBATTLE, KER, LORD KERR OF, v. 469-487.
Newbattle, Robert, styled lord Kerr of, v. 475.
— William, eldest son of 1st marquess of Lothian; styled lord, v. 479.
— master of, William, eldest son of Robert, lord Kerr of Newbattle; styled, v. 77, 479.
Newbigging of Newbigging, William, viii. 7.
— Ingelram, bishop of Glasgow, viii. 2.
— Margaret, wife of William Somerville, viii. 3.

Newbigging, Sir Walter de, viii. 3 *bis*.
NEWBOTLE, KER, LORD, v. 456-487.
Newbotle, Mark, first lord, iii. 97; v. 456.
—— —— his wife, Margaret Maxwell, v. 456.
NEWBURGH, LIVINGSTON, VISCOUNT OF, vi. 452-453.
Newburgh, James, first viscount of, vi. 452.
NEWBURGH, LIVINGSTON, EARL OF, vi. 446-460.
Newburgh, Charles, second earl of, vi. 453.
—— —— his wife, Frances Brudenell, vi. 453.
—— Charlotte Maria, wife of (1) Thomas Clifford, and (2) Charles Radcliffe; countess of, vi. 453.
—— James, first earl of, vi. 452; viii. 300.
—— —— his 1st wife, Katharine Howard, vi. 453.
—— —— his 2nd wife, Anne Poole, vi. 453.
NEWBURGH, RADCLIFFE, EARL OF, vi. 456-457.
Newburgh, Anthony James, fifth earl of, vi. 457.
—— —— his wife, Anne Webb, vi. 457.
—— James Bartholomew, fourth earl of, vi. 455, 456.
—— —— his wife, Barbara Kemp, vi. 457.
NEWBURGH, GIUSTINIANI, EARL OF, vi. 457-458.
Newburgh, Maria Cecilia Agatha Anna Josepha Laurentia Donata Melchiora Baldassara Gaspara, wife of Charles, 4th marquis Bandini and Rustano; countess of, vi. 458.
—— Vincent Joseph Philip Gratilianus James Gaspar Balthassar Melchior Dominicus, *de jure* sixth earl of, vi. 455, 457.
—— —— his wife, Maria Nicoletta Grillo di Mondragone, vi. 458.
NEWBURGH, GIUSTINIANI-BANDINI, EARL OF, vi. 458-460.
Newburgh, Carlo, ninth earl of, vi. 459.
—— —— his wife, Maria Lanza di Trabia, vi. 459.
—— Sigismund Nicholas Venantius Gaietano Francis, eighth earl of, vi. 458.
—— —— his wife, Maria Sophia Angelica Massani, vi. 459.
Newburgh, Dorothy Eyre, wife of col. Charles Leslie; self-styled countess of, vi. 456.
—— Francis Eyre, self-styled earl of, vi. 455.
—— Francis Eyre, self-styled earl of, vi. 456.
—— Thomas Eyre, self-styled earl of, ii. 500; vi. 456.
—— —— his wife, Margaret Kennedy, ii. 500.
NEWBURGH, BARRET, LORD BARRET OF, ii. 34-35.
Newburgh, Edward, lord Barret of, ii. 34.
—— —— his 1st wife, Jane Cary, ii. 35.
—— —— his 2nd wife, Katharine Fenn, ii. 35.
NEWBURY, STEWART, LORD STUART OF, v. 360-361.
Newcastle-under-Lyme, Henry (Pelham-Clinton), 5th duke of, iv. 395.
—— —— his wife, S. H. C. Douglas-Hamilton, iv. 395.
—— Thomas (Pelham), 1st duke of, v. 88.
NEWCASTLE-ON-TYNE, STEWART, EARL OF, v. 357.
Newcastle-on-Tyne, Ludovick, earl of, v. 357.
Newcastle-upon-Tyne, William (Cavendish), 1st marquess of, iii. 592.
—— Henry (Cavendish), 2nd duke of, ii. 207.
—— —— his wife, Frances Pierrepont, ii. 207.
—— William (Cavendish), 1st duke of, v. 361; vi. 466.
—— —— his 1st wife, Elizabeth Basset, vi. 466.
Newcomen, Thomas (Newcomen), 2nd viscount, ix. 82.
—— Theresa, wife of (1) R. H. Cockerell, and (2) Archibald William, 13th earl of Eglinton, iii. 463; ix. 82.
NEWHAVEN, CHEYNE, VISCOUNT OF, vi. 461-468.
Newhaven, Charles, first viscount of, vi. 466.
—— —— his 1st wife, Jane Cavendish, vi. 466.
—— —— his 2nd wife, Letitia Isabella Smith, vi. 467.
—— William, second viscount of, vi. 467.
—— —— his 1st wife, Elizabeth Thomas, vi. 468.
—— —— his 2nd wife, Gertrude Pierrepont, vi. 468.
Newlands of Drayton, Richard Bingham, major, v. 314.
—— of Newlands, Jasper, ii. 384.
—— Emily Augusta Mary, wife of lt.-col. F. T. Maitland, v. 314.
NEWLISTON, DALRYMPLE, LORD, viii. 149-164.
Newliston, John, first lord, viii. 149.
Newmarch, George, major-gen. R.E., i. 96.
—— Isabel, wife of lt.-col. A. Hamilton Gordon, i. 96.
Newport of Scupholm, John, viii. 413.
—— —— his wife, Juliana Murray, viii. 413.
Newry and Morne, Francis Jack Needham, styled viscount, ii. 565.
—— —— his wife, Anne Amelia Colville, ii. 565.
Newton, Sir David Falconer, lord president of the College of Justice, lord, iii. 580; v. 247.
—— of Bundray, James, vii. 71.

Newton of Croxton Park and Pickhill Hall, George Onslow, iii. 420.
— of Dalcoif, Archibald, v. 393.
— — James, vii. 71.
— of Irnham, Francis, viii. 597.
— of Newton, Archibald, viii. 444.
— — his wife, Christian Hay, viii. 444.
— — Richard, vi. 12.
— — his wife, Julian Hume, vi. 12.
— of the Priory and Charlton, Sir Henry, bart., iii. 400.
— — his wife, Elizabeth Murray, iii. 400.
— Cecilia Florence, wife of 8th earl of Dysart, iii. 420.
— Henry, son of Sir Henry N., Warwickshire, iii. 400 *n*.
— Henry Alfred, ii. 59.
— — his wife, Mary Geraldine Hamilton, ii. 59.
— Mary, wife of John Seton, viii. 597.
Nicholas, the son of Brice, priest of Kirriemuir, i. 165.
Nicholas, father of Stephen, vii. 527.
Nicholas, rector of the church of Crieff, viii. 243.
Nicholas, Thomas, iii. 54.
Nicholson of West Rainton, James, viii. 309.
— — Jean, wife of Thomas, 8th earl of Strathmore, viii. 309.
— Agnes, wife of 1st lord Elibank, iii. 510.
— Alexander, iii. 365; vi. 503.
— Frances Jacobina, wife of (1) G. J. Carnegie, and (2) H. B. W. Cochrane, iii. 365; vi. 503.
Nicol of Cony Hatch, John, v. 199.
— Margaret, wife of 3rd duke of Chandos, v. 199.
Nicoll, Patrick, merchant, Edinburgh, viii. 295.
Nicolls, Francis, of the Middle Temple, iii. 485.
— — his wife, Margaret Bruce, iii. 485.
Nicolson of Carnock, Sir George, 6th bart., vii. 91.
— — his 2nd wife, Mary Anne Colyear, vii. 91.
— — Helen, vi. 427.
— — Isabella, vi. 427.
— — Margaret, wife of Sir Thos. Nicolson of Kemnay, v. 175; vi. 427.
— — Sir Thomas, 1st bart., viii. 10.
— — Sir Thomas, 2nd bart., v. 175, 447.
— — his wife, Margaret Livingston, v. 447.
— — Sir Thomas, 3rd bart., vi. 426, 427.
— — his wife, Jean Napier, vi. 426.
— — Sir Thomas, 4th bart., vi. 427.
— — Sir Thomas, 5th bart., vii. 89.
— — Sir Walter Philip, 7th bart., vii. 91.
— of Cockburnspath, Sir James, iii. 510; ix. 122.
Nicolson of Cockburnspath, Sir James, ix. 82.
— — his wife, Magdalen Bruce, ix. 82.
— — Thomas, iii. 510.
— of Kemnay, Sir Thomas, 1st bart., v. 175, 176, 480.
— — his wife, Margaret Nicolson of Carnock, v. 175.
— of Lasswade, John, advocate, iv. 487 *bis*.
— of Plean, Thomas, viii. 10.
— of Tillicoultry, Sir John, vii. 89.
— — his wife, Sabina *or* Martha Colyear *alias* Robertson, vii. 89.
— — Sir Thomas, vii. 88 *n*., 89.
— Eleanora, wife of (1) Robert Boyd, and (2) John Craufurd of Craufurdland, v. 175; ix. 119.
— Isabel, wife of * Brisbane, ix. 120.
— James, bishop of Dunkeld, vii. 192.
— Margaret, wife of 3rd marquess of Lothian, v. 480; ix. 119, 131 *bis*.
— Marion, wife of Geo. Hay of Balhousie, v. 230.
— Sir Thomas, lord advocate, v. 230; viii. 372.
NIDDRY OF NIDDRY, HOPE, BARON, iv. 502-505.
Niddry of Niddry, John, first baron, iv. 502.
Nimmo, James, burgess of Edinburgh, iv. 93.
— — his wife, Christian Hamilton, iv. 92, 93.
— James, receiver general of excise, ii. 368; vi. 19.
— — his 1st wife, Mary Erskine, ii. 368.
— — his 2nd wife, Jean Hume Campbell, vi. 19.
NISBET, KER, LORD KERR OF, v. 466-487.
Nisbet, Robert, first lord Kerr of, v. 466.
— of Auchinroglin, Mariota, wife of John Lockhart, v. 496.
— of Bankhead, Alexander, v. 496.
— — his wife, Margaret Campbell, v. 496.
— of Cairnhill, John More, viii. 160.
— — his wife, Agnes Dalrymple, viii. 160.
— of Carfin, Archibald, ii. 55.
— — Archibald, iv. 592.
— — his wife, Grizel Carmichael, iv. 592.
— — Archibald, their son, iv. 592, 597.
— of Craigentinny, Alexander, viii. 30.
— of Dalzell, John, viii. 14.
— — his wife, Mary Somerville, viii. 14.
— — Robert, ii. 407.
— — Robert, ii. 407.
— — his wife, Margaret Dalzell, ii. 407.
— of Dirleton, Sir John, lord president of the Court of Session, i. 259; vi. 431; vii. 78, 81.
— — Mary, wife of (1) major Wm. Hay of Newhall, and (2) Walter Campbell of Shawfield, viii. 460.
— — William, ii. 25; vi. 116; vii. 389.

* Name unknown.

…et of Dirleton, William, ii. 44; viii. 460.
— his wife, Mary Hamilton of Pen…itland and Biel, ii. 44.
…of Fern, Mariota, wife of John Lockhart, 496.
…of Manderston, Philip, iii. 282.
…of Mauldsley, Archibald, iv. 597.
…of Nisbet, Philip, iii. 282; vii. 370.
— his wife, Helen Rutherfurd, vii. …0.
— Sir Philip, iv. 476.
…of Nisbetfield, John, W.S., vii. 83.
…of Restalrig, James, ii. 409.
…Agnes, wife of Sir John Dalzell, ii. 409; …. 53.
…Agnes, wife of Walter Scott of White…eld, vii. 83.
…Alice Anne, wife of George Ramsay …aitland, v. 315.
…Elizabeth, wife of Wm. Hamilton, ii. 55.
…Elizabeth, wife of Geo. Carlyle, ii. 391.
…George, fencing-master, iv. 35.
… — his wife, Elizabeth Ogilvy, iv. 35.
…Janet, wife of James Ruthven of …uthven, vii. 389.
…Jean, wife of 7th lord Banff, ii. 25.
…Jean, wife of Alexander, 6th earl of …incardine, iii. 489 *n*.
…Jean, wife of (1) Sir Wm. Scott of …arden, and (2) Sir Wm. Scott of Thirle…tane, vi. 431; vii. 78.
…Josiah, H.E.I.C.S., v. 315.
…Katherine, wife of (1) * Dickson of Bel…hester, and (2) Sir Henry Home of Herd…ig, iv. 475.
…Katharine, wife of Patrick Sinclair of Balgriggie, ix. 157.
…Mary, wife of Jas. Hamilton, ii. 55.
…Thomas, 3rd son of Sir Philip N., iv. 475.
…Wilhelmina, wife of David, 6th earl of Leven and 5th earl of Melville, vi. 116.
…isbet-Hamilton of Dirleton and Belhaven, Robert Adam Christopher, M.P., iii. 493.
— — his wife, Mary Bruce, iii. 493.
…ISBITTS, KER, LORD KERR OF, v. 477-487.
…isbitts, Robert, first lord Kerr of, 477.
…ITH, DOUGLAS, VISCOUNT OF, vii. 138-156.
…ith, William, first viscount of, vii. 138.
…ITHSDALE, MAXWELL, EARL OF, vi. 469-492.
…ithsdale, Elizabeth (Douglas), wife of (1) John, 8th lord Maxwell, (2) Alex. Stewart of Garlies, and (3) John Wallace; styled countess of, vi. 483.
— John, third earl of, iv. 416; v. 116; vi. 487.
— — his wife, Elizabeth Gordon, iv. 417; v. 116; vi. 487.
— Robert, first earl of, vi. 485.
— — his wife, Elizabeth Beaumont, vi. 485.
Nithsdale, Robert, second earl of, i. 228; iv. 416; vi. 487.
— Robert, fourth earl of, iv. 417; vi. 488.
— — his wife, Lucy Douglas, i. 206; vi. 488; ix. 13.
— William, fifth earl of, v. 131; vi. 488, 500.
— — his wife, Winifred Herbert, iv. 417; vi. 488.
— William, sixth earl of, v. 131; vi. 490.
— — his 1st wife, Katharine Stuart, vi. 490.
— — his 2nd wife, Anne Fox, vi. 490.
Niven of Monkredding, Thomas, iii. 439 *n*.
— Oswald, commander R.N., iv. 569.
— — his wife, Rose Gordon Carmichael, iv. 569.
Noble of Kinpunt and Eliston, Ralph, vi. 202.
— — Thomas, vi. 202.
— Agnes, wife of David de Graham of Dundaff, vi. 202.
— Margaret, wife of Wm. Sempill of Cathcart, vii. 534.
Noel, Alice, vii. 94.
— Bridget, wife of David, viscount of Milsington, vii. 93.
— Elizabeth, wife of Sir Jas. B. Burgess, ix. 31.
— Katharine Hamilton, wife of Sir James Carnegie of Southesk, viii. 90.
— William Frederick, colonel, iv. 386.
Noel-Edwards, Gerard, iv. 338.
— — his wife, Diana Middleton, baroness Barham, vi. 180.
Nonsuch, Barbara (Villiers), baroness, i. 31.
Norbury, Hector John (Graham-Toler), 3rd earl of, v. 419.
— — his wife, Stewart Lindsay Lindsay, v. 419.
Norcliffe of Langton, Fairfax, vii. 357.
— — Frances, wife of Sir John Wray, vii. 357.
— Sir Thomas, v. 10.
— — his wife, Dorothy Fairfax, v. 10.
Norfolk, Hugh le Bigod, earl of, vi. 288.
— Roger le Bigod, earl of, i. 5; vi. 288.
— — his wife, Isabella of Scotland, i. 5; vi. 288.
— Edward (Howard), 9th duke of, i. 412.
— Henry (Howard), 6th duke of, i. 55.
— Henry Charles (Howard), 13th duke of, ii. 311; viii. 362.
— — his wife, Charlotte Sophia Leveson Gower, viii. 362.
— Henry Fitzalan (Howard), 15th duke of, v. 516.
— — his 1st wife, Flora Paulyna Hetty Barbara Abney-Hastings, v. 516.
— — his 2nd wife, Gwendoline Mary Constable-Maxwell, iv. 423.
— Henry Granville (Fitzalan-Howard), 14th duke of, v. 485.

* Name unknown.

Norfolk, Thomas (Howard), 4th duke of, v. 157.
—— Thomas (Howard), 8th duke of, i. 412.
Norfolk, Simon de, brother of Walter, 3rd steward of Scotland, v. 137.
Norin of Monorgund, v. 329.
—— —— his wife, Forveleth, v. 329.
Norin, son of Norman the Constable, vii. 267.
Norman, son of Bertolf, vii. 265.
Norman, son of Malcolm; constable of Inverurie, vii. 266.
—— —— his wife, A., vii. 266.
Norman, Elizabeth Cecile Sophia, wife of G. J. Drummond, viii. 224.
—— F. J., in holy orders, viii. 224.
Normandy, Richard, duke of, ii. 428.
Normanton, James (Agar-Ellis), 3rd earl of, ii. 213.
Normanville, Sir John de, ii. 537.
—— Walran de, ii. 254.
—— Robert, iii. 561.
—— *, wife of Wm. Colville of Oxnam, ii. 537.
Norreys, Sir Edward, v. 86.
—— —— his wife, Elizabeth Pierrepont, v. 86.
Norris, Francis (Norris), 2nd baron, iii. 230.
—— Frederica Lilian, wife of E. R. B. Drummond, viii. 230.
North, Dudley (North), 3rd lord, ii. 35.
—— Charlotte, wife of lieut.-col. John Lindsay, i. 528.
—— Dorothy, wife of Richard, lord Dacre, ii. 35.
—— Maria, wife of 2nd marquess of Bute, ii. 310.
North and Grey, William (North), lord, iii. 519.
—— —— his wife, Maria Margaritta d'Ellemeet, iii. 519.
Northampton, William (de Bohun), earl of, iv. 226.
—— Spencer (Compton), 2nd earl of, vi. 486 *n.*
—— —— his wife, Mary Beaumont, vi. 486 *n.*
—— William (Compton), 4th marquess of, iii. 124.
Northcote, Sir Stafford, bart., viii. 38.
—— Eliza, wife of 11th earl of Strathmore and Kinghorne, viii. 312.
—— George Barons, rector of Feniton, iii. 46.
—— Isabel Katharine, wife of Alfred Lindsay, iii. 46.
—— *, colonel, viii. 312.
NORTHESK, CARNEGIE, EARL OF, vi. 493-508.
Northesk, David, second earl of, iii. 325; vi. 497.
—— —— his wife, Jean Maule, vi. 21, 497.
—— David, third earl of, vi. 499.
—— —— his wife, Elizabeth Lindsay, iii. 37; vi. 499.

* Name unknown.

Northesk, David, fourth earl of, vi. 500.
—— —— his wife, Margaret Wemyss, ii. 283; vi. 501; viii. 506.
—— David, fifth earl of, vi. 502.
—— David John, tenth earl of, vi. 507.
—— —— his wife, Elizabeth Boyle Hallowes, vi. 507.
—— George, sixth earl of, vi. 502.
—— —— his wife, Anne Leslie, vi. 115, 503.
—— George John, ninth earl of, vi. 506.
—— —— his wife, Elizabeth Elliot, vi. 507.
—— John, first earl of, vi. 493.
—— —— his 1st wife, Magdalen Haliburton, vi. 495.
—— —— his 2nd wife, Marjory Maule, vi. 495; vii. 13.
—— William, seventh earl of, vi. 504.
—— —— his wife, Mary Ricketts, vi. 505.
—— William Hopetoun, eighth earl of, vi. 506.
—— —— his wife, Georgiana Maria Elliot, vi. 506.
Northington, Robert (Henley), 1st earl of, iii. 408.
Northumberland, Gospatrick, earl of, iii. 241.
—— Henry, earl of, i. 4.
—— —— his wife, Ada de Warenne, i. 4.
—— Robert Comyn, earl of, i. 503; iii. 242 *bis.*
—— Siward, earl of, i. 1, 3; iv. 1; vi. 283.
—— Uchtred, earl of, iii. 241 *bis.*
—— Waltheof, earl of, ii. 369; iv. 507 *n.*
—— Algernon (Percy), 6th duke of, i. 499.
—— George (Percy), 5th duke of, ii. 303.
—— —— his wife, Louisa Harcourt Stuart, ii. 303.
—— Henry (Percy), 1st earl of, iii. 271; ix. 11.
—— —— his wife, Maud de Lacy, ix. 11.
—— Henry (Percy), 4th earl of, v. 145.
—— Henry (Percy), 9th earl of, v. 219.
—— Henry George (Percy), 7th duke of, i. 391.
—— —— his wife, Edith Campbell, i. 391.
—— Hugh (Percy), 2nd duke of, i. 496; ii. 305.
—— —— his 1st wife, Anne Stuart, ii. 305.
—— Thomas (Percy), 7th earl of, v. 64 *n.*
—— George (Fitzroy), illeg. son of king Charles II; earl and duke of, i. 31.
—— —— his wife, Catherine Wheatley, iii. 217.
Norter, Sir Robert, iii. 378.
—— *, wife of James, 1st lord Dunkeld, iii. 378.
Norton of Charlton, Sir Gregory, bart., v. 122, 123.
—— —— his wife, Martha *, iv. 123.
—— James, iv. 390.
—— John, merchant, London, iv. 76.
—— Marina, wife of Frederic Douglas-Hamilton, iv. 390.

* Name unknown.

Norton, Rebecca, wife of 4th lord Forbes of Pitsligo, iv. 76.
Norvell of Boghall, George, advocate, v. 247; ix. 85.
—— —— his wife, Marion Elphinstone, ix. 85.
—— of Boghall and Deans, George, v. 251.
—— —— his wife, Marjory Falconer, v. 251.
—— Katharine Margaret, wife of capt. Cosby Swindell, v. 251.
—— Mary, wife of (1) Sir D. Falconer of Newton, and (2) John Hume of Ninewells, v. 247.
Norway, Eric Magnusson, king of, i. 6; ii. 433.
—— —— his 1st wife, Margaret of Scotland, i. 6.
—— —— his 2nd wife, Isabel Bruce, i. 6; ii. 433.
—— Magnus iv., king of, v. 34.
Norwich, Edward (Denney), earl of, v. 219.
—— Henry (Howard), 2nd earl of, iv. 556 *n.*
NORWICH, GORDON, EARL OF, iv. 556-558.
Norwich, Alexander, first earl of, iv. 556.
—— George, second earl of, iv. 557.
Nottingham, Thomas (Mowbray), earl marshal of England, earl of, vi. 300.
—— Charles (Howard), 1st earl of, ii. 442; vi. 318.
—— —— his 2nd wife, Margaret Stewart, iv. 160; vi. 318.
—— Daniel (Finch), 2nd earl of, vii. 351.
Nudd, John, Surrey, i. 144; ix. 9.
—— —— his wife, Sarah Ann Allardice, i. 143.
Nugent, Lawrence, capt., ii. 491.
—— —— his wife, Katharine Kennedy, ii. 491.
—— Mary Frances, wife of James Hope-Wallace, iv. 503.
Nunburnholme, Charles Henry (Wilson), 1st baron, vii. 359.

OAKELEY, Charlotte Mary Atholl, wife of F. C. Drummond, viii. 235.
—— Sir Herbert, archdeacon of Colchester, i. 494; viii. 235.
—— —— his wife, Athole Keturah Murray, i. 494.
Oakes, Isabella Frances, wife of D. S. Carmichael-Smyth, iv. 569.
—— W. H., iv. 569.
Oates, Titus, i. 410, 411.
Obeirne, Thomas Lewis, bishop of Meath, vi. 325.
—— —— his wife, Jane Stewart, vi. 324.
O'Beolan, the family of, vii. 231 *n.*
—— of Carloway, Patrick, vii. 162.
—— Norman, vii. 162.
—— *, wife of Iye 'Roy' Mackay of Strathnaver, vii. 162.
* Name unknown.

O'BRIEN, COUNTESS OF ORKNEY, vi. 580-581.
O'Brien of Lemineagh, Sir Donogh, i. 56.
—— —— his wife, Lucia Hamilton, i. 56.
—— Anne, dau. of Anne, countess of Orkney, vi. 580.
—— Elizabeth, dau of Anne, countess of Orkney, vi. 580.
—— Frances, dau. of Anne, countess of Orkney, vi. 580.
—— Katharine, wife of 3rd earl of Clarendon, v. 359.
O'Cathan of Ulster, Guy, v. 37.
—— Agnes, wife of Angus 'Og,' 6th lord of the Isles, v. 37.
OCHILTREE, STEWART, LORD, vi. 511-520.
Ochiltree, Andrew, first lord, vi. 511.
—— —— his wife, Margaret Hamilton, vi. 511.
—— Andrew, second lord, vi. 512.
—— —— his 1st wife, Agnes Cunningham, vi. 512.
—— —— his 2nd wife, Margaret Cunningham, iv. 241; vi. 513.
—— Andrew, third lord, ii. 507; iv. 464; vi. 516.
—— —— his wife, Margaret Kennedy, vi. 516.
—— James, fourth lord, iv. 160; vi. 513, 517; ix. 144.
—— —— his 1st wife, Katharine McDowall, vi. 518.
—— —— his 2nd wife, Mary Livingstone, vi. 518.
—— William, fifth lord, vi. 519; ix. 145 *ter.*
—— master of, Andrew, eldest son of 2nd lord Ochiltree, vi. 514; ix. 144.
—— —— his wife, Margaret Stewart, vi. 515.
—— master of, Andrew, eldest son of 3rd lord Ochiltree, vi. 517.
—— —— his wife, Anne Stewart, vi. 517; ix. 144.
—— master of, William, eldest son of 4th lord Ochiltree, vi. 518.
OCHILTREE, COLVILL, LORD COLVILL OF, ii. 569-575.
Ochiltree, David, self-styled lord Colvill of, ii. 574.
—— Robert, first lord Colvill of, ii. 573.
—— Robert, second lord Colvill of, ii. 572, 573.
—— Robert, third lord Colvill of, ii. 574.
—— Robert, self-styled lord Colvill of, ii. 574.
—— of Carstoun and Steill, William, iii. 348.
—— —— his wife, Mary Bruce, iii. 348, 487.
Ochonochor, alleged ancestor of the families of Forbes, Urquhart, and Mackay, iv. 42.
Ochterlony of Bonhard and Knox, Patrick, vii. 18.
—— —— his wife, Euphemia Maule, vii. 18.
—— of the Guynd, John, vii. 17.
—— —— his wife, Katharine Maule, vii. 17.

Ochterlony of Kelly, Alexander, vi. 276; vii. 7.
—— his wife, Janet Maule of Grenefurde, vii. 7.
—— David, i. 288.
—— his wife, Isabel Arbuthnott, i. 288.
—— William, vi. 276; vii. 7.
—— William, v. 6.
—— his wife, Elizabeth Stewart, v. 6.
— of Ochterlony, Sir James, viii. 277.
—— James, the younger, ix. 110.
—— his wife, Agnes Betoun, ix. 110.
—— William, iii. 313.
—— his wife, Katharine Scrymgeour, iii. 313.
— Margaret, wife of Alex. Arbuthnott, i. 295.
— William, viii. 277.
—— his wife, Mariota Lyon, viii. 277.
O'Connell, Michael, i. 62.
—— his wife, Philippa Hamilton, i. 62.
O'Connor, alleged ancestor of the families of Forbes, Urquhart, and Mackay, iv. 42.
Octreda of Allerdale, wife of (1) Randolph de Lindesay, and (2) Wm. de Esseville, iii. 3, 245.
Octreda, wife of Waldeve, son of Gillemin, iii. 245.
Odard of Hodelm, i. 231; ii. 371, 377 *n.*
Odard, the sheriff, ii. 371.
Odard, father of Roger, ii. 377 *n.*
Odell, Fulke, vi. 463.
—— his wife, Elizabeth Webbe, vi. 463.
O'Donnell of Tyrconnel, Callough, ix. 20.
—— his wife, Katharine Maclean, ix. 20 *bis.*
O'Donell, *, alleged wife of Sir Wm. Hamilton of Manor Elieston, i. 41 *n.*
O'Duin, Diarmid, i. 318.
— Eva, i. 318.
— Paul 'an sporran,' i. 318.
Offley, Margery, wife of Jas. Leveson, i. 400.
— Mary, wife of rev. William Graham, vii. 103.
— William, Chester, i. 400.
Ogden, Richard, London, i. 402.
—— his wife, Anne Aston, i. 402.
Ogilvie of the Garth, St. Margaret's Inch, and Wester Craigs, Thomas, viii. 293.
— George Macartney, viii. 232.
— Zina Liliae, wife of M. C. Drummond, viii. 232.
— *see also* Ogilvy.
OGILVIE-GRANT, VISCOUNT OF REIDHAVEN, vii. 487-493.
OGILVIE-GRANT, EARL OF SEAFIELD, vii. 454-494.
OGILVIE-GRANT, BARON STRATHSPEY OF STRATHSPEY, vii. 491-494.
Ogilvie-Grant of Grant, George Henry, v. 369.

* Name unknown.

Ogilvie-Grant, Alexander Lewis Henry, vii. 490.
—— his wife, Hilda Annie Perry, vii. 490.
— Alice Elizabeth, wife of lord Walter C. Gordon Lennox, v. 369; vii. 490.
— Alison Jean, vii. 490.
— Caroline Louisa, vii. 493.
— Charles Randolph Mark, vii. 490.
— Eleanora, dau. of William Robert G., vii. 490.
— George Henry Essex, captain 42nd Highlanders, vii. 490.
—— his wife, Eleanora Gordon Cumming, vii. 490.
— George Randolph Seymour, vii. 490.
— Henry Oswin, 2nd West India regiment, vii. 490.
— Jane, wife of Sir E. W. Forestier-Walker, vii. 490.
— Lewis Alexander, Royal Horse Guards, vii. 489.
—— his wife, Georgina Maunsell, vii. 489.
— Maria Jane Anne Stuart, vii. 490.
— Marjorie Elspeth, vii. 490.
— Mary Louisa Eleanora, wife of H. M. Sperling, vii. 490.
— Muriel Frances Charlotte, wife of Geoffrey St. Quintin, vii. 490.
— Nina Caroline, vii. 493.
— Nina Geraldine, vii. 493.
— Robert Abercromby, captain Gordon Highlanders, vii. 492.
— Robert George, vii. 490.
— Sydney Montague, wife of rev. Wm. Rice, vii. 493; ix. 155.
— Trevor, vii. 493.
—— his wife, Alice Louisa Hardy-Johnston, vii. 493.
— William Robert, vii. 490.
—— his wife, Maud Louisa Pechell, vii. 490.
OGILVY OF AIRLIE, OGILVY, LORD, i. 114-132.
Ogilvy of Airlie, David, ninth lord, i. 126.
—— David, eleventh lord, i. 127.
—— David, twelfth lord, i. 130.
—— David Graham Drummond, thirteenth lord, i. 131.
—— David Lyulph Gore Wolseley, fifteenth lord, i. 132.
—— David William Stanley, fourteenth lord, i. 131.
—— James, first lord, i. 114; ix. 7.
—— his 1st wife, Mary Douglas, i. 114.
—— his 2nd wife, Helen Douglas, i. 114; vi. 222; ix. 7, 12, 137.
—— his 3rd wife, Jonet Lyle, i. 114.
—— James, third lord, i. 116; iii. 25, 26.
—— his wife, Isobel Lindsay, i. 116; iii. 25.

Ogilvy of Airlie, James, fourth lord, i. 117.
—— —— his wife, Elinor *or* Helen Sinclair, i. 117; vii. 572.
—— —— James, fifth lord, i. 118, 119; iv. 25, 26 *bis*. 371, 536.
—— —— his wife, Jean Forbes, i. 119; iv. 56.
—— —— James, sixth lord, i. 122.
—— —— his 1st wife, Jean Ruthven, i. 122; iv. 262; ix. 8.
—— —— his 2nd wife, Elizabeth Napier, i. 122; vi. 417.
—— —— James, seventh lord, i. 123.
—— —— his wife, Isobel Hamilton, i. 124.
—— —— James, eighth lord, i. 125; vii. 199.
—— —— John, second lord, i. 114, 116.
—— —— his wife, Marion *or* Jean Graham, i. 116; vi. 223.
—— —— John, tenth lord, i. 127.
OGILVY OF ALYTH AND LINTRATHEN, OGILVY, LORD, i. 123-132.
Ogilvy of Alyth and Lintrathen, James, first lord, i. 123.
OGILVY OF CULLEN, OGILVY, LORD, iv. 37-41.
Ogilvy of Cullen, James, first lord, iv. 37.
OGILVY OF DESKFORD, OGILVY, LORD, iv. 26-41.
Ogilvy of Deskford, James, second lord, iv. 27.
—— —— his 1st wife, Elizabeth Leslie, iv. 29.
—— —— his 2nd wife, Marion Cunningham, iv. 29.
—— —— Walter, first lord, iv. 26; ix. 89.
—— —— his 1st wife, Agnes Elphinstone, iii. 536; iv. 26.
—— —— his 2nd wife, Marie Douglas, iv. 26.
OGILVY OF DESKFORD AND CULLEN, OGILVY, LORD, iv. 37-41.
Ogilvy of Deskford and Cullen, James, first lord, iv. 37.
OGILVY OF DESKFORD AND INSCHEMAIRTENE, OGILVY, LORD, iv. 28-41.
Ogilvy, master of, James, eldest son of 4th lord Ogilvy of Airlie, i. 118.
—— —— his wife, Katharine Campbell, i. 118.
—— master of, James, eldest son of 6th lord Ogilvy of Airlie, i. 123; viii. 101.
OGILVY, EARL OF AIRLIE, i. 106-132.
OGILVY, LORD BANFF, ii. 1-26.
OGILVY, LORD DESKFORD, iv. 28.
OGILVY, EARL OF FINDLATER, iv. 16-41.
OGILVY, LORD OGILVY OF AIRLIE, i. 114-132.
OGILVY, LORD OGILVY OF ALYTH AND LINTRATHEN, i. 123-132.
OGILVY, LORD OGILVY of CULLEN, iv. 37.
OGILVY, LORD OGILVY OF DESKFORD, iv. 26-41.
OGILVY, LORD OGILVY OF DESKFORD AND CULLEN, iv. 37-41.
OGILVY, LORD OGILVY OF DESKFORD AND INSCHMARTINE, iv. 28-41.
OGILVY, VISCOUNT OF REIDHAVEN, iv. 37-41.
OGILVY, VISCOUNT SEAFIELD, iv. 37-41.
OGILVY, EARL OF SEAFIELD, iv. 37-41.
Ogilvy of Alweth, George, ii. 9.
—— —— Walter, ii. 14.
—— of Ardranich, John. v. 524.
—— of Ardun, Alexander, iv. 20.
—— of Auchindoun, Alexander, iv. 22.
—— —— Sir James, iv. 22.
—— —— James, iv. 25, 537.
—— of Auchinstank, Alexander, iv. 20.
—— of Auchiries, James, ii. 12, 16; iv. 76.
—— of Auchlevin, Alexander, iv. 20.
—— —— Sir Walter, i. 111; iv. 16.
—— —— his 1st wife, Isobel [?Durward], i. 111, 112.
—— —— his 2nd wife, Isobel Glen, i. 112; iv. 16.
—— —— Sir Walter, sheriff of Banff, i. 112; ii. 1; iv. 16.
—— —— his wife, Margaret Sinclair of Deskford, ii. 1; iv. 16, 17.
—— —— Sir Walter, sheriff of Inverness and Banff, ii. 1; iv. 17, 18 *bis*.
—— —— his wife, Margaret Edmondstone, ii. 2, 3.
—— of Auchterhouse, Sir Alexander, sheriff of Angus, i. 109; ii. 266; iv. 29.
—— —— his wife, Janet Gray, iv. 272.
—— —— Alexander, sheriff of Angus, i. 109; iii. 20; iv. 17.
—— —— Margaret, wife of Sir Jas. Stewart, earl of Buchan, i. 109; ii. 266; ix. 47.
—— of Auchterhouse, Sir Patrick, i. 109; vi. 276.
—— —— his wife, Christian Keith of Grandon, i. 109; vi. 37, 301.
—— —— Sir Walter, sheriff of Angus, i. 107, 108 *bis*.
—— of Baddynspink, Walter, ii. 7.
—— of Balhegno, James, advocate, iv. 64.
—— —— his wife, Mary Forbes, iv. 64.
—— of Balconquhaile, Sir James, iv. 18.
—— of Baldavy, William. ii. 3.
—— of Balfour, Sir James, iv. 18.
—— —— James, i. 296; iii. 187; iv. 283.
—— —— his 1st wife, Margaret Stewart, iii. 187.
—— —— his 2nd wife, Margaret Gray, iv. 283.
—— —— his 3rd wife, Katharine Arbuthnott, i. 296.
—— —— James, i. 295.
—— —— his wife, Margaret Arbuthnott, i. 295.
—— —— John, i. 296.
—— —— Oliver, son of 1st lord Ogilvy of Airlie and Helen Douglas; ancestor of the family of, vi. 223 *bis*; ix. 7 *bis*, 137.
—— —— his wife, Felicia Fentoun, ix. 7.
—— of Balgally, James, eldest son of Sir David O. of Inchmartine, iv. 31, 34.
—— —— his wife, Isabella Oliphant, iv. 31.
—— of Balhawal, Alexander, iv. 20.

Ogilvy of Balhawal, Sir Andrew, iv. 30.
—— —— Sir John, iv. 17.
—— —— Sir Walter, iv. 17.
—— of Balkello, Gilbert, vii. 194.
—— of Balkery, Alexander, iv. 20.
—— of Balmuto, Sir Andrew, iv. 30.
—— —— David, iii. 15, 18.
—— —— David, i. 110.
—— —— his wife, Christian Glen, i. 110.
—— of Balzeordie, Sir James, iv. 18.
—— of Banff, Sir George, ii. 10.
—— —— Sir George, ii. 15.
—— —— Walter, ii. 11, 14.
—— of Bankhead, Alexander, iv. 21.
—— of Barras, Sir David, iv. 31 *bis*.
—— —— George, vi. 59.
—— —— Sir George, 1st bart, i. 286.
—— —— his wife, Margaret Arbuthnott, i. 286.
—— of Bauchlaw, Alexander, iv. 20.
—— —— Sir James, iv. 18.
—— of Beaufort, Walter, sheriff-depute of Angus and Banff, i. 110; iv. 17; vii. 273.
—— —— his wife, Margaret Fenton, i. 110.
—— of Bellouch, Thomas, vii. 183.
—— of Birnes, James, ii. 13.
—— —— his wife, Elspeth Abernethie, ii. 9, 13.
—— —— John, son of Geo. O. of Carnowseis, ii. 12.
—— —— his wife, Jean Seton, ii. 12.
—— of Blacklaw, George, ii. 11.
—— of Blairshannoch, Alexander, iv. 20.
—— —— Sir James, iv. 18.
—— of Bogmuchalls, John, 3rd son of 4th earl of Huntly, vi. 22 *bis*.
—— of Easter Bogside, John, ix. 8.
—— of Boyne, Alexander, *error for* Walter, ii. 4 *n*.
—— —— Alexander, ii. 166; iv. 21, 26, 56.
—— —— his wife, Jane Gordon, ii. 166; iv. 539; viii. 344.
—— —— Archibald, heir-male of the family of, iv. 36.
—— —— George, ancestor of the family of, ii. 3 *bis*, 26; iv. 20.
—— —— James, ii. 13, 15.
—— —— his wife, Isobelle Ogilvy, ii. 13, 15.
—— —— Sir Patrick, iii. 452; vii. 475; ix. 81.
—— —— his 1st wife, Anna Grant, vii. 475.
—— —— his 3rd wife, Anne Montgomerie, iii. 452; ix. 81.
—— —— [Sir Walter], ix. 91.
—— —— his wife, Violet Forbes, iv. 74; ix. 91.
—— —— Sir Walter, ii. 1; vii. 434.
—— —— Walter, son of George O., ii. 4, 6, 7, 269; iv. 20.
—— —— Walter, son of James O., ii. 15.
—— —— Sir William, claimant to barony of Banff, ii. 26.
—— of Brodland, James, iv. 22.
Ogilvy of Cairnbulg, Patrick, colonel, iv. 121.
—— of Caputh, Sir Patrick, iv. 34.
—— of Carcary, Sir Walter, i. 111; iv. 16.
—— of Cardell, James, eldest son of Alex. O. of Deskford, iv. 21, 22, 26.
—— —— his 1st wife, Jonet Gordon, iv. 22, 25; v. 104.
—— —— his 2nd wife, Marion Livingston, iv. 25.
—— of Carnowseis, Sir George, ii. 10.
—— —— his wife, Beatrix Seton, ii. 11.
—— —— George, provost of Banff, ii. 11; vii. 440, 441.
—— —— his 1st wife, Margaret Ogilvy, ii. 11.
—— —— his 2nd wife, Barbara Fraser, ii. 11; vii. 440.
—— —— Sir George, 1st bart., ii. 12, 16.
—— —— his wife, Jean Gordon, ii. 12.
—— —— John, son of Sir William O. of Stratherne, ii. 4.
—— —— his wife, Elizabeth Dunbar, ii. 5.
—— —— Walter, ii. 8.
—— —— his wife, Helen Stewart, ii. 8; v. 7.
—— of Cassingray, James, iv. 35.
—— —— Sir Patrick, iv. 35.
—— of Castelfield, Alexander, iv. 20.
—— of Castelyairdis Rock, Alexander, iv. 21.
—— of Cleghorn, Sir David, iv. 31.
—— of Cleishberry, Christian, wife of (1) John Campbell of Lawers, and (2) P. Hepburn, ii. 142, 178.
—— of Clova, Sir David, M.P., i. 123 *n*., 124; ii. 28.
—— —— his wife, Margaret Hamilton, i. 124.
—— —— David, i. 124.
—— —— Donald, H.E.I.C.S., M.P., i. 129.
—— —— his wife, Maria Morley, i. 129.
—— —— Thomas, vii. 183.
—— —— Walter, 2nd son of 4th earl of Airlie, i. 127, 129, 314.
—— —— his 1st wife, Margaret Fullarton, i. 129; viii. 109; ix. 8.
—— —— his 2nd wife, Jean Ogilvy, i. 129.
—— —— Walter, i. 129.
—— —— his wife, Ellen Smith, i. 129.
—— —— Walter Donald Duncan, i. 129.
—— of Cluny, David, i. 121, 127; viii. 109 *bis*.
—— —— his wife, Elizabeth Fullarton, viii. 109.
—— —— James, 2nd son of Patrick O. of Muirtown, i. 121.
—— —— his wife, Katharine Nairne, i. 121; ix. 141.
—— —— James, i. 121.
—— —— Margaret, wife of 4th earl of Airlie, i. 121, 127.
—— of Collard, Alexander, iv. 25.
—— —— his wife, Barbara Ogilvy, iv. 25.
—— —— James, iv. 22.
—— of Craig, Gilbert, iv. 126.
—— —— his wife, Anne Crichton, iv. 126.

Ogilvy of Craig, John, 4th son of 1st lord Ogilvy of Airlie, i. 115.
—— —— Sir John, 2nd son of 5th lord Ogilvy of Airlie, i. 120, 122.
—— —— his 1st wife, Elizabeth Crichton, i. 120.
—— —— his 2nd wife, * Brown, i. 120.
—— —— Thomas, i. 117.
—— of Craigboyne, Walter, vi. 45.
—— —— his wife, Christian Keith, vi. 45.
—— of Crannoch, George, ii. 11.
—— —— Sir George, ii. 12.
—— of Cullen, Sir James, iv. 18.
—— of Darchadlie, Alexander, iv. 21.
—— of Denside, John, v. 4.
—— —— his wife, Isobel Stewart, v. 4.
—— of Deskford, Alexander, iv. 19, 20.
—— —— his 1st wife, Jonet Abernethy, iv. 22; vii. 409.
—— —— his 2nd wife, Elizabeth Gordon, iv. 22.
—— —— Sir James, customer of Banff, ii. 1; iv. 17, 20, 21, 22; vii. 570.
—— —— his 1st wife, Margaret Innes, iv. 18.
—— —— his 2nd wife, Margaret Chaumer, iv. 18.
—— —— John, 3rd son of 4th earl of Huntly, iv. 21, 22, 23.
—— —— Sir Walter, iv. 16.
—— —— his wife, Margaret Sinclair, iv. 16, 17.
—— —— Sir Walter, iv. 26.
—— —— his 1st wife, Agnes Elphinstone, iv. 26.
—— —— his 2nd wife, Marie Douglas, iv. 26; vi. 374.
—— of Wester Dron, Sir Andrew, iv. 30.
—— of Drummadertie, William, 2nd son of W. O. of Murie, iv. 35.
—— of Drummy, Patrick, iv. 32.
—— of Drumnakeith, Alexander, iv. 20.
—— of Drymme, Andrew, 3rd son of Patrick O. of Inchmartine, iv. 32.
—— of Dunbog, Sir Walter, vii. 274.
—— of Dunlugus, Sir George, ii. 8, 10; iv. 26; ix. 35.
—— —— his wife, Beatrix Seton, ii. 10, 11; viii. 583.
—— —— Sir George, ii. 15.
—— —— his 1st wife, Margaret Irvine, ii. 17.
—— —— his 2nd wife, Janet Sutherland, ii. 18.
—— —— Sir Walter, 4th son of Sir Walter O. of Boyne, ii. 67; iv. 21.
—— —— his wife, Alison Home, ii. 8; iv. 451.
—— —— Walter, provost of Banff, ii. 14.
—— —— his wife, Helen Urquhart, ii. 14.
—— of Durdie-Inglis, John, 2nd son of Patrick O. of Inchmartine, iv. 32.

* Name unknown.

Ogilvy of Durne, John, ii. 4, 6, 7, 9.
—— —— his wife, Elizabeth Dunbar, ii. 15.
—— of Ebrux, Gilbert, ix. 89.
—— of Erroll, Sir Patrick, iv. 34.
—— of Fettercairn, Sir Walter, vii. 274.
—— of Findachtie, Alexander, iv. 21.
—— —— Alexander, illeg. son of James O. of Ogilvy and Findlater, iv. 25.
—— of Findlater, Alexander, iv. 19, 20.
—— —— James, iv. 17, 20, 22.
—— —— James, the younger, iv. 19.
—— —— his wife, Agnes Gordon, iv. 531.
—— —— James, iv. 21, 537.
—— —— his 1st wife, Jonet Gordon, iv. 25.
—— —— his 2nd wife, Marion Livingston, iv. 25; v. 439.
—— —— Walter, iv. 16.
—— —— Walter, iv. 26, 538.
—— of Fingask, Sir John, i. 116; viii. 277 *n.*
—— —— his wife, Marion *, i. 116.
—— of Fordyce, Margaret, wife of Thos. Menzies, ii. 5.
—— of Forglen, Sir Alexander, 1st bart., lord of Session, i. 142; ii. 19, 22, 23.
—— —— his 1st wife, Mary Allardice, i. 142; ii. 23.
—— —— his 2nd wife, Mary Leslie, ii. 24; vi. 442.
—— —— Alexander, captain, ii. 22, 24.
—— —— his wife, Jane Frend, ii. 24.
—— of Friock, George, i. 122.
—— —— his wife, Elspet Montgomerie, i. 122.
—— —— James, i. 122.
—— of Geddes, Alexander, ii. 5.
—— —— George, ii. 3.
—— —— Sir William, ii. 3, 6.
—— —— his wife, Alison Roull, ii. 4.
—— of Glassaugh, Alexander, iv. 20.
—— —— Walter, 4th son of Sir James O. of Deskford, iv. 19.
—— of Glenfidich, Alexander, iv. 20.
—— of Glenmoy, William, i. 123 *n.*
—— of Grandon, Sir Patrick, i. 109, 112.
—— —— his wife, Christian Keith, i. 109; vi. 37.
—— of Grange of Airlie, James, iv. 35.
—— —— Sir Patrick, iv. 35.
—— of Holme, James, iv. 22.
—— of Hutton, Sir George, ii. 10.
—— of Inchdrewer, George, ii. 17.
—— of Inchleslie, Patrick, colonel, iv. 36; vi. 112.
—— of Inchmartin, Andrew, 3rd son of Sir Alex. O. of Auchterhouse; 1st laird, i. 110; iv. 29, 30, 31.
—— —— his wife, Marjory Glen, i. 110; iv. 29.
—— —— Archibald, v. 312, 313.
—— —— his wife, Jane Maitland, v. 312.

* Name unknown.

Ogilvy of Inchmartin, Sir David, 2nd laird, i. 110; iv. 30, 278.
—— his contracted wife, Euphemia Wemyss, viii. 483.
—— his wife, Mariota Hay, iv. 31 *bis*.
—— James, 3rd laird, iv. 31, 32.
—— his wife, Isabella Oliphant, iv. 31.
—— James, 11th laird, iv. 37; v. 317.
—— his wife, Elizabeth Maitland, v. 317.
—— Patrick, 4th laird, iv. 31, 32.
—— his 1st wife, Mariota Stewart, iv. 32; v. 4.
—— his 2nd wife, Elizabeth Kinnaird, iv. 32; v. 207.
—— Patrick, 6th laird, iv. 33, 279.
—— his 1st wife, Marion *or* Marjorie Gray, iv. 33, 262.
—— his 2nd wife, Elizabeth Butter, iv. 33.
—— his 3rd wife, Geilis Seton, iv. 34.
—— Patrick, the younger, iv. 34.
—— his wife, Margaret Halyburton, iv. 34.
—— Sir Patrick, 7th laird, ii. 187; iv. 34.
—— his wife, Anne *or* Agnes Campbell, ii. 187; iv. 31.
—— Sir Patrick, 8th laird, iv. 28, 29 *ter*, 35, 36.
—— his wife, Elizabeth Ogilvy, iv. 29, 35.
—— Patrick, colonel, 3rd son of 3rd earl of Findlater; 9th laird, iv. 36.
—— his wife, Elizabeth Montgomerie, iii. 452; iv. 36.
—— Patrick, colonel, 10th laird, iv. 36.
—— his wife, Mary Ogilvy, iv. 37.
—— William, 5th laird, iv. 32, 33; v. 206; 208; ix. 89.
—— his wife, Jonet Gray, iv. 33, 279.
— of Innerichney, George, ii. 9.
—— Mr. Thomas, ii. 9.
—— Walter, ii. 14.
— of Inshewan, John, i. 121.
—— his wife, Jane Ogilvy, i. 121.
—— John, i. 129.
—— John, i. 129.
— of Inverkeiler, John, 3rd son of 4th lord Ogilvy of Airlie, i. 118.
—— his wife, Katharine Strachan, i. 118.
—— John, i. 118.
—— his wife, Elizabeth Betoun, i. 118.
— of Inverkerech, Alexander, iv. 20.
— of Invernorth, Patrick, colonel, iv. 121.
— of Inverquharity, Alexander, iv. 522.
—— Sir David, vi. 495.
—— John, 3rd son of Sir Walter O. of Auchterhouse, i. 111.
—— John, i. 119.
—— his wife, Helen Ogilvy, i. 119.
—— Sir John, i. 111 *bis*.
Ogilvy of Inverquharity, Sir John, 4th bart., vi. 498.
—— his wife, Anne Carnegie, vi. 498.
—— Sir Reginald Heward Alexander, 10th bart., v. 214; ix. 122.
—— his wife, Olivia Barbara Kinnaird, v. 214.
— of Iroly, James, v. 523.
— of Keithmore, Alexander, iv. 20.
—— James, iv. 537.
— of Kempcairn, Alexander, 2nd son of 1st lord Ogilvy of Deskford, iv. 27.
—— his wife, Katharine Grant, vii. 468.
—— James, iv. 73.
— of Kettins, Patrick, i. 107.
— of Kilmundy, Gilbert, i. 106, 161.
— of Kincailze, James, iv. 22.
— of Kinnaird, Patrick, iv. 32.
— of Kinneff, Alexander, i. 110; iv. 275.
—— David, iii. 15, 18.
— of Kneck, Alexander, burgess of Banff, ii. 12, 15.
—— his wife, Marie Ogilvy, ii. 13, 15.
—— James, ii. 13.
—— his wife, Elspeth Abernethy, ii. 9, 13.
— of Knockdurn, Alexander, iv. 21.
— of Labethie, Alexander, iii. 319.
—— his wife, Margaret Graham, iii. 319.
— of Langmuir, Alexander, iv. 21.
— of Laverocklaw, John, v. 524.
— of Lintrathen, Sir John, i. 112, 113; iv. 17, 30, 71; vi. 221.
—— his 1st wife, Margaret *, i. 113; vi. 303.
—— his alleged wife, Marion Seton, i. 113.
—— his 2nd wife, Isobel Forbes, ix. 7.
—— Sir Walter, high treasurer, i. 111, 279; ii. 454; iv. 16.
—— his 1st wife, Isabel *, i. 111, 112.
—— his 2nd wife, Isabel Glen, i. 112.
— of Lenmay, Archibald, iv. 36.
—— Patrick, colonel, M.P., iii. 452; iv. 36; vii. 445.
—— his 1st wife, Elizabeth Baird, ix. 90.
—— his 2nd wife, Elizabeth Montgomerie, iv. 36.
— of Loyal, William, commander R.N. M.P., i. 129.
— of Lude, Patrick, iv. 33.
— of Lunan, George, vi. 182.
— of Marytoun, Janet of, viii. 49.
— of Melgund, Marion *or* Mariota, mistress of cardinal David Betoun, i. 115; iv. 539.
— of Mennnir, Alexander, iv. 20.
— of Milton, John, vi. 556.

* Name unknown.

Ogilvy of Milton, Mary, wife of (1) P. Meldrum of Leathers, and (2) Charles, 7th lord Oliphant, vi. 556.
— of Montcoffer, George, ii. 15.
— of Monycabock, Walter, ii. 7.
— of Moy, John, v. 524.
— of Muirton, George, created baron Ogilvy de Muirton in Germany, i. 121.
— — his wife, Euphrasia Veronica de Reichsperg, i. 121.
— — George Benedict, 2nd baron, i. 121.
— — his wife, Marie Anastasia de Brumath, i. 121.
— — James, i. 121; ix. 142.
— — his wife, Katharine Nairne, i. 121; ix. 141.
— — Patrick, 6th son of 5th lord Ogilvy of Airlie, i. 120.
— — his wife, Isabella Murray, i. 121.
— of Murie, Patrick, iv. 35.
— — William, 2nd son of Sir Patrick O. of Inchmartine, iv. 35.
— of Murkle, John, physician in Forfar, i. 129.
— — his wife, Margaret Ogilvy, i. 129.
— of Neve, Alexander, iv. 229 *n.*
— of Newbigging, John, 'in Invergowrie,' i. 123; ix. 8.
— — his wife, Agnes Napier, i. 123; iv. 282; vi. 417.
— of Newgrange, Francis, 7th son of 5th lord Ogilvy of Airlie, i. 121.
— — his 1st wife, Helen Gardin, i. 121.
— — his 2nd wife, Elizabeth Adamson, i. 121.
— — Sir James. i. 121.
— — his wife, Margaret Guthrie, i. 121.
— of Newtoun, David, 2nd son of Sir John O. of Lintrathen, i. 113.
— of Ogilvy, Alexander de, 1250, i. 107.
— — Alexander, 1309, i. 107.
— — Alexander, 1517, iv. 20.
— — David, 1427, vi. 276.
— — Gilbert, ancestor of the family of, i. 106, 161.
— — Gilbert, i. 106; vii. 194.
— — Sir James, iv. 18.
— — James, iv. 22, 25.
— — John de, i. 107.
— — John, sheriff-depute of Angus, i. 108.
— — Patrick de, i. 107.
— — Patrick of, i. 107, 108.
— — Thomas, iii. 321.
— — his wife, Margaret Heriot, iii. 321.
— — Walter de, i. 107.
— — Sir Walter, iv. 26.
— of Orde, Sir George, ii. 10.
— of Ordinhuiffis, John, iv. 22.
— of Oures, Walter, i. 109, 110; iii. 222; iv. 17.
— — his wife, Margaret of Fenton, i. 110.
Ogilvy of Paddoklaw, James, ii. 12, 16.
— of Panbride, iv. 522.
— of Peill, John, i. 118.
— of Persie, David, i. 297.
— — his wife, Margaret Arbuthnott, i. 297; ix. 16.
— of Petconochy, Sir David, iv. 30.
— of Pitmedy, Sir James, iv. 18.
— of Pitmowis, David, 3rd son of 5th lord Ogilvy of Airlie, i. 120.
— — his 1st wife, Martha MacCalzean, i. 120.
— — his 2nd wife, Nicolas Guthrie, i. 120.
— of Pitnacree, Patrick, iv. 33.
— of Pitpointie, John, iii. 311.
— — his wife, Elizabeth Scrimgeour, iii. 311.
— of Pittenbrinzeans, Alexander, iv. 21.
— of Powrie, Gilbert, 3rd son of 1st earl of Angus, i. 106, 161.
— — Sir Gilbert, v. 86.
— of Wester Powry, Patrick, i. 108.
— — his wife, Marjory, i. 108.
— — Walter of, i. 107.
— of Ratee, Ardwne and Bothquhanston, Elizabeth, dau. of Sir Jas. O. of Deskford, iv. 19; ix. 89.
— of Rothiemay, Archibald, iv. 36, 37.
— — James, iv. 37; v. 317.
— — his wife, Elizabeth Maitland, v. 317.
— of Sandlach, Alexander, iv. 20.
— of Sanquhar, John, ii. 4.
— — his wife, Elizabeth Dunbar, ii. 5.
— of Seafield, Alexander, iv. 21.
— of Smythstown, Alexander, iv. 21.
— of Strathardle, Sir David, iv. 30.
— — James, iv. 34.
— — Sir Patrick, iv. 34.
— of Stratherne, John, ii. 4, 6; iv. 20.
— — Sir Walter, ii. 7.
— — Sir William, ii. 3, 5, 6; iv. 20.
— of Templehall, David, iv. 32; ix. 89.
— — his wife, Christina Galychtlie of Ebrux, ix. 89.
— of Tullynacht, Alexander, iv. 21.
— of Wardropstoun, Sir John, iv. 17; vi. 221.
— — Sir Walter, iv. 17.
— of Westercraig, John, illeg. son of Thos. O., i. 117.
— — Thomas, 2nd son of 4th lord Ogilvy of Airlie, i. 117.
— — his 1st wife, Janet Fraser, i. 117; ix. 8.
— — his 2nd wife, Beatrix Chisholm, i. 117.
— of Woodfield, Alexander, iv. 21.
— Agnes, wife of Thomas Erskine, son of Sir Thos. E. of Erskine, i. 118; ix. 8.
— Agnes, wife of John Erskine of Dun, i. 119.

Ogilvy, Agnes, wife of F. Gordon, ii. 19.
— Agnes, wife of Sir Alex. Reid, ii. 24.
— Agnes, contracted to Sir D. Lindsay of Beaufort and Edzell, iii. 20.
— Agnes, wife of Thos. Gourlaw of Ballindane, iv. 32.
— Alexander, son of Sir Walter O. of Carcary, i. 111; iv. 16.
— Alexander, 5th son of Sir Walter O. of Lintrathen, i. 112.
— Alexander, 4th son of 1st lord Ogilvy of Airlie, i. 114.
— — his wife, Nicolas Stratoun, i. 114.
— Alexander, 5th son of 4th lord Ogilvy of Airlie, i. 118.
— Alexander, son of James, master of Ogilvy, i. 118.
— Alexander, in Gamrie, ii. 9.
— Alexander, master of Banff, ii. 25.
— Alexander, killed at Flodden, iv. 19.
— Alexander, 4th son of 1st lord Ogilvy of Deskford, iv. 27.
— Alexander, 4th son of Patrick O. of Inchmartine, iv. 32.
— Alexander, vi. 433.
— — his wife, Marcia Anne Symson Napier, vi. 433.
— Andrew, 3rd son of James O. of Inchmartin, iv. 31.
— Andrew, 3rd son of William O. of Inchmartine, iv. 33.
— Andrew, 2nd son of Patrick O., iv. 34.
— Anna, dau. of David O. of Pitmowis, i. 120.
— Anna, wife of Sir Geo. Allardice, i. 143; iv. 37; ix. 90 *bis*.
— Anne, wife of Sir John Wood of Bonnytoun, i. 126.
— Anne, dau. of Walter O. of Clova, i. 130.
— Anne, wife of James Law, ii. 21; ix. 35.
— Ann, wife of Andrew Hay, ii. 24.
— Anne, wife of (1) James (Douglas), earl of Buchan, and (2) Andrew, 7th lord Gray, ii. 271; iv. 27, 287; ix. 48 *bis*.
— Anne, dau. of John O. of Balbegno, iii. 351.
— Anne, wife of 8th earl of Glencairn, iv. 29, 248.
— Anne, wife of 2nd earl of Hopetoun, iv. 39, 497.
— Anne, wife of Sir Thomas Erskine of Dirleton, v. 86; ix. 116.
— Anne, wife of Robert Middleton of Balbegno, vi. 182.
— Anne, wife of Jas. Carnegie of Kinnoull, vi. 495.
— Annie Sarah, wife of Donald Ogilvy, i. 129.
— Anthony, abbot of Glenluce, i. 116.
— Archibald, 2nd son of 1st lord Ogilvy of Airlie, i. 114.
Ogilvy, Archibald, 3rd son of 3rd lord Ogilvy of Airlie, i. 116.
— Archibald, eldest son of Thos. O. of Westercraig, i. 117; ix. 8.
— Archibald, 4th son of 4th lord Ogilvy of Airlie, i. 118.
— Archibald, son of James, master of Ogilvy, i. 118.
— Archibald, 5th son of 5th lord Ogilvy of Airlie, i. 120.
— Archibald, 4th son of 6th lord Ogilvy of Airlie, i. 123.
— Archibald, son of 7th lord Banff, ii. 25.
— Arthur, illeg. son of Francis O. of Newgrange, i. 121.
— Barbara, illeg. dau. of James O. of Ogilvy, iv. 25.
— Barbara, wife of (1) Alex. Ogilvy of Collard, and (2) John Panton of Pitsmeddan, iv. 25.
— Beatrice, wife of Alex. Seton, ii. 14.
— Beatrix, wife of * Garden of Leys, i. 117.
— Bridget, dau. of Alex. O., ii. 24.
— Bruce Arthur Ashley, i. 132.
— Charles, 4th son of Walter O. of Clova, i. 129.
— Charles, v. 312.
— — his wife, Margaret Maitland, v. 312.
— Christian, *possible* wife of Sir John Wemyss of Kincaldrum, Reres and Wemyss, i. 110; viii. 482.
— Christian, wife of * Lindsay, i. 110.
— Christian, alleged wife of Sir Alex. Forbes of Pitsligo, i. 113.
— Christian, wife of Sir John Forbes of Pitsligo, iv. 26, 74.
— Christian, wife of (1) John Campbell of Auchreoch, and (2) P. Hepburn of Beinston, ii. 142, 178; v. 499.
— Christian, wife of James Moncur, iv. 32.
— Christian, dau. of David O. of Inchmartine, iv. 278.
— Christina, wife of Sir Jas. Ramsay of Bamff, i. 124.
— Clara, wife of Robert Fletcher, i. 124.
— Clementina Drummond, wife of James Rait, i. 130.
— Clementina Gertrude Helen, wife of 1st baron Redesdale, i. 131.
— David, son of Sir Walter O. of Carcary, i. 111; iv. 16.
— David, 4th son of Sir Walter O. of Lintrathen, i. 112.
— David, son of Donald O. of Clova, i. 129.
— David, capt. 4th Dragoons, ii. 25.
— David, 5th son of Patrick O. of Inchmartine, iv. 32.
— David, captain Scots Guards, vii. 373.
— — his wife, Jean Thoirs, vii. 374.
— Donald, 2nd son of Donald O. of Clova, i. 129.

* Name unknown.

Ogilvy, Dorothea Maria, i. 129.
—— Dorothea Sophia Elizabeth, i. 129.
—— Edward David Stuart, Yulgilbar, iv. 213.
—— Egidia, wife of John Moncrieff of Moncrieff, iv. 32.
—— Elizabeth, wife of Sir Patrick Keith of Innerugie, i. 114.
—— Elizabeth, wife of W. Wood of Bonnytoun, i. 116.
—— Elizabeth, wife of G. Gordon of Gight, i. 123.
—— Elizabeth, wife of Sir John Carnegy of Balnamoon, i. 125; viii. 61; ix. 8.
—— Elizabeth, wife of Wm. Leslie of Balquhain, ii. 7.
—— Elizabeth, illeg. dau. of Sir Walter O., ii. 10.
—— Elizabeth, wife of Geo. Meldrum, ii. 12.
—— Elizabeth, wife of (1) Henry Urquhart, (2) Wm. Leslie, and (3) Thos. Menzies, ii. 5, 13.
—— Elizabeth, wife of Sir James Dunbar of Westfield, iv. 20.
—— Elizabeth, wife of 2nd earl of Findlater, iv. 28, 29, 35.
—— Elizabeth, wife of John Sandilands, iv. 33.
—— Elizabeth, dau. of Patrick O., yr. of Inchmartine, iv. 34.
—— Elizabeth, wife of George Nisbet, iv. 35.
—— Elizabeth, wife of Alex. Innes of Feddcrate, iv. 35; ix. 89.
—— Elizabeth, wife of 6th earl of Lauderdale, iv. 38; v. 311; ix. 125.
—— Elizabeth, wife of (1) William Haliburton of Gask, and (2) David Rollo of Menmuir, vii. 183.
—— Elizabeth, wife of admiral John Maitland, v. 313.
—— Elizabeth, wife of John Grant of Freuchie, vii. 458.
—— Elizabeth, dau. of 4th earl of Airlie, ix. 8.
—— Elizabeth, wife of Alex. Irvine of Drum, ix. 89.
—— Elspet, wife of Patrick Dunbar, ii. 5.
—— Eupham, wife of Sir Wm. Murray of Blebo, i. 467.
—— Euphemia, dau. of David O. of Pitmowis, i. 120.
—— Francis, servant of Robert, 1st lord Boyd, v. 145.
—— Francis, 2nd son of col. Patrick O. of Lonmay and Inchmartine, iv. 36.
—— George, eldest son of Sir Alex. O. of Auchterhouse, i. 109.
—— George, 7th son of Sir Walter O. of Lintrathen, i. 112; iv. 16.
—— George, queen's limner, ii. 23.
—— —— his wife, Jean Meldrum, ii. 24.
—— George, in holy orders, 6th son of Sir Jas. O. of Deskford, iv. 19.
Ogilvy, George, brother of Alexander O. of Deskford, iv. 20.
—— George, advocate, iv. 38; ix. 90.
—— Gilbert, 2nd son of Sir Jas. O. of Deskford, iv. 19, 20.
—— Giles, wife of Robert Arbuthnott of that Ilk, i. 112, 279.
—— Grisel, dau. of John O. of Balbegno, iii. 351.
—— Griselda Johanna Helen, wife of James Cheape, i. 131.
—— Grace, wife of * Douglas, ii. 25.
—— Helen, wife of James, 5th lord Innermeath, i. 118; v. 6.
—— Helen, wife of John Ogilvy of Innerquharity, i. 119.
—— Helen, wife of 2nd earl of Airlie, i. 126; ii. 18.
—— Helen, wife of Sir John Gordon of Park, i. 126.
—— Helen, dau. of 3rd earl of Airlie, i. 127.
—— Helen, wife of John Wedderburn, i. 130.
—— Helen, dau. of Walter O. of Carnowseis, ii. 8.
—— Helen, wife of Wm. Gray, ii. 12.
—— Helen, wife of Sir R. Lauder, ii. 19.
—— Helen, wife of James Smollett, ii. 24.
—— Helen, wife of Roger Robertson of Ladykirk, ix. 8.
—— Helen Alice Willington, dau. of 8th earl of Airlie, i. 132.
—— Helen Susanna Catherine Gertrude, wife of G. A. Pepper-Stavely, i. 130; ix. 9 *bis*.
—— Henriette Anne Mary, wife of D. Stewart-Robertson, i. 129.
—— Henrietta Blanche, wife of col. H. M. Hozier, i. 131.
—— Henry, prebendary of Tulynestyn, ix. 7.
—— Herbert Kinnaird, W.S., iii. 496.
—— —— his wife, Christian Augusta Bruce, iii. 496.
—— Hew, 4th son of 3rd earl of Findlater, iv. 37; ix. 90.
—— Isabel, wife of (1) Patrick, 1st lord Glamis, and (2) Gilbert, 1st lord Kennedy, i. 112; ii. 454; viii. 271.
—— Isobel, wife of Alex. Stewart, earl of Buchan, i. 115; ii. 267.
—— Isobel, wife of David Strachan of Carmylie, i. 116.
—— Isabel, wife of Robt. Guthrie of Kinblethmont, i. 118.
—— Isabel, dau. of 1st earl of Airlie, i. 125; ix. 8.
—— Isobelle, wife of James O. of Boyne, ii. 13, 15.
—— Isobel, dau. of 2nd lord Banff, ii. 19.
—— Isobel, wife of Geo. Barclay, ii. 21.

* Name unknown.

Ogilvy, Isabel, wife of (1) Kenneth, 1st lord Mackenzie of Kintail, and (2) Sir John Seton of Barns, vii. 504.
— James, 2nd son of Sir Walter O. of Lintrathen, i. 112.
— James, eldest son of 4th lord Ogilvy of Airlie; master of Ogilvy, i. 118.
— James, 2nd son of David O. of Pitmowis, i. 120.
— James, 5th son of 6th lord Ogilvy of Airlie, i. 123.
— James, illeg. son of Wm. O., i. 123.
— James, 1729, i. 477.
— James, commendator of Dryburgh, ii. 5.
— James, 5th son of Sir Walter O. of Dunlugus, ii. 9.
— — his wife, Agnes Gordon, ii. 9.
— James, illeg. son of Sir Walter O. of Dunlugus, ii. 10.
— James, captain, ii. 22.
— James, eldest son of Sir Jas. O. of Deskford and Findlater, iv. 19.
— — his wife, Agnes Gordon of Drumnakeith, iv. 19.
— James, brother of Alexander O. of Deskford and Findlater, iv. 19, 20.
— James, 3rd son of Patrick O. of Inchmartine, iv. 34.
— James, eldest son of col. Patrick O. of Lonmay and Inchmartine, iv. 36.
— James, kinsman of Abernethy of Auchencloich, vii. 415.
— Jane, wife of John Ogilvy of Inshewan, i. 121.
— Janet, contracted to a son of Gordon of Midmar, i. 115.
— Janet, alleged wife of * Leighton of Ulyshaven, i. 116.
— Janet, wife of Wm. Forbes, ii. 13.
— Janet, wife of John Leith, ii. 19.
— Janet, wife of Mr. J. Willison, ii. 25.
— Janet, wife of (1) Hugh Forbes, and (2) W. Duff of Braco, iv. 38.
— Janet, wife of John Scrimgeour of Glassary, iii. 310.
— Janet, wife of John Kinnaird of Kinnaird, iv. 32; v. 205.
— Janet, wife of George Kinnaird of Inchture, v. 206.
— Janet, wife of Jas. Anderson, ix. 8.
— Jean, wife of Patrick George of Kynnell, i. 121.
— Jean, dau. of 6th lord Ogilvy of Airlie, i. 123.
— Jean, wife of Walter Ogilvy of Clova, i. 129; ix. 8.
— Jean, wife of Sir J. F. Fitzgerald, i. 129.
— Jean, dau. of Walter O. of Clova, i. 130.
— Jean, lady Brotherstone, i. 303.
— Jean, wife of Gordon of Badinscoth, ii. 18.

* Name unknown.

Ogilvy, Jean, dau. of 2nd lord Banff, ii. 19.
— Jean, wife of Sir G. Abercromby, ii. 25.
— Jean, wife of Dr. Patrick Hay of Rattray, v. 229.
— Jean Graham Drummond, wife of 9th viscount Arbuthnott, i. 130, 316.
— Johanna, dau. of 5th earl of Airlie, i. 128.
— John, 2nd son of 3rd lord Ogilvy of Airlie, i. 116.
— John, eldest son of David O. of Pitmowis, i. 120.
— John, governor to 3rd earl of Airlie, i. 126.
— John, capt. 1st regt. of Foot, i. 129.
— John, i. 280.
— — his wife, Margaret Arbuthnott, i. 280.
— John, 5th son of Sir Walter O. of Boyne, ii. 6.
— John, parson of Cruden, ii. 9; ix. 35.
— John, burgess of Banff, ii. 15.
— John, 3rd son of Sir Jas. O. of Deskford, iv. 19, 20.
— John, brother of Alexander O. of Deskford, iv. 20 *bis*.
— Mr. John, Jesuit, iii. 233, 505; v. 169; ix. 156.
— John, in Newtoun, iv. 33.
— John, 2nd son of 6th earl of Findlater, iv. 40.
— John, 1511, iv. 564 *n*.
— Jonet, wife of Wm. Gordon of Schivas, ii. 7.
— Jonet, wife of Alex. Abercromby of Birkenbog, iv. 19.
— Jonet, wife of John Kinnaird of Kinnaird, iv. 32; v. 205.
— Julia Clementina, wife of capt. K. B. Stuart, i. 129.
— Katharine, wife of Sir John Scrymgeour, iii. 326.
— Katharine, dau. of John O. of Balbegno, iii. 351.
— Katharine, wife of W. Crawfurd of Fedderet, iv. 19.
— Kitty Edith Blanche, dau. of 8th earl of Airlie, i. 132.
— Lynlph Gilchrist Stanley, D.S.O., i. 131.
— Mabell Griselda Esther Sudley, dau. of 8th earl of Airlie, i. 132.
— Magdalen, wife of Sir Alex. Fraser of Philorth, ii. 9; vii. 440.
— Malcolm, 5th son of 1st lord Ogilvy of Airlie, i. 114.
— Margaret, wife of Sir John Oliphant, i. 110.
— Margaret, wife of Silvester Rattray, i. 110.
— Margaret, wife of Sir Gilbert Ramsay of Bamff, i. 114; ix. 8.
— Margaret, wife of W. Wood of Bonnytoun, i. 116.

Ogilvy, Margaret, wife of Andrew Gray, i. 117.
— Margaret, wife of Sir D. Graham of Fintry, i. 118.
— Margaret, wife of (1) George, 5th earl Marischal, and (2) Sir A. Strachan of Thornton, i. 122; vi. 53.
— Margaret, dau. of 6th lord Ogilvy of Airlie, i. 123.
— Margaret, wife of Patrick Urquhart of Lethentie and Meldrum, i. 124, 125.
— Margaret, wife of (1) Alexander, 2nd lord Falconer, and (2) Patrick Lyall, i. 126; v. 249.
— Margaret, wife of Sir John Wedderburn, i. 128.
— Margaret, wife of John Ogilvy of Murkle, i. 129.
— Margaret, wife of 8th viscount Arbuthnott, i. 130, 314.
— Margaret, contracted to Sir Robert Stewart, i. 439.
— Margaret, dau. of Walter O. of Carnowseis, ii. 8.
— Margaret, wife of Geo. Ogilvy of Carnowseis, ii. 11.
— Margaret, wife of John Lyon, ii. 18; ix. 35.
— Margaret, dau. of 2nd lord Banff, ii. 19.
— Margaret, dau. of Sir Alex. O. of Forglen, ii. 24.
— Margaret, wife of (1) John, master of Buchan, and (2) Geo. Barclay of Barclay, ii. 269; ix. 48.
— Margaret, *mistake for* Anne, wife of (1) James (Douglas), earl of Buchan, and (2) Andrew, lord Gray, ii. 271; iv. 27, 287; ix. 48 *bis*.
— Margaret, wife of James Gordon of Lesmoir, iv. 22.
— Margaret, wife of Robert Munro of Foulis, iv. 25.
— Margaret, wife of Sir P. Hay of Megginch, iv. 33.
— Margaret, wife of Sir L. Grant of Grant, iv. 39; vii. 484.
— Margaret, wife of John Kinnaird of Kinnaird, v. 205.
— Margaret, wife of Sir John Oliphant of Aberdalgie, vi. 587 *n.*, 539.
— Margaret, wife of George Durie of Grange, vii. 373.
— Margaret, wife of Robert Carnegie of Balnabreich, viii. 58.
— Margaret. wife of Frederick Lyon of Scrogerfield, viii. 295.
— Margaret, wife of John Grant of Freuchie, vii. 458; ix. 89.
— Maria Anne, dau. of 6th earl of Airlie, i. 130.
— Marie, wife of W. Abernethy, ii. 9.
Ogilvy, Marie, wife of Alex. Ogilvy of Knock, ii. 13, 15.
— Marie, wife of Alex. Sutherland of Kinminitie, iii. 204.
— Marion, wife of Henry Stewart of Rosyth, i. 114.
— Marion, wife of Patrick Gordon of Haddo, i. 84; iv. 19.
— Marion, wife of (1) James, lord Coupar, and (2) John, 4th lord Lindores, i. 126; ii. 577; v. 385; ix. 59.
— Marion, dau. of Alexander O. of Ogilvy, iv. 22, 25.
— Marion, wife of George Forbes of Auchannasse, iv. 73.
— Marion *or* Mariota, 'domina de Melgund,' mistress of Cardinal David Betoun, i. 115; iv. 539.
— Marion *or* Mariota, wife of Patrick, 4th lord Gray, i. 118; iv. 281.
— Mariota, wife of William Forbes, iv. 71.
— Marjory, wife of David, 3rd earl of Crawford, i. 110; iii. 18; ix. 61.
— Marjorie, wife of Walter Tulloch, i. 110.
— Marjorie, wife of John Lyon of Haltoun of Esse, i. 116.
— Marjory, wife of Andrew Winton of Strathmartin, iv. 34.
— Marjorie, wife of Alex. Keith, ii. 5.
— Marjory, dau. of 2nd lord Banff, ii. 19.
— Marjorie, dau. of Alex. O. of Collard, iv. 25, 26.
— Mary, alleged wife of David Lyon of Cossins, i. 116.
— Mary, dau. of Walter O. of Clova, i. 130.
— Mary, wife of Ninian Dunbar, ii. 15.
— Mary, wife of (1) W. Innes, and (2) A. Sutherland, ii. 18.
— Mary, wife of John Forbes, ii. 19.
— Mary, wife of (1) John Joass, and (2) W. Hunter, ii. 21, 22.
— Mary, dau. of Sir Alex. O. of Forglen, ii. 24.
— Mary, wife of Alex. Murray, ii. 25.
— Mary, wife of (1) John George, 5th lord Banff, and (2) rev. Thos. Kemp, ii. 22; ix. 35.
— Mary, wife of Alex. Urquhart, iv. 19.
— Mary, wife of Sir John Grant of Freuchie, iv. 27; vii. 470.
— Mary, wife of col. P. Ogilvy of Inchmartine, iv. 36.
— Mary, wife of (1) * Leslie, and (2) George Barclay, iv. 37; ix. 90.
— Matilda, wife of (1) William Fenton, and (2) * Ramsay, i. 108.
— Maude Josepha, wife of Theodore Whyte, i. 131.

* Name unknown.

Ogilvy, Oliver, son of 1st lord Ogilvy of Airlie, vi. 223 *bis*; ix. 7.
—— Patrick, 6th son of Sir Walter O. of Lintrathen, i. 112; iv. 16.
—— Patrick, brother of Alexander O. of Deskford, iv. 20 *bis*.
—— Patrick, son of col. William O. iv. 34.
—— Patrick Julian Harry Stanley, i. 132.
—— Rebecca, wife of John Forbes, master of Pitsligo, iv. 76.
—— Robert, burgess of Banff, ii. 13.
—— —— his wife, Janet Baird, ii. 13.
—— Mr. Robert, minister of Methlick, vi. 183.
—— —— his wife, * Middleton, vi. 183.
—— Robert, cornet of Dragoons, ix. 89.
—— Sibil, wife of Sir John Falconer, v. 248.
—— Sophia, dau. of 7th lord Banff, ii. 25.
—— Susan, dau. of Walter O. of Cleva, i. 130.
—— Susanna, wife of Wm. Fullarton of Fullarton, viii. 109.
—— Theodosia Isabella, wife of E. L. D. Boyle, iv. 213; ix. 96.
—— Thomas, abbot of Cupar, i. 113.
—— Thomas, son of Thos. O. of Westercraig, i. 117.
—— Sir Thomas, gentleman pensioner of the privy chamber, i. 124; iv. 106.
—— —— his wife, Christian Ruthven, i. 124; iv. 105.
—— Thomas, Louvain, ii. 9.
—— Thomas, 3rd son of Geo. O. of Carnowseis, ii. 12.
—— Thomas, 2nd son of James O. of Inchmartine, iv. 31.
—— Thomas, 2nd son of Wm. O. of Inchmartine, iv. 33.
—— Thomas, 4th son of Patrick O. of Inchmartine, iv. 34.
—— Thomas, son of 1st lord Ogilvy of Airlie, ix. 8.
—— Walter, illeg. son of Walter O. of Oures, i. 110.
—— Walter, illeg. son of Sir Walter O. of Dunlugus, ii. 10.
—— William, 4th son of 5th lord Ogilvy of Airlie, i. 120.
—— William, 2nd son of 6th lord Ogilvy of Airlie, i. 123.
—— William, 3rd son of 1st lord Ogilvy of Deskford, iv. 27.
—— William, colonel, 2nd son of Patrick O. of Inchmartine, iv. 34.
—— William, v. 365.
—— —— his wife, Emily Mary Lennox, v. 365.
—— *, wife of Alex. Gordon of Cluny, ii. 9.
—— *, dau. of Patrick O., younger of Inchmartine, iv. 34.

* Name unknown.

Ogilvy-Dalgleish of Errol, Sir William, bart., iv. 36.
Ogle of Dissington, Thomas, i. 410.
—— Elizabeth, wife of Thos. Aston, i. 410.
—— Henry, v. 479.
—— —— his wife, Anne Ker, v. 479.
—— Sir Thomas, governor of Chelsea College, iii. 479.
—— Thomas, iii. 479.
—— —— his wife, Henrietta Bruce, iii. 479.
O'Grady of Plattenstown, George, vii. 392.
—— —— his wife, Jane Stewart Hore-Ruthven, vii. 392.
Ogston of Ogston, John, i. 278.
—— —— Walter, ii. 149; vii. 408.
—— —— his wife, * Abernethy, vii. 408.
—— Elizabeth, wife of Adam Hepburn of the Craigs, ii. 149; vii. 408.
—— Janet, wife of Jas. Crichton of Ruthven, v. 525.
O'Hara, Charles, iv. 594.
—— —— his wife, Mary Carmichael, iv. 594.
Olaf, king of Dublin, ii. 313.
Olaf, king of Man and the Isles, iv. 136; v. 29.
—— —— his wife, Affrica, iv. 136.
Olave, son of Somerled, v. 31.
Oldmixon, John William, lieut. R.N., viii. 310.
—— —— his wife, Anne Price, viii. 310.
Olifard of Abernethy, Walter, vi. 527.
—— of Arbuthnott, Osbert, i. 272; vi. 525.
—— —— Walter, i. 272; vi. 525.
—— of Barton Hanred, Thomas, vi. 524; ix. 145.
—— of Bothwell, Sir David, ii. 123.
—— —— Walter, justiciar of Lothian, ii. 123; vi. 528.
—— —— *, wife of Walter de Meravia, ii. 123; vi. 529.
—— of Collessie, Walter, vi. 527.
—— of Crailing and Smailholm, David, justiciar, vi. 523, 524, 535 *n.*; ix. 145.
—— —— David, vi. 528.
—— —— his wife, Dervorgilla, vi. 529.
—— —— Walter, vi. 526.
—— —— his wife, Christian of Strathearn, vi. 527; viii. 241.
—— —— Walter, vi. 527.
—— —— his wife, Isabel *, vi. 528.
—— of Invervack, William, i. 421; vi. 530, 534 *n.*, 536.
—— of Ketsby, Robert, *perhaps* ancestor of the family of, vi. 523.
—— of Lilford, Walter, vi. 526.
—— —— Walter, the younger, vi. 528.
—— —— William, vi. 522; ix. 145.
—— of Great Livesden, Andrew, vi. 524.
—— —— Ralph, vi. 524.
—— —— William, vi. 524.
—— of Osbornyston, Walter, vi. 528.
—— —— his wife, Ysabel, vi. 528.

* Name unknown.

Olifard of Overtono-Waterville, Sir William, vi. 522 *n.*
— of Rudmarley-Olifar, Robert, vi. 523.
— of Stilton, Hugo, vi. 523; ix. 145.
— of Strogeith, Walter, viii. 241.
— of Stokes, Hugh, vi. 522; ix. 145.
— of Yaxley, Stephen, vi. 523; ix. 145.
— Adam, vi. 530.
— — his wife, Halwis, vi. 530.
— David, alleged son of David O., vi. 526.
— David, 2nd son of Walter O., vi. 526, 527.
— David, Mill of Cadder, vi. 527 *n.*
— — his wife, Joanna, vi. 527 *n.*
— Elizabeth, sister of Sir William de O., vi. 533 *bis.*
— Fulco, the chaplain, vi. 526.
— Hugh, prisoner at Colchester, vi. 533 *n.*
— John, Huntingdonshire, vi. 523; ix. 145.
— Philip, son of David O., vi. 526.
— Sir Philip, brother of Sir William O., vi. 531.
— Robert, Herefordshire, vi. 523.
— Roger, Northamptonshire, vi. 522.
— Walter, prisoner at Winchester Castle, vi. 533 *n.*
— William, Huntingdonshire, vi. 523; ix. 145.
— William, alleged son of David O., vi. 526.
— William, *perhaps* younger son of David the justiciar, vi. 529.
— Sir William, brother of Sir Philip O., vi. 531.
— Sir William, commander of Stirling Castle, vi. 531.
— Sir William, ancestor of the lords Oliphant, vi. 534.
OLIPHANT, OLIPHANT, LORD, vi. 521-563.
Oliphant, Charles, seventh lord, vi. 554, 556.
— — his wife, Mary Ogilvy, vi. 556.
— David, of Bachilton; self-styled lord, vi. 562.
— Francis, tenth lord, vi. 555, 560.
— — his wife, Mary Linley, vi. 561.
— John, second lord, vi. 543.
— — his wife, Elizabeth Campbell, i. 335; vi. 543.
— John, of Bachilton; self-styled lord, vi. 562.
— Laurence, first lord, i. 333; iv. 30; vi. 540; vii. 184, 185.
— — his 1st wife, Isabel Hay, iii. 565; vi. 541.
— — his 2nd wife, Elizabeth Cuninghame, iii. 529; vi. 543.
— Laurence, third lord, iii. 201; vi. 544.
— — his wife, Margaret Sandilands, vi. 544; viii. 384.
— Laurence, fourth lord, ii. 339; vi. 546; viii. 189.
— — his wife, Margaret Hay, iii. 571; vi. 548.
Oliphant, Laurence, fifth lord, vi. 332, 551.
— — his wife, Lilias Drummond, vi. 551; viii. 217.
— Laurence, of Gask; created, by King James VIII., lord, vi. 563.
Oliphant, Patrick, sixth lord, vi. 333, 548, 552.
— — his 1st wife, Elizabeth Cheyne, vi. 553.
— — his 2nd wife, Margaret Menzies, vi. 554.
— — his 3rd wife, Mary Crichton, iv. 129; vi. 554.
— Patrick, eighth lord, vi. 556.
— William, ninth lord, vi. 555, 557.
— — his wife, Marie Magdeleine Elinga, vi. 559.
— William, 5th son of C. Oliphant of Langton; voted as lord, vi. 561.
— master of, Colin, 2nd son of 2nd lord Oliphant, vi. 543.
— — his wife, Elizabeth Keith, vi. 45, 543.
— master of, John, 2nd son of 4th lord Oliphant; styled, vi. 548.
— — his wife, Lilias Gray, iv. 283; vi. 548.
— master of, Laurence, eldest son of 4th lord Oliphant, vi. 374, 549.
— — his wife, Christian Douglas vi. 373, 550.
— master of, Patrick, elder son of John Oliphant of Newtyle; styled, vi. 548, 552.
OLIPHANT, LORD OLIPHANT, vi. 521-563.
Oliphant of Aberdalgie, Sir John, ii. 95 *n.*; iv. 257; vi. 215, 537.
— — his 1st wife, * Borthwick, ii. 95 *n.*
— — his 2nd wife, * Home, iv. 441.
— — Sir John, vi. 538.
— — his wife, Margaret Ogilvy, i. 110; vi. 539.
— — Sir Laurence, i. 110.
— — Sir Walter, i. 8.
— — his wife, Elizabeth Stewart, i. 8.
— — Walter, alderman of Perth, vi. 536.
— — his wife, Elizabeth Bruce, vi. 537.
— — Sir William, ancestor of the lords Oliphant, vi. 533; viii. 251.
— — Sir William, vi. 538.
— — his 2nd wife, Marion *, v. 430; vi. 537 *n.*, 538 *n.*
— of Archellie, James, vi. 539, 541.
— — Walter, vi. 544.
— of Ardargie, Ninian, ancestor of the family of, vi. 562 *n.*
— of Arniston, William, 3rd son of 3rd lord Oliphant, vi. 545.
— of Auchtertyre, Sir William, vi. 534.
— of Bachilton, David, self-styled lord Oliphant, vi. 562; ix. 146.
— — George, i. 466.

* Name unknown.

Oliphant of Bachilton, James, ancestor of the first family of, vi. 539.
—— —— Janet, wife of 8th lord Elibank, iii. 521; vi. 562.
—— —— John, v. 230 *bis*.
—— —— John, self-styled lord Oliphant, iii. 521; vi. 562.
—— of Balcraig, Sir William, vi. 534.
—— of Balgonie, Æneas, W.S., vi. 555.
—— —— William, v. 384; vi. 549.
—— —— his wife, Katharine Haliday, vi. 549.
—— of Ballied, Ninian, ancestor of the family of, vi. 562 *n*.
—— of Balmakcorne, George, 4th son of 1st lord Oliphant, vi. 542.
—— of Berridale, Andrew, vi. 542 *bis*; viii. 384.
—— —— Charles, vi. 542.
—— —— George, vi. 541.
—— —— William, vi. 541.
—— —— his wife, Christian Sutherland of Strabrock, iii. 195; vi. 541.
—— of Binzean, William, ancestor of the family of, vi. 544.
—— of Carsbank, Peter, eldest son of Peter O. of Turin, vi. 545.
—— of Carpow, John, 1st laird, vi. 549.
—— —— John, nephew of David O. of Bachilton, vi. 562.
—— of Cary, John, 1st laird, vi. 549.
—— —— John, 2nd laird, vi. 549.
—— of Cessfurd, Marion, wife of Sir Robert Graham of Kinpunt, vi. 215, 538.
—— of Condie, Laurence, 1st laird, ii. 570; vi. 544 *n*.
—— —— William, ancestor of the family of, vi. 544.
—— of Cranshaws, Sir John, vi. 538.
—— —— Sir William, vi. 534.
—— of Culteuchar, Ninian, vi. 549, 562.
—— —— his wife, Helen Oliphant, vi. 549.
—— of Drimmie, Patrick, grandson of 3rd lord Oliphant, vi. 545, 562.
—— of Dron, Thomas, iv. 272; vi. 538 *n*.
—— —— his wife, Elizabeth Buchanan, iv. 272.
—— of Drumdewan, George, i. 466.
—— of Duffus, George, iii. 195; vi. 541.
—— of Dupplin, Sir William, vi. 534.
—— of Freeland, Thomas, vi. 562.
—— of Gallery, Sir William, vi. 534.
—— of Gask, George, i. 546.
—— —— his 1st wife, Ann Malcolm, i. 546.
—— —— his 2nd wife, Jean Balfour, i. 546.
—— —— James, vi. 555, 557.
—— —— James Blair, vi. 563.
—— —— Sir Laurence, vi. 554, 561, 562, 563.
—— —— his wife, Lilias Oliphant, vi. 554.
—— —— Laurence, vi. 396.
—— —— his wife, Amelia Ann Sophia Nairn, vi. 396.
Oliphant of Gask, William, ancestor of the family of, vi. 544.
—— —— his wife, Margaret Oliphant, vi. 542.
—— —— William, 3rd son of 4th lord Oliphant, vi. 549.
—— —— his wife, Katharine Broun, vi. 549.
—— —— William, 2nd laird, vi. 549.
—— —— his wife, Katharine Haliday, vi. 549; ix. 145.
—— of Gasknes, Sir William, vi. 534.
—— of Glenlyon, Sir William, vi. 534.
—— of Glensaugh, vi. 534.
—— of Hazelhead, Malcolm, vi. 537.
—— —— Sir William, vi. 534.
—— —— Sir William, vi. 538 *n*.
—— —— his 2nd wife, Marion *, v. 430; vi. 537 *n*., 538 *n*.
—— of Hedderwick, John, vi. 543.
—— —— his wife, Elizabeth Campbell, i. 335; vi. 543.
—— —— Sir William, vi. 534.
—— of Heuchfield, John, vi. 545.
—— of Hillcairnie, Sir Walter, ancestor of the family of, vi. 537.
—— of Kellie, Sir Alexander, vi. 546; vii. 291.
—— —— his 1st wife, Katharine Leslie, vii. 291.
—— —— his 2nd wife, Katharine Oliphant, vi. 545.
—— —— Sir John, vii. 291.
—— —— Thomas, ancestor of the family of iv. 444.
—— —— Sir Walter, vi. 537.
—— of Kellie-mills, John, vi. 546 *n*.
—— —— Peter, vi. 546 *n*.
—— —— Sir Walter, ancestor of the family of, vi. 537.
—— of Little Kenny, Patrick, vi. 545.
—— of Kinneddar, William, ancestor of the family of, vi. 544.
—— of Kinpurnie, Sir William, vi. 534.
—— of Kirkhill, William, vii. 14.
—— —— his wife, Janet Maule, vii. 14.
—— of Langton, Charles, clerk of Session, vi. 545 *n*., 561.
—— —— [James], viii. 308.
—— of Mugdrum Island, William, v. 384.
—— of Muirhouse, Sir William, vi. 534.
—— of Murdocairnie, Sir Walter, ancestor of the family of, vi. 537.
—— of Newton, Sir George, vii. 202.
—— —— his wife, Margaret Rollo, vii. 202.
—— —— Sir James, 1st bart., vi. 562.
—— —— Laurence, vii. 194.
—— —— his wife, Mary Rollo, vii. 194.
—— —— William, vi. 542, 544.
—— —— Sir William, king's advocate, iv. 488, 566; vi. 562.

* Name unknown.

Oliphant of Newtyle, John, 2nd son of 4th lord Oliphant, vi. 548.
—— —— his wife, Lilias Gray, iv. 283; vi. 548.
—— —— Sir William, vi. 534.
—— of Ochtertyre, John, 2nd son of 4th lord Oliphant, vi. 548.
—— —— Sir William, vi. 534.
—— of Orchardmill, William, ancestor of the family of, vi. 544.
—— of Oures, Sir Laurence, i. 110.
—— of Pitheavlis, Janet, wife of 8th lord Elibank, iii. 521; vi. 562.
—— —— John, iii. 521.
—— of Pitkeathlie, Ninian, ancestor of the family of, vi. 562 *n*.
—— of Pitkorie, Sir Walter, vi. 537.
—— —— Sir William, vi. 534.
—— of Pitlochie, William, vi. 549; vii. 198.
—— of Pitmadie, Laurence, vii. 188.
—— of Pittendreich, Patrick, vi. 554.
—— —— his wife, Mary Crichton, iv. 129; vi. 554.
—— of Pittotter, Sir Walter, ancestor of the family of, vi. 537.
—— of Portnellan, Gilbert, son of Mary O., vi. 533 *n*.
—— of Prinlaws, Sir Walter, ancestor of the family of, vi. 537.
—— of Provostmains, Ninian, ancestor of the family of, vi. 562 *n*.
—— of Reid Inch, William, v. 384.
—— of Rossie, Robert, iv. 497.
—— —— Robert, viii. 112.
—— —— his wife, Susan Mary Elizabeth Tod, viii. 112.
—— —— William, ancestor of the family of, vi. 544.
—— of Soutartoun, William, ancestor of the family of, vi. 544.
—— of Southdean, vi. 522.
—— of Tomperran, William, ancestor of the family of, vi. 544.
—— of Turin, Peter, 1st laird, vi. 545.
—— —— his 1st wife, Jean Hepburn, vi. 545.
—— —— his 2nd wife, Agnes Collace, vi. 545; vii. 195.
—— —— Peter, 2nd laird, vi. 545, 549, 552.
—— —— Sir William, vi. 534.
—— of Nether Turin, Laurence, vi. 545.
—— of Over Turin, Patrick, vi. 545, 562.
—— of Ure, William, ancestor of the family of, vi. 544.
—— Agnes, wife of 7th lord Lindsay of the Byres, v. 401; vi. 550.
—— Alexander, Albany Herald, vi. 544 *n*.
—— —— his wife, Janet Oliphant, vi. 544 *n*.
—— Andrew, in Binzean, vi. 542.
—— Andrew, illeg. son of 6th lord Oliphant, vi. 556.
—— Anna, wife of James, lord Mordington, i. 202; vi. 332, 552.
Oliphant, Anna, wife of 7th lord Lindsay of the Byres, v. 401; vi. 550.
—— Anna, dau. of 6th lord Oliphant, vi. 556.
—— Caroline, wife of William, 4th lord Nairn, vi. 398.
—— Cecilia, wife of James Cochrane, iii. 350.
—— Charles, illeg. son of 8th lord Oliphant, vi. 557.
—— Charles, M.D., M.P., vi. 562 *n*.; viii. 308.
—— Christian, wife of Alex. Blair of Balthayock, vi. 539.
—— Christine, wife of (1) Thomas Graham of Boquhapple, and (2) Alex. Livingston of Terrinterran, vi. 150.
—— David, 4th son of John O. of Cary, vi. 549.
—— Elizabeth, wife of (1) William, 10th earl of Angus, and (2) James Hamilton, i. 201; vi. 549.
—— Elizabeth, wife of dean Alexander Murray, iii. 398.
—— Elizabeth, wife of Walter Stewart of Outlaw, vi. 555.
—— Elizabeth, wife of Jas. Hering of Tullibole, ix. 145.
—— Elspet, wife of Francis Hay of Balhousie, v. 230.
—— Euphame, wife of James Johnston of Westerhall, vi. 549.
—— Francis, captain Scots Guards, 4th son of 6th lord Oliphant, vi. 555.
—— —— his wife, Mary Reddall, vi. 555.
—— George, son of John O. of Bachilton, v. 230.
—— —— his wife, Rebecca Hay, v. 230.
—— George, 3rd son of Wm. O. of Gask, vi. 549.
—— George, preacher, Edinburgh, iii. 350.
—— Helen, dau. of Andrew O. of Berridale, vi. 542.
—— Helen, wife of Thomas Mowat, vi. 542.
—— Helen, wife of (1) Ninian Oliphant of Culteuchar, and (2) George Hay, vi. 549.
—— Helen, wife of (1) P. Murray of Woodend, and (2) rev. Andrew Rollo, vii. 198.
—— Isabel, wife of Sir John Scrymgeour, iii. 306; vi. 538.
—— Isabella, wife of James Ogilvy of Balgally and Inchmartin, iv. 31.
—— Isobel, dau. of 6th lord Oliphant, ix. 145.
—— James, son of Andrew O. in Binzean, vi. 542.
—— —— his wife, Katharine Oliphant, vi. 542.
—— James, 2nd son of Peter O. of Turin, vi. 545.
—— James, M.D., 2nd son of 7th lord Oliphant, vi. 556.

Oliphant, Janet, dau. of Wm. O. of Berridale, vi. 542.
— Janet, wife of Alex. Oliphant, Albany Herald, vi. 544 *n.*
— Janet, wife of Mr. James Govan, vi. 549.
— Jean, wife of 2nd earl of Hopetoun, iv. 497.
— Jean, wife of David Carmichael of Balmedie, iv. 566.
— Jean, wife of William Moncreiff of that Ilk, vi. 546.
— Jean, wife of Alex. Bruce of Cultmalundie, vi. 549.
— Mr. John, iii. 232.
— John, oldest son of 2nd lord Oliphant, iv. 258; vi. 543.
— — his contracted wife, Margaret Ruthven, iv. 258; vi. 543.
— Mr. John, 3rd son of Sir John O. of Aberdalgie, vi. 539.
— John, burgess of Perth, vi. 544.
— — his wife, Margaret Swinton, vi. 544.
— John, 2nd son of John O. of Newtyle, vi. 548, 552.
— Jonet, wife of (1) A. Moncrieff, and (2) Jas. Hepburne, ii. 155.
— Joseph, son of 9th lord Oliphant, ix. 145.
— Katharine, wife of James Oliphant, vi. 542.
— Katharine, wife of * Isoun, vi. 542.
— Katharine, wife of (1) Sir Alex. Oliphant of Kellie, and (2) Geo. Dundas of that Ilk, vi. 545.
— Katharine, wife of Andrew Miller, vi. 545 *n.*
— Katharine, dau. of Wm. O. of Gask, vi. 549.
— Katharine, wife of (1) James Wemyss, and (2) Hugh Hay, vi. 549.
— Laurence, 4th son of Wm. O. of Berridale, vi. 542.
— Laurence, abbot of Inchaffray, vi. 542, 562 *n.*
— Sir Laurence, major-general, vi. 544.
— Laurence, traveller, novelist, and mystic, vi. 544.
— Laurence, burgess of Perth, vi. 549.
— Laurence, lieut. Scots Guards, 2nd son of 6th lord Oliphant, iv. 131; vi. 554.
— — his wife, Magdalen Crichton, iv. 130; vi. 554.
— Lilias, wife of David Lundie of Balgonie, vi. 546.
— Lilias, wife of Sir Laurence Oliphant of Gask, vi. 554.
— Malcolm, brother of Sir John O. of Aberdalgie, iv. 257.

* Name unknown.

Oliphant, Margaret, contracted to George, master of Angus; wife of Sir John Elphinstone, i. 186; iii. 529; vi. 542.
— Margaret, wife of John Nairn of Mukkersy, vi. 390.
— Margaret, wife of Henry Wardlaw of Torry, vi. 539.
— Margaret, wife of Wm. Oliphant of Newton, vi. 542, 544.
— Margaret, wife of (1) Wm. Moray of Abercairnie, (2) Jas. Clephane of Hillcairnie, and (3) Ninian Bonar of Keltie, vi. 546.
— Margaret, wife of (1) Francis Menzies of Balgownie, and (2) Richard Irvine of Cairnfield, vi. 554.
— Margaret, wife of David Carmichael of Balmedie, iv. 566.
— Margaret Oliphant Wilson, the novelist; Mrs., vi. 537.
— Marie Jeanne Baptiste, wife of Louis Grenolias, sieur de Cournou, vi. 560; ix. 145.
— Marion, wife of Sir Robert Graham of Kinpunt, vi. 215, 538.
— Mary, mother of Gilbert O., vi. 533 *n.*
— Mary, wife of (1) Sir Simon Fraser of Oliver Castle, and (2) Richard Siward, vi. 533 *n.*; vii. 421.
— Mary, sister of 10th lord Oliphant, vi. 555.
— Mary, wife of James, 7th earl of Strathmore and Kinghorne, vi. 562 *n.*; viii. 308.
— Ninian, Mill of Mure, vi. 562 *n.*
— Robert, petitioner to queen Elizabeth, vi. 550 *n.*
— Thomas, portioner of Hilcairny, vi. 99.
— — his wife, Christian Melville, vi. 99.
— Thomas, 6th son of Peter O. of Turin, vi. 545.
— Walter, illeg. son of Wm. O. of Arniston, vi. 545 *n.*
— William, in Fordell, vi. 549.
— William, son of David O., vi. 549.
— William, 2nd son of Laurence, master of Oliphant, vi. 550 *n.*
— William, apprentice, Kirkcaldy, vi. 555.
— William, 5th son of Charles O. of Langton, vi. 561.
— — his wife, Margaret Dallas, vi. 562.
— William Henry, iii. 522.
— — his wife, Charlotte Murray, iii. 522.
— *, wife of James Drummond of Balloch, vi. 539.
— *, wife of George Gordon of Cochlarachie, vi. 542.
— *, wife of William Rollo of Duncrub, vii. 185.
Oliver of Hailes, son of Kylvert, vii. 419.

* Name unknown.

Oliver of Oliver Castle, vii. 418.
Oliver of Southdean, vi. 522.
—— Sir Richard, v. 346.
—— —— his wife, Isabel, v. 346.
—— Robert, their son, v. 346.
Ollens, Sara, wife of 4th lord Rutherfurd, vii. 381.
Ommaney, Sir Francis, gentleman usher to George IV., ii. 502.
—— John Orde, ii. 502.
—— —— his wife, Susanna MacTaggart of Ardwell, ii. 502.
—— Julia H., ii. 598 *n*.
—— Marianne Susanna, wife of Sir Mark J. MacTaggart-Stewart, ii. 502.
O'Neile, Gordon, i. 50 *n*.
—— Sir Phelim, i. 50; iv. 545.
—— —— his wife, Jean Gordon, i. 50; iv. 545.
O'Neill of Shanes Castle, Edward (O'Neill), 2nd baron, iii. 366.
—— —— his wife, Louisa Catherine Emma Cochrane, iii. 366.
—— Shane, i. 338; ix. 20.
—— Turlough Luinech, i. 338.
—— —— his wife, Agnes Campbell, i. 338.
Onslow, Arthur, serjeant-at-law, vi. 456.
—— —— his wife, Mary Eyre, vi. 456.
—— Elizabeth, wife of canon Hamilton, i. 63.
—— Richard, major-general, i. 63.
Opdebeck, *, Brussels, iv. 395.
—— —— his wife, S. H. C. Douglas-Hamilton, iv. 395.
Orabilis, *apparently* wife of (1) Robert de Quincy, (2) Adam, son of Duncan, and (3) Gilchrist, earl of Mar, iv. 6; v. 571.
Orange, Charlotte of Nassau, wife of duke de la Trimouille; princess of, iii. 383.
—— Henry, prince of, i. 522.
—— Maurice, prince of, ii. 122.
—— William of Nassau, prince of, i. 29.
—— —— his wife, Mary Stewart, i. 29.
—— William of Nassau, prince of, i. 29, 33.
—— —— his wife, Mary Stewart, i. 33.
ORANSAY, CAMPBELL, LORD, i. 379.
Oransay, Archibald, first lord, i. 378.
Orby of Croyland, Sir Charles, 2nd bart., viii. 459.
—— Elizabeth, wife of (1) brigadier-gen. John Hay, and (2) major-gen. R. Hunter, viii. 459; ix. 168.
Orde of Orde, Elizabeth, portioner, ii. 10.
Orde-Powlett, Henry Robert, ii. 530.
—— —— his wife, Henrietta Cathcart, ii. 530.
—— Ivy, ii. 530.
—— Jean Mary, wife of lieut.-col. A. M. Cathcart, ii. 529.
—— Kathleen Mary, wife of Sir L. Falkiner, ii. 530.

* Name unknown.

O'Reilly, Walter Frederick, lt.-col. 41st regt., C.B., vii. 357.
—— —— his wife, Harriet Charlwood, vii. 357.
Orellana y Revest, Ignacio do Loyala de Padua de, colonel, iii. 416.
ORKNEY, THE ANCIENT EARLS OF, ii. 313-320.
Orkney, Arngils Sunnesson, earl of, ii. 320.
—— —— his wife, Agneta of Caithness, ii. 320.
—— Erlend, earl of, ii. 315.
—— Gilbert, earl of, i. 164; ii. 317.
—— Harold Maddadsson, earl of, i. 416; ii. 315; iv. 6.
—— —— his 1st wife, Afreka, ii. 315; iv. 6.
—— —— his 2nd wife, Gormlath *or* Hvarflod, ii. 315.
—— Harold ungi, earl of, ii. 315.
—— John, earl of, ii. 316.
—— Saint Magnus, earl of, ii. 315.
—— Magnus, earl of, ii. 317.
—— Magnus, earl of, ii. 318.
—— Magnus, earl of, ii. 318.
—— Magnus, earl of, ii. 319.
—— —— his wife, Katharine, ii. 319.
—— Malise, earl of, ii. 319; viii. 252.
—— —— his wife, Marjorie Ross, ii. 320; vii. 236.
—— Matilda of; wife of Malise, 5th earl of Strathearn, ii. 318, 319; viii. 246, 252.
—— Paul, earl of, ii. 315.
—— Rognvald, earl of, ii. 315.
—— Sigurd Eysteinsson, earl of, ii. 313; vi. 280.
—— Sigurd Hlodversson, earl of, ii. 314; vi. 281.
—— Thorfinn Sigurdsson, earl of, i. 2; ii. 314.
—— —— his wife, Ingibiorg, i. 2.
—— William (5th earl of Sutherland), styled earl of, viii. 326.
ORKNEY, SINCLAIR, EARL OF, vi. 564-571.
Orkney, Henry, first earl of, ii. 320; vi. 568; ix. 102.
—— —— his wife, Jean Halyburton, iv. 333; vi. 569; ix. 102.
—— Henry, second earl of, iv. 82; vi. 570.
—— —— his wife, Egidia Douglas, iii. 164; vi. 570; ix. 146 *bis*.
—— William, third earl of, ii. 332; vi. 571; ix. 50.
—— —— his 1st wife, Elizabeth Douglas, ii. 265, 333; iii. 167.
—— —— his 2nd wife, Marjory Sutherland, ii. 334.
—— —— his 3rd wife, Jonet Yeman, ii. 336.
ORKNEY, STEWART, EARL OF, vi. 572-577.
Orkney, Patrick, second earl of, ii. 440; iii. 590; vi. 573, 575; ix. 146 *bis*.
—— —— his wife, Margaret Livingston, ii. 70; v. 443; vi. 576.

Orkney, Robert, first earl of, i. 24; ii. 440; iii. 531; vi. 572.
—— —— his wife, Jean Kennedy, ii. 471; vi. 573.
—— Henry, eldest son of Robert, 1st earl of Orkney; master of, ii. 440; vi. 573.
—— John, 2nd son of 1st earl of Orkney; master of, ii. 440; vi. 573.
ORKNEY, HAMILTON, EARL OF, vi. 578-584.
Orkney, Anne, wife of William (O'Brien), 4th earl of Inchiquin; countess of, vi. 580.
—— George, first earl of, i. 411 *n.*; iv. 382; vi. 578.
—— —— his wife, Elizabeth Villiers, vi. 579.
ORKNEY, O'BRIEN, COUNTESS OF, vi. 580-581.
Orkney, Mary, wife of 5th earl of Inchiquin; countess of, vi. 580.
—— Mary, wife of Thos. Fitzmaurice of Llewenny Hall; countess of, vi. 581.
ORKNEY, FITZMAURICE, EARL OF, vi. 581-584.
Orkney, Edward Walter, seventh earl of, vi. 583.
—— —— his wife, Constance Macdonald Gilchrist, vi. 583.
—— George William Hamilton, sixth earl of, vi. 583.
—— —— his wife, Amelia *, vi. 583.
—— Thomas John Hamilton, fifth earl of, vi. 581.
—— —— his wife, Charlotte Isabella Irby, vi. 582.
ORKNEY, HEPBURN, DUKE OF, ii. 161-167.
Orkney, James, duke of, i. 26; ii. 161; iv. 429.
Orleans, Anne Mary, wife of Victor Amadeus II., duke of Savoy; princess of, i. 29.
—— Mary Louisa, wife of Charles II., king of Spain; princess of, i. 29.
—— Philip, duke of, i. 29.
—— —— his wife, Henrietta Anna Maria Stewart, i. 29.
Orm, son of Ketel, iii. 245.
Orm, father of Laurence of Coventre and Dunlappie, v. 573; vi. 530.
Orm(e of Aberargie and Pitgrunzie, vii. 398.
—— of Abernethy, Balbirnie, and Inverarity, vii. 396.
—— of Mugdrum, George, v. 384.
—— of Pitgrunzie, George, vii. 398.
—— of Priorlethame, David, v. 405.
—— Helen, wife of P. Lindsay of Kirkforthar, v. 405.
—— Katharine, wife of Geo. Clephane of Carslogie, vi. 589.
—— Stephen, viii. 498.
—— —— his wife, Isobel Wemyss, viii. 497.
ORMELIE, CAMPBELL, LORD, ii. 203.

* Name unknown.

Ormelie, John, first lord, ii. 203.
ORMELIE, CAMPBELL, EARL OF, ii. 210.
Ormelie, John, first earl of, ii. 210.
Ormiston of Meredene, Nicol, ii. 589.
—— —— his wife, Agnes Quhitlaw, ii. 589.
—— of Ormiston, Andrew, viii. 378.
—— —— James, the 'Black Laird,' v. 64 *n.*; vii. 582.
—— —— his wife, Margaret Sinclair, vii. 582.
—— —— *, vii. 377.
—— —— his wife, Grisel Rutherfurd, vii. 377.
—— *, alleged wife of 3rd lord Lindores, v. 385.
—— *, husband of Mary Gibb, v. 388.
ORMOND, STEWART, MARQUESS OF, i. 155; vii. 245-246.
Ormond, Charles, 2nd son of king James VI.; marquess of, i. 155.
—— James, 2nd son of king James III.; marquess of, i. 21; vii. 245.
ORMOND, DOUGLAS, EARL OF, vi. 585-586.
Ormond, Hugh, 4th son of 7th earl of Douglas; earl of, i. 114, 235; iii. 174, 177; vi. 277, 585.
—— —— his wife, *, vi. 586.
ORMOND, DOUGLAS, EARL OF ANGUS AND, i. 206.
Ormond, Archibald, first earl of Angus and, i. 206.
Ormond, James, Abingdon, iv. 68.
—— Louisa, wife of 19th lord Forbes, iv. 68.
Ormonde, Thomas (Butler), 10th earl of, iii. 121.
—— Walter (Butler), 11th earl of, i. 43, 53; iii. 121.
—— James (Butler), 1st marquess of, iii. 122.
—— John (Butler), 2nd marquess of, viii. 237.
—— Charles (Butler), *de jure* duke of, iii. 123.
—— James (Butler), 1st duke of, i. 53, 57; iii. 122, 344.
—— James (Butler), 2nd duke of, iii. 123; viii. 304.
Orpen, Mary, wife of (1) John Travers, and (2) Wm. Mordaunt Maitland, v. 318.
—— Richard, in holy orders, v. 318.
Orr, Patrick, W.S., v. 416.
—— —— his wife, Margaret Caroline Lindsay, v. 416.
Orr-Ewing of Ballikinrain, Sir Archibald, 1st bart., iv. 221; vii. 359.
—— of Dunskey, Charles Lindsay, M.P., iv. 221; vii. 393.
—— —— his 1st wife, Beatrix Mary Leslie Hore-Ruthven, vii. 393.
—— —— his 2nd wife, Augusta Helen Elizabeth Boyle, iv. 221.
—— James Alexander, major, vii. 359.
—— —— his wife, Margaret Frances Susan Innes-Ker, vii. 359.

* Name unknown.

Orrery, George (Boyle), earl of, vi. 580.
—— —— his wife, Harriet Hamilton, vi. 580.
Orrock of Orrock, Alexander, viii. 494.
—— —— his wife, Elizabeth Wemyss, viii. 494.
—— —— James, vi. 86.
—— of Silliebalbie, Alexander, vi. 86.
—— Margaret, wife of David Wemyss, viii. 494.
—— Robert, vi. 86.
Osbert the Crusader, i. 274.
Osbert of Spaldington, viii. 4.
Osbert, prior of Paisley, vi. 26.
Osborn, Bridget, wife of Charles Fitz Charles, earl of Plymouth, i. 30.
OSBORNE, VISCOUNT DUNBLANE, iii. 301-302.
Osborne of Kiveton, Thomas (Osborne), 1st baron, iii. 301.
—— —— Sir Edward, iii. 301.
—— —— Sir Thomas, iii. 301.
—— Mary, wife of (1) Henry, 2nd duke of Beaufort, and (2) John, 4th earl of Dundonald, iii. 355.
OSEBURNE OF DUNBLANE, OSBORNE, VISCOUNT, iii. 301-302.
Oseburne of Dunblane, Perigrine, second viscount, iii. 302.
—— —— Thomas, first viscount, iii. 301.
Ossory, Thomas, eldest son of 1st duke of Ormonde; styled earl of, iii. 122.
—— —— his wife, Amelia de Beverwest, iii. 122.
Oswald of Auchincruive, Richard, 1st laird, ii. 521; v. 134.
—— —— Richard, younger of, ii. 500.
—— —— his wife, Mary Kennedy, ii. 500.
—— —— Richard, ii. 521.
—— —— Richard Alexander, iii. 462.
—— —— his wife, Lilias Montgomerie, iii. 462.
—— of Dunnikier, James Townsend, M.P., iii. 493.
—— —— Sir John, lieut.-gen., G.C.B., i. 493, 494.
—— —— his 1st wife, Charlotte Murray, i. 494.
—— —— his 2nd wife, Emily Jane Murray, i. 493.
—— of Lochinvar, Richard, v. 134.
—— Alexander, advocate, viii. 130.
—— —— his wife, Anne Dalrymple, viii. 130.
—— Elizabeth, wife of 7th earl of Elgin, iii. 493.
Oswell of Athellis, James, ii. 411.
—— —— his wife, Marion Craufurd, ii. 411.
Otley of Delaford, Brook Taylor, i. 315.
—— Anna Maria, wife of capt. Walter Arbuthnott, i. 315.
Ott, *, Madame de, alleged wife of baron Stuart de Decies, ii. 307.

* Name unknown.

Otterburn of Redhall, Sir Adam, ii. 77; viii. 490.
—— —— John, i. 444.
—— —— his wife, Joneta Stewart, i. 444.
—— John, official of Lothian, i. 152.
—— Margaret, wife of Sir John Wemyss of Wemyss, viii. 490.
—— Nicholas of, ambassador to Burgundy iii. 60.
Otway of Castle Otway, Henry, i. 492.
—— —— his wife, Sarah, baroness Braye, i. 492.
Otway-Cave, Catharine, wife of (1) Henry Murray, and (2) 3rd earl Beauchamp, i. 492.
Ouchterlony, James, bailie of Montrose, v. 249.
—— —— his wife, Jane Falconer, v. 249.
Oughton, Sir James A., K.B., i. 490 *n.*; viii. 140.
—— —— his wife, Mary Ross, viii. 140.
Ouseley, Frances Rhoda, wife of capt. James Terence Fitzmaurice, vi. 582.
—— Sir William Gore, K.C.B., vi. 582.
Overbury, Sir Thomas, v. 71.
Overstone, Samuel Jones (Loyd), lord, i. 524.
Owen of Penrhos, William Charles, viii. 161.
—— Agnes Raney, wife of Walter F. Dalrymple, viii. 161.
Owens, Sara, wife of 4th lord Rutherfurd, vii. 381.
OXENFOORD OF COUSLAND, DALRYMPLE, BARON, viii. 159-164.
Oxenfoord, John, first lord, viii. 159.
Oxford, Aubrey (de Vere), 20th earl of, i. 32.
—— Henry (de Vere), 18th earl of, i. 488; iii. 478.
—— —— his wife, Diana Cecil, iii. 478.
—— Edward (de Vere), 17th earl of, i. 488; v. 467.
—— John (de Vere), 14th earl of, i. 499.
Oxford and Mortimer, Edward (Harley), 2nd earl of, vi. 189.
—— —— Edward (Harley), 3rd earl of, viii. 224.
—— —— Robert (Harley), 1st earl of, v. 232.
OXFUIRD, MAKGILL, VISCOUNT OF, vi. 587-601.
Oxfuird, Christian, wife of Wm. Maitland self-styled viscountess of, v. 309; vi. 599.
—— Henrietta, wife of James Hamilton o Orbiston; self-styled viscountess of, vi 600.
—— James, first viscount of, vi. 595.
—— —— his 1st wife, Katharine Cockburn, vi. 596; ix. 147.
—— —— his 2nd wife, Christian Livingston, v. 191; vi. 598; ix. 147.
—— Robert, second viscount of, vi. 599.
—— —— his 1st wife, Henriet Livingston, v. 449; vi. 599.
—— —— his 2nd wife, Jean Ramsay, iii. 101; vi. 600; vii. 258.

Oxfuird, Robert, son of Christian Maitland-Makgill; self-styled viscount of, v. 309; vi. 600.
—— —— his wife, Janet Christie, v. 309.
—— master of, George Makgill, son of 2nd viscount of Oxfuird, vi. 599; ix. 147.
Oxnam, Ker, lord Kerr of, v. 477-487.
Oxnam, Robert, first lord Kerr of, v. 477.

Packington of Westwood, Sir John, K.B., v. 86.
—— —— his wife, Dorothy Smith, v. 86.
—— —— Sir John, bart., v. 377.
—— —— his wife, Frances Ferrers, v. 377.
Paganell, Agnes de, wife of Robert de Bruce of Skelton, ii. 429.
—— Foulk de, ii. 429.
Paget of Beaudesert, Henry (Paget), 2nd baron, iii. 609.
—— Caroline, wife of 5th duke of Lennox, v. 368.
—— Cecil Stratford, viii. 512.
—— —— his wife, Mary Frances Erskine-Wemyss, viii. 512.
—— Florence Cecilia, wife of (1) Henry, 9th earl of Loudoun, and (2) Sir G. Chetwynd, v. 515.
—— George, general, K.C.B., viii. 512.
—— Henry William, major-general, iv. 169.
—— Jane, wife of 8th earl of Galloway, iv. 170.
Paintland, Campbell, viscount of, ii. 203, 204.
Paintland, John, first viscount, ii. 203.
—— *see also* Pentland.
Paisley, Hamilton, lord, i. 39-74.
Paisley, Claud, 4th son of 2nd earl of Arran, first lord, i. 39; ix. 2.
—— —— his wife, Margaret Seton, i. 39; viii. 590.
—— James, eldest son of 2nd earl of Abercorn; styled lord, i. 49; iv. 381.
—— —— his wife, Katharine Lenthall, i. 49.
Paisley, Hamilton, baron of, i. 46.
Paisley, James, eldest son of Claud, lord Paisley; first baron of, i. 46.
—— James, second baron of, i. 48.
—— master of, James Hamilton, eldest son of Claud, lord Paisley, i. 46; v. 401.
—— —— his wife, Marion Boyd, i. 47; v. 167.
Pakenham, John, admiral R.N., iii. 415.
—— —— his wife, Frances Julia Peters, iii. 415.
Pakington, John Slaney, iv. 218.
—— —— his wife, Diana Boyle, iv. 218.
Palbitzki, Gustaff Adolph, baron and count marshal, iii. 213.
—— —— his wife, Anna Sutherland, iii. 213.
Palmer of Luckley Park, Charles Fysche, iv. 557.
—— —— his wife, Madelina Gordon, iv. 557.
—— of Nazing Park, George, col., ii. 59.
Palmer, Anne, wife of Thomas Lennard, earl of Sussex, i. 31.
—— Charlotte Maria, wife of col. R. W. Hamilton, ii. 59.
—— Edith Douglas, wife of 17th earl of Moray, vi. 327.
—— George, rear-admiral R.N., vi. 327.
—— Minnie Augusta, wife of (1) major E. A. Cook, and (2) George Charles Gordon-Lennox, v. 368.
—— Sir Thomas, prisoner in Scotland, vi. 481.
—— W. H., Tunbridge Wells, v. 368.
Palmerston, Henry John (Temple), lord, iii. 123.
—— —— his wife, Emily Mary Lambe, iii. 123.
Palmes, Brian, Naburn, iii. 293.
—— —— his wife, Anne Constable, iii. 293.
Panitar, *see* Pantar.
Panmure, Maule, earl of, vii. 1-27.
Panmure, George, second earl of, vii. 21; viii. 300.
—— —— his wife, Jean Campbell, v. 507; vii. 22.
—— George, third earl of, vii. 24.
—— —— his wife, Jean Fleming, vii. 24; ix. 148.
—— James, fourth earl of, vii. 22, 24; ix. 148.
—— —— his wife, Margaret Hamilton, iv. 383; vii. 26; ix. 104.
—— Patrick, first earl of, vii. 19.
—— his 1st wife, Frances Stanhope, vii. 20.
—— his 2nd wife, Mary Waldrum, vii. 20.
—— his 3rd wife, Mary Erskine, v. 622; vii. 20; ix. 133.
Panmure of Brechin and Navar, Maule, lord, vii. 24.
Panmure of Brechin and Navar, Fox, second lord, vii. 24.
—— —— William, first lord, iii. 104, 107; vii. 24; ix. 148.
—— —— his 1st wife, Patricia Heron Gordon, vii. 24; ix. 66.
—— —— his 2nd wife, Elizabeth Barton, vii. 24; ix. 66.
Panmure of Forth, Maule, earl of, vii. 23.
Panmure of Forth, William, earl of, iii. 103; vii. 22, 25; viii. 85, 553.
Pantar, David, bishop of Ross, ii. 339; v. 453; vii. 287, 289; ix. 63.
—— Patrick, secretary to king James IV., vii. 287 *n.*
Panter of Newmaoswalls, David, viii. 48.
—— —— his wife, * Kinnaird, viii. 48.
Panton of Pitmeddan, iii. 590.
—— —— John, iv. 25.
—— —— his wife, Barbara Ogilvy, iv. 25.
—— Isobel, wife of William King of Barra, iii. 590.

* Name unknown.

Papla, Thomas, servitor to John Stewart, master of Orkney, ii. 440.
PARBROATH, LINDSAY, LORD, iii. 35-51; v. 402-420.
Parbroath, John, first lord, iii. 35; v. 402.
Parish, Charles Woodbine, iv. 211; viii. 397.
—— his 1st wife, Frances Montgomerie Boyle, iv. 211.
—— his 2nd wife, Helen Jane Sandilands, viii. 397.
— Sir Woodbine, K.C.H., iv. 211.
Park of Gilbertfield, John, iv. 189.
—— his wife, Margaret Crawfurd, iv. 189.
— of Wiston, Mungo, iv. 582.
Parker of Aigburth, Alfred Traill, viii. 315.
— of Shenstone, Sir William, 1st bart., admiral R.N., G.C.B., vi. 385.
— Alfred Ernest, 10th Hussars, viii. 315.
—— his wife, Joan Issobel Margaret Bowes-Lyon, viii. 314.
— Charlotte Martha, wife of admiral Geo. Henry Douglas, vi. 385.
— John, capt. 66th regt., vii. 309.
—— his wife, Katharine Caroline Leslie, vii. 309.
— Maria, wife of 9th earl of Haddington, iv. 326.
— Matthew, iii. 292.
—— his 3rd wife, Anne Constable, iii. 292.
— *, iv. 273.
—— his wife, * Gray, iv. 273.
— Patrick, their son, iv. 273.
Parkes, Jane, wife of Robert A. Dalzell, ii. 417.
— Samuel, Cork, ii. 418.
Parkle of Linlithgow, James, ii. 323; vii. 319.
Parlby, Emma Marion, wife of col. W. C. W. Arbuthnott, i. 315.
— rev. John Hall, Manadon, i. 315.
Parma, Robert de Bourbon, duke of, iii. 6.
Parnell of Baldock, John, ii. 75.
— Mary, wife of 3rd lord Bellenden, ii. 75.
Parois, madame, governess to Mary, queen of Scots, viii. 540.
Parr, *, H.E.I.C.S., i. 492.
Parsons, Henry, rector of Sandhurst, iv. 212.
— Louisa Catherine, wife of col. Wm. Boyle, vi. 212.
Partington, Oswald, M.P., iii. 524.
—— his wife, Clara Isabel Murray, iii. 524.
Paston, Sir John, v. 148.
Paterson of Bannockburn, Sir Hugh, iv. 103; viii. 31.
—— his wife, Barbara Ruthven, iv. 103.
—— Sir Hugh, v. 629.
—— his wife, Jean Erskine, v. 629.

* Name unknown.

Paterson of Carpow, Peter Hay, iii. 522.
—— his wife, Marianne Oliphant Murray, iii. 522.
— of Castle Huntly, George, iv. 293.
—— his wife, Anne Gray, iv. 293.
— of Dynmure, Andrew, i. 550.
—— George, v. 403.
—— George, i. 545.
— of Eccles, Sir John, vi. 21, 22.
—— his wife, Anne Hume Campbell, vi. 21.
— of Kirktoun, James, advocate, iv. 292.
—— his wife, Katharine Gray, iv. 292.
—— Katharine, wife of lieut. J. Sharp, R.N., iv. 292.
— of Prestonhall, John, vii. 587.
—— his wife, Grizel St. Clair, vii. 587.
— Barbara, dau. of John P. of Prestonhall, vii. 587.
— Duncan, burgess of Stirling, viii. 170.
—— his wife, Marion Alexander, viii. 170.
— Elizabeth, wife of col. Alex. Mackenzie, vii. 510.
— Euphame, wife of (1) Gavin Wemyss, and (2) John Makgill, vi. 590.
— Isobel, wife of Robt. Bruce, i. 550; ix. 33.
— Jane Hay, wife of John Rollo, vii. 208.
— Janet, wife of Arthur Balfour, i. 545.
— John, bishop of Edinburgh, archbishop of Glasgow, vii. 587; viii. 495.
—— his wife, Margaret Wemyss, viii. 495.
— John, bishop of Ross, vii. 510.
— Katharine, wife of Edward Hope, iv. 486.
— Margaret, wife of Jas. Lindsay of Kilquhis, v. 403.
— Margaret, wife of John Thomson of Charleton, vii. 587.
— Robert, principal of Marischal College, viii. 55.
—— his wife, Agnes Carnegie, viii. 55.
— Robertson James, vii. 208.
— Samuel, librarian to marquess of Lansdowne, ix. 58.
—— his wife, Hamilton Lewis Kennedy, ix. 58.
— Samuel, claimant to title of Cassillis, ix. 57.
Paterson-Balfour-Hay of Leys, Carpow, and Randerstone, Edmund, v. 217.
Paterson-St. Clair of Dysart and Roslin, James, colonel, vii. 587, 589.
Paton of Grandholm, John, col., ii. 354.
— George, master in High School, Edinburgh, v. 366.
— Mary Anne, wife of W. P. Lennox, v. 366.
— Mary Louisa, wife of C. H. Sinclair, ii. 354.

Patrick of Caistron, son of Edgar the Dauntless, iii. 249.
Patrick of Greenlaw and the Hirsel, 2nd son of Gospatric, 3rd earl of Dunbar, iii. 250.
—— —— his wife, *probably* Cecilia Fraser iii. 251.
Patrick of Inverpeffray, iii. 305.
Patrick, son of Constantine of Goswyck, i. 421 *n*.
Patrick, abbot of Dunfermline, 1206, i. 423.
Patrick the clerk, 'son of the earl,' *perhaps* of Gospatric, 3rd earl of Dunbar, iii. 251.
Patrick, abbot of Kelso, v. 278.
Pattle, James, Bengal C. S., viii. 128.
—— Sophia, wife of Sir J. W. Dalrymple of North Berwick, viii. 128.
Paul, E., H.E.I.C.S., i. 316.
—— —— his wife, Caroline *, i. 316.
Paulet of Hinton St. George, Sir William, iii. 608.
—— Elizabeth, wife of Sir Wm. Cary, iii. 608.
—— Lilian Mary, wife of R. G. Erskine-Wemyss, viii. 512.
Paunceford, Rachel, wife of 7th earl of Kincardine, iii. 490.
—— Robert, Herefordshire, iii. 490.
Pawtoun, Isobel, wife of William King of Barra, iii. 590.
Payler of Thoraldby, Watkinson, v. 12.
—— —— his wife, Margaret Fairfax, v. 12.
—— Mary, wife of Thomas Ingram, v. 12.
Payniston, John de, Longniddry, ii. 586.
Payne, Frances Anne, wife of John Rollo, vii. 207.
—— Louisa, wife of major Henry Gordon, iv. 559.
Peach of Tockington, Samuel Peach, i. 494.
—— Emma Sarah, wife of John Murray-Aynsley, i. 494.
Peachey of Westdean, Sir James, iii. 112.
—— —— his wife, Georgina Caroline Scott, iii. 112.
Peacock, colonel, vii. 383.
—— —— his wife, Jean Rutherfurd, vii. 383.
Peake of Borough-on-the-Hill, Walter Ansell, colonel, D.S.O., vi. 387.
—— Winona Constance de Maraisville, wife of Archibald R. S. Douglas, vi. 387.
Pearson of Balmadies, James, i. 295.
—— —— his wife, Margaret Lindsay, i. 294.
—— of Kippenross, James, vii. 197.
—— —— his wife, Helen Rollo, vii. 197.
—— of Southall, Alexander, lord of Session, v. 406.
—— Anabel, wife of Mr. Wm. Bellenden, ii. 67.
—— Elizabeth, wife of D. Lindsay of Kirkforthar, v. 406.
—— Thomas, son of * P. of Lochlands, vii. 13.
—— —— his wife, Elizabeth Maule, vii. 13.

* Name unknown.

Pechell, Mark Robert, admiral R.N., vii. 490.
—— Maud Louisa, wife of William Robert Ogilvie-Grant, vii. 490.
Pedefer, Jeanne de, wife of (1) Alexander, 5th lord Livingston, and (2) Pierre de Joisel, seigneur de St. Remy, v. 439.
PEDWARDINE, HAY, BARON HAY OF, v. 232-239.
PEEBLES, DOUGLAS, VISCOUNT OF, vii. 145-147.
Peebles, William, first viscount of, vii. 145; viii. 376; ix. 151.
—— of Auchincreugh and Mainshill, James, eldest son of col. Alex. Cochrane of Auchincreugh, iii. 341.
—— of Dalqueich, John, vi. 367.
—— of Mainshill, Hugh, iii. 341.
—— —— Hugh, 2nd son of Jas. Cochrane of Auchincreugh, ix. 76.
—— —— Marion, wife of James Cochrane of Auchincreugh, iii. 341.
—— of Middleton and Skirling, Alexander, iv. 314.
—— Alexander, provost of Perth, vii. 198.
—— Eupheme, dau. of Jas. P. of Auchincreugh and Mainshill, iii. 342.
—— James, son of James P. of Auchincreugh and Mainshill, iii. 342.
—— Katharine, wife of Sir John Hamilton of Trabroun, iv. 314.
—— Katharine, wife of Laurence Rollo of Rossie, vii. 198.
Peel of Kemptown, Lawrence, v. 367.
—— —— his wife, Jane Lennox, v. 367.
—— Jonathan, M.P., lieut.-gen., ii. 500.
—— —— his wife, Alice Jane Kennedy, ii. 500.
—— Sir Robert, 1st bart., ii. 500.
—— Sir Robert, 3rd bart., viii. 472.
—— —— his wife, Emily Hay, viii. 472.
Peg, Katharine, mistress of king Charles II., dau. of Thos. P. of Yeldersley, i. 30, 31.
Pelham, Henrietta Anne, wife of 13th earl of Rothes, vii. 308.
—— Thomas H. W., i. 554.
—— —— his wife, Louisa Keith Bruce, i. 554.
Pelly of Upton, Sir Henry, viii. 518.
—— —— his wife, Lilian Harriet Charteris, viii. 518.
—— Constance Lilian, wife of 27th earl of Crawford, iii. 49.
Pembroke, Aymer de Valence, earl of, i. 429, 430, 509.
—— Gilbert de Clare, earl of, i. 5.
—— —— his wife, Marjory of Scotland, i. 5.
—— Marie de Pol, countess of, i. 430.
—— William de Valence, earl of, i. 509.
—— —— his wife, Joan de Monchensy, i. 509.
—— Herbert, earl of, ii. 306.
—— George Augustus (Herbert), 11th earl of, iii. 394.

Pembroke, William (Herbert), 3rd earl of, iv. 374.
Pen, Estelaine, mistress of 3rd lord Dunkeld, ix. 77.
Pencaitland, James Hamilton, lord, ii. 43.
—— of Pencaitland, Alice, v. 283.
—— —— John, v. 283.
Penicuik of that Ilk, David de, iii. 55.
Penn of Stoke Pogis, William, ii. 304.
—— Sophia Margaret Julian, wife of archbp. Wm. Stuart, ii. 304.
Pennington, *, lt.-col. Foot Guards, iii. 408.
—— Louisa Theodosia, wife of E. A. Drummond, viii. 230.
—— Margaret Maria Frances, wife of 24th earl of Crawford, iii. 44.
Penny of Arrad, James, viii. 159.
—— Margaret, wife of Sir North Hamilton Dalrymple of Cleland and Fordel, viii. 159.
Penrhyn of Llandegai, Edward Gordon (Douglas-Pennant), 1st baron, vi. 383.
Pentland, Alexander, in Carrington, iii. 506 *n.*
—— Dionis, captain, Edinburgh, iii. 506; viii. 389.
—— Margaret, wife of Sir Gideon Murray, iii. 506.
Penyston, Sir John, vi. 462.
—— —— his wife, Eleanor Chesham, vi. 462.
Pepdie of Dunglas, Nicola, wife of Sir Thomas de Home, iv. 444.
Pepper-Stavely, George Augustus, i. 130.
—— —— his wife, Helen Susanna Catherine Gertrude Ogilvy, i. 130.
Pepys, Sir Charles Leslie, vii. 307.
—— Henrietta, wife of 10th earl of Devon, vii. 307.
—— Sir Henry Leslie, vii. 307.
—— Sir Lucas, vii. 307.
—— —— his wife, Jane Elizabeth, countess of Rothes, vii. 307.
Perceval, Mary, wife of A. B. Drummond, viii. 229.
PERCY, MURRAY, BARON, i. 499.
Percy, John James Hugh Henry, baron, i. 499.
—— Henry (Percy), 4th lord, iii. 163, 165.
—— of Brackenthwaite, Henry, i. 233.
—— of Kildale, Walter de, iii. 5.
—— —— his wife, Christian *, iii. 5.
—— Emily Charlotte, wife of A. M. Drummond, viii. 225.
—— Emily Frances, wife of 1st lord Glenlyon, i. 496, 499.
—— Sir Henry, 'Hotspur,' iii. 156, 428.
—— Lucy, wife of James (Hay), viscount Doncaster, earl of Carlisle, v. 219.
—— Ralph, brother of 'Hotspur,' vi. 37.
—— Sir Ralph, i. 433.
—— —— his wife, Philippa of Atholl, i. 433.

* Name unknown.

Percy, Sir Thomas, i. 433.
—— —— his wife, Elizabeth of Atholl, i. 433.
—— Sir Walter, iv. 11.
Perkins of Lifford, Richard, i. 50.
—— —— his wife, Cecilia Hamilton, i. 50.
Perris, Elizabeth, wife of Alex. Hume Campbell, vi. 19; ix. 134.
Perry, Hilda Annie, wife of A. L. H. Ogilvie-Grant, vii. 490.
—— Hugh, alderman of London, ii. 35.
—— —— his wife, Katharine Fenn, ii. 35.
—— Sir Thomas Erskine, chief-justice of Bombay, vii. 490.
Pershall of Canwell, Sir William, i. 409.
—— —— his 2nd wife, Frances Aston, i. 409.
—— Arabella, wife of 3rd earl of Breadalbane, ii. 209.
—— Sir John, bart., ii. 209.
—— —— his wife, Charlotte Colepeper, ii. 209.
—— Sir Thomas, bart., ii. 209.
PERTH, DRUMMOND, EARL OF, vii. 28-62.
Perth, Charles Edward, thirteenth (attainted) earl of, vii. 60.
—— Edward, ninth (attainted) earl of, vii. 56.
—— George, fourteenth earl of, vi. 71, 72; vii. 60.
—— —— his 1st wife, Albertine von Rothberg Coligny, vii. 60.
—— —— his 2nd wife, Susan Henrietta Sewell, vii. 60.
—— James, first earl of, vii. 47, 48.
—— —— his wife, Isabella Seton, vii. 48; viii. 592.
—— James, third earl of, vii. 50, 346.
—— —— his wife, Anne Gordon, iv. 547; vii. 51; ix. 111, 149.
—— James, fourth earl of, vii. 51, 139.
—— —— his 1st wife, Jane Douglas, i. 205; vii. 53.
—— —— his 2nd wife, Lilias Drummond, vii. 50, 53; viii. 223, 415; ix. 149.
—— —— his 3rd wife, Mary Gordon, iv. 549; vii. 53.
—— James, fifth (attainted) earl of, vii. 53.
—— James, sixth (attainted) earl of, vii. 54.
—— James, tenth (attainted) earl of, vii. 57.
—— —— his wife, Rachel Bruce, iii. 490; vii. 57.
—— James, eleventh (attainted) earl of, vii. 58.
—— James Louis, twelfth (attainted) earl of, vii. 59.
—— John, second earl of, ii. 189; vii. 47, 48.
—— —— his wife, Jean Ker, vii. 49, 345.
—— John, seventh (attainted) earl of, vii. 54, 55.
—— John, eighth (attainted) earl of, vii. 53, 56.
—— William Huntly, fifteenth earl of, vii. 61; viii. 237.

PERTH, DRUMMOND, LORD, vii. 58-59.
Perth, James, lord, vii. 58.
—— his wife, Clementina Elphinstone, iii. 549; v. 502; vii. 59.
Perth, Drummond, duke of, (Jacobite creation), vii. 52-57.
— Edward, sixth titular duke of, vii. 56, 58.
—— his wife, Elizabeth Middleton, vi. 188; vii. 57, 58.
— James, first titular duke of, vii. 52.
—— his 1st wife, Jane Douglas, i. 205; vii. 53.
—— his 2nd wife, Lilias Drummond, vii. 50, 53; viii. 223, 415; ix. 149.
—— his 3rd wife, Mary Gordon, iv. 549; vii. 53.
— James, second titular duke of, vii. 53; ix. 150 *bis*.
—— his wife, Jean Gordon, vii. 53.
— James, third titular duke of, i. 483; iii. 79; vii. 54; viii. 357.
— John, fourth titular duke of, vii. 55.
— John, fifth titular duke of, vii. 53, 56.
—— his 1st wife, Marjory Gray of Ballegerno, vii. 56; ix. 150.
—— his 2nd wife, Mary Stuart, vii. 56; viii. 407.
Perthic, John de, ii. 504.
—— his wife, Cecilia Cathcart, ii. 504.
Petaw of Mauld, Gideon, ix. 110.
— Geneviève, wife of rev. John Gordon, ix. 110.
Petcary of Moneythin, Andrew, i. 108.
Peter, *, wife of (1) * Irving, and (2) John Campbell, i. 382.
— William, in holy orders, i. 60.
—— his wife, Harriot Hamilton, i. 60.
Peterborongh and Monmouth, Charles (Mordaunt), earl of, iv. 551.
Peters of Betchworth Castle, Henry, iii. 415.
— of Harefield, William Henry, iv. 390.
— Frances Julia, wife of (1) F. T. Tollemache, and (2) admiral John Pakenham, iii. 415.
— Harriette Amy Blackburne, wife of Alfred Douglas-Hamilton, iv. 390.
Petersfield, Louise Renée de Perrancoet de Kerouaille, baroness, v. 363.
PETERSHAM, MAITLAND, BARON, v. 305.
Petersham, John, baron, v. 350.
Petley of Riverhead, Charles, iii. 83.
— Jane, wife of (1) K. Mackenzie of Cromartie, and (2) D. Macleod of Geanies, iii. 83.
Petrie, Robert, ii. 562.
—— his wife, Elizabeth Colville, ii. 562.
Pett, Alison, wife of Archibald Primrose, vii. 212.
Pettie, James Stewart, styled lord, ix. 138.
Peyto of Chesterton, William, i. 405.
—— his wife, Eleanor Aston, i. 405.

* Name unknown.

Philip of Feodarg and Balcormok, vi. 170.
Philip, abbot of Jedburgh, iii. 424.
Philip, abbot of Scone, v. 203.
Philip, James, clerk to the Privy Council, vii. 218.
— Sir John, 1413, i. 235.
Philips of Weston, Sir George Richard, bart., ii. 358.
— John, viii. 182.
—— his wife, Mary Alexander, viii. 182.
— Louisa Georgiana, wife of 14th earl of Caithness, ii. 358.
— Louise V., wife of Jas. Campbell, ix. 45.
Philips-Lee of Binfield, William, viii. 182.
Philipson of Stobo Castle, Hylton, iii. 524.
—— his wife, Nina Charlotte Murray, iii. 524.
Phillippo, Helen Kate, wife of (1) A. J. D. S. St. Aubyn, and (2) P. J. Crichton-Stuart, ii. 309.
— J. C., M.D., Jamaica, ii. 309.
Philp, Ann, wife of Sir Wm. Dalrymple of Kelloch, viii. 123.
Pieris, Marie, wife of (1) George, 4th lord Seton, and (2) Pierre de Clovis, seigneur de Bryante, viii. 584.
Pierrepoint, Robert, Nottingham, iii. 400.
—— his wife, Anne Murray, iii. 400.
Pierrepont, of Holme Pierrepont, Sir Henry, v. 86.
— of Thoresby, Robert, vi. 468.
—— his wife, Elizabeth Evelyn, vi. 468.
— Elizabeth, wife of (1) Sir E. Norreys, and (2) Thomas, 1st earl of Kellie, v. 86.
— Frances, wife of Henry (Cavendish) 2nd duke of Newcastle, ii. 207.
— Frances, wife of John, earl of Mar, v. 632.
— Gertrude, wife of 2nd viscount of Newhaven, vi. 468.
— Mary, wife of E. Wortley-Montague, ii. 302.
— William, ii. 207.
Pilkington of Swinthwaite, Edward, iv. 419.
—— his wife, A. M. Constable-Maxwell, iv. 419.
—— James, iv. 419.
Piltoun, Peter Rollo, bishop of Dunkeld, lord of Session, lord, vii. 190.
Pincheon of Writtle, William, i. 410.
— Elizabeth, wife of 1st earl of Portland, i. 410.
Pinfold, C., ii. 307.
—— his wife, Maria A. C. Stuart, ii. 307.
Pinkeney of Wedon-Pinkeney, Sir Henry de, husband of Alicia de Lindsay, iii. 7.
—— Henry, their son, iii. 7.
—— Sir Henry, iii. 7, 10.
—— Sir Robert de, the Competitor, i. 5; iii. 6, 7.
—— Sir Robert de, iii. 7.
—— his wife, Christina, iii. 7.

Pinto, Paul, lessee of Hilderston silver mine, viii. 171.
Pirie of Waterton, Gordon, vii. 567.
—— Duncan Vernon, capt. 3rd Hussars, M.P., vii. 567.
—— —— his wife, Evelyn Courtenay Forbes-Sempill, vii. 567.
Pitcairn of Drongy, Henry, vi. 85.
—— —— his wife, Gelis Melville, vi. 85.
—— of Forthar, David, v. 404.
—— —— his wife, Isabella Durie, v. 404.
—— —— Henry, iii. 397; v. 396.
—— of Mondynes, Alexander, i. 291.
—— of Pitlour, Henry, vi. 590.
—— —— his wife, Lilias Makgill, vi. 590.
—— —— John, vi. 85.
—— of Pitcairn, Archibald, physician and poet, v. 89; viii. 407.
—— —— his 2nd wife, Elizabeth Stevenson, ix. 170.
—— —— David, viii. 198.
—— —— Henry, iii. 397; v. 396.
—— —— Henry, v. 405.
—— Barbara, wife of William Murray of Letter Bannachty, viii. 198; ix. 161.
—— David, minister of Dysart, ii. 51.
—— —— his wife, Katharine Hamilton, ii. 51.
—— Isabella, wife of Patrick, 4th lord Lindsay of the Byres, v. 396.
—— Janet, wife of 5th earl of Kellie, v. 89.
—— Jean, wife of D. Lindsay of Kirkforthar, v. 405.
—— Katharine, wife of John Arbuthnott of Mondynes, i. 291.
—— Katharine, wife of (1) Charles Cochrane, and (2) C. O. Cambridge, iii. 359.
—— Margaret, wife of David Murray of Dollerie, iii. 397.
—— Marjory, wife of John Lindsay of Kirkforthar, v. 404.
—— Robert, archdeacon of St. Andrews, commendator of Dunfermline, i. 464; ii. 571; iv. 282.
—— —— his wife, Eupheme Murray, i. 464.
—— *, major, Royal Marines, iii. 359.
Pitgrunzie of Pitgrunzie, Orm, ancestor of the family of, vii. 397.
—— Margaret of, wife of John of Lundors, vii. 398.
PITSLIGO, FORBES, LORD FORBES OF, iv. 69-76.
Pitsligo, Alexander, first lord Forbes of, iv. 75.
—— Alexander, second lord Forbes of, ii. 577; iv, 75.
—— Alexander, third lord Forbes of, iv. 64, 75.
—— Alexander, fourth lord Forbes of, iv. 75.
—— master of, John, only son of 4th lord Forbes of Pitsligo, iv. 76.
—— —— his wife, Rebecca Ogilvy, iv. 76.

* Name unknown.

Pitsligo of Agaes, John, v. 526.
Pitt-Rivers of Rushmore, A. H. Lane-Fox, general, vii. 155.
PITTENWEEM, STEWART, LORD, vii. 63-69.
Pittenweem, Frederic, lord, v. 348; vii. 68.
Place of Skelton Grange, Edward, i. 94.
—— —— his wife, Anne Gordon, i. 94.
Plantagenet, Cecilia, i. 333; iii. 22; iv. 449; vii. 325.
—— Geoffrey, count of Anjou, i. 2.
—— Joan, countess of Gloucester, wife of (1) Gilbert, earl of Clare, and (2) Ralph, lord Mounthermer, iv. 12.
Pleydell of Melbourne St. Andrew, Edmund Morton, vi. 326.
—— Cornelia, wife of lt.-col. Archibald Stewart, vi. 326.
Plowden, Anna Maria, wife of 9th earl of Dundonald, iii. 362.
—— Francis, LL.D., iii. 362.
Plumer of Blakesware, col. John, i. 62.
—— of Gilston Park, William, M.P., i. 64.
—— —— his wife, Jane Hamilton, i. 64.
—— Anne, wife of 7th earl of Abercorn, i. 62.
Plumer-Ward of Gilston Park, Robert, i. 64.
—— —— his wife, Jane Hamilton, i. 64.
Plymouth, Charles (FitzCharles), 1st earl of, i. 30.
—— —— his wife, Bridget Osborn, i. 30.
Pocklington, admiral, iv. 163.
—— Bridget, alleged wife of brigadier-general John Stewart of Sorbie, iv. 163.
Podolska, Elizabeth Busson de, wife of James, earl of Dirleton, iii. 130.
Poelnitz, Ernest, baron de, iv. 67.
—— —— his wife, Isabella Drummond Forbes, iv. 67.
Poiret, Elias, sieur de la Roche, iii. 77.
Poitiers, Charles, col. 61st regt., iii. 389.
—— Elizabeth Alicia, wife of capt. Virginius Murray, iii. 389.
Pol, Marie de, countess of Pembroke, i. 430.
Poland, Ladislas VII., king of, iv. 548.
—— —— his wife, Marie Louise de Gonzaga, iv. 548.
Pole, Anne de la, v. 553.
Polignac, Anne de, wife of Gaspard de Coligny, lord of Chatillon, iv. 317.
Pollisworth, Adam de, viii. 561.
—— —— his wife, Emma de Seton, vi. 199; viii. 561.
Pollock, Elizabeth, wife of col. Geo. Napier, vi. 433.
—— Robert, captain, vi. 433.
Pollok of Lismany, John, vii. 392.
—— of Pollok, 1401, ii. 506.
—— —— Charles, ii. 78.
—— —— his wife, Margaret Stewart, ii. 78.
—— —— John, son of Robert, vi. 473.

Pollok of Pollok, John, vii. 533 *n*.
—— —— his wife, Jonet Spreule, vii. 533.
—— —— John, vii. 535.
—— —— his wife, Margaret Sempill, vii. 535.
—— —— Robert, vi. 473.
—— —— his wife, Agnes Maxwell, vi. 473.
—— Zara Eileen, wife of capt. A. G. A. Hore-Ruthven, vii. 392.
POLMONT, HAMILTON, LORD, iv. 378-380.
Polmont, James, son of 2nd duke of Hamilton; styled lord, iv. 380.
—— William, lord, iv. 378.
Polson, Paul Mackay, ancestor of the family of, vii. 159.
POLWARTH, HUME, LORD, vi. 14-24.
Polwarth, Alexander, 3rd son of 1st earl of Marchmont; styled lord, vi. 18.
—— —— his wife, Margaret Campbell of Cessnock, vi. 19.
—— Alexander, son of 3rd earl of Marchmont; styled lord, vi. 22.
—— —— his wife, Annabella Yorke, vi. 23.
—— George, eldest son of 2nd earl of Marchmont; styled lord, vi. 19.
—— Patrick, first lord, vi. 12.
—— —— his wife, Grisell Ker, vi. 14.
—— Patrick, eldest son of 1st earl of Marchmont; styled lord, vi. 16.
—— —— his 1st wife, Elizabeth Hume, vi. 9, 16.
—— —— his 2nd wife, Jean Home, iv. 479; vi. 16.
POLWARTH, SCOTT, LORD, vii. 70-87.
Polwarth, Anne, *de jure* baroness, vii. 70.
—— Diana, wife of Walter Scott of Harden; *de jure* baroness, vii. 70, 83.
—— Henry Francis, seventh lord, vii. 85.
—— —— his wife, Georgina Baillie, iv. 323; vii. 85.
—— Hugh, sixth lord, vii. 84.
—— —— his wife, Harriet Bruhl, vii. 84.
—— Walter Hugh, eighth lord, ii. 237; vii. 86.
—— —— his wife, Mary Gordon, i. 98; vii. 86.
POLWARTH OF POLWARTH, REDBRAES, AND GREINLAW, HUME, LORD, vi. 14-24.
Polwarth of Polwarth, Redbraes and Greinlaw, Patrick, first lord, vi. 14.
—— of Beath, Adam de, vi. 199, 201.
—— —— his wife, Emma de Seton, vi. 199; viii. 561.
—— —— Adam de, son of above, vi. 201.
—— of Polwarth, Elizabeth, wife of Sir John St. Clair of Herdmanston, vii. 579.
—— —— Patrick de, vi. 201.
—— —— Sir Patrick, vii. 579.
Pomarão, James Francis Mason, count of, iii. 50.
Ponsonby, Frances Anna Georgiana, wife of 9th lord Kinnaird, v. 214; ix. 121.
Ponsonby, Helen Geraldine Maria, wife of 18th earl of Morton, vi. 386.
Pontefract, George Fitz Roy, baron, i. 31.
Poole, Anne, wife of 1st earl of Newburgh, vi. 453.
—— Sir Henry, vi. 453.
Poore, Francis Harwood, major, R.M.A., iv. 98.
—— —— his wife, Harriot Elizabeth Grimston, iv. 98.
—— Nina Mary Benita, wife of 13th duke of Hamilton, iv. 396.
—— Robert, major, iv. 396.
—— Robert Montagu, major 7th Hussars, iv. 389.
—— —— his wife, F. M. I. Douglas-Hamilton, iv. 389.
Poortugael, Hermina Clasina den Beer, wife of Æneas Mackay, vii. 172.
Pope, Alexander IV., v. 575.
—— Alexander VI., viii. 578.
—— Benedict XIII., v. 2, 3.
—— Clement VI., viii. 568.
—— Clement VII., ix. 2.
—— Eugenius IV., viii. 576.
—— Gregory XI., viii. 264 *n*.
—— John XXII., iii. 144; iv. 512.
—— Innocent IV., iii. 257.
—— Paul II., viii. 578 *n*.; ix. 42.
—— Pius II., viii. 577.
Pope, Alexander, the poet, vi. 20; vii. 511.
Popeley of Woolley Moorehouse, Francis, iii. 453.
—— Grace, wife of (1) Sir Thos. Wentworth, and (2) Alexander, 8th earl of Eglinton, iii. 453.
Portal of Freefolk, John, iii. 513.
—— Frances, wife of rev. D. R. Murray, iii. 513.
—— Katharine Charlotte, wife of F. W. Montagu Douglas Scott, ii. 246.
—— Melville, ii. 246.
Portarlington, George (Dawson-Damer), 5th earl of, ii. 499.
—— —— his wife, Emma Andalusia Kennedy, ii. 499.
—— John (Damer), 1st earl of, ii. 305.
—— —— his wife, Caroline Stuart, ii. 305.
Porteous of Halkshaw, Sir Patrick, vi. 430.
—— of Headschaw, vii. 75.
—— —— his wife, * Scott, vii. 75.
—— Janet, wife of Walter Scott of Gamescleuch, vi. 430.
—— John, captain, i. 374; viii. 205.
Porterfield of Comiston, Patrick, vi. 334.
—— —— his wife, Anna Douglas, vi. 334.
—— of Hapland, *, vi. 372.
—— —— his wife, Jean Douglas, vi. 372.
—— of Porterfield, Alexander, v. 175.
—— —— his wife, Katharine Boyd, v. 175.

* Name unknown.

Porterfield of Porterfield, William, iv. 238.
— Katharine, wife of Henry Balfour, i. 545.
— Marion, wife of Alex. Cunningham of Corsehill, iv. 238.
Portland, Jerome (Weston), 2nd earl of, v. 360.
— — his wife, Frances Stewart, v. 359.
— Richard (Weston), 1st earl of, i. 410.
— — his 1st wife, Elizabeth Pincheon, i. 410.
— William (Bentinck), 2nd duke of, vi. 189 *n.*
— — his wife, Margaret Cavendish Harley, vi. 189.
— William Henry (Bentinck), 3rd duke of, viii. 362.
Portman, William Henry Berkeley (Portman), 2nd viscount, vi. 122.
Portman of Bryanston, Edward Berkeley, viii. 224.
— of Orchard Portman, Sir Henry, v. 467.
— — his wife, Anne Stanley, v. 467.
— Emma Selina, wife of 11th earl of Leven, vi. 122.
— Henry Berkeley, ii. 499.
— — his wife, Emma Andalusia Kennedy, ii. 499.
— Marianne, wife of G. Drummond of Stanmore, viii. 224.
PORTMORE, COLYEAR, EARL OF, vii. 88-97.
Portmore, Charles, second earl of, vii. 94.
— — his wife, Julian Hele, vii. 94.
— David, first earl of, vii. 91.
— — his wife, Katharine Sedley, countess of Dorchester, vii. 93.
— Thomas Charles, fourth earl of, vii. 96.
— — his 1st wife, Mary Elizabeth Bertie, vii. 96.
— — his 2nd wife, Frances Murrells, vii. 96.
— William Charles, third earl of, vii. 95.
— — his wife, Mary Leslie, vii. 95, 306.
PORTMORE AND BLACKNESS, COLYEAR, LORD, vii. 92.
Portmore and Blackness, David, lord, vii. 92.
Portsmouth, John (Wallop), earl of, i. 104.
— Louise Renée de Perrancoet de Keroualle, duchess of, i. 32, 89; v. 362.
Portugal, kings of, Alfonso VI., i. 30.
— — John IV., i. 30.
— — Pedro II., i. 30.
Poultney of Misterton, Sir William, i. 31.
— Anne, wife of 1st duke of Cleveland, i. 31.
Pounden of Brownswood, Jeremiah Lonsdale, iv. 293.
— — his wife, Jane Stuart, iv. 293; vi. 328.
— Evelyn, baroness Gray, wife of J. M. Smith, iv. 293, 295.
Powell of Pen-y-bank, Anna Charlotta Maria, wife of lord Anne Hamilton, iv. 388.
— — Charles, iv. 388.
— Alice, wife of 2nd duke of Buccleuch, ii. 241.
— Harriet, wife of Kenneth, earl of Seaforth, vii. 513.
— Joseph, Westminster, ii. 241.
Power, Bonamy Mansell, Guernsey, vii. 24.
— — his wife, Elizabeth Barton, vii. 24.
— Christian, wife of capt. Wm. Boyle, iv. 194.
— Hew, merchant, iv. 194.
— John, major 29th regt., iii. 414.
— — his wife, Emilia Magdalen Louisa Sinclair, iii. 413.
— William, ii. 457.
— — his wife, Elizabeth Kennedy, ii. 457.
Powis, Edward (Herbert), 2nd earl, vi. 271.
— — his wife, Lucy Graham, vi. 271.
— William (Herbert), 1st marquess of, vi. 489; vii. 510.
Powle, Mary, wife of Sir Francis Cheyne, vi. 464.
— Sir Stephen, Stepney, vi. 464.
— Thomas, clerk of the Crown in Chancery, vi. 464.
Praebenda, Robert de, bishop of Dunblane, viii. 245 *n.*
Prange, Anton, viii. 82.
— Emilie, wife of Edward Hugo Carnegie, viii. 82.
Prannell, Henry, London, v. 357.
— — his wife, Frances Howard, v. 357.
Prat of Muiravonside, Margaret, wife of Sir Richard Melville of Melville, vi. 78.
— of Tynedale, Richard, vi. 78.
Pratt of Ryston Hall, Jermyn, in holy orders, iv. 210.
— Benjamin, D.D., dean of Down, i. 62.
— — his wife, Philippa Hamilton, i. 62.
— Blanche Eleanor Murray, wife of capt. James Boyle, iv. 210.
— Harriet, wife of John M. Maitland, v. 314.
— Joseph, in holy orders, v. 314.
Pratt-Barlow of Lynchmere House, Frank, vii. 452.
— Edward, 60th Rifles, vii. 452.
— — his wife, Marjory L. K. Fraser, vii. 452.
— Francis, iv. 211.
— — his wife, Agnes Margaret Boyle, iv. 210.
Prendergast, Sir Jeffrey, major-general, viii. 142.
— — his wife, Elizabeth Dalrymple, viii. 142.
Presles, marquis de, Intendant of Dauphiné, vi. 69.

Presmennan, Robert Hamilton, lord, ii. 42, 43.
PRESTON, GRAHAM, VISCOUNT OF, vii. 98-108.
Preston, Charles, third viscount of, vii. 107.
— — his wife, Anne Cox, vii. 108.
— Edward, second viscount of, vii. 107.
— — his wife, Mary Dalton, vii. 107.
— Richard, first viscount, vii. 104.
— — his wife, Anne Howard, vii. 106.
— William, self-styled viscount of, vii. 103.
PRESTON, EARL OF DESMOND, iii. 122.
PRESTON, LORD DINOWALL, iii. 117-125.
PRESTON, BARON DUMORE, iii. 112.
PRESTON, DOUGLAS, LORD DOUGLAS OF, i. 210.
Preston of Airdrie, John, vi. 497.
— — his wife, Marjorie Carnegie, vi. 497.
— of Wester Benyne, Sir William, ix. 67.
— of Cameron, George, iii. 27.
— — his wife, Isobel Lindsay, ii. 110; iii. 27.
— of Craigmillar, Sir George, 2nd son of Simon de P., iii. 118; ix. 67.
— — George, ii. 110.
— — Sir George, iv. 244.
— — his wife, Agnes Hay, iv. 244.
— — George, elder son of David P. of Whitehill, iii. 121.
— — Robert, iii. 120.
— — Simon de, sheriff of Lothian, 1st laird, iii. 118.
— — Sir Simon, i. 460.
— — his wife, Elizabeth Crichton, i. 460.
— — Simon, ii. 230.
— — his wife, Janet Betoun, ii. 230.
— — William, iii. 118.
— of Fentonbarns, John, iii. 120.
— of Formartin and Fyvie, Sir Henry de, ii. 540; iii. 11, 12; iv. 46.
— — his wife, Elizabeth Lindsay, iii. 11.
— — Mariota, wife of (1) A. Chisholm, and (2) Sir John Forbes, iv. 46.
— of Furness, Sir Thomas, iii. 299.
— of Gorton, Sir John de, ambassador to England, iii. 117; ix. 67 *bis*.
— — John, v. 406, 408.
— — his wife, Agnes Lindsay, v. 406, 408.
— — Sir Robert, lord of Session, iv. 436.
— — his 2nd wife, Margaret Bothwell, iv. 436.
— — Robert, v. 408.
— — his wife, Euphemia Preston, v. 408.
— — Sir William, iv. 438.
— of Haltree, Sir Richard, tutor of Whitehill, iii. 120, 121.
— of Leithinhopes, Sir James, v. 469.
— of Loganraw, Archibald, ix. 67.
— — Richard, ix. 67.
Preston of Loganraw, Simon, eldest son of Simon de P. iii. 118; ix. 67.
— — Thomas, ix. 67.
— of Morphet, Sir James, v. 469.
— of Myles, Christian, ix. 67.
— — Sir John, ix. 67.
— — Laurence, ix. 67.
— of Penicuik, Sir James, v. 469.
— — Sir John, president of the Court of Session, vi. 392.
— of Preston, George, son of David P. of Whitehill, iii. 121.
— — his wife, Jean Gibson, iii. 121.
— — Robert, iii. 120.
— — Sir Robert, lord of Session, iii. 121; iv. 436.
— — Sir Simon, ix. 67.
— — Simon, i. 464; iii. 27, 119; iv. 88.
— — his wife, Agnes Forrester, iv. 88.
— — Sir William, ix. 41.
— — his wife, Elizabeth Hepburne, ii. 149; ix. 41.
— of Prestonhill, Sir John, i. 570.
— — his wife, Margaret Elphinstone, i. 570.
— of Valleyfield, Archibald, vii. 543, 551.
— — Sir George, 1st bart., ii. 552; vi. 589; vii. 555.
— — his wife, Marian Sempill, vii. 555.
— — Sir George, 4th bart., iii. 349.
— — his wife, Anne Cochrane, iii. 349.
— — James, 1st laird, iii. 472; vi. 587.
— — James, v. 609.
— — his wife, Jean Erskine, v. 609.
— — Sir John, ix. 82.
— — John, ii. 550.
— — his wife, Grizel Colville, ii. 550.
— — Sir Robert, *error for* Sir John, iii. 486, 489.
— — Sir Robert, iii. 492.
— of Whitehill, Andrew, alleged ancestor of the family of, iii. 118; ix. 67.
— — Archibald, iii. 119.
— — David, iii. 120.
— — his 1st wife, Margaret Ker, iii. 120.
— — his 2nd wife, Susanna Colville, ii. 549; iii. 120.
— — George, iii. 121.
— — his wife, Jean Gibson, iii. 121.
— — John, iii. 120.
— — his wife, Jane Crichton, iii. 120.
— — Richard, iii. 119.
— — his wife, Helen Coutts, iii. 119.
— — Robert, iii. 121.
— — Thomas, iii. 118.
— — his wife, Alison *, iii. 119.
— — Thomas, his grandson, iii. 119.
— — his wife, Christian Seton, iii. 119; viii. 577 *n*.
— Agnes, wife of Francis Hepburn, iii. 121.

* Name unknown.

Preston, Anne, wife of 2nd baron Clifford of Chudleigh, iii. 299.
— Archibald, 2nd son of Thos. P. of Whitehill, iii. 119.
— Archibald, tutor to William P. of Craigmillar, iii. 118.
— Archibald, king's esquire, iii. 118 *n.*
— Barbara, wife of (1) Robert, master of Sempill, and (2) R. Mure of Caldwell, vii. 543.
— Elizabeth, dau. of Richard P. of Whitehill, iii. 120, 121.
— Elizabeth, wife of col. John Fullarton of Dudwick, viii. 108.
— Euphemia, wife of Robert Preston of Gorton, v. 406, 408.
— George, general, governor of Edinburgh Castle, iii. 358.
— Helen, wife of (1) Henry Forrester of Corstorphine, and (2) Wm. Borthwick of Soutra, iv. 90.
— Henry, Edinburgh, iii. 117.
— Isabel, wife of Sir Jas. Makgill of Rankeillor, vi. 589.
— James, chaplain of Hospital of St. Mary Magdalene, iii. 118.
— James, 2nd son of Richard P. of Whitehill, iii. 120.
— Mr. John, 2nd son of David P. of Whitehill, iii. 121.
— John, son of Simon de P. of Craigmillar, ix. 67.
— Katharine, wife of Robert Bruce of Blairhall, iii. 489.
— Katharine, wife of Robert Nairn of Mukkersy, vi. 392.
— Laurence of, i. 454 *n.*
— Lyulph de, iii. 117.
— Margaret, wife of William de Crichton of Gilberton, iii. 57; ix. 62, 67.
— Margaret, wife of Robert Bothwell, iv. 438.
— Margaret, wife of John Napier of Balcormo, vi. 408.
— Margaret, wife of John Makgill, vi. 587.
— Marion, wife of Jas. Murray of Pardewis, i. 464.
— Marion, dau. of John P. of Whitehill, iii. 120.
— Mary, wife of Mr. John Colville, ii. 552.
— Mary, wife of Geo. Bruce of Carnock, iii. 486.
— Nicol, Edinburgh, iii. 117.
— Simon, eldest son of Simon de P. of Craigmillar, iii. 118.
— Thomas, bailie of Edinburgh, iii. 118 *n.*
— William, Edinburgh, iii. 117.
Preston-Bruce of Valleyfield, Charles Dashwood, iii. 492, 495.
— — his wife, Harriet Elizabeth Rivers, iii. 492.
Preston-Bruce of Valleyfield, Robert, M.P., 2nd son of 8th earl of Elgin, iii. 495.
Prestonhall, Roderick Mackenzie, lord Justice-Clerk, lord, iii. 72.
Prestwood of Butterford, George, vii. 94.
— Julian, wife of Roger Hele of Halwell, vii. 94.
Prettyjohn, John, Barbados, v. 314.
— Katharine, wife of gen. F. Maitland, v. 314.
Price of Beckett, Barrington, colonel, viii. 311 *bis.*
— — his 1st wife, Mary Bowes, viii. 311.
— — his 2nd wife, Mary Thornhill, viii. 311.
— of Saintfield, Nicholas, vii. 511.
— — his wife, Maria Mackenzie, vii. 511.
— Anne, wife of (1) John Lyon, and (2) lieut. J. W. Oldmixon, viii. 310.
— Bartholomew, Linlithgow, iii. 611.
— Elizabeth, wife of Alexander Leslie, styled lord Newark, vi. 444.
Priestfield, Thomas Hamilton, senator of the College of Justice, lord, iv. 306.
PRIMROSE, PRIMROSE, VISCOUNT OF, vii. 109-111.
Primrose, Archibald, second viscount of, vii. 110.
— Hugh, third viscount of, vii. 111, 222, 223.
— — his wife, Anne Drelincourt, vii. 111.
— James, first viscount of, iii. 544; vii. 110.
— — his wife, Eleanor Campbell, v. 508; vii. 110.
PRIMROSE, PRIMROSE, LORD, vii. 221-229.
Primrose, Archibald, first lord, vii. 221.
PRIMROSE AND CASTLEFIELD, PRIMROSE, LORD, vii. 109-111.
Primrose and Castlefield, James, first lord, vii. 110.
PRIMROSE, LORD DALMENY, vii. 221-229.
PRIMROSE, BARON EPSOM OF EPSOM, ix. 152.
PRIMROSE, VISCOUNT OF INVERKEITHING, vii. 221-229.
PRIMROSE, VISCOUNT MENTMORE OF MENTMORE, ix. 152.
PRIMROSE, EARL OF MIDLOTHIAN, ix. 152.
PRIMROSE, LORD PRIMROSE, vii. 221.
PRIMROSE, VISCOUNT OF PRIMROSE, vii. 109-111, 221-229.
PRIMROSE, LORD PRIMROSE AND CASTLEFIELD, vii. 109-111.
PRIMROSE, EARL OF ROSEBERY, vii. 212-229.
PRIMROSE, BARON ROSEBERY OF ROSEBERY, vii. 225-229.
Primrose of Barcruik, James, vii. 213.
— of Barhill, James, vii. 213.
— — his wife, Margaret Maisterton, vii. 213.

Primrose of Barnbougle, Sir Archibald, 1st laird, vii. 219.
—— —— Sir James, vii. 219.
—— —— his wife, Elizabeth Sinclair, iii. 451; vii. 219.
—— of Burnbrae, Peter, ancestor of the family of, vii. 214.
—— of Carrington, Sir Archibald, lord Justice General, iv. 289; vii. 109, 218; viii. 77 *bis*.
—— —— his 1st wife, Elizabeth Keith, vi. 54; vii. 219.
—— —— —— his 2nd wife, Agnes Gray, iv. 289; vii. 219.
—— —— Sir James, vii. 110.
—— —— his wife, Eleanor Campbell, v. 508; vii. 110.
—— —— Sir William, clerk of Notaries, ii. 32; vii. 109, 219.
—— —— his wife, Mary *or* Anna Scott, vi. 431; vii. 109.
—— of Dalmeny, Sir Archibald, 1st laird, vii. 218.
—— —— Archibald, M.P., vii. 221.
—— —— his wife, Dorothea Cressy, vii. 222.
—— of Dunipace, Sir Archibald Foulis, vii. 220, 222.
—— —— his 1st wife, Margaret Fleming, vii. 220.
—— —— his 2nd wife, Mary Primrose, vii. 220, 222.
—— of Fodsmill, James, vii. 214.
—— of Kincardine, Peter, vii. 214.
—— of Leny, Everingham, vii. 222.
—— of Newlands, James, vii. 214.
—— of Wolmerston, Sir Archibald, v. 413.
—— Adam, vii. 215.
—— —— his wife, Jean Clayhills, vii. 215.
—— Agnes, wife of James Aitken of Middle Grange, vii. 213.
—— Agnes, dau. of Henry P., vii. 215.
—— Agnes, wife of Alexander Menteith, vii. 217.
—— Alexander, 5th son of James P., vii. 217.
—— Alice Jane, wife of (1) G. W. Mercer Henderson of Fordel, and (2) John Bellingham, vii. 227.
—— Alison, dau. of Archibald P., vii. 215.
—— Alison, wife of George Heriot, vii. 217.
—— Alison, dau. of James P., vii. 218.
—— Anne, wife of Henry Tufnell, vii. 227.
—— Archibald, dean, chamberlain of Culross, vii. 212.
—— —— his wife, Alison Pett, vii. 212.
—— Archibald, burgess of Edinburgh, vii. 215.
—— —— his wife, Christian Gillespie, vii. 215.
—— Archibald, his son, vii. 215.
Primrose, Archibald, writer, clerk of taxations and mines, vii. 215, 216.
—— —— his wife, Katharine Andro, vii. 215.
—— Archibald, his 2nd son, vii. 215.
—— Arthur John, Bengal C.S., vii. 226.
—— Bouverie Francis, C.B., vii. 226.
—— —— his wife, Frederica Sophia Anson, vii. 226.
—— Charlotte, wife of (1) Kenneth, 1st earl of Effingham, and (2) Thomas Holmes, vii. 225.
—— Charlotte Henrietta, wife of commr. Carlton Tufnell, vii. 227.
—— Christian, wife of 6th lord Torphichen, vii. 217; viii. 393.
—— Christian, dau. of James P., vii. 218.
—— Constance Evelyn, wife of 2nd lord Leconfield, vii. 227.
—— David, 4th son of Henry P., vii. 214.
—— —— his wife, Janet Blaw, vii. 214.
—— David, advocate, vii. 214.
—— —— his 1st wife, Marion Purdie, vii. 214.
—— —— his 2nd wife, Margaret Forrester, vii. 215.
—— —— his 3rd wife, Alison Logan, vii. 215.
—— —— his 4th wife, Christian Ross, vii. 215.
—— David, son of David P., advocate, vii. 215.
—— Dorothea, dau. of 1st earl of Rosebery, vii. 222.
—— Dorothea, wife of Sir Adam Inglis of Cramond, vii. 224.
—— Dorothea Arabella, wife of William Hervey, vii. 225.
—— Duncan, bailie in Culross, vii. 213.
—— —— his wife, Helen Smyth, vii. 213.
—— Duncan, chirurgeon to the king, vii. 213.
—— Duncan, brother of Gilbert P., vii. 214.
—— Edward, lieut. in earl of Morton's regt., vii. 213.
—— —— his wife, Elizabeth Merschell, vii. 213.
—— Edward Henry, col. Grenadier Guards, vii. 227.
—— Edward Neil, vii. 226.
—— Elizabeth, wife of 9th lord Elphinstone, iii. 545; vii. 110.
—— Elizabeth, wife of George Mackmoran, vii. 217.
—— Elizabeth, dau. of Sir James P. of Barnbougle, vii. 219.
—— Elizabeth, dau. of Sir Archibald P. of Carrington, vii. 220.
—— Euphame, in Leith, dau. of Henry P., vii. 215.
—— Euphame, wife of Sir George Bruce of Carnock, iii. 485; vii. 216; ix. 82.
—— Eupheme, dau. of James P., vii. 218.

Primrose, Francis, 4th son of Sir William P. of Carrington, vii. 109.
— Francis Archibald, vii. 226.
— — his wife, Jane King, vii. 226.
— Francis Ward, barrister-at-law, vii. 225.
— — his wife, Percy Gore, vii. 225.
— Frederica Mary, dau. of Bouverie P., vii. 227.
— George Anson, vice-admiral R.N., vii. 226.
— — his wife, Mary Cecilia Violet Kenny, vii. 226.
— Gilbert, chirurgeon to king James VI., iii. 317; vii. 213.
— — his wife, Alison Grahame, iii. 317; vii. 213.
— Gilbert, minister at Bordeaux and London, vii. 216.
— Gilbert, joint-clerk to the Privy Council, vii. 216.
— — his wife, Janet Foulis, vii. 216.
— Gilbert, major-general, vii. 220.
— Gilbert Edward, vii. 226.
— — his wife, Jessie Katharine Costelloe, vii. 226.
— Grisel, wife of (1) Francis, 8th lord Sempill, and (2) brig.-gen. R. Cunningham, vii. 221, 558.
— Harriet, wife of Sir John Dunlop, vii. 227.
— Harry, 2nd son of James P. of Barhill, vii. 213.
— Henry, Culross, vii. 212.
— Henry, burgess of Culross, vii. 214.
— — his wife, Margaret Reidoch, vii. 214.
— Henry, notary, Mauchline, vii. 214.
— — his wife, Bessie Rodger, vii. 214.
— Henry, mariner, vii. 214.
— Henry, 3rd son of Henry P., vii. 215.
— Sir Henry William, K.C.B., vii. 226.
— — his wife, Helen Mary M'Micking, vii. 226.
— James, elder son of Archibald P., vii. 215 *bis*.
— James, clerk to the Privy Council, vii. 216; viii. 26.
— — his 1st wife, Sibylla Miller, vii. 216.
— — his 2nd wife, Katharine Lawson, vii. 216.
— James, clerk to the Conservers of Peace, and to the Privy Council, vii. 217, 218.
— — his wife, Nicolas Mercer, vii. 217.
— Janet, wife of Gilbert Gourlay, vii. 217.
— Jean, wife of Hugh Montgomerie of Coilsfield, iii. 447; vii. 110.
— Jean, wife of James Christie, vii. 215.
— John, storekeeper, Edinburgh Castle, vii. 222.
— Katharine, wife of Alexander Couston, vii. 214.
— Katharine, dau. of Arch. P., vii. 215.
Primrose, Katharine, dau. of Archibald P., Edinburgh, vii. 215.
— Katharine, wife of Andrew Clayhills, vii. 216.
— Katharine, dau. of James P., vii. 217.
— Katharine, dau. of James P., vii. 218.
— Katharine, wife of Sir D. Carnegie of Pittarrow, vii. 220; viii. 77.
— Louisa, dau. of 4th earl of Rosebery, vii. 227.
— Magdalene, wife of George Robertson, vii. 218.
— Margaret, wife of Alexander, 9th earl of Caithness, ii. 346; vii. 222.
— Margaret, wife of George Hume of Kimmerghame, vi. 11; vii. 219.
— Margaret, dau. of 1st viscount of Primrose, vii. 110.
— Margaret, wife of James Coneway, vii. 213.
— Margaret, wife of Wm. Spottiswood of Foular, vii. 213.
— Margaret, wife of Thos. Young of Leny, vii. 217.
— Margaret, wife of Sir John Foulis of Ravelston, vii. 220.
— Margaret, dau. of Arch. P. of Burnbrae, ix. 82.
— Margaret Etrenne Hannah, wife of 1st marquess of Crewe, vii. 228.
— Margaret Sophia, vii. 226.
— Marion, wife of (1) David Gourlay, and (2) Sir A. Clerk of Pittencrieff, iii. 318; vii. 213.
— Marion, wife of Robert Coustoun, vii. 215.
— Marion, dau. of James P., vii. 218.
— Mary, dau. of Sir Archibald P. of Carrington, vii. 221.
— Mary, wife of 3rd lord Bargany, ii. 32; vii. 110; ix. 36.
— Mary, wife of Sir Archibald Foulis Primrose of Dunipace, vii. 220, 222.
— Mary, dau. of 2nd earl of Rosebery, vii. 224.
— Mary, wife of Henry John Shepherd, vii. 225.
— Mary Anne, dau. of 4th earl of Rosebery, vii. 227.
— Mary Katharine Constance, wife of Henry Walter Hope of Luffness, vii. 227.
— Mause, wife of Andrew Gibson, vii. 214.
— Nicolas, dau. of James P., vii. 217.
— Nicolas, dau. of James P., vii. 218.
— Mr. Peter, minister of Mauchline, vii. 213.
— Mr. Peter, minister of Crossmichael, vii. 213.
— Peter, 7th son of James P., vii. 217.
— Richard, 3rd son of 1st earl of Rosebery, vii. 222.
— Robert, envoy to Gustavus Adolphus, vii. 216.

Primrose, Sibylla, dau. of James P., vii. 217.
—— Sibyl Myra Caroline, wife of capt. C. J. C. Grant, vii. 228.
—— Thomas, 6th son of James P., vii. 217.
—— William, captain in Flemish wars, vii. 109.
—— William, advocate, vii. 110.
—— William, burgess of Dysart, vii. 212.
—— —— his wife, Margaret Sandis, vii. 212.
Pringle of Balmungo, George, ii. 103; iv. 105.
—— —— his 1st wife, Elspeth Ruthven, iv. 105.
—— —— his 2nd wife, Agnes Borthwick, ii. 103.
—— of Blyndlie, George, iv. 471.
—— —— his wife, Marion Pringle, iv. 471.
—— —— Robert, ii. 114.
—— of Buckholm, James, iii. 283.
—— of Crichton, Andrew, vii. 382.
—— of Galashiels, David, vii. 75.
—— —— his wife, Margaret Scott, vii. 75.
—— —— Sir James, vii. 75.
—— —— Jean, wife of Hugh Scott in Greenhead, vii. 75.
—— of St. Christopher's, Walter, viii. 145.
—— of Smailholm, David, iii. 281.
—— of Sticbell, Sir James, 4th bart., iv. 322.
—— —— Sir John, 5th bart., ii. 211; iv. 327; vii. 590.
—— —— his wife, Elizabeth Maitland Campbell, ii. 210.
—— —— Robert, 1st laird, ii. 235; v. 118.
—— —— Sir Robert, 1st bart., ii. 102.
—— of Torsonce, John, iii. 507.
—— of the Tynnes, James, iii. 283; ix. 32.
—— —— his wife, Agnes Forrester, i. 532; ix. 32.
—— of Whytbank, James, iii. 503; iv. 471.
—— —— his 1st wife, Marion Murray, iii. 503.
—— —— James, iv. 105.
—— of Wodehouse, James, iv. 471.
—— Andrew, minister at Castletoun, ii. 190.
—— Ann Crawfurd, wife of commr. Charles St. Clair, vii. 590.
—— Ann Young, wife of John Dalrymple, viii. 145.
—— Elizabeth, wife of Colin Campbell of Carwhin, ii. 190.
—— Elizabeth, wife of Sir Walter Murray of Livingstone, iii. 507.
—— John, ii. 235.
—— —— his wife, Margaret Scott, ii. 235.
—— Margaret, wife of Walter Rutherfurd, vii. 382.
—— Marion, wife of (1) Geo. Pringle, and (2) William Home, iv. 471; ix. 108.
—— Marion, wife of (1) Wm. Cairncross of Colmislie, and (2) Sir Andrew Ker of Cessford, vii. 334.
—— Mary, wife of Henry Borthwick of Pilmuir, ii. 102.
Pringle, Mary, wife of Geo. Baillie of Jerviswoode, ii. 211; iv. 322.
—— Mary Gavin, wife of Robert Baillie-Hamilton, iv. 327.
—— Robert, in Baitingbus, v. 118.
—— Robert, councillor-at-law, viii. 394.
—— —— his wife, Christian Sandilands, viii. 394.
Pritchard, Thomas, London, viii. 124.
—— —— his wife, Anne Dalrymple, viii. 124.
Proby, Baptist, dean of Lichfield, vii. 514.
—— Elizabeth Emma, wife of lord Claud Hamilton, i. 67.
—— Mary, wife of Francis, lord Seaforth, vii. 513.
Prodgers of Kington, Herbert, vii. 567.
—— Gwendolin Emily Mary, wife of 18th lord Sempill, vii. 567.
Prosser, George Augustus, iv. 388.
—— Lucretia, wife of admiral C. P. Hamilton, iv. 388.
Protheroe, Elizabeth, wife of Wm. Walters, ii. 238.
Prudence, 1st wife of Sir Patrick Murray of Redcastle, viii. 412.
Prussia, king of, Frederick II., the Great, vi. 62, 63, 64.
Pryse of Gogerddan, Sir Robert, iv. 265.
—— —— his wife, Mary Ruthven, iv. 265.
Psaraki, Alexandros, Crete, viii. 451.
—— Kalitza, wife of Robert Hay of Linplum, viii. 451.
Puckering of the Priory and Charlton, Sir Henry Newton, bart., iii. 400.
—— —— his wife, Elizabeth Murray, iii. 400.
Puckler, Francis, baron von, vii. 171.
—— Margaret, wife of brigadier-gen. Æneas Mackay, vii. 171.
Puer, Sir Robert, v. 518.
Pulteney of Bath, Daniel, iii. 517.
—— —— Frances, wife of Sir William Johnstone of Westerhall, iii. 517.
—— —— Sir James, bart., son of Sir Robert Murray of Hillhead, iii. 517.
—— —— his wife, Henrietta Laura (Pulteney), countess of Bath, iii. 517 *bis*.
—— —— Sir William, bart., 3rd son of Sir James Johnstone of Westerhall, iii. 517.
—— —— his 1st wife, Frances Pulteney, iii. 517.
Purdie of Kinnaldie, James, Islay Herald, vii. 214.
—— Marion, wife of (1) Wm. Marjoribanks, and (2) David Primrose, vii. 214.
Purdie, the grammarian, vii. 520.
Purgstall, Wenceslaus, count of, ii. 598.
—— —— his wife, Jane Anne Cranstoun, ii. 598.
Purves of Polwarth, Sir William, bart., vi. 19.

Purves of Purveshall, Sir Alexander, 5th bart., vi. 19, 21.
—— —— his wife, Catherine Le Blanc, vi. 19.
—— —— Sir William, 1st bart., iv. 479.
—— —— Sir William, 3rd bart., vi. 19.
—— —— Sir William, 4th bart., vi. 19.
—— —— his wife, Anne Hume Campbell, vi. 19, 21.
—— Anne, wife of 6th earl of Home, iv. 479.
—— Mr. George, minister of Glencorse, iv. 436.
—— —— his wife, Anna Bothwell, iv. 436.
—— Margaret, wife of Robert Makgill, lord of Session, vi. 590.
Pye of Wadley, Charles, major, 3rd Dragoons, ii. 89.
—— —— his wife, Mary Colt, ii. 89.
Pym of the Hasells, Francis, vi. 118.
—— —— his wife, Jane E. Leslie-Melville, vi. 118.
Pyngle of Longforgan, Adam de, viii. 264.

Quarantely, Elena, wife of Sir James Cunningham of Hassendean, iv. 225 *n.*
Quarrell, Richard, vii. 150.
—— —— his wife, Basilia Dawes, vii. 150.
Queen of Scots, Margaret, the Maid of Norway, i. 6, 7; iii. 258; v. 34.
—— —— Mary, i. 24, 25, 400; ii. 164, 166, 167; v. 157, 353, 354, 436, 437, 440, 528; vi. 370; vii. 122, 124, 283, 293, 411, 541; viii. 490, 585, 586.
Queens Consort of Scotland—
—— —— Æthelreda, dau. of Gospatric, earl of Northumberland and Dunbar, and wife of Duncan ii., i. 3; iii. 245.
—— —— Annabella, dau. of Sir John Drummond, and wife of Robert iii., i. 17; ii. 438; vii. 37; ix. 2.
—— —— Anne, dau. of Frederick ii. of Denmark and Norway, and wife of James vi., i. 27; iv. 264, 433, 580; viii. 493; ix. 99.
—— —— Anne, dau. of Edward (Hyde), earl of Clarendon, and 1st wife of James vii., i. 33.
—— —— Elizabeth, dau. of Richard de Burgh, earl of Ulster, and 2nd wife of Robert i., i. 8; vii. 234.
—— —— Elizabeth, dau. of Sir Adam Mure of Rowallan, and 1st wife of Robert ii. i. 15, 135; ix. 2.
—— —— Ermengarde, dau. of Richard, viscount de Bellomont, and wife of William the Lion, i. 5; vii. 399.
—— —— Euphemia, dau. of Hugh, earl of Ross, and 2nd wife of Robert ii., i. 16, 134, 436; vi. 297; vii. 181 *n.*, 236; viii. 263.
—— —— Henrietta Maria of Bourbon, dau. of Henry iv. of France, and wife of Charles i., i. 28.
Queens Consort of Scotland—
—— —— Ingibiorg, ?dau. of Thorfinn, earl of Caithness, and 1st wife of Malcolm iii., 'Ceannmor,' i. 2; ii. 314.
—— —— Isabella, dau. of John, earl of Surrey, and wife of John Baliol, i. 7.
—— —— Isabella, dau. of Donald, 10th earl of Mar, and 1st wife of Robert i., i. 8; v. 578.
—— —— Joan Plantagenet, dau. of John of England, and 1st wife of Alexander iii., i. 6; ii. 423, 430: iii. 252.
—— —— Joan Plantagenet, dau. of Edward ii. of England, and 1st wife of David ii., i. 9; iii. 145; iv. 141; ix. 1.
—— —— Joan, dau. of John Beaufort, 1st earl of Somerset, and wife of (1) James i., and (2) Sir James Stewart, the Black Knight of Lorn, i. 18, 450; ii. 141; iii. 564, 569; v. 2, 427.
—— —— Joleta of Dreux, 2nd wife of Alexander iii., i. 6; vi. 564.
—— —— Katherina, Infanta of Portugal, wife of Charles ii., i. 30.
—— —— Madeleine de Valois, dau. of Francis i. of France, and 1st wife of James v., i. 23.
—— —— Saint Margaret, dau. of Edward the Ætheling, and 2nd wife of Malcolm 'Ceannmor,' i. 2; viii. 476.
—— —— Margaret Plantagenet, dau. of Henry iii. of England, and 1st wife of Alexander iii., i. 6; iv. 9; vii. 400.
—— —— Margaret, dau. of Sir Malcolm Drummond, and wife of (1) John Logie of Logie, and (2) David ii., i. 9; ii. 262, 445; vi. 348; vii. 32.
—— —— Margaret, dau. of Christian i. of Denmark, and wife of James iii., i. 20; v. 144, 147, 638.
—— —— Margaret Tudor, eldest dau. of Henry vii. of England, and wife of James iv., i. 21, 26, 27; iv. 261; v. 150; vi. 166, 167.
—— —— Marie, dau. of Enguerand iii., baron de Coucy, and 2nd wife of Alexander ii., i. 6.
—— —— Maria, dau. of Arnold, duke of Guelders, and wife of James ii., i. 20; iii. 60; v. 604, 637.
—— —— Marie, dau. of Claude i. de Guise Lorraine, and 2nd wife of James v., i. 23; iv. 23; v. 527; vii. 122, 292; viii. 283, 585.
—— —— Mary Beatrice Eleanor D'Este, dau. of Alphonso, duke of Modena, and 2nd wife of James vii., i. 33; iii. 217.
—— —— Matilda, dau. of Waltheof, earl of Huntingdon, and wife of David i., i. 3.
—— —— Sybilla, illeg. dau. of Henry i. of England, and wife of Alexander i., i. 3.
—— —— Yolande, comtesse de Montfort, dau. of Robert iv., comte de Dreux, and 2nd wife of Alexander iii., i. 6; vi. 564.

QUEENSBERRY, DOUGLAS, EARL OF, vii. 134-156.
Queensberry, James, second earl of, vii. 135.
—— —— his 1st wife, Mary Hamilton, vii. 136.
—— —— his 2nd wife, Margaret Stewart, vii. 136; viii. 405; ix. 150.
—— William, first earl of, iii. 234; vii. 133; ix. 71.
—— —— his wife, Isobel Ker, v. 458; vii. 133.
—— William, third earl of, vii. 137.
—— —— his wife, Isabel Douglas, i. 205; vii. 140.
QUEENSBERRY, DOUGLAS, MARQUESS OF, vii. 138-156.
Queensberry, Archibald William, seventh marquess of, vii. 153.
—— —— his wife, Caroline Margaret Clayton, vii. 153.
—— Charles, third marquess of, vii. 143.
—— Charles, fifth marquess of, vii. 151.
—— —— his wife, Caroline Scott Montagu, ii. 243; vii. 152.
—— James, second marquess of, vii. 140.
—— John, sixth marquess of, vii. 153.
—— —— his wife, Sarah Douglas, vii. 150, 153.
—— John Sholto, eighth marquess of, vii. 154.
—— —— his 1st wife, Sibyl Montgomery, vii. 154.
—— —— his 2nd wife, Ethel Weedon, vii. 154.
—— Percy Sholto, ninth marquess of, vii. 155.
—— —— his wife, Anna Maria Walters, vii. 155.
—— William, first marquess of, v. 124; vii. 138.
—— —— his wife, Isabel Douglas, i. 205; vii. 140.
—— William, fourth marquess of, vii. 146.
QUEENSBERRY, DOUGLAS, DUKE OF, vii. 112-156.
Queensberry, Charles, third duke of, i. 211; vii. 142, 143; ix. 151.
—— —— his wife, Katharine Hyde, vii. 144.
—— James, second duke of, ii. 241; iv. 37; vii. 140.
—— —— his wife, Mary Boyle, vii. 142.
—— William, first duke of, i. 89; iii. 329; vii. 137, 145; viii. 422.
—— —— his wife, Isabel Douglas, i. 205; vii. 140; ix. 13.
—— William, fourth duke of, ii. 242, 485; vii. 146, 362; ix. 151.
QUEENSBERRY, DOUGLAS-SCOTT, DUKE OF, ii. 242-243.
Queensberry, Henry, fifth duke of, ii. 242; vii. 147.
QUEENSBERRY, MONTAGU-DOUGLAS-SCOTT, DUKE OF, ii. 244-249.
Queensberry, Charles William Henry, sixth duke of, ii. 244.
—— Walter Francis, seventh duke of, ii. 245.
—— William Henry Walter, eighth duke of, ii. 247; vii. 147.
Queuille, Anne de la, wife of John Stewart of Aubigny, v. 352.
—— François de la, v. 350, 352.
—— —— his 2nd wife, Anne de Rohan, v. 352.
—— Jacqueline de la, wife of Robert Stewart of Aubigny, v. 350.
QUHITCHESTER AND ESKDAILL, SCOTT, LORD SCOTT OF, ii. 234.
Quhitchester and Eskdaill, Walter, first lord Scott of. ii. 234.
Quhite, Andrew, N.P., ii. 336 *n.*
Quhytlaw of Quhytlaw, Mary, wife of Sir William Home, iii. 286.
—— Agnes, wife of (1) Nicol Ormiston, and (2) J. Cranstoun, ii. 589.
—— Isabella, wife of James Murray, i. 121.
Quincy, Elena de, wife of Alan de la Zouch, iv. 142.
—— Elizabeth, *or* Isabella, *or* Marjory, wife of Alex. Comyn, earl of Buchan, ii. 254; iv. 142.
—— Margaret, *or* Agnes, de, wife of William, earl of Ferrars and Derby, ii. 254; iv. 142.
—— Sir Robert de, iv. 6; v. 572.
—— —— his wife, Orabilis, iv. 6.
—— Roger de, constable of Scotland, earl of Winchester, ii. 585; iv. 142; viii. 562.
—— —— his wife, Elena of Galloway, iv. 142.

RADCLIFFE, EARL OF NEWBURGH, vi. 456-457.
Radcliffe of Ordsall, John, iii. 292.
—— Anne, dau. of 4th earl of Newburgh, vi. 457.
—— Barbara Joanna, dau. of Charlotte Maria, countess of Newburgh, vi. 455.
—— Charles, 3rd son of 2nd earl of Derwentwater, vi. 454, 456.
—— —— his wife, Charlotte Maria, countess of Newburgh, vi. 454.
—— Charlotte, dau. of Charlotte Maria, countess of Newburgh, vi. 455.
—— James Clement, major-general in French service, vi. 455.
—— —— his wife, Clementina *, vi. 455.
—— Jane, wife of Sir Ralph Constable, iii. 292.
—— Mary Frances Guillelma, wife of Francis Eyre, vi. 455.
Radnor, Jacob (Pleydell-Bouverie), 4th earl of, iv. 97.
—— —— his wife, Mary A. F. Grimston, iv. 97.

* Name unknown.

Radnor, John (Robartes), 1st earl of, vi. 467.
—— —— his wife, Letitia Isabella Smith, vi. 467.
—— William (Bouverie), 1st earl of, vii. 226.
Radulf, father-in-law of Conghal of Tullibardine, i. 453 *n.*
Radulph of Dundee, v. 242; vii. 6.
—— *see also* Randolph.
Rae of Eskgrove, Sir David, 2nd bart., ii. 89.
—— —— his wife, Helen Stewart, ii. 89.
—— of Pitsindie, Adam, iv. 490.
—— Helen, wife of Sir Thos. Hope of Kerse, iv. 490.
—— Helen, wife of Robert St. Clair, vii. 584.
Raeburn of Chesterfield, W., iii. 495.
—— —— his wife, Katharine Bruce Fernie, iii. 495.
Ragnald, wife of (1) Hlodver, (2) Harvard-Arsael, and (3) Liot, earl of Caithness, ii. 314.
Ragnhildis, wife of Somerled, lord of the Isles, v. 29, 30.
Rait of Anniston, Agnes, wife of H. A. Lindsay-Carnegie, vi. 496; viii. 113.
—— —— A. J., lieut.-col., C.B., i. 315.
—— —— his wife, Kathleen Georgina Arbuthnott, i. 315.
—— —— James, i. 130; vi. 496.
—— —— his wife, Clementina Drummond Graham, i. 130.
—— of Drumnagair, David, i. 284, 288.
—— —— his wife, * Arbuthnott, i. 287.
—— of Halgreen, *, i. 294, 299.
—— —— William, i. 294.
—— —— William, i. 304.
—— —— his wife, Janet Arbuthnott, i. 304.
—— Elizabeth, wife of David Arbuthnott, i. 294; ix. 16.
—— Elizabeth, wife of Robert Arbuthnott, i. 294.
—— *, wife of Patrick Arbuthnott of Chapelton, i. 299.
RAITH, MONIMAIL, AND BALWEARIE, MELVILLE, LORD, vi. 108-123.
Raith, Monimail, and Balwearie, George, first lord, vi. 108.
—— Alexander, eldest son of 1st earl of Melville; styled lord, vi. 109.
—— —— his wife, Barbara Dundas, vi. 109.
—— Thomas, provost of the College Church of Seton, viii. 589.
Ralph, 2nd abbot of Cupar, i. 417 *n.*
Ralston of Ralston, ii. 41.
—— —— his wife, Barbara Hamilton, ii. 41.
—— —— Gavin, iv. 201.
—— —— his wife, Jean Mure, iv. 201.
—— bishop of Dunkeld, iii. 60.
Ramey of Yarmouth, John, barrister-at-law, iv. 481.
—— Abigail Brown, wife of 9th earl of Home, iv. 481.

* Name unknown.

RAMSAY OF BARNS, RAMSAY, LORD, iv. 300.
Ramsay of Barns, John, lord, iv. 300.
RAMSAY OF CARRINGTON, RAMSAY, LORD, iii. 99-110.
Ramsay of Carrington, George, eldest son of 6th earl of Dalhousie; styled lord, iii. 103.
—— —— his wife, Jean Maule, iii. 103; vii. 23.
—— —— George, eldest son of 9th earl of Dalhousie; styled lord, iii. 106; ix. 66.
—— —— John Gilbert, eldest son of 14th earl of Dalhousie; styled lord, iii. 109.
—— —— William, first lord, iii. 99.
RAMSAY OF DALHOUSIE, RAMSAY, LORD, iii. 98.
Ramsay of Dalhousie, George, first lord, iii. 98; iv. 297, 300, 312.
—— —— his wife, Elizabeth *or* Margaret Douglas, iii. 97; vi. 370; ix. 66.
—— —— William, second lord, iii. 99.
—— —— his 1st wife, Margaret Carnegie, iii. 99; viii. 67.
—— —— his 2nd wife, Jocosa Apsley, iii. 99.
RAMSAY OF GLENMARK, RAMSAY, BARON, iii. 108-110.
Ramsay of Glenmark, Arthur George Maule, third baron, iii. 109.
—— —— George, first baron, iii. 108.
—— —— John William, second baron, iii. 109.
RAMSAY OF MELROSE, RAMSAY, LORD, iii. 98.
Ramsay of Melrose, George, second lord, iii. 98; iv. 300, 312.
—— —— John, first lord, iii. 97 *n.*; iv. 300.
RAMSAY, LORD BOTHWELL, ii. 132-134.
RAMSAY, EARL OF DALHOUSIE, iii. 87-110.
RAMSAY, MARQUESS OF DALHOUSIE, iii. 106-107.
RAMSAY, BARON DALHOUSIE OF DALHOUSIE CASTLE, iii. 106-107.
RAMSAY, VISCOUNT OF HADDINGTON, iv. 297-302.
RAMSAY, EARL OF HOLDERNESSE, iv. 301-302.
RAMSAY, BARON OF KINGSTON-UPON-THAMES, iv. 301.
RAMSAY, LORD MELROSE, iv. 300.
RAMSAY, LORD RAMSAY OF BARNS, iv. 300.
RAMSAY, LORD RAMSAY OF CARRINGTON, iii. 99-110.
RAMSAY, LORD RAMSAY OF DALHOUSIE, iii. 98.
RAMSAY, BARON RAMSAY OF GLENMARK, iii. 108-110.
RAMSAY, LORD RAMSAY OF MELROSE, iii. 98.
Ramsay of Abbotshall, Sir Andrew, iii. 452.
—— of Ardbekie, John, viii. 491.
—— —— his wife, Janet Trail, viii. 491.
—— of Auchterhouse, Sir Alexander, i. 108.
—— —— Isabel, alleged wife of Sir Walter Ogilvy, i. 108.

Ramsay of Balkery, Matilda de, wife of William de Fenton, i. 108.
— of Balmain, Sir Alexander, 5th bart., viii. 84.
— — Sir Alexander, 2nd bart. *of 2nd creation*, viii. 455.
— — Sir Charles, 3rd bart., ix. 123.
— — his 1st wife, Margaret Carnegie, vi. 495.
— — his 2nd wife, Elizabeth Falconer, ix. 123 *bis*, 124.
— — David, vi. 175; viii. 56.
— — his wife, Katharine Carnegie, viii. 56.
— — David, their son, viii. 56.
— — Sir David, 2nd bart.; vi. 182.
— — Sir Herbert, 5th bart., *of 2nd creation*, ii. 134; viii. 56.
— — Sir John, 1st laird, vii. 278.
— of Balnabreich, iii. 20.
— — his wife, Janet Lindsay, iii. 20.
— of Bamff, Sir George, vii. 447.
— — his wife, Eleanora Fraser, vii. 447.
— — Sir Gilbert, i. 114.
— — his wife, Margaret Ogilvy, i. 114; ix. 8.
— — Sir James Henry, 10th bart., i. 500.
— of East Barns, Sir John, iv. 300.
— of Barnton, George, ii. 53; v. 315.
— — his wife, Jean Hamilton, ii. 53.
— — Susan, wife of Alex. Gibson Maitland, v. 315.
— of Blackcraig, Robert, i. 553.
— of Brackmonth, David, viii. 489.
— — his wife, Grizel Wemyss, viii. 489.
— — John, i. 77.
— — his wife, Marjory Sandilands, i. 77.
— — William, i. 76.
— of Carnock, Sir Alexander, sheriff of Teviotdale, ii. 223; iii. 89, 90, 149; iv. 226; vi. 341; viii. 257; ix. 64.
— — his wife, * Lindsay, iii. 11.
— — Sir George, ii. 132; v. 401.
— of Carriden, George, 3rd son of 2nd earl of Dalhousie, iii. 100.
— — his wife, * Buckson, iii. 101.
— of Clarybald, James, iii. 93.
— of Clatto, David, iii. 95, 97 *bis*.
— — Elizabeth, wife of James Ramsay, iii. 95.
— — George, iii. 19.
— — Sir George, iii. 95, 97, 533.
— — James, 2nd son of George R. of Dalhousie, iii. 95.
— of Coalstoun, Susan Georgiana, wife of (1) Robert, baron Connemara, and (2) lt.-col. W. H. Briggs, iii. 107.
— of Cockpen, Sir Edmond de, iii. 88.
— — James, iii. 96, 97.
— — his wife, Helen Ramsay, iii. 96.
— — Malcolm, iii. 89.

* Name unknown.

Ramsay of Cockpen, Robert, iii. 92; iv. 86, 297.
— — his wife, Margaret Forrester, iv. 86.
— of Colluthie, Elizabeth, wife of David Carnegie of Panbride, viii. 53, 60.
— — John, vi. 406.
— — Sir William, iii. 158; iv. 13.
— — his 2nd wife, Isabella, countess of Fife, iv. 13.
— of Corstoun, ii. 132.
— — John, iv. 566.
— — his wife, Euphame Carmichael, iv. 566.
— of Crookston, Sir Alexander, ii. 97 *n.*
— of Dalhousie *or* Dalwolsy, Sir Alexander, son of Sir Alex. R. of Carnock, 5th laird, iii. 90; ix. 64, 65.
— — his wife, Katharine *, iii. 90.
— — Sir Alexander, auditor of Exchequer, 7th laird, ii. 97 *n.*; iii. 91, 93; v. 287.
— — his 1st wife, Christian *, iii. 91.
— — his 2nd wife, Margaret *, iii. 91.
— — Alexander, the younger, sheriff of Edinburgh, iii. 91, 92; ix. 65.
— — Alexander, 8th laird, iii. 92; iv. 297.
— — his wife, Elizabeth *or* Isabella Douglas, i. 178; iii. 92.
— — Alexander, 9th laird, iii. 92, 97; ix. 65.
— — his 1st wife, Elene Home, ix. 65.
— — his 2nd wife, Nicolas Ker, iii. 92.
— — George, 11th laird, ii. 157, 592; iii. 94.
— — his wife, Elizabeth Hepburn, iii. 95.
— — Sir George, 13th laird, iii. 95, 97; v. 401.
— — his wife, Margaret Douglas, iii. 97; ix. 66.
— — John, 12th laird, iii. 95, 96, 97.
— — his wife, Marion Bellenden, ii. 65; iii. 96.
— — Nicholas de, 10th laird, iii. 93.
— — his 1st wife, Isabella Livingston, iii. 93.
— — his 2nd wife, Christian Ross, iii. 93; vii. 252.
— — Sir Patrick, 4th laird, iii. 89, 117.
— — his wife, Margaret, iii. 89, 90.
— — Sir Robert, 6th laird, iii. 91; viii. 264.
— — his wife Agnes ?Bruce of Longforgan, viii. 264.
— — William, 1st laird, i. 107; iii. 88.
— — William, 2nd laird, iii. 88; ix. 64.
— — Sir William, 3rd laird, iii. 89; ix. 64.
— — Sir William, sheriff of Lothian; styled, iii. 90 *n.*; ix. 64.
— — his wife, Agnes, iii. 90 *n.*
— of Derchester, Alexander, iv. 297.
— — Robert, iv. 297, 298.
— of Edglaw, Alexander, iii. 95.

* Name unknown.

Ramsay of Edington, Sir George, iii. 97.
—— —— John, 2nd son of lord Ramsay of Dalhousie, iii. 98.
—— —— his wife, Egidia Kellie, iii. 98.
—— of Edmerisden, Robert, iii. 92; iv. 297.
—— of Elbothel, Walter, v. 392.
—— of Fascay, David, viii. 64.
—— of Forthar, John, viii. 480.
—— of Halhouse, George, iii. 91.
—— —— his wife, Christina de Valence, iii. 91.
—— of Hawthornden, Sir Alexander, ix. 64.
—— of Inverleith, David, ix. 65.
—— —— Robert, iii. 91.
—— —— Sir William, ix. 64, 65.
—— of Keryntoun, Alexander, iii. 90.
—— —— Sir Alexander, iii. 91.
—— —— James, ix. 65 *bis*.
—— —— Sir Patrick, iii. 90; ix. 65.
—— —— his wife, Margaret, iii. 90; ix. 65.
—— of Leuchars, Elizabeth, wife of David Carnegie, viii. 53, 60.
—— of Nether Liberton, Sir William, sheriff of Lothian, iii. 90 *n.*; ix. 64.
—— —— his wife, Agnes, iii. 90 *n.*
—— of Likbernard, George, iii. 91.
—— of Montfod, iii. 432.
—— of Newtonlees, Sir George, iv. 298.
—— of Odmeston, James, viii. 74.
—— of Panbride, *, vii. 9.
—— —— his wife, Isabel Maule, vii. 9.
—— —— Henry, vii. 10.
—— —— his wife, Isabel Maule, vii. 10.
—— of Panmure, David, vi. 501.
—— of Pitcruvie, ii. 132.
—— —— Janet, wife of 2nd lord Lindsay of the Byres, ii. 132; v. 394, 395.
—— —— Sir John, v. 395.
—— —— Walter, v. 395.
—— —— his wife, Isobel Wemyss, v. 395.
—— of Priorletham, John, vi. 102.
—— —— his wife, Agnes Melville, vi. 102.
—— of St. Monans, John, i. 77.
—— —— his wife, Marjorie Sandilands, i. 77.
—— of Easter Softlaw, Thomas, iv. 297.
—— of Wester Strath, David, viii. 56.
—— —— his wife, Katharine Carnegie, viii. 56.
—— of Swynisdene, Robert, iii. 91.
—— of Tannadyce, John, viii. 523.
—— —— his wife, Esota Fleming, viii. 523.
—— of Trarinzean, Sir John, ii. 459.
—— —— his wife, Janet Kennedy, ii. 459.
—— of Waughton, Sir Andrew, 1st bart., iii. 452.
—— —— his 2nd wife, Anne Montgomerie, iii. 452.
—— —— Sir Andrew, 2nd bart., iii. 452.
—— of Westhall, Edward, v. 604.
—— of Whitehill, James, iii. 97.
—— —— Sir James, iv. 437; v. 406.

* Name unknown.

Ramsay of Whitehill, Robert, ancestor of the family of, iii. 91.
—— of Wyliecleuch, Alexander, iv. 298.
—— —— Sir George, iii. 99 *n.*; iv. 298; ix. 100.
—— —— his wife, Margaret Ker, iii. 99 *n.*; iv. 299.
—— —— John, *perhaps* descended of, iii. 96 *n.*
—— —— Margaret, dau. of Robert R., iv. 298.
—— —— Robert, iv. 298.
—— —— Sir Robert, iv. 298.
—— —— Thomas, iv. 298.
—— —— his wife, Alison Home, iv. 298.
—— Adam, burgess of Perth, vi. 391.
—— —— his wife, Elizabeth *or* Isobel Davidson, vi. 391.
—— Agnes, wife of A. Riddell of that Ilk, iii. 96.
—— Agnes, wife of James Elphinstone of Elieston and Inverdovat, iii. 533.
—— Alexander, sheriff of Edinburgh, eldest son of Sir Alex. R. of Dalhousie, iii. 91, 92; ix. 65.
—— Alexander, in Carrington, iii. 94.
—— Alexander, 5th son of Sir Robt. R. of Wyliecleuch, iv. 299.
—— Mr. Alexander, minister of St. Giles, Edinburgh, ix. 9.
—— Alexander Robert Maule, R.N., iii. 109.
—— Alison, wife of Robt. Cranstoun, iv. 298.
—— Andrew, 4th son of lt.-gen. John R., iii. 104.
—— Andrew, 5th son of 8th earl of Dalhousie, iii. 105.
—— —— his wife, Rachel Cook, iii. 105; ix. 66.
—— Andrew, 6th son of Sir Robt. R. of Wyliecleuch, iv. 300.
—— Andrew, minister of Magdalen Chapel, Edinburgh, iv. 492.
—— Anne, wife of (1) John, earl of Dundee, and (2) Sir Henry Bruce, iii. 100, 315.
—— Anne, wife of 5th earl of Home, iii. 101; iv. 479.
—— Anne, dau. of 6th earl of Dalhousie, iii. 102.
—— Anne Finlay Anderson, wife of col. D. Ewart, iii. 105.
—— Bethia, wife of D. Lindsay of Kirkforthar, v. 406.
—— Charles, 2nd son of 9th earl of Dalhousie, iii. 106.
—— Charles, 2nd son of viscount Haddington, iv. 301.
—— Charles Fox Maule, iii. 109.
—— Charles Frederick, 2nd son of 6th earl of Dalhousie, iii. 102.
—— Charles Maule, lieutenant R.A., M.P., iii. 108.
—— —— his wife, Martha Estelle Garrison, iii. 109.

Ramsay, Charlotte, wife of col. Marcus Slade, ix. 66.
— Christian, wife of Romeo Arbuthnott, i. 307.
— Christian Dalhousie, iii. 105.
— Cuthbert, captain of Crichton Castle, ii. 157; iii. 94.
— — his 1st wife, Agnes Stewart, ii. 157, 267; iii. 94; ix. 65.
— — his 2nd wife, Janet Fleming, iii. 94.
— David, capt. R.N., ii. 353.
— David, parson of Foulden, iii. 91.
— David, 2nd son of James R. of Clatto, iii. 95; vi. 494.
— David, 4th son of lord Ramsay of Dalhousie, iii. 98.
— David, 6th son of lt.-gen. John R., iii. 104.
— David, captain 1st Foot, iii. 105.
— Dorothy, dau. of John R., iv. 299.
— Edith Christian, wife of Sir Jas. Fergusson of Kilkerran, iii. 107.
— Edward Bannerman, dean of Edinburgh, viii. 57.
— Elizabeth, wife of (1) Robert Watson, and (2) Jas. Sandilands of Cruvy, i. 76.
— Elizabeth, wife of Sir Alex. Boswell of Balmuto, iii. 92; ix. 65.
— Elizabeth, wife of (1) Thos. Edington, and (2) Lawrence Howburn, iii. 95, 96; ix. 65.
— Elizabeth, wife of Patrick Broun of Colstoun, iii. 96.
— Elizabeth, wife of 2nd lord Hawley, iii. 102, 103.
— Elizabeth, dau. of lt.-gen. John R., iii. 104.
— Elizabeth, wife of Sir Thos. Moncrieffe, iii. 105.
— Elizabeth, wife of Robert Cranstoun, iv. 298.
— Elizabeth, wife of Edmund Aston, iv. 299.
— Elizabeth, wife of John Middleton of Kilhill, vi. 175, 181.
— Elizabeth, wife of Andrew Middleton of Pitgarvie, vi. 182.
— Elizabeth, alleged wife of Sir John de Seton, viii. 569 *n.*
— Elizabeth, dau. of Sir William R. of Colluthie, ix. 46.
— Emma, alleged wife of Adam de Brus, ii. 428.
— Euphame, wife of James Rollo of Balbegie, vii. 191.
— Frances, wife of col. J. S. Sinclair, ii. 353.
— George, 2nd son of Sir Alexander R. of Dalhousie, iii. 93.
— George, grandson of Sir George R. of Wyliecleuch, iv. 299.
— — his wife, Mary Widdrington, iv. 299.
Ramsay, George Spottiswood, lieutenant R.A., iii. 108.
— Georgina, dau. of lt.-gen. John R., iii. 104.
— Georgina, dau. of 8th earl of Dalhousie, iii. 105.
— Georgina Harvey, wife of lt.-gen. Sir R. J. Hay, viii. 455.
— Helen, dau. of James R. of Clatto, iii. 95.
— Helen, wife of James Ramsay of Cockpen, iii. 96.
— Henry, 6th son of Nicholas R. of Dalhousie, iii. 94.
— Sir Henry, K.C.S.I., C.B., iii. 104.
— — his wife, Laura Lushington, iii. 104.
— Henry, H.E.I.C. Naval Service, iii. 105.
— Isobel, wife of R. Dickson of Peill, iv. 298.
— Jacob *or* James, gen.-major in Swedish service, ix. 100.
— — his wife, Isobel Spens, ix. 100.
— James, tutor of the Lowis, i. 118.
— James, 2nd son of Sir Patrick R. of Dalhousie, iii. 90.
— Sir James, 'the Black Ramsay,' defender of Hanau, iii. 96 *n.*
— James, 3rd son of lord Ramsay of Dalhousie, iii. 98.
— James, 3rd son of 1st earl of Dalhousie, iii. 99.
— James, colonel, 3rd son of 3rd earl of Dalhousie, iii. 101.
— James, colonel 2nd Foot, iii. 104.
— James, major-general Bengal army, iii. 104.
— — his wife, Hariet Charlotte Bennet, iii. 104.
— James, elder son of viscount Haddington, iv. 301.
— James, 4th son of 2nd earl of Dalhousie, ix. 66.
— Jane, wife of John Lovell, iv. 299.
— Jane, wife of Robt. More, ix. 100.
— Janet, dau. of lord Ramsay of Dalhousie, iii. 98.
— Janet, wife of Robert Douglas of Drumgarland, vi. 368.
— Janet, wife of Henry Napier, vi. 406.
— Jean, wife of John Kincaid of Warriston, iii. 96.
— Jean, dau. of 6th earl of Dalhousie, iii. 102.
— Jean, wife of Sir John Ruthven of Dunglass, iv. 103.
— Jean, dau. of George R. of Carriden, iii. 101.
— Jean, wife of (1) George, 11th lord Ross of Halkhead, and (2) Robert, viscount Oxfuird, iii. 101, 102; vi. 600; vii. 258; ix. 66 *ter.*

Ramsay, John, in Pitgormo, ii. 132.
—— —— his wife, Elizabeth Cant, ii. 132.
—— John, 3rd son of James R. of Clatto, iii. 95.
—— John, ancestor of Ramsays of Sweden, Finland and Russia, iii. 95 *n.*
—— John, 2nd son of 1st earl of Dalhousie, iii. 99, 102; ix. 66 *ter.*
—— —— his wife, Marjorie Spence, ix. 66.
—— John, capt. in the Scots Dutch, iii. 100.
—— John, asst. quartermaster-general in Scotland, iii. 104; ix. 66 *bis.*
—— —— his wife, Mary Delisle, iii. 104.
—— John, lieutenant-colonel H.E.I.C.S., iii. 104.
—— —— his wife, Kate Sinclair Laing, iii. 104.
—— John, grandson of Sir George R. of Wyliecleuch, iv. 299.
—— John, son of Sir Geo. R. of Wyliecleuch, iv. 299.
—— —— his wife, Alice *, iv. 299.
—— John, son of Wm. R., ix. 65.
—— Jonet, wife of D. Lindsay, bishop of Ross, iii. 19.
—— Jonet, dau. of Robt. R., iv. 298.
—— Jonet, dau. of Alex. R., sheriff of Edinburgh, ix. 65.
—— Katharine, wife of Patrick Balfour, i. 536.
—— Katharine, wife of Arch. Nairn, vi. 391.
—— Katharine Marjory, wife of John George, styled marquess of Tullibardine, i. 500.
—— Lucinda, dau. of 8th earl of Dalhousie, iii. 105.
—— Lydia, dau. of 2nd earl of Dalhousie, ix. 66.
—— Magdalen, dau. of 1st earl of Dalhousie, iii. 100.
—— Malcolm, 3rd son of 6th earl of Dalhousie, iii. 102.
—— Malcolm, deputy adj.-general in Scotland, iii. 103.
—— Margaret, wife of Thos. Bruce, i. 553.
—— Margaret, wife of Sir John Cranstoun, ii. 591; iii. 96.
—— Margaret, dau. of Sir Alexander R. of Dalhousie, iii. 93.
—— Margaret, wife of John Nasmyth, iii. 94.
—— Margaret, wife of Wm. Livingston of Kilsyth, iii. 98; v. 191.
—— Margaret, wife of Alex. Hoppringle, iv. 298; ix. 100.
—— Margaret, wife of Luke Collingwood, iv. 299.
—— Margaret, wife of Jas. Hoppringle of Hoppringle, iv. 299.
—— Marie, wife of (1) James Strachan of Inchtuthill, Fettercairn and Monboddo, and (2) Alexander Buchan of Auchmacoy, vi. 181.

* Name unknown.

Ramsay, Marion, wife of (1) Jas. Weir, and (2) Wm. Bannatyne, iii. 96.
—— Marjory de, wife of Sir David of Brechin, ii. 222.
—— Marjory, wife of (1) Jas. Erskine, earl of Buchan, and (2) Mr. Jas. Campbell, ii. 273; iii. 100; ix. 49.
—— Marjory, wife of Sir David Wemyss of Wemyss, viii. 479.
—— Mary, wife of Sir David of Brechin, ii. 222.
—— Mary, dau. of lt.-gen., John R., iii. 105.
—— Mary, wife of Jas. Hay of Drum, iii. 105.
—— Mary, wife of (1) John Baird, (2) John Mason, and (3) Henry Bothwell, iv. 437.
—— Mary, wife of Ralph Williamson, iv. 299.
—— Mary, dau. of John R., iv. 299.
—— Maud, dau. of lt.-gen. John R., iii. 105.
—— Michael, tutor to 10th earl of Eglinton, iii. 458.
—— Sir Neil, viii. 569 *n.*
—— Sir Nessus de, iii. 87.
—— Nicholas de, *c.* 1260, iii. 88.
—— Nicholas, Berwick-on-Tweed, iv. 299.
—— Nicol, son of Wm. R., ix. 65.
—— Patrick de, bishop of Aberdeen, iii. 88.
—— Patrick, 7th son of Sir Robt. R. of Wyliecleuch, iv. 300.
—— Patrick William Maule, iii. 109.
—— Peter, banker, Edinburgh, ii. 54.
—— —— his wife, Susan Mary Hamilton, ii. 54.
—— Peter de, bishop of Aberdeen, iii. 88.
—— Richard, son of Cuthbert R., iii. 94.
—— Robert, 5th son of 2nd earl of Dalhousie, iii. 101; ix. 66 *bis.*
—— Robert, eldest son of Sir Robt. R. of Wyliecleuch, iv. 298.
—— —— his wife, Isobel Dickson, iv. 298.
—— Robert, grandson of Sir George R. of Wyliecleuch, iv. 299.
—— Robert, vi. 496.
—— —— his wife, Susan Lindsay-Carnegie, vi. 496; viii. 113.
—— Robert, merchant, ix. 136.
—— —— his wife, Margaret Melville, ix. 136.
—— Robert Anderson, lieut.-col., iii. 104.
—— Ronald Edward Maule, iii. 109.
—— Simon de, iii. 87.
—— Thomas, 9th son of Sir Robt. R. of Wyliecleuch, iv. 299.
—— Walter, father-in-law of Sir David Wemyss, viii. 479.
—— William, son of John, lord Bothwell, ii. 134.
—— William de, *about* 1190, iii. 87.
—— William de, prior of St. Serf's, iii. 88.
—— William de, in tournament at Berwick, 1338, iii. 89.

Ramsay, William, banker, Edinburgh, ii. 53.
— — his wife, Betty Hamilton, ii. 53.
— William, 5th son of Sir Alex. R. of Dalhousie, iii. 91.
— William, 3rd son of Nicholas de R. of Dalhousie, iii. 93; ix. 65.
— — his wife, Janet Wycht, ix. 65.
— William, iii. 95; ix. 66 *bis*.
— William, brother of David R. of Clatto, iii. 97.
— William, captain, 4th son of 1st earl of Dalhousie, iii. 100.
— William, cornet, his son, iii. 100.
— William, 2nd son of 8th earl of Dalhousie; baron Panmure, iii. 104, 107.
— William, grandson of Sir George R. of Wyliecleuch, iv. 299.
— William, 8th son of Sir Robert R. of Wyliecleuch, iv. 300.
— William, son of Wm. R., ix. 65.
— William Maule, major-general Bengal army, iii. 104.
— *, father of Sir Patrick R. of Dalhousie, iii. 90.
— *, mother of William Borthwick of Collilaw, iii. 94.
— *, mother of John Gibson, iii. 94.
— *, killed at Pinkie, iii. 94, 95.
— *, wife of John Montgomerie of Bowhouse, iii. 432.
— *, wife of Edward Trotter, iv. 298.
Ramsay-Gibson-Maitland of Cliftonhall and Barnton, Sir Alexander Charles, 3rd bart., v. 315.
— — his wife, Thomasina Agnes Hunt, v. 315.
— — Sir James, 4th bart., v. 315, 321.
— — his wife, Fanny Lucy Fowke, v. 315.
Ramsden of Byrom, Sir John, 4th bart., v. 19.
— — his wife, Louisa Susannah Ingram-Shepherd, v. 19.
— — Sir John William, 5th bart., v. 19.
— — Sir William, 2nd bart., v. 15.
— of Rogerthorpe, William John Frescheville, iii. 44.
— — his wife, Mabel Lindsay, iii. 44.
— Edythe Mary, wife of capt. C. D. Hope, vii. 524.
— Frecheville, lieut.-col., v. 15.
— — his wife, Isabella Ingram, v. 15.
— George, captain 15th Hussars, v. 15.
— Richard, Siddinghurst, vii. 524.
Ramsey, Sir William de, 11th cent., ii. 428.
Ranald, John, in Carse Grange, v. 500.
Randall, Susan, wife of 3rd earl of Rosebery, vii. 224.
— William, Yarmouth, vii. 224.

* Name unknown.

Randerode, Marie van, wife of William van Hoorne, v. 588.
Randolph of Boncle, viii. 3.
Randolph of Dundee, v. 242; vii. 6.
Randolph of Kinguthin, v. 242.
RANDOLPH, EARL OF MORAY, vi. 286-295.
Randolph of Annandale, Sir Thomas, ii. 379.
— of Broxmouth, Sir Thomas, vi. 292.
— of Garlies, Sir Thomas, vi. 291.
— lord of the Isle of Man, Sir Thomas, vi. 292.
— of Morton, Sir Thomas, vi. 291.
— of Stichel, Sir Thomas, iv. 511; vi. 291 *bis*.
— of Strathdon, Sir Thomas, high chamberlain, ii. 433; vi. 289.
— — his wife, Isabel, vi. 290.
— Agnes, wife of Patrick, 9th earl of Dunbar, iii. 265, 266, 268, 269, 270; vi. 294.
— Isabel, wife of Sir William Murray, i. 215; vi. 291.
— Isobel, wife of Sir Patrick Dunbar, iii. 260, 266, 269, 270; vi. 295.
— Sir John, 2nd son of 1st earl of Moray, iii. 266, 269; vi. 294, 295.
— Sir Nicholas, vi. 289.
— Thomas, clerk to king Alexander II., sheriff of Dumfries, vi. 288.
— — his wife, Juliana, vi. 288.
— Thomas, English envoy, vii. 288.
Ranfurly, Thomas (Knox), 2nd earl of, ii. 304.
— — his wife, Mary Juliana Stuart, ii. 304.
Rankin of Fowlartoun of Corsby, v. 492.
— Gilbert, vii. 537.
Rannie, James, wine merchant, viii. 140.
— — his wife, Eleanora Jean Dalrymple, viii. 139.
RANNOCH, MURRAY, DUKE OF, i. 481-482.
Rannoch, William, 2nd son of 1st duke of Atholl; duke of, i. 481.
Ransom, Elizabeth, wife of 7th lord Kinnaird of Inchture, v. 212.
— Griffin, banker, London, v. 212.
Ranulf, son of Dunegal of Nithsdale, vi. 287.
— — his wife, Bethoc of Rowcastle, vi. 288.
Ranulph le Meschin, lord of Carlisle, ii. 369; iii. 243.
Rapp, general count, vi. 73.
— — his wife, Albertine de Rotberg, vi. 73.
Rarity, Isabel, mother of Sylvester Carnegie, vi. 502.
Rashleigh of Menabilly, William, ii. 92.
— — his wife, Katharine Stuart, ii. 92.
Ratcliffe, Elizabeth, wife of John, viscount of Haddington, iv. 301.
Rattray of Craighall Rattray, David, v. 230.

Rattray of Craighall Rattray, James, iii. 379.
—— his wife, Elizabeth Hay, iii. 379.
—— Patrick, viii. 218.
—— his wife, Anne Drummond, viii. 218.
—— Silvester, iv. 278.
—— his wife, Marjory Gray, iv. 278.
—— Thomas, bishop of Dunkeld, and primus, iii. 380.
— of Kincarrochy, Henry, ix. 98.
— of Rattray, Henry, iv. 260; ix. 98.
—— his wife, Barbara Ruthven, iv. 260.
—— Sir John, i. 443.
—— Silvester, i. 110.
—— his wife, Margaret Ogilvy, i. 110.
— Grizel, wife of John, 3rd earl of Atholl, i. 443; ix. 28 *bis*.
— Grizel, wife of George Knollis, vii. 251.
— Mr. James, minister at Alyth, i. 296.
— Margaret, wife of Jas. Arbuthnott of Blackstoun, i. 296.
Rauloc, *see* Rollock.
Ravelrig, John Maitland, lord of Session, lord, v. 310.
Ravenscroft of Wickham, George, viii. 408.
— Mary, wife of 7th earl of Traquair, viii. 408.
Rawdon, Francis (Rawdon Hastings), 1st earl of, v. 512.
Rawdon of Rawdon, Francis (Rawdon Hastings), 1st baron, v. 512.
— Sir Arthur, captain, i. 137; ix. 9.
—— his wife, Helen *or* Eleanor Graham, i. 137.
RAWDON-HASTINGS, EARL OF LOUDOUN, v. 512-515.
RAWDON-HASTINGS, VISCOUNT LOUDOUN, v. 512-517.
Rawdon-Hastings, Edith Maud, v. 516.
— Edward Hugh Hastings, v. 515.
— Elizabeth Frances, v. 516.
— Flora Anna, v. 516.
— Isabel Jacqueline, v. 516.
— Paulyn Charles James Reginald, v. 515.
Rawdon-Hastings-Abney-Hastings, Paulyn Francis Cuthbert, major, iv. 98; v. 515.
—— his wife, Maud Grimston, iv. 98.
Rawlins, Emmeline Fanny, wife of M. P. Drummond, viii. 225.
— Francis A., in holy orders, viii. 225.
Raymond of Belchamp Hall, Samuel, iii. 362.
— Isabella, wife of (1) John Mayne, and (2) Archibald, 9th earl of Dundonald, iii. 362.
Raynton, John de, iv. 332.
Reade of Shipton Court, Sir John Chandos, 7th bart., iii. 513.
—— his wife, Louisa Murray, iii. 513.
Reade, Anna Maria, wife of R. A. J. Drummond, viii. 235.
— Compton, viii. 235.
— Mary, wife of 12th viscount Falkland, iii. 617.
— Robert, New York, iii. 617.
— * betrothed to Mary Vanlore, viii. 181.
Reading of Dublin, Sir Robert, bart., i. 59.
—— his wife, Jane Hannay, i. 59.
— Elizabeth, wife of 6th earl of Abercorn, i. 59.
Réance, Pierre, comte de, ix. 3.
—— his wife, Margaret Hamilton, ix. 3.
REAY, MACKAY, LORD, vii. 157-179.
Reay, Alexander, eighth lord, vii. 177.
—— his wife, Marion Gall, vii. 177.
— Æneas, tenth lord, vii. 171, 178.
—— his wife, Mary Katharine Anna Jacoba Fagel, vii. 178.
— Donald, first lord, iv. 61; vii. 167.
—— his 1st wife, Barbara Mackenzie, vii. 168, 504.
—— his 2nd wife, Elizabeth Thomson, vii. 169.
—— his 3rd wife, Marjory Sinclair, vii. 169.
— Donald, fourth lord, vii. 176.
—— his 1st wife, Marion Dalrymple, ii. 32; vii. 176; viii. 131.
—— his 2nd wife, Christian Sutherland, vii. 176.
— Donald James, eleventh lord, vii. 178.
—— his wife, Fanny Georgina Jane Hasler, vii. 178.
— Eric, seventh lord, vii. 157 *n.*, 175, 177.
— Eric, ninth lord, vii. 178.
— George, third lord, vii. 170, 174; viii. 357.
—— his 1st wife, Margaret Mackay, vii. 174.
—— his 2nd wife, Janet Sinclair, vii. 174.
—— his 3rd wife, Mary Doull, vii. 175.
— George, fifth lord, vii. 176.
—— his 1st wife, Marion Mackay, vii. 176.
—— his 2nd wife, Elizabeth Fairley, vii. 176.
— John, second lord, vii. 169.
—— his 1st wife, Isabel Sinclair, vii. 170.
—— his 2nd wife, Barbara Mackay, vii. 170.
REAY OF DURNESS, MACKAY, BARON, vii. 178-179.
Reay of Durness, Donald James, baron, vii. 178.
Rectrude, wife of Ansold, lord of Maule, vii. 2.
Reddall, Jane, London, vi. 555.

* Name unknown.

Reddall, Mary, wife of capt. Francis Oliphant, vi. 555.
Reddik of Dalbeattie, John, i. 225.
—— —— his wife, Marion Maclellan, i. 225.
Redesdale, Algernon Bertram (Freeman-Mitford), 1st baron, i. 131.
—— —— his wife, Clementina Gertrude Helen Ogilvie, i. 131.
Redhouse, Andrew Hamilton, senator of the College of Justice, lord, iv. 307.
Redman, Sir Mathew, iii. 12.
Redpath of Redpath, William, vi. 587.
—— —— his wife, Margaret Makgill, vi. 587.
Reece, Elizabeth Anne, wife of Lydston Horton Leslie, vii. 310.
—— Robert, vii. 310.
Reed of Lochindorb, Simon, i. 510.
Reeve of Hendens, Sir Thomas, v. 389.
—— Jane, wife of 8th lord Lindores, v. 389.
—— Susanna, wife of (1) Richard French, and (2) rev. Wm. Graham, vii. 103.
—— *, captain, v. 417.
—— —— his wife, Jane Lindsay, v. 417.
—— *, Ashburnham, vii. 103.
Reginald, priest of Aberdalgie, vi. 530.
Reginald Mac Ruari of Kintail, vii. 237.
Reichsperg, Euphrasia Veronica von, wife of baron Ogilvy of Muirton, i. 121.
Reid of Aikenhead, John, iii. 474.
—— of Balmachie, David, captain, viii. 55.
—— of Barra, Sir Alexander, 2nd bart., ii. 24.
—— —— his wife, Agnes Ogilvy, ii. 24.
—— of Barskimming, Adam, vi. 514.
—— —— Janet, wife of Henry Stewart of Gogar, vi. 514.
—— of Collieston, Gilbert, viii. 57.
—— —— his wife, Jean Carnegie, viii. 57.
—— of Little Drumquhendill, Gilbert, viii. 57.
—— —— his wife, Jean Carnegie, viii. 57.
—— of Strathardle, iv. 260.
—— —— his wife, Isabel Ruthven, iv. 260.
—— Adam, iii. 195.
—— —— his wife, Christina Sutherland of Torboll, iii. 194.
—— Alaster, Strathardle, viii. 489.
—— —— his wife, Margaret Wemyss, viii. 489.
—— Alice, wife of James Stewart of Cardonald, iv. 156.
—— Alison, wife of Edward Bruce of Blairhall, iii. 474.
—— Elizabeth, wife of Sir G. Mackenzie of Grandvale, iii. 76.
—— Elizabeth, wife of Sir Gilbert Hay of Dronlaw, iii. 562; ix. 85.
—— George, viii. 124.
—— —— his wife, Jean Dalrymple, viii. 124.
—— George, bailie of Edinburgh, ix. 5.

* Name unknown.

Reid, Helen, wife of Alex. Acheson of Gosford, vi. 8.
—— James, chaplain, i. 197.
—— James, tutor of Aikenhead, v. 83.
—— —— his wife, Margaret Erskine, v. 83.
—— John, Greenwich, iii. 76.
—— Margaret, wife of Andrew Gray of Bullion, iv. 285.
—— Neville, vi. 436.
—— —— his wife, Caroline Napier, vi. 436.
—— Robert, bishop of Orkney, iv. 23; v. 527, 528; vii. 283, 462; viii. 542.
—— Walter, abbot of Kinloss, prior of Beauly, v. 528; vii. 462 *bis*.
REIDHAVEN, OGILVY, VISCOUNT OF, iv. 37-41.
Reidhaven, James, first viscount of, iv. 37.
REIDHAVEN, OGILVIE-GRANT, VISCOUNT OF, vii. 487-494.
Reidhaven, John Charles, styled viscount of, vii. 491.
—— —— his wife, Caroline Stuart, vii. 491.
Reidheuch of Aberlednoch, Isobel, wife of Alex. Murray, i. 462; ix. 28.
—— —— Margaret, wife of Henry Primrose, vii. 214.
—— —— Peter, i. 462; vii. 214.
—— Robert of, v. 329.
Rendlesham, Frederick William (Brook), 5th lord, iii. 463.
—— —— his wife, Egidia Montgomerie, iii. 463.
Rennald of Larnie, John, i. 307.
—— Janet, wife of Alex. Arbuthnott of Knox, i. 307.
Renny of Borrowfield, Robert, v. 252.
—— Julia, wife of 7th earl of Kintore, v. 252.
Renny-Strachan of Seaton and Tarrie, Thomas, viii. 87.
Renny-Strachan-Carnegie of Seaton and Tarrie, Claud Cathcart, viii. 87.
—— —— his wife, Mary Madeline Breakenridge, viii. 87.
—— —— John, captain, viii. 87.
—— —— his wife, Elizabeth Susan Grey, viii. 87.
—— —— Alan Bruce, advocate, viii. 87.
—— —— Dorothy Olivia, wife of David Horndon, viii. 87.
Renton of Billie, David, vii. 581.
—— —— David, vii. 582.
—— —— David, v. 377.
—— of Lamberton, John, iii. 457.
—— —— his wife, Susanna Montgomerie, iii. 457.
—— Anna, wife of 1st earl of Leven, v. 377.
—— Beatrix, wife of (1) Sir Wm. St. Clair of Herdmanston, (2) Wm. Crichton of Drylaw, and (3) E. Sinclair of Dryden, vii. 581.

Reoch of Freuchie, Patrick, vii. 455.
—— —— Patrick, his son, vii. 455.
Repas, Denis de, viii. 458.
Restalrig, Edward of, iii. 135.
—— John de, viii. 245.
—— —— his wife, Annabella of Strathearn, viii. 245.
—— Thomas of, iii. 135.
Revel, Henry, vii. 398.
—— —— his wife, Margaret de Abernethy, vii. 398.
Reventlow Criminil, count, viii. 511.
—— —— his wife, Isabella Harriet Jane Wemyss, viii. 511.
Revest, Dora Cleopatra Maria Lorenza, wife of rev. R. W. L. Tollemache, iii. 416.
Reynold, Robert, chaplain, viii. 106.
Reynolds of Elvetham, Sir Robert, viii. 182.
—— —— his wife, Priscilla Windham, viii. 182.
—— Eliza, wife of David Arbuthnott, i. 315.
—— Thomas Forbes, M.D., i. 315.
Rhett, Edward Loundes, iii. 606.
Rhind, Christian, wife of David Arbuthnott, i. 280.
Rhine, Charles Louis, count palatine of the, i. 27; v. 481.
—— Frederick v., count palatine of the, i. 27.
—— —— his wife, Elizabeth Stewart, i. 27.
Ribblesdale, Thomas (Lister), 2nd lord, viii. 231.
Ricardo of Bramley Park, Percy, v. 370.
—— Amy Mary, wife of 7th duke of Lennox, v. 370.
Riccart, David, i. 310.
—— —— his wife, Katharine Arbuthnott, i. 310.
RICCARTOUN, DOUGLAS, VISCOUNT OF, vii. 146-147.
Riccartoun, William, viscount of, vii. 146.
RICCARTOUN, HAMILTON, VISCOUNT OF, vii. 361-363.
Riccartoun, John, first viscount, vii. 361.
—— William, son of 1st earl of Ruglen; styled lord, vii. 362.
Riccio, David, iv. 260, 261; v. 399; vii. 253, 293.
Rice, Ellen Mary Margaret, wife of L. M. St. Clair, vii. 591.
—— William, rector of Sympson, ix. 155.
—— —— his wife, Sydney Montague Ogilvie-Grant, vii. 493; ix. 155.
—— William Roche, C.S.I., M.D., vii. 591.
Rich of Sonning, Sir William, 2nd bart., iii. 479.
—— —— his wife, Anne Bruce, iii. 479.
—— of Woodlands, John S., captain, vi. 383.
—— Agnes Julia, wife of (1) rev. C. Douglas of Earl's Gift, and (2) col. W. C. Gason, vi. 383.
Rich, Mary, wife of 1st earl of Breadalbane, ii. 205.
—— Nathaniel, colonel, v. 228, 468.
—— —— his wife, Elizabeth Ker, v. 468.
—— Sir Robert, v. 409.
Richard II., king of England, i. 147.
Richard of Chilham, i. 425.
—— —— his wife, Roesia of Dover, i. 425.
Richard of Dover, son of Richard FitzRoy, ix. 11.
—— —— his wife, Matilda, countess of Angus, ix. 11.
Richard their son, ix. 11.
Richard of Invertuyl, v. 202.
Richard of Invertuyl, son of John, v. 203.
Richard Fitz-Truite, ii. 372.
Richard, son of Richard Fitz-Truite, ii. 372.
Richard, son of Galfrid, son of Gunnild, vi. 79.
—— —— his wife, Alicia Melville, vi. 79.
Richard, son of Richard the smith, vi. 197.
Richard, abbot of Kelso, iii. 138.
Richard, bishop of Moray, 1187, i. 161; ii. 121.
Richard, bishop of St. Andrews, iv. 5, 6.
Richard, abbot of St. Colm, iii. 186.
Richard, abbot of Wetherall, ii. 369.
Richard the clerk, viii. 319 *n.*
Richards of Caerynwch, Richard, vi. 386.
—— Anna Maria Harriet, wife of bishop Arthur Gascoigne Douglas, vi. 386.
—— Eliza Jane, wife of Augustus Maitland, v. 314.
—— Ella Frances, wife of rev. Sydney George William Maitland, v. 322.
—— James, vicar of St. Peter's, Rochdale, v. 322.
—— William Page, D.D., v. 314.
RICHARDSON, LORD CRAMOND, ii. 578-584.
Richardson of Little Hockham and Stanfeild, William, ii. 581.
—— —— his wife, Abigail *, ii. 581.
—— of Honingham, Thomas, ii. 582.
—— —— his wife, Anna Salmon, ii. 582.
—— of Meldrumsheugh, Patrick, treasurer of Edinburgh, iv. 427.
—— of Smeatoun, Sir James, v. 458, 466; vii. 584.
—— —— his wife, Mary Ker, v. 458.
—— —— Sir James, vi. 598.
—— —— his wife, Anna Makgill, vi. 598.
—— —— James, v. 475.
—— —— his wife, Margaret Ker, v. 475.
—— of Stanfield, Sir Thomas, chief justice, ii. 578.
—— —— his wife, Elizabeth Beaumont, baroness Cramond, ii. 578.
—— —— Sir Thomas, master of Cramond, ii. 580.
—— —— his 1st wife, Elizabeth Hewett, ii. 581.
—— —— his 2nd wife, Mary Hanbury, ii. 581.
—— Angelica, dau. of 1st lord Cramond, ii. 583.

* Name unknown.

Richardson, Anne, dau. of Charles R., ii. 581.
— Charles, 3rd son of the master of Cramond, ii. 581.
— — his wife, Elizabeth Wiseman, ii. 581.
— Charles, their son, ii. 581.
— Edward, ii. 580 *n.*
— Edward, 8th son of the master of Cramond, ii. 582.
— Elizabeth, wife of R. Wood, ii. 580.
— Elizabeth, wife of R. Mansel *or* Mansfeild, ii. 582.
— Elizabeth, wife of Wm. Jermy, ii. 583.
— Henry, 5th son of the master of Cramond, ii. 581.
— Janet, wife of Francis Bothwell, iv. 427.
— Margaret, dau. of Charles R., ii. 581.
— Mary, wife of John Webb, ii. 580.
— Mary, wife of Sir John St. Clair of Herdmanston, vii. 584.
— Susan, dau. of Sir Thomas R., ii. 580.
— Ursula, wife of Sir W. Yelverton, ii. 580.
— Ursula, dau. of Charles R., ii. 581.
— William, Norfolk, ii. 579.
— — his wife, Agnes *, ii. 579.
Richardson-Robertson of Ballathie, Tulliebelton and Kinnaird, Robert, major-gen., C.B., vii. 209.
— — his wife, Martha Rollo, vii. 209.
Richerius, father of Gilbert, viii. 319 *n.*
Richieson, Agnes, wife of col. Alex. Cochrane of Auchincreugh, iii. 341.
Richmond, Conan IV., earl of, i. 4.
— — his wife, Margaret of Huntingdon, i. 4.
— John (de Dreux), 10th earl of, iii. 264.
RICHMOND, STEWART, EARL OF, v. 357.
Richmond, Ludovick, earl of, v. 357.
RICHMOND, LENNOX, DUKE OF, v. 363-371.
Richmond, Charles, first duke of, i. 32; v. 363.
— — his wife, Anne Brudenell, v. 363.
RICHMOND, STEWART, DUKE OF, v. 357.
Richmond, Ludovick, duke of, v. 357.
RICHMOND, STEWART, DUKE OF, v. 360-362.
Richmond, Charles, third duke of, i. 55; ii. 84; v. 360.
— — his 1st wife, Elizabeth Rogers, v. 361.
— — his 2nd wife, Margaret Banaster, v. 361.
— — his 3rd wife, Frances Teresa Stewart, ii. 84.
— Esme, second duke of, v. 360.
— James, first duke of, v. 360.
— — his wife, Mary Villiers, v. 360.
Richmond, Charles (Stuart), 1st duke of, iv. 203.
— Charles (Stuart), 3rd duke of, iii. 482.
— — his wife, Mary Bruce, iii. 482.
Richmond and Lennox, Charles (Stuart), 4th duke of, iv. 557.
— — his wife, Charlotte Gordon, iv. 557, 558; ix. 111.

* Name unknown.

Richmond and Lennox, Charles (Stuart), 5th duke of, i. 73.
— — Charles Henry (Stuart), 7th duke of, iv. 253.
Richmond, Georgina Katharine, wife of 10th lord Belhaven, ii. 60.
— Legh, ii. 60.
Ricketts of Longwood, William Henry, vi. 505.
— Edward Jervis, vi. 505 *n.*
— Mary, wife of 7th earl of Northesk, vi. 505.
Riddell of Cheesburn Grange, Edward, vi. 582.
— — his wife, A. M. Scrope, vi. 582.
— of Cranston Riddell, Hugo de, iii. 53.
— of Grange, John, i. 307.
— of Hayning, Andrew, ii. 409; vii. 148.
— — his wife, Jean Stuart, vii. 148.
— of Riddell, Andrew, iii. 96.
— — his wife, Agnes Ramsay, iii. 96.
— — Gervase, vii. 364.
— — James, vii. 71 *bis.*
— — John, vii. 80.
— — his wife, Agnes Scott, vii. 80.
— — Walter de, viii. 560.
— — Sir Walter, vii. 79.
— Agnes, wife of James Scott, vii. 79.
— Elizabeth, wife of Robt. Arbuthnott of Kirkbraehead, i. 307.
— Margaret, wife of Walter Scott of Sinton, vii. 71.
— Mary, wife of capt. F. Oliphant, vi. 555.
— Violet, wife of Sir Robt. Dalzell of Glenae, ii. 409.
— *, wife of Walter Scott, younger of Sinton, vii. 71.
Riddell-Carre of Cavers-Carre, Thomas Alexander, v. 53.
Ridgeway, Thomas (Ridgeway), lord, v. 83.
— of Fairlawn, Joseph, ii. 565.
— — his wife, Georgiana Clementina Colville, ii. 565.
Rig of Carberry, James, ii. 592.
— — Mungo, ii. 592.
— — his wife, Helen Cranstoun, ii. 592.
— John, merchant, Edinburgh, ii. 572.
— Patrick, Edinburgh, ix. 109.
— — his wife, Elizabeth Hope, ix. 109.
Rigge, John, minister at Strathmiglo, viii. 200.
— — his wife, Jean Murray, viii. 200.
RIPPON, DOUGLAS, BARON, vii. 141-144.
Rippon, James, first baron, vii. 140.
Rires, Margaret Beaton, wife of Arthur Forbes of Rires; styled lady, i. 445; viii. 541.
Ritchie of Busbie, James, iii. 449.
— — his wife, Frances Montgomerie, iii. 449.

* Name unknown.

Ritchie, Samuel, i. 145.
—— —— his wife, Margaret Barclay Allardice, i. 144; ix. 9.
Rivallon, brother of Alan the seneseal, i. 9.
Rivers, Anthony (Widvile), 2nd earl, i. 20.
—— Thomas (D'Arey), 1st earl, iii. 299.
—— John (Savage), 2nd earl, vii. 93.
—— of Stratbfieldsaye and Sudeley, William Horace (Pitt-Rivers), 3rd baron, iii. 492.
—— Harriet Elizabeth, wife of Charles Dashwood Bruee Preston, iii. 492.
Robartes, Charles, son of 1st earl of Radnor, vi. 467.
Robberds, Frederick Walter, M.A., vii. 565.
—— —— his wife, Caroline Ann Forbes, vii. 565.
Robeck, John Michael Henry, baron de, v. 367.
—— —— his wife, M. M. Lawless, v. 366.
Robert I., king of Seots, i. 7, 426; ii. 433, 435; iii. 139, 145; v. 35, 577, 579; vii. 234; viii. 248.
—— —— his 1st wife, Isabel of Mar, i. 8; v. 578.
—— —— his 2nd wife, Elisabeth de Burgh, i. 8; vii. 234.
Robert II., king of Scots, i. 9, 15; iii. 467.
—— —— his 1st wife, Elizabeth Mure, i. 16, 135; ix. 2.
—— —— his 2nd wife, Euphemia of Ross, i. 16, 134, 436; vi. 297; vii. 181 *n.*, 236; viii. 263.
Robert III., king of Seots, i. 17.
—— —— his wife, Annabella Drummond, i. 17; vii. 37.
Robert of Aehednapobbel, the chaplain, iv. 251.
Robert of Reidheugh, v. 329.
Robert of Serogis, vi. 199.
Robert, son of Maldred, iii. 241.
Robert, son of Wernebald of Kilmaurs, iv. 222.
Robert, son of Wernebald, iv. 223; vi. 170.
—— —— his wife, Riehenda, iv. 223.
Robert, grandson of Wernebald of Kilmaurs, iv. 223.
Robert, son of Maccus, vi. 469.
Robert, abbot of Melrose, ii. 229.
Robert, bishop of St. Andrews, iii. 241; iv. 5, 7; viii. 519.
Robert, bishop of Ross, iii. 424 *n.*
Robert, abbot of Kelso, iv. 565.
Robert, janitor of Kineardine, vii. 428.
ROBERTON, DOUGLAS, LORD DOUGLAS OF, i. 210-211.
Roberton, Archibald, lord Douglas of, i. 210.
—— of Earnock, James, ii. 405.
—— —— his wife, Cristine Dundas, ii. 405.
—— —— John, iv. 344.
Roberton of Earnoek, Simon, iv. 344.
—— —— his wife, *, dau. of David Fitzwalter, iv. 344.
—— Bartholomew, ii. 405.
—— James, elerk of Session, iii. 490.
—— —— his wife, Euphemia Burnett, iii. 490.
—— Janet, wife of William, 8th earl of Kincardine, iii. 490.
—— John, sheriff-clerk of Lanark, ii. 405.
—— —— his wife, Katharine Dalzell, ii. 405.
Roberts, Douglas Walkden, eaptain R.A., viii. 315.
—— —— his wife, Marjorie Effie Bowes-Lyon, viii. 315.
—— George, Grotton, viii. 122.
—— —— his wife, Francees Ellen Dalrymple, viii. 122.
—— H., Peekham Rye, v. 313.
—— John M., Bath, viii. 315.
—— Laura, wife of P. J. Maitland, v. 313.
—— major-general, viii. 123.
—— —— his wife, Jane Dalrymple, viii. 123.
Robertson of Aberdour, John, portioner, iii. 187.
—— of Auehinroath, William, ii. 354.
—— —— his wife, Elizabeth Sinclair, ii. 354.
—— of Auchleeks, Andrew de Atholia, aneestor of the family of, i. 419.
—— of Bishopmiln, James, ii. 354.
—— of Carronvale, Duncan Stewart, i. 129.
—— —— his wife, Henriette Anne Mary Ogilvy, i. 129.
—— of Drumaehin, Duncan, vi. 396.
—— —— his wife, Marjory *or* May Nairn, vi. 396.
—— of Dulcaben, vii. 88.
—— of Duncanzemere, Robert, vii. 207.
—— of Faseally, Alexander, v. 501.
—— —— his wife, Isobel Hay, v. 501.
—— —— Robert, ii. 200.
—— —— his wife, Mary Campbell, ii. 200.
—— of Inchmagranoch, Alexander, ii. 186.
—— of Ladykirk, Roger, ix. 8.
—— —— his wife, Helen Ogilvy, ix. 8.
—— of Logan House, William, iii. 108.
—— of Lude, Alexander, ii. 201.
—— —— his wife, Katharine Campbell, ii. 201.
—— —— James, vi. 396.
—— —— his wife, Margaret Mereer, vi. 396.
—— —— John, vi. 396.
—— —— his wife, Charlotte Nairn, vi. 396.
—— of Easter Moddervil, Robert, ii. 404.
—— of Monquaith, John, vi. 174.
—— of Strowan, vii. 88.
—— —— Alexander, 5th laird, i. 442; iii. 569; viii. 273.
—— —— his 1st wife, Elizabeth Lyon, viii. 273.
—— —— his 2nd wife, Elizabeth Stewart, i. 442.

* Name unknown.

Robertson of Strowan, Alexander, 12th laird, ii. 199; viii. 217.
—— —— his 1st wife, Katharine Drummond, viii. 217.
—— —— Alexander, 13th laird, iii. 331.
—— —— Andrew de Atholia, ancestor of the family of, i. 419.
—— —— his wife, * of Glenherthy and Tolykyne, i. 419.
—— —— Robert, ii. 177.
—— —— Robert, the younger, i. 442.
—— —— his wife, Margaret Stewart, i. 442.
—— of Thometayvoir in Fernan, Duncan, ii. 185.
—— of Tulliebelton, Richardson, lieut.-general, vi. 121.
—— —— his wife, Julia Louisa Leslie-Melville, vi. 121.
—— Alaster, Strathardle, viii. 489.
—— —— his wife, Margaret Wemyss, viii. 489.
—— Alexander, lieut. R.N., ii. 354.
—— —— his wife, Katharine Sinclair, ii. 354.
—— Christian, wife of A. Campbell of Lagvinshoch, ii. 186.
—— Elizabeth, wife of (1) Henry Stewart of Buchlyvie, and (2) John Wemyss of Cutkillhill, iii. 187; ix. 68.
—— George, goldsmith, vii. 218.
—— —— his, wife, Magdalen Primrose, vii. 218.
—— Janet, mistress of Robert Stewart of Strathdown, vi. 575.
—— *error for* Janet Thomson. wife of Henry Stenhouse, i. 547.
—— Julian, wife of Alex. Campbell of Lochdochart, ii. 199.
—— Margaret *or* Marie, wife of Sir C. Campbell of Glenurchy, ii. 177.
—— Margaret, wife of 7th earl of Erroll, iii. 569.
—— Margaret, wife of Alexander Middleton of Berrihill, vi. 174.
—— Patrick, col. of Livingston's Dragoons, ix. 29.
—— —— his wife, Anna Murray, ix. 29.
—— Sarah Frances, wife of 12th earl of Dalhousie, iii. 108.
—— Walter, vicar of Aberdour, ii. 160.
—— William Boyd, v. 152.
—— —— his wife, Ann Boyd of Trochrig, v. 152.
—— Wilhelmina, wife of John Ballantine Rollo, vii. 207.
—— *, vii. 88.
—— —— his wife, * Hay, vii. 88.
Robertson *alias* Colyear, Sir Alexander, 1st bart., vii. 89.
—— —— his wife, Jean Murray, vii. 90.
—— David, chamberlain to the prince of Orange, vii. 88.
—— —— his wife, Jean Bruce, vii. 89.

* Name unknown.

Robertson *alias* Colyear, David Alexander, vii. 89.
—— Jean, vii. 89.
—— Sabina *or* Martha, wife of Sir John Nicolson of Tillicoultry, vii. 89.
—— *, wife of Thos. Dunbar of Grange, vii. 89.
Robeson of Hallshill, Richard, iii. 341.
Robins, Mary Christina, wife of rev. G. D. Boyle, iv. 213; ix. 96.
—— William, Hagley, iv. 213.
Robinson of Farmingwood, Sir John, viii. 507.
—— —— Mary, wife of 3rd earl of Wemyss, viii. 507.
—— of Newton Garth, Leonard, iii. 291.
—— —— his wife, Mary Constable, iii. 291.
—— Emma Chambres, wife of Henry David Boyle, iv. 211.
—— Sir Frederic Philipse, lieut.-gen., G.C.B., governor of Tobago, iv. 388.
—— Hugh George, canon of York, iv. 211.
—— Maria Susannah, wife of H. C. J. Hamilton, iv. 388.
—— Thomas Bond Bird, rector of Milton, viii. 43.
—— —— his wife, Emily Charlotte Somerville, viii. 43.
Robson of Hownam, Thom, vii. 322.
—— John, chieftain of Clan Gunn, viii. 338.
—— —— his wife, * Gordon, viii. 338.
Roche, James, licenser of pedlars, i. 53.
Roche Chandre, Antoine de la, v. 350.
—— —— his wife, Anne Monypenny, v. 350; vi. 278 *n*.
Rochead of Inverleith, Sir James, viii. 143.
—— Janet, wife of (1) Alex. Murray of Melgund, and (2) Sir D. Dalrymple of Hailes, viii. 143.
Rochester, John (Wilmot), earl of, viii. 36.
—— Lawrence (Hyde), earl of, ii. 240; vii. 139.
—— Robert, 5th son of Sir Thos. Ker of Fernichirst; viscount, v. 69, 70 *bis*, 74.
Rochford, Frederick (Nassau), 3rd earl of, iv. 392.
—— Jane *or* Janet, wife of Malise, 1st earl of Menteith, vi. 144.
Rockville, Alexander Gordon, senator of the College of Justice, lord, i. 91; iii. 237.
Rodakowski, Ernest von, viii. 92.
—— —— his wife, Dora Susan Carnegie, viii. 92.
—— Joseph von, general, viii. 92.
—— —— his wife, countess Ottilie Wrangel, viii. 92.
Rodarc *or* Rodard, nephew of Alwin, 2nd earl of Lennox, v. 327.
Roderick of Garmoran, ancestor of Clan Ruari, v. 32.
Rodger, Bessie, wife of Henry Primrose, vii. 214.

* Name unknown.

lney, George Brydges (Rodney), admiral, st baron, ii. 91, 566.
- Fanny Mary, wife of 11th lord Blanyre, ii. 91.
- John, son of admiral lord R., ii. 91; v. 36.
- Katharine Henrietta, wife of Sir P. Stewart, ii. 90.
- Louisa Frederica, wife of lieut.-col. J. ?. Lennox, v. 366.
e of Mount Dunville Park, Henry, iv. 561.
- Charlotte D'Olier, wife of lord Granville Armyne Gordon, iv. 561.
esia of Dover, wife of Richard de Chilham, i. 425.
ger of Auldtoun, vii. 366.
ger of Drumelzier, son of Finlay, vii. 420.
ger, son of Udard, ii. 377.
ger, son of Gilbert, iii. 244.
— — his wife, Sigrid, iii. 244.
oger, prior of Paisley, v. 550.
oger, rector of Witfield, vii. 421.
oger, Lardenarius, viii. 3.
ogers of Brianstone, Richard, v. 361.
— A., vicar of Yarlington, iv. 172.
— Elizabeth, wife of (1) Charles (Cavendish), lord Mansfield, and (2) Charles, 6th duke of Lennox, v. 361.
— Elizabeth Louisa, wife of (1) J. S. Thompson, and (2) F. R. S. K. Stewart, iv. 171.
ogerson of Dumcrieff, John, vii. 209.
— Elizabeth, wife of 9th lord Rollo, vii. 209.
ohan, Anne de, wife of François de la Queuille, v. 352.
— Henri de, seigneur d'Espinay, v. 352.
Rokeby of Sandal, John, iii. 596.
Rolland, John, ix. 157.
— — his wife, Katharine Boswell, ix. 157.
Rolle of Stephenstoun, Sir John, K.B., iii. 479.
— John, iii. 479.
— — his wife, Christian Bruce, iii. 479.
— Mark George Kerr, vi. 386.
— — his wife, Gertrude Jane Douglas, vi. 386.
Rolleston, Launcelot, col., D.S.O., ii. 418.
— — his wife, Charlotte Emma Maud Dalzell, ii. 418.
Rollit, Sir Albert Kaye, viii. 364.
— — his wife, Mary Caroline Mitchell, viii. 364.
ROLLO OF DUNCRUB, ROLLO, LORD, vii. 180-211.
Rollo of Duncrub, Andrew, first lord, vii. 195.
— — his wife, Katharine Drummond, vii. 196; viii. 217.
— Andrew, third lord, vii. 202.
— — his wife, Margaret Balfour, i. 546; vii. 203; ix. 152.
Rollo, Andrew, fifth lord, vii. 205.
— — his 1st wife, Katharine Murray, i. 476; vii. 206.
— — his 2nd wife, Elizabeth Moray, vii. 206.
— James, second lord, vii. 200.
— — his 1st wife, Dorothea Graham, vi. 241; vii. 201.
— — his 2nd wife, Mary Campbell, i. 350; vii. 202.
— James, seventh lord, vii. 207.
— — his wife, Mary Aytoun, vii. 207.
— John, sixth lord, vii. 206.
— — his 1st wife, Cecilia Johnstone, vii. 206.
— — his 2nd wife, Mary Kennedy, vii. 206.
— — his 3rd wife, Jane Watson, vii. 206.
— John, eighth lord, vii. 208.
— — his wife, Agnes Greig, vii. 208.
— John Rogerson, tenth lord, vii. 209.
— — his wife, Agnes Bruce Trotter, vii. 209.
— Robert, fourth lord, vii. 204.
— — his wife, Mary Rollo, vii. 187, 204.
— William, ninth lord, vii. 209.
— — his wife, Elizabeth Rogerson, vii. 209.
— master of, John, eldest son of 3rd lord Rollo, vii. 203.
— master of, John, son of 5th lord Rollo, vii. 206.
— master of, William Charles Wordsworth, eldest son of 10th lord Rollo, vii. 209.
— — his wife, Mary Eleanor Hotham, vii. 209.
ROLLO, BARON DUNNING OF DUNNING AND PITCAIRNS, vii. 209-210.
ROLLO, LORD ROLLO OF DUNCRUB, vii. 180-211.
Rollo, Rollock, of Airlywicht, Andrew, vii. 189, 190.
— of Ardkelly, Andrew, vii. 184.
— of Ashgrove and Castlehill, Andrew Fitz-James Cunninghame Rollo Bowman Ballantine, vii. 207.
— — his wife, Annie Harriet Curzon Chalmers, vii. 207.
— — James Cunningham, vii. 207.
— of Bakak, Robert, vii. 189.
— of Balbegie, James, vii. 191; ix. 151.
— — his wife, Euphame Ramsay, vii. 191.
— — William, tutor of Gardin, vii. 188, 189, 190, 191.
— — his 2nd wife, Elizabeth Hay, v. 220; vii. 191; ix. 99.
— of Ballachie, David, iv. 275; vii. 10.
— — his wife, Elizabeth Gray, iv. 275; vii. 183.

Rollo, Rollock, of Ballingall, William, vii. 185.
— of Balkello, George, vii. 194.
— of Balloch or Ballachie, *see* of Bello.
— of Balnagown, Andrew, vii. 184.
— of Bannockburn, Andrew, vii. 197, 202.
— — Sir John, vii. 196.
— — his 1st wife, Isabella Cockburn, vii. 196.
— — his 2nd wife, Annabel Buchanan, vii. 197.
— — his 3rd wife, Helen St. Clair, vii. 198.
— — Hugh James Paterson, i. 307.
— — his wife, Helen Arbuthnott, i. 307.
— of Bello, David, 2nd laird, vii. 183.
— — his 1st wife, Elizabeth Gray, iv. 275; vii. 183.
— — his 2nd wife, Marjory Berclay, vii. 183.
— — David, 3rd laird, vii. 183.
— — his wife, Elizabeth Ogilvy, vii. 183.
— — David, 4th laird, vii. 183.
— — Marion, wife of Andrew Rollo of Duncrub, vii. 184, 188.
— — Robert, burgess of Dundee, 1st laird, vii. 182.
— of Corstoun, Andrew, 5th son of Andrew R. of Duncrub, vii. 188, 191.
— of Croftis, William, vii. 191.
— — his 2nd wife, Elizabeth Hay, vii. 191.
— of Duncrub, Andrew, 3rd laird, vii. 182, 184.
— — Andrew, 6th laird, vii. 187.
— — his wife, Marion Rollo of Menmuir, vii. 184, 188.
— — Sir Andrew, 9th laird, vii. 195.
— — his wife, Katharine Drummond, vii. 196.
— — Duncan, 2nd laird, vii. 182.
— — George, 7th laird, iii. 337 *n.*; vii. 188, 194; ix. 75.
— — his wife, Isobella Moncreiff, vii. 194.
— — James, 8th laird, vii. 188, 195.
— — his wife, Agnes Collace, vi. 545; vii. 195.
— — Sir James, 10th laird, vii. 200 *bis.*
— — his 1st wife, Dorothea Graham, vi. 241; vii. 201.
— — his 2nd wife, Mary Campbell, i. 350; vii. 202.
— — John, bailie of Perth, 1st laird, vii. 181.
— — Robert, 5th laird, vii. 186.
— — his wife, Jonet Graham, vii. 186.
— — William, 4th laird, vii. 185.
— — his wife, * Oliphant, vii. 185.
— of Dundee, George, vii. 189.
— — John, vii. 189.
— of Kirkton of Dunning, William, vii. 185.

* Name unknown.

Rollo, Rollock, of Park of Dunning, John, vii. 182.
— of Edindonyng, Andrew, vii. 188.
— of Findony, David, 2nd son of Andrew R. of Duncrub, vii. 184.
— — John, vii. 182.
— — William, vii. 185.
— of Garden, Andrew, vii. 190.
— — Sir Walter, tutor of Duncrub, vii. 188, 195.
— — his 1st wife, *, vii. 189.
— — his 2nd wife, Jean Stewart, v. 7; vii. 189, 190.
— of Kincledie, Andrew, vii. 196.
— — David, notary public, vii. 186.
— — his wife, Marion Livingstone, vii. 186.
— — David, vii. 196.
— of Kippans, Andrew, vii. 196.
— of Ladcathy, John, vii. 182.
— of Lawton, Sir Walter, tutor of Duncrub, vii. 188, 191.
— of Menmuir, David, 1st laird, vii. 183.
— — David, 2nd laird, vii. 183.
— — David, 3rd laird, vii. 183.
— — Marion, wife of Andrew Rollo of Duncrub, vii. 184, 188.
— of Monkisholm, James, vii. 191.
— — his wife, Margaret Goldman, vii. 191.
— of Muretoun, Robert, iv. 281; vii. 189.
— of Pitmadie, George, vii. 194.
— — John, advocate, sheriff-depute, vii. 189, 190.
— — his wife, Cristina Justice, vii. 190.
— — Thomas, advocate, vii. 187, 189 *bis.*
— — his wife, Annabel Forrester, vii. 187.
— — Walter, tutor of Duncrub, viii. 188.
— of Piltoun, John, advocate, sheriff-depute, vii. 189.
— — John, son of Peter R. of Pilton, vii. 190.
— — Peter, bishop of Dunkeld, lord of Session, vii. 188, 189, 191.
— — his 1st wife, Christian Cant, vii. 193.
— — his 2nd wife, Elizabeth Weston, vii. 193.
— — Peter, vii. 190.
— — his 1st wife, Elizabeth Haliburton, vii. 190.
— — his 2nd wife, Marie Stirling, vii. 190.
— of Polcak, Robert, vii. 189.
— of Powis, David, vii. 186.
— — his wife, Mariota Livingstone, vii. 187.
— — David, 2nd laird, vii. 187.
— — David, 1615, vii. 196.
— — Robert, vii. 200.
— — his wife, Jean Rollo, vii. 200.
— of Quhitbank, Andrew, vii. 184.

* Name unknown.

Rollo, Rollock, of Rossie, Andrew, vii. 196.
—— —— Laurence, 3rd son of 1st lord Rollo, vii. 198.
—— —— his wife, Katharine Peebles, vii. 198.
—— of Rossy Easter, Andrew, vii. 188.
—— —— George, vii. 194.
—— of Skeoch, Andrew, vii. 202.
—— —— Sir John, vii. 196, 202.
—— of Thanesland, James, vii. 195.
—— of Threepwood, Robert, vii. 181.
—— of Tillicoultry, Andrew, vii. 196.
—— of Woodside, Henry, 1st laird, minister in Edinburgh, vii. 187.
—— —— his wife, Helen Elphinstone, iii. 540; vii. 187.
—— —— Sir Henry, 3rd laird, vii. 187, 204.
—— —— his wife, Margaret Young, vii. 204.
—— —— Mary, wife of Robert, 4th lord Rollo, vii. 187, 204.
—— Agnes Katharine, wife of rev. R. M. Gore Browne, vii. 210.
—— Andrew, eldest son of Charles R., vii. 191.
—— —— his wife, Euphame Rollo, vii. 191; ix. 152.
——Mr. Andrew, minister of Duns, and Dunning, vii. 198.
—— —— his 1st wife, Isabella Lindsay, vii. 198.
—— —— his 2nd wife, Helen Oliphant, vii. 198.
—— —— his 3rd wife, Helen Mercer, vii. 198.
—— Andrew, elder son of Mr. Andrew R., vii. 198.
—— Anna, wife of Geo. Graham of Pitcairns and Monzie, vii. 197.
—— Anna, wife of (1) Wm. Mercer of Clavage, and (2) major Drummond of Pitcairns, vii. 200.
—— Anna, dau. of 5th lord Rollo, vii. 206.
—— Annabella, wife of Wm. Vest, vii. 207.
—— Annabella, wife of David Drummond of Invermay, vii. 197.
—— Archibald, 2nd son of James R. of Duncrub, vii. 195.
—— Archibald, major, 2nd son of 2nd lord Rollo, vii. 202.
—— Barbara, dau. of 7th lord Rollo, vii. 208.
—— Beatrix, wife of Oliver Sinclair of Quhitkirk, vii. 186.
—— Bernard Francis, vii. 210.
—— Cecilia Anne, wife of James Thomson, vii. 207.
—— Cecily Agatha Agnes, vii. 210.
—— Charles, burgess of Perth, vii. 191, 194.
—— Christian, dau. of Peter R. of Pilton, vii. 190.
—— Christian, dau. of Sir Walter R. of Garden, vii. 191.
—— Clement Sobieski, vii. 205.
—— —— his wife, Amelia Maria Irving, vii. 205.
Rollo, Rollock, Constance Agnes, vii. 210.
—— David, Edinburgh, vii. 198.
—— —— his wife, Bethia Laurie, vii. 198.
—— David, 3rd son of 3rd lord Rollo, vii. 203.
—— Eliza, wife of Dr. J. C. Howden, vii. 207.
—— Elizabeth, wife of Sir Thos. Maule of Panmure, vii. 10, 184.
—— Elizabeth, wife of Sir James Stewart of Ballechin, vii. 195.
—— Elizabeth Cecilia, wife of James C. Bruce of Balchristie, vii. 208.
—— Elspeth, dau. of Sir Walter R. of Garden, vii. 191.
—— Emilia, wife of Wm. Irving of Bonshaw, vii. 203.
—— Eric Norman, vii. 210.
—— —— his wife, Constance Maud Hohler, vii. 210.
—— Euphame, wife of Andrew Rollo, vii. 191; ix. 152.
—— George, eldest son of Sir Walter R. of Gardin, vii. 189.
—— George, 2nd son of William R. of Balbegie, vii. 191.
—— Gilbert de St. Croix, vii. 210.
—— —— his wife, Margaret Freda Evelyn Antrobus, vii. 210.
—— Glory Evelyn, vii. 210.
—— Gylla Constance Susan, vii. 210.
—— Helen, wife of James Pearson of Kippenross, vii. 197.
—— Henry, 2nd son of 4th lord Rollo, vii. 204.
—— —— his wife, Anne Ruthven, vii. 204, 388.
—— Herbert Evelyn, vii. 210.
—— Hercules, master in High School, Edinburgh, vii. 187.
—— Hugh James, W.S., vii. 187.
—— Humphrey, keeper of Kildrummy Castle, vii. 185.
—— —— his wife, Jonet Graham, vii. 186.
—— Humphrey, at Mill of Findon, vii. 194.
—— —— his wife, Christian Chalmer, vii. 194.
—— Humphrey, their son, vii. 194.
—— Isobel, wife of George Hay of Kirkland, v. 229; vii. 191.
—— Isabella, dau. of Sir John R. of Bannockburn, vii. 198.
—— Isobel, wife of James Blair of Corbs, vii. 199.
—— Isabell, wife of William Halliday of Tullibole, vii. 200.
—— Isabella, wife of Robert Johnstone of Wamphray, vii. 203.
—— Isobel, wife of John Aytoun of Inchdairnie, vii. 205.
—— Isabella, dau. of 7th lord Rollo, vii. 208.
—— Isobel, dau. of James R. of Balbegie, ix. 152.
—— James, provost of Dundee, vii. 182.
—— James, 4th son of 4th lord Rollo, vii. 204.
—— James, major, vii. 207.
—— —— his wife, Mary Anne Keogh, vii. 207.

Rollo, Rollock, James, 3rd son of 7th lord Rollo, vii. 208.
—— James Arthur, vii. 208.
—— Jane, wife of capt. Patrick Hunter, vii. 208.
—— Janet, wife of Andrew Blair of Rossie-ochil, vii. 194.
—— Jean, wife of Robert Balcanquhal, vii. 187.
—— Jean, wife of John Stewart of Killie-chassie, vii. 199.
—— Jean, wife of (1) Robert Rollo of Powis, and (2) John Drummond of Pitkellonie, vii. 200.
—— Jean, dau. of 3rd lord Rollo, vii. 203.
—— Jean, wife of capt. Robert Johnstone of Wamphray, vii. 205.
—— Jemima, vii. 207.
—— Jessie, wife of Archibald Currie, vii. 207.
—— Joanna, wife of Sir Alex. Innes of Cockstoun, vii. 198.
—— Joanna, wife of John Carmichael, vii. 206.
—— John, clerk of the diocese of Moray, notary, vii. 181 *n.*
—— John, barrack-master at Perth, vii. 205.
—— John, son of John Ballantine R., vii. 207.
—— —— his wife, Frances Anne Payne, vii. 207.
—— John, 3rd son of 8th lord Rollo, vii. 208.
—— —— his 1st wife, Jane Hay Paterson, vii. 208.
—— —— his 2nd wife, Jane Marshall, vii. 208.
—— John, his son, vii. 208.
—— —— his wife, Mary Maitland, vii. 208.
—— John Ballantine, vii. 207.
—— —— his 1st wife, Williamina Robertson, vii. 207.
—— —— his 2nd wife, Janet Gray, vii. 207.
—— John Eric Henry, vii. 210.
—— Jonet, dau. of William R. of Balbegie, vii. 191.
—— Malcolm Rogerson, vii. 210.
—— Margaret, wife of Wm. Drummond of Belliclon, vii. 194.
—— Margaret, wife of Sir John Drummond of Carnock, vii. 200.
—— Margaret, wife of Sir George Oliphant of Newton, vii. 202.
—— Margaret, wife of Richard Blyth, ix. 152.
—— Margaret Bowman, wife of (1) Joseph Harriman, and (2) C. E. N. Dörr, vii. 208.
—— Marion, wife of Sir James Bruce of Powfoulis, vii. 195.
—— Marion, wife of (1) Mr. Robert Forrest, and (2) James Bruce *or* Forsyth, vii. 197.
—— Marion, dau. of 1st lord Rollo, vii. 200.
Rollo, Rollock, Marjorie, wife of (1) Geo. Graham of Inchbrakie, and (2) John Graham of Balgowne, vii. 194.
—— Martha, wife of major-gen. Richardson Robertson, vii. 209.
—— Martha Hay Paterson, vii. 208.
—— Mary, wife of L. Oliphant of Newton, vii. 194.
—— Mary, dau. of 2nd lord Rollo, vii. 202.
—— Mary, dau. of Clement Sobieski R., vii. 205.
—— Mary, wife of D. Drummond of Pitkellonie, vii. 205.
—— Mary Isabella, wife of gen. Wm. Macpherson, vii. 207.
—— Mary, dau. of 7th lord Rollo, vii. 208.
—— Mary, wife of capt. R. K. Trotter, vii. 209.
—— Patrick, servitor to Sir T. Lyon of Auldbar, vii. 189.
—— Peter, captain, vii. 190.
—— —— his wife, Mary Stewart, i. 446, 448; vii. 191.
—— Robert, elder son of Andrew R. of Duncrub, vii. 185.
—— Robert, principal of Edinburgh University, vii. 187.
—— —— his wife, Helen Baron, vii. 187; ix. 151.
—— Robert, burgess of Dundee, vii. 191.
—— Robert, captain of 42nd regiment of Foot, vii. 205.
—— —— his wife, Janet Graeme, vii. 205.
—— Robert, general, vii. 209.
—— —— his wife, Harriet Anne Ferguson-Davie, vii. 209.
—— Robert Roger, vii. 207.
—— Robert William Ernest Hay, vii. 208.
—— Roger, R.A., collector of customs, Ayr, vii. 207.
—— —— his wife, Eliza Hunt, vii. 207.
—— Roger, their 3rd son, vii. 207.
—— Rosalind Mary Agnes, vii. 209.
—— Susanna, wife of Hugh Gillespie of Chirriebelly, vii. 204.
—— Thomas, legtd. son of David R. of Menmuir and Bello, vii. 184.
—— Thomas, advocate, vii. 187.
—— —— his 1st wife, Annabel Forrester, vii. 187.
—— —— his 2nd wife, Grizel Scott, ix. 151.
—— Torfrida Henrietta Louisa, vii. 210.
—— Umphra, at the mill of Findany, vii. 188, 194.
—— Walter, 2nd son of John R. of Pilton, vii. 190.
—— William, 2nd son of Robert R. of Duncrub, vii. 186.
—— Sir William, major under Montrose, vii. 199.
—— William Hereward Charles, vii. 210.
—— William Robert Dunbar, vii. 205.

, Rollock, Williamina Eliza, vii. 207.
wife of Collace of Balnamoon, vii.
wife of Walter Drummond of Broich
Balloch, vii. 186.
k, Adam, 1328, prisoner in England,
180.
Ienry, minister of the High Church,
nburgh, iii. 540; vii. 187.
ohn, bailie of Perth, clerk of the
ket, Edinburgh, vii. 181.
Robert, Kintore and Perth, vii. 181.
Walter, Perth, 1343, vii. 181.
Walter, illeg. son of bishop Peter R.
Pilton, vii. 193.
Villelmus de, esquire, vii. 180.
ee *also* Rollo.
s, Richard de, Normandy, vii. 180.
of Sacombe Park, Edward, viii. 36.
— his wife, Anne Wilmot, viii. 36.
illy of Huntington Park, Samuel
nry, viii. 91.
— his wife, Arabella Charlotte Cargie, viii. 91.
ney, Charles (Marsham), 4th earl of,
514.
— his wife, Frances Augusta Connce Mure-Campbell-Rawdon-Hastings,
514.
Robert (Marsham), 1st baron, iv. 595.
— his wife Elizabeth Shovel, iv. 595.
Charles (Marsham), 3rd earl of, ii. 245.
— his wife, Margaret Harriet Scott,
245.
ghe, Eustachius, Flemish saltmaker,
. 68.
ke, James, i. 32.
— his wife, Mary Tudor, i. 32.
se of Brynntirion, George Bradley, vi.
2.
Sarah Jane, wife of capt. Henry Warnder of Tregof, vi. 582.
th, Edward, Kilkenny, vi. 188.
er of Muffets, Robert, LL.D., v. 234.
— his wife, Henrietta Hay, v. 234.
y, son of the Green Abbot, v. 44.
of Sanquhar, Isabella, wife of William
Crichton, iii. 53, 219.
— Isabella, wife of John de Graham
Coldene, Dalkeith, and Crichton, iii. 54.
— *, wife of Richard Edgar, iii. 53, 219.
Robert de, i. 5.
— his wife, Isabella, i. 5.
William de, a Competitor, i. 5; ii. 505.
common, Robert (Dillon), 2nd earl of,
84.
— his 2nd wife, Dorothy Hastings,
83.
e of Ballivat, John, v. 246.
of Balvraid, John, ix. 70.
— his wife, Esther Sutherland, ix. 70.

* Name unknown.

Rose of the Holm, Alexander, vii. 461.
— of Kilravock, Hugh, 8th, iii. 194; iv. 18.
— — his 1st wife, Isabel Sutherland, iii. 194.
— — his 2nd wife, Margaret Gordon, iv. 526.
— — his 4th wife, Janet Innes, iii. 196.
— — Hugh, 9th, iv. 2, 3; v. 244.
— — Hugh, 10th, v. 244.
— — his wife, Katharine Falconer, v. 244.
— — Hugh, 12th, v. 543.
— — his wife, Magdalen Fraser, v. 543.
— — Hugh, 15th, iv. 62.
— — his 2nd wife, Mary Forbes, iv. 62.
— — Hugh, 17th, iii. 211; vii. 478.
— — his 1st wife, Elizabeth Grant, vii. 478.
— — Sir William, ii. 129.
— — his wife, Morella de Doune, ii. 129.
— — William, v. 530.
— of Montreal, Sir John, G.C.B., 1st bart., ii. 531.
— Alexander, bailie of Inverness, vii. 174.
— — his wife, Sibylla Mackay, vii. 174.
— David, son of Alex. R. of the Holm, vii. 461.
— — his wife, Agnes Grant, vii. 461.
— Edward Temple, capt. 10th Hussars, ii. 531.
— — his wife, Cecilia Cathcart, ii. 531.
— Frances Theodora, wife of 16th earl of Morton, vi. 385.
— George, secretary of State, vi. 20.
— Sir George Henry, G.C.H., vi. 20, 385.
— Henrietta, wife of Sir William Dunbar, iii. 211.
— John, in Keiss, ix. 51.
— Katharine, wife of (1) Jas. Grant of Ardneillie, and (2) Simon, 6th lord Lovat, v. 530; vii. 465.
— Katharine, wife of capt. James Sinclair, ix. 51.
— Lilias, wife of bishop Colin Falconer, v. 245.
ROSEBERY, PRIMROSE, EARL OF, vii. 212-229.
Rosebery, Archibald, first earl of, vii. 221.
— — his wife, Dorothea Cressy, vii. 222.
— Archibald John, fourth earl of, vii. 225.
— — his 1st wife, Harriet Bouverie, vii. 226.
— — his 2nd wife, Anne Margaret Anson, vii. 226.
— Archibald Philip, fifth earl of, vii. 227.
— — his wife, Hannah Rothschild, vii. 228.
— James, second earl of, vii. 222.
— — his wife, Mary Campbell, i. 382; vii. 223.

Rosebery, Neil, third earl of, vii. 224.
—— his 1st wife, Susan Randall, vii. 224.
—— his 2nd wife, Mary Vincent, vii. 224.
ROSEBERY, PRIMROSE, VISCOUNT OF, vii. 221-229.
Rosebery, Archibald, first viscount of, vii. 221.
ROSEBERY OF ROSEBERY, PRIMROSE, BARON, vii. 225.
Rosebery of Rosebery, Archibald John, first baron, vii. 225.
ROSEHILL, CARNEGIE, LORD, vi. 495-508.
Rosehill, David, eldest son of 6th earl of Northesk; styled lord, vi. 503; ix. 144.
—— his wife, Mary Cheer, vi. 503.
— David Ludovic George Hopetoun; styled lord, vi. 507.
— George, eldest son of 7th earl of Northesk; styled lord, vi. 505.
— John, first lord, vi. 495.
Roskelyn, Henry de, vi. 564.
Rospigliosi, prince Camillo, vi. 459.
—— his wife, Elena Maria Giustiniani-Bandini, vi. 459.
ROSS, THE ANCIENT EARLS OF, vii. 230-244.
Ross, Euphemia, wife of (1) Sir Walter Leslie, and (2) Alex. Stewart, earl of Buchan; countess of, ii. 260, 261, 262; vii. 238, 239, 271.
— Ferquhard, first earl of, iv. 224 *n.*; vii. 231.
— Florence III., count of Holland, earl of, vii. 231.
—— his wife, Ada of Scotland, i. 4.
— Gillanders, earl of, vii. 231.
— Hugh, fourth earl of, ii. 222; vii. 234, 235; ix. 152.
—— his alleged wife, Jean Stewart, i. 14.
—— his 1st wife, Matilda *or* Maud Bruce, ii. 435; vii. 236.
—— his 2nd wife, Margaret Graham, vi. 211; vii. 236.
— Malcolm MacEth, earl of, v. 30; vi. 285; vii. 158, 230.
—— his wife, * of the Isles, vii. 231.
— Sigurd Hlodversson, earl of, vi. 281.
— William, second earl of, vii. 233; viii. 323.
—— his wife, Jean Comyn, i. 505; vii. 233.
— William, third earl of, ii. 222; iv. 44; vii. 233; viii. 324.
—— his wife, Euphemia Graham (?), v. 579; vi. 204; vii. 235.
— William, fifth earl of, ii. 320; vii. 237; viii. 253, 254.
—— his wife, Mary Macdonald, v. 37; vii. 237.

* Name unknown.

ROSS, LESLIE, EARL OF, vii. 241-244.
Ross, Alexander, earl of, vii. 241, 273.
—— his wife, Isabel Stewart, i. 14[...] 242.
— Euphemia, dau. of Alexander, e[...] Ross; *de jure* countess of, v. 41; vi[...] 303, 304; vii. 242.
— Mary *or* Margaret, wife of Donald of the Isles; countess of, v. 41, 42; vi[...] 243.
— Walter, *de jure ux.* earl of, vii. 23[...] 430; viii. 263.
—— his wife, Euphemia, counte[...] Ross, vii. 239.
ROSS, MACDONALD, EARL OF, v. 41-47.
Ross, Alexander, lord of the Isles, ea[...] iii. 306; v. 522, 564; vii. 243; viii. 331.
— Angus Macdonald of Glengarry, cl[...] ant to earldom of, v. 564.
— Donald, lord of the Isles, *de jure* earl of, v. 40; vii. 242.
—— his wife, Mary *or* Margaret Le[...] countess of Ross, v. 41; vii. 243.
— John, lord of the Isles, earl of, iii. 181; iv. 526; v. 45, 244; vii. 498.
—— his wife, Elizabeth Livingston[...] 47, 431.
ROSS, STEWART, EARL OF, i. 155.
Ross, Charles, 2nd son of king James [...] earl of, i. 155.
— Henry, lord Darnley; earl of, i. 155.
— John, earl of Buchan; earl of, ii. [...] 449; vii. 243.
—— his wife, Elizabeth Douglas, ii. [...]
Ross, Robert Bruce, illeg. son of ki[...] Robert I.; alleged to have been creat[...] earl of, iii. 466.
ROSS, DOUGLAS, VISCOUNT OF, vii. 138-156.
Ross, William, first viscount of, vii. 138.
ROSS, STEWART, DUKE OF, vii. 245-246.
Ross, Alexander, 4th son of king James I[...] duke of, i. 21; vii. 246.
— James, 2nd son of king James III.; du[...] of, i. 21; ii. 151, 387; vii. 245.
ROSS OF HALKHEAD, ROSS, LORD, vii. 2[...] 263.
Ross of Halkhead, George, eleventh lor[...] vii. 257.
—— his 1st wife, Grizel Cochrane, i[...] 350; vii. 258.
—— his 2nd wife, Jean Ramsay, iii. 10[...] 102; vii. 258.
—— George, thirteenth lord, vii. 261.
—— his wife, Elizabeth Ker, v. 480; vi[...] 262.
—— James, fourth lord, vii. 252.
—— his wife, Jean Sempill, vii. 254.
—— James, sixth lord, vii. 255; vi[...] 28.
—— his wife, Margaret Scott, vi[...] 255.
—— James, seventh lord, vii. 256.

Ross of Halkhead, John, first lord, vii. 249.
—— his 1st wife, Marjory Mure, vii. 250.
—— his 2nd wife, Marion Baillie, vii. 250; viii. 12.
—— John, second lord, vi. 81; vii. 250.
—— his wife, Christian Edmonstone, vii. 251.
—— Ninian, third lord, vii. 251.
—— his 1st wife, Janet Stewart, v. 350; vii. 252; ix. 125.
—— his 2nd wife, Elizabeth Ruthven, iv. 259; vii. 252.
—— his 3rd wife, Elizabeth Stewart, vii. 252; ix. 126.
—— his 4th wife, Janet Montgomery, vii. 252.
—— Robert, fifth lord, vii. 254; viii. 390.
—— his wife, Jean Hamilton, vii. 255.
—— Robert, ninth lord, vii. 256.
—— William, eighth lord, vii. 256.
—— William, tenth lord, vii. 254, 257.
—— his 1st wife, Elizabeth Houston, vii. 257.
—— his 2nd wife, Helen Forrester, vii. 257; ix. 92.
—— William, twelfth lord, vii. 259.
—— his 1st wife, Agnes Wilkie, vii. 261.
—— his 2nd wife, Margaret Wharton, vii. 261.
—— his 3rd wife, Anne Hay, vii. 261; viii. 462.
—— his 4th wife, Henrietta Scott, vi. 431; vii. 261.
—— William, fourteenth lord, iv. 215; vi. 81; vii. 262.
— master of, Robert, eldest son of 3rd lord Ross of Halkhead, vii. 252.
—— his wife, Agnes Moncrief, vii. 252.
Ross of Hawkhead, Boyle, baron, iv. 216-219.
Ross of Hawkhead, George, first baron, iv. 216.
—— George Frederick, third baron, iv. 218.
—— James, second baron, iv. 218.
Ross, lord Ross of Halkhead, vii. 247-263.
Ross of Ardnel, Godfrey de, v. 138.
—— Reginald de, v. 138.
—— Robert de, v. 138.
— of Auchinbothy Wallace, Sir John, vii. 249.
— of Auchleskin, John, viii. 216.
— of Auchlossen, Robert, ix. 9.
— of Balkail, Alexander, viii. 140.
— of Balnagown, Alexander, iii. 195; vii. 160.
—— his wife, Dorothea Sutherland, iii. 195.
—— Alexander, ii. 338; vii. 500.
—— his 1st wife, Janet Sinclair, ii. 338.
—— his 2nd wife, Katharine Mackenzie, vii. 500.
Ross of Balnagown, Charles, general, M.P., 2nd son of 11th lord Ross of Halkhead, vii. 258.
—— Charles, M.P., 2nd son of 13th lord Ross of Halkhead, vii. 261, 262.
—— Sir David, vii. 161, 498; ix. 10.
—— his 2nd wife, Margaret Stewart, i. 153; ix. 9.
—— David, i. 470; viii. 346.
—— his 1st wife, Mary Gordon, viii. 346.
—— his 2nd wife, Annabella Murray, i. 470; ix. 29.
—— David, iii. 207; v. 533.
—— his wife, Mary Fraser, v. 533.
—— David, vi. 322; vii. 259.
—— his wife, Anne Stewart, vi. 322.
—— George, ii. 352; vii. 189, 468, 504; viii. 188, 346.
—— Hugh, 1st laird, 3rd son of Hugh, 4th earl of Ross, vii. 236, 238, 239.
— of Balneil, James, viii. 119.
— of Bladensburg of Rostrevor, Edmund James Thomas, iii. 47.
—— his wife, Alexina Frances Lindsay, iii. 47.
— of Bondynton of Lathame, John de, viii. 266.
— of Brownhill, George, vii. 64.
— of Buchan, Sir John, 2nd son of 3rd earl of Ross, ii. 260; vii. 235, 238; viii. 324.
—— his wife, Margaret Comyn, ii. 256, 260; vii. 235.
— of Craigie, John, viii. 277.
—— his wife, Agnes Lyon, i. 189; iv. 53; viii. 277.
—— John, iv. 124; v. 502; vii. 252 *n.*; viii. 188.
—— John, vi. 514; viii. 216.
—— Thomas, vi. 545.
—— his wife, Jean Hephurn, vi. 545.
— of Craigrossie, John, vii. 250.
— of Craigton, James, iii. 187.
—— his wife, Marjory Stewart, iii. 187; v. 5.
— of Denys, Sir John, vii. 249.
— of Galston, George, vii. 64.
—— George, vi. 598.
—— his wife, Christian Makgill, vi. 598.
—— John, v. 508.
—— his wife, Christian Campbell, v. 508.
— of Geanies, viii. 188.
— of Haining, *, vi. 514.
—— his wife, Margaret Wallace, v. 163; vi. 514.
—— Matthew, iv. 194.
—— his wife, Marion Boyle, iv. 194.
— of Hamelak, William, ii. 377, 378.
— of Hawkhead, Elizabeth, wife of 3rd earl of Glasgow, iv. 215; vi. 81; vii. 262; ix.

* Name unknown.

Ross of Hawkhead, Jean, wife of John Ross Mackye of Polgowan, iv. 215; vi. 81; vii. 262.
—— John, 1st laird, vii. 247.
—— Sir John, 2nd laird, ii. 397; vii. 248.
—— Sir John, 3rd laird, vii. 248.
—— Sir John, 4th laird, vii. 248.
—— his 1st wife, Marjory Mure, vii. 250.
—— his 2nd wife, Marion Baillie, vii. 250.
— of Hilton-Malar, John, iv. 124.
— of Invercarron, Walter, iii. 71.
— of Kilbride, Godfrey de, v. 138.
—— Reginald de, v. 138.
— of Kindeace, William, the younger, iii. 209.
— of Kinfauns, Hugh de, viii. 265.
—— John, iv. 272.
—— his wife, * Gray, iv. 272.
— of Kingedward, Euphemia, wife of Sir Alex. Stewart, earl of Buchan, ii. 262.
— of Lochintillow, Sir John, vii. 249.
— of Melville, Elizabeth, wife of 3rd earl of Glasgow, iv. 215; vi. 81; vii. 262; ix. 96.
—— Jean, wife of John Ross M'Kye, iv. 215; vi. 81; vii. 262.
—— Sir John, vi. 81; vii. 249, 250.
—— his wife, Christian Edmonstone, vii. 251.
—— Robert, vii. 250.
—— his wife, Agnes Melville, vii. 250.
— of Millanderdale, Gilbert, provost of the College Kirk of Maybole, vi. 595.
—— John, vi. 595.
—— his wife, Anna Makgill, vi. 595.
— of Montgrenan, Thomas, vii. 532.
— of Murieston, Sir William, iv. 91; vii. 254, 257.
—— his 1st wife, Elizabeth Houston, vii. 257.
—— his 2nd wife, Margaret Forrester, iv. 91; vii. 257.
— of Newriston, Sir William, vii. 257.
— of Ochtergavin, Christina, vi. 392.
—— Elizabeth, vi. 392.
—— John, vi. 392.
— of Philorth, Hugh, vi. 567.
— of Pitcalnie, Nicholas, vii. 189.
— of Portincross, Godfrey de, v. 138.
—— Reginald de, v. 138.
— of Rarichies, Hugh, 3rd son of Hugh, 4th earl of Ross, vii. 236.
— of Redeplowland, John de, viii. 266.
— of Starlaw, Sir John, vii. 249.
— of Stewarton, Godfrey de, vii. 247.
— of Torphin, William, vii. 257.
— of Tortreven, James, viii. 171.
—— John, vii. 251.
—— his wife, Christian Edmonstone, vii. 251.

* Name unknown.

Ross of Tortreven, John, illeg. son of 3rd lord Ross of Halkhead, vii. 252.
— of Torwoodheid, Sir William, iv. 91.
—— his wife, Margaret Forrester, iv. 91.
— of Walterstoun, John, vii. 249.
— of Wardlaw, Andrew, 1st laird, vii. 251.
—— James, viii. 390.
— of Werk, Robert, ii. 377.
—— William, ii. 377, 378.
— Agnes, wife of John Boyle of Kelburne, iv. 191.
— Agnes, wife of Archibald Campbell of Lawers, v. 502.
— Alice *or* Alison, wife of Sir John Melville of Carnbee, vii. 254.
— Anne, wife of 4th lord Balmerino, i. 570; ix. 34.
— Anna, dau. of 11th lord Ross of Halkhead, vii. 259.
— Anne, dau. of 12th lord Ross of Halkhead, vii. 261.
— Arthur, archbishop of St. Andrews and Glasgow, i. 545, 570.
— Barbara, wife of John Balfour, i. 545.
— C., v. 313.
—— his wife, Laura Maitland, v. 313.
— Christian, wife of (1) John Mure of Caldwell, (2) Nicholas Ramsay of Dalhousie, and (3) John Weir, iii. 93; vii. 252.
— Christian, wife of David Primrose, vii. 215.
— David, Calcutta, vii. 178.
—— his wife, Marion Gall, vii. 177.
— [David], judge of the Court of Session, lord Ankerville, vii. 178.
— Dorothea de, wife of Torquil M'Leod of Lewis, vii. 235.
— Dorothy, dau. of 4th lord Ross of Halkhead, vii. 254.
— Elizabeth, wife of Allan Lockhart of Cleghorn, vii. 254.
— Elizabeth, wife of Sir Thos. Sempill of Eliotstoun, vii. 530; ix. 152.
— Elizabeth, wife of 5th lord Fleming, vii. 252; viii. 544; ix. 152.
— Elspeth, wife of James Miller, vii. 255.
— Euphemia, wife of (1) John Randolph, 3rd earl of Moray, and (2) king Robert II., i. 16, 134, 436; vi. 297; vii. 236.
— Euphemia *or* Emelia, wife of (1) William, 3rd earl of Kilmarnock, and (2) John Murray, i. 477; v. 177; vii. 261; ix. 152.
— Euphemia de, wife of Walter de Moray of Duffus, ii. 122; vii. 232; viii. 321.
— Euphame, dau. of 11th lord Ross of Halkhead, vii. 259.
— Gelis, wife of James Auchinleck, iii. 336.
— George, 3rd son of 13th lord Ross of Halkhead, vii. 262.

Ross, Sir Godfrey, sheriff of Ayr and Lanark, v. 490; vii. 247; viii. 256.
— Godfrey, his eldest son, vii. 247.
— Grisel, wife of Sir Archibald Stirling of Keir, vii. 254.
— Grizel, wife of Sir Alex. Gilmour of Craigmillar, vii. 258.
— Grizel, wife of Sir James Lockhart of Carstairs, vii. 261; ix. 152.
— Helen, wife of John Blair of that Ilk, vii. 251.
— Helen, wife of Sir John Melville of Carnbee, vii. 254.
— Hugh, 3rd son of 2nd lord Ross of Halkhead, vii. 252.
— Isabella, contracted to Edward Bruce, i. 428; ii. 436; vii. 235.
— Isabella, wife of (1) John Sutherland, and (2) James Innes, iii. 207.
— Isobel, wife of George Munro of Foulis, vii. 160.
— James, merchant, Edinburgh, ix. 101.
— — his wife, Marion Hamilton, ix. 101.
— Jane, wife of major-gen. G. M. Carmichael-Smyth, iv. 572.
— Janet, wife of Sir Alex. Fraser of Cowie, ii. 261; vii. 239, 431.
— Janet, wife of K. Mackenzie of Scatwell, iii. 71.
— Janet, wife of 3rd lord Lovat, v. 526, 527.
— Janet, wife of (1) Monymusk of Monymusk, and (2) Sir Alex. Murray of Drumsergarth, vii. 237.
— Jean, wife of Robt. Stewart of Pitheveles, vi. 514; ix. 144 *bis*.
— Jean, wife of (1) Sir Jas. Sandilands of Calder, and (2) Henry Stewart of Craigiehall, vii. 254; viii. 389.
— Jean, wife of Sir Robt. Innes of Innes, vii. 256, 356; ix. 152.
— Jean, wife of 6th earl of Dalhousie, iii. 102; vii. 259.
— Jean, wife of Kenneth Mackenzie of Kintail, vii. 504.
— Joanna de, wife of Sir Alexander Fraser of Cowie, ii. 261; vii. 239, 431.
— John, pedagogue, iii. 576.
— John, 2nd son of Hugh, 4th earl of Ross, vii. 236.
— Katharine, wife of Harry Hamilton, ii. 44.
— Katharine, wife of Sir Wm. Sinclair, ii. 352.
— Katharine, wife of John Crichton of Rossie, ix. 70.
— Lilias, wife of Wm. Urquhart, sheriff of Cromarty, vii. 237.
— Margaret, wife of Andrew Murray of Balvaird, vii. 252 *n.*; viii. 188.
— Margaret, wife of Sir George Stirling of Keir, vii. 256.
Ross, Margaret, dau. of 11th lord Ross of Halkhead, vii. 259.
— Margaret, dau. of 13th lord Ross of Halkhead, vii. 262.
— Margaret, wife of (1) F. Kennedy of Knockdaw, and (2) James, 1st viscount of Stair, viii. 119.
— Maria, wife of Adam Stewart of Barskimming, vi. 514.
— Mariota de, wife of Alexander Sutherland of Dunbeath, vii. 244.
— Marjorie, wife of Malise, 8th earl of Strathearn, ii. 320; vii. 236, 238; viii. 254.
— Mary, wife of 1st duke of Atholl, i. 485; vii. 261; ix. 152.
— Mary, wife of John Hepburn of Waughton, vii. 256.
— Mary, dau. of 13th lord Ross of Halkhead, vii. 262.
— Mary, wife of (1) capt. John Dalrymple, and (2) Sir J. A. Oughton, viii. 140.
— Muriel, wife of (1) D. Grant of Rothiemurchus, and (2) D. Grant of Clurie, vii. 468.
— Robert, son of Sir John R. of Halkhead, vi. 81.
— — his wife, Agnes Melville of Melville, vi. 81.
— Robert, 2nd son of 5th lord Ross of Halkhead, vii. 255.
— Thomas, 3rd son of 2nd lord Ross of Halkhead, vii. 251.
— Sir Walter, slain at Bannockburn, vii. 235.
— William, Montrose, i. 309.
— — his wife, Margaret Arbuthnott, i. 309.
— William de, son of 5th earl of Ross, vii. 239.
— William, 2nd son of Sir Godfrey R., sheriff of Ayr, vii. 247.
— William, 4th son of 3rd lord Ross of Halkhead, vii. 252.
— *, wife of Roderick Mackenzie of Achilty, vii. 498.
Ross-Lockhart of Balnagowan, Sir James, vii. 263.
Rosse, Richard, first viscount, i. 54.
— — his 3rd wife, Elizabeth Hamilton, i. 54.
ROSSIE OF ROSSIE, KINNAIRD, BARON, v. 214.
Rossie of Rossie, George William Fox, first baron, v. 214.
— — his wife, Frances Anna Georgiana Spencer-Ponsonby, v. 214.
Rossie of Rossie, Patrick, v. 246.
— Isobel, wife of Robert Falconer of Drimmie, v. 246.
Rosslyn, Alexander (Wedderburn), 1st earl of, vii. 588.

* Name unknown.

Rosslyn, James (Erskine), 2nd earl of, vii. 588.
— James Alexander (St. Clair-Erskine), 3rd earl of, viii. 511.
— — his wife, Frances Wemyss, viii. 511.
— James Francis Harry (St. Clair-Erskine), 5th earl of, viii. 501, 511.
Rossmore, Warner William (Westenra), 2nd lord, viii. 514.
— — his wife, Augusta Charteris, viii. 514.
Rotberg, Albertine de, wife of (1) general comte Rapp, and (2) George, duc de Melfort, comte de Lussan, vi. 73.
Rothe, Michael, lieut.-general in French service, vi. 188.
— — his wife, Katharine Middleton, vi. 188.
— *, lieut.-general, comte de, iii. 614.
— — his wife, Lucy Cary, iii. 614.
Rotheri, mormaer of Mar, ii. 250.
Rotheric Beg of Carrick, vii. 29.
Rotherham of Much Waltham, John, viii. 37.
— Frances, wife of (1) Peter Curgenven, and (2) James, 12th lord Somerville, viii. 37.
ROTHES, LESLIE, EARL OF, vii. 264-311.
Rothes, Andrew, fifth earl of, vii. 65, 292; viii. 23; ix. 126.
— — his 1st wife, Grisel Hamilton, iv. 261; vii. 293; ix. 103.
— — his 2nd wife, Jean Ruthven, iv. 262; vii. 294.
— — his 3rd wife, Janet Durie, vii. 294.
— George, first earl of, vii. 274.
— — his 1st wife, Margaret Lundin, vii. 275.
— — his 2nd wife, Christian Halyburton, iv. 335; vii. 275.
— — his 3rd wife, Elizabeth Campbell, vii. 275.
— George, second earl of, iii. 310; vii. 277.
— — his wife, Jane *or* Janet Douglas, i. 178; vii. 278.
— George, fourth earl of, vii. 281; viii. 187.
— — his 1st wife, Margaret Crichton, iii. 67; vii. 281, 284.
— — his 2nd wife, Elizabeth Gray, iv. 277; vii. 285.
— — his 3rd wife, Agnes Somerville, vii. 285.
— — his 4th wife, Isobel Lundy, iii. 27; vii. 285.
— George William, thirteenth earl of, vii. 307.
— — his 1st wife, Henrietta Anne Pelham, vii. 308.
— — his 2nd wife, Charlotte Julia Campbell, vii. 308; ix. 153 *bis*.

* Name unknown.

Rothes, George William Evelyn, fifteenth earl of, vii. 309.
— — his wife, Louisa Morshead, vii. 309.
— George William Evelyn, sixteenth earl of, vii. 309.
— Henrietta Anderson Morshead, wife of George Waldegrave; countess of, vii. 309.
— Henrietta Anne, wife of George Gwyther; countess of, vii. 308.
— Jane Elizabeth, wife of (1) George Raymond Evelyn Glanville, and (2) Sir Lucas Pepys; countess of, vii. 307.
— John, sixth earl of, iv. 318, 319; vii. 297.
— — his wife, Anna Erskine, v. 622; vii. 299.
— John, seventh earl of, i. 563; v. 90, 379; vii. 299.
— — his wife, Anna Lindsay, iii. 37; vii. 301.
— John, ninth earl of, iv. 319; vii. 303.
— — his wife, Jean Hay, vii. 304; viii. 462.
— John, tenth earl of, vii. 305.
— — his 1st wife, Hannah Howard, vii. 306.
— — his 2nd wife, Mary Lloyd, vii. 306.
— John, eleventh earl of, vii. 306.
— — his wife, Jean Maitland, vii. 307.
— Margaret, wife of 5th earl of Haddington; countess of, iv. 319; vii. 302.
— Mary Elizabeth, wife of M. E. Haworth; countess of, vii. 308, 309.
— Norman Evelyn, nineteenth earl of, vii. 310.
— — his wife, Noëlle Lucy Martha Dyer Edwardes, vii. 310.
— William, third earl of, vii. 277, 278.
— — his wife, Jonet Balfour, vii. 278.
ROTHES, LESLIE, DUKE OF, vii. 301.
Rothes, John, duke of, i. 88; v. 381; vii. 301.
— — his wife, Anna Lindsay, iii. 37; vii. 301.
— master of, Andrew, son of 1st earl of Rothes, vii. 276.
— — his wife, Elizabeth *or* Marjory Sinclair, vii. 276, 278; ix. 50.
— master of, George, grandson of 1st earl of Rothes, vii. 275, 277.
— — his wife, Janet Douglas, i. 178; vii. 278.
— master of, James, eldest son of 5th earl of Rothes, vii. 295.
— — his 1st wife, Margaret Lindsay, v. 400; vii. 296.
— — his 2nd wife, Katharine Drummond, vii. 47, 296.
— master of, John, eldest, son of Andrew, master of Rothes, v. 276.
— — his wife, Janet Keith, v. 277; vi. 41.

Rothes, master of, Norman, eldest son of 4th earl of Rothes, iii. 67; vii. 282, 286, 292.
—— —— his wife, Isobel Lindsay, v. 398; vii. 286.
—— master of, Walter, alleged son of 2nd earl of Rothes, vii. 278 *n.*
ROTHESAY, STEWART, DUKE OF, vii. 312-313.
Rothesay, David, eldest son of king Robert III.; first duke of, i. 17, 147; iii. 161, 271, 275; v. 425; vii. 312; viii. 481.
—— —— his wife, Marjory Douglas, i. 18; iii. 163.
—— Henry Frederick, eldest son of king James VI.; prince of Wales, duke of, i. 27; iii. 370; iv. 432; v. 617; vii. 213.
—— James, eldest son of king James I.; duke of, i. 26, 155; vii. 313.
Rothschild of Mentmore, Meyer Amschel de, vii. 228.
—— Hannah, wife of 5th earl of Rosebery, vii. 228.
Rothwell, John Sutton, colonel R.A., iv. 211.
—— —— his wife, Henrietta Camilla Boyle, iv. 211.
Rouet-Smollett of Bonhill and Auchindennan, John, rear-admiral R.N., iv. 214.
—— —— his wife, Elizabeth Boyle, iv. 214.
Roule of Altonburn, Adam of, vii. 316.
—— of Fouleroule, Bernard de, vi. 567.
—— of Hindhope, Andrew, vii. 322.
—— of Molle, Adam de, iv. 330.
—— —— his wife, Johanna Haliburton *or* Wyschard, iv. 330.
—— of Plenderleith, Andrew, vii. 322.
—— of Primside, Adam, vii. 320.
—— —— Andrew, vii. 319, 321, 322.
—— —— George, vii. 319, 321.
—— —— his wife, Margaret Ker, vii. 321.
—— Alison, wife of Sir Wm. Ogilvy, ii. 3, 4, 6.
—— Richard de, viii. 3.
Route, John, v. 530.
Row of Bandeath, John, v. 249.
—— —— his wife, Euphame Falconer, v. 249; ix. 123.
Rowe, Anthony, iv. 95.
—— Charlotte, wife of 5th lord Forrester of Corstorphine, iv. 95, 96.
—— Isabella, wife of John Cockburn of Ormiston, iv. 96.
Rowley of Castleroe, John, v. 267.
—— —— his wife, Mary Gage, v. 267.
—— of Hill House, Sir Charles, 1st bart., admiral R.N., v. 235.
—— of Priory Hill, Charles, i. 526.
—— Anne, wife of rev. C. Lindsay, i. 526.
—— George Dawson, i. 526.
—— —— his wife, Caroline Frances Lindsay, i. 526.
Rowley, Louisa Burton, wife of 11th earl of Kinnoull, v. 235.
Roxburgh, Hugh, bishop of Glasgow, chancellor of Scotland, ii. 252; iii. 87.
ROXBURGHE, KER, LORD, vii. 341-360.
Roxburghe, Robert, first lord, vii. 341.
ROXBURGHE, KER, EARL OF, vii. 343-360.
Roxburghe, John, fifth earl of, vii. 350.
—— —— his wife, Mary Finch, vii. 351.
—— Robert, first earl of, iv. 27; v. 459 *bis*, 475; vii. 341.
—— —— his 1st wife, Margaret Maitland, v. 296; vii. 345.
—— —— his 2nd wife, Jean Drummond, vii. 47, 345.
—— —— his 3rd wife, Isabel Douglas, vi. 378; vii. 348.
—— Robert, third earl of, vii. 349; ix. 154, 168.
—— —— his wife, Margaret Hay, vii. 349; viii. 456.
—— Robert, fourth earl of, v. 477; vii. 349.
—— William, second earl of, ii. 72; vii. 50, 348.
—— —— his wife, Jean Ker, vii. 348 *bis*.
ROXBURGHE, KER, DUKE OF, vii. 314-352.
Roxburghe, John, first duke of, vii. 350.
—— John, third duke of, vii. 351.
—— Robert, second duke of, vii. 351.
—— —— his wife, Essex Mostyn, vii. 351.
ROXBURGHE, BELLENDEN-KER, DUKE OF, vii. 352-354.
Roxburghe, William, fourth duke of, vii. 352.
—— —— his 1st wife, Margaret Burroughs, vii. 353.
—— —— his 2nd wife, Mary Bechenoe, vii. 353.
ROXBURGHE, INNES-KER, DUKE OF, vii. 356-360.
Roxburghe, James, fifth duke of, vii. 356; ix. 154 *bis*.
—— —— his 1st wife, Mary Wray, vii. 357.
—— —— his 2nd wife, Harriet Charlwood, vii. 357.
—— James Henry Robert, seventh duke of, vii. 358.
—— —— his wife, Anne Emily Churchill, vii. 358.
—— James Robert, sixth duke of, vii. 357.
—— —— his wife, Susanna Stephanie Dalbiac, vii. 357.
—— Henry John, eighth duke of, vii. 359.
—— —— his wife, May Goelet, vii. 359.
—— master of, William, elder son of 1st lord Roxburghe, vii. 345.
Roy of Nenthorn, William, v. 316.
—— —— his wife, Isabella Maitland, v. 316.
—— Bessie, accused of witchcraft, iii. 590.
Rozas, José de, count of Castel Blanco, vi. 70.

Rozas, Margaret de, wife of don Joseph Ignaz de Vallabriga, ix. 135.
Royston, Sir James Mackenzie, 1st baronet, lord of Session, lord. iii. 72, 76.
Rudd of Thorne, Erick, in holy orders, iii. 213, 214.
— Eric, v. 417.
— — his wife, Emilia Lindsay, v. 417.
— Eric Sinclair James Sutherland, v. 417.
— Eric de Sioblade Sutherland, v. 417.
— — his wife, Jessie Forrester M'Arthur Moir, v. 417.
— Henry Ayton Lindsay, v. 417.
— Ian Forrester Sutherland, v. 417.
— James, rector of Newton Kyme and Full Sutton, iii. 213.
— — his wife, Elizabeth Sutherland, iii. 213.
— James Sutherland, iii. 213.
Rue, Jean, wife of Thomas Erskine, v. 92.
Rugeley of Dunton, Ralph, i. 400.
— Mary, wife of (1) Geo. Barbour, and (2) Wm. Aston, i. 400.
Ruggles-Brise, Harold Goodeve, Grenadier Guards, i. 501.
— — his wife, Dorothea Louisa Murray, i. 501.
RUGLEN, DOUGLAS, EARL OF, vii. 146-147.
Ruglen, William, third earl of, vii. 146, 362.
RUGLEN, HAMILTON, EARL OF, vii. 361-363.
Ruglen, Anne, wife of (1) William, 2nd earl of March, and (2) Anthony Sawyer; countess of, vii. 146, 362.
— John, first earl of, vii. 361, 518.
— — his 1st wife, Anne Kennedy, ii. 485; vii. 362.
— — his 2nd wife, Elizabeth Hutchinson, vii. 362.
Rule, Barbara, wife of John Kennedy of Craig, iii. 437.
— *see also* Roule.
Rumely, Alice de, wife of William Fitz-duncan, i. 3; ii. 375.
— Robert de, i. 3.
Rupert of the Rhine, prince, son of Frederick v., count Palatine, count von Simmern, i. 27; vi. 248; vii. 346.
Rushout, George, rev., 2nd son of 1st lord Northwick, iv. 170.
— — his wife, Caroline Stewart, iv. 170.
Rushworth of Farringdon Hill, Edward, iii. 516; viii. 146.
— — his wife, Katharine Holmes, iii. 516; viii. 146.
— Elizabeth, wife of James Patrick Murray, iii. 516.
— Mary, wife of Sir John Pringle Dalrymple, viii. 146.
Russell, Francis, eldest son of 5th earl of Bedford; styled lord, v. 67.
Russell, George, eldest son of capt. William R., vii. 358.
— — his wife, Charlotte Isabella Innes-Ker, vii. 358.
— Isabella, wife of (1) William Comyn of Kirkintilloch, and (2) Sir Edward Hastings, i. 507; vi. 129, 131.
— Janet, wife of Mr. John Colville, ii. 570.
— John, 2nd son of 2nd earl of Bedford; styled lord, i. 395.
— Sir John, 2nd husband of Isabella, countess of Menteith, i. 507; vi. 129.
— Louisa Jane, wife of 1st duke of Abercorn, i. 70.
— William, R.N., vii. 358.
Rutherford, *see* Rutherfurd.
RUTHERFURD, RUTHERFURD, LORD, vii. 364-384.
Rutherfurd, Alexander, self-styled lord, vii. 383.
— Andrew, first lord, vii. 373, 374.
— — his wife, Susanna Melville, vii. 375.
— Archibald, third lord, vii. 381.
— David (Durie), self-styled lord, vii. 374.
— George (Durie), self-styled lord, vii. 373.
— — his wife, Margaret Ogilvy, vii. 373.
— John, self-styled lord, vii. 377, 381, 383.
— — his wife, Isabel Ainslie, vii. 383.
— John (Anderson of Goland), self-styled lord, vii. 384.
— Robert, fourth lord, vii. 381; ix. 154.
— — his wife, Sara Owens *or* Ollens, vii. 381.
— Thomas, second lord, vii. 374, 380.
— — his wife, Christian Urquhart, vii. 380.
RUTHERFURD, LORD RUTHERFURD, vii. 364-384.
RUTHERFURD, EARL OF TEVIOT, vii. 374-375.
Rutherfurd of Bankend, John, ancestor of the family of, vii. 377.
— — his wife, Barbara Gladstanes, vii. 377.
— — William, vii. 380.
— of Barnhills, Dr. William, vii. 80.
— — his wife, Agnes Scott, vii. 80.
— of Capehope, Alexander, captain Royal Horse Guards, vii. 383.
— — Andrew David, portioner, vii. 383.
— — his wife, Margaret Rutherfurd, vii. 383.
— — James, vii. 367.
— — John, vii. 382.
— — his wife, Enphan Gledstanes, vii. 382.
— — John, portioner, vii. 382.
— — his wife, Janet Ainslie, vii. 382.
— — John, vii. 383.
— — his wife, Cecilia Bennet, vii. 383.

Rutherfurd of Capehope, John, captain Scots Grenadiers, claimant to the barony of Rutherfurd, vii. 377, 381, 383.
—— of Chatto, Adam, vii. 377.
—— —— his wife, Janet Rutherfurd, vii. 377.
—— —— George, 1st laird, vii. 369.
—— —— his wife, Jonet Rutherfurd, vii. 369.
—— —— Robert, 2nd laird, vii. 369.
—— —— his wife, Margaret Glendinwyn, vii. 370.
—— —— Robert, 3rd laird, vii. 370.
—— —— his wife, Janet *, vii. 370.
—— of Nether Chatto, John, vii. 375.
—— of Crailing, James, vii. 367.
—— of Dodington Mill, Sir Nicol, vii. 365.
—— —— his wife, Marjorie *, vii. 365.
—— of Eckford, William, vii. 368.
—— of Edgerston, James, vii. 367.
—— —— John, vii. 589.
—— —— John, vi. 115.
—— —— his wife, Mary Anne Leslie, vi. 115.
—— —— Richard, vii. 376; viii. 400.
—— —— his wife, Betty Rutherfurd, vii. 376.
—— —— Thomas, ancestor of the family of, vii. 367.
—— of Fairnilee, Robert, vii. 383.
—— of Farnington, Thomas, ancestor of the family of, vii. 368.
—— of Glennysland, Richard, vii. 370.
—— of Grubet, Mary, wife of Sir James Ker, v. 69.
—— —— Nicholas, v. 69.
—— —— his wife, Martha Stewart, v. 69.
—— —— Nicol, vii. 368.
—— —— his 1st wife, Margaret Charteris, vii. 368.
—— —— his 2nd wife, * Cranstoun, vii. 368.
—— of Grundisnuke, Thomas, vii. 376.
—— of Hardaneheid, John, vii. 377.
—— of Hundalee, John, ancestor of the family of, vii. 368.
—— —— John, vii. 368.
—— —— his wife, Janet Rutherfurd, vii. 368.
—— —— Mary, wife of Sir Jas. Ker of Crailing, v. 69.
—— —— Nicol, v. 69; vi. 516.
—— of Hunthill, Andrew, 5th laird, vii. 371.
—— —— his wife, Helen Rutherfurd, vii. 367, 371, 376.
—— —— Andrew, 10th laird, v. 191; vii. 380.
—— —— his wife, Margaret Livingston, v. 191; vii. 380; ix. 121.
—— —— George, 2nd laird, vii. 370.
—— —— his wife, Mariota *, vii. 371.
—— —— George, 4th laird, vii. 371.
—— —— John, 6th laird, vii. 339, 371, 375.
—— —— his 1st wife, Christine Hoppringle, vii. 375, 376.
—— —— his 2nd wife, Isobel Ker, vii. 339.

* Name unknown.

Rutherfurd of Hunthill, John, 'the Cock of Hunthill,' 7th laird, vii. 376.
—— —— his 1st wife, Agnes Kirktoun, vii. 376.
—— —— his 2nd wife, Grisel Home, vii. 377.
—— —— John, 9th laird, v. 76; vii. 379.
—— —— his wife, Alison Ker, v. 76; vii. 379.
—— —— John, 11th laird, vii. 380.
—— —— Robert, 1st laird, vii. 370.
—— —— his wife, Margaret Glendinning, vii. 370.
—— —— Thomas, 8th laird, ii. 592; vii. 377.
—— —— his 1st wife, Jean Cranstoun, ii. 592; vii. 378.
—— —— his 2nd wife, Alison Edmonstone, vii. 378.
—— —— Sir Thomas, 12th laird, vii. 374, 380.
—— —— his wife, Christian Urquhart, vii. 381.
—— —— Thomas, vii. 381.
—— —— William, 3rd laird, vii. 371.
—— of Huntlydene, Walter, vii. 382.
—— —— his wife, Margaret Pringle, vii. 382.
—— of Hyndhousefield and Howdenbraes, John, sheriff-depute of Roxburgh, vii. 377.
—— of Kirkraw, John, vii. 383.
—— of Langnewton, George, vii. 369.
—— —— his wife, Katharine Sele, vii. 369.
—— —— William, vii. 371.
—— of Lethbert, James, vii. 366.
—— of Littleheuch, Richard, 'Dickon draw the sword,' vii. 382.
—— —— his wife, Lilias Gladstanes, vii. 382.
—— —— William, vii. 382.
—— of Lynbrods, Walter, vii. 382.
—— of Philliphope, John, vii. 382.
—— of Quarrelholes, Robert, major-general, vii. 372.
—— —— William, vii. 372.
—— —— his wife, Giles Stewart, vii. 372; viii. 402.
—— —— William, vii. 373.
—— —— his wife, Margaret Guthrie, vii. 373.
—— of Redheugh, Walter, ancestor of the family of, vii. 369.
—— of Rutherford, Gregory, vii. 364.
—— —— Helen, wife of (1) Sir John Forman, (2) Sir Thomas Ker, (3) Andrew Rutherfurd, and (4) Patrick Home, vii. 367, 371, 376; viii. 399, 400.
—— —— Hugh, 1215, vii. 364.
—— —— Hugh, 1252, vii. 364.
—— —— James, eldest son of Sir Richard R., vii. 366.
—— —— James, warden of the Marches, vii. 330, 366.
—— —— his wife, Margaret Erskine, vii. 367.
—— —— Katharine, wife of James Stewart of Traquair, vii. 367; viii. 399.
—— —— Sir Nicholas, vii. 364.
—— —— Sir Nicholas, vii. 365.
—— —— his wife, Marjorie *, vii. 365.

* Name unknown.

Rutherfurd of Rutherfurd, Philip, the younger, ii. 228; vii. 367.
—— —— his wife, Elizabeth Ker, ii. 228; vii. 331, 367.
—— —— Richard, 1252, vii. 364.
—— —— Richard, vii. 366 *bis*.
—— —— Sir Richard, vii. 366; ix. 154.
—— —— his wife, Jean Douglas, vii. 366.
—— —— Richard, grandson of James R. of that Ilk, vii. 367; viii. 399.
—— —— Robert, 1st laird, vii. 364.
—— —— William, son of Richard R., vii. 317, 366.
—— —— William, his son, vii. 317; ix. 154.
—— of Sandystanys, George, vii. 369.
—— of Scraisburgh, George, vii. 370.
—— —— Robert, vii. 370.
—— of Swynside, James, vii. 367.
—— of Sunlaws, William, viii. 402.
—— of Wells, Helen, viii. 400.
—— —— Thomas, vii. 381.
—— of Wrightslands, Robert, major-general, governor of Majorca, vii. 372.
—— —— William, vii. 372.
—— of Yetholm, Nicol, vii. 368.
—— Adam, prior of anchorites in Over Anerum, vii. 369.
—— Adam, 3rd son of William R. of Littleheuch, vii. 382.
—— Andrew, 4th son of James R. of that Ilk, vii. 368.
—— Andrew, canon of Jedburgh, vii. 371.
—— —— his wife, * Douglas, vii. 371.
—— Andrew, 4th son of 'the Cock of Hunthill,' vii. 377.
—— Andrew, 3rd son of Thomas R. of Hunthill, vii. 377.
—— Andrew, tenant of Cockplays, vii. 382.
—— Andrew, 2nd son of William R. of Littleheuch. vii. 382.
—— Anna, wife of Mr. Thomas Abernethy, vii. 379.
—— Anna, wife of James Aitken, bishop of Galloway, vii. 379.
—— Archibald, ii. 541.
—— Archibald, canon of Jedburgh, vii. 371.
—— —— his wife, * Douglas, vii. 371.
—— Aymer, 2nd son of Sir Nicholas of R., vii. 365.
—— Betty, wife of Richard Rutherfurd of Edgerston, vii. 376.
—— Christian, wife of Sir Robert Ker of Caverton, vii. 329, 368.
—— Christine, wife of Robert Durie of Grange, vii. 373.
—— Christian, dau. of John R., provost of St. Salvator's College, vii. 374.
—— David, elder son of Mr. John R., vii. 372.
—— Elizabeth, wife of Walter Scott of Wauchope, vii. 383.

* Name unknown.

Rutherfurd, Elizabeth, wife of Andrew St. Clair of Herdmanston, vii. 589.
—— Elspeth, dau. of Thomas R. of Hunthill, vii. 378.
—— Eva, grand-dau. of Sir Nicholas of R., vii. 365.
—— George, 3rd son of 'the Cock of Hunthill,' vii. 377.
—— Gilbert, c. 1436, ii. 226.
—— Grizel, wife of Ormiston of Ormiston, vii. 377.
—— Grizel, wife of Adam Kirktoun of Stuartfield, vii. 378.
—— Helen, wife of Sir T. Borthwick, ii. 98; vii. 369.
—— Helen, wife of Philip Nisbet of Nisbet, vii. 370.
—— Helena, wife of Thomas Lewin of Amble, vii. 379.
—— Isabel, wife of Archibald Wilkie of Harlawmuir, vii. 373.
—— Isabel, dau. of John R. of Hunthill, vii. 376.
—— Isobel, wife of Alex. Burnet of Carlops, vii. 379.
—— James, son of John R., advocate, vii. 372.
—— Janet, wife of John Rutherfurd of Hundalie, vii. 368.
—— Janet, dau. of Mr. John R., vii. 372.
—— Janet, wife of Adam Rutherfurd of Chatto, vii. 377.
—— Jean, dau. of Thomas R. of Hunthill, vii. 378.
—— Jean, wife of col. Peacock, vii. 383.
—— John, professor of philosophy abroad, and provost of St. Salvator's College, St. Andrews, vii. 371.
—— —— his wife, Christian Forsyth, vii. 371.
—— John, minister of Denino, vii. 372.
—— —— his wife, Janet Inglis, vii. 372.
—— John, minister of Cupar, and Kilconquhar, etc., vii. 372.
—— —— his wife, Barbara Sandilands, vii. 372.
—— John, minister of Kirkden, vii. 372.
—— —— his wife, Isobel Auchmutie, vii. 372.
—— John, advocate, vii. 372.
—— —— his wife, Janet Muschett, vii. 372.
—— John, 2nd son of James R. of that Ilk, vii. 367.
—— Sir John, killed at Crevant, vii. 368.
—— Jonet, wife of George Rutherfurd of Chatto, vii. 369.
—— Katharine, wife of William Cockburn of Henderland, vii. 369.
—— Laurence, brother of George R. of Chatto, vii. 368.
—— Lilias, wife of Henry Ker of Graden, vii. 379.

Rutherfurd, Lilias, wife of Wm. Douglas of Plewland, ix. 154.
—— Margaret, wife of Ralph Ker of Primsideloch, v. 53.
—— Margaret, dau. of Sir Nicholas of R., vii. 365.
—— Margaret, wife of Hugh Wallace of Craigie, vii. 370.
—— Margaret, wife of David Auchmutie of Drumeldrie, vii. 372.
—— Margaret, wife of Wm. Elliot of Dinlayhyre, vii. 379.
—— Margaret, wife of Alexander Durham of Largo, vii. 380.
—— Margaret, wife of Andrew David Rutherfurd, vii. 383.
—— Margaret, wife of Charles Scott of Palace Hill, vii. 383.
—— Mariota, wife of William Rutherfurd, vii. 376.
—— Marjory, grand-dau. of Sir Nicholas of R., vii. 365.
—— Mary, wife of David Ainslie of Fala, vii. 376.
—— Percie, 5th son of 'the Cock of Hunthill, vii. 377.
—— Richard, alleged son of 'the Cock of Hunthill,' vii. 381.
—— Robert, 5th son of James R. of that Ilk, vii. 368.
—— Robert, governor of Ostend, count, vii. 373.
—— Robert, 7th son of 'the Cock of Hunthill,' vii. 377.
—— Robert, son of 4th lord Rutherfurd, vii. 381; ix. 154.
—— Robert, captain, 2nd son of Walter R. of Huntliedene, vii. 383.
—— 'Robin with the tod's tail,' vii. 368.
—— —— his 2nd wife, Joan Heton, vii. 368.
—— Samuel, minister of Anwoth, professor of divinity, v. 117, 118, 119, 170.
—— Steven, brother of John R. of Hunthill, vii. 376.
—— Steven, 6th son of 'the Cock of Hunthill,' vii. 376.
—— Thomas, 2nd son of Thos. R. of Hunthill, vii. 378.
—— Walter, eldest son of 'Dickon draw the sword,' vii. 382.
—— William, tutor of Langnewton, vii. 371.
—— —— his wife, Christian Armstrong, vii. 371.
—— William, ship-master, Leith, vii. 372.
—— —— his *probable* wife, Mariota Rutherfurd, vii. 376.
—— William, treasurer to the king of Spain, vii. 372.
—— William, 2nd son of 'the Cock of Hunthill,' vii. 377, 382.
—— William, 4th son of William R. of Littleheuch, vii. 382.
RUTHVEN, RUTHVEN, LORD, iv. 254-268.
Ruthven, Patrick, third lord, iv. 259, 261, 337.
—— —— his 1st wife, Janet Douglas, i. 193; iv. 261; viii. 399.
—— —— his 2nd wife, Janet Stewart, i. 443; iv. 261; ix. 98.
—— Patrick, M.D., 5th son of 1st earl of Gowrie; styled lord, iv. 264.
—— —— his wife, Elizabeth Woodford, iv. 265.
—— Patrick, solicitor, styled lord, iv. 265.
—— —— his 1st wife, Sarah Head, iv. 265.
—— —— his 2nd wife, Jane Macdannell, iv. 265.
—— William, first lord, iii. 20, 225; iv. 101, 257.
—— —— his 1st wife, Isobel Levington, iii. 19; iv. 258.
—— —— his 2nd wife, Christian Forbes, iv. 52, 101, 258.
—— William, second lord, iii. 338; iv. 101, 258, 259.
—— —— his wife, Janet Haliburton, iv. 259, 337.
—— William, fourth lord, iv. 263, 337; vi. 547; vii. 253.
—— —— his contr. wife, Mary Gray, iv. 263, 282.
—— —— his wife, Dorothea Stewart, iv. 263; vi. 268.
—— master of, Archibald, 4th son of 3rd lord Ruthven; styled, iv. 262; ix. 98.
—— master of, Patrick, eldest son of 3rd lord Ruthven, iv. 261.
—— —— his wife, Marion Gray, iv. 262, 282.
—— master of, William, eldest son of 1st lord Ruthven, iv. 259.
—— —— his 1st wife, Katharine Buttergask, iv. 259.
—— —— his 2nd wife, Jean Hepburn, iv. 259; ix. 41.
—— master of, William, 2nd son of 3rd lord Ruthven, iv. 262.
RUTHVEN OF ETTRICK, RUTHVEN, LORD, iv. 104-106.
Ruthven of Ettrick, Patrick, first lord, iv. 104.
—— —— his 1st wife, *, iv. 105.
—— —— his 2nd wife, Joanna Henderson, iv. 105.
—— —— his 3rd wife, Clara Berner, iv. 105.
RUTHVEN OF FREELAND, RUTHVEN, LORD, vii. 385-393.
Ruthven of Freeland, David, second lord, vii. 387.
—— —— Isabel, wife of James Johnstone of Graitney; baroness, vii. 387, 388.
—— —— James, fifth lord, vii. 388.
—— —— his 1st wife, Janet Nisbet, vii. 389.
—— —— his 2nd wife, Anne Stewart, ii. 301; iii. 550; vii. 389.

* Name unknown.

Ruthven of Freeland, James, sixth lord, vii. 390.
— — his wife, Mary Elizabeth Leslie, vi. 117; vii. 390.
— — James, seventh lord, vii. 390.
— — his wife, Mary Hamilton Campbell, vii. 390.
— — Jean, baroness, vii. 387.
— — Mary Elizabeth Thornton, wife of Walter Hore; baroness, vii. 391.
— — Thomas, first lord, iv. 260; vii. 385.
— — his wife, Isabel Balfour, i. 544; vii. 387.
— — Walter James, ninth lord, vii. 392.
— — his wife, Caroline Annesley Gore, vii. 392.
— — master of, Walter Patrick, eldest son of 9th lord Ruthven of Freeland, vii. 392.
— — his wife, Jean Leslie Lampson, vii. 392.
RUTHVEN, EARL OF BRENTFORD, iv. 104-106.
RUTHVEN, EARL OF FORTH, iv. 101-106.
RUTHVEN, EARL OF GOWRIE, iv. 254-268.
RUTHVEN, LORD RUTHVEN, iv. 254-268.
RUTHVEN, LORD RUTHVEN OF ETTRICK, iv. 104-106.
RUTHVEN, LORD RUTHVEN OF FREELAND, vii. 385-393.
Ruthven of Ballernach, Sir William, sheriff of St. Johnstoun, iv. 257.
— — Sir William, his son, iv. 257.
— of Ballindean *or* Bandon, Patrick, iii. 590.
— — William, 3rd son of 1st lord Ruthven, iv. 101, 258, 260 *bis*; ix. 92.
— — his wife, Agnes Crichton, iv. 101.
— — Sir William, 2nd laird, iv. 101, 102.
— — his wife, Katharine *or* Jean Stewart, iv. 102; v. 6.
— — William, 3rd laird, iv. 102; vii. 190.
— — his wife, Christian Barclay, iv. 102.
— of Blackferkill, William, iv. 101.
— of Burleigh, John, 2nd son of 1st earl of Gowrie, i. 534; iv. 264, 267.
— of Carse, Sir Francis, governor of Memel, iv. 102; ix. 92.
— — William, ancestor of the family of, iv. 258.
— of Cultmalundie, Sir Gilbert de, vi. 531.
— of Cultvainy and Drumdrane, Alexander, iv. 258.
— — John, *alias* Lindsay, legtd. son of 1st lord Ruthven, iii. 20; iv. 258.
— of Dunglass, Sir John, general, ii. 297; iv. 102; v. 378.
— — his 1st wife, Jean Ramsay, iv. 103.
— — his 2nd wife, Barbara Leslie, iv. 103; v. 378.
— — Sir William, iv. 103.
— — his wife, Katharine Douglas, i. 205; iv. 103.
Ruthven of Dunlugas, William, ancestor of the family of, iv. 258.
— of Forteviot, Archibald, general in Swedish service, iv. 262; ix. 98.
— — James, iv. 101, 260.
— of Freeland, Alexander, 5th son of 2nd lord Ruthven, iv. 101, 260; vii. 385.
— — his wife, Elizabeth Moncrieff, iv. 260.
— — Sir Thomas, iv. 260; vii. 385.
— — his wife, Isabel Balfour, i. 544; vii. 387.
— — William, iv. 260; vii. 385; ix. 98.
— — his wife, Isabella Fotheringham, iv. 260.
— of Gardyne, John, captain, 5th laird, iv. 102 *bis*; vii. 598.
— — his wife, Katharine Makgill, vii. 598.
— — Patrick, 3rd laird, iv. 102.
— — William, ancestor of the family of, iv. 101, 258.
— — William, 1st laird, iv. 102.
— — his wife, Christian Barclay, iv. 102.
— — William, 2nd laird, iv. 102 *bis*.
— — William, 4th laird, iv. 102.
— of Graitney, James, colonel of 3rd Foot Guards, vii. 388.
— — his wife, Isabel, baroness Ruthven, vii. 388.
— of Halieland, Alexander, 6th son of 3rd lord Ruthven, iv. 262; ix. 98.
— — his wife, Elizabeth Wemyss, ix. 99.
— of Kettins, William, 3rd son of 1st lord Ruthven, iv. 101, 258.
— of Kirchberg, Patrick, lieut.-general, governor of Ulm, iv. 104.
— of Kirktoun of Mailer, William, vii. 385.
— of Murchall, David, iv. 257; ix. 98.
— of Redcastle, Sir Francis, 1st bart., iv. 103.
— — his wife, Elizabeth Ruthven, iv. 103; vii. 387.
— — William, ancestor of the family of, iv. 258.
— of Ruthven, Alan de, son of Walter, i. 12 *n*.
— — his wife, Eva, dau. of Swan, i. 12.
— — Alan, iv. 255.
— — his wife, Cecilia de Maule, iv. 255; vii. 4.
— — Sir Gilbert, iv. 255.
— — James, vii. 388.
— — his 1st wife, Janet Nisbet, vii. 389.
— — his 2nd wife, Anne Stewart, vii. 389.
— — Sir John, sheriff of Perth, iv. 257.
— — Sir Patrick, sheriff-depute of Perth, iv. 257; vii. 40.
— — his wife, * Cranstoun, ii. 589; iv. 257.

* Name unknown.

Ruthven of Ruthven, Sir Walter, son of Alan, iv. 255, 256; v. 573 *n.*
—— —— his wife, Cecilia of Strathearn, iv. 255; viii. 244.
—— —— Walter, iv. 256.
—— —— Sir William, 2nd son of Sir Walter, i. 12; iv. 255, 256.
—— —— William, iv. 256.
—— —— William, iv. 256.
—— —— his wife, Johanna, iv. 256.
—— —— Sir William, sheriff of St. Johnstoun, iv. 257.
—— —— Sir William, hostage in England, iv. 257.
—— —— Sir William, conservator of the Three Years' Truce, iv. 257; vii. 40.
—— of Scone, John, iv. 267.
—— of Yair, Patrick, governor of Edinburgh Castle, iv. 104.
—— Alexander, captain, 3rd son of Sir Wm. R. of Ballindean, iv. 102; ix. 92.
—— Alexander, 3rd son of Sir John R. of Dunglass, iv. 103.
—— Alexander, 3rd son of Alex. R. of Freeland, iv. 260; ix. 98.
—— —— his wife, Agnes Adamson, ix. 98.
—— Alexander, master of Gowrie, iv. 264, 267; v. 85.
—— Annas, dau. of Alex. R. of Freeland, ix. 98.
—— Anne, wife of 11th lord Elphinstone, iii. 550; vii. 389.
—— Anne, wife of (1) Sir Wm. Cunynghame, and (2) Wm. Cunningham, vii. 387.
—— Anne, wife of (1) Henry Rollo, and (2) F. Bruce, vii. 205, 388.
—— Barbara, wife of Sir H. Paterson of Bannockburn, iv. 103.
—— Barbara, wife of Henry Rattray of Kincarrochy, iv. 260; ix. 98.
—— Barbara, wife of 5th lord Gray, iv. 261, 284.
—— Barbara, dau. of 1st earl of Gowrie, iv. 266.
—— Beatrix, wife of Sir John Home of Cowdenknowes, iv. 266, 475.
—— Beatrix, dau. of Alex. R. of Freeland, ix. 98.
—— Cecilia, wife of Sir D. Wemyss of Wemyss, iv. 260; viii. 493.
—— Cecilia, wife of Francis Bruce, iv. 262.
—— Charlotte Rebecca, vii. 390.
—— Christiana, wife of (1) Sir Thos. Ker, and (2) Sir Thos. Ogilvy, i. 124; iv. 106.
—— Christian, dau. of Wm. R. of Ballindean, iv. 101.
—— Christian, wife of Sir James Lundie, iv. 102.
—— Christian, dau. of Sir Wm. R. of Dunglass, iv. 103.
—— Christian, wife of William Lundin of that Ilk, iv. 261.
Ruthven, Christian, dau. of Sir John R. of Dunglass, ix. 92.
—— Clara, wife of (1) Andrew Dick, and (2) * Murray of Spot, iv. 94.
—— David, Bengal Civil Establishment. vii. 390.
—— Dorothea, wife of John Wemyss of Pittencrieff, iv. 266, 465; ix. 99.
—— Dorothy, wife of Jas. Ruthven in Feu, ix. 98.
—— Edward, 3rd son of James (Baillie), 2nd lord Forrester of Corstorphine, iv. 93.
—— —— his wife, Martha Temple, iv. 94.
—— Elizabeth, wife of (1) Sir Dugal Stewart of Bute, and (2) Robert M'Neill of Illandrow, ii. 297; ix. 50.
—— Elizabeth, wife of (1) William, 5th earl of Erroll, and (2) Ninian, 2nd lord Ross of Halkhead, iii. 568; iv. 259; vii. 252.
—— Elizabeth, dau. of Wm. R. of Ballindean, iv. 101.
—— Elizabeth, wife of Sir Francis Ruthven of Redcastle, iv. 103; vii. 387.
—— Elizabeth, wife of David Makgill of Rankeillor, iv. 260; vi. 589.
—— Elizabeth, dau. of Patrick R., iv. 265.
—— Elizabeth, wife of (1) Sir R. Gordon of Lochinvar, and (2) Hugh, 1st lord Campbell of Loudoun, iv. 266; v. 116, 118, 498; ix. 118 *bis*.
—— Elizabeth, dau. of Sir John R. of Dunglass, ix. 92.
—— Elizabeth, dau. of capt. Alex. R., ix. 92.
—— Elizabeth Maria, wife of Sir Robert Laurie of Maxwellton, vii. 389.
—— Elspeth, wife of (1) William Lundie, and (2) George Pringle, iv. 105.
—— George, precentor of Dunkeld, iv. 262.
—— Sir Gilbert de, 1262, vii. 4.
—— Gilbert, 2nd son of Sir William R. of Ruthven, iv. 256.
—— Harry, tutor of Freeland, iv. 260; ix. 98.
—— —— his wife, Bessie Mathow, ix. 98.
—— Helen, dau. of Sir John R. of Dunglass, iv. 103.
—— Henry, 3rd son of 2nd lord Ruthven, iv. 101, 260.
—— Isabel, wife of Sir Jas. Colville of Culross, ii. 553, 556; iv. 262.
—— Isobel, wife of John Murray of Wallaceton and Tibbermuir, iv. 259.
—— Isabel, wife of Reid of Strathardle, iv. 260.
—— Isabel, wife of (1) Sir R. Gordon, and (2) George, 1st lord Loudoun, iv. 266.
—— Isabel, wife of John Macdougall of Macdougall, vii. 389.
—— James, 4th son of Wm. R. of Ballindean and Gardyne, iv. 103.

* Name unknown.

Ruthven, James, illeg. son of 3rd lord Ruthven, iv. 262.
— James, precentor of Dunkeld, iv. 262, 264.
— James, 4th son of Sir John R. of Dunglass, ix. 92.
— James, in Feu, ix. 98.
— — his wife, Dorothy Ruthven, ix. 98.
— Jane, dau. of 6th lord Ruthven of Freeland, vii. 390.
— Janet, wife of Adam Stewart, prior of Charterhouse, i. 25; iv. 101.
— Janet, wife of 2nd lord Forrester of Corstorphine, iv. 93, 106.
— Janet, wife of (1) John Crichton of Strathord, and (2) Laurence Mercer of Meiklour, iv. 261.
— Janet, wife of Wade Toby Caulfield, vii. 389.
— Janet Anne, dau. of 6th lord Ruthven of Freeland, vii. 390.
— Jean, wife of 6th lord Ogilvy of Airlie, i. 122; iv. 266; ix. 8.
— Jean, wife of Laurence Mercer of Clavedge, iv. 260; ix. 98.
— Jean, wife of (1) Henry, 2nd lord Methven, and (2) Andrew, 5th earl of Rothes, iv. 262; vi. 169; vii. 294.
— John, eldest son of Sir John R. of Dunglass, iv. 103.
— John, captain R.N., commander of *Terpsichore*, vii. 389.
— John, son of Alex. R. of Freeland, ix. 98.
— Katharine, wife of Colin Campbell of Glenurchy, ii. 182; iv. 260; ix. 43.
— Katharine, dau. of 1st earl of Gowrie, ix. 99.
— Lilias, wife of David, 2nd lord Drummond, i. 469; iv. 260; vii. 46; ix. 149.
— Lilias, illeg. dau. of general Archibald R. of Forteviot, iv. 262.
— Lilias, dau. of 1st earl of Gowrie, iv. 266, 465; ix. 99.
— Margaret, wife of John Murray of Trewin, i. 457.
— Margaret, contracted to John Oliphant, and wife of (1) Alex. Stewart, earl of Buchan, (2) John Erskine, (3) Jas. Stewart of Ryland, and (4) Wm. Wood of Bonnytoun, ii. 267, 268; iv. 259; vi. 543; ix. 47.
— Margaret, dau. of Wm. R. of Ballindean, iv. 101.
— Margaret, dau. of Wm. R. of Ballindean and Gardyne, iv. 103.
— Margaret, wife of Sir Alexander Seton, iv. 256; viii. 569.
— Margaret, wife of Jas. Johnston of Elphinston, iv. 261.
— Margaret, wife of 4th earl of Montrose, iv. 266; vi. 241; ix. 99.
Ruthven, Margaret, alleged wife of Sir Walter Drummond of Stobhall, vii. 40.
— Margaret, wife of Jas. Henderson, ix. 92.
— Maria, wife of Geo. Hay of Naughton, iv. 260; ix. 98.
— Mariota, wife of (1) *, (2) Sir Patrick Edgar, and (3) Sir William of Home, iv. 255, 443.
— Mary, wife of (1) John Stewart, 5th earl of Atholl, (2) John Stewart, earl of Atholl, lord Innermeath, and (3) James Stewart, i. 446, 447; iv. 266; ix. 28 *bis*, 48.
— Mary, wife of Sir Robert Douglas of Ardit, iv. 103.
— Mary, wife of (1) Sir A. Van Dyck, and (2) Sir Robert Pryse, iv. 265.
— Patricia, dau. of 2nd lord Forrester of Corstorphine, iv. 94.
— Patrick, son of Alexander, lord Ettrick, iv. 105.
— Robert, grandson of 1st earl of Gowrie, iv. 265.
— Sophia, wife of 2nd duke of Lennox, iv. 266; v. 357.
— Stewart James, vii. 389.
— William, 4th son of 2nd lord Ruthven, iv. 101, 260.
— William, 4th son of 1st earl of Gowrie, iv. 264.
— William, 2nd son of 5th lord Ruthven of Freeland, vii. 389.
— Willielma, dau. of 6th lord Ruthven of Freeland, vii. 390.
— Wortley-Montagu, dau. of 5th lord Ruthven of Freeland, vii. 389.
— *, wife of Sir Patrick Edgar, iv. 255.
Rutland, Henry John Brinsley (Manners), 8th duke of, iii. 45.
— — his wife, Marion Margaret Violet Lindsay, iii. 45.
— John (Manners), 1st duke of, iii. 479.
— — his wife, Diana Bruce, iii. 479.
— John (Manners), 2nd duke of, iii. 412; vi. 268.
— John Henry (Manners), 5th duke of, vii. 229.
— John James Robert (Manners), 7th duke of, ii. 248; iii. 45.
Ryan of Derriweit Heights, Charles, ii. 247.
— Ada Mary, wife of admiral C. T. Montagu-Douglas-Scott, ii. 246.
Ryder, Cyril John, capt. King's Royal Rifle Corps, iv. 389.
— — his wife, I. F. U. I. Douglas-Hamilton, iv. 389.
Ryklynton, Alexander de, iii. 90.
Rymer, Nicholas, rector of Newton Kyme, iii. 601.
Rynd of Broxmouth, James, viii. 277.
— — his wife, Margaret Lyon, viii. 277.

* Name unknown.

Rynd of Carse, William, i. 122.
—— Alexander, page to 11th earl of Crawford, iii. 31.
—— Janet, wife of Sir Thos. Home of Langshaw, iv. 451.
—— Robert, ix. 59.
—— —— his wife, Margaret Ker, ii. 543; ix. 59.
Ryther of Ryther, Sir William, iii. 595.
—— Isabella, wife of Sir Guy Fairfax, iii. 595.

Sabine, abbot of Arbroath, ii. 217 *n.*
—— of Quinohall, Joseph, general, ii. 520.
—— *, captain, ii. 520.
—— —— his wife, Elizabeth Malyn, ii. 520.
Sackville, Anne, wife of 4th earl of Home, iv. 479.
—— Sir Edward, iii. 477.
Saddeler, Cyril, vii. 366.
Sadleir of Standon, Sir Ralph, i. 408; vii. 121.
—— —— Ralph, i. 408 *n.*, 410.
—— —— his wife, Anne Coke, i. 408 *n.*
—— —— Sir Thomas, i. 408.
—— —— his 2nd wife, Gertrude Markham, i. 408.
—— of Temple Dinesley, Lee, i. 406.
—— Anne, wife of Edw. Aston, i. 406.
—— Gertrude, wife of 1st lord Aston of Forfar, i. 408.
Sadler of Wester Softlaw, Robert, vi. 473.
St. Albans, Aubrey (de Vere), 6th duke of, iii. 414.
—— —— his 2nd wife, Louisa Grace Manners, iii. 414.
—— Aubrey, 7th duke of, iii. 414.
—— Charles (Beauclerk), 1st duke of, i. 32; vii. 224.
—— William Aubrey (de Vere), 9th duke of, iii. 616.
St. Aubyn, Arthur James Dudley Stuart, ii. 309.
—— —— his wife, Helen Kate Phillippo, ii. 309.
St. Clair of Berriedale and Glenurchy, Campbell, lord, ii. 203.
St. Clair of Berriedale and Glenurchy, John, lord, ii. 203.
—— of Bray, Alexander, vi. 567.
—— of Carfrae, Henry, vii. 577, 579.
—— —— Sir John, vii. 578.
—— —— William, vii. 584.
—— —— his wife, Christian Sinclair, vii. 584.
—— of Cessworth, Sir Walter, vii. 578.
—— —— Sir William, vii. 578.
—— of Dysart, James, general, viii. 588; viii. 358 *bis.*
—— —— James, *né* Paterson, colonel, vii. 587.
—— —— William, vii. 570.
—— of Estertyre, Alexander, vi. 567.

* Name unknown.

St. Clair of Gourton, Sir Henry, vi. 566.
—— of Herdmanston, Allan de, 2nd laird, vii. 577.
—— —— his wife, Matilda of Windsor, vii. 577.
—— —— Andrew, 21st laird, vii. 589.
—— —— his wife, Elizabeth Rutherford, vii. 589.
—— —— Charles, 20th laird, vi. 17, 21; vii. 585, 589.
—— —— his wife, Elizabeth Hume, vi. 17; vii. 589.
—— —— Charles, 22nd laird, lieut.-col., M.P., vii. 589.
—— —— his 1st wife, Mary Agnes Chisholm, vii. 590.
—— —— his 2nd wife, Isabella Mary Chatto, vii. 590.
—— —— Henry de, sheriff of Richard de Moreville; 1st laird, vii. 577.
—— —— Henry, 18th laird, vii. 586.
—— —— his wife, Barbara Cockburn, vii. 586.
—— —— James, general, 19th laird, vii. 588.
—— —— his wife, Janet Dalrymple, vii. 588; viii. 147.
—— —— John, 3rd laird, vii. 577.
—— —— John, 4th laird, vii. 578.
—— —— Sir John, 6th laird, iv. 333; vii. 578.
—— —— his wife, Margaret Sinclair, i. 170; vi. 567; vii. 578; ix. 11.
—— —— Sir John, 7th laird, i. 171; vii. 579.
—— —— his wife, Elizabeth Polwarth of Polwarth, vii. 579.
—— —— Sir John, 9th laird, ii. 399; vii. 579; viii. 574 *n.*
—— —— his wife, Isabel *, vii. 580.
—— —— John, the younger, iii. 280; vi. 1, 12 *n.*; vii. 580.
—— —— his wife, Katharine Home, iv. 448; vii. 580.
—— —— John, 11th laird, vii. 580; ix. 157 *bis.*
—— —— his wife, Marion Cockburn, vii. 581.
—— —— John, 13th laird, vii. 582; ix. 157.
—— —— his wife, Margaret Sinclair, vii. 582; ix. 158 *bis.*
—— —— Sir John, sheriff of Haddington, 15th laird, vii. 584.
—— —— his wife, Mary Richardson, vii. 584.
—— —— Sir John, M.P., 16th laird, vii. 584.
—— —— his wife, Elizabeth Sinclair, vii. 584.
—— —— John, 17th laird, vii. 577, 585.
—— —— his wife, Katharine Sinclair, vii. 577, 585.
—— —— Sir William, 5th laird, iv. 332; vii. 578.
—— —— Sir William, 8th laird, vii. 579; viii. 573.
—— —— his wife, Margaret, vii. 579.
—— —— Sir William, 10th laird, vi. 1; vii. 580; ix. 157.

* Name unknown.

St. Clair of Herdmanston, Sir William, 12th laird, vii. 581.
— — his wife, Beatrix Renton, vii. 581.
— — Sir William, 14th laird, vi. 595; vii. 583; ix. 158.
— — his wife, Sibil Cockburn, vi. 595; vii. 583.
— of Kimmerghame, Sir John, vii. 579.
— — his wife, Elizabeth of Polwarth, vii. 579.
— — Marion *or* Mariota, wife of (1) Geo. Home of Wedderburn, and (2) Geo. Ker of Samuelston, iii. 280; iv. 448; vi. 1, 12; vii. 580; ix. 157.
— — Sir William, vi. 1; vii. 580.
— of Longformacus, Gregory, alleged ancestor of the family of, vi. 565.
— — James, probable ancestor of the family of. vii. 578.
— — Sir John, ii. 355 *n.*
— — his wife, Frances Towers, ii. 355 *n.*
— — Sir Robert, 1st bart., ii. 31; iii. 451; vii. 219; viii. 177.
— — his 2nd wife, Margaret Alexander, viii. 177.
— of Wester Pencaitland, John, vii. 581.
— of Polwarth, Margaret, wife of Patrick Home, iii. 280; iv. 448; vi. 2; vii. 580.
— of Ravenscraig, James, general, vii. 588.
— — William, vii. 570.
— of Roslin, Alexander, vii. 558.
— — his wife, Jean Sempill, vii. 558.
— — Sir Henry, sheriff of Lanark, vi. 565.
— — his wife, Alice de Fenton, vi. 566.
— — James, iv. 131 *n.*
— — James, *né* Paterson, colonel, vii. 587.
— — James, general, M.P., ambassador, vii. 588.
— — his wife, Janet Dalrymple, vii. 588; viii. 147.
— — Sir John, vii. 584.
— — Sir Oliver, 2nd son of William, earl of Orkney and Caithness, ii. 334; iii. 226 *n.*; vii. 570; viii. 535, 578.
— — his wife, Margaret *or* Katharine Borthwick, ii. 107; viii. 431.
— — Sir William, justiciar of Galloway, keeper of Dunbar Castle, vi. 206, 564; viii. 418.
— — his wife, Amicia, vi. 565.
— — Sir William, son of Sir Henry St. C., vi. 566.
— — William, vi. 567; ix. 146.
— — his wife, Isabella of Strathearn, ii. 320; vi. 567.
— — Sir William, ii. 112.
— — Sir William, vii. 198, 584; viii. 178, 549.
— — William, the last laird, vii. 558.
St. Clair, of St. Ella's Lodge, Charles, commander R.N., vii. 590.
— — his 1st wife, Isabella Jane Home, vii. 590.
— — his 2nd wife, Ann Crawfurd Pringle, vii. 590.
— of Skedduay, William, major 1st Royal Scots, vii. 587.
— Ada, wife of Petrus de Haga of Bemersyde, vii. 577.
— Ada Jane, dau. of 16th lord Sinclair, vii. 592.
— Alexander, 2nd son of John S. of Herdmanston, vii. 581.
— Alexander, 4th son of John S. of Herdmanston, vii. 582.
— Alison, dau. of John S. of Herdmanston, vii. 583.
— Andrew, M.D., professor, vii. 585.
— — his wife, Elizabeth Drummond, vii. 585.
— Ann, dau. of 10th lord Sinclair, vii. 588.
— Annabel, wife of (1) Sir Robert Bisset, and (2) Sir David Wemyss, vi. 565.
— Archibald, commr. R.N., vii. 591.
— Archibald James Murray, master of Sinclair, vii. 591.
— — his wife, Violet Frances Murray-Kennedy, vii. 591.
— Barbara, dau. of George S., vii. 585.
— Beatrix, dau. of John S. of Herdmanston, vii. 583.
— Charles Henry Murray, capt. Seaforth Highlanders, vii. 592.
— Christian, dau. of William S. of Carfrae, vii. 584.
— David, 4th son of 10th lord Sinclair, vii. 587.
— Eleanor, dau. of Andrew S. of Herdmanston, vii. 589.
— Eleanor, dau. of 14th lord Sinclair, vii. 599.
— Elizabeth, dau. of Sir Wm. S. of Herdmanston, vii. 582.
— Elizabeth, dau. of Sir William S. of Herdmanston, vii. 584.
— Elizabeth, dau. of William S. of Carfrae, vii. 584.
— Elizabeth, dau. of Sir John S. of Herdmanston, vii. 584.
— Elizabeth, wife of 3rd earl of Wemyss, vii. 588; viii. 507.
— Elizabeth, wife of lt.-col. James Dalrymple, vii. 589; viii. 145.
— Euphame, dau. of Sir William S. of Herdmanston, vii. 584.
— George, eldest son of Oliver S. of Roslin, vii. 333.
— — his wife, Agnes Crichton, iii. 226 *n.*; vii. 333.
— George, 2nd son of Sir William S. of Herdmanston, vii. 583.

St. Clair, George, vii. 585.
—— —— his wife, Isabella Durham, vii. 585.
—— Georgina Violet, wife of major H. M. Davson, vii. 592.
—— Grizel, wife of John Paterson of Prestonhall, vii. 587.
—— Helen, wife of Sir John Rollo, vii. 198.
—— Henry, 5th son of 10th lord Sinclair, vii. 587.
—— Isobel, dau. of George S., vii. 585.
—— James, 3rd son of John S. of Herdmanston, vii. 581.
—— James, in Hiemurcroce, vii. 581.
—— James, 2nd son of Sir John S. of Herdmanston, vii. 584.
—— James Chisholme, Madras Civil Service, vii. 591.
—— Jane, dau. of John S. of Herdmanston, vii. 583.
—— Jane Elizabeth, wife of canon W. L. Feilden, vii. 590.
—— Jean, dau. of Sir William S. of Herdmanston, vii. 584.
—— Jean, dau. of Robert S., vii. 584.
—— Jean, wife of Sir John Forrester of Corstorphine, iv. 84; vi. 570.
—— Sir John, Minorca, vi. 502.
—— John, 2nd son of Sir Henry S. of Roslin, vi. 566.
—— John, son of Sir William S. of Roslin, vi. 567.
—— John, legtd. son of John S. of Herdmanston, vii. 581.
—— John, 2nd son of Sir William S. of Herdmanston, vii. 582.
—— John, M.D., Haddington, vii. 585.
—— John, 2nd son of John S. of Herdmanston, vii. 585.
—— John, 5th son of 14th lord Sinclair, vii. 590.
—— Katharine, wife of Sir John Erskine of Alva, vii. 587.
—— Lockhart Matthew, C.I.E., vii. 591.
—— —— his wife, Ellen Mary Margaret Rice, vii. 591.
—— Margaret, wife of (1) Thomas, 2nd earl of Angus, and (2) Sir John St. Clair of Herdmanston, i. 170; vi. 567; vii. 578; ix. 11.
—— Margaret, dau. of Sir William S. of Herdmanston, vii. 582.
—— Margaret, dau. of John S. of Herdmanston, vii. 583.
—— Margaret, dau. of Sir William S. of Herdmanston, vii. 584.
—— Margaret, dau. of Sir John S. of Herdmanston, vii. 584.
—— Margaret, wife of Sir William Baird, vii. 588.
—— Margaret Helen, wife of A. C. Fraser, vii. 592.
St. Clair, Marion, dau. of Sir John S. of Herdmanston, vii. 584.
—— Mary, wife of David M'Gill of Cranston Riddell, vi. 595; vii. 583.
—— Mary, wife of George Wilson, vii. 586.
—— Mary Agnes, dau. of 15th lord Sinclair, vii. 591.
—— Matthew, 6th son of 10th lord Sinclair, vii. 587.
—— Matthew, vi. 21; vii. 585.
—— —— his 1st wife, Margaret Home, ix. 158.
—— —— his 2nd wife, Margaret Carre of Nisbet, v. 53; vii. 585.
—— Matthew, lieut. 84th regiment, vii. 590.
—— Matthew, commander R.N., vii. 589.
—— Oliver, 3rd son of John S. of Herdmanston, vii. 582.
—— Patrick, brother of John S. of Herdmanston, ix. 157.
—— Robert de, vi. 564.
—— —— his wife, Eleanor de Dreux, vi. 564.
—— Robert, 3rd son of Sir John S. of Herdmanston, vii. 584.
—— —— his wife, Helen Rae, vii. 584.
—— Robert, governor of Tilbury, vii. 585.
—— Sibyl, dau. of Sir William S. of Herdmanston, vii. 584.
—— Susan, wife of F. D. Massy-Dawson, vii. 590.
—— Thomas, bailie of Orkney, vi. 567.
—— Thomas, 5th son of Sir John S. of Herdmanston, vii. 585.
—— William, bishop of Dunkeld, vi. 565; ix. 146.
—— William, 3rd son of Sir William S. of Herdmanston, vii. 583.
—— William, brother of John S. of Herdmanston, ix. 157.
—— *, wife of William Mollison, vii. 585.
—— *, two daus. of John S. of Herdmanston, ix. 157.
St. Clair-Erskine, Millicent Fanny, wife of 4th duke of Sutherland, iii. 85; viii. 364.
St. Clair, *see also* Sinclair.
St. Colme, Stewart, lord, vii. 394-395.
St. Colme, Henry, first lord, iii. 189; vi. 319; vii. 394; ix. 155.
—— —— his wife, Jean Stewart, i. 446; vii. 395.
—— James, second lord, vi. 320; vii. 395; ix. 155.
Ste. Hermione, Magdalene Silvie de, wife of col. Andrew Drummond, vi. 69.
Sainthill, Margaret, wife of Sir Hew Dalrymple, ii. 31; viii. 126.
—— Peter, surgeon, Garlickhill, ii. 31; viii. 126.
St. Hypolite, David Montolieu, baron de, iii. 512.
—— Lewis Charles Montolieu, baron de, iii. 520.

* Name unknown.

St. John, Frederick, colonel, v. 483.
—— —— his wife, Mary Ker, v. 483.
—— John de, ii. 505; iv. 12.
St. John-Mildmay of Moulsham, Sir Henry Carew, 4th bart., vii. 226.
—— —— his 1st wife, Charlotte Bouverie, vii. 226.
—— —— his 2nd wife, Harriet Bouverie, vii. 226.
St. Liz, Simon de, i. 3.
—— —— his wife, Matilda of Huntingdon, i. 3.
St. Quintin of Harpham, Sir William, iii. 454.
—— of Scampston Hall, lieut.-col. 17th Lancers, vii. 490.
—— Geoffrey, vii. 490.
—— —— his wife, Muriel Frances Charlotte Ogilvie-Grant, vii. 490.
—— Katharine, wife of (1) Michael Wentworth, (2) Sir John Kaye, (3) Henry Sandys, and (4) Alexander, 8th earl of Eglinton, iii. 454.
St. Vincent, John (Jervis), 1st viscount of, vi. 505 *n*.
Sale, Eleanor, wife of James, 3rd lord Dunkeld, iii. 381.
Salisbury, James (Cecil), 2nd marquess of, iv. 172.
—— James (Cecil), 4th earl of, iii. 129, 131.
—— Robert (Cecil), first earl of, iii. 475; viii. 411.
—— William (Cecil), 2nd earl of, i. 350; iii. 130; v. 228.
—— Hester Lynch, wife of (1) Henry Thrale, and (2) Gabriel Piozzi, iii. 549.
—— John, iii. 548.
Salkeld, Thomas, ii. 232.
Sallarie, Thomas de, Perth, viii. 267.
SALLWAY, DOUGLAS, EARL OF, vii. 143-144.
Sallway, Charles, earl of, vii. 143.
Salmon, Anna, wife of (1) R. Bourne, and (2) Thos. Richardson, ii. 582.
—— *, M.D., London, ii. 583.
Salting, Katharine Augusta Millicent, wife of George, lord Binning, iv. 328.
—— William Severin, iv. 328.
Saltonstall, Anne, wife of James, 2nd lord Torthorwald, ii. 394.
SALTOUN OF ABERNETHY, ABERNETHY, LORD, vii. 396-416.
Salteun of Abernethy, Alexander, fourth lord, vii. 409.
—— —— his wife, * Stewart, vii. 409.
—— Alexander, sixth lord, iv. 124, 125; vii. 411.
—— —— his 1st wife, Alison Keith, vi. 50; vii. 411.
—— —— his 2nd wife, Jean Johnstone, vii. 412.
—— Alexander, ninth lord, vii. 414, 442.

* Name unknown.

Saltoun, George, seventh lord, vii. 413.
—— —— his wife, Margaret Stewart, i. 445; vii. 413.
—— James, third lord, vii. 408.
—— John, eighth lord, ii. 85: vii. 413, 415; ix. 155.
—— —— his 1st wife, Magdalen Urquhart, vii. 414.
—— —— his 2nd wife, Elizabeth Stewart, vi. 318; vii. 414.
—— —— his 3rd wife, Anna Stewart, ii. 85; vii. 414.
—— Laurence, first lord, vii. 407.
—— —— his wife, Margaret *, vii. 407.
—— William, second lord, vii. 326, 408.
—— —— his 2nd wife, Isabella Borthwick vii. 408.
—— William, fifth lord, iii. 567; iv. 124; vii. 410.
—— —— his wife, Elizabeth Hay, iii. 567; vii. 411; viii. 434; ix. 86.
SALTOUN, FRASER, LORD, vii. 417-453.
Saltoun, Alexander, tenth lord, iv. 114; vii. 415, 441.
—— —— his 1st wife, * Forbes, vii. 443.
—— —— his 2nd wife, Elizabeth Seton, vii. 413, 443.
—— Alexander, twelfth lord, vii. 445.
—— —— his wife, Mary Gordon, i. 89; vii. 446.
—— Alexander, thirteenth lord, vii. 446.
—— Alexander, fifteenth lord, vii. 447.
—— —— his wife, Margery Fraser of Ness Castle, vii. 448.
—— Alexander, seventeenth lord, vii. 451.
—— —— his wife, Charlotte Evans, vii. 452.
—— Alexander George, sixteenth lord, vii. 433, 448.
—— —— his wife, Katharine Thurlow, vii. 449, 450.
—— Alexander William Frederick, eighteenth lord, vii. 452.
—— —— his wife, Mary Helena Bellew, vii. 453.
—— George, fourteenth lord, vii. 446.
—— —— his wife, Eleanor Gordon, vii. 447.
—— William, eleventh lord, vii. 444.
—— —— his wife, Margaret Sharpe, vii. 444.
—— master of, Alexander, son of 10th lord Saltoun, vii. 443.
—— —— his 1st wife, Ann Ker, v. 474; vii. 443.
—— —— his 2nd wife, Marion Cunningham, iv. 29, 247; vii. 444; ix. 97.
—— —— his 3rd wife, Sophia Erskine, v. 6; vii. 444.
—— master of, Alexander, eldest son of 12th lord Saltoun, vii. 446.
—— master of, Alexander Arthur, vii. 453
—— master of, William, 2nd son of Alexander, master of Saltoun, vii. 444.

* Name unknown.

Sampson, Thomas, lieut. 59th regiment, viii. 122.
—— —— his wife, Martha Hamilton-Dalrymple, viii. 122.
Samuel of Stobo, vii. 420.
Samuel, baron de, vi. 583.
—— —— his wife, Amelia, vi. 583.
Samuolston of Cousland, Samuelston and Stevenston, John, v. 489.
SANCHAR, DOUGLAS, EARL OF, vii. 138-156.
Sanchar, William, first earl of, vii. 138.
Sandbach of Broadway, John, i. 406.
—— —— his wife, Elizabeth Aston, i. 406.
Sandfoord, Dorothy, wife of (1) C. Crackenthorp, and (2) Arthur Balfour, i. 545.
Sandford of Birchington, Henry, ii. 582.
—— of Sandford, Thomas Hugh, iii. 43.
—— —— his wife, Alexina Lindsay, iii. 43.
—— Elizabeth, wife of Sir R. Gurney, ii. 582.
SANDILANDS, LORD ABERCROMBIE, i. 75-81.
SANDILANDS, LORD TORPHICHEN, viii. 378-398.
Sandilands of Abercrombie, Sir James, i. 79.
—— —— his 1st wife, Jean Lichtoun, i. 79.
—— —— his 2nd wife, Christian Fletcher, i. 80.
—— of Addiewell, Walter, viii. 396.
—— of Airth, Sir James, viii. 381.
—— of Braidshaw, John, ix. 4.
—— —— Thomas, ix. 4.
—— —— Walter, advocate, viii. 396.
—— of Brokland, James, i. 76.
—— of Calder, Sir James, viii. 378; ix. 163.
—— —— his wife, Eleanor Douglas, iii. 142; viii. 379.
—— —— Sir James, i. 173; iv. 563; viii. 380.
—— —— his wife, Joanna Stewart, i. 16; viii. 268, 381.
—— —— Sir James, iv. 564; viii. 381.
—— —— his wife, Jonet, viii. 382.
—— —— Sir James, i. 75; iii. 567; iv. 574, 575; viii. 383.
—— —— his 1st wife, Margaret Kinloch, viii. 382, 383.
—— —— his 2nd wife, Margaret Ker, i. 75; vii. 326; viii. 383.
—— —— Sir James, iv. 87; viii. 385.
—— —— his wife, Marion *or* Marjorie Forrester, iv. 87; viii. 385.
—— —— Sir James, viii. 388, 389.
—— —— his wife, Jean Ross, vii. 254; viii. 389.
—— —— Sir John, iv. 573; viii. 382.
—— —— his wife, Christian Dundas, viii. 383.
—— —— his alleged wife,* Somerville, viii. 6.
—— —— John, viii. 385.
—— —— his wife, Elizabeth Scrymgeour, iii. 307; viii. 385.

* Name unknown.

Sandilands of Calder, John, viii. 386, 387.
—— —— his 1st wife, Margaret Bartoun, viii. 388.
—— —— his 2nd wife, Janet Fleming, v. 436; viii. 388, 540.
—— of Camilty, James, viii. 390.
—— of Collessie, James, i. 76.
—— of Coustoun, Walter, viii. 392.
—— —— Walter, advocate, viii. 396.
—— —— his wife, Elizabeth Sandilands, viii. 396.
—— —— William, viii. 392.
—— —— his wife, Mary Easton, viii. 392.
—— —— William, viii. 392.
—— of Cremanan, Sir James, viii. 97.
—— of Cruvie, James, 2nd son of Sir James S. of Calder, i. 75; viii. 383, 384, 385.
—— —— his wife, Katharine Scot, i. 75.
—— —— James, 2nd laird, i. 76; iv. 33 *bis*.
—— —— his 1st wife, Elizabeth Meldrum, i. 76.
—— —— his 2nd wife, Janet Gray, i. 76; iv. 33; ix. 4.
—— —— his 3rd wife, Elizabeth Ramsay, i. 76.
—— —— James the younger, i. 76, 77; ix. 86.
—— —— his 1st wife, Elizabeth Betoun, i. 77.
—— —— his 2nd wife, Isabel Strang, i. 77.
—— —— William, i. 77.
—— —— his wife, Jean Bothwell, i. 78; ix. 4.
—— of Dalzell, Sir James, ii. 398; viii. 380.
—— of Erthbisset, Sir James, viii. 382.
—— of Ferniflat, Sir James, i. 79.
—— of Little Galway, Sir James, iv. 563.
—— of Gartcarron, John, viii. 384.
—— —— Peter, rector of Calder, viii. 384.
—— of Little Harwode, James, viii. 383.
—— of Hilderstoun, Walter, viii. 391.
—— —— William, tutor of Torphichen, viii. 391, 393.
—— —— his 1st wife, Grizel Bannatyne, viii. 391.
—— —— his 2nd wife, Elizabeth *, viii. 391.
—— of Kinghorn, Sir James, viii. 381.
—— —— William, i. 78.
—— of Kinloch, Sir James, viii. 75.
—— —— James, viii. 75.
—— of Largie, Sir James, i. 79.
—— of Methil, James, viii. 383.
—— —— his wife, Margaret Kinloch, viii. 383.
—— of Muirhousedykes, Walter, viii. 396.
—— of Petlair, James, i. 76; viii. 383.
—— —— William, i. 77.
—— of North Pittedle, John, ix. 4.
—— —— Peter, i. 76; ix. 4, 86.
—— —— his wife, Isobel Cuninghame, ix. 4.
—— of Rashiehill, John, ix. 4.

* Name unknown.

Sandilands of Rashiehill, John, ix. 4.
— of St. Monans, James, iv. 33, 279; viii. 384.
— — his wife, Janet Gray, iv. 33, 279.
— — Sir James, the younger, i. 78; ix. 4.
— — his wife, Agnes Carnegie, i. 78; viii. 67.
— — William, i. 78; iv. 431, 435.
— — his wife, Jean Bothwell, i. 78; iv. 431.
— of Sandilands, Sir James, viii. 378.
— — his wife, Eleanor Douglas, iii. 142; viii. 379.
— — Sir John, viii. 382.
— — his wife, Christian Dundas, viii. 383.
— of Scheillis, William, i. 78.
— of Slamannan, Sir James, constable of Blackness Castle, v. 444; vi. 236; viii. 388, 390.
— — his 1st wife, Jean Craufurd, viii. 389.
— — his 2nd wife, Barbara Napier, viii. 389.
— — Sir James, son of the Constable, viii. 389.
— of Southbello, John, viii. 385.
— of Torphin, James, viii. 383.
— of Weddersbie, James, i. 76.
— of Wiston, Sir James, viii. 378.
— Agnes, wife of James Drummond, viii. 386.
— Alexander, M.D., viii. 396.
— Alexander, Scots Greys, viii. 396.
— Alison, wife of Sir Alex. Boswell of Balmuto, viii. 385.
— Alison, wife of John Cockburn of Ormiston, viii. 386.
— Alison Margaret, viii. 398.
— Andrew, tutor of Torphichen, i. 77.
— — his wife, Euphemia Kinninmond, i. 77.
— Mr. Andrew, 3rd son of William S. of Cruvie, i. 78; ix. 4.
— Andrew, major, viii. 395.
— Anna, dau. of 1st lord Abercrombie, i. 81.
— Anna, dau. of Wm. S. of Hilderstoun, viii. 391.
— Anna, dau. of 4th lord Torphichen, viii. 392.
— Anna, dau. of Sir James S. of Slamannan, ix. 163.
— Anne, wife of Robert Menzies, viii. 177, 391.
— Barbara, wife of John Forbes of Rires, i. 176.
— Barbara, wife of (1) Thos. Dischington, and (2) Mr. John Rutherfurd, vii. 372.
— Charles, lieut. R.N., viii. 395.
— Christian, dau. of James S., i. 77.
— Christian, wife of Adam Bothwell of Pitcaly, i. 78.
Sandilands, Christian, wife of (1) D. Hepburn of Waughton, and (2) Andrew Anstruther of that Ilk, viii. 384.
— Christian, wife of R. Pringle, viii. 394.
— Christian, dau. of 7th lord Torphichen, viii. 395.
— David, 6th son of James S. of Cruvie, i. 77.
— David, 2nd son of Sir James S., i. 78.
— Douglas, 43rd regt., viii. 397.
— Elizabeth, wife of (1) David Forrester of Garden, and (2) John Shaw of Broich, i. 75; ix. 4.
— Elizabeth, dau. of James S., i. 77.
— Elizabeth, dau. of Wm. S. of Cruvie, i. 76.
— Elizabeth, wife of John Gibbeson, viii. 389; ix. 163.
— Elizabeth, wife of John Mowbray, viii. 389.
— Elizabeth, dau. of Wm. S. of Hilderstoun, viii. 391.
— Elizabeth, wife of 8th lord Torphichen viii. 396.
— Elizabeth, wife of P. Wemyss of Rumgay and Craighall, viii. 497.
— Eupham, dau. of John S. of Calder, viii. 388.
— Francis Robert, commander R.N., viii. 397.
— — his wife, Maud Bayard Wiggins, viii. 397.
— Frederick, viii. 389.
— George, 3rd son of Sir James S., i. 78.
— Grisel, wife of John Strang of Balcaskie, i. 77; ix. 4.
— Grizel, dau. of capt. Robert S., viii. 395.
— Grizel, dau. of 7th lord Torphichen, viii. 395.
— Helen, wife of Geo. Towers of Inverleith, i. 76.
— Helen Caroline, viii. 397.
— Helen Jane, wife of Charles Woodbine Parish, viii. 397.
— Henry, 5th son of 2nd lord Torphichen viii. 391.
— Hugh, 78th regt., viii. 396.
— Isobel, dau. of Wm. S. of Hilderstoun, viii. 391.
— Isabel, wife of Hugh Wallace of Elderslie, viii. 391.
— Isabel, wife of Sir Thos. Kirkpatrick of Closeburn, viii. 392.
— Isobel, wife of John Boswell of Balmuto, ix. 4.
— Sir James, eldest son of William S. of Cruvie, i. 78.
— — his wife, Agnes Carnegie, i. 78; viii. 67.
— James, assassinated near Dumbarton, viii. 382.

Sandilands, James, preceptor of Torphichen, viii. 386.
—— —— his wife, Janet Murray, vii. 387.
—— James, 3rd son of Wm. S. of Hilderstoun, viii. 391.
—— James, eldest son of 7th lord Torphichen, viii. 391.
—— James, captain 8th Hussars, viii. 397.
—— James, son of James S. and Eliz. Betoun, ix. 4.
—— James Bruce, viii. 397.
—— Janet, wife of Jas. Learmonth of Dairsie, i. 77.
—— Janet, dau. of 4th lord Torphichen, viii. 393.
—— Jean, dau. of William S. of Cruvie, i. 78; ix. 4.
—— John, parson of Hawick, i. 75.
—— —— his wife, Janet Craig, i. 75.
—— John, 3rd son of James S. of Cruvie, i. 77.
—— —— his wife, Elizabeth Ogilvy, i. 77; iv. 33.
—— John, 4th son of Wm. S. of Cruvie, i. 78.
—— John, i. 303.
—— —— his wife, Helen Arbuthnott, i. 303.
—— John, assassinated by P. Thornton, viii. 383.
—— John, 2nd son of Sir James S. of Slamannan, vii. 389.
—— John, rector of Coston, viii. 397.
—— —— his wife, Helen Hope, viii. 397.
—— John Hope, viii. 397.
—— —— his wife, Helen Mary Anne Tourle, viii. 397.
—— Katharine, wife of Adam Bothwell, i. 78; iv. 435; ix. 4.
—— Katharine, wife of Sir Robert Dalzell of Glenae, i. 79; ii. 409; ix. 5, 53.
—— Katharine, wife of D. Drummond of Cultmalindie, viii. 177, 394.
—— Katharine, dau. of 4th lord Torphichen, viii. 392.
—— Lilias, dau. of 6th lord Torphichen, viii. 394.
—— Magdalen, dau. of 6th lord Torphichen, viii. 395.
—— Margaret, dau. of John S., parson of Hawick, i. 75.
—— Margaret, dau. of James S., i. 77.
—— Margaret, wife of Sir Jas. Learmonth of Balcomie, i. 78.
—— Margaret, dau. of Sir James S., i. 79.
—— Margaret, wife of (1) Robt. Bruce of Auchinbowie, and (2) Laurence, 3rd lord Oliphant, vi. 544; vii. 544; viii. 384.
—— Margaret, wife of (1) Sir Jas. Dundas of Dundas, and (2) Wm. Wauchope of Niddrie, viii. 386.
—— Margaret, wife of H. Drummond of Riccartoun, viii. 388.
Sandilands, Margaret, dau. of Wm. S. of Hilderstoun, viii. 391.
—— Margaret, wife of Thos. Marjoribanks, viii. 393.
—— Marjory, lady St. Monans, wife of John Ramsay of Brackmonth, i. 77.
—— Marjory, dau. of Sir James S., i. 79.
—— Marjorie, wife of Adam Gordon, and mistress of Robert Stewart of Strathdown, vi. 575.
—— Mary, dau. of Wm. S. of Cruvie, i. 78.
—— Mary, wife of Joseph Douglas, viii. 389.
—— Mary, dau. of Wm. S. of Hilderstoun, viii. 391.
—— Mary, wife of Wm. Ramsay-Ramsay of Barnton, viii. 397.
—— Patrick, viii. 380.
—— —— his wife, Isabella *, viii. 380.
—— Patrick, commander H.E.I.C.S. Navy, viii. 395.
—— Peter, rector of Calder, viii. 384 *bis*.
—— Robert, 4th son of 2nd lord Torphichen, viii. 391.
—— Robert, captain, viii. 395.
—— —— his wife, Grizel Kirkpatrick, viii. 395.
—— Susanna, dau. of Wm. S. of Hilderstoun, viii. 391.
—— Susanna, dau. of capt. Robert S., viii. 395.
—— Thomas, tutor of St. Monans, i. 76.
—— Walter, 3rd son of 6th lord Torphichen, viii. 394.
—— Walter Alexander, viii. 398.
—— Wilhelmina Caroline, viii. 395.
—— William, 2nd son of Sir Wm. S., i. 78; ix. 4.
—— —— his wife, Katharine Cranstoun, ix. 4.
—— William, their son, ix. 4.
—— William, 2nd son of Wm. S. of Hilderstoun, viii. 391.
—— *, wife of George de Dalzell, ii. 398.
—— *, 1st wife of William Dishington of Ardross, viii. 384.
—— *, wife of Jas. Carstairs, ix. 4.
Sands, Warren Hastings, W.S., v. 416.
—— —— his wife, Harriet Lindsay, v. 416.
—— *, Buckinghamshire, ix. 71.
—— —— his wife, Anne Farmer, ix. 71.
Sandys of Doune Court, Henry, iii. 454.
—— —— his wife, Katharine St. Quintin, iii. 454.
—— of Graithwaite Hall, Myles, viii. 121.
—— —— his wife, Elizabeth Hamilton-Dalrymple, viii. 121.
—— of Miserden, Sir Miles, ii. 581.
—— —— his wife, Mary Hanbury, ii. 581.
—— of Roscommon, Robert, col., i. 401.
—— Edwyn, archbishop of York, iii. 295.
—— Margaret, wife of Thos. Aston, i. 401.

* Name unknown.

Sandys, Margaret, wife of Wm. Primrose, vii. 212.
Sanford of Minehead, John, vi. 445.
—— —— his wife, Jane Leslie, vi. 445.
Sankey, Francis F., M.D., iv. 213.
—— Frances Sydney, wife of capt. Robert Boyle, iv. 213; ix. 96.
SANQUHAR, CRICHTON, LORD CRICHTON OF, iii. 219-238.
Sanquhar, Robert, first lord Crichton of, iii. 222; v. 432; vi. 5.
—— Robert, second lord Crichton of, iii. 224; iv. 403, 405.
—— Robert, third lord Crichton of, i. 222; iii. 225; vii. 119.
—— Robert, fourth lord Crichton of, iii. 226.
—— Robert, sixth lord Crichton of, iii. 227, 229.
—— Robert, eighth lord Criehton of, iii. 230; vii. 130.
—— Robert, styled lord Crichton of, iii. 235.
—— William, fifth lord Crichton of, ii. 514; iii. 225, 226; vii. 539, 546; viii. 541.
—— William, self-styled lord Crichton of, iii. 232.
—— William, ninth lord Crichton of, ii. 393; iii. 128, 227, 232; v. 222; vii. 133.
—— William, tenth lord Crichton of, iii. 235.
—— William, eleventh lord Crichton of, iii. 236.
Sanseverino, Carlo, lt.-col., vi. 455.
—— —— his wife, Anne Clifford, vi. 455.
Sanshult of Doderhalts, James King, baron, iii. 593.
Santa Croce di Villa Hermosa, Charles, marquis, vi. 458.
—— —— his wife, Nicoletta Bandini, vi. 458.
Sapientia, wife of William of Carlyle, the younger, ii. 377.
Sardinia, Victor Amadeus, king of, i. 29.
—— —— his wife, Anne Mary of Orleans, i. 29.
Sarsfield of Lucan, William, i. 30.
—— —— his wife, Mary Walters, i. 31.
Sartoris of Hoppsford Hall, Jules Alexandre, captain, ii. 280.
—— Rosalie Louisa, wife of Shipley Gordon Stuart, 14th earl of Buchan, ii. 280.
Saunders of the Downes, Andrew, iv. 571.
—— Eva Maria, wife of lieut.-col. G. L. Carmichael, iv. 571.
—— William, iii. 604.
Sausse, Sir Matthew, chief-justice of Bombay, v. 547.
—— —— his wife, Charlotte Henrietta Fraser, v. 547.
Savage of Ardken, Henry, iii. 342.
—— Anne, wife of 2nd earl of Cardigan, iii. 299.
—— Joan, wife of col. Hugh Cochrane of Ferguslie, iii. 342.
Savage, Katharine, wife of Sir C. Sedley of Southfleet, vii. 93.
Savile of Copley, Sir John, i. 412.
—— Anne, wife of Charles, 4th earl of Elgin, iii. 482.
—— Sir Henry, governor of Pontefract Castle, iv. 153.
—— Sir Henry, provost of Eton, vi. 451 *n.*, 452 *n.*
—— —— his wife [Margaret Dacres], vi. 451 *n.*
—— Mary Elizabeth, wife of lord Thomas Howard, i. 412.
—— Sarah Elizabeth, V.A., wife of Sir Jas. Lindsay, K.C.M.G., iii. 44.
Savoy, Louis, duke of, 1447, i. 19.
—— Victor Amadeus II., duke of, i. 29.
—— —— his wife, Anne Mary of Orleans, i. 29.
Sawyer, Anthony, paymaster of the forces in Scotland, vii. 362.
—— —— his wife, Anne, countess of Ruglen, vii. 362.
—— Herbert, admiral R.N., iv. 496.
—— Susan Anne, wife of Charles Hope, R.N., iv. 496.
Saxe-Weimar, prince Edward of; field-marshal, v. 368.
—— —— his wife, Augusta Katharine Gordon-Lennox, v. 368.
Say of Saytun, viii. 559.
—— William de, i. 5.
—— —— his wife, Aufrica, i. 5.
Saye and Sele, John (Twisleton-Wykeham-Fiennes), 14th lord, v. 237.
—— —— his wife, Augusta Sophia Hay, v. 237.
Sayer, Frederick, captain, v. 236.
—— Harriet Lepel Dorothea, wife of H. C. F. Hay, v. 236.
Scarborough, Richard George (Lumley-Saunderson), 9th earl of, iii. 587.
—— Thomas (Lumley-Saunderson), 3rd earl of, vi. 580.
—— —— his wife, Frances Hamilton, vi. 580.
—— Anne, wife of Henry, 7th viscount Irvine, v. 17.
—— Charles, Windsor, v. 15, 17.
—— Elizabeth, wife of (1) F. Brace, and (2) Charles Ingram, v. 15, 17.
Scargehill, Warene de, vii. 578.
Scarlate of Greneland and Wester Clith, William, ii. 338.
Scarlet of Longforgan, Thomas, viii. 264.
Scarsdale, Francis, (Leeke), 1st earl of, iii. 614.
—— Nathaniel (Curzon), 1st lord, vii. 94.
—— —— his wife, Caroline Colyear, vii. 94.
Schankis of Stair, Reginald de, iii. 427.
—— —— his wife, Mariota of Stair, iii. 426.
—— *, wife of * Kennedy, iii. 427.

* Name unknown.

Schaw of Auchingouny, Sir James, iv. 337.
— of Dryfholme, John de, iii. 62.
— of Greenock, John, ii. 86.
— — his wife, Helen Houston, ii. 86.
— — Sir John, ii. 519; viii. 142.
— — his wife, Margaret Dalrymple, viii. 142.
— of Henristoune, John de, iii. 62.
— of Knockhill, William, vi. 150.
— — his wife, Marion Graham, vi. 150.
— of Sauchie [Sir Alexander], i. 24.
— — James, comptroller, vi. 223.
— — Sir James, captain of Stirling Castle, iv. 336, 337.
— — Sir James, v. 434; vi. 4.
— — his wife, Alison Hume, vi. 4.
— — Sir James, iii. 33; viii. 171.
— of Sauchieburn, Sir James, iv. 336.
— of Sornbeg, John, iv. 92.
— — his wife, Margaret Forrester, iv. 92.
— Helen, wife of (1) Robert Moubray, and (2) 1st lord Colville of Culross, ii. 557.
— Helen, wife of (1) Archibald Halyburton, (2) Patrick Hume of Polwarth, (3) Sir Patrick Houston, and (4) Sir Robert Hamilton of Fingaltoun, iv. 336; vi. 3.
— Isobel, wife of Alexander Hamilton of Innerwick, iv. 305.
— Isobel, wife of (1) John Buchanan of Arnprior, and (2) Thomas Graham of Boquhapple, vi. 150.
— Marion, wife of 8th lord Cathcart, ii. 519; ix. 58.
Scheppers, Alberic Joseph, iii. 416.
— Katharine, wife of A. C. Tollemache, iii. 416.
Schereinwood of Lenturk, John, v. 429.
Schevez, William, primate of Scotland, i. 441; v. 394.
Schivas of Schivas, *, wife of Robert Maitland, v. 283.
Schomberg, Frederick Herman, 1st duke of, iv. 287; v. 481.
Schubert of Viol, Carl von, i. 525.
— — his wife, Rhoda Lindsay, i. 525.
Schuster of the Grange, Samuel Leo, vi. 582.
— — his wife, Isabella Emma Elizabeth Fitzmaurice, vi. 582.
Schuyler, Arent, ii. 494.
— — his wife, Maria Walter, ii. 494.
— Katharine, wife of Archibald Kennedy of Pavonia, ii. 495.
— Peter, New Jersey, ii. 495.
— — his wife, Hester Walter, ii. 495.
Scobell of Down House, S. Z. T., v. 322.
— Edith, wife of capt. Alfred H. Maitland, v. 322.
SCONE, MURRAY, LORD, viii. 192-214.
Scone, David, first lord, i. 540; viii. 189 *n.*, 192.

* Name unknown.

Scone, Mungo David Malcolm, son of 6th earl of Mansfield; styled lord, viii. 214.
SCONE, MURRAY, LORD OF, viii. 193-214.
Scone, David, first lord of, viii. 193.
— James, third lord of, i. 229; viii. 197.
— Mungo, second lord of, viii. 196.
Scot of Allanhauch, Robert, iii. 501.
— of Balwearie, Sir James, vi. 103.
— — Michael, ii. 225 *n.*; ix. 121.
— — William, vi. 82, 83.
— — Sir William, iii. 471.
— — Sir William, i. 75; vi. 86.
— — Sir William, v. 396.
— — his wife, Isabel Lindsay, v. 396.
— — Sir William, ii. 515.
— of Craighall and Flacraig, Michael, ix. 121.
— of Dura, William, son of Sir Wm. S. of Balwearie, vi. 89.
— of Edenshead, Ann, wife of Charles Erskine, ii. 367.
— — Walter, son of Sir John S. of Scotstarvit, ii. 367.
— of Monzie, vii. 40.
— of Scotstarvit, David, i. 226, 523; viii. 204.
— — his 1st wife, Nicolas Grierson, viii. 204.
— — Sir James, the younger, vi. 497.
— — his wife, Marjorie Carnegie, vi. 497.
— — Sir John, ii. 367; iv. 246; v. 456, 458, 474; vi. 497; vii. 80; viii. 196.
— — Robert, ancestor of the family of, ii. 228.
— Agnes, wife of John Scott of Woll, vii. 79.
— Alexander, son of William S. of Balweary, iii. 471.
— — his wife, Elizabeth Lindsay, iii. 471.
— Elizabeth, wife of P. Kinnaird of Kinnaird, v. 205.
— John, versifier, vii. 109.
— Marjory, wife of 5th viscount of Stormont, i. 226.
— Robert, colonel, ii. 282.
— Robert, son of Robert S. of Allanhauch, iii. 500.
— Robert, lieutenant of the Tower of London, viii. 382.
— *, wife of Thomas Drummond of Drummonderinoch, vii. 40.
— *see also* Scott.
Scoto d'Agazano, Marc Antonio, i. 203.
SCOTT OF BUCCLEUCH, SCOTT, LORD, ii. 233.
Scott of Buccleuch, Walter, first lord, ii. 232.
— — his wife, Margaret Kerr, ii. 233; vii. 341.

* Name unknown.

Scott of Buccleuch, Walter, second lord, ii. 233; vii. 76.
—— his wife, Mary Hay, ii. 234.
SCOTT OF ESKDAILL, SCOTT, LORD, ii. 234.
Scott of Eskdaill, Francis, second lord, ii. 235.
—— Walter, first lord, ii. 233.
SCOTT OF QUHITCHESTER, SCOTT, LORD, ii. 234.
Scott of Quhitchester, Francis, second lord, ii. 235.
—— Walter, first lord, ii. 233.
SCOTT OF TINDALL, SCOTT, BARON, ii. 237, 241.
Scott of Tindall, Francis, second baron, ii. 241.
—— James, first baron, ii. 237.
SCOTT OF WHITCHESTER AND ESKDAILL, SCOTT, LORD, ii. 237-249.
Scott, George Henry, eldest son of 4th duke of Buccleuch; styled lord, ii. 244.
— James, first lord, ii. 237.
— John, eldest son of Francis, earl of Dalkeith; styled lord, ii. 242.
SCOTT, LORD ALEMOOR, ii. 237; vii. 80-81.
SCOTT, EARL OF BUCCLEUCH, ii. 234.
SCOTT, DUKE OF BUCCLEUCH, ii. 225-249.
SCOTT, LORD CAMPCASTELL, ii. 237; vii. 80-81.
SCOTT, EARL OF DALKEITH, ii. 237-249.
SCOTT, EARL OF DELORAINE, iii. 111-114.
SCOTT, EARL OF DONCASTER, ii. 237, 241.
SCOTT, LORD GOLDILANDS, iii. 111-114.
SCOTT, VISCOUNT OF HERMITAGE, iii. 111-114.
SCOTT, LORD POLWARTH, vii. 70-87.
SCOTT, LORD SCOTT OF BUCCLEUCH, ii. 233.
SCOTT, LORD SCOTT OF QUHITCHESTER AND ESKDAILL, ii. 234.
SCOTT, BARON SCOTT OF TINDALL, ii. 237, 241.
SCOTT, LORD SCOTT OF WHITCHESTER AND ESKDAILL, ii. 237.
SCOTT, EARL OF TARRAS, ii. 237; vii. 80-81.
Scott of Abbotsford, Sir Walter, 1st bart., ii. 244; iv. 422; vii. 79; viii. 31, 40, 41, 178 *n.*, 180.
— of Abbotshall, Thomas, vii. 252.
—— his wife, Agnes Moncrieff, vii. 252.
—— William, vi. 370, 372.
—— his wife, Margaret Durie, vi. 370.
— of Abington, Alexander, 2nd son of Sir Walter S. of Buccleuch, ii. 227.
— of Aikwood, Robert, ii. 591.
—— his wife, Marion Cranstoun, ii. 591.
— of Allanhaugh, Robert, 3rd son of David S. of Buccleuch, ii. 228; vi. 429.
— of Ancrum, Sir Patrick, bart., advocate, vii. 78.
—— his wife, Margaret Scott, vii. 78.
—— Sir William, bart., i. 144.
Scott of Ardross, Sir William, director of Chancery, ii. 85; iii. 346; iv. 309.
—— his 3rd wife, Jean Skene, ii. 85.
—— Sir William, 2nd laird, iv. 586; v. 402.
—— his wife, Helen Lindsay, v. 402.
— of Balcomie, John, general, M.P., iii. 581; vi. 327.
—— his wife, Mary Hay, iii. 581; ix. 70, 87.
— of Beechwood, Francis, 4th son of Walter S. of Harden, vii. 83.
—— his wife, Mary Don, vii. 83.
— of Benholm, David, viii. 82.
— of the Bog, George, i. 243.
— of Bonnytoun, Simon, vii. 75.
— of Bosworth Park, Charles Norman Lindsay, iii. 419.
—— his wife, Agnes Mary Manners Tollemache, iii. 419.
— of Bowhill, Charles, 2nd son of 2nd duke of Buccleuch, ii. 241.
— of Branxholm, David, eldest son of 'Wicked Wat' of Buccleuch, ii. 230.
—— Robert, ii. 226.
— of Branxholm and Buccleuch, David, ii. 227.
—— his alleged wife, * Somerville, viii. 9.
—— David, the younger, ii. 228.
—— his wife, Jane Douglas, i. 178; ii. 228; vii. 278.
—— Sir Walter, ii. 226.
—— his wife, Margaret Cockburn, ii. 227.
—— Sir Walter, ii. 228.
—— his wife, Elizabeth Kerr, ii. 228; vii. 331.
—— Sir Walter, 'Wicked Wat,' ii. 229; v. 58, 61, 63; vii. 119, 333, 336.
—— his 1st wife, Elizabeth Carmichael, ii. 230.
—— his 2nd wife, Janet Ker, ii. 230; v. 59; ix. 115.
—— Sir Walter, ii. 161, 231; v. 63, 64; vii. 336.
—— his wife, Margaret Douglas, i. 193; ii. 231; ix. 12, 46.
—— Sir Walter, 'the bold Buccleuch, ii. 232; iii. 505; vi. 430; vii. 73.
—— his wife, Margaret Ker, ii. 233.
— of Bundray, Robert, vii. 71.
— of Bunraw, Archibald, vii. 72. 78.
—— George, 2nd son of George S. of Sinton, vii. 72.
—— his wife, * Douglas, vii. 72.
— of Burellands, Stephen, ii. 226.
— of Burnhead, James, ancestor of the family of, ii. 227.
— of Callange, William, vi. 82.

* Name unknown.

Scott of Cannobie, David, 3rd son of 1st earl of Buccleuch, ii. 234.
—— of Over Cassock, William, vii. 76.
—— of Castlelaw, Stephen, son of Robt. S. of Murthockstoun, ii. 226.
—— of Clerkington, Lawrence, iv. 91.
—— —— Sir William, iii. 282.
—— of Comistoun, John, colonel, viii. 83.
—— —— his wife, Mary Carnegie, viii. 83.
—— of Cruikston, Sir Robert, viii. 287.
—— —— his wife, Mary Lyon, vi. 430; viii. 287.
—— of Dalkeith, Francis, ii. 235; vi. 377.
—— of Davington, Francis, 1st laird, vi. 430.
—— of Deephope, William, vii. 76.
—— of Dodbank, James, vii. 72.
—— of Dryhope, John, vii. 74.
—— of Dunfedling, Walter, vi. 375.
—— of Durachmore, William, vi. 82.
—— of Elerig, Walter, ii. 399.
—— of Elie, Sir William, director of Chancery, iii. 346.
—— of Erinscleuch, Sir Robert, vii. 76.
—— —— Sir William, vii. 76.
—— of Fingland, William, 3rd son of Robert S. of Thirlestane, vi. 430.
—— of Foulsheills, Andrew, ii. 235.
—— —— his wife, Janet Scott, ii. 235.
—— of Gala, Hugh, 2nd son of Walter S. of Harden; ancestor of the family of, vii. 75.
—— —— his wife, Jean Pringle of Galashiels, vii. 75.
—— of Gamescleuch, Walter, vi. 430.
—— —— his wife, Janet Porteous, vi. 430.
—— of Gamelscleuch, Sir William, vii. 76.
—— of Gilmanscleuch, James, vi. 429.
—— —— John, vi. 429.
—— —— his wife, Marion Douglas, vi. 429.
—— of Goldielands, Walter, illeg. son of Sir Walter S. of Buccleuch, ii. 230; vii. 74.
—— of Gorrenberry, John, legtd. son of 1st earl of Buccleuch, ii. 235; vii. 80.
—— —— John, vii. 83.
—— of Gramislaw, Walter, iii. 57.
—— of Haining, Robert, ii. 230.
—— —— his wife, Janet Scott, ii. 230, 590.
—— —— Thomas, vii. 339.
—— of Halcroft, Sir William, vii. 77.
—— of Harden, Hugh, 14th laird, vi. 22; vii. 84.
—— —— his wife, Harriet Bruhl, vii. 84.
—— —— John, 11th laird, vii. 82.
—— —— his wife, Jean Erskine, v. 88; vii. 82.
—— —— Robert, 2nd son of Walter S. of Synton; 1st laird, vii. 71, 73.
—— —— Robert, 9th laird, vii. 78, 82.
—— —— his wife, Jean Ker, vii. 78.
—— —— Walter, eldest son of Robert S. of Strickshaws; 2nd laird, vii. 71.
—— —— Walter, 4th laird, vii. 73.
Scott of Harden, Walter, 5th laird, 'Auld Wat,' vii. 73.
—— —— his 1st wife, Mary Scott, vii. 74.
—— —— his 2nd wife, Margaret Edgar, vii. 74.
—— —— Walter, 10th laird, vii. 82.
—— —— Walter, 12th laird, vii. 82.
—— —— his 1st wife, Agnes Nisbet, vii. 83.
—— —— his 2nd wife, Agnes Scott, vi. 428; vii. 83.
—— —— his 3rd wife, Ann Scott, vii. 83.
—— —— his 4th wife, Christian Ker, vii. 83.
—— —— Walter, 13th laird, ii. 22; vii. 70, 83.
—— —— his wife, Diana Hume Campbell, *de jure* baroness Polwarth, vi. 22; vii. 70, 83.
—— —— William, 2nd son of Robert S. of Stirkshaws; 3rd laird, vii. 72.
—— —— his wife, * Ker, vii. 73.
—— —— Sir William, 6th laird, vi. 431; vii. 75, 76.
—— —— his 1st wife, Agnes Murray, iii. 507; vii. 77.
—— —— his 2nd wife, Margaret Ker, vii. 77.
—— —— Sir William, 7th laird, v. 171; vii. 77; ix. 119.
—— —— his wife, Christian Boyd, v. 171; vii. 78.
—— —— Sir William, M.P., 8th laird, vii. 78.
—— —— his wife, Jean Nisbet, vi. 431; vii. 78.
—— of Harlawood, Walter, colonel, iii. 342; ix. 76.
—— —— his wife, Elizabeth Napier, iii. 342; ix, 76.
—— —— Walter, ix. 76.
—— of Harperrig, Lawrence, iv. 91.
—— of Harwood, Robert, vii. 79.
—— of Hassendean, James, ancestor of the family of, ii. 227.
—— of Highchester, Sir Gideon, 2nd son of Sir Walter S. of Harden, ii. 237; vii. 78, 79.
—— —— his wife, Margaret Hamilton, vii. 79.
—— —— Gideon, vii. 82.
—— —— his 1st wife, Anna Kinloch, vii. 82.
—— —— his 2nd wife, Mary Drummond, vi. 68; vii. 82; ix. 135.
—— of Hoscote, William, 1st laird, vii. 73, 76.
—— —— Sir William, vii. 76.
—— of Howcleuch, Sir Gideon, vii. 79.
—— of Howfuird, Francis, 4th son of Walter S. of Harden, vii. 75.
—— —— his wife, Isobel Scott, vii. 75.
—— —— Walter, vii. 75.
—— of Howpasley, Alexander, 2nd son of Sir Walter S. of Buccleuch, ii. 227; vi. 428.
—— —— Robert, vi. 428.
—— —— Walter, ii. 227.
—— —— *, 1615, vii. 132.
—— —— his wife, *, vii. 132.

* Name unknown.

Scott of Hundelshope, William, vii. 76.
— of Huntly, William, 'Will ill to haud,' vii. 71.
— of Huntlydene, Francis, vii. 382.
— of Iliston, Robert, vii. 78.
— — his wife, Jean Ker, vii. 78.
— of Kirkhope, Walter, vii. 74.
— of Kirkurd, David, eldest son of Sir Walter S. of Buccleuch, ii. 227.
— — James, 3rd son of Sir Walter S. of Buccleuch, ii. 227.
— — Walter, vii. 368.
— — Sir William, 2nd son of Sir Walter S. of Buccleuch, ii. 161, 230, 231; ix. 46.
— — his wife, Grisel Betoun, ii. 231; iii. 503; ix. 46.
— of Kirkwood, Sir William, vii. 77.
— of Langhope, Walter, vii. 74.
— — William, vii. 72.
— of Langshaw, Patrick, v. 474.
— of Logie, James, vi. 242 *n.*
— — Mary, wife of lieut.-gen. Sir John Hope, iv. 495.
— — Robert, iv. 495.
— of Lytchett Minster, Sir Edward Henry, 5th bart., v. 236.
— of Malleny, John, viii. 461.
— — his wife, Susan Hay, viii. 461.
— of Mangerton, Francis, illeg. son of 1st earl of Buccleuch, ii. 234.
— — William, illeg. son of 1st earl of Buccleuch, ii. 234.
— of Mertoun, Sir William, vii. 76.
— of Mollance, John Lindsay, iii. 419.
— of Monzie, Peter, vii. 44.
— of Mostyn, Walter, viii. 315.
— of Murthockstoun, Sir Michael, vii. 71 *n.*
— — Richard le, ii. 225.
— — Robert, ii. 225.
— — Robert, ii. 226.
— — Sir Walter, ii. 226.
— of Newburgh, Symon, ancestor of the family of, iv. 429.
— of Outarsyderigg, George, vii. 72.
— — his wife, Mary Gladstanes, vii. 72.
— — Walter, vii. 72.
— of Palace Hill, Charles, vii. 383.
— — his wife, Margaret Rutherfurd, vii. 383.
— of Pirnetados, Walter, vii. 74.
— — Sir William, vii. 76.
— of Pitlochie, viii. 201.
— of Pitscottie, William, vi. 82.
— — William, son of Sir Wm. S. of Balwearie, vi. 89.
— of Pittedie, viii. 201.
— of Poubudy, William, vii. 76.
— of Quylt, William, vii. 76.
— of Raeburn, Walter, 'Wat Wudspurs,' vii. 78, 79.
— — his wife, Anne Isabel Macdougall, vii. 79.
Scott of Rankilburn, Richard le, ii. 225.
— — Robert, ii. 225.
— — Robert, his grandson, ii. 226.
— — Sir Walter, ii. 225.
— of Roberton, Sir Gideon, vii. 79.
— — James, vii. 79.
— — Walter, 'Wat Wudspurs,' vii. 79.
— of Rossie, Patrick, i. 306.
— of Rysholm, Adam, iv. 185 *n.*
— — Robert, iv. 185 *n.*; ix. 14.
— of St. Leonards, Walter, ix. 76.
— of Satchels, James, 4th son of Walter S. of Synton, vii. 71.
— — Robert, vii. 72.
— — Walter, the author, vii. 71.
— of Scalloway and of Scottshall, Alexander, ancestor of the families of, v. 449.
— — his wife, Agnes Wauchope, v. 449.
— of Strickshaws, Stirches, Robert, 2nd son of Walter S. of Synton, vii. 71.
— — 'Watty burn the braes,' vii. 71.
— of Synton, Arcbibald, representative of the family of, vii. 72, 78.
— — Francis, 4th son of 'Auld Wat' of Harden, vii. 75.
— — his wife, Isobel Scott, vii. 75.
— — George, vii. 72.
— — his wife, Margaret Edmonston, vii. 72.
— — George, vii. 72, 75.
— — his wife, Mary Gladstanes, vii. 72, 75.
— — George, representative of the family of, vii. 72.
— — his wife, * Douglas, vii. 72.
— — Walter, vii. 70.
— — his 1st wife, Marjorie Cockburn, vii. 71.
— — his 2nd wife, Margaret Riddell, vii. 71.
— — Walter, his son, vii. 71.
— — his wife, * Riddell, vii. 71.
— — Walter, 'Watty burn the braes,' vii. 71.
— — Walter, 3rd son of 'Watty burn the braes,' vii. 72.
— — Walter, vii. 72.
— — his wife, Isobel Douglas, vii. 72, 75.
— — Sir William, representative of the family of, vii. 78.
— — his wife, Jean Nisbet, vii. 78.
— of Tanlawhill, Patrick, vi. 430 *ter.*
— of Tarras, William, vii. 76.
— of Thirlestane, Sir Francis, 1st bart., vi. 431.
— — his wife, Henrietta Ker, v. 475; vi. 431.
— — John, 1st laird, vi. 428.
— — his 1st wife, * Scott, vi. 429.
— — his 2nd wife, Marion Douglas, vi. 429.

* Name unknown.

Scott of Thirlestane, Sir John, 4th laird, vi. 430.
—— —— his wife, Eupham Young, vi. 430.
—— —— Patrick, 5th laird, vi. 430; vii. 80.
—— —— his wife, Isabel Murray, vi. 431.
—— —— Robert, 2nd laird, vi. 429.
—— —— his wife, Margaret Scott, ii. 230, 232; vi. 429.
—— —— Sir Robert, 3rd laird, vi. 430; vii. 76.
—— —— his 1st wife, Margaret Cranstoun, ii. 591; vi. 430.
—— —— his 2nd wife, Katharine Jardine, vi. 430.
—— —— Sir William, 2nd bart., vi. 428, 431; vii. 83.
—— —— his 1st wife, Elizabeth, mistress of Napier, vi. 428.
—— —— his 2nd wife, Jean Nisbet, vi. 431.
—— of Todschawhill, Walter, vii. 74.
—— of Tushielaw, Adam, v. 261.
—— —— Walter, ii. 230; vi. 430.
—— —— * vii. 75.
—— —— his wife, * Scott, vii. 75.
—— of Wamphray, Adam, son of Robert S., i. 239; iv. 185 *n.*; ix. 14.
—— —— Robert, i. 239.
—— —— his wife, Katharine Boyle, i. 239; iv. 185 *n.*
—— —— Robert, iv. 185 *n.*
—— of Wauchope, Walter, vii. 383.
—— —— his 1st wife, Elizabeth Rutherfurd, vii. 383.
—— of Whitchester, Robert, 3rd son of David S. of Buccleuch, ii. 228.
—— of Whitefield, Walter, 3rd son of Walter, earl of Tarras, vii. 82.
—— of Whitehaughbrae, Thomas, vii. 71.
—— of Whitehope, William, ii. 228.
—— of Whiterigge, Sir William, vii. 76.
—— of Whitslaid, Robert, ii. 233.
—— —— his wife, Jean Scott, ii. 233.
—— —— Walter, vii. 75.
—— —— Sir Walter, vii. 75; ix. 142.
—— —— his wife, Susanna Scott, ix. 142.
—— of Winterburgh, Symon, tutor of Thirlestane, vi. 429, 430.
—— of Woll, John, M.P., vii. 79.
—— —— his wife, Agnes Scot, vii. 79.
—— Adam, 2nd son of Alex. S. of Abington, ii. 227.
—— Agnes, wife of Gavin Wemyss, ii. 282.
—— Agnes, wife of Walter Scott of Whitefield and Harden, vi. 428; vii. 83.
—— Agnes, dau. of George S. of Sinton, vii. 72.
—— Agnes, wife of John Riddell, vii. 80.
—— Agnes, wife of (1) Sir Jas. Grant of Dalvey, and (2) Dr. Wm. Rutherfurd of Barnhills, vii. 80.
—— Agnes, dau. of Walter, earl of Tarras, vii. 82.

* Name unknown.

Scott, Alexander, goldsmith, Edinburgh, v. 449.
—— —— his wife, Agnes Wauchope, v. 449.
—— Anna, wife of (1) Sir Daniel Carmichael, and (2) Sir Robt. Sinclair, iv. 586.
—— Anna, wife of Sir Wm. Primrose of Carrington, vii. 109.
—— Anne, dau. of Anna, duchess of Buccleuch, ii. 239.
—— Anne, dau. of James, earl of Dalkeith, ii. 240.
—— Anne, dau. of 2nd duke of Buccleuch, ii. 241.
—— Anne, wife of col. Robert Cunningham, iv. 246.
—— Anne, wife of C. Baillie, iv. 322.
—— Anne, wife of capt. Gladstanes of Whitelaw, vii. 72.
—— Anne, dau. of Walter, earl of Tarras, vii. 82.
—— Anne, wife of Walter S. of Whitefield, vii. 83.
—— Anne, dau. of Walter S. of Whitefield and Harden, vii. 83.
—— Anne, dau. of Walter S. of Harden, vii. 84.
—— Anne Elizabeth, dau. of 4th duke of Buccleuch, ii. 244.
—— Archibald, captain; 2nd son of Walter S. of Sinton, vii. 72.
—— Blanche Alice, wife of 10th lord Elibank, iii. 523.
—— Campbell, 3rd son of Francis, earl of Dalkeith, ii. 242.
—— Caroline, dau. of Francis, earl of Dalkeith, ii. 242.
—— Caroline, wife of 6th marquess of Queensberry, ii. 243; vii. 152.
—— Cecily, wife of Charles Ker of Abbotrule, v. 474.
—— Charles Walter, eldest son of 6th lord Polwarth, vii. 84.
—— Charlotte, dau. of Anna, duchess of Buccleuch, ii. 239.
—— Charlotte, dau. of James, earl of Dalkeith, ii. 240.
—— Charlotte Albinia, wife of 4th earl of Courtown, ii. 244.
—— Christian, dau. of Walter S. of Sinton, vii. 72.
—— Christian, wife of William Ker of Chatto, vii. 78.
—— Christian, dau. of Walter S. of Whitefield and Harden, vii. 83.
—— Christina, mistress of 5th earl of Rothes, ix. 127.
—— David, 2nd son of David S. of Buccleuch, ii. 228.
—— —— his wife, Jane Douglas, i. 178; ii. 228.
—— David, 4th son of Sir Walter S. of Buccleuch, ii. 230.

Scott, David, 3rd son of George S. of Sinton, vii. 72 *bis*.
— David, 3rd son of Robert S. of Stirches, vii. 73.
— David, killed at Aberdeen, 1530, vii. 436.
— Diana, dau. of Walter S. of Harden, vii. 84.
— Edward John, Southsea, iii. 523.
— Elizabeth, wife of 4th earl of Balcarres, i. 523.
— Elizabeth, contr. to Thos. Ker, and wife of John Carmichael of Meadowflat, ii. 231; vii. 339.
— Elizabeth, wife of 2nd lord Cranstoun, ii. 233, 594.
— Elizabeth, wife of John, lord Erskine, ii. 234; v. 625.
— Elizabeth, wife of 10th earl of Home, ii. 243; iv. 482.
— Elizabeth, wife of Sir Andrew Ker of Greenhead, vii. 79.
— Elizabeth, dau. of Walter, earl of Tarras, vii. 82.
— Elizabeth, wife of Walter Chisholm, ix. 142.
— Elspeth, dau. of Walter S. of Synton, vii. 72.
— Esther, wife of (1) Elliot of Falnash, and (2) George Langlands of Langlands, vii. 75.
— Euphame, wife of 1st earl of Dundonald, iii. 346.
— Frances, wife of Archibald, lord Douglas of Douglas, i. 213; ii. 242.
— Francis, 5th son of Sir Gideon S. of Highchester, vii. 80.
— Francis, 5th son of Walter, earl of Tarras, vii. 82.
— Francis Winstone, viii. 315.
— — his wife, Ernestine Hester Maud Bowes-Lyon, viii. 315.
— George, apprentice saddler, vii. 72 *bis*.
— Georgina Caroline, wife of Sir James Peachey, lord Selsey, iii. 112.
— Gideon, 4th son of Sir Gideon S. of Highchester, vii. 80.
— Grizell, wife of (1) 7th lord Borthwick, and (2) Walter Cairncross, ii. 111, 112, 230.
— Grizel, wife of Thos. Rollock, ix. 151.
— Harriet Janet Sarah, wife of rev. E. Moore, ii. 245.
— Harriet Montagu, wife of 6th marquess of Lothian, ii. 244; v. 483.
— Helen, wife of 2nd lord Blantyre, ii. 85.
— Helen, wife of James Douglas, commendator of Melrose, vi. 372.
— Helen, dau. of Walter, earl of Tarras, vii. 82.
— Helen, wife of George Brown of Elliston, vii. 83.
— Henrietta, wife of N. Boyce, iii. 112.
Scott, Henrietta, wife of 12th lord Ross of Halkhead, vi. 431: vii. 261.
— Henry, 3rd son of James, duke of Monmouth and Buccleuch, ii. 239; iii. 111.
— Hugh, in Greenhead, 2nd son of Walter S. of Harden, vii. 74, 75.
— Isabella, wife of (1) Sir S. Carruthers, and (2) John Murray, ii. 228.
— Isabella, dau. of Anna, duchess of Buccleuch, ii. 239.
— Isabella, wife of Alex. Ireland, vi. 391.
— Isabella Mary, wife of P. F. Cust, ii. 245.
— James, C. S., ii. 103.
— James, 4th son of Francis, earl of Dalkeith, ii. 242.
— James, 4th son of Sir William S. of Harden, vii. 79.
— — his wife, Agnes Riddell, vii. 79.
— James Cospatrick, v. 487.
— — his wife, Isobel Alice Adelaide Ker, v. 487.
— Jane, dau. of 2nd duke of Buccleuch, ii. 241.
— Janet, wife of Sir Jas. Douglas of Drumlanrig, ii. 228.
— Janet, wife of (1) J. Cranstoun, and (2) Robert Scott of Haining, ii. 230, 590.
— Janet, wife of Sir Thos. Kerr of Fernihirst, ii. 231; v. 66, 69.
— Janet, wife of Andrew Scott of Foulsheills, ii. 235.
— Janet, wife of Thomas Scott, vii. 75.
— Janet, wife of John Murray in Eschiesteill, vii. 79.
— Janet, wife of John Hay of Smithfield, viii. 435.
— Jean, wife of Alex. Arbuthnott of Knox, i. 306.
— Jean, wife of (1) J. Cranston, and (2) R. Scott, ii. 230, 590.
— Jean, dau. of 1st lord Scott of Buccleuch, ii. 233.
— Jean, wife of Robert Scott of Whitslaid, ii. 233.
— Jean, wife of 1st marquess of Tweeddale, ii. 234, 236; viii. 454.
— Jean, wife of Sir Jas. Hay of Linplum, vi. 431; viii. 446.
— Jean, wife of Thomas Scott, vii. 75 *bis*.
— Jean, dau. of Walter S. of Whitefield, vii. 83.
— John, provost of Crichton, ii. 233.
— John, councillor-at-law, 2nd son of 3rd lord Deloraine, iii. 113.
— — his wife, Isabella Young, iii. 113.
— John, their son, iii. 113.
— John, captor of John Douglas of Balvany, iii. 175.
— John, vicar of Aberdour, vi. 355.
— John, son of Walter S. of Tushlelaw vi. 430.

Scott, John, chamberlain to the archbishop of Glasgow, vii. 71 *n.*
— John, 2nd son of George S. of Synton, vii. 72.
— John, 2nd son of Walter S. of Whitefield, vii. 83.
— John Douglas, 3rd son of 4th duke of Buccleuch, ii. 244.
— — his wife, Alicia Anne Spottiswoode, ii. 244.
— Katharine, wife of (1) James Sandilands of Cruvie, and (2) Wm. Wood of Bonnytoun, i. 75.
— Katharine Frances, dau. of 4th duke of Buccleuch, ii. 245.
— Lucy, wife of 10th earl of Moray, vi. 327.
— Margaret, wife of John Johnstone of that Ilk, i. 251; ii. 231.
— Margaret, wife of Sir J. Bellenden, ii. 65.
— Margaret, wife of James Haig of Bemersyde, ii. 228.
— Margaret, wife of Robert Scott of Thirlestane, ii. 230; vi. 429.
— Margaret, dau. of Sir Walter S. of Buccleuch, ii. 232.
— Margaret, wife of (1) James, 6th lord Ross, and (2) Alexander, 6th lord Eglinton, ii. 233; iii. 446; vii. 255, 257.
— Margaret, wife of John Pringle, ii. 235.
— Margaret, dau. of 2nd earl of Buccleuch, ii. 236.
— Margaret, wife of Sir. Alex. Home of Renton, iii. 282.
— Margaret, wife of James Gray of Buttergask, iv. 280.
— Margaret, wife of John Melville of Raith, vi. 103.
— Margaret, dau. of Walter S. of Gamescleugh, vi. 430.
— Margaret, wife of Sir Alex. Bannerman of Elsick, vi. 431.
— Margaret, wife of (1) David Pringle, and (2) Sir W. Macdougall of Makerston, vii. 75.
— Margaret, 'Maggie Fendy,' wife of Sir Gilbert Elliot of Stobs, vii. 75 *bis.*
— Margaret, wife of Sir Patrick Scott of Ancrum, vii. 78.
— Margaret, wife of Thos. Ker of Mersington, vii. 79.
— Margaret, wife of James Corbet of Tolcorse, vii. 80.
— Margaret, wife of Thos. Gordon, vii. 82; ix. 150.
— Margaret Nicolson, wife of Archibald Borthwick, ii. 103.
— Marion, wife of (1) Archibald Carruthers, and (2) Sir Adam Johnstone, i. 239.
Scott, Marion, wife of (1) * Scott, (2) Nicol Cairncross, and (3) Geo. Henderson of Fordel, ii. 65; ix. 37.
— Marion, wife of Patrick Borthwick, ii. 103.
— Marion, dau. of Walter S. of Gamescleugh, vi. 430.
— Marion, 'the flower of Yarrow,' wife of Walter Scott of Harden, vii. 74.
— Marjory, wife of Sir John Melville of Raith, vi. 82, 83.
— Mary, wife of Wm. Elliot of Lariston, ii. 232.
— Mary, dau. of 1st earl of Buccleuch, ii. 234.
— Mary, dau. of 2nd duke of Buccleuch, ii. 241.
— Mary, wife of 3rd earl of Courtown, ii. 243; ix. 46.
— Mary, wife of col. A. W. H. Hay, v. 236.
— Mary, wife of Sir Wm. Primrose of Carrington, vi. 431; vii. 109.
— Mary, 'the flower of Yarrow,' wife of Walter Scott of Harden, vii. 74.
— Mary, dau. of Gideon S. of Highchester, vii. 82.
— Mary, dau. of Walter, earl of Tarras, vii. 82.
— Patrick, burgess of Dundee, iv. 272.
— Richard, minister of Kirkbean, and of Ashkirk, vii. 72.
— Robert, son of Adam S. of Tushielaw, v. 261.
— Robert, younger son of William S. of Fingland, vi. 430.
— Robert, murdered by Andrew Crossar, vii. 71.
— Robert, 4th son of Walter S. of Synton, vii. 72.
— Simon, 2nd son of Walter S. of Gamescleugh, vi. 430.
— Susan, wife of George Carnegie of Pittarrow, viii. 82.
— Susanna, wife of Walter Scott of Whitslaid, ix. 142.
— Thomas, son of Walter S. of Whitslaid, vii. 75.
— — his wife, Janet *or* Jean Scott, vii. 75.
— Thomas, 3rd son of Sir Gideon S. of Highchester, vii. 80.
— Thomas, 4th son of Walter, earl of Tarras, vii. 82.
— Walter, eldest son of Walter S. of Harden, vii. 84.
— Walter, eldest son of David S. of Buccleuch, ii. 227.
— Walter, 3rd son of Sir Walter S. of Buccleuch, ii. 230.
— Walter, elder son of William S. of Fingland, vi. 430.

* Name unknown.

Scott, Walter, 3rd son of Patrick S. of Thirlestane, vi. 431.
—— Walter, in Essinside, 3rd son of Walter S. of Harden, vii. 74, 75.
—— —— his wife, Elspeth Hay, vii. 75.
—— Walter, eldest son of George S. of Synton, vii. 72.
—— William, receiver-gen. of Isle of Man, i. 493.
—— —— his wife, Charlotte Wilhelmina Murray, i. 493.
—— William, 4th son of David S. of Buccleuch, ii. 228.
—— William, 3rd son of John S. of Thirlestane, vi. 429.
—— William, 2nd son of Walter S. of Harden, vii. 73.
—— William, 2nd son of Sir Gideon S. of Highchester, vii. 80.
—— —— his wife, Jean Kirkaldy, vii. 80.
—— William, 3rd son of Walter S. of Whitefield, vii. 83.
—— Winifrede Agatha Tollemache, iii. 419.
—— *, wife of John Lindsay of Covington, ii. 228.
—— *, capt. 32nd regt., iv. 570.
—— —— his wife, Teresa Ann Morris, iv. 570.
—— *, wife of John Scott of Thirlestane, vi. 429.
—— *, dau. of Walter S. of Synton, vii. 71.
—— *, wife of Geddes of Kirkurd, vii. 75.
—— *, wife of Porteous of Headschaw, vii. 75.
—— *, wife of Scott of Tushielaw, vii. 75.
Scott-Montagu, Caroline, wife of 5th marquess of Queensberry, ii. 243; vii. 152.
—— Elizabeth, wife of 10th earl of Home, ii. 243; iv. 482.
—— Harriet, wife of 6th marquess of Lothian, ii. 244; v. 483.
—— Helen Cecil, ii. 246.
—— John Walter Edward, eldest son of 1st baron Montagu of Beaulieu, ii. 246.
—— —— his wife, Cecil Victoria Constance Kerr, ii. 246.
—— Rachel Cecily, wife of H. W. Forster, ii. 246.
—— Robert Henry, 2nd son of 1st baron Montagu of Beaulieu, ii. 246.
—— —— his wife, Alice *, ii. 246.
Scougall, Margaret, wife of R. Colville, ii. 546.
Scrogis, Robert of, vi. 199.
—— Simon of, vi. 199.
Scrope of Bolton, John (Scrope), 5th lord, iv. 449.
—— —— John (Scrope), 8th lord, iii. 294.
—— of Cockerington, Gervase, iii. 113.
—— of Danby, Simon, iii. 299.
—— —— Simon Thomas, vi. 582.

* Name unknown.

Scrope, Adela Mary, wife of (1) Edward Riddell, and (2) Alex. Temple Fitzmaurice, vi. 582.
—— Sir John le, i. 433.
—— —— his wife, Elizabeth of Atholl, i. 433.
—— Margaret, wife of Sir John Constable, iii. 294.
—— Mary, wife of (1) 2nd earl of Deloraine, and (2) Thos. Vivian, iii. 113.
SCRYMGEOUR, SCRYMGEOUR, LORD, iii. 313-315.
Scrymgeour, James, second lord, iii. 314.
—— John, first lord, iii. 313.
—— John, third lord, iii. 315.
SCRYMGEOUR, VISCOUNT DUDHOPE, iii. 313-315.
SCRYMGEOUR, EARL OF DUNDEE, iii. 303-315.
SCRYMGEOUR, LORD INVERKEITHING, iii. 315.
SCRYMGEOUR, LORD SCRYMGEOUR, 313-315.
Scrymgeour of Ardormy, John, iii. 310.
—— of Baldovan, Sir James, iii. 312.
—— of Ballagernoch, James, constable of Dundee, iii. 307.
—— —— James, iii. 309.
—— —— his wife, Elizabeth Scrymgeour, iii. 309.
—— —— John, iii. 309, 312.
—— —— Margaret, wife of Patrick Gray of Kingudy, iii. 310.
—— of Ballantor, John, ii. 310.
—— of Balmakewan, David, ix. 72, 73.
—— of Balmullo, John, iii. 310.
—— of Banvy and Balrudry, James, iii. 307.
—— —— Sir John, iii. 306.
—— of Wester Bowhill, John, vi. 105.
—— of Canons, John, constable of Dundee, iii. 313.
—— of Cartmore, David, ii. 240 *n.*
—— of Wester Cartmore, James, vi. 105.
—— —— his wife, Margaret Melville, vi. 105.
—— of Dudhope, Sir James, 1st laird, iii. 308.
—— —— James, 2nd laird, iii. 308.
—— —— Sir James, 5th laird, iii. 311.
—— —— John, 3rd laird, son of John S. of Glastre, iii. 310.
—— —— John, 4th laird, iii. 311.
—— of Dundee, Alexander, 1st laird, 'son of Colin,' iii. 304; ix. 72.
—— —— his wife, Tiphanie de Inchsyreth, ix. 72.
—— —— Alexander, 3rd laird, iii. 305.
—— —— his wife, Agnes of Glascoster, iii. 305.
—— —— James, 4th laird, iii. 305.
—— —— his wife, Egidia Maxwell, iii. 306.
—— —— James, 6th laird, iii. 306; ix. 72.
—— —— his 1st wife, Jonet Lyon, iii. 307.
—— —— his 2nd wife, Margaret Maitland, iii. 307; ix. 73.
—— —— Sir James, 7th laird, iii. 307; ix. 73.
—— —— his wife, Isobel Gray, iii. 308; iv. 277.

Scrymgeour of Dundee, James, 8th laird, iii. 308; ix. 73.
— — his 1st wife, Mariot Stewart, iii. 309; ix. 73.
— — his 2nd wife, Marion Wardlaw, ii. 145; iii. 309.
— — Sir James, 12th laird, ii. 83; iii. 311; viii. 289.
— — his 1st wife, Margaret Carnegie, iii. 313; viii. 57.
— — his 2nd wife, Magdalene Livingston, iii. 313; v. 439.
— — Sir John, 5th laird, iii. 306, 309 *bis*, 312; iv. 272; v. 287; ix. 73.
— — his 1st wife, Katharine Ogilvy, iii. 306.
— — his 2nd wife, Isobel Oliphant, iii. 306; vi. 538.
— — his 3rd wife, Marion Abernethy, iii. 306; v. 287, 289; ix. 73.
— — John, 9th laird, iii. 307, 309.
— — his wife, Janet Ogilvy, iii. 310.
— — John, 10th laird, iii. 310.
— — his wife, Isobel Cunninghame, iii. 311.
— — John, 11th laird, iii. 311, 312.
— — his wife, * Campbell, iii. 311.
— — John, 13th laird, ii. 83; iii. 313; viii. 64.
— — his wife, Margaret Seton, iii. 313.
— — Nicholas, 2nd laird, iii. 304.
— — Richard, constable of Dundee, ix. 72.
— of Fardill, David, 3rd son of Sir John S. of Dundee, iii. 306, 307 *bis*, 308, 310.
— — James, ii. 100; iii. 308, 312.
— — John, iii. 315 *n*.
— of Fordey, David, iii. 312 *bis*.
— — James, iii. 308.
— of Gallery, John, vi. 539.
— of Glassary, Alexander, constable of Dundee, iii. 305.
— — his wife, Agnes of Glassary, iii. 305.
— — James, iii. 306, 316; ix. 74.
— — John, iii. 307, 308 *bis*, 309; ix. 73 *bis*.
— — John, constable of Dundee, iii. 309.
— of Glaswell and Torbirnis, James, iii. 311.
— — John, iii. 312.
— — Walter, 3rd son of John S. of Glassary, iii. 308. 310.
— — his wife, Katharine Murray, iii. 310.
— of Glenquharite, John, iii. 310.
— of Gokelmure, John, iii. 310.
— of Gone, James, iii. 308.
— of Hallhill, John, iii. 310.
— of Henristoun, Alexander, iii. 307, 310.
— — James, 2nd son of John S. of Glassary, iii. 311.
— — John, v. 287; ix. 72.
— — his wife, Janet Stag, ix. 72.

* Name unknown.

Scrymgeour of Henristoun, John, their son, ix. 72.
— of Hilfield, James, eldest son of 1st viscount Dudhope, iii. 314.
— — Nicholas, iii. 305.
— of Inverkeithing, James, 'vexillator regis,' iii. 305.
— — James, constable of Dundee, iii. 306.
— — James, eldest son of 1st viscount Dudhope, iii. 314.
— of Mill of Kelly, John, iii. 313.
— of Kirklands of Inschyra, John, 2nd son of 1st viscount Dudhope, iii. 313.
— of Kirkton of Erlestrathichty, Elizabeth, wife of James Scrymgeour of Balgarno, iii. 308, 309; ix. 73.
— — James, constable of Dundee, iii. 308.
— — John, iii. 308, 309, 312.
— — John, iii. 309; vi. 590.
— — his wife, Jean Makgill, vi. 590.
— — John, iii. 315 *n*.
— of Lillok, Nicholas, iii. 307, 310.
— of Lumlethen and Crago, John, iii. 310.
— of Myres, James, iii. 312.
— — John, iii. 309, 312.
— of Pitnepie, Andrew, 4th son of 1st viscount Dudhope, iii. 314.
— of Rydgond, James, iii. 312.
— of Sonahard, David, iii. 307; ix. 73.
— — James, eldest son of David S. of Fardill, iii. 307.
— — James, constable of Dundee, iii. 308.
— — Sir James, constable of Dundee, iii. 312.
— of Southbello, James, viii. 385.
— of Strickmartin, Sir James, iii. 312.
— Agnes, wife of Peter Bruce of Earlshall, iii. 309; ix. 73.
— Alexander, 2nd son of Alex. S., constable of Dundee, iii. 305.
— Alexander, rector of Glassary, iii. 306, 307.
— Alexander, burgess and bailie of Dundee, iii. 312 *bis*.
— Alexander, brother of John S. of Glaswell, iii. 312.
— Alexander, 5th son of 1st viscount Dudhope, iii. 314.
— Alexander, captain, 2nd son of 2nd viscount Dudhope, iii. 314.
— Alexander, son of John S. of Fordell, iii. 315 *n*.
— Christian, wife of John Leslie, bishop of Ross, vii. 501.
— Clara, dau. of David S., iii. 314.
— David, son of David S. of Sonyhard, iii. 307.
— David, 3rd son of 1st viscount Dudhope, iii. 313.
— — his wife, Jean Cockburne, iii. 313.

Scrymgeour, Donald, 2nd son of John S., constable of Dundee, iii. 311.
— Egidia, wife of James Maitland of Auchinbreck, iii. 306; v. 287.
— Elizabeth, wife of John Sandilands, iii. 307; viii. 385.
— Elizabeth, wife of (1) Andrew Wintoun, and (2) John Ogilvie, iii. 311.
— Elizabeth, wife of Mr. John Murray, iii. 401.
— Elizabeth, wife of 4th lord Glamis, viii. 276.
— Elspeth, wife of John Campbell of Lundie, ix. 73.
— Gilbert, brother of John S. of Kirkton, iii. 312.
— Giles, wife of Thomas Spalding, iii. 308; ix. 73.
— Henry, W.S., v. 417.
— James, rector of Glassary, canon of Lismore, iii. 308, 310 *bis*.
— James, brother of Alex. S. of Henristoune, iii. 310.
— James, son of David S., Dundee, iii. 310.
— James, son of Robert S., iii. 312.
— James, 2nd son of John S. of Henristoun, ix. 72.
— James, 3rd son of James S. of Dundee, ix. 72.
— Jane, wife of Sir John Carnegie of Pittarrow, iii. 314; viii. 67.
— Janet, wife of 3rd lord Carlyle, ii. 388; iii. 308.
— Jean, wife of John Graham of Fintry, iii. 315; ix. 74.
— John, called 'Jack,' burgess of Dundee, iii. 307.
— John, brother of Alex. S. of Henristoun, iii. 307.
— John, macer, iii. 307, 308, 310.
— John, son of Sir John S. and Marion Abernethy, v. 287.
— John, 4th son of Sir John S. of Dundee, ix. 73.
— Katharine, wife of William Ochterlony, iii. 313.
— Magdalene, wife of Alexander Irvine of Drum, iii. 314; ix. 74.
— Margaret, wife of John Stewart, earl of Buchan, ii. 268; iii. 308.
— Margaret, wife of James Haliburton, iii. 313.
— Margaret. dau. of David S., iii. 314.
— Margaret, wife of Sir Thos. Thomson of Duddingston, iii. 314.
— Margaret, wife of lt.-col. James Alexander, viii. 180; ix. 73.
— Mariota, wife of Robert Arbuthnott of Arbuthnott, i. 282; iii. 307.
— Mary, wife of Peter Hay of Megginch, iii. 314.
Scrymgeour, Mary, dau. of 2nd viscount Dudhope, iii. 315; ix. 74 *bis*.
— Matilda, wife of Sir Robert Graham of Fintry, iii. 307, 316; vi. 218.
— Patrick, son of David S. of Sonyhard, iii. 307.
— Robert, son of David S. of Sonyhard, iii. 307.
— Robert, 3rd son of John S. of Glassary, iii. 311, 312.
— — his wife, Margaret Campbell, iii. 311; ix. 73 *bis*.
— Robert, 3rd son of 2nd viscount Dudhope, iii. 315.
— *, alleged wife of Sir Robert de Brus of Clackmannan, iii. 469.
— *, wife of William Fraser, Dundee, v. 520.
Scrymgeour-Wedderburn of Birkhill, Henry, v. 316.
— — his wife, Mary T. Maitland, v. 316.
— — Henry, hereditary standard-bearer in 1902, iii. 309; v. 307, 321 *n.*; ix. 73.
— of Wedderburn, Frederick Lewis, i. 316.
— — his wife, Helen Arbuthnott, i. 316.
Scudéry, Madeleine de, ix. 101.
SEAFIELD, OGILVY, VISCOUNT, iv. 37-41.
Seafield, James, first viscount, iv. 37.
SEAFIELD, OGILVY, EARL OF, iv. 37-41.
— James, first earl of, iv. 37.
— — his wife, Anne Dunbar, iv. 38.
— James, 2nd earl of, iv. 39.
— — his 1st wife, Elizabeth Hay, iv. 39.
— — his 2nd wife, Sophia Hope, iv. 39.
— James, third earl of, iv. 39.
— — his wife, Mary Murray, iv. 40; ix. 90.
— James, fourth earl of, iv. 40.
— — his wife, Cristina Teresa Murray, iv. 40; ix. 90.
SEAFIELD, OGILVIE-GRANT, EARL OF, vii. 454-494.
Seafield, Francis William, sixth earl of, vii. 486, 488.
— — his 1st wife, Mary Ann Dunn, vii. 489.
— — his 2nd wife, Louisa Emma Maunsell, vii. 489.
— Francis William, tenth earl of, vii. 492.
— — his wife, Ann Trevor Corry Evans, vii. 492.
— Ian Charles, eighth earl of, vii. 491.
— James, ninth earl of, vii. 489, 492.
— — his 1st wife, Caroline Louisa Evans, vii. 492.
— — his 2nd wife, Constance Helena Abercromby, vii. 492.
— — his 3rd wife, Georgina Adelaide Forestier-Walker, vii. 492.

* Name unknown.

Seafield, James, eleventh earl of, vii. 493.
——— his wife, Mary Elizabeth Nina Townend, vii. 493.
—— John Charles, seventh earl of, vii. 490.
—— —— his wife, Caroline Stuart, ii. 92; vii. 491.
—— Lewis Alexander, fifth earl of, vii. 487.
SEAFORTH, MACKENZIE, EARL OF, vii. 495-515.
Seaforth, Colin, first earl of, vii. 506.
—— —— his wife, Margaret Seton, iii. 372; vii. 507; ix. 77.
—— George, second earl of, vii. 504, 507.
—— —— his wife, Barbara Forbes, iv. 62; vii. 508; ix. 91.
—— Kenneth, third earl of, iii. 210; vii. 509.
—— —— his wife, Isabel Mackenzie, iii. 73, 210; vii. 509.
—— Kenneth, fourth earl of, vi. 14; vii. 510; ix. 156.
—— —— his wife, Frances Herbert, vii. 510.
—— William, fifth earl of, vii. 511.
—— —— his wife, Mary Kennet, vii. 511.
SEAFORTH, MACKENZIE, EARL OF, vii. 512-513.
Seaforth, Kenneth, earl of, vii. 512.
—— —— his 1st wife, Caroline Stanhope, vii. 513.
—— —— his 2nd wife, Harriet Powell, vii. 513.
SEAFORTH, MACKENZIE, LORD, vii. 513-514.
Seaforth, Kenneth, lord, vii. 513.
—— —— his wife, Mary Proby, vii. 513.
Seaforth, Kenneth (Mackenzie), marquess of, vii. 510.
Seale of Mount Boone, Sir John Henry, 1st bart., ii. 601.
—— —— his wife, Paulina Elizabeth Jodrell, ii. 601.
—— Elizabeth, wife of 10th lord Cranstoun, ii. 601.
Seaman, Jane, wife of rev. William Somerville, viii. 33.
—— Lionel, D.D., archdeacon of Taunton, viii. 33.
Seaton, Lachlan, sergeant 3rd Scots Guards, iv. 132.
—— Marjory, wife of (1) Lewis, 4th viscount Frendraught, and *perhaps* (2) George, 5th viscount Frendraught, iv. 132, 133 *n.*
—— Mary, dau. of Lachlan S., iv. 132.
—— *see also* Seton.
Sedley of Southfleet, Sir Charles, vii. 93.
—— —— his wife, Katharine Savage, vii. 93.
—— Katharine, countess of Dorchester, mistress of king James II. and VII., and wife of David, 1st earl of Portmore, vii. 93.
Segrave, Sir Geoffrey, iii. 426.
—— Sir John de, senr., ii. 127.
Seher, Janet de, wife of major-gen. Patrick Middleton, vi. 178.
Selby of Pasten, Gabriel, ii. 598.
—— —— his wife, Anne Cranstoun, ii. 598.
—— of Twizell, Sir William, iii. 598.
—— —— his wife, Ellen Fairfax, iii. 598.
—— Sir William, master of ordnance, ii. 232.
Sele, Katharine, wife of (1) George Rutherfurd, and *perhaps* (2) * Morris, vii. 369.
SELKIRK, DOUGLAS, EARL OF, vii. 516-525.
Selkirk, Charles, second earl of, vii. 516.
—— Dunbar, fourth earl of, vii. 361, 521.
—— —— his wife, Helen Hamilton, vii. 521.
—— Dunbar James, sixth earl of, vii. 524.
—— —— his wife, Cecely Louisa Egerton, vii. 524.
—— John, third earl of, vii. 361, 518.
—— —— his 1st wife, Anne Kennedy, ii. 485; vii. 362.
—— —— his 2nd wife, Elizabeth Hutchinson, vii. 362.
—— Thomas, fifth earl of, vii. 523.
—— —— his wife, Jean Wedderburn-Colvile, vii. 523.
—— William, 3rd son of 1st marquess of Douglas; first earl of, i. 205; iv. 27; vii. 516.
—— —— his wife, Anne, duchess of Hamilton, iv. 381; vii. 516.
Sellar, Marion, wife of Robert Broune, v. 166.
Sellick, *, husband of Katharine Graham, i. 140.
Selsey, James (Peachey), baron, iii. 112.
—— —— his wife, Georgina Caroline Scott, iii. 112.
Selwyn, George, vii. 147 *n.*
—— Townshend, rector of Kilmington, i. 492.
—— —— his wife, Charlotte Sophia Murray, i. 492.
Semarc of Chenies, Anne, vi. 462.
Semervilla, Guillelmus de, Evreux, viii. 1 *n.*
SEMPILL, SEMPILL, LORD, vii. 526-566.
Sempill, Anne, wife of Francis Abercromby, lord Glasfoord; baroness, iv. 181; vii. 558, 559.
—— Francis, styled lord, vii. 556.
—— —— his wife, Mary Mackenzie, vii. 556.
—— Francis, sixth lord, vii. 557.
—— —— his wife, Isabel Seton, vii. 557; viii. 600.
—— Francis, eighth lord, vii. 558.
—— —— his wife, Grisel Primrose, vii. 221, 558.
—— Francis, tenth lord, vii. 560.
—— Hugh, fifth lord, vii. 554.
—— —— his 1st wife, Anne Hamilton, i. 48; vii. 555.
—— —— his 2nd wife, Elizabeth Hay, iii. 577; vii. 555.

* Name unknown.

Sempill, Hew, twelfth lord, vii. 562.
—— —— his wife, Sarah Gaskell, vii. 562.
—— Hugh, fourteenth lord, vii. 564, 565.
—— —— his wife, Maria Mellish, vii. 565.
—— John, first lord, iii. 337, 529; vii. 250, 531.
—— —— his 1st wife, Margaret Colville, vii. 533.
—— —— his 2nd wife, Margaret Crichton, ii. 325; vii. 533.
—— John, eleventh lord, vii. 561.
—— John, thirteenth lord, vii. 563.
—— —— his wife, Janet Dunlop, vii. 564.
—— Maria Janet, wife of Edward Candler; baroness, vii. 565.
—— Robert, third lord, i. 38; vii. 538.
—— —— his contracted wife, Margaret Crichton, vii. 543.
—— —— his 1st wife, Isabel Hamilton, vii. 543.
—— —— his 2nd wife, Elizabeth Carlile, vii. 548.
—— Robert, fourth lord, iv. 195; vii. 254, 551.
—— —— his 1st wife, Agnes Montgomerie, iii. 442; vii. 552.
—— —— his 2nd wife, Johanna Everard, i. 40; vii. 553.
—— Robert, son of Archibald S. of Dykehead; styled lord, vii. 555.
—— —— his wife, Elizabeth *, vii. 556.
—— Robert, seventh lord, vii. 555, 557.
—— —— his wife, Anne Douglas, vi. 333; vii. 558; ix. 156.
—— Selkirk, fifteenth lord, vii. 565.
—— William, second lord, ii. 513, 514; vii. 535.
—— —— his 1st wife, Margaret Montgomery, iii. 437; vii. 536.
—— —— his 2nd wife, Elizabeth Arnot, vii. 536.
—— —— his 3rd wife, Marion Montgomery, iii. 437 *n.*; vii. 536.
—— master of, Robert, eldest son of 2nd lord Sempill, iii. 227; vii. 537.
—— —— his contr. wife, Margaret Crichton, vii. 543.
—— —— his wife, Isabel Hamilton, vii. 543.
—— master of, Robert, eldest son of 3rd lord Sempill, iv. 365; vii. 543.
—— —— his 1st wife, Elizabeth Hamilton, iv. 365 *n.*; vii. 543.
—— —— his 2nd wife, Barbara Preston, vii. 543.
—— master of, Robert, eldest son of 7th lord Sempill, vii. 558.
SEMPILL, FORBES-SEMPILL, LORD, vii. 566-568.
Sempill, John, eighteenth lord, vii. 567.
—— —— his wife, Gwendolin Emily Mary Prodgers, vii. 567.

* Name unknown.

Sempill, William, seventeenth lord, iv. 67; vii. 564, 566.
—— —— his 1st wife, Caroline Louisa Forbes, vii. 566.
—— —— his 2nd wife, Frances Emily Abercromby, vii. 566.
—— —— his 3rd wife, Mary Beresford Sherbrooke, vii. 567.
—— master of, William Francis, son of 18th lord Sempill, vii. 567.
SEMPILL, LORD SEMPILL, vii. 526-568.
Sempill of Thirdpart of Auchenames, William, sheriff-depute of Renfrewshire, vii. 537, 546.
—— —— his wife, Margaret Maxwell, vii. 538.
—— of Auchtermuchty, John, legtd. son of 3rd lord Sempill, v. 437; vii. 548.
—— of Barr, Francis, vii. 558.
—— of North Barr, Hew, vii. 562.
—— of Beltries, Francis, vii. 549.
—— —— his wife, Jane Campbell, vii. 549.
—— —— John, legtd. son of 3rd lord Sempill, v. 437; vii. 542, 548.
—— —— his wife, Marie Livingstone, v. 437; vii. 538, 548.
—— —— Sir James, ambassador to France, vii. 548.
—— —— his wife, Egidia Elphinstone, vii. 549.
—— —— Robert, vii. 549.
—— —— his wife, Marie Lyon, vii. 549; viii. 287.
—— —— Robert, sheriff-clerk of Renfrew, vii. 549.
—— —— his wife, Elizabeth Cochran, vii. 549.
—— of Bultrees, William, 1st laird, vii. 536.
—— of Bruntscheillis, Andrew, 2nd son of 3rd lord Sempill, iii. 228; vii. 544, 545.
—— —— his contracted wife, Margaret Crichton, iii. 228; vii. 539, 544.
—— —— his wife, Margaret Stirling, vii. 544.
—— —— Hew, vii. 544, 553.
—— —— John, 4th son of 3rd lord Sempill, vii. 542, 545.
—— —— William, elder son of Andrew S., vii. 544.
—— of Callan, Morton Pinckney, Dun Edin and Belwood, Edward, vii. 566.
—— —— his wife, Maria Janet, baroness Sempill, vii. 565.
—— of Carbery, Sir James, vii. 549.
—— of Carswells, Gabriel, vii. 533.
—— —— his wife, Jonet Spreule, vii. 533.
—— of Cassiltoun, Sir John, vii. 532.
—— of Castle Sempill, Sir William, sheriff of Renfrew, ii. 509; vii. 530.
—— —— his wife, Margaret *or* Marion Cathcart, ii. 509; vii. 530.
—— of Cathcart, Bryce, vii. 554.

Sempill of Cathcart, Gabriel, 3rd son of 1st lord Sempill, ii. 513; vii. 533.
—— —— his wife, Jonet Spreule, vii. 533.
—— —— Gabriel, vii. 534.
—— —— his wife, Margaret Spreule, vii. 534.
—— —— Gabriel, vii. 534.
—— —— his wife, Margaret Lindsay, vii. 534.
—— —— John, vii. 534.
—— —— his wife, Mariot Lindsay, vii. 534.
—— —— Thomas, vii. 535.
—— —— William, vii. 534.
—— —— his 1st wife, Marion Kirkcaldy, vii. 533.
—— —— his 2nd wife, Janet Montgomery, vii. 534.
—— —— his 3rd wife, Margaret Noble, vii. 534.
—— —— claimant to title of lord Sempill, vii. 559.
—— of Clook, Ninian, vii. 537.
—— of Craigbait, Gabriel, vii. 534 *bis*.
—— —— Hew, rector of the Scots College, Madrid, vii. 535, 544, 551, 553.
—— —— Robert, vii. 534, 553.
—— —— his wife, Grissel Montgomery, vii. 534.
—— —— William, vii. 533.
—— of Craiginfeoch, David, 2nd son of 2nd lord Sempill, vii. 537.
—— —— Francis, vii. 554.
—— —— John, vii. 537.
—— —— William, vii. 537.
—— of Cruikston, Robert, vii. 539.
—— of Little Cumbrae, John, legtd. son of 3rd lord Sempill, v. 437; vii. 548.
—— —— Robert, vii. 538.
—— of Dicbar, Sir John, vii. 532.
—— of Over Drumdelgie, John, legtd. son of 3rd lord Sempill, v. 437; vii. 538, 548.
—— —— his wife, Mary Livingston, v. 437; vii. 538, 548.
—— of Dykehead, Archibald, 4th son of 5th lord Sempill, vii. 555.
—— of Egliston, Thomas, vii. 528.
—— of Eliotstoun, Sir John, 3rd laird, ii. 286; vii. 527, 528.
—— —— John, 4th laird, vii. 529.
—— —— Sir John, 8th laird, vii. 531.
—— —— Sir Robert, 5th laird, vii. 529; ix. 156.
—— —— his wife, Elizabeth *, vii. 529.
—— —— Thomas, 2nd laird, vii. 528.
—— —— Sir Thomas, 7th laird, vii. 530.
—— —— his wife, Elizabeth Ross, vii. 530.
—— —— William de, steward of Renfrew, 1st laird, vii. 527.
—— —— Sir William, 6th laird, v. 552; vii. 530.
—— —— his wife, Margaret *or* Marion Cathcart, ii. 509; vii. 530.
—— —— his alleged wife, Agnes Montgomerie, iii. 432; vii. 530.

* Name unknown.

Sempill of Esperstoun, Alexander, vii. 528 *n.*
—— —— Robert, vii. 527 *n.*
—— of Fernynes, Sir Robert, vii. 529.
—— of Fulwood. *See* Semple of F.
—— of Glasfuird, Sir John, vii. 528.
—— —— Robert, vii. 557.
—— of Meikle Govane, James, vii. 544.
—— —— his wife, Sibella Glen, vii. 544.
—— of Greenside, Thomas, illeg. son of Robert, master of Sempill, vii. 544.
—— of Henderstoun Wester, Sir John, vii. 532.
—— of Kilbride, Sir John, vii. 528.
—— of Ladymure, Gabriel, vii. 533.
—— of Langside, Gabriel, ii. 513; vii. 533.
—— —— Hew, vii. 535; ix. 156.
—— —— Thomas, vii. 535.
—— of Largs, Robert de, vii. 526.
—— of Letterkenny, Sir William, 4th son of 4th lord Sempill, i. 52; vii. 554.
—— —— his wife, Anne Stewart, vii. 554.
—— of Lochwinnoch, Sir John, vii. 532.
—— of Longniddry, Thomas de, vii. 526.
—— of Millbank, James, vii. 544.
—— of Mylnbank, Robert, burgess of Renfrew, iv. 195.
—— —— his wife, Elizabeth Boyle, iv. 195.
—— of Mychelstoun, Sir William, vii. 530; ix. 156.
—— of Paidyeauch, Sir John, vii. 532.
—— of Paisley Abbey, Robert, i. 38; vii. 541.
—— of Wester Perthwike, John, vii. 529 *n.*
—— of Previk, William, vii. 535.
—— of Raite, William, vii. 527.
—— of Risdalemure, Sir John, vii. 532.
—— of Rossy, Sir William, vii. 530.
—— of Southannan, Sir Robert, vii. 529.
—— of Stewarton, John, legtd. son of 3rd lord Sempill, v. 437; vii. 548.
—— of Thankerton, Robert, vii. 539.
—— Anna, dau. of Archibald S. of Dykehead, vii. 556.
—— Anne, wife of * Hamilton, vii. 555.
—— Anne, wife of Dr. Adam Austin, vii. 563.
—— Annas, wife of Sir Archibald Stewart of Castlemilk, vii. 553.
—— Arthur, 2nd son of John S. of Beltries, vii. 550.
—— Barbara, wife of Sir Coll Lamont of Inveryne, vii. 553.
—— Bessie, dau. of Gabriel S. of Cathcart, vii. 535.
—— Clariadus, grandson of 2nd lord Sempill, vii. 538 *n.*
—— Dorathie, dau. of John S. of Beltries, vii. 550.
—— Dorothea, wife of Robert Montgomery of Skelmorlie, vii. 550.
—— Elizabeth, wife of (1) R. Graham, and (2) Robt. Lindsay, i. 512; iii. 318 *n.*; vii. 550.

* Name unknown.

Sempill, Elizabeth, wife of John Cochrane of Cochrane, iii. 338; ix. 75.
— Elizabeth, wife of 2nd lord Mordington, vi. 334; vii. 557.
— Elizabeth, wife of Sir Adam Mure of Caldwell, vii. 531.
— Elizabeth, wife of John Spreule of Coldoun, vii. 533 *n.*
— Elizabeth, wife of Sir Geo. Maxwell of Newark, vii. 550.
— Elizabeth, dau. of 7th lord Sempill, vii. 558.
— Elizabeth, wife of John Cochrane of Cochrane, ix. 76.
— Francelina, wife of Sir C. Hamilton of Killishandra, vii. 554.
— Francis, 2nd son of 1st lord Sempill, vii. 533.
— Francis, Jacobite agent in France, vii. 556.
— — his wife, Mary Mackenzie, vii. 511, 556.
— Francis, 2nd son of 14th lord Sempill, vii. 565.
— Gabriel, 2nd son of Gabriel S. of Craigbait, vii. 534, 535.
— George, 3rd son of capt. Robert S., vii. 556.
— George, colonel, vii. 562.
— — his 1st wife, Katharine Gordon, vii. 562.
— — his 2nd wife, Anne Clive, vii. 563.
— — his 3rd wife, Jane Butterworth, vii. 563.
— George, lieut. 78th Foot, vii. 564.
— Gilbert, brother of col. William S., vii. 551.
— Grizel, wife of John Blair of Blair, iii. 339; vii. 550.
— Grizell, wife of Jas. Hamilton of Stonehouse; mistress of archbishop Hamilton, iv. 362; vii. 545.
— Grissel, wife of John Logan of Raiss, vii. 554.
— H. C., Beltrees, New South Wales, iii. 391.
— Helen, wife of 3rd lord Cathcart, ii. 513; vii. 538.
— Helen, dau. of 3rd lord Sempill and Janet Leslie, vii. 551.
— Henrietta, dau. of capt. Robert S., vii. 556.
— Hugh, 2nd son of capt. Robert S., vii. 556.
— Hugh, captain of marines, vii. 563.
— Isobel, contracted to Robert Crawford; wife of George Chalmers, vii. 535.
— Isobel, wife of Jas. Hamilton of Kincavill, vii. 550.
— James, two legtd. sons of Ninian S. of Clook, vii. 537.
— James, 3rd son of 3rd lord Sempill, vii. 544.
Sempill, James, 2nd son of Francis S. of Beltries, vii. 549.
— James, 3rd son of Sir James S. of Beltries, vii. 550.
— James, 3rd son of 4th lord Sempill, vii. 553 *bis.*
— James, a Jesuit, 5th son of 5th lord Sempill, vii. 556.
— James, a Jesuit, 2nd son of 7th lord Sempill, vii. 558.
— Janet, dau. of 13th lord Sempill, vii. 565.
— Jean, wife of Sir John Stewart, sheriff of Bute, ii. 286; vii. 528.
— Jean, wife of 4th lord Ross of Halkhead, vii. 254, 550.
— Jean, wife of John Brisbane of Bishoptoun, vii. 554.
— Jean, dau. of Archibald S. of Dykehead, vii. 556.
— Jean, wife of Wm. Menzies of Pitfoddels, vii. 557.
— Jean, wife of Alex. Sinclair of Roslin, vii. 558.
— Jean, dau. of lord Glasfoord, vii. 560.
— Jean, dau. of 12th lord Sempill, vii. 563.
— Joanna, dau. of 13th lord Sempill, vii. 565.
— John, brother of 1st lord Sempill, vii. 531.
— John, 2nd son of William S. of Cathcart, vii. 534.
— John, captain, 3rd son of John S. of Beltries, vii. 550 *bis.*
— Jonet, wife of Sir John Stewart of Bute, ii. 286; vii. 528.
— Maldel, dau. of Gabriel S. of Cathcart, vii. 535.
— Margaret, wife of (1) John Houstoun of Houstoun, and (2) Robert Crawford of Kilbirny, vii. 531.
— Margaret, wife of (1) John Pollok of Pollok, and (2) Robt. Maxwell, vii. 535.
— Margaret, wife of (1) D. Hamilton of Broomhill, and (2) John Whitefoord of Whitefoord, vii. 547.
— Marion, wife of John Stewart, vii. 531.
— Marion, wife of George Maxwell, vii. 535.
— Marian, wife of Hugh Montgomery of Hazelhead, vii. 550.
— Marian, wife of Sir Geo. Preston of Valleyfield, vii. 555.
— Marianne, dau. of 12th lord Sempill, vii. 563.
— Mary, wife of Thos. Brisbane of Bishopstoun, vii. 530.
— Mary, alleged wife of Sir John Stirling of Keir, vii. 538.
— Mary, wife of Sir Colin Campbell of Ardkinglas, vii. 550.
— Peter, constable of Edinburgh Castle, vii. 538.

Sempill, Ralph, 5th son of 12th lord Sempill, vii. 563.
— Rebecca, dau. of 12th lord Sempill, vii. 563.
— Robert de, steward of the barony of Renfrew, vii. 526.
— Robert, 2nd son of William S. of Eliotstoun, vii. 527.
— Robert, 3rd son of William S. of Cathcart, vii. 534.
— Robert, 2nd son of Gabriel S. of Cathcart, vii. 535.
— Robert, captain in French regiments, heir male of the S. family, vii. 555; ix. 156, 157.
— — his wife, Elizabeth *, vii. 556.
— Robert, captain, 2nd son of lord Glasfoord, vii. 560.
— Sarah, wife of Patrick Crawfurd of Auchinames, vii. 563.
— Sarah, wife of Sir Wm. Forbes of Craigievar, vii. 564.
— Sarah, dau. of 14th lord Sempill, viii. 565.
— Susan, wife of lieut.-col. Samuel Hood Murray, iii. 391.
— Thomas, 2nd son of Robert de S. of Largs, vii. 527.
— William, 4th son of Sir James S. of Beltries, vii. 550.
— William, colonel, founder of the Scots College, Madrid, vii. 551.
— — his wife, Maria de Ledesma, vii. 551.
— William, 2nd son of 4th lord Sempill, vii. 553.
— William, 2nd son of Hugh, 5th lord Sempill, vii. 553, 555.
— *, wife of Wm. Fleming of Barrochan, vii. 550.
— *, illeg. dau. of 7th lord Sempill, ix. 156.
Semple of Fulwood, John, vii. 528 *n.*
— John, i. 185; iii. 338.
— — his wife, Margaret Douglas, i. 185.
— — *, iii. 340.
— *see* Sempill.
Senescal, Senescalli, *see* Stewart.
Senior, *, wife of William Leslie, vi. 445.
Seres of Inverallan, Patrick, vii. 456.
SETON, SETON, LORD, viii. 576-606.
Seton, George, 1st lord, i. 236; viii. 575.
— — his 1st wife, Margaret Stewart, ii. 265; viii. 576.
— — his 2nd wife, Christian Murray, i. 461; viii. 576.
— George, second lord, viii. 578.
— — his wife, Marion *or* Margaret Campbell, i. 334; viii. 579.
— George, third lord, viii. 580.
— — his wife, Jonet Hepburn, ii. 140; viii. 580.

* Name unknown.

Seton, George, fourth lord, viii. 581.
— — his 1st wife, Elizabeth Hay, viii. 436, 583.
— — his 2nd wife, Marie Pieris, viii. 584.
— George, fifth lord, ii. 9; v. 454; viii. 585.
— — his wife, Isabel Hamilton, viii. 588.
— George, eighth lord, viii. 593.
— George, eldest son of 3rd earl of Winton; styled lord, viii. 594 *bis.*
— — his wife, Henrietta Gordon, iv. 547; viii. 595.
— George, ninth lord, viii. 601.
— George, tenth lord, viii. 603.
— Ralph, styled lord, viii. 596.
— Robert, sixth lord, iii. 589; viii. 590.
— — his wife, Margaret Montgomerie, iii. 442; viii. 591.
— Robert, seventh lord, viii. 592.
— — his wife, Anna Maitland, v. 301; viii. 592.
— master of, George, eldest son of 5th lord Seton, viii. 588.
— master of, John, son of 1st lord Seton, v. 394, 554; viii. 577.
— — his wife, Christian Lindsay, iv. 235; v. 394; viii. 577.
— master of, Robert, 2nd son of 5th lord Seton, viii. 590.
— — his wife, Margaret Montgomerie, iii. 442; viii. 591.
SETON, EARL OF DUNFERMLINE, iii. 369-375.
SETON, LORD FYVIE, iii. 368-375.
SETON, EARL OF HUNTLY, iv. 521-523.
SETON, LORD KILWINNING, i. 541.
SETON, VISCOUNT OF KINGSTON, v. 195-198.
SETON, LORD SETON, viii. 576-606.
SETON, LORD URQUHART, iii. 370.
SETON, EARL OF WINTON, viii. 559-606.
Seton of Abercorn, Alexander, ancestor of the family of, viii. 573.
— — Sir Bruce Maxwell, 8th bart., iv. 525; viii. 497.
— — Sir Henry, 3rd bart., viii. 497.
— — his wife, Barbara Wemyss, viii. 497.
— — Sir Walter, iv. 493.
— of Aboyne, Sir Alexander, iv. 522.
— of Athelstaneford, George, viii. 594.
— — Sir John, viii. 596.
— of Badenoch, Sir Alexander, iv. 523.
— of Barns, Sir Alexander, ancestor of the family of, viii. 566.
— — George, i. 91.
— — James, colonel, i. 91.
— — James Alexander, viii. 589 *n.*
— — Sir John, 3rd son of 5th lord Seton, iii. 370; iv. 57; v. 263; viii. 588.
— — his wife, Anna Forbes, iv. 57; viii. 589.
— — Sir John, viii. 548.
— — his 2nd wife, Anna Fleming, v. 190; viii. 548.
— — his 3rd wife, Anna Home, vi. 9.

Seton of Barns, Sir John, iii. 577.
—— —— his wife, Margaret Hay, iii. 577.
—— of Beath, Emma, wife of Adam de Polwarth, vi. 199; viii. 561.
—— of Binning, George, viii. 579.
—— of Cariston, Christopher, v. 406.
—— —— Christopher, major 54th Foot, v. 408.
—— —— his wife, Katharine Lindsay, v. 408.
—— —— George, v. 414.
—— —— his wife, Elizabeth Lindsay, v. 414.
—— —— George, v. 407.
—— —— George, representative of the family of, viii. 583 *n.*
—— —— John, ancestor of the family of, viii. 581, 583.
—— —— his wife, Isabel Balfour of Carraldstoun, viii. 583.
—— of Clentis, George, viii. 582.
—— of Cockenzie, Robert, viii. 590.
—— of Culheg, Sir Henry, 4th bart., viii. 451.
—— —— his wife, Margaret Hay, viii. 451.
—— of Culcaigreis, Sir John, v. 263.
—— of Dundas, Sir Alexander, viii. 566.
—— of Echt, William, vii. 570.
—— of Elphinstone, Sir Alexander, viii. 566.
—— of Fausyde, Sir Alexander, viii. 566.
—— of Foulstruther, Sir Alexander, 3rd son of 1st earl of Winton, iii. 444, 445; viii. 591.
—— —— his 1st wife, Anna Livingston, iii. 446; v. 446.
—— —— John, viii. 581.
—— of Fyvie, George, i. 91.
—— —— James, colonel, i. 91.
—— of Gammilstoun, George, viii. 432, 435, 582.
—— of Gargunnock, Sir John, i. 43.
—— —— his wife, Margaret Hamilton, i. 43.
—— of Garleton, George, ancestor of the family of, viii. 594.
—— —— Sir George, 2nd bart., viii. 598.
—— —— his wife, Barbara Wauchope, viii. 599.
—— —— Sir George, 3rd bart., viii. 599, 600.
—— —— Sir John, 1st bart., viii. 596.
—— —— his wife, Christian Hume, viii. 596.
—— of Gogar, Sir Alexander, viii. 566.
—— of Gordon, Alexander, 2nd son of Sir William S. of Seton, ii. 223; iv. 69, 253, 518; v. 600; vi. 305, 309 *n.*; viii. 529, 572.
—— —— his wife, Elizabeth of Gordon, iv. 518; viii. 572 *bis.*
—— —— Sir Alexander, iv. 50, 521.
—— —— his 1st wife, Egidia Hay, iv. 524.
—— —— his 2nd wife, Elizabeth Crichton, iv. 524.
—— of Grange, Sir William, viii. 590.
—— of Greendykes, Robert, viii. 584.
—— of Hailes, George, viii. 594.
—— —— Sir George, iii. 452; iv. 36.
—— —— Robert, iii. 452.
—— —— his wife, Anne Montgomerie, iii. 452; iv. 36.
Seton of Halsington, Sir Alexander, viii. 566.
—— of Hertsheved, Sir Alexander, viii. 567.
—— of Innernytie, George, viii. 593.
—— of Kilcroich, Sir Alexander, lord of Session, vii. 14.
—— —— his wife, Marion Maule, vii. 14.
—— of Kilwinning, Sir Alexander, 3rd son of 1st earl of Winton, i. 541; viii. 591.
—— of Kirkliston, George, viii. 582.
—— of Kylesmure, Sir William, 5th son of 5th lord Seton, viii. 589, 593.
—— —— his wife, Agnes Stirling, viii. 590.
—— of Lambyngston, Sir Alexander, viii. 567.
—— of Langniddrie, George, viii. 593, 594.
—— of Meanie, James, iv. 117, 132.
—— of Mekylwardis, Alexander, iv. 69.
—— of Meldrum, Alexander, ancestor of the family of, iv. 521; viii. 573.
—— —— his wife, Elizabeth of Gordon, viii. 573.
—— —— Alexander, 1st laird, viii. 332 *n.*; ix. 93.
—— —— his wife, Muriel Sutherland, viii. 332 *n.*; ix. 69, 93.
—— —— Alexander, 3rd laird, iii. 589, 590 *bis*; iv. 54; vii. 163; ix. 91.
—— —— Alexander, 5th laird, vii. 412.
—— —— his 2nd wife, Jean Abernethy, vii. 412.
—— —— Alexander, the younger, iv. 112; vii. 413.
—— —— his wife, Christian Fraser, iv. 112.
—— —— Elizabeth, wife of John Urquhart of Craigfintry, iv. 112.
—— —— William, iv. 521.
—— —— his wife, Elizabeth Meldrum of that Ilk, iv. 521.
—— —— William, iv. 126.
—— —— his wife, Anne Crichton, iv. 126.
—— of Monylangain, Sir John, iii. 204.
—— of Mounie, Alexander, ancestor of the family of, viii. 573.
—— —— John, iii. 589.
—— of Mylis, Sir Alexander, viii. 566.
—— —— Robert, 4th son of 4th lord Seton, viii. 584.
—— of Myltoun, James, 5th son of 4th lord Seton, viii. 584.
—— of Newark, John, iv. 181.
—— of Niddrie, Sir Alexander, viii. 567.
—— —— William, iv. 80.
—— of West Niddrie, George, viii. 582.
—— of Northrig, Alexander, viii. 579.
—— —— his wife, Jonet Sinclair of Northrig, viii. 579.
—— of Olivestob, Sir Thomas, viii. 592.
—— —— his wife, Agnes *or* Anna Drummond, viii. 592.
—— of Panbride, Sir Alexander, iv. 522.
—— of Parbroath, Alexander, i. 461.
—— —— his wife, Helen Murray, i. 461.

Seton of Parbroath, Andrew, vii. 289.
—— —— David, comptroller of Scotland, iv. 283.
—— —— his wife, Marion Gray, iv. 282.
—— —— Sir David, ix. 73.
—— —— George, vi. 104; ix. 157.
—— —— his wife, Jean Sinclair, vi. 104; vii. 575; ix. 157.
—— —— Gilbert, vii. 289.
—— —— his wife, Helen Leslie, vii. 289.
—— —— Sir John, alleged ancestor of the family of, viii. 569 *n*.
—— of Pitmedden, Alexander, ancestor of the family of, viii. 573.
—— —— Alexander, ii. 14.
—— —— his wife, Beatrice Ogilvy, ii. 14.
—— —— James, ii. 15.
—— —— John, ii. 15.
—— —— Sir William Samuel, 9th bart., iv. 521.
—— of Pluscarden, Alexander, chancellor of Scotland, iii. 369; viii. 589.
—— of Queensferry, Sir Alexander, viii. 566.
—— of Redshiel, George, viii. 432, 435, 582.
—— of Richelkellach, Bertram de, viii. 562, 563.
—— of St. Germains, Sir Alexander, viii. 591.
—— —— George, W.S., viii. 592.
—— —— Sir John, viii. 592.
—— —— his wife, Margaret Kellie, viii. 592.
—— —— Robert, viii. 590.
—— of Scetun, Osbert de, viii. 559 *n*.
—— of Seton, Alexander de, ancestor of the family of, viii. 560.
—— —— Sir Alexander de, vi. 199; viii. 561.
—— —— Sir Alexander, son of Serlo de S., iii. 257; viii. 563.
—— —— Sir Alexander, the patriot, governor of Berwick, viii. 563; ix. 169.
—— —— his wife, Christian Cheyne, viii. 568.
—— —— Bartine *or* Bertram de, viii. 562, 563.
—— —— Sir George de, viii. 575.
—— —— his 1st wife, Margaret Stewart, ii. 265; viii. 576.
—— —— Sir John, iv. 83; viii. 573.
—— —— his wife, Katharine de St. Clair, iv. 519 *n*.; viii. 573.
—— —— Margaret, wife of Alan de Wyntoun, viii. 570; ix. 169.
—— —— Philip de, viii. 560.
—— —— his alleged wife, Alice *or* Helen of Dunbar, viii. 561.
—— —— his wife, Matilda Corbet, viii. 561.
—— —— Sir Serlo *or* Seyer de, viii. 562.
—— —— Sir William, ii. 223 *n*., 586; iv. 343, 518; viii. 571; ix. 46, 60, 170.
—— —— his 2nd wife, Jonet Fleming, ii. 223; iv. 519; viii. 529, 572; ix. 46.
—— —— Sir William, i. 236; viii. 574.
—— —— his wife, Janet Dunbar, i. 236; viii. 574.
Seton of Seton Manor, Sir Christopher de, ii. 425, 434; viii. 563.
—— —— his wife, Christiana de Brus, ii. 434; viii. 563.
—— —— Sir John de, viii. 564.
—— of Strathbogie, Sir Alexander, iv. 522.
—— of Thornton, John, viii. 300.
—— of Touch and Tullibody, Alexander, ancestor of the family of, viii. 573.
—— —— Sir Alexander, iv. 520, 521.
—— —— his 1st wife, Egidia Hay, i. 15; iv. 524.
—— —— his 2nd wife, Elizabeth Crichton, iv. 524.
—— —— Alexander, eldest son of 1st earl of Huntly, iv. 449, 525, 526.
—— —— his wife, Elizabeth Erskine, iv. 525; v. 607.
—— —— Sir Alexander, v. 432.
—— —— James, ii. 66; iii. 234.
—— —— John, ii. 594.
—— —— his wife, Barbara *or* Janet Cranstoun, ii. 594.
—— —— Sir Ninian, vi. 412.
—— —— his wife, Janet Chisholm, vi. 412.
—— —— Sir Walter, ii. 66; iv. 60; v. 612.
—— —— his wife, Elizabeth Erskine, v. 612.
—— of Travernent, Sir Alexander, viii. 566.
—— of Upcraigie, George, viii. 593.
—— of Urquhart, Alexander, 4th son of 5th lord Seton, iii. 369; viii. 589.
—— of Westercraigs, Sir Alexander, viii. 566.
—— of Whittinghame, Elizabeth, wife of Wm. Hay of Drumelzier, viii. 449.
—— of Winchelburgh, Alexander de, viii. 560.
—— —— Philip de, viii. 560.
—— of Windygowl, Sir Robert, bart., viii. 596, 600.
—— —— William, viii. 600.
—— of Winton, Alexander, ancestor of the family of, viii. 560.
—— Adam de, churchman, viii. 562 *n*.
—— Agnes, wife of 3rd lord Mordingtoun, v. 196; vi. 334.
—— Sir Alexander, styled master of Gordon, iv. 520, 521.
—— Sir Alexander, 4th son of 3rd earl of Winton, v. 195; viii. 595.
—— Alexander, 3rd son of 1st viscount of Kingston, v. 196.
—— Alexander, son of Sir Alex. S. of Parbroath, v. 394.
—— —— his wife, Katharine Lindsay, v. 394.
—— Alexander de, crusader, viii. 562 *n*.
—— Alexander, son of Christopher S., viii. 563 *n*.

Seton, Sir Alexander, killed at Kinghorn, viii. 567, 569.
—— —— his alleged wife, Margaret Murray, viii. 569 *n.*
—— Sir Alexander, master of the House of Torphichen, viii. 568.
—— Sir Alexander, grandson of Sir Alexander S. of Seton, viii. 569.
—— —— his wife, Margaret Ruthven, iv. 256; viii. 569.
—— Alexander, brother of 2nd lord Seton, viii. 577.
—— Alexander, brother of 4th earl of Winton, viii. 595; ix. 170.
—— Alexander, apprenticed to J. Jolly, viii. 598.
—— Andrew, in Ireland's regiment, viii. 599.
—— Anna, wife of Sir John Hamilton of Fingaltoun, iv. 343.
—— Anne, wife of Alexander, viscount of Fentoun, iii. 372; v. 86.
—— Ann, wife of 3rd lord Mordington, v. 196; vi. 334.
—— Anne, wife of John, 2nd earl of Traquair, viii. 406, 600.
—— Archibald, son of John S., viii. 577 *n.*
—— —— his wife, * Livingston, viii. 577 *n.*
—— Archibald, 'ane maister clerk,' viii. 577 *n.*
—— Archibald, 3rd son of 3rd lord Seton, viii. 581.
—— Arthur, 5th son of 1st viscount of Kingston, v. 196.
—— Barbara, dau. of 1st viscount of Kingston, v. 197.
—— Barbara, alleged wife of Sir Wm. Keith of Keith-Marischal, vi. 30; viii. 562 *n.*
—— Barbara, dau. of Sir George S. of Garleton, viii. 599.
—— Beatrix, wife of Sir Geo. Ogilvy, ii. 10, 11; viii. 583.
—— Charles, eldest son of 1st viscount of Kingston, v. 196.
—— Charles, 6th son of Sir John S. of Garleton, viii. 598.
—— Christell, a churchman, viii. 579 *n.*
—— Christian, wife of Thos. Preston of Whitehill, iii. 119; viii. 577 *n.*
—— Christiana, wife of George, 10th earl of Dunbar, iii. 273, 275; viii. 571; ix. 71, 169.
—— Christiana, wife of Norman Leslie of Rothes, vii. 273; viii. 574.
—— Christian, dau. of Sir John S. of Garleton, viii. 598.
—— Christian, wife of Hugh Douglas of Borg, viii. 577.
—— Christian, illeg. dau. of 5th earl of Winton, ix. 170.
—— Christopher, witness in 1247, viii. 563 *n.*
—— Christopher, brother of 4th earl of Winton, viii. 595.

* Name unknown.

Seton, Christopher, 3rd son of 3rd earl of Winton, viii. 595.
—— Christopher, 8th son of 3rd earl of Winton, viii. 596.
—— Christopher, 5th son of Sir John S. of Garleton, viii. 598.
—— Christopher, 2nd son of 4th earl of Winton, viii. 603.
—— Cristal, 2nd son of Sir Walter S. of Tullibody, ii. 66.
—— Dugal de, viii. 562.
—— Dugal, 2nd son of 1st lord Seton, viii. 576 *n.*
—— Eleanor, contr. to F. Douglas, and wife of Hugh, 6th lord Somerville, viii. 24, 583; ix. 170 *ter.*
—— Elizabeth, wife of Alexander, 9th lord of the Isles, iv. 521; v. 44.
—— Elizabeth, wife of capt. George Lindsay, v. 407.
—— Elizabeth, wife of Wm. Hay of Drumelzier, v. 197.
—— Elizabeth, wife of 7th earl Marischal, vi. 59; viii. 595.
—— Elizabeth, wife of (1) John Urquhart, and (2) 10th lord Saltoun, vii. 413, 443.
—— Emma, wife of Adam of Polwarth, vi. 199; viii. 561.
—— Euphemia, wife of (1) Patrick Hamilton, and (2) William, 1st visconnt of Air, iii. 234.
—— Euphame, wife of Robert Bennett, viii. 577 *n.*
—— Geills, wife of P. Ogilvy of Inchmartine, iv. 34.
—— George, tutor of Meldrum, iii. 589.
—— Sir George, 2nd son of 1st earl of Huntly, iv. 523, 525, 526.
—— George, 2nd son of 1st viscount Kingston, v. 196.
—— George, advocate, author of *The History of the Family of Seton*, viii. 560 *n.*, 583 *n.*
—— George, eldest son of Archibald S., viii. 577 *n.*
—— George, saddler, Bellingham, viii. 604.
—— George James, v. 408.
—— Grizel, dau. of 1st earl of Dunfermline, iii. 373.
—— Helenor, contr. to Francis Douglas, and wife of Hugh, 6th lord Somerville, viii. 24, 583; ix. 170 *ter.*
—— Henrietta, wife of (1) William, 5th earl of Wigtown, and (2) William, 18th earl of Crawford, iii. 37, 374; viii. 553; ix. 78.
—— Henry, 3rd son of Sir Alexander S. of Gordon, iv. 521.
—— Isobel, wife of (1) James, 1st earl of Perth, and (2) Francis, lord Stewart and Bothwell, ii. 173; vii. 48; viii. 592; ix. 149.
—— Isobel, wife of 1st earl of Lauderdale, iii. 372; v. 301.

Seton, Isabel, dau. of 1st viscount of Kingston, v. 197.
—— Isabel, wife of 6th lord Sempill, vii. 557; viii. 600.
—— James, 3rd son of Archibald S., viii. 577 *n.*
—— James, legtd. son of 2nd lord Seton, viii. 579 *n.*
—— James, 3rd son of 4th lord Seton, viii. 583.
—— James, lieut. in col. Keith's regt., viii. 599.
—— Janet, wife of Patrick Gordon of Braco, i. 85.
—— Janet, wife of George, 11th earl of Dunbar, iii. 275 *n.*; viii. 573.
—— Janet, wife of (1) John, 1st lord Haliburton, and (2) Edward Congalton, iv. 335; viii. 575.
—— Janet, wife of Sir Robert Keith, vi. 40; viii. 574.
—— Janet, wife of Thomas (Dunbar), 4th earl of Moray, vi. 305.
—— Janet, wife of James Hamilton of Samuelston, vii. 289.
—— Jean, wife of John Ogilvy of Birnes, ii. 12.
—— Jean, wife of 8th lord Hay of Yester, iii. 373; viii. 448; ix. 167 *bis.*
—— Jean, wife of Alex. Abercromby, iv. 181.
—— Jean, wife of 3rd lord Mordington, v. 196.
—— Jean, dau. of 3rd earl of Winton, viii. 601.
—— John, bailie in Bourtie to the abbey of Arbroath, iii. 590.
—— John, 6th son of 1st viscount of Kingston, v. 197.
—— John, 2nd son of Sir John S. of Garleton, v. 197; viii. 596.
—— —— his wife, Frances Neale, viii. 596.
—— Sir John, Scots Guards in France, 2nd son of John S., 1st of Careston, viii. 28; ix. 159.
—— John, viii. 567.
—— —— his wife, Mary Newton, viii. 597.
—— John, their son, viii. 597.
—— —— his wife, Mary Hughes, viii. 597.
—— Sir John, 4th son of Sir Alexander S. of Seton, viii. 569.
—— —— his alleged wife, Elizabeth Ramsay, viii. 569 *n.*
—— John, brother of 2nd lord Seton, viii. 577.
—— —— his wife, * Little, viii. 577 *n.*
—— John, bailie of Tranent, viii. 577 *n.*
—— John, 3rd son of 2nd lord Seton, viii. 579.
—— John, Jesuit, viii. 599.

* Name unknown.

Seton, John, illeg. son of 5th earl of Winton, ix. 170.
—— Jonet, wife of (1) Sir John Bellenden, and (2) John, 8th lord Forbes, ii. 64, 66; iv. 60, 61.
—— Katharine, wife of (1) Sir Alan Stewart of Darnley, and (2) Herbert, 1st lord Maxwell of Carlaverock, v. 348; vi. 475; viii. 575.
—— Katharine, wife of John Lindsay of Kirkforthar, v. 406.
—— Katharine, wife of Thomas (Dunbar), 4th earl of Moray, vi. 305.
—— Katharine, nun at Edinburgh, viii. 579.
—— Lilias, dau. of 1st earl of Dunfermline, iii. 373.
—— Lilias, alleged dau. of 5th earl of Winton, viii. 605.
—— Margaret, wife of lord Claud Hamilton, 1st baron Paisley, i. 39; viii. 590; ix. 2.
—— Margaret, wife of 1st earl of Seaforth, i. 519; iii. 372; vii. 507; ix. 77.
—— Margaret, wife of James Sutherland of Kinminitie, iii. 204.
—— Margaret, wife of 1st viscount Dudhope, iii. 313.
—— Margaret, wife of Thos. Fraser of Cairnbulg, iv. 117.
—— Margaret, wife of William Maitland of Lethington, v. 291; viii. 579.
—— Margaret, wife of W. Lindsay of Pyotston, v. 412.
—— Margaret, wife of Robert, 2nd lord Lyle, v. 554; viii. 577 *n.*, 578; ix. 132.
—— Margaret, wife of 10th earl of Dunbar, viii. 571; ix. 169.
—— Margaret, wife of (1) R. Logan of Restalrig, and (2) D. Hamilton of Ladyflat, viii. 583.
—— Margaret, dau. of 3rd earl of Winton, viii. 595.
—— Margaret, dau. of Sir John S. of Garleton, viii. 598.
—— Margaret, dau. of Sir George S. of Garleton, viii. 599.
—— Margaret, mistress of 4th viscount of Kenmure, ix. 118.
—— Marie, maid-of-honour to queen Mary, vii. 585.
—— Marion, alleged wife of Sir John Ogilvy of Lintrathen, i. 113.
—— Marion, wife of (1) Thomas *or* Arthur, master of Borthwick, (2) Hugh, 2nd earl of Eglinton, and (3) Alex. Graham of Wallastoun, ii. 108; iii. 439; vi. 229; viii. 581; ix. 39 *ter.*
—— Marion, wife of (1) John, 4th earl of Menteith, and (2) John, 10th earl of Sutherland, vi. 160; viii. 342, 583.
—— Martha, wife of William Maitland of Lethington, v. 291; viii. 579.

Seton, Mary, wife of 3rd earl of Carnwath, ii. 414; viii. 601.
— Mary, wife of John Arrat of Fofarty, viii. 562 *n.*, 598, 599.
— Mary, alleged dau. of 5th earl of Winton, viii. 605.
— Mary Katharine, wife of John Broadbent, viii. 597.
— Ralph, eldest son of John S., viii. 596.
— Robert, in French service, viii. 579.
— Robert, eldest son of 1st earl of Winton, viii. 593.
— Robert, 2nd son of John S., viii. 598.
— Robert, Jesuit at Aboyne, viii. 598.
— Sophia, wife of 1st lord Lindsay of Balcarres, i. 518; iii. 372.
— Thomas, cornet of Horse, iv. 132.
— Thomas, *perhaps* son of Philip de S., viii. 561.
— Thomas, hanged at Berwick, viii. 567, 568.
— Thomas, servant to king James IV. viii. 579 *n.*
— William, drowned at Berwick, viii. 568.
— William, man-at-arms in France, viii. 579.
— William, illeg. son of 2nd lord Seton, viii. 579 *n.*
— William, provost of the collegiate church of Seton, viii. 589.
Seton-Broadbent, James, viii. 597.
— — his wife, Sophia Francis Lee, viii. 598.
— Thomas George, viii. 598; ix. 170.
SETTRINGTON, STEWART, BARON, v. 357.
Settrington, Ludovick, baron, v. 357.
SETTRINGTON, LENNOX, BARON OF, v. 363-371.
Settrington, Charles, first baron of, i. 32; v. 363.
— Charles Henry, eldest grandson of 7th duke of Lennox; styled lord, v. 370.
Sewell of Athenry, Thomas Bermingham, vi. 73; vii. 60.
— Susan Henrietta, wife of (1) col. Burrowes, and (2) George, 14th earl of Perth, vi. 73; vii. 60.
— Sir W. H., lieut.-general, K.C.B., viii. 129.
— — his wife, Georgina Hacking Dalrymple, viii. 129.
Seymour of Tottenham and Savernake Forest, Elizabeth, wife of 3rd earl of Elgin, iii. 480.
— Anna Maria Jane, wife of William Tollemache, iii. 413.
— Augusta Georgiana Sophia, wife of Charles William Bruce, iii. 412 *n.*
— Frederick Charles William, iv. 560.
— — his wife, Mary Gordon, iv. 560.
— George, son of 1st marquess of Hertford, i. 64.
— — his wife, Isabella Hamilton, i. 64.
Seymour, Gertrude Frances, wife of col. J. F. D. Crichton-Stuart, ii. 309.
— Sir G. Hamilton, G.C.B., ii. 309.
— Jane, wife of Charles (Boyle), viscount Dungarvan, vii. 142.
— Victoria, wife of C. A. de Trafford, ii. 530.
— William, v. 355.
— — his wife, Arabella Stewart, v. 354.
Seymour-Conway, Anne, wife of Geo. Damer, i. 386; ix. 25.
Shaftesbury, Anthony (Cooper), 8th earl of, v. 96.
Shairp of Houston, John, advocate, 1st laird, vii. 68.
— — John, ix. 100.
— — his wife, Christian Hamilton, ix. 100.
Shannon, Elizabeth (Killegrew), viscountess, i. 30.
Sharp of Ballindoch, Sir William, ix. 51.
— — his wife, Margaret Dundas, ix. 51.
— of Chippenham Park, John, viii. 468.
— — his wife, Hannah Charlotte Hay, viii. 468.
— of Scotscraig, Sir James, bart., vi. 69.
— — his wife, Mary Drummond, vi. 68; vii. 82.
— — Sir William, v. 91.
— — his wife, Margaret Erskine, v. 91.
— — Sir William, v. 92.
— — his wife, Sophia Erskine, v. 92.
— of Stoneyhill, Sir James, bart., vii. 82.
— John, lieut. R.N., iv. 292.
Sharpe of Hoddam, Charles Kirkpatrick, v. 634.
— James, archbishop of St. Andrews, i. 520; iv. 248; v. 379; vii. 444.
— Margaret, wife of 11th lord Saltoun, vii. 444.
— Susan, wife of capt. James Floyer Erskine, v. 634.
— William, sheriff-clerk of Banff, ii. 16.
Shaw of Broich, John, i. 228; ix. 4.
— — his wife, Elizabeth Sandilands, i. 75; ix. 4.
— of Cambusmoir, Alexander, ii. 189.
— — Sir Henry, v. 501.
— — his wife, Marion Forrester, v. 501.
— of Dalton, John, ii. 493.
— — his wife, Helen Kennedy, ii. 493.
— of Ditton, Thomas, vi. 438.
— of Fetham, William, vii. 76.
— of Haylie, Sir John, ambassador to Denmark, iv. 152.
— — John, ii. 512.
— — his wife, Jean Cathcart, ii. 512.
— of Kenward, Sir John Gregory, bart., iv. 67.
— of Lethangie, John, ix. 4.
— — William, vii. 76; ix. 68.
— of Quylt, William, vii. 76.

Shaw of Welhurn Hall, John, v. 420.
—— Agnes, wife of Wm. Stewart, ix. 68.
—— Beatrice Mary, wife of Reginald Bethune, viscount Garnock, v. 420.
—— David, iii. 360.
—— Elizabeth, mistress of James v., i. 24.
—— Elizabeth, wife of John (Murray), 1st earl of Annandale, i. 228.
—— Elizabeth, wife of John Stewart of Dalswinton, iv. 151.
—— Elizabeth, wife of D. Livingston of Bantaskin, ix. 129.
—— George, abbot of Paisley, vii. 245.
—— George, Perth, viii. 202.
—— —— his wife, Rebecca Murray, viii. 202.
—— George, son of John S. of Lethangie, ix. 4.
—— Horatia, wife of 19th lord Forbes, iv. 67.
—— Isabella, wife of (1) major J. Leith, and (2) col. John Scott Napier, vi. 438.
—— James, iv. 573.
—— Margaret, wife of 4th lord Blantyre, ii. 86.
—— Margaret, wife of 13th earl of Crawford, iii. 33.
—— Margaret, wife of Walter Graham of Gartur, vi. 152; ix. 136.
—— Maria, wife of (1) Sir Jacob Wheate, bart., and (2) admiral A. F. I. Cochrane, iii. 360.
—— Mary Glencairn, wife of Claude D. J. Carmichael, iv. 573.
—— *, wife of Mr. George Ker, v. 53.
—— *see also* Schaw.
Shaw-Kennedy of Kirkmichael, John, ii. 493.
Shaw-Lefevre, Sir John George, K.C.B., i. 97.
—— Rachel Emily, wife of 1st baron Stanmore, i. 97.
Shaw Stewart of Greenock, Sir Michael, 6th bart., iii. 493.
—— Katharine Mary, V.A., wife of maj.-gen. Robert Bruce, iii. 493.
Shee of Dunmore, Sir George, bart., iii. 518 *n.*
—— —— his wife, Jane Young, iii. 518 *n.*
Sheffield, Katharine Sophia, wife of Joseph Cox of Stanford Vale, vii. 482.
—— Mary, wife of 2nd lord Fairfax, iii. 598.
Shepheard of Exning, Samuel, M.P., v. 18.
—— Frances, wife of Charles, 9th viscount Irvine, v. 18.
—— Frances Ingram, wife of lord William Gordon, iv. 554; v. 19.
Shepherd, Henry John, vii. 225.
—— —— his wife, Mary Primrose, vii. 225.
Sherard, Bennet, iii. 601.
Sherbrooke of Oxton Hall, Henry Porter, vii. 567.

* Name unknown.

Sherbrooke, Mary Beresford, wife of 17th lord Sempill, vii. 567.
Sheres, * seducer of Isobel Sempill, wife of Jas. Hamilton of Kincavil, vii. 551.
Sheridan, Thomas, viii. 470.
—— Thomas Brinsley, viii. 470.
—— Helen Selina, wife of (1) Price, 4th lord Dufferin and Clandeboye, and (2) George, earl of Gifford, viii. 470.
Sherwood, Anne, wife of D. S. Carmichael-Smyth, iv. 569.
—— J. D., major-general Bengal artillery, iv. 569.
Shewalton, David Boyle, senator of the College of Justice, lord, iv. 208.
—— Patrick Boyle, senator of the College of Justice, lord, iv. 177, 200, 204.
Shipley, Sir Charles, governor of Grenada, ii. 278.
—— Elizabeth Cole, wife of Henry David, 12th earl of Buchan, ii. 278.
Shireburn *or* Williams, Anne, i. 380, 381.
Shirley of Staunton Harold, Sir Seymour, bart., iii. 479.
—— —— his wife, Diana Bruce, iii. 479.
Shirreff, William Henry, rear-admiral R.N., iii. 513.
—— —— his wife, Elizabeth Ann Murray, iii. 513.
Short, Helen, wife of John Guthrie, vi. 159.
SHORTCLEUCH, DOUGLAS, LORD, iv. 381; vii. 516-525.
Shortcleuch, William, first lord, iv. 381; vii. 516.
Shovel of Crayford, Sir Cloudesley, admiral R.N., iv. 595, 596.
—— —— Elizabeth, wife of (1) Robert, 1st lord Romney, and (2) John, 3rd earl of Hyndford, iv. 595.
Shrewsbury, Henry John (Chetwynd-Talbot), 18th earl of, v. 485.
—— —— his wife, Sarah Elizabeth Beresford, v. 485.
Shrewsbury Herald, pursuivant of George, 10th earl of March, iii. 272.
Shuttleworth of Forcett, Robert, iv. 96.
—— Charles, in holy orders, iv. 96.
—— —— his wife, Mary Cockburn, iv. 96.
Sibbald of Balgony, Sir John, master of the Household, i. 177.
—— of Balmedie, Elizabeth *or* Isobel, wife of (1) George, 4th earl of Angus, (2) John Carmichael of Balmedie, and (3) Sir Robt. Douglas of Lochleven, i. 177; iv. 564; vi. 367.
—— of Kair, i. 283.
—— —— Andrew, i. 291.
—— —— his wife, Margaret Arbuthnott, i. 291.
—— of Moneythin, Thomas, i. 108.
—— James, parson of Arbuthnott, i. 283.

* Name unknown.

Sibbald, James, D.D., minister of New Aberdeen, i. 291.
— John, minister of Arbuthnott, i. 291.
— Sir Robert, M.D., vii. 446.
Sibilla, wife of Edward of Edlingham, iii. 247 *n.*, 248.
SIDLAW, LYON, LORD, viii. 299-317.
Sidlaw, Patrick, first lord, viii. 299.
Sidney, Sir Philip, i. 195.
— Emma, wife of (1) gen. Sir H. B. Edwardes, and (2) William Tollemache, iii. 413.
— James, Richmond Hill, iii. 413.
Sighterman, Christina Elisabeth, wife of Anthony Adrian, 8th lord Falconer of Halkerton, and 5th earl of Kintore, v. 251.
Sigrid *or* Sigarith, wife of (1) Waldeve of Allerdale, and (2) Roger, son of Gilbert, iii. 244.
Sigurd, son of Hlodver of Caithness, ii. 314.
Sigurd Eysteinsson, earl of Moray, Orkney, etc., ii. 313; vi. 281.
Sigurd Hlodversson, earl, ii. 314; vi. 281.
Simeon, Sir John, 3rd bart., ii. 565.
— — his wife, Katharine Dorothea Colville, ii. 565.
Simmern, Charles Louis, elector palatine, count zu, i. 27; v. 481.
— Charlotte, dau. of Frederick v., elector palatine; countess von, i. 28.
— Edward, 4th son of Frederick v., count von, i. 27.
— — his wife, Anne de Gonzaga, i. 27.
— Elizabeth, abbess of Hervorden, countess von, i. 28.
— Elizabeth Charlotte, wife of Philip, duke of Orleans; countess von, i. 27.
— Frederick v., count palatine of the Rhine, king of Bohemia, graf zu, i. 27.
— — his wife, Elizabeth Stewart, i. 27.
— Henrietta, wife of Sigismund Racoczy, prince of Transylvania; countess von, i. 28.
— Louise Hollandine, abbess of Maubisson, countess von, i. 28.
— Maurice, 3rd son of Frederick v., elector palatine; count von, i. 27.
— Philip, 5th son of Frederick, elector palatine; count von, i. 28.
— Rupert, 2nd son of Frederick v., elector palatine; count von, i. 27; vi. 248; vii. 346.
— Sophia, wife of Ernest Augustus, duke of Brunswick; countess von, i. 28.
Simon of Scrogis, son of Robert, vi. 199.
Simon, eldest son of Malcolm, 2nd earl of Atholl, i. 417.
Simon, bishop of Moray, ii. 121.
Simon, brother of Walter, 3rd high steward of Scotland, v. 136.
Simon, bishop of Whithorn, v. 256.
Simpson of Bradley, John, viii. 310.
— — his wife, Anne Lyon, viii. 310.
— Ada Twyford, wife of 13th earl of Lauderdale, v. 322.
— Elizabeth, wife of Jas. Wemyss of Caskieberran, ii. 281.
— Frances Josephine, wife of rev. C. R. Tollemache, iii. 416.
— Henry, Portobello, iii. 416.
— Henry Trail, rector of Adel, v. 322.
— Sir James, general, ii. 565.
SINCLAIR, SINCLAIR, LORD, vii. 569-592.
Sinclair, Andrew, *de jure* thirteenth lord, vii. 589.
— — his wife, Elizabeth Rutherford, vii. 589.
— Charles, *de jure* twelfth lord, vi. 17, 21; vii. 585, 589.
— — his wife, Elizabeth Hume, vi. 17; vii. 589.
— Charles, fourteenth lord, vii. 589.
— — his 1st wife, Mary Agnes Chisholm, vii. 590.
— — his 2nd wife, Isabella Mary Chatto, vii. 590.
— Charles William, sixteenth lord, v. 53; vii. 591.
— — his wife, Margaret Jane Murray, vii. 591.
— Henry, third lord, ii. 334; vii. 571.
— — his wife, Margaret Hepburn, ii. 150, 159; vii. 571.
— Henry, fifth lord, vii. 573.
— — his 1st wife, Janet Lindsay, v. 398; vii. 574.
— — his 2nd wife, Elizabeth Forbes, iv. 56; vii. 574.
— Henry, sixth lord, vii. 575.
— Henry, tenth lord, vii. 586.
— — his wife, Barbara Cockburn, vii. 586.
— James, seventh lord, vii. 575.
— James, *de jure* eleventh lord, vii. 587, 588.
— — his wife, Janet Dalrymple, vii. 588; viii. 147.
— James, fifteenth lord, vii. 591.
— — his wife, Jane Little, vii. 591.
— John, ninth lord, ii. 577; vii. 576.
— — his wife, Mary Wemyss, vii. 576; viii. 500.
— Patrick, eighth lord, vii. 574, 576.
— — his wife, Margaret Cockburn, vii. 576.
— William, first lord, ii. 334; vii. 569.
— William, 'the Waster,' second lord, ii. 333; vii. 569.
— — his wife, Christina Leslie, ii. 334; vii. 276, 570.
— William, fourth lord, ii. 338; vii. 572.
— — his 1st wife, Elizabeth Keith, vi. 45; vii. 573.
— — his alleged 2nd wife, Agnes Bruce, vii. 573; ix. 157.

Sinclair, master of, Archibald James Murray, elder son of 16th lord Sinclair, vii. 591.
—— his wife, Violet Frances Murray-Kennedy, vii. 591.
— master of, Henry, elder son of 4th lord Sinclair, vii. 573.
—— his wife, Janet Lindsay, v. 398; vii. 574.
— master of, James, eldest son of 5th lord Sinclair, v. 295; vii. 574.
—— his contr. wife, Marion Maitland, v. 295; ix. 157.
—— his wife, Isabella Leslie, vii. 294, 574.
— master of, John, eldest son of 10th lord Sinclair, vii. 586.
—— his 1st wife, Margaret Stewart, iv. 164; vii. 587; viii. 74.
—— his 2nd wife, Amelia Murray, i. 485; vii. 587.
SINCLAIR, BARON BARROGILL, ii. 358.
SINCLAIR, EARL OF CAITHNESS, ii. 332-359.
SINCLAIR, EARL OF ORKNEY, vi. 564-571.
SINCLAIR, LORD SINCLAIR, vii. 569-592.
SINCLAIR, LORD OF ZETLAND, vi. 568-571.
Sinclair of Aith, Arthur, ii. 571.
—— his wife, Margaret Colvill, ii. 571.
— of Auchdale, David, vi. 567.
— of Balgriggie, John, last laird, vii. 575.
—— Patrick, burgess of Dysart, vii. 574, 576.
—— his 1st wife, Katharine Nisbet, ix. 157.
—— his 2nd wife, Katharine Boswell, vii. 574.
— of Banks, James, vii. 187.
—— his wife, Annabel Forrester, vii. 187.
— of Barrock, George, ii. 353.
—— John, ii. 355; iii. 211.
—— his 2nd wife, Janet Dunbar, iii. 211.
— of Barrogill, James, ii. 352.
—— his wife, Elizabeth Leslie, ii. 352.
— of Blans, John, vii. 582 *bis*.
—— Sir John, vii. 584.
—— William, viii. 400.
—— his wife, * Stewart, viii. 400.
—— William, ii. 393.
—— his wife, Elizabeth Carlyle, ii. 391.
— of Brabster, Alexander, ii. 349.
—— his wife, Margaret Sinclair, ii. 349.
— of Bray, Alexander, vi. 567.
— of Brew, Olave, ii. 170.
— of Broynach, David, 2nd son of Sir Jas. S. of Murchil, ii. 341.
—— his 1st wife, * Sinclair, ii. 341.
—— his 2nd wife, Janet Ewing, ii. 341.
— of Brims, John, vii. 166.
—— his wife, Annas Mackay, vii. 166.
— of Brugh, Hugh, vi. 575.
—— his wife, Grizel Stewart, vi. 575.
— of Cannisbay, Sir James, ii. 352.

* Name unknown.

Sinclair of Carberry, William, vii. 570.
— of Catboll, Sir William, ii. 352.
—— his wife, Katharine Ross, ii. 352.
— of Cousland, Sir Oliver, vii. 570.
—— William, vii. 570.
— of Deskford and Findlater, Margaret, wife of Sir Walter Ogilvy, ii. 1; iv. 16, 17.
— of Dubbo, William, vii. 570.
— of Dun, Alexander, last laird, ii. 356.
—— David, illeg. son of 3rd earl of Caithness, ii. 338.
—— his wife, Margaret Calder of Dun, ii. 338.
—— John, ii. 338.
—— William, ii. 341.
—— *, vii. 165.
— of Dunbeath, Alexander, 2nd son of 2nd earl of Caithness, ii. 337; viii. 337.
—— his wife, Elizabeth Innes, ii. 337.
—— George, iv. 59.
—— his wife, Margaret Forbes, iv. 59.
—— Sir James, 1st bart., ii. 199.
—— his 2nd wife, Isobel Lumsden, ii. 199.
—— Sir John, v. 533.
—— his 2nd wife, Katharine Fraser, i. 305; iv. 118; v. 533.
—— Sir John R. G., 7th bart., ii. 59.
—— William, viii. 339.
—— his wife, Beatrice Gordon, viii. 339.
—— William, ii. 351.
— of Durran, James, ii. 353.
—— his 1st wife, Elizabeth Dunbar, ii. 353.
—— his 2nd wife, Dorothea Bruce, ii. 354.
—— John, ii. 353.
—— his wife, Elizabeth Sinclair, ii. 353.
—— Katharine, wife of capt. J. Worth, ii. 354.
—— Patrick, capt. R.N., ii. 353, 354.
—— his wife, Anne Sutherland, ii. 354.
—— Robert, 3rd son of Sir James S. of Mey, ii. 348, 353.
—— his wife, Anne Sinclair, ii. 348.
— of Earncraig, John, vi. 569.
— of Estertyre, Alexander, vi. 567.
— of Forss, Francis, 3rd son of 8th earl of Caithness, ii. 346.
—— his wife, Janet Morrison, ii. 346.
—— John, ii. 349.
—— his wife, Barbara Sinclair, ii. 349.
—— William, 2nd son of David S. of Dun, ii. 338.
— of Freswick, David, ii. 348, 355.
—— his wife, Barbara Sinclair, ii. 355.
—— James, ii. 348.
—— John, viii. 124.
—— his wife, Margaret Dalrymple, viii. 124.

* Name unknown.

Sinclair of Freswick, William, ii. 348.
—— his 1st wife, Elizabeth Sinclair, ii. 348.
—— his 2nd wife, Jean Cunningham, ii. 348.
—— William, ii. 349 *bis*.
— of Galwaldmoir, William, vi. 450.
—— his wife, Mary Livingston, vi. 450.
— of Goat, Lawrence, vi. 575.
—— his wife, Mary Stewart, vi. 575.
— of Greenland, Sir John, 3rd son of John, master of Caithness, ii. 342, 347.
—— his wife, Janet Sutherland, ii. 347.
— of Herbertshire, George, viii. 535; ix. 129.
—— Sir Oliver, vii. 570.
— of Highfield, George, ix. 105.
— of Keiss, Francis, 2nd son of 5th earl of Caithness, ii. 343, 345.
—— his wife, Elizabeth Fraser, ii. 343.
—— William, iii. 211.
—— his wife, Charlotte Sutherland, iii. 211.
—— Sir William, iii. 213.
— of Kinninmonth, Magnus, vii. 573.
—— his 1st wife, Marion Bruce, iii. 473; vii. 573.
—— his 2nd wife, Beatrix Sinclair, ix. 157.
— of Kirkton, John, Foud of Zetland, vi. 569.
—— his wife, Ingebiorg, vi. 569.
— of Latheron, Alexander, ii. 348.
—— his wife, Jean Cunningham, ii. 348.
—— James, ii. 349.
—— his wife, Frances Sinclair, ii. 349.
— of Loganhouse, John, vi. 569.
— of Longformacus, James, *probable* ancestor of the family of, vii. 578.
— of Lybster, Henry, ancestor of the family of, ii. 342.
— of Merchamyston, William, vi. 567.
— of Mey, George, 3rd son of 4th earl of Caithness, ii. 342, 351; viii. 343 *n.*; ix. 52.
—— his wife, Margaret Forbes, ii. 351; iv. 57.
—— Sir James, 1st bart., ii. 352.
—— his wife, Elizabeth Leslie, ii. 352; v. 384.
—— Sir James, 3rd bart., ii. 355.
—— his 1st wife, Frances Towers, ii. 355.
—— his 2nd wife, Jean Sinclair, ii. 343, 355.
—— Sir James, 4th bart., ii. 355.
—— his wife, Mary Sutherland, ii. 355; iii. 212.
—— Sir James, 5th bart., ii. 355.
—— his wife, Margaret Sinclair, ii. 355.
—— Sir James, 7th bart., ii. 356.
—— his wife, Jean Campbell, ii. 356.
—— Sir John, 6th bart., ii. 356; iii. 214.
—— his wife, Charlotte Sutherland, ii. 356; iii. 214.
Sinclair of Mey, William, 2nd son of 4th earl of Caithness, ii. 342, 351; ix. 51.
—— Sir William, eldest son of George S., ii. 351.
—— his wife, Katharine Ross, ii. 352.
—— Sir William, 2nd bart., ii. 355.
—— his wife, Margaret Mackenzie, ii. 355; vii. 509.
— of Morton, William, vi. 567.
— of Morton and Mortonhall, Sir Oliver, vii. 570.
— of Murchil, James, master of Caithness, ii. 340, 345; iv. 476; vii. 166.
—— his 1st wife, Elizabeth Stewart, ii. 340; vi. 574.
—— his 2nd wife, Grizel Crichton, ix. 51.
—— Sir James, ii. 340; ix. 51.
—— his 1st wife, Margaret Dundas, ii. 340; ix. 51.
—— his 2nd wife, Jean Stewart, ii. 340.
—— John, ii. 341, 345.
—— his wife, Janet Carmichael, ii. 345.
—— John, advocate, lord Murkle, ii. 345.
—— his wife, Anna MacKenzie, ii. 346; iii. 76.
— of Newburgh, David, vi. 567.
—— John, Foud of Zetland, vi. 569.
—— William, 'the Waster,' ii. 333; vii. 569.
— of Northfield, Francis, ii. 343.
— of Olrig, Charles, iii. 213.
—— his wife, Elizabeth Sutherland, iii. 213.
—— George, ii. 354.
— of Pentland, Sir Oliver, vii. 570.
— of Pitcairn, Oliver, ii. 62; iv. 427.
—— his wife, Katharine Bellenden, ii. 62; iv. 427.
— of Quhitkirk, Oliver, vii. 186.
—— his wife, Beatrix Rollo, vii. 186.
— of Ratter, Alexander, ii. 347.
—— James, ii. 347, 348.
—— his wife, Janet Bruce, ii. 348.
—— Sir John, 3rd son of John, master of Caithness, ii. 342, 347.
—— his wife, Janet Sutherland, ii. 347.
—— John, 3rd son of Sir John, ii. 347.
—— John, 4th laird, ii. 349.
—— his wife, Elizabeth Sinclair, ii. 349, 355.
—— John, 5th laird, ii. 349.
—— his wife, Janet Sinclair, ii. 349.
—— John, elder son of 5th laird, ii. 349.
—— William, eldest son of Sir John, ii. 347.
—— William, 3rd laird, ii. 348.
—— his 1st wife, Elizabeth Sinclair, ii. 348.
—— his 2nd wife, Jean Cunningham, ii. 348.
—— William, 6th laird, ii. 349.
—— his wife, Barbara Sinclair, ii. 350.

Sinclair of Reaster, James, ii. 348.
—— —— his wife, Janet Bruce, ii. 348.
—— of Scalloway, James, ii. 169 *n*.
—— of Scotscalder, John, ii. 350.
—— of Southdun, David, ii. 346; iii. 211.
—— —— his wife, Janet Sinclair, ii. 346.
—— —— Patrick, ii. 349.
—— of Spotts, Patrick, ix. 117.
—— —— his wife, Margaret Gordon, v. 105; ix. 117.
—— of Stamster, Alexander, 2nd son of 2nd earl of Caithness, ii. 337.
—— —— his wife, Elizabeth Innes, ii. 337.
—— of Stangergill, John, ii. 353.
—— of Stevenson, Sir John, bailie of Edinburgh, 1st bart., v. 171; vii. 584.
—— —— Sir John, 6th bart., ii. 347.
—— —— Sir Robert, 3rd bart., iii. 37.
—— —— his 1st wife, Helen Lindsay, iii. 37.
—— —— his 2nd wife, Anna Scot, iv. 586.
—— —— Sir Robert, 5th bart., viii. 456.
—— —— Sir Robert, 7th bart., iv. 557.
—— —— his wife, Madelina Gordon, iv. 557.
—— of Stirkoke, Francis, ancestor of the family of, ii. 343; vii. 169.
—— —— Francis, ii. 355.
—— —— his wife, Margaret *or* Barbara Sinclair, ii. 355.
—— of Sunnelishopes, John, vi. 569.
—— of Ulbster, George, viii. 357.
—— —— his wife, Janet Gordon, viii. 357.
—— —— Sir George, 2nd bart., iii. 413, 418.
—— —— his wife, Katharine Camilla Tollemache, iii. 418.
—— —— John, 2nd laird, vi. 577.
—— —— his 2nd wife, Katharine Stewart, vi. 577.
—— —— John, 4th laird, ii. 348.
—— —— his wife, Janet Sinclair, ii. 348.
—— —— John, 5th laird, viii. 124.
—— —— Sir John, 1st bart., ii. 356; iv. 218.
—— of Underhoull, William, ii. 169.
—— —— his wife, Margaret Stewart, ii. 169.
—— of Warsetter, *, ii. 388 *n*.
—— —— Sir William, 2nd son of 2nd lord Sinclair, vii. 570, 572.
—— —— his wife, Helen Gordon, vii. 570.
—— of Wells, John, viii. 370.
—— —— his wife, Beatrix Fokhart, viii. 370.
—— of Westray, Sir William, iv. 531.
—— —— his wife, Helen Gordon, iv. 531.
—— of Whitekirk, Henry, iv. 473.
—— of Wilston, William, vii. 570.
—— of Woodhall, George, lord Woodhall, ii. 347.
—— of Woodhouselee, Patrick, ix. 117.
—— —— his wife, Margaret Gordon, v. 105; ix. 117.
—— Ada Jane, vii. 592.
—— Agnes, wife of 3rd earl of Bothwell, ii. 159, 167; vii. 572.

* Name unknown.

Sinclair, Agnes, wife of John Mackay of Strathy, ii. 340; vii. 166; ix. 151.
—— Agnes, wife of (1) Andrew, 8th earl of Erroll, and (2) Alex. Gordon of Strathaven, ii. 342; iii. 571; iv. 541; ix. 51 *bis*.
—— Mr. Alexander, vicar of Legane, ii. 334.
—— Alexander, 3rd son of David S. of Dun, ii. 338.
—— Alexander, captain, iii. 213.
—— —— his wife, Elizabeth Sutherland, iii. 213.
—— Alexander Eric George, 91st regt., ii. 358.
—— Alexander Robert, ii. 59.
—— Amelia Anne, wife of R. E. Dudgeon, ii. 354.
—— Sir Andrew, Denmark, vii. 575.
—— —— his wife, Kirstine Kaas, vii. 575.
—— Annabella, wife of (1) Sir Robert Bisset, and (2) Sir D. Wemyss, viii. 478, 479.
—— Anne, wife of 1st earl of Cromartie, ii. 354; iii. 75; ix. 63.
—— Anne, wife of (1) Robert S. of Durran, and (2) John Campbell of Castlehill, ii. 348, 353.
—— Anne, wife of Sir John Swinton of Swinton, viii. 178.
—— Archibald, 4th son of 8th earl of Caithness, ii. 346.
—— Archibald, 3rd son of 3rd earl of Caithness, ix. 50.
—— Arthur, 7th son of William, earl of Orkney and Caithness, ii. 334.
—— Barbara, wife of John Sinclair of Forss, ii. 349.
—— Barbara, wife of William, 10th earl of Caithness, ii. 350.
—— Barbara, wife of David Sinclair of Freswick, ii. 355.
—— Barbara, wife of Francis Sinclair of Stirkoke, ii. 355.
—— Barbara, dau. of 5th lord Sinclair, vii. 575.
—— Barbara *or* Beatrix, wife of (1) 11th earl of Sutherland, and (2) Alex. Innes, ii. 342; viii. 344; ix. 51.
—— Beatrix, wife of James, 7th earl of Douglas, iii. 174, 178; vi. 571.
—— Beatrix, wife of Wm. Borthwick, ix. 38.
—— Beatrix, wife of Magnus Sinclair of Kinninmonth, ix. 157.
—— Charles Augustus, rector of Hempsted, ii. 359.
—— —— his wife, Marianne Harman, ii. 359.
—— Charles Home, H.M. Exchequer and Audit Office, ii. 354.
—— —— his wife, Mary Louisa Paton, ii. 354.
—— Charlotte Ann, wife of maj.-gen. A. Murray MacGregor, ii. 357.

Sinclair, Christian, wife of William St. Clair of Carfrae, vii. 584.
— Christina, wife of Iye 'Dhu' Mackay of Farr, vii. 165.
— Sir David, chamberlain of Ross and Ardmanach, ii. 335.
— David, 7th son of David S. of Dun, ii. 338.
— David, 3rd son of David S. of Broynach, ii. 341.
— — his wife, Margaret More, ii. 341.
— David, 4th son of 4th earl of Caithness, ii. 342.
— Diana, dau. of Norman Macleod S., ii. 359.
— Donald, Sarclet, ii. 341.
— Dorothea, wife of James, 2nd earl Fife, ii. 346.
— Edward, illeg. son of Sir William S. of Warsetter, ii. 338.
— Eleanor, wife of John Stewart, earl of Atholl, i. 442; ii. 334; ix. 27, 50.
— Elene, wife of (1) Sir J. Mowbray, and (2) Sir A. Hepburne, ii. 145.
— Elinor, wife of 4th lord Ogilvy of Airlie, i. 117; vii. 572.
— Elizabeth, wife of Sir Duncan Campbell of Glenorchy, i. 473; ii. 187; vii. 574, 575.
— Elizabeth, wife of * Houston of Houston, ii. 334.
— Elizabeth, dau. of David S. of Broynach, ii. 341.
— Elizabeth, wife of (1) Alex. Sutherland, and (2) Hugh Mackay, ii. 342; iii. 200, 201; vii. 166; ix. 51, 69, 151.
— Elizabeth, wife of 14th earl of Crawford, ii. 343; iii. 34.
— Elizabeth, wife of John Cunningham, ii. 348.
— Elizabeth, wife of Wm. Bruce, ii. 348.
— Elizabeth, wife of William Sinclair of Ratter, ii. 348.
— Elizabeth, wife of Wm. Robertson, ii. 354.
— Elizabeth, wife of Sir Wm. Sinclair of Dunbeath, ii. 355.
— Elizabeth, wife of John Sinclair of Ratter, ii. 349, 355.
— Elizabeth, wife of William Sinclair, ii. 356.
— Elizabeth, wife of Patrick Dunbar, iii. 277.
— Elizabeth, wife of John Sinclair of Durran, ii. 353.
— Elizabeth, wife of (1) Sir James Primrose, and (2) Francis Montgomerie, iii. 451; vii. 219.
— Elizabeth, wife of Sir John Drummond of Cargill, vi. 569; vii. 39.

* Name unknown.

Sinclair, Elizabeth, wife of John Glendonwyn, vii. 571.
— Elizabeth, wife of Andrew Leslie, master of Rothes, vii. 276, 278.
— Elizabeth, wife of Sir John St. Clair of Herdmanston, vii. 584.
— Elizabeth, wife of Wm. Hay of Lawfield and Spott, viii. 456.
— Elizabeth, dau. of 3rd lord Sinclair, vii. 572.
— Emilia Magdalen Louisa, wife of (1) H. B. Tollemache, and (2) major John Power, iii. 413.
— Eric George, R.N., ii. 357.
— Euphemia Helen, ii. 354.
— Euphemia Margaret, ii. 354.
— Euphemia Wilhelmina, ii. 359.
— Fanny Georgiana Elizabeth, ii. 358.
— Frances, wife of James Sinclair of Latheron, ii. 349.
— Francis, 2nd son of James S. of Murchil, ii. 340.
— — his wife, Janet Sutherland, ii. 340.
— Francis, 4th son of Sir John S. of Ratter, ii. 347.
— George, 5th son of William, earl of Orkney and Caithness, ii. 334.
— George, 6th son of David S. of Dun, ii. 338.
— George, major 65th regt., ii. 353.
— George, Writer to the Signet, ii. 353.
— — his wife, Elizabeth Sutherland, ii. 353.
— George, 2nd son of Sir William S. of Mey, ii. 355.
— — his wife, Margaret Moncreiff, ii. 355.
— George Arthur, Legal Dept., Board of Trade, ii. 359.
— George Sutherland, W.S., ii. 353.
— Hector, parson of Kilbride, vii. 119.
— Helen, wife of 4th lord Ogilvy of Airlie, i. 117; vii. 572.
— Helen, wife of Donald Mackay of Farr, vii. 164.
— Helen, dau. of 12th earl of Caithness, ii. 357.
— Helen, wife of Sir John Rollo of Bannockburn, vii. 198.
— Helen, wife of Andrew Kinninmont, vii. 575.
— Henry, 4th son of David S. of Dun, ii. 338.
— Henry, iv. 428.
— — his wife, * Bellenden, iv. 428; ix. 37.
— Henry, provost of Roslin, iv. 487.
— Henry, 6th son of 5th lord Sinclair, vii. 575.
— Henry, colonel, 2nd son of 8th lord Sinclair, vii. 576.
— Isabella, dau. of 10th earl of Caithness, ii. 350.

* Name unknown.

Sinclair, Isobel, dau. of Oliver S. of Pitcairns, iv. 427.
— Isabel, wife of 2nd lord Reay, vii. 170.
— Isabel, wife of Gilbert Gordon of Garty, viii. 337, 342.
— Jacobina, dau. of John S. of Ratter, ii. 349.
— James, son of Francis S., ii. 340.
— James, capt. H.E.I.C.S., ii. 341, 349.
— — his wife, Katharine Rose, ix. 51.
— James, lieut. R.N., ii. 354.
— Sir James, illeg. son of Sir William S. of Warsetter, ii. 338; vii. 572.
— James, lieut.-col., ii. 357.
— — his wife, Elizabeth Tritton, ii. 357.
— Jane, wife of Sir James Sinclair of Mey, ii. 343, 355.
— Jane, wife of Sir Wm. Dunbar, ii. 346.
— Jane, wife of Wm. Bothwell, iv. 434.
— Janet, wife of Wm. Borthwick, ii. 99.
— Janet, wife of Alex. Ross, ii. 338.
— Janet, wife of David Sinclair of Southdun, ii. 346.
— Janet, wife of Sir Stuart Threipland, ii. 346.
— Janet, wife of Walter Bruce of Ham, ii. 348.
— Janet, wife of John Sinclair of Ulbster, ii. 348.
— Janet, wife of John Sinclair of Ratter, ii. 349.
— Janet, wife of James Trail, ii. 350.
— Janet, wife of Jas. Buchanan, ii. 357.
— Janet, dau. of rev. Charles A. S., ii. 359.
— Janet, wife of 'the wicked master' of Crawford; styled countess of Crawford, iii. 26; vii. 572.
— Janet, wife of (1) Benjamin Dunbar, and (2) George, 3rd lord Reay, vii. 174.
— Jean, wife of John Hamilton, master of Bargany, ii. 31; viii. 177.
— Jean, wife of lieut.-capt. R. Campbell, ii. 198.
— Jean, wife of James Sutherland, ii. 353.
— Jean, wife of Alexander, master of Crawford, iii. 26; vii. 572.
— Jean, wife of Sir William Dunbar, iii. 211.
— Jean, wife of Sir John Forrester of Corstorphine, iv. 84: vi. 570.
— Jean, wife of (1) George Seton of Parbroath, and (2) Jas. Melville of Ardmnre, vi. 104; vii. 575; ix. 157.
— Jean, dau. of 10th earl of Caithness, ix. 52.
— John, supposed bishop of Caithness, ii. 335.
— John, archdeacon of Caithness, ii. 338.
— John, master of Caithness, ii. 338, 340.
— — his wife, Jean Hepburn, ii. 340.
— John, lieut.-col. in Swedish service, ii. 343.
Sinclair, John, illeg. son of 5th earl of Caithness, ii. 343.
— John, 2nd son of James S. of Ratter, ii. 348.
— John, master of Berriedale, ii. 343.
— — his wife, Jean Mackenzie, vii. 507.
— John, son of John S. of Durran, ii. 353.
— John, lieut. R.A., ii. 353.
— John, 5th son of James S. of Durran, ii. 354.
— John, capt. 79th Foot, ii. 356.
— John, styled lord Berriedale, eldest son of 12th earl of Caithness, ii. 356.
— John, 6th son of 12th earl of Caithness, ii. 357.
— — his wife, Maria Petronella Church, ii. 357.
— John, eldest son of Sir John S. of Stevenson, v. 171.
— — his wife, Isabel Boyd, v. 171.
— John, dean of Restalrig, v. 614 *n.*
— John Sutherland, lieut.-col. R.A., ii. 353.
— — his 1st wife, Marianne Gamble, ii. 353.
— — his 2nd wife, Frances Ramsay, ii. 353.
— — his 3rd wife, Euphemia Buchan, ii. 354.
— Jonet, wife of Wm. Sutherland of Dunbeath, ix. 51.
— Julia, wife of 4th earl of Glasgow, iv. 218; ix. 96 *bis.*
— Katharine, wife of Alexander, duke of Albany, i. 152; ii. 334.
— Katharine, dau. of William, earl of Orkney and Caithness, ii. 334.
— Katharine, wife of G. Manson, ii. 349.
— Katharine, wife of lieut. Alex. Robertson, R.N., ii. 354.
— Katharine, wife of Sir John de Seton, iv. 519 *n.*; viii. 573.
— Katharine, wife of Sir David Wemyss of that Ilk, vii. 572; viii. 488.
— Katharine, wife of Sir George Hamilton of Blackburn, vii. 574; ix. 157.
— Katharine, wife of John St. Clair of Herdmanston, vii. 577, 585.
— Kenneth, 3rd son of Sir James S. of Mey, ii. 355.
— Laurence, captain, Dysart, vii. 575.
— Lucy, dau. of Norman Macleod S., ii. 359.
— Madeline, wife of Wm. Middleton of Kincarden O'Neil, vi. 182.
— Magnus, 3rd son of 2nd lord Sinclair, vii. 571.
— Magnus, 4th son of 5th lord Sinclair, vii. 575.
— Margaret, wife of David Boswell of Balmuto, ii. 334.
— Margaret, wife of Wm. Sutherland, ii. 342; iii. 203.

Sinclair, Margaret, wife of William, lord Berriedale, ii. 343; vii. 574.
— Margaret, wife of John Smith, ii. 348.
— Margaret, wife of (1) Alex. Sinclair of Brabster, and (2) Mr. Alex. Gibson, ii. 349.
— Margaret, wife of P. Honeyman, ii. 354.
— Margaret, dau. of George S., ii. 355.
— Margaret, wife of Francis Sinclair of Stirkoke, ii. 355.
— Margaret, dau. of Sir James S. of Mey, ii. 355.
— Margaret, wife of Sir James Sinclair of Mey, ii. 355.
— Margaret, wife of rev. Wm. Leslie, ii. 356.
— Margaret, wife of John de Innerpeffer, iv. 332.
— Margaret, wife of Harie Home of Bedrule, iv. 473.
— Margaret, wife of James of Cragy, lord of Hupe, vi. 569.
— Margaret, wife of (1) John St. Clair of Herdmanston, and (2) James Ormiston of Ormiston, vii. 582.
— Margaret, wife of Patrick Crichton of Petlandy, ix. 70.
— Margaret Helen, ii. 359.
— Marie, wife of Sir John Home of Cowdenknowes, ii. 342; iv. 474, 476; ix. 51, 108.
— Marie, wife of D. Makgill of Cranstoun Riddell, vi. 595; vii. 583.
— Mariot, dau. of William, earl of Orkney and Caithness, ii. 334.
— Marjory, dau. of William, earl of Orkney and Caithness, ii. 334.
— Marjory, wife of Sir David Menzies of Weem, vi. 570.
— Marjorie, mistress of Patrick (Stewart), 2nd earl of Orkney, vi. 576.
— Marjory, wife of 1st lord Reay, vii. 169.
— Marjory, wife of Andrew Leslie, master of Rothes, vii. 276 *n*.
— Marjory, wife of Sir Alex. M'Culloch of Mertoun, ix. 157.
— Mary, wife of William, lord Berriedale, ii. 343; vii. 574.
— Mary, dau. of Sir Wm. S. of Mey, ii. 355.
— Mary, wife of Thos. Somerville of Carnwath, vi. 570; viii. 9.
— Mary Esmé, ii. 354.
— Mary Jessie, ii. 359.
— Mary Norman, ii. 353.
— Matthew, illeg. son of 3rd earl of Caithness, ix. 51.
— Meredith Isabel, ii. 359.
— Nicola, ii. 359.
— Nicola Helen Meredith, ii. 354.
— Norman Alexander, ii. 59.
— — his wife, Edith Lilian Hamilton, ii. 59.
Sinclair, Norman Macleod, ii. 359.
— — his wife, Lilian Higford, ii. 359.
— Olivia, ii. 359.
— Patrick, *familiaris servitor* to king James IV., iv. 469.
— — his wife, Elizabeth Stewart, iv. 469.
— Patrick Campbell, ii. 357.
— — his wife, Isabella M'Gregor, ii. 357.
— Richard, merchant in Thurso, ii. 356.
— Robert, capt., i. 546.
— — his wife, Anne Balfour, i. 546.
— Robert, 6th son of William, 1st earl of Orkney and Caithness, ii. 334.
— Robert, son of Wm. S, of Ratter, ii. 348.
— Robert, son of John S. of Durran, ii. 353.
— Robert, major, son of George S., ii. 354.
— Robert, iv. 428.
— — his wife, * Bellenden, iv. 428; ix. 37.
— Ronald Norman John Charles Udney, ii. 59.
— Sidney, wife of Sir John Dalrymple of Cousland, viii. 124.
— Susan, dau. of William, earl of Orkney and Caithness, ii. 334.
— Teresa, ii. 359.
— Thomas, 6th son of Sir John S. of Ratter, ii. 347.
— Thomas Buchan, ii. 354.
— William, 'the Waster,' eldest son of William, earl of Orkney and Caithness, ii. 333; vii. 569.
— — his wife, Christina Leslie, ii. 334; vii. 276, 570.
— William, legtd. son of 2nd earl of Caithness, ii. 337.
— William, elder son of 3rd earl of Caithness, ii. 338.
— William, styled lord Berriedale, eldest son of 5th earl of Caithness, ii. 343.
— — his wife, Margaret *or* Mary Sinclair, ii. 343; vii. 574.
— William, 2nd son of 10th earl of Caithness, ii. 350.
— William, 2nd son of Sir James S. of Mey, ii. 355.
— William, son of Sir James S. of Mey, ii. 356.
— — his wife, Elizabeth Sinclair, ii. 356.
— William, 3rd son of 1st earl of Orkney, vi. 569.
— William, rector of Olrig, vicar of Latheron, vii. 572.
— William, slain at Ostend, 1608, vii. 575.
— William Leigh Canning, ii. 357.
— Williamina, ii. 356.
— *, wife of David Sinclair of Broynach, ii. 341.
— *, wife of capt, John Ramsay, father of 6th earl of Dalhousie, iii. 100.
— *, wife of Cockburn of Skirling, vi. 570.

* Name unknown.

Sinclair, *, wife of Heron of Marieton, vi. 570.
Sinclair-Wemyss of Southdun, William, iii. 215.
— — his wife, Henrietta Dunbar, iii. 214.
— *see also* St. Clair.
Sinton of Sinton, Isabella, wife of Sir Edward Keith, vi. 33.
Siohlade, Charlotta Christina, wife of 3rd lord Duffus, iii. 212.
— Eric, governor of Gottenborg, iii. 212.
Siward, earl of Northumberland, son of Biorn, i. 1, 3; iii. 240.
Siward of Kellie, Helen, wife of Isaac Maxwell, vi. 533, 536.
— Richard, vi. 533; vii. 421.
— — his wife, Mary [Oliphant?], vi. 533 *n.*; vii. 421.
Skeffington, Richard, London, i. 405.
— — his wife, Godith *, i. 405.
Skelly, John, in holy orders, iv. 553.
— — his wife, Elizabeth Gordon, iv. 553.
Skelmersdale, Edward (Bootle-Wilbraham), 1st baron, iii. 49.
SKELTON, BRUCE, BARON BRUCE OF, iii. 478-483.
Skene of Wester Corse, James, iv. 110.
— of Curriehill, Sir James, lord president of the College of Justice, iii. 488.
— of Grange, vi. 496.
— of Hallyards, John, clerk of Session, ix. 84.
— — John, i. 477; vi. 590.
— — his wife, Margaret Makgill, vi. 590.
— of Northam, James, iv. 110.
— — his wife, Jean Lumsden, iv. 110.
— of Pitlurg, William Gordon Cuming, viii. 135.
— of Skene, Alexander, v. 204.
— — his wife, Mariota Kinnaird, v. 204.
— — Alexander, vii. 508.
— — Gilbert, iv. 51.
— — his wife, Christian Mercer, iv. 51.
— — James, iv. 108.
— — James, i. 184.
— — his wife, Joan Douglas, i. 184.
— Christian, wife of C. Elphinstone-Dalrymple, viii. 135.
— Helen, wife of (1) Sir Robert Bruce of Broomhall, (2) Sir Charles Erskine, and (3) Sir James Dundas of Arniston, iii. 488; v. 622.
— Jean, wife of Sir Wm. Scot, ii. 85.
— Katharine, wife of (1) Sir Jas. Anstruther, (2) major A. Whyte, and (3) capt. E. Murray, i. 477.
— Katharine, wife of Wm. Murray of Langhermiston, iii. 507; ix. 84 *bis*.
— Margaret, wife of John Carnegie of Boysack, vi. 496.

* Name unknown.

Skene, Mary, wife of George Mackenzie, vii. 508.
Skipwith, Frances, wife of (1) Ralph Constable, and (2) Ralph Ellerker, iii. 293.
— Margaret, wife of John Cheyne of Chendith, vi. 464.
— Thomas, St. Albans, vi. 464.
— Sir William, iii. 293.
Sklrlaw, Walter, bishop of Durham, iii. 12.
Skirving of Plewlandhill, John, vi. 42.
Skuli, 4th son of Thorfinn Skullsplitter, ii. 314.
SKUTTERSKELFE, CARY, BARON HUNSDON OF, iii. 616-617.
Slade, Marcus, col. 50th regt., ix. 66.
— — his wife, Charlotte Ramsay, ix. 66.
Slaney, Sir Stephen, lord mayor of London, i. 405.
— Stephen, his son, i. 405.
— — his wife, Katharine Aston, i. 405.
Sleigh, B. W. A., lieut.-col., v. 321.
— Charlotte Sarah, wife of major Frederick Henry Maitland, v. 321.
Slingsby of Redhouse, Sir Henry, v. 12.
— Eleanor, wife of Sir A. Ingram, v. 12.
Smart, Christina, wife of H. K. Cranstoun, ii. 598.
Smith of Bidborough, Sir John, vi. 467.
— of Blendon Hall, Oswald, viii. 314.
— of Braco, Patrick, i. 397.
— — his 2nd wife, Jean Stewart, i. 397.
— — Patrick, vi. 54.
— — his 1st wife, Anna Keith, vi. 54.
— of Capenhurst House, Robert, ii. 523.
— — his wife, Katharine Selina Cathcart, ii. 523.
— of Craigend, James, ii. 280.
— of Egton Bridge, Thomas, M.P., iii. 294.
— — his wife, Averilla Constable, iii. 294.
— of Grothill and King's Cramond, Sir John, provost of Edinburgh, iv. 288.
— of Woodhall Park, Samuel, M.P., vi. 118 *bis*.
— Abel, M.P., vi. 119.
— — his wife, Marianne Leslie-Melville, vi. 119.
— Dr. Adam, ii. 242.
— Agnes Graham, wife of David Stuart, 13th earl of Buchan, ii. 279.
— Alexander, i. 129.
— Anne, wife of gen. Alex. Grant of Grant, vii. 480.
— Anne Mary, wife of Dr. G. Hepburne-Scott, vii. 86.
— Charlotte, wife of Alex. Leslie-Melville of Branston Hall, vi. 118.
— Charlotte Rochfort, wife of Sir R. M. Jephson, ii. 501.
— Dorothy, wife of (1) Benedict Barnham, (2) Sir J. Packington, (3) Robert, 1st vis-

count Kilmorey, and (4) Thomas, 1st earl of Kellie, v. 86.
Smith, Egidia, wife of Sir Wm. Gray of Pittendrum, iv. 288.
— Ellen, wife of W. Ogilvy of Clova, i. 129.
— Ellen, wife of W. P. Lennox, v. 366.
— Frances Dora, wife of 13th earl of Strathmore and Kinghorne, viii. 314.
— Francis, rector of Tarrant Rushten, vi. 329.
— Gertrude Floyer, wife of 16th earl of Moray, vi. 329.
— Granville Roland Francis, Coldstream Guards, v. 254.
— — his wife, Blanche Catherine Keith-Falconer, v. 254.
— Henry, vi. 118.
— — his wife, Lucy Leslie-Melville, vi. 118.
— Henry Babington, C.S.I., iii. 496.
— — his wife, Elizabeth Mary Bruce, iii. 496.
— Humphrey, silk-mercer, Cheapside, v. 86.
— James Maclaren, iv. 295.
— — his wife, Evelyn Pounden, baroness Gray, iv. 295.
— Sir John, K.C.B., lt.-gen., ii. 501.
— John, v. 366.
— John, son of rev. Wm. S., ii. 348.
— — his wife, Margaret Sinclair, ii. 348.
— John, speaker of the House of Commons, vii. 480.
— J. C., Newport-on-Tay, vii. 86.
— Letitia Isabella, wife of (1) John, 1st earl of Radnor, and (2) Charles, 1st viscount of Newhaven, vi. 467.
— Peter, M.D., ii. 277.
— — his wife, Henrietta Erskine, ii. 277.
— Robert, Edinburgh, iv. 288.
— Sir Robert, governor of Rendsburg, vi. 445.
— Thomas Eustace, viii. 138.
— — his wife, Mary Martha Dalrymple, viii. 138.
— Tunstall, Baltimore, U.S.A., iii. 605.
— William, minister of Dunnet, ii. 348.
Smith-Gray, James Maclaren, iv. 295.
Smithson, Mary, wife of rev. James Atholl Cochrane, iii. 360.
Smollett of Bonhill, James, ii. 24.
— — James, ii. 24.
— — his wife, Helen Ogilvy, ii. 24.
— — John Rouet, rear-admiral, ii. 307.
— Elizabeth, wife of C. Villiers-Stuart, ii. 307.
— John, burgess of Dumbarton, vii. 544 *bis*.
Smyth of Aithernie, James, M.D., iv. 568.
— — his wife, Anne Watson, iv. 568.
Smyth of Gaybrook, Ralph, captain 17th Foot, viii. 44.
— — his wife, Selina Constance Somerville, viii. 44.
— — Robert, viii. 44.
Smythe of Methven, David, iii. 351.
— — his wife, Katharine Cochrane, iii. 351.
— — David, senator of the College of Justice, lord Methven, iii. 517; iv. 212.
— — his wife, Elizabeth Murray, iii. 517.
— — William, viii. 237.
Smyth(e, Corbetta, dau. of Wm. S., Shrewsbury, iii. 412.
— Helen, wife of Duncan Primrose, vii. 213.
— Jasper, Clackmannan, i. 548.
— — his wife, Agnes Bruce, i. 548.
— Katharine, grand-dau. of David S. of Methven, iii. 351; ix. 77.
— Katharine Campbell, wife of David Boyle of Shewalton, iv. 212.
— Margaret, wife of James Boyle, Glasgow, iv. 193.
— Margaret, wife of 10th viscount of Strathallan, viii. 237.
— Thomas, chaplain, St. Andrews, v. 402.
— William, apothecary, Shrewsbury, iii. 412.
Snowden of Oakland, Richard, iii. 604.
— Caroline Eliza, wife of (1) Albert Fairfax, and (2) Wm. Saunders, iii. 604.
Sobieska, Clementina, wife of James Francis Edward Stewart, 'Chevalier de St. George,' i. 35.
Sobieski, prince James, i. 35.
— John, king of Poland, i. 35.
Solph of Folcardistoun, iv. 565.
Solvathius, king of Scotland, iii. 133.
SOLWAY OF KINMOUNT, DOUGLAS, BARON, vii. 152.
Solway of Kinmount, Charles, baron, vii. 152.
Solza, Guardino de Colleoni Porto, count de, vi. 459.
— — his wife, Carolina Maria Giustiniani-Bandini, vi. 459.
Somerled, lord of the Isles, v. 28; vii. 230.
Somerset, Edward Adolphus (Seymour), 11th duke of, iii. 413; iv. 395.
— — his wife, Charlotte Douglas-Hamilton, iv. 395.
— John (Beaufort), 1st earl of, i. 18.
— Robert, 5th son of Sir Thos. Ker of Ferniehirst; earl of, v. 70, 75.
— — his wife, Francis Howard, v. 71.
— Edmund (Beaufort), 4th duke of, iii. 608.
— Henry (Beaufort), 5th duke of, iii. 608.

Somerset, William (Seymour), 2nd duke of, iii. 480; v. 355; vii. 142.
— William (Seymour), 3rd duke of, iii. 480.
— of Pauntley Court, Henry, i. 411.
— — his wife, Anne Aston, i. 411.
— Emily Blanch Charlotte, wife of 12th earl of Kinnoull, v. 237.
— Harriet Blanche, wife of 9th earl of Galloway, iv. 171.
— John, son of 1st marquess of Worcester, i. 411.
Somervell of Torbrex, Alexander, ii. 64.
— — his wife, Agnes Bellenden, ii. 64.
Somervile of Aston Somervile, Thomas, viii. 1.
— — his wife, Joan Aylesbury of Edstone, viii. 1.
— — William, the poet, viii. 32, 36, 38.
— of Edstone, William, author of *The Chase*, viii. 32, 36, 38.
— Edward, rector of Aston Somervile, viii. 39.
— Walter de, Staffordshire, viii. 1.
SOMERVILLE, SOMERVILLE, LORD, viii. 1-45.
Somerville, Aubrey John, eighteenth lord, viii. 38, 42, 44.
— Gilbert, seventh lord, viii. 25, 34; ix. 159.
— — his wife, Margaret Somerville, viii. 26.
— Hugh, fourth lord, viii. 15; ix. 159.
— — his 1st wife, Anne Hamilton, iv. 364; viii. 18.
— — his 2nd wife, Janet Maitland, v. 291; viii. 18.
— Hugh, sixth lord, viii. 22.
— — his contr. wife, Mary Beaton, viii. 24.
— — his wife, Eleanor Seton, viii. 24, 583; ix. 170 *ter*.
— Hugh, eighth lord, viii. 24, 26.
— — his wife, Margaret Hamilton, viii. 27.
— Hugh, seventeenth lord, viii. 44.
— James, fifth lord, iv. 365; viii. 20.
— — his 1st wife, Jean Hamilton, iv. 365; viii. 21; ix. 103.
— — his 2nd wife, Agnes Hamilton, iv. 361, 365; viii. 21.
— James, ninth lord, viii. 28.
— — his wife, Lilias Bannatyne, viii. 29.
— James, tenth lord, viii. 30.
— — his 1st wife, Martha Bannatyne, viii. 31.
— — his 2nd wife, Margaret Jamieson, viii. 31.
— James, eleventh lord, viii. 32.
— — his wife, Janet Murray, viii. 32; ix. 159.
Somerville, James, twelfth lord, viii. 33.
— — his 1st wife, Anne Bayntun, viii. 35, 36.
— — his 2nd wife, Frances Rotherham, viii. 37.
— James, thirteenth lord, viii. 39.
— John, second lord, viii. 11.
— — his 1st wife, Helen Hepburne, ii. 141; viii. 12.
— — his 2nd wife, Mariota Baillie, vii. 250; viii. 12.
— John, third lord, viii. 15.
— — his wife, Agnes Colquhoun, viii. 15.
— John Southey, fourteenth lord, viii. 38, 40.
— Kenelm, sixteenth lord, viii. 38, 42.
— — his wife, Frances Louisa Hayman, viii. 42.
— Mark, fifteenth lord, viii. 38, 42.
— William, first lord, viii. 9, 369.
— — his wife, Janet Mowat, viii. 10.
— master of, James, elder son of 7th lord Somerville, viii. 26.
— master of, William, baron of Carnwath, viii. 12.
— — his 1st wife, Marjorie Montgomerie, iii. 433; viii. 12.
— — his 2nd wife, Janet Douglas, vii. 117; viii. 12.
— master of, William, eldest son of Hugh, 6th lord Somerville, viii. 24; ix. 159 *bis*.
SOMERVILLE, LORD SOMERVILLE, viii. 1-45.
Somerville of Alrewas, viii. 1.
— of Aston Somervile, Aubrey John, viii. 44.
— — James, viii. 36.
— of Auchtermure, Mary, *perhaps* wife of * Hay of Locherworth and Yester, viii. 9; ix. 159 *bis*, 164 *bis*.
— of Braxfield, Alexander, ii. 402.
— — Gilbert, viii. 25.
— — Thomas, viii. 13.
— of Broomhill, John, parish clerk of Quothquan, viii. 18.
— of Broughton, Giles, wife of Thomas Weir of Blackwood, viii. 15.
— of Cambo, William, ancestor of the family of, viii. 6.
— of Cambusnethan, Sir James, ii. 27; viii. 26.
— — his wife, Helen Hamilton, ii. 27.
— — Sir James, viii. 29.
— — Sir John, ii. 150, 160; iv. 565; v. 155; viii. 12, 15.
— — his wife, Elizabeth *or* Katharine Carmichael, ii. 160, 168; iv. 565; viii. 14.

* Name unknown.

Somerville of Cambusnethan, John, 'Red Bag,' ii. 150; vi. 226; viii. 14, 15, 16.
—— —— his 1st wife, Janet Hepburne, ii. 150; viii. 13.
—— —— his 2nd wife, Margaret Graham, vi. 226; viii. 13.
—— —— John, ii. 64, 83; viii. 23.
—— —— his wife, Katharine Murray, ii. 83.
—— —— Thomas, v. 346; viii. 7.
—— —— his 1st wife, Janet Stewart, v. 346; viii. 9.
—— of Carnwath, Sir Thomas, 1296, viii. 4.
—— —— Sir Thomas, viii. 5.
—— —— his 1st wife, Elizabeth Douglas, vi. 344; viii. 5.
—— —— his 2nd wife, Maria de Vaus, viii. 5.
—— —— Thomas, ii. 399, 400; viii. 7; ix. 109.
—— —— his 1st wife, Janet Stewart, v. 346; viii. 7.
—— —— his 2nd wife, Elizabeth Keith, iv. 517; viii. 9; ix. 109.
—— —— his 3rd wife, Mary Sinclair, vi. 570; viii. 9.
—— —— Sir Walter, *of doubtful existence*, viii. 6 *n.*
—— —— William, *temp.* Malcolm IV., viii. 2.
—— —— William, his son, viii. 2.
—— —— Sir William, viii. 6.
—— —— his 1st wife, Katharine Halliday, viii. 6.
—— —— his 2nd wife, Giles Herring, viii. 6.
—— of Clifton, Sir John, son of William S. of Hedgeley, viii. 4 *n.*
—— of Comfortlee, Aubrey John, viii. 44.
—— of Corehouse, James, viii. 146.
—— of Croftlandhead, Gilbert, viii. 26.
—— —— his wife, Margaret Somerville, viii. 26.
—— of Dinder, Arthur Fownes, viii. 32, 33.
—— of Drishane, James, ancestor of the family of, viii. 22.
—— of Drum, Hugh, viii. 23.
—— —— Hugh, 10th son of 6th lord Somerville, viii. 24, 25, 26.
—— —— his wife, Margaret Hamilton, viii. 27.
—— —— James, viii. 28.
—— —— his wife, Lilias Bannatyne, viii. 29.
—— —— James, author of the *Memorie of the Somervilles*, viii. 30.
—— —— his 1st wife, Martha Bannatyne, viii. 31.
—— —— his 2nd wife, Margaret Jamieson, viii. 31.
—— —— James, viii. 32.
—— —— his wife, Janet Murray, viii. 32.
—— —— Thomas, viii. 5.
—— —— his wife, Katharine Straton, viii. 5.
—— of Edstone, James, viii. 36.
—— of Finnington, Giles, wife of Sir Robt. Logan of Restalrig, viii. 9.
Somerville of Gilmerton, Hugh, viii. 23.
—— —— Sir John, viii. 13.
—— —— Thomas, viii. 5.
—— of Girdwood, James, viii. 21, 43.
—— —— his wife, * Lindsay, viii. 22.
—— of Gladstanes, James, viii. 9.
—— —— his wife, * Gladstanes, viii. 9.
—— of Glenhove, John, vi. 154.
—— of Gutters, Hugh, viii. 23.
—— —— Thomas, viii. 5.
—— of Hedgeley, Sir John, viii. 4 *n.*
—— —— William de, viii. 4 *n.*
—— of Invertiel, Hugh, W.S., viii. 146.
—— of Kingledores, Sir John, viii. 13.
—— of Lanark, Thomas, viii. 24.
—— —— his wife, * Somerville, viii. 24.
—— of Linton, John *or* William, the dragon slayer, viii. 2.
—— —— Sir Thomas de, viii. 3.
—— —— Sir Thomas, viii. 5.
—— —— his 1st wife, Elizabeth Douglas, vi. 344; viii. 5.
—— —— his 2nd wife, Maria de Waus, viii. 5.
—— —— William de, *temp.* David I., viii. 2.
—— —— William, elder son of Sir Thomas S., viii. 4.
—— —— Sir William, viii. 6.
—— —— his 1st wife, Katharine Halliday of Moffat, viii. 6.
—— —— his 2nd wife, Giles Herring, viii. 6.
—— of Manuel, John, viii. 11.
—— —— Sir William, viii. 6.
—— of Mossmening, Giles, wife of Thos. Weir of Blackwood, viii. 15.
—— of Newbigging, Thomas, viii. 7.
—— —— William, viii. 10.
—— of Pavilion, Aubrey John, viii. 44.
—— —— John Southey, viii. 41.
—— —— Louisa Harriet, wife of col. Charles Stewart Henry, viii. 42.
—— of Pilrig's Mailling, James, viii. 28.
—— of Plean, David, viii. 10.
—— —— his wife, Christina Hepburne, viii. 10.
—— —— Sir David, iii. 531.
—— —— his wife, Elizabeth Elphinstone, iii. 531.
—— —— James, viii. 10.
—— —— Thomas, 2nd son of 1st lord Somerville, vii. 37; viii. 10.
—— —— his wife, Elizabeth of Airth, viii. 10.
—— —— Thomas, son of David S., viii. 10.
—— —— William, viii. 10.
—— —— *, viii. 22.
—— —— his wife, Agnes Somerville, viii. 22.
—— of Prestwickshaws, Janet, wife of John Symington, viii. 13.
—— —— Sir John, viii. 13.
—— —— Thomas, viii. 13.

* Name unknown.

Somerville of Quothquan, Sir John, 2nd son of 2nd lord Somerville, vi. 228; viii. 12, 15, 16.
—— —— his wife, Elizabeth Carmichael, iv. 565; viii. 14.
—— of Racklay, Thomas, viii. 9.
—— of Redpath, Aubrey John, viii. 44.
—— of Roberton, Sir John, viii. 13.
—— of Somerville, Gilbert, viii. 26.
—— —— his wife, Margaret Somerville, viii. 26.
—— of Spital, Hugh, 3rd son of 4th lord Somerville, viii. 19.
—— —— his wife, * Tweedie, viii. 19.
—— of Stenhouse, John, viii. 11.
—— of Tarbrax, John, viii. 23.
—— —— William, viii. 14.
—— of Tweedie, Hugh, viii. 14.
—— of Wichnour, Robert de, viii. 1.
—— of Wolfroddis, Hugh, viii. 22, 25.
—— —— his wife, Katharine Herries, viii. 25.
—— Agnes, wife of (1) John, 2nd lord Fleming, and (2) William, 3rd earl of Rothes, vii. 285; viii. 537.
—— Agnes, wife of (1) John Tweedie, and (2) William Murray of Romanno, viii. 19.
—— Agnes, wife of (1) * Somerville of Plean, viii. 22; ix. 163.
—— Alexander Neil, minister of Anderston Free Church, viii. 43.
—— Alison, contracted to H. Colquhoun of Luss, viii. 15.
—— Anne Vannam, wife of rev. Thomas Fownes, viii. 33.
—— Ann Wichnour, wife of capt. George Burges of Greyslee, viii. 38.
—— Augustus, viii. 38.
—— Christian, wife of Wm. Graham of Gartur, vi. 154.
—— Egidia, alleged wife of Herries of Terregles, iv. 403.
—— Elizabeth, wife of Archibald Campbell, yr. of Lochow, i. 332; viii. 12.
—— Elizabeth, wife of John Carmichael of Carmichael, iv. 577; viii. 19.
—— Elizabeth, wife of Robt. Dalzell of Dalzell, viii. 14 *n.*
—— Elizabeth, dau. of 11th lord Somerville, viii. 33.
—— Elizabeth, dau. of 12th lord Somerville, viii. 39.
—— Elizabeth Maria, dau. of capt. George S., viii. 33.
—— Elspeth, dau. of 6th lord Somerville, viii. 24.
—— Emily Charlotte, wife of rev. Thos. B. B. Robinson, viii. 43.
—— Euphemia, dau. of 11th lord Somerville, viii. 33.
—— Frances, wife of Wm. Booth Grey, viii. 38.

* Name unknown.

Somerville, Frederick Noel, lieut. Rifle Brigade, viii. 42.
—— Gavin, 2nd son of 8th lord Somerville, viii. 27.
—— George, adjutant-general in Scotland, viii. 32; ix. 159.
—— George, captain of dragoons, viii. 32.
—— —— his wife, Elizabeth Hickes, viii. 32.
—— Harriet, wife of 17th earl of Erroll, iii. 584; viii. 38.
—— Helen, wife of Sir John Jardine of Applegirth, viii. 12.
—— Helen, wife of 4th lord Boyd, v. 154, 155; viii. 14 *n.*
—— Hugh, son of Robert S., viii. 19.
—— Hugh, 5th son of 10th lord Somerville, viii. 32.
—— Hugh, major 16th Light Dragoons, viii. 37.
—— —— his 1st wife, Elizabeth Cannon Lethbridge, viii. 37.
—— —— his 2nd wife, Mary Digby, viii. 37.
—— Hugh, H.E.I.C.S., viii. 37.
—— —— his wife, Amicia Heming, viii. 37.
—— Isabella, wife of (1) Hew Dalrymple-Murray-Kynnynmond, and (2) Charles Murray, viii. 146.
—— James, son of Sir John S. of Quothquan, viii. 14 *n.*
—— James, illeg. son of William, master of Somerville, viii. 24; ix. 159.
—— James, eldest son of 10th lord Somerville, viii. 31.
—— —— his wife, Elizabeth Graham, viii. 31.
—— James, captain 68th regiment of Foot, viii. 33.
—— James, 2nd son of Sir James S., 6th baron of Cambusnethan, viii. 43.
—— James, slain c. 1526, viii. 385.
—— Janet, wife of William Cleland, viii. 11.
—— Janet, dau. of 6th lord Somerville, viii. 24.
—— Jean, wife of Robert Hamilton of Stoneypath, viii. 24.
—— Jean, wife of David Lindsay, and mistress of William, master of Somerville, viii. 24; ix. 159.
—— Jean, wife of James Tennant of Cairns, viii. 27.
—— Jean, wife of Jas. Livingston of Jerviswood, ix. 163.
—— John, ii. 403.
—— —— his wife Christian Dalzell, ii. 403.
—— Sir John, iv. 573; viii. 6 *n.*
—— —— his wife, Margaret Edmonston, viii. 6 *n.*
—— John de, clerk, viii. 4 *n.*
—— John, 3rd son of Sir Thomas S. of Linton, viii. 6.
—— John, rector of Liberton, viii. 22.
—— John, minister of Ednam, viii. 22.
—— —— his wife, Margaret Knox, viii. 22.

Somerville, John, 2nd son of James S., viii. 31.
— John, captain in United Provinces, viii. 31.
— — his wife, Anna Maria Susanna Hasill, viii. 31.
— John, 4th son of 11th lord Somerville, viii. 33.
— Julia Frances, wife of Sir E. W. Blackett of Matfen Hall, viii. 44.
— Julia Valenza, wife of Sir Francis Bond Head, viii. 38.
— Katharine, wife of Geo. Lauder of Halton, viii. 12.
— Margaret, alleged wife of Sir Gillascop Cambel, i. 319; viii. 3.
— Margaret, wife of Sir Archibald Campbell of Lochawe, i. 332; viii. 3.
— Margaret, wife of Sir Charles Murray of Cockpool, i. 224; viii. 19; ix. 13.
— Margaret, wife of (1) Sir R. Kirkpatrick of Closeburn, and *perhaps* (2) Thomas Ker of Kershaugh, v. 51 *n.*; viii. 9.
— Margaret, wife of Sir Robert Livingston of Drumry, viii. 10, 369.
— Margaret, wife of Sir Alex. Jardine of Applegirth, viii. 22.
— Margaret, wife of (1) Gilbert, 7th lord Somerville, and (2) Sir Jas. Muirhead of Lauchope, viii. 26.
— Margaret, wife of Sir Humphrey Colquhoun of Balvic, viii. 26.
— Margaret, dau. of 8th lord Somerville, viii. 27.
— Margaret, married dau. of 9th lord Somerville, viii. 29.
— Margaret, dau. of 10th lord Somerville, viii. 32.
— Marion, wife of Allan Lockhart, viii. 15.
— Mark, lieut. H.M.S. *Rochester*, viii. 33.
— Martha, dau. of James S., viii. 31.
— Mary, dau. of Sir John S. of Quothquan, vi. 228; viii. 14.
— Mary, wife of Ralph Weir of Blackwood, viii. 11.
— Mary, wife of Jas. Lockhart of Lee, viii. 12.
— Mary, wife of John Nisbet of Dalzell, viii. 14.
— Mary, wife of (1) James, 2nd lord Torphichen, and (2) Wm. Douglas of Pumpherston, viii. 26, 390; ix. 159.
— Mary, wife of rev. Charles Digby, viii. 38.
— Mary Agnes, wife of Sir Theophilus W. Biddulph, viii. 44.
— Michael, son of Sir John S. of Quothquan, viii. 14 *n.*
— Michael, 5th son of 4th lord Somerville, viii. 19.
— Nicolas, wife of 1st lord Blantyre, ii. 83.
Somerville, Patrick, 3rd son of 11th lord Somerville, viii. 33.
— Reginald Hugh, lieut. Welsh Fusiliers, viii. 38.
— Robert, 4th son of 4th lord Somerville, viii. 19.
— Robert, 2nd son of 6th lord Somerville, viii. 24.
— Robert, 2nd son of 7th lord Somerville, viii. 26.
— Selina Constance, wife of capt. Ralph Smyth, viii. 44.
— Sybil, dau. of James S. of Drum, viii. 29.
— Thomas Taylor, Tipton County, U.S.A., viii. 43.
— Walter, mythical ancestor of the family of, viii. 4 *n.*
— Walter Digby, viii. 38.
— William de, 1247, viii. 3.
— William de, 1281, viii. 3.
— — his wife, Margaret de Newbigging, viii. 3.
— William, vicar of Kirkbean, viii. 19.
— William, prebendary of Wells, viii. 32.
— — his wife, Jane Seaman, viii. 33.
— William, R.N., rector of Barford, viii. 37.
— — his wife, Charlotte Bagot, viii. 38.
— William Everard, in holy orders, viii. 38.
— *, dau. of William de S. of Linton, viii. 5.
— *, alleged wife of Sir Laurence Baird of Posso, viii. 6.
— *, alleged wife of Sir John Sandilands of Calder, viii. 6.
— *, alleged wife of Sir D. Scott of Branxholm, viii. 9.
— *, wife of John Hamilton of Newton, viii. 14.
— *, parson of Liberton, viii. 17.
— *, wife of Sir Jas. Lindsay of Pittardie, viii. 20.
— *, wife of Thos. Somerville of Lanark, viii. 24.
— *, married dau. of James S. of Drum, viii. 30.
Sotheby of Fairmead Lodge, William, F.R.S., ii. 54.
— — Charles, rear-admiral, R.N., ii. 54.
— — his wife, Jean Hamilton, ii. 54.
Soulis of Gilmerton, Sir William, claimant to Scottish throne, ii. 220; vi. 136; viii. 249, 250 *n.*
— — Sir John, the elder, ii. 212.
— — Sir John, son of Sir Nicholas S., ii. 256; viii. 250 *n.*
— Juliana de, alleged mother of William de Haya of Erroll, iii. 557 *n.*
— Sir Nicholas, the elder, viii. 250 *n.*

* Name unknown.

Somerville, Sir Nicholas, the Competitor, i. 6; ii. 256; viii. 250.
—— his wife, Margaret Comyn, ii. 256; viii. 250.
— Ranulph de, cupbearer to the king, iii. 555.
— Thomas, viii. 250 *n.*
— William, i. 427; viii. 250 *n.*
—— his wife, Ermengarde Durward, viii. 250 *n.*
— *, wife of John de Keith, vi. 33.
Soutar, George, son of John S., *alias* Johnstoun, ii. 154 *n.*
—— his wife, Annabella Hepburne, ii. 154 *n.*
Soutar, *alias* Johnstoun, John, in Banchrie, ii. 154 *n.*
Southampton, Henry (Wriothesley), earl of, viii. 366.
— Barbara (Villiers), countess of, i. 31.
— Charles (Fitz Roy), duke of, i. 31.
Southcote of Merstham, Sir John, i. 410.
—— his wife, Elizabeth Aston, i. 410.
SOUTHESK, CARNEGIE, EARL OF, viii. 46-93.
Southesk, Charles, fourth earl of, v. 309; viii. 72.
—— his wife, Mary Maitland, v. 309; viii. 72.
— Charles Noel, tenth earl of, viii. 92.
—— his wife, Ethel Mary Elizabeth Bannerman of Elsick, viii. 92.
— David, first earl of, i. 514; vi. 493; viii. 54, 64.
—— his wife, Margaret Lindsay, i. 514; viii. 66.
— David, *de jure* seventh earl of, viii. 86.
—— his wife, Agnes Murray Elliot, viii. 86.
— James, second earl of, viii. 67, 68.
—— his 1st wife, Mary Ker, ii. 412; vii. 346.
—— his 2nd wife, Janet Adamson, viii. 70.
— James, fifth earl of, iv. 164; viii. 73, 77.
—— his wife, Margaret Stewart, iv. 164; viii. 73.
— James, *de jure*, sixth earl of, viii. 83.
—— his wife, Christian Doig of Balzeordie and Cookston, viii. 85.
— James, *de jure* eighth earl of, viii. 88.
—— his wife, Charlotte Lysons, viii. 89.
— James, ninth earl of, viii. 90.
—— his 1st wife, Katharine Hamilton Noel, viii. 90.
—— his 2nd wife, Susan Katharine Mary Murray, iii. 394; viii. 91.
— Robert, third earl of, i. 79; iv. 290; viii. 70.
—— his wife, Anne Hamilton, iv. 380; viii. 71.

* Name unknown.

Southwell of Barham Hall, John, ii. 580.
—— his wife, Margaret Crofts, ii. 580.
— Sir Robert, ii. 442.
—— his wife, Elizabeth Howard, ii. 442.
Spain, Charles II., king of, i. 29; vii. 52.
—— his wife, Mary Louisa of Orleans, i. 29.
Spalding of Kinnalty, John, viii. 293.
— Thomas, iii. 308.
—— his wife, Giles Scrymgeour, iii. 308; ix. 73.
— William de, vi. 215.
Spang, Mr. William, v. 466 *n.*
Spearman, Edward Robert, C.M.G., vi. 583.
—— his wife, Mary Louisa Fitzmaurice, vi. 583.
Spedding of Mirehouse, Henry Anthony, iv. 172.
—— his wife, Jane Charlotte Stewart, iv. 172.
Spelman of Wickmer, William, vi. 186.
—— his wife, Elizabeth Middleton, vi. 186.
Spence of Unthank, Bernard, ii. 128.
— Frances Ingram, wife of (1) Marton Dalrymple of Fordel, and (2) rev. John Thomson of Duddingston, viii. 122.
— Marjorie, wife of capt. John Ramsay, ix. 66.
— Samuel, iv. 389.
— Sarah Julia, wife of C. H. Douglas-Hamilton, iv. 389.
— William, secretary to 9th earl of Argyll, i. 365.
SPENCER, VISCOUNT OF TEVIOT, viii. 366-367.
Spencer of Wormleighton, Robert (Spencer), 1st lord, viii. 366.
—— William, 2nd lord, viii. 366.
—— his wife, Penelope Wriothesley, viii. 366.
— of Althorp, Sir John, i. 406.
— of Spencer Coombe, Sir Robert, iii. 608.
— of Yarnton, Sir Thomas, 4th bart., viii. 366.
—— his wife, Jane Garrard, viii. 366.
— Anne, wife of James (Hamilton), earl of Arran, iv. 384.
— Caroline Louisa Elizabeth, wife of C. M. H. Forbes of Brux, iv. 67.
— George Augustus, lieut.-col., iv. 67.
— Jane, wife of Robert, viscount of Teviot, viii. 366.
— Margaret, wife of Thomas Cary, iii. 608.
— Margaret, dau. of William S., viii. 366.
— Mary, wife of Sir Edward Aston, i. 406.
— Muriel Emily, wife of lieut. A. L. O. Forbes-Sempill, vii. 567.
— Rachel, dau. of William S., viii. 366.
— Robert, M.P., viii. 366.
—— his wife, Jane Spencer, viii. 366.
— Walter, vicar of Welwyn, vii. 567.

Spencer, William, son of 2nd lord Spencer of Wormleighton, viii. 366.
Spencer-Churchill, Alfred, ii. 565.
—— Olivia, wife of lt.-col. A. E. W. Colville, ii. 565.
Spencer-Ponsonby, Frances Anna Georgiana, wife of 9th lord Kinnaird of Inchture, v. 215.
Spens of Bodum, iii. 20.
—— of Chirnside, Hugh, iii. 278.
—— of Kittedie and Craigsanquhar, James, v. 402.
—— of Lathallan, James, v. 402.
—— of Mairstoun, David, v. 399.
—— of Tulloch, George, iv. 125.
—— —— Robert, iv. 125.
—— —— his wife, Anna Crichton, iv. 125.
—— of Wormiston, David, v. 399; vii. 124.
—— —— Sir James, i. 561.
—— Elizabeth, wife of (1) Sir D. Lindsay of Beaufort and Edzell, and (2) John Anstruther, iii. 20.
—— Elspet, dau. of Robt. S. of Tulloch, iv. 125.
—— Grisel, wife of Jas. Bellenden, ii. 66.
—— Isobel, wife of gen.-major J. Ramsay, ix. 100.
—— James, count of Hoya, Swedish ambassador, ix. 100.
—— Thomas, bishop of Aberdeen, v. 144 *n.*
—— William, servitor to lord Scone, viii. 189.
—— —— his wife, Margaret Murray, viii. 189.
—— William George, ii. 105.
—— —— his wife, Mary Katharine Borthwick, ii. 105.
—— not proved to be descended from Duncan, earl of Fife, iv. 6.
Spenser of Rendlesham, Edward, iv. 392.
—— Anne, wife of (1) James, 5th duke of Hamilton, and (2) R. S. Nassau, iv. 392.
Sperling of Edgeworth Manor, Henry Maitland, vii. 490.
—— —— his wife, Mary L. E. Ogilvie-Grant, vii. 490.
Sperra, Malise, lord of Skaldale, vi. 568.
Spina, William, son of Hamo, i. 10.
—— —— his wife, Alicia Fitz-Alan, i. 10.
Spital of Leuchat, Alexander, v. 387.
—— —— James, v. 387.
—— —— his wife, Elizabeth Leslie, v. 387.
—— *, wife of John Leslie of Quarter, v. 387.
Spittal of Blairlogie, Henry, viii. 167.
—— —— his wife, Elizabeth Forbes, viii. 167.
Spoth of Boncle, Adam, viii. 3.
Spottiswood of Foular, William, vii. 213.
—— —— his wife, Margaret Primrose, vii. 213.
Spottiswoode of Spottiswoode, Alicia Anne, wife of lord John D. Scott, ii. 244.

* Name unknown.

Spottiswoode of Spottiswoode, John, i. 310.
—— —— his wife, Helen Arbuthnott, i. 310.
—— —— John, last laird, ii. 244.
—— —— William, vii. 75.
—— —— his wife, Margaret Edgar, vii. 74.
—— John, archbishop of St. Andrews, i. 540, 563; iii. 20, 98, 321 *n.*; vii. 193.
—— Sir Robert, i. 566; ii. 480; vi. 248.
Spreull of Cowdown, James, iii. 341.
—— of Coldoun, John, vii. 533.
—— —— his wife, Elizabeth Sempill, vii. 533 *n.*
—— Isobel, wife of (1) Peter Cochrane, and (2) Patrick Dunyng, ix. 75.
—— Jonet, wife of (1) John Pollok of Pollok, and (2) Gabriel Sempill of Cathcart, vii. 533.
—— Margaret, wife of Gabriel Sempill of Cathcart, vii. 534.
Sprott of Brighouse, Alexander, v. 417.
—— Mary, wife of Alex. M. Lindsay, v. 417.
Sproxtoune, Jane, wife of (1) Wm. Marwood, (2) Sir John Livingston of Kinnaird, and (3) Edward, 1st lord Gorges, vi. 451.
—— Richard, steward of the Star Chamber, vi. 451.
SPYNIE, LINDSAY, LORD, viii. 94-113.
Spynie, Alexander, first lord, i. 514; iii. 30; vii. 67; viii. 95.
—— —— his wife, Jean Lyon, i. 196; viii. 97, 291.
—— Alexander, second lord, iii. 34; v. 222; viii. 101.
—— —— his wife, Margaret Hay, v. 223; viii. 104.
—— George, third lord, i. 515; iii. 30; viii. 107.
—— Margaret, wife of William Fullarton of Fullarton; *de jure* baroness, viii. 108.
—— master of, Alexander Lindsay, eldest son of 2nd lord Spynie, viii. 104.
—— —— his wife, Jean Carnegie, i. 515; vi. 497; viii. 104.
Stacpoole, Cecile Elizabeth Margaret, wife of G. A. C. de Trafford, ii. 530.
—— Hubert, comte de, ii. 530.
Stafford, William (Howard), viscount, i. 411.
—— George (Leveson Gower), 2nd marquess of, viii. 361.
—— —— his wife, Elizabeth, countess of Sutherland, viii. 359.
—— George Granville, elder son of 4th duke of Sutherland; styled marquess of, viii. 364.
—— —— his wife, Eileen Gwladys Butler, ix. 163.
—— Granville (Leveson-Gower), 1st marquess of, iv. 166.
—— —— his wife, Susannah Stewart, iv. 166.
—— Thomas, iii. 608.
Stag, Janet, wife of John Scrymgeour of Henristoun, ix. 72.

STAIR, DALRYMPLE, VISCOUNT OF, viii. 118-164.
Stair, James, first viscount of, viii. 118.
—— —— his wife, Margaret Ross, viii. 119.
—— John, lord Justice-Clerk, secretary of state for Scotland; second viscount of, viii. 147.
STAIR, DALRYMPLE, EARL OF, viii. 114-164.
Stair, James, third earl of, iii. 237; viii. 150, 155; ix. 160.
—— John, secretary of state for Scotland, first earl of, iii. 236, 237; viii. 149.
—— —— his wife, Elizabeth Dundas of Newliston, viii. 149.
—— John, vice-admiral of Scotland, ambassador to Holland, and commander-in-chief, second earl of, viii. 149, 151; ix. 160.
—— —— his wife, Eleanor Campbell, v. 508; vii. 110; viii. 154; ix. 131.
—— John, fifth earl of, viii. 150, 156.
—— —— his wife, Margaret Middleton, viii. 157.
—— John, sixth earl of, viii. 157.
—— John, eighth earl of, viii. 121, 158.
—— —— his 1st wife, Harriet Johnson, viii. 159.
—— —— his 2nd wife, Adamina Duncan, viii. 159.
—— John Hamilton, tenth earl of, viii. 161.
—— —— his wife, Louisa Jane Henrietta Emily de Franquetot of Bargany, viii. 127, 161.
—— John Hew North Gustave Henry Hamilton, eleventh earl of, viii. 163.
—— —— his wife, Susan Harriet Grant-Suttie, viii. 163.
—— John William Henry, seventh earl of, viii. 157.
—— —— his 1st wife, Johanna Gordon, viii. 157.
—— —— his 2nd wife, Laura Manners, iii. 414; viii. 158.
—— North, ninth earl of, viii. 159.
—— —— his 1st wife, Margaret Penny, viii. 159.
—— —— his 2nd wife, Martha Willet Dalrymple, viii. 138, 160.
—— William, fourth earl of, iii. 237; viii. 150, 155.
—— —— his 1st wife, Anne Gordon, i. 90; viii. 156.
—— —— his 2nd wife, Anne Duff, viii. 156.
—— master of, Sir John Dalrymple, joint-secretary of state for Scotland; eldest son of 1st viscount of Stair, viii. 120, 148.
—— John of, son of Malcolm, iii. 426.
—— Malcolm of, son of Henry, iii. 426.
—— —— his wife, Marjorie Montgomerie, iii. 426.
—— Marie or Mariota of, wife of (1) *, and (2) Reginald de Schankis, iii. 426.

* Name unknown.

Stair, *, wife of * Kennedy, iii. 427.
Stallenge, *, vi. 574.
Stamford, George Harry (Grey), 6th earl of, viii. 514.
—— —— his wife, Henrietta Charlotte Elizabeth Charteris, viii. 514.
—— Harry (Grey), 3rd earl of, vi. 178.
—— Henry (Grey), 1st earl of, iii. 478.
Stamford and Warrington, George Harry (Grey), 5th earl of, viii. 38.
Stanhope, Charles (Stanhope), 3rd earl, viii. 211.
—— Philip (Stanhope), 2nd earl, ix. 101.
—— —— his wife, Grisell Hamilton, ix. 101.
—— Philip Henry (Stanhope), 4th earl, vii. 227.
Stanhope of Harrington, Charles (Stanhope) 2nd lord, vi. 452.
—— —— his wife, Dorothy Livingston, vi. 452; (*misnamed* Barret, ii. 34 *n.*).
—— —— John (Stanhope), 1st lord, iii. 403.
—— of Edlington and Grimston, Sir Edward, iii. 296.
—— —— his wife, Margaret Constable, iii. 296.
—— of Grimston, Sir Edward, vii. 20.
—— Caroline, wife of Kenneth, earl of Seaforth, vii. 513.
—— Elizabeth, wife of Sir Lionel Tollemache, iii. 403.
—— Elizabeth, wife of 4th earl of Strathmore and Kinghorne, viii. 304; ix. 162.
—— Frances, wife of Patrick Maule of Panmure, vii. 20.
—— James Hamilton, lieut.-col., viii. 211.
—— —— his wife, Frederica Louisa Murray, viii. 211.
—— Katharine Lucy Wilhelmina, wife of (1) Archibald, lord Dalmeny, and (2) Henry, 4th duke of Cleveland, vii. 227.
Stanley, William (Murray), viscount, vi. 395.
STANLEY, MURRAY, LORD MURRAY OF, i. 495-502.
STANLEY, MURRAY, BARON MURRAY OF, i. 495.
Stanley of Alderley, Edward John (Stanley), 2nd lord, i. 131.
—— of Cross Hall, Edward, v. 319.
—— —— his wife, Mary Maitland, v. 319.
—— of Hooton, Sir William, 5th bart., iv. 418.
—— —— Elizabeth, wife of Charles Maxwell-Constable, iv. 418.
—— Amelia Anne Sophia, wife of 1st marquess of Atholl, i. 475, 488.
—— Anne, wife of (1) Sir Henry Portman, and (2) Robert, 1st earl of Ancram, v. 466, 467.
—— Arthur Penrhyn, D.D., dean of Westminster, iii. 494.
—— —— his wife, Augusta Frederica Elizabeth Bruce, iii. 494.

* Name unknown.

Stanley, Charles, 3rd son of Wm. Haggerston-Maxwell-Constable, iv. 418.
—— —— his 1st wife, Elizabeth Stanley, iv. 418.
—— —— his 2nd wife, Mary Macdonald, iv. 418.
—— Henrietta Blanche, wife of 7th earl of Airlie, i. 131; ix. 9.
Stanmore, Arthur Hamilton-Gordon, 1st baron, i. 97.
—— —— his wife, Rachel Emily Shaw-Lefevre, i. 97.
Staples of Lissan, Sir Nathaniel Alexander, 10th bart., i. 525.
—— —— his wife, Elizabeth Lindsay Head, i. 525.
—— William Conolly, captain R.N., vi. 434.
—— —— his wife, Anna Louisa Stewart, vi. 434.
Stapleton of Wighill, Brian, iii. 292.
—— —— his wife, Margery Constable, iii. 292.
—— —— Robert, v. 13 *bis*.
—— —— his wife, Katharine Fairfax, v. 13.
—— —— Robert, iii. 601.
—— —— his wife, Dorothy Fairfax, iii. 601.
—— Henry, v. 13.
—— —— his wife, Ann Ingram, v. 13.
Staremberg, Maria Ernestina, wife of count Julius Hamilton; countess of, i. 48.
Starheved, Andrew, serjeant of Lanark, ii. 396.
Stark of Nether Auchinreoch, John, viii. 527.
—— —— William, viii. 527.
Starked, companion of the Bastard Heron, vii. 329.
Stede of Stedehill, Edwin, i. 58.
—— —— his wife, Elizabeth Hamilton, i. 58.
Steele, Annie, wife of A. R. Hamilton, ii. 57.
—— Sir T. M., K.C.B., commander of the forces in Ireland, iv. 210.
Stenhouse, Henry, schoolmaster at Inverkeithing, i. 547.
—— —— his wife, Janet Thomson, i. 547; ix. 33.
Stephen, king of England, i. 2.
Stephen, son of Nicholas, vii. 527.
Stephenson, Sir Henry Frederick, admiral R.N., vii. 452.
—— —— his wife, Charlotte E. E. Fraser, vii. 452.
Stepney of Prendergast, Sir John, iv. 265.
—— —— his wife, Justinia Van Dyck, iv. 265.
Stepney, Cowell, colonel, iv. 265.
Sterling, Harriet Theophila, wife of col. Wm. Middleton, vi. 179.
—— William, I.C.S., vi. 179.
Steuart of Allanbank, Sir John, 4th bart., viii. 123.
—— of Allanton, James, iv. 583.
—— —— his wife, Marion Carmichael, iv. 583; ix. 114.
—— —— Sir Walter, iv. 199; viii. 30.
Steuart of Dalguise, John, W.S., master of the Supreme Court of the Cape of Good Hope, iii. 522.
—— —— his wife, Janet Oliphant Murray, iii. 522.
—— of Goodtrees, Sir James, 1st bart., solicitor-general, ii. 276.
—— —— his wife, Anne Dalrymple, ii. 276; viii. 142.
—— of Grandtully, Archibald James Edward, i. 209, 211.
—— of Steuart's Lodge, John, brigadier-general, alleged ancestor of the family of, iv. 163.
—— —— his wife, Bridget Pocklington, iv. 163.
—— Anne Jane, wife of * Mower, ii. 101 *n*.
—— Elizabeth, wife of (1) col. Thos. Hamilton, and (2) Alex. Gibson, vi. 597.
—— Grizel, wife of Sir John Drummond of Logiealmond, vii. 50.
—— James, M.D., vi. 597.
—— James, father-in-law of 7th lord Elibank, iii. 520.
—— Katharine, wife of 7th lord Elibank, iii. 520.
—— Marion, wife of John Boyle of Kelburne, iv. 199.
—— Sholto Thomas, inf. son of Sir John S. of Grandtully, i. 210.
—— *see also* Stewart.
Stevenson of Dollan, David, vi. 505.
—— Charlotte, wife of J. J. Carnegie of Fair Oak, vi. 505.
—— Elizabeth, wife of Dr. Archibald Pitcairn, ix. 170.
—— Henry, husband of Katharine Constable, iii. 292.
—— William, chaplain to Isobel, lady St. Clair of Herdmanston, vii. 580.
Steward of Scotland, Alan, second High, i. 11, 12; iii. 424; v. 136.
—— —— his wife, Eva, i. 12; ix. 1.
—— Alexander, fourth High, i. 13; v. 31.
—— —— his wife, Jean of Bute, i. 13; v. 31.
—— James, fifth High, i. 13; iii. 9; iv. 224; v. 34; vii. 527.
—— —— his wife, Egidia de Burgh, i. 14, 322.
—— Robert, seventh High, i. 11, 15, 431; iii. 150, 151; v. 38, 344, 593; vii. 528.
—— —— his 1st wife, Elizabeth Mure, i. 15.
—— —— his 2nd wife, Euphemia Ross, i. 16; vii. 236.
—— Walter, first High, i. 10; iii. 422.
—— —— his wife, Eschyna de Molle, i. 11.
—— Walter, third High, i. 12; iii. 423, 425; v. 136, 332, 488.

* Name unknown.

Steward, Walter, sixth High, i. 14; iii. 11; v. 31; vii. 527; viii. 520, 521; ix. 1.
—— —— his 1st wife, Marjorie Bruce, i. 8, 14; vii. 526 *n.*
—— —— his 2nd wife, Isabella Graham, i. 41; vi. 197.
STEWART OF GARLIES, STEWART, BARON, iv. 167-173.
Stewart of Garlies, Alan Plantagenet, fourth baron, iv. 172.
—— —— John, first baron, iv. 167.
—— —— George, second baron, iv. 170.
—— —— Randolph, third baron, iv. 171.
—— —— Randolph Henry, fifth baron, iv. 172.
STEWART OF OYCHELTREE, STEWART, LORD, vi. 511-520.
Stewart of Oycheltree, Andrew, first lord, vi. 511.
—— —— his wife, Margaret Hamilton, vi. 511.
—— —— Andrew, second lord, vi. 512.
—— —— Andrew, third lord, vi. 516.
—— —— James, fourth lord, vi. 517; vii. 469.
—— —— William, fifth lord, vi. 519.
STEWART OF TRAQUAIR, STEWART, LORD, viii. 403-409.
Stewart of Traquair, John, first lord, viii. 403.
STEWART, LORD ABERNETHY, vi. 314.
STEWART, DUKE OF ALBANY, i. 146-155.
STEWART, EARL OF ANGUS, i. 169-171.
STEWART, LORD OF ANNANDALE, i. 151.
STEWART, LORD ARDMANOCH, i. 155.
STEWART, EARL OF ARDMANNACH, vii. 246.
STEWART, EARL OF ARRAN, i. 394-398.
STEWART, EARL OF ATHOLL, i. 436-448.
STEWART, LORD D'AUBIGNY, v. 356-362.
STEWART, LORD AUCHTERHOUSE, ii. 266.
STEWART, LORD AVANDALE, vi. 509-511.
STEWART, LORD BADENOCH, ii. 170.
STEWART, LORD BLANTYRE, ii. 77-93.
STEWART, LORD OF BRECHIN, vii. 246.
STEWART, EARL OF BUCHAN, ii. 262-270.
STEWART, LORD CABERSTON, viii. 403-409.
STEWART, EARL OF CAITHNESS, ii. 321-322.
STEWART, EARL OF CARRICK, ii. 438-442.
STEWART, LORD CLIFTON OF LEIGHTON-BROMSWOLD, v. 358-362.
STEWART, LORD DALKEITH, v. 356-362.
STEWART, LORD DARNLEY, ii. 168; v. 348-355.
STEWART, EARL OF DARNLEY, v. 356-362.
STEWART, LORD DOUNE, iii. 186-190.
STEWART, EARL OF EDERDALE, vii. 246.
STEWART, LORD FAILFORD, vi. 511.
STEWART, EARL OF FIFE, iv. 14-15.
STEWART, EARL OF GALLOWAY, iv. 145-173.
STEWART, EARL OF GARIOCH, v. 637.
STEWART, LORD GARLIES, iv. 160-173.
STEWART, LORD HAMILTON, i. 394-398.
STEWART, LORD INNERMEATH, v. 1-8.
STEWART, LORD KINCLAVEN, ii. 441.
STEWART, EARL OF LENNOX, v. 348-355.
STEWART, DUKE OF LENNOX, v. 344-362.
STEWART, LORD LINTON, viii. 403-409.
STEWART, EARL OF LITCHFIELD, v. 360-361.
STEWART, EARL OF MAR, v. 637-639; vi. 314.
STEWART, EARL OF MARCH, i. 151; v. 355, 362.
STEWART, LORD METHVEN, vi. 166-169.
STEWART, EARL OF MORAY, vi. 311-312.
STEWART, EARL OF MORAY, vi. 313-330.
STEWART, LORD OF NEVARE, vii. 246.
STEWART, EARL OF NEWCASTLE-UPON-TYNE, v. 357.
STEWART, LORD OCHILTREE, vii. 511-520.
STEWART, EARL OF ORKNEY, vi. 572-577.
STEWART, MARQUESS OF ORMOND, i. 155; vii. 245-246.
STEWART, LORD PITTENWEEM, vii. 63-69.
STEWART, EARL OF RICHMOND, v. 357.
STEWART, DUKE OF RICHMOND, v. 360-362.
STEWART, EARL OF ROSS, i. 155.
STEWART, DUKE OF ROSS, vii. 245-246.
STEWART, DUKE OF ROTHESAY, vii. 312-313.
STEWART, LORD ST. COLME, vii. 394-395.
STEWART, BARON SETTRINGTON, v. 357.
STEWART, BARON STEWART OF GARLIES, iv. 167-173.
STEWART, LORD STEWART OF OYCHELTREE, vi. 511-520.
STEWART, LORD STEWART OF TRAQUAIR, viii. 403-409.
STEWART, LORD STRATHEARN, vi. 314.
STEWART, EARL OF STRATHEARN, viii. 259-261.
STEWART, BARON STUART OF CASTLE STUART, vi. 326.
STEWART, LORD STUART OF NEWBURY, v. 360-361.
STEWART, LORD TARBOLTOUN, v. 356-362.
STEWART, EARL OF TRAQUAIR, viii. 399-409.
STEWART, LORD OF ZETLAND, vi. 572-577.
Stewart of Albany, Walter, 2nd son of Murdac, duke of Albany, i. 150; ii. 176; vi. 509; viii. 260.
—— of Ambrismore, James, ii. 290.
—— —— his 1st wife, Margaret Stewart, ii. 290.
—— —— his 2nd wife, Isobell Cuningham, ii. 290.
—— —— John, ii. 290.
—— —— his wife, Elizabeth Stewart, ii. 290.
—— —— Robert, 2nd son of Ninian S. of Bute, ii. 290.
—— —— his wife, Helen Stewart, ii. 290.
—— —— William, ii. 290.
—— —— his wife, Katharine Frisall, ii. 290.
—— of Angus, William, illeg. son of 2nd earl of Angus, i. 171; ix. 11.
—— of Annat, John, vi. 153.
—— —— his wife, Janet Graham, vi. 153.

Stewart of Annefield, John, 2nd son of Dougal S. of Blairhall, ii. 297.
— — his wife, Anne Stewart, ii. 297; vi. 325.
— of Appin, Sir James, ancestor of the family of, i. 13.
— — Dougal, 1st laird; son of John S., lord of Lorn, v. 4.
— — Duncan, ii. 200.
— — his wife, Jean Campbell, ii. 200.
— — John, ix. 20.
— — his wife, Katharine Maclean, ix. 20 *bis*.
— of Ardgowan, Sir James, v. 142.
— — Sir John, illeg. son of king Robert III., i. 18.
— — John, 1508, ii. 179.
— of Ardinho, James, 2nd son of John S. of Bute, ii. 293.
— — his wife, Elizabeth Bannatyne, ii. 293.
— — John, ii. 294.
— of Ardmaleish, Sir Dougal, 2nd bart., ii. 296.
— — Sir James, 1st bart., ii. 294.
— — John, sheriff of Bute, ii. 292.
— — Sir John, ii. 294.
— of Ardoch, Robert, i. 397.
— — his wife, Barbara Stewart, i. 397.
— of Ardvorlich, James 'beg,' ancestor of the family of, i. 151.
— — James, colonel, i. 139.
— of Arom, Sir Alexander, iv. 159.
— of Arthurle, Isabella, wife of Thomas Stewart of Minto, ii. 77.
— — Walter, ii. 77; iv. 151.
— — his wife, Janet Cameron, ii. 77.
— of Nether Ascog, James, ii. 293.
— — John, ii. 294.
— of Athol, Robert, illeg. son of 'the Wolf of Badenoch,' ii. 263.
— of Aubigny, Bernard, 3rd seigneur, v. 347, 350.
— — his 1st wife, Guillemette de Boucard, v. 347.
— — his 2nd wife, Anne de Maumont, v. 348.
— — Charles, 11th seigneur, v. 360.
— — Esme, 6th seigneur, v. 352, 355, 356.
— — his wife, Katharine de Balsac, v. 356.
— — George, 9th seigneur, v. 358.
— — his wife, Katharine Howard, v. 358.
— — Henry, 8th seigneur, v. 358.
— — Sir John, 1st seigneur, v. 346.
— — John, 2nd seigneur, v. 347.
— — John, 5th seigneur, v. 352.
— — his wife, Anne de la Queuille, v. 352.
— — Ludovic, 7th seigneur, v. 356.
— — Ludovic, 10th seigneur, v. 359.
Stewart of Aubigny, Robert, 4th seigneur, v. 348, 349.
— — his 1st wife, Anne Stewart, v. 348, 350.
— — his 2nd wife, Jacqueline de la Queuille, v. 350.
— of Aucharn, James, v. 540.
— of Auchingoun, Sir John, illeg. son of king Robert III., i. 18, 328, 331.
— of Auchinskeoch, Alexander, ii. 297.
— — his wife, Elizabeth Stewart, ii. 297.
— of Avandale, Alexander, son of Walter S. of Morphie, vi. 278, 510.
— of Badenoch, Alexander, 4th son of king Robert II., i. 16; ii. 263; vii. 241.
— — his wife, Euphemia, countess of Ross, vii. 239.
— of Balado, James, v. 93.
— — his wife, Penelope Erskine, v. 93.
— of Balcaskie, Sir Thomas, bart., lord of Session, iii. 76.
— — his wife, Jean Mackenzie, iii. 76; ix. 147.
— of Baldinneis, John, 2nd son of 4th lord Innermeath, v. 5.
— — his wife, Katharine Gray, v. 5.
— of Baldoran, Walter, 'bailie of Balquhidder,' ii. 177 *n.*; v. 187.
— — his wife, Katharine Campbell, ii. 177 *n.*
— — William, ii. 178.
— — his wife, Mariot Campbell, ii. 178.
— of Balinshangrie, Andrew, ancestor of the family of, ii. 286.
— of Ballechin, Sir James, iv. 34; vii. 195.
— — his 2nd wife, Elizabeth Rollo, vii. 195.
— — John, illeg. son of king James II., i. 20.
— — John, i. 475.
— — Patrick, iv. 34.
— — his wife, Elizabeth Butter, iv. 34.
— of Ballincreiff, Elizabeth, wife of John Hamilton, v. 344.
— of Ballintoy, Archibald, ii. 290.
— of Ballymoran, Thomas, vi. 154.
— — his wife, Margaret Graham, vi. 154.
— of Balvany, Sir James, i. 444 *n.*
— — Sir John, eldest son of the Black Knight of Lorn, i. 441.
— of Balzeqnhir, Sir Alexander, iv. 159.
— of Barclye, Walter, 2nd son of Alex. S. of Garlies, iv. 151, 152, 154; ix. 94.
— of Barnald, Archibald, 2nd son of Robert S. of Ambrismore, ii. 290.
— — Dugald, ii. 290.
— of Barquhill, Sir Alexander, eldest son of Sir Alex. S. of Garlies, iv. 156.
— — his wife, Katharine Herries, iv. 158.
— of Barre, Sir William, vii. 66.
— of Barscube, Matthew, v. 357.

Stewart of Barskimming, Adam, vi. 514.
—— —— his wife, Maria Ross, vi. 514.
—— —— Henry, vi. 514.
—— —— his wife, Janet Reid, vi. 514.
—— of Beath, Andrew, v. 393.
—— —— his wife, Marjory Lindsay, v. 393.
—— —— Sir James, 3rd son of 2nd lord Avondale, iii. 186; v. 395; vi. 511; ix. 68.
—— —— his wife, Margaret Lindsay, iii. 186; v. 4, 395.
—— of Birkenside, Euphemia, wife of 6th earl of Dunbar, iii. 267.
—— of Bishopstoun, Sir Alexander, iv. 159.
—— of Blackhall, Sir Archibald, M.P., vi. 246.
—— —— Sir Archibald, 1st bart., iv. 174.
—— —— his 1st wife, Anna Crawfurd, iv. 174.
—— —— James, the High Steward, iv. 340, 344.
—— —— James, v. 554.
—— —— his wife, Margaret Lyle, v. 554.
—— —— Sir John, illeg. son of king Robert III., i. 18, 331.
—— —— John, v. 553, 555.
—— —— his wife, Elizabeth Lyle, v. 553.
—— —— John, iv. 238.
—— —— John, vi. 325.
—— —— his wife, Anne Stewart, ii. 297; vi. 325.
—— of Blairhall, Dougal, 2nd son of Sir Dugal S. of Bute; lord of Session, ii. 297.
—— —— his wife, Mary Bruce, ii. 297.
—— —— James, i. 128; ii. 297.
—— —— his wife, Mary Crawford, ii. 297.
—— of Blairneill, *, wife of Thomas Fraser of Stoneywood, ix. 93.
—— of Blairquhan, Josias, ii. 487 *bis*.
—— of Bonkyl, Sir Alexander, i. 13, 169; v. 583.
—— —— Sir John, i. 13; iv. 146.
—— —— his wife, Margaret de Bonkyl, i. 13, 438; ii. 221.
—— —— Sir John, earl of Angus, i. 169.
—— —— his wife, Margaret Abernethy of Abernethy, i. 170.
—— of Bonnington, Josias, ii. 487 *bis*; vi. 515.
—— —— his wife, Mariota Finlayson, vi. 515.
—— of Bothwellmuir, James, iv. 371.
—— of Brankstane, William, vi. 518.
—— —— his wife, Jean Stewart, vi. 518.
—— of Brentwood, Thomas, vii. 64.
—— —— his wife, Isobel Henderson, vii. 64.
—— of Brighouse, Alexander, vi. 169.
—— of Brugh, Edward, ancestor of the family of, vi. 575.
—— of Buchlyvie, Henry, brother of 1st lord Doune, iii. 187; ix. 68.
—— —— his wife, Elizabeth Robertson, iii. 187; ix. 68.

* Name unknown.

Stewart of Bultrees, John, vii. 536.
—— of Burley, Sir John, illeg. son of king Robert II., i. 17.
—— of Burray, Sir Archibald, v. 386.
—— —— his wife, Margaret Stewart, v. 386.
—— —— Archibald, provost of Edinburgh, iii. 187.
—— —— his wife, Helen Aitchison, iii. 187; ix. 68.
—— —— Sir Archibald, 1st bart., iv. 159; ix. 94.
—— —— Barbara, wife of William Stewart of Mains, iii. 187; iv. 159.
—— —— Barbara, wife of (1) Sir Jas. Sinclair, and (2) Roderick Macleod, vi. 511, 574 *n*.
—— —— James, iii. 187.
—— —— his wife, Barbara MacLeod, iii. 187; ix. 68.
—— —— Sir James, iv. 568.
—— —— his wife, Anne Carmichael, iv. 568.
—— —— William, 2nd son of Sir Alex. S. of Garlies, iii. 187.
—— —— his wife, Barbara Stewart, iii. 187.
—— of Bute, Sir Dugal, 2nd bart., ii. 296.
—— —— his wife, Elizabeth Ruthven, ii. 297.
—— —— James, eldest son of the 'black' S., ii. 286.
—— —— James, son of Robert S. of Bute, ii. 286 *n*.
—— —— James, son of Wm. S. of Fennok, ii. 286 *n*., 287.
—— —— James, 5th sheriff, ii. 288.
—— —— Sir James, ii. 289, 291.
—— —— his 1st wife, Agnes Campbell, i. 338; ii. 292; ix. 20.
—— —— his 2nd wife, Marion Fairlie, ii. 292.
—— —— Sir James, 1st bart., ii. 287, 294.
—— —— his wife, Grizel Campbell, ii. 295.
—— —— Sir James, 3rd bart., ii. 298; iv. 201.
—— —— his wife, Agnes Mackenzie, ii. 298.
—— —— John 'the black,' illeg. son of king Robert II., i. 17; ii. 285.
—— —— his wife, Jonet Sympil, ii. 286; vii. 528.
—— —— John, ii. 292.
—— —— his 1st wife, Mary Campbell, ii. 293.
—— —— his 2nd wife, Finevola Macdonald, ii. 293.
—— —— his 3rd wife, Jean Blair, ii. 293.
—— —— Sir John, ii. 294.
—— —— his wife, Elizabeth Hepburn, ii. 294.
—— —— Ninian, ii. 289.
—— —— his 1st wife, * Campbell, ii. 289.
—— —— his 2nd wife, Jonet Dunlop, ii. 289.
—— —— his 3rd wife, Elizabeth Blair, ii. 289.
—— —— Robert, 3rd son of the 'black' S., ii. 286.
—— —— William, 2nd son of the 'black' S., ii. 287.
—— —— his wife, Margaret Stewart, ii. 287.

* Name unknown.

Stewart of Butteleis, Katharine, wife of William, 1st lord Monypenny, vi. 277, 278.
— of Caberstoun, Sir William, viii. 400.
— of Cally, Elizabeth, wife of Donald Lennox, v. 342.
— — Sir John, v. 342.
— of Calzebrochan, Andrew, ix. 70.
— — his wife, Margaret Crichton of Rossie, ix. 70.
— of Camnethan, Janet, wife of Thos. Somerville of Carnwath, v. 346.
— of Campsie, John, vi. 169.
— — his wife, Dorothea Stewart, vi. 169.
— of Cantraydown, Robert, vii. 457.
— of Cardney, Sir John, illeg. son of king Robert II., i. 17; vi. 215.
— of Cardonald, Alan, ii. 78; v. 350; vii. 532, 533.
— — his wife, Marion Stewart, v. 350.
— — James, ii. 81, 473; iii. 440; iv. 156; v. 350.
— — his wife, Alice Reid, iv. 156.
— — John, ii. 78.
— — his wife, Agnes Stewart, ii. 78.
— — Mary, wife of Robert Stewart, iv. 156.
— — Robert, 4th son of Sir Alex. S. of Garlies, iv. 156, 158.
— — his wife, Mary Stewart, iv. 156.
— of Careston, Sir John, viii. 61.
— of Carnsalloch, Sir John, iv. 84.
— — his wife, Marion Stewart, iv. 84.
— — Katharine, wife of Sir Herbert Maxwell, vi. 474.
— — Marion, wife of (1) Sir John Stewart, and (2) Sir John Forrester, iv. 150.
— of Carragan, William, ix. 56.
— — his wife, Jean Kennedy, ix. 56.
— of Castlemilk, Archibald, ii. 81.
— — his wife, Janet Stewart, ii. 81.
— — Sir Archibald, ii. 41; vii. 553; viii. 548.
— — his wife, Annas Sempill, vii. 553.
— — Archibald, the younger, viii. 548.
— — his wife, Mary Fleming, viii. 548.
— — Sir Archibald, 1st bart., iv. 589.
— — his wife, Mary Carmichael, iv. 589.
— — Sir John, iv. 149; v. 552.
— of Castle Stewart, Elizabeth, wife of John Gordon of Cardoness, iv. 162.
— — Walter, ancestor of the family of, v. 605.
— — William, colonel, 1st laird, iv. 155, 162.
— — William, 4th son of 2nd earl of Galloway, iv. 155, 162.
— — his wife, Elizabeth Gordon, iv. 162.
— — William, 5th laird, iv. 162, 163.
— — William, M.P., vii. 512.
— — his wife, Euphemia Mackenzie, vii. 512.
Stewart of Castramont, Montgomery Granville John, M.P., iv. 168.
— — his wife, Katharine Honeyman, iv. 168.
— of Catrine, Dugald, professor of moral philosophy, ii. 598.
— — his wife, Helen d'Arcy Cranstoun, ii. 598.
— of Clary, Anthony, parson of Penningham, iv. 155, 156, 162.
— — his wife, Barbara Gordon, iv. 155.
— of Clava, Robert, vii. 457.
— of Clawak, Alexander, vii. 434.
— of Cloichfoldich, Janet W. Maxwell, wife of W. B. S. Campbell, ii. 198.
— — Robert, ii. 198.
— of Clugston, Sir Alexander, eldest son of Sir Alex. S. of Garlies, iv. 155, 156.
— — Sir Alexander, iv. 154.
— of Cluny, John, i. 121; ix. 142.
— — Walter, i. 121; ix. 142.
— — his wife, Katharine Nairne, i. 121; ix. 141.
— of Coitland, Sir Alexander, iv. 158.
— of Coldingham, Francis, ii. 172; ix. 42.
— — Francis, captain, ix. 42.
— — John, ii. 171; ix. 72.
— — his wife, Anna Home, ix. 72.
— of Coltness, Sir James, 7th bart., viii. 512.
— — his wife, Frances Wemyss, viii. 512.
— of Concressault, Sir John, 1st seigneur, v. 346.
— — his wife, Elizabeth of Lennox, v. 341, 347.
— — John, 2nd seigneur, v. 347.
— — his wife, Beatrice d'Apchier, v. 347.
— of Conhaith, Sir Alexander, iv. 154.
— of Corrigan, Harry, i. 397.
— — Henry, 2nd son of earl of Arran, i. 397.
— — his wife, Margaret Horrie, i. 397.
— — James, i. 397.
— — William, major, i. 397.
— — his wife, Jane Stewart, i. 397; vi. 518.
— of Corsewell, Sir Alexander, iv. 160.
— — Sir James, 1st bart., iv. 161.
— of Cragy, John, ii. 399.
— of Craigiehall, Harry, tutor of Calder, vii. 254; viii. 389, 390.
— — his wife, Jean Ross, vii. 254; viii. 389.
— — John, ii. 509; iv. 86.
— — John, the younger, iv. 86.
— — his wife, Margaret Forrester, iv. 86.
— of Craigous, Robert, vii. 68.
— of Crostenterray, Henry, vii. 394.
— of Cruikston, Sir Alan, i. 13; iv. 303.
— — Sir Alexander, v. 345.
— — Sir John, iv. 303; v. 344 *bis*.
— — Sir Robert, i. 12.

Stewart of Culalay, Francis, 3rd son of 4th earl of Moray, vi. 321; ix. 139.
— of Culbeg, Robert, v. 625.
— — his wife, Annabella Erskine, v. 625.
— of Culteranich, Euphemia *or* Egidia, wife of Sir P. Graham of Dundaff, vi. 214.
— of Cultihill, William, 3rd son of Sir Alex. S. of Garlies, iv. 159.
— of Cumlodden, Sir William, G.C.B., lieut.-general, M.P., i. 221; iv. 167, 169.
— — his wife, Frances Douglas, iv. 168; vi. 383.
— of Cunningham, Sir John, i. 14.
— — Sir Walter, i. 14.
— of Daldar, Sir John, 5th son of Sir John S. of Bonkyl, i. 13.
— of Dalswinton, Sir Alexander, 3rd laird, iv. 151, 152.
— — his wife, Elizabeth Douglas, iv. 151.
— — Alexander, 4th laird, ix. 94.
— — his wife, Janet Gordon, v. 105; ix. 94.
— — Alexander, 5th laird, iv. 152.
— — his wife, Elizabeth Kennedy, iv. 152.
— — Sir Alexander, 6th laird, iv. 153.
— — his 1st wife, Katharine Crichton, iv. 155.
— — his 2nd wife, Margaret Dunbar, iv. 155.
— — his 3rd wife, Katharine Stewart, iv. 155.
— — Sir Alexander, 7th laird, iv. 158.
— — his 1st wife, Christian Douglas, iv. 159.
— — his 2nd wife, Elizabeth Douglas, i. 194; iv. 159.
— — Sir Alexander, 8th laird, iv. 159.
— — his wife, Grizel Gordon, iv. 159; v. 113.
— — John, vi. 474.
— — Sir John, iv. 149.
— — his wife, Marion Stewart, iv. 84, 149.
— — John, eldest son of Sir Alex. S. of Garlies, iv. 151.
— — his wife, Elizabeth Shaw, iv. 151.
— — Marion, wife of (1) Sir John Stewart of Jedworth, and (2) Sir John Forrester of Corstorphine, iv. 84, 149, 150 *bis*, 173 *n*.
— — Sir Walter, iv. 84, 149.
— — Sir William, iv. 150.
— of Dalzell, Sir Robert, son of Sir James S. of Pearston, v. 1.
— of Darnley, Sir Alan, i. 13; iv. 303.
— — Sir Alan, ii. 400, 401; v. 348; vii. 529; viii. 573 *n*., 575.
— — his wife, Katharine Seton, viii. 575.
— — Sir Alexander, 4th laird, iv. 145; v. 344, 345.
Stewart of Darnley, Sir Alexander, 5th laird, v. 345.
— — his 1st wife, * Turnbull, iv. 145; v. 345.
— — his 2nd wife, Janet Keith of Galston, iv. 345; v. 345; vi. 29.
— — Sir John, son of Sir Alan S., v. 344.
— — Sir John, constable of the Scots in France, i. 109; ii. 397; iv. 145, 146, 147, 150, 345; v. 345, 346.
— — his wife, Elizabeth of Lennox, v. 341, 347.
— — Sir John, 8th laird, iv. 151 *ter*; v. 348, 492.
— — his wife, Margaret Montgomerie, iii. 433; v. 349.
— — Walter, 2nd son of Sir Alan S. of Dreghorn, v. 344.
— of the Doill, David, iii. 195.
— — his wife, Christina Sutherland, iii. 194.
— of Doune, Sir James, son of 2nd lord Avandale, iii. 186.
— — his wife, Margaret Lindsay, iii. 186.
— — Sir James, commendator of St. Colme, i. 534; iii. 187.
— — his wife, Margaret Campbell, iii. 188.
— of Dreghorn, Sir Alan, 2nd son of Sir John S. of Bonkyl, i. 13; iv. 342; v. 344.
— — Alexander, 2nd son of Sir Alan S. of Darnley, v. 348; vii. 63.
— of Dormantside, Mungo, lieut. Garde Ecossaise, v. 351.
— of Ducarrick, John, viii. 555.
— — his wife, Elizabeth Fleming, viii. 555.
— of Dundaff, Matthew, v. 114.
— of Dundonald, Alexander, 4th High Steward, i. 13.
— — his wife, Jean Macdonald, i. 13.
— — Sir John, illeg. son of king Robert II., i. 17, 151.
— — his wife, Elizabeth Graham, vi. 218.
— of Dunduff, William, ix. 143.
— — his wife, Margaret Maxwell, vi. 483; ix. 143.
— — Sir William, 1st bart., vii. 554.
— of Duncarn, Archibald, 5th son of 4th earl of Moray, vi. 321; ix. 139.
— — his wife, Anna Henderson, vi. 321.
— — Sir Archibald, v. 386.
— — Charles, vi. 321; ix. 139 *ter*.
— — his 1st wife, Christina Bennet, vi. 321.
— — his 2nd wife, Jean Hamilton, vi. 321.
— of Durrisdeer, Sir James, 4th son of 5th High Steward, i. 14.
— — Sir Robert, son of Sir Jas. S. of Pearston, v. 1.
— — Robert, 2nd son of Sir Robt. S. of Innermeath, v. 1; vii. 114.
— — his wife, Janet of Argyll, v. 1.

* Name unknown.

Stewart of Eaglescairnie, Sir Patrick, G.C.M.G., ii. 90.
—— —— his wife, Katharine Henrietta Rodney, ii. 90.
—— of Eday, Henry, illeg. son of John, earl of Carrick, ii. 442.
—— —— his wife, Barbara Bannatyne, ix. 55.
—— —— Sir James, 4th son of 1st earl of Orkney, ii. 440; vi. 573, 576.
—— —— his 1st wife, Elizabeth Hamilton, ix. 146.
—— —— his 2nd wife, Margaret Lyon, vi. 574; viii. 288.
—— —— Robert, colonel, vi. 574; viii. 351.
—— —— his wife, Jean Gordon, viii. 351.
—— of Edgerston, John, viii. 400.
—— of Egilshay, William, colonel in Swedish service, vi. 575; ix. 59.
—— —— his 1st wife, * Bellenden, vi. 575.
—— —— his 2nd wife, Katharine Douglas, ix. 59.
—— of Eynhallew, George, legtd. son of 1st earl of Orkney, vi. 575.
—— of Emyrcreichan, Henry, vii. 394.
—— of Farr, Robert, bishop of Orkney, vi. 573; vii. 164.
—— of Fennok, William, 2nd son of the 'black' S. of Bute, ii. 286, 287.
—— —— his wife, Margaret Stewart, ii. 287.
—— —— William, his 2nd son, ii. 287.
—— of Fife, Robert, eldest son of Murdac, duke of Albany, i. 150; viii. 260; ix. 10.
—— —— Sir Walter, 2nd son of Murdac, duke of Albany, i. 150; ix. 10.
—— of Fincastle, James, ii. 187.
—— of Fintalloch, Archibald, ancestor of the family of, iv. 152 *bis*, 153, 155.
—— Archibald, iv. 154.
—— of the Forest, Sir William, ancestor of the Garlies family, iv. 148.
—— of Ferterkill, John, iv. 274, 275.
—— of Forthergill, John, 1473, iv. 30.
—— of Fort Stewart, Sir James, 7th bart., vi. 434.
—— of Gaithope, James, viii. 401.
—— —— Sir William, viii. 401.
—— of Galston, Sir Alexander, v. 345.
—— —— his 2nd wife, Janet Keith of Galston, iv. 345; v. 345; vi. 29.
—— —— Alexander, 3rd son of Sir Alex. S., v. 346.
—— —— Alexander, brother of 1st earl of Lennox, v. 348; vii. 63.
—— —— Alexander, son of Robert S., vii. 63.
—— —— Ludovic, vii. 64.
—— —— Robert, vii. 63.
—— —— Thomas, vii. 64.
—— —— his wife, Isobel Henderson, vii. 64.
—— —— Thomas, curator of 2nd duke of Lennox, v. 357; vii. 64, 67.

* Name unknown.

Stewart of Galston, William, the younger, iv. 192.
—— —— his wife, Janet Barclay, iv. 192.
—— of Garlies, Sir Alexander, 3rd laird, iv. 151; v. 105; ix. 94 *bis*.
—— —— his wife, Elizabeth Douglas, iv. 151.
—— —— Alexander, 4th laird, ix. 94.
—— —— his wife, Janet Gordon, v. 105; ix. 94.
—— —— Alexander, 5th laird, iv. 152.
—— —— his wife, Elizabeth Kennedy, iv. 152.
—— —— Sir Alexander, 6th laird, iv. 153, 173 *n.*; v. 107.
—— —— his 1st wife, Katharine Crichton, iv. 155.
—— —— his 2nd wife, Margaret Dunbar, iv. 155.
—— —— his 3rd wife, Katharine Stewart, iv. 155.
—— —— Sir Alexander, 7th laird, iv. 158.
—— —— his 1st wife, Christian Douglas, iv. 159; vii. 126; ix. 94 *bis*.
—— —— his 2nd wife, Elizabeth Douglas, i. 194; iv. 159.
—— —— Sir Alexander, 8th laird, iv. 159.
—— —— his wife, Grizel Gordon, iv. 160; v. 113.
—— —— Sir John, iv. 149.
—— —— his wife, Marion Stewart of Garlies, iv. 149, 150 *bis*.
—— —— Marion, wife of (1) Sir John Stewart, and (2) Sir John Forrester of Corstorphine, iv. 84, 149, 150 *bis*, 173 *n.*
—— —— Sir Walter, ancestor of the family of, i. 13.
—— —— Sir Walter, last of old line, iv. 149.
—— —— Sir William, iv. 150; ix. 94 *bis*.
—— —— his 1st wife, Elizabeth *, iv. 150.
—— —— his 2nd wife, Eupham Graham, iv. 150; vi. 151; ix. 94.
—— of Garth, David, general, i. 473 *n.*
—— —— Neil, i. 442.
—— —— his wife, Christian Stewart, i. 442.
—— of Girthon, Sir John, v. 342.
—— of Glasserton, Sir Alexander, iv. 154.
—— —— James Alexander, iv. 166; vii. 514.
—— —— his wife, Mary Frederica Elizabeth Mackenzie of Seaforth, vii. 514.
—— —— Keith, vice-admiral R.N., M.P., iv. 165, 170.
—— —— his wife, Georgina Isabella D'Aguilar, iv. 166.
—— —— Robert, 2nd son of 2nd earl of Galloway, iv. 161, 163.
—— —— his wife, Elizabeth Dunbar, iv. 161.
—— of Glassock, John, illeg. son of Alexander, lord Garlies, iv. 161.
—— of Glen, William, viii. 400.
—— of Glenluce, Sir Alexander, iv. 155.
—— of Glenmannoch, Sir Alexander, iv. 154.

* Name unknown.

Stewart of the Gloom, David, i. 110.
—— —— his wife, Christian Glen, i. 110.
—— of Graemsay, James, illeg. son of 1st earl of Orkney, vi. 575.
—— of Grandtully, Sir Alan, v. 141.
—— —— Alexander, 5th son of Sir John S. of Innermeath, v. 2, 141.
—— —— Sir James, ancestor of the family of, i. 13.
—— —— Sir John, son of Sir Thomas S., viii. 61.
—— —— Sir John, 3rd bart., i. 209; iii. 176, 517.
—— —— his 1st wife, Elizabeth Mackenzie, iii. 176.
—— —— his 2nd wife, Jane Douglas of Douglas, i. 209.
—— —— his 3rd wife, Helen Murray, iii. 517.
—— —— Sir John Archibald Drummond, 6th bart., vi. 328.
—— —— his wife, Jane Stuart, iv. 293; vi. 328.
—— Thomas, v. 3.
—— Thomas, i. 459.
—— —— his wife, Agnes Murray, i. 459.
—— —— Thomas, i. 461.
—— —— his wife, Margaret Murray, i. 461.
—— —— Sir Thomas, vi. 443; vii. 50.
—— —— William, i. 444.
—— —— his 2nd wife, Isobel *or* Elizabeth Stewart, i. 444.
—— —— Sir William, viii. 224.
—— of Grange Miltoun, William, iv. 365.
—— —— his wife, Janet Hamilton, iv. 365.
—— of Greenend, Alexander, 2nd son of Sir Alex. S. of Garlies, iv. 152.
—— —— his wife, Elizabeth Kennedy, iv. 152.
—— of the Grenan, Alexander, iv. 152.
—— —— his wife, Isabella Stewart, iv. 152.
—— —— Sir Alexander, iv. 155.
—— —— his wife, Katharine Stewart, iv. 155.
—— —— Alexander, grandson of Sir. Alex. S., 6th of Garlies, iv. 156, 158.
—— —— Montgomery Granville John, M.P., iv. 168.
—— of Grey, William, v. 348.
—— of Gogar, Henry, vi. 514.
—— —— his wife, Janet Reid of Barskimming, vi. 514.
—— of Halrig, John, vii. 68.
—— of Henriestoun, John, 'premier homme d'armes,' v. 350.
—— —— his 1st wife, Maria Sempill, v. 350; vii. 531.
—— —— his 2nd wife, Anne Monypenny, v. 350; vi. 278 *n*.
—— of Holy Cross Church, William, viii. 401.
—— of Hopcailzie-Wester, James, viii. 401.
—— —— Sir Robert, viii. 401.
—— —— his wife, Alice Cockburn, viii. 401.
—— of Horsburgh, James, viii. 401.
Stewart of Houstoun, Sir William, vii. 65.
—— —— his 1st wife, Erica *, vii. 68.
—— —— his 2nd wife, Isobel *or* Elizabeth Hepburn, vii. 68.
—— of How, David, vi. 575.
—— of Inchavan, Matthew, v. 554.
—— of Inchmarnock, John, ii. 294.
—— of Kirkland of Innerleithen, James, viii. 401.
—— of Innermeath, Sir John, v. 1, 2.
—— —— his wife, Isabel of Argyll, v. 2.
—— —— John 'Mourach,' v. 3.
—— —— Sir Robert, son of Sir James S. of Pearston, v. 1.
—— —— Robert, ii. 540; v. 2, 3.
—— —— his wife, Johanna Stewart, v. 3; ix. 10.
—— of Innernytie, John, v. 385; ix. 127.
—— —— his wife, Jean Leslie, v. 385; ix. 127.
—— —— Sir William, 2nd son of Sir William S. of Grandtully, viii. 223.
—— of Inverlunan, Alexander, illeg. son of king Robert II., i. 17.
—— of Mains of Invermay, Henry, vii. 394.
—— of Jedworth, John, alleged ancestor of the Garlies family, iv. 146.
—— —— Sir John, iv. 84, 149.
—— —— his wife, Marion Stewart of Dalswinton and Garlies, iv. 84, 149.
—— —— Sir William, 2nd son of Sir Alex. S. of Darnley, ii. 539; iv. 144, 145, 146, 150; v. 345; vii. 366.
—— —— his wife, Isabel, v. 346; ix. 93.
—— of Kelspokis, Alexander, ii. 291.
—— —— Robert, ii. 292.
—— of Kerremenoch, James, ii. 293.
—— —— John, ii. 294.
—— of Kilbride, James, illeg. son of king Robert III., i. 18.
—— of Kilcattan, Archibald, ii. 290.
—— —— James, 3rd son of Jas. S. of Bute, ii. 288.
—— —— his wife, Marabella Crawford, ii. 288.
—— —— John, ii. 288.
—— —— Ninian, 5th son of Ninian S. of Bute, ii. 288, 290.
—— —— his wife, Elizabeth Lindsay, ii. 290.
—— —— Ninian, grandson of Robt. S., ii. 290.
—— —— Robert, son of Ninian S. of Largobroughton, ii. 289 *n*., 290.
—— of Kilcoy, Sir James, vii. 502.
—— —— his wife, Jean Fraser, v. 543; vii. 502.
—— —— Katharine, wife of Robert Grant, vii. 465.
—— of Kilcreuchie, William, colonel, iv. 155, 162.
—— of Kildavanan, Alexander, 4th son of Ninian S. of Bute, ii. 290.
—— —— his wife, Elizabeth Tait, ii. 290.
—— —— Ninian, 5th son of Ninian S. of Bute, ii. 288, 290.

* Name unknown.

Stewart of Killeith, Sir James, captain; eldest son of James, earl of Arran, i. 397; ii. 474; iii. 506; vi. 363, 513, 515, 516, 517.
—— —— his 1st wife, Katharine M'Dowall, ii. 474.
—— of Killibroch, John, iv. 274, 275.
—— of Killiechassie, John, vii. 199.
—— —— his wife, Jean Rollo, vii. 199.
—— of Killinan, Henry, i. 397; vi. 169.
—— —— Sir John, vi. 513.
—— of Killislate, Walter, vi. 130.
—— of Kinclaven, Robert, eldest son of Murdac, duke of Albany, i. 150; ix. 10.
—— of Kinfauns, James, illeg. son of king Robert II., i. 17.
—— of Kingedward, John, ii. 264.
—— of Kintessock, Thomas, viii. 339.
—— of Kirkhill, Sir James, ii. 367; iv. 249.
—— —— Katharine, wife of 3rd lord Cardross, ii. 367; viii. 319 *n.*; ix. 52.
—— —— Sir Lewis, ii. 409.
—— —— his wife, Marion Arnot, ii. 409.
—— —— Nicolas, wife of 9th earl of Glencairn, iv. 249.
—— —— Sir William, ii. 367; iv. 249.
—— of Kirkmaho, Sir Alexander, iv. 154.
—— of Kirkmaiden, Sir Alexander, iv. 158.
—— of Kirktoun, Sir James, 1st bart., ii. 294.
—— —— Sir John, ii. 294, 295.
—— of Knightislands, Alexander, son of Sir Jas. S. of Bute, ii. 292.
—— of Ladywell, John, vi. 246.
—— of Laitheris, David, son of John S. of Redcastle, v. 6.
—— —— James, eldest son of 4th lord Innermeath, v. 6.
—— —— John, 2nd son of 4th lord Innermeath, v. 5.
—— —— his wife, Katharine Gray, v. 5.
—— of Largobroughton, Ninian, ii. 290.
—— of Lennox, Sir Walter, 2nd son of Murdac, duke of Albany, i. 150; ii. 176; v. 141, 605; vi. 509, 510; viii. 260; ix. 10.
—— —— his alleged wife, Janet Erskine, i. 150; vi. 510.
—— of Lesmurdie, Alexander, iv. 133.
—— —— his wife, Magdalen Crichton, iv. 133.
—— —— Francis, major-general, vii. 487.
—— —— his wife, Margaret Grant, vii. 487.
—— of Liddesdale, Sir Robert, vi. 340.
—— of Logierait, William, 4th son of 5th lord Innermeath, v. 7.
—— of Lorn, Isabel, wife of Colin, 1st earl of Argyll, i. 332; v. 3.
—— —— Sir James, ancestor of the family of, i. 13; v. 1.
—— —— Sir James, 'the Black Knight of Lorn,' i. 440; v. 2 *bis*, 3, 427.
—— —— his wife, queen Joan Beaufort, i. 18, 19; v. 2, 427; viii. 532.
Stewart of Lorn, Sir John, eldest son of Sir Robert S. of Innermeath, v. 1, 2.
—— —— his wife, Isobel of Argyll, v. 2.
—— —— John 'Mourach,' v. 3.
—— —— Jonet, wife of Sir Colin Campbell of Glenurchy, ii. 176; v. 4.
—— —— Marion, wife of Arthur Campbell of Otter, v. 4.
—— —— Robert, 2nd son of Sir Robert S. of Innermeath, v. 1.
—— —— his wife, Janet of Argyll, v. 1.
—— —— Robert, eldest son of Sir John S. of Innermeath, v. 3.
—— —— his wife, Johanna Stewart, v. 3; ix. 10.
—— of Halltoun of Luncartie, Robert, vi. 514.
—— —— his wife, Jean Ross, vi. 514.
—— of Mains, William, 3rd son of Sir Alex. S. of Garlies, iv. 159; ix. 94.
—— —— his wife, Barbara Stewart, i. 397; iii. 187; iv. 159.
—— of Melrose, James, viii. 399.
—— of Menteith, Robert, eldest son of Murdac, duke of Albany, i. 150.
—— of Methven, Sir John, constable and keeper of Dunbarton, i. 358.
—— —— his wife, Margaret Hamilton, i. 43; ix. 126.
—— of Middleton, Sir Robert, 5th son of 1st earl of Orkney, ii. 440; vi. 574, 576.
—— of Minto, Sir Alexander, iv. 154.
—— —— his 1st wife, Katharine Crichton, iv. 155.
—— —— his 2nd wife, Margaret Dunbar, iv. 155.
—— —— his 3rd wife, Katharine Stewart, iv. 155.
—— —— Sir John, provost of Glasgow, ii. 78.
—— —— his wife, Janet Fleming, ii. 78.
—— —— Sir John, keeper of Glasgow Castle, ii. 79, 405; iv. 154.
—— —— his 1st wife, Johanna Hepburn, ii. 80.
—— —— his 2nd wife, Margaret Stewart, ii. 81.
—— —— Sir John, last laird, ii. 81.
—— —— Sir Ludovic, iv. 247; vi. 258.
—— —— his wife, Elizabeth Cunningham, iv. 247; ix. 97 *bis*.
—— —— Sir Matthew, ii. 80, 405.
—— —— his 1st wife, Jonet Stewart, ii. 81.
—— —— his 2nd wife, Jean Colquhoun, ii. 81.
—— —— Sir Robert, ii. 78; viii. 538.
—— —— his wife, Janet Murray, ii. 79.
—— —— Thomas, 2nd son of Sir Wm. S. of Dalswinton, ii. 77; iv. 151.
—— —— his wife, Isabella Stewart, ii. 77; iv. 151.
—— —— Walter, ii. 81.
—— —— his wife, Christian Crawfurd, ii. 81.
—— —— Sir William, iv. 150.

Stewart of Moncastell, Henry, vii. 394.
—— —— Sir James, i. 534.
—— of Monkton, Sir William, vi. 513.
—— —— his wife, Helen Cunningham, vi. 513.
—— —— William, captain, ii. 393; vi. 513.
—— of Montgrenan, Alan, vii. 532.
—— of Morebattle, Thomas, 2nd son of Sir Wm. S. of Garlies, iv. 151.
—— —— Sir William, iv. 148.
—— of Morphie, Walter, legtd. son of Sir Walter S. of Lennox, i. 150; v. 605; vi. 509.
—— of Newark, John, colonel, ancestor of the family of, vi. 574.
—— of Newton, James, 2nd son of 2nd lord Ochiltree, i. 394; ii. 392; vi. 513.
—— —— Sir James, v. 543.
—— —— his wife, Jean Fraser, v. 543; vii. 502.
—— —— John, vii. 452.
—— —— Robert, 4th son of Sir Alex. S. of Darnley, v. 346.
—— of Ochiltree, Archibald, iii. 346.
—— of Oizon, John, v. 350.
—— —— his 1st wife, Maria Sempill, v. 350.
—— —— his 2nd wife, Anne Monypenny, v. 350.
—— —— William, 2nd son of 1st earl of Lennox, v. 348.
—— of Ormiston, Sir Alexander, iv. 154.
—— of Outlaw, James, ii. 15.
—— —— Walter, 2nd son of Thos. S. of Ryland, vi. 555.
—— —— his wife, Elizabeth Oliphant, vi. 555.
—— —— Walter, iv. 131.
—— —— his wife, Jean Crichton, iv. 131.
—— of Physgill, John, ancestor of the family of, iv. 155; ix. 94.
—— —— his wife, Margaret Stewart, ix. 94.
—— —— Robert Hathorn, viii. 455.
—— of Pittendreich, Francis, lieut.-col. of Honeywood's Dragoons, vi. 324.
—— —— his 1st wife, Helen *or* Eleanora Montgomerie, iii. 457; vi. 324; ix. 140.
—— —— his 2nd wife, *, vi. 324.
—— —— John, M.P., major-general, vi. 324.
—— —— his wife, Sybella Barbour, ix. 140.
—— of Pittenweem, Frederic, vii. 67, 68.
—— —— Sir William, v. 348; vii. 65; viii. 100.
—— —— his 1st wife, Erica *, vii. 68.
—— —— his 2nd wife, Isobel *or* Elizabeth Hepburn, vii. 68.
—— of Pittheveles, Robert, vi. 514.
—— —— his wife, Jean Ross, vi. 514; ix. 144 *bis*.
—— of Polcak, Sir Gilbert, ii. 202.
—— of Wester Polquharne, Josias, vi. 515.
—— of Easter Polquhairne, William, vi. 514.

* Name unknown.

Stewart of Powton, John, illeg. son of Sir Alex. S. of Garlics, iv. 159.
—— of Previck, Sir James, vi. 517.
—— of Railston, Sir John, 2nd son of 6th High Stewart, i. 14; viii. 421.
—— —— Sir Walter, i. 14; vi. 365.
—— of Ramalton, Sir William, 1st bart., vii. 554.
—— of Ravenstone, Robert, 2nd son of 2nd earl of Galloway, iv. 161; v. 125.
—— —— his wife, Elizabeth Dunbar, iv. 161.
—— —— William, iv. 162.
—— —— his wife, Elizabeth Gordon, iv. 162.
—— of Redcastle, David, v. 6.
—— —— John 'Mourach,' v. 3.
—— —— John, v. 3.
—— —— his wife, Elizabeth Beaton, iv. 282; v. 3.
—— —— John, 2nd son of 4th lord Innermeath, iv. 282; v. 5.
—— —— Robert, v. 491.
—— of Remiston, Robert, 2nd son of 2nd earl of Galloway, iv. 161, 163.
—— —— William, iv. 162.
—— of Roslane *or* Rosland, Andrew, son of John S. of Bute, ii. 286.
—— of Rossyth, Sir David, iii. 470.
—— —— Sir David, iii. 471.
—— —— his wife, Mariota Herries, iii. 471.
—— —— Sir David, vi. 367.
—— —— his wife, Margaret Douglas of Laidgreen, vi. 367.
—— —— David, v. 608.
—— —— his wife, Christian Erskine, v. 608.
—— —— George, the younger, vi. 591.
—— —— his wife, Rachel Makgill, vi. 591.
—— —— Henry, i. 114.
—— —— his wife, Marjorie *, i. 114.
—— —— his alleged wife, Marion Ogilvy, i. 114.
—— —— Henry, vi. 368.
—— —— his wife, Margaret Douglas, vi. 368.
—— —— James, vi. 421.
—— —— his wife, Margaret Napier, vi. 421.
—— —— Robert, 2nd son of Sir Robert S. of Innermeath; ancestor of the family of, v. 1.
—— —— his wife, Janet of Argyll, v. 1.
—— —— Robert, i. 464.
—— —— his wife, Euphemia Murray, i. 464; iv. 282.
—— of Rowehane, Sir Alexander, iv. 159.
—— of Rutherford, William, viii. 400.
—— of Ryland, James, iv. 259.
—— —— his wife, Margaret Ruthven, ii. 268; iv. 258.
—— —— James, ii. 15; ix. 85.
—— —— his wife, Janet Elphinstone, iii. 536; ix. 85.
—— —— Thomas, vi. 555.
—— —— Walter, ii. 13.
—— of Rynds, Frederic, vii. 69.

Stewart of St. Colm's Inch, Henry, vii. 394; ix. 154, 155.
— — his wife, Jean Stewart, i. 446; vii. 395.
— — Sir James. i. 340; iii. 186.
— of Sandhauch, Sir Andrew, 2nd illeg. son of 'the Wolf of Badenoch,' ii. 263.
— of Scotstownhill, Alexander, i. 153 *n.*
— of Seasyde, William, 3rd son of Sir Alex. S. of Garlies, iv. 159.
— of Shanbothy, Sir Robert, v. 257, 491.
— of Shawwood, John, i. 549.
— of Shillinglaw, James, viii. 401.
— — his wife, Katharine Ker, viii. 401.
— — James, son of Sir Robt. S., viii. 401.
— — Sir Robert, viii. 401, 402, 448.
— — his wife, Alice Cockburn, viii. 401.
— — William, viii. 399.
— of Sorbie, John, brigadier-general, M.P., iv. 163.
— — his alleged wife, Bridget Pockling-ton, iv. 163.
— of Southwick, Sir Mark J. Mactaggart, ii. 119, 502; viii. 145.
— of Springkell, John, ix. 41.
— of Stewarton, Sir Alexander, iv. 160.
— of New Stewarton, Sir William, i. 52; vii. 554.
— of Strabrock, Sir James, iv. 249.
— — Nicolas, wife of 9th earl of Glen-cairn, iv. 249.
— — Sir William, iv. 249.
— of Strathardle, John, iv. 30.
— of Strathdown, Robert, illeg. son of king James v., vi. 572.
— of Stuikis, James, iv. 34.
— — John, illeg. son of king James II., i. 20.
— — Patrick, iv. 34.
— — his wife, Elizabeth Butter, iv. 33.
— of Sunlaws, Thomas, 2nd son of Sir Wm. S. of Garlies, iv. 151.
— — Sir William, iv. 148.
— of Tantallon, James, Regent of Scot-land, i. 24; vi. 572.
— of Tarbolton, Sir John, eldest son of Sir Alan S., v. 344; vi. 198.
— — Sir John, v. 348.
— — his wife, Margaret Montgomerie, v. 348.
— — Sir Robert, i. 12.
— of Threapwood, Alan, provost of Edin-burgh, vii. 64.
— — his wife, Helen Baty, vii. 64.
— of Teviotdale, Sir William, iv. 148.
— of Tillicoultry, Sir Robert, 1st bart., lord of Session, ii. 296.
— — his 1st wife, Violet Hamilton, ii. 296.
— — his 2nd wife, Cecil Hamilton, ii. 44, 296; ix. 37.
Stewart of Tillicoultry, Sir Robert, 2nd bart., ii. 296.
— — his wife, Jean Calderwood, ii. 296.
— of Tonderghie, Walter, iv. 151.
— of Torbane, Alexander, 3rd son of Sir Alex. S. of Darnley, v. 346.
— of Traquair, James, legtd. son of James, 1st earl of Buchan, ii. 267; iv. 261; viii. 399.
— — his wife, Katharine Rutherford, vii. 367; viii. 399.
— — James, 3rd son of 2nd lord Avan-dale, iii. 186; viii. 400; ix. 68.
— — James, 6th laird, viii. 401.
— — his wife, Katharine Ker, viii. 401.
— — Sir John, captain of the Guard, vii. 375; viii. 400.
— — his wife, Janet Knox, viii. 400.
— — John, the younger, viii. 401, 402.
— — his wife, Margaret Stewart, vi. 515; viii. 402.
— — Sir John, M.P., P.C., viii. 402.
— — his wife, Katharine Carnegie, viii. 67, 405.
— — Louisa, dau. of 7th earl of Traquair, iv. 420; viii. 408.
— — Robert, viii. 400.
— — William, viii. 399.
— — his wife, Christian Hay, viii. 400, 434.
— — Sir William, M.P., viii. 400.
— of Tullos, Sir James, ii. 440; iv. 435; vi. 573, 576; viii. 287; ix. 55.
— — his 1st wife, Elizabeth Hamilton, ix. 146.
— — his 2nd wife, Margaret Lyon, vi. 574; viii. 288.
— of Tullynadies, John, son of Sir Robt. S. of Polcak, ii. 202.
— — his wife, Jean Campbell, ii. 201.
— of Urquhart, Robert, vii. 457.
— of Urrard, John, ii. 187.
— — his wife, Jean Stewart, ii. 187.
— — John, i. 361.
— — his wife, Susan Campbell, i. 361.
— of Wells, William, viii. 400.
— of Whitelaw, Henry, ii. 570.
— — his wife, * Colvill, ii. 570.
— — Hercules, ii. 169.
— — his wife, Mary Whitelaw, ii. 169.
— — Margaret, wife of (1) John Hamil-ton, and (2) John Hamilton, ii. 169; ix. 41.
— of Whithorn Priory, Sir Alexander, iv. 158.
— — Elizabeth, countess of Moray, iv. 158; vi. 316.
— — Margaret, iv. 158.
— of Wigtoun, Sir Alexander, iv. 154.
— Adam, prior of Charterhouse, illeg. son of king James v., i. 25; iii. 590; iv. 101; v. 353 *n.*
— — his wife, Janet Ruthven, iv. 101.

* Name unknown.

Stewart, Mr. Adam, 5th son of Sir Robt. S. of Minto, ii. 79.
—— Adam, illeg. son of John, earl of Carrick, ix. 55.
—— Agnes, mistress of king James IV., and wife of (1) Adam, 2nd earl of Bothwell, (2) Alexander, 3rd lord Home, (3) Robert, 5th lord Maxwell, and (4) Cuthbert Ramsay, i. 22; ii. 156, 267; iii. 94; vi. 480; ix. 2, 65, 107.
—— Agnes, wife of John Stewart of Cardonald, ii. 78.
—— Agnes, their dau., ii. 78.
—— Agnes, wife of John Wallace, ii. 81.
—— Agnes, dau. of Alexander, 2nd earl of Buchan, ii. 268.
—— Agnes, wife of Henry David (Erskine), 10th earl of Buchan, ii. 276; ix. 49.
—— Agnes, dau. of Sir Robert S. of Tillicoultry, ii. 296.
—— Agnes, wife of John, 4th lord Maxwell, iv. 152; vi. 478.
—— Agnes, wife of A. Agnew of Lochnaw, iv. 158.
—— Agnes, wife of William Edmonstone of Duntreath, v. 351.
—— Agnes, wife of John Boswell of Auchinleck, vi. 511.
—— Agnes, dau. of Robt. S. of Pittheveles, vi. 514.
—— Agnes, dau. of Andrew, master of Ochiltree, vi. 516.
—— Agnes, grand-dau. of James S. of Traquair, viii. 402.
—— Agnes, dau. of 1st lord Doune, ix. 68.
—— Alan, prebendary of Menmuir and Cruden, i. 439.
—— Alan, abbot of Crossraguel, ii. 472.
—— Alan, 3rd son of Robert S., lord of Lorn, v. 3 *bis*.
—— Alexander, canon of Glasgow, i. 17.
—— Alexander, inf. son of king James I., i. 19; ii. 96.
—— Alexander, archbishop of St. Andrews, illeg. son of king James IV., i. 22; v. 146; vii. 288 *n*.
—— Sir Alexander, 3rd son of Murdac, duke of Albany, i. 150.
—— —— his *possible* wife, Egidia Douglas of Nithsdale, iii. 164.
—— Alexander, prior of Whithorn, bishop of Moray, illeg. son of Alexander, duke of Albany, i. 152, 449; ii. 182; vii. 46 *n*.; ix. 10.
—— Alexander, illeg. son of the bishop of Moray, i. 153.
—— Alexander, legtd. son of the bishop of Moray, i. 153.
—— Alexander, tutor of Castlemilk, ii. 81.
Stewart, Sir Alexander, eldest son of 'the Wolf of Badenoch,' ii. 263; iii. 154; v. 587.
—— —— his 1st wife, Isabella, countess of Mar, iii. 153; v. 586.
—— —— his 2nd wife, Marie van Hoorne, v. 588.
—— Alexander, 2nd son of James, master of Buchan, ii. 269.
—— Alexander, 3rd son of William S. of Bute and Fennok, ii. 287.
—— Alexander, 5th son of 1st lord Doune, iii. 189; ix. 68.
—— Alexander, 3rd son of Sir Alex. S. of Darnley, iv. 145.
—— Sir Alexander, eldest son of Sir Alex. S. of Garlies, iv. 154, 155, 156.
—— —— his wife, Katharine Herries, iv. 158.
—— Alexander, master of Garlies, iv. 165.
—— Alexander, major-general, 3rd son of 9th earl of Galloway, iv. 171.
—— —— his wife, Adela Maria Loder, iv. 171.
—— Alexander, 4th son of John, 4th lord Innermeath, v. 6.
—— Alexander, 3rd son of Sir John S. of Darnley, v. 348.
—— Alexander, 3rd son of 1st earl of Lennox, v. 349.
—— Alexander, 4th son of 2nd lord Avandale, vi. 511.
—— Alexander, 5th son of 1st lord Blantyre, ix. 38.
—— Sir Alexander, diocese of Glasgow, ix. 155.
—— Amelia, wife of (1) Alex. Fraser, and (2) 19th earl of Crawford, iii. 38; v. 544; vi. 323.
—— Amelia, wife of Sir P. Halkett of Pitfirrane, vi. 325.
—— Andrew, eldest son of James, 5th High Stewart, i. 14; viii. 248.
—— Sir Andrew, 3rd son of Walter, 6th High Stewart, i. 15.
—— Andrew, son of Alexander, duke of Albany, i. 153.
—— Andrew, 3rd son of Robert, duke of Albany, i. 148; ii. 264.
—— Andrew, bishop of Moray, and St. Andrews, i. 441; vii. 249.
—— Andrew, canon of Dunkeld, abbot of Kelso, bishop of Caithness, high treasurer, i. 442; iii. 198; v. 54; viii. 335.
—— Andrew, M.D., minister of Bolton, ii. 90.
—— —— his wife, Margaret Stewart, ii. 90.
—— Andrew, 4th son of 3rd earl of Galloway, iv. 163.
—— Mr. Andrew, minister in Ireland, vi. 514; ix. 144.
—— —— his wife, Esther Wallace, ix. 144.

Stewart, Andrew, master of Ochiltree, vi. 514.
—— —— his wife, Margaret Stewart, vi. 168, 515.
—— Anna, wife of Archibald, earl of Angus and Ormond, i. 207; v. 359; ix. 13.
—— Anna, wife of 8th lord Saltoun of Abernethy, ii. 85; vii. 414.
—— Anna, wife of Gilbert Kennedy of Bargany, vi. 516.
—— Anna, wife of John Murdoch, vi. 519.
—— Anna, dau. of Sir William S. of Pittenweem, vii. 68.
—— Anna, dau. of 3rd lord Ochiltree, ix. 144.
—— Anna, dau. of 1st lord St. Colme, ix. 155.
—— Anna Louisa, wife of (1) capt. Staples, and (2) Richard Napier, vi. 434.
—— Annabella, wife of (1) Louis, count of Geneva, and (2) George, 2nd earl of Huntly, i. 19; iv. 528.
—— Annabel, dau. of the regent Moray, iii. 229; vi. 316.
—— Anne, wife of 5th earl of Airlie, i. 128.
—— Anne, wife of 2nd lord Castlestewart, i. 446; vi. 517; ix. 28, 144.
—— Ann, wife of (1) Alex. Bruce, and (2) Archd. Campbell, i. 549.
—— Anne, wife of Alex. Hay, ii. 88; viii. 450; ix. 38.
—— Anne, wife of Alex. Munro, ii. 296.
—— Anne, wife of (1) Alex. Macdonald, and (2) W. Campbell, ii. 296.
—— Anne, wife of John Steuart of Annefield and Blackhall, ii. 297; vi. 325.
—— Anne, wife of Jas. Kennedy of Blairquhan, ii. 487.
—— Anne, wife of A. Agnew of Lochnaw, iv. 161.
—— Anne, dau. of 5th earl of Galloway, iv. 164.
—— Anne, wife of 1st lord Jedburgh, v. 67, 72, 73; vi. 516.
—— Anne, wife of Robert Stewart, seigneur d'Aubigny, v. 348, 350.
—— Anne, wife of David Ross of Balnagown, vi. 322.
—— Anne, dau. of 9th earl of Moray, vi. 327.
—— Anne, wife of B. Crawfurd of Carse, vi. 511.
—— Anne, wife of Sir Wm. Sempill of Letterkenny, vii. 554.
—— Anne, dau. of 4th earl of Traquair, viii. 407.
—— Anne Harriet, wife of lord Spencer Chichester, iv. 169.
—— Arabella, wife of William Seymour, i. 22; v. 354.
—— Archibald, 3rd son of Ninian S. of Bute, ii. 290.
—— Archibald, W.S., iii. 76.
Stewart, Archibald, burgess of Edinburgh, iii. 189; ix. 68.
—— Archibald, 3rd son of 1st lord Doune, iii. 189.
—— Archibald, provost of Edinburgh, iii. 358.
—— Archibald, parson of Kirkmaho, iv. 152 *bis*, 153, 155.
—— Archibald, 2nd son of Sir John S. of Innermeath, v. 2, 3.
—— Archibald, son of Bernard S., v. 7.
—— Archibald, capt. R.N., 4th son of 7th earl of Moray, vi. 325.
—— Archibald, lieut.-col. Dorsetshire Militia, vi. 326.
—— —— his wife, Cornelia Pleydell, vi. 326.
—— Archibald, 3rd son of Robt. S. of Pittheveles, vi. 514.
—— Archibald Alan William John, viii. 112.
—— Arthur, inf. son of king James IV., i. 21.
—— Arthur, inf. son of king James V., i. 21; iii. 531; ix. 84.
—— Arthur, legtd. son of Sir Walter S. of Lennox, i. 150; vi. 509.
—— Barbara, wife of col. Stewart, i. 397.
—— Barbara, wife of James Menzies, i. 444; ix. 28.
—— Barbara, wife of Alex. Campbell, ii. 297.
—— Barbara, wife of (1) Sir Jas. Sinclair of Sanday, and (2) Roderick Macleod of Lewis, vi. 511.
—— Barbara, wife of H. Halcro of Halcro, vi. 574.
—— Barbara, dau. of 4th earl of Traquair, viii. 407.
—— Beatrix, alleged wife of Maldwin, earl of Lennox, i. 2.
—— Beatrix, dau. of James, 5th lord Innermeath, v. 7.
—— Bernard, 3rd son of Henry S. of Buchlyvie, iii. 187.
—— Bernard, 2nd son of Richard, 3rd lord Innerneath, v. 5.
—— Bernard, nephew of John, 6th lord Innermeath, v. 7.
—— Bernard, 7th son of 3rd duke of Lennox, v. 359.
—— Bethia, dau. of Sir Robert S. of Tillicoultry, ii. 296.
—— Bethia, dau. of 2nd lord Ochiltree, vi. 514.
—— Caroline, wife of rev. G. Rushout, iv. 170.
—— Caroline, dau. of 8th earl of Galloway, iv. 171.
—— Cecil, wife of E. Wright of Kersie, ii. 296.
—— Charles, major-gen. in Sweden, i. 397.
—— Charles, H.E.I.C.S., son of 7th lord Blantyre, ii. 89.

Stewart, Charles, barrister, son of 10th lord Blantyre, ii. 91.
— Sir Charles, K.B., lieut.-gen., ii. 304.
— — his wife, Louisa Bertie, ii. 304.
— Charles, 5th son of 9th earl of Moray, vi. 327.
— Charles Edward Louis Casimir, the young Chevalier de St. George, titular king Charles III., i. 35; iii. 481, 585; viii. 36, 360.
— — his wife, Louisa Maximiliana, princess of Stolberg-Guedern, iii. 481.
— Charles James, D.D., rector of Orton, bishop of Quebec, iv. 168.
— Charlotta Maria, inf. dau. of king James VII., i. 34.
— Charlotte, wife of John, 4th earl of Dunmore, iii. 389; iv. 166.
— Charlotte, wife of Sir Edward Crofton, iv. 169.
— Christian, wife of Neil Stewart of Garth, i. 442.
— Christian, wife of John Betoun of Balfour, i. 444.
— Christian, wife of Jas. Ogilvy, ii. 13.
— Christian, wife of Richard Douglas, ii. 270.
— Christian, wife of Sir James Dundas of Dundas, v. 2.
— Christian, wife of John Mouat of Hougaland, vi. 575.
— Christiana, wife of Cyrus Griffin, viii. 408.
— Christian, wife of Edward Withrington of Kirkington, ix. 42.
— David, eldest son of Walter, earl of Atholl, i. 438.
— David, 5th son of James, 6th lord Innermeath and earl of Atholl, i. 448.
— David, son of John S. of Craigiehall, ii. 509.
— — his wife, Helenor Cathcart, ii. 509.
— David, 4th son of Robert S., lord of Lorn, v. 3 *bis*.
— David, brother of Andrew, 3rd lord Avondale, iii. 530.
— — his wife, Isabella *or* Elizabeth Elphinstone, iii. 529.
— David, lieut. R.N., 3rd son of 8th earl of Moray, vi. 325.
— — his wife, Elizabeth Begg, vi. 326.
— David, canon of Ross, treasurer of Moray, ix. 133.
— Doratie, dau. of 4th lord Ochiltree, vi. 518.
— Dorothea, wife of 2nd earl of Tullibardine, i. 446, 471.
— Dorothea, wife of 1st earl of Gowrie, iv. 263; vi. 168.
— Dorothea, wife of John Stewart of Campsie, vi. 169.
Stewart, Dougal, captain, vii. 511.
— — his wife, Mary Mackenzie, vii. 511.
— Duncan, illeg. son of 'the Wolf of Badenoch,' ii. 263.
— Duncan, colonel 92nd Highlanders, viii. 112.
— — his wife, Emily Rose Lindsay, viii. 112.
— Edward, rector of Lamiston, vicar of Sparholt, iv. 169.
— Edward, bishop of Orkney, vi. 45.
— Edward Richard, brigade-major, M.P., 7th son of 7th earl of Galloway, iv. 168.
— — his wife, Katharine Charteris, iv. 169; viii. 514.
— Egidia, wife of Alexander de Meyners, i. 14.
— Egidia, wife of Sir Patrick Graham of Kincardine and Dundaff, i. 15.
— Egidia, wife of (1) Sir Jas. Lindsay of Crawford, (2) Sir Hugh of Eglinton, and (3) Sir Jas. Douglas of Dalkeith, i. 15; iii. 11, 428; vi. 348; ix. 80.
— Egidia, wife of Sir William Douglas of Nithsdale, i. 16; iii. 164.
— Egidia, dau. of king Robert III., i. 18.
— Eleanor, wife of Sigismund of Tirol, duke of Austria, i. 19; vi. 276; ix. 2.
— Eleanora, wife of Jean de l'Hôpital, comte de Choisy, i. 154.
— Elenor, wife of (1) William, 6th earl of Erroll, and (2) John, 10th earl of Sutherland, iii. 568; v. 353; viii. 342; ix. 86.
— Eleanor, wife of Dempster of Muiresk, ix. 48.
— Elena, wife of John Drummond, vii. 29.
— Elizabeth, wife of Maldwin, 3rd earl of Lennox, i. 12: v. 332.
— Elizabeth, wife of Sir William of Douglas, i. 13; iii. 140.
— Elizabeth, wife of Sir D. Lindsay, 1st earl of Crawford, i. 16; iii. 15.
— Elizabeth, wife of Thomas Hay, constable of Scotland, i. 16; iii. 561.
— Elizabeth, wife of Sir Jas. Douglas of Dalkeith, i. 18; vi. 350.
— Elizabeth, mistress of king James V., i. 25.
— Elizabeth, wife of Frederick V., count palatine of the Rhine, king of Bohemia, i. 27; v. 225, 444; vi. 251.
— Elizabeth, dau. of king Charles I., i. 29.
— Elizabeth, dau. of king James VII., i. 34.
— Elizabeth, wife of Malcolm Fleming of Biggar, i. 149: viii. 531, 532.
— Elizabeth, wife of Sir Alex. Hamilton of Ballencrieff and Innerwick, i. 170; iv. 304.
— Elizabeth, wife of 1st earl of Argyll, i. 332.

Stewart, Elizabeth, wife of 2nd earl of Argyll, i. 336; v. 350.
— Elizabeth, wife of (1) Hugh, 5th lord Fraser of Lovat, (2) Robert (Stewart), earl of Lennox and March, and (3) James (Stewart), earl of Arran, i. 396, 445; v. 355, 528, 529; ix. 28.
— Elizabeth, wife of Duncan Bayne of Tulloch, i. 397; vi. 513; ix. 26.
— Elizabeth, wife of (1) John (Stewart), 3rd earl of Lennox, and (2) Ninian, 3rd lord Ross of Halkhead, i. 442; v. 352; vii. 252; ix. 27.
— Elizabeth, wife of 2nd lord Gray, i. 442; iv. 276.
— Elizabeth, wife of (1) Thos. Innes of Elrick, and (2) Alex. Robertson of Strowan, i. 442; iii. 569.
— Elizabeth, wife of Robert Innes, i. 442.
— Elizabeth, wife of Kenneth Mackenzie of Kintail, i. 443; vii. 500.
— Elizabeth, wife of Mr. Walter Leslie, i. 448.
— Elizabeth, wife of Sir John Maxwell, ii. 79.
— Elizabeth, wife of capt. William Colquhoun, ii. 89.
— Elizabeth, wife of Jas. Cranstoun, ii. 172.
— Elizabeth, dau. of lord Stewart and Bothwell, ii. 173.
— Elizabeth, wife of John, master of Buchan, ii. 269; vi. 312; ix. 47, 138.
— Elizabeth, wife of A. Fraser of Muchalls, ii. 270.
— Elizabeth, wife of John Stewart of Ambrismore, ii. 290.
— Elizabeth, wife of N. Bannatyne of Kames, ii. 296.
— Elizabeth, wife of Alex. Stewart of Auchinskeoch, ii. 297.
— Elizabeth, wife of Francis I., duke of Brittany, ii. 326.
— Elizabeth, wife of James Sinclair of Murchil, ii. 340; vi. 574.
— Elizabeth, wife of Jas. Cranstoun, ii. 594.
— Elizabeth, wife of Robert Crichton, iii. 187.
— Elizabeth, wife of (1) Wm. Sutherland, and (2) Jas. Murray, iii. 199.
— Elizabeth, wife of John Macdonald, Kintyre, iii. 447.
— Elizabeth, wife of (1) John Bruce of Clackmannan, and (2) * Auchmuty, iii. 470; ix. 82.
— Elizabeth, wife of 2nd lord Elibank, iii. 510; viii. 405.
— Elizabeth, wife of John Fitzwalter *or* Hamilton, iv. 342.
— Elizabeth, wife of (1) W. Maxwell, (2) John Johnstone, and (3) Samuel Kirkpatrick, iv. 158, 415.
Stewart, Elizabeth, wife of (1) Mungo Home of Coldaneknollis, and (2) Patrick Sinclair, iv. 469; ix. 47.
— Elizabeth, dau. of Robt. S. of Ravenstone, iv. 162.
— Elizabeth, wife of John Hamilton of Ballencrieff, iv. 302.
— Elizabeth, wife of Wm. Ochterlony of Kelly, v. 6.
— Elizabeth, wife of David Gardin of that Ilk, v. 7.
— Elizabeth, wife of Sir Alex. Gordon of Kenmure, v. 103, 104.
— Elizabeth, wife of Sir John Colquhoun of Luss, v. 350.
— Elizabeth, wife of Sir Hugh Campbell of Loudoun, v. 351, 496.
— Elizabeth, dau. of 2nd duke of Lennox, v. 358.
— Elizabeth, wife of Henry, earl of Arundel, v. 359.
— Elizabeth, wife of Sir Geo. Campbell of Loudoun, v. 493.
— Elizabeth, wife of Sir Robert Lyle of Duchal, v. 552.
— Elizabeth, dau. of James, earl of Moray, vi. 312.
— Elizabeth, wife of 8th lord Saltoun of Abernethy, vi. 318; vii. 414.
— Elizabeth, wife of Alexander Grant of Grant, vi. 323; vii. 480.
— Elizabeth, wife of 2nd lord Newark, vi. 443.
— Elizabeth, legtd. dau. of 2nd lord Ochiltree, vi. 514.
— Elizabeth, alleged wife of Sir Wm. Douglas of Drumlanrig, vii. 114.
— Elizabeth, dau. of 2nd earl of Traquair, viii. 406.
— Elizabeth, dau. of 4th earl of Traquair, viii. 407.
— Elizabeth, dau. of Alex. S. of Garlies, ix. 94.
— Elizabeth Euphemia, wife of Wm. Phillips Inge, iv. 169.
— Ellen, wife of Sir David Baird, ii. 92.
— Emilia, wife of (1) Alex. Fraser of Strichen, and (2) John, 19th earl of Crawford, iii. 38; v. 544; vi. 323.
— Emily Octavia, wife of capt. F. A. J. Chichester, iv. 172.
— Emma Georgiana, wife of 2nd lord Tollemache of Helmingham, iv. 172.
— Euphemia, wife of Patrick, 6th earl of Dunbar, i. 12; iii. 256.
— Euphemia, wife of Alex. Murray of Broughton, i. 221; iv. 164.
— Euphemia, wife of (1) Patrick Graham of Dundaff, and (2) Sir Patrick Dunbar of Biel, iii. 260; viii. 260.

* Name unknown.

Stewart, Euphemia, dau. of 6th earl of Galloway, iv. 166.
—— Euphemia, dau. of 8th earl of Moray, vi. 325.
—— Evelyn, wife of 3rd marquess of Ailsa, ii. 92, 501.
—— Fanny Mary, wife of W. B. Ferrand, ii. 92.
—— Fitz Roy Somerset Keith, 6th son of 9th earl of Galloway, iv. 171.
—— —— his wife, Elizabeth Louisa Rogers, iv. 171.
—— Frances, wife of Sir Jas. Hamilton of Rosehall, ii. 42, 88.
—— Frances, wife of Jerome, 2nd earl of Portland, v. 359.
—— Frances Anne Emily, wife of 7th duke of Marlborough, vii. 358.
—— Frances Emily, wife of Archibald, styled earl of Cassillis, ii. 502.
—— Frances Teresa, wife of Charles, 6th duke of Lennox, i. 34; ii. 84; v. 361.
—— Francis, commendator of Kelso, ii. 170; vii. 337.
—— Francis, eldest son of Francis, earl of Bothwell, ii. 172.
—— —— his 1st wife, Isabella Seton, ii. 173; vii. 48; viii. 592.
—— Francis, 3rd son of 3rd duke of Lennox, v. 358.
—— Sir Francis, K.B., vice-admiral R.N., 2nd son of 2nd earl of Moray, vi. 318, 319; ix. 138.
—— Francis, son of lt.-col. Francis S. of Pittendreich, vi. 324.
—— Francis Archibald, vi. 326.
—— Frederick, 3rd son of earl of Arran, i. 397; vi. 513.
—— Frederick, 4th son of Francis, earl of Bothwell, ii. 172.
—— Gabriella, dau. of 1st duke of Lennox, iii. 444; v. 356.
—— George, 4th son of John, 6th lord Innermeath and earl of Atholl, i. 448.
—— George, 4th son of 5th earl of Galloway, iv. 164.
—— George, lieut. Lord Howe's regt., 5th son of 6th earl of Galloway, iv. 165.
—— George, brother of Matthew S. of Dundaff, v. 114.
—— George, 2nd son of 3rd earl of Moray, vi. 320; ix. 139.
—— George, 2nd son of 2nd earl of Traquair, viii. 406.
—— Georgiana, dau. of 7th earl of Galloway, iv. 169.
—— Georgiana Eliza, wife of Sir A. Buchanan, ii. 92.
—— Gertrude, wife of W. H. Gladstone, ii. 92.
—— Giles, wife of Alexander de Meyners, i. 14.
Stewart, Giles, wife of William Rutherfurd of Wrightslands, vii. 372; viii. 402.
—— Grace, wife of George Douglas of Cavers, vi. 327.
—— Grizel, wife of 11th earl of Crawford, i. 445; iii. 31; ix. 28 *bis*.
—— Grizzel, dau. of John S. of Ardmaleish, ii. 294.
—— Grizel, dau. of Robt. S. of Ravenstone, iv. 162.
—— Grizel, dau. of 5th lord Innermeath, v. 7.
—— Grizel, wife of 5th viscount of Kenmure, v. 125.
—— Grizel, wife of Sir R. Innes of Innes, vi. 318; vii. 356.
—— Grizel, wife of Hugh Sinclair of Brugh, vi. 575.
—— Guyonne, wife of Philippe de Brague, seigneur de Luat, v. 347.
—— Harie, M.D., 2nd son of Henry S. of Grandtully, ii. 102.
—— Harie, 3rd son of Francis, earl of Bothwell, ii. 172.
—— Harriet, wife of 9th duke of Hamilton, iv. 166, 394.
—— Helen, wife of Walter Ogilvy, ii. 8; v. 7.
—— Helen, wife of (1) John, 5th lord Lindsay of the Byres, and (2) Thos. Moncur, i. 443; v. 398; ix. 128.
—— Helen, wife of Sir John Macfarlane, i. 444; ii. 172.
—— Helen, wife of Thos. Hamilton, ii. 85.
—— Helen, wife of Jas. Muirhead, ii. 86.
—— Helen, wife of 10th lord Gray, ii. 88; iv. 292.
—— Helen, wife of Oliver Colt, ii. 89.
—— Helen, wife of Robert Stewart of Ambrismore, ii. 290.
—— Helen, wife of Andrew Lees, ii. 296.
—— Helen, wife of (1) William, 6th earl of Erroll, and (2) John, 10th earl of Sutherland, iii. 568, 569; v. 353; viii. 342; ix. 86.
—— Helen, wife of (1) William Gordon, (2) John Glendonwyn, and (3) Alexander M'Ghie, iv. 156; v. 108, 109; ix. 94.
—— Helen, wife of John Douglas of Stanhouse, iv. 159.
—— Helen, dau. of Robt. S. of Ravenstone, iv. 162.
—— Helen, illeg. dau. of lt.-gen. James S., iv. 164.
—— Helen, dau. of Robt. S. of Pittheveles, vi. 514.
—— Helen, wife of James Murray, M.D., viii. 202.
—— Helen Blanche, wife of W. C. Mellor, iv. 172.
—— Helenor, wife of (1) 6th earl of Erroll, and (2) 10th earl of Sutherland, iii. 568; v. 353; viii. 342.

Stewart, Henrietta, inf. dau. of king James VII., i. 33.
— Henrietta, wife of 11th earl of Glencairn, iv. 163, 250.
— Henriet, wife of Sir Hugh Campbell of Cawdor, vi. 321; ix. 139.
— Henrietta, wife of 1st marquess of Huntly, i. 50; iv. 544; v. 356.
— Henrietta, dau. of 4th earl of Traquair, viii. 407.
— Henrietta Anna Maria, wife of Philip, duke of Orleans, i. 29; ix. 2.
— Henrietta Caroline, wife of Algernon Turner, iv. 172.
— Henry, 2nd son of William S. of Mains, v. 226.
— Henry, major, 5th son of 7th earl of Moray, vi. 325.
— Henry Frederick, prince of Wales, i. 27; iii. 370; iv. 432; v. 617; vii. 213; viii. 171.
— Henry Holmes, rector of Porth-Kerry, viii. 91.
— — his wife, Beatrice Diana Cecilia Carnegie, viii. 91.
— Sir Herbert, V.C., K.C.B., major-general, iv. 169.
— Sir Hugh, 6th son of Sir John S. of Bonkyl, i. 13.
— Hugh, son of 5th lord Blantyre, ii. 88.
— Hugh, 2nd son of Sir Robert S. of Tillicoultry, ii. 296.
— Hugh, younger son of Sir John S. of Allanbank, viii. 123.
— — his wife, Christian Dalrymple, viii. 123.
— Hugh, 6th son of 7th earl of Moray, ix. 140.
— Ian Charles Lindsay, viii. 112.
— Isobel, wife of Thomas Randolph, earl of Moray, i. 13; vi. 294.
— Isabella, wife of (1) James, 2nd earl of Douglas, and (2) Sir John Edmonstone, i. 16; iii. 157.
— Isabella, wife of Francis I., duke of Brittany, i. 19; ii. 326.
— Isabella, dau. of king James VII., i. 33.
— Isobel, wife of (1) Alex. Leslie, earl of Ross, and (2) Sir Walter Haliburton of Dirleton, i. 149; iv. 334; v. 41; vii. 242.
— Isabel, wife of 1st earl of Argyll, i. 332; v. 3, 4.
— Isobel, wife of (1) Thos. Innes of Elrick, and (2) Alex. Robertson of Strowan, i. 442; iii. 569.
— Isabel, wife of Jas. Hering, i. 443.
— Isobel, wife of William Stewart of Grandtully, i. 444.
— Isabel, wife of (1) Sir Wm. Oliphant of Aberdalgy, and (2) Sir D. Murray of Gask, i. 455, 456 *n.*; v. 2.
— Isobel, dau. of James, master of Buchan, ii. 269.
Stewart, Isobel, wife of Ninian Bannatyne of Kames, ii. 297.
— Isabella, wife of Sir Geo. Mackenzie of Farnese, iii. 76.
— Isabel, wife of Sir Robert de Bruys of Clackmannan, iii. 468.
— Isabella, wife of Thomas Stewart of Minto, iv. 151.
— Isabella, wife of 5th viscount of Kenmure, iv. 162.
— Isobel, wife of John Ogilvy of Densyde, v. 4.
— Isabel, wife of Patrick Strachan, yr. of Glenkindie, v. 6.
— Isabel, wife of (1) Donald, 8th earl of Mar, (2) Geoffrey Moubray, (3) William Carsewell, and *perhaps* (4) * Baliol, v. 583.
— Isobel, wife of Duncan Macfarlane of that Ilk, vi. 512.
— Isabel, wife of Thos. Kennedy of Bargany, vi. 514.
— Isabel, dau. of 4th lord Ochiltree, vi. 518.
— Isobel, dau. of James S. of Traquair, viii. 402.
— Isabel, dau. of 2nd earl of Traquair, viii. 406.
— Isabel, dau. of 4th earl of Traquair, viii. 407.
— Isabel, wife of Neil, 2nd earl of Carrick, ix. 55.
— Isabel Maud, dau. of 9th earl of Galloway, iv. 172.
— Sir James, 'Mor,' 4th son of Murdac, duke of Albany, i. 17, 151; iv. 232.
— James, 2nd son of king James III.; commendator of Arbroath and Dunfermline, archbishop of St. Andrews, i. 21; v. 396; vii. 245.
— James, inf. son of king James IV., i. 21.
— James, inf. son of king James V., i. 23.
— James 'senior,' commendator of Melrose and Kelso, illeg. son of king James V., i. 24; ix. 2.
— James, legtd. son of king James V., prior of St. Andrews, earl of Moray, and regent of Scotland, i. 24; ii. 269; v. 613; vi. 313; ix. 48.
— James, 'tertius,' illeg. son of king James V., i. 24.
— James, 'Beg,' son of Jas. S., 'Mor,' i. 151.
— James, commendator of St. Colme, i. 340; iii. 187.
— — his wife, Margaret Campbell, i. 340; iii. 188.
— Sir James, eldest son of 1st lord Blantyre, ii. 83.
— — his wife, Dorothy Hastings, ii. 83.
— James, son of 5th lord Blantyre, ii. 88.
— James, capt. 30th Foot Guards, ii. 89.
— James, lt.-col., son of 11th lord Blantyre, ii. 91.

* Name unknown.

Stewart, James, illeg. son of 'the Wolf of Badenoch,' ii. 263.
— James, master of Buchan, ii. 269.
— — his wife, Christian Strang, ii. 269.
— James, his eldest son, ii. 269.
— — his wife, Mary Ruthven, iv. 165; ix. 48.
— James, 7th son of Ninian S. of Bute, ii. 291.
— James, 3rd son of Sir Robert S. of Tillicoultry, ii. 296.
— James, maj.-gen., ii. 307.
— James, 2nd son of John, viscount Mountstuart, ii. 308.
— — his wife, Hannah Tighe, ii. 309.
— James, abbot of Dryburgh, iii. 281.
— James, 5th son of Sir Alex. S. of Darnley, iv. 145.
— James, lieut.-general, M.P.; 2nd son of 5th earl of Galloway, iv. 164.
— James, 2nd son of 6th earl of Galloway, iv. 165.
— James, burgess of Glasgow, iv. 189.
— — his wife, Janet Boyle, iv. 189.
— James, 2nd son of Alex. S., yr. of Garlies, and Katharine Herries, iv. 408.
— James, 3rd son of 5th lord Innermeath, v. 6; vii. 18.
— — his wife, Margaret Maule, v. 7 *n.*; vii. 18.
— James, pedagogue to the Livingstons of Kilsyth, v. 189 *n.*
— James, 5th son of Sir Alex. S. of Darnley, v. 346.
— James, lieut.-col., deputy-governor of Fort George, vi. 325.
— James, prior of Mâcon, vi. 313.
— James, legtd. son of 1st earl of Orkney, vi. 574.
— James, minister of Holy Cross Church, Peebles, viii. 401, 444.
— James, viii. 295.
— — his wife, Cecilia Dunsmure, viii. 295.
— James, 4th son of Sir Alex. S. of Garlies, ix. 94.
— James Francis Edward, prince of Wales, 'Chevalier de St. George,' i. 34, 35.
— — his wife, Clementina Sobieska, i. 35.
— James Henry Keith, C.B., lieut.-col., M.P., iv. 169.
— — his wife, Henrietta Anne Madan, iv. 169.
— James William, 3rd son of lt.-col. Archibald S. vi. 327.
— Jane, wife of Sir Robert Hannay of Mochrum, i. 59.
— Jane, wife of adm. lord Geo. Stuart, ii. 307.
— Jane, wife of 6th duke of Marlborough, iv. 171.
— Jane, wife of rev. Thos. Lewis Obeirne, vi. 324.
Stewart, Jane Charlotte, wife of H. A. Spedding, iv. 172.
— Janet, wife of 3rd lord Fleming, and mistress of Henry II., king of France, i. 22; ii. 156; v. 439, 442; viii. 540; ix. 2.
— Janet, wife of David de Loen, i. 149; vi. 140.
— Janet, wife of Jas. Arbuthnott of that Ilk, i. 288, 443.
— Janet, wife of 6th earl of Argyll, i. 435; vi. 168; ix. 21.
— Janet, wife of (1) Alexander, master of Sutherland, (2) Sir Hew Kennedy, (3) Henry, lord Methven, (4) Patrick, lord Ruthven, and *possibly* (5) James Gray, i. 443; ii. 65; iv. 261, 263; vi. 167; viii. 338; ix. 28, 98 *bis*.
— [Janet], wife of John Hamilton of Udston, ii. 41.
— Janet, wife of Archibald Stewart of Castlemilk, ii. 81.
— Janet, dau. of Alexander, earl of Buchan, ii. 268.
— Janet, dau. of Sir Alex. S. of Darnley, iv. 145.
— Janet, wife of John Dunbar of Mochrum, iv. 152.
— Janet, wife of Jas. Kennedy of Culzean, iv. 159.
— Janet, wife of 3rd lord Ross of Halkhead, v. 350; vii. 252; ix. 125.
— Janet, wife of Thos. Somerville of Carnwath, v. 346; viii. 7.
— Janet, wife of Alexander, 5th lord Livingston, v. 435; ix. 129.
— Janet, wife of Lachlan M'Lean of Dowart, v. 589.
— Janet, wife of Jas. Chalmers of Corraith, vi. 514.
— Janet, wife of John Veitch of Dawick, viii. 402.
— Janet, wife of Thos. Charteris of Kinfauns, ix. 10.
— Janet, dau. of Alex. S. of Garlies, ix. 94.
— Janet, illeg. dau. of 2nd earl of Galloway, ix. 95.
— Janet, dau. of Robert S. of Pittheveles, ix. 144.
— Janet, wife of Andrew M'Dowell of Lefnoll, ix. 144.
— Jean, alleged dau. of Walter, 6th lord High Steward, and wife of Hugh, earl of Ross, i. 14.
— Jean, wife of (1) Sir John Keith, (2) Sir John Lyon, and (3) Sir Jas. Sandilands, i. 16; ii. 398; vi. 36; viii. 266, 268, 381.
— Jean, wife of 5th earl of Argyll, i. 25, 342; iv. 155; ix. 20, 21.
— Jean, wife of Jas. Arbuthnott of that Ilk, i. 288, 443.
— Jean, wife of (1) Hugh Halcro, and (2) P. Smith, i. 397.

Stewart, Jean, wife of 3rd earl of Huntly, i. 442; iv. 532; ix. 27.
— Jean, wife of Sir Robt. Gordon of Pitlurg, i. 442.
— Jean, wife of John Otterburn, i. 444; ix. 28.
— Jean, wife of Duncan Campbell, i. 445.
— Jean, wife of (1) Henry, lord St. Colme, and (2) Nicol Bellenden, i. 446; vii. 395; ix. 28.
— Jean, dau. of 1st lord Blantyre, ii. 85.
— Jean, wife of * Lindsay, ii. 85.
— Jean, wife of Robt. Elliot, ii. 172.
— Jean, wife of Sir D. Campbell, bart. of Glenurchy, ii. 185.
— Jean, wife of (1) Mr. Colin Campbell, and (2) John Stewart of Urrard, ii. 187.
— Jean, wife of Angus Campbell, ii. 296.
— Jean, wife of Sir Jas. Sinclair of Murchil, ii. 340.
— Jean, wife of (1) Patrick, 1st lord Lindores, and (2) Robert, 1st lord Melville, ii. 352; v. 383; vi. 99, 574.
— Jean, wife of 6th lord Lovat, iii. 189; v. 530; ix. 68.
— Jean, wife of Sir D. Bruce of Clackmannan, iii. 469; v. 3.
— Jean, wife of Wm. Ruthven of Ballindean, iv. 102; v. 6.
— Jean, wife of D. Garden of Leys, v. 6.
— Jean, wife of (1) Sir W. Rollock of Gardin, and (2) Sir Alex. Jardine of Applegarth, v. 7; vii. 189, 190; ix. 115.
— Jean, wife of Patrick Wood of Bonnytoun, vi. 168.
— Jean, wife of Gilbert Kennedy of Bargany, vi. 516.
— Jean, wife of William Stewart of Brankstane and Corrogan, vi. 518.
— Jean, wife of (1) Sir Jas. Young of Seaton, (2) major G. Crichton of Arbekie, and (3) F. Lyon of Brigtoun, vi. 574; viii. 296; ix. 146.
— Jean, dau. of 4th earl of Traquair, viii. 407.
— Jean, wife of John Campbell, ix. 55.
— Jean, illeg. dau. of 1st earl of Orkney, ix. 146.
— Jean, dau. of 1st lord St. Colme, ix. 155.
— Joanna, wife of (1) Sir John Keith, (2) Sir John Lyon, and (3) Sir Jas. Sandilands, i. 16; ii. 398; vi. 36; viii. 260, 268, 381.
— Joanna, wife of James Douglas of Dalkeith, 1st earl of Morton, i. 19, 176; vi. 277, 356.
— Joan, wife of Malcolm, 3rd lord Fleming, and mistress of Henry II. of France, i. 22; ii. 156; v. 439, 442; viii. 540; ix. 2.
— Joanna, wife of Robert Stewart of Innermeath, lord of Lorn, v. 3; ix. 10.

* Name unknown.

Stewart, John, 2nd son of Walter, 3rd High Stewart, i. 12.
— Sir John, 3rd son of James, 5th High Stewart, i. 14.
— Sir John, 2nd son of Sir John S. of Railston, i. 14.
— John, *afterwards* king Robert III., i. 15, 17.
— John, prior of Coldingham, legtd. son of king James V., i. 24; iii. 282; vi. 313; ix. 2.
— — his wife, Jean Hepburn, ii. 160; ix. 2.
— John, 2nd son of John, 6th lord Innermeath and earl of Atholl, i. 448.
— John, 2nd son of Sir John S. of Minto, ii. 81.
— — his wife, Elizabeth *, ii. 81.
— John, illeg. son of Sir John S. of Minto, ii. 81.
— Mr. John, 4th son of 1st lord Blantyre, ii. 85.
— John, advocate, ii. 88.
— John, 5th son of 7th lord Blantyre, ii. 89.
— John, commendator of Coldingham, 2nd son of Francis, earl of Bothwell, ii. 171.
— — his wife, Margaret Home, ii. 171.
— John, son of Hercules S. of Quhytlaw, ii. 169.
— John, 6th son of Ninian S. of Bute, ii. 291.
— John, master of Buchan, ii. 269.
— — his wife, Mary Stewart, iii. 269.
— John, eldest son of John S. of Craigiehall, iv. 86.
— — his wife, Margaret Forrester, iv. 86.
— John, provost of Glasgow, 2nd son of Sir John S. of Garlies, iv. 150.
— John, parson of Kirkmaho, iv. 154, 155.
— — his wife, Margaret Stewart, ix. 94.
— John, 4th son of 1st lord Doune, iii. 189.
— John, contracted to Christina Sutherland of Torboll, iii. 195.
— John, v. 37.
— — his wife, Finvola Macdonald, v. 37.
— John, elder son of Sir John S. of Cruikston and Darnley, v. 344.
— John, general of Horse, 6th son of 3rd duke of Lennox, v. 359.
— John, master of Methven, eldest son of 1st lord Methven, vi. 167.
— John, illeg. son of James, earl of Moray, vi. 312.
— John, 4th son of 4th earl of Moray, vi. 321.
— John, 3rd son of 5th earl of Moray, vi. 323.
— John, vi. 474.
— — his wife, Margaret de Cragy, vi. 474.

* Name unknown.

Stewart, John, burgess of Ayr, vi. 513.
—— —— his wife, Helen Cunningham, vi. 513.
—— John, of the Ochiltree family, vi. 513 *n.*
—— John, his son, Sweden, vi. 513 *n.*
—— John, 4th son of Andrew, master of Ochiltree, vi. 515.
—— John, viii. 405.
—— —— his wife, Katharine Stewart, viii. 405.
—— John, 4th son of 2nd earl of Traquair, viii. 406.
—— John, 2nd son of Henry S. of Buchlivie, ix. 68.
—— —— his wife, Esther Thomson, ix. 68.
—— John, son of Sir Alex. S., ix. 155.
—— —— his wife, Marion Abernethy, ix. 155.
—— John Morton, vi. 326.
—— Joneta, wife of John Otterburn, i. 144; ix. 28.
—— Jonet, wife of Sir Matthew Stewart of Minto, ii. 81.
—— Jonet, co-heiress of John S., ii. 81.
—— Jonet, wife of Sir C. Campbell, 1st of Glenurchy, ii. 176; v. 4.
—— Jonet, wife of (1) A. Campbell of Skipness, and (2) N. Bannatyne of Kames, ii. 288; ix. 19.
—— Katharine, *presumed* wife of Sir Robt. Logan of Restalrig, i. 16 *n.*
—— Katharine, wife of James, 3rd earl of Morton, i. 22; iii. 359, 361.
—— Katharine, inf. dau. of king James VII., i. 33.
—— Katharine, wife of (1) Sir Patrick Hamilton of Kincavil, and (2) D. Ross of Balnagowan, i. 153; iv. 354; ix. 10, 103 *bis.*
—— Katharine, wife of James Murray of Broughton, i. 221; iv. 166.
—— Katharine, wife of Jas. Arbuthnott, i. 296.
—— Katharine, wife of 6th lord Forbes, i. 442; iv. 53.
—— Katharine, wife of Wm. Rashleigh, ii. 92.
—— Katharine, wife of Alex. Murray, ii. 296.
—— Katharine, wife of Sir Wm. Ruthven of Ballindean, iv. 102; v. 6.
—— Katharine, wife of Sir Alex. Stewart of Garlies, iv. 155.
—— Katharine, dau. of 5th earl of Galloway, iv. 164.
—— Katharine, wife of Sir Jas. Graham of Netherby, iv. 169.
—— Katharine, wife of John Betoun of Balfour, v. 1.
—— Katharine, wife of 3rd earl of Morton, v. 146; vi. 359, 361.
—— Katharine, wife of (1) Henry, lord Ibracan, and (2) Sir Joseph Williamson, v. 358; ix. 126 *bis.*
Stewart, Katharine, wife of John Stewart of Duchray and Glenny, vi. 148.
—— Katharine, wife of 1st lord Monypenny, vi. 277, 278.
—— Katharine, wife of col. Duncan Campbell, vi. 515.
—— Katharine, dau. of 4th lord Ochiltree, vi. 518; ix. 145.
—— Katharine, wife of John Sinclair of Ulbster, vi. 577.
—— Katharine, wife of John Stewart, viii. 405.
—— Katharine, illeg. dau. of 1st earl of Orkney, ix. 146.
—— Katharine Laura, inf. dau. of king James VII., i. 33.
—— Keith, C.B., vice-admiral R.N., 4th son of 8th earl of Galloway, iv. 170.
—— —— his wife, Mary Caroline Fitzroy, iv. 171.
—— Keith Anthony, younger son of 11th earl of Galloway, iv. 173.
—— Leveson, 3rd son of 7th earl of Galloway, iv. 167.
—— Louisa, wife of 2nd lord Feversham, iv. 171.
—— Louisa, dau. of 4th earl of Traquair, viii. 407.
—— Louisa Maria Teresa, 'la Consolatrice,' i. 33; vi. 187.
—— Lucy, dau. of 2nd earl of Traquair, viii. 406.
—— Lucy, dau. of 4th earl of Traquair, viii. 406.
—— Lucy, dau. of 6th earl of Traquair, viii. 406.
—— Ludovic, cardinal, v. 359.
—— Ludovic, 6th son of 1st lord Blantyre, ix. 38.
—— Magdalen, wife of Thos. Hamilton of Redhouse, viii. 405.
—— Malcolm, 3rd son of Thos. S. of Minto, ii. 78.
—— Malcolm, 4th son of Sir Robt. S. of Minto, ii. 79.
—— Marcellina, wife of Sir D. Campbell of Lochow, i. 331; ii. 174; ix. 18.
—— Margaret, wife of Nigel of Galloway, earl of Carrick, i. 12; ii. 426.
—— Margaret, wife of Sir John Hay of Boyne and Enzie, i. 15.
—— Margaret, wife of John, 7th lord of the Isles, i. 16; v. 40.
—— Margaret, wife of Archibald, 4th earl of Douglas, duke of Touraine, i. 18; ii. 380; iii. 166; iv. 402.
—— Margaret, wife of Louis, dauphin of France, i. 19; ii. 540.
—— Margaret, dau. of king James II., i. 20; iii. 64, 65, 66.
—— Margaret, wife of (1) John, lord Gordon, and (2) Sir John Drummond of Inner-

peffray, i. 22; iv. 532; vii. 44 *bis*; ix. 149.
Stewart, Margaret, illeg. dau. of king James v., i. 25; iv. 462.
— Margaret, inf. dau. of king James VI. i. 28; v. 441.
— Margaret, wife of 4th earl of Aboyne, i. 104; iv. 166.
— Margaret, wife of Sir John Swinton, i. 149; ix. 10.
— Margaret, wife of (1) Patrick Hamilton of Kincavil, and (2) D. Ross of Balnagowan, i. 153; iv. 354; ix. 10, 103 *bis*.
— Margaret, wife of (1) P. Graham of Inchbrakie, and (2) C. Campbell of Glenurchie, i. 153; ii. 182; vii. 46 *n*.
— Margaret, countess of Angus, wife of Thomas, 9th earl of Mar, and mistress of 1st earl of Douglas, i. 171; iii. 153, 154; iv. 304; v. 585.
— Margaret, wife of Sir Duncan Campbell of Lochow, i. 331; ix. 18.
— Margaret, wife of Robt. Robertson, yr. of Strowan, i. 442.
— Margaret, wife of Sir Wm. Murray of Castleton, i. 442, 461.
— Margaret, wife of John Grant, i. 444; vii. 463.
— Margaret, wife of George, 7th lord Saltoun, i. 445; vii. 413.
— Margaret, dau. of James, 5th earl of Atholl, i. 446.
— Margaret, wife of Chas. Pollok, ii. 78.
— Margaret, co-heiress of John S., ii. 81.
— Margaret, wife of Sir John Stewart of Minto, ii. 81; v. 350.
— Margaret, wife of John Swinton, ii. 85.
— Margaret, dau. of 7th lord Blantyre, ii. 89.
— Margaret, wife of rev. Dr. Andrew Stewart, Bolton, ii. 90.
— Margaret, wife of (1) Wm. Sinclair, and (2) Wm. Bruce, ii. 169.
— Margaret, wife of Sir John Home of Renton, ii. 172.
— Margaret, wife of 5th lord Cathcart, ii. 172, 517; ix. 42 *bis*.
— Margaret, dau. of lord Stewart and Bothwell, ii. 173.
— Margaret, wife of Robert, 6th earl of Sutherland, ii. 263; viii. 330.
— Margaret, wife of Sir George Seton of Seton, 1st lord Seton, ii. 265; viii. 576.
— Margaret, wife of Sir Adrian Damaan of Birtewelte, ii. 269.
— Margaret, wife of William Stewart of Bute and Fennok, ii. 287.
— Margaret, wife of James Stewart of Ambrismore, ii. 290.
— Margaret, wife of Lennox of Woodhead, ii. 296.
Stewart, Margaret, wife of Dougal Lamont, ii. 297.
— Margaret, wife of Sir Matthew Mennes, ii. 442; ix. 55.
— Margaret, wife of Jas. Ogilvie of Balfour, iii. 187.
— Margaret, wife of Torquil MacLeod of Lewis, iii. 187.
— Margaret, dau. of 1st lord Doune, iii. 189; ix. 68.
— Margaret, wife of 1st lord Duffus, iii. 209; vi. 321; ix. 69, 139.
— Margaret, wife of 9th earl of Erroll, iii. 576; vi. 316; ix. 138 *bis*.
— Margaret, wife of P. M'Kie of Lurg, iv. 155.
— Margaret, wife of Sir John Clerk of Penicuik, iv. 163; ix. 95.
— Margaret, wife of John Crawford of Kilbirnie, 1st viscount Garnock, iv. 175.
— Margaret, wife of Sir Robert Crichton of Cluny, v. 7.
— Margaret, wife of (1) John, 2nd lord Fleming, and (2) Alex. Douglas of Mains, v. 351; viii. 530, 536 *bis*.
— Margaret, wife of Robert Algeo of Easter Walkinshaw, v. 355.
— Margaret, wife of (1) Sir Archd. Stewart of Burray, and (2) David, 5th lord Lindores, v. 386.
— Margaret, wife of Sir Hugh Campbell of Loudoun, v. 496.
— Margaret, wife of (1) Andrew Stewart, master of Ochiltree, and (2) Uchtred Macdowal of Garthland, vi. 168, 515.
— Margaret, wife of (1) Charles (Howard), earl of Nottingham, and (2) William, lord Monson of Castlemaine, vi. 318.
— Margaret, wife of P. Carnegie of Lour, vi. 498.
— Margaret, wife of James Whyte, vi. 513.
— Margaret, wife of (1) John Knox, and (2) Sir Andrew Ker of Faldonside, vi. 514.
— Margaret, wife of Thos. Kennedy of Bargany, vi. 515.
— Margaret, wife of John Stewart of Traquair, vi. 515; viii. 402.
— Margaret, wife of George Craufurd of Leifnorris, vi. 517.
— Margaret (?), wife of colonel Walter Stewart, vi. 518.
— Margaret, dau. of Sir James S. of Eday and Tullos, vi. 574.
— Margaret, wife of David, 2nd lord Drummond, vii. 45, 46.
— Margaret, wife of Jas. Chalmers of Gadgirth, vii. 64.
— Margaret, wife of 2nd earl of Queensberry, vii. 136; viii. 405; ix. 150.
— Margaret, wife of (1) James, 5th earl of Southesk, and (2) John, master of Sinclair, iv. 164; vii. 587; viii. 73.

Stewart, Margaret, wife of Sir John Drummond of Machany, viii. 223.
— Margaret, wife of (1) Jas. Murray of Falahill, and (2) G. Douglas of Bonjedward, viii. 400.
— Margaret, wife of Wm. Burnett of Barns, viii. 402.
— Margaret, dau. of 4th earl of Traquair, viii. 407.
— Margaret, wife of Sir John Hay of Tullibody, viii. 421.
— Margaret, dau. of 4th earl of Lennox, ix. 126.
— Margaret, wife of John Stewart, parson of Kirkmaho, ix. 155.
— Margaret, dau. of Jas. S. of Traquair, ix. 163.
— Margaret Anna, wife of David C. H. Dalrymple, viii. 145.
— Maria, wife of Sir Wm. Abernethy, i. 149; vii. 406.
— Maria, wife of John Kennedy of Blairquhan, vi. 517.
— Marie, dau. of 2nd lord Blantyre, ii. 85.
— Marie, wife of John Finlayson of Killeith, vi. 513; ix. 26.
— Marion, wife of Arthur Campbell of Otter, i. 333; v. 4.
— Marion, wife of Adam Maxwell of Southbar, ii. 78; vi. 476.
— Marion, wife of Wm. Cleland, ii. 81.
— Marion, wife of Jas. Stirling of Keir, ii. 88.
— Marion, dau. of 7th lord Blantyre, ii. 89.
— Marion, wife of Robert Crichton of Riccarton and Kinnoull, iii. 223; v. 350.
— Marion, wife of (1) Sir John Stewart of Jedworth, and (2) Sir John Forrester of Corstorphine, iv. 84, 149, 150 *bis*, 173 *n*.
— Marion, wife of Alan Stewart of Cardonald, v. 350.
— Marion, mistress of James (Stewart), earl of Moray, vi. 312.
— Marion, wife of James Tweedie of Drumelzier, viii. 399.
— Marion, contracted to Sir Thos. Ogilvy, ix. 47.
— Marion, wife of (1) John Cochrane, and (2) John Gibson, ix. 75.
— Mariota, wife of Arthur Campbell of Otter, i. 333; v. 4.
— Mariot, alleged wife of Sir C. Campbell, 1st of Glenurchy, ii. 176.
— Mariota, wife of Alex. Irvine of Drum, ii. 270; ix. 48.
— Mariot, wife of James Scrymgeour, constable of Dundee, iii. 309.
— Mariota, wife of Patrick Ogilvy of Inchmartine, iv. 32; v. 4.
— Mariota, mistress of Sir Jas. Hamilton of Finnart, iv. 362.
— Marjory, wife of (1) Roger Magven, (2) Sir A. Lindsay of Glenesk, and (3) Sir H. Douglas of Lochleven, i. 14; iii. 14; vi. 364.
Stewart, Marjorie, wife of (1) John, earl of Moray, and (2) Sir Alex. Keith of Grandown and Craibstone, i. 16; vi. 37, 301.
— Marjory, wife of (1) George (Douglas), 1st earl of Angus, (2) Sir W. Cunningham, (3) James Kennedy, (4) William, lord of Graham, and (5) Sir Wm. Edmonston, i. 18, 173; ii. 448; iv. 230; vi. 217, 218; ix. 2, 11 *bis*.
— Marjory, wife of Sir D. Campbell of Lochaw, 1st lord Campbell, i. 149, 331; ix. 18.
— Marjory, wife of Sir Colin Campbell of Glenorchy, i. 442; ii. 180.
— Marjorie, wife of Wm. Borthwick, ii. 102.
— Marjory, wife of (1) James Ross of Craigton, and (2) John Lindsay of Dowhill, iii. 187; v. 5.
— Marjorie, wife of David Lindsay of Vayne, v. 6.
— Marjory, wife of Sir Roger Aston, vi. 516.
— Martha, wife of Nicholas Rutherford of Hundalee, v. 69; vi. 516.
— Mary, wife of (1) George (Douglas), 1st earl of Angus, (2) Sir William Cunningham, (3) Sir James Kennedy of Dunure, (4) William, lord of Graham, and (5) Sir W. Edmonston of Culloden, i. 18, 173; ii. 448; iii. 316; iv. 230; vi. 217, 218; ix. 2, 11 *bis*.
— Mary, wife of Wolfart van Borselen, count of Grand Pré, and lord of Campvere, i. 19.
— Mary, wife of (1) Thomas Boyd, earl of Arran, and (2) James, 1st lord Hamilton, i. 20; iv. 352, 366; v. 143, 147, 148.
— Mary, wife of William, prince of Orange, i. 29.
— Mary, wife of William, prince of Orange, i. 33; ii. 238.
— Mary, wife of 9th earl of Argyll, i. 366; vi. 321; ix. 24, 139 *bis*.
— Mary, wife of 9th earl of Erroll, i. 445; iii. 576.
— Mary, wife of (1) James (Stewart), 2nd earl of Atholl, and (2) capt. Peter Rollock, i. 446, 448; vii. 191.
— Mary, dau. of 12th lord Blantyre, ii. 92.
— Mary, wife of John (Erskine), earl of Mar, ii. 365; v. 356, 620, 621.
— Mary, wife of Sir John Wemyss, iii. 189; viii. 498.
— Mary, wife of David King of Warbester, iii. 590.
— Mary, wife of Kenneth, lord Fortrose, iv. 165; vii. 512.

Stewart, Mary, wife of Alex. Cunningham of Corsehill, iv. 238.
— Mary, wife of 6th lord Gray, iv. 286; vi. 574.
— Mary, wife of Alex. Bothwell of Glencorse, iv. 435; vi. 574; ix. 106, 146.
— Mary, wife of Richard (Butler), styled earl of Arran, v. 360.
— Mary, wife of Jas. Grant of Freuchie, vi. 320; vii. 474; ix. 139 *bis*.
— Mary, dau. of 5th earl of Moray, vi. 323.
— Mary, wife of Lawrence Sinclair of Goat, vi. 575.
— Mary, illeg. dau. of Patrick, 2nd earl of Orkney, vi. 577.
— Mary, dau. of James S. of Traquair, viii. 402.
— Mary, dau. of 6th earl of Traquair, viii. 408.
— Mary, wife of admiral Jas. Hay of Belton, viii. 455.
— Mary Louisa, wife of C. E. S. Cooke, iv. 172.
— Matilda, wife of William Edmonston, i. 151.
— Matilda, wife of Sir William Lindsay of Rossie, iii. 14.
— Matthew, son of James S. of Cardonald, iii. 440.
— — his wife, Jehan Montgomerie, iii. 440.
— May, dau. of Sir Robt. S. of Tillicoultry, ii. 296.
— Nicholas *or* Nicol, son of Thos. S. of Minto, ii. 78.
— Nicolas, wife of Alex. Dunbar of Pankill, iv. 159.
— Nicolas, wife of John Gordon of Greenlaw, iv. 162; v. 125.
— Patrick, prior of Whithorn, 2nd son of 1st earl of Orkney, i. 25; vi. 573, 576.
— Patrick, parson of Muckersie, v. 7.
— Rachael, dau. of 4th lord Ochiltree, vi. 519.
— Sir Robert, 7th son of Sir John S. of Bonkyl, i. 13.
— Robert, inf. son of king Robert III., i. 18.
— Robert, commendator of Holyrood, prior of Whithorn, illeg. son of king James V., i. 24; ii. 65; iv. 429; vi. 576; ix. 2.
— Robert, 4th son of Robert, duke of Albany, i. 148; ii. 264; vii. 243.
— Sir Robert, grandson of Walter, earl of Atholl, i. 439.
— — his *supposed* wife, Margaret Ogilvy, i. 439.
— Robert, 5th son of Thos. S. of Minto, ii. 78.
— Robert, 3rd son of Sir Robt. S. of Minto, ii. 79.
Stewart, Robert, 2nd son of Sir Matthew S. of Minto, ii. 81.
— Robert, son of Sir John S. of Minto, ii. 81.
— Robert, minister of Bolton, ii. 90.
— — his wife, * Cockburn, ii. 90.
— Robert, 2nd son of Francis, lord Stewart and Bothwell, ii. 173; ix. 42.
— Robert, 4th son of James S. of Bute, ii. 288.
— — his wife, * Lamont, ii. 288.
— Sir Robert, son of Sir Robert S. of Durisdeer, iii. 468.
— Robert, 4th son of Sir Alex. S. of Darnley, iv. 145.
— Robert, citizen of Glasgow, iv. 150, 154.
— Robert, 6th son of 3rd earl of Galloway, iv. 163.
— Robert, 5th son of Robert S., lord of Lorn, v. 3 *bis*.
— Robert, 2nd son of James, 5th lord Innermeath, v. 6.
— — his wife, Janet Leslie, ix. 115.
— Robert, hostage in England, 2nd son of Sir John S. of Cruikston and Darnley, v. 344.
— Robert, bishop of Caithness, ii. 339, 351; v. 355; viii. 340.
— Sir Robert, legtd. son of 1st lord Ochiltree, vi. 512.
— Robert, ancestor of the earls Castlestuart, vi. 517.
— Robert, 3rd son of 4th lord Ochiltree, vi. 519.
— Robert, legtd. son of 1st earl of Orkney, vi. 574.
— Robert, illeg. son of Patrick, 2nd earl of Orkney, vi. 576 *bis*.
— Robert, 4th son of 4th earl of Traquair, viii. 407.
— Robert, Nevay, ix. 48.
— Ronald Robert, viii. 112.
— Sophia, wife of H. Bulkeley, ii. 84.
— Sophia, wife of col. the Hon. W. Bligh, iv. 170.
— Susan, wife of 5th duke of Marlborough, iv. 169.
— Susannah, wife of 1st marquess of Stafford, iv. 166.
— Susanna, dau. of Andrew, master of Ochiltree, vi. 168, 516.
— Thomas, archdeacon of St. Andrews, dean of Dunkeld, i. 17.
— Thomas, colonel, 2nd son of Sir John S. of Bute, ii. 294.
— Mr. Thomas, treasurer of Caithness, iii. 198.
— Thomas, 2nd son of Sir Alex. S. of Garlies, iv. 159; ix. 94.

* Name unknown.

Stewart, Thomas, illeg. son of Sir Alex. S., earl of Mar, v. 588, 620.
—— —— his wife, Elizabeth Douglas, ii. 265; iii. 167; v. 589.
—— Thomas, 2nd son of Alex. S. of Garlies, ix. 94.
—— Thomas, 6th son of 2nd lord Ochiltree, ix. 144.
—— Walter, 'Bailloch,' 3rd son of 3rd High Steward, i. 12; vi. 130.
—— —— his wife, Mary, countess of Menteith, vi. 127.
—— Walter, 2nd son of king Robert II., i. 15; iv. 13.
—— —— his wife, Isabella, countess of Fife, iv. 13.
—— Walter, illeg. son of king Robert II., i. 17.
—— Walter, in Clunie, 3rd son of John, earl of Atholl, i. 448.
—— Walter, son of Sir Robt. S. of Minto, ii. 79.
—— Walter, prior of Blantyre, ii. 81; iv. 159.
—— Walter, M.D., son of 1st lord Blantyre, ii. 84.
—— Walter, master of Blantyre, son of 12th lord Blantyre, ii. 92.
—— Walter, illeg. son of 'the Wolf of Badenoch,' ii. 263.
—— Walter, 2nd son of 1st lord Ochiltree, vi. 512; ix. 144.
—— Walter, colonel, son of William S. of Mains, vi. 518.
—— —— his wife, Margaret (?) Stewart, vi. 518.
—— Walter, 4th son of James S. of Traquair, viii. 402.
—— Walter John, colonel, 4th son of 9th earl of Galloway, iv. 171.
—— Watte, Arran, 1505, iv. 356.
—— William, illeg. son of Thomas, earl of Angus, i. 170.
—— Sir William, alleged son of James, earl of Arran, i. 397.
—— William, bishop of Aberdeen, ii. 77; iv. 152.
—— William, lt.-gen., son of 10th lord Blantyre, ii. 91.
—— Sir William, K.C.M.G., C.B., son of 11th lord Blantyre, ii. 91.
—— —— his wife, Georgina Tremenheere, ii. 91.
—— William, 8th son of Ninian S. of Bute, ii. 291.
—— William, 2nd son of Henry S. of Buchlivie, iii. 187.
—— —— his wife, Agnes Shaw, ix. 68.
—— Sir William, iii. 447 *n.*
—— —— his wife, Elizabeth Hamilton, iii. 447 *n.*
—— William, 6th son of Sir Alex. S. of Darnley, iv. 145; v. 346, 347.
Stewart, William, 5th son of Sir Alex. S. of Garlies, iv. 156.
—— William, adjutant to the marquess of Montrose, iv. 159.
—— William, 5th son of 3rd earl of Galloway, iv. 163.
—— William, captain 12th Dragoons, M.P., iv. 164.
—— William, 3rd son of Richard, 3rd lord Innermeath, v. 5.
—— William, 3rd son of John, 4th lord Innermeath, v. 6.
—— William, 5th son of Sir John S. of Innermeath, v. 427.
—— William, 5th son of 2nd lord Avandale, vi. 511.
—— —— his wife, Isobel Ker, vi. 511.
—— William, Sweden, vi. 512.
—— William, son of Sir Wm. S. of Monkton, vii. 513.
—— William, in Ayr, vi. 515.
—— —— his wife, Marion M'Alexander, vi. 515.
—— William, 2nd son of 4th earl of Traquair, viii. 406.
—— William, 3rd son of Sir Alex. S. of Garlies, ix. 94.
—— William Molloy, viii. 226.
—— —— his wife, Ellen Urquhart, viii. 226.
—— Winifred, dau. of 4th earl of Traquair, viii. 407.
—— *, alleged 1st wife of Sir Gilleaspock Cambel of Lochow, i. 327.
—— *, wife of Wood of Balbegno, i. 444.
—— *, 2nd son of Sir John S. of Minto, ii. 78.
—— *, alleged dau. of Sir John S. of Minto, and wife of * Crawford of Ferme, ii. 81.
—— *, 2nd son of Alexander S., earl of Buchan, ii. 268.
—— *, wife of Wm. Craigie of Gairsay, ii. 442.
—— *, wife of Sir Alexander de Lindsay, iii. 9, 11.
—— *, 1st wife of James Douglas of Balvany, iii. 174.
—— *, 2nd son of Sir Wm. S. of Jedworth, iv. 149.
—— *, contr. to Archibald, 6th earl of Angus, iv. 261; viii. 399; ix. 12.
—— *, illeg. dau. of king James V. and Elizabeth Beaton, iv. 462.
—— *, alleged wife of 1st lord Lindsay of the Byres, v. 3, 393.
—— *, alleged wife of Robert, 1st lord Erskine, v. 3, 604; ix. 115.
—— *, wife of Donald, lord of the Isles, v. 33; ix. 1.
—— *, alleged wife of John Melville of Raith, vi. 82.
—— *, wife of Alexander, 4th lord Saltoun of Abernethy, vii. 409; ix. 47.

* Name unknown.

Stewart, *, wife of William Sinclair of Blans, viii. 400.
—— *, wife of John Livingston of Hayning, ix. 145.
Stewart-Campbell of Cloichfoldich, William Bowie, W.S., ii. 198.
—— —— his 1st wife, Sarah Priscilla Fearnside, ii. 198.
—— —— his 2nd wife, Janet W. Maxwell Stewart of Cloichfoldich, ii. 198.
Stewart-Mackenzie of Seaforth, James Alexander, grandson of 6th earl of Galloway, iv. 166.
—— —— his wife, Mary Mackenzie of Seaforth, iv. 166; vii. 514.
—— James A., colonel, iv. 166.
—— Julia Charlotte Sophia, wife of (1) Arthur, 9th marquess of Tweeddale, (2) Sir J. R. Best, and (3) Sir Wm. Evans Gordon, ix. 168.
Stewart-Murray, Dorothea Louisa, wife of H. G. Ruggles-Brise, i. 501.
—— Evelyn, i. 501.
—— Helen, i. 501.
—— George, 3rd son of 7th duke of Atholl, i. 500.
—— James Thomas, 4th son of 7th duke of Atholl, i. 501.
—— John George, styled marquess of Tullibardine, i. 500.
Stewart-Richardson of Pitfour, Edward Austin, 15th bart., iii. 85.
—— —— his wife, Constance Hay-Mackenzie, iii. 85.
—— Ian Roy Hay, iii. 85.
Stewart-Robertson of Carronvale, Duncan, i. 129.
—— —— his wife, Henriette Anne Mary Ogilvy, i. 129.
STIRLING, ALEXANDER, VISCOUNT OF, viii. 173-174.
Stirling, William, first viscount of, iv. 196; viii. 173.
STIRLING, ALEXANDER, EARL OF, viii. 165-185.
Stirling, Alexander (Humphreys), self-styled earl of, viii. 184.
—— —— his wife, Fortunata Bartoletti, viii. 184.
—— Henry, third earl of, viii. 179, 181.
—— —— his wife, Mary Vanlore, viii. 181.
—— Henry, fourth earl of, viii. 181.
—— —— his 1st wife, Judith Lee, viii. 182.
—— —— his 2nd wife, Priscilla Windham, viii. 182.
—— Henry, fifth earl of, viii. 182.
—— —— his wife, Elizabeth Hoby, viii. 183.
—— William, first earl of, ii. 235, 558; viii. 170.
—— —— his wife, Janet Erskine, ii. 235; viii. 176.

* Name unknown.

Stirling, William, second earl of, viii. 177, 181.
—— William, self-styled earl of, viii. 183.
—— —— his wife, Sarah Livingston, viii. 184.
Stirling of Ardoch, Henry, vi. 163; vii. 188; viii. 168.
—— —— Sir Henry, bart., ii. 52.
—— of Auchyll, George, iii. 228.
—— —— his wife, Jean Crichton, iii. 228.
—— —— Walter, vi. 148.
—— —— his wife, Isobel Graham, vi. 148.
—— —— William, vi. 150.
—— of Baldoran, John, ii. 405.
—— —— his wife, Helen Dalzell, ii. 405.
—— of Ballenkeir, Robert, viii. 531.
—— —— his wife, Mariota Fleming, viii. 531.
—— of Balquhomry, Sir William, viii. 534.
—— —— his wife, Mariot Fleming, viii. 534.
—— of Breky, John, v. 523.
—— of Easter Breky, Peter, v. 520.
—— of Cadder, William, iii. 340 *n.*
—— of Coldoch, Archibald, ii. 200.
—— —— his wife, Marjory Campbell, ii. 200.
—— of Cragbrey, William, iii. 340 *n.*
—— of Craigbernard *or* Craigbarnet, Bernard, ancestor of the family of, v. 329.
—— —— Charles Campbell Graham, major 42nd Royal Highlanders, vi. 156.
—— —— his wife, Elizabeth Agnes Napier, vi. 156.
—— —— George, viii. 541.
—— —— John, vii. 409.
—— —— his wife, Margaret Abernethy, vii. 409.
—— —— John, vi. 155.
—— —— John, vi. 156.
—— —— Mungo, vi. 155.
—— of Edzell, Sir John, iii. 13.
—— —— Katharine, wife of Sir Alex. de Lindsay, iii. 13; ix. 61.
—— of Feodallis, James, vii. 188.
—— of Garden, Archibald, iii. 508.
—— —— his wife, Elizabeth Murray, iii. 508.
—— —— Sir John, iii. 508.
—— of Glenesk, Sir John, iii. 13.
—— —— Katharine, wife of Sir Alex. de Lindsay, iii. 13; ix. 61.
—— of Glorat, Bernard, ancestor of the family of, v. 329.
—— —— John, ix. 54.
—— of Herbertshire, William, iv. 95.
—— —— his wife, Lilias Forrester, iv. 95.
—— of Inverallon, Sir James, iv. 457.
—— of Keir, Sir Archibald, vii. 47, 254.
—— —— his 1st wife, Mary Drummond, vii. 47.
—— —— his 2nd wife, Grizel Ross, vii. 254.
—— —— Archibald, viii. 451.
—— —— his wife, Anne Hay, viii. 451.

Stirling of Keir, Sir George, v. 447; vi. 246, 424; vii. 256.
—— —— his 1st wife, Margaret Ross, vii. 256.
—— —— his 2nd wife, Margaret Napier, vi. 424.
—— —— his 4th wife, Margaret Livingston, v. 447.
—— —— Sir James, iv. 457; vi. 226, 232, 420.
—— —— his 2nd wife, Jean Chisholm, vi. 226.
—— —— James, ii. 42, 88.
—— —— his wife, Marion Stewart, ii. 88.
—— —— Sir John, ii. 325; iv. 457; vi. 4; vii. 538.
—— —— his contr. wife, Margaret Hume, vi. 4.
—— —— his alleged wife, Mary Sempill, vii. 538.
—— —— Sir John, ii. 366; v. 447.
—— —— his 1st wife, Margaret Livingston, v. 447.
—— —— his 2nd wife, Lilias Colquhoun, v. 308.
—— —— Lucas *or* Luke, ii. 178; iii. 279; vi. 215; vii. 274.
—— —— his wife, Marjorie Dunbar, iii. 279.
—— —— Sir William, iii. 470.
—— —— Sir William, i. 183, 334; ii. 324; viii. 534.
—— —— his 1st wife, Mariot Fleming, viii. 534.
—— —— his 2nd wife, Margaret Crichton, ii. 325; vii. 533.
—— —— William, iv. 293.
—— —— his 1st wife, Helen Gray, iv. 293.
—— of Kippendavie, Charles, i. 306.
—— —— his wife, Katharine Arbuthnott, i. 306.
—— —— John, viii. 397.
—— —— Patrick, i. 306.
—— of Wester Perthwike, Nicholas, vii. 529 *n*.
—— Agnes, wife of Sir Wm. Seton of Kylesmure, viii. 590.
—— Alexander de, 1234, vii. 232.
—— Christine, wife of Jas. Erskine of Little Sauchie and Balgownie, v. 609.
—— Elizabeth, wife of Adam Crichton of Ruthven, ii. 324.
—— Elizabeth, wife of 4th lord Elibank, iii. 512.
—— Elizabeth, mistress of canon Wm. Graham of Killearn, vi. 229.
—— Elizabeth, wife of John Napier of Merchiston, vi. 420.
—— George, surgeon, M.P., iii. 512.
—— Grisel, wife of Geo. Graham, vi. 163.
—— Henry of, illeg. son of David, earl of Huntingdon, i. 4; ii. 215.
—— Isabella, wife of John Hamilton, ii. 52.
—— James, 2nd son of Charles S. of Kippendavie, i. 306.
Stirling, Janet, wife of Sir David Bruce of Clackmannan, iii. 470.
—— John, brother of Henry S. of Ardoch, viii. 168.
—— —— his wife, Margaret Alexander, viii. 168.
—— Sir John, governor of Edinburgh Castle, viii. 325.
—— Katharine, wife of 5th earl of Angus, and mistress of 3rd lord Home, i. 183; iv. 456.
—— Katharine, wife of 8th earl of Crawford, iii. 27.
—— Lilias, wife of (1) John Murray of Touchadam, and (2) John Erskine of Carnock, ii. 366.
—— Margaret, wife of Sir H. Hamilton of Rosehall, ii. 42.
—— Margaret, wife of Sir C. Campbell, 1st of Glenurchy, ii. 175, 178.
—— Margaret, wife of Wm. Graham of Boquhapple, vi. 150.
—— Margaret, dau. of Sir George S. of Keir, vii. 256.
—— Margaret, wife of captain Andrew Sempill, vii. 544.
—— Margaret, wife of Wm. Dalzell of Chisholm, ix. 54.
—— Margaret Douglas, wife of 10th lord Torphichen, viii. 397.
—— Mary, wife of R. Graham of M'Keanston, vi. 155.
Stirling-Crawfurd of Milton, William Stuart, vi. 272.
—— —— his wife, Caroline Agnes Horsley-Beresford, vi. 272.
Stirling-Hamilton of Preston, Sir William, 10th bart., iv. 343.
Stirling-Home-Drummond-Moray of Abercairney, Charles, vii. 153.
—— —— his wife, Anne Georgina Douglas, vii. 153.
Stirling-Maxwell of Keir and Pollok, Sir William, 9th bart., vi. 120.
—— —— his 1st wife, Anna Maria Leslie-Melville, vi. 120.
Stirling-Stuart of Castlemilk, James, capt., ii. 279.
—— Katharine, wife of C. S. Gordon, ii. 279.
Stobo, Anabell of, vii. 420.
—— Eugene of, vii. 420.
—— Mariota of, vii. 420.
—— Samuel of, vii. 420.
Stock, Thomas, vii. 153.
—— —— his wife, Gertrude Georgina Douglas, vii. 153.
Stockdale of Green Hamerton, William, v. 165.
—— —— his wife, Dorothy Mill, v. 165.
—— Jane, wife of 6th lord Boyd, v. 165.
Stockton, Thomas, justice of the King's Bench, Ireland, i. 401.

Stockton, Ursula, wife of (1) Sir Wm. Aston, and (2) Sir C. Feilding, i. 401.
Stolberg-Guedern, Gustavus Adolphus, prince of, i. 35; iii. 481.
—— —— his wife, Elizabeth Philippina de Hornes, iii. 481.
—— Louisa Maximiliana, wife of prince Charles Edward Stewart, and princess of, i. 35; iii. 481.
Stoney, Andrew Robinson, lieut. 30th Foot, viii. 310.
—— —— his wife, Mary Eleanor Bowes, viii. 310.
Stopford, Edith Louisa, wife of adm. Sir W. R. Kennedy, ii. 497.
—— Edward, captain R.N., ii. 497.
STORMONT, MURRAY, VISCOUNT OF, viii. 186-214.
Stormont, Alan David, eleventh viscount of, viii. 213.
—— David, first viscount of, viii. 191.
—— —— his wife, Elizabeth Beaton, viii. 196.
—— David, fourth viscount of, i. 228, 229; viii. 201, 203.
—— —— his wife, Jean Carnegie, viii. 70, 197, 204.
—— David, fifth viscount of, viii. 204.
—— —— his wife, Marjory Scot, viii. 204.
—— David, sixth viscount of, viii. 205, 207.
—— —— his wife, Anne Stewart, viii. 207.
—— David, seventh viscount of, ii. 523; viii. 206, 208.
—— —— his 1st wife, Henrietta Frederica Bunau, viii. 208.
—— —— his 2nd wife, Louisa Cathcart, ii. 523; viii. 206, 209.
—— David William, eighth viscount of, viii. 209, 210.
—— —— his wife, Frederica Markham, viii. 210.
—— James, third viscount of, i. 228; viii. 197.
—— —— his wife, Jean Carnegie, viii. 70, 197.
—— Mungo, second viscount of, i. 228, 470; viii. 196, 200.
—— —— his 1st wife, Anna Murray, viii. 190, 197.
—— —— his 2nd wife, Anna Wemyss, viii. 197, 501.
—— William David, ninth viscount of, viii. 212.
—— —— his wife, Louisa Ellison, viii. 212.
—— William David, son of 4th earl of Mansfield; styled viscount of, viii. 212.
—— —— his wife, Emily Louisa MacGregor, viii. 212.
—— William David, tenth viscount of, viii. 213.
—— master of, Sir Mungo (Murray), 4th son of 1st earl of Tullibardine, i. 470; viii. 196, 197, 199.
Story, Richard, viii. 552.
—— —— his wife, Lilias Fleming, viii. 552.
Stourton, Charles (Stourton), 17th lord, iv. 420, 422.
STRABANE, HAMILTON, BARON OF, i. 48-73.
Strabane, Charles, sixth lord, i. 51.
—— —— his wife, Katharine Hamilton, i. 49, 52.
—— Claud, second lord, i. 47, 49.
—— —— his wife, Jean Gordon, i. 50; iv. 545.
—— Claud, fifth lord, i. 51.
—— George, fourth lord, i. 43, 50.
—— —— his wife, Elizabeth Fagan, i. 51.
—— James, first lord, i. 48.
—— —— his wife, Katharine Clifton, i. 49.
—— James, third lord, i. 50.
—— James, seventh lord, i. 58.
STRABANE, HAMILTON, VISCOUNT OF, i. 58-73.
—— James, first viscount of, i. 58.
—— —— his wife, Elizabeth Reading, i. 59.
—— James, second viscount of, i. 62.
—— —— his wife Anne Plumer, i. 62.
—— James, third viscount of, i. 64.
—— James, fifth viscount of, i. 68.
—— James, sixth viscount of, i. 72.
—— John James, fourth viscount of, i. 66.
STRABANE, HAMILTON, MARQUESS OF HAMILTON OF, i. 69-73.
Strabane, James, first marquess of Hamilton of, i. 69.
Strachan of Auchnagat, Michael, iii. 204.
—— of Balvousie, James, vii. 12.
—— —— his wife, Janet Maule, vii. 12.
—— of Benholm, Sir Alexander, vi. 55.
—— of Brigton, Alexander, i. 293.
—— —— his wife, Isobel Arbuthnott, i. 293.
—— of Carmyllie, Alexander, vii. 6, 7.
—— —— his wife, Christina Maule of Carmyllie, vii. 6.
—— —— Alexander, vii. 10.
—— —— his wife, Elizabeth Maule, vii. 10.
—— —— David, i. 116.
—— —— his wife, Isobel Ogilvy, i. 116.
—— —— David, iv. 283.
—— —— his wife, Isobel Gray, iv. 283.
—— —— Henry, vii. 7.
—— —— his wife, Ysota, vii. 7.
—— —— James, vii. 18.
—— —— his wife, Elizabeth Maule, vii. 18.
—— —— Thomas, iv. 279.
—— —— viii. 57.
—— —— his wife, Mary Carnegie, viii. 57.
—— —— vii. 12.
—— —— his 2nd wife, Agnes Maule, vii. 12.
—— of Culloden, vii. 458.
—— of Glenkindie, Alexander, iii. 323.
—— —— his wife, Margaret Graham, iii. 323.
—— —— [Patrick, the younger], v. 6.
—— —— his wife, Isabel Stewart, v. 6.
—— —— Thomas de, iv. 271.
—— of Inchtuthill, Fettercairn and Monboddo, James, vi. 181.
—— —— his wife, Marie Ramsay, vi. 181.
—— of Kilhill, Alexander, vi. 175.

Strachan of Monboddo, vi. 175.
— of Tarrie, Alexander, viii. 80.
— — his wife, Elizabeth Carnegie, viii. 80.
— of Thornton, Alexander, i. 199, 285; vi. 51 *bis*, 173, 174; viii. 187.
— — his wife, Isobel Keith, vi. 51.
— — Sir Alexander, 1st bart., vi. 53, 55, 175.
— — his 1st wife, Margaret Lindsay. i. 518.
— — his 2nd wife, Margaret Ogilvy, i. 122; vi. 53.
— — Sir James, vi. 181.
— — Sir John, vi. 51.
— — Robert, i. 199.
— — his wife, Sarah Douglas, i. 199.
— of Tibbertie, Andrew, i. 287.
— — his wife, Giles Arbuthnott, i. 287.
— Archibald, colonel, vi. 251.
— Elizabeth, wife of Andrew Arbuthnott of Fiddes and Pitcarles, i. 285.
— Euphame, wife of John Carnegie of Kinnaird, viii. 51.
— Isabella, wife of Andrew Drummond of Stanmore, viii. 224.
— James, Lower Tooting, vi. 496; viii. 111; ix. 144.
— Katharine, wife of John Ogilvy of Inverkeiler, i. 118.
— Katharine, wife of John Lindsay, iii. 20.
— Katharine, wife of John Middleton of Middleton, vi. 174.
— Katharine, wife of Robert Middleton of Caldhame, vi. 176.
— Marjorie, wife of Robert Gray of Drummalie, iv. 279.
— Marjory, wife of David Lyon of Letham, viii. 270.
— Mary Elizabeth, wife of James Fullarton Lindsay Carnegie of Boysack, vi. 496; viii. 111.
— Robert, in Kinkell, 2nd son of * S. of Monboddo, vi. 175.
— — his wife, Margaret Middleton, vi. 175.
— Sara, wife of Andrew Arbuthnott of Little Fiddes, ix. 16.
— Violet, wife of (1) Thomas Sutherland, and (2) George Gordon, iii. 204.
— *, wife of John Grant of Corriemony, vii. 458.
STRADICHTIE, LYON, LORD, viii. 299-317.
Stradichtie, Patrick, first lord, viii. 299.
Strahan, James Morgan, viii. 122.
— — his wife, Caroline Dalrymple, viii. 122.
Straiton of Fiddes, *, 1st laird, i. 276.
— — his wife, * Arbuthnott, i. 275.
— of Little Fiddes, George, i. 285.
— of Lauriston, i. 276, 278.

* Name unknown.

Straiton of Straiton, Alexander, i. 293.
— — his wife, Agnes Arbuthnott, i. 293.
— — George, i. 290, 293.
— *see also* Straton.
Straker, James, harrister-at-law, viii. 139.
— Marianne, wife of major Hew Dalrymple, viii. 139.
Strang of Balcaskie, George, yr., vii. 286.
— — his wife, Christian Wood, vii. 286.
— — John, i. 77; ii. 269.
— — John, i. 77.
— — his wife, Grisel Sandilands, i. 77.
— of Kilrenny, George, portioner, iv. 431.
— — his wife, Elizabeth Bothwell, iv. 431.
— of Pitcorthy, John, iii. 269, 537.
— — his wife, Cecilia Anstruther, iii. 269.
— — Walter, iii. 310.
— Christian, wife of James Stewart, master of Buchan, ii. 269.
— Isabel, wife of (1) James Sandilands, and (2) Ninian Bonar, i. 77.
— John, in Teasses, vii. 279 *n*.
— — his wife, Elizabeth Wemyss, vii. 279 *n*.
— Margaret, wife of William Primrose, vii. 212 *n*.
— Margaret, wife of Wm. Livingston, ix. 129.
STRANGE, MURRAY, LORD, i. 488.
Strange, Charlotte, baroness of, i. 490.
— James, lord, i. 488.
STRANGE, MURRAY, EARL, i. 495-502.
Strange, John, first earl, i. 495.
Strange, James, viii. 232.
— — his wife, Anne Dundas, viii. 232.
Strangeways of Fyfield, James, iv. 530.
— — his wife, Katharine Gordon, iv. 530.
— of Melbury Sampford, Thomas, iv. 392.
— Elizabeth, wife of 5th duke of Hamilton, iv. 392.
STRANRAER, DALRYMPLE, LORD, viii. 119-149.
Stranraer, James, first lord, viii. 119.
STRANRAER, DALRYMPLE, LORD, viii. 149-164.
Stranraer, John, first lord, viii. 149.
Stratford, Elizabeth, wife of vice-admiral J. R. D. Tollemache, iii. 410.
STRATHALLAN, DRUMMOND, VISCOUNT OF, viii. 215-238.
Strathallan, Andrew John, *de jure* seventh viscount of, viii. 233.
— James, third viscount of, viii. 222.
— James Francis Edward, fifth viscount of, viii. 233.
— — his wife, Euphemia Gordon, viii. 233; ix. 162 *bis*.
— James, *de jure* sixth viscount of, viii. 233.

Strathallan, James Andrew John Laurence Charles, eighth viscount of, viii. 229, 234.
—— —— his wife, Amelia Sophia Murray, i. 498; viii. 234.
—— James David, tenth viscount of, viii. 236.
—— —— his 1st wife, Ellen Thornhill, viii. 236.
—— —— his 2nd wife, Margaret Smythe, viii. 237.
—— William, first viscount of, v. 232, 325; viii. 220.
—— —— his wife, Elizabeth Johnston, viii. 222.
—— William, second viscount of, viii. 222; ix. 161.
—— —— his wife, Elizabeth Drummond, vi. 68; viii. 222; ix. 161.
—— William, fourth viscount of, viii. 224, 228.
—— —— his wife, Margaret Nairn, vi. 396; viii. 228.
—— William Henry, ninth viscount of, viii. 236.
—— —— his wife, Christina Maria Hersey Baird, viii. 236.
—— William Huntly, eleventh viscount of, viii. 237.
STRATHARDLE, MURRAY, EARL OF, i. 479-502.
Strathardle, John, first earl of, i. 479.
STRATHAVEN, GORDON, LORD OF, i. 102-105.
Strathaven, Charles, first lord of, i. 102.
STRATHAVEN, GORDON, LORD, iv. 549-558.
Strathaven, George, first lord, iv. 550.
Strathbogie, David of, 3rd son of Duncan, earl of Fife, i. 424; iv. 8.
—— David of, 8th earl of Atholl, i. 425.
—— David of, 10th earl of Atholl, i. 428; ii. 379.
—— —— his wife, Joan Comyn, i. 429, 509.
—— David of, 11th earl of Atholl, i. 430, 509.
—— David of, 12th earl of Atholl, i. 432.
—— John of, i. 424; iv. 8.
—— —— his *probable* wife, Ada, countess of Atholl, i. 424.
—— John of, 9th earl of Atholl, i. 425.
—— Laurence de, iv. 45.
—— Margaret de, alleged wife of John Mackenzie of Kintail, vii. 496.
STRATHBRAN, MURRAY, LORD, i. 481.
Strathbran, William, lord, i. 481.
Stratheach, Wallevus de, vii. 420.
STRATHEARN, THE ANCIENT EARLS OF, viii. 239-254.
Strathearn, Ferteth *or* Ferquhard, second earl of, v. 325 *n.*; viii. 240.
—— —— his wife, Ethne, viii. 241.
—— Gilbert, third earl of, i. 451; iii. 557; iv. 9; vii. 455 *n.*; viii. 241.
—— —— his 1st wife, Matilda d'Aubigny, viii. 242.
—— —— his 2nd wife, Ysenda of Abercairny, viii. 242.
Strathearn, John (de Warenne), earl of, viii. 253.
—— Malise, first earl of, viii. 239.
—— Malise, fifth earl of, i. 164, 451, 452; vi. 531; viii. 245.
—— —— his 1st wife, Marjory de Muschamp, viii. 246.
—— —— his 2nd wife, Matilda of Caithness, i. 164; ii. 317; viii. 246.
—— —— his 3rd wife, Emma [Comyn], ii. 256; viii. 246.
—— —— his 4th wife, Mary of Argyll, viii. 246.
—— Malise, sixth earl of, i. 426, 427; viii. 247, 251.
—— —— his wife, Agnes Comyn, viii. 249.
—— Malise, seventh earl of, viii. 251.
—— —— his 1st wife, *, viii. 251.
—— —— his 2nd wife, Joanna Menteith, i. 435; ii. 130; iii. 162; v. 581; vi. 132; viii. 251, 257, 327; ix. 27.
—— Malise, eighth earl of, ii. 318, 319; vi. 138, 568; viii. 252; ix. 64.
—— —— his wife, Marjorie Ross, vii. 236; viii. 254.
—— Robert, fourth earl of, i. 453 *n.*; viii. 242, 244.
STRATHEARN, MORAY, EARL OF, viii. 255-258.
Strathearn, Maurice, earl of, ii. 320 *n.*; vi. 132; viii. 253, 255.
—— —— his wife, Joanna Menteith, i. 435; ii. 130; iii. 162; v. 581; vi. 132; viii. 251, 257, 327; ix. 27.
STRATHEARN, STEWART, EARL OF, viii. 259-261.
Strathearn, David, son of king Robert II.; earl of, i. 16, 133, 134; ii. 321; iii. 14; vii. 182, 237; viii. 259.
—— —— his wife, * Lindsay, iii. 14; viii. 259.
—— Euphemia, wife of (1) Patrick Graham, and (2) Sir P. Dunbar of Biel; countess of, i. 134, 455; ii. 321; iii. 14, 260; v. 214; vi. 142; viii. 260; ix. 10 *bis*.
—— Robert, *afterwards* king Robert II.; earl of, i. 15; iv. 183; v. 99; vii. 236; viii. 259.
—— Walter, earl of Atholl; earl of, i. 16, 436; viii. 261.
STRATHEARN, GRAHAM, EARL OF, viii. 260.
Strathearn, Malise, earl of, i. 133; iv. 350; vi. 142; viii. 260.
—— Patrick, *de jure ux.* earl of, vi. 214; viii. 260.
—— —— his wife, Euphemia, countess of Strathearn, viii. 260.
—— William, earl of, i. 134, 135.
STRATHEARN, STEWART, LORD, vi. 314.
Strathearn, James, first lord, vi. 314.

* Name unknown.

Strathearn, Ada de, wife of Sir Wm. Murray, i. 453, 454 *n.*; ix. 28.
—— Agneta de, wife of Arngils Sunnesson, earl of Orkney, ii. 320.
—— Annabella de, wife of (1) John de Lestalrig, and (2) Sir P. Graham of Kincardine, vi. 207; viii. 245.
—— Cecilia de, wife of Walter Ruthven, iv. 255; viii. 244.
—— Cecilia de, dau. of 5th earl of Strathearn, viii. 247.
—— Christian de, wife of Walter Olifard of Crailing, vi. 527; viii. 241.
—— Ethne de, wife of David Hay of Erroll, iii. 557; viii. 244.
—— Eufamia de, an heir of Malise, 8th earl of Strathearn, ii. 320 *n.*
—— Gilchrist de, eldest son of Gilbert, earl of Strathearn, i. 451; viii. 242.
—— Sir Gilbert de, 3rd son of Robert, 4th earl of Strathearn, viii. 245.
—— Gilbert de, 2nd son of Malise, 6th earl of Strathearn, viii. 250.
—— Henry de, son of Malise, steward of Strathearn, i. 453 *n.*
—— Hugh de, prior of Inchaffray, viii. 244, 245 *n.*
—— Isabella of, wife of Wm. Sinclair of Roslin, ii. 320; vi. 567.
—— John de, iv. 443.
—— Sir Malise, steward of, i. 453.
—— —— his wife, Muriel of Tullibardine, i. 453 *n.*
—— Maria de, wife of Sir Nicholas Graham of Dalkeith and Abercorn, v. 577; vi. 195; viii. 247.
—— Mary de, wife of Sir John Johnstone, viii. 245.
—— Maria de, wife of Sir John Moray of Drumsargard, viii. 252, 255.
—— Matilda de, wife of Malcolm, earl of Fife, i. 451; viii. 244.
—— Matilda, wife of Wayland del Ard, ii. 320.
—— Matilda de, wife of Robert de Toeni, viii. 250.
—— Muriel de, wife of William, earl of Mar, v. 576; viii. 247.
—— Robert de, 2nd son of Malise, 5th earl of Strathearn, viii. 247.
—— Robert de, 3rd son of Malise, 6th earl of Strathearn, viii. 250.
—— *, wife of Guttorm Sperra, ii. 320.
Strathechin of Monycabock, Donald, viii. 530.
—— —— his wife, Annabel, viii. 530.
—— Isabel, wife of Sir D. Fleming, viii. 530.
—— Alexander de, vii. 6, 7.
—— —— his wife, Cristina Maule of Carmyle, vii. 6.

* Name unknown.

Strathechin, Henry of, vii. 7.
—— —— his wife, Ysota, vii. 7.
—— John de, vii. 6.
—— *see also* Strachan.
Strathmore, Lyon, earl of, viii. 261-310.
Strathmore, Charles, fourth earl of, viii. 295, 307.
—— —— his wife, Susan Cochrane, iii. 355; viii. 308.
—— James, fifth earl of, viii. 305, 308.
—— —— his wife, Mary Oliphant, viii. 308.
—— John, second earl of, viii. 303.
—— —— his wife, Elizabeth Stanhope, viii. 304.
—— John, third earl of, viii. 305.
—— Patrick, first earl of, viii. 299; ix. 6.
—— —— his wife, Helen Middleton, vi. 185; viii. 302.
—— Thomas, sixth earl of, viii. 305, 308.
—— —— his wife, Jean Nicolson, viii. 309.
Strathmore, Bowes, earl of, viii. 310-312.
Strathmore, John, seventh earl of, viii. 311.
—— —— his wife, Mary Millner, viii. 311.
—— John, eighth earl of, viii. 310.
—— —— his wife, Mary Eleanor Bowes of Streatlam, viii. 311.
Strathmore, Lyon-Bowes, earl of, viii. 312-313.
Strathmore, Thomas, ninth earl of, viii. 312.
—— —— his 1st wife, Mary Elizabeth Louisa Rodney Carpenter, viii. 312.
—— —— his 2nd wife, Eliza Northcote, viii. 312.
—— —— his 3rd wife, Marion Cheape, viii. 313.
—— Thomas George, tenth earl of, viii. 313.
—— —— his wife, Charlotte Maria Barrington, viii. 313.
Strathmore, Bowes-Lyon, earl of, viii. 313-317.
Strathmore, Claude, eleventh earl of, viii. 313.
—— —— his wife, Frances Dora Smith, viii. 314.
—— Claude George, twelfth earl of, viii. 315.
—— —— his wife, Nina Cecilia Cavendish-Bentinck, viii. 316.
Strathnairn, Sir James Ogilvy, styled lord of, iv. 18.
Strathnaver, Johanna, wife of Freskin de Moravia of Duffus; lady of, ii. 122, 316.
—— George, 2nd son of 13th earl of Sutherland; styled lord, iii. 204; viii. 351.
—— —— his wife, Jean Wemyss, i. 207, 544; ii. 283; iv. 77; viii. 352, 503.
—— John, eldest son of 13th earl of Sutherland; styled lord, viii. 350.
—— John, elder son of George, 14th earl of Sutherland; styled lord, viii. 352 *bis*, 353.
—— —— his 1st wife, Helen Cochrane, viii. 354.

Strathnaver, John, grandson of 15th earl of Sutherland; styled lord, viii. 356.
— William, son of John, 15th earl of Sutherland; styled lord, viii. 355.
— — his wife, Katharine Morison, viii. 356.
— William, grandson of 15th earl of Sutherland; styled lord, viii. 357.
— — his wife, Elizabeth Wemyss, viii. 358.
— master of, John Gordon, eldest son of William, lord Strathnaver, viii. 356.
— master of, William Gordon, son of John, lord Strathnaver, viii. 355.
STRATHSPEY OF STRATHSPEY, OGILVY-GRANT, BARON, vii. 491-493.
Strathspey, John Charles, first baron, vii. 491.
STRATHTAY, MURRAY, EARL OF, i. 479-502.
Strathtay, John, first earl of, i. 479.
Straton of Castlecary, Alexander, iv. 80.
— of Kirkside, Arthur, vi. 243.
— of Lauristoun, Alexander, iv. 277; vi. 171.
— — his wife, Isobel Gray, iv. 277.
— — Andrew, iv. 280.
— — George, iv. 72.
— — his wife, Christian Forbes, iv. 72.
— of Scotston, Arthur, vi. 243.
— of Straton, c. 1400, viii. 5.
— — Alexander, vii. 437.
— — his wife, Katharine Menzies, vii. 437.
— Katharine, wife of Thomas Somerville of Gilmerton, Drum, and Gutters, viii. 5.
— Nicolas, wife of (1) Laurence Middleton, and (2) Alexander Ogilvy, i. 114; vi. 171.
— Samuel, physician, Montrose, i. 306.
— — his wife, Jean Arbuthnott, i. 306.
— *see also* Straiton.
Streatfield of Chiddingston, Henry Dorrien, col., ii. 567.
— Ruby, wife of 2nd vis. Colville, ii. 567.
Stretton, John, minister at Foulis, viii. 187.
— — his wife, Janet Murray, viii. 187.
Strichen, Alexander Fraser of Strichen, judge of the Court of Session, lord, v. 545.
Strickland of Boynton, Sir William, bart., iii. 348.
— Anne, wife of (1) Ralph Constable, and (2) Edward Holme, iii. 291.
— Margaret, wife of Sir John Cochrane of Ochiltree, iii. 348.
— Sir Walter, iii. 291.
Strong, Clement, in holy orders, vi. 179.
— Katharine Anne, wife of C. J. Middleton, vi. 179.
Strother, Henry, sheriff of Northampton, viii. 422.
Stuardo, Giacomo, i. 30 *n.*
— Jacobo Errico de Bove, i. 30 *n.*
— — his wife, Teresa Corona, i. 30 *n.*
— Maria, i. 30 *n.*
STUART OF CASTLE STUART, STEWART, BARON, vi. 326.
Stuart of Castle Stuart, Francis, first baron, vi. 326.
STUART DE DECIES, STUART, BARON, ii. 307.
Stuart de Decies, Henry, baron, ii. 307.
STUART OF NEWBURY, STEWART, LORD, v. 360-361.
Stuart of Newbury, Charles, lord, v. 360.
— — Bernard, baron, v. 359.
STUART DE ROTHESAY, STUART, BARON, ii. 304.
Stuart de Rothesay, Charles, first baron, ii. 304.
STUART, MARQUIS OF ANGRA, ii. 304.
STUART, EARL OF BUTE, ii. 299-311.
STUART, MARQUESS OF BUTE, ii. 285-312.
STUART, BARON CARDIFF OF CARDIFF CASTLE, ii. 305.
STUART, LORD CUMRA, ii. 299.
STUART, LORD INCHMARNOCK, ii. 299.
STUART, VISCOUNT KINGARTH, ii. 299.
STUART, COUNT MACHICO, ii. 304.
STUART, VISCOUNT MOUNTJOY IN THE ISLE OF WIGHT, ii. 306.
STUART, LORD MOUNT STUART, ii. 299.
STUART, BARON MOUNT STUART OF WORTLEY, ii. 306.
STUART, BARON STUART DE DECIES, ii. 307.
STUART, BARON STUART DE ROTHESAY, ii. 304.
STUART, EARL OF WINDSOR, ii. 306.
Stuart d'Albanie, Charles Edward, iii. 585.
— — Charles Edward Hay, iii. 585.
— of Aldenham Abbey, William, vii. 492.
— — his wife, Georgina Adelaide Forestier Walker, vii. 492.
— of Ascog, John, iii. 520.
— of Blackbarony, John, iii. 520.
— of Dunearn, Charles, ii. 366.
— of Fettercairn, Sir John Wishart Belsches, bart., M.P., vi. 117.
— — his wife, Jane Leslie, vi. 117.
— of Glanderston, Sir John, iv. 192.
— — Margaret, wife of John Fraser of Knock, iv. 192.
— of Hoborne, Charles, general, ii. 304.
— of Inchbreck, *, c. 1595, i. 294.
— — Robert, i. 286.
— — his wife, Sara Arbuthnott, i. 286.
— of Inchbreck and Laithers, Alexander, i. 316.
— — his wife, Clementina Arbuthnott, i. 316.
— of Montford, Henry, ii. 307.
— — his wife, Cecilia Hammersley, ii. 307.
— of Schelinlaw, Sir Robert, vii. 148.
— of Tempsford Hall, William, ii. 304.
— of Torrance, Andrew, the historian, iv. 146.

* Name unknown.

Stuart of Torrance, Archibald, 3rd laird, iii. 359; vi. 21.
— of Traquair, Louisa, dau. of 7th earl of Traquair, iv. 420; viii. 408.
— of Whitecraigs, James, major-general, vi. 21.
— — his wife, Margaret Humo Campbell, vi. 21.
— Anne, wife of 5th lord Ruthven, ii. 300; vii. 389.
— Anne, wife of 2nd duke of Northumberland, ii. 305.
— Anne, wife of Richard Hay-Newton, viii. 461.
— Ann Grace, dau. of 10th earl of Moray, vi. 328.
— Arabella, wife of William Seymour, i. 22; v. 354.
— Archibald, 3rd son of 2nd earl of Bute, ii. 300.
— Archibald John Morton, vi. 327.
— Augusta, wife of capt. Andrew Corbet, ii. 305.
— Caroline, wife of 7th earl of Seafield, ii. 92; vii. 491.
— Caroline, wife of 1st earl of Portarlington, ii. 305.
— Sir Charles, K.B., lieut.-gen., 4th son of 3rd earl of Bute ii. 304.
— — his wife, Louisa Bertie, ii. 304.
— Sir Charles, ambassador, ii. 304.
— — his wife, Elizabeth Margaret Yorke, ii. 304.
— Charles, R.N., 4th son of 1st marquess of Bute, ii. 306.
— Charles, 72nd Highlanders; 6th son of 10th earl of Moray, vi. 328.
— Charlotte, wife of earl of Canning, ii. 304.
— Charlotte, wife of Sir W. J. Homan, ii. 307.
— Cornelia, wife of rev. W. H. A. Truell, vi. 327.
— Douglas Moray, vi. 327.
— Douglas Wynne, vi. 327.
— — his wife, Marcia Luttrell, vi. 327.
— Dudley Coutts, M.P., ii. 307.
— — his wife, Christina Alexandra Egypta Bonaparte, ii. 308.
— Edmund Luttrell, rector of Winterborne Houghton, vi. 327.
— — his wife, Elizabeth Jackson, vi. 327.
— Elizabeth, dau. of 2nd earl of Bute, ii. 300.
— Elizabeth Jane, wife of 4th marquess of Townshend, ii. 307.
— Emily Frances, wife of C. Abbott, ii. 307.
— Evelyn James, col., ii. 306.
— Frances, wife of 2nd earl of Harrowby, ii. 308.
— Frances Teresa, wife of 6th duke of Lennox, i. 34; ii. 84; v. 361.
Stuart, Frederick, M.P., 3rd son of 3rd earl of Bute, ii. 303.
— George, rear-admiral, ii. 307.
— — his wife, Jane Stewart, ii. 307.
— George Gray, in holy orders, vi. 327.
— Grace, wife of John Campbell of Stonefield, ii. 301.
— Helen, wife of 10th lord Gray, ii. 88; iv. 292.
— Henrietta, wife of 1st marquess of Huntly, i. 50; iv. 544; v. 356.
— Henry, M.P., ii. 304.
— Henry, 5th son of 1st marquess of Bute, ii. 306.
— — his wife, Gertrude Amelia Mason-Villiers, ii. 306.
— Herbert Windsor, ii. 303 *n.*, 306.
— Hermione Moray, vi. 327.
— James, capt. 85th regt., vi. 328.
— James Gray, vi. 327.
— Jane, wife of George, earl Macartney, ii. 305.
— Jane, wife of (1) Sir J. A. Drummond Stewart of Grandtully, and (2) Dr. J. L. Pounden of Brownswood, iv. 293; vi. 328.
— Jean, wife of Wm. Courtenay, ii. 301.
— Jean, wife of Thomas, 8th earl of Dundonald, ii. 359.
— Jean, wife of (1) A. Riddell of Hayning, and (2) Sir W. Douglas of Kelhead, vii. 148.
— John, 2nd son of 1st earl of Bute, ii. 299.
— John, lt.-col. Guards, viii. 461.
— John, his father, viii. 461.
— John James, capt. R.N., ii. 304.
— — his wife, Albinia Sullivan, ii. 304.
— Katharine, wife of Wm. Maxwell of Nithsdale, iv. 417; vi. 490; viii. 407.
— Kenneth Bruce, capt. 63rd regt., i. 129.
— — his wife, Julia Clementina Ogilvy, i. 129.
— Louisa, dau. of 3rd earl of Bute, i. 378; ii. 305.
— Louisa, wife of 3rd marquess of Waterford, ii. 304.
— Louisa, dau. of archbp. William S., ii. 304.
— Louisa, dau. of 10th earl of Moray, vi. 328.
— Margaret Jane, dau. of 10th earl of Moray, vi. 328.
— Maria Alicia Charlotte, wife of C. Pinfold, ii. 307.
— Mary, wife of Sir R. Menzies, ii. 300.
— Mary, wife of James, earl of Lonsdale, ii. 304.
— Mary, wife of John Erskine of Carnock, ii. 366.
— Mary, wife of John, 5th titular duke of Perth, vii. 56; viii. 407.
— Mary Juliana, wife of 2nd earl of Ranfurly, ii. 304.

Stuart, Patrick James Herbert, ii. 308.
—— —— his wife, Hannah Tighe, ii. 309.
—— Paul Amadeus Francis Coutts, ii. 308.
—— Robert, major, H.B.M. minister at Hayti, ii. 523.
—— —— his wife, Elizabeth Sarah Cathcart, ii. 523.
—— Sophia, wife of Henry Bulkeley, i. 34; ii. 84.
—— William, archbishop of Armagh, ii. 304; ix. 50.
—— —— his wife, Sophia Margaret Juliana Penn, ii. 304.
—— William, capt. R.N., son of 1st marquess of Bute, ii. 307.
—— —— his wife, Georgina Maude Cornwallis, ii. 307.
—— Williamina, wife of Sir Wm. Forbes of Pitsligo, vi. 117.
—— *, wife of David Arbuthnott of Findowrie, i. 294.
—— *, major-general, Scots Hollanders, iii. 358.
—— *see also* Stewart.
Stuart-Gray of Kinfauns Castle, Morton Gray, vi. 327.
—— —— his wife, Edith Douglas Palmer, vi. 327.
Stuart-Mackenzie of Rosehaugh, James, lord Privy Seal, i. 377, 378; ii. 300.
—— —— his wife, Elizabeth Campbell, i. 377.
Stuart-Wortley-Mackenzie, Cicely Susan, wife of 1st baron Montagu of Beaulieu, ii. 246.
—— George, R.N., ii. 303.
—— James Archibald, 2nd son of 3rd earl of Bute, ii. 303; ix. 50.
—— John, Coldstream Guards, ii. 303.
—— Louisa Harcourt, wife of George, earl of Beverley, ii. 303.
—— Mary, wife of Wm. Dundas, ii. 303.
Stuart-Menteath of Closeburn, Sir Charles Granville, 1st bart., v. 635.
Studdy of Waddeton Court, Henry, vii. 310.
—— Georgina Frances, wife of Martin Leslie Leslie, vii. 309.
Studholme, Fanny, wife of Alex. Boyle, iv. 210.
—— Michael, Waimate, New Zealand, iv. 210.
Stutteville of Torpenhow, Robert de, vii. 364.
Sudbury, Henry (Fitz-Roy), 1st baron, i. 31.
Sudeley, Charles Douglas Richard (Hanbury-Tracy), 4th baron, iii. 417.
—— —— his wife, Ada Maria Katharine Tollemache, iii. 417.
Sudley, Arthur (Saunders), eldest son of 2nd earl of Arran; styled viscount, i. 68.
Sueno, son of Thor, i. 12; iii. 2; iv. 254, 255.
Suffolk, John (De la Pole), duke of, vi. 540.

* Name unknown.

Suffolk, Henry (Howard), 10th earl of, iii. 614.
—— Henry Bowes (Howard), 11th earl of, vii. 103.
—— —— his wife, Katharine Graham, vii. 103.
—— Theophilus (Howard), 2nd earl of, i. 30; ii. 207; iii. 288; vi. 453.
—— —— his wife, Elizabeth Home, iii. 288.
Sullivan, Albinia, wife of capt. J. J. Stuart, ii. 304.
—— John, ii. 304.
Sully, Elizabeth de, wife of William de Brus, ii. 431.
—— Raymond de, ii. 431.
Sulyarde, Sir Thomas, vii. 261.
—— —— his wife, Margaret Wharton, vii. 261.
Sunderland, Charles (Spencer), 4th earl of, ii. 533.
—— —— his wife, Anne Churchill, ii. 533.
—— Henry (Spencer), 1st earl of, viii. 366.
—— Robert (Spencer), 2nd earl of, iv. 384.
—— Robert (Spencer), 3rd earl of, viii. 366.
SUNDRIDGE OF COOMBANK, CAMPBELL, BARON, i. 386-393.
Sundridge of Coombank, John, first baron, i. 386.
Sundrum, Alan, 3rd lord Cathcart, styled lord, ii. 513 *n.*
Surrey, John (Plantagenet), earl of, i. 7.
—— John (de Warenne), earl of, viii. 253.
—— William (de Warenne), 2nd earl of, i. 4.
Sussex, Robert (Ratcliffe), 13th earl of, iv. 301.
—— Thomas (Ratcliffe), 3rd earl of, v. 64.
—— Thomas (Lennard), earl of, i. 31.
—— —— his wife, Anne Palmer *or* Fitz-Roy, i. 31.
SUTHERLAND, SUTHERLAND, EARL OF, viii. 318-337.
Sutherland, Elizabeth, wife of Adam Gordon; countess of, iii. 196; viii. 334, 336.
—— John, seventh earl of, iii. 192; viii. 330.
—— —— his wife, Margaret Baillie, viii. 331.
—— John, eighth earl of, viii. 332.
—— —— his 1st wife, * Macdonald, viii. 334.
—— —— his 2nd wife, Fingola of Calder, viii. 334.
—— —— his 3rd wife, Katharine *, viii. 334.
—— John, ninth earl of, viii. 335.
—— Kenneth, fourth earl of, iii. 191; viii. 324.
—— —— his wife, Mary *or* Marjorie of Mar, v. 578; viii. 325.
—— Robert, sixth earl of, iii. 192; viii. 329.
—— —— his wife, Margaret Stewart, ii. 263; viii. 330.
—— William, first earl of, viii. 321.
—— William, second earl of, viii. 323.

* Name unknown.

Sutherland, William, third earl of, viii. 323.
—— William, fifth earl of, iii. 191; vi. 36; vii. 158; viii. 325.
—— —— his 1st wife, Margaret Bruce, i. 8; viii. 326, 327.
—— —— his 2nd wife, Joanna Menteith, vi. 133; viii. 251, 257, 327.
SUTHERLAND, GORDON, EARL OF, viii. 337-361.
Sutherland, Adam, *de jure ux.* earl of, iii. 196; iv. 530, 531; vii. 162, 570 *n.*
—— —— his wife, Elizabeth, countess of Sutherland, viii. 334, 336.
—— Alexander, eleventh earl of, vii. 165; viii. 343.
—— —— his 1st wife, Barbara *or* Beatrix Sinclair, ii. 342; viii. 344.
—— —— his 2nd wife, Jane Gordon, ii. 166; iv. 539; viii. 344.
—— Elizabeth, wife of George (Leveson Gower), viscount Trentham; countess of, vii. 177; viii. 360.
—— George, fourteenth earl of, viii. 351.
—— —— his wife, Jean Wemyss, i. 207, 544; ii. 283; iv. 77; viii. 352, 503.
—— John, tenth earl of, iii. 200; vii. 164; viii. 339.
—— —— his 1st wife, Elizabeth *or* Isobel Campbell, i. 338; viii. 342.
—— —— his 2nd wife, Helenor Stewart, v. 353; viii. 342; ix. 86.
—— —— his 3rd wife, Marion Seton, vi. 160; viii. 342.
—— John, twelfth earl of, viii. 346.
—— —— his wife, Agnes *or* Annas Elphinstone, iii. 539; viii. 347.
—— John, thirteenth earl of, iii. 207; vii. 168; viii. 348.
—— —— his 1st wife, Jean Drummond, vii. 48; viii. 350.
—— —— his 2nd wife, Anna Fraser, v. 533; viii. 350.
—— John, fifteenth earl of, viii. 353.
—— —— his 1st wife, Helen Cochrane, iii. 352; viii. 354.
—— —— his 2nd wife, Katharine Tollemache, iii. 405; viii. 355.
—— —— his 3rd wife, Frances *, viii. 355.
—— William, sixteenth earl of, iii. 213: viii. 357.
—— —— his wife, Elizabeth Wemyss, viii. 358, 508.
—— William, seventeenth earl of, viii. 358.
—— —— his wife, Mary Maxwell, viii. 359.
SUTHERLAND, SUTHERLAND - LEVESON-GOWER, DUKE OF, viii. 361-365.
Sutherland, Cromartie, fourth duke of, iii. 85; viii. 364.
—— —— his wife, Millicent Fanny St. Clair Erskine, viii. 364.

* Name unknown.

Sutherland, George, first duke of, viii. 361.
—— —— his wife, Elizabeth, countess of Sutherland, viii. 359.
—— George Granville, second duke of, viii. 362.
—— —— his wife, Harriet Elizabeth Georgiana Howard, viii. 362.
—— George Granville William, third duke of, viii. 363.
—— —— his 1st wife, Anne Hay-Mackenzie, countess of Cromartie, iii. 84; viii. 363.
—— —— his 2nd wife, Mary Caroline Mitchell, viii. 364.
—— master of, Alexander (Sutherland), eldest son of 7th earl of Sutherland, viii. 331.
—— master of, Alexander (Gordon), eldest son of Elizabeth, countess of Sutherland, iii. 198; vii. 162; viii. 338.
—— —— his wife, Janet Stewart, i. 443; viii. 338.
SUTHERLAND, LORD DUFFUS, iii. 191-215.
SUTHERLAND, EARL OF SUTHERLAND, viii. 318-337.
Sutherland of Backies, Kenneth, viii. 328.
—— of Berriedale, Alexander, vii. 165.
—— —— his wife, Jane Mackay, vii. 165.
—— —— William, iii. 193.
—— of Brichmond, William, iii. 196.
—— of Clyne, Alexander, 5th laird, iii. 205.
—— —— his wife, Mary Sutherland, iii. 204, 205.
—— —— Elizabeth, iii. 205.
—— —— Henrietta, iii. 205.
—— —— James, 4th laird, iii. 205.
—— —— James Murray, 6th laird, iii. 205.
—— —— John, 3rd son of William S. of Duffus; 1st laird, iii. 204.
—— —— John, 2nd laird, iii. 205.
—— —— Patrick, iii. 205.
—— of Croftcroy, James, advocate, iii. 204.
—— of Croystoun, Hutcheon, vii. 161.
—— —— *, wife of Neil 'Naverach' Mackay, vii. 161.
—— of Daldred, Alexander, viii. 332.
—— of Dalnamain, James, iii. 206.
—— of Dirlot, Alexander, vii. 161 *bis*; viii. 332, 333.
—— —— his wife, * Mackay, vii. 161.
—— of Drummoy, Kenneth, viii. 328, 329.
—— of Duffus, Alexander, 3rd laird, son of Henry S., iii. 192, 197, 220; viii. 330.
—— —— his wife, Muriel Chisholm, iii. 193.
—— —— Alexander, 8th laird, iii. 195, 197, 199, 200.
—— —— his wife, Janet Grant, iii. 201; vii. 46.
—— —— Alexander, the younger, ii. 342; iii. 201.
—— —— his wife, Elizabeth Sinclair, ii. 342.

* Name unknown.

Sutherland of Duffus, Alexander, 11th laird, iii. 207.
—— —— his 1st wife, Jean Mackenzie, iii. 209.
—— —— Christina, wife of (1) William Oliphant, (2) Sir Thomas Lundie, and (3) Sir Wm. Keith, iii. 194, 195; vi. 541; ix. 68, 69.
—— —— James, capt. 26th Foot, ix. 87.
—— —— John, elder son of Nicholas S., iii. 191.
—— —— Nicholas, 2nd son of 4th earl of Sutherland, iii. 191; vii. 159, 160; viii. 325.
—— —— his wife, Mary le Cheyne of Duffus, iii. 191; vii. 160.
—— —— William, 4th laird, iii. 194, 195.
—— —— his wife, Janet Innes, iii. 196.
—— —— William, 5th laird, iii. 196.
—— —— his wife, Janet Innes, iii. 197.
—— —— William, 6th laird, iii. 197, 203.
—— —— William, 7th laird, iii. 198, 203; v. 526.
—— —— his wife, Elizabeth Stewart, iii. 199.
—— —— William, 9th laird, iii. 203.
—— —— his 1st wife, Margaret Sinclair, ii. 342; iii. 203.
—— —— his 2nd wife, Margaret Mackintosh, iii. 204; ix. 69.
—— —— William, 10th laird, iii. 205.
—— —— his wife, Jean Grant, iii. 206; vii. 468.
—— of Dunbeath, Alexander, ii. 334; vi. 171; vii. 244; ix. 18.
—— —— his wife, Mariota of the Isles, vii. 244; ix. 18.
—— —— William, ix. 51.
—— —— his wife, Jonet Sinclair, ix. 51.
—— of Evelix, Hugh, lieutenant, iii. 202, 207.
—— —— his wife, Magdalene Clunes, iii. 202, 207.
—— —— James, iii. 202, 207.
—— —— his wife, Margaret Sutherland, iii. 202, 207.
—— —— William, iii. 199.
—— of Forss, Alexander, ii. 340.
—— —— George, claimant to earldom of Sutherland, viii. 329, 359.
—— —— John, ii. 353.
—— —— Kenneth, ancestor of the family of, viii. 328.
—— of Greeshop, Alexander, iii. 193.
—— —— his wife, Muriel Chisholm, iii. 193.
—— of Invercharron, John, captain, iii. 202.
—— of Inverhassie, William, iii. 206.
—— of Kinminitie, Alexander, 2nd laird, iii. 204.
—— —— his wife, Jean Forbes, iii. 204.
—— —— Alexander, 3rd laird, iii. 204; ix. 69.
—— —— his 2nd wife, Marie Ogilvy, ii. 18; iii. 204.
—— —— Alexander, 4th laird, iii. 204.
—— —— his wife, Elizabeth Edwards, iii. 204; ix. 63, 69.
Sutherland of Kinminitie, Alexander, 5th laird, iii. 204, 205.
—— —— James, tutor of Duffus; 1st laird, iii. 204, 207, 208.
—— —— his wife, Margaret Seaton, iii. 204.
—— —— John, lieutenant-colonel, iii. 207.
—— —— his wife, Isabella Ross, iii. 207.
—— —— William, iii. 207.
—— of Kinnauld, Hugh, ix. 69.
—— of Kinstearie, David, iii. 202.
—— —— James, 3rd son of Alex. S. of Duffus, iii. 201, 202.
—— —— his wife, Violet Fraser, iii. 202.
—— —— James, iii. 202.
—— —— John, iii. 202.
—— —— William, iii. 196.
—— —— his wife, Janet Innes, iii. 197.
—— —— William, iii. 202.
—— —— his wife, Margaret Innes, iii. 202.
—— of Langwell, James, iii. 211.
—— —— his wife, Rachel Dunbar, iii. 211.
—— —— Robert, ii. 354.
—— of Mosstowie, Alexander, ix. 69.
—— —— his 1st wife, Barbara Guthrie, ix. 69.
—— —— his 2nd wife, Marie Ogilvy, ii. 18; iii. 204.
—— of Pronsy, Angus, iii. 194, 197.
—— —— his wife, Christina *, iii. 194.
—— —— Christian, contr. to John Kinnaird; wife of (1) David Stewart of the Doill, and (2) Adam Reid, iii. 194; v. 205.
—— —— Hugh, iii. 194, 196.
—— —— his wife, Agnes M'Leod, iii. 194.
—— —— James, vii. 176.
—— —— his wife, Margaret Sutherland, vii. 176.
—— —— Nicholas, iii. 194.
—— —— William, iii. 196.
—— of Quarrelwood, William, iii. 195.
—— —— William, iii. 198; v. 526.
—— of Rearquhar, Christian, wife of John Sutherland, iii. 202; ix. 69.
—— —— James, iii. 202.
—— —— John, iii. 202.
—— —— his wife, Christian Sutherland, iii. 202.
—— —— John, his son, iii. 202.
—— —— William, iii. 202; ix. 69.
—— of Roscommon, William, iii. 211.
—— —— his wife, Helen Duff, iii. 211.
—— of Skelbo, Alexander, iii. 198.
—— —— William, iii. 200.
—— of Strabrock, Alexander, iii. 192.
—— —— his wife, Muriel Chisholm, iii. 193.
—— —— Alexander, son of William S., iii. 193.
—— —— Christian, wife of (1) Wm. Oliphant of Berridale, (2) Sir Thos. Lundin of Pratis, and (3) Sir Wm. Keith of Inverugie, iii. 194, 195; vi. 541; ix. 68, 69.

* Name unknown.

Sutherland of Strathnaver, William, vii. 163.
—— of Strathullie, Thomas, ancestor of the family of, viii. 331.
—— of Swinzie, James, ii. 353.
—— —— his wife, Jean Sinclair, ii. 353.
—— of Torboll, Alexander, iii. 192, 197; viii. 330.
—— —— Angus, iii. 194.
—— —— Christina, wife of (1) David Stewart, and (2) Adam Reid, iii. 194.
—— —— Henry, 2nd son of Nicholas S. of Duffus, iii. 192.
—— —— his wife, Margaret of Mureff, iii. 192.
—— —— Hugh, iii. 194, 196.
—— —— Nicholas, iii. 194.
—— Alexander, rector of Duffus, dean of Caithness, iii. 197, 198.
—— Alexander, 5th son of 2nd lord Duffus, iii. 211.
—— Alexander, son of John S. and Janet Dunbar, countess of Moray, vi. 306.
—— Alexander, *error for* John, eldest son of William, 5th earl of Sutherland, viii. 328.
—— Alexander, alleged son of Robert, 6th earl of Sutherland, viii. 330.
—— Alexander, 2nd son of John, 8th earl of Sutherland, viii. 334, 336.
—— —— his wife, * Mackay, vii. 162; viii. 335.
—— Alexander, ix. 115.
—— —— his wife, Marion Macdonald, ix. 115.
—— Angus, 'Hectorsone,' iii. 202.
—— Anna, wife of Patrick Grant of Clunie, iii. 207; vii. 470.
—— Anna, wife of baron Gustaff Adolph Palbitzki, iii. 213.
—— Anne, wife of Patrick Sinclair, ii. 354.
—— Anne, wife of Geo. Mackay of Skibo, iii. 214; vii. 175.
—— Axel *or* Axley, 2nd son of Eric, titular lord Duffus, iii. 213.
—— Charlotta, wife of baron Otto Gustaff Wrede, iii. 213; ix. 70.
—— Charlotte, wife of Sir John Sinclair of Mey, iii. 214.
—— Christian, wife of 4th lord Reay, vii. 176.
—— Christian, *error for* Margaret, wife of (1) James Sutherland of Pronsy, and (2) Sir John Gordon of Embo, vii. 176 *n.*
—— David, viii. 352; ix. 163.
—— Donald, 2nd son of Angus S. of Torboll, iii. 194.
—— Dorothea, wife of Alex. Ross, iii. 195.
—— Duncan, Kinauld, iii. 202.
—— —— his wife, Anne Clunes, iii. 202.
—— Elizabeth, wife of John, 3rd earl of Caithness, ii. 337; iii. 197.

* Name unknown.

Sutherland, Elizabeth, wife of Geo. Sinclair, ii. 353.
—— Elizabeth, wife of Archibald Douglas of Pittendreich, iii. 202; vi. 364.
—— Elizabeth, wife of Sir John Gordon of Embo, iii. 212; ix. 69.
—— Elizabeth, wife of (1) Alex. Sinclair, (2) Charles Sinclair, and (3) rev. James Rudd, iii. 213.
—— Esther, wife of John Rose, ix. 70.
—— Eustachia, wife of Gilbert Moray of Culbin, viii. 325.
—— Frances, dau. of 2nd lord Duffus, iii. 212.
—— Helen, wife of Sir Jas. Colquhoun of Luss, vii. 482; viii. 356.
—— Henrietta, wife of 4th earl of Linlithgow, iii. 209; v. 449.
—— Henrietta, dau. of 2nd lord Duffus, iii. 212.
—— Hugh, 2nd son of William S. of Kinstearie, iii. 202.
—— Isabel, wife of Hew Rose, iii. 194.
—— Isobel, wife of Sir Alexander Dunbar of Westfield, iii. 195; vi. 306.
—— Isabel, dau. of 2nd lord Duffus, ix. 70.
—— J. C. C., Calcutta, viii. 235.
—— James, tutor of Duffus, ii. 18.
—— James, son of Thomas S., iii. 204.
—— James, advocate, iii. 210.
—— —— his wife, Elizabeth Dunbar of Hempriggs, iii. 210.
—— James, capt. 26th Foot, iii. 214; ix. 70.
—— Jane, wife of Sir Alex. Abercromby, iii. 204.
—— Janet, wife of 1st lord Banff, ii. 18; iii. 205.
—— Janet, wife of Francis Sinclair, ii. 340.
—— Janet, wife of Sir John Sinclair of Greenland and Ratter, ii. 347.
—— Janet, wife of John Clunes of Neilston, iii. 202.
—— Janet, wife of Alexander Dunbar, viii. 332.
—— Jean, wife of James, viscount Maitland, iv. 249; v. 311.
—— John, 4th son of 2nd lord Duffus, iii. 211.
—— John, vi. 306.
—— —— his wife, Janet Dunbar, 'countess of Moray,' vi. 306.
—— John, eldest son of William, 5th earl of Sutherland, viii. 328.
—— Julia Mary, wife of Sir Edmund Drummond, viii. 235.
—— Katharine, wife of John Cuthbert, iii. 212.
—— Margaret, wife of James Sutherland of Evelix, iii. 202, 207.
—— Margaret, wife of James Irvine in Artomford, iii. 204.
—— Margaret, wife of col. Robert Monro, iii. 205.

Sutherland, Margaret, dau. of 1st lord Duffus, iii. 209.
— Margaret, dau. of Wm. S. of Roarquhar, ix. 69.
— Marie, dau. of 1st lord Duffus, ix. 69.
— Marjory, wife of William, earl of Orkney and Caithness, ii. 334.
— Mary, wife of Alex. Sutherland of Clyne, iii. 204, 205.
— Mary, wife of James Sinclair of Mey, iii. 212.
— Muriel, wife of (1) Alex. Seton of Meldrum, and (2) Andrew Fraser of Stonywood, iv. 109; viii. 332 *n.*; ix. 69, 93.
— Nicholas, 3rd son of Wm. S. of Duffus, iii. 200.
— Nicholas, 3rd son of John, 7th earl of Sutherland, viii. 331.
— Patrick, capt. Sutherland militia, iii. 205.
— Robert, alleged son of Robert, 6th earl of Sutherland, viii. 330.
— Robert, son of John, 7th earl of Sutherland, viii. 330.
— Robin, 4th son of 1st lord Duffus, ix. 69.
— Thomas, 2nd son of Alex. S. of Kinminitie, iii. 204.
— — his wife, Violet Strachan, iii. 204.
— Thomas, illeg. son of John, 7th earl of Sutherland, viii. 332.
— Walter, iii. 200.
— *, mother of Mr. Patrick Dunbar, iii. 201.
Sutherland-Dunbar of Latheronwheel, Robert, captain, iii. 214.
— Louisa, wife of Garden Duff, iii. 214.
SUTHERLAND-LEVESON-GOWER, DUKE OF SUTHERLAND, viii. 362-365.
Sutherland-Leveson-Gower, Alastair St. Clair, viii. 364.
— Albert, viii. 363.
— — his wife, Grace Abdy, viii. 363.
— Alexandra, iii. 85; viii. 364.
— Caroline, wife of 4th duke of Leinster, viii. 363.
— Constance Gertrude, wife of 1st duke of Westminster, viii. 363.
— Elizabeth Georgiana, wife of 8th duke of Argyll, i. 390; viii. 363.
— Evelyn, wife of 12th lord Blantyre, viii. 363.
— Florence, wife of Henry Chaplin, iii. 85; viii. 364.
— Frederick George, Rifle Brigade, viii. 362.
— Ronald Charles, viii. 363.
— Rosemary Millicent, viii. 364.
Suttie of Balgone, Sir James, 2nd bart., viii. 142.
— — his wife, Elizabeth Dalrymple, viii. 142.

* Name unknown.

Sutton, Mary, wife of 1st earl of Home, iv. 465, 466.
— Walter H., in holy orders, vii. 391.
— — his wife, Mary L. Hore-Ruthven, vii. 391.
— William, ii. 194.
— — his wife, Colin Maria Nairne Campbell, ii. 194.
Suze, Gaspard de Champagne, comte de la, iv. 317.
— — his wife, Henriette de Coligny, iv. 317.
Swan, father of Thor of Tranent, iv. 254.
Swan of Crawford, son of Thor of Tranent and Tippermuir, i. 12; iii. 2; iv. 254, 255.
Sweden, saint Bridget of, v. 391.
— Christina, queen of, v. 374, 376.
— Gustavus Adolphus, king of, v. 373.
Swift of Rotherham, Sir Robert, iii. 234, 235.
— — his wife, Ursula Barnham, iii. 235.
— lieut. in lord Cadogan's regt., i. 570.
— Mary, wife of Sir Robert Fielding, iii. 235.
— Penelope, wife of 2nd earl of Dumfries, iii. 235; ix. 71.
Swinburne of Swinburne, Sir Adam, vi. 197.
— — his wife, Idonea Graham, vi. 197.
— Algernon Charles, vi. 197 *n.*
— Sir John, Renfrew, iii. 425.
Swindell, Cosby, capt. 55th Foot, v. 251.
— — his wife, Catherine Margaret Norvell, v. 251.
Swinton of Abernethy, Alan de, vi. 527.
— of Arbuthnott, Hugo de, i. 272; vi. 525.
— of Collessie, Alan de, vi. 527.
— of Mersington, Sir Alexander, i. 552.
— of Swinton, Sir Alan de, i. 273.
— — Alan de, iii. 525.
— — Alan, his son, iii. 525.
— — Cospatrick de, i. 273; vi. 527.
— — Ernulf de, i. 273; iv. 507 *n.*
— — Sir John, i. 149; v. 585, 597; vii. 38.
— — his 1st wife, Margaret, countess of Mar, iii. 153; v. 585.
— — his 2nd wife, Margaret Stewart, i. 149.
— — Sir John, iii. 279.
— — his wife, Marjorie of Dunbar, iii. 279.
— — Sir John, iii. 279; vi. 538.
— — John, iii. 281.
— — his wife, Margaret Home, iii. 281.
— — John, iii. 285.
— — his wife, Katharine Lauder, iii. 285.
— — John, ii. 85.
— — his 1st wife, Margaret Stewart, ii. 85.
— — Sir John, viii. 178.
— — his 2nd wife, Anne Sinclair, viii. 178.
— — John, lord of Session, vi. 503.
— — Robert, viii. 442.
— — his 1st wife, Elizabeth Hay, viii. 442.

Swinton, Elizabeth, wife of lt.-col. Geo. Carnegie, vi. 503.
—— Hugo de, son of Cospatrick de S., i. 273.
—— John, son of Alan de S., iii. 525.
—— Margaret, wife of John Oliphant, Perth, vi. 544.
—— Mary, wife of (1) John Fletcher, and (2) James Bruce, i. 551.
—— Mary, dau. of Sir John S. of Swinton, viii. 178 *n.*
Swynfen, John, M.P., i. 410.
Sybilla, wife of king Alexander I., i. 3.
Sydenham of Brompton, Sir John, iv. 287.
—— —— his wife, Mary Guldeford, iv. 287; ix. 99.
Sydney, Thomas (Townshend), 1st viscount, ii. 244.
Sym, Alexander, advocate, commissary of Edinburgh, iv. 427.
—— —— his wife, Katharine Bothwell, iv. 427.
Syme, Agnes, wife of lt.-col. Charles Erskine, v. 628.
Symington, John, viii. 13.
—— —— his wife, Janet Somerville of Prestwickshaws, viii. 13.
Symmer of Balzeordie, George, i. 293.
—— —— George, i. 293.
—— —— his wife, Christian Arbuthnott, i. 293.
—— —— George, i. 294; iii. 322.
—— —— his wife, Margaret Grahame, i. 293; iii. 322.
—— —— Magdalen, wife of David Doig of Cookston, viii. 85.
—— Margaret, wife of Robert Arbuthnott of Mondynes, i. 291.
Symondstoun, Duncan of, ii. 586.
—— Thomas of, ii. 586.
Symple, *see* Sempill.
Symson of Concraig, Alexander, vi. 433.
—— Andrew, minister of Kirkinner, viii. 147.
—— Isobel, dau. of Mr. Patrick S., ii. 594.
—— Margaret, wife of major-gen. Mark Napier, vi. 433.
—— Patrick, minister of Stirling, ii. 594.
Syras, Adam de, iv. 5.

Tailor, Esther, wife of (1) D. Drummond, and (2) Sir George Melville, ix. 135.
Tailyefer of Barmagachan, Stephen, v. 259.
Tailliefere, John, ii. 333.
Tailziefeir, John, in Normangill, viii. 371.
—— —— his wife, Margaret Graham, viii. 371.
Tailzeour, John, parson of Cummertrees, vii. 124.
Tait, Elizabeth, wife of Alexander Stewart of Kildavanan, ii. 290.
Talbot, Charles (Chetwynd), 2nd earl, v. 485.
—— —— his wife, Frances Thomasine Lambart, v. 485.
Talbot of Falconhurst, John Gilbert, M.P., ii. 247.
—— Barbara, wife of 5th lord Aston of Forfar, i. 413; ix. 26.
—— Bertram, v. 486.
—— —— his wife, Victoria Alexandrina Montagu-Douglas-Scott, ii. 247; v. 486.
—— George, brother of 13th earl of Shrewsbury, i. 413.
—— —— his wife, Mary Fitz William, i. 413.
—— Richard, i. 509.
—— —— his wife, Elizabeth Comyn of Goodrich Castle, i. 509.
Talmash of Helmingham, Sir Lionel, bart., iii. 403.
—— —— his wife, Elizabeth Stanhope, iii. 403.
—— Elizabeth, wife of 1st duke of Argyll, i. 370; iii. 405.
—— *see also* Tollemache.
Tanfield, Elizabeth, wife of 1st viscount Falkland, iii. 610; ix. 88.
—— Sir Laurence, iii. 610.
Tankerville, Charles (Bennet), 6th earl of, iii. 109.
TANNADYCE, LYON, LORD, viii. 299-317.
Tannadyce, Patrick, first lord, viii. 299.
Tanner, James, i. 145.
—— —— his wife, Margaret Barclay Allardice, i. 145.
TARBAT, MACKENZIE, VISCOUNT OF, iii. 74-80.
Tarbat, George, first viscount of, iii. 74.
—— —— his 1st wife, Anna Sinclair, iii. 75.
—— —— his 2nd wife, Margaret, countess of Wemyss, iii. 77; viii. 504.
—— George, eldest son of 2nd earl of Cromartie; styled lord, iii. 78.
—— master of, John, eldest son of 1st viscount of Tarbat, iii. 77.
TARBAT OF TARBAT, HAY-MACKENZIE, VISCOUNT, iii. 84-86.
Tarbat of Tarbat, Anne, wife of 3rd duke of Sutherland; viscountess, iii. 84.
—— Roderick Grant, son of Sibell Lilian, countess of Cromartie; styled lord, iii. 85.
TARBOLTON, LENNOX, BARON, v. 363-371.
Tarbolton, Charles, first baron, v. 363.
TARBOLTON, STEWART, LORD, v. 356-362.
Tarbolton, Esme, first lord, v. 352.
Tarpley, Thomas Griffin, vii. 512.
—— —— his wife, Katharine Mackenzie, vii. 512.
TARRAS, SCOTT, EARL OF, ii. 237; vii. 80-81.
Tarras, Walter, eldest son of Sir Gideon Scott of Highchester; earl of, ii. 237; vii. 80.
—— —— his 1st wife, Mary, countess of Buccleuch, ii. 236; vii. 80.
—— —— his 2nd wife, Helen Hepburn, vii. 82.
TARVES, GORDON, LORD, i. 88-99.

Tarves, George, first lord, i. 88.
Tatham, Mary, wife of David Carmichael, iv. 568.
— William, rector of Wormingford, iv. 568.
Taunton, Henry (Labouchere), lord, ii. 309.
TAY, CAMPBELL, VISCOUNT OF, ii. 203.
Tay, John, first viscount of, ii. 203.
Taylor of Ardgillan Castle, Thomas Edward, M.P., iii. 417.
— — his wife, Louisa Harrington Murray, iii. 417.
— of Firby Hall, Edward H. Clough, i. 391.
— — his wife, Elizabeth Campbell, i. 391.
— of Kirktonhill, Robert, viii. 83.
— — his wife, Jean Carnegie, viii. 83.
— of Townhead and Abbotshall, John, M.D., H.E.I.C.S., iii. 449.
— Elizabeth, wife of Alexander Montgomerie of Annick Lodge, iii. 449.
— John, the Water Poet, vii. 468.
— Mariota, v. 435.
— Sir Richard Chambre Hayes, lieut.-general, G.C.B., viii. 472.
— — his wife, Jane Hay, viii. 472.
Telfer of Haircleugh, William, iv. 583.
— — his wife, Margaret Carmichael, iv. 583.
— of Redhouse, Alexander, iv. 92.
— — his wife, Margaret Forrester, iv. 92.
Tempest of Tong, John, iii. 596.
— Peter, vi. 342.
Temple, Richard (Nugent-Temple), 4th earl, v. 200.
— of the Nash, Sir Richard, 1st bart., G.C.S.I., i. 525.
— — his 2nd wife, Mary Augusta Lindsay, i. 525.
— of Stowe, William Stephen (Temple-Gore-Langton), 4th earl, iii. 522; v. 201.
— — Sir Thomas, 1st bart., ix. 3.
— Hester, wife of Sir John Lenthall, ix. 3.
— Martha, wife of Edward Ruthven, iv. 94.
Templemore, Arthur (Chichester), 1st lord, iv. 172.
Tenand, John, 'filius clerici,' viii. 49.
— Mariota, viii. 49.
Tennant of Cairns, James, viii. 27.
— — his wife, Jean Somerville, viii. 27.
Tennison, Margaret, wife of col. Richard Murray, i. 493.
— William, i. 493.
Tenterden of Hendon, Charles (Abbott), 1st baron, ii. 307.
— — Charles Stuart Aubrey, 3rd baron, ii. 307.
Terranuova, Bernard Stewart, duca de, v. 347.
TERREGLES, HERRIES, LORD HERRIES OF, iv. 398-424.
Terrick, Anne, wife of archdeacon Hamilton, ii. 50, 56.
Terrick, Richard, bishop of London, ii. 50.
TERRINYEAN, CAMPBELL, LORD, v. 506-517.
Terrinyean, John, first lord, v. 506.
Tervalt of Tervait, John, viii. 535.
— — his contracted wife, Isobel Fleming, viii. 535.
TEVIOT, SPENCER, VISCOUNT OF, viii. 366-367.
Teviot, Robert, viscount of, viii. 366.
— — his wife, Jane Spencer, viii. 366.
TEVIOT, LIVINGSTON, VISCOUNT, viii. 368-377.
Teviot, Thomas, viscount, i. 91; viii. 375; ix. 151.
— — his wife, Macktellina Walrave, viii. 376.
TEVIOT, RUTHERFURD, EARL OF, vii. 374-375.
Teviot, Andrew, earl of, v. 25; vii. 374, 379.
— — his wife, Susanna Melville, vii. 375.
Thacker, Anne, wife of E. W. T. Hamilton, ii. 56.
— John, Ascot, ii. 56.
Thackeray, Frederick Raynell, general, C.B., R.E., vi. 506.
— — his wife, E. M. Carnegie, vi. 506.
— Richmond Makepeace, iv. 569.
— — his wife, Anne Beecher, iv. 569.
— Thomas, headmaster of Harrow School, viii. 358.
— William Makepeace, viii. 358.
Thane of Edindonyng, Alexander, vii. 188, 195.
— of Thanesland, Alexander, vii. 195.
Thanet, Nicholas (Tufton), 1st earl of, iii. 297.
Tharp of Chippenham Park, Joseph, iii. 391.
— — his wife, Susan Murray, iii. 391.
Theobald the Fleming, Lesmahagow, iii. 133 *n*.
Thiboutat, marquis de, iii. 430.
Thimelby of Irnham, Sir John, i. 408, 409.
— Henry, i. 409.
— — his wife, Gertrude Aston, i. 409.
— Katharine, wife of Herbert Aston, i. 408.
— Richard, i. 408, 409.
THIRLESTANE, MAITLAND, LORD, v. 299-323.
Thirlestane, John, first lord, v. 298; vii. 342.
— — his wife, Jean Fleming, v. 300; viii. 542.
— John, second lord, v. 301.
— — his wife, Isobel Seton, iii. 372; v. 301.
THIRLESTANE AND BOLTON, MAITLAND, LORD, v. 302-323.
Thirlestane and Bolton, John, first lord, v. 302.
THIRLESTANE, MUSSELBURGH, AND BOLTON, MAITLAND, LORD, v. 305.
THIRLESTANE CASTLE, MAITLAND, LORD LAUDERDALE OF, v. 319-320.
Thirlestane, master of, John, son of 1st lord Thirlestane, v. 300.
— of Abertarff, Avicia, wife of Sir Richard Maitland, v. 278.

Thirlestane of Abertarff, Thomas de, v. 277.
—— —— his wife, Agnes, v. 277, 278.
—— Alan of, v. 277.
—— Eisi of, v. 277.
Thoirs, Sir David, vii. 137.
—— ——his wife, Margaret Douglas, vii. 137.
—— Jean, wife of capt. David Ogilvy, vii. 374.
Thomas, son of Thankard, vi. 198.
Thomas, son of Ranulf; sheriff of Dumfriesshire, vi. 288.
—— —— his wife, Juliana, vi. 289.
Thomas of Wenvoe, Edmond, vi. 468.
—— —— his wife, Mary Morgan of Ruperra, vi. 468.
—— of Ystrad, Ellen Katharine, wife of H. E. M. Lindsay, i. 527.
—— —— George, i. 527.
—— Elizabeth, wife of William, lord Cheyne, vi. 468.
Thomond, Barnaby (O'Brien), 6th earl of, iii. 231.
—— —— his wife, Anne Farmer, iii. 231.
—— Henry (O'Brien), 7th earl of, v. 359.
Thomson of Arduthie, James, i. 292, 303.
—— —— his wife, Katharine Arbuthnott, i. 292.
—— of Charleton, Grizel Maria, wife of col. John Anstruther, vii. 587.
—— —— John, vii. 587.
—— —— his wife, Margaret Paterson, vii. 587.
—— of Colmslie, James, merchant, vi. 151.
—— —— his wife, Katharine Lithgow, vi. 151.
—— of Duddingston, Sir Thomas, 1st bart., iii. 314 *bis*, 379.
—— —— his wife, Margaret Graham, iii. 314.
—— of Faichfield, Mr. William, iv. 113.
—— of Fiddes, James, i. 303.
—— of Kenfield, vi. 181.
—— Andrew, tailor, Edinburgh, iv. 89.
—— Elizabeth, wife of 1st lord Reay, vii. 169.
—— Esther, wife of John Stewart, ix. 68.
—— James, vii. 207.
—— —— his wife, Cecilia Anne Rollo, vii. 207.
—— Janet, wife of Henry Stenhouse, i. 547; ix. 33.
—— John, merchant, Dumfries, ii. 391.
—— —— his wife, Elizabeth Carlyle, ii. 391.
—— John, minister of Duddingston, viii. 122.
—— —— his wife, Frances Ingram Spence, viii. 122.
—— Margaret, wife of 2nd lord Dunkeld, iii. 379.
—— Margaret, wife of Robert Boyd, v. 174.
—— Robert, Greenwich, keeper of the queen's wardrobe, vii. 169.
—— Thomas, younger son of T. of Kenfield, vi. 181.
—— —— his wife, Phœbe Hammond, vi. 181.
Thomson, William, Annan, vii. 149.
—— *, reader of the kirk of Terregles, iv. 411.
—— *, wife of David Douglas, vii. 149.
Thompson of Ipston, William, viii. 229.
—— Elizabeth, wife of Charles Robert Lindsay, iii. 42.
—— J. Stanley, iv. 172.
—— —— his wife, Elizabeth Louisa Rogers, iv. 172.
—— Thomas William, iii. 42.
—— Winifred, wife of R. Drummond, viii. 229.
Thor, father of Swan, lord of Tippermuir, i. 12; iii. 2.
Thor of Tranent, son of Sweyn, iv. 254.
Thorfinn Sigurdsson, earl of Moray, Orkney, Caithness, and Sudrland, i. 2; ii. 314; vi. 280; viii. 318.
—— —— his wife, Ingibiorg, i. 2; ii. 314.
Thorfinn Skullsplitter, ii. 314.
Thorkell-Fostri, in Caithness, ii. 314.
Thorne of Uffculm, William, ii. 279.
—— Ann, wife of J. M'L. F. Erskine, ii. 279.
THORNHILL, DOUGLAS, LORD DOUGLAS OF, vii. 143-144.
Thornhill, Charles, lord Douglas of, vii. 143.
—— of Kingston Lisle, Edward, viii. 311.
—— Cudbert Bensley, C.S.I., viii. 236.
—— Ellen, wife of 10th viscount of Strathallan, vii. 236.
—— Mary, wife of (1) Geo. Bowes, and (2) B. Price, viii. 311.
—— Sarah Caroline, wife of Thomas Charles Bruce, iii. 494.
—— Sir Thomas, bart., iii. 494.
Thornhurst, Frances, wife of R. Jennings, ii. 532.
—— Sir Gifford, bart., ii. 533.
Thornton of Balgownie, Donald, viii. 300.
—— of Eassie, Donald, viii. 300.
—— of Thornton, vii. 432.
—— John, apostolic protonotary, viii. 527.
—— Patrick, assassin, viii. 383.
—— Thomas, Hull, iii. 291.
—— —— his wife, Jane Constable, iii. 291.
—— Walter de, ii. 505.
Thorstein the Red, son of Olaf, king of Dublin, ii. 313.
Thouars, Claude de la Trémouille, duke of, i. 475.
—— —— his wife, Charlotte of Nassau, i. 475; iii. 383.
Thrale of Streatham, Henry, iii. 548.
—— —— his wife, Hester Lynch Salisbury, iii. 548.
—— Hester Maria, wife of viscount Keith, iii. 548.
Threipland of Fingask, Sir Patrick, 1st bart., iii. 471; vi. 498.

* Name unknown.

Threipland of Fingask, Sir Stuart, M.D., 3rd bart., ii. 346.
—— —— his wife, Janet Sinclair, ii. 346.
—— Marjory, wife of P. Carnegie of Lour, vi. 498.
Throckmorton, Sir George, London, iii. 291.
—— Jane, wife of (1) Richard Etherington, and (2) Michael Constable, iii. 291.
—— Sir Nicholas, ii. 167.
Throndssön, Anna, betrothed to 4th earl of Bothwell, ii. 163.
—— Christopher, Norwegian admiral, ii. 163.
Thurles, James (Butler), styled lord, iii. 122.
—— Thomas (Butler), styled viscount, i. 53.
Thurlow, Edward (Thurlow), 1st baron, vii. 450.
—— Thomas John (Hovell-Thurlow), 4th baron, iii. 495.
—— —— his wife, Elma Cumming-Bruce, iii. 495.
—— Katharine, wife of 16th lord Saltoun, vii. 449, 450.
—— Thomas, in holy orders, viii. 310.
—— —— his wife, Frances Lyon, viii. 310.
Thursby, John, Madras Civil Service, iii. 390.
—— —— his wife, Anne *, iii. 390.
Thurstan, son of Leving of Levingston, v. 422.
Thwaites of Denton, Isabel, wife of Sir William Fairfax, iii. 596.
—— —— Thomas, iii. 596.
Thynne, Charlotte Anne, wife of 5th duke of Buccleuch, ii. 245.
TIBBERIS, DOUGLAS, VISCOUNT OF, vii. 143-144.
Tibberis, Charles, viscount of, vii. 143.
Tighe of Woodstock, William, ii. 309.
—— —— William Frederick Fownes, v. 367.
—— —— his wife, Louisa Maddelena Lennox, v. 367.
—— Hannah, wife of lord P. J. H. Crichton-Stuart, ii. 309.
Tildesley, Sir Thomas, governor of Lichfield, i. 409.
Tillicoultry, Sir Robert Stewart, bart., lord of Session, lord, ii. 296.
TILLIMET, MURRAY, LORD MURRAY OF, iii. 384.
TINDALL, SCOTT, BARON SCOTT OF, ii. 237-249.
Tindall, Francis, second baron Scott of, ii. 241.
—— James, first baron Scott of, ii. 237.
Tinmouth, James Fitz James, earl of, i. 34.
Tippermuir, Swan of, i. 12; iv. 254.
Tireman, Katharine, wife of lt.-col. John Carnegie, viii. 85.
—— *, sub-dean and prebendary of Chichester, viii. 85.

* Name unknown.

Tirol, Sigismond of, duke of Austria, i. 19.
—— —— his wife, Eleanor Stewart, i. 19; ix. 2.
TIRY, CAMPBELL, LORD, i. 369-393.
Tiry, Archibald, first lord, i. 369.
Tocketts of Tocketts, William, iii. 294.
—— —— his wife, Mary Constable, iii. 294.
Tod, Agnes, wife of Sir Archibald Forrester of Corstorphine, iv. 86.
—— Susan Mary Elizabeth, wife of Robert Oliphant of Rossie, viii. 112.
—— Thomas, judge of the Commissary Court, viii. 112.
—— —— his wife, Susan Lindsay, viii. 112.
Todd, Ann, wife of Alexander Middleton, vi. 177.
—— Anthony, secretary of General Post Office, v. 319.
—— Eleanor, wife of 8th earl of Lauderdale, v. 319; ix. 125.
Todrick, William, burgess of Edinburgh, iii. 66, 501; vii. 284 *n.*
—— —— his wife, Margaret Crichton, iii. 66; vii. 284.
Toeni, Ralph de, viii. 250.
—— Robert de, viii. 250.
—— —— his wife, Matilda de Strathearn, viii. 250.
Tollemache of Helmingham, John (Tollemache), 1st baron, iii. 410.
—— —— Wilbraham Frederick (Tollemache), 2nd lord, iv. 172.
—— —— his 1st wife, Emma Georgiana Stewart, iv. 172.
—— —— his 2nd wife, Mary Stuart Hamilton, i. 67.
TOLLEMACHE, EARL OF DYSART, iii. 406-420.
TOLLEMACHE, LORD OF HUNTINGTOWER, iii. 406-420.
Tollemache of Ballincor, Arthur Frederick Churchill, iii. 416.
—— —— his wife, Susan Eleanor Carter Campbell, iii. 416.
—— of Helmingham, John Richard Delap, son of major J. D. Halliday and lady Jane Tollemache; vice-admiral of the Red, iii. 410.
—— —— his wife, Elizabeth Stratford, iii. 410.
—— —— Sir Lionel, 2nd bart., iii. 403.
—— —— Sir Lionel, 3rd bart., iii. 403.
—— —— his wife, Elizabeth, countess of Dysart, iii. 403.
—— of Market Overton and Harrington, Charles, iii. 413.
—— —— his 1st wife, Frances Hay, iii. 413.
—— —— his 2nd wife, Gertrude Florinda Gardiner, iii. 413.
—— Ada Maria Catherine, wife of 4th lord Sudeley, iii. 417.
—— Adèle, dau. of Arthur Cæsar T., iii. 416.

Tollemache, Agatha Manners, wife of 3rd baron Westbury, iii. 420.
— Agnes Mary Manners, wife of Charles N. Lindsay Scott, iii. 419.
— Albert, Bengal Artillery, iii. 416.
— Algernon Grey, M.P., iii. 417.
— — his wife, Frances Louisa Tollemache, iii. 414.
— Anastasius Eugene, captain 22nd Foot, iii. 417.
— — his wife, Alice Elizabeth Cursham, iii. 417.
— Anna Maria, wife of Wilbraham, earl of Dysart, iii. 412.
— Arthur Hugh, iii. 413.
— Arthur Cæsar, lieut. 6th Dragoon Guards, iii. 415.
— — his wife, Catherine Scheppers, iii. 416.
— Arthur Lionel, iii. 416.
— — his wife, Emily Bryant, iii. 416.
— Augustus Francis, vicar of Whitwick, iii. 417.
— Caroline, wife of rev. R. W. L. Tollemache, iii. 415, 416.
— Caroline Magdalene, dau. of William, lord Huntingtower, iii. 418.
— Cecilia Eleanor, iii. 417.
— Clement Reginald, Government chaplain at Rangoon, iii. 416.
— — his wife, Frances Josephine Simpson, iii. 416.
— Cornelia Katharine, iii. 417.
— Elizabeth, wife of 1st duke of Argyll, i. 370; iii. 405.
— Elizabeth, wife of Sir R. S. Cotton, iii. 406.
— Ernest Celestine, vicar of Well, iii. 416.
— — his wife, Henrietta Maria Dixon, iii. 416.
— Felix Thomas, M.P., iii. 415.
— — his 1st wife, Sarah Grey, iii. 415.
— — his 2nd wife, Frances Julia Peters, iii. 415.
— Frances, dau. of 4th earl of Dysart, iii. 409.
— Frances Emily, dau. of William, lord Huntingtower, iii. 418.
— Frances Louisa, wife of (1) lieut. Geo. R. Halliday, and (2) A. G. Tollemache, iii. 414, 417.
— Frederick James, M.P., iii. 417.
— — his 1st wife, Sarah Maria Bomford, iii. 417.
— — his 2nd wife, Isabella Anne Forbes, iii. 417.
— George, R.N., H.M.S. *Modeste*, iii. 408.
— Grace, dau. of 3rd earl of Dysart, iii. 407.
— Henrietta, wife of Thomas Clutterbuck, iii. 407.
Tollemache, Henry Bertie, Scots Fusilier Guards, iii. 413.
— — his wife, Emilia Magdalen Louisa Sinclair, iii. 413.
— Hugh Francis, rector of Harrington, iii. 416.
— — his wife, Matilda Hume, iii. 416.
— Jane, wife of (1) John Delap Halliday, and (2) David George Ferry, iii. 410; ix. 80.
— John, R.N., captain H.M.S. *Zebra*, iii. 408.
— — his wife, Bridget Henley, iii. 408; ix. 79.
— John, *formerly* Manners, vii. 353.
— — his wife, Mary Bechinoe, iii. 413; vii. 353.
— Katharine, wife of John, marquess of Carnarvon, iii. 406.
— Katharine, wife of (1) James, lord Doune, and (2) John, 15th earl of Sutherland, iii. 405; vi. 323; viii. 355; ix. 79 *ter*.
— Katharine Camilla, wife of Sir G. Sinclair of Thurso, iii. 418.
— Katharine Eliza, iii. 416.
— Katharine Octavia, iii. 418.
— Laura, dau. of John Manners and Louisa, countess of Dysart, iii. 414.
— Laura, wife of Albert, comte de Lastic St. Jal, iii. 416.
— Laura Maria, wife of Rt. Hon. James Grattan, iii. 418.
— Lionel, capt. 76th Foot, iii. 413.
— Lionel Alexander Arthur, ix. 80.
— — his wife, Louisa Margaret Hope, ix. 80.
— Lionel Robert, ensign Coldstream Guards, iii. 409.
— Louisa, dau. of Arthur Cæsar T., iii. 416.
— Louisa Grace, wife of Joseph Burke, iii. 418.
— Louisa Harrington, wife of Rt. Hon. T. E. Taylor, iii. 417.
— Louisa Maria, iii. 417.
— Maria Eliza, wife of 1st marquess of Ailesbury, iii. 412 *n.*, 414.
— Mary, dau. of 3rd earl of Dysart, iii. 407.
— Mary Louisa Napoleona Manners, iii. 419.
— Matilda Anne Frances, wife of rev. G. E. Maunsell, iii. 417.
— Melanie Sophia, wife of R. L. Abrial, iii. 416.
— Ralph William Lyonel, rector of South Witham, iii. 415, 416.
— — his wife, Caroline Tollemache, iii. 415.
— Thomas, lieut.-gen., M.P., governor of the Isle of Wight, iii. 404.
— Thomas, ensign to lieut.-col. Willkins, iii. 405 *n.*

Tollemache, Wilbraham Francis, commander R.N., iii. 413.
—— his wife, Elizabeth Munro, iii. 413.
— William, capt. R.N., 3rd son of Sir Lionel T., iii. 405; viii. 71.
— William, R.N., lieut. H.M.S. *Repulse*, iii. 409; ix. 80.
— William, iii. 413.
—— his 1st wife, Anna Maria Jane St. Maur, iii. 413.
—— his 2nd wife, Emma Sidney, iii. 413.
— William James Felix, iii. 415.
Tonge, Francis Henry, capt. 62nd regiment, v. 254.
—— his wife, Madeleine Dora Keith-Falconer, v. 254.
Tooker of Chilcompton, William, i. 60.
—— his wife, Frances Hamilton, i. 60.
Toone, Maria Elizabeth, wife of 8th earl of Dysart, iii. 418.
— Sweeney, Keston Lodge, iii. 418.
TORPHICHEN, SANDILANDS, LORD, viii. 378-398.
Torphichen, James, first lord, viii. 386.
—— his wife, Janet Murray, viii. 386.
— James, second lord, i. 77; vii. 76; viii. 390.
—— his 1st wife, Elizabeth Heriot, viii. 390.
—— his 2nd wife, Mary Somerville, viii. 26, 390.
— James, third lord, viii. 391.
— James, seventh lord, viii. 394.
—— his wife, Jean Hume, vi. 17; viii. 394.
— James, ninth lord, viii. 396.
—— his wife, Anne Inglis, viii. 396.
— James, tenth lord, viii. 395, 396.
—— his wife, Margaret Douglas Stirling, viii. 397.
— James Walter, twelfth lord, viii. 397.
—— his wife, Ellen Frances Gordon, viii. 398.
— John, fourth lord, viii. 392.
—— his wife, Isabel Dundas, viii. 392.
— John, fifth lord, viii. 393.
— Robert, eleventh lord, viii. 397.
—— his wife, Helen Maitland, viii. 397.
— Walter, sixth lord, viii. 393; ix. 160.
—— his 1st wife, Jean Lindsay, i. 515; viii. 393.
—— his 2nd wife, Katharine Alexander, viii. 177, 393; ix. 160.
—— his 3rd wife, Anna Elphinstone, iii. 542; viii. 393.
—— his 4th wife, Christian Primrose, vii. 217; viii. 393.
— Walter, eighth lord, viii. 395.
—— his wife, Elizabeth Sandilands, viii. 396.
— master of, James Archibald Douglas, viii. 398.
Torphichen, master of, John Gordon, viii. 398.
Torphin, eldest son of Harald Maddadsson, earl of Caithness, ii. 316.
Torrie, Archibald, ii. 278.
— Jane Halliday, wife of Henry, lord Cardross, ii. 278.
TORRY, BRUCE, BARON BRUCE OF, iii. 486-497.
TORTHORWALD, DOUGLAS, LORD, ii. 392-394.
Torthorwald, James, first lord, ii. 392.
—— his wife, Elizabeth Carlyle of Torthorwald, ii. 391.
— James, second lord, ii. 393.
—— his 1st wife, Elizabeth Gordon, ii. 394; v. 113.
—— his 2nd wife, Anne Saltonstall, ii. 394.
TORTHORWALD, DOUGLAS, VISCOUNT OF, vii. 138-156.
Torthorwald, William, first viscount of, ii. 394 *n.*; vii. 138.
Toshoch of Monzie, Andrew, ii. 183.
— of Monzievaird, Alexander, i. 466; viii. 198.
—— his wife, Elizabeth Murray, viii. 198.
—— Andrew, ii. 200.
—— his wife, Katharine Campbell, ii. 200.
—— David, ii. 180.
—— his wife, Elizabeth Campbell, ii. 180.
—— David, son of Edward T., v. 504, 505; vi. 552.
—— Edward, v. 504.
—— his wife, Marjory Campbell, v. 504.
— of Pittenzie, John, ii. 186.
—— his wife, Margaret Campbell, ii. 186.
— Margaret, wife of Arch. Campbell, ii. 183.
Tostig Godwinsson, earl of Northumbria, iii. 241.
Tott, Jaqueline de, wife of Henry Hope, iv. 487.
TOTTENHAM, BRUCE, BARON BRUCE OF, iii. 481-483.
Touraine, Louis of Anjou, duke of, iii. 167.
TOURAINE, DOUGLAS, DUKE OF, iii. 166-172.
Touraine, Archibald, first duke of, iii. 166.
—— his wife, Margaret Stewart, i. 18; iii. 166.
— Archibald, second (titular) duke of, iii. 168; v. 289.
— William, third (titular) duke of, iii. 170.
Touris, *see* Towers.
Tourle, Helen Mary Anne, wife of John Hope Sandilands, viii. 397.
— Thomas, viii. 397.
Tovey, James, general, v. 416.
— Margaret Augusta, wife of major M. E. Lindsay, v. 416.

Tower, rev. Charles, ii. 57.
—— Fanny Elizabeth, wife of capt. H. G. Hamilton, ii. 57.
Towers of Dalry, George, i. 76.
—— —— Sir William, iii. 142.
—— —— his wife, Eleanor Douglas, iii. 142.
—— of Garmilton, Sir Alexander, viii. 501.
—— —— his wife, Jean Wemyss, vii. 21; viii. 501.
—— of Inverleith, George, i. 76.
—— —— his wife, Helen Sandilands, i. 76.
—— —— Sir George, viii. 501; ix. 153.
—— —— his wife, Jean Ker, viii. 501; ix. 153.
—— —— James, iii. 282.
—— —— his wife, Mariota Home, iii. 282.
—— —— Sir James, vi. 412.
—— —— his wife, Janet Chisholm, vi. 412.
—— —— Sir John, viii. 488.
—— —— Sir John, ii. 355.
—— of Towers, Gabriel, iv. 86.
—— —— Sir John, ii. 355.
—— —— William, iv. 86.
—— —— his wife, Janet Forrester, iv. 86.
—— Elizabeth, wife of Wm. Hepburne, ii. 139.
—— Elizabeth, mistress of Sir John Wemyss of Wemyss, viii. 492.
—— Frances, wife of Sir James Sinclair of Mey, ii. 355.
—— Frances, wife of Sir John Sinclair of Longformacus, ii. 355 *n.*
—— Mariota, wife of (1) Sir D. Wemyss of Wemyss, and (2) B. Hamilton of Bogwood, viii. 488.
—— Mary, wife of Ralph Ker, v. 51 *n.*
Towneley of Towneley, Charles, colonel, v. 368.
—— Emily Frances, wife of Alexander F. C. Gordon-Lennox, v. 368.
Townend, Joseph Henry, M.D., vii. 493.
—— Mary Elizabeth Nina, wife of 11th earl of Seafield, vii. 493.
Townshend, Charles (Townshend), 2nd viscount, iv. 203.
—— George (Townshend), 1st marquess, i. 377.
—— John (Townshend), 4th marquess, ii. 307.
—— —— his wife, Elizabeth Jane Stuart, ii. 307.
—— John Villiers Stuart (Townshend), 5th marquess, ii. 307.
—— John James Dudley Stuart (Townshend), 6th marquess, ii. 307.
—— Anne, wife of Richard Wilson, M.P., i. 377.
—— Charles, chancellor of the Exchequer, i. 377; ii. 242.
—— —— his wife, Caroline (Campbell), baroness Greenwich, i. 377; ii. 241.
—— Harriet Katharine, wife of 4th duke of Buccleuch, ii. 244.
Townshend, Thomas Charles, capt. 45th Foot, i. 377.
—— William John, capt. 59th and 41th Foot, i. 377.
Trabia e di Butera, Giuseppe, principe di, vi. 459.
—— Maria Lanza di, wife of 9th earl of Newburgh, vi. 459.
Tracy, John (Tracy), 3rd viscount, iv. 391.
Traherne of Coytraben, Morgan Popkin, viii. 231.
—— Caroline, wife of rev. M. Drummond, viii. 231.
Traill of Blebo, Alexander, viii. 491.
—— —— John, v. 404.
—— of Hobbister, James, advocate, ii. 350.
—— —— his wife, Janet Sinclair, ii. 350.
—— Janet, wife of (1) John Ramsay of Arbeikie, and (2) Sir John Wemyss of Wemyss, viii. 491.
—— Margaret, wife of (1) P. Lindsay, and (2) Archibald Hamilton, v. 412.
—— Patrick, v. 404.
—— —— his wife, Margaret Lindsay, v. 404.
—— Robert, minister of Elie, v. 170 *n.*
—— William, D.D., viii. 513.
—— —— his wife, Frances Charteris, viii. 513.
Transylvania, Sigismund Racoczy, prince of, i. 28.
—— —— his wife, Henriette von Simmern, i. 28.
TRAQUAIR, STEWART, EARL OF, viii. 399-409.
Traquair, Charles, fourth earl of, viii. 406.
—— —— his wife, Mary Maxwell, v. 88; vi. 488; viii. 406.
—— Charles, fifth earl of, viii. 407.
—— —— his wife, Theresa Conyers, viii. 408.
—— Charles, seventh earl of, viii. 408.
—— —— his wife, Mary Ravenscroft, viii. 408.
—— Charles, eighth earl of, viii. 409.
—— John, first earl of, i. 565; iv. 27, 585; viii. 402.
—— —— his wife, Katharine Carnegie, viii. 67, 405.
—— John, second earl of, viii. 405.
—— —— his 1st wife, Henrietta Gordon, iv. 547; viii. 406, 595; ix. 111.
—— —— his 2nd wife, Anne Seton, viii. 406, 600.
—— John, sixth earl of, viii. 408.
—— —— his wife, Christian Anstruther, viii. 408.
—— William, third earl of, viii. 406.
TRAQUAIR, STEWART, LORD STEWART OF, viii. 403-409.
Travell, Sir John Robert, viii. 355.
—— —— his wife, Frances *, viii. 355.
Travers of Fir Grove, John, v. 318.
—— —— his wife, Mary Orpen, v. 318.

* Name unknown.

Tredegar, Godfrey Charles (Morgan), 2nd baron, viii. 92.
Trefusis, Evelyn Anne, wife of Edward W. Douglas, vi. 385.
— Walter Randolph, col. Scots Guards, ii. 247.
— — his wife, Mary Charlotte Scott, ii. 247.
Tremenheere, George Borlase, maj.-gen., ii. 91.
— Georgina, wife of Sir Wm. Stewart, ii. 91.
Tremouille, Charlotte de la, wife of 7th earl of Derby, i. 475; iii. 382.
— Louis Stanislas Kostka, prince de la, iii. 390.
— — his wife, Augusta Murray, iii. 390.
— Claude de la, duc de Thouars, i. 475; iii. 383.
— — his wife, Charlotte of Nassau, iii. 383.
Trentham, George (Leveson Gower), eldest son of Granville, lord Gower; styled viscount, viii. 360.
— — his wife, Elizabeth, countess of Sutherland, viii. 359.
Tresham, Mary, wife of 2nd earl of Cardigan, iii. 298.
— Sir Thomas, iii. 298.
Trevanion, Hugh Charles, viii. 312.
Trevelyan, Sir George, v. 267.
— — his wife, Mary Gage, v. 267.
Trevor, Arthur William (Hill-Trevor), 2nd lord, vii. 452.
— — his wife, A. M. E. Fraser, vii. 452.
— George Arthur, capt. Royal Sussex regt., ii. 499.
— — his wife, Susan Funnell, ii. 499.
Trionfi, Augustin, marquis, vi. 458.
— — his wife, Elizabetta Bandini, vi. 458.
Tritton, Elizabeth, wife of lieut.-col. Jas. Sinclair, ii. 357.
— George, Westhill, Wandsworth, ii. 357.
Trotter of Ballindean, Robert Knox, col. 17th Lancers, vii. 209.
— — his wife, Mary Rollo, vii. 209.
— of Dreghorn, Archibald, v. 419.
— of Dyrham Park, John, ii. 57; v. 419.
— of Mortonhall, John, iv. 436.
— of Westville, Sir B. A. Coutts, bart., i. 92, 524.
— — his wife, Margaret Gordon, i. 92.
— Agnes Bruce, wife of 10th lord Rollo, vii. 209.
— Algernon R., capt. 2nd Life Guards, M.V.O., D.S.O., iii. 464.
— — his wife, Edith Mary Montgomerie, iii. 464.
— Anne, wife of lieut.-gen. Jas. Lindsay of Balcarres, i. 524.
— Coutts, wife of Sir H. Lindsay Bethune of Kilconquhar, v. 419.
Trotter, Edward, in Swinton Mylne Steill, iv. 298.
— — his wife, * Ramsay, iv. 298.
— James Stuart, lieut. R.N., v. 419.
— — his wife, Jane Coutts Lindsay, v. 419.
— Janet, wife of Alex. Bothwell of Glencorse, iv. 436.
— Martha, wife of C. F. Boyle, iv. 213.
— Martin, wife of W. J. Hamilton, ii. 57.
Troup of Craigie, William, iv. 270.
— Alison, wife of John Gray of Crichie, iv. 288.
— James, merchant, Edinburgh, iv. 288.
— John de, vi. 171.
Trubleville, Ralph de, vi. 527.
Truell, William Henry Augustus, Clonmannon, vi. 327.
— — his wife, Cornelia Stuart, vi. 327.
Truelock, George, archdeacon of Killala, iv. 571.
— Sarah Margaret, wife of David F. Carmichael, iv. 571.
Trumbull of Easthampstead Park, Sir William, viii. 182.
— — his 2nd wife, Judith Alexander, viii. 182.
Truro of Bowes, Sir Thomas Wilde, baron, iii. 392.
— — his 2nd wife, Augusta Emma D'Este, iii. 392.
Tucker, Ethel, wife of Archibald Lionel Lindsay, v. 420.
— William Austin, v. 420.
Tudor, Dorothy Susan, wife of major D. S. Carmichael-Smyth, iv. 571.
— Margaret, wife of (1) king James IV., (2) Archibald, 6th earl of Angus, and (3) Henry, 1st lord Methven, i. 21, 26, 27, 190, 192; iv. 261; v. 150, 353; vi. 166, 167; ix. 12.
— Mary, sister of king Henry VIII., iii. 480.
— Mary, illeg. dau. of king Charles II., wife of (1) Francis, earl of Derwentwater, (2) Henry Graham of Levens, and (3) James Rooke, i. 32; vii. 102.
— William, iv. 571.
Tufnell, Carlton, commander R.N., vii. 227.
— — his wife, Charlotte Henrietta Primrose, vii. 227.
— Frederick, rector of Sudbury, v. 96.
— — his wife, Frances Elizabeth Erskine, v. 96.
— Henry, M.P., vii. 227.
— — his wife, Anne Primrose, vii. 227.
Tufton of Hothfield, Sir John, 1st bart., iii. 297.
— — his 2nd wife, Christian Brown, iii. 297.
— Mary, wife of Henry, 1st viscount Dunbar, iii. 297.

* Name unknown.

Tughall, Robert, chamberlain of Berwick, vii. 317.
Tuite, Sir George, bart., iii. 362.
—— —— his wife, Janet Cochrane, iii. 362.
Tuke, Francis, in holy orders, viii. 227.
—— Mabel, wife of E. B. Drummond, viii. 227.
TULLIBARDINE, MURRAY, EARL OF (1606), i. 469-472.
Tullibardine, John, first earl of, i. 466, 469; viii. 410.
—— —— his wife, Katharine, *or* Margaret Drummond, i. 469; vii. 47; ix. 29.
—— William, second earl of, i. 470; viii. 410; ix. 29 *bis*.
—— —— his 1st wife, Cecilia Wemyss, i. 471; viii. 498.
—— —— his 2nd wife, Dorothy Stewart, i. 446, 471.
TULLIBARDINE, MURRAY, EARL OF (1628), viii. 410-415.
Tullibardine, Patrick, third earl of, i. 470, 471; viii. 411.
—— —— his 1st wife, Prudence *, viii. 412.
—— —— his 2nd wife, Elizabeth Dent, viii. 412.
—— James, fourth earl of, i. 474; iii. 573; viii. 414.
—— —— his 1st wife, Lilias Drummond, viii. 223, 414.
—— —— his 2nd wife, Anne Murray, i. 473; viii. 415.
—— —— his 3rd wife, Lilias Drummond, viii. 415.
TULLIBARDINE, MURRAY, EARL OF (1676), i. 474.
Tullibardine, John, fifth earl of, i. 474.
—— —— his wife, Amelia Anne Sophia Stanley, i. 475.
TULLIBARDINE, MURRAY, EARL OF (1696), i. 478.
Tullibardine, John, sixth earl of, i. 475, 478; iii. 354; iv. 37.
TULLIBARDINE, MURRAY, MARQUESS OF, i. 479-502.
Tullibardine, George Augustus Frederick John, sixth marquess of, i. 498.
—— James, second marquess of, i. 487; vii. 556 *n*.
—— John, first marquess of, i. 479.
—— John, eldest son of 1st duke of Atholl; styled marquess of, i. 480; ix. 29.
—— John, third marquess of, i. 489.
—— John, fourth marquess of, i. 495.
—— John, fifth marquess of, i. 498.
—— John George, eldest son of 7th duke of Atholl; styled marquess of, i. 500.
—— —— his wife, Katharine Marjory Ramsay, i. 500.
—— John James Hugh Henry, seventh marquess of, i. 499.

* Name unknown.

Tullibardine, William, 2nd son of 1st duke of Atholl; styled marquess of, i. 480.
—— master of, William Murray, eldest son of 1st earl of Tullibardine, i. 469.
TULLIBARDINE, MURRAY, LORD MURRAY OF, i. 469-501.
Tullibardine, Ada of, wife of Sir William Murray, i. 453, 454 *n.*; ix. 28.
—— Conghal of, i. 453 *n*.
—— Duncan of, i. 419.
—— Muriel of, wife of Sir Malise, steward of Strathearn, i. 453.
TULLIBODY, ALEXANDER, LORD ALEXANDER OF, viii. 173.
Tullideph of Tullideph, Walter, vi. 115.
—— Mary Margaret, wife of major-gen. Alexander Leslie, vi. 115.
Tullie, David, iv. 566.
—— —— his wife, Euphame Carmichael, iv. 566.
Tulloch of Bonnington, Dorothea, wife of Walter Wode, viii. 274.
—— of Montcoffer, Alexander, iv. 71.
—— —— his wife, * Forbes, iv. 71.
—— —— John, portioner, viii. 281.
—— —— his wife, Elizabeth Lyon, iv. 54; viii. 280.
—— of Tulloch, Walter, i. 110.
—— —— his wife, Marjorie Ogilvy, i. 110.
—— Elizabeth, dau. of John T., iv. 54.
Tullois of Pitkennetie, Thomas, v. 411.
Tunstall of Scargill and Wycliffe, Francis, iii. 298.
—— —— his wife, Cicely Constable, iii. 298.
—— Cuthbert, bishop of Durham, iv. 358.
Tunstall-Constable of Burton Constable, Cuthbert, nephew of last viscount Dunbar, iii. 298.
Turck, Johanna, wife of Sir Henry Livingston, vi. 449.
Turing of Foveran, Gilbert, i. 287.
—— —— his wife, Katharine Arbuthnott, i. 287.
—— —— Robert, viii. 56.
—— —— his wife, Helen Carnegie, viii. 56.
Turnbull of Bedrule, George, v. 59.
—— —— his wife, Janet Ker, ii. 230; v. 59.
—— —— Sir Thomas, iv. 472; v. 61; viii. 400.
—— —— Walter, iv. 473.
—— —— William, iv. 472.
—— —— his wife, Margaret Home, iv. 471.
—— of Bewlie, Robert, v. 73.
—— of Hassendean Bank, John, iv. 229.
—— of Minto, Sir John, 'out wyth swerd,' ii. 539; iv. 145, 147, 148, 150; vii. 366.
—— —— Walter, iv. 150.
—— Andrew, v. 69.
—— Esther, vii. 72.
—— James, advocate, ii. 277.
—— —— his wife, Erskine Monro, ii. 277.

* Name unknown.

Turnbull, John, inquisitor for Selkirk, 1467, iii. 499.
— Margaret, wife of Andrew Borthwick, ii. 103.
— Margaret, wife of Robert Frenche of Thornydikes, iv. 472.
— William, bishop of Glasgow, ii. 327; iii. 60.
— *, wife of Sir Alex. Stewart of Darnley, iv. 145; v. 345.
— *, wife of Wm. Cochrane, ix. 76.
Turner, Elizabeth, wife of Charles Cranstoun, ii. 599.
— John, a fencing-master, iii. 230.
— Sir James, v. 459, 460; viii. 180.
Turnor of Stoke Rochford, Edmund, iv. 561.
— — his wife, Mary Katharine Gordon, iv. 561.
— Algernon, C.B., iv. 172.
— — his wife, Henrietta Caroline Stewart, iv. 172.
Turnour, Sir Edward, vi. 60.
— — his wife, Isabel Keith, vi. 60.
Turstan, son of Leving, iii. 87.
Tweddell of Unthank Hall, John, viii. 123.
— Hannah, wife of general Samuel Dalrymple, viii. 123.
TWEEDDALE, HAY, EARL OF, viii. 447-474.
Tweeddale, John, first earl of, viii. 447; ix. 167 *bis*.
— — his 1st wife, Jean Seton, iii. 373; viii. 449; ix. 167 *bis*.
— — his 2nd wife, Margaret Montgomery, viii. 449.
— John, second earl of, viii. 451.
— — his wife, Jean Scott, ii. 234; viii. 451.
TWEEDDALE, HAY, MARQUESS OF, viii. 416-474.
Tweeddale, Arthur, ninth marquess of, viii. 472; ix. 168.
— — his 1st wife, Helena Eleanora Augusta de Kilemansegge, ix. 168.
— — his 2nd wife, Julia Charlotte Sophia Mackenzie, ix. 168.
— Charles, third marquess of, viii. 458, 462.
— — his wife, Susan Hamilton, iv. 382; viii. 462.
— George, fifth marquess of, viii. 465.
— George, sixth marquess of, viii. 463, 465.
— George, seventh marquess of, iv. 324; viii. 466.
— — his wife, Hannah Charlotte Maitland, v. 318; viii. 466.
— George, eighth marquess of, viii. 468; ix. 168.
— — his wife, Susan Montagu, viii. 470.
— John, first marquess of, viii. 453.
— — his wife, Jean Scott, ii. 234; viii. 451.

* Name unknown.

Tweeddale, John, second marquess of, iv. 38; viii. 456.
— — his wife, Mary Maitland, v. 306; viii. 458.
— John, fourth marquess of, viii. 464.
— — his wife, Frances Carteret, viii. 460, 464.
— William George Montagu, eleventh marquess of, viii. 473.
— William Montagu, tenth marquess of, viii. 470, 472.
— — his wife, Candida Louisa Bartolucci, viii. 473.
TWEEDDALE OF YESTER, HAY, BARON, viii. 473-474.
Tweeddale of Yester, William Montagu, first baron, viii. 473.
Tweedie of Dreva, Adam, vii. 73.
— of Drumelzier, James, viii. 19, 399, 431, 537.
— — his 1st wife, Elizabeth Hay, viii. 434 *bis*.
— — his 2nd wife, Marion Stewart, viii. 399.
— — James, vii. 126.
— — his wife, Janet Douglas, vii. 126.
— — James, vii. 73; viii. 401, 448, 448.
— — his wife, Elizabeth Hay, viii. 444 *bis*.
— — John, viii. 19 *bis*, 536, 538.
— of Frude, James, viii. 536, 538.
— — his contr. wife, * Fleming, viii. 537.
— — his wife, Katharine Fraser of Frude, viii. 537 *bis*.
— of Hopcailzo, John, viii. 19.
— — his wife, Agnes Somerville, viii. 19.
— Margaret, wife of Andrew Ker of Altonburn and Cessford, vii. 323 *bis*.
— *, vi. 349.
— — his wife, * Douglas, vi. 349.
— *, wife of Hugh Somerville, of Spital, viii. 19.
Tweedmouth, Dudley Coutts (Marjoribanks), baron, i. 98.
Twinning, Helen Martha, wife of vice-admiral Donald Mackay, vii. 175.
— William, Bengal Medical Service, vii. 175.
Twisden of Raydon Hall, Sir William, iii. 460.
— Frances, wife of (1) Archibald, 11th earl of Eglinton, and (2) Francis Moore, iii. 460; ix. 81 *bis*.
Tyllings, Sara, wife of Sir Alex. Livingston of Lethington, viii. 375.
Tyndall, John, LL.D., D.C.L., F.R.S., i. 67.
— — his wife, Louisa Charlotte Hamilton, i. 67.
Tynedale, Charles William Henry (Scott), baron, ii. 244.
Tyningham, Adam de, bishop of Aberdeen, iv. 108.

* Name unknown.

Tyningham, William, parson of Melville, vi. 80.
TYNNINGHAM, MURRAY, LORD MURRAY OF, i. 228.
Tyrconnel, George (Carpenter), 2nd earl of, vi. 445.
—— —— his wife, Frances Manners, vi. 445.
—— George (Carpenter), 3rd earl of, ix. 109.
—— Richard (Talbot), duke of, i. 54.
—— —— his wife, Frances Jennings, i. 54.
Tyrie of Drumkilbo, David, iii. 318; iv. 283.
—— —— his wife, Lilias Gray, iv. 283; vi. 548.
Tyringham of Tyringham, John, vi. 462.
—— —— his wife, Elizabeth Brudenell, vi. 462.
Tyrrel, Sir Charles, iv. 95.
—— Elizabeth, wife of capt. John Ferrester, R.N., iv. 95.
Tyrrell, Sir Toby, 3rd bart., vi. 466.
—— —— his wife, Lucy Barrington, vi. 465.
Tyrwhit, Mary, wife of Henry Constable, iii. 291.

UCHTRED, son of Waldeve of Tynedale, i. 3, 417.
—— —— his wife, Bethoc of Scotland, i. 3, 417.
Uchtred, son of Fergus, lord of Galloway, ii. 371.
Uchtred, son of Maldred, iii. 241.
Uchtred, earl of Northumberland, iii. 241 *bis*.
Uchtred, son of Liulph of Maccusteun, vi. 469.
Udard, father of Roger, ii. 377.
Udny of Udny, John, i. 302.
—— —— John, i. 89.
—— —— his wife, Martha Gordon, i. 89.
—— Juliana, wife of W. R. Hamilton, ii. 56.
Udwart, Nathaniel, iii. 377.
Ulgric of Galloway, iv. 135.
Ulkil, son of Maldred, iii. 241.
Ulster, James, 3rd son of king Charles I.; earl of, i. 32.
—— Richard de Burgh, earl of, i. 8, 322.
UMFRAVILLE, EARL OF ANGUS, i. 167-168.
Umfraville, Sir Gilbert de, i. 167.
—— —— his wife, Matilda, countess of Angus, i. 166, 167.
—— Gilbert de, his grandson, i. 168.
—— Sir Ingram de, ii. 219, 221.
Undwain, father of Maccus, vi. 469.
Unes, Meg, a witch, ii. 113.
Urchell, *, dau. of 5th lord Herries of Terregles, and wife of Sir John Graham of Orchell; styled lady, iv. 415; vi. 230.
Ure, John, minister of Leuchars, viii. 53.
—— of Pitsligo, William, i. 397.
—— —— his wife, Elizabeth Erskine, i. 397.

* Name unknown.

Urie, Margaret, wife of Henry Stewart of Killinnan, i. 397.
Urry, William, vii. 529.
Urquhart, Alexander Seton, senator of the College of Justice, lord, iii. 370.
URQUHART, SETON, LORD, iii. 370.
Urquhart, Alexander, lord, iii. 370.
—— of Burrisyards, Thomas, ii. 14.
—— of Old Craig, James, iv. 128.
—— of Craigfintrie, John, tutor of Cromarty, vii. 412, 443.
—— —— his 2nd wife, Jean Abernethy, vii. 412.
—— —— his 3rd wife, Elizabeth Seton of Meldrum, iv. 112; vii. 413, 443.
—— of Cromarty, Alexander, iv. 19.
—— —— his wife, Mary Ogilvy, iv. 19.
—— —— Alexander, vii. 412.
—— —— his wife, Beatrix Innes, vii. 412.
—— —— Sir Alexander, iv. 131.
—— —— Henry, ii. 13; vii. 414.
—— —— his wife, Elizabeth Ogilvy, ii. 13.
—— —— James, colonel, vi. 259.
—— —— John, vii. 509.
—— —— his wife, Barbara Mackenzie, vii. 509; ix. 156.
—— —— Jonathan, vi. 259.
—— —— his wife, Jean Graham, vi. 259.
—— —— Thomas, vii. 409.
—— —— his wife, Helen Abernethy, vii. 409.
—— —— Sir Thomas, ii. 15; vii. 412, 503.
—— —— his wife, Christian Elphinstone, iii. 540.
—— —— Sir Thomas, the author, vii. 169, 409.
—— —— Walter, ii. 14; vii. 500.
—— —— his 1st wife, Elizabeth Mackenzie, vii. 500.
—— —— William, vii. 237.
—— —— his alleged wife, Lilias de Ross, vii. 237.
—— —— Sir William, iv. 50.
—— —— his wife, Susanna Forbes, iv. 50.
—— —— William, iv. 71.
—— —— his wife, Isabel Forbes, iv. 71.
—— of Cullicudden, Thomas, vii. 503.
—— of Dunlugus, Sir Thomas, ii. 15.
—— of Fischerie, Thomas, vii. 409.
—— of Lethintie and Meldrum, Patrick, i. 124.
—— —— his wife, Margaret Ogilvy, i. 124.
—— of Meldrum, Adam, iv. 549.
—— —— his wife, Mary Gordon, iv. 549.
—— of Moncoffer, Sir Thomas, ii. 15.
—— of Newhall, Alexander, ii. 416.
—— Alexander de, constable of Ferres, v. 522.
—— Christian, wife of (1) Thomas, lord Rutherford, (2) James, 2nd viscount Frendraught, and (3) George Morrison, iv. 131 *bis*; vii. 380.
—— Ellen, wife of (1) F. B. Drummond, and (2) W. M. Stewart, viii. 226.

Urquhart, Grizel, wife of 5th earl of Carnwath, ii. 416.
—— Helen or Isobel, wife of W. Ogilvy, ii. 14.
—— Magdalen, wife of 8th lord Saltoun of Abernethy, vii. 414.
—— W. H., viii. 226.
Uspac Hakon, 3rd son of Dugall of Lorn, v. 30.
Uthred, father of Edulph of Eddleston, iii. 87.
Uvedale of Wickham, Sir William, iii. 610, 611.
—— Francis, iii. 610.
—— Susan, wife of Patrick Cary, iii. 610; ix. 88.
Uxbridge, Henry (Paget), 1st earl of, iv. 170.

Valance of Halhouse and Likbernard, Christina, wife of George Ramsay, iii. 91.
—— —— David de, iii. 91.
Valence, Agnes de, wife of Sir Hugh de Baliol, iv. 142.
—— Sir Aymer de, i. 509; ii. 219; iii. 560.
—— Johanna de, wife of 'the Red Comyn No. 2,' i. 509.
—— P. de, iii. 4.
—— William de, i. 509.
—— *see also* Valoniis.
Vall of Kilsyth, Robert de la, v. 424; viii. 522.
—— —— *, his daughter, v. 424.
Vallabriga, Joseph Ignaz de, ix. 135.
—— —— his wife, Margaret de Rozas, ix. 135.
Vallibus, John de, viii. 319 *n.*
—— *see also* Vaus.
Valoniis of Kilbride, Isobel de, wife of Sir David Comyn, i. 505; vii. 5.
—— —— Roger de, i. 505; vii. 5.
—— of Lochore, Sir Andrew de, viii. 481.
—— Christian de, wife of Peter de Maule, vii. 5.
—— Gunnora de, wife of Robert Fitzwalter, vii. 5.
—— Lora de, wife of Sir Henry Baliol, vii. 5.
—— Philip de, vii. 5, 364.
—— Robert de, i. 505.
—— William de, chamberlain of Scotland, vii. 5.
—— —— his wife, Loretta de Quincy, vii. 5.
Valrose, George Drummond, baron de, vi. 72; vii. 60.
—— Marie Louise Susan Edith Grace Drummond, baronne de, vi. 73.
Van Beest, Katharine, wife of capt. Chas. Boyd, ix. 119.

* Name unknown.

Van Borselen, Wolfart, count of Grandpré and lord of Campvere, i. 19; ii. 265 *n.*
—— —— his wife, Mary Stewart, i. 19; ii. 265 *n.*
Vandeleur, Boyle, colonel, iii. 616.
—— Emily Caroline, wife of col. J. H. Fraser, vii. 451.
—— John, colonel 10th Hussars, vii. 451.
Van der Borchens, Diliana, wife of James King of Birness and Dudwick, iii. 593.
Vanderbyl, Michael Servas, Cape of Good Hope, ii. 197.
—— —— his wife, Charlotte Elizabeth Campbell, ii. 197.
Vander-Graaff, Jacomina Gertrude, wife of Geo. Leslie, vi. 117.
—— William Jacob, governor of Java, vi. 117.
Van der Wyck, Alpheda Louise, wife of Barthold Mackay, vii. 173.
Vanden Bempde, Charlotte van Lore, wife of (1) James, 1st marquess of Annandale, and (2) col. John Johnstone, i. 268; ix. 15.
—— John, of Hackness, i. 268.
Van den Steen, Arnolda Margaret, wife of col. Donald Mackay, vii. 171.
Vandeput, Sir George, iii. 514.
Van Dyck, Sir Anthony, iv. 264, 265.
—— —— his wife, Mary Ruthven, iv. 265.
—— Justinia, wife of Sir John Stepney of Prendergast, iv. 265.
Vane, William (Vane), 2nd viscount, iv. 385.
—— —— his wife, Frances Hawes, iv. 384.
—— Anne, wife of (1) Charles Hope of Craigiehall, and (2) col. Geo. Monson, iv. 494.
—— Sir Ralph, iv. 470.
Van Enghuizen, Maria Adelheid van Heeckeren, wife of major-gen. Frans Mackay, vii. 171.
Van Haeften, Ursulina Philippina, wife of col. Æneas Mackay, vii. 171.
Van Leeuven, Maria, wife of Henry Balfour, i. 537.
Vanlore of Tylehurst, Sir Peter, bart., viii. 181.
—— Mary, wife of (1) Henry, 3rd earl of Stirling, and (2) col. John Blount, viii. 181.
Van Lynden, Elizabeth Wilhelmina, wife of baron Æneas Mackay, vii. 172.
—— Juliana Anna, wife of baron Theodoor Philip Mackay, vi. 172.
—— Margaretha Clara Franciska, wife of baron Johan F. H. J. E. Mackay, vii. 172.
Vannet, Jane Margaret, wife of George North Dalrymple, viii. 160.
Van Renesse, Anna Magdalena Frederica Henriette, wife of baron Barthold J. C. Mackay, vii. 171.

Van Rensselaar of New York, Patroon, ii. 495.
Van Rynhuyzen, Isabolla Constantia de Geer, wife of (1) Count de Quadt, and (2) major Donald Mackay, vii. 171.
Vans, Isabel, wife of George Murray of Broughton, i. 221.
— Sir John, v. 112.
— Margaret, wife of (1) John Glendonwyn of Drumrash, (2) James Gordon of Barncrosh, and (3) James Maxwell of Breconside, iv. 416; v. 112; ix. 118 *bis*.
Van Somelsdyke, Cornelius van Arsen, baron Somelsdyke, iii. 487.
— Veronica van Arsen, wife of 2nd earl of Kincardine, iii. 487.
Varnall, Peter, iii. 298.
Vasserot, *, father-in-law of George Hamilton, i. 58.
Vaughan of Woodstone, Thomas Wright, colonel, iv. 559.
— Charlotte Anne, wife of rev. lord George Gordon, iv. 559.
— Clare, wife of L. C. C. Lindsay, iii. 47.
— Francis B., colonel, iii. 47.
— Herbert, cardinal, iii. 47.
— Sir John, governor of Londonderry, i. 44.
— Sidney, wife of Sir Frederick Hamilton of Manor Hamilton, i. 44.
Vaus of Barnbarroch, Patrick, i. 252.
— — his wife, Grisel Johnstone, i. 252.
— — Sir Patrick, ii. 471.
— — his wife, Katharine Kennedy, ii. 471.
— — Robert, vi. 151.
— — his wife, Euphame Graham, vi. 151.
— of Blans, Elizabeth, vii. 584.
— of Dirleton, Christian, wife of John de Haliburton, ix. 102.
— — John de, vii. 6.
— — William de, iv. 332.
— — *, wife of Patrick Hepburn, yr. of Hailes, ii. 138.
— of Librack, Patrick, v. 264.
— — his wife, Margaret Maclellan, v. 264.
— of Many, John, ii. 64; viii. 53.
— — Margaret, wife of John Carnegie, viii. 53.
— Alexander, bishop of Caithness and Whitherne, viii. 576.
— Ethana de, wife of William de Maule of Panmure, vii. 6.
— Isabella, wife of John Acarsane of Glen, v. 106.
— John, husband of Margaret Dunbar, iii. 278.
— Margaret de, wife of Sir John Lyle, v. 551.

* Name unknown.

Vaus, Maria de, wife of Sir Thos. Somerville of Linton, viii. 5.
— *, wife of John Carnegie of Kinnaird, viii. 51.
Vavasour of Hazlewood, Sir Edward, iv. 422.
— Marcia, wife of 10th lord Herries of Terregles, iv. 422.
Veitch of Dawyck, John, viii. 402.
— — his wife, Janet Stewart, viii. 402.
— — Sir John, king's architect, iv. 586, 587.
— — William, viii. 531.
— — his wife, Mariota Fleming, viii. 531.
— — *, vii. 91.
— — his *supposed* wife, Mary Anne Colyear, vii. 91.
— of Eliock, George Douglas, ii. 416 *n.*
— — William, W.S., ii. 416.
— James, merchant, Dumfries, ii. 391.
— — his wife, Agnes Carlyle, ii. 391.
— William, minister of Dumfries, i. 365.
Vendôme, counts of, iv. 398.
— Jean, comte de, i. 154.
Ventry, Dayrolles Blakeney (de Moleyns), 4th lord, iv. 504.
Vere of Blackwood, Katharine, wife of Charles Hope of Craigiehall, iv. 494.
— — Sir William, iv. 494.
— of Stonebyres, Sir William, ii. 27.
— — his wife, * Hamilton, ii. 27.
— of Tilbury, Horatio (Vere), lord, iii. 599.
— Anne, wife of 3rd lord Fairfax, iii. 599.
— Diana, wife of 1st duke of St. Albans, i. 32.
— Elizabeth, wife of 6th earl of Derby, i. 488; v. 467.
— Sir Francis, captain of Portsmouth, viii. 412.
— — his wife, Elizabeth Dent, viii. 412.
— Sir Horace, iii. 599.
Verelst, Dirk Hubert, Dutch ambassador to Berlin, i. 91.
— — his wife, Sarah Lydia Diodati, i. 91.
Veremund, Richard, canon of St. Andrews, v. 575.
Vernatti, Anna Margaret, wife of F. Edwards of Welham Grove, iv. 385.
Vernon of Hanbury Hall, Sir Harry Foley, 1st bart., iv. 327.
— *, M.P. for Whitechurch, vii. 259.
Vernuz, Constance de, wife of Sir Adam de Gurdon, iv. 510.
— John de, iv. 510.
Verschoyle of Kilberry, Robert, viii. 230.
— Augusta, wife of capt. A. M. Drummond, viii. 230.
Verulam, Francis (Bacon), lord, ii. 558.

* Name unknown.

Verulam of Gorhambury, James Bucknall (Grimston), 1st baron, iv. 96.
—— —— James Walter (Grimston), 1st earl of, iv. 96, 97.
—— —— James Walter (Grimston), 2nd earl of, iv. 98; v. 515.
—— —— James Walter (Grimston), 3rd earl of, iv. 98.
Vesci of Sprouston, Eustace de, i. 5; iv. 330.
—— —— his wife, Margaret, i. 5.
—— William de, the Competitor, i. 5.
Veterepontе, William de, v. 277; viii. 319 *n*.
Vickers, Florence Evelyn, wife of W. H. Hamilton-Gordon, i. 97.
—— Thos. Edward, C.B., i. 97.
Vieane, Nicola, viii. 293.
Vienne, Jean de, admiral of France, i. 146, 234; iii. 155; vi. 299; viii. 329, 422.
Vigurus, Thomas, burgess of Roxburgh, vii. 366.
Vilage, colonel de, viii. 374.
Villiers, James Fitzgerald, eldest son of 1st earl of Grandison; styled lord, iii. 611.
—— of Brokesby, Sir Edward, vi. 378.
—— Augustus John, ix. 85.
—— —— his wife, Georgiana Augusta Henrietta Keith-Elphinstone, ix. 85.
—— Caroline Elizabeth, wife of (1) 1st marquess of Anglesey, and (2) 6th duke of Argyll, i. 388.
—— Charles, rector of Croft, iv. 98.
—— Charles Hyde, major Royal Horse Guards, vii. 359.
—— —— his wife, Victoria Alexandrina Innes-Ker, vii. 359.
—— Sir Edward, knight-marshal, ii. 207.
—— —— his 1st wife, Frances Howard, ii. 207.
—— Elizabeth, wife of Robert, 7th earl of Morton, vi. 378; ix. 141.
—— Elizabeth, wife of George (Hamilton), 1st earl of Orkney, vi. 579.
—— Gertrude Amelia, wife of lord Henry Stuart, ii. 306.
—— Gertrude Mary Amelia, wife of rev. R. Grimston, iv. 98.
—— Henrietta, wife of 2nd earl of Breadalbane, ii. 207.
—— Henry Windsor, son of lord Stuart de Decies, ii. 307.
—— Mary, wife of (1) Charles, lord Herbert, (2) James, 4th duke of Lennox, and (3) col. Thos. Howard, v. 360.
Villiers-Stuart of Castletown, William, ii. 307.
—— —— his wife, Katharine Cox, ii. 307.
—— of Dromana, Henry, M.P., ii. 306.
—— —— his alleged wife, Madam de Ott, ii. 307.
—— Charles, ii. 307.
—— —— his wife, Elizabeth Smollett, ii. 307.
Villiers-Stuart, Gertrude Amelia, dau. of lord Henry S., ii. 307.
Vincent of Barnborough Grange, Thomas, ii. 416.
—— of Stoke d'Abernon, Sir Francis, vii. 224.
—— Margaret, wife of 5th earl of Carnwath, ii. 416.
—— Mary, wife of 3rd earl of Rosebery, vii. 224.
—— Sir William, rector of Postwick, ii. 279.
—— —— his wife, Margaret Erskine, ii. 279.
Vipont, William de, v. 277; viii. 319 *n*.
Vismes, Elizabeth de, wife of rev. E. A. Drummond-Hay, v. 233.
—— William, count de, v. 233.
Vivian of Bosahan, Sir Arthur Pendarves, viii. 162.
—— —— his wife, Jane Georgina Dalrymple, viii. 162.
—— Thomas, iii. 113.
—— —— his wife, Mary Scrope, iii. 113.
Vost, William, vii. 207.
—— —— his wife, Annabella Rollo, vii. 207.
Vygh, baron, of the Snor and Appelenburg, vii. 171.
—— —— his wife, Frances Jacoba Mackay, vii. 171.

Wade, George, v. 484.
—— —— his wife, Frances Ker, v. 484.
Wadsworth, Elise, wife of C. A. Murray, iii. 393.
—— James, Geneseo, N.Y., iii. 393.
Wake, Margaret, wife of (1) John Comyn, and (2) Edmund of Woodstock, i. 510.
—— Thomas, lord of Liddell, i. 510.
Wakefield, John, lieut.-col. H.E.I.C.S., viii. 82.
—— Maria Priscilla, wife of Geo. Carnegie, viii. 82.
Wakeman of Beckford, William, iv. 419.
—— Edmund, iv. 419.
—— Theresa Apollonia, wife of Marmaduke Constable-Maxwell, iv. 419.
Walcher, bishop of Durham, iii. 242.
Waldegrave, Henry (Waldegrave), 1st lord, i. 34.
—— —— his wife, Henrietta FitzJames, i. 34.
—— William Frederick (Waldegrave), 8th lord, vii. 309.
Waldegrave-Leslie, George, vii. 309.
—— —— his wife, Henrietta, countess of Rothes, vii. 309.
Waldemar, king of Denmark, vi. 569.
Walden, Hay, viscount of, viii. 453-474.
Walden, Arthur, 2nd son of 8th marquess of Tweeddale; styled viscount of, viii. 472.
—— —— his 1st wife, Helena Eleanora Augusta de Kielmansegge, ix. 168.
—— —— his 2nd wife, Julia Charlotte Sophia Stewart-Mackenzie, ix. 168.

Walden, John, first viscount of, viii. 453.
Waldeve of Allerdale, 2nd son of 1st earl of Dunbar, iii. 243.
—— —— his wife, Sigrid, iii. 244.
Waldeve of Dundas, Inverkeithing, and Bassenthwaite, son of Gospatric, iii. 244.
Waldeve of Edlingham, son of Edward, iii. 248.
Waldeve of Tyndale, i. 504.
Waldeve, abbot of Croyland, iii. 244.
Waldeve, son of Alan of Allerdale, iii. 244.
Waldeve, son of Gillemin, iii. 245.
—— —— his wife, Octreda *or* Ethreda, iii. 245.
Waldeve, abbot of Melrose, iii. 254 *n.*
Waldeve, the clerk, rector of Dunbar, son of 6th earl of Dunbar, iii. 257.
Waldrum, Mary, wife of P. Maule of Panmure, vii. 20.
Wales, Caroline Elizabeth of Brunswick, wife of George, prince of, ix. 90.
—— James Francis, prince of, iii. 579.
—— Llewellyn, prince of, iv. 9.
Walker of Dalry, James, W.S., viii. 461.
—— —— his 1st wife, Jean Hay-Newton, viii. 461.
—— of Innerdovat, Dr. James, vi. 115.
—— —— his wife, Mary Leslie, vi. 115.
—— of Manor House, Bushey, Frederick Nathaniel, general, vii. 492.
—— Agnes, wife of vice-admiral Alex. Boyle, iv. 209.
—— Sir Baldwin Wake, admiral, bart., K.C.B., ii. 354.
—— —— his wife, Mary Katharine Sinclair Worth, ii. 354.
—— Georgina Adelaide Forestier, wife of (1) Wm. Stuart of Tempsford Hall, and (2) James, 9th earl of Seafield, vii. 492.
—— James, C.E., iv. 209.
—— Jane, wife of (1) Dalhousie Watherstone, and (2) Wm. Mordaunt Maitland, v. 318.
—— Margaret, wife of William Maitland, v. 309.
—— Sarah, wife of William Fairfax, iii. 600.
—— Thomas, major, Nassau, Bahamas, iii. 600.
—— Thomas, in holy orders, v. 318.
—— *, Westminster, v. 124 *n.*
—— *, Middlesex, ix. 48.
—— —— his wife, Dorothy Erskine, ix. 48.
Walker-Drummond of Hawthornden, Sir Francis, viii. 461.
Walkinshaw of Barrowfield, John, i. 36.
—— —— John, colonel, viii. 306.
—— of Walkinshaw, John, ii. 407.
—— —— his wife, Margaret Hamilton, ii. 407.
—— —— John, ii. 46.
—— Anne, wife of Jas. Hamilton, ii. 46.

* Name unknown.

Walkinshaw, Clementina Mary Sophia mistress of prince Charles Edward Stewart, i. 36.
—— Mary, wife of Wm. Hamilton of Leat, i. 42.
Wall, Joseph, Goree, vii. 512.
—— —— his wife, Frances Mackenzie, vii. 512.
Wallace, Thomas (Wallace), 1st lord, iv. 498, 503.
—— —— his wife, Jean Hope, iv. 498.
—— of Auchans, John, ii. 81.
—— —— his wife, Agnes Stewart, ii. 81.
—— of Cairnhill, iv. 187.
—— —— Sir John, ii. 518.
—— of Corsbie, William, minister of Failfuird, v. 165.
—— of Craigie, Elizabeth, ii. 506.
—— —— Hugh, ii. 512; vii. 370.
—— —— his wife, Margaret Rutherfurd, vii. 370.
—— —— Sir John, vi. 365, 585.
—— —— his wife, Margaret Douglas, vi. 365.
—— —— John, the younger, ii. 456.
—— —— his contr. wife, Marion Kennedy, ii. 456.
—— —— John, ii. 512.
—— —— his wife, Sibella Cathcart, ii. 512.
—— —— John, ii. 516.
—— —— John, iv. 241.
—— —— his wife, Margaret Cunningham, iv. 241; ix. 97.
—— —— Sir John, v. 497.
—— —— his wife, Margaret Campbell, v. 497.
—— —— Sir John, i. 194; iii. 175; iv. 159; vi. 483.
—— —— his 1st wife, Margaret Maxwell, vi. 483.
—— —— his 2nd wife, Elizabeth Douglas, iii. 175.
—— —— Matthew, ii. 509.
—— —— Sir Thomas, v. 494.
—— —— Sir Thomas, lord of Session, vi. 69.
—— —— Sir William, ii. 456; iii. 21.
—— —— his wife, Margaret Dunbar, iii. 21.
—— —— William, iii. 226.
—— —— his wife, Elizabeth Campbell of West Loudoun, iii. 226.
—— —— William, ii. 471; vii. 545.
—— —— his wife, Margaret Kennedy, ii. 471.
—— of Craigo and Carnhill, James, ii. 510 *n.*
—— —— William, ii. 510 *n.*
—— —— his wife, Elena Chalmer, ii. 510 *n.*
—— of Dundonald, John, ii. 81; iv. 158.
—— —— his alleged wife, Katharine Herries, iv. 158, 408.
—— —— his wife, Agnes Stewart, ii. 81.

Wallace of Elderslie, Hugh, viii. 391.
—— —— his wife, Isabel Sandilands, viii. 391.
—— —— Sir Malcolm, v. 490; viii. 522.
—— —— his wife, Margaret Crauford, v. 490.
—— —— Sir William, the patriot, i. 509; iii. 140, 301; v. 334, 490.
—— of Glentig, John, ii. 455.
—— of Helenton, William, advocate, ix. 97.
—— —— his wife, Elizabeth Cunningham, ix. 97.
—— of Showalton, Edward, iv. 200.
—— —— William, iv. 198.
—— —— his wife, Mary Boyle, iv. 198.
—— of Sundrum, Sir Duncan, ii. 506; iii. 142; viii. 380 *bis*.
—— —— his wife, Eleonora Douglas, ii. 437; iii. 142; ix. 55.
—— of Thornlie, John, ii. 458 *n*.
—— —— his wife, Katharine Kennedy, ii. 458 *n*.
—— Elene, wife of 1st lord Hailes, ii. 142.
—— Elizabeth, wife of 6th lord Boyd, v. 166.
—— Euphame, wife of Sir Robt. Colville, ii. 541.
—— Euphemia, wife of John, 1st earl of Melfort, vi. 69.
—— Esther, wife of Andrew Stewart, ix. 111.
—— Isabel, wife of David Boswell of Auchinleck, ii. 518.
—— Isobel, wife of Sir H. Campbell of Loudoun, v. 494.
—— James, son of John W., iv. 408 *n*.
—— Janet, wife of Alex. Kennedy of Glentig, ii. 456.
—— John, son of Wm. W. of Craigo, ii. 510 *n*.
—— John, tutor of Craigie, iv. 408.
—— Sir John, 1304, v. 138.
—— Katharine, wife of (1) Robert Barclay of Pearstoun, and (2) John Boyle of Ballikewin, iv. 187.
—— Margaret, wife of 4th lord Cathcart, ii. 516.
—— Margaret, wife of Jas. Colvill, ii. 574.
—— Margaret, wife of (1) * Ross of Hayning, and (2) col. David Boyd of Tourgill, v. 163; vi. 514.
—— Margaret, wife of 1st lord Lyle, v. 553.
—— Margaret, wife of Wm. Dalrymple of Stair, viii. 116.
—— Robert, bishop of the Isles, v. 564; ix. 97.
—— —— his wife, Anna Cunningham, ix. 97.
—— William, in Cassendilly, ii. 574.
—— William, son of John W., iv. 408.
—— *, wife of Sir Alan of Cathcart, ii. 505.
Walleis, Elizabeth, wife of William Constable, iii. 292.
—— Sir John, v. 138.

* Name unknown.

Walleis, William, co. Lincoln, iii. 292.
Wallingford, William (Knollys), viscount, v. 71.
Wallis, Katharine, wife of (1) Robert Barclay of Pearstoun, and (2) John Boyle of Ballikewin, iv. 187.
Wallop, Katharine, wife of col. Lockhart Gordon, i. 104; ix. 6 *bis*, 7.
Wallscourt, Joseph Henry (Blake), 1st lord, iii. 583.
Walmesley, Anne, wife of Sir Edward Osborne, iii. 301.
Walpole, Charlotte, wife of Lionel, 5th earl of Dysart, iii. 411; ix. 80.
—— Sir Edward, K.B., iii. 411.
—— Horace, i. 386; ix. 80, 82.
—— Maria, wife of (1) James, 2nd earl Waldegrave, and (2) prince William Henry, duke of Gloucester, iii. 411.
Walrave, Macktellina, wife of Thomas, viscount Teviot, viii. 376.
Walrond of Calder Park, Theodore, iv. 211.
—— Jane, wife of John Boyle, iv. 211.
Walsingham, William, iii. 608.
—— —— his wife, Joyce Denny, iii. 608.
Walter of Barrone, in Bute, ii. 286.
Walter of Culgask, son of Alan of Ruthven, iv. 255.
—— —— his wife, Cecilia of Strathearn, iv. 255.
Walter of Cultmalundie, son of Edgar, vi. 531.
Walter of Faslane, v. 330, 337.
—— —— his wife, Margaret, countess of Lennox, v. 330, 337.
Walter of Machan, son of Gilbert, i. 510.
Walter, son of Alan, 'dapifer regis,' ii. 503.
Walter, 2nd son of Sweyn of Crawford, iv. 255 *bis*.
Walter, bishop of Glasgow, v. 489.
Walter, son of Aldwyn, vi. 79.
Walter of Sarsden, Sir William, bart., iii. 479.
—— —— his wife, Mary Bruce, iii. 479.
—— of Stalbridge, Edward, M.P., iv. 95.
—— —— his wife, Harriet Forrester, iv. 95.
—— Harriet, wife of 3rd viscount Grimston, iv. 96.
—— Hester, wife of Peter Schuyler, ii. 495.
—— John, New York, ii. 495.
—— Maria, wife of (1) A. Schuyler, and (2) Archibald Kennedy, ii. 494.
—— Neville, in holy orders, i. 60.
—— —— his wife, Rachel Hamilton, i. 60.
—— Robert, New York, ii. 495.
Walters, Anna Maria, wife of 8th marquess of Queensberry, vii. 155.
—— Anne, wife of John Busfield, and aunt of Lucy Walters, i. 30.
—— Lucy, mistress of king Charles II., i. 30; ii. 238.

Walters, Mary, wife of (1) Wm. Sarsfield, and (2) Wm. Fanshaw, i. 30.
—— Thomas, vicar of Boyton, vii. 155.
—— William, Haverfordwest, ii. 238.
—— —— his wife, Elizabeth Protheroe, ii. 238.
Waltheof, earl of Huntingdon, i. 3.
Waltheof of Allerdale, 2nd son of 1st earl of Dunbar, iii. 243.
—— —— his wife, Sigrid, iii. 244.
Waltheof, abbot of Croyland, iii. 244.
Walton of Fole, James, i. 400.
—— Margery, wife of John Aston, i. 400.
—— John, viii. 139.
—— Rosina, wife of Campbell James Dalrymple, viii. 139.
WANDELL, DOUGLAS, LORD, iv. 77-79.
Wandell, Archibald, first lord, iv. 77.
—— Archibald, second lord, iv. 78.
Wantage, Robert (Lindsay), V.C., K.C.B., lord, i. 524.
—— —— his wife, Harriet Loyd Jones, i. 524.
Warbeck, Perkin, the pretender, iv. 530.
—— —— his wife, Katharine Gordon, iv. 530.
Warburton of Winnington, Thomas, i. 376.
—— Jane, wife of duke of Argyll and Greenwich, i. 376.
Ward, William Humble (Ward), 10th baron, i. 392.
—— Alice, wife of M. P. G. D. Drummond, viii. 225.
—— Joseph, London, i. 410 *n.*
—— Julia Susannah, wife of (1) A. H. A. Anson, and (2) bishop Claughton, i. 392.
—— William C., viii. 225.
Warde, George, H.E.I.C.S., i. 492.
—— —— his wife, Anne Amelia Dashwood, i. 492.
Wardlaw of Hownam, Henry, vii. 326.
—— of Kilbaberton, John, iii. 64; ix. 63.
—— —— his wife, Margaret Cockburn, iii. 64.
—— —— Robert, ix. 113.
—— —— his wife, Margaret Carmichael, ix. 113.
—— of Otterston, Elizabeth, wife of Walter Leslie of Cowcairnie, vii. 291.
—— —— Isabella, vii. 291.
—— of Pitreavie, Sir Henry, viii. 178.
—— of Riccarton, James, ii. 144.
—— —— William, vi. 417.
—— —— his wife, Abellina Napier, vi. 417.
—— of Spot, Henry, iii. 276 *n.*
—— of Torrie, Andrew, vii. 290.
—— —— his contr. wife, Beatrix Leslie, vii. 290.
—— —— Andrew, vii. 296.
—— —— his 1st wife, Agnes Leslie, vii. 296.
—— —— Henry, vi. 539; vii. 326.
—— —— his wife, Margaret Oliphant, vi. 539.
Wardlaw of Torrie, Henry, iv. 457; vii. 281, 546; ix. 83.
—— —— his contr. wife, Grisel Leslie, vii. 281.
—— —— his contr. wife, Agnes Murray, iii. 502; ix. 83.
—— —— his 1st wife, Alison Home, iv. 457.
—— —— John, iii. 309; vii. 281.
—— Agnes, wife of Alex. Colville, ii. 549.
—— Christian, wife of * de Hay of Locherworth, viii. 422.
—— Elizabeth, wife of David Melville, iii. 92.
—— Elizabeth, wife of Sir Anthony Alexander, viii. 179.
—— Helen, wife of Sir James Makgill, and *probably* dau. of Thomas W. of Foulford, vi. 587.
—— Henry, bishop of St. Andrews, iii. 275, 276; iv. 564.
—— Isobel, wife of Sir A. Hepburn, ii. 144.
—— James, advocate, vi. 593.
—— —— his wife, Isobel Cuninghame, vi. 593.
—— Jonet, sister of Henry W. of Spot, iii. 276 *n.*
—— Jonet, dau. of Henry W. of Spot, iii. 276 *n.*
—— Margaret, sister of Henry W. of Spot, iii. 276 *n.*
—— Margaret, wife of William Maitland of Thirlestane, v. 289.
—— Margaret, wife of Henry Makgill, vi. 591.
—— Marion, wife of (1) Jas. Scrimgeour, and (2) Sir A. Hepburne, ii. 145; iii. 309.
—— Robert, v. 403.
—— —— his wife, Martha Fernie, v. 402.
—— William, brother of Henry W. of Spot, iii. 276 *n.*
—— * wife of Sir John Carmichael of Carmichael, iv. 564.
Wardlaw-Ramsay of Whitehill, Robert, captain, iii. 43.
—— —— his wife, Anne Lindsay, iii. 43.
—— —— Robert Balfour, viii. 471.
—— —— his wife, Louisa Jane Hay, viii. 471.
—— R. E., captain, viii. 472.
Wardrop, James, M.D., viii. 138.
—— —— his wife, Margaret Dalrymple, viii. 138.
—— John of, v. 329.
—— —— his wife, Mary, v. 329.
Ware, Samuel Hibbert, M.D., i. 493.
—— —— his wife, Charlotte Wilhelmina Murray, i. 493.
Warenne of Coventre, Reginald de, vi. 530; vii. 398.
—— Ada de, wife of Henry, earl of Northumberland and Huntingdon, i. 4; viii. 560 *n.*

* Name unknown.

Warenne, Isabella de, wife of John Baliol, king of Scotland, i. 7.
— John de, earl of Surrey, i. 7.
— William de, 2nd earl of Surrey, i. 4.
Warin of Mira, ii. 376.
Waring of Lennel, Walter, captain, M.P., viii. 473.
— — his wife, Susan Elizabeth Clementine Hay, viii. 473.
Warnebald, father of Robert, vi. 170.
Warrand of Lentran, v. 546.
Warren, William, i. 536.
— — his wife, Anne Gouldsmith, i. 536.
— *, Cheshire, iii. 406.
— — his wife, Grace Wilbraham, iii. 406.
Warrender of Bruntsfield, Sir John, v. 320.
— — his wife, Julian J. Maitland, v. 320.
— of Lochend, Sir John, 2nd bart., vi. 432.
— — Sir John, 5th bart., iv. 328.
— — Sir Patrick, 3rd bart., viii. 128.
— Charlotte, wife of Sir John Dalrymple of North Berwick, viii. 128.
— Grizel, wife of capt. Charles Napier of Merchiston Hall, vi. 432.
— Helen Catherine, wife of 11th earl of Haddington, iv. 328.
Warwick, Francis (Greville), 1st earl of, iv. 167.
— — his wife, Elizabeth Hamilton, iv. 167.
— George (Greville), 2nd earl of, ii. 524.
— George (Greville), 4th earl of, viii. 516.
— — his wife, Anne Charteris, viii. 516.
— Sir Philip, ix. 93.
Washington, George, iii. 600, 603.
— Lawrence, iii. 600.
— Louisa, wife of 9th lord Fairfax, iii. 603.
— Susanna, wife of Reginald Graham of Nunnington, vii. 99.
— Warner, iii. 601, 603.
— Sir William, vii. 99.
Waterford, Henry (Beresford), 2nd marquess of, v. 485.
— Henry (Beresford), 3rd marquess of, ii. 304.
— — his wife, Louisa Stuart, ii. 304.
— Henry de la Poer (Beresford), 6th marquess of, vi. 400.
— — his wife, Beatrix Frances Fitzmaurice, vi. 400.
Wathen, Augustus, major 15th Hussars, vii. 308.
— — his wife, Elizabeth Jane Leslie, vii. 308.
Watherstone of Manderston, Dalhousie, v. 318.
— — his wife, Jane Walker, v. 318.
Watkins of Shotton Hall, Watkin James Yuille S., v. 420.
— — his wife, Muriel M. S. Lindsay, v. 420.

* Name unknown.

Watkins, William, Westminster, ii. 413.
— — his wife, Katharine Abingdon, ii. 413.
Watson of Aithernie, Alexander, iv. 568.
— — his wife, Margaret Lindsay, i. 516; iv. 568.
— — Anne, wife of Dr. James Smyth, iv. 568.
— of Bilton Park, George, ii. 492.
— — his wife, Clementina Kennedy, ii. 492.
— of Cranston, Thomas, v. 282.
— — William, v. 282.
— of Earnock, Sir John, 1st bart., ii. 58.
— of Gressiston, William, v. 282.
— of Muirhouse, John, vii. 175.
— — his wife, Anne Mackay, vii. 175.
— of Neilsland Sir John, ii. 58.
— of Quhylta, William, son of Mariota de Crag, v. 282.
— of Saughton, Charles, vi. 503.
— — his wife, Margaret Carnegie, vi. 503.
— — James, iv. 497.
— — his wife, Helen Hope, iv. 497.
— — James, vi. 386.
— of Southfield, Walter, i. 553.
— — his wife, Margaret Bruce, i. 553.
— of Traquair, Thomas, v. 282.
— of Turin, John, vi. 498.
— Alexander, merchant, Aberdeen, vii. 206.
— Alison, wife of P. Carnegie of Lour, vi. 498.
— Andrew, burgess of Aberdeen, v. 551.
— Charlotte, wife of the rev. Thos. Erskine, v. 634.
— David, viii. 78.
— — his wife, Katharine Carnegie, viii. 78.
— Elizabeth, wife of William Maitland of Traquair, v. 282.
— Georgina, wife of 9th lord Belhaven, ii. 58.
— Helen, wife of 17th earl of Morton, vi. 386.
— Jane, wife of 6th lord Rollo, vii. 206.
— Janet, wife of Edward Hope, iv. 486.
— John, W.S., founder of John Watson's Institution, viii. 78.
— Robert, i. 76.
— — his wife, Elizabeth Ramsay, i. 76.
— Sidney, ii. 499.
— — his wife, Ethel Mary Fowler, ii. 499.
— T. E., ix. 154.
Watson-Carnegie of Turin and Lour, Patrick, vi. 499.
— — his wife, Rachel Anne Forbes, vi. 499.
— Patrick Alexander, vi. 499.
— — his wife, Elizabeth Caroline Davidson, vi. 499.

Watson-Kennedy, Thomas Francis Archibald, lt.-col., ii. 499.
—— —— his wife, Ethel Mary Fowler, ii. 499.
Watson-Taylor of Erlestoke Park, Simon, viii. 471.
—— —— his wife, Hannah Charlotte Hay, viii. 471.
Watt of Rosehill, John, ii. 495 *n.*
Watts of Great Munden, Katharine, wife of Charles, 1st earl of Dunmore, iii. 384.
—— —— Richard, iii. 384.
—— —— his wife, Katharine Werden, iii. 384.
—— Ann, wife of 11th earl of Cassillis, ii. 495, 496.
—— John, New York, ii. 495.
—— —— his wife, * de Lancy, ii. 495.
—— Robert, New York, ii. 496.
Wauch, John, minister of Borrowstounness, iv. 92.
—— —— his wife, Christian Forrester, iv. 92.
Wauchope of Cakemuir, Francis, advocate, iv. 438.
—— —— his wife, Vere Bothwell, iv. 438.
—— —— Henry, iv. 438.
—— of Gleghornie, William, vi. 7.
—— of Keckmure, Adam, ix. 60.
—— of Niddrie-Marischal, Andrew, son of Sir John W., viii. 599.
—— Andrew, vi. 17; viii. 599.
—— —— his wife, Helen Hume, vi. 17.
—— —— Andrew, capt. 1st Dragoon Guards, vi. 21.
—— —— Archibald, vi. 591.
—— —— his wife, Rachel Makgill, vi. 591.
—— —— Sir John, v. 464; viii. 28.
—— —— his 2nd wife, Jean Ker, v. 464.
—— —— Robert, vii. 126.
—— —— his 2nd wife, Margaret Douglas, iii. 230; vii. 125.
—— —— William, viii. 436.
—— —— his wife, Beatrix Hay, viii. 436.
—— —— William, viii. 386.
—— —— his 2nd wife, Margaret Sandilands, viii. 386.
—— Agnes, wife of (1) Alex. Scott, and (2) George, 3rd earl of Linlithgow, v. 449.
—— Barbara, wife of Sir G. Seton of Garleton, viii. 599.
—— Euphemia, wife of Geo. Hay of Menzeon, ix. 166.
—— Francis, son of Francis W. of Cakemuir, iv. 438.
—— George, merchant burgess, Edinburgh, v. 449.
—— John, 3rd son of Andrew W. of Niddrie, vi. 21.
—— Margaret, wife of (1) Sir John Murray of Blackbarony, and (2 Henry Cranstoun, ii. 594; ix. 60.
—— Margaret, wife of Patrick Hume, vi. 7.

* Name unknown.

Wauchope, Robert, rear-admiral R.N., viii. 87.
—— —— his wife, Jane Carnegie, viii. 87.
—— William, 2nd son of Andrew W. of Niddrie, vi. 21.
—— William Andrew, viii. 87.
Waugh, Gilbert, lieut. 73rd regt., i. 493.
Waus, *see* Vaus.
Wauss, Sir Mawnys, provost of the church of Tain, iv. 23.
Wawane of Seggie, Christian, wife of (1) Andrew Mowbray, (2) Patrick, 5th lord Haliburton, and (3) William, 1st earl of Montrose, iv. 337; vi. 225; ix. 102, 137.
—— of Stevinston, Thomas, iv. 337.
Way, Magdalen, wife of the rev. Jas. Fleming, viii. 556.
—— Thomas, vicar-general of Ossory, viii. 556.
Weaver, William, Royal Horse Guards, vi. 335.
—— —— his wife, Mary Douglas, *suo jure* baroness Mordingtoun, vi. 335.
Webb of Welford, Joseph, vi. 457.
—— Anne, wife of 5th earl of Newburgh, vi. 457.
—— John, ii. 580.
—— —— his wife, Mary Richardson, ii. 580.
—— William, London, vii. 512.
—— —— his wife, Margaret Mackenzie, vii. 512.
Webb-Weston of Sutton Place, John, iv. 419.
—— —— his wife, Mary Maxwell-Constable, iv. 419.
Webbe, Elizabeth, wife of (1) Fulke Woodhull, and (2) Robert Cheyne, vi. 463.
—— George Allan, captain 15th Hussars, iii. 586.
—— John, gentleman-usher to Edward VI., vi. 463.
Webber, Amelia, wife of 8th lord Colville of Culross, ii. 563.
Webster, Alexander, D.D., iii. 349 *n.*
—— —— his wife, Mary Erskine, iii. 349 *n.*
Wedderburn of Ballindean, Sir John, 6th bart., i. 128; iv. 502.
—— —— his wife, Margaret Ogilvy, i. 128.
—— of Blackness, viii. 56.
—— —— Sir John, viii. 109.
—— —— his wife, Jean Fullarton, viii. 109.
—— of Gosford, Sir Peter, 1st bart., ii. 574.
—— of Wedderburn, J. L. Scrymgeour, i. 316.
—— —— his wife, Helen Arbuthnott, i. 316.
—— Alexander, lord chancellor, vii. 588.
—— Elizabeth, wife of (1) Archibald Campbell of Invertschie and Dunfallinch, and (2) Patrick Lyon, v. 500.
—— Janet, wife of Robert Ayton Colville, ii. 574.
—— Janet, wife of Sir Henry Erskine of Alva, vii. 587.

Wedderburn, John, Jamaica, i. 130.
—— —— his wife, Helen Ogilvy, i. 130.
—— Harry George, iv. 571.
—— —— his wife, Jane T. Carmichael, iv. 571.
—— Louisa Dorothea, wife of 4th earl of Hopetoun, iv. 502.
—— Marjorie, wife of Robert Carnegie of Leuchland, viii. 56.
—— Doctor, v. 380.
Wedderburn-Colvile of Inveresk, James, vii. 523.
—— Jean, wife of 5th earl of Selkirk, vii. 523.
Wedderspoon, Elizabeth, wife of Alex. Livingston of Westquarter, vi. 448.
—— Robert, burgess of Linlithgow, vi. 448.
Weedon, Edward Charles, vii. 154.
—— Ethel, wife of * de Courcy Adams, and bigamous wife of 8th marquess of Queensberry, vii. 154.
WEICK, CAMPBELL, LORD, ii. 203, 204.
Weick, John, first lord, ii. 203.
Weiller, Wilhelm, baron von, Heidelberg, ii. 497.
—— —— his wife, Frances Kennedy, ii. 497.
Weir of Birkhill, William, iv. 583.
—— of Blackwood, George, iii. 96.
—— —— his 1st wife, Margaret Weir, iii. 96.
—— —— Sir George, bart., iii. 488.
—— —— his 2nd wife, Helen Bruce, iii. 488.
—— —— James, iii. 96.
—— —— his wife, Marion Ramsay, iii. 96.
—— —— Katharine, wife of Charles Hope of Craigiehall, iv. 494.
—— —— Randolph, viii. 8, 11.
—— —— his wife, Mary Somerville, viii. 11.
—— —— Thomas, viii. 8.
—— —— Thomas, viii. 15.
—— —— his wife, Giles Somerville of Broughton and Mossmening, viii. 15.
—— —— Sir William, ix. 37.
—— —— his wife, Rachel Hamilton, ix. 37.
—— —— Sir William, iv. 494; viii. 408.
—— —— his 2nd wife, Christian Anstruther, viii. 408.
—— of Clowburn, Hugh, iv. 580.
—— —— his wife, Abigail Carmichael, iv. 580; ix. 113.
—— of Poniehill, William, iv. 583.
—— —— his wife, Katharine Carmichael, iv. 583.
—— of Stonebyres, James, iv. 589.
—— —— his wife, Rachel Carmichael, iv. 589.
—— —— William, viii. 371.
—— —— his wife, Isobel Cunningham, viii. 371.
—— William, the yr., ix. 14.
—— —— his wife, Janet Johnstone, i. 246; viii. 371; ix. 14.
—— —— William, iii. 96.

* Name unknown.

Weir, Cornelius, burgess of Edinburgh, iii. 509, 510.
—— John, vii. 252.
—— —— his wife, Christian Ross, vii. 252.
—— Katharine, wife of (1) Wm. Maxwell of Cavens, (2) Sir James Murray of Kilhaberton, and (3) Patrick, 1st lord Elibank, iii. 127, 509, 510.
—— Margaret, wife of Robt. Carlyle, ii. 386.
—— Margaret, wife of George Weir, iii. 96.
Weld of Lulworth Castle, Edward, i. 413.
—— —— his wife, Katharine Elizabeth Aston, i. 412.
—— Elizabeth Katharine, wife of 2nd lord Carrington, ii. 566.
Welles, John (de Welles), 5th lord, iii. 15.
Wellesley, Elizabeth, wife of Chichester Fortescue of Dromiskin, v. 482.
Wellington, Arthur Richard (Wellesley), 2nd duke of, viii. 472.
—— —— his wife, Elizabeth Hay, viii. 472.
Wells of Bickley, William, viii. 232.
—— of Holmwood, William, viii. 517.
—— —— his wife, Louisa Charteris, viii. 516.
—— Susannah, wife of rev. H. R. Drummond, viii. 232.
Welsh, Mr. John, the preacher, ii. 29; v. 117.
WEMYSS, WEMYSS, EARL OF, viii. 475-513.
Wemyss, David, second earl of, ii. 282; viii. 501.
—— —— his 1st wife, Anna Balfour, i. 544; viii. 503.
—— —— his 2nd wife, Helenor Fleming, viii. 503, 550; ix. 168.
—— —— his 3rd wife, Margaret Leslie, vii. 81, 299; viii. 503.
—— David, third earl of, ii. 283; viii. 506.
—— —— his 1st wife, Anna Douglas, vii. 140; viii. 507, 515.
—— —— his 2nd wife, Mary Robinson, viii. 507.
—— —— his 3rd wife, Elizabeth St. Clair, vii. 588; viii. 507.
—— James, fourth earl of, viii. 508.
—— —— his wife, Janet Charteris of Amisfield, viii. 509.
—— John, first earl of, viii. 500.
—— —— his wife, Jean Gray, iv. 286; viii. 500; ix. 168.
—— Margaret, wife of (1) James, lord Burntisland, and (2) George, 1st earl of Cromartie; countess of, ii. 282; iii. 77; viii. 504; ix. 49.
WEMYSS, WEMYSS-CHARTERIS, EARL OF, viii. 513-515.
Wemyss, Francis, *de jure* fifth earl of, viii. 509, 512.
—— —— his wife, Katharine Gordon, iv. 553; viii. 513.

Wemyss, Francis, sixth earl of, vii. 140; viii. 514.
—— —— his wife, Margaret Campbell, viii. 515.
WEMYSS, WEMYSS-CHARTERIS-DOUGLAS, EARL OF, viii. 515-518.
Wemyss, Francis, seventh earl of, viii. 516.
—— —— his wife, Louisa Bingham, viii. 516.
—— Francis, eighth earl of, viii. 517.
—— —— his 1st wife, Anne Frederica Anson, viii. 517.
—— —— his 2nd wife, Grace Blackburn, viii. 517.
WEMYSS OF ELCHO, WEMYSS, LORD, viii. 499-518.
Wemyss of Elcho, John, first lord, v. 533; viii. 499.
WEMYSS OF WEMYSS, WEMYSS-CHARTERIS, BARON, viii. 515-518.
Wemyss of Wemyss, Francis, first baron, viii. 514.
WEMYSS, LORD BURNTISLAND, ii. 281-284.
WEMYSS, LORD ELCHO, viii. 500-518.
WEMYSS, LORD METHIL, viii. 500-518.
WEMYSS, EARL OF WEMYSS, viii. 475-518.
WEMYSS, LORD WEMYSS OF ELCHO, viii. 499-518.
Wemyss of Ardargie, Sir David, viii. 478.
—— —— Sir John, viii. 485.
—— of Auchleven, David, viii. 484.
—— of Balbedie, Sir David, viii. 478.
—— of Balfarg, David, sheriff of Fife, viii. 494.
—— —— his wife, Mary Wemyss, viii. 494.
—— —— Sir James, viii. 494, 496.
—— —— Sir James, viii. 493.
—— of Balhall, Sir David, viii. 486.
—— —— John, viii. 485.
—— of Balhepburn, John, viii. 485.
—— of Ballinkillie and Ballinald, Sir David, viii. 486.
—— of Bogie, Sir James, viii. 493.
—— —— his 1st wife, Margaret Melville, vi. 102; viii. 494.
—— —— his 2nd wife, Elizabeth Durie, viii. 494.
—— —— Sir James, 1st bart., viii. 494, 496.
—— —— his wife, Anna Aytoun, viii. 496.
—— —— Sir James, 3rd bart., viii. 496.
—— —— Sir John, viii. 494, 495.
—— —— his 1st wife, Elizabeth Aytoun, viii. 496.
—— —— his 2nd wife, Margaret Johnston, viii. 496.
—— —— Sir John, 2nd bart., viii. 496.
—— —— his wife, Anne Lockhart, viii. 496.
—— of Wester Bogie, Henry, viii. 494.
—— of Burntisland, James, general, vi. 92.
—— —— Sir James, ii. 282; viii. 488.
—— —— his wife, Margaret, countess of Wemyss, ii. 283; viii. 504.
Wemyss of Cameron, Sir David, sheriff of Fife, viii. 477, 480, 481.
—— —— his 1st wife, Margaret *, viii. 477.
—— —— his 2nd wife, Isabel Crichton, viii. 477.
—— —— Duncan, viii. 477, 481.
—— —— John, viii. 477.
—— —— his wife, Amabilla de Anesly of Cameron, viii. 477.
—— —— Sir John, viii. 477, 481.
—— —— Sir Michael, viii. 477, 480.
—— of Cameron Mill, John, viii. 485.
—— —— James, viii. 487.
—— of Capuldrae, Sir David, viii. 478.
—— of Caskieberran, James, 2nd son of David W. of that Ilk, ii. 281; viii. 488.
—— —— his wife, Janet Durie, ii. 281.
—— —— James, his eldest son, ii. 281.
—— —— his wife, Elizabeth Simpson, ii. 281.
—— —— James, general of Artillery, ii. 281; ix. 49.
—— —— his wife, *, ii. 282.
—— of Clarylaw, David, iii. 278.
—— —— John, iii. 278.
—— —— his wife, Margaret Dunbar, iii. 278.
—— of Condland, Henry, viii. 494.
—— —— his 1st wife, Isabel Kirkaldy, viii. 495.
—— —— his 2nd wife, Margaret Durie, viii. 495.
—— —— Sir James, viii. 493.
—— of Craighall, Patrick, viii. 497.
—— of Cuttlehill, William, viii. 136.
—— —— his wife, Eleonora Dalrymple-Elphinstone, viii. 136.
—— of Dron, David, captain, viii. 488.
—— —— his 1st wife, Margaret Cunningham, viii. 488.
—— —— his 2nd wife, Janet Beaton, viii. 488.
—— —— his 3rd wife, Euphame Kinninmonth, viii. 489.
—— —— James, viii. 489.
—— —— his wife, Helen Lundy, viii. 489.
—— —— Sir John, viii. 485.
—— —— Robert, viii. 489.
—— of Wester Dron, Sir Michael, viii. 480.
—— of Dunipace, Sir David, viii. 486.
—— of Earl's Seat, James, viii. 492.
—— —— Robert, viii. 492.
—— —— his wife, Margaret Law, viii. 492.
—— of Eglisdikin, Sir David, viii. 478.
—— of Elcho, John, viii. 485.
—— of Fingask, David, ancestor of the family of, viii. 497.
—— —— David, ii. 573 *bis*; viii. 494.
—— —— his wife, Margaret Colvill, ii. 573.
—— of Foodie, David, ancestor of the family of, viii. 497.
—— of Glennistoun, Andrew, viii. 495.
—— —— James, viii. 495.

* Name unknown.

Wemyss of the Haugh, Sir John, viii. 485.
— of Hilldron, Sir David, viii. 486.
— of Inchmartin, David, iv. 29, 30; viii. 483.
— — John, iv. 30 *bis*.
— of Kilmany, Alexander, viii. 482.
— — Sir John, viii. 481.
— of Kincaldrum, Sir John, iv. 274; vi. 82; viii. 477 *bis*, 479, 480.
— of Kinnaird, John, viii. 485.
— of Kirkmichael, Sir David, viii. 486.
— of Lathockar, Alexander, ancestor of the family of, viii. 482.
— — James, vi. 549.
— — his wife, Katharine Oliphant, vi. 549.
— — Sir John, viii. 481.
— — Ronald, v. 414.
— of Easter Lathrisk, Robert, viii. 487.
— — his wife, Janet Symsoun, viii. 487.
— of Leuchars, Sir John, viii. 479.
— — Sir John, viii. 480.
— of Lochore, Sir David, viii. 478.
— of Lochhead, John, viii. 500.
— of Logie, 1592, i. 538.
— of Logie-Murdoch, Duncan, viii. 482.
— of Ludquharn, Duncan, v. 600.
— of Little Lun, John, viii. 485.
— of Markinch, Sir John, viii. 481.
— of Maw, John, viii. 500.
— of Methil, John, vi. 373.
— — his wife, Margaret Douglas, vi. 373.
— of Myrecairnie, Sir David, viii. 481.
— — Duncan, viii. 482.
— — Sir John, viii. 481.
— of Myrtoun, Sir John, viii. 481.
— of Newton, Andrew, viii. 497.
— — James, viii. 487.
— — Sir John, viii. 481.
— of Pirchock, Duncan, v. 600.
— of Wester Pitcaple, George, principal of St. Leonard's College, viii. 495.
— — his wife, Magdalene Lundie, viii. 495.
— of Pitconnochie, John, viii. 485.
— of Pitmiddil, David, iv. 29, 30.
— — Michael, tutor of Wemyss, viii. 482, 484.
— of Pittencrieff, Duncan, ancestor of the family of, viii. 482.
— — John, iv. 71 *n*.
— — his wife, Elizabeth Dishington, iv. 71 *n*.
— — John, iv. 266.
— — his wife, Dorothea Ruthven, iv. 266.
— — John, iv. 362; viii. 369.
— — his wife, Margaret Livingston, iv. 362; viii. 369.
— — Patrick, iv. 71 *n*.
— of Powguild, Gavin, 3rd son of Sir John W. of Wemyss, viii. 492.
— — his wife, Katharine Wemyss, viii. 492.
Wemyss of Wester Raith, John, viii. 477.
— of Rires, Duncan, iv. 519; v. 600; viii. 482.
— — his wife, Elizabeth Erskine, iv. 519; v. 600; viii. 482.
— — Elizabeth, wife of Arthur Forbes, iv. 71.
— — Sir John, iv. 274; vi. 82; viii. 477 *bis*.
— — his 2nd wife, Isabel Erskine, v. 592; viii. 482.
— — his *possible* 3rd wife, Christian Ogilvy, i. 110; viii. 482.
— — Sir Thomas, iv. 71.
— of Wester Rires, David, viii. 477.
— of Rumgay, Patrick, viii. 497.
— — his wife, Elizabeth Sandilands, viii. 497.
— of Strathardle, David, captain, viii. 489.
— — James, viii. 489.
— — John, vii. 408; viii. 485.
— — his wife, Christian Abernethy, vii. 408; viii. 485.
— — Robert, viii. 489.
— of Strathruddie, Sir David, viii. 478.
— of Wester Tarvit, Sir John, viii. 481.
— of Tillybreak, Grizel, wife of David Boswell of Glassmonth, viii. 485.
— — Sir John, viii. 481.
— of Unthank, David, viii. 492.
— — Gavin, 3rd son of Sir John W. of Wemyss, viii. 492.
— — his wife, Katharine Wemyss, viii. 492.
— — Gavin, vi. 590.
— — his wife, Euphame Paterson, vi. 590.
— of Wardropstoun, John, viii. 485.
— of Wemyss, Sir David, ambassador to Norway, viii. 478.
— — his 1st wife, Annabella Sinclair, viii. 478, 479.
— — his 2nd wife, Marjory Ramsay, viii. 479.
— — David, iv. 29, 30; v. 522; viii. 483; ix. 168.
— — his wife, Christian Douglas, viii. 483.
— — Sir David, iv. 278; viii. 486.
— — his 1st wife, Euphemia Lundy, viii. 487.
— — his 2nd wife, Janet Gray, iv. 278; viii. 487.
— — David, vi. 86, 87; viii. 487.
— — his 1st wife, Katharine Sinclair, vii. 572; viii. 488.
— — his 2nd wife, Mariota Towers, viii. 488.
— — David, 'with the Birken Flower,' ii. 281; iv. 261; viii. 493.
— — his wife, Cecilia Ruthven, iv. 260; viii. 493.

Wemyss of Wemyss, James, R.N., viii. 509.
—— —— his wife, Elizabeth Gordon, viii. 358, 510.
—— —— James Erskine, rear-admiral R.N., viii. 511.
—— —— his wife, Emma Hay, iii. 584; viii. 511.
—— —— Sir John, i. 451 *n.*; viii. 476.
—— —— Sir John, v. 592; viii. 480.
—— —— his 2nd wife, Isabella Erskine, v. 592; viii. 482.
—— —— his *possible* 3rd wife, Christian Ogilvy, i. 110; viii. 482.
—— —— Sir John, viii. 369, 484.
—— —— his 1st wife, Margaret Livingston, viii. 369, 484.
—— —— his 2nd wife, Heleu Dunbar, viii. 484.
—— —— Sir John, viii. 485.
—— —— his wife, Christian Abernethy, vii. 408; viii. 485.
—— —— Sir John, viii. 386, 489.
—— —— his 1st wife, Margaret Otterburn, viii. 490.
—— —— his 2nd wife, Janet Trail, viii. 491.
—— —— Sir John, admiral of the Forth, viii. 498.
—— —— his 1st wife, Margaret Douglas, viii. 498.
—— —— his 2nd wife, Mary Stewart, iii. 189; viii. 498.
—— —— Sir John, 1st bart., viii. 499.
—— —— his wife, Jean Gray, iv. 286; viii. 500.
—— —— Michael, ancestor of the family of, viii. 476.
—— —— Sir Michael, viii. 478.
—— —— his *probable* wife, * de Lochore, viii. 478.
—— —— Sir Michael, son of the ambassador, viii. 480.
—— —— William, major-general, viii. 510.
—— —— his wife, Frances Erskine, viii. 510.
—— of East Wemyss, *, wife of John Livingston of Drumry, viii. 368, 480.
—— —— *see also* Erskine-Wemyss of Wemyss.
—— of Wemyss Hall, David, viii. 492.
—— —— Gavin, ancestor of the family of, viii. 492.
—— of Wemyss-Tarvit, John, viii. 485.
—— Agnes, wife of Andrew Kinninmonth, viii. 486.
—— Agnes, wife of John Aytoun of Dynmure, viii. 491.
—— Andrew, 5th son of Sir John W. of Wemyss, ii. 336 *n.*; viii. 482.
—— Anna, wife of (1) Alex. Lindsay, and (2) Mungo, viscount Stormont, i. 514; viii. 197, 501.

* Name unknown.

Wemyss, Anna, wife of David, 3rd earl of Leven, ii. 283; vi. 112; viii. 506.
—— Anna, dau. of Thos. W., viii. 496.
—— Annabell, dau. of Thos. W., viii. 496.
—— Anne, wife of John Dalrymple-Hamilton, ii. 31; viii. 131, 512.
—— Barbara, wife of Sir H. Seton of Abercorn, viii. 497.
—— Beatrix, wife of Sir James Fraser of Brea, v. 531.
—— Cecilia, wife of 2nd earl of Tullibardine, i. 471; viii. 498.
—— Cecilia, wife of (1) A. Kinninmonth, and (2) Wm. Learmonth, viii. 497.
—— Charles, 3rd son of Sir John W. of Wemyss, viii. 485.
—— Charles, R.N., 5th son of James W. of Wemyss, viii. 510.
—— Charles, R.N., 4th son of William W. of Wemyss, viii. 511.
—— David, 7th son of Jas. W. of Caskieberran, ii. 281.
—— David, 2nd son of Jas. W. of Caskieberran, ii. 281.
—— David, eldest son of Sir John W. of Wemyss, vii. 295; viii. 498.
—— —— his wife, Elizabeth Leslie, vii. 295; viii. 498.
—— David, hostage for king David II., viii. 477.
—— David, eldest son of Robert W. of Easter Lathrisk, viii. 487.
—— David, eldest son of capt. David W. of of Dron, viii. 489.
—— Mr. David, 2nd son of Sir Jas. W. of Bogie, viii. 494.
—— —— his wife, Margaret Orrock, viii. 494.
—— David, burgess of Edinburgh, viii. 496.
—— —— his wife, Katharine Baillie, viii. 496.
—— David, 3rd son of 3rd earl of Wemyss, viii. 508.
—— David, H.E.I.C.S., viii. 510.
—— Duncan, 5th son of Jas. W. of Caskieberran, ii. 281.
—— Duncan, legtd. son of Sir John W. of Wemyss, viii. 492.
—— Elizabeth, contracted to James and Robert Colville, and wife of Alex. Wood of Lamlethan, ii. 557; viii. 497.
—— Elizabeth, wife of (1) Alexander Forbes of Pitsligo, and (2) Thomas Blair, iv. 71.
—— Elizabeth, wife of 1st lord Gray, iv. 273, 274; viii. 482.
—— Elizabeth, wife of John Strang, vii. 279.
—— Elizabeth, wife of (1) D. Balfour of Balbutby, and (2) Robert Carnegie, viii. 54, 491.
—— Elizabeth, dau. of Sir David W. of Wemyss, viii. 487.
—— Elizabeth, wife of William, 16th earl of Sutherland, viii. 358, 508.
—— Elizabeth, wife of Alex. Orrock of Orrock, viii. 495.

Wemyss, Elizabeth, dau. of David W., viii. 494.
— Elizabeth, dau. of Andrew W. of Glennistoun, viii. 495.
— Elizabeth, wife of (1) John Boswell, and (2) James Arnot, viii. 495.
— Elizabeth, dau. of Thomas W., viii. 496.
— Elizabeth, wife of John Aytoun, viii. 501.
— Elizabeth, wife of Alex. Ruthven of Halieland, ix. 99.
— Elizabeth Margaret, wife of Alex. Brodie of Arnhall, viii. 510.
— Euphame, wife of (1) Andrew Dunbar of Kilconquhar, (2) John Wemyss, and (3) David Carnegie of Kinnaird and Colluthie, iii. 278; viii. 61, 491; ix. 71.
— Euphemia, contr. wife of (1) W. Livingston of Drumry, and (2) Sir D. Ogilvy, iv. 30; viii. 369, 483.
— Euphame, wife of Peter Carmichael of Dron and Abernethy, iv. 565.
— Frances, wife of 3rd earl of Rosslyn, viii. 511.
— Frances, wife of Sir James Stewart Denholm of Coltness, viii. 512.
— Francis, captain 16th regt., viii. 510.
— Francis, lieut. R.N., viii. 511.
— Gavin, 8th son of Jas. W. of Caskieberran, ii. 281.
— Gavin, 3rd son of Jas. W. of Caskieberran, ii. 281.
— — his wife, Agnes Scott, ii. 281.
— Gavin, 2nd son of Sir John W. of Wemyss, viii. 485.
— George, partner with John Hope, viii. 497.
— Grizel, wife of (1) A. Kinninmonth, and (2) D. Ramsay, viii. 489.
— Grisel, dau. of Thomas W., viii. 496.
— Harry, vi. 494.
— Helen, wife of Hugh Dalrymple of Fordel, viii. 124, 512.
— Henry, bishop of Galloway, ii. 461.
— Isabel, dau. of Jas. W. of Caskieberran, ii. 281.
— Isobel, wife of (1) Alexander Forbes of Pitsligo, and (2) Thomas Blair, iv. 71.
— Isabella, wife of Hugh Fraser of Lovat, v. 522; viii. 483.
— Isobel, wife of 7th lord Fraser of Lovat, v. 532; viii. 499.
— Isobel, wife of (1) John Lundin of Lundin, and (2) Walter Ramsay of Pitcruvie, v. 395.
— Isobel, wife of (1) John Auchmoutie, and (2) Stephen Orme, viii. 497.
— Isabella Harriet Jane, wife of count Reventlow Criminil, viii. 511.
— James, brother of W. of Pittencrieff, viii. 489.
— — his wife, Margaret Wemyss, viii. 489.
Wemyss, James, legtd. son of David W. of Wemyss, viii. 489.
— James, parish clerk of Dysart, viii. 492.
— James, eldest son of Sir Jas. W. of Bogie, viii. 494.
— — his wife, Margaret Kinninmonth, viii. 494.
— James, elder son of Mr. David W., viii. 494.
— James, son of Dr. Ludovick W., viii. 495.
— James, 7th son of Sir James W. of Bogie, viii. 495.
— James, son of Thomas W., viii. 496.
— James, eldest son of James W. of Wemyss, viii. 510.
— James, Bengal Civil Service, viii. 510.
— — his wife, Caroline Charlotte Binfield, viii. 510.
— Janet, wife of 1st lord Colville of Ochiltree, ii. 573; viii. 499.
— Janet, dau. of James W. of Caskieberran, ii. 281.
— Janet, dau. of Mr. David W., viii. 494.
— Janet, wife of John Lundie of Easter Conland, viii. 494, 495.
— Jean, wife of (1) Archibald, earl of Angus and Ormond, and (2) George, 14th earl of Sutherland, i. 207, 544; ii. 283; iv. 77; viii. 352, 355, 503; ix. 13, 168.
— Jean, wife of Jas. Makgill of Rankeillor, vi. 588; viii. 497.
— Jean, wife of (1) Sir Alex. Towers, and (2) col. Harry Maule of Balmakellie, vii. 21; viii. 501.
— John, 3rd son of James W. of Caskieberran, ii. 281.
— John, 2nd son of lord Burntisland, ii. 283.
— John, lt.-governor of Edinburgh Castle, iii. 38.
— — his wife, Katharine Lindsay, iii. 38.
— John, son of Andrew W., ii. 336 *n.*; viii. 482.
— John, 4th son of Sir John W. of Wemyss, viii. 486.
— John, legtd. son of Robert W. of Easter Lathrisk, viii. 487.
— John, 2nd son of Sir John W. of Wemyss, viii. 491.
— John, viii. 492.
— — his wife, Eupheme Wemyss, viii. 492.
— John, illeg. son of Sir John W. of Wemyss, viii. 493.
— John, 2nd son of Mr. David W., viii. 494.
— John, godson to the earl of Rothes, viii. 504.
— John, 1547, ix. 103.
— — his wife, * Hamilton, ix. 103.

* Name unknown.

Wemyss, Jonet, wife of (1) Thos. Clephane, and (2) R. Boswell, viii. 489.
— Katharine, wife of (1) D. Carnegie of Craig, and (2) Sir A. Ker of Greenhead, viii. 67, 501; ix. 159.
— Katharine, illeg. dau. of Sir John W. of Wemyss, viii. 493.
— Katharine, wife of Sir John Haldane of Gleneagles, viii. 499.
— Katharine, dau. of Jas. W. of Wemyss, viii. 510.
— Ludovick, viii. 494.
— Ludovick, D.D., viii. 495.
— Margaret, wife of 4th earl of Northesk, ii. 283; vi. 501; viii. 506.
— Margaret, wife of 2nd lord Colville of Ochiltree, ii. 573.
— Margaret, wife of (1) Jas. Moncrieff, and (2) P. Lindsay, v. 414.
— Margaret, wife of Sir John Inchmartine of that Ilk, v. 592; viii. 480.
— Margaret, wife of Sir John Melville of Raith, vi. 89; viii. 486.
— Margaret, wife of 8th earl of Moray, vi. 325; viii. 508.
— Margaret, wife of James Wemyss, viii. 498.
— Margaret, wife of Alaster Reid *or* Robertson, viii. 489.
— Margaret, wife of D. Barclay of Collairnie, viii. 491.
— Margaret, wife of bishop John Paterson, viii. 495.
— Margaret, wife of (1) John Bethune of Blebo, and (2) Philip Hamilton of Kilbrachmont, viii. 496.
— Margaret, wife of Jas. Beaton of Creich, viii. 497.
— Margaret, dau. of 2nd earl of Wemyss, viii. 503.
— Marion, dau. of Jas. W. of Caskieberran, ii. 281.
— Mariota, wife of R. Fairlie of Braid, viii. 489.
— Mary, wife of John, 9th lord Sinclair, vii. 576; viii. 500.
— Mary, wife of David Wemyss of Balfarg, viii. 494.
— Mary, dau. of Thomas W., viii. 496.
— Mary, dau. of 2nd earl of Wemyss, viii. 504.
— Michael, captain, viii. 492.
— Patrick, 4th son of Jas. W. of Caskieberran, ii. 281.
— Patrick, legtd. son of David W. of Wemyss, viii. 489.
— Patrick, burgess of Dysart, viii. 489.
— Robert, 2nd son of Jas. W. of Caskieberran, ii. 281.
— Robert, in Caskieberran, viii. 487.
— — his wife, Janet Symsoun of Easter Lathrisk, viii. 487.
Wemyss, Robert, their 2nd son, viii. 487.
— Thomas, 6th son of Jas. W. of Caskieberran, ii. 281.
— Thomas, son of Duncan, viii. 477.
— Thomas, advocate, viii. 496.
— — his 1st wife, Christian Main, viii. 496.
— — his 2nd wife, Annabella Maxwell, viii. 496.
— Thomas, wife of Wm. Aytoun, viii. 496.
— Walpole, wife of Louis de Chastel, sieur de la Barthe, viii. 512.
— William, lieut.-general, clerk-marshal to prince Albert, viii. 511.
— — his wife, Isabella Hay, iii. 584; viii. 511.
— *, wife of John Livingston of Drumry, viii. 368, 480.
— *, wife of * Boswell of Balmuto, viii. 480.
— *, *proposed* wife of a nephew of Sir Andrew Ogilvy of Inchmartin, viii. 483.
— *, drowned at St. Andrews, viii. 495.
— *, mistress of James Wemyss, ix. 49.
Wemyss-Charteris, earl of Wemyss, viii. 513-515.
Wemyss-Charteris, baron Wemyss of Wemyss, viii. 515-518.
Wemyss-Charteris, *see* Charteris.
Wentworth, Henrietta Maria (Wentworth), baroness, ii. 240 *n*.
— of Wellesborough, Edward (Noel), 1st viscount, ix. 31.
— of Bretton, Sir Thomas, 1st bart., iii. 453.
— — his wife, Grace Popeley, iii. 453.
— of Woolley, Sir George, iii. 454, 598.
— — his wife, Anne Fairfax, iii. 597.
— Michael, iii. 454.
— — his wife, Katharine St. Quintin, iii. 454.
— Thérèse Maude St. Croix, wife of A. M. R. Douglas-Hamilton, iv. 390.
— W. B. C. A. P., capt. 78th Highlanders, iv. 390.
Werden of Cholmeaton, Sir John, 1st bart., iii. 385.
— — Robert, major-general, iii. 384.
— Katharine, wife of Richard Watts of Great Munden, iii. 384.
Werge, Margaret, wife of capt. W. H. C. Dalrymple, viii. 138.
— Oswald, lieut.-colonel, viii. 138.
Wernebald, ancestor of the family of Cunningham, iv. 222.
Werth, Hannah de, wife of John Cochrane of Waterside, iii. 350.
West, Diana, wife of lieut.-gen. Sir John Clavering, i. 387; vi. 436.
— Reginald, v. 236.
— — his wife, Ida Agnes Vane Hay, v. 236.

* Name unknown.

Westbury, Richard Pilkington (Bethell), 3rd baron, iii. 420.
—— —— his wife, Agatha Manners Tollemache, iii. 419.
Western, Anne, wife of 3rd earl of Marchmont, vi. 21.
—— Sir Thomas, vi. 21.
Westhall, David Dalrymple, lord of Session, lord, viii. 136.
Westmeath, George Frederick (Nugent), 7th earl of, iv. 503.
Westminster, Hugh Lupus (Grosvenor), 1st duke of, vii. 228; viii. 363.
—— —— his 1st wife, Constance Gertrude Sutherland-Leveson-Gower, viii. 363.
—— Richard (Grosvenor), 2nd marquess of, iii. 43; viii. 362.
—— —— his wife, Elizabeth Mary Leveson Gower, viii. 362.
Westminster, Murray, earl of, iii. 514.
Westminster, Alexander, 6th son of 4th lord Elibank; earl of, iii. 514.
Westmoreland, Charles (Fane), 3rd earl of, iii. 299.
—— —— his wife, Dorothy Brudenell, iii. 299.
—— Charles (Nevill), 6th earl of, v. 64.
—— Francis (Fane), 1st earl of, iv. 467.
—— John (Fane), 9th earl of, iv. 555.
—— —— his wife, Susan Gordon, iv. 555.
—— John (Fane), 11th earl of, iii. 124.
—— Henry (Nevill), 5th earl of, iii. 295.
—— Ralph (Nevill), 3rd earl of, iii. 183.
Weston, Elizabeth, wife of (1) John Fairlie, and (2) Peter Rollock, vii. 193.
—— Sir John de, guardian of Edward I.'s children, i. 509; vii. 427.
—— Mary, wife of 2nd lord Aston, i. 410.
Wetherspune of Brighouse, James, v. 439.
—— —— his wife, Helen Livingston, v. 439.
Weyland, Elizabeth Joanna, wife of 2nd earl of Verulam, iv. 98.
—— Richard, major, iv. 98.
Weyndis, Alexander of le, vii. 115.
Whalley, *, mistress of viscount Belhaven, ii. 37.
Wharncliffe of Wortley, Edward Montagu Stuart Granville (Montagu-Stuart-Wortley-Mackenzie), 3rd baron and 1st earl of, ii. 303.
—— —— James Archibald, 1st baron, ii. 303.
—— —— John, 2nd baron, ii. 246, 303.
Wharton, Philip (Wharton), 4th lord, vii. 261.
—— Thomas (Wharton), deputy-warden of the Marches, 1st lord, i. 222, 224, 244; vii. 17, 120.
—— Sir George, i. 367; ii. 84.
—— Margaret, wife of (1) major Dunch, (2) Sir T. Sulyarde, and (3) William, 12th lord Ross of Halkhead, vii. 261.
—— Mary, wife of (1) Jas. Campbell of Burnbank, and (2) col. Brierly, i. 367; ix. 24.

* Name unknown.

Wharwood, *, ix. 67.
—— —— his wife, Jane Maxwell, ix. 67.
Wheate, Sir Jacob, bart., captain R.N., iii. 360.
—— —— his wife, Maria Shaw, iii. 360.
Wheatley of Bracknell, Robert, iii. 217.
—— Anne, wife of 1st earl of Dumbarton, iii. 217.
—— Catharine, wife of (1) Thomas Lucy of Charlecote, and (2) George (Fitz Roy *or* Palmer), duke of Northumberland, iii. 217.
Wheeler, Brabazon, wife of lieut.-col. John Nairn, vi. 398.
Whetham, Thomas, major-general, iii. 358.
Whetle, Mary, wife of Sir J. Hanbury, ii. 581.
Whitbread of Southill, Samuel Charles, iii. 395.
—— Juliana, wife of 2nd earl of Leicester of Holkham, iii. 395.
Whitchester, Scott, lord of, ii. 237.
Whitchester, James, first lord, ii. 237.
—— —— his wife, Anna, countess of Buccleuch, ii. 237.
—— Walter John Montagu Douglas Scott, styled lord, ii. 248.
White of Ardarroch, John, v. 368.
—— —— his wife, Amelia Susannah *, v. 368.
White of Leixlip, Sir Nicholas, i. 51.
White of Maw, 1504, viii. 485.
—— —— Robert, vi. 95.
—— —— his wife, Katharine Melville, vi. 95.
—— of Walling Wells, Sir Thomas Wollaston, 2nd bart., v. 315.
—— of Wierton Grange, John Bazley, vii. 310.
—— —— his wife, Grace Leslie, vii. 310.
—— Anne, wife of C. Fagan of Feltrim, i. 51.
—— Archibald, stabler, Edinburgh, ii. 411.
—— Fanny Lucy Fowke, wife of Sir Jas. Ramsay-Gibson-Maitland, v. 315.
—— Sir John Chambers, vice-admiral R.N., K.C.B., viii. 141.
—— —— his 2nd wife, Charlotte Elizabeth Dalrymple, viii. 140.
—— Martha, wife of Charles, 5th earl of Elgin, iii. 491.
—— Sir Nicholas, seneschal of Wexford, v. 441.
—— Thomas, banker, London, iii. 491.
—— William, Aberdeen, iv. 71.
—— —— his wife, * Forbes, iv. 71.
Whitefoord of Blairquhan, Sir Adam, ii. 518.
—— —— his wife, Margaret Cathcart, ii. 518.
—— —— John, ii. 488.
—— of Milton, *, ii. 41.
—— of Whitefoord, James, iv. 581.
—— —— John, vii. 547.
—— —— his wife, Margaret Sempill, vii. 547.
—— —— Sir John, 2nd bart., viii. 140.
—— —— Sir John, 3rd bart., ii. 598.

* Name unknown.

Whitefoord of Whitefoord, Mary Ann, wife of H. K. Cranstoun, ii. 598.
— Helen, wife of J. Hamilton of Coltness, ii. 41.
— Jean, wife of capt. John Dalrymple, viii. 140.
— Walter, bishop of Brechin, i. 255; iv. 581.
— — his wife, Anna Carmichael, iv. 581; ix. 113.
Whitehead of Aston Somervile, John, viii. 44.
Whitelaw of Balmablare, James, iv. 335.
— of Newgrange, Alexander, iv. 280.
— — his wife, Geilis Gray, iv. 280.
— of Whitelaw, Mary, wife of (1) Hercules Stewart, and (2) Wm. Home, ii. 169.
— — Sir Patrick, i. 248.
— — his wife, Margaret Hamilton, i. 248; iv. 363.
— — Patrick, ii. 169.
Whiteside, Noel, ii. 59.
— R. Borras, ii. 59.
— — his wife, Lenore Agnes Watson Nisbet Hamilton, ii. 58.
Whitfield, Anne, wife of 3rd duke of Argyll, i. 380; ix. 24 *bis*.
— John, London, i. 403.
— Penelope, wife of Walter Aston, i. 403.
— Walter, major Royal Marines, i. 380; ix. 24.
Whitham, Abraham, consul-general of Majorca, iii. 516.
— Anne, wife of gen. James Murray of Beauport, iii. 516.
Whitla of Ben Eaden, George Alexander, capt. Royal Antrim Rifles, iv. 391.
— Mary Isabel Hammond, wife of C. R. S. Douglas-Hamilton, iv. 391.
Whitlaw, Isabella, wife of Andrew Ker of Romanno Grange and Fentoun, v. 454.
Whitmore of Apley Park, Thomas Charlton, vii. 152.
— — his wife, Louisa Anne Douglas, vii. 152.
— Edward, ensign in col. Lamb's regt., i. 516.
— — his wife, Janet Lindsay, i. 516.
Whitney, Perina, wife of John Cheyne of Chesham Bois, vi. 462.
— Sir Robert, vi. 462.
Whittier, Thomas Leigh, i. 307.
— — his wife, Margaret Arbuthnott, i. 307.
WHORLTON, BRUCE, BARON BRUCE OF, iii. 477-483.
Whytakers, Miles, keeper of the park of Theobalds, viii. 411.
Whyte of Estes Park, Theodore, i. 131.
— — his wife, Maude Josepha Ogilvy, i. 131.
Whyte, Andrew, major, lieut.-governor of Edinburgh Castle, i. 477.
— — his wife, Katharine Skene, i. 477.
— James, embroiderer, vi. 513.
— — his wife, Margaret Stewart, vi. 513.
Wichtane, Thomas, notary public, iii. 314 *n*.
Wickham of Parkhill, George Lamplugh, major Royal Horse Guards, iv. 561.
— — his wife, Elena Mary Gordon, iv. 561.
— of Roxby, William, v. 13.
— — his wife, Katharine Fairfax, v. 13.
— Henry, lieutenant-colonel, iv. 561.
— — his wife, Ethelreda Caroline, iv. 561.
Wicklow, Ralph Francis (Howard), 7th earl of, i. 73.
— — his wife, Gladys Mary Hamilton, i. 73.
— William (Howard), 4th earl of, iii. 46.
— — his wife, Cecil Frances Hamilton, iii. 46.
Widdrington, William (Widdrington), 4th lord, vii. 107.
— — his 2nd wife, Katharine Graham, vii. 104, 107.
— of Cheeseburn Grange, Sir Thomas, iii. 598.
— Mary, wife of (1) Geo. Ramsay, and (2) Wm. Delaval, iv. 299.
WIGAN OF HAIGH HALL, LINDSAY, BARON, iii. 43-51.
Wigan of Haigh Hall, Alexander William, second baron, iii. 47.
— — James, first baron, iii. 43.
— — James Ludovic, third baron, iii. 48.
Wiggins, Frederick Augustus, viii. 397.
— Maud Bayard, wife of commr. F. R. Sandilands, viii. 397.
Wiggons, Thomas, M.P., v. 212.
— — his wife, Margaret Kinnaird, v. 212.
Wight, Janet, wife of Wm. Ramsay, iii. 95.
Wigmore, *, wife of John Forrester of Corstorphine, iv. 85; ix. 92.
Wigram, Loftus, Q.C., M.P., vii. 524.
— — his wife, Katharine Jean Douglas vii. 524.
WIGTOWN, DOUGLAS, EARL OF, iii. 168.
Wigtown, Archibald, earl of, iii. 168; vii. 114; viii. 7.
WIGTOWN, FLEMING, EARL OF, viii. 519-524.
Wigtown, Malcolm, first earl of, iv. 226; v. 424; viii. 520.
— — his wife, Marjorie *, viii. 522.
— Marjorie, wife of William of Fawsyde; styled countess of, viii. 522, 523.
— Thomas, 2nd earl of, iii. 159; iv. 226; viii. 522, 523.
WIGTOWN, FLEMING, EARL OF, viii. 519-558.
Wigtown, Charles, seventh earl of, viii. 553, 555.

* Name unknown.

Wigtown, Charles Ross, self-styled earl of, viii. 548, 555, 556.
— John, first earl of, viii. 546.
— — his 1st wife, Lilias Graham, vi. 239; viii. 546; ix. 137.
— — his 2nd wife, Sarah Maxwell, i. 254; iv. 413; viii. 546.
— John, second earl of, ii. 360; viii. 549.
— — his wife, Margaret Livingston, v. 446; viii. 549.
— John, third earl of, viii. 551.
— — his wife, Jean Drummond, vii. 50; viii. 551; ix. 149.
— John, fourth earl of, viii. 552.
— — his wife, Anne Ker, vii. 348; viii. 552.
— John, sixth earl of, viii. 554.
— — his 1st wife, Margaret Lindsay, i. 522; viii. 554.
— — his 2nd wife, Mary Keith, vi. 62; viii. 554.
— — his 3rd wife, Euphame Lockhart, viii. 554.
— William, fifth earl of, viii. 552.
— — his wife, Henrietta Seton, iii. 374; viii. 553; ix. 78.
Wilbraham of Woodhey, Sir Thomas, 3rd bart., iii. 406.
— — his wife, Elizabeth Mitton, iii. 406.
— Grace, wife of (1) Lionel, 3rd earl of Dysart, and (2) * Warren, iii. 406.
Wildey, James, Oxford Militia, v. 135.
— Mary Anne, wife of 8th viscount of Kenmure, v. 135.
Wildman of Newstead Abbey, colonel, viii. 515.
— John, colonel, viii. 515.
— — his wife, Margaret Charteris, viii. 515.
Wilkes, John, iii. 514.
Wilkie of Foulden, Agnes, wife of 12th lord Ross of Halkhead, vii. 261.
— — Sir John, iv. 588; vii. 261.
— — his wife, Agnes Carmichael, iv. 588.
— — William, ancestor of the family of, iv. 585; viii. 372.
— of Harlawmuir, Archibald, vii. 373.
— — his wife, Isabel Rutherfurd, vii. 373.
— — Archibald, his son, vii. 373.
— Agnes, wife of Sir James Carmichael of Westraw, iv. 585.
— Bessie, wife of (1) Gavin Lockhart, and (2) Hugh Livingston, viii. 372.
— Mr. Harie minister of the Wemyss, ix. 49.
— Mr. Robert, minister at Douglas, and Glasgow, iv. 585.
Wilkieson, Elizabeth, wife of James Graham of Gartur, vi. 154.
— Philip, Balnabinch, vi. 154; ix. 136.
Wilkin, Andrew, burgess of Annan, i. 218.
— Mr. Robert, minister at Douglas, and Glasgow, iv. 585.
Wilkins, David, D.D., prebendary of Canterbury, iii. 602.
— Edith Belle, wife of C. A. Drummond, viii. 230.
— L. T., Southampton, viii. 230.
Wilkinson, Dr., Oxford, v. 468.
— — his wife, Vere Ker, v. 468.
— Thomas, viii. 310.
— — his wife, Mary Lyon, viii. 310.
Willes, Edward, bishop of Bath and Wells, viii. 33.
William I., 'the Lion,' king of Scots, i. 4, 5; v. 325.
— — his wife, Ermengarde de Bellomont, i. 5.
William III., king of Great Britain, i. 33.
— — his wife, Mary Stuart, i. 33.
William IV., king of Great Britain, ii. 499; iii. 585.
William of Greenlaw, son of Patrick, iii. 251, 254, 256; iv. 440.
— — his wife, M. the countess, iii. 251.
— — his alleged wife, Ada Dunbar of Home, iii. 254; iv. 440.
William 'Fitz-Duncan,' son of king Duncan II., i. 3; iii. 245.
William, son of Gilbert, 1st earl of Angus, i. 162.
William, abbot of Dunfermline, iii. 88, 525.
William, abbot of Melrose, iii. 422 *n.*
William, son of Edward, in Thirlstane, v. 280.
William, son of Thurstan of Levingston, v. 422.
William, father of Nes, v. 571.
William, father of Hugh of Kinmonth, vi. 529.
William, abbot of St. Germains, vii. 2.
William, 11th abbot of Cupar, vii. 268.
William, 2nd son of Gilbert, earl of Strathearn, viii. 242.
Williams of Beidehead, Robert, vi. 121.
— — his wife, Emily Maria Leslie-Melville, vi. 121.
— of Bodlonfa, R., v. 322.
— of Craig-y-Don, Thomas Pears, colonel, vii. 358.
— of Temple House, Peers, lieut.-col., M.P., iii. 463.
— Agar, New Zealand, ix. 95.
— — his wife, Phyllis Montgomery Boyle, ix. 95.
— Anne, Maidstone, i. 380.
— Anna Dering, wife of major-gen. F. C. Maitland, v. 313.
— Blanche Mary, wife of lt.-col. C. J. Innes-Ker, vii. 357.
— Gwendoline Lucy, wife of Frederick Colin, viscount Maitland, v. 322.

Williams, Nina Janet, wife of Seton Montolieu Montgomerie, iii. 463.
—— Stephen, barrister-at-law, v. 313.
—— *alias* Campbell, Archibald, i. 381.
—— William, lieut.-col. 3rd Foot Guards, i. 380, 381.
—— *alias* Shireburn, Anne, i. 380.
Williamson, Angus, ix. 123.
—— —— his wife, Marjorie Falconer, ix. 123.
—— Janet, wife of (1) John Lindsay, and (2) Geo. Meldrum, v. 412.
—— Sir Joseph, v. 359.
—— —— his wife, Katharine Stewart, baroness Clifton, v. 359.
—— Ralph, collector of customs, iv. 299.
—— —— his wife, Mary Ramsay, iv. 299.
Willington of Hurley, Waldive, i. 402.
—— Elizabeth, wife of Wm. Aston, i. 402.
Willis, James, India House, ii. 89.
—— —— his wife, Elizabeth Colt, ii. 89.
—— John Walpole, viii. 312.
—— —— his wife, Mary Isabella Lyon-Bowes, viii. 312.
Willison, James, in Elvanfoot, ix. 15.
—— —— his wife, Christian Johnstone, ix. 15.
—— John, minister of Forgandenny, ii. 25.
—— —— his wife, Janet Ogilvy, ii. 25.
Willock of Chapelton, George, i. 297.
—— of Magdalene Chapel, George, i. 297.
—— Mr. John, preacher, ii. 467.
Willoughby de Broke, lords, ii. 442.
—— de Eresby, Clementina, wife of Sir G. J. Heathcote; baroness, vii. 59.
—— —— Priscilla, wife of 1st lord Gwydyr; baroness, vii. 59.
—— —— Peter, baron, vii. 59.
—— —— his wife, Clementina Sarah Drummond, vii. 59.
—— —— Sir Robert, ix. 11.
—— Charles S. Heathcote Drummond, major, ii. 280.
—— —— his wife, Muriel Agnes Stuart Erskine, ii. 280.
—— Claude Henry Comaraich, lieut.-col. 9th Lancers, iii. 393.
—— —— his wife, Sybil Louisa Murray, iii. 393.
—— Joan, wife of Gilbert de Umfraville, 4th earl of Angus, ix. 11.
Wills of Northmore, Sir Frederick, 1st bart., iv. 389.
—— Edith Hamilton, wife of Percy S. Douglas-Hamilton, iv. 389.
Wilmot of Chaddesden, Sir Ralph Henry Sacheverel, 6th bart., v. 322.
—— —— his wife, Ada Marian Maitland, v. 322.
—— Anne, wife of Henry Bayntun of Spye Park, viii. 36.
Wilson of Croglin, John, ii. 411.
—— —— his wife, Margaret Dalzell, ii. 411.
Wilson of Plewlands, Euphemia, wife of Mr. David Lindsay, v. 406.
—— —— George, v. 406.
—— —— James, v. 406.
—— —— Samuel, v. 406.
—— of Stottencleugh, George, vi. 178.
—— Andrew, waulkmill of Crombie, ii. 573.
—— Elizabeth, wife of Geo. Middleton of Lethamdolls and Mosshall, vi. 178.
—— George, Edinburgh, vii. 586.
—— —— his wife, Mary St. Clair, vii. 586.
—— Guy Greville, vii. 359.
—— —— his wife, Isabel Innes-Ker, vii. 359.
—— James, burgess of Edinburgh, ii. 595.
—— John, burgess of Edinburgh, ii. 134.
—— —— his wife, Janet Napier, ii. 134.
—— Margaretta Maria, wife of rev. A. Drummond, viii. 232.
—— Sir Thomas, general, ii. 524.
—— Thomas, merchant, Edinburgh, vii. 586.
—— Sir Thomas Maryon, viii. 232.
Wiltshire, Thomas (Boleyne), earl of, iii. 608.
—— Alice, wife of P. Bowes-Lyon, viii. 315.
Wimund, bishop of the Isles, vii. 231.
Winchester, Roger (de Quincy), earl of, i. 107; viii. 562.
—— —— his 1st wife, Alianora of Galloway, ii. 254.
—— Robert (de Quincy), earl of, iv. 142.
—— his wife, Elena of Galloway, iv. 142.
—— John (Paulet), 14th marquess of, viii. 512.
Winchilsea, Daniel (Finch), 8th earl of, viii. 206.
—— George William (Finch-Hatton), 10th earl of, vi. 271; viii. 209.
—— —— his 1st wife, Georgina Charlotte Graham, vi. 271.
Windham of Pilsden Court, Sir Hugh, viii. 182.
—— Priscilla, wife of (1) Sir R. Reynolds, and (2) Henry, 4th earl of Stirling, viii. 182.
Windsor, Herbert Hickman (Windsor), viscount, ii. 306.
—— his wife, Alice Clavering, ii. 306.
WINDSOR, STUART, EARL OF, ii. 306-312.
Windsor, John, first earl of, ii. 306.
—— Charlotte Jane, wife of 1st marquess of Bute, ii. 306.
Wingfield, Sarah, wife of Sir Wm. Aston, i. 401.
—— Thomas, Shrewsbury, i. 401.
Winram of Liberton, George, iv. 308.
—— —— his wife, Agnes Hamilton, iv. 308.
Winter, father of Elsi of Thirlestane, v. 277.

Winterfield, Rachel, alleged wife of 1st lord Reay, and wife of capt. Thomas Kakyne, vii. 169; ix. 151.
Winterton, Edward (Turnour), 5th earl of, i. 71.
—— —— his wife, Georgiana Susan Hamilton. i. 71.
Winton, Roger (de Quincy), earl of, i. 107; ii. 254; viii. 562.
WINTON, SETON, EARL OF, viii. 559-606.
Winton, George, third earl of, iii. 373, 577; viii. 561 *n.*, 591, 593.
—— —— his 1st wife, Anne Hay, viii. 594.
—— —— his 2nd wife, Elizabeth Maxwell, iv. 416; viii. 595; ix. 106.
—— George, eldest son of Sir Geo. Seton of Garleton; styled earl of, viii. 600.
—— George, fourth earl of, iii. 442, 462; viii. 601; ix. 170.
—— —— his 1st wife, Mary Montgomerie, iii. 452; viii. 602.
—— —— his 2nd wife, Christian Hepburne of Addinstoun, viii. 602.
—— George, fifth earl of, viii. 603.
—— Robert, first earl of, viii. 591.
—— —— his wife, Margaret Montgomerie, iii. 442; viii. 591.
—— Robert, second earl of, viii. 592.
—— —— his wife, Anna Maitland, v. 301; viii. 592.
WINTON, MONTGOMERIE, EARL OF, iii. 462-465.
Winton, Archibald William, first earl of, iii. 462.
—— —— his 1st wife, Theresa Newcomen, iii. 463.
—— —— his 2nd wife, Adela Caroline Hariet Capel, iii. 463.
—— Archibald William, second earl of, iii. 463.
—— —— his wife, Sophia Theodosia Worsley, iii. 463.
—— George Arnulf, third earl of, iii. 464.
—— —— his wife, Janet Lucretia Cuninghame, iii. 464.
Wintoun of Andat, Ingram, v. 599.
—— of Stradichty-Martin, Andrew, iii. 311.
—— —— his wife, Elizabeth Scrymgeour, iii. 311.
—— of Strathmartin, Andrew, iv. 34.
—— —— his wife, Marjory Ogilvy, iv. 34.
—— —— Thomas, iv. 34.
—— of Wrychtishouses, Henry de, iv. 81.
Wiseman, Elizabeth, wife of Sir W. Hewett, ii. 581.
—— Elizabeth, wife of C. Richardson, ii. 581.
—— Richard, St. Lawrence Pountney, ii. 581.
—— Richard, deputy-bailie, iv. 48.
—— Sir William, bart., ii. 581 *n.*
Wishart of Aberdalgie, William, vi. 530 *n.*, 534 *n.*
—— of Balgillo, John, iv. 276.
—— of Balisycht, John, i. 199.
—— —— his wife, Jean Douglas, i. 199.
—— of Bondarge, Thomas, vii. 13.
—— —— his wife, Barbara Maule, vii. 13.
—— of Carnebeg, Andrew, v. 244.
—— —— his wife, Marjorie Falconer, v. 244; ix. 123.
—— of Clifton Hall, Sir George, i. 104.
—— of Glensaugh, William, bishop of St. Andrews, i. 427 *n.*; iv. 9, 10; vi. 203, 534 *n.*; vii. 423.
—— of Logie, *, vii. 13.
—— of Pittarrow, *, 1420, i. 278.
—— —— James, i. 282.
—— —— John, iv. 276; v. 243; vi. 172.
—— —— Sir John, i. 199; vi. 232.
—— —— John, i. 514.
—— —— his wife, Jean Douglas, i. 199.
—— of Plenderleith, Alicia, wife of Sir George de Abernethy, vii. 404.
—— —— William, vii. 405.
—— of Redhall, John, v. 243.
—— of Turin, William, bishop of St. Andrews, vi. 534 *n.*
—— Fergusia, wife of George Lockhart of Carnwath, i. 104.
—— Gilbert, son of W. of Logie, vii. 13.
—— —— his wife, Grisel Maule, vii. 13.
—— Margaret, wife of Robt. Arbuthnott of that Ilk, i. 282; ix. 15.
—— Margaret, wife of David Lindsay of Edzell, i. 514.
—— Marjorie, wife of Gilbert Middleton, vi. 172.
—— Robert, bishop of Glasgow, iv. 12; viii. 519.
Witfield, Beatrix de, vii. 421.
—— Robert de, vii. 421.
Withrington of Kirkington, Edward, ix. 42.
—— —— his wife, Christian Stewart, ix. 42.
Wod of Dunone, David, vi. 591.
—— —— his wife, Elizabeth Makgill, vi. 591.
Wodehouse, Charles Nourse, archdeacon of Norwich, iii. 584.
Wolfe, James, general, v. 540.
Wolfe-Murray of Cringletie, James, iii. 523.
Wollaston, Frederick, major, i. 307.
—— —— his wife, Josette Eliza Jane Arbuthnott, i. 307.
Wolverton, George Carr (Glynn), 1st lord, i. 391.
Wood of Balbegno, Andrew, i. 310.
—— —— his wife, Elizabeth Arbuthnott, i. 310.
—— —— Andrew, vi. 182.

* Name unknown.

Wood of Balhegno, Walter, iv. 111.
—— —— his wife, Isobel *or* Elizabeth Forbes, iv. 111.
—— —— c. 1550, i. 444.
—— —— his wife, * Stewart, i. 444.
—— of Bonnytoun, Sir Henry, i. 121; iii. 320; vi. 497.
—— —— Sir John, i. 126; vi. 495.
—— —— his wife, Anne Ogilvy, i. 126.
—— —— Patrick, vi. 168.
—— —— his wife, Jean Stewart, vi. 168.
—— —— Patrick, vi. 497.
—— —— his wife, Anna Carnegie, vi. 497.
—— —— William, i. 75; iv. 259.
—— —— his 1st wife, Margaret Ruthven, ii. 268; iv. 259.
—— —— his 2nd wife, Katharine Scot, i. 75.
—— of Bracon Ash, Robert, ii. 580.
—— —— his wife, Elizabeth Richardson, ii. 580.
—— of Craig, David, viii. 58.
—— of Dryfesdale, iii. 56, 68.
—— of Nether Gallowhill, William, iii. 357.
—— —— his wife, Katharine Cochrane, iii. 357.
—— of Forrenes, John, v. 244.
—— of Hardenwood, Henry, chaplain, vii. 320.
—— of Kinblethmont, Sir John, vi. 495.
—— of Lamlethan, Alexander, viii. 497.
—— —— his wife, Elizabeth Wemyss, viii. 497.
—— of Largo, Andrew, viii. 217.
—— —— his wife, Jean Drummond, viii. 217.
—— of Stonthall, Edward Robert, colonel, vii. 391.
—— Agnes, wife of Sir John Carnegie of Kinnaird, viii. 58.
—— Christian, wife of George Strang, and mistress of 4th earl of Rothes, vii. 286, 291.
—— Frederick George Lindley, iii. 48.
—— Helen, wife of Wm. Murray of Little Ardit, viii. 187.
—— Sir Henry, i. 31.
—— John, minister of St. Andrews, v. 414.
—— —— his wife, Helen Lindsay, v. 414.
—— John Philip, v. 314.
—— Marianne, wife of C. E. S. Here-Ruthven, vii. 391.
—— Mary, wife of 1st duke of Cleveland, i. 31.
—— Mary Isabella, wife of John Maitland, v. 314.
—— Walter, viii. 274.
—— —— his wife, Dorothea Tulloch of Bonyngtoun, viii. 274.
—— William, ix. 77.
—— —— his wife, Katharine Cochrane, ix. 77.

* Name unknown.

Wood, *, Drumlagair, i. 142.
—— —— his wife, Elizabeth Barclay, i. 142.
Woodford of Brightwell, Robert, iv. 265.
—— Elizabeth, wife of (1) Thomas, 1st baron Gerard, and (2) Patrick Ruthven, iv. 265.
—— lieut.-col., Gordon Fencibles, iv. 555.
—— —— his wife, Susan Gordon, iv. 555.
Woodforde, Samuel, R.A., viii. 41.
Woodhall, George Sinclair, senator of the College of Justice, lord, ii. 346.
—— of Balmanno, Adam Cunningham of Woodhall, senator of the College of Justice, lord, v. 248.
Woodhall, Thomas, major 12th regt., iii. 362.
—— —— his wife, Janet Cochrane, iii. 362.
Woodhull, Fulke, vi. 463.
—— —— his wife, Elizabeth Webbe, vi. 463.
Woodman of Fenzies, William, iv. 71.
—— —— his wife, * Forbes, iv. 71.
Worsley, Sophia Adelaide Theodosia, wife of 14th earl of Eglinton, iii. 463.
Worswick, John, Stafford, i. 402.
—— —— his wife, Anne Aston, i. 402.
Worth of Oakley, John, capt. R.N., ii. 354.
—— —— his wife, Katharine Sinclair of Durran, ii. 354.
—— Mary Catherine Sinclair, wife of Admiral Sir B. W. Walker, ii. 354.
Wortley-Mackenzie of Wortley and Rosehaugh, James Archibald, 2nd son of 3rd earl of Bute, ii. 303.
—— —— his wife, Margaret Cunynghame, ii. 303.
Wortley Montague of Wortley, Edward, ii. 302.
—— —— his wife, Mary Pierrepont, ii. 302.
—— —— Mary, wife of 3rd earl of Bute, and baroness Mountstuart of Wortley, ii. 302.
Wotton, Sir Henry, English ambassador, ii. 69.
Wray of Glentworth, Sir John, vii. 357.
—— —— his wife, Frances Norcliffe of Langton, vii. 357.
—— of Langton, Mary, wife of Sir James Innes of Innes, vii. 357.
Wrede, baron Otto Gustaff, ix. 70.
—— —— his wife, Charlotta Sutherland, iii. 213; ix. 70.
Wren of Binchester, Farren, viii. 309.
—— Mary Elizabeth, wife of Thos. Lyon, viii. 309.
Wright of Kersie, Edward, ii. 296.
—— —— his wife, Cecil Stewart, ii. 296.
—— Ann, wife of Walter Aston, i. 403; ix. 26.
—— Elizabeth, wife of Francis Cheyne, vi. 465.

* Name unknown.